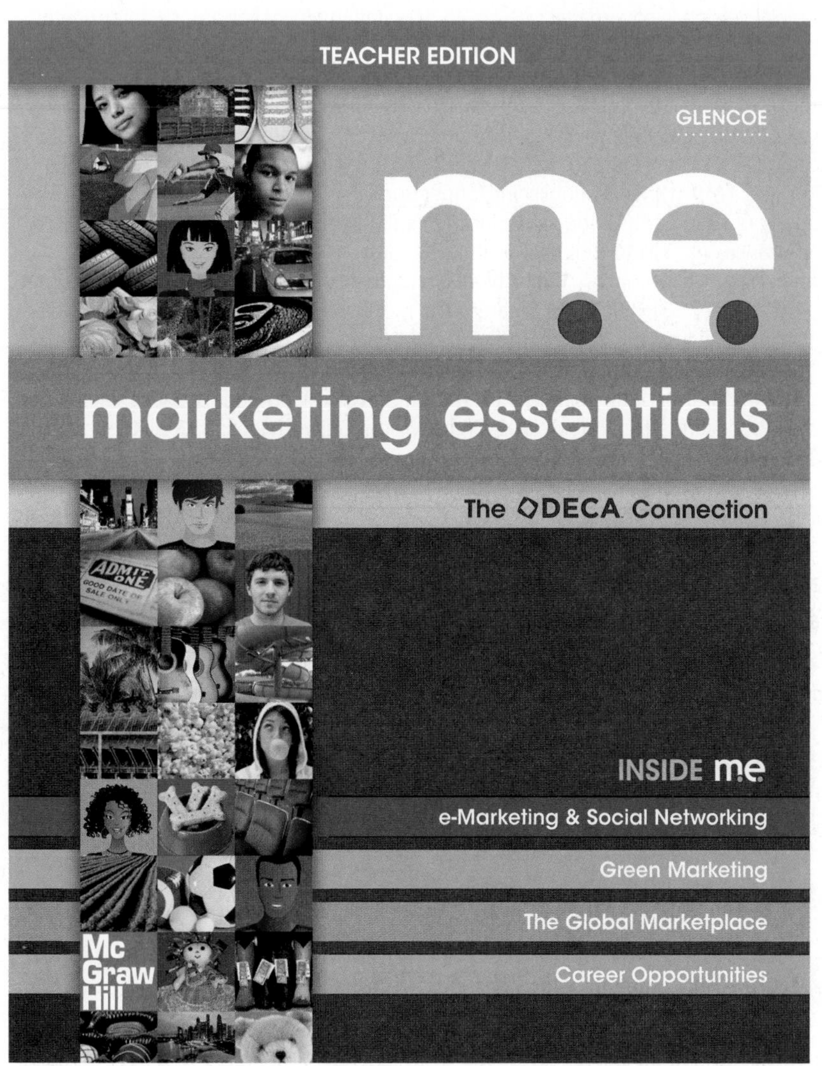

Lois Schneider Farese
Grady Kimbrell
Carl A. Woloszyk, Ph.D.

Bothell, WA • Chicago, IL • Columbus, OH • New York, NY

Photo Credits

All AMA logos are "Used by permission of American Marketing Association."
All DECA logos are "Used by permission of DECA Inc."
All Marketing Core graphics are "Used by permission. Copyright MBA Research, Columbus, Ohio."

Abbreviation key: MH=The McGraw-Hill Companies

Cover (from left to right, top to bottom)Rubberball Photography/Veer; (2 4 10 11 21 31)Karen Gonzalez/The McGraw-Hill Companies; (3)Image Source/Getty Images; (5)Digital Vision/Getty Images; (6)PhotoAlto Photography/Veer; (7)Nicholas Eveleigh/Getty Images; (8 14 25 30)giraffarte/iStockphoto; (9)fotog/Getty Images; (12 19)Flickr/Getty Images; (13 22 34)Photodisc/Getty Images; (15)Digitaler Lumpensammler/Getty Images; (16)Brand X Pictures/PunchStock; (17)Yellowdog Productions/Getty Images; (18)Image Source Photography/Veer; (20)Thomas Hawk/Getty Images; (23)Artville/Getty Images; (24)Hola Images/Getty Images; (26 29)Royalty-Free/CORBIS; (27)Miemo Penttinen/Getty Images; (28)Photo 24/Getty Images; (32) Kraig Scarbinsky/Getty Images; (33)Andrew Dernie/Getty Images; (35)Image Source/Alamy Images; (36) Used by permission of DECA Inc.; **TM9** (l)Ingram Publishing/SuperStock, (r)vario images GmbH & Co.KG/Alamy; **TM10** (l)Image property of Little Earth Productions, Inc., (r)giraffarte/iStockphoto; **TM24** Produced by Food Alliance, www.FoodAlliance.org.; **TM40** Bellurget Jean Louis/Getty Images; **TM42** BananaStock/JupiterImages; **TM57** Jupiter Images/Getty Images; **TM59** Noel Hendrickson/Getty Images; **TM63** Hill Street Studios/Getty Images; **21** Royalty-Free/CORBIS; **75** Jill Braaten/The McGraw-Hill Companies; **151** Photodisc/Getty Images; **221** Digital Vision/Getty Images; **287** Photodisc/Getty Images; **331** Ingram Publishing/Age Fotostock; **431** Keith Eng/The McGraw-Hill Companies; **499** Digital Vision/PunchStock; **571** Artville/Veer; **595** Royalty-Free/CORBIS; **607** Photodisc/Getty Images; **711** The McGraw-Hill Companies; **743** Digital Vision/Getty Images; **765** Rubberball Productions/Rubberball; **809** Digital Vision/Getty Images; **833** Jill Braaten/The McGraw-Hill Companies; **855** Artville/Getty Images; **907** Monkey Business Images/Cutcaster.

Notice: Information on featured companies, organizations, and their products and services is included for educational purposes only and does not present or imply endorsement of the *Marketing Essentials* program.

glencoe.com

Printed in the United States of America.

Send all inquiries to:
Glencoe/McGraw-Hill
4400 Easton Commons
Columbus, OH 43219

ISBN: 978-0-07-895313-2 (Teacher Edition)
MHID: 0-07-895313-8 (Teacher Edition)

Printed in the United States of America.

3 4 5 6 7 8 9 QDB/LEH 17 16 15 14 13 12 11

ABOUT THE AUTHORS

Lois Schneider Farese is a nationally recognized secondary marketing educator and DECA advisor from New Jersey. She has been involved in organizing and running New Jersey regional and state DECA conferences and has also participated as series director and event manager at state and national DECA conferences. The State Officer Action Team presented Farese with the Outstanding Service Award for her dedication, professionalism, and commitment to New Jersey DECA in 1993, 1996, and 1999, as well as with the Honorary Life Membership Award in 1990 for setting a new level of professionalism for local advisors. She was inducted into the DECA Hall of Fame in 1996. Farese was named "Teacher of the Year" in 1981 by the Marketing Education Association of New Jersey. In 1993 and 1999, the University of Richmond recognized Farese for her contributions to the intellectual growth and achievement of students who graduated from her marketing program. In 2000 Farese was the nominee from Northern Highlands Regional High School for the Princeton Prize for Distinguished Secondary School Teaching. Farese holds a bachelor's degree in business and distributive education and two master's degrees from Montclair State University in New Jersey.

Grady Kimbrell, a nationally recognized author and consultant on career education, began his career in education teaching high school business in Kansas. After relocating to Southern California, Kimbrell taught business courses and coordinated students' in-class activities with their on-the-job experience. He later directed the work experience program for the high schools of Santa Barbara, California. Kimbrell has served on numerous state instructional program committees and writing teams, designed educational computer programs, and produced educational films. Kimbrell holds degrees in business administration, educational psychology, and business education.

Carl A. Woloszyk is a professor emeritus from Western Michigan University with an extensive background in marketing education. He has served as a state department of education consultant for marketing and cooperative education, DECA and Delta Epsilon Chi state advisor, a career and technical administrator for a regional education service agency, and a secondary marketing teacher-coordinator. As a secondary marketing teacher-coordinator, he taught beginning and advanced marketing courses. His students have received numerous awards at district, state, and national DECA conferences. Woloszyk has served on the board of directors for DECA; he has been president of the Marketing Education Foundation and of the ACTE Cooperative Work Experience Education Association. He is a board member of the Michigan Marketing Educators' Association. He has received the Marketing Education Professional Award from the national Marketing Education Association for Exemplary Service to Marketing Education. Woloszyk holds a master's degree from Eastern Michigan University and an educational specialist degree in occupational education from the University of Michigan. He received his doctorate in business and distributive education from Michigan State University.

REVIEWERS AND CONTRIBUTORS

Priscilla McCalla
Professional Development Director (retired)
National DECA
Reston, VA

Jennifer Allen
Marketing Teacher
Wilson Central High School
Lebanon, TN

Shauna Binkerd
Business/Marketing Educator
Springville High School
Springville, UT

Rose M. Blevins
DECA Advisor/SkillsUSA Advisor
Kecoughtan High School
Hampton, VA

Diana Canton
Marketing Education Teacher/DECA Advisor
Cigarroa High School
Laredo, TX

Tracy Conley
Coolidge High School
Coolidge, AZ

Ron Cooper
Advisor Development
Washington DECA
Seattle, WA

Alana Eaton
Business Education Teacher
Kennard-Dale High School
Fawn Grove, PA

Michelle Gilbert
Marketing DECA Coordinator
Justin F. Kimball High School
Dallas, TX

Cassandra Jones
Marketing Education Teacher-Coordinator
Allen High School
Allen, TX

Shanna LaMar
Executive Director
Washington DECA
Seattle, WA

Ariana Langford
Har-Ber High School
Springdale, AR

Kit Lynch
Marketing Instructor
Gahanna Lincoln High School
Gahanna, OH

Michelle Stortzum
Marketing Instructor / LHS DECA Advisor
Lindbergh High School
St. Louis, Missouri

Shelly Stanton
Billings West High School
Billings, MT

James Walker Todd
Douglas MacArthur High School
San Antonio, TX

TABLE OF CONTENTS

TEACHER EDITION

INSIDE THE STUDENT EDITION

INSIDE THE TEACHER EDITION

PROGRAM RESOURCES

CLASSROOM SOLUTIONS

Begin the Unit

ACADEMICS INTEGRATED WITH 21ST CENTURY SKILLS

Marketing Essentials provides academic rigor in real-life skill settings by providing relevant activities correlated to national standards and integrating learning resources throughout each unit at the point of use.

Marketing Internship Project Preview At the beginning of each unit, a preview lets students know what is to come. Have students use the preview to think about how what they are learning applies to the project.

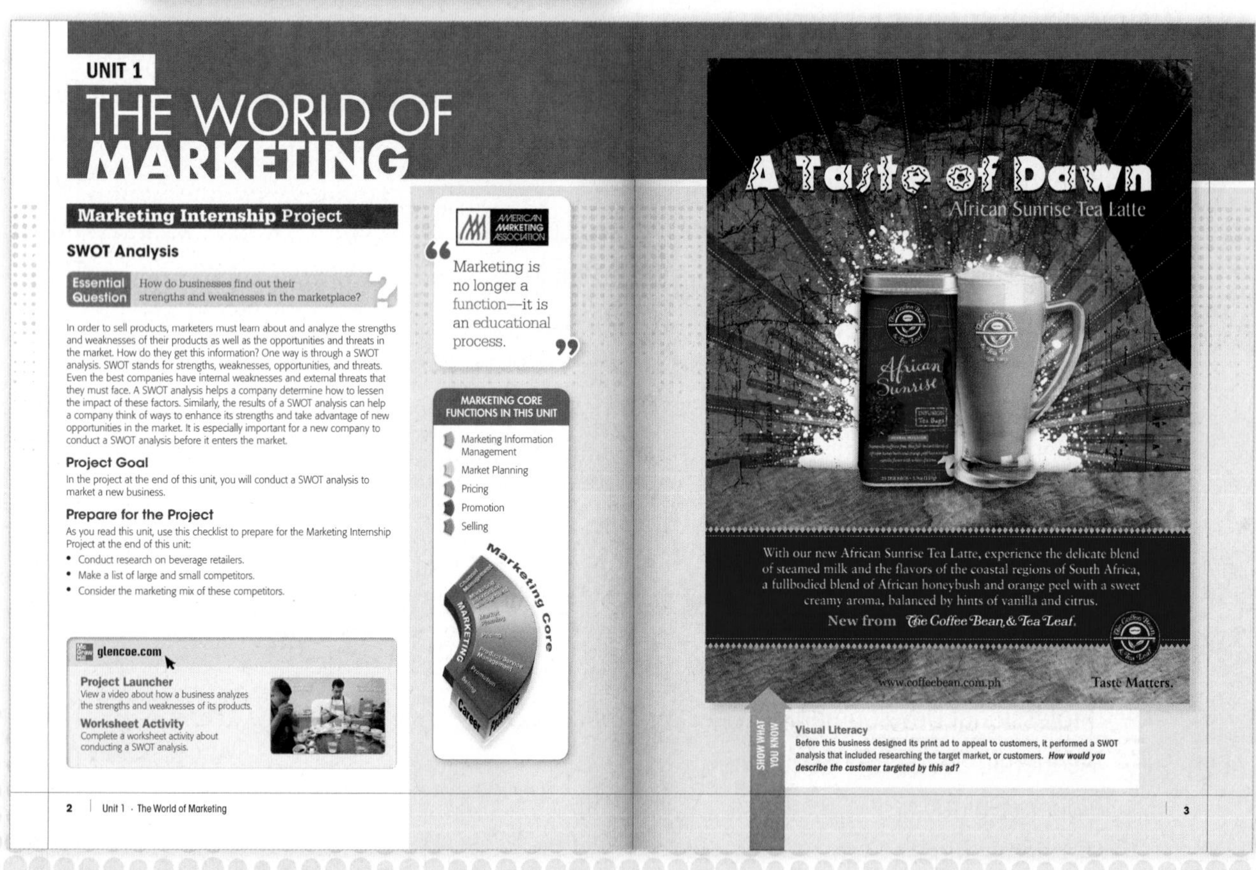

UNIT 1

THE WORLD OF **MARKETING**

Marketing Internship Project

SWOT Analysis

Essential Question How do businesses find out their strengths and weaknesses in the marketplace?

In order to sell products, marketers must learn about and analyze the strengths and weaknesses of their products as well as the opportunities and threats in the market. How do they get this information? One way is through a SWOT analysis. SWOT stands for strengths, weaknesses, opportunities, and threats. Even the best companies have internal weaknesses and external threats that they must face. A SWOT analysis helps a company determine how to lessen the impact of these factors. Similarly, the results of a SWOT analysis can help a company think of ways to enhance its strengths and take advantage of new opportunities in the market. It is especially important for a new company to conduct a SWOT analysis before it enters the market.

Project Goal

In the project at the end of this unit, you will conduct a SWOT analysis to market a new business.

Prepare for the Project

As you read this unit, use this checklist to prepare for the Marketing Internship Project at the end of this unit:

- Conduct research on beverage retailers.
- Make a list of large and small competitors.
- Consider the marketing mix of these competitors.

glencoe.com

Project Launcher
View a video about how a business analyzes the strengths and weaknesses of its products.

Worksheet Activity
Complete a worksheet activity about conducting a SWOT analysis.

AMERICAN MARKETING ASSOCIATION

"Marketing is no longer a function—it is an educational process."

MARKETING CORE FUNCTIONS IN THIS UNIT

- Marketing Information Management
- Market Planning
- Pricing
- Promotion
- Selling

Marketing Core
MARKETING
Career Pathways

A Taste of Dawn
African Sunrise Tea Latte
With our new African Sunrise Tea Latte, experience the delicate blend of steamed milk and the flavors of the coastal regions of South Africa, a fullbodied blend of African honeybush and orange peel with a sweet creamy aroma, balanced by hints of vanilla and citrus.
New from The Coffee Bean & Tea Leaf.
www.coffeebean.com.ph
Taste Matters.

SHOW WHAT YOU KNOW

Visual Literacy
Before this business designed its print ad to appeal to customers, it performed a SWOT analysis that included researching the target market, or customers. ***How would you describe the customer targeted by this ad?***

2 | Unit 1 · The World of Marketing

3

Online Resources such as videos and worksheet activities help students better understand how the unit material will relate to the project.

Understand the Marketing Skills that will be featured in the unit.

Show What You Know
By examining the photo at the beginning of the unit, students will begin to think about the topics covered in the unit. It visually guides the student with an engaging question to help interpret the meaning.

Begin the Chapter

BUILD STUDENTS' STUDY SKILLS WITH CHAPTER ACTIVITIES

Marketing Essentials chapters include activities designed to help students build their reading and writing skills and investigate chapter topics.

Discovery Project Encourage students to use their reading, writing, and research skills to create a project that previews topics they will learn in the chapter.

DECA Connection Students connect with others through role-playing and interview practice.

Chapter 1 | Section 1.1 Marketing and the Marketing Concept | Section 1.2 The Importance of Marketing | Section 1.3 Fundamentals of Marketing

marketing is all around us

SHOW WHAT YOU KNOW

Visual Literacy Whenever you see advertising in print, online, or on the street, marketing is in action. When you go shopping, marketing is present in displays. When you go on the Internet, marketing pops up in front of you. When you see trucks hauling products, marketing is taking place. All these activities are aspects of marketing. *What other activities have you observed that are part of marketing? How would you define marketing?*

Discovery Project

Keeping Customers

Essential Question How do businesses keep their customers?

Project Goal

Work with a partner to identify two businesses that cater to teenagers. One business should sell goods and the other services. Use the seven marketing functions—Channel Management, Marketing Information Management, Market Planning, Pricing, Product/Service Management, Promotion, and Selling—to explain how each business caters to its customers. How effective are those businesses in satisfying their customers' needs and wants? Develop a rating scale to present your findings.

Ask Yourself...

- Which two businesses will you study?
- How will you use the marketing functions to evaluate each business?
- How will you devise a rating scale?
- How will you present your findings?

Analysis and Interpretation Why is it important for businesses to follow the marketing functions?

glencoe.com

Activity
Get a worksheet activity about keeping customers.

Evaluate
Download a rubric that you can use to evaluate your project.

DECA Connection

DECA Event Role Play

Concepts in this chapter are related to DECA competitive events that involve either an interview or role play.

Performance Indicators The performance indicators represent key skills and knowledge. Your key to success in DECA competitive events is relating them to the concepts in this chapter.

- Explain the concept of marketing strategies.
- Explain the concept of markets and market identification.
- Explain the importance of promotion in the marketing mix.
- Describe marketing functions and related activities.
- Determine economic utilities created by business activities.

DECA Prep

Role Play Practice role playing with the DECA Connection competitive-event activity at the end of this chapter. More information about DECA events can be found on DECA's Web site.

Chapter 1 · Marketing Is All Around Us | 5

Explore the Photo Students can visually jumpstart their thinking about the chapter's main topics.

Online Resources Students can access project resources at this book's Online Learning Center.

Begin the Section

STRENGTHEN COMPREHENSION WITH READING GUIDES

To strengthen students' reading success, each section of ***Marketing Essentials*** begins with a Reading Guide. Students can preview section content, vocabulary words, and organize concepts through graphic organizers.

Academic Standards Students can see which academic standards are integrated into the content of each section.

Before You Read A pre-reading study tip will help your students be better prepared to learn the section's content.

Section Objectives By reading the Section Objectives and Main Idea, students will know what they can expect to learn in that section.

Vocabulary Students can check the Content and Academic Vocabulary lists for words they are not familiar with and look them up in the glossary in the back of the book.

Graphic Organizer A visual tool will help students organize and remember new content. You and your students can download printable graphic organizers from the *Marketing Essentials* Online Learning Center.

READING GUIDE

Before You Read

Connect Suppose you had to market yourself as a student. What are your strengths?

Objectives

- **Learn** how to conduct a SWOT analysis.
- **List** the three key areas of an internal company analysis.
- **Identify** the factors in a PEST analysis.
- **Explain** the basic elements of a marketing plan.

The Main Idea

A company looks at itself and the world around it to create a marketing plan for reaching goals.

Vocabulary

Content Vocabulary
- SWOT analysis
- PEST analysis
- marketing plan
- executive summary
- situation analysis
- marketing strategy
- sales forecasts
- performance standard

Academic Vocabulary

You will find these words in your reading and on your tests. Make sure you know their meanings.
- factors
- technology

Graphic Organizer

Draw or print a two-column chart to identify the seven elements of a marketing plan.

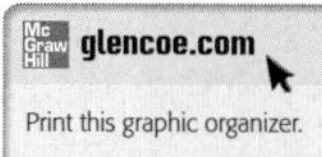

glencoe.com

Print this graphic organizer.

Marketing Plan

Element	Analysis
1.	
2.	
3.	
4.	
5.	
6.	
7.	

STANDARDS

ACADEMIC

English Language Arts

NCTE 1 Read texts to acquire new information.

Social Studies

NCSS VII B Production, Distribution, and Consumption Analyze the roles that supply and demand, prices, incentives, and profits play in determining what is produced and distributed in a competitive market system.

NCSS *National Council for the Social Studies*
NCTE *National Council of Teachers of English*
NCTM *National Council of Teachers of Mathematics*
NSES *National Science Education Standards*

Common Core Reading Determine central ideas or themes of a text and analyze their development; summarize the key supporting details and ideas.

MARKETING CORE FUNCTION

Market Planning

30 | Unit 1 · The World of Marketing

Study with Features

SKILLS STUDENTS CAN USE AT SCHOOL AND IN THE WORKPLACE

High-interest, colorful features in each chapter engage students, enhance their understanding of important concepts, and increase involvement with real-world situations. Features incorporate activities, such as projects and critical thinking questions that help students apply what they have learned.

World Market These features showcase marketing in countries all over the world.

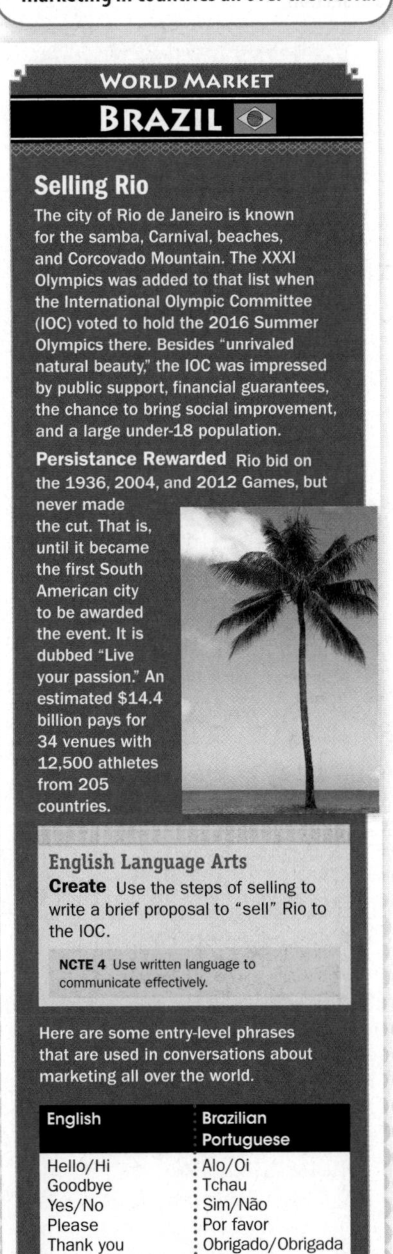

WORLD MARKET

BRAZIL

Selling Rio

The city of Rio de Janeiro is known for the samba, Carnival, beaches, and Corcovado Mountain. The XXXI Olympics was added to that list when the International Olympic Committee (IOC) voted to hold the 2016 Summer Olympics there. Besides "unrivaled natural beauty," the IOC was impressed by public support, financial guarantees, the chance to bring social improvement, and a large under-18 population.

Persistance Rewarded Rio bid on the 1936, 2004, and 2012 Games, but never made the cut. That is, until it became the first South American city to be awarded the event. It is dubbed "Live your passion." An estimated $14.4 billion pays for 34 venues with 12,500 athletes from 205 countries.

English Language Arts

Create Use the steps of selling to write a brief proposal to "sell" Rio to the IOC.

NCTE 4 Use written language to communicate effectively.

Here are some entry-level phrases that are used in conversations about marketing all over the world.

English	Brazilian Portuguese
Hello/Hi	Alo/Oi
Goodbye	Tchau
Yes/No	Sim/Não
Please	Por favor
Thank you	Obrigado/Obrigada
You're welcome	De nada

Hot Topic Students will learn facts about marketing as well as the tips and tricks that marketers use to make their work more successful.

Marketing Mix Businesses use social networking sites to promote their products and research new ones.

Marketing Case Study Students will learn how real-world companies successfully faced marketing challenges. Each of these features has a question that can help students connect what they have learned with other academic subjects.

MARKETING CASE STUDY

Adidas's Sales Automation

To prepare for a meeting with a customer, the Adidas® sales force usually checks inventory. But frustration would set in when some products were no longer available after a sale was made. A sales representative would have to call the customer to revise the order. Or, worse, phone customer service while on a sales call, interrupting the selling process. So, Adidas gave laptops to its sales staff so they could interface with the company's computer system to check real-time inventory.

Improving the Process

To improve on this solution, Adidas turned to AT&T™ and Atlas2Go, an automated sales-force application. The software program can run on a wireless BlackBerry® device. With this system, sales representatives check inventory on the spot while taking a customer's order. This improvement reduced frustration, errors, and the need to change orders. Another unforeseen benefit was the ability to spot product trends quickly.

Social Studies

Analyze Discuss how supply and demand resulted in sales representatives having immediate access to a company's inventory during the sales process.

NCSS VII B Production, Distribution, and Consumption Analyze the role that supply and demand, prices, incentives, and profits play in determining what is produced and distributed in a competitive market system.

The Green Marketer These features allow students to see how marketers promote green products and services to entice customers. Each of these features has a Green Marketer worksheet activity you and your students can download at this book's Online Learning Center.

Selling Eco-Fashion

Everything old is new again, at least in the world of eco-fashion. Turning yesterday's trash into today's ready-to-wear is the trend. Environmental entrepreneurs are developing businesses with earth-friendly names, such as "Save the Planet" and "Greenloop." They build their marketing plans around green products. They attract customers who want to do good as well as look good in clothes made from recycled wares and natural fibers.

Raw Material Worn tires and old denim take shape as ultra-cool sneakers. Fabric made from wood, bamboo, or corn turns into high-end haute couture. Reclaimed Coke® cans add sparkle when recycled as sequins. For the conscientious shopper, dressing "green" means wearing conviction with style.

English Language Arts

Create Think of an object at home that could be recycled as a product for a new business venture. Describe in writing the new product and business, along with the pros and cons of starting the new business.

NCTE 5 Use different writing process elements to communicate effectively.

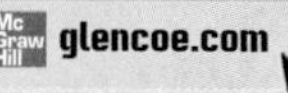

Get an activity on green marketing.

DIGITAL NATION

See You on Facebook

Social networking is growing exponentially, with tens of millions of new users every month. One of the most visited sites for connecting with friends is Facebook.com. The site is used not only for personal interaction, but also for marketing. Most major brands have pages on Facebook that allow users to become fans, receive special news and offers, and interact with company staff.

App Magic

Facebook made news by allowing users to write software applications (apps) that people can embed on their personal profiles. Companies create apps that engage users in fun activities, such as games, polls, and quizzes. Users can rate apps, become fans of them, and recommend them to their friends. This spreads the word about the company without the use of paid advertising. Facebook pages and apps are a growing part of many businesses' marketing plans.

Science

Evaluate Imagine you are working in the marketing department of a company that creates science related products. How can you use apps on social networking sites to reach your customers?

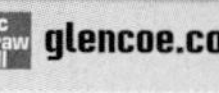

Get a Digital Nation Worksheet Activity.

Digital Nation Students can discover how using technology such as social networking, Web sites, and e-mail can help companies market their products and services. Each of these features has a Digital Nation worksheet activity that you can download at this book's Online Learning Center.

Career Chatroom These are brief interviews with marketing professionals. Students can find more information on marketing careers and career exploration activities at this book's Online Learning Center.

Career Chatroom

Peggy Masterson Kalter
President/CEO
The Masterson/SWOT Team

What do you do at work?

As a strategic marketing consulting company, we specialize in insight generation, brand positioning, portfolio management, and communications optimization. My job includes keeping clients satisfied and pleased with our work, and participating in the analysis phase and final delivery of our projects.

What is your key to success?

I treat each client's business as though it were my own. Simply put: I care. I've never lost business because I cared too much, but I have certainly kept and won business because of it.

What skills are most important to you?

Listening is a key skill for insight and strategy specialists. Other important skills include being able to think inductively instead of deductively; being able to connect the dots and see the big picture; and being able to focus on the core of a marketing issue, problem, or opportunity.

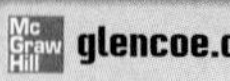

Read more about this career and get a Career Exploration Activity.

Review the Section

HAVE STUDENTS CHECK THEIR UNDERSTANDING

Each After You Read section review helps test students' understanding of the content before they reach the end of the chapter. Review Key Concept questions relate directly to the main topics of each section.

MARKETING AUDIT

The marketing process is ongoing. You can think of it as a circular pattern that continues through the three phases of the marketing process of planning, implementation, and control. The key question at the end of the process is, "Did we accomplish the objectives listed in the marketing plan within the boundaries of the plan?"

If the objectives are met, then the marketing plan can be deemed a success. If the answer to that question is that the objectives were not accomplished, then a company must determine the reasons and make adjustments.

This evaluation at the end of the marketing process is called a marketing audit. A marketing audit evaluates a company's marketing objectives, strategies, budgets, organization, and performance. It identifies problem areas in marketing operations as well as areas that proved to be successful in meeting objectives. Most companies typically conduct a formal marketing audit at least once every year, but informal reviews of the marketing plan happen on a continual basis. Because of the important feedback that a marketing audit provides, a company that regularly conducts marketing audits can be more flexible and responsive than a competitor that reviews its processes only every now and then.

After You Read Section 2.1

Review Key Concepts

1. **Explain** the four aspects of a SWOT analysis and tell how it fits into a marketing plan.
2. **List** the four areas that are investigated in PEST analysis and explain why the knowledge gained can be valuable to a company.
3. **Describe** how the marketing mix relates to the implementation of a marketing plan.

Review Students can check their understanding of the key concepts found in the section.

Practice Academics

English Language Arts

4. One of the statements below represents a goal that a company has established. The other represents an objective. Tell which is which and write a sentence or two explaining your choices.
   - To increase by one-third the amount of paper waste each store recycles within eight months.
   - To become a strong advocate for the environmental concerns of our customers and employees.

NCTE 3 Apply strategies to interpret texts.

Mathematics

5. A company's sales revenue at year end is $1,386,000. If the company's objective is to increase sales by 10 percent in the next year, what is its new sales goal in dollars?

Math Concept **Ways of Representing Numbers** An increase in a number can be represented by a percent greater than 100.

Starting Hints Think of next year's sales goal as 110 percent of this year's sales. Convert 110 percent to a decimal by moving the decimal point two places to the left. Multiply that decimal number by this year's sales revenue to find next year's sales goal in dollars.

NCTM Number and Operations Understand numbers, ways of representing numbers, relationships among numbers, and number systems

For help, go to the **Math Skills Handbook** located at the back of this book.

glencoe.com

Check your answers.

Chapter 2 · The Marketing Plan 41

Practice Academics Connect the section's content to academic skills with these cross-curricular activities.

Check Your Answers Students can go online and check their answers to ensure comprehension.

Review the Chapter

KNOW AND UNDERSTAND THE CHAPTER CONCEPTS

Each chapter ends with a four-page review and applications designed to help students recall, use, and expand on the concepts presented in the chapter.

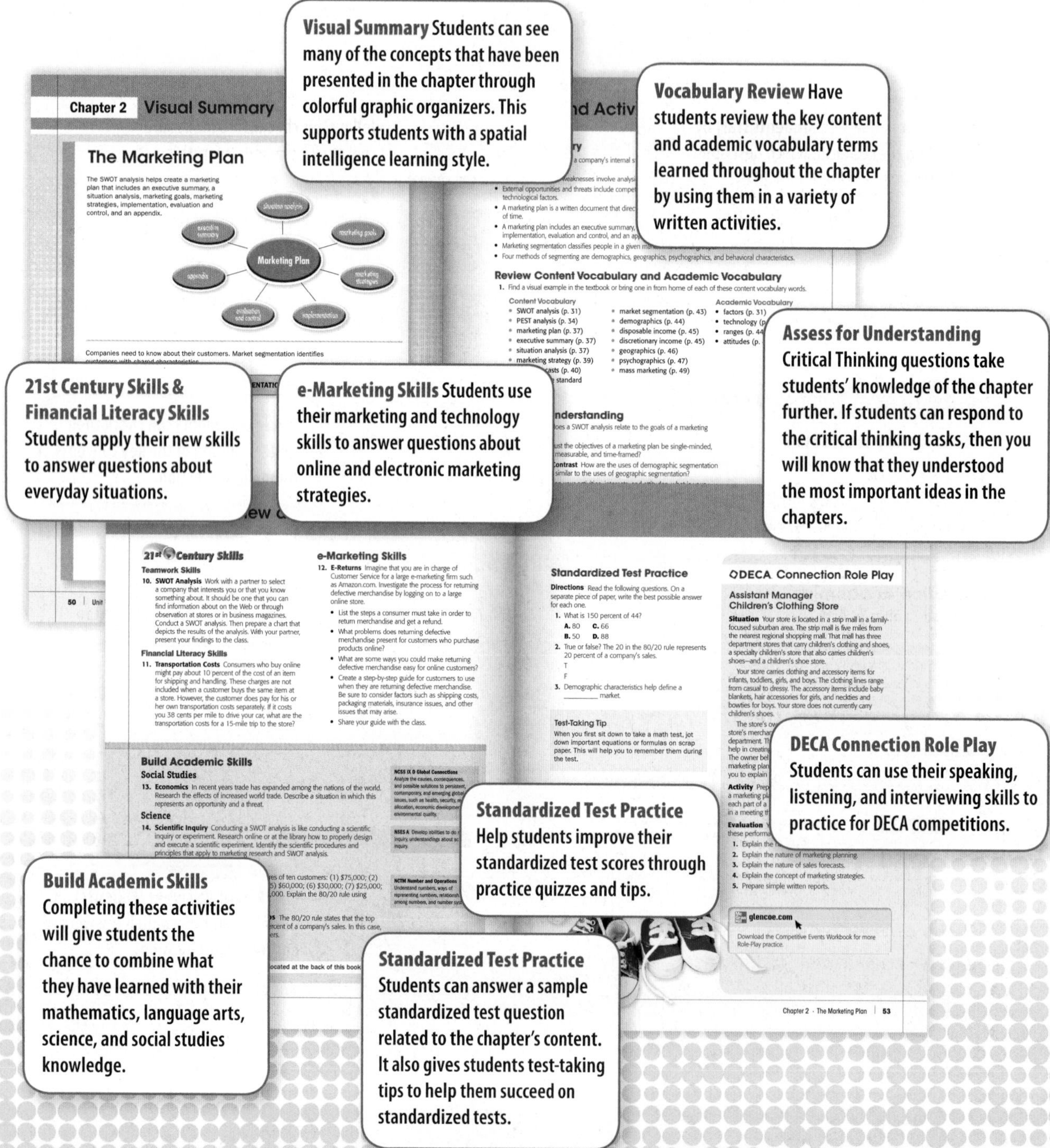

Visual Summary Students can see many of the concepts that have been presented in the chapter through colorful graphic organizers. This supports students with a spatial intelligence learning style.

Vocabulary Review Have students review the key content and academic vocabulary terms learned throughout the chapter by using them in a variety of written activities.

21st Century Skills & Financial Literacy Skills Students apply their new skills to answer questions about everyday situations.

e-Marketing Skills Students use their marketing and technology skills to answer questions about online and electronic marketing strategies.

Assess for Understanding Critical Thinking questions take students' knowledge of the chapter further. If students can respond to the critical thinking tasks, then you will know that they understood the most important ideas in the chapters.

DECA Connection Role Play Students can use their speaking, listening, and interviewing skills to practice for DECA competitions.

Standardized Test Practice Help students improve their standardized test scores through practice quizzes and tips.

Build Academic Skills Completing these activities will give students the chance to combine what they have learned with their mathematics, language arts, science, and social studies knowledge.

Standardized Test Practice Students can answer a sample standardized test question related to the chapter's content. It also gives students test-taking tips to help them succeed on standardized tests.

Close the Unit

PREPARE STUDENTS FOR COLLEGE AND CAREERS WITH PROJECT-BASED LEARNING

Each Marketing Internship Project integrates academic skills into a project-based format. Step-by-step directions allow learners to gain independence by completing the project at their own pace. All projects include a self-evaluation rubric.

Read the Scenario Students start by reading the scenario, which describes the project's background and explains what they will need to do.

Project Checklist Students can follow this checklist to make sure that they have done everything they need to complete their projects.

UNIT 1 **Marketing Internship Project**

SWOT Analysis for a Coffee and Tea Chain

Competition in the specialty coffee and tea market is hot. Is it too late for a new competitor to break into this lucrative market?

Scenario

An Italian coffee and tea chain is considering entering the specialty coffee market in the United States. Before making that investment, our client would like our firm to conduct a SWOT analysis. The Italian coffee chain has been successful in European and Asian markets because it has used its strengths and taken advantage of opportunities in these markets.

Each café's interior design is upscale with comfortable seating, artwork, and designer plates and cups. Exotic teas and specialty coffee offerings are priced in line with and below current competitors' offerings. Only high-grade coffee beans from selected coffee bean growers are used. The Italian cafés are trying to create a unique experience in coffee and tea drinking: coffee and tea should be savored.

The Skills You'll Use

Academic Skills Reading, writing, social studies, and researching

Basic Skills Speaking, listening, thinking, and interpersonal

Technology Skills Word processing, telecommunication, and Internet

NCTE 4 Use written language to communicate effectively.
NCTE 7 Conduct research and gather, evaluate, and synthesize data to communicate discoveries.

Your Objective

Analyze the current specialty coffee and tea market in order to help a client decide whether or not to enter the market.

STEP 1 Do Your Research

Go to the Internet or your school library. Find out about the coffee and tea specialty market in restaurants, cafés, and similar outlets in the United States.

As you conduct your research, answer these questions:

- Is the market growing or shrinking and why?
- What economic, political, socio-cultural or technological factors affect this market?
- Who makes up the target market of U.S. coffee drinkers and tea drinkers in terms of demographic, psychographic, geographic, and behavioral factors?
- How successful are the marketing mixes of competitors such as Starbucks®, Dunkin Donuts®, and McDonald's®?
- What are the strengths, weaknesses, opportunities, and threats for our client in the United States coffee and tea specialty market?

Write a summary of your research.

STEP 2 Plan Your Project

Now that you have completed your research, you need to begin planning your project.

- Conduct a SWOT analysis for the Italian café chain.
- Identify a potential target market in the United States for the Italian café chain.
- Write a report summarzing your SWOT analysis, identifying your target market, and explaining why you have chosen this target market.
- Suggest a marketing mix for the Italian café chain.
- Determine whether that market segment is big enough to support the Italian café chain.

54 | Unit 1 · The World of Marketing

STEP 3 Connect with Your Community

- Test your conclusions by conducting interviews with trusted adults in your community that match the target market you have identified. Ask questions about their habits.
- Take notes during the interviews, and transcribe your notes after the interviews.
- Observe customers in the competition's places of business and note how long they wait for service, how long they sit and drink their beverages, and what else they might be doing while drinking their beverages.

STEP 4 Share What You Learn

Assume your class is the committee from the Italian café chain.

- Share your findings in an oral presentation to your class. Be prepared to answer questions.
- Explain how businesses find out their strengths and weaknesses in the marketplace.
- Explain how businesses react to opportunities and threats in the marketplace.
- Make your recommendation and provide rationale for your decision.
- Use software to create a slide presentation to accompany your oral report. Include one slide in your presentation for each key topic in your written report.

STEP 5 Evaluate Your Marketing and Academic Skills

Your project will be evaluated based on the following:

- Knowledge of the specialty coffee and tea market
- Comprehensive SWOT analysis
- Proper use of marketing terminology
- Rationale for recommendation
- Organization and continuity of presentation
- Mechanics—presentation and neatness
- Speaking and listening skills

MARKETING CORE FUNCTIONS

Market Planning
Pricing

Marketing Internship Project Checklist

Plan

✓ Research current market conditions in the industry.
✓ Assess the strengths, weaknesses, opportunities, and threats a new competitor would face in this market.
✓ Identify a location to use as a test market for the new competitor.

Write

✓ Describe current market conditions in the industry.
✓ Explain how the results of the SWOT analysis help the new competitor understand the risks involved in the market.

Present

✓ Present the results of your SWOT analysis and justify your chosen location for the new competitor.
✓ Respond to questions posed by the audience.
✓ Consider the needs and experiences of the audience as you present research to your class.

glencoe.com

Evaluate Download a rubric you can use to evaluate your final project.

my marketing portfolio

Internship Report When you have completed your Marketing Internship Project and oral presentation, put your written report and printouts of key slides from your oral presentation in your marketing portfolio.

Analyze a Different Market and Company Select a different market (e.g., sports equipment, ice cream, cell phones, bicycles, vitamin-enriched water) and a company of your choice in that market. Conduct a SWOT analysis of that company. How effective is that company in following the marketing concept? Should that company pull out of that market or remain? If it should remain, make recommendations with regard to the company's marketing mix (product, place, price, and promotion). Prepare a written report and an oral presentation.

Unit 1 · The World of Marketing | 55

Help students to understand the **Academic, Basic, and Technology Skills** that will be used as the basis of the project.

Five Steps Each project has five steps: Research, Plan, Connect, Share, and Evaluate.

Unit Resources

GIVE STUDENTS AN EXPANDED VIEW OF UNIT TOPICS

Several teaching features are built in to the ***Marketing Essentials Teacher Edition*** to help you to explain and expand upon topics and ideas students will encounter in the unit. Refer back to these resources as students progress through the unit to refresh their memories.

Marketing Core Functions Introduce students to the marketing core functions within the unit as you introduce the unit topic. This will help students with their understanding of how each topic contributes to marketing ideas and functions.

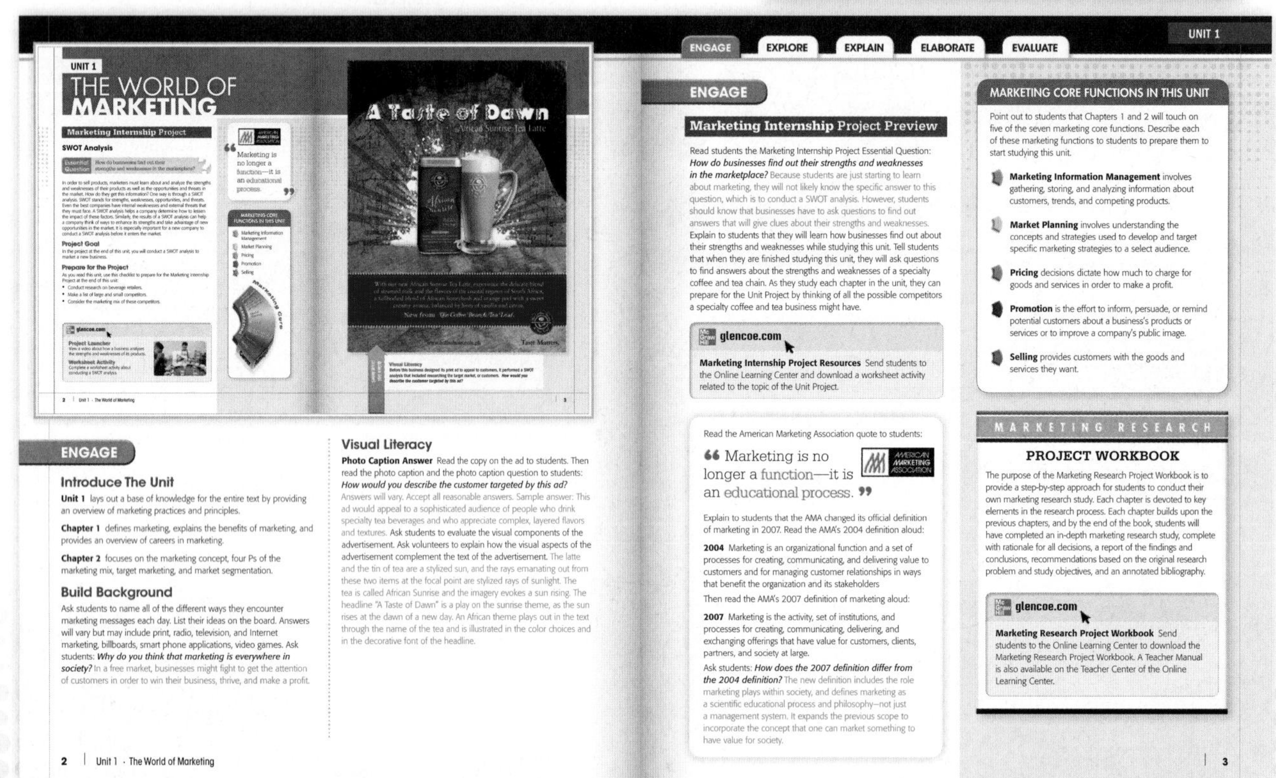

ENGAGE EXPLORE EXPLAIN ELABORATE EVALUATE

UNIT 1

UNIT 1
THE WORLD OF MARKETING

A Taste of Dawn

ENGAGE

Introduce The Unit

Unit 1 lays out a base of knowledge for the entire text by providing an overview of marketing practices and principles.

Chapter 1 defines marketing, explains the benefits of marketing, and provides an overview of careers in marketing.

Chapter 2 focuses on the marketing concept, four Ps of the marketing mix, target marketing, and market segmentation.

Build Background

Ask students to name all of the different ways they encounter marketing messages each day. List their ideas on the board. Answers will vary but may include print, radio, television, and Internet marketing, billboards, smart phone applications, video games. Ask students: ***Why do you think that marketing is everywhere in society?*** In a free market, businesses might fight to get the attention of customers in order to win their business, thrive, and make a profit.

Visual Literacy

Photo Caption Answer Read the copy on the ad to students. Then read the photo caption and the photo caption question to students: ***How would you describe the customer targeted by this ad?*** Answers will vary. Accept all reasonable answers. Sample answer: This ad would appeal to a sophisticated audience of people who drink specialty tea beverages and who appreciate complex, layered flavors and textures. Ask students to evaluate the visual components of the advertisement. Ask volunteers to explain how the visual aspects of the advertisement complement the text of the advertisement. The latte and the tin of tea are a stylized sun, and the rays emanating out from these two items at the focal point are stylized rays of sunlight. The tea is called African Sunrise and the imagery evokes a sun rising. The headline "A Taste of Dawn" is a play on the sunrise theme, as the sun rises at the dawn of a new day. An African theme plays out in the text through the name of the tea and is illustrated in the color choices and in the decorative font of the headline.

2 | Unit 1 · The World of Marketing

ENGAGE

Marketing Internship Project Preview

Read students the Marketing Internship Project Essential Question: ***How do businesses find out their strengths and weaknesses in the marketplace?*** Because students are just starting to learn about marketing, they will not likely know the specific answer to this question, which is to conduct a SWOT analysis. However, students should know that businesses have to ask questions to find out answers that will give clues about their strengths and weaknesses. Explain to students that they will learn how businesses find out about their strengths and weaknesses while studying this unit. Tell students that when they are finished studying this unit, they will ask questions to find answers about the strengths and weaknesses of a specialty coffee and tea chain. As they study each chapter in the unit, they can prepare for the Unit Project by thinking of all the possible competitors a specialty coffee and tea business might have.

glencoe.com

Marketing Internship Project Resources Send students to the Online Learning Center and download a worksheet activity related to the topic of the Unit Project.

Read the American Marketing Association quote to students:

"Marketing is no longer a function—it is an educational process."

AMERICAN MARKETING ASSOCIATION

Explain to students that the AMA changed its official definition of marketing in 2007. Read the AMA's 2004 definition aloud:

2004 Marketing is an organizational function and a set of processes for creating, communicating, and delivering value to customers and for managing customer relationships in ways that benefit the organization and its stakeholders

Then read the AMA's 2007 definition of marketing aloud:

2007 Marketing is the activity, set of institutions, and processes for creating, communicating, delivering, and exchanging offerings that have value for customers, clients, partners, and society at large.

Ask students: ***How does the 2007 definition differ from the 2004 definition?*** The new definition includes the role marketing plays within society, and defines marketing as a scientific educational process and philosophy—not just a management system. It expands the previous scope to incorporate the concept that one can market something to have value for society.

MARKETING CORE FUNCTIONS IN THIS UNIT

Point out to students that Chapters 1 and 2 will touch on five of the seven marketing core functions. Describe each of these marketing functions to students to prepare them to start studying this unit.

- **Marketing Information Management** involves gathering, storing, and analyzing information about customers, trends, and competing products.
- **Market Planning** involves understanding the concepts and strategies used to develop and target specific marketing strategies to a select audience.
- **Pricing** decisions dictate how much to charge for goods and services in order to make a profit.
- **Promotion** is the effort to inform, persuade, or remind potential customers about a business's products or services or to improve a company's public image.
- **Selling** provides customers with the goods and services they want.

MARKETING RESEARCH

PROJECT WORKBOOK

The purpose of the Marketing Research Project Workbook is to provide a step-by-step approach for students to conduct their own marketing research study. Each chapter is devoted to key elements in the research process. Each chapter builds upon the previous chapters, and by the end of the book, students will have completed an in-depth marketing research study, complete with rationale for all decisions, a report of the findings and conclusions, recommendations based on the original research problem and study objectives, and an annotated bibliography.

glencoe.com

Marketing Research Project Workbook Send students to the Online Learning Center to download the Marketing Research Project Workbook. A Teacher Manual is also available on the Teacher Center of the Online Learning Center.

3

Introduce the Unit gives you a preview of the topics students will learn in each unit's chapters. Build Background offers suggestions for you to access the students' prior knowledge of the unit topic.

Project Workbook Discover additional online and print resources that can help students grasp involved marketing concepts. These resources include the Marketing Research Project Workbook, which can be found on the Teacher Center at this book's Online Learning Center.

Chapter Resources

PREPARE STUDENTS FOR CHAPTER INFORMATION

Several teaching features are built in to the ***Marketing Essentials Teacher Edition*** to help you to explain and expand upon topics and ideas students will encounter in the chapter. Refer to these resources as students progress through the chapter.

Introduce the Chapter gives you a short list of the chapter's main topics. Discussion Starter activities help activate your students' prior knowledge of important chapter ideas.

Print Resources and Technology Toolbox allow you to quickly see the resources that are available to you to enhance student learning.

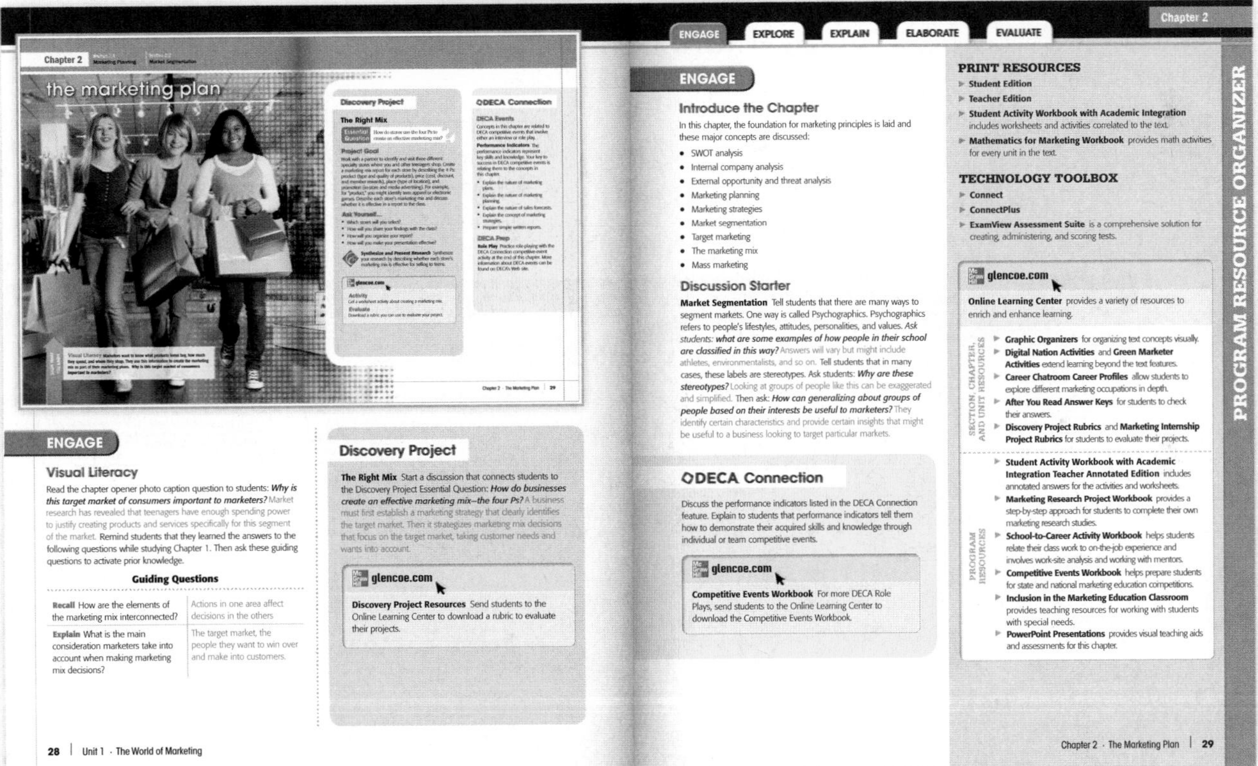

Chapter 2

the marketing plan

ENGAGE

Visual Literacy

Read the chapter opener photo caption question to students: ***Why is this target market of consumers important to marketers?*** Market research has revealed that teenagers have enough spending power to justify creating products and services specifically for this segment of the market. Remind students that they learned the answers to the following questions while studying Chapter 1. Then ask these guiding questions to activate prior knowledge.

Guiding Questions

Recall How are the elements of the marketing mix interconnected?	Actions in one area affect decisions in the others.
Explain What is the main consideration marketers take into account when making marketing mix decisions?	The target market, the people they want to win over and make into customers.

Discovery Project

The Right Mix Start a discussion that connects students to the Discovery Project Essential Question: ***How do businesses create an effective marketing mix—the four Ps?*** A business must first establish a marketing strategy that clearly identifies the target market. Then it strategizes marketing mix decisions that focus on the target market, taking customer needs and wants into account.

glencoe.com

Discovery Project Resources Send students to the Online Learning Center to download a rubric to evaluate their projects.

28 | Unit 1 · The World of Marketing

ENGAGE EXPLORE EXPLAIN ELABORATE EVALUATE

ENGAGE

Introduce the Chapter

In this chapter, the foundation for marketing principles is laid and these major concepts are discussed:

- SWOT analysis
- Internal company analysis
- External opportunity and threat analysis
- Marketing planning
- Marketing strategies
- Market segmentation
- Target marketing
- The marketing mix
- Mass marketing

Discussion Starter

Market Segmentation Tell students that there are many ways to segment markets. One way is called Psychographics. Psychographics refers to people's lifestyles, attitudes, personalities, and values. Ask students: ***what are some examples of how people in their school are classified in this way?*** Answers will vary but might include athletes, environmentalists, and so on. Tell students that in many cases, these labels are stereotypes. Ask students: ***Why are these stereotypes?*** Looking at groups of people like this can be exaggerated and simplified. Then ask: ***How can generalizing about groups of people based on their interests be useful to marketers?*** They identify certain characteristics and provide certain insights that might be useful to a business looking to target particular markets.

DECA Connection

Discuss the performance indicators listed in the DECA Connection feature. Explain to students that performance indicators tell them how to demonstrate their acquired skills and knowledge through individual or team competitive events.

glencoe.com

Competitive Events Workbook For more DECA Role Plays, send students to the Online Learning Center to download the Competitive Events Workbook.

PRINT RESOURCES

- Student Edition
- Teacher Edition
- **Student Activity Workbook with Academic Integration** includes worksheets and activities correlated to the text.
- **Mathematics for Marketing Workbook** provides math activities for every unit in the text.

TECHNOLOGY TOOLBOX

- Connect
- ConnectPlus
- **ExamView Assessment Suite** is a comprehensive solution for creating, administering, and scoring tests.

glencoe.com

Online Learning Center provides a variety of resources to enrich and enhance learning.

SECTION, CHAPTER, AND UNIT RESOURCES

- **Graphic Organizers** for organizing text concepts visually.
- **Digital Nation Activities** and **Green Marketer Activities** extend learning beyond the text features.
- **Career Chatroom Career Profiles** allow students to explore different marketing occupations in depth.
- **After You Read Answer Keys** for students to check their answers.
- **Discovery Project Rubrics** and **Marketing Internship Project Rubrics** for students to evaluate their projects.

PROGRAM RESOURCES

- **Student Activity Workbook with Academic Integration Teacher Annotated Edition** includes annotated answers for the activities and worksheets.
- **Marketing Research Project Workbook** provides a step-by-step approach for students to complete their own marketing research studies.
- **School-to-Career Activity Workbook** helps students relate their class work to on-the-job experience and involves work-site analysis and working with mentors.
- **Competitive Events Workbook** helps prepare students for state and national marketing education competitions.
- **Inclusion in the Marketing Education Classroom** provides teaching resources for working with students with special needs.
- **PowerPoint Presentations** provides visual teaching aids and assessments for this chapter.

PROGRAM RESOURCE ORGANIZER

Chapter 2 · The Marketing Plan | 29

Chapter Project Resources offer you tools for introducing these projects to students. Guiding questions lead students to better grasp marketing topics.

The Teacher and Student Centers of the *Marketing Essentials* Online Learning Center have unit, chapter, and section resources as well as program resources, including workbooks and inclusion strategies.

Section and Chapter Answers

ASSESS STUDENTS' UNDERSTANDING OF KEY CONCEPTS

In the Teacher Edition, you'll find answer keys for all unit Marketing Internship Projects, chapter Review and Activities, and section After You Read assessments.

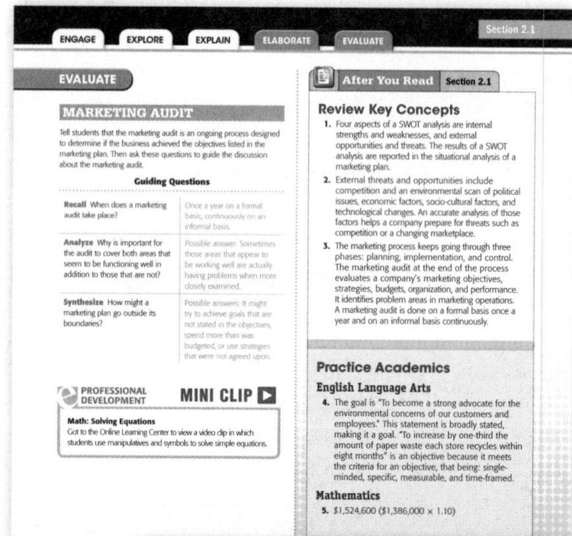

ENGAGE | EXPLORE | EXPLAIN | ELABORATE | EVALUATE — Section 2.1

EVALUATE

MARKETING AUDIT

Tell students that the marketing audit is an ongoing process designed to determine if the business achieved the objectives listed in the marketing plan. Then ask these questions to guide the discussion about the marketing audit.

Guiding Questions

Recall When does a marketing audit take place?	Once a year on a formal basis; continuously on an informal basis.
Analyze Why is important for the audit to cover both areas that seem to be functioning well in addition to those that are not?	Possible answer: Sometimes those areas that appear to be working well are actually having problems when more closely examined.
Synthesize How might a marketing plan go outside its boundaries?	Possible answers: It might try to achieve goals that are not stated in the objectives, spend more than was budgeted, or use strategies that were not agreed upon.

PROFESSIONAL DEVELOPMENT MINI CLIP

Math: Solving Equations
Got to the Online Learning Center to view a video clip in which students use manipulatives and symbols to solve simple equations.

After You Read Section 2.1

Review Key Concepts

1. Four aspects of a SWOT analysis are internal strengths and weaknesses, and external opportunities and threats. The results of a SWOT analysis are reported in the situational analysis of a marketing plan.
2. External threats and opportunities include competition and an environmental scan of political issues, economic factors, socio-cultural factors, and technological changes. An accurate analysis of those factors helps a company prepare for threats such as competition or a changing marketplace.
3. The marketing process keeps going through three phases: planning, implementation, and control. The marketing audit at the end of the process evaluates a company's marketing objectives, strategies, budgets, organization, and performance. It identifies problem areas in marketing operations. A marketing audit is done on a formal basis once a year and on an informal basis continuously.

Practice Academics

English Language Arts

4. The goal is "To become a strong advocate for the environmental concerns of our customers and employees." This statement is broadly stated, making it a goal. "To increase by one-third the amount of paper waste each store recycles within eight months" is an objective because it meets the criteria for an objective, that being: single-minded, specific, measurable, and time-framed.

Mathematics

5. $1,524,600 ($1,386,000 × 1.10)

Section Answer Key is given at the point of reference for each After You Read section review. Students can check their answers at the *Marketing Essentials* Online Learning Center.

Chapter Review and Activities answer key shows answers or sample answers for all activities included in the chapter review.

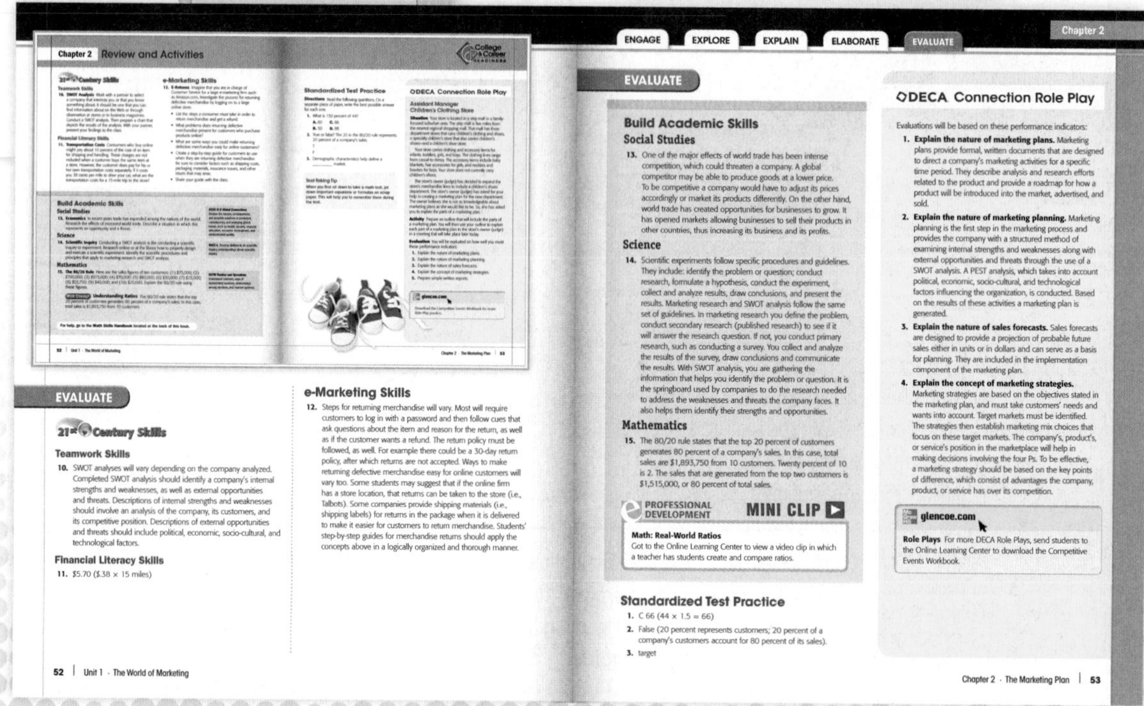

ENGAGE | EXPLORE | EXPLAIN | ELABORATE | EVALUATE — Chapter 2

EVALUATE

21st Century Skills

Teamwork Skills

10. SWOT analyses will vary depending on the company analyzed. Completed SWOT analysis should identify a company's internal strengths and weaknesses, as well as external opportunities and threats. Descriptions of internal strengths and weaknesses should involve an analysis of the company, its customers, and its competitive position. Descriptions of external opportunities and threats should include political, economic, socio-cultural, and technological factors.

Financial Literacy Skills

11. $5.70 ($.38 × 15 miles)

e-Marketing Skills

12. Steps for returning merchandise will vary. Most will require customers to log in with a password and then follow cues that ask questions about the item and reason for the return, as well as if the customer wants a refund. The return policy must be followed, as well. For example there could be a 30-day return policy, after which returns are not accepted. Ways to make returning defective merchandise easy for online customers will vary too. Some students may suggest that if the online firm has a store location, that returns can be taken to the store (i.e., Talbots). Some companies provide shipping materials (i.e., shipping labels) for returns in the package when it is delivered to make it easier for customers to return merchandise. Students' step-by-step guides for merchandise returns should apply the concepts above in a logically organized and thorough manner.

52 | Unit 1 · The World of Marketing

EVALUATE

Build Academic Skills

Social Studies

13. One of the major effects of world trade has been intense competition, which could threaten a company. A global competitor may be able to produce goods at a lower price. To be competitive a company would have to adjust its prices accordingly or market its products differently. On the other hand, world trade has created opportunities for businesses to grow. It has opened markets allowing businesses to sell their products in other countries, thus increasing its business and its profits.

Science

14. Scientific experiments follow specific procedures and guidelines. They include: identify the problem or question; conduct research, formulate a hypothesis, conduct the experiment, collect and analyze results, draw conclusions, and present the results. Marketing research and SWOT analysis follow the same set of guidelines. In marketing research you define the problem, conduct secondary research (published research) to see if it will answer the research question. If not, you conduct primary research, such as conducting a survey. You collect and analyze the results of the survey, draw conclusions and communicate the results. With SWOT analysis, you are gathering the information that helps you identify the problem or question. It is the springboard used by companies to do the research needed to address the weaknesses and threats the company faces. It also helps them identify their strengths and opportunities.

Mathematics

15. The 80/20 rule states that the top 20 percent of customers generates 80 percent of a company's sales. In this case, total sales are $1,893,750 from 10 customers. Twenty percent of 10 is 2. The sales that are generated from the top two customers is $1,515,000, or 80 percent of total sales.

PROFESSIONAL DEVELOPMENT MINI CLIP

Math: Real-World Ratios
Got to the Online Learning Center to view a video clip in which a teacher has students create and compare ratios.

Standardized Test Practice

1. C 66 (44 × 1.5 = 66)
2. False (20 percent represents customers; 20 percent of a company's customers account for 80 percent of its sales).
3. target

DECA Connection Role Play

Evaluations will be based on these performance indicators:

1. **Explain the nature of marketing plans.** Marketing plans provide formal, written documents that are designed to direct a company's marketing activities for a specific time period. They describe analysis and research efforts related to the product and provide a roadmap for how a product will be introduced into the market, advertised, and sold.
2. **Explain the nature of marketing planning.** Marketing planning is the first step in the marketing process and provides the company with a structured method of examining internal strengths and weaknesses along with external opportunities and threats through the use of a SWOT analysis. A PEST analysis, which takes into account political, economic, socio-cultural, and technological factors influencing the organization, is conducted. Based on the results of these activities a marketing plan is generated.
3. **Explain the nature of sales forecasts.** Sales forecasts are designed to provide a projection of probable future sales either in units or in dollars and can serve as a basis for planning. They are included in the implementation component of the marketing plan.
4. **Explain the concept of marketing strategies.** Marketing strategies are based on the objectives stated in the marketing plan, and must take customers' needs and wants into account. Target markets must be identified. The strategies then establish marketing mix choices that focus on these target markets. The company's, product's, or service's position in the marketplace will help in making decisions involving the four Ps. To be effective, a marketing strategy should be based on the key points of difference, which consist of advantages the company, product, or service has over its competition.

glencoe.com

Role Plays For more DECA Role Plays, send students to the Online Learning Center to download the Competitive Events Workbook.

Chapter 2 · The Marketing Plan | 53

Professional Development and Personalized Learning

OPPORTUNITIES FOR TEACHING AND LEARNING

Throughout the Teacher Edition pages, you'll find opportunities for developing your professional teaching skills and offering differentiated instruction for a variety of student learners.

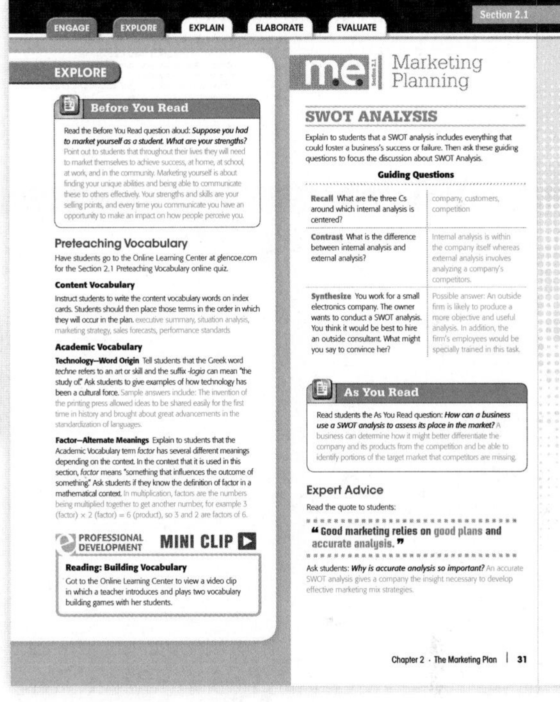

ENGAGE EXPLORE EXPLAIN ELABORATE EVALUATE Section 2.1

EXPLORE

Before You Read

Read the Before You Read question aloud: ***Suppose you had to market yourself as a student. What are your strengths?*** Point out to students that throughout their lives they will need to market themselves to achieve success, at home, at school, at work, and in the community. Marketing yourself is about finding your unique abilities and being able to communicate these to others effectively. Your strengths and skills are your selling points, and every time you communicate you have an opportunity to make an impact on how people perceive you.

Preteaching Vocabulary

Have students go to the Online Learning Center at glencoe.com for the Section 2.1 Preteaching Vocabulary online quiz.

Content Vocabulary

Instruct students to write the content vocabulary words on index cards. Students should then place those terms in the order in which they will occur in the plan. executive summary, situation analysis, marketing strategy, sales forecasts, performance standards

Academic Vocabulary

Technology—Word Origin Tell students that the Greek word *techne* refers to an art or skill and the suffix *-logia* can mean "the study of." Ask students to give examples of how technology has been a cultural force. Sample answers include: The invention of the printing press allowed ideas to be shared easily for the first time in history and brought about great advancements in the standardization of languages.

Factor—Alternate Meanings Explain to students that the Academic Vocabulary term *factor* has several different meanings depending on the context. In the context that it is used in this section, *factor* means "something that influences the outcome of something." Ask students if they know the definition of factor in a mathematical context. In multiplication, factors are the numbers being multiplied together to get another number, for example 3 (factor) × 2 (factor) = 6 (product), so 3 and 2 are factors of 6.

PROFESSIONAL DEVELOPMENT MINI CLIP

Reading: Building Vocabulary

Got to the Online Learning Center to view a video clip in which a teacher introduces and plays two vocabulary building games with her students.

m.e. Section 2.1 Marketing Planning

SWOT ANALYSIS

Explain to students that a SWOT analysis includes everything that could foster a business's success or failure. Then ask these guiding questions to focus the discussion about SWOT Analysis.

Guiding Questions

Recall What are the three Cs around which internal analysis is centered?	company, customers, competition
Contrast What is the difference between internal analysis and external analysis?	Internal analysis is within the company itself whereas external analysis involves analyzing a company's competitors.
Synthesize You work for a small electronics company. The owner wants to conduct a SWOT analysis. You think it would be best to hire an outside consultant. What might you say to convince her?	Possible answer: An outside firm is likely to produce a more objective and useful analysis. In addition, the firm's employees would be specially trained in this task.

As You Read

Read students the As You Read question: ***How can a business use a SWOT analysis to assess its place in the market?*** A business can determine how it might better differentiate the company and its products from the competition and be able to identify portions of the target market that competitors are missing.

Expert Advice

Read the quote to students:

"Good marketing relies on good plans and accurate analysis."

Ask students: ***Why is accurate analysis so important?*** An accurate SWOT analysis gives a company the insight necessary to develop effective marketing mix strategies.

Chapter 2 · The Marketing Plan | 31

Professional Development mini clip videos offer targeted professional development, and are correlated with unit, chapter, and section topics.

Mini Projects make universal access and personalized instruction easy. Suggestions and activities are offered for a variety of teaching strategies, including differentiated instruction to adapt lessons to a variety of learning types, extension projects to expand marketing knowledge, and enrichment to enhance chapter and section information.

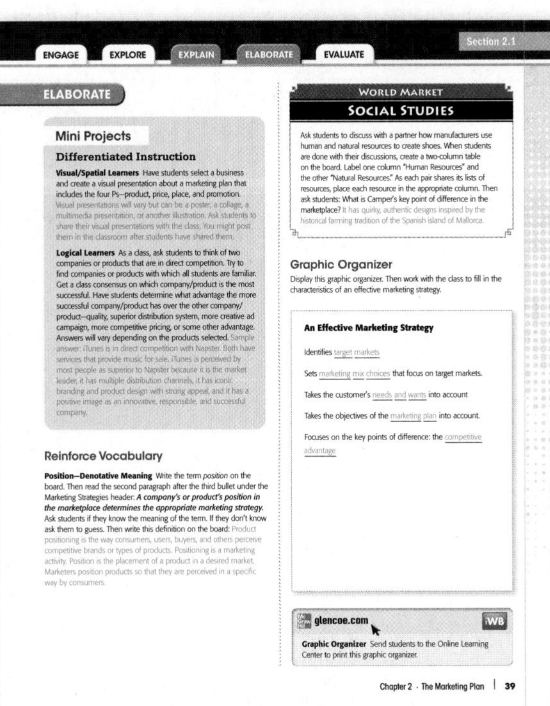

ENGAGE EXPLORE EXPLAIN ELABORATE EVALUATE Section 2.1

ELABORATE

Mini Projects

Differentiated Instruction

Visual/Spatial Learners Have students select a business and create a visual presentation about a marketing plan that includes the four Ps—product, price, place, and promotion. Visual presentations will vary but can be a poster, a collage, a multimedia presentation, or another illustration. Ask students to share their visual presentations with the class. You might post them in the classroom after students have shared them.

Logical Learners As a class, ask students to think of two companies or products that are in direct competition. Try to find companies or products with which all students are familiar. Get a class consensus on which company/product is the most successful. Have students determine what advantage the more successful company/product has over the other company/product—quality, superior distribution system, more creative ad campaign, more competitive pricing, or some other advantage. Answers will vary depending on the products selected. Sample answer: iTunes is in direct competition with Napster. Both have services that provide music for sale. iTunes is perceived by most people as superior to Napster because it is the market leader, it has multiple distribution channels, it has iconic branding and product design with strong appeal, and it has a positive image as an innovative, responsible, and successful company.

Reinforce Vocabulary

Position—Denotative Meaning Write the term *position* on the board. Then read the second paragraph after the third bullet under the Marketing Strategies header: ***A company's or product's position in the marketplace determines the appropriate marketing strategy.*** Ask students if they know the meaning of the term. If they don't know ask them to guess. Then write this definition on the board: Product positioning is the way consumers, users, buyers, and others perceive competitive brands or types of products. Positioning is a marketing activity. Position is the placement of a product in a desired market. Marketers position products so that they are perceived in a specific way by consumers.

WORLD MARKET SOCIAL STUDIES

Ask students to discuss with a partner how manufacturers use human and natural resources to create shoes. When students are done with their discussions, create a two-column table on the board. Label one column "Human Resources" and the other "Natural Resources." As each pair shares its lists of resources, place each resource in the appropriate column. Then ask students: What is Camper's key point of difference in the marketplace? It has quirky, authentic designs inspired by the historical farming tradition of the Spanish island of Mallorca.

Graphic Organizer

Display this graphic organizer. Then work with the class to fill in the characteristics of an effective marketing strategy.

An Effective Marketing Strategy

Identifies target markets

Sets marketing mix choices that focus on target markets.

Takes the customer's needs and wants into account

Takes the objectives of the marketing plan into account.

Focuses on the key points of difference: the competitive advantage

glencoe.com iWB

Graphic Organizer Send students to the Online Learning Center to print this graphic organizer.

Chapter 2 · The Marketing Plan | 39

Engage, Explore, Explain, Elaborate, Evaluate

USE THE FIVE ES TO BUILD STUDENT KNOWLEDGE

The Five Es method of instruction uses the principle that students gain knowledge by continuing to build upon previously learned concepts. ***Marketing Essentials Teacher Edition*** uses the Five Es throughout each chapter and section to ensure that students understand important concepts before moving on.

Explore Students build upon previous knowledge to explore scenarios, ideas, and vocabulary.

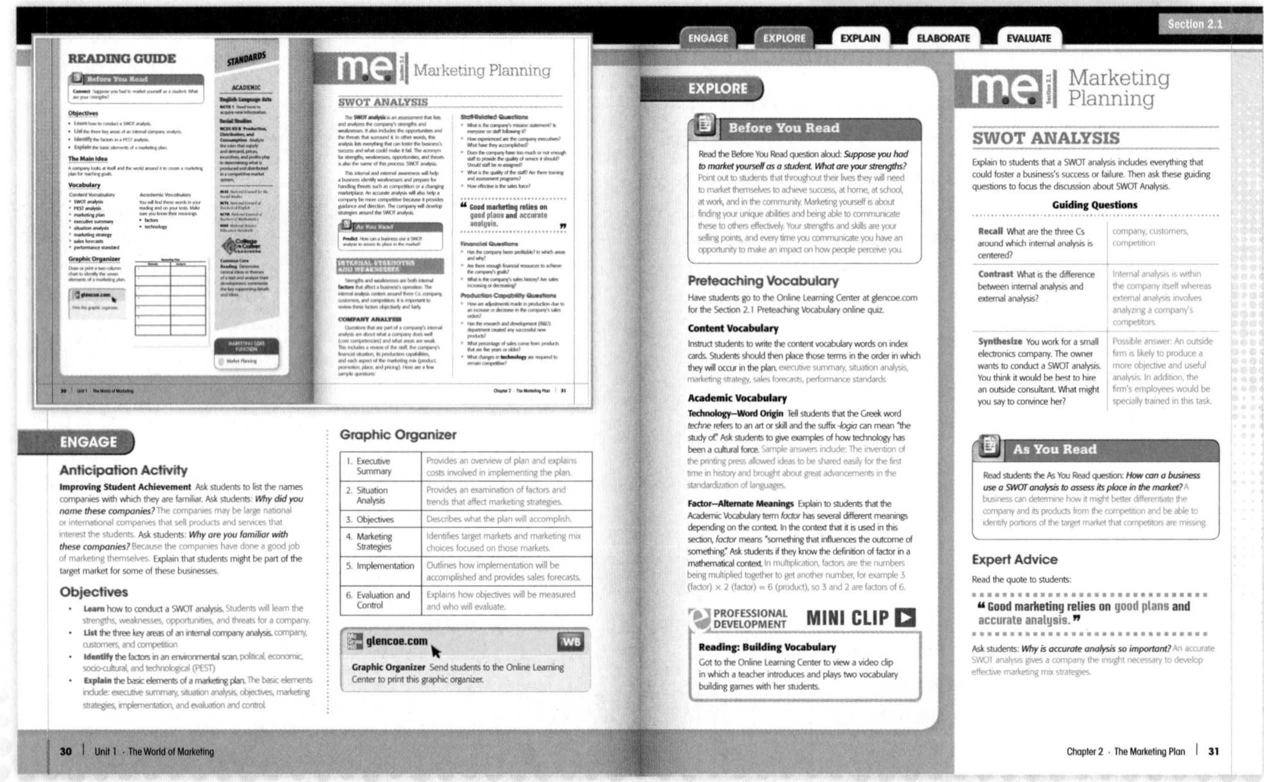

ENGAGE | EXPLORE | EXPLAIN | ELABORATE | EVALUATE

Section 2.1

ENGAGE

Anticipation Activity

Improving Student Achievement Ask students to list the names companies with which they are familiar. Ask students: ***Why did you name these companies?*** The companies may be large national or international companies that sell products and services that interest the students. Ask students: ***Why are you familiar with these companies?*** Because the companies have done a good job of marketing themselves. Explain that students might be part of the target market for some of these businesses.

Objectives

- **Learn** how to conduct a SWOT analysis. Students will learn the strengths, weaknesses, opportunities, and threats for a company.
- **List** the three key areas of an internal company analysis. company, customers, and competition
- **Identify** the factors in an environmental scan. political, economic, socio-cultural, and technological (PEST)
- **Explain** the basic elements of a marketing plan. The basic elements include: executive summary, situation analysis, objectives, marketing strategies, implementation, and evaluation and control.

Graphic Organizer

1. Executive Summary	Provides an overview of plan and explains costs involved in implementing the plan.
2. Situation Analysis	Provides an examination of factors and trends that affect marketing strategies.
3. Objectives	Describes what the plan will accomplish.
4. Marketing Strategies	Identifies target markets and marketing mix choices focused on those markets.
5. Implementation	Outlines how implementation will be accomplished and provides sales forecasts.
6. Evaluation and Control	Explains how objectives will be measured and who will evaluate.

glencoe.com WB

Graphic Organizer Send students to the Online Learning Center to print this graphic organizer.

30 | Unit 1 · The World of Marketing

EXPLORE

Before You Read

Read the Before You Read question aloud: ***Suppose you had to market yourself as a student. What are your strengths?*** Point out to students that throughout their lives they will need to market themselves to achieve success, at home, at school, at work, and in the community. Marketing yourself is about finding your unique abilities and being able to communicate these to others effectively. Your strengths and skills are your selling points, and every time you communicate you have an opportunity to make an impact on how people perceive you.

Preteaching Vocabulary

Have students go to the Online Learning Center at glencoe.com for the Section 2.1 Preteaching Vocabulary online quiz.

Content Vocabulary

Instruct students to write the content vocabulary words on index cards. Students should then place those terms in the order in which they will occur in the plan. executive summary, situation analysis, marketing strategy, sales forecasts, performance standards

Academic Vocabulary

Technology—Word Origin Tell students that the Greek word *techne* refers to an art or skill and the suffix *-logia* can mean "the study of." Ask students to give examples of how technology has been a cultural force. Sample answers include: The invention of the printing press allowed ideas to be shared easily for the first time in history and brought about great advancements in the standardization of languages.

Factor—Alternate Meanings Explain to students that the Academic Vocabulary term *factor* has several different meanings depending on the context. In the context that it is used in this section, *factor* means "something that influences the outcome of something." Ask students if they know the definition of factor in a mathematical context. In multiplication, factors are the numbers being multiplied together to get another number, for example 3 (factor) × 2 (factor) = 6 (product), so 3 and 2 are factors of 6.

PROFESSIONAL DEVELOPMENT **MINI CLIP**

Reading: Building Vocabulary

Got to the Online Learning Center to view a video clip in which a teacher introduces and plays two vocabulary building games with her students.

m.e. Section 2.1 Marketing Planning

SWOT ANALYSIS

Explain to students that a SWOT analysis includes everything that could foster a business's success or failure. Then ask these guiding questions to focus the discussion about SWOT Analysis.

Guiding Questions

Recall What are the three Cs around which internal analysis is centered?	company, customers, competition
Contrast What is the difference between internal analysis and external analysis?	Internal analysis is within the company itself whereas external analysis involves analyzing a company's competitors.
Synthesize You work for a small electronics company. The owner wants to conduct a SWOT analysis. You think it would be best to hire an outside consultant. What might you say to convince her?	Possible answer: An outside firm is likely to produce a more objective and useful analysis. In addition, the firm's employees would be specially trained in this task.

As You Read

Read students the As You Read question: ***How can a business use a SWOT analysis to assess its place in the market?*** A business can determine how it might better differentiate the company and its products from the competition and be able to identify portions of the target market that competitors are missing.

Expert Advice

Read the quote to students:

"Good marketing relies on good plans and accurate analysis."

Ask students: ***Why is accurate analysis so important?*** An accurate SWOT analysis gives a company the insight necessary to develop effective marketing mix strategies.

Chapter 2 · The Marketing Plan | 31

Engage The first step is to engage students in topics by connecting new ideas with past learning experiences. Activities in Engage sections are designed to anticipate topics and grab student interest as the lesson begins.

Engage, Explore, Explain, Elaborate, Evaluate

Explain To ensure that concepts have been learned, students should be asked to explain or demonstrate the ideas they have encountered in the chapter or section. Activities in the Explain section offer you ways to introduce in-depth information on marketing processes and skills.

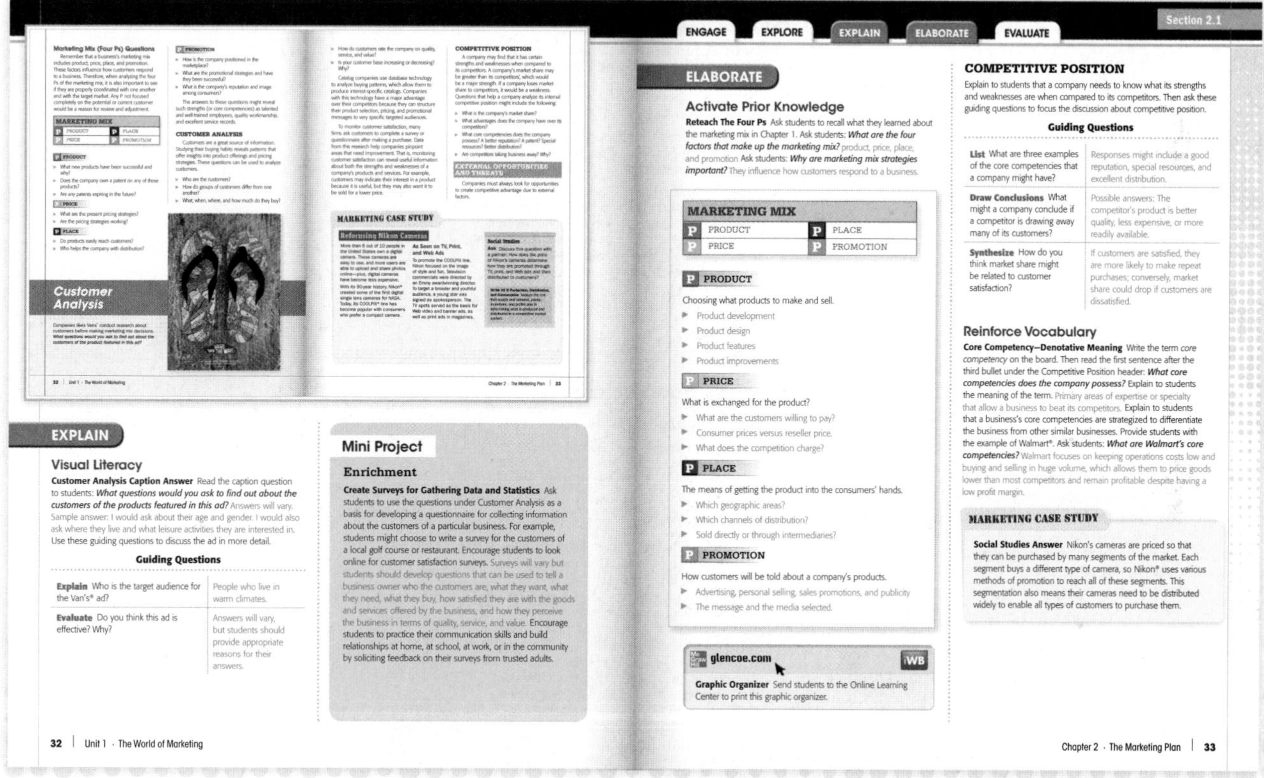

ENGAGE | EXPLORE | EXPLAIN | ELABORATE | EVALUATE

Section 2.1

EXPLAIN

Visual Literacy

Customer Analysis Caption Answer Read the caption question to students: ***What questions would you ask to find out about the customers of the products featured in this ad?*** Answers will vary. Sample answer: I would ask about their age and gender. I would also ask where they live and what leisure activities they are interested in. Use these guiding questions to discuss the ad in more detail.

Guiding Questions

Explain Who is the target audience for the Van's® ad?	People who live in warm climates.
Evaluate Do you think this ad is effective? Why?	Answers will vary, but students should provide appropriate reasons for their answers.

Mini Project

Enrichment

Create Surveys for Gathering Data and Statistics Ask students to use the questions under Customer Analysis as a basis for developing a questionnaire for collecting information about the customers of a particular business. For example, students might choose to write a survey for the customers of a local golf course or restaurant. Encourage students to look online for customer satisfaction surveys. Surveys will vary but students should develop questions that can be used to tell a business owner who the customers are, what they want, what they need, what they buy, how satisfied they are with the goods and services offered by the business, and how they perceive the business in terms of quality, service, and value. Encourage students to practice their communication skills and build relationships at home, at school, at work, or in the community by soliciting feedback on their surveys from trusted adults.

32 | Unit 1 · The World of Marketing

ELABORATE

Activate Prior Knowledge

Reteach The Four Ps Ask students to recall what they learned about the marketing mix in Chapter 1. Ask students: ***What are the four factors that make up the marketing mix?*** product, price, place, and promotion Ask students: ***Why are marketing mix strategies important?*** They influence how customers respond to a business.

MARKETING MIX	
P PRODUCT	P PLACE
P PRICE	P PROMOTION

P PRODUCT

Choosing what products to make and sell.

- Product development
- Product design
- Product features
- Product improvements

P PRICE

What is exchanged for the product?

- What are the customers willing to pay?
- Consumer prices versus reseller price.
- What does the competition charge?

P PLACE

The means of getting the product into the consumers' hands.

- Which geographic areas?
- Which channels of distribution?
- Sold directly or through intermediaries?

P PROMOTION

How customers will be told about a company's products.

- Advertising, personal selling, sales promotions, and publicity
- The message and the media selected.

glencoe.com iWB

Graphic Organizer Send students to the Online Learning Center to print this graphic organizer.

COMPETITIVE POSITION

Explain to students that a company needs to know what its strengths and weaknesses are when compared to its competitors. Then ask these guiding questions to focus the discussion about competitive position.

Guiding Questions

List What are three examples of the core competencies that a company might have?	Responses might include a good reputation, special resources, and excellent distribution.
Draw Conclusions What might a company conclude if a competitor is drawing away many of its customers?	Possible answers: The competitor's product is better quality, less expensive, or more readily available.
Synthesize How do you think market share might be related to customer satisfaction?	If customers are satisfied, they are more likely to make repeat purchases; conversely, market share could drop if customers are dissatisfied.

Reinforce Vocabulary

Core Competency—Denotative Meaning Write the term *core competency* on the board. Then read the first sentence after the third bullet under the Competitive Position header: ***What core competencies does the company possess?*** Explain to students the meaning of the term. Primary areas of expertise or specialty that allow a business to beat its competitors. Explain to students that a business's core competencies are strategized to differentiate the business from other similar businesses. Provide students with the example of Walmart®. Ask students: ***What are Walmart's core competencies?*** Walmart focuses on keeping operations costs low and buying and selling in huge volume, which allows them to price goods lower than most competitors and remain profitable despite having a low profit margin.

MARKETING CASE STUDY

Social Studies Answer Nikon's cameras are priced so that they can be purchased by many segments of the market. Each segment buys a different type of camera, so Nikon® uses various methods of promotion to reach all of these segments. This segmentation also means their cameras need to be distributed widely to enable all types of customers to purchase them.

Chapter 2 · The Marketing Plan | 33

Elaborate Once conceptual learning is confirmed, students can begin to elaborate on that fundamental knowledge by extending their use of marketing concepts.

Engage, Explore, Explain, Elaborate, Evaluate

Evaluate The After You Read answer key in the Evaluate section allows you to check student understanding of main ideas and ensure that students are ready to move on.

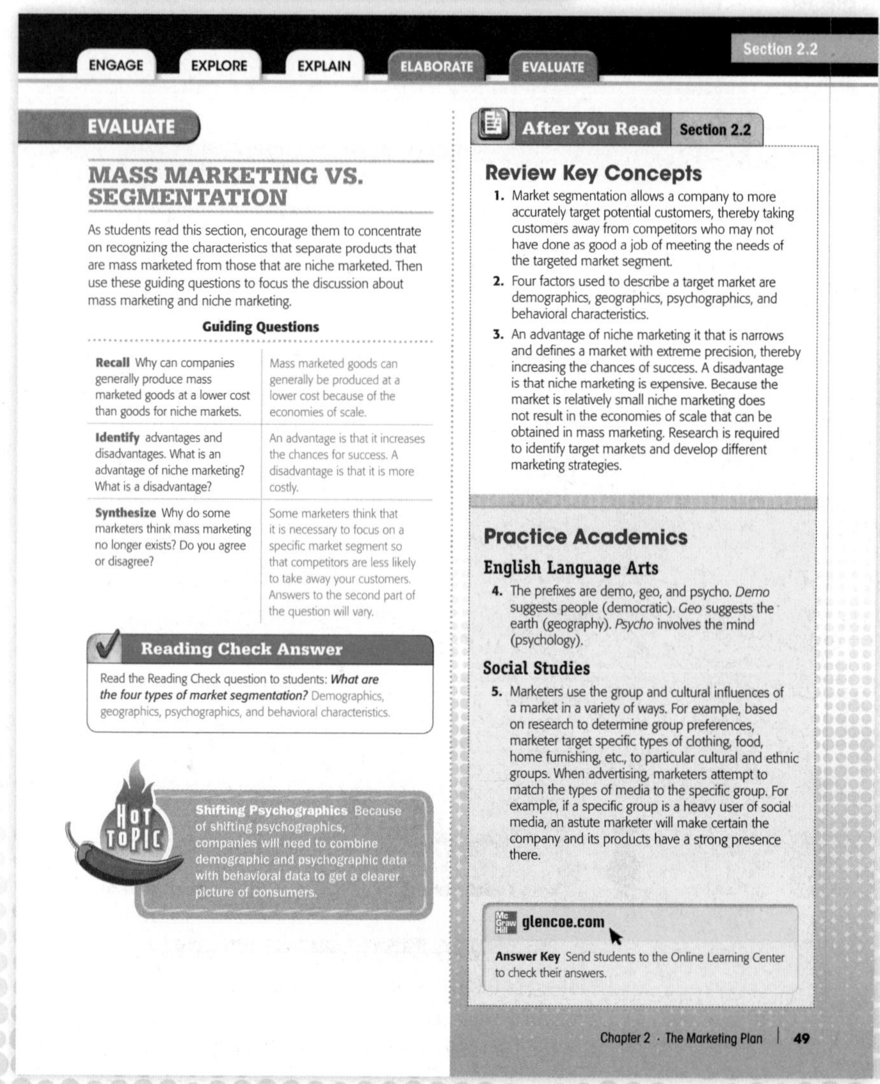
ENGAGE
EXPLORE
EXPLAIN
ELABORATE
EVALUATE
Section 2.2
EVALUATE
MASS MARKETING VS. SEGMENTATION
As students read this section, encourage them to concentrate on recognizing the characteristics that separate products that are mass marketed from those that are niche marketed. Then use these guiding questions to focus the discussion about mass marketing and niche marketing.
Guiding Questions
Recall Why can companies generally produce mass marketed goods at a lower cost than goods for niche markets.
Mass marketed goods can generally be produced at a lower cost because of the economies of scale.
Identify advantages and disadvantages. What is an advantage of niche marketing? What is a disadvantage?
An advantage is that it increases the chances for success. A disadvantage is that it is more costly.
Synthesize Why do some marketers think mass marketing no longer exists? Do you agree or disagree?
Some marketers think that it is necessary to focus on a specific market segment so that competitors are less likely to take away your customers. Answers to the second part of the question will vary.
Reading Check Answer
Read the Reading Check question to students: What are the four types of market segmentation? Demographics, geographics, psychographics, and behavioral characteristics.
HOT TOPIC
Shifting Psychographics Because of shifting psychographics, companies will need to combine demographic and psychographic data with behavioral data to get a clearer picture of consumers.
After You Read Section 2.2
Review Key Concepts
1. Market segmentation allows a company to more accurately target potential customers, thereby taking customers away from competitors who may not have done as good a job of meeting the needs of the targeted market segment.
2. Four factors used to describe a target market are demographics, geographics, psychographics, and behavioral characteristics.
3. An advantage of niche marketing it that is narrows and defines a market with extreme precision, thereby increasing the chances of success. A disadvantage is that niche marketing is expensive. Because the market is relatively small niche marketing does not result in the economies of scale that can be obtained in mass marketing. Research is required to identify target markets and develop different marketing strategies.
Practice Academics
English Language Arts
4. The prefixes are demo, geo, and psycho. Demo suggests people (democratic). Geo suggests the earth (geography). Psycho involves the mind (psychology).
Social Studies
5. Marketers use the group and cultural influences of a market in a variety of ways. For example, based on research to determine group preferences, marketer target specific types of clothing, food, home furnishing, etc., to particular cultural and ethnic groups. When advertising, marketers attempt to match the types of media to the specific group. For example, if a specific group is a heavy user of social media, an astute marketer will make certain the company and its products have a strong presence there.
glencoe.com
Answer Key Send students to the Online Learning Center to check their answers.
Chapter 2 · The Marketing Plan | 49

Student Activity Workbook

The Student Activity Workbook contains a variety of worksheets and activities correlated to each chapter in the text. These worksheets and activities will help reinforce the chapter content, increasing students' comprehension. The Student Activity Workbook offers students a chance to apply what they have learned and to use their critical thinking skills.

- Note-Taking
- Real-World Applications
- Study Skills
- DECA Connection Role Plays
- Academics Activities
- Chapter Vocabulary Activities
- Test-Taking

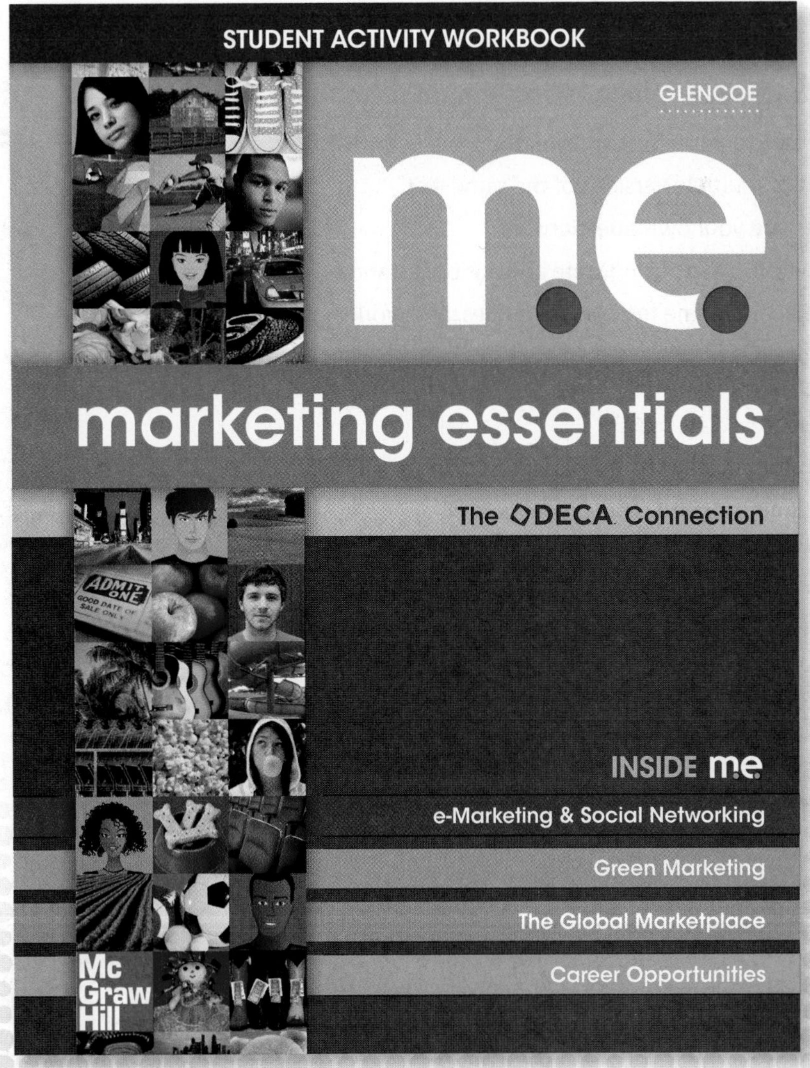

Technology Solutions

EXAMVIEW® ASSESSMENT SUITE

Streamline assessment from start to finish with the ExamView® Assessment Suite CD. This easy-to-use software allows teachers to customize and create unique quizzes, chapter tests, unit tests, midterm exams, and final exams. The ExamView® Assessment Suite works across platforms, on the Web, and across a local area network. It offers teachers a comprehensive solution that allows them to administer and score tests. The test banks, which are organized by unit and chapter, use a variety of question types to improve assessment.

Use the ExamView® Assessment Suite to:

- Create a paper test in fewer than five minutes.
- Print multiple versions of the same test.
- Create your own questions.
- Develop tests using state and national standards.
- Prepare online tests, study guides, and worksheets.

Use the ExamView® Test Manager to:

- Create a class roster.
- Automatically score a paper test using a scanner.
- Administer and score an online test.
- Prepare a variety of useful class and student reports.

VIRTUAL BUSINESS®

Virtual Business is an exciting visual business simulation to integrate into your business and personal finance classroom. By playing Virtual Business, your students will find learning how to run a real-world business energizing, motivating, and most importantly, educational. Correlations to Virtual Business lessons can be found in the teacher lesson plans.

McGraw Hill connect™ for the Student

If you have CONNECT online access then you can get supplementary resources for *Marketing Essentials* through CONNECT. This innovative Web-based program is designed to help students succeed in their coursework and in the workplace.

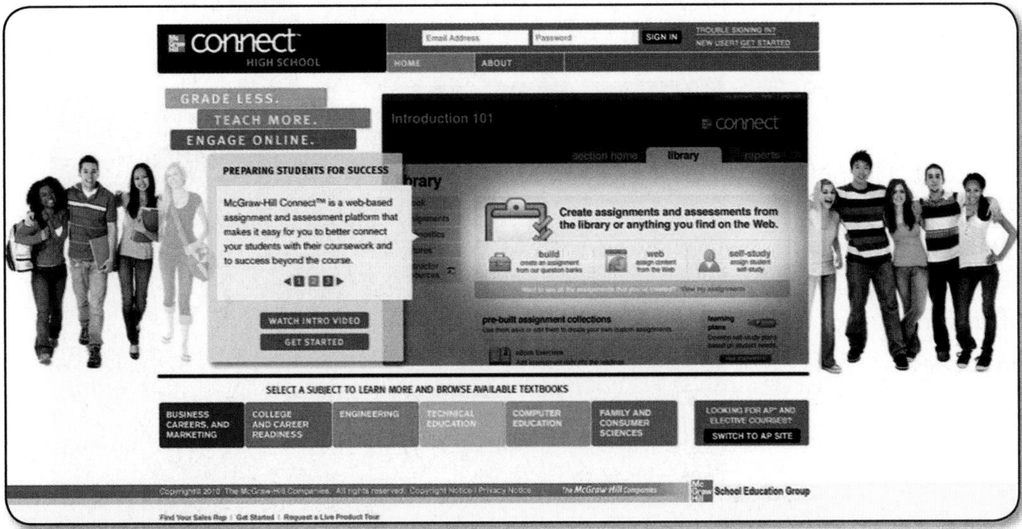

CONNECT

Students can use Connect to access the *Marketing Essentials* course home page.

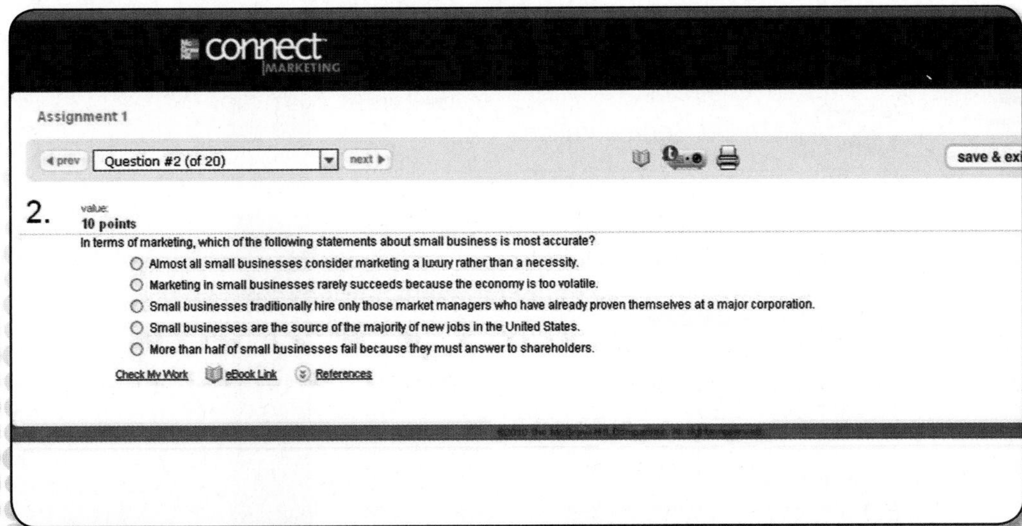

LEARN

- Complete homework online.
- Get immediate feedback on work.
- Link back to sections of the book to review marketing concepts.

EASY TO ACCESS!

CONNECT TO GLENCOE *MARKETING ESSENTIALS* AT MCGRAWHILLCONNECT.COM/K12

SUCCEED

Students can use CONNECT to access the *Marketing Essentials* Online Learning Center for these resources:

- Unit videos
- Self-checks
- Practice tests
- Chapter Summaries
- Chapter Visual Summaries with Content and Academic Vocabulary
- Chapter Graphic Organizers
- Chapter Games and Puzzles

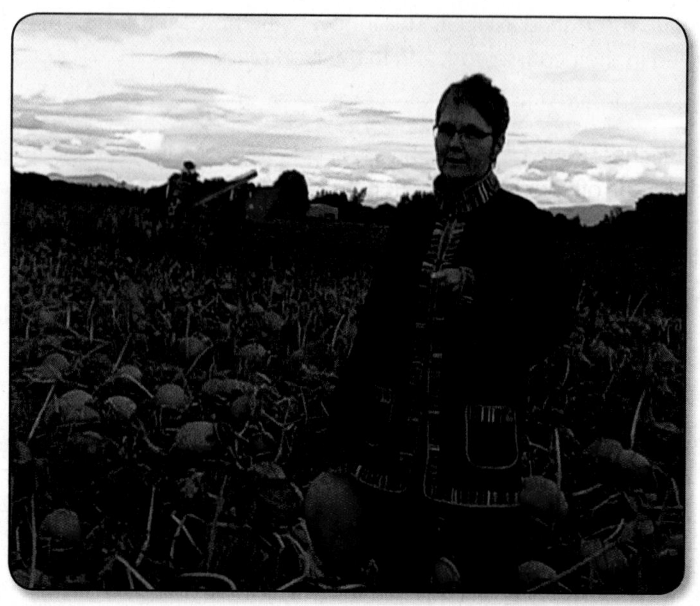

Access the eBook anywhere!

- Store class notes.
- Highlight and bookmark material online.
- Full book coverage, including all topics and every relevant figure from the textbook.

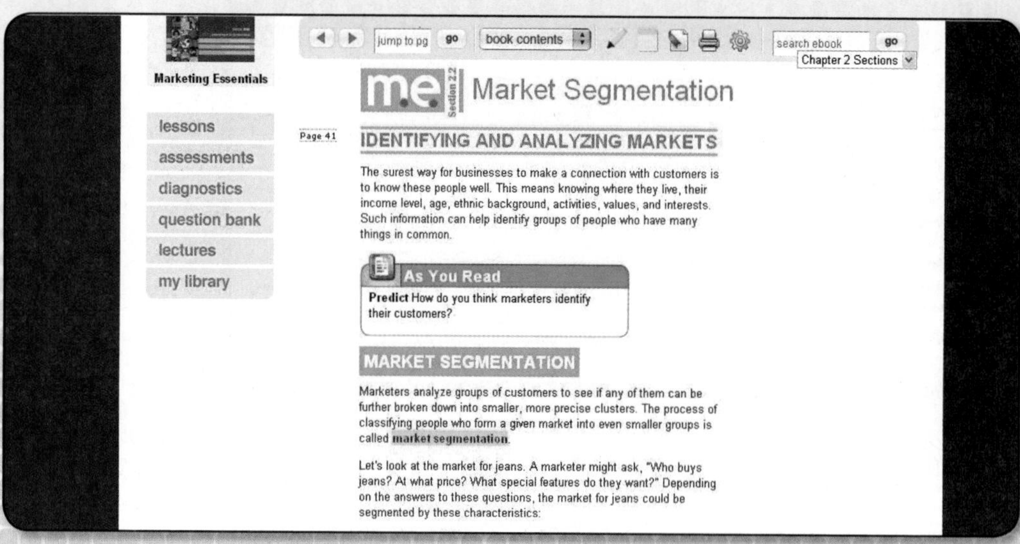

with ConnectPlus

McGraw Hill connect™ for the Teacher

CONNECT is an easy-to-use content-delivery platform that enables you to create, deliver, grade, and track results from your students.

PERSONALIZE

The Teacher Home page provides quick access to all of your course section tasks, communicating to your students and managing assignments for your class. From the Home page you can

- organize your assignments.
- access Web activities.
- subscribe to news feeds with course related news.
- add Web bookmarks to save important course related Web sites.
- post and manage messages to students.

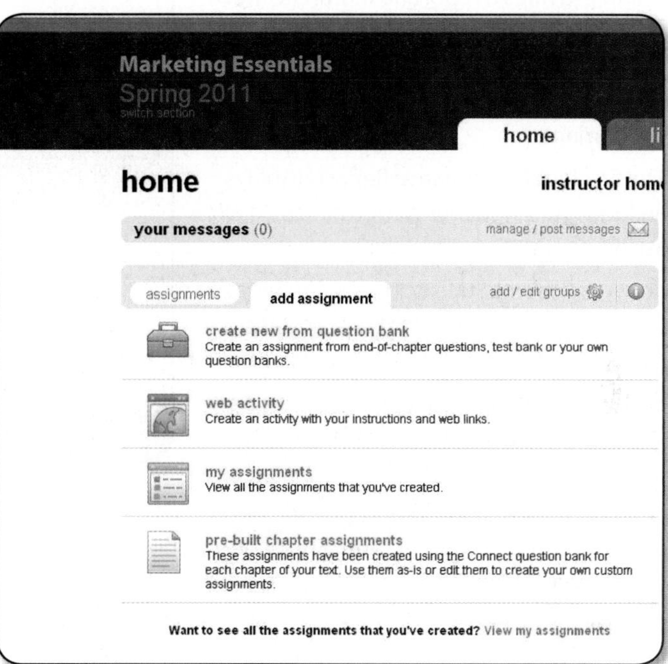

CREATE ASSIGNMENTS

CONNECT provides easy access to an Assignment Builder to allow you to create assignments from question banks or create your own questions. CONNECT provides several types of assignments including

- homework
- practice assignments
- quizzes
- exams

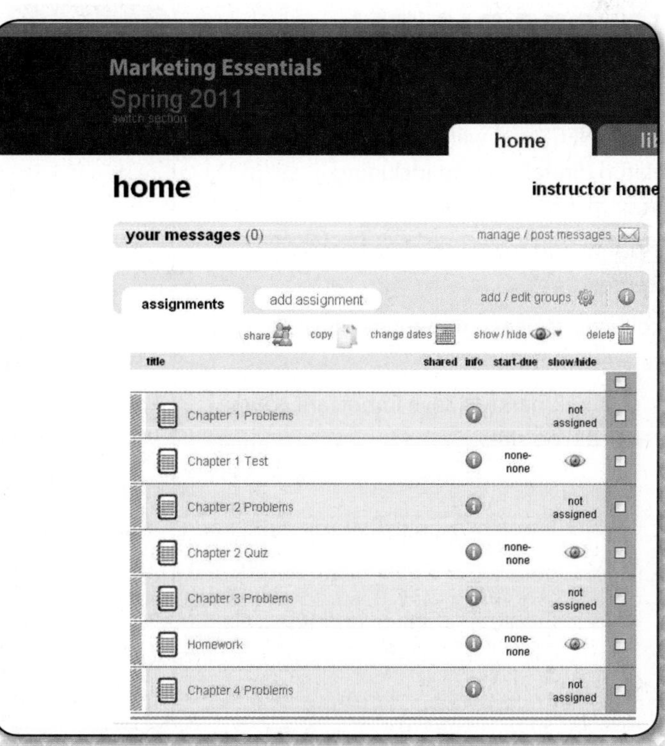

EVALUATE PERFORMANCE

Once your students have submitted their assignments, CONNECT automatically grades them and provides a reporting feature to view several types of customizable grade reports.

- The Assignment Results report provides a list of all students and their scores on each assignment.
- The Student Performance Report displays an individual student's performance on all assignments.
- The Assignment Statistics report provides a set of common assignment report statistics such as high score, low score, or mean score.
- The Item Analysis report provides statistics on each question within a single assignment.
- The Category Analysis report provides statistics on each content category among assignments.

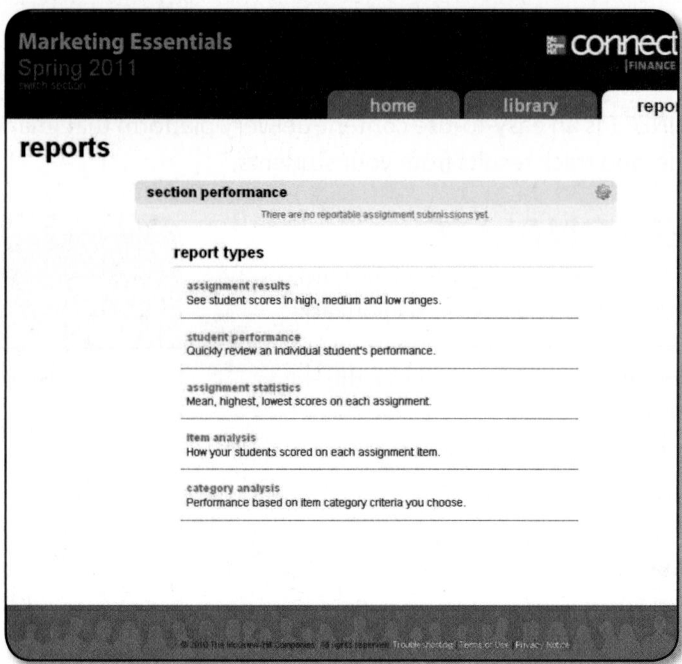

EXPLORE DIGITAL CONTENT

With CONNECT you will have access to a wealth of related digital content including

- your recorded lectures.
- student and teacher Online Learning Centers.
- collections of assignment banks and other related information.
- Web bookmarks to save important course related Web sites.

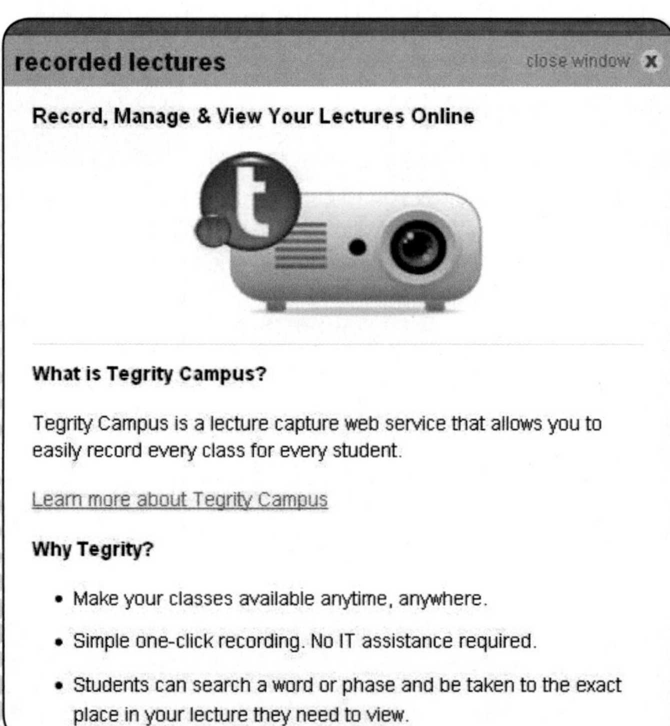

How to Access the Online Learning Center

If you are not using Connect online, follow these steps to access the textbook resources at the *Marketing Essentials* Online Learning Center.

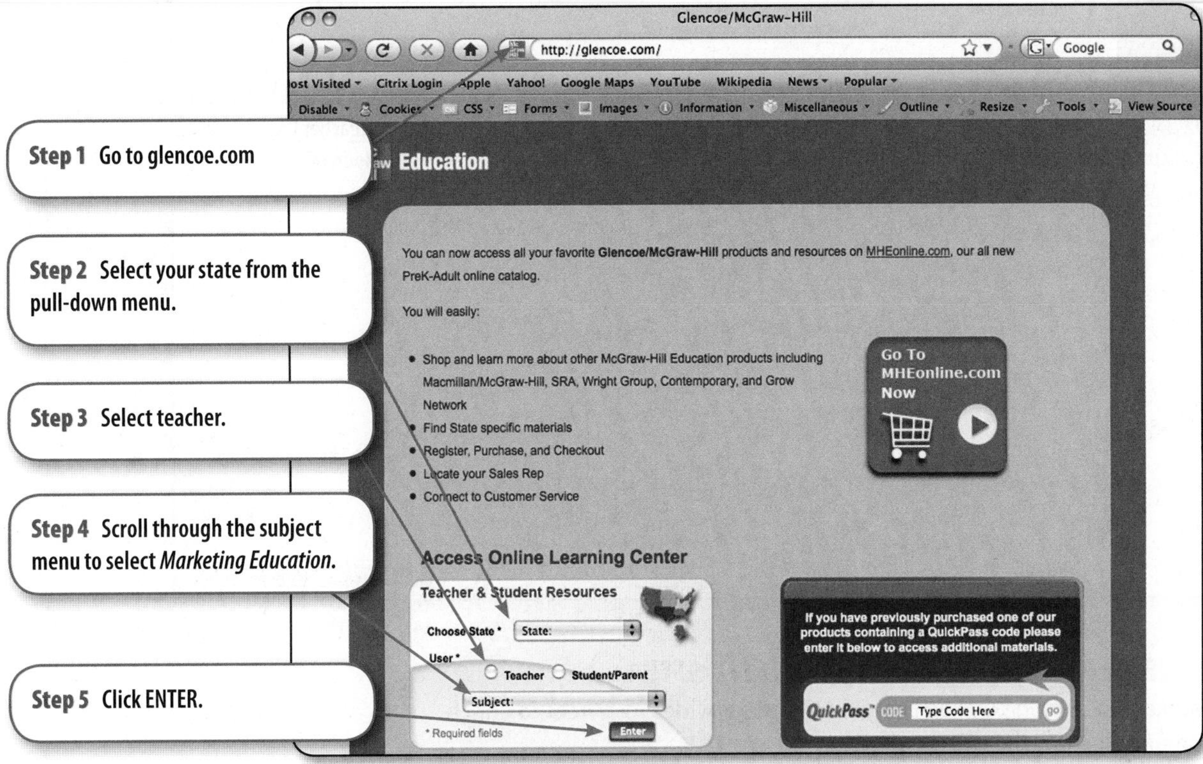

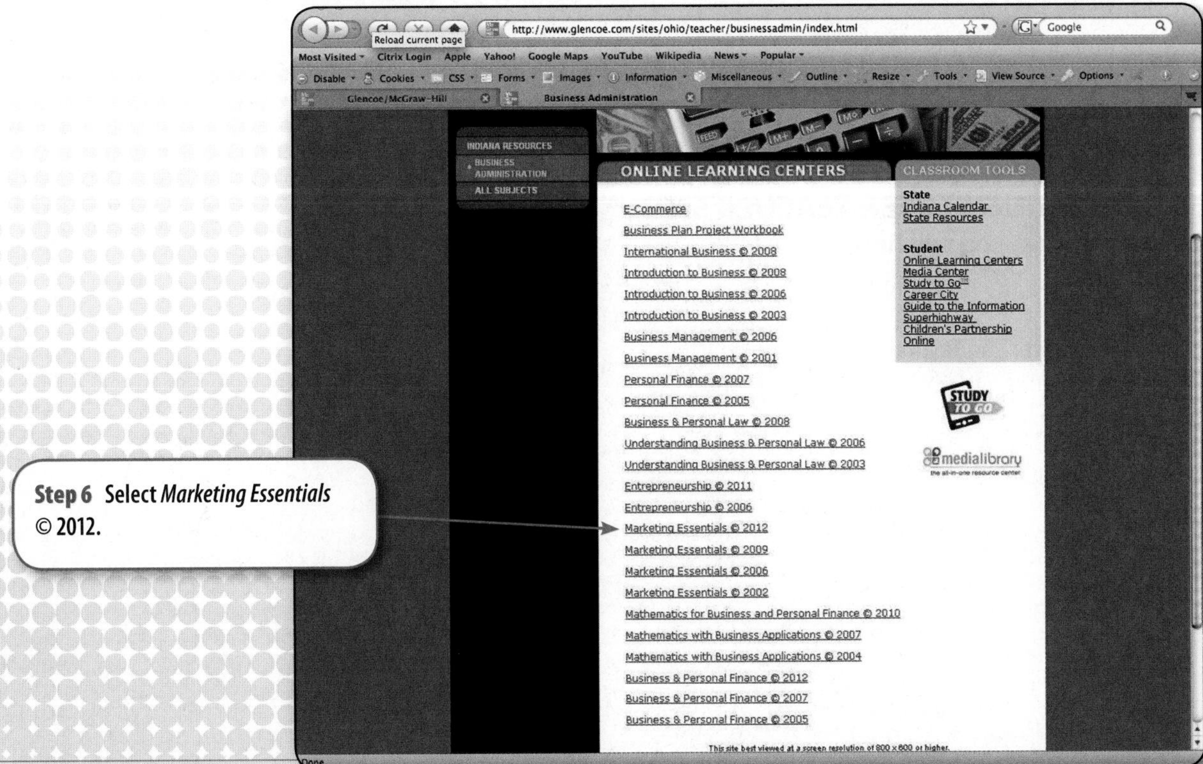

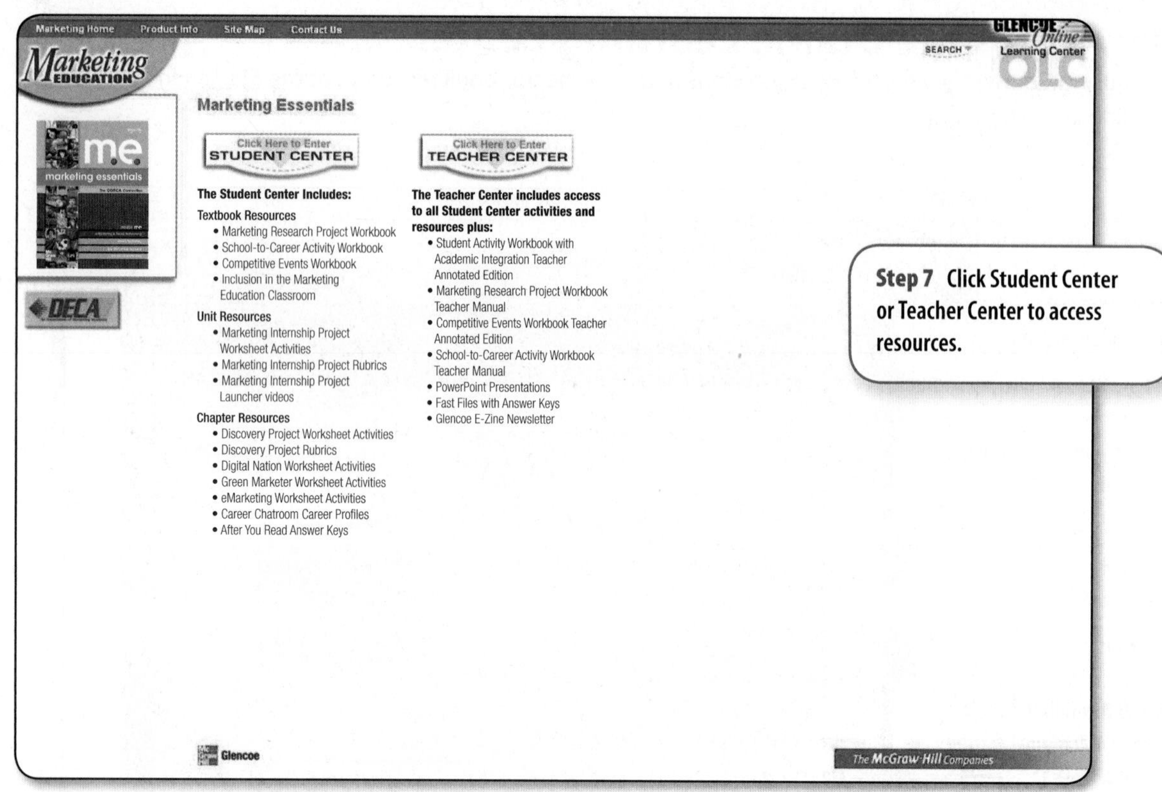

ONLINE LEARNING CENTER STUDENT SITE

The *Marketing Essentials* Online Learning Center provides resources to enrich and enhance learning.

The student site includes

- Lesson Summaries with Content Vocabulary and Academic Vocabulary
- Graphic organizers
- Interactive chapter practice tests
- Enrichment activities

ONLINE LEARNING CENTER TEACHER SITE

On the teacher site, you will find

- Lesson plans
- Rubrics
- Answers and answer suggestions
- Enrichment activities

Technology Resources on the Online Learning Center

These resources can be accessed on the *Marketing Essentials* Online Learning Center Teacher Center.

STUDENT ACTIVITY WORKBOOK WITH ACADEMIC INTEGRATION TEACHER ANNOTATED EDITION

The Student Activity Workbook with Academic Integration Teacher Annotated Edition includes annotated answers for all of the Workbook activities.

POWERPOINT® PRESENTATIONS

The PowerPoint® presentations provide visually motivating presentations that are helpful to both students and teachers. The presentations target key concepts by highlighting important text, providing graphic organizers, and utilizing visuals from the textbook.

Teachers can use the presentations to:

- Preview important concepts at the beginning of a new chapter or lesson
- Provide differentiated instruction for visual learners
- Create a customized learning experience for students

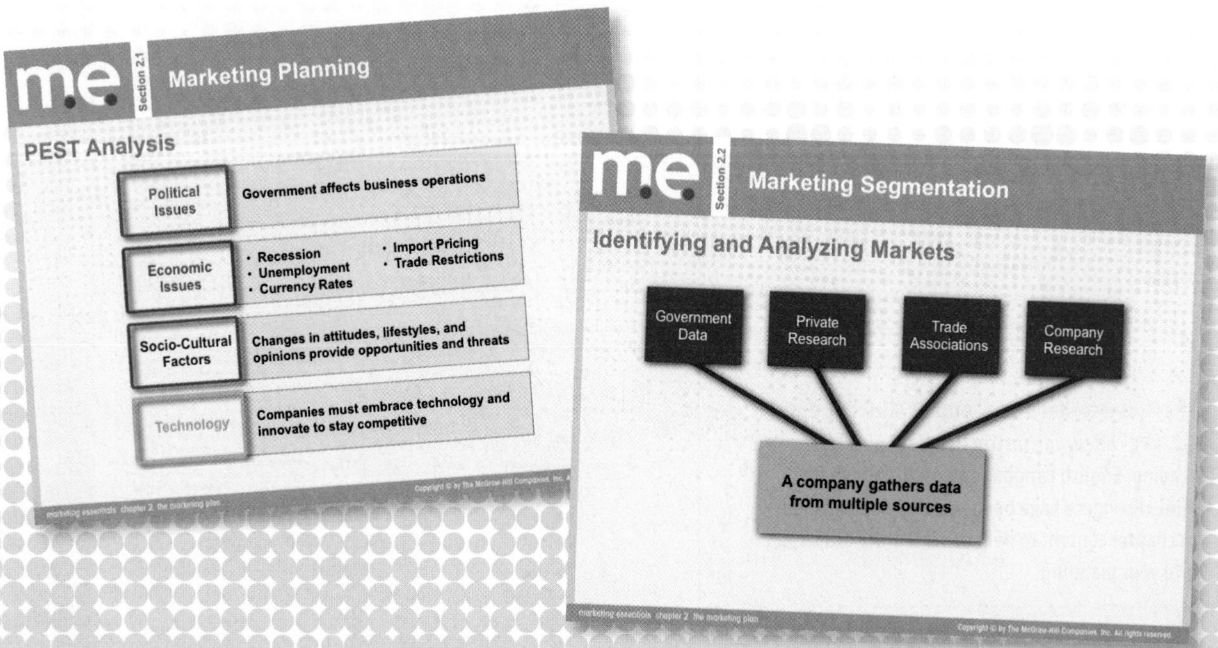

Glencoe and Professional Development

Perkins IV has placed more emphasis than ever on providing quality professional development for Career and Technology educators. The legislation mandates that the focus of professional development be the integration and reinforcement of academic competencies in order to improve student achievement. Specifically, Perkins requires measurements of students' academic success.

To support educators in their efforts to meet new professional development requirements, Glencoe now offers a new resource, *Glencoe's Online Professional Development for Integrating Academics.* This program offers a suite of online products designed to help teachers become more effective in teaching and reinforcing academic skills. The focus of this program is on instructional strategies that can help educators integrate challenging academic content seamlessly into their technical curriculum. These teaching strategies zero in on

- Math
- Reading
- English Language Arts
- Differentiated Instruction
- English Language Learners Instruction

GLENCOE'S ONLINE PROFESSIONAL DEVELOPMENT FOR INTEGRATING ACADEMICS

1. Professional Development Accredited Online Courses (Academic Credit available through Adams University)
2. Professional Development Web Site
3. Video Workshops
4. Mini-Clip Video Library
5. McGraw-Hill Experienced Consultants

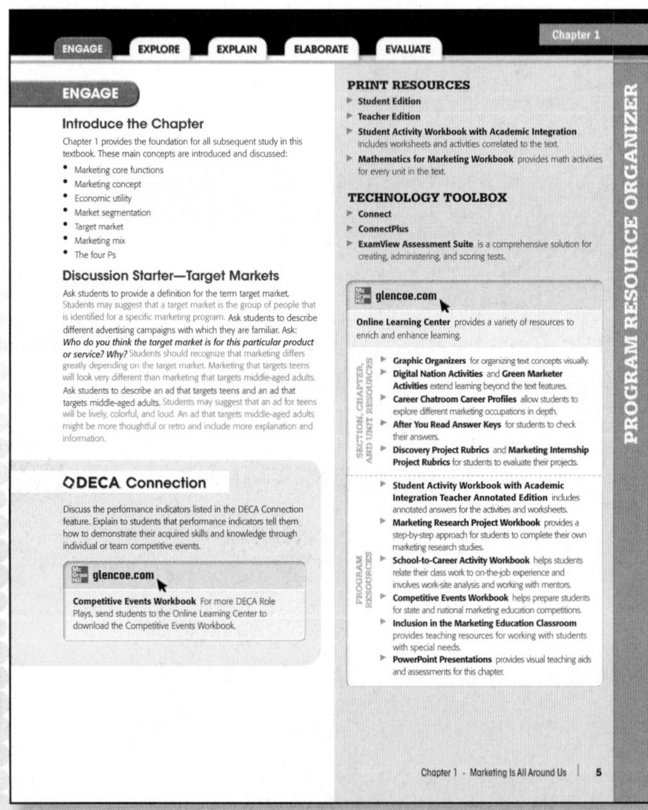

ENGAGE | EXPLORE | EXPLAIN | ELABORATE | EVALUATE

Chapter 1

ENGAGE

Introduce the Chapter

Chapter 1 provides the foundation for all subsequent study in this textbook. These main concepts are introduced and discussed:

- Marketing core functions
- Marketing concept
- Economic utility
- Market segmentation
- Target market
- Marketing mix
- The four Ps

Discussion Starter—Target Markets

Ask students to provide a definition for the term target market. Students may suggest that a target market is the group of people that is identified for a specific marketing program. Ask students to describe different advertising campaigns with which they are familiar. Ask: ***Who do you think the target market is for this particular product or service? Why?*** Students should recognize that marketing differs greatly depending on the target market. Marketing that targets teens will look very different than marketing that targets middle-aged adults. Ask students to describe an ad that targets teens and an ad that targets middle-aged adults. Students may suggest that an ad for teens will be lively, colorful, and loud. An ad that targets middle-aged adults might be more thoughtful or retro and include more explanation and information.

DECA Connection

Discuss the performance indicators listed in the DECA Connection feature. Explain to students that performance indicators tell them how to demonstrate their acquired skills and knowledge through individual or team competitive events.

glencoe.com

Competitive Events Workbook For more DECA Role Plays, send students to the Online Learning Center to download the Competitive Events Workbook.

PRINT RESOURCES

- **Student Edition**
- **Teacher Edition**
- **Student Activity Workbook with Academic Integration** includes worksheets and activities correlated to the text.
- **Mathematics for Marketing Workbook** provides math activities for every unit in the text.

TECHNOLOGY TOOLBOX

- **Connect**
- **ConnectPlus**
- **ExamView Assessment Suite** is a comprehensive solution for creating, administering, and scoring tests.

glencoe.com

Online Learning Center provides a variety of resources to enrich and enhance learning.

SECTION, CHAPTER, AND UNIT RESOURCES

- **Graphic Organizers** for organizing text concepts visually.
- **Digital Nation Activities** and **Green Marketer Activities** extend learning beyond the text features.
- **Career Chatroom Career Profiles** allow students to explore different marketing occupations in depth.
- **After You Read Answer Keys** for students to check their answers.
- **Discovery Project Rubrics** and **Marketing Internship Project Rubrics** for students to evaluate their projects.

PROGRAM RESOURCES

- **Student Activity Workbook with Academic Integration Teacher Annotated Edition** includes annotated answers for the activities and worksheets.
- **Marketing Research Project Workbook** provides a step-by-step approach for students to complete their own marketing research studies.
- **School-to-Career Activity Workbook** helps students relate their class work to on-the-job experience and involves work-site analysis and working with mentors.
- **Competitive Events Workbook** helps prepare students for state and national marketing education competitions.
- **Inclusion in the Marketing Education Classroom** provides teaching resources for working with students with special needs.
- **PowerPoint Presentations** provides visual teaching aids and assessments for this chapter.

PROGRAM RESOURCE ORGANIZER

Chapter 1 · Marketing Is All Around Us | 5

For further pricing and ordering information, go to mcgraw-hill-pd-online.com.

The Professional Development Mini Clip Video Library offers you instructional support for reading, English Language Learners, and math. Mini-clip videos have been selected and matched to chapter content to help you integrate academics into your planning.

National English Language Arts Standards

To help incorporate literacy skills (reading, writing, listening, and speaking) into *Marketing Essentials,* each chapter contains a listing of the language arts skills covered. These skills have been developed into standards by the *National Council of Teachers of English.*

National Council of Teachers of English Standards		
NCTE 1	Students read a wide range of print and non-print texts to build an understanding of texts, of themselves, and of the cultures of the United States and the world; to acquire new information; to respond to the needs and demands of society and the workplace; and for personal fulfillment. Among these texts are fiction and nonfiction, classic and contemporary works.	12, 30, 42, 70, 92, 122, 136, 164, 174, 198, 212, 218, 240, 284, 296, 372, 394, 404, 411, 418, 426, 440, 466, 475, 476, 481, 484, 492, 502, 514, 518, 523, 524, 529, 539, 556, 563, 564, 573, 674, 688, 695, 698, 706, 715, 716, 723, 726, 730, 737, 738, 745, 748, 752, 759, 760, 767, 770, 798, 803, 804, 811, 814, 818, 827, 838, 850, 861, 864
NCTE 3	Students apply a wide range of strategies to comprehend, interpret, evaluate, and appreciate texts. They draw on their prior experience, their interactions with other readers and writers, their knowledge of word meaning and of other texts, their word identification strategies, and their understanding of textual features (e.g., sound-letter correspondence, sentence structure, context, graphics).	11, 15, 16, 23, 26, 41, 49, 60, 69, 115, 146, 171, 242, 276, 289, 306, 316, 329, 404, 411, 414, 576, 626, 637, 698, 818, 828, 835, 838, 842, 849, 864
NCTE 4	Students adjust their use of spoken, written, and visual language (e.g., conventions, style, vocabulary) to communicate effectively with a variety of audiences and for different purposes.	6, 54, 87, 106, 132, 144, 158, 190, 201, 204, 232, 236, 252, 255, 259, 270, 288, 305, 313, 320, 325, 326, 333, 340, 348, 386, 433, 452, 459, 478, 486, 532, 578, 721, 772, 794, 866, 914
NCTE 5	Students employ a wide range of strategies as they write and use different writing process elements appropriately to communicate with different audiences for a variety of purposes.	197, 198, 205, 301, 347, 388, 501, 536, 543, 646, 778, 780
NCTE 7	Students conduct research on issues and interests by generating ideas and questions, and by posing problems. They gather, evaluate, and synthesize data from a variety of sources (e.g., print and non-print texts, artifacts, people) to communicate their discoveries in ways that suit their purpose and audience.	54, 66, 90, 106, 158, 173, 186, 232, 245, 256, 265, 268, 270, 281, 303, 388, 486, 578, 638, 643, 648, 662, 667, 700, 772, 804, 806, 822, 866, 914
NCTE 8	Students use a variety of technological and information resources (e.g., libraries, databases, computer networks, video) to gather and synthesize information and to create and communicate knowledge.	212, 217, 228, 364, 371, 379, 380, 462, 492, 662, 669, 678, 681, 700, 872, 879, 881, 888, 898, 900, 909
NCTE 9	Students develop an understanding of and respect for diversity in language use, patterns, and dialects across cultures, ethnic groups, geographic regions, and social roles	104, 193, 648, 662, 671
NCTE 12	Students use spoken, written, and visual language to accomplish their own purposes (e.g., for learning, enjoyment, persuasion, and the exchange of information).	190, 208, 225, 239, 248, 252, 353, 357, 383, 401, 422, 423, 431, 442, 498, 507, 544, 549, 552, 564, 566, 569, 604, 611, 612, 614, 688, 692, 709, 730, 736, 752, 756, 784, 787, 798, 801, 892, 895, 912

National Math Standards

Students also have opportunities to practice math skills indicated by standards developed by the *National Council of Teachers of Mathematics.*

National Council of Teachers of Mathematics Standards*		
Number and Operations	Understand numbers, ways of representing numbers, relationships among numbers, and number systems.	10, 11, 15, 23, 26, 41, 52, 69, 77, 80, 91, 101, 145, 151, 164, 172, 173, 183, 190, 197, 212, 218, 225, 232, 252, 255, 283, 289, 333, 347, 357, 360, 372, 379, 380, 411, 425, 589, 604, 610, 804, 811, 828, 835
	Understand meanings of operations and how they relate to one another.	104, 121, 132, 186, 459, 502, 507, 612, 619, 654, 661, 678, 687, 706, 715, 730, 737
	Compute fluently and make reasonable estimates.	12, 67, 129, 256, 261, 265, 305, 383, 403, 409, 451, 462, 475, 481, 484, 501, 510, 523, 528, 532, 556, 563, 584, 600, 622, 626, 632, 646, 698, 726, 738, 745, 748, 752, 759, 798, 803, 850, 854, 864, 888, 912
Algebra	Represent and analyze mathematical situations and structures using algebraic symbols.	156, 239, 313, 536, 543, 576, 770, 794, 814, 838, 850, 861, 872, 881
	Use mathematical models to represent and understand quantitative relationships.	174, 454, 818, 827, 842, 849
Geometry	Use visualization, spatial reasoning, and geometric modeling to solve problems.	268
Measurement	Understand measurable attributes of objects and the units, systems, and processes of measurement	228, 325, 336, 778, 783, 784, 791
	Apply appropriate techniques, tools, and formulas to determine measurements	198, 205, 316
Data Analysis and Probability	Formulate questions that can be addressed with data and collect, organize, and display relevant data to answer them.	153
	Develop and evaluate inferences and predictions that are based on data.	112
Problem Solving	Apply and adapt a variety of appropriate strategies to solve problems.	208, 245, 248, 292, 386, 552, 604, 611, 626, 637, 662, 671, 688, 695, 723, 760, 767, 892, 897
	Solve problems that arise in mathematics and in other contexts.	217, 364, 371, 376, 414, 499, 536, 544, 547, 549, 564, 573, 590, 592, 597, 629, 638, 643, 662, 666, 760, 765, 766, 842, 845, 882, 885, 898, 909
	Build new mathematical knowledge through problem solving.	436, 529, 674

National Science Standards

Activities in this text are correlated to the *National Science Education Standards* developed by the National Academy of Sciences.

National Science Education Standards		
Content Standard A		26, 52, 156, 316, 360, 469, 510, 552, 600, 622, 646
Content Standard E	Students should develop abilities of technological design, understandings about science and technology.	436, 440, 451, 462, 466, 476, 484, 514, 524, 532, 576, 678, 687, 716, 726, 738, 744, 748, 814
Content Standard F	Students should develop understanding of personal and community health; population growth; natural resources; environmental quality; natural and human-induced hazards; science and technology in local, national, and global challenges.	80, 146, 224, 228, 292, 336, 344, 823

National Social Studies Standards

Activities in *Marketing Essentials* relate to social studies standards developed by the *National Council for Social Studies.*

National Council for the Social Studies Standards		
I. CULTURE		
NCSS I A	Analyze and explain the ways groups, societies, and cultures address human needs and concerns.	6, 125, 426
NCSS I B	Predict how data and experiences may be interpreted by people from diverse cultural perspectives and frames of reference.	101, 706, 712
NCSS I C	Apply an understanding of culture as an integrated whole that explains the functions and interactions of language, literature, the arts, traditions, beliefs and values, and behavior patterns	208
NCSS I F	Interpret patterns of behavior reflecting values and attitudes that contribute or pose obstacles to cross-cultural understanding.	892, 896
II. TIME, CONTINUITY, AND CHANGE		
NCSS II B	Apply key concepts such as time, chronology, causality, change, conflict, and complexity to explain, analyze, and show connections among patterns of historical change and continuity.	850, 857
III. PEOPLE, PLACES, AND ENVIRONMENTS		
NCSS III G	Describe and compare how people create places that reflect culture, human needs, government policy, and current values and ideals as they design and build specialized buildings, neighborhoods, shopping centers, urban centers, industrial parks, and the like.	268, 418, 425, 433

III. PEOPLE, PLACES, AND ENVIRONMENTS *(continued)*		
NCSS III H	Examine, interpret, and analyze physical and cultural patterns and their interactions, such as land use, settlement patterns, cultural transmission of customs and ideas, and ecosystem changes.	778, 783
NCSS III K	Propose, compare, and evaluate alternative policies for the use of land and other resources in communities, regions, nations, and the world.	220
IV. INDIVIDUAL DEVELOPMENT AND IDENTITY		
NCSS IV C	Describe the ways family, religion, gender, ethnicity, nationality, socioeconomic status, and other group and cultural influences contribute to the development of a sense of self.	49, 527, 912
NCSS IV D	Apply concepts, methods, and theories about the study of human growth and development, such as physical endowment, learning, motivation, behavior, perception, and personality.	292, 336, 340
NCSS IV F	Analyze the role of perceptions, attitudes, values, and beliefs in the development of personal identity.	888
V. INDIVIDUALS, GROUPS, AND INSTITUTIONS		
NCSS V A	Apply concepts such as role, status, and social class in describing the connections and interactions of individuals, groups, and institutions in society.	248
NCSS V B	Analyze group and institutional influences on people, events, and elements of culture in both historical and contemporary settings.	122, 394, 403, 414, 510, 564, 570
NCSS V C	Describe the various forms institutions take, and explain how they develop and change over time.	129
NCSS V G	Analyze the extent to which groups and institutions meet individual needs and promote the common good in contemporary and historical settings.	8, 770
VI. POWER, AUTHORITY, AND GOVERNANCE		
NCSS VI B	Explain the purpose of government and analyze how its powers are acquired, used, and justified.	156, 784, 791, 882, 885
NCSS VI C	Analyze and explain ideas and mechanisms to meet needs and wants of citizens, regulate territory, manage conflict, establish order and security, and balance competing conceptions of a just society.	136, 145, 590, 597
NCSS VI D	Compare and analyze the ways nations and organizations respond to conflicts between forces of unity and forces of diversity	892, 897

VII. PRODUCTION, DISTRIBUTION, AND CONSUMPTION		
NCSS VII A	Explain how the scarcity of productive resources (human, capital, technological, and natural) requires the development of economic systems to make decisions about how goods and services are to be produced and distributed.	39, 60, 153
NCSS VII B	Analyze the role that supply and demand, process, incentives, and profits play in determining what is produced and distributed in a competitive market system.	30, 33, 42, 112, 121, 276, 280, 283, 284, 296, 306, 326, 348, 590, 596, 600, 622
NCSS VII D	Describe the relationships among the various economic systems such as households, business firms, banks, government agencies, labor unions, and corporations.	80, 132, 794
NCSS VII G	Compare basic economic systems according to how rules and procedures deal with demand, supply, prices, the role of government, banks, labor and labor unions, savings and investments, and capital.	80, 584, 589
NCSS VII F	Compare how values and beliefs influence economic decisions in different societies.	235, 612, 619
NCSS VII H	Apply economic concepts and reasoning when evaluating historical and contemporary social developments and issues.	77, 360
NCSS VII I	Distinguish between the domestic and global economic systems, and explain how the two interact.	70
VIII. SCIENCE, TECHNOLOGY, AND SOCIETY		
NCSS VIII A	Identify and describe both current and historical examples of the interaction and interdependence of science, technology, and society in a variety of cultural settings.	332, 378, 386
NCSS VIII E	Recognize and interpret varied perspectives about human societies and the physical world using scientific knowledge, ethical standards, and technologies from diverse world cultures.	654, 661, 674
NCSS IX C	Analyze and evaluate the effects of changing technologies on the global community.	95
NCSS IX D	Analyze the causes, consequences, and possible solutions to persistent, contemporary, and emerging global issues, such as health, security, resource allocation, economic development, and environmental quality.	52, 84, 91, 104, 186, 443
NCSS IX E	Analyze the relationships and tensions between national sovereignty and global interest, in such matters as territory, economic development, nuclear and other weapons, use of natural resources, and human rights concerns.	91, 92, 104
NCSS IX G	Describe and evaluate the role of international and multinational organizations in the global arena.	84
X. CIVIC IDEAS AND PRACTICES		
NCSS X D	Practice forms of civic discussion and participation consistent with the ideals of citizens in a democratic republic.	436, 468, 615, 798, 802, 874

National Council for the Social Studies, *Expectations of Excellence: Curriculum Standards for Social Studies (Washington, D.C.: NCSS, 1994).*

Pacing for Your Course

In the following pacing guide, you will find suggested time spans for each chapter in *Marketing Essentials*. Your own class and school schedules will ultimately determine the amount of time you devote to each lesson. For the following guide, a regular period is defined as one 45-minute class period, and a block period is defined as one 90-minute class period.

	Traditional Schedule 36 Week Course	Block Schedule 36 Week Course	Traditional Schedule 18 Week Course	Block Schedule 18 Week Course
Chapter/Unit	**Regular Period**	**Block Period**	**Regular Period**	**Block Period**
UNIT 1 THE WORLD OF MARKETING	1	.5	1	.5
Chapter 1 Marketing Is All Around Us	3	1.5	1	.5
Chapter 2 The Marketing Plan	3	1.5	1	.5
Unit 1 Marketing Internship Project	4	2	2	1
UNIT 2 ECONOMICS	1	.5	1	.5
Chapter 3 Political and Economic Analysis	3	1.5	1	.5
Chapter 4 Global Analysis	3	1.5	1	.5
Unit 2 Marketing Internship Project	4	2	2	1
UNIT 3 BUSINESS AND SOCIETY	1	.5	1	.5
Chapter 5 The Free Enterprise System	3	1.5	1	.5
Chapter 6 Legal and Ethical Issues	3	1.5	1	.5
Unit 3 Marketing Internship Project	4	2	2	1
UNIT 4 SKILLS FOR MARKETING	1	.5	1	.5
Chapter 7 Basic Math Skills	3	1.5	1	.5
Chapter 8 Communication Skills	3	1.5	1	.5
Chapter 9 Technology for Marketing	3	1.5	2	1
Chapter 10 Interpersonal Skills	3	1.5	2	1
Chapter 11 Management Skills	3	1.5	2	1
Unit 4 Marketing Internship Project	5	2.5	2	1
UNIT 5 SELLING	1	.5	1	.5
Chapter 12 Selling Overview	3	1.5	1	.5
Chapter 13 Beginning the Sales Process	3	1.5	1	.5
Chapter 14 Presenting the Product	3	1.5	2	1
Chapter 15 Closing the Sale	3	1.5	2	1
Chapter 16 Using Math in Sales	3	1.5	2	1
Unit 5 Marketing Internship Project	5	2.5	2	1
UNIT 6 PROMOTION	1	.5	1	.5
Chapter 17 Promotional Concepts and Strategies	3	1.5	1	.5
Chapter 18 Visual Merchandising and Display	3	1.5	1	.5
Chapter 19 Advertising	3	1.5	2	1
Chapter 20 Print Advertisements	3	1.5	2	1
Unit 6 Marketing Internship Project	5	2.5	2	1

	Traditional Schedule 36 Week Course	Block Schedule 36 Week Course	Traditional Schedule 18 Week Course	Block Schedule 18 Week Course
Chapter/Unit	**Regular Period**	**Block Period**	**Regular Period**	**Block Period**
UNIT 7 DISTRIBUTION	1	.5	1	.5
Chapter 21 Channels of Distribution	3	1.5	1	.5
Chapter 22 Physical Distribution	3	1.5	2	1
Chapter 23 Purchasing	3	1.5	2	1
Chapter 24 Stock Handling and Inventory Control	3	1.5	2	1
Unit 7 Marketing Internship Project	5	2.5	2	1
UNIT 8 PRICING	1	.5	1	.5
Chapter 25 Price Planning	3	1.5	1	.5
Chapter 26 Pricing Strategies	3	1.5	1	.5
Chapter 27 Pricing Math	3	1.5	2	1
Unit 8 Marketing Internship Project	5	2.5	2	1
UNIT 9 MARKETING INFORMATION MANAGEMENT	1	.5	1	.5
Chapter 28 Marketing Research	3	1.5	1	.5
Chapter 29 Conducting Marketing Research	3	1.5	1	.5
Unit 9 Marketing Internship Project	4	2	2	1
UNIT 10 PRODUCT AND SERVICE MANAGEMENT	1	.5	1	.5
Chapter 30 Product Planning	3	1.5	1	.5
Chapter 31 Branding, Packaging, and Labeling	3	1.5	1	.5
Chapter 32 Extended Product Features	3	1.5	2	1
Unit 10 Marketing Internship Project	4	2	2	1
UNIT 11 ENTREPRENEURSHIP AND FINANCE	1	.5	1	.5
Chapter 33 Entrepreneurial Concepts	3	1.5	1	.5
Chapter 34 Risk Management	3	1.5	1	.5
Chapter 35 Developing a Business Plan	3	1.5	2	1
Chapter 36 Financing the Business	3	1.5	2	1
Unit 11 Marketing Internship Project	5	2.5	2	1
UNIT 12 CAREER DEVELOPMENT	1	.5	1	.5
Chapter 37 Identifying Career Opportunities	3	1.5	1	.5
Chapter 38 Finding and Applying For a Job	3	1.5	1	.5
Unit 12 Marketing Internship Project	4	2	2	1

Raise the Bar and Help Students Clear It

ACADEMIC INTEGRATION

Academic skills are crucial for success both inside and outside the classroom. In addition to traditional academic skills, your students will need communication skills, interpersonal skills, and strong technology skills in order to succeed in the real world. Basic skills will support your students in completing the tasks that their jobs and lives will demand.

COLLEGE AND CAREER READINESS

The No Child Left Behind Act of 2001 called for 100 percent proficiency by the year 2014 in reading and math to raise graduation rates from high school. With publication of the Common Core State Standards by the National Governors Association and the Council of Chief State School Officers, many education advocacy groups are now focused on making students ready to achieve their goals—whether it is technical certifications, 2-year community colleges, or 4-year colleges and universities.

Regardless of the path taken after high school, it is critical that students master the core academic areas. Traditionally, these subjects have been defined as language arts, science, and mathematics. No Child Left Behind names the following academic subjects:

- English
- Reading/Language Arts
- Mathematics
- Science
- World Languages
- Civics and Government
- Economics
- Art
- History
- Geography

THE IMPORTANCE OF INTEGRATING ACADEMICS

In a recent survey of high school graduates—many of whom had gone directly to work rather than into postsecondary education—more than half the respondents said their high schools should have placed more emphasis on basic academic skills. Unfortunately, these students—like so many others—were not able to recognize the relevance of their course work while they were in high school. By explicitly integrating academic skills into the family and consumer sciences curriculum, you can make students aware of the connections between schoolwork and the real world.

Integrated learning offers the following additional benefits to students:

- It provides real-world learning and thus establishes patterns of lifelong learning.
- It improves the academic achievement of all students—including those who will begin their careers directly after high school, those who will go on to postsecondary education or training, and those who will obtain four-year college degrees and beyond.
- It helps students make realistic plans for their own careers and education.

Academics in the Business Curriculum

Integrate academic skills into the classroom as a regular part of your classroom activities. For example, by having students read class assignments and texts, write letters and reports, give presentations, and perform mathematics exercises, you are helping them improve their academic skills. Make expectations clear. For example, if you ask your students to prepare a written report, explain that grammar, spelling, and presentation will be evaluated along with subject content. These are skills that students will need for success in school and at work.

To integrate academics into your course, you must incorporate principles from other subjects in a way that students can understand either on a concrete level or in metaphoric terms. This type of teaching will help those students who learn best when they are exposed to a variety of examples.

Deliver Efficient Instruction to All Students

ACCOUNTABILITY

To ensure that schools meet state and federal requirements for yearly progress in raising student achievements, many states require testing for high school graduation. Accountability measures new to the Perkins reauthorization bill include

- academic proficiency as measured by the state criteria developed under NCLB;
- graduation rates, also as defined by NCLB;
- number of students to continue to postsecondary education;
- number of students to complete state or industry certification or licensure; and
- student achievement on assignments aligned with industry standards.

CONNECTION TO RELEVANCE

With the mandatory requirements for proven test scores and graduation numbers, how can we assure that our students are learning? Most educators agree it is by connecting the relevance of education to life.

The Association for Career and Technical Education past-president Bob Scarborough says the Perkins reauthorization "ensures we are providing all students with an education that will help them succeed in the workplace and in life."

The Rigor/Relevance Framework, developed at the International Center for Leadership in Education, illustrates leveled learning processes that enable students to perform high-level thinking. The learning process defines student performance in four sequential categories: acquisition, application, assimilation, and adaptation.

As educators, our goal is to teach students to adapt their acquired knowledge and skills in complex ways to any situations, known and unknown. As educators, we are committed to provide the connectivity between classroom learning and real-world application.

APPLICATIONS

Studies show that students understand and retain knowledge when they experience or apply it to relevant situations. The *Marketing Essentials* program is dedicated to meet the challenge. Every chapter in *Marketing Essentials* is filled with ways to engage students in experiential learning and to apply their knowledge to their lives.

Features designed to help students find the relevance in content include

- Marketing Internship Unit Project (featuring skills self-assessment, conducting research, marketing careers exploration, and connection to the community)
- Discovery Projects
- DECA Connection
- World Market
- Marketing Case Studies
- Green Marketer
- Digital Nation
- Career Chatroom
- Chapter Review and Activities, including 21st Century Skills, e-Marketing Skills, and DECA Connection Role Plays

The content and teaching strategies in *Marketing Essentials* are designed to help applied learning students acclimate into the real world and to prepare them for a career in the professional business world.

Designing Instruction for a Diverse Classroom

THE DIVERSE CLASSROOM

No two students enter a classroom with identical abilities, backgrounds, experiences, and learning preferences, yet they are all expected to master the curricular objectives. Teachers face the enormous challenge of designing instruction to better meet the diverse learning needs of students.

UNIVERSAL ACCESS AND UNIVERSAL DESIGN

Universal access and universal design, as well as differentiated instruction, provide a framework for professional educators to address the challenges and opportunities of a diverse classroom.

Universal Access

Universal Access (UA) means that all people have an equal opportunity to access information, products, and services. Universal access, from an educational perspective, means that all students have an equal opportunity to education. This means access to high-quality curriculum and instruction regardless of learning diversities. UA may involve the use of specialized technology and environments.

Universal Design

Universal Design (UD) has a foundation in architecture. UD originally focused on accessibility issues for individuals with disabilities. Current UD philosophy focuses on designs that support all individuals, not just individuals with disabilities. From an educational perspective, universal design makes instructional facilities, materials, and activities available so that all learners can achieve success. The key instructional element associated with UD is variety:

- A variety of teaching methods to deliver the content
- A variety of ways for students to interact with teachers and other students
- A variety of ways students can demonstrate their learning
- A variety of ways to assess and evaluate student learning

Differentiated Instruction

Differentiated Instruction (DI) is a planned, deliberate, sequential, and systematic instructional technique designed to maximize the learning and achievement of all students in the classroom. Because of the diversity in student learning abilities and preferences, instruction needs to be equally diverse. By recognizing and positively responding to diverse student backgrounds, languages, abilities, and learning preferences, teachers are better able to deliver instruction that creates opportunities for improved student learning and success within the framework of universal design.

FIVE KEY STEPS FOR DELIVERING DIFFERENTIATED INSTRUCTION

1 Know your students' learning profiles.

A student's learning profile may include information about learning disabilities, English language ability, learning preferences, customs, needs, interests, and background. To gather student learning profiles, record student inventories, take note of conversations, make observations, and connect with other education specialists. Use the Universal Access activities and suggestions found in *Marketing Essentials* to craft lessons to suit your students' needs.

2 Use a variety of instructional methods.

Differentiated instruction varies the way that learning expectations are delivered to the students. *Marketing Essentials* offers suggestions for modifying instructional delivery to include problem-solving activities, writing, models, demonstrations, and graphic organizers.

3 Provide ample opportunities for student/teacher and student/student interactions.

The varied use of small group, partner, and whole-class instruction provides a differentiated approach that can be used to support many needs, such as language skills, review, enrichment, or acceleration. Modify the independence of the activities in *Marketing Essentials* using group and partner activity suggestions throughout the book, Interpersonal and Collaborative Activities in the chapter reviews, and Guided Practice activities in the Teacher Edition Lesson Plans.

4 Allow students to demonstrate their learning with a variety of product options.

Students should be given the opportunity to demonstrate their learning in diverse ways. For example, some students who struggle with writing may prefer to demonstrate their learning orally (speech, skit, audio recording), visually (model, exhibit, poster, drawing), or through media applications (video, PowerPoint®, music). Use the many creative activities throughout *Marketing Essentials* as models for alternative product options.

5 Use varied methods to assess and evaluate student learning.

Student assessments should be varied and frequent. They should be formal (graded, such as a test or product) and informal (nongraded, such as observations or group questioning for progress monitoring). Self-assessments allow the students to judge their own progress. Assessments should also include a range of low- to high-level thinking and responding skills in both traditional and authentic assessment formats. Use the Self-Evaluation Rubrics, quizzes, critical thinking assignments, and discussion questions in *Marketing Essentials* to assess and evaluate student learning.

Delivering Instruction to Reach All Students

DIFFERENTIATED INSTRUCTION FOR ENGLISH LANGUAGE LEARNERS

Differentiated instruction is important in virtually all classrooms. It is critical in language-diverse classrooms, where many learning activities can be and should be modified and differentiated. Before determining what level of differentiation is needed for your English language learners (ELL), ask yourself two questions:

1. Which language proficiency level best describes my English language learners?

Many schools, districts, and/or states typically place their ELL students in one of several language proficiency levels. Each level offers suggested activity verbs that support student learning. The use of verb taxonomies for differentiating both the process and product of learning can be helpful to students. Use the verbs most appropriate for the students' proficiencies, as identified below:

Language Proficiency Levels

Beginning/Early Intermediate These students typically read English at 0–2.5 grade level. They may be able to write short simple paragraphs and identify main ideas and story characters.
Activity Verbs: tell, point, circle, underline, name, draw, change, describe, and discuss.

Intermediate These students read English at 2.6–3.5 grade level and can often write paragraphs and identify "wh" questions (who, what, when, where, and why).
Activity Verbs: apply, show, classify, modify, explain, solve, and demonstrate.

Early Advanced These students are near proficient. They read at 3.6–5.5 grade level and may be fluent in oral English. They often need help with academic and written English.
Activity Verbs: analyze, compare, contrast, criticize, examine, create, predict, design, manage, and prepare.

2. Is some degree of activity modification necessary to assure achievement and success?

Some activities may not need modification for ELL students, but many will need modification. There are three common ways to modify an activity:

- **Modify the Language Rigor**
  Change the activity verb to better align with the student's language proficiency.
- **Modify the Independence Rigor**
  Change the students' degree of independence to align with his/her needed support. For example, an activity that directs the students to complete a task "independently" could be changed to "with a partner."
- **Provide Product Options**
  Allow students to demonstrate their learning in multiple ways by asking them to write a report or poem; draw; orally explain; or create a game, poster, commercial, video, presentation, song, or cartoon. Students may also teach a lesson, build a model, construct a diagram, or conduct an experiment.

Prior to any activity modification, confirm that all associated vocabulary is clearly understood by all students. Whenever possible, activity modification should be supported by graphic organizers, such as T-charts, webs, sequence, hierarchical, cluster, vocabulary, and data charts.

Sample Activity Modified for ELL Students

W Writing Strategy

Make a List Ask students to create a list of questions to ask when evaluating an advertisement. Have them create a worksheet that they can fill out when looking at an advertisement that contains their questions and space to answer them.

Modified for Beginner/Early Intermediate Students

ELL Writing Strategy

As a class, ask students to think of questions to ask when evaluating an advertisement. Write each question on the board. Give the class an advertisement to evaluate. Walk students through each question as a class. Write their answers on the board.

Modified for Intermediate Students

ELL Writing Strategy

In small groups, have students list four questions to ask when evaluating an advertisement. Have students answer each question orally to their group as they evaluate an advertisement.

Modified for Early Advanced Students

ELL Writing Strategy

In pairs, have students list four questions to ask when evaluating an advertisement. Have them create a worksheet listing questions they can answer in writing when looking at an advertisement.

Meeting Special Needs

UNIVERSAL ACCESS AND UNIVERSAL DESIGN

Universal access and universal design, as well as differentiated instruction, provide a framework for professional educators to address challenges and opportunities of a diverse classroom.

Subject	Description	Sources of Information
English Language Learners	Certain students speak English as a second language, or not at all. Customs and behavior of people in the majority culture may be confusing for some of these students. Cultural values may inhibit some of these students from full participation in the classroom.	• *Teaching English as a Second Language* • *Mainstreaming and the Minority Child*
Students with Behavior Disorders	Students with behavior disorders deviate from standards or expectations of behavior and impair the functioning of others and themselves. These students may also be gifted or have learning disabilities.	• *Exceptional Children* • *Journal of Special Education*
Students with Visual Impairments	Students with visual impairments have partial or total loss of sight. Individuals with visual impairments are not significantly different from their sighted peers in ability range or personality. However, a visual impairment may affect cognitive, motor, and social development.	• *Journal of Visual Impairment and Blindness* • *Education of Visually Handicapped* • *American Foundation for the Blind*
Students with Hearing Impairments	Students with hearing impairments have partial or total loss of hearing. Individuals with hearing impairments are not significantly different from their hearing peers in ability, range, or personality. However, a chronic hearing impairment may affect cognitive, motor, social, and speech development.	• *American Annals of the Deaf* • *Journal of Speech and Hearing Research* • *Sign Language Studies*
Students with Physical Impairments	Students with physical impairments fall into two categories—those with orthopedic impairments (use of one or more limbs severely restricted) and those with other health impairments.	• *The Source Book for the Disabled* • *Teaching Exceptional Children*
Gifted Students	Although no formal definition exists, these students can be described as having above average ability, task commitment, and creativity. They rank in the top five percent of their classes. They usually finish work more quickly than other students and are capable of divergent thinking.	• *Journal for the Education of the Gifted* • *Gifted Child Quarterly* • *Gifted Creative/Talented*
Students with Learning Disabilities	Students with learning disabilities have a problem in one or more areas, such as academic learning, language, perception, social-emotional adjustment, memory, or ability to pay attention.	• *Journal of Learning Disabilities* • *Learning Disability Quarterly*

Tips for Instruction

- Remember that students' ability to speak English does not reflect their academic ability.
- Try to incorporate students' cultural experiences into your instruction. The help of a bilingual aide may be effective.
- Include information about different cultures in your curriculum to help build students' self-image.
- Avoid cultural stereotypes.
- Encourage students to share their cultures in the classroom.

- Work for long-term improvement; do not expect immediate success.
- Talk with students about their strengths and weaknesses, and clearly outline objectives.
- Structure schedules, rules, room arrangement, and safety for a conducive learning environment.
- Model appropriate behavior for students and reinforce proper behavior.

- Modify assignments as needed to help students become independent.
- Teach classmates how to serve as guides for students with visual impairments.
- Tape lectures and reading assignments for students with visual impairments.
- Encourage students to use their sense of touch; provide tactile models whenever possible.
- Verbally describe people and events as they occur in the classroom.

- Limit unnecessary noise in the classroom.
- Provide a favorable seating arrangement so students with hearing impairments can see speakers and read their lips (or interpreters can assist); avoid visual distractions.
- Write out all instructions on paper or on the board; overhead projectors enable you to maintain eye contact while writing.
- Avoid standing with your back to the window or light source.

- With the student, determine when you should offer aid.
- Help other students and adults understand students with physical impairments.
- Learn about special devices or procedures and if any special safety precautions are needed.
- Allow students to participate in all activities including field trips, special events, and projects.

- Emphasize concepts, theories, relationships, ideas, and generalizations.
- Let students express themselves in a variety of ways including drawing, creative writing, or acting.
- Make arrangements for students to work on independent projects.
- Make arrangements for students to take selected subjects early.

- Provide assistance and direction; clearly define rules, assignments, and duties.
- Allow for pair interaction during class time; utilize peer helpers.
- Practice skills frequently.
- Allow extra time to complete tests and assignments.

Eight Ways of Learning

Learning Style	Description	Likes to	Is Good at	Learns Best by
Verbal/ Linguistic Learner	Intelligence is related to words and language, written and spoken.	read, write, tell stories, play word games, and tell jokes and riddles.	memorizing names, dates, places, and trivia; spelling; using descriptive language; and creating imaginary worlds.	saying, hearing, and seeing words.
Logical/ Mathematical Learner	Intelligence deals with inductive and deductive thinking and reasoning, numbers, and abstractions.	perform experiments, solve puzzles, work with numbers, ask questions, and explore patterns and relationships.	math, reasoning, logic, problem solving, computing numbers mentally, moving from concrete to abstract, thinking conceptually, and organizing thoughts.	categorizing, classifying, and working with abstract patterns and relationships.
Visual/Spatial Learner	Intelligence relies on the sense of sight and being able to visualize an object, including the ability to create mental images.	draw, build, design, and create things, daydream, do jigsaw puzzles and mazes, watch videos, look at photos, and draw maps and charts.	understanding the use of space and how to get around in it, thinking in three-dimensional terms, and imagining things in clear visual images.	visualizing, dreaming, using the mind's eye, and working with colors and pictures.
Musical/ Rhythmic Learner	Intelligence is based on recognition of tonal patterns, including various environmental sounds, and on a sensitivity to rhythm and beats.	sing and hum, listen to music, play an instrument, move body when music is playing, and make up songs.	remembering melodies; keeping time; mimicking beat and rhythm; noticing pitches, rhythms, and background and environmental sounds; and differentiating patterns in sounds.	rhythm, melody, and music.
Bodily/ Kinesthetic Learner	Intelligence is related to physical movement and the brain's motor cortex, which controls bodily motion.	learn by hands-on methods, demonstrate skill in crafts, tinker, perform, display physical endurance, and challenge self physically.	physical activities such as sports, dancing, acting, and crafts.	touching, moving, interacting with space, and processing knowledge through bodily sensations.
Interpersonal Learner	Intelligence operates primarily through person-to-person relationships and communication.	have lots of friends, talk to people, join groups, play cooperative games, solve problems as part of a group, and volunteer help when others need it.	understanding people and their feelings, leading others, organizing, communicating, manipulating, and mediating conflicts.	sharing, comparing, relating, cooperating, and interviewing.
Intrapersonal Learner	Intelligence is related to inner states of being, self-reflection, metacognition, and awareness of spiritual realities.	work alone, pursue own interests, daydream, keep a personal diary or journal, and think about starting own business.	understanding self, focusing inward on feelings/dreams, following instincts, pursuing interests, setting goals, and being original.	working alone, doing individualized projects, engaging in self-paced instruction, and having own space.
Naturalistic Learner	Intelligence has to do with observing, understanding, and organizing patterns in the natural environment.	spend time outdoors and work with plants, animals, and other parts of the natural environment; good at identifying plants and animals and at hearing and seeing connections to nature.	measuring, charting, mapping, observing plants and animals, keeping journals, collecting, classifying, participating in outdoor activities.	visualizing, hands-on activities, bringing outdoors into the classroom, relating home/classroom to the natural world.

Is Good at...	Learns Best by...	Famous Learners
memorizing names, dates, places, and trivia; spelling; using descriptive language; and creating imaginary worlds.	saying, hearing, and seeing words	Maya Angelou—poet Abraham Lincoln—U.S. President and statesman Jerry Seinfeld—comedian Mary Hatwood Futrell—international teacher, leader, orator
math, reasoning, logic, problem solving, computing numbers, moving from concrete to abstract, thinking conceptually.	categorizing, classifying, and working with abstract patterns and relationships.	Stephen Hawking—physicist Albert Einstein—theoretical physicist Marilyn Burns—math educator Alexa Canady—neurosurgeon
understanding the use of space and how to get around in it, thinking in three-dimensional terms, and imagining things in clear visual images.	visualizing, dreaming, using the mind's eye, and working with colors and pictures.	Pablo Picasso—artist Maria Martinez—Pueblo Indian famous for black pottery Faith Ringgold—painter, quilter, and writer I. M. Pei—architect
remembering melodies; keeping time; mimicking beat and rhythm; noticing pitches, rhythms, and background and environmental sounds.	rhythm, melody, and music..	Henry Mancini—composer Marian Anderson—contralto Daniel Heifetz—violinist Paul McCartney—singer, song writer, musician
physical activities such as sports, dancing, acting, and crafts.	touching, moving, interacting with space, and processing knowledge through bodily sensations.	Marcel Marceau—mime Jackie Joyner-Kersey—Olympic gold medalist in track and field Katherine Dunham—modern dancer Dr. Christiaan Bernard—cardiac surgeon
understanding people and their feelings, leading others, organizing, communicating, manipulating, mediating conflicts.	sharing, comparing, relating, cooperating, and interviewing.	Jimmy Carter—U.S. President and statesman Eleanor Roosevelt—former first Lady Lee Iacocca—president of Chrysler Corporation Mother Teresa—winner of Nobel Peace Prize
understanding self, focusing inward on feelings/dreams, following instincts, pursuing interests, and being original.	working alone, doing individualized projects, engaging in self-paced instruction	Marva Collins—educator Maria Montessori—educator and physician Sigmund Freud—psychotherapist Anne Sexton—poet
measuring, charting, mapping, observing plants and animals, keeping journals, collecting, classifying, participating in outdoor activities.	visualizing, hands-on activities, bringing outdoors into the classroom, relating home/classroom to the natural world.	George Washington Carver—agricultural chemist Rachel Carson—scientific writer Charles Darwin—evolutionist John James Audubon—conservationist

How Can I Motivate My Students to Read?

As a teacher, your role is to help students make personal connections in order to answer the question, "Why do I need to learn this?" Emphasize that reading is not only a necessity for work and for life; it can also bring enjoyment and enlightenment.

Ask your students, "What role does reading play in your life?" You can open this discussion by modeling examples: I love historical biographies; I read menus and order meals in Spanish; I read magazines and access the Internet to stay up to date on my favorite sports teams.

Improving or Fine-Tuning Reading Skills Will Help Your Students:

- Improve grades
- Read faster and more efficiently
- Improve their study skills
- Remember more information accurately
- Improve their writing

The Reading Process

Good reading skills build on one another, overlap, and spiral in much the same way that a winding staircase goes around and around while leading readers to a higher place. The Reading Skills Handbook is designed to help your students find and use the tools to use before, during, and after reading.

Reading Strategies

- Identify, understand, and learn new words
- Understand why you read
- Take a quick look at the whole text
- Try to predict what you are about to read
- Take breaks during reading and ask questions about the text
- Take notes
- Keep thinking about what will come next
- Summarize

Vocabulary Development

Word identification and vocabulary skills are the building blocks of reading and writing. By learning to use a variety of strategies to build word skills and vocabulary, your students will become stronger readers.

USE CONTEXT TO DETERMINE MEANING

The best way for your students to expand and extend vocabulary is to read widely, listen carefully, and participate in a rich variety of discussions. When reading independently, students can often figure out the meanings of new words by looking at their context, or the other words and sentences that surround them.

PREDICT A POSSIBLE MEANING

Another way to determine the meaning of a word is to take the word apart. If a reader understands the meaning of the **base,** or **root,** part of a word, and knows the meanings of key syllables added either to the beginning or end of the base word, it becomes easy to figure out what the word means.

Word Origins Since Latin, Greek, and Anglo-Saxon roots are the basis for much of our English vocabulary, having some background in one of these languages can be a useful vocabulary tool. For example, astronomy comes from the Greek root *astro,* which means relating to the stars. *Stellar* also has a meaning referring to stars, but its origin is Latin. Knowing root words in other languages can help readers determine meanings, derivations, and spellings in English.

Prefixes and Suffixes A prefix is a word part that can be added to the beginning of a word. For example, the prefix *semi* means half or partial, so *semicircle* means half a circle. A suffix is a word part that can be added to the end of a word. Adding a suffix often changes a word from one part of speech to another.

Using Dictionaries A dictionary provides the meaning or meanings of a word. Look at the sample dictionary entry in the student edition Reading Skills Handbook to see what other information it provides.

Thesauruses and Specialized References A thesaurus provides synonyms and often antonyms. It is a useful tool to use to expand vocabulary. Remind students to check the exact definition of the listed words in a dictionary before using a thesaurus. Specialized dictionaries such the *Barron's Dictionary of Business Terms* or *Black's Law Dictionary* list terms and expressions not commonly included in a general dictionary. Many such dictionaries can be found online as well as in print.

Glossaries Many textbooks and technical works contain condensed dictionaries that provide an alphabetical listing of words used throughout the text and their specific definitions.

Recognize Word Meanings Across Subjects Words often have different meanings when used for different purposes. The word *product* may mean one thing in math and another in science. For example:

Math After you multiply the two numbers, explain how you arrived at the **product.**

Science One **product** of photosynthesis is oxygen.

Economics The Gross National **Product** is the total dollar value of goods and services produced by a nation.

How Can I Help My Students Understand What They Read?

Reading comprehension means understanding—deriving meaning from—what has been read. Using a variety of strategies can help improve comprehension and make reading more interesting and more fun.

READ FOR A REASON

To get the greatest benefit from reading, teach students to **establish a purpose for their reading.** In school, some of the reasons for reading are to:

- learn and understand new information
- find specific information
- review before a test
- complete an assignment
- prepare (research) before you write

As reading skills improve, you will notice that your students apply different strategies to fit the different purposes for reading. For example, a person reading for entertainment may read quickly, but reading to gather information or follow directions might require reading more slowly, taking notes, constructing a graphic organizer, or rereading sections of text.

DRAW ON PERSONAL BACKGROUND

Drawing on personal background, or activating prior knowledge, helps students connect their culture and experiences to their reading. Before introducing a new topic, you may want to encourage students to ask:

- What have I heard or read about this topic?
- Do I have any personal experience relating to this topic?

You can also set common background knowledge with discussion before reading. For example, to prepare students to read the novel *A Farewell to Arms,* you might lead a discussion about these common background themes:

- World War I
- Italy (You might ask a student to show the location of Italy on a map)
- Other Ernest Hemingway titles
- The Nobel Prize in literature

Having this historical background will help to set the scene for students as they read.

Using a KWL Chart A KWL chart is a good device for organizing information gathered before, during, and after reading. In the first column, students list what they already know, then list what they want to know in the middle column. They use the third column to review and assess what they learned. You or your students can add more columns to record places where they found information and places where they can look for more information.

K (What I already know)	W (What I want to know)	L (What I have learned)

Adjust Your Reading Speed Reading speed is a key factor in how well students understand what they read. Reading speed can vary depending on the purpose for reading.

Scanning means running one's eyes quickly over the material to look for words or phrases. Readers scan to find a specific piece of information.

Skimming means reading a passage quickly to find its main idea or get an overview. Skim a passage as a preview to determine what the material is about.

Reading for detail involves careful reading while paying attention to text structure and monitoring understanding. Readers read for detail to learn concepts, follow complicated directions, or prepare to analyze a text.

Previewing Strategies

- Read the title, headings, and subheadings of the selection.
- Look at the illustrations and notice how the text is organized.
- Skim the selection. Take a glance at the whole thing.
- Decide what the main idea might be.
- Predict what a selection will be about.

Techniques to Help Students Understand and Remember What They Read

PREVIEW

Previewing strategies help students begin at a visual level, then drill down to evaluate, predict, draw conclusions, and use contextual clues about what they will read.

PREDICT

As students read, they take educated guesses about story events and outcomes. They make predictions before and during reading. This helps them focus their attention on the text and that focus improves understanding.

DETERMINE THE MAIN IDEA

When students look for the main idea, they are looking for the most important statement in a text. Depending on what kind of text they read, the main idea can be located at the very beginning (news stories in a newspaper or a magazine) or at the end (scientific research document).

Encourage students to ask these questions to determine the main idea:

- What is each sentence about?
- Is there one sentence that is more important than all the others?
- What idea do the details support or point out?

Keep track of the text's structure (see below). Looking at headers and content structure will give students important clues about the main idea.

TAKING NOTES

Cornell Note-Taking System There are many methods for note taking. The **Cornell Note-Taking System** is a well-known method that can help students organize what they read. To the right is a note-taking activity based on the Cornell Note-Taking System.

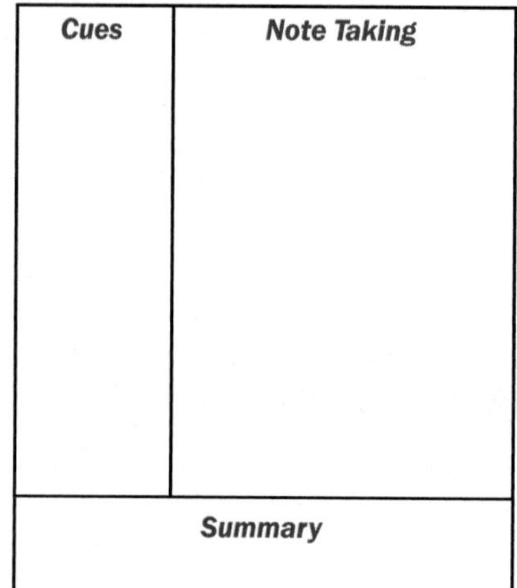

Graphic Organizers Using a graphic organizer to retell content in a visual representation will help students remember and retain content. Encourage students to make charts or diagrams to organize what they have read. Some good examples are:

Venn Diagrams A Venn diagram is a good way to organize information in a compare-and-contrast text structure. The outer portions of the circles show how two characters, ideas, or items contrast, or are different, and the overlapping part compares two things, or shows how they are similar.

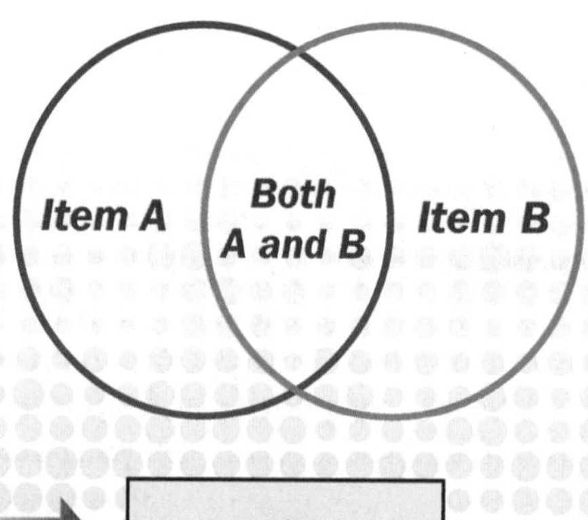

Flow Charts Students can track a sequence of events or cause and effect on a flow chart. Demonstrate how to arrange ideas or events in their logical, sequential order. Then, draw arrows between ideas to indicate how one idea or event flows into another.

Go to **glencoe.com** for more information about note taking and additional study tools.

VISUALIZE

Encourage students to try to form a mental picture of scenes, characters, and events as they read. This technique helps them to use the details and descriptions the author gives readers. If students can **visualize** what they read, they will become more interested and will remember the information better.

QUESTION

Tell students to ask questions about the text while they read. Encourage them to ask about the importance of the sentences they read, how the sentences relate to one another, whether they understand what they just read, and what they think is going to come next.

CLARIFY

Encourage students to try these techniques when they do not understand meaning (through questioning):

What to Do When You Do Not Understand

Reread confusing parts of the text.

- Diagram (chart) relationships between chunks of text, ideas, and sentences.
- Look up unfamiliar words.
- Talk through the text as if explaining it to someone else.
- Read the passage once more.

REVIEW

Make sure students take time to stop and review what they have read. Use note-taking outlines or other graphic organizers, charts, or visual aids.

MONITOR COMPREHENSION

Teach students to continue to check their understanding using the following two strategies:

Summarize Pause and state the main ideas of the text and the key supporting details. Try to answer the following questions: Who? What? When? Where? Why? How?

Paraphrase Pause, close the book, and try to retell what they have just read using their own words. It helps students to retell, or paraphrase reading into their own words.

Understanding Text Structure

Good writers do not just put together sentences and paragraphs; they organize their writing with a specific purpose in mind. That organization is called text structure. When students understand and follow the structure of a text, it is easier to remember the information they read. There are many ways text may be structured. Each type of structure usually makes use of some specific words. Teach students to watch for these **signal words.** They will help them follow the text's organization. (Remind them to use these techniques as they write.)

COMPARE AND CONTRAST

This structure shows similarities and differences between people, things, and ideas. This is often used to demonstrate that things that seem alike are really different, or vice versa.

Signal words: similarly, more, less, on the one hand/on the other hand, in contrast, but, however

CAUSE AND EFFECT

Writers use the cause-and-effect structure to explore the reasons for something happening and to examine the results or consequences of events.

Signal words: so, because, as a result, therefore, for the following reasons

PROBLEM AND SOLUTION

When writers organize text around the question "How?", they state a problem and suggest solutions.

Signal words: how, help, problem, obstruction, overcome, difficulty, need, attempt, have to, must

SEQUENCE

Sequencing tells readers in which order to consider thoughts or facts. Examples of sequencing are:

Chronological order refers to the order in which events take place.

Signal words: first, next, then, finally

Spatial order describes the organization of things in space (to describe the placement of objects in a room, for example).

Signal words: above, below, behind, next to

Order of importance lists things or thoughts from the most important to the least important (or the other way around).

Signal words: principal, central, main, important, fundamental

Thinking About Reading

It is important for students to think about what they are reading to get the most information from a text, to understand the consequences of what the text says, to remember the content, and to form their own opinions about what they read.

INTERPRET

Interpreting involves asking, "What is the writer really saying?" and then using what students already know to answer the question.

INFER

Writers do not always state exactly everything they want readers to understand. They sometimes imply certain information by providing clues and details. To infer involves using reasoning and experience to develop the idea, based on what an author implies, or suggests. What is most important when drawing inferences is to be sure that readers have accurately based their guesses on supporting details from the text. If students cannot point to a place in the selection to help back up an inference, encourage them to rethink that guess.

DRAW CONCLUSIONS

A conclusion is a general statement a reader can make and explain using reasoning or supporting details from a text.

ANALYZE

To understand persuasive nonfiction (a text that lists facts and opinions to arrive at a conclusion), readers must analyze statements and examples to see if they support the main idea. To understand an informational text, students need to keep track of how the ideas are organized to find the main points.

Hint: Have students use graphic organizers and note-taking charts.

DISTINGUISH BETWEEN FACTS AND OPINIONS

This is one of the most important reading skills students can learn. A fact is a statement that can be proven. An opinion is what the writer believes. A writer may support opinions with facts, but an opinion cannot be proven. For example:

Fact: California produces fruit and other agricultural products.

Opinion: California produces the best fruit and agricultural products.

EVALUATE

Remind students that to rely on accurate information, they will need to consider who wrote it and why. Where did the writer get information? Is the information one-sided? Can readers verify the information?

Reading for Research

To guide students in reading actively to research a topic, encourage them to follow these directions:

- Generate an interesting, relevant, and researchable question.
- Categorize that information.
- Evaluate the information.
- Organize information in a new way for a specific audience.
- Draw conclusions about the original research question.

What Is Academic English?

by Robin Scarcella, Ph.D.

Academic English is the language commonly used in business and education. It is the language used in academics, business, and courts of law. It is the type of English used in professional books, including textbooks, and it contains specific linguistic features that are associated with all disciplines. Proficiency in reading and using academic English is strongly related to long-term success in all parts of life.

WHAT IS ACADEMIC VOCABULARY?

By the time they complete elementary school, students should acquire the knowledge they will need to understand academic vocabulary. For example, in academic texts, a full 8% of the words are academic words. A basic 2,000-word vocabulary of high-frequency words makes up 87% of the words. Three percent are technical words that vary depending on the discipline. The remaining 2% are low-frequency words.

WHY SHOULD STUDENTS LEARN ACADEMIC VOCABULARY?

English language learners who have mastered a basic 2,000-word vocabulary are ready to acquire the majority of general words found in their texts and on standardized tests.

Knowledge of academic words, combined with continued acquisition of general words, can significantly boost an English learner's comprehension level of academic texts. English learners who learn and practice these words before they graduate from high school are likely to master academic material with more confidence and speed. They waste less time and effort in guessing words than those students who know only the basic 2,000 words that characterize general conversation.

ACADEMIC VOCABULARY AND ACADEMIC ENGLISH IN THE FAMILY AND CONSUMER SCIENCES CLASSROOM

Teachers can provide their students with rich samples of academic vocabulary and help students understand the academic English of their text. To develop academic English, students must have already acquired a large amount of basic proficiency in the grammar of everyday English.

Academic English should be taught within contexts that make sense. Academic English arises not only from a knowledge of linguistic code and cognition but also from social practices in which academic English is used to accomplish communicative goals. The acquisition of academic vocabulary and grammar is necessary to advance the development of academic English.

Tips for Teaching Academic Vocabulary

- **Expose Students to Academic Vocabulary**—Students learn academic vocabulary through use and in reading content. You do not need to call attention to all academic words students are learning because they will acquire them subconsciously.
- **Do Not Correct Students' Mistakes When Using Academic Vocabulary**—All vocabulary understanding and spelling errors are developmental and will disappear once the student reads more.
- **Help Students Decode the Words Themselves**—Once students learn the alphabet, they will be able to decode words. Decoding each word they do not recognize will help them more than trying to focus on sentence structure. Once they can recognize words, they can read authentic texts.
- **Do Not Ignore the English Learner in This Process**—These students can learn academic vocabulary before they are completely fluent in spoken English.
- **Helping Students Build Academic Vocabulary Leads to Broader Learning**—Students who have mastered the basic academic vocabulary are ready to continue acquiring words from the rest of the vocabulary groups. Use the Internet to find lists of appropriate vocabulary words.

Guidelines for Teaching Academic Vocabulary

There are a number of guidelines that teachers can follow when teaching academic English and vocabulary:

1. Use direct and planned instruction.
2. Employ models that have increasingly difficult language.
3. Focus attention on form by pointing out linguistic features of words.
4. Provide practice opportunities.
5. Motivate student interest and self-confidence.
6. Provide instructional feedback.
7. Use assessment tools on a regular basis.

PERFORMANCE-BASED ASSESSMENTS

One good way to present a performance assessment is in the form of an open-ended question.

- **Journals**—Students write from their own perspective on topics that affect their lives.
- **Letters**—Students write a letter from themselves to friends and family, or another audience.
- **Position Paper or Editorial**—Students explain a controversial issue and present their own opinions and recommendations, supported with strong evidence and convincing reasons.
- **Newspaper**—Students write stories from the perspective of a reporter.
- **Biographies and Autobiographies**—Students write about leaders either from the third person point of view (biography) or from the first person (autobiography).
- **Creative Stories**—Students integrate family and consumer sciences topics into a piece of fiction.
- **Poems and Songs**—Students follow the conventions of a particular type of song or poem as they tell about a topic or event.
- **Research Reports**—Students synthesize information from a variety of sources into a well-developed research report.

ORAL PRESENTATIONS

Oral presentations allow students to demonstrate their academic and topical literacy in front of an audience. Oral presentations are often group efforts, although this need not be the case.

- **Simulations**—Students hold simulations of actual events, such as a role play in a specific scenario.
- **Debates**—Students debate two or more sides of a policy or issue.
- **Interview**—Students conduct a mock journalism interview or job interview.
- **Oral Reports**—Students present the results of research efforts in a lively oral report. This report may be accompanied by visuals.
- **Skits and Plays**—Students use specific events or topics as the basis for a play or skit.

VISUAL PRESENTATIONS

Visual presentations allow students to demonstrate their understanding in a variety of visual formats. Visual presentations can be either group or individual projects.

- **Model**—Students make a model to demonstrate or represent a particular process.
- **Museum Exhibit**—Students create a rich display of materials around a topic. Typical displays might include models, illustrations, photographs, videos, writings, and presentation software.

- **Graph or Chart**—Students analyze and represent data in a line graph, bar graph, table, or other chart format.
- **Drawing**—Students represent an event or period through illustration, including cartoons.
- **Posters and Murals**—Posters and murals may include maps, time lines, diagrams, illustrations, photographs, and written explanations that reflect students' understanding of the information.
- **Videotapes**—Students film a video to show a simulation of an event.
- **Multimedia Presentation**—Students create a computer-generated presentation or slide show containing information and analysis.

HOW ARE PERFORMANCE ASSESSMENTS SCORED?

There are a variety of means used to evaluate performance tasks. Some or all of the following methods may be used:

- **Scoring Rubrics**—A scoring rubric is a set of guidelines for assessing the quality of a process and/or product. It sets out criteria used to distinguish acceptable responses from unacceptable ones, generally on a scale from excellent to poor. Rubrics may be used as guidelines as the students prepare their products. They are also commonly used for peer-to-peer assessment and self-assessment.
- **Models of Excellent Work**—Teacher-selected models of excellent work concretely illustrate expectations and help students set goals for their own projects.
- **Student Self-Assessment**—Common methods of self-assessment include ranking work in relation to the model, using a scoring rubric, and writing goals and then evaluating how well the goals have been met.
- **Peer or Audience Assessment**—Many of the performance tasks target an audience other than the classroom teacher. If possible, the audience of peers should give feedback. Have the class create rubrics for specific projects together.
- **Observation**—As students carry out their performance tasks, you may want to formally observe them at work. Start by developing a checklist, identifying all the specific behaviors and understandings you expect students to demonstrate. Then, observe students as they carry out performance tasks and check off behaviors as you observe them.
- **Interviews**—As a form of ongoing assessment, you may want to conduct interviews with students, asking them to analyze, explain, and assess their participation in performance tasks. When projects take place over an extended period of time, you can hold periodic interviews as well as exit interviews.

Test-Prep Strategies

Students can follow the steps below to prepare for the standardized assessments they are required to take.

- **Read About the Test**—Students can familiarize themselves with the format, the types of questions, and the amount of time they will have to complete the test. Emphasize that it is very important for students to budget their time during test-taking.
- **Review the Content**—Consistent study will help students build knowledge and understanding. If there are specific objectives or standards that are tested on the exam, help students review facts or skills.
- **Practice**—Provide practice, ideally with real tests, to build students' familiarity with the content, format, and timing of the real exam. Students should practice all the types of questions they will encounter on the test.
- **Pace**—Students should pace themselves differently depending on how the test is administered. As students practice, they should try to increase the number of questions they can answer correctly. If students have trouble with an item, they should mark it and come back to it later.
- **Analyze Practice Results**—Help students improve test-taking performance by analyzing their test-taking strengths and weaknesses. Help students identify what kinds of questions they found most difficult. Look for patterns in errors and tailor instruction to review the appropriate test-taking skills or content.

Test-Taking Strategies

It's not enough for students to learn facts and concepts. They must be able to show what they know in a variety of test-taking situations.

OBJECTIVE TESTS

Apply the following strategies to help students do their best on objective tests.

Multiple-Choice Questions

- Students should read the directions carefully to learn what answer the test requires—the best answer or the right answer. This is especially important when answer choices include "all of the above" or "none of the above."
- Students should watch for negative words, such as *not*, *except*, and *unless*.
- Students should try to mentally answer the question before answering.
- Students should eliminate answer choices that are obviously wrong.

True/False Questions

- It is important that students read the entire question before answering. For an answer to be true, the entire statement must be true. If one part of a statement is false, the answer should be marked false.
- Remind students to watch for words such as *all*, *never*, *every*, and *always*. Statements containing these words are often false.

Matching Questions

- Students should read through both lists before they mark any answers.
- Unless an answer can be used more than once, students should cross out each choice as they use it.
- Students can use grammar to find the right answer. When matching word/definition, the definition is often the same part of speech (noun, verb, adjective, or adverb) as the word.

ESSAY TESTS

Essay tests require students to provide thorough and well-organized written responses, in addition to telling what they know. Help students use these strategies on essay tests.

Read the Question

The key to writing successful essay responses lies in reading and interpreting questions correctly. Teach students to identify and underline key words to guide them in understanding what the question asks.

Plan and Write the Essay

Students should follow the writing process to develop their answer. Encourage students to follow these steps to plan and write their essays.

1. Map out an answer. Make lists, webs, or an outline to plan the response.
2. Decide on an order in which to present the main points.
3. Write an opening statement that directly responds to the essay question.
4. Write the essay. Expand on the opening statement. Support key points with specific facts, details, and reasons.
5. Write a closing statement that brings the main points together.
6. Proofread to check spelling, grammar, and punctuation.

Critical Thinking

One of the factors that determines students' success is their ability to deal with the varied demands of day-to-day life. This requires insightful decision making, creative problem solving, and interactions with diverse groups. Thus, teaching critical thinking equips your students with the skills necessary to achieve success.

Critical thinking skills are important for these reasons:

- They help students investigate their own problem-solving mechanisms.
- They help students find creative resolutions.
- They lead students to compare and contrast what they know with unknowns.
- They allow students to make decisions about their own learning while making them aware of their learning processes.

Cooperative Learning

Studies show that students learn faster and retain more information when they are actively involved in the learning process. Cooperative learning is one method that gets students actively involved in learning and at the same time allows for peer teaching.

In *Marketing Essentials,* students and teachers have a variety of materials to assist with cooperative learning activities. Many of the features and section and chapter assessment activities can be completed in a cooperative learning environment.

THE BENEFITS OF COOPERATIVE LEARNING

- Cooperative learning emphasizes working toward group goals rather than the traditional emphasis on individual competition and achievement.
- Students discover that not only must they learn the material themselves, but they are also responsible for helping everyone in the group learn the material.
- Cooperative learning increases academic achievement and develops essential social skills.
- Students learn valuable problem-solving, team-building, and creativity skills that transfer to real-world environments and situations.
- People who help each other and work together toward a common goal generally begin to feel more positive about themselves and each other.
- Students have the opportunity to perceive other students as colleagues rather than competitors. As a result, they recognize the value of helping others rather than working competitively.

Multicultural Education

Multicultural education incorporates the idea that all students—regardless of their gender and social class, and their ethnic, racial, or cultural characteristics—should have an equal opportunity to learn in school. Learning about other cultures concurrently with their own culture helps students recognize similarities and appreciate differences, without perceiving inferiority or superiority of one or the other. To foster cultural awareness:

- Recognize that all students are unique, having special talents and abilities.
- Promote uniqueness and diversity as positive traits.
- Know, appreciate, and respect the cultural backgrounds of your students.
- Use authentic situations to provide cultural learning and understanding.
- Make sure people of all cultures are represented fairly and accurately.
- Make sure that historical information is accurate and nondiscriminatory.
- Make sure that materials do not include stereotypical roles.
- Make sure there is gender equity.
- Welcome family and community involvement.
- Use current news stories, advertisements, or other forms of media to call students' attention to cultural differences that influence businesses, communities, and families.

Ethics

Helping students learn about ethical behavior and how to consider the effects of a decision before it is made are important life skills for your students preparing for the real world.

THE BENEFITS OF INTEGRATING ETHICS

The goal of teaching ethical decision-making skills is not to teach values. It is to help students clarify their ethical beliefs and learn how to evaluate ethical situations. Make your classroom a risk-free environment in which students can discuss issues and make ethical decisions. Students need to learn how to evaluate their actions and to ask questions such as, "Will I be proud of myself if I take this action?" and "Would I want others to know about my actions?"

THE ETHICAL DECISION MODEL

Your students will learn to analyze ethical situations better if they have a model to use in deliberating the issues that helps them to understand how a decision can affect others. Several decision models exist, but the basic steps for an ethical decision model are as follows:

1. Determine the ethical issue.
2. Identify the actions for handling the situation.
3. Identify the people affected by the situation.
4. Analyze how the situation affects the people involved.
5. Decide which of the actions to take.

TABLE OF CONTENTS

TABLE OF CONTENTS

TABLE OF CONTENTS

UNIT 6 PROMOTION 390

TABLE OF CONTENTS

UNIT 12 CAREER DEVELOPMENT 868

FEATURES TABLE OF CONTENTS

Project-Based Learning

These project-based features will help you get involved in the world of marketing. Each project includes a related worksheet activity and a rubric you can use to evaluate your work.

Marketing Internship Project

Discovery Project

Marketing in the Real World

It is important to know how marketing concepts actually work in business and global economies. These features will show you how real companies faced marketing challenges and how the economies in different countries and cultures can affect people around the world.

MARKETING CASE STUDIES

WORLD MARKET

Marketing with DECA

DECA prepares emerging leaders and entrepreneurs in marketing, finance, hospitality and management in high schools and colleges around the world. These features can help you prepare for DECA events and interact with other students.

DECA Connection Role Play

Online Connection!

Visit this book's Online Learning Center at glencoe.com for more DECA Role Plays.

What Do You Want to Be?

The world of marketing is a gateway to many different careers. These features allow you to learn about many different marketing-related careers and the skills and education you will need to get them.

Career Chatroom

glencoe.com

Learn more about these careers and complete a Career Exploration Activity.

Improve Your Marketing Skills

Do you know how to properly use social media for marketing? Can you promote products and services using green methods? These features will help you improve your digital and green marketing skills.

DIGITAL NATION

The GREEN Marketer

Thinking Creatively

Marketing professionals must be able to think creatively to solve problems. These Hot Topic features will help improve your understanding of important marketing concepts.

HOT TOPIC

McGraw Hill connect™

If your classroom has CONNECT online access then you can access supplementary resources for Marketing through CONNECT. This innovative Web-based program is designed to help you succeed in your coursework and in the workplace.

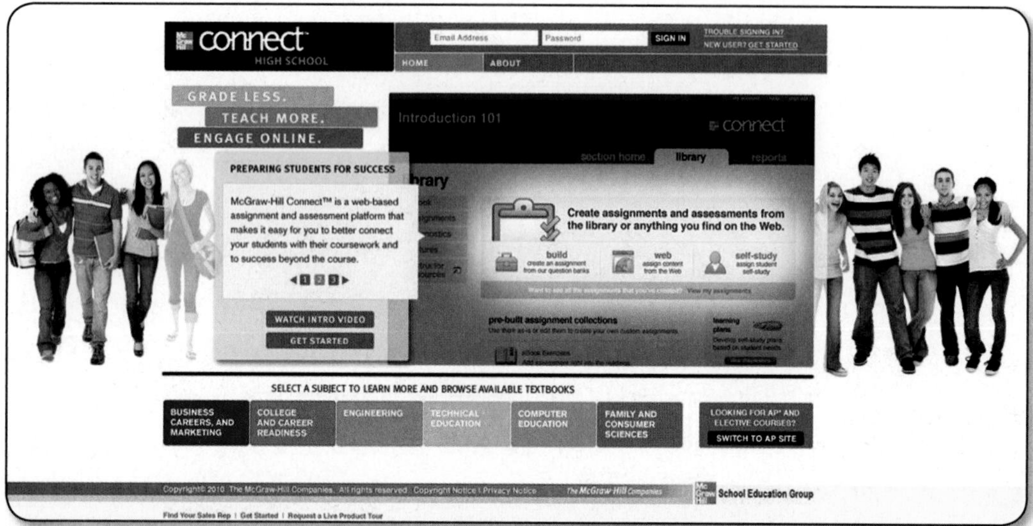

CONNECT

Use Connect to access your Marketing course home page.

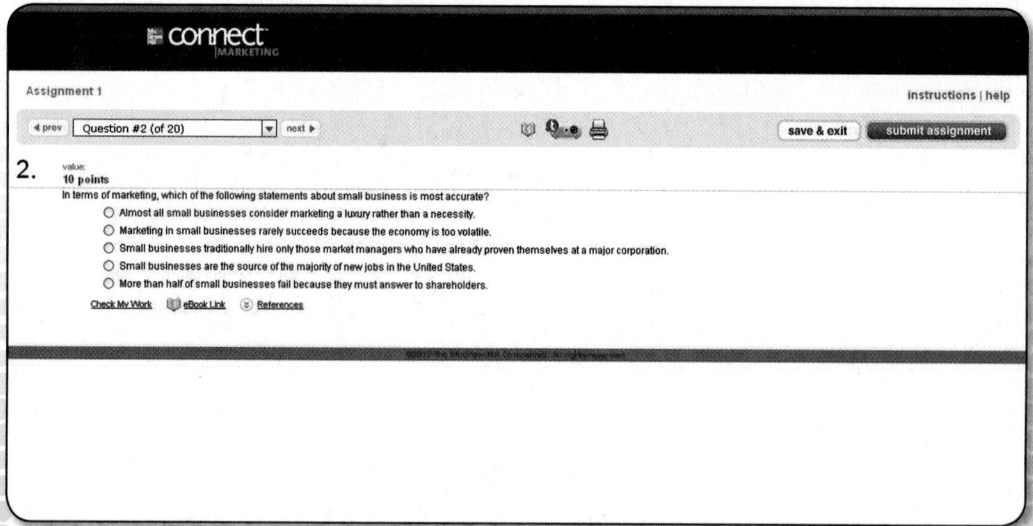

LEARN

- Complete your homework online.
- Get immediate feedback on your work.
- Link back to sections of the book to review accounting concepts.

Easy to access!

Connect to *Marketing Essentials* at mcgrawhillconnect.com/k12

SUCCEED

Use CONNECT to access the *Marketing Essentials* Online Learning Center for these resources:

- Unit videos
- Self-checks
- Practice tests
- Chapter Summaries
- Chapter Visual Summaries with Content and Academic Vocabulary
- Chapter Graphic Organizers
- Chapter Games and Puzzles

Access your eBook anywhere!

- Store class notes.
- Highlight and bookmark material online.
- Full book coverage, including all topics and every relevant figure from the textbook.

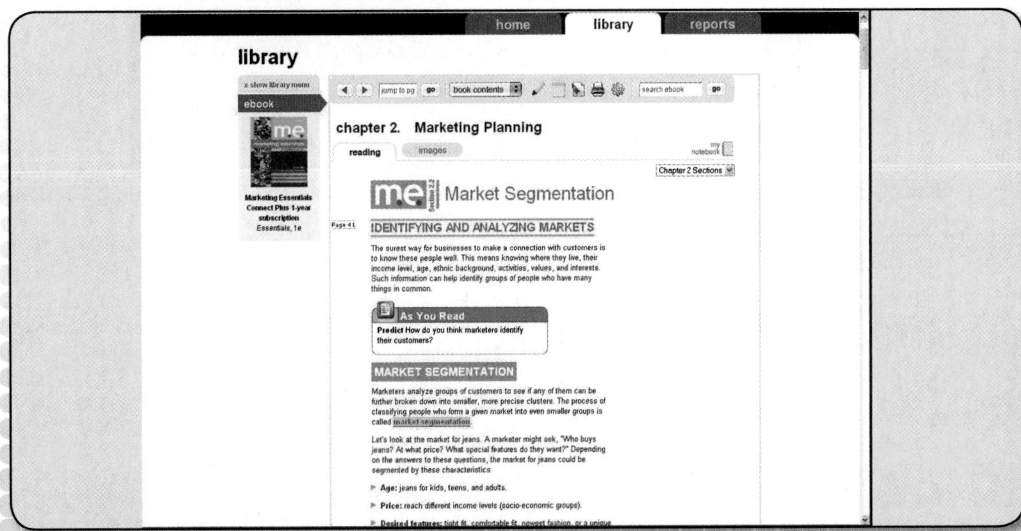

with ConnectPlus

Online Learning Center

Use the Internet to Extend Your Learning

Throughout the text, look for this icon that directs you to the Marketing Essentials Online Learning Center for more activities and information. Follow these steps to access the textbook resources at *Marketing Essentials'* Online Learning Center.

glencoe.com
Print this graphic organizer.

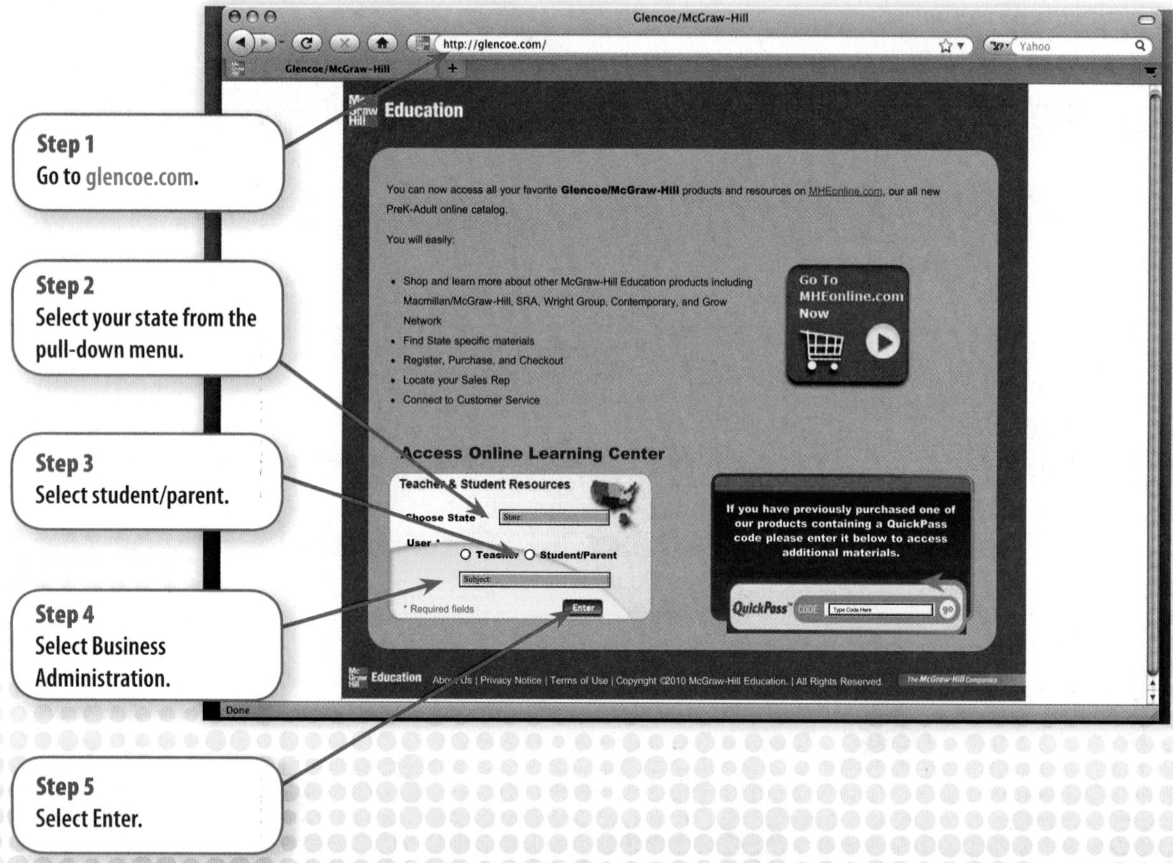

Step 1
Go to glencoe.com.
Step 2
Select your state from the pull-down menu.
Step 3
Select student/parent.
Step 4
Select Business Administration.
Step 5
Select Enter.
Glencoe/McGraw-Hill
http://glencoe.com/
Education
Go To MHEonline.com Now
Access Online Learning Center
Teacher & Student Resources
Student/Parent
Enter

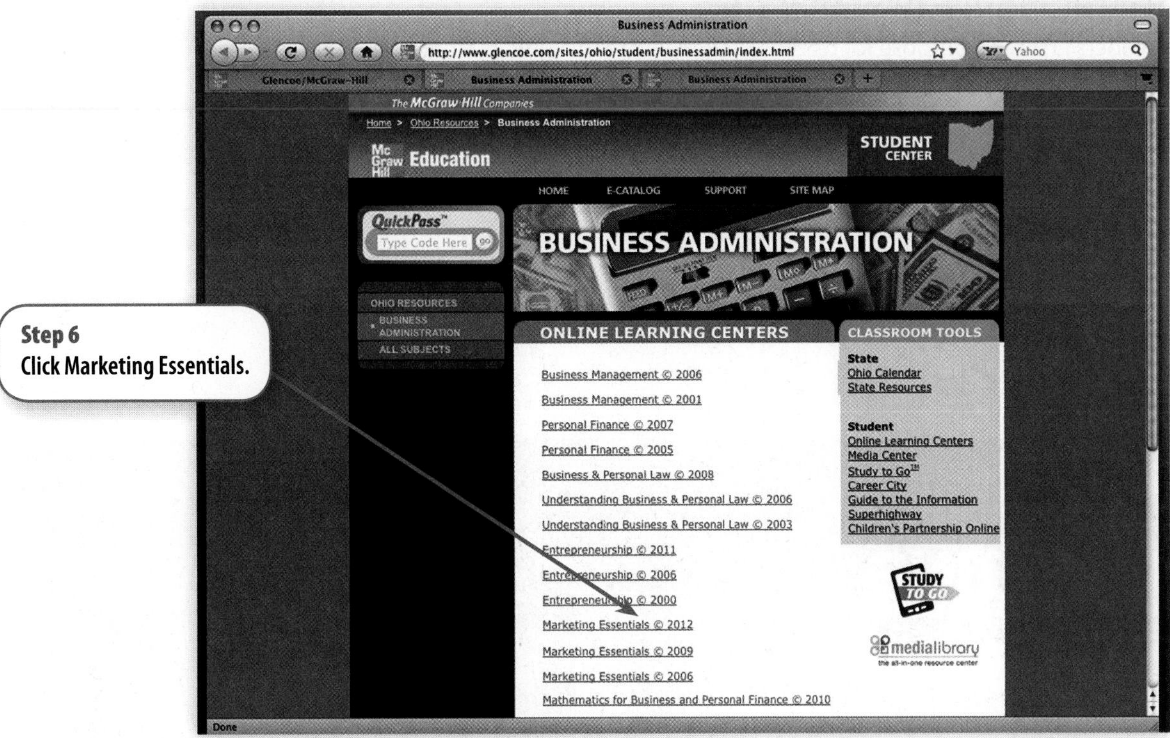

Step 6
Click Marketing Essentials.

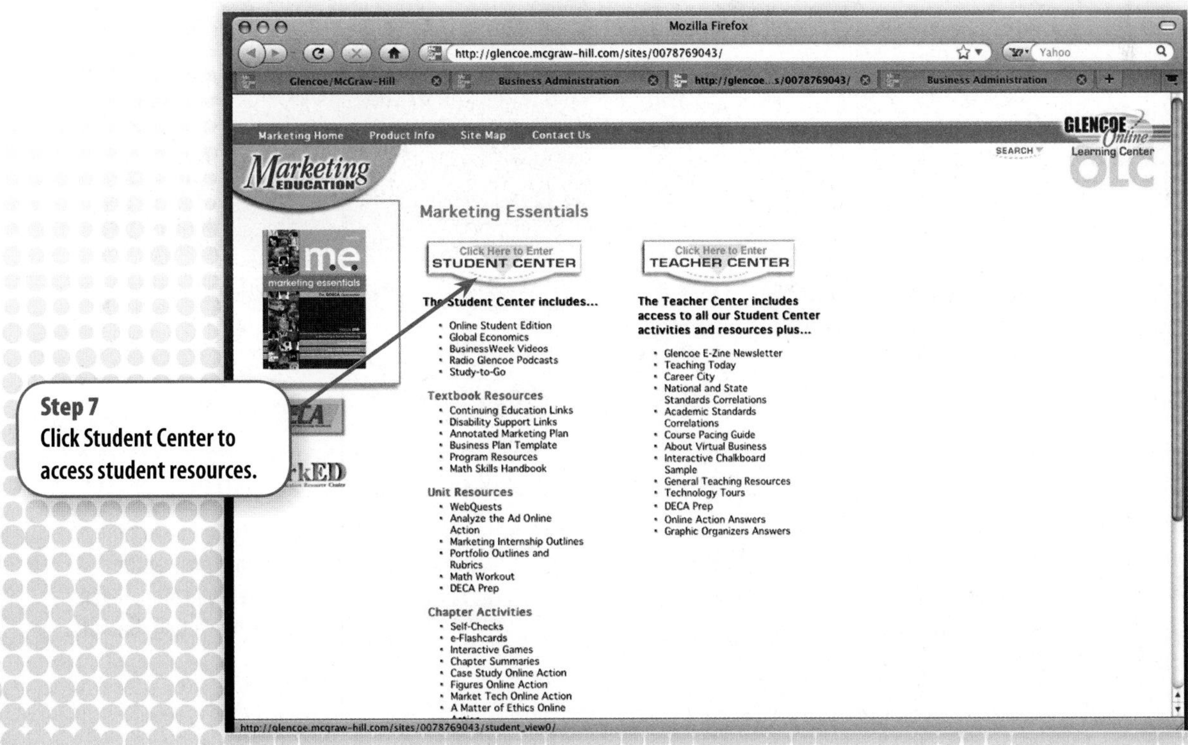

Step 7
Click Student Center to access student resources.

Begin the Unit

DISCOVER THE WORLD OF MARKETING

Successful readers first set a purpose for reading. Before you read a unit in ***Marketing Essentials,*** think about why you are reading this book, and consider how you might be able to use what you learn. ***Marketing Essentials*** teaches you the marketing skills you need to make plans for your future in the business workforce.

Preview the Project at the beginning of each unit. Use the preview to think about how what you are learning applies to the project.

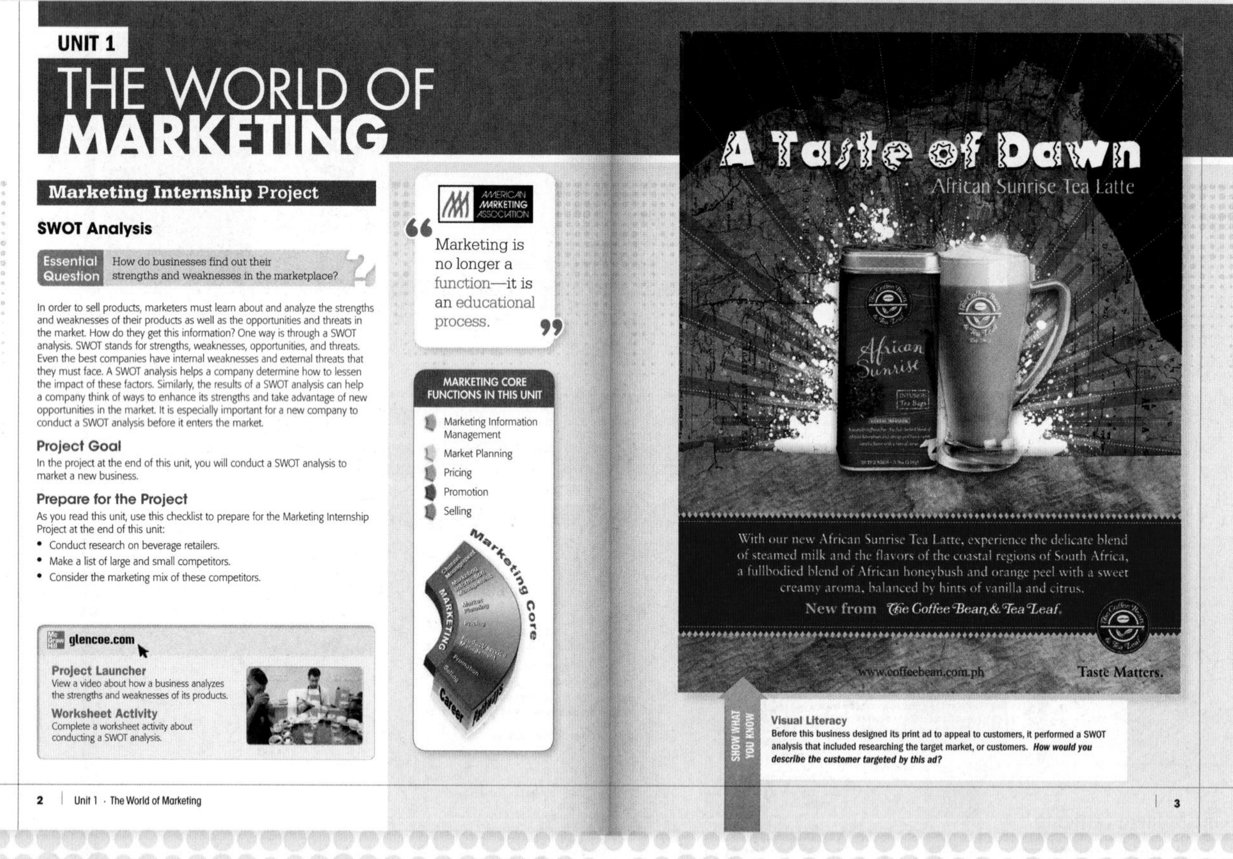

UNIT 1

THE WORLD OF MARKETING

Marketing Internship Project

SWOT Analysis

Essential Question: How do businesses find out their strengths and weaknesses in the marketplace?

In order to sell products, marketers must learn about and analyze the strengths and weaknesses of their products as well as the opportunities and threats in the market. How do they get this information? One way is through a SWOT analysis. SWOT stands for strengths, weaknesses, opportunities, and threats. Even the best companies have internal weaknesses and external threats that they must face. A SWOT analysis helps a company determine how to lessen the impact of these factors. Similarly, the results of a SWOT analysis can help a company think of ways to enhance its strengths and take advantage of new opportunities in the market. It is especially important for a new company to conduct a SWOT analysis before it enters the market.

Project Goal

In the project at the end of this unit, you will conduct a SWOT analysis to market a new business.

Prepare for the Project

As you read this unit, use this checklist to prepare for the Marketing Internship Project at the end of this unit:

- Conduct research on beverage retailers.
- Make a list of large and small competitors.
- Consider the marketing mix of these competitors.

glencoe.com

Project Launcher
View a video about how a business analyzes the strengths and weaknesses of its products.

Worksheet Activity
Complete a worksheet activity about conducting a SWOT analysis.

AMERICAN MARKETING ASSOCIATION

"Marketing is no longer a function—it is an educational process."

MARKETING CORE FUNCTIONS IN THIS UNIT

- Marketing Information Management
- Market Planning
- Pricing
- Promotion
- Selling

Marketing Core
MARKETING
Career Pathways
A Taste of Dawn
African Sunrise Tea Latte
With our new African Sunrise Tea Latte, experience the delicate blend of steamed milk and the flavors of the coastal regions of South Africa, a fullbodied blend of African honeybush and orange peel with a sweet creamy aroma, balanced by hints of vanilla and citrus.
New from The Coffee Bean & Tea Leaf.
www.coffeebean.com.ph
Taste Matters.

SHOW WHAT YOU KNOW

Visual Literacy
Before this business designed its print ad to appeal to customers, it performed a SWOT analysis that included researching the target market, or customers. ***How would you describe the customer targeted by this ad?***

2 | Unit 1 · The World of Marketing

3

Use Online Resources to help you better understand how the unit material will relate to the project.

Identify the Marketing Skills that will be featured in the unit.

Use the Photo to Predict the focus of the unit. Answer the question to help you prepare for learning new marketing concepts.

Begin the Chapter

What Is the Chapter All About?

The information in the chapter opener will help you prepare to learn about chapter topics by connecting what you already know to the information found in the chapter. Think about the businesses you have encountered in your own life. Do they have any similarities with those in your textbook?

Plan a short project to get ready for what you'll learn in the chapter.

Prepare for DECA through role-playing practice.

Chapter 2 | Section 2.1 Marketing Planning | Section 2.2 Market Segmentation

the marketing plan

Visual Literacy Marketers want to know what products teens buy, how much they spend, and where they shop. They use this information to create the marketing mix as part of their marketing plans. ***Why is this target market of consumers important to marketers?***

SHOW WHAT YOU KNOW

Discovery Project

The Right Mix

Essential Question How do stores use the four Ps to create an effective marketing mix?

Project Goal

Work with a partner to identify and visit three different specialty stores where you and other teenagers shop. Create a marketing mix report for each store by describing the 4 Ps: product (type and quality of products), price (cost, discount, and member rewards), place (type of location), and promotion (in-store and media advertising). For example, for "product," you might identify teen apparel or electronic games. Describe each store's marketing mix and discuss whether it is effective in a report to the class.

Ask Yourself...

- Which stores will you select?
- How will you share your findings with the class?
- How will you organize your report?
- How will you make your presentation effective?

Synthesize and Present Research Synthesize your research by describing whether each store's marketing mix is effective for selling to teens.

glencoe.com

Activity Get a worksheet activity about creating a marketing mix.

Evaluate Download a rubric you can use to evaluate your project.

DECA Connection

DECA Events

Concepts in this chapter are related to DECA competitive events that involve either an interview or role play.

Performance Indicators The performance indicators represent key skills and knowledge. Your key to success in DECA competitive events is relating them to the concepts in this chapter.

- Explain the nature of marketing plans.
- Explain the nature of marketing planning.
- Explain the nature of sales forecasts.
- Explain the concept of marketing strategies.
- Prepare simple written reports.

DECA Prep

Role Play Practice role-playing with the DECA Connection competitive-event activity at the end of this chapter. More information about DECA events can be found on DECA's Web site.

Chapter 2 · The Marketing Plan | 29

Explore the Photo to jumpstart your thinking about the chapter's big ideas.

Go online to find the rubric for evaluating your work and worksheet activities that connect you with the topics.

Begin the Section

Prepare with Reading Guides and Study Tools

Use the Reading Guide at the beginning of each section to preview what you will learn in the section. See if you can predict the information and skills you will learn in the section by using clues and information that you already know.

Before You Read asks you to think about one of the big ideas of the section.

Check Vocabulary lists for words you do not know. You can look them up in the glossary before you read the section.

Take Notes with graphic organizers. You can go online and print them to use as you read.

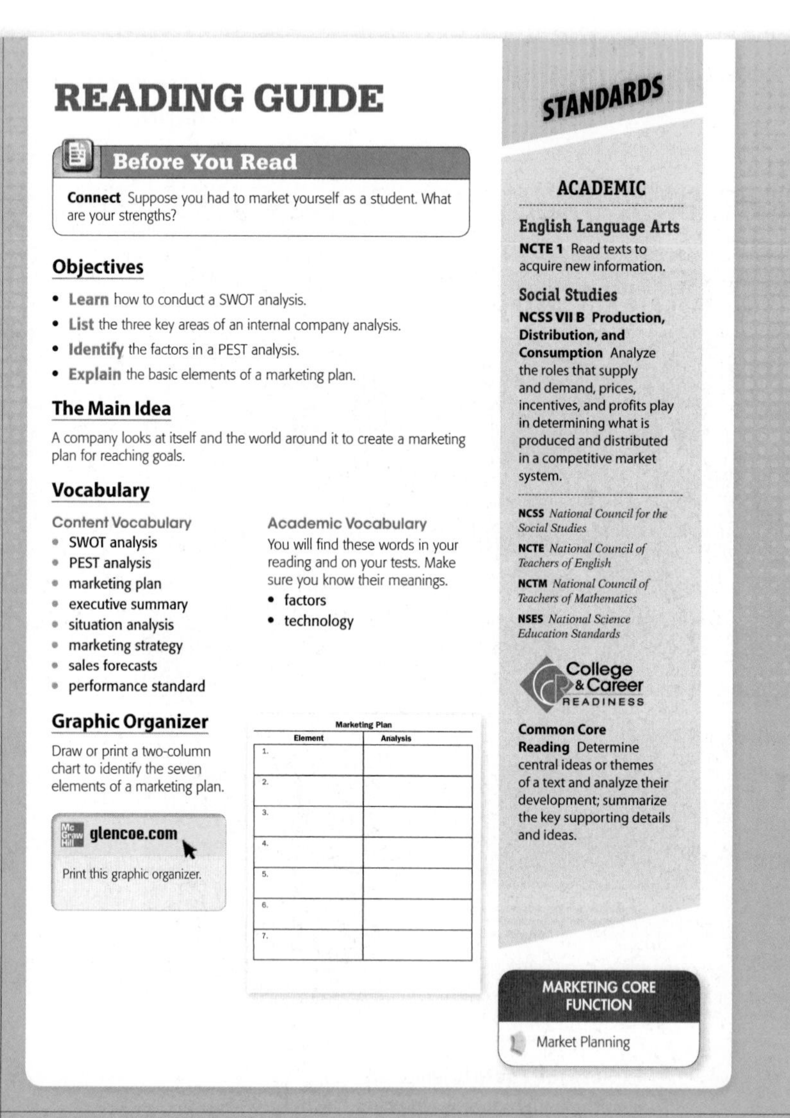

READING GUIDE

Before You Read

Connect Suppose you had to market yourself as a student. What are your strengths?

Objectives

- **Learn** how to conduct a SWOT analysis.
- **List** the three key areas of an internal company analysis.
- **Identify** the factors in a PEST analysis.
- **Explain** the basic elements of a marketing plan.

The Main Idea

A company looks at itself and the world around it to create a marketing plan for reaching goals.

Vocabulary

Content Vocabulary

- SWOT analysis
- PEST analysis
- marketing plan
- executive summary
- situation analysis
- marketing strategy
- sales forecasts
- performance standard

Academic Vocabulary

You will find these words in your reading and on your tests. Make sure you know their meanings.

- factors
- technology

Graphic Organizer

Draw or print a two-column chart to identify the seven elements of a marketing plan.

glencoe.com

Print this graphic organizer.

Marketing Plan

Element	Analysis
1.	
2.	
3.	
4.	
5.	
6.	
7.	

STANDARDS

ACADEMIC

English Language Arts

NCTE 1 Read texts to acquire new information.

Social Studies

NCSS VII B Production, Distribution, and Consumption Analyze the roles that supply and demand, prices, incentives, and profits play in determining what is produced and distributed in a competitive market system.

NCSS *National Council for the Social Studies*

NCTE *National Council of Teachers of English*

NCTM *National Council of Teachers of Mathematics*

NSES *National Science Education Standards*

College & Career READINESS

Common Core

Reading Determine central ideas or themes of a text and analyze their development; summarize the key supporting details and ideas.

MARKETING CORE FUNCTION

Market Planning

30 | Unit 1 · The World of Marketing

Study with Features

Skills You Can Use at School and in the Workplace

As you read, look for feature boxes throughout each chapter. These features build academic skills and critical thinking skills that relate to real-world marketing topics to prepare you for the workplace.

World Market These features showcase different companies from all over the world.

WORLD MARKET

SPAIN

Imagination Walks

For more than a decade, the Camper® footwear company, based on the Spanish island of Mallorca, has outsold other brands in Spain. Today the company is global with stores in London, Milan, New York, Paris, and Taipei, and sales topping $120 million in one year. The Camper concept that luxury is in simplicity has revolutionized the world of traditional shoemaking.

Camper Culture The Camper story began in 1877 with master shoemaker, Antonio Fluxa. The business passed down to his grandson Lorenzo Fluxa, who created the Camper brand in 1975. With quirky, authentic designs inspired by the farming tradition of Mallorca, "Camper" means "peasant." Fluxa's mission for Camper grew from "the historical and social changes that occurred in Spain during the 70s."

Social Studies

Collaborate Discuss with a partner how manufacturers use human and natural resources to create shoes.

NCSS VII A Production, Distribution, and Consumption Explain how the scarcity of productive resources (human, capital, technological, and natural) requires the development of economic systems to make decisions about how goods and services are to be produced and distributed.

Here are some entry-level phrases that are used in conversations about marketing all over the world.

English	Spanish
Hello	Hola
Goodbye	Adios
How are you?	¿Cómo está usted?
Thank you	Gracias
You're welcome	De nada

Hot Topic Learn the tips and tricks that marketers use to make their work more successful.

Marketing Mix Businesses use social networking sites to promote their products and research new ones.

Marketing Case Study Learn how real-world companies successfully faced marketing challenges. Each of these features has a question that can help you connect what you have learned with other academic subjects.

MARKETING CASE STUDY

Adidas's Sales Automation

To prepare for a meeting with a customer, the Adidas® sales force usually checks inventory. But frustration would set in when some products were no longer available after a sale was made. A sales representative would have to call the customer to revise the order. Or, worse, phone customer service while on a sales call, interrupting the selling process. So, Adidas gave laptops to its sales staff so they could interface with the company's computer system to check real-time inventory.

Improving the Process

To improve on this solution, Adidas turned to AT&T™ and Atlas2Go, an automated sales-force application. The software program can run on a wireless BlackBerry® device. With this system, sales representatives check inventory on the spot while taking a customer's order. This improvement reduced frustration, errors, and the need to change orders. Another unforeseen benefit was the ability to spot product trends quickly.

Social Studies

Analyze Discuss how supply and demand resulted in sales representatives having immediate access to a company's inventory during the sales process.

NCSS VII B Production, Distribution, and Consumption Analyze the role that supply and demand, prices, incentives, and profits play in determining what is produced and distributed in a competitive market system.

The Green Marketer These features allow you to see how marketers promote green products and services to entice customers. Each of these features has a green activity you can download at the *Marketing Essentials* Online Learning Center at glencoe.com.

Digital Nation Discover how using technology such as social networking, Web sites, and e-mail can help companies market their products and services. Each of these features has a question that can help you connect what you have learned with other academic subjects.

Career Chatroom Have you ever wondered how experts in the marketing field became successful? These interviews with marketing professionals provide insight into their success. More information about these careers can be found at the *Marketing Essentials* Online Learning Center at glencoe.com.

The GREEN Marketer

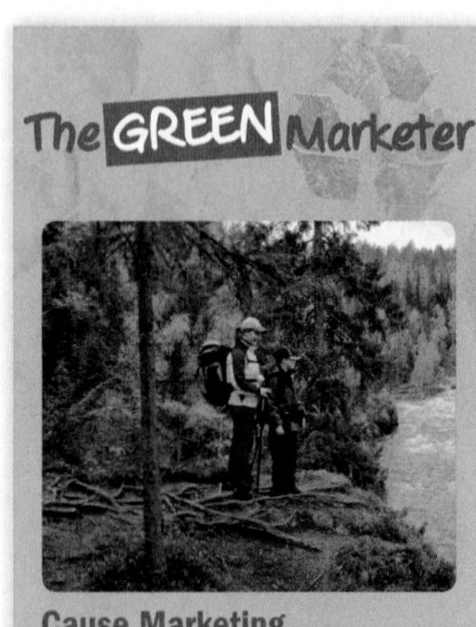

Cause Marketing

In cause marketing, for-profit companies team up with nonprofits to promote a social or environmental cause. In 2008, for example, Tripadvisor.com launched its "More Than Footprints" campaign, which invited Web visitors to vote on how the company should split a $1 million donation among five nonprofits, including Conservation International and the Nature Conservancy. Facebook posts, a video on the company's YouTube channel, and widgets on the charities' Web sites helped spread the word about the campaign.

Social Studies

Discuss Some people argue that cause marketing may cause consumers to cut their direct giving to charities that address human needs and concerns. How might this be the case? What are the benefits of cause marketing that are not part of direct giving to charities? Discuss your response with a partner and then share with the class.

NCSS I A Culture Analyze and explain the ways groups, societies, and cultures address human needs and concerns.

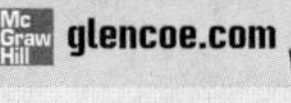
glencoe.com

Get an activity on green marketing.

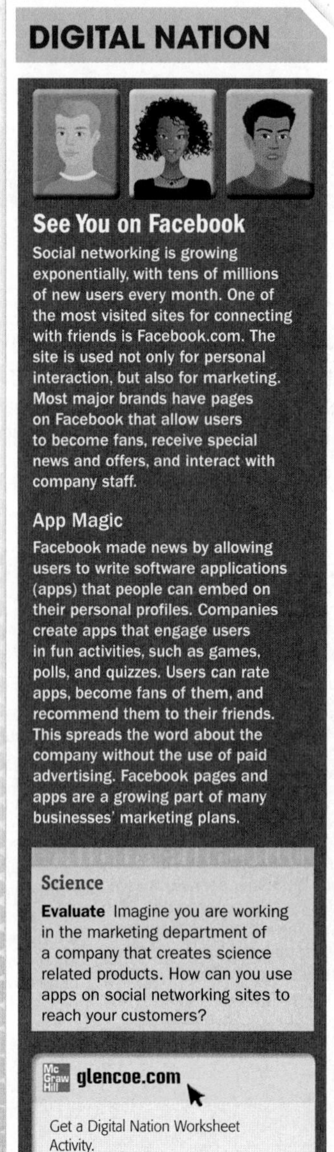

DIGITAL NATION

See You on Facebook

Social networking is growing exponentially, with tens of millions of new users every month. One of the most visited sites for connecting with friends is Facebook.com. The site is used not only for personal interaction, but also for marketing. Most major brands have pages on Facebook that allow users to become fans, receive special news and offers, and interact with company staff.

App Magic

Facebook made news by allowing users to write software applications (apps) that people can embed on their personal profiles. Companies create apps that engage users in fun activities, such as games, polls, and quizzes. Users can rate apps, become fans of them, and recommend them to their friends. This spreads the word about the company without the use of paid advertising. Facebook pages and apps are a growing part of many businesses' marketing plans.

Science

Evaluate Imagine you are working in the marketing department of a company that creates science related products. How can you use apps on social networking sites to reach your customers?

glencoe.com

Get a Digital Nation Worksheet Activity.

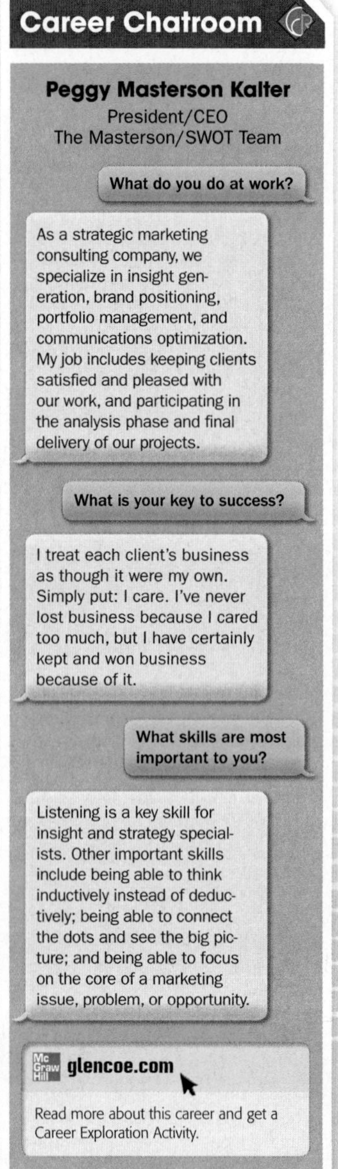

Career Chatroom

Peggy Masterson Kalter
President/CEO
The Masterson/SWOT Team

What do you do at work?

As a strategic marketing consulting company, we specialize in insight generation, brand positioning, portfolio management, and communications optimization. My job includes keeping clients satisfied and pleased with our work, and participating in the analysis phase and final delivery of our projects.

What is your key to success?

I treat each client's business as though it were my own. Simply put: I care. I've never lost business because I cared too much, but I have certainly kept and won business because of it.

What skills are most important to you?

Listening is a key skill for insight and strategy specialists. Other important skills include being able to think inductively instead of deductively; being able to connect the dots and see the big picture; and being able to focus on the core of a marketing issue, problem, or opportunity.

glencoe.com

Read more about this career and get a Career Exploration Activity.

Review the Section

Check Your Understanding with Self-Assessments

Use the After You Read self-assessment at the end of the section to monitor your understanding. Make sure that you can answer the questions in your own words before moving on in the text.

Confirm Your Understanding of key concepts and skills found in the section.

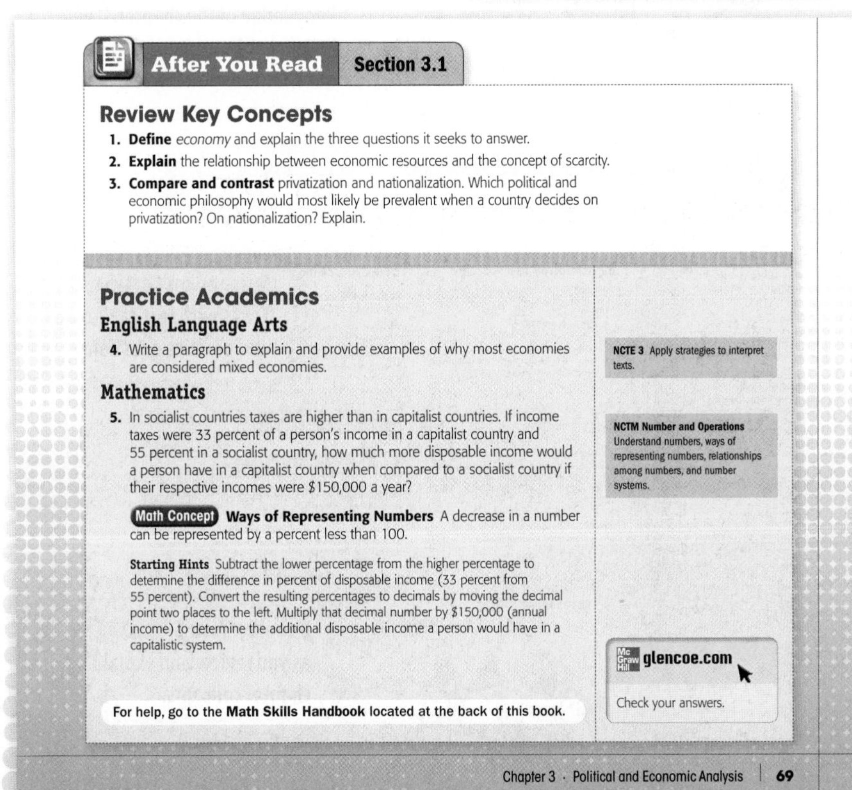

After You Read | Section 3.1

Review Key Concepts

1. **Define** *economy* and explain the three questions it seeks to answer.
2. **Explain** the relationship between economic resources and the concept of scarcity.
3. **Compare and contrast** privatization and nationalization. Which political and economic philosophy would most likely be prevalent when a country decides on privatization? On nationalization? Explain.

Practice Academics

English Language Arts

4. Write a paragraph to explain and provide examples of why most economies are considered mixed economies.

NCTE 3 Apply strategies to interpret texts.

Mathematics

5. In socialist countries taxes are higher than in capitalist countries. If income taxes were 33 percent of a person's income in a capitalist country and 55 percent in a socialist country, how much more disposable income would a person have in a capitalist country when compared to a socialist country if their respective incomes were $150,000 a year?

Math Concept **Ways of Representing Numbers** A decrease in a number can be represented by a percent less than 100.

Starting Hints Subtract the lower percentage from the higher percentage to determine the difference in percent of disposable income (33 percent from 55 percent). Convert the resulting percentages to decimals by moving the decimal point two places to the left. Multiply that decimal number by $150,000 (annual income) to determine the additional disposable income a person would have in a capitalistic system.

NCTM Number and Operations Understand numbers, ways of representing numbers, relationships among numbers, and number systems.

For help, go to the **Math Skills Handbook** located at the back of this book.

glencoe.com

Check your answers.

Chapter 3 · Political and Economic Analysis | 69

Check Your Answers online at the *Marketing Essentials* Online Learning Center at glencoe.com.

Practice Academic Skills related to marketing with these cross-curricular activities.

Review the Chapter

Know and Understand the Chapter Concepts

Review what you learned in the chapter and see how this learning applies to your other subjects and real-world situations.

Visualize the relationships among key concepts.

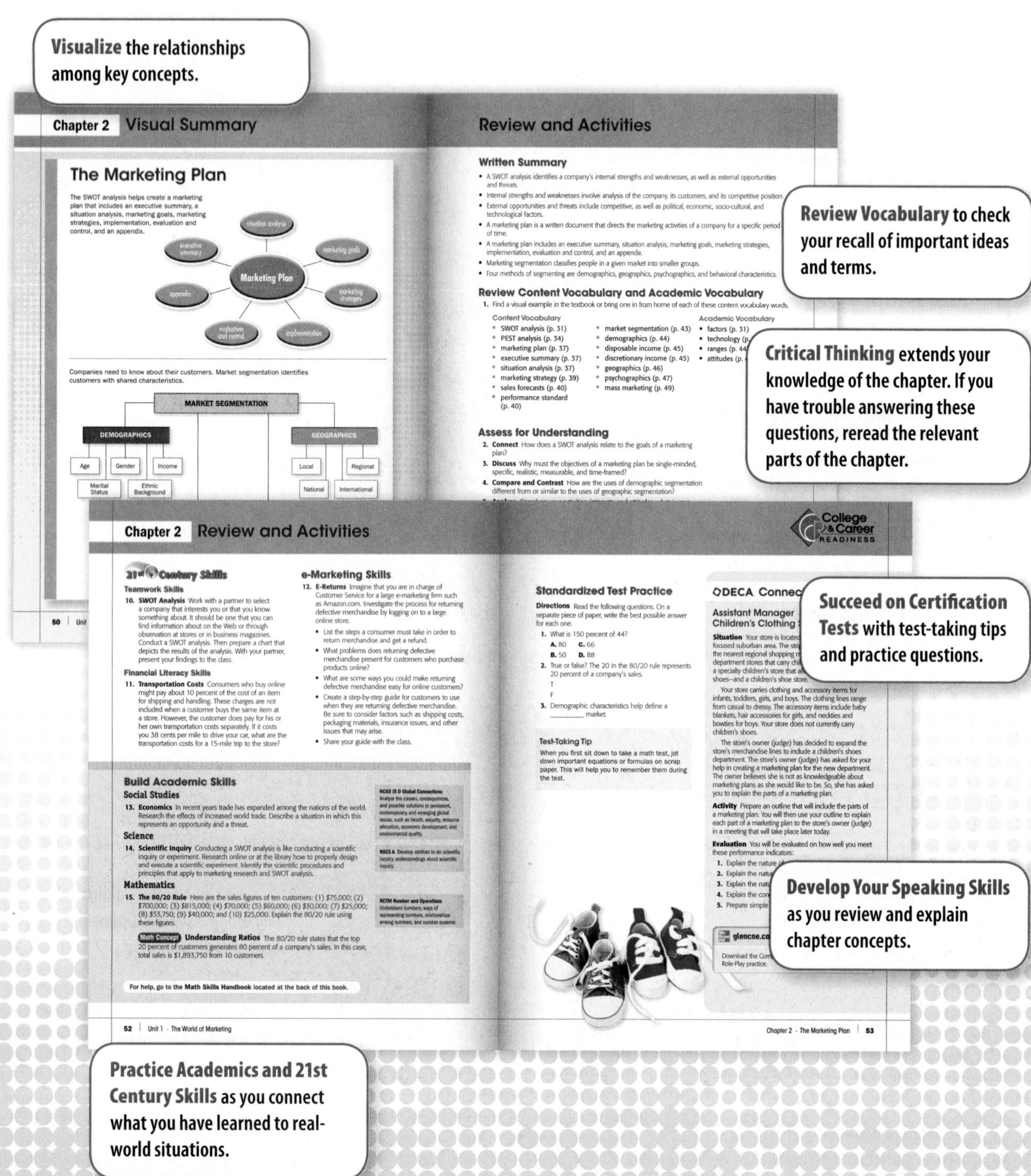

Review Vocabulary to check your recall of important ideas and terms.

Critical Thinking extends your knowledge of the chapter. If you have trouble answering these questions, reread the relevant parts of the chapter.

Succeed on Certification Tests with test-taking tips and practice questions.

Develop Your Speaking Skills as you review and explain chapter concepts.

Practice Academics and 21st Century Skills as you connect what you have learned to real-world situations.

Close the Unit

WHAT HAVE YOU LEARNED ABOUT MARKETING?

Every unit ends with a Marketing Internship Project that lets you apply an important skill from the unit. To complete each project, you will perform research, plan your project, connect with your community, create a report, and share what you have learned.

Read the Scenario, which describes the project's background and explains the project's goals.

Follow the Project Checklist to make sure that you have done everything to complete your project.

UNIT 1 Marketing Internship Project

SWOT Analysis
for a Coffee and Tea Chain

Competition in the specialty coffee and tea market is hot. Is it too late for a new competitor to break into this lucrative market?

Scenario

An Italian coffee and tea chain is considering entering the specialty coffee market in the United States. Before making that investment, our client would like our firm to conduct a SWOT analysis. The Italian coffee chain has been successful in European and Asian markets because it has used its strengths and taken advantage of opportunities in these markets.

Each café's interior design is upscale with comfortable seating, artwork, and designer plates and cups. Exotic teas and specialty coffee offerings are priced in line with and below current competitors' offerings. Only high-grade coffee beans from selected coffee bean growers are used. The Italian cafés are trying to create a unique experience in coffee and tea drinking: coffee and tea should be savored.

The Skills You'll Use

Academic Skills Reading, writing, social studies, and researching

Basic Skills Speaking, listening, thinking, and interpersonal

Technology Skills Word processing, telecommunication, and Internet

NCTE 4 Use written language to communicate effectively.
NCTE 7 Conduct research and gather, evaluate, and synthesize data to communicate discoveries.

Your Objective

Analyze the current specialty coffee and tea market in order to help a client decide whether or not to enter the market.

STEP 1 Do Your Research

Go to the Internet or your school library. Find out about the coffee and tea specialty market in restaurants, cafés, and similar outlets in the United States.

As you conduct your research, answer these questions:

- Is the market growing or shrinking and why?
- What economic, political, socio-cultural or technological factors affect this market?
- Who makes up the target market of U.S. coffee drinkers and tea drinkers in terms of demographic, psychographic, geographic, and behavioral factors?
- How successful are the marketing mixes of competitors such as Starbucks®, Dunkin Donuts®, and McDonald's®?
- What are the strengths, weaknesses, opportunities, and threats for our client in the United States coffee and tea specialty market?

Write a summary of your research.

STEP 2 Plan Your Project

Now that you have completed your research, you need to begin planning your project.

- Conduct a SWOT analysis for the Italian café chain.
- Identify a potential target market in the United States for the Italian café chain.
- Write a report summarizing your SWOT analysis, identifying your target market, and explaining why you have chosen this target market.
- Suggest a marketing mix for the Italian café chain.
- Determine whether that market segment is big enough to support the Italian café chain.

STEP 3 Connect with Your Community

- Test your conclusions by conducting interviews with trusted adults in your community that match the target market you have identified. Ask questions about their habits.
- Take notes during the interviews, and transcribe your notes after the interviews.
- Observe customers in the competition's places of business and note how long they wait for service, how long they sit and drink their beverages, and what else they might be doing while drinking their beverages.

STEP 4 Share What You Learn

Assume your class is the committee from the Italian café chain.

- Share your findings and be prepared to answer questions.
- Explain how businesses find out their strengths and weaknesses in the marketplace.
- Explain how businesses react to opportunities and threats in the marketplace.
- Make your recommendation and provide rationale for your decision.
- Use software to create a slide presentation to accompany your oral report. Include one slide in your presentation for each key topic in your written report.

STEP 5 Evaluate Your Marketing and Academic Skills

Your project will be evaluated based on the following:

- Knowledge of the specialty coffee and tea market
- Comprehensive SWOT analysis
- Proper use of marketing terminology
- Rationale for recommendation
- Organization and continuity of presentation
- Mechanics—presentation and neatness
- Speaking and listening skills

MARKETING CORE FUNCTIONS
Market Planning
Pricing

Marketing Internship Project Checklist

Plan
- ✓ Research current market conditions in the industry.
- ✓ Assess the strengths, weaknesses, opportunities, and threats a new competitor would face in this market.
- ✓ Identify a location to use as a test market for the new competitor.

Write
- ✓ Describe current market conditions in the industry.
- ✓ Explain how the results of the SWOT analysis help the new competitor understand the risks involved in the market.

Present
- ✓ Present the results of your SWOT analysis and justify your chosen location for the new competitor.
- ✓ Respond to questions posed by the audience.
- ✓ Consider the needs and experiences of the audience as you present research to your class.

glencoe.com
Evaluate Download a rubric you can use to evaluate your final project.

my marketing portfolio

Internship Report When you have completed your Marketing Internship Project and oral presentation, put your written report and printouts of key slides from your oral presentation in your marketing portfolio.

Analyze a Different Market and Company Select a different market (e.g., sports equipment, ice cream, cell phones, bicycles, vitamin-enriched water) and a company of your choice in that market. Conduct a SWOT analysis of that company. How effective is that company in following the marketing concept? Should that company pull out of that market or remain? If it should remain, make recommendations with regard to the company's marketing mix (product, place, price, and promotion). Prepare a written report and an oral presentation.

54 | Unit 1 · The World of Marketing

Unit 1 · The World of Marketing | 55

Apply the Academic, Basic, and Technology Skills that will be used as the basis of the project.

Build Your Own Marketing Portfolio with materials you created for your project.

PREPARE FOR ACADEMIC SUCCESS!

By improving your academic skills, you improve your ability to learn and achieve success now and in the future. The features and assessments in Marketing Essentials provide many opportunities for you to strengthen your academic skills.

NATIONAL ENGLISH LANGUAGE ARTS STANDARDS

To help incorporate literacy skills (reading, writing, listening, and speaking) into *Marketing Essentials,* each section contains a listing of the language arts skills covered.

NCTE 1 Students read a wide range of print and nonprint texts to build an understanding of texts, of themselves, and of the cultures of the United States and the world; to acquire new information; to respond to the needs and demands of society and the workplace; and for personal fulfillment. Among these texts are fiction and nonfiction, classic and contemporary works.
NCTE 2 Students read a wide range of literature from many periods in many genres to build an understanding of the many dimensions (e.g., philosophical, ethical, aesthetic) of human experience.
NCTE 3 Students apply a wide range of strategies to comprehend, interpret, evaluate, and appreciate texts. They draw on their prior experience, their interactions with other readers and writers, their knowledge of word meaning and of other texts, their word identification strategies, and their understanding of textual features (e.g., sound-letter correspondence, sentence structure, context, graphics).
NCTE 4 Students adjust their use of spoken, written, and visual language (e.g., conventions, style, vocabulary) to communicate effectively with a variety of audiences and for different purposes.
NCTE 5 Students employ a wide range of strategies as they write and use different writing process elements appropriately to communicate with different audiences for a variety of purposes.
NCTE 6 Students apply knowledge of language structure, language conventions (e.g., spelling and punctuation), media techniques, figurative language, and genre to create, critique, and discuss print and nonprint texts.
NCTE 7 Students conduct research on issues and interests by generating ideas and questions, and by posing problems. They gather, evaluate, and synthesize data from a variety of sources (e.g., print and nonprint texts, artifacts, people) to communicate their discoveries in ways that suit their purpose and audience.
NCTE 8 Students use a variety of technological and informational resources (e.g., libraries, databases, computer networks, video) to gather and synthesize information and to create and communicate knowledge.
NCTE 9 Students develop an understanding of and respect for diversity in language use, patterns, and dialects across cultures, ethnic groups, geographic regions, and social roles.
NCTE 10 Students whose first language is not English make use of their first language to develop competency in the English language arts and to develop understanding of content across the curriculum
NCTE 11 Students participate as knowledgeable, reflective, creative, and critical members of a variety of literacy communities.
NCTE 12 Students use spoken, written, and visual language to accomplish their own purposes (e.g., for learning, enjoyment, persuasion, and the exchange of information).

NATIONAL SCIENCE STANDARDS

The National Science Education Standards outline these science skills that you can practice in this text.

Unifying Concepts and Processes Students should develop an understanding of science unifying concepts and processes: systems, order, and organization; evidence, models, and explanation; change, constancy, and measurement; evolution and equilibrium; and form and function.
Content Standard A Students should develop abilities necessary to do scientific inquiry, understandings about scientific inquiry.
Content Standard B Students should develop an understanding of the structure of atoms, structure and properties of matter, chemical reactions, motions and forces, conservation of energy and increase in disorder, and interactions of energy and matter.
Content Standard C Students should develop understanding of the cell; molecular basis of heredity; biological evolution; interdependence of organisms; matter, energy, and organization in living systems; and behavior of organisms.
Content Standard D Students should develop an understanding of energy in the earth system, geochemical cycles, origin and evolution of the earth system, origin and evolution of the universe.
Content Standard E Students should develop abilities of technological design, understandings about science and technology.
Content Standard F Students should develop understanding of personal and community health; population growth; natural resources; environmental quality; natural and human-induced hazards; science and technology in local, national, and global challenges.
Content Standard G Students should develop understanding of science as a human endeavor, nature of scientific knowledge, historical perspectives.

NATIONAL MATH STANDARDS

You also have opportunities to practice math skills indicated by standards developed by the National Council of Teachers of Mathematics.

National Council of Teachers of Mathematics Standards for Grades 9–12

Number and Operations
Understand numbers, ways of representing numbers, relationships among numbers, and number systems.
Understand the meanings of operations and how they relate to one another.
Compute fluently and make reasonable estimates.
Algebra
Understand patterns, relations, and functions.
Represent and analyze mathematical situations and structures using algebraic symbols.
Use mathematical models to represent and understand quantitative relationships.
Analyze change in various contexts.
Geometry
Analyze characteristics of two- and three-dimensional geometric shapes and develop mathematical arguments about geometric relationships.
Use visualization, spatial reasoning, and geometric modeling to solve problems.
Measurement
Understand measurable attributes of objects and the units, systems, and processes of measurement.
Apply appropriate techniques, tools, and formulas to determine measurements.
Data Analysis and Probability
Formulate questions that can be addressed with data and collect, organize, and display relevant data to answer them.
Select and use appropriate statistical methods to analyze data.
Develop and evaluate inferences and predictions that are based on data.
Understand and apply basic concepts of probability.
Problem Solving
Apply and adapt a variety of appropriate strategies to solve problems.
Solve problems that arise in mathematics and in other contexts.
Build new mathematical knowledge through problem solving.
Monitor and reflect on the process of problem solving.

NATIONAL SOCIAL STUDIES STANDARDS

The National Council for the Social Studies is another organization that provides standards to help guide your studies. Activities in this text relate to these standards.

National Council for the Social Studies Curriculum Standards

I. Culture	
A Analyze and explain the ways groups, societies, and cultures address human needs and concerns.	E Demonstrate the value of cultural diversity, as well as cohesion, within and across groups.
B Predict how data and experiences may be interpreted by people from diverse cultural perspectives and frames of reference.	F Interpret patterns of behavior reflecting values and attitudes that contribute or pose obstacles to cross-cultural understanding.
C Apply an understanding of culture as an integrated whole that explains the functions and interactions of language, literature, the arts, traditions, beliefs and values, and behavior patterns.	G Construct reasoned judgments about specific cultural responses to persistent human issues.
D Compare and analyze societal patterns for preserving and transmitting culture while adapting to environmental or social change.	H Explain and apply ideas, theories, and modes of inquiry drawn from anthropology and sociology in the examination of persistent issues and social problems.
II. Time, Continuity, and Change	
A Demonstrate that historical knowledge and the concept of time are socially influenced constructions that lead historians to be selective in the questions they seek to answer and the evidence they use.	D Systematically employ processes of critical historical inquiry to reconstruct and reinterpret the past, such as using a variety of sources and checking their credibility, validating and weighing evidence for claims, and searching for causality.
B Apply key concepts such as time, chronology, causality, change, conflict, and complexity to explain, analyze, and show connections among patterns of historical change and continuity.	E Investigate, interpret, and analyze multiple historical and contemporary viewpoints within and across cultures related to important events, recurring dilemmas, and persistent issues, while employing empathy, skepticism, and critical judgment.
C Identify and describe significant historical periods and patterns of change within and across cultures, such as the development of ancient cultures and civilizations, the rise of nation-states, and social, economic, and political revolutions.	F Apply ideas, theories, and modes of historical inquiry to analyze historical and contemporary developments, and to inform and evaluate actions concerning public policy issues.
III. People, Places, and Environments	
A Refine mental maps of locales, regions, and the world that demonstrate understanding of relative locations, direction, size, and shape.	G Describe and compare how people create places that reflect culture, human needs, government policy, and current values and ideals as they design and build specialized buildings, neighborhoods, shopping centers, urban centers, industrial parks, and the like.
B Create, interpret, use, and synthesize information from various representations of the earth, such as maps, globes, and photographs.	H Examine, interpret, and analyze physical and cultural patterns and their interactions, such as land use, settlement patterns, cultural transmission of customs and ideas, and ecosystem changes.
C Use appropriate resources, data sources, and geographic tools such as aerial photographs, satellite images, geographic information systems (GIS), map projections, and cartography to generate, manipulate, and interpret information such as atlases, databases, grid systems, charts, graphs, and maps.	I Describe and assess ways that historical events have been influenced by, and have influenced, physical and human geographic factors in local, regional, national, and global settings.
D Calculate distance, scale, area, and density, and distinguish spatial distribution patterns.	J Analyze and evaluate social and economic effects of environmental changes and crises resulting from phenomena such as floods, storms, and drought.
E Describe, differentiate, and explain the relationships among various regional and global patterns of geographic phenomena such as landforms, soils, climate, vegetation, natural resources, and population.	K Propose, compare, and evaluate alternative policies for the use of land and other resources in communities, regions, nations, and the world.
F Use knowledge of physical system changes such as seasons, climate and weather, and the water cycle to explain geographic phenomena.	

National Council for the Social Studies, *Expectations of Excellence: Curriculum Standards for Social Studies (Washington, D.C.: NCSS, 1944).*

ACADEMIC STANDARDS

IV. Individual Development and Identity	
A Articulate personal connections to time, place, and social/cultural system.	**F** Analyze the role of perceptions, attitudes, values, and beliefs in the development of personal identity.
B Identify, describe, and express appreciation for the influence of various historical and contemporary cultures on an individual's daily life.	**G** Compare and evaluate the impact of stereotyping, conformity, acts of altruism, and other behaviors on individuals and groups.
C Describe the ways family, religion, gender, ethnicity, nationality, socioeconomic status, and other group and cultural influences contribute to the development of a sense of self.	**H** Work independently and cooperatively within groups and institutions to accomplish goals.
D Apply concepts, methods, and theories about the study of human growth and development, such as physical endowment, learning, motivation, behavior, perception, and personality.	**I** Examine factors that contribute to and damage one's mental health and analyze issues related to mental health and behavioral disorders in contemporary society.
E Examine the interaction of ethnic, national, or cultural influences in specific situations or events.	

V. Individuals, Groups, and Institutions	
A Apply concepts such as role, status, and social class in describing the connections and interactions of individuals, groups, and institutions in society.	**E** Describe and examine belief systems basic to specific traditions and laws in contemporary and historical movements.
B Analyze group and institutional influences on people, events, and elements of culture in both historical and contemporary settings.	**F** Evaluate the role of institutions in furthering both continuity and change.
C Describe the various forms institutions take, and explain how they develop and change over time.	**G** Analyze the extent to which groups and institutions meet individual needs and promote the common good in contemporary and historical settings.
D Identify and analyze examples of tensions between expressions of individuality and efforts used to promote social conformity by groups and institutions.	**H** Explain and apply ideas and modes of inquiry drawn from behavioral science and social theory in the examination of persistent issues and social problems.

VI. Power, Authority, and Governance	
A Examine persistent issues involving the rights, roles, and status of the individual in relation to the general welfare.	**F** Analyze and evaluate conditions, actions, and motivations that contribute to conflict and cooperation within and among nations.
B Explain the purpose of government and analyze how its powers are acquired, used, and justified.	**G** Evaluate the role of technology in communications, transportation, information-processing, weapons development, or other areas as it contributes to or helps resolve conflicts.
C Analyze and explain ideas and mechanisms to meet needs and wants of citizens, regulate territory, manage conflict, establish order and security, and balance competing conceptions of a just society.	**H** Explain and apply ideas, theories, and modes of inquiry drawn from political science to the examination of persistent ideas and social problems.
D Compare and analyze the ways nations and organizations respond to conflicts between forces of unity and forces of diversity.	**I** Evaluate the extent to which governments achieve their stated ideals and policies at home and abroad.
E Compare different political systems (their ideologies, structure, institutions, processes, and political cultures) with that of the United States, and identify representative political leaders from selected historical and contemporary settings.	**J** Prepare a public policy paper and present and defend it before an appropriate forum in school or community.

VII. Production, Distribution, and Consumption	
A Explain how the scarcity of productive resources (human, capital, technological, and natural) requires the development of economic systems to make decisions about how goods and services are to be produced and distributed.	**C** Consider the costs and benefits to society of allocating goods and services through private and public sectors.
B Analyze the role that supply and demand, prices, incentives, and profits play in determining what is produced and distributed in a competitive market system.	**D** Describe the relationships among the various economic institutions that comprise economic systems such as households, business firms, banks, government agencies, labor unions, and corporations.

E Analyze the role of specialization and exchange in economic processes.	**I** Distinguish between the domestic and global economic systems, and explain how the two interact.
F Compare how values and beliefs influence economic decisions in different societies.	**J** Apply knowledge of production, distribution, and consumption in the analysis of a public issue such as the allocation of health care or the consumption of energy, and devise an economic plan for accomplishing a socially desirable outcome related to that issue.
G Compare basic economic systems according to how rules and procedures deal with demand, supply, prices, the role of government, banks, labor and labor unions, savings and investments, and capital.	**K** Distinguish between economics as a field of inquiry and the economy.
H Apply economic concepts and reasoning when evaluating historical and contemporary social developments and issues.	
VIII. Science, Technology, and Society	
A Identify and describe both current and historical examples of the interaction and interdependence of science, technology, and society in a variety of cultural settings.	**D** Evaluate various policies that have been proposed as ways of dealing with social changes resulting from new technologies, such as genetically engineered plants and animals.
B Make judgments about how science and technology have transformed the physical world and human society and our understanding of time, space, place, and human-environment interactions.	**E** Recognize and interpret varied perspectives about human societies and the physical world using scientific knowledge, ethical standards, and technologies from diverse world cultures.
C Analyze how science and technology influence the core values, beliefs, and attitudes of society, and how core values, beliefs, and attitudes of society shape scientific and technological change.	**F** Formulate strategies and develop policies for influencing public discussions associated with technology-society issues, such as the greenhouse effect.
IX. Global Connections	
A Explain how language, art, music, belief systems, and other cultural elements can facilitate global understanding or cause misunderstanding.	**E** Analyze the relationships and tensions between national sovereignty and global interests, in such matters as territory, economic development, nuclear and other weapons, use of natural resources, and human rights concerns.
B Explain conditions and motivations that contribute to conflict, cooperation, and interdependence among groups, societies, and nations.	**F** Analyze or formulate policy statements demonstrating an understanding of concerns, standards, issues, and conflicts related to universal human rights.
C Analyze and evaluate the effects of changing technologies on the global community.	**G** Describe and evaluate the role of international and multinational organizations in the global arena.
D Analyze the causes, consequences, and possible solutions to persistent, contemporary, and emerging global issues, such as health, security, resource allocation, economic development, and environmental quality.	**H** Illustrate how individual behaviors and decisions connect with global systems.
X. Civic Ideals and Practices	
A Explain the origins and interpret the continuing influence of key ideals of the democratic republican form of government, such as individual human dignity, liberty, justice, equality, and the rule of law.	**F** Analyze a variety of public policies and issues from the perspective of formal and informal political actors.
B Identify, analyze, interpret, and evaluate sources and examples of citizens' rights and responsibilities.	**G** Evaluate the effectiveness of public opinion in influencing and shaping public policy developments and decision making.
C Locate, access, analyze, organize, synthesize, evaluate, and apply information about selected public issues—identifying, describing, and evaluating multiple points of view.	**H** Evaluate the degree to which public policies and citizen behaviors reflect or foster the stated ideals of a democratic republican form of government.
D Practice forms of civic discussion and participation consistent with the ideals of citizens in a democratic republic.	**I** Construct a policy statement to achieve one or more goals related to an issue of public concern.
E Analyze and evaluate the influence of various forms of citizen action on public policy.	**J** Participate in activities to strengthen the "common good," based upon careful evaluation of possible options for citizen action.

Reading Skills Handbook

Reading: What's in It for You?

What role does reading play in your life? The possibilities are countless. Are you on a sports team? Perhaps you like to read about the latest news and statistics in sports or find out about new training techniques. Are you looking for a part-time job? You might be looking for advice about résumé writing, interview techniques, or information about a company. Are you enrolled in an English class, an algebra class, or a business class? Then your assignments require a lot of reading.

Improving or Fine-Tuning Your Reading Skills Will:

- Improve your grades.
- Allow you to read faster and more efficiently.
- Improve your study skills.
- Help you remember more information accurately.
- Improve your writing.

The Reading Process

Good reading skills build on one another, overlap, and spiral around in much the same way that a winding staircase goes around and around while leading you to a higher place. This handbook is designed to help you find and use the tools you will need **before, during,** and **after** reading.

Strategies You Can Use

- Identify, understand, and learn new words.
- Understand why you read.
- Take a quick look at the whole text.
- Try to predict what you are about to read.
- Take breaks while you read and ask yourself questions about the text.
- Take notes.
- Keep thinking about what will come next.
- Summarize.

Vocabulary Development

Word identification and vocabulary skills are the building blocks of the reading and the writing process. By learning to use a variety of strategies to build your word skills and vocabulary, you will become a stronger reader.

Use Context to Determine Meaning

The best way to expand and extend your vocabulary is to read widely, listen carefully, and participate in a rich variety of discussions. When reading on your own, though, you can often figure out the meanings of new words by looking at their **context,** the other words and sentences that surround them.

Tips for Using Context

Look for clues like these:

- A synonym or an explanation of the unknown word in the sentence:
  Elise's shop specialized in millinery, or hats for women.
- A reference to what the word is or is not like:
  An archaeologist, like a historian, deals with the past.
- A general topic associated with the word:
  The cooking teacher discussed the best way to braise meat.
- A description or action associated with the word:
  He used the shovel to dig up the garden.

Predict a Possible Meaning

Another way to determine the meaning of a word is to take the word apart. If you understand the meaning of the **base,** or **root,** part of a word, and also know the meanings of key syllables added either to the beginning or end of the base word, you can usually figure out what the word means.

Word Origins Since Latin, Greek, and Anglo-Saxon roots are the basis for much of our English vocabulary, having some background in languages can be a useful vocabulary tool. For example, *astronomy* comes from the Greek root *astro,* which means "relating to the stars." *Stellar* also has a meaning referring to stars, but its origin is Latin. Knowing root words in other languages can help you determine meanings, derivations, and spellings in English.

Prefixes and Suffixes A prefix is a word part that can be added to the beginning of a word. For example, the prefix *semi* means "half" or "partial," so *semicircle* means "half a circle." A suffix is a word part that can be added to the end of a word. Adding a suffix often changes a word from one part of speech to another.

Using Dictionaries A dictionary provides the meaning or meanings of a word. Look at the sample dictionary entry on the next page to see what other information it provides.

Thesauruses and Specialized Reference Books A thesaurus provides synonyms and often antonyms. It is a useful tool to expand your vocabulary. Remember to check the exact definition of the listed words in a dictionary before you use a thesaurus. Specialized dictionaries such as *Barron's Dictionary of Business Terms* or *Black's Law Dictionary* list terms and expressions that are not commonly included in a general dictionary. You can also use online dictionaries.

Glossaries Many textbooks and technical works contain condensed dictionaries that provide an alphabetical listing of words used in the text and their specific definitions.

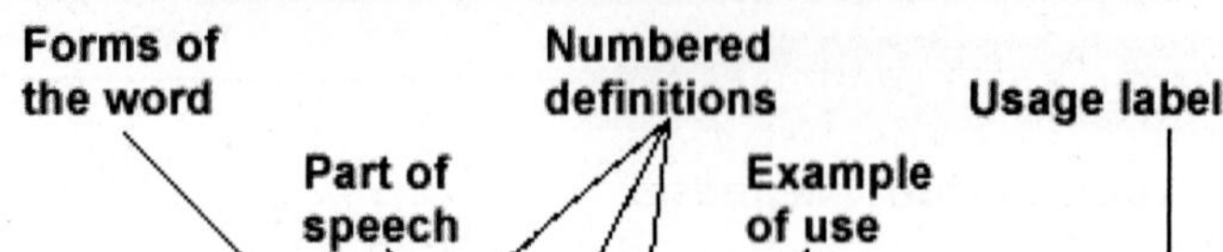

Dictionary Entry

Forms of the word | Numbered definitions | Usage label | Part of speech | Example of use

help (help) **helped** or *(archaic)* **holp**, **helped** or *(archaic)* **hol-pen, help-ing**. *v.t.* **1.** to provide with support, as in the performance of a task; be of service to: *He helped his brother paint the room.* ▲ also used elliptically with a preposition or adverb: *He helped the old woman up the stairs.* **2.** to enable (someone or something) to accomplish a goal or achieve a desired effect: *The coach's advice helped the team to win.* **3.** to provide with sustenance or relief, as in time of need or distress; succor: *The Red Cross helped the flood victims.* **4.** to promote or contribute to; further. *The medication helped his recovery.* **5.** to be useful or profitable to; be of advantage to: *It might help you if you read the book.* **6.** to improve or remedy: *Nothing really helped his sinus condition.* **7.** to prevent; stop: *I can't help his rudeness.* **8.** to refrain from; avoid: *I couldn't help smiling when I heard the story.* **9.** to wait on or serve (often with to): *The clerk helped us. The hostess helped him to the dessert.* **10. cannot help but.** *Informal* cannot but. **11. so help me (God).** oath of affirmation. **12. to help oneself to.** to take or appropriate: *The thief helped himself to all the jewels.* –*v.i.* to provide support, as in the performance of a task; be of service. –*n.* **1.** act of providing support, service, or sustenance. **2.** source of support, service, or sustenance. **3.** person or group of persons hired to work for another or others. **4.** means of improving, remedying, or preventing. [Old English *helpan* to aid, succor, benefit.] **Syn.** *v.t.* **1. Help, aid, assist** mean to support in a useful way. Help is the most common word and means to give support in response to a known or expressed need or for a definite purpose: *Everyone helped to make the school fair a success.* **Aid** means to give relief in times of distress or difficulty: *It is the duty of rich nations to aid the poor.* **Assist** means to serve another person in the performance of his task in a secondary capacity: *The secetary assists the officer by taking care of his corresponding.*

Idioms | Origin (etymology) | Synonyms

Recognize Word Meanings Across Subjects Have you learned a new word in one class and then noticed it in your reading for other subjects? The word might not mean exactly the same thing in each class, but you can use the meaning you already know to help you understand what it means in another subject area. For example:

Math Each digit represents a different place **value.**

Health Your **values** can guide you in making healthful decisions.

Economics The **value** of a product is measured in its cost.

Understanding What You Read

Reading comprehension means understanding—deriving meaning from—what you have read. Using a variety of strategies can help you improve your comprehension and make reading more interesting and more fun.

Read for a Reason

To get the greatest benefit from your reading, **establish a purpose for reading.** In school, you have many reasons for reading, such as:

- to learn and understand new information.
- to find specific information.
- to review before a test.
- to complete an assignment.
- to prepare (research) before you write.

As your reading skills improve, you will notice that you apply different strategies to fit the different purposes for reading. For example, if you are reading for entertainment, you might read quickly, but if you read to gather information or follow directions, you might read more slowly, take notes, construct a graphic organizer, or reread sections of text.

Draw on Personal Background

Drawing on personal background may also be called activating prior knowledge. Before you start reading a text, ask yourself questions like these:

- What have I heard or read about this topic?
- Do I have any personal experience relating to this topic?

Using a K-W-L Chart A K-W-L chart is a good device for organizing information you gather before, during, and after reading. In the first column, list what you already **know,** then list what you **want** to know in the middle column. Use the third column when you review and assess what you **learned.** You can also add more columns to record places where you found information and places where you can look for more information.

K (What I already know)	W (What I want to know)	L (What I have learned)

Adjust Your Reading Speed Your reading speed is a key factor in how well you understand what you are reading. You will need to adjust your speed depending on your reading purpose.

Scanning means running your eyes quickly over the material to look for words or phrases. Scan when you need a specific piece of information.

Skimming means reading a passage quickly to find its main idea or to get an overview. Skim a text when you preview to determine what the material is about.

Reading for detail involves careful reading while paying attention to text structure and monitoring your understanding. Read for detail when you are learning concepts, following complicated directions, or preparing to analyze a text.

Techniques to Understand and Remember What You Read

Preview

Before beginning a selection, it is helpful to **preview** what you are about to read.

Previewing Strategies

- Read the title, headings, and subheadings of the selection.
- Look at the illustrations and notice how the text is organized.
- Skim the selection: Take a glance at the whole thing.
- Decide what the main idea might be.
- Predict what a selection will be about.

Predict

Have you ever read a mystery, decided who committed the crime, and then changed your mind as more clues were revealed? You were adjusting your predictions. Did you smile when you found out that you guessed who committed the crime? You were verifying your predictions.

As you read, take educated guesses about story events and outcomes; that is, **make predictions** before and during reading. This will help you focus your attention on the text and it will improve your understanding.

Determine the Main Idea

When you look for the **main idea**, you are looking for the most important statement in a text. Depending on what kind of text you are reading, the main idea can be located at the very beginning (news stories in newspaper or a magazine) or at the end (scientific research document). Ask yourself the following questions:

- What is each sentence about?
- Is there one sentence that is more important than all the others?
- What idea do details support or point out?

Taking Notes

Cornell Note-Taking System There are many methods for note taking. The **Cornell Note-Taking System** is a well-known method that can help you organize what you read. To the right is a note-taking activity based on the Cornell Note-Taking System.

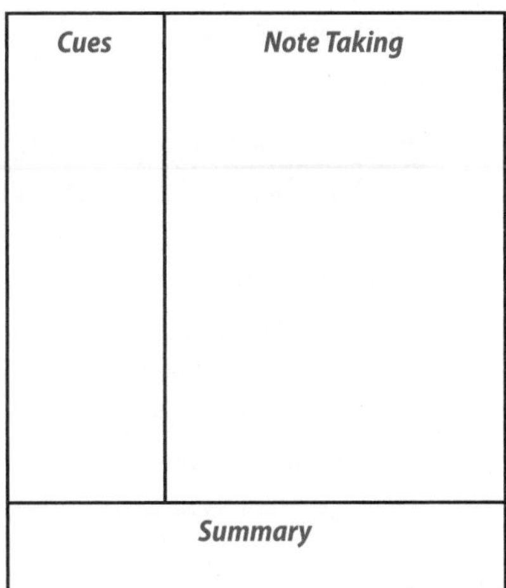

Graphic Organizers Using a graphic organizer to retell content in a visual representation will help you remember and retain content. You might make a **chart** or **diagram,** organizing what you have read. Here are some examples of graphic organizers:

Venn diagrams When mapping out a compare-and-contrast text structure, you can use a Venn diagram. The outer portions of the circles will show how two characters, ideas, or items contrast, or are different, and the overlapping part will compare two things, or show how they are similar.

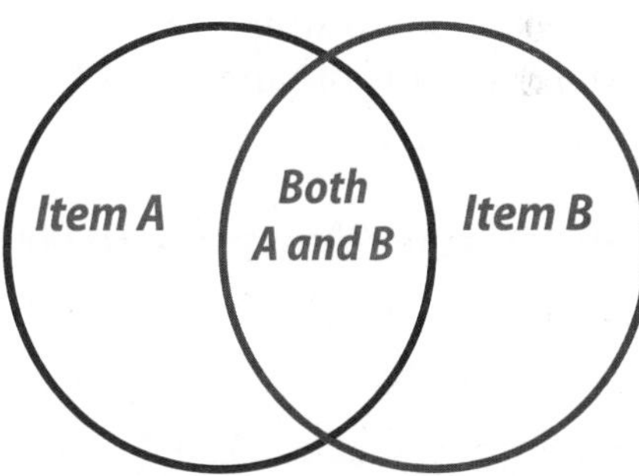

Flow charts To help you track the sequence of events, or cause and effect, use a flow chart. Arrange ideas or events in their logical, sequential order. Then, draw arrows between your ideas to indicate how one idea or event flows into another.

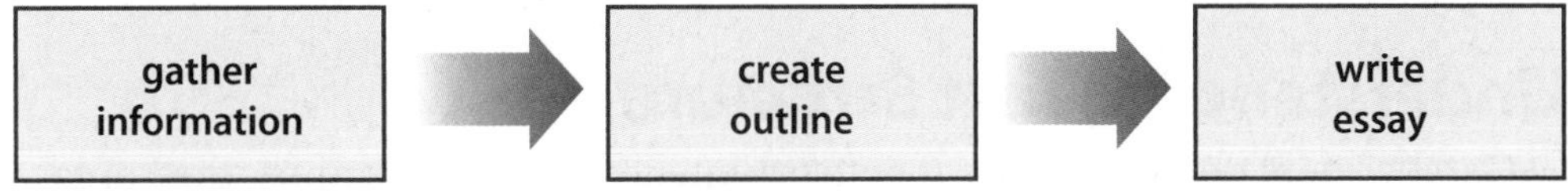

Visualize

Try to form a mental picture of scenes, characters, and events as you read. Use the details and descriptions the author gives you. If you can **visualize** what you read, it will be more interesting and you will remember it better.

Question

Ask yourself questions about the text while you read. Ask yourself about the importance of the sentences, how they relate to one another, if you understand what you just read, and what you think is going to come next.

Clarify

If you feel you do not understand meaning (through questioning), try these techniques:

What to Do When You Do Not Understand

- Reread confusing parts of the text.
- Diagram (chart) relationships between chunks of text, ideas, and sentences.
- Look up unfamiliar words.
- Talk out the text to yourself.
- Read the passage once more.

Review

Take time to stop and review what you have read. Use your note-taking tools (graphic organizers or Cornell notes charts). Also, review and consider your K-W-L chart.

Monitor Your Comprehension

Continue to check your understanding by using the following two strategies:

Summarize Pause and tell yourself the main ideas of the text and the key supporting details. Try to answer the following questions: Who? What? When? Where? Why? How?

Paraphrase Pause, close the book, and try to retell what you have just read in your own words. It might help to pretend you are explaining the text to someone who has not read it and does not know the material.

Understanding Text Structure

Good writers do not just put together sentences and paragraphs, they organize their writing with a specific purpose in mind. That organization is called text structure. When you understand and follow the structure of a text, it is easier to remember the information you are reading. There are many ways text may be structured. Watch for **signal words**. They will help you follow the text's organization (also, remember to use these techniques when you write).

Compare and Contrast

This structure shows similarities and differences between people, things, and ideas. This is often used to demonstrate that things that seem alike are really different, or vice versa.

Signal words: similarly, more, less, on the one hand / on the other hand, in contrast, but, however

Cause and Effect

Writers use the cause-and-effect structure to explore the reasons for something happening and to examine the results or consequences of events.

Signal words: so, because, as a result, therefore, for the following reasons

Problem and Solution

When they organize text around the question "how?" writers state a problem and suggest solutions.

Signal words: how, help, problem, obstruction, overcome, difficulty, need, attempt, have to, must

Sequence

Sequencing tells you in which order to consider thoughts or facts. Examples of sequencing are:

Chronological order refers to the order in which events take place.

Signal words: first, next, then, finally

Spatial order describes the organization of things in space (to describe a room, for example).

Signal words: above, below, behind, next to

Order of importance lists things or thoughts from the most important to the least important (or the other way around).

Signal words: principal, central, main, important, fundamental

Reading for Meaning

It is important to think about what you are reading to get the most information out of a text, to understand the consequences of what the text says, to remember the content, and to form your own opinion about what the content means.

Interpret

Interpreting is asking yourself, "What is the writer really saying?" and then using what you already know to answer that question.

Infer

Writers do not always state exactly everything they want you to understand. By providing clues and details, they sometimes imply certain information. An **inference** involves using your reason and experience to develop the idea on your own, based on what an author implies or suggests. What is most important when drawing inferences is to be sure that you have accurately based your guesses on supporting details from the text. If you cannot point to a place in the selection to help back up your inference, you may need to rethink your guess.

Draw Conclusions

A conclusion is a general statement you can make and explain with reasoning, or with supporting details from a text. If you read a story describing a sport where five players bounce a ball and throw it through a high hoop, you may conclude that the sport is basketball.

Analyze

To understand persuasive nonfiction (a text that discusses facts and opinions to arrive at a conclusion), you need to analyze statements and examples to see if they support the main idea. To understand an informational text (a text, such as a textbook, that gives you information, not opinions), you need to keep track of how the ideas are organized to find the main points.

Hint: Use your graphic organizers and notes charts.

Distinguish Facts from Opinions

This is one of the most important reading skills you can learn. A fact is a statement that can be proven. An opinion is what the writer believes. A writer may support opinions with facts, but an opinion cannot be proven. For example:

Fact: California produces fruit and other agricultural products.

Opinion: California produces the best fruit and other agricultural products.

Evaluate

Would you take seriously an article on nuclear fission if you knew it was written by a comedic actor? If you need to rely on accurate information, you need to find out who wrote what you are reading and why. Where did the writer get information? Is the information one-sided? Can you verify the information?

Reading for Research

You will need to **read actively** in order to research a topic. You might also need to generate an interesting, relevant, and researchable **question** on your own and locate appropriate print and nonprint information from a wide variety of sources. Then, you will need to **categorize** that information, evaluate it, and **organize** it in a new way in order to produce a research project for a specific audience. Finally, **draw conclusions** about your original research question. These conclusions may lead you to other areas for further inquiry.

Locate Appropriate Print and Nonprint Information

In your research, try to use a variety of sources. Because different sources present information in different ways, your research project will be more interesting and balanced when you read a variety of sources.

Literature and Textbooks These texts include any book used as a basis for instruction or a source of information.

Book Indices A book index, or a bibliography, is an alphabetical listing of books. Some book indices list books on specific subjects; others are more general. Other indices list a variety of topics or resources.

Periodicals Magazines and journals are issued at regular intervals, such as weekly or monthly. One way to locate information in magazines is to use the *Readers' Guide to Periodical Literature*. This guide is available in print form in most libraries.

Technical Manuals A manual is a guide or handbook intended to give instruction on how to perform a task or operate something. A vehicle owner's manual might give information on how to operate and service a car.

Reference Books Reference books include encyclopedias and almanacs, and are used to locate specific pieces of information.

Electronic Encyclopedias, Databases, and the Internet There are many ways to locate extensive information using your computer. Infotrac, for instance, acts as an online reader's guide. CD encyclopedias can provide easy access to all subjects.

Organize and Convert Information

As you gather information from different sources, taking careful notes, you will need to think about how to **synthesize** the information, that is, convert it into a unified whole, as well as how to change it into a form your audience will easily understand and that will meet your assignment guidelines.

1. First, ask yourself what you want your audience to know.
2. Then, think about a pattern of organization, a structure that will best show your main ideas. You might ask yourself the following questions:
   - When comparing items or ideas, what graphic aids can I use?
   - When showing the reasons something happened and the effects of certain actions, what text structure would be best?
   - How can I briefly and clearly show important information to my audience?
   - Would an illustration or even a cartoon help to make a certain point?

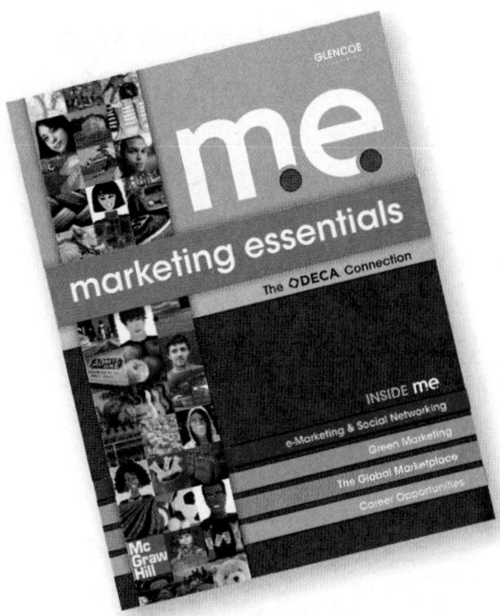

THE DECA CONNECTION

What is DECA?

DECA is a national association for students of marketing. It was formed in 1946 to improve the education of students in business subject areas, in particular marketing, entrepreneurship, and management.

DECA, which stands for the Distributive Education Clubs of America, offers students the opportunity to develop their leadership and professional skills. This is done through on-the-job experience, activities and projects sponsored by individual schools or chapters, and a series of competitive events in specific occupational areas. All activities apply the concepts of marketing to real-life situations. It is likely that DECA will be an integral part of your learning experience as you explore the world of marketing.

What is DECA's mission statement?

The mission of DECA is to enhance the co-curricular education of students with interests in marketing, management, and entrepreneurship. DECA helps students develop skills and competence for marketing careers, build self-esteem, experience leadership, and practice community service. DECA is committed to the advocacy of marketing education and the growth of business and education partnerships.

How can DECA help me?

Even though some activities may take time outside of school, DECA should be considered a co-curricular activity instead of an after-school activity. The basis for the projects and events will come from your classroom learning. Information from events that you take back to the classroom will enhance not only your learning experience, but that of your classmates as well. DECA also offers scholarships and other recognition awards to exceptional students. In general, success in DECA events is a positive addition to your résumé or portfolio.

DECA can help you:

- Develop strong leadership skills
- Understand the importance of making ethical decisions in your personal life and future career
- Focus on enhancing effective public speaking and presentation skills
- Understand the need for diversity in the global marketplace
- Enhance skills needed for a career in marketing or as an entrepreneur
- Increase your self-confidence when presenting or speaking in public
- Investigate career opportunities available in the marketing field
- Develop good social and business etiquette

What is DECA's mission statement?

Marketing Essentials is designed to prepare you for a career or further study in marketing. It is also helpful in preparing for DECA activities. You will notice that the DECA logo and DECA-approved activities are prominently featured throughout your book. The DECA Connection feature is modeled after DECA individual or team projects. It will help you apply knowledge learned in your marketing class. DECA activities can also enhance your classroom learning by helping you develop stronger communication and analytical skills.

DECA sponsors competitive events in 30 occupational areas, including:

- Apparel and Accessories Marketing Series
- Advertising Campaign Event
- Automotive Services Marketing Series
- Business Services Marketing Series
- E-Commerce Management Team Decision-Making Event
- Food Marketing Series, AL
- Financial Analysis Management Team Decision-Making Event
- Food Marketing Series, ML
- Full Service Restaurant Management Series
- Hospitality Services Management Team Decision-Making Event
- Hospitality and Recreation Marketing Research Event
- Marketing Management Series
- Quick Serve Restaurant Management Series
- Restaurant and Food Service Management Series
- Retail Merchandising Series
- Sports and Entertainment Marketing Series
- Sports and Entertainment Marketing Management Team Decision-Making Event
- Travel and Tourism Marketing Management Team Decision-Making Event
- Technical Sales Event

UNIT 1

The World of Marketing

PLANNING GUIDE AND RESOURCES

	Print	Digital
Unit 1 The World of Marketing		Unit 1 Fast Files: Marketing Internship Project Activity Connect Online Learning Center through glencoe.com
Chapter 1 **Marketing is All Around Us**	Student Activity Workbook: Chapter 1 DECA Connection Role Play; Chapter 1 Vocabulary Activity; Section Note Taking Activities; Chapter Academics Activity; Section Study Skills Activities; Section Real-World Applications Activities Mathematics for Marketing Workbook Marketing Research Project Workbook School-to-Career Activity Workbook	Unit 1 Fast Files: Chapter 1 Discovery Project Worksheet and Rubric; Chapter 1 Green Marketer Activity; Chapter 1 Digital Nation Activity; Section Graphic Organizers; Section Outlines with Key Terms and Definitions; Section Summaries ExamView Assessment Suite, Chapter 1 Connect Online Learning Center through glencoe.com
Chapter 2 **The Marketing Plan**	Student Activity Workbook: Chapter 2 DECA Connection Role Play; Chapter 2 Vocabulary Activity; Section Note Taking Activities; Chapter Academics Activity; Section Study Skills Activities; Section Real-World Applications Activities Mathematics for Marketing Workbook Marketing Research Project Workbook School-to-Career Activity Workbook	Unit 1 Fast Files: Chapter 2 Discovery Project Worksheet and Rubric; Chapter 2 Green Marketer Activity; Chapter 2 Digital Nation Activity; Section Graphic Organizers; Section Outlines with Key Terms and Definitions; Section Summaries ExamView Assessment Suite, Chapter 2 Connect Online Learning Center through glencoe.com

McGRAW-HILL PROFESSIONAL DEVELOPMENT

Perkins IV has placed more emphasis than ever on providing quality professional development for Career and Technology educators. The legislation mandates that the focus of professional development be the integration and reinforcement of academic competencies in order to improve student achievement. Specifically, Perkins requires measurements of students' academic success. McGraw-Hill answers the challenge for strong and effective professional development with a five-prong **Online Professional Development for Integrating Academics.**

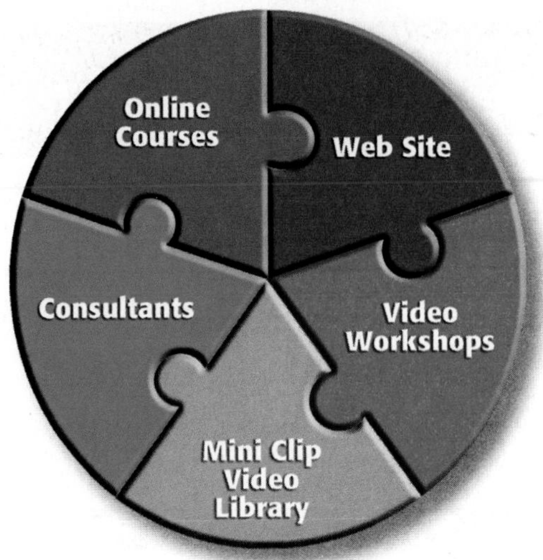

For pricing and ordering information contact your McGraw-Hill Sales Representative.

VIDEO LIBRARY

The McGraw-Hill Professional Development Mini-Clip Video Library, referenced for your convenience at the point of use, provides teaching strategies to strengthen academic and learning skills. Go to the Online Learning Center to view these professional development video clips for Unit 1:

Chapter 1: Marketing Is All Around Us

- **Reading: Prereading Strategies:** A teacher assesses prior knowledge about a text selection. (p. 7)
- **Reading: Options for Learning:** Teachers explain multiple ways to respond to a text. (p. 13)
- **ELL: Vocabulary Activities:** Students use synonyms, antonyms, and definitions in context. (p. 17)

Chapter 2: The Marketing Plan

- **Reading: Building Vocabulary:** A teacher introduces and plays two vocabulary building games with her students. (p. 31)
- **Math: Solving Equations:** Students use manipulatives and symbols to solve simple equations. (p. 41)
- **Reading: Strategic Readers:** A teacher discusses the characteristics of strategic readers. (p. 43)
- **ELL: Using Realia:** A teacher uses realia to make lesson concepts more real to students. (p. 45)
- **Math: Real-World Ratios:** A teacher has students create and compare ratios. (p. 53)

UNIT OVERVIEW

Sections	Objectives	Common Core State Standards College and Career Readiness
Section 1.1 **Marketing and the Marketing Concept**	• Describe the scope of marketing. • Describe each marketing core function. • Explain the marketing concept.	• **Reading** Determine central ideas or themes of a text and analyze their development; summarize the key supporting details and ideas.
Section 1.2 **The Importance of Marketing**	• Describe the benefits of marketing. • Explain the concept of utility. • Cite examples of utilities.	• **Reading** Read closely to determine what the text says explicitly and to make logical inferences from it; cite specific textual evidence when writing or speaking to support conclusions drawn from the text.
Section 1.3 **Fundamentals of Marketing**	• Describe how marketers use knowledge of the market to sell products. • Compare and contrast consumer and organizational markets. • Explain the importance of target markets. • Explain how each component of the marketing mix contributes to successful marketing.	• **Reading** Integrate and evaluate content presented in diverse formats and media, including visually and quantitatively, as well as in words.

Sections	Objectives	Common Core State Standards College and Career Readiness
Section 2.1 **Marketing Planning**	• Learn how to conduct a SWOT analysis. • List the three key areas of an internal company analysis. • Identify the factors in a PEST analysis. • Explain the basic elements of a marketing plan.	• **Reading** Determine central ideas or themes of a text and analyze their development; summarize the key supporting details and ideas.
Section 2.2 **Market Segmentation**	• Explain the concept of market segmentation. • Analyze a target market. • Differentiate between mass marketing and market segmentation.	• **Reading** Interpret words and phrases as they are used in a text, including determining technical, connotative, and figurative meanings, and analyze how specific word choices shape meaning or tone.

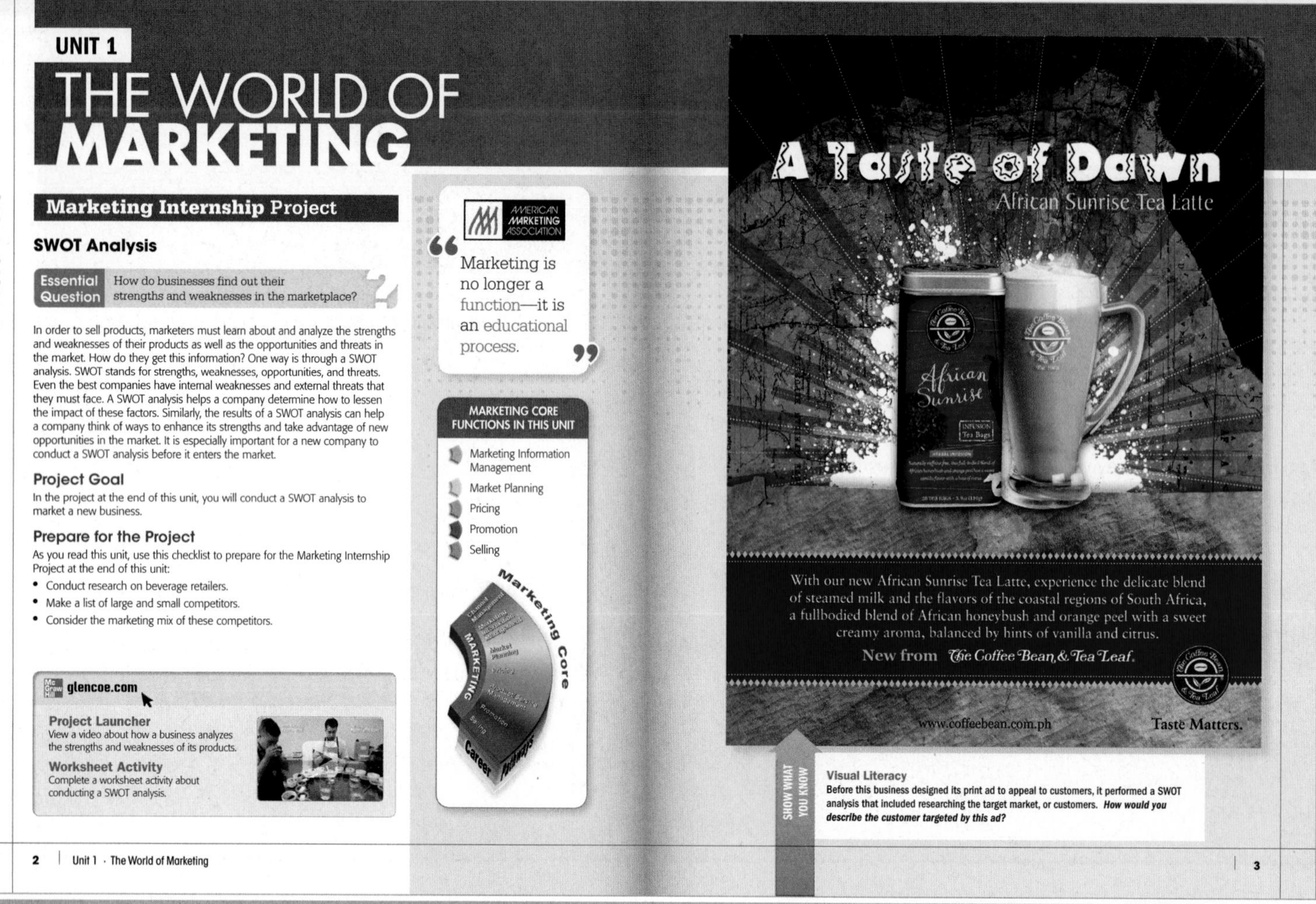

UNIT 1

THE WORLD OF MARKETING

Marketing Internship Project

SWOT Analysis

Essential Question How do businesses find out their strengths and weaknesses in the marketplace?

In order to sell products, marketers must learn about and analyze the strengths and weaknesses of their products as well as the opportunities and threats in the market. How do they get this information? One way is through a SWOT analysis. SWOT stands for strengths, weaknesses, opportunities, and threats. Even the best companies have internal weaknesses and external threats that they must face. A SWOT analysis helps a company determine how to lessen the impact of these factors. Similarly, the results of a SWOT analysis can help a company think of ways to enhance its strengths and take advantage of new opportunities in the market. It is especially important for a new company to conduct a SWOT analysis before it enters the market.

Project Goal

In the project at the end of this unit, you will conduct a SWOT analysis to market a new business.

Prepare for the Project

As you read this unit, use this checklist to prepare for the Marketing Internship Project at the end of this unit:

- Conduct research on beverage retailers.
- Make a list of large and small competitors.
- Consider the marketing mix of these competitors.

glencoe.com

Project Launcher
View a video about how a business analyzes the strengths and weaknesses of its products.

Worksheet Activity
Complete a worksheet activity about conducting a SWOT analysis.

AMERICAN MARKETING ASSOCIATION

"Marketing is no longer a function—it is an educational process."

MARKETING CORE FUNCTIONS IN THIS UNIT

- Marketing Information Management
- Market Planning
- Pricing
- Promotion
- Selling

Marketing Core
MARKETING
Career Pathways
A Taste of Dawn
African Sunrise Tea Latte
African Sunrise
With our new African Sunrise Tea Latte, experience the delicate blend of steamed milk and the flavors of the coastal regions of South Africa, a fullbodied blend of African honeybush and orange peel with a sweet creamy aroma, balanced by hints of vanilla and citrus.
New from The Coffee Bean & Tea Leaf.
www.coffeebean.com.ph
Taste Matters.

SHOW WHAT YOU KNOW

Visual Literacy
Before this business designed its print ad to appeal to customers, it performed a SWOT analysis that included researching the target market, or customers. ***How would you describe the customer targeted by this ad?***

ENGAGE

Introduce The Unit

Unit 1 lays out a base of knowledge for the entire text by providing an overview of marketing practices and principles.

Chapter 1 defines marketing, explains the benefits of marketing, and provides an overview of careers in marketing.

Chapter 2 focuses on the marketing concept, four Ps of the marketing mix, target marketing, and market segmentation.

Build Background

Ask students to name all of the different ways they encounter marketing messages each day. List their ideas on the board. Answers will vary but may include print, radio, television, and Internet marketing, billboards, smart phone applications, video games. Ask students: ***Why do you think that marketing is everywhere in society?*** In a free market, businesses might fight to get the attention of customers in order to win their business, thrive, and make a profit.

Visual Literacy

Photo Caption Answer Read the copy on the ad to students. Then read the photo caption and the photo caption question to students: ***How would you describe the customer targeted by this ad?*** Answers will vary. Accept all reasonable answers. Sample answer: This ad would appeal to a sophisticated audience of people who drink specialty tea beverages and who appreciate complex, layered flavors and textures. Ask students to evaluate the visual components of the advertisement. Ask volunteers to explain how the visual aspects of the advertisement complement the text of the advertisement. The latte and the tin of tea are a stylized sun, and the rays emanating out from these two items at the focal point are stylized rays of sunlight. The tea is called African Sunrise and the imagery evokes a sun rising. The headline "A Taste of Dawn" is a play on the sunrise theme, as the sun rises at the dawn of a new day. An African theme plays out in the text through the name of the tea and is illustrated in the color choices and in the decorative font of the headline.

ENGAGE

Marketing Internship Project Preview

Read students the Marketing Internship Project Essential Question: ***How do businesses find out their strengths and weaknesses in the marketplace?*** Because students are just starting to learn about marketing, they will not likely know the specific answer to this question, which is to conduct a SWOT analysis. However, students should know that businesses have to ask questions to find out answers that will give clues about their strengths and weaknesses. Explain to students that they will learn how businesses find out about their strengths and weaknesses while studying this unit. Tell students that when they are finished studying this unit, they will ask questions to find answers about the strengths and weaknesses of a specialty coffee and tea chain. As they study each chapter in the unit, they can prepare for the Unit Project by thinking of all the possible competitors a specialty coffee and tea business might have.

glencoe.com

Marketing Internship Project Resources Send students to the Online Learning Center to watch a video and download a worksheet activity related to the topic of the Unit Project.

Read the American Marketing Association quote to students:

“Marketing is no longer a function—it is an educational process.”

Explain to students that the AMA changed its official definition of marketing in 2007. Read the AMA's 2004 definition aloud:

2004 Marketing is an organizational function and a set of processes for creating, communicating, and delivering value to customers and for managing customer relationships in ways that benefit the organization and its stakeholders

Then read the AMA's 2007 definition of marketing aloud:

2007 Marketing is the activity, set of institutions, and processes for creating, communicating, delivering, and exchanging offerings that have value for customers, clients, partners, and society at large.

Ask students: ***How does the 2007 definition differ from the 2004 definition?*** The new definition includes the role marketing plays within society, and defines marketing as a scientific educational process and philosophy—not just a management system. It expands the previous scope to incorporate the concept that one can market something to have value for society.

MARKETING CORE FUNCTIONS IN THIS UNIT

Point out to students that Chapters 1 and 2 will touch on five of the seven marketing core functions. Describe each of these marketing functions to students to prepare them to start studying this unit.

- **Marketing Information Management** involves gathering, storing, and analyzing information about customers, trends, and competing products.
- **Market Planning** involves understanding the concepts and strategies used to develop and target specific marketing strategies to a select audience.
- **Pricing** decisions dictate how much to charge for goods and services in order to make a profit.
- **Promotion** is the effort to inform, persuade, or remind potential customers about a business's products or services or to improve a company's public image.
- **Selling** provides customers with the goods and services they want.

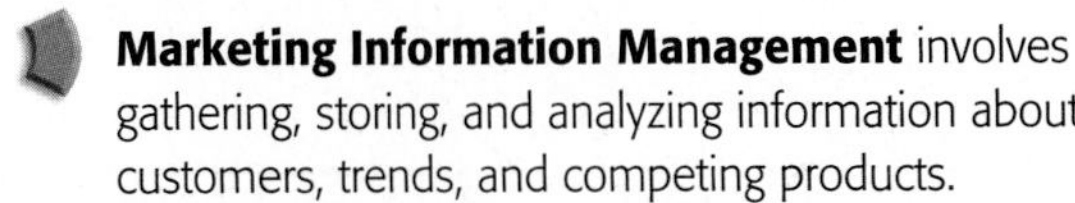
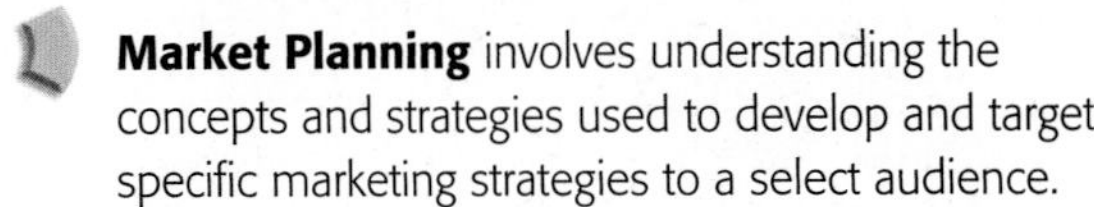

MARKETING RESEARCH PROJECT WORKBOOK

The purpose of the Marketing Research Project Workbook is to provide a step-by-step approach for students to conduct their own marketing research study. Each chapter is devoted to key elements in the research process. Each chapter builds upon the previous chapters, and by the end of the book, students will have completed an in-depth marketing research study, complete with rationale for all decisions, a report of the findings and conclusions, recommendations based on the original research problem and study objectives, and an annotated bibliography.

glencoe.com

Marketing Research Project Workbook Send students to the Online Learning Center to download the Marketing Research Project Workbook. A Teacher Manual is also available on the Teacher Center of the Online Learning Center.

Chapter 1 | Section 1.1 Marketing and the Marketing Concept | Section 1.2 The Importance of Marketing | Section 1.3 Fundamentals of Marketing

marketing is all around us

SHOW WHAT YOU KNOW

Visual Literacy Whenever you see advertising in print, online, or on the street, marketing is in action. When you go shopping, marketing is present in displays. When you go on the Internet, marketing pops up in front of you. When you see trucks hauling products, marketing is taking place. All these activities are aspects of marketing. ***What other activities have you observed that are part of marketing? How would you define marketing?***

Discovery Project

Keeping Customers

Essential Question How do businesses keep their customers?

Project Goal

Work with a partner to identify two businesses that cater to teenagers. One business should sell goods and the other services. Use the seven marketing functions—Channel Management, Marketing Information Management, Market Planning, Pricing, Product/Service Management, Promotion, and Selling—to explain how each business caters to its customers. How effective are those businesses in satisfying their customers' needs and wants? Develop a rating scale to present your findings.

Ask Yourself...

- Which two businesses will you study?
- How will you use the marketing functions to evaluate each business?
- How will you devise a rating scale?
- How will you present your findings?

Analysis and Interpretation Why is it important for businesses to follow the marketing functions?

glencoe.com

Activity
Get a worksheet activity about keeping customers.

Evaluate
Download a rubric that you can use to evaluate your project.

DECA Connection

DECA Event Role Play

Concepts in this chapter are related to DECA competitive events that involve either an interview or role play.

Performance Indicators The performance indicators represent key skills and knowledge. Your key to success in DECA competitive events is relating them to the concepts in this chapter.

- Explain the concept of marketing strategies.
- Explain the concept of markets and market identification.
- Explain the importance of promotion in the marketing mix.
- Describe marketing functions and related activities.
- Determine economic utilities created by business activities.

DECA Prep

Role Play Practice role playing with the DECA Connection competitive-event activity at the end of this chapter. More information about DECA events can be found on DECA's Web site.

Chapter 1 · Marketing Is All Around Us | 5

ENGAGE

Visual Literacy

Read the chapter opener photo caption questions to students: ***What other activities have you observed that are part of marketing? How would you define marketing?*** Students may mention television and radio commercials, flyers that come in the mail and newspaper, as well as pop-up ads on the Internet, and so on as marketing activities they have observed. Definitions of marketing might include selling products using advertising. Ask these guiding questions to activate prior knowledge. Write student generated questions produced during the discussion on the board and return to them throughout the chapter.

Guiding Questions

Explain How has marketing influenced your purchases?	Encourage students to share items they have purchased or wanted to purchase because of the way the items were marketed.
Make a Judgment In your opinion, what is the most effective form of marketing?	Sample answer: Students may feel that ads on television or the Internet are most effective.

Discovery Project

Keeping Customers Ask students if they have ever stopped going to a particular store or using a particular product. Ask why. Then ask them the Discovery Project Essential Question: ***How do businesses keep their customers?*** Students should be aware that businesses use a combination of marketing techniques and customer service to get and to keep their customers. Ask students to share what marketing techniques and customer service would keep them as a customer. Students might suggest such techniques as sales, competitive pricing, good warranties, and so on would help to keep them as a customer.

Discovery Project Resources Send students to the Online Learning Center to download a rubric to evaluate their projects.

ENGAGE

Introduce the Chapter

Chapter 1 provides the foundation for all subsequent study in this textbook. These main concepts are introduced and discussed:

- Marketing core functions
- Marketing concept
- Economic utility
- Market segmentation
- Target market
- Marketing mix
- The four Ps

Discussion Starter

Target Markets Ask students to provide a definition for the term target market. Students may suggest that a target market is the group of people that is identified for a specific marketing program. Ask students to describe different advertising campaigns with which they are familiar. Ask: ***Who do you think the target market is for this particular product or service? Why?*** Students should recognize that marketing differs greatly depending on the target market. Marketing that targets teens will look very different than marketing that targets middle-aged adults. Ask students to describe an ad that targets teens and an ad that targets middle-aged adults. Students may suggest that an ad for teens will be lively, colorful, and loud. An ad that targets middle-aged adults might be more thoughtful or retro and include more explanation and information.

DECA Connection

Discuss the performance indicators listed in the DECA Connection feature. Explain to students that performance indicators tell them how to demonstrate their acquired skills and knowledge through individual or team competitive events.

glencoe.com

Competitive Events Workbook For more DECA Role Plays, send students to the Online Learning Center to download the Competitive Events Workbook.

PRINT RESOURCES

- **Student Edition**
- **Teacher Edition**
- **Student Activity Workbook with Academic Integration** includes worksheets and activities correlated to the text.
- **Mathematics for Marketing Workbook** provides math activities for every unit in the text.

TECHNOLOGY TOOLBOX

- **Connect**
- **ConnectPlus**
- **ExamView Assessment Suite** is a comprehensive solution for creating, administering, and scoring tests.

glencoe.com

Online Learning Center provides a variety of resources to enrich and enhance learning.

SECTION, CHAPTER, AND UNIT RESOURCES

- **Graphic Organizers** for organizing text concepts visually.
- **Digital Nation Activities** and **Green Marketer Activities** extend learning beyond the text features.
- **Career Chatroom Career Profiles** allow students to explore different marketing occupations in depth.
- **After You Read Answer Keys** for students to check their answers.
- **Discovery Project Rubrics** and **Marketing Internship Project Rubrics** for students to evaluate their projects.

PROGRAM RESOURCES

- **Student Activity Workbook with Academic Integration Teacher Annotated Edition** includes annotated answers for the activities and worksheets.
- **Marketing Research Project Workbook** provides a step-by-step approach for students to complete their own marketing research studies.
- **School-to-Career Activity Workbook** helps students relate their class work to on-the-job experience and involves work-site analysis and working with mentors.
- **Competitive Events Workbook** helps prepare students for state and national marketing education competitions.
- **Inclusion in the Marketing Education Classroom** provides teaching resources for working with students with special needs.
- **PowerPoint Presentations** provides visual teaching aids and assessments for this chapter.

READING GUIDE

Before You Read

Connect When have you been influenced by marketing?

Objectives

- **Describe** the scope of marketing.
- **Describe** each marketing core function.
- **Explain** the marketing concept.

The Main Idea

To be a successful marketer, you need to understand the marketing skills, marketing core functions, and basic tools of marketing.

Vocabulary

Content Vocabulary
- marketing
- goods
- services
- marketing concept

Academic Vocabulary

You will find these words in your reading and on your tests. Make sure you know their meanings.
- create
- conduct

Graphic Organizer

Draw or print this umbrella graphic organizer to take notes about the marketing core functions.

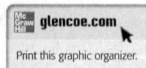

glencoe.com

Print this graphic organizer.

Selling

STANDARDS

ACADEMIC

English Language Arts

NCTE 4 Use written language to communicate effectively.

Social Studies

NCSS I A Culture Analyze and explain the ways groups, societies, and cultures address human needs and concerns.

NCSS *National Council for the Social Studies*

NCTE *National Council of Teachers of English*

NCTM *National Council of Teachers of Mathematics*

NSES *National Science Education Standards*

College & Career READINESS

Common Core

Reading Determine central ideas or themes of a text and analyze their development; summarize the key supporting details and ideas.

MARKETING CORE FUNCTION

Market Planning

Marketing and the Marketing Concept

m.e. Section 1.1

THE SCOPE OF MARKETING

You have been a consumer for many years, and you have made decisions about products you liked and did not like. As you study marketing, you will analyze what businesses do to influence consumers' buying decisions. That knowledge will help you begin to think like a marketer.

According to the American Marketing Association (AMA), "**marketing** is the activity, set of institutions, and processes for creating, communicating, delivering, and exchanging offerings that have value for customers, clients, partners, and society at large." It involves the process of planning, pricing, promoting, selling, and distributing ideas, goods, or services to **create** exchanges that satisfy customers. Note that marketing is a process. The AMA reviews the definition of marketing on a regular basis to make sure it conforms to current marketing practices. Thus, marketing is ongoing, and it changes. As a marketer, you need to keep up with trends and consumer attitudes.

As You Read

Connect Marketers track trends and consumer attitudes. What trends have you noticed in your experience as a teenager?

IDEAS, GOODS, AND SERVICES

Ideas, goods, and services are offerings. Politicians, for example, offer voters their platform or ideas in hopes of getting votes. **Goods** are tangible items that have monetary value and satisfy your needs and wants, such as cars, furniture, televisions, and clothing. Intangible items that have monetary value and satisfy your needs and wants are **services**. Intangible means you cannot physically touch an item.

Services involve a task, such as cooking a hamburger or cutting hair. Banks, dry cleaners, and accounting offices all provide economic services.

> "You already know a lot about marketing because it is all around you."

Every time someone sells or buys something, an exchange occurs in the marketplace. The marketplace is the commercial environment where exchanges occur. It is the world of shops, Internet stores, financial institutions, catalogs, and more.

SKILLS AND KNOWLEDGE

Marketing is one career cluster in business administration. The practice of marketing depends on many key areas of skill and knowledge. These areas are listed in the Marketing Core image on page 2 that introduces Unit 1. Many of the topics that you will study in *Marketing Essentials* are based on these areas of skill and knowledge:

- Business Law
- Communications
- Customer Relations
- Economics
- Emotional Intelligence
- Entrepreneurship
- Financial Analysis
- Human Resource Management
- Information Management
- Operations
- Professional Development
- Strategic Management

ENGAGE

Anticipation Activity

Improving Student Achievement Ask students to name the different types of advertising with which they are familiar. Have a volunteer list the types on the board. List catalogs, flyers, television and radio commercials, Internet ads, and so on. Point out to students that these are all types of marketing. Ask students: ***Why do you think there are so many different types of marketing?*** Marketers target different audiences with different types of ads.

Objectives

- **Describe** the scope of marketing. planning, pricing, promoting, selling, and distributing ideas, goods, services to create exchanges and satisfy customers
- **Describe** each marketing core function. channel management, marketing information management, market planning, pricing, product/service management, promotion, selling
- **Explain** the marketing concept. businesses should strive to satisfy customers' needs and wants while generating a profit

Graphic Organizer

1. Channel management	Decides how to get goods to customers
2. Marketing information management	gathers, stores, and analyzes customer trends, and competition
3. Market planning	Targets specific marketing strategies
4. Pricing	based on costs and on what competitors charge for the same product or service
5. Product/service management	Maintains, and improves product mix in response to market opportunities
6. Promotion	Informs current and potential customers about a business's products or services
7. Selling	Customers receive goods they want.

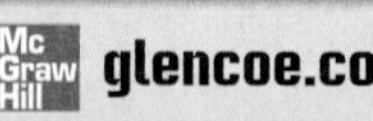

Graphic Organizer Send students to the Online Learning Center to print the graphic organizer.

EXPLORE

Before You Read

Read the Before You Read question aloud: ***When have you been influenced by marketing?*** Students may recognize that they are bombarded with advertising in newspapers and magazines, on buses and billboards, on television, and on the Internet. They may realize that advertising influences their choices even if they are not aware of it. Ask students to think about the last few purchases they made. Ask students: ***Why did you choose to buy your last purchase?*** Ask volunteers to share their answers. Students' answers will vary but should include marketing influences.

Preteaching Vocabulary

Have students go to the Online Learning Center at glencoe.com for the Chapter 1 Preteaching Vocabulary games.

Content Vocabulary

Instruct students to write a paragraph in which they discuss how the vocabulary terms are interrelated. *Marketing* involves planning, pricing, promoting, selling, and distributing *goods* (tangible items that have monetary value) and *services* (intangible items that have monetary value). The *marketing concept* implements marketing techniques to ensure customer satisfaction. Ask volunteers to share their paragraphs with the rest of the class.

Academic Vocabulary

Conduct—Synonyms Tell students that the Academic Vocabulary term *conduct* can be both a noun and a verb. Have students work together in pairs to develop a list of synonyms for the noun *conduct.* Synonyms may include: control, operation, direction, governance, oversight, guidance, management, regulation, administration, supervision. Then have them list synonyms for the verb *conduct.* Synonyms may include: control, direct, govern, transport, guide, handle, manage, lead, oversee, operate, regulate, run, administer, supervise. Ask students to determine which synonyms best fit the use of *conduct* in the text: Companies conduct research so they can be successful at marketing and selling their products. Answers might include: run, administer, direct, manage, and so on.

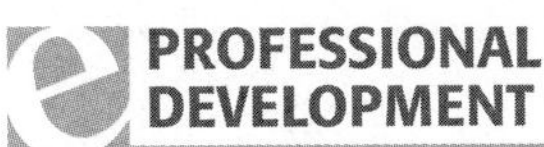

Reading: Prereading Strategies
Go to the Online Learning Center to view a video in which a teacher assesses prior knowledge about a text selection.

Section 1.1

Marketing and the Marketing Concept

THE SCOPE OF MARKETING

Explain to students that the scope of marketing includes many processes to create exchanges and satisfy customers. Then ask these guiding questions to focus the discussion about the scope of marketing.

Guiding Questions

Identify What are the three offerings in the scope of marketing?	Ideas, goods, and services
Explain What is an exchange in the marketplace?	An exchange occurs every time someone buys or sells something, such as in the commercial environment—banks and shops, on the Internet, catalogs, and so on.
Analyze the importance of business law, communications, and customer relations as skills and knowledge in marketing.	Possible answer: Business law is important for understanding a business's responsibilities. Communications convey ideas and information. Customer relations applies strategies to foster positive, ongoing relationships.

As You Read

Read students the As You Read question: ***Marketers track trends and consumer attitudes. What trends have you noticed in your experience as a teenager?*** Students will likely mention changing music styles, clothing styles, and video games. They may also mention cell and touch phones, MP3 players, laptops and touchpad computers.

Expert Advice

Read the quote to students:

> **"You already know a lot about marketing because it is all around you."**

Ask students: ***What marketing strategies do you see in the classroom or at home?*** Possible answers: company logos; print advertising; commercials on television and the Internet

Trustmarks: Green Seals of Approval

More and more companies are using trustmarks, packaging symbols that suggest that a product is greener or healthier than the competition. The three most recognized trustmarks are the recyclable symbol, the Energy Star label, and the USDA Organic seal. Energy Star and USDA Organic are awarded by the federal government, while the use of the recycling symbol is not regulated by law. That means anyone can use it to promote a product. Nonprofit organizations award many other trustmarks, such as the Rainforest Alliance Certified seal, in exchange for a fee. Each of these trustmarks tells consumers about the product's benefits.

Social Studies

Discuss Some trustmarks, such as the Smart Choices Program for healthy foods, are created by industry groups. Would you trust a seal created by the companies that use it on their products? Why or why not? Discuss your responses with a partner.

NCSS V G Individuals, Groups, and Institutions Analyze the extent to which groups and institutions meet individual needs and promote the common good in contemporary and historical settings.

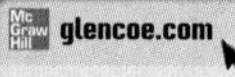

Get an activity on green marketing.

SEVEN MARKETING CORE FUNCTIONS

The marketing core includes seven functions. The image here also includes these functions. These functions define all the aspects that are part of the practice of marketing.

CHANNEL MANAGEMENT

Channel management, or distribution, is the process of deciding how to get goods into customer's hands. Physically moving and storing goods is part of distribution planning. The main methods of transportation are by truck, rail, ship, or air. Some large retail chains store products in warehouses for later distribution. Distribution also involves the systems that track products.

Companies may decide on several different channels of distribution, depending on whether the product is sold to individuals or businesses. The goal is to find the best way to get the product into the customer's hands based on his or her purchasing methods.

MARKETING INFORMATION MANAGEMENT

Good business and marketing decisions rely on good information about customers, trends, and competing products. Gathering this information, storing it, and analyzing it are all part of marketing information management. Companies **conduct** research so they can be successful at marketing and selling their products. They need to get information about their customers, their habits and attitudes, where they live, and trends in the marketplace. Marketers can use this information to create a marketing plan for their products.

MARKET PLANNING

Market planning involves understanding the concepts and strategies used to develop and target specific marketing strategies to a select audience. This function requires an in-depth knowledge of activities that involve determining information needs, designing data-collection processes, collecting data, analyzing data, presenting data, and using that data to create a marketing plan. The plan will include methods for reaching different types of customers.

PRICING

Pricing decisions dictate how much to charge for goods and services in order to make a profit. Pricing decisions are based on costs and on what competitors charge for the same product or service. To determine a price, marketers must also determine how much customers are willing to pay.

PRODUCT/SERVICE MANAGEMENT

Product/service management is obtaining, developing, maintaining, and improving a product or a product mix in response to market opportunities. Marketing research guides product/service management toward what the consumer needs and wants. New technology and trends influence product/service management as well.

PROMOTION

Promotion is the effort to inform, persuade, or remind current and potential customers about a business's products or services. Television and radio commercials are forms of promotion. This type of promotion is called advertising.

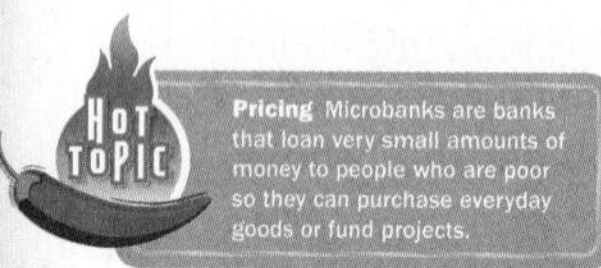

Pricing Microbanks are banks that loan very small amounts of money to people who are poor so they can purchase everyday goods or fund projects.

Promotion is also used to improve a company's public image. A company can show social responsibility by recycling materials or cleaning up the environment. Promotion concepts and strategies can help to achieve success in the marketplace.

SELLING

Selling provides customers with the goods and services they want. This includes selling in the retail market to you, the customer, and selling in the business-to-business market to wholesalers, retailers, or manufacturers.

Selling techniques and activities include determining client needs and wants and responding through planned, personalized communication. The selling process influences purchasing decisions and enhances future business opportunities.

Reading Check

Compare and Contrast What is the difference between goods and services?

Products Help Consumers Go Green

"We're using a sea of blue to become a lot greener"
POMPEIAN

The Pompeian® olive oil company uses methods that help reduce greenhouse gases by reducing fuel costs through shipping in bulk and switching to recyclable bottles. ***How can green initiatives like these help a business's profits as well as the environment?***

EXPLAIN

The GREEN Marketer

Social Studies Answer Ask students: *Would you trust a seal created by the companies that use it on their products? Why or why not?* No, I would not trust a green seal created by a company because the use of the seal may not be regulated by any official government organization. Yes, I would trust a green seal created a company because they are doing what they can for the environment and they want to keep their customers.

 glencoe.com 

Worksheet Activity Send students to the Online Learning Center to get a Green Marketer worksheet activity.

SEVEN MARKETING CORE FUNCTIONS

Tell students that the marketing core functions are the foundation on which marketing is developed. Then ask these guiding questions to focus the discussion about the marketing core.

Guiding Questions

Analyze Which of the functions focus on the consumer? Give examples.	All seven functions focus on the consumer. Sample examples include: promotion focuses on the consumer as it is designed to appeal to the consumer.
Predict What might happen if a company neglected one of the seven core functions?	The company would not focus on all aspects of marketing and would not have well-rounded marketing strategies.

ELABORATE

Mini Project

Enrichment

Research the Functions of Marketing Divide the class into seven collaborative groups. Assign each group one of the core functions. Have each group make a presentation about their assigned core function for a particular product or service that they researched. Encourage students to include visuals during their reports. Presentations will vary depending on the product or service and the core functions assigned and researched. Sample answer: Our group analyzed the core functions relevant to a new type of soccer ball that is promoted to youth soccer players. The function we researched was pricing, and during our research we found that this soccer ball was priced at a lower price point than most other soccer balls, this is likely due to the fact that it is marketed to young people who have less disposable income.

Graphic Organizer Point out the Marketing Core Functions illustration on the page. Tell students that this illustration shows one visual representation of the seven functions. Challenge students to think about the functions visually and come up with a new way to visually depict them, taking into account the relationships among the functions. Graphic organizers depicting the seven functions will vary but should represent that the functions are interconnected and equally important. A sample graphic organizer might depict the seven functions in a word web emanating from a central shape that says Marketing Core Functions. Accept all reasonable answers.

Graphic Organizer

Ask sudents to name the seven core marketing functions.

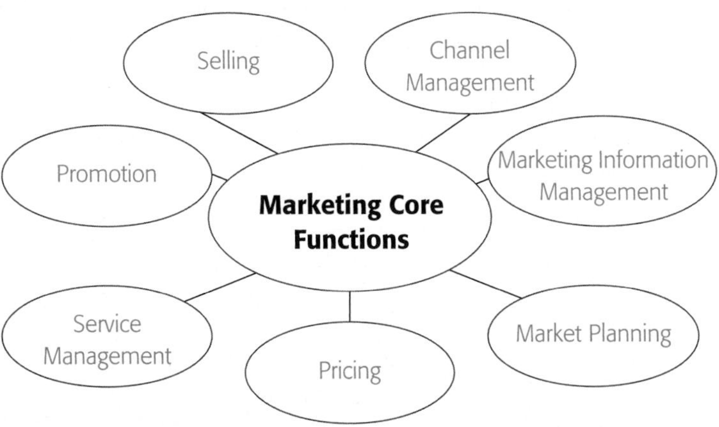

Graphic Organizer Send student to the Online Learning Center to print this graphic organizer.

Critical Thinking

To reinforce the concept of channel management, have students work with a partner to choose a product and research how that product is distributed. Remind students that distribution is the process of deciding the best way to get products to customers. Answers will vary depending on the product chosen by students. Possible answer: a Honda automobile is shipped by truck from the manufacturing plant in Japan to the sea port where it is loaded onto a ship and transported to a port in the United States. From the U.S. port it is shipped via truck or train to a local car dealership.

Pricing Have students research microbanks to learn what types of businesses receive loans and how the businesses fare over the long term. Students may also want to learn about the selection process microbanks use for companies receiving the loans.

Reading Check Answer

Read the Reading Check question to students: ***What is the difference between goods and services?*** Goods are tangible items that have monetary value and satisfy your needs and wants, such as a car or furniture. Services are intangible items that have monetary value and satisfy your needs and wants. Examples include a car wash or a house cleaning.

Visual Literacy

Social Benefits Caption Answer Read the photo caption question to students: ***How can green initiatives like these help a business's profits as well as the environment?*** Customers who feel strongly about environmental issues may be more likely to purchase products made by companies that promote green awareness, which would result in more profit for those businesses. Ask students: ***What methods does the ad use to persuade you to purchase the product or service?*** Possible answers may include attractive visuals, statement by the company's CEO, copy describing green initiatives, etc.

VIRTUAL BUSINESS

TARGETED MARKETING

Introduce students to the concept of targeted marketing using Knowledge Matters' Virtual Business Retailing visual simulation, *Targeted Marketing*. In this simulation, students will learn how to identify a target market and its characteristics.

THE MARKETING CONCEPT

The **marketing concept** is the idea that a business should strive to satisfy customers' needs and wants while generating a profit for the business. The focus is on the customer. After all, if customers do not buy a company's products, then it will go out of business.

The marketing concept holds that the desires and needs of the target market must be determined, anticipated, and satisfied in order to successfully achieve the goals of the producer. The best way to satisfy customers' needs is to stay in touch with them and monitor their purchasing behavior. The marketing concept is a philosophy. It makes the customer, and the satisfaction of his or her needs, the focal point of all business activities.

For an organization to be successful, all seven marketing core functions need to support the marketing concept. There are methods of satisfying customers' needs with regard to each marketing core function.

The people who are responsible for the marketing core functions must understand the marketing concept and reach for the same goal in order to send a consistent message to the customer. The message is that customer satisfaction is most important. Everyone in an organization needs to recognize that repeat customers keep a company in business. It is much more profitable for a company to hold on to existing customers than to search for new ones.

MARKETING CASE STUDY

Johnson & Johnson: Target Marketing

Research indicates that moms go online to get information about their newborn babies. Research also found that babies who are Hispanic represent 25 percent of babies born in the United States.

Media to Reach Moms

After analyzing these facts, Johnson & Johnson saw an opportunity to reach out to mothers who are Hispanic to sell its baby products. The company decided to create a Web site completely in Spanish, offering educational Webisodes that address concerns mothers have regarding their newborns. A few topics address the importance of touch in bonding with a newborn.

The product being introduced during this campaign was baby lotion. The message offers the benefits of touch in the development of a healthy baby.

To coordinate the campaign, Johnson & Johnson turned to Univision, a Spanish-language media company. It placed banner video ads on Univision's Web site, as well as ads on a variety of shows airing on its television network. A similar program was established in English so that mothers who are Hispanic could have a choice in language.

Social Studies

Math If Johnson & Johnson sold $12,949,847 of hand lotion in 2009 and $3,150,367 of that money was spent by mothers of children who are Hispanic, what percentage of Johnson & Johnson's profits were due to mothers who are Hispanic? Round to the nearest tenth.

NCTM Number and Operations Understand numbers, ways of representing numbers, relationships among numbers, and number systems.

CUSTOMER RELATIONSHIP MANAGEMENT

In the 21st century marketplace, a company's relationship with its customers is most important. It may be the main factor that determines whether a company is successful. Customer relationship management (CRM) is an aspect of marketing that combines customer information (through database and computer technology) with customer service and marketing communications. This combination allows companies to serve their customers as efficiently as possible.

By using CRM, companies are better able to understand their customers' purchasing patterns and demographics. An understanding of who its customers are and what they want to buy helps a company satisfy its customers' needs, optimize revenue, and generate more profit.

Computer databases contain information about customers who have purchased products from a company. Information from these databases is shared with the company's marketing professionals. Marketers analyze and interpret the information and search for trends and patterns in the data. These trends and patterns can serve as a company's inspiration to create new products or offer new services to meet customer needs.

Marketing professionals can also use forms of digital communication as part of CRM. A company can send emails or use posts on social networking sites to notify customers of new promotions and events that the company offers. Customers can also use email to contact the company with comments and questions about products and services. Effective communication between a company and its customers helps to keep customers satisfied and increase profits.

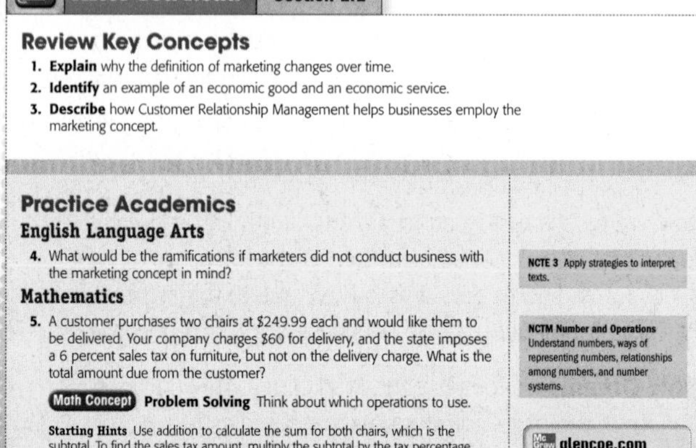

After You Read — Section 1.1

Review Key Concepts

1. **Explain** why the definition of marketing changes over time.
2. **Identify** an example of an economic good and an economic service.
3. **Describe** how Customer Relationship Management helps businesses employ the marketing concept.

Practice Academics

English Language Arts

4. What would be the ramifications if marketers did not conduct business with the marketing concept in mind?

NCTE 3 Apply strategies to interpret texts.

Mathematics

5. A customer purchases two chairs at $249.99 each and would like them to be delivered. Your company charges $60 for delivery, and the state imposes a 6 percent sales tax on furniture, but not on the delivery charge. What is the total amount due from the customer?

Math Concept **Problem Solving** Think about which operations to use.

Starting Hints Use addition to calculate the sum for both chairs, which is the subtotal. To find the sales tax amount, multiply the subtotal by the tax percentage. Add the sales tax amount to the delivery charge to find the total amount due.

NCTM Number and Operations Understand numbers, ways of representing numbers, relationships among numbers, and number systems.

For help, go to the **Math Skills Handbook** located at the back of this book.

glencoe.com

Check your answers.

ELABORATE

THE MARKETING CONCEPT

Ask students to rephrase the definition of marketing concept in their own words. Definitions should include the idea that a business must meet customer needs and wants. Ask these guiding questions about the marketing concept.

Guiding Questions

Identify What are the seven marketing core functions and how do they help a company's market concept?	core functions: channel management, marketing information management, market planning, pricing, product/service management, promotion, and selling; all satisfy customers' needs
Explain Why is it important that everyone in an organization recognize that repeat customers keep a company in business?	Every team member in the company is responsible to help keep customers returning to the business. Salespeople have more contact with customers and can determine their return.

MARKETING CASE STUDY

Math Answer 24% of Johnson & Johnson's profits were due to mothers who are Hispanic ($3,150,367 ÷ $12,949,847 = 0.24). **Extend the Concept** Ask students: ***Can you think of any other examples of companies reaching out to customers in the manner that Johnson & Johnson® chose to reach out to the Hispanic market?*** Sample answer: Old Spice reached out to teens with promotional messages targeted toward young people and free samples of their products to young athletes. As a result, the brand generated new found popularity. Ask students: Why should a company be very careful when planning marketing strategies designed to appeal to specific ethnic markets? Sample answer: In an attempt to appeal to the cultural needs of ethnic niches, stereotypes can be reinforced. Advertisers must be careful to make sure that the message they are sending is one that will not be misconstrued by some members of the niche ethnicity.

EVALUATE

CUSTOMER RELATIONSHIP MANAGEMENT

Ask students: ***In today's marketplace, do you think that customer relationships are important?*** Sample answer: Yes, there is competition for the customer's business and in how customers are treated. No, with so many customer services going online, customer interaction is not as important.

Then ask students these guiding questions to direct a discussion on customer relationship management:

Guiding Questions

Explain Why is it important to serve customers efficiently?	The more efficiently a customer can be served, the less time and money it costs the company.
Examine Why do companies collect information about customers' buying trends?	Companies use information about customers' buying trends to develop better relations and new products and services.
Synthesize Has the use of digital communications increased customer service?	Digital communications make customer issues faster to resolve. Face-to-face contact is not as important.

Reinforce Vocabulary

Trend—Denotative Meaning Write the term *trend* on the board. Discuss with students whether researching trends is important in developing new products. Ask students to provide definitions for the term *trend.* A trend is a general movement in one direction or a tendency to go in a particular direction.

Critical Thinking

Instruct students to create a brief survey in which they ask middle-aged and elderly people how advertising and customer service have changed. Students should develop a list of questions to ask. Students should compile the data they collect into a table. Working in groups, students could compile all class data into one table. Ask students: ***What trends, if any, do you see in the data?*** Trends may include such things as a de-personalization of customer service, too many advertisements in the mail and newspaper, and so on. Ask students: ***What conclusions might you draw from this information?*** Conclusions will vary. Students may determine that while advertising methods have improved, customer service has not necessarily improved.

After You Read Section 1.1

Review Key Concepts

1. Marketing is ongoing. Marketers must keep up with trends and consumer attitudes when trends and the customer base change over time. The AMA revises the definition of marketing to make sure it conforms to current practices in the marketplace.
2. Goods are tangible items that have monetary value and satisfy customers' needs and wants. Examples of economic goods are cars, furniture, electronics, and clothing. Services are intangible items that have monetary value and satisfy customers' needs and wants. Examples of economic services are banks, movie theaters, and accounting services.
3. Customer Relationship Management combines customer information (through database and computer technology) with customer service and marketing communications. This combination allows companies to serve their customers as efficiently as possible and makes them better able to satisfy customers' needs and generate a profit.

Practice Academics

English Language Arts

4. If marketers do not conduct business with the marketing concept in mind profits for the company will suffer. If the marketing concept is not followed, businesses would not be able to keep customers happy and will not return for repeat business. Businesses must satisfy customers' needs by staying in touch with them and monitoring their purchasing behavior.

Mathematics

5. The answer is $589.98 ($249.99 × 2 × 1.06 + $60).

 **glencoe.com** 

Answer Key Send students to the Online Learning Center to check their answers.

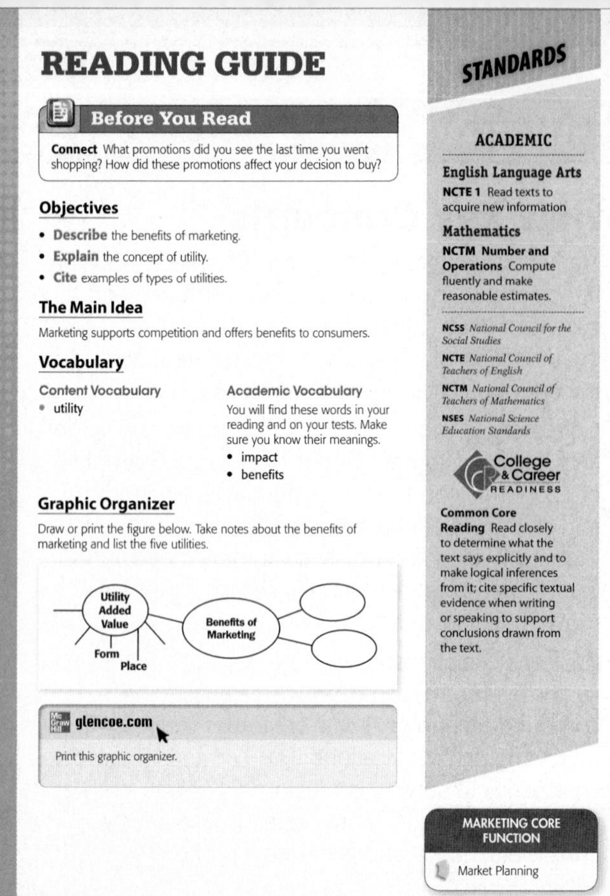

READING GUIDE

Before You Read

Connect What promotions did you see the last time you went shopping? How did these promotions affect your decision to buy?

Objectives

- **Describe** the benefits of marketing.
- **Explain** the concept of utility.
- **Cite** examples of types of utilities.

The Main Idea

Marketing supports competition and offers benefits to consumers.

Vocabulary

Content Vocabulary
- utility

Academic Vocabulary

You will find these words in your reading and on your tests. Make sure you know their meanings.
- impact
- benefits

Graphic Organizer

Draw or print the figure below. Take notes about the benefits of marketing and list the five utilities.

glencoe.com

Print this graphic organizer.

STANDARDS

ACADEMIC

English Language Arts
NCTE 1 Read texts to acquire new information

Mathematics
NCTM Number and Operations Compute fluently and make reasonable estimates.

NCSS National Council for the Social Studies
NCTE National Council of Teachers of English
NCTM National Council of Teachers of Mathematics
NSES National Science Education Standards

College & Career READINESS

Common Core
Reading Read closely to determine what the text says explicitly and to make logical inferences from it; cite specific textual evidence when writing or speaking to support conclusions drawn from the text.

MARKETING CORE FUNCTION

Market Planning

ECONOMIC BENEFITS OF MARKETING

The **impact** of marketing affects the economy and standard of living in countries around the world. Marketing is a global force. Marketing plays an important role in an economy because it provides the means for competition to take place. In a competitive marketplace, businesses try to create new or improved products at lower prices than their competitors. Those efforts force them to be efficient and responsive to consumers. In addition, businesses look for ways to add value to a consumer's shopping experience. There are many economic **benefits** of marketing to an economy and to consumers.

As You Read

Reflect How have you benefited from marketing?

NEW AND IMPROVED PRODUCTS

Marketing generates competition, which fosters new and improved products. Businesses always look for ways to satisfy customers' wants and needs to keep customers interested. This creates a larger variety of goods and services. For example, cell phones have become "smart phones." Their capabilities have evolved from simple to complex.

> **"Through the study of marketing, you will understand the importance of marketing and how much it affects you and other consumers."**

LOWER PRICES

Marketing activities increase demand, and this helps to lower prices. When demand is high, manufacturers can produce products in larger quantities. This reduces the unit cost of each product. This is because the fixed costs (such as the rent on a building) remain the same whether the company produces 1,500 units or 15,000 units. When a company produces a larger quantity of a product, it spends less per unit on fixed costs. The company can charge a lower price per unit, sell more units, and make more money.

Here is an example using a fixed cost of $300,000:

Scenario 1

1,500 units with $300,000 fixed costs

$300,000 ÷ 1,500 units = $200 per unit

Scenario 2

15,000 units with $300,000 fixed costs

$300,000 ÷ 15,000 units = $20 per unit

In Scenario 2, the fixed cost per unit is reduced by $18 ($20 – $2). If the original price was $95, the new price to customers would be $77.

In addition, when products become popular, more competitors enter the marketplace. To remain competitive, marketers find ways to lower their prices. Consider the personal computer market where computers have become smaller, lighter, more powerful, and a lot less expensive.

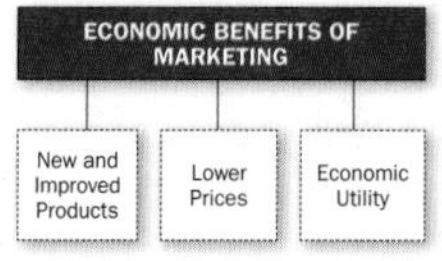

ENGAGE

Anticipation Activity

Have students name new products that are currently being advertised. Encourage students to describe what is new and different about these products. Ask students: ***Where did you get your information? Did it come from personal knowledge of the product or from advertisements? How did you hear about the product in the first place?*** Answers to the questions will vary but students should be aware that we usually hear about new products through advertising and much of what we know about products comes from advertising and marketing pieces.

Objectives

- **Describe** the benefits of marketing. new and improved products, lower prices, and added value or utility
- **Explain** the concept of utility. attributes of goods or services that make them capable of satisfying consumer's wants and needs
- **Cite** examples of types of utilities. form utility; place utility; time utility; possession utility; information utility

Graphic Organizer

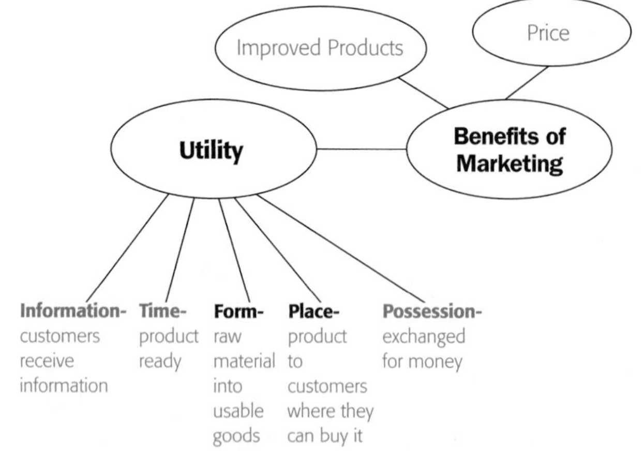

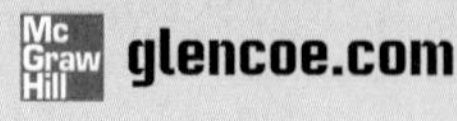

iWB

Graphic Organizer Send students to the Online Learning Center to print this graphic organizer.

EXPLORE

Before You Read

Read the Before You Read question aloud: ***What promotions did you see the last time you went shopping?*** posters in store windows, in-store displays denoting a sale, going out of business banners ***How did these promotions affect your decision to buy?*** Students should explain whether or not they purchased what was being promoted and tell why. Ask students: ***In general, do you tend to purchase items that are being promoted? Why or why not?*** Sample answer: Yes, if the item is on sale. No, I do not typically purchase promotional items.

Preteaching Vocabulary

Have students go to the Online Learning Center at glencoe.com for the Chapter 1 Preteaching Vocabulary games.

Content Vocabulary

Write the key term *utility* on the board. Explain to students that it comes from the Latin verb for *to use.* Tell students that when used in marketing *utility* has a specialized meaning. Ask a volunteer to locate the term in the glossary. A utility is an attribute of a product or service that makes it capable of satisfying consumers' wants and needs.

Academic Vocabulary

Impact—Usage Have students volunteer sentences in which they use the term *impact* (noun). Ask the class to determine whether the term was used correctly. Tell students that the term means the force of the impression that is made. Sample answers: The sales flyer made an *impact* on shoppers' buying habits. The Internet advertisement impacted the activity on the Web site.

Benefits—Usage Have students volunteer sentences in which they use the term *benefits.* Ask the class to determine whether the term was used correctly. Tell students that for the importance of marketing, a benefit is an advantage or something useful. Sample answers: The billboard announced the benefits of buying a hybrid automobile. Lower prices benefitted the store because customers bought more than one item.

Reading: Options for Learning
Go to the Online Learning Center to view a video in which teachers explain multiple ways to respond to a text.

The Importance of Marketing

ECONOMIC BENEFITS OF MARKETING

Tell students that as they become a part of the world of work and earn money, they will want to learn the benefits of marketing to help them spend their earnings wisely. There are a number of ways in which marketing can benefit the consumer. Ask these guiding questions to focus the discussion on the economic benefits of marketing.

Guiding Questions

Identify Who is affected by the impact of marketing?	People in countries all over the world are affected as economies and standards of living are impacted by marketing.
Summarize What is the benefit of competition?	Businesses create new or improved products at lower prices, forcing efficiency and responsiveness to consumers.
Explain What role does marketing play in an economy?	Marketing provides the means for competition to take place in the marketplace.

As You Read

Read students the As You Read question: ***How have you benefited from marketing?*** Answers will vary but should include benefits such as purchasing products for lower prices and being able to compare products made by different companies.

Expert Advice

Read the quote to students:

> **"Through the study of marketing, you will understand the importance of marketing and how much it affects you and other consumers."**

Ask students: ***In what ways does marketing affect you?*** Sample answers: paying lower prices for products, knowing when and where a product is available, learning about new and improved products

ECONOMIC UTILITY

The functions of marketing add value to a product. This added value in economic terms is called **utility**. Utilities are the attributes of goods or services that make them capable of satisfying consumers' wants and needs.

There are five economic utilities involved with all products: form, place, time, possession, and information. Although form utility is not directly related to marketing, much of what goes into creating new products, such as marketing research and product design, makes it an integral part of the marketing process.

FORM UTILITY

Form utility involves changing raw materials into usable goods or putting parts together to make them more useful. The manufacturing of products involves taking things of little value by themselves and putting them together to create more value. If you consider a zipper, a spool of thread, and several yards of cloth, each would have some value. However, the value would be greater if you put all three together to make a jacket.

Form utility involves making products that consumers need and want. Special features or ingredients in a product add value and increase its form utility. For example, electronic controls on the steering wheel of an automobile add value to the final product.

PLACE UTILITY

Place utility involves having a product where customers can buy it. Businesses study consumer shopping habits to determine the most convenient and efficient locations to sell products. Some businesses use a direct approach by selling products through catalogs or the Internet. Other businesses rely on retailers to sell their products at a physical store.

TIME UTILITY

Time utility is having a product or service available at a certain time of year or a convenient time of day. For example, some banks are open seven days a week with extended hours for drive-through operations. Some gas stations are open 24 hours a day. Retailers often have extended shopping hours during special promotions or holiday seasons. Marketers increase the value of products by having them available when consumers want them.

New Products

One of the major economic benefits of marketing is the proliferation of new and improved products. ***Why is it important for marketers to constantly update and improve their products?***

POSSESSION UTILITY

The exchange of a product for money is possession utility. Retailers may accept alternatives to cash, such as personal checks or debit cards, in exchange for their merchandise. They may even offer installment or layaway plans (delayed possession in return for gradual payment). In business-to-business situations, companies also grant credit to their customers. They may give them a certain period (for example, 30 days) to pay a bill. This adds value to the products they sell.

Possession utility is involved every time legal ownership of a product changes hands. Possession utility increases as purchase options increase. That is, the choice between using cash, credit, check, or another form of payment increases possession utility. The Internet also provides consumers with options to pay by providing secure sites where credit cards are accepted.

INFORMATION UTILITY

Information utility involves communication with the consumer. Salespeople provide information to customers by explaining the features and benefits of products. Displays communicate information, too. Packaging and labeling inform consumers about qualities and uses of a product. The label on a frozen food entrée tells you the ingredients, nutritional information, directions for preparation, and any safety precautions needed. Advertising informs consumers about products, tells where to buy products, and sometimes tells how much products cost.

Many manufacturers provide owners' manuals that explain how to use their products. Businesses also have Web sites where they provide detailed information about their companies and their products for customers.

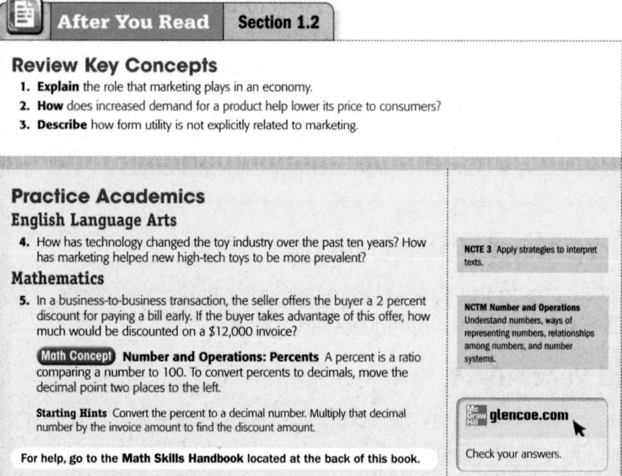

After You Read | **Section 1.2**

Review Key Concepts

1. **Explain** the role that marketing plays in an economy.
2. **How** does increased demand for a product help lower its price to consumers?
3. **Describe** how form utility is not explicitly related to marketing.

Practice Academics

English Language Arts

4. How has technology changed the toy industry over the past ten years? How has marketing helped new high-tech toys to be more prevalent?

Mathematics

5. In a business-to-business transaction, the seller offers the buyer a 2 percent discount for paying a bill early. If the buyer takes advantage of this offer, how much would be discounted on a $12,000 invoice?

Math Concept **Number and Operations: Percents** A percent is a ratio comparing a number to 100. To convert percents to decimals, move the decimal point two places to the left.

Starting Hints Convert the percent to a decimal number. Multiply that decimal number by the invoice amount to find the discount amount.

For help, go to the Math Skills Handbook located at the back of this book.

NCTE 3 Apply strategies to interpret texts.

NCTM Number and Operations Understand numbers, ways of representing numbers, relationships among numbers, and number systems.

glencoe.com

Check your answers.

14 | Unit 1 · The World of Marketing

Chapter 1 · Marketing Is All Around Us | 15

ELABORATE

Graphic Organizer

Display this graphic organizer. Ask students to provide details about the economic benefits of marketing.

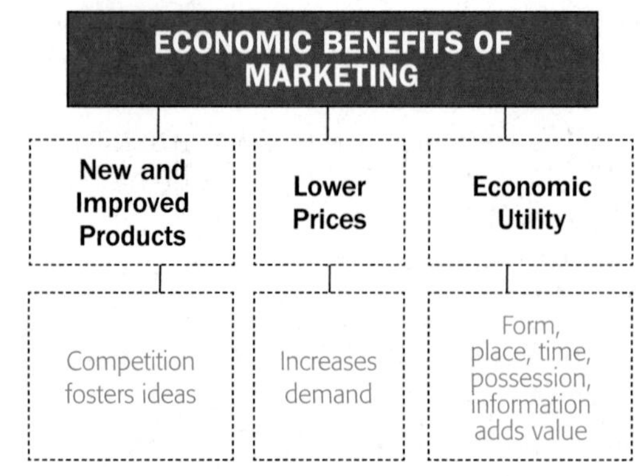

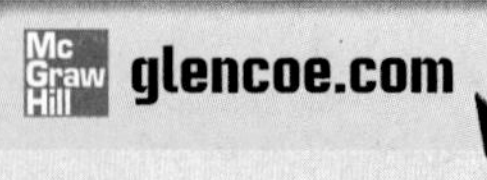

iWB

Graphic Organizer Send students to the Online Learning Center to print this graphic organizer.

Visual Literacy

New Products Caption Answer Read the caption question to students: ***Why is it important for manufacturers to constantly update and improve their products?*** Manufacturers must constantly update and improve their products because marketing creates competition. A larger variety of goods and services are developed as people desire upgraded features.

Mini Project

Enrichment

Research New Products Instruct students to research five products labeled new or improved. Students should record the name of the product and list what the manufacturer claims is new or improved about the product. Ask students to determine whether they believe the new or improved products were a result of consumer demand. Students should realize that all new or improved products are created to supply consumers' wants or needs (whether real or perceived to be real by the manufacturer).Sample answer: There are numerous improvements and new applications for tablet computers based on the latest technology.

EVALUATE

ECONOMIC UTILITY

Tell students that utilities are attributes of goods or services that make them capable of satisfying consumers. Then ask these guiding questions to focus the discussion about Economic Utility.

Guiding Questions

Identify What are the five economic utilities?	form utility, place utility, time utility, possession utility, information utility
Formulate Why is form utility not directly related to marketing?	When form utility involves changing materials or putting parts together to make them useful, individual parts are not marketed as the final product.
Appraise How are time and place utilities related?	Time utility cannot exist without place utility. If products are available to consumers at a certain time, but there is no place where they can buy them, products will not sell.

Mini Projects

Differentiated Instruction

Interpersonal Learners Ask students to work in groups to generate a short list of products that might be used in a classroom to determine: 1) Form utility 2) Place utility 3) Time utility 4) Possession utility 5) Information utility Sample answer: Product—textbook; 1) paper, ink, glue; 2) through sales representatives, at publishers' Web sites 3)before the start of school 4) purchase order from the district 5) visits from sales, mail flyers, online advertising

Gifted Learners Share an example of social responsibility being used as part of a company's marketing strategy. Have students present other examples where marketing and social responsibility combine. Sample answers: tuna companies that promote dolphin-safe fishing techniques, cleaning product companies that do not use chemicals, cosmetic companies that they do not test their products on animals.

After You Read — Section 1.2

Review Key Concepts

1. Marketing plays an important role in an economy because it provides the means for competition to take place. In a competitive marketplace, businesses try to create new or improved products at lower prices than their competitors. Those efforts force them to be efficient and responsive to consumers. In addition, businesses look for ways to add value to a consumer's shopping experience.
2. When demand is high, manufacturers can produce products in larger quantities. This reduces the unit cost of each product. This is because the fixed costs (such as the rent on a building) remain the same whether the company produces 1,500 units or 15,000 units. When a company produces a larger quantity of a product, it spends less per unit on fixed costs. The company can charge a lower price per unit, sell more units, and make more money.
3. Form utility is not directly related to marketing. However, much of what goes into creating products, such as marketing research and product design, makes it an integral part of the marketing process.

Practice Academics

English Language Arts

4. Answers will vary. A good example would be electronic games, such as the Wii System, which shows the effect of a player's physical action (hitting a golf ball, throwing a bowling ball) onto a screen and provides immediate feedback, evaluating the player's efforts. Marketing has helped in that endeavor by educating different target markets as to the benefits of the new game. This communication helped to increase sales to more customers who had never thought to buy such a product.

Mathematics

5. \$11,760 (Convert 2% to a decimal = 0.02. Multiply \$12,000 × 0.02 = \$240. Subtract \$12,000 – \$240 = \$11,760.)

glencoe.com

Answer Key Send students to the Online Learning Center to check their answers.

READING GUIDE

Before You Read

Connect What markets are you a part of?

Objectives

- **Describe** how marketers use knowledge of the market to sell products.
- **Compare and Contrast** consumer and organizational markets.
- **Explain** the importance of target markets.
- **Explain** how each component of the marketing mix contributes to successful marketing.

The Main Idea

The term *market* refers to all the people who might buy a product. The marketing mix is a combination of elements used to sell a product to a specific target market.

Vocabulary

Content Vocabulary
- market
- consumer market
- organizational market
- market share
- target market
- customer profile
- marketing mix

Academic Vocabulary

You will find these words in your reading and on your tests. Make sure you know their meanings.
- similar
- elements

Graphic Organizer

Draw or print these two diagrams. In the first diagram, write four terms about the concept of market. In the second diagram, write the four Ps of the marketing mix.

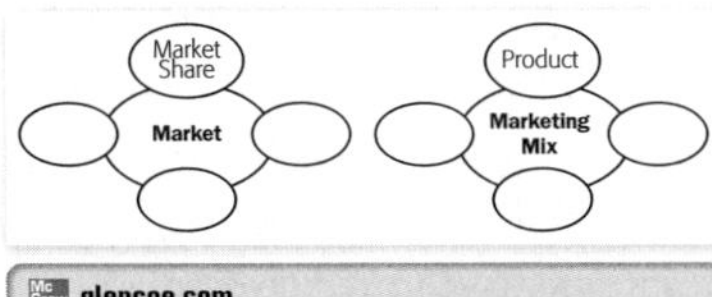

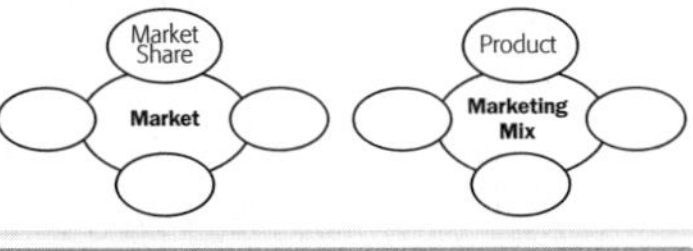

glencoe.com

Print this graphic organizer.

STANDARDS

ACADEMIC

English Language Arts

NCTE 3 Apply strategies to interpret texts.

NCSS *National Council for the Social Studies*

NCTE *National Council of Teachers of English*

NCTM *National Council of Teachers of Mathematics*

NSES *National Science Education Standards*

Common Core

Reading Integrate and evaluate content presented in diverse formats and media, including visually and quantitatively, as well as in words.

MARKETING CORE FUNCTION

Market Planning

m.e. Section 1.3 Fundamentals of Marketing

MARKET AND MARKET IDENTIFICATION

Remember these terms so you can use them correctly when discussing marketing principles and practices. These terms are used throughout this textbook. It is essential to learn the language that marketers use to communicate with each other.

Marketers design products to satisfy customers' needs and wants. They know not all customers may want their product or service. So they identify those people who want their product and who have the ability to pay for their product. All people who share **similar** needs and wants and who have the ability to purchase a given product are a **market**.

You could be part of the market for video games, but not be part of the market for an expensive car. Even though you may want an expensive car, you may not have the means to buy one. If you liked video games and had the resources to buy or rent them, you would be part of the video game market.

As You Read

Predict How do you think marketers decide where to sell their products?

CONSUMER VERSUS ORGANIZATIONAL MARKETS

There are different types of markets. A market can be described as a consumer market or an organizational market.

The **consumer market** consists of consumers who purchase goods and services for personal use. Consumers' needs and wants generally fall into a few categories that reflect their lifestyles. For the most part, consumers are interested in products that will save them money, make their lives easier, improve their appearance, create status in the community, or provide satisfaction.

The **organizational market** or business-to-business (B2B) market includes all businesses that buy products for use in their operations. This market includes transactions among businesses. The goals and objectives of business firms are somewhat different from those in the consumer market. Most goals and objectives relate to improving profits. Companies want to increase productivity, increase sales, decrease expenses, or increase efficiency.

> **"The marketing terminology in this section is the foundation for future work and study in marketing."**

Companies that produce goods and services for sale in the consumer market consider the reseller of their products to be part of the organizational market. The wholesaler who sells to the retailer is part of the organizational market. Therefore, the company needs to create two distinct marketing plans to reach each market.

MARKET SHARE

A market is further described by the total sales in a product category. Examples of categories are video games, televisions, cameras, ice cream, or soft drinks. For example, the Smartphone market (e.g., iPhones, Droids, and Blackberrys) could have sales of $15 billion, and the market for Blu-Ray DVD players could have total sales of $1.2 billion. The Smartphone or DVD player market includes sales through electronic or appliance stores, computer or office superstores, mass merchandisers, the Internet, and through catalog mail order.

ENGAGE

Anticipation Activity

Improving Student Achievement Ask students to name examples of recent marketing trends they have observed through the media or by watching others. organic foods, legal music downloading services, the miniaturization of portable electronics such as cell phones and MP3 players, social networking Web sites

Objectives

- **Describe** how marketers use knowledge of the market to sell products. Identify consumers who have the ability to pay
- **Compare and contrast** consumer and organizational markets. Consumer market: purchases for personal use. Organizational market: purchases for businesses.
- **Explain** the importance of target markets. All marketing strategies are directed to target markets.
- **Explain** how each component of the marketing mix contributes to successful marketing. The product must be developed for a target market and convenient for customers to purchase.

Graphic Organizer

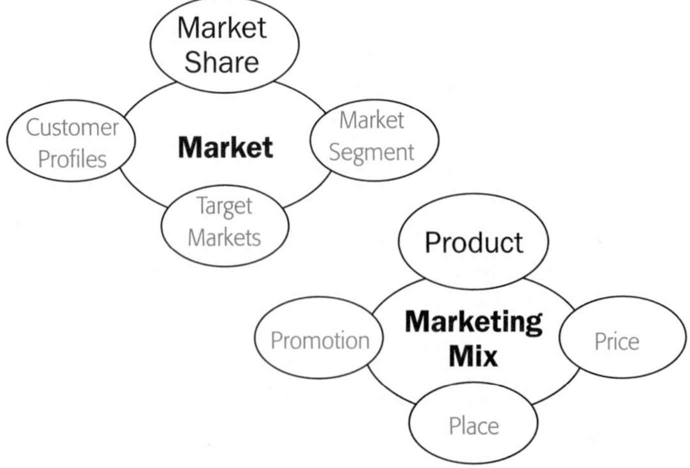

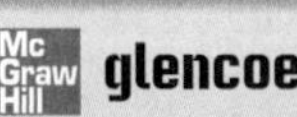

glencoe.com iWB

Graphic Organizer Send students to the Online Learning Center to print this graphic organizer.

EXPLORE

Before You Read

Read the Before You Read question aloud: ***What markets are you a part of?*** Possible answers: electronic devices and cell phones; food items such as pizza; clothing Ask students: ***Do you think about being part of a market when you are making purchases?*** Most students probably did not realize that they are part of various markets. Ask students: ***Do you think it is an advantage or disadvantage to be part of a market?*** Students should support their answers with a valid explanation.

Preteaching Vocabulary

Have students go to the Online Learning Center at glencoe.com for the Chapter 1 Preteaching Vocabulary games.

Content Vocabulary

Write the key term *customer profile* on the board. Tell students that a customer profile is a list of information about a target market, such as age, income level, ethnicity, lifestyle, and geographic residence. Ask students to explain why marketers would want to collect this information. The more information marketers have about customers, the better they can market their products.

Academic Vocabulary

Define the terms *similar* and *elements. similar*—having common elements or characteristics, alike; *elements*—parts Ask students to create sentences using the terms. The members of our class have similar buying habits. The MP3 music download market is one element of our buying trends.

Critical Thinking

Ask students: ***How would the needs of the consumer market differ from the needs of the business-to-business market?*** Consumer: supply personal needs and wants Business-to-business: purchases to increase productivity and sales

As You Read

Read the As You Read question aloud: ***How do you think marketers decide where to sell their products?*** Marketers must learn where their potential customers shop to determine where to sell their products. ***At what kinds of places do you typically shop? Why?*** Students may say they shop at neighborhood stores to buy locally or online so they can stay at home.

Fundamentals of Marketing

MARKET AND MARKET IDENTIFICATION

Tell students that as they study the fundamentals of marketing they will begin to think more like marketers rather than consumers. Ask these guiding questions to focus the discussion on market and market identification:

Guiding Questions

Define In your own words, what is the definition of *market?*	A market consists of people who share similar needs and wants and are capable of buying products.
Compare What is the difference between the consumer market and the organizational market?	The consumer market consists of consumers who purchase goods and services for personal use. The organizational, also known as business-to-business or B-to-B, market includes all businesses that buy products for their operations.
Analyze Why is it important for companies to know their market share?	Knowing the market share helps marketers analyze their competition and to better define their marketing strategies.

Expert Advice

Read the quote to students:

> **"The marketing terminology in this section is the foundation for future work and study in marketing."**

Ask students: ***What is meant by saying the terminology in this section is the foundation for future work and study in marketing?*** Students may realize the importance of the terminology they will learn in this section. They will understand that they need to learn the terms now to better understand what they will study later. Have student keep a word log of terms in this section, as well as words that they would like to explore further.

ELL: Vocabulary Activities
Go to the Online Learning Center to view a video in which students use synonyms, antonyms, and definitions in context.

A company's **market share** is its percentage of the total sales volume generated by all companies that compete in a given market. It may be represented in dollars or units. Knowing market share helps companies analyze their competition as well as their status in a given market. (See **Figure 1.1**.)

Market shares change all the time as new competitors enter the market and as the size of the market increases or decreases in volume. A company with a large market share can afford to take risks that other companies cannot. For example, it can develop new products that are more adventurous than its competitors because of its large market share.

MARKET SEGMENTATION

Businesses look for ways to sell their products to different consumers who may be potential customers. This involves segmenting, or breaking down, the market into smaller groups that have similar characteristics. Market segmentation is the process of classifying customers by specific characteristics. Marketers know that groups of people often buy the same products. They use this information to fine tune their approach to selling in that market.

TARGET MARKETS

The goal of market segmentation is to identify the group of people most likely to become customers. The group that is identified for a specific marketing program is the **target market**.

Target markets are very important because all marketing strategies are directed to them. When a business does not identify a target market, its marketing plan has no focus. Identifying the target market correctly is an important key to success.

FIGURE 1.1 Market Share

Who Leads in This Market? A company's percentage of total sales in a given market, such as the smart phone market, is its market share. ***What could cause a business's market share to change?***

U.S. Smartphone Market Share

- Research In Motion (RIM) 39%
- Apple iPhone 21.2%
- Palm 3.1%
- Motorola 7.4%
- Nokia 9.8%
- Others 19.5%

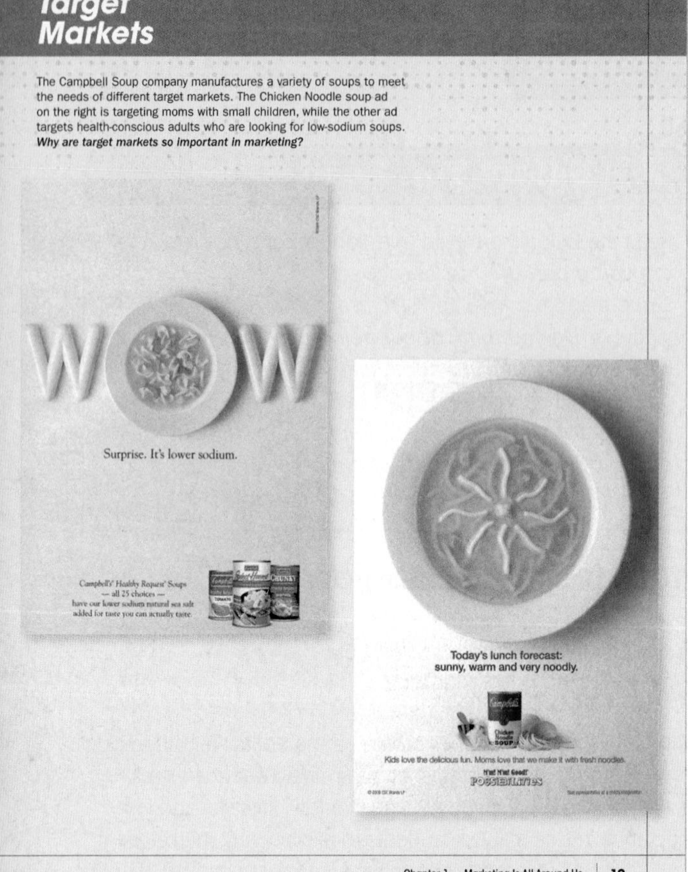

Target Markets

The Campbell Soup company manufactures a variety of soups to meet the needs of different target markets. The Chicken Noodle soup ad on the right is targeting moms with small children, while the other ad targets health-conscious adults who are looking for low-sodium soups. ***Why are target markets so important in marketing?***

EXPLORE

Visual Literacy

Figure 1.1 Caption Answer Read the figure caption question to students. *What could cause a business's market share to change?* Reasons could include new competition, a drop in manufacturing due to unavailability of raw materials or a natural disaster, failure to improve upon the product, or failure to respond to consumer demands. Use these guiding questions to discuss the concept of market share in more detail.

Guiding Questions

Investigate Why might consumers be interested in a company's market share?	Market share might be important to know for investing purposes. Also, some might feel that they can get the best product for the best price from the company that has the largest market share.
Hypothesize How do you think businesses use the concept of market share in their marketing?	Students may suggest that successful businesses make it a goal to try to maintain or grow their market share.

Mini Project

Enrichment

Understand Target Market and Market Segmentation

Divide students into small groups and tell them to imagine that a company that sells class rings has targeted their class. Have them list factors the company can use in its marketing effort based on their group. After groups have had time to create their lists, create a class list of factors. Ask students to determine the similarities and differences in the factors. Specific factors may vary however, in general the lists will include factors such as age, gender, and interests. Have the class generate ideas how a company might market the same product to :

- Males and females
- 10-year-olds and 20-year-olds
- Stay-at-home moms and business executives

Ideas should show how marketers try to interest different markets based on the interests of each market.

EXPLAIN

Mini Project

Differentiated Instruction

Visual and Kinesthetic Learners Bring to class a variety of magazines. Have students look through the magazines and study the advertisements. Based on the advertisements, have students determine the customer profile for readers of the magazine. Kinesthetic learners can tape advertisements to a wall or whiteboard and create categories for customers profiles. For example, according to *Seventeen* magazine's Web site, the magazine targets teen girls and young women interested in beauty, fashion, and entertainment.

Graphic Organizer

Display this graphic organizer. Ask students to suggest details to add to the subtopics.

Consumers purchase goods and services for personal use. Businesses that buy products for use in their operations
Consumer and Organizational Markets
Markets
Market Share
Market Segmentation
A company's percentage of the total sales volume in a given competitive market.
Classifying customers by characteristics

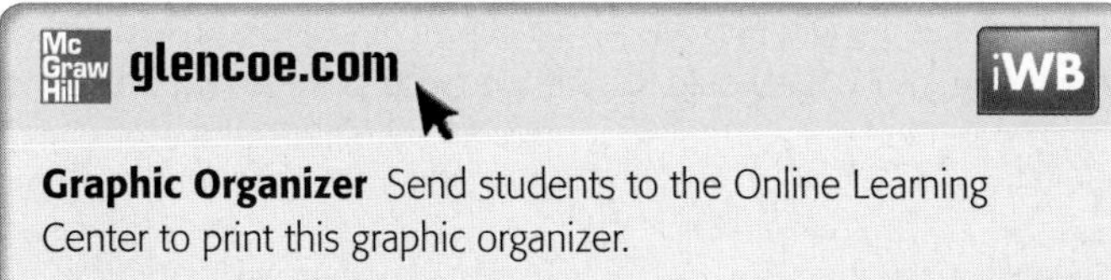
Mc Graw Hill glencoe.com
iWB

Graphic Organizer Send students to the Online Learning Center to print this graphic organizer.

Reading Check Answer

Read the Reading Check question to students: *How can you use a customer profile to learn about a business's target market?* Businesses research their target market's customer profiles to develop a clear picture of their target market.

Graphic Organizer

Have students use a graphic organizer similar to this table to develop their personal customer profile. They should fill in something for each category in the table. Sample answers are provided.

PERSONAL CUSTOMER PROFILE	
Age	17
Gender	Female
Income level	$500 per month
Marital status	Single
Ethnic background	Hispanic
Geographic residence	Urban—city center
Attitudes	Conservative, strong ethnic ties, family oriented, strong religious beliefs
Lifestyle	Focuses on family, school, church, helping the community
Behavior	Conservative, enjoys small-group and independent activities

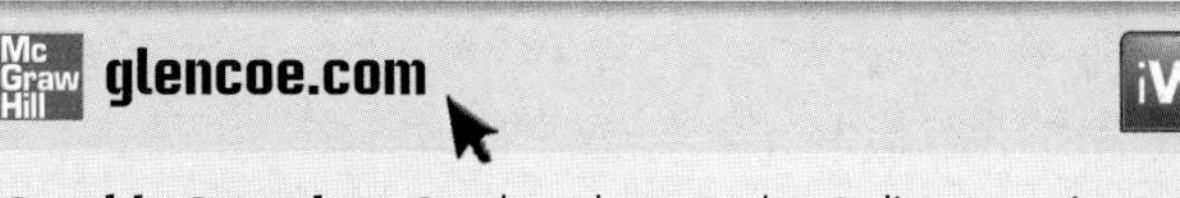
Mc Graw Hill glencoe.com
iWB

Graphic Organizer Send students to the Online Learning Center to print this graphic organizer.

Visual Literacy

Target Markets Caption Answer Read the caption question to students. *Why are target markets so important in marketing?* Target markets are important because all marketing strategies are directed to them. If a business does not identify the target market for a particular product, the marketing plan will have no focus. Identifying the target market correctly is an important key to success for any business.

Critical Thinking

Ask students to write an essay in which they identify a product that is typically marketed to a distinct group of people. Students should include a description of the product and a customer profile of the target market for the product. Students should analyze why this product is successful to this market. Essays will vary but should identify a product, a target market, and a customer profile. A sample answer might describe a riding lawn mower with a target market of people or places with large areas to mow such as golf courses, schools, and parks.

For example, consider the market for shoes. Everyone needs shoes for comfort and protection. Some people need shoes for athletics, work safety, or special occasions. There are also different shoe sizes for women, men, girls, and boys. If a company tries to sell the same type of shoe to all of these people, it will not be successful. It has not identified a target market.

MULTIPLE TARGET MARKETS

A product may have more than one target market. For example, manufacturers of children's cereal know that they need to target children and parents differently. They have two target markets: one is the children (consumers) who will be asking for the cereal and eating it; the other is the parents (customers) who need to approve of it and will be buying it. To reach the children, marketers might advertise on Saturday morning television programs specifically designed for children. The advertising message might be how much fun it is to eat this cereal. To reach parents, print advertising in magazines, such as *Family Circle* or *Parenting*, might be used, and the ad message might stress health benefits.

Advertising in the Consumer Market

This ad suggests that consumers should consider using State Farm insurance policies. ***How different would this ad look if the company were advertising insurance policies in the business market?***

CUSTOMER PROFILES

To develop a clear picture of their target market, businesses create a customer profile. A **customer profile** lists information about the target market, such as age, gender, income level, marital status, ethnic background, geographic residence, attitudes, lifestyle, and behavior. Marketers spend a lot of money and time on research to collect data so that they understand the characteristics of their target market's customer profile.

Reading Check

Respond How can you use a customer profile to learn about a business's target market?

MARKETING MIX

An easy and fun way to understand customer profiles of a target market is to look at magazines. If you thumb through a magazine's articles and advertisements, you will know who reads the publication. To see if you are correct about the target market, check out the magazine's Web site and view its media kit where you will find the reader profile. Magazines use the reader profile of its target market to convince advertisers that the customer profile matches their product's target market. As you can see, target markets are very important in marketing.

The **marketing mix** includes four basic marketing strategies called the four Ps: product, place, price, and promotion. Marketing professionals or businesses use these elements to communicate with and reach their intended target market. Marketers control decisions about each of the four Ps and base their decisions on the people they want to win over and make into customers. Because of the importance of customers, some would add a fifth "P" to the list: people. Marketers must first clearly define each target market before they can develop marketing strategies.

The importance of the target market (people) cannot be overemphasized. Marketers make decisions for the other four **elements** of the marketing mix based on the target market. They are interconnected. Each strategy involves making decisions about the best way to reach, satisfy, and keep customers and the best way to achieve the company's goals.

Let's look at what each marketing mix element involves, using a specific target market—the first "P" in the marketing mix. The target market is health-conscious adults who do not get their daily requirement of vegetables. Follow **Figure 1.2** (on page 22) to see each of the other Ps illustrated and explained for a vegetable/fruit juice.

PRODUCT

Product decisions begin with choosing what products to make and sell. Much research goes into product design. A product's features, brand name, packaging, service, and warranty are all part of the development. Companies also need to decide what to do with products they currently sell. In some cases, those products require updating or improvements to be competitive. By developing new uses or identifying new target markets, a company can extend the life of a product. V8 V-Fusion juice is a product developed for adults who do not like the taste of the original V8 juice, which is still on the market and has been for more than 75 years. The company developed flavors, such as Pomegranate Blueberry, Peach Mango, and Strawberry Banana, to reach out to the specific target market that wanted a tasty alternative to the original V8 juice. Package design included 46-ounce and 12-ounce bottles with bright colors that matched the juices' flavors.

PRICE

Price is what is exchanged for the product. Price strategies should reflect what customers are willing and able to pay. To that end, marketers must consider the price they will charge their organizational customers, including resellers. Pricing decisions also consider prices that the competition charges for comparable products.

Price strategies, therefore, include arriving at the list price or manufacturer's suggested retail price, as well as discounts, allowances, credit terms, and payment period for organizational customers. Originally, the manufacturer's suggested retail price for the V8 V-Fusion 46-ounce bottle was $3.89; and $1.79 for the 12-ounce size.

On occasion, a company may use special promotional pricing that would adjust the suggested retail price. Companies frequently use this technique to launch new products.

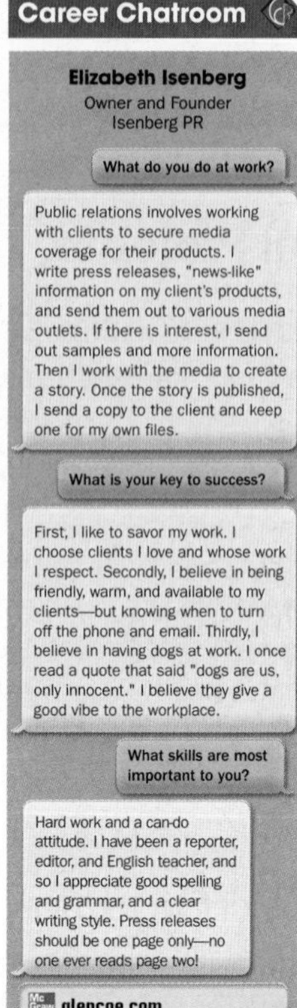

Career Chatroom

Elizabeth Isenberg
Owner and Founder
Isenberg PR

What do you do at work?

Public relations involves working with clients to secure media coverage for their products. I write press releases, "news-like" information on my client's products, and send them out to various media outlets. If there is interest, I send out samples and more information. Then I work with the media to create a story. Once the story is published, I send a copy to the client and keep one for my own files.

What is your key to success?

First, I like to savor my work. I choose clients I love and whose work I respect. Secondly, I believe in being friendly, warm, and available to my clients—but knowing when to turn off the phone and email. Thirdly, I believe in having dogs at work. I once read a quote that said "dogs are us, only innocent." I believe they give a good vibe to the workplace.

What skills are most important to you?

Hard work and a can-do attitude. I have been a reporter, editor, and English teacher, and so I appreciate good spelling and grammar, and a clear writing style. Press releases should be one page only—no one ever reads page two!

glencoe.com

Read more about this career and get a Career Exploration Activity.

EXPLAIN

Visual Literacy

Advertising in the Consumer Market Caption Answer Read the caption question to students: ***How different would this ad look if the company were advertising insurance policies to businesses?*** Answers will vary. The copy and the photo would reflect a different market and a different audience would be targeted.

Reinforce Vocabulary

Practice Key Terms Tell students that the key terms in this chapter are foundational to the study of marketing. To help students connect the marketing-related terms, consider playing word games in which you supply either the key term or the definition and have students supply the matching definition or term. Students can create their own crossword puzzles to share with the class.

MARKETING MIX

Ask these questions to focus the discussion about the marketing mix.

Guiding Questions

Identify What are the four basic marketing strategies of the marketing mix?	product, place, price, and promotion (the four Ps)
Explain Why would some marketers add a fifth P to the marketing mix? What would the P stand for?	Some might add a fifth P to represent people because of the importance of the employees and the customers of the business
Describe the four Ps.	Product—deciding what product to sell, developing the product's features, service; Price—what customers are willing to pay, what competition charges; Place—getting the product to customers; Promotion— advertising, sales promotion, publicity

ELABORATE

Career Chatroom

Use these questions to focus the discussion about the Career Chatroom feature.

Guiding Questions

Identify How does Elizabeth Isenberg define public relations?	working with clients to secure media coverage for their products, writing press releases
Explain What does Elizabeth Isenberg consider to be her key to success?	chooses clients she loves and respects, is friendly, warm, and available to clients, takes time for herself
Analyze What does Ms. Isenberg mean by saying "hard work and a can-do attitude" are important skills?	anticipating that you will need to work hard to succeed, telling yourself and others that you have the capabilities to do the job are necessary for success

Public Relations A company's existence and success can depend on how they are perceived by the public. A public relations specialist helps companies with their public image by writing press releases and other documents that tell what the company is doing and what it stands for. Ask students to further research the career of public relations specialist.

glencoe.com

Career Exploration Send students to the Online Learning Center to read more about this career and to get a Career Exploration Activity.

e MARKETING

Smartphone Apps

A smartphone is a mobile phone that has a computer operating system, software, web access, keyboard, and messaging capabilities, which permits the user to download a variety of applications, or apps. These applications open doors to allow both small and large businesses to attract new customers, communicate with current customers, and offer special customer services. Applications are downloaded on the smartphone. Marketers that want their presence on a smartphone create an application for it. Apple is now offering marketers the ability to advertise on their phone with the iAds platform. For example, an advertisement promoting Nissan's new electric car – the Leaf will be embedded in an application using the iAds platform. Apple's iAds platform offers video, graphics, and animation capabilities.

Innovate and Create

Ask students to share with the class the smartphone applications that they have seen or used themselves. Ask what advertisers might do to take advantage of Apple's iAds platform to reach them as potential customers. Those same advertisers may want to reach them on their smartphones.

Students may identify Apple's iTunes App Store as a site where they find apps for their iPhone. Cars, fast food restaurants, clothing stores, and electronic games are businesses that might take advantage of Apple's iAds platform to reach them by advertising on those apps. Marketers have zeroed in on how they can be connected with their customers wherever they happen to be – so marketing is all around us – wherever we go with our smartphones.

glencoe.com

eMarketing Worksheet Activity Send students to the Online Learning Center to download an eMarketing worksheet activity.

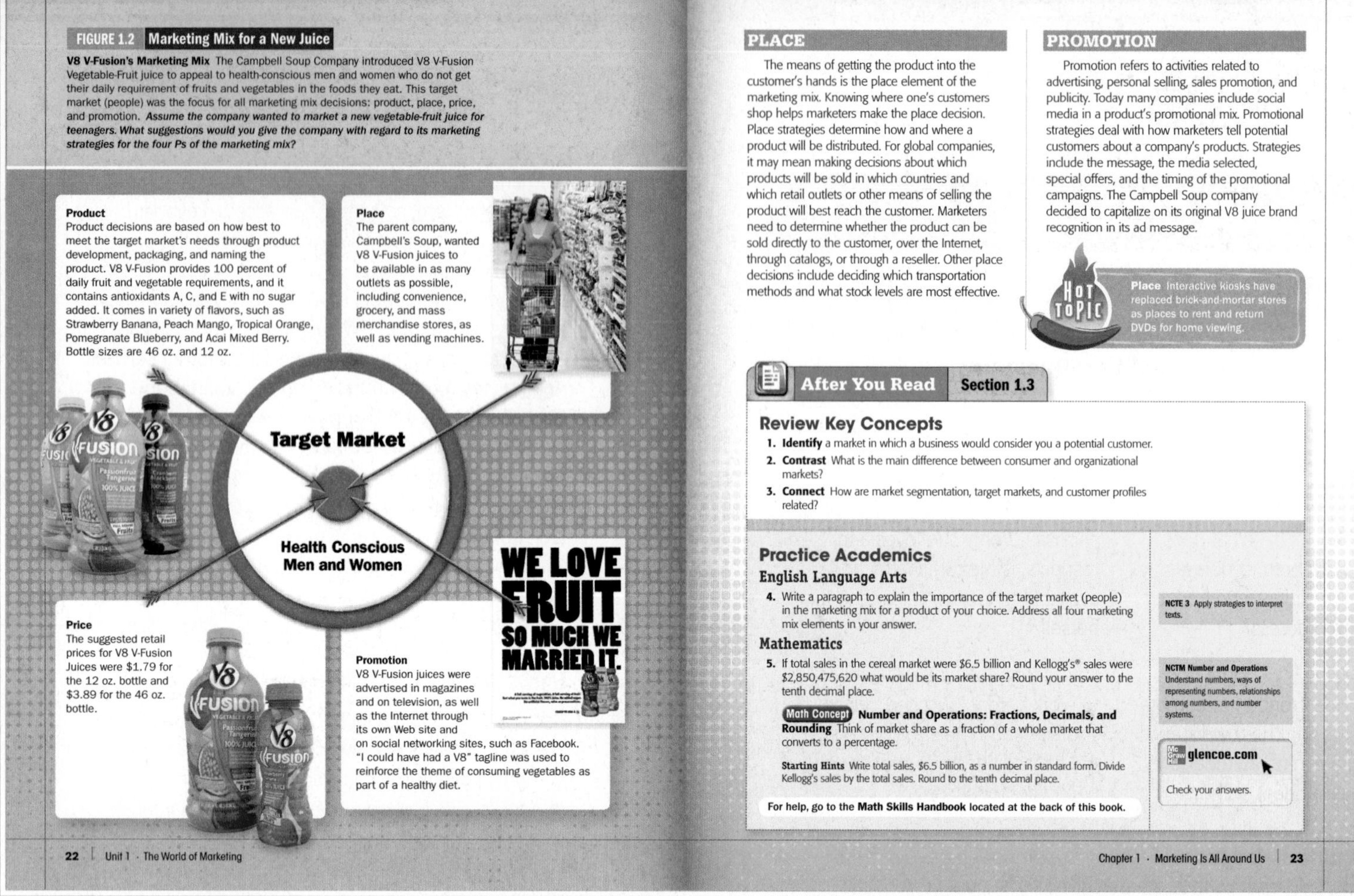

FIGURE 1.2 Marketing Mix for a New Juice

V8 V-Fusion's Marketing Mix The Campbell Soup Company introduced V8 V-Fusion Vegetable-Fruit juice to appeal to health-conscious men and women who do not get their daily requirement of fruits and vegetables in the foods they eat. This target market (people) was the focus for all marketing mix decisions: product, place, price, and promotion. ***Assume the company wanted to market a new vegetable-fruit juice for teenagers. What suggestions would you give the company with regard to its marketing strategies for the four Ps of the marketing mix?***

Product
Product decisions are based on how best to meet the target market's needs through product development, packaging, and naming the product. V8 V-Fusion provides 100 percent of daily fruit and vegetable requirements, and it contains antioxidants A, C, and E with no sugar added. It comes in variety of flavors, such as Strawberry Banana, Peach Mango, Tropical Orange, Pomegranate Blueberry, and Acai Mixed Berry. Bottle sizes are 46 oz. and 12 oz.

Place
The parent company, Campbell's Soup, wanted V8 V-Fusion juices to be available in as many outlets as possible, including convenience, grocery, and mass merchandise stores, as well as vending machines.

Target Market

Health Conscious Men and Women

Price
The suggested retail prices for V8 V-Fusion Juices were $1.79 for the 12 oz. bottle and $3.89 for the 46 oz. bottle.

Promotion
V8 V-Fusion juices were advertised in magazines and on television, as well as the Internet through its own Web site and on social networking sites, such as Facebook. "I could have had a V8" tagline was used to reinforce the theme of consuming vegetables as part of a healthy diet.

V8
FUSION
WE LOVE FRUIT SO MUCH WE MARRIED IT.

PLACE

The means of getting the product into the customer's hands is the place element of the marketing mix. Knowing where one's customers shop helps marketers make the place decision. Place strategies determine how and where a product will be distributed. For global companies, it may mean making decisions about which products will be sold in which countries and which retail outlets or other means of selling the product will best reach the customer. Marketers need to determine whether the product can be sold directly to the customer, over the Internet, through catalogs, or through a reseller. Other place decisions include deciding which transportation methods and what stock levels are most effective.

PROMOTION

Promotion refers to activities related to advertising, personal selling, sales promotion, and publicity. Today many companies include social media in a product's promotional mix. Promotional strategies deal with how marketers tell potential customers about a company's products. Strategies include the message, the media selected, special offers, and the timing of the promotional campaigns. The Campbell Soup company decided to capitalize on its original V8 juice brand recognition in its ad message.

HOT TOPIC **Place** Interactive kiosks have replaced brick-and-mortar stores as places to rent and return DVDs for home viewing.

After You Read Section 1.3

Review Key Concepts

1. **Identify** a market in which a business would consider you a potential customer.
2. **Contrast** What is the main difference between consumer and organizational markets?
3. **Connect** How are market segmentation, target markets, and customer profiles related?

Practice Academics

English Language Arts

4. Write a paragraph to explain the importance of the target market (people) in the marketing mix for a product of your choice. Address all four marketing mix elements in your answer.

NCTE 3 Apply strategies to interpret texts.

Mathematics

5. If total sales in the cereal market were $6.5 billion and Kellogg's® sales were $2,850,475,620 what would be its market share? Round your answer to the tenth decimal place.

Math Concept **Number and Operations: Fractions, Decimals, and Rounding** Think of market share as a fraction of a whole market that converts to a percentage.

Starting Hints Write total sales, $6.5 billion, as a number in standard form. Divide Kellogg's sales by the total sales. Round to the tenth decimal place.

For help, go to the **Math Skills Handbook** located at the back of this book.

NCTM Number and Operations Understand numbers, ways of representing numbers, relationships among numbers, and number systems.

glencoe.com Check your answers.

22 | Unit 1 · The World of Marketing

Chapter 1 · Marketing Is All Around Us | 23

ELABORATE

Visual Literacy

Figure 1.2 Caption Answer Read the caption question to students: *What suggestions would you give the company with regard to its marketing strategies for the four Ps of the marketing mix?* Possible answers: make the packaging more edgy for the teen market, focus on taste, charge less for the 12-ounce bottle To further discuss Figure 1.2, ask students the following guiding questions.

Guiding Questions

Identify What nutritional claims are made for V8 V-Fusion? Under which P are they listed?	V8 V-Fusion provides 100 percent of daily fruit and vegetable requirements, antioxidants A, C, and E with no sugar added–Product
Calculate Which suggested retail price for V8 offers the best price per ounce?	64-ounce bottle at $3.89 is $0.08 per ounce, 12-ounce bottle at $1.79 is $0.15 per ounce, 64-ounce bottle offers the best per-ounce price

Mini Project

Differentiated Instruction

Interpersonal Learners Divide the class into pairs. Ask students to carefully read the caption for Figure 1.2 and the text in the figure. Tell students that the Campbell Soup Company wants to market a new vegetable-fruit juice for teenagers. Have pairs rewrite the text in the figure to reflect the new vegetable-fruit juice. Sample answer: Product–packaging might include a neon colored label Place–sold in schools, video arcades, Internet cafés, convenience stores, vending machines Price–available in a 12-ounce bottle sold for $1.75 Promotion–to sponsor high school events and promote the new juice, ads in teen magazines, on the Internet

EVALUATE

PROMOTION

Graphic Organizer

Display this diagram. Ask students to name ways companies promote their products and services. Possible answers:

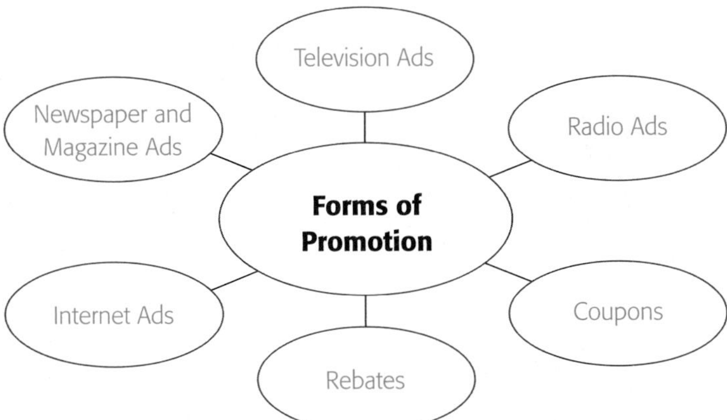

 glencoe.com  iWB

Graphic Organizer Send students to the Online Learning Center to print this graphic organizer.

Guiding Questions

Bring in a variety of advertisements and commercial clips. Answer the guiding questions for each advertisement.

Guiding Questions

What product or service is being promoted?	Answers will vary based on the product or service being promoted in the advertisement.
Who is the target audience for the advertisement?	Teenagers, middle-aged men, women, children, and so on.
Explain how you determined the target audience.	parents of young children, the ad is in a parenting magazine

 glencoe.com  iWB

Graphic Organizer Send students to the Online Learning Center to print this graphic organizer.

 After You Read **Section 1.3**

Review Key Concepts

1. Possible answers would be: fast food chains (i.e. McDonalds, Burger King), cell phones, jeans manufacturers, specific retail stores such as The GAP and Abercrombie & Fitch. These businesses carry items that appeal to teenagers, so teens are one of their target markets.
2. The consumer market consists of people who buy goods and services for personal use. In the organizational market, goods and services are purchased for use in a business operation.
3. Market segmentation helps marketers classify customers based on certain characteristics that can be used to develop customer profiles for a specific target market.

Practice Academics

English Language Arts

4. All answers must include the importance of the product, place, price, and promotion elements of the marketing mix appealing to and being directed to a specific target market. For example, if Gatorade was used as an example, the target market might be athletes who participate in strenuous sports and need hydration. The product's ingredients help restore the electrolytes needed for hydration and the flavors are fruity to appeal to the taste buds. Advertisements use popular professional athletes to promote the product and many professional teams use Gatorade as the team's drink. Gatorade can be found in convenience stores, grocery stores, vending machines, and snack bars. Price would be in line with other sports drinks currently on the market.

Mathematics

5. 44% (2,850,475,620 ÷ 6,500,000,000 = .44)

 glencoe.com 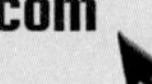

Answer Key Send students to the Online Learning Center to check their answers.

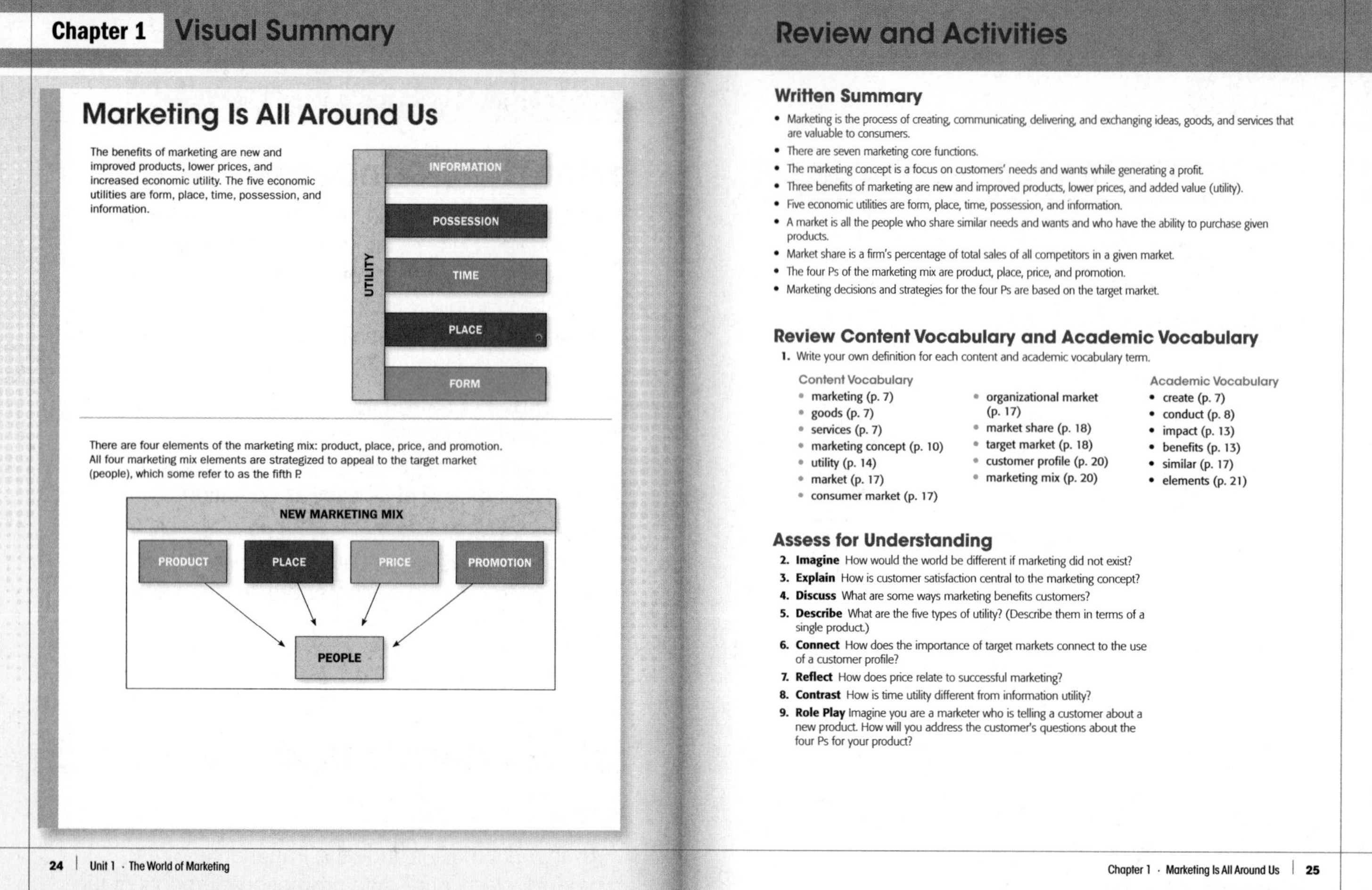

Chapter 1 Visual Summary

Marketing Is All Around Us

The benefits of marketing are new and improved products, lower prices, and increased economic utility. The five economic utilities are form, place, time, possession, and information.

There are four elements of the marketing mix: product, place, price, and promotion. All four marketing mix elements are strategized to appeal to the target market (people), which some refer to as the fifth P.

24 | Unit 1 · The World of Marketing

Review and Activities

Written Summary

- Marketing is the process of creating, communicating, delivering, and exchanging ideas, goods, and services that are valuable to consumers.
- There are seven marketing core functions.
- The marketing concept is a focus on customers' needs and wants while generating a profit.
- Three benefits of marketing are new and improved products, lower prices, and added value (utility).
- Five economic utilities are form, place, time, possession, and information.
- A market is all the people who share similar needs and wants and who have the ability to purchase given products.
- Market share is a firm's percentage of total sales of all competitors in a given market.
- The four Ps of the marketing mix are product, place, price, and promotion.
- Marketing decisions and strategies for the four Ps are based on the target market.

Review Content Vocabulary and Academic Vocabulary

1. Write your own definition for each content and academic vocabulary term.

Content Vocabulary
- marketing (p. 7)
- goods (p. 7)
- services (p. 7)
- marketing concept (p. 10)
- utility (p. 14)
- market (p. 17)
- consumer market (p. 17)
- organizational market (p. 17)
- market share (p. 18)
- target market (p. 18)
- customer profile (p. 20)
- marketing mix (p. 20)

Academic Vocabulary
- create (p. 7)
- conduct (p. 8)
- impact (p. 13)
- benefits (p. 13)
- similar (p. 17)
- elements (p. 21)

Assess for Understanding

2. **Imagine** How would the world be different if marketing did not exist?
3. **Explain** How is customer satisfaction central to the marketing concept?
4. **Discuss** What are some ways marketing benefits customers?
5. **Describe** What are the five types of utility? (Describe them in terms of a single product.)
6. **Connect** How does the importance of target markets connect to the use of a customer profile?
7. **Reflect** How does price relate to successful marketing?
8. **Contrast** How is time utility different from information utility?
9. **Role Play** Imagine you are a marketer who is telling a customer about a new product. How will you address the customer's questions about the four Ps for your product?

Chapter 1 · Marketing Is All Around Us | 25

EVALUATE

Visual Summary

Express Creativity Ask students to develop their own visual summary of a concept in the chapter. Encourage students to use different formats for their visual summaries, such as a storyboard, a timeline, a table, a tree diagram, or a word web. Visual summaries will vary depending on the concept depicted and the visual manner in which it is depicted. Questions to ask when assessing a visual summary include:

- Is the summary clear, economical, and simple?
- Are any important steps left out?
- Are steps or concepts arranged in the same order as the original?
- Does the summary reveal a pattern that connects the details?
- Does the summary locate and highlight the most important information?

Review Content Vocabulary and Academic Vocabulary

1. Sentences will vary. Sample answers:

When **marketing goods** and **services,** successful businesses follow the **marketing concept.**

Marketing helps to create **utility,** which makes customers satisfied with their purchases.

Teens are part of the soft drink **market.**

Computers can be marketed in the **consumer** and **organizational market.**

Product improvements can help businesses increase their **market share.** A **target market's customer profile** dictates how decisions are made in the **marketing mix.**

Marketing activities **create** competition, which helps to lower prices. It is a good idea to **conduct** research in order to determine the **impact** an advertising campaign may have on a target market.

One **benefit** of marketing is the role it plays in increasing demand for products, which helps to lower prices.

People of certain age tend to have **similar** wants and needs.

Some businesses consider the target market so important that they include "people" as one **element** of the marketing mix.

EVALUATE

Assess for Understanding

2. Answers will vary but may include: Without marketing people would not know about products, businesses would not know about customers' needs and wants. Products to supply customers' needs and wants would not be developed and sold, and so on.

3. If customers are not satisfied with a company's product or service, the company will not get the customer's repeat business. If customers do not purchase a company's products or services, the company will go out of business.

4. Marketing benefits customers in a number of ways including helping to ensure that the customer is heard and that their needs and wants are met at prices that are affordable. Marketing helps to keep the customer informed about new products and services and generates competition, which fosters new and improved products.

5. Student's answers should provide information similar to the following in terms of a single product. Utility is an economic term for value added to a product. Types of utilities include form (changing raw materials or putting parts together to make them more useful), place (having product where customers can buy it), time (having the product when customers want to buy it), possession (making it easy for customers to make a purchase), and information (communicating with customers regarding the features and benefits of a product).

6. Businesses create a customer profile to develop a clear picture of their target market. The customer profile lists information about the target market that businesses use so that they can understand the characteristics of their target market and better focus their marketing efforts directly at the target market.

7. Pricing of a product must reflect what customers are willing and able to pay. This information can be determined through the development of customer profiles of the target market for the product, which is part of marketing information management—one of the seven marketing core functions.

8. Time utility is having a product or service available at a certain time of year or a convenient time of day to suit the customer. Information utility involves dispersing information about services and products to customers through salespeople, displays, packaging, and labeling. Information utility informs customers as to where and when products and services are available.

9. Sample answers for the role play may include: Product—describing for the customer the product's features, brand name, packaging, and warranty; Price—discussing price strategies that reflect what customer's are willing and able to pay. Pricing should include suggested retail price and discounts, allowances, credit terms, and payment period for organizational customers; Place—the marketer should describe how the product will get into the customers' hands, which should include distribution, placement in retail outlets and other means of selling the product, and determining whether the product can be sold directly to customers; Promotion—the marketer should discuss with the customer the activities related to advertising, personal selling, sales promotion, and publicity for the product.

21st Century Skills

Teamwork Skills

10. **Target Markets** Work with a partner to demonstrate the importance of target markets. Prepare a customer profile for a product of your choice. Change the customer profile (age, income level, gender) to target a different audience. Explain all the changes that must be made in the marketing mix (product, place, price, and promotion) for the new target market (people). Prepare a written report and an oral presentation using presentation software.

Financial Literacy Skills

11. **Business Loans** A company took out a $9,000 loan in order to create a Web site. The interest on the loan is 5 percent for one year. The Web site generated enough business to pay back the loan in 9 months. What is the total amount of the check the owner will prepare to pay back the loan with interest?

Everyday Ethics

12. **Calling on Youth** Hello Kitty products are very popular with young girls. British retailer WH Smith and Sanrio, owner of Hello Kitty, want to find out how popular they are with young women. They have begun marketing the phones to women in their 20s and 30s. The problem is some advocates object to promoting adult products to children. They argue that all Hello Kitty products target 6- to 7-year-olds. Some believe that marketing products directly to children is unethical. What is your opinion on this topic? Discuss your response as a class and be sure to distinguish between customers and consumers.

e-Marketing Skills

13. **Social Media Marketing** Help a local business utilize social media to better communicate with its customers. Design an e-mail program or use other social media platforms to share new promotions and offerings with customers. Present your ideas in a written and an oral report.

Build Academic Skills

English Language Arts

14. **The Marketing Concept** Write a memo to the staff of a computer customer service center explaining the marketing concept. Stress their role in keeping customers satisfied. Be sure to use the correct format and check your grammar, spelling, and punctuation.

NCTE 3 Apply strategies to interpret texts.

Science

15. **Scientific Inquiry** Describe market share by conducting a survey of the cell phone service providers of 25 teens. Follow the procedures used for an experiment. Calculate the percentages and draw a pie chart to show the results of your survey. What do your findings suggest about the respective companies' market shares?

NSES A Develop abilities to do scientific inquiry, understandings about scientific inquiry.

Mathematics

16. **Calculating Market Share** Calculate Panasonic's market share if total sales in the LCD television market are $4,865,375,550 and Panasonic's sales are $1,798,450,782. Round your answer to the nearest tenth decimal place.

Math Concept **Computing Percentages** To solve this problem, use the following formula:

Company's Sales/Whole Market's Sales = Company's Market Share

NCTM Number and Operations Understand numbers, ways of representing numbers, relationships among numbers, and number systems.

For help, go to the Math Skills Handbook located at the back of this book.

Standardized Test Practice

Directions Read the following questions. On a separate sheet of paper write the best possible answer for each one.

1. In addition to people (target market), what are the elements of the marketing mix?
   - **A.** product, place, advertising, and sales
   - **B.** goods, services, ideas, and promotion
   - **C.** product, place, price, and promotion
   - **D.** form, place, time, and possession
2. True or False? All people who share similar needs and wants and who have the ability to purchase a given product are called a market.
   - T
   - F
3. Form, place, time, possession, and information are types of economic ________.

Test-Taking Tip

When you sit down to take a math test, jot down important equations or formulas on scrap paper. This way, you will not forget them during the test.

DECA Connection Role Play

Employee Cleaning Service

Situation Assume the role of employee of a recently opened cleaning service business. You have solid business experience and are experienced in the services provided by your new employer. The business provides a wide assortment of cleaning services targeted to a broad variety of businesses. The business offers cleaning services ranging from display window cleaning to daily interior cleaning and trash disposal. The business has been open for one month. Business has been good and cleaning contracts have exceeded the plan.

The business owner has asked you to help prepare a newspaper advertisement for the business. The purpose of the advertisement is to announce the opening of the business and the services your business provides. A fellow employee (judge) who has little business experience asks you why the business is planning an advertisement when the business is doing well.

Activity You are to briefly explain to the employee (judge) the role of advertising and promotion and the role they play in a business's overall marketing strategy. You are also to explain the role of marketing in general.

Evaluation You will be evaluated on how well you meet the following performance indicators:

1. Explain the concept of marketing strategies.
2. Explain the concept of market and market identification.
3. Explain the importance of promotion in the marketing mix.
4. Describe marketing functions and related activities.
5. Determine economic utilities created by business activities.

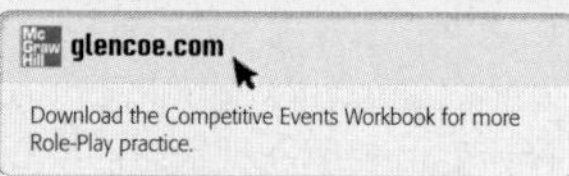

Download the Competitive Events Workbook for more Role-Play practice.

EVALUATE

Teamwork Skills

10. Presentations should reflect understanding of target markets and should include the profile for a product as it is currently marketed. Student pairs should change the customer profile with regard to at least one characteristic (i.e. age, income level, gender). Based on the changes made, the marketing mix (product, place, price, and promotion) strategies should reflect the new market.

Financial Literacy Skills

11. Answer is $9,337.50 (9 months divided by 12 months = .75; $9,000 × .05 = $450; $450 × .75 = $337.50; $9,000 + $337.50 = $9,337.50).

Everyday Ethics

12. Discussions may include businesses that target children as consumers often create images that portray their products as fun. When parents are the target market, companies highlight product qualities such as educational value. In the case of the Hello Kitty phone, a more mature audience would be the target. Some students may consider any type of marketing to children unethical.

e-Marketing Skills

13. The social media selected and the students' ideas with regard to how a local business can better communicate with its customers will vary. An example would be a program using e-mails. Students should include a way to obtain customers' e-mail addresses, possibly through a customer loyalty program. Promotions and offerings could be sent on a weekly basis to all customers in the loyalty program. More sophisticated programs could send promotions based on regular purchases.

EVALUATE

Build Academic Skills

English Language Arts

14. Memos to the staff of a computer customer service center must stress the staff's role in keeping customers satisfied. Here is a sample memo:

TO: Customer Service Staff
FROM: Student's Name
DATE: Current Date
RE: Customer Satisfaction & the Marketing Concept

The marketing concept is the idea that a business should strive to satisfy customers' needs and wants while generating a profit. You must understand the marketing concept to send a consistent message to the customer. The message is that the customer satisfaction is most important. You know that repeat customers keep a company in business. Be patient and work toward a satisfying solution to our customers' problems. You are our company in the customer's eyes.

Science

15. Survey results will vary. Check pie charts to see that the students calculated the percentages correctly and that they total 100 percent. When reporting their survey results, students should be able to identify the service provider with the highest market share based on their sample.

Mathematics

16. Panasonic has a market share of 37% ($1,798,450,782 ÷ $4,865,375,550 = 0.3696).

Standardized Test Practice

1. C. product, place, price, and promotion
2. True
3. utilities

DECA Connection Role Play

Evaluations will be based on these performance indicators:

1. **Explain the concept of marketing strategies.** A marketing strategy identifies target markets and sets marketing mix choices involving product, price, place, and promotion.
2. **Explain the concept of market and market identification.** A market includes all the people who share similar needs and wants. Markets include the consumer market, which consists of consumers who purchase for personal use and the organizational market, which includes business-to-business sales. Market identification includes market segmentation—breaking down the market into similar groups and classifying customers by specific characteristics. All marketing strategies are directed to the target market.
3. **Explain the importance of promotion in the marketing mix.** Promotion refers to activities related to advertising and publicity. Promotional strategies include the message, the media, special offers, and the timing of the promotional campaigns. The level of success can determine the success or failure of the business.
4. **Describe marketing functions and related activities.** Marketing Core: channel management—the process of deciding how to get goods into customers' hands; marketing information management—analyzing information about customers, trends, and competing products; market planning—understanding the concepts used to develop and target a select audience; pricing—how much to charge for goods and services to make a profit; product/service management—obtaining, developing, maintaining, and improving a product mix in response to market opportunities; promotion— informing current and potential customers about products; selling—provides customers with goods and services they want.
5. **Determine economic utilities created by business activities.** Economic utilities: form utility—changing raw materials into usable goods, putting parts together; place utility—having a product where customers can buy it; time utility—having a product at a certain time; possession utility—the exchange of a product for money; information utility—communication with the consumer.

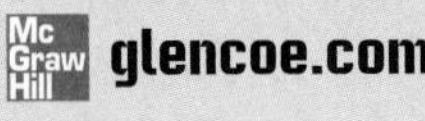

Role Plays For more DECA Role Plays, send students to the Online Learning Center to download the Competitive Events Workbook.

the marketing plan

SHOW WHAT YOU KNOW

Visual Literacy Marketers want to know what products teens buy, how much they spend, and where they shop. They use this information to create the marketing mix as part of their marketing plans. ***Why is this target market of consumers important to marketers?***

Discovery Project

The Right Mix

Essential Question How do stores use the four Ps to create an effective marketing mix?

Project Goal

Work with a partner to identify and visit three different specialty stores where you and other teenagers shop. Create a marketing mix report for each store by describing the 4 Ps: product (type and quality of products), price (cost, discount, and member rewards), place (type of location), and promotion (in-store and media advertising). For example, for "product," you might identify teen apparel or electronic games. Describe each store's marketing mix and discuss whether it is effective in a report to the class.

Ask Yourself...

- Which stores will you select?
- How will you share your findings with the class?
- How will you organize your report?
- How will you make your presentation effective?

Synthesize and Present Research Synthesize your research by describing whether each store's marketing mix is effective for selling to teens.

glencoe.com

Activity Get a worksheet activity about creating a marketing mix.

Evaluate Download a rubric you can use to evaluate your project.

DECA Connection

DECA Events

Concepts in this chapter are related to DECA competitive events that involve either an interview or role play.

Performance Indicators The performance indicators represent key skills and knowledge. Your key to success in DECA competitive events is relating them to the concepts in this chapter.

- Explain the nature of marketing plans.
- Explain the nature of marketing planning.
- Explain the nature of sales forecasts.
- Explain the concept of marketing strategies.
- Prepare simple written reports.

DECA Prep

Role Play Practice role-playing with the DECA Connection competitive-event activity at the end of this chapter. More information about DECA events can be found on DECA's Web site.

ENGAGE

Visual Literacy

Read the chapter opener photo caption question to students: ***Why is this target market of consumers important to marketers?*** Market research has revealed that teenagers have enough spending power to justify creating products and services specifically for this segment of the market. Remind students that they learned the answers to the following questions while studying Chapter 1. Then ask these guiding questions to activate prior knowledge.

Guiding Questions

Recall How are the elements of the marketing mix interconnected?	Actions in one area affect decisions in the others
Explain What is the main consideration marketers take into account when making marketing mix decisions?	The target market, the people they want to win over and make into customers.

Discovery Project

The Right Mix Start a discussion that connects students to the Discovery Project Essential Question: ***How do stores create an effective marketing mix?*** A business must first establish a marketing strategy that clearly identifies the target market. Then it strategizes marketing mix decisions that focus on the target market, taking customer needs and wants into account.

glencoe.com

Discovery Project Resources Send students to the Online Learning Center to download a rubric to evaluate their projects.

ENGAGE

Introduce the Chapter

In this chapter, the foundation for marketing principles is laid and these major concepts are discussed:

- SWOT analysis
- Internal company analysis
- External opportunity and threat analysis
- Marketing planning
- Marketing strategies
- Market segmentation
- Target marketing
- The marketing mix
- Mass marketing

Discussion Starter

Market Segmentation Tell students that there are many ways to segment markets. One way is called Psychographics. Psychographics refers to people's lifestyles, attitudes, personalities, and values. *Ask students:* ***what are some examples of how people in their school are classified in this way?*** Answers will vary but might include athletes, environmentalists, and so on. Tell students that in many cases, these labels are stereotypes. Ask students: ***Why are these stereotypes?*** Looking at groups of people like this can be exaggerated and simplified. Then ask: ***How can generalizing about groups of people based on their interests be useful to marketers?*** They identify certain characteristics and provide certain insights that might be useful to a business looking to target particular markets.

DECA Connection

Discuss the performance indicators listed in the DECA Connection feature. Explain to students that performance indicators tell them how to demonstrate their acquired skills and knowledge through individual or team competitive events.

glencoe.com

Competitive Events Workbook For more DECA Role Plays, send students to the Online Learning Center to download the Competitive Events Workbook.

PRINT RESOURCES

- **Student Edition**
- **Teacher Edition**
- **Student Activity Workbook with Academic Integration** includes worksheets and activities correlated to the text.
- **Mathematics for Marketing Workbook** provides math activities for every unit in the text.

TECHNOLOGY TOOLBOX

- **Connect**
- **ConnectPlus**
- **ExamView Assessment Suite** is a comprehensive solution for creating, administering, and scoring tests.

glencoe.com

Online Learning Center provides a variety of resources to enrich and enhance learning.

SECTION, CHAPTER, AND UNIT RESOURCES

- **Graphic Organizers** for organizing text concepts visually.
- **Digital Nation Activities** and **Green Marketer Activities** extend learning beyond the text features.
- **Career Chatroom Career Profiles** allow students to explore different marketing occupations in depth.
- **After You Read Answer Keys** for students to check their answers.
- **Discovery Project Rubrics** and **Marketing Internship Project Rubrics** for students to evaluate their projects.

PROGRAM RESOURCES

- **Student Activity Workbook with Academic Integration Teacher Annotated Edition** includes annotated answers for the activities and worksheets.
- **Marketing Research Project Workbook** provides a step-by-step approach for students to complete their own marketing research studies.
- **School-to-Career Activity Workbook** helps students relate their class work to on-the-job experience and involves work-site analysis and working with mentors.
- **Competitive Events Workbook** helps prepare students for state and national marketing education competitions.
- **Inclusion in the Marketing Education Classroom** provides teaching resources for working with students with special needs.
- **PowerPoint Presentations** provides visual teaching aids and assessments for this chapter.

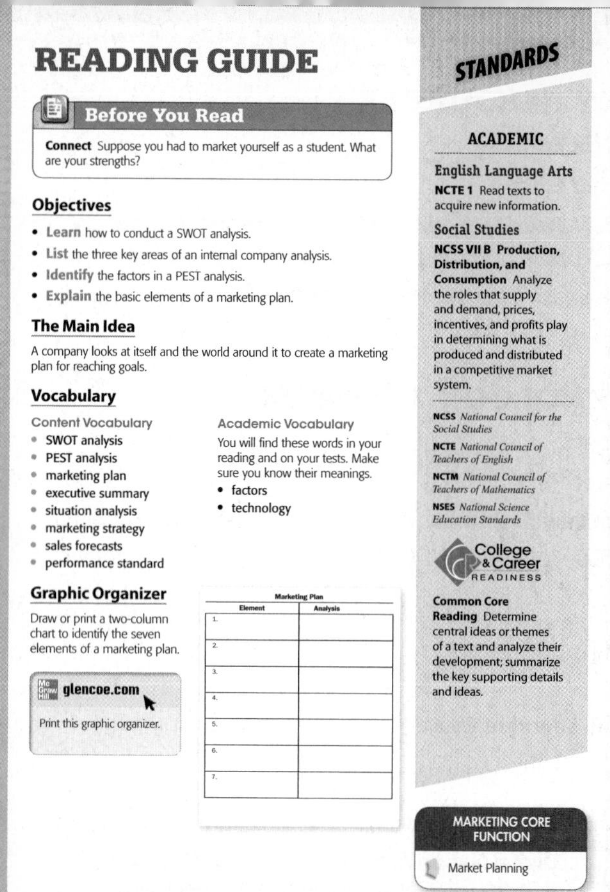

READING GUIDE

Before You Read

Connect Suppose you had to market yourself as a student. What are your strengths?

Objectives

- **Learn** how to conduct a SWOT analysis.
- **List** the three key areas of an internal company analysis.
- **Identify** the factors in a PEST analysis.
- **Explain** the basic elements of a marketing plan.

The Main Idea

A company looks at itself and the world around it to create a marketing plan for reaching goals.

Vocabulary

Content Vocabulary
- SWOT analysis
- PEST analysis
- marketing plan
- executive summary
- situation analysis
- marketing strategy
- sales forecasts
- performance standard

Academic Vocabulary

You will find these words in your reading and on your tests. Make sure you know their meanings.
- factors
- technology

Graphic Organizer

Draw or print a two-column chart to identify the seven elements of a marketing plan.

Marketing Plan

Element	Analysis
1.	
2.	
3.	
4.	
5.	
6.	
7.	

glencoe.com

Print this graphic organizer.

STANDARDS

ACADEMIC

English Language Arts

NCTE 1 Read texts to acquire new information.

Social Studies

NCSS VII B Production, Distribution, and Consumption Analyze the roles that supply and demand, prices, incentives, and profits play in determining what is produced and distributed in a competitive market system.

NCSS *National Council for the Social Studies*

NCTE *National Council of Teachers of English*

NCTM *National Council of Teachers of Mathematics*

NSES *National Science Education Standards*

College & Career READINESS

Common Core

Reading Determine central ideas or themes of a text and analyze their development; summarize the key supporting details and ideas.

MARKETING CORE FUNCTION

Market Planning

Section 2.1 Marketing Planning

SWOT ANALYSIS

The **SWOT analysis** is an assessment that lists and analyzes the company's strengths and weaknesses. It also includes the opportunities and the threats that surround it. In other words, this analysis lists everything that can foster the business's success and what could make it fail. The acronym for strengths, weaknesses, opportunities, and threats is also the name of this process: SWOT analysis.

This internal and external awareness will help a business identify weaknesses and prepare for handling threats such as competition or a changing marketplace. An accurate analysis will also help a company be more competitive because it provides guidance and direction. The company will develop strategies around the SWOT analysis.

As You Read

Predict How can a business use a SWOT analysis to assess its place in the market?

INTERNAL STRENGTHS AND WEAKNESSES

Strengths and weaknesses are both internal **factors** that affect a business's operation. The internal analysis centers around three Cs: company, customers, and competition. It is important to review these factors objectively and fairly.

COMPANY ANALYSIS

Questions that are part of a company's internal analysis are about what a company does well (core competencies) and what areas are weak. This includes a review of the staff, the company's financial situation, its production capabilities, and each aspect of the marketing mix (product, promotion, place, and pricing). Here are a few sample questions:

Staff-Related Questions

- What is the company's mission statement? Is everyone on staff following it?
- How experienced are the company executives? What have they accomplished?
- Does the company have too much or not enough staff to provide the quality of service it should? Should staff be re-assigned?
- What is the quality of the staff? Are there training and assessment programs?
- How effective is the sales force?

> "Good marketing relies on good plans and accurate analysis."

Financial Questions

- Has the company been profitable? In which areas and why?
- Are there enough financial resources to achieve the company's goals?
- What is the company's sales history? Are sales increasing or decreasing?

Production Capability Questions

- How are adjustments made in production due to an increase or decrease in the company's sales orders?
- Has the research and development (R&D) department created any successful new products?
- What percentage of sales come from products that are five years or older?
- What changes in **technology** are required to remain competitive?

ENGAGE

Anticipation Activity

Improving Student Achievement Ask students to list the names of companies with which they are familiar. Ask students: ***Why did you name these companies?*** The companies may be large national or international companies that sell products and services that interest the students. Ask students: ***Why are you familiar with these companies?*** Because the companies have done a good job of marketing themselves. Explain that students might be part of the target market for some of these businesses.

Objectives

- **Learn** how to conduct a SWOT analysis. Students will learn the strengths, weaknesses, opportunities, and threats for a company.
- **List** the three key areas of an internal company analysis. company, customers, and competition
- **Identify** the factors in a PEST analysis. political, economic, socio-cultural, and technological (PEST)
- **Explain** the basic elements of a marketing plan. The basic elements include: executive summary, situation analysis, objectives, marketing strategies, implementation, and evaluation and control.

Graphic Organizer

1. Executive Summary	Provides an overview of plan and explains costs involved in implementing the plan.
2. Situation Analysis	Provides an examination of factors and trends that affect marketing strategies.
3. Objectives	Describes what the plan will accomplish.
4. Marketing Strategies	Identifies target markets and marketing mix choices focused on those markets.
5. Implementation	Outlines how implementation will be accomplished and provides sales forecasts.
6. Evaluation and Control	Explains how objectives will be measured and who will evaluate.

glencoe.com

Graphic Organizer Send students to the Online Learning Center to print this graphic organizer.

EXPLORE

Before You Read

Read the Before You Read question aloud: ***Suppose you had to market yourself as a student. What are your strengths?*** Point out to students that throughout their lives they will need to market themselves to achieve success, at home, at school, at work, and in the community. Marketing yourself is about finding your unique abilities and being able to communicate these to others effectively. Your strengths and skills are your selling points, and every time you communicate you have an opportunity to make an impact on how people perceive you.

Preteaching Vocabulary

Have students go to the Online Learning Center at glencoe.com for the Chapter 2 Preteaching Vocabulary games.

Content Vocabulary

Instruct students to write the content vocabulary words on index cards. Students should then place those terms in the order in which they will occur in the plan. executive summary, situation analysis, marketing strategy, sales forecasts, performance standards

Academic Vocabulary

Technology—Word Origin Tell students that the Greek word *techne* refers to an art or skill and the suffix *-logia* can mean "the study of." Ask students to give examples of how technology has been a cultural force. Sample answers include: The invention of the printing press allowed ideas to be shared easily for the first time in history and brought about great advancements in the standardization of languages.

Factor—Alternate Meanings Explain to students that the Academic Vocabulary term *factor* has several different meanings depending on the context. In the context that it is used in this section, *factor* means "something that influences the outcome of something." Ask students if they know the definition of factor in a mathematical context. In multiplication, factors are the numbers being multiplied together to get another number, for example 3 (factor) × 2 (factor) = 6 (product), so 3 and 2 are factors of 6.

Reading: Building Vocabulary

Go to the Online Learning Center to view a video clip in which a teacher introduces and plays two vocabulary building games with her students.

Marketing Planning

SWOT ANALYSIS

Explain to students that a SWOT analysis includes everything that could foster a business's success or failure. Then ask these guiding questions to focus the discussion about SWOT Analysis.

Guiding Questions

Recall What are the three Cs around which internal analysis is centered?	company, customers, competition
Contrast What is the difference between internal analysis and external analysis?	Internal analysis is within the company itself whereas external analysis involves analyzing a company's competitors.
Synthesize You work for a small electronics company. The owner wants to conduct a SWOT analysis. You think it would be best to hire an outside consultant. What might you say to convince her?	Possible answer: An outside firm is likely to produce a more objective and useful analysis. In addition, the firm's employees would be specially trained in this task.

As You Read

Read students the As You Read question: ***How can a business use a SWOT analysis to assess its place in the market?*** A business can determine how it might better differentiate the company and its products from the competition and be able to identify portions of the target market that competitors are missing.

Expert Advice

Read the quote to students:

> **"Good marketing relies on good plans and accurate analysis."**

Ask students: ***Why is accurate analysis so important?*** An accurate SWOT analysis gives a company the insight necessary to develop effective marketing mix strategies.

Marketing Mix (Four Ps) Questions

Remember that a business's marketing mix includes product, price, place, and promotion. These factors influence how customers respond to a business. Therefore, when analyzing the four Ps of the marketing mix, it is also important to see if they are properly coordinated with one another and with the target market. Any P not focused completely on the potential or current customer would be a reason for review and adjustment.

P PRODUCT

- What new products have been successful and why?
- Does the company own a patent on any of those products?
- Are any patents expiring in the future?

P PRICE

- What are the present pricing strategies?
- Are the pricing strategies working?

P PLACE

- Do products easily reach customers?
- Who helps the company with distribution?

P PROMOTION

- How is the company positioned in the marketplace?
- What are the promotional strategies and have they been successful?
- What is the company's reputation and image among consumers?

The answers to these questions might reveal such strengths (or core competencies) as talented and well-trained employees, quality workmanship, and excellent service records.

CUSTOMER ANALYSIS

Customers are a great source of information. Studying their buying habits reveals patterns that offer insights into product offerings and pricing strategies. These questions can be used to analyze customers.

- Who are the customers?
- How do groups of customers differ from one another?
- What, when, where, and how much do they buy?
- How do customers rate the company on quality, service, and value?
- Is your customer base increasing or decreasing? Why?

Catalog companies use database technology to analyze buying patterns, which allow them to produce interest-specific catalogs. Companies with this technology have a major advantage over their competitors because they can structure their product selection, pricing, and promotional messages to very specific targeted audiences.

To monitor customer satisfaction, many firms ask customers to complete a survey or questionnaire after making a purchase. Data from this research help companies pinpoint areas that need improvement. That is, monitoring customer satisfaction can reveal useful information about both the strengths and weaknesses of a company's products and services. For example, customers may indicate their interest in a product because it is useful, but they may also want it to be sold for a lower price.

COMPETITIVE POSITION

A company may find that it has certain strengths and weaknesses when compared to its competitors. A company's market share may be greater than its competitors', which would be a major strength. If a company loses market share to competitors, it would be a weakness. Questions that help a company analyze its internal competitive position might include the following:

- What is the company's market share?
- What advantages does the company have over its competitors?
- What core competencies does the company possess? A better reputation? A patent? Special resources? Better distribution?
- Are competitors taking business away? Why?

EXTERNAL OPPORTUNITIES AND THREATS

Companies must always look for opportunities to create competitive advantage due to external factors.

Customer Analysis

Companies likes Vans® conduct research about customers before making marketing mix decisions. ***What questions would you ask to find out about the customers of the product featured in this ad?***

MARKETING CASE STUDY

Refocusing Nikon Cameras

More than 6 out of 10 people in the United States own a digital camera. These cameras are easy to use, and more users are able to upload and share photos online—plus, digital cameras have become less expensive.

With its 90-year history, Nikon® created some of the first digital single lens cameras for NASA. Today, its COOLPIX® line has become popular with consumers who prefer a compact camera.

As Seen on TV, Print, and Web Ads

To promote the COOLPIX line, Nikon focused on the image of style and fun. Television commercials were directed by an Emmy awardwinning director. To target a broader and youthful audience, a young star was signed as spokesperson. The TV spots served as the basis for Web video and banner ads, as well as print ads in magazines.

Social Studies

Ask Discuss this question with a partner: How does the price of Nikon's cameras determine how they are promoted through TV, print, and Web ads and then distributed to customers?

NCSS VII B Production, Distribution, and Consumption Analyze the role that supply and demand, prices, incentives, and profits play in determining what is produced and distributed in a competitive market system.

EXPLAIN

Visual Literacy

Customer Analysis Caption Answer Read the caption question to students: ***What questions would you ask to find out about the customers of the products featured in this ad?*** Answers will vary. Sample answer: I would ask about their age and gender. I would also ask where they live and what leisure activities they are interested in. Use these guiding questions to discuss the ad in more detail.

Guiding Questions

Explain Who is the target audience for the Van's® ad?	People who live in warm climates.
Evaluate Do you think this ad is effective? Why?	Answers will vary, but students should provide appropriate reasons for their answers.

Mini Project

Enrichment

Create Surveys for Gathering Data and Statistics Ask students to use the questions under Customer Analysis as a basis for developing a questionnaire for collecting information about the customers of a particular business. For example, students might choose to write a survey for the customers of a local golf course or restaurant. Encourage students to look online for customer satisfaction surveys. Surveys will vary but students should develop questions that can be used to tell a business owner who the customers are, what they want, what they need, what they buy, how satisfied they are with the goods and services offered by the business, and how they perceive the business in terms of quality, service, and value. Encourage students to practice their communication skills and build relationships at home, at school, at work, or in the community by soliciting feedback on their surveys from trusted adults.

ELABORATE

Activate Prior Knowledge

Reteach The Four Ps Ask students to recall what they learned about the marketing mix in Chapter 1. Ask students: ***What are the four factors that make up the marketing mix?*** product, price, place, and promotion Ask students: ***Why are marketing mix strategies important?*** They influence how customers respond to a business.

MARKETING MIX	
P PRODUCT	P PLACE
P PRICE	P PROMOTION

P PRODUCT

Choosing what products to make and sell.

- Product development
- Product design
- Product features
- Product improvements

P PRICE

What is exchanged for the product?

- What are the customers willing to pay?
- Consumer prices versus reseller price.
- What does the competition charge?

P PLACE

The means of getting the product into the consumers' hands.

- Which geographic areas?
- Which channels of distribution?
- Sold directly or through intermediaries?

P PROMOTION

How customers will be told about a company's products.

- Advertising, personal selling, sales promotions, and publicity
- The message and the media selected.

glencoe.com iWB

Graphic Organizer Send students to the Online Learning Center to print this graphic organizer.

COMPETITIVE POSITION

Explain to students that a company needs to know what its strengths and weaknesses are when compared to its competitors. Then ask these guiding questions to focus the discussion about competitive position.

Guiding Questions

List What are three examples of the core competencies that a company might have?	Responses might include a good reputation, special resources, and excellent distribution.
Draw Conclusions What might a company conclude if a competitor is drawing away many of its customers?	Possible answers: The competitor's product is better quality, less expensive, or more readily available.
Synthesize How do you think market share might be related to customer satisfaction?	If customers are satisfied, they are more likely to make repeat purchases; conversely, market share could drop if customers are dissatisfied.

Reinforce Vocabulary

Core Competency—Denotative Meaning Write the term *core competency* on the board. Then read the first sentence after the third bullet under the Competitive Position header: ***What core competencies does the company possess?*** Explain to students the meaning of the term. Primary areas of expertise or specialty that allow a business to beat its competitors. Explain to students that a business's core competencies are strategized to differentiate the business from other similar businesses. Provide students with the example of Walmart®. Ask students: ***What are Walmart's core competencies?*** Walmart focuses on keeping operations costs low and buying and selling in huge volume, which allows them to price goods lower than most competitors and remain profitable despite having a low profit margin.

MARKETING CASE STUDY

Social Studies Answer Nikon's cameras are priced so that they can be purchased by many segments of the market. Each segment buys a different type of camera, so Nikon® uses various methods of promotion to reach all of these segments. This segmentation also means their cameras need to be distributed widely to enable all types of customers to purchase them.

FIGURE 2.1 **Plan Success With SWOT Analysis**

Planning with SWOT The SWOT analysis helps a business and its employees organize factors that influence its success. ***What factor is the successful marketing of a competitor's product?***

SWOT

INTERNAL		EXTERNAL	
STRENGTHS	WEAKNESSES	OPPORTUNITIES	THREATS
• large market share • reputation for quality • creative product developers	• low profit • few employees	• competitors going out of business • strong economy • few direct competitors	• legal issues • decreasing amounts of natural resources

COMPETITION

To stay competitive, companies need to know what their competitors are doing at all times. Changes in a competitor's financial situation and problems in the marketplace can provide opportunities. For example, Starbucks became the largest coffee company in the world, but it relied heavily on U.S. sales. However, in 2008, due to a slowdown in consumer spending, consumers sought coffee at less expensive competitors.

Companies that conduct a SWOT analysis (See **Figure 2.1**) on an ongoing basis are in a better position to react and make adjustments to their marketing mix. To assist in this process, companies must continually scan the external environment.

PEST ANALYSIS

A **PEST analysis** is the scanning of outside influences on an organization. This is a methodical look at the world that typically includes four factors: political, economic, socio-cultural, and technological. Understanding how each of these areas is changing or is likely to change can lead to a better appreciation of potential opportunities or threats for the firm. An alert business owner may use a change in one of these four influences as an opportunity to be first to market products customers want.

POLITICAL ISSUES

Political issues center around government involvement in business operations. Companies must be alert to changes in laws and regulations that affect their industries. Global companies need to understand the political structure and regulations of each foreign country in which they conduct business. To assess potential political risks and new opportunities, it is important to see what changes are likely in the laws governing a business operation, as they will have an impact on marketing plans.

Here are a few examples of issues and current regulations in the United States that may affect certain industries in a positive way (opportunity) or in a negative way (threat):

- **Do Not Call Registry** This legislation requires telemarketers to drop from their lists home and cell phone numbers of registered consumers. This regulation forced many businesses to rethink their marketing strategies. Telemarketing companies had to adjust data files to comply with the law.
- **Downloading Music from the Internet** Illegal downloading of music created an industry of companies that provide legal downloading of music for a fee. This reduced revenue for traditional music stores, but has become an opportunity for other Internet retailers.

ECONOMIC FACTORS

The current state of the economy is of interest to all businesses: If the economy is robust, businesses are more likely to invest in new products and markets. An economy that is in a recession or slowing down sends a completely different message to the company's decision makers.

Upcoming marketing programs may be altered or scrapped altogether in a weak economy. Factors such as the unemployment rate, inflation, retail sales figures, productivity, and consumer confidence are tools to estimate the current status of the economy. The value of the dollar in relation to foreign currencies affects imports and exports. Import and export prices affect how a company buys and sells its products in the global market. It is necessary for companies to analyze the economy from local, national, and international perspectives. That way, they can adapt to changes in their local market as well as those in markets all over the world. Here are some economic factors marketers would consider as opportunities or threats:

- **Recession** An economy in recession poses a threat to nearly all companies. Most companies slow or stop plans for new facilities and often reduce research and development (R&D) efforts.
- **Unemployment** If unemployment figures decrease and consumer confidence increases, companies may see an opportunity to grow their businesses.
- **Currency Rates** Changes in foreign currency rates could be seen as a threat or an opportunity depending on whether this makes the company's products or services cheaper or more expensive in their foreign target market.
- **Import Pricing** Illegal dumping (selling imported products at a very low price) in a given market is a threat to all businesses in that industry.
- **Trade Restrictions** Changes in trade restrictions, such as lowering or raising tariffs (taxes) on imported goods, could be considered a threat or an opportunity, depending on where a company does business.

Companies cannot control these economic factors, so they must react to them in ways that create opportunities and diminish threats. For example, a company may develop a less expensive line of goods during a recession. It may also offer special promotions and discounts to attract customers to its business. It may also focus more on online retail opportunities when consumers are less willing to travel to shop.

When laws began to prohibit most free downloading of music, new businesses developed for legal music downloading. ***What products have become popular as a result of the downloading laws?***

EXPLAIN

Visual Literacy

Figure 2.1 Caption Answer Read the figure caption question to students. ***What factor is the successful marketing of a competitor's product?*** external threat Then ask students: ***What might happen if a company did not conduct SWOT analyses on a regular basis?*** It might not identify internal and external strengths, weaknesses, opportunities, and threats early enough to respond properly.

Critical Thinking

Ask students: ***Why is it important for a technology company to differentiate products and marketing messages using information about who will use the products and how the products are used?*** Technology companies often develop products that meet the specific needs of specific groups of customers. A technology company must speak to its various audiences based on their expertise. Some advertising messages need to be more sophisticated and detailed for experienced users, while novices would need simplified directions and explanations.

PEST ANALYSIS

Ask students what four factors the letters in the acronym PEST analysis represent. Political, economic, socio-cultural, and technological. Then ask these guiding questions to focus the discussion about political issues and economic factors.

Guiding Questions

Identify Cause and Effect Do you think consumer confidence might be related to unemployment rates? What kind of PEST factor does this scenario illustrate? Explain your answer.	If the unemployment rate goes up, consumer confidence is likely to go down because workers may worry that the economy is not stable and that they might lose their jobs. The relationship between unemployment rates and consumer confidence is an economic factor.
Synthesize A government begins placing tariffs on certain imported goods. What group is most likely to support such an effort? Why?	The companies in the country where the goods are being imported are most likely to support the tariff because it will make the prices of their goods more competitive in the marketplace.

ELABORATE

Graphic Organizer

Draw this diagram. Explain to students that there are many tools for evaluating the state of the economy. Then ask students to name the factors listed in the text. Write their answers in the graphic organizer.

 glencoe.com  iWB

Graphic Organizer Send students to the Online Learning Center to print this graphic organizer.

Visual Literacy

iOpportunity Caption Answer Read the photo caption question to students. ***What products have become popular as a result of downloading laws?*** New businesses were created that facilitate the legal and licensed purchase of music and other copyrighted materials. Then ask these guiding questions to focus the discussion about external opportunities and threats.

Guiding Questions

Identify Give an example of a change in a company's situation that might provide an opportunity for a competitor.	Possible answers: Changes in the company's financial situation or ownership; problems with the quality of one or more product.
Analyze Why is it vital that companies continually keep track of what their competitors are doing?	Companies must keep track of competitors' activities to react quickly and make adjustments to their marketing mix.
Evaluate How are external threats different from internal threats? Which do you think are more dangerous to a company's success in the marketplace?	External threats come from other companies; for example, another company may have lower prices. An internal threat comes from within a company, for example, having an inefficient distribution system.

e MARKETING

Social Network Advertising

Social networking started out as a way for people to connect with old friends, make new friends, and stay in touch with other people of similar interests via the Internet. Over time social networking has become an excellent way for businesses to make targeted and immediate contact with the masses.

Social ads in social networking sites are related to users' activities. Imagine this scenario: Rob, a Facebook user, just bought a new Chevrolet® truck. He took a picture of his new truck and posted it on his profile page. His friends receive regular updates on Rob's activities. Embedded in the update shared with his friends, there could be an image of a Chevy truck and a link to the Chevrolet Web site. The ad spreads among members of Rob's social network.

Innovate and Create

Ask students to work in small groups to create a scenario in which friends within a social network might influence the online buying behaviors of others in the group. Have each group present its ideas to the class. Answers will vary. Sample answer: A clothing company has a virtual fitting room on its Web site. This allows consumers to upload their picture and try different clothes on virtually to see how they may look before making a purchase. For users who value the opinion of their friends, the company could benefit from linking its online site to a social networking site where users may even get instant feedback from their friends before making a purchase.

 glencoe.com 

eMarketing Worksheet Activity Send students to the Online Learning Center to download an eMarketing worksheet activity.

DIGITAL NATION

See You on Facebook

Social networking is growing exponentially, with tens of millions of new users every month. One of the most visited sites for connecting with friends is Facebook.com. The site is used not only for personal interaction, but also for marketing. Most major brands have pages on Facebook that allow users to become fans, receive special news and offers, and interact with company staff.

App Magic

Facebook made news by allowing users to write software applications (apps) that people can embed on their personal profiles. Companies create apps that engage users in fun activities, such as games, polls, and quizzes. Users can rate apps, become fans of them, and recommend them to their friends. This spreads the word about the company without the use of paid advertising. Facebook pages and apps are a growing part of many businesses' marketing plans.

Science

Evaluate Imagine you are working in the marketing department of a company that creates science related products. How can you use apps on social networking sites to reach your customers?

glencoe.com

Get a Digital Nation Worksheet Activity.

SOCIO-CULTURAL FACTORS

A socio-cultural analysis is based on customers and potential customers. Changes in their attitudes, lifestyles, and opinions provide a multitude of opportunities and threats. Socio-cultural analysis examines changes in all demographic factors, such as age, income, occupation, education level, and marital status. Here are two examples of such changes:

- **Diversity** The United States is becoming a more ethnically and racially diverse country. Marketing plans need to meet this change.
- **Health** Obesity has become an issue in the United States, as it causes many health problems. Consumer advocates for healthier eating habits criticize fast food.

TECHNOLOGY

Changing technology may be a threat for one industry or company, but an opportunity for others. A perfect example is digital photography. To be competitive, traditional photo companies such as Kodak® are looking for ways to adapt to this new technology. Camera companies are making more digital cameras. Other companies are seizing the opportunity to capitalize on this new technology by developing products to support it. Printer companies like Epson® and Hewlett-Packard® have developed products to make it easy for consumers to print their own digital photographs.

EPSON®
EXCEED YOUR VISION

Companies that keep abreast of the newest technological breakthroughs, such as computer animation and satellite technology, can use that knowledge to be more competitive.

Reading Check

Recall What is a SWOT analysis?

WRITING A MARKETING PLAN

Marketing is a complicated activity that relies on many different tasks. For this reason, marketers create a marketing plan. A **marketing plan** is a formal, written document that directs a company's activities for a specific period of time. It details analysis and research efforts and provides a road map for how a product will enter the market, be advertised, and sold.

A marketing plan also communicates the goals, objectives, and strategies of a company's management team. The specifics let managers know their responsibilities, budget, and timelines for completion. A plan helps a company monitor a company's performance. A small retail business may develop a simple marketing plan for a year, but a large manufacturer would prepare a marketing plan that covers five years.

ELEMENTS OF A MARKETING PLAN

Marketing plans may differ from company to company. However, there are some basic elements that will be found in all marketing plans. Those elements include an executive summary, a situation analysis, marketing goals/objectives, marketing strategies, and implementation, as well as a system for evaluation and control. See **Figure 2.2** on page 38 for a complete outline of a marketing plan.

EXECUTIVE SUMMARY

An **executive summary** is a brief overview of the entire marketing plan. It briefly addresses each topic in the plan and gives an explanation of the costs involved in implementing the plan. The executive summary may also be used to provide information to people outside the organization, such as investors or business consultants.

SITUATION ANALYSIS

Situation analysis is the study of the internal and external factors that affect marketing strategies. The situation analysis takes stock of where the company or product has been, where it is now, and where it is headed. It also considers the external factors and trends that affect a company. The information from a company's SWOT and PEST analyses creates the basis for this portion of the marketing plan. The situation analysis can be done for a whole company, a business unit, a product line, or an individual product.

OBJECTIVES

Objectives let everyone know what the marketing plan will accomplish. They are based around the company's mission statement. To be useful, an objective must be single-minded (meaning it has only one topic for each objective), specific, realistic, measurable, and have a time frame.

- **Single-Minded** For example, you cannot include increasing sales and increasing profits in the same objective. Each topic needs to be a separate objective.
- **Specific** Specific means that the objective provides enough detail that there can be no misunderstanding. You cannot use, "to be better than a competitor" as an objective because what is "better" is vague.
- **Realistic** Realistic means the goal can be achieved by the company. It must take both its strengths and weaknesses into account.
- **Measurable** Measurable means that the objective includes a way to measure or evaluate the results. You cannot simply say you want to increase sales. You need to identify the percentage increase in dollar or unit sales to make that objective measurable. So, you could state, "to increase dollar sales by 15 percent as compared to the same time last year."
- **Time Framed** Finally, you must include a time frame, such as in six months, or as compared to last year's sales. You need a time frame to know if an objective was actually reached.

Marketing Mix Businesses use social networking sites to promote their products and research new ones.

EXPLAIN

DIGITAL NATION

Science Answer Read the Science Activity to students. Imagine you are working in the marketing department of a company that creates science-related products. ***How can you use apps on social networking sites to reach your customers?*** Answers will vary. Sample answer: You could begin by identifying any target markets that use social networking sites. Then you could create apps that feature the products used by this target market. The app could be a game that involves winning virtual prizes that are related to the products this target market purchases.

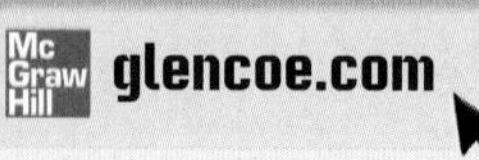

glencoe.com

Worksheet Activity Send students to the Online Learning Center to get a Digital Nation worksheet activity.

SOCIO-CULTURAL FACTORS

Tell students that companies that keep abreast of the newest socio-cultural trends and technological breakthroughs can use that knowledge to be more competitive. Then ask these guiding questions to focus the discussion about socio-cultural and technology factors.

Guiding Questions

List Name four demographic factors that might be examined in a socio-cultural analysis.	Age, income, occupation, education level, marital status are the four factors cited in the text. Explain to students that they will learn more about demographics in Section 2.2 of this chapter.
Identify Cause and Effect Why would it be important for an infant clothing manufacturer to be aware that the age of first-time parents is increasing?	Possible answer: More mature parents are likely to have more discretionary income, and therefore are likely to purchase more expensive clothing than younger parents.

ELABORATE

Mini Project

Differentiated Instruction

Verbal/Linguistic Learners Bring business newspapers or magazines to class and or have students read articles and identify political, economic, socio-cultural, and technological issues that could affect businesses. Assign students to work in small groups to discuss the types of businesses that would be affected, and how the issues might affect the businesses. Issues will vary depending on the articles selected. Sample group answer: We evaluated an article about the new water park that is being built downtown. Developers chose the location due to a large increase in the number of families with children living in the downtown area, which is a socio-cultural issue. The city government voted to give tax breaks to the business to encourage the company to build the park downtown, which is a political issue.

Reading Check Answer

Read the Reading Check question to students: ***What is a SWOT analysis?*** A SWOT analysis is an assessment of a company's strengths and weaknesses, as well as an understanding of the opportunities and threats in the market that may affect the company.

WRITING A MARKETING PLAN

Ask volunteers to read aloud the first two paragraphs under the header Writing a Marketing Plan. Then ask these guiding questions to focus the discussion about writing a marketing plan.

Guiding Questions

Recall What is the advantage of reading a marketing plan's executive summary?	It provides a brief overview of the entire plan without the detailed information contained in the remainder of the plan.
Compare How is a marketing plan similar to a road map?	Both provide a means of reaching a specified goal.

Graphic Organizer

Display this table on the board. Then work with the class to compose a marketing objective that follows the criteria set forth in the text. First write the objective. Then write notes about how the objective meets the criteria. A sample answer is provided.

Objective	To increase sales of bottled water at airport kiosks by 10% by the end of this year.
Single-minded	This objective has only one topic.
Specific	This objective is specific to bottled water sold at airport kiosks.
Realistic	This objective is realistic because the airport has the resources necessary to achieve the goal.
Measurable	This objective identifies the percentage increase required, making it measurable.
Time framed	This objective has a specific end date by which the objective must be achieved.

glencoe.com

Graphic Organizer Send students to the Online Learning Center to print this graphic organizer.

Marketing Mix Encourage students to discuss specific ways they have seen companies promote their products on social networking sites such as Facebook and Twitter.

FIGURE 2.2 **The Marketing Plan**

Elements of a Marketing Plan A marketing plan is an essential planning tool for a company. This outline lists the basic elements found in a marketing plan. ***How can a small company benefit from writing a marketing plan?***

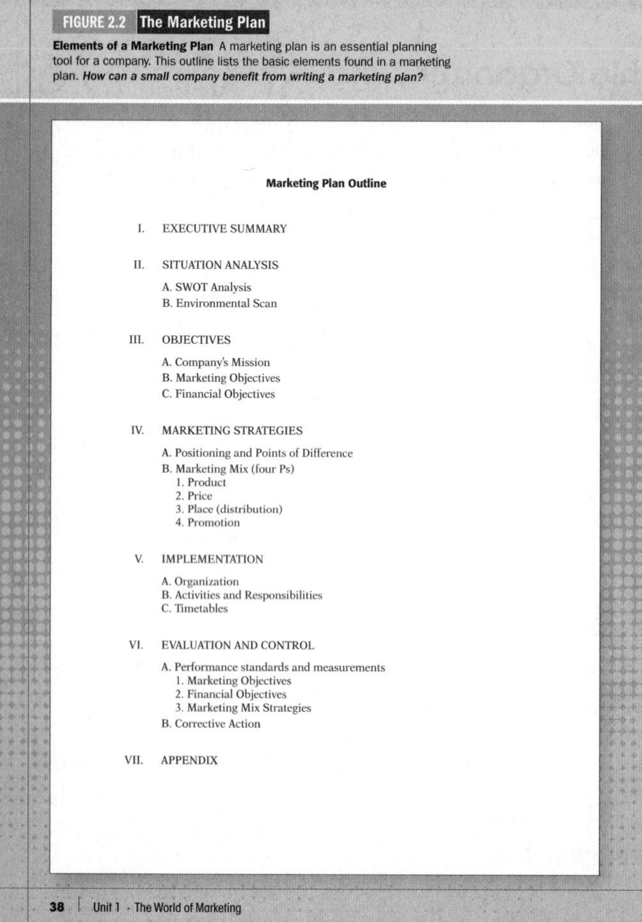

Marketing Plan Outline

I. EXECUTIVE SUMMARY

II. SITUATION ANALYSIS
- A. SWOT Analysis
- B. Environmental Scan

III. OBJECTIVES
- A. Company's Mission
- B. Marketing Objectives
- C. Financial Objectives

IV. MARKETING STRATEGIES
- A. Positioning and Points of Difference
- B. Marketing Mix (four Ps)
  - 1. Product
  - 2. Price
  - 3. Place (distribution)
  - 4. Promotion

V. IMPLEMENTATION
- A. Organization
- B. Activities and Responsibilities
- C. Timetables

VI. EVALUATION AND CONTROL
- A. Performance standards and measurements
  - 1. Marketing Objectives
  - 2. Financial Objectives
  - 3. Marketing Mix Strategies
- B. Corrective Action

VII. APPENDIX

A company's mission statement provides the focus for a firm's goals with its explanation of the company's core competencies, values, expectations, and vision for the future.

Marketing objectives must be in line with the organization's goals and mission. If an organization's goal is to double its business in five years, marketing objectives must coincide with that goal and provide the means to reach it.

When writing objectives, the need for specific and measurable goals is important. For example, if a marketing objective involves increasing a company's market share by a certain percentage, then a corresponding financial objective would provide an increase in sales to achieve that market share. The use of objectives helps a company determine if it has met its goals.

MARKETING STRATEGIES

A **marketing strategy** identifies target markets and sets marketing mix choices that focus on those markets. All strategies need to take the customer's needs and wants into account, as well as the objectives of the marketing plan.

A company's or product's position in the marketplace determines the appropriate marketing strategy. The positioning of the product or service will drive decisions for each of the four Ps.

An effective marketing strategy should be focused on the key points of difference. The key point of difference is the advantage a company, a product, or service has over its competition. The point of difference could be any of the following factors:

- The quality of the product
- A superior distribution system
- A more creative ad campaign
- A more competitive pricing structure

This competitive advantage is what will make the company successful. The marketing mix elements can help create points of difference with respect to competition.

Notice how each of these factors relates to one of the four Ps of the marketing mix. The company assesses whether to adjust each or every element of the marketing mix to emphasize its points of difference.

The results of both the situation analysis and the SWOT analysis should provide enough information to identify the specific target market and to suggest ideas to create the necessary point(s) of difference for the product to be competitive.

WORLD MARKET

SPAIN

Imagination Walks

For more than a decade, the Camper footwear company, based on the Spanish island of Mallorca, has outsold other brands in Spain. Today the company is global with stores in London, Milan, New York, Paris, and Taipei, and sales topping $120 million in one year. The Camper concept that luxury is in simplicity has revolutionized the world of traditional shoemaking.

Camper Culture The Camper story began in 1877 with master shoemaker, Antonio Fluxa. The business passed down to his grandson Lorenzo Fluxa, who created the Camper brand in 1975. With quirky, authentic designs inspired by the farming tradition of Mallorca, "Camper" means "peasant." Fluxa's mission for Camper grew from "the historical and social changes that occurred in Spain during the 70s."

Social Studies

Collaborate Discuss with a partner how manufacturers use human and natural resources to create shoes.

NCSS VII A Production, Distribution, and Consumption Explain how the scarcity of productive resources (human, capital, technological, and natural) requires the development of economic systems to make decisions about how goods and services are to be produced and distributed.

Here are some entry-level phrases that are used in conversations about marketing all over the world.

English	Spanish
Hello	Hola
Goodbye	Adios
How are you?	¿Cómo está usted?
Thank you	Gracias
You're welcome	De nada

EXPLAIN

Visual Literacy

Figure 2.2 Caption Answer Read the figure caption question to students: ***How can a small company benefit from writing a marketing plan?*** A small company can benefit from writing a marketing plan because it would allow it to organize its goals and objectives, as well as its marketing strategies around its customers' needs and wants. As those needs and wants change, a small company could revise its marketing plan accordingly. Having it in writing helps a small company stay focused on its company mission.

Critical Thinking

Ask students: ***Why must marketing objectives align with an organization's mission statement?*** Sample answer: a company's mission statement provides the focus for a firm's goals. If an organization's goal is to double its business in five years, marketing objectives that reflect the core competencies, values, expectations, and vision outlined in the mission statement will provide the focus needed to reach the objectives.

MARKETING STRATEGIES

Explain to students that a marketing strategy identifies target markets and sets marketing mix choices that focus on those markets. Then ask these guiding questions to focus the discussion about Marketing Strategies.

Guiding Questions

Recall What does the term *key point of difference* mean?	The term key point of difference refers to the advantage a company, a product, or a service has over its competition.
Analyze Why do you think that the company's mission is the first component under Objectives?	It is the first element under Objectives because the mission statement states the company's purpose and goals, which must be constantly kept in mind while developing a marketing plan.
Apply What do all marketing strategies need to take into account?	Customer needs and wants and the objectives of the marketing plan must be carefully considered when developing marketing strategies.

ELABORATE

Mini Projects

Differentiated Instruction

Visual/Spatial Learners Have students select a business and create a visual presentation about a marketing plan that includes the four Ps—product, price, place, and promotion. Visual presentations will vary but can be a poster, a collage, a multimedia presentation, or another illustration. Ask students to share their visual presentations with the class. You might post them in the classroom after students have shared them.

Logical Learners As a class, ask students to think of two companies or products that are in direct competition. Try to find companies or products with which all students are familiar. Get a class consensus on which company/product is the most successful. Have students determine what advantage the more successful company/product has over the other company/ product—quality, superior distribution system, more creative ad campaign, more competitive pricing, or some other advantage. Answers will vary depending on the products selected. Sample answer: iTunes is in direct competition with Napster. Both have services that provide music for sale. iTunes is perceived by most people as superior to Napster because it is the market leader, it has multiple distribution channels, it has iconic branding and product design with strong appeal, and it has a positive image as an innovative, responsible, and successful company.

Reinforce Vocabulary

Position—Denotative Meaning Write the term *position* on the board. Then read the second paragraph after the third bullet under the Marketing Strategies header: ***A company's or product's position in the marketplace determines the appropriate marketing strategy.*** Ask students if they know the meaning of the term. If they don't know ask them to guess. Then write this definition on the board: Product positioning is the way consumers, users, buyers, and others perceive competitive brands or types of products. Positioning is a marketing activity. Position is the placement of a product in a desired market. Marketers position products so that they are perceived in a specific way by consumers.

WORLD MARKET
SOCIAL STUDIES

Ask students to discuss with a partner how manufacturers use human and natural resources to create shoes. When students are done with their discussions, create a two-column table on the board. Label one column "Human Resources" and the other "Natural Resources." As each pair shares its lists of resources, place each resource in the appropriate column. Then ask students: What is Camper's key point of difference in the marketplace? It has quirky, authentic designs inspired by the historical farming tradition of the Spanish island of Mallorca.

Graphic Organizer

Display this graphic organizer. Then work with the class to fill in the characteristics of an effective marketing strategy.

An Effective Marketing Strategy

Identifies target markets

Sets marketing mix choices that focus on target markets.

Takes the customer's needs and wants into account

Takes the objectives of the marketing plan into account.

Focuses on the key points of difference: the competitive advantage

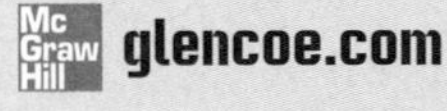

Graphic Organizer Send students to the Online Learning Center to print this graphic organizer.

IMPLEMENTATION

Implementation is putting the marketing plan into action and managing it. This means obtaining the financial resources, management, and staffing necessary to put the plan into action. A timetable shows when each part goes into play.

This part of the marketing plan outlines a schedule of activities, job assignments, **sales forecasts** (the projection of probable, future sales in units or dollars), budgets, details of each activity, and who will be responsible for each activity.

This phase of the plan requires excellent communication among members of the management team so that tasks are completed on a timely basis.

EVALUATION AND CONTROL

In the evaluation section of the marketing plan, measures that will be used to evaluate the plan are discussed. It is important to explain exactly how a specific objective will be measured and who will be responsible for providing that evaluation.

PERFORMANCE STANDARDS AND EVALUATION

A **performance standard** is an expectation for performance that reflects the plan's objectives. Performance standards are the measuring stick. These performance standards can help assess marketing objectives, financial objectives, and marketing mix strategies. As part of the planning process, the control section suggests actions that should be considered if objectives are not met. In the control phase, the company's goal is to reduce the gap between the planned performance standards and the actual performance.

Let's say sales did not reach the sales forecast numbers. One reason could be recent changes in economic conditions. In such a situation, a company may take corrective action and revise its sales forecast to be more realistic.

APPENDIX

The appendix is the section of the marketing plan that includes supplemental materials such as financial statements, sample ads, and other materials that support the plan.

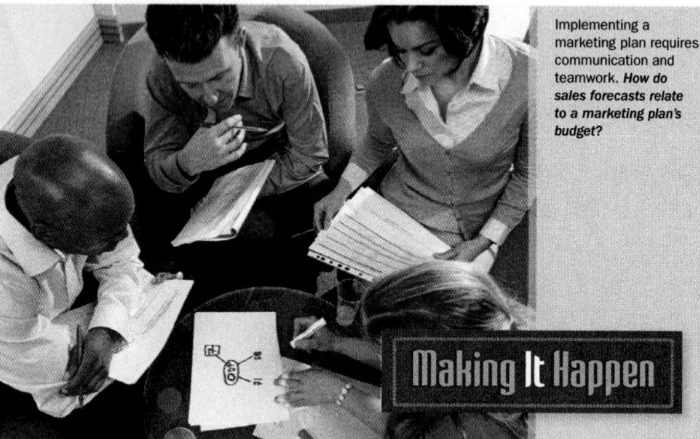

Implementing a marketing plan requires communication and teamwork. ***How do sales forecasts relate to a marketing plan's budget?***

MARKETING AUDIT

The marketing process is ongoing. You can think of it as a circular pattern that continues through the three phases of the marketing process of planning, implementation, and control. The key question at the end of the process is, "Did we accomplish the objectives listed in the marketing plan within the boundaries of the plan?"

If the objectives are met, then the marketing plan can be deemed a success. If the answer to that question is that the objectives were not accomplished, then a company must determine the reasons and make adjustments.

This evaluation at the end of the marketing process is called a marketing audit. A marketing audit evaluates a company's marketing objectives, strategies, budgets, organization, and performance. It identifies problem areas in marketing operations as well as areas that proved to be successful in meeting objectives. Most companies typically conduct a formal marketing audit at least once every year, but informal reviews of the marketing plan happen on a continual basis. Because of the important feedback that a marketing audit provides, a company that regularly conducts marketing audits can be more flexible and responsive than a competitor that reviews its processes only every now and then.

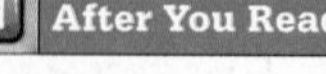

After You Read | **Section 2.1**

Review Key Concepts

1. **Explain** the four aspects of a SWOT analysis and tell how it fits into a marketing plan.
2. **List** the four areas that are investigated in PEST analysis and explain why the knowledge gained can be valuable to a company.
3. **Describe** how the marketing mix relates to the implementation of a marketing plan.

Practice Academics

English Language Arts

4. One of the statements below represents a goal that a company has established. The other represents an objective. Tell which is which and write a sentence or two explaining your choices.
   - To increase by one-third the amount of paper waste each store recycles within eight months.
   - To become a strong advocate for the environmental concerns of our customers and employees.

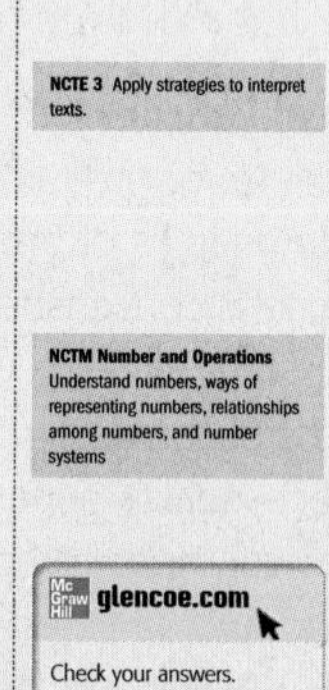

NCTE 3 Apply strategies to interpret texts.

Mathematics

5. A company's sales revenue at year end is $1,386,000. If the company's objective is to increase sales by 10 percent in the next year, what is its new sales goal in dollars?

Math Concept **Ways of Representing Numbers** An increase in a number can be represented by a percent greater than 100.

Starting Hints Think of next year's sales goal as 110 percent of this year's sales. Convert 110 percent to a decimal by moving the decimal point two places to the left. Multiply that decimal number by this year's sales revenue to find next year's sales goal in dollars.

NCTM Number and Operations Understand numbers, ways of representing numbers, relationships among numbers, and number systems.

For help, go to the **Math Skills Handbook** located at the back of this book.

glencoe.com

Check your answers.

ELABORATE

IMPLEMENTATION

Ask students to turn back to Figure 2.2 (page 38) and briefly review the information under the implementation sections of the outline. Then ask these questions to guide the discussion about implementation.

Guiding Questions

Explain What is the meaning of implementation in the context of a marketing plan?	Implementation means obtaining the financial resources, management, and staffing necessary to put the marketing plan into action.
Analyze Refer to Figure 2.2. How are items B and C under Implementation related to one another?	The activities and responsibilities in part B must be completed according to the timetables in part C.

Reinforce Vocabulary

Implementation—Word Origin Tell students that the root of the word *implementation* is *implement.* The word *implement* comes from the Latin word *implementum,* meaning "the action of filling up." Discuss how this Latin meaning could result in today's definition of *implement:* "to carry out." The expression "to fill up" can, in a general sense, mean "to fulfill" or "to complete" which by extension can mean "to carry out."

Visual Literacy

Making It Happen Caption Answer Read the photo caption question to students. ***How do sales forecasts relate to a marketing plan's budget?*** Sales forecasts are part of the marketing plan, along with a schedule of activities, job assignments, budgets, details of each activity and who will be responsible for each activity. Sales forecasts are important because they keep everyone focused on what needs to be done to reach those projected sales.

EVALUATE

MARKETING AUDIT

Tell students that the marketing audit is an ongoing process designed to determine if the business achieved the objectives listed in the marketing plan. Then ask these questions to guide the discussion about the marketing audit.

Guiding Questions

Recall When does a marketing audit take place?	Once a year on a formal basis; continuously on an informal basis.
Analyze Why is it important for the audit to cover both areas that seem to be functioning well in addition to those that are not?	Possible answer: Sometimes those areas that appear to be working well are actually having problems when more closely examined.
Synthesize How might a marketing plan go outside its boundaries?	Possible answers: It might try to achieve goals that are not stated in the objectives, spend more than was budgeted, or use strategies that were not agreed upon.

PROFESSIONAL DEVELOPMENT

MINI CLIP

Math: Solving Equations
Go to the Online Learning Center to view a video clip in which students use manipulatives and symbols to solve simple equations.

After You Read Section 2.1

Review Key Concepts

1. Four aspects of a SWOT analysis are internal strengths and weaknesses, and external opportunities and threats. The results of a SWOT analysis are reported in the situational analysis of a marketing plan.
2. External threats and opportunities include competition and an environmental scan of political issues, economic factors, socio-cultural factors, and technological changes. An accurate analysis of those factors helps a company prepare for threats such as competition or a changing marketplace.
3. The elements of the marketing mix (product, price, place, promotion) should be determined before the marketing plan can be implemented.

Practice Academics

English Language Arts

4. The goal is "To become a strong advocate for the environmental concerns of our customers and employees." This statement is broadly stated, making it a goal. "To increase by one-third the amount of paper waste each store recycles within eight months" is an objective because it meets the criteria for an objective, that being single-minded, specific, measurable, and time-framed.

Mathematics

5. $1,524,600 ($1,386,000 × 1.10)

glencoe.com

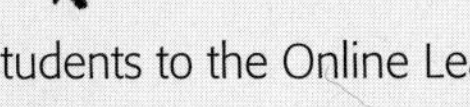

Answer Key Send students to the Online Learning Center to check their answers.

READING GUIDE

Before You Read

Connect Think of all the ways a marketer might describe you as a consumer. Begin with your age and gender, then get more specific about your shopping requirements.

Objectives

- **Explain** the concept of market segmentation.
- **Analyze** a target market.
- **Differentiate** between mass marketing and market segmentation.

The Main Idea

The key to marketing is to know your customer or target market. Market segmentation helps identify the target market.

Vocabulary

Content Vocabulary
- market segmentation
- demographics
- disposable income
- discretionary income
- geographics
- psychographics
- mass marketing

Academic Vocabulary

You will find these words in your reading and on your tests. Make sure you know their meanings.
- ranges
- attitudes

Graphic Organizer

Draw or print this chart to list different ways to segment markets and the reason each is used.

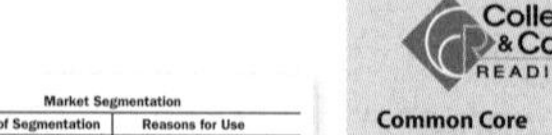

Market Segmentation	
Methods of Segmentation	Reasons for Use

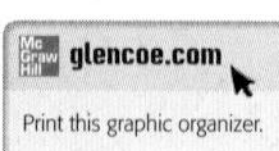

glencoe.com

Print this graphic organizer.

STANDARDS

ACADEMIC

English Language Arts

NCTE 1 Read texts to acquire new information.

Social Studies

NCSS VII B Production, Distribution, and Consumption Analyze the role that supply and demand, prices, incentives, and profits play in determining what is produced in a competitive market system.

NCSS *National Council for the Social Studies*
NCTE *National Council of Teachers of English*
NCTM *National Council of Mathematics*
NSES *National Science Education Standards*

College & Career READINESS

Common Core
Reading Interpret words and phrases as they are used in a text, including determining technical, connotative, and figurative meanings, and analyze how specific word choices shape meaning or tone.

MARKETING CORE FUNCTION

Market Planning

m.e. Section 2.2

Market Segmentation

IDENTIFYING AND ANALYZING MARKETS

The surest way for businesses to make a connection with customers is to know these people well. This means knowing where they live, their income level, age, ethnic background, activities, values, and interests. Such information can help identify groups of people who have many things in common.

As You Read

Predict How do you think marketers identify their customers?

MARKET SEGMENTATION

Marketers analyze groups of customers to see if any of them can be further broken down into smaller, more precise clusters. The process of classifying people who form a given market into even smaller groups is called **market segmentation**.

Let's look at the market for jeans. A marketer might ask, "Who buys jeans? At what price? What special features do they want?" Depending on the answers to these questions, the market for jeans could be segmented by these characteristics:

- **Age:** jeans for kids, teens, and adults.
- **Price:** reach different income levels (socio-economic groups).
- **Desired features:** tight fit, comfortable fit, newest fashion, or a unique design.

To meet the needs of the different market segments, jeans manufacturers develop a unique marketing mix, including different products, promotions, stores for distribution, and price points. For example, Levi's® jeans are available in relaxed fit, regular fit, 501 original, loose straight, loose boot cut, low-rise straight, and low-rise boot cut.

The next question marketers ask is: "Which of these segments should we target?" It is usually too costly to target all the potential target markets. So, it is very important to identify those markets in which the company has an advantage that enables it to survive against its competition over a long period of time. Marketers call this situation a sustainable competitive advantage.

GATHERING DATA

Companies study data generated by governments, private research firms, trade associations, and their own research to determine if a given target market is large enough to justify the expense.

> "Businesses look for ways to connect with current and potential customers. The surest way to make that connection is to know these people well."

For example, U.S. census data might reveal that there are enough teenagers to justify making jeans for that segment of the market. Additional research into teenagers would reveal more about this market segment. Their buying behavior, interests, activities, opinions about fashion, values, status, household income levels, ethnic background, and any other factor might help marketers create a customer profile. These factors help marketers gather demographic, geographic, psychographic, and behavioral information about each market segment.

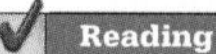

Reading Check

Recall What sources do marketers use to find data for their research?

ENGAGE

Anticipation Activity

Improving Student Achievement Ask students to brainstorm a list of different groups of people such as children, teens, athletes, and so on. Groups should not be based solely on age. Ask students: ***Would they market shoes in the same way to each group?*** Businesses would tailor the marketing message to the specific audience they want to reach. Tell students how businesses make decisions about how to market products to different groups of customers is part of marketing segmentation, which they will learn about in this section.

Objectives

- **Explain** the concept of market segmentation. Market segmentation is the process of classifying people who form a given market into even smaller groups.
- **Analyze** a target market. Students should use demographics, geographics, psychographics and product-related behavior.
- **Differentiate** between mass marketing and market segmentation. Mass marketing involves using a single marketing strategy to reach all customers; market segmentation involves marketing to smaller, more defined groups.

Graphic Organizer

Market Segmentation

Methods of Segmentation	Reasons for Use
Demographics	People with different personal characteristics have different needs and interests.
Geographics	People's needs vary depending on where they live.
Psychographics	Lifestyle has an impact on how money is spent.
Behavioral Characteristics	Behavioral characteristics influence shopping patterns.

 glencoe.com  

Graphic Organizer Send students to the Online Learning Center to print this graphic organizer.

EXPLORE

Before You Read

Read the Before You Read question aloud: ***Think of all the ways a marketer might describe you as a consumer. Begin with your age and gender, then get more specific about your shopping requirements.*** Answers will vary. Sample answer: I am an African-American male teenager who attends high school. I live in the West. I consider education and physical fitness to be very important and I plan to devote my career to environmental causes. I want to make the most of my money, so I always conduct research before making buying decisions.

Preteaching Vocabulary

Have students go to the Online Learning Center at glencoe.com for the Chapter 2 Preteaching Vocabulary games.

Content Vocabulary

Have students name those content vocabulary terms that identify ways in which a market can be segmented. demographics, geographics, psychographics

Academic Vocabulary

Range—Alternate Meanings Explain to students that the academic vocabulary term *range* means "a category defined by an upper and a lower limit." Ask students whether they know the definition of *range* in a musical context or a geographical context. Musical: the notes, from highest to lowest, that somebody's voice or a musical instrument can produce. Geographical: a number of mountains or hills forming a connected row or group.

Attitude—Denotative Meaning Tell students that consumers attitudes often change as they grow older and experience life. Ask students to look up the definition of *attitude* in the glossary. Attitude is a mental state involving beliefs, feelings, and values that determines your disposition to think and act in certain ways. Remind students that having a positive attitude can help them to achieve happiness and success at home, at work, at school, and in the community.

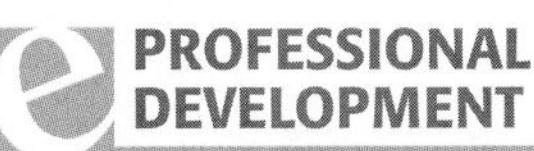

MINI CLIP

Reading: Strategic Readers
Go to the Online Learning Center to view a video clip in which a teacher discusses the characteristics of strategic readers.

Section 2.2

Marketing Segmentation

Expert Advice

Read the quote to students:

> **"Businesses need to connect with current and potential customers."**

Ask students: ***What does this quote have to do with market segmentation?*** In order for a company to survive and thrive, it must continue to use market segmentation-based research to identify markets to which it can sell its goods and services.

IDENTIFYING AND ANALYZING MARKETS

Remind students that virtually any group of people can be segmented in a variety of ways. Then use these guiding questions to focus the discussion about market segmentation.

Guiding Questions

Recall What are three ways you might segment the market for athletic shoes?	Sample answers: age, gender, purpose, price, desired features
Contrast What is the difference between the terms *target market* and *market segmentation?*	A target market is the group that is identified for a specific marketing program; market segmentation involves classifying people in a given market into even smaller groups.

As You Read

Read students the As You Read question: ***How do you think marketers identify their customers?*** Answers will vary. Sample answer: Marketers use market segmentation-based research to determine how to classify customers.

Reading Check Answer

Read the Reading Check question to students: ***What sources do marketers use to find data for their research?*** In addition to their own research, marketers use data generated by the government, private research firms, and trade associations.

Teens buy jeans, but so do many other people. ***How might a jeans ad for a teenager differ from a jeans ad for an adult?***

TYPES OF SEGMENTATION

The data marketers gather can be used to segment the market in various ways. There are four ways to segment the market. Customers can be segmented into groups based on demographics, geographics, psychographics, and behavioral characteristics.

DEMOGRAPHICS

Demographic factors help define a target market for a company wanting to sell its products. **Demographics** refer to statistics that describe a population in terms of personal characteristics such as age, gender, income, marital status, ethnic background, education, and occupation. See **Figure 2.3**.

AGE

Marketers can easily use age to segment the market by creating age **ranges**. The United States census provides information that might help in deciding on the age categories. Here are common labels used to segment the population by generation:

- **Baby Boom Generation** The 76 million babies born in the United States between 1946 and 1964 are known as the baby boomers. As baby boomers get older, their income and spending power increase. So, they are targets for all types of products, such as technological gadgets, cosmetics, and products to enhance lifestyle.
- **Generation X** (or the Baby Bust Generation) They followed the Baby Boom Generation. Most members of Generation X are children of dual-career households or divorced parents. They have been bombarded with media from an early age. They are savvy purchasers and skeptical consumers. To reach this group, marketers must use interesting images, hip music, and a sense of humor.
- **Generation Y** They are the sons and daughters of the later baby boomers. Generation Y is also known as the Echo Boomers or Millennium Generation. According to the U.S. Census, this group is more racially and ethnically diverse with spending power. Fashions and information get passed along via the Internet.

GENDER

Gender helps to create market segments as well. Jockey, at one time a men's underwear company, doubled its sales when it entered the women's market with Jockey® underwear for women. Products such as safety razors are also segmented by gender. The razors women use often have longer handles than those used by men. Electric razors are different for each gender as well. These differences are due to the different uses of razors by each gender, which means marketers need to have a different approach for men and women.

INCOME

Marketers want to know how much money people have to spend on different products. For this reason, they look at two types of income measurement: disposable income and discretionary income. **Disposable income** is the money left after taking out taxes. Marketers who produce and distribute products that are necessities are interested in changes in consumers' disposable income. **Discretionary income** is the money left after paying for basic living necessities such as food, shelter, and clothing. Marketers who sell luxury and premium products are interested in changes in consumers' discretionary income. During tough economic times, people have less discretionary income, so it is harder to market luxury items.

MARITAL STATUS

The U.S. Census indicates that there is currently a lower percentage of married couples in the United States compared to the percentage in the 1950s. Reasons for this reduction in married couples can be attributed to several factors. People are older when they get married for the first time. They are also living longer, divorcing more, and remarrying less. All of this information is useful to marketers. They can decide whether to market their products to married couples with children, single adults living together, or adults who live alone. You may have seen family-sized or individual-sized boxes of food at the grocery store. This product packaging is a result of demographic segmentation. Since parents need to provide food for their children, marketers created boxes that have more servings of food. Adults who live alone must buy smaller portions of perishable foods. They will not be able to eat all of their food before it spoils, so their buying patterns are different from families with children.

ETHNIC BACKGROUND

The U.S. population is becoming more multicultural and ethnically diverse, mainly due to increased immigration. The Caucasian population is declining relative to African-American, Hispanic, and Asian-American populations. It is essential for marketers to be aware of the multicultural nature of the modern United States.

FIGURE 2.3 Demographic Characteristics

Targeting a Market Demographic information relates to personal characteristics, such as age, gender, income, marital status, ethnic background, education, and occupation. Marketing plans are customized for the target market. ***Think of your demographic profile. What products would a marketer try to sell to you?***

By Age Marketers use age to segment and define the target market. They use age ranges, such as ages 15 to 18. Certain products are designed and marketed specifically to children, teens, or adults.

By Gender Many products are made for both men and women. However, products such as clothing and shoes are designed specifically by gender.

By Ethnicity With a diverse and multicultural population, the United States has many different ethnic market segments.

EXPLORE

Visual Literacy

Just for You Caption Answer Read the photo caption question to students: ***How might a jeans ad for a teenager differ from a jeans ad for an adult?*** An ad photo for a teenager would depict teens wearing jeans designed for teens in a setting typical to teens. An ad for jeans for adults would depict a different style of jeans modeled by an adult in an adult setting. Then use these questions to focus the discussion about how marketers segment markets for jeans.

Guiding Questions

List What demographic factors do companies take into account when marketing products such as jeans?	Age, gender, income, marital status, ethnic background.
Elaborate What do you think is going through this teen's mind while looking at the stacks of jeans?	Answers will vary. Possible answers: There are a lot of choices. I hope I can find the type I want in my size.

TYPES OF SEGMENTATION

After students read about the demographic factors of age and gender, ask them the guiding questions below. Then use these guiding questions to focus the discussion about the various types of segmentation.

Guiding Questions

Recall Who is included in the baby boom generation?	people born between 1946 and 1964
Analyze Why do you think humor is successful when marketing to Generation X?	Sample answer: Because these consumers are media savvy and skeptical; however humor can attract attention in ways that straightforward advertising cannot.
Elaborate What are some products that are segmented by gender? Why do you think market segmentation by gender occurs?	Sample answer: Some products are segmented because of preferences, like clothing fit, style, or scent.

EXPLAIN

DEMOGRAPHICS

Tell students that demographics refers to statistics that describe a population. Then use these guiding questions to focus the discussion about age, income, and marital status.

Guiding Questions

Explain Marketers of what types of products are most likely to see drops in their sales during tough economic times?	Marketers of luxury and premium products are most likely to see drops in their sales.
Analyze How do you think the fact that people are marrying at a later age might affect their purchases?	Possible answer: People who are single and have no children tend to have more discretionary income than married people who are likely to have children.
Synthesize What products and services might be different for people of different ethnic backgrounds?	Students will likely think of foods, but encourage them to think of other things like media offerings and home furnishings.

Reinforce Vocabulary

Demographics—Word Origin Tell students that *demos* is the Greek word for people and the suffix *graphy* can refer to writing about a specific subject. Based on this information, ask for a volunteer to provide a definition of *demographics.* Sample answer: writing about people. Compare student definitions to the textbook definition "statistics that describe a population."

Visual Literacy

Figure 2.3 Caption Answer Read the figure caption question to students: ***Think of your demographic profile. What products would a marketer try to sell to you?*** Answers will vary. Marketers might try to sell students products geared toward teens, such as music that appeals to this age group. Students also might state that marketers might target them for equipment and clothing for sports in which they are interested, electronic equipment such as games and cell phones.

Mini Projects

Extension

Marketing by Demographics Have students work individually to look through magazines and find and cut out three advertisements featuring different types of clothes marketed to three different target markets. Have students tape the pictures to a piece of paper, and under each picture, students should list the demographics of the targeted consumer. Display the pictures where the entire class can view them. Ads will vary but should target different markets. Encourage students to consider all of the demographic factors at play in the ads rather than focusing only on age and gender.

Research Generations Divide the class into three groups. Assign each group one of the following: Baby Boom Generation, Generation X, and Generation Y. Have students research the groups to find out the age ranges and how companies market their products or services to that group. Groups should prepare a presentation in which they share their findings with the rest of the class. Presentations will vary. Sample answers include: Products marketed to Baby Boomers would appeal to that generation's retirement lifestyle expectations. Products marketed to members of Generation X would appeal to that generation's media savvy nature. The oldest members of Generation X were born in 1965, so all members of that generation experienced the transition from an analog to a digital world. Products marketed to Generation Y often feature more diverse people and situations. Members of Generation Y are digital natives and they are more likely to take advantage of the power of technology in every aspect of their lives.

ELL: Using Realia
Go to the Online Learning Center to view a video clip in which a teacher uses realia to make lesson concepts more real to students.

GEOGRAPHICS

The term **geographics** refers to segmentation of the market based on where people live. To segment a market geographically, you can refer to local, state, regional, national, or even global markets. Geographic segmentation can also include population density (urban vs. suburban areas) and climate (warm vs. cold). It is well known that people who reside in a certain area generally share similar demographic characteristics, such as income, ethnic background, and education. Thus, geographic segmentation is often combined with demographic data to provide marketers with the information they need to make marketing decisions.

LOCAL, STATE, AND REGIONAL GEOGRAPHICS

A small independent restaurant segments its market on a local basis. It knows the geographic area from which it attracts most of its customers. The restaurant may very well have customers who dine there so frequently that they become known as regulars. Such a level of familiarity with customers allows the business owner to gain a detailed view of the restaurant's primary demographic. The restaurant can create menu offerings and set prices based on the known preferences of people who live nearby. This information can help the business provide the greatest appeal to its most likely customers.

Local and state geographics also play a very significant role in political campaigns. Politicians who want to reach their constituents know exactly where their voters live and what those voters' communities are like. Their campaigns compile data on the demographics of particular areas in order to learn the issues that matter most to the voters who live there. Political consultants conduct research to learn the income and education levels of their constituents, their ethnic and religious backgrounds, their average age, and how various segments of the population tended to vote in previous elections. Politicians can use this data to target the specific needs and interests of residents of the geographic areas they hope to represent.

Regional geographics can influence the way regional banks do business. Banks may study the geographical area to identify possible new branch sites. Demographic information, such as income levels in an area, helps in that decision-making process. Also, knowing the population of a certain geographic area helps banks develop correct marketing messages and staffing levels.

Food manufacturers and retailers have learned that people in certain geographic areas share similar tastes and may even use different terms to describe the same product. A sausage company had to change its ingredients to cater to both northeastern tastes and southeastern tastes. A slight change in its spices did the trick. Carbonated drinks may be referred to as either "pop" or "soda." Certain regions of a country may have different climates. A snowblower manufacturer would segment the market geographically to the northern region of the United States. Manufacturers and retailers of surfboards would segment their markets geographically around the nation's coasts. Another example involves cultural and language differences that require employees and advertisements to be bilingual.

NATIONAL AND GLOBAL GEOGRAPHICS

Large national and global companies create divisions within their organization in order to segment their markets geographically. If you visit a global company's Web site, like Unilever® or Pepsico®, you will be able to see the corporate subdivisions of the global company. For example Unilever's Web site has five regional divisions: Africa, Americas, Asia Pacific, Europe, and Middle East. Within those divisions, you can select specific countries. The language for each country is provided on its Web site, making it easy for its customers to research its products and services. It is interesting to note that products are developed for specific geographic areas. For example, Pepsico has several brands of potato chips to cater to specific geographic regions. You will find Lay's® brand potato chips in North America. In its international market you will find Walkers® Potato Crisps brand and Sabritas® brand of potato chips.

PSYCHOGRAPHICS

Psychographics involves grouping people with similar attitudes, interests, and opinions, as well as lifestyles and shared values. Consumer lifestyles include how people spend their time and money. Attitudes, values, and opinions require research to learn more about a group's personality traits and motivation. When psychographics is coupled with demographics, marketers can create a comprehensive customer profile. Its marketing programs can be tailored to reach the inner-most consumer motivations that influence purchases.

These characteristics require marketers to use special research techniques. They need to learn more about each group's personality traits and motivation. One special method involves hiring a marketing research firm to conduct research in small groups called focus groups. Sessions with these groups are recorded. This process allows researchers to study responses to questions and the interaction among participants. This method lends itself to in-depth analysis.

ATTITUDES AND OPINIONS

Consumers' **attitudes** and opinions are often created by changing times and personal experiences. Marketers study trends that evolve from these shared attitudes. Clothing manufacturers capitalize on fashion trends. Going "green" to save the environment is a trend that businesses have utilized to create new products and packaging.

Taking responsibility for one's health, eating healthier, and becoming physically fit are trend-setting issues for businesses. Food marketers are increasingly revamping their offerings to include more reduced-fat selections. Food manufacturers are also displaying lower calorie counts on their packaging. Small 100-calorie count packages of cookies and other treats help consumers control their calorie intake. Fast-food chains have created healthier menu options. The dairy industry capitalized on this trend by promoting skim milk and water instead of soda and other drinks high in sugar content in an ad campaign to help combat childhood obesity.

Marketers must also exercise caution when segmenting by psychographics. It is often difficult to predict whether new opinions, interests, and attitudes in the marketplace will result in short-lived fads or long-lasting trends. Due to the possibility of quickly changing consumer values and lifestyles, it is especially important for marketers to be sure of their market before they respond to every new shift in their customers' attitudes or opinions.

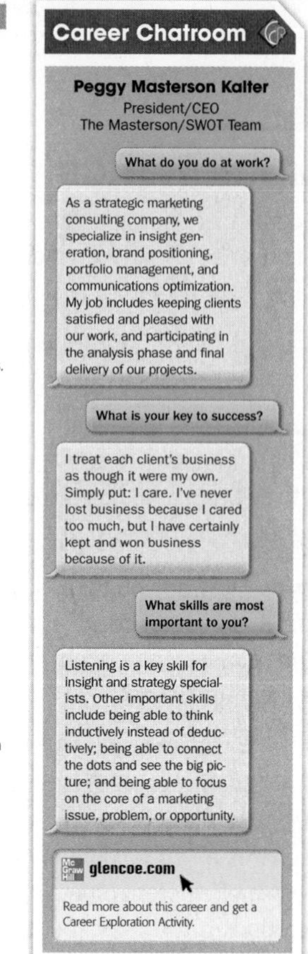

Career Chatroom
Peggy Masterson Kalter
President/CEO
The Masterson/SWOT Team
What do you do at work?
As a strategic marketing consulting company, we specialize in insight generation, brand positioning, portfolio management, and communications optimization. My job includes keeping clients satisfied and pleased with our work, and participating in the analysis phase and final delivery of our projects.
What is your key to success?
I treat each client's business as though it were my own. Simply put: I care. I've never lost business because I cared too much, but I have certainly kept and won business because of it.
What skills are most important to you?
Listening is a key skill for insight and strategy specialists. Other important skills include being able to think inductively instead of deductively; being able to connect the dots and see the big picture; and being able to focus on the core of a marketing issue, problem, or opportunity.
glencoe.com
Read more about this career and get a Career Exploration Activity.

EXPLAIN

GEOGRAPHICS

Ask students how they would classify themselves in terms of where they live. Write their responses on the board. Then use these guiding questions to focus the discussion about geographics.

Guiding Questions

Recall List five ways that markets can be segmented geographically.	Ways include locally, by state, by region, nationally, globally, by population density, by climate, etc.
Infer A company sells goose down ski jackets. How might geographic segmentation help marketers best reach potential customers?	Marketers would probably target colder regions and areas where skiing is popular, such as mountainous regions. They also might target geographic areas where consumers are more affluent as skiing tends to be an expensive pastime.

Build Global Perspective

Explain to students that geographic segmentation is an important consideration, particularly for multi-national and global businesses and brands. Many companies have regional and national marketing programs that alter their products, advertising, and promotion to meet the individual needs of geographic segments. Form students into small groups. Have each group choose a type of global business. Ask groups: Imagine that you are the marketing department of a company that does business on a global scale. How might you alter your products and services to appeal to different geographic segments? Have groups report their findings to the class. Answers will vary depending on the types of businesses students choose. Sample answer: We are the marketing department of a global restaurant chain. In India, we sell burgers made of lamb rather than beef because of the religious beliefs of the people from that geographic area. In Mexico, we offer chili sauce as a condiment to appeal to the population's appeal for the traditional tastes of Mexican cuisine. Throughout the West Coast, we offer low-fat versions of our meals to appeal to a large population of people from that area who tend to be health-conscious.

ELABORATE

Graphic Organizer

Display this table. Then ask students to provide examples of how they have seen local, regional, state, national, and global geographics come into play in different marketing campaigns. Answers will vary. Sample answers are provided.

GEOGRAPHIC SEGMENTATION	
Local	The family-owned pizza restaurant in town advertises discounts for local high school students.
Regional	A chain of three carpet stores in the metropolitan area offers free delivery to anyone living within 50 miles of the business.
State	A surfboard company concentrates its marketing in the state of California because that is where Americans enjoy surfing most.
National	A wireless communications company that offers services nationwide uses a national campaign to advertise in every state.
Global	The company selling the most popular smart phone uses the same ads around the world.

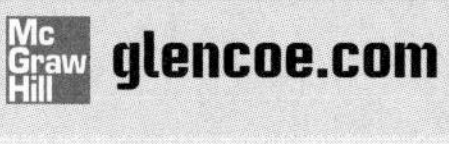

glencoe.com iWB

Graphic Organizer Send students to the Online Learning Center to print this graphic organizer.

PSYCHOGRAPHICS

Introduce the concept of psychographics by encouraging students to discuss their individual attitudes, interests, opinions, lifestyles, and values. Then use these guiding questions to focus the discussion about how marketers use psychographics to target markets.

Guiding Questions

Recall Why do marketers want to couple psychographics with demographics?	Coupling psychographics with demographics allows marketers to create a comprehensive customer profile that tries to reach the inner-most consumer motivations that influence purchases.
Analyze Do you think it is easier for a marketer to determine consumers' geographics or their psychographics? Why?	Geographics, because they are based on facts, whereas psychographics are based on attitudes, interests, and opinions, which are more subjective.

Graphic Organizer

Display this Venn diagram. Ask students to define and name characteristics of geographics and psychographics. Write their definitions in the appropriate circle, then ask them to name ways in which geographics and psychographics are similar. Write their ideas in the area where the circles overlap.

PSYCHOGRAPHICS	BOTH	GEOGRAPHICS
Based on people's attitudes, interests, opinions, lifestyles, and values	Grouping people by criteria Provides useful information	Based on where people live

glencoe.com iWB

Graphic Organizer Send students to the Online Learning Center to print this graphic organizer.

Career Chatroom

Use these questions to focus the discussion about the Career Chatroom feature.

Guiding Questions

Analyze Why do you think that Peggy Masterson Kalter says that she treats every client's business as though it were her own?	This approach would put the client at ease, knowing that she cares as much as the client does.
Predict If you wanted to become a member of the Masterson/SWOT Team, what kinds of skills would you work to develop?	adaptability, flexibility, and analytical skills; the ability to quickly grasp specific situations and understand how they might occur

glencoe.com

Career Exploration Send students to the Online Learning Center to read more about this career and to get a Career Exploration Activity.

INTERESTS AND ACTIVITIES

If you made a list of all your present activities and interests, you would come to realize just how many market segments can be identified by psychographics. Visit the magazine section of a bookstore. For each interest group and activity, you will find at least one magazine that represents a market segment. People who share common interests and activities often purchase similar products and services. In a fashion magazine, you will find advertisements for clothing, cosmetics, and accessories. Similarly, in a music magazine, you will find advertisements for albums, music players, and concerts or festivals. Use an Internet search engine to see consumer, trade, industry, and professional magazines to grasp the extent of interest groups available for market segmentation.

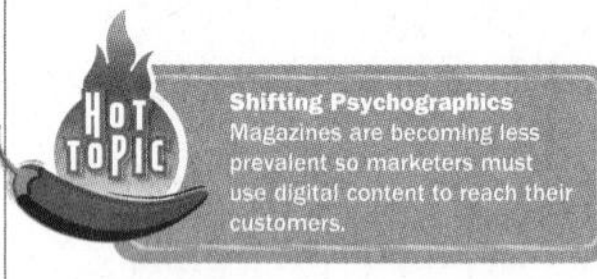

Shifting Psychographics Magazines are becoming less prevalent so marketers must use digital content to reach their customers.

PERSONALITIES AND VALUES

More advanced study of psychographics includes the study of personality characteristics and values. Abraham Maslow created a hierarchy of needs that helps define the personality and values of individuals at each stage of development. The five stages of needs are the following: survival, safety, love and belonging, esteem, and self-actualization. Marketers use those innermost desires in the hierarchy to sell their products. Ads for financial institutions offer individuals the means to retire and have enough money to realize their life's dreams (self-actualization). Certain clothing brands promote the need for belonging or self esteem. Greeting cards address the need for love and caring. Tires promise safety.

An offshoot of Maslow's hierarchy of needs is a research tool called VALS™. VALS identifies types of consumers based on their motivations (thinkers, achievers, experiencers, believers, strivers, and makers) and resources (innovators vs. survivors). This research helps businesses create consumer profiles.

BEHAVIORAL CHARACTERISTICS

Segmenting the market based on purchasing-related behavior involves analyzing your customers with regard to sales generated, shopping patterns, and purchase decision-making processes. Companies classify their customers according to the percentage of sales each group generates. Many businesses find that the 80/20 rule applies. The 80/20 rule means that 80 percent of a company's sales are generated by 20 percent of its loyal customers. This information helps businesses decide how to allocate their resources to each market segment. Some companies use loyalty programs to ensure that their customers keep buying the company's products. This method helps companies retain the customers that generate the most sales.

Astute marketers study consumer shopping patterns to determine usage rates. For example, Jupiter Research, a market research company, has determined that most teenagers spend about $50 a month on entertainment and that teenage girls spend 15 percent more on music than teenage boys spend. A company that markets products to teenagers might use this research to target more of their advertising toward teenage girls.

Companies have found that many consumers research products on the Internet before making a final purchase. As more and more consumers connect with others via social media and the Internet, marketers follow suit by utilizing that media to stay close to their customers. They recognize the need to create a presence in places where consumers look for product information. Also, this shift in decision-making means that companies need to make sure they offer helpful information about their products on the Internet. Often this can take the form of product reviews by customers themselves. Companies that have easy-to-use Web sites or interesting online promotions will be more likely to stay close to their customers.

Reading Check

Recall What are four types of market segmentation?

MASS MARKETING VS. SEGMENTATION

When products have universal appeal and few features to differentiate them from competitors, mass marketing is used. **Mass marketing** involves using a single marketing strategy to reach all customers.

An advantage of mass marketing is economies of scale. Companies can produce more products at lower costs because their product, promotion, pricing, or distribution does not change. The marketing plan is simplified. A disadvantage is competitors can identify specific unmet needs and wants of customers, and then steal those customers. Some marketers think mass marketing does not even exist any longer. They say it is more important to focus on various market segments. This type of broad approach ensures that a company can reach as many customers as effectively as possible. A mass marketing approach may reach all customers in a market, but it may not be as effective as segmented marketing.

NICHE MARKETING

Since most products can be segmented by demographics, psychographics, geographics, and behavioral characteristics, mass marketing is not as popular as it once was. One advantage of market segmentation is the ability to identify and target a very specific audience. Niche marketing narrows and defines a market with extreme precision, which increases the chances of a product's success. A disadvantage of niche marketing is the cost involved. Research is needed to identify target markets and develop different marketing strategies. For example, milk can have a number of target markets. The "Got Milk" campaign targets different segments with different themes through various media, including print ads, television spots, and Internet banners. If a particular product has multiple varieties and many target markets, then the production, packaging, and advertising of that product becomes more expensive.

After You Read | **Section 2.2**

Review Key Concepts

1. **Explain** how market segmentation can help a company increase its market share.
2. **Define** the four factors that are used to describe a target market.
3. **List** the advantages and disadvantages of niche marketing.

Practice Academics

English Language Arts

4. Identify the prefixes in demographics, geographics, and psychographics. Define each prefix in a sentence, and list two other words that use them.

Social Studies

5. How do marketers use the group and cultural influences of a market to sell their products?

NCTE 3 Apply strategies to interpret texts.

NCSS IV C Individual Development & Identity Describe the ways group and cultural influences contribute to the development of a sense of self

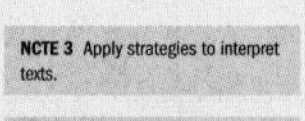

Check your answers.

For help, go to the **Math Skills Handbook** located at the back of this book.

ELABORATE

PERSONALITIES AND VALUES

Explain to students that understanding psychographics factors such as personalities and values is vital to effective marketing. Then use these guiding questions to focus the discussion about these psychographic factors.

Guiding Questions

Recall According to Maslow, what are the five stages of needs?	physiological, safety, love and belonging, esteem, and self-actualization
Contrast How are ads aimed at individuals' physiological needs different from those aimed at individuals' needs for love and belonging?	Answers will vary. Possible answer: Ads aimed at physiological needs might include basic clothing whereas those aimed at a person's need for love and belonging might promote items that help people feel they are part of a group, such as a shirt with the logo of a professional sports team.

BEHAVIORAL CHARACTERISTICS

Ask students to compare the behavioral characteristics with other characteristics they have learned about. Then use these guiding questions to focus the discussion about behavioral characteristics.

Guiding Questions

Explain What does the 80/20 rule state?	It states that 80 percent of a company's sales are generated by 20 percent of its customers.
Analyze A local restaurant has a program in which a customer receives a free dessert for every fourth dinner purchased. What type of program is this? What is its purpose?	It is a loyalty program. It is designed to retain those customers who are regular customers and generate the most sales.

EVALUATE

MASS MARKETING VS. SEGMENTATION

As students read this section, encourage them to concentrate on recognizing the characteristics that separate products that are mass marketed from those that are niche marketed. Then use these guiding questions to focus the discussion about mass marketing and niche marketing.

Guiding Questions

Recall Why can companies generally produce mass marketed goods at a lower cost than goods for niche markets.	Mass marketed goods can generally be produced at a lower cost because of the economies of scale.
Identify advantages and disadvantages. What is an advantage of niche marketing? What is a disadvantage?	An advantage is that it increases the chances for success. A disadvantage is that it is more costly.
Synthesize Why do some marketers think mass marketing no longer exists? Do you agree or disagree?	Some marketers think that it is necessary to focus on a specific market segment so that competitors are less likely to take away your customers. Answers to the second part of the question will vary.

Reading Check Answer

Read the Reading Check question to students: ***What are the four types of market segmentation?*** Demographics, geographics, psychographics, and behavioral characteristics.

Shifting Psychographics Because of shifting psychographics, companies will need to combine demographic and psychographic data with behavioral data to get a clearer picture of consumers.

After You Read Section 2.2

Review Key Concepts

1. Market segmentation allows a company to more accurately target potential customers, thereby taking customers away from competitors who may not have done as good a job of meeting the needs of the targeted market segment.
2. Four factors used to describe a target market are demographics, geographics, psychographics, and behavioral characteristics.
3. An advantage of niche marketing it that it narrows and defines a market with extreme precision, thereby increasing the chances of success. A disadvantage is that niche marketing is expensive. Because the market is relatively small niche marketing does not result in the economies of scale that can be obtained in mass marketing. Research is required to identify target markets and develop different marketing strategies.

Practice Academics

English Language Arts

4. The prefixes are demo, geo, and psycho. *Demo* suggests people (democratic). *Geo* suggests the earth (geography). *Psycho* involves the mind (psychology).

Social Studies

5. Marketers use the group and cultural influences of a market in a variety of ways. For example, based on research to determine group preferences, marketers target specific types of clothing, food, home furnishing, etc., to particular cultural and ethnic groups. When advertising, marketers attempt to match the types of media to the specific group. For example, if a specific group is a heavy user of social media, an astute marketer will make certain the company and its products have a strong presence there.

glencoe.com

Answer Key Send students to the Online Learning Center to check their answers.

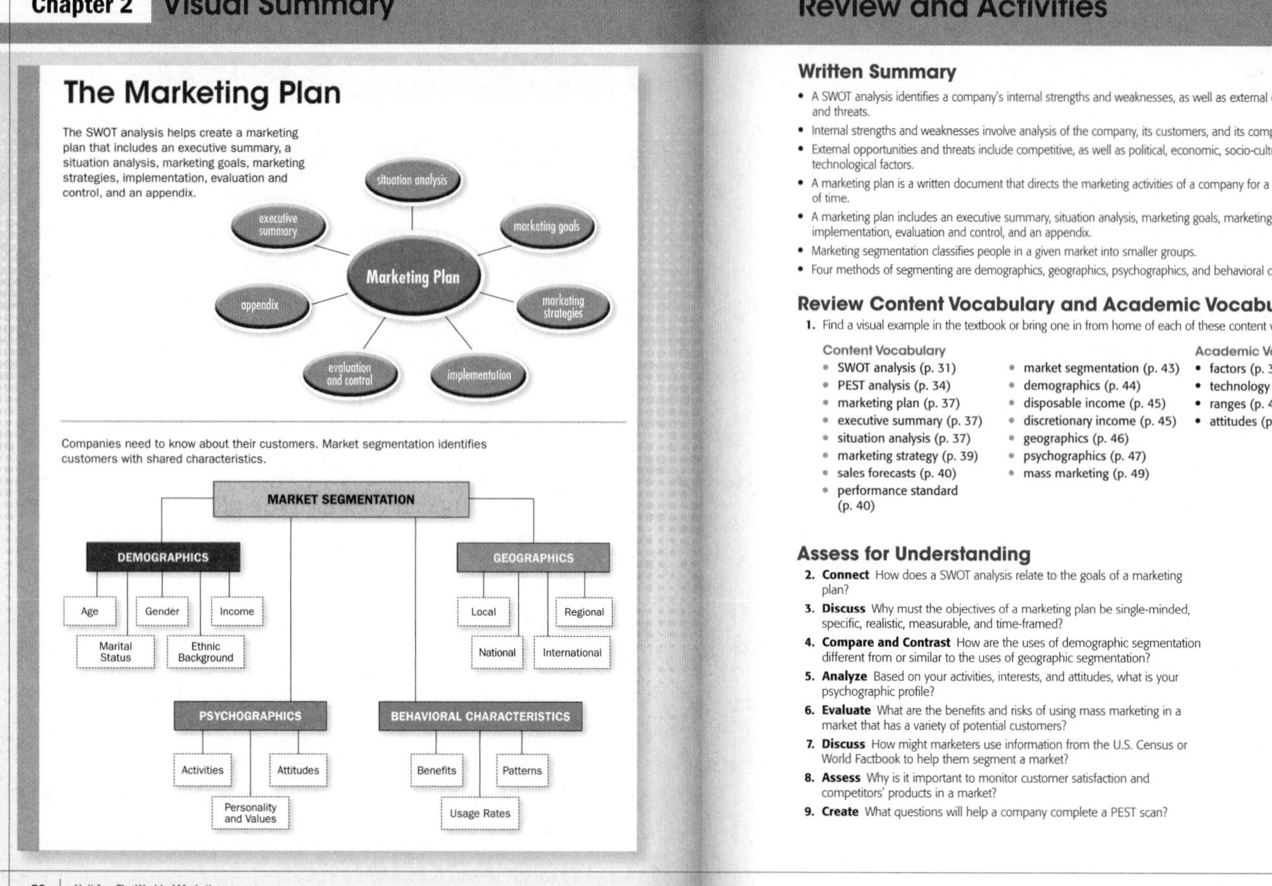

Chapter 2 Visual Summary

The Marketing Plan

The SWOT analysis helps create a marketing plan that includes an executive summary, a situation analysis, marketing goals, marketing strategies, implementation, evaluation and control, and an appendix.

Companies need to know about their customers. Market segmentation identifies customers with shared characteristics.

50 | Unit 1 · The World of Marketing

Review and Activities

Written Summary

- A SWOT analysis identifies a company's internal strengths and weaknesses, as well as external opportunities and threats.
- Internal strengths and weaknesses involve analysis of the company, its customers, and its competitive position.
- External opportunities and threats include competitive, as well as political, economic, socio-cultural, and technological factors.
- A marketing plan is a written document that directs the marketing activities of a company for a specific period of time.
- A marketing plan includes an executive summary, situation analysis, marketing goals, marketing strategies, implementation, evaluation and control, and an appendix.
- Marketing segmentation classifies people in a given market into smaller groups.
- Four methods of segmenting are demographics, geographics, psychographics, and behavioral characteristics.

Review Content Vocabulary and Academic Vocabulary

1. Find a visual example in the textbook or bring one in from home of each of these content vocabulary words.

Content Vocabulary
- SWOT analysis (p. 31)
- PEST analysis (p. 34)
- marketing plan (p. 37)
- executive summary (p. 37)
- situation analysis (p. 37)
- marketing strategy (p. 39)
- sales forecasts (p. 40)
- performance standard (p. 40)
- market segmentation (p. 43)
- demographics (p. 44)
- disposable income (p. 45)
- discretionary income (p. 45)
- geographics (p. 46)
- psychographics (p. 47)
- mass marketing (p. 49)

Academic Vocabulary
- factors (p. 31)
- technology (p. 31)
- ranges (p. 44)
- attitudes (p. 47)

Assess for Understanding

2. **Connect** How does a SWOT analysis relate to the goals of a marketing plan?
3. **Discuss** Why must the objectives of a marketing plan be single-minded, specific, realistic, measurable, and time-framed?
4. **Compare and Contrast** How are the uses of demographic segmentation different from or similar to the uses of geographic segmentation?
5. **Analyze** Based on your activities, interests, and attitudes, what is your psychographic profile?
6. **Evaluate** What are the benefits and risks of using mass marketing in a market that has a variety of potential customers?
7. **Discuss** How might marketers use information from the U.S. Census or World Factbook to help them segment a market?
8. **Assess** Why is it important to monitor customer satisfaction and competitors' products in a market?
9. **Create** What questions will help a company complete a PEST scan?

Chapter 2 · The Marketing Plan | 51

EVALUATE

Visual Summary

Express Creativity Ask students to develop their own visual summary of a concept in the chapter. Encourage students to use different formats for their visual summaries, such as a storyboard, a timeline, a table, a tree diagram, or a word web. Visual summaries will vary depending on the concept depicted and the visual manner in which it is depicted. Questions to ask when assessing a visual summary include:

- Is the summary clear, economical, and simple?
- Are any important steps left out?
- Are steps or concepts arranged in the same order as the original?
- Does the summary reveal a pattern that connects the details?
- Does the summary locate and highlight the most important information?

Review Content Vocabulary and Academic Vocabulary

1. Sentences will vary. Sample answers:

   A **marketing plan** includes an **executive summary, situation analysis** (which includes a **SWOT analysis** and **environmental scan** (PEST), as well as a **marketing strategy, sales forecast,** and **performance standards.**

   Market segmentation involves classifying people according to similar characteristics, such as **demographics** (which includes **disposable income,** and discretionary income), **geographics,** and **psychographics.**

   Mass marketing is the opposite of market segmentation because it involves using a single marketing plan to reach all customers. With market segmentation customers with similar needs and wants can be segmented and targeted.

   A **factor** that should be considered in marketing planning is **technology,** which changes frequently.

   You will find that a customer's **attitude** about a certain product can **range** from not at all satisfied to very satisfied.

EVALUATE

Assess for Understanding

2. The results of a company's SWOT analysis will give its marketers an idea of goals to create for the company. These goals are addressed in the marketing plan in the form of objectives. A company can identify strengths and opportunities through a SWOT analysis and use this information to create objectives in its marketing plan.

3. The objectives must be focused, specific, measurable, and time-framed because otherwise it will not be possible to determine whether the objectives have been met. For example, if an objective is to sell 10 percent more of a specific product to the Asian community, a time frame must be given to determine whether the objective has been met. If the objective is not properly stated, employees do not know what to strive for.

4. Demographic characteristics include: age, gender, income, marital status, and ethnic background. Geographic factors involve where people live. The similarity of people in a region is closely related to demographics. Geographical segments can also include local, regional, national, or even global markets.

5. Psychographic profiles will vary depending on the student. For example, a profile might include an interest in using products that do not damage the environment and in eating locally grown foods, the opinion that everyone should be involved in local government, and a lifestyle which values spending time with friends and family.

6. One of the major benefits of mass marketing is its low cost. With one product and one theme, manufacturing and promotions are less expensive. If the advertising is inexpensive, it may also be possible to reach enough potential customers with mass marketing even with a lot of wasted circulation. The use of mass marketing in such a market is risky because one approach may not be able to reach all potential customers effectively. In that case, the money spent would be lost on people who are not potential customers.

7. Marketers can use information from the U.S. Census to identify the size of particular market segments. The information in the U.S. Census will show marketers a variety of information about the age, gender, ethnicity, and location of possible market segments. *The World Factbook* can also be used to identify the size of particular market segments. *The World Factbook* organizes information by country. Information that might be useful for market segmentation includes population, number of people in specific age groups, average household income, climate, level of urbanization, ethnic groups, and so forth.

8. Monitoring customer satisfaction helps companies pinpoint areas that need improvement. Analyzing a company's competitive position helps to reveal its position in the marketplace in relation to its competitors. Market share is like a barometer of how well a company is doing in relation to its competitors. It lets a company know if it has increased or lost market share. If it has increased market share, the company knows that its marketing strategies are working. If it is losing market share it is a wake-up call. The company might change its marketing strategies in order to take business away from its competitors to increase its market share.

9. Companies can ask questions about current political issues, such as restrictions on manufacturing or distributing products. Economic concerns, such as a rising rate of unemployment or increasing taxes also need to be assessed. Questions about socio-cultural factors such as shifts in attitudes or outlooks can be asked. Finally, questions about technological advancements for consumers will help marketers complete a PEST scan.

Chapter 2 Review and Activities

21st Century Skills

Teamwork Skills

10. **SWOT Analysis** Work with a partner to select a company that interests you or that you know something about. It should be one that you can find information about on the Web or through observation at stores or in business magazines. Conduct a SWOT analysis. Then prepare a chart that depicts the results of the analysis. With your partner, present your findings to the class.

Financial Literacy Skills

11. **Transportation Costs** Consumers who buy online might pay about 10 percent of the cost of an item for shipping and handling. These charges are not included when a customer buys the same item at a store. However, the customer does pay for his or her own transportation costs separately. If it costs you 38 cents per mile to drive your car, what are the transportation costs for a 15-mile trip to the store?

e-Marketing Skills

12. **E-Returns** Imagine that you are in charge of Customer Service for a large e-marketing firm such as Amazon.com. Investigate the process for returning defective merchandise by logging on to a large online store.
    - List the steps a consumer must take in order to return merchandise and get a refund.
    - What problems does returning defective merchandise present for customers who purchase products online?
    - What are some ways you could make returning defective merchandise easy for online customers?
    - Create a step-by-step guide for customers to use when they are returning defective merchandise. Be sure to consider factors such as shipping costs, packaging materials, insurance issues, and other issues that may arise.
    - Share your guide with the class.

Build Academic Skills

Social Studies

13. **Economics** In recent years trade has expanded among the nations of the world. Research the effects of increased world trade. Describe a situation in which this represents an opportunity and a threat.

NCSS IX D Global Connections Analyze the causes, consequences, and possible solutions to persistent, contemporary, and emerging global issues, such as health, security, resource allocation, economic development, and environmental quality.

Science

14. **Scientific Inquiry** Conducting a SWOT analysis is like conducting a scientific inquiry or experiment. Research online or at the library how to properly design and execute a scientific experiment. Identify the scientific procedures and principles that apply to marketing research and SWOT analysis.

NSES A Develop abilities to do scientific inquiry, understandings about scientific inquiry.

Mathematics

15. **The 80/20 Rule** Here are the sales figures of ten customers: (1) $75,000; (2) $700,000; (3) $815,000; (4) $70,000; (5) $60,000; (6) $30,000; (7) $25,000; (8) $53,750; (9) $40,000; and (10) $25,000. Explain the 80/20 rule using these figures.

Math Concept **Understanding Ratios** The 80/20 rule states that the top 20 percent of customers generates 80 percent of a company's sales. In this case, total sales is $1,893,750 from 10 customers.

NCTM Number and Operations Understand numbers, ways of representing numbers, relationships among numbers, and number systems.

For help, go to the **Math Skills Handbook** located at the back of this book.

Standardized Test Practice

Directions Read the following questions. On a separate piece of paper, write the best possible answer for each one.

1. What is 150 percent of 44?
   A. 80 **C.** 66
   B. 50 **D.** 88
2. True or false? The 20 in the 80/20 rule represents 20 percent of a company's sales.
   T
   F
3. Demographic characteristics help define a __________ market.

Test-Taking Tip

When you first sit down to take a math test, jot down important equations or formulas on scrap paper. This will help you to remember them during the test.

DECA Connection Role Play

Assistant Manager Children's Clothing Store

Situation Your store is located in a strip mall in a family-focused suburban area. The strip mall is five miles from the nearest regional shopping mall. That mall has three department stores that carry children's clothing and shoes, a specialty children's store that also carries children's shoes—and a children's shoe store.

Your store carries clothing and accessory items for infants, toddlers, girls, and boys. The clothing lines range from casual to dressy. The accessory items include baby blankets, hair accessories for girls, and neckties and bowties for boys. Your store does not currently carry children's shoes.

The store's owner (judge) has decided to expand the store's merchandise lines to include a children's shoes department. The store's owner (judge) has asked for your help in creating a marketing plan for the new department. The owner believes she is not as knowledgeable about marketing plans as she would like to be. So, she has asked you to explain the parts of a marketing plan.

Activity Prepare an outline that will include the parts of a marketing plan. You will then use your outline to explain each part of a marketing plan to the store's owner (judge) in a meeting that will take place later today.

Evaluation You will be evaluated on how well you meet these performance indicators:

1. Explain the nature of marketing plans.
2. Explain the nature of marketing planning.
3. Explain the nature of sales forecasts.
4. Explain the concept of marketing strategies.
5. Prepare simple written reports.

glencoe.com

Download the Competitive Events Workbook for more Role-Play practice.

52 | Unit 1 · The World of Marketing

Chapter 2 · The Marketing Plan | 53

EVALUATE

21st Century Skills

Teamwork Skills

10. SWOT analyses will vary depending on the company analyzed. Completed SWOT analysis should identify a company's internal strengths and weaknesses, as well as external opportunities and threats. Descriptions of internal strengths and weaknesses should involve an analysis of the company, its customers, and its competitive position. Descriptions of external opportunities and threats should include political, economic, socio-cultural, and technological factors.

Financial Literacy Skills

11. $5.70 ($.38 × 15 miles)

e-Marketing Skills

12. Steps for returning merchandise will vary. Most will require customers to log in with a password and then follow cues that ask questions about the item and reason for the return, as well as if the customer wants a refund. The return policy must be followed, as well. For example there could be a 30-day return policy, after which returns are not accepted. Ways to make returning defective merchandise easy for online customers will vary too. Some students may suggest that if the online firm has a store location, that returns can be taken to the store (i.e., Talbots). Some companies provide shipping materials (i.e., shipping labels) for returns in the package when it is delivered to make it easier for customers to return merchandise. Students' step-by-step guides for merchandise returns should apply the concepts above in a logically organized and thorough manner.

EVALUATE

Build Academic Skills

Social Studies

13. One of the major effects of world trade has been intense competition, which could threaten a company. A global competitor may be able to produce goods at a lower price. To be competitive a company would have to adjust its prices accordingly or market its products differently. On the other hand, world trade has created opportunities for businesses to grow. It has opened markets allowing businesses to sell their products in other countries, thus increasing its business and its profits.

Science

14. Scientific experiments follow specific procedures and guidelines. They include: identify the problem or question; conduct research, formulate a hypothesis, conduct the experiment, collect and analyze results, draw conclusions, and present the results. Marketing research and SWOT analysis follow the same set of guidelines. In marketing research you define the problem, conduct secondary research (published research) to see if it will answer the research question. If not, you conduct primary research, such as conducting a survey. You collect and analyze the results of the survey, draw conclusions and communicate the results. With SWOT analysis, you are gathering the information that helps you identify the problem or question. It is the springboard used by companies to do the research needed to address the weaknesses and threats the company faces. It also helps them identify their strengths and opportunities.

Mathematics

15. The 80/20 rule states that the top 20 percent of customers generates 80 percent of a company's sales. In this case, total sales are $1,893,750 from 10 customers. Twenty percent of 10 is 2. The sales that are generated from the top two customers is $1,515,000, or 80 percent of total sales.

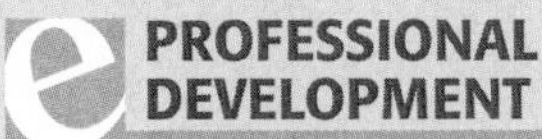

Math: Real-World Ratios
Go to the Online Learning Center to view a video clip in which a teacher has students create and compare ratios.

Standardized Test Practice

1. C 66 ($44 \times 1.5 = 66$)
2. False (20 percent represents customers; 20 percent of a company's customers account for 80 percent of its sales).
3. target

DECA Connection Role Play

Evaluations will be based on these performance indicators:

1. **Explain the nature of marketing plans.** Marketing plans provide formal, written documents that are designed to direct a company's marketing activities for a specific time period. They describe analysis and research efforts related to the product and provide a roadmap for how a product will be introduced into the market, advertised, and sold.
2. **Explain the nature of marketing planning.** Marketing planning is the first step in the marketing process and provides the company with a structured method of examining internal strengths and weaknesses along with external opportunities and threats through the use of a SWOT analysis. A PEST analysis, which takes into account political, economic, socio-cultural, and technological factors influencing the organization, is conducted. Based on the results of these activities a marketing plan is generated.
3. **Explain the nature of sales forecasts.** Sales forecasts are designed to provide a projection of probable future sales either in units or in dollars and can serve as a basis for planning. They are included in the implementation component of the marketing plan.
4. **Explain the concept of marketing strategies.** Marketing strategies are based on the objectives stated in the marketing plan, and must take customers' needs and wants into account. Target markets must be identified. The strategies then establish marketing mix choices that focus on these target markets. The company's, product's, or service's position in the marketplace will help in making decisions involving the four Ps. To be effective, a marketing strategy should be based on the key points of difference, which consist of advantages the company, product, or service has over its competition.
5. **Prepare simple written reports.** Reports should contain details about how to expand the product line, and be organized in a logical way. Each paragraph in the report should focus on one main idea, and all the sentences in the paragraph should support the main idea. Reports should be free of grammar and spelling errors.

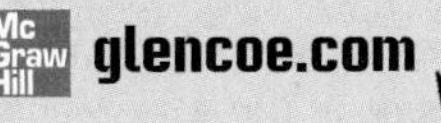

Role Plays For more DECA Role Plays, send students to the Online Learning Center to download the Competitive Events Workbook.

UNIT 1 **Marketing Internship Project**

SWOT Analysis
for a Coffee and Tea Chain

Competition in the specialty coffee and tea market is hot. Is it too late for a new competitor to break into this lucrative market?

Scenario

An Italian coffee and tea chain is considering entering the specialty coffee market in the United States. Before making that investment, our client would like our firm to conduct a SWOT analysis. The Italian coffee chain has been successful in European and Asian markets because it has used its strengths and taken advantage of opportunities in these markets.

Each café's interior design is upscale with comfortable seating, artwork, and designer plates and cups. Exotic teas and specialty coffee offerings are priced in line with and below current competitors' offerings. Only high-grade coffee beans from selected coffee bean growers are used. The Italian cafés are trying to create a unique experience in coffee and tea drinking: coffee and tea should be savored.

The Skills You'll Use

Academic Skills Reading, writing, social studies, and researching

Basic Skills Speaking, listening, thinking, and interpersonal

Technology Skills Word processing, telecommunication, and Internet

NCTE 4 Use written language to communicate effectively.
NCTE 7 Conduct research and gather, evaluate, and synthesize data to communicate discoveries.

Your Objective

Analyze the current specialty coffee and tea market in order to help a client decide whether or not to enter the market.

STEP 1 Do Your Research

Go to the Internet or your school library. Find out about the coffee and tea specialty market in restaurants, cafés, and similar outlets in the United States.

As you conduct your research, answer these questions:

- Is the market growing or shrinking and why?
- What economic, political, socio-cultural or technological factors affect this market?
- Who makes up the target market of U.S. coffee drinkers and tea drinkers in terms of demographic, psychographic, geographic, and behavioral factors?
- How successful are the marketing mixes of competitors such as Starbucks®, Dunkin Donuts®, and McDonald's®?
- What are the strengths, weaknesses, opportunities, and threats for our client in the United States coffee and tea specialty market?

Write a summary of your research.

STEP 2 Plan Your Project

Now that you have completed your research, you need to begin planning your project.

- Conduct a SWOT analysis for the Italian café chain.
- Identify a potential target market in the United States for the Italian café chain.
- Write a report summarizing your SWOT analysis, identifying your target market, and explaining why you have chosen this target market.
- Suggest a marketing mix for the Italian café chain.
- Determine whether that market segment is big enough to support the Italian café chain.

STEP 3 Connect with Your Community

- Test your conclusions by conducting interviews with trusted adults in your community that match the target market you have identified. Ask questions about their habits.
- Take notes during the interviews, and transcribe your notes after the interviews.
- Observe customers in the competition's places of business and note how long they wait for service, how long they sit and drink their beverages, and what else they might be doing while drinking their beverages.

STEP 4 Share What You Learn

Assume your class is the committee from the Italian café chain.

- Share your findings in an oral presentation to your class. Be prepared to answer questions.
- Explain how businesses find out their strengths and weaknesses in the marketplace.
- Explain how businesses react to opportunities and threats in the marketplace.
- Make your recommendation and provide rationale for your decision.
- Use software to create a slide presentation to accompany your oral report. Include one slide in your presentation for each key topic in your written report.

STEP 5 Evaluate Your Marketing and Academic Skills

Your project will be evaluated based on the following:

- Knowledge of the specialty coffee and tea market
- Comprehensive SWOT analysis
- Proper use of marketing terminology
- Rationale for recommendation
- Organization and continuity of presentation
- Mechanics—presentation and neatness
- Speaking and listening skills

MARKETING CORE FUNCTIONS

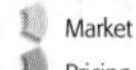

Market Planning
Pricing

Marketing Internship Project Checklist

Plan

- ✓ Research current market conditions in the industry.
- ✓ Assess the strengths, weaknesses, opportunities, and threats a new competitor would face in this market.
- ✓ Identify a location to use as a test market for the new competitor.

Write

- ✓ Describe current market conditions in the industry.
- ✓ Explain how the results of the SWOT analysis help the new competitor understand the risks involved in the market.

Present

- ✓ Present the results of your SWOT analysis and justify your chosen location for the new competitor.
- ✓ Respond to questions posed by the audience.
- ✓ Consider the needs and experiences of the audience as you present research to your class.

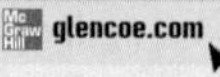

Evaluate Download a rubric you can use to evaluate your final project.

my marketing portfolio

Internship Report When you have completed your Marketing Internship Project and oral presentation, put your written report and printouts of key slides from your oral presentation in your marketing portfolio.

Analyze a Different Market and Company Select a different market (e.g., sports equipment, ice cream, cell phones, bicycles, vitamin-enriched water) and a company of your choice in that market. Conduct a SWOT analysis of that company. How effective is that company in following the marketing concept? Should that company pull out of that market or remain? If it should remain, make recommendations with regard to the company's marketing mix (product, place, price, and promotion). Prepare a written report and an oral presentation.

EVALUATE

Anticipation Activity

Project Objective Read the project objective aloud to students: ***Analyze the current specialty coffee and tea market in order to help a client decide whether to enter the market.*** Then ask students to think about what they learned about SWOT analyses in Unit 1. Remind them of these key points:

- Strengths and opportunities are positive internal factors.
- Weaknesses and threats are negative internal and external factors or trends.

Ask students: ***What is the goal of a SWOT analysis?*** The goal is to match the company's strengths to market opportunities resulting from emerging trends or voids in your competitors' product or service offerings, eliminate or overcome any weaknesses, and minimize any threats.

Ask students: ***Why should you create a customer profile before you make your marketing mix decisions?*** The customer profile drives the choice of target markets. Without a clear understanding of your customer profile and your target market, you cannot make effective marketing mix decisions.

Graphic Organizer

Display this diagram. Ask students to name places in their communities where people can buy coffee. Possible answers:

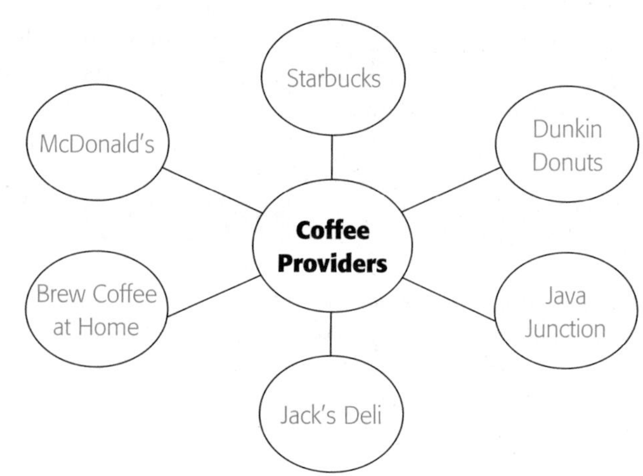

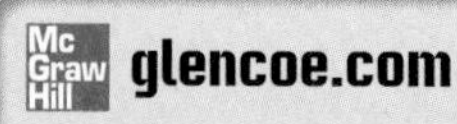

Graphic Organizer Send students to the Online Learning Center to print this graphic organizer.

EVALUATE

STEP 1 Do Your Research

Tell students that there are many places to find information they can use to develop their SWOT analyses. Students can use library and Internet resources, but they should also talk to people in the community. Encourage students to seek the opinions and ideas of trusted people they know. Other people can bring new perspectives and ideas about strengths, weaknesses, opportunities, and threats as well as economic, political, socio-cultural and technological factors that affect the specialty coffee and tea market.

STEP 2 Plan Your Project

Students should create a detailed customer profile before choosing their target markets because the customer profile will drive the target market choice. Students should explain why they chose the target market and provide information about segmentation of their chosen market. Students' explanation of the marketing mix they have chosen should include all four Ps: product, price, place, and promotion.

STEP 3 Connect with Your Community

Explain to students that connecting with members of the community is a great way to build relationships. Tell them that young people who have relationships with caring and competent adults are more likely to achieve success in life than those who do not. Encourage students to take part in opportunities for adults to serve as mentors, coaches, advocates, and advisors, both formally and informally.

STEP 4 Share What You Learn

Students should present their ideas in a written report and oral presentation with presentation software. They should have at least one slide in their presentation for each key topic in the written report. Encourage students to speak clearly, use appropriate grammar and vocabulary, and actively engage the audience by making and maintaining eye contact and using movement (facial expressions, posture, gestures) to focus attention and interest.

STEP 5 Evaluate Your Marketing and Academic Skills

Have students use the Marketing Internship Project Checklist to help them to plan, write, and present their reports. Exemplary written reports will include information that clearly supports a central thesis, a single, distinct focus, generally well-developed ideas, well-phrased sentences that flow smoothly and are varied in length and structure, consistently precise word choice, and few, if any, errors in grammar, spelling, and mechanics.

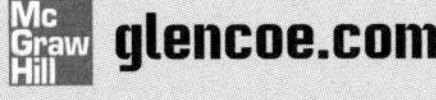

Evaluation Rubric Send students to the Online Learning Center to get a rubric to evaluate their projects.

Culminating Activity

Explain to students that one way to make a SWOT analysis more detailed is to take a closer look at the business environment. Often, opportunities arise as a result of a changing business environment that would affect a SWOT analysis. Ask students: ***Can you think of any examples of opportunities that have been created due to a changing business environment?*** Answers will vary. Sample answers include: New trends often develop, and sometimes these new trends cause the demand to outpace the supply of quality options. For example, when the trend toward healthy eating first emerged, there were not very many choices for healthful fast-food snacks. Many fast-food businesses seized the opportunity to provide such options, and now healthful fast-food options are widespread. Sometimes a customer segment becomes more powerful and predominant, but their needs are not being fully met. For example, the Hispanic population in the United States was not a widely targeted market until the 1990s. The market of Hispanic consumers has grown dramatically and, as the Hispanic population has grown, more and more businesses have targeted this market, which has strong characteristics of a cohesive community of like-minded individuals.

my marketing portfolio

Internship Report Have students put their written reports and printouts of key slides from their oral presentations in their marketing portfolio.

Analyze a Different Market and Company Direct students to select a different market and a company of their choice in that market and conduct a SWOT analysis of that company. Students' completed analyses should include all of the elements and answer all of the questions included in the Marketing Internship Project on this page. This additional activity can build relevance for students who are motivated to learn about other specific businesses and industries. Relevance shifts the focus to what motivates individual students to learn.

2

PLANNING GUIDE AND RESOURCES

	Print	Digital
Unit 2 Economics		Unit 2 Fast Files: Marketing Internship Project Activity Connect Online Learning Center through glencoe.com
Chapter 3 Political and Economic Analysis	Student Activity Workbook: Chapter 3 DECA Connection Role Play; Chapter 3 Vocabulary Activity; Section Note Taking Activities; Chapter Academics Activity; Section Study Skills Activities; Section Real-World Applications Activities Mathematics for Marketing Workbook Marketing Research Project Workbook School-to-Career Activity Workbook	Unit 2 Fast Files: Chapter 3 Discovery Project Worksheet and Rubric; Chapter 3 Green Marketer Worksheet; Chapter 3 Digital Nation Activity; Section Graphic Organizers; Section Outlines with Key Terms and Definitions; Section Summaries ExamView Assessment Suite, Chapter 3 Connect Online Learning Center through glencoe.com
Chapter 4 Global Analysis	Student Activity Workbook: Chapter 4 DECA Connection Role Play; Chapter 4 Vocabulary Activity; Section Note Taking Activities; Chapter Academics Activity; Section Study Skills Activities; Section Real-World Applications Activities Mathematics for Marketing Workbook Marketing Research Project Workbook School-to-Career Activity Workbook	Unit 2 Fast Files: Chapter 4 Discovery Project Worksheet and Rubric; Chapter 4 Green Marketer Activity; Chapter 4 Digital Nation Activity; Section Graphic Organizers; Section Outlines with Key Terms and Definitions; Section Summaries ExamView Assessment Suite, Chapter 4 Connect Online Learning Center through glencoe.com

McGRAW-HILL PROFESSIONAL DEVELOPMENT

Perkins IV has placed more emphasis than ever on providing quality professional development for Career and Technology educators. The legislation mandates that the focus of professional development be the integration and reinforcement of academic competencies in order to improve student achievement. Specifically, Perkins requires measurements of students' academic success. McGraw-Hill answers the challenge for strong and effective professional development with a five-prong **Online Professional Development for Integrating Academics.**

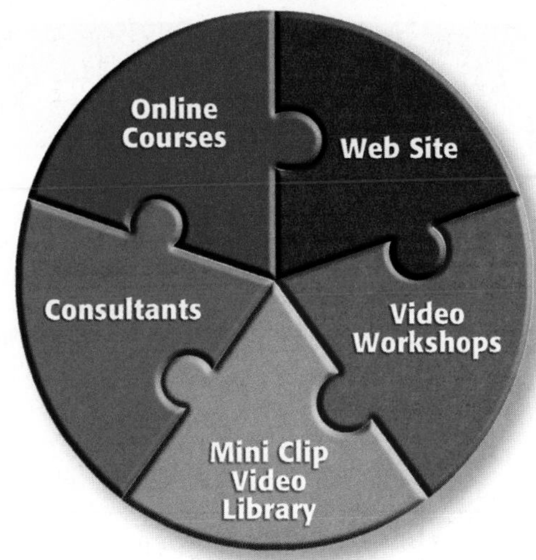

For pricing and ordering information contact your McGraw-Hill Sales Representative.

VIDEO LIBRARY

The McGraw-Hill Professional Development Mini-Clip Video Library, referenced for your convenience at the point of use, provides teaching strategies to strengthen academic and learning skills. Go to the Online Learning Center to view these professional development video clips for Unit 2:

Chapter 3: Political and Economic Analysis

- **Reading: Connecting the Pieces:** A teacher helps students develop predictions and inferences. (p. 61)
- **Reading: Differentiated Instruction:** An educator discusses elements of a differentiated classroom. (p. 63)
- **ELL: Language Practice:** Students of varying language proficiencies work together to review the content they have just read. (p. 65)
- **Reading: Flexible Grouping:** Teachers use flexible groupings and partner-sharing to encourage and promote discussion. (p. 69)
- **Reading: Guided Instruction:** A teacher helps students identify major and minor details. (p. 75)

Chapter 4: Global Analysis

- **Reading: Guided Instruction:** A teacher helps students identify major and minor details. (p. 85)
- **ELL: Elaborating on Student Responses:** A teacher uses explanatory language to elaborate on a student response and helps place it in the broader context of the lesson. (p. 87)
- **Reading: Strategic Readers:** An author discusses the characteristics of strategic readers. (p. 89)
- **Reading: Vocabulary:** An author describes the critical importance of academic language. (p. 93)

UNIT OVERVIEW

Sections	Objectives	Common Core State Standards College and Career Readiness
Section 3.1 **What is an Economy?**	• Explain the concept of an economy. • Discuss how scarcity and factors of production affect the economy. • Compare and contrast how traditional, market, and command economies answer the three basic economic questions. • Explain why most economies are mixed. • Identify examples of different political and economic philosophies.	• **Reading** Interpret words and phrases as they are used in a text, including determining technical, connotative, and figurative meanings, and analyze how specific word choices shape meaning or tone.
Section 3.2 **Understanding the Economy**	• List the goals of a healthy economy. • Explain how an economy is measured. • Analyze the key phases of the business cycle.	• **Reading** Integrate and evaluate content presented in diverse formats and media, including visually and quantitatively, as well as in words.

Sections	Objectives	Common Core State Standards College and Career Readiness
Section 4.1 **International Trade**	• Describe the benefits of international trade. • Discuss the balance of trade. • Compare and contrast three types of trade barriers. • Discuss three significant trade agreements and alliances.	• **Reading** Determine central ideas or themes of a text and analyze their development; summarize the key supporting details and ideas.
Section 4.2 **The Global Marketplace**	• List forms of international trade. • Identify political, economic, socio-cultural, and technological factors that affect international business. • Understand global marketing strategies.	• **Reading** Integrate and evaluate content presented in diverse formats and media, including visually and quantitatively, as well as in words.

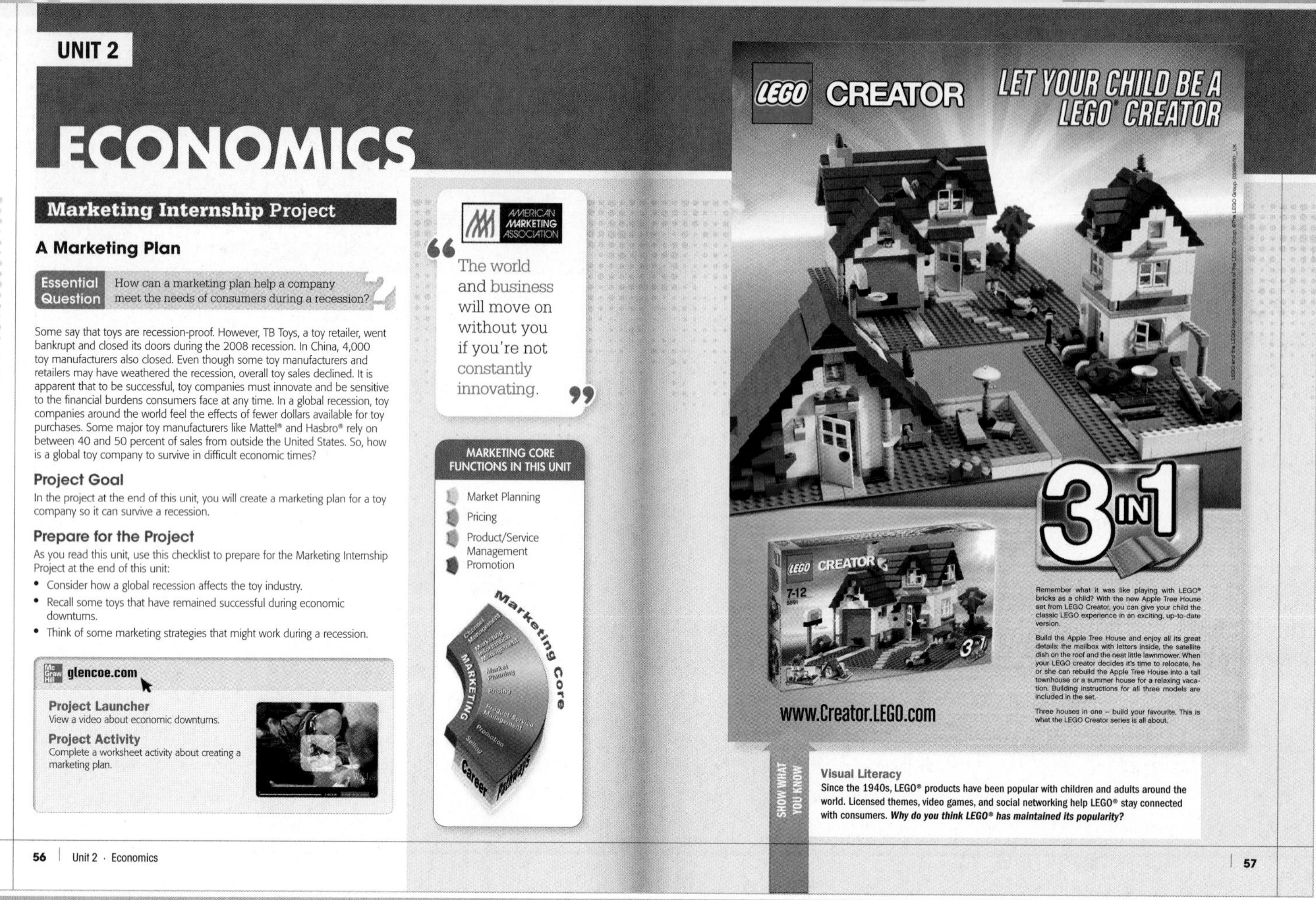
UNIT 2

ECONOMICS

Marketing Internship Project

A Marketing Plan

Essential Question How can a marketing plan help a company meet the needs of consumers during a recession?

Some say that toys are recession-proof. However, TB Toys, a toy retailer, went bankrupt and closed its doors during the 2008 recession. In China, 4,000 toy manufacturers also closed. Even though some toy manufacturers and retailers may have weathered the recession, overall toy sales declined. It is apparent that to be successful, toy companies must innovate and be sensitive to the financial burdens consumers face at any time. In a global recession, toy companies around the world feel the effects of fewer dollars available for toy purchases. Some major toy manufacturers like Mattel® and Hasbro® rely on between 40 and 50 percent of sales from outside the United States. So, how is a global toy company to survive in difficult economic times?

Project Goal

In the project at the end of this unit, you will create a marketing plan for a toy company so it can survive a recession.

Prepare for the Project

As you read this unit, use this checklist to prepare for the Marketing Internship Project at the end of this unit:

- Consider how a global recession affects the toy industry.
- Recall some toys that have remained successful during economic downturns.
- Think of some marketing strategies that might work during a recession.

glencoe.com

Project Launcher
View a video about economic downturns.

Project Activity
Complete a worksheet activity about creating a marketing plan.

AMERICAN MARKETING ASSOCIATION

"The world and business will move on without you if you're not constantly innovating."

MARKETING CORE FUNCTIONS IN THIS UNIT
- Market Planning
- Pricing
- Product/Service Management
- Promotion

SHOW WHAT YOU KNOW

Visual Literacy
Since the 1940s, LEGO® products have been popular with children and adults around the world. Licensed themes, video games, and social networking help LEGO® stay connected with consumers. ***Why do you think LEGO® has maintained its popularity?***

56 | Unit 2 · Economics

57

ENGAGE

Introduce the Unit

Unit 2 discusses basic principles of economic and political systems.

Chapter 3 examines different types of economies, including the free or private enterprise system, and develops key economic concepts, such as resources and the ways in which economies are evaluated.

Chapter 4 compares the private enterprise system with other economic systems and their related political systems.

Build Background

Tell students that business has become increasingly global. Have students name different businesses or companies that are global. List their answers on the board. Some answers may include McDonald's®, Xbox®, Nike® shoes and athletic wear, automobile makers such as Honda®, Toyota®, or Volkswagen®. Ask students: ***What are some reasons for the growth of global business?*** Answers may include modern transportation, communication, immigration, and Internet sales result in increased international communication and commerce.

Visual Literacy

Photo Caption Answer Read the copy on the ad to students. Then read the photo caption and the photo caption question to students: ***Why do you think LEGO® has maintained its popularity?*** Answers will vary. Accept all reasonable answers. Sample answer: This product not only appeals to children, but to older consumers as well in many countries, as users can build items that are specific to their own cultures. It is durable so that it can last a long time without need for replacement for years. Also, family members, friends, and students can play with it together, or individuals can play with it alone. Ask students to evaluate the visual components of the advertisement. Ask volunteers to explain how the visual aspects of the advertisement complement the text of the advertisement. Answers will vary but may note that the bright primary colors of red, blue, and yellow are appealing and attention-getting for most children and adults. The simplicity of the single image allows the viewer to focus on the creative structure created by the LEGO blocks. The solitary logotype with the word "LEGO" echoes simplicity, focusing attention on the product itself as the brief slogan highlights imagination.

ENGAGE

Marketing Internship Project Preview

Read students the Marketing Internship Project Essential Question: ***How can a marketing plan help a company meet the needs of consumers during a recession?*** Because students are just starting to learn about marketing and economic systems and conditions, they will likely not know the specific answer to this question, which is how to develop a marketing plan with provisions to compensate for an economic downturn. However, students should know that doing business in a difficult economy requires innovative marketing strategies for a company and its products to succeed. Explain to students that they will learn about free enterprise, competition, profit, risk, and types of economic systems while studying this unit. Tell students that when they are finished studying this unit, they will ask questions to find answers about toy companies doing business globally during a recession. As they study each chapter in the unit, they can prepare for the Unit Project by thinking of some toys that have remained successful despite tough economic times.

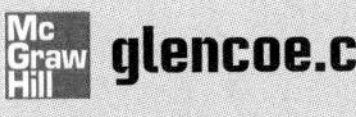

Marketing Internship Project Resources Send students to the Online Learning Center to watch a video and download a worksheet activity related to the topic of the Unit Project.

Read the American Marketing Association quote to students:

> “The world and business will move on without you if you're not constantly innovating.”

AMERICAN MARKETING ASSOCIATION

Explain to students that the AMA's Resource Library provides information through articles and other resources that address current trends in marketing.

Global Technology Marketing strategies must adapt to current trends and economic conditions in different countries as business is increasingly global. Ask students: ***What product trends have dominated the market? What trends do you expect to see in the future?*** Sample answer: the expansion of e-books and social networking, along with the convergence of cell phone technology. Green awareness among consumers intensified. Future trends might include other alternative energy sources, remote workplaces, and telecommuting.

MARKETING CORE FUNCTIONS IN THIS UNIT

Point out to students that Chapters 3 and 4 will touch on four of the seven marketing core functions. Describe each of these marketing functions to students to prepare them to start studying this unit.

- **Market Planning** involves understanding the concepts and strategies used to develop and target specific marketing strategies to a select audience.
- **Pricing** decisions dictate how much to charge for goods and services in order to make a profit.
- **Promotion** is the effort to inform, persuade, or remind potential customers about a business's products or services or to improve a company's public image.
- **Product/Service Management** involves obtaining, developing, maintaining, and improving a product or a product mix in response to marketing opportunities.

MARKETING RESEARCH

PROJECT WORKBOOK

The purpose of the Marketing Research Project Workbook is to provide a step-by-step approach for students to conduct their own marketing research study. Each chapter is devoted to key elements in the research process. Each chapter builds upon the previous chapters, and by the end of the book, students will have completed an in-depth marketing research study, complete with rationale for all decisions, a report of the findings and conclusions, recommendations based on the original research problem and study objectives, and an annotated bibliography.

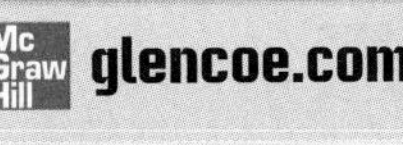

Marketing Research Project Workbook Send students to the Online Learning Center to download the Marketing Research Project Workbook. A Teacher Manual is also available on the Teacher Center of the Online Learning Center.

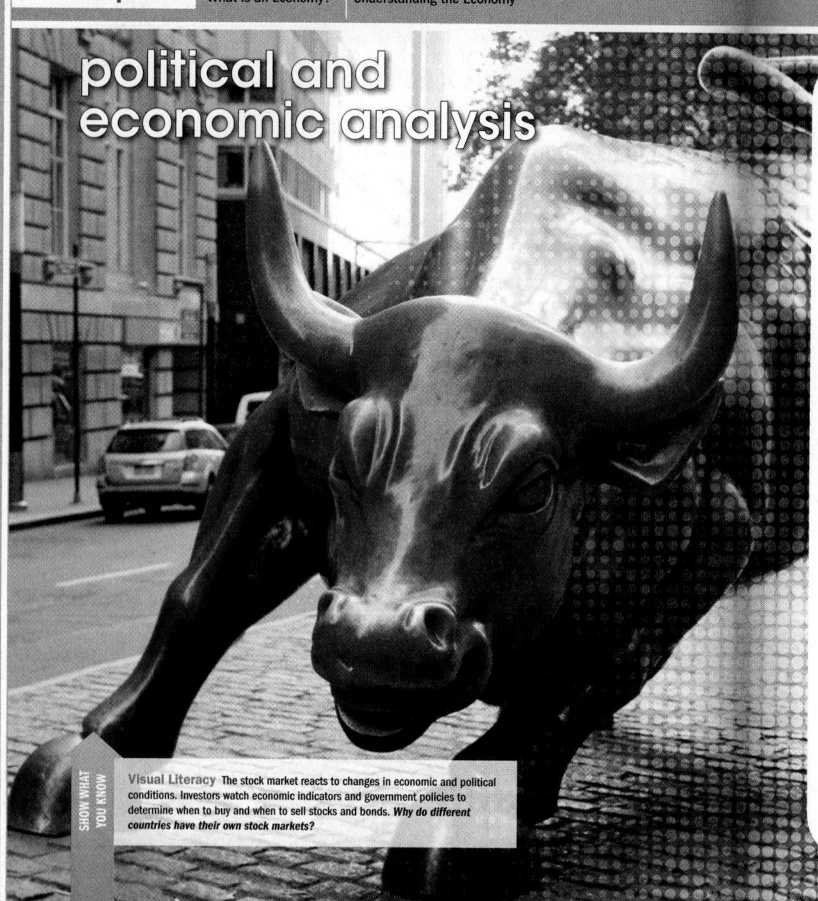

SHOW WHAT YOU KNOW

Visual Literacy The stock market reacts to changes in economic and political conditions. Investors watch economic indicators and government policies to determine when to buy and when to sell stocks and bonds. ***Why do different countries have their own stock markets?***

Discovery Project

Risks and Rewards

Essential Question How will you invest the money you have saved?

Project Goal

Work with a partner to study economic indicators, such as unemployment rate, Consumer Price Index, and Gross Domestic Product to determine the current state of the United States economy. Study any pending government actions that may affect the economy in the near future. Then decide how you would invest $100,000. Conduct a SWOT analysis to determine which company or companies you think will be successful. Provide rationale for your decisions.

Ask Yourself...

- Where will you find information on the economy and government policies?
- Where will you find information on companies that may be successful?
- How will you use this information to help you decide how to invest your money?
- How will you present your investment decisions with supporting rationale?

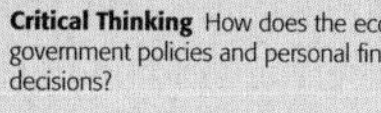

Critical Thinking How does the economy affect government policies and personal financial decisions?

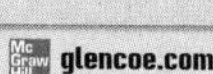 glencoe.com

Activity
Get a worksheet activity about economic risks and rewards.

Evaluate
Download a rubric you can use to evaluate your project.

DECA Connection

DECA Event Role Play

Concepts in this chapter are related to DECA competitive events that involve either an interview or role play.

Performance Indicators The performance indicators represent key skills and knowledge. Your key to success in DECA competitive events is relating them to the concepts in this chapter.

- Explain the concept of economic resources.
- Explain the types of economic systems.
- Examine the relationship between government and business.
- Discuss the role government agencies play in the food marketing industry.
- Determine the impact of business cycles on business activities.

DECA Prep

Role Play Practice role playing with the DECA Connection competitive-event activity at the end of this chapter. More information about DECA events can be found on DECA's Web site.

ENGAGE

Visual Literacy

Read the chapter opener photo caption question to students: ***Why do different countries have their own stock markets?*** Students may suggest answers such as countries can regulate the markets, people can invest more easily, etc. Ask these guiding questions to activate prior knowledge. Write student generated questions produced during the discussion on the board and return to them throughout the chapter.

Guiding Questions

Explain Why is it important that global companies understand the political system of each foreign country in which they conduct business?	Government goals and regulations can greatly affect a company's risks and opportunities. For example, new laws regarding imports can affect what a company can sell in a foreign country.
Draw Conclusions Which country will probably have more niche marketing: one with a high standard of living or a low standard of living? Why?	In general, countries with a high standard of living will have more niche marketing because of consumers' greater discretionary income.

Discovery Project

Risks and Rewards Direct students to the Discovery Project Essential Question: ***How will you invest the money you have saved?*** Possible answer: I will invest in companies that are doing well in the marketplace and are providing products and services that are popular among people of all age groups. Ask students: ***Where will you find information on the economy and government policies?*** government websites Ask students where they will find information on companies that may be successful. Possible answers: companies' annual reports and websites, search engines Ask students: ***How will you use this information to help you decide how to invest your money?*** Possible answer: I will compare information to determine growth patterns. Ask students How they will present investment decisions with supporting rationale. charts, graphs, SWOT analyses

 glencoe.com 

Discovery Project Resources Send students to the Online Learning Center to download a rubric to evaluate their projects.

ENGAGE

Introduce the Chapter

In this chapter, different political and economic systems are discussed and compared and these major concepts are presented:

- Economic resources
- Scarcity
- Traditional economies
- Market economies
- Command economies
- Capitalism
- Communism
- Socialism
- Developing economies
- Economic measurements
- The business cycle

Discussion Starter

Entrepreneurship Ask students: ***What characteristics do you think a good entrepreneur would have?*** Possible answers: self-motivated, good problem-solver, willing to take risks Tell students that an entrepreneur has been defined as "a person who looks at a problem and sees an opportunity." Ask students: ***Do you think this is a good definition? Why or why not?*** Yes, because many people can manage an existing business, but entrepreneurs excel at recognizing how a business can successfully meet needs and wants.

DECA Connection

Discuss the performance indicators listed in the DECA Connection feature. Explain to students that performance indicators tell them how to demonstrate their acquired skills and knowledge through individual or team competitive events.

 **glencoe.com** 

Competitive Events Workbook For more DECA Role Plays, send students to the Online Learning Center to download the Competitive Events Workbook.

PROGRAM RESOURCE ORGANIZER

PRINT RESOURCES

- **Student Edition**
- **Teacher Edition**
- **Student Activity Workbook with Academic Integration** includes worksheets and activities correlated to the text.
- **Mathematics for Marketing Workbook** provides math activities for every unit in the text.

TECHNOLOGY TOOLBOX

- **Connect**
- **ConnectPlus**
- **ExamView Assessment Suite** is a comprehensive solution for creating, administering, and scoring tests.

 **glencoe.com**

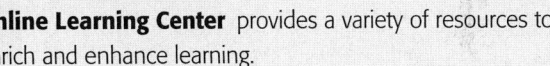

Online Learning Center provides a variety of resources to enrich and enhance learning.

SECTION, CHAPTER, AND UNIT RESOURCES

- **Graphic Organizers** for organizing text concepts visually.
- **Digital Nation Activities** and **Green Marketer Activities** extend learning beyond the text features.
- **Career Chatroom Career Profiles** allow students to explore different marketing occupations in depth.
- **After You Read Answer Keys** for students to check their answers.
- **Discovery Project Rubrics** and **Marketing Internship Project Rubrics** for students to evaluate their projects.

PROGRAM RESOURCES

- **Student Activity Workbook with Academic Integration Teacher Annotated Edition** includes annotated answers for the activities and worksheets.
- **Marketing Research Project Workbook** provides a step-by-step approach for students to complete their own marketing research studies.
- **School-to-Career Activity Workbook** helps students relate their class work to on-the-job experience and involves work-site analysis and working with mentors.
- **Competitive Events Workbook** helps prepare students for state and national marketing education competitions.
- **Inclusion in the Marketing Education Classroom** provides teaching resources for working with students with special needs.
- **PowerPoint Presentations** provides visual teaching aids and assessments for this chapter.

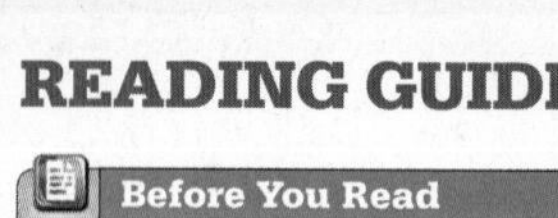

READING GUIDE

Before You Read

Connect How do economic decisions and policies affect your daily life?

Objectives

- **Explain** the concept of an economy.
- **Discuss** how scarcity and factors of production affect the economy.
- **Compare and contrast** how traditional, market, command economies answer the three basic economic questions.
- **Explain** why most economies are mixed.
- **Identify** examples of different political and economic philosophies.

The Main Idea

An economy is a nation's method for making economic choices that involve how it will use its resources to produce and distribute goods and services to meet the needs of its population.

Vocabulary

Content Vocabulary
- economy
- resources
- factors of production
- infrastructure
- entrepreneurship
- scarcity
- traditional economy
- market economy
- command economy

Academic Vocabulary

You will find these words in your reading and on your tests. Make sure you know their meanings.
- approaches
- theory

Graphic Organizer

Draw or print a diagram like this to record similarities and differences among market and command economies.

Market Economy
Both
Command Economy

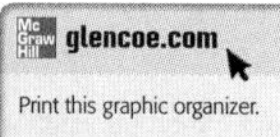

glencoe.com

Print this graphic organizer.

STANDARDS

ACADEMIC

English Language Arts

NCTE 3 Apply strategies to interpret texts.

Social Studies

NCSS VII A Production, Distribution, and Consumption Explain how the scarcity of productive resources (human, capital, technological, and natural) requires the development of economic systems to make decisions about how goods and services are to be produced and distributed.

NCSS *National Council for the Social Studies*
NCTE *National Council of Teachers of English*
NCTM *National Council of Teachers of Mathematics*
NSES *National Science Education Standards*

College & Career READINESS

Common Core

Reading Interpret words and phrases as they are used in a text, including determining technical, connotative, and figurative meanings, and analyze how specific word choices shape meaning or tone.

MARKETING CORE FUNCTION

Market Planning

me. Section 3.1

What Is an Economy?

WHAT CREATES AN ECONOMY?

An **economy**, or economic system, is the organized way a nation provides for the needs and wants of its people. Countries with different economic systems have different **approaches** when making choices. A country's economic resources determine economic activities, such as manufacturing, buying, selling, transporting, and investing. Broad categories of economic resources that are common to all nations affect how business is done across the world.

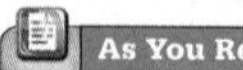

As You Read

Predict How are products manufactured and transported through the economy?

ECONOMIC RESOURCES

Economic **resources** are all the things used in producing goods and services. Economists use the term **factors of production** when they talk about these resources. Factors of production are comprised of land, labor, capital, and entrepreneurship. Tangible economic resources include land and capital. Intangible economic resources include labor and entrepreneurship.

LAND

Land includes everything contained in the earth or found in the seas. Coal and crude oil are natural resources. So is a lake and all of the living things in it. Trees and plants, as well as the soil in which they grow, are natural resources. These natural resources are used as the raw material for making goods and creating services. Some countries' climate and geography are perfect for attracting tourists. Switzerland is a destination for skiing and mountain landscapes. So, the tourist trade is a viable industry that helps support its economy.

> "A nation chooses how to use its resources to produce and distribute goods and services."

LABOR

Labor refers to all the people who work. Labor includes full- and part-time workers, managers, and professional people in both the private and public sectors. Companies may spend a lot of money training employees because a well-trained labor force is an asset to a company. Economies with well-educated and well-trained labor have an advantage. A country with such a labor force can use its own citizens for jobs. It does not have to search for employees in other countries.

CAPITAL

Capital includes money to start and operate a business. It also includes the goods used in the production process. Factories, office buildings, computers, and tools are all considered capital resources. Raw materials that have been processed into a more useful form (such as lumber or steel) are considered capital. Without capital, a business would not have the funds or the resources needed to develop, to advertise, and to transport goods. Capital includes **infrastructure**, which is the physical development of a country. This includes its roads, ports, sanitation facilities, and utilities, especially telecommunications. These things are necessary for the production and distribution of goods and services in an economy. For example, an international business needs dependable phone and Internet service. Companies that ship goods need to be able to reach their customers.

ENGAGE

Anticipation Activity

Accessing Prior Knowledge Ask students: ***Do you think a country's political system affects how its economy functions? Why or why not?*** The type of political system affects how economic decisions are made and who makes them.

Objectives

- **Explain** the concept of an economy. An economy is a way of organizing the use of a nation's resources.
- **Discuss** how scarcity and factors of production affect the economy. Scarcity and factors of production force nations to make choices depending on their unique needs.
- **Compare and contrast** how traditional, market, and command economies answer economic questions. Either the government or consumers make decisions about what to produce, how to produce, and who gets that which is produced.
- **Explain** why most economies are mixed. Most economies meet needs using a combination of approaches.
- **Identify** examples of different political and economic philosophies. capitalism, communism, socialism

Graphic Organizer

Market Economy Consumers decide what will be produced by their purchases, businesses decide how, possession of money decides who makes purchases

Both Market and Command Economies Limited by economic resources—land, labor, capital, entrepreneurship

Command Economy Government decides what to produce, how to produce, who gets that which is produced

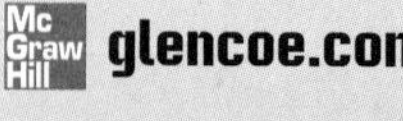

glencoe.com

iWB

Graphic Organizer Send students to the Online Learning Center to print this graphic organizer.

EXPLORE

Before You Read

Read the Before You Read question aloud: ***How do economic decisions and policies affect your daily life?*** Encourage students to take a broad view of this topic, including discussing not only their personal decisions, but also how government policies affect their lives. For example, government regulations on auto safety and gasoline mileage affect what vehicles are manufactured.

Preteaching Vocabulary

Have students go to the Online Learning Center at glencoe.com for the Chapter 3 Preteaching Vocabulary games.

Content Vocabulary

Read aloud the content vocabulary words with the class. Discuss how prefixes can be used to change the meanings of words. Point out that infrastructure has the prefix *infra-*, which means "under" or "below." An infrastructure is an underlying foundation or framework. Ask students: ***What are some examples of sentences using the word*** **infrastructure?** Possible answer: The city raised taxes to pay for expansions to its infrastructure.

Academic Vocabulary

Approaches—Denotative Meaning Explain that many words have both concrete and abstract meanings. The noun *approaches* can be used in a concrete or abstract way. Ask students to provide an example of each. Answers will vary. Sample answers: Concrete: The approaches to the government building were carefully guarded. Abstract: Our approaches to solving the problem were very different. As students read, have them determine whether *approaches* is used in its concrete or abstract sense in this section.

Theory—Word Origin Tell students that the word *theory* comes from the Greek word *theōría*, which means "viewing or contemplating." Ask students: ***How is this Greek word related to the definition of theory as "a plausible or scientifically acceptable principle offered to explain phenomena"?*** Possible answer: When determining whether a theory is true, we contemplate it and examine it in a variety of ways.

PROFESSIONAL DEVELOPMENT **MINI CLIP**

Reading: Connecting the Pieces
Go to the Online Learning Center for a video clip in which a teacher helps students develop predictions and inferences.

Section 3.1

What Is an Economy?

WHAT CREATES AN ECONOMY?

Emphasize that a country's economic actions are controlled by its economic resources. To focus discussion on this topic, ask students these guiding questions.

Guiding Questions

Recall Name a factor of production that a nation might be able to control. Name one that it cannot control.	Able to control: training of workforce; Cannot control: natural resources such as oil.
Contrast From an economic resource standpoint, how is steel different from iron ore?	Iron ore is a natural resource (land). Steel contains processed iron ore (capital).
Synthesize Many countries have never installed telephone lines. How has satellite technology affected their need to do so today? What does this say about the development of infrastructure?	Satellites and other wireless technologies have allowed countries to forgo traditional phone lines; delaying some infrastructures allows nations to implement more advanced ones.

As You Read

Read students the As You Read question: ***How are products manufactured and transported through the economy?*** Answers will vary. Encourage students to think about products with which they are familiar. Discuss why some products are more difficult to manufacture and transport than others. For example, computers require highly specialized manufacturing conditions and milk must be transported in refrigerated trucks.

Expert Advice

Read the quote to students:

> **"A nation chooses how to use its resources to produce and distribute goods and services."**

Ask students: ***What do you think would happen if a nation was able to produce the goods its people needed, but was unable to distribute them?*** The goods would not be used and people might suffer.

ENTREPRENEURSHIP

Entrepreneurship refers to the skills of people who are willing to invest their time and money to run a business. Entrepreneurs organize factors of production to create the goods and services that are part of an economy. They are the employers of a population.

People who are constantly thinking of new ideas can be good entrepreneurs. It takes more than a good idea, though. An entrepreneur must also have the skills needed to run a business. A good imagination and a capacity for hard work are the qualities all entrepreneurs have.

Entrepreneurs can make major contributions to the economy. Innovations in transportation and communications led to much of the growth and change in the U.S. during the twentieth century.

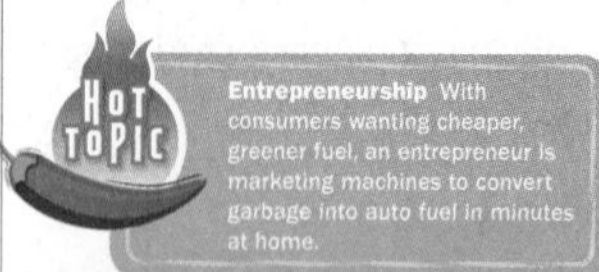

Entrepreneurship With consumers wanting cheaper, greener fuel, an entrepreneur is marketing machines to convert garbage into auto fuel in minutes at home.

SCARCITY

Different economies have different amounts of economic resources. The United States has an educated labor force, a great deal of capital, an abundance of entrepreneurs, and many natural resources. Most underdeveloped nations are not that fortunate. They might have natural resources to spare but not the capital or the skilled labor to develop them.

Even the United States, with its wealth of economic resources, cannot meet the needs and wants of all its citizens. Many citizens live below poverty level. Businesses go bankrupt on a regular basis. It is apparent that nations have unlimited wants and needs for growth and development but limited resources to meet them. The difference between wants and needs and available resources is called **scarcity**. Scarcity forces nations to make economic choices. For example, entrepreneurs in underdeveloped nations may not have much money or resources. They will need capital or raw materials so they can start a business. The scarcity in their country can make it hard to be successful.

Reading Check

Recall What are the four economic resources?

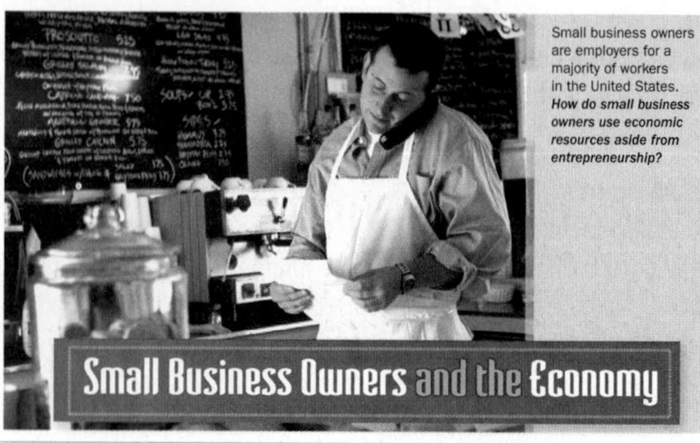

Small business owners are employers for a majority of workers in the United States. ***How do small business owners use economic resources aside from entrepreneurship?***

TYPES OF ECONOMIC SYSTEMS

Nations must answer these three basic economic questions about how to use limited economic resource to get the goods and services the country needs.

1. **What** goods and services should be produced?
2. **How** should the goods and services be produced?
3. **For whom** should the goods and services be produced and distributed?

Economists have studied the way nations answer the three basic economic questions and have classified economic systems into three broad categories: traditional, market, and command economies. However, no economy is purely traditional, market, or command. Elements of all three systems are found in all economies. Learning the characteristics of the pure form of each economic system will make it easier to classify and categorize information about them.

TRADITIONAL ECONOMIES

In a **traditional economy**, habits, traditions and rituals answer the basic questions of what, how, and for whom. The answers are often based on cultural or religious practices and ideals that have been passed from one generation to the next. Typically, these activities involve subsistence farming, animal gathering, tool making, and other activities used to provide food, shelter, and clothing.

1. What? In a traditional economy there is little choice about what to produce. People produce what they need to survive. They use the natural resources in their habitat to do so.
2. How? Traditional societies are underdeveloped. They produce what they need with simple, handmade tools and their ingenuity. People use the techniques they learned from their ancestors.
3. For whom? Traditional economic systems have a sense of community. Any excess food or other items that are made are traded among the residents.

MARKET ECONOMIES

In a pure **market economy**, there is no government involvement in economic decisions. Individuals and companies own the means of production and businesses compete for consumers. The government lets the market answer the three basic economic questions.

1. What? Consumers decide what should be produced in a market economy through the purchases that they make. Products that do not satisfy consumers' needs are not purchased and are not successful. They are no longer sold.
2. How? Businesses in a market economy decide how to produce goods and services. They must produce quality products at lower prices than their competitors. It is necessary for them to find the most efficient way to produce their goods and services and the best way to encourage customers to buy these products.
3. For whom? In a market economy, the people who have more money are able to use it as a medium of exchange to buy more goods and services. To obtain money, people are motivated to work and invest the money they make.

Tourism Contributes to an Economy

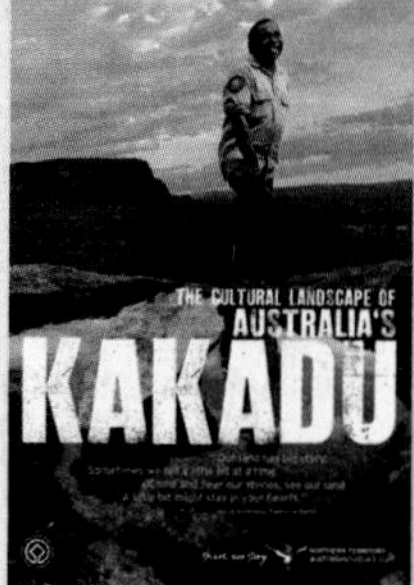

A country's natural economic resources can help build its economy through tourism. ***Choose a country and explain the economic resources or factors of production that make it a good vacation spot or site for opening a business.***

EXPLAIN

Visual Literacy

Small Business Owners and the Economy Caption Answer Read the figure caption question to students: ***How do small business owners use economic resources aside from entrepreneurship?*** They use natural resources to build products and stores, hire labor to work in their businesses, spend capital to start and operate businesses, etc. Then ask students: ***Do you think the kinds of economic resources used by small businesses are different from those used by large companies?*** Possible answer: No, because both require land, labor, capital, and entrepreneurship.

Critical Thinking

Ask students: ***Do you think labor or entrepreneurship is the more important economic resource?*** Possible answer: Both are equally important and necessary in order for an economy to meet the needs and wants of its people.

SCARCITY

Explain to students that scarcity is at the heart of how economic systems function. Ask the following questions to help students further understand economic scarcity.

Guiding Questions

List What are three economic resources that the United States possesses?	The United States has an educated labor force, a great deal of capital, an abundance of entrepreneurs, and many natural resources
Analyze Even in countries with great economic resources, not everyone's wants and needs are met. Why is this?	In all nations, regardless of wealth, economic resources are limited.

Reading Check Answer

Read the Reading Check question to students: ***What are the four economic resources?*** land, labor, capital, entrepreneurship

ELABORATE

Reinforce Vocabulary

Scarcity—Alternate Meanings Ask students what the word *scarcity* means to them. Possible answer: something that is hard to find or in short supply. Tell students that *scarcity* has a very specific meaning to economists: "the difference between wants and needs and available resources." Remind students that many words have specialized meanings when used in a particular discipline.

DIFFERENT TYPES OF ECONOMIC SYSTEMS

Read aloud the three basic questions nations must ask. Ask students: ***Does the order of these questions matter? Why or why not?*** Yes, because these questions build on one another. To further explore this topic, ask the following guiding questions.

Guiding Questions

Explain What determines who obtains available goods and services in a market economy?	whether people have money
Analyze Why do economists continue to categorize national economic systems even though all economies are actually blends?	Categorizing an economic system as "leaning toward a market economy," for example, helps economists make certain generalizations.
Judge Do you think it would be possible for a purely traditional economy to exist today? What do you think would be necessary for there to be such an economy?	Accept all reasonable answers. It might be possible, but the society would have to live separately from outside influences.

Visual Literacy

Tourism Contributes to an Economy
Read aloud the directions: ***Choose a country and explain the economic resources or factors of production that make it a good vacation spot or a good site for opening a business.*** Answers will vary depending on the country chosen, but students should name the specific economic resources that make the country a good vacation spot or a place that will support successful businesses.

Mini Projects

Differentiated Instruction

Logical Learners Bring in a collection of advertisements that tout an economic resource that a region possesses. Create a three-column table. Label the first column: "Economic Resource," the second column: "What Does Ad Say About this Resource," and the third column: "How Effective Is this Ad?" Have students complete the chart. Ask students: ***Do you think the type of economic resource affects how people respond to an ad? For example, is an ad that emphasizes a state's beautiful lakes going to appeal to people more strongly than one that emphasizes its strong telecommunications facilities?*** Sample answers: businesspeople often look for locations with specific infrastructural features instead of beautiful surroundings. Emphasize that advertisers promoting a region's economic resources must have a clear understanding of their target audience. Then, have students extend the chart by adding a column, labeled "Who Is the Target Audience for this Ad?"

Visual/Spatial Learners Organize students into small groups. Each group should pick a specific economic resource of your state. If necessary, encourage students to conduct research on the Internet or other appropriate sources to learn more about possible options. Students should then work together to create an advertisement emphasizing the importance of their chosen resource. Have students create a poster showing their ads. Students then present their ads to the class. Advertisements should explain to the reader the importance of a specific economic resource. The image should reinforce this message, perhaps by tying the resource to some symbol of the state, such as a historical landmark. When students evaluate one another's ads, encourage them to discuss whether the ad's message is clearly presented, and the audience is clearly defined.

Kinesthetic Learners With the class, create a list of three to five economic resources for your region. Divide students into three to five small groups. Designate one of the resources that the class identified to each group. Students will work together to create a skit promoting the benefits of their resource. Student groups should perform their skits to the class, school, or local community. Skits should include stage directions and props. The finished skits should show the economic benefits of that resource to the region and to your state.

Reading: Differentiated Instruction
Go to the Online Learning Center for a video clip in which an educator discusses elements of a differentiated classroom.

COMMAND ECONOMIES

A **command economy** is a system in which a country's government makes all economic decisions regarding what, how, and for whom goods and services will be produced and distributed. In this system, the government controls the factors of production and makes all decisions about their use. The government is responsible for answering the three basic economic questions.

1. What? One person (often a dictator) or a group of government officials (a central planning committee) decides what products are needed based on what they believe is important.
2. How? Since the government owns the means of production, it runs all businesses. It decides how goods and services will be produced. It controls all job opportunities and workers' benefits. In some cases, the government tells people where they will work and how much they will get paid.
3. For whom? The government decides who will receive what is produced. In principle, wealth is shared equally among all people to ensure that everyone's basic needs are met. The idea is that all people are equal and are offered the same opportunities. The government provides subsidies for housing and food, medical care, education, and jobs.

MIXED ECONOMIES

No economy is purely a traditional, market, or command economy. Every economy has influences that make it at least somewhat mixed. The United States is considered a mixed economy with leanings toward a market economy. In a pure market economy, there is no government interference at all. However, there is some government involvement in the U.S. economy through the laws and regulations that businesses must follow. There are also regulations to protect our food, air, and water supplies, and to protect consumers from unsafe products. There are labor laws that determine at what age people can start working, and the minimum wage they earn. The U.S. government provides social programs for those who need help, such as welfare and Medicaid for the poor and Medicare for the elderly.

The state of the economy in the United States is a divisive issue. Since it is a mixed economy, some people think it is too close to a pure market economy. Other people think it is too close to a command economy. This division was seen clearly as a result of the government's role in addressing the recession in the late 2000s.

Reading Check

Contrast How do a command economy and a market economy answer the three basic economic questions differently?

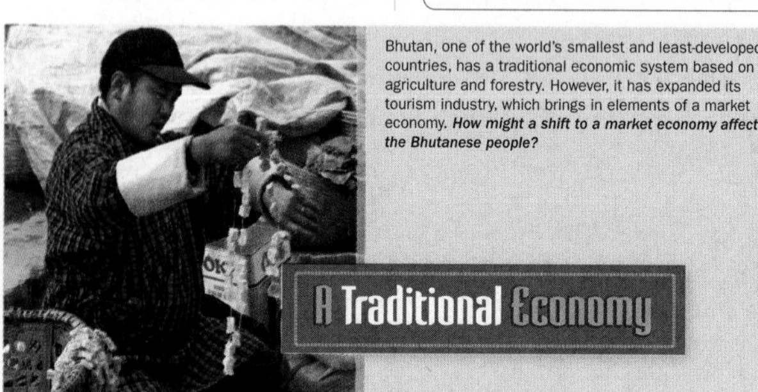

Bhutan, one of the world's smallest and least-developed countries, has a traditional economic system based on agriculture and forestry. However, it has expanded its tourism industry, which brings in elements of a market economy. ***How might a shift to a market economy affect the Bhutanese people?***

POLITICAL AND ECONOMIC PHILOSOPHIES

All economies in the world today are mixed. However, it is possible to distinguish between them. A meaningful economic classification depends on how much a government is involved with the free market. The three political philosophies that have shaped world economies are capitalism, communism, and socialism.

CAPITALISM

Capitalism is a political and economic philosophy characterized by marketplace competition and private ownership of businesses. It is the same as free enterprise or private enterprise. An advantage of capitalism is that successful employers and employees prosper.

CHARACTERISTICS OF A CAPITALIST COUNTRY

Government in a capitalist society is also concerned about its people and cares for those who cannot care for themselves. The number of social services, however, does not match that of a socialist country.

The government also has some involvement in the free market. The government has policies and laws that affect the market. It must keep a balance between regulating too much and too little.

POLITICAL FOUNDATIONS OF CAPITALISM

The political system most frequently associated with capitalism is democracy. Nations that practice democracy believe that political power should be in the hands of the people. There is usually more than one political party from which to choose representatives to run the government in a democratic country. People in a democracy are free to elect those candidates who agree with their philosophy on how the government and the economy should be run. The United States and Japan are two examples of countries that are classified as capitalist and have a democratic form of government.

COMMUNISM

Communism is a social, political, and economic philosophy in which the government, usually authoritarian, controls the factors of production. There is no private ownership of property or capital. The **theory** behind these practices is that goods owned in common (by the government representing the community as a whole) are available to a classless society on an as-needed basis. People are given jobs that fit their abilities. They are then given the goods that fit their needs.

CHARACTERISTICS OF A COMMUNIST COUNTRY

In a communist country all people who are able to work are assigned jobs. Theoretically, there is no unemployment. Employees who do not go to work continue to get paid under this system.

The government decides the type of schooling people will receive and also tells them where to live. Housing accommodations are assigned according to need. Food and housing subsidies keep prices low, so everyone has a place to live and food to eat. Medical care is free.

However, there is little or no economic freedom associated with communism. In this system there is no financial incentive for people to increase their productivity. People who would like to be entrepreneurs are not able to start their own businesses.

EXAMPLES OF COMMUNIST COUNTRIES

There are very few communist countries left in the world today. The economies of such countries have collapsed in recent years. The few countries that can still be classified as communist include Cuba and North Korea. China, which is still politically dominated by a communist party, is allowing more and more free enterprise practices. Vietnam and Laos are also following that path.

EXPLAIN

Reading Check Answer

Read the Reading Check question to students: ***How do a command economy and a market economy answer the three basic economic questions differently?*** (1) Command: Government decides what is produced; Market: Consumers decide. (2) Command: Government decides how goods and services will be produced; Market: Private businesses decide. (3) Command: Government decides who will receive what is produced; Market: People who have money can make purchases.

Visual Literacy

A Traditional Economy Caption Answer Read the figure caption question to students: ***How might a shift to a market economy affect the Bhutanese people?*** Companies from outside the country would be more likely to enter the marketplace, opening the Bhutanese people to a variety of external influences. Ask: ***What goods and services do you think would thrive in each economy?*** Possible answer: Traditional: foods and clothing related to religious celebrations; Market: appliances, more tools.

MIXED ECONOMIES

To help students better understand mixed economies, present the following guiding questions.

Guiding Questions

Recall What are some ways that the U.S. government is involved in the economy?	environmental regulations, labor laws, social programs
Analyze What groups of people do you think might want the United States economy to be closer to a pure market economy? Why?	Possible answer: Business people who are restricted by government regulations might think their businesses would be more successful without government regulations.
Judge Give an example of a labor law that you think would be appropriate for a government to make. Give an example of a labor law that you think would be overly restrictive.	Sample answer: Appropriate labor law: young children are not allowed to work. Overly restrictive labor law: labor unions can require all workers to join their union.

ELABORATE

Graphic Organizer

To help students understand how market economies answer the three economic questions, complete this cause-and-effect graphic organizer.

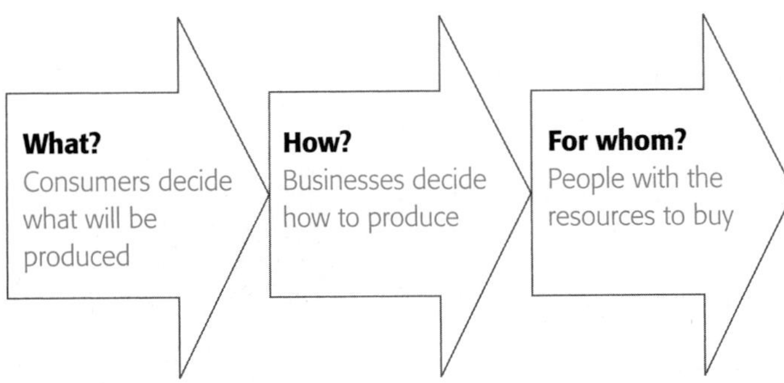

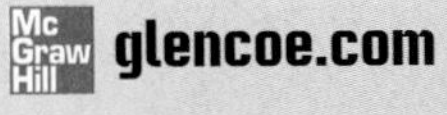 glencoe.com  iWB

Graphic Organizer Send students to the Online Learning Center to print this graphic organizer.

Reinforce Vocabulary

Command Economy—Connotative Meaning Read aloud the first sentence under the "Command Economies" heading. Explain that this is the word's denotation—its actual meaning. The term *command economy* also has a specific connotative meaning: "an economy that is strictly controlled."

PROFESSIONAL DEVELOPMENT **MINI CLIP**

ELL: Language Practice
Go to the Online Learning Center to view a video in which students of varying language proficiencies work together to review the content they have just read.

VIRTUAL BUSINESS

BUSINESS PLAN ANALYSIS

Introduce the concept of business plan analysis to students using Knowledge Matters' Virtual Business Retailing visual simulation, *Business Plan Analysis*. In this simulation, students will study business plans and explore the reasons for preparing a business plan.

POLITICAL AND ECONOMIC PHILOSOPHIES

Remind students of the basic types of economic systems. Tell students they will now learn about different types of political and economic philosophies. Ask these guiding questions to focus the discussion on these philosophies.

Guiding Questions

Recall What is the main factor that should be taken into account when classifying a nation's economy?	the extent to which the government is involved in the economy
Apply If you were a worker in a communist country, how do you think you would respond if you were required to work overtime without receiving any additional benefits?	Possible answer: Because there would be no additional economic reward for the overtime work, I would be resentful and try to avoid it if possible.
Analyze Why do democratic governments often lean toward capitalism?	Democracies believe political power should be in the hands of the people rather than the government.

Mini Projects

Differentiated Instruction

Interpersonal Learners Divide students into three groups. Assign each group one of the three economic systems. Tell each group to imagine that they are the leaders of a small developing nation. The nation has natural resources of fresh water and natural gas and its major agricultural products are corn, soybeans, and citrus fruits. Direct groups to use their economic systems to make decisions regarding what to produce and how to produce it. Have groups share their decisions with the class. Answers will vary. Students should adhere to the philosophies of their system in making decisions. In a market economy, consumers should decide what is produced from the available resources whereas in the command economy, the leaders decide.

Verbal/Linguistic Learners Tell students that the current idea of a communist state grew out of economic conditions in which great wealth and privilege was concentrated in the hands of very few people. Have students research the history of communism in one of these countries: China, North Korea, the former Soviet Union, or Cuba. They then should give an oral presentation on how that political or economic system differs or differed from the ideal. Presentations will vary, but should present specific ways in which the country's government fails/failed to reach the communist ideal.

The GREEN Marketer

Preventing Green Fatigue

Tired of ads about eco-friendly products? You may be suffering from green fatigue—confusion and skepticism caused by marketing claims about products' green benefits. Some of these claims are true. Others are examples of "greenwashing," or making a product sound more environmentally friendly than it really is. In response to the rising tide of greenwashing, the Federal Trade Commission has developed rules about environmental claims. All claims, whether specific or implied (suggested), must be backed by scientific evidence.

English Language Arts/Writing

Investigate Locate a product that makes a specific or implied environmental claim. Identify the scientific evidence the company offers, either on the packaging or on its Web site, to support the claim. Explain in one paragraph whether you think the claim is valid.

NCTE 7 Conduct research and gather, evaluate, and synthesize data to communicate discoveries.

glencoe.com

Get an activity on green marketing.

SOCIALISM

Socialism is a term that originally referred to a system on its way to the communist ideal of a classless society. Today, most countries that are defined as socialist have democratic political institutions. They differ from capitalist nations in the increased amount of government involvement in the economy. The main goal is to meet basic needs for all and to provide employment for many.

CHARACTERISTICS OF A SOCIALIST COUNTRY

Socialist countries tend to have more social services to ensure a certain standard of living for everyone. Medical care and education are free or inexpensive. These countries have systems for pensions and elderly care. Businesses and individuals pay much higher taxes than those in capitalist countries. These taxes contribute to financing government services.

EXAMPLES OF SOCIALIST COUNTRIES

The government runs key industries and makes economic decisions. State-controlled, noncompetitive companies are often found in industries such as telecommunications, natural resources (such as gas, water, and power), transportation, and banking. Canada, Germany, and Sweden are generally characterized as having socialist elements in their economies.

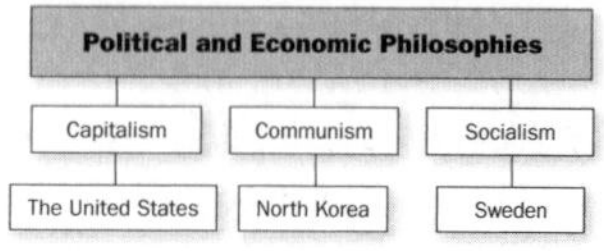

ECONOMIES IN TRANSITION

The breakup of the former Soviet Union provides a good example of societies making the change from command to market economies. For example, prior to the breakup, Poland owned approximately 80 percent of the country's productive assets. After the breakup it only owned 55 percent. Poland welcomed private investors that wanted to buy its state-run factories, which were inefficient and nonproductive. When governments sell their state-owned businesses, they are privatized. Most Eastern European countries that were once communist satellites moved toward global market economies and more democratic forms of government.

PRIVATIZATION VERSUS NATIONALIZATION

Privatization refers to the process of governments selling government-owned businesses to private individuals or businesses. This process generates much-needed revenue for the governments involved. It also demonstrates a high level of commitment to making the transition to a market system.

Countries that have socialist elements often have increasing costs for their national health care and retirement programs. In these cases, privatization can help them balance their budgets. For example, Great Britain sold its national phone company, national steel company, national sugar company, and several other national companies.

Another example of a company that used privatization is British Airways. Since its privatization in 1987, the company has been increasing exponentially and has become a very popular airline in Europe.

The opposite of privatization is nationalization. Nationalization occurs when the government takes over a privately-held company. The transfer of ownership may be due to an economic crisis, a political upheaval, or a change in government policy.

Consider Cuba for example. It is a communist country. In 1960, Cuba nationalized all foreign businesses. This means that Cuba no longer has companies from other countries that provide goods and services to Cubans.

MARKETING CASE STUDY

Retailing in a Shifting Economy

Beginning in 2008, there was a global recession. Industrialized countries around the world were committing money to bail out failing banks and instituting economic stimulus packages. In the United States, a 2008 tax rebate was issued to consumers ranging from $600 to $1,200. The Emergency Economic Stabilization Act of 2008 was enacted to shore up financial institutions' "troubled assets." The American Recovery and Reinvestment Act of 2009 was enacted to create jobs and increase consumer spending.

Businesses Respond to a Failing Economy

To increase business, some retailers offered consumers 10 percent more if they would buy a store gift card with their 2008 rebate check. A new consumer trend for careful spending started during the recession.

Dollar stores and warehouse food stores (e.g., Costco® and Walmart®) benefited, while traditional supermarkets and restaurants suffered. Shoppers were buying pasta and other foods to eat at home.

Businesses had to change their marketing strategies. For example, J. Crew® reduced its $118 ballet flats to $98. Starbucks® , known for its high-priced coffee, began offering a $3.95 deal that included a sandwich and coffee. High-end fashion apparel companies were selling more in their outlet stores than in high-end retail stores. As an alternative to costly car ownership, Hertz® created a car-sharing program. Users pay a membership fee and hourly or monthly rates when they rent an auto.

Math

Compute In 2008, the U.S. population was 304,059,724. That same year, 130,425,121 consumers received the rebate from the economic stimulus package. What percent of U.S. citizens received the rebate? Round your answer to the nearest tenth.

NCTM Number and Operations Compute fluently and make reasonable estimates.

EXPLAIN

The GREEN Marketer

English Language Arts/Writing Answer Paragraphs should have logical organization and refer to information obtained through investigation.

glencoe.com

Worksheet Activity Send students to the Online Learning Center to get a Green Marketer worksheet activity.

SOCIALISM

Ask students: ***What do you think of when you hear the word socialism?*** Possible answer: a society that provides a large number of social services such as free health care. Ask the following guiding questions to help students further understand socialism.

Guiding Questions

Recall What is the main goal of a socialist society?	The main goal is to meet the basic needs of all citizens and to provide employment for as many citizens as possible.
Analyze Why are taxes high in socialist countries?	Governments provide a large number of services.

ELABORATE

Graphic Organizer

To summarize the different political and economic philosophies, have the class work together to complete the diagram by listing the characteristics of each philosophy.

Political and Economic Philosophies

Capitalism	Communism	Socialism
• marketplace competition • private ownership of business • successful employers and employees prosper • some social services • some government regulations	• usually authoritarian • controls factors of production • assigned jobs • goods given according to need • no financial incentive to increase productivity	• more government involvement in economy and social services • tax rates high • government may run key industries • government makes many economic decisions

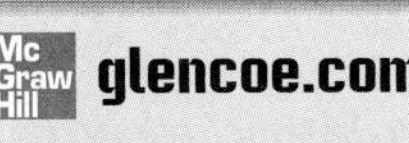

iWB

Graphic Organizer Send students to the Online Learning Center to print this graphic organizer.

ECONOMIES IN TRANSITION

To help students understand the complexities of economic transitions, present these guiding questions.

Guiding Questions

Describe How did ownership of Poland's productive assets change after the breakup of the Soviet Union?	Government ownership decreased by approximately 25%.
Generalize In today's world, do you think more nations are switching from command to market economies or from market to command economies? Why?	Countries are tending toward market economies; they appear to better meet the needs of the largest number of people.

Mini Project

Enrichment

Write a Letter to the Editor Tell students that they are citizens in a small country where a dictator has just been overthrown. Instruct students to write a letter to the editor of a local newspaper explaining what type of political system and economic system they would like their new country to have. Sample letter: I think we should have a democratic government in which we elect officials to represent us. For many years, we have been controlled by a dictator who made all the political and economic decisions. As we can see from the success of other democracies, sharing the power among all citizens is the best way to achieve fairness. We should gradually work toward having a free market as this is the best way to making sure the greatest number of people's needs are met. However, we also should institute safeguards to protect those people, such as the handicapped and elderly, who are unable to take care of themselves.

PRIVATIZATION VERSUS NATIONALIZATION

Explain to students that a private company is one that is not owned by the government. To help students understand the differences between privatization and nationalization, ask the following questions.

Guiding Questions

Recall What happened to foreign businesses in Cuba in 1960?	Foreign businesses were nationalized; the government owned these businesses.
Defend In which of these cases do you think a country's citizens want a company to nationalize? (1) The industry is ignoring government regulations regarding environmental safeguards; (2) there is no competition, so consumers feel over charged.	Sample answer: I think citizens would be more upset about overly high prices because the money comes directly out of their pockets.

MARKETING CASE STUDY

Math Answer 30%

Natural Economic Resources

Countries with the right mix of sun and fertile ground have many farms. In the United States, California's natural resources are perfect for farming fruits, vegetables, nuts, and grapes. ***How do your state's economic resources benefit its economy?***

BIGGER, BETTER BERRIES.

Recognized Worldwide For Superior Berries.

Grown under the golden California sun, Well-Pict berries grow big as all outdoors thanks to the fertile valleys and cool coastal breezes our West Coast fields offer all year round. Known around the globe for their bigger-than-life taste, color and aroma. Well-Pict's sizeable flavor is unmatched in the industry. Just one bite, and your customers are sure to leave their heart with Well-Pict.

WELL-PICT BERRIES

www.wellpict.com USA 831-722-3871

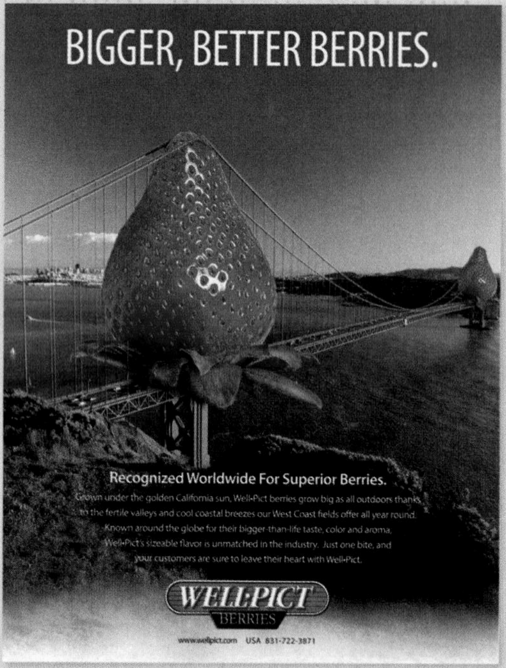

In 2008 Hugo Chavez, the President of Venezuela, nationalized foreign oil companies. He has also nationalized telephone, electricity, steel, and cement companies during his reign. Chavez uses the revenue generated from these companies to support government-sponsored programs for his people.

DEVELOPING ECONOMIES

Developing economies are mostly poor countries with little industrialization. They are trying to become more prosperous and develop their infrastructure. Much of their success depends on improving the education levels of their labor force. Directing and using foreign investments efficiently will also contribute to their success.

Chad, a country in central Africa, is a good example of a developing economy. It is a traditional economy based on agriculture and livestock farming. Cotton, cattle, and gum arabic are its primary exports. However, with an oil field and pipeline project paid for by foreign investors, Chad has begun to develop its oil reserves for export. This investment will help generate much-needed funds for this poor nation to use to improve its infrastructure and develop its labor resources.

After You Read | **Section 3.1**

Review Key Concepts

1. **Define** *economy* and explain the three questions it seeks to answer.
2. **Explain** the relationship between economic resources and the concept of scarcity.
3. **Compare and contrast** privatization and nationalization. Which political and economic philosophy would most likely be prevalent when a country decides on privatization? On nationalization? Explain.

Practice Academics

English Language Arts

4. Write a paragraph to explain and provide examples of why most economies are considered mixed economies.

Mathematics

5. In socialist countries taxes are higher than in capitalist countries. If income taxes were 33 percent of a person's income in a capitalist country and 55 percent in a socialist country, how much more disposable income would a person have in a capitalist country when compared to a socialist country if their respective incomes were $150,000 a year?

Math Concept **Ways of Representing Numbers** A decrease in a number can be represented by a percent less than 100.

Starting Hints Subtract the lower percentage from the higher percentage to determine the difference in percent of disposable income (33 percent from 55 percent). Convert the resulting percentages to decimals by moving the decimal point two places to the left. Multiply that decimal number by $150,000 (annual income) to determine the additional disposable income a person would have in a capitalistic system.

For help, go to the **Math Skills Handbook** located at the back of this book.

NCTE 3 Apply strategies to interpret texts.

NCTM Number and Operations Understand numbers, ways of representing numbers, relationships among numbers, and number systems.

glencoe.com Check your answers.

ELABORATE

Visual Literacy

Natural Economic Resources Caption Answer Read the caption question: ***How do your state's economic resources benefit its economy?*** Sample answer: New Jersey is called the Garden State because its farmland provides large quantities of fruit and vegetables. These economic resources provide citizens with employment and government income from taxes. Ask students for examples of how these economic resources benefit their local communities and possibly their own families. Sample answer: If a region's paper mills draw workers, local businesses thrive when they are patronized by these workers.

Graphic Organizer

Display this T-chart. Ask: ***How do these two economic resources compare?*** Sample answers:

Labor	Entrepreneurship
requires people	requires people
refers to work	refers to skills
workforce is economic resource	ideas are economic resource

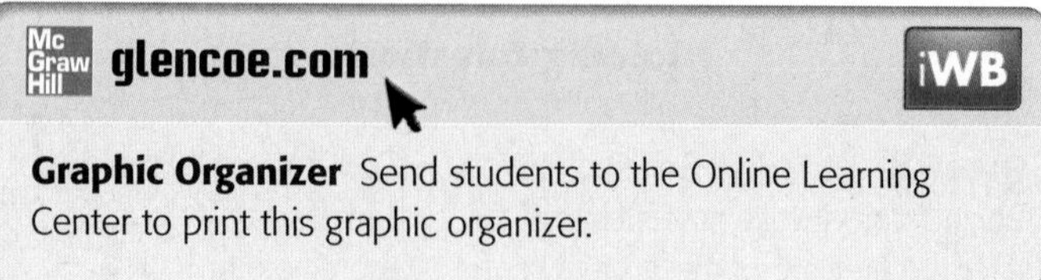

EVALUATE

Mini Project

Extension

Prepare a Presentation on German Reunification Explain that East Germany, founded in 1949, experienced more than four decades under a Soviet Union-imposed command economy. East Germany's standard of living, technology, and productivity fell far behind that of its western counterparts. When it was reunified with West Germany in 1990, it faced many challenges in trying to catch up with other democracies. Have students work in groups of three or four to research these challenges. Each group should then prepare a presentation on the challenges faced by Germany upon reunification. In their presentations, students should discuss challenges faced by the reunified Germany in helping the eastern portion catch up with other European democracies. Challenges included: Unemployment became much higher than in western Germany, and the needs of eastern Germany's economy weighed down the western portion. A significant portion of western Germany's gross domestic product continues to be transferred to the east each year, which is a massive drain on the nation's economy.

PROFESSIONAL DEVELOPMENT **MINI CLIP**

Reading: Flexible Grouping
Go to the Online Learning Center to view a video in which teachers use flexible groupings and partner-sharing to encourage and promote discussion.

Critical Thinking

Ask students: ***Why do you think the United States government chose to give a tax rebate to consumers in 2008 and then later enact the American Recovery and Reinvestment Act of 2009? What might have happened if these actions had been taken in reverse order?*** The tax rebate was enacted first because officials believed this was a better method of quickly getting additional money into the economy. The 2009 act involved the creation of new jobs, which is seen as a more long-term method of pumping money into the economy.

After You Read — Section 3.1

Review Key Concepts

1. An economy is the organized way a nation provides for the needs and wants of its people. Three questions are: (1) What goods and services should be produced? (2) How should goods and services be produced? (3) For whom should goods and services be produced?
2. The difference between wants and needs of a country's people and available economic resources is scarcity. Economic resources are all the things used in producing goods and services. They include land, labor capital, and entrepreneurship. A nation must choose how to use those resources to produce and distribute the goods and services for its people. Countries have varying amounts of resources. Some have fertile land for farming, but limited capital. Others may have limited natural resources, but they compensate with a highly educated labor force.
3. Privatization is when a country sells its state-run businesses. Nationalization occurs when a government takes over a privately-held company. Privatization would be more prevalent in a country moving toward a capitalistic philosophy. Nationalization would be more prevalent in a country moving toward a communistic philosophy.

Practice Academics

English Language Arts

4. All economies are mixed. No economic system is purely traditional, market, or command. Some countries allow the marketplace to decide what will be produced by consumers' purchases. There are government regulations to protect people. Businesses must adhere to safety and environmental concerns. Some countries provide socialist benefits such as Medicare and Medicaid in the United States.

Mathematics

5. \$33,000 more spending money in a capitalistic country. (55 percent − 33 percent = 22 percent. \$150,000 × 0.22 = \$33,000).

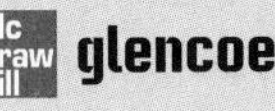

glencoe.com

Answer Key Send students to the Online Learning Center to check their answers.

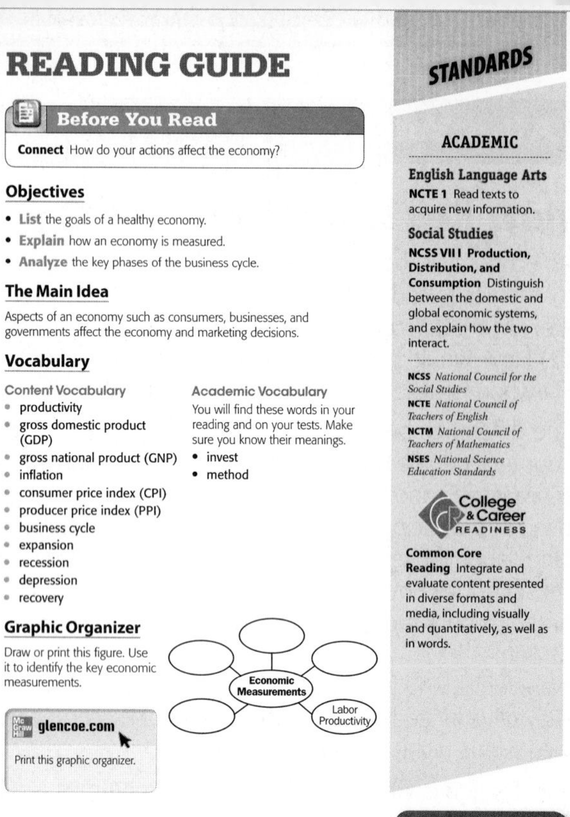

READING GUIDE

Before You Read

Connect How do your actions affect the economy?

Objectives

- **List** the goals of a healthy economy.
- **Explain** how an economy is measured.
- **Analyze** the key phases of the business cycle.

The Main Idea

Aspects of an economy such as consumers, businesses, and governments affect the economy and marketing decisions.

Vocabulary

Content Vocabulary
- productivity
- gross domestic product (GDP)
- gross national product (GNP)
- inflation
- consumer price index (CPI)
- producer price index (PPI)
- business cycle
- expansion
- recession
- depression
- recovery

Academic Vocabulary

You will find these words in your reading and on your tests. Make sure you know their meanings.
- invest
- method

Graphic Organizer

Draw or print this figure. Use it to identify the key economic measurements.

Economic Measurements
Labor Productivity

glencoe.com

Print this graphic organizer.

STANDARDS

ACADEMIC

English Language Arts

NCTE 1 Read texts to acquire new information.

Social Studies

NCSS VIII Production, Distribution, and Consumption Distinguish between the domestic and global economic systems, and explain how the two interact.

NCSS *National Council for the Social Studies*
NCTE *National Council of Teachers of English*
NCTM *National Council of Teachers of Mathematics*
NSES *National Science Education Standards*

College & Career READINESS

Common Core
Reading Integrate and evaluate content presented in diverse formats and media, including visually and quantitatively, as well as in words.

MARKETING CORE FUNCTION

Market Planning

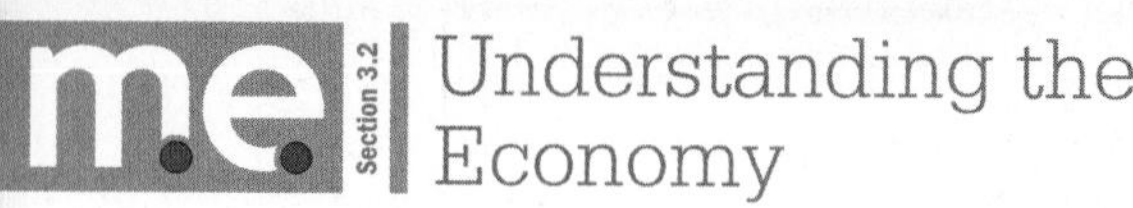

THE ECONOMY AND MARKETING

An understanding of how to measure an economy and what factors contribute to economic strength or weakness is essential. It is only then that you can appreciate how the economy, consumers, businesses, and government influence each other.

As You Read

Evaluate What effect do your actions have on the economy?

GOALS OF A HEALTHY ECONOMY

A healthy economy has three goals: increase productivity, decrease unemployment, and maintain stable prices. All nations analyze their economies to keep track of how well they are meeting these goals. This analysis allows businesses, consumers, and governments to make appropriate economic decisions.

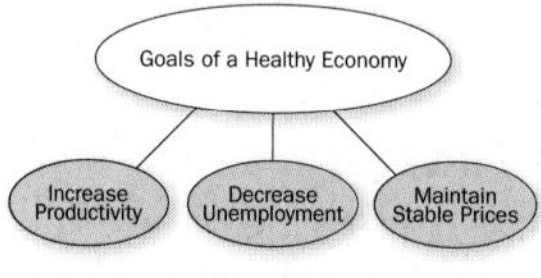

ECONOMIC MEASUREMENTS

Accurate information about an economy is essential to determining whether it is meeting its goals. The key economic measurements that nations routinely use to analyze their economic strength are labor productivity, gross domestic product, standard of living, inflation rate, and unemployment rate.

LABOR PRODUCTIVITY

Productivity is output per worker hour that is measured over a defined period of time, such as a week, month, or year. Businesses can increase their productivity in a number of ways. They can **invest** in new equipment or facilities that allow their employees to work more efficiently. Providing additional training or financial incentives can also boost staff productivity. Businesses can also reduce their work force and increase the responsibilities of the workers who remain. This makes an organization more financially efficient and more effective. Higher productivity improves a company's profit.

> "If you want to perform a useful SWOT analysis, you need to consider the economic measures that will influence your market planning."

Specialization and division of labor are key concepts related to increasing productivity. An assembly line is an example of specialization and division of labor whereby each part of a finished product is completed by a person who specializes in one aspect of its manufacturing. The theory behind this **method** of production is that the work can be completed faster and more efficiently when people specialize in certain areas. This method also makes it easier for companies to identify issues with their products. They know where and how each part of the product is made. They can use this information to find out what went wrong when the product was made.

ENGAGE

Anticipation Activity

Ask students: ***Do you think the economy in the United States today is healthy?*** Answers will vary depending on students' individual perceptions, which may relate to their own personal economic situations or may reflect the reality of the national economic situation. Possible answers: The economy is bad because it is hard to find a job in my town and people are not spending as much money as they used to spend. The economy is good because new businesses are opening and lots of people seem to have money to spend.

Objectives

- **List** the goals of a healthy economy. increase productivity, decrease unemployment, maintain prices
- **Explain** how an economy is measured. labor productivity, gross domestic product, gross national product, standard of living, inflation rate, unemployment rate
- **Analyze** the key phases of the business cycle. expansion, recession, trough, recovery

Graphic Organizer

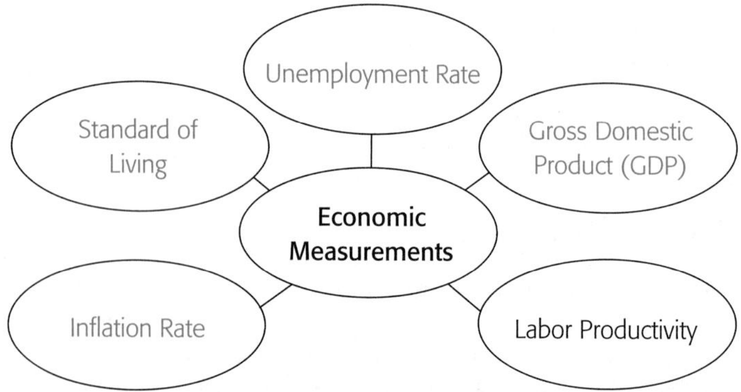

glencoe.com

Graphic Organizer Send students to the Online Learning Center to print this graphic organizer.

EXPLORE

Before You Read

Read the Before You Read question aloud: ***How do your actions affect the economy?*** Possible answer: I recently bought an old truck, but gas and repairs are expensive. I have had to reduce the amount I spend.

Preteaching Vocabulary

Have students go to the Online Learning Center at glencoe.com for the Chapter 3 Preteaching Vocabulary games.

Content Vocabulary

Write the following content vocabulary words on the board: *gross domestic product, gross national product, consumer price index, producer price index.* Ask students: ***What is an acronym?*** An acronym is a term formed from the initial letters of a name or term. Then ask: ***What are the acronyms for each of these terms?*** GDP, GNP, CPI, PPI

Academic Vocabulary

Invest—Denotative Meaning Write the word *invest* on the board. Explain that one meaning of the word *invest* is: "to commit money or other resources to gain a financial return." Ask: ***Why is investing vital to a market economy?*** Businesses require economic resources to grow and thrive.

Graphic Organizer

Have students give examples of the three goals of a healthy economy.

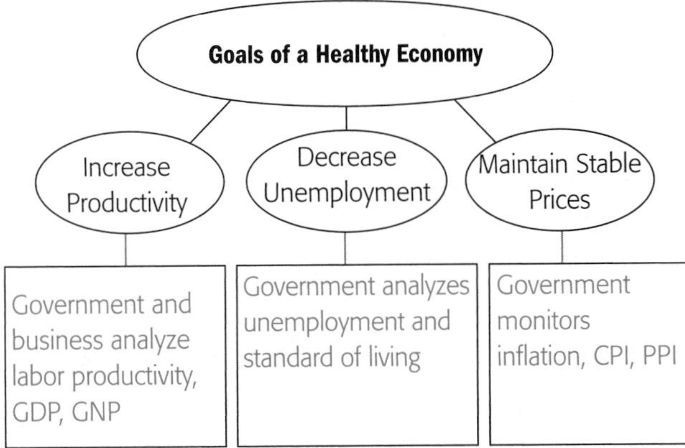

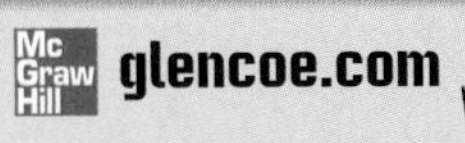

Graphic Organizer Send students to the Online Learning Center to print this graphic organizer.

THE ECONOMY AND MARKETING

Ask these guiding questions to help students understand the importance of having a productive workforce.

Guiding Questions

Recall What are two ways a business can increase its efficiency?	invest in new facilities, provide additional training or financial incentives, reduce work force; increase responsibilities of remaining workers
Apply Give an example of how specialization can improve efficiency.	Possible answer: Many dentists employ dental hygienists, freeing the dentist to perform other work.

As You Read

Read students the As You Read question: ***What effect do your actions have on the economy?*** Possible answer: The kinds of goods and services I purchase, whether or not I work, how productive I am at work, whether I drive, take public transportation, ride a bike—all affect the economy. Then ask: ***Do you think businesses respond to the ways in which you and your friends spend your money? Why or why not?*** Possible answer: Yes, because they make the clothing styles we like available to buy.

Expert Advice

Read the quote to students:

> **"If you want to perform a useful SWOT analysis, you need to consider the economic measures that will influence your market planning."**

Remind students that a SWOT analysis involves looking at both internal strengths and weaknesses and external opportunities and threats. Ask: ***Which of the economic measures might influence a SWOT analysis? How?*** If a home electronics business sees that the unemployment rate is increasing, it might conclude that the demand for high-end home entertainment centers, might decrease.

GROSS DOMESTIC PRODUCT

Most governments study productivity by keeping track of an entire nation's production output. Today the principal way of measuring that output in the United States is gross domestic product. **Gross domestic product (GDP)** is the output of goods and services produced by labor and property located within a country. The U.S. Bureau of Economic Analysis publishes a report on the United States' GDP.

The GDP is made up of private investment, government spending, personal spending, net exports of goods and services, and change in business inventories (see **Figure 3.1**). Private investment includes spending by businesses for things like equipment and software. It also includes home construction. Government spending includes money spent by local, state, and federal governments. This money is spent on social services and also construction projects. Personal spending includes all the money consumers spend on goods and services for their own use.

Expanding inventories show that businesses are producing goods that are being stored in their warehouses—that adds to the GDP. Inventories that are shrinking indicate that people are buying more than what was actually produced, so you subtract that figure from the GDP.

As a review, here is the calculation for GDP: Add private investment, government spending, and personal spending. Then either add a trade surplus or subtract a trade deficit. After that, add expanding inventories or subtract shrinking inventories.

Since 1991, the United States has been using GDP as its primary measurement of productivity. Before 1991, it used a measurement called gross national product. **Gross national product (GNP)** is the total dollar value of goods and services produced by a nation, including goods and services produced abroad by U.S. citizens and companies. There is a significant difference between GNP and GDP. The GNP counts the country responsible for production. With GDP, the country where the production takes place is more important.

FIGURE 3.1 Gross Domestic Product

Here is a look at what makes up the United States' GDP. These numbers do not add up to 100% because two items shrink the economy's total production. When we import more than we export, the resulting trade deficit is subtracted from the GDP. Expanding inventories add to the GDP. Shrinking inventories subtract from the GDP. ***Of what significance is GDP when evaluating the health of a country's economy?***

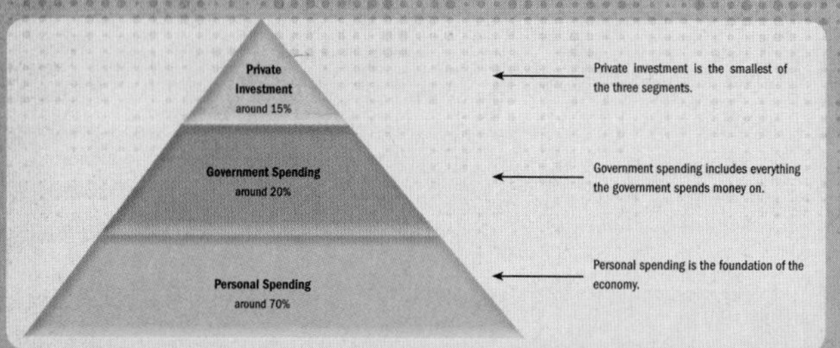

Private Investment around 15%
Government Spending around 20%
Personal Spending around 70%
Private investment is the smallest of the three segments.
Government spending includes everything the government spends money on.
Personal spending is the foundation of the economy.

What Is Produced Where

BMW®, a German car manufacturer, produces cars in Germany that are exported and sold in the United States. BMW has also built factories in North America. ***If you buy a car manufactured by BMW in South Carolina, is this car part of the U.S. GDP? Is the same car also part of the U.S. GNP?***

For example, Ford® is a U.S. corporation. It has a plant in England that produces cars. The portion of Ford's production that occurs in England is included in the U.S. GNP, but not in its GDP. The portion of Ford's production that occurs in England is part of England's GDP, but not its GNP.

STANDARD OF LIVING

A country's standard of living is a measurement of the amount and quality of goods and services that a nation's people have. It is a number that reflects their quality of life. To calculate the standard of living, you divide the GDP or GNP of a country by its population. This calculation gives you the amount of GDP or GNP per person. (Rates measured per person are also known as per capita measurements.) Most industrialized nations enjoy a high standard of living because they have a high level of production.

Some marketers also look at additional factors to get a broader picture of a nation's standard of living. Some countries provide more social services for their citizens. Social benefits, such as free education and health care provided by the government, may be reviewed. The number of households per 1,000 inhabitants with durable goods, such as washing machines, refrigerators, dishwashers, and autos, can be included in the analysis. High levels of social services and durable goods mean that a country has a high standard of living.

INFLATION RATE

Inflation refers to rising prices. A low inflation rate (1 to 5 percent each year) is good because it shows that an economy is stable. Double-digit inflation (10 percent or higher) hurts an economy. When inflation is that high, money loses its value. The period from the mid-1960s to the early 1980s was a highly inflationary period. Prices tripled in the United States during that time. People who live on a fixed income such as a monthly Social Security check are especially hurt by high inflation.

Controlling inflation is one of a government's major goals. When inflation starts to go up, many governments raise interest rates to discourage borrowing money. The result is slower economic growth, which helps to bring inflation down. Two measures of inflation used in the United States are the consumer price index and the producer price index. The **consumer price index (CPI)** measures the change in price over a period of time of 400 specific retail goods and services used by the average urban household. It is also called the cost of living index. Food, housing, utilities, transportation, and medical care are a few of its components. The CPI excludes food and energy prices, which tend to be unpredictable. The **producer price index (PPI)** measures wholesale price levels in the economy. Producer prices generally get passed along to the consumer. When there is a drop in the PPI, it is generally followed by a drop in the CPI.

EXPLAIN

GROSS DOMESTIC PRODUCT

The GDP is our nation's best measurement of total production output. Ask the following questions to focus the discussion of GDP.

Guiding Questions

Identify What government agency is responsible for reporting the U.S. GDP?	U.S. Bureau of Economic Analysis
Interpret A year ago, a company had $55 million of goods in its warehouses; today it has $58 million. What does this change indicate and how does it affect the GDP?	It indicates that the company is producing more goods than consumers are buying. This will cause an increase in the GDP.
Validate Why do you think the United States government switched from using the GNP to the GDP?	Possible answer: the GDP is a more accurate reflection of what is produced in the U.S. and is a better indicator of the economy's health

Reinforce Vocabulary

Inflation—Analogies Read the sentence at the beginning of the Inflation Rate section: ***Inflation refers to rising prices.*** Ask: ***How is economic inflation similar to inflating a balloon?*** In both cases, sizes are increasing. Discuss that making analogies between economic terms and real-world objects can help you remember the terms and their meaning.

Visual Literacy

Figure 3.1 Caption Answer Read the caption question to students: ***Of what significance is GDP when evaluating the health of a country's economy?*** GDP helps evaluate a country's economy by providing insight into government involvement, private investment, and consumer confidence by showing the percent of the GDP contributed by each one. It helps in gauging the health of the economy by indicating whether it is growing or shrinking.

ELABORATE

Graphic Organizer

Have students fill in the graphic organizer with examples of the three types of goods and services that make up the GDP.

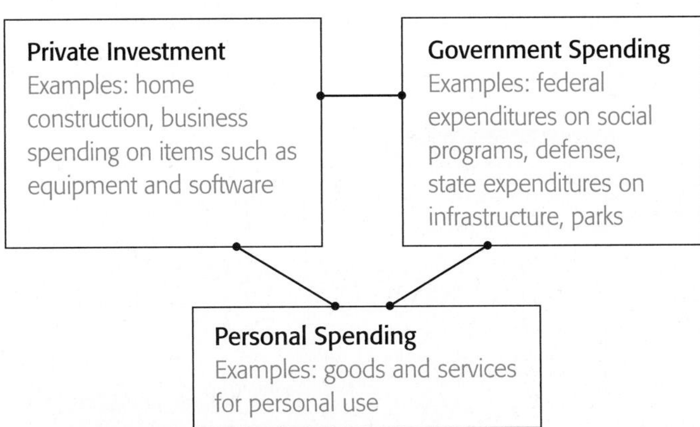

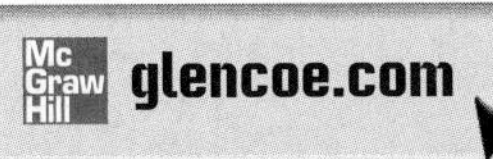

Examples: federal expenditures on social programs, defense, state expenditures on infrastructure, parks

iWB

Have students go to the Online Learning Center to print this graphic organizer.

STANDARD OF LIVING

Ask: ***What does a country's standard of living measure?*** Possible answers: It is a measurement of the amount and quality of goods and services that a nation's people have. Use the following guiding questions to explore this topic.

Guiding Questions

Recall How is a nation's standard of living calculated?	One method is to divide the GDP by the population.
Draw Conclusions Do you think a nation's GDP would positively or negatively correlate with its standard of living? Why?	In general, it would positively correlate because when a nation produces more, its workers' purchasing ability rises.

Visual Literacy

What Is Produced Where Caption Answer Read the caption question to students: ***If you buy a car manufactured by BMW® in South Carolina, is this car part of the U.S. GDP? Is the same car also part of the U.S. GNP?*** It would be part of the GDP, but not the GNP.

INFLATION RATE

Ask: ***What are some things that affect the quality of your life?*** Possible answers: amount of money I have to spend, my home, my friends. Use the following guiding questions to explore this topic.

Define In your own words, give the definition for *inflation.*	Possible answer: Inflation refers to an increase.
Explain Why does the government try to discourage borrowing money?	Possible answer: The government controls inflation by raising the interest rate. This slows the economic growth and may help to bring inflation down.
Analyze When wholesale price levels decline, what happens to the cost of living index?	Possible answer: The cost of living index, also known as the CPI, will realize a drop in retail goods and services when wholesale prices, measured by the PPI, drop.

Graphic Organizer

To help students compare the consumer price index (CPI) and the producer price index (PPI), display this Venn diagram. Ask students: ***How do these two economic measures compare?*** Possible answers:

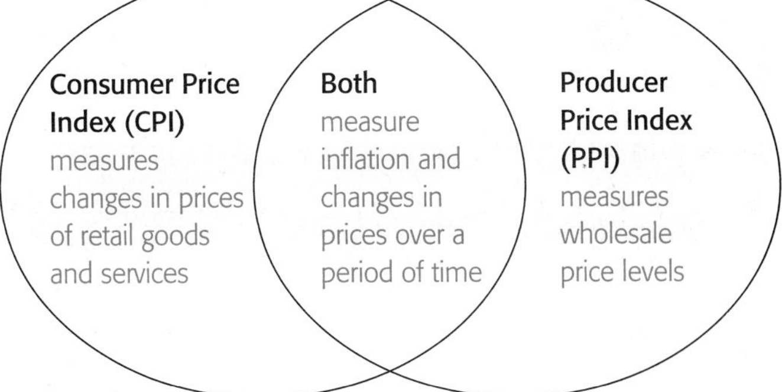

Consumer Price Index (CPI)
measures changes in prices of retail goods and services
Both
measure inflation and changes in prices over a period of time
Producer Price Index (PPI)
measures wholesale price levels

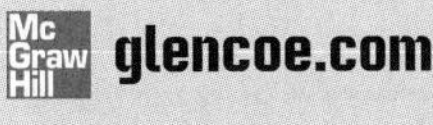

Have students go to the Online Learning Center to print this graphic organizer.

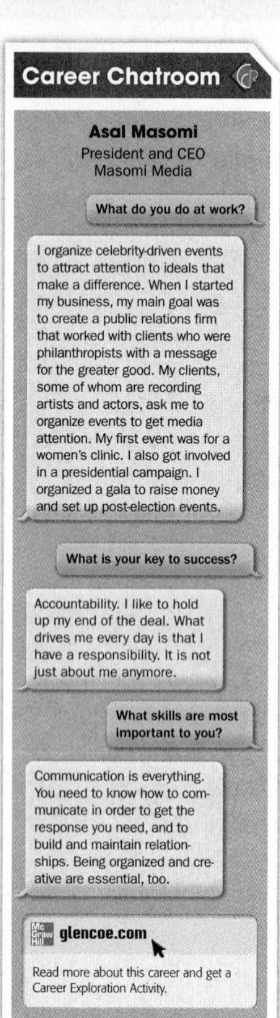

Career Chatroom
Asal Masomi
President and CEO
Masomi Media
What do you do at work?
I organize celebrity-driven events to attract attention to ideals that make a difference. When I started my business, my main goal was to create a public relations firm that worked with clients who were philanthropists with a message for the greater good. My clients, some of whom are recording artists and actors, ask me to organize events to get media attention. My first event was for a women's clinic. I also got involved in a presidential campaign. I organized a gala to raise money and set up post-election events.
What is your key to success?
Accountability. I like to hold up my end of the deal. What drives me every day is that I have a responsibility. It is not just about me anymore.
What skills are most important to you?
Communication is everything. You need to know how to communicate in order to get the response you need, and to build and maintain relationships. Being organized and creative are essential, too.
glencoe.com
Read more about this career and get a Career Exploration Activity.

UNEMPLOYMENT RATE

All nations chart unemployment, or jobless rates. The higher the unemployment rate, the greater the chances are of slow economic times. The lower the unemployment rate, the greater the chances are of an economic expansion. This is true because when more people work, there are more people spending money and paying taxes. Businesses and government both take in more money. The government does not have to provide as many social services.

HOT TOPIC **Unemployment** High unemployment does not always mean that there are no jobs available. Rather, many workers may not be qualified for the jobs that are available.

OTHER ECONOMIC INDICATORS AND TRENDS

The Conference Board provides additional indicators to help economists evaluate the performance of the U.S. economy. The Conference Board is a private business research organization that is made up of businesses and individuals who work together to assess the state of the economy. Three Conference Board indicators are the consumer confidence index, the consumer expectations index, and the jobs index. The jobs index measures consumers' perceptions regarding the number of jobs available. Consumers are polled to see how they feel about personal finance, economic conditions, and buying conditions. Retail sales are studied to see whether consumer confidence polls match consumer actions in the marketplace. Along those same lines, the rate of housing starts is reviewed, as are sales of trucks and autos. These are big purchases that tend to be affected by the economy and interest rates.

Wages and new payroll jobs provide additional information about the strength of the economy at any given point in time. When everyone is employed, supply and demand theory predicts that wages should increase due to the shortage of workers. Economists study these factors, because they may affect inflation and other economic indicators.

Reading Check

Identify What are the key economic measurements?

THE BUSINESS CYCLE

History shows that sometimes an economy grows, which is called expansion, and at other times it slows down, which is called contraction. These recurring changes in economic activity are called the **business cycle** (see **Figure 3.2**). The business cycle includes the following key phases: expansion, recession, trough, and recovery. After recovery, expansion begins again.

Expansion is a time when the economy is flourishing. It is sometimes referred to as a period of prosperity. Across the nation, there is low unemployment. More goods and services are produced and purchased. Consumers spend a lot of money that fuels the economy. An expansion is a good time for new businesses to start up or expand their operations. Expansion continues until it reaches a peak. A peak signifies the end of expansion and the beginning of a recession.

A **recession** is a period of economic slowdown that lasts for at least two quarters of a year, or six months. Financial experts call periods of three months "quarters." The National Bureau of Economic Research (NBER) defines a recession as a significant decline in activity spread across the economy. To be considered a recession, this decline must last more than a few months.

During a recession, companies reduce their workforces and consumers have less money to spend. A reduced workforce results in higher unemployment. When more consumers are out of work, they have less money to spend. Since consumers are spending less, producers respond by making fewer goods and services. Companies cut back on research and development (R&D) of new products. Future plans for expanding business operations are generally put on hold.

FIGURE 3.2 The Four Key Phases of the Cycle

Throughout history, economies have followed a pattern of expansion and contraction called the business cycle. There are four phases in the business cycle: expansion (ended by a peak), recession, trough, and recovery. The length and intensity of each of the phases depends on many factors such as wars, natural disasters, and industrial innovation. ***In which phase is the United States today?***

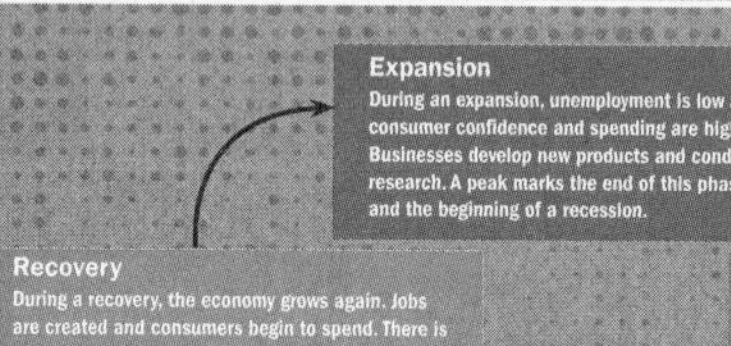

74 | Unit 2 · Economics

Chapter 3 · Political and Economic Analysis | 75

EXPLAIN

Career Chatroom

Explain What does Masomi mean by the term *accountability?*	To be responsible and hold up your end of any deals.
Infer How do you think Masomi feels about his clients? On what do you base your opinion?	He wants to work with "philanthropists for the greater good." He feels these people are concerned about others.
Evaluate Do you agree with Masomi's statement that "Communication is everything"? Why or why not?	Without communication, you cannot maintain relationships and achieve goals; being organized is essential.

glencoe.com

Career Exploration Send students to the Online Learning Center to read more about this career and to get a Career Exploration Activity.

HOT TOPIC **Unemployment** Ask students: ***Based on this information, what can you do to reduce your chances of being unemployed at times when unemployment rates are high?***

Reading Check Answer

Read the Reading Check question to students: ***What are the key economic measurements?*** gross domestic product (GDP), standard of living, consumer price index (CPI), producer price index (PPI), unemployment rate Provide students with scenarios in which they must identify the proper indicator. Ask students: ***What indicator would you use to determine if employers were hiring more workers?*** unemployment rate

ELABORATE

THE BUSINESS CYCLE

Ask students: ***What is an example of a cycle in nature?*** Possible answers: seasons of the year, water cycle Ask students the following questions to focus discussion on the business cycle.

Guiding Questions

List What are three words or phrases you might associate with the expansion phase of the business cycle?	Possible answers: growth, wealth, new jobs, increased spending
Draw Conclusions Why is a circular structure used to illustrate the business cycle?	It behaves in a circular fashion, without end.
Elaborate Why do you think the lowest point of the business cycle is called the "trough"?	A narrow channel or depression is often referred to as a trough; the business cycle's trough is similar to such a depression.

Reinforce Vocabulary

Expansion—Word Origins Explain that *expansion* is a form of the word *expand*, which comes from the Latin *expandere*, which means "to spread." Read this sentence from the textbook: ***Expansion is a time when the economy is flourishing***. Ask: ***What does the word flourishing mean in this context?*** doing well, growing, expanding

Visual Literacy

Figure 3.2 Caption Answer Read the question to students: ***In which phase is the United States today?*** Accept all reasonable answers as long as the student provides rationale backed up with information about current economic indicators. Ask students: ***How can the current phase of the business cycle best be determined?*** Possible answer: The current phase can best be determined through researching economic indicators. Generally, it is not until the beginning of the next phase that economists determine the last phase.

MINI CLIP

Reading: Guided Instruction
Go to the Online Learning Center to view a video in which a teacher helps students identify major and minor details.

e MARKETING

Online Government

Online government refers to all the Web sites available in federal, state, and local governments. All prominent agencies in the federal government have Web sites. If you do a search you can recognize a government Web site by its address, which ends in .gov. You can access an enormous amount of useful information regarding laws, rulings, and the economy from government sources. As a case in point, a new CARD Act legislation has had an impact on stores that sell gift cards. There are new regulations regarding fees and expiration dates. Businesses that offer general purpose reloadable prepaid cards (i.e. from Visa® or MasterCard®) are not included in that legislation, so they are targeting gift card customers; especially parents of teens. Parents also like the idea of a prepaid card for use in an emergency and as a replacement for carrying money.

Innovate and Create

Have students select a government Web site that has information of interest to a business owner. Have students work in groups to select pertinent information to target customers with a new ad message that would be beneficial to a specific business. Accept all reasonable ad messages as long as they are connected to research conducted on a government Web site. For example, students may elect to visit the Consumer Product Safety Commission's Web site to find products that have been recalled by a competitor. They can use that information to create an ad message that addresses the safety of their product.

glencoe.com

eMarketing Worksheet Activity Send students to the Online Learning Center to download an eMarketing worksheet activity.

Recessions can end relatively quickly or last for a long time. According to the NBER, a recession begins immediately after the economy reaches a peak of activity. It ends as the economy reaches its trough. A trough is when the economy reaches the lowest point in a recession. After this point is reached, economic activity begins to rise. The NBER studies indicators in the economy to determine the start of a recession. However, it is not always easy to identify when an economy has moved out of the trough.

A **depression** is a period of prolonged recession. During a depression, it becomes nearly impossible to find a job, and many businesses are forced to shut down. During a depression, consumer spending is very low, unemployment is very high, and production of goods and services is down significantly. Poverty results because so many people are out of work and cannot afford to buy food, clothing, or shelter. The Great Depression of the early 1930s best illustrates this aspect of the business cycle.

Recovery is the term that signifies a period of renewed economic growth following a recession or depression. This is where the cycle begins again with economic expansion. The GDP begins to increase. During this stage, business picks up, people find jobs, and the demand for goods increases. As more goods are needed, production increases. Businesses begin to grow and hire new employees. As jobs increase, consumers have more money to spend, furthering recovery with an upward economic climb. Recovery is characterized by reduced unemployment, increased consumer spending, and moderate expansion by businesses. Periods of recovery differ in length and strength.

FACTORS THAT AFFECT BUSINESS CYCLES

Business cycles are affected by the actions of businesses, consumers, and the government. In turn, businesses, consumers, and the government are affected by business cycles. Businesses tend to react to business cycles by expanding their operations during periods of recovery or expansion. They may also react by cutting back their operations during periods of recession.

During an expansion businesses may invest in new properties, equipment, and inventories, and hire more employees.

Economists study indicators to identify the changing phases of the economy's business cycle. Theses indicators help the government and businesses predict the future of the economy. The predictions are used to make business and economic decisions.

When the economy moves into a recession, businesses may lay off employees. Businesses also cut back inventories to match lowered demand for products in a recession or depression. This has a ripple effect in the economy as business suppliers lose revenue.

During a period of recession, consumers' biggest fear is losing their jobs. Another big fear is a decrease in wages. These fears result in a loss of consumer confidence in the economy. This change reduces consumer spending. Reduced consumer spending causes businesses to reduce their operations in response to lower demand.

The opposite is true during periods of prosperity and recovery. During those periods, consumers are more optimistic. They spend more money on material goods and luxury items. Businesses will also respond by producing more goods. This cycle shows how important consumers are to an economy. Consumer spending accounts for more than-two thirds of the U.S. GDP.

GOVERNMENT'S INFLUENCE ON BUSINESS CYCLES

A government influences business cycles through its policies and programs. Taxation has a strong effect on what happens in an economy. As the government requires more money to run programs, higher taxes are needed. When taxes are raised, businesses and consumers have less money to fuel the economy. When the economy needs a boost, the government may cut taxes or reduce interest rates. Lower taxes and interest rates give businesses and consumers more money to spend and invest. The government may also use tax money to fund various programs. Government spending can help spark a depressed economy in which other activity is very slow.

When an economy worsens, the Federal Reserve generally responds by lowering interest rates. This practice makes borrowing money more affordable, which encourages businesses and consumers to spend. Mortgage rates are affected because the commercial banks' prime lending rate reflects the Federal Reserve's funding rate. For example, when the federal funds rate was at one percent, the prime lending rate was around four percent. At the same time, mortgage rates were between five and six percent. Lower mortgage rates serve as an incentive for consumers to buy homes and borrow money for other major purchases. If inflation becomes a problem, interest rates might be increased to discourage buying on credit.

Other actions governments can take to spark economic growth are illustrated by efforts in the United States in 2008–2009. Under President George W. Bush in 2008, the government issued tax rebates to taxpayers to encourage consumer spending. His administration also enacted the Emergency Economic Stabilization Act of 2008 to help troubled banks. The following year, President Barack Obama signed the American Recovery and Reinvestment Act of 2009, which was a $787 billion economic stimulus package. The U.S. government took these dramatic actions to try to spur consumption and shore up the financial sector. The goal was to revive an economy that was in its worst recession in 70 years.

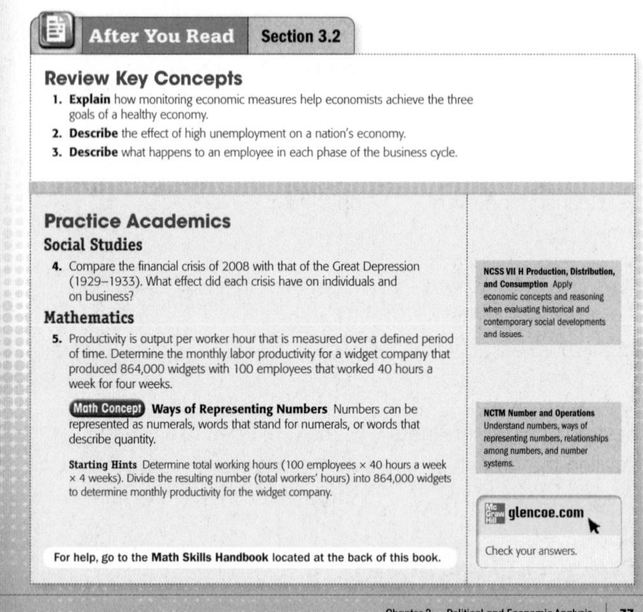

After You Read | **Section 3.2**

Review Key Concepts

1. **Explain** how monitoring economic measures help economists achieve the three goals of a healthy economy.
2. **Describe** the effect of high unemployment on a nation's economy.
3. **Describe** what happens to an employee in each phase of the business cycle.

Practice Academics

Social Studies

4. Compare the financial crisis of 2008 with that of the Great Depression (1929–1933). What effect did each crisis have on individuals and on business?

Mathematics

5. Productivity is output per worker hour that is measured over a defined period of time. Determine the monthly labor productivity for a widget company that produced 864,000 widgets with 100 employees that worked 40 hours a week for four weeks.

Math Concept **Ways of Representing Numbers** Numbers can be represented as numerals, words that stand for numerals, or words that describe quantity.

Starting Hints Determine total working hours (100 employees × 40 hours a week × 4 weeks). Divide the resulting number (total workers' hours) into 864,000 widgets to determine monthly productivity for the widget company.

For help, go to the **Math Skills Handbook** located at the back of this book.

NCSS VII H Production, Distribution, and Consumption Apply economic concepts and reasoning when evaluating historical and contemporary social developments and issues.

NCTM Number and Operations Understand numbers, ways of representing numbers, relationships among numbers, and number systems.

glencoe.com

Check your answers.

ELABORATE

FACTORS THAT AFFECT BUSINESS CYCLES

Ask these questions to focus the discussion of the business cycle.

Guiding Questions

Recal During a recession, what is the average person's greatest fear?	losing his or her job
Contrast How is a depression different from a recession?	A depression lasts longer and has a larger decrease in economic activity.
Synthesize The executives at a television manufacturer increased production because they believed the economy was in recovery. Now they have large quantities of TVs in their warehouses. Why do you think they have this overstock condition?	Possible answer: Consumer confidence may not yet have increased so consumer spending may not have picked up. Alternately, the executives could have been wrong about the economy being in a recovery phase.

Reinforce Vocabulary

Recovery—Denotative Meaning *Recovery is the term that signifies a period of renewed economic growth following a recession or depression.* Ask: ***Based on this sentence, what would you expect to happen during a recovery?*** Companies would increase production, jobs would increase, consumers would make more purchases.

Mini Project

Differentiated Instruction

Intrapersonal Learners Instruct students to conduct research to learn about people's lives during the Great Depression. They may want to read books such as Studs Terkel's: *Hard Times: An Oral History of the Great Depression.* Then have students write an essay in which they imagine being a high school student at that time. Encourage them to be as specific as possible about their daily lives. Students' essays will vary. Perhaps their fathers' lost their jobs, they wore old clothes that were heavily patched, and they only ate meat a couple of times a week.

EVALUATE

Graphic Organizer

Ask for volunteers to give an example of how each factor affects the business cycle and how the business cycle affects that factor.

Factors Affecting the Business Cycle		
Factor	**How Can this Factor Affect the Business Cycle?**	**How Can the Business Cycle Affect this Factor?**
Businesses	Businesses tend to expand operations during a recovery phase, hastening economic improvement.	Being in a recession can lead to reduced consumer spending resulting in a reduction in sales.
Consumers	Decreases in consumer spending can lead to recession.	Consumers might find wages increasing during recovery or expansion.
Government	The government might issue rebates to spur spending and encourage economic expansion.	In a recession, tax income might be reduced, forcing government to examine expenditures.

 **glencoe.com** 

Have students go to the Online Learning Center to print this graphic organizer.

Mini Project

Extension

Prepare Radio Interview on the Great Depression
Organize students into pairs. Tell them that they are going to prepare a radio interview. One person will be the interviewer and the other person an economics professor at a local university. The interviewer should ask the professor questions concerning the causes of the Great Depression. Encourage students to conduct research on these causes and then prepare a list of questions to be asked during the interview. Have each pair present their interview to the class. Interviews will vary. Commonly agreed-upon causes include the stock market crash of 1929, which in part was caused by people buying on margin, runs on banks causing many banks to fail, reduced spending by consumers, extreme drought in the Dust Bowl, and the Smoot-Hawley Tariff which resulted in a decrease in foreign trade.

 **After You Read** Section 3.2

Review Key Concepts

1. Monitoring economic measures helps economists quickly notice changes in productivity, employment, and prices, and determine when the government should respond to changing conditions; for example, by lowering interest rates to spur the economy.
2. High unemployment has a negative effect on a nation's economy. The unemployed cannot make purchases so companies produce less and cut back on capital projects. Tax revenue decreases. Unemployment benefits cause state governments to reduce spending.
3. During an expansion, jobs are readily available and wages typically increase; employees can move from one job to another fairly easily. In a recession, employees may be laid off and finding another job can be difficult. In a trough, jobs are typically scarce, but may gradually become more plentiful. In a recovery, more jobs become available as the economy grows and workers may see their wages increase, enabling them to increase their standards of living.

Practice Academics

Social Studies

4. During the Great Depression, the stock market crashed. Banks failed. People defaulted on loans and lost their homes and farms. FDR's New Deal established programs such as the Securities and Exchange Commission. The FDIC was established, which insures bank deposits. Due to these and other government policies, the 2008 financial crisis was not as bad as the Great Depression. The housing market plummeted and foreclosures increased. An economic stimulus plan helped spur the economy. The Emergency Economic Stabilization Act of 2008 provided up to $700 billion to financial institutions.

Mathematics

5. 5.4 output per worker hour (100 employees × 40 hours × 4 weeks = 160,000; 864,000 divided by 16,000 = 5.4)

 **glencoe.com**

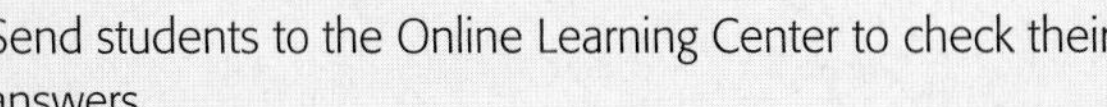

Send students to the Online Learning Center to check their answers.

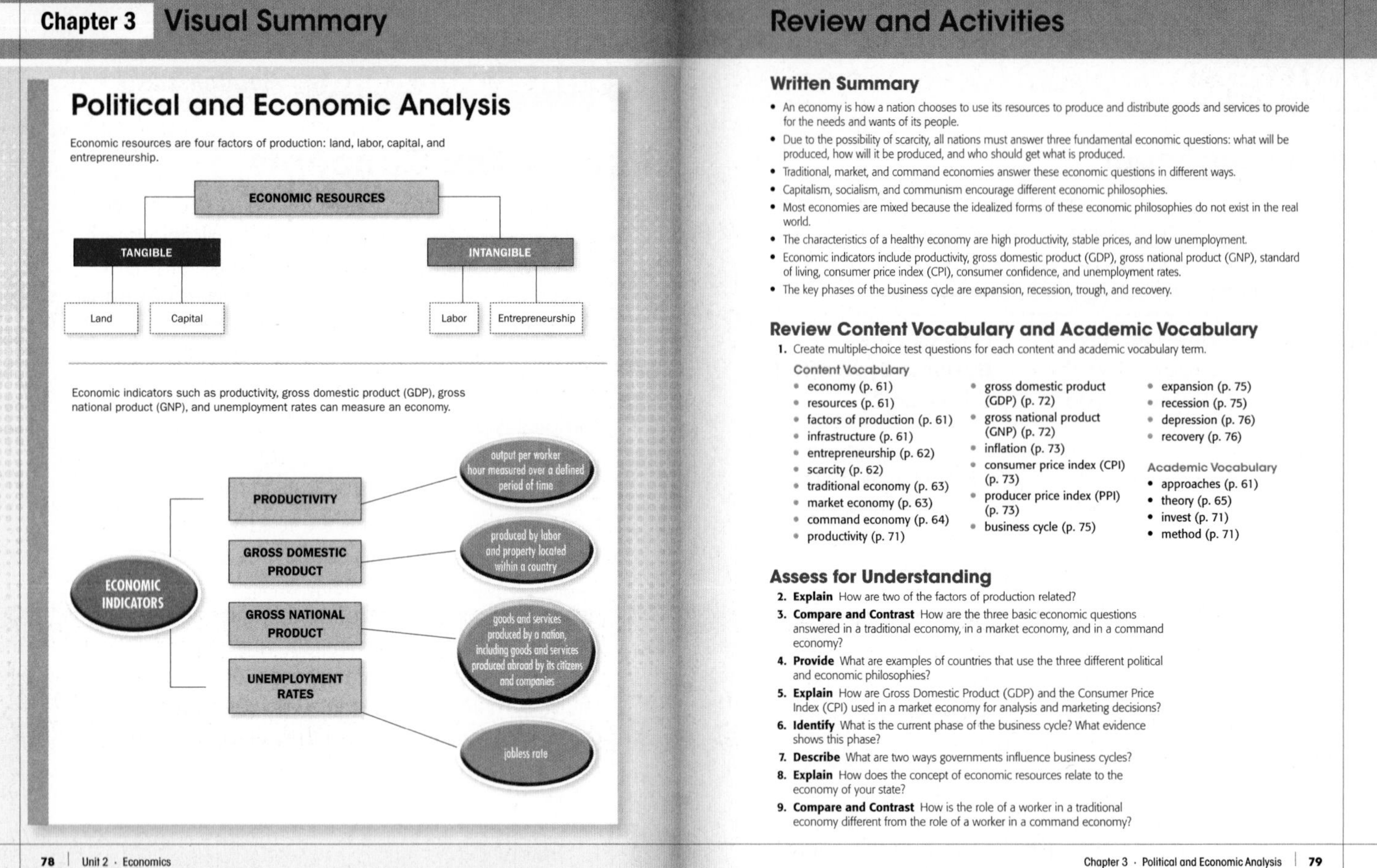
Chapter 3 Visual Summary

Political and Economic Analysis

Economic resources are four factors of production: land, labor, capital, and entrepreneurship.

Economic indicators such as productivity, gross domestic product (GDP), gross national product (GNP), and unemployment rates can measure an economy.

78 | Unit 2 · Economics

Review and Activities

Written Summary

- An economy is how a nation chooses to use its resources to produce and distribute goods and services to provide for the needs and wants of its people.
- Due to the possibility of scarcity, all nations must answer three fundamental economic questions: what will be produced, how will it be produced, and who should get what is produced.
- Traditional, market, and command economies answer these economic questions in different ways.
- Capitalism, socialism, and communism encourage different economic philosophies.
- Most economies are mixed because the idealized forms of these economic philosophies do not exist in the real world.
- The characteristics of a healthy economy are high productivity, stable prices, and low unemployment.
- Economic indicators include productivity, gross domestic product (GDP), gross national product (GNP), standard of living, consumer price index (CPI), consumer confidence, and unemployment rates.
- The key phases of the business cycle are expansion, recession, trough, and recovery.

Review Content Vocabulary and Academic Vocabulary

1. Create multiple-choice test questions for each content and academic vocabulary term.

Content Vocabulary
- economy (p. 61)
- resources (p. 61)
- factors of production (p. 61)
- infrastructure (p. 61)
- entrepreneurship (p. 62)
- scarcity (p. 62)
- traditional economy (p. 63)
- market economy (p. 63)
- command economy (p. 64)
- productivity (p. 71)
- gross domestic product (GDP) (p. 72)
- gross national product (GNP) (p. 72)
- inflation (p. 73)
- consumer price index (CPI) (p. 73)
- producer price index (PPI) (p. 73)
- business cycle (p. 75)
- expansion (p. 75)
- recession (p. 75)
- depression (p. 76)
- recovery (p. 76)

Academic Vocabulary
- approaches (p. 61)
- theory (p. 65)
- invest (p. 71)
- method (p. 71)

Assess for Understanding

2. **Explain** How are two of the factors of production related?
3. **Compare and Contrast** How are the three basic economic questions answered in a traditional economy, in a market economy, and in a command economy?
4. **Provide** What are examples of countries that use the three different political and economic philosophies?
5. **Explain** How are Gross Domestic Product (GDP) and the Consumer Price Index (CPI) used in a market economy for analysis and marketing decisions?
6. **Identify** What is the current phase of the business cycle? What evidence shows this phase?
7. **Describe** What are two ways governments influence business cycles?
8. **Explain** How does the concept of economic resources relate to the economy of your state?
9. **Compare and Contrast** How is the role of a worker in a traditional economy different from the role of a worker in a command economy?

Chapter 3 · Political and Economic Analysis | 79

EVALUATE

Visual Summary

Express Creativity Ask students to develop their own visual summary of a concept in the chapter. Encourage students to use different formats for their visual summaries, such as a storyboard, a timeline, a table, a tree diagram, or a word web. Visual summaries will vary depending on the concept depicted and the visual manner in which it is depicted. Questions to ask when assessing a visual summary include:

- Is the summary clear, economical, and simple?
- Are any important steps left out?
- Are steps or concepts arranged in the same order as the original?
- Does the summary reveal a pattern that connects the details?
- Does the summary locate and highlight the most important information?

Review Content Vocabulary and Academic Vocabulary

1. The **economy** of a country is based on its economic **resources,** which are referred to as f**actors of production.** A highly developed **infrastructure** is found in most industrialized countries. **Entrepreneurship** involves risk-taking. **Scarcity** is the principle behind how countries make economic decisions. In a **traditional economy,** work involves tasks for self-sufficiency. In a **market economy** consumers determine what will be produced. In a **command economy** economic decisions are made by the government. The **productivity** of workers in the United States is high. The United States used **gross domestic product (GDP)** to measure productivity. Before using GDP, the United States used **gross national product (GNP).** Sky-rocketing **inflation** is bad for an economy. The **consumer price index (CPI)** and **producer price index (PPI)** are indicators of inflation. The **business cycle** goes through several phases including: **expansion,** peak, **recession,** and **recovery.** A devastating recession is called a **depression.** The **approach** a country takes when making economic decisions depends on its philosophy about government intervention in business. One **theory** suggests that the government run all important industries. Consumers can **invest** in a company by buying its stock. One **method** of helping an economy is to cut taxes so consumers have more money to spend.

EVALUATE

Assess for Understanding

2. Answers will vary depending on the factors of production chosen. Sample answer: Capital and land are related because natural resources (land) are usually necessary to create finished products. Capital is required to build the factories, machinery, etc., required to transform these natural resources.

3. The three economic questions are: What goods and services should be produced? How should they be produced? For whom should they be produced and distributed? In a traditional economy, habits, traditions, and rituals answer the basic questions of what, how, and for whom. Traditional economies are generally found in underdeveloped nations. In a pure market economy, the government lets businesses and consumers decide what, how, and for whom. Consumers decide through the purchases they make and businesses respond by producing the items consumers want. To get the goods they want, consumers work to obtain the money to make those purchases. In a command economy, the country's government makes all economic decisions regarding what, how, and for whom goods and services will be produced and distributed.

4. Capitalist: Japan; Communist: North Korea; Socialist: Canada.

5. Gross Domestic Product (GDP) is used in a market economy to show the output of goods and services produced by labor and property located within a country. It consists of private investment, government spending, personal spending, net exports of goods and services, and changes in business inventories. It is a good indicator of the country's productivity and the health of its economy. The Consumer Price Index (CPI) measures the change in price over a period of time of some 400 specific retail goods and services used by the average urban household. The CPI provides marketers with information on inflation. Both measures can help the government and economists decide whether policies such as limiting imports or lowering interest rates should be implemented.

6. Answers will vary depending on the current state of the economy. Sample answer: During the past two years, the economy has been in a recession in which unemployment was relatively high and employers were not expanding their businesses. Consumer confidence was low and there was minimal spending. However, economic indicators show that the recession is not worsening, and, in fact, may be slightly lessening. There has been a slight decrease in the unemployment rate in the last few months and the standard of living has been stable. Because of these factors, it appears we may be in a trough and are possibly getting ready to enter a recovery period.

7. Two ways governments influence business cycles are by their policies and programs. When the economy needs a boost, the government might lower taxes, reduce interest rates, or institute federally funded programs to spark a depressed economy. If inflation becomes a problem, interest rates might be increased to discourage buying on credit.

8. Answers will vary depending on the state. Montana has a variety of natural resources such as minerals that attract mining businesses. Large amounts of open grassland make Montana suitable for grazing cattle and sheep. Its mountains, clear streams and lakes, and abundant wildlife attract tourists.

9. In a traditional economy, most workers make their living doing what they need to survive, such as farming, herding animals, and building shelters. Skills are passed on from one generation to the next. In a command economy, the government may tell workers what jobs they will perform and provides any needed training. Workers are provided subsidies for necessities such as food, housing, and medical care.

21st Century Skills

Teamwork Skills

10. **Analyze Government Policies** Work with a team to analyze the impact of the current U.S. government's monetary and fiscal policies on businesses and consumers. Prepare a written report using a word processing program and an oral report using presentation software.

Communication Skills

11. **Specialized and Organized Labor Debate** Research labor unions in the United States. Debate the advantages and disadvantages of specialized and organized labor.

Everyday Ethics

12. **Economic Judgments** In 2008, three auto company executives flew to Washington, D.C., to ask for government funding during a recession. These executives were criticized for using company-owned jets instead of the cars their companies manufacture. When they returned to Washington, D.C., for a second time, all three executives drove in company autos. Other criticism during the recession involved companies that paid excessive executive salaries and bonuses with federal funds. So, in 2009, legal safeguards limited executive salaries and bonuses for companies that received new government funding. Investigate government limits on executive compensation. Write a paragraph on your opinion about that policy.

e-Marketing Skills

13. **Government Web Sites** Research United States government Web sites to determine the current phase of the business cycle. Search sites that provide information on U.S. productivity, balance of trade, inflation, and unemployment. Based on your findings, would you suggest that marketers invest more or less money on product expansion; increase or decrease prices; and increase or decrease research and development?

Build Academic Skills

Social Studies

14. **Economic Analysis** Use the U.S. Bureau of Economic Analysis Web site to find information on the GDP. Chart the percentage of GDP attributed to government spending over the past ten years in the United States. Use your chart to make a statement about how government spending has changed in this period. Explain your statement to demonstrate your understanding of different political and economic systems.

NCSS VII D Production, Distribution, and Consumption Describe relationships among the various economic institutions that comprise economic systems such as households, business firms, banks, government agencies, labor unions, and corporations. **NCSS VII G Production, Distribution, and Consumption** Compare basic economic systems according to how rules and procedures deal with demand, supply, prices, the role of government, banks, labor and labor unions, savings and investments, and capital.

Science

15. **Natural Resources** Explore the natural resources in a developing country to determine how those resources are being used for its population. Discuss your findings with a partner.

NSES F Develop understanding of personal and community health; population growth; natural resources; environmental quality; natural and human-induced hazards; science and technology in local, national, and global challenges.

Mathematics

16. **Inflation and Deflation** During inflationary periods the cost of living is higher than during a deflationary period. During a stable price period, assume the weekly food bill was $125. If inflation goes up to 15 percent, what would be the weekly food bill? If deflation occurred by the same 15 percent what would be the weekly food bill?

Math Concept **Understanding Percentages** Multiply the $125 food bill by 115 percent to determine the weekly food bill during an inflationary period.

NCTM Numbers and Operations Understand numbers, ways of presenting numbers, relationship among numbers, and number systems.

For help, go to the **Math Skills Handbook** located at the back of this book.

Standardized Test Practice

Directions Read the following questions. On a separate sheet of paper write the best possible answer for each one.

1. What are recurring changes in economic activity called?
   A. expansion
   B. recession
   C. business cycle
   D. depression
2. True or false? Privatization is the same as nationalization.
   T
   F
3. The output per worker hour defined over a measure of time is ________.

Test-Taking Tip
When answering multiple-choice questions, ask yourself if each option is true or false.

DECA Connection Role Play

Retail Store Manager
Food Store Chain

Situation You are a retail store manager for a food store chain. The corporate office is reviewing all stores due to the current recession. The community serviced by this store has an unemployment rate that is higher than the national rate. Consumer confidence is down. The demographics of the customer base have changed with a greater influx of lower income families, many of whom receive government subsidies. Based on the current measures of the economy and your store's particular situation, what changes in product selection or store policy do you recommend?

The corporate office is sending a representative (judge) to your store to meet with you regarding your store's operation.

Activity Prepare a report noting recommendations you believe would be helpful in making your store more profitable during this economic recession. Use that report when meeting with the representative from the corporate office (judge).

Evaluation You will be evaluated on how well you meet these performance indicators:

- Explain the concept of economic resources.
- Explain the types of economic systems.
- Examine the relationship between government and business.
- Discuss the role government agencies play in the food marketing industry.
- Determine the impact of business cycles on business activities.

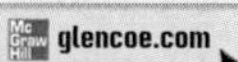 **glencoe.com**

Download the Competitive Events Workbook for more Role-Play practice.

EVALUATE

Teamwork Skills

10. The students' written and oral reports should address U.S. government's monetary and fiscal policies and their effect on economic decisions made by businesses and consumers. It should address the relationship between business and government. For example, if the government cut interest rates and provides $8,000 for first time home buyers, those policies would help real estate businesses sell more homes because consumers would more likely to be able to buy a new home.

Communication Skills

11. Pros for labor unions (organized labor) would be job security and fair wages for a fair day's work. The ability to negotiate contracts is another positive aspect. Specialization allows workers to do their respective jobs well. Cons for organized labor are not all workers perform their best. Employment contracts protect workers who do not perform well. They are costly to employers.

Everyday Ethics

12. Answers will vary. Students should write a paragraph discussing their opinions about the legal limitations on executive compensation. Sample answer: While people in these industries might say that these executives earn their salaries by their ability to increase company revenues, the compensations have been so out-of-line with what other workers receive that it seems appropriate to place some limits on them. Many workers were deeply hurt by the recession, so it is only fair that executives should also take the consequences of downturns in the economy.

e-Marketing Skills

13. Student's research from the United States government Web sites should be cited in their report with regard to U.S. productivity, balance of trade, inflation, and unemployment. If those economic indicators are good, they should suggest that marketers invest in their businesses and in research and development. If those economic indicators are poor, they should suggest decreasing prices and money spent on research and development. If the economic indicators show that the economy is not in the recovery or expansion phase of the business cycle, businesses should cut back on capital spending and possibly lay off workers as production is cut back.

EVALUATE

Build Academic Skills

Social Studies

14. Answers depend on the current GDP in relation to past GDP percentages of government spending. From 2004 to 2007 the percentage was 18.7 percent to 18.8 percent. In 2008 and 2009, the percentage increased to around 20 percent. Students should go to the Bureau of Economic Analysis (BEA) Web site and view the tables for GDP. They should then divide the figure for government spending by total GDP to get the actual percentage for each year and use the results to generate a chart. Students should conclude with a statement indicating their understanding of different political and economic systems. Sample statement: An increase in government spending in relation to GDP indicates increasing socialist tendencies in the government.

Science

15. Accept all reasonable answers. For example, Zambia's natural resources include soil for farming maize, sorghum, groundnuts, as well as mining minerals such as copper, cobalt, zinc, and lead. Copper mining was successful in Zambia once the country privatized the mines in 2000. Capital investments and high copper prices helped increase copper production. Domestic food supplies have improved with education and capital investments.

Mathematics

16. During inflation the $125 weekly food bill would be $143.75 ($125 × 1.15). During deflation the $125 weekly food bill would be $106.25 ($125 × .85).

Standardized Test Practice

1. C business cycle
2. False (Privatization is selling off government-owned properties while nationalization is when a government takes over privately-held companies.)
3. Gross Domestic Product–GDP

DECA Connection Role Play

Evaluations will be based on these performance indicators:

1. **Explain the concept of economic resources.** Tangible economic resources are land, labor, and capital, while an intangible resource is entrepreneurship. Resources from the earth include coal, crude oil, and trees. The geography and climate of a region are economic resources. A well-trained labor force is an asset to a company, because it may increase production. Capitalism includes the goods used in the production process such as machinery and tools as well as the raw materials. Entrepreneurship refers to the skills to organize materials.
2. **Explain the types of economic systems.** In a traditional economy, culture plays a part in the type of goods produced and who receives them. In a market economy, individuals and companies make decisions and compete for consumers. In command economies, the government controls all production matters. The United States is considered a mixed economy.
3. **Examine the relationship between government and business.** Capitalism is private ownership and competition. Businesses and the government are concerned with individuals. In a communist society, the government assigns jobs, there is no private ownership, and citizens are given goods from the government. Socialist countries have increased government involvement in business but they also provide opportunities for private ownership.
4. **Discuss the role that government agencies play in the food marketing industry.** Businesses must comply with laws governing the sale and production of food. The Food and Drug Administration (FDA) and the United States Department of Agriculture (USDA) oversee food safety. There are laws regarding labeling of food products and advertising claims. The FDA can order businesses to recall tainted or dangerous food and medicine.
5. **Determine the impact of business cycles on business activities.** An expansion features high production and profits along with low unemployment. A recession is an economic slowdown in which unemployment increases. A depression occurs when a recession does not end for an extensive period. Recovery involves renewed growth and renewed employment opportunities.

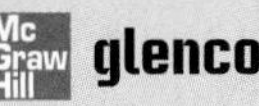

glencoe.com

Role Plays For more DECA Role Plays, send students to the Online Learning Center to download the Competitive Events Workbook.

global analysis

SHOW WHAT YOU KNOW

Visual Literacy Globalization has created new markets for all products. It has also changed how business is done. ***What challenges and opportunities do you see for global businesses?***

Discovery Project

Marketing in an Emerging Country

Essential Question How would you select an emerging country to market a product and what marketing strategy would you use?

Project Goal

Select a product to sell in an emerging nation. An emerging nation is a country that is developing into an industrialized nation. Conduct a PEST analysis on a minimum of two countries to determine which country is better suited for the product. Provide rationale for your selection and note any problems you may have to address. Prepare an advertising message and explain your plan for marketing the product in that country. Use a word processing program to prepare a written report. Use presentation software to prepare visuals for your oral presentation to the class.

Ask Yourself...

- What products do consumers need in emerging countries?
- In which nation would you have a chance of success?
- How will you address differences in language and culture in your marketing plan?
- How will you decide on what to include in the advertising message?
- What marketing strategy should you use?

Think Critically What opportunities and threats are apparent in emerging countries as a market for consumer products?

glencoe.com

Activity
Get a worksheet activity about globalization.

Evaluate
Download a rubric you can use to evaluate your project.

DECA Connection

DECA Event Role Play

Concepts in this chapter are related to DECA competitive events that involve either an interview or role play.

Performance Indicators The performance indicators represent key skills and knowledge. Your key to success in DECA competitive events is relating them to the concepts in this chapter.

- Explain the nature of global trade.
- Discuss the impact of cultural and social environments on global trade.
- Assess global trends and opportunities.
- Discuss the global environment in which businesses operate.
- Identify considerations in implementing international marketing strategies.

DECA Prep

Role Play Practice role-playing with the DECA Connection competitive-event activity at the end of this chapter. More information about DECA events can be found on DECA's Web site.

ENGAGE

Visual Literacy

Read the chapter opener photo caption question to students: ***What challenges and opportunities do you see for global businesses?*** Possible answers: political factors (trade restrictions/trade agreements), economic factors (poor standard of living/high standard of living, labor force, taxes), social and cultural factors (language, religion), technological factors (phone system, Internet access). Then ask these guiding questions to activate prior knowledge.

Guiding Questions

Identify How might trade with other countries affect answers to the three basic questions nations consider in deciding how to use their economic resources?	Countries have to consider their trading partners. Some goods and services may not be produced if they are imported, while others might be produced for export.
Explain Why are the goals of an economy important in international trade?	A country's economy has an impact on the other countries with which they trade goods and services.

Discovery Project

Marketing in an Emerging Country Start a discussion that connects students to the Discovery Project Essential Question: ***How would you select an emerging country to market a product and what marketing strategy would you use?*** Remind students of the PEST analysis that they studied in Chapter 2. Tell them that they can use the same factors to evaluate a country's marketing opportunities and threats in the international market. A global environmental scan includes analysis of political (P) and economic (E) factors, socio-cultural (S) differences and technological (T) levels.

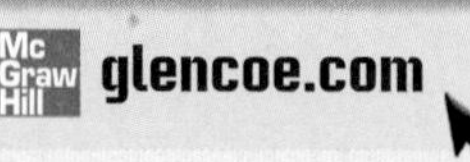

Discovery Project Resources Send students to the Online Learning Center to download a rubric to evaluate their projects.

ENGAGE

Introduce the Chapter

Chapter 4 explains the basics of international trade and doing business in the global marketplace. These major concepts are discussed:

- Interdependence of nations
- Absolute advantage and comparative advantage
- Benefits of international trade
- Balance of trade
- Trade barriers
- Trade agreements and alliances
- Importing and exporting
- Licensing, contract manufacturing, and joint ventures
- Foreign direct investment
- Multinationals and mini-nationals
- Political, economic, socio-cultural, and technological factors
- Globalization, adaptation, and customization

Discussion Starter

Interdependence of Nations Tell students that in the 1960s, social commentator Marshall McLuhan coined the term *global village* to refer to the contemporary world where electronic communications made all the people on earth neighbors. Ask students: ***Do you think that this description is more or less true today? Why or why not?*** Students should realize that since the 1960s the countries of the world have become more dependent on each other. Ask students: ***What items do you use that come from other countries?*** Students may mention food items such as fruit from countries in Central and South America or electronics from Japan and China.

DECA Connection

Discuss the performance indicators listed in the DECA Connection feature. Explain to students that performance indicators tell them how to demonstrate their acquired skills and knowledge through individual or team competitive events.

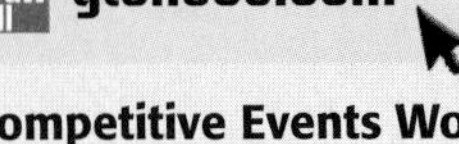

glencoe.com

Competitive Events Workbook For more DECA Role Plays, send students to the Online Learning Center to download the Competitive Events Workbook.

PRINT RESOURCES

- **Student Edition**
- **Teacher Edition**
- **Student Activity Workbook with Academic Integration** includes worksheets and activities correlated to the text.
- **Mathematics for Marketing Workbook** provides math activities for every unit in the text.

TECHNOLOGY TOOLBOX

- **Connect**
- **ConnectPlus**
- **ExamView Assessment Suite** is a comprehensive solution for creating, administering, and scoring tests.

glencoe.com

Online Learning Center provides a variety of resources to enrich and enhance learning.

SECTION, CHAPTER, AND UNIT RESOURCES

- **Graphic Organizers** for organizing text concepts visually.
- **Digital Nation Activities** and **Green Marketer Activities** extend learning beyond the text features.
- **Career Chatroom Career Profiles** allow students to explore different marketing occupations in depth.
- **After You Read Answer Keys** for students to check their answers.
- **Discovery Project Rubrics** and **Marketing Internship Project Rubrics** for students to evaluate their projects.

PROGRAM RESOURCES

- **Student Activity Workbook with Academic Integration Teacher Annotated Edition** includes annotated answers for the activities and worksheets.
- **Marketing Research Project Workbook** provides a step-by-step approach for students to complete their own marketing research studies.
- **School-to-Career Activity Workbook** helps students relate their class work to on-the-job experience and involves work-site analysis and working with mentors.
- **Competitive Events Workbook** helps prepare students for state and national marketing education competitions.
- **Inclusion in the Marketing Education Classroom** provides teaching resources for working with students with special needs.
- **PowerPoint Presentations** provides visual teaching aids and assessments for this chapter.

READING GUIDE

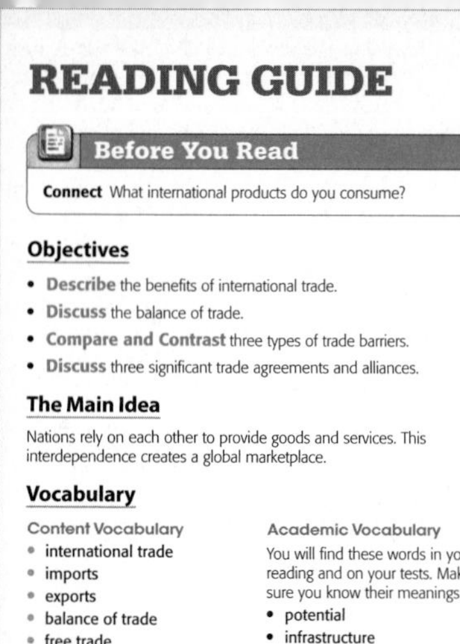

Before You Read

Connect What international products do you consume?

Objectives

- **Describe** the benefits of international trade.
- **Discuss** the balance of trade.
- **Compare and Contrast** three types of trade barriers.
- **Discuss** three significant trade agreements and alliances.

The Main Idea

Nations rely on each other to provide goods and services. This interdependence creates a global marketplace.

Vocabulary

Content Vocabulary
- international trade
- imports
- exports
- balance of trade
- free trade
- tariff
- quota
- embargo
- protectionism
- World Trade Organization (WTO)
- North American Free Trade Agreement (NAFTA)
- European Union (EU)

Academic Vocabulary

You will find these words in your reading and on your tests. Make sure you know their meanings.
- potential
- infrastructure

Graphic Organizer

Draw or print this chart to help you organize key concepts related to international trade.

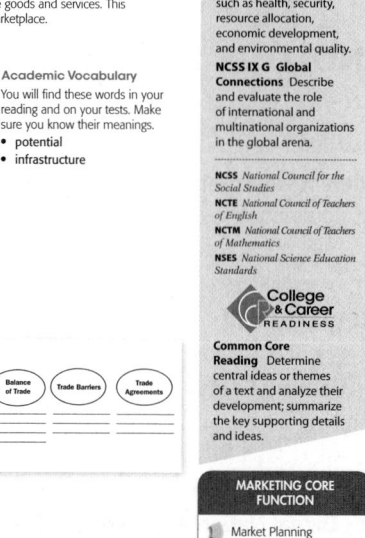

Balance of Trade | Trade Barriers | Trade Agreements

glencoe.com

Print this graphic organizer.

STANDARDS

ACADEMIC

English Language Arts

NCTE 1 Read texts to acquire new information.

Social Studies

NCSS IX D Global Connections Analyze the causes, consequences, and possible solutions to persistent, contemporary, and emerging global issues, such as health, security, resource allocation, economic development, and environmental quality.

NCSS IX G Global Connections Describe and evaluate the role of international and multinational organizations in the global arena.

NCSS *National Council for the Social Studies*
NCTE *National Council of Teachers of English*
NCTM *National Council of Mathematics*
NSES *National Science Education Standards*

College & Career READINESS

Common Core Reading Determine central ideas or themes of a text and analyze their development; summarize the key supporting details and ideas.

MARKETING CORE FUNCTION

Market Planning

m.e. Section 4.1 International Trade

NATURE OF INTERNATIONAL TRADE

The global marketplace exists because countries need to trade with one another. It continues to expand because of the reduction of trade restrictions throughout the world. This new global marketplace makes all people and businesses in the world not only **potential** customers but also potential employees or employers.

International trade is the exchange of goods and services among nations. **Imports** are goods and services purchased from other countries. Conversely, **exports** are goods and services sold to other countries. These exchanges occur between businesses, but they are controlled by the governments of the countries involved.

As You Read

Consider How would your life be different if countries did not exchange products?

INTERDEPENDENCE OF NATIONS

Most countries do not produce or manufacture all the goods and services they need. They get some of their goods and services from other nations. This economic interdependence happens because each country possesses unique resources and capabilities. The principle of economic interdependence is fundamental to marketing in a global environment.

> "The global marketplace is here to stay."

ABSOLUTE ADVANTAGE AND COMPARATIVE ADVANTAGE

Some nations tend to specialize in certain areas. They specialize in products that they can produce most efficiently due to available resources in their countries.

ABSOLUTE ADVANTAGE

An absolute advantage occurs when a country has economic resources that allow it to produce a product at a lower unit cost than any other country. For example, Brazil has an absolute advantage in coffee over most other countries. In this case, it is clear that Brazil will export its coffee to other countries in the global marketplace.

COMPARATIVE ADVANTAGE

Some countries have an absolute advantage in more than one product. They must compare the unit cost of each product. Then they decide which ones to produce and which ones to import.

The United States has a comparative advantage in producing high-tech products because of its **infrastructure**, raw materials, and educated work force. Products include airplanes, computers, high-tech machinery, entertainment, and telecommunications.

Some emerging nations have large, unskilled labor forces available at low costs. Labor-intensive industries—ones that rely on labor as opposed to machinery—do well in these countries. Emerging nations can produce labor-intensive toys, clothing, and shoes at a lower unit cost than most industrialized nations. They have a comparative advantage when manufacturing these goods. It is more cost-effective for high-wage countries like the United States to buy those items from emerging nations.

ENGAGE

Anticipation Activity

Ask students: ***How might consumers react if many commonly used imported products were no longer available?*** Students will likely suggest that consumers would be upset and would try to find replacement items that were available.

Objectives

- **Describe** the benefits of international trade. International trade results in high-quality products with lower prices
- **Discuss** the balance of trade. Balance of trade is the difference in value between a country's imports and exports
- **Compare and Contrast** three types of trade barriers. tariff–tax on imports; quota–limits units or monetary value of a product; embargo–ban on goods
- **Discuss** three significant trade agreements and alliances. World Trade Organization–coalition for international trade; North America Free Trade Agreement–agreement with Canada, the U.S., Mexico; European Union–trading bloc

Graphic Organizer

Balance of Trade	Trade Barriers	Trade Agreements
Difference between imports/exports; Positive balance-exports more than imports; Negative balance-trade deficit; Trade deficit reduces revenue	Tariffs Quotas Embargoes	North American Free Trade Agreement, European Union, World Trade Organization,

glencoe.com iWB

Graphic Organizer Send students to the Online Learning Center to print this graphic organizer.

EXPLORE

Before You Read

Read the Before You Read question aloud: ***What international products do you consume?*** If students don't know what international products they consume, have them look for the "Made in" tag in clothing and other textiles, the label on fruit, and "Product of" labels or engravings on electronic products and automobiles. Ask students whether they are surprised at the number of products that come from other countries.

Preteaching Vocabulary

Have students go to the Online Learning Center at glencoe.com for the Chapter 4 Preteaching Vocabulary games.

Content Vocabulary

Have students create a table with the heads "International Trade," "Trade Barriers," and "Trade Agreements and Alliances." Have students put the content vocabulary terms under the head where it fits best. International Trade: international trade, imports, exports, balance of trade, free trade. Trade Barriers: tariff, quota, embargo, protectionism. Trade Agreements and Alliances: World Trade Organization, North American Free Trade Agreement, European Union.

Academic Vocabulary

Infrastructure—Defining Words Ask students to divide the term *infrastructure* into its root word and prefix. The root word is *structure* and the prefix is *infra*. Have students find the meanings of the root word and prefix and try to develop a definition for *infrastructure* using those meanings. A *structure* is something that is made up of various parts that are put together in a particular way. *Infra* means beneath or below. A possible definition is a structure that is below something. The actual definition for *infrastructure* as used in this section is the physical development of a country, including its roads, ports, sanitation facilities, and utilities.

PROFESSIONAL DEVELOPMENT MINI CLIP

Reading: Guided Instruction

Go to the Online Learning Center to view a video in which a teacher helps students identify major and minor details.

Section 4.1 International Trade

NATURE OF INTERNATIONAL TRADE

Ask these guiding questions to help students focus on the nature of international trade.

Guiding Questions

Apply What might be an example of two people being interdependent on each other?	An employer needs an employee for a business to function. The employee needs the employer to earn wages for living expenses.
Contrast What is the difference between absolute advantage and comparative advantage?	Absolute: when a country has economic resources that allow it to produce a product at the lowest unit cost; Comparative: when a country has resources to produce multiple products at the lowest unit cost

As You Read

Read students the As You Read question: ***How would your life be different if countries did not exchange products?*** Encourage students to look at the labels on their clothing or in their books to find where things were made or printed and to think of the products that they use every day like electronics that originate in other countries. Ask students: ***Do you think prices would remain the same if products that typically come from other countries were manufactured in the United States?*** Students may be aware that one of the reasons products are imported from other countries is that the cost is lower than if the products were made or manufactured in the U.S.

Expert Advice

Read the quote to students:

"The global marketplace is here to stay."

Ask students: ***Do you agree or disagree with this statement?*** Most, if not all, students should realize that this statement is true. As long as people continue to need and want products that must be imported from other countries, the global marketplace will continue to exist.

BENEFITS OF INTERNATIONAL TRADE

Consumers, producers, workers, and nations benefit from international trade in different ways. Consumers benefit from the competition that the foreign companies offer. This competition encourages the production of high-quality goods with lower prices. The variety of goods increases as more producers market their goods in other countries. Individuals have more options when making purchasing decisions.

Many producers today expand their business by conducting operations in other countries. Hewlett-Packard®, IBM®, and H.J. Heinz® report that over 50 percent of their sales are made overseas. About one-third of the profits of U.S. businesses come from international trade and foreign investments. As a result, businesses that want to be successful should consider using international trade. Even small businesses sell products that are used all over the world.

Workers also benefit from international trade. Increased trade leads to higher employment rates both at home and abroad. For example, according to the U.S. Chamber of Commerce, Toyota®, a Japanese company, has generated 500,000 jobs in the United States. Thousands of U.S. manufacturing firms employ workers because they have a strong export business.

Nations as a whole benefit from international trade. Increased foreign investment in a country often improves the standard of living for that country's people. Individuals have more options to choose from when making purchasing decisions. Economic alliances among nations often solidify political alliances that foster peace.

Reading Check

Contrast What is the difference between absolute advantage and comparative advantage?

Brazil is the largest producer of coffee in the world, so it has an absolute advantage over all other countries. China produces rice. ***Does China have an absolute advantage or comparative advantage over the United States in the production of rice?***

GOVERNMENT INVOLVEMENT IN INTERNATIONAL TRADE

All nations control and monitor their trade with businesses in other countries. The U.S. government monitors imports through the customs division of the U.S. Treasury Department. All goods that enter the United States from another country are subject to search and review by U.S. customs officials. Other countries also check incoming goods. All U.S. citizens and businesses must meet the customs requirements of foreign countries when exporting goods.

BALANCE OF TRADE

Nations must keep track of their international trade to be aware of their economic status. The difference in value between exports and imports is called **balance of trade**. A trade surplus occurs when a nation exports more than it imports.

A negative balance of trade, or trade deficit, occurs when a nation imports more than it exports.

TRADE DEFICIT

The large U.S. trade deficit may seem surprising because the United States is the world's biggest exporter. Some analysts believe this situation exists because Americans purchase more goods and services than do people of other nations. Others believe that the United States is now focusing more on providing services, making it more economical to import goods that were once domestically manufactured. The textile trade is a perfect example of this trend. Most apparel sold in the United States is imported from foreign countries, many of which are located in Asia. For example, the United States has a huge trade deficit with China in the area of textiles.

MARKETING CASE STUDY

Global Philanthropists

A global nonprofit venture capital firm called Acumen Fund is helping people in developing nations. It finds out what small villagers need and then researches a simple solution. The problems generally fall into three categories: health, water, and housing. Acumen uses the donations it receives to invest and loan money to companies in those developing countries. Then the companies can produce the needed products and services.

Global Solutions

In Africa, malaria is a major health problem. Acumen financed an existing business: A to Z Textile Mills of Tanzania. This helped the company create a specially designed bed net with an insecticide. The insecticide kills mosquitoes that spread malaria.

In India, where water is scarce, an inexpensive drip-irrigation kit was designed to help farmers. An Indian company started with Acumen financing was created to help provide information to poor rural residents about health, pensions, and government resources. The business model consists of information-hub kiosks equipped with computers, modems, digital cameras, and fax machines. Villagers pay a small fee for each transaction. They can apply for loans or look for jobs. These information kiosks can now be found all over India's countryside.

English Language Arts/Writing

Investigate Research developing countries around the world and select one country to support. Write a letter to Acumen recommending a specific project the company should consider.

NCTE 4 Use written language to communicate effectively.

EXPLAIN

Visual Literacy

Absolute Advantage Caption Answer Read the caption question to students: ***Does China have an absolute advantage or comparative advantage over the United States in the production of rice?*** China would have an absolute advantage over the United States because it has the land, climate, work force, and economies of scale to produce much more rice than the United States.

Reading Check Answer

Read the Reading Check question to students: ***What is the difference between absolute advantage and comparative advantage?*** An absolute advantage occurs when a country has economic resources that allow it to produce a product at a lower unit cost than any other country. A comparative advantage occurs when a country has an absolute advantage in more than one product and must compare the unit cost of each product to determine which ones to produce and which ones to import.

BENEFITS OF INTERNATIONAL TRADE

Explain to students that a country's involvement in international trade has the potential to benefit companies and individuals. Use these guiding questions to help students better understand this concept.

Guiding Questions

Explain How do countries benefit from international trade?	Increased foreign investment in a country often increased the standard of living, individuals have more choices when purchasing items, and trade agreements often solidify political alliances and that contribute to peace between countries.
Relate How do individuals and companies benefit from international trade?	Consumers benefit from low prices caused from competition. Workers benefit from higher employment rates associated with international trade. Companies can expand their international trade, increasing profits.

ELABORATE

Activate Prior Knowledge

Ask students: ***How does having absolute advantage in a product help to keep consumer costs down?*** Absolute advantage helps to ensure that products are being produced at the lowest cost possible. This allows consumers to purchase products at the lowest price possible. Ask students: ***What might happen to a country's absolute advantage if the unit cost to produce the product increases?*** The absolute advantage could be lost to another country that could produce the product at a lower per unit cost.

Graphic Organizer

Ask students to give brief answer to the question: ***What are the benefits of international trade?*** Ask students to offer examples of each benefit. Sample answers:

International Trade

Benefits	Examples
High-quality goods	Electronics, cars.
Lower prices	Clothing, textiles
Larger profits	McDonalds, KFC
Higher employment	China, India
Improved standard of living	China, India
More purchasing options	U.S. consumers

 **glencoe.com** 

Graphic Organizer Send students to the Online Learning Center to print this graphic organizer.

Mini Project

Enrichment

Research Human Rights and International Trade Inform students that when engaging in international trade, many U.S. companies take into account ethical consideration such as whether the efficiency of production is dependent on an oppressive government, low wages, or poor working conditions for the labor force. Have students research human rights and international trade and give a presentation on their findings. Presentations will vary depending on the issues and countries researched. Presentations should clearly explain whether governments are violating human rights in an attempt to increase profits and income by participating in international trade and what measures are being taken to rectify the violations.

GOVERNMENT INVOLVEMENT IN INTERNATIONAL TRADE

Tell students that it is necessary for governments to be involved in international trade. Individual businesses that import products would not be able to search and review all of the products imported. Then ask these guiding questions to focus the discussion on government involvement in international trade.

Guiding Questions

Identify What is the outcome of an unfavorable balance of trade?	This reduces a country's revenue and can result in debt and increased unemployment.
Explain What does the following statement mean? The United States has a huge trade deficit with China in textile trade.	The United States imports more textiles from China than it exports textiles to China.
Assess Which of the following options is better? A. A country imports more than it exports. B. A country exports more than it imports.	B. It is better when a country exports more than it imports because it means that the country's businesses are selling more abroad than its consumers are buying from foreign producers.

MARKETING CASE STUDY

English Language Arts/Writing Answer Accept all reasonable recommendations for specific projects for a poverty-stricken country that Acumen should consider. For example, in Africa, any type of medicine or promotional campaign to rid a country from a prevalent disease may be suggested. Health, water, and housing topics are all acceptable as possible suggestions.

ELL: Elaborating on Student Responses

Go to the Online Learning Center to view a video clip in which a teacher elaborates on a student response using explanatory language.

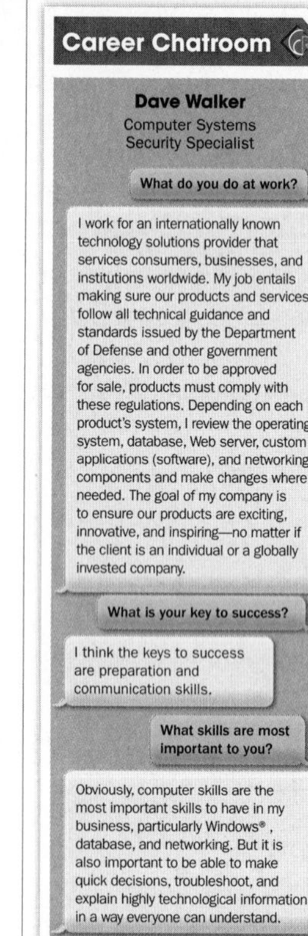
Career Chatroom

Dave Walker
Computer Systems Security Specialist

What do you do at work?

I work for an internationally known technology solutions provider that services consumers, businesses, and institutions worldwide. My job entails making sure our products and services follow all technical guidance and standards issued by the Department of Defense and other government agencies. In order to be approved for sale, products must comply with these regulations. Depending on each product's system, I review the operating system, database, Web server, custom applications (software), and networking components and make changes where needed. The goal of my company is to ensure our products are exciting, innovative, and inspiring—no matter if the client is an individual or a globally invested company.

What is your key to success?

I think the keys to success are preparation and communication skills.

What skills are most important to you?

Obviously, computer skills are the most important skills to have in my business, particularly Windows®, database, and networking. But it is also important to be able to make quick decisions, troubleshoot, and explain highly technological information in a way everyone can understand.

glencoe.com

Read more about this career and get a Career Exploration Activity.

NEGATIVE CONSEQUENCES OF A TRADE DEFICIT

An unfavorable balance of trade reduces a nation's revenue. When more money leaves a country than enters it, that country is in debt, or is a debtor nation. To survive as a debtor nation, the United States relies on foreign investors who buy U.S. securities. Another effect of a negative balance of trade can be increased unemployment. People may lose their jobs as foreign competitors take business away from domestic firms. If domestic businesses do not become competitive, they will fail.

TRADE BARRIERS

Many countries around the world favor and practice **free trade**. This is the commercial exchange between nations that is conducted on free market principles without any regulations. However, a nation's government may impose trade barriers or restrictions when it wants to limit trade. These controls restrict the flow of goods and services among nations. The three main types of trade barriers are tariffs, quotas, and embargoes.

TARIFFS

A **tariff** (sometimes called a duty) is a tax on imports. Tariffs may be used to produce revenue for a country. Revenue-producing tariffs were used in the United States as a primary source of government income before the federal income tax was established in 1913. These revenue-producing tariffs still exist today, but they can be as low as 25 cents per item or pound.

Another type of tariff is protective. A protective tariff is generally high. Its purpose is to increase the price of imported goods so that domestic products can compete with them. Protective tariffs can prevent foreign businesses from trading with the United States. This would protect domestic jobs and new domestic industries from foreign competition, especially from foreign nations that might not practice completely ethical and fair trade.

QUOTAS

An import **quota** limits either the quantity or the monetary value of a product that may be imported. For example, the U.S. government could place a quota on foreign automobiles, limiting the number that may be imported. This would control the number of cars entering the United States from other countries.

In theory, such a measure would give U.S. auto manufacturers a better chance to sell cars.

Sometimes one trading partner voluntarily puts quotas on exports to improve its relations with another country. In the 1980s, Japan placed quotas on its auto exports to the United States to improve trade relations between the two nations.

EMBARGOES

An **embargo** is a total ban on specific goods coming into and leaving a country. A government can impose an embargo for health reasons. The U.S. government embargoed Chilean grapes in 1989 as a precaution after inspectors found poisoned fruit in a shipment. That embargo was lifted within a week. In another example, China imposed a two-year embargo on U.S. beef in 2004 due to the "Mad Cow" disease scare.

Embargoes are more often used for political reasons. Such embargoes based on political differences can last for a very long time. The United States lifted its 20-year embargo on Vietnam in 1994 so that trade relations could start again between the two nations. The U.S. embargo against Cuba—imposed in 1960 when Fidel Castro created a communist state—still remains in effect. In 2000, President Clinton signed a law that relaxed restrictions on food sales to Cuba. As a result, the United States has become Cuba's main source of food products.

PROTECTIONISM

Trade regulations can have many political and economic consequences. **Protectionism** is a government's establishment of economic policies that systematically restrict imports in order to protect domestic industries. Protectionism is the opposite of free trade. Imposing tariffs, quotas, and embargoes are three methods of practicing protectionism.

Under protectionism, a country chooses to conduct very little trade. It is as if the country has many embargoes against other countries. A protectionist country must rely largely on its own resources to meet the needs of its population. This can be difficult for countries that do not have many natural resources.

PROTECTIONISM AND SUBSIDIES

A government can accomplish the same goal by subsidizing domestic industries. This allows them to be more competitive against foreign competition. For example, the United States and Europe subsidize their farmers. Those subsidies allow them to overproduce products that they can sell or donate overseas. All excess output can then be sold internationally at very low prices. Naturally this displeases foreign competitors, who cannot compete with those low prices in the global marketplace. In 2009 a "Buy American" clause was included in the 2009 United States stimulus package. It was seen by many trading partners as a subsidy and an example of protectionism.

PROTECTIONISM AND RETALIATION

Sometimes, when one country imposes a tariff or quota, the other country retaliates. For example, in 2009, the United States imposed a 35 percent tariff on automobile tires made in China. After that tariff was announced, China responded by threatening to impose a higher tariff on chicken produced in the United States. In such situations, each country may complain that the other is engaging in unfair trade practices. A cycle of tariffs or quotas followed by retaliation may result in what economists and financial experts call a "trade war."

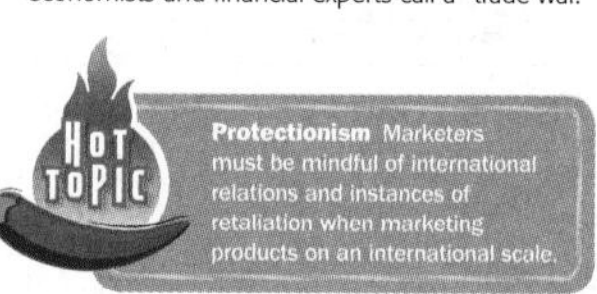

HOT TOPIC
Protectionism Marketers must be mindful of international relations and instances of retaliation when marketing products on an international scale.

88 | Unit 2 · Economics

Chapter 4 · Global Analysis | 89

EXPLAIN

Career Chatroom

Use these questions to focus the discussion about the Career Chatroom feature.

Guiding Questions

Analyze Why would Dave Walker think that preparation and communication skills are the key to success?	He has a highly-skilled, technical job that requires many years of training. He must be able to communicate clearly to ensure that clients are receiving exactly what they need and are paying for.
Synthesize How is Dave Walker's key to success linked to the ability to troubleshoot?	It is important to be prepared with appropriate background knowledge that allows you to respond quickly when decisions are needed to solve problems.

Graphic Organizer

Display this graphic organizer. Ask students to define each term.

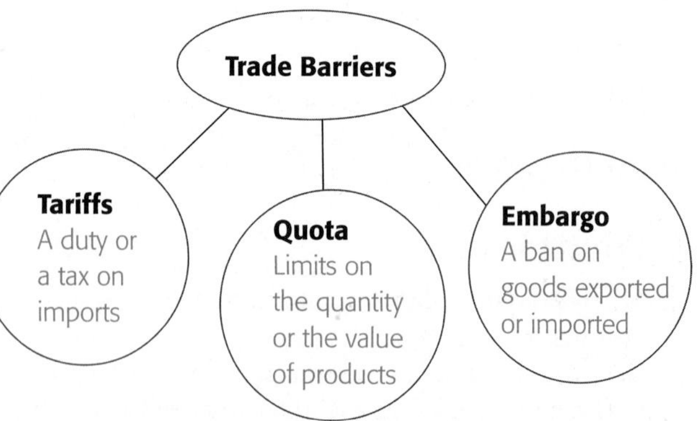

A ban on goods exported or imported

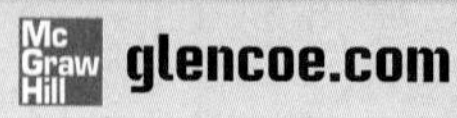

Graphic Organizer Send students to the Online Learning Center to print this graphic organizer.

ELABORATE

TRADE BARRIERS

Tell students that in order to limit competition from other countries, governments develop trade barriers or restrictions. Then ask these guiding questions to focus the discussion on trade barriers.

Guiding Questions

Compare and Contrast Explain the uses of each type of trade barrier.	Tariffs may be used to product revenue for a country. Protective tariffs may increase the price of imported products so that domestic products can compete. Quotas control the amount of a product that enters the country so that domestic producers can compete. Embargoes are imposed for health reasons or political reasons.
Analyze How is protectionism the opposite of free trade?	Free trade is the commercial exchange of products between nations that is conducted on free market principles without restrictions. Protectionism is a government's establishment of economic policies, which systematically restrict imports in order to protect domestic industries. Protectionism is the opposite of free trade because it limits and imposes costs upon free trade.

Reinforce Vocabulary

Impose—Synonyms Ask students to read the paragraph under the head Trade Barriers. Then say: ***Based on its use in this paragraph, provide a synonym for the word* impose.** Students may suggest *set* or *decree* as synonyms.

Subsidizing—Synonyms Have a volunteer read aloud the first paragraph under the head Protectionism and Subsidies. Ask students to provide a synonym for *subsidized.* Synonyms might include the words *financed, funded,* or *underwritten.*

MINI CLIP

Reading: Strategic Readers

Go to the Online Learning Center to view a video in which an author discusses the characteristics of strategic readers.

Protectionism Encourage students to research the history and consequences of real-world protectionism. Research should include the history and an analysis of the consequences to both sides.

Critical Thinking

Tell students that when the United States ended its trade embargo on Vietnam in 1995, American products could be sold there. The Coca-Cola® company flew a 30-foot-tall inflatable bottle to a Vietnamese celebration, and PepsiCo® placed a giant photo of a Pepsi can in the main part of Ho Chi Minh City. Ask students: ***What do you suppose the purpose of these public relations ads might have been?*** Students may suggest that the purpose was to attract consumers to the product in a new market.

Mini Projects

Differentiated Instruction

Interpersonal Learners Divide the class into small groups. Tell students the following: A government can impose a trade sanction, or penalty, on other countries, usually by adding tariffs. Then ask groups to discuss this question: ***Do you think there are good reasons to do this?*** Ask groups to share their answers to the question. Some students may feel it is unfair for more prosperous countries to claim this advantage to promote their products. Other may feel there are times when tariffs or sanctions can be a political advantage, to retaliate, or to encourage a country's industry.

Students with Learning Disabilities/Gifted Learners Create small groups that include both students with learning disabilities and gifted learners. Have students work together to ensure that they all understand and can explain trade barriers—tariffs, quotas, embargoes, and protectionism.

Intrapersonal Learners Instruct students to write a thesis statement and include supporting details about the legitimacy of the embargo that limits trading with Cuba. Statements will vary—students might provide information about the original purpose of the embargo and the effect it has had since its beginning in 1963.

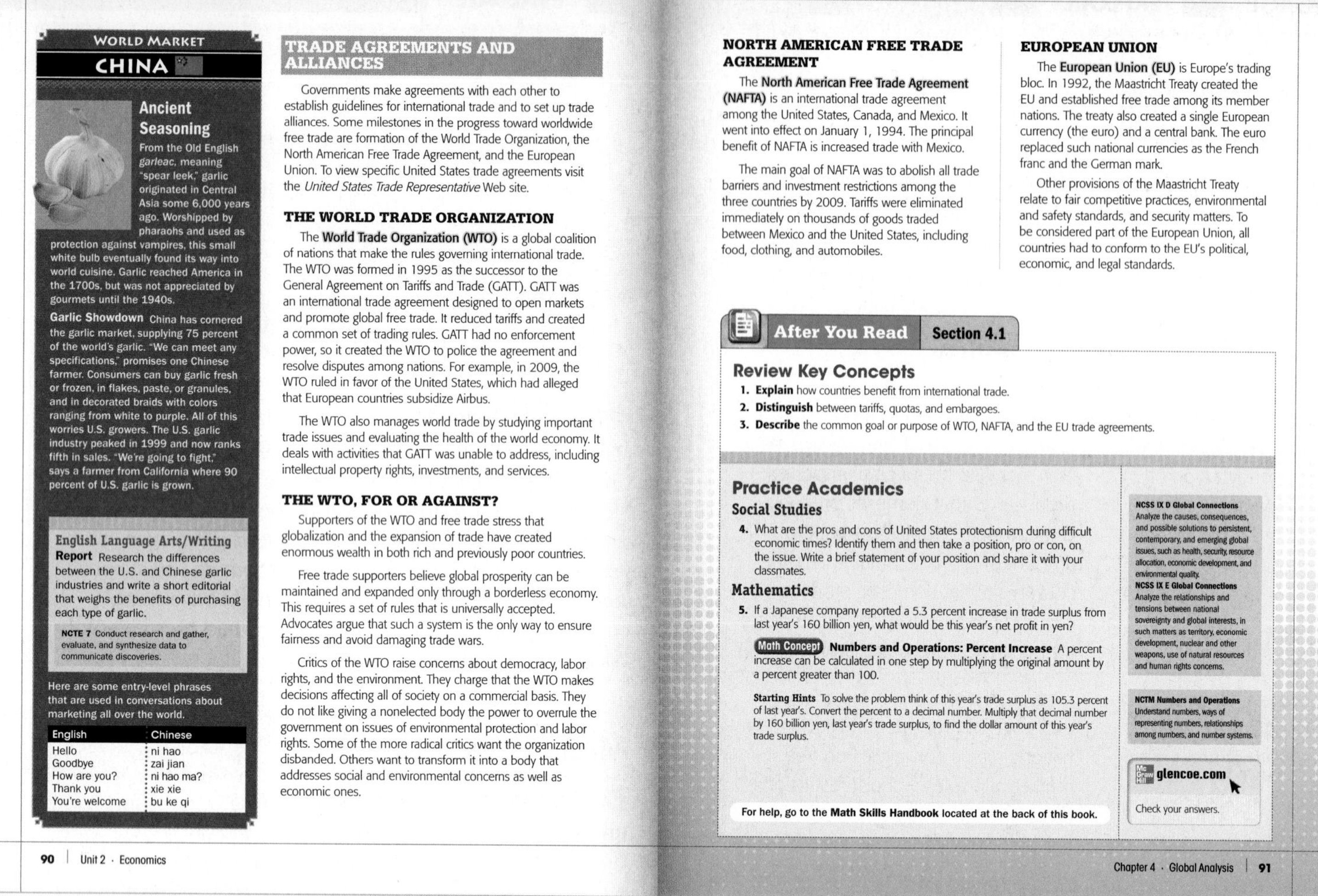

WORLD MARKET

CHINA

Ancient Seasoning From the Old English *garleac,* meaning "spear leek," garlic originated in Central Asia some 6,000 years ago. Worshipped by pharaohs and used as protection against vampires, this small white bulb eventually found its way into world cuisine. Garlic reached America in the 1700s, but was not appreciated by gourmets until the 1940s.

Garlic Showdown China has cornered the garlic market, supplying 75 percent of the world's garlic. "We can meet any specifications," promises one Chinese farmer. Consumers can buy garlic fresh or frozen, in flakes, paste, or granules, and in decorated braids with colors ranging from white to purple. All of this worries U.S. growers. The U.S. garlic industry peaked in 1999 and now ranks fifth in sales. "We're going to fight," says a farmer from California where 90 percent of U.S. garlic is grown.

English Language Arts/Writing

Report Research the differences between the U.S. and Chinese garlic industries and write a short editorial that weighs the benefits of purchasing each type of garlic.

NCTE 7 Conduct research and gather, evaluate, and synthesize data to communicate discoveries.

Here are some entry-level phrases that are used in conversations about marketing all over the world.

English	Chinese
Hello	ni hao
Goodbye	zai jian
How are you?	ni hao ma?
Thank you	xie xie
You're welcome	bu ke qi

TRADE AGREEMENTS AND ALLIANCES

Governments make agreements with each other to establish guidelines for international trade and to set up trade alliances. Some milestones in the progress toward worldwide free trade are formation of the World Trade Organization, the North American Free Trade Agreement, and the European Union. To view specific United States trade agreements visit the *United States Trade Representative* Web site.

THE WORLD TRADE ORGANIZATION

The **World Trade Organization (WTO)** is a global coalition of nations that make the rules governing international trade. The WTO was formed in 1995 as the successor to the General Agreement on Tariffs and Trade (GATT). GATT was an international trade agreement designed to open markets and promote global free trade. It reduced tariffs and created a common set of trading rules. GATT had no enforcement power, so it created the WTO to police the agreement and resolve disputes among nations. For example, in 2009, the WTO ruled in favor of the United States, which had alleged that European countries subsidize Airbus.

The WTO also manages world trade by studying important trade issues and evaluating the health of the world economy. It deals with activities that GATT was unable to address, including intellectual property rights, investments, and services.

THE WTO, FOR OR AGAINST?

Supporters of the WTO and free trade stress that globalization and the expansion of trade have created enormous wealth in both rich and previously poor countries.

Free trade supporters believe global prosperity can be maintained and expanded only through a borderless economy. This requires a set of rules that is universally accepted. Advocates argue that such a system is the only way to ensure fairness and avoid damaging trade wars.

Critics of the WTO raise concerns about democracy, labor rights, and the environment. They charge that the WTO makes decisions affecting all of society on a commercial basis. They do not like giving a nonelected body the power to overrule the government on issues of environmental protection and labor rights. Some of the more radical critics want the organization disbanded. Others want to transform it into a body that addresses social and environmental concerns as well as economic ones.

90 | Unit 2 · Economics

NORTH AMERICAN FREE TRADE AGREEMENT

The **North American Free Trade Agreement (NAFTA)** is an international trade agreement among the United States, Canada, and Mexico. It went into effect on January 1, 1994. The principal benefit of NAFTA is increased trade with Mexico.

The main goal of NAFTA was to abolish all trade barriers and investment restrictions among the three countries by 2009. Tariffs were eliminated immediately on thousands of goods traded between Mexico and the United States, including food, clothing, and automobiles.

EUROPEAN UNION

The **European Union (EU)** is Europe's trading bloc. In 1992, the Maastricht Treaty created the EU and established free trade among its member nations. The treaty also created a single European currency (the euro) and a central bank. The euro replaced such national currencies as the French franc and the German mark.

Other provisions of the Maastricht Treaty relate to fair competitive practices, environmental and safety standards, and security matters. To be considered part of the European Union, all countries had to conform to the EU's political, economic, and legal standards.

After You Read | **Section 4.1**

Review Key Concepts

1. **Explain** how countries benefit from international trade.
2. **Distinguish** between tariffs, quotas, and embargoes.
3. **Describe** the common goal or purpose of WTO, NAFTA, and the EU trade agreements.

Practice Academics

Social Studies

4. What are the pros and cons of United States protectionism during difficult economic times? Identify them and then take a position, pro or con, on the issue. Write a brief statement of your position and share it with your classmates.

Mathematics

5. If a Japanese company reported a 5.3 percent increase in trade surplus from last year's 160 billion yen, what would be this year's net profit in yen?

Math Concept **Numbers and Operations: Percent Increase** A percent increase can be calculated in one step by multiplying the original amount by a percent greater than 100.

Starting Hints To solve the problem think of this year's trade surplus as 105.3 percent of last year's. Convert the percent to a decimal number. Multiply that decimal number by 160 billion yen, last year's trade surplus, to find the dollar amount of this year's trade surplus.

For help, go to the **Math Skills Handbook** located at the back of this book.

NCSS IX D Global Connections Analyze the causes, consequences, and possible solutions to persistent, contemporary, and emerging global issues, such as health, security, resource allocation, economic development, and environmental quality.

NCSS IX E Global Connections Analyze the relationships and tensions between national sovereignty and global interests, in such matters as territory, economic development, nuclear and other weapons, use of natural resources and human rights concerns.

NCTM Numbers and Operations Understand numbers, ways of representing numbers, relationships among numbers, and number systems.

glencoe.com

Check your answers.

Chapter 4 · Global Analysis | 91

ELABORATE

THE WORLD TRADE ORGANIZATION

Ask students these guiding questions to focus the discussion on the World Trade Organization.

Guiding Questions

Recall Why was the WTO created?	It was created to police the international trade agreement designed to open markets and promote global free trade.
Pro and Con What are the arguments for and against the WTO?	Arguments for: globalization and the expansion of trade have created wealth in both rich and previously poor countries; a system of universally accepted rules is necessary for global prosperity Arguments against: decisions that affect democracy, labor rights, the environment, and society should not be based solely on commerce; the power to overrule member governments is too much power.

Mini Project

Enrichment

Role Play Have students work together in groups to prepare a skit in which they play the roles of ambassadors of two or more countries that are engaged in a dispute over trade barriers. One student in each group can play the role of mediator. Suggest a dispute regarding a tariff recently imposed by one country on a trading partner (another country) and the trading partner's method of retaliation (for example, imposing a tariff or quota on a different product). Skits will vary. Look for student understanding that trade barriers imposed by one country often create problems with free trade and that the trading partner often retaliates with its own trade barriers. For example, if the United States increases a tariff on automobiles made in Japan, Japan might retaliate by imposing a tariff or quota on products it imports from the U.S., such as wheat, beef, or machinery.

EVALUATE

Mini Project

Enrichment

Create Surveys to Collect Data Tell students they will conduct a survey about the effect NAFTA has had on the people of the United States. Students should create a list of questions to ask at least five different people. Sample questions: Do you think NAFTA has had a positive effect on the people of the United States? Why or why not? Students should try to survey different types of people such as business owners, blue-collar workers, and so on. After students have collected their data, have them analyze the results. Ask: ***What conclusions can you draw about the effect NAFTA has had on the people of the United States?*** Students' conclusions will vary. Answers to the survey questions will differ because people in different parts of the country have been affected in different ways.

Graphic Organizer

Tell students that the European Union (EU) consists of a number of democratic European countries committed to working together for peace and prosperity. EU countries still make many of their own economic decisions, but they leave other decisions to Europe-wide institutions such as the European Parliament and the European Central Bank. Display this T-chart and lead the class in a discussion about why countries might or might not want to become a part of the European Union. Sample answers:

European Union Membership

Pros	Cons
• Gives smaller countries more clout with larger countries • Makes trade easier with a common currency • Helps with economic and political stability	• Relinquishes some powers of the individual countries to the EU • Makes decisions for member countries • Makes decisions that are not always in the best interest of all of the member countries.

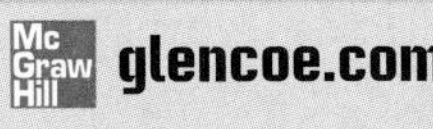

glencoe.com iWB

Graphic Organizer Send students to the Online Learning Center to print this graphic organizer.

After You Read — Section 4.1

Review Key Concepts

1. Increased foreign investment in a country often improves the standard of living for the country's people. Individuals have more options to choose from when making purchasing decisions. Economic alliances among nations often solidify political alliances that foster peace.
2. A tariff is a tax on imports. A quota limits either the quantity or the monetary value of a product that may be imported. An embargo is a total ban on specific goods coming into and leaving a country (typically imposed for health or political reasons).
3. The common goal or purpose of WTO, NAFTA, and the EU trade agreements is to reduce trade restrictions and increase free trade among nations.

Practice Academics

Social Studies

4. Accept all reasonable answers. Some pros of U.S. protectionism are protecting U.S. industries and U.S. workers. Some cons of U.S. protectionism are breaking existing trade agreements with other countries, retaliation from trading partners, creating higher prices for consumers by reducing competition, and creating strained relationships with foreign countries.

Mathematics

5. 68.48 billion yen ($160 \times 1.053 = 168.48$)

glencoe.com

Answer Key Send students to the Online Learning Center to check their answers.

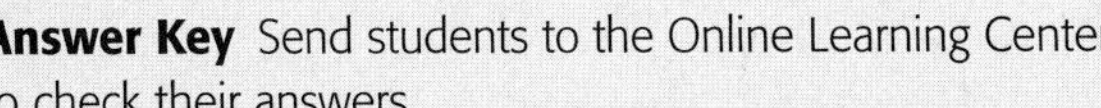

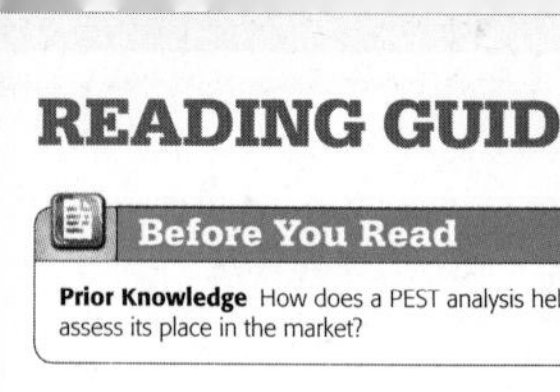

READING GUIDE

Before You Read

Prior Knowledge How does a PEST analysis help a company assess its place in the market?

Objectives

- **List** forms of international trade.
- **Identify** political, economic, socio-cultural, and technological factors that affect international business.
- **Understand** global marketing strategies.

The Main Idea

Besides language barriers, there are many other factors that must be considered for doing international business.

Vocabulary

Content Vocabulary
- licensing
- contract manufacturing
- joint venture
- foreign direct investment (FDI)
- multinationals
- mini-nationals
- globalization
- adaptation
- customization

Academic Vocabulary
You will find these words in your reading and on your tests. Make sure you know their meanings.
- proprietary
- corporate

Graphic Organizer

Draw or print this chart to list factors that affect international businesses.

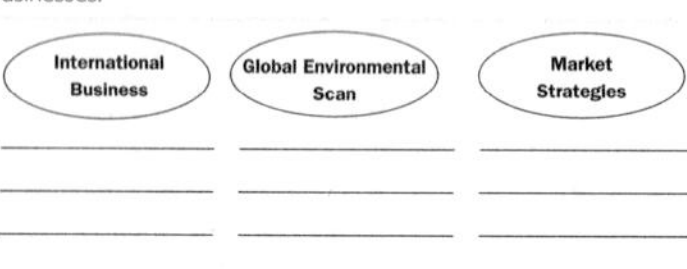

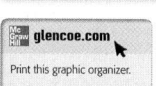

Print this graphic organizer.

ACADEMIC

English Language Arts
NCTE 1 Read texts to acquire new information.

Social Studies
NCSS IX E Global Connections Analyze the relationships and tensions between national sovereignty and global interests, in such matters as territory, economic development, nuclear and other weapons, use of natural resources and human rights concerns.

NCSS *National Council for the Social Studies*
NCTE *National Council of Teachers of English*
NCTM *National Council of Teachers of Mathematics*
NSES *National Science Education Standards*

Common Core
Reading Integrate and evaluate content presented in diverse formats and media, including visually and quantitatively, as well as in words.

The Global Marketplace

DOING BUSINESS INTERNATIONALLY

The global marketplace has been growing with the increased acceptance of capitalism around the world, advances in technology such as Internet connections, and the reduction of trade barriers. Global news coverage is instantaneous, connecting people throughout the world. These factors have encouraged businesses to venture into foreign countries. In this section, you will see what it takes for a business to become a global player.

Trade agreements by governments set the guidelines for businesses to operate in the global marketplace. Getting involved in international trade can mean importing, exporting, licensing, contract manufacturing, joint ventures, or foreign direct investment. Each of these options offers a different level of risk and control. **Figure 4.1** (page 94) shows how the profit potential increases as the level of financial commitment, risk, and marketing control increase for each market entry option.

As You Read

Connect What risks are involved in trying to learn a new skill?

IMPORTING

Importing involves purchasing goods from a foreign country. A domestic company that wants to expand its product selections can begin importing goods. Products imported for the U.S. market must meet the same standards as domestic products, including those imposed by the Food and Drug Administration. If these standards are met, most products can be imported without prior government approval.

A quota can limit entry of certain goods into the country. Quotas exist on agriculture, food products, and other merchandise. Once a quota is reached for a certain item, no more of that item may enter the country. Any shipment in excess of the quota is quarantined by U.S. Customs. Because understanding importing policies can be difficult, U.S. businesses usually hire customs brokers—specialists licensed by the U.S. Treasury Department. Customs brokers know the laws, procedures, and tariffs governing imports. They handle over 90 percent of all imports because of the complex procedures involved.

“What does it take to become a global player?”

EXPORTING

A domestic company that wishes to enter into the global marketplace with minimal risk and control might consider exporting. Domestic companies that want to export their goods and services can get help from the United States government through its Internet export portal and at its BuyUSA Web site.

LICENSING

Licensing involves letting another company, or licensee, use a trademark, patent, special formula, company name, or some other intellectual property for a fee or royalty. This type of market entry has its pros and cons. With licensing, a foreign company makes the product using the information or guidelines provided by the licensor. If the product is a success in the foreign country, the licensor has gained entry with minimal risk. If the product fails, the licensor will have a harder time trying to enter the market in the future.

ENGAGE

Anticipation Activity

Ask students: ***What product or service would you market from what specific country?*** Students should respond with an existing product or service or be able to describe a new product or service they would like to develop.

Objectives

- **List** forms of international trade. Importing, exporting, licensing, contract manufacturing, joint ventures, foreign direct investment, multinationals, and mini-nationals.
- **Identify** political, economic, socio-cultural, and technological factors that affect international business. government stability, infrastructure, labor force, employee benefits, standard of living, foreign exchange rate, symbols, holidays, systems of measurement; the Internet; broadcast media
- **Understand** global marketing strategies. globalization, adaptation, customization

Graphic Organizer

International Business	Global Environmental Scan	Market Strategies
Importing, Exporting, Licensing; Contract Manufacturing, Joint Ventures; Foreign Direct Investment; Multinationals, Mini-Nationals	Political Factors, Economic Factors, Socio-Cultural Factors, Technological Factors	Globalization, Adaptation, Customization

Graphic Organizer Send students to the Online Learning Center to print this graphic organizer.

EXPLORE

Before You Read

Read the Before You Read question aloud: ***How does a PEST analysis help a company assess its place in the market?*** Understanding how political, economic, socio-cultural, and technological factors are changing or likely to change can help companies develop a better appreciation of potential opportunities or threats. Ask students whether they think a PEST analysis would be important for companies involved in international trade. Students should recognize that a PEST analysis is important for all companies.

Preteaching Vocabulary

Have students go to the Online Learning Center at glencoe.com for the Chapter 4 Preteaching Vocabulary games.

Content Vocabulary

Have students create a table with the heads "Forms of International Trade" and "Global Marketing Strategies." Have students put the content vocabulary terms under the head where it fits best. Forms of International Trade: licensing, contract manufacturing, joint venture, foreign direct investment (FDI), multinationals, mini-nationals. Global Marketing Strategies: globalization, adaptation, customization.

Academic Vocabulary

Proprietary—Word Origin Tell students that the term *proprietary* is from Middle English, Old French, and Latin and has similar meanings in each language: owner of property, of a property owner, and ownership, respectively. Ask a volunteer to use a dictionary to find the definition of *proprietary. Proprietary* means "exclusive ownership." Ask students to create sentences in which they use the term *proprietary.* When doing business internationally, proprietary information must sometimes be shared. It was a proprietary, or exclusively owned, hospital.

Corporate—Derivatives Provide students with this definition for the term *corporate:* "configured into an association that has the rights, privileges, and liabilities of an individual." Ask students to think of words that are derived from *corporate.* Words may include corporation, corporative, corporatize, corporatism.

Reading: Vocabulary
Go to the Online Learning Center for a video in which an author describes the importance of academic language.

The Global Marketplace

DOING BUSINESS INTERNATIONALLY

Ask these guiding questions to help students focus on doing business internationally.

Guiding Questions

Analyze How have advances in technology encouraged businesses to venture into foreign countries?	Communicating instantaneously with people in other countries makes businesses feel that they would be able to manage a company in another country more easily.
Differentiate What is the difference between imports and exports?	Imports: purchased goods from a foreign country; Exports: selling goods produced in one country to foreign countries.

As You Read

Read students the As You Read question: ***What risks are involved in trying to learn a new skill?*** Depending on the skill, the risks could range from physical to financial. Ask students what types of risks they think companies might have if they decide to market their products internationally. Students should recognize that financial risks would be the greatest risks for companies deciding to do business internationally.

Expert Advice

Read the quote to students:

"What does it take to become a global player?"

Ask students how they would answer the question. Finances, connections, understanding of the target culture; Knowing the political, economic, socio-cultural, and technological factors in the area where business is to be transacted is also important.

A special type of licensing is franchising. In a franchise agreement, a franchisor grants the franchisee the rights to operate under the company name. The agreement involves following specific guidelines for operation to foster a unified image of the franchisor. Many fast-food chains, like McDonald's®, Wendy's®, and Burger King®, have franchised operations in foreign countries. Even though these companies are operating in different countries, there are elements of their stores, menus, and service that are the same.

CONTRACT MANUFACTURING

Contract manufacturing has become popular as emerging countries offer facilities, know-how, and inexpensive labor. **Contract manufacturing** involves hiring a foreign manufacturer to make products according to a company's specifications. The finished goods are either sold in that country or exported. Many U.S. companies that sell clothing, toys, golf clubs, and computers use contract manufacturers in emerging countries to manufacture their products.

The major benefit is lower wages, which allow companies to be more competitive in their pricing. One of the pitfalls of contract manufacturing is that **proprietary** information must be given to these companies. Golf clubs are an example. In China, molds of new golf club heads have been stolen by workers and sold to counterfeiters. The counterfeit clubs are then sold as copies or knockoffs in the United States and abroad for much less than the brand-name clubs.

JOINT VENTURES

A **joint venture** is a business enterprise that a domestic company and a foreign company undertake together. In some countries, foreign investors are not permitted to own 100 percent of a business. If a company wants to conduct business in those countries, it must find a local business partner, thus creating a joint venture. This is often a good idea even when it is not mandated by law. Domestic business partners know the market and procedures for conducting business in their own country.

FIGURE 4.1 Doing Business Internationally

Level of Risk and Control International trade includes importing, exporting, licensing, contract manufacturing, joint ventures, and foreign direct investment. Each of these options involves a different level of risk and control. ***What advice would you give to a small or medium-sized company interested in international trade?***

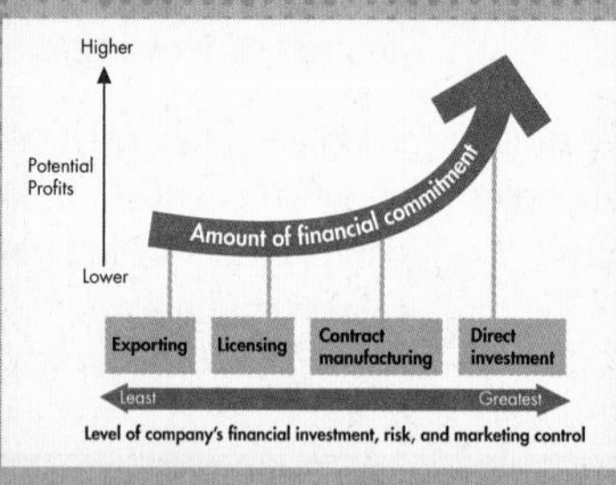

As an example of a joint venture, consider Viacom, Inc.® It owns CBS, Nickelodeon, and MTV, and it has a minority share in a joint venture with Shanghai Media Group. That means Viacom has operations in both the United States and China.

FOREIGN DIRECT INVESTMENT

All the joint ventures described above are considered foreign direct investments. A **foreign direct investment (FDI)** is the establishment of a business in a foreign country. It can take many forms and is used for many purposes.

Sometimes that may involve no more than setting up an office with a staff to maintain a presence in that country. Higher levels of direct investment involve acquisitions of existing foreign companies and construction of facilities such as manufacturing plants and retail stores. Honda®, a Japanese company, has invested in several countries. It has foreign direct investment of approximately $9 billion in North America. In the United States, Honda has eight manufacturing plants and several other related businesses in various states.

MULTINATIONALS AND MINI-NATIONALS

Multinationals are large corporations that have operations in several countries. About one-third of the world's private-sector assets are controlled by more than 37,000 transnational corporations. These corporations have more than 170,000 foreign affiliates. The affiliates are companies that do business in international markets.

Apple® Inc., Procter and Gamble®, Unilever®, Nike®, PepsiCo®, and Coca Cola® are multinational firms. Nike has manufacturing operations in more than 50 countries. The products from these operations are sold in more than 160 countries. **Mini-nationals** are midsize or smaller companies that have operations in foreign countries.

Multinationals and mini-nationals are different from domestic businesses because of how they generate revenue. Multinationals make their money from foreign investments in factories, offices, and other facilities abroad. All these investments are referred to as FDIs. The difference between multinationals and mini-nationals is their size.

Reading Check

Contrast How is franchising different from foreign direct investment?

DIGITAL NATION

The iPhone Conquers the Globe

Apple® Computers launched the iPhone to long lines and big headlines in the U.S. on June 29, 2007. Within a year the product was available in 27 countries, including Australia, Japan, and Mexico, and had sold over 14 million units.

International Challenges

When it introduced the iPhone on the international market, Apple set up exclusive distribution deals with a single cell carrier in each country. Then legislation in several nations forced a halt to such exclusive deals. The company quickly switched its strategy. Apple began to distribute the iPhone through a variety of cell carriers, which boosted sales. By 2010 the iPhone dominated the smart phone market everywhere except Asia and Africa. International sales are growing faster than U.S. sales.

Social Studies

Collaborate Discuss with your class how Apple was able to effectively analyze and evaluate the way its technology was used in the international market.

NCSS IX C Global Connections Analyze and evaluate the effects of changing technologies on the global community.

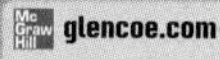

glencoe.com

Get a Digital Nation activity.

EXPLAIN

Visual Literacy

Figure 4.1 Caption Answer Read the figure caption question to students. ***What advice would you give to a small or medium-sized company interested in international trade?*** Advice will vary. Students may suggest that the company needs to determine how much risk they are willing to take and how much control they are willing to give to others before deciding what kind of international trade they want to become involved in. Smaller companies and those who want minimal risk should look into exporting. Higher levels of risk come with licensing, contract manufacturing and direct investment. Ask students to imagine that they are business owners. Ask: ***How much risk would you be willing to take to become involved in international trade? Explain your reasoning.*** Students' answers will vary depending on the students' willingness to take risks. Students should give reasons for their decisions.

Mini Project

Extension

Agree or Disagree Ask students: ***Should intellectual property, such as ideas, written work, and so on, be protected and licensed in the same way that products are?*** Have students who say "yes" to this question stand on one side of the room and have students who say "no" stand on the other side of the room. Those who are undecided should stand in the middle. Ask someone on the "yes" side to give a reason for their thinking. If their reasoning makes someone on the "no" side change their mind or convinces someone in the middle, have the person on the "no" side or person in the middle move to the "yes" side. Then have someone on the "no" side provide a reason for their feelings. If their reasoning convinces someone on the "yes" side to change their mind or convinces someone in the middle, have those people move to the "no" side. Continue the activity until all students have shared their reasons and there is no more movement from one side to the other.

ELABORATE

Critical Thinking

Explain to students that the United States has laws designed to create a safe workplace and to provide a certain amount of pay. Some companies have moved operations to other countries where wages are lower and there are fewer restrictions. Ask students: ***What have you heard about this practice of some U.S. companies moving their operations to other countries?*** Students may say that they have heard that U.S. jobs are lost because of this practice. They may also have heard that companies make a bigger profit when they move their operations to other countries. It can mean that companies can charge less for their products. It may also mean that the quality of the products is compromised.

Mini Project

Extension

Internet Research Ask students: ***Are you surprised to learn that foreign businesses invest in manufacturing facilities and retail stores in the United States?*** Students' answers will vary. Most likely will not be aware that foreign companies are involved in many U.S. businesses. Explain that many corporations have global branches and interests. have students use the Internet to research foreign companies that have operations in the United States. Students' research should answer such questions as: What country is the company from? What products or services do they sell? How many U.S. citizens are employed by the company? Students should give three-minute presentations on their findings. Presentations should be well-organized and answer at least the questions listed above. You may want to have students share their opinions of the practice of foreign businesses having ownership in U.S. companies.

Graphic Organizer

Discuss with students the relationship between contract manufacturing and knockoffs. Ask students: ***What might happen when knockoffs are sold?*** Possible answers:

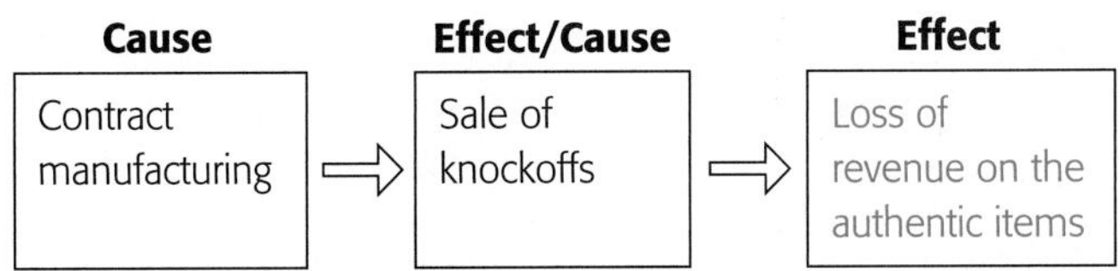

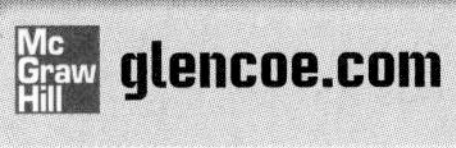

iWB

Graphic Organizer Send students to the Online Learning Center to print this graphic organizer.

MULTINATIONALS AND MINI-NATIONALS

Ask these guiding questions to focus the discussion on multinationals and mini-nationals.

Guiding Questions

Explain How are multinationals and mini-nationals different from domestic businesses?	Multinationals and mini-nationals are different from domestic businesses because of how they generate revenue. They make their money from foreign investments.
Analyze Apple Inc.®, Procter and Gamble®, Unilever®, Nike®, PepsiCo®, and Coca Cola® are multinational firms. What characteristics do they share?	Possible answers: the products these companies produce cross social boundaries. These companies' products appeal to consumers wherever they are sold.

Reading Check Answer

Read the Reading Check question to students: ***How is franchising different from foreign direct investment?*** In a franchise agreement, a franchisor grants the franchisee the rights to operate under the company name. The agreement involves following specific guidelines for operation to foster a unified image of the franchisor. A foreign direct investment is the establishment of a business in a foreign country. Since the foreign direct investment is not opening a business under another company's name, it does not have to operate under specific company guidelines.

DIGITAL NATION

Social Studies Answer Apple® was able to realize that providing their iPhones through multiple providers would increase sales. The government restrictions actually helped Apple rather than hurting them.

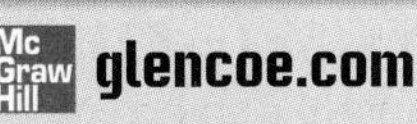

Worksheet Activity Send students to the Online Learning Center to get a Digital Nation worksheet activity.

GLOBAL ENVIRONMENTAL SCAN

Recall the factors involved in a PEST analysis (See Chapter 2). These factors can be used to evaluate a country's marketing opportunities and threats in the international market. A global environmental scan includes analysis of political and economic factors, socio-cultural differences, and technological levels.

POLITICAL FACTORS

Political factors include a government's stability, its trade regulations and agreements, and any other laws that impact a company's operation.

GOVERNMENT STABILITY

A government's stability is an important factor when considering international business operations. If there are changes in the government, investors become wary. For example, when Luiz Inacio Lula da Silva, a left-wing politician, won Brazil's presidential election in 2002, stock prices plunged. Stocks regained strength when businesses saw that President Da Silva supported continued economic reform.

TRADE REGULATIONS AND LAWS

A business must keep abreast of new trade regulations, which can force companies to reconsider doing business in a country. Changes in trade regulations include review of trade agreements, tariffs, and laws to protect intellectual property rights and foreign direct investment. For example, on January 1, 2004 the United States-Chile Free Trade Agreement went into force. Under this agreement, Chile must adopt stronger standards for the protection of intellectual property rights. This means that Chile must adopt rules similar to those in the United States for copyrights, trademarks, patents, and trade secrets.

Domestic laws must be followed by foreign marketers. For example, Sweden does not permit advertising to children, and war toys cannot be advertised in Greece. These regulations are important for toy retailers, such as Toys "R" Us®.

Microlending

The concept of microlending is a growing field of interest in international business. Premal Shah founded Kiva, a company that facilitates investors' lending small amounts of money to people in emerging countries to help them get their businesses up and running. ***How might the practice of microlending be incorporated into a global PEST scan?***

ECONOMIC FACTORS

Key economic factors relevant to starting a business in another country include infrastructure, the quality and cost of labor, employee benefits, taxes, the standard of living, and foreign exchange rates. In addition, economic stability of that nation should be considered.

INFRASTRUCTURE

Things like undependable telephone service or inadequate roads would rule out a location for some businesses. Yet these same infrastructure factors would be an opportunity for companies involved in building roads, energy plants, and telecommunications systems. For example, Poland and the Czech Republic had to carry out environmental cleanup to meet the entry requirements for membership in the European Union. U.S. companies that have expertise in that area could partner with companies in Poland and the Czech Republic to help them with these projects.

LABOR FORCE

The quality and cost of a labor force is another important element in the decision to enter the market in another country. The educational and skill levels of the workers, as well as the customary wages and employment laws are important pieces of information. For example, India has been supporting technology education and now has a pool of highly qualified workers whose wages are lower than those for similar workers in the United States. U.S. companies like AOL®, Yahoo!®, and Google® have recognized this opportunity. They now look to India for computer programming and other computer-related expertise.

EMPLOYEE BENEFITS

In most countries, employers must pay for mandated employee benefits in addition to employees' wages. Many companies do not invest in France because of its labor policies. France restricts the work week to 35 hours and requires companies to consult with employees before downsizing or restructuring. Payroll taxes and employee benefits are high. The cost of hiring a new employee is higher in France than in many countries.

TAXES

Other costs include taxes on property and profits. Countries that want to attract foreign investment may offer reduced taxes for a period of time as an incentive.

Switzerland has been known for its low **corporate** taxes since 1997. In 2008 additional tax incentives were introduced. As a result of these tax breaks, Switzerland has experienced a significant growth in foreign direct investment. Some large companies, like Procter & Gamble®, McDonalds®, Kraft Foods®, Nissan®, Starbucks®, and Google®, have their European headquarters in Switzerland.

STANDARD OF LIVING

Standard of living can be a consideration if a business is considering a country as a market.

When Honda entered China's consumer market, it recognized that most Chinese people could not afford cars. The company targeted the motorcycle market instead and was very successful.

The number of middle-income workers is increasing in poorer nations. This increases the demand for all types of ordinary consumer goods. U.S. products like soaps, detergents, breakfast cereals, snack foods, cell phones, and soft drinks are gaining popularity among consumers in emerging nations.

FOREIGN EXCHANGE RATE

The foreign exchange rate is the price of one country's money currency if purchased with another country's currency. Exchange rates vary every business day. The exchange rate for a nation's currency based on the U.S. dollar is an important factor to consider.

Changes in a nation's currency exchange affect businesses that sell abroad. If the dollar strengthens in value against other currencies, that means it costs more yen, euros, or pesos to buy one dollar. It also means it costs more yen, euros, or pesos to buy one dollar's worth of U.S.-made products. If the U.S. dollar is devalued, U.S. products are more attractive in the global marketplace.

EXPLAIN

Activate Prior Knowledge

Reteach the PEST Analysis Ask students: ***What does the acronym PEST stand for?*** P stands for political factors, E stands for economic factors, S stands for socio-cultural factors, and T stands for technology. Ask: ***What is a PEST analysis used for?*** A PEST analysis is used to gain a better understanding of potential opportunities or threats to a company.

Visual Literacy

Microlending Caption Answer Read the photo caption question to students. ***How might the practice of microlending be incorporated into a global PEST scan?*** Answers may include: microlending might be considered along with the economic factors of a country. If microlenders are helping businesses to start in the country, that would be a positive factor for the country's economy.

GLOBAL ENVIRONMENTAL SCAN

Remind students that in Chapter 2 they studied the PEST analysis in relation to a company doing business in their own country. Then ask these questions to guide the discussion about a global PEST analysis for companies desiring to conduct international business.

Guiding Questions

Determine Why must companies desiring to conduct international business become familiar with a country's trade regulations and laws?	Companies must be aware of the trade regulations because they will help to determine whether the company can afford to do business in the country. They must be familiar with the laws.
Synthesize Why is it important to study the infrastructure of a country before doing business there?	Understanding the infrastructure can help a company determine whether they can sell their products in that country.

ELABORATE

Mini Projects

Extension

Imagine Ask students to imagine that they have just become employed in a marketing job. The company they work for is considering marketing its product, a new brand of toothpaste, in foreign markets. Ask students to give an example of the political and economic factors, socio-cultural differences, and technological levels they might consider before marketing this item in foreign markets. Political factors—students might consider whether toothpaste would be considered a food item and fall under trade regulations for foods. Economic factors—they might consider whether the country's people would be able to afford what might be considered a luxury item. Socio-cultural factors—they may consider whether dental hygiene is important in the target country. Technology—they might consider whether the product packaging will need to be altered if the country uses a different measurement system.

Research Tell students that they have been asked to conduct an environmental scan to determine whether it would be profitable to sell an electric razor their company produces in the foreign market. Tell students to choose a foreign country and conduct an environmental scan for that country. Students' research should include information on the political, economic, socio-cultural, and technological factors associated with the country. Presentations should include a recommendation as to whether or not the razor should be marketed in the country.

Labor Force Ask students why the company cut production. Students may suggest that when the economy is bad, people do not make purchases of luxury items such as diamonds. Then ask students by what percentage production was cut. Production was cut by approximately 55%.

Visual Literacy

Insuring Business in Another Country Caption Answer Read the photo caption question to students. ***What kinds of risks might a company encounter in a foreign country?*** Risks requiring insurance in a foreign country might be similar to the insurance most companies buy normally: liability for law suits filed by employees or customers due to accidents, natural disasters, and robberies; and life insurance for owners.

Graphic Organizer

Ask students to name the factors of a global environmental scan and the elements that make up the factors. Write their responses in the graphic organizer. Possible answers:

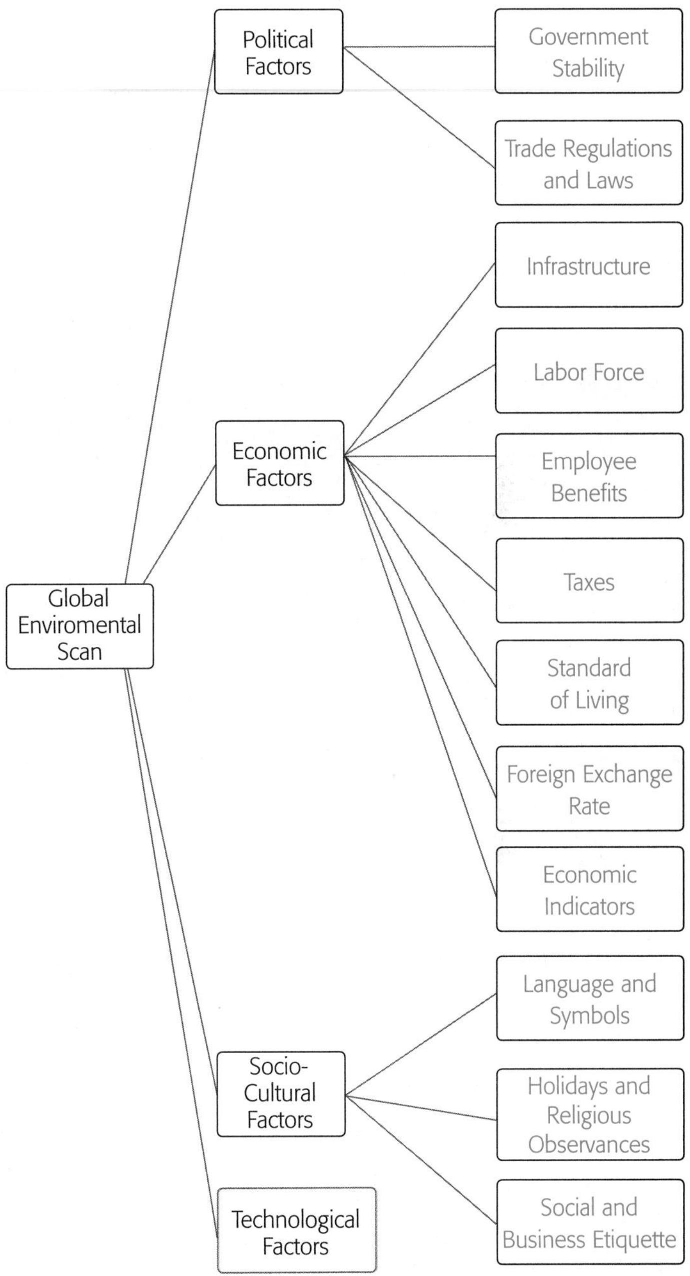

Mc Graw Hill **glencoe.com**

Graphic Organizer Send students to the Online Learning Center to print this graphic organizer.

ECONOMIC INDICATORS

Economic indicators used to evaluate a country's economic stability are the same for all nations. You can study inflation, unemployment, and business failure rates to determine how stable a nation's economy is. Interest rate data and retail sales figures also offer information on economic stability.

SOCIO-CULTURAL FACTORS

Before conducting business in a foreign country, a cross-cultural analysis should be performed. It should include socio-cultural factors such as language, symbols, holidays, religious observances, and social and business etiquette.

Differences in language and customs make international trade more challenging than doing business domestically. Cultural symbols are often different. In the United States, the number 13 is considered unlucky. In China and Japan, the number four is unpopular because it relates to death. Marketers should consider such symbols.

Holidays and religious observances are part of a country's culture too. In India, the cow is sacred, so no beef is sold there. Marketers must heed these cultural differences when creating, naming, packaging, and advertising products.

Social and business etiquette is critical when doing business abroad. A common practice in one nation may take on a different meaning elsewhere. Gift giving is another area of concern. A gift may be considered part of business etiquette in some countries. However, it might be considered an illegal bribe in the United States.

TECHNOLOGICAL FACTORS

Technology is changing the ways that businesses can get involved in international trade. Studying a country's technology means taking into consideration even the most basic factors such as measurement systems and electric voltage standards.

It is important to take a thorough look at the use of computers, faxes, voicemail, wireless phones, and the Internet. A visit to the CIA's *World Fact Book* Web site provides information about the number of telephones (land lines and mobile), radio and television broadcast stations, and Internet users in a given country. These facts must be considered if a company is trying to do business in another country.

Reading Check

Interpret How can infrastructure be an opportunity as well as a threat to foreign investment?

Insuring Business in another Country

This ad suggests that businesses need to consider buying insurance to cover risks in a foreign country. ***What kinds of risks might a company encounter in a foreign country?***

GLOBAL MARKETING STRATEGIES

In planning and making decisions about the four Ps (see Chapter 1) of the marketing mix, global marketers need to consider all the factors that were analyzed as part of the PEST analysis. There are three marketing strategies marketers can use when selling abroad. **Globalization** means complete standardization. New product development and complete customization are also options. **Figure 4.2** (p. 100) shows examples of the global marketing strategies for product and promotion decisions.

GLOBALIZATION

Globalization is selling the same product and using the same promotion methods in all countries. Globalization is mass marketing on a global scale. Very few products can use this marketing strategy.

HOW GLOBALIZATION WORKS

Companies can use the same product and same promotion if they have found a common need across cultures. Benefits of globalization are global brand recognition and reduced marketing costs. A company only has to design one logo and one ad campaign. A challenge is that it is difficult to translate words and phrases so they have the same intended meaning in different countries.

GLOBALIZATION EXAMPLES

Coca-Cola® and other soft drink companies can use a globalization marketing strategy by offering the same version of their products. They can use the same advertising message in countries around the world. Another example of a company that answers common needs across the globe is Microsoft®. Users need computer programs to function in different languages, but the basic applications remain the same. This is also true of Internet search engines.

The success of e-commerce has increased the power of globalization in some instances, particularly where technology is involved.

ADAPTATION

Companies study the characteristics of a country and find ways to target consumers with similar needs and wants. That often requires adapting their products or promotions. Sometimes only the product is changed, while in other cases, only the promotion is changed. **Adaptation** is a company's use of an existing product or promotion from which changes are made. These changes better suit the characteristics of a country or region. This type of market segmentation has the advantage of addressing very specific cultural tastes and interests, which makes market acceptance more reliable. When compared to globalization there is a slight increase in marketing costs. There is also an increase in research and development, which may be considered a disadvantage.

PRODUCT ADAPTATION

Changing a product to meet different consumer needs or to reflect the cultural differences in a foreign market is product adaptation. In some cases, a product's brand name is changed. For example, Unilever's® Sunsilk hair products are called Seda (which means silk) in Latin America. In addition, Sunsilk's ingredients are formulated to match consumers' needs (in this case, typical hair types and styles) in different countries.

PROMOTION ADAPTATION

A promotion adaptation strategy involves changing the advertising message to reflect the values, familiar images, and cultural differences in a foreign market. The change may be as simple as using a popular model or star from a respective country in the different ads. In some cases, the advertising is changed in order to adhere to specific government regulations. For example, McDonald's must use adults in its advertising in Sweden, where advertising to children is prohibited.

EXPLAIN

SOCIO-CULTURAL FACTORS

Ask these guiding questions to focus the discussion on socio-cultural factors.

Guiding Questions

Identify What socio-cultural factors should a company consider before marketing their products in a foreign country?	language, symbols, holidays, religious observances, social and business etiquette
Determine Why would Starbucks® not want to market a four-pack of frappuccino in China?	The number four is unpopular in China because it relates to death.

Reading Check Answer

Read the Reading Check question to students: ***How can infrastructure be an opportunity as well as a threat to foreign investment?*** For some companies a threat might translate into an opportunity for other companies. For example, an area that does not have a dependable water supply would present a challenge for a company that wanted to sell garden hoses and sprinkler systems. However, a water well-digging company might see the area as an opportunity.

ELABORATE

GLOBAL MARKETING STRATEGIES

Tell students that when companies decide to market their products in foreign countries, they often have to make changes to the products or to the promotion for the product. Then ask these guiding questions to focus the discussion about global marketing strategies.

Guiding Questions

Recall What is adaptation?	a company's use of an existing product or promotion with changes to better suit the country or region
Explain How does globalization work?	Companies use the same product and same promotion if they have found a common need across cultures.
Apply Ask students to think of one product that could be marketed through globalization.	Possible answers: globalization—cell phones, iPods, MP3 players, computers.

Graphic Organizer

Ask students to name the three marketing strategies and to provide information about each strategy.

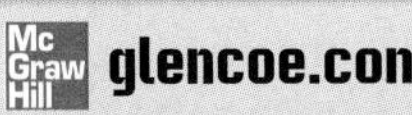

iWB

Graphic Organizer Send students to the Online Learning Center to print this graphic organizer.

e MARKETING

Web Globalization

Web Globalization refers to Web sites that cater to more than one country. A global Web site supports more than one language and reflects a local country's culture. Thus, there is internationalization and localization. For example Google offers its search services in over 125 languages. Not all businesses support that many languages. However, if a company wants to go global, it needs to have its marketing messages translated in the countries where it operates. For example General Mills® sells its products in over 100 countries. Its Web sites for each country must be translated into that country's language or languages. Its advertising messages and product packages must be translated as well. The exact same product may go by different names. For example, Unilever® sells Promise Margarine™ in the United States and sells the same product under the Becel® brand name and Flora® brand name in different countries.

Innovate and Create

Search the Internet for examples of Web globalization by visiting the Web sites of international companies. What similarities and difference did you notice in the way companies created internationalization and localization? While reviewing the different international companies, look for examples of the following marketing strategies: globalization, product adaptation, promotion adaptation, and customization. Share you findings with classmates. Student's observations may differ. Similarities may include: doing business in more than one country, translations into the country's language(s), and a site map that allows you to find products and home offices of the main offices for the company. Differences may be in the way the site map is constructed—there may be separate Web Sites for each country or there may be links for each country or links for the international brands. For example, if you look at the Häagen Dazs® brand of ice cream from General Mills, you will see examples of product and promotional adaptation through the different products and flavors; as well as different Web site designs for each country where Häagen Dazs is sold. Customization might be easier to find at an international food company where certain food products are popular in one region or country, but not in others.

eMarketing Worksheet Activity Send students to the Online Learning Center to download an eMarketing worksheet activity.

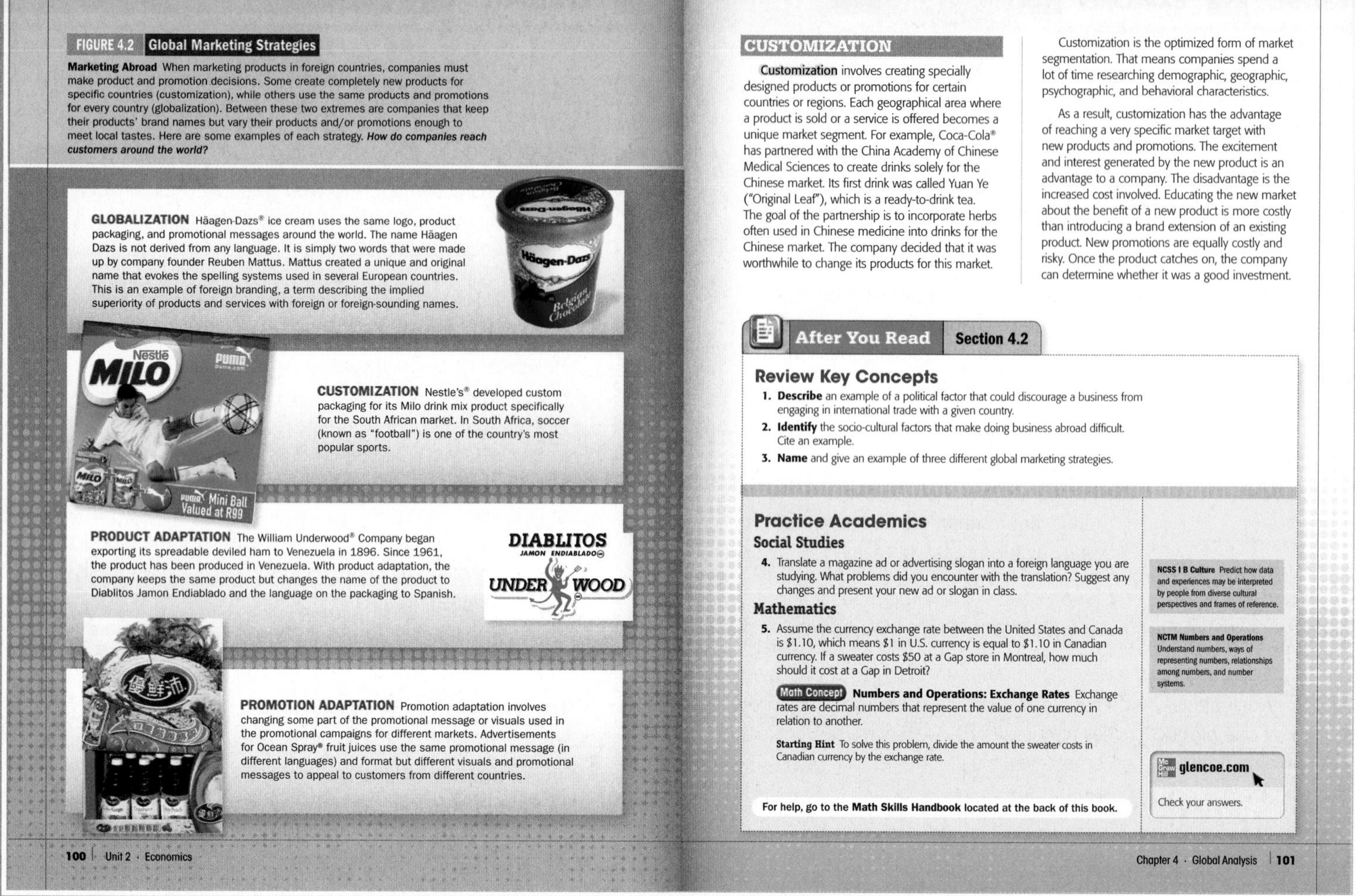

FIGURE 4.2 Global Marketing Strategies

Marketing Abroad When marketing products in foreign countries, companies must make product and promotion decisions. Some create completely new products for specific countries (customization), while others use the same products and promotions for every country (globalization). Between these two extremes are companies that keep their products' brand names but vary their products and/or promotions enough to meet local tastes. Here are some examples of each strategy. ***How do companies reach customers around the world?***

GLOBALIZATION Häagen-Dazs® ice cream uses the same logo, product packaging, and promotional messages around the world. The name Häagen Dazs is not derived from any language. It is simply two words that were made up by company founder Reuben Mattus. Mattus created a unique and original name that evokes the spelling systems used in several European countries. This is an example of foreign branding, a term describing the implied superiority of products and services with foreign or foreign-sounding names.

CUSTOMIZATION Nestle's® developed custom packaging for its Milo drink mix product specifically for the South African market. In South Africa, soccer (known as "football") is one of the country's most popular sports.

PRODUCT ADAPTATION The William Underwood® Company began exporting its spreadable deviled ham to Venezuela in 1896. Since 1961, the product has been produced in Venezuela. With product adaptation, the company keeps the same product but changes the name of the product to Diablitos Jamon Endiablado and the language on the packaging to Spanish.

PROMOTION ADAPTATION Promotion adaptation involves changing some part of the promotional message or visuals used in the promotional campaigns for different markets. Advertisements for Ocean Spray® fruit juices use the same promotional message (in different languages) and format but different visuals and promotional messages to appeal to customers from different countries.

100 | Unit 2 · Economics

CUSTOMIZATION

Customization involves creating specially designed products or promotions for certain countries or regions. Each geographical area where a product is sold or a service is offered becomes a unique market segment. For example, Coca-Cola® has partnered with the China Academy of Chinese Medical Sciences to create drinks solely for the Chinese market. Its first drink was called Yuan Ye ("Original Leaf"), which is a ready-to-drink tea. The goal of the partnership is to incorporate herbs often used in Chinese medicine into drinks for the Chinese market. The company decided that it was worthwhile to change its products for this market.

Customization is the optimized form of market segmentation. That means companies spend a lot of time researching demographic, geographic, psychographic, and behavioral characteristics.

As a result, customization has the advantage of reaching a very specific market target with new products and promotions. The excitement and interest generated by the new product is an advantage to a company. The disadvantage is the increased cost involved. Educating the new market about the benefit of a new product is more costly than introducing a brand extension of an existing product. New promotions are equally costly and risky. Once the product catches on, the company can determine whether it was a good investment.

After You Read | **Section 4.2**

Review Key Concepts

1. **Describe** an example of a political factor that could discourage a business from engaging in international trade with a given country.
2. **Identify** the socio-cultural factors that make doing business abroad difficult. Cite an example.
3. **Name** and give an example of three different global marketing strategies.

Practice Academics

Social Studies

4. Translate a magazine ad or advertising slogan into a foreign language you are studying. What problems did you encounter with the translation? Suggest any changes and present your new ad or slogan in class.

Mathematics

5. Assume the currency exchange rate between the United States and Canada is $1.10, which means $1 in U.S. currency is equal to $1.10 in Canadian currency. If a sweater costs $50 at a Gap store in Montreal, how much should it cost at a Gap in Detroit?

Math Concept **Numbers and Operations: Exchange Rates** Exchange rates are decimal numbers that represent the value of one currency in relation to another.

Starting Hint To solve this problem, divide the amount the sweater costs in Canadian currency by the exchange rate.

For help, go to the **Math Skills Handbook** located at the back of this book.

NCSS I B Culture Predict how data and experiences may be interpreted by people from diverse cultural perspectives and frames of reference.

NCTM Numbers and Operations Understand numbers, ways of representing numbers, relationships among numbers, and number systems.

glencoe.com

Check your answers.

Chapter 4 · Global Analysis | 101

ELABORATE

Visual Literacy

Figure 4.2 Caption Answer Read the caption question to students. ***How do companies reach customers around the world?*** Companies may decide which marketing strategies to use when marketing products in foreign countries based on the needs and wants of the customer being targeted. If the needs and wants are universal in nature, like having fun, globalization would work. If the product is completely unique to that foreign country, then customization would be used. If a segment of the market is being targeted, then market segmentation in the form of product adaptation or promotion adaptation would be used. Ask students to give their opinions on the effectiveness of each of the ads in the figure. Have them provide real-life examples as well as their own first impression. Then divide the class into small groups and have them discuss and defend their opinions. Ask volunteers to share their examples and first impressions with the class. Class members might ask questions that would help the volunteers better define their thoughts.

Activate Prior Knowledge

Reteach Global Marketing Strategies Ask students to explain the differences among globalization, adaptation, and customization. In globalization, the product is sold as is, without modification for particular countries. In adaptation, the product or the promotion of it is changed to suit the country. Customization is the creating of an entirely new product for a specific foreign market.

Reinforce Vocabulary

Promotion—Multiple Meanings Ask students how they have heard the term *promotion* used. Some students will likely mention its use in advertising and others may mention its use to describe students moving from one grade to a higher grade. Tell students that when used in this text, *promotion* refers to decisions about advertising, personal selling, sales promotion, and publicity used to attract potential customers.

Critical Thinking

Divide the class into small groups. Ask each group to answer the question: ***Why do food and food products lend themselves well to product adaptation?*** Then ask groups to share their answers with the rest of the class. Food preferences vary by culture. Adaptations may occur when new ways are developed to store or process foods.

EVALUATE

CUSTOMIZATION

Tell students that often, products or their promotions must be specially designed to sell in different countries or regions. Then use these guiding questions to focus the discussion about customization.

Guiding Questions

Explain What are demographic, geographic, psychographic and behavioral characteristics?	Demographics: statistics that describe a population in age, gender, income, marital status, ethnic background Geographics: segmentation of the market based on where people live Psychographics: grouping people with similar attitudes,opinions, lifestyles, shared values Behavioral: analyzing shopping patterns decision-making processes.
Analyze Why would a company try to adapt an existing product or promotion before turning to customization?	Customization is very costly. The company must educate the new market about the benefits of a new product and create new promotions.

WORLD MARKET
ENGLISH LANGUAGE ARTS/ WRITING

Ask students to research the differences between the U.S. and Chinese garlic industries and to write a short editorial that weighs the benefits of purchasing each type of garlic. After students have completed their research and written the editorials, ask volunteers to share their editorials with the rest of the class. Ask students: ***How do you think U.S. growers will "fight" to stay on top of the garlic market?*** Students may suggest that farmers will look at new farming techniques that will increase production without raising costs. They might look into stronger marketing campaigns or work together against foreign competition, and so on.

After You Read — Section 4.2

Review Key Concepts

1. Accept all reasonable examples. Some plausible answers are: Political ideology (i.e., Communist Cuba), government stability, (overthrow of a government), trade regulations (quotas or high tariffs), and any other laws that affect a company's operations, such as taxes, restrictions on advertising or poor legal recourse in cases of piracy.
2. Socio-cultural factors that make doing business abroad difficult include differences in language and symbols, holidays and religious observances, social and business etiquette. Accept all reasonable examples. One example is McDonald's® in India does not sell beef burgers, instead they sell mutton burgers. Translating advertising messages into a foreign language could be problematic, "Nova" in Spanish means "no go" which is not what you want to say about an automobile.
3. Globalization, adaptation (product and promotion), and customization are three different types of global marketing strategies. Accept all reasonable examples. An example of globalization is Coca Cola® brand Coke which uses the same advertising message around the world. An example of product adaptation is Unilever's® Sunsilk hair products which are formulated to match consumers' needs (prevalent hair types) in different countries. An example of promotion adaptation is McDonald's advertising in Sweden to only adults because advertising to children is prohibited. Customization is creating a product solely for one country or region, such as Yuan Ye, ready-to-drink tea for the Chinese market.

Practice Academics

Social Studies

4. Translations, problems encountered, suggested changes, and new ads should be reviewed to see if the same advertising message is communicated.

Mathematics

5. \$45.45 (\$50 divided by \$1.10 = \$45.45)

 glencoe.com 

Answer Key Send students to the Online Learning Center to check their answers.

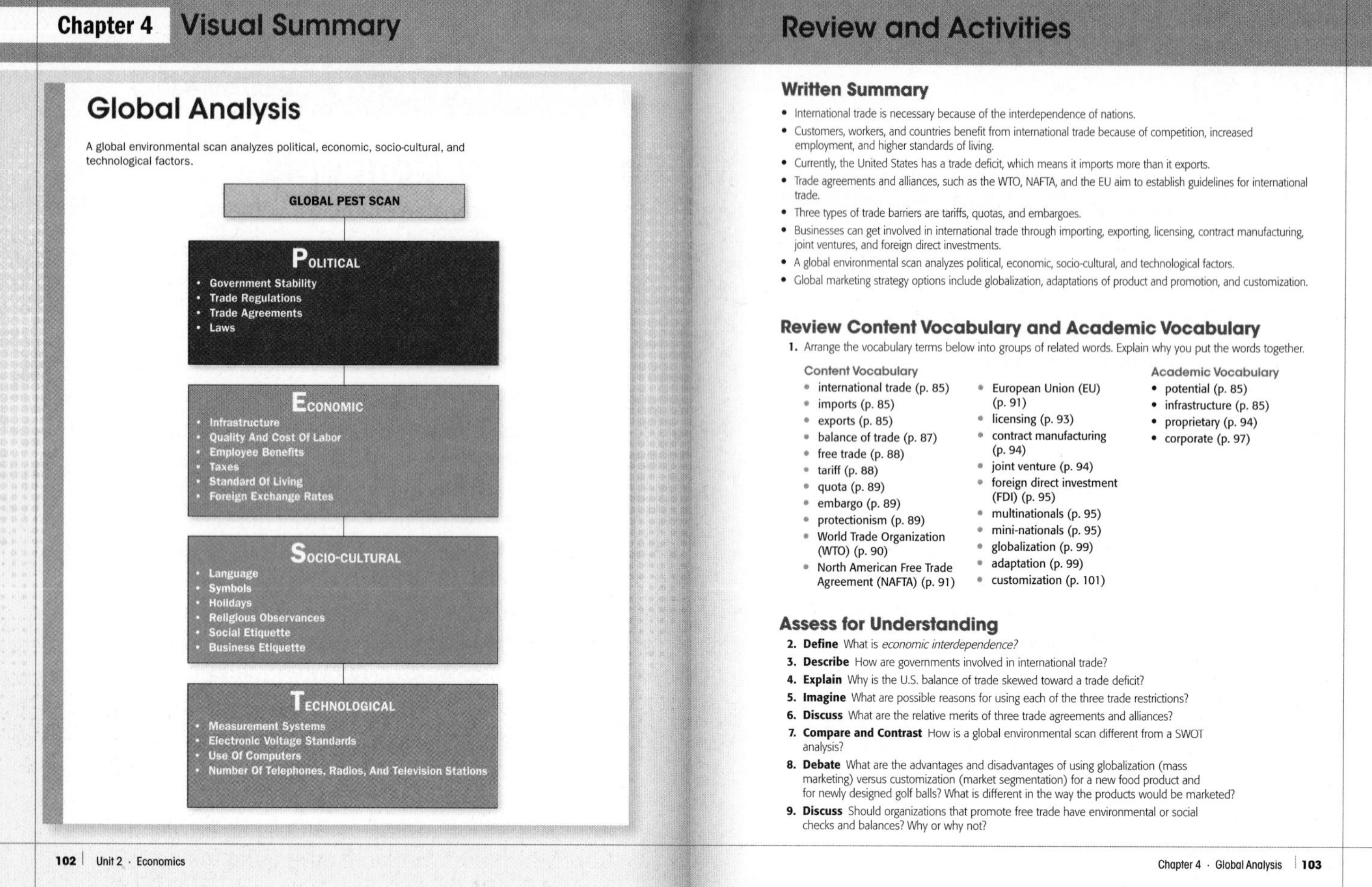

Chapter 4 Visual Summary

Global Analysis

A global environmental scan analyzes political, economic, socio-cultural, and technological factors.

GLOBAL PEST SCAN
POLITICAL
• Government Stability
• Trade Regulations
• Trade Agreements
• Laws
ECONOMIC
• Infrastructure
• Quality And Cost Of Labor
• Employee Benefits
• Taxes
• Standard Of Living
• Foreign Exchange Rates
SOCIO-CULTURAL
• Language
• Symbols
• Holidays
• Religious Observances
• Social Etiquette
• Business Etiquette
TECHNOLOGICAL
• Measurement Systems
• Electronic Voltage Standards
• Use Of Computers
• Number Of Telephones, Radios, And Television Stations

102 | Unit 2 · Economics

Review and Activities

Written Summary

- International trade is necessary because of the interdependence of nations.
- Customers, workers, and countries benefit from international trade because of competition, increased employment, and higher standards of living.
- Currently, the United States has a trade deficit, which means it imports more than it exports.
- Trade agreements and alliances, such as the WTO, NAFTA, and the EU aim to establish guidelines for international trade.
- Three types of trade barriers are tariffs, quotas, and embargoes.
- Businesses can get involved in international trade through importing, exporting, licensing, contract manufacturing, joint ventures, and foreign direct investments.
- A global environmental scan analyzes political, economic, socio-cultural, and technological factors.
- Global marketing strategy options include globalization, adaptations of product and promotion, and customization.

Review Content Vocabulary and Academic Vocabulary

1. Arrange the vocabulary terms below into groups of related words. Explain why you put the words together.

Content Vocabulary
- international trade (p. 85)
- imports (p. 85)
- exports (p. 85)
- balance of trade (p. 87)
- free trade (p. 88)
- tariff (p. 88)
- quota (p. 89)
- embargo (p. 89)
- protectionism (p. 89)
- World Trade Organization (WTO) (p. 90)
- North American Free Trade Agreement (NAFTA) (p. 91)
- European Union (EU) (p. 91)
- licensing (p. 93)
- contract manufacturing (p. 94)
- joint venture (p. 94)
- foreign direct investment (FDI) (p. 95)
- multinationals (p. 95)
- mini-nationals (p. 95)
- globalization (p. 99)
- adaptation (p. 99)
- customization (p. 101)

Academic Vocabulary
- potential (p. 85)
- infrastructure (p. 85)
- proprietary (p. 94)
- corporate (p. 97)

Assess for Understanding

2. **Define** What is *economic interdependence?*
3. **Describe** How are governments involved in international trade?
4. **Explain** Why is the U.S. balance of trade skewed toward a trade deficit?
5. **Imagine** What are possible reasons for using each of the three trade restrictions?
6. **Discuss** What are the relative merits of three trade agreements and alliances?
7. **Compare and Contrast** How is a global environmental scan different from a SWOT analysis?
8. **Debate** What are the advantages and disadvantages of using globalization (mass marketing) versus customization (market segmentation) for a new food product and for newly designed golf balls? What is different in the way the products would be marketed?
9. **Discuss** Should organizations that promote free trade have environmental or social checks and balances? Why or why not?

Chapter 4 · Global Analysis | 103

EVALUATE

Visual Summary

Express Creativity Ask students to develop their own visual summary of a concept in the chapter. Encourage students to use different formats for their visual summaries, such as a storyboard, a timeline, a table, a tree diagram, or a word web. Visual summaries will vary depending on the concept depicted and the visual manner in which it is depicted. Questions to ask when assessing a visual summary include:

- Is the summary clear, economical, and simple?
- Are any important steps left out?
- Are steps or concepts arranged in the same order as the original?
- Does the summary reveal a pattern that connects the details?
- Does the summary locate and highlight the most important information?

Review Content Vocabulary and Academic Vocabulary

1. **Imports** are products that a country buys from other countries. **Exports** are products sold to other countries. When exports are more than imports a nation has a negative **balance of trade.** Trade agreements encourage **free trade.** A **tariff** can be imposed to protect domestic industries. When a **quota** is reached no more goods in that category may enter the country. An **embargo** may be instituted for political or health reasons. **Protectionism** is the opposite of free trade. The **World Trade Organization** was established as the successor to the General Agreement on Tariffs and Trade (GATT). The **North American Free Trade Agreement** is between the United States, Canada, and Mexico. The **European Union** is Europe's trading bloc. **Licensing** involves letting another company use a trademark, patent, special formula, company name or some other intellectual property for a fee or royalty. **Contract manufacturing** is used to take advantage of inexpensive labor in foreign countries. **Joint ventures** are often required by foreign governments if a business wants to operate in that country. **Foreign direct investment** may be an office, manufacturing facility, or retail operation in a foreign country. Apple Inc, Procter and Gamble, and Unilever are **multinationals**. **Mini-nationals** are smaller companies that have operations in foreign countries.

EVALUATE

Review Content Vocabulary and Academic Vocabulary *(continued)*

Globalization is a marketing strategy that can be considered mass marketing on a global scale. Product and promotion **adaptation** are methods used to appeal to potential customers in foreign markets. **Customization** is market segmentation whereby a unique product is designed specifically for a geographical foreign market segment. You have the **potential** to become a marketer. The **infrastructure** of a nation is one factor in an environmental scan. **Proprietary** information should not be divulged by employees. **Corporate** taxes should be considered when considering setting up shop in a foreign country.

Assess for Understanding

2. Most countries do not produce or manufacture all the goods and services they need. They get some of their goods and services from other nations. This economic interdependence happens because each country has unique resources and capabilities.

3. Governments are involved in international trade by controlling and monitoring trade with foreign countries. Governments sign trade agreements with countries to encourage free trade and impose tariffs, quotas, or embargoes that restrict trade.

4. The United States balance of trade is skewed toward a trade deficit because more goods are imported than exported.

5. *Tariffs* may be used to produce revenue for a country and to increase the price of imported goods so that domestic products can compete with them. *Quotas* are used to limit the monetary value or quantity of products that can be imported to control the number of products that enter the U.S. market from other countries. *Embargoes* are total bans on specific goods for health or political reasons.

6. The *World Trade Organization* makes and enforces the rules governing international trade and manages world trade by studying important trade issues and evaluating the health of the world economy. The *North American Free Trade Agreement* eliminated tariffs on thousands of goods traded between Mexico and the U.S. and was to get rid of all trade barriers among Canada, Mexico, and the U.S. by 2009. The *European Union* established free trade among member nations, a single European currency, fair competitive practices, environmental and safety standards, and security measures.

7. The main difference between a global environmental scan and a SWOT analysis is that the global environmental scan is used to evaluate a country's marketing opportunities and threats while a SWOT analysis is used to evaluate a company's marketing opportunities and threats. A global environmental scan takes into consideration: political factors, such as government stability and trade laws and regulations; economic factors such as a country's infrastructure, labor force, employee benefits, taxes, standard of living, foreign exchange rate, and economic indicators; socio-cultural factors, such as language and symbols, holidays and religious observances, as well as social and business etiquette; and technological factors, such as use of computers and Internet capabilities. A SWOT analysis lists and analyzes a company's strengths and weaknesses and includes the opportunities and the threats that could affect a company.

8. Accept all reasonable responses during the debate. Advantages of globalization are global brand recognition and reduced marketing costs. A disadvantage is that it is difficult to translate words and phrases so they have the same intended meaning in different countries. It is more plausible to use globalization with a golf ball than a food product because golf rules and the sport is played the same way around the world. Golfers have the same common need that transcends different cultures–they want to improve their game.

Customization is the optimum in market segmentation. As such, it has the advantage of reaching a very specific market target with new products and promotions. The excitement and interest generated by the "newness" is an advantage to a company. The disadvantage involves the costs involved in developing new products and the risk of failure. A food product is better suited for customization because of the inherently different tastes and cultures.

9. Students may discuss either side of this issue. Those who feel that organizations that promote free trade should have environmental or social checks and balances may say that currently, free trade organizations make decisions based on economic factors only and do not take into consideration environmental or social issues. Those who do not think free trade organizations should have environmental or social checks and balances might argue that having those checks and balances would severely limit the participation of some countries in the free market.

21st Century Skills

Teamwork Skills

10. **International Trade Benefits** Work in a group to prepare an oral presentation to explain international trade to a foreign language class in your school. Include an explanation and examples of why it is important, its benefits and disadvantages, and what government measures affect or regulate it. Also include what business ventures foster it and why learning a foreign language is beneficial for pursuing a career in the global marketplace. Present your findings in a written outline, using word processing software, and create an oral presentation, using presentation software. Cite your sources.

Technology Applications

11. **Global Recession** Research the global recession in 2008–2009 and how it affected business activities in one country. Consider how that country's balance of trade, foreign direct investment, and GDP were affected. Use word processing software, charts, and graphs to prepare a short report on your findings.

e-Marketing Skills

12. **Global Scan** Visit the Web site for the CIA's World Fact Book to conduct a global environmental scan for a country of your choice. Decide if it is a country where you could sell American-made products or if it is a country where you might want to have goods manufactured. Consider the following questions as you complete your research:
    - Are any of your competitors in the market in this country?
    - What are the risks of exporting as compared to foreign direct investment (FDI)?
    - What will you need to do to distinguish your product from others in the country?
    - What resources (human, capital, and natural) will you need?

Build Academic Skills

Social Studies

13. **Embargo on Cuba** The United States placed a trade embargo on Cuba in 1962. Research how that embargo has changed between 2000 and 2009. What U.S. companies benefited from those changes? If the embargo was lifted completely, what U.S. companies would find business opportunities in Cuba?

NCSS IX D Global Connections Analyze the causes, consequences, and possible solutions to persistent, contemporary, and emerging global issues, such as health, security, resource allocation, economic development, and environmental quality.
NCSS IX E Global Connections Analyze the relationships and tensions between national sovereignty and global interests, in such matters as territory, economic development, nuclear and other weapons, use of natural resources and human rights concerns.

English Language Arts

14. **Diversity and the Global Marketplace** Prepare a brief presentation that addresses the impact and value of diversity in the marketplace, as well as how diversity affects marketing in a global marketplace. Include specific examples in your oral presentation.

NCTE 9 Develop an understanding of diversity in language use across cultures.

Mathematics

15. If the exchange rate is 13 Mexican pesos for one U.S. dollar, how many pesos would you get for $5,000? Research prices for items such as food and lodging in Mexico. How many days could you afford to stay in Cancun? Use a spreadsheet program to present a report on the daily costs of your trip.

Math Concept **Choosing an operation** To solve this problem, multiply the U.S. dollar amount by the number of pesos it is worth.

NCTM Number and Operations Understand the meanings of operations and how they relate to one another.

For help, go to the **Math Skills Handbook** located at the back of this book.

Standardized Test Practice

Directions Read the following questions. On a separate piece of paper, write the best possible answer for each one.

1. Assume the exchange rate between the United States dollar and Euro is .77, which means that $1 is equal to .77 Euros. How much would $50 be worth in Euros?
   A. $27.00 **C.** $38.50
   B. $77.00 **D.** $88.50
2. **True or False** Adaptation and customization are examples of mass marketing on a global scale.
   T
   F
3. _________ is when a government establishes economic policies that restrict imports in order to protect domestic industries.

Test-Taking Tip

When working on a test, keep things moving along. Work on a problem until you get stuck. Think about it for a minute or two, and if nothing comes to mind, then drop it and go on to another problem.

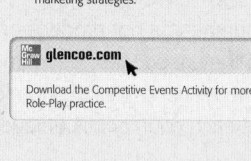

DECA Connection Role Play

Intern
Advertising Agency

Situation Assume the role of an intern in a global advertising agency. A new client is an educational toy company that is considering marketing its goods abroad. This client has had great success with its products in the domestic market. However, this company is unsure whether its toys will be successful across the globe.

Since this company has not marketed its products internationally, its employees do not know about the concepts of licensing, contract manufacturing, franchising, joint venture, and foreign direct investment. You may not need to explain the differences between each of these concepts. However, you will need to make a recommendation to the company about how it should do business internationally.

Activity You are to prepare an outline of a presentation to your mentor (judge). Include the pros and cons of international trade and the challenges that companies face when marketing toys in a foreign country.

Evaluation You will be evaluated on how well you meet the following performance indicators:

- Explain the nature of global trade.
- Discuss the impact of cultural and social environments on global trade.
- Assess global trends and opportunities.
- Discuss the global environment in which businesses operate.
- Identify considerations in implementing international marketing strategies.

glencoe.com

Download the Competitive Events Activity for more Role-Play practice.

EVALUATE

Teamwork Skills

10. **International Trade Benefits** Possible answers include an explanation and examples of why international trade is important, its benefits and disadvantages, what government measures affect or regulate it, what business ventures foster it, and why learning a foreign language is beneficial for pursuing a career in the global marketplace.

Technology Applications

11. **Global Recession** Accept reports that address the financial crisis in 2008–2009, particularly the effects of the sub-prime mortgage collapse in the United States on the housing and banking industries and investment and mortgage companies. Unemployment went up. Consumer confidence and spending went down. Most industrialized countries were affected by the crisis. The U.S. provided bailout money for automakers. Many European nations nationalized banks. Stock markets around the world responded negatively. Many companies went bankrupt.

e-Marketing Skills

12. **Global Scan** Accept all reasonable environmental scans for the countries students research at the CIA's Web site. Also, see if the students' analyses regarding the sale of American-made products in that country or the country as a site to have goods manufactured are reasonable. Students should answer the following questions in their research: Are any of your competitors in the market in this country? What are the risks of exporting as compared to foreign direct investment (FDI)? What will you need to do to distinguish your product from others in the country? What resources (human, capital, and natural) will you need?

EVALUATE

Build Academic Skills

Social Studies

13. Embargo on Cuba In 2000, the U.S. government allowed U.S. companies to sell meat, grain, and medical equipment to Cuba. Farmers and manufacturers of medical equipment benefited. In 2009 President Obama eased sanctions to allow visits to Cuba and to allow telecommunications companies to do business in Cuba. If the embargo is lifted completely, companies like Caterpillar® and other companies involved in construction would benefit, as Cuba's infrastructure needs a lot of work.

English Language Arts

14. Diversity and the Global Marketplace The presentations should address the impact and value of diversity, as well as how diversity affects marketing in a global marketplace. Accept all reasonable examples. Diversity helps companies grow their businesses by developing products for specific segments of the market. Companies that address diversity must market their products differently by changing the product to reflect the cultural mores or tastes of different people. Their advertising messages must be translated into different languages. For example companies that market food products in India may add the spice curry to the ingredients to appeal to Indian's taste buds. Promotional messages for products sold in Mexico must be written in Spanish.

Mathematics

15. You would get 65,000 pesos for $5,000 at the exchange rate of 13 pesos per one U.S. dollar. Students should use the Internet to research rental fees and the cost of food in Cancun, Mexico. Daily costs should be presented using a spreadsheet program.

Standardized Test Practice

1. C $38.50 (multiply .77 × $50)
2. False (Globalization is mass marketing on a global scale).
3. Protectionism

DECA Connection Role Play

Evaluations will be based on these performance indicators:

1. **Explain the nature of global trade.** This new global marketplace makes people and businesses in the world potential customers and potential employees or employers. International trade is the exchange of goods and services among nations. Imports are goods and services purchased from other countries. Exports are goods and services sold to other countries.
2. **Discuss the impact of cultural and social environments on global trade.** Language and cultural differences make international trade challenging. In China and Japan, the number four relates to death. Marketers in these countries who sell products as a package should consider groups other than four. Religious observances are part of a country's culture. In India, the cow is sacred, so no beef is sold there. Fast-food companies like McDonald's® adapt by selling chicken, fish, and mutton burgers. Social and business etiquette is important when doing business abroad. A gift may be considered part of business etiquette in the Far East; however, it might be considered illegal in the United States or Canada.
3. **Assess global trends and opportunities.** In recent years the global marketplace has been growing with the increased acceptance of capitalism, advances in technology, and the reduction of trade barriers. Global news coverage is instantaneous.
4. **Discuss the global environment in which businesses operate.** Most countries do not produce all the goods and services they need. They get some of these from other nations. This economic interdependence happens because each country possesses unique resources. Some nations tend to specialize in products they produce efficiently due to available resources. Some emerging nations have unskilled labor forces at low costs. Labor-intensive industries do well in these countries.
5. **Identify considerations in implementing international marketing strategies.** Globalization is mass marketing on a world scale. Adaptation is an existing promotion with changes to better suit a country. Customization is specially designed products for certain countries.

Mc Graw Hill **glencoe.com**

Role Plays For more DECA Role Plays, send students to the Online Learning Center to download the Competitive Events Workbook.

UNIT 2 **Marketing Internship Project**

A Marketing Plan for a Recession-Proof Toy

What was your favorite childhood toy? Do you think it was recession-proof?

Scenario

You work for a toy manufacturer that sells toys in different countries. There is a global recession, which does not appear to be ending soon. Mattel® Inc. and Hasbro® Inc., large global toy manufacturers, have lowered their sales projections. Walmart® created its own doll line to sell for $5 and cut the prices of other toys. Toy departments at K-Mart® and Sears'® look for toys that will sell. Spin Master® makes popular Bakugan™ products, and another small toy manufacturer came out with a tiny robotic hamster that retails for $10.

The owner of your company has put together a committee of employees from the design, production, and marketing departments. Each member of the team is expected to come up with an idea for a new recession-proof toy and marketing plan for it.

The Skills You'll Use

Academic Skills Reading, writing, social studies, researching, and analyzing

Basic Skills Speaking, listening, thinking, and interpersonal

Technology Skills Word processing, presentation, spreadsheet, telecommunication, the Internet

NCTE 4 Use written language to communicate effectively.
NCTE 7 Conduct research and gather, evaluate, and synthesize data to communicate discoveries.

Your Objective

Design a toy and create a marketing plan for it so that it can be successful in any economic environment.

STEP 1 Do Your Research

Conduct research to find out about toy companies that have created popular toys that have captured the imagination of the public. Also, conduct research about how economic factors have affected the toy industry. As you conduct your research, answer these questions:

- What political, economic, socio-cultural, and technological factors affected the toy industry during a recent recession?
- What marketing strategies were used by toy companies that did well during a recession?
- What toys appeal to children all over the world?
- What global issues have to be considered when designing a new toy?

Write a summary of your research.

STEP 2 Plan Your Project

Now that you have completed your research, you need to begin planning your project.

- Conduct a PEST analysis.
- Design a new toy by making a drawing or a model.
- Write a marketing plan for your new toy. Include the PEST analysis, objectives, and marketing strategies.
- Include suggestions for your plan's implementation, execution, and evaluation.
- Use your knowledge of economics, business cycles, and the global marketplace to make a plan for how to sell your ideas to the committee.

STEP 3 Connect with Your Community

- Share your design idea with trusted adults and children to gauge their interest in your toy.
- Ask children to identify the features they enjoy in the toys they have.
- Find similar information about consumers of toys in different countries.

STEP 4 Share What You Learn

Assume your class is the committee the owner established to come up with new toy ideas.

- Present your toy design and marketing ideas in an oral presentation. Be prepared to answer questions.
- Explain how toy companies can meet the needs of consumers during a recession.
- Provide rationale for your project with supporting research.
- Present your complete marketing plan in a written format using word processing software.
- Use software to create a slide presentation to accompany your oral report. Include one slide for each key topic in your marketing plan.

STEP 5 Evaluate Your Marketing and Academic Skills

Your project will be evaluated based on the following:

- Knowledge of global recessions and the toy industry
- Knowledge of economics, business cycles, and global marketing strategies
- Toy design and marketing plan
- Rationale for recommendation
- Organization and continuity of presentation
- Mechanics—presentation and neatness
- Speaking and listening skills

MARKETING CORE FUNCTIONS

- Market Planning
- Pricing
- Product/Service Management
- Promotion

Marketing Internship Project Checklist

Plan
- ✓ Conduct research on toys and recessions.
- ✓ Design a toy and marketing plan for it.
- ✓ Use the results of a PEST analysis to inform your marketing plan.

Write
- ✓ Describe what happens to the toy industry during a recession.
- ✓ Explain how the results of the PEST analysis will help the committee decide whether to develop your toy.

Present
- ✓ Present the new toy design and the rationale behind your marketing plan.
- ✓ Respond to questions posed by the audience.
- ✓ Consider the needs and experiences of the audience as you present research to your class.

glencoe.com

Evaluate Download a rubric you can use to evaluate your final project.

my marketing portfolio

Internship Report When you have completed your Marketing Internship Project and oral presentation, put your written report and printouts of key slides from your oral presentation in your Marketing Portfolio.

Marketing Plan for a Recession Select a different market and a company of your choice in that market. For example, imagine that you work for a hotel chain that has locations around the world. A global recession is affecting your firm significantly. Conduct research and create a marketing plan for your hotel chain to weather this recession. How have hotels survived in other recessions? What marketing strategies do hotels use? How does your research support your proposed marketing plan? How will you use your knowledge of economics, business cycles, and global marketing strategies to create an effective plan? Prepare a written report and an oral presentation.

106 | Unit 2 · Economics

Unit 2 · Economics | 107

EVALUATE

Anticipation Activity

Project Objective Read the project objective aloud to students: ***Design a toy and create a marketing plan for it so that it can be successful in any economic environment.*** Then ask students to think about what they learned in Unit 2 regarding economic systems and how the state of an economy can affect business and productivity. Remind them of these key points:

- A PEST analysis is an environmental scan that considers political, economic, social, and technological factors.
- The environmental scan is used to evaluate marketing opportunities or threats.

Ask students: ***What is the goal of the PEST analysis?*** Understanding how these four areas may be changing can lead to a better appreciation of potential opportunities or threats. Recognizing a change in one of these aspects can open the door to a new opportunity for developing and marketing a new product.

Ask students: ***Why should you consider consumers of similar products around the world?*** Knowing attitudes, lifestyles, and opinions of consumers can help you understand consumer preferences for similar products in many markets.

Graphic Organizer

Display this table. Then ask students to list any number of favorite toy features that consumers might name. Write down the ideas on the chart. Possible answers:

Favorite Toy Features
Good design
Makes sounds
Has motion
Admired by others
Easy to use
Inexpensive
Safe, not toxic
Not boring

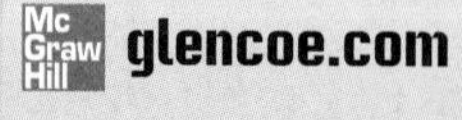

iWB

Graphic Organizer Send students to the Online Learning Center to print this graphic organizer.

EVALUATE

STEP 1 Do Your Research

Tell students that there are many places to find information they can use to develop their product and marketing plan. Students can use library and Internet resources, but they should also talk to people in the community. Encourage students to seek the opinions and ideas of trusted people they know. Other people can bring new perspectives and ideas about political, economic, socio-cultural, and technological factors that affect the toy market and what appeals to children globally.

STEP 2 Plan Your Project

Students should create thorough environmental scans before designing a new toy to sell. Students should explain why they chose the design and provide information about the marketing plan. Students' explanation of the marketing plan should include the PEST analysis, objectives, and marketing strategies, and reflect knowledge of economics, business cycles, and the global marketplace.

STEP 3 Connect with Your Community

Explain to students that in Step 3 of this project they will connect with members of the community. Tell them that young people who have relationships with caring, responsible, and competent adults are more likely to achieve success in life than those who do not. Encourage students to take part in opportunities for trusted adults to serve as mentors, coaches, advocates, and advisors, both formally and informally.

STEP 4 Share What You Learn

Students should present their ideas in a written report and oral presentation with presentation software. They should have at least one slide in their presentation for each key topic in the written report. Encourage students to speak clearly, use appropriate grammar and vocabulary, and actively engage the audience by making and maintaining eye contact and using movement (facial expressions, posture, gestures) to focus attention and interest.

STEP 5 Evaluate Your Marketing and Academic Skills

Have students use the Marketing Internship Project Checklist to help them to plan, write, and present their reports. Exemplary written reports will include information that clearly supports a central thesis, a single, distinct focus, generally well-developed ideas, well-phrased sentences that flow smoothly and are varied in length and structure, consistently precise word choice, and few, if any, errors in grammar, spelling, and mechanics.

Evaluation Rubric Send students to the Online Learning Center to get a rubric to evaluate their projects.

Culminating Activity

Remind students that changes in other countries might result in changes in economic stability and policy in the United States, both of which can affect business. Ask students: ***Can you think of major changes in other countries that have affected the economy in the United States?*** Answers will vary. Sample answers may include: The threat of several European countries, including Greece, Spain, and Portugal, defaulting on their government loan payments in 2010 was a factor in the U.S. stock market and other global stock markets losing ground in volatile trading, making people insecure and reluctant to invest. The resulting drop in the stock market as well as other factors reinforced consumers' aversion to spending money on non-essential products manufactured by businesses.

my marketing portfolio

Internship Report Have students put their written reports and printouts of key slides from their oral presentations in their marketing portfolio.

Marketing Plan for a Recession Direct students to select a hotel chain as their model, and then to conduct research and create a marketing plan for the hotel chain to weather a global recession. Students' completed research and marketing plans should include all of the elements and answer all of the questions included in the Marketing Internship Project on this page. This additional activity can build relevance for students who are motivated to learn about other specific business and industries. Relevance shifts the focus to what motivates individual students to learn.

PLANNING GUIDE AND RESOURCES

	Print	Digital
Unit 3 Business and Society		Unit 3 Fast Files: Marketing Internship Project Activity Connect Online Learning Center through glencoe.com
Chapter 5 **The Free Enterprise System**	Student Activity Workbook: Chapter 5 DECA Connection Role Play; Chapter 5 Vocabulary Activity; Section Note Taking Activities; Chapter Academics Activity; Section Study Skills Activities; Section Real-World Applications Activities Mathematics for Marketing Workbook Marketing Research Project Workbook School-to-Career Activity Workbook	Unit 3 Fast Files: Chapter 5 Discovery Project Worksheet and Rubric; Chapter 5 Green Marketer Activity; Chapter 5 Digital Nation Activity; Section Graphic Organizers; Section Outlines with Key Terms and Definitions; Section Summaries ExamView Assessment Suite, Chapter 5 Connect Online Learning Center through glencoe.com
Chapter 6 **Legal and Ethical Issues**	Student Activity Workbook: Chapter 6 DECA Connection Role Play; Chapter 6 Vocabulary Activity; Section Note Taking Activities; Chapter Academics Activity; Section Study Skills Activities; Section Real-World Applications Activities Mathematics for Marketing Workbook Marketing Research Project Workbook School-to-Career Activity Workbook	Unit 3 Fast Files: Chapter 6 Discovery Project Worksheet and Rubric; Chapter 6 Green Marketer Activity; Chapter 6 Digital Nation Activity; Section Graphic Organizers; Section Outlines with Key Terms and Definitions; Section Summaries ExamView Assessment Suite, Chapter 6 Connect Online Learning Center through glencoe.com

McGRAW-HILL PROFESSIONAL DEVELOPMENT

Perkins IV has placed more emphasis than ever on providing quality professional development for Career and Technology educators. The legislation mandates that the focus of professional development be the integration and reinforcement of academic competencies in order to improve student achievement. Specifically, Perkins requires measurements of students' academic success. McGraw-Hill answers the challenge for strong and effective professional development with a five-prong **Online Professional Development for Integrating Academics.**

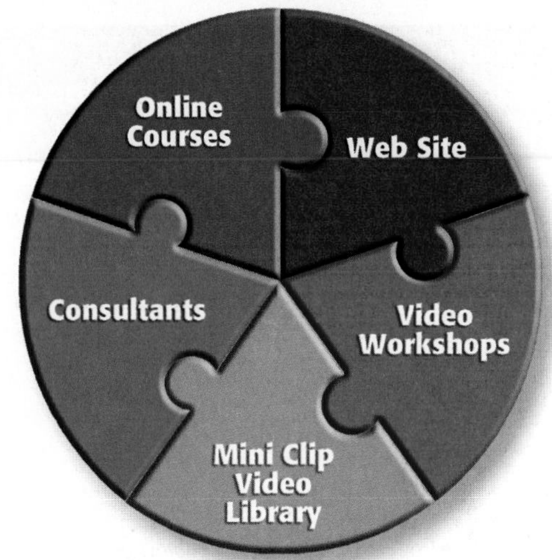

For pricing and ordering information contact your McGraw-Hill Sales Representative.

VIDEO LIBRARY

The McGraw-Hill Professional Development Mini-Clip Video Library, referenced for your convenience at the point of use, provides teaching strategies to strengthen academic and learning skills. Go to the Online Learning Center to view these professional development video clips for Unit 3:

Chapter 5: The Free Enterprise System

- **Reading: Standards-Based Instruction:** An educator and author discusses standards-based instruction. (p. 117)
- **Reading: Planning for Future Instruction:** Teachers plan for future instruction by developing learning strategies for nonfiction text. (p. 119)

Chapter 6: Legal and Ethical Issues

- **ELL Scaffolding Question:** Students learn appropriate verbal responses to a series of scaffolded questions. (p. 145)
- **Reading: On Workshops:** An author and educator discusses the "Workshop Approach" to teaching. (p. 153)
- **Math: Real-World Ratios:** A teacher has students create and compare ratios. (p. 157)

UNIT OVERVIEW

Sections	Objectives	Common Core State Standards College and Career Readiness
Section 5.1 **Traits of Private Enterprise**	• Explain the characteristics of the free enterprise system. • Distinguish between price and nonprice competition. • Explain the theory of supply and demand.	• **Reading** Integrate and evaluate content presented in diverse formats and media, including visually and quantitatively, as well as in words.
Section 5.2 **Business Opportunities**	• Compare for-profit and nonprofit organizations. • Distinguish between public and private sectors. • List the major types of businesses in the organizational market. • List the major functions of business.	• **Reading** Read closely to determine what the text says explicitly and to make logical inferences from it; cite specific textual evidence when writing or speaking to support conclusions drawn from the text.

Sections	Objectives	Common Core State Standards College and Career Readiness
Section 6.1 **Government and Laws**	• Explain the role of government in the private enterprise system. • Identify federal regulatory agencies and laws that protect consumers, workers, investors, and the environment. • Provide examples of the impact of government on business.	• **Reading** Determine central ideas or themes of a text and analyze their development; summarize the key supporting details and ideas.
Section 6.2 **Social Responsibilities and Ethics**	• Provide examples of a business's social responsibilities. • Explain the concept of business ethics. • Apply guidelines for ethical behavior.	• **Reading** Interpret words and phrases as they are used in a text, including determining technical, connotative, and figurative meanings, and analyze how specific word choices shape meaning or tone.

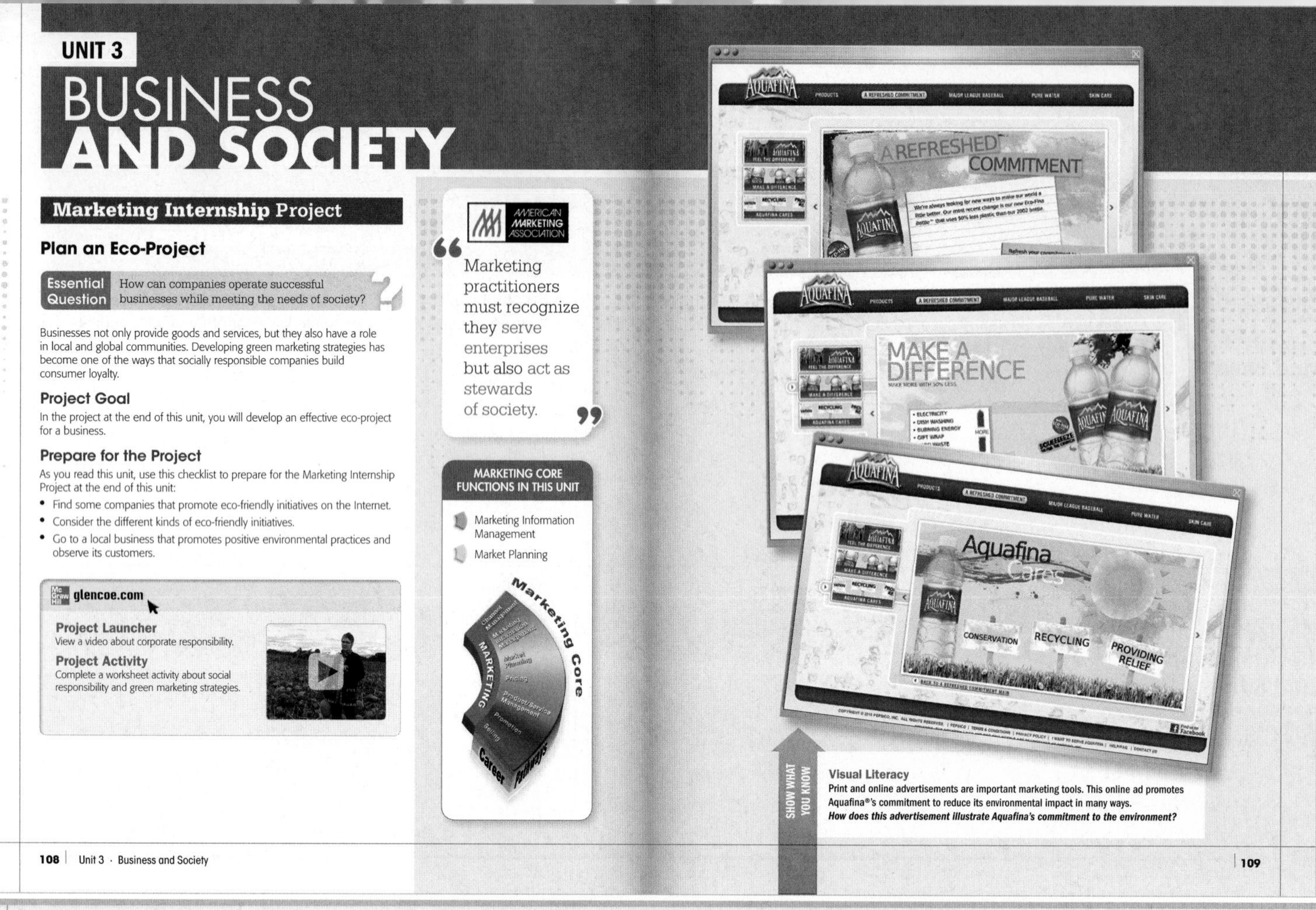

UNIT 3

BUSINESS AND SOCIETY

Marketing Internship Project

Plan an Eco-Project

Essential Question How can companies operate successful businesses while meeting the needs of society?

Businesses not only provide goods and services, but they also have a role in local and global communities. Developing green marketing strategies has become one of the ways that socially responsible companies build consumer loyalty.

Project Goal

In the project at the end of this unit, you will develop an effective eco-project for a business.

Prepare for the Project

As you read this unit, use this checklist to prepare for the Marketing Internship Project at the end of this unit:

- Find some companies that promote eco-friendly initiatives on the Internet.
- Consider the different kinds of eco-friendly initiatives.
- Go to a local business that promotes positive environmental practices and observe its customers.

glencoe.com

Project Launcher
View a video about corporate responsibility.

Project Activity
Complete a worksheet activity about social responsibility and green marketing strategies.

AMERICAN MARKETING ASSOCIATION

"Marketing practitioners must recognize they serve enterprises but also act as stewards of society."

MARKETING CORE FUNCTIONS IN THIS UNIT

- Marketing Information Management
- Market Planning

Visual Literacy
Print and online advertisements are important marketing tools. This online ad promotes Aquafina®'s commitment to reduce its environmental impact in many ways.
How does this advertisement illustrate Aquafina's commitment to the environment?

108 | Unit 3 · Business and Society

109

ENGAGE

Introduce the Unit

Unit 3 explores international business and the basic functions of business.

Chapter 5 focuses on the private or free enterprise system as an economic system in the United States and examines economies in the global marketplace.

Chapter 6 discusses government's role in regulating business and protecting consumers, and outlines types of businesses and their social responsibilities to society.

Build Background

Ask students to list ways in which private businesses in the United States can demonstrate responsibility to society. Ask students: ***How would you define the U.S. private enterprise system?*** Answers will vary. Sample answer: The private or free enterprise system in the United States encourages individuals to start and operate their own businesses.

Visual Literacy

Photo Caption Answer Read the copy on the ad to students. Then read the photo caption and the photo caption question to students: ***How does this advertisement illustrate Aquafina's commitment to the environment?*** Answers will vary. Accept all reasonable answers. Sample answer: The image of the water bottle focuses attention on packaging. In this case, the company has designed an eco-friendly bottle using 50 percent less plastic than its previous bottles, saving 75 million pounds of plastic annually. By clicking the link on this Web page, the viewer finds multiple tips on saving energy, from dish washing and lighting to using the phone. Ask students to evaluate the visual components of the advertisement. Ask volunteers to explain how the visual aspects of the advertisement complement the text of the advertisement. The fresh blue sky and green grass provide the backdrop for the image of the "Eco-Fina" bottle, emphasizing refreshing water bottled in an environmentally aware package. The text "A Refreshed Commitment" reinforces the visual message that this company has a serious green initiative. The index card provides more helpful information for eco-conscious consumers using a simple, no-frills design.

ENGAGE

Marketing Internship Project Preview

Read students the Marketing Internship Project Essential Question: ***How can companies operate successful businesses while meeting the needs of society?*** Because students are just starting to learn about the private enterprise system and how businesses demonstrate social responsibility, they will likely not know the specific answer to this question, which is to develop socially responsible business practices and initiatives. Students may know that operating a successful business can be compatible with being socially responsible. In addition, many ethical business practices may be mandated by law. Explain to students that they will learn how businesses demonstrate socially responsible practices while studying this unit. Tell students that when they are finished studying this unit, they will develop a business initiative for a sports footwear company. As they study each chapter in the unit, they can prepare for the Unit Project by thinking about eco-friendly initiatives.

 **glencoe.com** 

Marketing Internship Project Resources Send students to the Online Learning Center to watch a video and download a worksheet activity related to the topic of the Unit Project.

Read the American Marketing Association quote to students:

AMERICAN MARKETING ASSOCIATION

> “Marketing practitioners must recognize they serve enterprises but also act as stewards of society.”

Read to students the three ethical norms from the AMA's Statement of Ethics:

As Marketers, we must:
1. Do no harm.
2. Foster trust in the marketing system.
3. Embrace ethical values.

Ask students: ***What do these Ethical Norms mean?***

1. Consciously avoiding harmful actions or omissions, embodying high ethical standards, and adhering to laws.

2. Striving for good faith and fair dealing, avoiding deception in product design, pricing, communication, and distribution.

3. Building relationships and consumer confidence in the integrity of marketing, affirming Ethical Values.

MARKETING CORE FUNCTIONS IN THIS UNIT

Point out to students that Chapters 5 and 6 will touch on two of the seven marketing core functions. Describe each of these marketing functions to students to prepare them to start studying this unit.

 **Marketing Information Management** involves gathering, storing, and analyzing information about customers, trends, and competing products.

 **Market Planning** involves understanding the concepts and strategies used to develop and target specific marketing strategies to a select audience.

MARKETING RESEARCH PROJECT WORKBOOK

The purpose of the Marketing Research Project Workbook is to provide a step-by-step approach for students to conduct their own marketing research study. Each chapter is devoted to key elements in the research process. Each chapter builds upon the previous chapters, and by the end of the book, students will have completed an in-depth marketing research study, complete with rationale for all decisions, a report of the findings and conclusions, recommendations based on the original research problem and study objectives, and an annotated bibliography.

 **glencoe.com** 

Marketing Research Project Workbook Send students to the Online Learning Center to download the Marketing Research Project Workbook. A Teacher Manual is also available on the Teacher Center of the Online Learning Center.

Chapter 5 | Section 5.1 Traits of Private Enterprise | Section 5.2 Business Opportunities

the free enterprise system

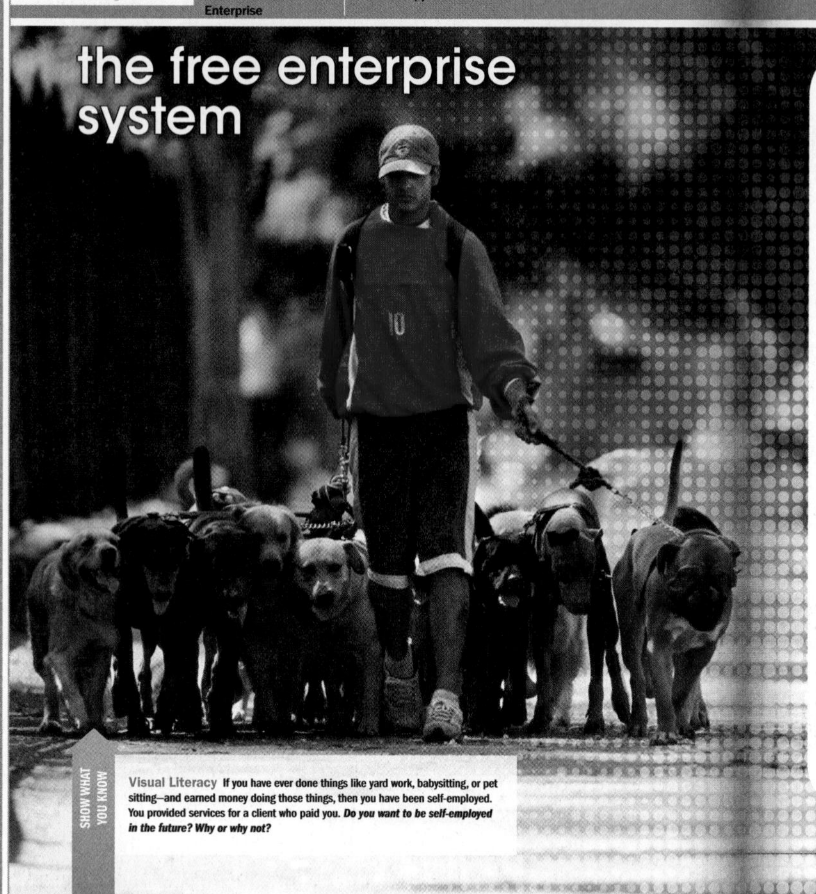

SHOW WHAT YOU KNOW

Visual Literacy If you have ever done things like yard work, babysitting, or pet sitting—and earned money doing those things, then you have been self-employed. You provided services for a client who paid you. ***Do you want to be self-employed in the future? Why or why not?***

Discovery Project

Being Self-Employed

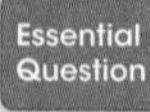

Essential Question What are the advantages and disadvantages to being self-employed?

Project Goal

Interview someone who is self-employed. Self-employed individuals are entrepreneurs who engage in private enterprise because they own their businesses. The person may be self-employed as a plumber, an electrician, a doctor, an insurance broker, or an owner of an auto repair shop, an accounting firm, a flower shop, a bakery, or a candy store.

Ask Yourself...

- How will you find a self-employed person in your community?
- How should you approach the person to ask for an interview?
- What questions will give you helpful information during the interview?
- How will you present information you learned during the interview?

Analyze and Interpret Assess the opportunities and problems entrepreneurs have in a market-oriented economy.

glencoe.com

Activity
Get a worksheet activity about self-employment.

Evaluate
Download a rubric you can use to evaluate your project.

DECA Connection

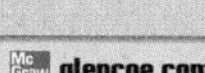

DECA Event Role Play

Concepts in this chapter are related to DECA competitive events that involve either an interview or role play.

Performance Indicators The performance indicators represent key skills and knowledge. Your key to success in DECA competitive events is relating them to the concepts in this chapter.

- Explain the concept of the free enterprise system.
- Explain the concept of competition.
- Explain the principles of supply and demand.
- Identify factors affecting a business's profit.
- Describe types of business activities.

DECA Prep

Role Play Practice role-playing with the DECA Connection competitive-event activity at the end of this chapter. More information about DECA events can be found on DECA's Web site.

ENGAGE

Visual Literacy

Read the chapter opener photo caption question to students: ***Do you want to be self-employed in the future? Why or why not?*** Negative reasons: afraid of risk, don't have the necessary money, do not want that much responsibility Positive reasons: enjoy their work, work the hours they want, possibly make more money. Then ask these guiding questions to activate prior knowledge.

Guiding Questions

Describe How does a market economy answer the three basic economic questions of "What? How? and For Whom?"	What? Consumers determine what should be produced. How? Businesses decide how to produce goods and services. For whom? People who have money to spend.
Identify What three factors have led to the growth of the global marketplace?	growth of capitalism around the world, advances in transportation and communication technologies, reduction of trade barriers

Discovery Project

Being Self-Employed To encourage students to think about what it means to work for yourself, read the Discovery Project Essential Question: ***What are the advantages and disadvantages to being self-employed?*** Advantages: You are your own boss; you might work in a field that you are knowledgeable about; you have the potential for making more money. Disadvantages: You have all the responsibility; work long hours; business might fail.

glencoe.com

Discovery Project Resources Send students to the Online Learning Center to download a rubric to evaluate their projects.

EXPLORE

Introduce the Chapter

In this chapter, these issues related to private enterprise are discussed:

- Basic principles of private enterprise
- Intellectual property rights
- Importance of competition
- Types of risks businesses face
- Role of profit in the free enterprise system
- Theory of supply and demand
- Difference between for-profit and nonprofit organizations
- Roles of the public and private sectors
- Major types of businesses in the organizational market
- Major functions of business

Discussion Starter

Recognizing a Private Enterprise System Remind students that a private enterprise system is one in which ordinary people can own their own business. Ask students: ***If you just came to the United States from a foreign country, what things would tell you that our marketplace is primarily free-enterprise?*** Possible answers: The large number of stores, both chain stores and local businesses; the vast assortment of goods available in these stores; ads that list prices and proclaim their products as being better than others; coupons, discounts, etc., that encourage consumers to patronize a specific store.

DECA Connection

Discuss the performance indicators listed in the DECA Connection feature. Explain to students that performance indicators tell them how to demonstrate their acquired skills and knowledge through individual or team competitive events.

glencoe.com

Competitive Events Workbook For more DECA Role Plays, send students to the Online Learning Center to download the Competitive Events Workbook.

PROGRAM RESOURCE ORGANIZER

PRINT RESOURCES

- **Student Edition**
- **Teacher Edition**
- **Student Activity Workbook with Academic Integration** includes worksheets and activities correlated to the text.
- **Mathematics for Marketing Workbook** provides math activities for every unit in the text.

TECHNOLOGY TOOLBOX

- **Connect**
- **ConnectPlus**
- **ExamView Assessment Suite** is a comprehensive solution for creating, administering, and scoring tests.

glencoe.com

Online Learning Center provides a variety of resources to enrich and enhance learning.

SECTION, CHAPTER, AND UNIT RESOURCES

- **Graphic Organizers** for organizing text concepts visually.
- **Digital Nation Activities** and **Green Marketer Activities** extend learning beyond the text features.
- **Career Chatroom Career Profiles** allow students to explore different marketing occupations in depth.
- **After You Read Answer Keys** for students to check their answers.
- **Discovery Project Rubrics** and **Marketing Internship Project Rubrics** for students to evaluate their projects.

PROGRAM RESOURCES

- **Student Activity Workbook with Academic Integration Teacher Annotated Edition** includes annotated answers for the activities and worksheets.
- **Marketing Research Project Workbook** provides a step-by-step approach for students to complete their own marketing research studies.
- **School-to-Career Activity Workbook** helps students relate their class work to on-the-job experience and involves work-site analysis and working with mentors.
- **Competitive Events Workbook** helps prepare students for state and national marketing education competitions.
- **Inclusion in the Marketing Education Classroom** provides teaching resources for working with students with special needs.
- **PowerPoint Presentations** provides visual teaching aids and assessments for this chapter.

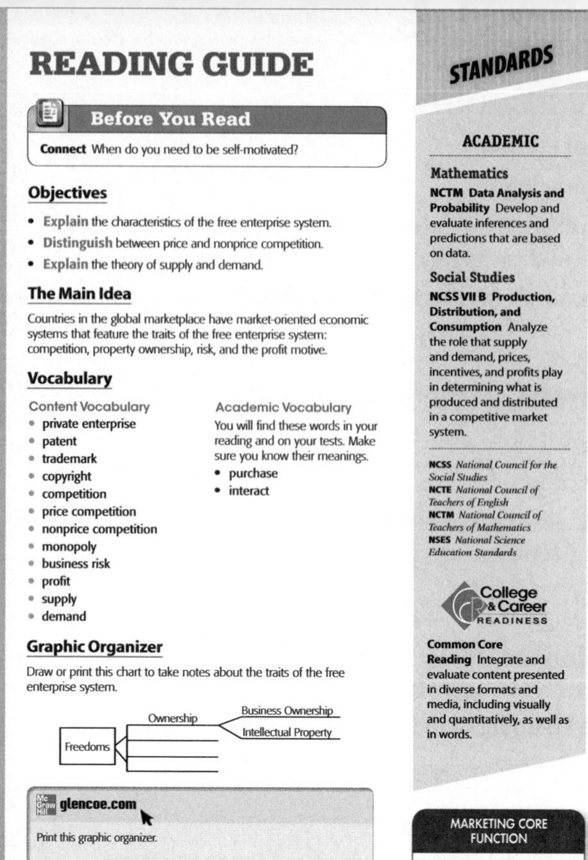

READING GUIDE

Before You Read

Connect When do you need to be self-motivated?

Objectives

- **Explain** the characteristics of the free enterprise system.
- **Distinguish** between price and nonprice competition.
- **Explain** the theory of supply and demand.

The Main Idea

Countries in the global marketplace have market-oriented economic systems that feature the traits of the free enterprise system: competition, property ownership, risk, and the profit motive.

Vocabulary

Content Vocabulary
- private enterprise
- patent
- trademark
- copyright
- competition
- price competition
- nonprice competition
- monopoly
- business risk
- profit
- supply
- demand

Academic Vocabulary

You will find these words in your reading and on your tests. Make sure you know their meanings.
- purchase
- interact

Graphic Organizer

Draw or print this chart to take notes about the traits of the free enterprise system.

Freedoms — Ownership — Business Ownership / Intellectual Property

glencoe.com

Print this graphic organizer.

STANDARDS

ACADEMIC

Mathematics

NCTM Data Analysis and Probability Develop and evaluate inferences and predictions that are based on data.

Social Studies

NCSS VII B Production, Distribution, and Consumption Analyze the role that supply and demand, prices, incentives, and profits play in determining what is produced and distributed in a competitive market system.

NCSS *National Council for the Social Studies*
NCTE *National Council of Teachers of English*
NCTM *National Council of Teachers of Mathematics*
NSES *National Science Education Standards*

College & Career READINESS

Common Core
Reading Integrate and evaluate content presented in diverse formats and media, including visually and quantitatively, as well as in words.

MARKETING CORE FUNCTION

Market Planning

Traits of Private Enterprise

Section 5.1

BASIC PRINCIPLES

The founders of the United States defined freedom of choice as rights that are central to our society. Consumers have the freedom to **purchase** goods and services. They make these purchases with the income they earn. This income is earned from their wages and salaries at their jobs. If a consumer owns a business, income can also come from the profits of that business.

People can then invest their money in banks to earn interest or in businesses to earn dividends. All these freedoms are part of a market-oriented economic system. They are fundamental to the concept of private enterprise. **Private enterprise** is business ownership by ordinary people, not the government. It is the basis of a market-oriented economy. Private enterprise is also known as free enterprise.

The basic elements of the free enterprise system include the freedom to own property, the freedom to compete, the freedom to take risks, and the freedom to make a profit. People are encouraged to start and operate their own businesses as a part of the free enterprise system. These businesses are part of a competitive system that has no involvement from the government.

The marketplace determines prices through the interaction of supply and demand. If the supply of a product exceeds the demand, the price tends to drop. If demand is greater than supply, the price tends to go up. The government does not set prices or distribute goods and services.

The market-oriented economic system in the United States is modified because the government intervenes from time to time. It issues rules and regulations for businesses and also directly intervenes on a limited basis. It does this to protect citizens. For example, during the recession in 2008–2009, the United States government intervened in businesses such as banks and the auto industry. The government did this because it was determined that some business practices needed to be regulated.

As You Read

Apply Consider the experiences of a self-employed person you know as you read about free enterprise.

You can opt to use your personal interest in something to open your own business. ***How is this choice a defining part of free enterprise?***

ENGAGE

Anticipation Activity

Tell the class that their assignment is to agree on a place to go to lunch. Ask: ***How might you decide? Give some specific reasons you would choose one place over another.*** Possible answers: a place that offers food they like, where their friends work, that is inexpensive. Then discuss that these kinds of decisions are at the heart of free enterprise.

Objectives

- **Explain** the characteristics of a private enterprise. Businesses are owned by individuals. Consumers decide what businesses to support by deciding what to purchase.
- **Distinguish** between price and nonprice competition. Price competition: based on what businesses charge. Nonprice competition: factors such as having a wide selection of goods, giving customers excellent service, and providing fast delivery.
- **Explain** the theory of supply and demand. Supply and demand interact to determine the price customers are willing to pay.

Graphic Organizer

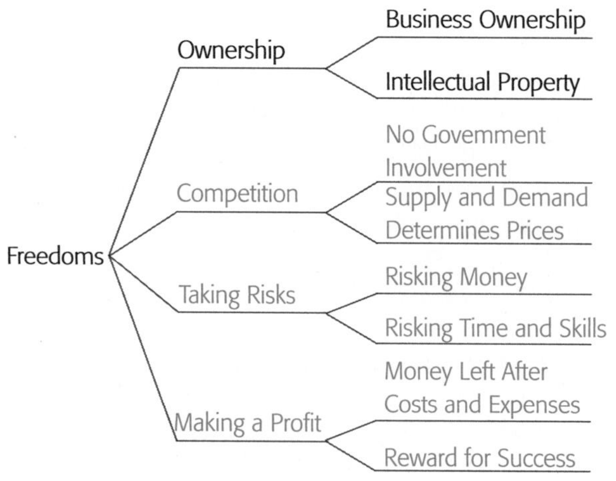

glencoe.com

iWB

Graphic Organizer Send students to the Online Learning Center to print this graphic organizer.

EXPLORE

Before You Read

Read the Before You Read question aloud: ***When do you need to be self-motivated?*** Possible answer: If you are not earning money to meet your own personal goals, you need another motivation, such as feeling that you accomplished something worthwhile. This is often a factor in volunteer work, such as cleaning up neighborhoods or helping children with their schoolwork.

Preteaching Vocabulary

Have students go to the Online Learning Center at glencoe.com for the Chapter 5 Preteaching Vocabulary games.

Content Vocabulary

Tell students that three of the content vocabulary terms are related to intellectual property rights. Have students work individually to skim this section and locate these three words. patent, trademark, copyright They have students write down each word's definition.

Academic Vocabulary

Purchase—Denotative Meaning Read aloud this sentence: *Consumers have the freedom to purchase goods and services.* Ask students: ***What does* purchase *mean in this sentence?*** to buy or to pay for Ask: ***Is* purchase *used as a noun or a verb?*** verb Then ask: ***What would be an example of a sentence using* purchase *as a noun?*** Possible answer: I made a purchase at the shoe store. Ask: ***What does it mean in this sentence?*** a buy, an acquisition

Interact—Prefixes Ask: ***What prefix does this word have?*** inter- Then ask: ***What do you think this prefix means?*** between Ask: ***Based on this, what do you think* interact *might mean?*** to act between one another Instruct students to watch for this word as they read and determine whether this meaning is correct.

Critical Thinking

Ask: ***What is a traditional economy?*** one in which goods and services are based on tradition and survival needs Ask: ***Do you think private enterprise could do well in a traditional society? Why or why not?*** Accept all answers that are well thought out. Basically, skills are passed from one generation to another. Therefore, if your parent prospered as a shoemaker, you probably will do the same.

me. Section 5.1 | Traits of Private Enterprise

BASIC PRINCIPLES

Private enterprise, which is the basis of this chapter, is based on the concept of a market economy. To focus the discussion on the basic principles behind private enterprise, ask students these guiding questions.

Guiding Questions

Recall How do consumers get the money they use to purchase goods and services?	They use income earned from wages and salaries or profits from businesses they own.
Apply What are three ways that people can use their money? How do you use your own money?	Spend it on goods and services, invest it, or start a business. Possible answers: I spend most of my money but am saving some money each month to buy a car.
Analyze Is the market-oriented system in the United States a true free enterprise system? Why or why not?	No, because government interferes in business in a variety of ways, for example, by preventing monopolies and instituting safety measures.

As You Read Answer

Read students the As You Read assignment: ***Consider the experiences of a self-employed person you know as you read about free enterprise.*** Explain to students that because we live in a country with a free enterprise system, people are free to earn a living by owning a business. However, they also can lose their business if they cannot earn enough money to make a living.

Visual Literacy

Your Choice Caption Answer Read the figure caption question to students: ***How is this choice a defining part of free enterprise?*** It provides everyone with the opportunity to own their own business by doing something of interest to them. It allows for the "American Dream" of being an entrepreneur and truly enjoying what you do.

You may or may not decide to invest your money in a company listed on the New York Stock Exchange. ***What are the pros and cons of investing in company stocks?***

Being a Stockholder

OWNERSHIP

In the free enterprise system, people are free to own property, such as cars, computers, and homes. They can also own natural resources such as oil and land. You can buy anything you want as long as it is not prohibited by law. You can also do what you want with your property. You can give it away, lease it, sell it, or use it for yourself. If you engage in the free enterprise system, you try to make money from your property ownership.

> " Freedoms found in private enterprise make it enticing to be a business owner. "

BUSINESS OWNERSHIP

The free enterprise system encourages individuals to own businesses. In the United States, there are some restrictions on how and where those businesses may operate. Businesses may be restricted in where they can locate. These restrictions come in the form of zoning laws.

Most businesses are zoned so that they are far away from areas that are zoned for private housing. Manufacturers may be forced to comply with environmental and safety measures. They need to make products in a way that does not hurt the environment or endanger their employees.

There are many types of business. People who start and operate their own businesses are called entrepreneurs. Others support business by investing their money in parts or shares of a company. These shares of a business are called stocks and the investors are called stockholders. There are preferred stocks and common stocks. Common stockholders have voting rights so they can influence management policies. Preferred stockholders do not have voting rights. However, when a company earns money, they receive payments sooner than common stockholders. Company stocks are bought and sold daily. When a company is doing well, stock prices generally increase as more people want to buy that stock.

INTELLECTUAL PROPERTY RIGHTS

Intellectual property rights are protected. That means that a product or idea a person creates or invents is legally protected from being copied. Patents, trademarks, copyrights, and trade secrets are intellectual property rights.

If you get a **patent** on an invention, you alone own the rights to that item or idea. To ensure that protection, you would apply for a utility patent in the U.S. Patent and Trademark Office. If the patent is granted, you would have the exclusive rights to make, use, or sell that invention. The patent on your invention would protect it for up to 20 years. During this time, anyone who wanted to manufacture your product would have to pay you for its use through a licensing agreement.

A **trademark** is a word, name, symbol, sound, or color that identifies a good or service. It cannot be used by anyone but the owner. Unlike a patent, a trademark can be renewed forever, if it is being used by a business.

Trademarks A Chinese company owns the trademark "i-phone," so Apple cannot use "iPhone" to market that product in China.

A **copyright** involves anything that is authored by an individual, such as writings (books, magazine articles, etc.), music, and artwork. It gives the author the exclusive right to reproduce or sell the work. A copyright is usually valid for the life of the author plus 70 years.

A trade secret is information that a company keeps and protects for its use only. However, it is not patented. For example, Coca-Cola's® formula for Coke is a trade secret that is not protected by a patent, but the company guards the information.

When a company wants to use another's name, symbol, creative work, or product, it must get permission to do so and pay a fee for the use. A licensing agreement protects the originator's name and products. A T-shirt manufacturer might be granted a licensing agreement with the National Football League (NFL) so that it can produce T-shirts with NFL logos on them. The company will have to pay NFL Properties a fee for this permission. It will also have to agree to certain standards to protect the NFL's reputation. In addition, the NFL has control over all teams' logos and how the teams can use them.

COMPETITION

The free enterprise system encourages businesses to attract new customers and keep old ones. Other businesses try to take those same customers away. This struggle for customers is called **competition**.

Competition is an essential part of the free enterprise system. It is one of the ways the free enterprise system benefits consumers. Competition forces businesses to produce better-quality goods and services at reasonable prices.

MARKETING CASE STUDY

Instant Photo Nostalgia

The Polaroid® Company stopped production of its instant film on December 31, 2008, for its 60-year old Polaroid brand instant cameras. Loyal users of the iconic camera were so upset they flocked to a Web site called SavePolaroid.com. Web site visitors could share their nostalgic stories. One of the Web site founders wrote, "Watching a Polaroid picture develop is like watching a memory form right before your eyes."

Polaroid Responds to Consumers

In January 2009 Polaroid introduced the Polaroid PoGo™ Instant Digital Camera. The digital camera is combined with an instant printer. Camera users can select, crop, edit, and print the digital photos instantly. Special inkless paper is used for the 2 × 3-inch sticky-backed photos. With the new technology the photos are completely developed when they leave the printer. The fun of shaking the photos until they dry is gone.

English Language Arts/Writing

Discuss What risk did Polaroid take when it stopped production of the film used in its traditional instant camera knowing it still had a strong following of consumers? Share your opinion with a partner and then discuss the topic as a class.

NCTE 3 Apply strategies to interpret texts.

EXPLAIN

Visual Literacy

Being a Stockholder Caption Answer Read this question to students: ***What are the pros and cons of investing in company stocks?*** Pros: become a part owner in the company; if a common stockholder you can vote; often pay dividends, can make money when selling stocks if your selling price is higher than the purchase price. Cons: involve risk; difficulty selecting the right stocks; no guarantee that the company you invest in will be profitable; if economy is weak, the value of your stock may go down and if you choose to sell the stock, you will lose money.

Reinforce Vocabulary

Patent—Word Origin Tell students that the word *patent* originally came from the Latin word *patēre*, which means "open." Its present day meaning is "having exclusive rights to make and sell an invention for a specified period of time."

Expert Advice

Read the quote to students:

> " Freedoms found in private enterprise make it enticing to be a business owner. "

Ask students: ***What are some of these freedoms?*** Possible answers: be your own boss, decide how the business is run and money it spent, possibly decide the hours you work ***In what ways might owning your own business take away some of your freedom?*** You might be required to work specific hours, you might have to work long hours and be on-call all the time, you might have a lot of worries and stress if the business does not do well.

VIRTUAL BUSINESS

RISKS AND SURPRISES

Introduce the concept of risks and surprises to students using Knowledge Matters' Virtual Business Retailing visual simulation, *Risks and Surprises*. In this simulation, students will learn about the types of risks that businesses face and how to manage them.

ELABORATE

BUSINESS OWNERSHIP

Ask these guiding questions to focus on business ownership.

Guiding Questions

Differentiate What is an advantage to owning common stock? To owning preferred stock?	Common stock: Holders have voting rights and can influence management policies. Preferred stock: If a company earns money, preferred stockholders receive payments earlier.
Appraise Why do most cities and towns have zoning laws that prevent businesses from locating in residential areas?	Most people do not want their homes to be near businesses. Business districts tend to be noisy and typically have more traffic than residential areas.

Graphic Organizer

Display the Venn Diagram. Have the class work together to fill in the similarities and differences.

Patent Own rights to an invention, which can be an item or idea; exclusive rights for up to 20 years
Trademark Own rights to a word, name, symbol, sound, or color that identifies a good or service; no time limit
protection
Copyright Own exclusive rights to reproduce or sell a writing authored by an individual, time limit is life of the author plus 70 years

glencoe.com iWB

Graphic Organizer Send students to the Online Learning Center to print this graphic organizer.

INTELLECTUAL PROPERTY RIGHTS

To help students in understanding intellectual property rights and how these rights affect companies, focus on these guiding questions.

Guiding Questions

Define What are the four types of intellectual property rights?	patents, trademarks, copyrights, trade secrets
Explain What must a company do if it wants to print a professional baseball team's logo on baseball caps and sell these caps commercially?	obtain a licensing agreement from the owner of the logo, pay a specified fee, adhere to other requirements
Predict What do you think would happen if patents did not exist? Why?	Some people might be hesitant to spend time and money in developing products if anyone can declare ideas their own

MARKETING CASE STUDY

English Language Arts/Writing Answer
The risk Polaroid took was that the company faced the loss of its loyal customer base when it stopped production of the film used in its traditional camera.

HOT TOPIC

Trademarks Tell students that some organizations have begun making inroads into establishing international copyright law. For example, the World Intellectual Property Organization (WIPO), which is among the United Nation's family of organizations, administers what is commonly known as the "Madrid System." Over 80 countries are members of the Madrid System, which provides a centralized method of registering a trademark.

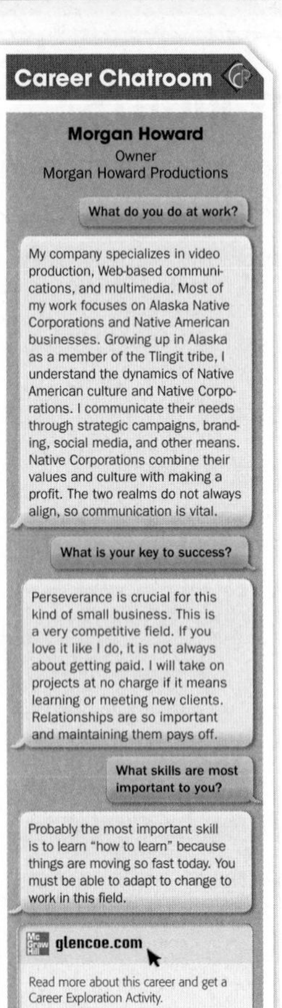
Career Chatroom

Morgan Howard
Owner
Morgan Howard Productions

What do you do at work?

My company specializes in video production, Web-based communications, and multimedia. Most of my work focuses on Alaska Native Corporations and Native American businesses. Growing up in Alaska as a member of the Tlingit tribe, I understand the dynamics of Native American culture and Native Corporations. I communicate their needs through strategic campaigns, branding, social media, and other means. Native Corporations combine their values and culture with making a profit. The two realms do not always align, so communication is vital.

What is your key to success?

Perseverance is crucial for this kind of small business. This is a very competitive field. If you love it like I do, it is not always about getting paid. I will take on projects at no charge if it means learning or meeting new clients. Relationships are so important and maintaining them pays off.

What skills are most important to you?

Probably the most important skill is to learn "how to learn" because things are moving so fast today. You must be able to adapt to change to work in this field.

glencoe.com

Read more about this career and get a Career Exploration Activity.

Businesses constantly look for ways to develop new products and improve old ones to attract new customers. Competition results in a wider selection of products from which to choose. The results of these efforts increase the nation's output of goods and services, as well as its standard of living.

There are two basic strategies that businesses use to compete: price competition and nonprice competition.

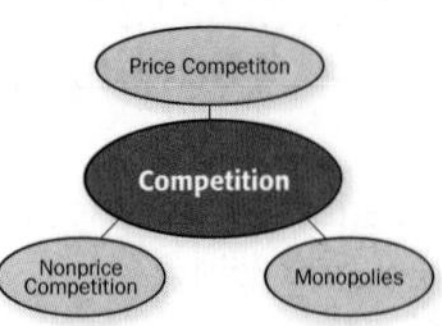

PRICE AND NONPRICE COMPETITION

Price competition focuses on the sale price of a product. The assumption is that, all other things being equal, consumers will buy the products that are lowest in price.

The marketing strategies used by Walmart® and Southwest Airlines® are examples of price competition. Both use their low prices as their competitive advantage. Companies that run sales and offer rebates are using price competition. A $5,000 cash-back offer by an auto manufacturer and a retailer's one-day sale that offers a 15 percent discount storewide are examples of price competition.

In **nonprice competition**, businesses choose to compete on the basis of factors that are not related to price. These factors include the quality of the products, service, financing, business location, and reputation. Some nonprice competitors also stress the qualifications or expertise of their personnel. Businesses that use nonprice competition may charge more for products than their competitors do.

Examples of nonprice competition in advertising programs stress a company's reliability, tradition, market knowledge, and special services. Free shipping and same-day delivery are examples of nonprice competition.

These examples of price and nonprice competition seem to suggest that businesses adopt one strategy or the other. In our value-oriented society, however, it is not uncommon for businesses to try to do both. As competition increases, you may see more price-oriented competitors offering services they have never offered in the past.

MONOPOLIES

When there is no competition and one firm controls the market for a given product, a monopoly exists. A **monopoly** is exclusive control over a product or the means of producing it.

Monopolies are not permitted in a market-oriented economic system because they prevent competition. A company can charge whatever it wants because there is no chance of price competition from another company. It can also control the quality of a product and who gets it. These nonprice factors cannot be challenged by other companies either. Without competition, there is nothing to stop a company from acting without regard to customers' wants and needs.

One of the most publicized monopoly cases in recent history involved Microsoft®, the computer software company. A federal judge declared Microsoft's Windows operating system a monopoly. Its technology dominance was said to have stifled innovation. The judge ruled that the situation was unfair to consumers and Microsoft's competitors. The ruling found that Windows' dominance was harmful to the free enterprise system.

The U.S. government has allowed a few monopolies to exist. These monopolies exist mainly in industries where it would be wasteful to have more than one firm. These regulated monopolies, however, are on the decline.

Utility companies, such as gas and electric companies, have been deregulated. This practice allows customers to choose their own electric and gas suppliers. The government still controls gas and electric companies' prices, but it imposes price restrictions that prevent the formerly regulated monopolies from charging excessive prices.

Along with the benefits that come from competition and private ownership of property, businesses also face risk. **Business risk** is the potential for loss or failure. As the potential for earnings gets greater, so does the risk. Putting money in the bank with guaranteed interest rates is less risky than investing in the stock market. Simply starting a company is a risk.

If you wanted to open your own business, you would probably put your savings into the enterprise. You make money if the business is successful; but if the business fails, you lose all your savings. One out of every three businesses in the United States fails after one year of operation.

Businesses also run the risk of being sued or having their name tarnished from bad publicity. This bad publicity may not even be accurate, but it can still be very damaging. Natural disasters could also ruin a business. While these events cannot be prevented, businesses must do everything they can to manage risks.

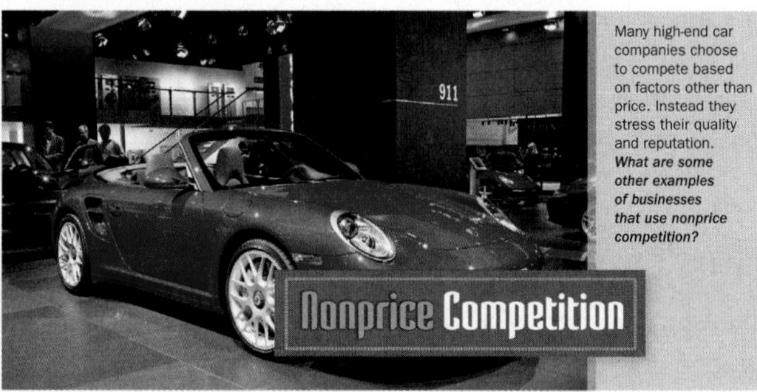

Many high-end car companies choose to compete based on factors other than price. Instead they stress their quality and reputation. ***What are some other examples of businesses that use nonprice competition?***

EXPLAIN

Career Chatroom

Focus the discussion by asking these guiding questions.

Guiding Questions

Recall For what groups does Morgan Howard mainly work?	Alaska Native Corporations, Native American businesses
Make Judgments Howard says his most important skill is to learn "how to learn." Do you agree with this statement?	Business and technology are changing quickly. Everyone must continually work to learn new skills.

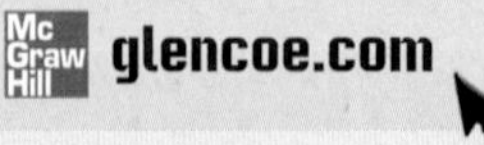

Career Exploration Send students to the Online Learning Center to find more information about this career and get a Career Exploration activity.

Graphic Organizer

To help students understand price versus nonprice competition, display this table. Ask students: ***What are some examples of how price competition and nonprice competition affect what you buy?***

Price Competition
tennis racket on sale 30 miles away, made a special trip

Purchases
Sporting Equipment

Nonprice Competition
bought bicycle from local shop because they offer repairs

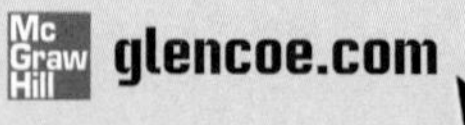

Graphic Organizer Send students to the Online Learning Center to print this graphic organizer.

ELABORATE

Graphic Organizer

Ask students: ***What is a monopoly?*** Exclusive control over a product or the means of producing it. Display the cause-and-effect diagram on the board. Discuss with students that having complete control over a product is against the basic premise of a free marketplace.

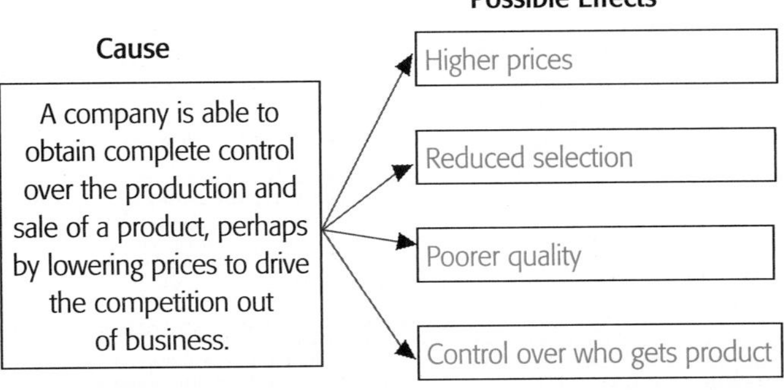

 glencoe.com 

Graphic Organizer Send students to the Online Learning Center to print this graphic organizer.

Mini Project

Extension

Examining a Product's Failure Have students conduct research to locate a product that failed within a year of introduction. Students should investigate the events that led up to this failure and reasons why it occurred. Students should present background about the product and explore reasons for its failure. Presentations will vary depending on the product, but should explain the product and summarizing the events leading up to its failure.

PROFESSIONAL DEVELOPMENT **MINI CLIP**

Reading: Standards-Based Instruction

Go to the Online Learning Center to view a video in which an educator/author discusses standards-based instruction.

RISK

Remind students that risk is always present in business. It important that businesspeople are aware of their risks so they can take steps to minimize them. To focus the discussion on risk, present these guiding questions.

Guiding Questions

Define What does the term *business risk* mean?	any potential for loss or failure
Analyze Why do you think that one out of three small businesses fails after one year of operation?	Unsuccessful businesses may underestimate the competition, expenses, or the difficulties in keeping customers.
Deduce What can happen if a company is sued or is tarnished by bad publicity?	Customers might go elsewhere, even if the lawsuit is unjustified or the publicity is untrue.

Critical Thinking

Refer to the diagram. Ask: ***What is an example of this relationship between risks and rewards?*** If a manufacturer moves its plants to a foreign country, it may be able to make greater profits because it can lower employee pay. However, the manufacturer is also taking greater risks because it has fewer controls over the factory, may have unexpected problems with the local government, and so forth.

 glencoe.com

Graphic Organizer Send students to the Online Learning Center to print this graphic organizer.

Visual Literacy

Nonprice Competition Caption Answer Read the question to students: ***What are some other examples of businesses that use nonprice competition?*** Businesses that compete on factors other than price include home builders, providers of legal services, health care providers, manufacturers of high-end electronics, and so on.

VIRTUAL BUSINESS

RISKS AND SURPRISES

Introduce the concept of risks and surprises to students using Knowledge Matters' Virtual Business Retailing visual simulation, *Risks and Surprises*. In this simulation, students will learn about the types of risks that businesses face and how to manage them.

When an industry develops and profits are growing, more people enter that industry. This increases competition and the risk of failure for individual firms. When there are more companies in a market for the same product, they must compete for customers in the same market. Those companies that cannot compete effectively will face the possibility of failure.

You may have read of businesses closing operations in an effort to reduce losses and become more competitive. For example, Levi Strauss & Co® closed its manufacturing plants in North America and now contracts with foreign manufacturers to make its garments.

Risk is also involved in the development of new products. Product introductions are costly and risky. Up to 85 percent of new products fail in the first year. It is difficult to assess the need for a product that does not exist yet. Some products that failed quickly include Harley Davidson® perfume, Gerber® Singles for adults, and Bic® underwear produced by the disposable pen company.

Bankruptcy

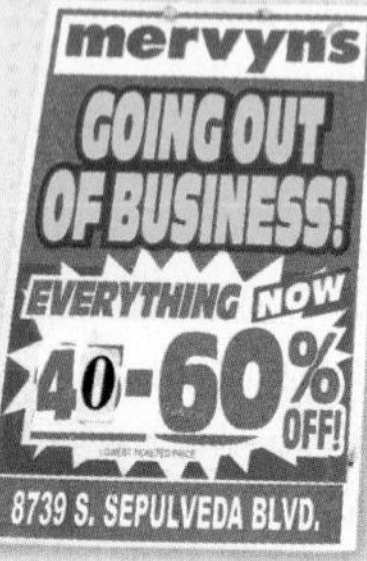

After over 50 years in business, Mervyn's (or Circuit City®) filed for bankruptcy and was forced to close its doors. A deep recession and stiff competition led to the company's demise. ***How do you think this company's failure affected its employees, the communities where they were located, and its competitors?***

PROFIT

Profit is the money earned from conducting business after all costs and expenses have been paid. Profit is often misunderstood. Some people think the money a business earns from sales is its profit. That is not true. The range of profit for most businesses is one percent to five percent of sales. The remaining 95 to 99 percent goes to pay costs, expenses, and business taxes.

Profit is the motivation for taking the risk of starting a business. It is the reward for taking that risk. It is also the reward for satisfying the needs and wants of customers and consumers. Businesses may use their profits to pay owners or stockholders, or they may elect to reinvest those profits in their businesses.

Profits are good for our economy in many ways. The concept of profit is the driving force in a market-oriented economic system. It encourages people to develop new products and services in the hope of making a profit. Without profit, few new products would be introduced.

Profit remains high when sales are high and costs are kept low. This encourages companies to work in an efficient way that helps to conserve precious human and natural resources. Profits provide money for a company to keep its facilities and machinery up-to-date. Then the business can produce goods more efficiently.

ECONOMIC COST OF UNPROFITABLE FIRMS

An unprofitable business faces many problems. One of the first things businesses do when their profits decline is to lay off employees. Stockholders in unprofitable companies can lose money if the stock value falls below what they paid for it. As more investors sell their stock in the poorly performing company, the company has fewer resources with which to conduct business.

Government also suffers when business profits decline. Poorly performing businesses pay less money to the government in taxes. When businesses lay off workers, there is a rise in unemployment. This causes an increase in the cost of social services and puts more stress on such agencies.

ECONOMIC BENEFITS OF SUCCESSFUL FIRMS

Profitable businesses hire more people. Employees may have higher incomes, better benefits, and higher morale. Investors earn money from their investments, which they spend or reinvest. Vendors and suppliers make more money, too. As employment and profits climb, the government makes more money from taxation of individuals and businesses. Companies and individuals are also more likely to donate to charities when they are doing well.

Remember that profitable companies attract competition, which is beneficial to the consumer. To satisfy consumers' wants and needs, they try to offer new products, the lowest prices, the highest quality, and the best service.

When people earn higher incomes, they have more money to spend. There is increased demand not only for expensive products such as cars, homes, and luxury products, but also for services provided by a variety of businesses, from hair salons to travel agencies.

SUPPLY AND DEMAND

In a market-oriented economy, supply and demand determine the prices and quantities of goods and services produced. To understand how prices are determined, you have to understand how supply and demand interact. See **Figure 5.1** (p. 120).

Supply is the amount of goods producers are willing to make and sell. The law of supply is the economic rule that price and quantity supplied move in the same direction. This means that as prices rise for a good, the quantity supplied generally rises. As the price falls, the quantity supplied by sellers also falls. Thus, suppliers want to supply a larger quantity of goods at higher prices so their businesses can be more profitable.

Demand refers to consumer willingness and ability to buy products. The law of demand is the economic principle that price and demand move in opposite directions. As the price of a good increases, the quantity of the good demanded falls. As the price falls, demand for the good increases.

When supply and demand **interact** in the marketplace, conditions of surplus, shortage, or equilibrium are created. These conditions often determine whether prices will go down, up, or stay the same.

SURPLUSES

Surpluses of goods occur when supply exceeds demand. If the price of a product is too high or seems unreasonable to most customers in the marketplace, the customers may decide not to buy it. Their decisions will affect the market. Businesses lower prices to encourage people to buy more of the product. They may run sales or special promotions to entice customers to buy the product.

One of the best examples of surpluses can be found in the produce section of a supermarket. Peaches, apples, broccoli, bananas, and other produce may be priced very low one week due to supply. When a given crop is in season, there is often an excess supply. The result is that farmers lower their prices to sell large quantities. Supermarkets that buy large quantities of the crop at the low price do the same. The surplus of produce affects the price of produce for producers, sellers, and consumers.

You can see how a produce shortage affects produce prices. When there is a poor season for growing oranges, you will find that the price of oranges is higher. For produce, extreme weather conditions such as a drought, flood, or freezing weather can affect the supply. However, when the product in question is a necessity, customers will pay the price determined by the market.

SHORTAGES

When demand exceeds supply, shortages of products occur. When shortages occur, businesses can raise prices and still sell their merchandise. An oil shortage increases the price of gasoline, so consumers who want to drive their vehicles pay the higher price. In many cases it is against the law to increase the price of a product or service during a shortage if the shortage is caused by a natural disaster, like a hurricane.

EXPLAIN

Visual Literacy

Bankruptcy Caption Answer Read the figure caption question to students: ***How do you think this company's failure affected its employees, the communities where they were located, and its competitors?*** Employees lost their jobs, communities lost tax revenue, and competitors benefitted by gaining new customers.

Critical Thinking

Explain that when Circuit City® went bankrupt in 2009, it was the second largest electronics store, after Best Buy®. Best Buy was left with little competition from other bricks-and-mortar stores. Ask students: ***What advantage did this give Best Buy?*** Because of lack of competition, sales increased. Then ask: ***Do you think there might have been any disadvantages? If so, what might they be?*** Yes, because businesses often do best when they have strong competitors who challenge them.

PROFIT

Remind students that profit is the reward for the risks businesspeople take. To look more closely at profit, focus on these guiding questions.

Guiding Questions

Predict If you had just started a small business that was making a profit, what do you think you would do with this money?	Possible answer: Most owners who are just starting a small business reinvest any profits back into the business in order to improve it.
Evaluate How important is it to our economy that most businesses make a profit? How do we all benefit from their success?	It is very important. The potential for making a profit encourages people to develop new products and services that benefit us all. Profitable businesses also tend to employ more workers.

ELABORATE

SUPPLY AND DEMAND

Tell students that the theory of supply and demand is the foundation of the free market. To focus on how supply and demand affects the workings of the marketplace, ask these guiding questions.

Guiding Questions

Explain What is the theory of supply?	the economic rule that price and quantity supplied move in the same direction
Predict The price of a movie ticket goes from $7.00 to $8.50. What should happen to the demand for these tickets?	Demand for movie tickets should go down.
Interpret Why would an economist say that "Supply and demand are inversely related to one another"?	Because as one goes up, the other goes down. (The word *inverse* means *opposite*.)

Mini Project

Enrichment

Simulate a Business Venture To emphasize the concepts of risk and profit, have students simulate starting a new business: making and selling T-shirts to other students at their school. Each student has $200 of imaginary money to invest or keep. Ask students how much of their $200 they are willing to invest in this venture. Emphasize that if the business is a success, those who invested the most will receive the greatest profit. Start by asking for $200 investments. If there are few or none of these, begin to gradually lower the price. When done, encourage students to discuss how they chose the amount they were willing to invest. Ask: ***Were you afraid you might lose the $200 if you invested it? Were you hopeful you would make a lot of money?*** Students' attitudes and willingness to take risks will influence their decisions. Some might say that they invested a lot because they thought the T-shirts would be popular whereas others might say that there would be too much competition.

SURPLUSES

Explain that businesses try to avoid surpluses and shortages, both of which can lead to problems. Then ask these guiding questions.

Guiding Questions

List What are some synonyms for surplus?	excess, oversupply, extra
Analyze What are two common causes of surpluses?	More items are produced than needed, the price is too high

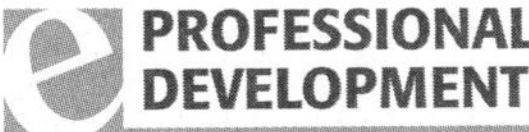

MINI CLIP

Reading: Planning for Future Instruction
Go to the Online Learning Center to view a video in which teachers plan for future instruction by developing learning strategies for nonfiction text.

SHORTAGES

To further explore shortages, ask these guiding questions.

Guiding Questions

Give Examples What is an example of a situation in which a shortage is caused by a change in supply? A change in demand?	Supply: The orange crop is damaged by frost, so grocery stores have fewer oranges. Demand: After a hurricane, consumers rush to buy plywood to board up broken windows.
Construct You manage a home improvement store. Your area has just been hit by a flood. Building supplies quickly become in short supply. Would you raise prices to profit from this shortage? Why or why not?	Possible answer: No, because it would be unethical to take advantage of a situation in which consumers have no choice but to pay the higher price. Plus it would probably lead to bad publicity for the store.
Break Down How do shortages affect businesses?	Businesses can raise prices and still sell products.

VIRTUAL BUSINESS

SUPPLY AND DEMAND

Introduce the concept of supply and demand to students using Knowledge Matters' Virtual Business Retailing visual simulation, *Supply and Demand*. In this simulation, students will learn about the factors of supply and demand and what happens in businesses when these factors are out of balance.

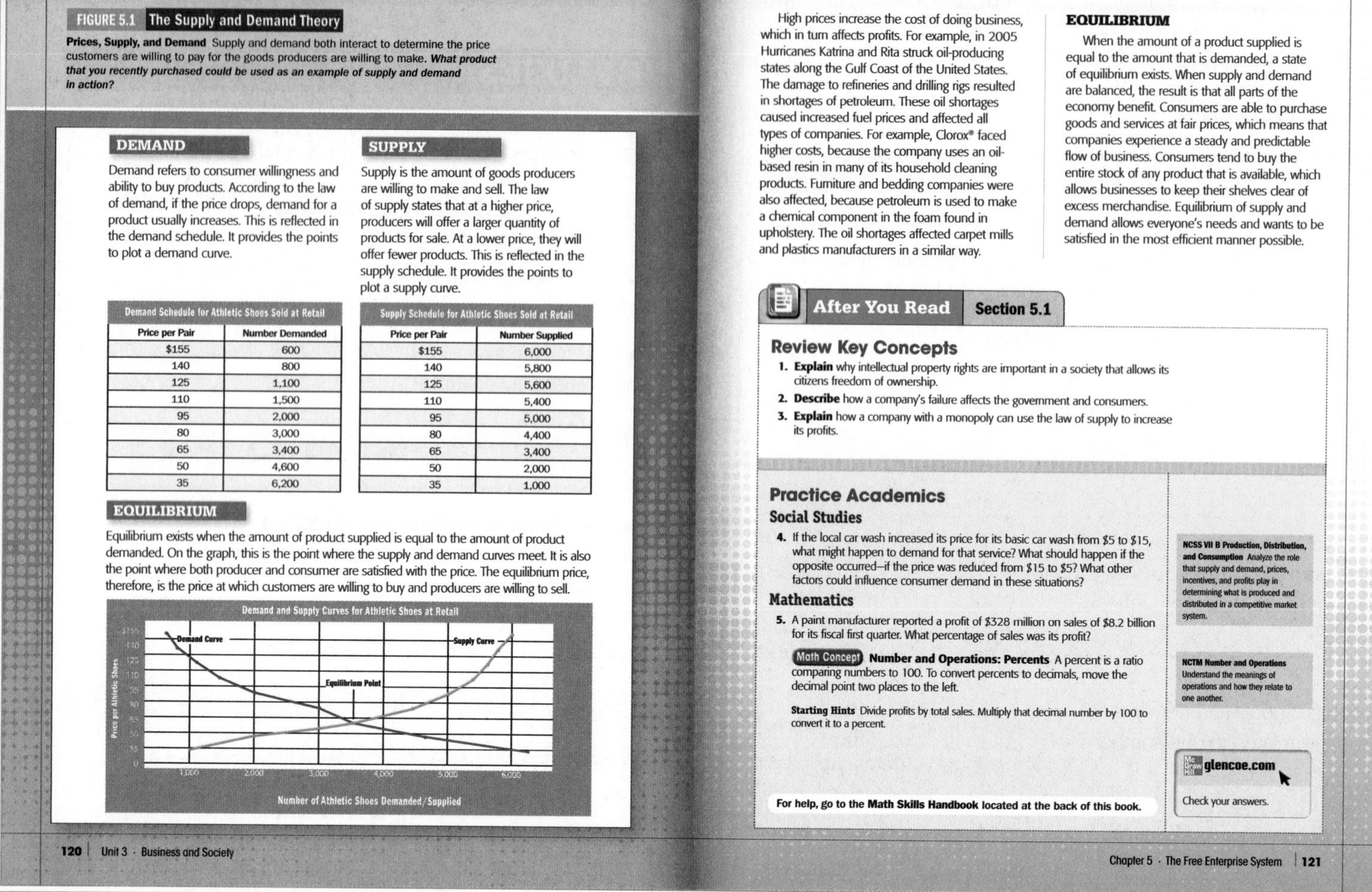

FIGURE 5.1 The Supply and Demand Theory

Prices, Supply, and Demand Supply and demand both interact to determine the price customers are willing to pay for the goods producers are willing to make. ***What product that you recently purchased could be used as an example of supply and demand in action?***

DEMAND

Demand refers to consumer willingness and ability to buy products. According to the law of demand, if the price drops, demand for a product usually increases. This is reflected in the demand schedule. It provides the points to plot a demand curve.

SUPPLY

Supply is the amount of goods producers are willing to make and sell. The law of supply states that at a higher price, producers will offer a larger quantity of products for sale. At a lower price, they will offer fewer products. This is reflected in the supply schedule. It provides the points to plot a supply curve.

Demand Schedule for Athletic Shoes Sold at Retail

Price per Pair	Number Demanded
$155	600
140	800
125	1,100
110	1,500
95	2,000
80	3,000
65	3,400
50	4,600
35	6,200

Supply Schedule for Athletic Shoes Sold at Retail

Price per Pair	Number Supplied
$155	6,000
140	5,800
125	5,600
110	5,400
95	5,000
80	4,400
65	3,400
50	2,000
35	1,000

EQUILIBRIUM

Equilibrium exists when the amount of product supplied is equal to the amount of product demanded. On the graph, this is the point where the supply and demand curves meet. It is also the point where both producer and consumer are satisfied with the price. The equilibrium price, therefore, is the price at which customers are willing to buy and producers are willing to sell.

High prices increase the cost of doing business, which in turn affects profits. For example, in 2005 Hurricanes Katrina and Rita struck oil-producing states along the Gulf Coast of the United States. The damage to refineries and drilling rigs resulted in shortages of petroleum. These oil shortages caused increased fuel prices and affected all types of companies. For example, Clorox® faced higher costs, because the company uses an oil-based resin in many of its household cleaning products. Furniture and bedding companies were also affected, because petroleum is used to make a chemical component in the foam found in upholstery. The oil shortages affected carpet mills and plastics manufacturers in a similar way.

EQUILIBRIUM

When the amount of a product supplied is equal to the amount that is demanded, a state of equilibrium exists. When supply and demand are balanced, the result is that all parts of the economy benefit. Consumers are able to purchase goods and services at fair prices, which means that companies experience a steady and predictable flow of business. Consumers tend to buy the entire stock of any product that is available, which allows businesses to keep their shelves clear of excess merchandise. Equilibrium of supply and demand allows everyone's needs and wants to be satisfied in the most efficient manner possible.

After You Read Section 5.1

Review Key Concepts

1. **Explain** why intellectual property rights are important in a society that allows its citizens freedom of ownership.
2. **Describe** how a company's failure affects the government and consumers.
3. **Explain** how a company with a monopoly can use the law of supply to increase its profits.

Practice Academics

Social Studies

4. If the local car wash increased its price for its basic car wash from $5 to $15, what might happen to demand for that service? What should happen if the opposite occurred—if the price was reduced from $15 to $5? What other factors could influence consumer demand in these situations?

Mathematics

5. A paint manufacturer reported a profit of $328 million on sales of $8.2 billion for its fiscal first quarter. What percentage of sales was its profit?

Math Concept **Number and Operations: Percents** A percent is a ratio comparing numbers to 100. To convert percents to decimals, move the decimal point two places to the left.

Starting Hints Divide profits by total sales. Multiply that decimal number by 100 to convert it to a percent.

NCSS VII B Production, Distribution, and Consumption Analyze the role that supply and demand, prices, incentives, and profits play in determining what is produced and distributed in a competitive market system.

NCTM Number and Operations Understand the meanings of operations and how they relate to one another.

For help, go to the **Math Skills Handbook** located at the back of this book.

glencoe.com

Check your answers.

ELABORATE

Visual Literacy

Figure 5.1 Caption Answer Read the figure caption question to students: ***What product that you recently purchased could be used as an example of supply and demand in action?*** Accept all reasonable answers. Possible answer: Students may have paid a high price for concert tickets for a band that is currently extremely popular. To focus discussion on the interaction between the supply and demand curves, ask these guiding questions.

Guiding Questions

Define How would you define equilibrium point?	point where supply and demand meet
Synthesize Explain that the theory of supply and demand can only be applied if other things remain unchanged. Describe a scenario in which both average income and price of gas go up. Supply and demand states that gas usage then should go down. Ask: Do you think this will necessarily be true?	Not necessarily, because the increase in income means consumers have more spending power. Therefore, gas usage may not drop, and could even rise.

Activate Prior Knowledge

Reteach the Different Types of Economic Systems Have students think back to what they learned in Chapter 3. Ask: ***What are the different types of economic systems?*** traditional, market, command, mixed Explain that students are now going to learn about the theory of supply and demand, which states that supply and demand interact in different ways to affect whether a surplus, a shortage, or equilibrium is reached. Ask: ***Does the theory of supply and demand affect all types of economies? Why or why not?*** No, supply and demand only affects a market economy in which consumers decide what should be produced and businesses decide how it is to be produced. In a traditional economy, supply and demand are based on survival needs, cultural practices, and tradition. In command economies, the government controls supply and demand.

Reinforce Vocabulary

Demand—Alternate Meanings Write the word *demand* on the board. Explain to students that, like many words, *demand* can be used as either a noun or verb. Read aloud the first sentence in the third paragraph under the Supply and Demand header: ***Demand refers to consumer willingness and ability to buy products.*** Ask: ***Does this sentence use* demand *as a noun or a verb?*** noun Ask: ***What do you think* demand *means when used as a verb?*** to insist upon, to call for urgently Ask: ***What is an example of a sentence using* demand *as a verb?*** Answers will vary. Sample answer: I demand to know where you went last night.

EVALUATE

Mini Projects

Enrichment

Write a True/False Quiz Have students work independently to develop a 10-question true/false quiz about supply and demand. Then organize students into pairs. Each person should take their partner's quiz. When they are done, students should go over the questions together. Students should write true/false quizzes that ask question about the theory of supply and demand. Sample question: *Surpluses of building supplies often occur during natural disasters such as hurricanes, causing the price of supplies to drop. (False)*

Learn About How Shortages Affect People's Lives Instruct students to work in groups of three or four to research shortages of items in a particular region or country over a specific period of time. You might give the example of food, nylon, and fuel shortages for domestic use during World War II. Another example you might put forth would be the shortage of H1N1 flu vaccines in 2009. Have interested students choose a specific shortage and research the effects of the shortage along with how individuals, governments, and organizations responded to the shortage. They should share their finding in an informal oral presentation. Students' reports will depend on the shortage they choose. For example, during World War II, many everyday items, including fuel oil, gasoline, sugar, meat, shoes, firewood, and coal were rationed. Because of the extensive needs of the war effort, the U.S. government controlled supply and demand. Families received ration books that determined how much of each rationed item they could receive. To avoid hoarding, the stamps in the ration books were only valid for a limited time. The government produced posters and other promotional materials emphasizing that, by practicing rationing, everyone was supporting the war effort. Even though most people were willing to suffer shortages to win the war, there was still a black market where people could buy rationed goods at higher prices.

VIRTUAL BUSINESS

FINANCING

Introduce students to the concept of financing using Knowledge Matters' Virtual Business Retailing visual simulation, *Financing*. In this simulation, students will learn about and evaluate different financing methods to finance their start-up business.

After You Read — Section 5.1

Review Key Concepts

1. Individuals have used their time, creativity, and skills to develop intellectual property, just as others have used their time and skills to make products or to provide services. Therefore, intellectual property deserves to be protected just like other things that people produce.
2. A company's failure affects the government because it then receives fewer tax dollars. In addition, it may have to pay unemployment benefits to laid-off workers. It affects consumers because they then have fewer choices. If another company then has a monopoly, prices might go up.
3. The company can decrease the supply to raise the demand and therefore the price can be increased resulting in profits going up.

Practice Academics

Social Studies

4. The demand for a basic car wash would go down if the price went from \$5 to \$15. If the price went from \$15 to \$5, the demand would go up. Other factors that could influence consumer demand in these situations might be the weather (rainy or snowy season), location of the car wash, competition, and the quality of the car wash.

Mathematics

5. Four percent. (\$328 million divided by \$8.2 billion = .04 = 4%).

 glencoe.com 

Send students to the Online Learning Center to check their answers.

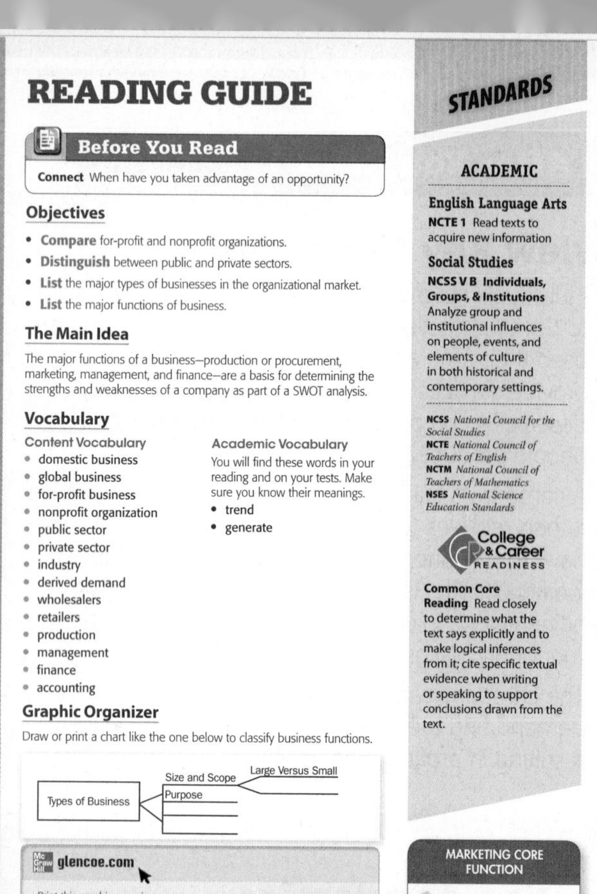

READING GUIDE

STANDARDS

Before You Read

Connect When have you taken advantage of an opportunity?

Objectives

- **Compare** for-profit and nonprofit organizations.
- **Distinguish** between public and private sectors.
- **List** the major types of businesses in the organizational market.
- **List** the major functions of business.

The Main Idea

The major functions of a business—production or procurement, marketing, management, and finance—are a basis for determining the strengths and weaknesses of a company as part of a SWOT analysis.

Vocabulary

Content Vocabulary
- domestic business
- global business
- for-profit business
- nonprofit organization
- public sector
- private sector
- industry
- derived demand
- wholesalers
- retailers
- production
- management
- finance
- accounting

Academic Vocabulary
You will find these words in your reading and on your tests. Make sure you know their meanings.
- trend
- generate

Graphic Organizer

Draw or print a chart like the one below to classify business functions.

Types of Business — Size and Scope — Large Versus Small; Purpose

glencoe.com

Print this graphic organizer.

ACADEMIC

English Language Arts
NCTE 1 Read texts to acquire new information

Social Studies
NCSS V B Individuals, Groups, & Institutions Analyze group and institutional influences on people, events, and elements of culture in both historical and contemporary settings.

NCSS *National Council for the Social Studies*
NCTE *National Council of Teachers of English*
NCTM *National Council of Teachers of Mathematics*
NSES *National Science Education Standards*

College & Career READINESS

Common Core
Reading Read closely to determine what the text says explicitly and to make logical inferences from it; cite specific textual evidence when writing or speaking to support conclusions drawn from the text.

MARKETING CORE FUNCTION

Market Planning

122 | Unit 3 · Business and Society

Section 5.2

Business Opportunities

TYPES OF BUSINESS

In the free enterprise system, there are many opportunities to invest or work in many different types of businesses. In order to view those opportunities, it is a good idea to start by classifying businesses. To understand their differences, you will need to know the terminology associated with business classification. Keep in mind that a business may be classified in more than one category. A business can be categorized by its size and scope, by its purpose, and by its place within the industry.

As You Read

Classify Select a business in your community and categorize it by size, purpose, and place in the industry.

SIZE AND SCOPE

One of the easiest ways to describe a business is by its size. Is it large or small? The scope of a business refers to the extent of its business operation. Some businesses serve a small neighborhood, while others do business globally.

LARGE VERSUS SMALL BUSINESSES

A small business is one that is operated by only one or a few individuals. It generally has fewer than 100 employees. A large business is usually considered one that employs more than 1,000 people.

Nationwide, there are millions of small businesses. This category also contains many brick-and-mortar and Internet companies that often start off with small budgets and staffs. About 95 percent of all U.S. businesses are classified as small businesses. These types of businesses employ more than half of the private-sector (nongovernment) work force.

DOMESTIC VERSUS GLOBAL

A business that sells its products only in its own country is considered a **domestic business**. Because a domestic business limits its scope of operation to one country, its opportunities for growth are limited to customers within that country.

A **global business** sells its products in more than one country. The use of the Internet, along with faster transportation and financial transfers, makes it easier to do business globally. Products produced in one country are more easily sold around the world. The **trend** among large and small businesses is toward a more global market.

> "You have many opportunities to invest and work in different types of businesses."

PURPOSE

A business exists to serve the needs of its customers in order to make a profit. The purpose of a business is to produce goods or provide a service, and profits are what is left over after all costs and expenses have been paid. However, there are other organizations that function like a business but have different purposes. To understand these differences in purpose, we need to distinguish between for-profit businesses and nonprofit organizations. We must also understand the similarities and differences between public and private enterprise. It is interesting to note that some private enterprises can be nonprofit, and some public enterprises aim to earn a profit.

Chapter 5 · The Free Enterprise System | 123

ENGAGE

Anticipation Activity

Write the names of these businesses and organizations on the board: Sierra Club, McDonald's, Food and Drug Administration, and City Council. Also list the name of a local business. Ask students: ***How do these businesses and organizations compare?*** All provide products or services, but they differ in the types of products and services.

Objectives

- **Compare** for-profit and nonprofit organizations. For-profit: seek to make a profit from operations. Nonprofit: use money they make to fund causes identified in their charters.
- **Distinguish** between public and private sectors. Public sector: most local, state, and federal agencies. Private sector: not associated with any government agency.
- **List** the major types of businesses in the organizational market. extractors, construction and manufacturing businesses, wholesalers, retailers, service-related firms
- **List** the major functions of business. production and procurement, marketing, management, finance and accounting

Graphic Organizer

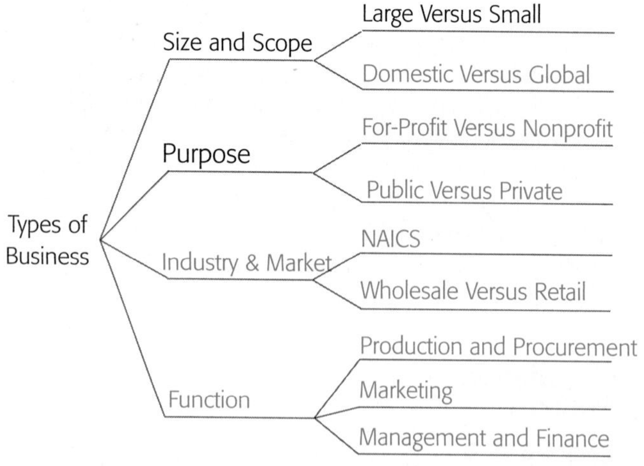

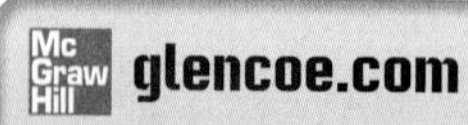

glencoe.com

Graphic Organizer Send students to the Online Learning Center to print this graphic organizer.

EXPLORE

Before You Read

Read the Before You Read question aloud: ***When have you taken advantage of an opportunity?*** Answers will vary. Possible answer: My parents looked into having a lawn care company mow our grass, but it was more than they wanted to pay. So they started paying me a slightly smaller amount to do the mowing. I realized this could be a profitable business, so I made arrangements with several neighbors to also mow their grass. Discuss with students that one characteristic of entrepreneurs is that they are always keeping their eyes open for consumer needs that are not being met. Ask: ***Do you see any ways in which the needs of the students in this school are not being met? How might an entrepreneur meet these needs?*** Possible answer: An entrepreneur might start a business serving lunches to students from a mobile fast-food truck.

Preteaching Vocabulary

Have students go to the Online Learning Center at glencoe.com for the Chapter 5 Preteaching Vocabulary games.

Content Vocabulary

Write the following content vocabulary words on the board: *domestic business, global business, for-profit business, nonprofit organization, public sector, private sector, industry, derived demand, wholesalers, retailers, production, management, finance, accounting*. Encourage students to use their prior knowledge to answer: ***What two terms are used to indicate whether an organization is connected with the government?*** public sector and private sector Ask: ***What two terms indicate whether a company does business internationally?*** domestic business and global business

Academic Vocabulary

Trend—Context Read this sentence to students: *A new trend is for women to wear longer skirts.* Ask: ***Based on its context, what do you think the word* trend *means?*** tendency, inclination Then read the last sentence under the Domestic Versus Global header: *The trend among large and small businesses is toward a more global market.* Ask: ***How might you reword this sentence so that it does not use the word* trend?** Both large and small businesses are tending to have a more global market.

Generate—Word Origin Tell students that *generate* comes from the Latin *generare*, which means to "bring about" or "produce."

Business Opportunities

TYPES OF BUSINESS

Ask these guiding questions to focus the discussion of different classification methods.

Guiding Questions

Recall How many employees does a company typically need to have to be considered a larger business?	more than 1,000
Deduce How do you think the Internet is affecting the trend toward a more global market?	It encourages companies to market internationally because it provides an immediate, inexpensive means of communicating.
Decide Can you think of a situation in which you would rather deal with a small, local business than a large global business?	Possible answer: If I wanted to know about the ingredients used at a restaurant, I would rather deal with a locally owned café than with a global chain such as McDonald's.

As You Read

Read students the As You Read question: ***Select a business in your community and categorize it by size, purpose, and place in the industry.*** Accept all reasonable answers. For example, a local house-cleaning business with ten employees would be a small, domestic, for-profit service business.

Expert Advice

Read the quote to students:

"You have many opportunities to invest and work in different types of businesses."

Have students list reasons why this statement is true. Write the reasons on the board and encourage students to discuss each one. Possible reasons: We live in a democracy with a relatively free marketplace. We are developing the skills needed to compete in this marketplace. We are obtaining a good education. The Internet provides access to a wide variety of current information, such as the sources needed for research on making investment decisions and locating job opportunities.

FOR-PROFIT VERSUS NONPROFIT ORGANIZATIONS

A **for-profit business** seeks to make a profit from its operations. A **nonprofit organization** functions like a business but uses the money it makes to fund the cause identified in its charter. Nonprofit organizations **generate** revenue through gifts and donations. Some sell goods or services. This generates income. Nonprofit organizations usually do not have to pay taxes on their income, but they have expenses. They pay employees and rent for their office space. Other expenses may include supplies, printing, and postage for letters sent requesting donations. The American Red Cross, Girl and Boy Scouts of America®, DECA, and other nonprofit organizations try to generate more income than expenses, just like a for-profit business. However, unlike profit-oriented businesses, nonprofit organizations use that extra money for their cause. Although there are many unpaid volunteers, a staff of paid workers is often also needed to manage the operation of a nonprofit organization.

PUBLIC VERSUS PRIVATE

In addition to charities, other organizations operate like businesses, but are not intended to earn a profit. Most local, state, and federal government agencies and services fall into this category. Take schools and libraries for example. Their main purpose is to provide service to the people in the country or community in which they operate. At the federal level, there are military agencies, like the Army and the Air Force; social agencies, like Social Security and Medicare; and regulatory agencies, like the Food and Drug Administration and the Environmental Protection Agency. Government-financed agencies like these are part of the **public sector**. Businesses not associated with government agencies are part of the **private sector**.

Public and Private The Public Company Accounting Oversight Board, created by the Sarbanes-Oxley Act of 2002, is considered a private organization that has some public functions.

Public-sector organizations purchase one-third of all goods and services sold in the United States each year. Think about all the products and supplies purchased in the operation of your public school system. Can you see why businesses seek out customers in the public sector?

American Red Cross

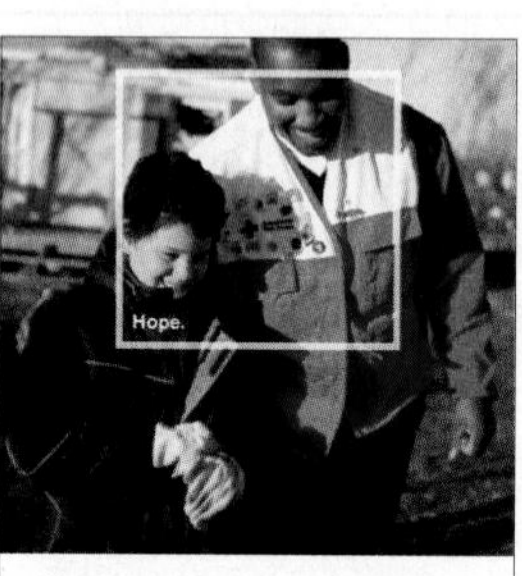

Hope.
When Heartbreak Turns to Hope, You're There.
Down the street, across the country, around the world—you help save the day. Every day.
When you give blood or provide a hot meal to a disaster victim, train in first aid or help a member of our military, you reach out your hand. It's at that moment—when heartbreak turns to hope—that you're there through the American Red Cross.
We need you now more than ever.
Support disaster relief today. Visit redcross.org.
American Red Cross
1-800-RED CROSS | redcross.org

The American Red Cross is a nonprofit organization that has employees and volunteers. You will see its efforts at natural disasters, providing help to people in their time of need. ***As a nonprofit organization, how does it get the funds it needs to pay its employees, run the organization, and provide that assistance?***

INDUSTRY & MARKETS

Businesses are often classified according to the industry they represent, the products they sell, and the markets they target. The government provides a system for classifying types of business by industry and sector. Products and markets are classified according to intended use. All of these classifications are interrelated with relation to the customers served.

NAICS

According to the U.S. Department of Labor, an **industry** consists of a group of establishments primarily engaged in producing or handling the same product or group of products or in rendering the same services. For 60 years, the U.S. government used the Standard Industrial Classification (SIC) system to collect data on businesses and analyze the U.S. economy. However, rapid changes in services and technology made a new system necessary. The United States, Canada, and Mexico jointly developed the North American Industry Classification System (NAICS). In a nutshell, it states that "establishments that do similar things in similar ways are classified together." NAICS uses a six-digit coding system to classify all economic activity into 20 industry sectors. For example, the information sector includes the industries involved in communications, publishing, and motion picture and sound recording, as well as Internet companies. Some of the subcategories of the Internet industry are Web search portals, Internet publishing and broadcasting, electronic shopping, and electronic auctions. The information in the NAICS can be helpful to businesses looking for new marketing opportunities. It is also helpful to people who want to find employment or invest in those sectors.

CONSUMER, ORGANIZATIONAL, AND SERVICE MARKETS

As you read in Chapter 2, the consumer market consists of customers who buy goods for personal use. The organizational market consists of business customers who buy goods for use in their operations. The two are interrelated because of the economic concept of derived demand. **Derived demand** in the organizational market is based on, or derived from, the demand for consumer goods and services.

When consumers decide to buy more automobiles, dealers need more cars. This means auto manufacturers will need an increased supply of auto components, such as tires, radios, batteries, and electronic parts. Companies that make such parts experience an increased demand as a result of consumer decisions to buy more cars.

The GREEN Marketer

Cause Marketing

In cause marketing, for-profit companies team up with nonprofits to promote a social or environmental cause. In 2008, for example, Tripadvisor.com launched its "More Than Footprints" campaign, which invited Web visitors to vote on how the company should split a $1 million donation among five nonprofits, including Conservation International and the Nature Conservancy. Facebook posts, a video on the company's YouTube channel, and widgets on the charities' Web sites helped spread the word about the campaign.

Social Studies

Discuss Some people argue that cause marketing may cause consumers to cut their direct giving to charities that address human needs and concerns. How might this be the case? What are the benefits of cause marketing that are not part of direct giving to charities? Discuss your response with a partner and then share with the class.

NCSS I A Culture Analyze and explain the ways groups, societies, and cultures address human needs and concerns.

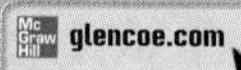

glencoe.com

Get an activity on green marketing.

EXPLAIN

Visual Literacy

American Red Cross Caption Answer Read the figure caption question to students: ***As a nonprofit organization, how does it get the funds it needs to pay its employees, run the organization, and provide that assistance?*** The American Red Cross gets its funds through charitable donations by individuals and companies

Public and Private Tell students that the Sarbanes-Oxley Act was enacted in response to several major corporate scandals, such as those involving Enron and WorldCom. Ask students: ***Why do you think it was particularly important for Congress to place controls on public companies by establishing the Public Company Accounting Oversight Board?***

PURPOSE

Ask students these guiding questions to focus on these two groups' purposes.

Guiding Questions

Identify What are three public services you use? What are three private services you use?	Public services: school, library, police and fire protection, city buses. Private services: music lessons, car repair services, gym, hair stylists
Compare How is the purpose of a for-profit business different from the purpose of a nonprofit organization?	For-profit: works to make a profit Nonprofit: uses any extra money to support its cause.
Evaluate What do you expect from a nonprofit organization to which you contribute? What do you expect from a for-profit company whose goods you purchase?	Possible answer: I expect the nonprofit organization to spend my contributions for the cause. I expect the for-profit company to give me a good quality product that will meet my needs.

ELABORATE

INDUSTRY AND MARKETS

Discuss with students that businesses can be classified according to the industry they belong to, what they sell, and who they sell it to. Ask these guiding questions to focus the discussion on these classification methods.

Guiding Questions

State What is the purpose of the North American Industry Classification System?	to classify all economic activity into one of 20 industry sectors
Determine Provide an example of how a purchase you recently made affected derived demand.	Possible answer: I bought a pair of athletic shoes recently. The manufacturer had to obtain the raw materials from a supplier, which is an example of a derived demand.
Analyze How might the NAICS be helpful to businesses? How might it be helpful to individuals?	might help businesses find new marketing opportunities, might help individuals who want to find employment in a specific area

Mini Projects

Enrichment

Examine a Nonprofit Organization Ask student for examples of nonprofit organizations and list them on the board. Possible answers: Sierra Club, humane societies, UNICEF, homeless shelters, Special Olympics, and student vocational organizations (such as DECA). Instruct students to choose one of these nonprofit organizations. Have students access their organization's Web site (or another appropriate source) and read about the organization's purpose and accomplishments. Students should write an essay discussing why someone might choose to work for this organization rather than a business that makes a profit. Student essays will vary. Reasons might include idealism, ethics, personal satisfaction, to help others, and so forth.

Reinforce Vocabulary

Derived demand—Denotative meaning Write the term *derived demand* on the board. Explain that a demand that is "derived" is based on another factor. As an example, describe a print shop that buys paper from the manufacturer. This derived demand exists because the print shop must have these supplies to meet its customers' needs.

The GREEN Marketer

Social Studies Answer Students' opinions will vary. Cause marketing might result in consumers reducing their direct giving because they feel they have already supported a worthy cause. Benefits include that consumers might support causes that they would not have otherwise supported and consumers might become aware of these causes because of promotions. Use these guiding questions to discuss this topic in more detail.

Guiding Questions

Describe What are some of the channels that Tripadvisor.com uses to promote its "More Than Footprints" campaign?	company Web site, Facebook, YouTube, widgets on charities' Web sites
Critique What is the primary benefit that a for-profit company gets from being involved in cause marketing?	It may encourage socially responsible consumers to purchase their products.

glencoe.com

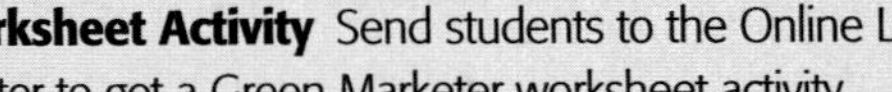

Worksheet Activity Send students to the Online Learning Center to get a Green Marketer worksheet activity.

CONSUMER, ORGANIZATIONAL, AND SERVICE MARKETS

To help focus the discussion on different markets, ask these guiding questions.

Guiding Questions

Identify A wholesaler supplies computers to retail stores. From what type of business would the wholesaler purchase computers?	typically the manufacturer
Analyze What category of the organizational market would a farmer belong in? Why?	extractors, they use the earth to produce a crop that is sold on to a food processor.
Synthesize Why do you think wholesalers generally refuse to sell to individual consumers?	wholesalers only sell goods in large quantities

Due to the relationship between consumer and organizational demand, organizational companies look for opportunities to increase their business by studying consumer trends. Businesses that are service-related function in both consumer and organizational markets.

Businesses that are involved in the organizational market include extractors, construction and manufacturing businesses, wholesalers, retailers, and service-related firms.

Extractors are businesses that take something from the earth or its water supply. They include agriculture, forestry, fishing, and mining businesses. The products they extract are sold primarily to other businesses.

Construction companies build structures such as houses, office buildings, and manufacturing plants. Manufacturing involves producing goods to sell to other manufacturers or to wholesalers and retailers.

Wholesalers obtain goods from manufacturers and resell them to organizational users, other wholesalers, and retailers. Wholesalers are also called distributors. **Retailers** buy goods from wholesalers or directly from manufacturers and resell them to the consumer. For the most part, retailers cater to the consumer market.

Service-related businesses are companies that provide intangible products to satisfy needs and wants of consumers and businesses. Consumer services include such things as dry cleaning, hair styling, entertainment (movies and theater), transportation, and insurance. It also includes personal needs, such as lawn-cutting, child care, and housekeeping.

Business services follow the same concept. That is why some firms specialize in accounting, marketing, management, insurance, shipping, and finance. There are also professional services—those provided by professionals such as doctors, dentists, and lawyers.

Internet-related services, such as Web portals, Web-casting, Web site design, and Web advertising have created opportunities that did not exist many years ago. For example, e-commerce (short for "electronic commerce") is the buying and selling of products through the use of electronic networks. Even traditional retailers adapt their marketing to e-commerce, resulting in the term *e-tailing*.

Reading Check

Compare What is the difference between retailers and wholesalers?

THE FUNCTIONS OF BUSINESS

Regardless of the type of business, there are four main functions involved in an organization's operation. They are production or procurement, marketing, management, and finance. The ways each business performs these activities may differ. However, all four are essential for running a business or organization. The success of business is dependent on how well these activities are coordinated, managed, and performed.

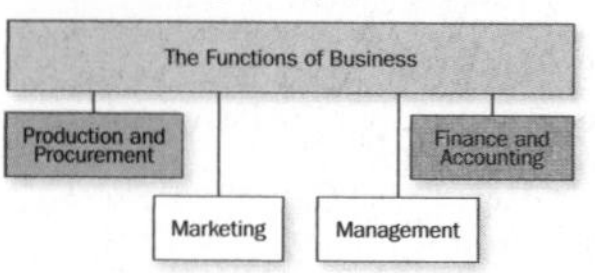

A company that has a great product but is poorly managed will not succeed. A company will also fail if it lacks the resources to pay for experienced personnel or to maintain inventory levels so products are available for sale. Poor financial record keeping can lead to poor management decisions, which may result in poor performance. If inaccurate accounting causes investors to believe that a company is more profitable than it really is, a corporation's reputation may be damaged. That in turn can lead to bad publicity and lower stock prices. Thus, the four business functions must be viewed in relation to one another. As you evaluate the strengths and weaknesses conducted during a SWOT analysis, review all four activities.

PRODUCTION AND PROCUREMENT

The process of creating, growing, manufacturing, or improving on goods and services is called **production**. A farmer grows wheat. Ford® Motor Company manufactures cars. Van conversion companies improve newly manufactured vans to make them more suitable for a driver who is disabled. Production, as a function of business, is found in industries. Such industries include farming, mining, forestry, manufacturing and service-related operations.

When evaluating this function of business in a SWOT analysis, look for innovation, speed to market, efficiency, and level of success with products. Company leaders focus on efficient production and consider many situations that may affect it, such as the law of diminishing returns. This law states that if one factor of production is increased while others remain the same, overall returns will decrease after a certain point. Companies that want to be leaders in an industry produce the most innovative products and do so before their competitors. Efficiency helps to keep prices down and sales up, which makes for a profitable company.

Hewlett-Packard® is one of the nation's largest patent holders. It has 15,000 patents in the United States and 25,000 worldwide. It adds about 1,500 new patents per year. Anything that is not patented is protected by trade secrets. As a result, it is an industry leader in information technology (IT).

PROCUREMENT

Procurement involves buying materials, products, and supplies needed to run a business. Manufacturing businesses need raw materials and parts to make the goods they sell. For example, clothing companies buy fabric, thread, buttons, and zippers. Procurement is sometimes referred to as sourcing because it involves researching suppliers, negotiating prices, and following through on purchases made. A SWOT analysis would involve evaluation of inventory management of the supplies needed to keep production at full capacity at all times. Buying the right quality materials at the right price would factor into that evaluation as well.

Retail and wholesale businesses buy ready-made products and resell them. A supermarket (retailer) buys cans of soup, fresh produce, frozen foods, dairy products, and the other non-food items for resale. Most of these products were purchased from manufacturers, while a few may have been purchased from wholesalers.

SWOT ANALYSIS, WHOLESALERS AND RETAILERS

In a SWOT analysis, you evaluate wholesalers and retailers on their merchandising ability. The five rights of merchandising are having the right goods, having them at the right time, having them in the right place, having them at the right price, and having them in the right quantity.

Predicting customer demand and product preferences is a difficult task, as is determining the price at which those products will sell.

MARKETING

All activities from the time a product leaves the producer or manufacturer until it reaches the final consumer are considered marketing activities.

All types of business, regardless of size, scope, intended purpose, and products sold use marketing activities in their operations. Manufacturers, service operations, wholesalers, and retailers buy goods for use in their operations and sell their finished products to customers.

All related marketing activities support the buying and selling functions. For example, research helps to determine what products to make or purchase, as well as how to price and promote them. Promotion educates customers about a company's products and is used to stimulate sales.

The Groupe Danone, a Paris food company has spent millions of dollars on research and development to find the right mix of ingredients for functional foods. Product development was based on science and clinical studies. Research results produced products like Danone's Activa and DanActive. Both are yogurts with special bacteria that have health benefits. These probiotic yogurts were marketed with higher prices than regular yogurts and succeeded in the marketplace.

126 | Unit 3 · Business and Society

Chapter 5 · The Free Enterprise System | 127

EXPLAIN

Graphic Organizer

Display this graphic organizer. Have the class choose a business and give examples of how each of these functions might be applied.

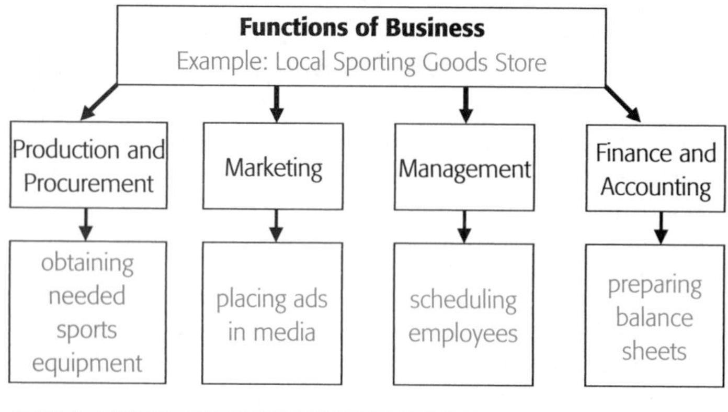

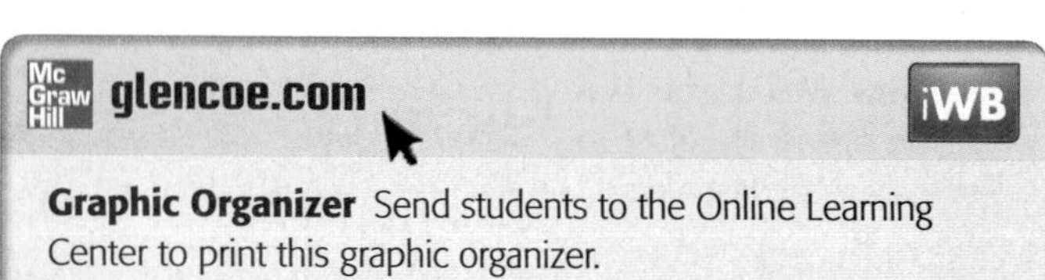

Graphic Organizer Send students to the Online Learning Center to print this graphic organizer.

Reading Check Answer

Read the Reading Check question to students: ***What is the difference between retailers and wholesalers?*** Wholesalers obtain goods from manufacturers and resell them. Retailers buy goods from wholesalers or manufacturers and resell to the consumer.

VIRTUAL BUSINESS

FINANCIAL STATEMENTS

Introduce the concept of financial statements to students using Knowledge Matters' Virtual Business Retailing visual simulation, *Financial Statements*. In this simulation, students will learn that business owners must have accurate and timely information about the financial status of their business to make the best decisions.

ELABORATE

PRODUCTION AND PROCUREMENT

To focus the discussion on production and procurement, ask these guiding questions.

Guiding Questions

Explain Why is procurement sometimes called sourcing?	the procurer must research suppliers, negotiate prices, then make purchases
Summarize In your own words, explain the law of diminishing returns.	For example, if too many workers are hired to work on an assembly line, employee productivity will eventually decrease. The reason is that only so much can be produced in a given period of time, based on the amount of materials and machinery that are available.
Assess If you were evaluating the strengths of a manufacturer in production, what would you assess?	innovation, speed to market, efficiency, levels of quality, levels of success with products

Knowledge Matters

VIRTUAL BUSINESS

ANALYZING THE COMPETITION

Introduce the concept of analyzing the competition to students using Knowledge Matters' Virtual Business Retailing visual simulation, *Analyzing the Competition*. In this simulation, students will learn how to determine who the competition is, competitive analysis, and how competition affects a business.

e MARKETING

E-tailing

E-tailing (electronic retailing) refers to selling goods and services online. It is a form of direct distribution from business to consumer (B2C). Some e-tailers are found only on the Internet, such as Amazon.com®. Other e-tailers also maintain traditional stores (Walmart®, Sears®, and Kohls®, for example). E-tailers that maintain only a Web site have fewer expenses than brick-and-mortar establishments that also offer online shopping. Pure e-tailers' expenses are warehousing, shipping, sales, and service. Brick-and-mortar e-tailers also incur expenses involved in running the physical store, such as visual merchandising, staffing, rent, utilities, and maintenance.

Innovate and Create

Have students work in groups to create a Web site for a new pure e-tailing business. Have them research the competition and incorporate the principles of free enterprise (competition, ownership, risk, and profit) into their reports. You may want to assign students a business category so they have to compete. Criteria for evaluation may include creativity, functionality, and ease of navigation. Criteria for the reports must include a discussion of the principles of free enterprise and competition. Student should also discuss how they think they can make a profit and still handle costs and expenses (salaries, cost of goods sold, utilities, rent, insurance, marketing, etc.). Finally, students should discuss the risks they may face (financial losses, the possibility of bankruptcy, legal expenses, etc.) and how to mitigate those risks (e.g., purchasing insurance).

glencoe.com

eMarketing Worksheet Activity Send students to the Online Learning Center to download an eMarketing worksheet activity.

In a SWOT analysis, you evaluate the four Ps of the marketing mix and how well they focus on the intended target market(s). They should also be reviewed in relation to the company's objectives and sales performance.

MANAGEMENT

Management is the process of achieving company goals by effective use of resources through planning, organizing, and controlling.

Management determines the corporate culture, ethics, and mission or vision for a firm. These include the way a company goes about doing business, values and principles that guide behavior, and a description of long-range goals.

Planning involves establishing company objectives and strategies to meet those objectives. The planning process involves setting goals and then determining the best way to meet them.

Organizing involves specific operations, such as scheduling employees, delegating responsibilities, and maintaining records.

Controlling has to do with overseeing and analyzing operating budgets to suggest the most cost-effective measures for a company to follow. Analysis of financial reports, such as cash-flow and profit and loss statements, is part of controlling.

A SWOT analysis evaluates the personnel who run a company. Important indicators are the levels of expertise of the CEO (or owner in a smaller operation) as well as the firm's key managers.

FINANCE AND ACCOUNTING

Finance is the function of business that involves money management. **Accounting** is the discipline that keeps track of a company's financial situation. If you want to analyze a company's finances, you would study its balance sheet, profit and loss statement, and cash-flow statement.

BALANCE SHEET

A balance sheet reports a company's assets, liabilities, and owner's equity. Assets are things a company owns. Liabilities represent money owed by a business to its creditors.

If most of a company's assets have not been paid for yet, a company's financial situation is not positive. For example, if a company had assets of $100,000 and liabilities of $75,000, its owner's equity is only $25,000. In this case, creditors own more of the company than the owners.

PROFIT AND LOSS STATEMENTS

Profit and loss statements reflect the ongoing operations of a firm. They include income from sales revenue and investments, as well as costs and expenses of doing business.

A profitable company generates more income than it pays out for costs of goods and expenses to run the business. When a business suffers a loss, its costs and expenses exceed its revenue.

FINANCIAL STATEMENTS AND THE SWOT ANALYSIS

In a SWOT analysis, all three types of financial statements can provide important information regarding how well a business is doing financially.

A profitable business with high owner's equity allows a company to grow. It can invest in more research and development that can lead to new products and more efficient methods of producing them. A profitable business can also expand its operations by building new facilities or acquiring other businesses.

Buying Fresh Foods

Many food and drink companies emphasize the fresh or natural qualities of their products. ***What business function do the products in this ad perform? What function of business is involved with supermarkets that purchase these products?***

After You Read | **Section 5.2**

Review Key Concepts

1. **Discuss** the significance of small businesses to the U.S. economy.
2. **Explain** why DECA is classified as a nonprofit organization.
3. **List** What information is reported in a company's balance sheet? In its profit and loss statement?

Practice Academics

Social Studies

4. Research a nonprofit organization to determine how it began and how it derives its income. What percentage of its donations is spent on its cause and what percentage is spent on administration? Share your findings in a written report and an oral presentation.

NCSS V C Individuals, Groups, & Institutions Describe the various forms institutions take, and explain how they develop and change over time.

Mathematics

5. What is the owner's equity of a company that has assets of $750,000 and liabilities of $200,000?

Math Concept **Theory Problem Solving: Using Formulas** The accounting equation defines a company's worth as its assets minus liabilities.

NCTM Number and Operations Compute fluently and make reasonable estimates.

For help, go to the **Math Skills Handbook** located at the back of this book.

glencoe.com Check your answers.

ELABORATE

Activate Prior Knowledge

Review the Characteristics of a SWOT Analysis As students read, they should review the SWOT analysis to identify strengths and weaknesses for each of the business functions.

Visual Literacy

Buying Fresh Foods Caption Answer Read the figure caption question to students: ***What business function do the products in this ad perform? What function of business is involved with supermarkets that purchase these products?*** Production; Procurement: when supermarkets purchase packaged goods.

Graphic Organizer

Display the following chart. Reinforce the characteristics of a SWOT Analysis for internal strengths and weaknesses.

SWOT

INTERNAL	
STRENGTHS	**WEAKNESSES**
Production and procurement: innovation, efficiency	Production and procurement: poor quality
Marketing: product is competitively priced	Marketing: no online marketing
Management: owner is knowledgeable	Management: managers use employees' time ineffectively
Finance and accounting: owner reinvests profits in company	Finance and accounting: creditors own a sizable portion of the company

glencoe.com

iWB

Graphic Organizer Send students to the Online Learning Center to print this graphic organizer.

EVALUATE

Graphic Organizer

Display the following diagram. Complete the second row by providing a description of each.

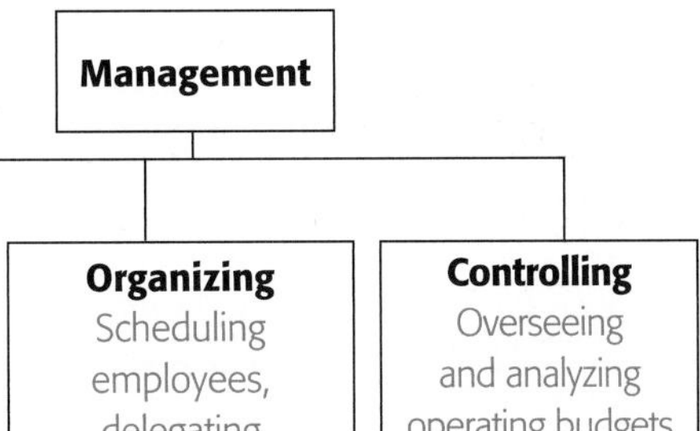

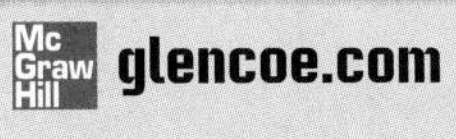

glencoe.com iWB

Graphic Organizer Send students to the Online Learning Center to print this graphic organizer.

FINANCE AND ACCOUNTING

Ask these guiding questions to encourage the discussion of this topic.

Guiding Questions

Identify What documents can analyze a company's finances?	balance sheet, profit and loss statement, cash-flow statement
Contrast How are assets different from liabilities?	Assets: things the company owns; Liabilities: money owed by the company to its creditors.
Conclude the value of a company you are buying that has assets of $350,000 and liabilities of $320,000.	Assets are only $20,000 more than its liabilities; the owner has little equity in the business and its worth may be low.

After You Read Section 5.2

Review Key Concepts

1. Over 95 percent of U.S. businesses are classified as small business and they employ over half of the private-sector work force, which makes them significant to the U.S. economy.
2. DECA is classified as a nonprofit organization because the revenue it generates from dues, the products it sells, and the donations it receives ar used to support the function of the organization.
3. Balance sheet: assets, liabilities, and owner's equity. Profit and loss statement: income, cost of goods sold, and expenses.

Practice Academics

Social Studies

4. Accept all reasonable answers for nonprofit organizations. All reports should include the following: how it began, how it derives its income, what percentage of its donations is spent on its cause and what percentage is spent on administration of the organization. One example is Play for P.I.N.K., which began in 1996 with the goal of raising funds for breast cancer research. It accepts donations from grass roots fund-raising events. According to its Web site, the fund raising events include: "golf and tennis tournaments, equestrian events, card games, knitting circles, even spa days!" All funds raised (100%) are donated to The Breast Cancer Research Foundation. Administrative costs are covered by Bloomberg's, which underwrites the organization.

Mathematics

5. Owner's equity is $550,000 ($750,000 – $200,000 = $550,000).

glencoe.com

Answer Key Send students to the Online Learning Center to check their answers.

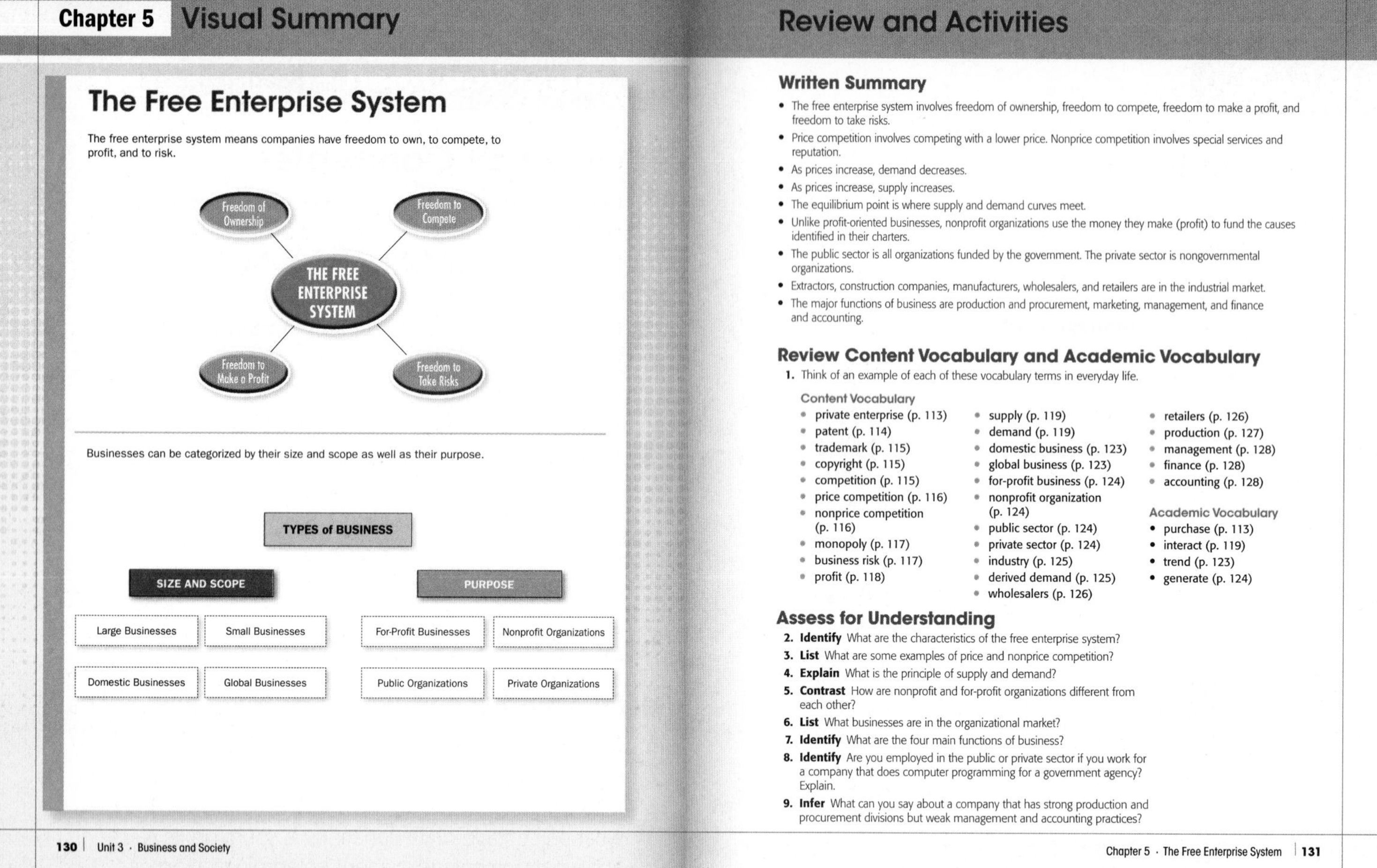

Chapter 5 Visual Summary

The Free Enterprise System

The free enterprise system means companies have freedom to own, to compete, to profit, and to risk.

Businesses can be categorized by their size and scope as well as their purpose.

130 | Unit 3 · Business and Society

Review and Activities

Written Summary

- The free enterprise system involves freedom of ownership, freedom to compete, freedom to make a profit, and freedom to take risks.
- Price competition involves competing with a lower price. Nonprice competition involves special services and reputation.
- As prices increase, demand decreases.
- As prices increase, supply increases.
- The equilibrium point is where supply and demand curves meet.
- Unlike profit-oriented businesses, nonprofit organizations use the money they make (profit) to fund the causes identified in their charters.
- The public sector is all organizations funded by the government. The private sector is nongovernmental organizations.
- Extractors, construction companies, manufacturers, wholesalers, and retailers are in the industrial market.
- The major functions of business are production and procurement, marketing, management, and finance and accounting.

Review Content Vocabulary and Academic Vocabulary

1. Think of an example of each of these vocabulary terms in everyday life.

Content Vocabulary

- private enterprise (p. 113)
- patent (p. 114)
- trademark (p. 115)
- copyright (p. 115)
- competition (p. 115)
- price competition (p. 116)
- nonprice competition (p. 116)
- monopoly (p. 117)
- business risk (p. 117)
- profit (p. 118)
- supply (p. 119)
- demand (p. 119)
- domestic business (p. 123)
- global business (p. 123)
- for-profit business (p. 124)
- nonprofit organization (p. 124)
- public sector (p. 124)
- private sector (p. 124)
- industry (p. 125)
- derived demand (p. 125)
- wholesalers (p. 126)
- retailers (p. 126)
- production (p. 127)
- management (p. 128)
- finance (p. 128)
- accounting (p. 128)

Academic Vocabulary

- purchase (p. 113)
- interact (p. 119)
- trend (p. 123)
- generate (p. 124)

Assess for Understanding

2. **Identify** What are the characteristics of the free enterprise system?
3. **List** What are some examples of price and nonprice competition?
4. **Explain** What is the principle of supply and demand?
5. **Contrast** How are nonprofit and for-profit organizations different from each other?
6. **List** What businesses are in the organizational market?
7. **Identify** What are the four main functions of business?
8. **Identify** Are you employed in the public or private sector if you work for a company that does computer programming for a government agency? Explain.
9. **Infer** What can you say about a company that has strong production and procurement divisions but weak management and accounting practices?

Chapter 5 · The Free Enterprise System | 131

EVALUATE

Visual Summary

Express Creativity Ask students to develop their own visual summary of a concept in the chapter. Encourage students to use different formats for their visual summaries, such as a storyboard, a timeline, a table, a tree diagram, or a word web. Visual summaries will vary depending on the concept depicted and the visual manner in which it is depicted. Questions to ask when assessing a visual summary include:

- Is the summary clear, economical, and simple?
- Are any important steps left out?
- Are steps or concepts arranged in the same order as the original?
- Does the summary reveal a pattern that connects the details?
- Does the summary locate and highlight the most important information?

Review Content Vocabulary and Academic Vocabulary

1. Sample answers: **Private enterprise** is found in a market-oriented economy. **Patents, trademarks,** and **copyrights** are intellectual property rights. There are two types of **competition: price competition** and **nonprice competition.** In a **monopoly** there is no competition. **Business risk** is inherent in private enterprise. **Profit** is the reward for being successful. **Supply** and **demand** determine price in a market-oriented economy. **Domestic businesses** are found in your own country. **Global business** is more prevalent now due to the Internet. The hair salon is an example of a **for-profit business**. The American Red Cross is a **nonprofit organization**. My teacher is employed in the **public sector**. I am employed in the **private sector**. Communications is an example of one **industry** in NAICS. It is important for organizational markets to study consumer trends because of the concept of **derived demand**. **Wholesalers** and **retailers** buy goods for resale. **Production**, **management**, and **finance** are three of the four functions of business. **Accounting** is financial recordkeeping. I plan to **purchase** a new pair of sneakers. Supply and demand **interact** to determine price. A current fashion **trend** is black-and-white clothing. You can **generate** sales by offering a discount.

EVALUATE

Assess for Understanding

2. The characteristics of private enterprise are: ownership of property (personal and a business), competition, risks, and profit.

3. An example of price competition might be Southwest Airlines' low prices in relation to its competitors. Examples of nonprice competition might include extraordinary service and high quality food in a five-star restaurant and 24-hour repair service from a heating and cooling company.

4. Supply and demand theory states that prices are determined in the marketplace based on how supply and demand interact with one another, creating conditions of surplus, shortage, or equilibrium.

5. The difference between nonprofit and for-profit organizations is how any money earned is used. In a nonprofit organization, the money earned is used to support the cause. In a for-profit organization, the money earned can be kept by the owner or reinvested in the business.

6. Businesses in the organizational market include: extractors, construction and manufacturing businesses, wholesalers, retailers, and service-related firms.

7. The four main functions of business are: production or procurement, marketing, management, and finance and accounting.

8. You are employed in the private sector because you work for a private enterprise that sells its services to a government agency.

9. It would probably have a good product to sell and be capable of making enough to meet demand, but would not be able to effectively market the product nor determine appropriate prices, keep track of expenditures, etc.

Chapter 5 Review and Activities

21st Century Skills

Communication Skills

10. Learn about Business Interview five adults to learn about their jobs and the companies that employ them. Ask questions about their job responsibilities to determine in which main function of business they work. Identify whether the companies that employ them are domestic or global in scope and if they are in the private or public sector. Identify their NAICS classification. Prepare a table using a word processing program to report your findings in an organized manner. Share your findings with classmates in an oral presentation.

Financial Literacy Skills

11. How Much Profit? If your company has sales of $5,877,700, costs of $2,938,850, and expenses of $2,762,519, does it make a profit or suffer a loss? What is the dollar amount of the profit or loss? What percentage of sales does the profit or loss represent?

Everyday Ethics

12. Comparative Advertisements Advertisers that make direct comparisons with competitors may be misleading or using puffery. For example, a Subway ad compared its foot-long sandwich to a Big Mac and claimed its sandwich had "less fat." What it did not say in the ad is that the sandwich had "more sodium, carbohydrates, calories, and sugar than the Big Mac." The FTC ordered Subway to stop those misleading ads. An example of puffery might be a statement such as "America's favorite pasta" because "favorite" is a word that has no standard by which to be measured. Review an advertisement that makes a comparison with a competitor. Does the ad include any research to support its claims? Note whether the ad is misleading or uses puffery. Share your findings with classmates.

e-Marketing Skills

13. Patents on the Web Visit the Web site for the U.S. Patent Office to learn more about the different types of patents. Write a short report on them and note the difference in length of time each is granted.

Build Academic Skills

English Language Arts

14. Planning for Demand Write two paragraphs about how a business may or may not chose to use supply and demand theory when establishing prices for limited supplies that consumers need before or after a natural disaster, such as a flood, hurricane or tornado.

NCTE 4 Use written language to communicate effectively.

Social Studies

15. The International Economy and Business Research how companies responded to the global economic crisis in the late 2000s. Provide specific examples of bankrupt companies and marketing strategies of companies that remained in business. Share your findings with the class.

NCSS VII D Production, Distribution, and Consumption Describe relationships among the various economic institutions that comprise economic systems such as households, business firms, banks, government agencies, labor unions, and corporations.

Mathematics

16. Profit from Sales Determine the profit a company makes with sales of $3,540,200, costs of $1,820,600, and expenses of $1,078,575. What percentage of sales does the profit represent? Round your answer to the tenth decimal place.

Math Concept **Number and Operations: Choosing an operation** The profits of a company equal total sales minus any operating expenses.

NCTM Number and Operations Understand the meanings of operations and how they relate to one another.

For help, go to the **Math Skills Handbook** located at the back of this book.

132 | Unit 3 · Business and Society

Standardized Test Practice

Directions Read the following questions. On a separate sheet of paper write the best possible answer for each one.

1. What is the net worth of a company with assets of $12,555,000 and liabilities of $11,633,000?
   A. $9,200
   B. $922,000
   C. $9,265,631
   D. $24,188,000
2. **True or False?** A trademark protects a company's invention from being used by another company without permission.
   T
   F
3. If you want to analyze a company's finances, you would study its balance sheet, profit and loss statement, and __________ statement.

Test-Taking Tip

Taking tests can be stressful. Stay relaxed. If you begin to get nervous, take a few deep breaths slowly to relax yourself, and then get back to work.

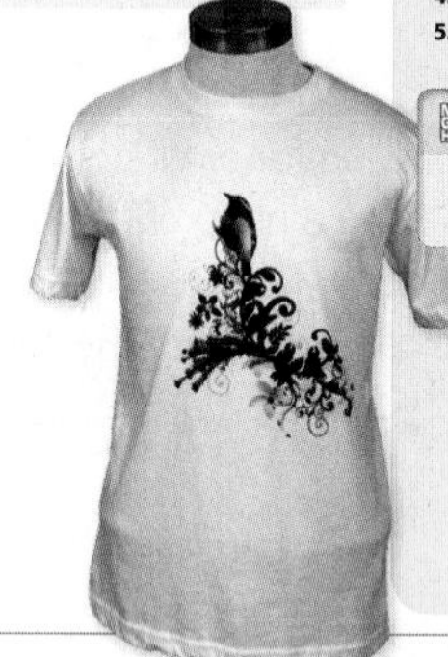

DECA Connection Role Play

Company Owner
Internet T-Shirt Company

Situation You are to assume the role of an owner of an Internet T-shirt company. You have been successful for the last two years with your T-shirt designs and marketing plan. At present your Internet sales have been approximately $1,000,000. Costs and expenses totaled 85 percent of sales, so you have made a profit before taxes. Your current net worth is around $400,000.

Now you want to open a brick and mortar retail T-shirt store. To do so, you need to convince investors that you understand the basics of the free enterprise system and the economics involved in business. You need a minimum of $200,000 to open the store. You are hoping to get ten investors to contribute $20,000 each.

Activity You are to meet with a potential investor (judge) who expects you to discuss and justify your business proposal.

Evaluation You will be evaluated on how well you meet the following performance indicators:

1. Explain the concept of the free enterprise system.
2. Explain the concept of competition.
3. Explain the principles of supply and demand.
4. Identify factors affecting a business's profit.
5. Describe types of business activities.

glencoe.com

Download the Competitive Events Workbook for more Role-Play practice.

Chapter 5 · The Free Enterprise System | 133

EVALUATE

21st Century Skills

Communication Skills

10. Learn about Business Accept all reasonable reports. Check to be sure students followed the directions by preparing a table.

Graphic Organizer Send student to the Online Learning Center to print this graphic organizer.

Financial Literacy Skills

11. How Much Profit? It makes a profit of $176,331, which is three percent of sales.($2,938,850 + $2,762,519 = $5,701,369 costs and expenses; $5,877,700 – $5,701,369 = $176,331. Net profit of $176,331 divided by sales of $5,877,700 = .03 = 3%.)

Everyday Ethics

12. Comparative Advertisements Findings will vary depending on the advertisement being examined. Students should state whether the ad's comparison information is backed up by research, is misleading, or uses puffery.

e-Marketing Skills

13. Patents on the Web The difference between the two patents as described at the U.S. Government Patent Web site is as follows:

"The Difference Between Design and Utility Patents In general terms, a "utility patent" protects the way an article is used and works (35 U.S.C. 101), while a "design patent" protects the way an article looks (35 U.S.C. 171). Both design and utility patents may be obtained on an article if invention resides both in its utility and ornamental appearance. While utility and design patents afford legally separate protection, the utility and ornamentality of an article are not easily separable. Articles of manufacture may possess both functional and ornamental characteristics."

EVALUATE

Build Academic Skills

English Language Arts

14. Accept all reasonable answers. The gist of the paragraphs should address the limited supply of items needed after a natural disaster with regard to supply and demand theory. Some students who do research may even introduce the concept of price gouging, which is when a business prices needed items unreasonably high to take advantage of the disaster. Price gouging is illegal in many states. Also, consumers may remember the business's actions and elect not to do business with that company in the future. So, that company may risk losing future sales once the disaster is over. In the same situation, businesses may opt not to take advantage of consumers and sell those needed items at their regular price. In that case, even though demand was high and supplies were limited, prices would remain the same.

Social Studies

15. Accept all reasonable answers. Some bankrupt companies may include local businesses, as well as some of chain store operations such as Circuit City (electronics), Mervyns (department store), Linens & Things (specialty retailer). Marketing strategies of companies that remained in business included lower prices and special promotions to encourage customers to shop and buy. Restaurants offered buy one meal and get one free or for half price. Luxury goods manufacturers, like Coach, introduced several less expensive designs and cut their gross margins. For example, Coach reduced its $325 handbags to $285 ***(Business Week,*** October 19, 2009, "Coach's Winning Bag of Tricks.")

Mathematics

16. The company made a 1.8% profit. ($3,540,200 – [$1,820,600 + $1,078,575]) / $3,540,200 = 0.1810702

Standardized Test Practice

1. B $922,000 (assets $12,555,000 less liabilities of $11,633,000

2. False (the definition is that of a patent, not a trademark)

3. cash flow

DECA Connection Role Play

Evaluations will be based on these performance indicators.

1. **Explain the concept of the free enterprise system.** Free enterprise is business ownership by ordinary people, not the government.
2. **Explain the concept of competition.** Competition is the struggle for companies to take customers away from one another. It is an essential part of private enterprise and benefits consumers because in order to remain competitive, businesses must produce better-quality goods and services at reasonable prices.
3. **Explain the principles of supply and demand.** Supply is the amount of goods producers are willing to make and sell. The principle of supply is the economic rule that price and quantity supplied move in the same direction. Demand refers to consumers' willingness and ability to buy products. The principle of demand states that price and demand move in opposite directions.
4. **Identify factors affecting a business's profit.** Factors affecting a business's profit include cost of materials, consumer demand, supply, competition, and government regulation.
5. **Describe types of business activities.** Business activities are production or procurement, marketing, management, and finance. The ways each business performs these activities may differ. However, all four are essential to running a business or organization. The success of a business is dependent on how well these activities are coordinated, managed, and performed.

Mc Graw Hill **glencoe.com**

Role Plays For more DECA Role Plays, send students to the Online Learning Center to download the Competitive Events Workbook.

Chapter 6 | Section 6.1 Government and Laws | Section 6.2 Social Responsibilities and Ethics

legal and ethical issues

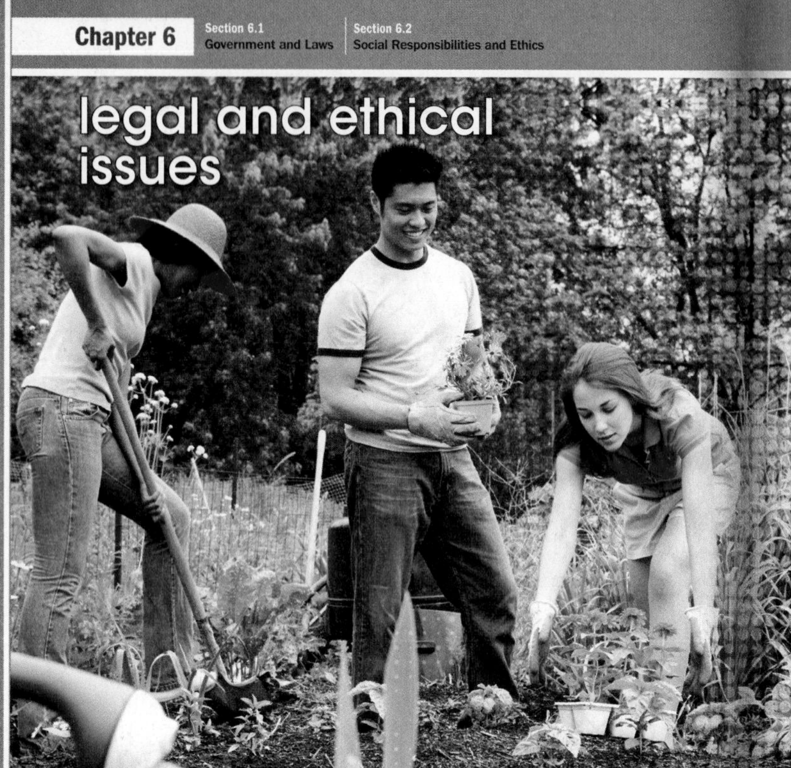

SHOW WHAT YOU KNOW

Visual Literacy All types of businesses can demonstrate social responsibility in different ways. For example, providing local and sustainable food products can support a community and also serve the environment. ***How might a mobile restaurant benefit your community?***

Discovery Project

Social Responsibility Begins With You

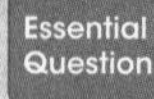

Essential Question What are companies doing to support social causes and how can you help?

Project Goal

Work with a partner to research companies that support causes important to you and your friends and family. The causes can be related to charitable donations, safe driving, environmental efforts, or other socially responsible acts. Select at least two companies to present. Explain what they do to support their causes. Evaluate the effectiveness of their efforts in supporting that cause. Identify how you can support their efforts.

Ask Yourself...

- Which causes are most important to you and your partner?
- Which companies are involved with those causes?
- What should you include in your description of their efforts to support the cause?
- How will you evaluate the companies' social responsibility efforts?
- What can you do to support their efforts?
- How will you present the information you researched?

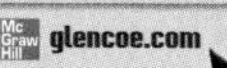

Synthesize and Present Research Synthesize your research by describing how each company is socially responsible in your presentation.

glencoe.com

Activity
Get a worksheet activity about social responsibility.

Evaluate
Download a rubric you can use to evaluate your project.

DECA Connection

DECA Event Role Play

Concepts in this chapter are related to DECA competitive events that involve either an interview or role play.

Performance Indicators The performance indicators represent key skills and knowledge. Your key to success in DECA competitive events is relating them to the concepts in this chapter.

- Explain the nature of business ethics.
- Explain the role of business in society.
- Discuss the nature of law and sources of law in the United States.
- Describe legal issues affecting businesses.
- Describe the United States' judicial system.

DECA Prep

Role Play Practice role-playing with the DECA Connection competitive-event activity at the end of this chapter. More information about DECA events can be found on DECA's Web site.

ENGAGE

Visual Literacy

Read the chapter opener photo caption question to students: ***How might a mobile restaurant benefit your community?*** It can help with fund raising efforts and emergencies such as fires or natural disasters. It can help feed the homeless and provide food service to rural communities. Ask these guiding questions to activate prior knowledge.

Guiding Questions

Recall What is competition?	the struggle between companies for business
Predict What might happen if an economy allowed monopolies?	no choice for consumers, prices would go up, quality might go down.
Analyze Why is nonprice competition important to businesses? How can businesses engage in nonprice competition?	It allows businesses to differentiate themselves based on quality, location, and reputation. Community involvement is one nonprice way to compete.

Discovery Project

Social Responsibility Begins With You To encourage students to begin thinking about social responsibility, read aloud the Discovery Project Essential Question: ***What are companies doing to support social causes and how can you help?*** Accept all reasonable answers. Encourage students to give specific examples. Perhaps they could participate in a public waterways cleanup day sponsored by a sporting goods store or collect food from grocery stores to take to the local food pantry. Encourage students to be creative in their ideas.

glencoe.com

Discovery Project Resources Send students to the Online Learning Center to download a rubric to evaluate their projects.

ENGAGE

Introduce the Chapter

In this chapter, issues related to social responsibility and ethics are discussed:

- Government's role as service provider
- Government regulatory agencies that protect consumers
- Government regulatory agencies that protect workers
- Government regulatory agencies that protect investors
- Government regulatory agencies that protect the environment
- Benefits offered by businesses to workers
- Ways companies work toward protecting the environment
- Ethical issues related to marketing functions

Discussion Starter

Workplace Safety Explain to students that there are many ways that the government attempts to protect workers. For example, there are extensive regulations regarding the use of forklifts in warehouses. Ask students: ***Why do you think the government has taken on the responsibility of making these regulations?*** Sample answer: Many accidents were occurring because businesses were not taking adequate safety measures. Ask students: ***If you managed a business such as a home improvement store, do you think you would like or dislike these regulations? Why?*** Sample answers: Yes, because I would know keeping workers safe would be beneficial for everyone. No, because I think the business could do an adequate job of making its own rules.

DECA Connection

Discuss the performance indicators listed in the DECA Connection feature. Explain to students that performance indicators tell them how to demonstrate their acquired skills and knowledge through individual or team competitive events.

glencoe.com

Competitive Events Workbook For more DECA Role Plays, send students to the Online Learning Center to download the Competitive Events Workbook.

PROGRAM RESOURCE ORGANIZER

PRINT RESOURCES

- **Student Edition**
- **Teacher Edition**
- **Student Activity Workbook with Academic Integration** includes worksheets and activities correlated to the text.
- **Mathematics for Marketing Workbook** provides math activities for every unit in the text.

TECHNOLOGY TOOLBOX

- **Connect**
- **ConnectPlus**
- **ExamView Assessment Suite** is a comprehensive solution for creating, administering, and scoring tests.

glencoe.com

Online Learning Center provides a variety of resources to enrich and enhance learning.

SECTION, CHAPTER, AND UNIT RESOURCES

- **Graphic Organizers** for organizing text concepts visually.
- **Digital Nation Activities** and **Green Marketer Activities** extend learning beyond the text features.
- **Career Chatroom Career Profiles** allow students to explore different marketing occupations in depth.
- **After You Read Answer Keys** for students to check their answers.
- **Discovery Project Rubrics** and **Marketing Internship Project Rubrics** for students to evaluate their projects.

PROGRAM RESOURCES

- **Student Activity Workbook with Academic Integration Teacher Annotated Edition** includes annotated answers for the activities and worksheets.
- **Marketing Research Project Workbook** provides a step-by-step approach for students to complete their own marketing research studies.
- **School-to-Career Activity Workbook** helps students relate their class work to on-the-job experience and involves work-site analysis and working with mentors.
- **Competitive Events Workbook** helps prepare students for state and national marketing education competitions.
- **Inclusion in the Marketing Education Classroom** provides teaching resources for working with students with special needs.
- **PowerPoint Presentations** provides visual teaching aids and assessments for this chapter.

READING GUIDE

Before You Read

Discuss What effect does the government have on your life?

Objectives

- **Explain** the role of government in the private enterprise system.
- **Identify** federal regulatory agencies and laws that protect consumers, workers, investors, and the environment.
- **Provide** examples of the impact of government on business.

The Main Idea

In the U.S. private enterprise system, the government plays a role in safeguarding its principles and the welfare of its citizens.

Vocabulary

Content Vocabulary

- Food and Drug Administration (FDA)
- Consumer Product Safety Commission (CPSC)
- Equal Employment Opportunity Commission (EEOC)
- Occupational Safety and Health Administration (OSHA)
- Securities and Exchange Commission (SEC)
- Environmental Protection Agency (EPA)
- Federal Trade Commission (FTC)

Academic Vocabulary

You will find these words in your reading and on your tests. Make sure you know their meanings.

- structure
- administration

Graphic Organizer

Draw or print this chart to take notes about the U.S. government and its role in the private enterprise system.

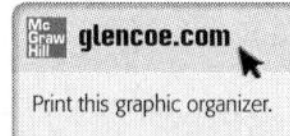

glencoe.com

Print this graphic organizer.

STANDARDS

ACADEMIC

English Language Arts

NCTE 1 Read texts to acquire new information.

Social Studies

NCSS VI C Power, Authority, & Governance Analyze and explain ideas and mechanisms to meet needs and wants of citizens, regulate territory, manage conflict, establish order and security, and balance competing conceptions of a just society.

NCSS *National Council for the Social Studies*
NCTE *National Council of Teachers of English*
NCTM *National Council of Teachers of Mathematics*
NSES *National Science Education Standards*

College & Career READINESS

Common Core
Reading Determine central ideas or themes of a text and analyze their development; summarize the key supporting details and ideas.

MARKETING CORE FUNCTION

Market Planning

me. Section 6.1

Government and Laws

THE ROLES OF GOVERNMENT

Government actions have a great impact on business and its operations. Thus, it is important to understand how government functions and how it affects businesses. The stability of a government, the stability of its **structure**, and the stability of its legal system are always part of the analysis of any business (the environmental scan). The government plays the roles of provider of services, customer, regulator, enforcer of private (free) enterprise, and monitor of the economy. Government laws and regulations affect business.

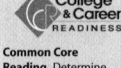

As You Read

Predict How do you think the government affects business?

STRUCTURE OF THE UNITED STATES GOVERNMENT

The United States government has three branches. They are the executive, legislative, and judicial branches. The power to make changes that affect the country is split between the branches. This system of checks and balances prevents any one branch of government from becoming too powerful. Similar branches of government exist at the state and local levels. Business owners and trade groups must follow the actions and directives of all branches and levels of government, because they all affect business operations.

> **"The stability of a government and its policies shape the political climate of a country."**

EXECUTIVE BRANCH

The executive branch of the federal government includes the Office of the President; Executive Departments (Interior, Commerce, Defense), as well as independent agencies and corporations, boards, commissions, and committees; and quasi-official agencies. Each president's **administration** has different programs that impact business.

The U.S. Department of Agriculture (USDA) is an agency that is part of the executive branch. It provides the inspection, grading, and certification of beef, lamb, and pork, for example. The meat grades are used as a marketing tool by retailers and restaurants to distinguish the better cuts from less expensive ones. The USDA also provides a grading service for dairy products.

Where to Find Government Information

To find out about current legislation or information about government programs, you can go to the U.S. government Web site. There is even a special section for topics of interest to teens. ***Why might you visit the government Web site?***

ENGAGE

Anticipation Activity

Improving Student Achievement Ask students: ***What are the three branches of the United States government?*** Legislative, executive, judicial Then ask: ***Which branch enacts federal laws and regulations?*** legislative ***What branch do you think has the most impact on businesses?*** The legislative branch, because it makes the laws that businesses must follow.

Objectives

- **Explain** the role of government in the private enterprise system. provider, customer, regulator, enforcer, monitor
- **Identify** federal regulatory agencies and laws that protect consumers, workers, investors, and the environment. Consumers: FDA; workers: OSHA; investors: SEC; Environment: EPA.
- **Provide** examples of the impact of government on business. protects consumers from unfair practices; protects against anti-competitive mergers; studies the impact of federal actions

Graphic Organizer

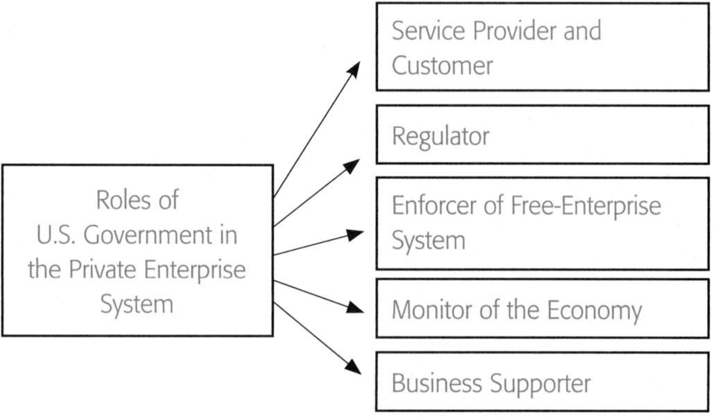

 **glencoe.com** 

Graphic Organizer Send students to the Online Learning Center to print this graphic organizer.

ENGAGE

Before You Read

Read the Before You Read question aloud: ***What effect does the government have on your life?*** Many laws affect workplaces, such as safety regulations, how many hours a week a student is allowed to work, minimum wage laws, and anti-discrimination laws. Ask students to give examples of laws created by local, state, and federal governments. State governments make the laws regarding driver's licenses; local governments establish zoning laws; the federal government decides environmental laws.

Preteaching Vocabulary

Have students go to the Online Learning Center at glencoe.com for the Chapter 6 Preteaching Vocabulary games.

Content Vocabulary

Read aloud the content vocabulary words to the class: ***Food and Drug Administration (FDA), Consumer Product Safety Commission (CPSC), Equal Employment Opportunity Commission (EEOC), Occupational Safety and Health Administration (OSHA), Securities and Exchange Commission (SEC), Environmental Protection Agency (EPA), Federal Trade Commission (FTC).*** Point out that many of these agencies have the word *commission* in their names. Ask a volunteer to look up *commission* in a dictionary and read aloud the definition that best applies. a government agency having legislative, executive, and judicial powers Explain to students that these agencies need these powers to carry out the duties assigned to them.

Academic Vocabulary

Structure—Word Origin Explain that the word *structure* comes from the Latin *structus*, which means "to heap up or build." Explain that in this chapter, *structure* is not used to mean a physical building but rather the theoretical organization of the government.

Administration—Denotative Meaning Read the following sentence under the Executive Branch heading: ***Each president's administration has different programs that impact business.*** The noun *administration* refers to only the executive branch of the government and not the legislative or judicial branches.

Government and Laws

THE ROLES OF GOVERNMENT

To focus the discussion, present these guiding questions.

Guiding Questions

Contrast Why did the founders of our government establish a system of checks and balances?	to keep one of the branches from becoming overly powerful
Synthesize What might happen if a company establishes a branch in a country with an unstable government?	Possible answer: The government might be overthrown and the business taken over by the new government.

As You Read

Read students the As You Read question: ***How do you think the government affects business?*** Possible answers: Signs stating that a government agency has inspected the premises for compliance with health regulations; maximum occupancy signs, and so on.

Expert Advice

Read the quote to students:

> **"The stability of a government and its policies shape the political climate of a country."**

Ask students to name characteristics of a stable government. feel safe; transferring power is done in an orderly fashion, prices remain constant, necessary goods and services are available Tell students that a stable government not only shapes a country's political climate, it also shapes its economic climate.

Visual Literacy

Where to Find Government Information Caption Answer Read the caption question to students: ***Why might you visit the government Web site?*** Teens might visit government Web sites to obtain information on any of these topics: driver's licenses, education (e.g., federally funded student aid), environmental consciousness, health, safety, jobs, volunteering, money, travel.

LEGISLATIVE BRANCH

The legislative branch of the U.S. government is the U.S. Congress. It is made up of the Senate and the House of Representatives. There are two senators for each state. The number of members of the House of Representatives depends on the size of each state. The members of Congress debate and vote on laws and regulations. Lobbyists try to influence the votes on bills that affect their interests. Lobbyists are not part of the legislative branch, however. They simply try to affect what laws are passed by Congress.

For example, some politicians, farm groups, and the Consumer Federation of America lobbied for mandatory country-of-origin labeling (COOL) on meat products. The mandatory labeling was part of the 2002 and 2008 farm bills. COOL became effective on March 16, 2009.

All types of meat, fish (shellfish and frozen), and fresh fruits and vegetables, as well as some nuts and ginseng must be labeled with their country of origin. Retailers that sell these food products must notify customers about the country of origin for all these products. The use of COOL is just one way the legislative branch affects how goods and services are bought and sold.

JUDICIAL BRANCH

The judicial branch of government interprets, applies, and administers the laws of the United States. The judicial system consists of a network of courts at all levels of government. When the legislative or executive branches enact laws or regulations that negatively affect businesses, those businesses may appeal to the judicial branch of government. Any court decision may create opportunities for some and threats to others. In 2004, four regional telephone companies (Verizon®, BellSouth®, Qwest® Communications, and SBC® Communications) appealed part of the Telecommunications Act of 1996. It required them to make their phone networks available to competitors at heavy discounts. Congress sided with the telephone companies. This provision was originally established to combat the near-monopoly of regional companies.

The Recording Industry Association of America (RIAA), a trade group, brought copyright infringement suits against more than 30,000 individuals for illegally downloading music. In 2006, FreePeers Inc.®, the company that distributes BearShare™ file-sharing software, paid a $30 million settlement to major music labels.

food Safety

The USDA, a government agency founded in 1862 by President Abraham Lincoln, controls the safety and quality of meat, poultry, and egg products. ***What do you think this USDA inspector is looking for when inspecting this food?***

THE ROLES OF SERVICE PROVIDER AND CUSTOMER

The government spends a lot of money to carry out its responsibility to ensure the safety and general welfare of United States citizens. Close to one-third of the country's gross domestic product is due to government spending.

To keep the country safe, the Department of Homeland Security spends money on border protection, disaster recovery, and on other measures such as airport security. To improve the country's infrastructure, the federal, state, and local governments fund the construction of roads and bridges.

Businesses that provide products and services for any government installation, project, or institution must adhere to certain guidelines. Why? Because it is taxpayers' money that the government is spending.

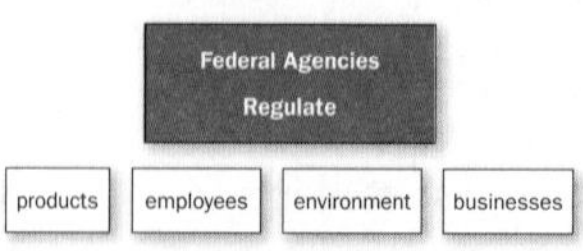

Federal Agencies
Regulate
products
employees
environment
businesses

THE ROLE OF REGULATOR

In the United States, most laws are designed to protect the safety, health, and welfare of individuals. At the federal, state, and local levels, these laws are carried out by government agencies.

The government acts as a regulator to protect consumers, employees, investors, and the environment and this affects businesses. Note that businesses must comply or suffer the legal consequences.

PROTECTING CONSUMERS

At the state and local levels, government agencies are involved with consumer protection. People who perform certain services, such as hairstylists, manicurists, and electricians, must be licensed. Local zoning laws about where homes, businesses, and farms can be located protect real estate investments and quality of life for residents.

Health departments inspect restaurants and other food-handling businesses to protect consumers. If a business fails these inspections, it is cited and required to correct the problems identified. Failure to do so can result in closure of the business.

DIGITAL NATION

Can the Spam

Spam messages, or unsolicited bulk e-mail, are sent by the billions each day. The federal law known as the CAN-SPAM Act tries to cut down on the negative effects of spam by setting rules for all commercial e-mail. These rules include:

- The "from" line, including the e-mail address, must identify the business sending the message.
- The subject line must be true to the content of the message.
- Offers in the e-mail must be truthful.
- Every message must include the sender's physical mailing address.
- Every message must clearly specify how recipients can opt out of future messages.
- Requests to opt out must be honored within ten days.

CAN-SPAM does not require senders to have permission to send commercial e-mail. However, most companies protect their reputation by only sending e-mail to people who have specifically asked for it.

English Language Arts/Writing

Locate a commercial e-mail message sent to you or a family member. Identify whether all of the CAN-SPAM requirements are met. Discuss your findings and the ethics of spam with your class.

glencoe.com

Get a Digital Nation Activity.

EXPLAIN

LEGISLATIVE BRANCH

Ask these guiding questions to guide the discussion.

Guiding Questions

Analyze Why do you think farm groups want mandatory country-of-origin labeling on meat and fresh fruits and vegetables?	So consumers can see that products were shipped from outside the U.S. and buy U.S. products instead.
Synthesize Imagine that you are a member of Congress. What kinds of lobbyists do you think would try to influence your voting?	Lobbyists tend to come from industries or interests with power in a specific jurisdiction.

Visual Literacy

Food Safety Caption Answer *What do you think this USDA inspector is looking for when inspecting this food?* facility cleanliness, temperature, how the meat is packaged, foul odor, unusual color, bacteria

Graphic Organizer

Display this graphic organizer. Ask students: *What is the primary duty of each of these branches?*

Branches of Government

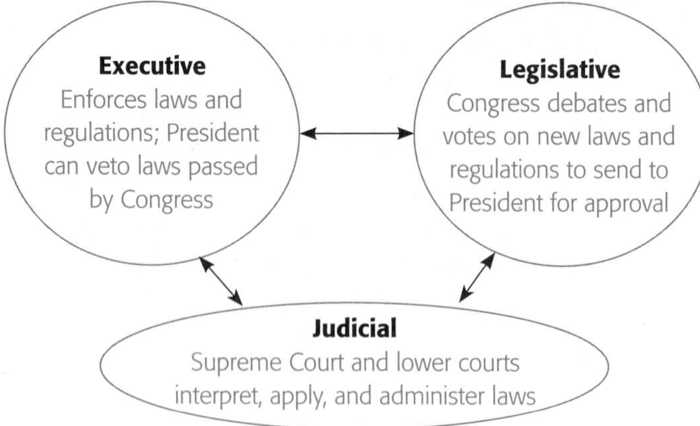

Executive
Enforces laws and regulations; President can veto laws passed by Congress
Legislative
Congress debates and votes on new laws and regulations to send to President for approval
Judicial
Supreme Court and lower courts interpret, apply, and administer laws

Mc Graw Hill
glencoe.com
iWB

Graphic Organizer Send students to the Online Learning Center to print this graphic organizer.

ELABORATE

Activate Prior Knowledge

Reteach Components of the Gross Domestic Product Explain that because the government is accountable to the taxpayers for this money, it is vital that it be spent wisely.

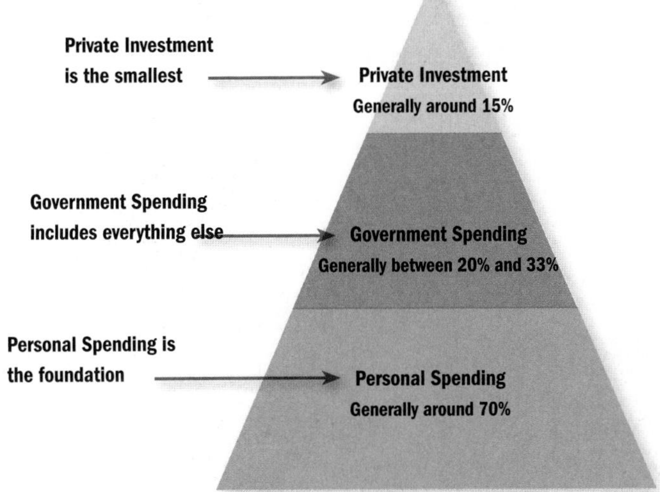

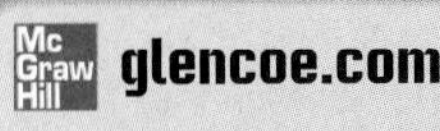

Graphic Organizer Send students to the Online Learning Center to print this graphic organizer.

THE ROLES OF SERVICE PROVIDER AND CUSTOMER

To further discuss this topic, present these guiding questions.

Guiding Questions

Enumerate What percentage of the GDP is a result of government spending?	close to one-third
Summarize What is the primary goal of the Department of Homeland Security?	to keep citizens and infrastructure safe by providing border protection, disaster recovery, airport security
Predict What might happen if strict business guidelines were not established by the government?	businesses might try to overcharge the government or the goods and services might not meet quality standards

PROTECTING CONSUMERS

Focus the discussion on how government regulations attempt to protect consumers by asking these questions.

Guiding Questions

Analyze Why do you think determining the safety of toys and other products for infants and children is especially difficult?	Possible answer: It is hard to speculate what children might do with an object (i.e., chew on it). Children and infants do not understand the dangers involved.
Evaluate Tobacco products contain government warning labels. Do you think these warnings keep people from smoking? Why?	Possible answer: Yes, I think they might discourage some people because they do not want to die or suffer serious health consequences.

DIGITAL NATION

English Language Arts/Writing Answer Read the assignment to the students. When they have finished analyzing their e-mail messages, have students share their findings. Findings will vary. Students might find missing or non-functioning unsubscribe links, misleading or confusing subject lines, and a missing physical mailing address. Then use these guiding questions to focus the discussion about SPAM.

Guiding Questions

Analyze Why do most companies only send e-mail to those people who have requested it?	to protect their reputations and not annoy their customers
Evaluate Would you purchase an item from a business that violated the CAN-SPAM Act? Why or why not?	Example: an e-mail that offers a promotional code for 20% off, but the code does not work when applied to a purchase.

Mc Graw Hill glencoe.com 

Worksheet Activity Send students to the Online Learning Center to get a Digital Nation worksheet activity.

The Food and Drug Administration and the Consumer Product Safety Commission are two federal agencies that protect consumers. The **Food and Drug Administration (FDA)** regulates the labeling and safety of food, drugs, and cosmetics sold throughout the United States. It is responsible for the Nutrition Facts labels that are found on food packages. It monitors these labels to ensure that they are accurate.

The FDA approves new products and reviews products already on the market. For example, in 2004 the FDA banned an herbal stimulant *ephedra* because of health risks associated with products that contain that ingredient. In 2007, a new law required manufacturers to notify the FDA if there were any problems with dietary supplement pills. In 2009, the FDA found that some dietary supplement pills for weight loss contained hidden ingredients that could be harmful. One of the hidden ingredients was a pharmaceutical drug called *bumetanide*. Its inclusion in the weight-loss drug violated the law for supplements. The FDA issued alerts, and makers of those pills voluntarily recalled them.

In recent years, contaminated foods have also been addressed by the FDA. Food-borne illnesses come from tainted foods, such as peanut butter, cookie dough, and spinach and other produce. The risk of contamination causes the public to worry about unsafe foods (**Figure 6.1**). The government responds to those fears by passing legislation to give the FDA more oversight and power.

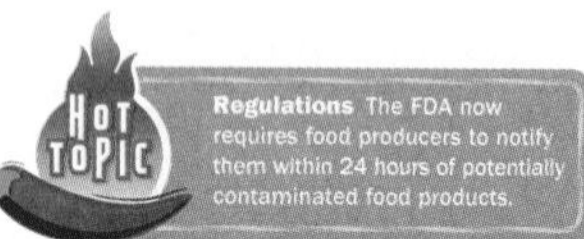

Regulations The FDA now requires food producers to notify them within 24 hours of potentially contaminated food products.

The **Consumer Product Safety Commission (CPSC)** is responsible for overseeing the safety of products such as toys, electronics, and household furniture. The CPSC is not responsible for oversight of food, drugs, cosmetics, medical devices, tobacco products, firearms and ammunition, motor vehicles, pesticides, aircraft, boats, and fixed-site amusement rides.

The CPSC was established under the Consumer Product Safety Act of 1972. That act gives the commission the authority to set standards for products that are considered hazardous. It also gives the commission the power to recall dangerous products. Product recalls are published at the CPSC Web site and communicated through radio and television announcements.

The Consumer Product Safety Commission covers many areas. It also enforces the Federal Hazardous Substances Act, the Flammable Fabrics Act, the Poison Prevention Packaging Act, and the Refrigerator Safety Act. The prime concern with these acts is the safety of children. It is a good idea for businesses to test products before marketing them to the public. Businesses should also keep up with new guidelines for labeling their products, especially regarding directions for safe use. An incident resulting from unsafe use can affect a company's reputation in the market. Businesses label their products with warnings and instructions so that consumers use them correctly.

PROTECTING WORKERS

The Equal Employment Opportunity Commission and the Occupational Safety and Health Administration are among the groups responsible for protecting employees at the federal level. Companies also must comply with minimum wage standards and other laws and regulations established by state and federal governments. One such regulation is the Family and Medical Leave Act. Other acts protect employees who report illegal practices by their employers. These laws protecting whistle-blowers are covered later in this section.

The **Equal Employment Opportunity Commission (EEOC)** is responsible for the fair and equitable treatment of employees with regard to hiring, firing, and promotions. Some of the laws it enforces are Title VII of the Civil Rights Act, the Equal Pay Act of 1963, the Age Discrimination in Employment Act of 1967 (ADEA), Sections 501 and 505 of the Rehabilitation Act of 1973, Titles I and V of the Americans with Disabilities Act of 1990 (ADA), and the Civil Rights Act of 1991. These laws prevent companies from discriminating against employees due to race, age, ability, gender, and other factors.

FIGURE 6.1 **The Government's Role in Protecting our Food**

Food-borne Illness The United States food industry is considered safe due to government regulations and cooperation from the food industry. However, food-borne illnesses can still occur. When contaminated food is not noticed, people get sick and can even die from tainted food. ***Why might it be difficult for the government to ensure food safety?***

SPINACH OUTBREAK IN 2006 In 2006, fresh bagged spinach was contaminated with Escherichia coli (E.coli) bacteria. The spinach was traced to a farm in California, but the actual cause for the contamination could not be identified. The processing plant that sold the bagged spinach was not responsible for the contamination. Since that business sold the spinach to food stores and restaurants, the recall involved 26 states. E. coli outbreaks in the United States are most often found in leafy greens and other fresh produce.

PEANUT SALMONELLA OUTBREAK OF 2009 An extensive recall of tainted peanut-containing products in 2009 covered 46 states. It affected manufacturers of peanut-containing products who purchased an ingredient from the Peanut Company of America. The recall involved brownies, cakes, candy, cereal, cookies, donuts, ice cream, snack bars, and pet foods. All of these products were tainted with Salmonella bacteria. Interestingly, jars of peanut butter from major national brands were not recalled.

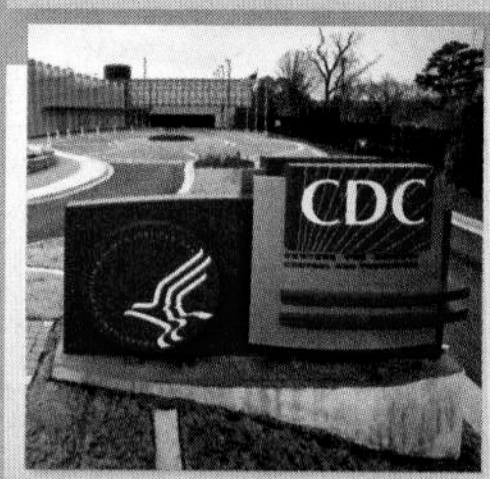

THE CDC The Center for Disease Control and Prevention (CDC), part of the U.S. Department of Health and Human Services, is involved in the investigation of food-borne illnesses. This agency works with the Food and Drug Administration (FDA) and state health agencies. The government's recall Web site explains how often food recalls are initiated by responsible companies. The Food Safety Enhancement Act of 2009 helps the FDA to prevent food-borne illness. It creates measures to ensure food safety in the United States.

EXPLAIN

Regulations Ask students: Why do you think the *FDA requires that it receive notification within 24 hours?* Then ask: If contaminated food has already been sold, what do you think is the best *way to get this information to consumers?*

Graphic Organizer

Display this diagram. As you discuss the FDA and the CPSC, have students name the similarities and differences among these agencies.

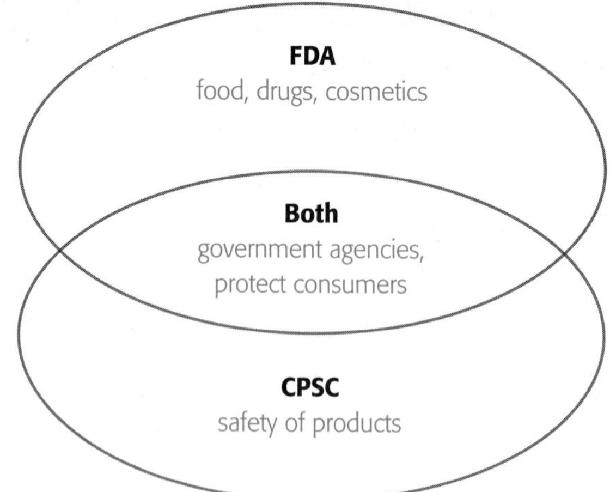

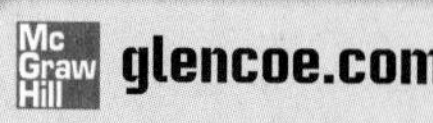

Graphic Organizer Send students to the Online Learning Center to print this graphic organizer.

ELABORATE

Reinforce Vocabulary

Securities and Exchange Commission (SEC)—Denotative Meaning. Explain to students that in this situation the word *securities* refers to stocks and bonds. Stocks allow the purchaser to buy a portion of a corporation whereas bonds represent loans to a private or government corporation.

Critical Thinking

Ask students: ***When used by manufacturers, what does the word recall mean?*** a public call for the return of a product that may be defective or contaminated Then ask: ***Do you think issuing a recall damages a manufacturer's reputation? Why or why not?*** Answers will vary. Possible answer: If the public sees the manufacturer as being honest and quick in issuing the recall, I do not think its reputation will be damaged.

Mini Project

Differentiated Instruction

Visual Learners Instruct students to work individually to choose a product recall that involved the FDA. Students should conduct research to learn about this event. Based on what they learn, students should prepare an illustrated time line of what happened during the recall. For example, the time line might first show how the problem came to light, then show television newscasters reporting on it, and so forth. The time line should show any changes that took place because of this recall. The time line should conclude with any changes that came about because of the incident.

Interpersonal Learners Have students conduct an interview with a person who performs a service, such as a hairstylist or plumber. Students should ask the person what kinds of government regulations he or she must follow. For example, is licensing required? Students should differentiate between federal, state, and local regulations. Student interviews can be presented to the class in a variety of ways, including podcasts, video clips, or class presentations. Students should list each regulation the interviewee is required to follow, along with its purpose, and report the information to the class.

PROTECTING WORKERS

Ask these guiding questions to focus the discussion on worker protections.

Guiding Questions

Recall What agency is responsible for making certain that employers do not discriminate based on gender?	Equal Employment Opportunity Commission (EEOC)
Draw Conclusions Why do you think it is necessary for laws to require fair treatment for hiring practices? For promotions?	Without the law, companies might hire fairly, but only promote those individuals with certain characteristics, such as certain age or gender.
Synthesize How do you think the Family and Medical Leave Act has changed the workplace?	Workers who have sick family members are more at ease because they can take time off.

Visual Literacy

Figure 6.1 Caption Answer Read the figure caption question to students: ***Why might it be difficult for the government to ensure food safety?*** Sample answers: there is an enormous quantity of food available and government resources are limited; with items such as fresh produce, only a small percentage might be tainted; not all contamination is easily detectable. Explain that often the exact cause of a particular type of contamination is never determined. This occurred with the E. coli contamination of spinach in 2006. Ask students: ***Why would government regulators be particularly concerned about these cases?*** If they are not able to determine the cause, they will not be able to prevent contaminations in the future.

Businesses must adhere to the health and safety policies established by the United States Department of Labor. The **Occupational Safety and Health Administration (OSHA)** sets guidelines for workplace safety and environmental concerns. It also enforces those regulations. For example, construction workers must wear hard hats for protection.

The Family and Medical Leave Act (FMLA) of 1993 requires employers that qualify to grant eligible employees up to a total of 12 work weeks of unpaid leave during any 12-month period. This leave is given for one or more of the following reasons: the birth and care of the newborn child of the employee; placement with the employee of a son or daughter for adoption or foster care; to care for an immediate family member (spouse, child, or parent) with a serious health condition; or to take medical leave when the employee has a serious health condition.

PROTECTING INVESTORS

The **Securities and Exchange Commission (SEC)** regulates the sale of securities (stocks and bonds). It is responsible for issuing licenses to brokerage firms and financial advisers. It also investigates any actions among corporations, such as mergers, that affect the value of stocks. This protects investors from deceptive practices. The SEC requires that all information about a corporation that is given to investors is truthful. This protects the investor and the corporation.

Companies whose shares are traded on the stock exchange must publish the company's annual report.

A company prospectus must also be provided. A prospectus is a document offered to potential investors when they are making a decision about whether to invest in a company. Corporations must prepare an annual report at least once a year to show its investors how the company has performed. On a more frequent basis, such corporations report their profits and stock dividends for publication in the media.

PROTECTING THE ENVIRONMENT

The **Environmental Protection Agency (EPA)** was established in 1970 to protect human health and our environment. Its responsibilities include monitoring and reducing air and water pollution. It oversees recycling and hazardous waste disposal.

For example, the 1970 Clean Air Act was amended in 1990 to make it more effective. In 2004, new rules to improve air quality were added. One of those rules involves stricter pollution controls on diesel engines used in industries such as construction, agriculture, and mining. Two other industries that will have similar emission standards are makers of diesel locomotives and marine diesel engines.

Environmental laws cover problems such as acid rain, asbestos, lead poisoning, mercury, mold, ozone depletion, pesticides, radon, and littering.

Hard Hats Required

Construction workers and engineers visiting construction sites must wear hard hats for protection. ***Why is worker safety important for companies?***

For example, new laws regarding distribution of advertising materials went into effect on April 1, 2001. A company can be fined if it distributes advertising materials inappropriately.

ENFORCER OF THE PRIVATE-ENTERPRISE SYSTEM

The **Federal Trade Commission (FTC)** has the responsibility of enforcing the principles of a private enterprise system and protecting consumers from unfair or deceptive business practices. As an independent agency, it reports to Congress on its actions. Its commissioners are nominated by the president and confirmed by the Senate. The FTC runs three bureaus: the Bureau of Consumer Protection; the Bureau of Competition; and the Bureau of Economics.

BUREAU OF CONSUMER PROTECTION

The Bureau of Consumer Protection is responsible for enforcing consumer protection laws and trade regulation rules. It investigates individual companies and industry-wide operations. In addition, it initiates lawsuits against companies that violate these laws and regulations. There are six divisions with special responsibilities: advertising, enforcement, financial, marketing, international, and planning and information.

- The Advertising Division enforces truth-in-advertising laws. It makes sure that any claims a company makes in an advertisement can be fulfilled by the product or service.
- The Enforcement Division enforces laws involving the Internet; the Postal Service; textile, wool, fur, and care labeling; and energy use. For example, clothing labels must identify fabric content, country of origin, and care instructions.
- The Financial Practices Division covers the Truth-In-Lending Act, as well as leasing and privacy issues. This division helps consumers make informed choices when they are applying for credit cards or loans.
- The Marketing Practices Division is responsible for responding to fraudulent activities and scams. This division enforces the Telemarketing Sales Rule, the 900-Number Rule, the Funeral Rule, and the Magnuson-Moss Act.
- The International Division of Consumer Protection promotes consumer confidence in the international marketplace.
- The Division of Planning and Information provides information and help for consumers who report identity theft and other fraud-related complaints.

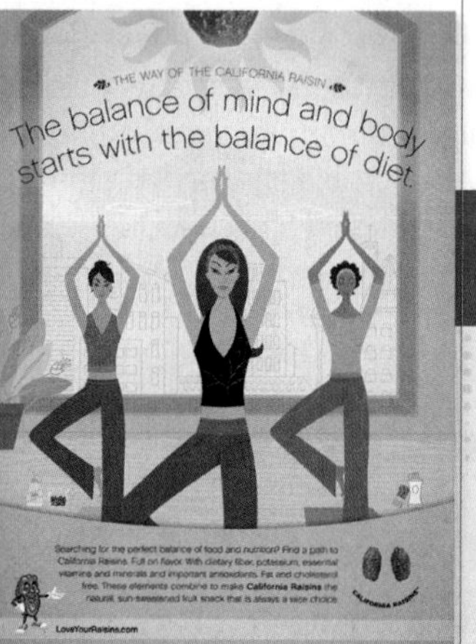

Raisins: Good for Your Health

This ad provides information about the nutritional value of raisins. ***What concerns might the FDA and FTC have about the content of advertisements for food?***

EXPLAIN

PROTECTING THE ENVIRONMENT

Present these guiding questions to focus the discussion.

Guiding Questions

Infer Based on the information given, why do you think the Clean Air Act was amended in 1990?	the quality of the environment was not as good as authorities thought
Develop What are some other legal methods to control littering?	fining for littering, requiring deposits, requiring recycling

Visual Literacy

Hard Hats Required Caption Answer Read the figure caption question to students: *Why is worker safety important for companies?* Employees tend to work harder when they feel protected; accidents can be very expensive; if workers take time off due to injuries, there may be legal consequences.

Graphic Organizer

Use this graphic organizer to lead a discussion of the SEC.

iWB

Graphic Organizer Send students to the Online Learning Center to print this graphic organizer.

EXPLAIN

Graphic Organizer

To help students understand the different divisions of the Bureau of Consumer Protection, display the following table.

Bureau of Consumer Protection

Division	**Purpose**
Advertising Division	enforces truth-in-advertising laws; makes sure advertisement claims can be fulfilled
Enforcement Division	ensures compliance with laws involving the internet, postal service, textile, wool, fur, and care labeling
Financial Practices Division	covers the truth-in-lending act; helps consumers make informed choices when applying for credit cards or loans
Marketing Practices Division	responds to fraudulent activities and scams; enforces rules such as the telemarketing sales and funeral rules
International Division of Consumer Protection	promotes consumer confidence in the international marketplace
Division of Planning and Information	helps consumers get needed information; provides help lines for reporting identify theft, fraud-related complaints

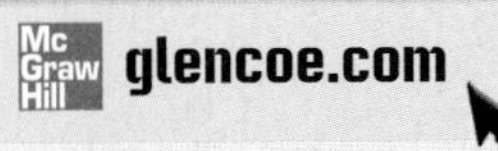

Graphic Organizer Send students to the Online Learning Center to print this graphic organizer.

Mini Project

Differentiated Instruction

Logical Learners Instruct students to examine the care instructions on two different garments and write a paragraph evaluating the instructions. For example, were the instructions clear? Did they use simple words that almost anyone could understand? Was there any missing information? Paragraphs will vary. Students should evaluate the care instructions on two garments, indicating whether they thought they were clear and complete.

Visual Literacy

Raisins: Good for Your Health Caption Answer Read the figure caption question to students: *What concerns might the FDA and FTC have about the content of advertisements for food?* whether the claims made in the ads are true

Graphic Organizer

Display the following graphic organizer. Ask students to describe each of these acts.

Sherman Antitrust Act
Outlaws contracts and agreements that limit trade or competition in interstate commerce

Hart-Scott-Rodino Amendment
Requires companies to inform federal government before planning a merger

Federal Trade Commission Act
Prohibits unfair methods of competition

Robinson-Patman Act
Prohibits price discrimination

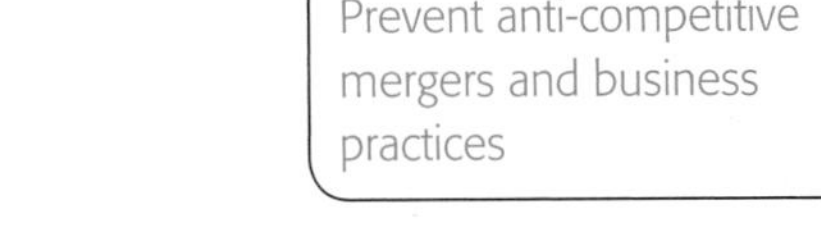

Goal:
Prevent anti-competitive mergers and business practices

Graphic Organizer Send students to the Online Learning Center to print this graphic organizer.

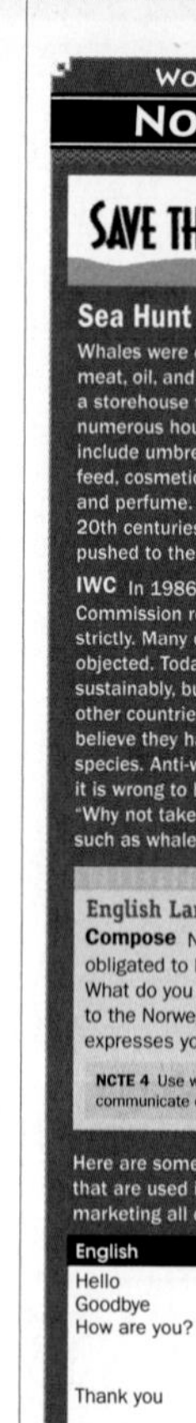

WORLD MARKET
NORWAY

SAVE THE WHALES

Sea Hunt

Whales were once valued mainly for meat, oil, and bone. Now they are a storehouse for the production of numerous household products. These include umbrella spokes, candles, animal feed, cosmetics, vitamin supplements, and perfume. In the late 19th and early 20th centuries, many whale species were pushed to the edge of extinction.

IWC In 1986, the International Whaling Commission regulated whaling more strictly. Many countries signed on. Norway objected. Today Norway hunts whales sustainably, but at a higher rate than other countries. Norwegian whalers believe they have the right to hunt this species. Anti-whaling groups believe that it is wrong to hunt whales. They ask, "Why not take part in a lucrative industry such as whale *watching*?"

English Language Arts/Writing

Compose Norway is not legally obligated to honor the whale ban. What do you think? Compose a letter to the Norwegian Prime Minister that expresses your position on the issue.

NCTE 4 Use written language to communicate effectively.

Here are some entry-level phrases that are used in conversations about marketing all over the world.

English	Norwegian
Hello	Hallo/Hei
Goodbye	Ha det bra
How are you?	Hvordan har du det? (Vŭr/done hăr doo dă)
Thank you	Mange takk (Mŭng/yā tŭck)
You're welcome	Vær så god (Vă-shī-goo)

BUREAU OF COMPETITION

The FTC's antitrust responsibilities involve prevention of anti-competitive mergers and business practices. Some of the acts that the bureau enforces include the following:

- The Federal Trade Commission Act prohibits unfair methods of competition.
- The Sherman Antitrust Act (1890) outlawed all contracts and agreements that would limit trade or competition in interstate commerce. It also prevents one company from undercharging for an item or service in order to put the competition out of business. This practice is known as *predatory pricing.*
- The Clayton Antitrust Act (1914) reduced loopholes in the Sherman Antitrust Act and covered mergers and acquisitions.
- The Hart-Scott-Rodino Amendment to the Clayton Act (1976) requires companies to notify antitrust agencies before planning a merger.
- The Robinson-Patman Act (1936) prohibits price discrimination, the practice of selling the same goods or services to different customers for different prices.

Distribution laws also fall under the FTC's jurisdiction. Several states have similar laws. The growth of the Internet and e-commerce makes these laws especially relevant. One example of distribution law is the sale of tobacco products to minors. It is illegal to sell tobacco products or distribute samples to underage customers. Retailers that do not comply with the law can be fined or arrested.

BUREAU OF ECONOMICS

The Bureau of Economics studies the impact of its actions on consumers and reports its findings to Congress, to the executive branch, and to the public. Its reports cover antitrust, consumer protection, and regulation. In certain instances, it may also provide information on pending bills' legislation.

MONITOR OF OUR ECONOMY

To ensure economic stability of the United States, the government monitors our economy and controls our monetary supply through the Federal Reserve System. This is our nation's central bank. When the Federal Reserve Board of Governors thinks that the economy is moving too fast or too slowly, it reacts to correct the problem. When prices are going up too fast, the board may increase interest rates to slow economic activity. Higher interest rates discourage borrowing money and expansion by businesses. The Federal Reserve Board of Governors might also lower interest rates during a slow economic period. This practice encourages people to invest or borrow money.

BUSINESS SUPPORTER

The Small Business Administration (SBA) is a United States government agency that provides support to small businesses. The role of the SBA is to encourage the free enterprise system by providing counseling and educational materials to prospective business owners. Additional support comes in the form of loan guarantees for some business owners who cannot get conventional loans. Since its founding in 1953, the SBA has provided billions of dollars in loans and guarantees to thousands of companies, making it the largest financial backer of business in the U.S.

INTERNATIONAL ISSUES

Governments in other countries may not provide the legal protection or infrastructure necessary to ensure that businesses operate in a safe and secure manner. Thus, it is important to analyze the U.S. government's role in promoting free enterprise and its ability to enforce those principles overseas. For example, lower labor costs have led many U.S. businesses to set up factories in China. However, limited intellectual property protection and a complicated legal system also make China a challenging place for companies to market and sell U.S. products.

After You Read | **Section 6.1**

Review Key Concepts

1. **Identify** five roles the government plays in a private enterprise system.
2. **Compare and contrast** the roles of the three bureaus run by the Federal Trade Commission.
3. **Describe** how antitrust laws promote healthy competition in a private enterprise system.

Practice Academics

Social Studies

4. Research the Credit Card Accountability, Responsibility, and Disclosure (CARD) Act of 2009. Explain its main principles. Note the requirements necessary for young people who wish to carry their own credit cards. Include your opinion about the marketing and distribution of credit cards to teenagers and young adults. How would you have liked the law to read for teenagers? Defend your ideas objectively.

NCSS VI C Power, Authority, & Governance Analyze and explain ideas and mechanisms to meet needs and wants of citizens, regulate territory, manage conflict, establish order and security, and balance competing conceptions of a just society.

Mathematics

5. The Truth in Lending legislation requires banks and other lending institutions to clearly disclose their annual interest rates. If the monthly interest rate on an outstanding credit card is 2.5 percent, what is the annual interest rate?

Math Concept **Number and Operations: Percents** A percent is a ratio comparing numbers to 100. To convert percents to decimals, move the decimal point two places to the left.

Starting Hints To solve the problem, multiply the percent value of the monthly interest rate by 12, the number of months in a year.

NCTM Number and Operations Understand numbers, ways of representing numbers, relationships among numbers, and number systems.

For help, go to the **Math Skills Handbook** located at the back of this book.

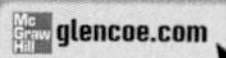

glencoe.com

Check your answers.

ELABORATE

WORLD MARKET
ENGLISH LANGUAGE ARTS/WRITING

Discuss with students that countries are not legally obligated to follow International Whaling Commission bans. Ask students: ***What power might you have over countries that refuse to honor International Whaling Commission bans? Do you think it is a good idea to use this power? Why or why not?*** Students might suggest not purchasing goods made with whale products or avoiding purchases of goods from countries that do not abide by the commission. Answers to the second part will vary. Some may suggest that whales be protected at all costs or they may become extinct. Others may suggest that economies that depend on whale products should be allowed to continue their practices.

MONITOR OF OUR ECONOMY

Ask these guiding questions to focus the discussion of the Federal Reserve System.

Guiding Questions

Recall What group runs the Federal Reserve System?	Board of Governors
Predict What might the Federal Reserve System do if it wants to encourage businesses to expand?	lower interest rates
Synthesize The Federal Reserve System is an independent government agency and does not have to ask Congress for funding. Do you think this is a good idea?	Yes, because this independence allows the Fed to make financial decisions that are vital to our nation's economy with less outside interference or consequences.

EVALUATE

Mini Projects

Differentiated Instruction

Visual/Spatial Learners Tell students to imagine that they are going to start a small business. They should choose a business in which they are interested, such as lawn care or pet grooming. Students should then go to the Small Business Administration Web site to find out the kinds of help the SBA can offer. Students should then create a poster explaining how the SBA can help them. Students' posters will vary depending on the business they choose, but should indicate specific ways the SBA can help. For example, the SBA site provides instructions on developing a business plan, how to obtain financial assistance, and forums where they can share information and experiences with others.

Intrapersonal Learners Have students work individually to write down a scenario. The response to the scenario should be the name of a regulatory agency. For example, if the scenario were "A paint manufacturing company is illegally dumping chemical waste into a river," the response would be the EPA (the agency that deals with this issue). Have students read aloud their questions to the class and ask volunteers to answer them. Students should each develop and present a scenario that is answered by giving the name of one of the regulatory agencies discussed in this section, such as the EPA, OSHA, or the FTC.

PROFESSIONAL DEVELOPMENT **MINI CLIP**

ELL Scaffolding Question Go to the Online Learning Center for a video in which students learn appropriate verbal responses to a series of scaffolded questions.

After You Read Section 6.1

Review Key Concepts

1. The five roles the government plays in a free enterprise system are provider of services, customer, regulator, supporter of private (free) enterprise, and monitor of the economy.
2. All three are concerned with enforcing the principles of the private-enterprise system and protecting consumers, but the ways in which they accomplish this differ. The Bureau of Consumer Protection is responsible for protecting consumers from businesses that violate laws and regulations; the Bureau of Competition is responsible for preventing anti-competitive mergers and business practices; the Bureau of Economics studies the impact of FTC actions on consumers.
3. Because these laws are designed to prevent anti-competitive mergers and business practices, they make certain that goods and services are priced competitively.

Practice Academics

Social Studies

4. The main goals of the CARD Act of 2009 are to protect consumers, make the language used to communicate with consumers easier to understand, make sure consumers are not taken advantage of, and make sure credit card companies are held accountable for their actions. The bill is designed to restrict the ability of teens and young adults to get credit cards. If they want a credit card, their parents must co-sign for it. Accept all reasonable answers with regard to students' opinions about this legislation.

Mathematics

5. The annual interest rate is 30 percent. (2.5 × 12)

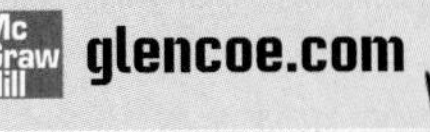

Answer Key Send students to the Online Learning Center to check their answers.

READING GUIDE

Before You Read

Judge Why do you think it is a good idea for companies to be socially responsible?

Objectives

- **Provide** examples of a business's social responsibilities.
- **Explain** the concept of business ethics.
- **Apply** guidelines for ethical behavior.

The Main Idea

Socially responsible and civic-minded businesses are concerned with their workers, customers, communities, and the environment. Business ethics are part of social responsibility and play a role in decisions made by businesses.

Vocabulary

Content Vocabulary

- flextime
- telecommuting
- Ad Council
- green marketing
- ethics
- Better Business Bureau
- price gouging
- whistle blowing

Academic Vocabulary

You will find these words in your reading and on your tests. Make sure you know their meanings.

- role
- policy

Graphic Organizer

Draw or print this outline to organize information on social responsibility, ethics in business, and the guidelines for ethical behavior. Link key concepts together for each topic.

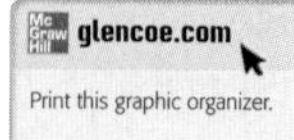

glencoe.com

Print this graphic organizer.

STANDARDS

ACADEMIC

English Language Arts
NCTE 3 Apply strategies to interpret texts.

Science
NSES F Develop an understanding of environmental quality.

NCSS *National Council for the Social Studies*
NCTE *National Council of Teachers of English*
NCTM *National Council of Teachers of Mathematics*
NSES *National Science Education Standards*

College & Career READINESS

Common Core
Reading Interpret words and phrases as they are used in a text, including determining technical, connotative, and figurative meanings, and analyze how specific word choices shape meaning or tone.

MARKETING CORE FUNCTION

Market Planning

Section 6.2 Social Responsibilities and Ethics

BUSINESS AND SOCIAL RESPONSIBILITY

Corporate scandals and unethical behavior have a negative effect on consumer confidence and the image of a company. It is essential to see the **role** of business in society not only as provider of goods and services, but also as a participant in the society at large.

Anyone can choose to go into business in a private enterprise system, but everyone must abide by local, state, and federal laws that apply to businesses. Some of those laws encourage fair business practices. Others protect consumers, workers, investors, and the environment.

Apart from following the law, should businesses have any further social responsibility? Some business owners feel they should. They believe the business's role in society includes actions affecting its employees, its consumers, its communities, and the environment. These civic-minded businesses set themselves apart from others on the basis of management's vision of their role in the workplace, marketplace, community, and environment.

As You Read

Connect Think of two business practices that demonstrate social responsibility and ethics.

IN THE WORKPLACE

Many businesses recognize their employees' needs outside the workplace and try to accommodate these needs. In so doing, they create a friendly workplace environment. Some employee benefits offered by socially responsible companies include flextime, telecommuting, extended family leave, on-site child care, health care benefits, and time off with pay.

FLEXTIME

Flextime allows workers to choose their work hours. Possible arrangements include early start/early finish (7 A.M.–3 P.M.), late start/late finish (10 A.M.–6 P.M.), and even four-day workweeks (four 9- or 10-hour days, followed by a 3-day weekend).

> "Social responsibility and ethics are part of business and marketing plans."

TELECOMMUTING

Telecommuting involves working at home, usually on a computer. Employees can send completed tasks by e-mail or mail-in disk. Telecommuting helps reduce office space requirements. Because these employees do not have to commute, this benefit is also good for the environment. It reduces gas consumption.

EXTENDED FAMILY LEAVE

Some companies offer employees family leave with pay in addition to the time required by the Family and Medical Leave Act. In some cases, the time off could be as long as one year. Such a **policy** allows companies to retain valued employees. These employees are encouraged to stay with a company that allows such flexibility.

ON-SITE CHILD CARE

On-site child care has grown in popularity with the increase in two-income families. Some employers have expanded it to include on-site schools and on-site clinics for children who are ill. Any form of the benefit tends to reduce employee absenteeism and employee turnover.

ENGAGE

Anticipation Activity

Improving Student Achievement Ask students: ***What does the word ethics mean to you?*** Sample answer: doing what is right even when it is not easy. Then have volunteers provide an example of when they behaved ethically. Sample answers: return extra change when a cashier makes a mistake; never allow a classmate to copy test answers or homework; always download music legally. Explain to students that in this section they will learn about ethical standards for business.

Objectives

- **Provide** examples of business's social responsibilities. Businesses offer employees benefits such as flextime, on-site child care, and health care insurance.
- **Explain** the concept of business ethics. doing what is right, being truthful and fair, following rules and laws
- **Apply** guidelines for ethical behavior. provide accurate information, engage in self-regulation, avoid price gouging and unethical selling practices, follow proper procedures

Graphic Organizer

- Business and Social Responsibility
  - Workplace: Flextime, Telecommuting, Health Care Benefits
  - Marketplace: Provide Information, Employ Self-Censorship, Respond to Consumer Concerns
  - Business Ethics: Consumerism, Marketing Practices
  - Community and Environment: Support Community Causes, Engage in Green Marketing

glencoe.com iWB

Graphic Organizer Send students to the Online Learning Center to print this graphic organizer.

EXPLORE

Before You Read

Read the Before You Read question aloud: *Why do you think it is a good idea for companies to be socially responsible?* civic-minded and ethical behavior makes the company appear to be socially responsible and honest in their customers' eyes, which makes customers feel good about doing business with the company

Preteaching Vocabulary

Have students go to the Online Learning Center at glencoe.com for the Chapter 6 Preteaching Vocabulary games.

Content Vocabulary

Write the following content vocabulary words on the board: *flextime, telecommuting, Ad Council, green marketing, ethics, Better Business Bureau, price gouging, whistle blowing.* Assign these content vocabulary words to student pairs. Have the pairs find the words in context, define them, and then present their words and definitions to the class.

Academic Vocabulary

Role—Use Prior Knowledge Ask students: *Have you ever been in a play? What role did you have?* Answers will vary. Ask students: *What does the word* role *mean in this situation?* a part played by an actor Then read the second sentence on this page: *It is essential to see the role of business in society not only as provider of goods and services, but also as a participant in the society.* Ask students: *Do you think* role *means the same in this sentence as a role in a play?* It has a similar meaning because in the text the word role refers to the part that businesses play in our society.

Policy—Denotative Meaning Tell students that policy consists of management or procedure based primarily on material interests. For example, a store might establish a policy concerning when to accept returned merchandise.

As You Read

Read students the As You Read question: *Think of two business practices that demonstrate social responsibility and ethics.* Examples of social responsibility include businesses sponsoring fund-raising projects, green marketing, or working with government agencies. Ethical business practices include recalling unsafe products, charging fair prices, and advertising truthful claims.

Social Responsibility

BUSINESS AND SOCIAL RESPONSIBILITY

Graphic Organizer

Display the graphic organizer. Ask students to give examples.

Employee Benefit	Example of When Benefit Might Be Useful
Flextime	A parent wants to start work early so he can be done when school gets out.
Telecommuting	An employee must move 120 miles from her place of work.
Extended Family Leave	A worker has an elderly parent who has had surgery.
On-Site Child Care	A parent wants to eat lunch with her child.
Health Care Benefits	A child must have her tonsils removed.
Time Off with Pay	A worker wants to take a vacation to Alaska.

 glencoe.com 

Graphic Organizer Send students to the Online Learning Center to print this graphic organizer.

Expert Advice

Read the quote to students:

“Social responsibility and ethics are part of business and marketing plans.”

Ask students: *Why do you think it is vital that social responsibility and ethics be an integral part of any business and marketing plan?* Businesses need to make decisions that they will be comfortable with and will help them develop strong, positive relationships.

HEALTH CARE BENEFITS

With rising health care costs, health care insurance paid for by employers is a major employee benefit. Some health care benefits cover employees and their dependents, and may extend into retirement.

TIME OFF WITH PAY

Time off with pay includes vacations, sick days, and personal days. Paid vacations are generally part of an employee's contract. The time allotted for the paid vacation is generally based on the length of time an employee has been with the company.

IN THE MARKETPLACE

Consumers are the focus of companies that follow the marketing concept. These businesses are concerned about consumers' perceptions of a company and about issues that impact consumers.

PROVIDING INFORMATION

Socially responsible companies work with the government and consumer groups to provide important information to consumers. The National Consumers League and the FDA created a public education campaign about the safe and proper use of over-the-counter pain relievers.

The **Ad Council** is a nonprofit organization that helps produce public service advertising campaigns for government agencies and other qualifying groups.

EMPLOYING SELF-CENSORSHIP

The Federal Communications Commission (FCC) establishes standards for broadcasting. Beyond those regulations, network executives establish their own policies for self-regulation. Many channels have no-advocacy policies. Each station reviews commercials that might be considered controversial. If a commercial is not socially acceptable, is inaccurate, or poses a legal liability, station management may reject it.

RESPONDING TO CONSUMER CONCERNS

Socially responsible companies look for ways to respond to consumers' concerns. For example, a U.S. government report identified obesity as a major social problem. As a result, many companies sought solutions that promote good health.

IN THE COMMUNITY

United States companies provide community support in many ways. Multi-nationals consider how they affect the global community.

Many local businesses support community efforts. You may know of a local business that funds a Little League team or that sponsors a holiday food drive for the needy.

Many large companies support community causes as well. Ben & Jerry's®, the ice cream manufacturer, donates 7.5 percent of its pretax earnings to needy people and groups that strive for social change and environmental protection. Newman's Own® food company donates its profits and royalties after taxes to educational and charitable causes.

The United Nations World Business Council for Sustainable Development (WBCSD), a coalition of international companies, has a mission "to provide business leadership as a catalyst for change toward sustainable development, and to promote the role of eco-efficiency, innovation, and corporate social responsibility."

IN THE ENVIRONMENT

Socially responsible companies are concerned about our environment. They have programs that work toward saving Earth for future generations.

Alternatives to the traditional transportation fuels of gasoline and diesel fuel are being developed. Some fuels create less pollution than gasoline. These "clean fuels" can include alcohol, electricity, natural gas, and propane.

In **green marketing**, companies engage in the production and promotion of environmentally safe products. Such products may be labeled *ozone-safe, recyclable, environmentally friendly,* or *biodegradable.* Green marketing helps companies build consumer loyalty. Many consumers are willing to pay more for products that are environmentally friendly. Green products are not always more expensive.

Reading Check

Describe What are some benefits of responsible business practices?

Addressing the Issues

Many companies are developing marketing plans that include corporate social responsibility efforts on many fronts. ***How do businesses and markets benefit from community-oriented market plans?***

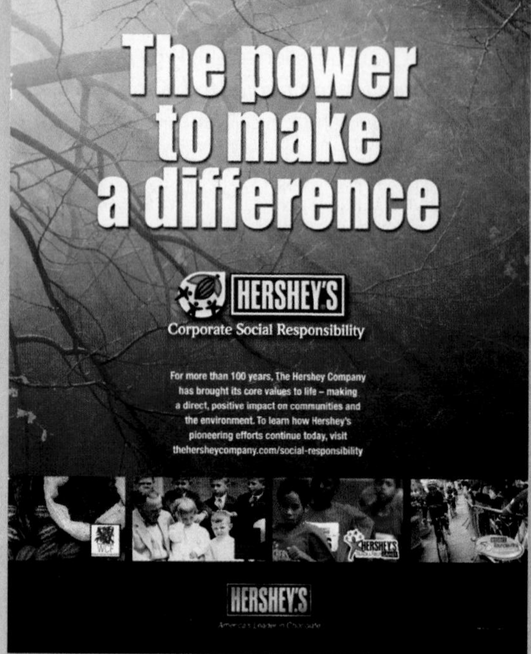

The power to make a difference
HERSHEY'S
Corporate Social Responsibility
For more than 100 years, The Hershey Company has brought its core values to life – making a direct, positive impact on communities and the environment. To learn how Hershey's pioneering efforts continue today, visit thehersheycompany.com/social-responsibility
HERSHEY'S

EXPLAIN

IN THE MARKETPLACE

Use these guiding questions to focus the discussion on how ethical behavior can be implemented in the marketplace.

Guiding Questions

Identify What is the purpose of the Ad Council?	helps produce public service advertising campaigns for government agencies and qualifying groups
Analyze Do you think it is important for broadcasters to engage in self-censorship? Why or why not?	Possible answer: Yes, because standards of what is acceptable may vary in different parts of the country.
Infer What do you think is meant by the sentence "Many channels have no-advocacy policies?" Why do you think this is?	Advocacy groups push for a certain point of view, such as being against people wearing animal fur. Many channels think these issues are overly controversial.

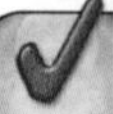

Reading Check Answer

Read the Reading Check question to students: ***What are some benefits of responsible business practices?*** Employees feel they are acting ethically and protecting the earth for future generations; consumers may be loyal to companies they believe behave responsibly; companies may be able to save money by using recycled materials.

ELABORATE

IN THE ENVIRONMENT

Ask these questions to guide the discussion about social responsibility and the environment.

Guiding Questions

Predict During what phase of the business cycle do you think companies are most likely to expand their green marketing?	during the expansion phase, when sales are high, companies have more money to invest in change and new products
Apply Imagine you are head of manufacturing for a bicycle company. You want to build bicycle frames out of recycled metals. What might you say to support your idea?	Emphasize that using recycled materials is good for the environment and may save money. Bicyclists might be more likely to buy from a company that shares their values.

Reinforce Vocabulary

Green Marketing—Connotative Meaning Why do you think green marketing has the word "green" in its name? Why, for example, is it not called "brown marketing" or "red marketing"? Green connotes living things; green marketing is designed to protect living things;

Mini Project

Enrichment

Examining Ad Council Campaigns Tell students that the Ad Council produces a wide variety of public service campaigns. Have students go to the Council's website and watch some of these campaigns. They then should pick the one they think is most effective in promoting social responsibility. Students should give a presentation in which they show the class the campaign, explain its purpose, and explain why they think this campaign does a good job of promoting social responsibility.

Visual Literacy

Addressing the Issues Caption Answer Read the figure caption question to students: ***How do businesses and markets benefit from community-oriented marketing plans?*** Businesses are seen as being good citizens and might possibly realize an increase in sales because of consumers who choose their products over others. Both businesses and markets reap the benefits of being involved in a community that cares for people and has a cleaner environment.

Mini Projects

Enrichment

Creating a Contest that Encourages Environmentalism Tell students that some companies have developed contests to encourage customers to be environmentally conscious. For example, Levi Strauss & Company® (makers of Levi jeans) recently had a contest that gave $10,000 to the creator of "the most innovative and sustainable way to air-dry your clothes." Have students work in small groups to develop a similar contest for a company of their choosing. The contest should encourage environmentalism and be related to the company's products. Have students create an ad that promotes this contest and could be posted on the company's Facebook page. Ads will vary, but should be entertaining, promote environmentalism, be related to the company's products, and be appropriate for the company's social network page.

Promoting Green Cleaning Products Have students go to a supermarket or discount store and locate a cleaning product that claims to be "green." Tell students to compare this product to similar "non-green" products. Have students create a television ad to present to the class. The ad should emphasize why this product is more environmentally friendly than similar products. Ads will vary, but should state specific reasons why their product is more environmentally friendly than other similar products. For example, the container may be made of recycled material or the ingredients may be non-toxic.

BUSINESS ETHICS

A major aspect of social responsibility is business ethics. **Ethics** are guidelines for good behavior. Ethical behavior is based on knowing the difference between right and wrong—and doing what is right. Ethical behavior is truthful and fair. It takes into account the well-being of everyone. There is often a fine line between legal issues and ethical issues, especially when cultural differences are involved. Ethical businesses also follow the laws.

ETHICS AND CONSUMERISM

Consumerism involves the relationship of marketing to a company's customers. It is the societal effort to protect consumer rights by putting legal, moral, and economic pressure on business. Individual consumers, consumer groups, government, and socially responsible business leaders share this effort. The greatest growth in consumerism took place from the early 1960s until about 1980.

President John F. Kennedy's Consumer Bill of Rights states that consumers have four basic rights:

- To be informed and protected against fraud, deceit, and misleading statements, and to be educated in the wise use of financial resources
- To be protected from unsafe products
- To have a choice of goods and services
- To have a voice in product and marketing decisions made by government and business

ETHICS IN MARKETING

Consumerism and corporate scandals have caused businesses to address many ethical issues. Some issues involve marketing in general, as well as its specific functions and activities. Ethical principles are important in business. They reflect the management of the company and the trust between a company and its stakeholders.

SELF-REGULATION

Ethical companies are proactive. They join organizations that help to create an ethical business environment. One such organization is the **Better Business Bureau** (BBB). Established in 1912, the BBB is a nonprofit organization that promotes self-regulation among businesses. To be a member of the BBB, a business must "agree to follow the highest principles of business ethics and voluntary self-regulation, and have a proven record of marketplace honesty and integrity." The BBB has a strict Code of Advertising as well.

Ethical companies subscribe to the American Marketing Association's (AMA) Code of Ethics. The Code addresses honesty and fairness as well as rights and duties in all areas of marketing and organizational relationships.

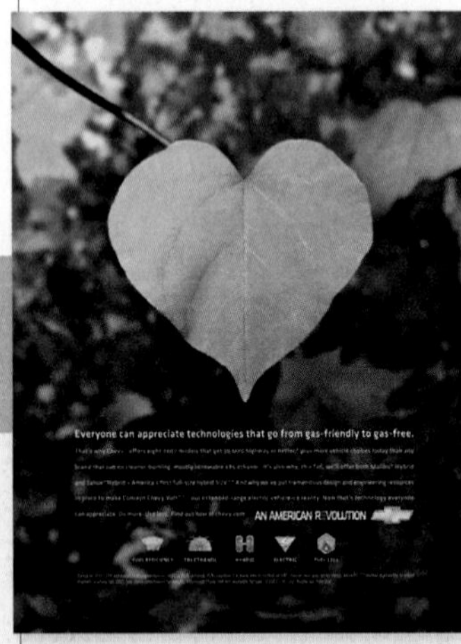

Socially Responsible Businesses

This advertisement shows how businesses can use their technology to save energy. ***Why might all types of businesses be interested in using their resources responsibly?***

ETHICAL ISSUES RELATED TO MARKETING FUNCTIONS

There are ethical issues that involve marketing functions such as pricing, management of marketing information, and selling.

Price Gouging

Price gouging is pricing products unreasonably high when the need is great or when consumers do not have other choices.

In the pharmaceutical industry, patented prescription drugs are granted monopoly status for a period of time. The pricing of the drug during that time is an area of dispute. The companies argue that high prices are due to time and money spent on research and development. Many consumer groups think this is a case of price gouging. They say it is unfair for consumers to pay high prices for drugs they need to stay alive.

Some states have laws that govern price gouging during disasters, like hurricanes or tornadoes. Products in high demand, such as hotel rooms, bottled water, flashlights, food, and fuel, are often priced higher due to the unusual demand created by the catastrophe.

Marketing Information

Industries that maintain customer databases containing personal information have a responsibility to keep that information private. Banks, doctors, and marketing research companies must not share that information with anyone unless you give them permission to do so. Product research and marketing research must report findings honestly by disclosing all the facts involved in the research design and results.

MARKETING CASE STUDY

Tide's "Loads of Hope" campaign

Laundry detergent brand Tide® launched its "Loads of Hope" campaign, a cleverly named program that goes into areas struck by natural disasters and provides free laundry service to the victims. The program started after Hurricane Katrina, when the program's "CleanTruck" went into the hardest hit areas and did more than 20,000 loads of laundry for those who had been hurt by the storm.

Reaching out through social media

The Loads of Hope program also did an interesting experiment in March 2009. It wanted to find out how best to market through social media. Tide hosted a "Digital Night," 40 social media experts were challenged to sell as many t-shirts as possible through social media by the end of the night. When it was all over, the winning team sold $50,000 worth of t-shirts—and Tide matched that amount, giving the money to charity.

Math

If the second-place team on Digital Night sold 15 percent fewer shirts than the team that won, how much money did the second-place team earn?

NCTM Number and Operations Understand numbers, ways of representing numbers, relationships among numbers, and number systems.

EXPLAIN

BUSINESS ETHICS

To focus the discussion on business ethics, use these guiding questions.

Guiding Questions

Explain What is the basis for ethical behavior?	knowing the difference between right and wrong
Analyze Why was the Consumer Bill of Rights created?	Many individuals, organizations, and the government felt that consumers were being taken advantage of and wanted to place legal, moral, and economic pressure on businesses.
Evaluate How can membership in the Better Business Bureau help businesses? How can it help consumers?	Potential customers may be more likely to patronize the business. Consumers can identify businesses that agree to the BBB guidelines.

Visual Literacy

Socially Responsible Businesses Caption Answer Read the figure caption question to students: ***Why might all types of businesses be interested in using their resources responsibly?*** Sample answers: to reduce waste and protect the environment, to save money, to be seen as socially responsible.

Reinforce Vocabulary

Ethics—Word Origin Explain that *ethics* comes from the Greek word *ēthikē*. *Ēthikē* is derived from the Greek words *ēthikos* (ethical) and *ēthos* (character). Ask students: ***Why do you think the word ethics comes in part from the Greek word ethos?*** A person with positive ethical standards shows good character.

Activate Prior Knowledge

Reteach the Elements of a Marketing Plan Review the Marketing Plan Outline. Then ask: ***What are some ways that social responsibility and ethical behavior can be integrated into a Marketing Plan?*** Encourage students to make notes during the class discussion. Under the Environmental Scan, competitors' weaknesses in this area could be presented; under Positioning and Points of Difference, socially responsible behavior, such as using recycled and biodegradable materials, could be emphasized.

ELABORATE

Graphic Organizer

Display this diagram to encourage students to discuss the reasons for price gouging.

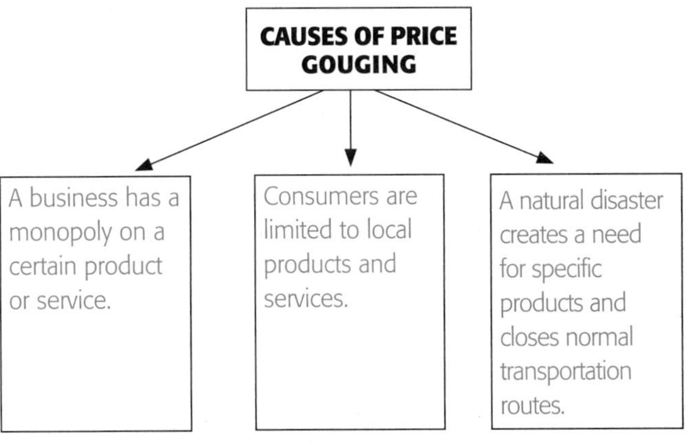
CAUSES OF PRICE GOUGING
A business has a monopoly on a certain product or service.
Consumers are limited to local products and services.
A natural disaster creates a need for specific products and closes normal transportation routes.

glencoe.com

iWB

Graphic Organizer Send students to the Online Learning Center to print this graphic organizer.

MARKETING CASE STUDY

Math Answer The second place team would have sold $42,500 worth of t-shirts.

Use these questions to discuss how Tide® uses its "Loads of Hope" campaign to demonstrate social responsibility.

Explain What is the purpose of the "Loads of Hope" campaign?	provides free laundry service to victims
Draw Conclusions What does the success of Tide's social media campaign tell you?	it is vital for businesses to have a presence in various social mediums

e MARKETING

Internet Crime and Permission Marketing

The issue of Internet crime has become such a major problem that the U.S. government has an Internet Crime Complaint Center. Its definition of Internet crime is "any illegal activity involving one or more components of the Internet, such as Web sites, chat rooms, and/or e-mail." Internet crimes related to marketing involve fraud, copyright infringement, identity theft, and spam. Fraud often involves payment for services that are never performed or products that are not delivered. Copyright infringement occurs when authors and entertainers are not paid because their work was illegally downloaded. Identity theft occurs when hackers break into a company's computer operations and steal personal data or when consumers provide personal information not knowing it will be used for illegal purposes. Spam is unsolicited e-mail or spamdexing on a search engine. Marketers that want to legally use the Internet to send information to customers ask customers if they want to "opt in" or "opt out" from receiving information from them via the Internet. Thus, consumers give businesses "permission" to communicate with them in permission marketing.

Innovate and Create

Discuss the ramifications of Internet crime and the future of Internet marketing. How may legitimate businesses be affected if Internet crime continues to increase and spammers become more sophisticated? Have students conduct a survey of at least 20 students with regard to e-mail spam and spamdexing. Ask if they receive e-mails from businesses. If they do, continue the survey by asking them to recall how they "opted in" or "opted out" from receiving e-mails from companies from which they have made purchases. Ask if they ever bought something after spamdexing (visited search engine and was sent to an unrelated link). Have students tally the results and report their findings in oral and written reports.

Warning!

glencoe.com

eMarketing Worksheet Activity Send students to the Online Learning Center to download an eMarketing worksheet activity.

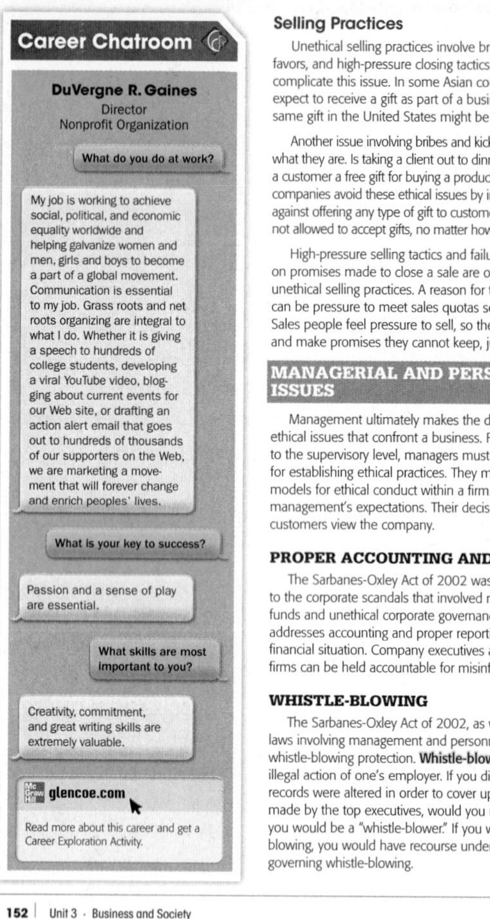

Career Chatroom

DuVergne R. Gaines
Director
Nonprofit Organization

What do you do at work?

My job is working to achieve social, political, and economic equality worldwide and helping galvanize women and men, girls and boys to become a part of a global movement. Communication is essential to my job. Grass roots and net roots organizing are integral to what I do. Whether it is giving a speech to hundreds of college students, developing a viral YouTube video, blogging about current events for our Web site, or drafting an action alert email that goes out to hundreds of thousands of our supporters on the Web, we are marketing a movement that will forever change and enrich peoples' lives.

What is your key to success?

Passion and a sense of play are essential.

What skills are most important to you?

Creativity, commitment, and great writing skills are extremely valuable.

glencoe.com

Read more about this career and get a Career Exploration Activity.

Selling Practices

Unethical selling practices involve bribes, kickbacks, favors, and high-pressure closing tactics. Cultural differences complicate this issue. In some Asian countries, businesspeople expect to receive a gift as part of a business relationship. The same gift in the United States might be considered a bribe.

Another issue involving bribes and kickbacks is defining what they are. Is taking a client out to dinner a bribe? Is giving a customer a free gift for buying a product a kickback? Some companies avoid these ethical issues by imposing strict rules against offering any type of gift to customers. Their buyers are also not allowed to accept gifts, no matter how inexpensive they are.

High-pressure selling tactics and failure to follow through on promises made to close a sale are other examples of unethical selling practices. A reason for this unethical behavior can be pressure to meet sales quotas set by management. Sales people feel pressure to sell, so they hound customers and make promises they cannot keep, just to make a sale.

MANAGERIAL AND PERSONNEL ISSUES

Management ultimately makes the decisions about major ethical issues that confront a business. From the top level to the supervisory level, managers must take responsibility for establishing ethical practices. They must become role models for ethical conduct within a firm. Employees follow management's expectations. Their decisions impact how customers view the company.

PROPER ACCOUNTING AND REPORTING

The Sarbanes-Oxley Act of 2002 was passed in response to the corporate scandals that involved misuse of company funds and unethical corporate governance. This legislation addresses accounting and proper reporting of a corporation's financial situation. Company executives and their consulting firms can be held accountable for misinformation.

WHISTLE-BLOWING

The Sarbanes-Oxley Act of 2002, as well as many other laws involving management and personnel issues, include whistle-blowing protection. **Whistle-blowing** is reporting an illegal action of one's employer. If you discovered that financial records were altered in order to cover up personal purchases made by the top executives, would you report it? If you did, you would be a "whistle-blower." If you were fired for whistle-blowing, you would have recourse under several federal laws governing whistle-blowing.

Making a decision to be a whistle-blower involves personal ethics. Employees who face such decisions find it easier to report offenses when a company has specific guidelines for making ethical decisions and a way to report these offenses.

GUIDELINES FOR ETHICAL BEHAVIOR

Companies with an interest in ethical business behavior develop guidelines to help employees make ethical decisions. People make the decisions, so business ethics are related to personal ethics. There are specific steps you can take and questions to ask to guide you through the process of making decisions involving ethical issues.

To make the right choices, employees should follow these steps:

1. Get the facts.
2. Identify all parties concerned.
3. Think of all your alternatives.
4. Evaluate your alternatives by asking yourself:
   - Is it in compliance with the law?
   - Does it go against company policy?
   - How does it affect everyone involved?
   - Is it right, fair, and honest?
   - Will it build good will for the company?
   - Am I comfortable with it?
   - How will it hold up to public scrutiny?

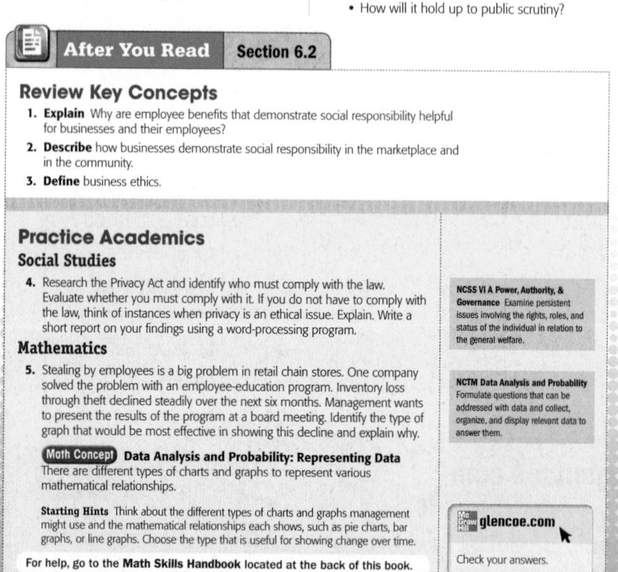

After You Read Section 6.2

Review Key Concepts

1. **Explain** Why are employee benefits that demonstrate social responsibility helpful for businesses and their employees?
2. **Describe** how businesses demonstrate social responsibility in the marketplace and in the community.
3. **Define** business ethics.

Practice Academics

Social Studies

4. Research the Privacy Act and identify who must comply with the law. Evaluate whether you must comply with it. If you do not have to comply with the law, think of instances when privacy is an ethical issue. Explain. Write a short report on your findings using a word-processing program.

Mathematics

5. Stealing by employees is a big problem in retail chain stores. One company solved the problem with an employee-education program. Inventory loss through theft declined steadily over the next six months. Management wants to present the results of the program at a board meeting. Identify the type of graph that would be most effective in showing this decline and explain why.

Math Concept **Data Analysis and Probability: Representing Data** There are different types of charts and graphs to represent various mathematical relationships.

Starting Hints Think about the different types of charts and graphs management might use and the mathematical relationships each shows, such as pie charts, bar graphs, or line graphs. Choose the type that is useful for showing change over time.

For help, go to the **Math Skills Handbook** located at the back of this book.

NCSS VI A Power, Authority, & Governance Examine persistent issues involving the rights, roles, and status of the individual in relation to the general welfare.

NCTM Data Analysis and Probability Formulate questions that can be addressed with data and collect, organize, and display relevant data to answer them.

glencoe.com

Check your answers.

ELABORATE

Career Chatroom 

Focus the Career Chatroom discussion concerning DuVergne R. Gaines by asking students these guiding questions.

Guiding Questions

Explain What ways does Gaines spread the word?	speeches, videos, blogs, emails
Analyze Why are writing skills so valuable?	Writing is an essential part of communication. People who write well are likely to be taken seriously.

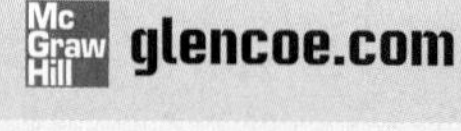

Career Exploration Send students to the Online Learning Center to find more information about this career and to get a Career Exploration activity.

Reinforce Vocabulary

Whistle-Blowing—Origin Remind students that whistle-blowing is reporting illegal actions of one's employer. Ask students: ***Why do you think this term includes the word*** **whistle?** Sample answer: Officials, such as referees, often blow whistles to indicate conduct that is against the rules. Tell students that before modern policing methods, officers carried whistles that they blew to draw attention to individuals who were breaking the law.

EVALUATE

MANAGERIAL AND PERSONNEL ISSUES

Ask students these guiding questions to focus the discussion on managerial and personnel issues.

Guiding Questions

Identify What are three unethical selling practices?	Unethical selling practices include bribes, kickbacks, favors, and high-pressure closing tactics.
Draw Conclusions Why does it fall on the shoulders of a business's management to demonstrate ethical behavior?	Employees follow management's example.
Evaluate Do you think that whistle-blowing laws are necessary? Why or why not?	Yes, because whistle-blowers are reporting the illegal activities of their employers and, if not protected, they could be fired or suffer other serious consequences.

Mini Project

Extension

Examining a Whistle-Blower Instruct students to conduct research on a specific whistle-blower. Sources might include magazines, books, the Internet, and even television shows and movies. Have students write an essay that briefly summarizes what this person did and why. Then have them discuss whether they would have done the same in similar circumstances. For example, in 1996, Jeffrey Wigand exposed that the tobacco industry had known for decades that tobacco products were addictive and life-threatening. Students might conclude that they would have done the same as Wigand because people's health was at risk.

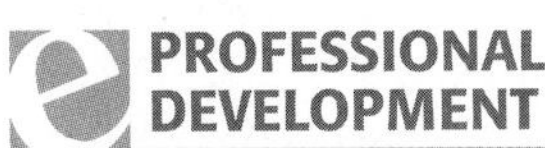

MINI CLIP

Reading: On Workshops
Go to the Online Learning Center for a video in which an author and educator discusses the "Workshop Approach" to teaching.

After You Read Section 6.2

Review Key Concepts

1. These benefits simplify employees' lives and aid them in times of difficulty, so they increase the chances that employees will remain at a job. They are helpful to businesses because they have less employee turnover. The businesses' reputation is improved because they are seen as being concerned with the welfare of their workers.
2. In the marketplace, businesses provide information, employ self-censorship, and respond to consumer concerns. In the community, businesses support community efforts (e.g., sponsor sports teams, food drives, and so on.), contribute money to worthy causes, and promote sustainable development.
3. Business ethics are guidelines for good behavior. Ethical businesses are honest and fair with everyone—workers, consumers, and the communities in which they operate.

Practice Academics

Social Studies

4. Accept all reasonable reports that reflect adequate research of the Privacy Act. Students might learn that even they may have to comply with the Privacy Act if they collect information about others on their own computers or do so for an employer. According to the government's Web site, "Agency and bureau managers, Privacy Act Officers, systems managers—and you" are responsible for complying with the law. Instances of when privacy is an ethical issue includes when an employee knows proprietary information, such as the markup on products or the profit made by a privately owned company. In both these instances, the employee should not divulge such information to others. Accept other reasonable ethical privacy examples.

Mathematics

5. A line graph would be most appropriate. It would clearly indicate theft over time and show how it had declined over the last six months.

glencoe.com

Answer Key Send students to the Online Learning Center to check their answers.

Chapter 6 Visual Summary

Legal and Ethical Issues

Socially responsible businesses address issues in the workplace, marketplace, community, and environment.

SOCIAL RESPONSIBILITY

- Workplace: Health Care; Time Off with Pay; Flextime; Telecommuting; Extended Family Leave; On-Site Child Care
- Marketplace: Providing Information; Employing Self-Censorship; Responding to Consumer Concerns
- Community: Local Businesses; International Businesses; Large Companies
- Environment: Cleaner Fuel; Green Marketing

Review and Activities

Written Summary

- The government plays a critical role in enforcing private enterprise and providing for the health, safety, and welfare of its citizens.
- The Food and Drug Administration (FDA) and the Consumer Product Safety Commission (CPSC) are two federal agencies that protect consumers.
- The Equal Employment Opportunity Commission (EEOC) and the Occupational Safety and Health Administration (OSHA) protect employees.
- The Securities and Exchange Commission (SEC) protects investors and the Environmental Protection Agency (EPA) protects the environment.
- The Federal Trade Commission (FTC) promotes private enterprise and protects consumers from unfair or deceptive business practices.
- Socially responsible businesses have policies and programs that address issues in the workplace, marketplace, community, and environment.
- Business ethics are guidelines for good behavior.
- Some guidelines for ethical behavior include getting the facts, identifying all parties concerned, thinking of alternatives, and evaluating alternatives.

Review Content Vocabulary and Academic Vocabulary

1. Label each of these vocabulary terms as a noun, verb, or adjective.

Content Vocabulary

- Food and Drug Administration (FDA) (p. 140)
- Consumer Product Safety Commission (CPSC) (p. 140)
- Equal Employment Opportunity Commission (EEOC) (p. 140)
- Occupational Safety and Health Administration (OSHA) (p. 142)
- Securities and Exchange Commission (SEC) (p. 142)
- Environmental Protection Agency (EPA) (p. 142)
- Federal Trade Commission (FTC) (p. 143)
- flextime (p. 147)
- telecommuting (p. 147)
- Ad Council (p. 148)
- green marketing (p. 148)
- ethics (p. 150)
- Better Business Bureau (p. 150)
- price gouging (p. 151)
- whistle blowing (p. 152)

Academic Vocabulary

- structure (p. 137)
- administration (p. 137)
- role (p. 147)
- policy (p. 147)

Assess for Understanding

2. **Decide** How closely should the government monitor food production?
3. **Compare and Contrast** How do federal regulatory agencies protect consumers, workers, investors, and the environment?
4. **Discuss** Why is it important for the Federal Reserve to regulate and enforce private enterprise?
5. **Sequence** What is the chain of events that might result from a company's decision to offer its employees flextime and telecommuting?
6. **Connect** How is the use of price gouging connected to antitrust concerns?
7. **Describe** Why is it important for businesses to be proactive about ethical practices?
8. **Consider** Are you a whistle blower if you know your employer is doing something illegal or unethical? Explain your decision objectively.
9. **Imagine** What if one of the laws or ethical practices described in this chapter did not exist? How would this absence affect marketing?

EVALUATE

Visual Summary

Express Creativity Ask students to develop their own visual summary of a concept in the chapter. Encourage students to use different formats for their visual summaries, such as a storyboard, a timeline, a table, a tree diagram, or a word web. Visual summaries will vary depending on the concept depicted and the visual manner in which it is depicted. Questions to ask when assessing a visual summary include:

- Is the summary clear, economical, and simple?
- Are any important steps left out?
- Are steps or concepts arranged in the same order as the original?
- Does the summary reveal a pattern that connects the details?
- Does the summary locate and highlight the most important information?

Review Content Vocabulary and Academic Vocabulary

1. **Food and Drug Administration (FDA)**—noun; **Consumer Product Safety Commission (CPSC)**—noun; **Equal Employment Opportunity Commission (EEOC)**—noun; **Occupational Safety and Health Administration (OSHA)**—noun; **Securities and Exchange Commission (SEC)**—noun; **Environmental Protection Agency (EPA)**—noun; **Federal Trade Commission (FTC)**—noun; **flextime**—noun; **telecommuting**—verb; **Ad Council**—noun; **green marketing**—noun; **ethics**—noun; **Better Business Bureau**—noun; **price gouging**—verb; **whistle blowing**—verb; **structure**—noun; **administration**—noun; **role**—noun; **policy**—noun;

EVALUATE

Assess for Understanding

2. Answers will vary. Sample answer: I think the government should check all food to make certain it is safe to eat, for example not contain any harmful bacteria. It also should make certain that it is properly labeled. For example, if a package says it contains 100 percent beef, it should contain nothing else.

3. Consumers: FDA regulates labeling and safety of food, drugs, and cosmetics; CPSC oversees safety of products such as toys and electronics; Bureau of Economics works to protect against price gouging that can occur when monopolies develop; local zoning laws protect the value of residential property. Workers: OSHA regulates workplace safety; EEOC is responsible for the fair and equitable treatment of employees. Investors: SEC regulates the sale of securities, investigates any actions among corporations that affect the value of stocks, and requires companies on the stock exchange to publish a prospectus and an annual report. Environment: EPA monitors air and water pollution and oversees recycling and hazardous waste disposal.

4. It is important for the FTC to regulate and enforce private enterprise so that all companies have the opportunity to compete and succeed in the marketplace.

5. Employees might begin working at home and adjusting their hours to suit their family schedules, outside interests, and other responsibilities they may have, such as volunteering at a local school or library. For example, a telecommuter may choose to work Saturday mornings so that she can take Thursday afternoons off to volunteer at a local hospital.

6. When a company, or small group of companies, controls the production and/or distribution of a particular product or service, they also can control the price and often will raise it higher than would occur in a competitive marketplace. This causes price gouging to occur.

7. When a corporate scandal or unethical behavior on the part of a business becomes known, consumers develop a very poor image of the company and may choose to take their business elsewhere. When companies are civic-minded, they are seen as being good citizens, and consumers may go out of their way to buy from them. Unethical behavior may also be illegal, leading to problems with the government.

8. Accept all reasonable answers. Students should defend their decisions objectively with regard to whistle blowing. Some will feel it is their duty to do so and note that they are protected under the law. Others will note the fear of reprisals for being a whistle-blower, especially if the company is hurt so badly that it might have to close down and all employees lose their jobs.

9. Answers will vary depending on the law or ethical practice chosen. For example, if companies could develop monopolies, they could control an entire market and charge consumers whatever they wanted, leading to extremely unfair pricing practices.

College & Career READINESS

21st Century Skills

Teamwork Skills

10. Carbon Footprint Work in a group to research and report on a variety of socially responsible business efforts with regard to the environment. Look at carbon footprint efforts, green marketing, packaging, and other eco-friendly measures. Create an oral presentation using presentation software.

Financial Literacy Skills

11. Minimum Payment A credit card company offers an annual percentage rate of 21 percent. The balance on your credit card is $1,000, and the minimum payment due is $100. If you make the minimum payment, what will the balance on your credit card be the next month, assuming you did not make any new purchases?

e-Marketing Skills

12. Research Skills Imagine that you are the financial controller for a large business. You have recently reviewed your business' profits and you were happy to find more money than you expected. After consulting with the board of directors and your company's CEO, you have decided to donate the money to charity. Research a charity that you think your business should support.

- Describe your business and its role in the market.
- Identify the charity your business should support.
- Justify your choice of charity.
- Explain your business' marketing efforts required for the suggested charity.
- Create an advertisement that shows the partnership between your business and the charity.

Build Academic Skills

Social Studies

13. Government Bailout In 2008 and 2009, the U.S. government took measures to shore up the financial sector and the auto industry. It bailed out both industries with taxpayers' money. Research the factors that led up to these extreme measures, note the companies involved, and any controversies that occurred. Discuss these bailouts with regard to the role of government in a private enterprise system. Present your findings in a written report.

NCSS VI B Power, Authority, & Governance Explain the purpose of government and analyze how its powers are acquired, used, and justified.

Science

14. Music and Technology Research how recorded music was played from the 1950s to present day. Create a timeline to show the way music lovers enjoyed their favorite tunes during each decade. Discuss the role technology played in the transformation of music. What legal and ethical issues caused problems in that transformation? Report your findings in a written report and use presentation software to present your findings to the class.

NSES A Develop abilities necessary to do scientific inquiry, understandings about scientific inquiry.

Mathematics

15. The Price of Recycling If the local recycling plant pays $0.10 per pound for aluminum cans, how many pounds of cans would it take to get $25?

Math Concept **Using Algebraic Symbols** Write an equation using an algebraic symbol for the unknown quantity before solving the problem.

NCTM Algebra Represent and analyze mathematical situations and structures using algebraic symbols.

For help, go to the **Math Skills Handbook** located at the back of this book.

Standardized Test Practice

Directions Read the following questions. On a separate sheet of paper write the best possible answer for each one.

1. Which government agency is responsible for overseeing the safety of toys?
   A. Food & Drug Administration
   B. Federal Trade Commission
   C. Consumer Product and Safety Commission
   D. Occupational Safety and Health Administration
2. True or false? The Better Business Bureau is a government agency.
   T
   F
3. The Consumer Bill of Rights was established by ________.

Test-Taking Tip

Study for tests over a few days or weeks and continually review class material. Do not wait until the night before and then try to learn everything at once.

DECA Connection Role Play

Manager
Auto Parts Store

Situation Assume the role of manager of a locally owned auto parts store. Earlier this week you learned that your business computer system was hacked, and some customer credit information was accessed. You have since installed a state-of-the-art safeguard system to better protect customer information. This system is designed to scramble customer information so that it is useless to thieves. The system also makes it much more difficult to hack your business computers.

You are notifying your customers that their credit card information may have been stolen. You are explaining the situation and how it is being handled to a part-time employee (judge). The employee (judge) asks why it is so important to notify all of the customers since there is a chance they will not be affected by the data theft.

Activity You are to explain to the employee (judge) that you have an ethical responsibility to protect customer information. You must further explain that customer trust is essential to operate a successful business, and that it is in your best interest to be honest with your customers about the situation.

Evaluation You will be evaluated on how well you meet the following performance indicators:

1. Explain the nature of business ethics.
2. Explain the role of business in society.
3. Discuss the nature of law and sources of law in the United States.
4. Describe legal issues affecting businesses.
5. Describe the United States' judicial system.

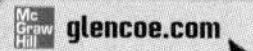

Download the Competitive Events Workbook for more Role-Playing practice.

EVALUATE

Teamwork Skills

10. Evaluate the group's oral presentation based on the variety of examples presented of socially responsible business efforts: carbon footprint efforts, green marketing, packaging, and other eco-friendly measures. Examples: if consumers donate $5 or more to Feeding America, Kellogg Company® will give them cereal coupons equal to $5; HP® provides packaging for consumers to return used ink cartridges; Sprint® has eco-friendly accessories such as solar-powered charges and carrying cases made from recycled materials; Nike® is experimenting with old sneakers to make soles for new sneakers; local businesses offer incentives for shoppers to purchase reusable bags; many companies have reduced packaging or changed the materials used for packaging; many companies offer e-billing to reduce paper use.

Financial Literacy Skills

11. The balance on the credit card the next month would be $915.75. (monthly interest rate is 1.75 percent; 21% divided by 12; $\$1000 - \$100 = \$900 \times 1.0175 = \$915.75$).

e-Marketing Skills

12. Accept all reasonable ideas concerning the business's efforts to benefit the selected charity. Sample answer: A company that manufactures and sells women's clothing at local department stores might decide to support research to find a cure for breast cancer. For example, they might sponsor a local "Walk for the Cure," advertise the walk, provide the needed supplies, and so on. Ads might include posters and newspaper advertisements that provide information about how to join the walk, the importance of the research, and mention the sponsoring company's commitment to the cause.

EVALUATE

Build Academic Skills

Social Studies

13. Reports should touch on the bailout of American International Group, Inc. (AIG), bank bailouts, and auto industry bailouts for General Motors and Chrysler. Legislation allowed taxpayers' money to be used for these bailouts called Troubled Asset Relief Program (TARP). The Treasury Department spent $700 billion in the financial crisis. Citigroup and Bank of America took advantage of TARP funds. Controversies relating to these bailouts included excessive executive pay and bonuses in companies receiving TARP funds and auto executives flying on private jets to Washington D.C. It is not the government's role to intervene in private enterprise, however it has happened in the past (i.e., 1971 Lockheed, 1980 Chrysler, Airline industry after the terrorist attacks on September 11, 2001).

Science

14. 1950: music was recorded on vinyl records in three speeds and sizes [12 inch format–78 rpm (ended in 1956); 7 inch format 45 rpm; albums at 33 1/3 rpm]. By 1988, Compact Disk (CD) sales were greater than vinyl sales. 1990s music was recorded digitally. Apple Computer Company introduced the iPod portable music player. Consumers could download music from the Internet. Downloading music without paying for it broke copyright laws. The Recording Industry Association of American (RIAA) sued individuals and Internet companies that were part of the piracy. There are still ethical questions about digital copying of music. Questions that still arise: Is it ethical to make several copies of a CD? Is it legal to make copies and sell them?

Mathematics

15. It would take 250 pounds. ($25 divided by $.10 = 250 pounds)

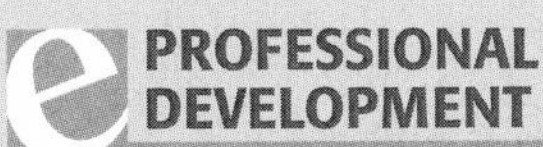

Math: Real-World Ratios
Go to the Online Learning Center to view a video clip in which a teacher has students create and compare ratios.

Standardized Test Practice

1. C. Consumer Product Safety Commission
2. False
3. President John F. Kennedy

DECA Connection Role Play

Evaluations will be based on these performance indicators:

1. **Explain the nature of business ethics.** Business ethics are essentially guidelines for good behavior, and are based on knowing the difference between right and wrong. Ethical behavior is truthful and fair and takes into account everyone's well-being.
2. **Explain the role of business in society.** The role of business in society is not only as a provider of needed goods and services, but also as a participant in society at large. Businesses must obey the law. Most people believe businesses should behave ethically when involved in actions that affect their employees, consumers, communities, and the environment.
3. **Discuss the nature of law and sources of law in the United States.** The nature of law is to institute rules and regulations that provide for an orderly society and the fair and just treatment of individuals, the protection of the environment, and so forth. Laws can be enacted at the federal, state, and local level. At the federal level, members of the U.S. Congress debate and vote on laws and regulations.
4. **Describe legal issues affecting businesses.** Legal issues affecting businesses include laws that control how goods and services are bought and sold, both within the country and globally; regulatory laws designed to protect the safety, health, and welfare of individuals and the environment; laws regulating competition among businesses; copyright laws, and so forth.
5. **Describe the United States' judicial system.** The judicial branch interprets, applies, and administers the laws of the United States. It consists of a network of courts at all levels of government.

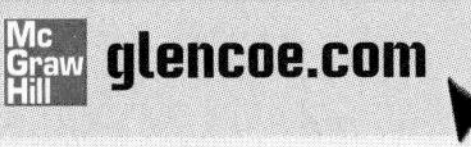

Role Plays For more DECA Role Plays, send students to the Online Learning Center to download the Competitive Events Workbook.

UNIT 3 **Marketing Internship Project**

An Eco-Project
for a Sports Footwear Company

Businesses around the world are becoming environmentally aware and "going green." How can a company become eco-friendly?

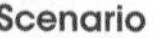

Scenario

You work for a sports footwear company. Your new CEO came from a company that was involved with the World Business Council for Sustainable Development (WBCSD). Since membership in the WBCSD is by invitation only, companies that want to join must already be engaged in projects that help save the planet. Having a commitment to the environment is in line with the WBCSD's mission. A partnership with Live Earth is an example of an eco-friendly initiative.

Your CEO wants your company to develop an environmental program and also apply for membership in the WBCSD.

The Skills You'll Use

Academic Skills Reading, writing, social studies, researching, and analyzing

Basic Skills Speaking, listening, thinking, and interpersonal

Technology Skills Word processing, presentation, telecommunications, and the Internet

NCTE 4 Use written language to communicate effectively.
NCTE 7 Conduct research and gather, evaluate, and synthesize data to communicate discoveries.

Your Objective

Your objective is to develop an effective eco-project (initiative) for your company, a global manufacturer of sports footwear.

STEP 1 Do Your Research

Go to the Internet or your school library. Find out about different companies involved in eco-friendly projects. Then devise an idea for your own project for your company. As you conduct your research, answer these questions:

- What costs are associated with your project?
- What are the political, economic, socio-cultural, and technological factors (PEST analysis) that may affect your project?
- Is your project both legal and ethical worldwide?
- What role does the U.S. government play in environmental protection?
- What are the basic qualifications for invitation to the WBCSD?

Write a summary of your research.

STEP 2 Plan Your Project

Now that you have completed your research, you need to begin planning your project.

- Conduct a PEST analysis.
- Write a marketing plan for your eco-friendly project, including the PEST analysis, objectives, and marketing strategies.
- Provide rationale for your project with supporting research.
- Include suggestions for your project's implementation, execution, and evaluation.
- Use your knowledge of the private enterprise system, the government's role, types of businesses, and the U.S. legal system to be sure your project is appropriate.

STEP 3 Connect with Your Community

- Observe green marketing initiatives by local businesses and global companies.
- Interview a small business owner who engages in eco-friendly business practices. Tell the business owner about your ideas for your project and ask for feedback.
- Test your ideas by conducting interviews with other trusted adults at home, at school, at work, or in your community. Ask for feedback.
- Revise your project plans as needed to incorporate any good feedback or constructive criticism.

STEP 4 Share What You Learn

Assume your class is a board of the company's top executives that will be in charge of implementing the environmental initiative.

- Present your findings in an oral presentation and be prepared to answer questions.
- Explain how companies can operate successful businesses while meeting the needs of society.
- Describe the requirements for invitation to the WBCSD.
- Use software to create a slide presentation to accompany your oral report. Include one slide for each topic in your marketing plan.

STEP 5 Evaluate Your Marketing and Academic Skills

Your project will be evaluated based on the following:

- Knowledge of current eco-projects in the real world of business
- Research to support your selection of eco-project features
- Creativity and interest in your eco-project
- Organization and continuity of presentation
- Mechanics—presentation and neatness
- Speaking and listening skills

MARKETING CORE FUNCTION
Market Planning

Marketing Internship Project Checklist

Plan
- ✓ Research current eco-friendly trends in your company's market.
- ✓ Use the results of a PEST analysis to inform your market plan for the initiative.
- ✓ Consider how complex it will be to implement the initiative internally.

Write
- ✓ Describe current eco-projects in your company's industry.
- ✓ Explain how the results of the PEST analysis will help your company's leaders decide whether to commit to this initiative.

Present
- ✓ Present your marketing plan and justify its implementation.
- ✓ Respond to questions posed by the audience.
- ✓ Consider the needs and experiences of the audience as you communicate your research with your class.

glencoe.com

Evaluate Download a rubric you can use to evaluate your final project.

my marketing portfolio

Internship Report Once you have completed your Marketing Internship Project and oral presentation, put your written report and a few printouts of key slides from your oral presentation in your Marketing Portfolio.

Research and Develop a Marketing Plan Do research and create a marketing plan for another socially conscious issue a company may support. Consider projects involving health-related issues, homelessness, disaster relief, or a local issue. Does your research provide the rationale to support the issue? How engaging and creative is your plan? Does it meet the criteria set forth in the objectives of the marketing plan? How will you implement and evaluate the plan? Prepare a written report and an oral presentation.

EVALUATE

Anticipation Activity

Project Objective Read the project objective aloud to students: ***Develop an effective eco-project (initiative) for your company, a global manufacturer of sports footwear.*** Then ask students to think about what they learned about global business, social responsibility in business, and ethics in marketing in Unit 3. Remind them of these key points:

- Socially responsible businesses demonstrate concern through initiatives for positive change in the environment, workplace, and community.
- Businesses in most countries are regulated by their governments to varying degrees.

Ask students: ***What is the purpose of developing an environmental initiative?*** Creating an environmental initiative can boost a company's public image to consumers. Many consumers consciously do business with companies that practice social responsibility.

Ask students: ***Why should you research the legality and ethicality of your project worldwide?*** Ethics are guidelines for good behavior, based on knowing the difference between right and wrong. However, there can be differences between ethics and the law, especially if there are cultural differences involved from one country to another.

Graphic Organizer

Display this diagram. Ask students to list the kinds of environmental issues that could be addressed by a business's eco-friendly project. Possible answers:

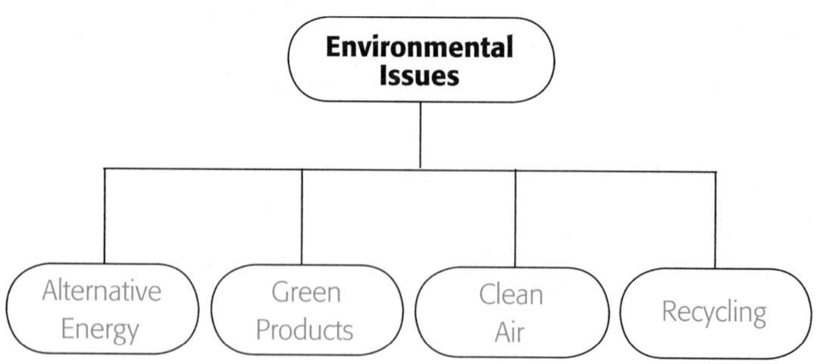

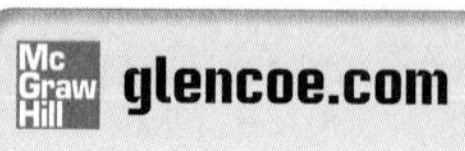

glencoe.com

iWB

Graphic Organizer Send students to the Online Learning Center to print this graphic organizer.

EVALUATE

STEP 1 Do Your Research

Tell students that there are many places to find information they can use to develop their eco-projects for a global sports footwear company. Students can use library and Internet resources, but they should also talk to people in the community. Encourage students to seek the opinions and ideas of trusted people they know. Other people can bring new perspectives and ideas about environmental initiatives undertaken at other companies as well as the PEST and legal factors.

STEP 2 Plan Your Project

Students should create a detailed PEST analysis before choosing their eco-projects and writing their marketing plans. Students should explain why they chose their projects and provide information on their market. Students' explanation of the marketing plan should include the PEST analysis, objectives, and marketing strategies, and reflect knowledge of the private enterprise system, the government's role, types of businesses, and the U.S. legal system.

STEP 3 Connect with Your Community

Explain to students that connecting with members of the community is a great way to build relationships. Tell them that young people who are capable of building relationships with caring, responsible, and competent adults are more prepared to achieve success in life. Encourage students to take part in opportunities for trusted adults to serve as mentors, coaches, advocates, and advisors.

STEP 4 Share What You Learn

Students should present their ideas in a written report and oral presentation with presentation software. They should have at least one slide in their presentation for each key topic in the written report. Encourage students to speak clearly, use appropriate grammar and vocabulary, and actively engage the audience by making and maintaining eye contact and using movement (facial expressions, posture, gestures) to focus attention and interest.

STEP 5 Evaluate Your Marketing and Academic Skills

Have students use the Marketing Internship Project Checklist to help them to plan, write, and present their reports. Exemplary written reports will include information that clearly supports a central thesis, a single, distinct focus, generally well-developed ideas, well-phrased sentences that flow smoothly and are varied in length and structure, consistently precise word choice, and few, if any, errors in grammar, spelling, and mechanics.

glencoe.com

Evaluation Rubric Send students to the Online Learning Center to get a rubric to evaluate their projects.

Culminating Activity

Explain to students that one way marketers can promote socially responsible initiatives, such as initiatives focusing on the environment or social issues, is through public service announcements (PSAs) aired on television, radio, or via the Internet on videos and podcasts. Ask students: ***What are some examples of PSAs and how do they benefit the cause and/or the sponsor?*** Answers will vary. Accept all reasonable answers. Sample answer might be NBA Cares is the league's social responsibility initiative that builds on the NBA's tradition of addressing important social issues (nutrition, Special Olympics, children's health and fitness) in the United States and around the world.

my marketing portfolio

Internship Report Have students put their written reports and printouts of key slides from their oral presentations in their marketing portfolio.

Research and Develop a Marketing Plan Direct students to select a socially conscious issue for a company to support, and then do research and create a marketing plan around this issue. Students' completed marketing plan for the initiative should include all of the elements and answer all of the questions included in the Marketing Internship Project on this page. This additional activity can build relevance for students who are motivated to learn about other specific business and industries. Relevance shifts the focus to what motivates individual students to learn.

UNIT 4 Skills for Marketing

PLANNING GUIDE AND RESOURCES

	Print	Digital
Unit 4 Skills for Marketing		Unit 4 Fast Files: Marketing Internship Project Activity Connect Online Learning Center through glencoe.com
Chapter 7 **Basic Math Skills**	Student Activity Workbook: Chapter 7 DECA Connection Role Play; Chapter 7 Vocabulary Activity; Section Note Taking Activities; Chapter Academics Activity; Section Study Skills Activities; Section Real-World Applications Activities Mathematics for Marketing Workbook Marketing Research Project Workbook School-to-Career Activity Workbook	Unit 4 Fast Files: Chapter 7 Discovery Project Worksheet and Rubric; Chapter 7 Green Marketer Activity; Chapter 7 Digital Nation Activity; Section Graphic Organizers; Section Outlines with Key Terms and Definitions; Section Summaries ExamView Assessment Suite, Chapter 7 Connect Online Learning Center through glencoe.com
Chapter 8 **Communication Skills**	Student Activity Workbook: Chapter 8 DECA Connection Role Play; Chapter 8 Vocabulary Activity; Section Note Taking Activities; Chapter Academics Activity; Section Study Skills Activities; Section Real-World Applications Activities Mathematics for Marketing Workbook Marketing Research Project Workbook School-to-Career Activity Workbook	Unit 4 Fast Files: Chapter 8 Discovery Project Worksheet and Rubric; Chapter 8 Green Marketer Activity; Chapter 8 Digital Nation Activity; Section Graphic Organizers; Section Outlines with Key Terms and Definitions; Section Summaries ExamView Assessment Suite, Chapter 8 Connect Online Learning Center through glencoe.com
Chapter 9 **Technology for Marketing**	Student Activity Workbook: Chapter 9 DECA Connection Role Play; Chapter 9 Vocabulary Activity; Section Note Taking Activities; Chapter Academics Activity; Section Study Skills Activities; Section Real-World Applications Activities Mathematics for Marketing Workbook Marketing Research Project Workbook School-to-Career Activity Workbook	Unit 4 Fast Files: Chapter 9 Discovery Project Worksheet and Rubric; Chapter 9 Green Marketer Activity; Chapter 9 Digital Nation Activity; Section Graphic Organizers; Section Outlines with Key Terms and Definitions; Section Summaries ExamView Assessment Suite, Chapter 9 Connect Online Learning Center through glencoe.com
Chapter 10 **Interpersonal Skills**	Student Activity Workbook: Chapter 10 DECA Connection Role Play; Chapter 10 Vocabulary Activity; Section Note Taking Activities; Chapter Academics Activity; Section Study Skills Activities; Section Real-World Applications Activities Mathematics for Marketing Workbook Marketing Research Project Workbook School-to-Career Activity Workbook	Unit 4 Fast Files: Chapter 10 Discovery Project Worksheet and Rubric; Chapter 10 Green Marketer Activity; Chapter 10 Digital Nation Activity; Section Graphic Organizers; Section Outlines with Key Terms and Definitions; Section Summaries ExamView Assessment Suite, Chapter 10 Connect Online Learning Center through glencoe.com
Chapter 11 **Management Skills**	Student Activity Workbook: Chapter 11 DECA Connection Role Play; Chapter 11 Vocabulary Activities; Section Note Taking Activities; Chapter Academics Activity; Section Study Skills Activities; Section Real-World Applications Activities Mathematics for Marketing Workbook Marketing Research Project Workbook School-to-Career Activity Workbook	Unit 4 Fast Files: Chapter 11 Discovery Project Worksheet and Rubric; Chapter 11 Green Marketer Activity; Chapter 11 Digital Nation Activity; Section Graphic Organizers; Section Outlines with Key Terms and Definitions; Section Summaries ExamView Assessment Suite, Chapter 11 Connect Online Learning Center through glencoe.com

McGRAW-HILL PROFESSIONAL DEVELOPMENT

Perkins IV has placed more emphasis than ever on providing quality professional development for Career and Technology educators. The legislation mandates that the focus of professional development be the integration and reinforcement of academic competencies in order to improve student achievement. Specifically, Perkins requires measurements of students' academic success. McGraw-Hill answers the challenge for strong and effective professional development with a five-prong **Online Professional Development for Integrating Academics.**

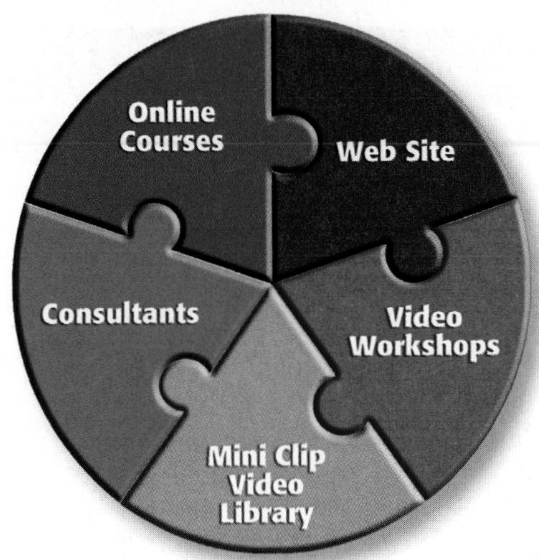

For pricing and ordering information contact your McGraw-Hill Sales Representative.

VIDEO LIBRARY

The McGraw-Hill Professional Development Mini-Clip Video Library, referenced for your convenience at the point of use, provides teaching strategies to strengthen academic and learning skills. Go to the Online Learning Center to view these professional development video clips for Unit 4:

Chapter 7: Basic Math Skills

- **Mathematics: Understanding Fractions:** An algebra teacher discusses the importance of fraction concepts in pre-algebra instruction. (p. 165)
- **Math: Communication in Mathematics:** An expert explains the importance of student communication in the mathematics classroom. (p. 175)
- **Mathematics: Ways of Working—Solving Equations:** A teacher uses partner work and whole group instruction to build understanding of the equation-solving process. (p. 179)

Chapter 8: Communication Skills

- **Reading: Attentive Reading:** A teacher uses read aloud and direct questioning to help her students identify elements of a persuasive essay. (p. 191)
- **ELL: Words in Action:** Students act out vocabulary words. (p. 195)
- **ELL: Direct Vocabulary Instruction:** Students create vocabulary cards. (p. 199)

Chapter 9: Technology for Marketing

- **Reading: Building Vocabulary:** A teacher introduces and plays vocabulary-building games with students. (p. 213)
- **Math: Understanding Fractions:** An algebra teacher discusses the importance of fraction concepts in pre-algebra instruction. (p. 225)

Chapter 10: Interpersonal Skills

- **Reading: Connecting the Pieces:** A teacher assesses ways to help students develop predictions and inferences. (p. 233)

Chapter 11: Management Skills

- **Reading: Differentiated Activities:** A teacher models ways to create vocabulary cards that support different learning styles. (p. 253)
- **Reading: Scaffolding Questions:** A teacher uses a series of questions to lead a student to an appropriate verbal response. (p. 263)
- **Reading: Connecting the Pieces:** A teacher helps students develop predictions and inferences. (p. 264)

UNIT OVERVIEW

Sections	Objectives	Common Core State Standards College and Career Readiness
Section 7.1 **Math Fundamentals**	• Express numbers with letters, using commas and hyphens. • Explain fractions. • Perform basic math operations with decimal numbers and round answers. • Convert fractions to decimal equivalents.	• **Reading** Interpret words and phrases as they are used in a text, including determining technical, connotative, and figurative meanings, and analyze how specific word choices shape meaning or tone.
Section 7.2 **Interpreting Numbers**	• Use a calculator to solve math problems. • Convert percentages to decimals and decimals to percentages. • Read graphs used to present mathematical skills.	• **Reading** Integrate and evaluate content presented in diverse formats and media, including visually and quantitatively, as well as in words.
Section 8.1 **Defining Communication**	• Define effective verbal and nonverbal communication. • Explain the role of listening in communication. • Explain why awareness of cultural differences is important. • Define reading for meaning.	• **Writing** Produce clear and coherent writing in which the development, organization, and style are appropriate to task, purpose, and audience.
Section 8.2 **Speech and Writing**	• Explain how to organize and present your ideas. • Demonstrate professional telephone communication skills. • Explain how to write effective business letters and persuasive messages.	• **Reading** Write informative/explanatory texts to examine and convey complex ideas and information clearly and accurately through the effective selection, organization, and analysis of content.
Section 9.1 **Computer Applications**	• Identify nine types of computer applications. • Explain how computer applications are used in business and marketing.	• **Writing** Conduct short as well as more sustained research projects based on focused questions, demonstrating understanding of the subject under investigation.
Section 9.2 **Technology and Marketing**	• Describe the computer software programs that are influencing and reshaping marketing. • Explain how the Internet and the World Wide Web can increase business productivity.	• **Writing** Produce clear and coherent writing in which the development, organization, and style are appropriate to task, purpose, and audience.

Sections	Objectives	Common Core State Standards College and Career Readiness
Section 10.1 **Personal Interactions**	• Identify the personal traits necessary for ethical action in the workplace. • List important interpersonal skills. • Perform effectively in diverse environments. • Manage conflicts by using appropriate negotiation skills.	• **Writing** Produce clear and coherent writing in which the development, organization, and style are appropriate to task, purpose, and audience.
Section 10.2 **Leadership and Teamwork**	• Discuss how to receive and handle customer complaints. • Identify skills needed to be a good team member and provide leadership. • List six aspects of successful teamwork.	• **Reading** Interpret words and phrases as they are used in a text, including determining technical, connotative, and figurative meanings, and analyze how specific word choices shape meaning or tone.
Section 11.1 **Management Structures**	• Explain how horizontally organized companies differ from vertically organized companies. • Name the three levels of management in a vertically organized company. • Explain how a self-management team functions.	• **Writing** Conduct short as well as more sustained research projects based on focused questions, demonstrating understanding of the subject under investigation.
Section 11.2 **Management Functions**	• Name three functions of management. • Describe the management techniques used by effective managers. • Explain how to manage employees properly.	• **Writing** Produce clear and coherent writing in which the development, organization, and style are appropriate to task, purpose, and audience.

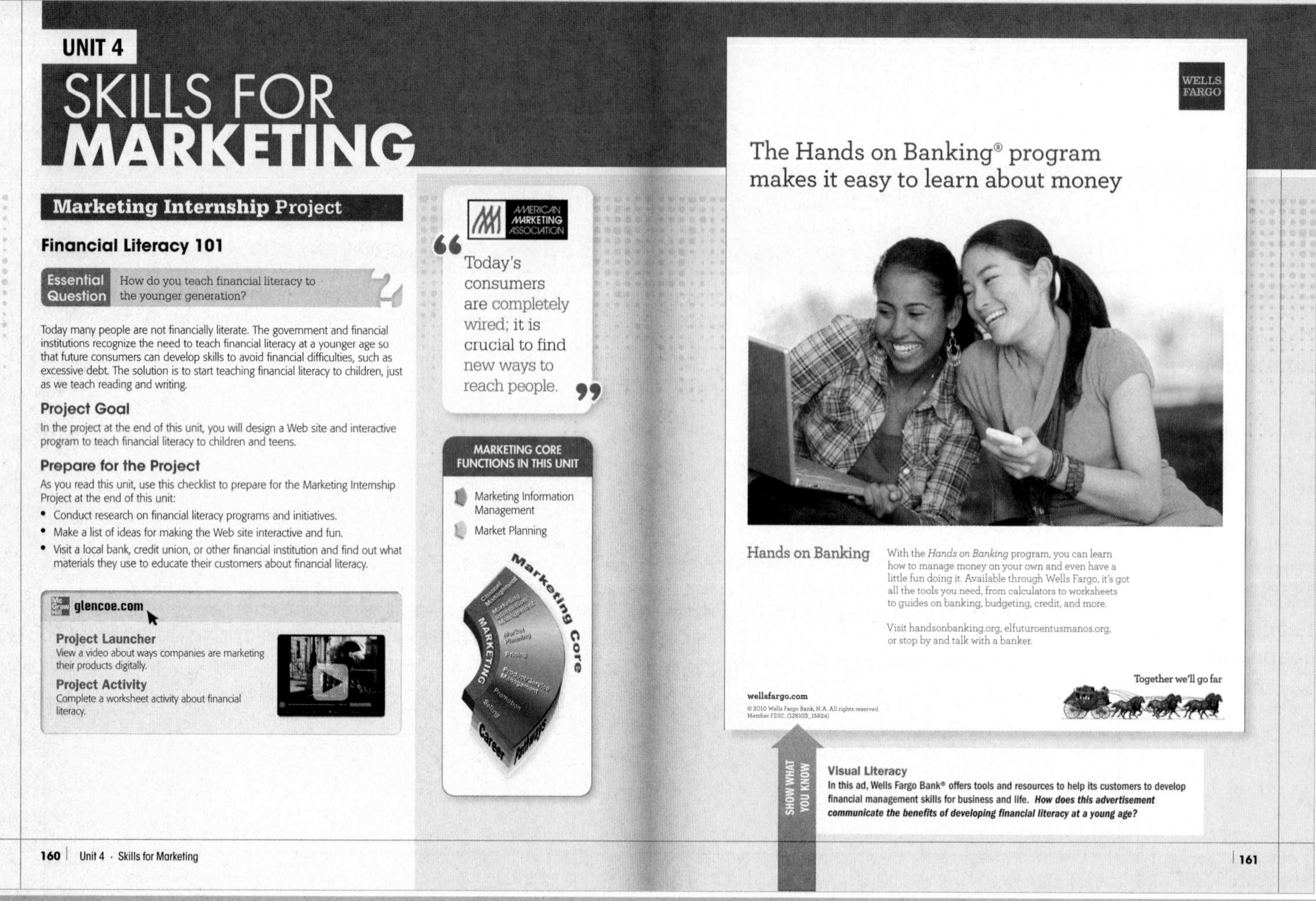

UNIT 4

SKILLS FOR MARKETING

Marketing Internship Project

Financial Literacy 101

Essential Question How do you teach financial literacy to the younger generation?

Today many people are not financially literate. The government and financial institutions recognize the need to teach financial literacy at a younger age so that future consumers can develop skills to avoid financial difficulties, such as excessive debt. The solution is to start teaching financial literacy to children, just as we teach reading and writing.

Project Goal

In the project at the end of this unit, you will design a Web site and interactive program to teach financial literacy to children and teens.

Prepare for the Project

As you read this unit, use this checklist to prepare for the Marketing Internship Project at the end of this unit:

- Conduct research on financial literacy programs and initiatives.
- Make a list of ideas for making the Web site interactive and fun.
- Visit a local bank, credit union, or other financial institution and find out what materials they use to educate their customers about financial literacy.

glencoe.com

Project Launcher View a video about ways companies are marketing their products digitally.

Project Activity Complete a worksheet activity about financial literacy.

AMERICAN MARKETING ASSOCIATION

"Today's consumers are completely wired; it is crucial to find new ways to reach people."

MARKETING CORE FUNCTIONS IN THIS UNIT

- Marketing Information Management
- Market Planning

SHOW WHAT YOU KNOW

Visual Literacy
In this ad, Wells Fargo Bank® offers tools and resources to help its customers to develop financial management skills for business and life. ***How does this advertisement communicate the benefits of developing financial literacy at a young age?***

160 | Unit 4 · Skills for Marketing

161

ENGAGE

Introduce the Unit

Unit 4 introduces the concepts of business, marketing, and technology along with the basic skills necessary for success.

Chapter 7 provides a review of basic mathematical skills.

Chapter 8 focuses on communication skills.

Chapter 9 discusses current technologies used in marketing.

Chapter 10 focuses on teamwork and interpersonal skills.

Chapter 11 explains management functions and techniques.

Build Background

Ask students to identify different skills they think would be important for a marketing career. List their ideas on the board. Answers will vary but may include computer/Internet skills, communication skills, interpersonal skills. Ask students: ***What courses might be most beneficial for pursuing a career in marketing?*** Typical courses might include English, mathematics, statistics, computer courses, business courses, public speaking, courses related to a specialty such as sports marketing.

Visual Literacy

Photo Caption Answer Read the copy on the ad to students. Then read the photo caption and the photo caption question to students: ***How does this advertisement communicate the benefits of developing financial literacy at a young age?*** Answers will vary. Accept all reasonable answers. Sample answer: This ad represents two older teenaged girls, probably about to embark on financial independence. The text in the ad indicates that learning about money can be easy and fun, and not just for adults. Ask students to evaluate the visual components of the advertisement. Ask volunteers to explain how the visual aspects of the advertisement complement the text of the advertisement. The photograph shows two girls who are laughing and having fun with what they are doing on their mobile devices. The photo fits in with the text in the ad that says that the *Hands On Banking* program can be easy and fun to learn.

ENGAGE

Marketing Internship Project Preview

Read students the Marketing Internship Project Essential Question: ***How do you teach financial literacy to the younger generation?*** Students should know that learning math and the basics of saving and investing at a young age can be valuable in the future. The specific answer to this question is to make financial literacy accessible to young people through educational programs. Explain to students that they will learn about basic math, technology, and communication skills while studying this unit. Tell students that when they are finished studying this unit, they will design a financial literacy Web site for children and teens. As they study each chapter in the unit, they can prepare for the Unit Project by thinking of ideas for making a Web site fun and informative.

glencoe.com

Marketing Internship Project Resources Send students to the Online Learning Center to watch a video and download a worksheet activity related to the topic of the Unit Project.

Read the American Marketing Association quote to students:

“Today's consumers are completely wired; it is crucial to find new ways to reach people.”

Explain to students that the AMA's Resource Library provides information on integrating technology into marketing plans. Because consumers are “wired,” technology enables new ways to reach target markets.

Facebook A defacto standard in social media marketing, the opportunities to build sales are plentiful.

Twitter Twitter has rapidly become the hot tool for marketing and communications.

E-Mail There are billions of users.

Blogs Literally millions of blogs exist and many cater to unique micro-niches.

Ask students: ***What are some other examples of how technology is used in marketing?*** Web sites and video sharing site are examples of technology used in marketing.

MARKETING CORE FUNCTIONS IN THIS UNIT

Point out to students that Chapters 7, 8, 9, 10, and 11 will touch on two of the seven marketing core functions. Describe each of these marketing functions to students to prepare them to start studying this unit.

Marketing Information Management involves gathering, storing, and analyzing information about customers, trends, and competing products.

Market Planning involves understanding the concepts and strategies used to develop and target specific marketing strategies to a select audience.

MARKETING RESEARCH

PROJECT WORKBOOK

The purpose of the Marketing Research Project Workbook is to provide a step-by-step approach for students to conduct their own marketing research study. Each chapter is devoted to key elements in the research process. Each chapter builds upon the previous chapters, and by the end of the book, students will have completed an in-depth marketing research study, complete with rationale for all decisions, a report of the findings and conclusions, recommendations based on the original research problem and study objectives, and an annotated bibliography.

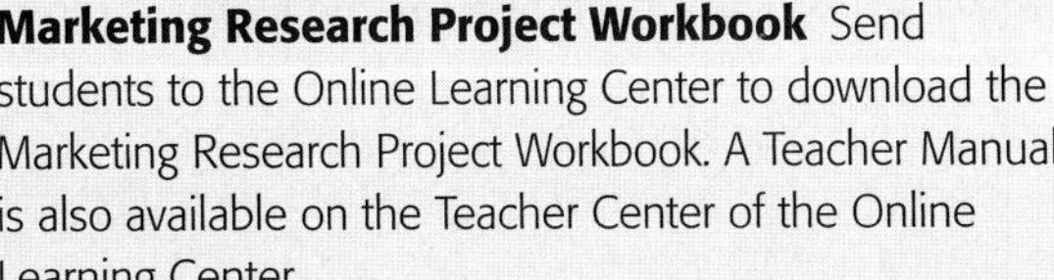
glencoe.com

Marketing Research Project Workbook Send students to the Online Learning Center to download the Marketing Research Project Workbook. A Teacher Manual is also available on the Teacher Center of the Online Learning Center.

basic math skills

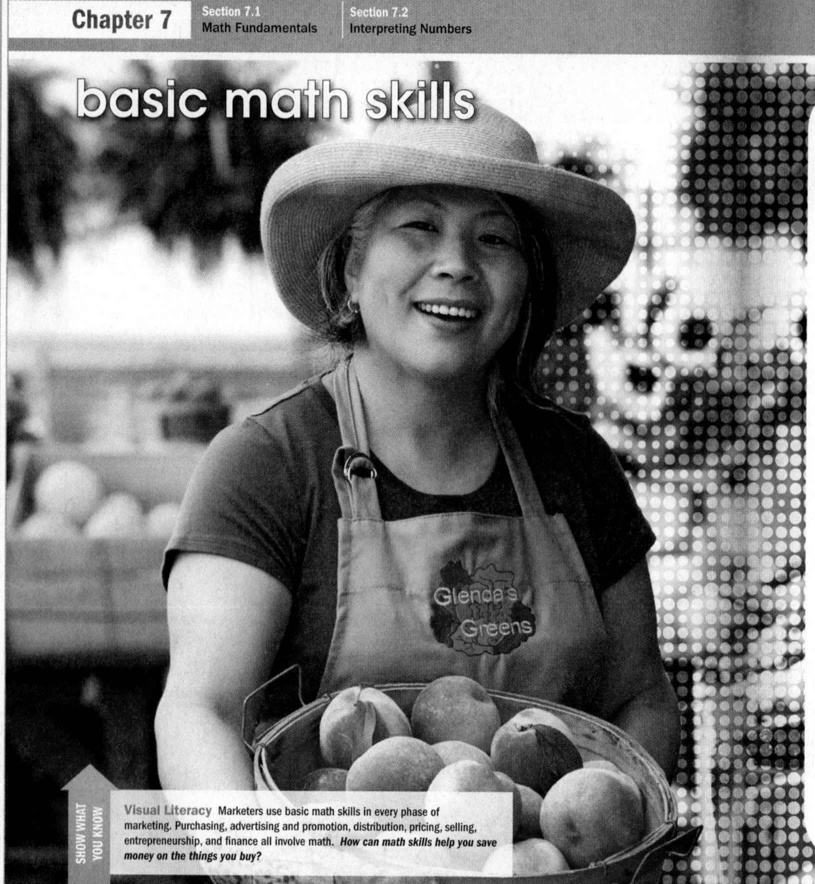

SHOW WHAT YOU KNOW

Visual Literacy Marketers use basic math skills in every phase of marketing. Purchasing, advertising and promotion, distribution, pricing, selling, entrepreneurship, and finance all involve math. ***How can math skills help you save money on the things you buy?***

Discovery Project

Using Basic Math Every Day

Essential Question How do marketers use basic math skills?

Project Goal

Assume that you are employed in a camera store that sells computers, printers, and software, as well as cameras and photographic accessories. Data shows that the profit margin on major categories of products and supplies sold for the past year was as follows: cameras at 25 percent, lenses at 27 percent, memory cards at 28 percent, batteries at 19 percent, printers at 26 percent, printer ink at 30 percent, and photo paper at 33 percent. Identify a trend or pattern in the data. Consider the different ways to display this data in a graph. Present information to your class that emphasizes the trend or pattern you identified.

Ask Yourself...

- How might this information affect the store's advertising program?
- How would the total sales in dollars in each category also affect advertising?
- What is the most effective way to present this data?
- What trends or patterns do you see in the data?

Problem Solving What additional data would be helpful for making advertising decisions?

Activity
Get a worksheet activity about basic math skills.

Evaluate
Download a rubric you can use to evaluate your project.

DECA Connection

DECA Event Role Play

Concepts in this chapter are related to DECA competitive events that involve either an interview or role play.

Performance Indicators The performance indicators represent key skills and knowledge. Your key to success in DECA competitive events is relating them to the concepts in this chapter.

- Demonstrate problem-solving skills.
- Develop a personal budget.
- Set financial goals.
- Maintain financial records.
- Demonstrate responsible behavior.

DECA Prep

Role Play Practice role-playing with the DECA Connection competitive-event activity at the end of this chapter. More information on DECA events can be found on DECA's Web site.

ENGAGE

Visual Literacy

Read the chapter opener photo caption question to students: ***How can math skills help you save money on the things you buy?*** Possible answers: Basic math skills can help you figure which product is the best buy by figuring unit costs and discounts. They can help you track money so that you don't end up short. Ask students the following guiding questions to activate prior knowledge.

Guiding Questions

Recall Can you describe a time when you saved money by using your math skills?	Possible answer: I determined that the regular price of one brand was less than the sale price of another.
Explain In what ways have you seen adults you know use basic math skills in their daily lives?	Answers may include paying bills, balancing a bank account, totalling costs while shopping, or creating a home budget.

Discovery Project

Using Basic Math Every Day Start a discussion that connects students to the Discovery Project Essential Question: ***How do marketers use basic math skills?*** Marketers use math skills in predicting or estimating potential sales or products, budgeting the cost of a marketing campaign, helping to price products and services competitively, overseeing the budget for staff, and managing accounts for customers.

glencoe.com

Discovery Project Resources Send students to the Online Learning Center to download a rubric to evaluate their projects.

ENGAGE

Introduce the Chapter

In this chapter, these basic math skills are discussed:

- Whole numbers
- Fractions
- Decimal numbers
- Operations with decimal numbers
- Surface measurements
- Calculators
- Ten-key by sight or touch
- Percentages
- Charts and graphs
- Algebraic thinking
- Descriptive statistics

Discussion Starter

Ten-Key Calculators Tell students that ten-key calculators have been popular for many years with people who have to enter many numbers rapidly. Ask students: ***Have you ever used the keypad on your computer keyboard?*** Students may or may not have used the key pad. Encourage those who have to share their experiences with the rest of the class. Ask: ***Were you able to use the keypad without looking?*** Answers will depend on students' experiences. If possible, provide students with practice using a ten-key calculator or the keypad on a computer keyboard. Encourage students to practice entering numbers without looking.

DECA Connection

Discuss the performance indicators listed in the DECA Connection feature. Explain to students that performance indicators tell them how to demonstrate their acquired skills and knowledge through individual or team competitive events.

glencoe.com

Competitive Events Workbook For more DECA Role Plays, send students to the Online Learning Center to download the Competitive Events Workbook.

PRINT RESOURCES

- **Student Edition**
- **Teacher Edition**
- **Student Activity Workbook with Academic Integration** includes worksheets and activities correlated to the text.
- **Mathematics for Marketing Workbook** provides math activities for every unit in the text.

TECHNOLOGY TOOLBOX

- **Connect**
- **ConnectPlus**
- **ExamView Assessment Suite** is a comprehensive solution for creating, administering, and scoring tests.

glencoe.com

Online Learning Center provides a variety of resources to enrich and enhance learning.

SECTION, CHAPTER, AND UNIT RESOURCES

- **Graphic Organizers** for organizing text concepts visually.
- **Digital Nation Activities** and **Green Marketer Activities** extend learning beyond the text features.
- **Career Chatroom Career Profiles** allow students to explore different marketing occupations in depth.
- **After You Read Answer Keys** for students to check their answers.
- **Discovery Project Rubrics** and **Marketing Internship Project Rubrics** for students to evaluate their projects.

PROGRAM RESOURCES

- **Student Activity Workbook with Academic Integration Teacher Annotated Edition** includes annotated answers for the activities and worksheets.
- **Marketing Research Project Workbook** provides a step-by-step approach for students to complete their own marketing research studies.
- **School-to-Career Activity Workbook** helps students relate their class work to on-the-job experience and involves work-site analysis and working with mentors.
- **Competitive Events Workbook** helps prepare students for state and national marketing education competitions.
- **Inclusion in the Marketing Education Classroom** provides teaching resources for working with students with special needs.
- **PowerPoint Presentations** provides visual teaching aids and assessments for this chapter.

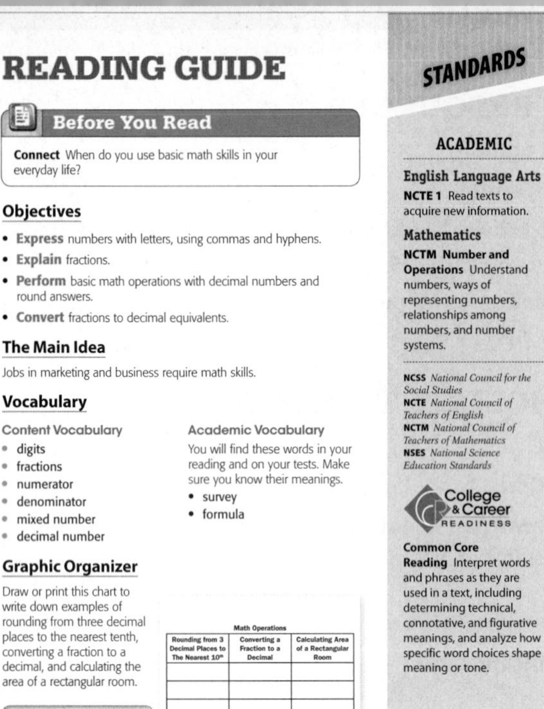

READING GUIDE

Before You Read

Connect When do you use basic math skills in your everyday life?

Objectives

- **Express** numbers with letters, using commas and hyphens.
- **Explain** fractions.
- **Perform** basic math operations with decimal numbers and round answers.
- **Convert** fractions to decimal equivalents.

The Main Idea

Jobs in marketing and business require math skills.

Vocabulary

Content Vocabulary
- digits
- fractions
- numerator
- denominator
- mixed number
- decimal number

Academic Vocabulary

You will find these words in your reading and on your tests. Make sure you know their meanings.
- survey
- formula

Graphic Organizer

Draw or print this chart to write down examples of rounding from three decimal places to the nearest tenth, converting a fraction to a decimal, and calculating the area of a rectangular room.

Math Operations

Rounding from 3 Decimal Places to The Nearest 10th	Converting a Fraction to a Decimal	Calculating Area of a Rectangular Room

glencoe.com

Print this graphic organizer.

STANDARDS

ACADEMIC

English Language Arts

NCTE 1 Read texts to acquire new information.

Mathematics

NCTM Number and Operations Understand numbers, ways of representing numbers, relationships among numbers, and number systems.

NCSS *National Council for the Social Studies*
NCTE *National Council of Teachers of English*
NCTM *National Council of Teachers of Mathematics*
NSES *National Science Education Standards*

College & Career READINESS

Common Core

Reading Interpret words and phrases as they are used in a text, including determining technical, connotative, and figurative meanings, and analyze how specific word choices shape meaning or tone.

MARKETING CORE FUNCTION

Pricing

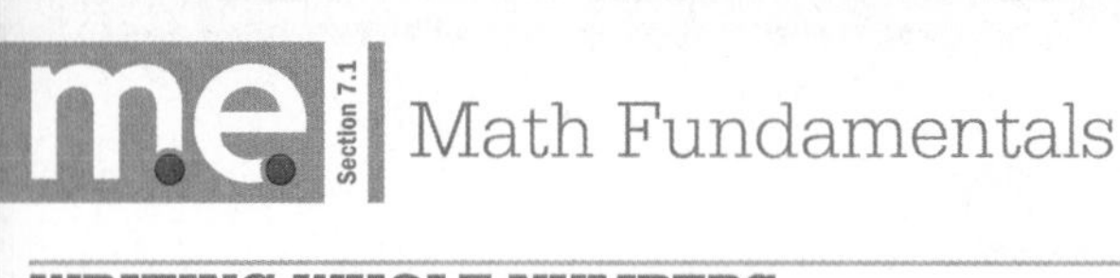

WRITING WHOLE NUMBERS

Our numbering system is composed of ten basic symbols called **digits**: 0, 1, 2, 3, 4, 5, 6, 7, 8, and 9. Each digit represents a number and can be combined to represent larger numbers, such as 25; 186; 5,749; and 46,732.

A company must know how many products are in its warehouse to do inventory.

The numbers in the previous paragraph are all whole numbers because they can be written without fractions or decimals. Each digit in a whole number represents how many of something. The digit on the far right represents the number of ones. The next digit to the left represents the number of tens. So, in the number 25, there are five ones and two tens.

As You Read

Analyze Consider the relationships of fractions, decimal numbers, and percentages to marketing.

Knowing the place name for each digit and for groups of digits is necessary for reading numbers and writing them in words. You use this skill, for example, when you write a check. The check format requires that amounts be written in both numbers and words. Follow these five steps when you read whole numbers or write them in words:

1. Separate the number into groups of three digits: units, thousands, and millions. Very large numbers may include groups of digits for billions, trillions, and even higher groups.

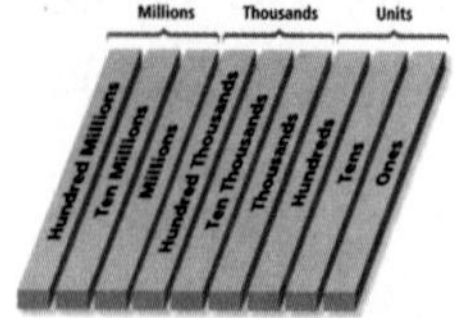

2. Separate the groups with commas.

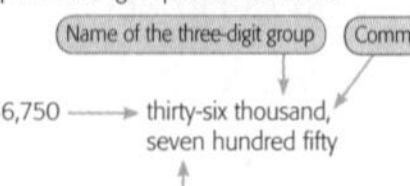

3. When writing the names of whole numbers, never use the word *and*.

360 → three hundred sixty

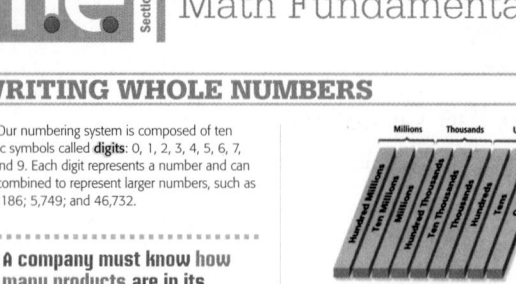

4. Use hyphens in numbers less than 100 that are written as two words.

29 → twenty-nine

Use a hyphen.

5. When a three-digit group is made up of only zeros, do not write the name of the group.

3,000,375 → three million, three hundred seventy-five

Reading Check

Recall When will you need to write numbers in numbers and words?

ENGAGE

Anticipation Activity

Improving Student Achievement Ask students: *What math skills would you need to know to run a business?* knowing how to add and subtract money (to track income), being able to figure percentages (to calculate discounts), multiplying decimals (to figure salaries). Explain to students that they will be learning about writing numbers, fractions, decimals, and calculating surface measurements.

Objectives

- **Express** numbers with letters, using commas and hyphens. Example: 34,345,227 = thirty-four million, three hundred forty-five thousand, two hundred twenty-seven
- **Explain** fractions. Fractions are numbers used to describe or compare parts of a whole (numerator—number of parts being considered; denominator—how many parts are in the whole).
- **Perform** basic math operations with decimal numbers and round answers. Example: $3.44 \times 5.4 = 18.576 = 18.6$; $26.221 \div 12.2 = 2.149 = 2.2$
- **Convert** fractions to decimal equivalents. Example: $\frac{3}{4} = 0.75$; $\frac{4}{5} = 0.8$

Graphic Organizer

Examples will vary. Sample examples:

Math Operations

Rounding from 3 Decimal Places to the Nearest 10th	Converting a Fraction to a Decimal	Calculating Area of a Rectangular Room
4.789 = 4.8	$\frac{1}{8} = 0.125$	12 ft. long, 9 ft. wide = 12 × 9 = 108 sq. ft.
774.123 = 774.1	$\frac{2}{5} = 0.4$	20 ft. long, 18 ft. wide = 20 × 18 = 360 sq. ft.
62.455 = 62.5	$\frac{2}{3} = 0.667$	35 ft. long, 30 ft. wide = 35 × 30 = 1,050 sq. ft.

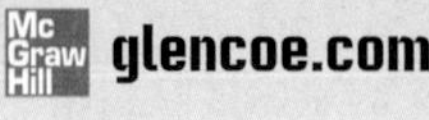

iWB

Graphic Organizer Send students to the Online Learning Center to print this graphic organizer.

EXPLORE

Before You Read

Read the Before You Read question aloud: ***When do you use basic math skills in your everyday life?*** Ask a volunteer to write students' answers on the board. Students may say that they use math when following recipes, when counting out money or receiving change for a purchase, when calculating how much ten gallons of gas will cost, when determining whether they have enough money to purchase two sweaters, and so on. Ask: ***Do you think there will ever be a time in your life when you won't need to know basic math skills?*** Most students should realize that basic math skills are used throughout one's life.

Preteaching Vocabulary

Have students go to the Online Learning Center at glencoe.com for the Chapter 7 Preteaching Vocabulary games.

Content Vocabulary

Have students write one or more sentences using the Content Vocabulary terms *fractions*, *numerator, denominator,* and *mixed number*. Sentences should explain what the terms mean and how the terms are related. Fractions are used to describe or compare parts of a whole. The top number of the fraction, or the numerator, tells how many parts are being considered. The bottom number of the fraction, the denominator, tells how many parts are in the whole. A mixed number is made up of a whole number and a fraction.

Academic Vocabulary

Survey—Contextual Meaning Display the following sentence: The marketing research department of a soap company did a *survey*. Ask students: ***Based on the way it is used in this sentence, what is the meaning of the term* survey?** a research study to collect data for a particular purpose

Formula—Alternate Meanings Explain to students that the term *formula* is used to mean a mathematical equation. Ask: ***What other meanings of the term* formula *are you familiar with?*** Possible answer: chemical recipes

Mathematics: Understanding Fractions
A teacher discusses the importance of fraction concepts.

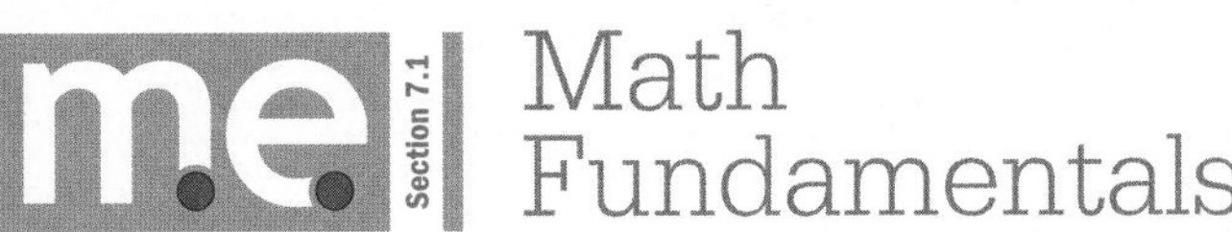

WRITING WHOLE NUMBERS

Tell students that in marketing, knowledge of whole numbers is important. Whole numbers are made up of the ten basic digits. Ask these guiding questions to focus the discussion about whole numbers.

Guiding Questions

Explain why the following numbers are whole numbers: 27, 92, 11,145, 8,704, 3	These are whole numbers; they are written without fractions or decimals.
Apply How would you write 23,654,786 in words?	Twenty-three million, six hundred fifty-four thousand, seven hundred eighty-six
Demonstrate Where would you place commas in the following number? 23984761256498	23,984,761,256,498
Analyze In the following number, which digit is in the tens place? The thousands place? 23,659	5 is in the tens place; 3 is in the thousands place.

As You Read

Read students the As You Read question: ***Consider the relationships of fractions, decimal numbers, and percentages to marketing.*** Fractions—market research; decimals—pricing, purchasing, selling, and finance; and percentages—advertising and promotion.

Expert Advice

Read the quote to students:

> **"A company must know how many products are in its warehouse to do inventory."**

Ask students: ***Why is it important for a company to know how many products it has in its warehouse?*** It needs to know how many products to order to be able to fill future orders for customers.

Reading Check Answer

Read the Reading Check question to students: ***When will you need to write numbers in numbers and words?*** This is needed when writing checks.

FRACTIONS

The marketing research department of a soap company did a **survey**. They found that two thirds of the people who bought their new dish detergent thought it did a better job than the competition. This means that for every three people surveyed, two were pleased with the new product and one was not. Many jobs in business, especially in marketing, require a good understanding of fractions.

Fractions are numbers used to describe or compare parts of a whole. The top number, the **numerator**, represents the number of parts being considered. The bottom number, the **denominator**, represents how many parts in a whole. For example, the shaded area in the rectangle below is $\frac{3}{5}$ (three fifths) of the total rectangle.

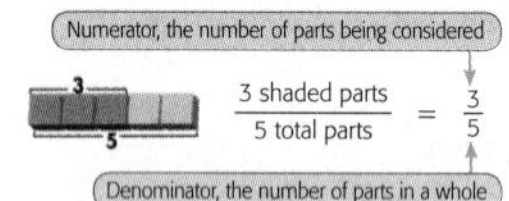

In the example below, the number of circles is $\frac{2}{7}$ (two sevenths) of the total number of shapes.

$\frac{\text{2 circles}}{\text{7 shapes}} = \frac{2}{7}$

Here are more examples illustrating the same principle.

$\frac{\text{Number of shaded parts}}{\text{Total number of parts}} = \frac{3}{8}$

$\frac{\text{3 shaded parts}}{\text{Total number of parts}} = \frac{3}{3} = 1$

One whole circle is shaded.

$\frac{\text{5 shaded triangles}}{\text{4 triangles in a square}} = \frac{5}{4}$ of a square

A fraction can describe a number greater than 1.

When the numerator is greater than the denominator, the fraction describes a number greater than one. It can be written as a **mixed number**, which is a whole number and a fraction.

$\frac{6}{5} = 1\frac{1}{5}$ ← Mixed number

Numerator is greater than denominator.

PRACTICE 1

What fraction of each shape is shaded?

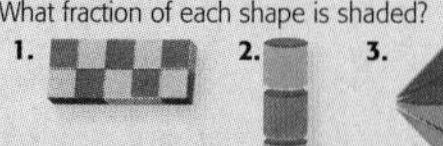

Answer each question with a fraction:

6. If you spend eight hours a day sleeping, what fraction of the day are you asleep?
7. You have saved $75 of the $250 you need to buy a new printer. What fraction of the money do you still need to save?
8. A class has 12 females and 18 males. What fraction of the class is female?
9. If one-third of your family's income is spent on housing, what fraction is left for other expenses?
10. Seventy-five cents represents what fraction of one dollar?

Check answers to all practice sets.

Reading Check

Recall What is the name for a fraction that has a greater numerator than its denominator?

DECIMAL NUMBERS

A **decimal number** is another way to write a fraction or mixed number whose denominator is a power of 10 (10, 100, 1000, etc.). The decimal number 5.3 means $5 + 0.3$ or $5 + \frac{3}{10}$ or $5\frac{3}{10}$. The decimal number 935.47 can be broken down as $900 + 30 + 5 + \frac{4}{10} + \frac{7}{100}$.

Knowing place names is necessary for reading decimals and writing them in words. Decimal place names apply to digits to the right of the decimal point.

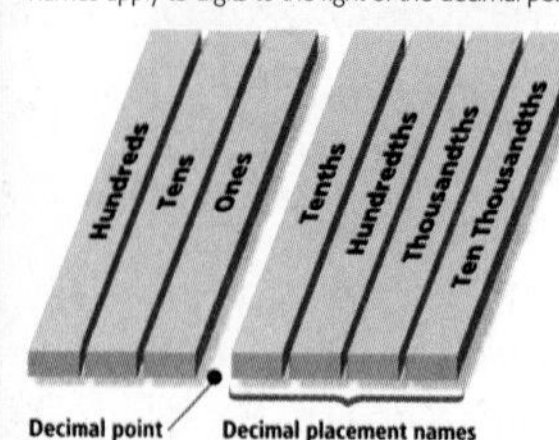

To read a decimal number or write it in words, follow these steps. Use 15.083 as an example.

1. Begin with the whole number to the left of the decimal point *(fifteen)*.
2. Read or write *and* for the decimal point.
3. Read or write the number to the right of the decimal point as a whole number *(eighty-three)*.
4. Use the name of the decimal place of the final digit *(thousandths)*.

The result is *fifteen and eighty-three thousandths.*

You may also hear decimal numbers read using the whole number and the names of the digits in the decimal places. In this method, *point* stands for the decimal point. For example, 9.7 could also be read as *nine point seven;* 15.083 might be read as *fifteen point zero eight three.*

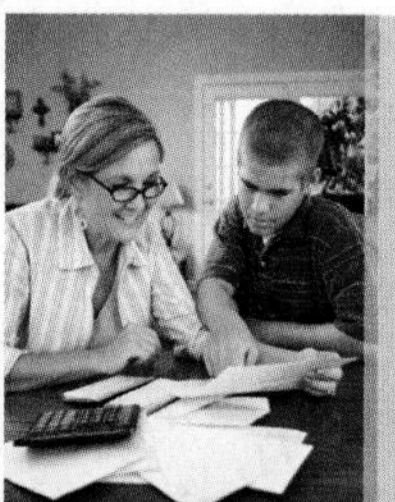

More and more people pay bills online or use electronic funds transfer, but writing checks is still an essential skill. On a check, the amount must be written in words and as a decimal number. ***What other math skills are required to manage a checking account?***

Representing Numbers

WRITING NUMBERS

Why is it important for you to know how to write decimals and fractions and to understand the relationship between the two?

The relationship between decimals and fractions is important for writing checks. After writing the amount as a decimal, you must write it again. This time it is in words for the dollars and a fraction for the cents. (See **Figure 7.1** on p. 168.)

PRACTICE 2

Write the decimals in words. Write the money amounts in words for dollars and fractions for cents. Write the words in decimals.

1. 7.8
2. 0.4
3. 33.67
4. 0.083
5. $87.40
6. $639.89
7. $132.07
8. Six thousand, one hundred sixty-four and eight tenths
9. Four hundred four and seven hundredths
10. Seven hundred twenty-one dollars and thirty-seven cents

Reading Check

Apply What are two ways of reading *14.20?*

EXPLAIN

Mini Project

Differentiated Instruction

Gifted Students/Students with Learning Disabilities

Divide the class into groups containing a mix of gifted students and students with learning disabilities. Have student groups write a number of fractions and take turns identifying: numerator, denominator, and mixed numbers. Ask: ***Which number is the numerator? Which is the denominator?*** Answers will vary depending on the fractions. Then have students write fractions and draw shaded figures that represent the fractions.

Reading Check Answer

Read the Reading Check question to students: ***What is the name for the fraction that has a larger numerator than its denominator?*** The fraction describes a number greater than one and is called a mixed number.

PRACTICE 1 ANSWERS

1. $\frac{5}{10} = \frac{1}{2}$
2. $\frac{1}{3}$
3. $\frac{2}{4} = \frac{1}{2}$
4. $\frac{11}{16}$
5. $\frac{8}{8}$ or 1
6. $\frac{8}{24} = \frac{1}{3}$
7. $\frac{75}{250} = \frac{3}{10}$; you would need to save $\frac{7}{10}$
8. $\frac{12}{30} = \frac{2}{5}$
9. $\frac{2}{3}$
10. $\frac{75}{100}$ or $\frac{3}{4}$

ELABORATE

DECIMAL NUMBERS

Explain to students that decimal numbers are a part of their everyday lives. They will need to be familiar with them in order to understand how they are used in marketing as well as other areas of their lives. Then ask these guiding questions to focus the discussion on decimal numbers.

Guiding Questions

Identify What is the place name of the underlined number? (Display these numbers, underlining the appropriate number.) A. 44.15 B. 387.4 C. 9,782.137 D. 497.4498 E. 59.495	A. hundredths B. tenths C. ones D. ten thousandths E. thousandths
Explain How would you read aloud these numbers? (Write the following numbers on the board.) A. 3,498.223 B. 47.29 C. 987.1245 D. 449.3 E. 9,824.246	A. three thousand, four hundred ninety-eight and two hundred twenty-three thousandths B. forty-seven and twenty-nine hundredths C. nine hundred eighty-seven and one thousand, two hundred forty-five ten thousandths D. four hundred forty-nine and three tenths E. nine thousand, eight hundred twenty-four and two hundred forty-six thousandths

Mini Projects

Enrichment

Practice Decimals Have students make flashcards and write different decimal numbers on each. Then have pairs take turns showing their partner a flashcard. Then, ask: ***What, if any, problems did you have in reading the decimal numbers?*** Offer more practice by writing additional decimal numbers on the board.

Survey Managers Conduct a survey in which students interview business managers about the math skills they require of their employees. Have students figure the percentage of the class that has each math skill listed on the board. Percentages will vary depending on the types of businesses surveyed.

PRACTICE 2 ANSWERS

1. Seven and eight-tenths
2. Four-tenths
3. Thirty-three and sixty-seven hundredths
4. Eighty-three thousandths
5. Eighty-seven and $\frac{40}{100}$ dollars
6. Six hundred thirty-nine and $\frac{89}{100}$ dollars
7. One hundred thirty-two and $\frac{7}{100}$ dollars
8. 6,164.8
9. 404.07
10. $721.37

Reading Check Answer

Read the Reading Check question to students: ***What are two ways of reading 14.20?*** (1) fourteen and twenty hundredths; (2) fourteen point two zero.

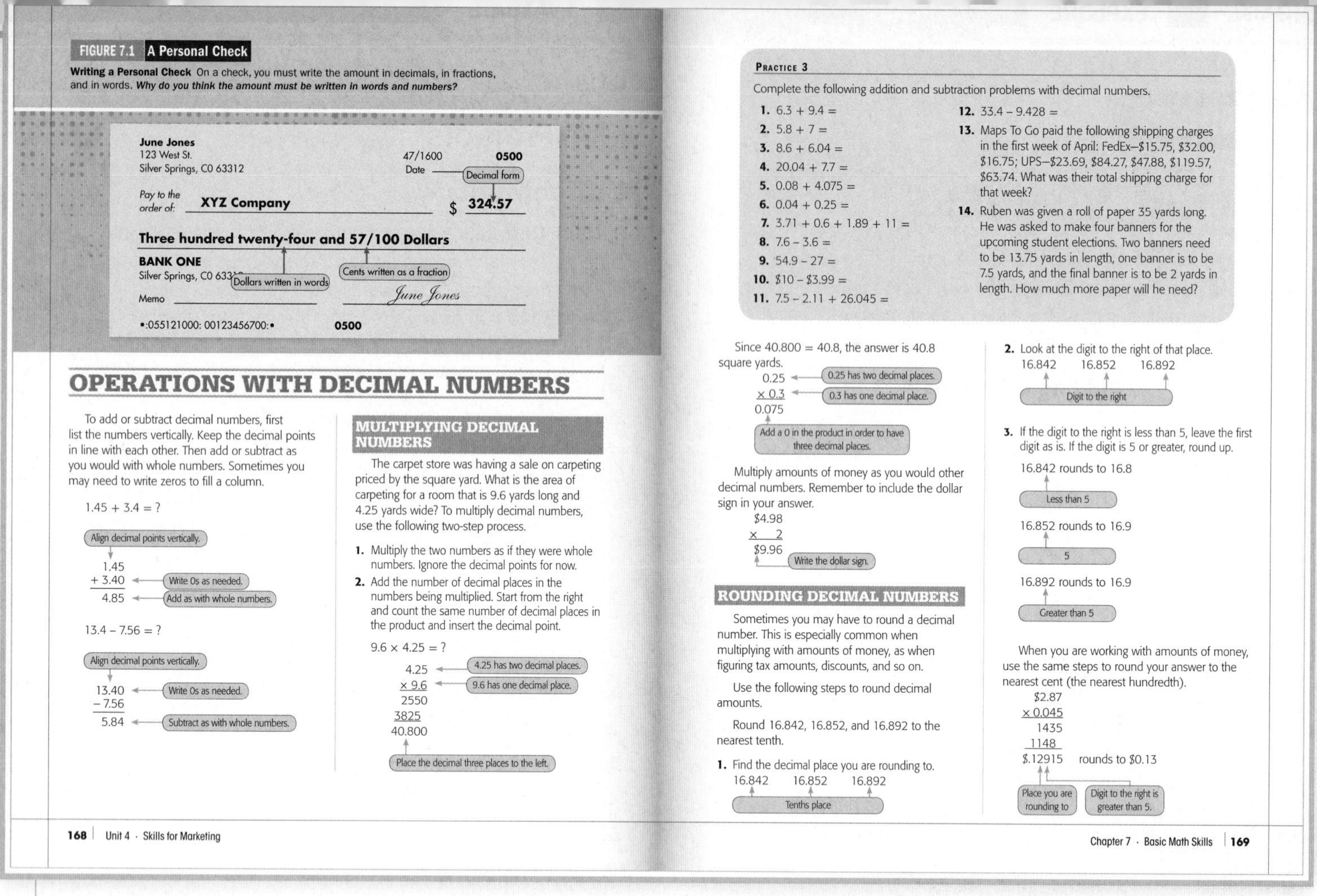

FIGURE 7.1 A Personal Check

Writing a Personal Check On a check, you must write the amount in decimals, in fractions, and in words. ***Why do you think the amount must be written in words and numbers?***

June Jones
123 West St.
Silver Springs, CO 63312

47/1600 0500
Date ______ (Decimal form)

Pay to the order of: XYZ Company $ 324.57

Three hundred twenty-four and 57/100 Dollars

BANK ONE
Silver Springs, CO 63312 (Dollars written in words) (Cents written as a fraction)

Memo ______ *June Jones*

•:055121000: 00123456700:• 0500

OPERATIONS WITH DECIMAL NUMBERS

To add or subtract decimal numbers, first list the numbers vertically. Keep the decimal points in line with each other. Then add or subtract as you would with whole numbers. Sometimes you may need to write zeros to fill a column.

1.45 + 3.4 = ?

(Align decimal points vertically.)

```
  1.45
+ 3.40   ← Write 0s as needed.
  4.85   ← Add as with whole numbers.
```

13.4 − 7.56 = ?

(Align decimal points vertically.)

```
  13.40  ← Write 0s as needed.
 − 7.56
   5.84  ← Subtract as with whole numbers.
```

MULTIPLYING DECIMAL NUMBERS

The carpet store was having a sale on carpeting priced by the square yard. What is the area of carpeting for a room that is 9.6 yards long and 4.25 yards wide? To multiply decimal numbers, use the following two-step process.

1. Multiply the two numbers as if they were whole numbers. Ignore the decimal points for now.
2. Add the number of decimal places in the numbers being multiplied. Start from the right and count the same number of decimal places in the product and insert the decimal point.

9.6 × 4.25 = ?

```
   4.25  ← 4.25 has two decimal places.
 × 9.6   ← 9.6 has one decimal place.
  2550
 3825
 40.800
```

(Place the decimal three places to the left.)

Since 40.800 = 40.8, the answer is 40.8 square yards.

```
  0.25  ← 0.25 has two decimal places.
 × 0.3  ← 0.3 has one decimal place.
 0.075
```

(Add a 0 in the product in order to have three decimal places.)

Multiply amounts of money as you would other decimal numbers. Remember to include the dollar sign in your answer.

```
  $4.98
 ×   2
  $9.96
```

(Write the dollar sign.)

ROUNDING DECIMAL NUMBERS

Sometimes you may have to round a decimal number. This is especially common when multiplying with amounts of money, as when figuring tax amounts, discounts, and so on.

Use the following steps to round decimal amounts.

Round 16.842, 16.852, and 16.892 to the nearest tenth.

1. Find the decimal place you are rounding to.
   16.842 16.852 16.892 (Tenths place)
2. Look at the digit to the right of that place.
   16.842 16.852 16.892 (Digit to the right)
3. If the digit to the right is less than 5, leave the first digit as is. If the digit is 5 or greater, round up.
   16.842 rounds to 16.8 (Less than 5)
   16.852 rounds to 16.9 (5)
   16.892 rounds to 16.9 (Greater than 5)

When you are working with amounts of money, use the same steps to round your answer to the nearest cent (the nearest hundredth).

```
   $2.87
 × 0.045
   1435
  1148
 $.12915   rounds to $0.13
```

(Place you are rounding to) (Digit to the right is greater than 5.)

PRACTICE 3

Complete the following addition and subtraction problems with decimal numbers.

1. 6.3 + 9.4 =
2. 5.8 + 7 =
3. 8.6 + 6.04 =
4. 20.04 + 7.7 =
5. 0.08 + 4.075 =
6. 0.04 + 0.25 =
7. 3.71 + 0.6 + 1.89 + 11 =
8. 7.6 − 3.6 =
9. 54.9 − 27 =
10. $10 − $3.99 =
11. 7.5 − 2.11 + 26.045 =
12. 33.4 − 9.428 =
13. Maps To Go paid the following shipping charges in the first week of April: FedEx—$15.75, $32.00, $16.75; UPS—$23.69, $84.27, $47.88, $119.57, $63.74. What was their total shipping charge for that week?
14. Ruben was given a roll of paper 35 yards long. He was asked to make four banners for the upcoming student elections. Two banners need to be 13.75 yards in length, one banner is to be 7.5 yards, and the final banner is to be 2 yards in length. How much more paper will he need?

168 | Unit 4 · Skills for Marketing

Chapter 7 · Basic Math Skills | 169

EXPLAIN

Visual Literacy

Figure 7.1 Caption Answer Read the figure caption question to students. ***Why do you think the amount must be written in words and numbers?*** Students may suggest that sometimes it is difficult to read hand-written numbers so writing the amounts as words and numbers can help clarify messy writing. Then have students practice filling in checks.

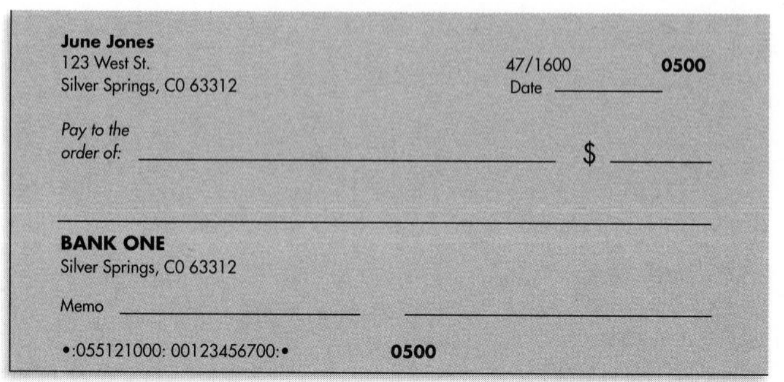
June Jones
123 West St.
Silver Springs, CO 63312

47/1600 0500
Date ______

Pay to the order of: ______ $ ______

BANK ONE
Silver Springs, CO 63312

Memo ______

•:055121000: 00123456700:• 0500

OPERATIONS WITH DECIMAL NUMBERS

Tell students that the most common use of decimal numbers is in working with money. It is important to know how to add, subtract, multiply, and divide decimals to keep track of a budget and to determine best buys. Then ask students these guiding questions to focus the discussion on operations with decimal numbers.

Guiding Questions

List three steps for adding or subtracting decimals.	1. List the numbers vertically. 2. Keep the decimal points in line with each other. 3. Add or subtract as you would with whole numbers.
Explain When might you need to round a decimal?	when multiplying amounts of money, such as figuring taxes or discounts
Draw Conclusions Why is it important to understand how to add and subtract decimal numbers when dealing with money?	Money amounts are stated in decimals. If you don't know them, you may make mistakes and think you have more or less money than you actually have.

ELABORATE

PRACTICE 3 ANSWERS

1.	15.7	**8.**	4
2.	12.8	**9.**	27.9
3.	14.64	**10.**	$6.01
4.	27.74	**11.**	31.435
5.	4.155	**12.**	23.972
6.	0.29	**13.**	$403.65
7.	17.2	**14.**	2 yards

Mini Projects

Extension

Add and Subtract Decimals Bring to class a newspaper ad for a clothing store. Tell students they have $200 to spend on items in the ad. Have them prepare a budget that lists which products they will buy and the quantity of each. They should include the subtotal for each product and the grand total. Sample answer: 2 shirts @ $19.99 = $39.98; 3 pairs of pants @ $24.75 = $74.25; 1 pair of shoes @ $49.99; 1 jacket @ $37.00. $200.00 − 39.98 − 74.25 − 49.99 − 35.00 = $0.78.

Multiply Decimals Bring to class a newspaper ad for a grocery store. Ask students to choose a product and calculate the price if they bought two of the product. Then have them calculate the cost to buy 10 of the product. To give students additional practice, repeat the activity with different numbers. Sample answers: A can of high-energy drink costs $1.39; two cans cost $2.78; 10 cans cost $13.90.

Critical Thinking

Ask students: ***How might rounding numbers affect business applications such as sales data, purchase orders, or pricing?*** Ask volunteers to share their thoughts with the class. Sample answers: Rounding in any of these situations can give unrealistic numbers and cause errors in tracking cash inflow and outflow for the business.

Visual Literacy

Representing Numbers Caption Answer Read the photo caption question to students. ***What other math skills are required to manage a checking account?*** Students should know that they must add and subtract in the check register to keep track of income and outflow. Ask: ***What might happen if you did not add and subtract correctly in your check register?*** Answers will vary but students should realize that if mistakes are made in the check register, they will not have an accurate account of how much money they have on hand. This could cause them to spend more than they actually have, which could cost them a penalty with the bank.

Mini Project

Enrichment

Cooperative Learning Divide the class into groups. Each group will develop five assigned word problems that use the skills dividing decimal numbers and converting fractions to decimals. Problems should be based on a company's finances. Within the groups, students should determine who will take on the role of leader, who will act as secretary, and roles for the other group members. When groups have finished developing their problems, they should exchange problems with another group. Each group should then solve the problems they have received. Original groups will be responsible to check that their problems were answered correctly and to offer help if they were not answered correctly. Problems and answers will vary depending on the problems developed by the groups. Ensure that each group member contributes to the group activity.

Practice 4

Complete the following multiplication problems with decimal numbers. Round any money amounts to the nearest cent.

1. 4.8 × 8
2. 26.3 × 2.04
3. 5.14 × .5
4. 27.26 × 0.49
5. 9.5 × .0001
6. 3.87 × 10 =
7. 0.687 × 100 =
8. 12.345 × 1,000 =
9. Gasoline costs $3.52 per gallon when you pay with a credit card, but $3.47 when you pay with cash. How much do you save on a 12-gallon purchase if you pay with cash?
10. Every month you deposit $75 into a savings account for insurance costs. Your insurance expenses for this year were four equal payments of $219.50. How much remained in your savings account after the last payment?
11. Your phone company charges a $3.95 monthly long distance service fee plus $0.05 per minute for long distance phone calls. How much will you pay if you have 646 minutes of long distance calls for the month?

DIVIDING DECIMAL NUMBERS

Division of decimal numbers is similar to division of whole numbers. Follow the steps below to divide decimal numbers.

1. Set up the division problem as you would with whole numbers.

   69.7 divided by 1.724 = 1.724)69.7

2. Shift the decimal point in the divisor so that the divisor becomes a whole number. The divisor is the number you are dividing by. Then shift the decimal point in the dividend the same number of decimal places. The dividend is the number to be divided. Write zeros in the dividend, if necessary, in order to place the decimal point.

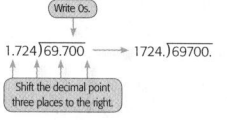

   Write 0s.

   1.724)69.700 → 1724.)69700.

   Shift the decimal point three places to the right.

3. Place a decimal point in the answer space directly above its new position in the dividend. Then divide as with whole numbers.

   Place the decimal point in the answer.

   1724.)69700.

You may need to write extra zeros after the decimal point in order to complete the division.

40.429 rounds to 40.43 (rounded to nearest hundredth)

```
        40.429
1724.)69700.000
       6896
        7400
        6896
         5040
         3448
         15920
         15516
           404   ← Remainder is 404.
```

Some decimal answers will continue infinitely as you write zeros to the right of the decimal point. *Repeating decimals* will repeat a number or pattern of numbers.

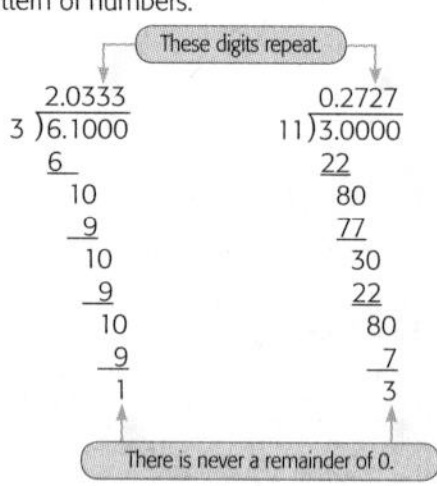

CONVERTING FRACTIONS TO DECIMALS

Decimals are easier than fractions to add, subtract, multiply, and divide. To convert any fraction to a decimal, simply divide the numerator by the denominator.

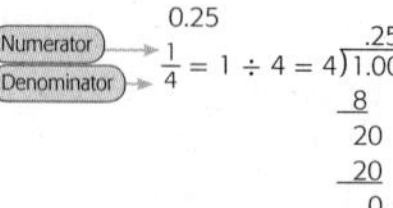

Practice 5

Complete the following division problems. Round answers to the nearest thousandth.

1. 514 ÷ 15 =
2. 38.6 ÷ 3.7 =
3. 3.865 ÷ 8.25 =
4. 7.8 ÷ 0.035 =
5. 0.01 ÷ 2 =
6. 4.002 ÷ 0.75 =
7. If you are paid $11.02 per hour, how many hours must you work to pay for a computer that is priced at $495.90?
8. Compare the cost of Brand X and Brand Y laundry detergent. Which is the better buy? Brand X is $6.59 for 64 ounces. Brand Y is $10.79 for 96 ounces.

```
                  0.666
2/3 = 2 ÷ 3 = 3)2.000
                 1 8
                   20
                   18
                    20
                    18
                     2
```

There is never a remainder of 0.

In its decimal form, $\frac{2}{3}$ is a repeating decimal. When working with repeating decimals, you may round to the nearest hundredth in most cases. Thus, $\frac{2}{3} = 0.67$.

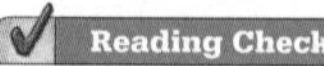

Apply Why are decimals more common than fractions when expressing values related to money?

MARKETING CASE STUDY

GEICO Campaign

The insurance company GEICO has always been known for humorous and innovative advertising campaigns. GEICO's ads often point out how consumers can save money easily. GEICO brought us ad campaigns that featured the GEICO gecko, as well as the cavemen who are offended when something is described as "so easy, even a caveman could do it." In a more recent ad campaign begun in 2009, GEICO featured the "Kash" character.

The character of Kash is a stack of money, with two eyes on top—literally the money you could be saving if you switched to GEICO. The stack of bills usually appears out of nowhere and surprises people. Many of GEICO's ads play slightly on the fear and uneasiness a customer might feel when spending too much money.

English Language Arts/Writing

The Kash ads work by implying to viewers that they are wasting their money. Consider the pros and cons of this direct approach. Write a brief response that establishes your opinion on this topic.

NCTE 3 Apply strategies to interpret texts.

EXPLAIN

Practice 4 Answers

1. 38.4
2. 53.652
3. 2.57
4. 13.3574
5. 0.00095
6. 38.7
7. 68.7
8. 12,345
9. $0.60
10. $22.00
11. $36.25

DIVIDING DECIMAL NUMBERS

Ask these guiding questions to focus the discussion about dividing decimal numbers.

Guiding Questions

Recall What are the names of the three parts of a division problem?	The number being divided into is the dividend; the number doing the dividing is called the divisor; the answer is the quotient
Explain What are the steps to divide decimal numbers?	1) Set up the division problem as you would with whole numbers. 2) Shift the decimal point in the divisor so that the divisor becomes a whole number. Shift the decimal point in the dividend the same number of places. If necessary, write zeroes in the dividend to place the decimal point correctly. 3) Place a decimal point in the answer directly above its new position in the dividend.

ELABORATE

Graphic Organizer

Display a diagram like the one below. Then ask students to name the steps in rounding decimals.

Rounding Decimal Numbers
1. Find the decimal place you are rounding to.
2. Look at the digit to the right of that place.
3. If the digit to the right is less than 5, leave the first digit as is. If the digit is 5 or greater, round up.

 **glencoe.com** 

Send students to the Online Learning Center to print this graphic organizer.

Critical Thinking

Ask students to think of reasons why it is easier to add, subtract, multiply, and divide decimals than fractions. Students may suggest that dealing with numerators and denominators and having to find common denominators and reducing fractions takes a lot more time and effort than working with decimals. Ask: ***Are there any cases in which it would be easier to work with fractions?*** Students may suggest that when working with recipes and measurements, it is easier to work with fractions.

Practice 5 Answers

1. 34.267	**5.** 0.005
2. 10.432	**6.** 5.336
3. 0.468	**7.** 45 hours
4. 222.857	**8.** Brand X is a better buy.

Reading Check Answer

Read the Reading Check question to students: ***Why are decimals more common than fractions when expressing values related to money?*** Money amounts are stated in terms of decimals.

CONVERTING FRACTIONS TO DECIMALS

0
1

Graphic Organizer

Display the number line. Write various fractions on small pieces of paper. Distribute the pieces of paper to the class. Have students take turns placing their fractions on the number line. Now have students convert the fraction to a decimal. Have them try again to place their number. Ask: ***Was it easier to place the numbers as fractions or as decimals?*** Students will likely say it was easier to place the decimals.

Send students to the Online Learning Center to print this graphic organizer.

MARKETING CASE STUDY

English Language Arts/Writing Answer Students' responses will vary depending on their opinion about the direct approach Geico uses in their marketing campaigns. Students should state their position clearly, and use facts to back up their position. Paragraphs should be well-written and have no spelling or grammar errors.

Mini Project

Extension

Calculate Tax Have students "shop" online for books, CDs, or DVDs. Tell students they will purchase five of the product. Then tell them that there is a 7.5 percent sales tax on the cost of the purchase. Have students calculate the price of the items plus the sales tax. For further practice, repeat the activity with other products, quantities, and taxes. Sample answer: five CDs @ \$9.95 = \$49.75; \$49.75 + (49.75 × .075) = \$49.75 + 3.73 = \$53.48.

Web Searches That Give Back

What if you could help the environment just by doing a Web search? Search engines such as GoodSearch and EveryClick donate some of the money they collect from advertisers to the charity of your choice. Charity shopping portals such as iGive and WeCare partner with online merchants. These merchants donate a small amount of each purchase made through the portal to charity.

Little by Little A penny per search may not seem like a lot of money. However, the combination of these small contributions on a large scale results in a significant amount of money. Searchers who share their experience on the site with their friends increase the potential for more contributions to the charities. These word-of-mouth recommendations happen on a large scale on the Internet. This results in more traffic to the search engine and more contributions to the charities.

Mathematics

A charity search engine donates one penny to the Environmental Defense Fund for each search performed. Use the following search totals to determine how much money the charity earned in the past year: First Quarter: 123,987 searches; Second Quarter: 319,546 searches; Third Quarter: 250,983 searches; Fourth Quarter: 299,419 searches. Create a bar graph that displays these totals and the total amount earned by the charity.

NCTM Number and Operations Understand numbers, ways of representing numbers, relationships among numbers, and number systems.

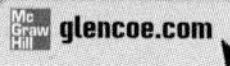
glencoe.com

Get an activity on green marketing.

CALCULATING SURFACE MEASUREMENTS

When planning to install new carpeting or to use space in an office, warehouse, or retail store, you will need to calculate the area of floor surface. The area of a surface is the number of squares of a certain measure that the surface covers.

If you measure the length and width in feet, the area will be expressed in square feet. If you measure in inches, the area will be expressed in square inches.

To compute the area of a rectangle or square, multiply the length of one side by the length of the side next to it. The shorter length is commonly called the width. The formula for the area of a rectangle is

$A = l \times w$

where *A* stands for area, *l* for length, and *w* stands for width.

The **formula** for the area of a square is really the same, but because there is no difference in the length and width, it may be written

$A = s^2$

where *A* stands for area and *s* stands for side.

Formulas in Business Webcasters, agreeing to pay royalties for music streamed online, use formulas to calculate payments.

BUSINESS APPLICATIONS OF SURFACE MEASUREMENTS

Calculating surface is a business skill that retailers use to figure out the floor space they need or how this space can be rearranged. It is also necessary for anybody who sells, distributes, or manufactures products that need to have an exact area measurement. For example, how would you go about deciding how much fabric you would need to reupholster a sofa?

You would measure each area that needs to be covered. You would then have several geometric shapes with perimeter measurements. With that information, you could calculate the area measurement of each shape and add them to find the amount of fabric needed.

Practice 6

The owner of a retail store wishes to replace the carpeting. The store measures 92 feet long and 50 feet wide. The new carpet is priced at $35 per square yard and sales tax is 8 percent. Calculate the surface area of the floor, and estimate the cost of material to replace the carpet, including sales tax. (Remember that there are nine square feet in one square yard.)

After You Read — Section 7.1

Review Key Concepts

1. **Write** the whole number 3,010,049 in words, using commas and hyphens correctly.
2. **Round** $6.875 to the nearest cent and to the nearest dollar.
3. **Convert** the fraction $\frac{1}{8}$ to its decimal equivalent.

Practice Academics

English Language Arts

4. Research careers that require good basic math skills, and write one or more paragraphs describing how math is used in these careers.

Mathematics

5. Explain why the decimal number 6.25 correctly represents $6.25 when talking about money, but does not correctly represent 6 hours and 25 minutes when talking about time.

Math Concept **Ways of Representing Numbers** The value of a digit in a number depends on the number system used and the value of the place in which it appears.

Starting Hints To solve this problem, think about the different number systems we use. For example, how many hundredths, tenths, ones, and tens are there in a decimal or money amount like 34.56 and $34.56? What does each digit mean in 3 hours and 4 minutes? Think about the place value of each digit in each number.

For help, go to the **Math Skills Handbook** located at the back of this book.

NCTE 7 Conduct research and gather, evaluate, and synthesize data to communicate discoveries.

NCTM Number and Operations Understand numbers, ways of representing numbers, relationships among numbers, and number systems.

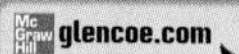
glencoe.com

Check your answers.

ELABORATE

The GREEN Marketer

Mathematics Answers

First Quarter: **$1,239.87 (123,987 × $0.01)**

Second Quarter: **$3,195.46 (319,546 × $0.01)**

Third Quarter: **$2,509.83 (250,983 × $0.01)**

Fourth Quarter: **$2,994.19 (299,419 × $0.01)**

glencoe.com

Activity Worksheet Send students to the Online Learning Center to get a Green Marketer worksheet activity.

Practice 6 Answers

$19,320.00 (92 × 50 = 4,600 sq. ft.; 4,600 ÷ 9 = 511.1 sq.yd.; 511.1 × $35 = $17,888.50; $17,888.50 × 1.08 = $19,319.58)

EVALUATE

CALCULATING SURFACE MEASUREMENTS

Tell students that calculating surface measurements is a necessary skill for those who need to know the exact area of a space or item. Then ask these questions to guide the discussion about surface measurements.

Guiding Questions

Apply What is the area of a warehouse that is 17 yards long and 13 yards wide? State the final answer in square feet.	$A = 17 \times 13 = 221$ sq. yd.; $221 \times 9 = 1{,}989$ sq. ft.
Analyze Give examples for when you might calculate an area in square inches, square feet, square yards, or square miles.	For example, if you are going to cover a wall in gold leaf for an advertisement, and gold leaf is sold by the square inch, you would figure the area of the wall in square inches so you would not have to spend any more money than necessary.

Formulas in Business The formulas figure a percentage of the Webcasters revenues, which are gained by advertisers and subscribers. Ask students whether they subscribe to any Webcasts.

After You Read Section 7.1

Review Key Concepts

1. Three million, ten thousand, forty-nine
2. Rounded to the nearest cent: $6.88; to the nearest dollar: $7.00
3. 0.125 ($1 \div 8 = 0.125$)

Practice Academics

English Language Arts

4. Students may research careers such as bank teller, cashier, accountant, and so on. Paragraphs should focus on one main idea and all sentences in the paragraph should support the main idea. Transitions should be used to show connections between ideas.

Mathematics

5. $.25 is $\frac{25}{100}$ as there are 100 cents in a dollar; an hour has only 60 minutes, so a .25 portion of an hour would only be $\frac{25}{60}$ or .4167.

glencoe.com

Answer Key Send students to the Online Learning Center to check their answers.

READING GUIDE

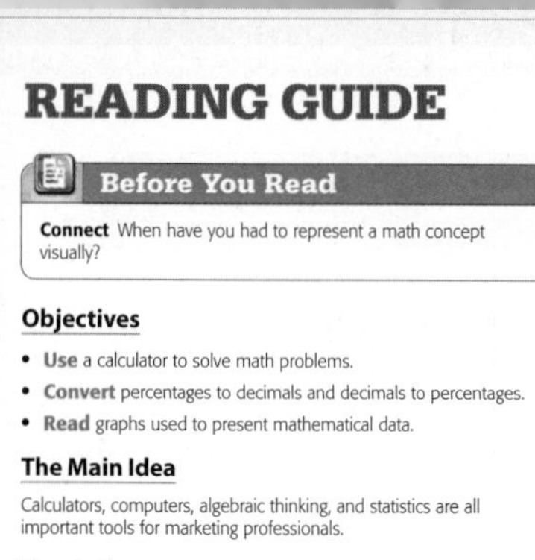

Before You Read

Connect When have you had to represent a math concept visually?

Objectives

- **Use** a calculator to solve math problems.
- **Convert** percentages to decimals and decimals to percentages.
- **Read** graphs used to present mathematical data.

The Main Idea

Calculators, computers, algebraic thinking, and statistics are all important tools for marketing professionals.

Vocabulary

Content Vocabulary

- RPN
- percentage
- bar graph
- line graph
- circle graph
- pie chart

Academic Vocabulary

You will find these words in your reading and on your tests. Make sure you know their meanings.

- estimate
- percent

Graphic Organizer

Draw or print this chart to write an example of calculating tax on a sale, estimating a gratuity, and illustrating or comparing data.

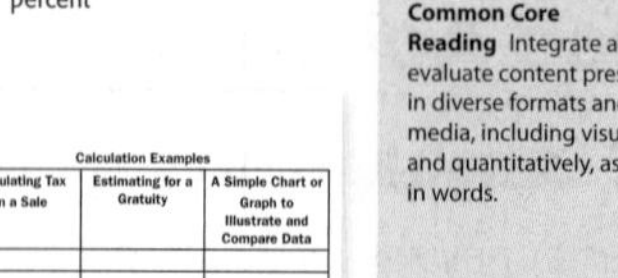

Calculation Examples

Calculating Tax on a Sale	Estimating for a Gratuity	A Simple Chart or Graph to Illustrate and Compare Data

glencoe.com

Print this graphic organizer.

STANDARDS

ACADEMIC

English Language Arts

NCTE 1 Read texts to acquire new information.

Mathematics

NCTM Algebra Use mathematical models to represent and understand quantitative relationships.

NCSS *National Council for the Social Studies*
NCTE *National Council of Teachers of English*
NCTM *National Council of Teachers of Mathematics*
NSES *National Science Education Standards*

College & Career READINESS

Common Core

Reading Integrate and evaluate content presented in diverse formats and media, including visually and quantitatively, as well as in words.

MARKETING CORE FUNCTION

Selling

m.e. Section 7.2 Interpreting Numbers

USING A CALCULATOR

Many people use calculators to pay bills, create budgets, and balance their checkbooks. There are two basic types of calculators. The most widely used type uses algebraic logic to enter numbers. This is the type of calculator used in the problems in this section.

The other type uses **RPN**, an entry method in which the operators follow the operands. Using RPN, you enter the first amount and press the enter key, then the second amount, and then the operation (added to, subtracted from, multiplied by, or divided into the first amount). If you have a calculator that uses RPN, read the instruction book that accompanies your calculator very carefully. You will get a very different answer if you enter numbers as if using algebraic logic.

> "Calculators simplify the computation that is common in both the business world and in people's personal lives."

If you expect to be hired in sales or any other marketing job, you will almost certainly use a calculator. Besides simply knowing which buttons to press, you will be expected to work accurately. You will need to know how to work with fractions and amounts of money. You also need to have an understanding of how the calculator computes with multiple operations.

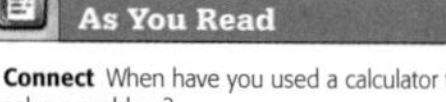

As You Read

Connect When have you used a calculator to solve a problem?

ESTIMATE, THEN OPERATE

Many people follow the guess-and-check method. They **estimate** first, and then enter the problem in the calculator. Finally, they check the displayed answer against the estimate.

388 + 995 = ?

Estimate: 400 + 1,000 = 1,400

Enter the problem:

3 8 8 + 9 9 5 = 1,383

Displayed answer

Check: 1,383 is close to the estimate of 1,400.

480 × 112 = ?

Estimate: 500 × 100 = 50,000

Enter the problem:

4 8 0 × 1 1 2 = 53,760

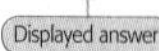

Displayed answer

Check: 53,760 is close to the estimate of 50,000.

It is important to estimate your answers when you use a calculator. You may make errors when entering numbers or operations. It is a good idea to have an estimate of the answer in mind. For example, if you are expecting an answer of about 300, you will know something is wrong if the displayed answer on your calculator is 3,300.

You should check the display after you enter each number and operation. If you make an error, press the Clear Entry key CE to remove the last entry. Suppose you want to multiply 5.8 × 7.2, but you enter 5 . 8 × 7 2. Press CE to delete the last two keystrokes. Then you can reenter the second number correctly. The first number will remain in the calculator. Press the Equals key = and the answer will be displayed: 41.76.

ENGAGE

Anticipation Activity

Improving Student Achievement Tell students to imagine that one of the Internet-based ads they have developed has received the following number of hits over a six month period: January–1,098; February–1,735; March–2,112; April–2,045; May–2,254; June–2,549. Tell students that they need to share this data with the customer the ad was developed for. Ask: ***How would you display this data so that the customer can easily understand it?*** Students may suggest percentages, bar graphs, line graphs, circle graphs, and pie charts.

Objectives

- **Use** a calculator to solve math problems. Example: Enter 5.132 × 7.8; press equal sign; answer: 40.0296.
- **Convert** percentages to decimals and decimals to percentages. Examples: 73% = 73 ÷ 100 = 0.73; 0.06 = 0.06 × 100 = 6%
- **Read** graphs used to present mathematical data. Students learn to read and make bar graphs, line graphs, circle graphs, and frequency tables to display various types of data.

Graphic Organizer

Examples will vary. Sample examples:

Calculation Examples

Calculating Tax on a Sale	Estimating for a Gratuity	A Simple Chart or Graph to Illustrate and Compare Data
New car price: $15,995. Sales tax: 6.5%. Calculation: $15,995 × 0.065 = $1,039.68	Cost of dinner: $57.72. Gratuity: 15%. Calculation: Round $57.72 to $60; $60 × 0.15 = $9.00.	**Sales** (pie chart) ■ 1st Qtr ■ 2nd Qtr ■ 3rd Qtr ■ 4th Qtr

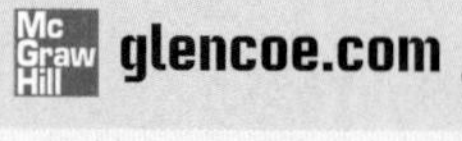

glencoe.com iWB

Graphic Organizer Send students to the Online Learning Center to print the graphic organizer.

EXPLORE

Before You Read

Read the Before You Read question aloud: ***When have you had to represent a math concept visually?*** Students might suggest that they had to represent math concepts visually when displaying data for a survey for a social studies project, when calculating math problems, when displaying information at work, and so on. Ask: ***Do you think it is easier to understand math concepts when displayed visually? Why or why not?*** Students will likely say that it is easier to understand math concepts (or any concepts) when displayed visually because visuals are generally easier to understand than words.

Preteaching Vocabulary

Have students go to the Online Learning Center at glencoe.com for the Chapter 7 Preteaching Vocabulary games.

Content Vocabulary

Challenge students do online research to find what RPN stands for. RPN stands for Reverse Polish Notation. Then ask: ***What are the similarities among bar graph, line graph, circle graph, and pie chart?*** Students should realize that all of these are methods to visually present mathematical data.

Academic Vocabulary

Estimate—Multiple Usages Tell students that the term *estimate* can be used as both a verb and a noun. As a verb, it means "to roughly determine or approximate value, extent, or size." As a noun, it means "an approximate or rough calculation as to value or size." Ask students to give examples of the use of *estimate* as both a verb and a noun. Examples might include: Will you please estimate how much tip we should leave? The estimate for the repair of the car was $245.

Percent—Word Origin Tell students that the word *percent* is from the Latin word *centum*, which means "one hundred." Percent means one part in a hundred. Ask students: ***Give the percentage that would be equal to a whole object.*** 100%. ***How much would 1% be equal to?*** 1% is equal to one part in a hundred.

PROFESSIONAL DEVELOPMENT MINI CLIP

Math: Communication in Mathematics
Go to the Online Learning Center for a video in which an expert explains the importance of student communication in the mathematics classroom.

Interpreting Numbers

USING A CALCULATOR

Explain to students that using calculators to help figure math problems has become a part of life for many people. The uses for calculators range from helping to keep a check register up to date to figuring how much carpet is needed for the bedroom. Then ask these guiding questions to focus the discussion about using calculators.

Guiding Questions

Identify What type of logic do most calculators use?	algebraic logic
Explain Why is it important to check the calculator's display after you make each entry?	so you only need to correct that entry if you made a mistake; otherwise, you would have to reenter the entire problem
Estimate Use estimation to calculate these problems: 49 + 72; 143 − 44; 487 × 11; 987 ÷ 199	49 + 72 = 50 + 70 = 120; 143 − 44 = 140 − 40 = 100; 487 × 11 = 500 × 10 = 5,000; 987 ÷ 199 = 1000 ÷ 200 = 5

Expert Advice

Read the quote to students:

"Calculators simplify the computation that is common in both the business world and in people's personal lives."

Ask students: ***What is a computation?*** A computation is another word for calculation. Ask: ***What kinds of computations are done in both the business world and in people's personal lives?*** Students may suggest the obvious: addition, subtraction, multiplication, and division or they may suggest such things as calculating budgets or income and outflow.

As You Read

Read students the As You Read question: ***When have you used a calculator to solve a problem?*** Students will likely mention that they have used calculators during math class. Some may say that they use them at home to figure their weekly or monthly budget. Others might say they use them at work for various reasons. Ask: ***How does a calculator make figuring math problems easier?*** Students will likely say that it makes it much faster to perform the calculations.

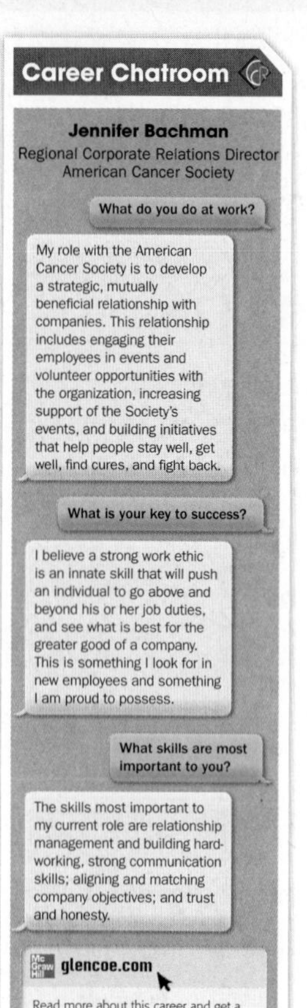

Career Chatroom

Jennifer Bachman
Regional Corporate Relations Director
American Cancer Society

What do you do at work?

My role with the American Cancer Society is to develop a strategic, mutually beneficial relationship with companies. This relationship includes engaging their employees in events and volunteer opportunities with the organization, increasing support of the Society's events, and building initiatives that help people stay well, get well, find cures, and fight back.

What is your key to success?

I believe a strong work ethic is an innate skill that will push an individual to go above and beyond his or her job duties, and see what is best for the greater good of a company. This is something I look for in new employees and something I am proud to possess.

What skills are most important to you?

The skills most important to my current role are relationship management and building hard-working, strong communication skills; aligning and matching company objectives; and trust and honesty.

glencoe.com

Read more about this career and get a Career Exploration Activity.

HOW TO MAKE ENTRIES

You can ignore leading zeros (as in 0.6 or 0.375) and trailing zeros (as in 9.250 or 41.500).

Number	Keystrokes Entered	Display
0.785	[.] [7] [8] [5]	0.785
5.10	[5] [.] [1]	5.1

For mixed numbers or fractions, convert the fractions to decimal form first. To enter $5\frac{1}{4}$, first enter [1] [÷] [4]. Then add the whole number by entering [+] [5].

For money problems, include the dollar sign. You may also have to round the displayed answer to the nearest cent.

Display	Answer Written as Money Amount
5.25	$5.25
25.368216	$25.37 (Round to nearest cent)
76514.1	$76,514.10

You can perform a series of calculations on more than two numbers. When only addition and subtraction are involved, the calculator will perform these operations as they are entered.

[8] [.] [6] [+] [1] [1] [.] [9] [−] [3] [.] [6] [2] [=] 16.88

When only multiplication and division are involved, the calculator will perform these operations as they are entered.

[7] [7] [5] [÷] [5] [×] [1] [.] [9] [6] [=] 303.8

Calculations that involve addition or subtraction with multiplication or division are more complex. You will need to check how your calculator performs these operations. Most calculators will do the operations as they are entered.

6 + 4 × 6 will be calculated as

|6 + 4| × 6 =

10 × 6 = 60

6 × 4 + 6 will be calculated as

|6 × 4| + 6 =

24 + 6 = 30

4 × 2 + 1 ÷ 3 will be calculated as

|4 × 2| + 1 ÷ 3 =

|8 + 1|

9 ÷ 3 = 3

TEN-KEY BY SIGHT OR TOUCH

Ten-key calculators have been popular for many years. They use algebraic entry. Most computer keyboards have a 10-key keypad along the right side of the board. (There are actually more than 10 keys; the 10-key name refers to the digits 0 through 9.) With practice, you can learn to operate a 10-key keypad by touch, just as you learned to type the alphabetic characters on a keyboard by touch. This allows very fast operation and is a valuable skill for online point-of-sale entries, accounting, using spreadsheet programs, and other computer-related applications.

While learning to use a 10-key keypad, keep your fingers close to the home row of keys. On a 10-key keypad, these are the 4, 5, and 6 keys. Try to keep your arm, wrist, and hand in a straight line. Do not rest your wrist on your desk or the counter. Relax your fingers and press the keys lightly. Frequent, short periods of practice are most effective in developing speed with accuracy. Courses for developing skill on a 10-key keypad are available at many community colleges and on the Internet.

Reading Check

Recall Why should you estimate before you calculate?

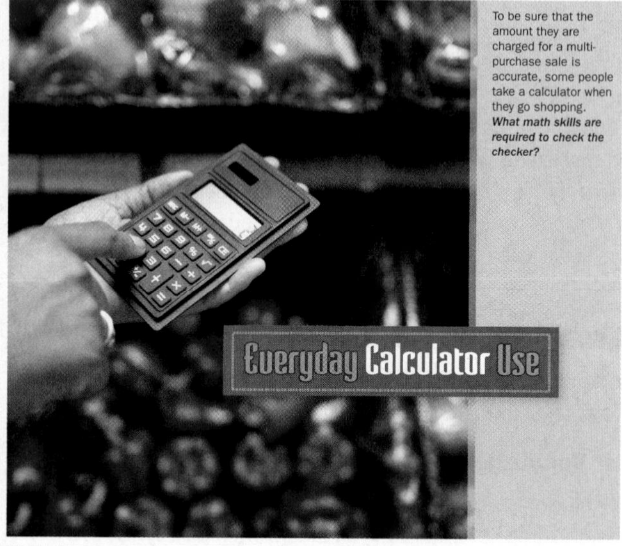

To be sure that the amount they are charged for a multi-purchase sale is accurate, some people take a calculator when they go shopping. ***What math skills are required to check the checker?***

EXPLAIN

Career Chatroom

Use these questions to focus the discussion about the Career Chatroom feature.

Guiding Questions

Analyze What is work ethic?	working for company's good
Interpret How does trust help companies?	builds relationships based on strong communication

 **glencoe.com** 

Career Exploration Send students to the Online Learning Center to find more information about this career and to get a Career Exploration activity.

Critical Thinking

Tell students that when solving a problem that has more than one operation, mathematicians have agreed upon an order in which to do the operations to make sure that there is just one answer to a series of computations. First, simplify within the parentheses, and then multiply and divide from left to right, and finally add and subtract from left to right. Write this problem on the board: $5\,(4 + 3) + 8 \div (6 - 2) =$ Tell students to solve the problem using the method you just described. $5\,(7) + 8 \div 4 = 35 + 2 = 37$ Ask: ***What steps did you use to solve the problem?*** Students should restate the steps mentioned above: simplify within the parentheses, multiply from left to right, add and subtract from left to right.

ELABORATE

Graphic Organizer

Display the diagram. Have students compare and contrast calculators that use algebraic logic and those that use RPN. Possible answers:

Algebraic Logic	RPN
When using calculators that use algebraic logic, you enter the numbers and operators in the order they appear in the problem. For example: 225 ÷ 25 × 4 = (in that order)	When using calculators that use RPN, the amounts are entered first and the operators are entered last. For example: 225 ÷ 25, would be entered 225 25 ÷

 glencoe.com 

Graphic Organizer Send students to the Online Learning Center to print this graphic organizer.

Reading Check Answer

Read the Reading Check question to students: ***Why should you estimate before you calculate?*** Estimating gives you an idea of what the answer will be. This can help you double-check the answer you get on the calculator if it is way off from your estimate.

Visual Literacy

Everyday Calculator Use Caption Answer Read the caption question to students: ***What math skills are required to check the checker?*** Multiplication skills are necessary to determine the cost when more than one of an item is purchased. Addition skills are necessary to add the costs of all items for a total.

TEN-KEY BY SIGHT OR TOUCH

Guiding Questions

Identify What is the guess-and-check method of operating a calculator?	estimating first, entering the problem, checking answer against estimate
Analyze How will frequent practice on the ten-key keypad help you?	Frequent practice will help develop and reinforce speed and accuracy.

e MARKETING

Going Paperless

Small tablet computers, such as Apple's® iPad help businesses go paperless. "Paperless" means that paper is replaced with technology. Companies implement paperless functions to save on the cost of paper and printing supplies, as well as time saved by the elimination of a paper trail. E-mail certainly has helped businesses reduce paper costs. Another example is a warehouse operation in which time spent inputting data into a computer from paper records is eliminated by entering the data directly onto an iPad. In a hair salon, owners provided iPads to customers to use while waiting during treatments; thus replacing the cost of magazine subscriptions. Companies that deliver merchandise use computer tablets to collect electronic signatures when items are delivered; track the location of the truck via GPS, and can even be equipped to show photos in the company's catalog to entice customers to purchase accessories.

Innovate and Create

(A) Have students assume that United States companies spent approximately $8 billion on paper last year. One company estimated that it saved $100,000 in paper costs in one year when it replaced paper processing with computer tablets. How many companies would have to save $100,000 to cover the annual cost of paper used in the United States in one year? (A) 80,000 companies ($8B divided by $100,000 = 80,000). (B) Have students research the cost of an Apple iPad to see how much money has to be invested by a company to equip 50 delivery persons with high end iPads. (B) Depending on the current price of an iPad, the total for 50 will vary. In 2010 iPads prices ranged from $500 to a little over $800 depending on the model required. (C) Calculate the net savings from the $100,000 savings from going paperless. (C) To calculate the savings, deduct the cost of the iPads from $100,000. For example, since it is a business operation let's assume that the price of that model is $800. The savings would be $60,000 (50 × $800 = $40,000; $100,000 - $40,000 = $60,000). (D) Brainstorm other uses for computer tablets in marketing to cut down on expenses. (D) Other uses for computer tablets in marketing will vary. Accept all reasonable answers. Some uses may include: creating and making sales presentations; preparing sales proposals on the spot; checking inventory; and providing status reports and scheduling changes.

eMarketing Worksheet Activity Send students to the Online Learning Center to download an eMarketing worksheet activity.

PERCENTAGES

Two **percent** of a company's revenue goes to pay for insurance. This means that $2 of every $100 that comes in goes to pay for insurance.

Percentage is a number expressed as parts per 100. Thus, a number expressed as a percentage represents the number of parts per 100.

To write a whole number or a decimal number as a percentage, multiply it by 100. A simple way to do this is to move the decimal point two places to the right.

Move the decimal point two places to the right.

$0.70 = 0.7 \times 100 = 70\%$ or $0.70 = 70\%$

$0.05 = 0.05 \times 100 = 5\%$ or $0.05 = 5\%$

$2.5 = 2.5 \times 100 = 250\%$ or $2.50 = 250\%$

Write 0s as needed.

You can use a calculator to do this operation.

[.] [7] [×] [1] [0] [0] [=] 70 = 70%

[2] [.] [5] [×] [1] [0] [0] [=] 250 = 250%

CONVERTING FRACTIONS TO PERCENTAGES

To write a fraction or mixed number as a percentage, first convert the fraction to decimal form. Do this by dividing the numerator by the denominator. If there is a whole number, add it to the converted fraction. Then multiply by 100. You can use a calculator to do this operation.

$\frac{1}{2}$ = [1] [÷] [2] [×] [1] [0] [0] [=] 50 = 50%

$\frac{3}{8}$ = [3] [÷] [8] [×] [1] [0] [0] [=]
37.5 = 37.5%

$4\frac{2}{5}$ = [2] [÷] [5] [+] [4] [×] [1] [0] [0] [=]
440 = 440%

CONVERTING PERCENTAGES TO DECIMALS

Sometimes it may be easier to complete a math problem by changing a percentage to a decimal. You can change a percentage to a decimal number by dividing by 100. A simple way to do this is to move the decimal point two places to the left.

Move the decimal point two places to the left.

$24.8\% = 24.8 \div 100 = .248$ or $24.8\% = 0.248$

$0.5\% = 0.5 \div 100 = 0.005$ or $0.5\% = 0.005$

Write 0s as needed.

You can use a calculator to do this operation.

12.6% = [1] [2] [.] [6] [÷] [1] [0] [0] [=] 0.126

1.4% = [1] [.] [4] [÷] [1] [0] [0] [=] 0.014

You can also convert a percentage with a fraction or mixed number to a decimal by using a calculator.

$7\frac{1}{4}\%$ = [1] [÷] [4] [+] [7] [÷] [1] [0] [0] [=]
0.0725

PERCENTAGE PROBLEMS

Percentage problems are often encountered in marketing jobs. For example, you may be asked to figure a gratuity, a discount amount, or the amount of sales tax. You may have to figure the total selling price, including the tax. You may be asked to figure the percentage of commission on your total sales.

Most percentage problems will involve finding a percentage of a number. To do that, multiply the decimal equivalent of the percentage by the number.

Decimal equivalent of $5\frac{1}{2}\%$

$5\frac{1}{2}\%$ of $35 = 0.055 × $35

of tells you to multiply.

Follow these steps to solve percentage problems.

1. Estimate the answer.
2. Translate the problem into a math statement.
3. Do the calculations.
4. If necessary, round money amounts to the nearest cent.
5. Check your answer.

Three types of percentage problems are explained below. Solve the first problem by estimating the answers. Solve the other problems with a calculator.

1. Suppose you and three friends have enjoyed dinner at a restaurant. When the waiter brings the check, you decide to treat your friends and pay for dinner. To figure the gratuity (tip), you will not need to dig out a calculator because you know how to estimate. The total on the check is $98.58, including tax. You know that a 15 percent gratuity is usual, so you round the total to $100. You know that 10 percent of $100 is $10, and 15 percent is $1\frac{1}{2}$ times 10 percent. Your estimate for the gratuity is $15, and a good estimate is all that is needed. You leave $115.
2. Suppose you have sold a set of golf clubs listed at $395.99 to someone eligible for a 15% discount. How much in dollars and cents will you allow as a discount on the golf clubs?
   - *First: Estimate the answer*. Round the list price to $400. Figure that 10% of $400 is $40. Since 15% is $1\frac{1}{2}$ times 10%, estimate the discount at about $60 ($1\frac{1}{2}$ times $40).
   - *Second: Translate the problem into a math statement.*

     15% of $395.99 = 0.15 × $395.99
   - *Third: Do the calculations.*

     0.15 × $395.99 = $59.3985
   - *Fourth: Round the answer to the nearest cent, if necessary.* $59.3985 rounds to $59.40
   - *Finally: Check the answer against your estimate.* The amount $59.40 is reasonably close to the estimate of $60. The discount is $59.40.
3. If sales tax is $6\frac{1}{2}\%$, how much tax should you collect on the sale of the golf clubs? Before you can figure the tax, you have to find out the net selling price.

   List price – discount = net price

   $395.99 – $59.40 = $336.59

Now you can proceed, following the guidelines given above.

- *Estimate*: Round $6\frac{1}{2}$ % to 7% and $336.59 to $300. A 7% sales tax means that $7 tax is collected on every $100 in sales. So you can estimate the tax to be $21 (3 × $7).
- *Translate*: $6\frac{1}{2}$ % of $336.59 = 0.065 × $336.59
- *Calculate*: 0.065 × $336.59 = $21.8784
- *Round*: $21.8784 rounds to $21.88
- *Check*: $21.88 is reasonably close to the estimate of $21. The sales tax to be collected is $21.88.

Reading Check

Apply How would you use percentages to calculate the tip at a restaurant?

EXPLAIN

PERCENTAGES

Ask these guiding questions to focus the discussion about percentages.

Guiding Questions

Describe How do you change a fraction into a percentage?	Divide the numerator by the denominator, and then multiply the decimal by 100.
Solve You have purchased a new computer for $795. Sales tax for your state is 6.5% and local tax is 3.5%. What would be the total cost of your computer?	Convert sales tax to a decimal number by dividing by 100. 6.5 ÷ 100 = 0.065; 3.5 ÷ 100 = 0.035. Multiply the decimal by the price of the computer: $795 × 0.065 = $51.68; $795 × 0.035 = $27.83. Add the sales tax to the cost of the computer: $795 + $51.68 + $27.83 = $874.51. Alternative solution: total the tax amounts (10%), convert to a decimal (0.10) and multiply by $795. The answer is $79.50. Add $795 + $79.50 = $874.50

Mini Project

Enrichment

Percentages in Everyday Life To help students better understand the widespread use of percentages in everyday life, bring in examples of real-life percentages, such as sales tax on a receipt, ads for interest rates on loans, a card showing tipping amounts, and so on. Then divide the class into groups of two or three and have each group make a list of different school, home, work, or other situations in which percentages are used. Have groups write out on paper two scenarios that involve calculating percentages. Have groups exchange problems and practice solving the percentage problems. After students have had time to work, lead a discussion about any problems they may have had when calculating percentages. Scenarios may include calculating sales tax, tipping a server, calculating interest on a loan, and so on.

ELABORATE

Graphic Organizer

Display the table and ask students to calculate the missing numbers.

Converting Fractions and Percentages

Fraction	Percentage	Decimal
$\frac{1}{2}$	50%	0.50
$\frac{5}{8}$	62.5%	0.625
$\frac{5}{7}$	71%	0.71
$\frac{83}{100}$	83%	0.83
$\frac{1}{4}$	25%	0.25
$3\frac{3}{8}$	337.5%	3.375
$\frac{1}{5}$	20%	0.2
$\frac{7}{1000}$	.7%	0.007
$\frac{11}{40}$	27.5%	0.275
$\frac{3}{20}$	15%	0.15

Graphic Organizer Send student to the Online Learning Center to print this graphic organizer.

Mini Projects

Extension

Research Sales Tax Assign students to do online research to find local sales taxes. Have students write a summary of their findings. Summaries should include the amount of the tax and what items are taxable. Students should locate the best sources for information and take notes as they do their research.

PERCENTAGE PROBLEMS

Tell students that in the marketing business, percentages are used frequently. They may be used to calculate discounts, sales tax, and so on. Then ask these guiding questions to focus the discussion about percentage problems.

Guiding Questions

Identify What are the steps to solving percentage problems?	1. Estimate the answer. 2. Translate the problem into a math statement. 3. Do the calculations. 4. If necessary, round money amounts to the nearest cent. 5. Check your answer.
Calculate Follow the steps to solving percentage problems to calculate the answer to this problem: There is an 8% delivery charge on a set of DVDs that sells for \$145. What is the delivery charge?	1. Estimate: Round 8% to 10% and round \$145 to \$150. 10% of \$150 is \$15. 2. Translate: 8% of \$145 = 0.08 × \$145 3. Calculate: 0.08 × \$145 = \$11.60 4. Round: No need to round. 5. Check: \$11.60 is close to the estimate of \$15.

Reading Check Answer

Read the Reading Check question to students: *How would you use percentages to calculate the tip at a restaurant?* Answers will vary. Students may suggest that they would simply calculate 15% of the total bill by multiplying 0.15 × the total. Others may estimate by rounding the bill and then calculating 10% of the bill and then half again as much (another 5%).

Mathematics: Ways of Working—Solving Equations
A teacher uses partner work and whole group instruction to build understanding of the equation-solving process.

READING CHARTS AND GRAPHS

In marketing, people need to use numbers to describe market trends, growth of sales, and other data. Graphs present such information in a way that is easier to understand. It is easy to tell that one bar is longer than another or that a line is going up or down. It is harder to try to understand data by reading lists of multiple numbers. A graph shows the relationship between two or more kinds of data.

BAR GRAPHS

A **bar graph** is a drawing made up of parallel bars whose lengths correspond to what is being measured. The bar graph in **Figure 7.2** shows the percent of people who own cell phones by different age groups. The bottom of the graph lists the age groups. Each group is represented by a bar of a certain height. There is a vertical line along the left side of the graph. It shows the percentage of individuals in each age group who own cell phones. The bar graph provides a clear visual representation of this data.

To find out the percentage of 12- to 17-year-olds who own cell phones, draw an imaginary line across the top of the bar for that age group. Then note where that line intersects the left side of the graph. The result is 48 percent.

LINE GRAPHS

Another kind of graph you have probably seen is a line graph. A **line graph** is a line (or lines) that joins points representing changes in a quantity over a specific period of time. It is very useful for charting sales, prices, profits, output, and things that people expect to change over time. The information can help predict future trends so that businesses can make plans to prepare for them.

The line graph in **Figure 7.2** charts changes in cell phone subscribers and fixed line (land line) subscribers over a 12-year period. Along the bottom of the graph are the years. Along the left side are the percentages of cell phone and fixed line subscribers. As you can see by following the lines, cell phone use increased steadily during that time period. Fixed line use peaked in 2006 and has declined somewhat since then. This kind of information can help marketers determine how to market their products. It can also help stores decide how much merchandise to order for the following year.

FIGURE 7.2 Bar Graph, Line Graph, and Pie Chart

How to Use Charts and Graphs Bar graphs, line graphs, and circle, or pie graphs are used to display different kinds of data. Here is how to choose the best type of graph to show your data. ***How are graphs used?***

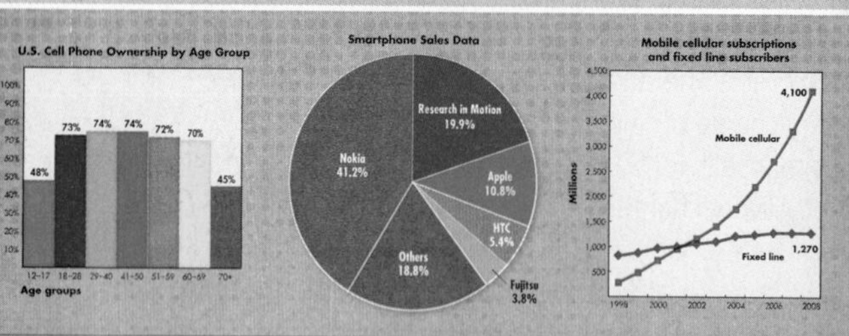

FIGURE 7.3 Main Reasons for Using the Web

Frequency Tables Display Counts Frequency tables are used to show counts for particular categories or intervals. This frequency table shows the number of Web-site uses, or hits, by purpose of visit. ***What was the most frequent purpose for using the Web? How might marketers use this information?***

Purpose for Use	Count or Frequency of Uses	Percent of Responses
Education	2,020	16%
Shopping	1,725	13%
Entertainment	1,977	15%
Work	2,168	17%
Communication	1,165	9%
Personal information	2,421	19%
Time-wasting	1,219	9%
Other	286	2%
Total responses	**12,981**	**100%**

CIRCLE GRAPHS

A **circle graph** is a pie-shaped figure that shows the relative sizes of the parts of a whole. Pie graphs can show the costs of different aspects of manufacturing, a department's budget, or how income from sales is used by a company.

Circle graphs offer an easy way to understand how a whole relates to its parts. A circle graph is better known as a **pie chart**, because it looks like a pie that is cut into slices of relative sizes. Pie charts allow companies to see how successful they were compared to other companies. They can use this information to assess their place in the market.

The pie chart in **Figure 7.2** shows a percentage breakdown of smartphone sales among the manufacturers. Without reading the numbers, you can see which company has the largest share of the smartphone market.

FREQUENCY TABLES

A frequency table lists numbers, fractions, or percentages for different intervals. It can reveal information for things like consumer buying behavior. For example, the frequency table in **Figure 7.3** shows information about different uses of the Web.

PRACTICE 7 (PROJECT)

The information in the following frequency table is data from a survey by age group on the uses of the Web. Based on this information, create a bar graph for the age ranges of 11–20 and 21–25.

PRIMARY USE OF THE INTERNET

	Percentage of Responses	
	Ages 11–20	**Ages 21–25**
Education	17%	16%
Shopping	8%	12%
Entertainment	19%	17%
Work	8%	15%
Communication	12%	10%
Personal Information	16%	17%
Time-wasting	16%	11%
Other	4%	2%
Total responses	100%	100%

Reading Check

Apply When would you use a pie chart instead of a bar graph to display data?

EXPLAIN

READING CHARTS AND GRAPHS

Ask students these guiding questions to focus the discussion on reading charts and graphs.

Guiding Questions

Define What is a bar graph?	a drawing made up of parallel bars lengths corresponding to what is being measured
Compare and Contrast the use of bar graphs and line graphs.	Bar graphs: used to compare numerical facts Line graphs: used to compare data over time

Visual Literacy

Figure 7.2 Caption Answer Read the caption question to students: ***How are graphs used?*** Graphs are used in a variety of ways. Basically they are used to show the relationship between two or more kinds of data. This can be done using line graphs, bar graphs, and circle graphs.

Reinforce Vocabulary

Analyze Words Preview the following words by reading them in context in this section. *Parallel* (first paragraph under Bar Graphs). Ask: ***What does* parallel *mean?*** *Parallel* means that two lines are always the same distance apart and never meet. *Variable* (first paragraph under Algebraic Thinking). Ask: ***What does the term* variable *mean?*** *Variable* means able to change. They are used to represent numbers we are not sure of or numbers that will change.

ELABORATE

Visual Literacy

Figure 7.3 Caption Answer Read the caption question to students: ***What was the most frequent use for the Web?*** To locate personal information was the most frequent use for the Web. Then read: ***How might marketers use this information?*** to place ads for products and services, to determine the types of sites used to gather personal information

Graphic Organizer

Display the pie chart and elicit students' opinions about the main reasons people use the Web.

Main Reasons for Using the Web

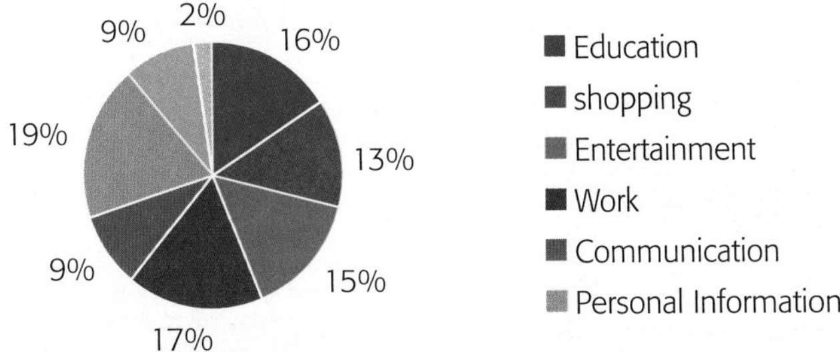

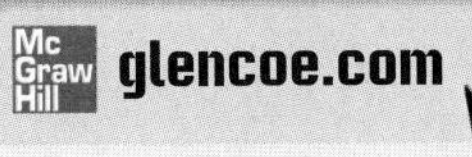
glencoe.com

Send students to the Online Learning Center to print this graphic organizer.

Reading Check Answer

Read the Reading Check question to students: ***When would you use a pie chart instead of a bar graph to display data?*** Students may say they would use a pie chart to show the relative sizes of the parts of a whole. For example, they might use one to show the percentage of students who are going to attend specific colleges as compared to all students who are going to attend college.

Practice 7 Answers (Project)

Student graphs should reflect appropriate percentages.

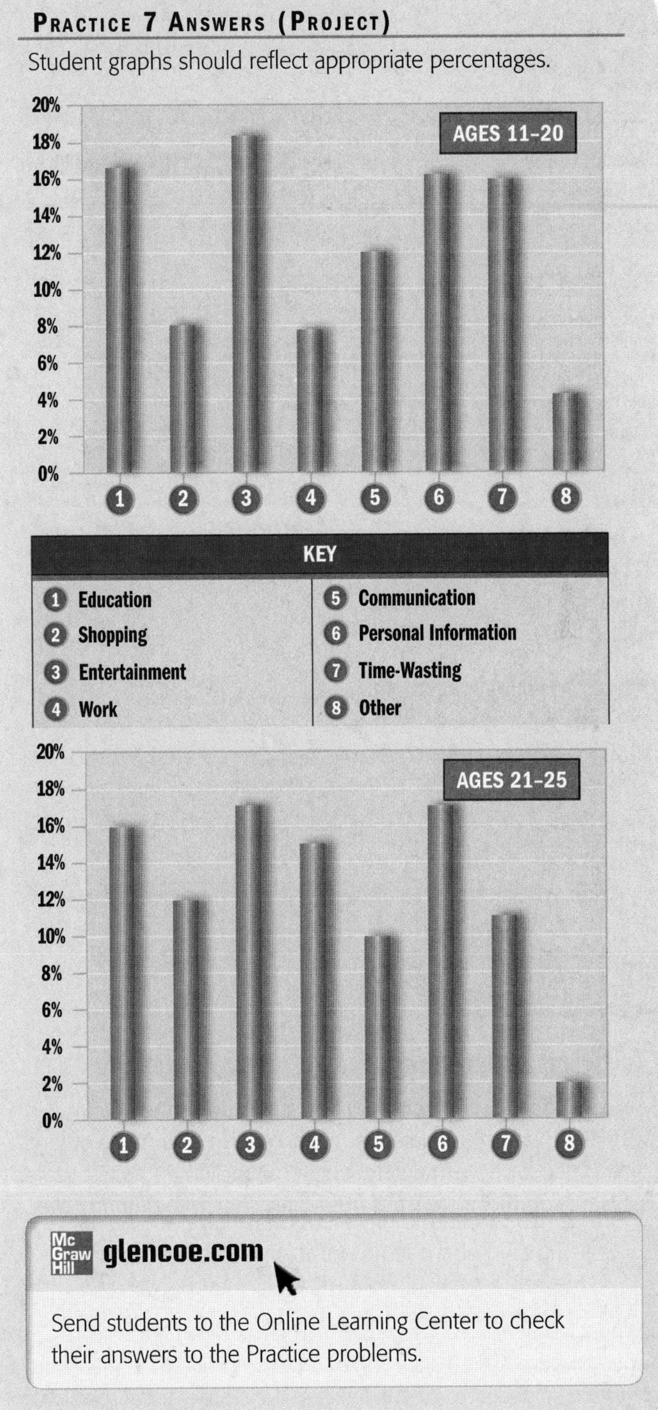

glencoe.com

Send students to the Online Learning Center to check their answers to the Practice problems.

ALGEBRAIC THINKING

Charts and graphs help organize information so we can analyze it and make decisions. But how do we analyze numbers to make sense of them? We use algebraic thinking to look for patterns and relationships. These patterns are called functions in mathematics. We also use symbols to represent variables, which are numbers we are not sure of or those that will change. For example, Asami, a marketing analyst, finds that 30 percent of those who buy a new car will purchase four new tires after two years. Asami's company needs to plan ahead. She wants to know how many tires this group will purchase three years from now.

Asami lets n stand for the number of new cars purchased next year, and t stand for the number of tires purchased in three years. Then, she writes an equation: $t = n \times 30\% \times 4$. So, if she estimates that 1 million new cars are sold next year, she knows that this group will purchase $1{,}000{,}000 \times 0.30 \times 4 = 1.2$ million tires in three years.

Reading Check

Recall What is a variable?

DESCRIPTIVE STATISTICS

Statistics are used to describe and summarize data. It makes the data more meaningful and easier to understand.

If you read the sports page of your local newspaper, you know something about statistics. Professional baseball, basketball, and football standings indicate the ranking of teams by games won and lost. They also show the percentage of wins for each team. Box scores for a baseball game include statistics on each team member's times at bat, hits, runs batted in, and runs scored.

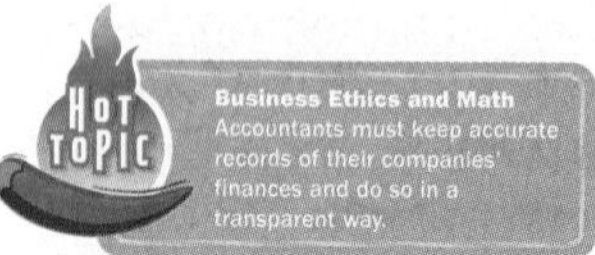

Business Ethics and Math Accountants must keep accurate records of their companies' finances and do so in a transparent way.

BUSINESS APPLICATIONS OF DESCRIPTIVE STATISTICS

In business, statistics are used in analyzing data. For example, Naoki is doing a study to track how many people use the Internet to make purchases. He collects data on thousands of people and uses statistics to find the following measures:

- The distribution
- The central tendency
- The dispersion

The distribution is a summary of the frequency of values for a variable such as age. This may be presented in a frequency distribution table that lists the percentage of customers making Internet purchases by age group.

Customers by Age	Percentage
12–17	48%
18–28	73%
29–40	74%
41–50	74%
51–59	72%
60-69	70%
70 and up	45%

The central tendency of a distribution is an estimate of the center of the distribution. Here are the three main estimates of central tendency:

- Mean
- Median
- Mode

The mean, also known as the *average*, is the most common way of describing central tendency. The mean is computed by adding up all the values and dividing by the number of values. Thus, the average of the values 4, 8, 13, 28, 35, 44, and 56 is 188 divided by 7 = 26.86, rounded to 27.

The median is the exact middle of a set of values. The median in the set of values above is 28. Notice that it is very close to the mean of 27. If there are an even number of values, the median is the mean of the two middle values.

The mode is the most frequently occurring value. You would not look for a mode in a set of only seven values, but it can be useful when there is a large number of values.

For example, you take a final exam in your marketing class. When the exams are corrected and graded, the scores range from 65 to 95. No more than two students receive the same score, except that 5 students scored 81. Thus, 81 is the mode.

Dispersion is the spread of values around the central tendency. The simplest way to measure the dispersion is with the range. The range is the highest value minus the lowest value. With final exam scores between 65 and 95, the range is 30. This is how far the scores are dispersed from the center of the scores.

After You Read **Section 7.2**

Review Key Concepts

1. **Calculate** the decimal equivalent of $\frac{2}{3}$. Round to the nearest thousandth.
2. **Determine** the decimal equivalent of 25 percent. What is the percentage equivalent of 1?
3. **Explain** how graphs are helpful in representing numerical data. What are three common forms of graphic representation?

Practice Academics

Social Studies

4. Use the Internet to learn about and define the CPI (Consumer Price Index) and the inflation rate. Draw a line graph representing the inflation rate over a recent ten-year period.

Mathematics

5. Employees who work overtime are usually paid time-and-a-half. This term means they are paid one-and-a-half times as much per hour as usual. How do you write time-and-a-half as a percentage? If your regular pay rate is $18 per hour, how much is your hourly rate for overtime?

Math Concept **Number and Operations: Representing Numbers** Fractions can be converted to decimal numbers or percents.

Starting Hints To solve this problem, write the expression "time-and-a-half" as 1.5, the decimal number. Multiply the decimal 1.5 by 100 to convert it to a percentage. Multiply the regular pay rate by the percentage to determine the over-time pay rate.

For help, go to the **Math Skills Handbook** located at the back of this book.

NCTM Number and Operations Understand numbers, ways of representing numbers, relationships among numbers, and number systems.

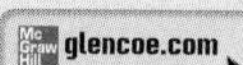

glencoe.com

Check your answers.

ELABORATE

Critical Thinking

Provide students with a list of 30 test scores. Have them work together in pairs to calculate the mean, median, and mode of the scores. Then have them determine the dispersion of the test scores. Ask: ***How can these statistics help a teacher in evaluating the effectiveness of a test?*** Sample answer: The mean will provide the class average for the test scores, the median will show the exact middle of the scores, and the mode will show which score showed up most frequently. The dispersion will show how far the scores are dispersed from the median. For example, the higher the mean, the better the students did on the test and the smaller the dispersion, the closer they were to the median score.

Reading Check Answer

Read the Reading Check question to students: ***What is a variable?*** A variable is numbers we are not sure of or those that will change.

Business Ethics and Math Ask students: ***What does it mean to keep books in a transparent way?***

Mini Project

Extension

Conduct a Survey Have students conduct a survey about people's preferences. The survey might look at people's tastes in music, for example. To survey people's tastes in music, the survey might list a number of different types of music and ask people to rank the list in order of their favorites. After students have collected their data, have them construct a frequency table and a graph to present their results. Results will vary. Ask students to share their tables and graphs with the class and discuss the results.

EVALUATE

DESCRIPTIVE STATISTICS

Ask these guiding questions to focus the discussion about descriptive statistics.

Guiding Questions

Identify What is one reason for using statistics?	One reason to use statistics is that it makes the data more meaningful and easier to understand.
Explain What are the distribution, the central tendency, and the dispersion?	distribution—summary of the frequency of values for a variable; central tendency—estimate of the center of the distribution, often defined by the mean, median, and mode; dispersion—the spread of values around the central tendency

Graphic Organizer

Display this diagram. Ask students to provide the terms to fill in the organizer.

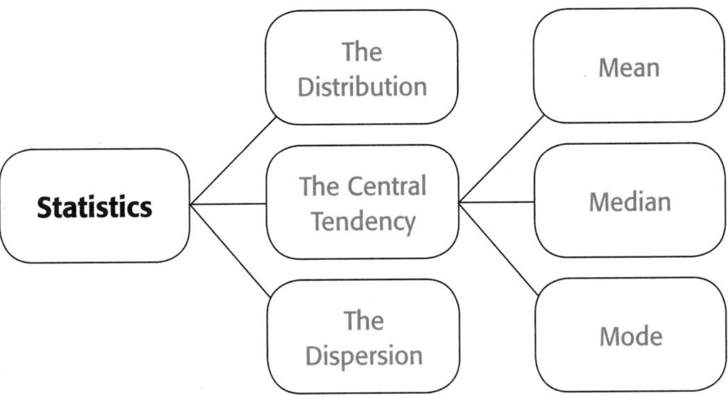

Graphic Organizer Send student to the Online Learning Center to print this graphic organizer.

After You Read Section 7.2

Review Key Concepts

1. The decimal equivalent of $\frac{2}{3}$, rounded to the nearest thousandth, is 0.667.
2. The decimal equivalent of 25% is .25; the percentage equivalent of 1 is 100%.
3. Graphs present information in a way that is easy to understand. Three common forms of graphic representation are bar graphs, line graphs, and circle graphs.

Practice Academics

Social Studies

4. The Consumer Price Index (CPI) is a measure of the average change over time in the prices urban consumers pay for goods and services. Inflation is a process of rising prices.

Mathematics

5. Time-and-a-half, written as a percentage, is 150%. If the regular pay rate is $18 per hour, then time-and-a-half would be $27 per hour.

glencoe.com

Answer Key Send students to the Online Learning Center to check their answers.

Basic Math Skills

Basic math skills such as using whole numbers, decimals, and fractions have a variety of applications in business.

MATH FUNDAMENTALS
WHOLE NUMBERS
FRACTIONS
DECIMALS
Inventory
Human Resources
Sales Forecasts
Market Share
Finance
Accounting
Payroll

Charts and graphs present data in a way that is easier to understand than series of numbers.

U.S. Cell Phone Ownership by Age Group
Age groups

Mobile cellular subscriptions and fixed line subscribers
Mobile cellular
Fixed line
Millions

Smartphone Sales Data
Nokia 41.2%
Research In Motion 19.9%
Apple 10.8%
NTC 5.4%
Fujitsu 3.8%
Others 18.8%

Written Summary

- When reading numbers, writing numbers, and writing checks, it is necessary to know the placement name for each digit and for groups of digits.
- A fraction is a number used to describe a part of a whole amount.
- A decimal number is a fraction or mixed number whose denominator is a power of 10.
- Rounding decimal numbers is common when multiplying with amounts of money, as when figuring tax, discounts, and gratuities.
- To convert a fraction to a decimal, divide the numerator by the denominator.
- There are two basic types of calculators.
- The more commonly used type of calculator uses the algebraic entry system.
- The other type of calculator uses the reverse-entry system.
- Charts and graphs present data in a way that is easier to understand than a long series of numbers.
- Charts and graphs are used to describe market trends, growth of sales, and other data.

Review Content Vocabulary and Academic Vocabulary

1. Arrange the vocabulary terms below into groups of related words. Explain why you put the words together.

Content Vocabulary
- digits (p. 165)
- fractions (p. 166)
- numerator (p. 166)
- denominator (p. 166)
- mixed number (p. 166)
- decimal number (p. 167)
- RPN (p. 175)
- percentage (p. 178)
- bar graph (p. 180)
- line graph (p. 180)
- circle graph (p. 181)
- pie chart (p. 181)

Academic Vocabulary
- survey (p. 166)
- formula (p. 172)
- estimate (p. 175)
- percent (p. 178)

Assess for Understanding

2. **Justify** Why is it important to know how to use algebraic operations by hand when calculators are available?
3. **Compare** When would you use fractions to present information? When would you use decimals for the same purpose?
4. **Contrast** What are the rules for adding or subtracting decimal numbers and the rules when multiplying and dividing decimal numbers?
5. **Identify** When have you seen percentage used? How would the presentation of this information change if the percentage was converted to a decimal? A fraction?
6. **Discuss** Why is it important to estimate your answer when using a calculator?
7. **Connect** How are the uses of different types of graphs connected to different measures of central tendency?
8. **Contrast** What are the different uses for bar graphs, line graphs, and circle graphs in business?
9. **Imagine** How can you share information about a changing market share to an audience that has difficulty with fractions, percentages, and decimals?

EVALUATE

Visual Summary

Express Creativity Ask students to develop their own visual summary of a concept in the chapter. Encourage students to use different formats for their visual summaries, such as a storyboard, a timeline, a table, a tree diagram, or a word web. Visual summaries will vary depending on the concept depicted and the visual manner in which it is depicted. Questions to ask when assessing a visual summary include:

- Is the summary clear, economical, and simple?
- Are any important steps left out?
- Are steps or concepts arranged in the same order as the original?
- Does the summary reveal a pattern that connects the details?
- Does the summary locate and highlight the most important information?

Review Content Vocabulary and Academic Vocabulary

1. Groups will vary. Sample answers:

   Group A—terms related to fractions: digits, fractions, numerator, denominator, mixed number, survey.

   Group B—terms related to calculators: RPN, estimate.
   Group C—terms related to percentages: decimal number, percentage, percent.

   Group D—terms related to charts and graphs: bar graph, line graph, circle graph, pie chart.

   Group E—method of computing surface area: formula.

EVALUATE

Assess for Understanding

2. It is important to know how to do algebraic operations by hand so that you know how to enter the information into the calculator.

3. When writing checks, the amount of the check is written first as a decimal, then as words for the dollars and a fraction for the cents.

4. To add or subtract decimal numbers, first list the numbers vertically, keeping the decimal points in line with each other. Then add or subtract as you would with whole numbers. To multiply decimal numbers, 1) multiply the two numbers as if they were whole numbers, 2) add the number of decimal places in the two numbers being multiplied, 3) working from the right, count off the same number of decimal places in the product and insert the decimal point. To divide decimal numbers, 1) determine whether the divisor is a decimal; if it is, move the decimal point to the right until the divisor is a whole number; 2) move the decimal point of the dividend the same number of places; 3) divide as usual; 4) place the decimal point in the answer directly above the decimal point in the dividend.

5. Student's answers may include: percentages are used to figure gratuities, discounts, or the amount of sales tax. When converting a percentage to a decimal or fraction, the presentation of the information would change as in this example: $75\% = 0.75 = \frac{3}{4}$.

6. It is important to estimate your answers when using a calculator because you may make errors when entering numbers or operations, so it is a good idea to have an estimate of the answer in mind.

7. Different types of graphs, especially line graphs and frequency tables, can be used to display measures of central tendency.

8. Answers may include: A bar graph can be used to show comparisons between and among numbers such as the percentages of people, divided by age groups, who make online purchases. Line graphs shows changes in quantity over a period of time. These types of graphs can be used to track sales of particular items over time. Circle graphs show how a part is related to a whole. These can be used to show where a company stands in sales in relation to other companies.

9. Students should recognize that a line graph is a good visual way to present information about a changing market share. The audience could tell by the line how the market is changing without having to deal with fractions, percentages, or decimals.

21st Century Skills

Problem-Solving Skills

10. **Calculating Estimates of Central Tendency** Suppose students in your class had the following scores on a final examination: 54, 56, 57, 59, 60, 62, 66, 69, 71, 73, 74, 76, 79, 82, 84, 85, 85, 85, 87, 89, 90, 91, 92, 93, and 94.
    A. What is the mean?
    B. What is the median?
    C. What is the mode?

Financial Literacy Skills

11. **Reaching a Savings Goal** Suppose that you have a part-time job, and you have saved $200 toward your goal of buying a new computer priced at $2,500. How much more will you have to save? If you can save $75 each week, how long will it take to save enough to buy the computer?

Everyday Ethics

12. **Hard Times and Hard Numbers** During the summer, a well-known hotel offers luxury rooms at $150 a night. In order to offer such a low price, hotel executives have to lay off hundreds of housekeepers who make $15 an hour. Then they hire new temporary housekeepers who make $8 an hour. Representatives of the hotel say that bad economic times make it necessary to lose staff in order to save money and give customers fair prices. But only veteran housekeepers, the lowest-paid staffers, are laid off. Write a one-page response to this situation that discusses whether it is cost-effective or ethical to lay off the lowest-paid employees of a company.

e-Marketing Skills

13. **Starting an Online Business** Imagine that a wealthy relative has offered to provide you with start-up costs up to $50,000 to set up your own online business. Research the costs associated with starting the e-business of your choice. Prepare a pie chart showing how much money should be allocated for each type of cost.

Build Academic Skills

Social Studies

14. **Economics** The global economy has expanded trade between the United States and many countries in recent years. Locate information about the dollar value of goods imported and exported in a recent year. (Hint: If you are using the Internet, use key words such as *top ten U.S. export and import partners.*) Draw a bar graph depicting the dollar value of imports from the top six countries.

NCSS IX D Global Connections Analyze the causes, consequences, and possible solutions to persistent, contemporary, and emerging global issues, such as health, security, resource allocation, economic development, and environmental quality.

English Language Arts

15. **Population Growth and Environmental Quality** Some researchers state that human population growth is the greatest threat to the world's environment. Use the Internet to research U.S. and world population growth in recent years and forecasts for population growth in the future. Also, research the effects of population growth on availability of food and water, fisheries, and forests. Then prepare a line graph showing the relationship of population to these resources.

NCTE 7 Conduct research and gather, evaluate, and synthesize data to communicate discoveries.

Mathematics

16. **Using a Calculator** Use a calculator to solve the following problem: Your local sales tax is 8.25 percent. What would be the tax on an item that sold for $35?

Math Concept **Number and Operations: Rounding** Numbers that end with the digits 5 through 9 are rounded up. Round down if the number ends with 4 or less.

NCTM Number and Operations Understand the meanings of operations and how they relate to one another.

For help, go to the **Math Skills Handbook** located at the back of this book.

Standardized Test Practice

Directions Read the following questions. On a separate piece of paper, write the best possible answer for each one.

1. What is the product of $259 × .0875 expressed in the correct form of measure?
   A. $22.66
   B. $22.67
   C. $26.66
   D. $26.67
2. True or false? When dividing decimal numbers, some answers will continue infinitely.
   T
   F
3. A ________ graph is a good choice for charting sales, prices, profits, and things that change over time.

Test-Taking Tip

Begin studying for a test a week or more before the test. Reviewing your textbook and notes for 20 or 30 minutes a day is far more effective than studying two or three hours on the night before a test.

DECA Connection Role Play

High School Marketing Student

Situation Assume the role of a high school marketing student. You have been hired for your first job. You are looking forward to working and earning money. You must develop a budget for yourself so that you can make wise use of your money. You will save a portion of your take-home pay from each paycheck. Part of your savings will be set aside for your future college expenses. Another part will be used to buy a laptop computer. You also have expenses that must be considered that include gas for your car, entertainment, clothing, and spending money.

You have been working on your personal budget. Make notes of realistic amounts for your planned savings and expenses. Use the amount of $160 as your weekly take-home pay to calculate the amounts you will budget for savings and the expenses listed above. Your best friend (judge) knows you are working on your personal budget. Your friend (judge) asks you why you are doing so much planning.

Activity You are to explain to your friend (judge) the importance of setting financial goals and managing your money in order to achieve them. You are to also explain the role a written budget plays in helping you achieve your goals. Use the figures you calculated for the budget items as examples.

Evaluation You will be evaluated on how well you meet the following performance indicators:

1. Demonstrate problem-solving skills.
2. Develop a personal budget.
3. Set financial goals.
4. Maintain financial records.
5. Demonstrate responsible behavior.

Download the Competitive Events Workbook for more Role-Play practice.

186 | Unit 4 · Skills for Marketing

Chapter 7 · Basic Math Skills | 187

EVALUATE

Problem Solving Skills

10.

A. The mean is 76.52.

B. The median is 79.

C. The mode is 85.

Financial Literacy Skills

11. You will need to save an additional $2,300. It will take 31 weeks to save the rest of the money.

Everyday Ethics

12. Students may suggest that it is not ethical to lay off the lowest-paid employees. They probably have the fewest marketable skills and will have the most difficulty finding a new job. They might also suggest that it is not necessarily cost-effective to lay off the lowest paid employees. Hiring and training new staff will add to the company's costs. A better solution might be to lose some of the middle management.

e-Marketing Skills

13. Pie charts will vary but may include such items as equipment, furnishings, facility, inventory, supplies, employees, product development, operating costs.

EVALUATE

Build Academic Skills

Social Studies

14. Students' answers will vary depending on data collected. Sample answer:

Dollar Value of Imports to U.S., Jan.–April, 2010

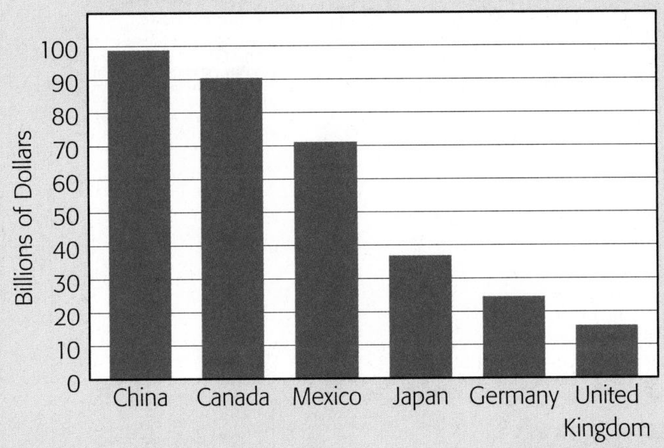

English Language Arts

15. Students' research may vary. Line graphs should show population growth as it relates to availability of food and water and its effects on fisheries and forests. General trends show that the population will continue to increase over the years and with responsible use of resources and technology, food and water sources can be maintained and expanded to support the growing population.

Mathematics

16. The cost per lemon is $0.33. However, customers buying only one lemon would be charged $0.34. Whenever a price cannot be divided evenly for a single item that is priced in multiples, a business should round up regardless of the usual mathematical rules for rounding.

Standardized Test Practice

1. A $22.66
2. True
3. line

DECA Connection Role Play

Evaluations will be based on these performance indicators:

1. **Demonstrate problem-solving skills.** Students should write about a situation in which they demonstrate their problem-solving skills. Situations may include determining how much money to put away for a new computer and still have enough money for regular expenses. Or, it might include having to budget for an unexpected expense like two new tires for the car.
2. **Develop a personal budget.** Personal budgets will vary but should be based on an income of $160 per week. Budget items may include fixed expenses such as car insurance, variable expenses such as clothing or books, and unexpected items such as a medical expense. Budgets should also include money put into savings to meet future financial goals and money set aside for emergencies.
3. **Set financial goals.** Financial goals are the purposes you want to accomplish with your money. What you do with your money today will affect your ability to achieve your financial goals in the future. Following a practical budget can help you achieve your financial goals and develop wise financial habits.
4. **Maintain financial records.** Spreadsheets should include all income (salary and interest income) and all outflow (savings funds, emergency funds, fixed expenses, and variable expenses). Budget numbers will be based on an income of $160 per week; expenses will vary.
5. **Demonstrate responsible behavior.** Demonstrations will vary but may include students providing examples of how they kept to their budget for a number of months–not making any unnecessary purchases and actually putting money into savings accounts.

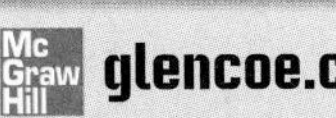

Role Plays For more DECA Role Plays, send students to the Online Learning Center to download the Competitive Events Workbook.

communication skills

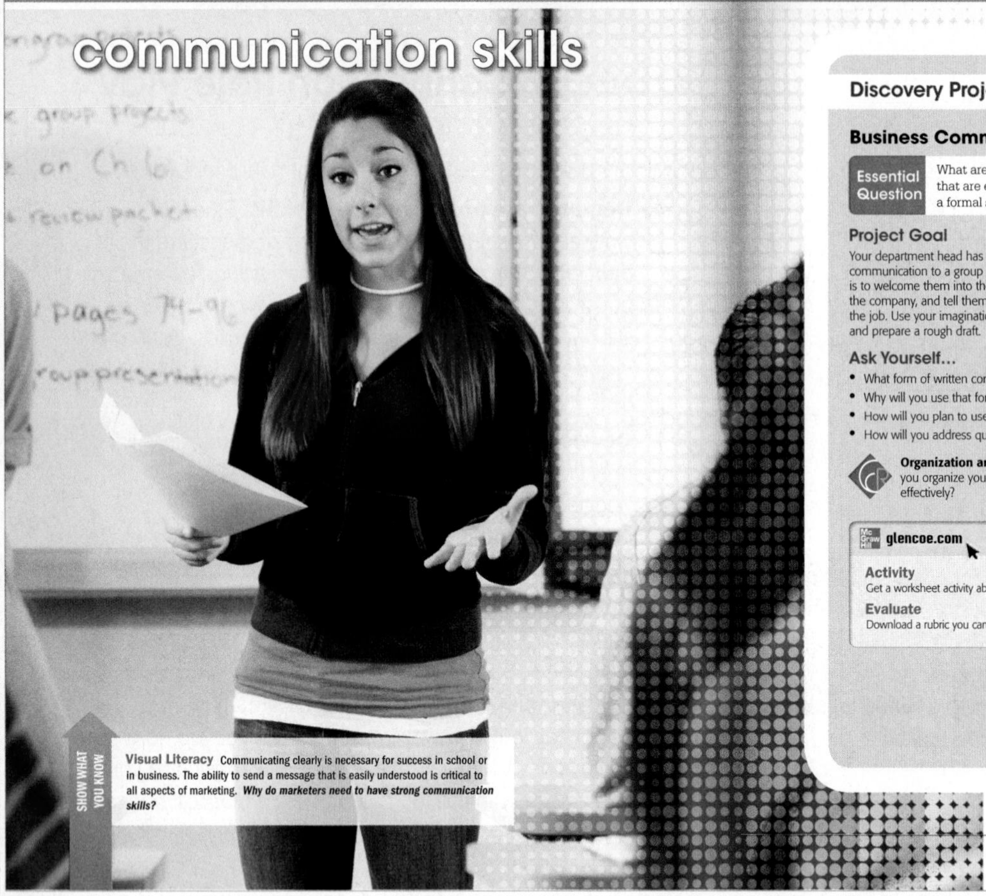

Visual Literacy Communicating clearly is necessary for success in school or in business. The ability to send a message that is easily understood is critical to all aspects of marketing. *Why do marketers need to have strong communication skills?*

Discovery Project

Business Communication

Essential Question What are four basic patterns that are effective for structuring a formal speech?

Project Goal

Your department head has asked you to prepare a written communication to a group of new employees. The purpose is to welcome them into the company, inform them about the company, and tell them what is expected of them on the job. Use your imagination, make up a company name, and prepare a rough draft.

Ask Yourself...

- What form of written communication will you use?
- Why will you use that form of communication?
- How will you plan to use language effectively?
- How will you address questions they might have?

Organization and Communication How will you organize your thoughts to communicate effectively?

glencoe.com

Activity Get a worksheet activity about business communication.

Evaluate Download a rubric you can use to evaluate your project.

DECA Connection

DECA Event Role Play

Concepts in this chapter are related to DECA competitive events that involve either an interview or role play.

Performance Indicators The performance indicators represent key skills and knowledge. Your key to success in DECA competitive events is relating them to the concepts in this chapter.

- Extract relevant information from written material.
- Prepare simple written reports.
- Organize information.
- Participate in a staff meeting.
- Make oral presentations.

DECA Prep

Role Play Practice role-playing with the DECA Connection competitive-event activity at the end of this chapter. More information on DECA events can be found on DECA's Web site.

ENGAGE

Visual Literacy

Read the chapter opener photo caption question to students: ***Why do marketers need to have strong communication skills?*** Communicating clearly is necessary for the success of marketers. The ability to send a message that is easily understood by the market is critical to all aspects of marketing—from advertising to sales to customer service.

Activate Prior Knowledge

Remind students that in Chapter 1 they learned about the seven marketing core functions—channel management, marketing information management, market planning, pricing, product/service management, promotion, and selling. Ask students: ***What is the marketing core function of promotion?*** Promotion is the effort to inform, persuade, or remind current and potential customers about a business's products or services. Then ask: ***What role does communication play in promotion?*** Students should realize that promotion cannot happen without communication. Marketers inform, persuade, and remind by communicating orally through television or radio ads, and through written communication in magazine, Internet, and newspaper ads.

Discovery Project

Business Communication Start a discussion that connects students to the Discovery Project Essential Question: ***What are four basic patterns that are effective for structuring a formal speech?*** (1) enumeration—listing items in order; (2) generalization—a statement that is accepted as true by most people; (3) cause and effect—demonstrates that one event or situation is the cause of another; and (4) compare and contrast—new ideas are explained by showing how they are similar to or different from the ideas listeners already know.

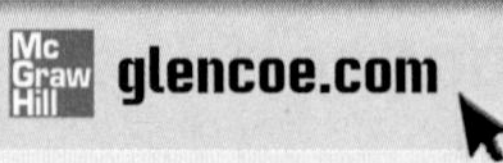

Discovery Project Resources Send students to the Online Learning Center to download a rubric to evaluate their projects.

ENGAGE

Introduce the Chapter

In this chapter, communications skills are explained and these major concepts are discussed:

- The communication process
- Channels, feedback, barriers, and setting
- Techniques for effective listening
- Barriers to listening for understanding
- Reading
- Techniques for effective speaking
- Speaking formally
- Basic considerations of writing
- Developing a writing style
- Forms of written communication
- Meetings and parliamentary procedure

Discussion Starter

The Importance of Communication Ask students to give examples of people working together for a common goal. Answers may include sports teams, musicians in a band, firefighters, or social activists. Then ask: ***How important is communication to the people in these examples? Can a team work effectively if there is no communication?*** Students should realize that in all of these examples, communication is extremely important. If members of sports teams do not communicate, there may be two people trying to do the same thing or no one doing what needs to be done. If firefighters do not communicate, both they and the people they are protecting could come to harm.

DECA Connection

Discuss the performance indicators listed in the DECA Connection activity. Explain to students that performance indicators tell them how to demonstrate their acquired skills and knowledge through individual or team competitive events.

glencoe.com

Competitive Events Workbook For more DECA Role Plays, send students to the Online Learning Center to download the Competitive Events Workbook.

PROGRAM RESOURCE ORGANIZER

PRINT RESOURCES

- **Student Edition**
- **Teacher Edition**
- **Student Activity Workbook with Academic Integration** includes worksheets and activities correlated to the text.
- **Mathematics for Marketing Workbook** provides math activities for every unit in the text.

TECHNOLOGY TOOLBOX

- **Connect**
- **ConnectPlus**
- **ExamView Assessment Suite** is a comprehensive solution for creating, administering, and scoring tests.

glencoe.com

Online Learning Center provides a variety of resources to enrich and enhance learning.

SECTION, CHAPTER, AND UNIT RESOURCES

- **Graphic Organizers** for organizing text concepts visually.
- **Digital Nation Activities** and **Green Marketer Activities** extend learning beyond the text features.
- **Career Chatroom Career Profiles** allow students to explore different marketing occupations in depth.
- **After You Read Answer Keys** for students to check their answers.
- **Discovery Project Rubrics** and **Marketing Internship Project Rubrics** for students to evaluate their projects.

PROGRAM RESOURCES

- **Student Activity Workbook with Academic Integration Teacher Annotated Edition** includes annotated answers for the activities and worksheets.
- **Marketing Research Project Workbook** provides a step-by-step approach for students to complete their own marketing research studies.
- **School-to-Career Activity Workbook** helps students relate their class work to on-the-job experience and involves work-site analysis and working with mentors.
- **Competitive Events Workbook** helps prepare students for state and national marketing education competitions.
- **Inclusion in the Marketing Education Classroom** provides teaching resources for working with students with special needs.
- **PowerPoint Presentations** provides visual teaching aids and assessments for this chapter.

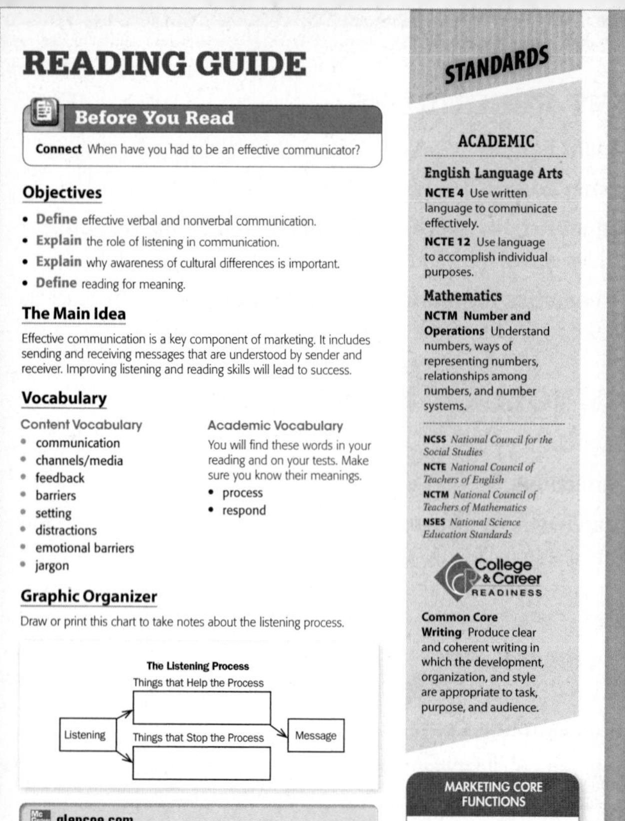

READING GUIDE

Before You Read

Connect When have you had to be an effective communicator?

Objectives

- **Define** effective verbal and nonverbal communication.
- **Explain** the role of listening in communication.
- **Explain** why awareness of cultural differences is important.
- **Define** reading for meaning.

The Main Idea

Effective communication is a key component of marketing. It includes sending and receiving messages that are understood by sender and receiver. Improving listening and reading skills will lead to success.

Vocabulary

Content Vocabulary
- communication
- channels/media
- feedback
- barriers
- setting
- distractions
- emotional barriers
- jargon

Academic Vocabulary

You will find these words in your reading and on your tests. Make sure you know their meanings.
- process
- respond

Graphic Organizer

Draw or print this chart to take notes about the listening process.

glencoe.com

Print this graphic organizer.

STANDARDS

ACADEMIC

English Language Arts

NCTE 4 Use written language to communicate effectively.

NCTE 12 Use language to accomplish individual purposes.

Mathematics

NCTM Number and Operations Understand numbers, ways of representing numbers, relationships among numbers, and number systems.

NCSS *National Council for the Social Studies*
NCTE *National Council of Teachers of English*
NCTM *National Council of Teachers of Mathematics*
NSES *National Science Education Standards*

College & Career READINESS

Common Core
Writing Produce clear and coherent writing in which the development, organization, and style are appropriate to task, purpose, and audience.

MARKETING CORE FUNCTIONS
- Marketing Information Management
- Selling

Section 8.1 Defining Communication

THE COMMUNICATION PROCESS

Communication is the **process** of exchanging messages between a sender and a receiver. These messages contain information, ideas, or feelings. The skills used to send and receive these messages are called communication skills. They include listening, reading, speaking, and writing. These skills allow a speaker or writer to present a message clearly and concisely. This allows a listener or reader to understand it easily.

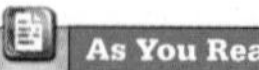

As You Read

Consider What are the differences between listening and reading and between speaking and writing?

CHANNELS OR MEDIA

Channels, or **media**, are the avenues through which messages are delivered. Examples include face-to-face conversations, telephone calls, text and instant messages, written memos, letters, reports, e-mail, and online chat and messaging through social networking sites. Channels differ in terms of how much content they can carry, the speed with which the message is delivered, cost of the message, and its quality. The choice of medium depends on the relative importance of these factors in the delivery of the message.

FEEDBACK

A receiver's response to a message is known as **feedback**. For example, if your boss asks you to post a report on the company Web site, you will probably ask some questions about what to include and when to post it. Feedback allows participants to clarify the message. It also ensures that all parties understand its meaning.

BARRIERS

Barriers are obstacles that interfere with the understanding of a message. They can be verbal barriers, such as vague or unclear language or a language or dialect that is unfamiliar to the receiver. For example, some people use the words *soda, pop, soda pop,* or even something else to describe the same drink. Marketers need to make sure the language they are using is appropriate for and understandable by their audiences. This applies to cross-cultural marketing as well. For example, the Spanish language has many dialects. People from different Spanish-speaking countries, such as Cuba, Mexico, Spain, and the Dominican Republic, often use different Spanish words to express the same concept. Businesses that try to target customers who are Hispanic must know about these cultural backgrounds.

> "Effective communication is vital in every aspect of business."

SETTING

The **setting** is where communication takes place. It includes place, time, sights, and sounds. It can be a barrier to communication. A salesperson at an electronics store may find it difficult to explain the features of a video camera to a customer if the music department across the aisle has a stereo playing at full volume.

Reading Check

Recall What are the four elements of the communication process?

ENGAGE

Anticipation Activity

Improving Student Achievement Ask students to name the different ways they communicate each day. Have a volunteer display the responses. Possible answers: face-to-face, cell phone, e-mail, texting, tweeting, and social networking. Then ask: ***Which of these represent spoken communication and which represent written communication?*** Spoken—face-to-face and phone; written—texting, e-mailing, tweeting, and posting. Tell students that learning to communicate effectively is important in both personal life and business.

Objectives

- **Define** effective verbal and nonverbal communication. Verbal—speaking, listening; nonverbal—writing, body language.
- **Explain** the role of listening in communication. It is the process of recognizing, assimilating, and evaluating what is heard.
- **Explain** why awareness of cultural differences is important. Businesses compete globally; their messages must be clear and appropriate for different cultures.
- **Define** reading for meaning. Read carefully, learn new words, search for answers, analyze and evaluate information.

Graphic Organizer

The Listening Process

Things that Help the Listening Process

Listening → identify the purpose, look for a plan, give feedback, search for a common interest, evaluate the message, listen for more than verbal content, listen for a conclusion, take notes → Message

Things that Stop the Listening Process

distractions, emotional barriers, planning a response

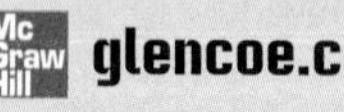

glencoe.com iWB

Graphic Organizer Send student to the Online Learning Center to print this graphic organizer.

EXPLORE

Before You Read

Read the Before You Read question aloud: ***When have you had to be an effective communicator?*** Possible answers: presenting oral reports for a school assignment or speeches when running for a school office; during a job interview; providing directions.

Preteaching Vocabulary

Have students go to the Online Learning Center at glencoe.com for the Chapter 8 Preteaching Vocabulary games.

Content Vocabulary

Display the Content Vocabulary terms and go over each word with students. Ask students to predict what the meaning of the term is. Then share the actual meanings with the class. communication—process of exchanging messages; channels or media—avenues through which messages are delivered; feedback—receiver's response to a message; barriers—obstacles that interfere with the understanding of a message; setting—where communication takes place; distractions—things that compete with the message for the listener's attention; emotional barriers—biases against the sender's opinions that prevent a listener from understanding; jargon—specialized vocabulary used by members of a particular group

Academic Vocabulary

Process—Examples Ask volunteers to orally present sentences in which they use the term *process*. Sentences should show that the students understand the meaning of the term. Possible answers: The process for baking a cake includes following a recipe. You must use a prescribed process to successfully download music files to your MP3 player. It was difficult to process so much information at one time. If students are unclear about the meaning of *process*, explain that it is a way of doing something. As a verb, it can also mean "to absorb information."

Respond—Examples Ask students to write sentences using the term *respond* to show their understanding of its meaning. Possible answers: I did not respond to the party invitation. She responded to my e-mail immediately.

Reading: Attentive Reading
Go to the Online Learning Center for a video in which a teacher uses read aloud and direct questioning to help her students identify elements of a persuasive essay.

Defining Communication

THE COMMUNICATION PROCESS

Ask these guiding questions to focus student discussion.

Guiding Questions

Identify What skills are included in communication skills?	listening, reading, speaking, writing
Apply What are some common barriers to communication among individuals from different cultures?	Physical—clothing or ornaments that obscure eyes, face; Linguistic—use of slang; Cultural—body language
Synthesize While commercials and print ads are effective, a phone solicitation or online ad can result in an immediate response. What are some drawbacks of sales pitches that ask consumers to make a quick decision?	Many potential customers may feel they need more time before making a decision.

As You Read

Read the question aloud: ***What are the differences between listening and reading and between speaking and writing?*** When listening, feedback is often given to the speaker; when reading, this is not usually the case. When writing, it is easier to change your message than it is when you are speaking.

Expert Advice

Read the quote to students:

> **"Effective communication is vital in every aspect of business."**

Share with students the Greek proverb: "To speak much is one thing, to speak well, another." Ask: ***How does this Greek proverb relate to the quote in your textbook?*** Communication does not necessarily need to be lengthy to be effective.

Reading Check Answer

Read the Reading Check question to students: ***What are the four elements of the communication process?*** The four elements of the communication process are listening, reading, speaking, and writing.

LISTENING

Listening for understanding is one of the most valuable communication skills. Listening is an active mental process. It involves recognizing, assimilating, assessing, and evaluating what is heard. (See **Figure 8.1** on page 195 for a list of barriers to listening.) Listening plays an important role when handling customer complaints, understanding feedback, recognizing clients' needs, and following directions.

HOT TOPIC
Listening
Usually, taking notes while listening will help you remember details, but in brief conversations note taking can interfere with communication.

TECHNIQUES FOR EFFECTIVE LISTENING

Listening, like all skills, must be learned. Effective listening is comprised of eight core components—purpose, plan, feedback, common interest, evaluate, listen, conclusion, and note taking. Practicing the listening techniques in this section will help you to improve your listening skills and become a more effective listener.

IDENTIFY THE PURPOSE

Prepare to listen by learning and reviewing the purpose of the communication. Managers planning a group meeting send out an agenda in advance so everyone will know the meeting's purpose. When a customer sets up a meeting, understand the meeting's purpose to be prepared to **respond** to the customer's questions.

LOOK FOR A PLAN

When you listen to a structured speech, think about how the speaker has organized the presentation. Be alert at the beginning of the speech because the speaker may give an outline of the main ideas of the talk. If you see a structure or pattern, it will be easier to see how the different parts of the message fit together. Face-to-face conversations are often informal and unplanned, so just stay focused on the message instead of thinking about structure.

GIVE FEEDBACK

When you are speaking about business, listen carefully, and then give feedback to show whether you have understood the message. Without interrupting, you can nod your head, smile, or frown. Look for an opportunity to ask questions when the speaker pauses or completes his or her point. Think through what has been said.

Many cultures use different gestures to show respect or greeting. ***What are some gestures that you use to demonstrate greeting or respect?***

Cultural Norms

Summarize your understanding of the message. Acknowledge your understanding respectfully or ask the speaker for clarification if you are uncertain.

When a speaker is giving instructions, it may be better to interrupt with questions than to wait for a pause. That way, a confusing point can be clarified and you can follow the remainder of the directions. However, before interrupting, be sure that the speaker is comfortable with this approach.

SEARCH FOR A COMMON INTEREST

Effective listening is easier when you are interested in the ideas being discussed. If you find the subject boring and are tempted to tune out, resist the temptation. Nodding and repeating key words will help you stay focused and let the speaker know that you are interested. Tuning out can become a bad habit and can cause you to miss important information.

EVALUATE THE MESSAGE

It is important to know how to respond appropriately to a message. You must evaluate it. For example, if a customer shares a personal point of view with you, even if you disagree, it would be inappropriate to make a sudden judgment. Doing so could be destructive to your relationship. Instead, try to see the message from the speaker's point of view. Listen carefully and try to understand the new information even if it conflicts with your view. Relax and do not become defensive. Recognize that the other person's experience may be unlike yours. Different experiences may cause differences in perception. Ask polite but probing questions to understand the message better. Try to identify any parts of the speaker's message with which you agree.

LISTEN FOR MORE THAN VERBAL CONTENT

Listen for more than just words in the speaker's message. What is communicated by the speaker's rate of speech, pitch, volume, and voice quality?

Awareness of cultural differences will help in the understanding of vocal cues. In the United States and other Western countries, including Canada, Australia, and Great Britain, speakers are expected to look at and speak directly to listeners. In many Asian countries, however, speakers show respect by averting their eyes, speaking in soft tones, and approaching their subject indirectly. A speaker in Canada who wants to say "No" will simply say "No." In Korea, a person who wants to communicate the same message may say, "That might be very difficult." Both statements mean "No," but the messages reflect cultural differences.

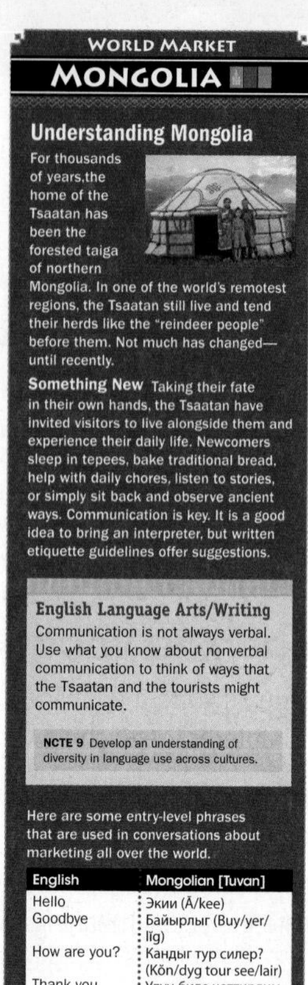

WORLD MARKET

MONGOLIA

Understanding Mongolia

For thousands of years,the home of the Tsaatan has been the forested taiga of northern Mongolia. In one of the world's remotest regions, the Tsaatan still live and tend their herds like the "reindeer people" before them. Not much has changed—until recently.

Something New Taking their fate in their own hands, the Tsaatan have invited visitors to live alongside them and experience their daily life. Newcomers sleep in tepees, bake traditional bread, help with daily chores, listen to stories, or simply sit back and observe ancient ways. Communication is key. It is a good idea to bring an interpreter, but written etiquette guidelines offer suggestions.

English Language Arts/Writing

Communication is not always verbal. Use what you know about nonverbal communication to think of ways that the Tsaatan and the tourists might communicate.

NCTE 9 Develop an understanding of diversity in language use across cultures.

Here are some entry-level phrases that are used in conversations about marketing all over the world.

English	Mongolian [Tuvan]
Hello	Экии (Ă/kee)
Goodbye	Байырлыг (Buy/yer/lĭg)
How are you?	Кандыг тур силер? (Kŏn/dyg tour see/lair)
Thank you	Улуу-биле четтирдим (oo/loo bĕ/lĕ chĕt/tur/dĭm)
You're welcome	Ажырбас (Ăzh/yr-băs)

EXPLAIN

Activate Prior Knowledge

Listening Experiences Ask students: ***Have you ever been in a situation when a sales clerk or other employee talked too much?*** Ask volunteers to share their experiences. Then ask: ***Have you ever had a sales clerk who listened too much?*** If students are uncertain what is meant by "listened too much," tell them that it's not likely that a sales clerk will listen too much—the more one listens, the better able he or she should be to help meet the customer's needs because listening will generally provide more knowledge or information that can help the clerk give the customer exactly what he or she wants. Tell students that President Calvin Coolidge once said, "Nobody ever listened himself out of a job." Ask: ***Do you think this is true? How might someone "listen himself out of a job"?*** Students may suggest that if someone only listens and never acts, he may "listen himself out of a job."

Listening Ask students: ***Do you think it is useful to take notes during a conversation? Why or why not?*** Ask students: ***Have you ever been so focused on taking notes that you did not realize the teacher asked you a question? Did this make communication difficult?***

Visual Literacy

Cultural Norms Caption Answer Read the caption question to students: ***What are some gestures that you use to demonstrate greeting or respect?*** Answers may include shaking hands, kissing on the cheek, hugging, winking, nodding, saluting, and bowing. Have students practice appropriate classroom gestures. Ask: ***Which greeting felt most comfortable? Why?*** Some may prefer handshakes because they are comfortable with touching others. Others may prefer nods or bows because they are not comfortable touching others.

ELABORATE

LISTENING

Ask students whether they find it easy or difficult to listen. Ask: ***What do you have the most difficulty listening to?*** Students may suggest that they find it difficult to listen to long speeches or lectures or to people they disagree with. Tell students that there are techniques to use to make a better, more effective, listening experience. Then use these guiding questions to focus the discussion on listening.

Guiding Questions

Describe What are eight techniques for effective listening?	Identify the purpose, look for a plan, give feedback, search for a common interest, evaluate the message, listen for more than verbal content, listen for a conclusion, and take notes are techniques for effective listening.
Apply Imagine that you and a friend are in a noisy darkened room. Your friend is upset and trying to explain why. How can you be a good listener?	Students might suggest that they employ the following techniques to help them focus on the message: identify the purpose, give feedback, evaluate the message, listen for more than verbal content, and listen for a conclusion.
Analyze Why is listening considered to be an active mental process?	Listening involves recognizing, assimilating, assessing, and evaluating what is heard.

Mini Project

Extension

Critical Thinking Write the phrase "listening is more than hearing" on the board. Ask students to share what they think the phrase means. Students may suggest that you can hear things—birds singing, water running, cars going by, people talking—but to listen you have to pay attention to what you are hearing, you have to focus your thought process. Ask students to share situations in which they "hear" and situations in which they "listen." Answers may include: "I listen when my parents tell me to do something." "I hear my little sister telling about her day at school." "I listen to the explanations in algebra class." "I hear the bus driver telling students to be quiet."

WORLD MARKET

ENGLISH LANGUAGE ARTS/WRITING

Ask students to imagine what it would be like to be a Tsaatan villager in charge of welcoming tourists and showing them around the village. Then have students form pairs. One student acts the role of the villager, and the other student should play the role of a tourist. Challenge them to communicate with each other without speaking. Ask: ***What was easy about this process?*** Possible answers: It was easy to smile and nod greetings, and to use simple sign language like pointing and demonstrating how to do something. ***What was difficult or impossible to express?*** Possible answers: It was difficult to ask for more information, and impossible to have an actual discussion about anything.

Mini Project

Enrichment

Self Rating Display the table. Have students think of typical listening experiences such as a class lecture, a guest speaker, a talk at a religious center, a political speech, and so on. Then have them rate themselves as listeners.

	Always	Almost Always	Sometimes	Almost Never	Never
Do you identify the purpose of what you are listening to?					
Do you look for a plan when listening?					
Do you provide the speaker with feedback?					
Do you search for a common interest?					
Do you evaluate the message?					
Do you listen for more than verbal content?					
Do you listen for a conclusion?					
Do you take notes?					

glencoe.com

Graphic Organizer Send students to the Online Learning Center to print this graphic organizer.

Career Chatroom

Tali Pressman
Managing Director
Cornerstone Theater Company

What do you do at work?

Working at a mid-size, not-for-profit theater company means that each staff person wears many hats. I wear the management and fundraising hats—managing the organization's operations and finances, the Board of Directors, and supervising the staff to make sure each facet of the organization runs smoothly. I am also responsible for raising funds to keep the company open and thriving, and for creating excellent community-engaged theater.

What is your key to success?

I am passionate about my work and make strong, informed choices. I think that the key to success is communication—this means speaking so people can hear you and truly listening to others. Mindful, intentional communication has helped me create a lasting and growing network of colleagues.

What skills are most important to you?

Strong writing and editing skills are a must. Active listening, the ability to collaborate with others, and planning are necessary when working as part of a team and when building relationships with funders and other supporters.

glencoe.com

Read more about this career and get a Career Exploration Activity.

LISTEN FOR A CONCLUSION

Listen carefully for the speaker's conclusion. You may want to take action based on it. Do not jump to your own conclusion before the speaker has finished presenting the facts that support his or her conclusion. Be prepared to check your understanding by asking well-thought-out questions. If the situation is a formal one, wait to ask questions at the right time. Intelligent questions indicate not only interest but also respect for the speaker's work.

TAKE NOTES

Try to identify a plan in the presentation of formal meetings. Then structure your notes according to the plan. Take notes on the main points presented at business meetings. Important points are often preceded by signal words such as *first, second, next, then, another, therefore,* and *thus.* If there is a summary at the end of the meeting, listen carefully and check your notes to make sure you understood the main ideas.

BARRIERS TO LISTENING FOR UNDERSTANDING

A barrier to receiving a message can be environmental, such as a plane flying overhead or a cell phone ringing loudly. It may involve attitudes and characteristics of the listener. Some common barriers include the following:

- **Distractions** **Distractions** are things that compete with the message for the listener's attention. These can include noises, conversations, and competing thoughts. One way to overcome distractions is to move away from them.
- **Emotional barriers** **Emotional barriers** are biases against the sender's opinions that prevent a listener from understanding. Poor listeners close their minds to things with which they disagree. Good listeners always listen with an open mind.
- **Planning a response** Planning a response occurs when the receiver of the message stops listening and begins to think about what to say next. A person cannot focus on the message and plan a response at the same time.

Listeners must avoid or overcome any barriers to concentrate on the message.

Reading Check

Explain Why is listening a good communication skill?

FIGURE 8.1 Barriers to Listening

Listen Carefully Barriers to listening interfere with communication. They prevent the listener from receiving and understanding the messages sent to them. ***How can you be a good listener?***

DISTRACTIONS Distractions interfere with the ability to listen well. You may be distracted by thoughts about another subject. Focus your attention on the speaker's words.

EMOTIONAL BARRIERS When you have a negative emotional reaction to something someone says, it prevents you from concentrating on what is being said. To overcome this barrier, try to keep an open mind.

PLANNING A RESPONSE If you are trying to figure out what to say when another person is still speaking, you will not take in all that he or she is saying. To overcome this barrier, listen carefully until the other person has finished, and then respond.

194 | Unit 4 · Skills for Marketing

Chapter 8 · Communication Skills | 195

EXPLAIN

Career Chatroom

Focus the discussion by asking these guiding questions.

Guiding Questions

Analyze How does Tali Pressman use communication in her work?	supervising staff members, managing the board of directors, soliciting funds.
Predict If Tali Pressman hired an assistant, what skills would the assistant need?	writing, editing, listening, collaboration, planning, and teamwork

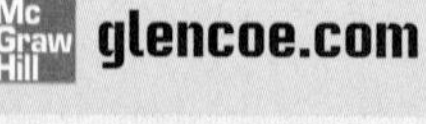

glencoe.com

Career Exploration Send students to the Online Learning Center to find more information about this career and to get a Career Exploration activity.

Mini Project

Differentiated Instruction

Kinesthetic Learners Divide the class into groups of three or four. Have each group create and present one or more skits on dealing with common diversity issues in the workplace such as racial issues, physical disability issues, disparity between men and women, or personality conflicts. Skits should present a problem and a possible solution. Skits should emphasize the use of communication, especially listening, in trying to resolve the workplace issues. Students should exhibit good listening skills in the skits. Now have some of the groups present skits in which they do not show good listening skills. In these skits, students should not pause to listen. They should present nonverbal communication, and they should not acknowledge understanding. Ask the class to identify what should have been done differently. Students should suggest that the people in the skits should have used better listening skills such as pausing, giving nonverbal feedback, and acknowledging understanding.

ELABORATE

Reading Check Answer

Read the Reading Check question to students: ***Why is listening a good communication skill?*** Listening promotes communication by helping listeners and readers to understand information more easily. Listening plays an important role in handling customer complaints, understanding feedback, recognizing clients' needs, and following directions.

Visual Literacy

Figure 8.1 Read the caption question to students. ***How can you be a good listener?*** Good listeners identify the purpose of what they are listening to, look for a plan, give feedback, search for a common interest, evaluate the message, listen for more than verbal content, listen for a conclusion, and take notes. They do not allow distractions, emotional barriers, or planning a response to interfere with their listening. Then ask these guiding questions to focus the discussion about barriers to listening.

Guiding Questions

List What are three barriers to listening?	distractions, emotional barriers, planning a response
Apply Imagine that you are listening to a lecture. The instructor has asked that questions and comments be held until the end of the lecture. The instructor made a point you would like to respond to but you must wait. What would you do?	Possible answers: continue listening and taking notes and hope to remember the comment when the time comes; jot down the question in the margin of their notes so they won't forget to ask later.
Analyze When you have a negative emotional reaction to something someone says, it prevents you from concentrating on what the message is. How can you keep an open mind to try to overcome this barrier?	Keeping an open mind means not evaluating what the speaker is saying based on your own feelings. Trying to listen and understand without making a judgment is difficult but necessary.

Critical Thinking

Tell students that attitudes in listening are important. When you have a positive attitude toward someone, you remain open and receptive. If you have a negative attitude, you become closed and critical, no matter how hard you try to listen. Ask: ***How can you maintain a positive attitude in situations when you are angry, disappointed, or uncomfortable?*** Students may suggest letting their anger, disappointment, or discomfort go and trying to focus on the words of the speaker rather than on the situation or what has happened to cause the negative feelings.

Mini Project

Differentiated Instruction

English Language Learners Divide the class into six groups. Assign each of the barriers to listening—distractions, emotional barriers, planning a response—to two different groups. Each group should develop a skit that demonstrates the barrier they have been assigned. The barriers can be demonstrated in very obvious ways or in more subtle ways. If time and interest allow, students might use simple props, costumes, and so on. After students have had time to prepare, have them present the skits to the class. As you introduce the skits, do not tell which barrier is being demonstrated. After each skit, ask the class to identify which barrier was demonstrated. Ask the class for suggestions on how to overcome the barriers. List their suggestions on the board. Suggestions for overcoming distractions may include moving away from them; suggestions for overcoming emotional barriers may include listening with an open mind; and suggestions for overcoming planning a response may include focusing on the message and waiting to respond.

Students with Learning Disabilities Bring to class a variety of articles from newspapers and magazines. Have students practice listening for meaning as you read aloud paragraphs from the articles. Then have students write short paraphrases of the articles. Ask volunteers to read their paraphrases to the class. Have the class evaluate how closely the paraphrase captures the meaning of the article.

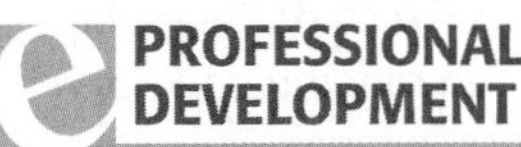

ELL: Words in Action Go to the Online Learning Center to view a video clip in which students act out vocabulary words.

READING

Reading, like listening, is an active mental process of receiving and understanding a message. Reading skills are essential for all jobs. In fact, they are usually needed to get a job in the first place. Applicants must read online job postings and help-wanted ads. In the workplace, reading skills are needed to interpret information in schedules, graphs, training manuals, letters, memos, e-mails, and reports.

KNOW THE PURPOSE OF YOUR READING

Many of the techniques for effective listening also apply to reading. For instance, it is helpful when reading to

- look for a plan
- search for an interest
- evaluate the message

A valuable technique for building good reading skills is to keep in mind the purpose for your reading. Good readers know *why* they are reading. When you read a novel, magazine, or newspaper, typically your purpose is reading for pleasure. You are hoping to simply enjoy what you are reading, so can read as fast or as slowly as you want.

When you read a job application form or a company memo, you have to read more carefully because you have a different purpose. This is information that is important to know in order to do your job well. Every word must be read carefully to ensure that you gain a complete understanding. You can accomplish this by using strategies that help you read for meaning.

Reading for Meaning
Focus
Summarize
Connect
Visualize
Build Vocabulary

READING FOR MEANING

Reading for meaning requires that a person read carefully. He or she must figure out the meaning of new words, search for answers, and analyze and evaluate information—often in a short period of time.

Most job-related reading assignments involve reading for meaning. For example, you may be required to search for sources online or read through a large report to find information about marketing trends. Another job-related reading task is checking facts.

There are five strategies that can improve the ability to read for meaning:

1. **Focus your mind.** The mind does not focus on a subject automatically. It must be trained. Monitoring your thoughts when you read can keep you focused. Think about how each paragraph relates to your purpose for reading.
2. **Summarize as you read.** As you finish each paragraph and section of the text, mentally review what you have just read and summarize it. If you do not understand the text, go over it again. If it is still unclear, jot down a question so that you can follow up on it later.
3. **Make connections.** Think about how the material relates to ideas or information with which you are familiar.
4. **Form mental pictures.** Try to form pictures of the people, places, things, and situations described. This can help you remember the material in a meaningful way.
5. **Build your vocabulary.** You may come across words that are unfamiliar when reading. Skipping over these words may cause you to miss key points in the message. Try to figure out the meaning by the way the word is used in the sentence. Use a dictionary and learn how to use the thesaurus and dictionary included in office computer software. Looking up words will improve your vocabulary and your understanding.

In job-related reading, you may come across **jargon**, a specialized vocabulary used by members of a particular group. Because these words or meanings are not commonly used, they are often not listed in standard dictionaries. If you do find a dictionary entry for a word that is often used as jargon, the definition given may not match the way it is used in a professional setting.

For example, when *market* is used by people who work in marketing, it is an example of jargon because it has a specific meaning for marketers. In the dictionary, *market* may be defined as "any place where business is conducted." To marketing professionals, however, *market* means "a group of people or organizations that share a need for a particular product and have the willingness and ability to pay for it."

Learning the jargon used in your field will make it easier for you to do job-related reading. You will be able to better understand information that relates to your profession. Asking questions about the way specific terms are used will help you familiarize yourself with words not found in the dictionary. Once you learn the jargon, you will be able to effectively communicate with others in your field.

You can expect to exchange job-related text messages and e-mails with co-workers, supervisors, customers, and suppliers. In addition to understanding the jargon used in your job, you will also need to learn the keyboard shortcuts and abbreviations specific to your company's business. You will find that these communication skills are vital to doing any job well.

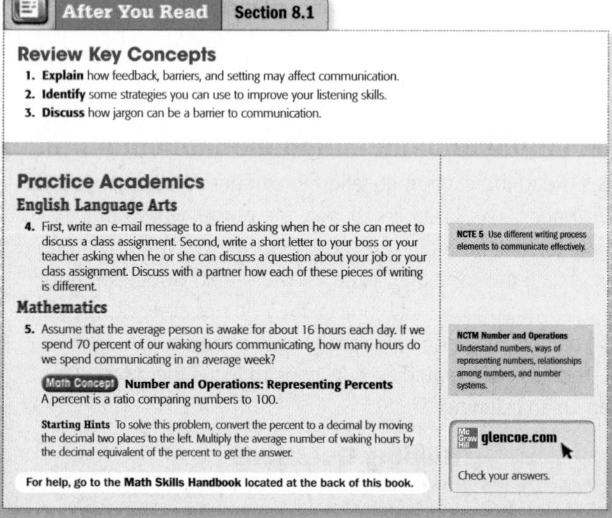

After You Read | **Section 8.1**

Review Key Concepts

1. **Explain** how feedback, barriers, and setting may affect communication.
2. **Identify** some strategies you can use to improve your listening skills.
3. **Discuss** how jargon can be a barrier to communication.

Practice Academics

English Language Arts

4. First, write an e-mail message to a friend asking when he or she can meet to discuss a class assignment. Second, write a short letter to your boss or your teacher asking when he or she can discuss a question about your job or your class assignment. Discuss with a partner how each of these pieces of writing is different.

NCTE 5 Use different writing process elements to communicate effectively.

Mathematics

5. Assume that the average person is awake for about 16 hours each day. If we spend 70 percent of our waking hours communicating, how many hours do we spend communicating in an average week?

NCTM Number and Operations Understand numbers, ways of representing numbers, relationships among numbers, and number systems.

Math Concept **Number and Operations: Representing Percents** A percent is a ratio comparing numbers to 100.

Starting Hints To solve this problem, convert the percent to a decimal by moving the decimal two places to the left. Multiply the average number of waking hours by the decimal equivalent of the percent to get the answer.

For help, go to the **Math Skills Handbook** located at the back of this book.

glencoe.com Check your answers.

ELABORATE

Reinforce Vocabulary

Ask students to provide examples of jargon. Students may mention terminology and acronyms associated with online networking sites, text messaging, surfing, and computers.

Critical Thinking

Ask students: ***What do reading and listening have in common?*** Reading and listening are both active mental processes that involve trying to understand a message. Then ask students to recall the primary elements of communication: senders, receivers, messages, channels, feedback, barriers, and setting. Ask: ***Which of the primary elements of communication are included in reading and listening experiences?*** All of the primary elements of communication are included in reading and listening experiences. Students may not mention feedback as being part of a reading experience. Tell them that immediate feedback may not be possible, but you can write letters to editors of newspapers and to publishers if you agree or disagree with something you have read.

Graphic Organizer

Display this diagram. Ask students to provide details for each of the strategies for reading for meaning. Sample answers:

Reading for Meaning
Focus Think about how each paragraph relates to your purpose for reading.
Summarize Mentally review what you have just read, go over it again if you do not understand what you have read.
Connect Ask yourself: How does the material relate to what I already know?
Visualize Form pictures of the people, places, things, and situations described.
Build Vocabulary Use context or a dictionary to figure out the meanings of words you do not know.

Graphic Organizer Send student to the Online Learning Center to print this graphic organizer.

EVALUATE

Mini Projects

Enrichment

Read for Meaning Bring to class examples of reading material such as newspapers, novels, store catalogs, and news or entertainment magazines. Tell students you are going to test their ability to read for meaning. Then ask them to skim a page or article for one minute. At the end of one minute, ask: ***How would you summarize the article?*** Answers will vary depending on the articles read and on how well students read the articles. Ask: ***What techniques did you use to read for meaning?*** Students may mention their own techniques or they may mention the techniques listed in the text—focus your mind, summarize as you read, make connections, form mental pictures, build your vocabulary.

Reading Online Ask students to visit the Web site of a local or national newspaper. Tell them to compare the news, entertainment, sports, business, ads and other sections, and identify their different purposes. Ask: ***How is each section read differently?*** Sample answer: News is read carefully with the intent to learn, to know what is going on around you; entertainment and sports are read for fun; business is read for information; and ads are read to learn where to buy necessities for the best price. Ask students to share their answers with the class.

Mock Interviews Have students work in pairs to conduct mock interviews as though they were on a television talk show. One student should start as the interviewer and the other as the interviewee. The interviewer should prepare questions to ask. Both the interviewer and interviewee should practice giving feedback, using both verbal and nonverbal techniques. Then have students switch roles. Ask: ***Was it difficult to stay focused on the interview questions? Why or why not?*** Students may suggest that there were distractions in the classroom or they just weren't interested in the activity. Ask: ***How did receiving feedback make you feel?*** Some students may say they appreciated the feedback because it made them feel like the other person was really paying attention and interested in the conversation. Others may feel offended by criticism.

After You Read — Section 8.1

Review Key Concepts

1. Feedback allows participants to clarify the message and it ensures that all parties understand the meaning of the communication. Barriers interfere with the understanding of the message being communicated. A setting can be a barrier to communication when, for example, the setting is too noisy for the listener to hear and understand what is being communicated.
2. Strategies include: identifying the purpose of the communication; looking for the plan or organization of a structured speech; giving verbal or nonverbal feedback to the speaker; searching for a common interest in the ideas being discussed; evaluating the message so you know how to respond to it; listening for more than verbal content through the speaker's rate of speech, pitch, volume, and voice quality; listening for a conclusion rather than jumping to your own conclusion; taking notes that are structured according to the plan in the presentation.
3. Jargon is a specialized vocabulary used by members of a particular group. Jargon can be a barrier if used to communicate to people who are not in the group. Those people likely would not understand the jargon and so it would become a barrier to communication.

Practice Academics

English Language Arts

4. E-mail messages and letters will vary. Students may suggest that the letter is a more formal type of communication. The letter would also be written more formally because it is written to a superior while the e-mail is written to a peer.

Mathematics

5. 78.4 hours [$7 \times (16 \times .70) = 7 \times 11.2 = 78.4$]

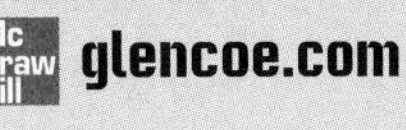

Answer Key Send students to the Online Learning Center to check their answers.

READING GUIDE

Before You Read

Share When have you had to change the way you spoke or wrote for different audiences?

Objectives

- **Explain** how to organize and present your ideas.
- **Demonstrate** professional telephone communication skills.
- **Explain** how to write effective business letters and persuasive messages.

The Main Idea

Speaking and writing are ways to send messages. Building professional speaking and writing skills will ensure that your messages are communicated successfully.

Vocabulary

Content Vocabulary
- persuade
- enumeration
- generalization

Academic Vocabulary

You will find these words in your reading and on your tests. Make sure you know their meanings.
- enhance
- sequence

Graphic Organizer

Draw or print this chart to write speaking tips in one circle and writing tips in the other. Write tips for both in the overlapping space.

Print this graphic organizer.

STANDARDS

ACADEMIC

English Language Arts

NCTE 1 Read texts to acquire new information.

NCTE 5 Use different writing process elements to communicate effectively.

Mathematics

NCTM Measurement Apply appropriate techniques, tools, and formulas to determine measurements.

NCSS *National Council for the Social Studies*
NCTE *National Council of Teachers of English*
NCTM *National Council of Teachers of Mathematics*
NSES *National Science Education Standards*

Common Core
Writing Write informative/explanatory texts to examine and convey complex ideas and information clearly and accurately through the effective selection, organization, and analysis of content.

MARKETING CORE FUNCTIONS

Marketing Information Management

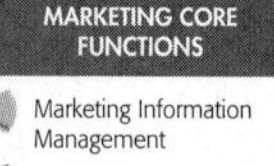
Promotion

m.e. Section 8.2 Speech and Writing

SPEAKING

People use speech to answer the telephone, to ask questions, and to discuss plans at meetings. In marketing, speaking has applications in customer relations, presenting marketing plans, and television advertising. Speaking is an important part of most aspects of business and marketing, so it is important to know how to speak effectively.

As You Read

Consider How is talking with your friends different from presenting to your class?

SHOW RESPECT

In most business situations, the most important rule is to show courtesy and respect for others. Whether handling a customer complaint or addressing a coworker at a meeting, maintain a friendly tone and always use proper grammar and vocabulary.

KNOW THE PURPOSE

As with listening and reading, it is helpful when speaking to know your purpose. Most often, speaking is done to inform, persuade, or entertain.

- **Inform**—Conversations with customers and general business meetings are held to inform others—to pass on information. When speaking to inform, be clear and concise—get to the point.
- **Persuade**—Marketing involves sending messages that convince others to change how they think or what they do. To **persuade** someone is to convince that person to change an opinion in order to get him or her to do what you want. Before you prepare to speak, identify your listeners' needs. Then talk about how you, your company, or your product can meet those needs. Persuasive speaking is also important in conflict resolution, when there is a need to present a point of view or suggest a solution.
- **Entertain**—Sometimes the purpose of speaking is to entertain others. Salespeople frequently need to entertain clients or customers. It is not necessary to be a comedian to joke and tell stories. This kind of informal speaking helps create a comfortable atmosphere, build friendships, and improve customer relations.

USING YOUR VOICE AND NONVERBAL CUES

Good communicators use their voices effectively, changing their tone and pace to improve delivery. Some people, such as news or sports commentators, have a natural talent for delivery. With practice, you too can improve communication by better controlling your voice.

> "Speaking is an important part of most jobs."

Nonverbal cues that can **enhance** presentation are body language and eye contact. When speaking, maintain eye contact with your listeners as much as possible.

SPEAKING FORMALLY

Effective speaking strategies are even more important in formal settings. Whether the speech is used to present a marketing plan to your marketing department or to give a speech to an audience of 500 people, the guidelines are the same. A good speech has a formal structure or organization. It begins with an opening statement that summarizes the topics to be covered. It ends with a concluding statement that reviews these topics. In between, four basic patterns can be used to structure the message. Visual aids often accompany the words spoken.

ENGAGE

Anticipation Activity

Improving Student Achievement Ask students to name their favorite writers. Ask a volunteer to display students' responses. Students may mention magazine columnists, newspaper reporters, bloggers, or novelists. Then ask: ***What is it about the writer's style or work that you like?*** Possible answers: a casual, easy-to-read style or a bold, in-your-face style; some may like the writer's honesty and integrity. Ask students: ***Do you use similar styles in your own writing?*** Answers will vary as some students may or may not be aware of their writing style.

Objectives

- **Explain** how to organize and present your ideas. Ways described in the text include numeration; generalization with examples; cause and effect; and compare and contrast
- **Demonstrate** professional telephone communication skills. Use a cheerful but formal greeting; convey all necessary information; take a message and repeat it to make sure it is correct.
- **Explain** how to write effective business letters and persuasive messages. Know your audience, purpose, and subject.

Graphic Organizer

Tips for Effective Communication

Effective Speaking
- Show respect
- Use voice effectively
- Structure the message
- Enumeration
- Generalization with examples
- Cause and effect
- Compare and contrast

Speaking/Writing
- Know the purpose
- Organize your thoughts

Effective Writing
- Know your audience
- Know your subject
- Develop a writing style
- Use language effectively

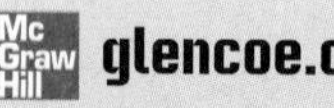

iWB

Graphic Organizer Send student to the Online Learning Center to print this graphic organizer.

EXPLORE

Before You Read

Read the Before You Read question aloud: ***When have you had to change the way you spoke or wrote for different audiences?*** Students may suggest that they change the way they talk when speaking to their friends, parents, grandparents, supervisors, teachers, and so on. They may have to change the way they write when texting, blogging, writing thank-you notes, or writing an essay.

Preteaching Vocabulary

Have students go to the Online Learning Center at glencoe.com for the Chapter 8 Preteaching Vocabulary games.

Content Vocabulary

Enumeration—Word Origin Write the Content Vocabulary term *enumeration* on the board. Ask: ***Is any part of the term familiar to you?*** Students may mention that part of the term looks like part of the word *number.* Tell students that both the words *enumeration* and *number* come from a Latin word (*numerous*) that means "to count." Ask students: ***What other words can you think of that may have come from this same Latin word?*** Answers may include: enumerate, numeral, numerate, numerator, numerical, and so on. Tell students that the term *enumeration* means "to list items in order."

Generalization—Contextual Meaning Write the following sentence on the board: She made a *generalization* that everyone agreed with. Ask: ***Based on its use in this sentence, what do you think the word* generalization *means?*** Students may suggest that it means "a general statement or conclusion."

Academic Vocabulary

Have students use each of the Academic Vocabulary terms in an original, written sentence. Sentences will vary. Students should try to capture the meaning of the terms *enhance* and *sequence* in their sentences. Ask: ***What Content Vocabulary term can also be considered an Academic Vocabulary word if used in a different context?*** Students may recognize that *generalization* is used both as a reading strategy and also to summarize or evaluate information and long passages.

PROFESSIONAL DEVELOPMENT **MINI CLIP**

ELL: Direct Vocabulary Instruction In this video, students create vocabulary cards.

Speech and Writing

SPEAKING

Explain to students that speaking is used in all aspects of their lives. Knowing the correct way to ask questions, provide directions, and discuss topics at meetings is very important to finding and keeping a job in marketing as well as other businesses.

Guiding Questions

Identify What are the three most common reasons for speaking?	The three most common reasons are to inform, persuade, and entertain.
Analyze Why is it important to show courtesy and respect to customers and coworkers?	When customers feel disrespected, they may stop doing business with the company. When coworkers do not respect one another, working conditions are often unpleasant.

As You Read Answer

Read students the As You Read question: ***How is talking to your friends different from presenting to your class?*** Students may suggest that they speak informally with their friends, using slang and jargon. When giving a presentation, students should know to use more formal speech and avoid slang and jargon.

Expert Advice

Read the quote to students:

"Speaking is an important part of most jobs."

Ask students: ***What jobs can you think of where speaking is not part of the job?*** Have a volunteer display responses for the class. The list will likely be quite short. Students may mention mimes or musicians (although they would need to speak well when being interviewed for a job.) Tell students that even though speaking may not be an important part of a job, it is still necessary to speak well for interviews, with coworkers, and so on. Ask students who have jobs: ***What role does speaking play in your job?*** Possible answers: food service—taking orders from customers and giving orders to the cooking staff; retail—talking with customers in person and on the phone; babysitting—giving directions to the child and keeping parents informed.

ENUMERATION

Enumeration is listing items in order. This strategy is often used when giving directions or explaining a process with steps. Use signal words, such as *first, second, third,* or *next,* to help the listener. These signal words show the relationship between what you have already said and what you will say next.

GENERALIZATION WITH EXAMPLES

Many speakers use generalizations to make a point. A **generalization** is a statement that is accepted as true by most people. Speakers support generalizations with evidence and examples. This creates confidence in the listener. For example, when you make a general statement, such as "Most people would rather have a PDA than a plain cellular phone," you could support the claim with evidence. For example, "A Gallup poll on consumer preferences found that 75 percent of ordinary cell-phone users plan to replace their phones with a PDA smartphone when they need a new phone."

Using evidence to support your generalizations also helps your listeners remember the main points. Signal words, such as *for instance* and *for example,* will help get your point across.

CAUSE AND EFFECT

When you present an issue in terms of cause and effect, you attempt to demonstrate that one event or situation is the cause of another. For example, you can show how implementing your marketing plan will allow the client to meet a sales goal. This pattern can be used effectively to persuade the listener. Use signal words or phrases, such as *therefore, consequently,* and *as a result* to help the listener understand the **sequence.**

COMPARE AND CONTRAST

Another pattern often used to persuade a listener is compare and contrast. In this pattern, new ideas are explained by showing how they are similar to or different from the ideas listeners already know. This approach is particularly useful when working in cross-cultural situations. Signal words or phrases such as *similarly, however, nevertheless,* and *on the other hand,* help to make the differences and similarities clear.

SPEAKING ON THE TELEPHONE

In most telephone conversations, your listener cannot see you. That means you cannot rely on facial expressions and body language to get your message across. The message is communicated only by voice, so a pleasant voice is very important.

Whether calling or answering, greet the other person in a cheerful but formal way. For example, you might say, "Customer Relations, this is Maria. How may I help you?" This greeting signals to the caller that he or she has reached the right number. Use a pleasant tone, enunciate clearly, and speak directly into the mouthpiece. Speak loudly enough for the other person to hear, but do not shout. Be courteous and respectful. Never interrupt when the other person is speaking. These guidelines are especially important when using a cellular phone, as sound quality often is not as clear as on land lines.

Speaking on the Phone While video phones allow people to see each other as they speak, it is still important to be clear and direct while you speak on any kind of phone.

It is also necessary that you convey all the necessary information. It may be a good idea to write down key points before a phone call. Telephone customer service representatives and telemarketers use scripts.

Be prepared to take a message. Note the time of the call, the caller's name and message, and the return phone number. Repeat the telephone number to the caller to make sure it is correct. Most companies make use of voice mail so that callers may leave a message when the person is unavailable.

Reading Check

Contrast How is enumeration different from generalization?

WRITING

Much business and marketing communication is in written form. A written message is necessary when there is a large volume of material and presenting it verbally would be impractical. Writing is also necessary when a permanent record of the communication is required. For instance, legal documents, manuals describing company policy, and letters confirming the terms of a deal are all written.

Writing takes more time and thought than a conversation. One advantage of writing a message rather than speaking it is that there is more time to organize the message. If your future is in marketing, you will need to develop effective business correspondence skills to write letters, e-mail, memos, and reports.

Each of these requires correct grammar, spelling, punctuation, and formatting. Marketing writing may also include print ads, scripts, and packaging.

BASIC CONSIDERATIONS IN WRITING

As with listening, reading, and speaking, it is important to know the reason for writing. The following are three basic considerations in writing:

1. **Know your audience.** Before you begin writing, think about who will receive your message. What do you know about them? Do they have the same experiences as you? Why will they read your message? What do they know about the subject? Answering these questions will help you to write a meaningful message.

MARKETING CASE STUDY

Gatorade® Simplifies with "G"

Few things are more iconic in the world of sports than Gatorade. Weary football players drink it from paper cups on the sidelines and excited players dump a cooler of it on their coach's head to celebrate victories. One of Gatorade's rebranding campaigns switched the focus to the amazing things athletes can do when they drink Gatorade. A part of that campaign involved simplifying the name down to simply "G."

A Call-to-Action

Gatorade flavors have traditionally had names like *Rain* or *X-Factor*, but under the rebranding, those names were switched to "calls-to-action." For instance, "Be Tough," "No Excuses" or "Bring It." Print ads show athletes in various poses, next to the letter G. On the bottles themselves, the name has also been simplified to the letter "G," alongside a redesigned lightning bolt logo.

English Language Arts/Writing

Compose Gatorade conveys a message about its product by showing athletes in action next to the letter "G." Translate the impact of this image into words. Discuss whether it is more effective to describe the image or capture its message visually.

NCTE 4 Use written language to communicate effectively.

EXPLAIN

Critical Thinking

Tell students that many of today's marketing jobs require the ability to communicate clearly over the telephone. Ask: ***Have you ever received a marketing phone call?*** For those who answer yes, say: ***Give a general critique of the calls you have received. What makes a good sales call?*** Students' answers and critiques will vary. Critiques may include the time of day telemarketers call, which may interrupt a meal or favorite TV show; the long introductions telemarketers often use before getting to the point of their call; and the "come-ons" telemarketers often use to get you to stay on the line, such as the promise of a prize or reward. A good sales call identifies the caller and purpose of the call in the first few seconds as well as the way in which the call may interest the person who answers. Ask students to work in pairs to create a script of successful and unsuccessful telemarketing phone conversations. Then ask students to role play their scenarios to the class. Role playing scenarios will vary. Students should be prepared to evaluate what was successful in the role plays, and what would be an effective change.

HOT TOPIC

Speaking on the Phone Ask students: ***Have you ever spoken on a video phone or through an Internet connection with a camera? If so, how was the experience different from talking over a regular phone?*** Then ask: ***Was it more or less important to use good telephone etiquette?***

Reading Check Answer

Read the Reading Check question to students: ***How is enumeration different from generalization?*** Enumeration is the process of listing items in order; a generalization is a statement that is accepted as true by most people.

ELABORATE

Mini Projects

Extension

Mobile Phones Tell students that in many states it is illegal to talk on a cell phone while driving. Have students research the technological options for hands-free cell phone use and compile a list of devices with their prices and features. Ask: ***Which devices would you recommend? Why?*** Devices may include Bluetooth headsets, speaker phones, OnStar, and so on. Students' recommendations will vary but should be supported with factual information.

Communication Practice Divide the class into pairs and assign the following roles: (1) a businessperson talking to a potential client and a creditor talking to a customer who is late with a payment; (2) a musician talking between songs during a concert and a musician talking to a lawyer; (3) an athlete talking to opponents during a game and an athlete talking to the coach during practice. Have pairs of students volunteer to act out these role plays for the entire class. After each role play, ask the class: ***How does the communication change from one scenario to another?*** Answers will vary, but students may suggest that a businessperson may be more friendly when talking to a new customer than when talking to someone who owes money. A musician would probably speak less formally during a concert than when talking to a lawyer. An athlete may be less cordial or more intense when talking to an opponent than he or she would be with a coach. Remind students that effective communication always involves showing respect.

Speaking on the Telephone Have the class work in pairs to practice talking on the phone. Each pair should write a dialog for a phone conversation with one person calling an office to leave a message and the other person answering the phone and taking the message. The dialogs should follow good telephone etiquette. The person taking the message should ask for pertinent information such as name, phone number, and reason for calling. Ask pairs to deliver their dialogs for the class. Ask the class to analyze the dialogs constructively.

Following Rules Tell students that you are going to conduct a class meeting to discuss the statement "people should eat more fruit" and to determine how to enforce the statement. During the meeting, follow the order of business as closely as possible. You might have students take turns being in charge of the meeting. After the meeting, ask: ***Was this the first formal meeting you have participated in? If not, what other formal meetings have you participated in?*** Students' answers will vary depending on whether they have attended formal meetings. You might have students share their experiences from other meetings.

Graphic Organizer

Display the chart. Have students provide a list of television programs and should include dramas, news, infomercials, sitcoms, reality, sports, and so on. Then ask: ***What is the purpose of each of the programs listed? Is the purpose to inform, persuade, or entertain?***

	PURPOSE		
Program	**Inform**	**Persuade**	**Entertain**

glencoe.com 

Graphic Organizer Send students to the Online Learning Center to print this graphic organizer.

BASIC CONSIDERATIONS IN WRITING

Ask these guiding questions to focus the discussion on writing.

Guiding Questions

Identify What are some considerations in writing?	know your audience, know your purpose, and know your subject.
Extend What does it mean to "know" your audience? Why is this important?	determine what you know about the person(s) receiving your message so as to grab their interest

MARKETING CASE STUDY

English Language Arts/Writing Answer Students' ads will vary. They should target a specific audience, draw attention to the product, arouse interest in the product, create desire, and cause action. Ads should appeal to people's feelings but be truthful. Ask yourself these questions while grading the ads: Does the ad promote? Does it provide facts and opinions to persuade the audience? Does it appeal to people who may not be interested? Discuss with students whether it is more effective to describe the image with words or to capture its meaning visually.

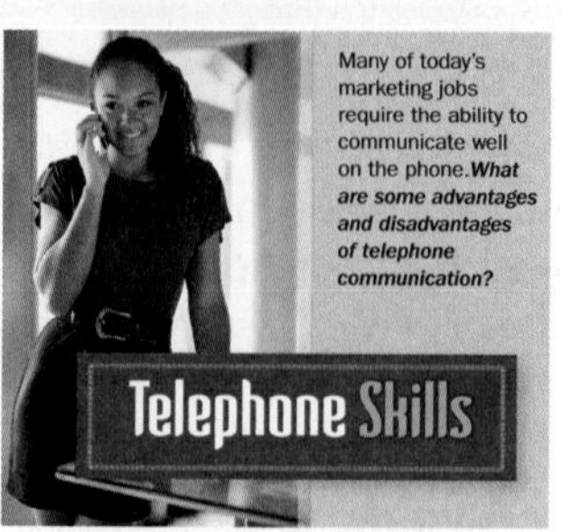

Many of today's marketing jobs require the ability to communicate well on the phone. ***What are some advantages and disadvantages of telephone communication?***

2. **Know your purpose.** Why are you writing? Most of your marketing writing is done to inform, confirm, inquire, answer, or persuade. Marketing messages are often written to persuade. Some messages combine two or more purposes.
3. **Know your subject.** To write effective messages, you need in-depth knowledge and you must know how to relate what you know to what the customer wants to know. You may be well educated on certain subjects, but almost every new assignment will require further research.

DEVELOPING A WRITING STYLE

Writing style differs from industry to industry. The executives of a company generally establish the company's writing style. It usually includes guidelines on when to use formal and informal communication. As you read company letters, official e-mail, memos, and reports, you will gain a feel for how the firm wishes to present itself to clients.

In formal business writing, it is generally best to use a direct yet respectful conversational style. Whether writing to inquire, inform, or persuade, your writing should be crisp, clear, and easy to read. Be professional, but do not use big words to impress others. Use the grammar and spelling checkers on your word processing program to fix common errors. Always review your writing one final time to ensure that all errors are corrected.

If you sometimes overlook mistakes, ask a colleague to proofread your work.

Personalize your message by using the name of the person who will receive it. When writing to someone outside your company, be formal until you have developed a relationship in which it would be appropriate to be more informal and personal in your writing.

You may want to use jargon in your messages to people in your professional field. However, when writing to a mixed audience, it is best to avoid jargon. If jargon is necessary, clearly define any technical words.

USE LANGUAGE EFFECTIVELY

Pay attention to the words and phrases used by your clients, vendors, and associates. If they are different from the ones you generally use, translate your ideas and feelings into language that makes sense to them. Using the words and phrases familiar to your audience in your communications can be a powerful persuasive technique.

ORGANIZE YOUR THOUGHTS

Construct your persuasive message in three parts:

1. an opening paragraph
2. a persuasive body
3. a concluding paragraph

In the opening paragraph, grab your readers' attention. State clearly why you are writing and involve them in some way, perhaps addressing them using *you* if appropriate.

Begin each body paragraph with a topic sentence. Follow with three to five sentences in which you develop a single point. Use connectives, such as *therefore* and *so you see.* Ethical writing requires honesty, so be sure to acknowledge any significant point of view that may differ from your own. There is nothing wrong with presenting evidence showing that your view is more likely to result in the desired outcome. If you can, quote a recognized expert or survey to add support for your case. Try to create a vivid image to help your reader see your point of view.

Your concluding paragraph should be positive and interesting. It should strongly support the message outlined in your introduction. Restate the points made in the body. Cite the evidence in support of each point. Emphasize the overall reason your position, product, or service is worth considering. Finally, state exactly what action should be taken next to achieve the mutually acceptable outcome.

FORMS OF WRITTEN COMMUNICATION

Most business writing is in the form of letters, e-mail, memos, and reports. Each of these formats follows its own very specific rules of style.

LETTERS

Written communication with people outside the company is usually done with business letters or e-mail. Letters are the more formal of the two. They are used for purposes such as official announcements, thank yous, and confirmations of business transactions. In direct-mail marketing, targeted letters are often written addressing the needs or interests of specific groups.

E-MAIL

E-mail is the method of choice for fast, informal communication with those inside and outside the company. Marketers often use e-mail for informal contacts between the firm and the client. E-mail has the advantage of speed over other forms of written communication. With e-mail, files can be attached to, or sent along with, the message.

While e-mail norms differ between companies, a typical interoffice e-mail contains the following:

- An informative subject title
- A traditional (not personal) greeting
- A concise, clearly stated body
- A statement regarding the type of response needed
- A formal closing and signature (For the signature, type your name, company, address, phone and fax number, and e-mail address.)

Although e-mail has a reputation for speed and informality, it is important to remember that, like all written communication, it leaves a permanent record. Business e-mails are official documents. They are the property of the company or firm.

Many companies have strict e-mail policies. The following rules are found in most e-mail policies:

- Save only essential e-mail.
- Do not forward e-mail without the sender's express permission.
- Seek permission, and then use extreme care when forwarding confidential e-mails.
- Use only copyrighted materials that you have permission, or have paid, to use.
- Do not use company computers for personal e-mail except as specifically allowed.

When writing business e-mail, follow the guidelines for business writing described above. Compose your messages carefully, and use conventional business language and style. One difference is that e-mail messages tend to be shorter and more concise than letters.

MEMOS

In most businesses, e-mail, instant messaging, and even texting have, to a considerable extent, replaced the use of memos. A memorandum, or memo, is a written message to someone in the company. It is usually brief and covers only one subject. Most memos are written in a simple format that has a standard set of headings. The standard headings include the sender's and receiver's names, the date, the subject, and a message in paragraph form. Correct grammar, spelling, and punctuation are as important in a memo as in letters and reports.

EXPLAIN

Visual Literacy

Telephone Skills Caption Answer Read the photo caption question to students. ***What are some advantages and disadvantages of telephone communication?*** Advantages may include: being able to communicate from almost anywhere and not having to dress up to have a conversation. Disadvantages may include: not being able to see the person you are talking to so you cannot rely on body language and facial expressions to help get your point across. Ask: ***Would you rather communicate face-to-face or by telephone? Why?*** Students' answers will vary but should be supported with sound reasoning.

Critical Thinking

Tell students that different businesses will have different writing styles. For example, a financial services business' press release will have a very different tone from a recording company's announcement about a new music release. Ask: ***Why do you think the tones would be different?*** Students may suggest that the tones would be different because the audiences would be different. The tone for a financial services business will need to be more formal for its client base, while the tone for a recording company would be less formal and more exciting for its customer base.

Mini Project

Enrichment

Techniques for Effective Listening Have students watch a televised interview. It can be hard news, entertainment, or a talk show. Ask them to take notes about feedback given by the interviewer. Both verbal and nonverbal communication should be recorded. Then ask them to watch the feedback given by the person being interviewed. Ask: ***Is the feedback given by the person being interviewed different than the feedback given by the interviewer?*** Depending on the type of interview, students may suggest that the interviewer is more relaxed and providing more positive feedback than the person being interviewed.

ELABORATE

DEVELOPING A WRITING STYLE

Ask these guiding questions to focus the discussion on developing a writing style.

Guiding Questions

Explain What is one way you can use language effectively?	In your communications to clients, vendors, and associates, use words and phrases that are used by them. If necessary, translate your ideas and feelings into language that makes sense to them.
Analyze What are the parts of a persuasive message?	opening paragraph—state clearly why you are writing; body—present evidence that supports your point of view, paragraphs consist of a topic sentence and supporting sentences; concluding paragraph—restate main points and ask for a call to action

Graphic Organizer

Display this graphic organizer. Ask students to provide details.

Written Communication

Letters, E-mail, Memos

Letters: more formal than e-mail; used for official announcements, thank yous, confirmations; often written to address group interests.

E-mail: fast, informal; files can be attached; leaves a permanent record; follow company rules about e-mail.

Memos: used in business; brief, covers one topic; grammar, spelling, punctuation important.

Business Reports

Business Reports: cover lengthy topics; prepared by multiple people; organization; may include charts and graphs.

Company Publications

Company Publications: for employees only; may include newsletters; may be on Web site; often written by communications department.

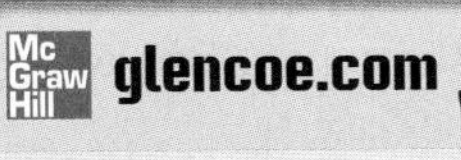

iWB

Graphic Organizer Send student to the Online Learning Center to print this graphic organizer.

e MARKETING

E-Mail Marketing and Twitter

E-mail marketing is electronic mail for commercial purposes. Special discounts, coupons and other promotions; as well as any information about the company can be disseminated via e-mail. Twitter is a private company offering its subscribers the ability to write and read messages in real time. A customer can tweet a business to share a good or bad experience; a business can tweet its customers with information about new products or services. A tweet is limited to 140 characters. Messages can be received on computers or mobile phones. As an information network, Twitter has become an excellent source for customer feedback. Businesses are able to gather marketing intelligence by following customers' tweets. Customers may offer suggestions, such as new product designs, new flavors for food products, new packaging, and new advertising concepts.

Innovate and Create

Ask students to list all the e-mail marketing and business "tweets" they receive. Ask students to compare and contrast e-mail marketing and Twitter. To demonstrate the differences, ask students to bring in sample e-mail messages and business "tweets" to create a bulletin board display or collage on poster board. To culminate the project, have students write a "tweet" (140 characters) to a business they frequent to share a recent experience—good or bad. Also have them create an e-mail marketing piece for a restaurant in your community. As an added bonus, have students pose as marketers that create e-mail marketing programs for businesses. Ask them to role play with a restaurant owner (you or another student) to convince the owner to begin an e-mail marketing program for its customers. Students should use the sample e-mail marketing piece in their presentation. Their tweets should be evaluated on the basis of their ability to communicate a message in 140 or fewer characters. The e-mail marketing piece should offer relevant information to the customer and some type of incentive to visit the restaurant. Incentives may be discount coupons or special promotions such as free dessert with any full-course entrée. The role play could be evaluated on the basis of the student's ability to fully explain the e-mail marketing program and its benefits to the restaurant owner.

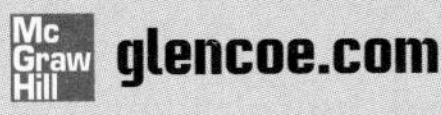

eMarketing Worksheet Activity Send students to the Online Learning Center to download an eMarketing worksheet activity.

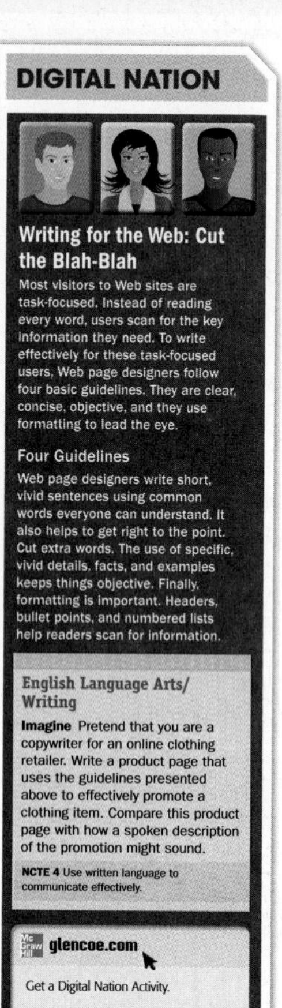
DIGITAL NATION

Writing for the Web: Cut the Blah-Blah

Most visitors to Web sites are task-focused. Instead of reading every word, users scan for the key information they need. To write effectively for these task-focused users, Web page designers follow four basic guidelines. They are clear, concise, objective, and they use formatting to lead the eye.

Four Guidelines

Web page designers write short, vivid sentences using common words everyone can understand. It also helps to get right to the point. Cut extra words. The use of specific, vivid details, facts, and examples keeps things objective. Finally, formatting is important. Headers, bullet points, and numbered lists help readers scan for information.

English Language Arts/Writing

Imagine Pretend that you are a copywriter for an online clothing retailer. Write a product page that uses the guidelines presented above to effectively promote a clothing item. Compare this product page with how a spoken description of the promotion might sound.

NCTE 4 Use written language to communicate effectively.

glencoe.com

Get a Digital Nation Activity.

BUSINESS REPORTS

Business reports usually cover lengthy topics, such as yearly sales, survey results, or problems that need attention. Some, called "in-house reports," are meant to be read only by company employees. Others, such as reports to stockholders, are written for a wider audience and are more formal. An in-house report can be written by a company department to let management know the results of a project, or a report might move from one department to another. For example, the sales department may produce a report to tell the design department how customers like a product. Several people may give input to produce the report, but one person is usually responsible for writing the final document.

Many of the techniques used in preparing a speech are also appropriate in preparing a report. Enumeration, generalization with example, cause and effect, and compare and contrast are patterns of organization that work well for reports. A simple report can be brief, perhaps as short as one page. Complex reports include more data and may use a variety of charts and graphs.

COMPANY PUBLICATIONS

Many companies produce internal publications for their employees, such as newsletters or employee handbooks of policies and procedures. These are often available online at password-protected pages on the company Web site. (Publishing them online saves money and conserves paper.) Some companies produce external publications, such as promotional brochures about the company or its products. A communications department writes internal publications, while a marketing department writes external publications.

MEETINGS AND PARLIAMENTARY PROCEDURE

Parliamentary procedure is a structure for holding group meetings and making decisions. DECA, for example, uses this structure for its meetings. Parliamentary procedure favors the opinion of the majority of a group, but the viewpoint of the minority is not overlooked. Parliamentary procedure has a very specific structure.

A QUORUM

A quorum is a proportion of the membership required to conduct official business. It may be a set number of members, such as 20. A quorum may also be a certain percentage of the membership, such as 51 percent.

ORDER OF BUSINESS

The meeting follows a standard order of business, which is called an agenda. The standard format for a meeting is as follows

1. **Call to order** This statement alerts all members that the meeting is beginning and that they should be quiet.
2. **Minutes of the meeting** The secretary reads the minutes, which are a written record that outlines the decisions made at the last meeting.
3. **Treasurer's report** The treasurer reports the money received since the last meeting, the money spent, and the current balance.
4. **Committee reports** Each committee presents a report to let the entire membership know what has been done and what else is left to do.
5. **Old business** Any issues that were discussed but were not decided on become old business.
6. **New business** New ideas are brought up at the end of the meeting.
7. **Adjournment** This is the official end of the meeting. The secretary records the time of adjournment in the minutes.

THE MOTION

After being allowed to speak by the chairperson, a member makes a motion, or proposal. Another member must second the motion. After discussion, a vote is taken on the motion.

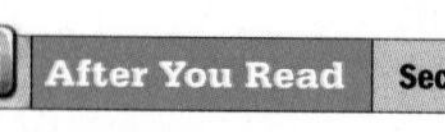

Review Key Concepts

1. **Describe** how each of the most common purposes for speaking might be used in a business situation.
2. **Explain** the nature of effective verbal communication and why written messages have some advantages over spoken messages.
3. **Explain** the importance of using correct grammar, spelling, punctuation, and formatting when writing effective business correspondence.

Practice Academics

English Language Arts

4. Imagine you need to share your company's new waste management policies with your employees. Write a memo about the policies and summarize it orally to a partner. Have your partner read your memo and discuss how reading and listening to the memo was different.

Mathematics

5. Communication on the Internet travels at the speed of light—186,000 miles per second. How long would it take an e-mail to travel 5,000 miles? Round your answer to the nearest one-thousandth of a second.

Math Concept **Measurement: Process** Apply appropriate techniques, tools, and formulas to determine measurements.

Starting Hints To solve this problem, divide the distance 5,000 miles by the travel speed of communication on the Internet, 186,000 miles per second, to determine the amount of time it takes for that e-mail to travel.

For help, go to the Math Skills Handbook located at the back of this book.

NCTE 5 Use different writing process elements to communicate effectively.

NCTM Measurement Apply appropriate techniques, tools, and formulas to determine measurements.

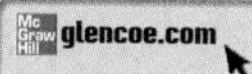

Check your answers.

ELABORATE

DIGITAL NATION

English Language Arts/Writing Answer Read the English Language Arts/Writing Activity to students: Pretend that you are a copywriter for an online clothing retailer. Write a product page that uses the guidelines presented above to effectively promote a clothing item. Compare this product page with how a spoken description of the promotion might sound. Product pages should avoid vague claims and wordy "marketese" and should instead focus on specific, vivid, quantifiable information about the characteristics and advantages of the product.

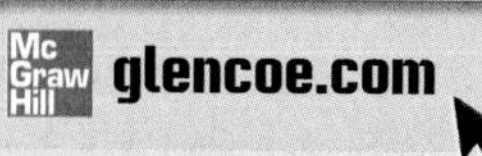

Worksheet Activity Send students to the Online Learning Center to get a Digital Nation worksheet activity.

MEETINGS AND PARLIAMENTARY PROCEDURE

Tell students that parliamentary procedure is a very structured method for holding meetings. Then ask these guiding questions to focus the discussion on parliamentary procedure.

Guiding Questions

Describe What is a quorum?	A quorum is the proportion of a membership needed to conduct official business.
Propose Why would it be important for a majority to allow the minority position time to state their viewpoint?	Students may suggest that it is part of the democratic principle that everyone gets to state their point of view; even though you are in the majority this time, you may be in the minority next time; and members of the minority may make points that have not been considered by members of the majority.

EVALUATE

Graphic Organizer

Display this diagram. Ask students to provide the standard format for a meeting. Write their answers in the seven circles.

 **glencoe.com** 

Graphic Organizer Send student to the Online Learning Center to print this graphic organizer.

Mini Project

Extension

Developing Guidelines Ask students if they perceive parliamentary procedure to be an awkward structure that might actually get in the way of communication rather than streamlining or enabling communication. Have them develop variations on the rules or make new rules for running meetings. Ask students to make guidelines for their systems and share them with the class. Have volunteers demonstrate their systems during a class meeting. Ask class members to offer a constructive critique of the systems demonstrated. Students' guidelines will vary, but should focus on ways to improve communication within the group or class.

 **After You Read** **Section 8.2**

Review Key Concepts

1. Inform—Conversations with customers and general business meetings are held to inform others. Persuade—Marketing involves sending messages that convince, or persuade, others to change how they think or what they do. Entertain—Salespeople frequently need to entertain clients or customers.
2. Effective verbal communication always shows courtesy and respect for others. Verbal communication also has a purpose, usually to inform, persuade, or entertain. Writing a message allows more time to organize the message and get the wording just the way you want it. Writing also allows for a permanent record of the information being communicated.
3. Students may suggest that correct grammar, spelling, punctuation, and formatting should always be used when writing business correspondence. Business correspondence represents the sender and the company the sender works for. Ensuring that grammar, spelling, punctuation, and formatting are correct shows that the sender cares, is professional and respectful, and pays attention to details, which is good business practice.

Practice Academics

English Language Arts

4. It is brief and covers only one subject (in this case, new waste management policies), it is written in a simple format with heads such as the sender's and receiver's names, the date, the subject, and includes a message in paragraph form. Discussions about how reading and listening to the memo differ will vary but students may suggest that listening requires greater concentration while reading allows you to take your time to focus on the message.

Mathematics

5. 0.027 of a second (5,000 ÷ 186,000 = 0.027)

 **glencoe.com** 

Answer Key Send students to the Online Learning Center to check their answers.

Communication Skills

The communication process includes channels, barriers, feedback, and setting.

Feedback

Channel

Barrier

Setting

Written Summary

- Communication is effective when the speaker or writer presents the message clearly and concisely so that the listener or reader can understand it easily.
- Listening is especially important when communicating with customers' complaints and needs.
- The global economy has brought new pressures on companies to communicate with customers and vendors around the world.
- Overcoming cultural barriers to listening with understanding is now more important than ever.
- As the volume of information to be absorbed increases, reading for meaning—the ability to differentiate what is important from what is not—is becoming an important business skill.
- Most business and marketing jobs require the ability to communicate a message clearly, concisely, and courteously by speaking and writing.
- It is especially important to communicate effectively on the telephone because the listener cannot see you.
- The patterns used to organize a formal speech also apply to writing.
- Persuasion is used to convince others of the value or importance of an idea or thing.
- The simplest and often most effective way to persuade others is to learn their needs and propose a way to fulfill them.

Review Content Vocabulary and Academic Vocabulary

1. Write each of the vocabulary terms below on an index card, and the definitions on separate index cards. Work in pairs or small groups to match each term to its definition.

Content Vocabulary
- communication (p. 191)
- channels/media (p. 191)
- feedback (p. 191)
- barriers (p. 191)
- setting (p. 191)
- distractions (p. 194)
- emotional barriers (p. 194)
- jargon (p. 197)
- persuade (p. 199)
- enumeration (p. 200)
- generalization (p. 200)

Academic Vocabulary
- process (p. 191)
- respond (p. 192)
- enhance (p. 199)
- sequence (p. 200)

Assess for Understanding

2. **Discuss** Why is it important to have awareness of cultural differences when doing business?
3. **Suggest** What are some ways to break down one of the barriers to effective listening?
4. **Weigh** What are the pros and cons of using the telephone for business communication?
5. **Compare and Contrast** What is similar and different about the way a business writes a memo with the way you write an essay for school?
6. **Evaluate** What writing style did you use in an assignment you completed for another class?
7. **Imagine** When might jargon confuse an audience? How can this problem be overcome?
8. **Revise** How can you improve a previous assignment to include persuasion, enumeration, or generalization?
9. **Discuss** Are you more comfortable with written or oral communication?

EVALUATE

Visual Summary

Express Creativity Ask students to develop their own visual summary of a concept in the chapter. Encourage students to use different formats for their visual summaries, such as a storyboard, a timeline, a table, a tree diagram, or a word web. Visual summaries will vary depending on the concept depicted and the visual manner in which it is depicted. Questions to ask when assessing a visual summary include:

- Is the summary clear, economical, and simple?
- Are any important steps left out?
- Are steps or concepts arranged in the same order as the original?
- Does the summary reveal a pattern that connects the details?
- Does the summary locate and highlight the most important information?

Review Content Vocabulary and Academic Vocabulary

1. Terms and definitions may include:
   communication—the process of exchanging messages between a sender and a receiver
   channels/media—the avenues through which messages are delivered
   feedback—a receiver's response to a message
   barrier—an obstacle that interferes with the understanding of a message
   setting—where communication takes place, including place, time, sights, and sounds
   distraction—something that competes with the message for the listener's attention
   emotional barrier—a bias against a sender's opinions that prevent a listener from understanding
   jargon—a specialized vocabulary used by members of a particular group
   persuade—to convince someone to change an opinion in order to get him or her to do what you want
   enumeration—a listing of items in order
   generalization—a statement that is accepted as true by most people
   process—a particular course of action intended to achieve a result
   respond—to reply or show a response or a reaction to something
   enhance—to increase, to make better or more attractive
   sequence—an order of steps; serial arrangement in which things follow in logical order or recurrent pattern

EVALUATE

Assess for Understanding

2. Marketing and other business professionals need to make sure the language they are using is appropriate to and able to be understood by their audience. For example, people from different Spanish-speaking countries, such as Cuba, Mexico, Guatemala, Spain, and the Dominican Republic often use different Spanish words to express the same concept. Different cultures also have different gestures to show respect or greeting.

3. Barriers to listening include distractions, emotional barriers, and planning a response. One way to overcome distractions is to move away from them. Emotional barriers can be overcome by listening with an open mind. Paying attention and waiting until the message is complete can help to overcome the barrier of planning a response.

4. Pros may include: the telephone makes it easy to communicate with people all over the world and people can often be reached any time of the day or night. Cons may include: the listener cannot see you so you cannot rely on facial expressions and body language to get your point across. The message is communicated only by voice, so a cheerful voice is very important.

5. Similarities may include: both should cover only one topic and correct grammar, spelling, and punctuation are important. Differences may include: memos are usually very brief and they are written in a simple format that has a standard set of headings. Essays have a format that is very different from memos; essays are also much longer than memos.

6. Students may mention using a formal or conversational writing style or writing to inquire, inform, or persuade.

7. Jargon may confuse an audience that is not part of the particular group the jargon relates to. If it is necessary to use jargon, defining or explaining it can help solve the confusion. If possible, do not use jargon with people who are not part of the group.

8. To include persuasion in a previous assignment, you should identify your reader's needs and then try to convince them to change their opinion so that they agree with you. Enumeration can be added to a written assignment in a number of ways such as listing steps or using signal words such as first, second, or next. A generalization or statement that most people accept as true, can be added and supported with evidence and examples.

9. Students' answers will vary depending on whether they are more comfortable with written or oral communication. Students should discuss the reasons behind their feelings.

Chapter 8 Review and Activities

21st Century Skills

Communication Skills

10. **Preparing a Formal Speech** You have been asked to speak at a state marketing conference on the topic *New Technology for Marketing.* Research current products that would interest people in the marketing field. Prepare an outline of your speech and indicate how you might use enumeration, generalization with examples, cause and effect, or compare and contrast patterns in your presentation.

Financial Literacy Skills

11. **Budgeting** Your paycheck does not seem to last until the next payday even now. You do not know where all the money goes. A budget will help you get more for your money. The first step is to keep a list of every dollar you spend in the next two weeks. Record how you spent this money and identify how you can save more.

e-Marketing Skills

12. **Designing a Web Page** Partner with a classmate to design an order form that customers can use to order merchandise from a company that sells casual clothing. Each partner should contribute ideas. Include all of the information that you would need from a customer to fill an order. Use the following questions to help you design your Web page:
    - What types of casual clothing does your store sell?
    - How will customers know whether the clothes fit them if they cannot try them on first?
    - Can the order form be printed out, written on, and sent through the mail, or does it need to be completed entirely online? How does your choice of approach meet your customers' needs?
    - What happens if an item is out of stock?
    - How can customers contact the company with questions about their order?

Build Academic Skills

Social Studies

13. **Culture** Research differences in how people from cultures outside of the United States communicate when speaking. Consider such differences in how those from other cultures greet one another, and whether and how they shake hands, make eye contact, or gesture. Write a half-page report about your findings.

NCSS I C Culture Apply an understanding of culture as an integrated whole that explains the functions and interactions of language, literature, the arts, traditions, beliefs and values, and behavior patterns.

English Language Arts

14. **Writing** Imagine that you are composing a press release for your business. Write three versions of the press release. In one, write the press release so that an elementary school student can understand it. In another, write the press release so that your peers can understand it. In the final paper, write the press release so that your market share can understand it. Compare the writing styles in each press release and discuss the effectiveness and appropriateness of each.

NCTE 12 Use language to accomplish individual purposes.

Mathematics

15. **Find Total Cost** You have been asked to make arrangements for an off-site meeting for your company. A local hotel charges $250 to rent a conference room for a half day and $400 for a full day. The hotel charges $18 per person for each lunch served and $35 per person for each dinner served. How much will it cost to rent the conference room for two and one-half days and to provide lunch and dinner for 16 people for two days?

NCTM Problem Solving Apply and adapt a variety of appropriate strategies to solve problems.

Math Concept **Problem Solving: Multi-Step Problems** When a word problem involves multiple steps and is confusing, outline the information you know before you solve.

For help, go to the **Math Skills Handbook** located at the back of this book.

Standardized Test Practice

Directions Read the following questions. On a separate piece of paper, write the best possible answer for each one.

1. When listening, you will learn more if you pay close attention to the speaker's
   A. rate of speech
   B. pitch
   C. volume
   D. all of the above
2. True or false? Planning a response is a very common block to listening.
   T
   F
3. Nonverbal cues that can enhance your presentation are body language and ______ ______.

Test-Taking Tip

Arrive early and do not talk to other students just before you enter the room to avoid being distracted.

DECA Connection Role Play

Employee
Fast-Food Restaurant

Situation Assume the role of experienced employee of a franchise fast-food hamburger restaurant. The restaurant's corporate office has decided to begin offering healthier menu options that will be available in one month. The healthier menu options will include three new entrée salads. The new salads include tossed salad greens with tomato and cucumber slices, Caesar salad, and Greek salad with green pepper and cucumber slices. All salads will cost $3.99. Grilled chicken is available as an optional topping for an additional $1.99. Salad dressings include the choice of vinaigrette, low-fat Thousand Island, Caesar dressing, and low-fat Caesar dressing.

Your manager (judge) has given you a written description of the new menu items. The manager (judge) has also asked you to prepare a description of the new salad items and the reasons they are being added to the menu. You will make your presentation to the staff at the next staff meeting.

Activity You are to prepare an outline of the information you will present at the staff meeting. Be prepared to answer staff questions. You are to review your presentation with your manager (judge) before the staff meeting.

Evaluation You will be evaluated on how well you meet the following performance indicators:

1. Extract relevant information from written material.
2. Prepare simple written reports.
3. Organize information.
4. Participate in a staff meeting.
5. Make oral presentations.

glencoe.com

Download the Competitive Events Workbook for more Role-Play practice.

208 | Unit 4 · Skills for Marketing

Chapter 8 · Communication Skills | 209

EVALUATE

21st Century Skills

Communication Skills

10. Students' research may focus on Internet-based products such as Facebook and Twitter that have become popular with marketers. Students' outlines may suggest using enumeration to provide a list of reasons for using the product; generalization with examples could be used to indicate that most people use the Internet and therefore would be likely to run across the ads at some point; using cause and effect, the speech could explain how the product would enhance or improve the customer's life; and the speech could compare and contrast competitor's products with your own product.

Financial Literacy Skills

11. Budgets should show students' income and how they spent their money. They should include a list of types of expenses such as clothing, transportation, food, school supplies, and so on. Students should identify areas where they can cut back and save money.

e-Marketing Skills

12. Web page designs for the order forms will vary. The order form should address types of clothing, measurement and fit issues, whether it is printable, out-of-stock items, and contacting customer service. The form should also have an area for the customer's personal information and how the order will be paid for.

EVALUATE

Build Academic Skills

Social Studies

13. Students' answers will vary but may include such information as in Japan handshaking is done frequently, often along with bowing; however, in Kuwait only male strangers meeting for the first time shake hands. Reports should contain cohesive paragraphs that contain a topic sentence and sentences that support the topic sentence. Reports should be free of grammar and spelling errors.

English Language Arts

14. Students' press releases will vary. There should be an obvious difference in the vocabulary and reading level in the three releases. The release for elementary school children should use fewer words and be easy to read. Press releases for peers and marketers should contain language and vocabulary that is appropriate for the level and purpose.

Mathematics

15. \$2,746 [(\$400 × 2 + \$250) + 2(16 × \$18 + 16 × \$35) = \$1,050 + \$1,696 = \$2,746]

Standardized Test Practice

1. D all of the above
2. True
3. eye contact

DECA Connection Role Play

Evaluations will be based on these performance indicators:

1. **Extract relevant information from written material.** Outlines should include an accurate description of the three salads based on the written material received from the manager. Outlines should include all information that is relevant to adding the new salads to the menu.
2. **Prepare simple written reports.** Reports should contain details about the new salads, including ingredients and options, and be organized in a logical way. Each paragraph in the reports should focus on one main idea and all the sentences in the paragraph should support the main idea. Reports should be free of grammar and spelling errors.
3. **Organize information.** Outlines should be organized in a logical manner. For example: when describing the salads, the student should explain each salad separately to be sure coworkers understand what is in each salad. Things that are common to all salads—price, optional chicken, and salad dressings—may be grouped together.
4. **Participate in a staff meeting.** If possible, set up a mock staff meeting in which students present their outlines in an oral presentation to other "staff" members. Students should come prepared to ask and answer questions relevant to adding the three new salads to the menu of the fast-food restaurant.
5. **Make oral presentations.** Presentations should be developed with the audience in mind. The presenter should speak clearly and audibly and maintain eye contact with the audience. The speaker should engage the audience as much as possible and should have a definite beginning, middle, and end to the presentation. Presentations might include visuals to reinforce the concepts presented.

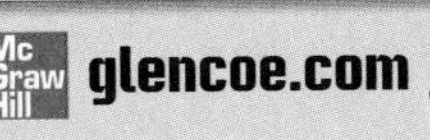

Role Plays For more DECA Role Plays, send students to the Online Learning Center to download the Competitive Events Workbook.

technology for marketing

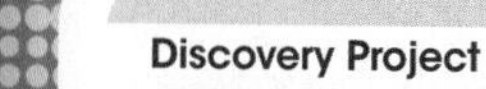

SHOW WHAT YOU KNOW

Visual Literacy Advances in technology have brought about the most productive period in United States and world history. Fast and powerful computer applications make it easy to do business and communicate with people all over the world. ***What opportunities and challenges does fast-paced global communication present?***

Discovery Project

Software Applications

Essential Question How has computer technology increased productivity?

Project Goal

Assume that you are an employee at a popular bicycle shop that sells products and does repairs. Because of your background in technology, your boss has asked you to make recommendations for upgrading software applications for the store. Presently, the only software used by the store includes two older programs for word processing and billing. Use your imagination regarding what would benefit the store. Research types of software programs on the Internet. Then recommend which types of programs should be considered as well as one or two brand names of programs.

Ask Yourself...

- What key words will you use to initiate your research?
- How will you determine the needs of the store that can by solved with new software?
- How could discussing the software needs and possible products with another employee help you with your project?

Problem Solving What criteria will you use when selecting software products to recommend?

glencoe.com

Activity
Get a worksheet activity about marketing technology.

Evaluate
Download a rubric you can use to evaluate your project.

DECA Connection

DECA Event Role Play

Concepts in this chapter are related to DECA competitive events that involve either an interview or role play.

Performance Indicator The performance indicators represent key skills and knowledge. Your key to success in DECA competitive events is relating them to the concepts in this chapter.

- Describe the use of technology in operations.
- Explain the impact of technology on retailing
- Explain the use of technology in customer relationship management.
- Describe the scope of the Internet.
- Demonstrate Web-search skills.

DECA Prep

Role Play Practice role-playing with the DECA Connection competitive-event activity at the end of this chapter. More information on DECA events can be found on DECA's Web site.

ENGAGE

Visual Literacy

Read the chapter opener photo caption question to students: ***What opportunities and challenges does fast-paced global communication present?*** Opportunities: providing a wide range of channels for sharing information over long distances and the ability to advertise on a global level. Challenges: being required to implement new technologies fast enough to remain competitive and counteracting threats to online communications by hackers and viruses. To activate prior knowledge, ask students: ***What is customer relationship management?*** It is the aspect of marketing that combines customer information (through database and computer technology) with customer service and marketing communications. Explain that customer relationship management software, along with many other current technologies, helps businesses remain competitive in the global marketplace.

Discovery Project

Software Applications To encourage students to consider the significance of technology in business, ask students the Discovery Project Essential Question: ***How has computer technology increased productivity?*** One way in which computer technology has increased productivity is by gathering and storing vast amounts of data and then manipulating it in an endless variety of ways. Virtually all job responsibilities in business depend on computer technology to help get the work done well with less human labor. Programs for word processing, database storage, spreadsheet operations, desktop publishing, graphics and design, and presentations all increase productivity. Businesses can communicate at very little cost, and social networks provide unlimited opportunities for creative marketers.

glencoe.com

Discovery Project Resources Send students to the Online Learning Center to download a rubric to evaluate their projects.

ENGAGE

Introduce the Chapter

Chapter 9 discusses the technology, including computer software, that is used in marketing. These main concepts are introduced and discussed:

- Types of software applications
- Communications programs
- Point-of-sale systems
- Integrated marketing software
- Interactive systems
- Search engines
- Electronic mail
- Web-site development
- E-commerce
- Online learning

Discussion Starter

Effective Marketing and Computer Technology Have students think of different types of marketing campaigns they have seen in the past few months. Examples might include billboard campaigns; television and Internet commercials; and Web site, e-mail, and Facebook contests. Ask: ***What is the most creative marketing campaign you have seen recently?*** Answers will vary. Encourage students to discuss those campaigns that caught their attention. Then ask: ***Were computers and communications technology used in this campaign? If so, how?*** Sample answers: Yes, the campaign was on the Internet, so communications technology was used. It was on a Web site and was created using software that integrated graphics and video in attention-grabbing ways.

DECA Connection

Discuss the performance indicators listed in the DECA Connection feature. Explain to students that performance indicators tell them how to demonstrate their acquired skills and knowledge through individual or team competitive events.

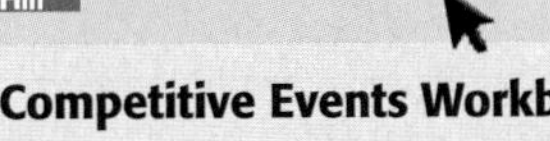

glencoe.com

Competitive Events Workbook For more DECA Role Plays, send students to the Online Learning Center to download the Competitive Events Workbook.

PRINT RESOURCES

- **Student Edition**
- **Teacher Edition**
- **Student Activity Workbook with Academic Integration** includes worksheets and activities correlated to the text.
- **Mathematics for Marketing Workbook** provides math activities for every unit in the text.

TECHNOLOGY TOOLBOX

- **Connect**
- **ConnectPlus**
- **ExamView Assessment Suite** is a comprehensive solution for creating, administering, and scoring tests.

glencoe.com

Online Learning Center provides a variety of resources to enrich and enhance learning.

SECTION, CHAPTER, AND UNIT RESOURCES

- **Graphic Organizers** for organizing text concepts visually.
- **Digital Nation Activities** and **Green Marketer Activities** extend learning beyond the text features.
- **Career Chatroom Career Profiles** allow students to explore different marketing occupations in depth.
- **After You Read Answer Keys** for students to check their answers.
- **Discovery Project Rubrics** and **Marketing Internship Project Rubrics** for students to evaluate their projects.

PROGRAM RESOURCES

- **Student Activity Workbook with Academic Integration Teacher Annotated Edition** includes annotated answers for the activities and worksheets.
- **Marketing Research Project Workbook** provides a step-by-step approach for students to complete their own marketing research studies.
- **School-to-Career Activity Workbook** helps students relate their class work to on-the-job experience and involves work-site analysis and working with mentors.
- **Competitive Events Workbook** helps prepare students for state and national marketing education competitions.
- **Inclusion in the Marketing Education Classroom** provides teaching resources for working with students with special needs.
- **PowerPoint Presentations** provides visual teaching aids and assessments for this chapter.

READING GUIDE

Before You Read

Connect How do you use computers to help with routine tasks?

Objectives

- **Identify** nine types of computer applications.
- **Explain** how computer applications are used in business and marketing.

The Main Idea

Careers in marketing require an understanding and skillful use of computers and several types of software.

Vocabulary

Content Vocabulary

- word-processing programs
- database programs
- accounting programs
- spreadsheet programs
- desktop publishing programs
- graphics and design programs
- presentation software
- home page
- hypertext markup language (HTML)
- communications programs
- Wi-Fi

Academic Vocabulary

You will find these words in your reading and on your tests. Make sure you know their meanings.

- analyze
- edit

Graphic Organizer

Draw or print this chart to note the nine types of software discussed in this section.

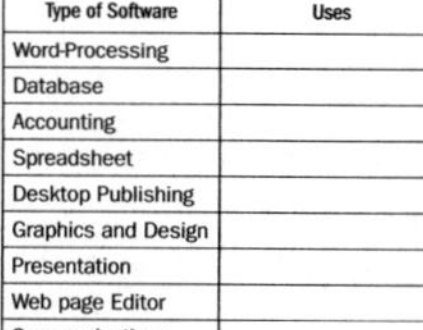

Type of Software	Uses
Word-Processing	
Database	
Accounting	
Spreadsheet	
Desktop Publishing	
Graphics and Design	
Presentation	
Web page Editor	
Communications	

Print this graphic organizer.

STANDARDS

ACADEMIC

English Language Arts

NCTE 1 Read texts to acquire new information.

NCTE 8 Use information resources to gather information and create and communicate knowledge.

Mathematics

NCTM Number and Operations Understand numbers, ways of representing numbers, relationships among numbers, and number systems.

NCSS *National Council for the Social Studies*
NCTE *National Council of Teachers of English*
NCTM *National Council of Teachers of Mathematics*
NSES *National Science Education Standards*

Common Core
Writing Conduct short as well as more sustained research projects based on focused questions, demonstrating understanding of the subject under investigation.

MARKETING CORE FUNCTIONS

- Marketing Information Management
- Promotion

212 | Unit 4 · Skills for Marketing

m.e. Section 9.1 | Computer Applications

TYPES OF APPLICATIONS

For personal use, daily planners and calendar applications manage time. Financial software manages money. Some applications serve as address books, while others help manage photos. For business use, virtually all businesses use computer applications. Medical offices use programs to schedule patients and track billing. Hotels use applications to manage room assignments and generate bills. Software is constantly being written, tested, and marketed to meet business needs.

As You Read

Predict What computer applications do you think marketers use?

WORD-PROCESSING PROGRAMS

Word-processing programs are applications that create text documents that may contain a few graphics. The benefits of a word-processing program include being able to determine the format of a document and see on screen exactly how the document will look when printed out. This is called "WYSIWYG," which stands for "What You See Is What You Get." Word-processing programs help develop more effective business correspondence by correcting and editing mistakes in spelling, grammar, punctuation, and formatting.

These programs also provide accurate word counts and add design elements, among many other features. The most common word-processing program is Microsoft Word®. There are many others, even free word-processing programs that you can find by searching the Internet. Businesses use word-processing programs to do the following:

- Write letters and memos.
- Produce research papers and reports.
- Develop business and marketing plans.
- Write contracts.
- Take notes and record meeting minutes.
- Create announcements.
- Create product manuals.

> "There is a computer application for just about every purpose imaginable."

DATABASE PROGRAMS

Database programs are applications that store and organize information. Database programs allow users to sort, find, filter, and organize information. A database can hold information about a company's products, orders, shipments, and customers. The power of a database is its ability to link that information together. Common database software includes Filemaker Pro®, Microsoft Access®, and 4D®. Database programs are available online, too, and some are free. Marketers use database programs to help with the following business needs:

- Maintain customer lists for automated mass mailings.
- Keep information about guests and vendors for parties and events.
- Catalog furniture and assets for insurance records.
- Manage time and track billable hours.
- Catalog personnel records.
- Scan the Internet to find suppliers and customers.
- Track the searches and purchases of clients visiting Web sites.

Chapter 9 · Technology for Marketing | 213

ENGAGE

Anticipation Activity

Improving Student Achievement Assign students the task of surfing the Web for ten minutes and keeping a list of ads and promotions they encounter. Students' lists will vary but are likely to include many different types of online ads for many different companies. Discuss the lists as a class. Emphasize that this type of marketing relies on computer technology.

Objectives

- **Identify** nine types of computer applications. word-processing, database, accounting, spreadsheet, desktop publishing, graphics, presentation, Web-page editing, and communications programs
- **Explain** how computer applications are used in business and marketing. Word processers: write letters, reports; database programs: store and manipulate data; accounting: collect and present financial data; spreadsheet programs: organize, calculate, and analyze numerical data; web-page editors: create and maintain Web sites; communications programs: share information over networks, and so on.

Graphic Organizer

Types of Software	Uses
Word-Processing	Create and modify text documents
Database	Store and organize information
Accounting	Store and process financial records
Spreadsheet	Organize, calculate, analyze data
Desktop Publishing	Manipulate both text and graphics
Graphics and Design	Create and modify images
Presentation	Create slide shows, presentations
Web page Editor	Create Web pages
Communications	Communicate via computers

glencoe.com

iWB

Graphic Organizer Send students to the Online Learning Center to print this graphic organizer.

EXPLORE

Before You Read

Read the Before You Read question aloud: ***How do you use computers to help with routine tasks?*** I use word processors for homework and reports and a Web-page editor to update the site for a club that I'm in. I use a Web browser to surf the Web, conduct research for school reports, and e-mail and instant messaging to talk with friends. Then ask: ***Would you be able to complete these tasks if you did not use a computer?*** I would be able to complete some of them, such as doing homework, but it would take more time. However, without a Web browser, I would not be able to access material on the Internet. To talk to friends, I'd have to use a phone or handwritten notes.

Preteaching Vocabulary

Have students go to the Online Learning Center at glencoe.com for the Chapter 9 Preteaching Vocabulary games.

Content Vocabulary

Have students examine the names of programs listed under Content Vocabulary. Discuss how they think each type of program got its name. For example, word-processing programs are used for entering and manipulating words; therefore they "process" these words.

Academic Vocabulary

Analyze—Denotative Meaning Write the word *analyze* for students to read. Explain that *analyze* means "to examine critically, so as to bring out its essential elements." Read this sentence: ***Spreadsheet programs can organize, calculate, and analyze numerical data.*** Ask: ***What are some ways you might analyze a list of 20 employee salaries?*** to determine their average, to determine largest and smallest salary

Edit—Synonyms Write the word *edit* for the students to read. Read this sentence: ***Word processing programs enable users to edit text.*** Ask students to suggest synonyms for *edit.* change, alter, modify, revise, correct

MINI CLIP

Reading: Building Vocabulary
Go to the Online Learning Center to view a video in which a teacher plays vocabulary-building games with students.

Computer Applications

As You Read

Read students the As You Read question: ***What computer applications do you think marketers use?*** e-mail, word processors, Web browsers, database and spreadsheet programs, presentation software

WORD-PROCESSING PROGRAMS

Ask these guiding questions to focus the discussion about word-processing programs.

Guiding Questions

Analyze What is the major advantage of WYSIWYG word processors?	They allow you to see how your document will appear when printed.
Infer How might creating a template help a business?	documents are standardized, contain same basic information

Expert Advice

Read the quote to students:

"There is a computer application for just about every purpose imaginable."

Have students identify a small business, such as an auto repair shop. Ask: ***What kind of specialized software might this business need?*** It might need a database designed to track customer repairs.

DATABASE PROGRAMS

Ask these guiding questions to focus the discussion about database programs.

Guiding Questions

Analyze How is a computer-based database more useful than filing cabinets?	It can be entered, modified, retrieved, organized, and analyzed much more quickly.
Elaborate How would having a database simplify creating a mass mailing to a company's clients?	Information, such as a company name, could automatically be taken from a database and placed in a form letter.

Suppose you are using a database of your company's mailing list. That mailing list contains the names and addresses of more than 3,000 customers. With one keystroke, the database can alphabetize the list by last name, group the addresses by ZIP code, or display only those customers who use post office boxes. Including purchase histories in the database allows you to quickly pull up a list of all customers who made purchases during a certain month or who purchased a certain dollar amount of merchandise.

Open-Source Applications Some software developers create programs that are free for anyone to use and develop.

ACCOUNTING PROGRAMS

The purpose of accounting is to collect and present financial data. **Accounting programs** can store and retrieve financial records and process all business transactions automatically. They can also provide an immediate and accurate picture of a company's financial status at any time. Accounting software is available for small businesses, large businesses, and every size of business in between. The most popular accounting program for small and medium-sized businesses is Intuit QuickBooks®.

Most large companies use an integrated computer system known as *Enterprise Resource Planning* (ERP). Before ERP, such functions as human resources, customer relations, supply chain management, manufacturing functions, and warehouse management each had a separate accounting program. ERP integrates data and processes of all functions of a business into a single database.

Accounting software is available for specific industries, such as manufacturing, shipping, medicine, law, and many others. Some businesses have their own custom accounting software written to their specifications.

SPREADSHEET PROGRAMS

Spreadsheet programs can organize, calculate, and **analyze** numerical data. With spreadsheets, you can perform financial and scientific calculations, organize numeric information, illustrate data with charts and graphs, and create professional-looking reports. Spreadsheets graphically display the relationship of data in the form of charts and graphs. It is often easier for people to understand charts than raw data. Microsoft Excel® is the most popular spreadsheet program. Businesspeople use spreadsheets to perform the following tasks:

- Develop a budget.
- Analyze financial performance.
- Track loans or mortgages.
- Track stock and bond performance.
- Schedule projects.
- Manage business assets.
- Produce profit and loss statements.
- Calculate and produce a payroll.
- Track client/customer responses.
- Build relationship marketing.
- Track sales and service.

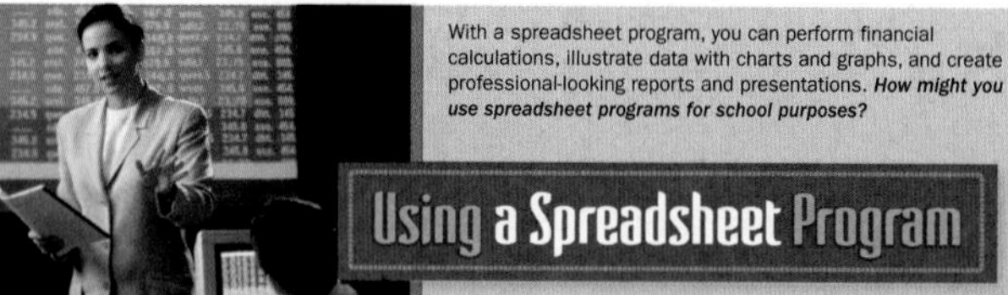

With a spreadsheet program, you can perform financial calculations, illustrate data with charts and graphs, and create professional-looking reports and presentations. ***How might you use spreadsheet programs for school purposes?***

Using a Spreadsheet Program

A spreadsheet consists of a grid of rows and columns. Users enter data and formulas into cells on the grid. The program performs calculations with speed and accuracy not possible by hand or with a calculator. When you change one piece of information, the spreadsheet automatically updates all related numbers. For example, you can see how adjusting the price of a product would affect sales, taxes, and the overall budget.

DESKTOP PUBLISHING PROGRAMS

Part word processor and part graphics application, **desktop publishing programs** enable users to **edit** and manipulate both text and graphics in one document. Desktop publishing software can produce documents that are creative, attractive, professional, and easy to read. The two most popular commercial programs are Adobe InDesign® and QuarkXPress®. Marketers use desktop publishing in the following ways:

- Create layouts for newsletters, books, brochures, and advertisements.
- Create professional-looking forms, such as invoices and project planning sheets.
- Create product manuals.

GRAPHICS AND DESIGN PROGRAMS

Graphics and design programs are software applications for creating and modifying images. Designers can create graphic elements themselves with the drawing tools provided by the software. Or, they can use photos and ready-made artwork, such as Clip art. These images are usually grouped together in categories like business, food, sports, people, places, animals, cartoons, and holidays. There are dozens of graphics programs, with some of the most common being Adobe Photoshop®, Adobe Illustrator®, CorelDRAW®, and Flash®. Marketers and businesses can use graphics programs to do the following:

- Design marketing promotion materials.
- Create logos and letterheads.
- Illustrate floor plans and furniture arrangements.
- Create professional-looking illustrations and photographic prints.
- Create images for presentations or for Web pages and Internet ads.

PRESENTATION SOFTWARE

Presentation software produces slide shows or multimedia presentations. This software helps users organize ideas and concepts to be presented in a meeting. Businesses and marketers can use presentation software to help with these tasks:

- Prepare verbal and visual information for meetings.
- Present and discuss ideas interactively via the Internet with clients in other cities or countries.
- Create slide shows using pictures or Web pages.
- Add voice narration to accompany visual material.

Presentation software can incorporate a series of slides, film clips, and streaming video. Presentations can include text, bulleted lists, graphs, photographs, and screen shots. It can even include interactive problem and decision situations. Voice narration can create a feeling of a live meeting even if participants are not together.

Software Programs

Many popular software programs are excellent for doing business tasks, but some are not. Research different products before you go shopping for a program. ***What are some advantages and disadvantages of buying and downloading software online?***

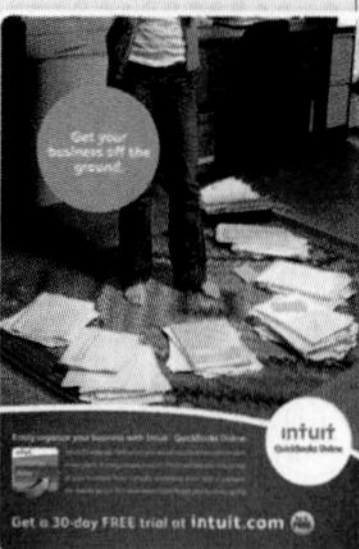

EXPLAIN

ACCOUNTING PROGRAMS

Ask these guiding questions to focus class discussion on the purpose and functions of accounting software.

Guiding Questions

Analyze How has ERP changed the way large companies perform accounting tasks?	ERP has allowed these functions to be integrated into a single system.
Infer Why do you think a large company might have customer accounting software written to its own specifications rather than use ERP?	One possible answer is that there is currently no commercial software that meets all of the company's needs.

Mini Project

Differentiated Instruction

Gifted Learners Have students investigate the open-source software (OSS) movement. In their research, they should learn about the goals of the movement, any requirements for software to be considered open source, and the types of open-source programs available. They may want to examine the Web site opensource.org to obtain an introduction to this topic. If possible, students should download a business-oriented open-source program and evaluate it. Students then should write a one- to two-page report discussing open-source software. Reports will vary, but students should thoughtfully discuss the goals of the OSS movement and the requirements for software to be considered open source. For example, if a user modifies an open-source program, the source code for the modified version must be freely available. Students also should discuss the kinds of open source software available.

ELABORATE

SPREADSHEET PROGRAMS

Ask these guiding questions to focus the discussion about spreadsheet programs.

Guiding Questions

Compare and Contrast How is spreadsheet software different from accounting software?	Accounting software processes business transactions automatically. Spreadsheet software is designed to perform numeric operations
Apply A spreadsheet calculates the total wholesale cost of a hundred items. What happens if you change the cost of one item?	The spreadsheet will automatically update the total wholesale cost based on the new cost of the changed item.

HOT TOPIC
Open-Source Applications Discuss with students that software developers have created many programs that users (including businesses) can download and use for free, saving them money.

Visual Literacy

Using a Spreadsheet Program Caption Answer Read the caption question to students: ***How might you use spreadsheet programs for school purposes?*** I might use it to keep track of my study time for each class, or to create charts to be used in class reports and presentations. For example, if I needed to write an economics report about increased U.S. imports over the past one hundred years, I might use a spreadsheet program to generate a line graph.

Activate Prior Knowledge

Reteach the Function of Business Use this graphic to help students recall the four main functions of business. As they learn about different types of computer software, encourage them to think about how each might be used in these functions.

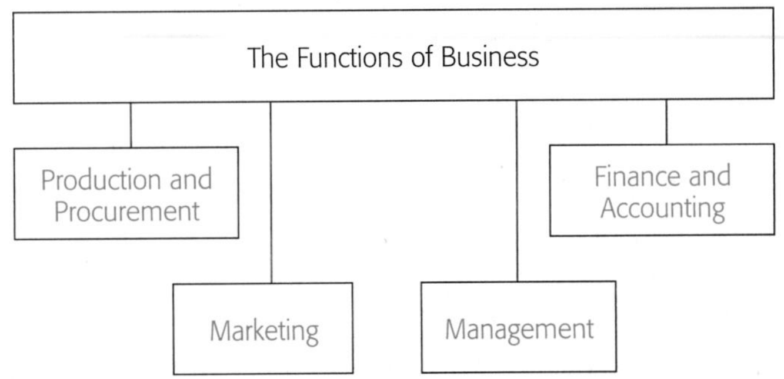

PRESENTATION SOFTWARE

Explain that presentation software is a great way to provide an audience with information in an interesting format. Ask these guiding questions to focus the discussion on presentation software.

Guiding Questions

Draw Conclusions A company executive must give a short, year-end review of sales activity. In past years, the executive distributed written reports. This year, the executive is considering presenting a slide show at a company meeting. What advantages might the slide show have?	Employees will find it more difficult to ignore the presentation than a printed report. The information might be easier to understand. Videoconferencing could be used to allow people who are not physically present to watch it.
Analyze A slide show that explains the features of a new product is to be presented at a sales meeting. Do you think a narration should be recorded and integrated into the show? Why?	Recorded narration provides consistency and makes the show self-contained. However, a live narrator can stop the slide show to answer questions, and is more likely to keep the audience's attention.

Visual Literacy

Software Programs Caption Answer Read the caption question to students: ***What are some advantages and disadvantages of buying and downloading software online?*** Advantages include that you can have the software immediately, and software may be available online that cannot be purchased locally. Disadvantages include that you do not receive a disk containing the software. This can make it more difficult to reinstall the software at a later time or on a different computer if necessary.

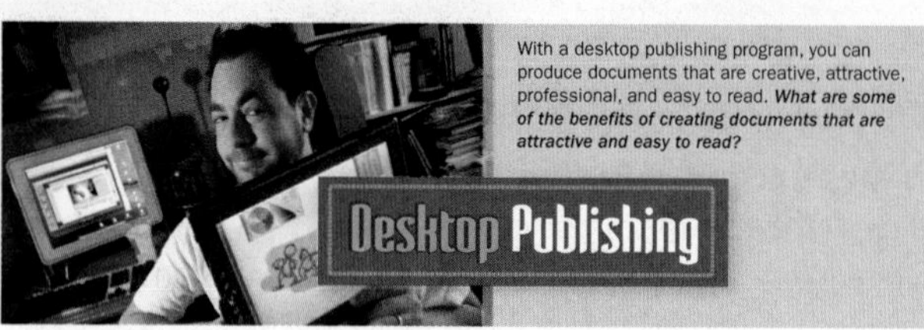

With a desktop publishing program, you can produce documents that are creative, attractive, professional, and easy to read. ***What are some of the benefits of creating documents that are attractive and easy to read?***

As global interaction in the business world increases, programs like this simplify communication and cut down on travel time. Some examples of presentation software programs are Microsoft PowerPoint® and Apple Keynote®.

WEB-PAGE EDITORS

The Internet has become an integral part of our world. Many businesses use their Web sites to promote their companies and products and to stay connected to their customers.

Web sites feature a **home page**, which is the entry point for a Web site. It gives general information to introduce the company, person, or product. The home page has links to other pages containing additional information, such as product details and contact information. The home page can also link to an online store or other interactive resources.

Creating a Web page used to require writing very specific, detailed, and complicated code, called **hypertext markup language (HTML)**. Today Web-editing programs enable people to create Web pages as if they were using a word processor or a desktop publishing program. Some of the most popular of these applications are Macromedia® Dreamweaver® and Microsoft FrontPage®.

COMMUNICATIONS PROGRAMS

Communications programs enable users to communicate with other users through their computers. The key to using any communication software is connecting to a network.

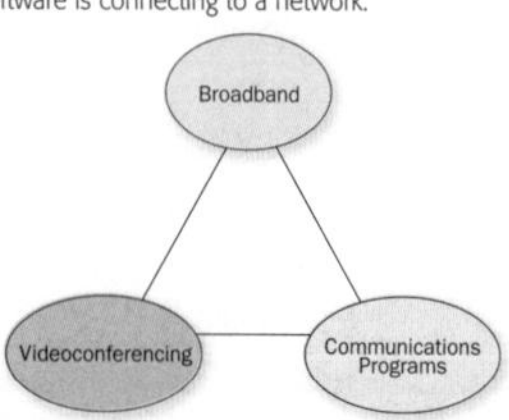

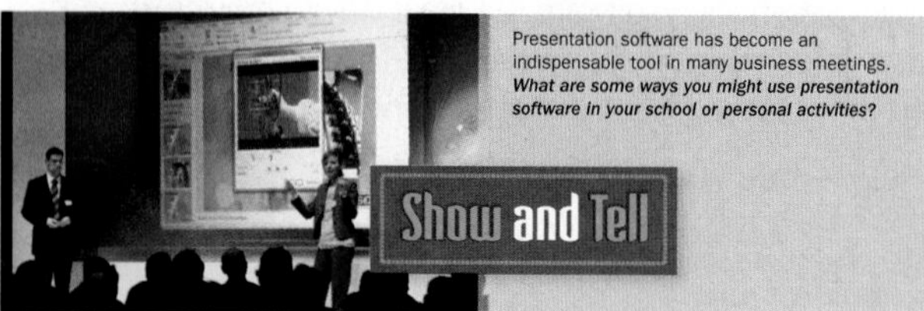

Presentation software has become an indispensable tool in many business meetings. ***What are some ways you might use presentation software in your school or personal activities?***

BROADBAND AND WIRELESS (G3) TECHNOLOGY

Broadband technology allows information to move through cable TV or special DSL phone lines. It transmits large amounts of data at very high speeds. Broadband allows audio chat or video conferencing to take place in real time (without delay) and complex Web pages to load in seconds.

Wireless routers provide Internet connectivity without a physical connection. This technology, called **Wi-Fi** (*wireless fidelity*), creates a wireless Internet connection with radio frequencies.

Third and fourth generation (3G and 4G) technology uses mobile phones to transmit data wirelessly. With a connector plugged into a USB port, a computer can connect to the Web from any location where there is cell-phone coverage. This popular technology will continue to grow as the technology moves into more countries and becomes cheaper to use.

VIDEOCONFERENCING

Videoconferencing has many advantages. Its greatest professional advantage is that it can reduce the need for expensive business travel. Travel time and expenses can be dramatically reduced by holding videoconferences rather than meeting in person.

COMMUNICATIONS PROGRAMS

Communications programs include e-mail software such as Microsoft Outlook® and Apple Mail®; instant-messaging software such as AOL Instant Messenger®; and videoconferencing software such as Apple iChat® and Skype®.

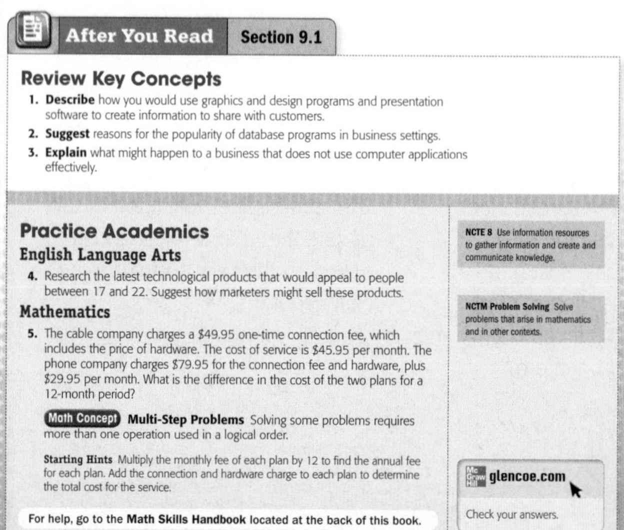

After You Read | **Section 9.1**

Review Key Concepts

1. **Describe** how you would use graphics and design programs and presentation software to create information to share with customers.
2. **Suggest** reasons for the popularity of database programs in business settings.
3. **Explain** what might happen to a business that does not use computer applications effectively.

Practice Academics

English Language Arts

4. Research the latest technological products that would appeal to people between 17 and 22. Suggest how marketers might sell these products.

NCTE 8 Use information resources to gather information and create and communicate knowledge.

Mathematics

5. The cable company charges a $49.95 one-time connection fee, which includes the price of hardware. The cost of service is $45.95 per month. The phone company charges $79.95 for the connection fee and hardware, plus $29.95 per month. What is the difference in the cost of the two plans for a 12-month period?

NCTM Problem Solving Solve problems that arise in mathematics and in other contexts.

Math Concept **Multi-Step Problems** Solving some problems requires more than one operation used in a logical order.

Starting Hints Multiply the monthly fee of each plan by 12 to find the annual fee for each plan. Add the connection and hardware charge to each plan to determine the total cost for the service.

For help, go to the **Math Skills Handbook** located at the back of this book.

glencoe.com
Check your answers.

ELABORATE

Visual Literacy

Desktop Publishing Caption Answer Read the caption question to students: ***What are some of the benefits of creating documents that are attractive and easy to read?*** The primary advantage is that customers (or others receiving the document) are more likely to read it. Then ask: ***Imagine that you see an advertisement in a printed magazine. What might attract your attention to it?*** Sample answer: It contains information I'm interested in and has attention-grabbing photos or images.

Critical Thinking

After students have read the section on Web-page editors, ask volunteers to talk about their favorite Web sites. Ask: ***What do you like most about them, in terms of both content and aesthetics?*** Answers will depend on personal taste, but may include that the content is up-to-date and easy to use and that they contain interesting graphics.

WEB-PAGE EDITORS

Ask these guiding questions to focus the discussion about web-page editing programs.

Guiding Questions

Recall What is the purpose of a home page?	an entry point for a Web site; contains a company overview, links
Evaluate How do Web-page editors simplify developing pages?	Programs such as Dreamweaver generate the code for Web pages automatically.

Visual Literacy

Show and Tell Caption Answer Read the caption question to students: ***What are some ways you might use presentation software in your school or personal activities?*** Answers may include: create slide shows to accompany classroom reports; present information, including text, graphics, and photos for a club or athletic event.

EVALUATE

COMMUNICATIONS PROGRAMS

Fast, efficient communication among businesses has been made possible by networking combined with the use of communications software. To encourage students to discuss the different types of communications programs, ask these guiding questions.

Guiding Questions

Explain Why is it necessary to have access to a network to use communications software?	You need a means of sending the message, whether you are sending it thousands of miles on the Internet or on a wireless network within your own home or office.
Advantages and Disadvantages Why might a company promote the use of videoconferencing rather than having its employees travel to corporate meetings? What disadvantages might there be to this plan?	Advantages—to save money and employee time. Disadvantages—it requires specific hardware and software and people cannot interact in exactly the same ways as when they are physically together.
Infer How has the widespread availability of Wi-Fi changed the way in which people use computers and the Internet?	People can work anywhere. Wi-Fi is available, whether at an airport or a local coffee shop.

Mini Project

Enrichment

Developing a Scenario Have students work individually to write a scenario in which a business has a specific challenge. This challenge can be solved by one of the types of programs discussed in this section. A company needs to create an employee brochure explaining its retirement plans and will use a desktop publishing program.

After You Read Section 9.1

Review Key Concepts

1. Answers will vary depending on the information being shared. For example, if you wanted to present the features of a communications device, such as a cell phone, you could use a desktop publishing program to create a document that includes a photo of the phone and then use a graphics program to label its components. You could place text describing the phone's features at the bottom of the document. Presentation software could be used to present information in a variety of formats, including bulleted lists, demonstrations in the form of short video clips, and charts and graphs that visually explain numeric data.
2. A database program stores and organizes information. In a business that gathers a large amount of information, such a program greatly increases both the speed and accuracy of information retrieval. The software allows data to be retrieved according to a wide variety of criteria, which is extremely useful in analyzing sales trends, preparing targeted marketing campaigns, and so on.
3. The business might be using outdated, incomplete, and inaccurate information to make marketing decisions. It would not be able to keep up with other companies when servicing its customers. For example, its Web site might be poorly designed and not provide all the features customers expect when making buying decisions.

Practice Academics

English Language Arts

4. For example, when marketing the latest smart phones, a company might use Facebook and Twitter to allow current users to share their experiences with the phones.

Mathematics

5. $49.95 + (45.95 \times 12) = 601.35$; $79.95 + (29.95 \times 12) = 439.35$; $601.35 - 439.35 = 162$

glencoe.com

Answer Key Send students to the Online Learning Center to check their answers.

READING GUIDE

Before You Read

Connect What everyday activities would you do differently if you could not use the Internet or computers?

Objectives

- **Describe** the computer software programs that are influencing and reshaping marketing.
- **Explain** how the Internet and the World Wide Web can increase business productivity.

The Main Idea

The Internet and technological innovations are providing businesses with new marketing opportunities to offer better service to customers.

Vocabulary

Content Vocabulary
- Enterprise Resource Planning (ERP)
- World Wide Web
- Internet
- hypertext transfer protocol (HTTP)
- uniform resource locator (URL)
- firewall
- site map

Academic Vocabulary

You will find these words in your reading and on your tests. Make sure you know their meanings.
- consists
- link

Graphic Organizer

Draw or print this chart to write in the five types of specialized computer technology that marketers use.

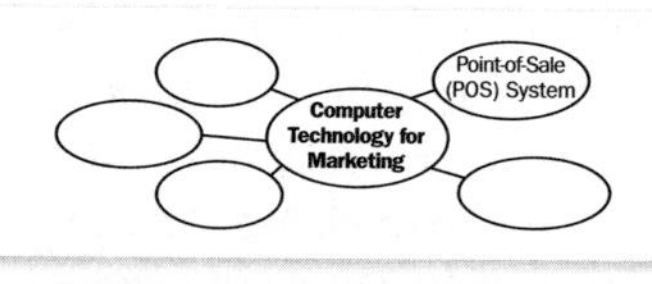

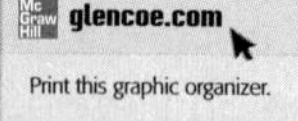

Print this graphic organizer.

STANDARDS

ACADEMIC

English Language Arts
NCTE 1 Read texts to acquire new information.

Mathematics
NCTM Number and Operations Understand numbers, ways of representing numbers, relationships among numbers, and number systems.

NCSS *National Council for the Social Studies*
NCTE *National Council of Teachers of English*
NCTM *National Council of Teachers of Mathematics*
NSES *National Science Education Standards*

College & Career READINESS

Common Core
Writing Produce clear and coherent writing in which the development, organization, and style are appropriate to task, purpose, and audience.

MARKETING CORE FUNCTIONS
- Marketing Information Management
- Promotion

m.e. Section 9.2 | Technology and Marketing

TECHNOLOGY FOR MARKETING

Today marketing software includes point-of-sale systems, interactive touch-screen computers, interactive TV, just-in-time schedulers, customer relationship management, and enterprise resource planning systems.

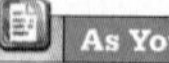

As You Read

Connect What are some ways you have used technology to make purchases?

POINT-OF-SALE SYSTEMS

A common use of computers in retailing is the point-of-sale (POS) system. This system **consists** of cash registers and peripherals, such as scanners, touch screens, handheld checkout devices, printers, and electronic kiosks. Scanners feed information directly from merchandise tags or labels into a computer to update inventory. See Chapter 16 for more information on POS systems.

> “Computer and software applications are shaping the way marketers conduct business.”

INTEGRATED MARKETING SOFTWARE

For a company to be truly successful, it must be tuned in to its customers needs and wants. Managing the relationships the company has with its customers is at the core of a business strategy called customer relationship management (CRM). This strategy now employs technology to gather and analyze customer information, including viewing customers' sales histories, and customizing promotions for particular groups of customers that a company wants to target.

New CRM applications are Internet-enabled, fully integrated Web-service applications. A customer can place an order online. The customer can also check the progress of the order either on the Web or by telephone. A company, in turn, can track all of that information in order to better serve its customers.

In addition to tracking the business the customer is doing with the company, it can suggest other products the customer may want to purchase. Through "cookies" stored in the customer's computer, it can generate ads for other Web sites targeting the customer's interests. CRM can also track the customer's satisfaction level at each step in the sales process.

Point-of-Sale Checkout

Point-of-sale systems (POS) serve the same purpose as cash registers, but they also scan bar codes, update inventory, and track information that can be helpful in store management. ***What stores do you shop in where POS systems are used? What stores do you shop where a POS system is not used?***

ENGAGE

Anticipation Activity

Improving Student Achievement Have students collaborate to create a list of places where they have seen Web site addresses listed. Answers may include: cereal boxes, athletic events, festivals, and billboards. Ask: ***Why do you think marketers would encourage this type of Web site placement?*** These locations are highly visible and have viewers who may be interested in visiting the sites.

Objectives

- **Describe** the computer software programs that are influencing and reshaping marketing. CRM: allows companies to capture customer information, engage in custom promotions; ERP: integrates the various functions involved in business management
- **Explain** how the Internet and the World Wide Web can increase business productivity. They allow employees, customers, and vendors to communicate in effective, time-saving ways.

Graphic Organizer

- Computer Technology for Marketing
  - Integrated Marketing Software
  - Point-of-Sale (POS) System
  - The Clickstream
  - Interactive Television
  - Interactive Touch-Screen Computers

iWB

Graphic Organizer Send students to the Online Learning Center to print this graphic organizer.

EXPLORE

Before You Read

Read the Before You Read question aloud: ***What everyday activities would you do differently if you could not use the Internet or computers?*** Instead of purchasing specialized items on the Web, I would have to place my order using the company's printed catalog. I wouldn't be able to IM my friends or e-mail my teachers with homework questions, so I would either have to wait until I saw them or call them on the phone. I would have to go to the library to conduct research for school reports.

Preteaching Vocabulary

Have students go to the Online Learning Center at glencoe.com for the Chapter 9 Preteaching Vocabulary games.

Content Vocabulary

Ask for volunteers to offer definitions for the terms in the Content Vocabulary list. As students read this section, encourage them to add to or modify these definitions as appropriate.

Academic Vocabulary

Consists—Denotative Meaning Point out that the word *consists* is commonly used with *of*, as in this statement: ***The POS system consists of cash registers and peripherals.*** Explain that in this case, *consists* means "is composed" or "is made up of."

Link—Usage Display these two sentences: ***Each metal link is joined together to create the chain. The home page has a link to the "Contact Us" page.*** Ask: ***How is the use of* link *similar in these two sentences?*** Both are about a link being used to join things together.

Expert Advice

Read the quote to students:

> **"Computer and software applications are shaping the way marketers conduct business."**

Ask students: ***Twenty years ago, how do you think a salesperson who traveled most of the time kept track of customer information?*** The salesperson would probably have relied on printouts of customers' sales history. He or she may also have used index cards to keep track of other information such as personal facts about the customer.

Section 9.2 Technology and Marketing

TECHNOLOGY FOR MARKETING

Ask these guiding questions to focus the discussion about technology for marketing.

Guiding Questions

Analyze Why do many major retailers depend on customer relationship management applications to help them maintain connections with their customers?	These applications capture customers' sales histories and other information that allows the company to customize promotions to increase sales and form a bond.
Judge A sporting goods Web site sees that you have purchased golf equipment. It sends this information to its partners, who begin sending you targeted promotions on high-end golf clubs. Do you see this as a service or a nuisance? Why?	I would see it as a service because I like to know about the latest advances in golf.

As You Read Answer

Read the As You Read question aloud: ***What are some ways you have used technology to make purchases?*** I have used kiosks with touch screens to purchase tickets and order items from catalogs, and at discount and grocery stores I've checked out using point-of-sale systems.

Visual Literacy

Point-of-Sale Checkout Caption Answer Read the caption question to the students: ***What stores do you shop in where POS systems are used?*** Student answers will vary based on their shopping experiences. Students should identify POS systems such as barcodes, cash registers, or other ways to instantly update inventory at point of sale. ***What stores do you shop in where a POS system is not used?*** If the stores where students shop do not have a POS system, have students suggest easy ways that the store's owner could implement a POS system.

The GREEN Marketer

E-Mail Marketing: Saving Trees

E-mail is a cheaper, faster, and more environmentally friendly way to reach customers than traditional print mail. It is quick to produce and send. It does not require paper, ink, or fuel for transportation. Offering customers the option to switch from print to e-mail for statements, bills, and other communications helps companies save money and create an environmentally aware image.

Mining Data

For marketers, e-mail is also a rich source of market information. By studying what links customers click in e-mail, marketers can discover what they are interested in and what kinds of offers motivate them to buy. Marketers can use this information to create new advertisements or products that will interest their customers.

Social Studies

Imagine Brainstorm a few ideas for technology such as email that can be used to replace print or personal communication. Describe how these changes would affect the use of resources by people around the world.

NCSS III K People, Places, & Environments Propose, compare, and evaluate alternative policies for the use of land and other resources in communities, regions, nations, and the world.

glencoe.com

Get an activity on green marketing.

ENTERPRISE RESOURCE PLANNING (ERP)

Enterprise resource planning (ERP) software is used to integrate all parts of a company's business management, including planning, manufacturing, sales, marketing, invoicing, payroll, inventory control, order tracking, customer service, finance, and human resources. Both CRM and ERP applications can help generate marketing reports and solve marketing problems.

INTERACTIVE TOUCH-SCREEN COMPUTERS

A touch screen is a computer display screen that responds to human touch. This allows the user to interact with the computer by touching words or pictures on the screen. (See **Figure 9.1**.) Many PDAs, such as Apple's iPhone®, use touchscreen technology.

Interactive computers are on shelves in retail stores and in stand-alone kiosks at malls and airports. Computer-assisted transactions are well suited for products, goods, and services that are fairly standard and receptive to programmable decision making. Costly or complex products need a degree of personal contact that is not possible without a salesperson.

INTERACTIVE TELEVISION

Interactive TV systems use satellite technology and computer hardware and software to make the TV function like a computer. Advertisers like the idea of interactive television because consumers can instantly get more information about products through their TVs. Some shopping channels offer the ability to buy merchandise using the TV's remote control.

THE CLICKSTREAM

Interactive TV also benefits marketers because of the click stream. Every click of the remote control goes into a database for later analysis. From this data, an idea of individual viewers and what motivates them emerges. Programmers can use this data to monitor viewers' reactions to content and then use that information in the future. Over time marketers can develop psychological profiles of individual viewers that provide an enormous amount of information.

Reading Check

Analyze When are computer-assisted transactions and programmable decision making not suitable for customers?

FIGURE 9.1 Marketing with Interactive Technology

Conversing with a Computer Interactive technology provides a way to have a conversation with a computer. It is changing the way products and services are marketed. It has also made sales and ordering more streamlined and efficient. Let's look at some ways interactive technology is used in marketing. ***Why is it important for marketers to know how to use interactive technology?***

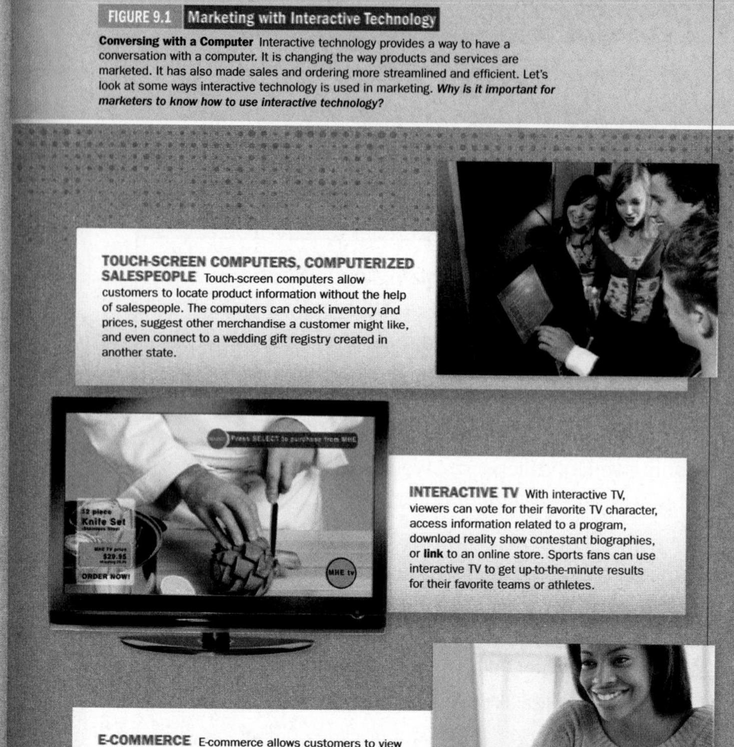

TOUCH-SCREEN COMPUTERS, COMPUTERIZED SALESPEOPLE Touch-screen computers allow customers to locate product information without the help of salespeople. The computers can check inventory and prices, suggest other merchandise a customer might like, and even connect to a wedding gift registry created in another state.

INTERACTIVE TV With interactive TV, viewers can vote for their favorite TV character, access information related to a program, download reality show contestant biographies, or **link** to an online store. Sports fans can use interactive TV to get up-to-the-minute results for their favorite teams or athletes.

E-COMMERCE E-commerce allows customers to view products, compare prices, and order—all at the click of a mouse. They can compare prices and styles at hundreds of online stores in a matter of minutes without leaving home. Information supplied when placing orders is captured in a database and used by a marketer to generate future sales.

EXPLAIN

The GREEN Marketer

Social Studies Answer Students may mention that tasks, such as paying bills, filing taxes, applying for college or loans, and sending letters or invitations, can be done electronically instead of using print or personal communication. This can result in positive changes like saving natural resources and individuals' time. However, this method might have negative effects, such as a risk to data security and lack of personal interaction. Ask students: ***Would you rather receive a printed catalog or an e-mail invitation to visit a Web site that sells the same products? Why?*** Answers will vary. Sample answer: The e-mail and Web site, because it saves paper and I do not have to store the catalog for future reference. Also, the Web site is likely to be updated regularly.

INTERACTIVE TOUCH-SCREEN COMPUTERS

Ask these guiding questions to focus the discussion.

Guiding Questions

List What are some devices that commonly used touch screens?	smart phones and PDAs, ATMs, POS systems such as those at libraries and retail stores.
Make a Judgment When performing a task online, would you prefer to use a touch screen or a mouse? Why?	Many people prefer touch screens because they think they are faster and more natural.

Reading Check Answer

Read the Reading Check question to students: ***When are computer-assisted transactions and programmable decision making not suitable for customers?*** When customers are buying complex products or products that are costly, programmed decision-making isn't as well suited as personal contact with a salesperson.

ELABORATE

Visual Literacy

Figure 9.1 Marketing with Interactive Technology Read the caption question to the students: ***Why is it important for marketers to know how to use interactive technology?*** Keeping up with technology is vital to being competitive because consumers and businesses will purchase goods from companies that can provide the most innovative and convenient services.

Critical Thinking

Discuss with students that interactive television is used in hotels to allow guests to order movies, play video games, and check out from the hotel. Ask: ***Why do you think such technology might have started in the hospitality industry***? Answers may include that hotels had to provide this service in order to remain competitive.

Mini Projects

Enrichment

Explaining the Advantages of Kiosks Tell students that their job is to sell kiosks that provide gift-registry functions. Customers, such as engaged couples and expectant parents, use the kiosk to enter a list of gifts they want. Gift-givers then select from the list and the kiosk's database is automatically updated. Have students prepare a presentation for gift shops and department stores that explains the advantages of purchasing a gift-registry kiosk. If possible, encourage students to locate a local gift-registry kiosk (or a similar type of kiosk) to better understand the features it provides. Student presentations should emphasize the advantages that such a kiosk can provide to a retail store. Advantages include: they save personnel time and simplify storing, updating, and retrieving gift information.

Ordering the Perfect Jeans Discuss with students that one way in which marketers have appealed to consumers is to allow them to use e-commerce Web sites and interactive technology to order custom-fit jeans at a reasonable price. Have students research an e-commerce site that provides this service. Have students present a brief oral report discussing how the process is completed. Students should report on a Web site of their choosing that allows customers to order custom-fit jeans. Sites such as makeyourownjeans.com allow customers to enter their measurements and then select from various fabrics, styles, and embellishments. The custom jeans are then mailed to the customer.

e MARKETING

Cloud Computing

Cloud Computing is virtual computing services offered by vendors. Many IT administrative tasks can now be outsourced through cloud computing services offered by Google®, Amazon®, and other upstart companies. For example, SalesForce.com offers cloud services for customer relationship management. Companies that subscribe can implement applications to support their sales force without the need for in-house servers and employees to do that job. Expense reporting, lead generation, and sales analysis can be performed by a cloud computing company. A pharmaceutical company can hire cloud servers to crunch scientific data from its scientists around the world. That same task would have required purchase of more than 20 computer servers. Thus, the benefits of cloud computing are: considerably lower costs, speed, and more flexibility as you only pay for services needed. Also, companies do not have to invest in capital expenditures for multiple servers and additional employees to provide those IT services.

Innovate and Create

Have students brainstorm ideas on what tasks can be outsourced using cloud computing services. Compile a list of those options and then rank them in a priority order based on what might be most beneficial to a firm to least beneficial. Support sales force with Customer Relationship Management; Back-up files for companies; Control e-mail spam and virus protection; Conduct data analysis—marketing research companies use cloud computing to analyze data from various sites where research is taking place; Create a more interactive Web site that allows customers to interface with each other or with employees; Develop computerized employee training programs; Design more exciting presentations for the staff; Provide real-time research and information to upper management via Internet data mining; Create exciting virtual business meetings; Conduct market research.

glencoe.com

eMarketing Worksheet Activity Send students to the Online Learning Center to download an eMarketing worksheet activity.

THE WORLD WIDE WEB

Although the terms are often used synonymously, the **World Wide Web** and the **Internet** are actually two different things. The Web is a part of the Internet and is a collection of interlinked electronic documents. These pages are viewed with a browser. A browser is any piece of software that tells the computer what Web content to display. Web pages contain links that prompt the browser to load a new page.

Researcher Tim Berners Lee invented the technology behind the Web. He developed the **hypertext transfer protocol (HTTP)** that links documents together. He also developed the **uniform resource locator (URL)**, which is the protocol used to identify and locate Web pages on the Internet. It is also known as a *Web address.*

Today there are billions of pages on the Web. Hundreds of thousands of new Web pages are added every week. Because the World Wide Web does not have a system for locating or categorizing content, companies have developed an assortment of Web directories and search engines to help users find what they want.

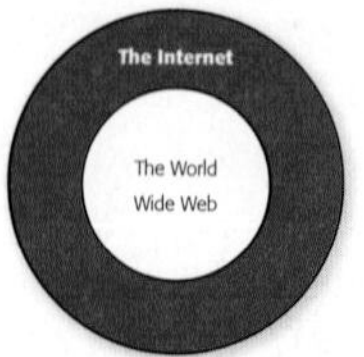

SEARCH ENGINES

Two of the most popular search engines are Google® and Yahoo!®. Google is by far the largest with a database of more than a trillion URLs. Many of the most useful and common Web pages are known to all search engines, but there are also many sites and pages identified only by one or two search engines. Always check other search engines to find sites missed by Google and Yahoo!.

Search engines try to return results that relate well to your search terms. But they are also designed to make money for the company. To do that, search engines will place paid advertisers near or high up in the search results listings. Ads may also appear alongside your search results.

ELECTRONIC MAIL

E-mail represents another revolutionary change prompted by the development of the Internet. E-mail is popular because it is delivered immediately. Also, the sender and receiver do not have to be available at the same time.

For example, an appliance store employee can e-mail an order for new merchandise to a shipper in a different time zone. The shipper can acknowledge the order when the employee arrives at work, and the merchandise can be prepared for shipment almost immediately.

One annoying aspect of using e-mail is the high number of messages from sources unknown to you. These messages are known as *spam.* All e-mail programs have filters that sort out spam, usually placing it in a separate folder, such as "junk mail." The CAN-SPAM law, passed by Congress in 2003, bans certain spamming techniques and requires senders to include a valid address. Although the law has made it easier to install filters to block spam, unwanted e-mail is still a problem.

HOT TOPIC
Protecting Digital Data
Cyberattacks on 27 South Korean commercial and government Web sites in September 2009 temporarily jammed over half of them.

Another misuse of e-mail is phishing, which is an attempt to get you to share personal information. This is more of a problem on personal computers used at home than at the workplace. An example is an e-mail that appears to be from your bank. It includes your bank's logo, name, and address—everything that makes it look like an official request from your bank for information. You should not provide information to such requests as they are attempts to gain information that could be used to commit fraud. Banks do not request information in this way.

INTRANETS AND EXTRANETS

An intranet is a private, secure network, usually within a company or organization that contains proprietary company data and can be accessed only by internal users. Some businesses have developed networks for their customers, employees, partners, and suppliers. These networks, called extranets, enable customers to access data stored on an internal server. A firewall protects the security of sensitive information. A **firewall** is a hardware and software checkpoint for all requests for inputs of data, incoming and outgoing. The firewall reviews the message to make sure that the data content is safe and acceptable for others to view.

WEB-SITE DEVELOPMENT

A business develops a Web site as a convenient and far-reaching way to inform customers, potential employees, business partners, and even investors about the company and the products it offers. A Web site can also enable the business to sell its products, to provide related resources, and to handle services and inquiries after the sale.

Any Web site's domain name comes from the Internet Corporation for Assigned Names and Numbers (ICANN). The domain name is the part of a URL that identifies a server or service provider. Top-level domains are three-letter extensions, which follow the dot in a Web address. Examples of top-level generic domains include *.com* and *.biz* for businesses and *.org* for nonprofit organizations.

Companies should plan to incur several costs to develop Web sites, including domain name registration, development and maintenance of the Web site, and subscription to a server (if one is not available in-house).

Most business Web sites have similar components that include the following: a branding logo, content, a shopping cart for electronic purchases, a secured payment system for purchases, and general policies related to privacy, shipping, returns, and collection of sales taxes. Many business Web sites also include links to sites run by other divisions of the same company as well as site maps to aid in navigation.

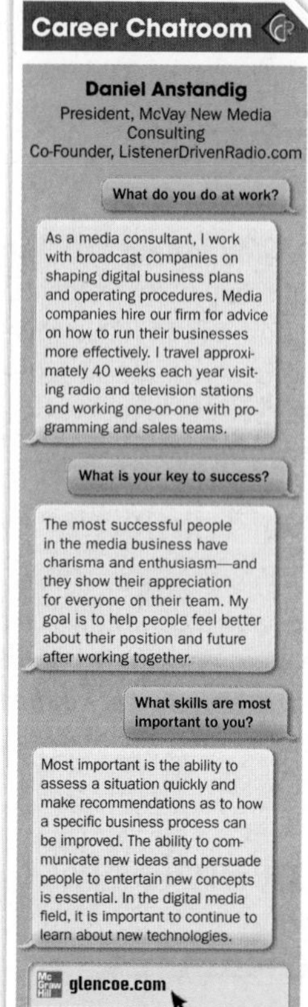

Career Chatroom
Daniel Anstandig
President, McVay New Media Consulting
Co-Founder, ListenerDrivenRadio.com
What do you do at work?
As a media consultant, I work with broadcast companies on shaping digital business plans and operating procedures. Media companies hire our firm for advice on how to run their businesses more effectively. I travel approximately 40 weeks each year visiting radio and television stations and working one-on-one with programming and sales teams.
What is your key to success?
The most successful people in the media business have charisma and enthusiasm—and they show their appreciation for everyone on their team. My goal is to help people feel better about their position and future after working together.
What skills are most important to you?
Most important is the ability to assess a situation quickly and make recommendations as to how a specific business process can be improved. The ability to communicate new ideas and persuade people to entertain new concepts is essential. In the digital media field, it is important to continue to learn about new technologies.
glencoe.com
Read more about this career and get a Career Exploration Activity.

222 | Unit 4 · Skills for Marketing

Chapter 9 · Technology for Marketing | 223

EXPLAIN

Graphic Organizer

Display this target diagram. Discuss the Internet and its vastness.

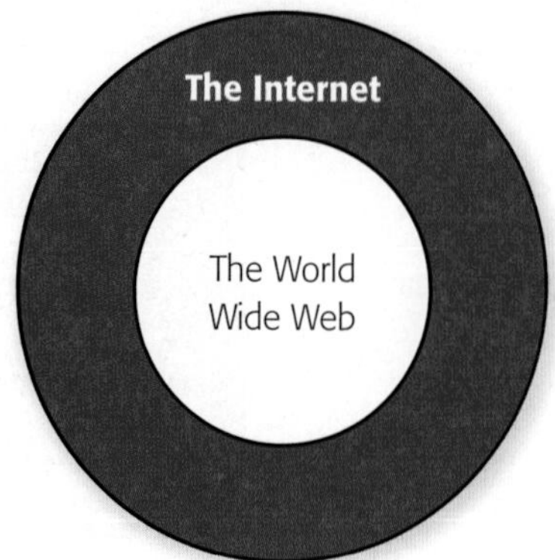

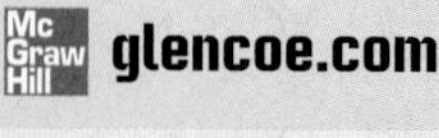

iWB

Graphic Organizer Send students to the Online Learning Center to print this graphic organizer.

SEARCH ENGINES

Ask these guiding questions to focus the discussion.

Guiding Questions

Explain When locating topic information, why is it best to use different search engines?	Different search engines may locate different web pages.
Analyze What can determine which sites are returned at the top of the results listing? Why is this?	Search engines will place paid advertisers high on the results listing because search engines are designed to make money for their owners.

Protecting Digital Data Ask students: ***What might happen if a company were to have all its data destroyed, for example, in a natural disaster such as flood?***

ELABORATE

ELECTRONIC MAIL

E-mail provides a convenient way for businesses to communicate with one another and with their customers. Ask these guiding questions to focus the discussion on electronic mail.

Guiding Questions

Explain What are two major reasons for e-mail's popularity?	It is delivered immediately, and the sender and receiver do not have to be available at the same time.
Summarize Why was the CAN-SPAM law enacted? What does the law state?	It was enacted because users were annoyed by receiving junk e-mail. It bans all spamming techniques and requires senders to include a valid address.

Graphic Organizer

Display this Venn diagram and use it to compare an Intranet and the Internet.

Intranet
- Contains proprietary company data
- Can only be accessed internally

Both
- Privately created
- Secure
- Created using same standards as the Internet

Internet
- Can be accessed by authorized outsiders, such as vendors
- Allows access to data on internal servers

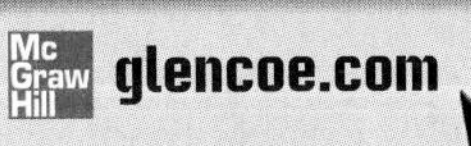

glencoe.com iWB

Graphic Organizer Send students to the Online Learning Center to print this graphic organizer.

Reinforce Vocabulary

Firewall—Usage Discuss that in some business districts, many companies may occupy a single building. Explain that in construction, a firewall is a fireproof wall designed to keep flames from spreading from one part of a building to another. When the Internet first began, companies' data often became contaminated, either accidentally or maliciously. Today, hardware and software firewalls are used to protect data in much the same way as a physical firewall protects a business from being damaged by a nearby blaze.

Career Chatroom

Focus the Career Chatroom discussion concerning Daniel Anstandig by asking students these guiding questions.

Guiding Questions

Explain Why do media companies hire ListenerDrivenRadio.com?	They want to get advice on how to run their businesses more effectively.
Analyze Why do you think Daniel Anstandig says that the successful people in his business have enthusiasm?	Enthusiastic people can express their thoughts in a way that will encourage others.
Infer Why does Anstandig say "The ability to communicate new ideas and persuade people to entertain new concepts is essential"?	If you cannot get people to incorporate your ideas and concepts, you will not be able to help them run their businesses more effectively.

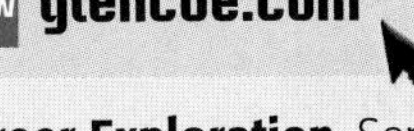

glencoe.com

Career Exploration Send students to the Online Learning Center to find more information about this career and to get a Career Exploration activity.

Mini Project

Extension

Examining the Importance of Hyperlinks Discuss with students that the ability to create hyperlinks (or simply links) is what really led to the enormous growth of the web. Have students write a brief report on the history of hyperlinks. In their reports, they should discuss the concept of "just-in-time" information and how hyperlinks are related to it. Students should write a report discussing that the term *hyperlink* was first used in the mid-1960s by Ted Nelson and his associates. Actual hyperlinks were first used to move about within a single document by a programming team led by Douglas Engelbart. Hyperlinks allow an enormous amount of information to be available online. The beauty of the concept is that the user only needs to access information when and if it is needed (hence the concept of just-in-time information.)

When developing a Web site, the designer creates a site map. A **site map** outlines what can be found on each page within the Web site. This concept in Web-site design is known as *global navigation.* The site map guides a viewer to the desired information and provides links to different parts of the Web site.

A Web-site designer prepares a layout grid for every page within a Web site. Layout grids identify all the Web-page elements, such as the title of the page, the branding logo, the placement of banner ads, the content, related links, and a navigation bar for movement within the site.

E-COMMERCE

E-commerce is the process of conducting business transactions on the Internet. E-commerce sales figures have risen dramatically over the years.

As e-commerce grows, it is redefining the relationship between the seller and the buyer. E-commerce can exist B2B (business to business) or B2C (business to consumer). Web markets differ from traditional markets in that they are always open for business—24 hours a day, seven days a week. Also, they are not affected by costly middlemen and distribution channels.

Suppliers all over the globe can compete if they can deliver the quality, price, quantity, and service demanded by the customer and are deemed trustworthy financially and ethically.

PROTECTING DIGITAL DATA

Digital data is not always safe. Sometimes a hard disk crashes and the data stored on it cannot be retrieved. Sometimes files are accidentally deleted, or files become corrupted and cannot be read. Optical disks and USB flash drives provide for convenient, portable backup of files. Portable external hard drives can be stored off-site and are easy to retrieve and access.

Computer files are vulnerable to viruses, worms, spyware, and malware. Viruses and worms can destroy your data. Spyware and malware can track all your online activity and collect personal information or force you to visit certain sites. To protect your data, you should back up your files regularly, use reputable anti-virus and anti-spyware software, and install a computer firewall.

Reading Check

Recall What is the difference between an intranet and an extranet?

MARKETING CASE STUDY

The Orbitz Hovercraft

The online travel-booking site Orbitz has some stiff competition, so it added a feature that automatically issues refunds to travelers if the price of a flight or hotel room goes down after they buy their tickets. To publicize the new feature, Orbitz built a quirky ad campaign around a man in a hovercraft who delivers the rebate checks.

Delivering the Benefit

In one ad, a man is watering his lawn when the hovercraft lands. When he asks the pilot why he did not just mail him the check, he replies, "Sir ... we have a hovercraft!" Another ad sees the check delivered to golfers on a golf course. Both ads use quirky, dry humor to catch the attention of viewers.

Science

Discuss Think of the technology required to make this program possible. Share with a partner how Orbitz might keep track of the various prices involved to make the refund system work.

NSES F Develop understanding of science and technology in local, national, and global challenges.

ONLINE LEARNING

Many courses of study are available online. In fact, you have many courses from which to choose. Many colleges and universities now offer courses online that can lead to a two-year (AA) degree or a four-year degree (BA). Many working adults enroll in courses to advance their careers and they complete their studies at home.

There are hundreds of course offerings listed on various Web sites. Some of these offerings include marketing-related classes in the following seven areas:

- Marketing
- Business Administration
- Financial Planning
- Small Business and Entrepreneurship
- Graphic Design and Multimedia
- Accounting
- Web Design and Animation

Private schools, colleges, and universities throughout the United States are adding more online courses every year. The costs for online courses are generally less than for attending classes in person.

After You Read — Section 9.2

Review Key Concepts

1. **Describe** how specialized computer systems are used for marketing.
2. **Distinguish** between uses of the Internet and uses of the World Wide Web for business.
3. **Explain** why it is important for businesses to protect their data.

Practice Academics

English Language Arts

4. Write an e-mail message to a vendor asking for specifications of a new printer that your company plans to market. Use your own knowledge of printers to help construct your message.

NCTE 12 Use language to accomplish individual purposes.

Mathematics

5. The following ratio shows the total Internet sales for one particular shoe company as compared to the total Internet shoe sales for the industry: $364,840/$2,168,760. What percent of the total Internet shoe sales does this particular company have? Round your answer to the nearest whole percent.

NCTM Number and Operations Understand numbers, ways of representing numbers, relationships among numbers, and number systems.

Math Concept **Ways of Representing Numbers** A ratio compares two numbers. Ratios can be expressed as fractions. When the comparison is a part of a whole, the numerator of the fraction usually represents the part, and the denominator represents the whole.

Starting Hints To solve this problem, divide the numerator by the denominator of the ratio to get a decimal. Multiply the decimal by 100 to get the percent. Round your answer to the nearest whole percent.

For help, go to the **Math Skills Handbook** located at the back of this book.

glencoe.com — Check your answers.

ELABORATE

E-COMMERCE

Ask these guiding questions to focus the discussion on e-commerce.

Guiding Questions

Predict Can you predict future trends?	Predictions will vary and may include new technology.
Draw Conclusions How do you think e-commerce got its name?	Electronic commerce is conducted by using electronic equipment, such as computers and networks.

Reading Check Answer

Read the Reading Check question to students: *What is the difference between an intranet and an extranet?* Intranets are private, secure networks, usually within an organization that contain proprietary company data and can be accessed only by internal users. Extranets are networks for a company's customers, employees, partners, and suppliers.

MARKETING CASE STUDY

Science Answer Partners should discuss the technology Orbitz® needs to make this refund system work. This ad campaign is a classic example of a consumer benefit that would not have been feasible just a few years ago. The Orbitz computer system must check databases to continually compare prices for flights and hotel rooms to determine whether they have dropped. If a price has been lowered, the system must use the information in the customer database to issue a refund.

EVALUATE

Graphic Organizer

Display this graphic organizer. Ask students to suggest ways in which data can be damaged or lost, and write down their answers.

glencoe.com iWB

Graphic Organizer Send students to the Online Learning Center to print this graphic organizer.

ONLINE LEARNING

Ask these guiding questions to focus the discussion about online learning.

Guiding Questions

Analyze Why might adults choose to enroll in online courses?	they may not have an appropriate school nearby; the cost is generally less.
Elaborate What do you think might be some disadvantages to online learning?	You do not get to interact directly with your classmates or your teacher. Some courses may not be available online.

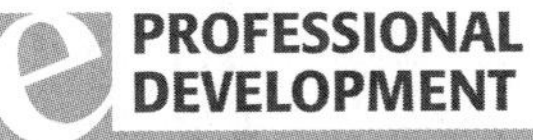
PROFESSIONAL DEVELOPMENT **MINI CLIP**

Math: Understanding Fractions
Go to the Online Learning Center to view a video clip in which an algebra teacher discusses the importance of fraction concepts in pre-algebra instruction.

After You Read Section 9.2

Review Key Concepts

1. Point-of-sale systems perform the functions of cash register in addition to performing other tasks, such as updating inventories. Integrated marketing software simplifies keeping track of customers' sales histories, customizing promotions, and allowing customers to place orders online. Interactive touch-screen computers are used in retail stores and stand-alone kiosks and allow customers to interact with the computer system by touching onscreen words or images. Interactive TV uses software, hardware, and satellite technology to allow the television to function as a computer. This capability can provide features such as allowing customers to use the TV's remote control to make shopping channel purchases.
2. The World Wide Web is part of the Internet. The Internet has additional components, such as e-mail, which allow companies to efficiently communicate with vendors and customers. The Web provides interactivity that allows customers to make online purchases and search for needed information. Web sites can integrate graphics and video to enhance the shopping experience. All of these capabilities make the Web ideal for e-commerce.
3. Data is one of the most valuable assets a company has. A loss of data can cause a business to fail because of loss of records such as customer files, past sales information, and employee data. Files must be protected against accidental corruption and malicious forces such as viruses and worms.

Practice Academics

English Language Arts

4. The e-mail might request information such as the printer's wholesale price or whether it can automatically print two-sided documents..

Mathematics

5. 17% (364,840/2,168,760 = 0.168, which rounds to 17%)

glencoe.com

Send students to the Online Learning Center to check their answers.

Chapter 9 Visual Summary

Technology for Marketing

Business needs are fulfilled by computer software applications for communications, accounting and record keeping, publishing, design, and presentation.

COMPUTER APPLICATIONS

Business Needs	Communications	Accounting and Record Keeping	Publishing	Design	Presentation
How They Are Met	• Word Processing Programs • Email and IM Programs	• Database Programs • Accounting Programs • Spreadsheet Programs	• Desktop Publishing Programs • Web-page Editing Programs	• Graphics and Design Programs • Web-page Editing Programs	• Presentation Software • Web-page Editing Programs

The World Wide Web is used in many ways in the workplace. Businesses search for information on the Internet, send and receive emails, develop and design Web sites, buy and sell products, and protect their private information from harm.

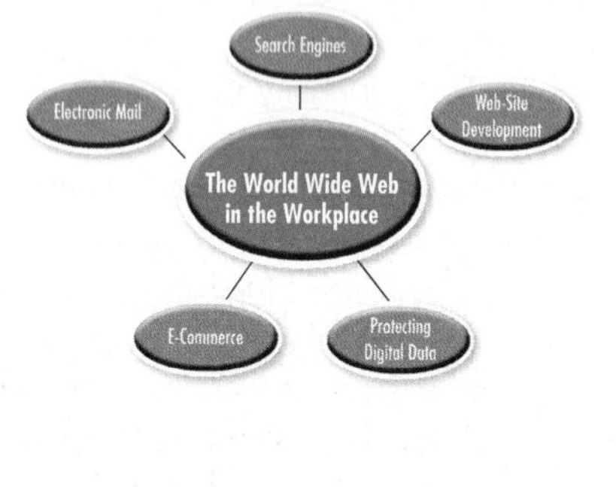

Review and Activities

Written Summary

- Computer software applications satisfy business needs for communication, word processing, accounting and record keeping, publishing, and graphic design.
- Broadband and wireless technology, videoconferencing, and communication programs help businesses stay in touch with each other.
- Computer technologies developed especially for marketing fulfill needs in the areas of point-of-sale systems, integrated marketing programs, interactive touch-screen computers, interactive TV, and the Internet.
- The World Wide Web is one part of the Internet.
- Business done on the Internet is called e-commerce.
- Companies need to be careful to protect their digital data on the Internet.

Review Content Vocabulary and Academic Vocabulary

1. Arrange the vocabulary terms below into groups of related words. Explain why you put the words together.

Content Vocabulary

- word-processing programs (p. 213)
- database programs (p. 213)
- accounting programs (p. 214)
- spreadsheet programs (p. 214)
- desktop publishing programs (p. 215)
- graphics and design programs (p. 215)
- presentation software (p. 215)
- home page (p. 216)
- hypertext markup language (HTML) (p. 216)
- communications programs (p. 216)
- Wi-Fi (p. 217)
- enterprise resource planning (ERP) (p. 220)
- World Wide Web (p. 222)
- Internet (p. 222)
- hypertext transfer protocol (HTTP) (p. 222)
- uniform resource locator (URL) (p. 222)
- firewall (p. 223)
- site map (p. 224)

Academic Vocabulary

- analyze (p. 214)
- edit (p. 215)
- consists (p. 219)
- link (p. 221)

Assess for Understanding

2. **Describe** What are some ways marketers use spreadsheet programs?
3. **Explain** How are graphics and design programs used in marketing?
4. **Determine** Which type of program would you use to share information with a group of people who are far from you? What are the benefits to this approach?
5. **Discuss** What opportunities and difficulties are presented by the use of interactive technology for marketing?
6. **Create** How would you use the Internet to market a local company?
7. **Judge** What are the benefits and risks associated with e-commerce?
8. **Connect** How does the use of the Internet for marketing purposes relate to segmented marketing?
9. **Distinguish** What is the difference between a firewall and antivirus software?

EVALUATE

Visual Summary

Express Creativity Ask students to create a visual summary that illustrates a concept in the chapter. Encourage students to use different formats for their visual summaries, such as an illustrated poster, a Venn diagram or a collage of screen captures from different software applications. Visual summaries will vary depending on the concept depicted. Questions to ask when assessing a visual summary include:

- Is the summary clear, economical, and simple?
- Are any important steps or concepts left out?
- Are steps or concepts arranged in the same order as the original?
- Does the summary reveal a pattern that connects the details?
- Does the summary locate and highlight the most important information?

Review Content Vocabulary and Academic Vocabulary

1. Students should arrange the vocabulary terms into groups of related words. Possible groups:
Types of computer applications—word-processing programs; database programs; accounting programs; spreadsheet programs; desktop publishing programs; graphics and design programs; presentation software. **World Wide Web**—Internet; hypertext transfer protocol (HTTP); uniform resource locator (URL); firewall; site map.

EVALUATE

Assess for Understanding

2. Marketers might use spreadsheet programs to develop and manage budgets, analyze the financial performance of campaigns, schedule projects, track responses to campaigns, and build relationship marketing.

3. Marketers use graphics and design programs to design marketing promotional materials; create logos; illustrate floor plans; create illustrations and photographic prints; and create images for presentations, Web pages, and Internet ads.

4. Sample answer: I could use videoconferencing to communicate with them. Presentation software could be used to create a slide show or multimedia presentation that shares specific information long-distances. A major benefit of using videoconferencing software to communicate is that it saves travel time and money.

5. Opportunities: interactive technology for marketing can be used virtually anywhere and reduce the need for employees. Difficulties: customers have little guidance in the decision-making process and therefore may make decisions that do not meet their needs. In addition, interactive technology requires extensive hardware and software to set up and must be maintained. Also, some customers may find it intimidating and refuse to use it.

6. Sample answer: I would place ads on sites that potential customers are likely to see, I would create a Web site with information about the company, such as contact information, product information, and so on, and I would create a Facebook page for the company.

7. Advantages of e-commerce include: cost savings because no physical store or showroom is needed, little or no need for middlemen, the business is open 24 hours a day, seven days a week and is accessible around the globe. The risks include that the company does not have the same kind of physical contact with customers as a bricks-and-mortar store has. Customers cannot physically examine products and the customer has to wait to receive the product.

8. Even if a segmented market is very small, an e-commerce company can still be successful because it can market its products to the entire world.

9. A firewall is software and/or hardware that checks to make certain all incoming and outgoing messages are checked to make certain the content is safe and acceptable for others to view. Anti-virus software, on the other hand, attempts to locate and remove any viruses (malicious software) it finds in data files.

21st Century Skills

Social Responsibility Skills

10. Recycling Technology In the past, many people tossed their old computers, monitors, and printers, in the garbage. Today people are more socially responsible. Make a list of the places that will accept these articles for recycling. Share your class's list with the school so that any old computers and peripherals are reused or recycled.

Financial Literacy Skills

11. Take-Home Pay You started a new job recently, and today you received your first paycheck. It was quite a bit less than you expected. When you were hired, you were told that you would earn $12 an hour. Over the first two weeks, you worked 30 hours, so you thought you would be paid $360. You asked your boss about it, and she simply said the difference was taken out for deductions. What does that mean? What deductions can legally be taken out of your paycheck? How are these deductions used?

Everyday Ethics

12. Green Eggs with SPAM You visit a new Mom & Pop café that holds weekly drawings for free treats and prizes. It requires signing up with your email address. The café promises not to share your information with any outside parties, but you start receiving a lot of spam after signing up. Even if a company promises not to sell your email address, it is possible for spammers to access the company's computers if they are not secure. Discuss with your class whether it is ethical for the restaurant to keep running this promotion.

e-Marketing Skills

13. Touchscreen Technology Research touchscreen technology. Find out what products are available and the differences between them. Answer the following questions:

Is this technology feasible for a medium-sized hardware store with 30 employees?

What is the range of costs for a single touchscreen checkout system?

How does this technology prevent theft?

Build Academic Skills

Science

14. Technology Use the Internet to research the technical qualities and specifications of a computer peripheral product, such as a printer or scanner, and provide your recommendation of the best product for the cost.

NSES F Develop understanding of science and technology in local, national, and global challenges.

English Language Arts

15. Research and Reporting Most businesses use computers built on the PC platform, but Macintosh (Apple) computers have made gains in the U.S. market. Research these two platforms for ease of use, reliability, customer service, available software, and expected cost over five years. Read articles on the Internet and in computer magazines. Write a recommendation for which computer system you think a local business should use.

NCTE 8 Use information resources to gather information and create and communicate knowledge.

Mathematics

16. Faster than Fast A millisecond (ms) is a unit of time used to describe how long it takes a computer to complete an operation. 1 second = 1,000 ms. If a computer can execute 35 operations per millisecond, how many operations can it complete in one minute? (60 seconds per minute)

NCTM Measurement Understand measurable attributes of objects and the units, systems, and processes of measurement.

Math Concept **Measurement** Measure objects and apply units, systems, and processes of measurement.

For help, go to the **Math Skills Handbook** located at the back of this book.

Standardized Test Practice

Directions Read the following questions. On a separate piece of paper, write the best possible answer for each one.

1. When you want to store a lot of information, you would probably choose the following type of program:
   A. word-processing
   B. accounting
   C. database
   D. none of the above
2. True or false? Spam can be an annoying aspect of using e-mail.
   T
   F
3. A good method of backing up computer files is to use an external _________ _________.

Test-Taking Tip
If there is time, quickly read through the test for an overview before you begin.

DECA Connection Role Play

Partner Bookstore

Situation Assume the role of new partner in a family-owned bookstore. You recently purchased a share in a bookstore that has been owned by a relative (judge). The store specializes in the mystery genre and locating signed books and first editions. The bookstore has been in operation for over 50 years and has been successful in the past. In recent years sales have declined, but the store has remained open because of loyal customers and the services it provides.

Before you purchased the partnership, you studied the operation and noted changes that would need to be made to improve the store's competitive position, attract new customers, and provide better overall customer service. You also secured agreement from the other owner to institute those changes. The most important change you plan to make is to add up-to-date technologies in the store.

Activity You are to make an outline of the technology additions you are planning, the uses of each, and how each will benefit the store's operation. You will then explain the information from your outline to your partner (judge).

Evaluation You will be evaluated on how well you meet the following performance indicators:

1. Describe the use of technology in operations.
2. Explain the impact of technology on retailing.
3. Explain the use of technology in customer relationship management.
4. Describe the scope of the Internet.
5. Demonstrate Web-search skills.

glencoe.com

Download the Competitive Events Workbook for more Role-Play practice.

EVALUATE

Social Responsibility Skills

10. Lists will vary depending on the local places that will accept old electronic equipment for recycling. Some organizations that retrain workers will accept such equipment, remove any working parts for reuse, and responsibly recycle the remaining components. Some landfills will accept electronic equipment, often for a small fee.

Financial Literacy Skills

11. Various taxes and other fees are allowed to be deducted. These include federal income tax, FICA (Federal Insurance Contributions Act), state taxes, and any local taxes. Federal income taxes are used to support the federal government while state and local taxes are used to support those entities. FICA consists of the taxpayer contributions to Social Security and Medicare.

Everyday Ethics

12. Student opinions will vary. Many people believe that a business should not collect personal information, such as customers' email addresses, unless it has the ability to protect the information from unauthorized access and use. This is particularly true when the company has promised not to share information. Smaller companies frequently are not aware of the dangers they may encounter when storing this type of data nor may they have the capability to properly protect the data.

EVALUATE

e-Marketing Skills

13. Results of students' research will vary. In general, to set up a touchscreen POS system, a hardware store would need a variety of peripherals, including the actual touchscreens, cash drawers, credit card terminals, and printers for receipts. Systems commonly cost in the $3,000 to $5,000 range. While such a system would be feasible for a medium-sized hardware store, the capital layout would probably be greater than most stores of this size would undertake. Some POS systems have cameras to reduce theft. Because these transactions are closely tracked throughout the system, they can help reduce employee theft.

Build Academic Skills

Science

14. Recommendations will vary depending on the peripheral product chosen and the purpose for which it will be used. For example, a laser printer that will be used by a single person in a small office need not have the same speed or durability as one that will be placed on a network and shared by a department of a dozen workers. A black-and-white laser printer for a single worker can cost $200–$400, while a larger one can cost several times that amount. If color printing is desired, the cost can be even higher.

English Language Arts

15. Preferences for a computer that is built on the PC platform as compared with a Macintosh computer depends on a variety of factors. Generally speaking, Macintosh computers and their peripherals are more expensive, but many people believe they are more user-friendly and some reports have found them to be more reliable. Most important is that businesses make certain that the systems they purchase can run all of the software they need.

Mathematics

16. 2,100,000 operations in one minute (35 × 1000 × 60)

Standardized Test Practice

1. C (database)

2. True

3. hard drive (or flash drive)

DECA Connection Role Play

Evaluations will be based on these performance indicators:

1. **Describe the use of technology in operations.** Database programs store and organize information, manage vendor and customer records, track inventories, catalog, track purchases of clients visiting Web sites, etc. Accounting programs store financial records and process all business transactions automatically. Spreadsheet programs organize, calculate, and analyze numerical data. Web-page editors are used to create Web sites and e-commerce sites. Broadband and wireless technologies allow users to send e-mail and share data over company networks and the Internet. Videoconferencing allows workers to hold meetings over networks.
2. **Explain the impact of technology on retailing.** Point-of-sale systems use scanners to directly enter information from merchandise tags into a computer to create bills and update inventory. Integrated marketing software captures customer information and allows users to view sales histories and customize promotions. Enterprise Resource Planning (ERP) allows businesses to integrate all parts of management, including planning, marketing, invoicing, payroll, human resources, etc.
3. **Explain the use of technology in customer relationship management.** Customer relationship management (CRM) technology captures customer information, views, sales histories, and customizes promotions. Most CRM applications are Internet-enabled, allowing customers to place orders and communicate with the company online. Based on ordering history, a business can recommend appropriate products.
4. **Describe the scope of the Internet.** E-commerce allows customers, vendors, etc., to communicate quickly and efficiently. Web sites can be updated more quickly than printed catalogs, allowing quick access to new products and inventory information. POS systems integrate sales information with the ordering process, allowing businesses to have adequate, but not excessive, inventory on hand at all times.
5. **Demonstrate web-search skills.** Search engines allow users to enter specific terms and return a listing of sites containing these terms.

glencoe.com

Role Plays For more DECA Role Plays, send students to the Online Learning Center to download the Competitive Events Workbook.

interpersonal skills

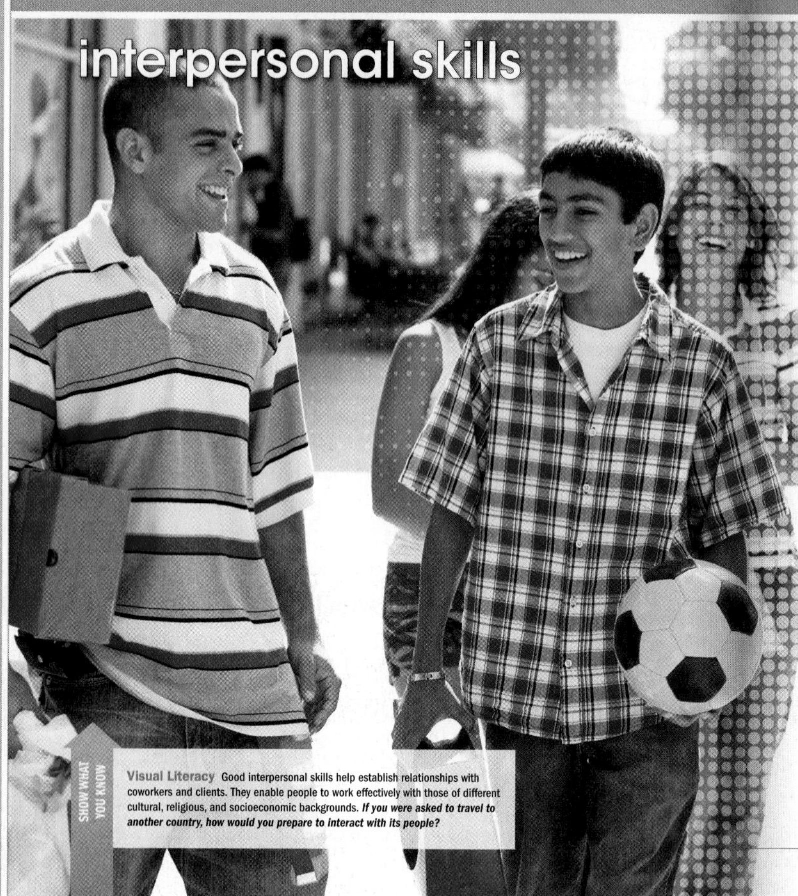

SHOW WHAT YOU KNOW

Visual Literacy Good interpersonal skills help establish relationships with coworkers and clients. They enable people to work effectively with those of different cultural, religious, and socioeconomic backgrounds. ***If you were asked to travel to another country, how would you prepare to interact with its people?***

Discovery Project

Interpersonal Relationships

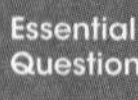

Essential Question Why are ethics, managing conflict, and teamwork important parts of interpersonal relationships?

Project Goal

You will soon be given responsibility for handling customer complaints. Your boss has asked you to develop a procedure to follow when dealing with customer complaints. Research ideas to include in your plan. You may want to search for how to handle customer complaints. Then prepare a one- or two-page plan outlining a step-by-step procedure for handling customer complaints.

Ask Yourself...

- What kinds of complaints do your customers usually have?
- What would likely be a good first step in handling a complaint?
- Would location make a difference in how effective you might be in handling a complaint?

Analysis What criteria will you use to guide your selection of items to include in your procedure document?

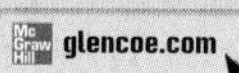

glencoe.com

Activity
Get a worksheet activity about interpersonal relationships.

Evaluate
Download a rubric you can use to evaluate your project.

DECA Connection

DECA Event Role Play

Concepts in this chapter are related to DECA competitive events that involve either an interview or role play.

Performance Indicators The performance indicators represent key skills and knowledge. Your key to success in DECA competitive events is relating them to the concepts in this chapter.

- Foster positive working relationships
- Explain the use of feedback for personal growth.
- Demonstrate ethical work habits.
- Identify desirable personality traits important to business.
- Describe the nature of emotional intelligence.

DECA Prep

Role Play Practice role-playing with the DECA Connection competitive-event activity at the end of this chapter. More information on DECA can be found on DECA's Web site.

ENGAGE

Visual Literacy

Read the chapter opener photo caption question to students: ***If you were asked to travel to another country, how would you prepare to interact with its people?*** discuss the topic with someone who has previously had business meetings in that country; conduct research online or in libraries Ask these guiding questions to activate prior knowledge.

Guiding Questions

Explain Why is awareness of cultural differences important?	Businesses compete globally. Messages must be understood by different cultural backgrounds.
Analyze What character trait is shown when a person learns about another culture before visiting the country?	Answers may vary, but respect should be mentioned.

Discovery Project

Interpersonal Relationships Ask students the Discovery Project Essential Question: ***Why are ethics, managing conflict, and teamwork important parts of interpersonal relationships?*** People who practice ethical behavior usually gain the trust of coworkers and clients. Conflict can often cause decreased efficiency and must be properly managed, usually through negotiation. Teamwork is critical to the success of companies, societies, and civilizations. Ask: ***How can ethics, managing conflicts, and teamwork help an employee deal with a customer complaint?*** Students may suggest that honesty is necessary when dealing with complaints; conflict management can help when faced with an irate customer; and knowing when to ask for help from coworkers can help diffuse a tense situation.

glencoe.com

Discovery Project Resources Send students to the Online Learning Center to download a rubric to evaluate their projects.

ENGAGE

Introduce the Chapter

Chapter 10 provides an overview of the key personal traits, interpersonal skills, and elements of teamwork that facilitate job success. These main concepts are introduced and discussed:

- Building good relationships
- Ethics in the workplace
- Managing conflict
- Interpersonal skills in marketing
- Teamwork
- Leadership skills

Discussion Starter

Interpersonal Skills

Tell students that with factors such as immigration and people retiring later in their careers, the workplace can be very diverse. Workers must have good interpersonal skills to be able to handle the diverse workplace. Ask: ***What are good interpersonal skills?*** Students may mention such things as politeness, concern, respect, honesty, friendliness, ability to communicate, and so on. Ask volunteers to give examples of interactions they have had with people of different age groups, genders, cultures, and backgrounds. Students' examples will vary depending on how much they have interacted with people in the groups mentioned. Encourage students to share positive as well as negative interactions. Then ask: ***How would you describe the qualities of someone you think demonstrates good interpersonal skills?*** Qualities will vary; students may mention kindness, empathy, respect, and so on.

DECA Connection

Discuss the performance indicators listed in the DECA Connection feature. Explain to students that performance indicators tell them how to demonstrate their acquired skills and knowledge through individual or team competitive events.

glencoe.com

Competitive Events Workbook For more DECA Role Plays, send students to the Online Learning Center to download the Competitive Events Workbook.

PROGRAM RESOURCE ORGANIZER

PRINT RESOURCES

- **Student Edition**
- **Teacher Edition**
- **Student Activity Workbook with Academic Integration** includes worksheets and activities correlated to the text.
- **Mathematics for Marketing Workbook** provides math activities for every unit in the text.

TECHNOLOGY TOOLBOX

- **Connect**
- **ConnectPlus**
- **ExamView Assessment Suite** is a comprehensive solution for creating, administering, and scoring tests.

glencoe.com

Online Learning Center provides a variety of resources to enrich and enhance learning.

SECTION, CHAPTER, AND UNIT RESOURCES

- **Graphic Organizers** for organizing text concepts visually.
- **Digital Nation Activities** and **Green Marketer Activities** extend learning beyond the text features.
- **Career Chatroom Career Profiles** allow students to explore different marketing occupations in depth.
- **After You Read Answer Keys** for students to check their answers.
- **Discovery Project Rubrics** and **Marketing Internship Project Rubrics** for students to evaluate their projects.

PROGRAM RESOURCES

- **Student Activity Workbook with Academic Integration Teacher Annotated Edition** includes annotated answers for the activities and worksheets.
- **Marketing Research Project Workbook** provides a step-by-step approach for students to complete their own marketing research studies.
- **School-to-Career Activity Workbook** helps students relate their class work to on-the-job experience and involves work-site analysis and working with mentors.
- **Competitive Events Workbook** helps prepare students for state and national marketing education competitions.
- **Inclusion in the Marketing Education Classroom** provides teaching resources for working with students with special needs.
- **PowerPoint Presentations** provides visual teaching aids and assessments for this chapter.

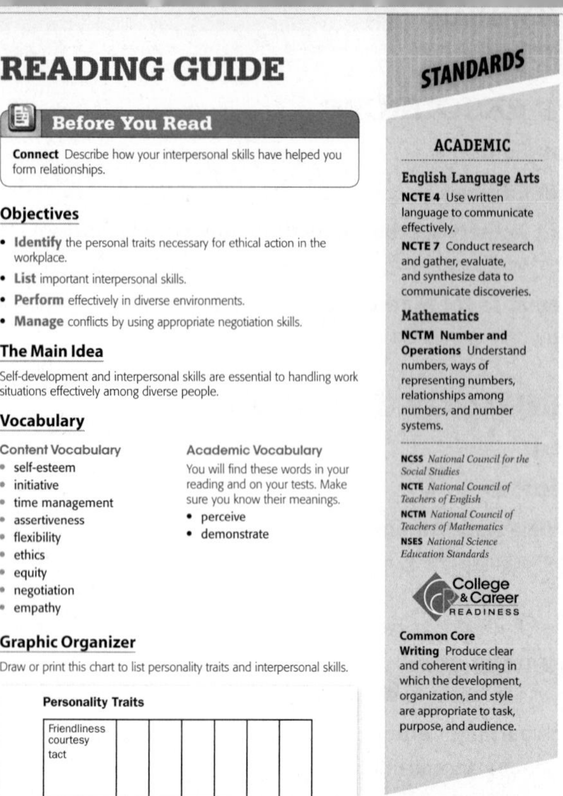

READING GUIDE

Before You Read

Connect Describe how your interpersonal skills have helped you form relationships.

Objectives

- **Identify** the personal traits necessary for ethical action in the workplace.
- **List** important interpersonal skills.
- **Perform** effectively in diverse environments.
- **Manage** conflicts by using appropriate negotiation skills.

The Main Idea

Self-development and interpersonal skills are essential to handling work situations effectively among diverse people.

Vocabulary

Content Vocabulary
- self-esteem
- initiative
- time management
- assertiveness
- flexibility
- ethics
- equity
- negotiation
- empathy

Academic Vocabulary

You will find these words in your reading and on your tests. Make sure you know their meanings.
- perceive
- demonstrate

Graphic Organizer

Draw or print this chart to list personality traits and interpersonal skills.

Personality Traits

Friendliness courtesy tact						

glencoe.com

Print this graphic organizer.

STANDARDS

ACADEMIC

English Language Arts

NCTE 4 Use written language to communicate effectively.

NCTE 7 Conduct research and gather, evaluate, and synthesize data to communicate discoveries.

Mathematics

NCTM Number and Operations Understand numbers, ways of representing numbers, relationships among numbers, and number systems.

NCSS *National Council for the Social Studies*
NCTE *National Council of Teachers of English*
NCTM *National Council of Teachers of Mathematics*
NSES *National Science Education Standards*

College & Career READINESS

Common Core
Writing Produce clear and coherent writing in which the development, organization, and style are appropriate to task, purpose, and audience.

MARKETING CORE FUNCTION

Selling

232 | Unit 4 · Skills for Marketing

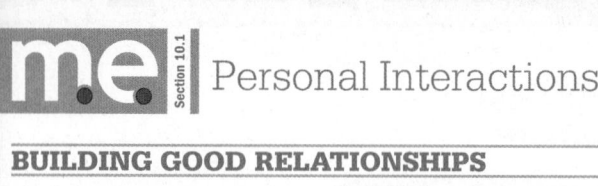

me. Section 10.1 Personal Interactions

BUILDING GOOD RELATIONSHIPS

A positive self-image, an understanding of the rules of acceptable behavior, and an awareness of different cultural, religious, and socioeconomic backgrounds are some of the factors involved in building good relationships.

As You Read

Predict How does acceptable behavior relate to awareness of different cultural backgrounds?

SELF-ESTEEM AND SELF-AWARENESS

Self-awareness is how you **perceive** yourself. **Self-esteem** is how you perceive your worth or value as a person. It is one of the basic building blocks of successfully interacting with others. Having an awareness of your self-esteem is important because it allows you to believe in yourself and improves your attitude at work.

How do you **demonstrate** self-esteem in the workplace? When you value yourself and know how you would like to be treated, it allows you to treat others the same way—with respect, friendliness, and patience. You need to do more than just talk about the way you would like to be treated.

Another way you show self-esteem is in your work habits and grooming. Dressing appropriately and behaving in a confident yet courteous way shows that you respect yourself and your work. Arriving at work on time shows that you value yourself as a professional.

Setting goals for your career and personal development is an aspect of self-awareness and self-esteem. You cannot get anywhere if you do not know where you are headed. Share these goals with your manager so he or she can assist you in your career development.

POSITIVE ATTITUDE

Your attitude is your mental outlook, which shapes the way you view people and situations. People with a positive attitude welcome a difficult assignment as a challenge. They look for something positive even when they experience setbacks. They also accept constructive criticism as a way to improve. Their attitude is a model for other workers. It can inspire them to do the best work they can do.

> "Successfully interacting with others and developing good human relations depends on many factors."

INITIATIVE AND RESPONSIBILITY

Initiative means taking action and doing what needs to be done without being asked. If you come up with a new idea, initiative allows you to act on it. Demonstrating initiative shows that you are interested and enthusiastic.

Accepting responsibility means that you are willing to be held accountable for your actions. After taking the initiative to begin a job, you must accept responsibility for completing it. Employers and customers value responsible employees because they fulfill their promises and do what is expected of them. An employee who takes initiative and is responsible is reliable. Employers, coworkers, and customers know they can depend on someone who can be counted on to take action and follow through.

Chapter 10 · Interpersonal Skills | 233

ENGAGE

Anticipation Activity

Improving Student Achievement Tell students to recall a time they worked with a group. Ask: ***What skills do you need to work effectively with a group?*** patience, understanding, self-control, and so on

Objectives

- **Identify** the personal traits necessary for ethical action in the workplace. honesty, respect, fairness, equity
- **List** important interpersonal skills. positive self-image, understanding rules of behavior, awareness of cultural, religious, and socioeconomic backgrounds
- **Perform** effectively in diverse environments. Learn about others' interests and experiences to improve understanding; good working relationships are based on mutual understanding.
- **Manage** conflicts by using appropriate negotiation skills. show respect, define the problem, seek various solutions, collaborate, be reliable, preserve the relationship

Graphic Organizer

Personality Traits

Friendliness Courtesy Tact	Self-esteem Self-awareness	Positive attitude Initiative	Responsibility Self-control Creativity
Time management Stress management	Assertiveness Flexibility	Honesty Respect	Fairness Equity

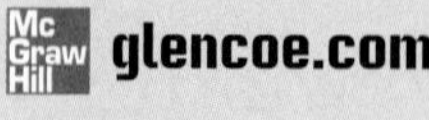

Graphic Organizer Send students to the Online Learning Center to print this graphic organizer.

EXPLORE

Before You Read

Read the Before You Read question aloud: ***Describe how your interpersonal skills have helped you form relationships.*** Students may not be aware of what interpersonal skills are, but they should recognize that such things as friendliness, attitude, courtesy, and tact are essential in forming relationships. Ask students to think about their relationships. Ask: ***What interpersonal skills do the other people in your relationships have?*** Ask volunteers to share their answers. Answers will vary but may include skills such as those mentioned above, as well as communication and leadership skills, empathy, and cooperation.

Preteaching Vocabulary

Have students go to the Online Learning Center at glencoe.com for the Chapter 10 Preteaching Vocabulary games.

Content Vocabulary

Instruct students to write a paragraph in which they discuss how the vocabulary terms are interrelated. Paragraphs will vary but students should recognize that all of the Content Vocabulary terms have to do with personal and interpersonal traits and relationships. Students may suggest that all of these are desirable traits that help to make relationships (personal and work-related) easier to deal with and develop. Ask volunteers to share their paragraphs with the rest of the class.

Academic Vocabulary

Perceive—Word Study Ask students what they think the Academic Vocabulary term *perceive* means. To perceive means to become aware of or to gain understanding of. Then ask students to name any words they believe are related to *perceive.* Answers may include perception, percept, perceptible, perceptive, and perceptual.

Demonstrate—Examples Ask students what the Academic Vocabulary term *demonstrate* means. To demonstrate means to show or give examples of. Ask volunteers to show their understanding of the term by demonstrating something.

PROFESSIONAL DEVELOPMENT **MINI CLIP**

Reading: Connecting the Pieces
A teacher assesses ways to help students develop predictions and inferences.

Personal Interactions

BUILDING GOOD RELATIONSHIPS

Explain to students that the ability to build good relationships is important not only for one's personal life, but also for a person's success in the workplace.

Guiding Questions

List What are some of the factors involved in building good relationships.	an understanding of the rules of acceptable behavior; an awareness of different cultural, religious, and socioeconomic backgrounds
Explain Why is a positive attitude important in the workplace?	A positive attitude can be an example for other employees and may inspire them to do their best.
Predict Why would an employer want an employee to accept responsibility?	An employee who accepts responsibility is willing to be held accountable for his or her actions. Responsible employees typically keep their promises.

As You Read

Read students the As You Read question: ***How does acceptable behavior relate to awareness of different cultural backgrounds?*** If a person is aware of cultural differences, his or her behavior will reflect that and will be acceptable (or not offensive) to the person from another culture.

Expert Advice

Read the quote to students:

> **“Successfully interacting with others and developing good human relations depends on many factors.”**

Ask students: ***What factors do you think are responsible for successful interactions with others?*** Possible answers: understanding other cultures, empathy, friendliness, politeness, and so on.

SELF-CONTROL

People who exercise self-control take careful, measured steps and do not act on impulse or emotion. Self-control in the workplace allows you to stop and analyze a situation before reacting to it emotionally.

This skill is very important when handling conflict. Self-control and orderly behavior inspire confidence in customers and in coworkers. People who cannot control themselves tend to be perceived as overly emotional, irresponsible, inattentive, and uninterested in the customer. They may not be taken seriously.

CREATIVITY

Creativity is the ability to use the imagination to invent. Creativity is used in marketing to think of new products and to develop new ways to present products. It also allows you to find new ways of doing your job. Creativity can help you analyze problems from a new and fresh perspective.

TIME MANAGEMENT

Time management means budgeting your time to accomplish tasks on a certain schedule. Time-management principles involve establishing goals, setting deadlines, allocating enough time for each task, tackling the most difficult task first, and being realistic. In order to be effective in your work, you must be able to use time wisely. Managing time well is an example of responsible behavior. To manage your time, follow these guidelines:

1. Make a list of the tasks you need to complete.
2. Determine which task is most important considering your time frame.
3. Continue to rank the tasks.
4. Create a schedule based on your list.

When you are working on one task, do not let yourself worry about another one. You may, however, be able to work on more than one task at a time. Managing multiple tasks at once is called multitasking.

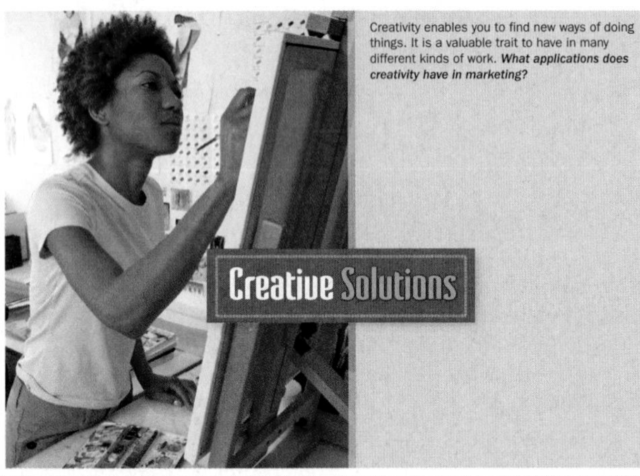

Creativity enables you to find new ways of doing things. It is a valuable trait to have in many different kinds of work. ***What applications does creativity have in marketing?***

STRESS MANAGEMENT

Stress is a reaction to outside pressure. It can have mental or physical effects. An example of mental stress might be your reaction if your manager asked you to prepare an extensive research report on competing products by 9:00 A.M. the next day when you already had plans to study for an upcoming exam all evening.

Stress can also have physical effects. It can energize, motivate, and excite us. The negative aspects of stress, though, are often harmful. Stress-related anxiety can trigger various physical reactions, collectively called the "fight-or-flight" mechanism. This can result in an increased heart rate and an aroused mental state. Reactions like this can become dangerous when they occur too often.

Research suggests that a hormone released by bodies under stress suppresses the immune system and can lead to long-term health problems. Highly stressed people catch colds and flu more often than those who can handle or relieve their stress. Learning to manage stress is a valuable workplace skill.

STRESS RELIEF

Researchers who have studied stress agree that three main elements help prevent stress: regular exercise, a balanced diet, and enough sleep. They also suggest engaging in recreation, making reasonable compromises, and accepting what you cannot change. At work, taking a minute to breathe deeply and consciously relax is a good stress reducer. Maintaining a sense of humor when things get tense also helps. When you are dealing with stress away from work, try getting a massage or watching a television program or movie. Getting involved in activities you enjoy, such as sports, reading, or listening to music, is a good way to relieve stress. Helping someone in need can help relieve stress by putting things in perspective.

ASSERTIVENESS

Assertiveness is standing up for what you believe. People will respect you if you can be assertive without being pushy or aggressive. Show confidence and speak with authority. For example, suppose you are working with a client who ridicules your opinion. In a very professional and respectful way, you should reassert your contribution. Be sure to point out its strengths in a clear and precise manner. Offer support for any claim that you make. Valid evidence will put you in a strong position to influence others. Assertiveness is a skill that takes time to learn. Confidence in being assertive comes with experience and practice.

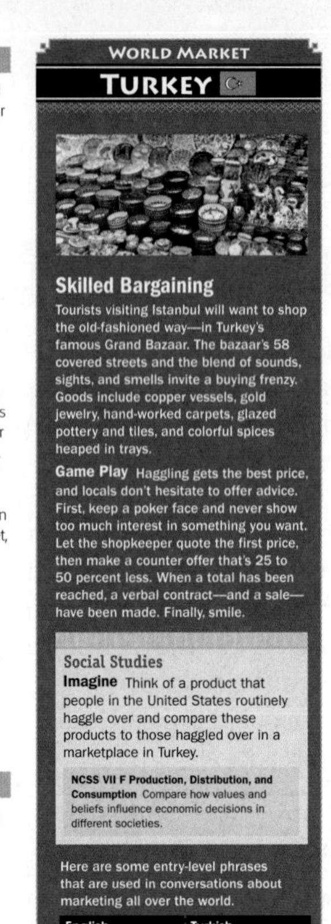

WORLD MARKET

TURKEY

Skilled Bargaining

Tourists visiting Istanbul will want to shop the old-fashioned way—in Turkey's famous Grand Bazaar. The bazaar's 58 covered streets and the blend of sounds, sights, and smells invite a buying frenzy. Goods include copper vessels, gold jewelry, hand-worked carpets, glazed pottery and tiles, and colorful spices heaped in trays.

Game Play Haggling gets the best price, and locals don't hesitate to offer advice. First, keep a poker face and never show too much interest in something you want. Let the shopkeeper quote the first price, then make a counter offer that's 25 to 50 percent less. When a total has been reached, a verbal contract—and a sale—have been made. Finally, smile.

Social Studies

Imagine Think of a product that people in the United States routinely haggle over and compare these products to those haggled over in a marketplace in Turkey.

NCSS VII F Production, Distribution, and Consumption Compare how values and beliefs influence economic decisions in different societies.

Here are some entry-level phrases that are used in conversations about marketing all over the world.

English	Turkish
Hello	merhaba
Goodbye	güle
Yes/No	evet/hayir
Thank you	tesekkür ederim
You're welcome	buyrun

EXPLAIN

Mini Project

Enrichment

Interview Businesspeople Have students interview the owner or manager of a local business. Students should ask the owner or manager to list the interpersonal skills they feel are necessary in order for coworkers to have effective working relationships. Then have students create a graphic that compares the answers they received with the interpersonal skills listed in Section 10.1. Ask students to create a Venn diagram or similar graphic to compare the interpersonal skills listed in the text, the interpersonal skills listed by the owner or manager, and the interpersonal skills that are common to both. Diagrams will vary but should clearly show a comparison of interpersonal skills listed by the owner or manager as well as those listed in the text.

Visual Literacy

Creative Solutions Caption Answer Read the caption question to students: *What applications does creativity have in marketing?* Creativity can be used to develop marketing campaigns. Use these guiding questions to discuss creativity in more detail.

Guiding Questions

Analyze Are there any jobs that would not benefit from creativity? Explain.	Some may think all jobs can benefit from creativity. Others may believe that routine tasks should not be done creatively.
Evaluate Creativity enables you to find new ways of doing things. Would this always be a good thing?	It might cost the company more money to do some jobs in a different way.

Time Management Encourage students to discuss specific ways in which they might manage their time effectively. List students' suggestions on the board.

ELABORATE

Graphic Organizer

Display this diagram. Tell students that they are a member of a start-up marketing company. List skills they would want their employers and their employees to have. In the middle intersection, have them list skills similar to both.

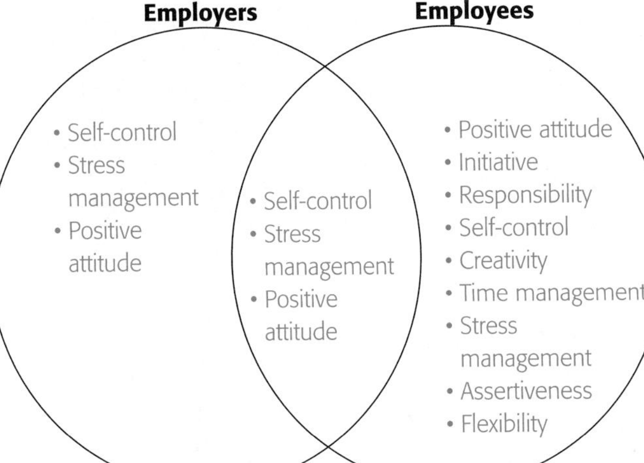

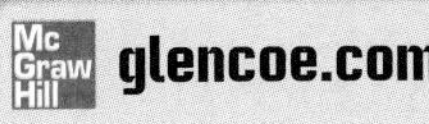 glencoe.com  iWB

Graphic Organizer Send students to the Online Learning Center to print this graphic organizer.

Reading Check Answer

Read the Reading Check question to students: ***Why is awareness of your self-esteem important in the workplace?*** Self-esteem allows you to successfully interact with others, believe in yourself, and improve your attitude at work.

WORLD MARKET
SOCIAL STUDIES

Ask students if they know what the word *haggling* means. To haggle means to bargain over the price of something. Tell students that haggling is not as common in the United States as it is in some other countries. Then ask students to think of a product that people in the United States might haggle over. In the United States people may haggle over the price of cars, houses, antiques, or when shopping at garage sales. Then ask: ***How do the items people in the United States haggle over compare to the items people in Turkey haggle over?*** Shoppers in the U.S. may haggle when they buy expensive items. In Turkey, where haggling is a social as well as business practice, people haggle over less valuable goods, especially one-of-a-kind handmade items like carpets, crafts, artwork, and antiques. These are items that do not have a standardized market.

Mini Project

Enrichment

Research Stress Management Tell students that many companies offer employees massage therapy, yoga, and other forms of stress relief. Such activities can cost considerable time and money for the company. Ask: ***Why do you think companies might be willing to pay for stress relief for their employees?*** Students may suggest that healthy and happy workers are more productive, and these stress-relieving incentives may increase company loyalty. They may also reduce the number of stress-related illnesses or injuries. Have students conduct research to learn more about the stress relief techniques listed above, or another stress relief technique of their choice. Students should write a one-page report of their research results. Ask volunteers to demonstrate the stress relief techniques they learned during their research.

Critical Thinking

Ask students to contrast assertiveness with aggression. If time allows, ask students to share their personal experiences with each. Assertiveness is standing up for what you believe, and not being afraid to state a concern or opinion; aggression is being hostile. Tell students that being assertive does not mean you are always right. It is just as important for individuals to admit when they are wrong as it is for them to stand up for what they believe is right.

DIGITAL NATION
Protecting Reputations
Web-savvy companies want to know what their customers are saying about them on Twitter, YouTube, Facebook, MySpace, Yelp, and blogs. To get answers, many turn to reputation-monitoring services that help them track, use, and respond to customer concerns and complaints published on the Web.
Tracking Tweets
Reputation-monitoring services crawl the Web looking for references to a company. Then they use software to evaluate the references. Companies can use this information to uncover what people like and dislike about them. Companies can also respond directly to angry customers before their complaints spread further across the Web.
English Language Arts
Evaluate Imagine that you are in charge of public relations for your company. You have recently discovered that someone has been repeatedly and unfairly criticizing your company's products online. Create a brief press release that explains the truth about your company's products and services.
NCTE 4 Use written language to communicate effectively.
glencoe.com
Get a Digital Nation Activity.

FLEXIBILITY

Flexibility allows you to adapt to changing circumstances. A flexible person can learn from others, accept criticism, and grow. To develop flexibility, listen with an open mind. Be willing to try new approaches.

As you will see in the next section, flexibility will help you be a productive team member. Businesses value employees with this trait because flexibility enables a business to move forward and adapt to changing markets.

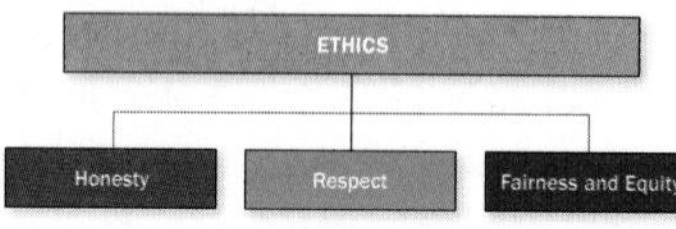

ETHICS IN THE 21ST-CENTURY WORKPLACE

Ethics are the basic values and moral principles that guide the behavior of individuals and groups. In most cultures, ethical behavior includes honesty, integrity, and a sense of fair play. Ethical behavior also means treating all people with respect. People who practice ethical behavior usually gain the trust of coworkers and clients.

ETHICS

Honesty | Respect | Fairness and Equity

HONESTY

Honesty in the workplace is an important part of ethical behavior. It includes telling the truth, maintaining confidentiality, and not spreading gossip. Respect for company property and making an effort to prevent theft are other aspects of workplace honesty.

Honesty is the basis for trust, which is essential to a good business relationship. People who are honest display strong personal integrity. Integrity is the quality of always behaving according to the moral principles that you believe in, so that people respect and trust you.

RESPECT

The number-one rule when speaking to business clients or customers is to show respect. That applies to interactions with coworkers as well. You demonstrate respect by listening with an open mind to the other person's point of view, then addressing any differences of opinion with courtesy and tact. This is especially important if there is a disagreement or conflict, for instance, when handling a customer complaint. While it may not always be easy to be courteous and pleasant, practice showing respect to others. They will admire your character and look forward to interacting with you in the future.

FAIRNESS AND EQUITY

People expect to be treated the way others are treated. **Equity** means that everyone has equal rights and opportunities. Never give special privileges to an employee for reasons that are unrelated to his or her work performance.

Sometimes a business establishes standards to maintain fairness. Equality is also protected through both federal and state laws. Such standards and laws can prevent discrimination in procedures such as hiring and firing. For example, employment laws forbid discrimination due to gender, age, religion, or national origin. Federal laws include the Americans with Disabilities Act of 1990, which protects qualified individuals with disabilities from discrimination. If an employee believes that he or she has been the victim of discrimination, the employee can file a complaint with the United States Equal Employment Opportunity Commission (EEOC).

AVOIDING STEREOTYPES

It is very important to become aware of any prejudices we may have and to eliminate them. Take some time to reflect on your own interests, experiences, and background. A person's interests often reflect his or her values. Our experiences shape how we think and view the world. You can understand other people better by making an effort to learn about their interests and experiences. By adopting this perspective, you will find it much easier to understand others, and they will be much more likely to understand you. Mutual understanding is a major factor in good communication. Positive workplace relationships and success in marketing are based on mutual understanding and respect.

Interpret Why is it important to be ethical in the workplace?

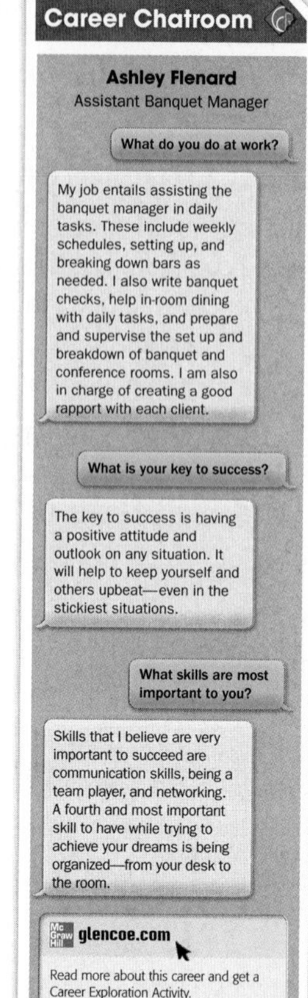

Career Chatroom
Ashley Flenard
Assistant Banquet Manager
What do you do at work?
My job entails assisting the banquet manager in daily tasks. These include weekly schedules, setting up, and breaking down bars as needed. I also write banquet checks, help in-room dining with daily tasks, and prepare and supervise the set up and breakdown of banquet and conference rooms. I am also in charge of creating a good rapport with each client.
What is your key to success?
The key to success is having a positive attitude and outlook on any situation. It will help to keep yourself and others upbeat—even in the stickiest situations.
What skills are most important to you?
Skills that I believe are very important to succeed are communication skills, being a team player, and networking. A fourth and most important skill to have while trying to achieve your dreams is being organized—from your desk to the room.
glencoe.com
Read more about this career and get a Career Exploration Activity.

EXPLAIN

DIGITAL NATION

English Language Arts Answer Read the English Language Arts Activity to students: Imagine that you are in charge of public relations for your company. You have recently discovered that someone has been repeatedly and unfairly criticizing your company's products online. ***Create a brief press release that explains the truth about your company's products and services.*** Press releases will vary. Students should determine what type of products and/or services their company provides and then explain in at least two paragraphs the benefits of their products and/or services.

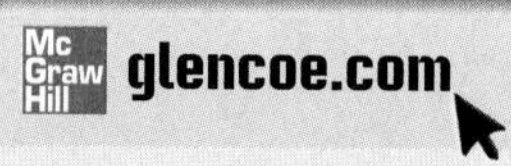

Worksheet Activity Send students to the Online Learning Center to get a Digital Nation worksheet activity.

ETHICS IN THE 21ST-CENTURY WORKPLACE

Graphic Organizer

Display this graphic organizer. As you discuss honesty, respect, fairness and equity, ask students to provide examples of when they experienced these values in a business situation. Fill in as many examples as time allows.

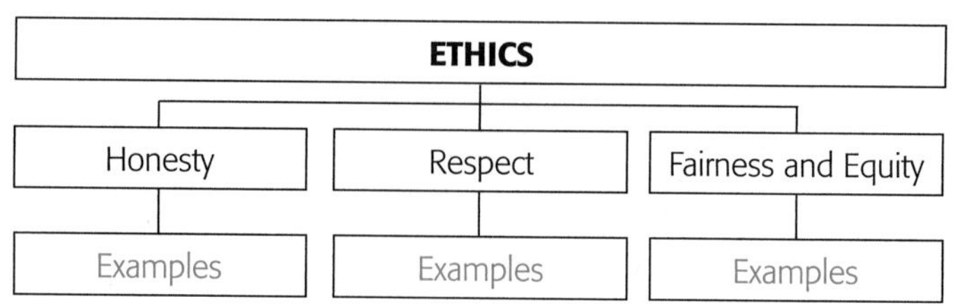

iWB

Graphic Organizer Send students to the Online Learning Center to print this graphic organizer.

ELABORATE

Mini Project

Extension

Research Ethical Behavior Tell students that ethical behavior in the workplace is a hot topic. Point out scandals that have rocked the loan industry, banking, car manufacturers, and Wall Street, and oil spills that have caused billions of dollars in damage. Tell them about textile manufacturers that use sweat shop labor in other countries. Explain that these are examples of how unethical behavior has far-reaching, devastating consequences and can damage or destroy a company. Have students research cases such as those listed, or find their own examples of recent situations involving unethical behavior. Have them describe how companies have acted to regain the public's trust. Have them compare large-scale cases to more personal ones that an individual worker might face. Invite students to share their findings with the class. As a class, discuss what can be learned from such events.

Critical Thinking

Ask students: ***What can consumers do to affect a company's unethical practices?*** Answers may include asking the company to change its practices, boycotting its goods or services, and publicizing unethical or illegal acts. Ask students: ***Have you ever seen people boycotting a store? If so, what was your reaction?*** Some students may say the boycott caused them to avoid patronizing the store. Others may say the boycott did not affect them at all.

Reinforce Vocabulary

Equity—Historical Aspect Write the term *equity* for students to view. Ask a volunteer to read the second paragraph under the head Fairness and Equity on page 237. Ask students: ***How are equity and discrimination related?*** Equity is the absence of discrimination. Ask: ***What are some discrimination issues that have occurred in the United States?*** Students may suggest such things as not allowing women to vote, limited rights for African Americans, legal vs. illegal immigration, limiting what people with disabilities can do, and so on. Then ask: ***Why is equity in the workplace important?*** Answers will vary but may include: it is illegal to discriminate against others; discrimination limits the pool of talent; equity means a wider variety of opinions and creative input.

Career Chatroom

Use these questions to focus the discussion about the Career Chatroom feature.

Guiding Questions

Explain What does Ashley Flenard consider to be the key to success?	According to Ashley Flenard, the key to success is having a positive attitude and outlook on any situation.
Predict Why is it important to develop a good rapport with each client?	Developing a good rapport with each client can help to ensure that the client will give you repeat business and tell others about your company.
Synthesize Ashley Flenard lists being a team player as an important skill. What is the connection between being a team player and ethics?	Team players must be honest with fellow employees and they must show respect to fellow employees. They will strive to be fair and show equity to the people they work with.

glencoe.com

Career Exploration Send students to the Online Learning Center to read more about this career and to get a Career Exploration Activity.

Reading Check Answer

Read the Reading Check question to students: ***Why is it important to be ethical in the workplace?*** People who practice ethical behavior in the workplace usually gain the trust of coworkers and clients. The workplace would be difficult to work in if coworkers did not trust each other, and clients would not return if they did not trust the employees.

Mini Project

Differentiated Instruction

Students with Learning Disabilities To reinforce learning, discuss conflict. Ask: ***What are simple techniques for conflict resolution?*** Show respect, recognize the problem, seek solutions, collaborate, keep the relationship

MANAGING CONFLICT

Like stress, conflict in the workplace can be productive or counterproductive. Counterproductive conflict can cause lost time and resources as well as a decrease in efficiency. Productive conflict can energize a person, group, or organization. However, successfully managing conflict requires understanding, skill, knowledge, and experience.

CONFLICT AND NEGOTIATION

Companies can help prevent conflict by creating an atmosphere in which all employees are accepted despite their differences in beliefs, values, backgrounds, or experiences. However, no company can completely prevent conflict in the workplace. When conflicts arise, they must be negotiated.

Negotiation is the process of working with the parties in conflict to find a resolution. Negotiating requires a willingness to work together. The key to any successful negotiation is clear communication. As you learned in Chapter 8, there are four basic skills involved in the communication process: listening, reading, speaking, and writing. Negotiation involves two of these communication skills: listening and speaking.

SPEAKING

The first step in negotiation is defining as clearly as possible the problem as each person sees it. Facts and feelings must be presented from each individual's perspective. This usually goes more smoothly when "I statements" are used. For example, avoid the aggressive tone in "You make me mad when you. . . ." Instead, say, "I become upset when you. . . ." Instead of saying "Your description of the problem is confusing," say, "I am confused about what the problem is."

Avoid placing blame because it puts people on the defensive. Participants should take some time to plan ahead what they will say. If possible, set a time and place to meet that is convenient for everyone involved. A quiet, neutral place with limited distractions is ideal.

LISTENING

Listening is an active process in which all of your attention is focused on the speaker. Encourage the speaker to share his or her feelings and thoughts. Maintaining eye contact with the speaker shows that you are interested and want to understand what is being said. Planning a response before the speaker's point is made is a distraction that can cause misunderstandings.

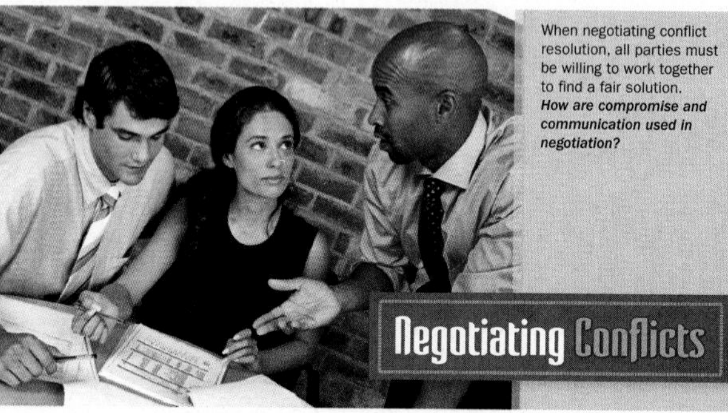

When negotiating conflict resolution, all parties must be willing to work together to find a fair solution. ***How are compromise and communication used in negotiation?***

Try to empathize, or show empathy, with the person who is speaking. **Empathy** is an understanding of a person's situation or frame of mind. Remember that people of different ages, genders, cultures, and abilities may have had experiences that are unfamiliar to you. Do not make the mistake of assuming that certain viewpoints and behaviors are universal. There are many people in the world with ideas that are very different from yours.

Six simple techniques for negotiating conflict resolution can be helpful:

1. Show respect.
2. Recognize and define the problem.
3. Seek a variety of solutions.
4. Collaborate.
5. Be reliable.
6. Preserve the relationship.

The problem is solved only when both sides reach a common understanding and agreement about what actions are to be taken. Never assume you understand the other person without asking some verification questions. For example, you might ask, "Is this what you meant by. . . ?" or "Did I understand correctly when. . . ?" These types of questions make sure that everyone understands everyone else's point of view. This level of understanding is essential for conflict management.

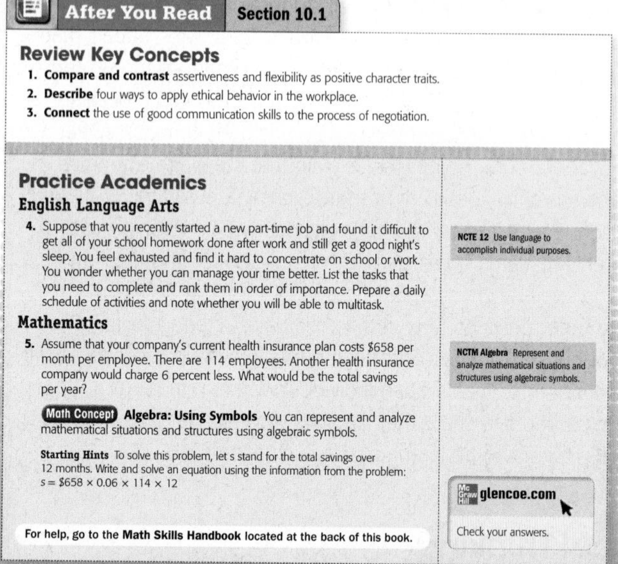

After You Read | **Section 10.1**

Review Key Concepts

1. **Compare and contrast** assertiveness and flexibility as positive character traits.
2. **Describe** four ways to apply ethical behavior in the workplace.
3. **Connect** the use of good communication skills to the process of negotiation.

Practice Academics

English Language Arts

4. Suppose that you recently started a new part-time job and found it difficult to get all of your school homework done after work and still get a good night's sleep. You feel exhausted and find it hard to concentrate on school or work. You wonder whether you can manage your time better. List the tasks that you need to complete and rank them in order of importance. Prepare a daily schedule of activities and note whether you will be able to multitask.

NCTE 12 Use language to accomplish individual purposes.

Mathematics

5. Assume that your company's current health insurance plan costs $658 per month per employee. There are 114 employees. Another health insurance company would charge 6 percent less. What would be the total savings per year?

NCTM Algebra Represent and analyze mathematical situations and structures using algebraic symbols.

Math Concept **Algebra: Using Symbols** You can represent and analyze mathematical situations and structures using algebraic symbols.

Starting Hints To solve this problem, let s stand for the total savings over 12 months. Write and solve an equation using the information from the problem: $s = \$658 \times 0.06 \times 114 \times 12$

For help, go to the **Math Skills Handbook** located at the back of this book.

glencoe.com

Check your answers.

ELABORATE

Visual Literacy

Negotiating Conflicts Read the caption question to students: ***How are compromise and communication used in negotiation?*** During negotiation, both sides may need to compromise, or give in on some of their demands, for a solution to be reached. Clear communication is the key to successful negotiation. Use these guiding questions to discuss negotiation in more detail.

Guiding Questions

Apply What are some examples of conflict resolution? You can refer to any instances you may have studied in history class.	Examples may include treaties between warring countries.
Analyze Can a conflict be resolved if all sides are not willing to work together?	No. Negotiating requires a willingness to work together, which is accomplished through clear communication.

MANAGING CONFLICT

Activate Prior Knowledge

Communication Skills Remind students that negotiation requires clear communication skills—especially listening and speaking skills. Have students recall and name elements for listening for meaning and elements for speaking well (refer to Chapter 8). Have students create a T-chart or a two-column chart and label the left column *Listening* and the right column *Speaking.* Under each head students should list elements for listening and for speaking. Answers may include: listening—identify the purpose, look for a plan, give feedback, search for a common interest, evaluate the message, listen for more than verbal content, listen for a conclusion, take notes; speaking—show respect, know the purpose, use voice and nonverbal cues, enumerate the speaker's points, provide examples, determine cause and effect, compare and contrast.

EVALUATE

Graphic Organizer

Display this T-chart. Discuss with students the appropriate tone of negotiation. In the left column, write a negative statement that might be heard in a workplace. Have students suggest a more positive way of saying the same thing. You might have students suggest both the negative and positive statements. Possible answers:

Negative Statement	Positive Statement
You really messed up the order.	Going forward, let's double check orders before sending them.
I can't believe you couldn't answer the customer's questions.	Take some time to familiarize yourself with the products so in the future you can answer customer's questions.
That was a really stupid thing to do.	Please take time to think through what you do before you do it to make sure there are no negative consequences.

 glencoe.com 

Graphic Organizer Send students to the Online Learning Center to print this graphic organizer.

Mini Project

Differentiated Instruction

Kinesthetic Learners Discuss with students the importance of empathy in marketing. Remind them that empathy is an understanding of a person's situation or frame of mind. Tell students that unless they understand their market, they cannot communicate effectively with potential clients. Divide the class into groups of two or three students. Ask groups to think of ways to better understand their markets. Have them select one of those ways and create a short presentation or role play explaining or acting out their choice. Choices for presentations and role plays will vary but may include spending time with members of the market, conducting focus groups, or hiring consultants.

 **After You Read** Section 10.1

Review Key Concepts

1. Assertiveness is standing up for what you believe. You can be assertive without being pushy or aggressive. People will respect you for being true to what you believe. It is important in the workplace to stand up for what you believe and to be ready to act on it. Flexibility allows you to adapt to changing circumstances. Flexibility is necessary in the workplace because things are always changing.
2. Ethical behavior can be applied in the workplace through (1) honesty, which includes telling the truth, maintaining confidentiality, and not spreading gossip; (2) respect, which includes treating customers and coworkers with courtesy and tact; (3) fairness, which means treating everyone the same way; and (4) equity, which means that everyone has equal rights and opportunities.
3. Negotiation, the process of working together with parties in conflict to find a resolution, involves the basic communication skills of speaking and listening. Speaking allows the parties to define the problem clearly and listening shows that the parties are interested and want to understand what is being said. Both of these skills are essential to the negotiation process.

Practice Academics

English Language Arts

4. Schedules will vary; students may use a grid to list days of the week across the top and tasks down the left side. Tasks should be listed in order of their importance.

Mathematics

5. The savings would be $54,008.64 per year ($s = \$658 \times 0.06 \times 114 \times 12 = \$54,008.64$).

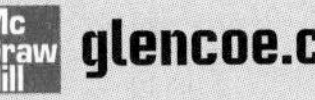 

Answer Key Send students to the Online Learning Center to check their answers.

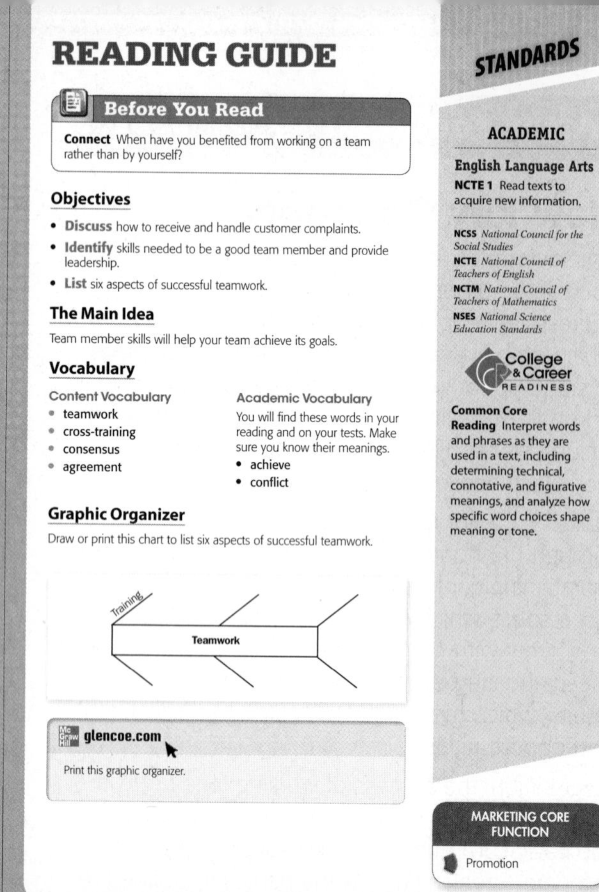

READING GUIDE

Before You Read

Connect When have you benefited from working on a team rather than by yourself?

Objectives

- **Discuss** how to receive and handle customer complaints.
- **Identify** skills needed to be a good team member and provide leadership.
- **List** six aspects of successful teamwork.

The Main Idea

Team member skills will help your team achieve its goals.

Vocabulary

Content Vocabulary
- teamwork
- cross-training
- consensus
- agreement

Academic Vocabulary

You will find these words in your reading and on your tests. Make sure you know their meanings.
- achieve
- conflict

Graphic Organizer

Draw or print this chart to list six aspects of successful teamwork.

glencoe.com

Print this graphic organizer.

STANDARDS

ACADEMIC

English Language Arts

NCTE 1 Read texts to acquire new information.

NCSS *National Council for the Social Studies*
NCTE *National Council of Teachers of English*
NCTM *National Council of Teachers of Mathematics*
NSES *National Science Education Standards*

College & Career READINESS

Common Core
Reading Interpret words and phrases as they are used in a text, including determining technical, connotative, and figurative meanings, and analyze how specific word choices shape meaning or tone.

MARKETING CORE FUNCTION

Promotion

INTERPERSONAL SKILLS IN MARKETING

As an employee, you should be familiar with your company's basic procedures in responding to customers. Know when to refer the customer to a manager or when a question involves information that your department does not have.

As You Read

Connect Consider the skills you have and need to be a good team member.

ADDRESSING CUSTOMERS' CONCERNS

To respond promptly and intelligently to customer concerns, you need to be familiar with company procedures. These procedures can be part of a company manual. They may also be shared with you in a presentation after you are hired. You should know how to handle the following situations:

- **Requests and questions**—You will need to learn the proper procedures for handling customer requests and questions. You will also need to know what you should say to customers if you cannot answer their questions yourself.
- **Directions**—You will need to be able to give clear and concise directions to your store or office. Local customers may be able to use informal directions, such as "our store is three blocks past the public garden on the right." Out-of-town customers will need more specific directions.
- **Management's role**—You will need to know under what circumstances a manager should be called to talk to a customer.
- **Business policies**—You will need to be able to explain business policies to customers. These may include return or exchange procedures and the company policy on checks or credit cards.

ADDRESSING CUSTOMERS' COMPLAINTS

Most customers never let the company or store know they have a complaint. Only 4 to 8 percent of customers who have a concern or complaint share their problem with the company. If a customer brings you a concern, it is important to deal with it and attempt to rectify the problem right away. Moreover, you have an opportunity to learn something that may help you improve the service you provide. You may also be able to prevent damage to the company and stop the problem from recurring.

Complaints cover a range of issues. Some are genuine errors on the part of the company, such as a faulty product or a bad service experience. Others stem from misunderstandings, such as poorly written directions on a product's package. The customer may even suggest how the company can improve its service.

> "Good working relationships between employees and customers or clients depend on the interpersonal skills of employees."

Since so few customers share their complaints, it is important to take these customers seriously. If you solve a problem for one customer, there is a chance that you have solved the same problem for many other customers who did not speak up. Seeking customer satisfaction always benefits a company in the long run.

ENGAGE

Anticipation Activity

Improving Student Achievement Have students discuss a time they worked in a team. Ask: ***What was your experience like?*** As students recount their stories, have them write down descriptors about the interpersonal skills of the people they worked with. Ask volunteers to share their team experiences with the class.

Objectives

- **Discuss** how to receive and handle customer complaints. Listen, take the customer aside, repeat, get help, and establish a plan.
- **Identify** skills needed to be a good team member and provide leadership. Make team goals top priority, listen actively, build positive group dynamics, follow up on assignments, work to resolve conflicts, respect team members, and inspire others to get involved.
- **List** six aspects of successful teamwork. Training, team planning, team goals, assigning roles, agreements, and shared responsibility/shared leadership.

Graphic Organizer

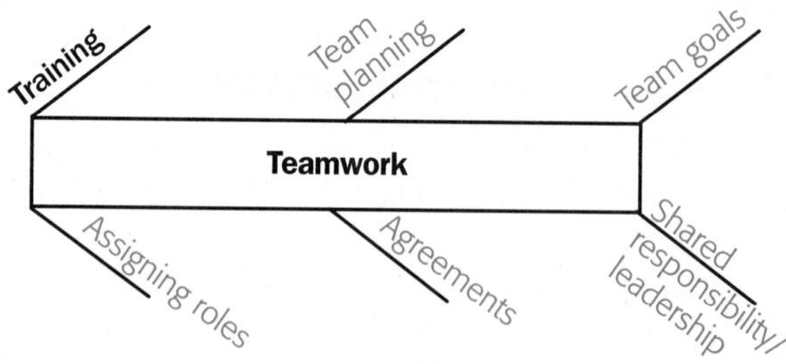

iWB

Graphic Organizer Send students to the Online Learning Center to print this graphic organizer.

EXPLORE

Before You Read

Read the Before You Read question aloud: ***When have you benefitted from working on a team rather than by yourself?*** Students' answers may include when they had a difficult job to complete or when they needed a variety of skills that they did not have. Students may also use examples from participation in team sports. Ask: ***Would you describe the teamwork experience as positive or negative? Why?*** Answers will vary. Students should recognize the benefits of teamwork in spite of issues that arise when working with others.

Preteaching Vocabulary

Have students go to the Online Learning Center at glencoe.com for the Chapter 10 Preteaching Vocabulary games.

Content Vocabulary

Cross-training—Current Usage Write the term *cross-training* on the board. Ask students: ***What comes to mind when you hear the term*** cross-training? Students likely will mention the use of the term in sports—engaging in a variety of athletic activities to promote well-rounded physical fitness. The term is also used to describe athletic shoes used for that purpose. Tell students that when associated with teamwork, *cross-training* means "being trained to do many different activities." Ask: ***How are the two uses of the term similar?*** Students may mention that both uses involve doing a variety of activities.

Academic Vocabulary

Achieve and Conflict—Predict Meanings Write the terms *achieve* and *conflict* on the board. Ask students to predict the meanings of the terms. *Achieve* means "to accomplish." A *conflict* is a disagreement. Ask: ***How do you think these terms might be related to teamwork?*** Students' answers will vary but may include: when working as part of a team it is easier to achieve your goals; when working as part of a team, conflicts can arise. Ask volunteers to use both Academic Vocabulary terms in a sentence that shows their understanding of the terms. Sentences will vary but should show usage consistent with the meanings of the terms. Sample: After resolving the conflict about whether or not to have co-leaders, the team was able to achieve its first of many goals.

Leadership and Teamwork

INTERPERSONAL SKILLS IN MARKETING

Tell students that interpersonal skills are necessary in all aspects of life. When they become part of the working world, interpersonal skills become even more important. Ask these guiding questions to focus the discussion on the interpersonal skills needed in marketing.

Guiding Questions

Identify What are four situations you will need to know to be able to respond promptly and intelligently to customer concerns?	how to handle requests, questions, and complaints; how to give directions; management's role; business policies
Predict Why do you think only 4 to 8 percent of customers who have a concern or complaint share their problem with the company?	The customer does not want to take the time to handle the issue. They do not think the issue will be resolved in an advantageous manner. It is easier to take one's business to another store.

As You Read

Read students the As You Read question: ***Consider the skills you have and need to be a good team member.*** Students' answers will vary but may include: tact, leadership, perspective, experience, cooperation, and a sense of humor.

Expert Advice

Read the quote to students:

> **"Good working relationships between employees and customers or clients depend on the interpersonal skills of employees."**

Ask students: ***As a customer, have you ever had a bad experience with an employee?*** Allow students to share experiences they have had. Ask: ***What do you feel was the cause of the issue?*** Students may suggest that the issue was due to an uninformed employee, an employee with a bad attitude, or a misunderstanding. Ask: ***How, if at all, was the issue resolved?*** Answers may include: money was returned or merchandise was exchanged; one party or the other apologized; or a manager got involved. Unresolved issues may have led to phone calls, letters, or emails to management, or taking business elsewhere.

Your company should develop a procedure to follow when dealing with customer complaints. Here are some guidelines for this procedure:

Listen
Take the customer aside
Repeat
Get help
Establish a plan

- **Listen.** First, listen completely and openly to the customer's complaint so that you are sure you understand it.
- **Take the customer aside.** If the customer is talking loudly, try to take him or her aside—if possible, into a separate room. A sales counter or desk can seem like a barrier. Standing side by side in a quiet place may ease the tension.
- **Repeat.** When appropriate, repeat the facts of the complaint to show the customer that you understand the details of the situation from his or her perspective. If you can explain what caused the problem for the customer, state your explanation clearly. Do not place blame on anyone.
- **Get help.** If you feel you need assistance from a coworker or a supervisor, let the customer know this and seek assistance promptly. Any time a customer is behaving aggressively, get help immediately.
- **Establish a plan.** Try to reach an agreement with the customer about the next course of action. Suggest action that is consistent with the company's policy. Then be absolutely certain to follow through on the action agreed upon.

Reading Check

Explain Why is it important for all marketing employees to know how to address customer concerns?

MARKETING CASE STUDY

MLB's "Beyond Baseball" Campaign

Baseball is a popular sport in the United States, but it is also a major cultural force that goes beyond the game itself. The marketers at Major League Baseball (MLB) realized this and channeled that spirit into a new ad campaign called "This is Beyond Baseball," which included a 30-minute TV special and a series of 20 commercials.

Fan Feedback

While traditional sports marketing involves focusing on the players, the new MLB campaign focuses on the fans. In one commercial, "Beyond Optimism," a series of fans of various teams expresses how confident they are that their team is going to make it all the way to the post-season. The tone of the commercial emphasizes that each spring is a "fresh start," and a new baseball season is lifted up as a positive event for fans.

English Language Arts

Ask Discuss with a partner whether it is more effective for MLB to focus on the fans rather than the players in this series of advertisements. Have each partner take a different side of the discussion and then share with the class.

NCTE 3 Apply strategies to interpret texts.

TEAMWORK

A team is a group of people who work together to achieve a common goal. **Teamwork** is work done by a group of people to achieve a common goal.

Teamwork is becoming increasingly important in the business world. According to football coach Vince Lombardi, "Individual commitment to a group effort—that is what makes a team work, a company work, a society work, a civilization work." This commitment includes many behaviors and attitudes. It is important for team members to keep these behaviors and attitudes in mind. The following descriptions are six important aspects of teamwork. (See **Figure 10.1** on page 244.)

HOT TOPIC

Teamwork Working as a team is a 21st Century skill that is becoming more and more important as businesses move to horizontally integrated organizations.

TRAINING

To be an effective team member, you must have training for all the tasks you will perform. You have probably heard of cross-training in sports. **Cross-training** means preparing to do many different activities.

On the job, people are cross-trained for many tasks on a team. This gives the team flexibility and diverse strengths. Every worker has different abilities. A company's workers can train each other to turn weaker skills into strengths. Work becomes more enjoyable when you know you will not be doing the same activity every day.

TEAM PLANNING

Before you start working on a project, make a plan as a team. Team planning involves setting goals, assigning roles, making agreements, sharing responsibility, and giving feedback. These practices will allow all members of the team to work together effectively.

TEAM GOALS

Team members must be involved in defining a goal in order to feel committed to it. This results in greater company loyalty and stronger team spirit. If team members know that their input is valued and considered, they will work harder to meet a goal.

Members should reach a consensus about goals. A **consensus** is a decision about which all members of a team approve. Therefore, all team members must be allowed to state their opinions. The final agreement may require team members to make a compromise. Being flexible as an individual helps you learn to compromise as a team member. It is likely that every individual on a team will have to compromise at some point. It is important for a team to keep this shared compromise in mind.

ASSIGNING ROLES

Team projects often work more smoothly if the team appoints a leader who coordinates tasks. Each person on the team needs to know which part of the process he or she is responsible for each day. Members are usually assigned tasks based on their skills and experience. These role assignments can change as the project evolves. This possibility of change is one reason cross-training is so valuable. It makes it easier for team members to change roles if necessary.

AGREEMENTS

An **agreement** is a specific commitment that each member makes to the group. When team members make agreements, the team becomes stronger and more cohesive. A team's agreements must be consistent with its goals.

It is important that each team member feel connected to the company's goals as well as to the team's goals. This connection is known as team loyalty. Team loyalty and positive peer pressure help to encourage people to keep their agreements. Members of the team will be more likely to make agreements if there is a high level of team loyalty.

EXPLAIN

Graphic Organizer

Display this diagram. Ask students to provide facts about addressing customers' complaints. Sample answers are provided below:

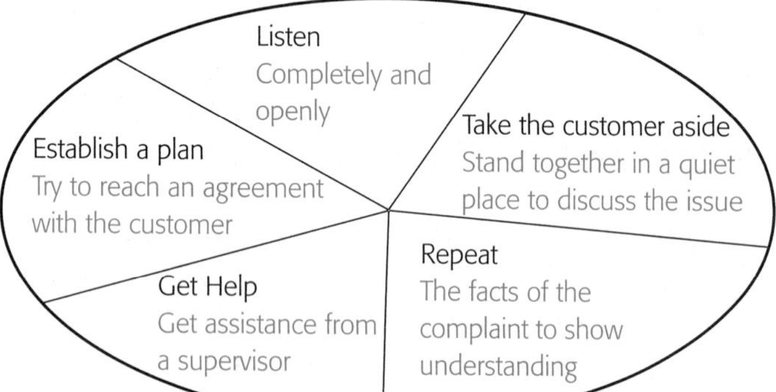

Listen
Completely and openly
Take the customer aside
Stand together in a quiet place to discuss the issue
Repeat
The facts of the complaint to show understanding
Get Help
Get assistance from a supervisor
Establish a plan
Try to reach an agreement with the customer

glencoe.com

iWB

Graphic Organizer Send students to the Online Learning Center to print this graphic organizer.

MARKETING CASE STUDY

English Language Arts Some students may feel it is more effective for MLB to focus on the fans rather than the players because the fans are the ones spending the money. Others may feel that the players are more important since the fans go to the games to see them play. Students should share their reasons for their feelings.

Reading Check Answer

Read the Reading Check question to students: ***Why is it important for all marketing employees to know how to address customer concerns?*** Quick and appropriate responses to a concern may lead to improved service and may prevent damage to the company's reputation.

ELABORATE

TEAMWORK

Ask students: ***What kinds of teams have you been a part of?*** Students will likely mention sports teams and possibly teams at work, or they might have been part of a team that put together a theatrical production. After students have had a chance to respond, ask these guiding questions to focus the discussion on teamwork.

Guiding Questions

List What are six important aspects of teamwork?	training, team planning, team goals, assigning roles, agreements, shared responsibilities and shared leadership
Analyze Why is it important for team members to make agreements?	When team members make a commitment to a team through an agreement, the team becomes stronger and more cohesive.
Synthesize What is the relationship between team planning and team goals? What is the relationship between team planning and assigning roles?	Setting team goals and assigning roles are both part of team planning and help to ensure that all team members will work together effectively.

Teamwork Encourage students to conduct research to learn more about horizontally integrated organizations and how they empower their workers through a decentralized and team-oriented workplace.

Critical Thinking

After students have read the section on training, tell them that there are companies that organize motivational speaking events geared toward professionals from all types of businesses. Often, the speakers are star athletes and coaches. Ask: ***What do you think successful people from the world of sports can offer to people in the workforce?*** Answers will vary but may include lessons in leadership, teamwork, tenacity, and attitude. Then, ask students to work in groups to create a mock motivational training. Each group should create a list of qualities of successful teams. Groups should also research what motivates certain groups and what training would be most effective. Student groups should present their mock trainings to the class.

e MARKETING

Weblog (blog)

A Weblog, also known simply as a "blog," is special type of Web site that is updated frequently by the author. Anyone can start a blog and share it with friends and the community at large on the Internet. A "blogosphere" is a community of bloggers with similar interests. For example, there are blogospheres for music, entertainment, finance, health, travel, pets, and so on. Businesses can use blogs to communicate with customers. The CEO of a company may use a blog to share the company's philosophy, update everyone on new policies or company goals. For example, take the design of a new automobile. A customer might post a comment on the CEO's blog about being dissatisfied with the design. The CEO (blogger) can then respond to that comment and perhaps mention other improvements that were made to the auto and note that the company is still working on the issue noted by the viewer's comment.

Individual bloggers in various blogospheres may inadvertently help businesses by posting positive comments about a product or service. Those comments can provide free publicity for a company and even help to start a favorable trend that could help the image of a company and the sales of its products. However, bloggers can also attack a company which could create negative publicity. Many companies have employees or outside vendors search the Internet to look for comments made by individual bloggers about their firms. That data information mining is useful in market planning.

Innovate and Create

Have students create their own blogs, either for fun or for a business purpose. In order to attract viewers to a blog, the topic needs to be interesting to others. Suggest a "Back to School" blog or another topic of interest to students for their blogosphere community. Have students write a blog and create entries for five days. Each day have other students react to the blog as viewers. Evaluate the blogger's content and tone in the messages posted each day. Include in the criteria their effectiveness with regard to tact, empathy, and self-control when reacting to viewers' comments.

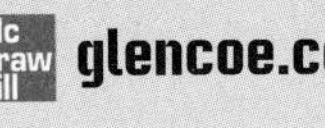

eMarketing Worksheet Activity Send students to the Online Learning Center to download an eMarketing worksheet activity.

SHARED RESPONSIBILITY AND SHARED LEADERSHIP

Shared responsibility means that each member must feel responsible for the whole team's efforts. If there is a problem during a project, all team members need to assess how they may be able to solve it. A team member who says the phrase, "that's not my job" is not being a responsible team member. Team leaders must work to develop each team member's sense of ownership.

Shared leadership allows all team members to perform some management functions. There will be times when team members have to respond to issues quickly. They may not have time to discuss the issue with the team leader, or the team leader may not be available. Team members need to feel confident to take care of issues independently if it is necessary to do so.

FEEDBACK

When giving feedback, make sure you are respectful. If you are overly critical, the feedback will not serve its purpose. Instead, it will alienate the team member being evaluated. Feedback is most effective when it identifies a behavior or attitude that can be changed. It also helps to give an example or model of this behavior or attitude.

Reading Check

Recall How is cross-training essential to teamwork?

FIGURE 10.1 Teamwork

Succeed Together As many businesses move away from a top-down management style toward a team approach, it is important for employees to understand how a team works and what is expected of individual members. ***What are some of the interpersonal skills that you need to be a valuable team member?***

Training Each member of a team needs to keep up with the team. This means having the necessary skills to do your job and staying current with the best practices in your field.

Team Planning Teams are usually assigned projects. Planning how to carry out those projects is the team's responsibility. Teams often include individuals with different strengths. For example, an advertising team may include an illustrator, a copywriter, a production coordinator, and a marketing specialist.

Team Goals The team sets goals. For an advertising team, that might mean completing a new ad or an entire advertising campaign by a certain date. Team goals must be aligned with the goals of the company.

Delegation/Agreements Members of the team are assigned different tasks, depending on their skills. Each team member agrees to complete the assigned task. On an advertising team, the graphic artist lays out graphics on a computer, the copywriter develops slogans and copy, and the production coordinator works with outside vendors.

Shared Responsibility/Leadership Everyone on the team shares responsibility for achieving the team's goal. Members of the team usually select a manager, or owner, to keep track of schedules and handle any difficulties that arise.

LEADERSHIP SKILLS

One definition of leadership is helping members of a group **achieve** their goals. Leaders need self-confidence and a willingness to take the initiative to solve new or unusual problems. Leaders need problem-solving, social judgment, and communication skills to define the problem, gather information, analyze the problem, and generate plans for a solution. Good leaders understand people and social systems and are able to motivate others to work together. **Conflict** resolution helps members of a group work together. A team can only be as successful as its members. For a team to be successful, it is important that each member is willing and able to work to achieve the team's goals.

BEING A VALUABLE TEAM MEMBER

What makes a person a good team member?

- Make the team's goals your top priority.
- Listen actively and offer suggestions.
- Build positive group dynamics with team members.
- Communicate with team members.
- Follow up on assignments.
- Work to resolve conflicts among team members.
- Respect the members of your team.
- Try to inspire others to get involved.
- Think creatively and present your ideas with enthusiasm.

After You Read Section 10.2

Review Key Concepts

1. **Define** teamwork and explain how it applies to the business world.
2. **List** the personal strengths and interpersonal skills required of a good leader.
3. **Identify** personal traits and interpersonal skills that make a person a good team member.

Practice Academics

English Language Arts

4. Conduct research to identify a current example of teamwork in the workplace. Share this information with your class and discuss how it might apply to the classroom.

Mathematics

5. A marketing company currently orders 370 boxes of pens each year at \$4.50 per box. A new office supply company offers a deal for you to switch to their company. The new supply company will give you 15 free boxes of pens if your company orders pens from them. If you order from the new supply company, how much money will your company save?

Math Concept **Problem Solving** Monitor and reflect on the process of mathematical problem solving.

Starting Hints The problem tells you how many boxes of pens are ordered each year, how many boxes of pens the new supply company will give you for free, and the cost of one box of pens. Calculate the cost savings by multiplying the cost per box by the number of boxes your company will be given for free.

For help, go to the **Math Skills Handbook** located at the back of this book.

NCTE 7 Conduct research and gather, evaluate, and synthesize data to communicate discoveries.

NCTM Problem Solving Apply and adapt a variety of appropriate strategies to solve problems.

glencoe.com

Check your answers.

ELABORATE

Visual Literacy

Figure 10.1 Caption Answer Read the caption question to students: ***What are some of the interpersonal skills that you need to be a valuable team member?*** Answers may include tact, leadership, perspective, experience, and a sense of humor. Use this guiding question to discuss the figure in more detail.

Guiding Question

Imagine You are part of a team that must come up with a new advertising campaign. What are some specific examples for each of the five aspects of teamwork that might be used in implementing the campaign?

training—learning to operate the computer; team planning—determining that the team leader will communicate with the computer manufacturer; team goals—the first of two ads will be completed in two weeks; delegation/agreements—team members assigned to write copy, create art/videos, test ad with consumers; shared responsibility and leadership—all team members participate in the ad campaign

Reading Check Answer

Read the Reading Check question to students: ***How is cross-training essential to team work?*** Cross-training gives the team flexibility and diverse strengths. Every worker has different abilities. A company's workers can train each other to strengthen weaker skills. Work becomes more enjoyable when you know you will not be doing the same thing every day.

Critical Thinking

Ask students: ***When providing feedback, why is it important to be respectful?*** If feedback is given with a critical attitude it tends to alienate the person receiving the feedback. It is important to be respectful so the feedback will be accepted and acted upon. The most helpful feedback identifies a behavior or attitude that can be changed and provides an example or model of the behavior or attitude.

EVALUATE

LEADERSHIP SKILLS

Tell students that the most effective team leaders must have the initiative and self-confidence necessary to lead a team. The best leaders lead by example and care about the people on their team. Ask these guiding questions to focus the discussion about leadership skills.

Guiding Questions

Recall What is leadership?	Leadership helps members of a group achieve their goals.
Determine Which of the eight traits of a valuable team member do you think is most important? Why?	Students should choose one of the following and explain why they believe it is most important to being a good team member: making the team's goals top priority, listening, building positive group dynamics, communicating, following up, working to resolve conflicts, respecting team members, and trying to inspire others.
Analyze How can conflict be a good thing for a team?	If the conflict is resolved in a positive manner, it can help make the team stronger.

Graphic Organizer

Display this diagram. Ask students: ***What tasks go into serving a customer?*** Write students' answers in the graphic organizer. Then ask: ***How can the failure of one team member slow or damage the entire process?*** Students may suggest that if a server does not take the order correctly, the meal cooked and delivered would be wrong, and the customer would be disappointed.

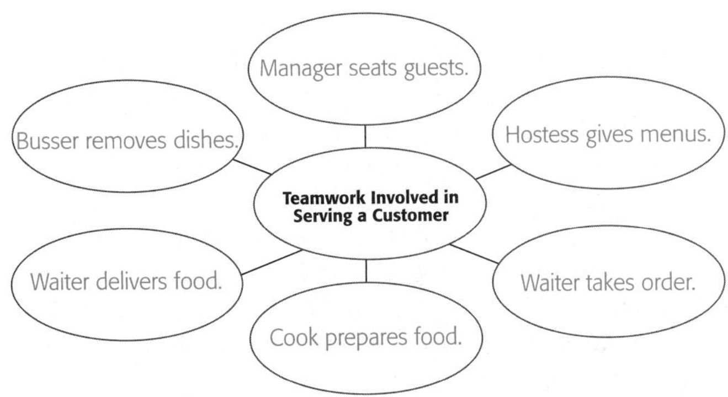

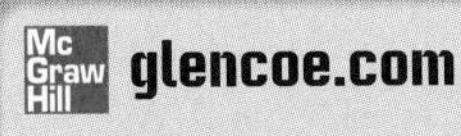 glencoe.com  iWB

Graphic Organizer Send students to the Online Learning Center to print this graphic organizer.

After You Read — Section 10.2

Review Key Concepts

1. Teamwork is done by a group of people who work together to achieve a common goal. It is becoming increasingly important in the business world as more businesses move to horizontally integrated organizations.
2. Personal strengths and interpersonal skills needed by a good leader include self-confidence, initiative, creativity, the ability to motivate team members, conflict resolution skills, problem solving, social judgment, and communication skills.
3. Personal traits and interpersonal skills required by a good team member include: making the team's goals top priority, listening, building positive group dynamics, communicating, following up, working to resolve conflicts, respecting team members, and trying to inspire others to become involved.

Practice Academics

English Language Arts

4. Research will vary but may include examples such as marketing teams, firefighters, police officers, software development teams, pit crews, flight crews, boat crews, and so on. Students may suggest that the examples may be applied in the classroom by assigning different classroom tasks to different class members so that all tasks are covered. They might also suggest that teamwork can be applied to interactive group work in the classroom.

Mathematics

5. \$67.50 (\$4.50 × 15 = \$67.50)

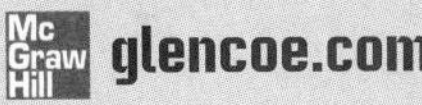 glencoe.com

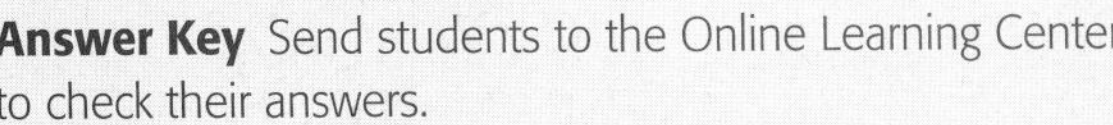

Answer Key Send students to the Online Learning Center to check their answers.

Chapter 10 Visual Summary

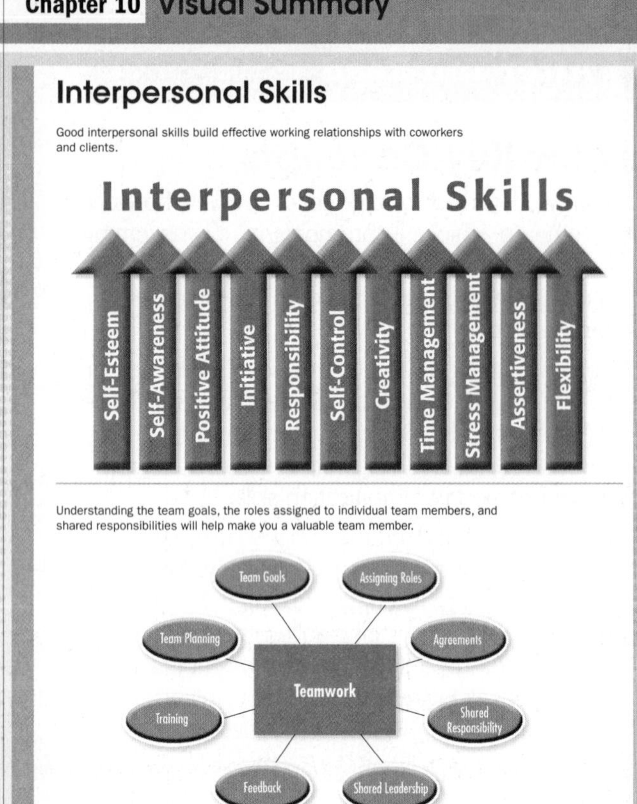

246 | Unit 4 · Skills for Marketing

Review and Activities

Written Summary

- Good interpersonal skills are necessary for building effective working relationships with coworkers and clients.
- Personality traits such as assertiveness and creativity can help people work effectively with others.
- Ethical behavior in today's workplace involves demonstrating respect for people of diverse backgrounds.
- Conflict negotiation requires good communication skills.
- Teamwork means a group of people work together toward a goal.
- Understanding the team goals, the roles assigned to individual team members, and shared responsibilities will help make you a valuable team member.

Review Content Vocabulary and Academic Vocabulary

1. Write a memo introducing yourself to the class. Use each of the following vocabulary terms in your memo.

Content Vocabulary
- self-esteem (p. 233)
- initiative (p. 233)
- time management (p. 234)
- assertiveness (p. 235)
- flexibility (p. 236)
- ethics (p. 236)
- equity (p. 237)
- negotiation (p. 238)
- empathy (p. 239)
- teamwork (p. 243)
- cross-training (p. 243)
- consensus (p. 243)
- agreement (p. 243)

Academic Vocabulary
- perceive (p. 233)
- demonstrate (p. 233)
- achieve (p. 245)
- conflict (p. 245)

Assess for Understanding

2. **Explain** Which personality traits might help you become a better friend and coworker?
3. **Explain** Why is initiative important in good working relationships?
4. **Describe** How can asking about others' interests and experiences help to prevent bias?
5. **Identify** What is the one thing that a team must do before it can begin its work?
6. **Discuss** How can sharing responsibility and leadership be helpful in achieving team goals?
7. **List** What are the five conventions that can help teams overcome obstacles?
8. **Describe** What are the characteristics of a team that works well in business? Why?
9. **Create** What are some positive teamworking behaviors you practice?

Chapter 10 · Interpersonal Skills | 247

EVALUATE

Visual Summary

Express Creativity Ask students to develop their own visual summary of a concept in the chapter. Encourage students to use different formats for their visual summaries, such as a storyboard, a timeline, a table, a tree diagram, or a word web. Visual summaries will vary depending on the concept depicted and the visual manner in which it is depicted. Questions to ask when assessing a visual summary include:

- Is the summary clear, economical, and simple?
- Are any important steps left out?
- Are steps or concepts arranged in the same order as the original?
- Does the summary reveal a pattern that connects the details?
- Does the summary locate and highlight the most important information?

Review Content Vocabulary and Academic Vocabulary

1. Memos will vary. Sample answer: Let me share with you some things that may help us work well together as classmates. I have a healthy **self-esteem** and I enjoy taking **initiative**. I have good **time management** skills and can be **assertive** when necessary. My **flexibility** allows me to adapt to changing situations and my strong **ethics** in such areas as honesty, respect, fairness, and **equity** help me get along well with others. I am good in **negotiations** because I listen and have **empathy** for others. I have strong **teamwork** skills such as **cross-training**, which prepares me to do many different activities. I believe team goals should be reached by a **consensus** of all team members. I believe team members should make commitments to the group through **agreements**. I **perceive** myself as one who can **demonstrate** my strengths as a member of a team and help the team **achieve** its goals with a minimum of **conflict**.

EVALUATE

Assess for Understanding

2. Personality traits may include: self-esteem, self-awareness, positive attitude, initiative, responsibility, self-control, creativity, time management, stress management, assertiveness, and flexibility.

3. Initiative shows that you are enthusiastic about your work and can do what needs to be done without being asked.

4. Asking about others' interests and experiences helps you understand them better, which can help prevent bias.

5. Before a team can act, it must have clearly defined goals.

6. Sharing responsibility and leadership helps employees feel more powerful because they have a part in making decisions.

7. Students should list five of these conventions that can help a team overcome obstacles. Conventions include making the team's goals top priority, listening and offering suggestions, building positive group dynamics, communicating with team members, following up on your work, resolving conflicts among team members, respecting other team members, and inspiring other employees to get involved.

8. A team that works well in business will have appropriate training, which allows for flexibility; planning as a team will make the team more effective; defining goals as a team fosters team loyalty; assigning roles helps team members know their specific responsibilities; making agreements helps the team become stronger and more cohesive; sharing responsibility helps to develop each team member's sense of ownership; shared leadership helps team members feel confident to take care of issues independently.

9. Answers may include: Making the team's goals top priority; listening actively and offering suggestions; building positive group dynamics with team members; communicating with team members; following up on assignments; working to resolve conflicts among team members; respecting other team members; inspiring others to get involved; thinking creatively and presenting ideas with enthusiasm.

21st Century Skills

Problem-Solving Skills

10. **Managing Conflict** Think of a conflict that you have observed in the past (but do not use names) or create a story about a conflict. Then prepare instructions for the most effective steps to take in managing this conflict.

Financial Literacy Skills

11. **Managing Credit** You have decided that you need a new computer to help get your homework done. The total cost is $840. You decide to charge it on a credit card. The interest rate is 18 percent, so the minimum monthly payment the first month is $33.60. If you only pay the minimum each month, about how long will it take to pay for the computer?

e-Marketing Skills

12. **Re-Selling on the Web** You have heard about people who buy and sell products via online auction sites on the Web. So you and a friend are exploring the idea as a way of earning some money. What research and planning will you do to determine whether this is an idea worth pursuing? Here are some questions to consider:
    - How will you keep track of money?
    - How will you ship products?
    - Who will pay for shipping?
    - What products will you sell?
    - How can you be sure your products will sell?
    - Where will you find products to sell?

Build Academic Skills

Social Studies

13. **Interactions Among People, Groups, and Institutions** Talk with four people you know from different places or in different ways. Ask them about their interests (hobbies or what they like to do in their spare time). After you have spoken with each person, identify the role each plays in society and in their work or school group.

NCSS V A Individuals, Groups, & Institutions Apply concepts such as role, status, and social class in describing the connections and interactions of individuals, groups, and institutions in society.

English Language Arts

14. **Reading and Writing** Conduct research on one of the following topics related to interpersonal skills: 1) ethics in the workplace, 2) managing conflict, or 3) teamwork on the job. Write a half-page summary about what you learned from your reading.

NCTE 12 Use language to accomplish individual purposes.

Mathematics

15. **Discounted Pricing** Math is a basic skill for team members. Your boss asks you to determine how much will be discounted from the price of a computer that has a list price of $1,499 and a discount of 15 percent. What answer would you give her?

NCTM Problem Solving Apply and adapt a variety of appropriate strategies to solve problems.

Math Concept **Problem Solving: Process** You can solve this problem by figuring the dollar amount of the discount and then subtracting it from the total. Or you can subtract the discounted percentage from 100 and multiply that percent by the total.

For help, go to the **Math Skills Handbook** located at the back of this book.

Standardized Test Practice

Directions Read the following questions. On a separate piece of paper, write the best possible answer for each one.

1. When addressing customer complaints, a good procedure would include:
   A. listening
   B. taking the customer to a quiet location
   C. repeating facts the customer states
   D. all of the above
2. True or false? Self-awareness is how you perceive yourself.
   T
   F
3. Conflict resolution helps members of a group work ___________________.

Test-Taking Tip
Look through the test and answer the easy questions first. Then you will know about how much time to allow for the more difficult questions.

DECA Connection Role Play

Manager
Travel Agency

Situation Assume the role of manager of a travel agency. The travel agency specializes in putting together custom tour packages for travel groups. Your upcoming 14-day tour of China has been very popular. The tour package includes airfare from your location, transfers, hotel accommodations, and admission to scheduled tourist destinations. The tour is expensive and each reservation requires a $1,500 non-refundable deposit. The tour is completely sold out with several customers on a waiting list for any cancellations. The China tour is scheduled to depart in six weeks.

One of your regular customers has booked two reservations for the China tour. The customer has come to the agency to tell the booking agent (judge) that he/she must cancel both of the tour reservations because of a family illness. The customer has also requested a refund on the deposit. The agent (judge) has followed company policy and explained that the deposit is non-refundable. The customer is upset and promising to find another travel agency. The agent (judge) has asked to discuss the situation with you and would like for you to consider making an exception and refund the customer's deposit.

Activity You are to decide whether or not to refund the customer's deposit and explain the reasons for your decision to the travel agent (judge).

Evaluation You will be evaluated on how well you meet the following performance indicators:

1. Foster positive working relationships.
2. Explain the use of feedback for personal growth.
3. Demonstrate ethical work habits.
4. Identify desirable personality traits important to business.
5. Describe the nature of emotional intelligence.

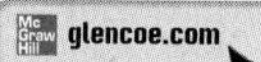

Download the Competitive Events Workbook for more Role-Play practice.

EVALUATE

21st Century Skills

Problem-Solving Skills

10. Students' descriptions or stories about a conflict will vary. Instructions for the most effective steps to take in managing a conflict will also vary but should include techniques similar to those listed in the text: (1) show respect; (2) recognize and define the problem; (3) seek a variety of solutions; (4) collaborate; (5) be reliable; (6) preserve the relationship.

Financial Literacy Skills

11. 30 months ($840 × 18% = 840 × .18 = 151.20; 840 + 151.20 = 991.20; $991.20 ÷ $33.60 = 29.5 = 30 months)

e-Marketing Skills

12. Answers will vary but should answer the questions posed in the text: How will you keep track of money? Sample answer: open a business bank account. How will you ship products? Sample answer: UPS or the U.S. Postal Service. Who will pay for shipping? Sample answer: customers. What products will you sell? Sample answer: gently used items, like baby clothes and CDs. How can you be sure your products will sell? Sample answer: research similar products. Where will you find products to sell? Sample answer: friends, family, swap meets, yard sales, garage sales, discount stores. Students should use proper grammar, spelling, and punctuation.

EVALUATE

Build Academic Skills

Social Studies

13. Roles identified will vary but should be based on the conversation with the individual, his or her hobbies and interests, and how these would fit in society or work or school. Students should consider the different roles that make up society, the workplace, and school and how the interests could help to fill those roles.

English Language Arts

14. Depending on which topic students choose to write about, reports should demonstrate an understanding of ethics in the workplace, managing conflict, or teamwork on the job. Reports should be written using proper grammar, spelling, and punctuation. Students should cite their sources in the report.

Mathematics

15. \$224.85 will be discounted from the price. ($\$1,499 \times 15\% = 1499 \times .15 = 224.85$)

Standardized Test Practice

1. D all of the above
2. True
3. together

DECA Connection Role Play

Evaluations will be based on these performance indicators:

1. **Foster positive working relationships.** Factors such as self-esteem, self-awareness, positive attitude, initiative, responsibility, self-control, creativity, time management, stress management, assertiveness, and flexibility may be discussed and/or demonstrated during completion of the activity.
2. **Explain the use of feedback for personal growth.** Feedback that identifies a behavior or attitude that can be changed or provides an example or model of a positive behavior or attitude can be used for personal growth. Students should recognize that positive feedback can be used to change their own behaviors and attitudes.
3. **Demonstrate ethical work habits.** Ethics are the basic values and moral principles that guide the behavior of individuals and groups. Students should demonstrate such ethical behaviors as honesty, respect, fairness, and equity.
4. **Identify desirable personality traits important to business.** Students should identify personality traits important to business such as friendliness, courtesy, tact, positive self-esteem, positive attitude, initiative, responsibility, self-control, creativity, time management, stress management, assertiveness, and flexibility, as well as honesty, respect, fairness, and equity.
5. **Describe the nature of emotional intelligence.** Students should be aware that emotional intelligence refers to the ability to recognize and control one's emotions. Emotional intelligence can also mean controlling the emotions of others and groups. Being aware of the emotions of oneself and others and being able to control the emotions in a positive way can be a real asset in the business world.

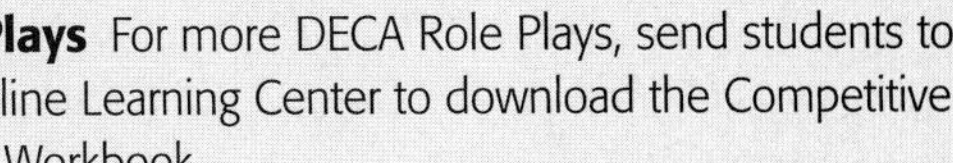

glencoe.com

Role Plays For more DECA Role Plays, send students to the Online Learning Center to download the Competitive Events Workbook.

management skills

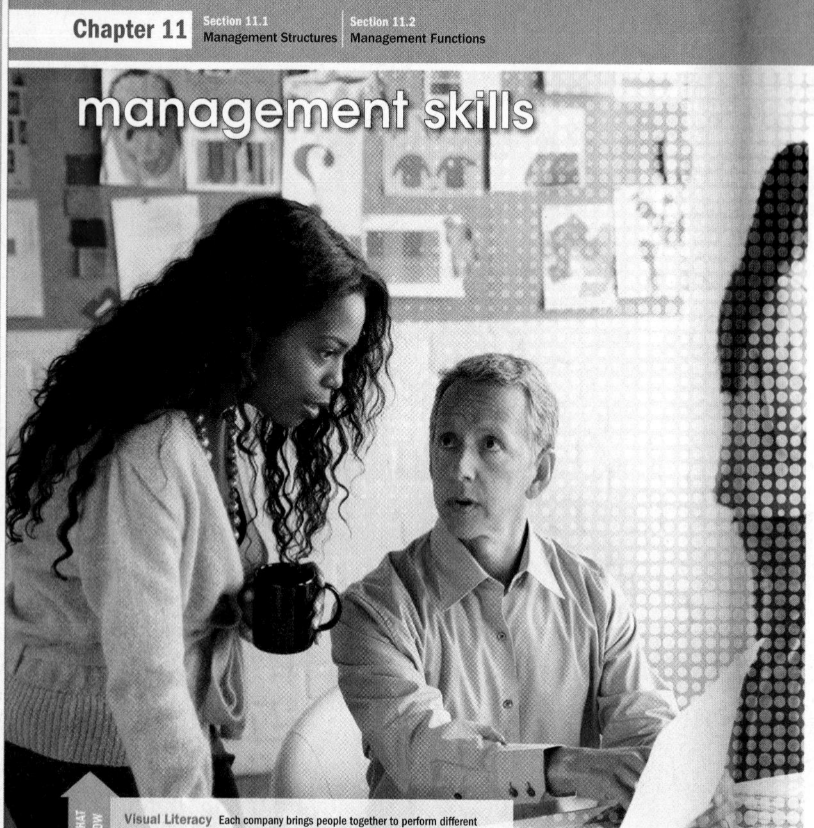

SHOW WHAT YOU KNOW

Visual Literacy Each company brings people together to perform different jobs, but everyone works toward the common goal of business success. Managers plan, organize, and control human resources, technology, and materials. ***What are some skills that a manager would need to have?***

Discovery Project

Management Styles

Essential Question What are several different management styles, and why are they effective?

Project Goal

Work with a partner to research and make a list of various management styles and associated skills. Identify three different types of small businesses in your area. Find out the names and contact information of a manager at each business. Interview the manager at each business, asking which management style best describes the way he or she interacts with employees. Write a report describing each management style. Include descriptions of each small business and its product.

Ask Yourself...

- How will you find businesses and managers in your community?
- What questions will you ask the managers?
- How will you describe your findings in your report?
- How will you present your report?

Synthesize and Present Research Synthesize your research and findings by writing a report that distinguishes between the management styles.

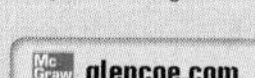

glencoe.com

Activity
Get a worksheet activity about management styles.

Evaluate
Download a rubric you can use to evaluate your project.

DECA Connection

DECA Event Role Play

Concepts in this chapter are related to DECA competitive events that involve either an interview or role play.

Performance Indicators The performance indicators represent key skills and knowledge. Your key to success in DECA competitive events is relating them to concepts in this chapter.

- Explain the concept of management.
- Explain the role of ethics in human resources management.
- Demonstrate responsible behavior.
- Explain the nature of staff communication.
- Make oral presentations.

DECA Prep

Role Play Practice role-playing with the DECA Connection competitive-event activity at the end of this chapter. More information on DECA events can be found on DECA's Web site.

ENGAGE

Visual Literacy

Read the chapter opener photo caption question to students: ***What are some skills that a manager would need to have?*** Students' answers might include: be a good listener, be able to give clear directions, and treat people fairly. Ask these guiding questions. Write student generated questions produced during the discussion on the board and return to them throughout the chapter.

Guiding Questions

Describe Give an example of each of these functions of management: planning, organizing, controlling.	planning—establish strategies for increasing sales by 8 percent; organizing—schedule employee hours; controlling—analyze quarterly operating budget
Analyze What are two questions that should be asked when analyzing management?	Questions might include: Do all managers follow the mission statement? Have executives met clearly established goals?

Discovery Project

Management Styles Explain to students that managers must plan, organize, and control a company's resources. Ask those students who have paying jobs to raise their hands. Then ask this group: ***Do you think your supervisor is a good manager? Why or why not?*** Sample answer: Yes, because he/she clearly explains what work I am supposed to do. Then ask students the Discovery Project Essential Question: ***What are several different management styles, and why are they effective?*** Students should recognize that some managers are more authoritarian in that they tell workers exactly what to do and how to do it. Other managers are more democratic, allowing workers considerable freedom as long as they accomplish their assigned tasks.

glencoe.com

Discovery Project Resources Send students to the Online Learning Center to download a rubric to evaluate their projects.

ENGAGE

Introduce the Chapter

Chapter 11 provides students with an overview of management structures and styles. These main concepts are introduced and discussed:

- Vertical organization
- Horizontal organization
- Organization by process
- Customer organization
- Effective management techniques
- Employee motivation
- Hiring and training employees
- Handling employee complaints and grievances

Discussion Starter

Have students consider the following scenario: A shoe factory loses all communication with its managers. No e-mail, Internet access, cell phones, or faxes can get through. Ask students: ***How long do you think the factory could remain functional under these circumstances? Why?*** Students should agree that a business, like any team, cannot function without communication from its leadership because it would not know its purpose or role in the company's plans. Ask: ***Based on this scenario, what do you think is the most important function of management?*** Possible answer: Managers must help workers see that they are part of a team that is working together to fulfill a company's mission statement.

DECA Connection

Discuss the performance indicators listed in the DECA Connection feature. Explain to students that performance indicators tell them how to demonstrate their acquired skills and knowledge through individual or team competitive events.

glencoe.com

Competitive Events Workbook For more DECA Role Plays, send students to the Online Learning Center to download the Competitive Events Workbook.

PRINT RESOURCES

- **Student Edition**
- **Teacher Edition**
- **Student Activity Workbook with Academic Integration** includes worksheets and activities correlated to the text.
- **Mathematics for Marketing Workbook** provides math activities for every unit in the text.

TECHNOLOGY TOOLBOX

- **Connect**
- **ConnectPlus**
- **ExamView Assessment Suite** is a comprehensive solution for creating, administering, and scoring tests.

glencoe.com

Online Learning Center provides a variety of resources to enrich and enhance learning.

SECTION, CHAPTER, AND UNIT RESOURCES

- **Graphic Organizers** for organizing text concepts visually.
- **Digital Nation Activities** and **Green Marketer Activities** extend learning beyond the text features.
- **Career Chatroom Career Profiles** allow students to explore different marketing occupations in depth.
- **After You Read Answer Keys** for students to check their answers.
- **Discovery Project Rubrics** and **Marketing Internship Project Rubrics** for students to evaluate their projects.

PROGRAM RESOURCES

- **Student Activity Workbook with Academic Integration Teacher Annotated Edition** includes annotated answers for the activities and worksheets.
- **Marketing Research Project Workbook** provides a step-by-step approach for students to complete their own marketing research studies.
- **School-to-Career Activity Workbook** helps students relate their class work to on-the-job experience and involves work-site analysis and working with mentors.
- **Competitive Events Workbook** helps prepare students for state and national marketing education competitions.
- **Inclusion in the Marketing Education Classroom** provides teaching resources for working with students with special needs.
- **PowerPoint Presentations** provides visual teaching aids and assessments for this chapter.

READING GUIDE

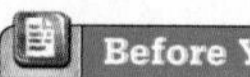

Before You Read

Connect When do you have to manage your time or your resources?

Objectives

- **Explain** how horizontally organized companies differ from vertically organized companies.
- **Name** the three levels of management in a vertically organized company.
- **Explain** how a self-management team functions.

The Main Idea

Two types of management structures are vertical and horizontal or a combination of both.

Vocabulary

Content Vocabulary
- management
- vertical organization
- top management
- middle management
- supervisory-level management
- horizontal organization
- empowerment

Academic Vocabulary

You will find these words in your reading and on your tests. Make sure you know their meanings.
- resource
- individual

Graphic Organizer

Draw or print this chart to take notes on the types of business organization.

glencoe.com

Print this graphic organizer.

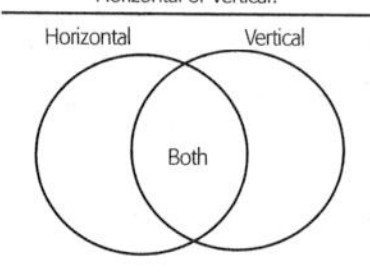

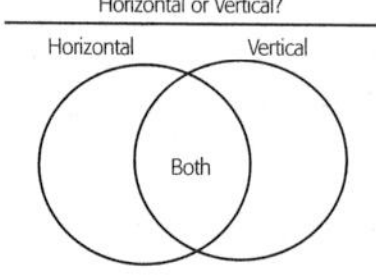

STANDARDS

ACADEMIC

English Language Arts

NCTE 4 Use written language to communicate effectively.

NCTE 12 Use language to accomplish individual purposes.

Mathematics

NCTM Number and Operations Understand numbers, ways of representing numbers, relationships among numbers, and number systems.

NCSS *National Council for the Social Studies*
NCTE *National Council of Teachers of English*
NCTM *National Council of Teachers of Mathematics*
NSES *National Science Education Standards*

College & Career READINESS

Common Core Writing Conduct short as well as more sustained research projects based on focused questions, demonstrating understanding of the subject under investigation.

MARKETING CORE FUNCTION

Marketing Information Management

m.e. Section 11.1 Management Structures

LEADERSHIP IN THE 21ST CENTURY

New leaders come from diverse backgrounds. Global competition is creating companies and managers who are united by common goals and ideals. Business leaders in the United States and around the world expect many changes in the coming years as a result of globalization.

As You Read

Predict What is the difference between vertical and horizontal organization?

TYPES OF MANAGEMENT STRUCTURE

Management is the business function of planning, organizing, and controlling all available resources to achieve company goals. To facilitate effective management, businesses are most often organized either vertically or horizontally.

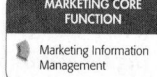

VERTICAL ORGANIZATION

For a long time, the role of management was to keep an eye on workers. In large, traditional companies, managers reported to higher levels of management. Managers were responsible for the proper operation of a particular department. Though updated and more worker friendly than in the past, the traditional vertical organization remains today. A **vertical organization** is a hierarchical, up-and-down organizational structure in which the tasks and responsibilities of each level are clearly defined.

Management Levels

In the vertically organized company, there are three basic levels of management: top management, middle management, and supervisory-level management.

Those who make decisions that affect the whole company are **top management**. CEO (chief executive officer), president, COO (chief operating officer), CFO (chief financial officer), and vice president are some of the top-management titles. They manage people and the structure of the company. The functions of top (or executive) management include setting a direction for the company as a whole, identifying **resources** and methods for meeting goals, and controlling the systems and structures of the company.

> "Managers utilize human resources, technology, and material resources."

Employees at the **middle management** level implement the decisions of top management. Middle management plans how the departments under them can work to reach top management's goals. They are supervised by the organization's top management. However, middle management's role involves implementation more than it does supervision. They monitor the effectiveness of the plans they implement.

In **supervisory-level management**, managers supervise the employees who actually carry out the tasks determined by middle and top management. Supervisors assign duties, monitor day-to-day activities in their department, and evaluate the work of production or service employees. Supervisors also set priorities for their departments, work to keep within budgets, and monitor their teams' workflow. The performance of their departments is supervised by middle management.

ENGAGE

Anticipation Activity

Improving Student Achievement Tell students that companies have different organization structures, and that they employ managers with a variety of management styles. Ask: ***Do you think the way a company's management is organized matters to the average worker?*** Some students might say that most workers don't care; others may say that workers want to know how the company makes decisions and sets goals.

Objectives

- **Explain** how horizontally organized companies differ from vertically organized companies. vertical organization—hierarchical structure-managers direct workers; horizontal organization—self-managing teams share decision making
- **Name** the three levels of management in a vertically organized company. top, middle, and supervisory-level management
- **Explain** how a self-management team functions. The team gathers and analyzes information and takes collective action.

Graphic Organizer

Horizontal	Both	Vertical
• Teams • Fewer staff • Self-managing Organized by process	• Provides structure • Provides planning, controlling functions • Works to meet goals	• Three management levels • Organized by function • Workers closely supervised

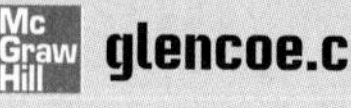

glencoe.com

Graphic Organizer Send students to the Online Learning Center to print this graphic organizer.

EXPLORE

Before You Read

Read the Before You Read question aloud: ***When do you have to manage your time or your resources?*** Possible answers: manage time when doing homework or studying for a test; manage resources when deciding how to spend money. Ask students: ***What do you think might happen if you did a poor job of managing your time?*** grades may suffer; not enough time for extracurricular activities

Preteaching Vocabulary

Have students go to the Online Learning Center at glencoe.com for the Chapter 11 Preteaching Vocabulary games.

Content Vocabulary

Instruct students to skim this section to determine which three Content Vocabulary terms are related to vertical organization. top management, middle management, supervisory-level management Have students write a paragraph explaining how these three terms are interrelated. Sample paragraph: In a vertical organization, top management sets the goals, middle management determines how to implement the goals, and supervisory-level management assigns workers to carry out the day-to-day tasks needed to reach the goals.

Academic Vocabulary

Individual—Denotative Meaning Tell students that *individual* means "a particular being or thing as distinguished from a group or species." As an example, read aloud this sentence: ***The sales team is concerned with the wants and needs of the individual who buys shoes at the store.*** Ask: ***What part of speech is* individual *in this sentence?*** noun Then read aloud this sentence: ***The individual items are priced at 20 percent off.*** Ask: ***What part of speech is* individual *in this sentence?*** adjective

Resource—Word Origin Explain that the word *resource* comes from Old French and means "relief or relieve," and from the Latin resurgere, which means "to rise again." Ask students: ***How would you describe a resourceful person?*** Someone who knows how to create something from unexpected supplies.

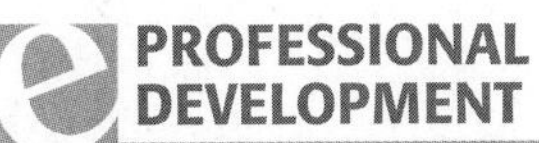

PROFESSIONAL DEVELOPMENT

MINI CLIP

Reading: Differentiated Activities
Go to the Online Learning Center to view a video clip in which a teacher models ways to create vocabulary cards that support different learning styles.

Management Structures

LEADERSHIP IN THE 21ST CENTURY

To focus the discussion on management and leadership, ask students these guiding questions.

Guiding Questions

Identify What type of organization has a hierarchical structure?	vertical organization
Contrast In a vertical organization, how is middle management different from supervisory-level management?	Middle managers implement the plans of top management; supervisor-level managers supervise employees who carry out the tasks determined by upper-level managers
Evaluate What characteristics do you think a member of top level management should have?	Possible answers: able to think of imaginative ways to compete in the marketplace, able to inspire workers at all levels

As You Read

Read students the As You Read question: ***What is the difference between vertical and horizontal organization?*** vertical organization—a chain-of-command, hierarchical structure where the tasks and responsibilities of each level of the organization are clearly defined; horizontal—top management shares decision-making with self-managing teams of workers who set their own goals and make their own decisions

Expert Advice

Read the quote to students:

> **"Managers utilize human resources, technology, and material resources."**

Ask students: ***How do you think managing human resources is different from managing material resources?*** When you manage material resources, you must know about the cost and capabilities of each resource.

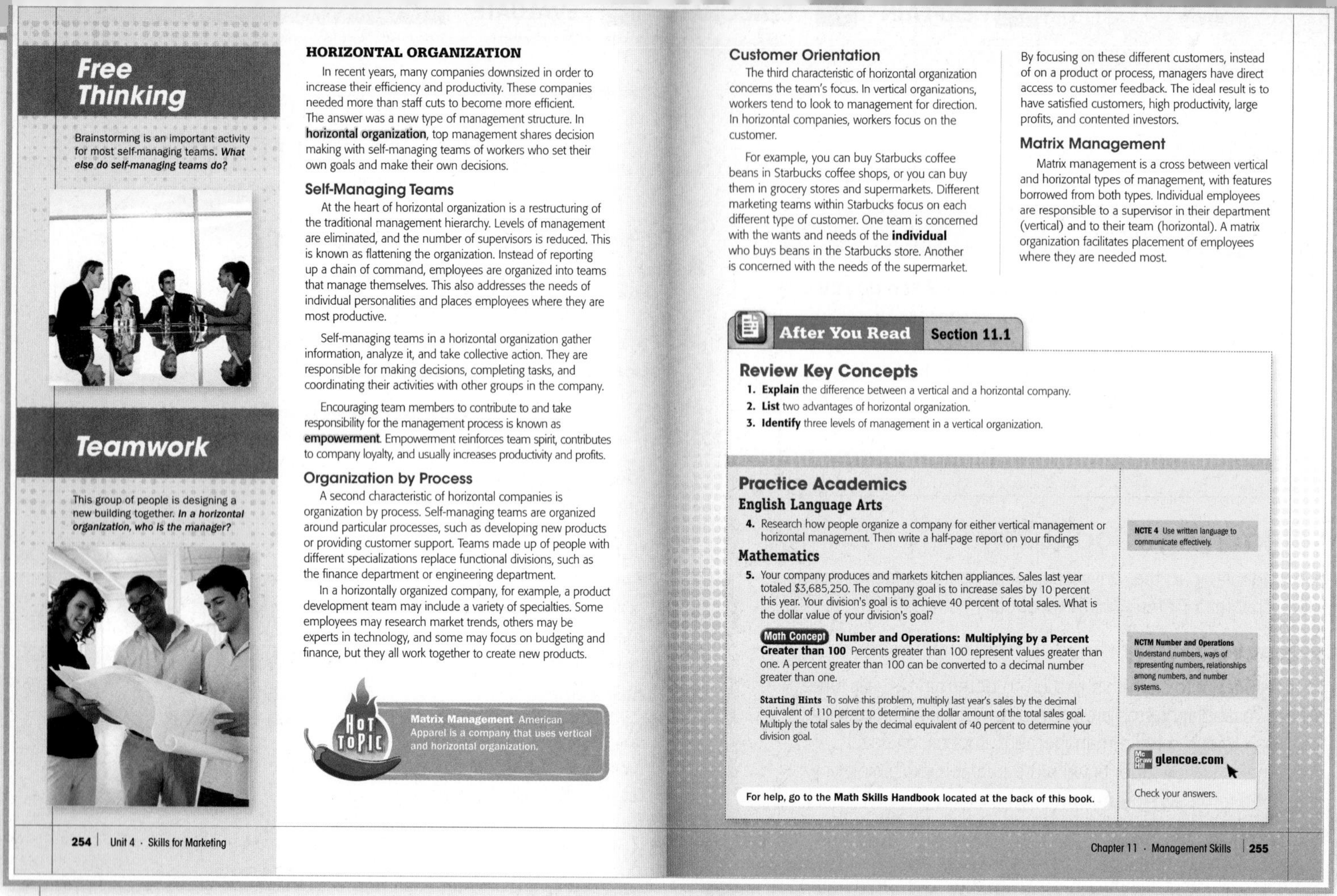

Free Thinking

Brainstorming is an important activity for most self-managing teams. ***What else do self-managing teams do?***

Teamwork

This group of people is designing a new building together. ***In a horizontal organization, who is the manager?***

HORIZONTAL ORGANIZATION

In recent years, many companies downsized in order to increase their efficiency and productivity. These companies needed more than staff cuts to become more efficient. The answer was a new type of management structure. In **horizontal organization**, top management shares decision making with self-managing teams of workers who set their own goals and make their own decisions.

Self-Managing Teams

At the heart of horizontal organization is a restructuring of the traditional management hierarchy. Levels of management are eliminated, and the number of supervisors is reduced. This is known as flattening the organization. Instead of reporting up a chain of command, employees are organized into teams that manage themselves. This also addresses the needs of individual personalities and places employees where they are most productive.

Self-managing teams in a horizontal organization gather information, analyze it, and take collective action. They are responsible for making decisions, completing tasks, and coordinating their activities with other groups in the company.

Encouraging team members to contribute to and take responsibility for the management process is known as **empowerment**. Empowerment reinforces team spirit, contributes to company loyalty, and usually increases productivity and profits.

Organization by Process

A second characteristic of horizontal companies is organization by process. Self-managing teams are organized around particular processes, such as developing new products or providing customer support. Teams made up of people with different specializations replace functional divisions, such as the finance department or engineering department.

In a horizontally organized company, for example, a product development team may include a variety of specialties. Some employees may research market trends, others may be experts in technology, and some may focus on budgeting and finance, but they all work together to create new products.

HOT TOPIC **Matrix Management** American Apparel is a company that uses vertical and horizontal organization.

Customer Orientation

The third characteristic of horizontal organization concerns the team's focus. In vertical organizations, workers tend to look to management for direction. In horizontal companies, workers focus on the customer.

For example, you can buy Starbucks coffee beans in Starbucks coffee shops, or you can buy them in grocery stores and supermarkets. Different marketing teams within Starbucks focus on each different type of customer. One team is concerned with the wants and needs of the **individual** who buys beans in the Starbucks store. Another is concerned with the needs of the supermarket.

By focusing on these different customers, instead of on a product or process, managers have direct access to customer feedback. The ideal result is to have satisfied customers, high productivity, large profits, and contented investors.

Matrix Management

Matrix management is a cross between vertical and horizontal types of management, with features borrowed from both types. Individual employees are responsible to a supervisor in their department (vertical) and to their team (horizontal). A matrix organization facilitates placement of employees where they are needed most.

After You Read — Section 11.1

Review Key Concepts

1. **Explain** the difference between a vertical and a horizontal company.
2. **List** two advantages of horizontal organization.
3. **Identify** three levels of management in a vertical organization.

Practice Academics

English Language Arts

4. Research how people organize a company for either vertical management or horizontal management. Then write a half-page report on your findings

NCTE 4 Use written language to communicate effectively.

Mathematics

5. Your company produces and markets kitchen appliances. Sales last year totaled $3,685,250. The company goal is to increase sales by 10 percent this year. Your division's goal is to achieve 40 percent of total sales. What is the dollar value of your division's goal?

Math Concept **Number and Operations: Multiplying by a Percent Greater than 100** Percents greater than 100 represent values greater than one. A percent greater than 100 can be converted to a decimal number greater than one.

Starting Hints To solve this problem, multiply last year's sales by the decimal equivalent of 110 percent to determine the dollar amount of the total sales goal. Multiply the total sales by the decimal equivalent of 40 percent to determine your division goal.

NCTM Number and Operations Understand numbers, ways of representing numbers, relationships among numbers, and number systems.

For help, go to the **Math Skills Handbook** located at the back of this book.

glencoe.com

Check your answers.

ELABORATE

Visual Literacy

Free Thinking Caption Answer Read the caption question to students: ***What else do self-managing teams do?*** They gather information and analyze it in order to make good decisions, assign tasks to members depending on their skills and the project's needs, and try to address the needs of individual personalities.

Critical Thinking

Describe two companies for the students. The first is a factory that makes furniture. Employees work on an assembly line where each performs a specific task. The second is a business that develops Web sites for nonprofit organizations. Groups of six to eight programmers work together to develop each site. Ask students: ***What kind of organizational structure do you think might work for each of these businesses? Why?*** Possible answers: Because jobs are well defined in the factory, a vertical structure with clear lines of authority might work well. A horizontal structure might work best at the Web development business because programmers are organized by project and must interact closely with one another.

Visual Literacy

Teamwork Caption Answer Read the caption question to students: ***In a horizontal organization, who is the manager?*** Each team works as a unit to manage itself. Ask students to think about which type of organization—horizontal or vertical—would best suit their own personality. Have volunteers share their thoughts.

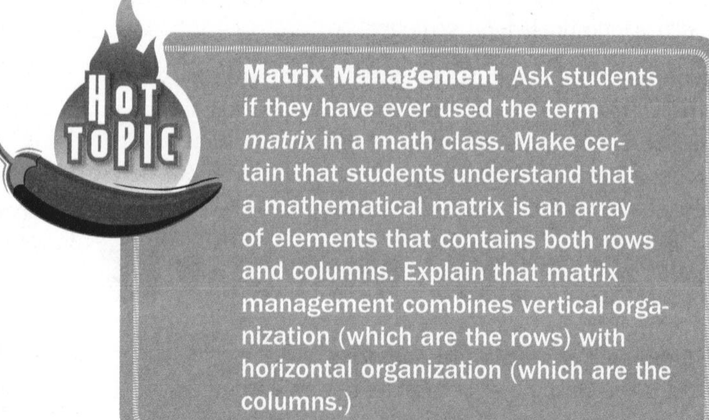

HOT TOPIC
Matrix Management Ask students if they have ever used the term *matrix* in a math class. Make certain that students understand that a mathematical matrix is an array of elements that contains both rows and columns. Explain that matrix management combines vertical organization (which are the rows) with horizontal organization (which are the columns.)

EVALUATE

Reinforce Vocabulary

Empowerment—Root Word Write the word *empowerment* on the board. Underline *power.* Explain that the root word of *empowerment* is *power.* Ask for a volunteer to look up the meaning of *power.* ability to produce an effect Tell students that the prefix *em-* means "to cause to be" and the suffix *-ment* means "a state or condition." Therefore, *empowerment* can be defined as "the state of being able to produce an effect." Explain that if people have empowerment, they can have an effect on their environment.

HORIZONTAL ORGANIZATION

Discuss with students that an increasingly competitive global marketplace has forced companies to become more "lean." Ask these guiding questions to focus the discussion on horizontal organization.

Guiding Questions

Explain Why is switching from vertical to horizontal organization called "flattening the organization"?	The management structure has fewer levels, but each level is broader.
Analyze From the company's point of view, what is an advantage to horizontal organization?	The company saves money because there are fewer managers, and productivity typically increases as employees feel more empowered.
Critique Do you think horizontal organization could work in a high school? Why or why not?	Answers will vary. Some may think that students should be more involved in decision-making; others may think students need hierarchical organization.

Mini Project

Differentiated Instruction

Logical Learners Organize students into pairs. Each pair should work together to establish a fictitious business that has a vertical organization. Students should then create a skit in which they are both members of top management. One manager supports the current hierarchical organization while the other wants to switch to a horizontal organization. In their skits, students should state specific reasons for their positions. Encourage them to use illustrations. Each student should demonstrate an understanding of their role and present advantages of their organizational method.

After You Read Section 11.1

Review Key Concepts

1. A vertical organization is a chain-of-command, hierarchical structure where the tasks and responsibilities of each level of the organization are clearly defined. In a horizontal organization, top management shares decision-making with self-managing teams of workers who set their own goals and make their own decisions.
2. Personnel costs are reduced in a horizontal organization because fewer managers are required. Members of self-managed teams are empowered as they are given authority to make their own decisions, complete their tasks, and coordinate their activities with other groups within the company.
3. The three levels are top management, middle management, and supervisory-level management.

Practice Academics

English Language Arts

4. Students should write a half-page report explaining how a company can be organized for either vertical management or horizontal management. For vertical management, the titles and functions of each position must be established. For example, the CFO (chief financial officer) would be in charge of all financial operations. Those middle managers that report to each top management person must then be established. Under this level are the supervisors who report to each middle manager. For horizontal management, employees should be organized into teams by process, rather than function. For example, in a sporting goods store, all employees who are responsible for customer service would be part of one team. These teams would be self-managing, making their own decisions and prioritizing their tasks.

Mathematics

5. $1,621,510 ([3,685,250 × 1.10] × 0.40)

Answer Key Send students to the Online Learning Center to check their answers.

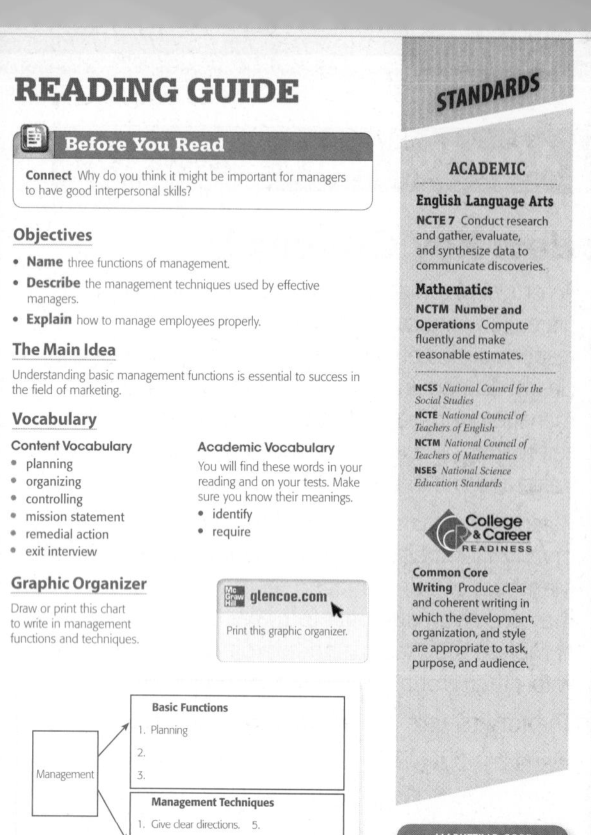

READING GUIDE

Before You Read

Connect Why do you think it might be important for managers to have good interpersonal skills?

Objectives

- **Name** three functions of management.
- **Describe** the management techniques used by effective managers.
- **Explain** how to manage employees properly.

The Main Idea

Understanding basic management functions is essential to success in the field of marketing.

Vocabulary

Content Vocabulary
- planning
- organizing
- controlling
- mission statement
- remedial action
- exit interview

Academic Vocabulary

You will find these words in your reading and on your tests. Make sure you know their meanings.
- identify
- require

Graphic Organizer

Draw or print this chart to write in management functions and techniques.

glencoe.com

Print this graphic organizer.

Management	Basic Functions	
	1. Planning	
	2.	
	3.	
	Management Techniques	
	1. Give clear directions.	5.
	2.	6.
	3.	7.
	4.	8.

STANDARDS

ACADEMIC

English Language Arts

NCTE 7 Conduct research and gather, evaluate, and synthesize data to communicate discoveries.

Mathematics

NCTM Number and Operations Compute fluently and make reasonable estimates.

NCSS National Council for the Social Studies
NCTE National Council of Teachers of English
NCTM National Council of Teachers of Mathematics
NSES National Science Education Standards

College & Career READINESS

Common Core

Writing Produce clear and coherent writing in which the development, organization, and style are appropriate to task, purpose, and audience.

MARKETING CORE FUNCTION

Marketing Information Management

Section 11.2

Management Functions

WHAT MANAGERS DO

Management decisions affect all employees. This means that communicating and motivating people are two of the most important management skills.

As You Read

Consider When have you seen or heard about these management styles in action?

BASIC MANAGEMENT FUNCTIONS

Whether a company is organized vertically or horizontally, the management functions remain the same. All managers perform certain basic functions of planning, organizing, and controlling, as outlined in **Figure 11.1** on page 258.

Planning involves setting goals and determining how to reach them. **Organizing** includes establishing a time frame in which to achieve the goal, assigning employees to the project, and determining a method for approaching the work. **Controlling** is the process of setting standards and evaluating performance.

All three of these management functions involve making decisions. Following a formal decision-making process can be helpful when making complicated decisions.

The decision-making process usually includes these steps:

1. Define the problem.
2. **Identify** the options available.
3. Gather information and determine the consequences of each option.
4. Choose the best option.
5. Take action.
6. Evaluate the results.

PLANNING

Good management planning is realistic, comprehensive, and flexible. It includes plans for the short- and long-range uses of people, technology, and material resources.

> "Managers make decisions in addition to supervising and directing the actions of others."

To be effective, a management plan should be a written statement that identifies resources that can be used to meet a given goal. The plan should be clear and direct. When completed, the plan should be distributed to and discussed with everyone who is involved.

ORGANIZING

Organizing is a coordinated effort to reach a company's planning goals. It involves assigning responsibility, establishing working relationships, hiring staff to carry out the work, and directing the work of employees. Some companies set up staffing as a separate function. Staffing involves recruiting, hiring, training, and evaluating workers.

CONTROLLING

Controlling is the process of comparing a plan with actual performance. It involves three activities: setting standards, evaluating performance according to those standards, and solving problems in the evaluation. Some companies designate *directing* as a separate function. The purpose of directing is to influence the behavior of employees so that they are effective in helping the company achieve its goals.

ENGAGE

Anticipation Activity

Improving Student Achievement Divide the class into three groups. Tell them they have five minutes to design a school flag. Afterwards, ask: ***Who did the planning? Were specific people assigned certain tasks? Were there leaders?*** Answers will vary but students should recognize that tasks involving more than one person involve organization, planning, and leadership.

Objectives

- **Name** three functions of management. planning, organizing, and controlling
- **Describe** the management techniques used by effective managers. give clear directions, treat employees fairly, be firm when necessary, set a good example, delegate, foster teamwork
- **Explain** how to manage employees properly. Managers should give clear directions, be ethical, and set a good example. They should make certain everyone understands his or her job and how their work will be evaluated.

Graphic Organizer

Management	Basic Functions	
	1. Planning 2. Organizing 3. Controlling	
	Management Techniques	
	1. Give clear directions.	5. Set a good example.
	2. Be consistent.	6. Delegate responsibility.
	3. Treat employees fairly.	7. Foster teamwork.
	4. Be firm when necessary.	8. Be ethical.

Graphic Organizer Send students to the Online Learning Center to print this graphic organizer.

EXPLORE

Before You Read

Read the Before You Read question aloud: ***Why do you think it might be important for managers to have good interpersonal skills?*** Managers need to give clear directions to workers; they often deal with difficult issues in a way that does not result in resentment or hard feelings.

Preteaching Vocabulary

Have students go to the Online Learning Center at glencoe.com for the Chapter 11 Preteaching Vocabulary games.

Content Vocabulary

Ask students to predict the meaning of each term. As students read, have them check to determine whether their predictions were correct.

Academic Vocabulary

Identify—Synonyms Ask students to suggest synonyms for *identify*. recognize, name, classify Read aloud ***I was able to identify the woman as my neighbor.*** Ask: ***Which of these synonyms can best replace identify in this sentence?*** recognize Encourage students to understand the subtle differences between these synonyms.

Mini Project

Differentiated Instruction

Visual Learners Organize students into groups of two or three. Have them define a decision that one of them must make. For example, they may be having difficulty balancing a part-time job with practice for the tennis team. Have students use the steps on page 257 to reach a decision. They then should create a poster that graphically illustrates how they reached their decision. Posters should graphically illustrate the decision-making process. For example, the process may be drawn like a ladder, with the first step being a definition of the problem, the second step illustrating each of the potential options (for example, playing tennis with teammates or earning money at work), and so on.

Section 11.2 Management Functions

WHAT MANAGERS DO

Ask these guiding questions to focus the discussion on the tasks involved in management.

Guiding Questions

Analyze A self-managed group creates a time line for developing an advertising campaign. Which type of management function is this? Why?	It is part of organizing because the team is establishing the time frame for reaching a particular goal.
Apraise What might happen if a manager does a poor job of controlling?	Workers might not have a clear understanding of the company's standards or if they are meeting those standards.

As You Read Answer

Read students the As You Read question: ***When have you seen or heard about these management styles in action?*** Answers will likely include experiences they have had at part-time jobs or events they have heard about. For example, a restaurant worker may have been given clear guidelines about cleanliness standards, dress codes, break policies, and so on.

Expert Advice

Read the quote to students:

> **“Managers make decisions in addition to supervising and directing the actions of others.”**

Display the two responsibilities of management stated here: making decisions and supervising and directing others. Ask students: ***In a company that's vertically organized, who has each of these responsibilities?*** making decisions—top management; supervising and directing—supervisory-level management

Before setting standards, many companies compose a **mission statement**, which is a description of the ultimate goals of a company. A mission statement summarizes why a company exists. It identifies goods or services offered and the target market.

After a company establishes goals in a mission statement, it adopts standards that are consistent with the goals. Here are some examples of standards:

- Financial standards—profit, cash flow, sales
- Employee standards—productivity, professional conduct, dress
- Customer satisfaction standards—sales returns, customer complaints, repeat business, referrals
- Quality control standards—production line checks for defects in materials or workmanship, repair requests, recalls
- Environmental standards—policies and practices that conserve resources and avoid damaging or polluting the natural environment

Managers use standards to evaluate both company and individual performance. When performance does not meet established standards, managers must identify and solve the problem.

EFFECTIVE MANAGEMENT TECHNIQUES

Whether you become a supervisor in a traditionally organized vertical company or a member of a self-managing team, you will need to develop management skills. The most effective management techniques are usually a matter of common sense.

GIVE CLEAR DIRECTIONS

Directing others **requires** good communication skills. Good communication is necessary at every level of management. Even the best employees will not be productive if they do not know what they are expected to do. A supervisor should give all the direction required for each job and encourage employees to ask questions about instructions if they are not clear.

FIGURE 11.1 Management Functions

Three Basic Functions Managers plan, organize, and control. Here are the management functions required of the manager, or owner, of a marketing team developing an ad campaign for a new car. In this case, the company structure is horizontal. ***What skills are necessary to be a manager?***

Planning In this stage, the team develops a plan covering the entire life of the ad campaign, from market research to tracking the campaign's effectiveness. The manager of the team must be sure that the team's plans and goals are aligned with the company's plans.

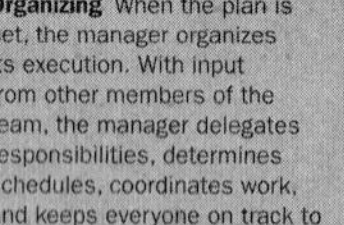

Organizing When the plan is set, the manager organizes its execution. With input from other members of the team, the manager delegates responsibilities, determines schedules, coordinates work, and keeps everyone on track to meet team goals.

Controlling When the project is complete, the manager should determine its effectiveness. If it was not successful, the manager must find out what went wrong.

BE CONSISTENT

If you have decided that a job must be completed in a certain way, make sure that all employees follow this standard. Do not make exceptions unless there is a good reason to do so.

TREAT EMPLOYEES FAIRLY

Set reasonable standards of performance and apply those standards to everyone. However, you should always consider the employees' points of view when making decisions. Listen to suggestions from your employees, and consider acting on them. Take time to explain your reasoning if you believe an employee is wrong. Employees will be more productive when treated fairly.

BE FIRM WHEN NECESSARY

Each situation requiring disciplinary action is different. A friendly suggestion may be all that is needed to get most employees on the right track. With others, you may have to be direct and firm. Give appropriate directions and be certain the employee understands your expectations.

Sometimes employee problems are caused by the inappropriate behavior of one employee toward another. In this case, have a discussion with the employees to solve the problem. Listen to what both parties have to say and be reasonable but firm.

SET A GOOD EXAMPLE

Set a good example in everything you do on the job. Doing this one simple thing will make your supervisory job much easier.

DELEGATE RESPONSIBILITY

Some supervisors and middle managers do too much work themselves. If a manager is taking work home almost every night, it usually means resources are not being managed well. The manager may not be delegating enough tasks to capable employees with lighter workloads who are willing to do more.

Organize your work responsibilities and then decide which ones you can delegate to others. Decide which employee can best handle each task. Take time to teach employees how to do new tasks. Monitor and evaluate the tasks that have been delegated. This will allow you more time to concentrate on the most important tasks.

HOT TOPIC
Responsibility Being too remote and working in isolation are common leadership blind spots that can impair an organization.

MARKETING CASE STUDY

FedEx: "We Understand"

Recessions take a serious toll on businesses everywhere. FedEx adapted its marketing strategy to address uncertainty that many companies feel during an economic downturn. In early 2009, it launched the "We Understand" campaign. This campaign reminded people "that FedEx understands . . . and offers solutions for . . . the various needs of our customers."

Emotional and Financial Appeal

The campaign used emotional appeal to show people how FedEx products and services help them do better business and survive tough economic times. Ads from the campaign also used humor to attempt to cut through pessimism. The campaign also demonstrated that FedEx services are less expensive than competitors' services.

English Language Arts

Research Research what type of management structure FedEx uses. Write a paragraph about how FedEx management might train employees to implement a campaign like "We Understand."

NCTE 4 Use written language to communicate effectively.

EXPLAIN

EFFECTIVE MANAGEMENT TECHNIQUES

Ask these guiding questions to focus the discussion about effective management techniques.

Guiding Questions

Draw Conclusions Why is it important for supervisors to be consistent?	If employees receive unequal treatment, they might not feel part of a team.
Interpret What might happen if a supervisor refuses to delegate responsibility to those under him, but rather takes on an extremely heavy work load?	Employees might feel that the supervisor does not trust them; supervisor might become fatigued and start doing poor-quality work.

Visual Literacy

Figure 11.1 Caption Answer Read the caption question to students: ***What skills are necessary to be a manager?:*** be a good communicator, be able to develop a clear plan on how to reach goals and organize the plan's execution, be able to evaluate the plans' effectiveness once it's completed. To focus the discussion, present these guiding questions.

Guiding Questions

Explain How is a company's mission statement related to the planning function?	A plan must specifically state how the mission statement's goals are to be accomplished.
Analyze What are specific ways that a manager can build team spirit while a plan is being executed?	clearly explain what is expected, assign tasks based on abilities and personalities, delegate responsibilities

EXPLAIN

Reinforce Vocabulary

Require—Usage Have students volunteer sentences in which they use a form of the term *require*. For each sentence, ask the class to determine whether the term is used correctly. Tell students that the term can mean "to need," "to demand, or "to compel." Sample sentences: The project requires $200 to complete. The company requires all employees to wear an identification badge. The contract required a signature.

Graphic Organizer

Display this graphic organizer that illustrates the three functions of management. Ask students to name at least three responsibilities under each of these functions.

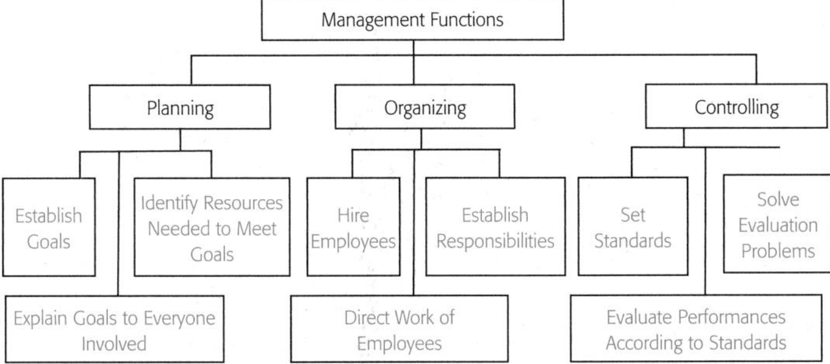

 glencoe.com 

Graphic Organizer Send students to the Online Learning Center to print this graphic organizer.

MARKETING CASE STUDY

English Language Arts Answer Paragraphs should explain that FedEx has always emphasized to employees that the company's goals center around customer needs. FedEx has continually worked to integrate systems and technologies it has developed and allow the customer to access these. With the "We Understand" campaign, FedEx managers could emphasize that employees must strive to see challenges from the customer's point of view and then work with the customer in developing a solution that meets everyone's needs.

VIRTUAL BUSINESS

STAFFING

Introduce students to the concept of staffing using Knowledge Matters' Virtual Business Retailing visual simulation, *Staffing*. In this simulation, students will learn that the hiring and managing of employees is a crucial part of a store's success.

e MARKETING

On-site Web Analytics

On-site web analytics is a tool used to evaluate the effectiveness of a web site by collecting, measuring and analyzing data generated by Web site visitors. Software can be used to count the number of hits a Web site receives, as well as how visitors navigate the site. Conversion rates can also be studied, which shows when visitors take positive action, such as signing up for a newsletter or purchasing goods. All data mined and reports generated from web analytics can be used by management to decide on the overall effectiveness of the company's online presence. It can help management decide what action, if any, is needed to improve the company's Web site.

Innovate and Create

Select two Web sites of competing companies for students to evaluate based on ease of navigation, visual appeal, and information relevancy. Assign different competing Web sites so reports are varied. Suggested competing Web site are two pharmacies (i.e., CVS® and Walgreens®), two supermarkets (i.e., A&P® and Stop & Shop®), and two clothing stores (Old Navy® and Buckle®). Have them share their evaluations and suggestions for improvement in two separate one-page written reports (one for each company's management). Students should include information on how this evaluation process would be improved if they had on-site web analytics to justify their recommendations. Have students share their findings and suggestions in an oral report. Use the following rubric to evaluate the students' two written reports:

Criteria – The written report	Possible Points for 1st Company	Points Earned for 1st Company	Possible Points for 2nd Company	Points Earned for 2nd Company
Effectively evaluated ease of navigation	10		10	
Effectively evaluated visual appeal	10		10	
Effectively evaluated information relevancy	10		10	
Included suggestions for Web site improvement	10		10	
Included suggestion for the need for web analytics to justify recommendations	10		10	
Total Points	50		50	

 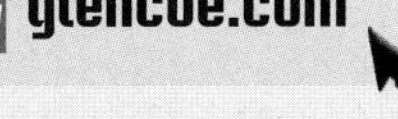

eMarketing Worksheet Activity Send students to the Online Learning Center to download an eMarketing worksheet activity.

FOSTER TEAMWORK

As mentioned earlier, teamwork is especially important in horizontally organized companies. As a manager or group owner, you can foster teamwork in a number of ways. Encourage team members to step outside their areas of specialization and learn about other aspects of the process for which they are responsible. Try to promote honest discussion before decisions are made. Listen respectfully to the comments and opinions of other team members, and encourage others in the group to do likewise. Respond to the comments and concerns of team members to develop a feeling of trust. Treat all team members equally. A team will not succeed if some members are treated unfairly.

BE ETHICAL

Ethical behavior involves understanding how your actions affect others and striving to make honest and just decisions. Management is responsible for promoting ethical behavior by example.

MANAGEMENT STYLES

Management style is the overall type of leadership used by a manager. The two basic management styles are *authoritarian* and *democratic*. All other styles are variations of one of these or a combination of both. An authoritarian manager makes all the decisions. Communication is mostly from top down. A democratic manager allows employees to take part in decision-making. Communication flows in both directions.

Variations of the two basic management styles include *participatory* and *teamwork*. In a participatory team, directions are given by management, but employees may complete a task without close supervision. In the *teamwork* variation, management allows employee teams to decide how best to complete a project.

Still other variations of management style used in some companies are *discussion management* and *delegating style*. In discussion management, managers meet frequently with employees about how tasks should be accomplished. In the delegating style, managers assign tasks to employees who they believe can complete them.

Different workplaces and situations call for different management styles. Diverse personalities, too, can make one management style more effective than another. Most managers strike a balance somewhere between authoritarian and democratic styles, and then adjust their style according to company objectives and the situation.

EMPLOYEE MOTIVATION

Motivating employees is a key skill for any manager. The more people feel that they are appreciated, the harder they work. Managers should provide frequent feedback to employees and formally evaluate them each year. Identifying long-term goals and rewarding employees who help meet them are important ways to motivate those whom you manage.

REWARDS

It is important to reward smart work, not busy work. A person who looks busy may not necessarily be getting the work done. To get results, reward results.

Identify those workers who value not only speed but quality. Ask them to suggest ways to improve job performance.

Enthusiastic long-term employees are the key to success in most companies. Reward loyalty by investing in continuing education for employees and promoting from within. Also, praise employees for their good ideas and successes. Employees who feel appreciated for their hard work are likely to continue to feel motivated to do a good job.

ENCOURAGE CREATIVITY

A reasonable amount of conformity is necessary in every company in order to maintain standards, but do not let conformity stifle creativity. Encourage employees to be creative, and remind them that they will not be penalized for mistakes. Sometimes, it is necessary to take risks when being creative.

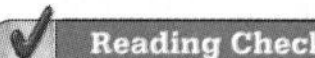
Reading Check

Recall What are the basic management styles and variations?

HUMAN RESOURCES

Without effective managers, team members, and employees, the best technology and material resources would be of little value to a business. Most companies have a human resources (HR) department that handles recruitment, hiring and firing, training, and other employee matters. Employee records are maintained in a file within the human resources office. These include records of an employee's hiring, participation in training programs, performance evaluations, disciplinary action, and awards.

RECRUITING

Recruiting is the process of electing employees from a pool of applicants. Employees can be recruited from a number of different sources. Some include current employees, walk-in applicants, media advertising, state employment services, public and private employment agencies, schools, and the Internet.

CURRENT EMPLOYEES

Job openings should be posted where all employees can see them. The notice should include the job title and duties, qualifications, contact name, and sometimes the salary. Current employees are a good source for referrals.

WALK-INS

Some applicants walk into the human resources office and ask to be considered for a job. Some companies now accept electronic "walk-ins" on their Web sites and at their hiring kiosks. Walk-ins usually complete an application form and may be given information on jobs that might soon become available. They might take the company's employment tests.

MEDIA ADVERTISING

Most companies use media advertising in newspapers and on the Internet to recruit applicants. Advertisements that do not disclose the name of the company are usually not very effective. The nature of the job and required qualifications should be clearly indicated in an advertisement.

Advertising on online job boards can be expensive. Social networking Web sites are increasingly used to locate potential employees and often cost nothing to use.

STATE EMPLOYMENT SERVICES

State employment offices provide screening and testing of prospective applicants. State offices and private employment agencies try to match listings of applicants with job openings. State or public agency services are free, but private agencies charge a fee when an applicant is hired.

The GREEN Marketer

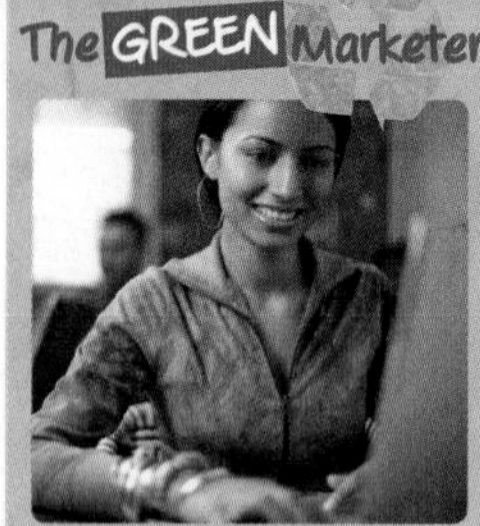

Telecommuting for Greener Productivity

Telecommuting can be good for workers and the environment. It reduces emissions created by driving to work. Another benefit is that it cuts down on traffic gridlock, especially in urban areas. Telecommuting often goes hand-in-hand with a flexible work schedule, which boosts workers' morale and helps them balance work and family responsibilities.

Perk for Employees Companies that allow telecommuting also have an edge in attracting top job candidates. Some 14 million Americans telecommute at least one day a week, and the number is growing.

Mathematics

Calculate Ray works from home one day a week. He lives 13.5 miles from his office, and his car gets 24 miles per gallon of gas. How many gallons of gas will Ray save each week, thanks to telecommuting? How much would he save if his car only got 18 miles per gallon?

NCTM Number and Operations Compute fluently and make reasonable estimates.

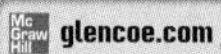
glencoe.com

Get an activity on green marketing.

EXPLAIN

Mini Project

Differentiated Instruction

Kinesthetic Learners Organize students into groups. Each group should conduct research on the Internet to locate team building activities. Students should engage in the team building activity as a group, and then demonstrate a team building activity, preferably one with movement and physical activity, for the class. When all groups have finished presenting their team building activities, encourage the class to discuss how successful they think these activities were in fostering team spirit. Students should choose a team building activity that will foster a sense of unity and encourage team members to want to help one another succeed. Pick two of the group activities that the class will vote on. Label a section of the room for each activity. For example, the West wall of the classroom would be the scavenger hunt. Have students, individually, move the the section of the room of the activity that they are voting for. The class completes the winning activity.

Graphic Organizer

Display this diagram. Ask students to list management techniques.

Techniques		Result
Giving Clear Directions		
Being Consistent		
Treating Employees Fairly	=	**Motivated and Productive Employees**
Being Firm When Necessary		
Setting a Good Example		
Being Ethical		
Fostering Teamwork		

glencoe.com

iWB

Graphic Organizer Send students to the Online Learning Center to print this graphic organizer.

ELABORATE

MANAGEMENT STYLES

Ask these guiding questions to focus the discussion about management styles.

Guiding Questions

Contrast How is communication different in a democratic rather than an authoritarian management style?	democratic—communication flows in both directions; authoritarian—mostly top down
Predict What type of person would perform best under an authoritarian management style? Under a delegating style?	authoritarian—one who needs clear and complete directions; delegating—one who is a self-starter

Graphic Organizer

Display this web. Fill in the ovals with student suggestions.

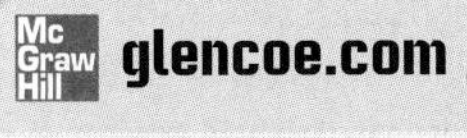
glencoe.com  iWB

Graphic Organizer Send students to the Online Learning Center to print this graphic organizer.

HUMAN RESOURCES

Present these guiding questions to focus the discussion about human resources.

Guiding Questions

Identify What records does a human resources office maintain?	Employee hirings, training program participation, performance evaluations, disciplinary actions, awards
Synthesize What companies would most likely recruit applicants online?	Companies looking for applicants who are comfortable communicating online.

The GREEN Marketer

Mathematics Answer If the car gets 24 miles per gallon, he would save 5.625 gallons of gas a week. If it gets 18 miles per gallon, he would save 7.5 gallons. Use these guiding questions to discuss this topic in more detail.

Guiding Questions

Analyze How does telecommuting help the environment?	Emissions are reduced; there is less traffic.
Apply If you were a young professional with two preschool-age children, what might be an advantage of telecommuting?	Advantage: You could take care of a sick child.

glencoe.com 

Activity Worksheet Send students to the Online Learning Center to download a Green Marketer worksheet activity.

SCHOOLS

High schools can be a good source for jobs that do not require specialized skills. Vocational and technical schools are sources for applicants who have learned a variety of specialized skills. Colleges are the source for applicants with higher-level skills.

DISCRIMINATION AND THE LAW

Laws against discrimination govern employers and recruitment agencies. These laws apply before an employee is hired. It is important to avoid discriminatory remarks and actions in all recruiting efforts. Federal law prohibits employers from discriminating on the basis of race, color, religion, gender, national origin, age, sexual orientation, or disability. The U.S. Equal Employment Opportunity Commission enforces and regulates these laws.

HIRING NEW EMPLOYEES

For the employer, the purpose of the interview is to determine whether an individual has the skills and abilities to perform well on the job.

Before managers interview job applicants, they must follow all the laws that govern the hiring process. They should be aware of which kinds of questions are illegal or unacceptable.

It is a good idea to conduct at least two interviews with applicants who seem well qualified. It is also a good idea to have at least two people interview final applicants. Ask only questions that are job related. If you are interviewing more than one applicant for the same job, ask each one exactly the same questions in exactly the same order. You need to allow the applicant to ask questions, too. It is the interviewer's responsibility to explain such things as wages and benefits.

Before hiring an applicant, most employers do some pre-employment testing. It may include an aptitude test to predict how well an applicant can perform certain tasks. Some companies give personality tests. Many companies ask prospective employees to be tested for illegal drugs.

ORIENTATION AND TRAINING PROGRAMS

Orienting new employees includes more than simply training them for their positions. It is important to make new employees feel valued and welcome and to familiarize them with the working environment. Orientation may take as little as a couple of hours or as long as a few days.

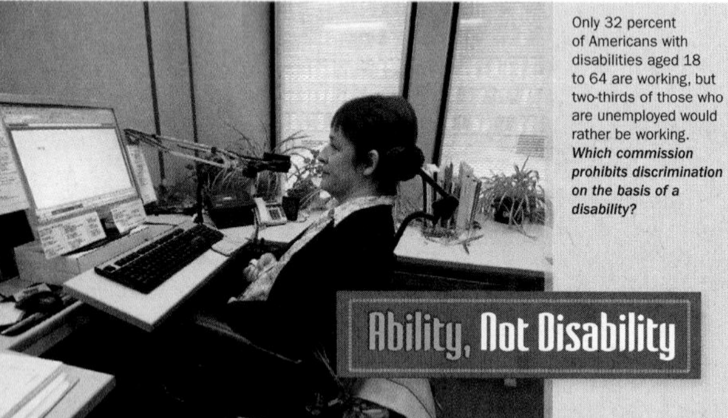

Only 32 percent of Americans with disabilities aged 18 to 64 are working, but two-thirds of those who are unemployed would rather be working. ***Which commission prohibits discrimination on the basis of a disability?***

The Interview

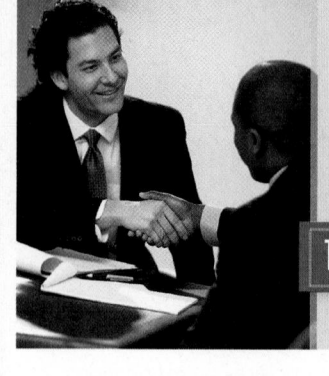

For the company, the purpose of a job interview is to determine whether an applicant can perform well on the job. ***As a manager, how would you prepare to interview several applicants for the same job?***

Orientation commonly includes the following:

- Tour of the company facilities and introductions to coworkers
- Description of the company's history, mission, and values
- Training on use and routine maintenance of equipment, such as point-of-sale systems, product scanners, computers, and printers
- Information on locations of facilities
- Information about payroll, benefits, and various company policies

All new employees need on-the-job training. As a supervisor, you may train new employees yourself or delegate this task to an experienced employee. Make sure that all job duties are explained and that new employees understand how to complete them.

SCHEDULING EMPLOYEES

Employee scheduling is the process of determining which employees should work at what times. Very small companies can handle the scheduling of employees quite simply without any special computer program. Today, though, most companies use some type of computer scheduling.

HANDLING COMPLAINTS AND GRIEVANCES

Employee complaints or grievances should be taken just as seriously as customer complaints. Most employee complaints fall into one of three categories: other employees, the quality of the company's product or service, or their own work situation.

Complaints about other employees should be handled with care and discretion. Conflicts in the workplace can damage morale and productivity. Some employees care about the quality of the company's products and bring problems to the attention of management. The employee who has complained should be kept informed at every step.

When a complaint involves the employee's work situation, gather the facts, report the findings to the employee who has complained, and make your decision. Then clearly explain to the employee the reasons and nature of your decision.

In most business situations, a grievance is considered more serious than a complaint. Agreements between management and labor unions almost always include a procedure for processing a complaint against the company.

EXPLAIN

HIRING NEW EMPLOYEES

Explain to students that the importance of making good hiring decisions cannot be overemphasized because these employees might work for the company for many years to come. Then use these guiding questions to focus the discussion about hiring new employees.

Guiding Questions

Recall What is the purpose of a job interview?	to determine whether the applicant has skills and abilities to perform well on the job
Summarize What are three tips to follow when conducting an interview?	Only ask questions that are job related; ask each applicant the same questions in the same order; have at least two interviewers for final applicants; allow applicants to ask questions; do not ask illegal questions.

Visual Literacy

Ability, Not Disability Caption Answer Read the caption question to students: ***Which commission prohibits discrimination on the basis of a disability?*** U.S. Equal Employment Opportunity Commission Discuss with students that it is illegal to take into account certain types of personal characteristics, such as physical abilities, sex, race, and religion, when hiring individuals. According to the U.S. government, the exception is when a specific characteristic is "a bona fide occupational qualification." Explain that "bona fide" means genuine or legitimate. Then ask: ***In what situations might it be legitimate to require that an applicant be a female?*** Possible answers: an acting position that requires a woman, a women's restroom attendant, a trainer at an all-women's gym.

Critical Thinking

Inform students that employees in human resources have access to information that other workers do not have. For example, human resources will keep on file an employee's personal information, performance evaluations, and disciplinary actions. Ask: ***What qualities should a person working in human resources possess?*** Tactful, discreet, ethical, aware of boundaries, able to keep personal information private.

ELABORATE

ORIENTATION AND TRAINING PROGRAMS

Explain that the word *orientation* refers to the process of making someone familiar with a particular situation. Then ask these guiding questions to focus the discussion on orientation and training programs.

Guiding Questions

Analyze Why might a supervisor delegate the training of a new employee to an experienced employee?	Possible answers: The experienced employee might be more knowledgeable about the specific task; supervisors should delegate whenever possible.
Predict How might a company be affected if an employee is properly trained for his position but the company's mission statement and values have not been explained to him?	Possible answer: The employee would not understand how his or her job fit into the overall company goals, and therefore might not feel motivated to work at the highest level.

Reading: Scaffolding Questions
Go to the Online Learning Center to view a video clip in which a teacher uses a series of questions to lead a student to an appropriate verbal response.

Visual Literacy

The Interview Caption Answer Read the caption question to students: ***As a manager, how would you prepare to interview several applicants for the same job?*** become familiar with the specific skills and abilities required for the position; talk with experienced workers who performed the same or similar jobs; create a clearly written detailed list of interview questions and make certain none of the questions were illegal; read over any résumés and cover letters submitted by applicants. Then ask: ***What might happen if you were poorly prepared to interview the applicants?*** Possible answer: The company might suffer for many years because the person hired was not the best choice; the company might miss out on hiring an applicant who would have excelled.

HANDLING COMPLAINTS AND GRIEVANCES

Use these guiding questions to focus the discussion on handling employee complaints and grievances.

Guiding Questions

Explain What should companies do to simplify handling complaints about an employee's salary?	Companies should have a pay range for each job and a way to deviate from that range for outstanding work.
Analyze Why should employee complaints be taken as seriously as customer complaints?	If employee complaints are ignored, workplace morale can suffer and productivity can go down.

Mini Projects

Extension

Investigating Laws Concerning Interviewing Employees Have students work in pairs to develop a written set of job interview questions for a position of their choice. Remind students that only job-related questions should be asked. Have students conduct research to determine what questions would be illegal (such as those related age, unless a person's age is relevant to the position.) When students are done writing their questions, have them take turns using the questions to interview one another. Students should write a list of job interview questions. All questions should be clearly stated, apply directly to the skills needed for the position, and follow the law. For example, questions related to religion may be asked if the individual would be working as a leader in a specific religious organization. However, if religion has nothing to do with the position, such questions would be illegal.

Using Teamwork to Develop a Solution Organize students into groups of four or five. Tell them that they work at a factory that operates 24 hours a day, every day of the year. Employees work 10-hour days, four days a week. Currently, there is considerable dissatisfaction because many employees request the same vacation time during the holidays. Some employees feel that those who have worked there longer always get the days off they request, leaving new employees to work the holidays. Give the groups 15 minutes to develop a solution they think is fair. Ask each group to report their solution to the class. Have the class critique the solutions. Students may choose to give points to each worker that can be redeemed for holiday time. Workers who have been there longer might get more points. Taking off some holidays will require more points.

Career Chatroom

Flash Shelton
Owner/President
Just Fix It, Inc.

What do you do at work?

We do home repair and remodel work for residential and commercial properties. Besides managing the business, meeting with customers, and following up on jobs, I am always thinking of ways to bring in new customers and keep the ones I *have* happy. To market the business, we use ads in phonebooks and on the Internet. Our Web site and involvement with community events are good sources of advertising, too.

What is your key to success?

Being successful requires knowledge, skills in management, networking, communication and marketing, customer service, reliability, trustworthiness, and a great imagination.

What skills are most important to you?

Overall knowledge of the job and good management skills are essential. You need drive and determination. Customer service and people skills are key. Another important skill is the ability to hire good help. Finally, take pride in what you do—it's not *just* a job.

glencoe.com

Read more about this career and complete a Career Exploration Activity.

ASSESSING EMPLOYEE PERFORMANCE

Assessment enables a manager to develop better workers and a more efficient and profitable company. In many companies, newly hired employees are placed on probation for a period of three to six months. Near the end of the probationary period, the employee is evaluated. If performance is satisfactory, the employee's status is changed to permanent. Usually, all employees are evaluated yearly. In many companies, the employee completes a self-evaluation form, and the supervisor completes the same form on the employee. Then a meeting is scheduled so that the supervisor and the employee can compare and discuss any differences in opinion.

REMEDIAL ACTION

It is the supervisor's responsibility to discuss substandard performance with the employee. Sometimes, remedial action is necessary. **Remedial action** is a means of encouraging appropriate workplace behavior in order to improve employee performance. Two approaches to remedial action are preventive discipline and corrective discipline.

PREVENTIVE DISCIPLINE

Preventive discipline focuses on managing employees in a way that prevents behavior that might require directly disciplining an employee. Its purpose is to encourage employees to follow the rules. Preventive discipline techniques might include involving employees in setting standards, encouraging employees to meet standards, and communicating standards clearly. It is also helpful to implement methods for controlling absences and to implement training programs in self-discipline and the recognition and prevention of workplace harassment.

CORRECTIVE DISCIPLINE

In some cases, corrective discipline is necessary. This usually begins with a verbal warning and an explanation of what will be required. Next is a written warning to the employee with a copy for the employee's personnel file. If the problem is not resolved, the third action is suspension from work without pay. The suspension usually lasts from one to five days and comes with a warning that if the problem is not corrected, the employee may be fired.

Corrective counseling is sometimes effective. This involves a discussion between the employee and a human resources counselor about the problem and what must be done to correct it.

DISMISSING EMPLOYEES

Most companies have to face the task of firing an employee for poor performance or bad behavior. Before this decision is made, certain procedures must be followed. A supervisor or manager must give the employee verbal and written warnings. This informs the employee that his or her performance or behavior is not acceptable. These warnings should be included on the employee's performance assessment form in the personnel file. The employee may be placed on probation and given time to change. When a decision is made to dismiss a worker, a letter of dismissal should be written, along with separate checks for final salary and severance pay.

THE EXIT INTERVIEW

When an employee leaves the company, an **exit interview** is arranged that will allow the employee and manager to get feedback. Exit interviews are often conducted with human resources rather than with the employee's supervisor. An employee always has the right not to participate in an exit interview.

An employee who is leaving voluntarily may have feedback on work conditions. If the employee is being dismissed, the reason should be discussed in the exit interview. Usually, an employee will be given advance notice of termination. As a manager, you must decide whether to have the employee continue working or leave immediately.

After You Read — Section 11.2

Review Key Concepts

1. **List** the three functions of management.
2. **Explain** the meaning of delegating responsibility.
3. **Discuss** the purpose of assessing employee performance.

Practice Academics

English Language Arts

4. As manager of your department, you have noticed that one of your employees has been complaining quite a bit. Complaints range from the lack of recent wage increases to dissatisfaction with the work situation to gripes about another employee whistling on the job. Discuss with a partner how you might address the situation or the employee.

NCTE 7 Conduct research and gather, evaluate, and synthesize data to communicate discoveries.

Mathematics

5. Grocery store clerks are negotiating with their company management for a 6.5-percent increase in their hourly wage. The average hourly wage of a clerk is $14.75. The company has 35 clerks who each work a 40-hour week, 50 weeks per year. The clerks receive a two-week paid vacation each year. What would the pay raise cost per year?

NCTM Number and Operations Compute fluently and make reasonable estimates.

Math Concept **Number and Operations: Computation** Fluent computation requires a logical sequence of steps.

Starting Hints To solve this problem, multiply the hourly wage by the decimal equivalent of 6.5 percent to find the increase in wages the employees want. Multiply the number of employees by the number of hours worked each week, 40, to determine the total number of hours worked by all the employees.

For help, go to the **Math Skills Handbook** located at the back of this book.

glencoe.com Check your answers.

264 | Unit 4 · Skills for Marketing

Chapter 11 · Management Skills | 265

ELABORATE

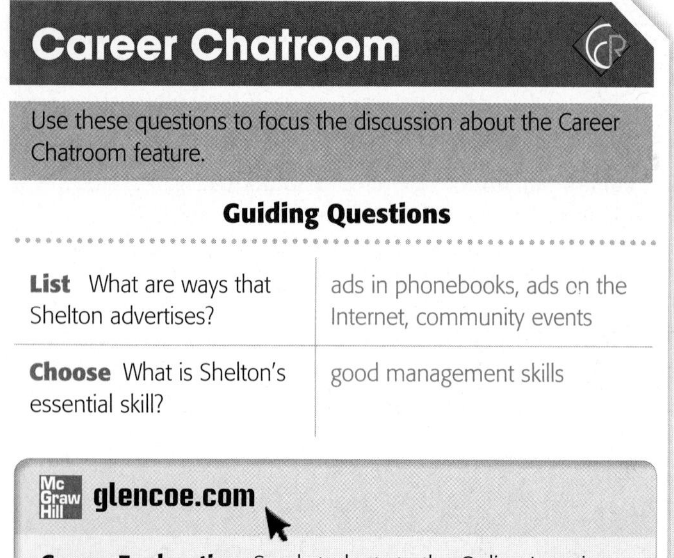

Career Chatroom

Use these questions to focus the discussion about the Career Chatroom feature.

Guiding Questions

List What are ways that Shelton advertises?	ads in phonebooks, ads on the Internet, community events
Choose What is Shelton's essential skill?	good management skills

glencoe.com

Career Exploration Send students to the Online Learning Center to find more information about this career and to get a Career Exploration Activity.

Reinforce Vocabulary

Remedial Action—Denotative Meaning Write *remedial* on the board. Read aloud this sentence: Remedial action is a means of encouraging appropriate workplace behavior. Tell students that *remedial* means "concerned with the correction of a faulty habit." Then ask for a definition of *remedial* when used in the workplace. something that is done to help an employee improve

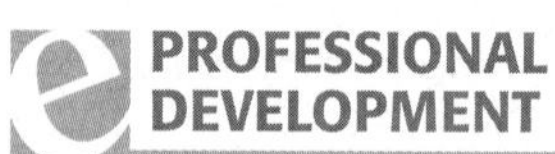

Reading: Connecting the Pieces
In this video clip a teacher helps students develop predictions and inferences.

Critical Thinking

Create an informal panel of three judges. Form two teams to debate whether preventative or corrective discipline is more effective. Student debate teams should offer arguments and facts to prove that their discipline is more effective. Have judges decide which team gave the better argument.

EVALUATE

Graphic Organizer

Display the organizer. Ask students to list the two types of remedial action discussed in this section. Then ask them to list characteristics of each.

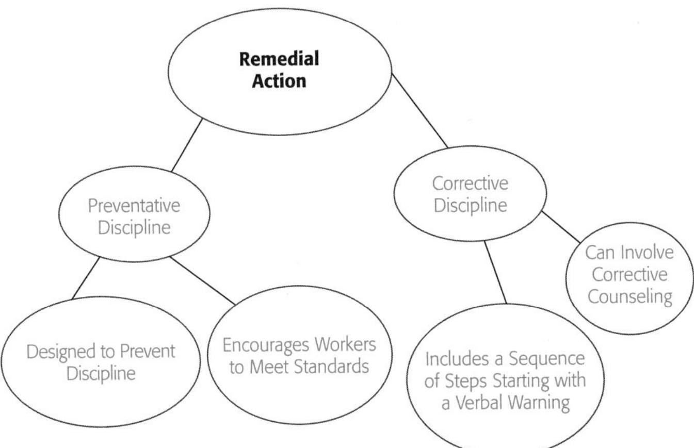

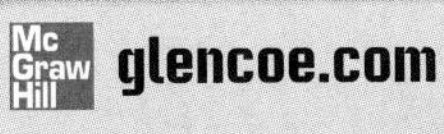

glencoe.com iWB

Graphic Organizer Send students to the Online Learning Center to print this graphic organizer.

DISMISSING EMPLOYEES

Ask these guiding questions to focus the discussion about dismissing employees.

Guiding Questions

Recall What procedures are followed before an employee is dismissed?	A verbal warning is given first, then a written warning. Suspension without pay and corrective counseling may also occur.
Infer Why do you think it is vital that procedures that occur before an employee is dismissed be documented?	It is important to have documentation in case there are questions in the future concerning why the employee was dismissed.
Support Why do you think it is necessary to provide separate checks to cover a dismissed worker's final wage or salary and severance pay?	Answers will vary but students should provide a rationale to support their argument. Possible answer: The separate checks would be necessary because they would be recorded differently for accounting purposes.

After You Read Section 11.2

Review Key Concepts

1. The three functions of management are planning, organizing, and controlling.
2. Delegating means giving jobs or duties to other people to do, rather than trying to do everything yourself.
3. The purpose of assessing employee performance is to develop better workers and a more effective and profitable company.

Practice Academics

English Language Arts

4. Responses will vary. Students might suggest they talk with the employee about why he or she seems to be unhappy with the current work situation. They might find there is an underlying situation that both they and the employee can work toward correcting. At least the employee would know that the supervisor is concerned about him or her.

Mathematics

5. \$69,888 (\$14.75 × 0.065 = \$0.95875; \$0.96 × 35 × 40 × 52 = \$69,888)

glencoe.com

Send students to the Online Learning Center to check their answers.

Chapter 11 Visual Summary

Management Skills

Vertically organized companies have top management, middle management, and supervisory-level management. Horizontal companies have top and middle management and self-managed teams.

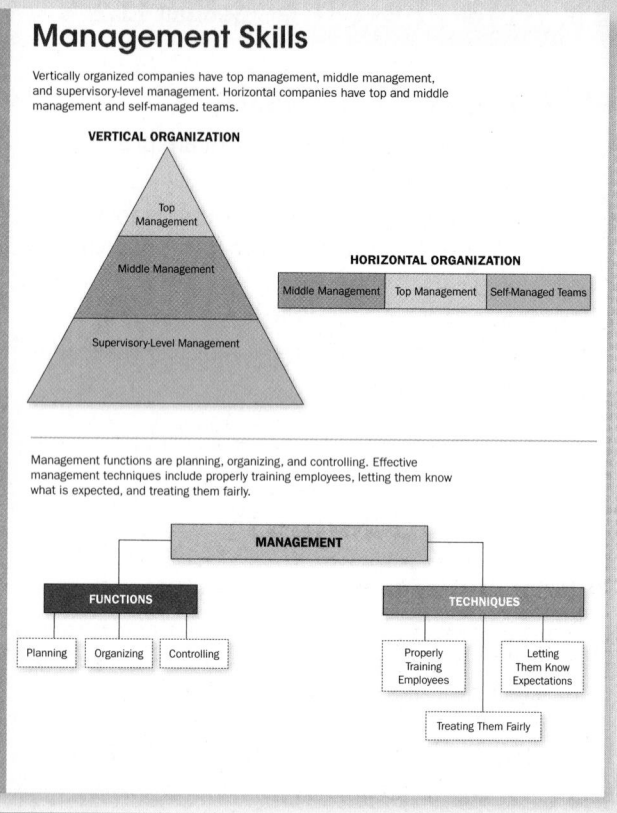

VERTICAL ORGANIZATION

Top Management

Middle Management

Supervisory-Level Management

HORIZONTAL ORGANIZATION

Middle Management | Top Management | Self-Managed Teams

Management functions are planning, organizing, and controlling. Effective management techniques include properly training employees, letting them know what is expected, and treating them fairly.

MANAGEMENT

FUNCTIONS: Planning, Organizing, Controlling

TECHNIQUES: Properly Training Employees, Letting Them Know Expectations, Treating Them Fairly

Review and Activities

Written Summary

- The global marketplace will influence the kind of leadership companies will need in the future.
- Businesses are organized in one of two ways: vertically or horizontally.
- Traditional, vertically organized companies have three levels of management: top management, middle management, and supervisory-level management.
- Horizontal companies have top and middle management. Horizontally organized companies have self-managed teams that set their own goals and make their own decisions.
- Basic management functions are planning, organizing, and controlling.
- Effective management techniques involve properly training employees, letting them know what is expected of them, and treating them fairly.
- In case of poor performance or unacceptable behavior, the employee should receive warnings, which should be included in the employee's personnel file. A letter of dismissal should be given to the employee at dismissal time, along with the final salary amount due.

Review Content Vocabulary and Academic Vocabulary

1. Create multiple-choice test questions for each content and academic vocabulary term.

Content Vocabulary
- management (p. 253)
- vertical organization (p. 253)
- top management (p. 253)
- middle management (p. 253)
- supervisory-level management (p. 253)
- horizontal organization (p. 254)
- empowerment (p. 254)
- planning (p. 257)
- organizing (p. 257)
- controlling (p. 257)
- mission statement (p. 258)
- remedial action (p. 264)
- exit interview (p. 265)

Academic Vocabulary
- resource (p. 253)
- individual (p. 255)
- identify (p. 257)
- require (p. 258)

Assess for Understanding

2. **Contrast** What is the difference between horizontally organized and vertically organized companies?
3. **Identify** What are three levels of management?
4. **Describe** How does a self-managed team function?
5. **Consider** How do the three functions of management affect employees?
6. **Imagine** What are the benefits of the six management techniques used by effective managers?
7. **Create** What would you include in an orientation program for your school?
8. **Consider** How can a company benefit from empowerment?
9. **Compose** How would you notify an employee that he or she needs remedial action? Write your response.

EVALUATE

Visual Summary

Express Creativity Ask students to create a visual summary that illustrates a concept in the chapter. Encourage students to use different formats for their visual summaries, such as a storyboard, a timeline, a cause-and-effect diagram, or a slide show. Visual summaries will vary depending on the concept depicted. Questions to ask when assessing a visual summary include:

- Is the summary clear, economical, and simple?
- Are any important steps or concepts left out?
- Are steps or concepts arranged in the same order as the original?
- Does the summary reveal a pattern that connects the details?
- Does the summary locate and highlight the most important information?

Review Content Vocabulary and Academic Vocabulary

1. Multiple-choice test questions will vary. Sample questions for the first two vocabulary terms:

1. A vertically organized company has three levels of ________.
   a. empowerment
   b. management
   c. resources
   d. teams
   Correct answer: B (management)
2. In a ________, the company has a hierarchical structure and each level's responsibilities are clearly defined.
   a. horizontal organization
   b. supervisory-level management organization
   c. top management organization
   d. vertical organization
   Correct answer: D (vertical organization)

EVALUATE

Assess for Understanding

2. In horizontally organized companies, the traditional hierarchy of management present in vertically organized companies is flattened and replaced by teams that manage themselves.

3. Levels of management are top management, middle management, and supervisory-level management.

4. Self-managing teams set their own goals and make their own decisions rather than being told what to do by a supervisor. They are organized by process and are customer oriented.

5. Planning—affects employees by setting specific goals and providing a path by which employees can help in reaching these goals. Organizing—affects employees because it assigns them specific tasks and provides guidance for completing these tasks. Controlling—affects employees by setting standards they are expected to meet and evaluations to provide them with feedback.

6. These techniques lead workers to produce a better quality product or service because they understand what is expected of them; they feel they are being treated fairly; they are responsible for their actions; and they have a sense of responsibility toward their coworkers and the company at large. Employees who enjoy their jobs stay longer, which saves on training costs. Overall, having productive, capable employees increases company profits.

7. Answers may include: set up the orientation program so that new students would feel welcome and valued; ask the heads of the school, including the principal, to give short speeches describing the school, why these new students will enjoy attending it, the kinds of academic and nonacademic programs available; arrange for students to be given tours in small groups led by students familiar with the school, the classrooms, cafeteria, gym, and music facilities; students would be encouraged to ask questions during the tour; arrange small discussion groups to share their thoughts and concerns; assign a "buddy," a student who was already familiar with the school, to each new student.

8. A company can benefit from empowerment because a strong sense of team spirit and company loyalty generally leads to employees producing more and higher-quality work, which increases profits.

9. Responses will vary. Sample response: I would clearly state why the employee needs remedial action. For example, if the employee failed to meet a specific standard, I would cite that standard. I would explain how the employee's behavior needs to change, the time frame in which this change needs to take place, and any follow-up procedures that will occur. I would encourage the employee to share his or her thoughts on this subject, listen carefully, and respond appropriately.

21st Century Skills

Leadership Skills

10. **Management and Motivation** A week ago you were promoted to a supervisory level in charge of 20 employees that manufacture electric motors. On the first day you noticed that there were problems, but you decided to observe for a few days as you plan what action to take. Some workers are sloppy in their work, some seem unsure about how to perform certain tasks, and there is general disharmony in the group. What are some actions that you will take to improve production, behavior, and harmony? Share suggestions with a partner.

Financial Literacy Skills

11. **Sales Projections** Your company produces and markets electronic equipment. Sales last year totaled $2,776,540. The company goal is to increase sales by 5 percent this year. Your division goal is to achieve 20 percent of total sales. What is the dollar value of your division goal?

Everyday Ethics

12. **Taking Charge** You are a cashier at a clothing store. Your manager tells you she must go out of town for the weekend, and that you will be in charge of the store while she is away, but you will not receive extra pay. She says if anyone asks to speak to a manager to say you are the manager. Is it ethical to tell customers that you are the manager, even if you are a substitute manager? Discuss what you would do in this situation and why.

e-Marketing Skills

13. **Feasibility Study** You are the manager of a small computer and electronics store. The owner has asked that you research the feasibility of setting up an online business that would be operated from your store. Research this topic and write your recommendations.

Build Academic Skills

Social Studies

14. **Business Locations** An automobile company is considering opening a new assembly plant in your state. The plant would add about 10,000 new jobs and require workers of all education and training levels. What part of the state would you suggest and why? Share a list of reasons for your selection.

English Language Arts

15. **Workplace Environment** Select a clothing store that carries clothing you like. Research and write about ethical policies the company follows in terms of working conditions for employees.

Mathematics

16. **Plan Office Space** Calculate the square feet of space required to organize an office area to accommodate six employees. Each cubicle will be 25 square feet. Plan for three cubicles on each side of the office (for a total of six cubicles) and a 4-foot wide hallway down the middle of the office.

Math Concept **Geometry: Calculating Area** The formula for area is length times width. Area is always measured in square units, such as square feet.

NCSS III G People, Places, & Environments Describe and compare how people create places that reflect culture, human needs, government policy, and current values and ideals as they design and build specialized buildings, neighborhoods, shopping centers, urban centers, industrial parks, and the like.

NCTE 7 Conduct research and gather, evaluate, and synthesize data to communicate discoveries.

NCTM Geometry Use visualization, spatial reasoning, and geometric modeling to solve problems.

For help, go to the **Math Skills Handbook** located at the back of this book.

Standardized Test Practice

Directions Read the following questions. On a separate piece of paper, write the best possible answer for each one.

1. Self-managed teams are part of which type of organization?
   A. traditional
   B. vertical
   C. horizontal
   D. none of the above
2. Since 2009, it has been illegal to fire employees.
   T
   F
3. When an employee leaves a company, the human resources department will usually arrange a(n) ________.

Test-Taking Tip
If time allows, review both questions and answers so you can avoid misreading a question.

DECA Connection Role Play

Manager
Bicycle Store

Situation Assume the role of newly hired manager of a bicycle store. The store sells and services a wide range of bicycles for individuals who enjoy cycling as a hobby. The store also sells a comprehensive selection of cycling accessories that include bike helmets, gloves, water bottles, and clothing. Eight sales associates who are all experienced cyclists staff the store. The staff is knowledgeable about the bicycles and accessories the store sells.

Store sales are acceptable, but not great, and staff morale is low. The shop's owner (judge) has hired you to improve sales and staff morale. You have had a discussion with each of the sales associates to get to know each of them and to try to discover the reasons for the low morale. You have learned that many of the sales associates feel that the previous manager did not appreciate their efforts and that their ideas regarding the shop were not taken seriously. You have determined that improving staff morale will help motivate the staff and lead to improved store sales.

Activity You are to outline some ways to improve staff morale. Once you have outlined your ideas you are to present them to the shop's owner (judge) before presenting them at this week's staff meeting.

Evaluation You will be evaluated on how well you meet the following performance indicators:

1. Explain the concept of management.
2. Explain the role of ethics in human resources management.
3. Demonstrate responsible behavior.
4. Explain the nature of staff communication.
5. Make oral presentations.

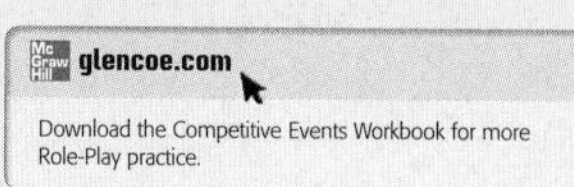

Download the Competitive Events Workbook for more Role-Play practice.

EVALUATE

Leadership Skills

10. Students' suggestions will vary. Because employees have been allowed to continue with their unprofessional behavior over a period of time, it is important to realize that changes also will have to take place gradually. Being honest but considerate in sharing your concerns with workers is vital. Explain that you realize everyone requires occasional refresher courses in procedures and that you are going to arrange for everyone to receive them. Requiring everyone to receive this training will show that you are fair and will treat everyone equally. Setting the example of being open and honest will encourage others to do the same and should increase harmony and a willingness to cooperate with the group.

Financial Literacy Skills

11. $583,073.40 ([$2,776,540 × .05] × 0.20)

Everyday Ethics

12. Responses will vary, but students should provide thoughtful reasons for their opinions. Some students will state it is okay to say they are the manager because that is what their manager instructed them to do. Others may feel this is unethical and misleading. In this case, they should immediately explain to the manager, in a straightforward manner, their discomfort with being placed in this position.

e-Marketing Skills

13. Students' recommendations will vary. Students should write a specific recommendation concerning setting up an online store based on research they have conducted. For example, students might state that they think setting up an online business would not be a good decision because there are already several large online stores that sell electronics at very low prices. These large stores have a much wider selection of electronics than they could offer. One reason the local store has thrived is because it provides high-quality installation and repair services, which would be virtually impossible with the online store unless the customers were local.

EVALUATE

Build Academic Skills

Social Studies

14. Student answers will vary depending on the state. Students might state that the assembly plant should be in or near a large metropolitan area because of the size of the required workforce. The area should have a potential workforce whose members have a wide variety of education and training backgrounds. It also should be near appropriate transportation resources so that raw materials can be transported in and finished goods can be transported out.

English Language Arts

15. Students should research the ethical policies in terms of working conditions at a clothing store. For example, the store might require that employees not work more than a certain number of hours a week, get a lunch hour, and get paid breaks. The store might have a policy concerning the fair treatment of all workers, regardless of their gender, race, or ethnicity. It also might have a written policy stating the steps employees should take if they feel that their supervisor is treating them unfairly.

Mathematics

16. 210 square feet ([25 × 6] + [4 × 15])

Standardized Test Practice

1. C horizontal
2. False
3. exit interview

DECA Connection Role Play

Evaluations will be based on these performance indicators:

1. **Explain the concept of management.** Management is the business function of planning, organizing, and controlling all available resources to achieve company goals. Businesses are typically organized either vertically or horizontally to achieve these goals. In a vertical organization, there is a hierarchical, up-and-down structure. Horizontal organization involves top management sharing decision-making with self-managing teams of workers who set their own goals and make their own decisions. Horizontal organization encourages workers to take responsibility for their own productivity.
2. **Explain the role of ethics in human resources management.** In human resources management, ethical behavior involves understanding how your actions affect others and striving to make honest and justified decisions for those under your supervision. It is important that employee complaints be taken just as seriously as customer complaints and that there be appropriate channels for dealing with them. Not showing favoritism, listening to employees' concerns, and making changes when appropriate are all signs of ethical behavior.
3. **Demonstrate responsible behavior.** Responsible behavior involves setting goals and then working to meet them. It also involves being trustworthy, consistent and dependable, and behaving ethically and treating people fairly and equally.
4. **Explain the nature of staff communication.** It is important that those individuals who supervise others, such as the owner of the bike shop, listen carefully to the concerns and ideas of the staff. When communicating with employees, supervisors must state their expectations and goals clearly. They must encourage teamwork by being supportive and respectful of all staff.
5. **Make oral presentations.** Students should be able to make a well organized oral presentation to the shop owner in which they explain their ideas for improving sales and staff morale at the bicycle shop.

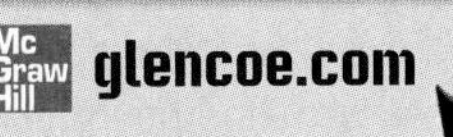

Role Plays For more DECA Role Plays, send students to the Online Learning Center to download the Competitive Events Workbook.

UNIT 4 **Marketing Internship Project**

Financial Literacy 101

to Teach Money Smarts

How much money do you have in your savings account, and what do you plan to do with it?

Scenario

Research indicates that close to 50 percent of high-school-aged teens are not financially literate. In the future, pensions are not going to be available to the younger generation as they may be replaced with 401(k) accounts. Stories abound about college students who charge so much money to credit cards that they get themselves in debt that lasts long after graduation.

As part of a statewide initiative, the local chamber of commerce has commissioned your company to create a Web site with an interactive program to make learning financial literacy fun and effective for young children and teens.

The Skills You'll Use

Academic Skills Reading, writing, social studies, researching, and analyzing

Basic Skills Speaking, listening, thinking, and interpersonal

Technology Skills Word processing, presentation, spreadsheet, telecommunication, and the Internet

NCTE 4 Use written language to communicate effectively.
NCTE 7 Conduct research and gather, evaluate, and synthesize data to communicate discoveries.

Your Objective

Design a fun-filled, interesting, and interactive "Financial Literacy 101" Web site that teaches children and teens about financial literacy.

STEP 1 Do Your Research

Conduct research to identify financial literacy programs that currently exist online. For example, search for national campaigns designed to help teens. Also search for credit unions and banks that sponsor financial literacy programs. As you conduct your research, answer these questions:

- What is the definition of financial literacy?
- What topics are included in financial literacy programs?
- How do financial literacy programs target young people?
- Which parts of the financial literacy programs will young people find interesting?

Write a summary of your research.

STEP 2 Plan Your Project

Now that you have completed your research, you need to begin planning your project.

- Conduct a survey of your peers to evaluate their financial literacy.
- Determine topics to be included in the financial literacy Web site.
- Design storyboards for a Web site that invites young people to learn about how to handle their own finances now and in the future.
- Plan interactive aspects of the Web site so that it is fun and interesting and young people will want to use it.
- Think about indicators that you can use to measure whether your program is effective.
- Use your knowledge of mathematics, communication skills, technology, and interpersonal skills to design an effective financial literacy program.

STEP 3 Connect with Your Community

- Gather published financial literacy materials from local banks and other financial institutions.
- Interview one or more trusted adults at home, at school, at work, or in your community about financial literacy. Consider talking to a business teacher at your school or ask a politician what financial literacy initiatives are being considered by the government.
- Takes notes during your interviews, and transcribe your notes after the interviews.

STEP 4 Share What You Learn

Assume your class is a committee from the Chamber of Commerce that will be in charge of approving the content of the financial literacy program.

- Present your project plan in an oral presentation. Be prepared to answer questions.
- Define financial literacy and explain its importance.
- Explain how to teach financial literacy skills to the younger generation.
- Present your Web-site design storyboards.
- Provide rationale for your ideas and your Web-site design.
- Use software to create a slide presentation to accompany your oral report.

STEP 5 Evaluate Your Marketing and Academic Skills

Your project will be evaluated based on the following:

- Knowledge of financial literacy and currently available programs
- Web-site design and interactive program for financial literacy
- Research to support your selection of topics and program features
- Organization and continuity of presentation
- Mechanics—presentation and neatness
- Speaking and listening skills

MARKETING CORE FUNCTIONS

Marketing Information Management
Market Planning

Marketing Internship Project Checklist

Plan

✓ Research financial literacy and explain its importance.
✓ Research currently available financial literacy programs.
✓ Design plans for an interactive Web site that teaches financial literacy.

Write

✓ Write a summary of your research.
✓ Explain why an interactive Web site about financial literacy is important.

Present

✓ Present research that supports the topics included in a financial literacy program.
✓ Present the design for your Web site.
✓ Suggest evaluation tools to measure the effectiveness of the program.

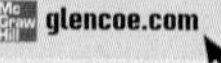

Evaluate Download a rubric you can use to evaluate your final project.

my marketing portfolio

Internship Report Once you have completed your Marketing Internship Project and oral presentation, put your written report and a few printouts of key slides from your oral presentation in your Marketing Portfolio.

Teen Driving Safety Program According to the National Highway Traffic Safety Administration, 35 percent of teen fatalities are due to motor vehicle accidents. Allstate Insurance Company cites additional facts: "Nearly 5,000 young people die in car crashes every year. Another 300,000 teens are injured in car crashes each year." Your firm wants to lower those statistics. What kind of interactive Web site can you design to help in that endeavor? What topics should be included and how can they be demonstrated? Prepare a written report and an oral presentation.

270 | Unit 4 · Skills for Marketing

Unit 4 · Skills for Marketing | 271

EVALUATE

Anticipation Activity

Project Objective Read the project objective aloud to students: ***Design a fun-filled, interesting, and interactive "Financial Literacy 101" Web site that teaches children and teens about financial literacy.*** Then remind students of these key points:

- Basic math skills are important in both personal and professional life.
- By applying technology and communication skills, you can develop Web sites that reach many people.

Ask students: ***What are some everyday math skills for financial literacy?*** Basic math skills include writing numbers in words, understanding and converting fractions, performing operations with decimals, using a calculator, performing percentage/decimal conversions, and reading graphs presenting mathematical data.

Ask students: ***What are some basic financial activities?*** Activities may include writing checks, balancing checking accounts, creating a budget, paying bills for rent and food, managing credit, purchasing online, paying bills online, getting a loan, and saving and/or investing money.

Graphic Organizer

Display this graphic organizer. Then ask students to name places in their communities and on the Internet to find financial literacy materials and information. Write down their ideas in the web. Answers will vary. Possible answers:

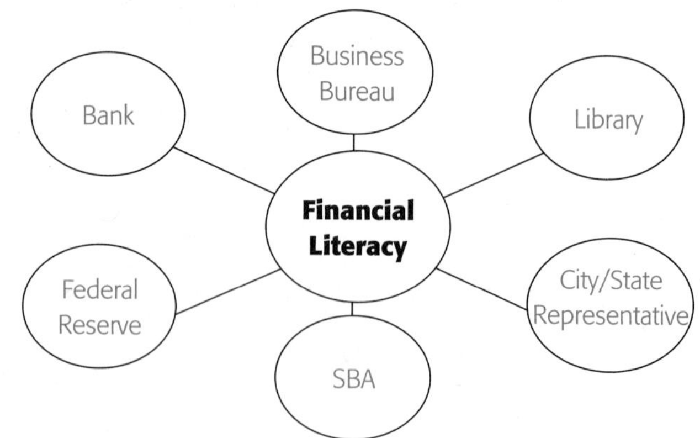

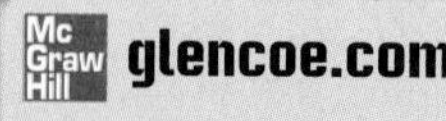

iWB

Graphic Organizer Send students to the Online Learning Center to print this graphic organizer.

EVALUATE

STEP 1 Do Your Research

Tell students that there are many places to find information they can use to develop their financial literacy Web sites. Students can use library and Internet resources, but they should also talk to people in the community. Encourage students to seek the opinions and ideas of trusted people they know.

STEP 2 Plan Your Project

Students should conduct a survey to evaluate users' needs and determine important topics before designing an interactive Web site. Students should explain why they chose their design and topics and provide indicators to measure the program's effectiveness. Students' explanation of the financial literacy Web site should include a discussion of mathematics, communication skills, technology, and interpersonal skills.

STEP 3 Connect with Your Community

Explain to students that connecting with members of the community is a great way to build relationships. Tell them that young people who build relationships with caring, responsible, and competent adults are more likely to achieve success in life. Encourage students to take part in opportunities for trusted adults to serve as mentors, coaches, advocates, and advisors, both formally and informally.

STEP 4 Share What You Learn

Students should present their ideas in a written report and oral presentation with presentation software. They should have at least one slide in their presentation for each key topic in the written report. Encourage students to speak clearly, use appropriate grammar and vocabulary, and actively engage the audience by making and maintaining eye contact and using movement (facial expressions, posture, gestures) to focus attention and interest.

STEP 5 Evaluate Your Marketing and Academic Skills

Have students use the Marketing Internship Project Checklist to help them to plan, write, and present their reports. Exemplary written reports will include information that clearly supports a central thesis, a single, distinct focus, generally well-developed ideas, well-phrased sentences that flow smoothly and are varied in length and structure, consistently precise word choice, and few, if any, errors in grammar, spelling, and mechanics.

glencoe.com

Evaluation Rubric Send students to the Online Learning Center to get a rubric to evaluate their projects.

Culminating Activity

Explain to students that one way to design a Web site is to start with making a site map. Many Web sites for companies and organizations include a link to the site map on the sidebar or top banner menu. Have students find an example of a site map of a Web site of their choice, possibly one that is similar to their design. Ask students: ***What is the purpose of the site map? How can it help in the design process?*** It outlines what can be found on each page within the Web site and presents global navigation. It guides viewers to whatever information they choose and provides direct links to all parts of the Web site. When creating a Web site, having a site map can provide an overview of the project and help the designer organize all components in the most effective and logical order for navigation. It can also serve as a checklist for components when the design is completed.

my marketing portfolio

Internship Report Have students put their written reports and printouts of key slides from their oral presentations in their marketing portfolio.

Teen Driving Safety Program Direct students to determine information and topics to present to teens in order to improve teen driving statistics, and then design a basic Web site with a report and presentation to help reach that goal. Students' completed Web-site plans should include all of the elements and answer all of the questions included in the Marketing Internship Project on this page. This additional activity can build relevance for students who are motivated to learn about other specific business and industries. Relevance shifts the focus to what motivates individual students to learn.

UNIT 5 Selling

PLANNING GUIDE AND RESOURCES

	Print	Digital
Unit 5 Selling		Unit 5 Fast Files: Marketing Internship Project Activity Connect Online Learning Center through glencoe.com
Chapter 12 **Selling Overview**	Student Activity Workbook: Chapter 12 DECA Connection Role Play; Chapter 12 Vocabulary Activity; Section Note Taking Activities; Chapter Academics Activity; Section Study Skills Activities; Section Real-World Applications Activities Mathematics for Marketing Workbook Marketing Research Project Workbook School-to-Career Activity Workbook	Unit 5 Fast Files: Chapter 12 Discovery Project Worksheet and Rubric; Chapter 12 Green Marketer Activity; Chapter 12 Digital Nation Activity; Section Graphic Organizers; Section Outlines with Key Terms and Definitions; Section Summaries ExamView Assessment Suite, Chapter 12 Connect Online Learning Center through glencoe.com
Chapter 13 **Beginning the Sales Process**	Student Activity Workbook: Chapter 13 DECA Connection Role Play; Chapter 13 Vocabulary Activity; Section Note Taking Activities; Chapter Academics Activity; Section Study Skills Activities; Section Real-World Applications Activities Mathematics for Marketing Workbook Marketing Research Project Workbook School-to-Career Activity Workbook	Unit 5 Fast Files: Chapter 13 Discovery Project Worksheet and Rubric; Chapter 13 Green Marketer Activity; Chapter 13 Digital Nation Activity; Section Graphic Organizers; Section Outlines with Key Terms and Definitions; Section Summaries ExamView Assessment Suite, Chapter 13 Connect Online Learning Center through glencoe.com
Chapter 14 **Presenting the Product**	Student Activity Workbook: Chapter 14 DECA Connection Role Play; Chapter 14 Vocabulary Activity; Section Note Taking Activities; Chapter Academics Activity; Section Study Skills Activities; Section Real-World Applications Activities Mathematics for Marketing Workbook Marketing Research Project Workbook School-to-Career Activity Workbook	Unit 5 Fast Files: Chapter 14 Discovery Project Worksheet and Rubric; Chapter 14 Green Marketer Activity; Chapter 14 Digital Nation Activity; Section Graphic Organizers; Section Outlines with Key Terms and Definitions; Section Summaries ExamView Assessment Suite, Chapter 14 Connect Online Learning Center through glencoe.com
Chapter 15 **Closing the Sale**	Student Activity Workbook: Chapter 15 DECA Connection Role Play; Chapter 15 Vocabulary Activity; Section Note Taking Activities; Chapter Academics Activity; Section Study Skills Activities; Section Real-World Applications Activities Mathematics for Marketing Workbook Marketing Research Project Workbook School-to-Career Activity Workbook	Unit 5 Fast Files: Chapter 15 Discovery Project Worksheet and Rubric; Chapter 15 Green Marketer Activity; Chapter 15 Digital National Activity; Section Graphic Organizers; Section Outlines with Key Terms and Definitions; Section Summaries ExamView Assessment Suite, Chapter 15 Connect Online Learning Center through glencoe.com
Chapter 16 **Using Math in Sales**	Student Activity Workbook: Chapter 16 DECA Connection Role Play; Chapter 16 Vocabulary Activities; Section Note Taking Activities; Chapter Academics Activity; Section Study Skills Activities; Section Real-World Applications Activities Mathematics for Marketing Workbook Marketing Research Project Workbook School-to-Career Activity Workbook	Unit 5 Fast Files: Chapter 16 Discovery Project Worksheet and Rubric; Chapter Green Marketer Activity; Chapter 16 Digital Nation Activity; Section Graphic Organizers; Section Outlines with Key Terms and Definitions; Section Summaries ExamView Assessment Suite, Chapter 16 Connect Online Learning Center through glencoe.com

McGRAW-HILL PROFESSIONAL DEVELOPMENT

Perkins IV has placed more emphasis than ever on providing quality professional development for Career and Technology educators. The legislation mandates that the focus of professional development be the integration and reinforcement of academic competencies in order to improve student achievement. Specifically, Perkins requires measurements of students' academic success. McGraw-Hill answers the challenge for strong and effective professional development with a five-prong **Online Professional Development for Integrating Academics.**

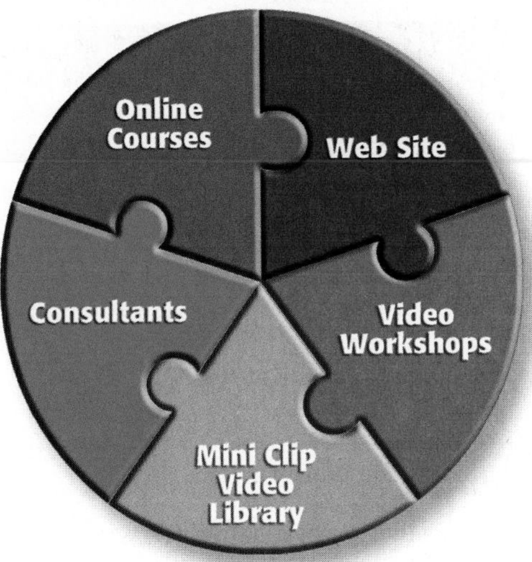

For pricing and ordering information contact your McGraw-Hill Sales Representative.

VIDEO LIBRARY

The McGraw-Hill Professional Development Mini-Clip Video Library, referenced for your convenience at the point of use, provides teaching strategies to strengthen academic and learning skills. Go to the Online Learning Center to view these professional development video clips for Unit 5:

Chapter 12: Selling Overview
- **ELL: Low-Risk Environment:** An author discusses a low-risk environment for learning. (p. 278)

Chapter 13: Beginning the Sales Process
- **ELL: Language Practice:** Students work together to review new content. (p. 297)
- **ELL: Direct Vocabulary Instruction:** Students create vocabulary cards to build a dictionary. (p. 307)

Chapter 14: Presenting the Product
- **Reading: Strategies for Student Achievement:** Teachers discuss strategies for helping all learners meet curriculum standards. (p. 321)
- **ELL: Accessing Prior Knowledge:** A teacher helps students make connections between what they already know and the topic of an upcoming reading selection. (p. 333)

Chapter 15: Closing the Sale
- **ELL: Elaborating on Student Responses:** A teacher elaborates on a student response. (p. 345)
- **ELL: Academic Language:** Two experts discuss the importance of addressing academic language. (p. 346)
- **ELL: Comprehension and English Language Learners:** An author discusses comprehension strategies for English language learners. (p. 350)

Chapter 16: Using Math in Sales
- **Reading: Strategic Readers:** An author discusses the characteristics of strategic readers. (p. 366)
- **ELL: Content Vocabulary:** A teacher provides students with opportunities to practice their academic vocabulary. (p. 373)

UNIT OVERVIEW

Sections	Objectives	Common Core State Standards College and Career Readiness
Section 12.1 **The Sales Function**	• Explain the purpose and goal of the selling function. • Discuss how selling is related to the marketing concept. • Describe Customer Relationship Management. • Analyze sales trends and technology. • Summarize sales management responsibilities. • Explain legal and ethical sales issues.	• **Writing** Conduct short as well as more sustained research projects based on focused questions, demonstrating understanding of the subject under investigation.
Section 12.2 **Sales Careers**	• Define personal selling. • Identify sales positions. • List the steps in the sales process. • Analyze how customers make buying decisions. • Evaluate selling as a career option.	• **Writing** Produce clear and coherent writing in which the development, organization, and style are appropriate to task, purpose, and audience.
Section 13.1 **Preliminary Activities**	• Explain how salespeople get ready to sell. • List sources of product information. • Explain feature-benefit selling and how it creates selling points. • Identify consumer buying motives. • List prospecting methods and explain how prospects are qualified.	• **Writing** Conduct short as well as more sustained research projects based on focused questions, demonstrating understanding of the subject under investigation.
Section 13.2 **First Steps of a Sale**	• Demonstrate how to properly approach a customer to open a sale. • Differentiate between organizational and retail sales approaches. • List three retail sales approach methods. • Discuss when and how to determine customer needs.	• **Writing** Produce clear and coherent writing in which the development, organization, and style are appropriate to task, purpose, and audience.
Section 14.1 **Product Presentation**	• Describe the goal of the product presentation. • Explain how products are selected for the presentation. • Explain what to say during the product presentation. • List techniques that help create effective product presentations.	• **Writing** Produce clear and coherent writing in which the development, organization, and style are appropriate to task, purpose, and audience.
Section 14.2 **Objections**	• Distinguish objections from excuses. • Explain why you should welcome objections in the sales process. • Explain the five buying decisions on which common objections are based. • Demonstrate the general four-step method for handling customer objections. • List seven methods of answering objections and identify when each should be used.	• **Reading** Interpret words and phrases as they are used in a text, including determining technical, connotative, and figurative meanings, and analyze how specific word choices shape meaning or tone.

Sections	Objectives	Common Core State Standards College and Career Readiness
Section 15.1 **How to Close a Sale**	• Identify customer buying signals. • List a few tips for closing a sale. • Decide on appropriate specialized methods for closing a sale.	• **Writing** Produce clear and coherent writing in which the development, organization, and style are appropriate to task, purpose, and audience.
Section 15.2 **Customer Satisfaction**	• Explain the benefits of suggestion selling. • List the rules for effective suggestion selling. • Demonstrate appropriate specialized suggestion selling methods. • Discuss strategies for maintaining and building a clientele. • Explain the importance of after-sale activities and customer service. • Discuss what salespeople can do to plan for future sales.	• **Writing** Write informative/explanatory texts to examine and convey complex ideas and information clearly and accurately through the effective selection, organization, and analysis of content.
Section 16.1 **Sales Transactions**	• List all types of retail sales transactions. • Process purchases, returns, and exchanges. • Generate and process sales documentation. • Calculate sales tax, discounts, and shipping charges.	• **Writing** Conduct short as well as more sustained research projects based on focused questions, demonstrating understanding of the subject under investigation.
Section 16.2 **Cash Registers**	• Name the functions of cash registers and point-of-sale (POS) terminals. • Explain the uses for Universal Product Codes (UPCs). • Make change.	• **Reading** Integrate and evaluate content presented in diverse formats and media, including visually and quantitatively, as well as in words.
Section 16.3 **Purchasing, Invoicing, and Shipping**	• Prepare purchase orders and invoices. • Explain shipping terms.	• **Reading** Determine central ideas or themes of a text and analyze their development; summarize the key supporting details and ideas.

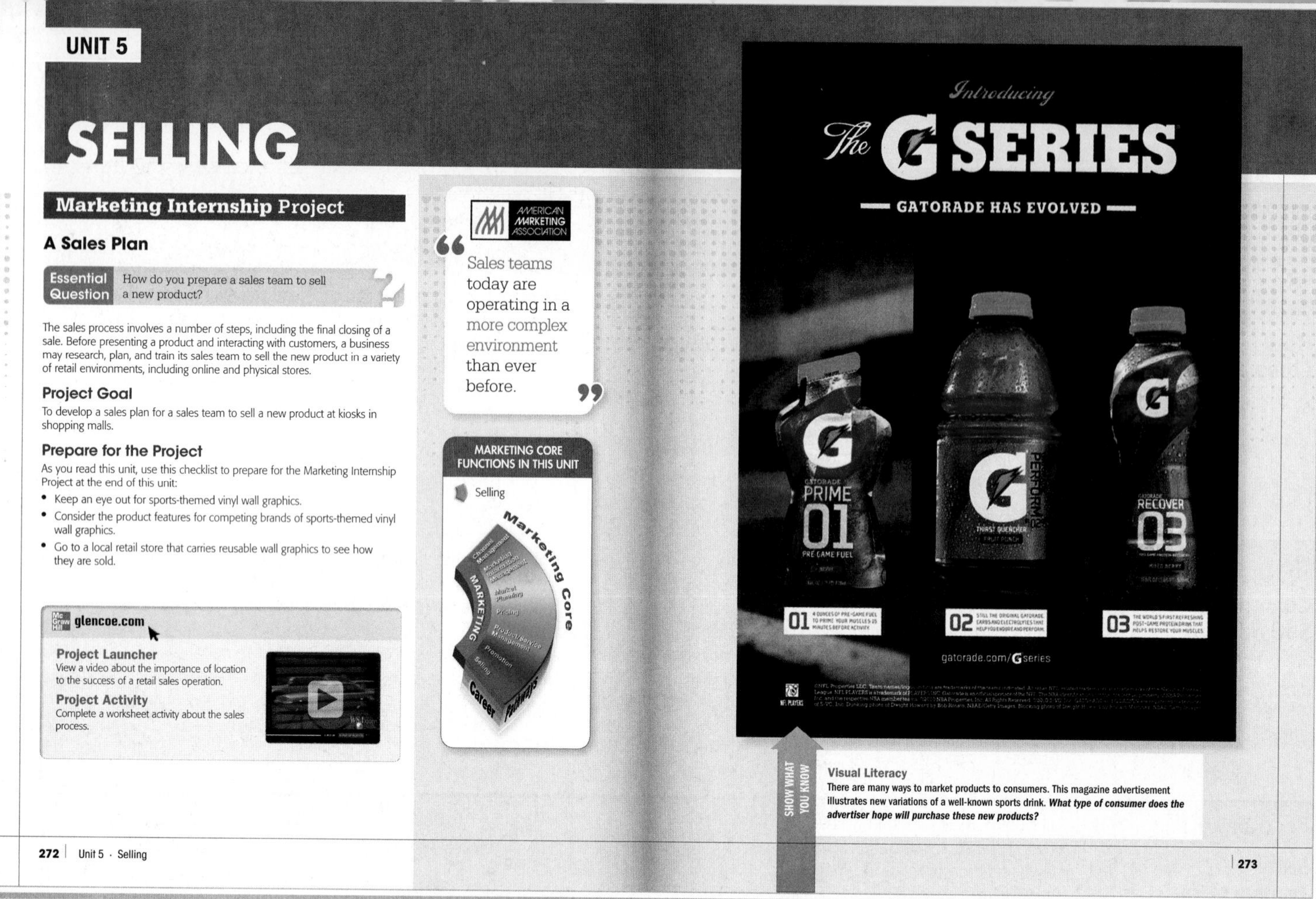
UNIT 5

SELLING

Marketing Internship Project

A Sales Plan

Essential Question How do you prepare a sales team to sell a new product?

The sales process involves a number of steps, including the final closing of a sale. Before presenting a product and interacting with customers, a business may research, plan, and train its sales team to sell the new product in a variety of retail environments, including online and physical stores.

Project Goal
To develop a sales plan for a sales team to sell a new product at kiosks in shopping malls.

Prepare for the Project
As you read this unit, use this checklist to prepare for the Marketing Internship Project at the end of this unit:

- Keep an eye out for sports-themed vinyl wall graphics.
- Consider the product features for competing brands of sports-themed vinyl wall graphics.
- Go to a local retail store that carries reusable wall graphics to see how they are sold.

glencoe.com

Project Launcher
View a video about the importance of location to the success of a retail sales operation.

Project Activity
Complete a worksheet activity about the sales process.

AMERICAN MARKETING ASSOCIATION

"Sales teams today are operating in a more complex environment than ever before."

MARKETING CORE FUNCTIONS IN THIS UNIT

Selling

Visual Literacy
There are many ways to market products to consumers. This magazine advertisement illustrates new variations of a well-known sports drink. ***What type of consumer does the advertiser hope will purchase these new products?***

SHOW WHAT YOU KNOW

272 | Unit 5 · Selling

273

ENGAGE

Introduce the Unit

Unit 5 examines aspects of the selling function of marketing.

Chapter 12 teaches how to prepare for making a sale by providing an overview of the selling process.

Chapter 13 introduces the initial steps of the sale—approaching customers and determining needs.

Chapter 14 explains the principles and practices of presenting the product and handling customers' objections.

Chapter 15 focuses on closing the sale, suggestion selling, and relationship marketing.

Chapter 16 reviews and teaches the mathematics involved in retail and business-to-business selling.

Build Background

Ask students if they think selling is a *learned* or a *natural* skill. List their responses on the board in two columns. Have students discuss the reasons for their answers. Answers will vary, but many will say that people can learn how to sell, as evidenced by this unit's content. Ask students: ***How important is the sales process for a business?*** A business that does not succeed in selling its products, regardless of their quality, will fail.

Visual Literacy

Photo Caption Answer Read the copy on the ad to students. Then read the photo caption and the photo caption question to students: ***What type of customer does the advertiser hope will purchase these new products?*** Answers will vary. Accept all reasonable answers. Sample answer: This advertiser is likely to be targeting athletic customers who are conscientious about how their bodies perform before, during, and after a sporting event. The target customer is someone who might consider themselves athletically "evolved." Ask students to evaluate the visual components of the advertisement. Ask volunteers to explain how the visual aspects of the advertisement complement the text of the advertisement. The photograph shows the three bottles of Gatorade to depict the ad's headline—The "G Series." The lightning bolt on the G implies strength. The colors red, black, and silver used in the ad and on the packaging also imply strength and power.

ENGAGE

Marketing Internship Project Preview

Read students the Marketing Internship Project Essential Question: ***How do you prepare a sales team to sell a new product?*** Because students are just starting to learn about selling, they will likely not know the specific answer to this question, which is to develop a sales plan for a sales team to sell products. However, students should know that training a sales team takes planning and knowledge of the new product. Explain to students that they will learn about several steps involved in making a sale while studying this unit. Tell students that when they are finished studying this unit, they will ask create a training plan for new sales employees selling sports wall graphics at malls. As they study each chapter in the unit, they can prepare for the Unit Project by thinking about the product features and potential markets for various types of vinyl wall graphics.

 glencoe.com

Marketing Internship Project Resources Send students to the Online Learning Center to watch a video and download a worksheet activity related to the topic of the Unit Project.

Read the American Marketing Association quote to students:

"Sales teams today are operating in a more complex environment than ever before."

Explain to students that the AMA's Resource Library provides information through articles and resources that address the functions of marketing. Content about the selling function discusses the retail market and the complexities of selling in the business-to-business (B2B) market:

Team Selling Many companies have shifted to a team-based selling approach. Team performance is a complex function of many different processes.

Sales Decisions Sales decisions consist of a series of interrelated processes, including: (1) determining the role of personal selling; (2) allocating selling effort to customers; (3) setting salesforce size; (4) designing sales territories; and (5) managing the salesforce.

Ask students: ***What might be the difference between retail selling and organizational selling?*** Retail selling involves sales at a store or online. Organizational selling may take place at a manufacturer's showroom, a customer's place of business, or online.

MARKETING CORE FUNCTIONS IN THIS UNIT

Point out to students that Chapters 12, 13, 14, 15, and 16 will touch on one of the seven marketing core functions. Describe this marketing function to students to prepare them to start studying this unit.

 **Selling** is offering customers in any market the right product or service, and requires intense business development to employ concepts and strategies that work.

MARKETING RESEARCH

PROJECT WORKBOOK

The purpose of the Marketing Research Project Workbook is to provide a step-by-step approach for students to conduct their own marketing research study. Each chapter is devoted to key elements in the research process. Each chapter builds upon the previous chapters, and by the end of the book, students will have completed an in-depth marketing research study, complete with rationale for all decisions, a report of the findings and conclusions, recommendations based on the original research problem and study objectives, and an annotated bibliography.

 glencoe.com 

Marketing Research Project Workbook Send students to the Online Learning Center to download the Marketing Research Project Workbook. A Teacher Manual is also available on the Teacher Center of the Online Learning Center.

selling overview

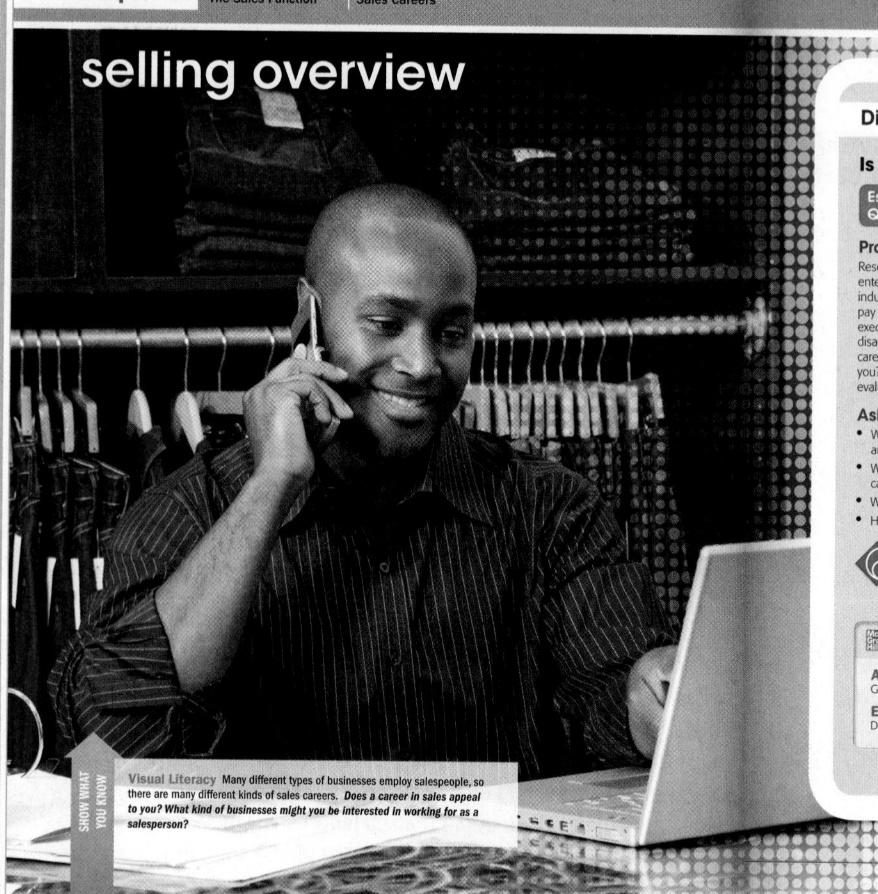

SHOW WHAT YOU KNOW

Visual Literacy Many different types of businesses employ salespeople, so there are many different kinds of sales careers. ***Does a career in sales appeal to you? What kind of businesses might you be interested in working for as a salesperson?***

Discovery Project

Is a Career in Selling for You?

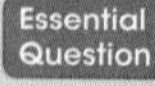

Essential Question What aspects of selling interest you?

Project Goal

Research some sales career options in all types of business enterprises (e.g., Internet, retail, manufacturing, and service industries). Investigate the employment requirements, pay scales, and benefits for entry level as well as the executive-management level. Research the advantages and disadvantages of a selling career. Which aspects of a selling career interest you, and which aspects do not appeal to you? Write a report that summarizes your research and your evaluation of selling as a career.

Ask Yourself...

- Where will you find employment requirements, pay scales, and benefits for different sales employment levels?
- What are the advantages and disadvantages of a selling career?
- What aspects of a selling career interest you?
- How will you present your findings?

Synthesize and Present Research Synthesize your research by writing a report that summarizes your research and your evaluation of selling as a career.

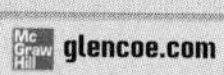

glencoe.com

Activity
Get a worksheet activity about sales careers.

Evaluate
Download a rubric you can use to evaluate your project.

DECA Connection

DECA Event Role Play

Concepts in this chapter are related to DECA competitive events that involve either an interview or role play.

Performance Indicators The performance indicators represent key skills and knowledge. Your key to success in DECA competitive events is relating them to concepts in this chapter.

- Explain the nature and scope of the selling function.
- Explain the selling process.
- Explain business ethics in selling.
- Describe the use of technology in the selling function.
- Explain the nature of sales management.

DECA Prep

Role Play Practice role-playing with the DECA Connection competitive-event activity at the end of this chapter. More information on DECA events can be found on DECA's Web site.

ENGAGE

Visual Literacy

Read the chapter opener photo caption questions to students: ***Does a career in sales appeal to you? What kind of businesses might you be interested in working for as a salesperson?*** Answers will vary Students will likely choose businesses that cater to young people. Then ask these guiding questions.

Guiding Questions

Identify What are the seven marketing core functions?	channel management, marketing information management, market planning, pricing, product/service management, promotion, selling
Apply What kinds of ethical behaviors should salespeople exhibit to gain customers' trust?	honesty, respectfulness of others and their ideas, fairness and equity in their dealings

Discovery Project

Is a Career in Selling for You? To encourage students to consider whether they might be interested in working in sales, ask them the Discovery Project Essential Question: ***What aspects of selling interest you?*** Explain that the word *aspect* means *facet* or *feature*. Student pairs should come up with a list of three or four aspects of sales that they think they would enjoy. interacting with customers, helping customers make choices that are suited to them, making money, being in a fun environment

 glencoe.com 

Discovery Project Resources Send students to the Online Learning Center to download a rubric to evaluate their projects.

ENGAGE

Introduce the Chapter

Chapter 12 provides students with an introduction to the importance of selling as a marketing function and to the wide variety of potential sales careers. These main concepts are introduced and discussed:

- Purpose of sales
- Sales trends and technology
- CRM software
- Sales management
- Types of sales positions available
- Steps in a sale
- Categories of customer decision making

Discussion Starter

Experiences with Salespeople Have students write a paragraph describing a memorable experience they have had with a salesperson. The experience can be either positive or negative. Encourage students to be as descriptive as possible when writing about their experience. Ask for volunteers to read aloud their paragraphs to the class. Ask: ***Why do people often remember their experiences with salespeople?*** Possible answer: because a good salesperson can make the experience pleasant and help us find a product or service that meets our needs, but a bad one can cost us a lot of money and aggravation. Then ask: ***If you gave one tip to a new salesperson on how to be successful, what would it be?*** Possible answers: listen to the customer's wants and needs, do not pressure the customer, and put yourself in the customer's place

DECA Connection

Discuss the performance indicators listed in the DECA Connection feature. Explain to students that performance indicators tell them how to demonstrate their acquired skills and knowledge through individual or team competitive events.

glencoe.com

Competitive Events Workbook For more DECA Role Plays, send students to the Online Learning Center to download the Competitive Events Workbook.

PROGRAM RESOURCE ORGANIZER

PRINT RESOURCES

- **Student Edition**
- **Teacher Edition**
- **Student Activity Workbook with Academic Integration** includes worksheets and activities correlated to the text.
- **Mathematics for Marketing Workbook** provides math activities for every unit in the text.

TECHNOLOGY TOOLBOX

- **Connect**
- **ConnectPlus**
- **ExamView Assessment Suite** is a comprehensive solution for creating, administering, and scoring tests.

glencoe.com

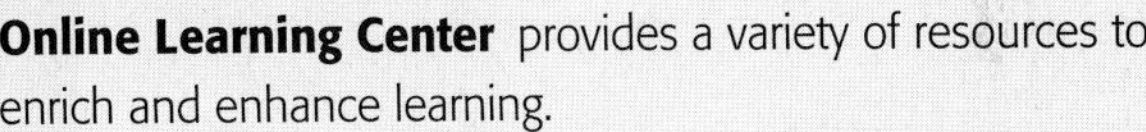

Online Learning Center provides a variety of resources to enrich and enhance learning.

SECTION, CHAPTER, AND UNIT RESOURCES

- **Graphic Organizers** for organizing text concepts visually.
- **Digital Nation Activities** and **Green Marketer Activities** extend learning beyond the text features.
- **Career Chatroom Career Profiles** allow students to explore different marketing occupations in depth.
- **After You Read Answer Keys** for students to check their answers.
- **Discovery Project Rubrics** and **Marketing Internship Project Rubrics** for students to evaluate their projects.

PROGRAM RESOURCES

- **Student Activity Workbook with Academic Integration Teacher Annotated Edition** includes annotated answers for the activities and worksheets.
- **Marketing Research Project Workbook** provides a step-by-step approach for students to complete their own marketing research studies.
- **School-to-Career Activity Workbook** helps students relate their class work to on-the-job experience and involves work-site analysis and working with mentors.
- **Competitive Events Workbook** helps prepare students for state and national marketing education competitions.
- **Inclusion in the Marketing Education Classroom** provides teaching resources for working with students with special needs.
- **PowerPoint Presentations** provides visual teaching aids and assessments for this chapter.

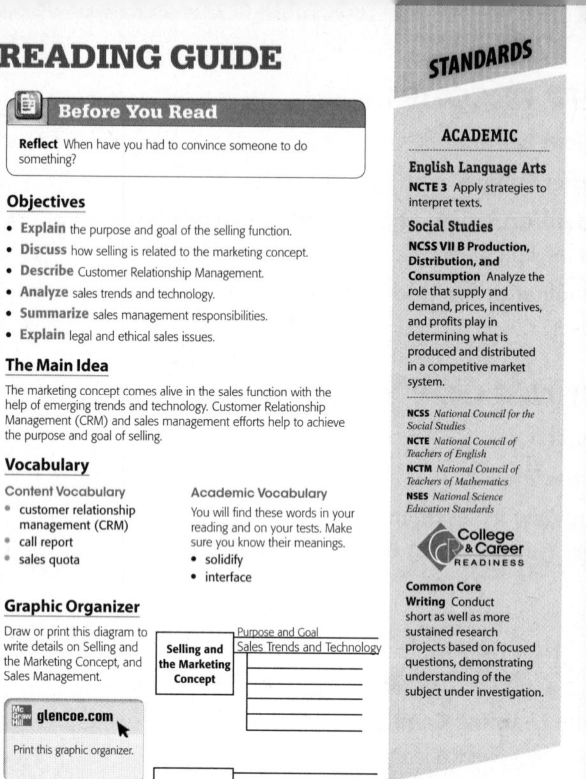

READING GUIDE

Before You Read

Reflect When have you had to convince someone to do something?

Objectives

- **Explain** the purpose and goal of the selling function.
- **Discuss** how selling is related to the marketing concept.
- **Describe** Customer Relationship Management.
- **Analyze** sales trends and technology.
- **Summarize** sales management responsibilities.
- **Explain** legal and ethical sales issues.

The Main Idea

The marketing concept comes alive in the sales function with the help of emerging trends and technology. Customer Relationship Management (CRM) and sales management efforts help to achieve the purpose and goal of selling.

Vocabulary

Content Vocabulary
- customer relationship management (CRM)
- call report
- sales quota

Academic Vocabulary

You will find these words in your reading and on your tests. Make sure you know their meanings.
- solidify
- interface

Graphic Organizer

Draw or print this diagram to write details on Selling and the Marketing Concept, and Sales Management.

glencoe.com

Print this graphic organizer.

STANDARDS

ACADEMIC

English Language Arts

NCTE 3 Apply strategies to interpret texts.

Social Studies

NCSS VII B Production, Distribution, and Consumption Analyze the role that supply and demand, prices, incentives, and profits play in determining what is produced and distributed in a competitive market system.

NCSS *National Council for the Social Studies*
NCTE *National Council of Teachers of English*
NCTM *National Council of Teachers of Mathematics*
NSES *National Science Education Standards*

College & Career READINESS

Common Core

Writing Conduct short as well as more sustained research projects based on focused questions, demonstrating understanding of the subject under investigation.

MARKETING CORE FUNCTION

Selling

Section 12.1

The Sales Function

SELLING AND THE MARKETING CONCEPT

Selling is an important marketing function. Why? Because selling generates the revenue that a business needs to operate. Successful companies have loyal customers. Loyal customers provide steady revenue for a company. They may recommend the company to others. This personal recommendation helps businesses grow. It is the sales division in a company that performs most of the tasks to find new customers, make sales, and keep current customers satisfied.

As You Read

Connect How do companies try to make you a loyal customer?

PURPOSE AND GOAL

The purpose of selling is to help customers make satisfying buying decisions, with the goal of creating ongoing, profitable relationships with them. As such, it is the essence of the marketing concept—businesses satisfying customers' needs and wants while making a profit. To make a profit, business must generate sales. Businesses' revenues are based on sales. This revenue is critical to keeping a company in business.

The marketing concept has created a customer-centered focus that companies have embraced. Departments coordinate their functions to help the sales function succeed. The marketing, customer service, and technology departments all work together to support sales efforts. Their respective activities ensure customer satisfaction.

For example, a potential customer may visit a company's Web site and request product information.That request may be directed to the customer service department for a response, with a copy to the sales department for follow-up. With the information obtained from the customer service staff, the sales staff is better prepared to satisfy the customer's request.

> "No company can stay in business if its products do not sell."

SALES TRENDS AND TECHNOLOGY

Marketers know that identifying the needs of customers and satisfying them can be profitable. However, only recently have firms made a dedicated effort to use **customer relationship management (CRM)**. This system involves finding customers and keeping them satisfied.

CRM has flourished due to new computer technology. Businesses have a tremendous amount of information about their customers at their finger tips. Company Web sites and e-mails have helped businesses communicate with customers on a frequent basis. Computer software has revolutionized the sales function. Let's look at some of the emerging trends and technologies that affect marketing and specifically help CRM.

WEB SITES AND SOCIAL MEDIA

Many companies have their own Web sites that provide product information. Some are designed for online purchases, while others tell visitors where a product may be purchased. To connect with the visitors who are customers or potential customers, companies often provide relevant educational information about topics of interest to visitors to the site. Some include fun, interactive games.

ENGAGE

Objectives

- **Explain** the purpose and goal of the selling function. The purpose and goal is to help customers make satisfying buying decisions.
- **Discuss** how selling is related to the marketing concept. Customers must be satisfied with their purchases in order for a business to generate current and future revenue.
- **Describe** customer relationship management.. CRM is a system that involves finding customers and keeping them satisfied.
- **Analyze** sales trends and technology. CRM is thriving because of new technology, such as Web sites, social media, e-mail.
- **Summarize** sales management responsibilities. plan, organize, and control sales functions; hire and train sales staff
- **Explain** legal and ethical sales issues. Commission sales and sales quotas can create pressure on sales staff to produce sales. If not taught properly in selling ethics and legal issues, sales associates may engage in hardsell tactics and possibly even purposely mislead customers.

Graphic Organizer

Selling and the Marketing Concept
- Purpose and Goal
- Sales Trends and Technology
  - Web Sites & Social Media
  - E-Mail
  - Customer Loyalty Programs
  - Computer Software
  - Mobile Devices
  - Partnerships

Sales Management
- Company Policies
- Training
- Compensation & Sales Quotas
- Legal and Ethical Issues
  - Sales Pressure
  - Sales Contracts
  - Sales Regulations

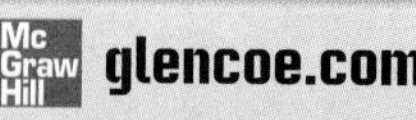

Graphic Organizer Send students to the Online Learning Center to print this graphic organizer.

EXPLORE

Before You Read

Read the Before You Read question aloud: ***When have you had to convince someone to do something?*** Possible answers: I needed someone's help with my homework; I had to get someone to cover my shift at work.

Preteaching Vocabulary

Have students go to the Online Learning Center at glencoe.com for the Chapter 12 Preteaching Vocabulary games.

Content Vocabulary

Instruct students to create stem sentences using each of the Content Vocabulary words. Have them trade their sentences with a partner and complete each other's sentences.

Academic Vocabulary

Interface—Prefixes Explain to students that the prefix *inter-* means "between" or "among." Ask students for examples of words using this prefix. interact, international, Internet, interstate Explain that when used as a verb, *interface* means "to connect between or among several devices, such as computer systems."

Activate Prior Knowledge

Reteach the Marketing Concept To help students recall the discussion of the marketing concept from Chapter 1, display the following diagram.

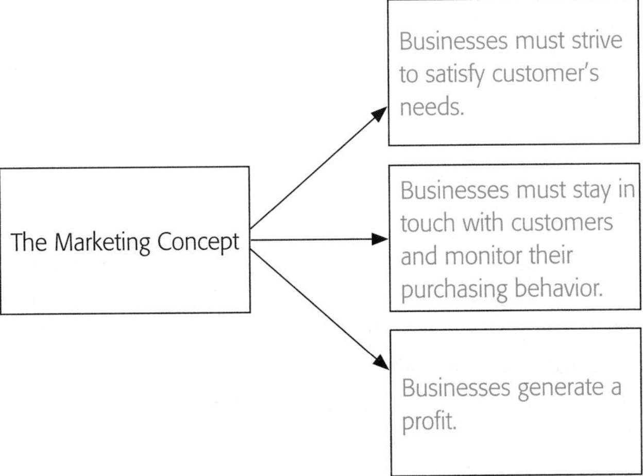
The Marketing Concept
Businesses must strive to satisfy customer's needs.
Businesses must stay in touch with customers and monitor their purchasing behavior.
Businesses generate a profit.

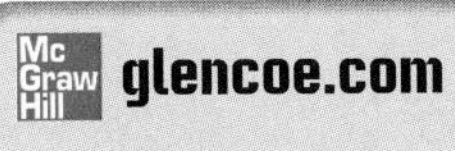 **glencoe.com** iWB

Graphic Organizer Send students to the Online Learning Center to print this graphic organizer.

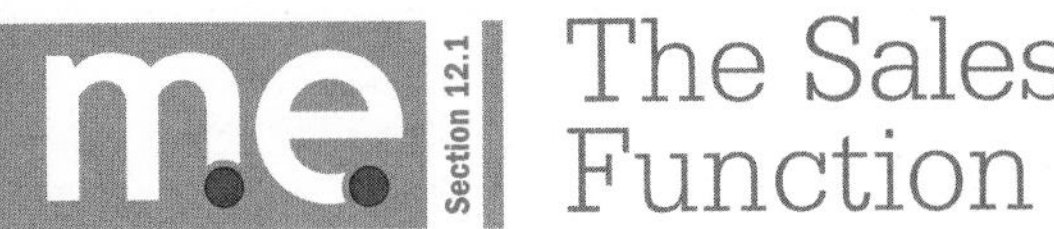
m.e.
Section 12.1

The Sales Function

SELLING AND THE MARKETING CONCEPT

Ask these guiding questions to focus the discussion.

Guiding Questions

Contrast How is finding new customers different from keeping current customers satisfied?	Finding new customers involves making them aware of how products can meet their needs.
Elaborate Imagine you are a real estate agent who helps families purchase homes. Why would you want to establish ongoing relationships?	Possible answer: I would want them to use my services again if they bought another home and to encourage their friends and coworkers to use my services.

As You Read

Read students the As You Read question: ***How do companies try to make you a loyal customer?*** Possible answer: by selling products that meet my needs, that are well made, and which are reasonably priced

Expert Advice

Read the quote to students:

"No company can stay in business if its products do not sell."

WEB SITES AND SOCIAL MEDIA

Ask these guiding questions to focus the discussion.

Guiding Questions

Analyze On the Lowe's® Web site, you can learn how to do everything from fixing a leaky faucet to building a deck. Why do you think the company puts such effort into providing extensive how-to information?	It increases the chances that Web site visitors will buy their home improvement supplies from Lowe's because they will see the company as being knowledgeable and supportive.
Evaluate Do you think it is a good idea for companies to allow customers to place product reviews on their Web sites? Why or why not?	Even though some of the reviews may be negative, it is a good idea because they provide useful information.

These encourage customers to return to the site frequently. All effective Web-site designs include the principles of selling that you will learn in this unit. For customers who need personal assistance, a Web site may offer contact information to speak with a salesperson.

Many businesses participate in social media sites, such as Facebook and Twitter. Both of these sites help companies stay in touch with their customers by receiving and sending business communications. Company Web sites and social media outlets allow companies to be accessible to potential customers nationally and globally.

E-MAIL

Another technology that helps in sending and receiving business communication is e-mail. E-mails are an efficient way to prepare written communication. E-mails can be used to thank customers for their orders and to address customer service issues. Businesses and customers can track orders and delivery status quickly and easily via e-mail. Thus, communication between companies and their customers can be quick and efficient, which helps to **solidify** relationships even after a sale is made.

Through extensive databases that keep track of customer purchases, companies are able to send targeted e-mails to their customers. The targeted e-mails update customers regarding new promotions and new products that fit their needs based on their past purchases. This information technology tool helps marketing efforts to create sales. There are a variety of software programs and companies that offer this service to businesses.

CUSTOMER LOYALTY PROGRAMS

To keep customers loyal, some companies offer special rewards programs to their regular customers. Airlines offer frequent flier programs. Pharmacies give their loyal customers discounts based on their level of purchases each month. Credit card companies, like American Express® and Capital One®, offer points based on purchases that can be redeemed for goods and services. E-mailed questionnaires with prize entries or advance notice of special sales are other methods marketers have developed to create and reinforce loyalty. Manufacturers offer special pricing programs and other incentives to customers who generate a certain amount of sales volume.

COMPUTER SOFTWARE

Computer software for the sales function is available for all types of businesses. Some companies purchase software that can be customized for their business. Others may subscribe to CRM services offered by Web-based companies. For example, Oracle® CRM OnDemand and salesforce.com host customer relationship management services. Other software companies specialize in a variety of sales-related areas, such as sales automation, sales territory management, sales forecasting, and management of compensation and incentive programs.

MOBILE DEVICES

Salespeople today are very connected. They can send and receive business communications while away from the office. Their mobile devices or laptops can be programmed to **interface** with their company's computer system. While visiting with a customer, a sales representative can check on the customer's past purchases, product availability, price changes, and more.

PARTNERSHIPS

Some companies become partners in an effort to solve a customer's problem. Oracle and IBM® were partners in an effort to design an Oracle CRM system for Konica Minolta® Business Solutions U.S.A. The result was improved collaboration with the direct sales force. Sales lead generation and follow-up were made easier and more efficient.

To successfully maintain sales accounts, company sales representatives must stay in contact with customers. Sales representatives act as partners or consultants for their customers. For example, a manufacturer of artificial knees or hips may have a sales representative present in the operating room during a medical procedure in case a question or problem comes up. In addition to developing expertise about the products, a sales representative for a medical supply company also goes through extensive medical training. This traning allows a sales representative to answer any questions the customer may have about a product's specifications and how it can be used.

By examining successful partnerships in business and elsewhere, marketers have discovered that enduring relationships are built on trust and commitment, and require a lot of time and effort to maintain.

Reading Check

Define What is customer relationship management?

Company Web Sites

Companies have several ways of selling their products to consumers. In this ad for Lucky Brand® Jeans, readers are provided the Web site address for this brand where they can shop online or find a store that carries this brand. ***Why would a company sell its products online and also in retail stores?***

Promoting Loyalty

CVS/pharmacy has a special program called "ExtraCare®," the largest retail rewards program in the U.S. ExtraCare offers automatic savings, personalized coupons, and other incentives to customers who opt-in. ***Why do you think companies use loyalty programs?***

278 | Unit 5 · Selling

Chapter 12 · Selling Overview | 279

EXPLAIN

Visual Literacy

Company Web Sites Caption Answer Read the caption question to students: ***Why would a company sell its products online and also in retail stores?*** The two methods of selling products typically appeal to different types of customers. Customers who are pressed for time and know what they want are likely to purchase on the Web. Customers who need the guidance of a salesperson, want to actually see and touch the product, or who need the product immediately, are more likely to go to a brick-and-mortar store.

Reinforce Vocabulary

Sales Quota—Word Origin Explain that the word quota comes from the Latin quota pars, which means "how great a part?" Therefore, sales quota means the portion or share of total sales assigned to each member of a sales team.

Critical Thinking

Ask a volunteer to go to Facebook and examine the contents of the UGG shoes page. Ask the student to tell the class about some of the page's contents. Possible answer: The wall contains messages from people who love their UGGs. There are also photos of people wearing UGGs. Ask students: ***How do you think this content affects the selling of UGGs?*** It probably increases the sale of UGGs because it gets people talking about UGGs, which shows potential customers how popular they are.

ELL: Low-Risk Environment

Go to the Online Learning Center to view a video in which an author discusses a low-risk environment for learning.

ELABORATE

Visual Literacy

Promoting Loyalty Caption Answer Read the caption question to students: ***Why do you think companies use loyalty programs?*** Companies offer special rewards programs to customers to make them feel special and keep their business.

Critical Thinking

Ask students: ***Have you ever belonged to a customer loyalty program?*** Ask for a volunteer to explain a program in which he or she participates. Then ask: ***Does belonging to this loyalty program affect whether or not you buy this company's product?*** Possible answer: Yes, because I get discounts on some products, plus a free gift on my birthday. Students should be aware that businesses have loyalty programs in the hope that they will encourage customers to buy more of their products.

Reading Check Answer

Read the Reading Check question to students: ***What is customer relationship management?*** CRM consists of a variety of trends and technologies, such as Web sites, social media, e-mail, mobile devices, and specialized computer software, that help a business to find customers and keep them satisfied. Then ask: ***Why do you think CRM software is becoming increasingly popular?*** Customers expect salespeople to have answers to their questions immediately and, to be successful, sales managers must continually keep track of the performance of their staff. CRM software provides an across-the-company integrated approach to efficiently performing these tasks.

E-MAIL

Ask these guiding questions to focus the discussion on e-mail.

Guiding Questions

List A customer orders a book from a Web-based book store. What are some e-mails from the company that the customer might receive in response to this order?	order confirmation, a message that the order has been shipped, and a request for feedback on the quality of the service
Make a Judgment Imagine you have a service issue with an online book store. Would you rather go to the company's Web site to chat with a service representative or deal with the problem via e-mail? Why?	Answers will vary. Possible answer: I would rather go to the Web site to chat with the representative because I would probably get a response more quickly.

Critical Thinking

Tell students that in 2010, SuperShoes.com instituted a Twitter-based Bingo contest to highlight new products. The game required players to share images of various shoes, which encouraged participants to discuss the company's products. Winners got a free pair of new shoes. The company reported an increase in Web sales of 150 percent. Ask students: ***Why do you think this Bingo contest was so successful?*** It got more people to visit the store's site and generated buzz about the company's products, which usually leads to increased sales.

Mini Project

Extension

Researching CRM Software Have students choose a specific type of CRM software, such as Oracle CRM On Demand, NetSuite, or SAP CRM. Students should conduct research to learn about the capabilities of the application they have chosen. Students should then give a presentation in which they try to sell their chosen software to a company. They may want to create a slide show so that they can visually explain the software and include visuals such as screen captures to illustrate the software's functions. Students should create a presentation in which they try to sell CRM software to a company. The presentation should focus on a specific type of CRM software and explore its features. For example, Oracle CRM On Demand increases the productivity of sales managers and representatives by automating and managing sales information, enhancing sales lead management and tracking, and providing an integrated solution for executing and analyzing marketing campaigns.

SALES MANAGEMENT

Sales management establishes the guidelines and policies for the sales team. Sales managers plan, organize, and control the sales function. They establish the structure of the sales organization. During planning, sales managers prepare and monitor sales budgets, establish realistic sales forecasts and quotas for certain divisions, and supervise individual sales personnel.

It is the job of sales management to hire and train members of a company's sales staff and assign them to specific territories. The managers analyze sales reports, hold sales meetings, and design compensation plans and incentive programs to motivate the sales staff. The sales staff's performance and ethical and legal conduct is monitored by sales managers. Sales managers also meet with management of other divisions to collaborate and develop new sales opportunities. Input from sales about what customers want can help in the development of new products.

COMPANY POLICIES

Company policies and goals must be communicated to the sales staff by sales management. For example, a company may have a goal of increasing market share by 10 percent in the coming year. To do so, the company needs to sell more of its products. That goal must be communicated to the sales staff. To reach that goal, an atmosphere of teamwork and integrity among workers would be necessary. Other company policies are created to ensure that personnel are performing their tasks effectively. For example, sales personnel may be required to complete call reports each time they visit a customer. A **call report** is a written report that documents a sales representative's visit with a customer. It includes customer information for the company database, the purpose and outcome of the visit, as well as any follow-up that is necessary.

MARKETING CASE STUDY

Adidas's Sales Automation

To prepare for a meeting with a customer, the Adidas® sales force usually checks inventory. But frustration would set in when some products were no longer available after a sale was made. A sales representative would have to call the customer to revise the order. Or, worse, phone customer service while on a sales call, interrupting the selling process. So, Adidas gave laptops to its sales staff so they could interface with the company's computer system to check real-time inventory.

Improving the Process

To improve on this solution, Adidas turned to AT&T™ and Atlas2Go, an automated sales-force application. The software program can run on a wireless BlackBerry® device. With this system, sales representatives check inventory on the spot while taking a customer's order. This improvement reduced frustration, errors, and the need to change orders. Another unforeseen benefit was the ability to spot product trends quickly.

Social Studies

Analyze Discuss how supply and demand resulted in sales representatives having immediate access to a company's inventory during the sales process.

NCSS VII B Production, Distribution, and Consumption Analyze the role that supply and demand, prices, incentives, and profits play in determining what is produced and distributed in a competitive market system.

Sales Management
- Company Policies
- Training
- Compensation and Sales Quota
- Legal and Ethical Issues

TRAINING

A four-step process is often used by sales managers who are ultimately responsible for training new sales personnel. The four steps are explanation, demonstration, trial, and critique. The person conducting the training first explains and then demonstrates a sales technique. In the next step, the new sales associate performs the newly learned task or demonstrates product knowledge in a role-playing format. The final step involves constructive criticism by the trainer. This sales training program works well for all steps in the sales process. It reinforces sales techniques and emphasizes the marketing concept with new and veteran sales associates.

COMPENSATION AND SALES QUOTAS

Salespeople are compensated by straight commission, straight salary, or salary plus commission. Some field sales staff also receive benefits, such as a company car and expense account. Company policies govern what is covered under the expense account.

Commission salespeople get paid only when they sell something. Salaried salespeople get paid a set amount, regardless of how much they sell. Salary plus commission salespeople generally have a set salary, and their commission rate is lower than the rate received by salespeople who are paid only commission.

Regardless of the method of compensation, sales managers often establish sales quotas. A **sales quota** is a dollar or unit sales goal set for the sales staff to achieve in a specified period of time. Sales managers make sales forecasts based on sales reports to predict what sales can be expected in the future. Managers must regularly monitor sales reports to see if quotas are being met. Some companies offer incentives to salespeople to encourage them to meet—and even exceed—their quotas. Incentives could include recognition, a gift, and/or a monetary bonus.

DIGITAL NATION

Nike's Social Network

Social networking is helping Nike® build customer loyalty. Nike+ is a specialized computer program that allows Nike to sponsor and track runs in many cities with runners registering online. To participate, a runner must purchase a $29 Nike iPod Sport Kit sensor. When a run is completed, the contestant uploads the information from their run onto the Nike Web site. In essence, all the runners in all the cities competed with each another in that Nike-sponsored run.

Sales-Related Products

In addition to the Nike+iPod Sports Kits, runners have purchased Nike+SportBands. These devices look like watches. Runners that prefer these devices can still participate in the Nike-sponsored runs around the world. Of course, loyal customers can also buy Nike running shoes and backpacks.

English Language Arts

Research Watch for competitors to build on Nike's success with their own sensors and means of keeping track of sports data in a social networking community. What makes social networking so effective in building customer loyalty? Investigate how other athletic apparel companies have used social networking.

NCTE 7 Conduct research and gather, evaluate, and synthesize data to communicate discoveries.

glencoe.com

Get a Digital Nation activity.

EXPLAIN

MARKETING CASE STUDY

Social Studies Answer Salespeople found themselves in the position of having already made a sale, only to later learn that the product was no longer available. They then had to contact the customer to revise the order, opening the possibility that the customer would cancel it. Because of this situation, Adidas® realized it was vital for field sales representatives to have immediate access to the company's inventory during the sales process so they were assured that the goods being ordered were in stock. This enabled them to complete the sales order with confidence.

TRAINING

Ask these guiding questions to focus the discussion on training.

Guiding Questions

Analyze Why is role playing vital to this type of training?	Salespeople learn to be successful primarily by practicing. Role playing provides a safe way of learning the sales process.
Apply What is meant by the term constructive criticism? Give an example of how a sales manager might provide constructive criticism.	Constructive criticism is feedback that the new sales associate can use to become a better salesperson. Examples will vary.

ELABORATE

Graphic Organizer

To provide an overview of the topics covered under Sales Management, display this graphic organizer. Ask students to name the four topics under Sales Management and write these in the boxes on the second level. Then ask for examples of issues related to each topic and use these to fill in the boxes on the third level. Possible answers:

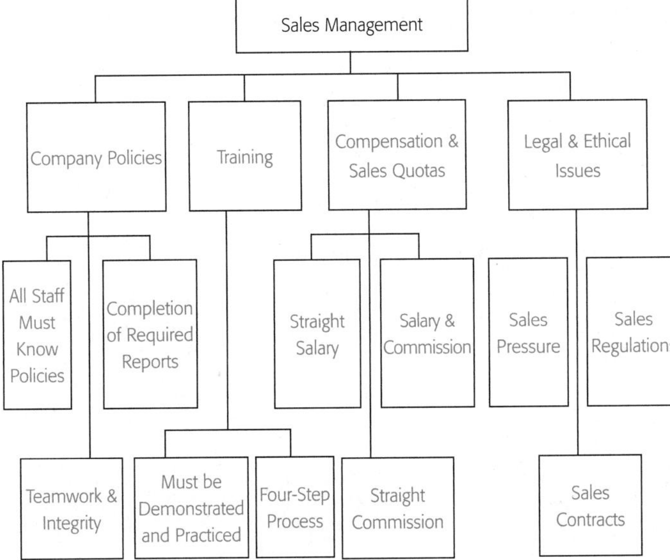

iWB

Graphic Organizer Send students to the Online Learning Center to print this graphic organizer.

COMPENSATION AND SALES QUOTAS

To focus the discussion on how companies compensate their sales force, ask these guiding questions.

Guiding Questions

Draw Conclusions Which of the three compensation methods do you think is the most risky? Which do you think can potentially lead to the greatest income? Why?	Straight commission is the riskiest but can lead to the greatest income. When salespeople work on straight commission, they only get income from their sales, their income potential unlimited.
Infer How might having a sales quota affect the behavior of a salesperson?	It might cause the salesperson to be more aggressive, and even suggest products that do not properly meet the customer's needs.

Mini Project

Enrichment

Applying the Four-Step Process Organize students into pairs. Tell them they are going to create a skit. One partner should play the role of a sales manager and use the four steps presented here to train the other, a new sales associate, on how to use a specific device, such as an iPod, or GPS device. The trainee should then demonstrate what was learned. The sales manager then offers the trainee constructive criticism. Students should present skits that follow a four-step training process in which a sales manager trains a new sales associate in the use of an electronic device. After the sales associate demonstrates what he or she learned, the manager should offer a critique that provides positive suggestions for improving performance.

Digital Nation

English Language Arts Answer Social networking is effective in building customer loyalty because the participants all share a common interest. Nike® created a "runner's community" with its sports kit sensor and sponsorship of runs, which allows runners from all over the world to compete against one another. Social networking is effective in building loyalty because customers feel a connection between one another due to their common interests. Ask these guiding questions to further explore Nike's use of social networking.

Guiding Questions

Analyze Nike+ presents numerous challenges for runners, such as one contest to see which team can run the most miles over a specific time period. How do these types of contests strengthen the social network?	They build a strong sense of team allegiance and a feeling of common purpose. Nike's goal is to have this sense of community translate into loyalty to the Nike brand.
Infer Many of the Nike+ activities result in money being given to international charities. Why do you think Nike supports these efforts?	Nike+ wants to demonstrate that it has the same kinds of concerns as its customers, resulting in the customer identifying with Nike's values.

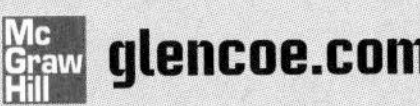

Worksheet Activity Send students to the Online Learning Center to get a Digital Nation worksheet activity.

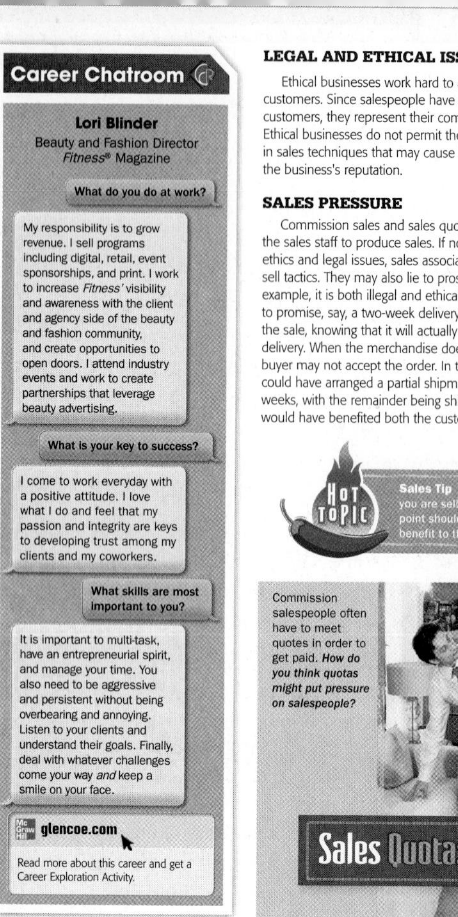

Career Chatroom

Lori Blinder
Beauty and Fashion Director
Fitness® Magazine

What do you do at work?

My responsibility is to grow revenue. I sell programs including digital, retail, event sponsorships, and print. I work to increase *Fitness'* visibility and awareness with the client and agency side of the beauty and fashion community, and create opportunities to open doors. I attend industry events and work to create partnerships that leverage beauty advertising.

What is your key to success?

I come to work everyday with a positive attitude. I love what I do and feel that my passion and integrity are keys to developing trust among my clients and my coworkers.

What skills are most important to you?

It is important to multi-task, have an entrepreneurial spirit, and manage your time. You also need to be aggressive and persistent without being overbearing and annoying. Listen to your clients and understand their goals. Finally, deal with whatever challenges come your way *and* keep a smile on your face.

glencoe.com

Read more about this career and get a Career Exploration Activity.

LEGAL AND ETHICAL ISSUES

Ethical businesses work hard to acquire and keep new customers. Since salespeople have direct contact with customers, they represent their company and its reputation. Ethical businesses do not permit their salespeople to engage in sales techniques that may cause legal problems or damage the business's reputation.

SALES PRESSURE

Commission sales and sales quotas can create pressure on the sales staff to produce sales. If not taught properly in selling ethics and legal issues, sales associates may engage in hard-sell tactics. They may also lie to prospective customers. For example, it is both illegal and ethically wrong for a salesperson to promise, say, a two-week delivery of an order, just to make the sale, knowing that it will actually take four weeks for delivery. When the merchandise does not arrive on time, the buyer may not accept the order. In this case, the salesperson could have arranged a partial shipment to be delivered in two weeks, with the remainder being shipped later. That solution would have benefited both the customer and the company.

HOT TOPIC **Sales Tip** Regardless of what you are selling, your main selling point should be the greatest benefit to the customer.

Sales Quotas

Commission salespeople often have to meet quotes in order to get paid. ***How do you think quotas might put pressure on salespeople?***

SALES CONTRACTS

It is important to remember that a sales order or purchase order is a legal agreement. It is a contract between the buyer and seller that is signed by both parties. It contains all the elements of a legal contract: an offer, an acceptance, consideration (price and terms), competent parties (buyer and seller), legal form, and legal subject matter.

A sales contract specifies what product or service is being offered, how much, and at what price. When the buyer signs the contract, it becomes a binding agreement to purchase the product or service at the price shown on the contract. The contract typically also contains language that spells out any guarantee or warranty that goes with the purchase.

SALES REGULATIONS

In certain selling situations, such as real estate, the buyer is given a set period of time, perhaps 24 to 48 hours, in which the agreement can be canceled without penalty.

Another aspect of a sales contract is full disclosure of the facts. In a contract providing services, all services and materials that will be used should be clearly identified. Pricing information must be accurate and based on services actually performed. In real estate dealings, full disclosure of all potentially negative factors (e.g., mold, termites, radon) must be disclosed by the seller.

Sales regulations protect the buyer against fraudulent or unethical selling practices. They give the buyer confidence that the item being purchased matches the seller's description.

After You Read **Section 12.1**

Review Key Concepts

1. **Explain** the purpose and goal of selling.
2. **Discuss** which trends and technologies help businesses with customer relationship management.
3. **Explain** the role that sales management plays in the sales process.

Practice Academics

Social Studies

4. Why must salespeople follow ethical sales practices and know about sales contracts? What are the ramifications if they do not?

Mathematics

5. Assume a salesperson has earned $35,000 as a base salary, plus 5 percent commission on sales of $800,000. Determine the salesperson's income for the year.

Math Concept **Ways of Representing Numbers** An increase in a number can be represented by a percent greater than 100.

Starting Hints Convert the 5 percent to a decimal. Multiple sales by .05 (5 percent) to determine the salesperson's commission for the year. Add the commission to the base salary to determine the salesperson's yearly income.

NCSS VII B Production, Distribution, and Consumption Analyze the role that supply and demand, prices, incentives, and profits play in determining what is produced and distributed in a competitive market system.

NCTM Number and Operations Understand numbers, ways of representing numbers, relationships among numbers, and number systems.

glencoe.com

Check your answers.

For help, go to the **Math Skills Handbook** located at the back of this book.

ELABORATE

Career Chatroom

Focus the discussion by asking these guiding questions.

Guiding Questions

Explain How do you create trust?	One way to create trust is to demonstrate integrity.
Synthesize Why is an entrepreneurial spirit necessary?	Entrepreneurs are innovative and can think creatively about clients' needs.

 **glencoe.com** 

Career Exploration Send students to the Online Learning Center to find more information about this career and to get a Career Exploration activity.

Sales Tip Ask students: *How might applying sales pressure to customers backfire on a salesperson?*

Visual Literacy

Sales Quotas Caption Answer Read the caption question to students: ***How do you think sales quotas might put pressure on salespeople?*** Sales quotas require salespeople to meet certain sales numbers within a time period. If sales quotas aren't met, salespeople might lose income, employment hours, or even their jobs.

EVALUATE

Graphic Organizer

Display this graphic organizer. Have students suggest examples of legal and ethical behavior. Possible answers:

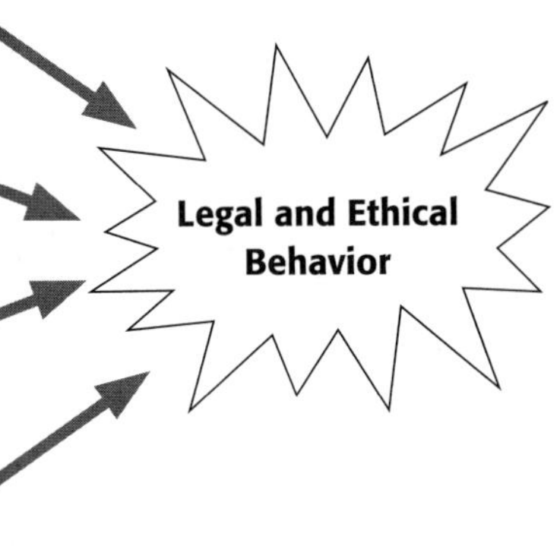
Do not engage in hard-sell tactics.
Do not make promises you cannot keep.
Remember that sales orders and purchase orders are legal documents.
Follow all laws and sales regulations.
Legal and Ethical Behavior

Mc Graw Hill
glencoe.com

iWB

Graphic Organizer Send students to the Online Learning Center to print this graphic organizer.

Mini Project

Differentiated Instruction

English Language Learners Draw this table on the board.

Word	Definition	Sample Sentence
Reputation	Overall quality as judged by people in general	The business worked hard to protect its reputation.
Tarnish	Bring disgrace on; damage	Companies can tarnish their reputations by treating customers poorly.

Review these terms with the class. Organize students into pairs. Each pair should copy this table onto a sheet of paper. They then should add at least six more words to the table. They should choose words from under "Legal and Ethical Issues." Students tables should correctly define each word and contain a sample sentence that properly uses that word.

After You Read Section 12.1

Review Key Concepts

1. The purpose of selling is to help customers make satisfying buying decisions with the goal of creating ongoing, profitable relationships with them.
2. Company Web sites, targeted customer e-mails, customer loyalty programs, computer sales software, mobile devices, and partnerships between businesses help with CRM.
3. Sales management establishes the guidelines and policies under which sales people function. Sales managers plan, organize, and control the sales function.

Practice Academics

Social Studies

4. Salespeople must follow ethical sales practices and know about sales contracts and regulations because they represent their company. As such, their actions impact the company legally and ethically, and they affect the company's reputation in the business community.

Mathematics

5. \$75,000 (\$800,000 × .05 = 40,000 + \$35,000)

Mc Graw Hill
glencoe.com

Answer Key Send students to the Online Learning Center to check their answers.

READING GUIDE

Before You Read

Connect What type of product would you enjoy selling? Why?

Objectives

- **Define** personal selling.
- **Identify** sales positions.
- **List** the steps in the sales process.
- **Analyze** how customers make buying decisions.
- **Evaluate** selling as a career option.

The Main Idea

An understanding of the purpose of selling and the different levels of customer decision making can help salespeople determine how they will perform the steps of a sale.

Vocabulary

Content Vocabulary

- personal selling
- organizational selling
- cold call
- telemarketing
- extensive decision making
- limited decision making
- routine decision making

Academic Vocabulary

You will find these words in your reading and on your tests. Make sure you know their meanings.

- pre-sold
- perquisite

Graphic Organizer

Draw or print this chart to make three lists that include sales positions, the seven steps of a sale, and the three levels of consumer decision making.

Sales Positions	Steps of a Sale	Customer Decision Making
Retail businesses	A - Approach	Extensive
	N - Needs determined	L
	P -	R
	O -	
	C -	
	S & R -	

glencoe.com

Print this graphic organizer.

STANDARDS

ACADEMIC

English Language Arts

NCTE 1 Read texts to acquire new information.

Social Studies

NCSS VII B Production, Distribution, and Consumption Analyze the role that supply and demand, prices, incentives, and profits play in determining what is produced and distributed in a competitive market system.

NCSS *National Council for the Social Studies*
NCTE *National Council of Teachers of English*
NCTM *National Council of Teachers of Mathematics*
NSES *National Science Education Standards*

College & Career READINESS

Common Core
Writing Produce clear and coherent writing in which the development, organization, and style are appropriate to task, purpose, and audience.

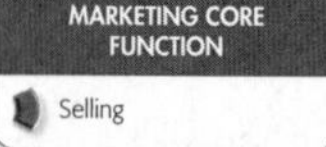

MARKETING CORE FUNCTION

Selling

m.e. Section 12.2 Sales Careers

PERSONAL SELLING

Personal selling is any form of direct contact between a salesperson and a customer. The key factor that sets it apart from other forms of promotion is the two-way communication between the seller and the buyer. Sales positions may have different titles, such as sales representative or account executive. Look in the "Help Wanted" or "Jobs" section of a print or online newspaper under "Sales Positions" to see the various names associated with a sales career. Regardless of the sales title, salespeople follow certain steps in the sales process. These steps are based on how customers make their buying decisions.

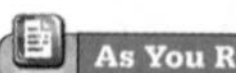

As You Read

Connect How might your need for sales assistance change for different products?

TYPES OF SALES POSITIONS

Salespeople work in retail businesses, industrial businesses, service businesses, telemarketing firms, nonprofit organizations, and Internet companies. As you read about these business categories, analyze the respective sales positions in order to see which ones interest you.

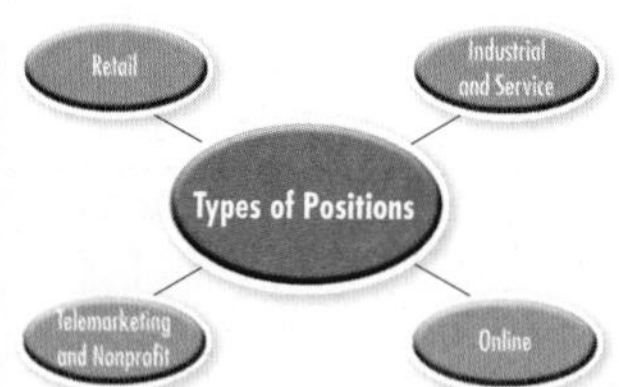

RETAIL BUSINESSES

Retail selling is unique because customers come to the store. Non-personal selling techniques, such Internet Web sites, advertising, and displays, help to create store traffic. Retail customers are **pre-sold** due to these promotional efforts. The salesperson's job involves simply offering customer service. When retail customers are not pre-sold, they require a salesperson's assistance to help them make a buying decision.

> "Personal selling involves two-way communication between the buyer and seller."

INDUSTRIAL AND SERVICE BUSINESSES

Manufacturers, wholesalers, and many service businesses (banks, advertising agencies, insurance companies, consulting firms) are involved with organizational sales.

Organizational selling involves sales exchanges that occur between two or more companies or business groups. The sales process may take place in the seller's showroom or company headquarters (inside sales) or at a customer's place of business (field or outside sales).

When the sales exchange occurs at a customer's place of business, it is up to the salesperson to make contact with the customer. Sales representatives will call to make an appointment prior to a visit. In other cases, sales representatives may make a **cold call**, which means they will visit without an appointment.

ENGAGE

Anticipation Activity

Improving Student Achievement Ask students: *How important is it to you to get advice from a salesperson when making a purchase?* It varies depending on the product. For large purchases, I like to get information and advice from a salesperson.

Objectives

- **Define** personal selling. Personal selling is direct contact between a salesperson and a customer.
- **Identify** sales positions. retail, industrial, service, telemarketing, nonprofit, Internet
- **List** the steps in the sales process. approach the customer, determine needs, present the product, overcome objections, close the sale, perform suggestion selling, build relationships
- **Analyze** how customers make buying decisions. product familiarity and cost, degree of perceived risk and value
- **Evaluate** selling as a career option. Evaluations will vary but should recognize that sales careers have a high income potential.

Graphic Organizer

Sales Positions	Steps of a Sale	Customer Decision Making
Retail businesses	A–Approach	Extensive
Industrial businesses	N–Needs determined	Limited
Service businesses	P–Present the product	Routine
Telemarketing firms	O–Overcome objections	
Nonprofit organizations	C–Close the sale	
Internet companies	S & R–Suggestion selling & Build relationships	

glencoe.com

iWB

Graphic Organizer Send students to the Online Learning Center to print this graphic organizer.

EXPLORE

Before You Read

Read the Before You Read question aloud: ***What type of product would you enjoy selling? Why?*** Answers will vary. Sample answer: I'd love to sell skateboards, gear for skating, and skate clothes because this is my number-one hobby. I know about all the latest features, the differences between the various brands of boards, and which are best for beginners, experienced skaters, and so on.

Preteaching Vocabulary

Have students go to the Online Learning Center at glencoe.com for the Chapter 12 Preteaching Vocabulary games.

Content Vocabulary

Have students work individually to write a quiz that contains four true-or-false statements that use the Content Vocabulary. Instruct students to take one another's quizzes. Students should discuss any questions that they answered incorrectly.

Academic Vocabulary

Perquisite—Short Forms of Words Write *perquisite* for students to view. Under it, write the word *perk.* Tell students that both have the same meaning—"a financial benefit that is provided in addition to a regular salary or commission." Explain that *perk* is short for *perquisite.* Many words have short forms. Ask students to list some examples. telephone: phone; facsimile: fax; submarine: sub

As You Read

Read the As You Read question aloud: ***How might your need for sales assistance change for different products?*** Accept all reasonable answers. Some answers will note the familiarity with or complexity and price of the item as the reasons for different levels of sales assistance. Then ask: ***Think of a recent situation in which you required the assistance of a salesperson. What kind of help did you ask for? Were you pleased with the help you received?*** Answers will vary. Possible answer: I was unable to locate a specific product or needed help in understanding how different products varied from each other.

Sales Careers

PERSONAL SELLING

Ask these guiding questions to focus the discussion about personal selling.

Guiding Questions

Contrast How are inside sales different from field sales?	inside sales: take place at the seller's place of business; field sales: salesperson goes to the customer
Analyze How do you think the skills a retail salesperson needs might be different from those of someone who is in organizational selling?	Retail salespeople generally do not have the same level of education, training, and experience required of organizational salespeople.

Graphic Organizer

Use the graphic organizer to provide an overview of sales positions.

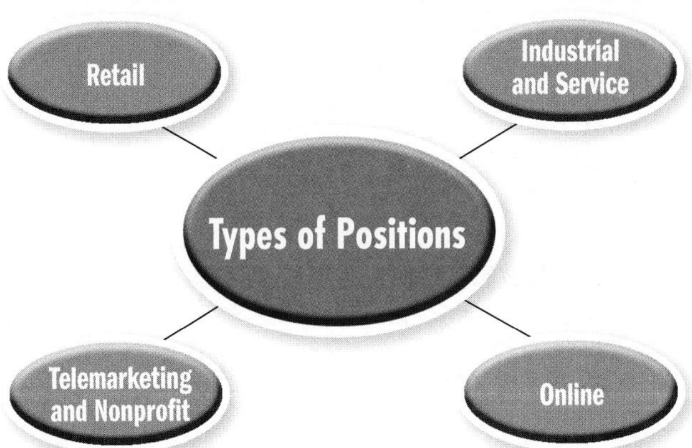

Expert Advice

Read the quote to students:

> **"Personal selling involves two-way communication between the buyer and seller."**

Ask students: What are examples of one-way communications that you use? radio, television Ask: ***What are examples of two-way communications?*** Examples include talking with someone in person, talking on the phone, texting, Skyping, or Tweeting.

TELEMARKETING AND NONPROFIT

Telemarketing is telephone solicitation to make a sale. Consumer goods and services that are commonly sold over the telephone include magazine or newspaper subscriptions and long-distance telephone services. Service contracts for newly purchased appliances, televisions, and computers are also sold over the telephone. Products that are purchased on a regular basis by businesses, such as cleaning supplies or office supplies like computer or copy paper, may be sold through telemarketing. Also, many nonprofit organizations use telemarketing to solicit donations.

In 2003, U.S. Congress passed legislation making it more difficult for telemarketers to operate. The law prohibits telemarketers from calling any phone number that has been registered with the national Do Not Call Registry, established by the Federal Communications Commission. This law significantly reduces the number of people telemarketers may contact.

INTERNET WEB SITES AND SALES

Many Internet Web sites have supporting sales staff to handle customers who call to place an order. The sales support staff must know sales techniques to help callers make a buying decision.

Companies that have a presence on the Internet (e.g., Google, Yahoo!, Bing, and Amazon) sell advertising space to generate revenue. They have sales employees who solicit that business.

STEPS OF A SALE

The sales process involves solving your customer's problems with your product. Salespeople play a vital role in this process. They gather information about customers, advise them about which products would best suit their needs, and then lead them to a decision to buy.

Depending on the customer's decision-making process, salespeople may or may not go through all the seven steps of a sale (see **Figure 12.1**).

1. **Approach the customer**—greeting the customer face-to-face
2. **Determine needs**—learning what the customer is looking for in order to decide what products to show and which product features to present first in the next step of the sale
3. **Present the product**—educating the customer about the product's features and benefits, as well as its advantages over the competition
4. **Overcome objections**—learning why the customer is reluctant to buy, providing information to remove that uncertainty and helping the customer to make a satisfying buying decision
5. **Close the sale**—getting the customer's positive agreement to buy
6. **Perform suggestion selling**—suggesting additional merchandise or services that will save your customer money or help your customer better enjoy the original purchase
7. **Build relationships**—following up by creating a means of maintaining contact with the customer after the sale is completed

Telemarketing

Telemarketing is a type of sales position that uses telephone solicitation to sell products or services. ***How do you think the Do Not Call Registry has changed the use of telemarketing?***

The other chapters in this unit discuss in more detail various selling principles and techniques for each step in the sales process.

CUSTOMER DECISION MAKING

Some customers need no help from salespeople, and others require significant time and effort. There are three distinct types of decision making—extensive, limited, and routine. How a person makes a decision is affected by the following factors:

- Previous experience with the product and company
- How often the product is purchased
- The amount of information necessary to make a wise buying decision
- The importance of the purchase to the customer
- The perceived risk involved in the purchase (such as, uncertainty about how the product will work)
- The time available to make the decision

EXTENSIVE DECISION MAKING

Extensive decision making is used when there has been little or no previous experience with an item. This category includes goods and services that have a high degree of perceived risk, are very expensive, or have high value to the customer. For a business, products in this category include expensive manufacturing machinery or land for a new building site. At the individual level, a consumer who is buying a first car or home will use extensive decision making.

LIMITED DECISION MAKING

Limited decision making is used when a person buys goods and services that he or she has purchased before but not regularly. There is a moderate degree of perceived risk involved, and the person often needs some information before buying the product.

FIGURE 12.1 The Steps of a Sale

Remembering the Steps A mnemonic device, such as ANPOCS, can help you remember the steps of a sale. ***How do the final two steps add value to a sale that has been closed?***

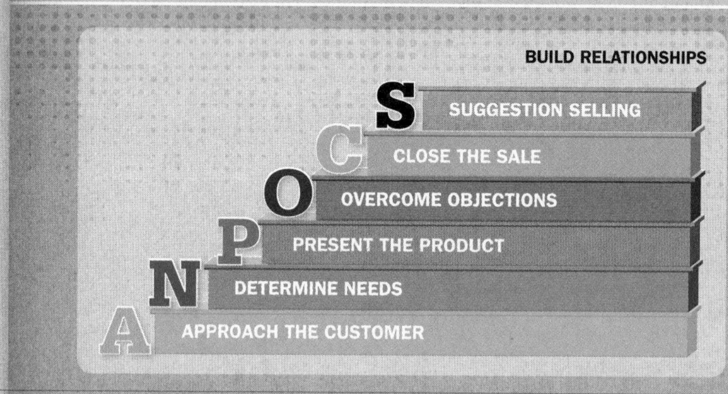

EXPLAIN

TELEMARKETING AND NONPROFIT

Ask these guiding questions to focus the discussion.

Guiding Questions

Identify Cause and Effect Why do you think Congress passed the legislation that created the Do Not Call Registry?	Consumers were getting annoyed with large numbers of telemarketing calls and put pressure on lawmakers to provide a way to stop them.
Apply If you were hiring workers for a telemarketing company, what kind of individuals would you look for?	Sample answer: I would hire people who are well spoken, persuasive, and who do not become discouraged easily.

Reinforce Vocabulary

Telemarketing–Identifying Word Components Write the word *telemarketing* for students to view. Ask students: What are the two basic components of this word? tele and marketing Ask: What does *tele* mean? having to do with the telephone Remind students that marketing is the process of exchanging products and services of value between two individuals or groups. The word *telemarketing* refers to using the phone to engage in this process.

Visual Literacy

Telemarketing Caption Answer Read the caption question to students: ***How do you think the Do Not Call Registry has changed the use of telemarketing?*** The registry has significantly affected the ability of telemarketing firms to do their jobs effectively.

ELABORATE

Build Background

Use the graphic in Figure 12.1 to discuss the steps of a sale.

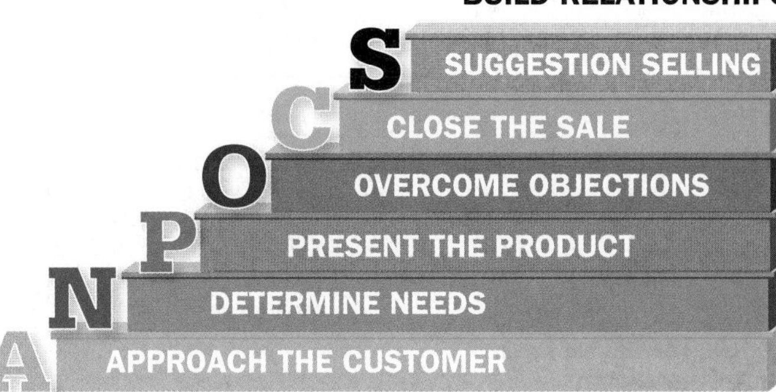

Visual Literacy

Figure 12.1 Caption Answer Read the caption question to students: ***How do the final two steps add value to a sale that has been closed?*** They emphasize that the salesperson wants to make certain that the customer will continue to be happy with the buying decision. Ask students: ***In what situations do you think it is most important for a salesperson to build an ongoing relationship with a customer? Why?*** When the customer makes regular purchases from the salesperson, it is important that the relationship continues to meet the customer's needs so that he or she will not go elsewhere.

STEPS OF A SALE

Ask these guiding questions to focus the discussion about the steps of a sale.

Guiding Questions

Classify Best Buy® has a slogan that states "Buy a laptop, get a geek." During what step should this be explained?	This would be explained during the Present the Product step.
Apply You work at an electronics store. A customer has just purchased a laptop from you. What might you do at this point to build a relationship with this customer?	You might learn that the customer will soon want to buy a color printer for the laptop, and suggest that you would be happy to help the customer make this decision.

e MARKETING

High Capacity Color Barcode

Microsoft® developed the High Capacity Color Barcode (HCCB), which is an identification device with embedded detailed product information, as well as the ability for customers to interact with it. Microsoft's version of HCCB is Microsoft Tag. Audiovisual publishers embraced this new technology because it allows them to provide customers with the information they need to make an informed purchase decision. For example when customers scan the HCCB they can learn about a DVD's ratings, parental control, pricing, contests, and promotions. This interactive technology requires cell phones with color cameras to work. Watch for HCCBs in various media, such as television, magazine ads, movie posters, and other platforms, as well as on product packaging. HCCBs look like colored triangles arranged on a grid.

Innovate and Create

Engage students in a discussion regarding the use of HCCBs as a sales tool. What role can HCCBs play in preselling customers and selling products online? What information should be provided to customers in the embedded code? How would people know to scan the HCCB seen in a magazine ad? How can HCCBs be used during the selling process when interacting with customers? What additional technology might be needed in brick and mortar stores to make use of HCCBs on the selling floor? Since customers decide to scan HCCBs they have already indicated an interest in the product. Any additional information about the product could presell them so they seek out the product in a brick and mortar store or make an online purchase if that option is made available. Answers will vary regarding the information to be embedded in the code depending on the product or service. Some generic information may include the price, sizes, colors, availability, where the product can be purchased, promotions, discounts, and invitations to be added to that company's social media platforms (i.e., Facebook, Twitter). During the selling process when interacting with customers, salespeople could be given devices to scan the HCCBs to show customers the information embedded in the code. Thus, HCCBs would act as a sales aid.

 **glencoe.com** 

eMarketing Worksheet Activity Send students to the Online Learning Center to download an eMarketing worksheet activity.

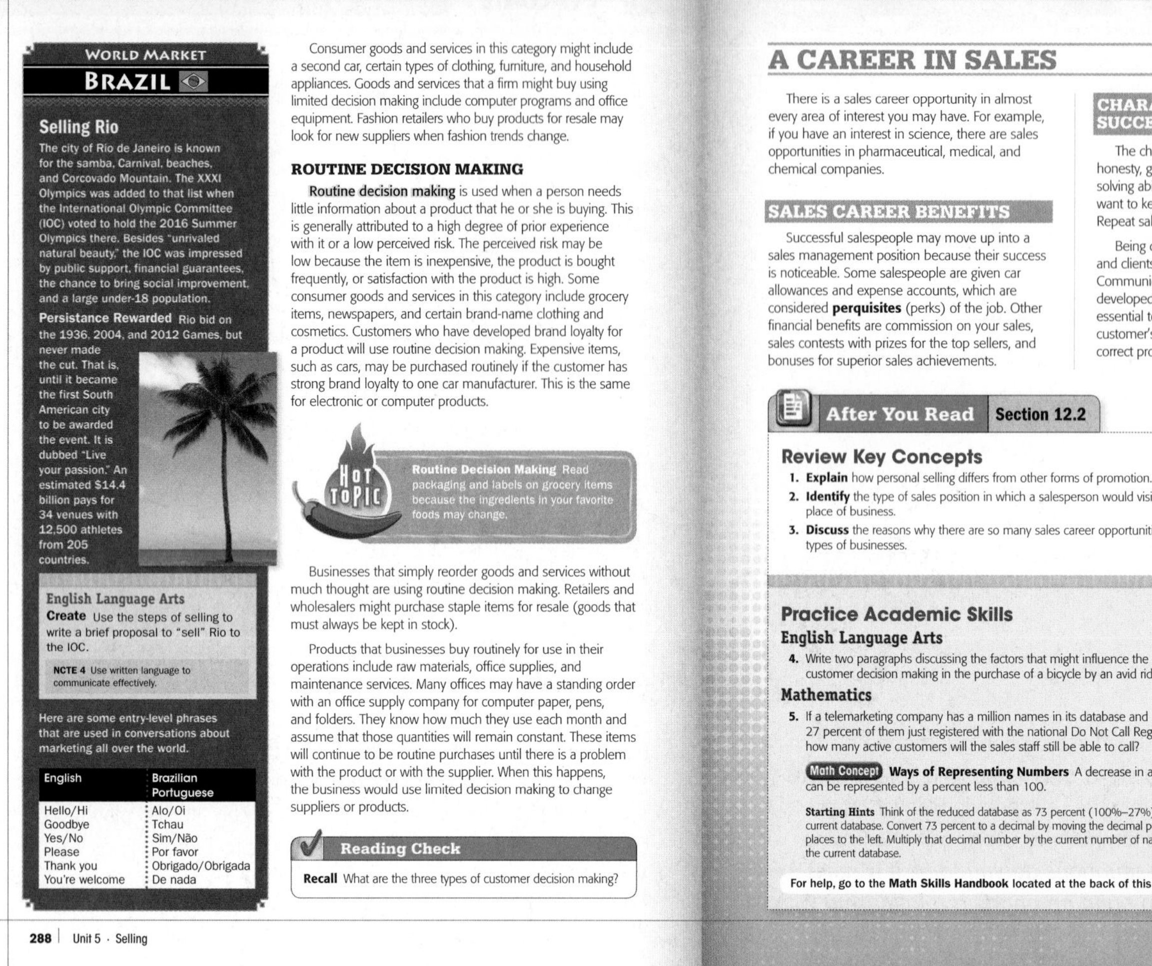

WORLD MARKET

BRAZIL

Selling Rio

The city of Rio de Janeiro is known for the samba, Carnival, beaches, and Corcovado Mountain. The XXXI Olympics was added to that list when the International Olympic Committee (IOC) voted to hold the 2016 Summer Olympics there. Besides "unrivaled natural beauty," the IOC was impressed by public support, financial guarantees, the chance to bring social improvement, and a large under-18 population.

Persistance Rewarded Rio bid on the 1936, 2004, and 2012 Games, but never made the cut. That is, until it became the first South American city to be awarded the event. It is dubbed "Live your passion." An estimated $14.4 billion pays for 34 venues with 12,500 athletes from 205 countries.

English Language Arts

Create Use the steps of selling to write a brief proposal to "sell" Rio to the IOC.

NCTE 4 Use written language to communicate effectively.

Here are some entry-level phrases that are used in conversations about marketing all over the world.

English	Brazilian Portuguese
Hello/Hi	Alo/Oi
Goodbye	Tchau
Yes/No	Sim/Não
Please	Por favor
Thank you	Obrigado/Obrigada
You're welcome	De nada

Consumer goods and services in this category might include a second car, certain types of clothing, furniture, and household appliances. Goods and services that a firm might buy using limited decision making include computer programs and office equipment. Fashion retailers who buy products for resale may look for new suppliers when fashion trends change.

ROUTINE DECISION MAKING

Routine decision making is used when a person needs little information about a product that he or she is buying. This is generally attributed to a high degree of prior experience with it or a low perceived risk. The perceived risk may be low because the item is inexpensive, the product is bought frequently, or satisfaction with the product is high. Some consumer goods and services in this category include grocery items, newspapers, and certain brand-name clothing and cosmetics. Customers who have developed brand loyalty for a product will use routine decision making. Expensive items, such as cars, may be purchased routinely if the customer has strong brand loyalty to one car manufacturer. This is the same for electronic or computer products.

HOT TOPIC **Routine Decision Making** Read packaging and labels on grocery items because the ingredients in your favorite foods may change.

Businesses that simply reorder goods and services without much thought are using routine decision making. Retailers and wholesalers might purchase staple items for resale (goods that must always be kept in stock).

Products that businesses buy routinely for use in their operations include raw materials, office supplies, and maintenance services. Many offices may have a standing order with an office supply company for computer paper, pens, and folders. They know how much they use each month and assume that those quantities will remain constant. These items will continue to be routine purchases until there is a problem with the product or with the supplier. When this happens, the business would use limited decision making to change suppliers or products.

Reading Check

Recall What are the three types of customer decision making?

A CAREER IN SALES

There is a sales career opportunity in almost every area of interest you may have. For example, if you have an interest in science, there are sales opportunities in pharmaceutical, medical, and chemical companies.

SALES CAREER BENEFITS

Successful salespeople may move up into a sales management position because their success is noticeable. Some salespeople are given car allowances and expense accounts, which are considered **perquisites** (perks) of the job. Other financial benefits are commission on your sales, sales contests with prizes for the top sellers, and bonuses for superior sales achievements.

CHARACTERISTICS OF SUCCESSFUL SALESPEOPLE

The characteristics of effective salespeople are honesty, good interpersonal skills, and problem-solving ability. Salespeople must be honest if they want to keep their customers for years to come. Repeat sales are necessary for success in sales.

Being comfortable speaking with customers and clients makes the selling job much easier. Communication and interpersonal skills can be developed by practicing them. Problem-solving is essential to sales because you need to assess a customer's situation in order to recommend the correct product or solution to a problem.

After You Read **Section 12.2**

Review Key Concepts

1. **Explain** how personal selling differs from other forms of promotion.
2. **Identify** the type of sales position in which a salesperson would visit a customer's place of business.
3. **Discuss** the reasons why there are so many sales career opportunities in different types of businesses.

Practice Academic Skills

English Language Arts

4. Write two paragraphs discussing the factors that might influence the level of customer decision making in the purchase of a bicycle by an avid rider.

NCTE 3 Apply strategies to interpret texts.

Mathematics

5. If a telemarketing company has a million names in its database and 27 percent of them just registered with the national Do Not Call Registry, how many active customers will the sales staff still be able to call?

NCTM Number and Operations Understand numbers, ways of representing numbers, relationships among numbers, and number systems.

Math Concept **Ways of Representing Numbers** A decrease in a number can be represented by a percent less than 100.

Starting Hints Think of the reduced database as 73 percent (100%–27%) of its current database. Convert 73 percent to a decimal by moving the decimal point two places to the left. Multiply that decimal number by the current number of names in the current database.

For help, go to the **Math Skills Handbook** located at the back of this book.

glencoe.com

Check your answers.

288 | Unit 5 · Selling

Chapter 12 · Selling Overview | 289

ELABORATE

WORLD MARKET
ENGLISH LANGUAGE ARTS

The proposal should follow the seven steps of a sale. First, they need to let the IOC know they are interested in having the 2016 Olympics in Rio de Janeiro. Next, they must determine the exact needs of the Olympics and how they will meet those needs. They must overcome any feelings the IOC might have about their inability to come through with their promises. To close the sale, they must get the IOC's agreement to hold the Olympics in Rio. They should emphasize the special features Rio can offer that other venues may not be able to provide, such as a large under-18 population and a fun atmosphere. They can then follow up by keeping the IOC informed about what they are doing to uphold their end of the contract.

ROUTINE DECISION MAKING

Ask these guiding questions to focus the discussion about routine decision making.

Guiding Questions

Draw Conclusions A consumer goes to the supermarket to buy laundry detergent, but the store is out of his brand. He buys a similar product. Why is he comfortable making this decision?	The consumer saw a low degree of perceived risk.
Predict A consumer routinely buys a specific brand of fabric softener. It appears that the softener is giving her son a rash. What will the consumer do?	engage in limited decision making and try a brand that is fragrance-free

Routine Decision Making Ask students: *What kinds of risks are there in routine decision making?*

EVALUATE

Reading Check Answer

Read the Reading Check question to students: ***What are the three types of customer decision making?*** extensive decision making, limited decision making, routine decision making

Graphic Organizer

Display this Venn diagram. Ask students to list the characteristics. Possible answers:

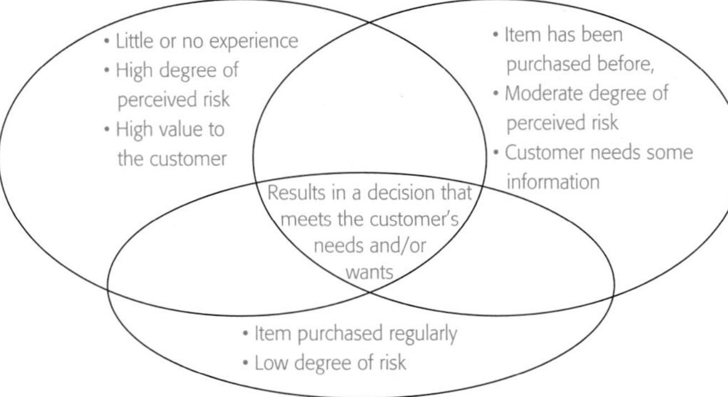

 glencoe.com  iWB

Graphic Organizer Send students to the Online Learning Center to print this graphic organizer.

A CAREER IN SALES

Ask these guiding questions to focus the discussion on careers in sales.

Guiding Questions

Explain Why is being a good problem solver at the heart of being a successful salesperson?	Successful salespeople determine how their products or services can solve customers' problems.
Apply You are a salesperson for a stapler manufacturer with a reputation for quality. The company has come out with a fashionable new stapler, but you know the quality is below average. What would you do?	I would discourage my customers from purchasing the product and steer them toward staplers I thought were of better quality. I also would inform my sales manager about my concerns.

After You Read Section 12.2

Review Key Concepts

1. Personal selling involves two-way communication between the buyer and seller; other forms of promotion are one-way.
2. Field (outside) sales involves a salesperson visiting a customer's place of business. Manufacturing, wholesaling, and some service businesses employ field sales representatives.
3. Since all companies make money by selling products and/or services, sales career opportunities can be found virtually everywhere. Because being a good salesperson requires specialized skills, there are always positions open for successful individuals.

Practice Academics

English Language Arts

4. The factors that might influence the level of customer decision making in the purchase of a bicycle by an avid rider include: previous experience with a specific brand or bicycle model, product research conducted on the Internet and through discussions with other avid riders, a change in the customer's needs, and time available to make the purchase, especially if the current bicycle is not functioning.

Mathematics

5. The sales staff could still call 730,000 active customers (100% − 27% = 73%; .73 × 1,000,000).

 glencoe.com

Answer Key Send students to the Online Learning Center to check their answers.

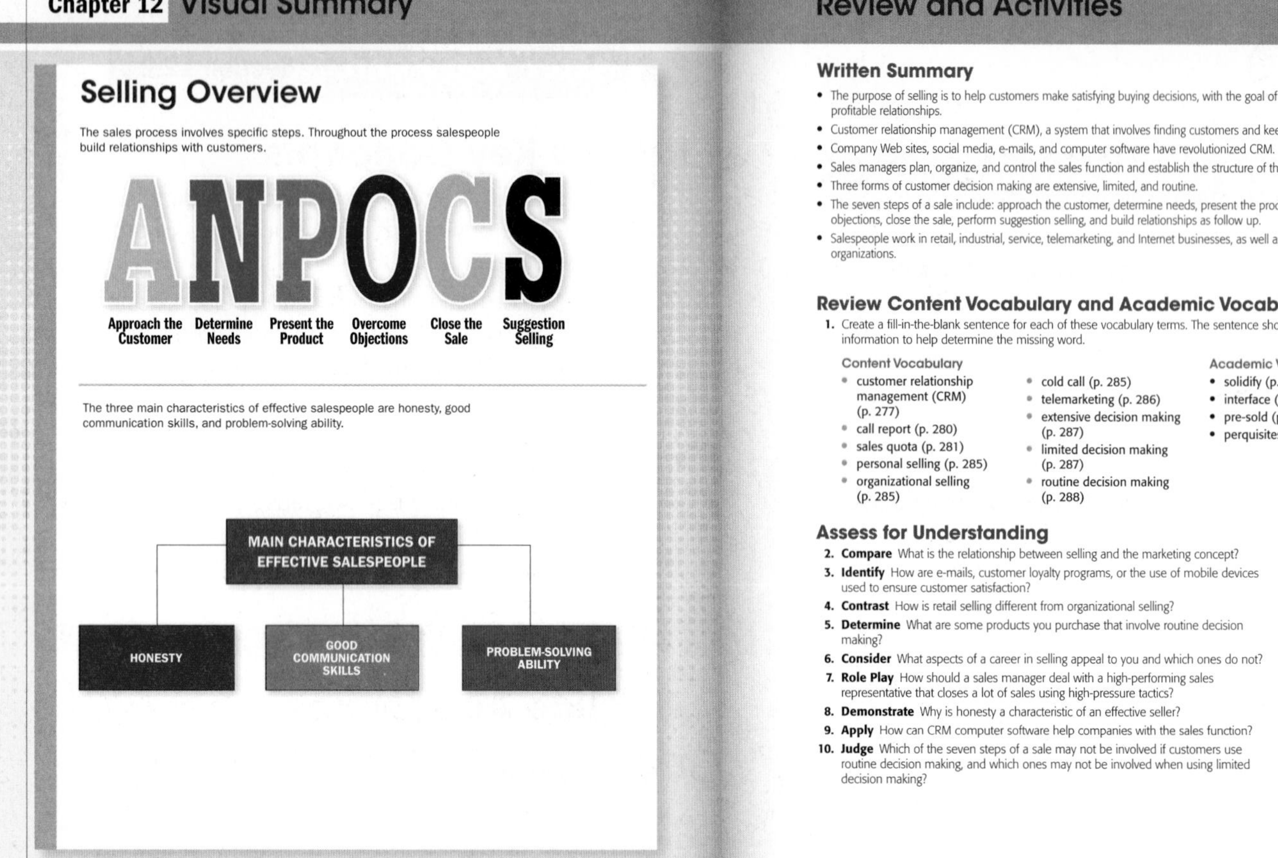

Chapter 12 Visual Summary

Selling Overview

The sales process involves specific steps. Throughout the process salespeople build relationships with customers.

The three main characteristics of effective salespeople are honesty, good communication skills, and problem-solving ability.

Review and Activities

Written Summary

- The purpose of selling is to help customers make satisfying buying decisions, with the goal of creating ongoing, profitable relationships.
- Customer relationship management (CRM), a system that involves finding customers and keeping them satisfied.
- Company Web sites, social media, e-mails, and computer software have revolutionized CRM.
- Sales managers plan, organize, and control the sales function and establish the structure of the sales organization.
- Three forms of customer decision making are extensive, limited, and routine.
- The seven steps of a sale include: approach the customer, determine needs, present the product, overcome objections, close the sale, perform suggestion selling, and build relationships as follow up.
- Salespeople work in retail, industrial, service, telemarketing, and Internet businesses, as well as nonprofit organizations.

Review Content Vocabulary and Academic Vocabulary

1. Create a fill-in-the-blank sentence for each of these vocabulary terms. The sentence should contain enough information to help determine the missing word.

Content Vocabulary
- customer relationship management (CRM) (p. 277)
- call report (p. 280)
- sales quota (p. 281)
- personal selling (p. 285)
- organizational selling (p. 285)
- cold call (p. 285)
- telemarketing (p. 286)
- extensive decision making (p. 287)
- limited decision making (p. 287)
- routine decision making (p. 288)

Academic Vocabulary
- solidify (p. 278)
- interface (p. 279)
- pre-sold (p. 285)
- perquisites (p. 289)

Assess for Understanding

2. **Compare** What is the relationship between selling and the marketing concept?
3. **Identify** How are e-mails, customer loyalty programs, or the use of mobile devices used to ensure customer satisfaction?
4. **Contrast** How is retail selling different from organizational selling?
5. **Determine** What are some products you purchase that involve routine decision making?
6. **Consider** What aspects of a career in selling appeal to you and which ones do not?
7. **Role Play** How should a sales manager deal with a high-performing sales representative that closes a lot of sales using high-pressure tactics?
8. **Demonstrate** Why is honesty a characteristic of an effective seller?
9. **Apply** How can CRM computer software help companies with the sales function?
10. **Judge** Which of the seven steps of a sale may not be involved if customers use routine decision making, and which ones may not be involved when using limited decision making?

EVALUATE

Visual Summary

Express Creativity Ask students to create a visual summary that illustrates a concept in the chapter. Encourage students to use different formats for their visual summaries, such as a storyboard, a timeline, a cause-and-effect diagram, or a slide show. Visual summaries will vary depending on the concept depicted. Questions to ask when assessing a visual summary include:

- Is the summary clear, economical, and simple?
- Are any important steps or concepts left out?
- Are steps or concepts arranged in the same order as the original?
- Does the summary reveal a pattern that connects the details?
- Does the summary locate and highlight the most important information?

Review Content Vocabulary and Academic Vocabulary

1. Customer relationship management is a trend that has flourished due to improved technologies. Call reports prepared by salespeople are reviewed by sales management. A sales quota can put pressure on a salesperson. Personal selling is unlike other promotional activities due to direct contact with customers. Organizational selling can be found in manufacturing companies, service companies, and wholesaling firms. A cold call is risky because your prospective customer may not be available at that time. Telemarketing activities have been reduced due to the "Do Not Call Registry" legislation. Three levels of decision making are extensive decision making, which occurs when there is little or no previous experience with the item; limited decision making, when a person has previously purchased the item, but does not do so regularly; and routine decision making, where the person needs no guidance in making the purchasing decision. It is a good idea to shake hands after making a sale to solidify the agreement. Different computer programs and people from different departments often interface with one another. The customer was pre-sold on a new smart phone after seeing it advertised on television. Having a company credit card to take customers to lunch is a perquisite in some sales positions.

EVALUATE

Assess for Understanding

2. Selling is at the heart of the marketing concept because businesses have the goal of satisfying customers' needs and wants while making a profit. Businesses cannot make a profit without generating sales.

3. E-mails targeting customers based on their previous purchases, customer loyalty programs that reward customers for their purchases, and mobile devices that help sales representatives quickly and efficiently place customers' orders and check on order status all help to ensure that the customers' needs are met as efficiently as possible.

4. Organizational selling requires more advanced training and is more sophisticated and more lucrative than retail selling.

5. Answers will vary, but might include situations in which the student always purchases the same type of product or brand, such as energy drinks, snack foods, small clothing items such as socks, and school supplies.

6. Answers will vary.

7. When meeting with the sales representative, the sales manager should stress sales ethics and the need for repeat business, both of which would be in jeopardy if the sales representative were to continue using high-pressure tactics.

8. Honesty is important in selling because making the sale is only the first step in building an ongoing and hopefully long relationship with a customer. Being dishonest in order to make one sale does not benefit the salesperson in the long run.

9. CRM software helps sales representatives and managers manage customer information and sales territories, follow current orders, check inventories, conduct sales forecasting, and so on.

10. In routine decision making, the steps that may not be involved are determining needs, presenting the product, and handling objections, because the customer is pre-sold and knows exactly what he or she wants. In limited decision making, all the steps may be involved, because information is needed to make decisions.

21st Century Skills

Teamwork Skills

11. **Everyday Ethics** Why do you think salespeople are sometimes depicted in movies as dishonest? With a partner, research sales ethics in business magazines, on the Web or through interviews with salespeople. Make a list of the characteristics of ethical salespeople. Use that list to prepare a simple "Code of Sales Ethics." Present your code to the class.

Financial Literacy Skills

12. **Compensation Options** Which sales compensation offer do you prefer? You can opt to get paid either a yearly salary of $50,000 *or* an 8-percent commission on all sales you close. The sales territory you would be assigned has historically generated $800,000 in sales. If sales remain the same, what would you earn in commission? What would your commission be if sales were to drop by 15 percent next year in your territory because of a weak economy? Choose one of the compensation options and explain why you selected that plan.

e-Marketing Skills

13. **Online Sales** Find a consumer products company that has a Web site where it sells its products online. Find another company that has a Web site that directs customers to retail stores to buy its products. How are the Web-site designs different? Why do you think some companies sell online while others do not? In your opinion, which type of company Web site is more effective and why? Suggest changes that could make the other more effective. Here are some factors to consider:
    - How profitable is the company?
    - What shipping options does the company offer?
    - Where is the company located? (Even online companies have physical locations.)
    - How are the sales teams different for each company?

Build Academic Skills

Social Studies

14. **Self-Analysis** List and analyze your personal interests and abilities to see if they match the characteristics of effective salespeople. How could you test your sales ability?

Science

15. **Technology for Selling** Sales managers use technology on a regular basis to monitor sales results. Research online computer software programs available to sales managers to help them with their work. Look for emerging technologies in marketing. Start with companies that offer CRM programs, as well as sales territory analysis, sales forecasting, and any other technological tools that would benefit them or their sales staff. Write a short report on your findings.

Mathematics

16. **Sales Costs** What percentage of sales revenue goes to the cost of sales for the XYZ company? XYZ offers salary plus commission and bonuses for sales personnel who reach their sales quotas. It has eight salespeople, each earning a base salary of $45,000 plus a 2-percent commission on sales. Sales were $3 million, and bonuses totaled $30,000 for the year.

Math Concept **Problem Solving** First, determine total sales costs for the XYZ company. Add the cost of sales bonuses to the cost of the base salaries of the sales personnel and their respective commission to get total sales costs.

For help, go to the **Math Skills Handbook** located at the back of this book.

NCSS IV D Individual Development & Identity Apply concepts, methods, and theories about the study of human growth and development, such as physical endowment, learning, motivation, behavior, perception, and personality.

NSES F Develop understanding of personal and community health; population growth; natural resources; environmental quality; natural and human-induced hazards; science and technology in local, national, and global challenges.

NCTM Problem Solving Apply and adapt a variety of appropriate strategies to solve problems.

Standardized Test Practice

Directions Read the following questions. On a separate piece of paper, write the best possible answer for each one.

1. What is 6 percent of $675,000?
   A. $64,500
   B. $48,000
   C. $40,500
   D. $45,000
2. Personal selling involves two-way communication between a buyer and seller.
   T
   F
3. The purpose of selling is to help customers make satisfying buying decisions with the goal of creating ________, ________ relationships with them.

Test-Taking Tip
Taking tests can be stressful. If you begin to get nervous, take a few deep breaths slowly and relax.

DECA Connection Role Play

Sales Representative Apparel Manufacturer

Situation To earn a $100 bonus at the end of each month as a sales representative, your sales must exceed $310,000. Only goods that are actually shipped count toward the sales quota. To date, your sales are $283,780.

You just met with one of your steady customers who placed a $50,000 order with the stipulation that delivery of the goods must be in two months from today's date. Company policy requires that you must get permission from your sales manager to extend the date of shipping. If you do not get permission for the extension, the goods will be shipped immediately, which is company policy. If you do get the extension, you will not reach your sales quota for the month. You need the bonus to pay bills. This sales order will also help your manager reach the sales goals set by upper-level management.

What will you do? The customer is waiting to hear back from you regarding the delivery extension before finalizing the order. You must meet with your sales manager (judge) to explain your customer's request for the delivery extension.

Activity Make a decision on how you think the order should be processed. Prepare notes on what you will say to your sales manager. You will then use your notes when you actually meet with your customer (judge).

Evaluation You will be evaluated on how well you meet these performance indicators:

1. Explain the nature and scope of the selling function.
2. Explain the selling process.
3. Explain business ethics in selling.
4. Describe the use of technology in the selling function.
5. Explain the nature of sales management.

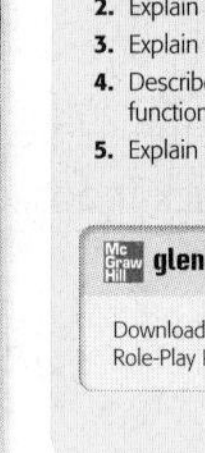

glencoe.com

Download the Competitive Events Workbook for more Role-Play Practice.

EVALUATE

21st Century Skills

Teamwork Skills

11. Accept all reasonable responses for the "Code of Sales Ethics." Some of the following traits will likely be included in the code: honesty, integrity, fairness, working toward meeting customer needs, and empathy.

Financial Literacy Skills

12. Some may opt for the yearly salary of $50,000 to be safe, while others may opt for straight commission. The calculations show that compensation would be greater with the projected straight commission options. ($800,000 × .08 = $64,000 straight commission if sales remain the same; $800,000 × .85 = $680,000 × .08 = $54,400 if sales decrease by 15%).

e-Marketing Skills

13. A Web site that directs visitors to a local store to make purchases, but does not allow for online sales, is likely to focus primarily on product features. A Web site that allows online purchases will allow customers to choose from available inventory and delivery methods, accept a variety of payment methods, and so on. Many customers prefer to make online purchases, primarily because of the time savings and wide product availability. However, other companies feel that allowing online purchases lowers sales at bricks-and-mortar stores, and can make it difficult for these stores to remain in business. In addition, some companies feel that it is important for their customers to have direct input from a qualified salesperson in order to have a positive buying experience.

EVALUATE

Build Academic Skills

Social Studies

14. Accept all reasonable answers. For example, students might say they tend to be shy around strangers, which could create a problem in personal selling. Ways students can test their sales ability might include working on a fundraiser that requires them to ask for donations or to sell a product or service. They also could use the sales techniques they learned in this course at a part-time job where they deal directly with customers.

Science

15. Student reports should discuss computer software, including CRM software, that provides features such as sales territory analysis, sales forecasting, customer return reports, and so on. Some companies, such as North American Systems International, provide software that can be customized to meet the company's specific needs. Sample modules that can be added to the software include CRM, MRP (materials resource planning), and supply chain management software. Because the modules are created by a single software developer, they work together seamlessly to provide a customizable, unified method of meeting customer needs.

Mathematics

16. The percentage of sales revenue that comes from the cost of the sales function is 15 percent. When you add the straight salary for 8 salespeople $360,000 (8 × $45,000 = $360,000); the commission at $60,000 ($3 million × 0.02), and total bonuses of $30,000 for the year, you get total costs of $450,000; $450,000 divided by $3 million equals 0.15 = 15%).

Standardized Test Practice

1. C $40,500

2. True

3. ongoing, profitable

DECA Connection Role Play

Evaluations will be based on these performance indicators:

1. **Explain the nature and scope of the selling function.** Selling generates revenue that businesses need to operate. Selling involves helping customers make satisfying buying decisions, with the goal of creating ongoing, profitable relationships with them in order to make a profit.
2. **Explain the selling process.** The selling process involves learning about the customer's needs and wants and working to satisfying these needs and wants in order to generate a profit. Doing so leads to loyal customers, resulting in steady revenue. Loyal customers will recommend the company to others, thereby helping the company grow, further increasing profits.
3. **Explain business ethics in selling.** Ethical behavior in selling does not allow salespeople to engage in sales techniques that may cause legal problems or tarnish the business's reputation. Salespeople must tell customers the truth and not make promises they cannot fulfill. Sales orders and purchase orders are legal agreements that both buyers and sellers must abide by.
4. **Describe the use of technology in the selling function.** One popular computer technology is customer relationship management (CRM), which involves finding customers and keeping them satisfied. It organizes customer information, such as order history, and makes it accessible to salespeople. Company Web sites are useful in providing product information and allowing customers to make online purchases. Many businesses now participate in social media sites, such as Facebook and Twitter, which allow them to be accessible to potential customers around the world. E-mail is an efficient method of communicating with customers via written messages, thanking them for their orders, addressing various customer service issues, etc.
5. **Explain the nature of sales management** Sales management establishes guidelines and policies for the sales team. Sales managers plan, organize, and control the sales function and set up the structure of the sales organization. Managers prepare and monitor sales budgets, realistic sales forecasting, and sales quotas.

glencoe.com 

Role Plays For more DECA Role Plays, send students to the Online Learning Center to download the Competitive Events Workbook.

beginning the sales process

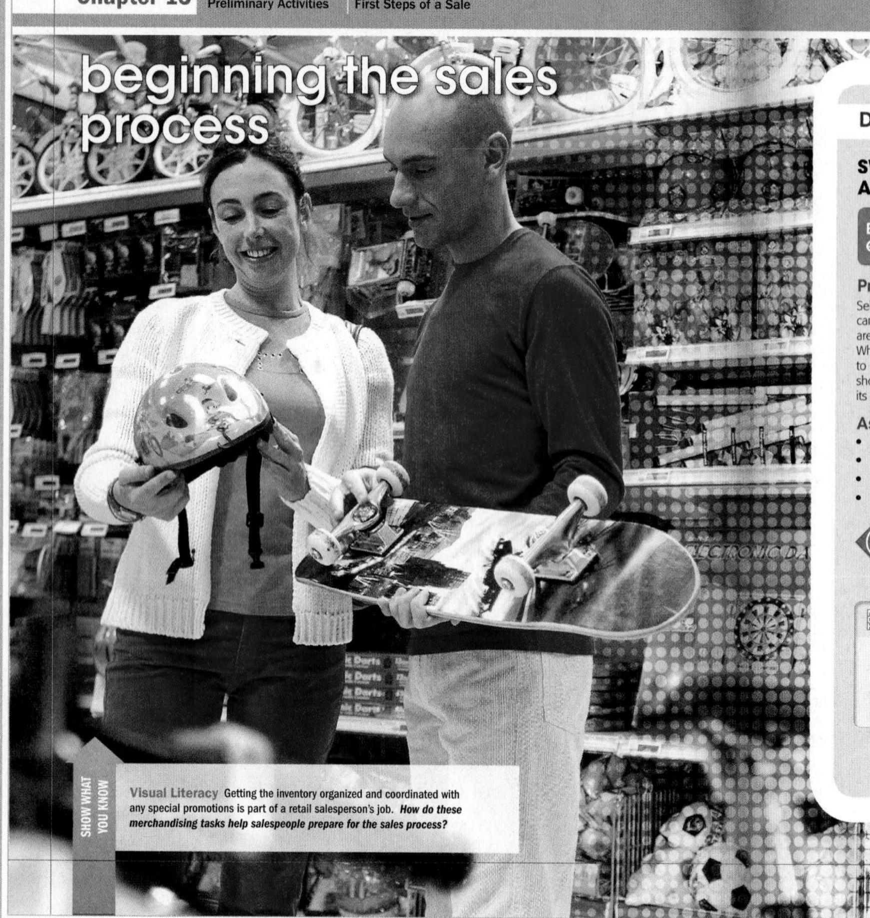

SHOW WHAT YOU KNOW

Visual Literacy Getting the inventory organized and coordinated with any special promotions is part of a retail salesperson's job. ***How do these merchandising tasks help salespeople prepare for the sales process?***

Discovery Project

SWOT Analysis for an Athletic Shoe

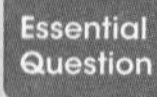

Essential Question Why is product information and knowledge of the competition so important in preparing for selling?

Project Goal

Select an athletic shoe to research. Learn everything you can about the shoe. How is it constructed? What materials are used in its construction? Is there a patent on its design? What is its retail price? What special features would appeal to prospective customers? Research a competing athletic shoe to see if the shoe you selected has an advantage over its competition.

Ask Yourself...

- How will you find information about athletic shoes?
- How will you select the specific athletic shoe to research?
- How will you find a competing athletic shoe?
- How will you present your findings?

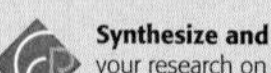

Synthesize and Present Research Synthesize your research on a competing athletic shoe and present your findings on whether the shoe you selected has an advantage over its competition.

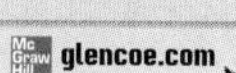

glencoe.com

Activity
Get a worksheet activity about conducting a SWOT analysis.

Evaluate
Download a rubric you can use to evaluate your project.

DECA Connection

DECA Event Role Play

Concepts in this chapter are related to DECA competitive events that involve either an interview or role play.

Indicators The performance indicators represent key skills and knowledge. Your key to success in DECA competitive events is relating them to concepts in this chapter.

- Acquire product information for use in selling.
- Analyze product information to identify product and features.
- Establish relationship with client/customer.
- Prepare for the sales presentation.
- Analyze customer needs.

DECA Prep

Role Play Practice role-playing with the DECA Connection competitive-event activity at the end of this chapter. More information on DECA events can be found on DECA's Web site.

ENGAGE

Visual Literacy

Read the chapter opener photo caption question to students: ***How do these merchandising tasks help salespeople prepare for the sales process?*** Working on special sales promotions and related merchandise provide a wealth of information salespeople can use to locate merchandise quickly, explain new sales promotions, and answer any questions that customers may have. Then ask these guiding questions.

Guiding Questions

Identify Who plans, organizes, and establishes the structure of the sales organization?	Sales managers
Explain What is the purpose of selling?	help customers make satisfying buying decisions, with the goal of creating profitable relationships

Discovery Project

SWOT Analysis for an Athletic Shoe Ask students if they have ever gone to purchase a product and were disappointed in the salesperson's knowledge of the product. Ask them to explain what they did. Then ask them the Discovery Project Essential Question: ***Why is product information and knowledge of your competitors so important in preparing for selling?*** Salespeople must know about their products so they can match products to customers' needs and wants. They must know about competitors' products so they are prepared when a customer asks them to compare their product to a competitor's product.

glencoe.com

Discovery Project Resources Send students to the Online Learning Center to download a rubric to evaluate their projects.

ENGAGE

Introduce the Chapter

Chapter 13 introduces students to the steps of the sales process. These main concepts are introduced and discussed:

- Product knowledge
- Industry trends and competition
- Merchandising
- Product features
- Customer benefits
- Selling points
- Customer buying motives
- Prospecting techniques
- Organizational selling
- Retail selling
- Determining needs

Discussion Starter

Product Knowledge Tell students that the first step in getting ready to sell is to acquire knowledge about the product(s) you are going to sell. Ask: ***How would you go about gaining knowledge about the products you are going to sell?*** Experience, published materials and Web sites, and training are the three main ways to learn product knowledge. Ask students: ***Do you think it is important to know about the competition's products? Why or why not?*** Students should recognize that it is important to know about the competition's products so they can be compared to their own products if a customer asks.

DECA Connection

Discuss the performance indicators listed in the DECA Connection feature. Explain to students that performance indicators tell them how to demonstrate their acquired skills and knowledge through individual or team competitive events.

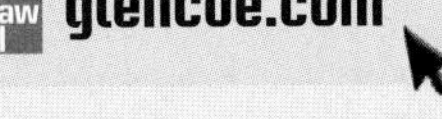

Competitive Events Workbook For more DECA Role Plays, send students to the Online Learning Center to download the Competitive Events Workbook.

PROGRAM RESOURCE ORGANIZER

PRINT RESOURCES

- **Student Edition**
- **Teacher Edition**
- **Student Activity Workbook with Academic Integration** includes worksheets and activities correlated to the text.
- **Mathematics for Marketing Workbook** provides math activities for every unit in the text.

TECHNOLOGY TOOLBOX

- **Connect**
- **ConnectPlus**
- **ExamView Assessment Suite** is a comprehensive solution for creating, administering, and scoring tests.

glencoe.com

Online Learning Center provides a variety of resources to enrich and enhance learning.

SECTION, CHAPTER, AND UNIT RESOURCES

- **Graphic Organizers** for organizing text concepts visually.
- **Digital Nation Activities** and **Green Marketer Activities** extend learning beyond the text features.
- **Career Chatroom Career Profiles** allow students to explore different marketing occupations in depth.
- **After You Read Answer Keys** for students to check their answers.
- **Discovery Project Rubrics** and **Marketing Internship Project Rubrics** for students to evaluate their projects.

PROGRAM RESOURCES

- **Student Activity Workbook with Academic Integration Teacher Annotated Edition** includes annotated answers for the activities and worksheets.
- **Marketing Research Project Workbook** provides a step-by-step approach for students to complete their own marketing research studies.
- **School-to-Career Activity Workbook** helps students relate their class work to on-the-job experience and involves work-site analysis and working with mentors.
- **Competitive Events Workbook** helps prepare students for state and national marketing education competitions.
- **Inclusion in the Marketing Education Classroom** provides teaching resources for working with students with special needs.
- **PowerPoint Presentations** provides visual teaching aids and assessments for this chapter.

READING GUIDE

Before You Read

Consider Do you think everyone who buys an item has the same reasons for buying it? Why or why not?

Objectives

- **Explain** how salespeople get ready to sell.
- **List** sources of product information.
- **Explain** feature-benefit selling and how it creates selling points.
- **Identify** consumer buying motives.
- **List** prospecting methods and explain how prospects are qualified.

The Main Idea

Getting ready to sell involves preliminary activities that help salespeople with the sales process, such as learning about the product, industry, and customer, to develop effective selling points.

Vocabulary

Content Vocabulary

- merchandising
- feature-benefit selling
- product features
- physical features
- extended product features
- customer benefits
- selling points
- buying motives
- rational motives
- emotional motives
- patronage motives
- prospecting
- prospect
- referrals
- endless-chain method
- cold canvassing

Academic Vocabulary

- shadowing
- longevity

Graphic Organizer

Draw or print this outline of the preliminary activities associated with the sales process.

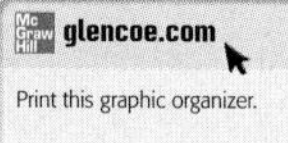

glencoe.com

Print this graphic organizer.

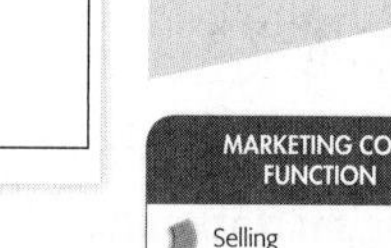

I. Getting ready to sell	II. Feature-Benefit Selling	III. Prospecting
A. Product Knowledge 1. 2. 3. B. C.	A. Product Features 1. 2. 3. B. C. D. E. Customer Buying Motives 1. 2. 3. 4.	A. Prospecting Techniques 1. 2. 3. B.

STANDARDS

ACADEMIC

English Language Arts

NCTE 1 Read texts to acquire new information.

Social Studies

NCSS VII B Production, Distribution, and Consumption Analyze the role that supply and demand, prices, incentives, and profits play in determining what is produced in a competitive market system.

NCSS *National Council for the Social Studies*
NCTE *National Council of Teachers of English*
NCTM *National Council of Teachers of Mathematics*
NSES *National Science Education Standards*

College & Career READINESS

Common Core

Writing Conduct short as well as more sustained research projects based on focused questions, demonstrating understanding of the subject under investigation.

MARKETING CORE FUNCTION

Selling

m.e. Section 13.1 Preliminary Activities

GETTING READY TO SELL

To be successful in sales, salespeople do their homework. They gather information about their products, industry trends, and competition. In retail situations, salespeople also perform tasks involved with merchandising.

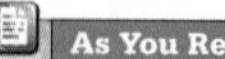

As You Read

Connect Analyze your backpack or a piece of clothing you are wearing. Find information on or in the product that might be useful in developing a selling point for it.

PRODUCT KNOWLEDGE

Salespeople must know their products so they can match them to customers' needs and wants. Product knowledge is essential when educating consumers and demonstrating a product. It is easy to gain product knowledge if you know where to locate product information. Sources of product information include experience with the product, published materials, Web sites, and formal training.

EXPERIENCE

Using a product is the best source of direct experience. Some businesses offer discounts to their salespeople to encourage them to use their merchandise. You can also get experience with a product by studying display models or visiting a manufacturing facility to see how it is made. Friends, relatives, coworkers, and customers can tell you about their experience with a product too.

PUBLISHED MATERIALS AND WEB SITES

Product information is found on Web sites and in published materials such as, labels, user manuals, manufacturer warranties and guarantees, catalogs, and promotional materials. Manufacturers and suppliers provide additional information and training materials in many cases. Web sites of manufacturers, retailers, and wholesalers provide an opportunity to view and study products.

> "Work associated with selling begins before a salesperson speaks with a client or a customer."

TRAINING

Formal training may be the best way to educate salespeople on certain products. Most industrial salespeople receive product knowledge through training sessions. Some salespeople spend months attending classes and **shadowing** experienced salespeople before selling on their own.

In retail settings, training is likely to be less structured. Information might be shared informally to the sales staff as new merchandise is received or selected for promotion. Some of the training materials may be provided by the supplier.

INDUSTRY TRENDS AND COMPETITION

Salespeople read periodicals to keep up with competitors and trends. Salespeople in the apparel industry read *Women's Wear Daily*, while those in the food industry read *Supermarket News*. All industries have trade publications related to their industry.

Standard & Poor's is a company that offers a trade reports by industry. It is available in college and public libraries and online.

ENGAGE

Anticipation Activity

Improving Student Achievement Ask volunteers to share poor sales experiences as customers. Ask: ***How could the situation have been improved?*** a salesperson with more training might have improved the situation

Objectives

- **Explain** how salespeople get ready to sell. gather information about products, industry trends, competition
- **List** sources of product information. experience, published materials, Web sites, formal training
- **Explain** feature-benefit selling and how it creates selling points. Matching the characteristics of a product to a customer's needs helps customers understand how the product meets his or her unique needs.
- **Identify** consumer buying motives. rational motives, emotional motives, patronage motives
- **List** prospecting methods and explain how prospects are qualified. customer referrals, cold canvassing, employer leads

Graphic Organizer

I. Getting Ready to Sell	II. Feature-Benefit Selling	III. Prospecting
A. Product Knowledge 1. Experience 2. Published Materials and Web Sites 3. Training B. Industry Trends and Competition C. Merchandising	A. Product Features 1. Basic Features 2. Physical Features 3. Extended Product Features B. Customer Benefits C. Selling Points D. Advantages E. Customer Buying Motives 1. Rational Motives 2. Emotional Motives 3. Patronage Motives 4. Multiple Motives	A. Prospecting Techniques 1. Customer Referrals 2. Cold Canvassing 3. Employer Sales Leads B. Qualifying Prospects

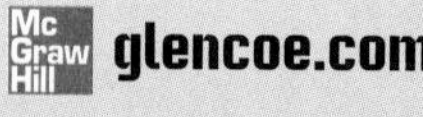

glencoe.com

Graphic Organizer Send students to the Online Learning Center to print this graphic organizer.

EXPLORE

Before You Read

Read the Before You Read question aloud: ***Do you think everyone who buys an item has the same reasons for buying it? Why or why not?*** Depending on the item purchased, other customers may or may not have the same reasons for buying it. Students should be able to defend their answers either way. For example, every car is purchased as a means of transportation; however, any one car may be selected for a variety of reasons, such as gas mileage, style, standard features, or performance.

Preteaching Vocabulary

Have students go to the Online Learning Center at glencoe.com for the Chapter 13 Preteaching Vocabulary games.

Content Vocabulary

Divide the class into pairs or groups of three or four. Have each group write definitions for the Content Vocabulary terms. Students should locate the definitions in dictionaries or the glossary in the back of the text. Then have groups write a sentence for each term. Sentences will vary but should show an understanding of the terms. Ask volunteers to share their sentences with the class.

Academic Vocabulary

Shadowing—Practical Application Ask students if they have ever had the opportunity to shadow someone. Ask: ***What was the experience like? What did you do?*** Some students may have had the opportunity to shadow their parent at work or had a different shadowing experience. Allow students to share their experiences. Ask: ***What did you learn from your shadowing experience?*** Students may suggest that they realized how hard their parent worked, that they would not be interested in doing what their parent does for a living, and so on.

MINI CLIP

ELL: Language Practice
Go to the Online Learning Center to view a video in which students work together to review new content.

GETTING READY TO SELL

Tell students that they may think their days of doing homework will end when they finish school. Salespeople must take time to learn about the products they sell and how to work with customers. Then ask these guiding questions to focus the discussion about getting ready to sell.

Guiding Questions

Explain Why is it necessary for a salesperson to have product knowledge?	Salespeople must know their products so they can match the products to the customer's needs.
Analyze Why would some salespeople need to spend months attending classes and shadowing experienced salespeople before selling on their own?	Some products are so complex it takes a considerable amount of time and effort to learn what is necessary to help customers.

As You Read

Read students the As You Read question: ***Analyze your backpack or a piece of clothing you are wearing. Find information on or in the product that might be useful in developing a selling point for it.*** Students should explain how the function benefits the customer. For example, a selling point on a backpack may be a protective interior section for holding a laptop.

Expert Advice

Read the quote to students:

"Work associated with selling begins before a salesperson speaks with a client or a customer."

Ask students: ***What work must a salesperson do before speaking with a client?*** Salespeople must learn about the products they are going to sell and they must learn how to help meet the customer's needs.

A Source of Product Information

Hang tags, packaging, and labels provide a wealth of information about the special features of a product and how they function. ***Why do manufacturers include so much information on hang tags and product packaging?***

Effective and knowledgeable salespeople research their competition to be prepared when customers ask them to compare their product with a competitor's. A visit to a competitor's Web site can provide a wealth of information about its products and policies. If a company does not have a Web site, salespeople can try to secure a competitor's catalog and price list. They also might purchase a competitor's product and examine it. It is a good idea to prepare a SWOT analysis (strengths, weaknesses, opportunities, threats) when you gather information on competitors to see how their products compare to your products.

MERCHANDISING

Merchandising involves coordination of sales and promotional plans with buying and pricing. You are already familiar with merchandising seen in fast-food establishments with special sales promotions. These restaurants give away small toys related to a current movie or popular character with the purchase of a child's meal. Signs and a display of the toys are visible in the fast-food restaurant. All order takers are familiar with the promotion. The same effort is made in all retail operations and other businesses that run promotions.

The right place, time, price, and quantity are considered when displaying products. These factors are essential to effective merchandising.

Products being promoted are generally moved to a location in the retail store that is visible. When running a sale or promotion, retailers must be sure that they have a sufficient quantity of products available. They will need to arrange to restock products frequently. If supplies run out during a promotion, not only will sales will be lost, but customers will be unhappy.

Signs explaining the promotion should be visible throughout the store. Window and interior displays should be updated as part of visual-merchandising activities. Price tags should be updated and computer systems adjusted with the new promotional pricing. To ensure maximum return, store managers work closely with the sales staff to organize and coordinate these tasks in a timely manner. Getting all of these preparations done on time will allow sales personnel to spend time with customers.

Reading Check

Contrast How is training different in industrial selling and retail selling?

Salespeople must learn all they can about trends, competition, and changes occurring in their field. ***What do you observe about people on the street and at your school that would help you sell a new fashion trend?***

FEATURE-BENEFIT SELLING

Matching the characteristics of a product to a customer's needs and wants is a concept called **feature-benefit selling**. This concept is the basis for developing the selling points used in the sales presentation. Why? Because many people believe that customers do not buy products; rather, they buy what the products will do for them. Consumers purchase leather shoes for their appearance, easy care, comfort, and **longevity.** They purchase computers for increased productivity. People buy insurance for emotional and financial security.

Salespeople work on constructing selling points for their product by using the feature-benefit selling concept. All the information researched on their product, industry trends, and competition is used to develop the selling points. An understanding of the customer's buying motives helps to establish the right priority for the selling points to include in the sales presentation. Let's take a closer look at how feature-benefit selling creates effective selling points and advantages over the competition.

PRODUCT FEATURES

The first step in preparing selling points is to study a company's products and sales policies. They are the foundation for building effective selling points. **Product features** are basic, physical, or extended attributes of the product or purchase.

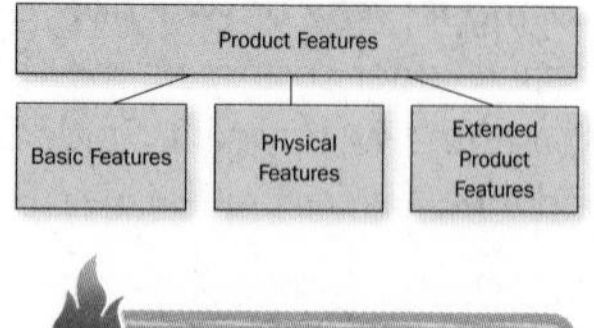

HOT TOPIC **Feature-Benefit Selling** Regardless of what you are selling, your main selling point should be the greatest benefit to the customer.

BASIC FEATURE

The most basic feature of a product is its intended use. A person buys an automobile for transportation and buys a watch to tell time. Basic product features are apparent and, therefore, generally accepted without question. So, salespeople do not have to spend time explaining basic product features unless the product is new and unusual. For example, an inventor of a new product would have to explain how to use the invention. The very first automobile was in this category. New technologies today fit in this category as well. When a product is new, explaining why customers would need such a product requires educating them about its intended use.

EXPLAIN

Visual Literacy

A Source of Product Information Caption Answer Read the caption question to students: ***Why do manufacturers include so much information on hang tags and product packaging?*** The information provided on hang tags and product packaging allows both salespeople and customers to learn about the product. Then ask these guiding questions about sources of product information.

Guiding Questions

List What are five types of published materials that provide product information?	labels, user manuals, manufacturer warranties/guarantees, catalogs, promotional materials
Analyze Why is using a product the best source of direct experience?	This gives the salesperson a first-hand understanding of the product. This allows the salesperson to speak from an experienced point of view.

Reading Check Answer

Read the Reading Check question to students: ***How is training different in industrial selling and retail selling?*** Most industrial salespeople receive product knowledge through training sessions. Some spend months attending classes and shadowing experienced salespeople before selling on their own. In retail settings, training may be brief, and it often happens on the job. Information might be shared informally to the sales staff as new merchandise is received or selected for promotion.

Critical Thinking

Have students visit a fast-food restaurant or a retail store that is currently offering a promotion. Ask students to look at the different aspects of the promotion and talk to servers about it. Have students write a half-page analysis of the promotion Analyses should discuss the physical aspects of the promotion and the server's knowledge about the promotion.

ELABORATE

Visual Literacy

Industry Trends Caption Answer Read the caption question to students: ***What do you observe about people on the street and at your school that would help you sell a new fashion trend?*** Observations may include the variety (or lack of variety) among the people they observed, or they may notice which items seem to be the most popular among students. Ask: ***How could these observations help you sell a new fashion trend?*** An observant salesperson will know how to appeal to the age group and social status of customers.

FEATURE-BENEFIT SELLING

Ask these guiding questions to focus the discussion about feature-benefit selling.

Guiding Questions

Identify What is the first step in preparing selling points?	Study a company's products and sales policies.
Explain In what way is feature-benefit selling connected to the concept of selling points?	Feature-benefit selling is the basis for developing the selling points used.
Analyze What is the meaning of the phrase, "Many people believe that customers do not buy products; they buy what the products will do for them"?	It illustrates that you don't purchase a book because you want a book, you purchase it because it can provide information or entertainment.

Reinforce Vocabulary

Longevity—Denotative Meaning Ask students what the root word for the term *longevity* is. Students should recognize that it is *long.* Ask students if they can guess the meaning of the term. Answers will vary but should include something about being long. Tell students that the term is from the Latin term *longus,* which means "long." The term *longevity* means "long life or duration." Ask a volunteer to read the first paragraph under the head Feature-Benefit Selling.

Graphic Organizer

Display this diagram. Ask students to provide examples for each type of product features. Possible answers:

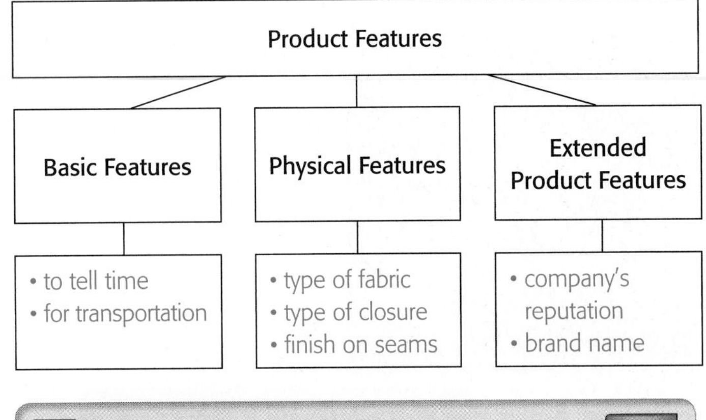

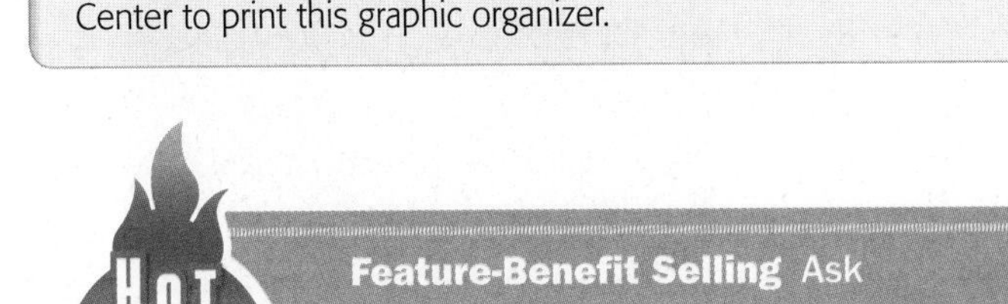

Graphic Organizer Send students to the Online Learning Center to print this graphic organizer.

HOT TOPIC

Feature-Benefit Selling Ask students to think about recent purchases they have made. Ask: ***What was the main selling point for the purchase?***

Critical Thinking

Tell students that people make purchases for many different reasons. Some of those reasons are practical and satisfy a need such as saving time or money. Other reasons may be more emotional such as to fill a desire (not necessarily a need). Write the terms *Basic Features, Physical Features,* and *Extended Product Features* for students to view. Ask students: ***How would you classify each type of feature—practical or emotional? Why?*** basic features fill practical needs while physical and extended product features fulfill emotional desires.

Identifying Product Features and Benefits

The information in this product insert visually identifies the product features and some of their corresponding benefits for FL-AIR 4 suitcases. ***What are two extended product features that you would need to know in order to sell this product effectively?***

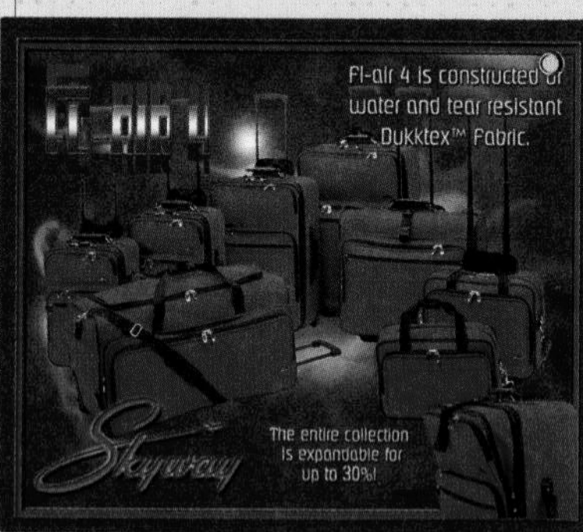

Fl-air 4 is constructed of water and tear resistant Dukktex™ Fabric.
The entire collection is expandable for up to 30%!

Designed for Function, Constructed To Last!
Zero-Gravity Construction

PHYSICAL FEATURES

Physical features of a product are tangible attributes that help explain how a product is constructed. For a jacket, its physical attributes are the fabrics used for the outer shell and insulation, as well as the type of collar, pockets, closure (buttons, snaps, or zipper), and sleeve design. How the seams are finished off and the garment's sizes are also physical attributes.

EXTENDED PRODUCT FEATURES

Extended product features are intangible attributes related to the sale of a product that customers find important. For example, customers might consider the reputation of a company or brand name of a product to be an extended feature. This may be true because there is reduced risk in doing business with a well-established company and brand. Significant company policies include warranties, guarantees, extended service contracts, financing, and customer service availability. Promotional support provided by a supplier to help sell a product is an extended feature found in organization sales situations. The price of a product is an extended product feature, which may be one of its most important features.

CUSTOMER BENEFITS

Customer benefits are the advantages or personal satisfaction a customer will get from a good or service. It is a salesperson's job to analyze product features from the customer's point of view. The first step in this analysis is to view the product feature in terms of how it functions. For example, air pockets in the heel of a running shoe (product feature) cushion the impact on pavement (function). Translating that information into a personal consumer benefit requires knowing what the customer values. In the case of the running shoe, the air pockets (feature), which cushions the impact on pavement (function), give the wearer more comfort when running or walking and help to protect the foot from injury (benefits).

SELLING POINTS

A **selling point** is created by noting the function of a product feature and explaining how it benefits a customer. Selling points are the result of the product analysis used in feature-benefit selling. If you review a well-designed catalog or Web site, you will see selling points in print. When communicating with customers in person, selling points form the foundation for the sales presentation. It is a good idea to practice writing selling points as *selling sentences.*

The GREEN Marketer

Understanding the Green Consumer

Green consumers are not all the same. With a variety of demographics, they represent all age brackets, income levels, and ethnic backgrounds. They are motivated to make purchases according to different wants and needs. Some are concerned about health; others about the environment, fair trade, or their kids' well-being; and still others about saving energy to save money.

Shades of Green Green consumers also come in different shades, from "deep greens," consumers who always put the environment first, to "light greens," who pick green options only when they are convenient and budget-friendly. Marketers must be aware of these shades of green and all of the ones in between if they want to be successful.

English Language Arts

Create Browse a supermarket for a food or cleaning product that is environmentally friendly. Write 50 words for an in-store display that will appeal to as many green consumer needs and segments as possible.

NCTE 5 Use different writing process elements to communicate effectively.

Get an activity on green marketing.

ELABORATE

Visual Literacy

Identifying Product Features and Benefits Caption Answer Read the caption question to students: ***What are two extended product features that you would need to know in order to sell this product effectively?*** Answers may include two of the following: brand name, warranty, guarantee, and price. Then ask these questions to guide the discussion about product features and benefits.

Guiding Questions

List What are three types of product features?	basic, physical, extended
Contrast How are basic features, physical features, and extended product features different?	Basic: intended uses of a product. Physical: attributes that help explain how a product is constructed. Extended: intangible attributes important to the customer.

Mini Project

Extension

Research Product Features Instruct students to research the features of five products.They should present the information in a table similar to the one below. Tables will vary depending on the products researched.

Product	Basic Features	Physical Features	Extended Product Features

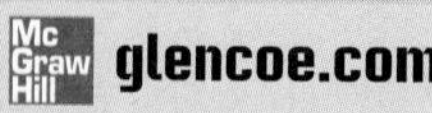

iWB

Graphic Organizer Send students to the Online Learning Center to print this graphic organizer.

ELABORATE

Graphic Organizer

Display this Venn diagram. Have students choose a product such as a car. Then ask students: ***What might be some selling points in a retail sales situation for the car? What might be some selling points in an organizational selling situation for the car?*** Possible answers:

Retail Sales	Both	Organizational Sales
• Lower price for end-of-year sale • Extended warranty • Several models and colors to choose from • Excellent gas mileage • Low maintenance • Free oil change for first year	• Price • Manufacturer's warranty • Fuel efficiency • Color, model availability	• More cars bought, lower price • Factory warranty on all models • Fuel efficient for frugal customers • Many colors and models available • Quick delivery, no shipping fees

 glencoe.com 

iWB

Graphic Organizer Send students to the Online Learning Center to print this graphic organizer.

VIRTUAL BUSINESS

MERCHANDISING

Introduce students to the concept of merchandising using Knowledge Matters' Virtual Business Retailing visual simulation, *Merchandising*. In this simulation, students will explore merchandising and its importance to store sales and profits.

The GREEN Marketer

English Language Arts Answer Read the English Language Arts Activity to students: ***Browse a supermarket for a food or cleaning product that is environmentally friendly. Write 50 words for an in-store display that will appeal to as many green consumer needs and segments as possible.*** Students' answers will vary, depending on the product they choose. Displays may contain words and phrases such as: concerned about health, environmentally friendly, fair trade, well-being, save energy and save money, easy and convenient to use, easy on the wallet, and so on. Ads should contain at least 50 words and be free of spelling errors.

 glencoe.com 

Worksheet Activity Send students to the Online Learning Center to get a Green Marketer worksheet activity.

Mini Projects

Differentiated Instruction

Linguistic Learners Instruct students to choose a product with which they are familiar. Then have them write at least five selling points for the product for a retail situation (selling points should be based on students' knowledge of the product). Have students write a brief analysis of how effective they believe the selling points would be for the majority of buyers and why they feel the way they do. Selling points will vary depending on the product students choose and on their own determination of what points are important to emphasize. Analyses should be thoughtful, and students should determine objectively whether the selling points would be effective with the majority of buyers and why they think so.

Kinesthetic Learners Divide the class into pairs. Have each pair write a skit in which one of the students is a retail salesperson and the other student is a customer. Students should determine the product to be sold/purchased, and write selling points for the salesperson to use. Students should also write questions the customer might ask the salesperson about the product. Skits will vary, but the selling points and questions should demonstrate considerable thought. Ask students to share their skits with the class.

Here are a few examples of effective selling points that may be used in retail and organizational sales situations.

- **Retail sales situation**
  - Customer: man or woman looking for jeans
  - Product: a pair of jeans
  - Selling point: The soft cotton denim fabric has 1 percent spandex (feature), which allows the jeans to stretch (function) and makes them comfortable to wear (benefits).
- **Organizational sales situation**
  - Customer: operations manager for an ice cream manufacturer
  - Product: insulated jacket
  - Selling point: The insulation in this garment (feature) is effective in cold temperatures (function), so it will protect your workers and allow them to perform at maximum efficiency while working in the freezer (benefits).

ADVANTAGES

In feature-benefit selling, salespeople also must consider their competition. Let's say your competitor uses inferior fabrics. Your garment uses better fabric. The advantage in this case can be used as a major benefit. Your higher-quality garment will last longer than your competitor's product. All advantages over your competition become selling points for your product.

CUSTOMER BUYING MOTIVES

To determine effective customer benefits for product features, it is a good idea to learn what motivates customers to buy. **Buying motives** are reasons a customer buys a product. As such, they influence buying behavior and buying decisions. Understanding customer motivation is not an easy task. Customers are not always aware of their inner motivations. Even when they are, they may not communicate them to you. As you gain experience in sales, you will get a better feel for reading customers' motives, which can be classified as rational, emotional, or patronage. To make the salesperson's task even more difficult, these motives may be combined or different for the same product. The difficulty depends on the customer and the sales situation.

RATIONAL MOTIVES

Rational motives are conscious, logical reasons for a purchase. Rational motives include product dependability, time or monetary savings, product quality, and good customer service. Customers are often interested in products because of rational motives. For example, customers may say they are looking for a dependable automobile with a history of excellent customer service.

EMOTIONAL MOTIVES

Emotional motives are feelings experienced by a customer through association with a product. Emotional motives are feelings such as social approval, fear, power, love, and prestige. Social approval may be one of the reasons that customers buy certain brands of cars, clothing, or accessories. Customers are generally reluctant to share their emotional motives for making a purchase. You may have to tactfully incorporate emotional motives into a sales presentation. Life insurance is a product that evokes emotions.

PATRONAGE MOTIVES

Patronage motives are reasons for remaining a loyal customer of a company. Currently satisfied customers possess patronage motives. Trust and confidence have been established through past experiences. Patronage motives make it easy to sell a company's products.

MULTIPLE MOTIVES

Most buying decisions involve a combination of motives. For example, people buy car tires for dependability (rational motive) and fear because they care about the safety of loved ones (emotional motive). Two customers could have different motivations for buying the same product. One person may buy shoes for comfort (rational motive), while another may buy the same shoes to make a fashion statement (emotional motive).

Reading Check

Recall What are three ways by which product features can be identified?

PROSPECTING

Looking for new customers is called **prospecting**. A **prospect**, or a sales lead, is a potential customer.

A potential customer may be a business or an individual. For example, a manufacturer of golf accessories would consider a newly opened retail golf shop as a prospect or sales lead. The person responsible for doing the buying for that store's golf accessories would also be considered a prospect or lead.

Prospecting is especially important in organizational selling situations. Service-related businesses and retailers search for new business opportunities by prospecting too. Any salesperson or business that wants to expand a customer base might use some of the following prospecting techniques.

PROSPECTING TECHNIQUES

There are several techniques and practices employed by salespeople and businesses to generate sales leads. They include customer referrals, cold canvassing, and employer-generated leads.

CUSTOMER REFERRALS

Satisfied customers are excellent sources for finding new customers. Sales representatives ask their customers for **referrals**—the names of other people who might buy the product. Referrals open the market to potential customers whom a salesperson might not have reached without a recommendation. When salespeople ask previous customers for names of potential customers, they are using the **endless chain method**. The endless chain method helps companies construct and maintain a list of prospects. Some companies offer discounts or gifts to customers who give referrals.

MARKETING CASE STUDY

Olympus: Selling Medical Technology

Olympus is known for making digital cameras for consumers. It also produces medical cameras for doctors that integrate high-definition television (HDTV) signals for improved image quality. The tiny camera at the end of a flexible scope can move around in the body, allowing a doctor to see from many angles. This device assists surgeons performing "laparoendoscopic single-site surgery," a less risky operation using a very small incision to remove a damaged organ or a tumor.

Competing Advantages

Olympus was first to introduce HDTV in its "videoscopes." Another competitor is Stryker, a company that also sells artificial hips and knees. HDTV medical cameras cost more than non-HDTV cameras. Competitors selling non-HDTV cameras can use price as a selling point. In addition, hospitals must upgrade their monitors and other devices to accommodate HDTV technology, which can be costly.

English Language Arts

Research Conduct research on competing medical video cameras. Write a selling point for an Olympus HDTV medical camera, noting the feature, function, and benefit.

NCTE 7 Conduct research and gather, evaluate, and synthesize data to communicate discoveries.

ELABORATE

CUSTOMER BUYING MOTIVES

Ask students to think about a recent purchase they made. Have them write down the reasons they chose the product they did. Then ask these guiding questions about customer buying motives.

Guiding Questions

List What are three types of customer buying motives?	rational, emotional, patronage
Analyze How might customers confuse emotional motives with rational motives?	Some people feel that such things as social approval and prestige are rational motives that need to be considered.

Mini Project

Extension

Survey Salespeople Have students survey salespeople and ask about the reasons people make purchases. Students should survey salespeople who sell average-priced products such as toasters or coffee makers, and people who sell expensive items such as jewelry, cars, or high-end electronics. Have students keep a list of the reasons the salespeople give, and then put the reasons into the following categories: Rational, Emotional, and Patronage. After students have categorized the reasons, ask: ***Was it difficult or easy to categorize all of the reasons? Explain your answer.*** Answers will vary. Sample answer: It was difficult because some of the reasons could be put into more than one category. If time allows, make a class list of all the reasons provided by salespeople and categorize the list by Rational, Emotional, and Patronage.

ELABORATE

Reading Check Answer

Read the Reading Check question to students: ***What are the three ways by which product features can be identified?*** Product features include: basic features, physical features, and extended product features.

PROSPECTING

Ask these guiding questions to focus the discussion on prospecting.

Guiding Questions

Identify What is another term for a prospect?	sales lead or potential customer
Explain Who are potential customers?	businesses or individuals that are not yet customers of the company or business

Graphic Organizer

Display this table. Ask students to rank these prospecting methods in order from most effective to least effective. After students determine the order of the list, ask volunteers to explain why they think some methods are more effective than others.

Method	Ranking
Family	
Friends	
Television	
Radio	
Internet	
Newspapers	
Magazines	
Posters	
Flyers	

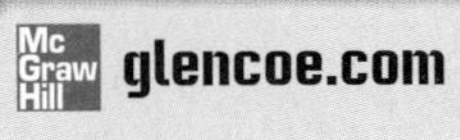

iWB

Graphic Organizer Send students to the Online Learning Center to print this graphic organizer.

MARKETING CASE STUDY

English Language Arts Answer Accept all selling points that incorporate a feature, function, and benefit for an Olympus HDTV medical camera. For example, high definition television (HDTV) signals into its medical camera (feature) improves the image quality (function), which allows surgeons to perform operations by using a very small incision to remove an organ or a tumor. This type of surgery reduces a patient's recovery time and the risks generally associated with surgery (benefits). Then tell students: According to the article, hospitals must upgrade their monitors and other devices to accommodate HDTV technology. Ask: ***How might the sellers of HDTV cameras turn this into an advantage?*** Sample answer: The camera companies might "bundle" the camera with the monitors and other technology required into one package at one price. They might also offer free technical assistance with the entire package.

Critical Thinking

Have students select a business and prospect for new customers. They might use the library and Internet to find tradeshows, journals, organizations, and other sources that may provide leads for new customers. Have students create an outline that lists the sources and their potential. Outlines will vary but should contain the sources—tradeshows, journals, organizations, and so on—and their potential. Students will have to use their knowledge to determine potential. Then, students should choose the best two outlines that have the greatest imagined potential for a new customer base. Have students analyze what their next steps would be. Students should also explain why these two prospect plans for new customers are more effective than other outlines. Make a list of the attributes that are most helpful, and the strategies in the outlines that weren't as effective to bring in new customers. Student choices will vary. Students should be able to distinguish, based on what they know, why these plans will be more effective than other outline plans. Criteria lists should show analysis and thought as to what will bring in, and what will deter or prohibit, a new customer base.

COLD CANVASSING

Cold canvassing is a process of locating as many potential customers as possible without checking leads beforehand. Cold canvassing is also sometimes called "blind prospecting" because it is a hit-and-miss method. One example is a real estate agent going door-to-door in a neighborhood, asking people if they would like to sell their homes. Another example of cold canvassing is a stockbroker selecting names from a telephone book at random and calling them. Insurance salespeople look through newspapers for birth announcements, while caterers and florists may check out engagement announcements. Use of trade directories, such as the *Thomas Register of American Manufacturers*, can be useful for organizational sales representatives. In addition, commercial lists of prospects can be purchased and used for cold canvassing. An Internet search engine can provide a huge selection of sales-lead companies that specialize in different industries.

EMPLOYER SALES LEADS

Some firms employ entire telemarketing teams to generate leads for their sales staffs. They also attend trade shows, where they display products for review by buyers in the industry. Interested buyers provide information for follow-up. Leads are categorized by territory and passed along to the sales staff. In some cases, customer service representatives may qualify, or evaluate, the leads for the professional sales staff. They do this by calling the prospects to see if they meet certain qualifications. Leads can be generated and qualified by using the Internet and the Web site of a prospective corporate customer.

QUALIFYING PROSPECTS

Once sales leads are generated, they need to be qualified before any sales effort is made. There are three important questions to ask in order to properly evaluate a sales lead. The following questions will help determine whether a prospect meets the qualifications for a sales call:

- Does the prospective customer (an individual, company, or organization) need the product or service?
- If the prospect is a company or an organization, who is authorized to make a purchase? Does the salesperson have an appointment with a person who has that authority?
- Does the prospective customer have the financial resources to pay for the product or service?

Salespeople can use the process of cold canvassing get help generating leads by going door-to-door. ***What other prospecting techniques might a real-estate agent use to generate leads?***

Finding New Customers

ANSWERS TO QUESTIONS

To find answers to these "three basic questions to evaluate a sales lead, " company customer-service representatives or salespeople have to make inquiries and do some background research. In some cases, a simple phone call may be all that is necessary to determine whether a lead needs a particular product.

For example, a manufacturer of work uniforms specializes in clothing designed to be worn by workers who spend time in cold environments. The apparel company's salespeople may ask leads whether they have any employees who work outdoors in the winter. They may also ask leads whether they employ people who work in refrigerated warehouses or freezer boxes. If the answer to these questions is "no," the lead should be considered a dead end. If a lead answers "yes," then it might be a potential customer.

The next questions might be: "How many employees work in those cold environments?" and "Who in the company is responsible for purchasing employees' work clothing?" The answers to these questions can reveal how much apparel the prospect might need and give the salesperson the name of a person to contact.

Additional research is necessary to determine whether the potential customer has the ability to pay its bills. Sales representatives can read the company's annual reports or subscribe to the database listings of a firm like Dun & Bradstreet®, which monitors businesses' financial situations. If a company has a need for the product and has a good credit rating, it would be a qualified prospect.

The research done during prospecting can become the basis of a strong sales presentation when meeting a qualified prospect face-to-face.

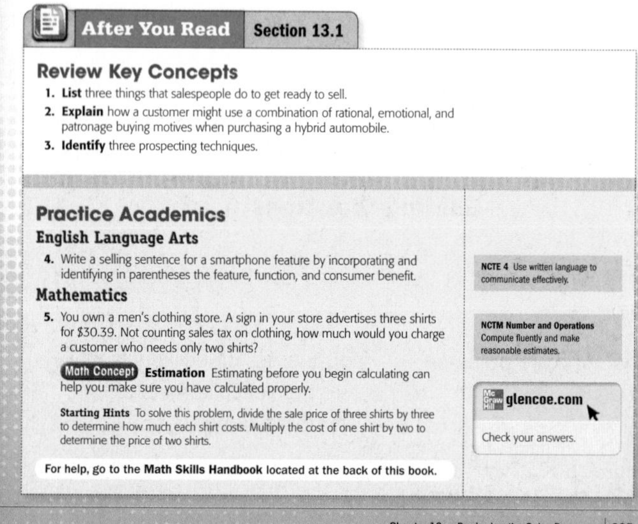

After You Read | **Section 13.1**

Review Key Concepts

1. **List** three things that salespeople do to get ready to sell.
2. **Explain** how a customer might use a combination of rational, emotional, and patronage buying motives when purchasing a hybrid automobile.
3. **Identify** three prospecting techniques.

Practice Academics

English Language Arts

4. Write a selling sentence for a smartphone feature by incorporating and identifying in parentheses the feature, function, and consumer benefit.

NCTE 4 Use written language to communicate effectively.

Mathematics

5. You own a men's clothing store. A sign in your store advertises three shirts for $30.39. Not counting sales tax on clothing, how much would you charge a customer who needs only two shirts?

Math Concept **Estimation** Estimating before you begin calculating can help you make sure you have calculated properly.

Starting Hints To solve this problem, divide the sale price of three shirts by three to determine how much each shirt costs. Multiply the cost of one shirt by two to determine the price of two shirts.

NCTM Number and Operations Compute fluently and make reasonable estimates.

glencoe.com

Check your answers.

For help, go to the **Math Skills Handbook** located at the back of this book.

ELABORATE

Visual Literacy

Finding New Customers Caption Answer Read the photo caption question to students: ***What other prospecting techniques might a real-estate agent use to generate leads?*** Subscribing to a lead-generating service supplies the salesperson with the name and contact information of potential clients. Then ask these guiding questions to focus the discussion on methods of prospecting.

Guiding Questions

Explain What is the endless chain method?	Salespeople ask previous or current customers for potential customers.
Compare How are customer referrals and employer sales leads similar?	Both techniques provide the salesperson with contact information of a potential customer.

Critical Thinking

Ask students if they or their parents have ever been contacted by a salesperson who said they got their name from a friend. Ask: ***Were you or your parents interested in the product or service being sold?*** Answers will vary depending on individual experiences. Ask: ***Did you feel this was a good way to contact potential customers? Why or why not?*** Some students may say yes because it meant that a friend thought they would enjoy the product. Others may say no because it's intrusive. Ask: ***What type of prospecting technique is this?*** It is the customer referral method (also known as the endless chain method). Then ask students to imagine that they are salespeople and to consider which type of prospecting technique they would prefer to use: cold canvassing or the endless chain method. Then ask them to explain why. The endless chain method is easier because it allows you to use the name of a current or previous customer to get your foot in the door.

EVALUATE

Graphic Organizer

Display this chart. Ask students to provide facts for each of the three types of prospecting techniques—customer referrals, cold canvassing, and employer sales leads. Sample answers:

Prospecting Techniques

Customer Referrals	Cold Canvassing	Employer Sales Leads
• recommendations from customers • endless chain method	• called "blind prospecting" • locates customers without leads • hit or miss	• telemarketers and trade shows • customers have indicated some interest in products

glencoe.com

Graphic Organizer Send students to the Online Learning Center to print this graphic organizer.

QUALIFYING PROSPECTS

Tell students that finding sales prospects is only the beginning of the prospecting process. Company representatives must make sure the potential customer is a good candidate for their products or services. Ask students these guiding questions to direct a discussion on qualifying prospects.

Guiding Questions

Identify What are three basic questions used to evaluate a sales lead?	Does the prospective company or individual need this product or service? Who in the organization has the authority to buy? Does the prospective company have the financial resources to pay?
Evaluate Why should leads be qualified before any sales effort is made?	If it turns out that the company or individual does not need the product, it would be a waste of the time to contact the lead.

After You Read Section 13.1

Review Key Concepts

1. To get ready to sell, salespeople must gather information about their products, industry trends, and the competition.
2. A sample explanation: rational motive—buying a hybrid automobile will help save on gas consumption and cost less money to operate; emotional motive—buying a hybrid automobile will help save the environment for my children and grandchildren; patronage motive—I've been very satisfied buying cars from this manufacturer for years; I expect their hybrid will be good quality.
3. Prospecting techniques include customer referrals, cold canvassing, and employer sales leads.

Practice Academics

English Language Arts

4. Sample answer: The slide-out keyboard (feature) provides full QWERTY keys (function) for faster text messaging (benefit).

Mathematics

5. The answer is \$20.26 (\$30.39 ÷ 3 × 2 = \$20.26).

glencoe.com

Answer Key Send students to the Online Learning Center to check their answers.

READING GUIDE

Before You Read

Predict Why is asking a customer "May I help you?" not an effective way to begin a sale in a retail environment?

Objectives

- **Demonstrate** how to properly approach a customer to open a sale.
- **Differentiate** between organizational and retail sales approaches.
- **List** three retail approach methods.
- **Discuss** when and how to determine customer needs.

The Main Idea

The actual sales presentation begins when you approach customers to open the sale and determine their needs.

Vocabulary

Content Vocabulary
- greeting approach
- service approach
- merchandise approach
- nonverbal communication
- open-ended question

Academic Vocabulary

You will find these words in your reading and on your tests. Make sure you know their meanings.
- rapport
- astute

Graphic Organizer

Draw or print this outline of this section's content.

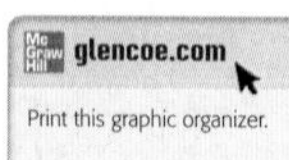

Print this graphic organizer.

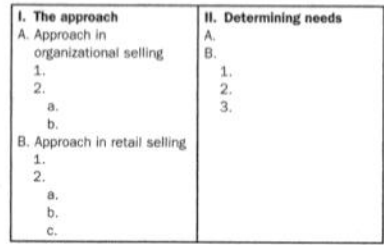

STANDARDS

ACADEMIC

English Language Arts

NCTE 3 Apply strategies to interpret texts.

Social Studies

NCSS VII B Production, Distribution, and Consumption Analyze the role that supply and demand, prices, incentives, and profits play in determining what is produced and distributed in a competitive market system.

NCSS *National Council for the Social Studies*
NCTE *National Council of Teachers of English*
NCTM *National Council of Teachers of Mathematics*
NSES *National Science Education Standards*

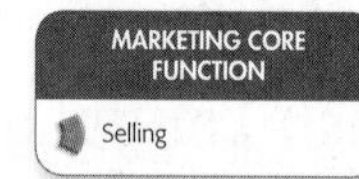

Common Core

Writing Produce clear and coherent writing in which the development, organization, and style are appropriate to task, purpose, and audience.

MARKETING CORE FUNCTION

Selling

First Steps of a Sale

Section 13.2

THE APPROACH

The approach, also known as the *sales opening*, is the first face-to-face contact with the customer. Salespeople can make or break a sale during their first few minutes with a customer. They must learn how to properly approach a customer to open a sale. The approach sets the mood for the other steps of the sale. Its purpose is to establish **rapport** (a positive relationship) with the customer whether for organizational or retail selling.

In order to achieve an effective sales opening, salespeople must remember to do the following:

- Treat customers as individuals. Never stereotype a person because of age, sex, race, religion, appearance, or any other characteristic.
- Be aware of the customer's personality and buying style. Some customers like to do business quickly. Others prefer a methodical pace.
- Show interest in the customer by maintaining good eye contact and showing friendliness.
- Learn and use the customer's name to personalize the sale when possible.
- Grab the customer's attention. Incorporate a theme in the approach that is related to the presentation and the customer's buying motives.
- Recognize that sales approaches differ in organization selling and retail selling situations.

As You Read

Predict How does the approach differ depending on the sales situation?

ORGANIZATIONAL SELLING

In organizational selling, salespeople usually make an appointment prior to making a sales call. This ensures that their customers have time to meet with them. Some may not call in advance. When they arrive without notice, they are "cold calling." The likelihood of being seen by the customer diminishes. When cold calling, it is a wise practice to ask customers if it is a good time to see them. This courtesy is appreciated by busy businesspeople.

> "You can make or break a sale during the approach."

ARRIVE EARLY

Field sales representatives should always arrive early for a sales call. This allows the salesperson to gather his or her thoughts. It also shows professionalism and courtesy because it ensures the salesperson will not be late for the sales call. In some cases, it allows the salesperson to observe the customer's place of business. Here are a few examples of how to make use of observations.

- If your customer is a retail store buyer, you can spend time walking through the store to see which competing brands are carried. You can also observe customers in the store to see if they appear to be part of your product's target market.
- If you sit in the waiting room for a purchasing agent in a manufacturing facility, you can read all the plaques on the walls and any industry or company literature on display. These items may be helpful in your approach as well as other steps of the sale.
- In the customer's office, you may observe something that will help you establish rapport. It might be a college plaque, a sports trophy, a painting, or something else that uncovers your customer's interests. For example, if the customer keeps golf clubs in his or her office, making small talk about this interest during the initial approach can help the salesperson to establish rapport with the customer.

ENGAGE

Anticipation Activity

Improving Student Achievement Ask students to share different methods salespeople have used to learn what they needed. Answers may include asking questions or listening.

Objectives

- **Demonstrate** how to properly approach a customer to open a sale. In organizational sales, arrive early and greet and engage the customer. In retail sales, carefully time the approach and use the greeting, service, or merchandise approach.
- **Differentiate** between organizational and retail sales approaches. Organizational: salespeople make appointment Retail: salespeople meet customers cold
- **List** three retail approach methods. greeting, service, and merchandise or theme methods
- **Discuss** when and how to determine customer needs. In organizational sales: when qualifying a prospect. In retail sales: during or immediately after the approach.

Graphic Organizer

I. The approach	**II. Determining needs**
A. Approach to organizational selling 1. Arrive early 2. Greet and engage customer a. Engaging a current customer b. Engaging a new customer B. Approach in retail selling 1. Timing the retail approach 2. Retail approach methods a. Greeting approach b. Service approach c. Merchandise or theme approach	A. When to determine needs B. How to determine needs 1. Observing 2. Listening 3. Questioning

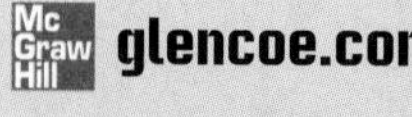

iWB

Graphic Organizer Send students to the Online Learning Center to print this graphic organizer.

EXPLORE

Before You Read

Read the Before You Read question aloud: ***Why is asking a customer "May I help you?" not an effective way to begin a sale in a retail environment?*** This is a "yes or no" question to which customers will often say "No, thank you, I am just looking." Ask: ***Have you ever been asked this question? If so, what was your response?*** Answers will likely depend on whether the student was just looking and did not want or need help from the salesperson.

Preteaching Vocabulary

Have students go to the Online Learning Center at glencoe.com for the Chapter 13 Preteaching Vocabulary games.

Content Vocabulary

Divide the class into pairs or small groups. Have pairs brainstorm and demonstrate examples of nonverbal communication. Nonverbal communication may include facial expressions, hand motions, eye movement, gestures, and so on. Then ask pairs to demonstrate examples of open-ended questions. Open-ended questions should be structures so that they require more than just "yes" or "no" answers.

Academic Vocabulary

Rapport—Word Origin Tell students that the term *rapport* originates from the French *raporter,* which means "to bring back." Inform students that rapport is a relationship generally built on mutual trust. Ask: ***How does the phrase "to bring back" relate to the definition of* rapport?** Students might suggest that a relationship built on mutual trust will bring one person back to another.

MINI CLIP

ELL: Direct Vocabulary Instruction
Go to the Online Learning Center to view a video in which students create vocabulary cards to build a dictionary.

First Steps of a Sale

Section 13.2

THE APPROACH

Ask these guiding questions to focus the discussion about the first step of the sale.

Guiding Questions

Summarize What are six things a salesperson must do to achieve an effective sales opening?	treat customers as individuals, be aware of the customer's buying style; show interest in the customer; learn and use the customer's name; grab the customer's attention; recognize that sales approaches are different
Analyze Why is organizational selling usually done by appointment?	Arranging appointments ensures that customers have time for a meeting. Without calling ahead, the likelihood of a meeting occuring drops.

As You Read

Read students the As You Read question: ***How does the approach differ depending on the sales situation?*** In organizational sales, the salesperson calls on the customer and has information about the customer before the initial approach. In retail sales, the customer typically comes into a store, and the salesperson generally has no prior information on the customer..

Expert Advice

Read the quote to students:

> **"You can make or break a sale during the approach."**

Ask students why the initial approach is so important in sales. Answer: The initial approach sets the tone and begins the communication between the salesperson and the customer. It is the first step in establishing rapport with the customer. Then ask: ***What could turn a customer off during the initial approach?*** Answers will vary. Responses may include: a salesperson who has a weak greeting or who does not make eye contact; a salesperson who is not properly groomed or who has bad breath; a salesperson who is too aggressive.

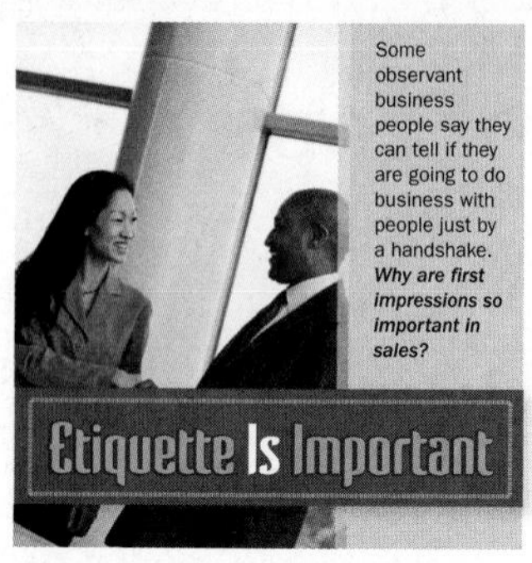

Some observant business people say they can tell if they are going to do business with people just by a handshake. ***Why are first impressions so important in sales?***

Etiquette Is Important

GREET AND ENGAGE CUSTOMER

The first step in the initial approach involves proper business etiquette. The salesperson greets the customer by name and introduces him- or herself and the company with a firm handshake and a smile. After the proper greeting and introductions, the next statement or question should engage the customer.

Engaging a Current Customer

When meeting with customers you visit frequently, you can be more personal. Comments on recent events in the customer's industry or personal recollections about the customer's family, interests, or hobbies can create a smooth meeting. This technique puts the customer at ease and helps open lines of communication.

Learning what is appropriate to say regarding personal matters is critical. When personal conversation is not appropriate, you can still engage in small talk to establish a relationship with the customer.

Engaging a New Customer

As noted, any common interest shared between the salesperson and the customer may also be used to engage the customer. That common interest might range from a personal connection (e.g. graduated from the same college) to sports-related passions (e.g. participant or fan).

You can also use information gathered during prospecting to create an opening statement. It is best to pick a theme that is related to the presentation and the customer's buying motives. For example, "When I spoke with you last week, you indicated an interest in looking at new golf accessories to enhance your current assortment." You can also use current topics in the industry with a new customer. For example, "According to *Supermarket News*, food stores that are going green are attracting new customers. My company has the products that will help you take advantage of that growing trend." Topics that are always of interest to organizational customers include reducing costs, increasing productivity, improving profits, and generating more business.

RETAIL SELLING

In most retail selling situations, the salespeople do not know customers prior to meeting them. The exception occurs when retail salespeople have steady customers whom they know well. In both cases, timing and type of approach are important.

TIMING THE RETAIL APPROACH

Timing the approach depends on the types of customers and on the products being sold. When customers are in an obvious hurry, you should approach them quickly. When customers seem undecided, it is best to let them look around before making the approach. Many customers prefer to shop around before buying. They appreciate salespeople who show interest while allowing them to make their own decisions. These casual lookers will seek help when they need it.

RETAIL APPROACH METHODS

There are three methods to use for the initial retail approach: greeting, service, and merchandise or theme. You must evaluate the selling situation and the type of customer to determine which method is best. In some cases, you may use one, two, or all three approaches as part of your sales opening.

Greeting Approach

With the **greeting approach**, the salesperson welcomes the customer to the store. This lets the customer know that the salesperson is available for questions or assistance. This can be simple. For example, simply greet a customer with "Good morning." If a frequent customer arrives, using the customer's name in the approach makes the customer feel important.

When you greet the customer, it is important to use a rising tone in your voice. Regardless of whether the customer responds in a friendly manner, it is extremely important for the salesperson to smile and continue to be friendly.

After greeting the customer, pause for a few seconds. Out of courtesy, most customers will respond. If they need help, they will tell you how you can assist them. If they are just looking, they will let you know. The greeting approach establishes a positive atmosphere and opens the lines of communication. It can also be incorporated easily into the other two retail approach methods.

Service Approach

With the **service approach**, salespeople ask customers if they need assistance. One way to use this method is to ask, "How may I help you?" An open-ended question such as this one offers the customer a greater opportunity to respond with more than "yes" or "no." The wrong way to use the service approach is to ask, "May I help you?" This question is ineffective because customers will often say, "No, thank you, I am just looking." That customer response ends communication between the customer and salesperson.

Merchandise or Theme Approach

With the **merchandise approach**, or theme approach, the salesperson makes a comment or asks questions about a product in which the customer shows an interest. You may say something about the product's features and benefits or typical customer buying motives. It should give the customer some information that is not immediately apparent to the eye.

Focus the conversation on the customer's interest. With a jacket, you might say, "That children's jacket comes in several other colors." If you have no indication of the exact interest, you can talk about the item's popularity, its unusual features, or its special values. You can also ask a question, such as "Is that the size you need?" or "Were you looking for a comfortable children's jacket?" This themed approach is effective in retail sales because it focuses attention on the product and the sales presentation. It increases customer interest and could encourage a purchase. In addition, customers may not see the desired style, size, or color on the selling floor. The merchandise approach lets the customer know what is available.

Reading Check

Recall What are three methods of retail approaches?

In retail stores, salespeople must judge when to approach customers and which retail sales method is most appropriate to use. ***How would you know when you should approach a customer in a retail shoe store?***

The Right Approach

EXPLAIN

Visual Literacy

Etiquette Is Important Caption Answer Read the photo caption question to students: ***Why are first impressions so important in sales?*** It is often said first impressions are lasting impressions. If you get off to a bad start with customers they may not give you a chance to complete your sales presentation because they have already decided that they are not going to do business with you. Then ask these guiding questions to focus the discussion on etiquette in selling.

Guiding Questions

Explain What is the proper way to meet and greet an organizational customer?	greet the customer by name; introduce himself or herself by name; identify the company; offer a firm handshake
Analyze How might a customer react to a salesperson's weak handshake?	Customers might decide on the spot that they will not do business with that salesperson.

Critical Thinking

Tell students that when approaching a customer, the salesperson generally has these purposes in mind: to open a conversation, to establish a rapport with the customer, and to focus on the product. Ask: ***Which purpose do you think is most important? Why?*** Since all three purposes are important to the approach, any answer is acceptable as long as the student provides proper rationale. Sample answer: Opening conversation is most important because the other two purposes cannot be accomplished without communication.

Reinforce Vocabulary

Astute—Synonyms Have students look up the term *astute* in a thesaurus or dictionary to find synonyms. Write the synonyms students find for the class to view. Go over the terms to ensure students' understanding. Synonyms might include: shrewd, smart, perceptive, wise, intelligent, and so on.

ELABORATE

RETAIL SELLING

Ask students if they could be considered a "regular customer" at any store or food service location. If so, ask: ***How do the salespeople in the store treat you?*** They greet me with a smile, they know me by name, and they have my "usual" ready by the time I get to the register. Then ask students these guiding questions to focus the discussion about sales approaches.

Guiding Questions

Explain Why is timing important in the retail sales approach?	Salespeople need to know whether customers are in a hurry and need help now or whether they want to look around; if the salesperson approaches too late or too early, he or she could jeopardize a sale.
Compare and Contrast How are the three retail approach methods (greeting approach, service approach, and merchandise or theme approach) different?.	The greeting approach is passive and allows the customer to initiate questions. The service approach focuses on asking if the customer needs assistance. In the merchandise or theme approach, the salesperson asks the customer questions and offers information about the product of interest.

Mini Project

Enrichment

Research Sales Techniques Inform students that there are professional journals to help salespeople be successful. Have students go to a library or go online to look up issues of *Selling Power, Sales and Marketing Management,* or other periodicals about selling. Have them read articles about the approach in retail sales and create a half-page report. Ask students to share their findings with the class. Then ask students: ***Can salespeople who are in totally different industries use the same journals about selling?*** Students should recognize that the selling process is similar, even if the products—such as clothing and electronics—are not.

Reading Check Answer

Read the Reading Check question to students: ***What are three methods of retail approaches?*** Approaches include: greeting approach, service approach, and merchandise or theme approach.

Visual Literacy

The Right Approach Caption Answer Read the photo caption question to students: ***How would you know when you should approach a customer in a retail shoe store?*** You would have to judge the interest level of the customer by his or her nonverbal communication, for example, whether the customer is looking for a specific shoe or just browsing.

Graphic Organizer

Display this diagram. Ask students to provide facts for each of the three retail approach methods. Possible answers:

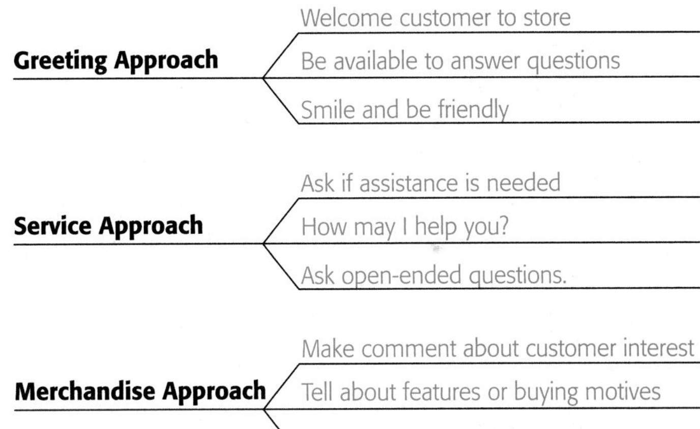
Greeting Approach
Welcome customer to store
Be available to answer questions
Smile and be friendly
Service Approach
Ask if assistance is needed
How may I help you?
Ask open-ended questions.
Merchandise Approach
Make comment about customer interest
Tell about features or buying motives
Focus on customer's interest

glencoe.com iWB

Graphic Organizer Send students to the Online Learning Center to print this graphic organizer.

Critical Thinking

Discuss with students the primary role of the salesperson in the selling process. The primary role of the salesperson is to gather information about the customer, advise the customer about which products best suit his or her needs, and lead to a decision to buy. Have students role play scenarios where a salesperson successfully gathers information from the customer and situations where the salesperson fails to gather information, and ultimately, loses the customer.

DETERMINING NEEDS

To make your sales presentation meaningful to your customers, you need to know their needs early in the sales process. This step in the sales process is important because it is the foundation of the marketing concept, which stresses the importance of satisfying customer's needs and wants. It is the salesperson's job to uncover their customers' problems or reasons for wanting to buy. In some instances, their motives or needs may be quite obvious, but that is not always the case. It is your job to determine those needs so you can offer one or more solutions. The solutions will come from the features and benefits of your product or company policies.

WHEN TO DETERMINE NEEDS

The sooner you know your customer's needs, the easier it is to build your sales presentation around the selling points that are important to your customer. In organizational selling situations, customers' needs can be determined when qualifying a prospect, which is well before ever meeting the customer. With loyal customers, a review of sales records and buying patterns before making an appointment to visit with the customer may shed some light on current needs.

In retail sales situations, the earliest you can determine your customers' needs is during or immediately after the approach. The service and merchandise approaches lend themselves to asking customers a question about their needs. With the greeting approach, the very next step would be to ask customers a question to uncover their reasons for visiting the store.

In both situations, the salesperson should continue determining needs throughout the sales process. Why? Because as customers learn more about the product, their needs and wants may change. Think of determining needs as peeling away layers of information that you need to get to the heart of something. In some cases, the original needs are based on limited information about a product. Once customers learn that they can check the scores of their favorite sports team from a certain cell phone model, their needs may shift. They may view the Internet connection feature of the cell phone as something they want, too. Thus, their original needs changed once they had more knowledge about the capabilities of a cell phone model they originally thought they wanted. It is important to assess what customers tell you they need or want in a product at the beginning of the sales process. After they learn more about a product's features and benefits, reassess their new needs and wants.

HOW TO DETERMINE NEEDS

To be an effective salesperson, you need to be **astute** in determining customers' needs and wants. Three methods that will help you become astute in determining customers' needs are observing, listening, and questioning. Each technique provides the salesperson with necessary information during the entire sales process. Thus, they are used in conjunction with one another.

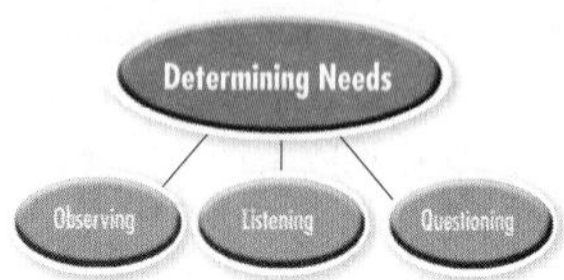

OBSERVING

As previously noted, observation can be helpful in organizational sales situations when visiting customers in their places of business. Anything observed in the business may provide insight into what a customer needs.

In all selling situations, seasoned salespeople learn to read their customers by observing them. **Nonverbal communication** is expressing oneself without the use of words. Facial expressions, hand motions, eye movement, and other forms of nonverbal communication can give you clues about a customer's interest in a product. For example, the length of time a customer looks at or handles a product in a store can give you an initial idea about their level of interest in the product. How long a customer holds the product during a sales presentation (if at all) can indicate how strongly he or she feels about the product. At the other end of the spectrum, a raised eye brow or frown may communicate dislike for a product's feature.

The key to observing is the proper selection of facts. You want only those facts that are important to the sales process. Avoid stereotyping people or drawing conclusions from your observations before getting additional facts. For example, a person dressed in shabby clothes may be more financially secure than someone dressed in more expensive-looking clothing.

LISTENING

Listening is one of the most important interpersonal skills you need to practice in selling. Giving customers your undivided attention and listening with empathy are two specific skills that will encourage your customers to talk freely. They will feel you are truly listening.

During conversations with your customers, you can pick up clues about their needs and wants. That information will be helpful for the product presentation. Here is an example:

Customer: "My copier is ten years old. It prints black-and-white copies. When I need color copies, I take my work to a copy center and pay for them. As my business grows, I find that I need color copies more and more."

From these statements, you have learned that the customer is looking for a quality color copier for business use. Since the copier is for a small but growing business, upgraded and advanced features may be important to this customer.

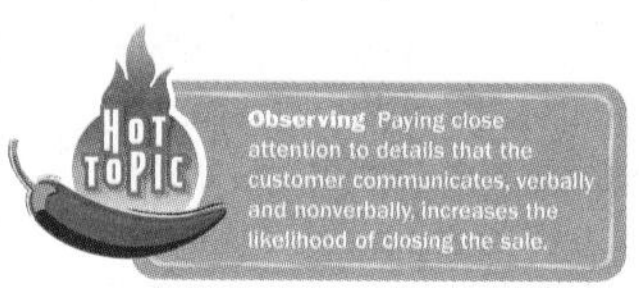

HOT TOPIC
Observing Paying close attention to details that the customer communicates, verbally and nonverbally, increases the likelihood of closing the sale.

QUESTIONING

Before you can listen to customers, you must get them talking. One way of engaging a customer in conversation is to ask questions.

Not all customers can clearly express their needs and motives when making a purchase. In such a situation, well-chosen questions can help you uncover needs and buying motives while putting the customer at ease.

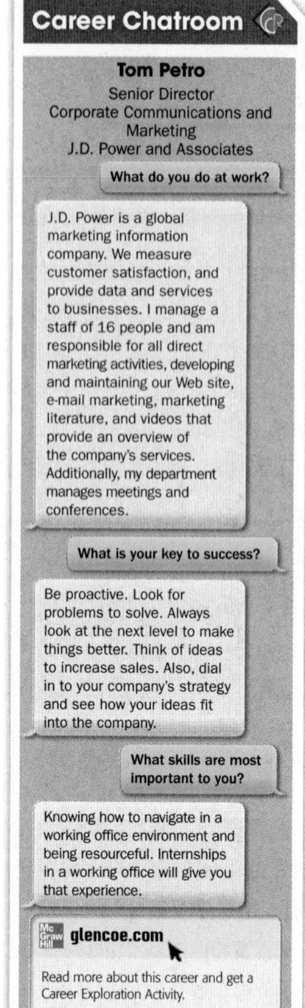

310 | Unit 5 · Selling

Chapter 13 · Beginning the Sales Process | 311

ELABORATE

DETERMINING NEEDS

Ask these guiding questions to focus the discussion on determining customer's needs.

Guiding Questions

Examine When is the best time to determine a customer's needs?	In organizational sales, the best time to determine needs is when qualifying a prospect; In retail situations, needs are typically determined during or shortly after the approach.
Explain Why is it important for a salesperson to continue to assess the customer's needs throughout the sales process?	The more the salesperson can learn about the customer and his or her needs, the more successful he or she will be in meeting those needs.

Graphic Organizer

Display this web. Ask students to provide facts for each of the methods for determining customers' needs. Possible answers:

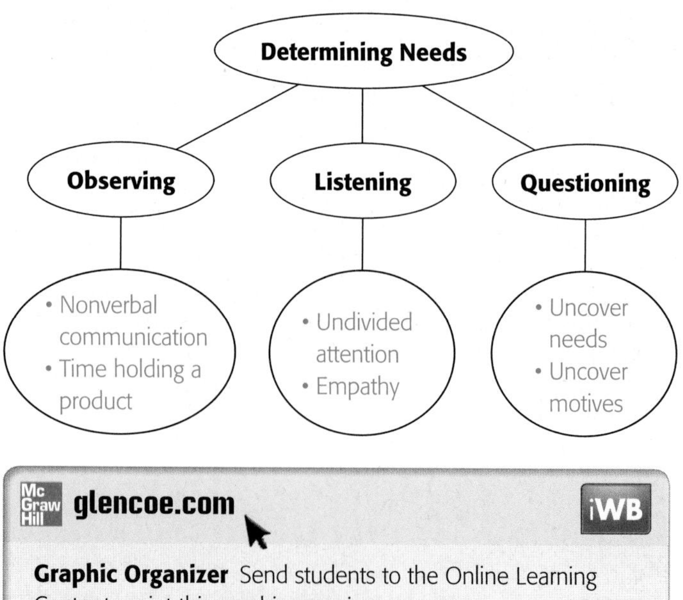

glencoe.com iWB

Graphic Organizer Send students to the Online Learning Center to print this graphic organizer.

ELABORATE

Reinforce Vocabulary

Loyal—Usage Ask a student to read the first paragraph under the section called When to Determine Needs. Ask students: ***What does it mean to be a loyal customer?*** Loyal customers return to the same store, possibly even to the same salesperson, because they were happy with the service they received.

Career Chatroom

Use these questions to focus the discussion about the Career Chatroom feature.

Guiding Questions

Explain What parts of Mr. Petro's job are directly related to marketing?	developing and maintaining the company's website, e-mail marketing, marketing literature, and developing videos that provide product overviews
Analyze How might looking for problems to solve help you progress in your career?	Managers look for employees who are problem solvers and who are proactive. This will save time and money in the long run.

 **glencoe.com** 

Career Exploration Send students to the Online Learning Center to read more about this career and to get a Career Exploration activity.

Mini Project

Differentiated Instruction

Interpersonal Learners Divide the class into small groups. Have students create profiles of different types of customers such as one who is in a hurry, one who has to buy a gift but does not know what to get, or someone who has time to spend looking around at all the different product offerings. Have groups answer the following question in their profiles: ***How can you identify the different types of customers?*** Profiles should include a description of the different types of customers and an answer to the question posed that is similar to the following: Observing nonverbal communication, listening to their conversations or comments, and asking questions are all good ways to identify the different types of customers.

e MARKETING

Viral and Affiliate Marketing

Viral e-marketing is a technique that e-marketers use to connect with potential customers via current customers. For example, you may send an e-mail to your friends and at the bottom of the e-mail an advertiser includes a tagline that invites them to try out your e-mail service. If each friend responds positively to the tagline, more customers may be generated. All responders that join may repeat the process and thereby "recruit" new customers for the e-mail provider. Hot Mail had success with this technique in India where it became the leading e-mail service without doing much of anything else. Another way of generating leads is through affiliate marketing, whereby one Web site will send viewers to another Web site. The affiliates are rewarded by the business getting the referrals, which are potential customers.

Innovate and Create

Compare viral and affiliate e-marketing with prospecting using the endless chain method (customer referrals) and cold canvassing. Explain how a blog service provider could generate customer leads for itself and other companies. Write a catchy tagline to generate new leads for a Blog service to demonstrate the viral e-marketing technique. The endless chain method relies on customer referrals whereby a customer provides names of potential customers to a company. In essence the customer acts as an endorser of the product and helps to open the door for the salesperson. In cold canvassing, no prior contacts are involved. Salespeople find prospects on their own and so it is hit or miss. Viral e-marketing and affiliate marketing are more closely aligned with the endless chain method than cold canvassing because in each case referrals are the basis of the technique. A blog service provider can provide a link that the blog visitor can click on to visit the home page of the blog service provider to sign up or a link to companies that specialize in preparing effective blogs, whereby acting as an affiliate. The catchy taglines will vary. All should encourage the visitor to click on the link to the blog service provider's Web site.

eMarketing Worksheet Activity Send students to the Online Learning Center to download an eMarketing worksheet activity.

When you begin determining needs, first ask general questions about the intended use of the product and any previous experience with it. Build your questions around words like *who, what, when, where, how,* and *why.* You might ask the following questions of a prospective customer who wants to purchase a copier:

- What type of copier are you presently using?
- Why is that copier not meeting your needs?
- How many copies will you be making every week or month?
- Do you need a copier to also serve as a printer?

How to Refine Questions

Once you have an idea about the customer's general needs, then you can ask more specific questions relating to the product. These might include inquiries about size, color, and any special features desired. In the case of the copier, you might ask questions about the need to enlarge or reduce the size of the original and whether the customer needs to collate or staple copies. Does the customer want to make color copies or will a copier that makes only black-and-white copies be sufficient? Does the customer plan to use the copier at home or for business purposes? You may need to find out how soon the product is needed, what kind of space it will be housed in, and whether the customer might need to have the copier delivered. The more you know about a customer's problems and needs, the better. This knowledge helps in the process of coming up with solutions to customers' problems and needs.

Questioning is a very important skill and must be done carefully. Always be sure to keep in mind that customers may be very protective of their privacy. Privacy concerns may include cost and price. For example, customers can get upset when asked, "How much money do you want to spend?" A customer may not want to share details about his or her budget or financial situation. Whenever possible, it is better to ask how a customer intends to use a product and to discuss any past experience that person might have had with something similar. Those kinds of details keep the focus on the customer, the product, and how best the salesperson can help. That information should be enough to help most customers select a product that not only suits their specific needs but also fits within their personal price range.

Reading Check

Predict How do you think salespeople determine their customers' needs?

Business relies on documents.
Documents rely on TASKalfa.
Productivity is: TASKalfa
KYOCERA

Determining Needs

Printers come in many sizes. Depending on a business' needs, there is a printer to fit those needs. ***How do questions you would ask a customer who uses printers at home differ from the questions you would ask a customer who uses printers for business?***

Question Do's and Don'ts

Here are some other "do's and don'ts" guidelines for questioning customers:

1. Do ask open-ended questions that encourage customers to do the talking. **Open-ended questions** are those that require more than a "yes" or "no" answer.
   For example, you could ask, "What do you dislike about the copier you're presently using?" The answer to such a question will provide valuable information about a customer's needs.
2. Do ask clarifying questions to make sure you understand customers' needs.
   To do this, use opening lines such as: "Let me see whether I understand what you want," or, "Am I correct in assuming that you're looking for a product that can . . .?"
3. Don't ask too many questions in a row. This will make customers feel as if they are being cross-examined.
   Give the customer plenty time to answer any questions you might have, and be sure to listen carefully and respond thoughtfully. A good salesperson learns how to develop a professional yet conversational manner.
4. Don't ask questions that might embarrass customers or put them on the defensive.
   For example, when selling skis, it is often necessary to determine the customer's weight, but a customer may feel uncomfortable giving this information. In such a situation, you might have the various weight classes listed. Then you can simply ask which is the customer's category. In this way, you avoid having to ask the person, "How much do you weigh?"

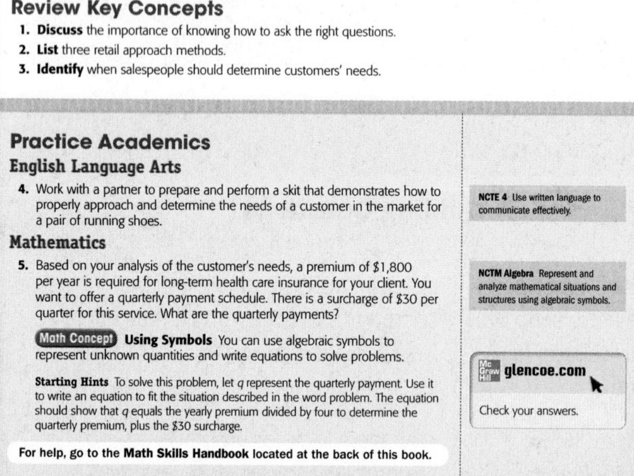

After You Read **Section 13.2**

Review Key Concepts

1. **Discuss** the importance of knowing how to ask the right questions.
2. **List** three retail approach methods.
3. **Identify** when salespeople should determine customers' needs.

Practice Academics

English Language Arts

4. Work with a partner to prepare and perform a skit that demonstrates how to properly approach and determine the needs of a customer in the market for a pair of running shoes.

NCTE 4 Use written language to communicate effectively.

Mathematics

5. Based on your analysis of the customer's needs, a premium of $1,800 per year is required for long-term health care insurance for your client. You want to offer a quarterly payment schedule. There is a surcharge of $30 per quarter for this service. What are the quarterly payments?

NCTM Algebra Represent and analyze mathematical situations and structures using algebraic symbols.

Math Concept **Using Symbols** You can use algebraic symbols to represent unknown quantities and write equations to solve problems.

Starting Hints To solve this problem, let *q* represent the quarterly payment. Use it to write an equation to fit the situation described in the word problem. The equation should show that *q* equals the yearly premium divided by four to determine the quarterly premium, plus the $30 surcharge.

For help, go to the **Math Skills Handbook** located at the back of this book.

glencoe.com Check your answers.

ELABORATE

Critical Thinking

Read the following scenario to students: You are one of two salespeople working in a gift shop. It is almost time to close and a couple walks in. They begin to look at the books, t-shirts, and other gift items. If they are going to buy something, you do not mind staying open late. If they are just looking around, you would rather close the store and go home. Ask: ***How should you approach and handle this situation?*** they might ask the customers if they might like to buy something; If the answer is "No, we are just looking," the salesperson might politely remind the customers that the store is closing in five minutes.

Visual Literacy

Determining Needs Caption Answer Read the caption question to students: ***How do questions you would ask a customer who uses printers at home differ from the questions you would ask a customer who uses printers for business?*** Questions for a home printer user might seek to learn how often the printer would be used, what it would be used for (photos, documents, homework), and who would use it (children and/or adults). Questions for a business printer user might ask how many copies per day/week/month would be made, how many people would use the printer, whether color printing is needed, and so on.

Knowledge Matters

VIRTUAL BUSINESS

ANALYZING THE COMPETITION

Introduce the concept of analyzing the competition to students using Knowledge Matters' Virtual Business Retailing visual simulation, *Analyzing the Competition*. In this simulation, students will learn how to determine who the competition is, competitive analysis, and how competition affects a business.

EVALUATE

Graphic Organizer

Display this chart. Ask students to imagine that they work at a appliance store and they are trying to sell a microwave oven. Have them provide examples for the question do's and don'ts. Possible questions:

	Do's	Don'ts
Open-ended questions	What do you dislike about the microwave you own?	Do you like the microwave you have now?
Qualifying questions	Am I correct in assuming that you would like a microwave very similar to the one you have now?	So, you want another microwave, right?
Number of questions	Tell me what features you would like your microwave to have.	What size microwave do you want? Do you want a carousel in the microwave? Should it have a browning rack? Is color important?
Sensitive questions	What functions on your current microwave do you use most often?	How much can you afford to pay for a new microwave?

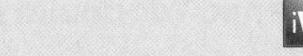

glencoe.com iWB

Graphic Organizer Send students to the Online Learning Center to print this graphic organizer.

Mini Project

Enrichment

Role Play Sales Situations Ask students to imagine that they are salespeople at a nursery specializing in orchids. These are very difficult to grow. Have students create tactful questions that can be asked to determine whether a customer knows how to care for the orchids they are buying. Role plays will vary but techniques for questioning and refining questions should be apparent in the role plays.

After You Read — Section 13.2

Review Key Concepts

1. Asking the right questions gets the customer talking and allows the salesperson to zero in on the customer's needs and wants.
2. Retail approach methods include the greeting approach, the service approach, and the merchandise or theme approach.
3. In organizational sales, the needs should be determined when qualifying a prospect. In retail sales, the needs should be determined during or immediately after the approach.

Practice Academics

English Language Arts

4. All skits should demonstrate one of the appropriate retail sales approaches and the proper order of questioning to determine a customer's needs in the sale of a pair of running shoes. The first question should be general (are you looking for an athletic shoe for yourself? What type of athletic shoe are you looking for (running shoe), what running shoe brand are you presently using? As the skit progresses the questions should get more specific regarding special requirements, size, and color.

Mathematics

5. \$480 (\$1,800 ÷ 4 + \$30 = \$480)

 **glencoe.com** 

Send students to the Online Learning Center to check their answers.

Chapter 13 Visual Summary

Beginning the Sales Process

Finding new customers can be achieved through three prospecting methods: customer referrals, cold canvassing, and employer sales leads.

WAYS OF FINDING CUSTOMERS
- CUSTOMER REFERRALS
- COLD CANVASSING
- EMPLOYER SALES LEADS

The approach in organizational selling is different from that in retail selling.

ORGANIZATIONAL SELLING	RETAIL SELLING
Arrive Early	Timing the Approach
Greet and Engage Customer	Method of Approach

314 | Unit 5 · Selling

Review and Activities

Written Summary

- To prepare for a sale, salespeople study products, industry trends, and competition.
- Matching the characteristics of a product to a customer's needs and wants is feature-benefit selling. Customers may have rational and emotional motives for buying.
- A prospect or lead is a potential customer.
- The approach step of the sales process can make or break the sale.
- The three purposes of the approach are to begin a conversation, build a relationship, and focus on the product.
- The three retail sales approaches are service, greeting, and merchandise.
- Determining needs is a step in the sales process that should begin as soon as possible and continue throughout the process.
- Three methods to determine needs are observing, listening, and asking questions.

Review Content Vocabulary and Academic Vocabulary

1. Write each of the vocabulary terms below on an index card, and the definitions on separate index cards. Work in pairs or small groups to match each term to its definition.

Content Vocabulary
- merchandising (p. 298)
- feature-benefit selling (p. 299)
- product features (p. 299)
- physical features (p. 301)
- extended product features (p. 301)
- customer benefits (p. 301)
- selling points (p. 301)
- buying motives (p. 302)
- rational motives (p. 302)
- emotional motives (p. 302)
- patronage motives (p. 302)
- prospecting (p. 303)
- prospect (p. 303)
- referrals (p. 303)
- endless-chain method (p. 303)
- cold canvassing (p. 304)
- greeting approach (p. 308)
- service approach (p. 309)
- merchandise approach (p. 309)
- nonverbal communication (p. 310)
- open-ended question (p. 313)

Academic Vocabulary
- shadowing (p. 297)
- longevity (p. 299)
- rapport (p. 307)
- astute (p. 310)

Assess for Understanding

2. **Identify** What are the sources of product information?
3. **Explain** How does feature-benefit selling create selling points?
4. **Describe** Why are customers' buying motives sometimes difficult to determine?
5. **Evaluate** What would you do with a customer who has been loyal in the past but now has new needs?
6. **Role-Play** What would you say in your approach to a customer who is standing in front of a specific television set? Explain why you elected to use that retail approach method.
7. **Generate** What types of questions would you ask to determine a customer's needs?
8. **Communicate** How can you use nonverbal communication to express an idea to someone? Demonstrate by doing.
9. **Role-Play** What would you say to clarify a customer's needs if that customer told you she was looking for an athletic shoe that did not look like an athletic shoe?

Chapter 13 · Beginning the Sales Process | 315

EVALUATE

Visual Summary

Express Creativity Ask students to create a visual summary that illustrates a concept in the chapter. Encourage students to use different formats for their visual summaries, such as a storyboard, a timeline, a cause-and-effect diagram, or a slide show. Visual summaries will vary depending on the concept depicted. Questions to ask when assessing a visual summary include:

- Is the summary clear, economical, and simple?
- Are any important steps or concepts left out?
- Are steps or concepts arranged in the same order as the original?
- Does the summary reveal a pattern that connects the details?
- Does the summary locate and highlight the most important information?

Review Content Vocabulary and Academic Vocabulary

1. Students should work with a partner or in small groups to practice matching the Content and Academic Vocabulary terms with their definitions. Students should use the definitions provided in the Glossary at the back of the text.

EVALUATE

Assess for Understanding

2. Sources of product information include: personal and others' experience with the product, published materials and Web sites, as well as formal training.

3. A selling point is created by noting the function of product feature and explaining how it benefits a customer, thus the concept of feature-benefit selling.

4. Customer buying motives are often difficult to determine because two customers may have different buying motives for the same product. Customers are not always aware of their inner motivations and even when they are, they may not communicate them to you.

5. I would assess the customer's new needs by asking pertinent questions when making the appointment and when speaking with the customer when we meet face-to-face. By doing that, I would be prepared to meet the customer's changing needs with solutions, which is a salesperson's job.

6. Merchandise or themed approach would be most effective because the customer has already shown an interest in a specific product. However, you could also justify using the greeting or service approach.

7. Types of questions to ask to determine a customer's needs include: open-ended questions that encourage customers to do the talking and clarifying questions to make sure you understand the customer's needs. You should not ask too many questions in a row and should not ask questions that might embarrass customers or put them on the defensive.

8. Demonstrations may include the use of facial expressions, hand motions, eye movements and other forms of nonverbal communication to express an idea.

9. Example clarifying question: Am I correct in assuming you're looking for an athletic shoe that can also be worn with casual attire? Other clarifying questions may begin with "Let me see if I understand . . ."

21st Century Skills

Communication Skills

10. **Writing to Sell** Write a sales letter to prospective customers. The purpose of the letter is to get them to make an appointment to see you in person so you can discuss your party planning services. Include a minimum of three selling points in your letter. Be sure to add a means of contacting you to follow up.

Financial Literacy Skills

11. **Assessing the Cost** You have decided to buy a list of sales leads for your small business. You buy a list of sales leads for $2,500. Of the 500 sales leads in that list, only 65 percent of them had the correct addresses, and only 20 percent of those leads became qualified prospects. What is the cost per qualified prospect?

Everyday Ethics

12. **Selling Credit** Credit card companies catch consumers' attention by promising low fixed-interest rates. However, rates can go up again for a variety of reasons. Although Congress has stepped in to help regulate credit card practices, interest rates have increased for many people. Explain whether you think it is ethical to offer a certain credit rate to "sell" customers, and then later raise it, even if a customer has complied with all terms in good faith.

e-Marketing Skills

13. **Determining Needs Online** Evaluate the Web site of a company that sells computers. Try to determine how the Web-site design is set up to determine customers' needs. What options are presented on the opening page? What is the next option presented to the online customer? What principles of questioning to determine needs did you observe in the design and content of that Web site?

Build Academic Skills

English Language Arts

14. **Selling Points** Choose a consumer product you might sell. Study all related product information, industry trends, and competition. Prepare five selling points for that item to demonstrate your knowledge of feature-benefit selling and customer buying motives.

NCTE 3 Apply strategies to interpret texts.

Science

15. **Scientific Inquiry** Write ten questions in the proper sequence for a product of your choice. Then answer those questions two different ways to demonstrate how two customers looking at the same product might have different needs.

NSES A Develop abilities necessary to do scientific inquiry, understandings about scientific inquiry.

Mathematics

16. **Managing Travel Time** You are stuck in traffic, and you are going to be late for your first meeting with a potential customer. You are traveling at 15 miles an hour and have 7 miles to go. If it is 8:30 a.m., at what time can you expect to arrive if you keep traveling at that speed?

NCTM Measurement Apply appropriate techniques, tools, and formulas to determine measurements.

Math Concept **Using Formulas** Rate (r), time (t), and distance (d) are related according to the formula $rt = d$. If you know two of the quantities, you can find the third using this formula.

For help, go to the **Math Skills Handbook** located at the back of this book.

Standardized Test Practice

Directions Read the following questions. On a separate sheet of paper write the best possible answer for each one.

1. A promotional flyer states, "Buy one purse and get a second one (of the same value or less) for half price." What is the cost for two purses priced at $21.99 and $25.99?
   A. $34.99
   B. $35.99
   C. $36.99
   D. $37.99
2. The endless chain method of prospecting involves customer referrals.
   T
   F
3. When you explain the function and customer benefit of a product feature, you are creating a ________ ________ for the product.

Test-Taking Tip

After you begin taking a math test, jot down important equations or formulas on scrap paper. This will help you to remember them as you take the test.

DECA Connection Role Play

Salesperson
Shoe Store

Situation You are a sales trainee (participant) in a retail store that sells footwear. New stock has just arrived. As you look through the material sent by the manufacturer that is in the shoe box, you find the following information: padded collar and tongue, leather upper, patented heel design, heel cushioning, arch support, comfort support system, and lightweight sole has millions of air bubbles. This walking shoe comes in both men's and women's styles and regular, narrow, and wide widths. It is available in black, brown, and beige. As part of your sales training, you are expected to prepare selling points for this new shoe, and practice the sales opening and determining needs steps of the sales process.

Activity In ten minutes the store manager (judge) will test your product knowledge about this new walking shoe to see if you can identify the product's features and benefits. Then you will be asked to practice the sales opening and determining needs steps of the sales process. You are to assume that a customer has stopped to look at the display of these new walking shoes.

Evaluation You will be evaluated on how well you meet these performance indicators:

1. Acquire product information for use in selling.
2. Analyze product information to identify product and features.
3. Establish relationship with client/customer.
4. Prepare for the sales presentation.
5. Analyze customer needs.

glencoe.com

Download the Competitive Events Workbook for more Role-Play practice.

EVALUATE

Communication Skills

10. Sales letters will vary, but all should include the proper format and be addressed to a prospective customer. The content of the letter must include a minimum of three selling points for the party planning service and the means for customers to contact a sales representative of the party planning service.

Financial Literacy Skills

11. $38.46 (500 × .65 = 325; 325 × .2 = 65; $2,500 ÷ 65 = $38.4615 per qualified lead).

Everyday Ethics

12. Some students may suggest that since the credit card companies are not breaking the law by raising interest rates, their actions are ethical. Others may feel that raising the interest rate when the customer has complied with all terms in good faith is not ethical. If the customer has held up his or her end of the agreement, the credit card company should hold up theirs.

e-Marketing Skills

13. Most students will recognize that one of the first options on the Web site will be "Home or Business." Once viewers select the appropriate option, they are directed to a page that identifies the products sold, where they select from a menu—laptops or desktops (also noted are other products). Once that selection is made (general question), they are given additional options related to specific features of the product. Thus, the Web site follows the principles of asking general questions about intended use before asking specific questions.

EVALUATE

Build Academic Skills

English Language Arts

14. The five selling points will vary but should include information about the product's basic features, physical features, and extended product features. Selling points should also cover consumer buying motives such as rational motives, emotional motives, patronage motives, and multiple motives.

Science

15. Sample questions include: What type of refrigerator do you have now? Why is that refrigerator not meeting your needs? How will you be using the refrigerator–in your home kitchen or for a business? How much space do you need in your refrigerator? Do you need equal space in the refrigerator and freezer sections? How large can the refrigerator be? Who will be using the refrigerator? What extras such as ice and water on the door are you interested in? Is saving energy important to you? Does the refrigerator need to match other appliances? Answers will vary–students should answer the questions based on the perspectives of two different customers.

Mathematics

16. You can expect to arrive at 8:58 ($7 \div 15 = 0.467$; $0.467 \times 60 = 28.02$; $8{:}30 + 28 = 8{:}58$).

Standardized Test Practice

1. C $36.99 ($25.99 + 50% of $21.99 = $36.99)
2. True
3. selling point

DECA Connection Role Play

Evaluations will be based on these performance indicators:

1. **Acquire product information for use in selling.** In addition to reviewing the published materials contained with the product, product information can be found on the company's Web site, and learned through formal training.
2. **Analyze product information to identify product and features.** Manufacturers' information identifies these features: padded collar and tongue, leather upper, patented heel design, heel cushioning, arch support, comfort support system, lightweight sole has millions of air bubbles. This walking shoe comes in both men's and women's styles and regular, narrow, and wide widths. It is available in black, brown, and beige.
3. **Establish relationship with client/customer.** Treat customers as individuals. Never stereotype a person because of age, sex, race, religion, appearance, or any other characteristic. Be aware of the customer's personality and buying style. Show interest in the customer by maintaining good eye contact and showing friendliness. Learn and use the customer's name to personalize the sale when possible. Incorporate a theme in the approach.
4. **Prepare for the sales presentation.** Background preparation for the sales presentation includes gaining product knowledge, learning about industry trends and competition, learning product features and customer benefits, developing selling points and advantages. With the retail customer the salesperson should engage the customer through a greeting, service, or merchandise/theme approach; determine the customer's needs; and match the right product to the customer's needs.
5. **Analyze customer needs.** There are three basic methods–observing, listening, and questioning–to help the salesperson determine the customer's needs. Observing–facial expressions, hand motions, eye movement, and other forms of nonverbal communication can give clues as to a customer's needs. Listening–giving customers your undivided attention and listening with empathy will encourage your customers to identify their needs and wants. Questioning–well-chosen questions can help determine a customer's needs.

glencoe.com

Role Plays For more DECA Role Plays, send students to the Online Learning Center to download the Competitive Events Workbook.

Chapter 14 Section 14.1 Product Presentation | Section 14.2 Objections

presenting the product

SHOW WHAT YOU KNOW

Visual Literacy Some products are sold to customers for personal use, while others are sold for business use. For product presentation to be effective, you must know the customer's intended use for the product. ***How might you decide which product features to communicate to this customer during product presentation?***

Discovery Project

Selling Back-to-School Products

Essential Question How do you present and sell electronic products for back-to-school customers?

Project Goal

Assume that you work in a store that sells electronics. You must train other sales associates on effective product presentations for the back-to-school market. Anticipate questions or concerns that the sales associates should expect from back-to-school customers. Create a training session for these associates to use.

Ask Yourself...

- Which products should be included in the sales training?
- What questions and concerns are often asked by customers who purchase these products?
- How will you prepare for the training session?
- What product presentation skills will you demonstrate in your training?

Synthesize and Present Develop a training session for sales associates on the presentation of electronic products for the back-to-school market.

glencoe.com

Activity
Get a worksheet activity about product presentation.

Evaluate
Download a rubric you can use to evaluate your project.

DECA Connection

DECA Event Role Play

Concepts in this chapter are related to DECA competitive events that involve either an interview or role play.

Performance Indicators The performance indicators represent key skills and knowledge. Your key to success in DECA competitive events is relating them to concepts in this chapter.

- Demonstrate product knowledge.
- Convert customer/client objections into selling points.
- Recommend specific products.
- Demonstrate initiative.
- Provide legitimate responses to inquiries.

DECA Prep

Role Play Practice role-playing with the DECA Connection competitive-event activity at the end of this chapter. More information on DECA events can be found on DECA's Web site.

Chapter 14 · Presenting the Product | 319

ENGAGE

Visual Literacy

Read the chapter opener photo caption question to students: ***How might you decide which product features to communicate to this customer during product presentation?*** It is necessary to learn the customer's intended use for the product before selecting a few samples that match those needs. You can learn a customer's needs by asking questions about needs, uses, and so on. Then ask these guiding questions.

Guiding Questions

Recall What sources can be used to learn product knowledge?	experience (self and others), published materials and Web sites, and training
Explain What are the three ways of determining the needs of customers?	observing—facial expressions, hand motions, eye movements; listening—pick up clues; questioning—ask who, what, when, where, why, and how

Discovery Project

Selling Back-to-School Products Start a discussion that connects students to the Discovery Project Essential Question: ***How do you present and sell electronic products for back-to-school customers?*** Asking a few questions about a customer's previous experience with the product would help the salesperson determine how to explain the features and benefits using terminology that matches the customer's level of experience.

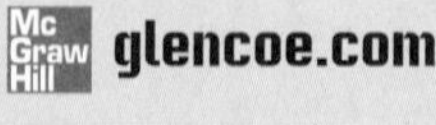

Discovery Project Resources Send students to the Online Learning Center to download a rubric to evaluate their projects.

ENGAGE

Introduce the Chapter

Chapter 14 covers two essential aspects of the sales process: product presentation and responding to objections. These main concepts are introduced and discussed:

- The goal of the product presentation
- Selecting products for the presentation
- What to say during a product presentation
- Creating effective product presentations
- Distinguishing objections from excuses
- Dealing with objections
- Five buying decisions related to customer objections
- Four-step method for handling customer objections
- Seven methods for answering objections

Discussion Starter

Product Knowledge Tell students that selling a product such as a high-end computer relies on both product features and emotional aspects of decision making. A salesperson must be able to relate to the customer on all these levels in order to close the sale. Ask: ***How can determining needs help a salesperson do a better job at selling a computer?*** After determining a customer's needs, the salesperson can present computer models that will most likely appeal to that customer. Tell students that making a major purchase, such as a computer, requires more consideration and thought than making a minor purchase. People tend to do more research before purchasing expensive items. Ask: ***How do you think the Internet has changed the way people shop for products?*** Students should realize that many people use the Internet to research products before buying. The customer often has a considerable amount of product knowledge.

DECA Connection

Discuss the performance indicators listed in the DECA Connection feature. Explain to students that performance indicators tell them how to demonstrate their acquired skills and knowledge through individual or team competitive events.

glencoe.com

Competitive Events Workbook For more DECA Role Plays, send students to the Online Learning Center to download the Competitive Events Workbook.

PROGRAM RESOURCE ORGANIZER

PRINT RESOURCES

- **Student Edition**
- **Teacher Edition**
- **Student Activity Workbook with Academic Integration** includes worksheets and activities correlated to the text.
- **Mathematics for Marketing Workbook** provides math activities for every unit in the text.

TECHNOLOGY TOOLBOX

- **Connect**
- **ConnectPlus**
- **ExamView Assessment Suite** is a comprehensive solution for creating, administering, and scoring tests.

glencoe.com

Online Learning Center provides a variety of resources to enrich and enhance learning.

SECTION, CHAPTER, AND UNIT RESOURCES

- **Graphic Organizers** for organizing text concepts visually.
- **Digital Nation Activities** and **Green Marketer Activities** extend learning beyond the text features.
- **Career Chatroom Career Profiles** allow students to explore different marketing occupations in depth.
- **After You Read Answer Keys** for students to check their answers.
- **Discovery Project Rubrics** and **Marketing Internship Project Rubrics** for students to evaluate their projects.

PROGRAM RESOURCES

- **Student Activity Workbook with Academic Integration Teacher Annotated Edition** includes annotated answers for the activities and worksheets.
- **Marketing Research Project Workbook** provides a step-by-step approach for students to complete their own marketing research studies.
- **School-to-Career Activity Workbook** helps students relate their class work to on-the-job experience and involves work-site analysis and working with mentors.
- **Competitive Events Workbook** helps prepare students for state and national marketing education competitions.
- **Inclusion in the Marketing Education Classroom** provides teaching resources for working with students with special needs.
- **PowerPoint Presentations** provides visual teaching aids and assessments for this chapter.

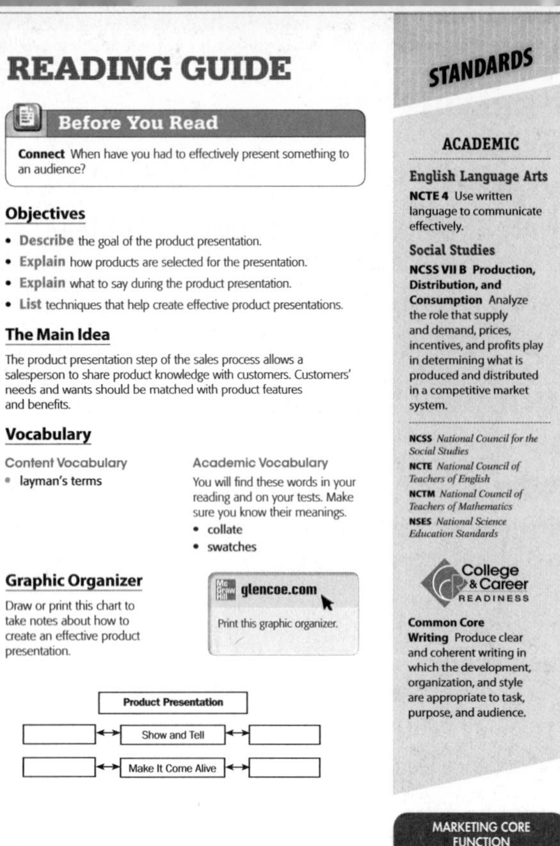

READING GUIDE

Before You Read

Connect When have you had to effectively present something to an audience?

Objectives

- **Describe** the goal of the product presentation.
- **Explain** how products are selected for the presentation.
- **Explain** what to say during the product presentation.
- **List** techniques that help create effective product presentations.

The Main Idea

The product presentation step of the sales process allows a salesperson to share product knowledge with customers. Customers' needs and wants should be matched with product features and benefits.

Vocabulary

Content Vocabulary
- layman's terms

Academic Vocabulary

You will find these words in your reading and on your tests. Make sure you know their meanings.
- collate
- swatches

Graphic Organizer

Draw or print this chart to take notes about how to create an effective product presentation.

glencoe.com 

Print this graphic organizer.

Product Presentation
Show and Tell
Make It Come Alive

STANDARDS

ACADEMIC

English Language Arts

NCTE 4 Use written language to communicate effectively.

Social Studies

NCSS VII B Production, Distribution, and Consumption Analyze the role that supply and demand, prices, incentives, and profits play in determining what is produced and distributed in a competitive market system.

NCSS *National Council for the Social Studies*
NCTE *National Council of Teachers of English*
NCTM *National Council of Teachers of Mathematics*
NSES *National Science Education Standards*

College & Career READINESS

Common Core
Writing Produce clear and coherent writing in which the development, organization, and style are appropriate to task, purpose, and audience.

MARKETING CORE FUNCTION

Selling

m.e. Section 14.1

Product Presentation

ORGANIZING THE PRODUCT PRESENTATION

When you do a puzzle, you analyze the various parts by shape and size. You might select the straight-edged pieces to use for the frame. When you sell, you analyze your customer's needs and buying motives. Then you use that information to begin framing your product presentation. The goal of the product presentation is to effectively present the features and benefits of a product that best match your customer's needs and buying motives.

As You Read

Consider How can you hold a customer's interest throughout the sales process?

SHOW AND TELL

Your first decision in the product presentation step of the sale is what product or products to show your customer. Then you must think about what you are going to say and how you are going to say it. This is the step of the sale in which you have the opportunity to share your expertise with the customer. You have put a lot of preparation into learning about the product you sell and how to communicate its selling points. This preparation will assist you now. Remember, you are the expert, and you have the solutions to your customer's problems and needs.

WHICH PRODUCTS DO YOU SHOW?

After you have learned the customer's intended use of a product, you should be able to select a few samples that match those needs. You may select technically advanced cameras for customers who want a camera for professional use. Novice customers might want fully automatic cameras.

When your product selection is not exactly accurate, ask questions to get the feedback you need to select a different model or style. Determining customer's needs occurs throughout the sales process.

> "Selling is, in many ways, like putting together a jigsaw puzzle."

WHAT PRICE RANGE SHOULD YOU OFFER?

Sometimes you will not know the customer's price range. Your knowledge of the intended use may be insufficient to determine a price range. In these cases, begin by showing a moderately priced product. You can move up or down in price once you begin to get the customer's feedback.

If you are offering consulting services or a quote on a major project, such as a kitchen renovation, you may need to get some idea of the customer's budget. In that case, you can provide the customer with a price range. For example, "Our fees range from $100 for our basic service up to $500 for our premium services." This technique will help you discover your customer's price range without asking "How much did you want to spend?"

It is not a good idea to introduce price early in the product presentation unless it is a major selling point. This is because you need time to show your clients or customers how valuable your product is to them. You know that if a product is something that you would really need and want, price becomes less of a factor in a purchase decision.

ENGAGE

Anticipation Activity

Improving Student Achievement Remind students about approaching the customer and determining needs. Ask: ***If you worked in a gift shop, how would approaching the customer and determining the customer's needs affect your product presentation?*** This part of the selling process will help you to show them the right gifts for the right person.

Objectives

- **Describe** the goal of the product presentation. The goal is to match customer needs to product features and benefits.
- **Explain** how products are selected for the presentation. First determine the customer's needs and wants, then use that information to select products
- **Explain** what to say during the product presentation. Present selling points then explain how features meet needs.
- **List** techniques that help create effective product presentations. displays, customer involvement, holding the customer's attention

Graphic Organizer

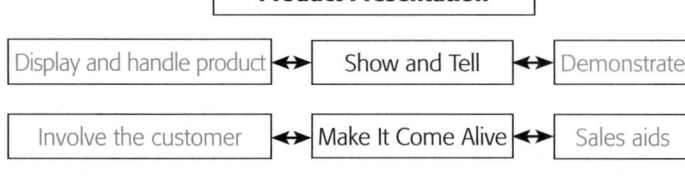

Product Presentation

Display and handle product	↔ Show and Tell ↔	Demonstrate
Involve the customer	↔ Make It Come Alive ↔	Sales aids

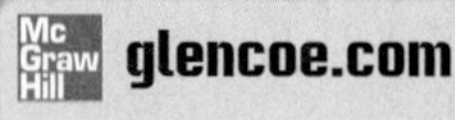

Graphic Organizer Send students to the Online Learning Center to print this graphic organizer.

EXPLORE

Before You Read

Read the Before You Read question aloud: ***When have you had to effectively present something to an audience?*** Answers may include speeches or presentations given in school, in clubs, or at work. Ask students: ***How did you prepare for your presentation?*** Students may mention that they studied necessary material and practiced beforehand.

Preteaching Vocabulary

Have students go to the Online Learning Center at glencoe.com for the Chapter 14 Preteaching Vocabulary games.

Content Vocabulary

Tell students that a layman is a nonprofessional who would not understand the jargon of a particular profession. Ask: ***What do you think layman's terms are?*** Students may recognize that layman's terms are words that someone who is not a professional would understand.

Academic Vocabulary

Collate–Demonstration Bring to class some cards or papers that can be put into alphabetical order or ordered in another obvious way. Ask a student to do that task. Tell students that this is a demonstration of *collating.* Ask: ***What do you think collating has to do with presenting a product?*** When giving a presentation, it is important to have materials in the order in which they are needed.

Swatches–Demonstration Bring to class different swatches of fabric or paint to show students. Ask students: ***If you worked in a fabric store or paint store, how might having swatches available help your product presentation?*** Seeing different types of fabric and different colors of paint can be very helpful to the customer, who will be able to see the full variety of products the store has available.

PROFESSIONAL DEVELOPMENT

MINI CLIP

Reading: Strategies for Student Achievement
Go to the Online Learning Center for a video in which teachers discuss strategies for helping all learners meet curriculum standards.

Product Presentation

ORGANIZING THE PRODUCT PRESENTATION

Ask students these guiding questions about organizing a product presentation.

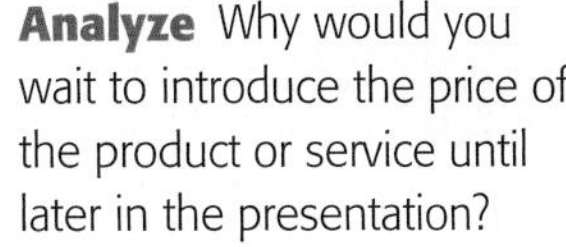

Guiding Questions

Identify What is the first decision that must be made when preparing a product demonstration?	The first decision is what product or products to show the customer.
Explain In what way is a sales presentation like a jigsaw puzzle?	Puzzle pieces must be analyzed before putting them in the correct position. Customer needs and buying motives must be analyzed to find the right product fit.
Analyze Why would you wait to introduce the price of the product or service until later in the presentation?	You want to convince the customer that he or she needs the product before introducing the price.

As You Read

Read students the As You Read question: ***How can you hold a customer's interest throughout the sales process?*** The more you know about a product and your customer, the easier it is to relate product features to a customer's needs and wants. Knowing a customer's main concerns helps you decide how best to present the product features.

Expert Advice

Read the quote to students:

> **"Selling is, in many ways, like putting together a jigsaw puzzle."**

Ask students: ***Do you agree or disagree with this statement? Why?*** Some may see the selling process as a jigsaw puzzle, which must be analyzed and put together in the right way. Others may see it as a step-by-step process.

HOW MANY PRODUCTS SHOULD YOU SHOW?

To avoid overwhelming your customer, show no more than three products at a time. It is difficult for most people to remember all the features of more than three items during a presentation. When a customer wants to see more than three, put away the displayed products in which the customer shows no interest.

HOT TOPIC
Show and Tell Provide useful information to the customer, and teach him or her to use the product, thereby enhancing its value.

WHAT DO YOU SAY?

In this step of the sales process, present the product's selling points. Educate customers by explaining how the product's features relate to their respective needs. Use highly descriptive adjectives and active verbs when describing product features. Avoid generalized descriptions, such as *nice, pretty,* and *fine.*

Avoid using slang and terms that have double meanings. For example, when selling an expensive suit to a corporate executive, you should not say something like, "You look cool in that suit." In such a situation, it would be more appropriate to point out the fine fabric used in the suit or the quality of the tailoring.

When selling industrial products, you can use the appropriate jargon to communicate with industrial buyers at their level of expertise. As you may recall from Chapter 8, jargon is specialized vocabulary used by members of a particular group. If you know the meanings of the terms used by your customers, you will be able to address their needs more professionally and effectively.

When selling products to retail customers, you should use layman's terms. **Layman's terms** are words the average customer can understand. If you are selling electronics, instead of talking about motherboards and processors, you could say, "This computer is fast and reliable."

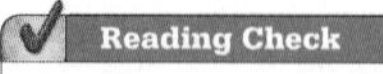

Identify What is the goal of product presentation?

In some businesses, salespeople rely on showroom displays for their product presentations. Displays help show off a product in a setting or in use. ***What businesses rely on displays to showcase their product? How do salespeople use those displays for their product presentations?***

PLAN THE PRESENTATION

Planning is necessary for an effective product presentation. Consider how you will present the product to the customer and how you will demonstrate its selling points. What sales aids will add to your presentation? Finally, how will you involve the customer?

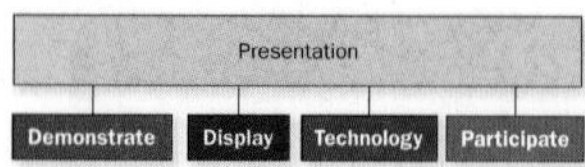

PRESENTING AND DEMONSTRATING THE PRODUCT

The way you physically present a product to the customer presents an image of its quality. Handle it with respect and use hand gestures to show the significance of certain features. For example, when presenting an expensive ring or watch to a customer, you might place it on a velvet pad rather than directly on a glass display counter.

Demonstrating the product in use helps to build customer confidence. This is especially true if you are selling an item that requires manipulation or operation, such as a camera, computer, or smartphone. To demonstrate the features of a copier, you might show how it can enlarge or reduce a document as well as **collate** and staple multiple copies. The capabilities of computer software products can be easily demonstrated directly on a computer.

USING DISPLAYS AND SALES AIDS

In retail selling situations, product displays can help in the product presentation. Mannequins give salespeople the opportunity to show how a complete outfit might look on the customer. When selling china, silverware, and glasses, a complete table-setting display gives customers an idea of how those products would look in their own homes. Manufacturers also display their products in their own showrooms to make it easier for their salespeople to sell.

When it is impractical to display or demonstrate the actual product or when you want to emphasize certain selling points, you can use sales aids in your presentations. Sales aids may include samples, fabric **swatches**, reprints of magazine and newspaper articles, audiovisual aids, and scaled models.

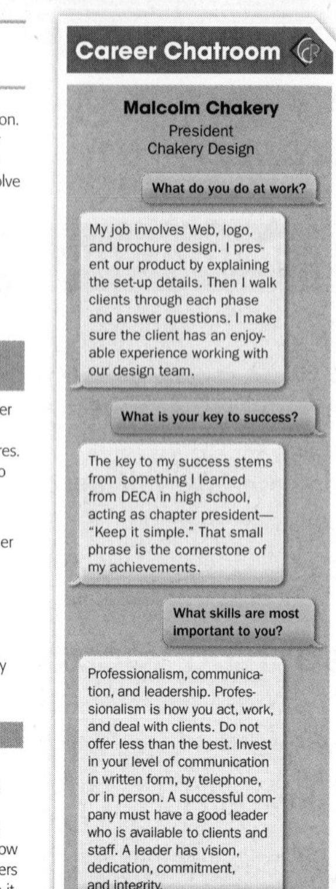

EXPLAIN

Visual Literacy

Displays Caption Answer Read the caption questions to students: ***What businesses rely on displays to showcase their product?*** stores that sell furniture, kitchen cabinets, replacement windows and doors, carpeting, and businesses that sell high-tech products ***How do salespeople use those displays for their product presentations?*** Salespeople use displays to involve customers in the sale and to demonstrate their products.

VIRTUAL BUSINESS

MERCHANDISING

Introduce students to the concept of merchandising using Knowledge Matters' Virtual Business Retailing visual simulation, *Merchandising*. In this simulation, students will explore merchandising and its importance to store sales and profits.

Show and Tell Ask students to bring to class a product with which they are very familiar. Ask them to demonstrate the product and to teach a classmate who is unfamiliar with the product how to use it. Have the class constructively critique the demonstrations.

Reading Check Answer

Read the Reading Check question to students: ***What is the goal of product presentation?*** The goal of product presentation is to effectively present the features and benefits of a product that best match your customer's needs.

ELABORATE

PLAN THE PRESENTATION

Ask these guiding questions to focus the discussion on planning the product presentation.

Guiding Questions

Analyze Why would demonstrating a product as it is actually used help to build customer confidence?	If the customer sees the salesperson using the product, they will think that they, too, can successfully operate the product.
Plan How would you display a living room sofa to best show its features?	Students may suggest that they would display it in a living room setting with chairs, end tables, coffee table, lamps, and so on.
Predict If you went to a customer's business to show the new paint colors your company has developed, how would you display the colors?	Students may suggest that they would take a portfolio showing color combinations in real-life settings, and swatches of the new colors.

Graphic Organizer

Display this diagram. Ask students to provide details about each of the items in the second row. Possible answers:

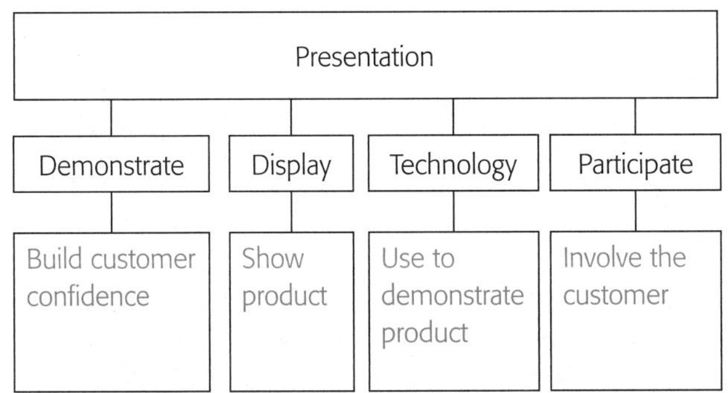

iWB

Graphic Organizer Send students to the Online Learning Center to print this graphic organizer.

Critical Thinking

Tell students that computer presentation software can be used as a sales aid. Discuss with students possible reasons that computer presentation software is playing an increasingly important role in product presentations. Ask: ***Why do you think computerized presentations are so popular?*** the portability of laptops for in-store presentations, the fact that most businesses have computers and can play presentations on a CD-ROM or via the Internet, and presentation software can be used on both PCs and Macs.

Career Chatroom

Use these questions to focus the discussion about the Career Chatroom feature.

Guiding Questions

Compare How is Mr. Chakery's job similar to a sales presentation?	Presenting and explaining the product and answering questions use the same skills for both
Analyze How does Mr. Chakery's phrase, "Keep it simple," apply to a sales presentation?	Not overwhelming the customer by showing too many products or offering too much information is important in a sales presentation.

glencoe.com

Career Exploration Send students to the Online Learning Center to read more about this career and to get a Career Exploration Activity.

Photographs, drawings, graphs, charts, specification sheets, customer testimonials, and warranty information can also be used as sales aids. Organizational sales representatives who sell machinery, industrial components, or other business-related technology may use high-tech, multimedia presentations. For example, computer-aided design can be used to show products in three-dimensional views. It may have the ability to rotate the product and highlight special features. Videos can show a product in use.

For a riding lawnmower, you could show the customer articles in magazines that rate its performance. You could also use any complimentary letters or testimonials from satisfied customers as a sales aid, or share the warranty the manufacturer offers. These sales tactics help consumers build confidence in the company because they show that the company stands behind its products. If you were selling this product to retailers for resale purposes, you may even want to use samples of the lawnmower's blade to demonstrate its effectiveness and durability. You might also show a video to demonstrate its ease of operation, safety features, and high-quality construction.

Be creative when determining which sales aids will help you in your particular product presentation. Manufacturers of industrial ovens might show a video of how quickly and efficiently the oven performs. Insurance salespeople might use graphs and charts to show how dividends will accumulate or to compare the benefits of one policy to another. They might even use a computer to personalize the presentation of that information for each customer and show different policy plans for that person.

INVOLVING THE CUSTOMER

It is best to get the customer physically involved with the product as soon as possible in the sales presentation. Appeal to the customers' five senses. You could have your customers hold and swing golf clubs, and try on and walk around in a pair of shoes. Allow customers to feel the ease of using a computer keyboard or mouse and listen to the sound quality and see the vivid colors on a television. Customers will want to test-drive an automobile or taste and smell food products. Some cosmetic companies offer free makeovers so a customer can see how the products enhance their appearance.

Allowing customers to try a product or service lets them participate in the sale. ***Why is it so important to get a product into the customer's hands or involve the customer in some other way during the sales presentation?***

You can also involve your customer verbally during the sales presentation by confirming selling points. Ask a question that is guaranteed to produce a positive response. You might say, "This jacket is wind and water resistant. Don't you think that feature will come in handy on an outdoor trip?" Pause for the customer's answer. If you get the customer's agreement on several selling points, you know you are on the right track with the selected product.

HOLDING THE CUSTOMER'S ATTENTION

When you involve a customer in the sale, you help him or her make intelligent buying decisions. You also help yourself because the customer is generally more attentive when doing more than just listening to what you say.

If you are losing your customer's attention, ask a simple question. Regaining your customer's attention is essential if you are to continue with the sales presentation. The key is keeping the customer involved.

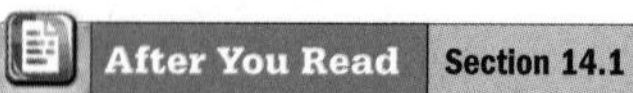

After You Read — Section 14.1

Review Key Concepts

1. **Explain** how to identify which priced product you should show when you cannot determine a customer's intended price range.
2. **Explain** how you might involve the customer in a product presentation about a high-tech product.
3. **Describe** how to involve a customer in the product presentation when selling fresh bread and pastries to a restaurant.

Practice Academics

English Language Arts

4. Write a detailed plan that covers the product presentation for a product of your choice. For at least one product feature, include what you will say, how you will demonstrate that feature, what sales aids you will use, how you will use them, and how you will involve your customer.

NCTE 4 Use written language to communicate effectively.

Mathematics

5. You work in a fabric store. A customer wants to buy 15 feet of wool fabric. If the price per yard is $16.50, how much do you charge?

Math Concept **Measurement** Measure objects and apply units, systems, and processes of measurement.

Starting Hints To solve this problem, divide 15 by 3 to convert the amount of feet into the amount of yards. Multiply $16.50 by the number of yards the customer wants to determine the total price.

NCTM Measurement Understand measurable attributes of objects and the units, systems, and processes of measurement.

For help, go to the **Math Skills Handbook** located at the back of this book.

glencoe.com

Check your answers.

324 | Unit 5 · Selling

Chapter 14 · Presenting the Product | 325

ELABORATE

Visual Literacy

Try It Out Caption Answer Read the caption question to students: ***Why is it so important to get a product into the customer's hands or involve the customer in some other way during the sales presentation?*** It gives the customer first-hand experience with the product, and it helps create an ownership mentality. It also keeps the customer interested in the sales presentation.

Mini Project

Extension

Research Customer Involvement Have students research different types of retail stores where customers are allowed to try products. Ask students to take note of special accommodations that must be made for customers to try the products. Have students share their findings with the class. Answers may include a fitting room for trying on clothing, listening stations for CDs or other forms of music, or an artificial putting green for trying out golf clubs, electronic gadgets that customers can try out, fragrances and cosmetics samples to test, and so on. Then tell students that some kitchenware stores offer cooking classes that allow customers to use specialized items that they may never try otherwise. Encourage students to think of similar classes offered by other types of businesses. Building supply and hardware stores offer do-it-yourself classes in which participants use tools they may not have used before. Fabric stores offer sewing classes. Computer stores offer training. Ask: ***How do businesses benefit from offering classes?*** Businesses benefit because customers are introduced to other products.

EVALUATE

Graphic Organizer

Display the diagram. Ask students to provide examples of items that can be used as sales aids during a product presentation. Possible answers:

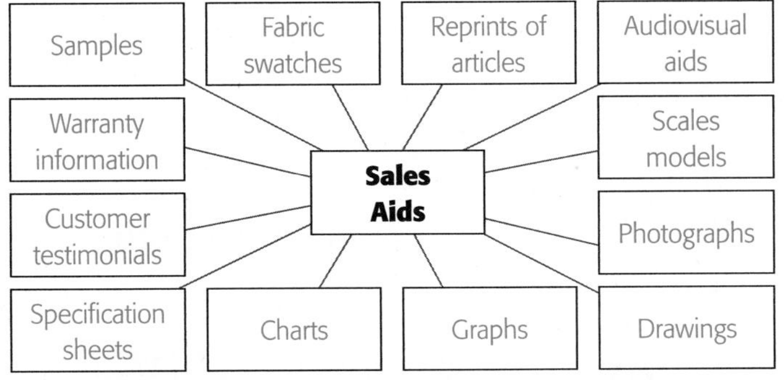

iWB

Graphic Organizer Send students to the Online Learning Center to print this graphic organizer.

Critical Thinking

Discuss with students the pros and cons of demonstrating products to customers. Ask students: ***How does the extra interaction allow a salesperson to learn more about the customer's needs and wants?*** Students may suggest that it allows more time and more conversation with the customer, which can help to better determine needs and wants. Then ask: ***What difficulties or challenges might demonstrating a product present to a salesperson?*** Students may mention the difficulty of demonstrating a product out of the context in which it is meant to be used. They might suggest that demonstration of a product requires the salesperson to be more knowledgeable about his or her products. If the product is of below-average quality, it might also do more harm than good to the selling process.

After You Read **Section 14.1**

Review Key Concepts

1. Show the medium-priced item so you can go up in price or down in price once you get feedback from the customer.
2. After giving a basic demonstration, have the customer use the product. Give directions and have the customer follow them so they can see and feel how the product operates.
3. To sell fresh bread and pastries to a restaurant, you must have the customer taste the products.

Practice Academics

English Language Arts

4. Plans will vary depending on the product. However, all plans must include: at least one product feature, what they would say, how they would demonstrate that feature, what sales aids they would use, how they would use them, and how they would involve the customer. They also should incorporate sample dialogue when appropriate.

Mathematics

5. The answer is \$82.50 ($15 \div 3 \times \$16.50 =$ \$82.50).

glencoe.com

Answer Key Send students to the Online Learning Center to check their answers.

READING GUIDE

Before You Read

Connect When have you had to respond to an objection?

Objectives

- **Distinguish** objections from excuses.
- **Explain** why you should welcome objections in the sales process.
- **Explain** the five buying decisions on which common objections are based.
- **Demonstrate** the general four-step method for handling customer objections.
- **List** seven methods of answering objections and identify when each should be used.

The Main Idea

Objections are helpful in the sales process because they provide an opportunity to further determine customers' needs and problems. Objections are easily managed when you know the basis for them.

Vocabulary

Content Vocabulary
- objections
- excuses
- objection analysis sheet
- substitution method
- boomerang method
- superior-point method
- third-party method

Academic Vocabulary

You will find these words in your reading and on your tests. Make sure you know their meanings.
- paraphrase
- compensate

Graphic Organizer

Draw or print this chart to take notes about ways to handle objections.

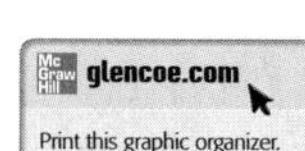

glencoe.com

Print this graphic organizer.

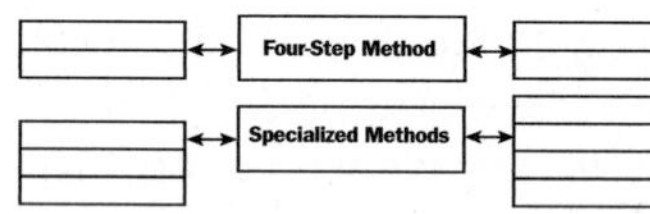

STANDARDS

ACADEMIC

English Language Arts

NCTE 4 Use written language to communicate effectively.

Social Studies

NCSS VII B Production, Distribution, and Consumption Analyze the role that supply and demand, prices, incentives, and profits play in determining what is produced and distributed in a competitive market system.

NCSS National Council for the Social Studies
NCTE National Council of Teachers of English
NCTM National Council of Teachers of Mathematics
NSES National Science Education Standards

College & Career READINESS

Common Core

Reading Interpret words and phrases as they are used in a text, including determining technical, connotative, and figurative meanings, and analyze how specific word choices shape meaning or tone.

MARKETING CORE FUNCTIONS

Selling

m.e. Section 14.2

Objections

UNDERSTANDING OBJECTIONS

Objections are concerns, hesitations, doubts, complaints, or other reasons a customer has for not making a purchase. Objections should be seen as positive. They give feedback and an opportunity to present more information to the customer.

Anticipate and plan potential answers to objections. This will help you feel more confident in your responses to customers. Then select the most appropriate method for handling those objections to promote success.

> "Objections should be welcomed in sales."

Objections can be presented as questions or statements. An example of a question would be: "Do you carry any other brands?" A statement would be: "These shoes don't fit me." For questions, simply answer the question posed. For statements, you may need more selling expertise.

Excuses are reasons given when a customer has no intention of buying. In retail sales situations, the most common excuse is: "I am just looking." When you are faced with that statement, be polite and courteous. Encourage customers to look around and ask you any questions they may have.

In organizational sales situations, clients may simply refuse to see the salesperson. In that case, it is best to leave a business card and ask to see the person at a more convenient time.

It can be difficult to distinguish between objections and excuses. A statement or question that seems to be an excuse may be an objection. For example, "I didn't plan to buy today" may really mean "I don't like the styles you have available." When you suspect that may be the case, ask additional questions to get to the real reason for the disinterest in your product or products.

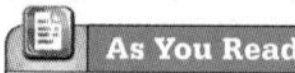

As You Read

Predict What are methods salespeople use to handle objections?

Objections should be welcomed. However, some objections may be excuses instead. ***How can a salesperson determine if a customer is giving an objection or an excuse?***

ENGAGE

Objectives

- **Distinguish** objections from excuses. Objections are concerns, hesitations, doubts, complaints, or other reasons for not making a purchase. Excuses are reasons given when a customer has no intention of buying.
- **Explain** why you should welcome objections in the sales process. Objections are feedback that provides an opportunity to present more information to the customer.
- **Explain** the five buying decisions on which common objections are based. need, product, source, price, and time
- **Demonstrate** the general four-step method for handling customer objections. listen carefully, acknowledge the objections, restate the objections, answer the objections
- **List** seven methods of answering objections and identify when each should be used. substitution, boomerang, question, superior point, denial, demonstration, third party

Anticipation Activity

Improving Student Achievement Ask students if they have ever gone shopping without any intention of buying. Ask: ***What responses did you give to salespeople who asked if they could help you?*** Write students' responses for students to view. Have student groups discuss how a salesperson should address each of the responses.

Graphic Organizer

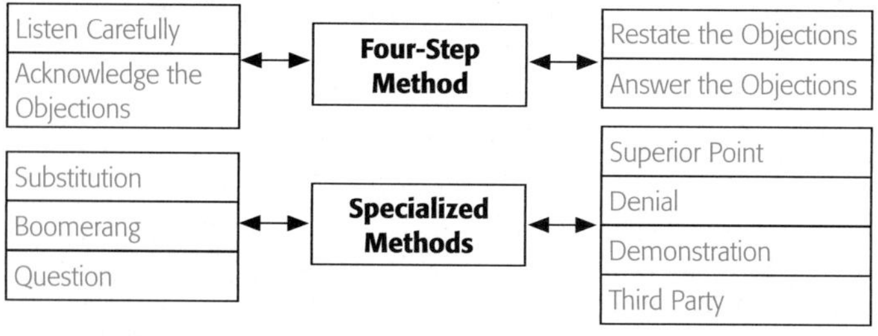

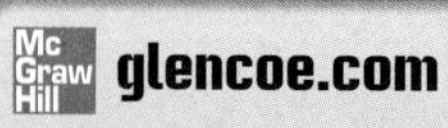

glencoe.com

Graphic Organizer Send students to the Online Learning Center to print this graphic organizer.

EXPLORE

Before You Read

Read the Before You Read question aloud: ***When have you had to respond to an objection?*** Most answers will not involve sales situations. Students will likely mention objections from parents, siblings, friends, teachers, and so on. Ask: ***How did you handle the objections?*** Some students may be honest enough to say they did not handle them well and ended up in an argument. Others may mention positive ways they handled the objections, such as asking for clarification or not taking it personally. Ask: ***In a sales situation, what might happen if you end up getting into an argument with a customer?*** Answers may include: you will lose the sale, the customer may file a complaint, and you may get reprimanded or even lose your job.

Preteaching Vocabulary

Have students go to the Online Learning Center at glencoe.com for the Chapter 14 Preteaching Vocabulary games.

Content Vocabulary

Have students make an aid for studying the Content Vocabulary terms by folding a sheet of paper lengthwise to make a pamphlet. With the folded edge to the left, students should write the vocabulary terms in a list on the front of the pamphlet. On the inside of the pamphlet, students should write the definitions of the terms. Students can use the pamphlet to self-test by looking at the term and then opening the pamphlet to see if they knew the correct definition.

Academic Vocabulary

Paraphrase—Usage Write the term *paraphrase* for students to view. Ask: ***What is the definition of this term?*** Paraphrase means to restate something, usually in a shorter form. Have students practice paraphrasing by asking them to read a paragraph from the text and then paraphrase it.

Compensate—Usage Write the term *compensate* for students to view. Ask a student to look up the meaning of the term and share it with the rest of the class. To make amends; or to pay someone for a loss or for work completed. Ask volunteers to use the term in original sentences.

Section 14.2

Objections

UNDERSTANDING OBJECTIONS

Tell students that we usually do not like to hear objections, much less deal with them. However, salespeople must get used to hearing objections and learn how to handle them. Ask these guiding questions to focus the discussion on objections.

Guiding Questions

Apply How would you respond to the following objection: In what other fabrics is the sofa available?	Show swatches, photos, catalogs, or, if available, another sofa or piece of furniture that features an alternate fabric.
Distinguish How would you handle an objection differently from an excuse?	Sample answer: Objections should be answered to the best of the salesperson's ability. Excuses should be questioned to gain insight into what the problem might actually be.

As You Read

Read students the As You Read question: ***What are methods salespeople use to handle objections?*** Salespeople use substitution, boomerang, question, superior point, denial, demonstration, and third party to handle objections.

Expert Advice

Read the quote to students:

> **"Objections should be welcomed in sales."**

Ask students: ***Do you agree that objections should be welcome? Why or why not?*** Students may suggest that handling objections allows a salesperson to erase a customer's doubts about a product or service.

Visual Literacy

Objections vs. Excuses Caption Answer Read the caption question to students: ***How can a salesperson determine if a customer is giving an objection or an excuse?*** The salesperson can ask questions to reveal the true nature of the statement.

PLAN FOR OBJECTIONS

Objections can occur at any time during the sales process and should be answered promptly. A customer who must wait to hear responses to questions or concerns will become preoccupied with the objection. When that happens, you may lose the customer's attention and confidence.

Objections can guide you in the sales process by helping you redefine the customer's needs and determine when the customer wants more information. A customer may say, "This item is very expensive." What the person may really mean is: "Tell me why this product costs so much." This objection not only lets you know why the customer is reluctant to buy, but also gives you an opportunity to bring out additional selling points.

So, you should welcome objections. They are not necessarily the sign of a lost sale. Research shows a positive relationship between customer objections and a successful sales outcome.

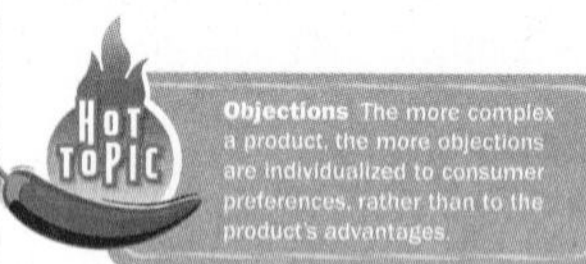

HOT TOPIC
Objections The more complex a product, the more objections are individualized to consumer preferences, rather than to the product's advantages.

You can prepare yourself for most objections that might occur in a sales situation by completing an **objection analysis sheet**, a document that lists common objections and possible responses to them. The actual objections may be slightly different from those you anticipated. However, thinking of responses can give you an idea of how to handle other objections.

You can incorporate anticipated objections into your product presentation so they do not become objections. You must be cautious about this, however. You do not want to include so many objections in your product presentation that you introduce doubt, especially if none existed before. Saying "I guess you're worried about the safety of this snowmobile," may introduce a fear that was not a previous concern.

A better way to handle the same situation would be to emphasize the safety features of the vehicle. You might say, "The suspension on this snowmobile is specially designed to keep it stable. It's very safe to operate."

COMMON OBJECTIONS

When you list general customer objections, you will see that they fall into certain categories. Most objections are based on five key decisions the customer must make before buying—decisions about need, product, source, price, and time. This is true for both retail and organizational sales situations. The actual objections will vary because of the difference in purchase motivation. Retail customers generally are making a purchase for personal use. Business-to-business customers are buying for a company's operation. Wholesalers and retailers are buying for resale purposes.

The following are examples of customer objections. They provide a starting point for the creation of an objection analysis sheet.

NEED

Objections related to need usually occur when the customer does not have an immediate need for the item. They may happen when the customer wants the item but does not truly need it. A supermarket owner may say, "I just don't have enough shelf space for another cereal brand." A comment, such as "I like these sandals, but I really don't need another pair," is an objection based on a conflict between a need and a want.

PRODUCT

Objections based on the product are more common. They include concerns about things such as ease of use, quality, color, size, or style. "I don't buy 100-percent cotton shirts because they have to be ironed" is a product objection.

SOURCE

Objections based on source often occur due to negative past experiences with the firm or brand. A customer might say, "The last time I placed an order with your company, I received it two weeks after the promised date."

PRICE

Objections based on price are more common with high-quality, expensive merchandise. You might hear statements such as "That's more than I wanted to spend."

TIME

Objections based on time reveal a hesitation to buy immediately. These objections are sometimes excuses. Customers usually have a real reason for not wanting to make a purchase on the spot. A customer might say, "I think I'll wait until July to buy those sandals when you have your summer sale."

You will probably hear many different kinds of objections once you begin selling. You should note them for future reference.

FOUR-STEP METHOD FOR HANDLING OBJECTIONS

Successful salespeople have learned to use a very basic strategy when answering all objections or complaints. It consists of four basic steps: listen, acknowledge, restate, and answer.

LISTEN CAREFULLY

Remember to be attentive, maintain eye contact, and let the customer talk. Also watch for nonverbal cues in order to interpret the true meaning of what is being said.

ACKNOWLEDGE THE OBJECTIONS

Acknowledging objections demonstrates that you understand and care about the customer's concerns. Show empathy for the customer's problem. Some common statements used to acknowledge objections include the following: "I can see your point" or "Other customers have asked us the same question."

MARKETING CASE STUDY

IBM's Presentation Centers

IBM® has designed "client centers" around the world to impress customers with technology and consulting services. Customers are brought to the facilities for sales presentations. The entire experience is planned, from when they are picked up at the airport to the actual product presentations. This approach ensures that all clients are treated in a professional manner with customer satisfaction as the focal point. What to say and when to say it is mapped out for the sales staff. The timing of product demonstrations and sales pitches is based on IBM's research.

Hands-On Presentation

At IBM's Industry Solution Lab, future technology is displayed alongside current technology. Clients can also interact with technology for different industries. This hands-on experience makes a day-long sales meeting engaging and more meaningful than just watching PowerPoint® presentations.

English Language Arts

Evaluate Do you think salespeople can handle customer objections effectively in these sales presentations? Discuss with your class.

NCTE 3 Apply strategies to interpret texts.

EXPLAIN

PLAN FOR OBJECTIONS

Ask these guiding questions to focus the discussion on planning for objections.

Guiding Questions

Explain Why should objections be answered promptly?	If a customer has to wait to receive an answer to an objection, he or she will probably become preoccupied with the objection, and the salesperson will lose the customer's attention and confidence.
Analyze How can an objection analysis sheet help a salesperson respond to objections?	This document helps salespeople plan ahead by listing objections and possible responses to them.

Critical Thinking

Divide the class into small groups. Have each group choose a type of business to simulate. Then have them to pick a product and create an objection analysis sheet for the product listing at least five objections and ways to address them. After groups have had time to prepare, have two groups work together—one group will offer objections and the other group will use their objection analysis sheets to answer the objections. Ask the groups to determine how well their objection analysis sheets worked.

Objections Have students analyze the Hot Topic statement. Ask: ***Why would a more complex product lead to more individualized objections?***

ELABORATE

Graphic Organizer

Display this diagram. Ask students to act as customers and provide objections. Possible answers:

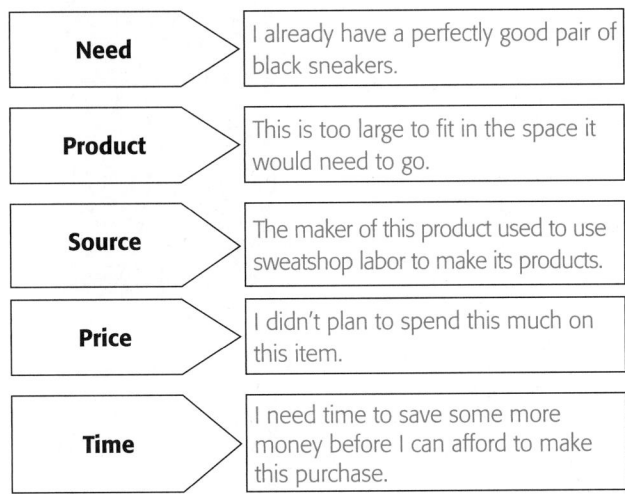

Need	I already have a perfectly good pair of black sneakers.
Product	This is too large to fit in the space it would need to go.
Source	The maker of this product used to use sweatshop labor to make its products.
Price	I didn't plan to spend this much on this item.
Time	I need time to save some more money before I can afford to make this purchase.

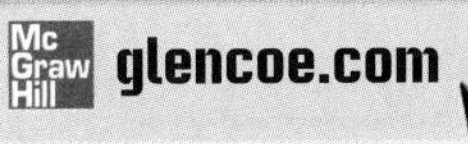

iWB

Graphic Organizer Send students to the Online Learning Center to print this graphic organizer.

MARKETING CASE STUDY

English Language Arts Answer Responses may include: Client centers get the clients undivided attention because they are away from distractions that might occur at the client's place, and IBM products can be displayed more effectively at client centers. Salespeople have more time to handle objections. They also have had time to prepare for objections.

Mini Projects

Differentiated Instruction

Interpersonal Learners Divide the class into pairs. Have members of each pair practice restating the objection by taking turns being the customer and the salesperson. The customer will make an objection and the salesperson will restate it. Emphasize to students the importance of paraphrasing and measuring one's tone so you don't sound incredulous, mocking, or condescending. If time allows, have pairs role play their sales situation for the class. Have the class critique whether the salesperson accurately restated the objection and whether he or she sounds incredulous, mocking, or condescending when restating the objection. Ask the class to offer solutions or suggestions to the salesperson.

Kinesthetic Learners Divide the class into pairs or small groups. Tell students that the four-step method for handling objections—listen carefully, acknowledge the objections, restate the objections, and answer the objections—can be used in situations not related to business. Have pairs of students develop role plays that are not business related in which they use the four-step method. Ask pairs to present their role plays to the class. Possible situations include: a parent objecting to a teen going out on a school night; a friend objecting to your choice of movie when going to the theater together.

Critical Thinking

Ask students if they have ever watched or participated in a debate. Have them recall aspects of the debate. List their responses for the class to view. Ask students: ***How can debates build skills in handling objections?*** Explain that during a debate, after a person gives a statement, he or she faces a rebuttal and is given a chance to respond. Ask: ***How is this similar to a salesperson handling a customer's objections?*** Salespeople anticipate and plan answers to customers' objections. Doing so increases the chances of completing a sale.

These acknowledgments make customers feel that their objections are understandable, valid, and worthy of further discussion. This does not mean that you agree with the customers, but it acknowledges the objection. Disagreeing with customers, or saying, "You're wrong," will put customers on the defensive, and you might lose the sale.

RESTATE THE OBJECTIONS

To be sure you understand a customer's objection, restate it in one of the following ways:

"I can understand your concerns. You feel that. . . . Am I correct?"

"In other words, you feel that. . ."

"Let me see if I understand. You want to know more about. . ."

Do not repeat the customer's concerns word for word. Instead, **paraphrase** the objections. A customer might say, "The style is nice, but I don't like the color." You could paraphrase the objection by asking, "Would you be interested in the jacket if we could find your size in another color?"

ANSWER THE OBJECTIONS

Answer each objection tactfully. Never answer with an air of superiority or suggest that the person's concern is unimportant.

Think of yourself as a consultant, using the objections to further define or redefine the customer's needs. In some cases, you will have to get to the bottom of the specific objection before answering it completely. For example, before answering the price objection, revisit the features on the more expensive model. Then see if the customer's needs can be met with a less expensive model.

SPECIALIZED METHODS OF ANSWERING OBJECTIONS

There are seven specialized methods for answering objections: substitution, boomerang, question, superior point, denial, demonstration, and third party.

Listening carefully is the best way to understand objections. Being attentive and making eye contact shows that you are listening. ***How would you show a customer that you understand his or her objection?***

Answering Objections: Substitution; Boomerang; Question; Superior Point; Denial; Demonstration; Third Party

SUBSTITUTION

Sometimes a customer is looking for a specific brand or model of a product that you do not carry. Or maybe the customer does not like the product you show. In any of those cases, you may want to use the **substitution method**, which involves recommending a different product that would still satisfy the customer's needs. Assume a customer says, "I don't like the way this dress looks on me." In this case, you may want to suggest a different style that is more becoming on your customer.

BOOMERANG

An objection can be returned to the customer in the same way that a boomerang returns to the thrower. The **boomerang method** brings the objection back to the customer as a selling point. Here is an example:

Customer: This ski jacket is so lightweight. It can't possibly keep me warm.

Salesperson: The jacket is so light because of an insulation material called Thinsulate. The manufacturer guarantees that Thinsulate will keep you warmer than other fiberfill insulation, without the bulk and extra weight.

When using the boomerang method, you must be careful not to sound as if you are trying to outwit the customer. Use a friendly, helpful tone to explain how the objection is really a selling point.

QUESTION

The question method is a technique in which you question the customer to learn more about his or her objections. To uncover their real objection, you can simply ask, "Why do you feel that way?" Their answer may unearth a lot of information that will reveal the real reason for the objection. A customer may say, "I don't like receiving my e-mails on a mobile phone."

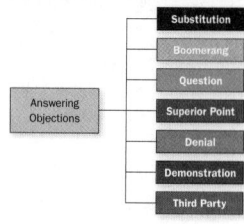

DIGITAL NATION

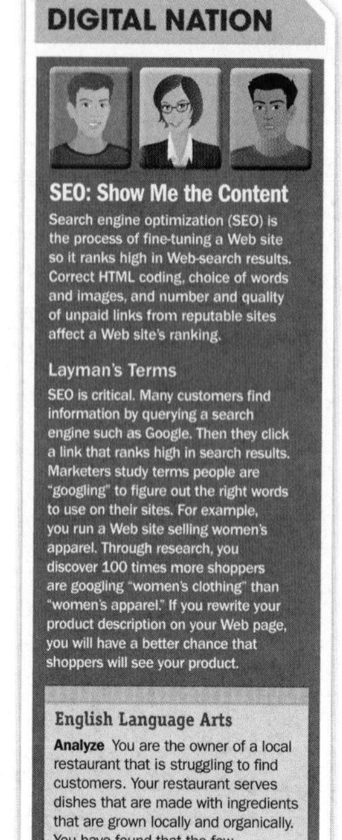

SEO: Show Me the Content

Search engine optimization (SEO) is the process of fine-tuning a Web site so it ranks high in Web-search results. Correct HTML coding, choice of words and images, and number and quality of unpaid links from reputable sites affect a Web site's ranking.

Layman's Terms

SEO is critical. Many customers find information by querying a search engine such as Google. Then they click a link that ranks high in search results. Marketers study terms people are "googling" to figure out the right words to use on their sites. For example, you run a Web site selling women's apparel. Through research, you discover 100 times more shoppers are googling "women's clothing" than "women's apparel." If you rewrite your product description on your Web page, you will have a better chance that shoppers will see your product.

English Language Arts

Analyze You are the owner of a local restaurant that is struggling to find customers. Your restaurant serves dishes that are made with ingredients that are grown locally and organically. You have found that the few customers that come to your store did not know about your Web site. Create a series of recommended modifications to your site that would rank higher in search engine results.

glencoe.com

Get a Digital Nation Activity.

EXPLAIN

Visual Literacy

Listening to Objections Caption Answer Read the caption questions to students: ***How would you show a customer that you understand her objection?*** by listening to the customer's concerns, being attentive, showing eye contact, looking for nonverbal gestures

Reinforce Vocabulary

Practice Key Terms Tell students that the key terms in this chapter are foundational to the study of marketing. To help students connect the marketing-related terms, consider playing word games in which you supply either the key term or the definition, and have students supply the matching definition or term.

Critical Thinking

Have student pairs compare and contrast the boomerang method with the superior-point method of handling objections. In the boomerang method, the salesperson turns a negative comment into a positive one. In the superior-point method, the salesperson responds with a different positive comment.

SPECIALIZED METHODS OF ANSWERING OBJECTIONS

Ask these questions to focus the discussion about methods for answering objections.

Guiding Questions

Identify What are seven specialized methods for answering objections?	substitution, boomerang, question, superior point, denial, demonstration, and third party
Explain What is the substitution method of answering objections?	If the product a customer wants doesn't meet that person's needs, the salesperson suggests a different product that will meet those needs.
Contrast How is the boomerang method of answering objections different from the question method?	The boomerang method returns the customer's objection back to them as a selling point. The question method seeks to learn more information from the customer to better meet that person's needs.

ELABORATE

Graphic Organizer

Display this diagram. Ask students to provide a brief description of each method for answering objections. Possible answers:

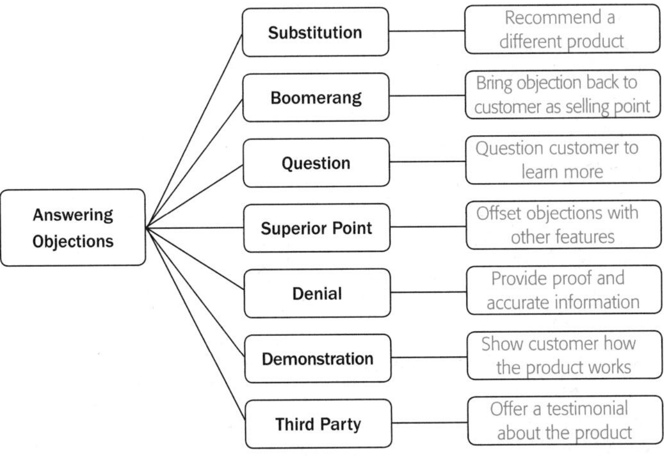
Answering Objections
Substitution
Recommend a different product
Boomerang
Bring objection back to customer as selling point
Question
Question customer to learn more
Superior Point
Offset objections with other features
Denial
Provide proof and accurate information
Demonstration
Show customer how the product works
Third Party
Offer a testimonial about the product

glencoe.com iWB

Graphic Organizer Send students to the Online Learning Center to print this graphic organizer.

DIGITAL NATION

English Language Arts Answer Read the English Language Arts Activity to students. ***You are the owner of a local restaurant that is struggling to find customers. Your restaurant serves dishes that are made with ingredients that are grown locally and organically. You have found that the few customers that come to your store did not know about your Web site. Create a series of recommended modifications to your site that would rank higher in search engine results.*** Answers should follow the guidelines stated in the article, such as figuring out the right words to use on the Web site that will get more hits.

glencoe.com

Worksheet Activity Send students to the Online Learning Center to get a Digital Nation worksheet activity.

e MARKETING

Selling via Digital Tech Savvy

Burberry®, a luxury clothing company, is tech savvy. Its ad campaign lets users drag and rotate models to see how accessories look in motion. Since 2009, Burberry has presented its fashion show online in 3D. Customers can place orders during and after the show. Items ordered are delivered in six to eight weeks. Sears® ran a promotion called "Campus Connection" where Web site viewers could shop for products and place them in a virtual dorm room.

Innovate and Create

Have students think of all businesses that would benefit from digital savvy to present products in an interesting way in order to generate online sales. What features of the product could be rotated, dragged, and zoomed. How could this same technology support the sales force too? Real estate agents and vacation sites can use digital savvy by showing virtual tours of homes and resorts. Automobile manufacturers, electronics, and high-tech machines could benefit from digital savvy too. Parts of a product could be shown in 3D and rotated to show all sides of the product as well as the product's functions. Demonstrations could be performed using videos. The product could be presented in various settings, depending upon the customer's needs. Since these products may be expensive, all this technology could help presell a customer and could also be used by the sales force when making a presentation to a customer offsite via a laptop computer or smartphone.

S
M
Lg

glencoe.com

eMarketing Worksheet Activity Send students to the Online Learning Center to download an eMarketing worksheet activity.

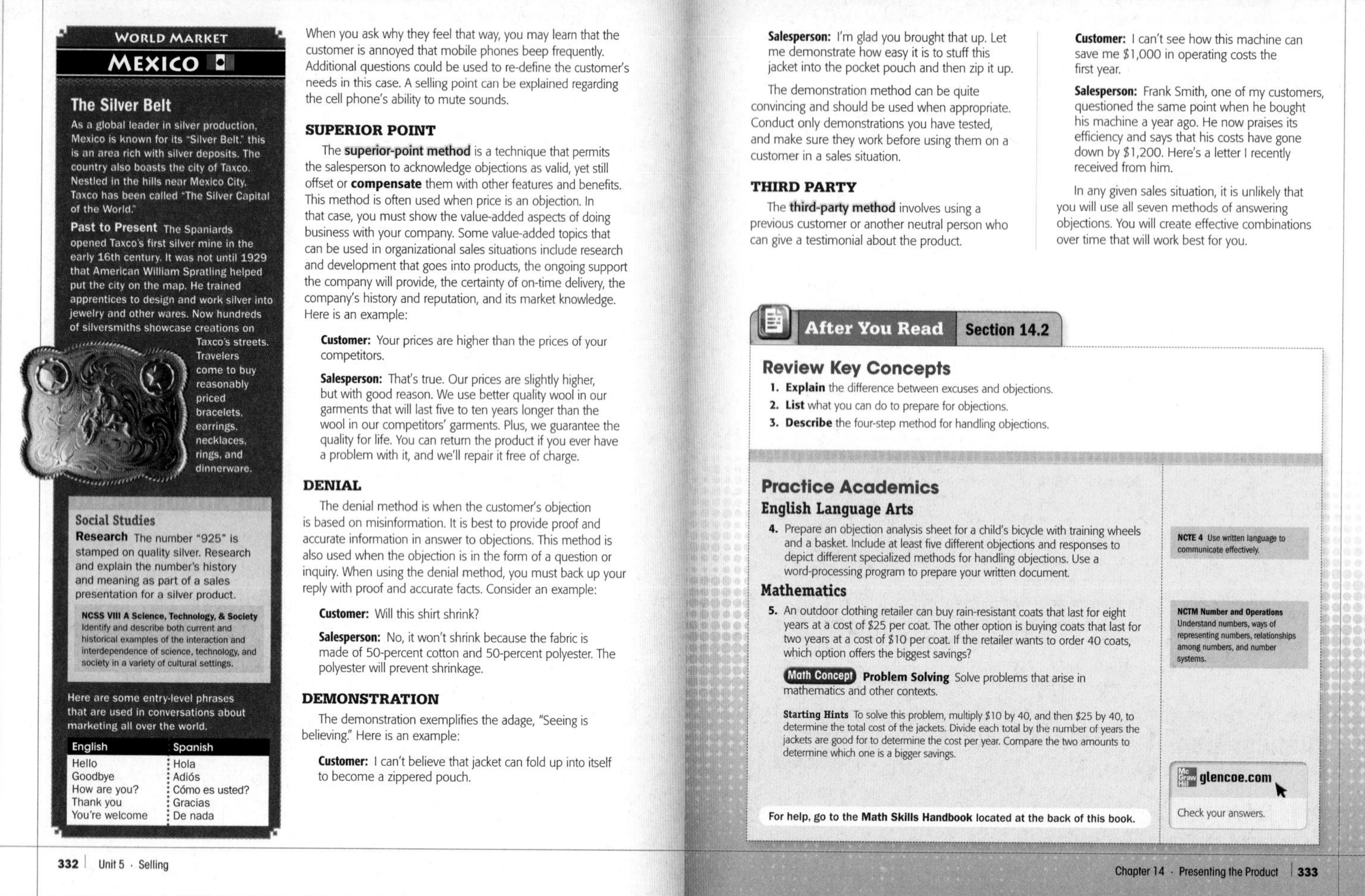

WORLD MARKET

MEXICO

The Silver Belt

As a global leader in silver production, Mexico is known for its "Silver Belt," this is an area rich with silver deposits. The country also boasts the city of Taxco. Nestled in the hills near Mexico City, Taxco has been called "The Silver Capital of the World."

Past to Present The Spaniards opened Taxco's first silver mine in the early 16th century. It was not until 1929 that American William Spratling helped put the city on the map. He trained apprentices to design and work silver into jewelry and other wares. Now hundreds of silversmiths showcase creations on Taxco's streets. Travelers come to buy reasonably priced bracelets, earrings, necklaces, rings, and dinnerware.

Social Studies

Research The number "925" is stamped on quality silver. Research and explain the number's history and meaning as part of a sales presentation for a silver product.

NCSS VIII A Science, Technology, & Society Identify and describe both current and historical examples of the interaction and interdependence of science, technology, and society in a variety of cultural settings.

Here are some entry-level phrases that are used in conversations about marketing all over the world.

English	Spanish
Hello	Hola
Goodbye	Adiós
How are you?	Cómo es usted?
Thank you	Gracias
You're welcome	De nada

When you ask why they feel that way, you may learn that the customer is annoyed that mobile phones beep frequently. Additional questions could be used to re-define the customer's needs in this case. A selling point can be explained regarding the cell phone's ability to mute sounds.

SUPERIOR POINT

The **superior-point method** is a technique that permits the salesperson to acknowledge objections as valid, yet still offset or **compensate** them with other features and benefits. This method is often used when price is an objection. In that case, you must show the value-added aspects of doing business with your company. Some value-added topics that can be used in organizational sales situations include research and development that goes into products, the ongoing support the company will provide, the certainty of on-time delivery, the company's history and reputation, and its market knowledge. Here is an example:

Customer: Your prices are higher than the prices of your competitors.

Salesperson: That's true. Our prices are slightly higher, but with good reason. We use better quality wool in our garments that will last five to ten years longer than the wool in our competitors' garments. Plus, we guarantee the quality for life. You can return the product if you ever have a problem with it, and we'll repair it free of charge.

DENIAL

The denial method is when the customer's objection is based on misinformation. It is best to provide proof and accurate information in answer to objections. This method is also used when the objection is in the form of a question or inquiry. When using the denial method, you must back up your reply with proof and accurate facts. Consider an example:

Customer: Will this shirt shrink?

Salesperson: No, it won't shrink because the fabric is made of 50-percent cotton and 50-percent polyester. The polyester will prevent shrinkage.

DEMONSTRATION

The demonstration exemplifies the adage, "Seeing is believing." Here is an example:

Customer: I can't believe that jacket can fold up into itself to become a zippered pouch.

Salesperson: I'm glad you brought that up. Let me demonstrate how easy it is to stuff this jacket into the pocket pouch and then zip it up.

The demonstration method can be quite convincing and should be used when appropriate. Conduct only demonstrations you have tested, and make sure they work before using them on a customer in a sales situation.

THIRD PARTY

The **third-party method** involves using a previous customer or another neutral person who can give a testimonial about the product.

Customer: I can't see how this machine can save me $1,000 in operating costs the first year.

Salesperson: Frank Smith, one of my customers, questioned the same point when he bought his machine a year ago. He now praises its efficiency and says that his costs have gone down by $1,200. Here's a letter I recently received from him.

In any given sales situation, it is unlikely that you will use all seven methods of answering objections. You will create effective combinations over time that will work best for you.

After You Read Section 14.2

Review Key Concepts

1. **Explain** the difference between excuses and objections.
2. **List** what you can do to prepare for objections.
3. **Describe** the four-step method for handling objections.

Practice Academics

English Language Arts

4. Prepare an objection analysis sheet for a child's bicycle with training wheels and a basket. Include at least five different objections and responses to depict different specialized methods for handling objections. Use a word-processing program to prepare your written document.

NCTE 4 Use written language to communicate effectively.

Mathematics

5. An outdoor clothing retailer can buy rain-resistant coats that last for eight years at a cost of $25 per coat. The other option is buying coats that last for two years at a cost of $10 per coat. If the retailer wants to order 40 coats, which option offers the biggest savings?

Math Concept **Problem Solving** Solve problems that arise in mathematics and other contexts.

Starting Hints To solve this problem, multiply $10 by 40, and then $25 by 40, to determine the total cost of the jackets. Divide each total by the number of years the jackets are good for to determine the cost per year. Compare the two amounts to determine which one is a bigger savings.

NCTM Number and Operations Understand numbers, ways of representing numbers, relationships among numbers, and number systems.

For help, go to the **Math Skills Handbook** located at the back of this book.

glencoe.com

Check your answers.

332 | Unit 5 · Selling

Chapter 14 · Presenting the Product | 333

ELABORATE

WORLD MARKET

SOCIAL STUDIES

Answer Have students research the number "925" and explain the number's history and meaning as part of a sales presentation for a silver product. 925 is a rating that means the silver is 92.5% pure, which is called sterling silver. Students should use this information in their sales presentations for a silver product. Ask: ***How might you prove to a skeptical customer that the silver is sterling?*** The salesperson could show the 925 stamp on the piece and then do an online search to find an explanation of the number.

Critical Thinking

Ask students to share about a time they experienced a salesperson being overly aggressive. Ask: ***Did the experience make you want to return to the store? Why or why not?*** Students might say they would not return. Others may say it had no effect on their return.

Build Global Perspective

Tell students that in many countries salespeople have very different method of selling. In some cultures bartering and haggling are the common ways to do business. Ask students: ***How would you define bartering?*** Bartering means to exchange goods or services or to negotiate the terms of a sale or other transaction. ***How would you define haggling?*** Haggling means to argue over a price. Ask students whether they think the specialized methods of answering objections would be useful or effective in a sales culture of bartering or haggling. the specialized methods of answering objections would be useful and effective used with both bartering and haggling. No matter the sales technique—bartering, haggling, or personal sales—the customer's objections must be answered.

EVALUATE

Mini Projects

Enrichment

Conduct Product Demonstrations Have students choose a product to demonstrate. Allow them time to develop and practice so they can conduct the demonstration without errors. Then have them imagine that a customer has just said, "I don't believe it works as easily as you say it does." Have students respond to the objection by conducting a demonstration of their product. You might have students work in pairs on this project so that during the demonstration, the "salesperson" can have the "customer" participate in the demonstration.

Compare Testimonials Ask students: ***What is a testimonial?*** A testimonial is a recommendation by someone. Ask students if they are familiar with uses of testimonials other than in the third-party method. Some students may be aware that testimonials are common in advertisements. Ask: ***Is the purpose of testimonials used in advertisements different from the purpose of testimonials used in the third-party method?*** Students should realize that both uses of testimonials are basically the same; they are used to help sell a product or service.

Practice Objections Have students role play that they are customers at a department store, and ask them to come up with six reasons not to purchase certain items. Afterward, have the students pretend to be salespeople. Ask the class to: (1) distinguish objections from excuses; and (2) come up with four-step responses to the objections. Have volunteers act out the objections and excuses in class.

PROFESSIONAL DEVELOPMENT **MINI CLIP**

ELL: Accessing Prior Knowledge
Go to the Online Learning Center for a video in which a teacher helps students make connections between what they already know and an upcoming reading selection.

After You Read — Section 14.2

Review Key Concepts

1. Excuses are reasons given when a customer has no intention of buying; while objections are concerns, hesitations, doubts, or other honest reasons for not making a purchase.
2. To prepare for objections, you can prepare an objection-analysis sheet which lists common objections and possible responses to those objections.
3. The four-step method for handling objections is as follows: (1) listen carefully; (2) acknowledge the objection; (3) restate the objection; and (4) answer the objection.

Practice Academics

English Language Arts

4. All work should include at least five different objections and responses to depict different specialized methods for handling objections. Some common objections students may include are: price is too high (use superior point—It is a little higher priced than other models, however it is made of ... which makes it more durable and provides more stability and comfort); not sure if the child is ready for a bicycle (question method—Why do you feel that way?); I don't like the color of this bike (substitution—It also comes in other colors, such as ...); do I have to put this bicycle together? (direct denial—No, we assemble the bicycle when you purchase it.); I don't know if this basket on the front of the bike is necessary (boomerang – That is the one feature that sets this bicycle apart from the others. Your child will use that basket often when riding the bicycle to and from school.).

Mathematics

5. Buying 40 jackets at $25 each offers the biggest savings. [($25 × 40 = $1,000 ÷ 8 = $125 per year); ($10 × 40 = $400 ÷ 2 = $200 per year)]

 **glencoe.com** 

Send students to the Online Learning Center to check their answers.

Chapter 14 Visual Summary

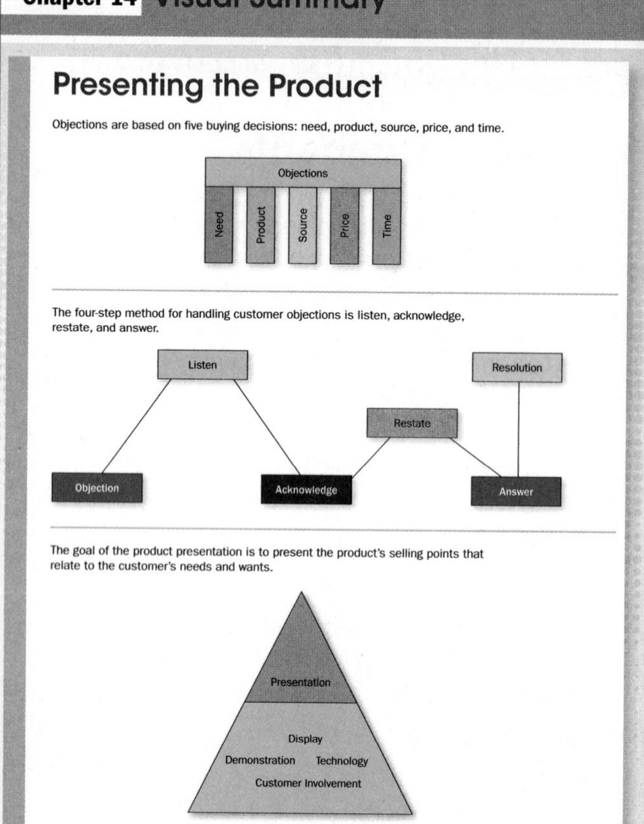

Presenting the Product
Objections are based on five buying decisions: need, product, source, price, and time.
Objections
Need
Product
Source
Price
Time
The four-step method for handling customer objections is listen, acknowledge, restate, and answer.
Listen
Resolution
Restate
Objection
Acknowledge
Answer
The goal of the product presentation is to present the product's selling points that relate to the customer's needs and wants.
Presentation
Display
Demonstration
Technology
Customer Involvement

334 | Unit 5 · Selling

Review and Activities

Written Summary

- The goal of product presentation is to match a customer's needs and wants to a product's features and benefits.
- When selecting products to show, consider customer needs and price range, and limit selection to three items.
- To make your product presentation lively and effective, handle the product with respect, demonstrate product features, involve the customer, and use sales aids.
- Objections are reasons for not buying or doubts that occur during a sales presentation.
- Objections can help clarify a customer's needs and provide an opportunity to introduce additional selling points.
- Objections are based on five buying decisions: need, product, source, price, and time.
- Four steps for handling customer objections are listen, acknowledge, restate, and answer.
- Seven specific methods for handling objections include substitution, boomerang, question, superior point, denial, demonstration, and third party.

Review Content Vocabulary and Academic Vocabulary

1. Think of an example of each of these vocabulary terms in everyday life.

Content Vocabulary
- layman's terms (p. 322)
- objections (p. 327)
- excuses (p. 327)
- objection analysis sheet (p. 328)
- substitution method (p. 331)
- boomerang method (p. 331)
- superior-point method (p. 332)
- third-party method (p. 333)

Academic Vocabulary
- collate (p. 323)
- swatches (p. 323)
- paraphrase (p. 330)
- compensate (p. 332)

Assess for Understanding

2. **Identify** What is the goal of the product presentation step in the sales process?
3. **Explain** What techniques help create an effective product presentation?
4. **Rephrase** How can you explain the features of a high-tech product such as a digital camera to someone who has never used one before?
5. **Discuss** How do objections help in the sales process?
6. **Create** What objections would you have to purchasing a new pair of shoes right now?
7. **Role-Play** Use the boomerang or superior point method to respond to a customer's objection for a product of your choice.
8. **Evaluate** How can you help an employee who does not always explain a product's features in layman's terms?
9. **Contrast** What makes objections different from excuses?

Chapter 14 · Presenting the Product | 335

EVALUATE

Visual Summary

Express Creativity Ask students to create a visual summary that illustrates a concept in the chapter. Encourage students to use different formats for their visual summaries, such as a storyboard, a timeline, a cause-and-effect diagram, or a slide show. Visual summaries will vary depending on the concept depicted. Questions to ask when assessing a visual summary include:

- Is the summary clear, economical, and simple?
- Are any important steps or concepts left out?
- Are steps or concepts arranged in the same order as the original?
- Does the summary reveal a pattern that connects the details?
- Does the summary locate and highlight the most important information?

Review Content Vocabulary and Academic Vocabulary

1. She explained the complex technology in **layman's terms.** He offered several **excuses** for not wanting the purple shirt. Dad prepared an **objection analysis sheet** before informing the children that they could no longer afford to attend private school. Elise used the **substitution method** to encourage her daughter to buy a warmer coat. The salesperson used the **boomerang method** to overcome the customer's **objections** to the light-weight, insulated shoes. The **superior-point method** proved valuable as Eric convinced the customer of the superiority of the product. The salesperson used the **third-party method** when she told the customer that she has one customer who buys this same pair of running shoes every time she needs a new pair. He **collated** the documents to make sure they were in order. The **swatches** showed a variety of different fabrics. The salesperson **paraphrased** the customer's needs and wants. Having a sun roof in the car **compensates** for it not being a convertible.

EVALUATE

Assess for Understanding

2. The goal of the product presentation step in the sales process is to match product features to customers' needs, wants, and buying motives.

3. Techniques to create an effective product presentation include: presenting and demonstrating product features; using displays and sales aids; involving the customer in the sales presentation; and holding the customer's attention.

4. When describing high-tech products such as digital cameras to someone who has never used one, it is best to explain the use of the camera in layman's terms, or words that the average customer can understand.

5. Objections help in the sales process by redefining the customer's needs and wants and giving salespeople the opportunity to introduce additional selling points.

6. Objections may include one or more of the following: need, product, source, price, or time.

7. Examples may include: Boomerang method—Customer: These hiking shoes are too lightweight to be durable. Salesperson: They are lightweight to make hiking easier on your feet, but they are made of a very durable yet lightweight composite material. Superior-point method—Customer: You don't carry as many models of this product as your competitor. Salesperson: No, we don't. We only carry the models that we feel give our customers the best value for their money.

8. Answers may include having the salesperson explain the product features and interrupting or asking for clarification every time he uses a technical term that most customers would not understand.

9. Objections are concerns, hesitations, doubts, complaints, or other reasons a customer has for not making a purchase. Excuses are given when a customer has no intention of buying.

21st Century Skills

Teamwork Skills

10. Business-to-Business Work with a team to prepare a product presentation for a business-to-business product. It can be sold for resale purposes or used in the operation of a business. Consider products such as retail apparel, machine parts for manufacturing, or business consulting services. Share your product presentation with the class.

Financial Literacy Skills

11. Return on Investment In order to sell products that are purchased for resale, you must show customers their projected return on investment (ROI). The ROI is based on the difference in *percentage* between the price you charge resellers and the price they charge their customers. Calculate the ROI for the following products. Assume the products were sold using the Manufacturer's Suggested Retail Price (MSRP).

Product	Quantity	Unit Price	MSRP	ROI
Video Games	3,000	$6.65	$14.99	___
CDs	1,000	$4.75	$ 9.99	___

e-Marketing Skills

12. Product Demo Services Research companies on the Internet that provide product demonstration services to businesses. What services and technologies would help a company sell its products in the following situations? Take the position of a sales representative in each situation. Write a proposal to your manager that includes which services and technologies you will need. Be sure to explain how these resources will support your ability to sell well.

a. A frozen food company will be exhibiting at a trade show and wants potential customers to taste its new products.

b. A firm wants to show its products in three dimensions to illustrate specific product features.

c. A manufacturer wants to digitally demonstrate its machinery in use to potential customers.

Build Academic Skills

Social Studies

13. Handling Objections How can you use the methods for handling objections for situations you may encounter in your personal life? Provide an example.

NCSS IV D Individual Development & Identity Apply concepts, methods, and theories about the study of human growth and development, such as physical endowment, learning, motivation, behavior, perception, and personality.

Science

14. Make a Chart You work as a sales associate for a global electronics retailer. Select two competing products to compare regarding their features and prices. Make a chart that shows this comparison for use in the product-presentation step of the sales process. Share your chart with classmates and be prepared to answer their questions and handle objections from them.

NSES F Develop understanding of personal and community health; population growth; natural resources; environmental quality; natural and human-induced hazards; science and technology in local, national, and global challenges.

Mathematics

15. Calculate the Customer Price Your customer wants to buy 20 square yards of carpet for one room of a house that measures 5 yards by 4 yards, and 12 square yards of carpet for another room that measures 3 yards by 4 yards. The price per square foot of carpet is $8.25. How much would you charge the customer?

Math Concept **Converting Units** 1 yard is equal to 3 feet. Divide the number of feet to determine the number of yards, and then multiply the number of yards to convert to feet.

NCTM Measurement Understand measurable attributes of objects and the units, systems, and processes of measurement.

For help, go to the **Math Skills Handbook** located at the back of this book.

Standardized Test Practice

Directions Read the following questions. On a separate sheet of paper write the best possible answer for each one.

1. Which of the following statements should not be used in the product presentation of a formal overcoat?
   - **A.** This jacket is made of a special fabric that repels water.
   - **B.** The fabrics used in this jacket make it machine washable.
   - **C.** You look totally awesome in that jacket.
   - **D.** The specially designed sleeves in this jacket give you full range of motion.
2. It is a good idea to have customers handle a product and respond to questions in order to involve customers in the product presentation step of the sales process.

   T

   F
3. In the __________ method for answering objections, the objection is converted into a selling point.

Test-Taking Tip

If you are reading too much into a question, skip it and try to answer it later with fresh eyes.

DECA Connection Role Play

Manager
Gourmet Produce Department

Situation You are the manager of the produce department in your local grocery store. In the next month, your department will begin to carry a limited number of exotic tropical fruit varieties. The new fruit varieties are ones that have not been carried by food stores in your area. Your gourmet store is able to stock these tropical fruits because the produce buyer has made an exclusive arrangement with a group of fruit growers on several Caribbean islands. Some of the tropical fruits that the store will have in stock include carambola, guava, and passion fruit. These new tropical fruit varieties will be carried as introductory items and in small quantities.

You have determined that proper presentation of the tropical fruit varieties will help to familiarize customers with the new varieties and help to sell them better, thereby making the introduction a success. Your idea for introducing the new produce items is to have a produce department employee demonstrate the handling of each variety, offer tasting samples of each, and have recipes available that feature each of the new produce items.

Activity You are planning to approach the store manager (judge) to describe your idea for introducing the new tropical fruit varieties and seek approval for implementing your ideas. You are to include in your discussion the fact that your ideas include the three basic methods of proper product presentation.

Evaluation You will be evaluated on how well you meet the following performance indicators:

1. Demonstrate product knowledge.
2. Convert customer/client objections into selling points.
3. Recommend specific products.
4. Demonstrate initiative.
5. Provide legitimate responses to inquiries.

glencoe.com

Download the Competitive Events Workbook for more Role-Play practice.

EVALUATE

21st Century Skills

Teamwork Skills

10. Product presentations for B2B products will vary depending on the product selected. Evaluate the presentation based on its effectiveness. Students should demonstrate the product's features, use sales aids, and involve the customer.

Financial Literacy Skills

11. Video games: 125%; CDs: 110% [Video games: 3000 × 6.65 = $19,950 investment; 3000 × $14.99 = $44,970; difference between $44,970 – $19,950 = $25,020; ROI = 125 percent] [CDs: $9.99 – $4.75 = $5.24; ROI $5.24 divided by $4.75 = 110 percent]

e-Marketing Skills

12. a. A company that provides trained personal demonstrators should be used for the frozen food company that will be exhibiting at a trade show and wants potential customers to taste its new products.

b. A company that provides computer-assisted design should be selected for the company that wants to illustrate product features in 3D.

c. A company that provides videos or virtual tours should be selected for a manufacturer that wants to digitally demonstrate its machinery to potential customers.

EVALUATE

Build Academic Skills

Social Studies

13. Accept all reasonable answers. Several students may acknowledge using these methods during a job interview. Others may see the benefits of learning how to tactfully respond to questions or situations that involve differing points of view between themselves and their friends, siblings, parents and employers.

Science

14. Charts will vary depending upon the products selected. However all charts should include two competing products that compare the respective features and prices.

Mathematics

15. $2,376 [20 + 12 = 32; 32 × 9 (the number of square feet in one square yard) = 288; 288 × $8.25 = $2,376]

Standardized Test Practice

1. C You look totally awesome in that jacket.

2. True

3. boomerang

DECA Connection Role Play

Evaluations will be based on these performance indicators:

1. Demonstrate product knowledge. In this step of the presentation, the produce manager should present the product's selling points. He or she should educate the store manager by explaining how the product's features relate to their customers' needs and wants. The produce manager should use highly descriptive adjectives and active verbs when describing product features and avoid generalized descriptions, such as nice, pretty, and tasty.

2. Convert customer/client objections into selling points. Anticipate and plan potential answers to any objections that might arise by completing an objection analysis sheet. Common objections involve need, product, source, price, and time. Incorporate anticipated objections into your product presentation. Use the four-step method for handling objections: listen carefully, acknowledge the objections, restate the objections, and answer the objections. Also use the specialized methods of handling objections: substitution, boomerang, question, superior point, denial, demonstration, and third party. Encourage customers to ask you any questions they might have.

3. Recommend specific products. To avoid overwhelming the customer, the produce manager should show no more than three products at a time, in this case carambola (star fruit), guava, and passion fruit. It is difficult for most people to remember all the features of more than three items during a presentation. If the store manager wants to see more than those three types of fruit, the produce manager should be ready with more choices.

4. Demonstrate initiative. The fact that the produce manager desires to present new fruit choices to the store manager for consideration, shows initiative. The presentation should capitalize on that by being upbeat, interesting, visual, and pleasant.

5. Provide legitimate responses to inquiries. The produce manager should be prepared to answer questions about need, product, source, price, and time. He should listen carefully, acknowledge any objections or inquiries, and provide clear and direct answers.

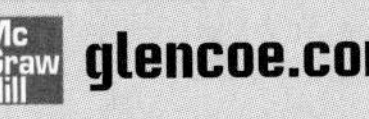

Role Plays For more DECA Role Plays, send students to the Online Learning Center to download the Competitive Events Workbook.

closing the sale

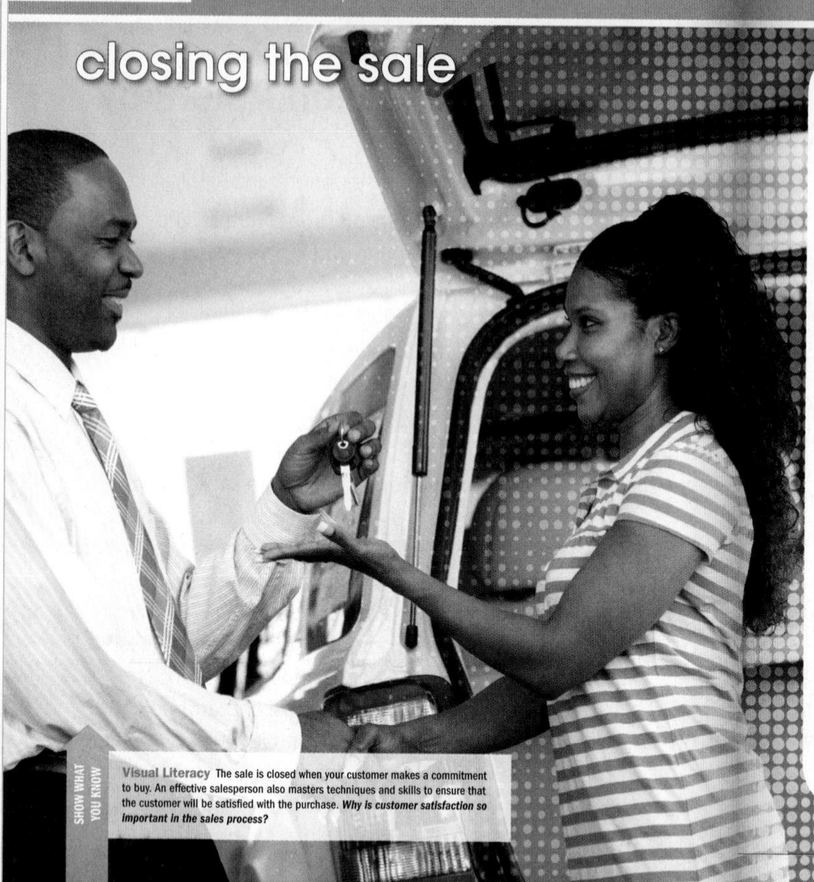

SHOW WHAT YOU KNOW

Visual Literacy The sale is closed when your customer makes a commitment to buy. An effective salesperson also masters techniques and skills to ensure that the customer will be satisfied with the purchase. ***Why is customer satisfaction so important in the sales process?***

Discovery Project

Closing the Sale and Customer Satisfaction

Essential Question How do you close a sale and make a steady customer?

Project Goal

Working with two partners, assume you are a salesperson in the home furnishings department of a retail store. For the next sales meeting, you have been asked to conduct a role play. It will demonstrate how to sell to customers who want to renovate or redecorate their homes. The role play focuses on do-it-yourself projects. Your goal is to sell the products that customers need to complete their projects. You must also explain a strategy to use to make them loyal customers. You are expected to emphasize closing the sale, customer satisfaction strategies, and follow-up.

Ask Yourself...

- What questions does someone who is renovating their home ask?
- Which sales techniques will you include in your role plays?
- How can you monitor the customer's satisfaction?
- How will you present the role plays?

Role Play Present your role play about selling to customers who want to renovate or redecorate their homes. Emphasize closing the sale, customer satisfaction strategies, and follow-up.

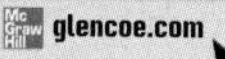

glencoe.com

Activity
Get a worksheet activity about closing the sale.

Evaluate
Download a rubric you can use to evaluate your project.

DECA Connection

DECA Event Role Play

Concepts in this chapter are related to DECA competitive events that involve either an interview or role play.

Performance Indicators The performance indicators represent key skills and knowledge. Your key to success in DECA competitive events is relating them to concepts in this chapter.

- Close the sale.
- Demonstrate suggestion selling.
- Explain the role of customer service as a component of selling relationships.
- Explain key factors in building a clientele.
- Plan follow-up strategies for use in selling.

DECA Prep

Role Play Practice role-playing with the DECA Connection competitive-event activity at the end of this chapter. More information on DECA events can be found on DECA's Web site.

ENGAGE

Visual Literacy

Read the chapter opener photo caption to students: ***Why is customer satisfaction so important in the sales process?*** Satisfied customers will return, and they may recommend the products and services. Businesses rely on repeat sales to be successful. Ask students: ***What is the most important thing a store can do to make you a satisfied customer?*** The store must have what I want or need to buy. Then ask these guiding questions.

Guiding Questions

Identify What are the three types of decision making that customers use when choosing what to buy?	extensive decision making, limited decision making, routine decision making
Analyze Why do ethical businesses forbid their salespeople from using hard-sell tactics to close a sale?	Customers do not like sales pressure. They probably will not return to the business and might tell others about their negative experience.

Discovery Project

Closing the Sale and Customer Satisfaction Ask students: ***Do you think a happy customer will be a steady customer?*** Answers will vary. If a customer needs the product regularly and is happy with a store, the customer will probably return regularly. To encourage students to think about the importance of how a sale is closed, ask them the Discovery Project Essential Question: ***How do you close a sale and make a steady customer?*** Answers may include: Customers must feel that the salesperson helped them purchase a product that meets their needs, that they made a wise decision, and that they received good value for their money.

glencoe.com

Discovery Project Resources Send students to the Online Learning Center to download a rubric to evaluate their projects.

ENGAGE

Introduce the Chapter

Chapter 15 discusses the techniques involved in closing a sale. These main concepts are introduced and discussed:

- Timing the close
- Tips for closing the sale
- Specialized closing methods
- Maintaining a positive attitude when failing to close
- Benefits of suggestion selling
- Rules and methods for suggestion selling
- After-sales activities
- Customer service
- Planning future sales

Discussion Starter

Making the Close Lead a discussion about closing a sale. Talk with students about the difficulty of identifying when a customer is ready to make a purchase. Ask: ***If you were a salesperson, what clues would you look for that a customer was ready to make a buy?*** Answers may include: the customer asks questions, makes eye contact, is engaged in the conversation, and shows signs of agreeing with the salesperson, such as head nodding. Remind students that closing a sale is how a business generates revenue. It is ideally the beginning of a lasting relationship. Ask students: ***When do you think a salesperson should start thinking about closing a sale?*** The sale should be closed as soon as the salesperson sees signs that the customer is ready to buy. Not doing so can lead to customer indecision and a lost sale.

DECA Connection

Discuss the performance indicators listed in the DECA Connection feature. Explain to students that performance indicators tell them how to demonstrate their acquired skills and knowledge through individual or team competitive events.

glencoe.com

Competitive Events Workbook For more DECA Role Plays, send students to the Online Learning Center to download the Competitive Events Workbook.

PRINT RESOURCES

- **Student Edition**
- **Teacher Edition**
- **Student Activity Workbook with Academic Integration** includes worksheets and activities correlated to the text.
- **Mathematics for Marketing Workbook** provides math activities for every unit in the text.

TECHNOLOGY TOOLBOX

- **Connect**
- **ConnectPlus**
- **ExamView Assessment Suite** is a comprehensive solution for creating, administering, and scoring tests.

glencoe.com

Online Learning Center provides a variety of resources to enrich and enhance learning.

SECTION, CHAPTER, AND UNIT RESOURCES

- **Graphic Organizers** for organizing text concepts visually.
- **Digital Nation Activities** and **Green Marketer Activities** extend learning beyond the text features.
- **Career Chatroom Career Profiles** allow students to explore different marketing occupations in depth.
- **After You Read Answer Keys** for students to check their answers.
- **Discovery Project Rubrics** and **Marketing Internship Project Rubrics** for students to evaluate their projects.

PROGRAM RESOURCES

- **Student Activity Workbook with Academic Integration Teacher Annotated Edition** includes annotated answers for the activities and worksheets.
- **Marketing Research Project Workbook** provides a step-by-step approach for students to complete their own marketing research studies.
- **School-to-Career Activity Workbook** helps students relate their class work to on-the-job experience and involves work-site analysis and working with mentors.
- **Competitive Events Workbook** helps prepare students for state and national marketing education competitions.
- **Inclusion in the Marketing Education Classroom** provides teaching resources for working with students with special needs.
- **PowerPoint Presentations** provides visual teaching aids and assessments for this chapter.

READING GUIDE

Before You Read

Reflect What questions do you ask of salespeople when you are shopping?

Objectives

- **Identify** customer buying signals.
- **List** a few tips for closing a sale.
- **Decide** on appropriate specialized methods for closing a sale.

The Main Idea

At a certain point in the sales process, your customer will be ready to make a purchase. In this section, you will learn how to close a sale.

Vocabulary

Content Vocabulary
- closing the sale
- buying signals
- trial close
- which close
- standing-room-only close
- direct close
- service close

Academic Vocabulary
You will find these words in your reading and on your tests. Make sure you know their meanings.
- commit
- perseverance

Graphic Organizer

Draw or print this chart to identify information you need to know in order to close a sale.

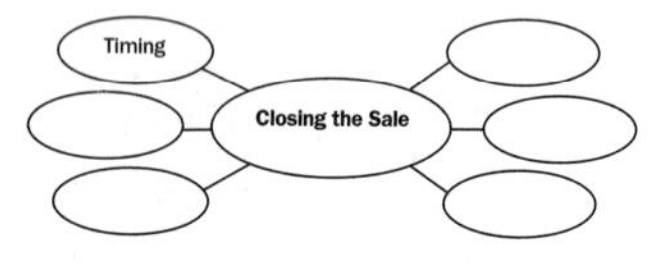

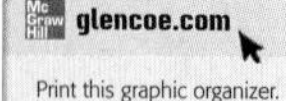
glencoe.com

Print this graphic organizer.

STANDARDS

ACADEMIC

English Language Arts
NCTE 4 Use written language to communicate effectively.

Social Studies
NCSS IV D Individual Development & Identity Apply concepts, methods, and theories about the study of human growth and development, such as physical endowment, learning, motivation, behavior, perception, and personality.

NCSS *National Council for the Social Studies*
NCTE *National Council of Teachers of English*
NCTE *National Council of Teachers of Mathematics*
NSES *National Science Education Standards*

Common Core
Writing Produce clear and coherent writing in which the development, organization, and style are appropriate to task, purpose, and audience.

MARKETING CORE FUNCTION
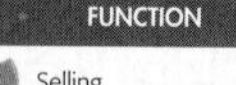
Selling

m.e. Section 15.1 How to Close a Sale

CLOSING CONCEPTS AND TECHNIQUES

Closing the sale is obtaining positive agreement from the customer to buy. All your efforts up to this step of the sale have involved helping your customers make buying decisions.

To close a sale, salespeople need to recognize when a customer is ready to buy. Sometimes it is so natural that the customer closes the sale for you. In many situations, however, the customer waits for the salesperson to close the sale.

As You Read

Predict What can salespeople do to make closing the sale more effective?

TIMING THE CLOSE

Some customers are ready to buy sooner than other customers; therefore, you must be flexible. You might show a customer a product and almost immediately detect an opportunity to close the sale. Other times, you may spend an hour with customers and still find that they are having difficulty making a decision.

You should never feel pressured to complete an entire sales presentation just because you planned it that way. The key to closing sales is customer readiness.

BUYING SIGNALS

When attempting to close a sale, look for **buying signals**, the things customers say or do to indicate a readiness to buy. These signals may be nonverbal and include facial expressions and body language. You know customers are ready to buy when they say, "This is exactly what I was looking for." Other comments that may be clues about their readiness include: "Do you have these same shoes in black?" "When would I be able to get delivery?" When a customer has mentally decided on the purchase, it is time to close the sale.

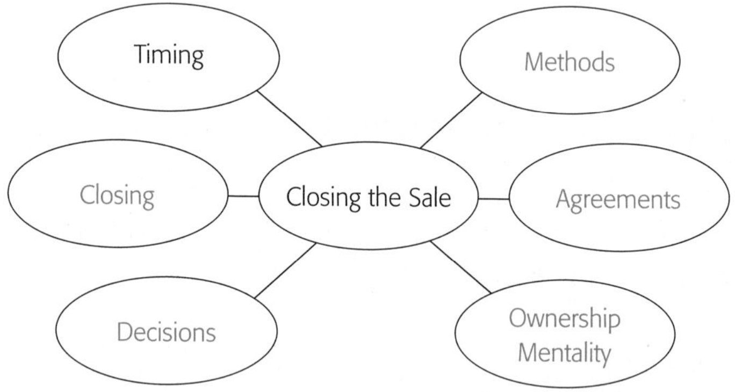

Determining when a customer is ready to buy is sometimes difficult for a novice salesperson. ***Looking at this photo, what customer cues might suggest that it is time to close the sale?***

ENGAGE

Anticipation Activity

Improving Student Achievement Have students work on a collaborative list of reasons to explain why a customer will decide to buy. Reasons may include fulfilling a need, getting a good deal, impulse. Then ask: ***What is the most common reason you make purchases?*** Answers may include wanting or needing a product or service.

Objectives

- **Identify** customer buying signals. smiling, positive comments about the object, ownership comments, admiring the object
- **List** a few tips for closing a sale. Close when you see buying signals, stop showing additional merchandise when customer cannot make a decision, create ownership mentality, get minor agreements, and pace your approach.
- **Decide** on appropriate specialized methods for closing a sale. Which close: get customer to decide between two items; Standing-room-only close: short supply; Direct close: strong buying signals

Graphic Organizer

Timing — Closing the Sale
Methods — Closing the Sale
Closing — Closing the Sale
Agreements — Closing the Sale
Decisions — Closing the Sale
Ownership Mentality — Closing the Sale

glencoe.com **iWB**

Graphic Organizer Send students to the Online Learning Center to print this graphic organizer.

EXPLORE

Before You Read

Read the Before You Read question aloud: ***What questions do you ask of salespeople when you are shopping?*** Students might say they ask salespeople to demonstrate the product or describe its features. If it is clothing, they might ask for a different size or color. They also might ask about fabric content and care instructions. For more expensive items, they may ask about payment plans.

Visual Literacy

Customer Readiness Caption Answer Read the caption question to students: ***Looking at this photo, what customer cues might suggest that it is time to close the sale?*** The couple is pausing to gaze intently at the ring. The young woman is holding the ring in front of them to display it. Both are smiling.

Preteaching Vocabulary

Have students go to the Online Learning Center at glencoe.com for the Chapter 15 Preteaching Vocabulary games.

Content Vocabulary

Write the term *closing the sale* for students to read. Have students work with a partner to determine as many different definitions as they can for the word *close*. to shut; to block against entry; to stop operation of; to bring to an end or complete; to bring or bind together; to reduce to nothing. Then ask: ***Which of these definitions applies to closing the sale?*** to bring to an end or complete

Academic Vocabulary

Commit—Contextual Meaning Write the following sentence for the class to read: ***Customers will most likely tell you why they are not ready to commit to buying.*** Ask students: ***Based on this sentence, what do you think* commit *means?*** agree, consent

Perseverance—Suffixes Write the word *persevere* for students to read. Explain that it means "to persist in a state or undertaking in spite of opposition or discouragement."

How to Close a Sale

Section 15.1

CLOSING CONCEPTS AND TECHNIQUES

Ask these guiding questions to focus the discussion on the concepts and techniques used in the closing process.

Guiding Questions

Explain In order to effectively close a sale, what must a salesperson be able to do?	The salesperson must be able to recognize when the customer is ready to buy.
Draw Conclusions Why do you think that customers often wait for the salesperson to close the sale?	Answers may include: Customers might have difficulties making buying decisions, or they might be waiting for the salesperson's affirmation that they are making the correct choice.

As You Read

Read students the As You Read question: ***What can salespeople do to make closing the sale more effective?*** Possible answers: time the close for when the customer is ready; keep the customer from becoming overwhelmed by too many choices, come to minor agreements during the selling process, and avoid threatening words or hard-sale tactics.

Expert Advice

Read the quote to students:

> **"Closing the sale is based on customer readiness to buy."**

Ask: ***Have you ever had a salesperson push you to make a buying decision when you were not ready? If so, what did you do?*** Yes, I felt pressured and annoyed. I went to a different store. Then ask: ***Have you ever had a salesperson go on about the features of a product after you had already decided to buy it? If so, what did you do?*** Yes. I was bored and in a hurry, but let the salesperson complete the sales pitch. However, I plan to avoid going to that salesperson in the future.

TRIAL CLOSE

You may attempt a trial close to test the readiness of a customer and your interpretation of a positive buying signal. A **trial close** is an initial effort to close a sale.

Trial closes are beneficial for two reasons. For one, if the trial close does not work, you will still learn from the attempt. Customers will most likely tell you why they are not ready to **commit** to buying. On the other hand, if the trial close does work, you will reach your goal of closing the sale. In both cases, you are in an excellent position to continue with the sales process.

TIPS FOR CLOSING THE SALE

Professional salespeople recognize closing opportunities, help customers make a decision, and create an ownership mentality for the customer. They rely on proven and tested techniques. They often use the techniques discussed in the following pages. You will find it easier to attempt trial closes and close more sales if you use these techniques. As you learn to be a salesperson, you will want to avoid saying or doing a few things when closing a sale.

RECOGNIZE CLOSING OPPORTUNITIES

Having a major obstacle removed usually makes a customer receptive to buying the product or service. You can also use effective product presentations to close the sale. Dramatic product presentations often prove important selling points and excite the customer about owning the product. Take advantage of high customer interest at these times and attempt to close.

HELP CUSTOMERS MAKE A DECISION

When a customer is having difficulty making a buying decision, stop showing additional merchandise. You should also narrow the selection of items by removing those products that are no longer of interest to the customer. You can do this by asking, "Which of these items do you like the least?" Once you reduce the selection to two items, you can help a customer decide by summarizing the major features and benefits of each product. You can also explain any advantages or disadvantages of each item being considered. Both methods help you to focus the decision making on important considerations.

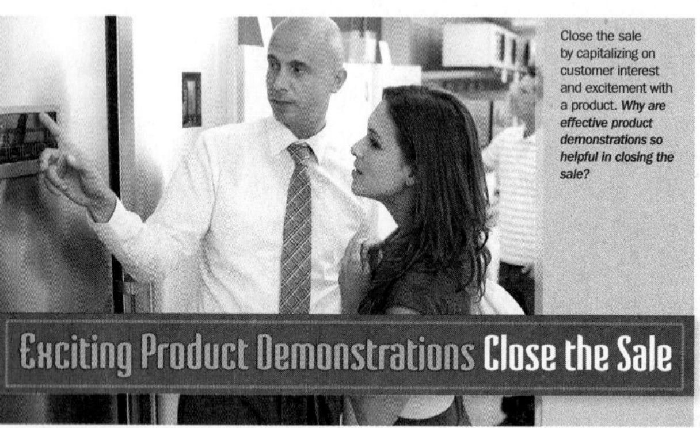

Close the sale by capitalizing on customer interest and excitement with a product. ***Why are effective product demonstrations so helpful in closing the sale?***

CREATE AN OWNERSHIP MENTALITY

Use words that indicate ownership, such as *you* and *your*. When presenting selling points, you might say, "You will appreciate these waterproof hiking shoes on your next hiking trip when it starts to rain." Using *you* and *your* when explaining selling points helps customers visualize themselves owning those products. Your selling points become more personal and therefore more effective in helping customers develop an ownership mentality.

AVOID THREATENING WORDS

When possible avoid words, like *now* and *today* because they have the connotation of having to act immediately. Customers may feel too much pressure in making a buying decision and may change their mind altogether. This approach may accidentally trigger an objection related to time that the customer did not have before.

GET MINOR AGREEMENTS

Solicit minor agreements on selling points that you know your customer has observed or experienced. For example, "Those newly designed golf shoes are comfortable, aren't they?"

When you get positive reactions from your customer throughout the sales process, that same positive frame of mind will help create a natural closing.

PACE YOUR CLOSING

If you think the customer is ready to make a buying decision, stop talking about the product. At that point, close the sale. Continuing to talk about a product after a customer's readiness is apparent may annoy that customer. It may even cause you to lose the sale.

On the other hand, do not rush a customer into making a buying decision. Be patient, courteous, polite, and helpful, and always remember that your primary interest is customer satisfaction.

SPECIALIZED METHODS FOR CLOSING THE SALE

Attempt to close the sale as soon as you recognize a buying signal. Your method for doing this depends on the selling situation. Certain selling situations warrant the use of specialized methods, including the which close, standing-room-only close, direct close, and service close methods.

When customers are overwhelmed with too many options, it is difficult for them to make a buying decision. ***If a customer has five pairs of shoes to try on and wants to see more shoes, what should the salesperson do?***

EXPLAIN

Activate Prior Knowledge

Reteach the Steps of a Sale Use this graphic to help students recall the steps of a sale as discussed in Chapter 12. Tell students that in this chapter they will learn about closing a sale, suggestion selling, and building relationships.

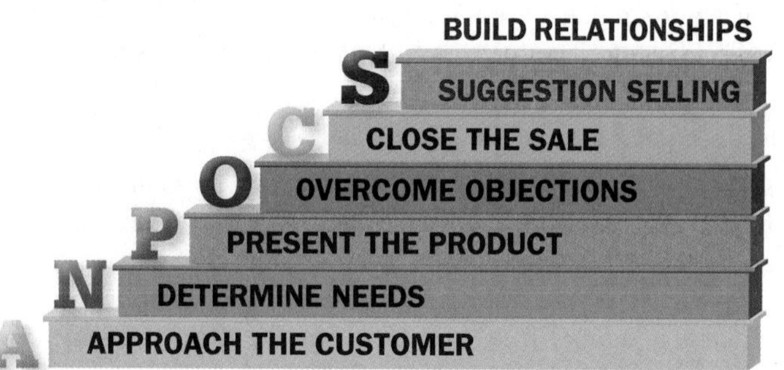

Visual Literacy

Exciting Product Demonstrations Close the Sale Caption Answer Read the caption question to students: ***Why are effective product demonstrations so helpful in closing the sale?*** Exciting product demonstrations are convincing, grab the customer's attention, and help to remove any doubt the customer may have regarding a product's capabilities. Ask students: ***For what types of products are demonstrations especially helpful?*** Answers may include: electronic equipment such as computers, cameras, televisions, and surround-sound systems; home appliances such as vacuum cleaners and food processors, and similar devices.

Reinforce Vocabulary

Trial Close—Denotative Meaning Read this sentence aloud: ***You may attempt a trial close to test the readiness of the customer.*** Explain that in this case, the word trial means preliminary, test, or experimental. Therefore, a trial close is an experimental close or a test close.

ELABORATE

Visual Literacy

Too Many Options Doom a Sale Caption Answer Read the caption question to students: ***If a customer has five pairs of shoes to try on and wants to see more shoes, what should the salesperson do?*** The salesperson should get the customer to eliminate at least two pairs of shoes by saying, "Which pairs do you like the least?" These pairs should be put away. The salesperson can then proceed to get one or two more pairs for the customer to try on. Encourage students to think about how children make decisions. Experienced parents and caregivers give children only a few choices; this helps keep them from being overwhelmed. The same is true for shoppers. The successful salesperson knows that customers appreciate having the buying process simplified for them.

TIPS FOR CLOSING THE SALE

Being able to use established tips for closing a sale is valuable to any salesperson. To focus the discussion on tips for closing a sale, ask these guiding questions.

Guiding Questions

Describe What is the first thing a salesperson should do when a customer cannot decide among several items?	Stop showing additional merchandise.
Predict A customer is having a difficult time deciding whether to buy a digital camera. The salesperson starts pressuring the customer by saying that there are only a few of these cameras left, even though this is not true. How might the customer respond?	The customer might refuse to make a decision because of feeling overly pressured. The pressure might even trigger an objection the customer did not previously have.

Critical Thinking

Ask students how they think the increasingly diverse marketplace affects the art of closing the sale. Answers will vary. Customers of different ages need to be handled differently. For example, a younger person just starting out on his or her own might need more help comparing the features of cleaning products and household appliances. Customers of different cultures also require the salesperson to be more skilled. For example, in some cultures, salespeople are expected to behave aggressively when closing a sale—if they do not, the customer may think the salespeople do not believe in their product. In other cultures, salespeople must behave very submissively toward customers and never push them.

Mini Projects

Differentiated Instruction

Kinesthetic Learners Have students work independently to choose a product to sell to the class. An important part of this selling process should be an effective demonstration of the product. Encourage students to choose a product with which they are familiar and that they can demonstrate in a fairly dramatic way—one that will influence customers to make a purchase. Students may want to engage a classmate to help with the demonstration. Students should effectively demonstrate the benefits of the product and inspire their "customers" to want to purchase it. Students should answer any questions their classmates have and work to overcome any objections that may be voiced.

Gifted Learners Discuss with students that because of various technological advances, marketers will frequently state that "geography is history." Therefore, it is crucial that salespeople understand the culture in which they are working. Have students research the characteristics of closing a sale in a specific culture. Questions to consider might include: ***Is pressuring the customer acceptable? Are men and women treated differently in the marketplace? How fast can you pace your close? Is haggling over the price customary?*** Students should prepare an oral presentation on the acceptable way to close a sale in their chosen culture. Student presentations should explain ways in which closing a sale in the chosen culture is different. For example, in China, establishing a relationship between buyer and seller is crucial and customers routinely haggle to lower a selling price. Sellers may agree to a price so low that they do not make a profit, just to keep the customer coming back to them.

The GREEN Marketer

TerraCycle™ Grows Greener

TerraCycle, Inc., is one of a number of eco-friendly companies in today's marketplace. Its products, packaging, and product use are all eco-friendly. For TerraCycle's all-natural plant food, the company uses organic waste to feed worms. Then the worms' waste is processed and used to make an all-natural plant food that is packaged in recycled soda bottles. To acquire these bottles, TerraCycle relies on fund-raising efforts by schools and nonprofit organizations.

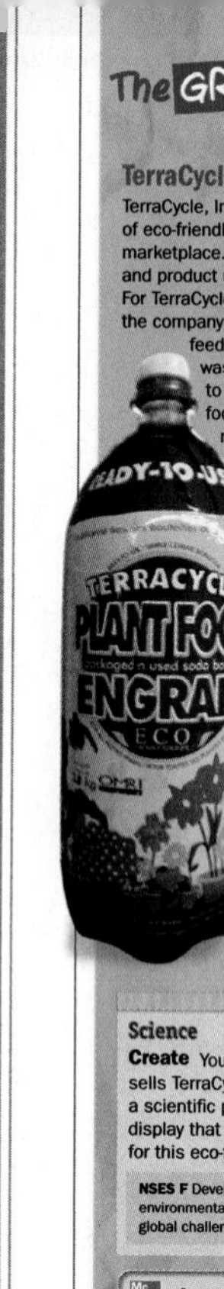

Good Results TerraCycle Plant Food is exceptional in that it outperforms synthetic plant food products in many ways and is safe to use. The product is sold in retail stores, such as Walmart®, Home Depot®, Whole Foods,® Ace Hardware®, Do It Best®, and True Value®, with a 100-percent satisfaction guarantee.

Science

Create You work in a store that sells TerraCycle Plant Food. Think of a scientific product demonstration or display that would help close the sale for this eco-friendly product.

NSES F Develop understanding of environmental quality in local, national, and global challenges.

glencoe.com

Get an activity on green marketing.

WHICH CLOSE

The **which close** is a closing method that encourages a customer to make a decision between two items. If you follow the tips for closing a sale, you will remove unwanted items to bring the selection down to two. Compare the selling points of each item, and then ask the customer, "Which one do you prefer?" This method makes it easier for a customer because only one simple decision must be made.

STANDING-ROOM-ONLY CLOSE

The **standing-room-only close** is a method used when a product is in short supply or when the price will be going up in the near future. This close should be used only when the situation honestly calls for it because it may be perceived as a high-pressure tactic. In many situations, a salesperson can honestly say, "I'm sorry, but I can't promise that I'll be able to make you this same offer later."

The standing-room only approach is often used in selling high-demand real estate. Customers must often be prompted to act on a hot property that will be off the market quickly. They also may be prompted to act if an item is advertised at a low price and there is a limited supply at that price. For example, "The item you like is part of a special promotion. It is the last one we have in your size."

Again, keep in mind that this approach can turn off a customer if he or she feels that you are pressuring them into a sale. Always be tactful and courteous to the customer in these situations.

DIRECT CLOSE

The **direct close** is a method in which you ask for the sale. You would use the direct close method when the buying signal is very strong. Here is one example of dialogue to use when using a direct close approach to a sales situation: "Can I assume that we're ready to talk about the details of your order?" "It appears you like everything I have shown you. Now we just need to discuss the quantity you will need."

You can use a statement like the one above and replace "quantity" with other specifics of the order, such as delivery, shipping terms, or special instructions. Positive statements by the customer to direct close approaches let you know that the customer is ready to buy. You can continue closing the order by addressing the specifics of the order.

In a retail situation, you might simply ask a question regarding payment, such as: "How would you like to pay for this purchase—cash, check, or credit card?"

The customer in this photo likes the product but is hesitant about buying it because it is a gift. ***Which specialized closing method would work best in this situation?***

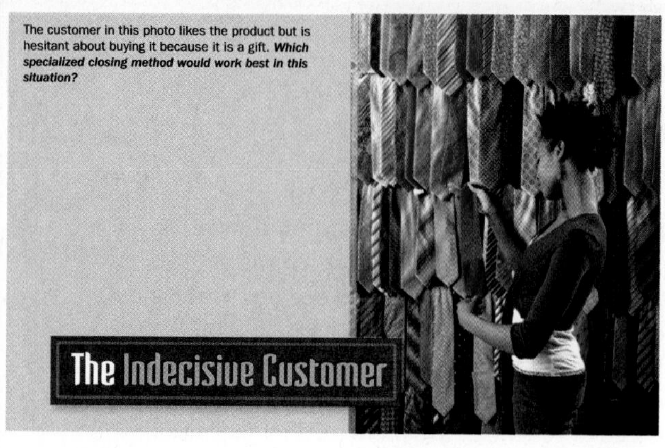

The Indecisive Customer

SERVICE CLOSE

Sometimes you may run into obstacles or instances that require special services to close the sale. The **service close** is a method in which you explain services that overcome obstacles or problems. Such services include gift wrapping, a return policy, special sales arrangements, warranties and guarantees, and bonuses or premiums. You might want to explain the store's return policy when a customer hesitates but seems to be willing to make the purchase anyway. This is an especially good idea when a customer is purchasing the item as a gift for someone else.

Special sales arrangements are used to close the sale when the customer needs help paying for the item or order.

The Service Close in Business-to-Business Situations

In an organizational selling situation, the sales representative would talk about the terms of the sale, discussing points such as when payment is expected. For example, payment could be due 30 or 60 days after the date of the invoice.

Customers may also need information about credit terms to help them decide to buy. In other cases, customers may need a sample to try out before purchasing large quantities. Sometimes offering a sampling program is beneficial if it is a new purchase or the buyer is changing vendors. The buyer needs proof that your product is a better substitute for the one currently being used.

The Service Close in Retail

In a retail selling situation, the use of credit and checks as well as special buying plans, such as layaway, can be suggested. When a customer questions the quality of the merchandise, perhaps you can explain that a warranty, or guarantee, is offered on the product. When your business offers the same quality merchandise at the same price as your competitors' price, your service may be the only factor that affects the buying decision.

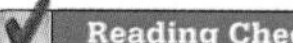

Reading Check

Analyze Why is it important for salespeople to help customers make decisions?

EXPLAIN

The GREEN Marketer

Science Answer The store might create a display of Terracycle Plant Food in a large container. Earth worms could be living in the plant food, showing that living things thrive there. Use these guiding questions to discuss.

Guiding Questions

Explain What are some reasons that TerraCycle says it is better than competitors?	safe to use and; outperforms synthetic plant foods
Analyze How does TerraCycle demonstrate that it supports local communities?	It relies on fundraising efforts to acquire recycled soda bottles for packaging.

Critical Thinking

Ask students: ***Has a salesperson ever used the standing-room-only close with you? If so, how did you respond?*** Responses will vary. If the reason expressed by the salesperson seemed legitimate (such as a short-term sale), the student may have been grateful. However, if the salesperson seemed to be pressuring the student, they may have responded negatively by not purchasing the product. Why must the standing-room-only close be used with great care? Most customers do not like to feel pressured and may withdraw from making the purchase.

Reinforce Vocabulary

Standing-room-only close—Use Prior Knowledge Ask students: ***What does the term*** standing-room-only ***mean?*** an event is so crowded that all seats are taken, so you have to stand to see the event Then ask: ***Based on this information, what do you think a standing-room-only close is?*** a close emphasizing that the customer better purchase the product quickly because there is little room for additional buyers

ELABORATE

Graphic Organizer

Display this graphic organizer. Have students suggest four specialized closing methods. Possible answers:

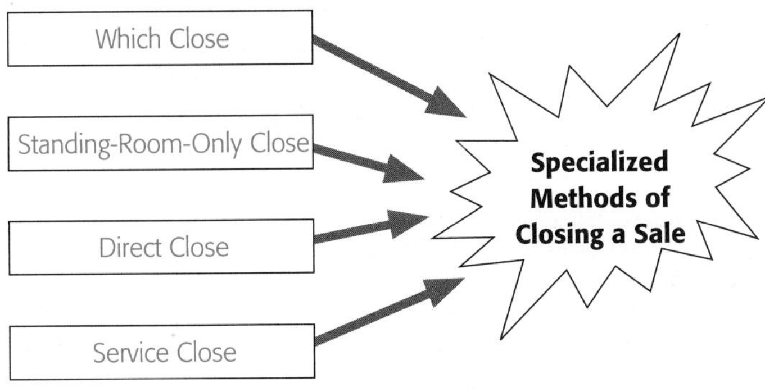

 glencoe.com  iWB

Graphic Organizer Send students to the Online Learning Center to print this graphic organizer.

Visual Literacy

The Indecisive Customer Caption Answer Read the caption question to students: ***Which specialized closing method would work best in this situation?*** Because the customer is buying for someone other than herself, such as a male friend or relative, the service close would probably work best. The salesperson could explain the store's return policy, emphasizing that the recipient can easily return the tie if it is not to his liking. Ask students: ***Do you think a direct close would work in this situation? Why or why not?*** Possible answer: Probably not, because the customer is concerned that she might choose a tie that the recipient will not like. To use a direct close may cause her to decide that she should not make the purchase and get something else as a gift.

SERVICE CLOSE

Ask these guiding questions to encourage students to discuss the service close.

Guiding Questions

Contrast How is a service close different from a direct close?	Direct close—salesperson asks the customer for the sale. Service close—salesperson offers the customer a specific reason to close.
Apply You are a salesperson at a car dealership. What are three different types of services you might offer to encourage customers to close?	special financing offers, warranties, promotional deals with discounts, deals on car maintenance such as free oil changes

Reading Check Answer

Read the Reading Check question to students: ***Why is it important for salespeople to help customers make decisions?*** Many people fear making the wrong decision, and therefore have a very difficult time making any decision. The salesperson is in an ideal position to guide customers to a decision that will meet their needs.

ELL: Elaborating on Student Responses
Go to the Online Learning Center to view a video clip in which a teacher elaborates on a student response.

Mini Projects

Differentiated Instruction

Logical Learners Set this scene for students: You are a sales associate for an electronics shop. It is the last day of the week and you are $400 short of your weekly sales quota. You have just spent 30 minutes with a couple who is looking for a flat-screen television. They are having difficulty choosing between a model that is on sale for $449 and another model priced at $499. At this point, your supervisor asks you to take a lunch break because she expects the store to be busy in half an hour. Have students write a one-page paper in which they identify at least three options in the above situation. Have students select the option they believe is best and explain their decision in a one-page paper. Options might include taking a break, making a trial close, handing the customers off to another salesperson, or continuing to help the customers and asking for a break after the busy period. This allows them to pursue closing the sale, perhaps by discussing the warranties more thoroughly (service close) or explaining that the $449 television will only be on sale for a few more days. (standing-room-only close). Students should explain that the goal is to reach a conclusion that satisfies everyones needs.

Kinesthetic Learners. Assign pairs one of the following specialized closing methods: which close, standing-room-only close, direct close, or service close. Have students create skits incorporating their assigned type of close. One student should be the customer and the other the salesperson. When each pair is done, have the class provide feedback. Each pair should perform a skit in which the salesperson uses the specified closing method. The class should provide feedback, discussing the effectiveness of the salesperson's closing method.

FAILURE TO CLOSE THE SALE

Do not assume that every sales presentation should end in a sale. Even the best salespeople can sell to only a fraction of their prospects.

You should also not take a failure to close the sale personally. The customer had reasons for not buying your product at that time. It is possible that your product did not meet your customer's needs. In that case, you would not have closed the sale anyway. In other cases, the customers may not need your product at that time but may in the future.

How do you handle a failed closing and what can you learn from it? Let's take a look at what you can do in a retail sales situation and in an organizational sales situation. Also, let's see how feedback can help you and your company.

MAINTAIN A POSITIVE ATTITUDE

The attitude of the salesperson who has not made the sale should be no different than the attitude of the successful salesperson. It is very important for the salesperson to smile and be friendly after failing to make a sale. Customers appreciate a sincere salesperson who has their best interest in mind.

You will have many more opportunities for success, particularly if you treat your customers with courtesy and respect. Be positive and leave the door open for future opportunities.

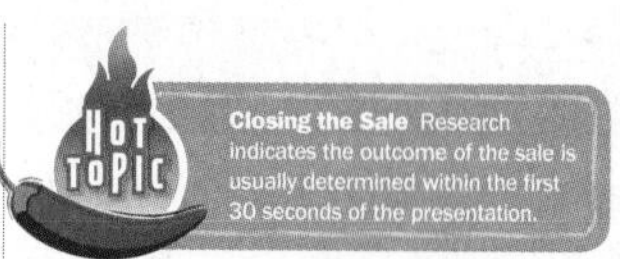

Closing the Sale Research indicates the outcome of the sale is usually determined within the first 30 seconds of the presentation.

IN RETAIL SALES

In a retail setting, invite the customer to shop in your store again. In some cases, your store simply may not have had the product the customer needed at that time. Customers who are treated nicely, even when they do not buy something, remember that experience and will return on another occasion. Thus, you will have a second chance to satisfy their needs and wants.

IN ORGANIZATIONAL SALES

Not all sales calls require a closing. Business-to-business salespeople may negotiate on large accounts for months before closing the sale. So, the first few sales calls may be building blocks upon which you develop a relationship and learn more about your customers' needs and wants. During that process, you become a partner and consultant in solving your customers' problems and satisfying their needs.

In organizational selling situations, it is not uncommon for buyers to be convinced by a sales presentation but not yet ready to buy. In such a situation, it is extremely important that the salesperson leave an opening for a return sales call. However, if you clearly sense an impending turndown, it is better to make a graceful exit and leave the possibility for a future sales call. In both cases, leave a business card with those prospects. Research suggests that **perseverance** is the way to succeed. So, remember every sales contact has the potential to become a successful sale in the future.

In some business-to-business selling situations, the buyer may have some feelings of guilt. These feelings could be due to their rejection of your sales proposition in favor of a competitor's.

This is especially true when you and the buyer have established a good relationship. In such a case, the buyer may respond to an appeal for consideration in the next order.

If you have established excellent rapport with the buyer, you may be able to ask him or her what factors led to the decision to buy from another source. An appeal for constructive criticism may work for you if you have earned the buyer's respect from past interactions.

FEEDBACK

Experienced salespeople capitalize on defeat and come away from an unsuccessful selling experience with something to show for it. A customer who does not make a purchase is still a prospect for future business. Be alert to what purchases today's non-buyer may make in the future.

It is important to get feedback on why a customer did not buy. Try to learn what factor or factors influenced that decision. You may learn that the factors were out of the buyer's control. For example, a new company policy or budgetary constraints may be the reason for not buying. Or you may learn that the buyer is purchasing a competitor's product because of its lower price.

Any feedback you receive can help you and your company in the future. For example, information obtained may help your company decide on future products, pricing, and marketing policies. Your company may learn a customer's opinion about what it needs to do to outsell competitors in the marketplace. The call report you complete will have all those details in it for management to review and act upon.

One popular misconception about selling is that salespeople are born, not made. It is true that effective salespeople possess certain behavioral characteristics. These characteristics include confidence, problem-solving abilities, honesty, and a sincere desire to be helpful.

However, success in selling is the result of training, apprenticeship, and experience. Learning one's products and how to handle various situations comes with experience and hard work.

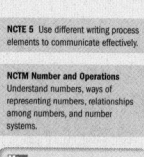

After You Read **Section 15.1**

Review Key Concepts

1. **Contrast** getting minor agreements with pacing your closing.
2. **Describe** what you would say when closing the sale to create an ownership mentality.
3. **Identify** the specialized method you would use to close the sale in this situation: A customer is interested in an item but wants to wait to purchase it when it goes on sale.

Practice Academics

English Language Arts

4. Write a dialogue between two people closing a sale in either a retail or an organizational setting.

Mathematics

5. To close the sale, you offer layaway as an option, which requires a 20-percent deposit. What would the required deposit be on a $1,099 television?

Starting Hints To solve this problem, convert 20 percent to a decimal by moving the decimal point two places to the left. Multiply $1,099 by the decimal number to determine the amount of the deposit.

For help, go to the **Math Skills Handbook** located at the back of this book.

NCTE 5 Use different writing process elements to communicate effectively.

NCTM Number and Operations Understand numbers, ways of representing numbers, relationships among numbers, and number systems.

glencoe.com

Check your answers.

ELABORATE

Graphic Organizer

To help students understand the role of feedback when a salesperson fails to close, display this diagram.

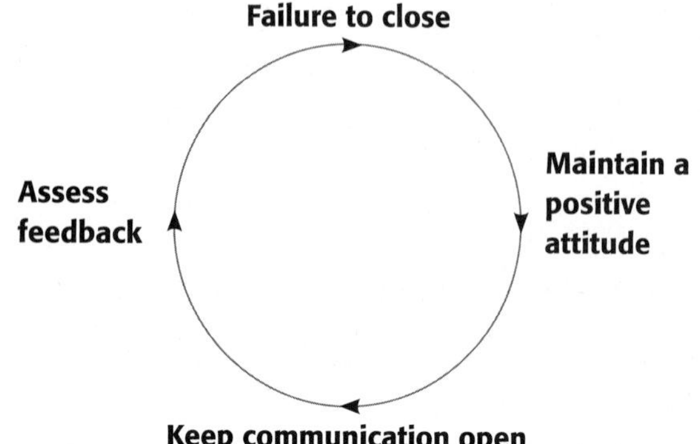

glencoe.com

Graphic Organizer Send students to the Online Learning Center to print this graphic organizer.

FAILURE TO CLOSE THE SALE

Ask these guiding questions to focus the discussion.

Guiding Questions

Recall Why should a salesperson not take the failure to close a sale personally?	product may not meet customer needs; the product may cost too much
Evaluate "The attitude of the salesperson who has not made the sale should be no different than that of the successful salesperson." Do you think this is possible?	It is possible if the salesperson believes there may be other opportunities to make sales in the future. It is also important not to take failure to close a sale personally.

MINI CLIP

ELL: Academic Language

Go to the Online Learning Center for a video in which experts discuss the importance of addressing academic language.

EVALUATE

Closing the Sale Ask students to reflect on whether the **outcome of a sale is determined within 30 seconds of the presentation.**

Critical Thinking

Have students look once again at the feedback diagram on page 346. Ask: ***Which of these four steps do you think would be the most difficult for you? Why?*** Sample answer: "Maintain a positive attitude" because I would be very discouraged if I went for a long time without being able to close a sale. Then ask: ***What are some ways that a salesperson can maintain a positive attitude?*** Possible answer: By talking with other salespeople who have been in the same situation, and continuing to practice sales techniques.

Mini Project

Enrichment

Providing Encouragement to a Salesperson Have the students imagine that they are sales managers at a bicycle shop. One of their salespeople has a solid record of sales, but lately has had a hard time closing sales. Instruct students to write an encouraging one-page letter to this salesperson. In the letter, they should list at least three of the points discussed under "Failure to Close the Sale." The letter might begin by stating that even the best salespeople close only a fraction of their sales and that everybody goes through challenging periods. Those salespeople who are successful are the ones who persevere. The student might want to mention the salesperson's good qualities, such as always being friendly even when a sale is not closed.

After You Read — Section 15.1

Review Key Concepts

1. Getting minor agreements involves having the customer concur with you on selling points that they have noticed. By doing this, you build a foundation of positive interactions throughout the selling process that naturally leads to the closing. Getting minor agreements is a good approach during the time the customer is making the buying decision. However, if you see that the customer is ready to make a buying decision, you should stop using any sales tactics—doing so might annoy the customer, who at this point is ready to proceed with the transaction.
2. To create an ownership mentality, use words like "you" and "your." You should use language that indicates to the person that the product is already theirs.
3. The standing-room-only close should be used. For example, you might say "There is a limited inventory of that item and it may be sold out before the sale even takes place."

Practice Academics

English Language Arts

4. The student should write a dialogue between two people closing either a retail sale or an organizational sale. Following is a sample of two people closing a retail sale. Salesperson: Would you prefer the maroon or red shirt? Customer: I think I'll take the red one. Salesperson: How would you like to pay for it? Customer: I'll use my debit card.

Mathematics

5. \$219.80 (\$1099 × .20)

glencoe.com

Answer Key Send students to the Online Learning Center to check their answers.

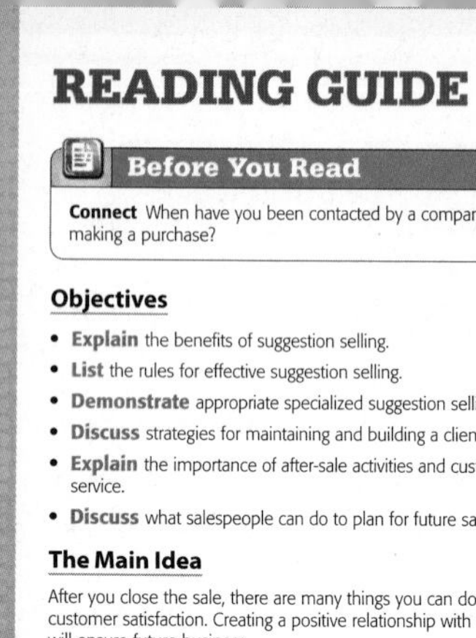

READING GUIDE

Before You Read

Connect When have you been contacted by a company after making a purchase?

Objectives

- **Explain** the benefits of suggestion selling.
- **List** the rules for effective suggestion selling.
- **Demonstrate** appropriate specialized suggestion selling methods.
- **Discuss** strategies for maintaining and building a clientele.
- **Explain** the importance of after-sale activities and customer service.
- **Discuss** what salespeople can do to plan for future sales.

The Main Idea

After you close the sale, there are many things you can do to enhance customer satisfaction. Creating a positive relationship with customers will ensure future business.

Vocabulary

Content Vocabulary
- suggestion selling

Academic Vocabulary
You will find these words in your reading and on your tests. Make sure you know their meanings.
- appreciated
- volume

Graphic Organizer

Draw or print this chart to summarize key points for suggestion selling and for building a clientele.

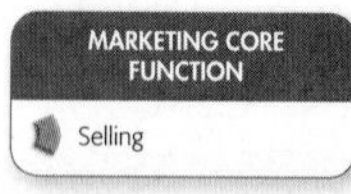

glencoe.com

Print this graphic organizer.

STANDARDS

ACADEMIC

English Language Arts
NCTE 4 Use written language to communicate effectively.

Social Studies
NCSS VII B Production, Distribution, and Consumption Analyze the role that supply and demand, prices, incentives, and profits play in determining what is produced and distributed in a competitive market system.

NCSS *National Council for the Social Studies*
NCTE *National Council of Teachers of English*
NCTM *National Council of Teachers of Mathematics*
NSES *National Science Education Standards*

Common Core
Writing Write informative/explanatory texts to examine and convey complex ideas and information clearly and accurately through the effective selection, organization, and analysis of content.

MARKETING CORE FUNCTION
Selling

m.e. Section 15.2 Customer Satisfaction

SUGGESTION SELLING

Maintaining and building a clientele is crucial for future sales. The actual sale is just the beginning of a relationship with the customer. To keep customers, it is important to make a good impression, get to know your customers, and provide excellent customer service. One significant part of this process is suggestion selling.

Suggestion selling is selling additional goods or services to the customer. It involves selling other items to customers that will ultimately save time and money or make the original purchase more **appreciated**. It is important to the sales process because it helps to improve customer satisfaction, and it increases sales for the business.

Consider the customer who buys an electronic toy for a child, takes it home, and only then realizes that batteries are needed for it to function. That means another trip to the store before the child can play with the toy. The salesperson might have had a sure sale with a suggestion to buy batteries.

As You Read

Predict What makes some companies better than others in creating loyal customers?

BENEFITS OF SUGGESTION SELLING

Suggestion selling benefits the salesperson, the customer, and the company. You benefit because customers will want to do business with you again, so your sales will increase. Since salespeople are often evaluated according to their sales figures, you will be viewed as an effective salesperson. Your customers benefit because they are pleased with their purchase. The company benefits because the time and cost involved in suggestion selling is less than the cost of making the original sale.

Selling is a process of persuasion, so the principles of persuasion apply to it. A counter clerk at McDonald's will ask you whether you would like a drink, French fries, or a hot apple pie with your meal. The clerk is using a suggestion selling approach.

> “The actual sale is the beginning of a relationship with a customer.”

Consider the two purchases in the following chart. The second purchase includes an extra item suggested by the salesperson. Note that the extra time spent on suggestion selling significantly increased the firm's net profits. Expenses rose, but not in proportion to the sales **volume**. There are two reasons for this. First, less time and effort are needed for suggestion selling compared to the initial sale. Second, certain business expenses (such as utilities and rent) remain the same despite the extra sales activity.

Purchase 1		Purchase 2	
Pants	$75	Pants	$75
		Shirt	$35
Total	$75	Total	$110
Cost of goods	–$37	Cost of goods	–$55
Gross Profit	$38	Gross Profit	$55
Expenses	–$12	Expenses	–$15
Net profit	$26	Net profit	$40

ENGAGE

Objectives

- **Explain** the benefits of suggestion selling. Benefits include: salesperson gains loyal customer, company makes money, customer more satisfied
- **List** the rules for effective suggestion selling. Do it only after customer is committed; keep customer's point of view in mind; make suggestion definite; show item; make suggestion positive
- **Demonstrate** appropriate specialized suggestion selling methods. Know how to perform cross-selling and up-selling and how to draw attention to special sales opportunities.
- **Discuss** strategies for maintaining and building a clientele. Process order efficiently, reassure client of wise buying choice, thank client, make sure order is properly filled, and follow up.
- **Explain** the importance of after-sale activities and customer service. Because they are satisfied, clients are more likely to become loyal customers.
- **Discuss** what salespeople can do to plan for future sales. Keep client file, evaluate their sales efforts, and analyze feedback.

Anticipation Activity

Improving Student Achievement Have students imagine that they work at a men's clothing store. Ask: ***After a customer buys a suit, what items can be sold to that customer through suggestion selling?*** ties, shirts, tie pins, cuff links, belts, socks

Graphic Organizer

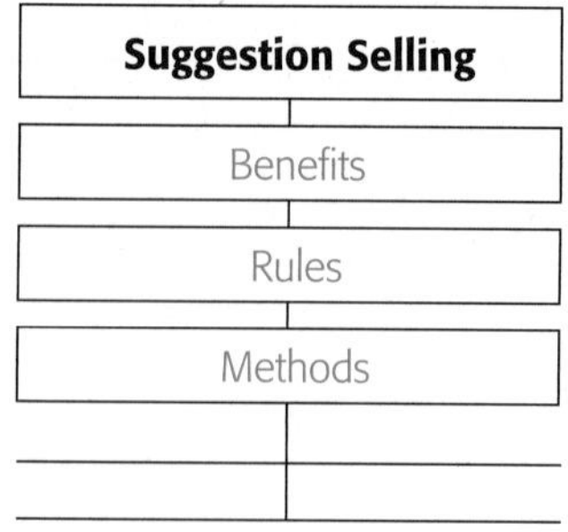

Graphic Organizer Send students to the Online Learning Center to print this graphic organizer.

EXPLORE

Before You Read

Read the Before You Read question aloud: ***When have you been contacted by a company after making a purchase?*** Most students will have been thanked via e-mail after making an online purchase. However, fewer will have been contacted after buying items at a bricks-and-mortar store. ***Then ask: What was the purpose of this follow-up contact?*** to show appreciation for being a customer; to provide information about shipping (in the case of online or catalog sales); to advertise new items or other items of interest; and to encourage future sales.

Preteaching Vocabulary

Have students go to the Online Learning Center at glencoe.com for the Chapter 15 Preteaching Vocabulary games.

Content Vocabulary

Write the word *suggestion* for the class to read. Have students work individually to write a definition of *suggestion.* Ask for volunteers to share their definitions. attempting to influence a person's physical or mental state by a thought or idea Discuss that the word can be difficult to define because it involves influencing the way that people think and act. In many instances, this type of influence is the ultimate goal of the salesperson. Explain that when engaging in suggestion sales, the salesperson is trying to influence the customer's purchase.

Academic Vocabulary

Appreciate—Word Origins Write the word *appreciate* for students to read. Explain that it comes from the Medieval Latin word *appretiāre*, which means "to value or prize." Ask students: ***How is this definition related to our definition of appreciate?*** *Appreciate* means "to grasp the worth or significance of," which means that we value or prize something.

Volume—Use Prior Knowledge Ask students: ***What does the word* volume *mean when used in a science or math class?*** In math and science, *volume* refers to the amount of space that is occupied.

As You Read

Read the As You Read question aloud: ***What makes some companies better than others in creating loyal customers?*** Possible responses: quality of products, wide range of choices, good service, personal attention, and satisfaction with previous shopping experiences and with the staff.

Customer Satisfaction

SUGGESTION SELLING

Present these guiding questions to focus the discussion about suggestion selling.

Guiding Questions

Analyze Think of a time when a salesperson suggested you buy a second product to go with the one you were buying. If so, were you happy with the decision?	I bought a laptop and the salesperson suggested I also buy a printer. I did not buy it because I wanted to conduct research first. However, a week later I returned to the store and bought a printer.
Synthesize How might a small store encourage its salespeople to engage in suggestion selling?	by offering incentives and bonuses for those who are successful in suggestion selling; by offering training and role-playing activities

Graphic Organizer

Display this graphic organizer to emphasize suggestion selling.

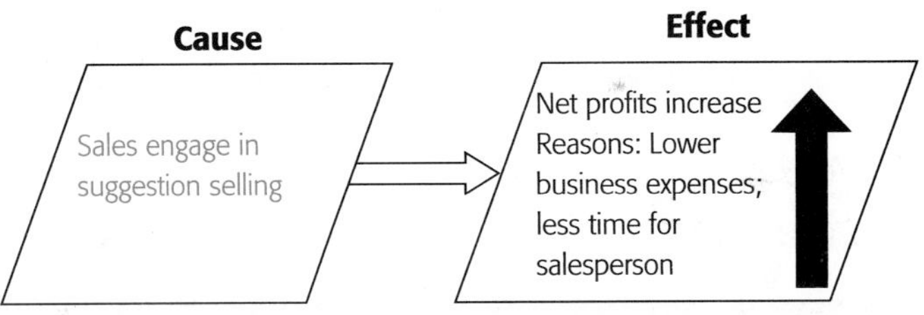
Cause
Effect
Sales engage in suggestion selling
Net profits increase
Reasons: Lower business expenses; less time for salesperson

 **glencoe.com** 

Graphic Organizer Send students to the Online Learning Center to print this graphic organizer.

Expert Advice

Read the quote to students:

"The actual sale is the beginning of a relationship with a customer."

Ask students: ***Do you think developing a strong customer relationship is more important in retail sales or organizational sales? Why?*** relationships are important in organizational sales because corporate buyers tend to stay with vendors for long periods of time.

RULES FOR SUGGESTION SELLING

Here are five basic rules for suggestion selling:

1. **Use suggestion selling after the customer has made a commitment to buy but before payment is made or the order written.** Introducing additional merchandise before the sale has been closed can create pressure for the customer. The only exception to this rule involves products whose accessories are a major benefit. If you are showing a retailer a new type of video game system, you may need to tell the retailer about the exciting new video games that will be sold in conjunction with that new system.
2. **Make your recommendation from the customer's point of view and give at least one reason for your suggestion.** You might say, "For your child to enjoy this toy immediately, you'll need two AAA batteries."
3. **Make the suggestion definite.** In most cases, general questions invite a negative response. Do not ask, "Will that be all?" Instead say, "This oil is recommended by the manufacturer for this engine."
4. **Show the item you are suggesting.** Merely talking about it is not enough. In many cases, the item will sell itself if you let the customer see and handle it. You may place a matching purse next to the shoes the customer has just decided to buy, adding some commentary. You might say, "This purse matches your shoes perfectly, doesn't it?"
5. **Make the suggestion positive.** You could say, "Let me show you the matching top for those slacks. It will complete the outfit beautifully." You would certainly never say, "You wouldn't want to look at scarves for your new coat, would you?" Such a negative statement shows a lack of enthusiasm or a lack of confidence on the part of the salesperson.

SUGGESTION SELLING METHODS

Suggestion selling methods are: offering related merchandise, recommending larger quantities, and calling attention to special sales opportunities. **Figure 15.1** shows examples of different ways to use suggestion selling.

OFFERING RELATED MERCHANDISE

Suggesting related merchandise, also known as *cross-selling*, increases the use or enjoyment of the customer's original purchase. Cross-selling is probably the easiest suggestion selling method. The related merchandise can be a good or service. For example, accessory items can be sold with the original purchase—perhaps a tie to match a new suit or a service contract for a new appliance.

RECOMMENDING LARGER QUANTITIES

Suggesting a larger quantity is often referred to as *up-selling*. This method works in retail settings when selling inexpensive items or when savings in money or time and convenience are involved. You may tell a customer who wants to buy one pair of socks, "One pair costs $4, but you can buy three pairs for $10.

In organizational sales situations, the salesperson may suggest a larger quantity so that the customer can take advantage of lower prices or special considerations like free shipping.

CALLING ATTENTION TO SPECIAL SALES OPPORTUNITIES

Salespeople are obligated to communicate special sales opportunities to their customers.

In retail sales, routinely inform your customer of the arrival of new merchandise. You could comment on a special sale by explaining, "We're having a one-day sale on all items in this department. You might want to look around before I process your purchase."

In organizational sales situations, sales representatives show new items to their customers after they have completed the sale of merchandise requested. Thus, the salesperson has an opportunity to establish a rapport with the customer before introducing new merchandise.

Reading Check

Identify Describe a scenario in which you would use up-selling.

FIGURE 15.1 Suggestion Selling

Suggestion-selling involves selling other items to customers that will ultimately save time and money or make the original purchase more enjoyable. Let's see how suggestion selling methods might be used by a sales representative that sells goods and services for pets.

UP-SELLING A salesperson who sold these dogsled harnesses may suggest larger quantities to make a customer eligible for special discounts.

CROSS-SELLING The salesperson should suggest related items of merchandise. For dogsled owners, dog grooming services might be suggested.

SPECIAL SALES OPPORTUNITIES When a company runs a special promotion on products unrelated to the original purchase, or wants to introduce a new product or service, like pet photography, it is up to the sales representative to share that information with the customer. These might be suggested after making the original sale.

EXPLAIN

RULES FOR SUGGESTION SELLING

Ask these guiding questions to focus the discussion on the rules for suggestion selling.

Guiding Questions

Explain Generally speaking, the salesperson should not engage in suggestion selling until after the customer has committed to a purchase. What is the exception to this rule?	when product accessories are a major benefit to the original purchase item
Analyze Why should the salesperson always try to show the item being suggested?	Seeing the item allows the customer to visualize how it enhances the original purchase—this is particularly true with clothing items.

Critical Thinking

Ask: ***Can you think of any cases where it is not ethical to suggest buying larger quantities of a product?*** When items tend to spoil or deteriorate quickly, the customer or client should not be encouraged to purchase more than can safely be used.

PROFESSIONAL DEVELOPMENT **MINI CLIP**

ELL: Comprehension and English Language Learners
Go to the Online Learning Center for a video that discusses comprehension strategies for English language learners.

ELABORATE

Critical Thinking

Have students share their experiences with after-sales activities, such as follow-up calls and e-mails from online retailers. Students may have received thank-you messages from Web sites, information about when their purchases will arrive, and advertisements for sales on similar products or accessories. Have students discuss whether such actions make it more likely for them to give return business. If a follow-up e-mail tells me about a sale where I might save money, I will probably check to see what is available; otherwise, I just ignore follow-up activities.

Reading Check Answer

Read the Reading Check question to students: ***Describe a scenario in which you would use up-selling?*** Answers will vary. Sample answers: I might remind a customer that they could save a dollar on paper towels if they purchased three packages instead of one.

Visual Literacy

Figure 15.1 Suggestion Selling Discuss with students that salespeople who are good at suggestion selling are able to put themselves in the customer's place. Describe for students a scenario in which an 18-year-old goes to an auto supply store to look at seat covers for a used pick-up truck he has purchased. Ask students: ***If you were a salesperson in this store, how might you use suggestion selling to help this new owner?*** Encourage students to be creative in their responses. Possible answers: The salesperson may note that the customer is looking at some low-end seat covers and suggest slightly more expensive ones that are stain repellent and have a more durable fabric. The salesperson might also show related items, such as steering wheel covers that match the seat covers.

Mini Projects

Enrichment

Identifying Suggestion Selling Opportunities Have students research cultural, religious, or national holidays, such as Rosh Hashanah, Cinco de Mayo, Ramadan, Kwanzaa, Christmas, Valentine's Day, Mother's Day, and Father's Day. Ask them to create a calendar listing these holidays and others on which special foods are eaten and/or gifts are given or exchanged. Have students write a one- to two-page report about how a business of their choice can use these events to increase sales. In the report, students can discuss how the business might use suggestion selling to encourage customers to make additional purchases. Student's reports will vary, but should discuss how a specific business can use suggestion selling to encourage purchases related to various holidays. For example, if a customer was purchasing a ham to serve for Christmas dinner, the salesperson might suggest they also purchase sweet potatoes, applesauce, and other side dishes that are traditionally served on Christmas as an accompaniment to ham.

Learning How to Influence People Discuss with students that in order to be good at suggestion selling, you must be able to establish a rapport with the client so that they will value your opinions. One of the oldest and most widely read books on this topic is Dale Carnegie's *How to Win Friends and Influence People.* Tell students that even though the book was first published in 1937, it has invaluable knowledge that can help people build stronger relationships today. It is especially applicable to salespeople because their sales will increase if their customers value their opinions. Have students read this relatively short book and then write a persuasive essay explaining why they think salespeople can benefit from the information and tips it provides. Students should write a persuasive essay explaining why this book could be helpful to salespeople, particularly in the area of suggestion selling. Tips such as being genuinely interested in others and listening intently to their needs and opinions are at the core of succeeding in sales.

MAINTAINING AND BUILDING A CLIENTELE

Making a sale is the first step in maintaining and building a clientele. Maintaining a clientele is necessary for repeat sales, which are necessary for businesses to be successful. Also, satisfied customers often help generate new customers by telling others about their positive experiences. It also costs more to find new customers than it costs to keep current customers satisfied. Positive customer- or client-relations require a lot of attention after the sale. After-sale activities by the sales and customer service staff, as well as planning for future sales, are key factors in building a clientele.

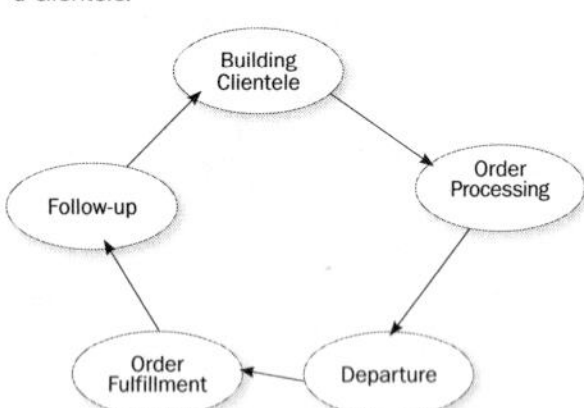

AFTER-SALES ACTIVITIES

The time you spend with your customer after a sale is just as important, if not more important, than the time you spent making the sale. After-sale activities include order processing, departure, order fulfillment, and follow-up. All these activities need to be handled in such a way that the customer wants to do business with you again. Satisfied customers become steady customers, which is a goal in selling: to generate repeat business.

ORDER PROCESSING

In retail selling, bag the merchandise with care. Products such as glassware may require individual wrapping before bagging. Expensive clothing may be left on hangers and enclosed in special bags made for that purpose. Work quickly to bag your customer's merchandise and complete the payment process.

In business-to-business sales, complete the paperwork quickly and accurately. Review the order with your customer and leave the customer with a copy of it along with your business card.

DEPARTURE

Before customers depart or before you leave your clients' offices, reassure your clientele of their wise buying choices. If an item needs special care or specific instructions, take the time to educate your customer about it. You may want to remind the customer, for example, that to get the best results from a Teflon-coated frying pan, it should be preheated. When selling new automobiles, this would be a good time to show your customers how to work some of the electronic devices, such as the GPS system. This extra time spent with customers helps ensure customer satisfaction.

Always thank your customers. Even when a customer does not buy, express your gratitude for the time and attention given to you. Invite customers back to the store, or ask for permission to call again in the near future.

ORDER FULFILLMENT

In organizational selling situations, order fulfillment is based on the purchase order or sales order. If a purchase order involves special instructions, salespeople need to communicate those special instructions to other company employees. This helps to ensure that everything is done to the customer's precise specifications. For example, salespeople may alert the shipping department when part of an order is to be shipped to different locations or at different times. Salespeople may speak directly with the manufacturing manager regarding specifications for embroidery of a customer's name on employee uniforms. The salesperson's attention to these details can avoid potential problems with the current sale and future sales.

In a retail store, order fulfillment is a simple process of the customer paying for merchandise and carrying it away.

In telemarketing or online sales, order fulfillment gets more complicated. It includes taking the order, financial processing (such as credit card information), picking the right product, packing it well, and shipping it according to the customer's preference. In some companies, fulfillment also includes customer service, technical support, managing inventory, and handling returns and refunds. Success often depends as much on appropriate fulfillment strategies as it does on having the right product at the right price. Some of the most successful online retailers have established their own fulfillment centers to ensure prompt delivery. Amazon.com, BarnesandNoble.com, and Dell® Computer all have their own fulfillment centers. Another approach is to outsource fulfillment to a third party.

Cross-Selling

Selling related merchandise is an easy method of suggestion selling. ***What is the key to suggesting related merchandise, as clearly identified in this L.L. Bean catalog page?***

MARKETING CASE STUDY

Selling Fitness at Equinox

Equinox Fitness is an upscale fitness club with locations in several U.S. cities. Its original system of developing and following up on leads was paper-based. Frustration with the outdated sales system created a high turnover of sales staff. It was clear that selling fitness memberships had to move into the computer age.

Microsoft Solution

Equinox had a lot of information about its customers, so it knew its target market. But it needed a boost, provided by the Microsoft Gold Certified Partner, Customer Effective. This system improved the process of member applications, while gathering data for sales presentations. Equinox also created its own Equinox Selling Process (ESP), a sales training tool for staff at its clubs. ESP provides sales techniques and support to help the sales staff close membership sales.

English Language Arts

Evaluate Discuss with a partner the risks and benefits involved in making a system-wide change to an established selling process. What are the advantages of using modern technology if the trade-off is having to retrain the entire sales force?

NCTE 12 Use language to accomplish individual purposes.

352 | Unit 5 · Selling

Chapter 15 · Closing the Sale | 353

EXPLAIN

Graphic Organizer

Display this diagram as an overview of after-sales activities. Add notes to the bottom row as you discuss with the class.

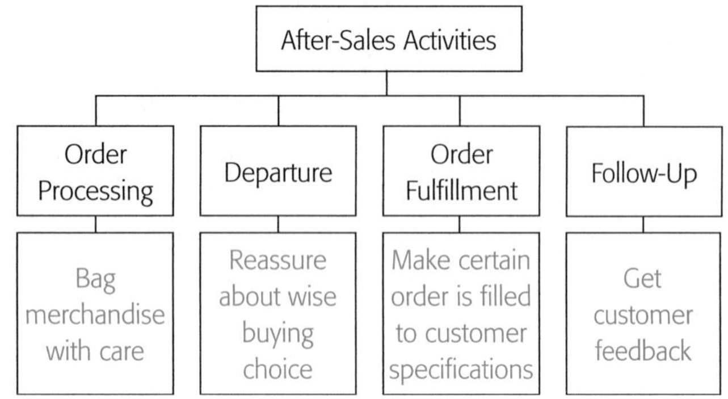

iWB

Graphic Organizer Send students to the Online Learning Center to print this graphic organizer.

Visual Literacy

Cross-Selling Caption Answer Read the caption question to students: ***What is the key to suggesting related merchandise, as clearly identified in this catalog page?*** The products must be closely related to the merchandise being purchased. They should be products that are likely to be needed by the owner of the purchased product. Bring in an item with which students are familiar, such as athletic shoes or a soccer jersey. Ask for volunteers to write items that could be cross-sold with this item. Possible answers for athletic shoes: appropriate socks, cleaning supplies for athletic shoes, clothing for sports activities

Critical Thinking

Describe for students this scenario: A homeowner purchases new carpet for a family room. A couple of days after the carpet layers have finished their work, the homeowner receives a call from the salesperson who sold her the carpet. The salesperson asks to visit the customer at her convenience. The salesperson then carefully examines the carpet and says how nice it looks in the family room. The next day the homeowner tells her neighbor that she had never had a carpet salesperson follow-up by inspecting the finished job. Ask students: ***How do you think this might affect the salesperson's future sales?*** Not only is this homeowner likely to seek out this salesperson the next time she needs to make a carpet purchase, her neighbor might do the same.

ELABORATE

AFTER-SALES ACTIVITIES

Ask these guiding questions to focus the discussion on after-sales activities.

Guiding Questions

Analyze In business-to-business sales, the salesperson should leave the customer a copy of the order. Why is this step important?	The customer may need to refer to the order for information, such as delivery date. The customer can also double-check the order when more time is available.
Predict Which of these companies is more likely to need additional help after a sale takes place: A corporation ordering a year's supply of copy paper or an engineering firm ordering components for a bridge that will go over a river?	The engineering firm because such a project has many components—it is likely some components will need to be exchanged, more will have to be added, and so on.

Graphic Organizer

Display this graphic organizer. Discuss the different categories of businesses that must fulfill orders.

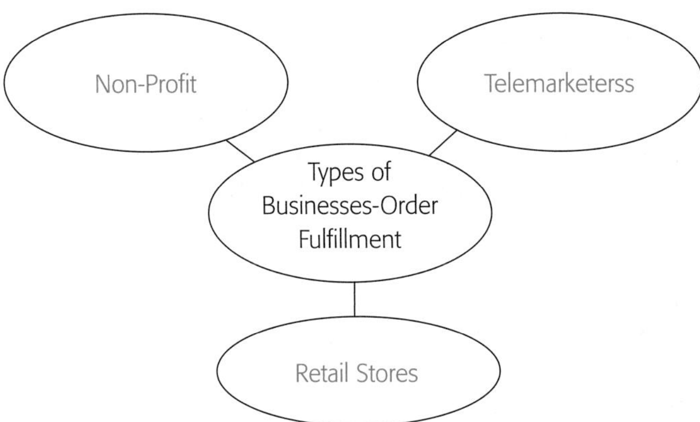

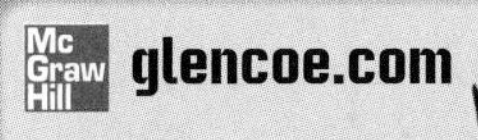

iWB

Graphic Organizer Send students to the Online Learning Center to print this graphic organizer.

MARKETING CASE STUDY

English Language Arts Answer
Students should discuss with a partner the advantages of having a computer-based system for processing member applications and gathering sales information. Important advantages include that a computer-based system is much easier to update and can be shared among multiple users at the same time. It provides sophisticated sales training tools and support for closing membership sales. The system also greatly simplifies spotting and analyzing membership trends.

Extend Have students use the Internet to research the advantages of being a member of the Microsoft Partner Network and discuss what they learn. Microsoft states that it can supply tools to support companies through the business cycle.

Mini Projects

Enrichment

Creating a Poster on Cross-Selling Locate a variety of catalogs or Web sites that use cross-selling to suggest related purchases that might interest customers. For example, a women's clothing site might suggest jewelry or scarves that go with a specific dress. Have students print or cut out these examples of cross-selling. Have them use these images to create a poster that explains cross-selling. The poster should include a title and a brief definition of cross-selling. Place posters where the entire class can view them. Student posters should contain examples of cross-selling that illustrate how catalogs and Web sites use these techniques to increase sales.

Deciding Whether to Outsource or Establish Own Fulfillment Center Tell students that they work for a Web site that sells sports memorabilia. Up until now, the company has outsourced fulfillment to a third party. However, the owner is now thinking about having the company establish its own fulfillment center. The owner has asked their opinion about this idea. Instruct students to write a one-page report in which they discuss the pros and cons of the company setting up its own fulfillment center. At the end of their reports, students should state the route they believe the company should take. Pros may include: the company would have more control over the process and orders might be filled more quickly. In addition, it might be less expensive. Cons may include: it takes a lot of time and effort to set up a fulfillment center, it detracts from the company's primary mission, and the company must provide warehouse space for the product. At the end of the report, the student should analyze the options and make a decision either for or against setting up an in-house fulfillment center.

This allows a company to concentrate its efforts on marketing the products. The goal in all forms of order fulfillment is to make the customer happy.

FOLLOW-UP

The follow-up includes making arrangements to follow through on all promises made during the sales process. It also includes checking on your customer's satisfaction with his or her purchase. Here are a few follow-up ideas:

- Call the shipping department to confirm a special delivery date.
- Check to make sure that delivery occurs as promised.
- Call the customer and explain any delay.
- Phone customers a week or two after the purchase to see if they are happy with the selection.
- Send a thank-you note with your business card attached.

CUSTOMER SERVICE

The role of customer service cannot be emphasized enough as a part of developing selling relationships. Salespeople do their job generating new customers. Customer service is needed to keep those customers happy. Businesses recognize the importance of customer service.

Employees provide excellent customer service to maintain their clientele. Customer service has many dimensions. It includes offering a variety of special services and handling customer complaints.

OFFERING SPECIAL SERVICES

Many customer services are designed to keep customers loyal by providing ongoing communication with them and help after the sale. Some of these special services include e-mail and social media interaction, online support, special retail and vendor services, and customer training.

E-Mail and Social Media

Businesses have recognized the benefits of keeping communication lines open with customers on an ongoing basis. Some use e-mail to provide customers with information regarding new products and special promotions on a regular basis. Businesses are legally required to get permission to send customers email. Customers must "opt-in" and agree to receive the emails. A business must also give customers the opportunity to "opt-out" if they no longer want to get emails from the company.

Social media opportunities include weblogs (blogs), Facebook®, Twitter®, and other Internet platforms that permit businesses to create a dialogue with customers on a frequent basis.

Proper handling of after-sale activities helps to ensure customer satisfaction with the entire shopping experience. ***What else should the salesperson do before the customer departs?***

Customer Satisfaction

The goal of customer service, whether handled by a customer service department or by the salesperson, is customer satisfaction and retention. ***Why is customer service an important part of sales?***

Company CEOs may blog about new products and services. Facebook and Twitter allow companies to interact with customers. Businesses on Facebook may create games or other special activities to engage customers. Customers' comments recorded on Facebook and Twitter often get responses from the company. This ongoing dialogue between the customer and the company provides customers with a personal response. It also helps companies address unforeseen problems they may not have discovered otherwise.

Online Customer Support

Many retailers and manufacturers offer answers to frequently asked questions (FAQs) on their respective Web sites. Their Web sites may also provide a link to a customer service center. This link allows customers to ask questions and receive replies via e-mail or a phone call from a customer service representative. This online customer support is extremely useful with products that require installation or manipulation.

Special Retail Services

Many retailers offer a bridal and/or baby registry. Engaged couples and expecting parents select items they like, and that list is made available to anyone who wants to buy them gifts. In some auto dealerships, specific customer service representatives are assigned to each customer to handle appointments and questions with auto problems and regular servicing. Merchandise returns and customer inquiries are often handled by a special customer service department.

Special Vendor Services

Large retailers may require vendors to provide additional services as part of their sales agreement. Some of those services may include keeping track of retail inventory, providing merchandising services, restocking promotional materials, and designing packages to meet their shelf-space requirements. A retailer that is very important to a vendor may employ its own staff whose sole responsibility is servicing that one big account.

Customer Training

When a product is purchased by a company that requires instruction before using it, hands-on training may be provided to customers. Apple®, Inc., offers everyone who purchases an Apple computer one year of free training.

More advanced instruction may be offered to companies when a new computer software program is installed. Key employees may attend classes provided by the vendor. Instead of formal classes at the company's headquarters, the training may be held in the customer's place of business or at a convenient location for the customer.

Manufacturers that sell products for resale may provide training materials to retailers' and wholesalers' sales staff. Computer-aided instruction, videos, training manuals, and other items may be used to educate the retail sales staff about a product's features and benefits. The manufacturer's sales representative may also provide personal instruction about how to handle customer questions and possible objections.

EXPLAIN

FOLLOW-UP

Follow-up completes the cycle which hopefully leads to future sales. To focus on follow-up activities, present these guiding questions to the class.

Guiding Questions

Recall What should the salesperson do if there in an unexpected delay in shipping?	Immediately inform the customer.
Infer What message is a salesperson sending the customer when the salesperson carefully carries through on all promises made during the sales process?	The salesperson is reliable and values the customer's business.
Apply If you were a salesperson, what would you say in a thank-you note to a customer?	I would thank the customer and mention her wise buying decision, and I would say that I was looking forward to another opportunity to help her.

Critical Thinking

The fourth follow-up step is to call the customer for feedback one or two weeks after delivery. Why would the salesperson want to wait this length of time? Some customers are busy and may not be able to examine the order immediately. Others may need time to determine whether the purchase is working for them.

Visual Literacy

After-Sale Activities Caption Answer Read the caption question to students: ***What else should the salesperson do before the customer departs?*** The salesperson should reiterate that the customer has made a good buying decision and remind that person of any special instructions regarding the product. The salesperson may also want to obtain information such as name, address, phone number, and e-mail address for the business's database for future follow-up. However, most important of all is to offer a sincere thank you, regardless of whether the customer made a purchase or not.

ELABORATE

CUSTOMER SERVICE

Explain to students that customer service covers everything from handling complaints to offering online product support. Ask these guiding questions to focus the discussion on customer service.

Guiding Questions

List What are three customer services designed to help customers and keep them loyal?	online support, special retail and vendor services, customer training, handling customer complaints
Apply You are a salesperson for a local electronics store. Your store offers no training in using the computers or computer software that you sell. What might you say to encourage your manager to begin offering such training?	Sample answer: Classes for using computers and computer software will encourage consumers to buy from our store. In addition, many of the chain stores offer such training, so we need to offer it to remain competitive.

Visual Literacy

Customer Satisfaction Caption Answer Read the caption question to students: ***Why is customer service an important part of sales?*** Providing good customer service tells customers that the company and the salesperson value their patronage. It sets the stage for long-term relationships and helps cement existing ones. Then ask: ***What special challenges might there be in providing good customer service when communicating over the phone?*** Possible answer: It is often easier to establish a personal rapport when face-to-face with someone because you can use nonverbal gestures and body language to establish the relationship. People who provide phone service must use other methods, such as tone of voice and being especially good listeners.

Mini Project

Enrichment

Examining a Commercial Web Site's Customer Support Instruct students to choose a commercial Web site and investigate its customer support services. Students may want to create a slide show to accompany their presentations. Students should give an oral presentation explaining the customer support services provided by their Web site. For example, the site may have a list of frequently asked questions (FAQs). Other support services might include an explanation of return policies and how to arrange next-day deliveries.

e MARKETING

Collaborative Filtering

With collaborative filtering, purchase patterns can be discerned based on previous purchases by an individual or by customers that purchase similar products. Companies use collaborative filtering to make recommendations when a customer purchases a product. Collaborative filtering is an effective form of suggestion selling because data indicate that the customer may be interested in the suggested item(s). Amazon® and some other online catalog companies use collaborative filtering. For example, when you purchase a book on Amazon, you are directed to view a few additional books based on your previous purchases or based on what other customers who purchased that book have purchased in the past.

Innovate and Create

Discuss the effectiveness of collaborative filtering as a form of suggestion selling. Why do you think the additional items are suggested after customers have made a commitment to buy but before they conduct their final online check out? What other methods of suggestion selling have you seen in practice online; especially on Amazon.com? For an online clothing e-tailer create the means for suggestion selling to take place before the final check out process. Decide what suggestion selling methods will work best for a clothing e-tailer. Collaborative filtering is an effective form of suggestion selling because the suggested items are based on previous purchases. For example, if a customer has purchased many books by the same author and a new book by that author is now available, it is a strong possibility that the customer will be interested in purchasing it. It is a good practice to conduct suggestion selling after there is a commitment to buy so you don't overwhelm a customer. To make the suggestion relevant you should give a reason why you are suggesting it (i.e., to complete an outfit, based on previous purchases may be interested in ...). With an online e-tailer, showing related merchandise such as accessories on a model (possibly one in the catalog) could create effective suggestion selling. Related merchandise and larger quantities of merchandise (buy one get the second one for half price) and new arrivals can all be used effectively when conducting suggestion selling for an online clothing e-tailer. .

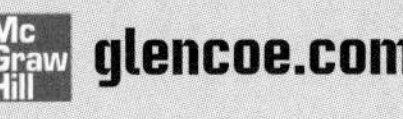

eMarketing Worksheet Activity Send students to the Online Learning Center to download an eMarketing worksheet activity.

Career Chatroom

Nadja Specht
Chief Marketer
Nuvota, LLC

What do you do at work?

I teach small business owners marketing fundamentals, using plain language, through marketing workshops, coaching, and consulting. This allows those who are unfamiliar with new terms and technology to understand how they can use today's marketing tools to attract customers. I want clients to get the marketing knowledge they need to make decisions independently so they can sell their products effectively.

What is your key to success?

It helps to have a great education, the right professional experiences, and to learn from mistakes. Beyond that, the key is to follow my instincts, believe in myself, and have endurance.

What skills are most important to you?

Analytical thinking: being detail-oriented and comfortable with number crunching. Conceptual thinking: not getting overwhelmed by details and unknowns, but creating a high-level conceptual framework. Emotional intelligence: being able to listen and adapt to clients' different personalities and needs to deliver quality service.

glencoe.com

Read more about this career and get a Career Exploration Activity.

HANDLING CUSTOMER COMPLAINTS

A manufacturer often has customer service representatives that handle telephone and e-mail customer complaints. Many companies also provide 800 numbers so customers can easily contact them with questions or complaints.

In business-to-business sales, customer complaints should be relayed to the sales representatives responsible for those customers. In some cases, the personal attention of the sales representative is required to ensure complete customer satisfaction and to maintain good relations with the customer.

How these complaints are handled is crucial to maintaining clientele. Customers expect immediate action when they file complaints. Positive customer-client relations require compassionate and understanding customer service personnel and sales associates who are problem solvers. The main goal is customer satisfaction.

In some cases, going the extra mile may be needed to keep a customer. For example, if a customer complains that a product is defective, you may have to replace it or offer a full refund. If the wrong product was delivered, you may have to use an overnight delivery service to get the product to the customer in time. In essence, you need to do whatever is necessary (within reason) to solve the problem and make the customer happy.

PLANNING FUTURE SALES

Successful salespeople strive to develop relationships with their customers and work to improve their sales techniques. Getting to know a customer personally is helpful when making future sales calls. To become an effective salesperson, self-evaluation is imperative.

KEEPING A CLIENT FILE

You can use the time immediately after the sale to plan for your next encounter with the customer. Take notes on your conversation with the customer. Keep this in a file for future reference. In retail sales, note a customer's preference in color, style, and size, as well as the person's address and telephone number. In business-to-business selling, record personal information on the buyer's marital status, children, and hobbies to assist with future sales visits. Record changes in buying patterns that may lead to future sales. Note any future service dates for appliances or cars so that you can send a reminder when the time comes. Be sure to inform your company of any changes you uncover, such as changes in personnel responsible for buying, as well as address or telephone changes, so that company files can stay up to date.

EVALUATE YOUR SALES EFFORTS

Even if your company has a formal method of reviewing your efforts, you should conduct your own evaluation. In your evaluation, consider the following:

- What were the strong points of your sales presentation?
- How could you have improved your performance?
- What would you do differently next time?
- What can you do now to solidify your relationship with your customer if you made the sale?

Asking yourself these questions can help you improve your selling skills as well as your business skills in general. They will enable you to look forward to your next sales opportunity. That kind of attitude will help you become more effective with each sales contact. It will also help you become more successful in building a strong relationship with your customers.

Some businesses send questionnaires or call customers to check on how well they were treated by the sales and service staff. The results of these surveys are passed on to salespeople so they can improve their sales techniques.

After You Read — Section 15.2

Review Key Concepts

1. **Explain** how suggestion selling benefits the salesperson, company, and customer.
2. **Name** three related items that could be used for suggestion selling after a customer's decision to buy a tent for camping purposes.
3. **Discuss** what a salesperson should do as a follow-up to a sale.

Academic Skills

English Language Arts

4. Assume you are training a new salesperson. Prepare a written plan that covers suggestion selling, after-sale activities, and planning for future sales. Use a product of your choice to provide examples of related merchandise to suggest and examples of how to build a relationship with customers after the sale.

NCTE 12 Use language to accomplish individual purposes.

Mathematics

5. You sold a $460 item via the Internet to a European customer, a Japanese customer, and a customer in New Zealand. Use the chart below to calculate the total amount due for the product with duties and customs for each of the three customers.

	Europe	Japan	New Zealand
Duties & Customs	20%	9%	50%

Math Concept **Ways of Representing Numbers** A percentage can be represented by a number that is less than one.

Starting Hints To solve this problem, convert each of the percents to a decimal by moving the decimal point two places to the left, or divide them by 100. Multiply $460 by each of the decimals to determine the duties and customs charges for each country. Add the duties and custom charges of each country to $460 to determine the total cost for each customer.

For help, go to the **Math Skills Handbook** located at the back of this book.

NCTM Number and Operations Understand numbers, ways of representing numbers, relationships among numbers, and number systems.

glencoe.com

Check your answers.

ELABORATE

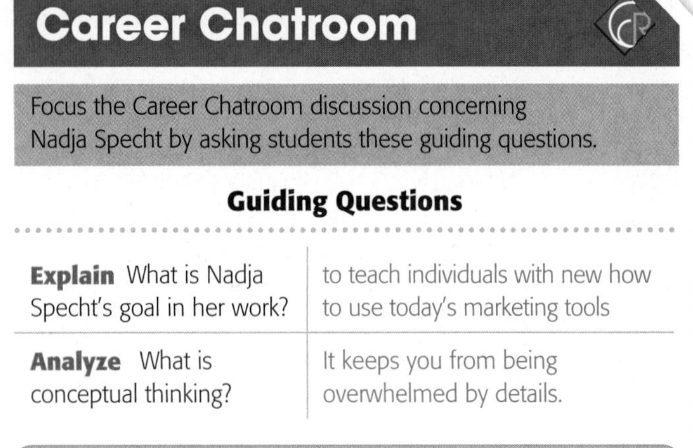

Career Chatroom

Focus the Career Chatroom discussion concerning Nadja Specht by asking students these guiding questions.

Guiding Questions

Explain What is Nadja Specht's goal in her work?	to teach individuals with new how to use today's marketing tools
Analyze What is conceptual thinking?	It keeps you from being overwhelmed by details.

glencoe.com

Career Exploration Send students to the Online Learning Center to find more information about this career and to get a Career Exploration activity.

KEEPING A CLIENT FILE

Explain to students that keeping a client file can serve to refresh the salesperson's memory before meeting with a customer. Ask these guiding questions to help students explore the advantages of maintaining a customer file.

Guiding Questions

Describe What kind of information might a clothing boutique salesperson keep on customers?	color, style, and size preferences, customer's address, e-mail address, and phone number; some personal information might be included
Infer Why might a salesperson's client database contain information on the client's hobbies?	Being able to talk about a client's interests establishes rapport. At the corporate level, salespeople may bring small gifts, and providing a gift related to a hobby shows thoughtfulness.

EVALUATE

EVALUATE YOUR SALES EFFORTS

Effective, objective evaluation can improve everyone's performance, not just those of people in sales. Ask these guiding questions to focus the discussion on self-evaluation.

Guiding Questions

Explain What are four points salespeople might consider when evaluating their sales performance?	What are strong points? How can they improve? What would they do differently next time? How can they solidify their relationship with the customer?
Summarize Why should you always evaluate your own sales efforts, even if your company has a formal method of reviewing your work?	Objective self-evaluation can help keep you on track toward reaching your goals. Your managers (and others who evaluate your efforts) may not have the same goals or insights that you possess.
Draw Conclusions Why do you think an appliance store might send out questionnaires to customers asking them to evaluate its salespeople?	The managers might want to determine how well salespeople are meeting customer needs and make adjustments accordingly. They also might want to provide feedback to salespeople so they can improve their methods of selling.

Mini Project

Extension

Creating a Customer Database Explain that today's corporate salesperson keeps client information in a database, typically stored on their personal laptop. This can be one of the most valuable assets the salesperson possesses. Have students create a database that contains appropriate information on each client a company might have. If students have the ability, they can create the database using software such as Microsoft Access. If database software is not available, they may choose to use a spreadsheet program, such as Microsoft Excel. Students should create a client database either on paper or using appropriate software. Each client record should contain appropriate information, such as the client's full name, address, telephone number, e-mail address(es), and any additional contact information. Notes on recent conversations and past buying patterns should be included. Some databases may also include the buyer's marital status, children's names, and information about hobbies and personal interests.

After You Read — Section 15.2

Review Key Concepts

1. Suggestion selling benefits the salesperson in that the customer will want to do business with the salesperson again and the salesperson will have higher sales figures. It benefits the company since the time and cost involved in suggestion selling is less than the cost of making the original sales and therefore net revenues will increase. It benefits customers because they will be more pleased with the original purchase because they will have what they need to be able to use it.
2. Accept all reasonable answers. Some related camping items include: sleeping bags, backpacks, camper tools, folding chairs, cots, folding tables, nylon rope, lantern, flashlight, tent fan, and hammock.
3. As a follow-up to a sale, salespeople should make arrangements to follow through on all promises made during the sales process. They also should check on the customer's satisfaction with the purchase, as well as delivery of the merchandise and send a thank you note with a business card attached.

Practice Academics

English Language Arts

4. Students should prepare a written plan of how they would train a new salesperson. Students should use a product of their choice as an example for activities such as suggestion selling. In the suggestion selling portion of the plan, students should discuss its benefits, list the five suggestion selling rules, and provide examples of cross-selling, up-selling, and promoting special sales opportunities. Students should then discuss after-sales activities, such as order processing, thanking the customer, and making certain the order is properly filled. Lastly, the student should present specific examples of how to build an on-going relationship, such as notifying the customer of any delivery delays, calling for feedback, and writing a thank you note.

Mathematics

5. European customer: $552 (460 × 1.20); Japanese customer: $501.40 ($460 × 1.09); New Zealand customer: $690 ($460 × 1.50)

glencoe.com

Answer Key Send students to the Online Learning Center to check their answers.

Closing the Sale

Four specialized methods for closing a sale are: which close, standing-room-only close (SRO), direct close, and service close.

Closing the Sale
Which Close
SRO Close
Direct Close
Service Close

Suggestion selling is important because it helps generate more sales revenue for a company and helps to create more satisfied customers.

Suggestion Selling Methods
Cross-Selling
Calling Attention to Special Sales
Up-Selling

Written Summary

- Customer buying signals help a salesperson determine a customer's readiness to buy.
- Close the sale as soon as the customer is ready to buy.
- Use success in answering objections or presenting a product as an opportunity to close.
- Help customers make a decision and create an ownership mentality.
- Four specialized methods for closing a sale include: the direct close, the which close, the standing-room-only close, and the service close.
- Suggestion selling helps generate sales revenue and create satisfied customers.
- Three specialized suggestion-selling methods include the following: offering related merchandise, or cross-selling; selling larger quantities, or up-selling; and calling attention to special sales opportunities.
- After-sales activities are important for maintaining and building a clientele. They include order processing, departure, order fulfillment, follow-up, customer service, keeping client files, and evaluating sales efforts.

Review Content Vocabulary and Academic Vocabulary

1. Use each of these vocabulary words in a written sentence.

Content Vocabulary
- closing the sale (p. 341)
- buying signals (p. 341)
- trial close (p. 342)
- which close (p. 344)
- standing-room-only close (p. 344)
- direct close (p. 344)
- service close (p. 345)
- suggestion selling (p. 349)

Academic Vocabulary
- commit (p. 342)
- perseverance (p. 346)
- appreciated (p. 349)
- volume (p. 349)

Assess for Understanding

2. **Identify** What are customer buying signals?
3. **Justify** Which specialized closing method(s) would you use when a customer does not have enough cash to make the purchase today?
4. **Discuss** Why is suggestion selling an important part of the sales process?
5. **Explain** Why is using suggestion selling before closing the sale a problem?
6. **Write** What would you include in a follow-up letter to a new customer?
7. **Discuss** How can effective customer service influence the retention of clientele?
8. **Define** What are the definitions of the terms *direct close* and *service close*?
9. **Plan** How would you maintain and build clientele for a company that has a few electricians who are hired for jobs with contractors and many more electricians who handle maintenance and repairs for businesses and residences?

EVALUATE

Visual Summary

Express Creativity Ask students to create a visual summary that illustrates a concept in the chapter. Encourage students to use different formats for their visual summaries, such as an illustrated poster, a Venn diagram or a photo collage. Visual summaries will vary depending on the concept depicted. Questions to ask when assessing a visual summary include:

- Is the summary clear, economical, and simple?
- Are any important steps or concepts left out?
- Are steps or concepts arranged in the same order as the original?
- Does the summary reveal a pattern that connects the details?
- Does the summary locate and highlight the most important information?

Review Content Vocabulary and Academic Vocabulary

1. **Closing the sale** should be a natural part of the sales process. **Buying signals** can include both verbal and nonverbal cues. You should use a **trial close** to test your customer's readiness to buy. The **which close** helps a customer decide between two items. Only use the **standing-room-only** close if there really is a limited supply. The **direct close** is best used when you are confident the customer is ready to buy. If you encourage a customer to make a purchase by saying that the item will be gift wrapped for free, you are making a **service close.** When you ask a customer if she would like to look at scarves to go with a new blouse, you are practicing **suggestion selling.** When closing a sale, you get a customer to **commit** to the terms of the sale. **Perseverance** is a trait that successful salespeople demonstrate. Customers **appreciate** a salesperson that is understanding and helpful. Suggestion selling helps to increase sales **volume.**

EVALUATE

Assess for Understanding

2. Customer buying signals can be verbal comments that indicate a readiness to buy, and nonverbal actions, such as a smile, using ownership words, or holding the item for a long time.

3. Answers will vary depending on what options the business might have to offer such as special buying plans, like layaway. Businesses selling larger items frequently allow the customer to apply for a credit card; if the card is granted and customers charge the item to the card, they may be allowed to pay for it over a specific period of time, such as a year, without being charged interest.

4. Suggestion selling is important because it leads to increased sales at less cost for the business and it increases the salesperson's success. In addition, it improves customer satisfaction because the customer will be better able to use the newly purchased product.

5. Introducing additional merchandise or other information before the sale is closed can confuse the customer and make it more difficult to make the close.

6. Items to include in a follow-up letter to a new customer include: reiterating how much you enjoyed doing business with the customer and look forward to doing more business in the future; discussing any additional support, such as helpful Web sites, that the customer might want to access; and explaining again any delivery and payment arrangements that have been made.

7. Effective customer services, such as online support, special retail services (such as bridal and baby registries), and vendor services (such as inventory management and merchandising), as well as customer training, can influence retention by helping customers use their time more efficiently and successfully meet their needs. Customers realize that the business has helped them to be successful and come back because they want to continue this pattern.

8. Direct close: Directly asking the customer to buy the item, asking how they will pay for the item, asking what quantity they want, and so on. Service close: Explaining a service that might overcome obstacles that are in the way of a customer making a purchase. Straightforward return policies, warranties and guarantees, bonuses or premiums, layaway plans, and plans that allow the customer to pay for purchases over time can all be used in making a service close.

9. Answers will vary. Sample answer: I would make certain that when new electrical work is done, the business or homeowner is informed that the company also provides maintenance and repair services. I also would try to get feedback on the job directly from the customer. I would consider providing a once-a-year inspection service in which an electrician would examine the building for potential problems. This service could either be free or at a very low cost. The idea would be to keep customers in touch with the company so that if they required additional electrical work, our company would be the first they called.

21st Century Skills

Communications Skills

10. Role Play With another student playing the role of a customer, perform a role play in which you demonstrate how you would sell a product of your choice to an individual customer. Be sure to close the sale and conduct suggestion selling as part of the role play presentation. Finalize the sale by taking payment and packaging the product.

Financial Literacy Skills

11. What's Your Commission? You take an order from an organizational customer that includes the following items: 35 boots @ $49.50 each, 70 gloves @ $8.50 each, and 25 jackets @ $65 each. This order qualifies for a 5-percent discount. Determine your 8-percent commission on this sale. Try using a spreadsheet program to display your calculations.

Everyday Ethics

12. House Accounts A salesperson closes the sale on one of the biggest accounts she has ever landed. It has potential to grow bigger. The vice president of sales congratulates her and then proceeds to explain a company policy regarding *house accounts:* All large accounts are reclassified as house accounts and are serviced by the vice president. This policy ensures continuity and provides large accounts with special attention. The sales rep would earn commission on the initial sale, but not on future sales for this account. Do you think this selling policy is ethical? Why or why not?

e-Marketing Skills

13. Online Suggestion Selling Visit two online companies that sell snowboards and find products that can be used for suggestion selling. Share your opinion on how effective these companies are at suggestion selling. What improvements to the Web site would you suggest to increase sales of additional merchandise?

Build Academic Skills

Social Studies

14. Economics In a recessionary period, what can companies do to help salespeople close more sales? Research the most recent recession and provide examples of what two companies have done to help close sales.

NCSS VII H Production, Distribution, and Consumption Apply economic concepts and reasoning when evaluating historical and contemporary social developments and issues.

Science

15. Applied Technology Research at least two different online sales companies to identify and evaluate the strategies used to close a sale and provide online customer support. How do these practices differ between consumer and organizational customers?

NSES A Develop abilities necessary to do scientific inquiry, understandings about scientific inquiry.

Mathematics

16. Managing Time Sara is a sales associate for a telecommunications company. She attends an average of 21 client meetings each month. Her manager has recently asked sales associates to increase the number of client meetings they have each month by 30 percent. How many meetings will Sara then have?

NCTM Number and Operations Understand numbers, ways of representing numbers, relationships among numbers, and number systems.

Math Concept **Relationships Among Numbers: Percents** To determine the percent of a number, for example 25 percent of 50, multiply the number (50) by the decimal equivalent of the given percent (0.25). If a value is increased by a certain percent, add the two values together.

For help, go to the **Math Skills Handbook** located at the back of this book.

Standardized Test Practice

Directions Read the following questions. On a separate piece of paper, write the best possible answer for each one.

1. Which of the following sales tactics is not considered effective suggestion selling?
   A. Up selling—suggesting a larger quantity to save money or time
   B. Cross selling—suggesting related merchandise
   C. Special sales—suggesting products on sale or new items
   D. Down selling—suggesting products the customer does not need
2. It is a good idea to use words like "I" and "me" when you are trying to create an ownership mentality for your customers.
   T
   F
3. A _________ close is the initial effort to close a sale.

Test-Taking Tip
Budget your time, making sure you have enough time to answer all the questions on a test.

DECA Connection Role Play

Assistant Manager Men's Clothing Store

Situation You are the assistant manager of an independent, upscale men's clothing store. Store sales have been declining. Top management believes that the decline in sales is because the sales associates are not well trained in closing the sale, suggesting related items, or developing an on-going relationship with customers.

Activity You are to prepare a training plan for the sales staff that demonstrates how to close the sale, how to suggest additional merchandise, and what can be done as a follow-up to keep customers loyal. The store's regional manager (judge) wants to see your plan before you present it at the next staff meeting.

Evaluation You will be evaluated on how well you meet the following performance indicators:

- Close the sale.
- Demonstrate suggestion selling.
- Explain the role of customer service as a component of selling relationships.
- Explain key factors in building a clientele.
- Plan follow-up strategies for use in selling.

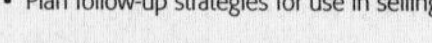

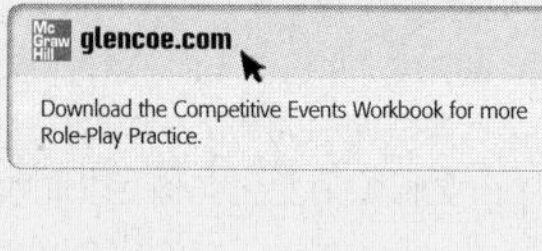

glencoe.com

Download the Competitive Events Workbook for more Role-Play Practice.

EVALUATE

21st Century Skills

Communication Skills

10. Students should role play selling an item of their choice to a fellow student, who plays the part of the customer. Students should properly close the sale and then engage in suggestion selling, possibly by offering related merchandise or telling customers about current sales. Students should ask the customer about the type of payment, take the payment, and package the product appropriately.

Financial Literacy Skills

11. $300.39 commission (35 × 49.50 = 1,732.50; 70 × $8.50 = $595; 25 × $65 = 1,625; 1,732.50 + 595 + 1,625 = $3.952.50; $3,952.50 × .95 = $3,754.875 = $3,754.88; $3,754.88 × .08 commission rate = $300.39).

Everyday Ethics

12. Accept all reasonable answers. Some students will think the sales policy is unfair to the salesperson who opened the account. Whether the practice is unethical is another question. If the policy was in effect before the situation occurred, then it would not be unethical. If the policy was established after the fact, then it may be considered unethical. Many executives justify these types of rules by saying the individual salesperson does not have the resources to manage such a large account. In addition, by having the account managed by an executive, the company is indicating to the customer the extent to which they value the account.

e-Marketing Skills

13. All reports should compare the two Web sites with regard to their effectiveness in providing customers with suggestions to complete their on-line purchase. For example, REI.com encourages the customers to purchase a lifetime $20 REI membership which entitles them to an annual refund that is typically 10 percent of qualifying purchases. However, there is no other suggestion selling. REI might consider placing ideas about related products, such as snowboard bindings, snowboard boots, and related gear.

EVALUATE

Build Academic Skills

Social Studies

14. Students should research the most recent recession and write about what two specific companies have done to help close sales. Student's responses will vary depending on the companies chosen. Many tech companies, for example, chose not to slash prices, because doing so tends to devalue the product in the consumer's eye. Instead, these companies chose to offer additional services, such as a longer warranties or free technical support. Kmart® advertised it was giving a 20 percent discount off 1,500 food and household items from Kmart's various store brands.

Science

15. Student answers will vary depending on the sites chosen, but students should evaluate the strategies used by the two sites to close sales and provide online customer support. Closing a sale online is typically a straightforward process. The customer opens the shopping cart, which contains the purchased items. The customer must supply needed information, such as a shipping address, payment method, shipping method, and so on. The customer may be asked if they have any coupons, special instructions, and so on. After all information is supplied, the customer submits the order and receives an on-screen thank you. In addition, a thank you e-mail is typically sent. This e-mail may contain a tracking number that lets the customer determine where the order is currently located in the shipping process. Many sites provide online help in which the customer can "chat" with a customer service representative to get answers to more specific questions.

Mathematics

16. Rounded up, the number of meetings would be 28. (21 + [21 × .30] = 27.3), rounded up to 28

Standardized Test Practice

1. D (Down selling—suggesting products the customer does not need)
2. False
3. trial

DECA Connection Role Play

Evaluations will be based on these performance indicators:

1. **Close the sale.** To close a sale, the salesperson must be able to judge the customer's readiness to buy, and determining which closing method will be most appropriate.
2. **Demonstrate suggestion selling.** When demonstrating suggestion selling, the salesperson offers other items to the customer that will ultimately save time and money or make the original purchase more appreciated and useful. Be sure to make recommendations from the customer's point of view, and be sure your suggestions are positive. When done correctly, suggestion selling improves customer satisfaction and increases sales, thereby enhancing revenues.
3. **Explain the role of customer service as a component of selling relationships.** Good customer service makes customers feel they made a wise buying decision. Making a sale is only the first step in maintaining and building a clientele. The order must be processed quickly and accurately; before the customer leaves, reaffirm the wisdom of the customer's decision; and later on, follow-up to make certain the order was delivered as promised.
4. **Explain key factors in building a clientele.** Key factors in building a clientele include ensuring that orders are processed and filled as promised, not making promises you cannot keep, following up to check on customer satisfaction, writing thank-you notes, etc.
5. **Plan follow-up strategies for use in selling.** Follow-up strategies include confirming delivery, calling the customer to explain any schedule changes or delays, and contacting customers after the purchase (and delivery) to check on their satisfaction with their selection, and sending a thank-you note with your business card attached.

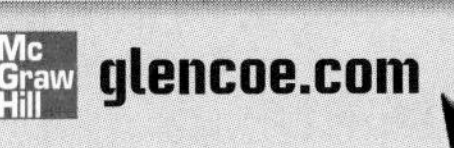

Role Plays For more DECA Role Plays, send students to the Online Learning Center to download the Competitive Events Workbook.

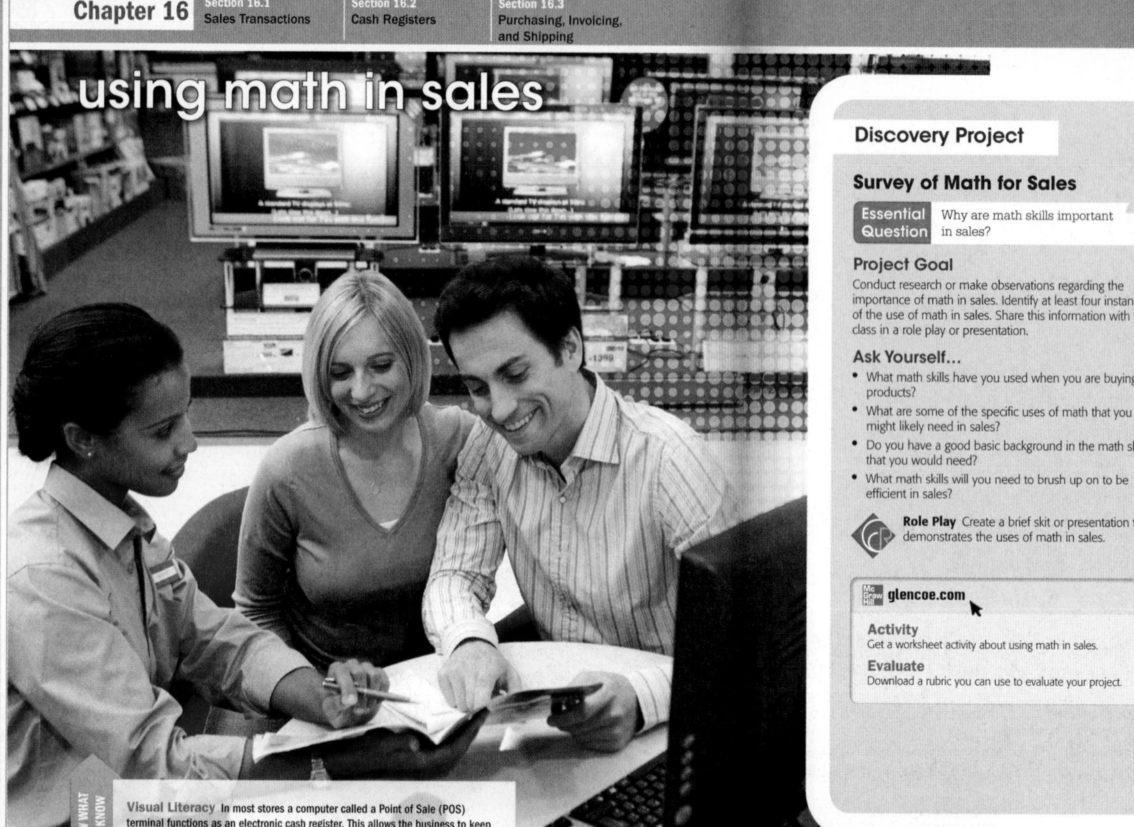

Chapter 16 | Section 16.1 Sales Transactions | Section 16.2 Cash Registers | Section 16.3 Purchasing, Invoicing, and Shipping

using math in sales

SHOW WHAT YOU KNOW

Visual Literacy In most stores a computer called a Point of Sale (POS) terminal functions as an electronic cash register. This allows the business to keep track of sales, inventory, and new merchandise. ***How many stores where you shop do not use electronic cash registers?***

Discovery Project

Survey of Math for Sales

Essential Question Why are math skills important in sales?

Project Goal

Conduct research or make observations regarding the importance of math in sales. Identify at least four instances of the use of math in sales. Share this information with your class in a role play or presentation.

Ask Yourself...

- What math skills have you used when you are buying products?
- What are some of the specific uses of math that you might likely need in sales?
- Do you have a good basic background in the math skills that you would need?
- What math skills will you need to brush up on to be efficient in sales?

Role Play Create a brief skit or presentation that demonstrates the uses of math in sales.

glencoe.com

Activity
Get a worksheet activity about using math in sales.

Evaluate
Download a rubric you can use to evaluate your project.

DECA Connection

DECA Event Role Play

Concepts in this chapter are related to DECA competitive events that involve either an interview or role play.

Performance Indicators The performance indicators represent key skills and knowledge. Your key to success in DECA competitive events is relating them to concepts in this chapter.

- Describe the use of technology in operations.
- Calculate miscellaneous charges.
- Select the best shipping method.
- Demonstrate systematic behavior.
- Organize information.

DECA Prep

Role Play Practice role-playing with the DECA Connection competitive-event activity at the end of this chapter. More information on DECA events can be found on DECA's Web site.

Chapter 16 · Using Math in Sales | 363

ENGAGE

Visual Literacy

Read the chapter opener photo caption question to students: ***How many stores where you shop do not use electronic cash registers?*** Answers will vary, but students will likely say that there are very few stores that do not use electronic cash registers. Ask: ***Which do you think would be more likely to use an electronic cash register: a local coffee shop or a chain coffee shop? Why?*** The chain store, because it can share information among branches and can afford the more expensive equipment. Then ask these guiding questions.

Guiding Questions

Calculate a Fraction You spent $25 of your $150 paycheck on snacks. What fraction is this?	$\frac{1}{6}$
Calculate a Percent You spent $25 of your $150 paycheck on snacks. What percent is this?	16.67 percent

Discovery Project

Survey of Math for Sales To help students understand why they need to hone their math skills, ask them the Discovery Project Essential Question: ***Why are math skills important in sales?*** Have the class come up with ways in which math is used in sales. Write these items on the board for students to view. Possible answers: calculating the total amount owed on sales checks, taxes, cost of an item on sale, employee salaries, and invoice and purchase order totals. Emphasize that even though today's electronic cash registers and business-oriented computer software can perform many of these math calculations automatically, there are still times when salespeople must rely on their own skills.

glencoe.com

Discovery Project Resources Send students to the Online Learning Center to download a rubric to evaluate their projects.

ENGAGE

Introduce the Chapter

Chapter 16 provides students with information on business transactions and the use of math in sales. These main concepts are introduced and discussed:

- Types of retail sales
- Sales tax
- Returns, exchanges, allowances
- Functions of cash registers
- Universal product codes
- Trends in business sales transactions
- Making change
- Purchase orders and invoices
- Delivery arrangements

Discussion Starter

Completing the Sales Transaction Ask students to think about what happens when they buy something. Ask: ***Do you pay cash, write a check, or use a debit card or credit card? What determines how you pay?*** Responses will vary. Students may say that they pay cash because they do not have a checking account or debit or credit card. Some may use debit cards or credit cards so they do not have to carry as much cash. The payment method may vary depending on the amount. For example, students may pay cash for small items but use debit cards for larger ones. Then ask: ***What do you do with your receipts? Why?*** Responses will vary. Many students will say they simply throw them away. Others may keep them in case they want to return the item or to get reimbursed by their parents. Tell students that this chapter will teach them more about sales transactions and the procedures used to perform them.

DECA Connection

Discuss the performance indicators listed in the DECA Connection feature. Explain to students that performance indicators tell them how to demonstrate their acquired skills and knowledge through individual or team competitive events.

 **glencoe.com** 

Competitive Events Workbook For more DECA Role Plays, send students to the Online Learning Center to download the Competitive Events Workbook.

PRINT RESOURCES

- **Student Edition**
- **Teacher Edition**
- **Student Activity Workbook with Academic Integration** includes worksheets and activities correlated to the text.
- **Mathematics for Marketing Workbook** provides math activities for every unit in the text.

TECHNOLOGY TOOLBOX

- **Connect**
- **ConnectPlus**
- **ExamView Assessment Suite** is a comprehensive solution for creating, administering, and scoring tests.

 **glencoe.com** 

Online Learning Center provides a variety of resources to enrich and enhance learning.

SECTION, CHAPTER, AND UNIT RESOURCES

- **Graphic Organizers** for organizing text concepts visually.
- **Digital Nation Activities** and **Green Marketer Activities** extend learning beyond the text features.
- **Career Chatroom Career Profiles** allow students to explore different marketing occupations in depth.
- **After You Read Answer Keys** for students to check their answers.
- **Discovery Project Rubrics** and **Marketing Internship Project Rubrics** for students to evaluate their projects.

PROGRAM RESOURCES

- **Student Activity Workbook with Academic Integration Teacher Annotated Edition** includes annotated answers for the activities and worksheets.
- **Marketing Research Project Workbook** provides a step-by-step approach for students to complete their own marketing research studies.
- **School-to-Career Activity Workbook** helps students relate their class work to on-the-job experience and involves work-site analysis and working with mentors.
- **Competitive Events Workbook** helps prepare students for state and national marketing education competitions.
- **Inclusion in the Marketing Education Classroom** provides teaching resources for working with students with special needs.
- **PowerPoint Presentations** provides visual teaching aids and assessments for this chapter.

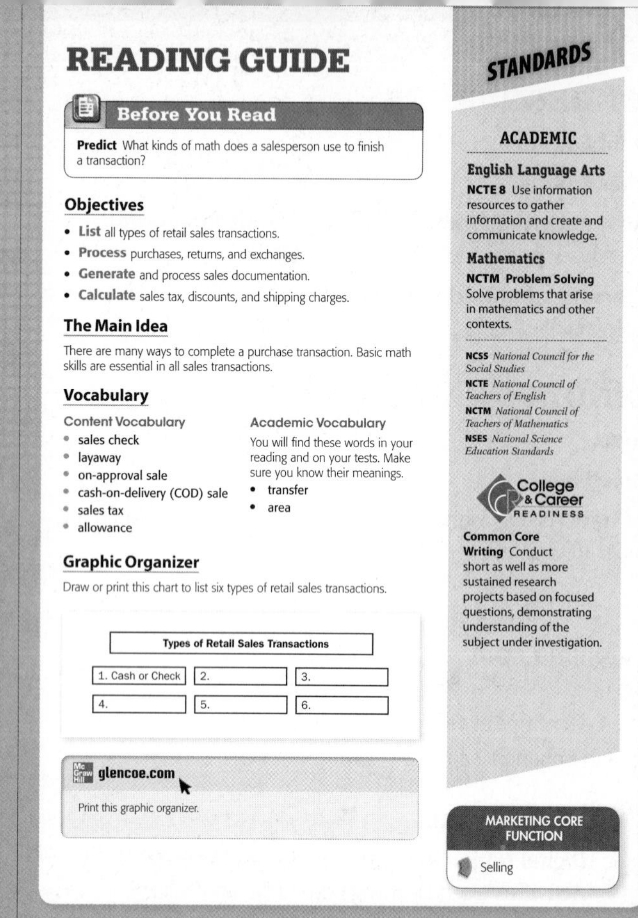

READING GUIDE

Before You Read

Predict What kinds of math does a salesperson use to finish a transaction?

Objectives

- **List** all types of retail sales transactions.
- **Process** purchases, returns, and exchanges.
- **Generate** and process sales documentation.
- **Calculate** sales tax, discounts, and shipping charges.

The Main Idea

There are many ways to complete a purchase transaction. Basic math skills are essential in all sales transactions.

Vocabulary

Content Vocabulary
- sales check
- layaway
- on-approval sale
- cash-on-delivery (COD) sale
- sales tax
- allowance

Academic Vocabulary

You will find these words in your reading and on your tests. Make sure you know their meanings.
- transfer
- area

Graphic Organizer

Draw or print this chart to list six types of retail sales transactions.

Types of Retail Sales Transactions		
1. Cash or Check	2.	3.
4.	5.	6.

glencoe.com

Print this graphic organizer.

STANDARDS

ACADEMIC

English Language Arts

NCTE 8 Use information resources to gather information and create and communicate knowledge.

Mathematics

NCTM Problem Solving Solve problems that arise in mathematics and other contexts.

NCSS *National Council for the Social Studies*
NCTE *National Council of Teachers of English*
NCTM *National Council of Teachers of Mathematics*
NSES *National Science Education Standards*

College & Career READINESS

Common Core
Writing Conduct short as well as more sustained research projects based on focused questions, demonstrating understanding of the subject under investigation.

MARKETING CORE FUNCTION

Selling

364 | Unit 5 · Selling

Section 16.1 Sales Transactions

TYPES OF RETAIL SALES

Most retail sales will use cash, debit, or credit card sales for consumer goods. However, you may deal with layaway (or will-call) sales, on-approval sales, and cash-on-delivery (COD) sales. You will also handle returns, exchanges, allowances, sales tax, and shipping charges.

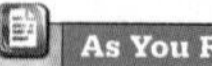

As You Read

Connect List the differences in handling various methods of payment.

CASH OR CHECK SALES

A cash sale is a transaction in which the customer pays with cash or a check. When the customer uses cash, you record the transaction on the register, give the customer change and a receipt, and wrap the item. When a customer writes a check, you may need to verify his or her identity by requesting a driver's license or another form of identification. You will have to learn the policy of your employer about accepting checks.

SALES CHECKS

A **sales check** is a written record of a sales transaction. It includes such information as the date of the transaction, the items purchased, the purchase prices, sales tax, and the total amount due. It is valuable to a customer as a receipt.

A complete sales check shows the customer's name, address, and phone number. It may have the time of the sale and the name of the salesperson. Handwritten sales checks are less common than printed ones. Some businesses still use them. The transaction is recorded in a sales-check book that has at least two copies of each form. One copy is given to the customer. One is kept by the business as a record of the sale.

MATH SKILLS FOR HANDWRITTEN SALES CHECKS

Math is necessary when preparing handwritten sales checks. The five steps of this process are shown in **Figure 16.1** on page 366. Occasionally, you will not be given a unit price, and you will need to calculate it on your own. This occurs when items are sold in multiple quantities, such as three reams of paper for $18. To find the selling price of one item in an instance like this, you divide the total price by the number of items: One ream of paper in this example would be $6 ($18 ÷ 3).

When the result of the division is uneven, any fraction of a cent is rounded up and charged to the customer. The price of one ream of paper when three reams are $16.99 is calculated as follows: $16.99 ÷ 3 = $5.6633 or $5.67.

"As a salesperson or cashier, you will handle several types of sales transactions."

DEBIT CARD SALES

Businesses that have an encrypted, or coded, personal identification number (PIN) pad can ask customers whether they would like to pay with debit or credit. Customers who choose "debit," key in their private PIN. The terminal then dials out and checks to see whether there are enough funds in the customer's account to pay for the sale. If so, the funds are transferred to the merchant's account. The customer does not need to sign a sales draft.

Chapter 16 · Using Math in Sales | 365

ENGAGE

Objectives

- **List** all types of retail sales transactions. cash, debit, credit card, layaway (will-call), on-approval, cash-on-delivery (COD)
- **Process** purchases, returns, and exchanges. Purchases: use cost per item, number of items, and sales tax (if any) to calculate total cost. Returns: determine amount paid and sales tax (if any). Give customer the money or a credit, as appropriate. Exchanges: calculate difference and either return that amount or obtain that amount from customer, as necessary.
- **Generate** and process sales documentation. Verify that the date of transaction, items purchased, purchase prices, sales tax, and total amount due are on sales documentation.
- **Calculate** sales tax, discounts, and shipping charges. Multiply discount by number of items, subtract from total; multiply total sales by tax rate; calculate shipping and add to total.

Anticipation Activity

Improving Student Achievement Divide the class into small groups of two or three. Have each group discuss their employers' policies (or ones they have observed as customers) about paying for purchases with each of the following: cash, checks, debit cards, or credit cards. Have the groups report their findings to the class.

Graphic Organizer

Types of Retail Sales Transactions		
1. Cash or Check	2. Debit	3. Credit card
4. Layaway	5. On-approval	6. Cash-on-delivery

iWB

Graphic Organizer Send students to the Online Learning Center to print this graphic organizer.

EXPLORE

Before You Read

Read the Before You Read question aloud: ***What kinds of math does a salesperson use to finish a transaction?*** Kinds of math can include addition, subtraction, multiplication, and division. Then ask: ***How do you think a salesperson's need for math has changed over the last 200 years? Why?*** Today's electronic cash registers perform math for the cashier; however, there may still be situations in which employees must do math by hand. Two hundred years ago, cashiers had to be fast and accurate at math because they had to perform calculations manually.

Preteaching Vocabulary

Have students go to the Online Learning Center at glencoe.com for the Chapter 16 Preteaching Vocabulary games.

Content Vocabulary

Tell students to write a multiple choice question for each of these three words. Have students answer one another's questions. The three terms are: layaway, on-approval sale, and cash-on-delivery (COD) sale. Students should write a multiple choice question for each of these words that demonstrates an understanding of each term.

Academic Vocabulary

Transfer—Alternate Meanings Explain to students that the word *transfer* can have several meanings. Write the following sentences. Have students come up with an appropriate meaning for each situation:

1. Please transfer the car seat to the minivan. meaning: *move, relocate*
2. Transfer the car title to the new owner. meaning: *hand over, sign over*
3. When manually processing a credit card, you can use a mechanical imprinter to transfer the customer's name and account number to the sales slip. meaning: *copy*

Area—Synonyms Remind students that a synonym is a word that has the same, or nearly the same, meaning as another word. Read aloud this sentence from the chapter: ***Removing merchandise from stock and keeping it in a separate storage area until the customer pays for it is called layaway.*** Ask students to list synonyms for *area* as it is used in this sentence. Possible answers: location, spot, section

Section 16.1 Sales Transactions

TYPES OF RETAIL SALES

Ask these guiding questions to focus the discussion on commonly available types of retail sales.

Guiding Questions

Explain When using a debit card, what must customers enter into the terminal?	their private PIN
Apply Give an example of a situation in which you might ask for an allowance when shopping at a retail store.	Answers will vary. Possible answer: I would ask for an allowance if a pair of boots had a broken or missing lace or the seam of a shirt had come partly unsewn.

As You Read

Read students the As You Read question: ***List the differences in handling various methods of payment.*** Cash: Cashier takes the money and gives the customer any change; Checks: Cashier must follow the store's procedures for accepting checks; Debit card: Customer must enter PIN; Credit card: Customer generally must sign.

Expert Advice

Read the quote to students:

> **"As a salesperson or cashier, you will handle several types of sales transactions."**

Ask students: ***Which of these types of payments do you think would be most difficult for a salesperson or cashier to handle: Cash, check, debit card, credit card? Why?*** Answers will vary. Possible answer: Cash, because the cashier must be careful to make the correct change and is held accountable if there is a mistake. Then ask: ***Which do you think is the easiest? Why?*** Answers will vary. Possible answer: Debit card, because the customer must enter a PIN, so the cashier does not have to do anything. In addition, the bank checks to make certain there are sufficient funds to cover the purchase.

FIGURE 16.1 Sales Check—Multiple Purchases

Adding Complexity The basic sales check becomes more complicated when the customer buys several items or several units of one item. ***How can you be sure that the final sales check is accurate?***

Step 1—Multiply unit price times quantity for each item and extend the amounts to the last column. Remember that the last two digits on the right are cents. Place a decimal point to their left, or enter them to the right of the vertical line dividing the last column into two unequal parts.

Step 2—Add item amounts to arrive at the merchandise subtotal. Enter this figure on the appropriate line.

Step 3—Calculate sales tax or look it up in a tax table. The buyer must pay sales tax on all retail sales totals. It is a percentage of the merchandise subtotal. In most states, food and prescription medicine are exempt from sales tax, as are shipping charges.

Step 4—Calculate shipping charges. You need to decide if you will use U.S. mail or a specific express mail carrier.

Step 5—Add subtotal, tax, and shipping to get the purchase total. This is the amount the customer will pay.

ODEL'S CAMERA, INC.
1329 Walnut Street • Santa Barbara, CA 93101

NEW CUSTOMER ☐ YES ☐ NO — DATE 6/17/--
NAME Joe Bundy
COMPANY The Daily Times
ADDRESS
CITY & STATE
PHONE (RESIDENCE) — PHONE (OTHER)
SOLD BY — TYPE OF SALE: CASH | CHECK ? | C.O.D. | CARD TYPE | ACCOUNT | PURCHASE ORDER NO.

CODE	QTY	DESCRIPTION	PRICE	AMOUNT	
6T	1	Olympus digital camera	399.00	399	00
4B	10	Batteries	2.80	28	00
	8	Cleaning cloths	3.00	24	00
			HANDLING	—	—
			SUB TOTAL	451	00
			TAX	31	57
			SHIPPING	—	—
			TOTAL AMOUNT	482	57
			PAID	500	00
			BALANCE	17	43
				7932	

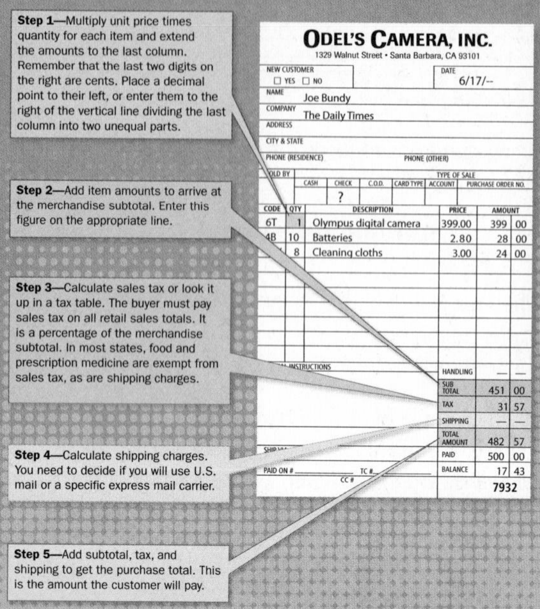

ADVANTAGES OF DEBIT CARD PAYMENTS

The bank that issues the debit card charges the merchant a flat rate per sale, such as $0.59 per sale, regardless of the amount of the sale. Debit cards are a convenience to many customers who prefer not to use a credit card. It also benefits those who do not carry either a checkbook or large amounts of cash or who cannot get approval for a credit card. Most merchants prefer payment by debit card to payment by check because they have access to the money much sooner. There is also no risk of delays in payment due to insufficient funds. The cost to the merchant is less than when the customer pays with a credit card.

CREDIT CARD SALES

Statistics show that by accepting credit cards, businesses can increase sales by as much as 40 percent. Primarily because of this potential for increased sales, most businesses today accept one or more of the major credit cards. These cards are Visa®, MasterCard®, American Express®, and Discover®.

CREDIT CARD PAYMENT ON THE INTERNET

Credit cards are also the most frequently used method of payment for Internet purchases. For safety reasons, the payment data (card number, expiration date, security code, cardholder's identity) sent via the Internet are encrypted. This makes it more difficult for unauthorized individuals to gain access to a customer's card numbers. Many Internet sites also allow the consumer to make purchases with a gift certificate that has a security code the customer must enter.

CREDIT CARD PAYMENT COSTS TO THE MERCHANT

If a company accepts credit cards, it pays a fee to the bank or agency that handles the billing and recordkeeping for each card transaction processed. This fee is a percentage of credit sales based on a sliding scale, which means that it varies according to the size of the store account and how the charges are processed.

Suppose one store had Visa sales of $100,000 in one month and another store had Visa sales of only $2,000 in that same month. The company with the sales of $100,000 would pay a smaller percentage for handling.

DIGITAL NATION

Making Online Purchases Safe

Identity theft and credit card theft are concerns for many online shoppers. In fact, a 2009 study showed that half of all shoppers have abandoned an online order because they were worried that an online retail Web site might not be secure. This represents billions of dollars in lost sales.

Encryption and Secure Connections Reputable online businesses transmit customers' personal and financial information using encryption, or data scrambling. Only authorized users who have the correct "key" can unscramble the data. Data security "trustmarks," such as those from TRUSTe and VeriSign, demonstrate that an online store is secure against data theft. Secure e-commerce sites also use an "HTTP secure" connection. A Web page with a secure connection for purchases has the letters "https" at the beginning of its Web address.

English Language Arts

Evaluate Visit an e-commerce Web site. What information does the company offer about its security practices? Place an item in the shopping cart and look for trustmarks on the checkout page. Does the site seem secure? Discuss your findings with the class.

glencoe.com

Get a Digital Nation Activity.

EXPLAIN

Visual Literacy

Figure 16.1 Caption Answer Read the caption question to students: ***How can you be sure that the final sales check is accurate?*** You can double-check your math, either on paper or with a calculator. Ask students: ***How is the subtotal different from the total?*** The total has the sales tax and shipping charges, if any, added to it. Then ask students: ***What does the amount listed under BALANCE indicate?*** amount of money that should be returned to the customer

Mini Project

Differentiated Instruction

Interpersonal Learners Bring to class or create several examples of sales checks. Divide students into groups and have them label the parts of one of the sales checks. Have students share their labeled sales checks with the class. Each group should label all appropriate components of their sales check, including information such as date of transaction, items purchased, purchase prices, sales tax, and the total amount due.

Critical Thinking

Ask students: ***Is it better to pay for purchases using cash or credit?*** Ask students to explain their responses. Reasons will vary. Possible advantages to using cash: You do not have to worry about sending a check to the credit card company, and you do not have to worry about accumulating a larger bill than you are able to pay. Possible advantages to using a credit card: You do not have to carry cash, which can be lost or stolen; you can establish a credit record if you make such purchases responsibly.

Reading: Strategic Readers

Go to the Online Learning Center to view a video clip in which an author discusses the characteristics of strategic readers.

ELABORATE

ADVANTAGES OF DEBIT CARD PAYMENTS

Ask these guiding questions to focus the discussion on the advantages of debit cards.

Guiding Questions

Recall What charges does a merchant pay when a customer uses a debit card?	The bank that issued the debit card charges the merchant a flat fee, such as $0.59 per sale.
Analyze Why might you choose to pay for your purchases with a debit card rather than paying with cash?	Possible answer: to avoid having to carry around large amounts of cash. If cash is lost or stolen, it cannot be replaced; a debit card offers a certain amount of security.
Apply You manage a small bookstore and are deciding whether to accept debit cards. You currently accept only cash or checks. Would you start accepting debit cards? Why or why not?	Sample answer: Yes, because I would have access to the money more quickly than with a check and there would be no risk of insufficient funds. In addition, accepting debit cards would be a convenience for my customers.

CREDIT CARD SALES

Discuss with students that credit cards are a fast, convenient way of paying for purchases. Ask these guiding questions to focus the discussion on credit card sales.

Guiding Questions

Explain What is the main reason for a business to accept credit cards?	Sales can increase up to 40 percent.
Analyze Why are credit cards the most common method of paying for Internet purchases?	It is easy to send the needed information online, and no money or printed documents need to change hands.
Infer Why do you think merchants are charged a flat fee for debit card usage whereas they must pay a percentage based on a sliding scale for credit card usage?	Possible answer: The debit card charge is based on processing costs incurred by the bank. However, with a credit card, money is actually being loaned to the customer.

DIGITAL NATION

English Language Arts Answer
Students should discuss their findings concerning the security of a specific e-commerce Web site. The discussion will vary depending on the site chosen. For example, Amazon.com states that it uses Secure Sockets Layer (SSL) software to encrypt information that is input by customers. In addition, it protects credit card numbers by using only the last four digits when confirming the order and prevents unauthorized access to an account by requiring a password. The shopping cart Web page has a "lock" symbol in the lower-right corner and the letters "https" at the beginning of its address. All of these features signal a secure Web site.

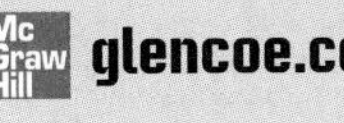

Worksheet Activity Send students to the Online Learning Center to get a Digital Nation worksheet activity.

Mini Project

Differentiated Instruction

Visual Learners Have students ask their parents or other adults to estimate the percentage of purchases they make using cash, check, debit card, and credit card. Students should work individually to create a pie chart illustrating these results. The pie chart should be appropriately titled and labeled. Students may want to use a spreadsheet program to create their charts. When completed, have students share their results with the class. Students should create a clearly-labeled pie chart that shows the percentage of purchases the chosen adults made with cash, check, debit card, or credit card.

HOW ARE CREDIT CARD PAYMENTS PROCESSED?

For many businesses, the amount of each credit card sale is electronically deposited in the business's bank account as the sale is made. A credit card sales check, or receipt, is issued by the cash register. The credit card company deducts its service charges from the store's bank account.

Practice 1: Credit Card Fees

Calculate the impact credit card fees would have on the business described below.

1. At Carol's Pearls and Stones, Visa sales are usually between $13,000 and $15,000 per month. The Visa handling charge is a sliding scale. For $10,000 to $14,999, it charges 3 percent of sales; for $15,000 to $19,999, 2.5 percent; and for $20,000 to $29,999, 2 percent. That means that for a purchase of $22,000, Visa collects a fee of 3 percent on the first $14,999, a fee of 2.5 percent on the next $5,000, and a fee of 2 percent on the remaining $2,001. Visa collects a total of $614.97.
   a. Carol had $15,500 in Visa sales in one month. How much more did she earn than if sales had been $14,300?
   b. How much would Carol have earned in that month if her shop had made $21,000 in Visa sales?
2. Carol has decided to accept the Diners Club card at her shop. The handling charges are 1 percent higher than those for Visa at each sales level. If Carol had $19,000 in Diners Club sales, how much more would she pay in handling fees than she would have for the same amount in Visa sales?
3. Carol had $13,600 in cash sales, $14,800 in Diners Club sales, and $15,200 in Visa sales one month. What were her net sales after handling charges?

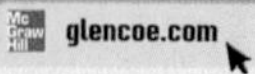
glencoe.com

Check your answers to all Practice sets.

The store normally has access to the customers' payment funds the next day. However, some businesses opt to have credit card fees deducted monthly.

Today businesses rarely take manual credit card slips to the bank. Most businesses process manual credit card sales over the phone, using an automated system provided by their bank. This can also be done by keying in the credit card and sales information directly into their credit card terminal.

GETTING CREDIT AUTHORIZATION

While credit cards are a convenient alternative to more traditional forms of payment, some fraud is always possible. Many retail businesses set a floor limit, a maximum amount a customer is allowed to charge to a credit card. This practice protects them against losses due to the use of stolen or fake credit cards. Illicit charges are disputed by the true cardholder and the credit card company. The store is liable for only the amount of the floor limit.

Fraud Users of stolen credit cards test the card by making small purchases, a practice that can alert the company that the card may have been stolen.

Most modern cash registers include an integrated credit authorizer. An electronic credit authorizer can also be a device that reads data encoded on credit cards. The sales clerk inputs the amount of the sale into the device. The data is then transmitted to a computer, which returns an approval or disapproval in less than a minute.

RECORDING CREDIT OR DEBIT CARD SALES

As a salesperson in retail business, you will probably process many credit card sales. If the transaction is manual, you write the information on the sales check by hand or use a mechanical imprinter to **transfer** the customer's name and account number to the sales slip. You give one copy to the customer and keep one for the seller. Another copy goes to the bank or credit card agency. Electronic recording of credit card sales is so common that it has almost completely replaced manually prepared sales checks.

LAYAWAY SALES

Removing merchandise from stock and keeping it in a separate storage **area** until the customer pays for it is called **layaway**, or will-call. The customer makes a deposit on the merchandise and agrees to pay for the purchase within a certain time period. The customer receives the merchandise when the bill is fully paid. If it is not paid for within the time period, the goods are returned to stock. The deposit is not refunded.

ON-APPROVAL SALES

An **on-approval sale** is an agreement that allows a customer to take merchandise (usually clothing) home for further consideration. Some department and specialty stores extend this special privilege to their regular customers. If the goods are not returned within an agreed-upon time, the sale is final. The customer must then send a check or return to the store to pay for the merchandise. Credit card information may be taken from the customer so that the sale can be processed if the customer decides to keep the item. This is a safe way for retailers to handle on-approval sales because there is much less risk involved.

CASH-ON-DELIVERY SALES

A **cash-on-delivery (COD) sale** is a sales transaction that occurs when a customer pays for merchandise at the time of delivery. Because the customer must be present to receive the merchandise being delivered, COD sales are not as efficient as other types of sales transactions.

Reading Check

Summarize What are the different types of retail sales transactions?

FIGURE 16.2 Refund Slip

Refund Policy Most businesses give customers refunds or exchanges under certain circumstances. ***Why do stores often insist that customers have a sales receipt before giving a refund?***

BFF Fashions — REFUND SLIP

STORE NO.	DATE	ITEM RETURNED	AMOUNT
	2---	SKIRT	45 00
NAME Stacy McClintock			
ADDRESS 777 Seaview Lane			
CITY & STATE Marblehead, MA 01945			
TELEPHONE NO. 781-882-0252		TAX	3 15
CUSTOMER'S SIGNATURE Stacy McClintock		TOTAL AMOUNT	48 15
EMPLOYEE NO. 6P	AUTHORIZED BY G. Smith	REASON FOR RETURN Wrong color	

No refunds after 30 days; No refunds without receipt

368 | Unit 5 · Selling

Chapter 16 · Using Math in Sales | 369

EXPLAIN

Answers to Practice 1

1. a. $1,166.50; b. $20,405.01
2. $190.00
3. $42,553

Fraud Ask a volunteer to read aloud the Hot Topic statement. Ask students: ***Based on this information, what can credit card holders do to reduce their chances of being the victims of fraud?***

Mini Project

Extension

Researching Credit Card Offers Have students conduct research to learn about available credit cards. Students should work individually to choose one of these credit cards to investigate. They should determine the requirements for obtaining the card and the period in which payment must be made in order to avoid interest payments. Students also should determine what interest rate will be charged on any balance that is not paid within the specified time. When completed, have the class share what they learned. The class should work to determine which of the cards they believe offers the consumer the best deal. Students should share the results of their research on a particular card by explaining the requirements for obtaining the card, when payment is due in order to avoid interest payments, and the interest rate on any remaining balance. Students should work together to evaluate the various cards.

ELABORATE

Reinforce Vocabulary

Layaway—Examine Word Components Write the word *layaway* for students to view. Tell students that dividing a word into components can help in determining its meaning. Ask: ***What two words are contained in layaway?*** *lay* and *away* Explain that these two words might lead you to believe that layaway involves putting something aside for a special purpose. In fact, it means to place aside merchandise until the buyer pays for it in full.

Graphic Organizer

Display this table and ask volunteers to fill in the advantages and disadvantages of the various types of retail sales.

Type of Retail Sale	Advantages	Disadvantages
Cash	Customer: Won't overspend Retailer: Gets money immediately	Customer: May need to carry large amounts of cash Retailer: Must handle cash
Debit card	Customer: Won't overspend Retailer: Receives money immediately	Customer: Money taken from account immediately Retailer: Must pay a fee
Credit card	Customer: Billed later Retailer: Increases sales	Customer: May overspend Retailer: Must pay percentage
Layaway	Customer: Only pays a deposit Retailer: Keeps merchandise until entirely paid for	Customer: Doesn't get merchandise immediately Retailer: Must store items until paid for
On-approval	Customer: Has more time to make a decision Retailer: Provides a service to customers	Customer: Must return merchandise if decides not to buy Retailer: Does not get money until later and the merchandise may be returned
Cash-on-delivery	Customer: Does not pay until delivery Retailer: Provides a service to customers	Customer: Must pay a fee Retailer: Does not receive payment until delivery

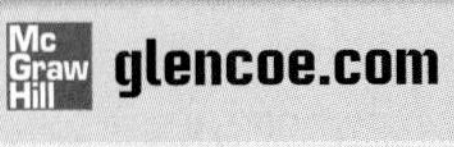

iWB

Graphic Organizer Send students to the Online Learning Center to print this graphic organizer.

Visual Literacy

Figure 16.2 Caption Answer Read the caption question to students: ***Why do stores often insist that customers have a sales receipt before giving a refund?*** Possible answers: to verify that the item was not stolen; the customer might have purchased the item at a different store; the item might have been on sale, in which case the store would only refund the sale price. Ask: ***Why do you think it is important for businesses to keep track of the reasons items are returned?*** So businesses can track customer likes and dislikes; so they can check to see if the item is defective in some way.

Critical Thinking

Describe for students the owner of a local jewelry store who spends considerable time collecting state sales tax. Competing businesses on the Internet do not charge sales tax. Ask students: ***How do you think the owner feels about this situation?*** The owner would feel that the Internet businesses have an unfair advantage. Encourage students to debate this complex topic.

Mini Project

Enrichment

Learning about State Sales Tax Have students work independently to research your state's (or another state of your choosing) sales tax. Students should then write a paragraph explaining the tax percentage, any exempt items, and so on. Paragraphs should explain the sales tax rate along with any exempt items, such as food and clothing.

VIRTUAL BUSINESS

PURCHASING

Introduce students to the concept of purchasing using Knowledge Matters' Virtual Business Retailing visual simulation, *Purchasing*. In this simulation, students will learn that purchasing inventory for a store is an important and complicated job.

SALES TAX

A **sales tax** is a percentage fee imposed by the government on the retail price of an item or service. Sales tax rates differ from state to state. State taxes are sometimes combined with local charges.

WHO PAYS SALES TAX?

Sales tax is paid only by the final user, or the individual customer who, in most cases, is also the consumer. It does not apply to goods bought for resale. Consumers pay the cost of sales taxes.

A sales tax is a regressive tax. This means that the tax rate decreases as the amount subject to taxation increases. It is assessed at a flat rate that applies to persons of all income levels. Thus, a low-income person and a person with a higher income may pay the same sales tax on the same item, but the lower-income person is paying a higher percentage of his or her income in making the purchase. For this reason, some states exempt certain items, such as food, clothing, or medication from sales tax. Sales to the U.S. government are never subject to sales tax.

SALES TAX ON THE INTERNET

In the past several years, Internet sales have soared, and some states feel that they should have an easier time collecting tax on all state-to-state sales, including online sales.

The government does not want to put unreasonable burdens on small businesses that sell goods and services through the Internet. Most of these mom-and-pop businesses do not have the computer software needed to apply each state's unique tax policies to every transaction. But then states complain that they cannot expect residents to keep perfect records of all their Internet transactions and then to voluntarily pay the states the taxes that are owed. If a company does not have a physical presence (buildings, offices) in a state, then it is not required to collect sales taxes on retail purchaes to customers in that state. Legislation is periodically considered that would establish an Internet sales tax collection system.

RETURNS, EXCHANGES, AND ALLOWANCES

A return is merchandise brought back for a cash refund or credit. Most businesses are happy to make exchanges because they want their customers to be satisfied. (See **Figure 16.2** on page 369.)

An **allowance** is a partial return of the sale price for merchandise that the customer has kept. These are usually given when there is a defect in the merchandise, such as a missing button.

Each of these situations requires a different type of sales transaction. Some businesses adopt a policy of no returns. However, most believe that accepting returns is an important part of good customer relations. Some businesses accept returns but only offer store credit. This credit can be used to pay for other merchandise from the same business instead of a cash refund. A transaction that involves returning an item for a replacement with the same price is an even exchange.

HANDLING SALES TAX FOR RETURN OR EXCHANGE TRANSACTIONS

Suppose Carmen decides that she wants a less expensive computer than the one she just received for her birthday. The original computer was priced at $1,149 (plus sales tax of 8.75 percent). Carmen wants to exchange it for one priced at $895. To handle this transaction, you refund the difference, $254, plus the sales tax on $254. This procedure is reversed for a customer who wants to exchange an item for one that is more expensive. The customer pays the extra cost and tax of the item.

Consider how a sales check is prepared. Each item is not taxed individually in multiple purchases. Instead, the subtotal is used to calculate the sales tax. First, find the item being returned and calculate the difference between that item and the item the customer is taking in exchange. Then determine the difference in tax on the two amounts. Tax is due only on the difference between the two items.

PRACTICE 2

How much will be returned to or paid by the customer in each of the following cases? Assume a sales tax rate of 7 percent.

1. Mr. Williams returned a $330 lamp that did not produce enough light. He chose another style priced at $225. How much will you return to him?
2. Mrs. Crawford returned a $159 printer because it was defective. She chose another model priced at $229. How much more will you charge her?

SHIPPING CHARGES

Not all purchases can be bought and carried home: Some items may be too bulky, and others are purchased via the telephone or the Internet. Shipping is necessary and adds separate charges. Because delivery charges are generally exempt from sales tax, they are added after the sales tax has been calculated. The cost of shipping merchandise depends on the service used, the weight of the shipment, and the distance it is being shipped.

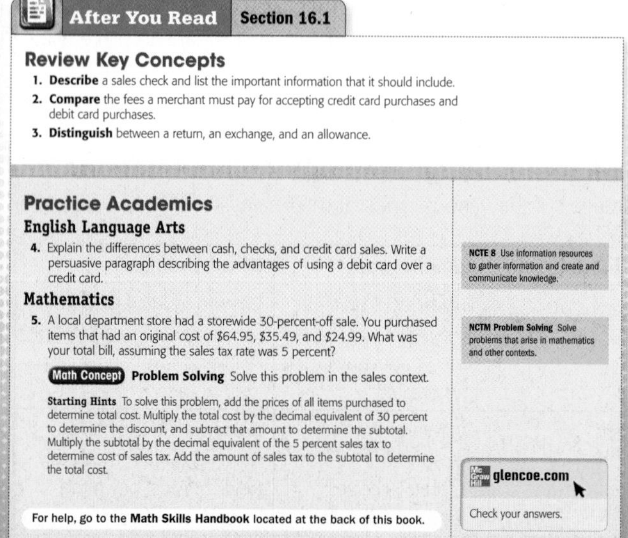

After You Read | **Section 16.1**

Review Key Concepts

1. **Describe** a sales check and list the important information that it should include.
2. **Compare** the fees a merchant must pay for accepting credit card purchases and debit card purchases.
3. **Distinguish** between a return, an exchange, and an allowance.

Practice Academics

English Language Arts

4. Explain the differences between cash, checks, and credit card sales. Write a persuasive paragraph describing the advantages of using a debit card over a credit card.

NCTE 8 Use information resources to gather information and create and communicate knowledge.

Mathematics

5. A local department store had a storewide 30-percent-off sale. You purchased items that had an original cost of $64.95, $35.49, and $24.99. What was your total bill, assuming the sales tax rate was 5 percent?

NCTM Problem Solving Solve problems that arise in mathematics and other contexts.

Math Concept **Problem Solving** Solve this problem in the sales context.

Starting Hints To solve this problem, add the prices of all items purchased to determine total cost. Multiply the total cost by the decimal equivalent of 30 percent to determine the discount, and subtract that amount to determine the subtotal. Multiply the subtotal by the decimal equivalent of the 5 percent sales tax to determine cost of sales tax. Add the amount of sales tax to the subtotal to determine the total cost.

For help, go to the **Math Skills Handbook** located at the back of this book.

glencoe.com

Check your answers.

ELABORATE

SALES TAX

Ask these guiding questions to focus the discussion on sales tax.

Guiding Questions

Analyze Why is sales tax considered a regressive tax?	It is charged at a flat rate. Low-income people pay at the same rate as those with a higher income.
Evaluate Many states have tax-free periods before the beginning of school in the fall. During this period, consumers may be able to purchase school supplies, clothing, computers, and so on, without paying state sales tax. Do you think this is a good idea? Why or why not?	Answers will vary. Sample answer: Yes, because it helps low-income families to save money when purchasing the items their children need for school.

Critical Thinking

Discuss the rules involving sales tax on the Internet. In most cases, a business is only required to collect state sales tax if it has one or more brick-and-mortar stores in that state. Consumers are supposed to report their Internet purchases to the state and voluntarily pay sales tax on these items. Ask students: ***Do you think most consumers voluntarily pay sales tax on Internet purchases? Why?*** Possible answer: No, most will not pay sales tax because they know that the state will not force them to pay.

Reinforce Vocabulary

Allowance—Alternate Meanings Ask students: ***What do you think the word*** allowance ***means?*** Possible answer: a sum of money regularly given to an individual, such as a weekly allowance. Explain that while this definition is correct, allowance also has another meaning: a reduction from a list price or other stated price. Retailers often grant allowances when there is relatively minor damage to goods.

EVALUATE

SHIPPING CHARGES

Because shipping charges can significantly increase the cost of an item, it is important to understand them. Ask students these guiding questions to focus the discussion on shipping charges.

Guiding Questions

Recall What three factors determine the cost of shipping an item?	the service used, the weight of the shipment, and the distance it is being sent
Analyze What is the main reason that the use of shipping for consumer-purchased goods has increased dramatically over the last 20 years?	Internet purchases

Mini Project

Enrichment

Investigating Shipping Costs for Online Purchases Have each student select an online store and find out how that store calculates shipping costs. Students should learn about the different shipping options the store offers and how the costs of these options vary. Ask students to present their findings to the class. Answers will vary depending on which online stores students investigated. Students should present their findings concerning the shipping options available at the online store they chose. They should explain each option and its costs, and compare these costs.

Answers to Practice 2

1. $112.35
2. $74.90

After You Read Section 16.1

Review Key Concepts

1. A sales check is a written record of a sales transaction and should include information such as the date of the transaction, the items purchased, the purchase prices, sales tax, and the total amount due.
2. For a debit card, the bank charges the merchant a flat fee, regardless of the amount. With credit cards, the merchant pays a percentage of the sale based on a sliding scale which varies based on the size of the store account and how the charges are processed.
3. Return: merchandise brought back for a cash refund or credit. Exchange: merchandise switched for another item. Allowance: A partial return of the sale price for merchandise that the customer has kept, often because of a minor defect.

Practice Academics

English Language Arts

4. Cash involves the customer giving money in exchange for the purchase. When writing checks, customers are instructing their bank to transfer the specified amount from the customer's bank account. In a credit card transaction, the amount is added to the customer's monthly credit card bill. With credit cards, when the money is transferred to the business's account varies, but it may be transferred as the sale is made. Students should write a persuasive paragraph describing the advantages of a debit card over a credit card. The primary advantage is that the customer cannot overspend. With a debit card, customers are using their own money rather than borrowing money from a credit card company.

Mathematics

5. $92.19 ($64.95 + 35.49 +24.99) × 0.70 × 1.05

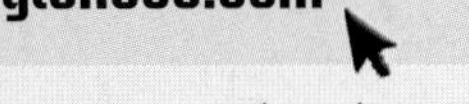

Answer Key Send students to the Online Learning Center to check their answers.

READING GUIDE

Before You Read

Predict What are some functions performed by cash registers and point-of-sale terminals?

Objectives

- **Name** the functions of cash registers and point-of-sale (POS) terminals.
- **Explain** the uses for Universal Product Codes (UPCs).
- **Make** change.

The Main Idea

The cash register or point-of-sale (POS) station is a cashier's most important tool in completing a sales transaction.

Vocabulary

Content Vocabulary
- Universal Product Code (UPC)
- point-of-sale (POS) system
- till
- opening cash fund

Academic Vocabulary

You will find these words in your reading and on your tests. Make sure you know their meanings.
- automatically
- concentrate

Graphic Organizer

Draw or print this chart to list three methods of entering information into an electronic cash register and three safeguards against theft.

Electronic Cash Registers		
Methods of Entering Information		
1.	2.	3.
Safeguards Against Theft/Counterfeiting		
1.	2.	3.

glencoe.com

Print this graphic organizer.

STANDARDS

ACADEMIC

English Language Arts

NCTE 1 Read texts to acquire new information.

Mathematics

NCTM Number and Operations Understand numbers, ways of representing numbers, relationships among numbers, and number systems.

NCSS *National Council for the Social Studies*
NCTE *National Council of Teachers of English*
NCTM *National Council of Teachers of Mathematics*
NSES *National Science Education Standards*

College & Career READINESS

Common Core
Reading Integrate and evaluate content presented in diverse formats and media, including visually and quantitatively, as well as in words.

MARKETING CORE FUNCTION

Selling

me. Section 16.2 Cash Registers

CASH REGISTERS AND THEIR MAIN FUNCTIONS

After the sale of a product or service is finalized, the sale is considered closed. In most businesses, cash registers can perform the function of recording the closed sale.

All cash registers, from the simplest to the most complex, perform these three basic sales transaction functions:

1. **Recording sales** Cash registers provide a convenient way to enter information about a sale. This usually includes the department, the type of transaction, the salesperson, the amount of the sale, and the form of payment (cash, check, credit card, debit card, or gift certificate). The salesperson also enters the amount of money given by the customer. The cash register computes the amount of change that the customer receives.
2. **Storing cash and sales documents** Cash registers provide a convenient, organized way to keep cash, personal checks, credit sales checks, and refund slips. Coupons and other sales-related documents may also be kept in the cash register drawer.
3. **Providing receipts** Cash registers **automatically** provide a receipt for the customer. This is the customer's record of the sale and proof of payment. Customers are advised to hold on to sales receipts in the event that they might want to return an item for refund or exchange. Sales receipts are also used by customers who may be able to write off certain purchases on their income taxes.

As You Read

Contrast List the key differences between the methods of recording sales.

THE ELECTRONIC CASH REGISTER

Most businesses today utilize sophisticated electronic cash registers that perform multiple functions in addition to the three basic functions of recording sales, storing cash and sales documents, and providing receipts. These may include figuring sales tax, calculating discounts, subtracting and crediting returns, determining the amount due back to the customer, tracking inventory, and, in some instances, automatically reordering stock.

> "For accounting and tax purposes, a closed sale must be recorded."

ENTERING DATA INTO AN ELECTRONIC CASH REGISTER

Salespeople can enter transaction data into an electronic cash register in several ways:

- **Optical scanning** Supermarkets and other retailers have improved their efficiency in recording sales transactions by installing optical scanners at checkout counters. Salespeople drag items across a scanner that can read the bar codes on the product packaging. If the scanner cannot read a code, the salesperson must key the information manually. Some retailers have installed scanners that customers can use to scan the items they are purchasing.
- **Electronic wand entry** Many retailers (especially department and clothing stores) use electronic wands to enter sales transactions. The salesperson moves the point of the wand across the data printed on a tag attached to the product.

ENGAGE

Objectives

- **Name** the functions of cash registers and point-of-sales (POS) terminals. cash registers: recording sales, storing cash and sales documents, providing receipts; POS terminals: same as cash registers, except they also capture information about the transactions and apply it to different functions
- **Explain** the uses for Universal Product Codes (UPCs). update inventory, maintain customer information for credit checking and marketing
- **Make** change. Start at the amount of the purchase. Count out the amount to yourself. As you give the change to the customer, announce the starting amount, hand each coin or bill and announce the new amount.

Anticipation Activity

Improving Student Achievement Bring several empty boxes to class to serve as "cash drawers" and a sufficient supply of "play" coins and currency. Have students count out the opening cash funds for each draw. Suggest $100 in coins and currency. Have students work in groups to set up their drawers and practice cash payments.

Graphic Organizer

Electronic Cash Registers		
Methods of Entering Information		
1. Optical scanning	2. Electronic wand entry	3. Manual key entry
Safeguards Against Theft/Counterfeiting		
1. Close cash drawer between transactions	2. Lock drawer when leaving it	3. Become familiar with currency

glencoe.com iWB

Graphic Organizer Send students to the Online Learning Center to print this graphic organizer.

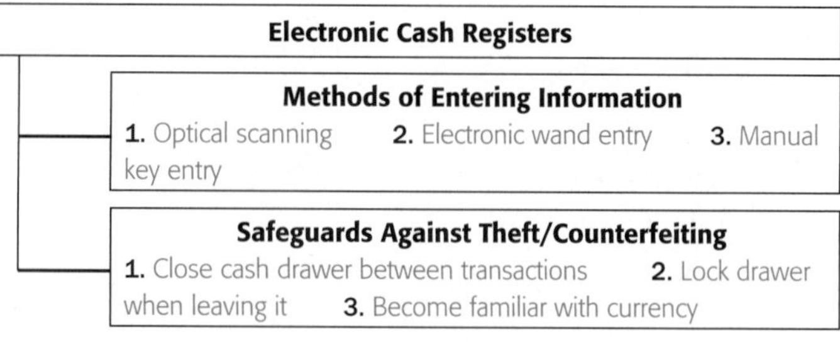

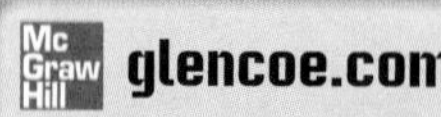

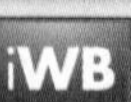

EXPLORE

Before You Read

Read the Before You Read question aloud: ***What are some functions performed by cash registers and point-of-sale terminals?*** recording sales, storing cash and various sales documents such as credit card receipts; providing receipts for customers; calculating sales tax and discounts; determining change owed to customer; tracking inventory Then ask students: ***What invention led to the capabilities of today's electronic cash registers?*** the invention of the computer and its integration with the functions of a traditional cash register

Preteaching Vocabulary

Have students go to the Online Learning Center at glencoe.com for the Chapter 16 Preteaching Vocabulary games.

Content Vocabulary

Divide the class into five teams. Assign each team one of the four Content Vocabulary terms. Have teams predict the meaning of their term and write the prediction for the class to view. Keep this list displayed so students can see how close their definitions were to the actual definitions as they work through the chapter.

Academic Vocabulary

Automatically—Using Suffixes Explain that *automatic* means "acting spontaneously or unconsciously." Write *automatically* for students to view, and underline the *-ly*. Explain that the suffix *-ly* means "having the characteristics of." Therefore, the adverb *automatically* means "having the characteristics of being done spontaneously or without conscious thought."

Concentrate—Denotative Meaning Read aloud this sentence to the students: ***You need to concentrate when making change.*** In this case, *concentrate* means "pay close attention" or "focus." Explain that *concentrate* is used in other ways that also have the same general meaning of "focusing." Read this sentence: ***The Vietnamese population is concentrated around Mount Pleasant.*** Explain that in this case, concentrated means "focused around" or "centered around."

PROFESSIONAL DEVELOPMENT **MINI CLIP**

ELL: Content Vocabulary
Go to the Online Learning Center to view a video clip in which a teacher provides students with opportunities to practice their academic vocabulary.

Section 16.2

Cash Registers

CASH REGISTERS AND THEIR MAIN FUNCTIONS

Present these guiding questions to focus the discussion on cash registers and their functions.

Guiding Questions

Analyze How do electronic cash registers simplify reordering stock?	They can keep track and total the items purchased and make this information available for reordering. Some systems will even automatically contact vendors to reorder items based on customer purchases.
Solve Problems What problem might a home improvement store have if the store used scanners that required each item to be dragged across them? How could this problem be overcome?	Some items might be too large or heavy to be dragged across the scanner bed. Hand-held scanners can overcome this problem.

As You Read

Read the As You Read question aloud: ***List the key differences between the methods of recording sales.*** Methods of recording sales include dragging a product across a scanner to read its barcode, using electronic wands to access data printed on packaging or on tags attached to products, or manually entering sales transactions, often by keying in the Universal Product Code.

Expert Advice

Read the quote to students:

"For accounting and tax purposes, a closed sale must be recorded."

Ask students: ***In this quote, what does the word* closed *mean?*** completed, finished Then ask: ***What might happen in a store where, because of cashier error, about 5 percent of sales were not recorded?*** The business's accounting would be wrong. This would make it impossible to determine gross sales, keep track of inventory, spot sales trends, calculate the sales tax owed to the state government, and so on.

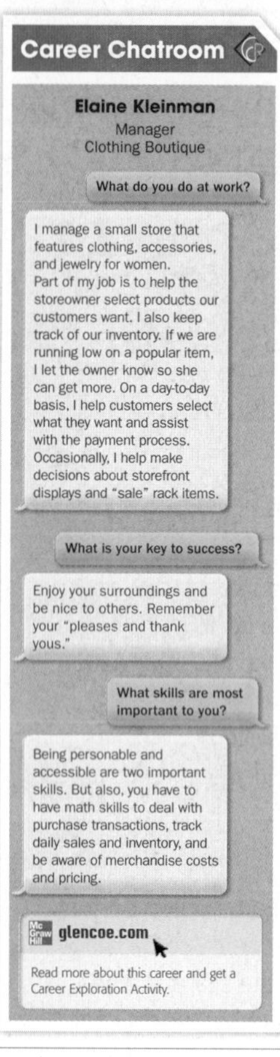

Career Chatroom
Elaine Kleinman
Manager
Clothing Boutique
What do you do at work?
I manage a small store that features clothing, accessories, and jewelry for women. Part of my job is to help the storeowner select products our customers want. I also keep track of our inventory. If we are running low on a popular item, I let the owner know so she can get more. On a day-to-day basis, I help customers select what they want and assist with the payment process. Occasionally, I help make decisions about storefront displays and "sale" rack items.
What is your key to success?
Enjoy your surroundings and be nice to others. Remember your "pleases and thank yous."
What skills are most important to you?
Being personable and accessible are two important skills. But also, you have to have math skills to deal with purchase transactions, track daily sales and inventory, and be aware of merchandise costs and pricing.
glencoe.com
Read more about this career and get a Career Exploration Activity.

- **Manual key entry** Even with electronic cash registers, some businesses have their salespeople enter sales transactions manually, often by keying in a Universal Product Code (UPC) using the register keys. All registers provide a numeric keyboard for entry in case other input devices do not function properly.

UNIVERSAL PRODUCT CODES

A **Universal Product Code (UPC)** is a combination barcode and number used to identify a product and manufacturer. Every item a manufacturer sells must have a different item number. For example, different sizes of the same garment and different sizes of containers of the same product must have distinct UPC codes.

UPCs have two parts: the UPC number and the machine-readable barcode. Barcodes, consisting of a series of vertical bars, are symbols printed on tags or on product packaging. The UPC number is the series of digits above or below the barcode.

The last number of the code is a check digit that is based on all the other digits: Every time a scanner reads an item, it uses a formula to calculate the check digit. If the calculated check digit does not match the check digit it reads, the scanner signals that the item needs to be rescanned. After the coded information is scanned and entered into a register, it can be transferred to a computer for further processing.

Many electronic cash registers are linked to computers as part of a POS (point-of-sale) system. Using the data, the computer can update inventory records with each sale and automatically reorder items in short supply. It stores customer information and makes it available for credit-checking or marketing purposes. It can also print out financial statements, sales trends, and sales personnel productivity reports.

POS systems have screens that show the names of items scanned and their prices. These displays are usually elevated and angled so customers can easily see the information. After all of the items have been scanned and totaled and tax has been added, the display will show the total amount of the sale. When the customer makes payment, the amount tendered and the change due the customer are then displayed.

Reading Check

Recall What functions, in addition to the basic functions, can electronic cash registers perform?

CURRENT TRENDS

Several technologies have emerged, changing the way business sales transactions are conducted and recorded. Several retailing chains offer their customers the option of using a self-service checkout. In a self-service lane at a typical grocery store, customers scan their own merchandise and weigh their own produce. They then enter payment in a self-service cash register, which allows them to pay with cash or with a credit or debit card.

Self-Service Grocery stores use self-service cash registers that allow customers to scan and bag their items.

INTEGRATION OF POINT-OF-SALE INFORMATION

A **point-of-sale (POS) system** combines a cash register with a computer, making it possible to capture information about the transaction at the time of the sale, and to then apply it to different functions. POS information is used to trigger replenishment of stock and manufacturing of replacement merchandise.

For example, imagine a Saturday afternoon at a store in Atlanta, Georgia. At the store, a teenage shopper purchases a size 8 plaid skirt. The clerk processes the transaction at a POS terminal.

On the following Monday afternoon, in Hong Kong, a computer technician downloads the information about the sale. On Wednesday, a factory worker in Hong Kong pulls the same size skirt off the assembly line and boxes it to be shipped to Atlanta. The skirt arrives at the store and is restocked on the sales rack by the following Saturday.

All this happens automatically without anyone at the Atlanta store having to fill out an order for a replacement. The point-of-sale system makes inventory tracking, reordering, and restocking an almost fully automated process.

RADIO FREQUENCY IDENTIFICATION

Another technology for sales transactions is radio frequency identification (RFID). With RFID, radio frequencies are used to read labels on products. An RFID tag is placed on cases and pallets by the manufacturer, who then labels each item with an Electronic Product Code (EPC). The tags are read by a radio-signal reading machine as a customer passes his or her cart through checkout. This technology makes it possible to read all the items in a cart simultaneously while they are still in the cart.

THE CASH DRAWER

Currency and checks collected as part of sales transactions are deposited in the till. The **till** is the cash drawer of a cash register. On most cash registers, the till can be opened only during a transaction. This feature is a security measure that prevents access to the cash drawer except during the course of a sale.

CASH DRAWER ARRANGEMENT

Usually, the till has ten compartments—five in the back of the cash drawer and five in the front. Although some companies vary the arrangement, bills are usually kept in the back of the drawer and coins in the front.

In the section for bills, the first compartment on the left often remains empty. It is reserved for checks or other special items. The second compartment contains $20 bills, the third has $10 bills, and the fourth $5 bills. The last compartment on the right is used for $1 bills. If a customer uses a larger bill, such as a $50 bill or a $100 bill, many businesses require that it be checked with a head cashier or a manager prior to being placed under the tray, where it is more secure.

In the section for coins, the first compartment on the left is used for silver dollars and half-dollars. The next compartment is for quarters, the following one for dimes, and the one after that for nickels. The last compartment on the right is for pennies.

EXPLAIN

Career Chatroom

Focus the Career Chatroom discussion concerning Elaine Kleinman by asking students these guiding questions.

Guiding Questions

List What are tasks that Ms. Kleinman performs?	helps owner select products, tracks inventory, helps customers
Analyze What does it mean to be"accessible"?	being easy to talk to, not in a rush, available

 **glencoe.com** 

Career Exploration Send students to the Online Learning Center to read more about this career and to get a Career Exploration Activity.

UNIVERSAL PRODUCT CODES

The use of UPCs has revolutionized the retail world. Ask these guiding questions to focus the discussion on Universal Product Codes.

Guiding Questions

Draw Conclusions Why do you think a UPC contains both a barcode and a printed number?	While most retail stores use scanners to read barcodes, there may be instances where this process does not work. In these cases, the cashier can manually enter the printed number.
Synthesize How might a point-of-sale system make customer information available for credit checking?	Possible answer: The system might be programmed to keep track of customers who have previously written checks with insufficient funds. The cashier could then be alerted to not accept checks from these customers.

ELABORATE

Reading Check Answer

Read the Reading Check question to students: ***What functions, in addition to the basic functions, can electronic cash registers perform?*** Electronic cash registers can figure sales tax, calculate discounts, subtract and credit returns, determine amount due back to customer, track inventory, and automatically reorder stock.

Self-Service Ask students: ***Have you ever used a self-service cash register? If so, did you like using it? What were the advantages? Were there any disadvantages?***

INTEGRATION OF POINT-OF-SALE INFORMATION

Ask these guiding questions to focus the discussion on the integration of POS information.

Guiding Questions

Explain What two things are combined to create a POS system?	a cash register and a computer
Analyze How can POS systems be used to automate reordering?	When a customer makes a purchase, the POS system updates the store's inventory and automatically notifies the supplier when replacement merchandise is needed. The supplier gets all the needed information and ships the required merchandise.
Infer What is the primary advantage of RFI technology?	It can read an entire collection of merchandise at once.

e MARKETING

QR Code—A Hardlink

A QR Code is a "quick response" barcode that can be read by scanning it with a scanning device or a mobile phone equipped with scanning capabilities. The QR Codes contain information pertinent to a product or a hard link to direct the user to a product's Web site. It is a great marketing tool. Napkins in fast food restaurants may have a QR code that can be scanned with nutritional information about menu selections. Retailers can include QR codes on receipts and directly on products like eye glasses. Since the QR Code can store a lot of information, all the details of a product can be part of the code. When products are sold the checkout person can scan the product's QR Code to provide management with detailed sales reports. For example when a customer buys a pair of glasses, all the details about the customer's prescription, the frame, color, manufacturer, and price can be retrieved and used to analyze eye glass sales.

Innovate and Create

How might QR Codes be used by physicians, supermarkets, clothing stores, appliance retailers, and movie theaters? Have students brainstorm all the data that could be generated from QR Codes for sales management purposes. Have students research the similarities and differences between QR Codes and High Capacity Color Barcodes (HCCB), such as Microsoft Tags? Physicians could use QR Codes to direct patients to their Web site to make appointments on their mobile phones or to find information on prescription drugs. Supermarket carts with built in scanners could scan products as customers put products into the cart. Clothing stores could use QR Codes to keep track of products sold so the fast-moving items can be reordered quickly. Appliance retailers could use QR codes attached to products for warranty registration and servicing. Movie theaters could affix QR codes to posters of upcoming attractions so when scanned more information about the movie and when it will be coming to that theater can be provided. When researching the similarities and differences between QR Codes and HCCBs students will learn that QR Codes are less expensive but that they cannot provide as much information as HCCBs. The obvious difference is that QR Codes are in black and white, while HCCBs are in color so only mobile phones with color can access HCCBs.

glencoe.com

eMarketing Worksheet Activity Send students to the Online Learning Center to download an eMarketing worksheet activity.

This arrangement facilitates the process of making change, because the bill and coin compartments are related and in descending order of value. Each pair has at least one digit in common. The $20 bills are behind the quarters ($.25). The $10 bills are behind the dimes ($.10). The $5 bills are behind the nickels ($.05), and the $1 bills are behind the pennies ($.01).

OPENING CASH FUND

At the beginning of each business day, the manager or another designated person places a limited amount of money in the cash register, which is called the **opening cash fund**. This fund consists of the coins and currency, or cash, for the register for a given day's business. The opening cash fund, which is used by the store to give change to customers when they pay for goods, is also known as the *change fund*. To verify the fund, the assigned person counts the coins and currency and places them, one denomination at a time, into the correct compartment in the cash drawer.

As the coins and currency are counted, the amount is written down, and then checked against the amount planned for the register. The change fund is "even" when the two amounts match exactly. When there is more than planned, the fund is "over." If there is less than planned, the fund is "short." An opening cash fund that is short or over should be reported immediately to the person who supplied the money. Then it can be corrected or accounted for prior to the start of business transactions for that day.

MAKING CHANGE

A salesperson who handles a large number of cash transactions may run short of certain denominations during the business day. Check your cash register from time to time in between transactions. You or your manager can exchange larger bills for smaller ones and any coins you might need. This procedure can prevent delays in making change when customers are waiting.

MARKETING CASE STUDY

Wendy's Nutritional Options

Wendy's® saw an opportunity to target cost-conscious consumers who also like nutritional fast-food choices. On the company's Web site, there is a section that features a variety of nutritional menu items. Some of these items include chili, side salads, and oranges.

Healthy Choices

The Wendy's Web site also shows various ways customers can have meals that are under 550 calories. There are options for consumers who want a meal that costs around five dollars. In addition, customers can see choices that combine fries and another menu item for less than 550 calories.

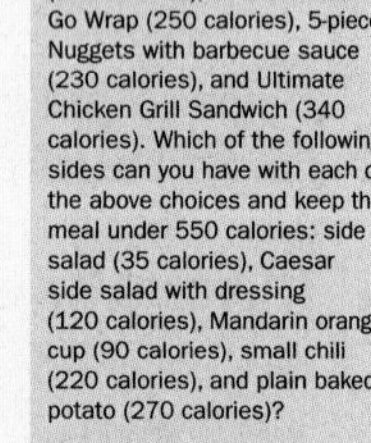

You know when it's real.®

Mathematics

Compute Consider the following menu options: Jr. Bacon Cheeseburger (310 calories), Grilled Chicken Go Wrap (250 calories), 5-piece Nuggets with barbecue sauce (230 calories), and Ultimate Chicken Grill Sandwich (340 calories). Which of the following sides can you have with each of the above choices and keep the meal under 550 calories: side salad (35 calories), Caesar side salad with dressing (120 calories), Mandarin orange cup (90 calories), small chili (220 calories), and plain baked potato (270 calories)?

NCTM Problem Solving Solve problems that arise in mathematics and in other contexts.

PRACTICE 3: MAKE CHANGE

How would you make or arrange for change in the following situations using the smallest number of bills and coins possible?

1. A customer gives you a $50 bill and a coupon worth $1 off one item to pay for a $23.19 purchase. What change would you give her?
2. A customer is buying two CDs that total $25.09, including tax. The smallest bills that he has are two $20 bills. What is your response?
3. A customer gives you $30.25 for a $21.25 purchase. How would you count back the change?
4. You are a cashier at Caldwell Drugstore, and a customer gives you $10.55 to pay for a purchase of $3.55. Count the customer's change back to him. Why did he give you the change along with the $10 bill?

glencoe.com

Check your answers to all Practice sets.

USING A POS SYSTEM

A POS system with a customer display makes it easy to count the correct change. Suppose the total amount of the purchase is $16.65, and the customer pays with $20 in cash. You enter this information into the register, and the customer display then shows the amount of change that is due. In this case, the register shows that the customer is due back $3.35 in change for a $16.65 purchase.

Select change from the cash drawer beginning with the largest denomination, taking out three $1 bills, a quarter, and a dime. The display shows the customer the amount of change that is due, so all you have to do is say, "$3.35," as you hand the change and receipt to the customer. If your POS includes a coin dispenser, the quarter and dime will automatically fall into a cup or tray connected to the cash register. All you have to do then is to hand the customer three $1 bills and the receipt as you say the full amount, "$3.35."

USING A NON-POS SYSTEM

If your cash register does not have a customer display showing the change due, begin by announcing the total amount of the sale, and then count up to the amount tendered. In doing this, be thorough and accurate, and follow these five steps:

1. Once the transaction has been entered in the cash register, announce to the customer the total amount of the sale. You might say, "That will be $16.65."
2. Announce the amount tendered when the customer offers payment in cash, saying, for example, "Out of a $20 bill."
3. Place the $20 bill on the cash drawer ledge and leave it there until you have given change to the customer. This eliminates most disputes over amount tendered.
4. Count silently while removing change from the cash drawer. The most common method is to count up from the purchase price, taking out smaller denominations of coins and currency first. Use as few coins as possible in making change for a customer.
5. Count aloud when handing the change to the customer and say, "That's $16.65 out of $20. $16.75 (giving the customer a dime), $17 (giving a quarter), $18, $19, and $20 (giving three $1 bills, one at a time)."

Many customers avoid accumulating small change by tendering an odd amount of change to pay for their purchases. A customer who wants to get rid of a quarter, a dime, and four pennies might give you $20.39 for a sales total of $18.39. You would use the $.39 to cancel out the "odd cents" of the sale and give change for the $20 bill. The customer would then get back an even $2. The same customer might also tender $20.50, in which case you would count the odd cents first, starting at $18.39. In this latter case, the customer would get $2.11 back in change.

SALES TALLY

Salespeople and cashiers who use a cash register must account for the day's sales and money at the end of the business day. This process goes by a number of names, including *balancing the cash* and *balancing the till*.

EXPLAIN

Activate Prior Knowledge

Reteach Estimating Remind students that when performing calculations, it is a good practice to always estimate your result first and then perform the actual arithmetic. Estimating helps to avoid any major errors. Use the following examples from Chapter 7 page 175 to provide practice in estimating.

$$388 + 995 = ?$$

Estimate: $400 + 1{,}000 = 1{,}400$

Enter the problem:

[3] [8] [8] [+] [9] [9] [5] [=] **1,383**

Displayed answer

Check: 1,383 is close to the estimate of 1,400.

$$480 \times 112 = ?$$

Estimate: $500 \times 100 = 50{,}000$

Enter the problem:

[4] [8] [0] [×] [1] [1] [2] [=] **53,760**

Displayed answer

Check: 53,760 is close to the estimate of 50,000.

OPENING CASH FUND

Ask these guiding questions to focus the discussion on the opening cash fund.

Guiding Questions

Summarize What should the cashier do if the opening cash fund is not "even"?	The cashier should immediately report any discrepancies.
Predict You are given an opening cash fund of $1 in pennies, $5 in nickels, $10 in quarters, and $25 in $5 bills. What problem will this cause?	Since you have not been given any $1 bills, you will have difficulties making change for some purchase amounts.

MARKETING CASE STUDY

Mathematics Answer

Jr. Bacon Cheeseburger: side salad, Caesar side salad, Mandarin orange cup; Grilled Chicken Go Wrap: any side; 5-piece Nuggets: any side; Ultimate Chicken Grill Sandwich: side salad, Mandarin orange cup

ELABORATE

MAKING CHANGE

Making correct change is an important task in many sales jobs. Ask these guiding questions to lead the discussion on making change.

Guiding Questions

Identify Cause and Effect What might happen if a cashier takes a $10 bill from a customer and places it in the cash drawer rather than on the cash drawer ledge?	There might be a misunderstanding concerning the amount the customer gave the cashier. For example, the customer might say it was a $20 bill instead of a $10 bill.
Apply If you worked in a clothing boutique, what steps would you follow to balance the till at the end of the day?	count the money in the till, fill out a closing balance report; send money, report, register tape to management

Answers to Practice 3

1. One penny, a nickel, three quarters, two $1 bills (or a $2 bill), a $5 bill, and a $20 bill.
2. Ask if the customer has $.09 in change or at least a dime.
3. By disregarding the exact change provided, the cashier is less likely to get confused. Disregard the $.25 and simply say, "That's $21 out of $30; twenty-two, twenty-three, twenty-four, twenty-five (counting back four $1 bills, one at a time), and $30 (giving back $5)."
4. "That's $3.55 out of $10.75; $.65, $.75 (handing back two dimes)," then say, "That leaves $3 out of $10; $4, $5 (handing back two $1 bills), and $10 (handing back a $5 bill)." By tendering the $.75, the customer reduces the amount of small change to be returned to him.

Mini Project

Extensions

Create a Change Making Guide Tell students they will create a handout that teaches cashiers and salespeople how to make change. The handout should provide step-by-step instructions. When done, students should trade their handouts with a partner. The partner should provide feedback by determining if the change-making instructions are correct and complete. Students should create an attractive handout that contains clear, complete, and accurate instructions for how to make change.

Graphic Organizer

To help in the discussion of making change when using a non-POS system, display this diagram. Review the steps in making change. Then repeat the steps using specific amounts. For example, you might state that the customer has given the cashier $5.24 for a $2.24 purchase.

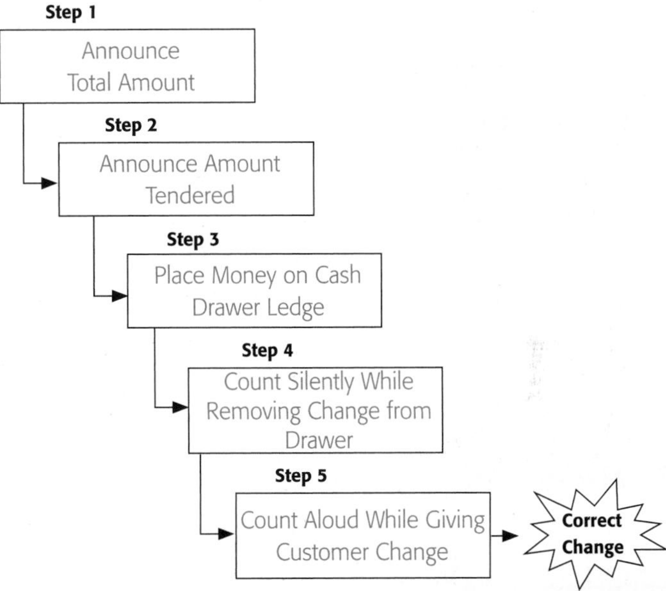

iWB

Graphic Organizer Send students to the Online Learning Center to print this graphic organizer.

Mini Project

Differentiated Instruction

Kinesthetic Learners Begin by making certain students understand the importance of good customer service when giving change. Then organize students into pairs. Instruct students to create a skit in which one person is the customer and the other a cashier. Have students practice giving out change for various amounts of money. In addition, students should practice various scenarios, such as the customer interrupting the cashier during the process and the customer disputing the amount of change given. Skits should demonstrate the importance of being attentive and always providing good service while giving change. The cashier should be able to calculate the correct change required based on the amount tendered from the customer.

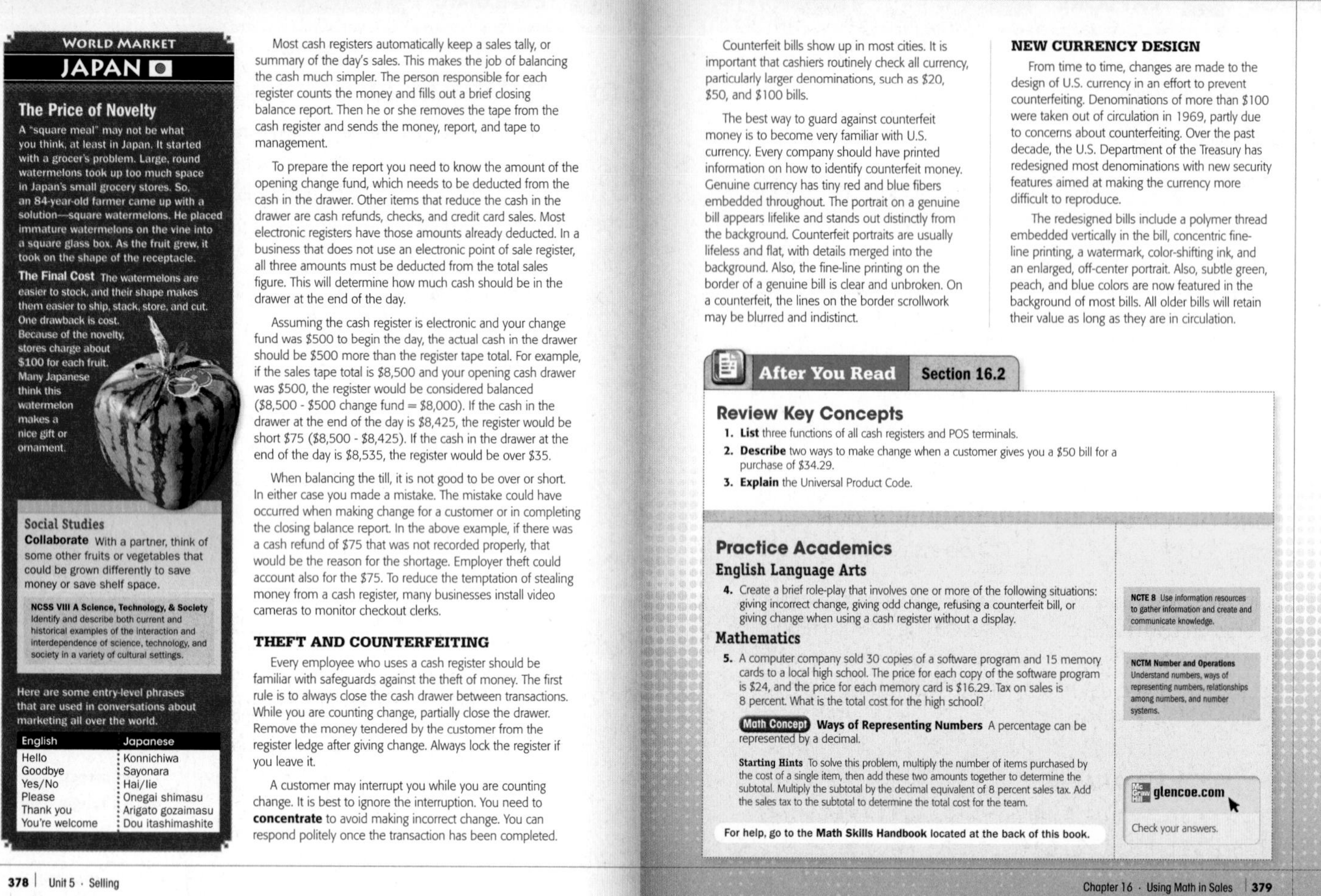

WORLD MARKET

JAPAN

The Price of Novelty

A "square meal" may not be what you think, at least in Japan. It started with a grocer's problem. Large, round watermelons took up too much space in Japan's small grocery stores. So, an 84-year-old farmer came up with a solution—square watermelons. He placed immature watermelons on the vine into a square glass box. As the fruit grew, it took on the shape of the receptacle.

The Final Cost The watermelons are easier to stock, and their shape makes them easier to ship, stack, store, and cut. One drawback is cost. Because of the novelty, stores charge about $100 for each fruit. Many Japanese think this watermelon makes a nice gift or ornament.

Social Studies

Collaborate With a partner, think of some other fruits or vegetables that could be grown differently to save money or save shelf space.

NCSS VIII A Science, Technology, & Society Identify and describe both current and historical examples of the interaction and interdependence of science, technology, and society in a variety of cultural settings.

Here are some entry-level phrases that are used in conversations about marketing all over the world.

English	Japanese
Hello	Konnichiwa
Goodbye	Sayonara
Yes/No	Hai/Iie
Please	Onegai shimasu
Thank you	Arigato gozaimasu
You're welcome	Dou itashimashite

Most cash registers automatically keep a sales tally, or summary of the day's sales. This makes the job of balancing the cash much simpler. The person responsible for each register counts the money and fills out a brief closing balance report. Then he or she removes the tape from the cash register and sends the money, report, and tape to management.

To prepare the report you need to know the amount of the opening change fund, which needs to be deducted from the cash in the drawer. Other items that reduce the cash in the drawer are cash refunds, checks, and credit card sales. Most electronic registers have those amounts already deducted. In a business that does not use an electronic point of sale register, all three amounts must be deducted from the total sales figure. This will determine how much cash should be in the drawer at the end of the day.

Assuming the cash register is electronic and your change fund was $500 to begin the day, the actual cash in the drawer should be $500 more than the register tape total. For example, if the sales tape total is $8,500 and your opening cash drawer was $500, the register would be considered balanced ($8,500 - $500 change fund = $8,000). If the cash in the drawer at the end of the day is $8,425, the register would be short $75 ($8,500 - $8,425). If the cash in the drawer at the end of the day is $8,535, the register would be over $35.

When balancing the till, it is not good to be over or short. In either case you made a mistake. The mistake could have occurred when making change for a customer or in completing the closing balance report. In the above example, if there was a cash refund of $75 that was not recorded properly, that would be the reason for the shortage. Employer theft could account also for the $75. To reduce the temptation of stealing money from a cash register, many businesses install video cameras to monitor checkout clerks.

THEFT AND COUNTERFEITING

Every employee who uses a cash register should be familiar with safeguards against the theft of money. The first rule is to always close the cash drawer between transactions. While you are counting change, partially close the drawer. Remove the money tendered by the customer from the register ledge after giving change. Always lock the register if you leave it.

A customer may interrupt you while you are counting change. It is best to ignore the interruption. You need to **concentrate** to avoid making incorrect change. You can respond politely once the transaction has been completed.

Counterfeit bills show up in most cities. It is important that cashiers routinely check all currency, particularly larger denominations, such as $20, $50, and $100 bills.

The best way to guard against counterfeit money is to become very familiar with U.S. currency. Every company should have printed information on how to identify counterfeit money. Genuine currency has tiny red and blue fibers embedded throughout. The portrait on a genuine bill appears lifelike and stands out distinctly from the background. Counterfeit portraits are usually lifeless and flat, with details merged into the background. Also, the fine-line printing on the border of a genuine bill is clear and unbroken. On a counterfeit, the lines on the border scrollwork may be blurred and indistinct.

NEW CURRENCY DESIGN

From time to time, changes are made to the design of U.S. currency in an effort to prevent counterfeiting. Denominations of more than $100 were taken out of circulation in 1969, partly due to concerns about counterfeiting. Over the past decade, the U.S. Department of the Treasury has redesigned most denominations with new security features aimed at making the currency more difficult to reproduce.

The redesigned bills include a polymer thread embedded vertically in the bill, concentric fine-line printing, a watermark, color-shifting ink, and an enlarged, off-center portrait. Also, subtle green, peach, and blue colors are now featured in the background of most bills. All older bills will retain their value as long as they are in circulation.

After You Read **Section 16.2**

Review Key Concepts

1. **List** three functions of all cash registers and POS terminals.
2. **Describe** two ways to make change when a customer gives you a $50 bill for a purchase of $34.29.
3. **Explain** the Universal Product Code.

Practice Academics

English Language Arts

4. Create a brief role-play that involves one or more of the following situations: giving incorrect change, giving odd change, refusing a counterfeit bill, or giving change when using a cash register without a display.

NCTE 8 Use information resources to gather information and create and communicate knowledge.

Mathematics

5. A computer company sold 30 copies of a software program and 15 memory cards to a local high school. The price for each copy of the software program is $24, and the price for each memory card is $16.29. Tax on sales is 8 percent. What is the total cost for the high school?

Math Concept **Ways of Representing Numbers** A percentage can be represented by a decimal.

Starting Hints To solve this problem, multiply the number of items purchased by the cost of a single item, then add these two amounts together to determine the subtotal. Multiply the subtotal by the decimal equivalent of 8 percent sales tax. Add the sales tax to the subtotal to determine the total cost for the team.

NCTM Number and Operations Understand numbers, ways of representing numbers, relationships among numbers, and number systems.

For help, go to the **Math Skills Handbook** located at the back of this book.

glencoe.com

Check your answers.

ELABORATE

WORLD MARKET
SOCIAL STUDIES

Answer Ideas will vary. Carrots and zucchini could be grown in long rectangular tubes so that they would stack neatly on top of one another. Other round fruit, such as apples and peaches, would take less shelf space if forced to grow in rectangular or cube shapes.

Extend Ask students: ***Can you think of any other marketing ideas for unusually shaped fruits or vegetables?*** They could make novelty gifts for holidays. Melons could be shaped like hearts or Hershey's kisses and sold as Valentine's Day gifts.

THEFT AND COUNTERFEITING

Because U.S. currency is seen around the world as being highly desirable, it is especially vulnerable to theft and counterfeiting. Ask these guiding questions to investigate this topic.

Guiding Questions

List What are three safeguards to follow to prevent theft from a cash drawer?	close drawer between transactions; when counting change, partially close the drawer; always lock register when you leave it
Infer Why do you think it is especially important that cashiers check bills of larger denominations to make certain they are genuine?	It is more profitable for counterfeiters to create larger bills than smaller ones.
Apply You are a cashier in the middle of making change when a customer asks you a question. How do you respond?	Continue making change. When you are done, politely answer the customer's question.

EVALUATE

Critical Thinking

Ask students: ***Why do you think some stores and other businesses will not accept currency larger than $20 bills?*** Answers will vary, but could include the following: Accepting larger bills forces you to keep more change in the cash drawer, which is a security risk. Mandating that only smaller bills be accepted is an employee theft deterrent because it is easier for management to keep track of a smaller amount of money in the till. The risk of getting a counterfeit bill increases with larger bills, such as $50s and $100s. Because creating reasonably good counterfeit bills is a complex process, counterfeiters are less likely to spend their time creating $5s and $10s.

Mini Projects

Enrichment

Avoiding Con Artists Have students conduct research to learn about techniques con artists use at the cash register. Students should then write a brief report on what they learn. Make the reports available for the class to read. Students' reports should include various strategies con artists use on unsuspecting cashiers. For example, a common strategy is to ask the cashier for change for a $5 bill. Once change is given, another request is made, and then another. By the time the requests are finished, the con artist is richer, and the clerk may not even realize there is a problem until the drawer is balanced.

Training Cashiers to Identify Counterfeit Currency Tell students that they are managers of a convenience store. On several occasions, store employees have accidentally accepted counterfeit bills. As managers, they have been assigned the task of creating a presentation to train employees in identifying counterfeit bills. In their training sessions, they should emphasize the importance of cashiers becoming accustomed to the look and feel of U.S. currency. They also should explain the steps in identifying genuine bills. Students may want to prepare a slide show to accompany their training sessions. Students should give a presentation in which they explain how to identify genuine U.S. currency. For example, they should explain the importance of becoming familiar with the distinct "feel" of genuine currency and demonstrate how to look for tiny red and blue fibers embedded throughout the bill. They should discuss that the bill should have fine-line printing that is clear and unbroken on its border. In addition, the portrait should appear lifelike. Students also should demonstrate how to identify the micro-printed security thread that can be seen when newer bills are held up to the light.

After You Read — Section 16.2

Review Key Concepts

1. All cash registers and POS terminals can perform three basic functions: (1) record sales, (2) storing cash and sales documents, and (3) provide receipts.
2. Two ways to make change when a customer tenders a $50 bill for a purchase of $34.29 are: (1) Using a POS system with a customer display, you count out the change shown on the display, beginning with the largest denomination, hand the change to the customer and say aloud "$15.71" as you hand the change to the customer; (2) If the cash register does not have a customer display showing the change due, begin by announcing the total amount of the sale and then count up to the amount tendered. This involves the five steps listed on page 377 of the text.
3. The Universal Product Code (UPC) is a combination barcode and number used to identify a product and manufacturer.

Practice Academics

English Language Arts

4. Students should role-play one of these situations: giving incorrect change, giving odd change, refusing a counterfeit bill, or giving change when using a cash register without a display. When role-playing, students should always demonstrate good customer service techniques.

Mathematics

5. $1,041.50 ([24 × 30] + [16.29 × 15] × 1.08)

glencoe.com

Send students to the Online Learning Center to check their answers.

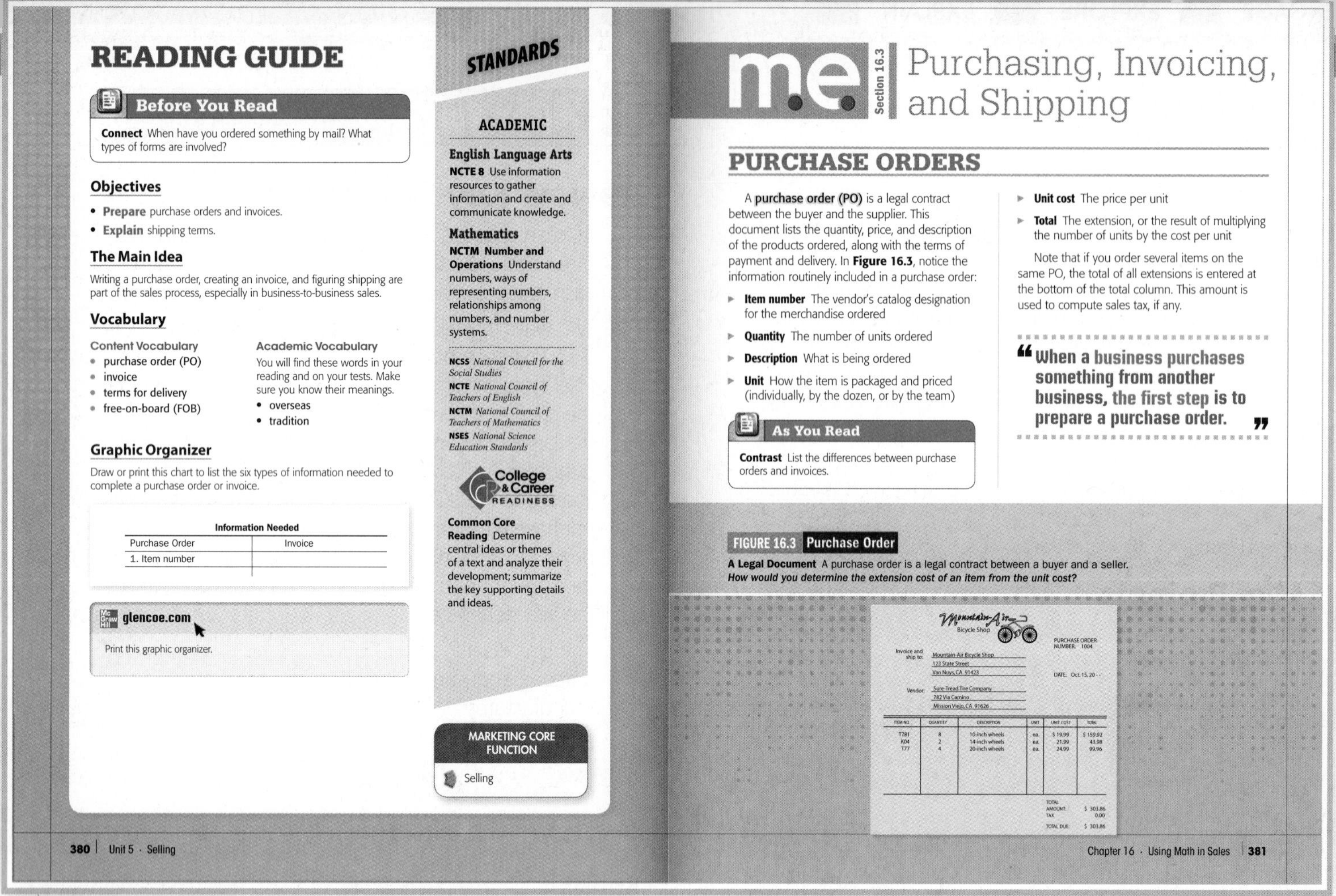

READING GUIDE

Before You Read

Connect When have you ordered something by mail? What types of forms are involved?

Objectives

- **Prepare** purchase orders and invoices.
- **Explain** shipping terms.

The Main Idea

Writing a purchase order, creating an invoice, and figuring shipping are part of the sales process, especially in business-to-business sales.

Vocabulary

Content Vocabulary
- purchase order (PO)
- invoice
- terms for delivery
- free-on-board (FOB)

Academic Vocabulary

You will find these words in your reading and on your tests. Make sure you know their meanings.
- overseas
- tradition

Graphic Organizer

Draw or print this chart to list the six types of information needed to complete a purchase order or invoice.

Information Needed	
Purchase Order	Invoice
1. Item number	

glencoe.com

Print this graphic organizer.

STANDARDS

ACADEMIC

English Language Arts
NCTE 8 Use information resources to gather information and create and communicate knowledge.

Mathematics
NCTM Number and Operations Understand numbers, ways of representing numbers, relationships among numbers, and number systems.

NCSS *National Council for the Social Studies*
NCTE *National Council of Teachers of English*
NCTM *National Council of Teachers of Mathematics*
NSES *National Science Education Standards*

College & Career READINESS

Common Core
Reading Determine central ideas or themes of a text and analyze their development; summarize the key supporting details and ideas.

MARKETING CORE FUNCTION
Selling

m.e. Section 16.3 Purchasing, Invoicing, and Shipping

PURCHASE ORDERS

A **purchase order (PO)** is a legal contract between the buyer and the supplier. This document lists the quantity, price, and description of the products ordered, along with the terms of payment and delivery. In **Figure 16.3**, notice the information routinely included in a purchase order:

- **Item number** The vendor's catalog designation for the merchandise ordered
- **Quantity** The number of units ordered
- **Description** What is being ordered
- **Unit** How the item is packaged and priced (individually, by the dozen, or by the team)
- **Unit cost** The price per unit
- **Total** The extension, or the result of multiplying the number of units by the cost per unit

Note that if you order several items on the same PO, the total of all extensions is entered at the bottom of the total column. This amount is used to compute sales tax, if any.

As You Read

Contrast List the differences between purchase orders and invoices.

> "When a business purchases something from another business, the first step is to prepare a purchase order."

FIGURE 16.3 Purchase Order

A Legal Document A purchase order is a legal contract between a buyer and a seller. ***How would you determine the extension cost of an item from the unit cost?***

Mountain-Air Bicycle Shop

PURCHASE ORDER NUMBER: 1004

Invoice and ship to: Mountain-Air Bicycle Shop, 123 State Street, Van Nuys, CA 91423

DATE: Oct. 15, 20 - -

Vendor: Sure-Tread Tire Company, 782 Via Camino, Mission Viejo, CA 91626

ITEM NO.	QUANTITY	DESCRIPTION	UNIT	UNIT COST	TOTAL
T781	8	10-inch wheels	ea.	$ 19.99	$ 159.92
K04	2	14-inch wheels	ea.	21.99	43.98
T77	4	20-inch wheels	ea.	24.99	99.96

TOTAL AMOUNT: $ 303.86
TAX: 0.00
TOTAL DUE: $ 303.86

ENGAGE

Anticipation Activity

Improving Student Achievement Give groups of students a blank purchase order and catalog or Web site for office supplies. Have them imagine they work in a small office and need to buy copy paper, file folders, pens, and notebooks. Ask students to use the PO to order enough supplies for one month. Stress that the PO must contain all needed information.

Objectives

- **Prepare** purchase orders and invoices. PO: Enter item number, quantity, description, unit, unit cost, extension. Total extensions, add any sales tax. Invoice: Create itemized list of goods, terms of sale, total, taxes and fees, amount due.
- **Explain** shipping terms. FOB: price includes delivery at seller's expense to a specified point. FOB destination: goods belong to seller until destination; seller pays for shipping. FOB shipping point: buyer pays for shipping, is responsible for goods in transit. FOB destination charges reversed: Goods belong to buyer only when received; buyer pays transportation charges.

Graphic Organizer

Information Needed

Purchase Order	Invoice
1. Item number	1. Prices of goods
2. Quantity	2. Terms of sale
3. Description	3. Total
4. Unit	4. Taxes
5. Unit cost	5. Fees
6. Total	6. Amount due

Graphic Organizer Send students to the Online Learning Center to print this graphic organizer.

EXPLORE

Before You Read

Read the Before You Read question aloud: ***When have you ordered something by mail? What types of forms were involved?*** Answers will vary. Sample answer: I ordered some decorations for a graduation party from a catalog. I had to fill out a table listing the items, item numbers, quantities, and so on. I had to calculate the total and also the shipping charges. I also had to enter the shipping address. I enclosed a check to pay for the items. Then ask: ***How is this similar to making a purchase on the Internet? How is it different?*** Sample answer: It's similar in that I had to provide the same types of information. It's different because I had to manually write in the information, rather than using the keyboard to enter it. On the Internet, the total and the shipping charges are calculated for me. When filling out the mail-order form, I had to manually calculate these amounts.

Preteaching Vocabulary

Have students go to the Online Learning Center at glencoe.com for the Chapter 16 Preteaching Vocabulary games.

Content Vocabulary

Have students name the two content vocabulary terms that are used when specifying who will pay shipping fees. terms of delivery, free-on-board (FOB)

Academic Vocabulary

Overseas—Denotative Meaning Explain that this word means "beyond or across a sea or ocean." Ask students to name some countries that are overseas in relation to the United States. Egypt, China, France, Turkey, Russia, India.

Tradition—Word Origin Explain to students that the word *tradition* comes from the Latin word *traditio,* which means "handing over" or "handing down."

As You Read

Read the As You Read question aloud: ***List the differences between purchase orders and invoices.*** purchase orders are issued by the buyer; invoices are issued by the seller; a purchase order (PO) contains the quantity, price, description of the products, and terms for payment; the invoice is an itemized list of goods and the terms of the sale

Section 16.3

Purchasing, Invoicing, and Shipping

PURCHASE ORDERS

Ask these guiding questions to focus the discussion on purchase orders.

Guiding Questions

Analyze Why is it necessary that the invoice contain each item's number?	Items may vary in minor ways that may not be indicated in the description.
Apply Each ream of paper contains 500 sheets. You order 12,000 sheets of paper. The cost is \$4.50 a ream. How much will this paper cost?	You will order 24 units. The cost will be \$108.00 (24 × 4.50).

Expert Advice

Read the quote to students:

"When a business purchases something from another business, the first step is to prepare a purchase order."

Remind students that these transactions are called "business-to-business" transactions. A detailed purchase order (PO) is filled out.

Visual Literacy

Figure 16.3 Caption Answer Read the caption question to students: ***How would you determine the extension cost of an item from the unit cost?*** multiply the unit cost by the quantity Then ask: ***What would be the extension cost for item T781 if the quantity was 20 (instead of 8)?*** \$399.80 (\$19.99 × 20)

INVOICES

For vendors—those who sell to other businesses—the equivalent form of a purchase order is the invoice. The calculations on both forms are very similar to those performed on sales checks by retail salespeople.

When filling an order based on a PO, a vendor includes an invoice with the delivered merchandise. An **invoice** is an itemized list of goods that includes prices, terms of sales, total, taxes and fees, and amount due. The invoice item numbers, quantities, unit costs, and extensions are correct when they match the PO.

DATING TERMS

Dating terms state when a bill must be paid and the discount for paying early. Ordinary dating occurs when the dating terms are based on the invoice date. Consider, for example, ordinary dating of 2/10, net 30. This means there will be a 2-percent discount if the buyer pays within 10 days and that the invoice total must be paid within 30 days.

SHIPPING

As in retail sales transactions, shipping charges are not subject to tax. Therefore, you should add those shipping charges after the tax is calculated.

Shipping services vary greatly from international companies that specialize in shipping goods **overseas** to the U. S. Postal Service's (USPS) regular mail service.

PARCEL POST

Parcel post is one type of standard surface package delivery that is offered by the U.S. Postal Service. Parcel post is a good option if there is time to take packages to the post office and if the customer is willing to wait for a delivery.

CASH ON DELIVERY (COD)

With COD (cash on delivery) shipping, the postal carrier will collect the amount due from the customer and forward it to the business, which must prepay the shipping charges. The amount due from the customer may include the total for both the merchandise and the shipping costs. The customer must pay a fee for the COD service, which varies depending on the amount collected.

Up to $500 may be collected on delivery by a USPS postal carrier. Many businesses prefer using UPS for COD shipments. This is because UPS does not limit the amount that can be collected at delivery to $500, and the shipping charges do not have to be prepaid.

Private package-delivery companies and the USPS's Express Mail service compete vigorously with each other in the extremely competitive overnight delivery market. ***Can you name some private delivery companies?***

DELIVERY ARRANGEMENTS

Part of the selling arrangement negotiated between a buyer and seller involves delivery. This is an important negotiation point in many business-to-business transactions. By **tradition**, the issues are who will pay for delivery and when change of title (ownership) will take place. The final delivery arrangement made between the buyer and seller is called **terms for delivery**. It is part of most agreements in business-to-business sales.

FOB (free on board) means that the price for goods includes delivery at the seller's expense to a specified point and no farther. The terms for delivery are all variations of FOB. There are four options: FOB destination; FOB shipping point, FOB factory freight paid; and FOB destination charges reversed.

1. **FOB destination** The title or ownership of the goods remains with the seller until the goods reach their destination. The seller pays the transportation charges and assumes the responsibility for the condition of the goods until they arrive at the buyer's place of business.
2. **FOB shipping point** The buyer pays the shipping cost and is responsible for losses for damages that occur in transit.
3. **FOB factory freight prepaid** The goods become the property of the buyer at the factory. The seller, however, pays the shipping charges.
4. **FOB destination charges reversed** The merchandise becomes the buyer's only when the goods are received. The buyer pays for the transportation charges. If the goods are lost or damaged in transit, the buyer's investment is protected because the goods do not yet belong to the buyer.

After You Read | **Section 16.3**

Review Key Concepts

1. **Identify** the party who issues a purchase order (PO) in business-to-business sales.
2. **Define** the term *extension* and explain its calculation on a purchase order.
3. **Explain** the term *2/10, net 30.*

Practice Academics

English Language Arts

4. You are the buyer for a company that sells computer games. Your boss has asked you to design a new logo and prepare a new slogan for the company purchase orders. Sketch the logo and slogan.

Mathematics

5. Calculate the extensions for these purchases: 50 reams of printer paper at $5.95 each, 36 pens at $2.20 each, and 24 printer cartridges at $32 each.

Math Concept **Estimation** Estimating before you begin calculating can ensure that you have calculated properly.

Starting Hints To solve this problem, multiply the number of each unit purchased by the cost of each, the extension of each item.

For help, go to the **Math Skills Handbook** located at the back of this book.

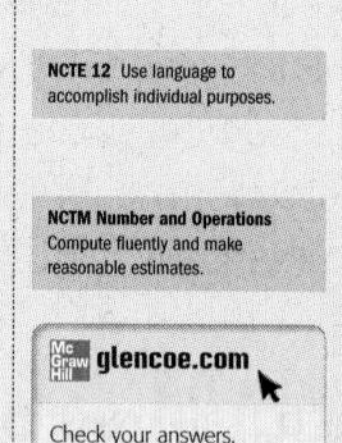

NCTE 12 Use language to accomplish individual purposes.

NCTM Number and Operations Compute fluently and make reasonable estimates.

glencoe.com

Check your answers.

ELABORATE

INVOICES

Ask these guiding questions to focus the discussion on invoices.

Guiding Questions

Recall What does the term *vendor* mean?	a business that sells to other businesses
Apply What does an ordinary dating of 1.5/14, net 45 mean?	there will be a 1.5 percent discount if buyer pays in 14 days; invoice must be paid in 45 days.

SHIPPING

Retailers who ship goods must have a clear understanding of the advantages and disadvantages of the various alternatives. Ask these guiding questions to focus discussion on shipping options.

Guiding Questions

Recall Why are shipping charges always listed on an invoice after the sales tax is calculated?	Shipping charges are not subject to sales tax.
Compare Why do many businesses prefer to use UPS rather than the U.S. Postal Service for COD shipments?	A USPS postal carrier can only collect a maximum of $500 for COD shipments, while UPS has no limit. In addition, the USPS requires shipping charges to be prepaid while UPS does not.

EVALUATE

DELIVERY ARRANGEMENTS

To help students understand the different types of FOB delivery arrangements, display this chart. Ask students to provide definitions for each type.

Free on Board

FOB Destination	**FOB Shipping Point**	**FOB Factory Freight Prepaid**	**FOB Destination Charges Reversed**
Goods belong to seller until destination and the seller pays for shipping.	Buyer pays for shipping and is responsible for goods in transit.	Goods become property of buyer at factory, but seller pays shipping charges.	Goods belong to buyer only when received; buyer pays shipping charges.

Mc Graw Hill **glencoe.com**  iWB

Graphic Organizer Send students to the Online Learning Center to print this graphic organizer.

Mini Projects

Extensions

Designing a Purchase Order Form Tell students to come up with an imaginary retail store. Explain that they have been asked to use word processing software to design a purchase order form for this store. Tell them to think of an appropriate name and logo for the store which will appear at the top of the form. The form should contain places for all information shown in Figure 16.3. Remind students to leave adequate space for the needed information to be inserted into the form. The form should contain the store's name and logo, along with places for all information shown in Figure 16.3.

Writing Invoices Create a variety of purchase orders. Organize students into groups and provide each group with a purchase order. The group should work to create an invoice for the purchase order provided to them. When finished, have students discuss anything that was difficult about writing the invoices. The students should write invoices to match the purchase orders they were given. Students should make certain all needed information is provided, including an itemized list of goods with prices, terms of sale, total, taxes and fees, and amount due.

 **After You Read** Section 16.3

Review Key Concepts

1. In business-to-business sales, the buyer issues a purchase order (PO).
2. The extension is the result of multiplying the number of units by the cost per unit.
3. The terms 2/10, net 30 mean that there will be a 2 percent discount if paid within 10 days, and the invoice total must be paid within 30 days.

Practice Academics

English Language Arts

4. The student should sketch a logo and slogan that would be appropriate for the purchase order for a company that sells computer games.

Mathematics

5. \$297.50 (50 × \$5.95); \$79.20 (36 × \$2.20); 768 (24 × \$32)

Mc Graw Hill **glencoe.com** 

Send students to the Online Learning Center to check their answers.

Chapter 16 Visual Summary

Using Math in Sales

Types of sales transactions include cash sales, debit card sales, credit card sales, layaway sales, on-approval sales, COD sales, returns, exchanges, and allowances.

Cash registers perform many functions and are used for various purposes in sales.

Review and Activities

Written Summary

- Sales transactions may be cash sales, debit card sales, credit card sales, layaway sales, on-approval sales, COD sales, returns, exchanges, and allowances.
- Sales tax and shipping charges are normally added to the total price of the products sold.
- Many retail businesses use electronic cash registers linked to computers as a point-of-sale (POS) system.
- Electronic cash registers display the amount of change to be returned to the customer.
- A purchase order includes the item number, quantity, description, unit, unit cost, and total (or extension) for each item ordered.
- When filling an order, a vendor prepares an invoice with the delivered merchandise.

Review Content Vocabulary and Academic Vocabulary

1. Write your own definition for each content and academic vocabulary term.

Content Vocabulary
- sales check (p. 365)
- layaway (p. 369)
- on-approval sale (p. 369)
- cash-on-delivery (COD) sale (p. 369)
- sales tax (p. 370)
- allowance (p. 370)
- Universal Product Code (UPC) (p. 374)
- point-of-sale system (POS) (p. 375)
- till (p. 375)
- opening cash fund (p. 376)
- purchase order (PO) (p. 381)
- invoice (p. 382)
- terms for delivery (p. 383)
- free-on-board (FOB) (p. 383)

Academic Vocabulary
- transfer (p. 368)
- area (p. 369)
- automatically (p. 373)
- concentrate (p. 378)
- overseas (p. 382)
- tradition (p. 383)

Assess for Understanding

2. **Identify** What are six types of retail sales transactions?
3. **Describe** How would you describe sales checks to a new sales associate?
4. **Explain** What is the arrangement of currency and coins in a cash register drawer?
5. **Define** What is a Universal Product Code (UPC)?
6. **List** What are two rules for safeguarding money at the cash register?
7. **Discuss** What terms for delivery would you use for an expensive gift for a friend?
8. **Contrast** What is the difference between a purchase order and an invoice?
9. **Role-Play** How might you deal with a customer who does not have a receipt and wants to make a return?

EVALUATE

Visual Summary

Express Creativity Ask students to create a visual summary that illustrates a concept in the chapter. Encourage students to use different formats for their visual summaries, such as a storyboard, a table, or a word web. Visual summaries will vary depending on the concept depicted. Questions to ask when assessing a visual summary include:

- Is the summary clear, economical, and simple?
- Are any important steps left out?
- Are steps or concepts arranged in the same order as the original?
- Does the summary reveal a pattern that connects the details?
- Does the summary locate and highlight the most important information?

Review Content Vocabulary and Academic Vocabulary

1. Definitions will vary. Sample definitions:
Sales check Written record of a sales transaction.
Layaway Process in which the customer makes a deposit on merchandise and then receives the merchandise when the bill is fully paid.
On-approval sale Agreement that allows the customer to take the merchandise home for further consideration.
Cash-on-delivery sale Customer pays for merchandise when it is delivered.
Sales tax Percentage fee levied by the government on the sale of goods and services.
Allowance Partial return of the sale price for merchandise that the customer has kept.
Universal Product Code (UPC) Combination bar code and number used to identify a product and manufacturer.
Point-of-sale (POS) system Combines a cash register and a computer.
Till Cash drawer of a cash register.
Opening cash fund The limited amount of money placed in a cash register at the beginning of each business day.
Purchase order (PO) Legal contract between a buyer and a supplier.
Invoice An itemized list of goods that includes prices, terms of sales, total, taxes and fees, and amount due.

EVALUATE

Assess for Understanding

2. Six types of retail sales transactions are cash or check sales, debit card sales, credit card sales, layaway sales, on-approval sales, and cash-on-delivery sales.

3. A sales check is a written record of a sales transaction that includes such information as the date of the sale, the items purchased, the purchase prices, sales tax, and the total amount due.

4. In a cash drawer, the bills are usually kept in the back of the drawer and coins in the front. In the section for bills, the first compartment on the left often remains empty. It is reserved for checks or other special items. The second compartment contains $20 bills, the third $10 bills, and the fourth $5 bills. The last compartment on the right is used for $1 bills. In the section for coins, the first compartment on the left is used for dollars and half-dollars. The next compartment is for quarters, the following one for dimes, and the one after that for nickels. The last compartment on the right is for pennies.

5. UPC stands for Universal Product Code. It is a combination bar code and number used to identify a product and manufacturer.

6. To safeguard money in a cash register, always close the cash drawer between transactions. While you are counting change, partially close the drawer. Remove the money tendered by the customer from the register ledge after giving change. You should always lock the register if you leave it. A customer may interrupt you while you are counting change. It is best to ignore the interruption. You need to concentrate to avoid making incorrect change. You can respond politely once the transaction has been completed.

7. You would want FOB destination so that the seller would be responsible for the goods until they arrived to you.

8. A purchase order is created by the buyer for goods being ordered, while an invoice is created by the seller to indicate the amount due.

9. Students should role-play how they would deal with a customer who wants to make a return but does not have a receipt. They should explain the store's policy concerning returns without a receipt. Some stores give store credit for these types of returns, while others do not allow returns if the customer has no receipt.

Chapter 16 Review and Activities

21st Century Skills

Communication Skills

10. **Convincing the Boss** You are the buyer in a women's specialty clothing shop. Almost every day someone comes into the shop and asks for a particular brand of shoe. Your manager has not carried that brand of shoe because he does not like doing business with the company. You have calculated how much money the store is losing by not carrying the shoes. Write an e-mail to your manager that explains how much more income the store would gain if it carried the shoes.

Financial Literacy Skills

11. **Business Loan** You are planning to open a bicycle shop. You will need a loan for $15,000 to get started. A bank will loan you the money at 6 percent, with payments for 5 years of $289.99 per month. A credit union will loan you the money at 5.5 percent, with payments for 5 years of $286.52 per month. What will be the total cost over 5 years for each loan?

e-Marketing Skills

12. **Customer Satisfaction** Your company is considering expanding its e-marketing division. Your boss has asked you to research how satisfied customers are with their online buying experience. Use your own online buying experiences and ask others for ideas, and then prepare a questionnaire to be circulated to learn the level of satisfaction with purchasing goods online. Here are some ideas to consider:
    - How will you measure customer satisfaction?
    - What technological resources does your company have?
    - When will the questionnaire be shared with customers?
    - How will the questionnaire's results be shared with customers?

Build Academic Skills

Social Studies

13. **Digital Archives** Use the Internet to research the history of digital-scanning technology and its use. Use presentation software to create a report on your findings.

NCSS VIII A Science, Technology, & Society Identify and describe both current and historical examples of the interaction and interdependence of science, technology, and society in a variety of cultural settings.

English Language Arts

14. **Forms of Payment** Most retail stores accept cash, checks, debit cards, and credit cards. In the stores where you shop, ask if all these forms of payment are accepted and which is the most popular and least popular with customers. Then write a half-page (or more) report summarizing your findings.

NCTE 4 Use written language to communicate effectively.

Mathematics

15. **Calculating Total Cost** You prepare a purchase order for the following items: 214 T-shirts at $14.85 each, 68 shirts at $19.99 each, 95 jackets at $20.80 each, and 45 jackets at $23.40 each. What is the total cost of the merchandise if no sales tax is added?

    Math Concept **Multi-Step Problems** Outline the information you know before you solve this word problem. List the information you know and decide how to use it to solve the problem.

NCTM Problem Solving Apply and adapt a variety of appropriate strategies to solve problems.

For help, go to the **Math Skills Handbook** located at the back of this book.

Standardized Test Practice

Directions Read the following questions. On a separate piece of paper, write the best possible answer for each one.

1. Which of the following is NOT a type of retail sales transaction?
   A. Cash
   B. Debit card
   C. Credit card
   D. UPC
2. An RFID tag makes it possible to read all the items in a cart simultaneously while they are all still in the cart.
   T
   F
3. Currency and checks collected in sales transactions are deposited in the ________.

Test-Taking Tip

When studying for a test from a textbook, re-read the chapter summaries. They do a good job of summarizing important points.

DECA Connection Role Play

Accountant
Wholesale Gift Warehouse

Situation You work as an accountant in the accounting department of a wholesale business that sells gift items to retail businesses. You have been working at this job for two months. During this time you have been diligent about learning all that you can about your new position and performing your job duties to the best of your abilities.

Your supervisor (judge) has noticed your hard work and conscientious approach to your job. Your supervisor (judge) is considering assigning you some more advanced duties. Before doing so, your supervisor (judge) wants to be certain that you understand purchase orders and invoices, their purposes, their similarities, their differences, and how extensions and other charges are calculated. Therefore, your supervisor (judge) has asked you to discuss that information in a meeting that will take place later today.

Activity You are to prepare any notes that you will need for the meeting to discuss purchase orders and invoices. Once you have completed your preparation, you will meet with your supervisor (judge).

Evaluation You will be evaluated on how well you meet the following performance indicators:

1. Describe the use of technology in operations.
2. Calculate miscellaneous charges.
3. Select the best shipping method.
4. Demonstrate systematic behavior.
5. Organize information.

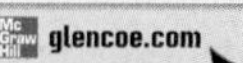

Download the Competitive Events Workbook for more Role-Play practice.

EVALUATE

Communication Skills

10. Students should write a concise e-mail in which they explain that a large number of customers are requesting the brand of shoes that the store does not carry. In the e-mail, students should emphasize their estimate of how much money the store is losing by not carrying the product.

Financial Literacy Skills

11. The cost over 5 years for a $15,000 bank loan at 6% would be $17,399.40 ($289.99 × 60 [5 years × 12 months/year] = $17,399.40). The cost over 5 years for a $15,000 credit union loan at 5.5% would be $17,191.20 ($286.52 × 60 [5 years × 12 months/year] = $17,191.20).

e-Marketing Skills

12. Students should prepare a questionnaire to evaluate how satisfied customers are with their online buying experiences. Students should carefully analyze how they want to evaluate customer satisfaction. Appropriate questions might include:
    - Overall, how would you rate your experience using our site to make an online purchase?
    - How easy was it to find the item you wanted to purchase?
    - Did the site contain enough information on the items in which you were interested? If not, what additional information would you want?
    - What method of payment did you use?
    - Did you receive your order in a timely fashion and was it correct?

    Students also should discuss their company's technological resources and how and when they will share the questionnaire results with the customers.

EVALUATE

Build Academic Skills

Social Studies

13. Students should use presentation software to share the history of digital-scanning technology with the class. Scanning technology was used in 1925 to scan and then wire photos for use by the news media. Color scanning was patented in 1937. NASA transmitted scanned images from the moon to the Earth in the late 1960s. The business world started using scanning technology for faxes. Early technologies were analog, but with the growth of the computer, digital technologies quickly took over. Scanning began to be used in medicine for CAT scans and MRIs. The scanning of products using UPC codes started in the mid-1970s, and expanded rapidly.

English Language Arts

14. Students should write an error-free half-page (or more) report summarizing the forms of payment the store accepts. The report should also discuss which forms of payment are the most popular and the least popular.

Mathematics

15. $7,566.22 ([214 × 14.85] + [68 × 19.99] + [95 × 20.80] + [45 × 23.40])

Standardized Test Practice

1. D (UPC)
2. True
3. till

DECA Connection Role Play

Evaluations will be based on these performance indicators:

1. **Describe the use of technology in operations.** Cash registers provide three basic sales transaction functions: recording sales, storing cash and sales documents, and providing receipts. In addition, most electronic cash registers can figure sales tax, calculate discounts, subtract and credit returns, and determine the amount due back to the customer. Point-of-sale (POS) systems combine the functions of a cash register with a computer. For example, POS systems can automatically reorder stock when inventory drops to a specified level. Many stores use optical scanners or electronic wands to read a product's UPC. The system uses the UPC not only to determine the product's price, but also to perform such tasks as updating inventory. The POS system can also print out financial statements, sales trends, and sales personnel productivity reports.
2. **Calculate miscellaneous charges.** The student should be able to properly add additional charges to the order, such as any sales tax, shipping charges, and so forth.
3. **Select the best shipping method.** The shipping method selected depends on factors like distance, weight of the shipment, type of items, etc. If a shipment is going overseas, an international company that specializes in importing and exporting can be used. The U.S. Postal Service provides a variety of services, including standard surface package delivery and Express Mail. Private companies providing delivery service include Federal Express, UPS, and DHL Express. With COD shipping, the amount due is collected from the customer by the carrier. FOB means that the price for goods includes delivery at the seller's expense to a specified point and no farther.
4. **Demonstrate systematic behavior.** Students should be able to perform tasks such as completing sales transactions, handling returns and exchanges, using POS systems, and completing purchase orders and invoices in a methodical and systematic way.
5. **Organize information.** The student is able to properly enter and organize information on sales transaction documents such as sales checks and on documents such as purchase orders, invoices, and shipping documents.

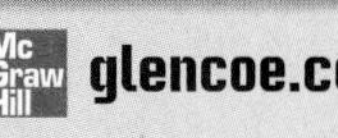

Role Plays For more DECA Role Plays, send students to the Online Learning Center to download the Competitive Events Workbook.

UNIT 5 **Marketing Internship Project**

A Sales Plan for a Sports Product

Selling is easy when you believe in your product. Sports products have a track record of success.

Scenario

The sports world has inspired products of all types for fans, from sports clothing and bobblehead dolls to wall graphics of popular athletes and sports teams. For example, Fathead® vinyl wall graphics cost between $19.99 and $99.99 and are sold via a Web site and through retailers, such as Target®. The price of these graphics depends on size and the popularity of the athlete.

Your company has decided to market its own line of vinyl wall graphics. The products are made of high-quality vinyl and adhesive for the same price as Fathead. Your company has its own Web site and is opening kiosks in shopping malls. For products to sell in kiosks, your sales staff must be well trained.

The Skills You'll Use

Academic Skills Reading, writing, social studies, researching, and analyzing

Basic Skills Speaking, listening, thinking, and interpersonal

Technology Skills Word processing, presentation, spreadsheet, telecommunication, and the Internet

NCTE 5 Use different writing process elements to communicate effectively.
NCTE 7 Conduct research and gather, evaluate, and synthesize data to communicate discoveries.

Your Objective

To create a training plan for new sales employees that will be selling your company's reusable wall graphics in a shopping mall kiosk.

STEP 1 Do Your Research

Go to the Internet to conduct research about reusable vinyl wall graphics. For example, visit Fathead's Web site and other wall-graphic sites to see the variety of wall graphics sold and their major selling points. As you conduct your research, answer these questions:

- How and where are removable vinyl wall graphics used?
- What are the features and benefits of vinyl wall graphics?
- Who are the prospective customers for wall graphics?
- How are wall graphics currently marketed?

Write a summary of your research.

STEP 2 Plan Your Project

Now that you have completed your research, you need to begin planning your project.

- Create a table of information comparing your products' selling points with the selling points of your competition.
- Write a sample script to demonstrate how to approach a customer, to determine the customer's needs, and to respond when confronted with customer objections.
- Develop an exciting product presentation that covers the major selling points, involves customers, and makes use of sales aids.
- Provide possible scenarios for closing the sale and suggestion selling.

STEP 3 Connect with Your Community

- Interview one or more trusted adults at home, at school, at work, or in your community to see if they own wall graphics. Find out what they like and dislike about them.
- Look for examples of wall graphics on autos, in school, and other public places.
- Visit a retail store that carries wall graphics to see how they are priced and merchandised.

STEP 4 Share What You Learn

Assume your class is a committee comprised of the vice president of sales and experienced sales representatives who must approve your sales training program.

- Present your sales training plan in an oral presentation. Be prepared to answer questions.
- Present your plan in a written report.
- Use software to create a slide presentation to accompany your oral report. Include one slide for each key topic found in the written report.

STEP 5 Evaluate Your Marketing and Academic Skills

Your project will be evaluated based on the following:

- Knowledge of the sales process and effective selling techniques
- Knowledge of reusable wall graphic products
- Completeness of the sales training plan, including an evaluation rubric
- Organization and continuity of presentation
- Mechanics—presentation and neatness
- Speaking and listening skills

MARKETING CORE FUNCTION
Selling

Marketing Internship Project Checklist

Plan
- ✓ Conduct research on reusable wall graphic companies and how they are marketed.
- ✓ Design an effective sales training program for new sales associates.

Write
- ✓ Summarize your research.
- ✓ Write a report detailing your sales plan.
- ✓ Write a sample script to demonstrate how to approach a customer, to determine the customer's needs, and to respond when confronted with customer objections.

Present
- ✓ Present your sales training plan.
- ✓ Present sample dialogue for each step of the sale.
- ✓ Present suggested sales aids for use in the kiosks.

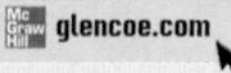

Evaluate Download a rubric you can use to evaluate your final project.

my marketing portfolio

Internship Report Once you have completed your Marketing Internship Project and oral presentation, put your written report and a few printouts of key slides from your oral presentation in your Marketing Portfolio.

Selling Wall Graphics in the Organizational Market Your employer sells removable vinyl wall coverings to businesses for window and point-of-purchase displays. They come in widths of 30, 48, 60, and 75 inches and lengths of 75, 150, and 300 inches in a variety of textures. They are flame and smoke certified. Prepare a written and oral sales plan for an upcoming trade show where you will work at your company's exhibit. What will you say and do during the sales process? What sales aids will be needed? How will you evaluate your efforts?

EVALUATE

Anticipation Activity

Project Objective Read the project objective aloud to students: ***Create a training plan for new sales employees who will be selling your company's reusable wall graphics in a shopping mall kiosk.*** Then ask students to think about personal selling, feature-benefit selling, and the steps of the sale in Unit 5. Remind them of these key points:

- Personal selling involves direct communication between a salesperson and a customer.
- Feature-benefit selling requires a salesperson to know a product's features, and then match them with the customer's needs and wants.
- The steps of selling begin with approaching the customer and end with building relationships.

Ask students: ***What is the goal of a sales training plan?*** The goal is to disseminate product information to sales staff and establish consistent guidelines for selling to achieve a successful outcome.

Ask students: ***What should you know about your product's features?*** You should know its basic features, or intended use; physical features that differ from competing products; and extended features such as warranties, service, and financing. Knowing features facilitates matching the product with customers' needs and wants.

Graphic Organizer

Display this graphic organizer. Ask students to name the steps.

1. Approach The Customer
2. Needs Determined
3. Present Product
4. Overcome Objections
5. Close The Sale
6. Suggestion Selling

Build Relationships

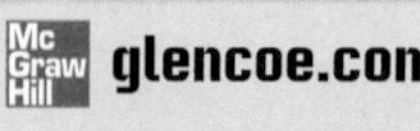

Graphic Organizer Send students to the Online Learning Center to print this graphic organizer.

EVALUATE

STEP 1 Do Your Research

Tell students that there are many places to find information they can use to learn about the product features to integrate into their selling plans. Students can use library and Internet resources, but they should also talk to people in the community. Encourage students to seek the opinions and ideas of trusted people they know. Other people can bring new perspectives and ideas about popular selling points, ways to approach customers and determine customer needs as well as their perceptions about the vinyl wall graphics market.

STEP 2 Plan Your Project

Students should create a list of selling points compared with those of the competition before writing a sample script to demonstrate how to sell to customers. Students should explain why they chose their product presentation and the particular selling points. Students' explanation of their scenarios should also include closing the sale and suggestion selling.

STEP 3 Connect with Your Community

Explain to students that connecting with members of the community is a great way to build relationships. Tell them that young people who have relationships with caring, responsible, and competent adults are more likely to achieve success in life than those who do not. Encourage students to take part in opportunities for adults to serve as mentors, coaches, advocates, and advisors, both formally and informally.

STEP 4 Share What You Learn

Students should present their ideas in a written report and oral presentation with presentation software. They should have at least one slide in their presentation for each key topic in the written report. Encourage students to speak clearly, use appropriate grammar and vocabulary, and actively engage the audience by making and maintaining eye contact and using movement (facial expressions, posture, gestures) to focus attention and interest.

STEP 5 Evaluate Your Marketing and Academic Skills

Have students use the Marketing Internship Project Checklist to help them to plan, write, and present their reports. Exemplary written reports will include information that clearly supports a central thesis, a single, distinct focus, generally well-developed ideas, well-phrased sentences that flow smoothly and are varied in length and structure, consistently precise word choice, and few, if any, errors in grammar, spelling, and mechanics.

glencoe.com

Evaluation Rubric Send students to the Online Learning Center to get a rubric to evaluate their projects.

Culminating Activity

Explain to students that evaluation or assessment during a training period is an effective way to improve a process—in this case, the sales process. Sales managers who train sales personnel can evaluate a salesperson's skill during a four-step training process: (1) explanation; (2) demonstration; (3) trial; and (4) critique. Sales associates get the opportunity to make specific improvements in the way they sell products during training. Ask students: ***How would you explain each of the four steps for training sales staff?*** First, the trainer explains, and then demonstrates a sales technique. Next, the sales associate performs the newly learned technique and demonstrates product knowledge in a role-playing format before finally applying this knowledge and skill to a real-world sales transaction. Following that, the trainer provides constructive criticism as needed to improve the process.

my marketing portfolio

Internship Report Have students put their written reports and printouts of key slides from their oral presentations in their marketing portfolio.

Selling Wall Graphics in the Organizational Market Direct students to select a business in the organizational market for which they would like to market wall graphics. Have them prepare written and oral sales plans for an upcoming trade-show exhibit. Students' completed plans and should include all of the elements and answer all of the questions included in the Marketing Internship Project on this page. This additional activity can build relevance for students who are motivated to learn about other organizational market businesses and industries. Relevance shifts the focus to what motivates individual students to learn.

UNIT 6

Promotion

PLANNING GUIDE AND RESOURCES

	Print	Digital
Unit 6 Promotion		Unit 6 Fast Files: Marketing Internship Project Activity Connect Online Learning Center through glencoe.com
Chapter 17 **Promotional Concepts and Strategies**	Student Activity Workbook: Chapter 17 DECA Connection Role Play; Chapter 17 Vocabulary Activity; Section Note Taking Activities; Chapter Academics Activity; Section Study Skills Activities; Section Real-World Applications Activities Mathematics for Marketing Workbook Marketing Research Project Workbook School-to-Career Activity Workbook	Unit 6 Fast Files: Chapter 17 Discovery Project Worksheet and Rubric; Chapter 17 Green Marketer Activity; Chapter 17 Digital Nation Activity; Section Graphic Organizers; Section Outlines with Key Terms and Definitions; Section Summaries ExamView Assessment Suite, Chapter 17 Connect Online Learning Center through glencoe.com
Chapter 18 **Visual Merchandising and Display**	Student Activity Workbook: Chapter 18 DECA Connection Role Play; Chapter 18 Vocabulary Activity; Section Note Taking Activities; Chapter Academics Activity; Section Study Skills Activities; Section Real-World Applications Activities Mathematics for Marketing Workbook Marketing Research Project Workbook School-to-Career Activity Workbook	Unit 6 Fast Files: Chapter 18 Discovery Project Worksheet and Rubric; Chapter 18 Green Marketer Activity; Chapter 18 Digital Nation Activity; Section Graphic Organizers; Section Outlines with Key Terms and Definitions; Section Summaries ExamView Assessment Suite, Chapter 18 Connect Online Learning Center through glencoe.com
Chapter 19 **Advertising**	Student Activity Workbook: Chapter 19 DECA Connection Role Play; Chapter 19 Vocabulary Activity; Section Note Taking Activities; Chapter Academics Activity; Section Study Skills Activities; Section Real-World Applications Activities Mathematics for Marketing Workbook Marketing Research Project Workbook School-to-Career Activity Workbook	Unit 6 Fast Files: Chapter 19 Discovery Project Worksheet and Rubric; Chapter 19 Green Marketer Activity; Chapter 19 Digital Nation Activity; Section Graphic Organizers; Section Outlines with Key Terms and Definitions; Section Summaries ExamView Assessment Suite, Chapter 19 Connect Online Learning Center through glencoe.com
Chapter 20 **Print Advertisements**	Student Activity Workbook: Chapter 20 DECA Connection Role Play; Chapter 20 Vocabulary Activity; Section Note Taking Activities; Chapter Academics Activity; Section Study Skills Activities; Section Real-World Applications Activities Mathematics for Marketing Workbook Marketing Research Project Workbook School-to-Career Activity Workbook	Unit 6 Fast Files: Chapter 20 Discovery Project Worksheet and Rubric; Chapter 20 Green Marketer Activity; Chapter 20 Digital Nation Activity; Section Graphic Organizers; Section Outlines with Key Terms and Definitions; Section Summaries ExamView Assessment Suite, Chapter 20 Connect Online Learning Center through glencoe.com

McGRAW-HILL PROFESSIONAL DEVELOPMENT

Perkins IV has placed more emphasis than ever on providing quality professional development for Career and Technology educators. The legislation mandates that the focus of professional development be the integration and reinforcement of academic competencies in order to improve student achievement. Specifically, Perkins requires measurements of students' academic success. McGraw-Hill answers the challenge for strong and effective professional development with a five-prong **Online Professional Development for Integrating Academics.**

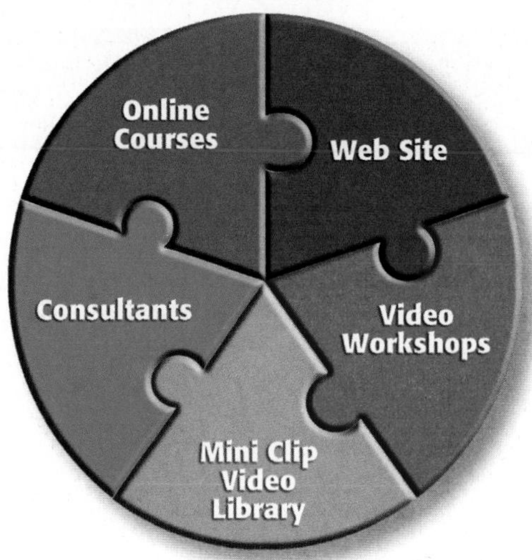

For pricing and ordering information contact your McGraw-Hill Sales Representative.

VIDEO LIBRARY

The McGraw-Hill Professional Development Mini-Clip Video Library, referenced for your convenience at the point of use, provides teaching strategies to strengthen academic and learning skills. Go to the Online Learning Center to view these professional development video clips for Unit 6:

Chapter 17: Promotional Concepts and Strategies

- **Reading: Modeling Reading:** Students practice fluency. (p. 395)
- **Reading: Fluency Development:** Different instructional strategies are used to develop reading fluency. (p. 405)

Chapter 18: Visual Merchandising and Display

- **ELL: Vocabulary Activities:** Students practice vocabulary using synonyms, antonyms, definitions, and words in context. (p. 419)
- **Reading: Strategies for Student Achievement:** Teachers discuss strategies to meet curriculum standards. (p. 423)
- **ELL: Accessing Prior Knowledge:** A teacher helps students make connections with what they already know and what they will read. (p. 428)

Chapter 19: Advertising

- **Reading: Differentiated Instruction:** An author discusses elements of a differentiated classroom. (p. 441)
- **ELL: Words and Pictures:** A teacher uses words and media examples to help students learn new vocabulary. (p. 453)

Chapter 20: Print Advertisements

- **ELL: Previewing a Text:** A teacher points out strategies to increase comprehension. (p. 467)
- **Reading: Obstacles to Achievement:** Teachers work together to help students master specific standards. (p. 470)
- **Reading: Strategic Readers:** An author discusses strategic readers. (p. 477)

UNIT OVERVIEW

Sections	Objectives	Common Core State Standards College and Career Readiness
Section 17.1 **The Promotional Mix**	• Explain the role of promotion in business and advertising. • Identify types of promotion. • Distinguish between public relations and publicity. • Explain the elements of a news release. • Describe the concept of the promotional mix.	• **Reading** Determine central ideas or themes of a text and analyze their development; summarize the key supporting details and ideas.
Section 17.2 **Types of Promotion**	• Define sales promotion. • Explain the use of promotional tie-ins, trade sales promotions, and loyalty marketing programs.	• **Reading** Interpret words and phrases as they are used in a text, including determining technical, connotative, and figurative meanings, and analyze how specific word choices shape meaning or tone.
Section 18.1 **Display Features**	• Explain the concept and purpose of visual merchandising. • Identify the elements of visual merchandising. • Describe types of display arrangements. • Understand the role of visual merchandisers on the marketing team.	• **Reading** Read and comprehend complex literary and informational texts independently and proficiently.
Section 18.2 **Artistic Design**	• List the five steps in creating a display. • Explain how artistic elements function in display design. • Describe the importance of display maintenance.	• **Writing** Produce clear and coherent writing in which the development, organization, and style are appropriate to task, purpose, and audience.

Sections	Objectives	Common Core State Standards College and Career Readiness
Section 19.1 **Advertising Media**	• Explain the concept and purpose of advertising in the promotional mix. • Identify the different types of advertising media. • Discuss the planning and selection of media.	• **Reading** Determine central ideas or themes of a text and analyze their development; summarize the key supporting details and ideas.
Section 19.2 **Media Rates**	• Identify media measurement techniques. • Explain techniques used to evaluate media. • Summarize how media costs are determined. • Explain promotional budget methods.	• **Writing** Produce clear and coherent writing in which the development, organization, and style are appropriate to task, purpose, and audience.
Section 20.1 **Elements of Advertising**	• Discuss how advertising campaigns are developed. • Explain the role of an advertising agency. • Identify the main components of print advertisements.	• **Reading** Integrate and evaluate content presented in diverse formats and media, including visually and quantitatively, as well as in words.
Section 20.2 **Advertising Layout**	• Explain the principles of preparing an ad layout. • List advantages and disadvantages of using color in advertising. • Describe how typefaces and sizes add variety and emphasis to print advertisements.	• **Writing** Produce clear and coherent writing in which the development, organization, and style are appropriate to task, purpose, and audience.

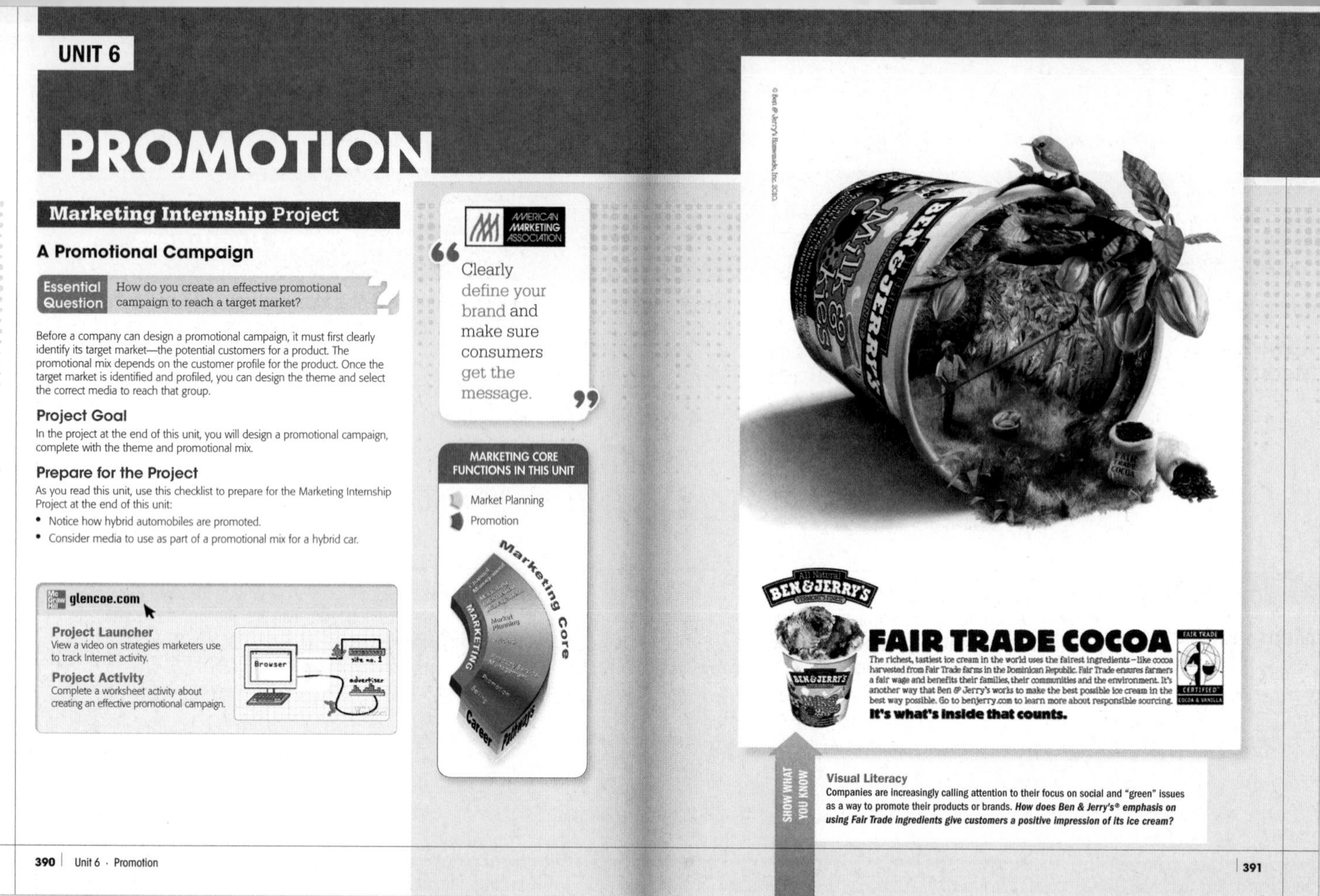

UNIT 6

PROMOTION

Marketing Internship Project

A Promotional Campaign

Essential Question How do you create an effective promotional campaign to reach a target market?

Before a company can design a promotional campaign, it must first clearly identify its target market—the potential customers for a product. The promotional mix depends on the customer profile for the product. Once the target market is identified and profiled, you can design the theme and select the correct media to reach that group.

Project Goal

In the project at the end of this unit, you will design a promotional campaign, complete with the theme and promotional mix.

Prepare for the Project

As you read this unit, use this checklist to prepare for the Marketing Internship Project at the end of this unit:

- Notice how hybrid automobiles are promoted.
- Consider media to use as part of a promotional mix for a hybrid car.

glencoe.com

Project Launcher View a video on strategies marketers use to track Internet activity.

Project Activity Complete a worksheet activity about creating an effective promotional campaign.

AMERICAN MARKETING ASSOCIATION

"Clearly define your brand and make sure consumers get the message."

MARKETING CORE FUNCTIONS IN THIS UNIT

Market Planning
Promotion

SHOW WHAT YOU KNOW

Visual Literacy
Companies are increasingly calling attention to their focus on social and "green" issues as a way to promote their products or brands. ***How does Ben & Jerry's® emphasis on using Fair Trade ingredients give customers a positive impression of its ice cream?***

390 | Unit 6 · Promotion

391

ENGAGE

Introduce the Unit

Unit 6 explores promotional strategies for selling goods and services or developing a business image.

Chapter 17 examines the concept of promotion and promotional strategies.

Chapter 18 focuses on visual merchandising and display concepts.

Chapter 19 discusses the different types of advertising media and how to calculate media costs.

Chapter 20 examines advertising campaign development, the role of advertising agencies, and the elements of print/online advertisements.

Build Background

Ask students to name promotional activities used by companies. Answers may include print and online advertisements, special events, displays, commercials, online videos, and product placement in movies and TV shows. Ask students: ***Why do you think businesses spend a lot of money on promotional activities?*** Through promotional activities, businesses can showcase their goods and services in order to inform and persuade consumers to buy their products.

Visual Literacy

Photo Caption Answer Read the copy on the ad to students. Then read the photo caption and the photo caption question to students: ***How does Ben & Jerry's® emphasis on using Fair Trade ingredients give customers a positive impression of its ice cream?*** Answers will vary. Accept all reasonable answers. Sample answer: Ben & Jerry's attitude toward responsible sourcing and its use of fair trade products gives customers a positive impression because fair trade ensures that farmers get a fair price for their coffee, which improves their standard of living. Ask students to evaluate the visual components of the advertisement. Ask volunteers to explain how the visual aspects of the advertisement complement the text of the advertisement. The image on the ad shows a scene going on inside of the ice cream container: a farmer working the land, harvesting fair trade beans. The text says "It's what's inside that counts." This implies that the quality of the ingredients that go into making the product is important. The illustration of the scene inside the container plays on this slogan.

ENGAGE

Marketing Internship Project Preview

Read students the Marketing Internship Project Essential Question: ***How do you create an effective promotional campaign to reach a target market?*** Because students are just starting to learn about promotions, they will likely not know the specific answer to this question, which is identify a target market, create a customer profile, and design a theme to inform a promotional campaign. However, students should know that it is important to know the customers because their preferences will influence decisions about promotions. Explain to students that they will learn about the strategies and media that businesses use to promote products while studying this unit. Tell students that when they are finished studying this unit, they will ask questions to find answers that will inform a promotional campaign for hybrid automobiles. As they study each chapter in the unit, they can prepare for the Unit Project by thinking of how hybrid automobiles are promoted and by talking to people who own hybrid automobiles.

glencoe.com

Marketing Internship Project Resources Send students to the Online Learning Center to watch a video and download a worksheet activity related to the topic of the Unit Project.

Read the American Marketing Association quote to students:

"Clearly define your brand and make sure consumers get the message."

Explain to students that the AMA's Resource Library provides information through articles and resources that address the functions of marketing. Content about the promotion function focuses on promotional strategies designed "to communicate with targeted audiences."

Defined Brand Good communication offers the best chance for potential customers to buy a product. It begins with a clearly defined brand. The brand definition serves as a foundation upon which all marketing activities are built. To define a brand, marketers should consider the company's mission, demographics, competition, and visual brand image.

Elements of Branding Visual brand elements include a logo, name, slogan, and any design that is recognizable.

Ask students: ***What are some methods used to "make sure consumers get the message"?*** Messages must be customized for the target market.

MARKETING CORE FUNCTIONS IN THIS UNIT

Point out to students that Chapters 17, 18, 19, and 20 will touch on two of the seven marketing core functions. Describe each of these marketing functions to students to prepare them to start studying this unit.

Market Planning involves understanding the concepts and strategies used to develop and target specific marketing strategies to a select audience.

Promotion is the effort to inform, persuade, or remind potential customers about a business's products or services or to improve a company's public image.

MARKETING RESEARCH

PROJECT WORKBOOK

The purpose of the Marketing Research Project Workbook is to provide a step-by-step approach for students to conduct their own marketing research study. Each chapter is devoted to key elements in the research process. Each chapter builds upon the previous chapters, and by the end of the book, students will have completed an in-depth marketing research study, complete with rationale for all decisions, a report of the findings and conclusions, recommendations based on the original research problem and study objectives, and an annotated bibliography.

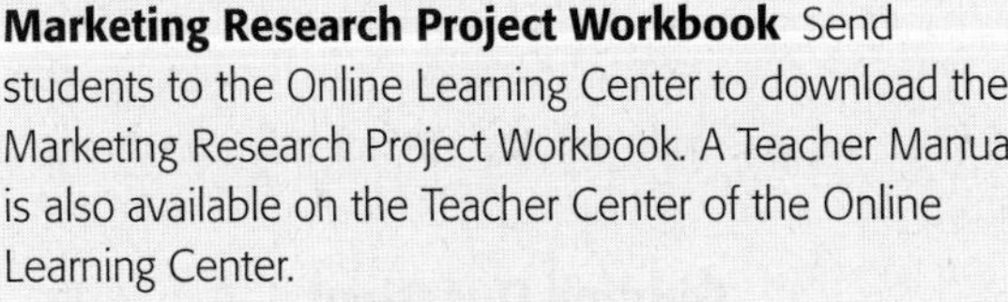
glencoe.com

Marketing Research Project Workbook Send students to the Online Learning Center to download the Marketing Research Project Workbook. A Teacher Manual is also available on the Teacher Center of the Online Learning Center.

promotional concepts and strategies

SHOW WHAT YOU KNOW

Visual Literacy Businesses promote themselves to create a favorable image, attract customers, build product awareness, and create sales. Promotion includes advertising, direct marketing, personal selling, public relations, and sales promotions. ***What unique promotional activities have you observed recently?***

Discovery Project

Promoting Products

Essential Question What makes a promotion successful?

Project Goal
Imagine you work for a marketing agency that represents a sports beverage company. You have been assigned to develop a promotional plan to attract young people (ages 16–25) to the product. Create a promotional mix by using advertising, direct marketing, sales promotions, and public relations activities. Your plan should include specific examples of how each type of promotion will be used to reach your target market.

Ask Yourself...
- How will you identify the specific product to promote to teens and young adults?
- How will you use advertising, direct marketing, sales promotion, and public relations activities to promote the product?
- How will you organize your promotional plan?
- How will you present your promotional plan?

Organize and Present Organize your information into a promotional plan for the product, and use presentation software to present your plan.

glencoe.com

Activity
Get a worksheet activity about promoting products.

Evaluate
Download a rubric you can use to evaluate your project.

DECA Connection

DECA Event Role Play
Concepts in this chapter are related to DECA competitive events that involve either an interview or role play.

Performance Indicators The performance indicators represent key skills and knowledge. Your key to success in DECA competitive events is relating them to concepts in this chapter.
- Explain the role of promotion as a marketing function.
- Plan displays and themes with management.
- Create displays.
- Create promotional signs.
- Coordinate activities in the promotional mix.

DECA Prep
Role Play Practice role-playing with the DECA Connection competitive-event activity at the end of this chapter. More information on DECA events can be found on DECA's Web site.

ENGAGE

Visual Literacy

Read the chapter opener photo caption question to students: ***What unique promotional activities have you observed recently?*** television commercials, creative flyers, interesting pop-up ads on the Internet, or a "sign spinner" twirling a sign on a street corner Ask these guiding questions to focus students' attention on promotional activities.

Guiding Questions

Explain How do promotional activities influence your purchases?	Sample answer: A good promotion will capture my interest in a product or service and persuade me to look into it more closely. Some students may say that they are not influenced by promotional activities
Make a Judgment In your opinion, what is the most effective form of promotion? Why?	Possible answer: advertisements on TV and the Internet are most effective because they have such a large, widespread audience.

Discovery Project

Promoting Products Ask students the Discovery Project Essential Question: ***What makes a promotion successful?*** Students may be aware that a promotion is successful when it achieves the goals that were set for the promotion. However, the bottom line for the success of a promotion is that it attracts current and new customers and generates revenue for the company. Ask students to share what promotional activities would keep them as a customer. Students might suggest such activities as sales promotions, coupons, frequent shopper rewards, and so on.

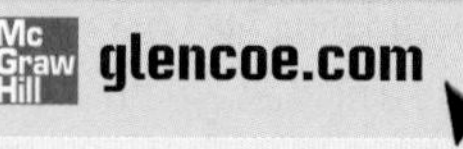

Discovery Project Resources Send students to the Online Learning Center to download a rubric to evaluate their projects.

ENGAGE

Introduce the Chapter

This chapter explores the concept of the promotional mix. These main concepts are introduced and discussed:

- Promotion in marketing
- Types of promotion in the promotional mix
- The concept of a promotional mix
- Developing a promotional mix
- Personal selling
- Advertising
- Direct marketing
- Sales promotion
- Public relations
- Trade promotions
- Consumer promotions
- Promotional budget

Discussion Starter

Promotions in Marketing Tell students that there are many different types of promotion used in marketing. Ask students to offer examples for each type of promotions with which they are familiar. Students may be familiar with television, radio, and Internet advertisements, in-home and in-store demonstrations, direct mail or electronic mail, coupons, and company-sponsored walks or runs to raise money for charitable organizations. Ask: ***Which type do you think is most effective? Why?*** In-store or in-home demonstrations are effective because you can immediately evaluate the quality and performance of a product.

DECA Connection

Discuss the performance indicators listed in the DECA Connection feature. Explain to students that performance indicators tell them how to demonstrate their acquired skills and knowledge through individual or team competitive events.

 **glencoe.com** 

Competitive Events Workbook For more DECA Role Plays, send students to the Online Learning Center to download the Competitive Events Workbook.

PROGRAM RESOURCE ORGANIZER

PRINT RESOURCES

- **Student Edition**
- **Teacher Edition**
- **Student Activity Workbook with Academic Integration** includes worksheets and activities correlated to the text.
- **Mathematics for Marketing Workbook** provides math activities for every unit in the text.

TECHNOLOGY TOOLBOX

- **Connect**
- **ConnectPlus**
- **ExamView Assessment Suite** is a comprehensive solution for creating, administering, and scoring tests.

 **glencoe.com** 

Online Learning Center provides a variety of resources to enrich and enhance learning.

SECTION, CHAPTER, AND UNIT RESOURCES

- **Graphic Organizers** for organizing text concepts visually.
- **Digital Nation Activities** and **Green Marketer Activities** extend learning beyond the text features.
- **Career Chatroom Career Profiles** allow students to explore different marketing occupations in depth.
- **After You Read Answer Keys** for students to check their answers.
- **Discovery Project Rubrics** and **Marketing Internship Project Rubrics** for students to evaluate their projects.

PROGRAM RESOURCES

- **Student Activity Workbook with Academic Integration Teacher Annotated Edition** includes annotated answers for the activities and worksheets.
- **Marketing Research Project Workbook** provides a step-by-step approach for students to complete their own marketing research studies.
- **School-to-Career Activity Workbook** helps students relate their class work to on-the-job experience and involves work-site analysis and working with mentors.
- **Competitive Events Workbook** helps prepare students for state and national marketing education competitions.
- **Inclusion in the Marketing Education Classroom** provides teaching resources for working with students with special needs.
- **PowerPoint Presentations** provides visual teaching aids and assessments for this chapter.

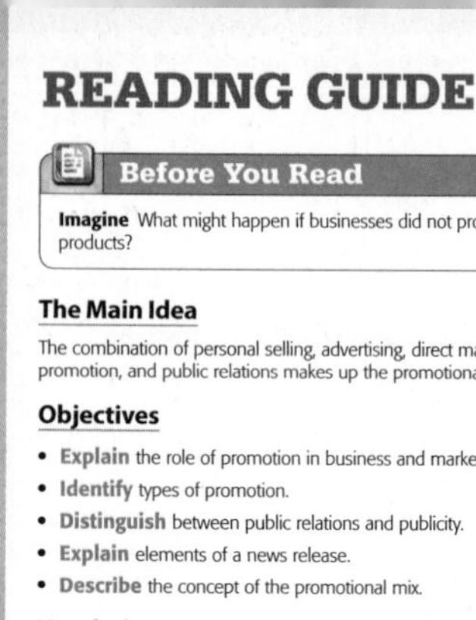

READING GUIDE

Before You Read

Imagine What might happen if businesses did not promote their products?

The Main Idea

The combination of personal selling, advertising, direct marketing, sales promotion, and public relations makes up the promotional mix.

Objectives

- **Explain** the role of promotion in business and marketing.
- **Identify** types of promotion.
- **Distinguish** between public relations and publicity.
- **Explain** elements of a news release.
- **Describe** the concept of the promotional mix.

Vocabulary

Content Vocabulary
- promotion
- product promotion
- institutional promotion
- promotional mix
- advertising
- direct marketing
- social media
- sales promotion
- public relations
- news release
- publicity
- push policy
- pull policy

Academic Vocabulary

You will find these words in your reading and on your tests. Make sure you know their meanings.
- via
- target

Graphic Organizer

Draw or print this chart and write examples for each different type of promotion.

glencoe.com

Print this graphic organizer.

Promotional Mix: Product Promotion | Institutional Promotion

STANDARDS

ACADEMIC

English Language Arts

NCTE 1 Read texts to acquire new information.

Social Studies

NCSS V B Individuals, Groups, & Institutions Analyze group and institutional influences on people, events, and elements of culture in both historical and contemporary settings.

NCSS *National Council for the Social Studies*
NCTE *National Council of Teachers of English*
NCTM *National Council of Teachers of Mathematics*
NSES *National Science Education Standards*

College & Career READINESS

Common Core
Reading Determine central ideas or themes of a text and analyze their development; summarize the key supporting details and ideas.

MARKETING CORE FUNCTION

Promotion

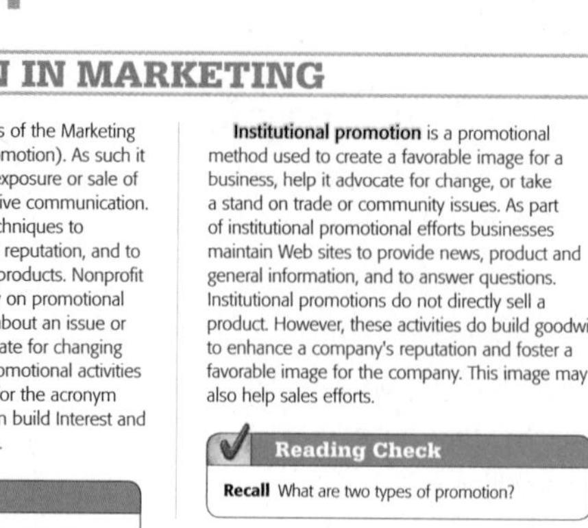

me. Section 17.1 The Promotional Mix

PROMOTION IN MARKETING

Promotion is one of the four Ps of the Marketing Mix (Product, Place, Price, & Promotion). As such it is any activity that helps in the exposure or sale of a product. Promotion is persuasive communication. Companies use promotional techniques to enhance their public image and reputation, and to persuade people to value their products. Nonprofit and charitable organizations rely on promotional activities to educate the public about an issue or cause. They also use it to advocate for changing laws or policies. The goals of promotional activities are summarized by the phrase for the acronym AIDA—first attract Attention, then build Interest and Desire, and finally ask for Action.

As You Read

Contrast Distinguish between the different types of promotion.

Product promotion is a promotional method used by businesses to convince prospects to select their goods or services instead of a competitor's brands. Promotional activities explain the major features and benefits of the product, identify where it is sold, advertise sales, answer customer questions, and introduce new offerings. Product promotion also helps businesses foster good relations with existing customers. These positive relations enhance customer loyalty.

> "Companies use promotion to build awareness and inform people about their products."

Institutional promotion is a promotional method used to create a favorable image for a business, help it advocate for change, or take a stand on trade or community issues. As part of institutional promotional efforts businesses maintain Web sites to provide news, product and general information, and to answer questions. Institutional promotions do not directly sell a product. However, these activities do build goodwill to enhance a company's reputation and foster a favorable image for the company. This image may also help sales efforts.

Reading Check

Recall What are two types of promotion?

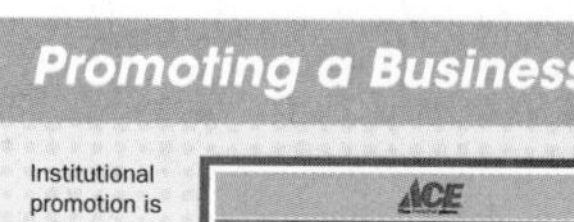

Promoting a Business

Institutional promotion is an important type of promotion. *How does endorsement by a research company benefit a business?*

ENGAGE

Anticipation Activity

Improving Student Achievement Ask: *Why do you think there are so many different types of promotion?* so marketers can target audiences

Objectives

- **Explain** the role of promotion in business and marketing. to inform people about products and services
- **Identify** types of promotion. personal selling, advertising, direct marketing, sales promotion, public relations
- **Distinguish** between public relations and publicity. Publicity is one aspect of public relations.
- **Explain** elements of a news release. Answers to *Who, What, When, Where* and *Why* questions
- **Describe** the concept of the promotional mix. combining selling, advertising, sales promotion, direct marketing, public relations

Graphic Organizer

Display the graphic organizer. Have students find an example to go with each element.

Promotional Mix

Product Promotion	Institutional Promotion
• personal selling	• public relations
• advertising	• company Web site
• sales promotion	• community involvement
• direct marketing	• charity involvement

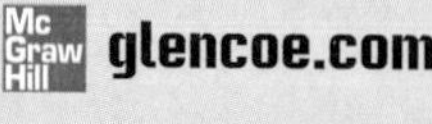

glencoe.com

iWB

Graphic Organizer Send students to the Online Learning Center to print this graphic organizer.

EXPLORE

Before You Read

Read the Before You Read question aloud: ***What might happen if businesses did not promote their products?*** Business efforts to boost sales would be very limited. Without promotion, customers would receive little information and have little incentive to purchase products and services. The number of customers would be limited to those who visit the company and learn about products and services from contact with previous customers.

Preteaching Vocabulary

Have students go to the Online Learning Center at glencoe.com for the Chapter 17 Preteaching Vocabulary games.

Content Vocabulary

Distribute dictionaries or have students use the glossary in their textbook. Tell students to write a definition for each Content Vocabulary term listed on page 394 and to use each term in a sentence. Definitions should match those given in the dictionary or the text glossary. Sentences will vary but should show an understanding of the terms.

Academic Vocabulary

Via—Word Origin Tell students that the Academic Vocabulary term *via* comes from the Latin *viā,* which means "road." Tell students that *via* is used to mean "by way of" or "by means of." Have students write sentences using the term *via.* Sample sentence: We came to Los Angeles via San Francisco.

Target—Prior Knowledge Ask students to recall the use of the term *target* in Chapter 1. Tell students that this knowledge will serve them well while studying Chapter 17, as the term *target* is used in the same way—to identify a particular group. Ask: ***Why is an understanding of target markets important to marketing and promotional strategies?*** Students should recall that all marketing strategies are directed to target markets.

PROFESSIONAL DEVELOPMENT

MINI CLIP

Reading: Modeling Reading Go to the Online Learning Center to view a video in which students practice fluency.

Section 17.1

The Promotional Mix

PROMOTION IN MARKETING

Ask students these guiding questions to focus the discussion.

Guiding Questions

Identify Why do companies use promotions?	to enhance their public image; to persuade people
Analyze What is the intended outcome of product promotion?	to convince prospects to select the company's goods or services; to foster good relationships

As You Read

Read students the As You Read question: ***Distinguish between the different types of promotion.*** Product promotion: to convince prospects to select their goods and services over a competitor's; Institutional promotion: to create a favorable image; Sales promotion: represents all marketing activities.

Expert Advice

Read the quote to students:

> **"Companies use promotion to build awareness and inform people about their products."**

Ask students: ***What would happen if a company did not use promotion?*** no one would know about the company

Reading Check Answer

Read the Reading Check question to students: ***What are two types of promotion?*** product promotion and institutional promotion

Visual Literacy

Promoting a Business Caption Answer Read the photo caption question to students: ***How does endorsement by a research company benefit a business?*** An objective endorsement by an outside research firm helps create a positive image, adds credibility, and sets a business apart from its competitors. .

TYPES OF PROMOTION IN THE PROMOTIONAL MIX

The **promotional mix** is the cost-effective combination of personal selling, advertising, direct marketing, sales promotion, and public relations strategies used to reach company goals. Each of the five basic categories in the promotional mix plays a vital role in promoting businesses and their products.

Through advertising, direct marketing, sales promotion, and public relations, companies communicate with customers in many ways other than direct contact. Personal selling, on the other hand, requires direct personal contact with the customer.

PERSONAL SELLING

Personal selling requires sales representatives to generate and maintain direct contact with prospects and customers. Direct contact like this can take the form of personal meetings, in-home demonstrations, e-mail and telephone correspondence.

Personal selling is one of the most expensive forms of promotion. Typically, personal selling takes place after other promotional activities have been tried.

ADVERTISING

Advertising is a form of nonpersonal promotion in which companies pay to promote ideas, goods, or services. These promotions are presented through a variety of media outlets.

Advertising can be found everywhere, on billboards, business cards, brochures, Internet, magazines, newspapers, phone directories, grocery store receipts, radio, television, sports arenas, cars and buses, restaurant menus, and Web sites. With advertising, a company engages in a one-way communication to the customer and prospective customer.

DIRECT MARKETING

Direct marketing is a type of promotion that companies use to address individuals directly and not through a third party medium (such as television, radio, or the Internet). One traditional form of direct marketing is direct mail, which is sent **via** standard mail to a home or business. Another form is telemarketing in which customers are called on the phone and asked directly for goods or services.

Direct marketing is a special type of advertising. *How does direct marketing differ from advertising?*

Promotions are also done through e-marketing to reach consumers who use the Internet to shop and research information. E-marketing is any promotion that is delivered via the Internet. It includes search engine marketing (paid search), Web site optimization, e-mail marketing, mobile phone applications (apps), and the use of social media.

Social media is electronic media that allows people with similar interests to participate in a social network. Social networks, such as Facebook®, MySpace®, LinkedIn®, YouTube®, and Twitter®, help businesses reach prospective customers.

The goals of direct marketing are to generate sales or leads for sales representatives to pursue. Direct marketing gives recipients an incentive to respond by visiting a store or Web site, calling a toll-free number, returning a form, or sending an e-mail. Targeted customers receive special offers or incentives, such as money-off coupons, limited-time sales, special merchandise offers, loyalty points for future purchases, and free delivery.

Both print and electronic direct marketing allow a business to engage in one-way communication with its customers about product announcements, special promotions, bulletins, customer inquiries, and order confirmations. However, as a result of consumer complaints about unwanted electronic direct mailings, Congress passed the CAN-SPAM Act of 2003. This act requires senders of unsolicited commercial e-mail to give recipients a way to opt out of e-mails. It also prohibits the use of deceptive subject lines and headers. In addition, it requires businesses to provide valid return addresses on their e-mails.

The Federal Trade Commission banned many pre-recorded, automated telemarketing solicitations, or "robocalls," in 2009. However, certain automated calls from charitable organizations, politicians, and healthcare providers are permitted. Telephone calls made by humans for selling products and services are also allowed unless the phone number is listed on the National Do Not Call Registry.

SALES PROMOTION

According to the American Marketing Association (AMA), **sales promotion** represents all marketing activities—other than personal selling, advertising, and public relations—that are directed at business or retail customers to boost sales. Sales promotions include coupons, money-off promotions, competitions, product samples, and point-of-purchase displays. The objectives of sales promotions are to increase sales, inform potential customers about new products, and create a positive business or corporate image.

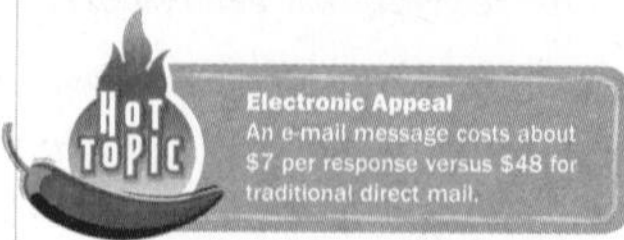

Electronic Appeal
An e-mail message costs about \$7 per response versus \$48 for traditional direct mail.

PUBLIC RELATIONS

Public relations (PR) activities help an organization to influence a target audience. Public relations campaigns try to influence general opinion and create a favorable public image for a person, organization, or a company, its products, or its policies. An example is a campaign to encourage business to sponsor the Children's Miracle Network, a national network of children's hospitals. Sponsors are featured in publications, print ads, mentioned during radio fund-raisers, and also help distribute paper miracle balloons for customer donations at local outlets. Public relations staff try to cultivate a positive image with reporters who may cover a specific industry.

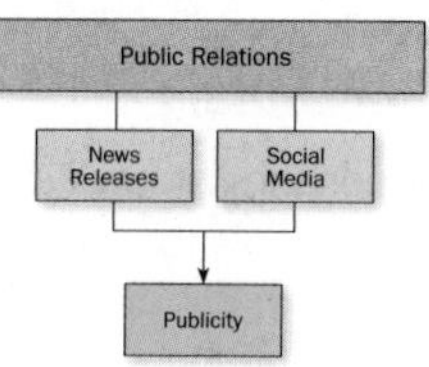

EXPLAIN

Visual Literacy

Targeting Your Customers Caption Answer Read the photo caption question to students: ***How does direct marketing differ from advertising?*** Direct marketing gives recipients an incentive to respond by visiting a store or Web site, calling a toll-free number, returning a form, or sending an e-mail. With advertising, a company engages in a one-way communication to the prospect or customer. Ask: ***What forms does direct marketing take?*** printed direct mail, electronic mail, and telemarketing calls Ask: ***What forms does advertising take?*** billboards, business cards, brochures, Internet, magazines, newspapers, phone directories, radio, television, sports arenas, vehicles, Web sites

TYPES OF PROMOTION IN THE PROMOTIONAL MIX

Explain to students that the promotional mix is a combination of advertising, sales, selling, promotion, direct marketing, and public relations strategies used to reach company goals. Ask students these guiding questions to focus on types of promotion in the promotional mix.

Guiding Questions

List What are the five basic categories of promotion in the promotional mix?	personal selling, advertising, direct marketing, sales promotion, public relations
Compare How are direct marketing and sales promotion similar?	Both include incentives such as money-off promotions; both want increased sales.

ELABORATE

Electronic Appeal Encourage students to research the costs for companies to promote their products on Web sites and social networking sites such as Facebook and Twitter. Discuss with students what types of products might be promoted on these sites, and what types of products might not be promoted on these sites.

Critical Thinking

Ask students to discuss why a business might use a promotional mix rather than relying on just one form of promotion. Since different types of promotion appeal to and reach different members of a target audience, using several types of promotion allows a business to appeal to and reach a larger audience.

Mini Projects

Extension

Understanding Direct Marketing Bring to class examples of flyers that have been sent to residential addresses. Have student groups study the flyers and create a direct mail advertisement for one of the following services: car sales or service, personal grooming products, pet care products, nutritional supplements, dentistry, or take-out food. Ask: ***What information needs to be included on the flyers?*** Information should include the product or service advertised, where and when the product or service is available, and the company selling the product or service.

Understanding Sales Promotion Ask students to recall a time an ad convinced them to purchase the product being advertised. Have students write an essay explaining why the ad was effective.Essays will vary but should include sound reasoning for why the ad influenced students to buy a product.

Understanding Advertising Tell students that the advertising firm they work for has asked them to come up with a creative, fun tagline to promote a client's new line of eco-friendly bottled water. Divide the class into small groups and have each group come up with a tagline. Then have the class vote on the best tagline. Taglines will vary but should get across the idea of eco-friendly bottled water in a creative and fun way.

Graphic Organizer

Display this chart. Students should locate and review a residential flyer, Internet ad, and a television ad and fill in the requested information. Sample answers:

	Product or Service	Availability	Seller	Target Audience
Residential Ad	Tires for all types of vehicles	Sale July 7–14	Roll-In Tires	People with vehicles
Internet Ad	Cars	Check local dealer	Name-brand car	Internet savvy people who drive
Television Ad	Ab exerciser	While supplies last	Flab-Free Zone	People who want to get into shape

Graphic Organizer Send students to the Online Learning Center to print this graphic organizer.

Critical Thinking

Lead students in a discussion on advertising approaches by asking the following question: ***When it comes to advertising a product, is the product's spokesperson or the general theme of the advertisement more important to you than the product itself?*** Have students explain their opinions. some students may think the spokesperson is most important because he or she lends credibility to the product or service. Others may think the general theme is most important because of the way it presents the product and captures customers' attention.

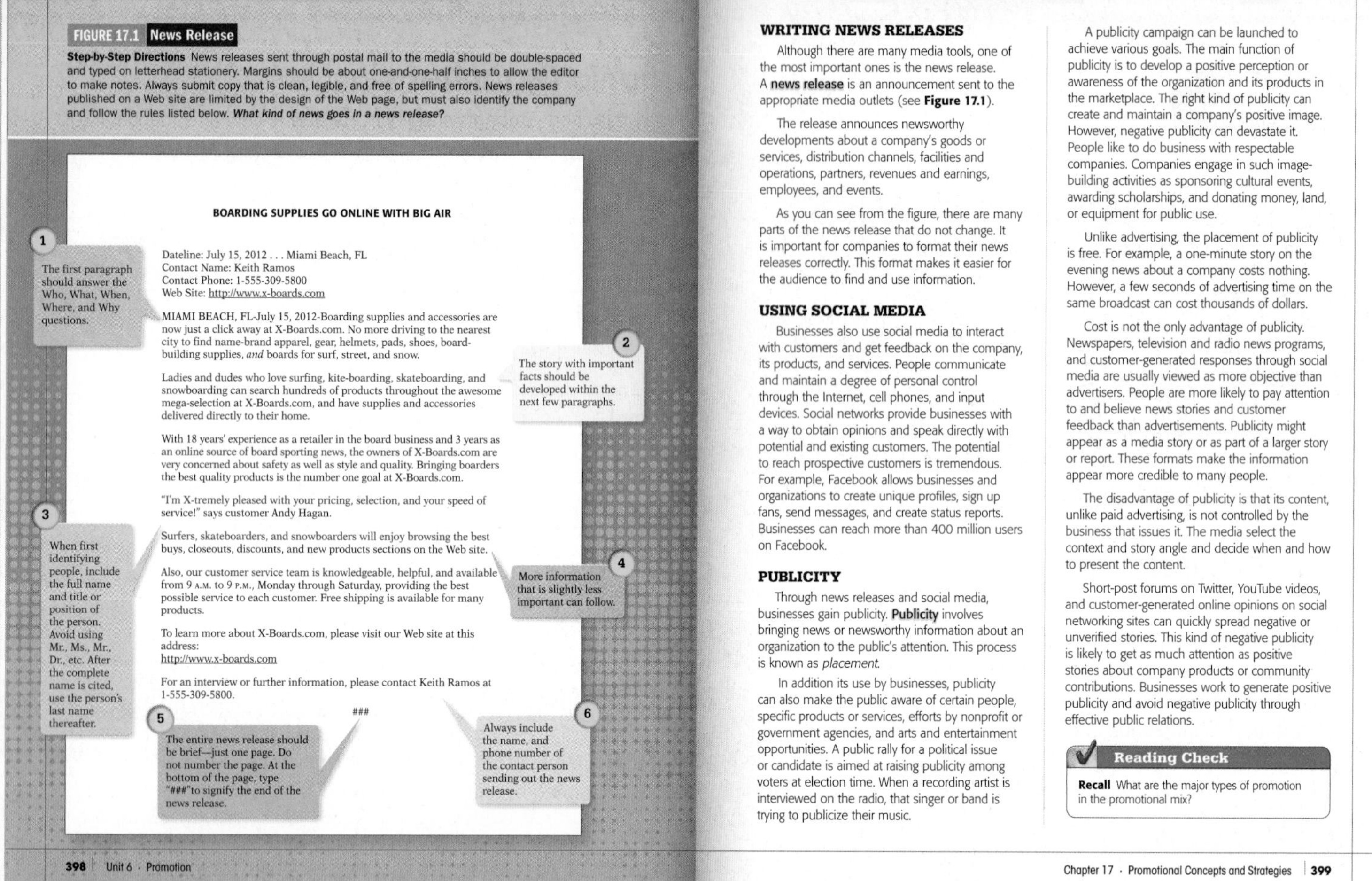

FIGURE 17.1 News Release

Step-by-Step Directions News releases sent through postal mail to the media should be double-spaced and typed on letterhead stationery. Margins should be about one-and-one-half inches to allow the editor to make notes. Always submit copy that is clean, legible, and free of spelling errors. News releases published on a Web site are limited by the design of the Web page, but must also identify the company and follow the rules listed below. ***What kind of news goes in a news release?***

BOARDING SUPPLIES GO ONLINE WITH BIG AIR

Dateline: July 15, 2012 . . . Miami Beach, FL
Contact Name: Keith Ramos
Contact Phone: 1-555-309-5800
Web Site: http://www.x-boards.com

MIAMI BEACH, FL-July 15, 2012-Boarding supplies and accessories are now just a click away at X-Boards.com. No more driving to the nearest city to find name-brand apparel, gear, helmets, pads, shoes, board-building supplies, *and* boards for surf, street, and snow.

Ladies and dudes who love surfing, kite-boarding, skateboarding, and snowboarding can search hundreds of products throughout the awesome mega-selection at X-Boards.com, and have supplies and accessories delivered directly to their home.

With 18 years' experience as a retailer in the board business and 3 years as an online source of board sporting news, the owners of X-Boards.com are very concerned about safety as well as style and quality. Bringing boarders the best quality products is the number one goal at X-Boards.com.

"I'm X-tremely pleased with your pricing, selection, and your speed of service!" says customer Andy Hagan.

Surfers, skateboarders, and snowboarders will enjoy browsing the best buys, closeouts, discounts, and new products sections on the Web site.

Also, our customer service team is knowledgeable, helpful, and available from 9 A.M. to 9 P.M., Monday through Saturday, providing the best possible service to each customer. Free shipping is available for many products.

To learn more about X-Boards.com, please visit our Web site at this address:
http://www.x-boards.com

For an interview or further information, please contact Keith Ramos at 1-555-309-5800.

###

1
The first paragraph should answer the Who, What, When, Where, and Why questions.
2
The story with important facts should be developed within the next few paragraphs.
3
When first identifying people, include the full name and title or position of the person. Avoid using Mr., Ms., Mr., Dr., etc. After the complete name is cited, use the person's last name thereafter.
4
More information that is slightly less important can follow.
5
The entire news release should be brief—just one page. Do not number the page. At the bottom of the page, type "###"to signify the end of the news release.
6
Always include the name, and phone number of the contact person sending out the news release.

WRITING NEWS RELEASES

Although there are many media tools, one of the most important ones is the news release. A **news release** is an announcement sent to the appropriate media outlets (see **Figure 17.1**).

The release announces newsworthy developments about a company's goods or services, distribution channels, facilities and operations, partners, revenues and earnings, employees, and events.

As you can see from the figure, there are many parts of the news release that do not change. It is important for companies to format their news releases correctly. This format makes it easier for the audience to find and use information.

USING SOCIAL MEDIA

Businesses also use social media to interact with customers and get feedback on the company, its products, and services. People communicate and maintain a degree of personal control through the Internet, cell phones, and input devices. Social networks provide businesses with a way to obtain opinions and speak directly with potential and existing customers. The potential to reach prospective customers is tremendous. For example, Facebook allows businesses and organizations to create unique profiles, sign up fans, send messages, and create status reports. Businesses can reach more than 400 million users on Facebook.

PUBLICITY

Through news releases and social media, businesses gain publicity. **Publicity** involves bringing news or newsworthy information about an organization to the public's attention. This process is known as *placement*.

In addition its use by businesses, publicity can also make the public aware of certain people, specific products or services, efforts by nonprofit or government agencies, and arts and entertainment opportunities. A public rally for a political issue or candidate is aimed at raising publicity among voters at election time. When a recording artist is interviewed on the radio, that singer or band is trying to publicize their music.

A publicity campaign can be launched to achieve various goals. The main function of publicity is to develop a positive perception or awareness of the organization and its products in the marketplace. The right kind of publicity can create and maintain a company's positive image. However, negative publicity can devastate it. People like to do business with respectable companies. Companies engage in such image-building activities as sponsoring cultural events, awarding scholarships, and donating money, land, or equipment for public use.

Unlike advertising, the placement of publicity is free. For example, a one-minute story on the evening news about a company costs nothing. However, a few seconds of advertising time on the same broadcast can cost thousands of dollars.

Cost is not the only advantage of publicity. Newspapers, television and radio news programs, and customer-generated responses through social media are usually viewed as more objective than advertisers. People are more likely to pay attention to and believe news stories and customer feedback than advertisements. Publicity might appear as a media story or as part of a larger story or report. These formats make the information appear more credible to many people.

The disadvantage of publicity is that its content, unlike paid advertising, is not controlled by the business that issues it. The media select the context and story angle and decide when and how to present the content.

Short-post forums on Twitter, YouTube videos, and customer-generated online opinions on social networking sites can quickly spread negative or unverified stories. This kind of negative publicity is likely to get as much attention as positive stories about company products or community contributions. Businesses work to generate positive publicity and avoid negative publicity through effective public relations.

Reading Check

Recall What are the major types of promotion in the promotional mix?

EXPLAIN

Visual Literacy

Figure 17.1 Caption Answer Read the figure caption question to students: ***What kind of news goes in a news release?*** News releases contain news about a company. Then ask these guiding questions to guide the discussion about news releases.

Guiding Questions

Analyze Why is it important to include the name, address, and phone number of the contact sending out the news release?	If someone wants more information, he or she can contact the person listed on the news release.
Predict What might happen if a company issued a six-page news release?	Recipients may not give it the attention they would give a to-the-point news release.

Critical Thinking

After students have read the news release in Figure 17.1, tell them to imagine that they are reporters for a newspaper. The news release in Figure 17.1 has come across their desk and their job is to write a news story based on the company's announcement in the news release. First, have the class brainstorm different angles from which they might approach the story. Then have students write a half-page news story based on the news release. News stories will vary but should follow the facts provided in the news release. The stories should approach the company's announcement from a particular angle and should be written in Standard English using good grammar and correct spelling. Ask volunteers to share their stories with the rest of the class. As a follow up to this activity, have students find a press release or news release about a company, product, or service that interests them. Have them share their releases in small groups.

ELABORATE

Graphic Organizer

Display this table. Ask students: ***What is social media?*** Social media is electronic media that allows people with similar interests to participate in a social network. Then say: ***Name some social networks.*** Social networks include Facebook®, MySpace®, LinkedIn®, YouTube®, and Twitter®. Ask students to indicate whether or not they use these social networking sites. Put the number of users and nonusers in the appropriate spaces on the graphic organizer. Ask students to explain why they do or do not use the sites. Answers will vary, but encourage students to be honest in their explanations. Ask: ***Why do you think that companies and businesses use these services?*** with the number of users of these sites, companies that post on the sites can potentially broaden their customer base and increase their revenue.

Social Network	Use	Do Not Use
Facebook®		
MySpace®		
LinkedIn®		
YouTube®		
Twitter®		

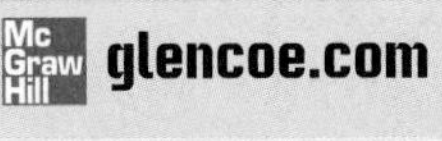
glencoe.com iWB

Graphic Organizer Send students to the Online Learning Center to print this graphic organizer.

Critical Thinking

Ask students to think of some examples of good publicity. Ask: ***What are some ways in which companies can react to their competitors' successful promotional activities?*** Students may suggest that competitors do a similar promotional activity, or they might send out a press release with an exciting announcement.

VIRTUAL BUSINESS

PROMOTION

Introduce students to the concept of promotion using Knowledge Matters' Virtual Business Retailing visual simulation, *Promotion*. In this simulation, students will learn that promotion is the way in which stores actively communicate with their customers.

Reading Check Answer

Read the Reading Check question to students: ***What are the major types of promotion in the promotional mix?*** personal selling, advertising, direct marketing, sales promotion, public relations

Mini Projects

Differentiated Instruction

English Language Learners Instruct students to think of a company with which they are familiar. It might be a local company or a national company. Have students create a list of five possible public relations efforts the company might take to promote its reputation and to get its name out to the public. Encourage the students to be creative with their ideas. Sample answers may include: writing news releases, advertising on social media networks, taking out radio and television commercial spots, distributing company-imprinted balloons at the Little League games, or participating in a fund raiser for heart disease research.

Interpersonal Learners Divide the class into small groups. Have each group discuss ideas for creating a better institutional image for the school. Each group should come up with at least one viable idea. After groups have come up with their ideas, have them share the ideas with the rest of the class. Have the class select the top two or three ideas and then submit those ideas to the student council for consideration. Students' ideas may include painting the school name or mascot on the football stadium bleachers, decorating the hallways with art from the school art classes, and so on.

Gifted Learners Tell students that in recent history, there have been a number of highly publicized cases in which public relations efforts helped to counter bad publicity. Have students research one case of damage control and write a half- to one-page report. Reports should describe the situation, the company, the bad publicity, and all major public relations efforts taken to overcome it. Reports should contain unified paragraphs, which focus on one main idea. All sentences in each paragraph should support the main idea and students should use transition words to connect their thoughts. Reports should be free of grammatical and spelling errors.

FIGURE 17.2 **Developing a Promotional Mix**

Strategies to Reach the Goal The promotional activities that marketers choose for promoting a particular product form the promotional mix. ***How do the elements in a promotional mix work together?***

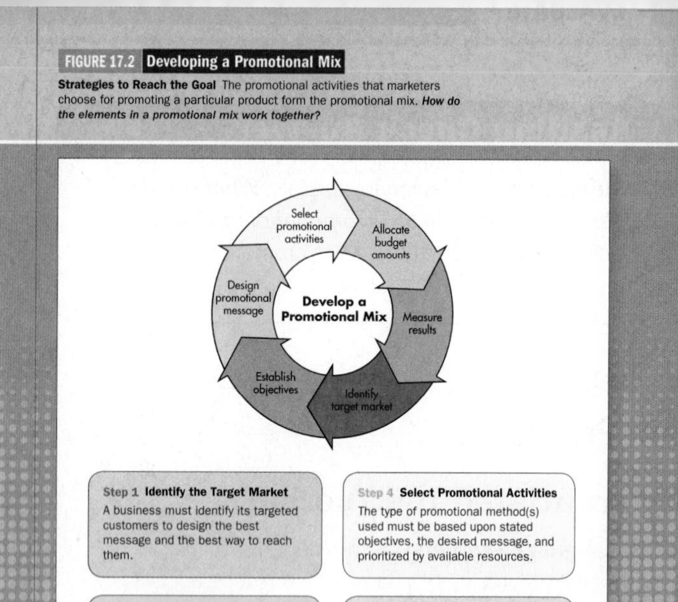

Step 1 Identify the Target Market
A business must identify its targeted customers to design the best message and the best way to reach them.

Step 2 Establish Objectives
A promotional mix must have objectives to accomplish, such as to create brand awareness, introduce a new product, build an image, or generate more sales.

Step 3 Design Promotional Message
Appropriate images or words should be selected to communicate with the target market. The selected message will largely dictate the format used, such as graphics, sound, electronic or print messages, or personal sales presentations.

Step 4 Select Promotional Activities
The type of promotional method(s) used must be based upon stated objectives, the desired message, and prioritized by available resources.

Step 5 Allocate Budget Amounts
A promotion budget should be based upon the "ideal" promotional mix and can include all promotional methods or a selected number based upon available resources.

Step 6 Measure Results
Promotional methods and the results achieved must be continually evaluated. The results will determine whether the planned activities should continue or be revised to meet objectives.

THE CONCEPT OF PROMOTIONAL MIX

Most businesses use more than one type of promotion to achieve their promotional goals. They use a cost-effective mix of promotional strategies that include advertising, selling, sales promotion, direct marketing, and public relations strategies. This mix assures them that their product will be widely recognized.

Once a product is recognized, it is easier to sell. These sales generate revenue for the company. It uses this revenue to offset the cost of using the promotional strategies. Companies learn which strategies are most effective in their promotional mix through this process.

How do companies develop a promotional mix? A business establishes a promotional mix by following a process that begins with identifying the **target** market. This process continues through a series of steps and ends with the company measuring the results of the mix. **Figure 17.2** shows the process in developing a promotional mix. It is represented as a cycle because a promotional mix must be on-going and continuous. The strategies in the mix are designed to complement one another. Information that is learned in one cycle of the mix is applied to the next cycle.

MARKETING CASE STUDY

Ladies and Gentlemen . . . The Beatles: Rock Band!

The popular music video game Rock Band® got a high-profile reintroduction with "The Beatles: Rock Band." In this game, players take on the roles of the Fab Four. It was not only the first Beatles game, it was also the first time the band's music became available in digital format. This allowed for some special advertising opportunities.

From Liverpool to You

Ads for the game utilized artful images from the game itself. The game features colorful animations of the band and how the musicians changed over time. A commercial also showed everyday people inserted into iconic parts of Beatles imagery. One ad showed people walking across Abbey Road. The promotion also referenced the new Beatles boxed CD sets, which were released at the same time as the game.

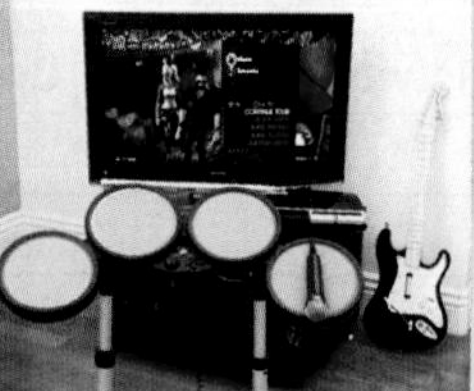

English Language Arts

Collaborate With a partner, create a basic promotional mix for this product, incorporating creative, nontraditional ideas. Present your ideas to the class using presentation software or poster boards.

NCTE 12 Use language to accomplish individual purposes.

EXPLAIN

Visual Literacy

Figure 17.2 Caption Answer Read the figure caption question to students: ***How do the elements in a promotional mix work together?*** The elements work together to communicate information and attract attention to particular audiences about images, products, and issues. Then ask these guiding questions to focus the discussion.

Guiding Questions

Analyze Why is identify the target market the first step in developing a promotional mix?	You must identify the target market to be able to develop the promotions to reach the market.
Determine Why is the development of a promotional mix circular?	it is an ongoing process; constant adjustments make the mix effective.

MARKETING CASE STUDY

English Language Arts Answer Students' promotional mixes for the game Rock Band® will vary. Remind students that they should include all the steps of the promotional mix. Ask: ***Which was the most difficult step to develop?*** Answers may include designing the promotional message or allocating budget amounts. Ask: ***Which was the easiest step to develop?*** Students may suggest that selecting promotional activities is the easiest and most fun step in the process.

ELABORATE

THE CONCEPT OF THE PROMOTIONAL MIX

Ask these guiding questions to guide the discussion about the concept of promotional mix.

Guiding Questions

Determine Why is it important for a product or service to be widely recognized?	A product or service widely recognized, is easier to sell.
Distinguish What is the difference between a promotional message and a promotional activity?	Promotional message: made up of appropriate images or words that communicate with the market; Promotional activity: based on the message

Mini Project

Enrichment

Types of Promotion Divide the class into teams of five or six members. Ask each team to create a business that sells products to high school students. Teams should assign each member to one of the five types of promotion (personal selling, advertising, direct marketing, sales promotion, and public relations) to develop ideas for a promotional mix. Assign a reporter to record the ideas of his or her team. Have each team present an oral report on their promotional strategies for their business. personal selling—having a sales representative talk with teens in off-campus places such as the mall, and distribute free samples of their product; advertising—in teen magazines or on teen-focused Web sites; direct marketing—sending e-mail ads to teens; sales promotion—positioning a point-of-purchase display in areas frequented by teens; public relations—the company purchasing a new score board for the local high school's football field

Graphic Organizer

Display the graphic organizer. Discuss with students the six steps that go into developing a promotional mix.

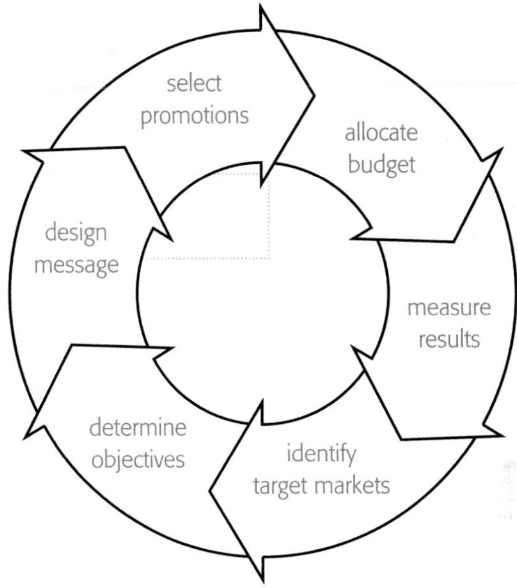

Graphic Organizer Send students to the Online Learning Center to print this graphic organizer.

Critical Thinking

To reinforce the concepts of public relations and publicity, ask students to share unfavorable news stories about someone famous or about a well-known product or company. Ask: ***Can publicity sometimes do more harm than good?*** Students may include stories about negative publicity such as product recalls or legal problems. Students should recognize that publicity can be harmful when it points out negatives rather than positives. Ask students whether they have ever seen commercials that point out the negatives in a competing product or a politician. Ask: ***Do you think this type of advertising is ethical or in good taste? Why or why not?*** Some students may feel that these types of commercials are not in good taste and are unethical and should not be allowed. Others may think it is acceptable to point out the negatives in a competitor as long as they are truthful.

For example, the process starts with a target market. Imagine that you work for a company that designs, manufacturers, and sells hiking equipment. It has national name brand recognition. Your company plans to introduce a totally new and improved lightweight backpack. Since your objectives are to introduce a new product, build awareness and create sales, your message must reach hikers and outdoor enthusiasts about the benefits of buying your new product. Your promotional mix must include methods for meeting all of these goals.

The marketing department selects the best promotional activity to reach the target market. It then develops a budget for advertising, direct marketing, and sales promotional activities. The selected promotional activities must complement one another, and they must be able to reach the potential market. They must also be realistic in terms of the budget for the promotion.

Advertising and direct marketing create awareness of a business's product. At the same time, public relations helps cultivate a favorable image and brand recognition. Sales promotional activities stimulate sales, reinforce advertising, and support selling efforts. Finally, personal selling builds on all of these previous efforts by completing the sale. Your company's budget will give you an idea of how to fund each of these areas of promotion.

Elements of the promotional mix must be coordinated. For example, national advertising should be reinforced by local promotional efforts. Many consumer product manufacturers give or sell retailers decorations or in-store displays to reinforce a national campaign. The national and local efforts need to be communicated to the store personnel. Being made aware of any coupons, rebates, contests, and featured promotional items allows staff to encourage customer participation.

When promoted products are not available as advertised or the selling staff is uninformed about a promotion, sales are lost and customers are dissatisfied. If these employees are informed of such promotions, they will be able to more effectively engage their customers. This engagement leads to more sales and more revenue.

The total promotional mix and each strategy in the mix must be measured on how well they met the objectives. The results determine whether promotional strategies are revised, improved, or discontinued.

PROMOTIONAL BUDGET

In large companies, the marketing department has many roles. It determines the promotional mix, establishes the budget, allocates resources, coordinates the campaign, supervises any outside resources, and measures the results.

It is important to consider all aspects of the promotional mix when developing the promotional budget. Determining the ideal budget is difficult. Often, a promotional budget is based on a percentage of sales. Other times, it is based on an estimate of what competitors spend on advertising, direct marketing, and sales promotion. There is no precise way to measure exact results of spending promotional dollars. This lack of precision makes it difficult to determine the ideal amount for the promotional budget. Its overall success is usually based upon whether the total effort led to increased sales.

It is vital for companies to study the effects of their promotional mix. It is like an experiment. They need to isolate a variable and monitor its effects. After the promotion is done, the company can assess the impact of the promotion and make a plan for the next time around.

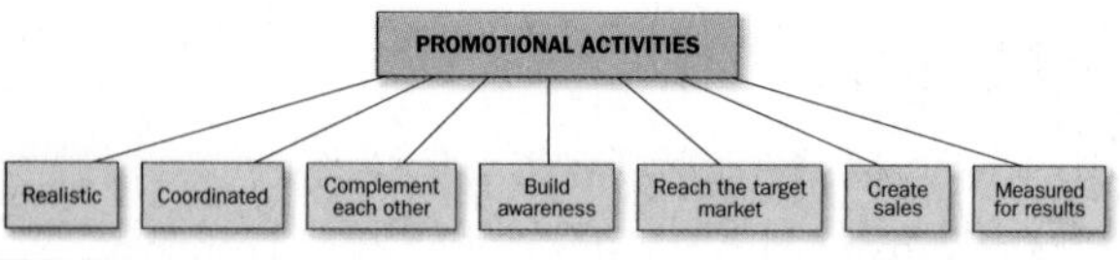

402 | Unit 6 · Promotion

THE PUSH-PULL CONCEPT

Manufacturers often develop a promotional mix for each segment of the distribution channel. To promote a product to large retailers that sell its products, a manufacturer might want to use a mix of advertising, personal selling, and trade discounts. This type of promotion, known as the **push policy**, is used with partners in the distribution channel. The manufacturer pushes the product through the distribution channel to the retailer. The main purpose of the promotion is to convince a retailer to stock the products being promoted.

This strategy is especially useful at trade shows and exhibitions, where cross-promoting is possible. It is a helpful strategy for manufacturers whose products do not have strong brand identity.

The same manufacturer might use a different promotional mix of local and national advertising, in-store displays, sales promotion, and public relations to reach consumers. The **pull policy** directs promotional activities toward consumers. The idea is to entice (or pull) the consumer into the store (or Web site) to buy the product. A typical pull marketing strategy would be to offer "half-off" deals or clearance sales.

This pull policy of promotion is designed to create consumer interest and demand. Consumer demand pulls the product through the distribution channel by encouraging wholesalers and retailers to carry a product. As mentioned, this strategy relies heavily on consumer advertising, premiums, samples, in-store displays, and demonstrations.

Section 17.1

Review Key Concepts

1. **Explain** why promotion is an important marketing function.
2. **Identify** when to use product and institutional promotion.
3. **Contrast** the push and pull policies in promotional mixes.

Practice Academics

Social Studies

4. Customer-driven responses on Web sites, such as Facebook®, MySpace®, and Twitter®, are changing the way businesses promote goods and services. Investigate the concept of social media and its effect on business. Write a paragraph on how business responds to customer-driven comments.

Mathematics

5. An outdoor apparel company has established a promotional budget of $1,000 to be spent in the following manner: $300 for a print advertisement in an outdoor magazine; $450 for an online advertisement campaign; $150 for premiums (decal stickers imprinted with the company name); $100 donation to a local outdoor program for children to build public relations. What percentage of the total budget is spent on each promotional category?

Math Concept **Number and Operations** Estimate before computing your answer to be sure your calculations are accurate.

Starting Hints To solve this problem, divide each dollar amount spent by the total dollar amount of the promotional budget, $1,000, to get a decimal. Multiply the decimal by 100 to determine what percent of the budget each category requires.

For help, go to the **Math Skills Handbook** located at the back of this book.

NCSS V B Individuals, Groups, & Institutions Analyze group and institutional influences on people, events, and elements of culture in both historical and contemporary settings.

NCTM Number and Operations Compute fluently and make reasonable estimates.

glencoe.com

Check your answers.

Chapter 17 · Promotional Concepts and Strategies | 403

ELABORATE

Critical Thinking

Tell students that in order to boost sales, a restaurant chain introduced a "mystery envelope" promotion. Customers received an envelope after dining at the restaurant. However, the envelope had to be returned unopened the following month to redeem the prize inside. Prizes ranged from free menu items to a trip to Las Vegas. Ask students: ***Would this type of promotion appeal to you? Why or why not?*** Some may enjoy the thrill of the unknown; others may be annoyed about having to come back at a certain time. Tell students that the promotion was so successful the restaurant runs it twice a year. The redemption rate is about 15% and the ROI is around 900%. Ask: ***Would this type of promotion work for all businesses and products?*** this type of promotion likely would not work well at a car dealership or an appliance store.

THE PUSH-PULL CONCEPT

Ask students these guiding questions to focus the discussion about push-pull policies.

Guiding Questions

Differentiate What is the difference between the push policy and the pull policy?	Push policy: used with partners in the distribution channel; Pull policy: directs promotional activities toward consumers
Predict What are you more likely to encounter, the push policy or the pull policy?	Students, and all consumers, are likely to encounter the pull policy.

EVALUATE

Graphic Organizer

After students have completed the section on The Concept of Promotional Mix display this graphic organizer. Instruct students to locate at least two different ads for the same product or service. Ads can be from television, radio, Internet, billboards, magazines, and newspapers. Students should indicate the location of the ads and compare and rate the ads according to the criteria in the table below. Students will need to predict whether the ads created sales and were measured for results. Sample:

	Ad #1	Ad #2	Ad #3
Realistic			
Coordinated			
Complement each other			
Build awareness			
Reach the target market			
Create sales			
Measured for results			

glencoe.com

Graphic Organizer Send students to the Online Learning Center to print this graphic organizer.

Mini Project

Differentiated Instruction

Students with Learning Disabilities Reinforce students' understanding of the elements of the promotional mix by referring them to Figure 17.2 on page 400. Have students restate the information in their own words and identify any words they are not familiar with. Then, have students create a flow chart of each step. Steps should be labeled. Direct students to find images or create simple drawings to show a visual example for the labeled steps. Students should explain their flow charts to a peer tutor or small learning group and have their audience ask questions on how the example reflects the promotional mix depicted.

After You Read Section 17.1

Review Key Concepts

1. Promotion is an important marketing function, because it is used to inform, persuade, or remind people about a company's products and its image.
2. Product promotion is used to convince people to buy or use a certain product. For example, if a company has come out with a new product, they would use product promotion to make people aware of the product. Institutional promotion does not directly sell a product, but is used to create a favorable image, which can result in sales. For example, a company develops a Web site for customers to learn more about the company's environmental and social responsibility initiatives.
3. The push concept depends on the manufacturer to get distribution channel members to purchase products. It relies on a mix of personal selling, advertising and buying discounts. The pull concept directs promotion to potential consumers or relies on advertising geared to consumers and consumer sales promotions such as coupons, premiums, samples, and demonstrations.

Practice Academics

Social Studies

4. Answers will vary, but many companies employ social media directors or have instituted an internal process to receive and respond to both positive and negative customer-generated responses and opinions about a company's products and services.

Mathematics

5. Print advertisement in an outdoor magazine = 30% ($300 ÷ 1000 = .30); online advertisement campaign = 45% ($450 ÷ 1000 = .45); premiums = 15% ($150 ÷ 1000 = .15); donation to a local outdoor program for children = 10% ($100 ÷ 1000 = .10)

glencoe.com

Answer Key Send students to the Online Learning Center to check their answers.

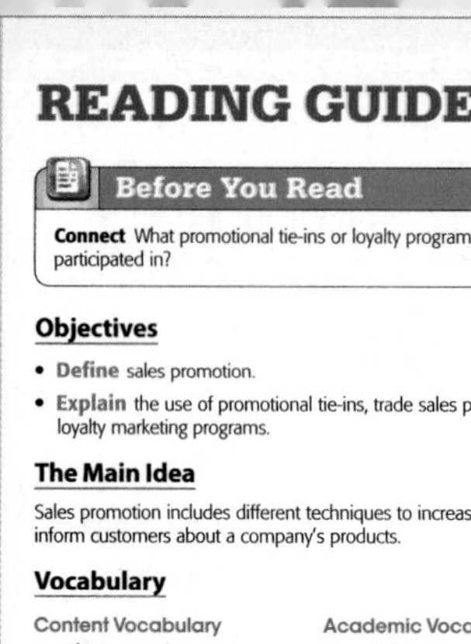

READING GUIDE

STANDARDS

Before You Read

Connect What promotional tie-ins or loyalty programs have you participated in?

Objectives

- **Define** sales promotion.
- **Explain** the use of promotional tie-ins, trade sales promotions, and loyalty marketing programs.

The Main Idea

Sales promotion includes different techniques to increase sales and inform customers about a company's products.

Vocabulary

Content Vocabulary
- sales promotions
- trade promotions
- consumer promotions
- coupons
- premiums
- incentives
- promotional tie-ins
- loyalty marketing programs
- kiosks

Academic Vocabulary

You will find these words in your reading and on your tests. Make sure you know their meanings.
- distribution
- register

Graphic Organizer

Draw or print this chart to list examples for different types of sales promotions.

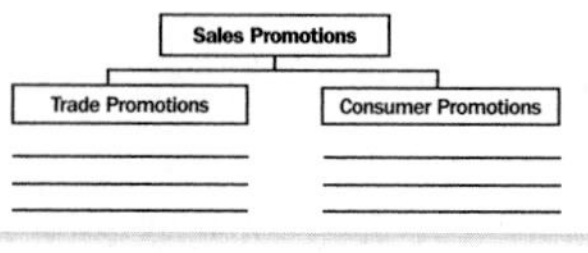

Print this graphic organizer.

ACADEMIC

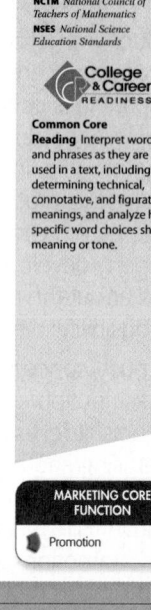

English Language Arts

NCTE 1 Read texts to acquire new information.

NCTE 3 Apply strategies to interpret texts.

NCSS *National Council for the Social Studies*
NCTE *National Council of Teachers of English*
NCTM *National Council of Teachers of Mathematics*
NSES *National Science Education Standards*

College & Career READINESS

Common Core
Reading Interpret words and phrases as they are used in a text, including determining technical, connotative, and figurative meanings, and analyze how specific word choices shape meaning or tone.

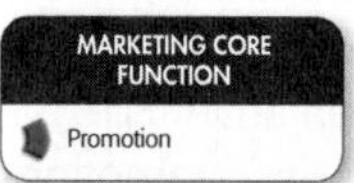

SALES PROMOTION

Sales promotions are incentives that encourage customers to buy products or services. Sales promotions build brand awareness, encourage customers to try a new product, increase purchases by current customers, or reward customer loyalty. Sales promotions are usually supported by advertising activities that include trade promotions and consumer promotions.

As You Read

Consider How might you promote a product that you like?

TRADE PROMOTIONS

Trade promotions are sales promotion activities designed to get support for a product from manufacturers, wholesalers, and retailers. More money is actually spent on promoting to businesses than to consumers. Major trade promotions include promotional allowances, cooperative advertising, slotting allowances, sales force promotions, and trade shows and conventions. Good business ethics require that trade promotional payments and awards be offered in a uniform manner. It also requires that terms be clearly spelled out and that no one is penalized for not achieving the goals. These requirements ensure that trade promotions are conducted fairly.

Trade Promotions	
Allowances	Quotas
Advertising	Trade Shows

PROMOTIONAL ALLOWANCES

Promotional allowances represent cash payments or discounts given by manufacturers to wholesalers or retailers for performing activities to encourage sales. For example, promotional allowances are sometimes used to encourage wholesalers or retailers to stock a large quantity of a product. The cash payment or price discount gives wholesalers and retailers an incentive to sell, so they are more likely to promote the product.

“Sales promotions may be either business-to-business (B2B) or business-to-consumer (B2C) activities.”

COOPERATIVE ADVERTISING

A manufacturer supports the retailer by helping to pay for the cost of advertising its product locally. This practice is known as *cooperative advertising.*

SLOTTING ALLOWANCES

A slotting allowance is a cash premium paid by a manufacturer to a retailer to help the retailer cover the costs of placing the manufacturer's product on the shelves. Slotting allowances can range from a few thousand dollars to several million dollars per product. In addition to buying space in the store, slotting allowances also pay for a retailer's discount specials on a product, charges for store shelves, penalties for poor sales, store advertising, and display costs.

ENGAGE

Anticipation Activity

Improving Student Achievement Ask students: ***How have promotional activities or strategies convinced you to buy or not buy a product?*** Students should present examples of times they were influenced to buy—or not buy—from a store based on its promotional activities.

Objectives

- **Define** sales promotion. Sales promotion represents all marketing activities that are used to stimulate purchasing and sales.
- **Explain** the use of promotional tie-ins, trade sales promotions, and loyalty marketing programs. Promotional tie-ins involve arrangements between one or more retailers or manufacturers. Trade sales promotions solicit support from manufacturers, wholesalers, and retailers. Loyalty marketing programs reward customers for their business.

Graphic Organizer

Sales Promotions

Trade Promotions	Consumer Promotions
allowances	coupons, premiums, deals,
advertising	incentives, samples, tie-ins,
quotas	cross selling, sponsorships,
sales force promotions	product placement,
trade shows	loyalty programs, displays

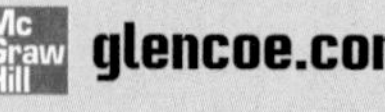

Graphic Organizer Send students to the Online Learning Center to print this graphic organizer.

EXPLORE

Before You Read

Read the Before You Read question aloud: ***What promotional tie-ins or loyalty programs have you participated in?*** Students may mention fast-food promotions or frequent flyer mileage programs.

Preteaching Vocabulary

Have students go to the Online Learning Center at glencoe.com for the Chapter 17 Preteaching Vocabulary games.

Content Vocabulary

Divide the class into nine groups. Assign one Content Vocabulary term to each group. Have the groups learn the meanings of the terms and develop a plan to teach the meaning of the term to the rest of the class. Allow time for each group to teach their term to the class.

Academic Vocabulary

Distribution—Root Word Write the term *distribution* on the board. Ask: ***What is the root word of* distribution?** distribute ***What does the word* distribute *mean?*** Distribute means "to divide and dispense, or supply." Ask: ***Based on the meaning of* distribute, *what does the word* distribution *mean?*** Distribution is the act of dividing and dispensing items.

Register—Usage Read the following sentence to students: Many consumers register online to make a purchase or to receive a discount from a marketer. Ask: ***How is the term* register *used in the sentence?*** It is used as a verb. Ask: ***What does it mean to register?*** To register means "to enter information necessary to receive an intended service" (make a purchase, receive a discount, and so on). Have students write original sentences using *register* as a verb. Sample sentences: I have to register for college classes in just a few months. When I turn 18, I will register to vote.

MINI CLIP 

Reading: Fluency Development
Go to the Online Learning Center for a video on different instructional strategies used to develop reading fluency.

Types of Promotion

SALES PROMOTION

Ask the guiding questions to focus the discussion of sales promotions.

Guiding Questions

Explain What are the benefits of sales promotions?	build brand awareness, encourage customers to try a new product, increase purchases by current customers, reward customer loyalty
Differentiate How do trade promotions differ from consumer promotions?	Trade promotions are sales promotions activities designed to gain support for a product from manufacturers, wholesalers, and retailers. Consumer promotions are sales strategies that encourage consumers to buy.

As You Read

Read students the As You Read question: ***How might you promote a product that you like?*** Students may suggest that if they like a product they recommend it to others, or they might wear clothing that displays the company logo.

Expert Advice

Read the quote to students:

"Sales promotions may be either business-to-business (B2B) or business-to-customer (B2C) activities."

Ask students: ***How might business-to-business sales promotions benefit you?*** Students may recognize that if a business can purchase a product at a reduced rate, they can pass that savings on to consumers.

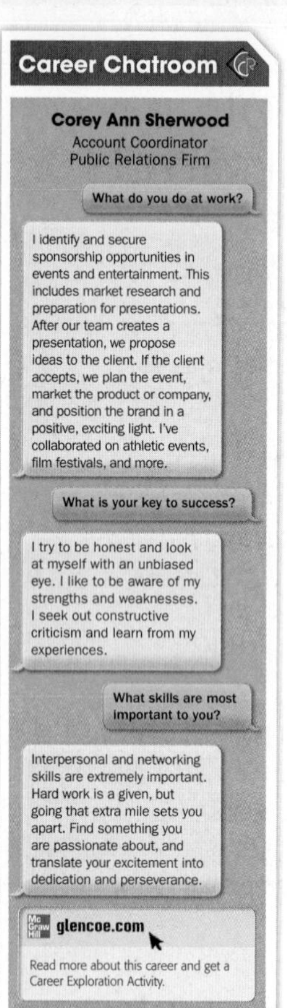

Career Chatroom

Corey Ann Sherwood
Account Coordinator
Public Relations Firm

What do you do at work?

I identify and secure sponsorship opportunities in events and entertainment. This includes market research and preparation for presentations. After our team creates a presentation, we propose ideas to the client. If the client accepts, we plan the event, market the product or company, and position the brand in a positive, exciting light. I've collaborated on athletic events, film festivals, and more.

What is your key to success?

I try to be honest and look at myself with an unbiased eye. I like to be aware of my strengths and weaknesses. I seek out constructive criticism and learn from my experiences.

What skills are most important to you?

Interpersonal and networking skills are extremely important. Hard work is a given, but going that extra mile sets you apart. Find something you are passionate about, and translate your excitement into dedication and perseverance.

glencoe.com 

Read more about this career and get a Career Exploration Activity.

SALES FORCE PROMOTIONS

Sales force promotions are awards given to dealers and employees who successfully meet or exceed a sales quota. Such quotas can apply to a specific period of time, such as a month, one day, or a year, or for a product or line of products.

Sales force promotions vary, but they may include cash bonuses or prizes such as merchandise or travel awards.

TRADE SHOWS AND CONVENTIONS

Trade shows and conventions showcase a particular line of products. One of the largest trade shows is the annual Consumer Electronics Show in Las Vegas, which attracts more than 190,000 manufacturers, retailers, product engineers, and developers. Many participating companies invest millions of dollars in their display booths. Trade shows provide businesses with opportunities to introduce new products, encourage increased sales of existing products, meet customers and partners in the **distribution** chain, and gain continued company and product support.

Reading Check

Analyze Why are trade promotions effective?

CONSUMER PROMOTIONS

Consumer promotions are sales strategies that encourage customers and prospects to buy a product or service. Consumer promotions support advertising, personal selling, and public relations efforts. Major consumer sales promotion devices include coupons, premiums, deals, incentives, product samples, sponsorships, promotional tie-ins, product placement, loyalty marketing programs, and point-of-purchase displays.

COUPONS

Coupons are certificates that entitle customers to cash discounts on goods or services. Manufacturers use coupons to introduce new products, to enhance the sales of existing products, and to encourage retailers to stock and display both. Coupons are placed on or inside product packages, in newspapers, and magazines.

Increasingly, companies use strategies to drive consumers to download and print online coupons. For example, a food manufacturer runs a summer online coupon program in partnership with supermarkets. Printed or online coupons are available for a limited time, and their value expires after a certain date.

Stores that accept coupons send them to the manufacturers' headquarters or to a clearinghouse to be sorted and passed along to redemption centers. The centers, in turn, reimburse the stores for the face value of each coupon plus a handling charge of about eight cents per coupon. The centers then bill the manufacturers.

HOT TOPIC
Coupons Starting in 2008, Groupon offered deal-of-the-day coupons for certain stores if enough customers in one city signed up to use them.

PREMIUMS

Premiums or giveaways are low-cost items given to consumers at a discount or for free. They are designed to increase sales by building product loyalty and attracting new customers. They can also persuade nonusers to switch brands.

The fundamental concept behind premium marketing is that people will be more motivated to buy a product when they are offered an added-value gift in exchange. Three types of popular consumer premiums are factory packs, traffic builders, and coupon plans.

Factory packs, or in-packs, are free gifts placed in product packages or as a container premium. This form of premium is especially popular with cereal manufacturers. Toy companies can cross-market or cross-sell their products with cereal companies. Children who eat the cereal and play with the toys will have a positive impression of both companies.

Traffic builders are low-cost premiums, such as pens, key chains, pocket calendars, and coffee mugs. They are given away to consumers for visiting a new store or attending a special event.

Each time a customer uses the premium, he or she is reminded of the company and the experience. This practice can foster positive feelings for the company. Some of these premiums also feature contact information for the company so it is easier for the customer to get in touch.

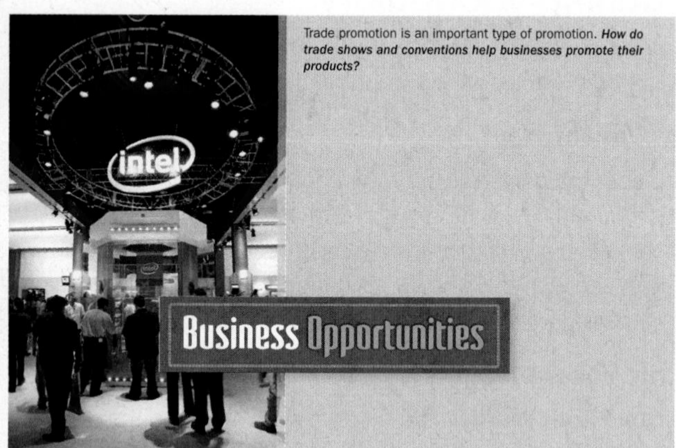

Trade promotion is an important type of promotion. ***How do trade shows and conventions help businesses promote their products?***

EXPLAIN

Career Chatroom

Use these questions to focus the discussion.

Guiding Questions

Explain What is Corey Ann Sherwood's job?	She secures sponsorships, conducts market research, and positions brands.
Analyze What does "going that extra mile sets you apart" mean?	When you put in more effort, clients see that you are willing to do more for them than other firms.

 **glencoe.com** 

Career Exploration Send students to the Online Learning Center to read more about this career and to get a Career Exploration Activity.

Reading Check Answer

Read the Reading Check question to students: ***Why are trade promotions effective?*** Trade promotions are effective because the wholesalers, manufacturers, and retailers gain monetary benefit from the promotions. Then they are able to pass along savings to consumers, and that keeps the consumers happy and coming in to make more purchases.

Critical Thinking

Ask students to brainstorm the types of promotions they frequently encounter. Ask a volunteer to write students' responses on the board. Answers may include: discounts, coupons, free offers, gifts, and so on. Have students find examples of promotion activities and bring them in to share with the class. Then, students should partner to create a promotional activity for your class. Have all pairs present their promotions to you and other faculty. Choose the best promotion for your classroom. Student pairs should be creative, know their target audience (you), and understand what the promotional activity will portray about the benefits to your class and classroom.

ELABORATE

Graphic Organizer

Display this graphic organizer. Have students fill in the three different types of premiums and give a brief description of each. Ask: ***What is a drawback to providing premiums to customers?*** Customers may think the premiums are disposable. Flooding customers with too many premiums increases the chances that the premiums will be discarded.

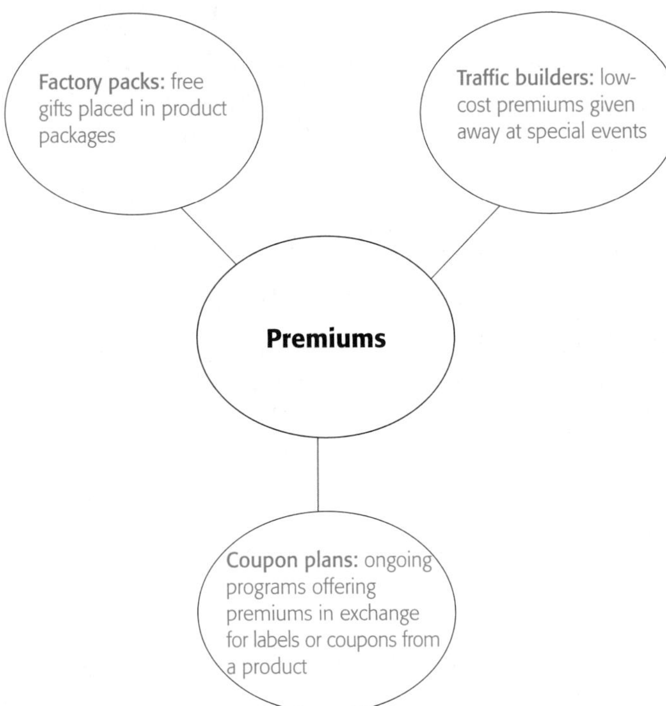
Factory packs: free gifts placed in product packages
Traffic builders: low-cost premiums given away at special events
Premiums
Coupon plans: ongoing programs offering premiums in exchange for labels or coupons from a product

Mc Graw Hill
glencoe.com iWB

Graphic Organizer Send students to the Online Learning Center to print this graphic organizer.

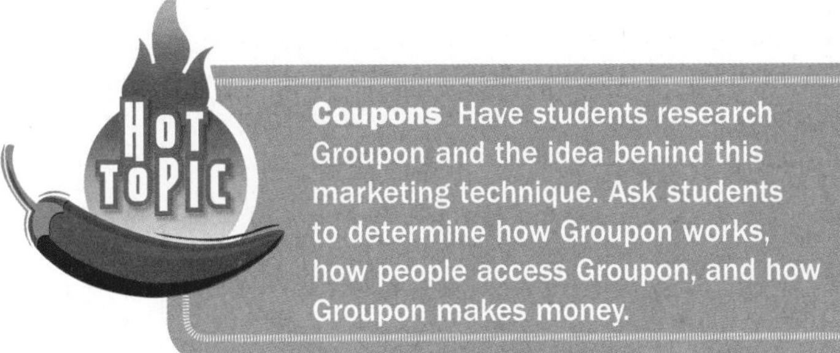
HOT TOPIC

Coupons Have students research Groupon and the idea behind this marketing technique. Ask students to determine how Groupon works, how people access Groupon, and how Groupon makes money.

Visual Literacy

Business Opportunities Caption Answer Read the figure caption question to students: ***How do trade shows and conventions help businesses promote their products?*** Trade shows and conventions provide businesses with opportunities to introduce new products, encourage increased sales of existing products, meet customers and partners in the distribution chain, and gain continued company and product support. Then ask these guiding questions to reinforce students' learning about promotions.

Guiding Questions

Compare How are trade promotions and consumer promotions similar?	Both offer monetary incentives to purchase a product.
Contrast How are trade promotions and consumer promotions different?	Trade promotions are designed to get support for a product from manufacturers, wholesalers, retailers. Consumer promotions are sales strategies to encourage customers to buy.

Mini Project

Enrichment

Research Premiums Share with students the following scenario: The high school booster club needs to sell t-shirts at the local events. Ask students to brainstorm possible ideas for how to offer low-cost premiums with the shirts. Write their ideas for all students to view. Divide the class into small groups and have each group choose one or two of the suggested premiums. Groups should conduct preliminary research to see how much it would cost to order 500 premium items in order to give them away with the shirts. Groups should also contact local vendors for approximate quotes on the premiums. Have groups present this information and their vendor recommendations in a one-page report. Reports will vary but should provide the requested information (prices for 500 premium items and a vendor recommendation) in a format that is well written and easy to understand.

Coupon plans are ongoing programs offering a variety of premiums in exchange for labels or coupons obtained from a product. A customer might send a manufacturer three soup-can labels in exchange for a recipe book. This exchange tells the company not only that their customers want recipes but also which products they purchase. If a soup company never received labels in the mail for one of its products, it would know not to market these products in association with this promotion.

One drawback to using premiums is that customers may think they are disposable. It is important for a company to not flood customers with too many premiums. This practice increases the chances that the premiums will be discarded.

DEALS

Deals or price packs offer short-term price reductions that are marked directly on the label or package, such as a retailer selling T-shirts for $10.50 each for one or $6 each for two or more. A deal might also "bundle" two-related products together, such as a free wing chair with a purchase of a discounted sofa.

INCENTIVES

Incentives are generally higher-priced products, awards, or gift cards that are earned and given away through contests, sweepstakes, special offers, and rebates. Businesses use incentives to promote many products because they create customer excitement and increase sales.

Contests are games or activities that require the participant to demonstrate a skill. Contest winners win such prizes as scholarships, vacations, and money. Many companies, such as McDonald's®, Kellogg's®, Kraft® Foods, and General Mills® have product promotions in the form of Internet games. Incentives are often offered to collect points in exchange for other games or gifts.

Sweepstakes are games of chance. (By law in most states, no purchase is necessary in order to enter a contest or sweepstakes.)

Special offers and rebates are discounts offered by businesses to customers who purchase an item during a given time period. Manufacturers and retail stores frequently use special offers and rebates to encourage customers to buy their products. Increasingly, a traditional marketer will offer an incentive for consumers to go online and **register** to make a purchase or receive a discount from a marketer.

Product samples are especially important when promoting new products. ***Can you think of some products that make good product samples?***

Stonyfield Farm Organic
Yummy Yogurt Samples

Product Samples

PRODUCT SAMPLES

Another form of consumer sales promotion is the product sample. A product sample is a free trial size of a product sent through the mail, distributed door-to-door, or given away at retail stores and trade shows. Detergents, toothpastes, shampoos, deodorants, and colognes are frequently promoted this way. Samples are especially important in promoting new products. Drug manufacturers frequently give samples to doctors and dentists so their patients can try new products.

SPONSORSHIP

Sponsors often negotiate the right to use their logos and names on retail products to enhance their corporate image. The sponsoring company pays a fee for rights to promote itself, its products or services at an event (such as a concert), with a group (such as a NASCAR® car racing team), with a person (such as a well-known basketball player), or at a physical site (such as a stadium).

Obtaining naming rights at a particular location is a high-profile promotional effort. A title sponsor is an organization that pays to have its name incorporated into the name of the sponsored location, such as The Home Depot® Center or a U.S. Olympic Training site on the publicly owned campus of California State University. Sponsorship deals must be able to withstand public and media scrutiny. The effectiveness of the particular sponsorship is measured by the response of those who actually view the title or logo.

PROMOTIONAL TIE-INS, CROSS-PROMOTION, CROSS-SELLING

Promotional tie-ins, also known as *cross-promotion* and *cross-selling* campaigns, are activities that involve sales promotions between one or more retailers or manufacturers.

Partners combine their advertising and sales promotional activities to conduct a promotion that will create additional sales for each partner. Promotional tie-ins can be complex and involve several companies. For example, Jack in the Box® teamed with Dr. Pepper® on a promotional tie-in directed at video gamers. Customers who bought combo meals received game pieces on drinks for prizes including GameStop® gift cards, Xbox 360® consoles, and several game rooms equipped with home theaters and recliners.

Another good example of promotional tie-ins can be found in breakfast cereals and at fast-food restaurants. When a blockbuster animated feature is about to hit theaters, a movie studio often cross-promotes the film by offering ticket discounts in cereal boxes or toys with kids' meals.

Green Premiums

At many eco-friendly companies, promotional premiums have been dropped in favor of clever, environmentally friendly alternatives. Popular eco-premiums range from organic-cotton tote bags and recycled-paper notepads to biodegradable golf tees and mouse pads that are crafted from old tires. Some companies even donate to a choice of charities instead of offering flashy and expensive premiums to high-profile clients. Green premiums both promote a company and give it a positive image.

Mathematics

Calculate Assume the cost of a traditional premium is $0.75 per premium and the cost of an eco-friendly premium is $1.10 per premium. Calculate the difference in price for 12,000 units of each premium as a dollar amount and as a percentage. Which option would you choose to promote your company?

NCTM Number and Operations Compute fluently and make reasonable estimates.

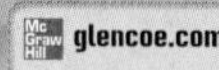
glencoe.com

Get an activity on green marketing.

EXPLAIN

Visual Literacy

Product Samples Caption Answer Read the question: ***Can you think of some products that make good product samples?*** Students will likely mention food, beverages, toys, or games. Ask: ***What types of product samples have you tried?*** Answers may include food and beverages in grocery stores, digital music samples, or trial software. Ask: ***Did the product samples encourage you to buy the product? Why or why not?*** Answers will vary. Some may say they wouldn't have bought the product if they hadn't tried the sample.

VIRTUAL BUSINESS

ADVANCED PROMOTION

Introduce the concept of advanced promotion using Knowledge Matters' Virtual Business Retailing visual simulation, *Advanced Promotion*. In this simulation, students will learn about additional sales and merchandise promotion activities that a storeowner or manager can use to attain the stated goals of a sales promotion.

SPONSORSHIP

Ask students these guiding questions to focus the discussion about sponsorship.

Guiding Questions

Define What is a title sponsor?	A title sponsor is an organization that pays to have its name incorporated into the name of the sponsored location, such as The Home Depot® Center.
Explain What is the difference between cross-selling and sponsorship?	Cross-selling is a promotion that involves promotional arrangements between one or more retailers or manufacturers. Sponsorship involves the promotion of a company in association with a property.

ELABORATE

Graphic Organizer

After students have completed the section about Consumer Promotions, have them fill in this graphic organizer with examples of each type of consumer promotion. Sample answers:

Consumer Promotions

Coupons	Premiums	Deals	Incentives
Magazine Online	Discounted Traffic builders	Short-term price reduction	Contests Sweepstakes
Product Samples	**Sponsorship**	**Tie-Ins, Cross-Promotion, Cross-Selling**	**Product Placement**
Toothpaste Shampoo Deodorant	Concert Car racing team Basketball player	Jack in the Box® teamed with Dr. Pepper®	Television series Movie Sporting event
Loyalty Programs	**Online Loyalty Programs**	**Point-of-Purchase Displays**	
Frequent buyer Reward Frequent shopper	Yahoo awards points to buyers	High-traffic areas Promote impulse purchases	

 **glencoe.com** 

iWB

Graphic Organizer Send students to the Online Learning Center to print this graphic organizer.

The GREEN Marketer

Mathematics Answer Traditional premium: $0.75 × 12,000 = $9,000. Eco-friendly premium: $1.10 × 12,000 = $13,200. Difference: $4,200 or 46%. Ask students: ***Which option would you choose to promote your company?*** Students who are concerned about the environment will likely choose the eco-friendly premium. Students who are not concerned about ecology will choose the traditional premium.

 **glencoe.com** 

Worksheet Activity Send students to the Online Learning Center to get a Green Marketer worksheet activity.

e MARKETING

Digital Coupons and "Groupons"

Digital coupons have increased significantly with the popularity of social media, such as Facebook and Twitter. Research indicates that product promotions using digital coupons increased 84 percent in one year on retailer Web sites. Manufacturers have partnered with retailers by providing coupons on retailers' Web sites to encourage customers to visit the stores. Digital "groupons" are communal coupons that require a certain number of people to participate in order for the coupon to be honored. The premise is that people interested in the coupon will try to persuade friends to sign up. Digital groupons are often sponsored by a local newspaper for small local businesses by creating a groupon site to which people can subscribe. Subscribers receive e-mail alerts for each new Groupon Coupon Event, which may include restaurants, retailers, and/or service businesses.

Innovate and Create

Have students work in groups to design a Web site for Groupon Coupon Events for local businesses in their community. Tell them they are hosting the site. Have them select the businesses and the criteria required for the coupon to be honored. Ask them to include their ideas for generating subscribers for the Groupon Coupon Web site and for soliciting businesses to participate in the promotions. Have students prepare a written and oral report to share their projects with classmates. Accept all reasonable projects that include a Web site design that allows subscribers to sign-up for Groupon Events. Evaluate their ideas for generating subscribers and businesses for the various Groupon promotions. Ideas may include having signs in the participating local businesses explaining the Groupon Events and information on how to become a subscriber. To solicit businesses, students can stress the multiplier factor with regard to having subscribers encouraging others to sign up so the "group" can take advantage of the digital coupons from the participating local businesses. The criteria for honoring the groupons should be a specific number of subscribers who sign up for a specific promotion event offered by a local business or businesses. The digital coupons should include some type of special offer, such as a discount or a free product or service.

 **glencoe.com** 

eMarketing Worksheet Activity Send students to the Online Learning Center to download an eMarketing worksheet activity.

PRODUCT PLACEMENT

Product placement is a consumer promotion that involves the verbal mention or appearance of a brand-name product in a television series, movie, or sporting event. It can even happen in a commercial for another product. For example, on the *American Idol* television series, the Ford Focus® was shown and the Sprint Nextel® phone was used as a prop. Product placement has increased on television shows because technology allows viewers to fast forward through paid commercials. One example of product placement in a movie took place in the Tom Hanks' movie *Cast Away* where FedEx® packaging and a Wilson® soccer ball were prominently featured. Both companies received international exposure.

LOYALTY MARKETING PROGRAMS

Loyalty marketing programs, also known as *frequent buyer, reward,* or *frequent shopper programs,* reward customers by offering incentives for repeat purchases.

The airline industry instituted one of the first such promotions, the frequent flyer program. These programs reward customers with free air travel once they have accumulated a designated amount of travel miles. Hotel industry chains, such as Hilton®, Hyatt®, and Marriott®, have adopted frequent guest programs in which consumers can earn free lodging by spending a designated dollar amount on lodging.

Customer loyalty means that customers are so satisfied with a brand or retailer that they continue to buy that brand or patronize that business even when they have others from which to choose. Most loyalty marketing programs do not cost anything for participation. However, large warehouse chains, such as Costco®, BJ's®, and Sam's Club®, require a membership fee for their loyalty cards that entitle the customer to large discounts.

Large and small businesses in many industries have adopted loyalty marketing programs. Hallmark®, a greeting card and gift chain, has *Crown Rewards*®. Customers can earn points for dollars spent and trade them for certificates on future purchases. Many local restaurants use simple loyalty cards that entitle frequent users to a free meal after a set number of purchases.

Grocery chains have also implemented loyalty programs. Customers who sign up for a frequent shopper card can accumulate points for every purchase. These points can then be applied to discounts on future shopping trips, or for stores that have gas stations, savings on fuel purchases.

Interacting with Customers

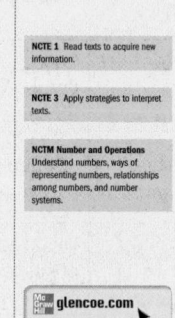

Kiosks allow customers to obtain product information. ***How do kiosks help businesses interact with customers?***

ONLINE LOYALTY MARKETING PROGRAMS

Online versions of loyalty programs have also become popular. The Internet search engine Yahoo! awards points to users who buy from certain retailers or visit certain Web sites. Yahoo! also negotiated with the airline industry to allow consumers to convert their points into frequent flyer miles. This arrangement benefits both Yahoo! and the airlines.

Companies can also use email to notify loyal customers of exclusive sales. They may also be directed to special online-only discounts or given a chance to try new products first.

POINT-OF-PURCHASE DISPLAYS

Point-of-purchase displays are displays designed primarily by manufacturers to hold and display their products. They are usually placed in high-traffic areas and promote impulse purchases. By exposing potential customers firsthand to a company's products, point-of-purchase displays stimulate sales and serve as in-store advertising.

Kiosks are point-of-purchase displays that are stand-alone structures. Web-based or display-screen kiosks disseminate information to customers. Store kiosks offer new ways to interact with the sales staff, provide opportunities for cross-selling, and improve customer service.

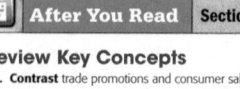

After You Read | **Section 17.2**

Review Key Concepts

1. **Contrast** trade promotions and consumer sales promotions.
2. **Contrast** contests, sweepstakes, special offers, and rebates.
3. **Explain** why a business would want product placement in entertainment media.

Practice Academics

English Language Arts

4. Conduct research to identify advantages and disadvantages for companies that seek naming rights for publicly financed or owned buildings such as stadiums, hospitals, or schools. Identify and label the advantages and disadvantages in a two-column table and share this information with your class.

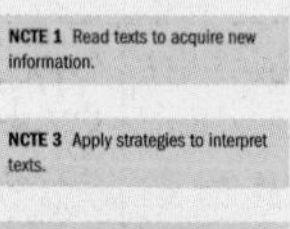

NCTE 1 Read texts to acquire new information.

NCTE 3 Apply strategies to interpret texts.

Mathematics

5. Promotional discounts are given to stores by manufacturers to place their products in preferred locations in the store and to display their products in store windows. A ski manufacturer sells a local ski shop 35 pairs of their new skis for $7,000, which is a discount of $2,625. What is the percentage of the discount given to the store? (Round your answer to the nearest whole percent.)

NCTM Number and Operations Understand numbers, ways of representing numbers, relationships among numbers, and number systems.

Math Concept **Number and Operations** A decimal can be multiplied by 100 to be represented by a percentage.

Starting Hints To solve this problem, subtract the discount amount from the purchase amount of each item to determine the net cost. For each item, divide the discount dollar amount by the purchase amount to get a decimal. Multiply each decimal by 100 to get the percent discount.

For help, go to the Math Skills Handbook located at the back of this book.

glencoe.com

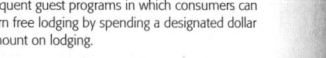

Check your answers.

ELABORATE

Mini Project

Extension

Create Promotion Logs Have students collect a week's worth of coupons and other premiums delivered in the newspaper, magazines, and mail. Have them create a descriptive log of these promotional items. It might include the type of consumer promotion, duration of the offer, notes on its visual appeal, and so on. Have students share their logs with the class. To extend this activity, ask students to locate promotions online and on television to include in their logs. Ask students: ***Which types of promotions are easiest to use? Why?*** Students may prefer going online to retrieve coupons, others may like watching television to learn what stores are having sales, and some may like to clip coupons out of newspapers or magazines.

Visual Literacy

Interacting With Customers Caption Answer Read the caption question to students: ***How do kiosks help businesses interact with customers?*** Web-based or display screen kiosks allow businesses to disseminate information to customers. Ask the guiding questions to focus the discussion on interacting with customers.

Guiding Questions

Explain What is a kiosk?	A kiosk is a point-of-purchase display that is a stand-alone structure.
Apply How can kiosks benefit a business?	by providing opportunities for cross-selling and to elicit customer feedback

EVALUATE

Critical Thinking

Ask students: ***What is a promotional tie-in?*** Promotional tie-ins are activities that involve sales promotions between one or more retailers or manufacturers. Then ask: ***What are some of the purposes of promotional tie-ins?*** Promotional tie-ins are designed to stimulate customer response to a product offered. They combine the resources of each partner in the arrangement and enable companies to reach customers and prospects within market segments that they have in common. They share costs and capitalize on the brand awareness of popular consumer or business-to-business brands.

Mini Projects

Differentiated Instruction

Students with Learning Disabilities Divide the class into groups of four or five students. Be sure that students with learning disabilities are distributed among the groups. Have group members work together to make sure all members can answer the following: ***Give examples of the locations where a sponsor might be found.*** physical site—stadium, hospital, museum, performing arts center; event—concert, film festival, boat race; group—car racing team; person—professional athlete ***Give examples of trade promotions and consumer promotions.*** trade promotions—promotional allowances, cooperative advertising, slotting allowances, sales force promotions, buying allowances, trade shows and conventions; consumer promotions—cross-selling, coupons, premiums, incentives, samples, sponsorship, product placement, loyalty marketing programs, and point-of-purchase displays

Gifted Learners Ask students to take photos of point-of-purchase displays in different places such as the mall, inside clothing stores and grocery stores, and so on. Create a photo gallery with the photos. Students should write a brief description of where the display is located (such as near the checkout counter, by the soft drinks, and so on) and attach it to the photo. Number the photos and have students critique them based on how effective they think the displays are. Critiques can be brief but should discuss the reasoning behind effectiveness.

After You Read — Section 17.2

Review Key Concepts

1. Trade promotions are sales promotion activities designed to gain manufacturers', wholesalers', and retailers' support for a product. Examples include promotional allowances, cooperative advertising, slotting allowances, sales force promotions, buying allowances, trade shows and conventions. Consumer sales promotion activities are designed to encourage individual customers to buy a product. Examples include cross selling, coupons, premiums, incentives, samples, sponsorship, product placement, loyalty marketing programs, and point of purchase displays.
2. Contests and sweepstakes are different types of games. Contests require participants to demonstrate a skill; sweepstakes are games of chance. Special offers and rebates are discounts offered by manufacturers to customers who purchase a product or service during a given time period.
3. Product placement allows viewers to see the product used or hear it discussed in an actual situation in an entertainment medium potentially viewed by millions. Because technology allows viewers to skip over paid TV advertisements or leave the area when ads are playing, product placement ensures that the product will at least be seen.

Practice Academics

English Language Arts

4. Advantages: name and logo builds brand awareness; positive publicity when the name of a sponsored facility appears. Disadvantages: high initial cost of sponsorship; annual long-term payments to continue naming rights; potential conflicts.

Mathematics

5. 27% ($2,625 ÷ $9,625 = .27)

 glencoe.com 

Answer Key Send students to the Online Learning Center to check their answers.

Chapter 17 Visual Summary

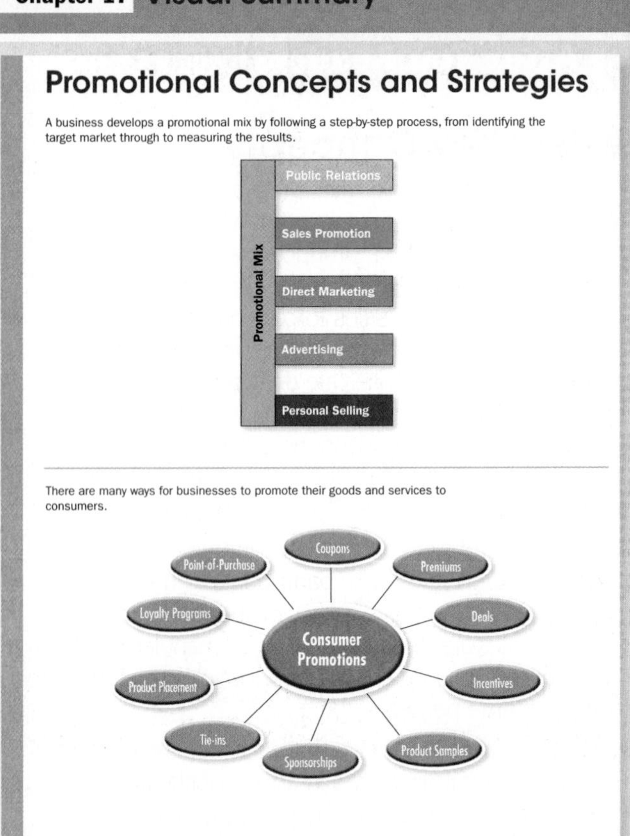

412 | Unit 6 · Promotion

Review and Activities

Written Summary

- Promotion is any form of communication a business uses to inform, persuade, or remind people about its products and its image.
- A promotional mix is the cost effective combination and use of five strategies, advertising, selling, sales promotion, direct marketing, and public relations, to reach objectives.
- Public relations create a positive image about a business, its products, or its policies.
- Publicity tries to place positive information about a business in the media. It is not advertising because it is free.
- Sales promotion is a short-term incentive given to encourage consumers to buy a product or service.
- Sales promotions can be classified either as trade promotions or consumer sales promotions.

Review Content Vocabulary and Academic Vocabulary

1. Create a fill-in-the-blank sentence for each of these vocabulary terms. The sentence should contain enough information to help determine the missing word.

Content Vocabulary

- promotion (p. 395)
- product promotion (p. 395)
- institutional promotion (p. 395)
- promotional mix (p. 396)
- advertising (p. 396)
- direct marketing (p. 396)
- social media (p. 397)
- sales promotion (p. 397)
- public relations (p. 397)
- news release (p. 399)
- publicity (p. 399)
- push policy (p. 403)
- pull policy (p. 403)
- sales promotions (p. 405)
- trade promotions (p. 405)
- consumer promotions (p. 406)
- coupons (p. 406)
- premiums (p. 407)
- incentives (p. 408)
- promotional tie-ins (p. 409)
- loyalty marketing programs (p. 410)
- kiosks (p. 411)

Academic Vocabulary

- via (p. 396)
- target (p. 401)
- distribution (p. 406)
- register (p. 408)

Assess for Understanding

2. **Explain** What is the purpose of promotion in marketing?
3. **Imagine** How might aggressive direct marketing affect public relations?
4. **Contrast** What is the difference between public relations and publicity?
5. **Draft** What new product will your company's press release introduce?
6. **Compare** What is similar about trade promotions and consumer promotions?
7. **Apply** When developing a promotional mix, at what stage will you consider push and pull policies?
8. **Consider** Why are sales promotions generally limited-time opportunities?
9. **Discuss** What are the purposes of promotional tie-ins, trade show promotions, and loyalty marketing programs?

Chapter 17 · Promotional Concepts and Strategies | 413

EVALUATE

Visual Summary

Express Creativity Ask students to develop their own visual summary of a concept in the chapter. Encourage students to use different formats for their visual summaries, such as a storyboard, a timeline, a table, a tree diagram, or a word web. Visual summaries will vary depending on the concepts depicted. Questions to ask when assessing summary:

- Is the summary clear, economical, and simple?
- Are any important steps left out?
- Are steps or concepts arranged in the same order as the original?
- Does the summary reveal a pattern that connects the details?
- Does the summary highlight the most important information?

Review Content Vocabulary and Academic Vocabulary

1. Sample fill-in-the-blank sentences: There are two basic types of promotion—product promotion and institutional promotion; each type involves advertising, personal selling, sales promotion, and public relations. The promotional mix is made up of personal selling, advertising, direct marketing, sales promotion, and public relations, which includes writing news releases, using social media, and publicity. Push policy promotes products to partners in the sales channel. Pull policy directs promotional activities toward consumers. Sales promotions are incentives that encourage customers to buy products or services and include trade promotions and consumer promotions, which include such things as coupons, premiums, promotional tie-ins, and loyalty marketing programs. Kiosks are point-of-purchase stand-alone structures. Advertising is often sent via regular mail to a target market. Companies sometimes distribute samples door-to-door or allow customers to register online.

EVALUATE

Assess for Understanding

2. Promotion is any form of communication a business uses to inform, persuade, or remind people about its products, services, and its image. Companies rely on promotion to inform people about their products and services.

3. Aggressive direct marketing may negatively affect public relations. For example, customer complaints about unwanted electronic direct mailings resulted in the CAN-SPAM Act of 2003, which allows recipients to opt out of receiving e-mails.

4. Public relations activities foster a favorable image about a business, its products, or its policies. Publicity brings news or newsworthy information about a company or organization to the public's attention.

5. Products introduced in the press release will vary. Important elements in a news release include the following: (1) the first paragraph answers the *Who*, *What*, *When*, *Where* and *Why* questions; (2) the story is developed after first paragraph; (3) identification of the full name and title of the person in press release; (4) less important information follows after person identification; (5) one- to two-page press releases are preferred; and (6) always include name, address, and phone number of contact person sending out the release.

6. Trade promotions are sales promotion activities designed to gain manufacturers' wholesalers' and retailers' support for a particular product. Consumer promotions are sales strategies that encourage customers and prospects to buy a product or service. Both are designed to gain attention and support for a product or service.

7. Push and pull policies would be considered during Step 4 when selecting promotional activities.

8. Sales promotions are limited-time opportunities to coincide with the promotional budgeting process which is usually developed for periods of less than a year. Short or limited time promotions encourage potential customers to act quickly to take advantage of the incentives being offered and are designed to boost immediate sales for the business offering the promotions.

9. Promotional tie-ins or cross-selling involve sales promotional arrangements between two or more businesses designed to boost sales for both. Trade promotions are sales promotion activities designed to gain the support of manufacturers, wholesalers, and retailers for a particular product. Examples include slotting allowances, buying allowances, trade shows and conventions, and sales incentives. Loyalty marketing programs are frequent buyer programs designed to reward customers for patronizing a particular business.

21st Century Skills

Social Responsibility Skills

10. **Targeting Kids?** Many manufacturers of consumer products and large restaurant chains offer Internet games or "advergames." These advergames for children can be fun and enjoyable, though they do promote a company's products to kids. Discuss the possible objections parents or caregivers might have to these games.

Financial Literacy Skills

11. **Coupon Promotions** Online coupons are a popular type of sales promotion. A food manufacturer has introduced a new pecan-and-almond nut-cluster snack. You obtain a manufacturer's online coupon for $1 off the snack that retails for $7.99. The store also has a sale and the snack is being offered at $6.49 for a limited time. What percentage discount would you receive if you used the coupon during the sale?

Everyday Ethics

12. **Name Game** David met Goliath in a Malaysian court case, McCurry v. McDonald's. Located in Kuala Lumpur, McCurry was a small local restaurant serving traditional Indian dishes. McDonald's believed that using the prefix "Mc" was too similar to its name. But after eight years of legal affairs, Malaysia's highest court ended the case in favor of McCurry. The publicity was great promotion for McCurry and many could not understand why McDonald's filed suit. What do you think?

e-Marketing Skills

13. **Online Entrepreneurship** Imagine that you are a store manager of a retail store. The owner has asked you to provide a rationale for starting an online store. Gather this information for the owner:
    - Projections for growth of online shopping.
    - Reasons for the growth of online shopping.
    - Ways your store can achieve growth in online shopping.

Build Academic Skills

English Language Arts

14. **Member Benefits** Loyalty marketing programs, also known as *frequent shopper, frequent buyer, rewards,* or *incentive programs,* are offered by companies in many different industries. Identify a few companies that offer loyalty marketing programs. Analyze the name of each program and suggest reasons the company may have chosen that particular name.

NCTE 3 Apply strategies to interpret texts.

Social Studies

15. **Promoting Ideals** Companies assist with activities that benefit the civic, social, and cultural life of a community. Examples include partnerships with nonprofit organizations, such as Habitat for Humanity®, or sponsorships of events like the Special Olympics®. Research corporate Web sites, annual reports, magazines, or library resources to identify a company that uses institutional promotion. Present your findings to the class orally by describing the company and its sponsored activities that are examples of institutional promotion.

NCSS V B Individuals, Groups, & Institutions Analyze group and institutional influences on people, events, and elements of culture in both historical and contemporary settings.

Mathematics

16. **Promotional Spending** A large amount of money is spent on promotional activities in the United States every year. The average budget breaks down as follows: 50 percent for advertising, 30 percent for sales promotion, and 20 percent for trade promotion. Use these percentages to calculate the amount a company will spend on each type of promotion if its overall budget is $400,000.

NCTM Problem Solving Solve problems that arise in mathematics and in other contexts.

Math Concept **Problem Solving: Computing Percentages** When determining what percentage the dollar amount is of another dollar amount, start by dividing the smaller amount by the larger amount.

For help, go to the **Math Skills Handbook** located at the back of this book.

Standardized Test Practice

Directions Read the following questions. On a separate piece of paper, write the best possible answer for each one.

1. Which of the following is a form of nonpersonal promotion in which companies pay to promote ideas, goods, or services in a variety of media outlets?
   A. Advertising
   B. Public Relations
   C. Personal Selling
   D. Sales Promotions
2. Direct marketing is a type of advertising that sends a promotional message to a mass audience.
   T
   F
3. Incentives to encourage customers to buy products or services are known as ________.

Test-Taking Tip

Though your first answers may often be correct, do not be afraid to change an answer if, after you think about it, you believe it is incorrect.

DECA Connection Role Play

Promotions Manager Beach Resort

Situation You work as promotions manager of a small beachside resort on a Caribbean island. The resort has been in business for more than 30 years. The owners and management have maintained the buildings and grounds in a state of near perfection. All of the guest rooms have been recently refurbished. The resort also offers guests many amenities, including an indoor pool, outdoor salt-water pool, spa, gourmet restaurant, casual restaurant, tennis courts, access to golf, and many others.

The resort has enjoyed near capacity bookings during the winter months. The winter months are the resort's prime season. It is very important that the resort have as many bookings as possible during these months. Most of your customers during the winter months are from northern areas and fly down to your island to stay for a week or longer.

During the past few years, your winter season bookings have consistently fallen short of expectations. The management team has noted a correlation between the decrease in bookings and warmer than usual winters in the northern areas where your customers reside. The resort's general manager (judge) feels that now is the time to promote the resort to help increase prime season bookings. The general manager (judge) has asked you to recommend some promotional ideas to help achieve this goal.

Activity You are to outline your promotional ideas, and then make recommendations to the resort general manager (judge) that will help increase prime-season bookings.

Evaluation You will be evaluated on how well you meet the following performance indicators:

1. Explain the role of promotion as a marketing function.
2. Plan displays and themes with management.
3. Create displays.
4. Create promotional signs.
5. Coordinate activities in the promotional mix.

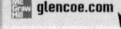

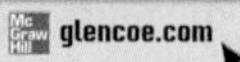
glencoe.com

Download the Competitive Events Workbook for more Role-Play practice.

EVALUATE

21st Century Skills

Social Responsibility Skills

10. Acceptable answers should include a statement on whether advergames directed at children are or are not ethical and include the reasoning behind their opinion. Objections from parents might include: the sites should add a no purchase necessary provision to play, privacy clauses, and information on better decision-making skills for nutrition.

Financial Literacy Skills

11. The discount would be 15.4% off the sale price.

Everyday Ethics

12. Some may be in favor of McCurry, the underdog; others may be in favor of McDonald's® and agree that the names are too similar. They might also point out that McCurry gained from the publicity of the court case. Students should support their comments with sound reasoning. Comments should use correct grammar and be free of spelling errors.

e-Marketing Skills

13. Students' research should show that online shopping will likely become more popular and achieve growth in the future. The reasons behind this prediction include the fact that the new generation of spenders is more tech savvy than previous generations and is more comfortable with using technology to do their shopping. Ways a store can achieve growth in online shopping will vary but may include conducting online marketing surveys, providing online coupons and other incentives, and so on.

EVALUATE

Build Academic Skills

English Language Arts

14. Answers will vary depending on the companies students choose, but answers should include the name of the company, the name of its loyalty rewards program, and an analysis of why the company might have chosen the name for its program. For example, the name Rewards Program might tell the customer that the more they spend the more they will be rewarded by the company.

Social Studies

15. Answers will vary but should include the name of the company and a list of its corporate sponsorships and activities. Examples include participation in the United Fund®, The American Red Cross®, area food banks, housing programs, athletic and scholarship programs, mentoring programs, and matching employee donations to charities.

Mathematics

16. $200,000 would be spent for advertising; $120,000 would be spent for sales promotion; and $80,000 would be spent for trade promotion.

Standardized Test Practice

1. A Advertising
2. False
3. sales promotions

DECA Connection Role Play

Evaluations will be based on these performance indicators:

1. **Explain the role of promotion as a marketing function.** Promotion, as a marketing function, involves decisions about advertising, personal selling, sales promotion, and public relations. Promotion is persuasive communication used by companies to enhance their public image and to persuade people to value their products or services.
2. **Plan displays and themes with management.** The promotional mix is the cost-effective combination of personal selling, advertising, direct marketing, sales promotion, and public relations strategies used to reach company goals. The process of establishing a promotional mix starts with identification of the target market for a particular product or service. Displays and themes should be coordinated and reinforce a consistent message.
3. **Create displays.** Point-of-purchase displays are designed primarily by manufacturers to hold and display their products. These displays serve as in-store advertising and stimulate sales by exposing potential customers firsthand to a company's products. Kiosks are stand-alone, often interactive point-of-purchase displays that disseminate information to customers. Displays are also used at trade shows and conventions to showcase a line of products.
4. **Create promotional signs.** Advertising is a form of nonpersonal promotion in which companies pay to promote ideas, goods, or services. Promotional signs are a form of advertising displayed on billboards, on cars and buses, at public transit stops, in store windows, inside stores, and in other locations. Promotional signs are a form of one-way communication between a business and potential customers.
5. **Coordinate activities in the promotional mix.** Elements of the promotional mix must be coordinated. National advertising should be reinforced by local promotional efforts. At the local retail level, the national and local efforts need to be communicated to the store personnel. Staff should be made aware of any coupons, rebates, contests, and featured promotional items. If these employees are informed of such promotions, they will be able to more effectively engage their customers.

Role Plays For more DECA Role Plays, send students to the Online Learning Center to download the Competitive Events Workbook.

visual merchandising and display

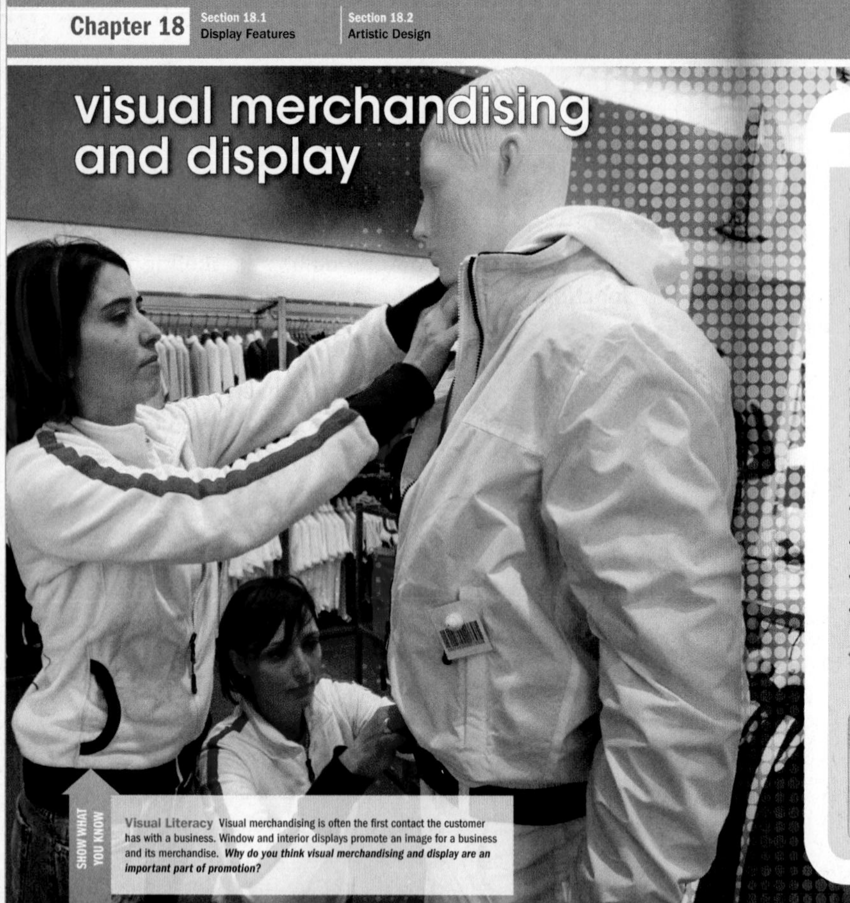

SHOW WHAT YOU KNOW

Visual Literacy Visual merchandising is often the first contact the customer has with a business. Window and interior displays promote an image for a business and its merchandise. ***Why do you think visual merchandising and display are an important part of promotion?***

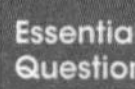

Discovery Project

The Right Presentation

Essential Question How do stores use their space to project an image and to present their products?

Project Goal

Work with a partner to visit a store where you and your friends shop. Create a visual merchandising and display report for the store by observing the store and interviewing a store supervisor. Develop a written report by describing the four elements of visual merchandising: storefront, (types of signs, marquee, entrances, and window displays), store layout (layout of selling space, location of storage space, location and use of personnel space, description of services in customer space), store interior (graphics, signage, color, sound, lighting, fixtures), and interior displays (types of interior displays).

Ask Yourself...

- What store will you identify to investigate in your community?
- How will you arrange transportation and schedule the necessary time for the visit?
- What staff member will you interview to obtain information?
- How will you organize your written report?

Synthesize and Present Research Synthesize your research and present your design ideas, using the four elements of visual design for attracting teen shoppers.

glencoe.com

Activity
Get a worksheet activity about visual merchandising.

Evaluate
Download a rubric you can use to evaluate your project.

DECA Connection

DECA Event Role Play

Concepts in this chapter are related to DECA competitive events that involve either an interview or role play.

Performance Indicators The performance indicators represent key skills and knowledge. Your key to success in DECA competitive events is relating them to concepts in this chapter.

- Explain the use of visual merchandising in retailing.
- Create displays.
- Create promotional signs.
- Plan visual merchandising activities.
- Plan/schedule displays/themes with management.

DECA Prep

Role Play Practice role-playing with the DECA Connection competitive-event activity at the end of this chapter. More information on DECA events can be found on DECA's Web site.

ENGAGE

Visual Literacy

Read the chapter opener photo caption question to students: ***Why do you think visual merchandising and display are an important part of promotion?*** They attract customers, create a desired business image, and promote interest in products and services. Then ask these guiding questions.

Guiding Questions

Describe What are three objectives of sales promotions such as point-of-purchase displays?	Objectives include: increase sales, tell potential customers about new products, and create a positive image.
Analyze Why do companies use promotional techniques?	These techniques enhance a company's public image and reputation and persuade people to value their products.

Discovery Project

The Right Presentation Have students think of a store where they enjoy shopping. Ask: ***What image do you think this store projects? Why?*** Possible answer: I think the store projects the image of being action-oriented and fun because it has displays showing young people using sports equipment together. Then ask students the Discovery Project Essential Question: ***How do stores use their space to project an image and present their products?*** Students should be aware that stores use their space to project a specific image that appeals to their target customers. To be successful, their products must be an integral part of the image they are projecting.

glencoe.com

Discovery Project Resources Send students to the Online Learning Center to download a rubric to evaluate their projects.

ENGAGE

Introduce the Chapter

Chapter 18 provides students with an overview of the importance of visual merchandising as a promotional strategy. These main concepts are introduced and discussed:

- Role of visual merchandisers
- Elements of the storefront
- Store layout and interior design
- Display design and preparation
- Decorative and functional props
- Types of display settings
- Artistic elements used in displays, such as color and balance
- Display maintenance

Discussion Starter

Developing an Image Have students imagine they are entering their favorite store. It can be anything from a coffee shop to a high-end shoe store. Then ask: ***What appeals to you about this store? How does it make you feel when you enter it?*** Answers will vary, but might include that students feel like they are going to enjoy themselves and that they are looking forward to seeing what the store has to offer. They may be drawn to certain products or to an intangible ambience. Then ask: ***What is it about the store that makes you want to shop or browse there?*** Students may say that it offers products they like and that they find the store attractive, cheerful, and welcoming. Discuss with students that stores work hard to project an image that will attract their target customers.

DECA Connection

Discuss the performance indicators listed in the DECA Connection feature. Explain to students that performance indicators tell them how to demonstrate their acquired skills and knowledge through individual or team competitive events.

glencoe.com

Competitive Events Workbook For more DECA Role Plays, send students to the Online Learning Center to download the Competitive Events Workbook.

PRINT RESOURCES

- **Student Edition**
- **Teacher Edition**
- **Student Activity Workbook with Academic Integration** includes worksheets and activities correlated to the text.
- **Mathematics for Marketing Workbook** provides math activities for every unit in the text.

TECHNOLOGY TOOLBOX

- **Connect**
- **ConnectPlus**
- **ExamView Assessment Suite** is a comprehensive solution for creating, administering, and scoring tests.

glencoe.com

Online Learning Center provides a variety of resources to enrich and enhance learning.

SECTION, CHAPTER, AND UNIT RESOURCES

- **Graphic Organizers** for organizing text concepts visually.
- **Digital Nation Activities** and **Green Marketer Activities** extend learning beyond the text features.
- **Career Chatroom Career Profiles** allow students to explore different marketing occupations in depth.
- **After You Read Answer Keys** for students to check their answers.
- **Discovery Project Rubrics** and **Marketing Internship Project Rubrics** for students to evaluate their projects.

PROGRAM RESOURCES

- **Student Activity Workbook with Academic Integration Teacher Annotated Edition** includes annotated answers for the activities and worksheets.
- **Marketing Research Project Workbook** provides a step-by-step approach for students to complete their own marketing research studies.
- **School-to-Career Activity Workbook** helps students relate their class work to on-the-job experience and involves work-site analysis and working with mentors.
- **Competitive Events Workbook** helps prepare students for state and national marketing education competitions.
- **Inclusion in the Marketing Education Classroom** provides teaching resources for working with students with special needs.
- **PowerPoint Presentations** provides visual teaching aids and assessments for this chapter.

READING GUIDE

Before You Read

Connect What memorable visual displays have you seen at stores?

Objectives

- **Explain** the concept and purpose of visual merchandising.
- **Identify** the elements of visual merchandising.
- **Describe** types of display arrangements.
- **Understand** the role of visual merchandisers on the marketing team.

The Main Idea

Visual merchandising and displays are important promotional strategies to sell products and services, attract potential customers, and create a desired business image.

Vocabulary

Content Vocabulary
- visual merchandising
- display
- storefront
- marquee
- store layout
- fixtures
- point-of-purchase displays (POPs)
- interactive kiosk

Academic Vocabulary

You will find these words in your reading and on your tests. Make sure you know their meanings.
- project
- concept

Graphic Organizer

Draw or print a scorecard like the one below to list the key features of each visual merchandising element.

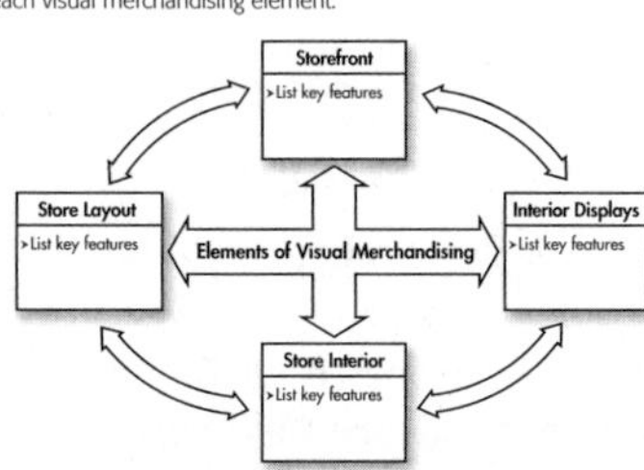

STANDARDS

ACADEMIC

English Language Arts

NCTE 1 Read texts to acquire new information.

Social Studies

NCSS III G People, Places, & Environments Describe and compare how people create places that reflect culture, human needs, government policy, and current values and ideals.

NCSS *National Council for the Social Studies*
NCTE *National Council of Teachers of English*
NCTM *National Council of Teachers of Mathematics*
NSES *National Science Education Standards*

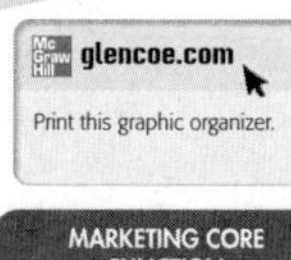

Common Core
Reading Read and comprehend complex literary and informational texts independently and proficiently.

glencoe.com

Print this graphic organizer.

MARKETING CORE FUNCTION

Promotion

m.e. Section 18.1 Display Features

VISUAL MERCHANDISING AND DISPLAY

Visual merchandising coordinates all of the physical elements in a place of business to **project** an image to customers. Visual merchandising attracts customers, creates a desired business image, and promotes interest in products or services.

The term *visual merchandising* is sometimes used interchangeably with the term *display*, but they are not the same. Display is a much narrower **concept** and makes up only one element of visual merchandising. **Display** refers to the visual and artistic aspects of presenting a product or service to a target group of customers to encourage a purchase. Visual merchandising, by contrast, includes the visual and artistic aspects of the entire business environment. Keep this distinction in mind when you read about these concepts.

As You Read

List Think of a product you recently purchased at a store and list the visual merchandising elements that were used to attract buyers.

Successful businesses create distinct, clear, and consistent images for their customers. A good image sets a business apart from its competition. This image is made up of a unique blend of store characteristics, location, products, prices, advertising, public relations, and personal selling.

An image can include the design and layout of the store, its logo and signage, the unique lines of merchandise the store carries, the design of the store's Web site, a distinct promotional or ad campaign, and a targeted base of shoppers. A store's image should highlight what sets it apart from the competition. A good image will attract positive attention and loyal customers.

This chapter primarily focuses on visual merchandising in retail stores. However, manufacturers and wholesalers also use visual merchandising to sell their products. Visual merchandising is used extensively in manufacturers' showrooms and at trade shows and other conventions.

> "The appearance of buildings and store interiors are promotional strategies to sell products and services."

THE ROLE OF VISUAL MERCHANDISERS

Visual merchandisers are responsible for the total merchandise or service presentation that helps to build the overall business or brand image. They design, create, and maintain the design elements of the building and displays. As active members of the marketing team, they promote a business's image and sales of its products or services.

As with all aspects of marketing, the goal of visual merchandisers is to attract customers to a store or business and keep them coming back. A visual merchandiser creates a selling space that is inviting and engaging and which allows customers to enjoy their shopping experience.

Reading Check

Explain Why is a display considered part of visual merchandising?

ENGAGE

Anticipation Activity

Improving Student Achievement Discuss with students the importance of making a good first impression. The ask students: ***What do you usually notice first when you look at the exterior of a store?*** store name, store logo, exterior colors, and window displays

Objectives

- **Explain** the concept and purpose of visual merchandising. Visual merchandising coordinates the physical elements of a business location to project an image for the purpose of attracting customers and promoting interest in products or services.
- **Identify** the elements of visual merchandising. storefront, store layout, store interior, and interior displays
- **Describe** types of display arrangements. architectural, closed, open, point-of-purchase, store decorations
- **Understand** the role of visual merchandisers on the marketing team. The role is to build the overall business or enhance the brand by using integrated design elements.

Graphic Organizer

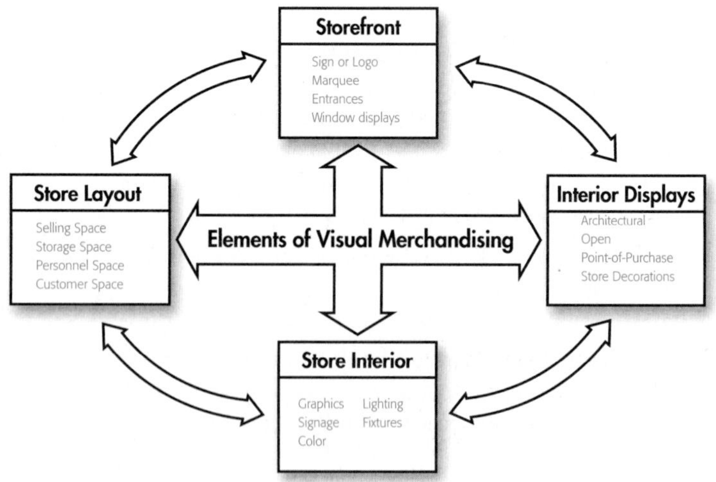

 **glencoe.com** 

Graphic Organizer Send students to the Online Learning Center to print this graphic organizer.

EXPLORE

Before You Read

Read the Before You Read question aloud: ***What memorable visual displays have you see at stores?*** Many complex and memorable visual displays revolve around holidays, seasonal themes, and newly introduced products. ***What was it about these displays that made them particularly memorable to you?*** attention-getting movement and/or music; large size; interesting and colorful components; attractive displays

Preteaching Vocabulary

Have students go to the Online Learning Center at glencoe.com for the Chapter 18 Preteaching Vocabulary games.

Content Vocabulary

Write the content vocabulary term *visual merchandising* on the board. Ask students what *visual* means. having to do with sight Then ask what *merchandising* means. the promotion of the sale of merchandise or goods Discuss that visual merchandising includes all the visual components of a store that encourage the customer to make purchases.

Academic Vocabulary

Project—Synonyms Read aloud this sentence: ***Visual merchandising coordinates all the physical elements in a place of business to project an image to customers.*** Ask: ***Based on this sentence, what are some synonyms of project?*** present, put forth, set forth Reread this sentence using each of the proposed synonyms. Discuss with students whether these sentences have the same meaning as the original one.

Concept—Denotative Meaning Write the word *concept* on the board. Tell students that *concept* means "idea, notion, or thought." Have students come up with sentences using *concept.* The engineers and designers are collaborating on the new concept car for next year's auto show.

ELL: Vocabulary Activities
Go to the Online Learning Center to view a video clip in which students practice using synonyms, antonyms, definitions, and words in context.

Section 18.1

Display Features

VISUAL MERCHANDISING AND DISPLAY

Ask these guiding questions to focus the discussion about visual merchandising and display.

Guiding Questions

Distinguish Why are visual merchandisers vital to retail stores?	They create the design elements of the overall location and the displays it contains.
Evaluate Which of these characteristics differentiates a restaurant: the quality of the food or the service?	Some may think that the food distinguishes a restaurant most. Others may think that the difference is the wait staff.

As You Read

Read students the As You Read question: ***Think of a product you recently purchased at a store and list the visual merchandising elements that were used to attract buyers.*** Sample answer: I recently bought batteries at the checkout counter—the display's placement attracted me to buy batteries, which I needed but I would have otherwise forgotten to buy.

Expert Advice

Read the quote to students:

“The appearance of buildings and store interiors are promotional strategies to sell products and services.”

Ask students: ***What is most appealing as you approach a store?*** Answers will vary. Students might say that store interiors that are designed for teens are appealing.

Reading Check Answer

Read the Reading Check question to students: ***Why is a display considered part of visual merchandising?*** A display is considered to be one element of visual merchandising because displays attract customers' attention, create a desire, and help to enhance product sales.

ELEMENTS OF VISUAL MERCHANDISING

The goal of visual merchandising is to create a positive shopping experience that will compel customers to return. Merchandisers consider four elements as key to achieving this goal: storefront, store layout, store interior, and interior displays. These elements lead customers into a store and keep them there once they have entered.

STOREFRONT

The exterior of a business is known as the *storefront.* The **storefront** includes a store's sign or logo, marquee, outdoor lighting, banners, planters, awnings, windows, and the exterior design, ambiance, landscaping, and lighting of the building. Consider The Home Depot® stores, for example. They are typically large buildings with bold graphics, bright orange signs, a convenient location near a highway, and a large, well-lit parking lot that provides easy access for customers. Unique storefronts build brand identity and help a company distinguish itself from its competitors and surrounding stores.

SIGNS

Outdoor signs are designed to attract attention, advertise a business, and project brand identity. The design of the sign should be original and easily recognizable. The name, letters, logo, materials, and colors used help create the store's desired image. An upscale clothing store might use an elegant script font in signage. A toy store, such as Toys 'R' Us®, uses bright primary colors to emphasize a youthful and playful image in its logo.

MARQUEE

A **marquee** is a canopy that extends over a store's entrance. Marquees are built over theater entrances, where names of the latest plays or movies are displayed. Marquees also can show the store's name, key products, hours of operation, phone number, and URL address. A company can exploit this highly visible space for advertising.

ENTRANCES

Entrances are usually designed with customer convenience and store security in mind. Smaller stores normally have only one entrance, while larger stores have several. The average midsize business needs at least two entrances. One is on the street for pedestrians and another is next to the parking lot for patrons who drive.

Types of entrances include revolving, push-pull, electronic, and climate-controlled entrances. Climate-controlled entrances are often found in indoor shopping malls. Each of these entrances projects a certain image. Electronically controlled sliding doors suggest a practical, self-service business. Push-pull doors with fancy metal or wooden push plates or bars suggest a full-service establishment.

Storefront Design

Businesses use exterior design features such as signs, logos, marquees, lighting, and various landscaping features. ***Why do you think large retail chains develop standardized storefronts?***

Attracting Attention

Effective window displays get shoppers' attention. ***Why are display windows useful for visual merchandising?***

WINDOW DISPLAYS

Display windows are especially useful for visual merchandising. Window displays attract prospects, create excitement for the products on display, and initiate the selling process. Customers who window shop are often drawn into stores by their window displays.

STORE LAYOUT

Store layout refers to ways that stores use floor space to facilitate and promote sales and serve customers. A typical store layout divides a store into four distinct spaces:

- **Selling space** is used for interior displays, wall and floor merchandise, product demonstrations, self-service and informational kiosks, sales transactions, and aisles for customer traffic flow.
- **Storage space** is for items that are kept in inventory or stockrooms. Customers do not see these items unless they ask to see an alternate version of a product that is in the selling space.
- **Personnel space** is allocated to store employees for office space, lockers, lunch breaks, and restrooms. These areas are marked with signs so that customers will not enter.
- **Customer space** is designed for the comfort and convenience of the customer and may include sandwich, soda, and coffee shops, in-store restaurants, seating, lounges, and recreation areas for children.

Store-layout planners and visual merchandisers decide how much selling space to allow for the entire floor space of the store. These planners also determine the type of interior and window displays to use for products and related items. They design specific customer traffic patterns to encourage browsing and impulse shopping.

STORE INTERIOR

Once the general placement of merchandise has been determined, store personnel can develop the visual merchandising approaches for the building's interior. Mannequins, decorations, comfortable seating, and innovative props are all valuable tools for creating a memorable shopping experience. The selection of floor and wall coverings, lighting, colors, store fixtures, interior signage, and graphics powerfully impact the customers' shopping experience and their image of the store.

The Importance of Customer Space

Many quick-serve restaurant chains design and include recreational areas as part of their store layout. ***What are the benefits for restaurants that create this type of customer space?***

EXPLAIN

STOREFRONT

To focus the discussion on the storefront, ask these guiding questions.

Guiding Questions

List What are three purposes of outdoor signs?	attract attention, advertise the business, project brand identity
Generalize Do you think the kind of bold signage that appears on a Home Depot® or Walmart® would be suitable for an exclusive clothing boutique? Explain your answer.	Probably not. In order to attract its target customers, the signage for this store should consist of a more elegant and stylized font, more muted colors, and so on.
Apply What kinds of information might an ice cream shop have on its marquee?	Possible answers: store name, logo or other graphic, types of ice cream sold, hours, URL address.

Visual Literacy

Storefront Design Caption Answer Read the caption question to students: ***Why do you think large retail chains develop standardized storefronts?*** so that customers can readily recognize them, even from a distance Ask students: ***Have you ever been on a trip with a 4- to 8-year-old when it is time to eat? What typically happens?*** Children often spot the familiar signage and logos associated with their favorite fast-food restaurants, even from a distance, and they want to stop there.

Reinforce Vocabulary

Marquee—Word Origin Write the word *marquee* on the board. Explain that *marquee* comes from the French word *marquis,* which means "large tent." Over the years, it came to mean a canopy over the entrance to a hotel or theater. While some marquees are still made of canvas (or a similar material), many of today's marquee's contain digital displays. Ask: ***What is the advantage of having a digital marquee?*** The information presented can be changed easily.

ELABORATE

STORE LAYOUT

Tell students that because retail space is often at a premium, stores must be laid out in a way that is both efficient and attractive to the customer. To focus the discussion of store layout, ask these guiding questions.

Guiding Questions

Apply You are designing the floor plan for a new book store. Because of a lack of floor space, you are going to have to either eliminate the coffee shop or reduce the product shelf space by 15 percent. What would you do?	Reducing the shelf space would probably reduce sales, which could make it more difficult to show a profit. However, the coffee shop draws in customers and encourages them to stay longer to browse.
Contrast How are traffic patterns in a department store typically different from those in a supermarket? Why do you think this is?	Supermarkets typically are arranged in a grid; department stores are set up to encourage shoppers to interact with merchandise and displays.

Mini Projects

Differentiated Instruction

Visual Learners Instruct students to examine the entrances of two different types of stores. In a presentation, students should answer these questions: ***How attractive were signs, logos, and other visuals? How did the traffic flow into and out of each store? Were they handicapped accessible?*** The presentations should discuss differences in traffic patterns. For example, a home improvement store would be designed for convenience and would be more likely to contain large entrances that building supplies could fit through. With a flower shop, customers might come in through a single, focused entry point.

Logical Learners Organize students into small groups. Provide students with the floor plan of an average-sized retail store. Have each group divide the floor space into four distinct spaces: selling space, storage space, personnel space, and customer space. Instruct the groups to color-code each type of space. The groups should then compare their results with one another. Each group should determine what parts of the floor plan fall into each of the four distinct spaces. They should color-code each type of space, perhaps by using a colored pencil to shade that area.

Visual Literacy

Attracting Attention Caption Answer Read the caption question to students: ***Why are display windows useful for visual merchandising?*** Display windows attract the attention of people who are walking by and otherwise might not have stopped to shop in the store. Well-designed display windows project a distinct image of the store and its merchandise, and they attract target customers. Then ask: ***Why do you think this store uses mannequins that do not have facial features rather than ones that are more realistic looking?*** Possible answers: They want to appeal to customers who are interested in more innovative, cutting-edge fashion; faceless mannequins are not equated with a particular ethnic group or standard of beauty, and are therefore more universally appealing.

Critical Thinking

Ask students: ***How is customer space similar to personnel space?*** Both need restrooms and space to sit and relax. ***How are they different?*** While employees need a regular lunchroom, possibly with a microwave, refrigerator, and vending machines, customers may or may not have a place to purchase a cup of coffee or a snack. Employees need office space and possibly lockers. Some stores provide recreational areas for customers' children.

Visual Literacy

The Importance of Customer Space Caption Answer Read the caption question to students: ***What are the benefits for restaurants that create this type of customer space?*** Because children enjoy the play area, they will encourage parents to take them there. It provides a chance for parents to relax, talk to each other, read the paper, and eat a meal while their children play in a safe environment. ***Why do you think more family restaurants do not have these recreational areas?*** Possible answer: They are expensive to build and maintain and require a considerable amount of space; safety and liability considerations.

Critical Thinking

Present this scenario to the students: You are in a mall that just opened. Even though you have never been in this mall, you can tell what kinds of stores you want to check out, and you know which ones you will pass up. ***What is it about the inside and outside of the stores that determines whether or not you will enter?*** Answers will vary. Many students may be drawn to young adult- and teen-oriented displays and music, cutting-edge designs, and high-energy sales associates, and disinterested in stores that appeal to other age groups. Students should recognize that even in malls, storefronts and interiors are carefully designed to attract their target customers.

Businesses also use earth-friendly systems and fixtures to appeal to socially conscious consumers and to save on operating costs. "Green" awareness is the focus on reducing environmental damage by reducing energy costs, recycling scarce resources, and adopting practices to protect and improve the Earth's environment. For example, retail chains and quick-service eateries nationwide have installed tables and chairs made from recycled materials. Newly built Kohl's® department stores use recycled materials and have onsite recycling and water-saving fixtures with its Green Scene initiative.

Green Stores Buildings can be LEED certified, which means they are Leaders in Energy and Environmental Design.

GRAPHICS, SIGNAGE, COLOR, AND SOUND

Interior graphics and signage help promote a particular product brand and a specific line of products. They also provide directions to various departments or assist with a special promotional campaign, such as a demonstration, special sale, or a holiday promotion.

Interior graphics and signage are important in today's self-service environment. Box stores, mega-stores, and super centers, such as Costco® and Sam's Club®, develop giant signs, graphics, and banners to assist customers. Overhead digital signage, including in-house TV networks, is also found in many grocery stores and larger stores. Digital signage communicates product promotions and periodic public service announcements.

Point-of-purchase graphics are interior features that can decorate walls, windows, shelves, ceilings, and floors to reinforce product and store image. These interior features can also display merchandise.

MARKETING CASE STUDY

5 Gum: Interactive Display

To promote the launch of its 5® Gum brand in France, Wrigley® created a colorful "augmented reality" application that invites users to create their own custom music and video mixes. The 5 Mixer allows users to scratch like a DJ by manipulating printed symbols in front of a Webcam. Different onscreen markers represent different flavors of the gum.

Digital Display

This high-tech, cutting-edge campaign plays heavily on the "cool factor" associated with music-mixing and real-time interaction with a Web site. Anybody with an inkjet printer and a Webcam can take part. People can make music with no experience or special equipment. This audio-visual interactive display extends the 5 brand to entirely new audiences.

English Language Arts

Analyze How can engaging the customer's artistic creativity create a positive association with the brand being marketed? How might Wrigley® visually modify this audio-visual campaign for different countries? Discuss your responses with a partner.

NCTE 12 Use language to accomplish individual purposes.

For example, clothing can be displayed high on the walls, and sports equipment can be suspended from ceilings. This technique has the advantages of saving space and attracting customers with unique and higher-than-eye-level views.

Different colors and color schemes appeal to different types of customers. Specialty stores catering to teens might favor bright colors and lighting. Stores catering to adults might choose subdued colors and soft lighting to create a more subtle effect.

Background music and sound in stores can set a particular mood, encourage customers to shop, and be used to announce special product offerings. Sound can also reinforce a particular brand, business image, or target a particular customer.

LIGHTING

Lighting draws attention to store areas and specific products. Large warehouse stores often choose fluorescent or high-intensity discharge lighting. High-end, prestige retailers might install expensive chandeliers. Some specialty stores use newer lighting technologies, such as light-emitting diodes (LED) and compact fluorescent lighting (CFL). Stores might also choose certain lighting options for environmental reasons as well. For example, Starbucks® stores use LED lighting, which lowers operating costs and reduces energy consumption.

FIXTURES

The principal installations in a store are the fixtures. **Fixtures** are permanent or movable store furnishings that hold and display merchandise. Basic types of fixtures include display cases, tables, counters, floor and wall shelving units, racks, bins, stands, and even seating areas. Fixtures are strategically placed to maximize sales. For example, brightly colored front counters attract impulse purchases of competitively priced items, such as candy and magazines.

A business cultivating an upscale image might enhance its fixtures by painting them or covering them with textured materials (e.g., carpeting, fabric, cork, or reed). A business catering to discount buyers uses basic and unadorned shelf fixtures. The width of a store's aisles is related to its fixtures. The width of aisles and positioning of the fixtures and displays influence traffic patterns and buying behavior.

Many clothing stores have added comfortable seating areas near fitting rooms for people who might be waiting on a friend or family member who is trying on clothing. These seating areas give the store more of an upscale atmosphere.

WORLD MARKET

ITALY

Italian Taste

The icy treat known as *gelato*, Italian for *frozen*, has been the favorite of Italians since the 16th century. Created for nobility, the recipe reached the Italian citizens and was handed down through generations. Enjoyed worldwide today, gelato is a symbol of Italian pride.

World of Variety The best gelato depends on "honest" ingredients: milk, sugar, pure flavorings, seasonal fruit, and nuts. The result is creamier than ice cream with half the fat. Gelato is typically displayed in rows of eye-popping colors with mouth-watering flavors, from almond to *zabalone* (custard).

English Language Arts

Create You are opening a gelato shop. Sketch a layout of the store and display of the products, including the color scheme. Explain the reasons behind your designs.

NCTE 12 Use language to accomplish individual purposes.

Here are some entry-level phrases that are used in conversations about marketing all over the world.

English	Italian
Hello	Salve
Goodbye	Arrivederci
How are you?	Come stai?
Thank you	Grazie
You're welcome	Prego

glencoe.com

Get an activity on global marketing.

EXPLAIN

Green Stores Have students imagine that they are the managers of a retail store. Ask them how important it would be to inform their customers that the store's building was LEED certified.

Critical Thinking

Ask students: ***How might the music played in a department store be different from a store that sells urban fashions?*** A department store would be likely to play conservative or mainstream pop music, whereas a store that sells urban fashions would be more likely to play hip-hop or alternative rock music.

MARKETING CASE STUDY

English Language Arts Answer Student discussions might include that in the future, consumers will associate 5 Gum with the fun and success they had when pretending to be a DJ. Since this interactive display made users feel "cool," they would associate the gum with this same feeling. Integrating the onscreen markers with the different flavors of gum provided a strong mental connection that would likely continue to cause participants to remember these flavors. Wrigley could visually modify the audio-visual campaign for different countries by replacing the existing music with local favorites and modifying the appearance of the interface as needed. They also could change the gum colors and flavors to suit local preferences.

ELABORATE

GRAPHICS, SIGNAGE, COLOR AND SOUND

Ask these guiding questions on graphics, signage, color, and sound.

Guiding Questions

Recall What kind of interior graphics might a large supermarket have?	overhead digital signage, signs listing items in aisles, in-house TV
Synthesize If you were designing a gift shop catering to affluent adults, what kind of lighting would you use?	soft, restful lighting designed to relax customers and encourage them to spend time browsing

PROFESSIONAL DEVELOPMENT MINI CLIP

Reading Strategies for Student Achievement
Go to the Online Learning Center to view a video in which teachers discuss strategies to meet curriculum standards.

FIXTURES

To focus the discussion on fixtures, present these guiding questions.

Guiding Questions

List Give five examples of fixtures that the typical retail store would have.	display cases, tables, counters, floor and wall shelving units, racks, bins, stands
Apply What might a jewelry store do to enhance the appearance of a display of gold rings set with gemstones?	They might cover it with a soft, textured, neutral fabric to contrast with the hardness and brightness of the rings.

Knowledge Matters

VIRTUAL BUSINESS

PROMOTION

Introduce students to the concept of promotion using Knowledge Matters' Virtual Business Retailing visual simulation, *Promotion*. In this simulation, students will learn that promotion is the way in which stores actively communicate with their customers.

WORLD MARKET
ENGLISH LANGUAGE ARTS

Students should sketch a layout of the store with an appropriate traffic pattern that takes customers in front of the prominently displayed gelato and then to small tables, possibly next to large glass windows. In order to focus on the gelato, store fixtures should be simple with clean lines. Because the gelato comes in "eye-popping" colors, the colors of the store should be light and neutral, possibly an off-white. White projects a clean image, which is vital to a store that sells a high-end food product aimed at people who want food created with wholesome ingredients.

Mini Projects

Extension

Learning About Lighting Tell students that all lights create color—there is no such thing as clear white light. Kelvin color temperature is used to rate the color of light produced by LED (light emitting diode) lights. The higher the Kelvin number, the bluer the light becomes. For example, 1200 Kelvin (K) produces a yellow color similar to that of a candle flame whereas 6500K is similar to bright daylight. Have students conduct research on the Internet or other appropriate source to learn about Kelvin color temperature. They then should write a brief report explaining this concept and how different lighting should be used in different types of displays. Student reports should discuss how Kelvin color temperature is used to rate lights. They should explain that the higher the Kelvin number, the bluer the light. Therefore, if designers want to create a warm glow, such as in a romantic room lit by a fireplace, they would use a light with a relatively low Kelvin number. To create the feeling of a bright, sunny day at the beach, they would use lighting with a higher Kelvin number.

Creating a Mood Talk with students about different types of hair salons or hair stylists. They might include salons geared toward low-cost services, trendy salons catering to a young crowd interested in current fashion, and more conservative salons catering to older adults who want more business-appropriate styles. Have student groups visit salons that fall in different categories. Groups should compare each salon's graphics, signage, use of color, lighting, and fixtures. Student groups should prepare a chart comparing these components in the two stores. Student charts should compare the ambience of the different types of salons. For example, they may note that the more trendy salons use bright, attention-getting colors while the conservative salons tend toward neutrals. Fixtures, particularly in the customer areas, may also vary considerably.

INTERIOR DISPLAYS

Interior displays show merchandise, provide customers with information, encourage customers to shop, reinforce advertisements, and promote a store's image. About one out of every four sales is generated by an interior display. There are five types of interior displays: architectural displays, closed displays, open displays, point-of-purchase displays, and store decorations.

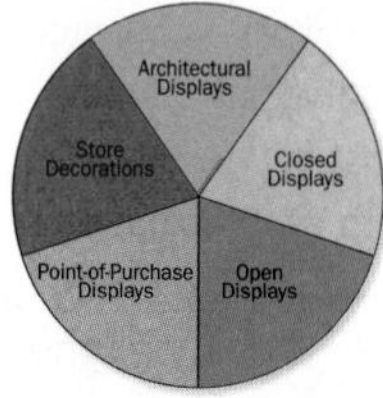

ARCHITECTURAL DISPLAYS

Architectural displays are model rooms that show customers how merchandise can be arranged in their homes. Examples include kitchens, bedrooms, and living rooms. This displays take up a considerable amount of room, so not all stores are able to use these kinds of displays.

CLOSED DISPLAYS

Closed displays allow customers to see but not handle merchandise without assistance from a salesperson. Closed displays are used for valuable items, such as jewelry, electronic devices, and other high-value items where theft, security, or breakage is a concern.

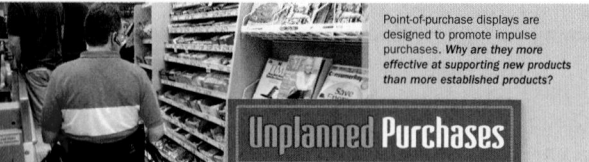

OPEN DISPLAYS

Open displays allow customers to handle and examine the merchandise without the help of a salesperson. Shelves, counters, and tables for food and hardware items can function as open displays. Open displays are an efficient way to sell products, so they have an important place in today's self-service selling environment.

POINT-OF-PURCHASE DISPLAYS

Point-of-purchase displays (POPs) are stand-alone structures that serve as consumer sales promotion devices. Most POPs are manufactured units with bold graphics and signage. They hold, display, and dispense products or provide information. Point-of-purchase displays encourage immediate purchases.

POPs that display products can be temporary, semi-permanent, and permanent. Temporary units are used for a short period of time and are normally not restocked after the featured merchandise is sold. An example is Hickory Farms® sausage and cheese kiosks for the winter holiday season. Semi-permanent units are used for themed promotions and are restocked for up to a year. Permanent units are designed for repeat usage over time. Vending machines for candy, beverages, snack items, and Automatic Teller Machines (ATMs) are examples of permanent point-of-purchase units.

POPs also provide services, directions to locate products, and offer tips on product usage. Examples include computer touch screens for digital-photo processing stands and gift registries. Blood-pressure testing stations, menu-planning units, and cosmetic stations to match a customer's preferences, coloring, and skin type are all POPs.

Unplanned Purchases

Point-of-purchase displays are designed to promote impulse purchases. ***Why are they more effective at supporting new products than more established products?***

Interactive Kiosks

Interactive kiosks are interactive point-of-purchase displays that are free-standing, full-service retail locations. They are actually computer terminals that provide information access via electronic methods. Kiosks are placed in a variety of locations such as stores, businesses, shopping malls, and airports. They can be operated year-round or on a seasonal basis. They play a growing role in point-of-sale and self-serve merchandising. Interactive Web-based kiosks have pedestal-mounted, high-tech screens. Immediate product availability, online ordering capabilities for out-of-stock or larger items, and more reliable technology have led to increased popularity. Examples include interactive kiosks for DVD rentals, music, video games, postal services, digital photographs, airline tickets, and concert and theater tickets.

STORE DECORATIONS

Store decorations are displays that may coincide with seasons or holidays. Bold and colorful banners, signs, and props create the appropriate atmosphere to encourage related holiday purchases.

Items such as clothing are difficult to showcase in a closed display. The cosmetic department uses many types of displays. Items such as brushes and accessories may be part of an open display. Other items could be contained in a closed display to prevent customers from sampling them inappropriately. Point-of-purchase displays may serve as product or service information sources. In the case of interactive Web-based kiosks, they dispense products. Interior displays complement one another and create a positive, interactive buying experience.

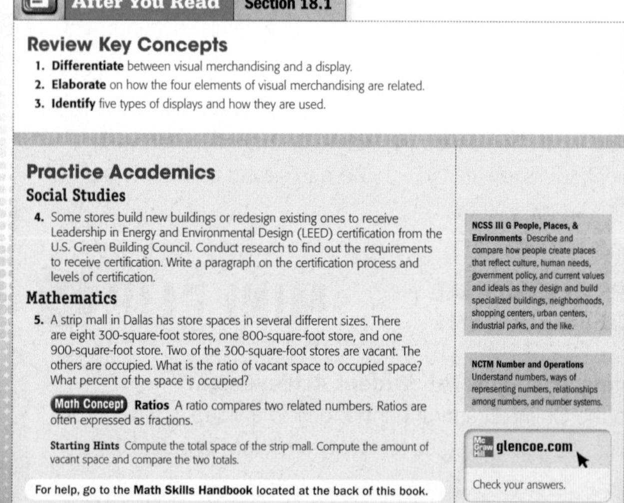

After You Read | **Section 18.1**

Review Key Concepts

1. **Differentiate** between visual merchandising and a display.
2. **Elaborate** on how the four elements of visual merchandising are related.
3. **Identify** five types of displays and how they are used.

Practice Academics

Social Studies

4. Some stores build new buildings or redesign existing ones to receive Leadership in Energy and Environmental Design (LEED) certification from the U.S. Green Building Council. Conduct research to find out the requirements to receive certification. Write a paragraph on the certification process and levels of certification.

Mathematics

5. A strip mall in Dallas has store spaces in several different sizes. There are eight 300-square-foot stores, one 800-square-foot store, and one 900-square-foot store. Two of the 300-square-foot stores are vacant. The others are occupied. What is the ratio of vacant space to occupied space? What percent of the space is occupied?

Math Concept **Ratios** A ratio compares two related numbers. Ratios are often expressed as fractions.

Starting Hints Compute the total space of the strip mall. Compute the amount of vacant space and compare the two totals.

For help, go to the **Math Skills Handbook** located at the back of this book.

NCSS III G People, Places, & Environments Describe and compare how people create places that reflect culture, human needs, government policy, and current values and ideals as they design and build specialized buildings, neighborhoods, shopping centers, urban centers, industrial parks, and the like.

NCTM Number and Operations Understand numbers, ways of representing numbers, relationships among numbers, and number systems.

glencoe.com

Check your answers.

ELABORATE

INTERIOR DISPLAYS

Ask students these guiding questions to focus the discussion of types of interior displays.

Guiding Questions

Analyze What types of stores are most likely to have architectural displays? Why?	Furniture stores and home improvement stores are likely to have architectural displays because these displays allow customers to see how items might look in their homes.
Apply Give an example of a situation in which a grocery store might use a temporary point-of-purchase display.	display candy hearts for Valentine's Day; windshield ice scrapers at the start of winter

Graphic Organizer

Use this graphic organizer to provide an overview of the different types of interior displays. Ask: ***Which type of display would you use if you were interested in protecting valuable merchandise?*** closed display Then ask: ***Which type is likely to generate the most sales?*** point-of-purchase display

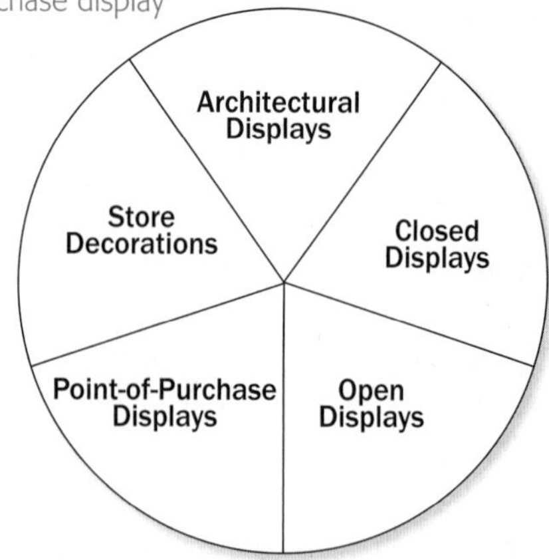

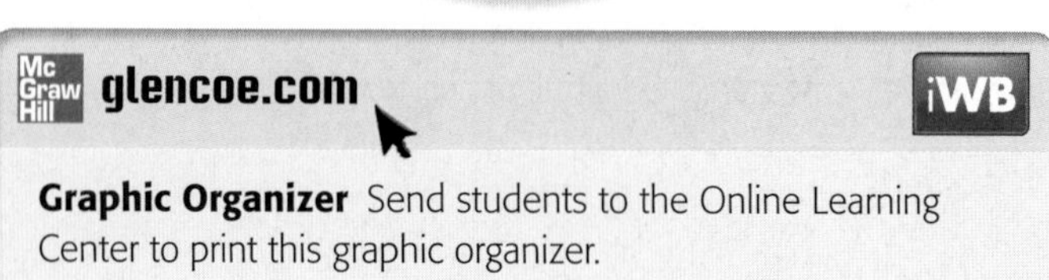

glencoe.com

iWB

Graphic Organizer Send students to the Online Learning Center to print this graphic organizer.

EVALUATE

Visual Literacy

Unplanned Purchases Caption Answer Read the caption question to students: ***Why are they more effective at supporting new products than more established products?*** Customers will seek out established products if they need them, but they might not know about new products. However, if they see them prominently displayed, they may want to try them. Explain to students that manufacturers and vendors typically pay to have their merchandise placed in point-of-purchase displays. Ask: ***If you were a manufacturer who had just released a new product, would you pay to have it placed in such a display.*** Possible answer: Probably, because the high degree of visibility should lead to increased sales.

Mini Project

Differentiated Instruction

Visual Learners Have students visit a retail store that has at least 20 interior displays. (If students select a large store, they should focus on one department within the store.) Instruct students to create a pie chart showing the percentage of each type of these displays the store has: architectural displays, closed displays, open displays, point-of-purchase displays, and store decorations. For example, if the store (or department within the store) has a total of 60 displays and 12 of them are closed displays, the store has 20 percent closed displays. Remind students to label all components of their pie chart. Students should examine the interior displays in their chosen store (or store department), categorize the displays, and determine the percentage of each type of display. They then should use this data to create a properly labeled pie chart.

Critical Thinking

Ask: ***What kinds of interactive kiosks have you used?*** Answers will vary, but might include ATMs, DVD rental kiosks, store or mall directory kiosks, and kiosks for checking in at airports, buying movie or concert tickets, or editing and printing photos. Ask: ***What advantage do these kiosks provide retailers?*** They save on employee expenses. ***What disadvantages do they have?*** Possible answer: The customer does not get the personal attention that comes from a well-trained salesperson, and typically a kiosk only offers a limited number of choices.

After You Read Section 18.1

Review Key Concepts

1. Visual merchandising encompasses all the visual elements of the selling environment. Display relates only to those visual and artistic elements that present the product to a target group of customers.
2. All four elements work together to create an overall image designed to appeal to the target customer. The storefront leads the customers into the store and other elements, such as layout and interior displays, encourage them to stay there and purchase items.
3. Architectural displays are model rooms that show how merchandise might look in customers' homes. Closed displays allow customers to look at, but not handle merchandise, unless they get the assistance from a salesperson. Open displays allow customers to handle merchandise without the assistance of a salesperson. Point-of-purchase displays are stand-alone structures that encourage immediate purchases. Store decorations are displays that may coincide with seasons or holidays.

Practice Academics

Social Studies

4. Certifications are awarded by the U.S. Green Building Council and four levels of certification can be received: platinum (the highest), gold, silver, and "certified." Certification means that the physical building has met standards identified by the council to be classified as a "green building."

Mathematics

5. The ratio of vacant space to occupied space is 6:35 (600:3500). About 85.4 percent of the space is occupied. ([8 × 300] + 800 + 900 = 4,100 sq. ft.; 2 × 300 = 600 sq. ft.; 600/4,100 or 6/41; 6 ÷ 41 = 0.146 or 14.6%, 100% – 14.6% = 85.4% .)

 **glencoe.com** 

Answer Key Send students to the Online Learning Center to check their answers.

READING GUIDE

Before You Read

Predict What personal traits and technical skills do you need to design an effective store display?

Objectives

- **List** the five steps in creating a display.
- **Explain** how artistic elements function in display design.
- **Describe** the importance of display maintenance.

The Main Idea

Visual merchandisers must know the rules of artistic design to create displays that enhance sales, attract customers, and sustain customer loyalty.

Vocabulary

Content Vocabulary
- props
- color wheel
- complementary colors
- adjacent colors
- triadic colors
- focal point
- proportion
- formal balance
- informal balance

Academic Vocabulary

You will find these words in your reading and on your tests. Make sure you know their meanings.
- equip
- principles

Graphic Organizer

Draw or print this process chart to list in order the steps to create a display.

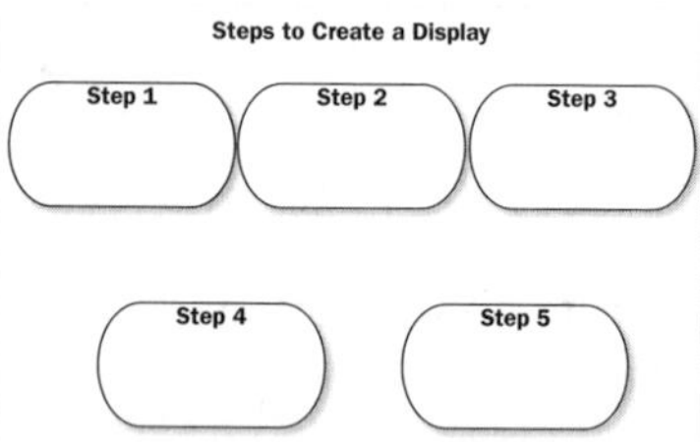

STANDARDS

ACADEMIC

English Language Arts
NCTE 1 Read texts to acquire new information.

Social Studies
NCSS I A Culture Analyze and explain the ways groups, societies, and cultures address human needs and concerns.

NCSS National Council for the Social Studies
NCTE National Council of Teachers of English
NCTM National Council of Teachers of Mathematics
NSES National Science Education Standards

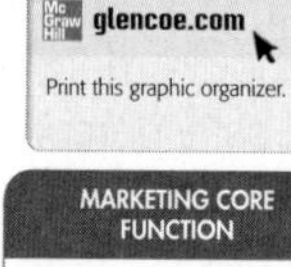

Common Core
Writing Produce clear and coherent writing in which the development, organization, and style are appropriate to task, purpose, and audience.

glencoe.com

Print this graphic organizer.

MARKETING CORE FUNCTION

Promotion

m.e. Section 18.2 Artistic Design

DISPLAY DESIGN AND PREPARATION

Visual merchandisers help companies to attract customers and sell products. They have a limited amount of time to do this. Having a limited time frame to attract customers means that a business must plan its displays carefully. They must be targeted so that they appeal to customers.

Displays must be sensitive to individual perceptions, appeal to targeted customers, and support the overall business image. Failing to support the image of the business can be a huge problem. Consider a traditional clothing store. If it started using abstract displays of trendy merchandise, it might gain new customers. However, it would run the risk of losing loyal customers who preferred its old design choices.

When planning and preparing displays, retailers and merchandisers must be sensitive to cultural and ethnic diversity. Many companies employ marketing specialists in cross-cultural and ethnic design to adapt displays to a target market. All display design and selection involves five steps.

As You Read

Consider What design skills do you have that would help you create a display?

STEP 1: SELECT MERCHANDISE FOR DISPLAY

The merchandise selected will determine the theme and all other supporting elements of the display. Display merchandise must also be visually appealing as well as contemporary to attract customers. New, popular, and best-selling products are often selected for display. The merchandise on display must also be appropriate for the season, its target audience, and for the store's geographic location.

STEP 2: SELECT THE TYPE OF DISPLAY

The merchandise selected for display determines the type of display to use and **equip**. There are four basic kinds of displays: displays that feature just one product; displays that feature similar products; displays that feature related products; and displays that feature an assortment or cross-mix of products.

A *one-item display* is best for a single-item product promotion of advertised specials or a newly developed product. An example might be an Apple® iPod set on a show box with a promotional logo. One-item displays are usually created for a single product promotion or an advertised special.

> "In the retail environment, a display has about four to six seconds to attract a customer's attention, create a desire, and sell the product."

Similar-product displays show one kind of product but feature several brands, sizes, or models. An example would be a display of digital cameras by different manufacturers. This type of display allows customers to compare products.

A *related-product display* features products that are meant to be used together. An apparel store's related-product display might feature casual-wear. Shirts, pants, sweaters, and shoes would all be included. These displays are designed to entice customers to buy more than one item.

ENGAGE

Anticipation Activity

Improving Student Achievement Discuss the four types of displays. Divide students into four groups. Using items in the classroom, have groups brainstorm creative ideas for a display type: one-item, similar-products, related-products, and assortment. Display ideas will vary. Encourage students to think of creative ideas that will attract viewers attention to the products featured in the displays.

Objectives

- **List** the five steps in creating a display. (1) select merchandise; (2) select type of display; (3) choose setting; (4) manipulate artistic elements; (5) evaluate completed display
- **Explain** how artistic elements function in display design. artistic elements—direct viewer's attention; color—emotionally engage customers; proportion and balance—make the display attractive
- **Describe** the importance of display maintenance. Regular maintenance keeps merchandise attractive to customers.

Graphic Organizer

Steps to Create a Display

- **Step 1** Select merchandise for display
- **Step 2** Select the type of display
- **Step 3** Choose a setting
- **Step 4** Manipulate the artistic elements
- **Step 5** Evaluate the completed display

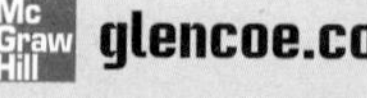

Graphic Organizer Send students to the Online Learning Center to print this graphic organizer.

EXPLORE

Before You Read

Read the Before You Read question aloud: ***What personal traits and technical skills do you need to design an effective store display?*** Personal traits: good communication skills; initiative; goal-setting skills; have an interest in design; be able to work independently, but also as a team member if required. Technical skills: knowledge of artistic design; ability to follow written and verbal directions; and excellent customer service skills.

Preteaching Vocabulary

Have students go to the Online Learning Center at glencoe.com for the Chapter 18 Preteaching Vocabulary games.

Content Vocabulary

Write the term *color wheel* on the board. Below it, write *complementary colors, adjacent colors,* and *triadic colors.* Explain that these terms all relate to the color wheel. Have students skim the Color portion of the chapter and then write a brief paragraph explaining these relationships. complementary: two colors opposite one another; adjacent: two colors next to one another; triadic: three colors evenly spaced on the wheel

Academic Vocabulary

Equip—Denotative Meaning Write the word *equip* on the board. Explain that *equip* means "to furnish" or "to make ready." Ask a volunteer to read aloud the first sentence under Step 2: ***The merchandise selected for display determines the type of display to use and equip.*** Then read it aloud using the word *furnish* in place of *equip.* Ask: ***Does this sentence have the same meaning?*** yes ***How might you equip a display?*** by positioning the needed products, fixtures, decorative elements, and so on in the display

As You Read

Read the As You Read question aloud: ***What design skills do you have that would help you create a display?*** Answers may include the ability to recognize how lines and color can be used to attract viewers' attention; a sense of how balance and proportion can be used to make a display that is pleasing to the eye and focuses on the merchandise.

Artistic Design

DISPLAY DESIGN AND PREPARATION

Ask these guiding questions to focus the discussion about display design and preparation.

Guiding Questions

Recall What characteristics should a display have?	be sensitive to perceptions, appeal to target customers, support business image
Synthesize You are a merchandiser. For a housewares display, you must choose between a new type of food processor and a popular heavy-duty mixer.	new type of food processor because the display can help customers become aware of the product

Expert Advice

Read the quote to students:

> **"In the retail environment, a display has about four to six seconds to attract a customer's attention, create a desire, and sell the product."**

Hold up a picture of a store display for six seconds. Ask: ***What did you see in the display?*** Answers will vary but many students will say that it is difficult to remember specifics about the items in the display.

VIRTUAL BUSINESS

ADVANCED PROMOTION

Introduce the concept of advanced promotion using Knowledge Matters' Virtual Business Retailing visual simulation, *Advanced Promotion*. In this simulation, students will learn about additional sales and merchandise promotion activities that a storeowner or manager can use to attain the stated goals of a sales promotion.

Assortment or cross-mix displays feature a collection of different or unrelated product lines placed on counters in the main aisles of a store. They are typically used by supermarkets, discount stores, and large mass-merchandising stores. This type of display has a special appeal to bargain hunters.

Props, or properties, are objects that hold the merchandise on display or support the display setting. Props are not for sale and are classified as decorative or functional. *Decorative props* include floor coverings and wall treatments, while *functional props* include items that hold the merchandise, such as shelves or hangers.

STEP 3: CHOOSE A SETTING

Displays can be presented in different settings. The setting depends on the image the business wants to project. The three types of settings are realistic, semi-realistic, and abstract.

A realistic setting depicts a room, area, or recognizable locale. The scene could be a restaurant, a park, or a party. Functional props, such as tables, chairs, plants, risers, books, dishes, and mannequins, provide the details.

A semi-realistic setting suggests a room or locale but leaves the details to the viewer's imagination. Decorative props, such as, a cardboard sun, a beach towel, a surfing poster, and a small sprinkling of sand would be enough to create the rest of the beach scene in the customer's mind. Businesses use semi-realistic settings when either space or budgets do not permit realistic settings.

An abstract setting does not imitate or even try to imitate reality. It focuses on form and color rather than on reproducing actual objects. Wide bands of torn colored paper placed as an accent behind or around merchandise can create an attractive abstract visual image that has little or nothing to do with reality.

Abstract settings are gaining popularity. They do not require large amounts of storage space for props. Remember that stores may have props for a variety of seasonal promotions. These props can occupy a lot of space in the store's storage space. Also, abstract settings often use inexpensive everyday objects. Display specialists often use materials such as cardboard, paper, string, yarn, ribbon, and paint to create abstract settings.

The merchandise on display must be appropriate for the target market. ***What are the four basic types of displays?***

Display Design

STEP 4: MANIPULATE THE ARTISTIC ELEMENTS

The artistic elements of a display include line, color, shape, direction, texture, proportion, balance, motion, and lighting. These **principles** of display influence your perception without you knowing it.

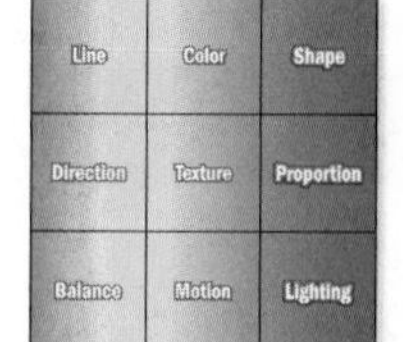

LINE

Lines within displays can direct the viewer's attention. Various types of lines create different impressions. Straight lines suggest stiffness and control, while curving lines suggest freedom and movement. Diagonal lines give the impression of action. Vertical lines project height and dignity. Horizontal lines convey confidence.

COLOR

Color selection is a critical step in developing displays. Colors are important because they can emotionally engage a customer to make a purchase decision. The colors selected for a display should contrast with those on the walls, floors, and fixtures around them. For example, a store decorated in pastels should feature displays that use darker, stronger colors.

FIGURE 18.1 **The Color Wheel**

Color Matters The color wheel is structured to show both similarities and differences in color. Effective displays use colors that draw customers' attention but do not compete with the product. ***How would you use this wheel to create complementary color harmony?***

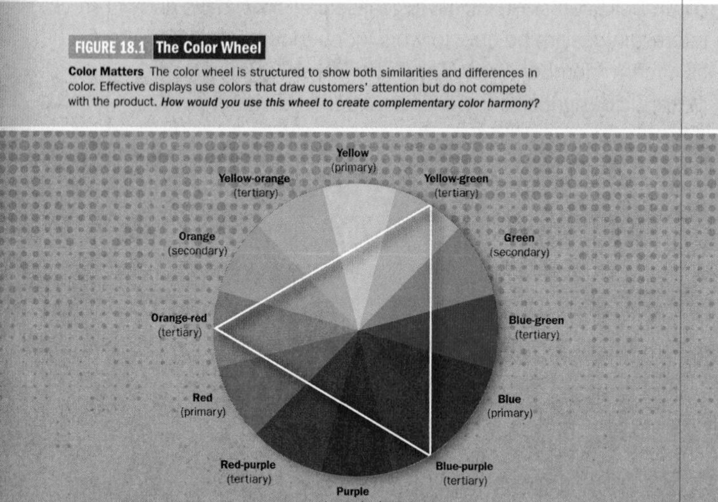

EXPLAIN

Visual Literacy

Display Design Caption Answer Read the caption question to students: ***What are the four basic types of displays?*** (1) single-item product displays; (2) similar-product displays; (3) related-product displays; (4) assortment or cross-mix displays Ask students: ***What are the three types of settings that stores use for displays?*** (1) realistic settings; (2) semi-realistic settings; (3) abstract settings

ELL: Accessing Prior Knowledge

Go to the Online Learning Center to view a video clip in which a teacher helps students make connections with what they already know and what they will read.

Critical Thinking

Read aloud the following statement from the book: ***Stores create festive displays to emotionally involve shoppers so they feel better about spending money.*** Ask students: ***Do you think problems might occur if shoppers come to associate spending money with feeling good?*** Such an association might lead some people to spend more than they can afford.

VIRTUAL BUSINESS

ADVANCED MERCHANDISING

Introduce the concept of advanced merchandising using Knowledge Matters' Virtual Business Retailing visual simulation, Advanced Merchandising. In this simulation, students will learn about the types of store layouts and considerations for merchandise placement.

ELABORATE

STEP 3: CHOOSE A SETTING

To focus the discussion on choosing an appropriate setting, ask these guiding questions.

Guiding Questions

State What are two major advantages of an abstract display?	They do not require large amounts of storage space and they often use inexpensive, everyday objects.
Contrast How is a semi-realistic display different from a realistic one?	A realistic display depicts an actual location, such as a room or a park; a semi-realistic setting suggests the location, but does not contain all the details.
Distinguish You are preparing an abstract setting that should suggest autumn. How might you create it?	Possible answer: You might use paper in fall colors torn into irregular shapes and overlapping in a random fashion to represent fall leaves.

Mini Project

Enrichment

Creating a Semi-Realistic Display Setting Organize students into pairs. Explain to students that they are going to create a semi-realistic display setting. Have students locate an existing realistic display setting, perhaps at a local mall or department store. Tell students that they are store merchandisers, but are on a limited budget. They have been assigned the task of recreating their chosen display in an inexpensive, semi-realistic way. Students may use any available, inexpensive materials to do so. For example, they may want to create a collage of items on a large poster board. While their display can appear considerably different from the original, it should have the same "feel" and project a similar image. Have each pair share their completed displays with the class. Student displays will vary, but should be semi-realistic and use inexpensive materials. For example, if an original display showed mannequins in full skiing gear standing around drinking hot chocolate, the semi-realistic display might have an image of snow-covered mountains in the background, with cardboard skis and poles, and ski hats and mittens made from colorful scraps of cloth arranged in front.

STEP 4: MANIPULATE THE ARTISTIC ELEMENTS

Ask these guiding questions to focus the discussion on manipulating artistic elements.

Guiding Questions

Describe What kind of impression can be created by use of diagonal lines?	a sense of action
Synthesize Why do you think wavy and curvy lines create a sense of freedom and movement, while straight lines suggest control?	Wavy and curvy lines are associated with nature, such as the natural curvature of mountains and the waves of the ocean, which people may see as free and unpredictable. Straight lines may be seen as rigid.

Visual Literacy

Figure 18.1 Caption Answer Read the caption question to students: ***How would you use this wheel to create complementary color harmony?*** Choose a color you want to use, and then locate the color on the opposite side of the wheel, which is its complement. Ask: ***How do two complementary colors relate to each other?*** They create high contrast. Then ask: ***How is this different from the relationship that adjacent colors have with each other?*** adjacent colors blend well

Graphic Organizer

Display this color wheel. Have students choose two complementary colors, two adjacent colors, and three triadic colors.

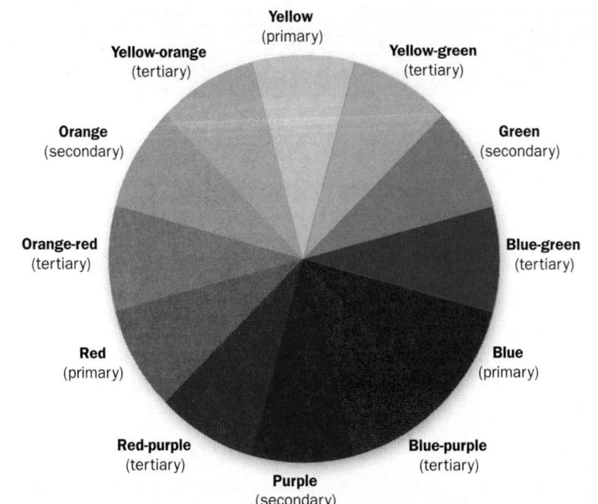

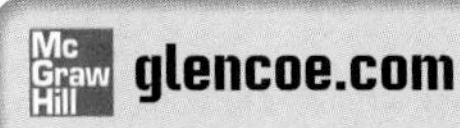

Graphic Organizer Send students to the Online Learning Center to print this graphic organizer.

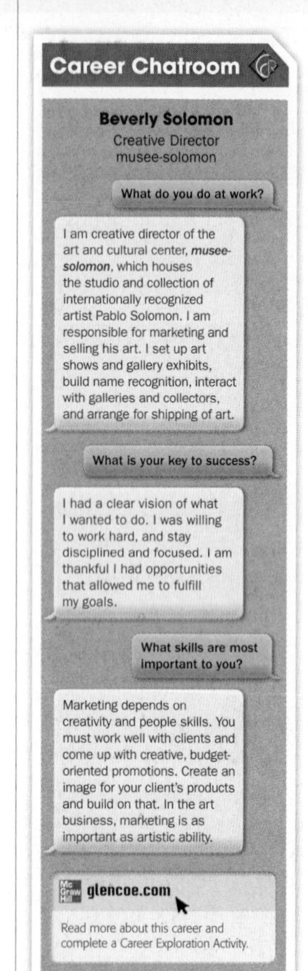

Career Chatroom
Beverly Solomon
Creative Director
musee-solomon
What do you do at work?
I am creative director of the art and cultural center, musee-solomon, which houses the studio and collection of internationally recognized artist Pablo Solomon. I am responsible for marketing and selling his art. I set up art shows and gallery exhibits, build name recognition, interact with galleries and collectors, and arrange for shipping of art.
What is your key to success?
I had a clear vision of what I wanted to do. I was willing to work hard, and stay disciplined and focused. I am thankful I had opportunities that allowed me to fulfill my goals.
What skills are most important to you?
Marketing depends on creativity and people skills. You must work well with clients and come up with creative, budget-oriented promotions. Create an image for your client's products and build on that. In the art business, marketing is as important as artistic ability.
glencoe.com
Read more about this career and complete a Career Exploration Activity.

The standard **color wheel**, shown in **Figure 18.1** on page 431, illustrates the relationships among colors. **Complementary colors** are opposite each other on the color wheel and create high contrast. Red and green, blue and orange, and yellow and purple are examples of pairs of complementary colors.

Adjacent colors, also called "analogous colors," are located next to each other on the color wheel and share the same undertones. Successive adjacent colors (such as yellow-orange, yellow, and yellow-green) form families, or groups of colors, that blend well with each other.

Triadic colors involve three colors equally spaced on the color wheel, such as red, yellow, and blue. Triadic color harmony, as shown by the triangle on the color wheel in **Figure 18.1** on page 429, creates vivid and contrasting colors. Triadic color schemes can be achieved by rotating the triangle within the color wheel.

Color and color groups create specific moods and feelings, such as calmness or excitement. Colors from the warm side of the color wheel, such as red and yellow, convey a festive mood that works well with lower-priced merchandise. These colors must be used cautiously. Their contrast is so great that it can detract from the merchandise and even irritate customers. This problem can usually be avoided by varying the shades of the colors somewhat to lessen their contrast. It is important to make sure they keep their warmth and friendliness too. Colors from the cool side of the color wheel, such as blue and green, represent calm and refinement. They are often associated with higher-priced merchandise.

Customers' expectations about color are also important in planning displays. Customers have come to expect certain color schemes at certain times of the year. Earth tones are more common in fall, while bright colors and pastels are common in spring. Customers' reactions to colors are also important. Red evokes excitement, so it should not be used in a display that is designed to convey calmness.

SHAPE

Shape refers to the physical appearance, or outline, of a display. Shape is determined by the props, fixtures, and merchandise used in the display. Display units might resemble squares, cubes, circles, and triangles. Displays that have little or no distinct shape, known as *mass displays*, are also an option. Dollar stores, discounters, and supermarkets often use mass displays to display large quantities and to indicate low price.

DIRECTION

A good display directs the viewer's eye to the merchandise, moving a viewer's attention seamlessly from one part of the display to another. This smooth visual flow is called "direction." Effective displays create direction by using techniques such as color, repetition, and lighting patterns. These displays also create direction by arranging merchandise in a pattern that guides a customer's eye.

Effective displays should also have a **focal point**, an area in the display that attracts attention first, above all else. A good method of creating an effective focal point is to build the display elements in a triangular shape. The focal point is created by placing the strongest shape at the top, or apex, of the imaginary triangle in the display. A viewer's eyes will naturally travel to the strongest shape within a display. This arrangement helps keep the eyes moving up and over the merchandise. Displays that lack a focal point are said to be unfocused. Typically, an unfocused display contains too many items, too many shapes, or too many props outside the imaginary triangle.

TEXTURE

Texture is the look of the surfaces in a display. It can be smooth or rough. The contrast between the textures used in a display creates visual interest. Products that are smooth, such as flatware, should be placed against backgrounds or props that are rough. This contrast allows the products to "pop," or stand out from the backgrounds where they are placed.

PROPORTION

Proportion refers to the relationship between and among objects in a display. The merchandise should always be the primary focus of a display. Props, graphics, and signs should be in proportion to the merchandise. They should not dominate the display.

BALANCE

Display designers also pay attention to balance when creating displays. They place large items with large items and small items with small items to create **formal balance** in a display. When a large item is on one side of a display, an equally large item should be on the other side for balance. The opposite effect can also be appealing to customers. To create **informal balance**, designers place several small items with one large item within the display. An example of an informal display would be an adult mannequin placed next to several shallow baskets of flowers that are elevated on a prop to the mannequin's height.

430 | Unit 6 · Promotion

Chapter 18 · Visual Merchandising and Display | 431

EXPLAIN

Career Chatroom

Ask students these guiding questions.

Guiding Questions

Explain What are Beverly's responsibilities?	managing exhibits, building name recognition, interacting with collectors
Analyze Why is merchandising needed?	Merchandising is important because art displays must be appealing for patrons to make purchase.

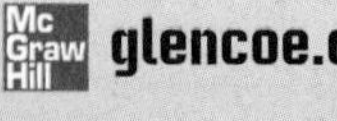

glencoe.com

Career Exploration Send students to the Online Learning Center to read more about this career and to get a Career Exploration Activity.

Reinforce Vocabulary

Complementary Colors—Homophones Write the words *complementary* and *complimentary* on the board. Explain that these words are homophones because they sound the same. However, complementary, when used with color, refers to colors that "complete" or enhance one another. Complimentary refers to expressing admiration or approval. Encourage students to use the terms complementary color and complimentary color in sentences. Complementary colors create high contrast. Yellow is a complimentary color for your skin tone.

Focal Point—Usage Explain that the term *focal point* is used in situations other than design. Ask students to come up with a variety of sentences that use the term. Write the sentences on the board. Then ask the class to determine whether each sentence uses focal point correctly. Sample sentences: The court house was the focal point of public life. The game's focal point was the halftime show.

ELABORATE

Graphic Organizer

Display this table. As you discuss each of these artistic elements, ask for suggestions to complete the Description and Example columns. Possible answers:

Element	Description	Example
Shape	Physical appearance or outline of a display	Square, circle, triangle
Direction	Way viewer's eye is moved	Repetition, lighting, pattern of organization
Texture	Surfaces in a display	Rough, smooth
Proportion	Relationships between display objects	Sizing merchandise so that it dominates
Balance	A sense of visual equality	Formal, informal

 glencoe.com 

Graphic Organizer Send students to the Online Learning Center to print this graphic organizer.

DIGITAL NATION

English Language Arts Answer Read the English Language Arts activity to the students: Find two websites that sell a similar product. Examine the layout, colors, and the use of motion. ***What image or personality does each site convey, and why?*** Students should cite specific elements of the sites' designs, such as the use of video or motion graphics, color scheme, type of images, position of elements, and use of text. Ask these guiding questions.

Guiding Questions

List What are some of the visual elements of a Web site?	layout, color, balance, proportion, motion
Explain What is one technique used to test Web sites?	Multivariate testing: Visitors are asked to evaluate two designs.

 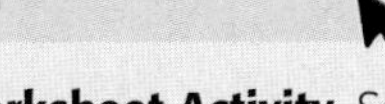

Worksheet Activity Send students to the Online Learning Center to get a Digital Nation worksheet activity.

e MARKETING

Digital Video Sharing

YouTube®, a subsidiary of Google®, is a free digital video sharing community. YouTube videos can be seen worldwide. Viewers can watch and comment on videos; as well as provide their own videos to share with the YouTube community. Businesses can share their messages with the global marketplace in a video format, making YouTube an excellent marketing tool. InVideo ads or YouTube video ads can be used. Or marketers can sponsor contests to connect with target market. For example, Visa® ran a campaign on the YouTube Channel for soccer fans. During the FIFA World Cup, soccer fans were able to share their support for their favorite teams by viewing, uploading, and sharing videos of goal calls. They also held a tournament titled, "Visa Watch Your Way To Brazil" sweepstakes with the prize being a trip to the 2014 FIFA World Cup in Brazil. To keep everyone involved, weekly prizes were added, such as $100 Visa gift cards.

Innovate and Create

Disney® created a new store prototype with lots of interactive features. It has touch screen kiosks so customers can view the store and products in 3D. They also can see video clips, articles, and social media feeds, which can be shared with friends by using their mobile phones to connect via e-mail, Twitter® and Facebook®. After telling students about Disney's new prototype stores, have them brainstorm ideas for Disney to utilize YouTube as a means to promote its new prototype stores. Accept all reasonable ideas. Some ideas may include ad videos of children playing in the new stores with the new technology, as well as videos of children sharing comments about their interactive experiences. The social media feeds that customers can share with friends could include a contest or sweepstakes to win Disney products or trips to Disney World. For example, each YouTube video feed customers share with friends via e-mail, Twitter, or Facebook gives them an entry into the sweepstakes.

eMarketing Worksheet Activity Send students to the Online Learning Center to download an eMarketing worksheet activity.

MOTION

Motion is playing an increasingly important role in display design. Animation can be achieved through the use of motorized fixtures, mannequins, and props. Mechanical mannequins have been used for years in holiday displays. Motion should be used sparingly to accentuate merchandise, not overpower it.

LIGHTING

Proper lighting is critical to attractive displays. Spotlights, floodlights, and rotating, colored, or flashing lights can highlight individual items. Lighting can help make merchandise appear more attractive. It is recommended that display lighting be two to five times stronger than a store's general lighting. Colored lighting in displays can create dramatic effects. Lighting used with reflective items, such as crystal, jewelry, and fine china, needs careful attention. The lighting in a fine housewares department would be much different than the lighting in a teen clothing department.

The lighting in the dressing rooms is not part of a display, but it should be considered. Dressing-room lighting that is glaring and unflattering will negatively affect a consumer's buying decisions. This is true even if the merchandise was lit appropriately in the display on the sales floor.

STEP 5: EVALUATE THE COMPLETED DISPLAY

Do the displays enhance the store's image, appeal to customers, and promote the product in the best possible way? Was a theme creatively applied? Were the color and signage appropriate? Was the result pleasing? These are just some of the questions that visual merchandisers consider when evaluating the effectiveness of displays.

Reading Check

Recall List in order the five steps used to create a display.

Displays have a limited time frame to attract customers. ***Do you think that this store's window display would catch the attention of the customers it is targeting? Why?***

DISPLAY MAINTENANCE

Once a display has been constructed, it needs to be maintained and eventually dismantled. Individual businesses have different policies regarding the duration of displays or how long they stay up. Some businesses, such as electronics stores, change out certain displays once a week to accommodate newly released items. Most businesses check their displays daily for damage, displacements, or missing items caused by customer handling and purchases. Folded and stacked clothing items in a display should be organized and restocked frequently. One of the first steps in dismantling a display is to organize, label, and pack or reshelve stock.

Proper display maintenance can keep the merchandise fresh and attractive to customers. Poor maintenance can create a negative image not only of the merchandise but also of the store. Display fixtures and props should be cleaned and merchandise dusted on a regular basis. Customers are not likely to be enthusiastic about purchasing items that are displayed on dusty or dirty fixtures. A customer may also ignore or pass by a display that is poorly stocked or appears disorganized. A final step in dismantling a display is to repair, replace, or discard damaged display materials. Any new stock that had been on display must also be returned to its proper place in the store.

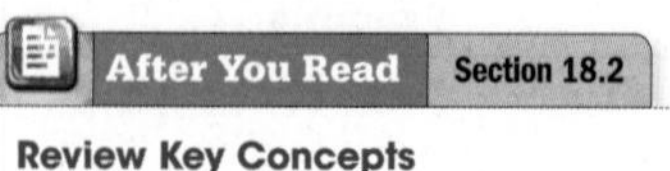

After You Read **Section 18.2**

Review Key Concepts

1. **Explain** why the first step in display preparation is so important.
2. **Differentiate** between decorative and functional props.
3. **Describe** how formal balance and informal balance are achieved in a display.

Practice Academics

English Language Arts

4. Compose a letter to a local business. In your letter, describe how the store's display is effective or how it could be improved. Provide suggestions and examples.

NCTE 4 Use written language to communicate effectively.

Social Studies

5. Visit a boutique store to observe point-of-purchase displays (POPs). Ask permission to sketch a display on a poster board. Ask the store owner why and how product display choices were made. Annotate your sketch with the comments and answers.

NCSS III G People, Places, & Environments Describe and compare how people create places that reflect culture, human needs, government policy, and current values and ideals as they design and build specialized buildings, neighborhoods, shopping centers, urban centers, industrial parks, and the like.

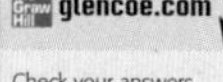

glencoe.com

Check your answers.

ELABORATE

Critical Thinking

Ask: ***What might be an advantage to using motion in a display?*** attracts interest, suggests action, helps explain the product Then ask: ***What might be a disadvantage?*** it can distract from the focal point

Visual Literacy

Display Design Caption Answer Read the caption question to students: ***Do you think this store's window display would catch the attention of the customers it is targeting? Why?*** Possible answer: Yes because of the prominent display of wedding dresses, lighting element of pink and red hearts, and pink color in store front.

Reading Check Answer

Read the Reading Check question to students: ***List in order the five steps used to create a display.*** (1) select merchandise for display; (2) select type of display; (3) choose setting; (4) manipulate artistic elements; (5) evaluate display

Critical Thinking

Discuss that this section primarily presented designing visual displays. Ask: ***What other senses might a display engage?*** smell, touch, hearing, taste Then ask: ***How might a display engage each of these senses?*** Smell: the display could project scents, for example, if it was designed to sell candles or home fragrances, it could allow customers to sample different scents. Touch: the display could allow customers to touch and compare fabrics, such as different types of towels or bed linens. Hearing: the display could include music appropriate for the product—for example, if the display contained western clothing, it could play country-western music. Taste: grocery stores and specialty food stores often have displays in which food and drink samples are offered to shoppers.

VIRTUAL BUSINESS

MERCHANDISING

Introduce students to the concept of merchandising using Knowledge Matters' Virtual Business Retailing visual simulation, Merchandising. In this simulation, students will explore merchandising and its importance to store sales and profits.

EVALUATE

DISPLAY MAINTENANCE

Remind students that creating a display is only the beginning. The display requires regular maintenance. To focus the discussion on the importance of maintaining displays, present these guiding questions.

Guiding Questions

Analyze Imagine your department contains two types of displays. One type shows mannequins playing golf, tennis, and other sports. The other type contains sports clothes stacked on shelves. Which type of display do you think will require more maintenance? Why?	The one containing clothes because they will quickly become disarrayed as customers go through the clothes.
Synthesize Have you ever seen a store display that was dirty, missing parts, or broken? Did it affect your attitude toward the store? Explain your answer.	Answers will vary. Possible answer: I thought the store must not be very well managed.

Graphic Organizer

Display this graphic organizer. Have students suggest questions that should be asked when evaluating a display. Possible answers:

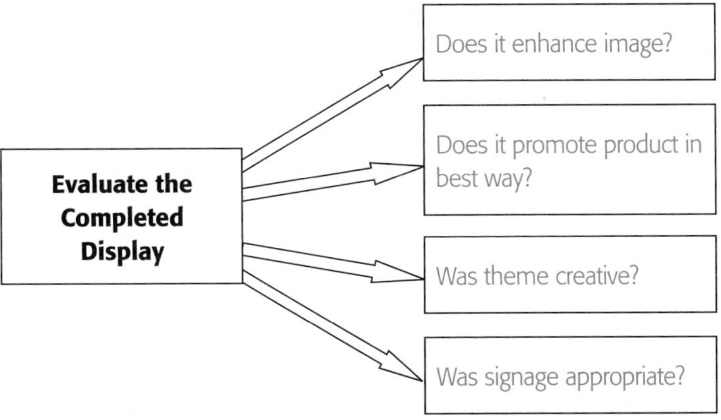
Evaluate the Completed Display
Does it enhance image?
Does it promote product in best way?
Was theme creative?
Was signage appropriate?

glencoe.com
iWB

Graphic Organizer Send students to the Online Learning Center to print this graphic organizer.

After You Read Section 18.2

Review Key Concepts

1. Selecting the merchandise is important because it will determine the theme and the other elements of the display.
2. Decorative props include such things as floor coverings, wall treatments, and backgrounds to create an interesting setting. Functional props serve a useful purpose and include items for holding merchandise such as mannequins, racks, and shirt forms.
3. Formal balance is achieved by placing large items with large items and small items with small items. Informal balance is achieved by balancing a large item with several smaller ones in a display.

Practice Academics

English Language Arts

4. Accept all reasonable paragraphs which focus on a specific store display and explain how its effectiveness could be improve. For example, students could explain how the display lacked balance and/or proportion, the focal point was unclear, the colors were a little too harsh for the type of merchandise, and so on.

Social Studies

5. Student posters should contain a sketch of a point-of-purchase display from a local boutique. The sketch should be annotated with comments about the display, such as its purpose, ease-of-use, and the degree to which it was actually used by store customers.

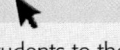

glencoe.com

Answer Key Send students to the Online Learning Center to check their answers.

Visual Merchandising and Display

Elements of visual merchandising that create a positive customer experience are storefront, store layout, store interior, and interior displays.

Storefront → Positive Customer Experience
Store Layout → Positive Customer Experience
Store Interior → Positive Customer Experience
Interior Displays → Positive Customer Experience

Prescribed steps and principles for artistic design help create effective displays that attract customers and keep them coming back.

Artistic Design Steps

① Select merchandise for display.
② Select the type of display.
③ Choose a setting.
④ Manipulate the artistic elements.
⑤ Evaluate the completed display.

Written Summary

- Visual merchandising is an important part of a business's total promotional mix.
- Visual merchandising must be coordinated with advertising, direct marketing, personal selling, and sales promotion efforts.
- Visual merchandising and in-store displays help to sell products, build brand image, and create store image.
- The four elements of visual merchandising that create a positive customer experience are storefront, store layout, store interior, and interior displays.
- Types of interior displays include architectural displays, store decorations, open displays, closed displays, and point-of-purchase displays.
- Businesses create effective displays by using prescribed steps and principles for artistic design to attract customers for new and repeat business.

Review Content Vocabulary and Academic Vocabulary

1. Write each of the vocabulary terms below on an index card, and the definitions on separate index cards. Work in pairs or small groups to match each term to its definition.

Content Vocabulary
- visual merchandising (p. 419)
- display (p. 419)
- storefront (p. 420)
- marquee (p. 420)
- store layout (p. 421)
- fixtures (p. 423)
- point-of-purchase displays (POPs) (p. 424)
- interactive kiosk (p. 425)
- props (p. 428)
- color wheel (p. 430)
- complementary colors (p. 430)
- adjacent colors (p. 430)
- triadic colors (p. 430)
- focal point (p. 431)
- proportion (p. 431)
- formal balance (p. 431)
- informal balance (p. 431)

Academic Vocabulary
- project (p. 419)
- concept (p. 419)
- equip (p. 427)
- principle (p. 429)

Assess for Understanding

2. **Describe** What is the concept and purpose of visual merchandising?
3. **Identify** What are the types of display arrangements?
4. **Summarize** What role do visual merchandisers play on the marketing team?
5. **Create** How will you follow the five steps in creating an effective display for a business?
6. **Elaborate** How do artistic elements function in designing displays?
7. **Compose** How should employees dismantle a display once it is done being used? Write a step-by-step guide.
8. **Role Play** What design elements will you and a business partner consider as you plan a display in your store?
9. **Evaluate** How could an environmentally friendly approach benefit your store?

EVALUATE

Visual Summary

Express Creativity Ask students to develop their own visual summary of a concept in the chapter. Encourage students to use different formats for their visual summaries, such as a storyboard, a timeline, a table, a tree diagram, or a word web. Visual summaries will vary depending on the concept depicted. Questions to ask when assessing a visual summary include:

- Is the summary clear, economical, and simple?
- Are any important steps left out?
- Are steps or concepts arranged in the same order as the original?
- Does the summary reveal a pattern that connects the details?
- Does the summary locate and highlight the most important information?

Review Content Vocabulary and Academic Vocabulary

1. Definitions will vary. Sample definitions:
   Visual merchandising Involves coordinating all the physical elements in a place of business to project an image to customers.
   Display Visual and artistic aspects of presenting a particular product or service to a target group of customers to encourage a purchase.
   Storefront Entire exterior of a business.
   Marquee Canopy that extends over the store's entrance.
   Store layout Way a business uses its floor space; designed to serve customers and encourage them to buy.
   Fixtures Permanent or movable store furnishings that hold and display merchandise.
   Point-of-purchase displays (POPs) Stand-alone structures that serve as consumer sales promotion devices.
   Interactive kiosk Interactive point-of-purchase display that are free-standing, full-service retail locations.
   Props Items that hold merchandise on display or support the display setting.
   Color wheel Circular diagram structured in such a way that it shows both similarities and differences among colors.

EVALUATE

Assess for Understanding

2. Visual merchandising coordinates all of the physical elements in a place of business to project an overall image to customers. The purpose of visual merchandising is to attract customers, create a desired business image, and promote interest in products and services.

3. Types of display arrangements are architectural displays, store decorations, open displays, closed displays, and point-of-purchase displays.

4. Visual merchandisers design, create, and maintain design elements of the building and displays.

5. To create an effective display for a business, you need to select appropriate merchandise for the display, select a display, choose a display setting, manipulate artistic elements, and evaluate the display for effectiveness.

6. Artistic elements in a display attract interest and motivate potential customers to make a purchase decision.

7. Steps in dismantling a display after stock has been removed include: Step 1, repair damaged areas of a display; Step 2, replace missing signs or hardware and other display components that are broken or no longer functioning; and Step 3, discard or recycle areas of the display that can not be repaired or reused.

8. Students should role play discussing design elements in a display for their store. Partners should discuss and incorporate elements such as the use of line to direct attention, colors to emotionally engage customers, shape, direction, texture, proportion, balance, motion, and lighting.

9. Many customers are increasingly aware of the green movement to reduce negative environmental impact. They are also more willing to support companies that practice earth-friendly and environmentally friendly practices.

21st Century Skills

Problem-Solving Skills

10. **Window Display** Work with a classmate to select a product or product category that interests the team. Use a poster board to sketch a potential window display for the selected item(s). You must identify the product or product category, type of setting for the product, functional and decorative props, and appropriate signage to use with your display.

Financial Literacy Skills

11. **Display Tool Box** You have been asked to order and assemble a display with the following items from a local store: scissors and stapler $15.15; a glue gun $9.95; a tape measure $5.49; razor blades and utility knife $5.49, paper towels and window spray $3.49; small tools (hammer, screwdriver and pliers) $15.65; and a notebook and a pad of paper, $2.95. Assume a sales tax of 6 percent. What will be the total cost of these items for your employer?

e-Marketing Skills

12. **Interactive Kiosks** Imagine that you work with digital signage for a large visual merchandising firm that wants to introduce digital signage to large-volume grocery stores. You have been asked to explain the idea to the management team of the grocery stores. Write a paragraph answering these questions:
    - How is digital signage used in product promotion?
    - What are the advantages of digital signage for this type of environment?
    - What are the disadvantages of digital signage for this type of environment?
    - Which local stores use digital signage?
    - How can you learn from these stores' use of digital signage?

Build Academic Skills

Social Studies

13. **Institutional Displays** Work with a partner to design and create an institutional display for a local charity, volunteer, or non-profit agency. The team must identify and research the organization, its goals and objectives, and suggest ideas for a possible interior display. When finished, present a summary of your research and how the display might appear to the class.

NCSS X D Civic Ideals & Practices Practice forms of civic discussion and participation consistent with the ideals of citizens in a democratic republic.

Science

14. **Science and Technology** Retailers desire lighting that highlights merchandise but also reduces energy and replacement costs. Conduct research on the technology of compact fluorescent lights (CFL) or light-emitting diodes (LED) lighting and the potential applications for visual merchandising and display. Recommend a way to incorporate these lighting systems into a local store.

NSES E Develop abilities of technological design, understandings about science and technology.

Mathematics

15. **Calculate Budgeted Expenses** Charlie owns a company that makes all-natural soap. Last year he spent 2 percent of the company's profits ($84,300) to get good placement on the shelves of grocery stores. This year he will only be able to spend $1,000 on the placement in grocery stores. What is the percent decrease? (Round your answer to the nearest whole percent.)

NCTM Problem Solving Build new mathematical knowledge through problem solving.

Math Concept **Mixed Numbers** When determining the value of a certain percent of the whole, convert the percent to a decimal by dividing it by 100, or move the decimal point two places to the left.

For help, go to the **Math Skills Handbook** located at the back of this book.

Standardized Test Practice

Directions Read the following questions. On a separate piece of paper, write the best possible answer for each one.

1. Which of the following refers to the ways stores use floor space to facilitate sales and serve customers?
   A. Interior displays
   B. Storefront
   C. Store interior
   D. Store layout
2. Point-of-purchase displays are a consumer sales promotion device.
   T
   F
3. Colors found opposite each other on the color wheel are called _________ colors.

Test-Taking Tip

When taking a test, keep moving along. Think about a problem for a minute or two, and if no answer comes to mind, then go on to the next problem. Come back to the other one later.

DECA Connection Role Play

Assistant Manager Clothing Store

Situation You are the assistant manager of a locally owned clothing store that sells merchandise targeted to teens and young adults. The store is located in a family friendly suburban area situated in a strip shopping center three miles from a large high school. Other businesses in the center include a music store, fast-food restaurant, grocery store, and drug store. Your store's merchandise consists mostly of casual clothing, some dressier items, and accessory items.

It is now mid-summer, approaching the back-to-school shopping season. The first shipment of back-to-school clothing is due to arrive soon. The store manager (judge) has decided it is time to plan storewide back-to-school visual merchandising. The store manager (judge) has asked for your help and ideas with the planning of the back-to-school visual merchandising. You will meet with the store manager (judge) later today to discuss your ideas. This meeting will focus on planning store signage and merchandise displays.

Activity You are to make notes about your ideas for the back-to-school store signage and merchandise displays. You will then meet with the store manager (judge) to present your ideas for the back-to-school store signage and merchandise displays.

Evaluation You will be evaluated on how well you meet the following performance indicators:

1. Explain the use of visual merchandising in retailing.
2. Create displays
3. Create promotional signs.
4. Plan visual merchandising activities.
5. Plan/schedule displays/themes with management.

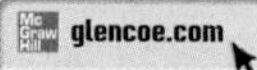

Download the Competitive Events Workbook for more Role-Play practice.

EVALUATE

Problem-Solving Skills

10. While the products will differ, each student team must select a product or line of products, the decorative and functional props to use, and the appropriate signage for the window display. For example, students may choose to create a window display that contains clothes from their favorite clothing store, such as Abercrombie & Fitch® or Buckle®. If they choose Buckle, they might create a sketch of a window display showing three or four young-looking mannequins lounging in an interesting spot, such as the porch of an old farm house with peeling paint, wearing jeans and t-shirts from Buckle. The goal would be to capture Buckle's look, which is described on their Web site as being vintage with a trendy attitude.

Financial Literacy Skills

11. $61.66 ([15.15 + 9.95 + 5.49 + 5.49 + 3.49 + 15.65 + 2.95] × 1.06 = $61.66)

e-Marketing Skills

12. Digital signage is used in product promotion in a variety of ways such as product or service advertising, to have conversations about products through social media such as Twitter and blogs, marketing research, for in-house networks, and as a vehicle to offer coupons. Advantages include that their content can be easily changed, they can be used for special sales and incentives, they can involve motion and are highly engaging, and they can be used for product information and public service announcements. Disadvantages include that some customers ignore the messages and consider them to be an annoyance that interferes with the shopping experience. They also can be relatively expensive. Answers to the last two parts of the question will vary.

EVALUATE

Build Academic Skills

Social Studies

13. Accept all reasonable answers that include a description of the charity, volunteer, or non-profit agency, its goals and objectives, and ideas for an interior display. An example of a non-profit agency that could be used is NAMI, National Alliance on Mental Illness. Its goal is to educate Americans about mental illness, offer resources to those in need, and insist that mental illness become a high national priority. The institutional display might be built around a NAMI money-raising effort, such as a run-walk at a local park. The display might explain the purpose and goals of NAMI and explain how individuals and groups can register to participate in the run-walk.

Science

14. Accept all reasonable answers which include a scientific explanation of either CFL or LED lighting technologies. LED (light emitting diode) lighting, for example, is extremely energy efficient, long-lasting, and produces more light per watt than incandescent bulbs. An LED contains a semiconductor that emits visible light when electrical current passes through it. Because they are solid-state devices, LEDs are much more resistant to breakage than CFLs or incandescent bulbs. LEDs make colors appear brilliant and vibrant, which is important in many retail settings. Applications for visual merchandising include focusing on specific merchandise, creating a particular mood, and incorporation into both outdoor and indoor settings.

Mathematics

15. 41% ($1 - 1000/[84300 \times 0.02] = 0.41 = 41\%$)

Standardized Test Practice

1. D Store layout
2. True
3. Complementary

DECA Connection Role Play

Evaluations will be based on these performance indicators:

1. **Explain the use of visual merchandising in retailing.** Visual merchandising is used to coordinate all the physical elements in a business and project a clear, distinct, and consistent image to the customer that sets the business apart from its competitors.
2. **Create displays.** Students should be able to create store displays such as window displays and interior displays that are appropriate for a clothing store that targets teens and young adults. These displays include architectural displays, closed displays, open displays, point-of-purchase displays, and store decorations. Each type has specific purposes for which it is useful.
3. **Create promotional signs.** Students should be able to create promotional signs appropriate for a clothing store that targets teens and young adults. Creating promotional signs includes the signs that appear on the store's exterior, such as the main store sign or logo, marquees, banners, etc. Exterior signs are designed to attract attention, often use bold graphics and may project brand identity. Marquees can display promotional information, such as the store's hours of operation and the URL address.
4. **Plan visual merchandising activities.** The first step in visual merchandising is to select the merchandise for display. New, popular, and best-selling projects are often selected. The target audience, the season, and the store's geographic location should all be taken into account in the planning process. The next step is to select the type of display, such as a one-item display, similar-product display, or related-product display. The third step is to choose a setting. Settings can be realistic, semi-realistic, or abstract. The fourth step is put the elements together, paying attention to artistic principles such as line, color, shape, proportion, balance, and lighting. .
5. **Plan/schedule displays/themes with management.** Students should be able to work with management to plan/schedule displays/themes. Displays and themes are often coordinated with the seasons and holidays, so careful timing is important. In addition, displays and themes throughout the store should be coordinated to present a unified image.

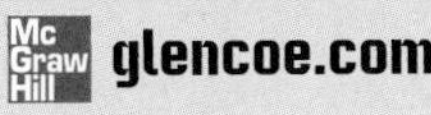

Role Plays For more DECA Role Plays, send students to the Online Learning Center to download the Competitive Events Workbook.

advertising

SHOW WHAT YOU KNOW

Visual Literacy There are many types of advertising to match the needs and budgets of large and small businesses. Advertising media comes in many forms and is shown in many places. ***How do you think a business decides what to spend and where to advertise its goods and services?***

Discovery Project

The Advertising Plan

Essential Question How does a business create an advertising plan?

Project Goal

Work with a classmate to select a good or service to promote. Develop a one-year advertising plan and a written report that includes a description of your target audience, the media that will be used for advertising, the costs of each advertising medium, and an estimated budget for each month and a whole year. Your advertising plan must be appropriate for your geographical location and reflect the types of media available with realistic costs.

Ask Yourself...

- What is your good or service and your target audience?
- What media will you select to use in your advertising plan?
- How will you determine media costs and a budget for the advertising plan?
- How will you organize the advertising plan and written report?

Organize and Interpret What types of advertising will be the most effective in reaching your target audience?

glencoe.com

Activity
Get a worksheet activity about advertising.

Evaluate
Download a rubric you can use to evaluate your project.

DECA Connection

DECA Event Role Play

Concepts in this chapter are related to DECA competitive events that involve a comprehensive test and either an interview or role play.

Performance Indicators The performance indicators represent key skills and knowledge. Your key to success in DECA competitive events is relating them to concepts in this chapter.

- Explain types of advertising media.
- Analyze a sales promotional plan.
- Develop an advertising campaign.
- Calculate media costs.
- Prepare a promotional budget.

DECA Prep

Role Play Practice role-playing with the DECA Connection competitive-event activity at the end of this chapter. More information on DECA events can be found on DECA's Web site.

Chapter 19 · Advertising | 439

ENGAGE

Visual Literacy

Read the chapter opener photo caption question to students: ***How do you think a business decides what to spend and where to advertise its goods and services?*** Businesses may use percentage of sale, all you can afford, follow the competition, or objective and task methods to determine how much to spend. They look at their target audience to determine the best media to use to reach the audience with their advertisements. Then ask these guiding questions.

Guiding Questions

Explain What is advertising?	a form of nonpersonal promotion in which companies pay to promote ideas, goods, or services in a variety of media outlets
Analyze How is advertising a one-way conversation with the customer?	Customers cannot respond to the advertising as in a conversation. They can only respond by buying the product or service.

Discovery Project

The Advertising Plan Ask students to share some of the different types of advertisements they have seen or heard. print media such as newspaper and magazines, broadcast media such as television and radio, Internet advertising, specialty media such as giveaways, in-store advertising Then ask them the Discovery Project Essential Question: ***How does a business create an advertising plan?*** Businesses must determine whether the campaign will be promotional or institutional. They consider which types of media to use in their advertising campaign—print, broadcast, Internet, specialty, in-store, new media—to reach their target. They must develop a budget for their campaign.

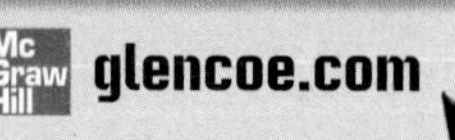

Discovery Project Resources Send students to the Online Learning Center to download a rubric to evaluate their projects.

ENGAGE

Introduce the Chapter

Chapter 19 introduces advertising and its purposes, and explains the different types of media. These main concepts are introduced and discussed:

- Promotional and institutional advertising
- Mass advertising
- Print media
- Broadcast media
- Internet advertising
- Specialty media
- Media measurement
- Media rates
- Promotional budget

Discussion Starter

Effective Advertising Post several print ads around the classroom. Include a mix of promotional and institutional ads with different target markets. Have students look at the ads, then close their eyes and tell which ads they remember best. Ask: ***What makes the ad memorable?*** Students may suggest the images, a catch phrase, or bright colors. Bring to class recorded television and radio ads. Play them for students and ask: ***Which ads are the most memorable? Why?*** catchy tunes, clever scripts, humor, and so on. Ask: ***What is the purpose of advertising?*** to attract buyers Ask: ***Would any of these ads persuade you to purchase the product or service advertised? Why or why not?*** Answers will vary but should be thoughtful and genuine.

DECA Connection

Discuss the performance indicators listed in the DECA Connection feature. Performance indicators tell them how to demonstrate their acquired skills and knowledge through competitive events.

glencoe.com

Competitive Events Workbook For more DECA Role Plays, send students to the Online Learning Center to download the Competitive Events Workbook.

PRINT RESOURCES

- **Student Edition**
- **Teacher Edition**
- **Student Activity Workbook with Academic Integration** includes worksheets and activities correlated to the text.
- **Mathematics for Marketing Workbook** provides math activities for every unit in the text.

TECHNOLOGY TOOLBOX

- **Connect**
- **ConnectPlus**
- **ExamView Assessment Suite** is a comprehensive solution for creating, administering, and scoring tests.

glencoe.com

Online Learning Center provides a variety of resources to enrich and enhance learning.

SECTION, CHAPTER, AND UNIT RESOURCES

- **Graphic Organizers** for organizing text concepts visually.
- **Digital Nation Activities** and **Green Marketer Activities** extend learning beyond the text features.
- **Career Chatroom Career Profiles** allow students to explore different marketing occupations in depth.
- **After You Read Answer Keys** for students to check their answers.
- **Discovery Project Rubrics** and **Marketing Internship Project Rubrics** for students to evaluate their projects.

PROGRAM RESOURCES

- **Student Activity Workbook with Academic Integration Teacher Annotated Edition** includes annotated answers for the activities and worksheets.
- **Marketing Research Project Workbook** provides a step-by-step approach for students to complete their own marketing research studies.
- **School-to-Career Activity Workbook** helps students relate their class work to on-the-job experience and involves work-site analysis and working with mentors.
- **Competitive Events Workbook** helps prepare students for state and national marketing education competitions.
- **Inclusion in the Marketing Education Classroom** provides teaching resources for working with students with special needs.
- **PowerPoint Presentations** provides visual teaching aids and assessments for this chapter.

READING GUIDE

Before You Read

Connect What effective advertisements have you seen recently?

Objectives

- **Explain** the concept and purpose of advertising in the promotional mix.
- **Identify** the different types of advertising media.
- **Discuss** the planning and selection of media.

The Main Idea

Advertising is an important element of promotion. Businesses advertise to promote their ideas, goods, and services.

Vocabulary

Content Vocabulary

- advertising
- promotional advertising
- institutional advertising
- media
- print media
- transit advertising
- broadcast media
- Internet advertising
- podcast
- blogs
- specialty media
- media planning

Academic Vocabulary

You will find these words in your reading and on your tests. Make sure you know their meanings.

- region
- networks

Graphic Organizer

Draw or print this chart to organize your notes about the types of media used for advertising.

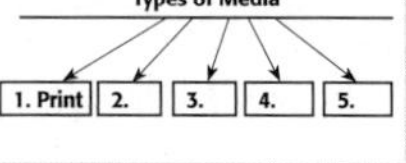

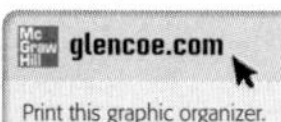

Print this graphic organizer.

STANDARDS

ACADEMIC

English Language Arts

NCTE 1 Read texts to acquire new information.

Science

NSES E Develop abilities of technological design, understandings about science and technology.

NCSS *National Council for the Social Studies*
NCTE *National Council of Teachers of English*
NCTM *National Council of Teachers of Mathematics*
NSES *National Science Education Standards*

Common Core
Reading Determine central ideas or themes of a text and analyze their development; summarize the key supporting details and ideas.

MARKETING CORE FUNCTION

Promotion

Section 19.1

Advertising Media

ADVERTISING AND ITS PURPOSE

Advertising is nonpersonal promotion which promotes ideas, goods, or services by using a variety of media. The average city dweller is exposed to more than 3,000 advertising messages every day. Advertisers control the message, where it will be seen or heard, and how often it will be repeated.

Depending on its purpose, marketers can use advertising to introduce a new business or change a company image. Advertising can also promote a new product or an existing one, encourage the use of a particular service, or encourage business-to-business transactions.

As You Read

Classify How would you classify the advertisements you have seen in the past week?

PROMOTIONAL AND INSTITUTIONAL ADVERTISING

There are two main types of advertising: promotional and institutional. **Promotional advertising** is advertising designed to increase sales. The targets of promotional advertising can be either consumers or business-to-business customers. Sometimes promotional advertising encourages potential customers to ask for information, call for appointments, participate on the Internet, or enter a retail store.

Promotional advertising generates leads or develops prospects that can lead to a purchase and increased sales for a business. Promotional advertising is an effective way to support direct selling, visual merchandising and display, and other sales promotion activities.

Institutional advertising is advertising designed to create a favorable image for a company and foster goodwill in the marketplace. Companies often perform public service advertising and underwrite the cost of ads to help community and nonprofit groups promote their services or projects. Institutional advertising does not directly increase sales. However, by connecting its name to a worthy cause, a company creates a good impression with potential customers.

> "Advertising is everywhere—television, radio, magazines, stores, Internet, billboards, schools, sports arenas, and even on highway road signs."

MASS ADVERTISING

Mass advertising enables companies to reach large numbers of people with their messages. Certain media, such as television and radio, lend themselves to mass advertising. Thanks to today's sophisticated technology, advertisers can also carefully target their messages to select audiences. This is known as targeted advertising. Advertising demonstrates the features and benefits of a good or service. As a result, advertising encourages business customers and general consumers to buy products.

Reading Check

Contrast How are promotional advertising and institutional advertising different?

ENGAGE

Anticipation Activity

Improving Student Achievement Ask students to name some characteristics of infomercials. talk-show format; celebrities; product demonstrations; testimonials; various incentives Ask: ***What types of products are advertised on infomercials?*** exercise equipment, kitchen appliances, cosmetics, cleaning products, gardening tools, and so on

Objectives

- **Explain** the concept and purpose of advertising in the promotional mix. concept: introduce a new business, change a company image, promote a new product, advertise an existing one; purpose: to increase sales
- **Identify** the different types of advertising media. print, broadcast, Internet, specialty, in-store, and new media
- **Discuss** the planning and selection of media. Answer such questions as: Can the medium present the product and the appropriate business image? Will the medium get the desired response rate?

Graphic Organizer

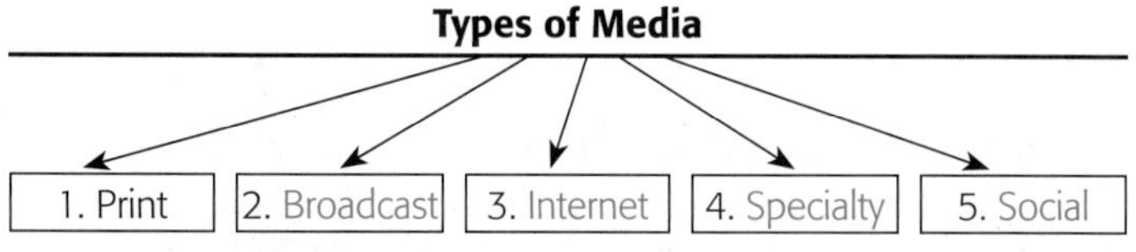

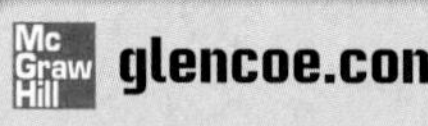

Graphic Organizer Send students to the Online Learning Center to print this graphic organizer.

ENGAGE

Before You Read

Read the Before You Read question aloud: ***What effective advertisements have you seen recently?*** Students should provide examples of several different types of advertising media, including broadcast, print, Internet, specialty, and new media. They may provide specific product examples as well. Ask: ***Why do you think the ads are effective?*** Students may suggest that the ads attract buyers through the use of humor, emotion, and persuasion.

Preteaching Vocabulary

Have students go to the Online Learning Center at glencoe.com for the Chapter 19 Preteaching Vocabulary games.

Content Vocabulary

Divide the class into three groups. Assign three of the Content Vocabulary terms to each group. Tell group members to discuss the terms and to come up with a good definition for each term. Then have groups teach the terms and their meanings to the rest of the class. Groups might create puzzles for the class or have a game show format. Allow the students to use their creativity. You might follow up this activity with a brief quiz to assess the effectiveness of the teaching.

Academic Vocabulary

Region—Synonyms Ask students to provide synonyms for the term *region.* Synonyms may include: area, territory, zone, district, state, county, state, province, and so on. Ask: ***How is the term* region *related to advertising?*** Students may recall from their study of Chapter 2 that geographics (segmentation of the market based on where people live) is a big part of marketing and advertising. Advertising campaigns are often designed to focus on a target area or region.

Networks—Usage Ask students if they have heard the term *networks.* Ask: ***In what context have you heard this term used?*** Students will probably mention the cell phone and smart phone networks, social networks, television networks, and job network. Ask: ***What is a network?*** A network is a group of connected companies, people, or organizations that work together.

Reading: Differentiated Instruction
Go to the Online Learning Center to view a video in which an author discusses elements of a differentiated classroom.

Advertising Media

ADVERTISING AND ITS PURPOSE

Ask these guiding questions to focus the discussion.

Guiding Questions

Discuss What are the two main types of advertising?	Promotional advertising is designed to increase sales. Institutional advertising is designed to create a favorable image for a company and foster goodwill in the marketplace.
Analyze What are the different purposes of advertising?	Introduce a new business, change a company image, promote a new product or existing one, encourage the use of a particular service, encourage business-to-business transactions

As You Read

Read students the As You Read question: ***How would you classify the advertisements you have seen in the past week?*** Students should be able to give examples of several different types of advertising media, such as broadcast, print, online, specialty, and new media.

Expert Advice

Read the quote to students:

> **“Advertising is everywhere—television, radio, magazines, stores, Internet, billboards, schools, sports arenas, and even on highway road signs.”**

Ask students: ***What advertisements do you see in the classroom or at home?*** company logos on school equipment; logos and brand images on the clothing of fellow students; print advertising; commercials

Reading Check Answer

Read the Reading Check question to students: ***How are promotional advertising and institutional advertising different?*** promotional advertising: designed to increase sales; institutional advertising: designed to create a favorable image for a company

TYPES OF MEDIA

Media are the agencies, means, or instruments used to convey advertising messages to the public. The four general categories of advertising media are print, broadcast, Internet, and specialty. The advertising message and the target audience determine the type of media that is used.

TYPE	EXAMPLE
Print	Newspaper
Broadcast	Television
Internet	Opt-in e-mail
Specialty	Giveaways

PRINT MEDIA

Print media includes advertising in newspapers, magazines, direct mail, signs, and billboards. This is one of the oldest and most effective types of advertising.

NEWSPAPER ADVERTISING

Newspapers continue to be an important advertising outlet for many consumer-oriented products and services. It is estimated that 50 percent of households in the United States subscribe to a newspaper. Advertisers want their ads to be seen, so high numbers of readers are very important. Newspapers offer a variety of advertising options, including the ad size, its location, and the frequency of ad insertions. This flexibility enables companies to select the options that best suit their budgets and advertising goals.

MARKETING CASE STUDY

Under Armour Shoes!

Under Armour® is known for manufacturing clothing and accessories for athletes. However, the company needed a marketing campaign to announce the launch of its new footwear line. The company developed the "Athletes Run" campaign, which featured appearances from a number of world-class athletes. The campaign focused on the concept that "all runners are athletes and all athletes run."

Celebrating Training

The ads aired on TV networks watched by athletes. They spotlighted the effort and dedication that goes into becoming great at a sport. The spots included professional athletes such as Brandon Jacobs of the New York Giants, soccer star Heather Mitts, Jeff Samardzija of the Chicago Cubs, Olympic volleyball player Nicole Branagh, and others.

English Language Arts/Writing

In addition to magazine and TV ads aimed at athletes, what are some other media this brand might use for advertisements? Create a brief ad for the new footwear line and explain how the company will use it.

NCTE 12 Use language to accomplish individual purposes.

Daily and Weekly Newspapers

There are more than 1,600 paid circulation daily newspapers in the United States and several thousand local weekly papers as well. These local papers provide a timely way for companies to reach their target audiences. Many retailers and local companies rely on daily newspapers to advertise their goods and services.

Shoppers and Alternative Newspapers

Another type of local paper is called a "shopper." Shoppers contain minimal editorial content, and they are often delivered free to residents in specific areas. In many larger cities, "alternative weeklies" are also available for free but are usually not home-delivered. Unlike shoppers, they often focus on local entertainment information, movie, music, and restaurant reviews, as well as alternative political comments or stories. Shoppers and alternative newspapers both offer opportunities for local advertisements.

National Newspapers

National newspapers, such as *USA Today®* and *The Wall Street Journal®*, are distributed throughout the country. Advertisers can purchase ad space in the newspaper to reach the entire national circulation or buy less expensive space targeted only to a specific **region** or city. Most local and national papers have online editions and sell advertising space for both printed and digital formats.

Advantages

What are the advantages of newspaper advertising? Because a newspaper's distribution is known, advertisers can target their advertising to people living in certain areas or with certain interests. A newspaper may even offer different neighborhood sections within the same city.

Responses to newspaper ads and coupon sales are dated and easily tracked. The cost of newspaper advertising remains relatively low because paper, print quality, and printing costs are lower than the same costs for magazines and direct mail.

Disadvantages

Newspaper advertising does have limitations, however. Some newspapers are sold to subscribers outside a business's target market. Also, newspapers have a limited shelf life because they are read and then thrown away each day. Many newspapers are printed with black ink or may also include a limited number of color pages. Newspaper ads are less visually appealing than those found in colorful magazines and direct mail. Also, newspaper circulation and daily readership continues to decline, especially among younger consumers who obtain product information from other media sources such as the Internet.

Going Viral

Viral marketing is a type of Web marketing that encourages people to share messages with friends. Viral campaigns often feature videos or games, plus tools for sharing them on Facebook and other social sites.

E-Green Marketing Viral marketing helps environmental groups spread messages widely for little money. For example, Greenpeace's "Kleercut" campaign encouraged Kleenex® to stop using wood from old-growth forests. It used online action kits, a Flickr® group, videos on YouTube and MySpace, and Web badges to gain the attention of people from around the world.

Social Studies

Evaluate Kimberly-Clark, the maker of Kleenex® , and Greenpeace announced they would work together to preserve old-growth forests. How might such an agreement benefit Kimberly-Clark? Discuss possible benefits and risks with a partner.

NCSS IX D Global Connections Analyze the causes, consequences, and possible solutions to persistent, contemporary, and emerging global issues, such as health, security, resource allocation, economic development, and environmental quality.

glencoe.com

Get an activity on green marketing.

EXPLAIN

MARKETING CASE STUDY

English Language Arts/Writing Answer Students' answers may include: billboards, especially those near sports complexes; Internet advertising; specialty media might also be used to advertise the new line of athletic shoes. Students' ads will vary but should contain information about the product and focus on a target market of athletes. Explanations should clearly define how the company would use the advertisement. Ask: ***What media do you think would be the most effective for advertising the new line of athletic shoes? Why?*** Possible answer: Television would be most effective because of the high number of sports channels and programs available. It is reasonable to assume that viewership is high, so the ad would reach a lot of potential customers. Social media might also be effective because runners may belong to social networks or be fans of this company's Facebook® page.

TYPES OF MEDIA

Tell students that they are in contact with many different types of media every day. Then ask these guiding questions to focus the discussion on media.

Guiding Questions

Define What is the meaning of the term *media*?	the agencies, means, or instruments used to convey advertising messages to the public
Analyze Why might companies choose to advertise in newspapers?	Advertisers can target people living in certain areas or with certain interests; responses to newspaper ads and coupon sales are dated and easily tracked; the cost of newspaper advertising remains relatively low.

ELABORATE

Mini Project

Enrichment

Write an Expository Essay Ask students to think about an instance when a print advertisement, such as a department store sale ad, influenced their decision to purchase a product advertised. Then have them think about a time when a newspaper ad made them less interested in a product. Ask: ***What elements of advertisements did or did not appeal to you? Why?*** Have students write their answer in a one-page expository essay. Essays will vary but should determine and define their audience, define their purpose, explain the main idea in a clear thesis statement, list facts as supporting details, and focus on cause-effect relationships between facts. Essays should be free of grammar and spelling errors.

Graphic Organizer

Display this diagram. Ask students to provide as many advantages and disadvantages as possible for using newspapers for advertising purposes. Possible answers:

Newspaper Advertising

Advantages	Disadvantages
• Distribution is known. • Targets people living in certain areas • Responses to ads and coupons are easily tracked. • Cost is relatively low.	• Some sold to subscribers outside target market zone • Limited shelf life • Limited color availability • Ads are less appealing than those found in magazines or direct mail. • Circulation and readership continues to decline.

glencoe.com

iWB

Graphic Organizer Send students to the Online Learning Center to print this graphic organizer.

Graphic Organizer

Display this diagram. Ask students to provide as many examples as possible for the different types of media. Possible answers:

Types of Media	
Type	**Examples**
Print	Newspaper; Magazine, Direct-mail, Directory, Outdoor, Transit
Broadcast	Television; Radio
Internet	Opt-in e-mail; Banner and search engine, Rich-media and video, Social-media
Specialty	Giveaways; Appointment books, Calendars, Magnets, Pens, Pencils
Other	In-store; New media, iPods®, Cell phones, Laptops, Video games

glencoe.com

iWB

Graphic Organizer Send students to the Online Learning Center to print this graphic organizer.

The GREEN Marketer

Social Studies Answer Read the Social Studies Activity to students: Kimberly-Clark, the maker of Kleenex, and Greenpeace announced they would work together to preserve old-growth forests. ***How might such an agreement benefit Kimberly-Clark?*** It might open up a whole new set of prospective customers who want to do business with companies that are conscious of the environment and are taking steps to preserve it.

glencoe.com

Worksheet Activity Send students to the Online Learning Center to get a Green Marketer worksheet activity.

MAGAZINE ADVERTISING

There are more than 19,000 magazine publications that are distributed locally, regionally, or nationally. They can be published as weeklies, monthlies, and quarterlies. Many magazines are now published in online formats and provide new advertising opportunities for marketers. *Newsweek*, *Time*, and *TV Guide* are examples of national weekly magazines. Regional magazines are usually developed to serve the needs of a metropolitan area or region. *Blue Ridge Country* is an example of a regional magazine. Some national magazines have regional, state, and city editions.

Consumer Magazines

Magazine publications can also be classified as consumer or business-to-business. Consumer magazines, such as *Car and Driver*, *Entertainment Weekly*, *Seventeen*, *Sports Illustrated*, and *Reader's Digest*, are developed for personal pleasure or interest. Advertisers can target their audiences by studying the characteristics of a magazine's subscribers.

Business-to-Business Magazines

Business-to-business magazines, also known as trade publications, interest professionals in specific fields. Examples include *Advertising Age*, *Mass Market Retailers*, and *Women's Wear Daily*. These publications are cost effective for advertisers who want to reach a target audience with little wasted circulation.

Advantages

Consumer and business-to-business magazines have longer life spans than newspapers. People tend to keep magazines for a more extended period of time. Keeping them longer increases the chance that the magazines and their ads will be reread or passed along to others. People also read magazines more slowly and thoroughly than newspapers. Magazines with digital color photography and powerful graphics have better quality images than newspapers. They produce powerful and more memorable advertising messages. Magazines also offer a variety of presentation formats, including full-page ads, two-page spreads, gatefolds (a page folded into itself), return cards, and heavy stock inserts.

Disadvantages

There are disadvantages to magazine advertising. The cost of advertisements in magazines is higher than newspaper advertisements. The deadline for submitting advertising material is several weeks or months before actual publication. Advance deadlines limit flexibility in making day-to-day or weekly adjustments in the advertising message, if market conditions change.

DIRECT-MAIL ADVERTISING

Direct mail or direct marketing is a highly focused form of advertising. The two types of direct marketing are printed direct mail (sent to a home or business) and electronic direct mail (delivered to an e-mail address).

Direct mail marketing is a good way to keep current customers aware of new products, services, and upcoming sales. It is also a cost-effective way to generate leads and qualify prospective customers.

Printed direct-mail advertising takes many forms, including newsletters, catalogs, coupons, samplers, price lists, circulars, invitations to special sales or events, letters, and more. Large retailers and manufacturers send direct-mail catalogs and price lists to current and prospective customers.

Advantages

Direct-mail advertising enables advertisers to be highly selective about who receives the mailing and when the person receives it. The success of direct-mail advertising depends on careful selection of the target audience. Direct mail is most effective with existing customers. However, in order to grow and increase market share, a company must find new customers.

Direct-mail advertisers seek new customers first by analyzing their existing customers to build a customer profile. Then they acquire the names of people or organizations that fit the same profile. Direct-marketing specialty firms sell lists of people's mailing addresses, phone numbers, and e-mail addresses. Names can be sorted according to many different demographic criteria to match the profile of a business's existing customers.

Direct-mail advertisers have a wide choice of printed advertisement formats—letters, catalogs, and postcards—limited only by postal regulations. Direct mail also includes electronic advertising campaigns. This flexibility enables direct mailers to test various creative approaches and obtain valuable results for perfecting future campaigns.

Disadvantages

There are disadvantages to direct mail. It yields a low level of response in relation to the number of items sent. An average return or redemption rate of 1 to 3 percent for printed direct mail is typical. Poorly planned and executed direct-mail campaigns yield less than a one-half percent response.

Direct mail also has an image problem. Many people think of printed or electronic direct-mail advertising as junk mail. The cost of printed direct mailing can be high because it includes producing and printing each piece of the mailing, collating it, buying mailing lists, and paying for postage to send it.

DIRECTORY ADVERTISING

The best example of a directory that accepts advertising is the telephone directory. In the *White Pages*, businesses and residents receive a free alphabetical listing of their phone numbers and addresses.

In the *Yellow Pages*, businesses pay for an alphabetical listing and, if desired, a display ad. The listings and ads appear under general category headings. Switchboard® is an online Internet-based version of the *Yellow Pages*. Consumers can find a business and maps with directions. The digital version provides advertising opportunities using interactive display ads. Advertisers can adjust their information, offers, or messages. In contrast, printed versions must remain the same until a directory is reprinted and distributed.

Directory advertising has some unique advantages. It is relatively inexpensive and can be used to target all demographic groups. For example, 99 percent of adults in the United States are familiar with the *Yellow Pages*. Printed directories are usually kept for at least a year or until another one is provided.

OUTDOOR ADVERTISING

Local, regional, and national businesses use outdoor signs for advertising. There are two types of outdoor signs: non-standardized and standardized. Nonstandardized outdoor signs are used by companies at their places of business or in other locations throughout the community. An example is a sign displaying a company's logo at the entrance to its office building.

Standardized outdoor signs, or billboards, are purchased from advertising companies. Billboards have standard sizes that are designed to be viewed from more than 50 feet away. Digital technologies have been integrated into some billboards, so that they appear as flat-screen televisions with impressive images. Billboard displays can use lights, moving parts, attachments and Bluetooth® technologies to attract attention. These types of billboards are common in densely populated metropolitan areas.

Billboards are classified by size. Called "bulletins," the largest of this type of billboard is 14 feet by 48 feet. Smaller versions are called "posters." Posters are outdoor panels and come in various sizes. They are changed three to four times each year. Bulletins are advertising signs placed along major highways that are changed every six months to a year.

Advantages and Disadvantages

Outdoor advertising is highly visible and relatively inexpensive. It provides a 24-hour a-day, 7-days-a-week message, and can be located to reach a specific geographical area. Drawbacks of outdoor advertising include limited viewing time and increasing government regulations. Outdoor advertising is usually restricted to highways, secondary roads, and areas zoned for commercial and industrial uses.

TRANSIT ADVERTISING

Transit advertising is advertisement seen on public transportation. It includes printed posters inside buses, taxis, and trains, as well as ads on public benches, bus-stop shelters, kiosks, and newsstands. Station advertising is seen near or in subways and in airline, bus, ferry, and railroad terminals.

EXPLAIN

Critical Thinking

As a class, discuss the differences between mass advertising and targeted advertising. Mass advertising enables companies to reach large numbers of people with their messages. Targeted advertising targets the messages to select audiences. Have students develop a list of mass advertisements and targeted advertisements. Answers will vary, but an example might include a TV or radio ad for a shoe store as a mass advertisement and a magazine ad promoting trendy shoes for teens as a targeted advertisement. Poll the class on their interests and their buying characteristics. As a class, decide on a product to market. Each group, organized by the poll of interests tallied, should create an advertisement for one of the target groups identified by the polling. Share the advertising campaigns with the class. In groups, develop a list of mass advertisements and targeted advertisements. For example, the class may choose shoes to create target market advertising. One target group may be all athletes, in which case the advertisement for that target group might focus on sports.

Mini Project

Enrichment

Analyze Advertisements Divide the class into pairs. Give each pair a number of magazine advertisements. Have the pairs determine the type of magazine the ads came from and the target market for the ads. Then have them describe the format, the colors used, and the paper stock the ads are printed on. Have pairs choose one of the ads that promotes a specific product, such as a computer. Have them identify the target market for the ad and then have them adapt the advertisement for a different target market. Have pairs share their revised ads with the class. Ask the class to determine the target audience for the ad. Students might select a computer ad that targets young people by highlighting the variety of designs available, and adapt it to target a more mature audience by focusing on such things as ease of use and ergonomic layout.

ELABORATE

Graphic Organizer

Display this diagram. Ask students to name the advantages and disadvantages of the print media listed. Possible answers:

Print Media	Advantages	Disadvantages
Newspapers	Distribution is known; Target people living in certain areas; Coupons easily tracked; Cost is relatively low	Some sold to subscribers outside target market; Limited shelf life; Limited color availability; Ads are less appealing than those found in magazines or direct mail; Circulation declines
Magazines	Longer life span than newspapers; Better quality graphics; Variety	Cost; Deadline limits flexibility to make change based on market
Direct-mail	Can send to select population; Can purchase mailing lists; Wide choice of printed advertisement formats; Flexibility	Yields low level of response; Image problems—"junk mail"; Cost
Directory	Relatively inexpensive; Can target all demographic groups; Printed directories kept for a year	Printed version can only be changed when reprinted
Outdoor	Highly visible; Relatively inexpensive; Provides messages 24/7; Can be located in specific geographic area	Limited viewing time; Increasing government regulations; Restricted to highways, secondary roads, commercial/ industrial zones
Transit	Reaches a wide and captive audience; Economical; Defined market of travelers	Difficult to target specific markets

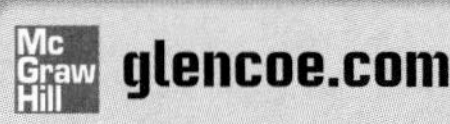

iWB

Graphic Organizer Send students to the Online Learning Center to print this graphic organizer.

Critical Thinking

Bring in a pile of direct mail. Discuss with students the perception of this stack of direct mail. Ask: ***Is the term "junk mail" appropriate? Why or why not?*** Students may suggest that it is appropriate because it can pile up very quickly and it is generally unwanted. Ask students to suggest different types of direct mail they have received. Answers may include catalogs, newsletters, invitations to special events, and so on. Ask: ***Have you ever been persuaded to purchase a product because of direct mail?*** Answers will vary. Ask volunteers to share their stories.

Tell students that all print advertising is only as effective as the customer response. Ask: ***What is customer response?*** Customer response occurs when customers see or hear an advertisement and they are prompted to seek out the product or service. Ask these guiding questions to focus the discussion about advertising.

Guiding Questions

Explain What are the disadvantages of advertising in magazines?	Cost is higher than newspaper ads; deadline is weeks or months before publication, which limits flexibility in making changes to the ad if market conditions change.
Analyze Why do most people consider direct-mail advertising as junk mail?	People receive unsolicited advertisements for products they may or may not use. It wastes their time looking over the ads and it fills the waste bin or recycle bin with unwanted paper.

Reinforce Vocabulary

Transit Advertising—Word Origin The word *advertising* has its root in the Latin word *advetere,* which means "to pay attention." The word *transit* is a Latin form of the word *transire,* which translates to mean "to go." Have students create slogans to promote transit advertising by rrearranging the Latin meaning of this term.

Broadcast media—Usage The adjective *broadcast* was first documented in the late 1700's to refer to scattering or casting in all directions. The word *media* is the plural form of *medium,* which means "a form of communication or avenue in which messages are delivered." Have one group of students create a list of adjectives that are synonyms of *broadcast.* Have a different group of students generate a list of plural nouns that are synonyms of *media.* Then, have both groups combine the terms to create a new list of terms that could take the place of *broadcast media.*

Almost everyone is familiar with the advertising on public transportation. ***What are some advantages of transit advertising?***

Transit advertising reaches a wide and sometimes captive audience. This type of advertising is economical and has a defined market of people who are traveling.

BROADCAST MEDIA

Broadcast media encompass radio and television. By age 66, the average person spends nearly ten years watching 2 million television commercials and almost six years listening to the radio. You can see why advertising through broadcast media is popular. Most of the 1,700 commercial television stations are affiliated with one of the major **networks**—ABC, CBS, NBC, or Fox. In addition, there are about 11,600 local cable systems. Network and cable television has mass appeal and is found in nearly all American households.

TELEVISION ADVERTISING

Most television advertisements are 30- or 60-second spots. An exception is the infomercial, which is a 30- or 60-minute advertisement. Infomercials promote products, such as cookware, exercise equipment, and appliances, using a talk-show type setting. Viewers can order the advertised merchandise by calling a phone number, visiting a Web site, or writing to an address.

Network television is the ultimate mass-advertising medium for many businesses because it combines all these elements—sight, sound, action, and color—to produce a compelling advertising message. As a result, television is a very effective medium for demonstrating a product's features and benefits. Cable television allows advertisers to target their advertising messages to audiences with a specific interest, such as history, music, sports, or travel.

Businesses can use local television advertising to market their products or services to a specific geographic area. Local companies can also place commercials inside network programming delivered by cable providers. "Smart" television systems allow viewers to push a button during a commercial to request more information. Use of this technology has become increasingly popular among political candidates at election time.

HOT TOPIC
Television Habits On average, households with annual income under $30,000 watch 5 hours and 20 minutes per day, while those with income over $100,000 watch 3 hours and 40 minutes per day.

There are some disadvantages to television advertising. It has the highest production costs of any type of media and a high cost for the TV time purchased. Production costs for a network TV commercial average more than $400,000. Prime-time and special-event costs are high. A 30-second ad for the Super Bowl costs about $3 million.

Smaller companies cannot usually afford network-television advertising, or they must buy time in less desirable time slots. Another disadvantage is that many viewers change stations, leave the room, or use devices that allow them to view commercial-free programming.

RADIO ADVERTISING

Radio is a medium that can be heard just about anywhere. It is also a timely medium. Radio advertisers can update or change their advertising messages daily or hourly. Radio has the immediacy of newspapers without the high production costs of television. More than 10,000 AM and FM radio stations reach 96 percent of all people age 12 and over in a given week. This ability to reach a wide audience makes radio an extremely efficient and cost-effective advertising medium.

Radio advertisers can carefully target their audiences when they select the station on which to broadcast their ads. Most radio station programming already targets a specific segment of the radio listening market.

Radio advertisements are presented in 10-, 20-, 30-, or 60-second time periods. These messages are effective in encouraging people to buy because an announcer or actors—along with background music, jingles, slogans, and sound effects—can add excitement, drama, or humor.

However, goods or services can only be described, not seen. Advertisers cannot rely on visual involvement to hold a listener's attention. That is why a catchy jingle is important. Radio advertisements also have a short life span.

INTERNET ADVERTISING

Internet advertising is a form of advertising that uses either e-mail or the World Wide Web. It is still a modest part of overall advertising spending, but it is growing steadily. Examples include opt-in e-mail ads, banner ads, pop-up ads, search engine ads, and rich-media video ads. These ads are

Billboard Advertising

Large billboards can use spectacular displays with lights, attachments, and moving parts to attract attention. ***What are the benefits of outdoor advertising?***

EXPLAIN

Visual Literacy

Transit Advertising Answer Read the caption question to students: ***What are some advantages of transit advertising?*** reaches a large audience, other than those who use public transportation, economical To focus your discussion on transit advertising, ask these guiding questions.

Guiding Questions

List Name some examples of advertising found on public transportation?	printed posters inside buses and taxis; digital and print advertising on trains; ads on public benches and kiosks; ads on newstands and bus stops; digital and audio advertisements at airports
Analyze What are possible disadvantages of transit advertising?	Rural areas or towns with sparse populations may not require or provide public transit.

Mini Project

Enrichment

Survey Outdoor and Transit Advertising Assign students to survey the outdoor advertising and transit advertising in your area. If possible, have students take photos of the ad to share. Have students compile the information they collect in a table similar to the one below Have students share their findings with the rest of the class. Possible answers:

	Ad #1	Ad #2	Ad #3
Where is the ad located?	Main St. and 8th Ave.		
What type of ad is it?	Billboard		
What product or service is featured?	Car		
Do you think the ad is effective? Why or why not?	Yes; it's located next to a car lot.		

ELABORATE

BROADCAST MEDIA

Broadcast media is an effective way of getting a message out to many people at the same time. It is a very effective medium for advertising. Ask these guiding questions to focus the discussion on broadcast media.

Guiding Questions

Explain What is meant by saying that radio is a timely medium?	Radio advertisers can change or update their advertising messages daily or hourly.
Analyze Why would television advertisers not change their advertisements daily or hourly?	The cost would prohibit it.
Determine If so many viewers leave the room, change stations, or use devices that allow them to watch commercial-free television, is television advertising effective?	Businesses and companies would not spend money on television advertising if it were not effective.

Mini Project

Differentiated Instruction

Musical Learners Play songs with vocals from a variety of different styles. As students listen, have them write down images, words, and emotions that are inspired by the music. Ask: ***What do you think the musician's purpose was in "speaking" to the audience in the song?*** Students might suggest the musician was trying to evoke an emotion, share a personal story, make a political or social statement, or make the audience feel like singing or dancing. Ask: ***What role might music play in advertising?*** Music can be used to evoke emotions or create sentimental feelings that might inspire the listener to purchase the product or service being advertised. Play some television or radio ads for students. Encourage students to listen carefully to the ad. Ask: ***Does the ad use music? If so, what feelings does the music evoke in you? Would this make you more likely to purchase this product or service?*** Answers will be based on students' own observations and feelings. Help students to understand that music evokes emotions and emotions cause us to do things we might not do under normal circumstances. Advertisers use this knowledge to influence us to purchase their products.

Critical Thinking

Work together as a class to develop a chart of television viewing and radio listening. Use the following questions to gain information for the chart.

- How much television do you watch per week (hours)?
- How much radio do you listen to per week (hours)?
- Which television shows do you regularly watch?
- Which radio stations do you regularly listen to?
- Name a television or radio jingle you know.

Have students write the answers to the questions on a sheet of paper. Then compile the class results into a television and radio viewing/listening chart to display for the students. Discuss the results with the class. Ask: ***How many advertisements do you think you hear or watch per week? Do you think these advertisements influence what you spend your money on? Why or why not?*** Encourage students to think critically about the effectiveness of television and radio advertisements on their own behavior. Tell students that money spent on television and radio advertisements often has a good return on investment.

Television Habits Ask students to analyze why they think families with lower incomes watch more television than families with higher incomes. Have students discuss how this might impact television advertising.

Visual Literacy

Billboard Advertising Caption Answer Read the photo caption question to students: ***What are the benefits of outdoor advertising?*** Outdoor advertising is highly visible and relatively inexpensive. It displays the message 7 days a week, 24 hours a day, and it can be located to reach a specific geographical area. Ask students: ***Why do you think billboard advertising is usually restricted to highways, secondary roads, and areas zoned for commercial and industrial uses?*** Students may suggest that the billboards are not necessarily attractive, and they block views so people in residential or downtown areas do not appreciate them.

increasingly combined with animation, video, and sound with interactive features to deliver more exciting advertising messages. Another area of Internet advertising is social marketing. This involves customer-generated feedback generated when a company invites consumers to submit comments and advertising ideas about the company's products.

OPT-IN E-MAIL ADS

Electronic direct-mail advertising is sent via e-mail. Today most advertising of this type is sent to prequalified groups of people. This is known as opt-in e-mail because recipients requested it or authorized it. Many of these e-mails provide links so that the recipient can click through to a company's Web site. This enables most companies to track exactly how many people visit their site by clicking on the link in the e-mail. It is also cost-effective and easy to update with personalized messages for each recipient.

BANNER AND SEARCH ENGINE ADS

Most online advertising appears as banner or display ads. Banner ads come in various shapes and sizes, but usually as a rectangle seen at the top, bottom, or side of a Web page.

Some advertisers use pop-up banner ads, which are TV-like spots that pop up between Web pages. They can also be inserted in audio or video streams, either live or on-demand. A viewer clicks on the ad to get to the advertiser's Web site—or to close the ad window to resume Internet use.

Search engine ads appear while using a search engine, such as on Google®, Bing®, or MSN Search®. These ads are short text lines that appear and direct the user to an advertiser's Web site. Advertisers can buy search terms that appear if a term is mentioned in the search results.

Online advertisers have found that bold colors, top-of-page placement, animation, calls to action, and limited frequency of exposures all help increase the number of visitors to Web sites.

But even using these techniques, online advertisers report response rates as low as 0.3 percent. In other words, for every 1,000 banner ads, only three in 1,000 users click on the online ad to visit the advertiser's Web site.

RICH-MEDIA AND VIDEO ADS

Rich-media banner ads combine animation, video, and sound with interactive features. Podcasting began as a way to listen to music from an electronic MP3 file in a digital music player, such as an iPod® device. A **podcast** can now be any brief digital broadcast that includes audio, images, and video delivered separately or in combination. Podcast ads provide additional opportunities for Internet advertisers.

Rich-media banner and video ads provide instant, detailed feedback about how much time viewers spend watching or listening to the ads. Rich-media and video ads entice viewers to make an online purchase or to submit their demographic data in real time. These ads generate better brand recognition and higher sales than do static online ads.

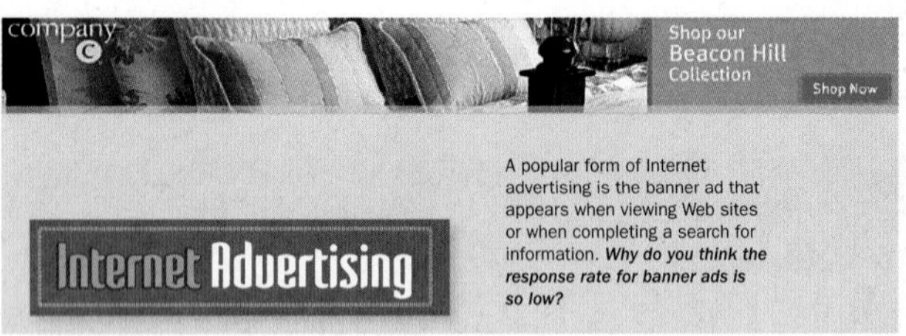

A popular form of Internet advertising is the banner ad that appears when viewing Web sites or when completing a search for information. ***Why do you think the response rate for banner ads is so low?***

SOCIAL-MEDIA ADVERTISING

Large companies use social media to get across their advertising messages. These companies invite consumers to interact with their products, often through personal blogs. **Blogs** are personal Web sites where individuals share thoughts, pictures, and comments with visitors.

Sometimes companies encourage ideas and opinions for advertising messages, read product blogs, generate or share videos about their product, or establish business pages on social media networks. Companies use social networks in the belief that people trust the opinions of their friends or peers. Therefore, product endorsement through social networks boosts overall product image and sales.

Examples of social-media advertising include the National Football League asking fans to submit Super Bowl ad ideas; Johnson & Johnson® using a YouTube® channel linked to the Olympics; and Coca-Cola®, Starbucks® or Pizza Hut® having business pages on Facebook®. Social media, such as Twitter®, MySpace®, and Facebook, allow companies opportunities to interact with their target audience.

These interactions allow companies to develop advertising messages, create customer profiles, develop sales leads, provide special offers, and maintain customer feedback. This informs them of the image and performance of their products.

SPECIALTY MEDIA

Specialty media, also known as *giveaways* or *advertising specialties*, are relatively inexpensive useful products that are imprinted with the company's name, message, or logo.

To be successful as advertising tools, specialty items must be practical, used frequently, and displayed in locations with high visibility. Common items that fit this description are appointment books, calendars, magnets, pens, pencils, shirts, caps, and bags. Specialty items carry the identity of the business sponsoring them and an advertising message.

Disadvantages include limited distribution of items and advertising to people who would never consider buying the product or patronizing the business.

Companies often have business pages on popular social-networking Web sites. ***What are the advantages for businesses to participate in social-network marketing?***

EXPLAIN

VIRTUAL BUSINESS

PROMOTION

Introduce students to the concept of promotion using Knowledge Matters' Virtual Business Retailing visual simulation, *Promotion*. In this simulation, students will learn that promotion is the way in which stores actively communicate with their customers.

ADVANCED PROMOTION

Introduce the concept of advanced promotion using Knowledge Matters' Virtual Business Retailing visual simulation, *Advanced Promotion*. In this simulation, students will learn about additional sales and merchandise promotion activities that a storeowner or manager can use to attain the stated goals of a sales promotion.

Visual Literacy

Internet Advertising Caption Answer Read the photo caption question to students: ***Why do you think the response rate for banner ads is so low?*** Possible answers: Most people just ignore them; they have other reasons for using the Internet and they don't want to be distracted. Ask students: ***Do you pay attention to banner ads on the Internet? Why or why not?*** Some students might say that they might click on banner ads that relate to something they are looking for or something that interests them.

Critical Thinking

Remind students that banner and search-engine ads have a very low response rate. Ask: ***Why do you think rich-media and video ads generate better brand recognition and higher sales than the static online ads?*** the rich-media and video ads are more interesting to watch and therefore gain more attention; They are also more difficult to ignore. If people spend more time looking at the ads because of the interest level, they might learn more about the product or service and gain a deeper interest in it.

ELABORATE

Reinforce Vocabulary

Podcast—Usage Remind students that podcasts are digital multimedia files that can be downloaded to MP3 players and computers. Podcasts can include audio, images, and video. Ask: ***Have you ever downloaded and listened to or watched a podcast? If so, what was the content of the podcast? What was your impression of this type of media?*** Some students may be familiar with podcasts; others may not have used one. Impressions will vary—students who downloaded them for personal use may have more favorable impressions than those who have downloaded them for school purposes.

Blogs—Usage Ask a volunteer to read the first paragraph under the head Social-Media Advertising on page 449. Tell students that blogs are biographical Web logs, a term which is shortened to *blogs.* These are considered to be a type of diary in which people share their thoughts, photos, and so on. Ask: ***Do you have a blog? Have you ever read a blog?*** Ask students what might have replaced blogs in recent years. Social-networking sites such as Facebook® and MySpace® have replaced blogs for many people.

Graphic Organizer

Display this web. Ask: ***With what types of Internet advertising are you familiar?*** Students' answers will vary depending on their exposure to the Internet and the different types of ads. Ask students to share their favorite type of Internet advertising. Possible answers:

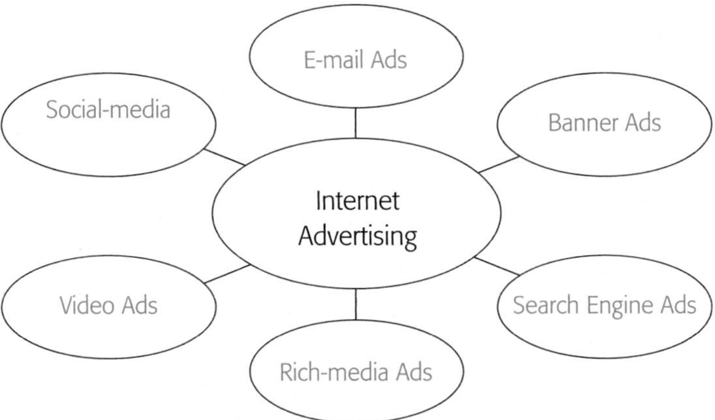

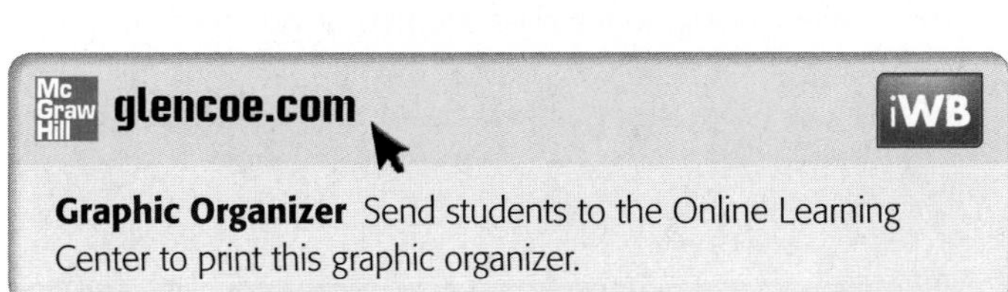

Graphic Organizer Send students to the Online Learning Center to print this graphic organizer.

Mini Projects

Enrichment

Survey Internet Users Have students conduct surveys about Internet advertising. Students should develop a survey with questions that ask about the subject's Internet use (e.g., casual or work related), and whether they pay attention to Internet advertisements. Surveys should ask whether subjects are familiar with opt-in e-mails, banner and search engine ads, rich-media and video ads, and social-media advertising. Surveys should also ask which, if any, of the ads appeal to or have influenced the subject. Have students display their results in a table or similar graphic organizer that clearly shows the information collected. Survey results should be graphically displayed and include answers to all of the survey questions. Have students share their results in a brief oral report to the class.

Create an Internet Advertisement Have student groups collaborate to create an Internet advertisement. Ads can be opt-in e-mail, banner, search-engine, rich-media, video, or social media. The software available for students' use may dictate what types of ads students can create. If appropriate software is not available, have students write out a script for their ads including descriptions for any videos, photos, and so on that would be included in the ads. Have groups present their ads to the class. Ask the class to determine the type of Internet ad groups have created. Ads will vary depending on the creativity of group members and available resources. Presentations should include graphics if possible or complete descriptions of the ads.

Visual Literacy

Joining a Social Network Caption Answer Read the photo caption question to students: ***What are the advantages for businesses to participate in social-network marketing?*** The customer interaction encouraged by advertising on social-networking pages allows companies to develop advertising messages, to create customer profiles, to develop sales leads, to provide special offers, and to maintain customer feedback about the image and performance of their products. Ask students: ***Do you interact with advertising on social-networking pages? If so, in what way?*** Students' answers will vary but may include offering ideas and opinions for advertising messages or writing product blogs.

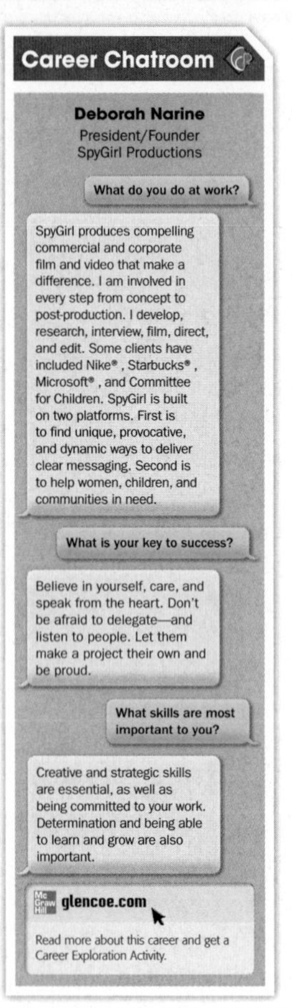
Career Chatroom

Deborah Narine
President/Founder
SpyGirl Productions

What do you do at work?

SpyGirl produces compelling commercial and corporate film and video that make a difference. I am involved in every step from concept to post-production. I develop, research, interview, film, direct, and edit. Some clients have included Nike®, Starbucks®, Microsoft®, and Committee for Children. SpyGirl is built on two platforms. First is to find unique, provocative, and dynamic ways to deliver clear messaging. Second is to help women, children, and communities in need.

What is your key to success?

Believe in yourself, care, and speak from the heart. Don't be afraid to delegate—and listen to people. Let them make a project their own and be proud.

What skills are most important to you?

Creative and strategic skills are essential, as well as being committed to your work. Determination and being able to learn and grow are also important.

glencoe.com

Read more about this career and get a Career Exploration Activity.

OTHER ADVERTISING MEDIA

Businesses are constantly creating innovative and unusual means of transmitting their messages to potential customers. Examples include:

- Ad-supported TV screens at airports, gas stations, health clubs, and subways
- Digital billboards at sports arenas
- On-screen movie theater ads
- Messages on diaper-changing stations, trash cans, bathroom stalls, elevators, and even hot-air balloons.

IN-STORE ADVERTISING

Increasingly, retailers are using in-store advertising techniques. These include:

- Ceiling and floor graphics
- Electronic shelf ads
- Supermarket-cart displays
- Instant-coupon machines

These techniques—as well as kiosks, sound systems, and closed-circuit television networks—advertise products within stores.

NEW MEDIA

New media advertising is interactive and Internet-driven. It uses new electronic media devices, such as Web-enabled small-screen iPods®, cell phones, laptops, and video games to reach an increasingly mobile population. Advertisers go to those places on the Internet where they can find their target customers: websites, blogs (Web logs), vlogs (video logs), visual and audio newscasts, RSS news feeds, and social networking sites (Facebook®, Twitter®).

Improved ways to access the Internet continue to provide marketers with creative advertising opportunities to market their goods and services. This includes Third-Generation (3G) and Fourth-Generation (4G) wireless networks, Voice-Over-Internet Protocol (VOIP) telephony, Home Networking, and Wi-Fi.

Reading Check

Identify What are five types of media used for advertising?

450 | Unit 6 · Promotion

MEDIA PLANNING AND SELECTION

Media planning is the process of selecting the appropriate advertising media and deciding the time or space in which ads should appear to accomplish a marketing objective. To select and compare different types of media, companies use media-planning software, media-cost data, and audience information. The choice of a particular advertising medium ultimately depends on the product to be advertised and the demographics and lifestyles of the target audience. The size of the advertising budget and the types of media available in the geographical area are also factors.

To establish the media plan and select the right medium to use, advertisers must ask and answer three basic questions:

1. Can the medium present the product and the appropriate business image?
2. Can the desired customers be targeted with the medium?
3. Will the medium get the desired response rate?

The media plan provides the opportunity to present a compelling message and project the desired business image to the target market.

After You Read Section 19.1

Review Key Concepts

1. **Determine** which form of advertising would most likely be used by a small company with a limited budget.
2. **Identify** potential drawbacks with using the two types of broadcast media.
3. **Connect** the practice of media planning to the concept of market segmentation.

Practice Academics

Science

4. Scientists are researching how the brain responds to the effects of colors, logos, product features, smell, touch, music, and jingles used in advertising messages. Conduct research on the science of neuromarketing. Choose an advertisement and identify how one of its features is related to neuromarketing.

NSES E Develop abilities of technological design, understandings about science and technology.

Mathematics

5. Assume that total Internet advertising revenue by format was $16.9 billion for one year. What advertising revenue amounts were generated in each format category, if search-engine ads represented 40 percent, display ads 22 percent, rich media and videos 7 percent, and e-mail 2 percent?

NCTM Number and Operations Compute fluently and make reasonable estimates.

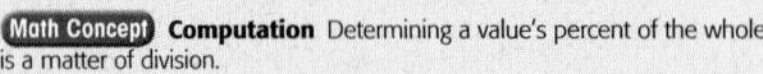

Math Concept **Computation** Determining a value's percent of the whole is a matter of division.

Starting Hints To solve this problem, divide the amount spent for each medium by the total amount spent on advertising to get a decimal number. Then multiply the decimal point and determine the percent.

For help, go to the **Math Skills Handbook** located at the back of this book.

glencoe.com

Check your answers.

Chapter 19 · Advertising | 451

ELABORATE

Career Chatroom

Use these questions to focus the discussion about the Career Chatroom.

Guiding Questions

Explain What does "Don't be afraid to delegate" mean?	You should feel confident that coworkers will do a good job.
Analyze Why is it wise to "believe in yourself"?	you need have the confidence to take chances

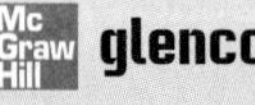

glencoe.com

Career Exploration Send students to the Online Learning Center to read more about this career and to get a Career Exploration Activity.

Mini Project

Extension

Research Giveaways Tell students they work for a company of their choice and have $1,000 in their advertising budget to spend on giveaways. Have students conduct online research into the different types of products companies and businesses can purchase to give away to customers and potential customers. Items should be able to be branded with the company's name and/or logo. Have students determine how best to spend their $1000 on giveaways. Then have students present their findings to the class. Students should present a breakdown of their spending. They might include a mockup or picture of the giveaway item(s) they choose for their giveaways.

Reading Check Answer

Read the Reading Check question to students: ***What are five types of media used for advertising?*** print, broadcast, Internet, specialty, and social media

EVALUATE

Mini Project

Enrichment

Scavenger Hunt Divide the class into teams of two or three students. Assign teams to locate examples of in-store advertising. Students should list the type of advertising and the store in which they found an example. Students answers should include a type of store advertising—ceiling and floor graphics, electronic shelf ads, supermarket cart displays, instant-coupon machines, kiosks, sound systems, and closed-circuit television networks—and the store in which they found the advertising.

MEDIA PLANNING AND SELECTION

Ask students: ***What is media planning?*** Media planning is the process of selecting the appropriate advertising media and deciding the time or space in which ads should appear to accomplish a marketing objective. Then ask students these guiding questions to focus the discussion about media planning and selection.

Guiding Questions

Identify What do companies use to select and compare different types of media?	media-planning software, media-cost data, and audience information
Discuss What questions must be answered before an advertising medium is selected and the media plan is established?	Can the medium present the product and the appropriate business image? Can the desired customers be targeted with the medium? Will the medium get the desired response rate?
Analyze Why is it important for an advertising medium to get the desired response rate?	If the desired response rate is not achieved, the desired ROI will not be achieved.

After You Read — Section 19.1

Review Key Concepts

1. Print advertising in the form of newspaper would likely be the best value for a small company with a limited budget. Through newspaper ads, the company could target local customers or those with interests that might connect them to the company.
2. Drawbacks for television advertising include: high production costs, and viewers often change stations or leave the room during commercials, or use devices that allow them to view commercial-free programming. Drawbacks for radio advertising include: goods or services can only be described, not seen and radio ads have a short life span.
3. Market segmentation—the process of classifying people who form a given market into even smaller groups—is a part of media planning. The demographics and lifestyles of the target audience must be considered during media planning.

Practice Academics

Science

4. Accept all reasonable responses to how various advertising characteristics such as color, sound, smell, and touch affect brain waves and purchasing decisions made by consumers. Students should also discuss the concept of neuromarketing, which uses medical technologies such as MRIs to measure changes in brain activity when the subject is viewing different types of advertisements. Discussions should also include an understanding of how the brain works and how this information might lead to more effective advertising.

Mathematics

5. Search-engine ads: $6,760,000,000; display ads: $3,718,000,000; rich-media and videos: $1,183,000,000; e-mail: $338,000,000

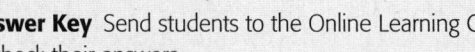

glencoe.com

Answer Key Send students to the Online Learning Center to check their answers.

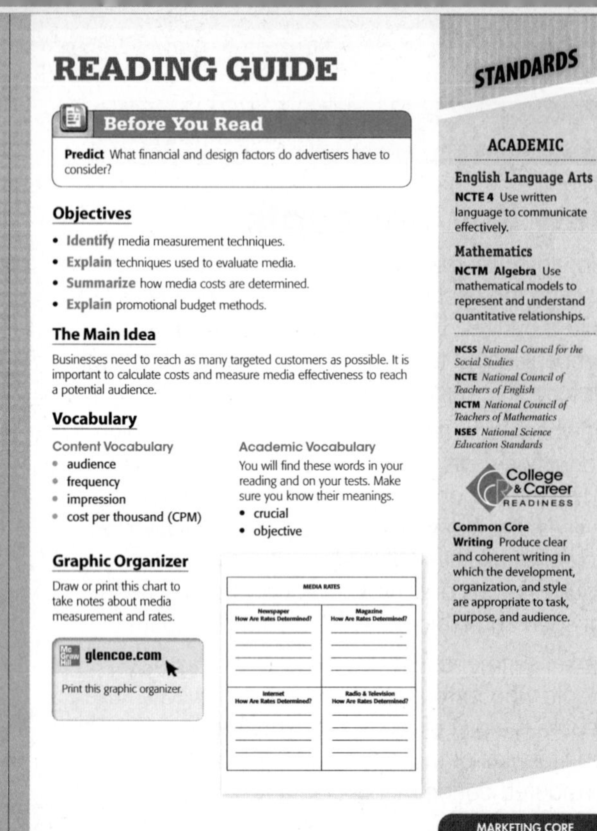

READING GUIDE

Before You Read

Predict What financial and design factors do advertisers have to consider?

Objectives

- **Identify** media measurement techniques.
- **Explain** techniques used to evaluate media.
- **Summarize** how media costs are determined.
- **Explain** promotional budget methods.

The Main Idea

Businesses need to reach as many targeted customers as possible. It is important to calculate costs and measure media effectiveness to reach a potential audience.

Vocabulary

Content Vocabulary
- audience
- frequency
- impression
- cost per thousand (CPM)

Academic Vocabulary

You will find these words in your reading and on your tests. Make sure you know their meanings.
- crucial
- objective

Graphic Organizer

Draw or print this chart to take notes about media measurement and rates.

glencoe.com

Print this graphic organizer.

STANDARDS

ACADEMIC

English Language Arts

NCTE 4 Use written language to communicate effectively.

Mathematics

NCTM Algebra Use mathematical models to represent and understand quantitative relationships.

NCSS *National Council for the Social Studies*
NCTE *National Council of Teachers of English*
NCTM *National Council of Teachers of Mathematics*
NSES *National Science Education Standards*

College & Career READINESS

Common Core Writing Produce clear and coherent writing in which the development, organization, and style are appropriate to task, purpose, and audience.

MARKETING CORE FUNCTION

Promotion

Section 19.2

Media Rates

MEDIA MEASUREMENT

Media planners must consider the correct medium to use for advertising, its costs, and how to measure overall advertising effectiveness. To understand media measurement, you need to become familiar with several key terms.

The number of homes or people exposed to an ad is called the **audience**. The audience for print media is the total number of readers per issue.

Readership in print media is measured by surveys or estimated by circulation. The audience figure is normally higher than its circulation because more than one person can read a single issue of a printed newspaper or magazine.

From an advertiser's point of view, the audience figure better reflects the actual number of people exposed to an ad. **Frequency** is the number of times an audience sees or hears an advertisement.

> **"Everyone knows that it pays to advertise, but the questions are "How well?" and "Was it worth the cost?""**

A single exposure to an advertising message is an **impression**. Online media measurement is measured through surveys and computer software tracking systems to calculate the number of people who view a particular ad.

When advertisers buy time on television or radio or space in print or online, they typically hope for the largest audience, greatest frequency, and most impressions possible. This helps ensure that their products or services are exposed to as many potential customers as possible.

Television media measurement is based upon data collected by ACNielsen Media Research® for a sample of TV viewers in more than 200 TV markets. This data is gathered through the use of either diaries filled out by sample households or set-top meters attached to televisions or cable or satellite boxes. The most important measurement of viewing behavior occurs during what are called "sweeps months" four times a year—in February, May, July, and November.

The Arbitron Company® similarly measures radio advertising in more than 260 markets. To determine radio listenership, Arbitron has sample households fill out diaries describing what stations they listened to and when they tuned in. Arbitron also collects data on listening behavior by means of cell-phone-sized Portable People Meters. The meter records data whenever the person wearing it is exposed to encoded signals from radio stations, regardless of their location.

Cost per thousand (CPM) is the media-measurement cost of exposing 1,000 readers or viewers to an advertising impression. (The "M" in CPM stands for *mille*, which is the Latin word for 1,000.) Cost per thousand is the comparison tool used to determine the effectiveness of different types of broadcast, print, and digital media.

It is important to know whether you are spending your advertising dollars effectively. Knowing the potential audience, how frequently your advertisement will be seen, and its CPM can tell you whether the rates charged by various media are right for your advertising budget.

As You Read

Predict How do businesses measure the effectiveness of their advertising media?

452 | Unit 6 · Promotion

Chapter 19 · Advertising | 453

ENGAGE

Anticipation Activity

Improving Student Achievement Write the two headings *Print* and *Broadcast* for the class to view. Ask students: ***What factors would influence the advertising rates for these types of media?*** Print—amount and location of space, timing, color; Broadcast—amount of air time, production costs, time of day.

Objectives

- **Identify** media measurement techniques. print: surveys and circulation estimation; online audiences: surveys and software tracking systems; television and radio audiences: meter data
- **Explain** techniques used to evaluate media. Cost per thousand is used to determine the effectiveness of different types of media.
- **Summarize** how media costs are determined. Costs vary by time, type of media, geographical location, and audience.
- **Explain** promotional budget methods. The methods include percentage of sales, all you can afford, following the competition, and the objective and task method.

Graphic Organizer

MEDIA RATES	
Newspaper How Are Rates Determined? Classified ad or display ad Amount of space Timing Location of ad	**Magazine** How Are Rates Determined? Circulation Type of readership Production techniques
Internet How Are Rates Determined? Display format CPM rate based on views Paid listings at portal sites Per-click rates Pay-for-sale advertising	**Radio & Television** How Are Rates Determined? Network radio, national spot-radio, or local radio Time of day

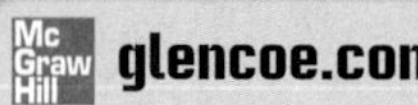

Graphic Organizer Send students to the Online Learning Center to print this graphic organizer.

EXPLORE

Before You Read

Read the Before You Read question aloud: ***What financial and design factors do advertisers have to consider?*** Financial factors: time, space, location, audience. Design factors: production rates and display format. Ask: ***Why is it important to understand the financial and design factors before beginning an advertising campaign?*** everything dealing with the cost of the campaign must be considered before actually beginning the campaign

Preteaching Vocabulary

Have students go to the Online Learning Center at glencoe.com for the Chapter 19 Preteaching Vocabulary games.

Content Vocabulary

Write the key term *impression* for the class to view. Explain to students that it comes from the Middle English word for *to imprint.* Tell students that when used in advertising, *impression* has a specialized meaning. Ask a volunteer to locate the term in the glossary and to read the definition aloud. An impression is a single exposure to an advertising message.

Academic Vocabulary

Crucial—Synonyms Have students use a dictionary or a thesaurus to look up synonyms for the Academic Vocabulary term *crucial.* As students offer synonyms, ask a volunteer to write them for the rest of the class to view. Possible answers include: important, critical, essential, vital, key, central, and fundamental. Now ask volunteers to use the term in a sentence. Possible answer: The audience is crucial to advertisers.

Objective—Synonyms Write the term *objective* for the class to view. Ask students to provide a definition for the term. An *objective* is something a person or company plans to achieve. Ask: ***What are some synonyms for the term objective?*** goal, aim, purpose, reason, point Have students find the Objectives for Section 19.2 on page 452 of their text. Ask: ***How do the objectives listed here relate to the meaning of the term objective?*** They are the goals for the section.

PROFESSIONAL DEVELOPMENT **MINI CLIP**

ELL: Words and Pictures
Go to the Online Learning Center to view a video clip in which a teacher uses words and media examples to help students learn new vocabulary.

Media Rates

MEDIA MEASUREMENT

Tell students that there are a number of decisions that must be made before developing advertising. Ask these guiding questions to focus the discussion on measuring the effectiveness of advertising.

Guiding Questions

Explain In media measurement, what is meant by an audience?	the number of homes or people exposed to an ad
Analyze Why is it important to know how many impressions an ad has?	Knowing the number of impressions allows advertisers to track the number of people who view a particular ad.
Determine Why might advertisers choose to air advertisements during the "sweeps months"?	Advertisers might believe that more people watch television during those months, and therefore gain more exposure to their advertisements.

As You Read

Read students the As You Read question: ***How do businesses measure the effectiveness of their advertising media?*** Cost per thousand (CPM)—the media measurement cost of exposing 1,000 readers or viewers to an advertising impression—is the comparison tool used to determine the effectiveness of different types of media.

Expert Advice

Read the quote to students:

> **"Everyone knows that it pays to advertise, but the questions are "How well?" and "Was it worth the cost?""**

Ask students: ***What do you think is the most effective way to determine the effectiveness of advertising?*** increased customer interest, increased sales, and so on ***In the quote above, what does the question "How well?" refer to?*** How effective was the advertising? Did it increase sales, if so, by how much? Tell students that it is important that the cost of advertising not exceed the effectiveness.

MEDIA RATES

To reach customers, advertisers use a set format that is defined in terms of time (e.g., 30-second TV commercial) or space (e.g., half-page newspaper ad). Media costs vary greatly, not just by type of media but also by geographical location and audience. For example, a quarter-page newspaper ad in a large city daily newspaper costs four to eight times more than the same-sized ad costs in a small-town weekly. It is virtually impossible to quote exact rates for each type of media advertising.

Businesses research rates for specific newspapers and magazines by visiting individual Web sites or by looking up rates in various publications from the Standard Rate and Data Service®.

Another important service for both advertisers and print media is provided by the Audit Bureau of Circulations® (ABC). Print media publishers subscribe to the ABC to verify their circulation figures. A circulation audit is **crucial** to publishers because it enables them to verify circulation numbers to advertisers. Circulation figures are important selling points when publications want to attract and retain their advertisers.

NEWSPAPER RATES

Newspaper advertising rates are divided into two categories depending on whether the ad is a classified ad or a display ad.

Classified ads are grouped, or classified, into specific categories, such as help wanted, real estate, personals, or auto sales. They are effective for selling everything from services to houses to job openings. People or businesses that buy classified ads usually pay by the word or line of type.

Display ads enable the advertiser to depict the product or service being advertised. Advertisers use a mix of art or photographs, headlines, copy, and a signature or logo of the product or business. Display ads are generally larger than classified ads. Their cost is based upon the amount of space used and the ad's position in the newspaper.

Newspapers quote display advertising rates by the column inch. A column inch is an area that is one-column wide by one-inch deep. If a newspaper quotes a column-inch rate, you simply multiply the number of columns by the number of inches to determine the total number of column inches. Then multiply the total column inches by the rate. For example, if the rate for a column inch is $17, then a single ad (called an "insertion") that measures three columns by four inches long will cost $204.

$17 × 3 columns × 4 inches = $204

Newspaper Advertising Rates
- Factors that Affect Rates
- Comparing Rates

FACTORS THAT AFFECT RATES

The open rate, or noncontract rate, represents the basic charge for a minimum amount of advertising space. The open rate, referred to as the noncontract rate, is used for infrequent advertisers. It is the highest rate charged for a display ad.

Advertising rates also vary depending on when an advertisement will appear in a paper. A newspaper may charge a Monday-through-Thursday rate of $29 per column inch, a Friday rate of $30, a Saturday rate of $32, and a Sunday rate of $35 per column inch.

The location of an ad is another factor. Display ads are usually sold at run-of-paper rates. Run-of-paper allows the newspaper to choose where to run an ad in the paper. For a higher rate, advertisers can run ads in guaranteed or preferred locations, such as the back cover. The use of color also affects the advertising rate. Color ads are sold at a higher price than black-and-white ads. The frequency of advertising lowers the amount charged. Businesses that advertise in the newspaper may contract to guarantee the newspaper that they will use a certain amount of space for a specified time period. They are granted contract rates, which are discounted from the open rate.

Contracts can be written in a number of ways. A yearly frequency contract guarantees that an advertiser will use a minimum number of column inches each week for 52 weeks. A bulk-space contract guarantees that a minimum number of inches will be used when the advertiser chooses within a 12-month period.

COMPARING RATES

The cost per thousand (CPM) measurement is useful in comparing the cost of advertising to reach 1,000 readers in one newspaper with the cost of advertising to reach 1,000 readers in another newspaper. The comparison is made by using the following formula:

Cost of the Ad × 1,000/Circulation = CPM

Suppose the cost of an ad in the *Times* is $500, and the paper has a circulation of 500,000. Its CPM would be calculated as follows:

$500 × 1,000/500,000 = $500,000/500,000 = $1 per 1,000 readers

Suppose the cost of an ad in the *Tribune*, a competing paper, is $600, and the paper has a circulation of 300,000. Its CPM would be calculated as follows:

$600 × 1,000/300,000 = $600,000/300,000 = $2 per 1,000 readers

All other things being equal, an advertiser would probably choose the *Times* over the *Tribune*. Of course, all other things might not be equal. The *Tribune's* circulation could include more of the advertiser's target market, or the paper could offer a special ad placement. CPM is a convenient measure that enables advertisers to compare costs.

MAGAZINE RATES

Magazine rates are based on circulation, the type of readership, and production techniques. To calculate the actual cost of magazine advertising, you need to become familiar with terms found on magazine advertising rate cards. These terms include bleed, black-and-white rates, color rates, full-color, premium position, and discounts. (See **Figure 19.1**, page 457.)

Bleed means that half- or full-page ads are printed to the very edge of the page, leaving no white border. Magazines generally charge between 15 to 20 percent extra for bleeds.

The lowest rates that magazines offer for display ads are black-and-white rates for black-and-white advertisements. Color rates are offered for color ads. Each time a magazine adds color to an ad, the rates increase. Four-color advertisements, also called full-color are the most expensive to buy.

Premium position refers to ad placement. Ads placed in premium spot, such as on the back cover or the inside of the first page, cost more.

Magazines quote display advertising rates by the color type and position of the advertisement. ***Why would a full-page, black and white ad cost more than a half-page full-color ad?***

ENGAGE

MEDIA RATES

Ask students what factors they think affect media rates. Students might suggest the different types of media, the time of day, the circulation, and so on. Tell students that there are a number of factors including geographical location that determine media rates. Ask these guiding questions to focus the discussion on media rates.

Guiding Questions

Identify What are the factors that affect rates?	open rate or noncontract rate, timing, location of ad, color, frequency, space
Distinguish What is the difference between classified ads and display ads?	Classified ads are word-only ads grouped into categories. Display ads use pictures and words and take up more space than classified ads.
Analyze Why would a business research rates for specific magazines?	For example: a motorcycle shop would advertise in a motorcycle magazine.

Critical Thinking

Understand Concepts Explain to students that advertising rates vary greatly, which makes it difficult to quote exact rates for each type of media advertising. Ask: ***How might you find this type of information?*** gathering a number of rates for each type of media Ask students to decide which type of newspaper advertising would best promote the following products or services. Possible answers:

- Puppies for sale (classified ad)
- Gardening help wanted (classified ad)
- New cars for sale (display ad)
- New apartment complex now renting (display ad)
- Scout leader wanted (classified ad)

EXPLORE

Graphic Organizer

Display this organizer. Ask students to name the factors that affect newspaper advertising rates. Then, have students provide facts about comparing newspaper advertising rates. Possible answers:

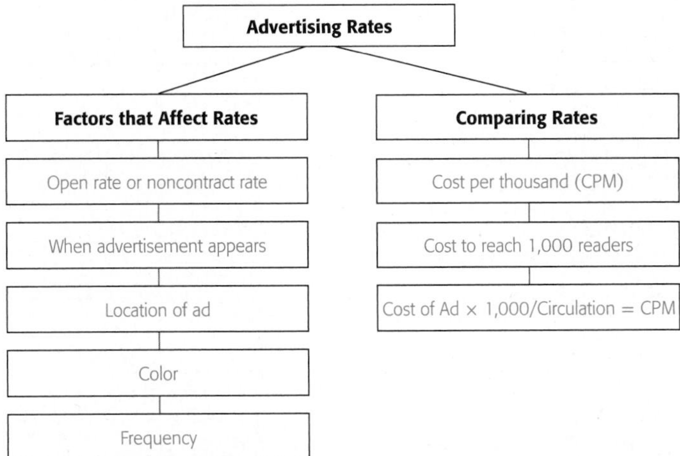

Advertising Rates
Factors that Affect Rates
Open rate or noncontract rate
When advertisement appears
Location of ad
Color
Frequency
Comparing Rates
Cost per thousand (CPM)
Cost to reach 1,000 readers
Cost of Ad × 1,000/Circulation = CPM

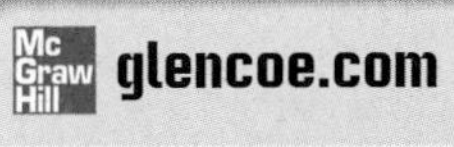

glencoe.com

iWB

Graphic Organizer Send students to the Online Learning Center to print this graphic organizer.

Mini Project

Extension

Online Advertising Have students find print ads for a particular product or service and then find a similar product or service advertised online. Have students create a T-chart in which they list similarities and differences between the ads. Lists should include such things as differences between the types of promotion and their effect on the audience. Ask students to share their lists with the class. If time allows, create a class list with input from the entire class.

MAGAZINE RATES

Ask students: ***Why might the rates to advertise in magazines be higher than the rates to advertise in newspapers?*** Magazines are typically not published as frequently as newspapers. The glossy paper used in magazines is more expensive than the paper used in newspapers. Then ask students these guiding questions to direct a discussion on ad rates in magazines.

Guiding Questions

Explain What is meant by premium position?	Premium position refers to ad placement. Ads placed in premium positions, such as the back cover, cost more.
Analyze Why might a customer choose to have a full-page with bleed rather than without?	Sample answers: the customer might not like the framed look of a full-page ad that does not bleed. Bleed pages look more modern and sophisticated.

Activate Prior Knowledge

Create an Advertisement Have students use the knowledge they have accumulated from the text to create an original advertisement for a product or service of their choice. They should take into consideration the target audience and choose an appropriate media in which to advertise. Have students share their finished advertisements with the class. Ask the class to identify the target audience and the media for the ad. Advertisements should contain as much detail as possible. Target audience and media should be identifiable.

Critical Thinking

Ask students: ***What is the total advertising cost for 8 inches per week of advertising in the Presque Isle County Advance Newspaper at the open rate of $5.80?*** $46.40 ($5.80 × 8 = $46.40) Now divide the class into pairs and have each member of the pair use the rate information provided to create additional problems. Have pairs exchange problems to solve.

Visual Literacy

Magazine Rates Caption Answer Read the caption question to students: ***When might a full-page, black and white ad cost more than a half-page full color ad?*** Ads are rated by black and white ads per size and color ads per size. If a full-page black and white ad is placed in a prime location, such as at the back cover or on the inside first page, it may cost more than a full color half-page ad.

RATE DISCOUNTS

Frequency discounts are offered to advertisers who run the same ad several times during the year. The magazine may publish an entire schedule of rates for the number of times during the year that an advertiser contracts to advertise. The rate per issue decreases as the frequency increases.

Another discount is a commission—a percentage of sales given by the magazine to the advertising agency for placing the ad for the advertiser. A typical commission is 15 percent.

Take a look at the rate card. You would calculate the cost of a full-page, four-color advertisement with bleed as follows:

$23,300	1 page, four-color rate
× .15	
$ 3,495	extra cost for bleed
$23,300	1 page, four-color rate
+ 3,495	
$26,795	for 1 page, four-color, with bleed

An ad agency placed the ad and it took the commission and the cash discount. The total cost of the above ad to the agency would be as follows:

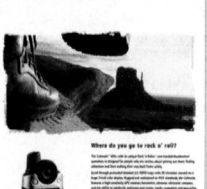

$26,795.00	1 page, four-color, with bleed
× .15	ad agency's commission
$ 4,019.25	
$ 26,795.00	1 page, four-color, with bleed
− 4,019.25	agency's commission
$ 22,775.75	net cost of ad to agency after commission
× .02	cash discount percentage if paid within 10 days of invoice
$ 455.52	cash discount
$22,775.75	net cost of ad to agency after commission
− 455.52	cash discount
$22,320.23	net cost to advertising agency for one full-page, four-color ad with bleed after cash discount and agency commission

As with newspapers, the CPM is used to compare the cost of advertising in several magazines. If a magazine has a circulation of 2 million and charges $35,000 for a full-page, black-and-white ad, the CPM would be $17.50.

$$\$35{,}000 \times 1{,}000/2{,}000{,}000 = \$17.50$$

A Premium Location

This ad appeared in a premium position of a consumer magazine—on the back cover. ***Why are higher rates charged for premium advertisements?***

INTERNET RATES

Internet advertising rates are based on the type of display format desired. Options include banner ads (mini, mid-page, vertical, horizontal, floating, expandable), rich-media ads, pop-up and pop-under ads. Online ad rates are set on a CPM rate based on page views. Rates vary based on the volume of monthly page views.

Additional online advertising options include paid listings at portal sites, sponsorship of Web sites, and newsletters sold on a flat-fee basis. Per-click rates are often used in search engine and opt-in e-mail advertisements.

Pay-for-sale advertising is another online option. It is used when e-marketers sign up other businesses to share a link or display ads. These businesses often sell related products. Commissions are paid to the other businesses as a percentage of sales only when sales are made through the affiliated link.

FIGURE 19.1 Magazine Rate Card

Ad rates are based on color. ***Based on this magazine rate card, what is the cost of a half-page, four-color ad paid in ten days from the issuance of the invoice?***

General Rates

RATE BASE: Rates based on a yearly average of 1,100,000 net paid A B C
A member of the Audit Bureau of Circulation

SPACE UNITS	BLACK & WHITE	BLACK & ONE COLOR	FOUR COLOR
1 page	$16,000	$19,630	$23,300
2 columns	11,620	14,560	18,170
½ page	10,130	13,550	17,200
1 column	5,920	9,530	12,180
½ column	3,020		
Covers			
Second Cover			$25,520
Third Cover			23,300
Fourth Cover			27,020

BLEED CHARGE: 15%
AGENCY COMMISSION: 15%
CASH DISCOUNT: 2% 10 days, net 30 days

Bleed accepted in color, black & white, and on covers, at an additional charge of 15%. No charge for gutter bleed in double-page spread.

Premium Positions: A 10% premium applies to advertising units positioned on pages 1, 2, and 3. A surcharge of 5% applies to bleed units in premium positions.

Rate Change Announcements will be made at least two months in advance of the black & white closing date for the issue affected. Orders for issues thereafter at rates then prevailing.

ISSUANCE AND CLOSING DATES

A. On sale date approximately the 15th of month preceding date of issue.

B. Black & white, black & one color, and four-color closing date, 20th of the 3rd month preceding date of issue. Example: Forms for August issue close May 20th.

C. **Orders for cover pages noncancellable. Orders for all inside advertising units are noncancellable 15 days prior to their respective closing dates.** Supplied inserts are noncancellable the 1st of the 4th month preceding month of issue. Options on cover positions must be exercised at least 30 days prior to four-color closing date. If order is not received by such date, cover option automatically lapses.

ENGAGE

RATE DISCOUNTS

Publishers have devised rate discounts to encourage advertisers to do repeat business with the magazine. Ask these guiding questions to focus the discussion about rate discounts.

Guiding Questions

Explain How does a frequency discount work?	The rate per issue decreases as the frequency of advertising increases.
Analyze How is a commission discount different from a frequency discount?	Frequency discounts are given to advertisers based on the number of times they advertise. Commissions are a percentage of sales given to an advertising agency for placing an ad.

Visual Literacy

A Premium Location Caption Answer Read the caption question to students: ***Why are higher rates charged for premium advertisements?*** Ads placed in premium positions get more attention from the readers. For example, if a reader does not look at an entire magazine, he or she will likely still see the advertisement on the back cover. Because advertisers can almost be certain that customers will see their ads placed in a premium location, they are charged more for the location.

Critical Thinking

After students have read the section on magazine rates, ask them to imagine that they are planning to run an ad in a popular teen magazine and want to get the best value for their advertising dollars. Have students answer these questions about their ad: What is the size of the ad? How many colors will be used? What is the ad's preferred position? Then have students explain their decisions. Students should recognize how the use of size, color, and position will affect the success of their ads.

EXPLORE

Visual Literacy

Figure 19.1 Caption Answer Read the caption question to students: ***Based on this magazine rate card, what is the cost of a half-page, four-color ad paid in ten days from the issuance of the invoice?*** $16,856 ($17,200 × .02 = 344; $17,200 – 344 = $16,856) Then ask these guiding questions about the magazine rate card.

Guiding Questions

Identify What is the cost of a half-page black and white ad?	$10,130
Calculate What is the difference between a one-page, four-color ad and half-page, four-color ad?	$6,100 ($23,300 – 17,200 = $6,100)
Draw Conclusions Based on the answer to the Calculate question above, what can you conclude about pricing?	The one-page, four-color ad is a better bargain than the half-page, four-color ad. You get twice the advertisement space for much less than twice the money.
Contrast What is the difference between the closing dates on the magazine rate card and the deadlines for the newspaper in the Figure 19.1 on page 457?	The magazine ads close three months before it is published, while the newspaper deadlines are only a few days in advance.

Reinforce Vocabulary

Review Definitions Write these terms for the class to view:

- **bleed** (half- or full-page ads are printed to the very edge of the page, leaving no white border)
- **black-and-white rates** (lowest magazine rates, offered for black-and-white advertisements)
- **color rates** (offered for color ads; each time a color is added, the price increases)
- **premium position** (ad placement such as the back cover or inside the front page)
- **discounts** (price breaks offered for running ads multiple times or a percentage of sales given to an advertising agency for placing an ad)

Ask students to use the terms in original sentences. Sentences will vary but should demonstrate an understanding of the terms.

e MARKETING

Online Interactive Advertising

Online interactive advertising gets customers and potential customers involved with a product or a company brand through active participation. The interactive experience has customers returning to a company's Web site over and over again. In some cases advertisers have partners that complement their brand involved in the unique experiences and/or prizes. For example, Mazda® partnered with "DriverVille," a virtual game where avatars race cars and win Driver Bucks that they can use to purchase virtual products for their cars. Mazda offers a mini-game within DriverVille, which is a digital version of Mazda Raceway.

Innovate and Create

Discuss the pros and cons of interactive advertising. Have students create an online interactive advertising campaign for a product or company of their choice. The aim of the interactive experience is to have customers involved for more than one day and to offer some type of reward for their participation. Suggest that students think of companies or social media platforms that complement their chosen product or company. The criteria for evaluating the students' interactive advertising campaigns should be: includes an interactive experience that is engaging so customers want to return; offers rewards; lasts for more than one day; is creative—has an interesting theme; and is realistic. The pros of interactive advertising are the excitement generated for the brand and long-term engagement of customers in the experience; thus keeping the brand in the forefront of the customer's mind and projecting a positive image for the brand. The cons are the additional expenses involved and the risk that the interactive experience may flop. If it is not successful and other companies were involved in the ad campaign, two or more companies may experience negative outcomes.

glencoe.com 

eMarketing Worksheet Activity Send students to the Online Learning Center to download an eMarketing worksheet activity.

RADIO RATES

When purchasing radio time, a business needs to decide what kind of radio advertising to use. There are three options: network radio advertising, national spot-radio advertising, and local radio advertising. It is important to know the difference between spot-radio and spot commercials. Spot radio refers to the geographical area an advertiser wants to reach with its advertising. Spot commercials are advertising messages of one minute or less that can be carried on network radio or spot radio.

Businesses with a national customer base usually choose network radio advertising or national spot-radio advertising. Network radio advertising is broadcast from a network studio to all affiliated radio stations throughout the country. Network radio advertising allows advertisers to broadcast ads, special programs, and radio talk shows simultaneously to several markets.

The following radio airtimes are listed from most expensive to least expensive:

- Class AA: Morning drive time: 6 A.M. to 10 A.M.
- Class A: Evening drive time: 4 P.M. to 7 P.M.
- Class B: Home worker time: 10 A.M. to 4 P.M.
- Class C: Evening time: 7 P.M. to midnight
- Class D: Nighttime: midnight to 6 A.M.

Rates are higher during early morning and late afternoon listening times, also called "drive times." Radio stations also offer less costly, run-of-schedule (ROS) airtimes. ROS airtime allows a radio station to decide when to run the ad. Weekday and weekend rates, weekly package plans, and discounts differ from station to station.

TELEVISION RATES

Advertising rates for television also vary with time of day. It is more expensive, for example, to advertise during the prime time hours of 7 P.M. to 10 P.M. than during other hours. The rates charged for other time slots, such as day (9 A.M. to 4 P.M.), late fringe (10:35 P.M. to 1:00 A.M.), or overnight (1 A.M. to 5 A.M.) are lower due to smaller numbers of viewers. Advertisers try to play their messages during the time slots that enable them to reach the most customers.

Reading Check

Infer Why is it virtually impossible to compare advertising rates from different media?

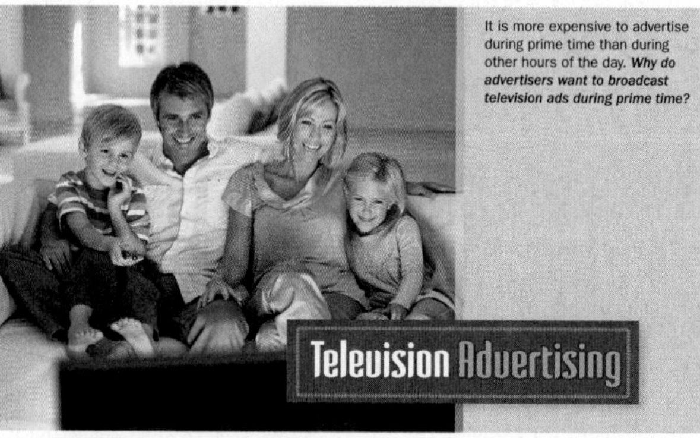

It is more expensive to advertise during prime time than during other hours of the day. ***Why do advertisers want to broadcast television ads during prime time?***

PROMOTIONAL BUDGET

The promotional budget considers not only the cost for developing and placing or airing advertising, but also the cost of staffing the department or advertising campaign. The advertiser must consider short- and long-term benefits of the effort. There are four common promotional budgeting methods:

1. **Percentage of Sales** In this method, the budget is based on a percentage of past or anticipated sales. For example, the current budget for advertising might be 5 percent of last year's sales, or 5 percent of projected sales for the coming season. In either case, the advertising budget is tied to figures that could be too high or too low for the current market condition.
2. **All You Can Afford** With this method, the business first pays all expenses, then applies the remainder of funds to promotional activities. This method is often used for only a short time. It is popular in small businesses. The **objective** is to build sales and reputation quickly.
3. **Following the Competition** With this method, an advertiser matches its competitor's promotional expenditures or prepares a budget based on the competitor's market share. A drawback is that it is based on only the competitor's objectives.
4. **Objective and Task** With this method, the company determines goals, identifies the steps to meet goals, and determines the cost for promotional activities to meet the goals. This is the most effective method because it focuses on the company's goals and how it will reach them.

After You Read Section 19.2

Review Key Concepts

1. **Contrast** possible ad rates for a small weekly newspaper with a large daily newspaper.
2. **Explain** how CPM determines the rates television and radio stations charge for advertising.
3. **Suggest** a reason that following the competition is not the best model for creating a promotional budget.

Practice Academics

English Language Arts

4. In the percentage-of-sales method, a business builds the advertising budget on a percentage of past or anticipated sales. Think of reasons this approach may not work in a slow economy. Create a brief dialogue between two or more members of a company who are discussing the use of this method in a slow economy.

NCTE 4 Use written language to communicate effectively.

Mathematics

5. What is CPM for a magazine that has a circulation of 1.7 million and charges $35,000 for a full-page, black-and-white advertisement?

Math Concept **Operations** The CPM is the cost per thousand, and is used to determine the cost of advertising per 1,000 people in an audience.

Starting Hints To solve this problem, multiply the cost of the ad by 1,000. Divide the number obtained from multiplying the cost by 1,000 by the total audience to determine the CPM.

NCTM Number and Operations Understand the meanings of operations and how they relate to one another.

For help, go to the **Math Skills Handbook** located at the back of this book.

glencoe.com Check your answers.

458 | Unit 6 · Promotion

Chapter 19 · Advertising | 459

ELABORATE

Reading Check Answer

Read the Reading Check question to students: ***Why is it virtually impossible to compare advertising rates from different media?*** For example, magazine rates are based on circulation, the type of readership, and production techniques. Internet advertising is based on the type of display format the customer desires such as banner ad, rich-media ads, pop-up ads, and so on.

Graphic Organizer

Acquire recordings of radio advertisements for four radio airtimes. After students have listened to all advertisements, conduct a class discussion. Ask questions such as: ***What types of products were advertised at the different times? Why do you think this is the case?*** different products are advertised at different times because of the number of listeners, some products may not be advertised during hours when children might be listening

Air Time	Product	Description
Class A		
Class B		
Class C		
Class D		

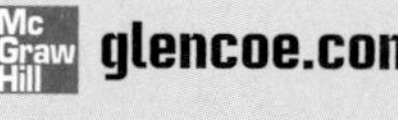

Graphic Organizer Send students to the Online Learning Center to print this graphic organizer.

EVALUATE

Critical Thinking

Divide the class into small groups to discuss the following questions: ***Why is using several different forms of media the best way to advertise a product or business?*** You have the potential to reach more people because not everyone uses all forms of media. If you rely on just one or two forms, you will miss potential customers. ***When might it be most effective and appropriate to use just one medium for all advertising?*** Small, local businesses might be better off using just one medium for advertising because of the expense and the local audience.

Graphic Organizer

Display this diagram. Ask students to name the four common promotional budgeting methods. Then ask: ***How would you describe each of the different methods?*** Percentage of Sale—based on a percentage of past or anticipated sales, tied to figures that could be too high or too low for current conditions; All You Can Afford—company pays all expenses first and applies the remainder to the promotional activities, popular in small businesses; Following the Competition—advertiser matches its competitor's promotional expenditures or prepares a budget based on the competitor's market share; Objective and Task—company determines goals, considers the necessary steps to meet goals, and determines the cost for promotional activities to meet the goals.

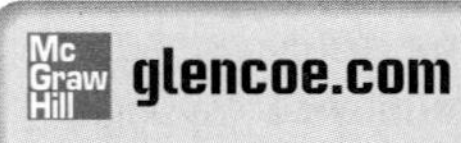

Graphic Organizer Send students to the Online Learning Center to print this graphic organizer.

After You Read Section 19.2

Review Key Concepts

1. With all things except circulation being equal, comparing rates using cost per thousand (CPM) measurement, it would cost less to advertise in a large daily newspaper. For example: Cost of ad for both papers = $500. Circulation for small weekly newspaper = 10,000. Circulation for large daily = 200,000. Calculate: small weekly newspaper ($500 × 1,000/10,000 = $50 per 1,000 readers. Large daily newspaper ($500 × 1,000/200,000 = $2.50.
2. CPM is the cost of exposing 1,000 viewers or listeners to an advertising impression. For television and radio, as the number of viewers or listeners increases, the cost of the advertising increases, so the CPM increases.
3. Possible answer: The competition's goals may be very different than your goals. Following the competition's advertising will likely not help you reach your goals.

Practice Academics

English Language Arts

4. The percentage of sales method is based upon sales. If sales are down, this method might be counterproductive, since less money is spent on advertising. Advertising activities tends to boost sales. This method allocates less money on advertising when more advertising activities should occur to increase sales.

Mathematics

5. $20.59 ($35,000 × 1,000 ÷ 1,700,000 = $20.588 = $20.59)

Answer Key Send students to the Online Learning Center to check their answers.

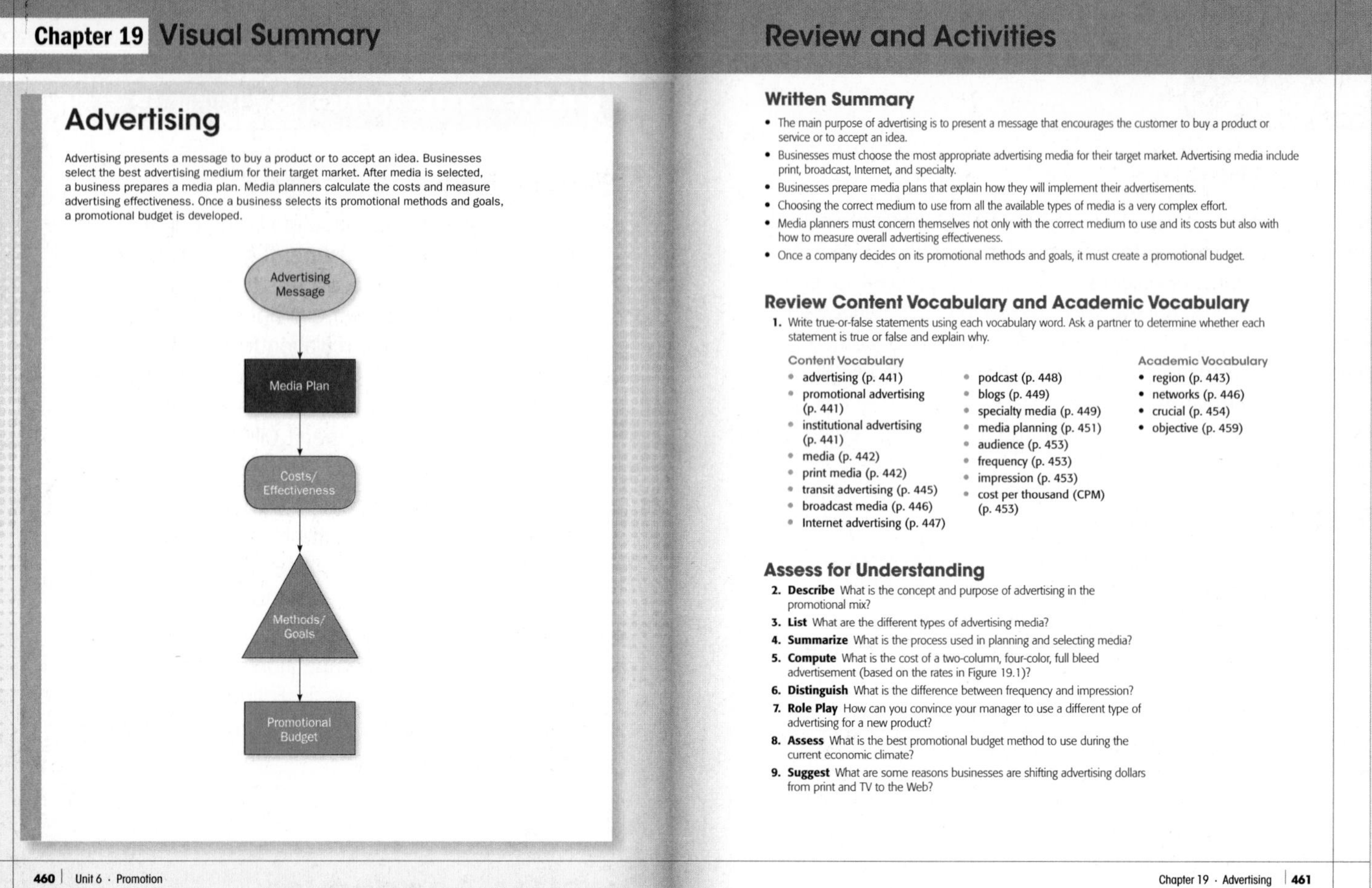
Chapter 19 Visual Summary

Advertising

Advertising presents a message to buy a product or to accept an idea. Businesses select the best advertising medium for their target market. After media is selected, a business prepares a media plan. Media planners calculate the costs and measure advertising effectiveness. Once a business selects its promotional methods and goals, a promotional budget is developed.

460 | Unit 6 · Promotion

Review and Activities

Written Summary

- The main purpose of advertising is to present a message that encourages the customer to buy a product or service or to accept an idea.
- Businesses must choose the most appropriate advertising media for their target market. Advertising media include print, broadcast, Internet, and specialty.
- Businesses prepare media plans that explain how they will implement their advertisements.
- Choosing the correct medium to use from all the available types of media is a very complex effort.
- Media planners must concern themselves not only with the correct medium to use and its costs but also with how to measure overall advertising effectiveness.
- Once a company decides on its promotional methods and goals, it must create a promotional budget.

Review Content Vocabulary and Academic Vocabulary

1. Write true-or-false statements using each vocabulary word. Ask a partner to determine whether each statement is true or false and explain why.

Content Vocabulary
- advertising (p. 441)
- promotional advertising (p. 441)
- institutional advertising (p. 441)
- media (p. 442)
- print media (p. 442)
- transit advertising (p. 445)
- broadcast media (p. 446)
- Internet advertising (p. 447)
- podcast (p. 448)
- blogs (p. 449)
- specialty media (p. 449)
- media planning (p. 451)
- audience (p. 453)
- frequency (p. 453)
- impression (p. 453)
- cost per thousand (CPM) (p. 453)

Academic Vocabulary
- region (p. 443)
- networks (p. 446)
- crucial (p. 454)
- objective (p. 459)

Assess for Understanding

2. **Describe** What is the concept and purpose of advertising in the promotional mix?
3. **List** What are the different types of advertising media?
4. **Summarize** What is the process used in planning and selecting media?
5. **Compute** What is the cost of a two-column, four-color, full bleed advertisement (based on the rates in Figure 19.1)?
6. **Distinguish** What is the difference between frequency and impression?
7. **Role Play** How can you convince your manager to use a different type of advertising for a new product?
8. **Assess** What is the best promotional budget method to use during the current economic climate?
9. **Suggest** What are some reasons businesses are shifting advertising dollars from print and TV to the Web?

Chapter 19 · Advertising | 461

EVALUATE

Visual Summary

Express Creativity Ask students to develop their own visual summary of a concept in the chapter. Encourage students to use different formats for their visual summaries, such as a storyboard, a timeline, a table, a tree diagram, or a word web. Visual summaries will vary depending on the concept depicted. Questions to ask when assessing a visual summary include:

- Is the summary clear, economical, and simple?
- Are any important steps left out?
- Are steps or concepts arranged in the same order as the original?
- Does the summary reveal a pattern that connects the details?
- Does the summary locate and highlight the most important information?

Review Content Vocabulary and Academic Vocabulary

1. **Advertising** promotes ideas, goods, or services through media. (T) There are only two types of advertising, **promotional advertising** and **institutional advertising**. (F These are two main types of advertising.) **Print media** is one of many types of **media** used to convey advertising messages to the public. (T) **Transit advertising** is seen on public transportation. (T) Radio and television are considered **Internet advertising**. (F They are **broadcast advertising**.) **Podcasts** and **blogs** are personal Web sites. (F Blogs are personal Web sites, podcasts are brief digital broadcasts.) **Specialty media** includes giveaways and advertising specialties. (T) **Media planning** is one method used to achieve marketing objectives. (T) The **audience** is a single exposure to an advertising message. (F An impression is a single exposure.) The number of people exposed to an ad is the **frequency**. (F The number of people is the audience.) **Impression** is the number of times an audience sees an advertisement. (F Frequency is the number of times an audience sees an ad.) **Cost per thousand** is the media measurement cost exposing 1,000 readers/viewers to an advertising impression. (T) Advertisers target a specific **region**, sometimes by using one of the major **networks**. (T) A promotional budget is **crucial** to meeting advertising **objectives.** (T)

EVALUATE

Assess for Understanding

2. Advertising is any paid form of nonpersonal promotion of ideas, goods, or services by an identified sponsor. The purpose of advertising is to sell products, services or ideas to a targeted audience.

3. Types of advertising media include: print media, broadcast media, online media, specialty media, and other media.

4. Selection of media involves the use of media planning software, media cost data, and audience information. To determine the right media to use a business must insure that the media presents the desired product and business image; the proper audience is targeted, and the medium gets the desired results.

5. \$20.59 is the cost per thousand—CPM [35,000 × 1,000 = 35,000,000 ÷ 1,700,000 = 20.588 = \$20.59]

6. *Frequency* is the number of times an audience sees or hears an advertisement. An *impression* is a single exposure to an advertising message.

7. To convince your manager to use a different type of advertising for a new product, you must first have positive answers to these questions: Can the medium present the product and the appropriate business image? Can the desired customers be targeted with the medium? Will the medium get the desired response rate?

8. While answers may vary, the objective and task method is the most effective in any economic climate because it focuses on the company's goals and how it will reach them.

9. Businesses are switching from print and TV for a variety of reasons. Acceptable answers include: online media target a specific audience, allow for customer interaction, provide for better tracking of the message (number of visitors can be recorded); and different formats, such as rich media and streamed videos can be incorporated into the ads. These advantages are often obtained at a lower cost per thousand than TV and newspaper advertising.

Chapter 19 Review and Activities

21st Century Skills

Communication Skills

10. **Interview** Contact and schedule an interview with the owner or manager of a local business. Identify the types of advertising used by the business. You must develop an introduction to use before the interview, an interview script, a one-page summary of the answers, and a thank-you letter after the interview.

Financial Literacy Skills

11. **Click-Through** Internet advertising rates are based on the type of display format the customer wants. Ads rates are normally based upon the number of viewer click-throughs per thousand. Calculate the number of impressions for each of these ads:

Type of Ad	Click-Through Rate	Number of Impressions/thousand
Expandable banner	0.3 percent	
Floating Ad	5.0 percent	
Floating expandable	1.4 percent	
Push-down banner	0.3 percent	

Everyday Ethics

12. **Texting and Driving** Mobile technology may be lethal—at least on the road. A nationwide study reports that nearly 6,000 people were victims of drivers who were distracted by using cell phones and other similar devices. The U.S. Transportation Secretary said it is "an epidemic, and it seems to be getting worse each year." Make a list of three basic rules for drivers who have these devices. Write a public service announcement (PSA) for radio, highlighting your rules.

e-Marketing Skills

13. **Social Networking** Imagine that you work for a company that is considering purchasing a business page on a social-networking Web site. Conduct research on the concept of social networking and personal blogs. You have been asked to summarize your findings. Include the following in your report:
   - List the benefits of having a business page on a social network Web site.
   - Identify some disadvantages of social networks and personal blogs.

Build Academic Skills

English Language Arts

14. **Communication Skills** Some television content is developed for babies and toddlers. Parents may be tempted to use TV viewing as an electronic babysitter, as there are so many children's TV shows, DVDs, and videos available. Conduct research on responsible ways to handle television viewing. Create a public service announcement that gives parents tips for how to watch TV with young children.

NCTE 8 Use information resources to gather information and create and communicate knowledge.

Science

15. **Science and Technology** Some people believe that Internet advertising and online shopping has advantages for protecting the environment. Develop a one-page outline with broad topic headings, such as "Energy," "Resources," and "Social Benefits." List some possible ways to save valuable resources or recycle them as a result of using Internet advertising versus print advertising.

NSES E Develop abilities of technological design, understandings about science and technology.

Mathematics

16. **CPM Calculations** Calculate the CPM for an ad that costs $12,000 in a magazine that has a circulation of 8,500,000 people. (Round your answer to the nearest cent.)

NCTM Number and Operations Compute fluently and make reasonable estimates.

Math Concept **Computation** Computing the CPM for ads in certain publications involves multiplication and division.

For help, go to the **Math Skills Handbook** located at the back of this book.

Standardized Test Practice

Directions Read the following questions. On a separate sheet of paper, write the best possible answer for each one.

1. Which of the following is a type of media that includes advertising in newspapers, magazines, and direct mail?
   A. Broadcast media
   B. Online media
   C. Print media
   D. Specialty media
2. The number of homes or people exposed to an advertising message is called the "frequency."
   T
   F
3. The media cost of exposing 1,000 readers or viewers to an advertising impression is known as the ________.

Test-Taking Tip
Concentration can reduce anxiety when you are taking a test. Pay close attention to one question at a time.

DECA Connection Role Play

Owner
Paint and Wallpaper Store

Situation Your store will open for business in one month. It is located in the downtown area of a mid-sized town. The population of your trade area is a mix of young professionals without children and families with young children.

Your store will stock paints manufactured by a national company that is known for its high quality and wide variety of colors. Your stock will also include wallpaper produced by high-quality manufacturers who make both traditional and contemporary wallpaper designs. You will also sell all the accessories and tools necessary for both professionals and amateurs to complete their projects.

You want your store to have a successful start. You know that you must let potential customers know about your store and the merchandise you sell. You are thinking about launching a small advertising campaign to introduce your store. Your promotional budget is limited. You must plan carefully and get the most from your advertising dollars. You are planning to meet with a friend (judge) who has much experience in advertising to ask for guidance and advice.

Activity Make notes about your ideas for a small advertising campaign to introduce the store. List the objectives of the campaign and several types of advertising media you are considering. You will discuss your ideas with your friend (judge).

Evaluation You will be evaluated on how well you meet the following performance indicators:

1. Explain types of advertising media.
2. Analyze a sales promotional plan.
3. Develop an advertising campaign.
4. Calculate media costs.
5. Prepare a promotional budget.

glencoe.com

Download the Competitive Events Workbook for more Role-Play practice.

EVALUATE

Communication Skills

10. Students' answers should include the following: name of the business, a strategy to contact and schedule an interview, a description of the advertising media used, an introduction to use before the interview, an interview script, a one-page summary of the answers, and a thank you letter.

Financial Literacy Skills

11.

Type of Ad	Click-through Rate	Number of Impressions/thousand
Expandable banner	0.3 percent	3/1,000 (.003 × 1,000)
Floating Ad	5.0 percent	50/1,000 (.05 × 1,000)
Floating expandable	1.4 percent	14/1,000 (.014 × 1,000)
Push-down banner	0.3 percent	3/1,000 (.003 × 1,000)

Everyday Ethics

12. Rules will vary but may include: Do not talk on your cell phone while driving unless you have a hands-free set. Do not make calls on your cell phone while driving if it involves dialing a number. Do not text while driving, ever! Public service announcements should highlight the rules in an interesting and possibly entertaining way.

e-Marketing Skills

13. Benefits: Membership on a social network such as Twitter®, MySpace®, and Facebook® can allow companies opportunities to interact with their target audience, help develop advertising messages, create customer profiles, develop sales leads, provide special offers, and maintain customer feedback about the image and performance of their products. Disadvantages: the possibility of stories and experiences on social networks and blogs that might give a negative image of the company and its products, false or misleading information can travel like a virus and cause short- and long-term harm to a company.

EVALUATE

Build Academic Skills

English Language Arts

14. Some possible responses are: Watch TV with your children, remove TVs from kids' bedrooms; limit parental viewing time as an example for children; set limits on the amount of viewing allowed; use common sense on what types of material children watch; discuss TV programs with children to be sure they understand what they are watching; answer questions children may have about the content of the programs.

Science

15. Outlines may include topics such as: reduction in greenhouse gases since less energy is used for transportation to stores; reduction in the amount of paper used for advertising in newspapers and magazines (fewer trees consumed); less money spent on advertising, which possibly could be re-directed to socially responsible business practices.

Mathematics

16. $1.41 ([$12,000 × 1,000] ÷ 8,500,000 = $1.41)

Standardized Test Practice

1. C Print media
2. False (It is called the audience.)
3. Cost per thousand (CPM)

DECA Connection Role Play

Evaluations will be based on these performance indicators:

1. **Explain types of advertising media.** Print media: newspapers, magazines, direct-mail, directory, outdoor, and transit. Broadcast media: television and radio advertising. Internet advertising: opt-in e-mail ads, banner and search engine ads, rich-media and video ads, and social-media advertising. Specialty media, or giveaways, are relatively inexpensive useful items featuring an advertiser's name or logo. Other advertising media includes in-store ads and new media, which utilize iPods®, cell phones, laptops, and video games.
2. **Analyze a sales promotional plan.** Use the Cost Per Thousand (CPM) to compare the cost of reaching 1,000 readers in print media and CPM to compare the cost of reaching viewer or listeners in broadcast media. You can also use CPM to determine the cost of reaching potential customers who use Internet media.
3. **Develop an advertising campaign.** Advertising campaigns will vary but students should consider which types of media to use in their advertising campaign—print, broadcast, Internet, specialty, in-store or new media. They should also develop a budget for their campaign.
4. **Calculate media costs.** In newspapers the cost to advertise depends on whether the ad is a display or classified. Display ad rate are based on column inches. If an ad measures 20 column inches and the rate per column inch is $5.00, the ad would cost $100 (20 x $5). Magazine rates are quoted in black and white with increase rates for each color added. For newspapers and magazines rates for premium positions are higher.
5. **Prepare a promotional budget.** In preparing the budget, students should consider the cost of staffing the advertising campaign as well as the cost for developing and placing or airing advertising. Students should also consider one: percentage of sales, all you can afford, following the competition, and objective and task.

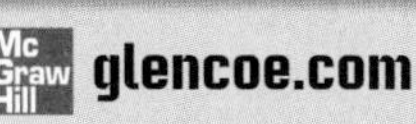

Role Plays For more DECA Role Plays, send students to the Online Learning Center to download the Competitive Events Workbook.

print advertisements

SHOW WHAT YOU KNOW

Visual Literacy Print advertisements have the ability to attract attention and help sell goods and services. Writing style, design, and the images in ads depend on the product and where the print ad appears. ***Think of a print ad you have seen recently. What makes it effective?***

Discovery Project

The Print Advertisement

Essential Question What key components make a print advertisement effective?

Project Goal

You and a classmate are employed at a sporting goods store. You and your partner must design a print advertisement for a product offered by the store. Your ad must include a headline, advertising copy, an illustration, and a signature. Develop your print advertisement and prepare a brief class presentation explaining the reasons for its design and why you believe the ad is effective.

Ask Yourself...

- What is your product and its target market?
- What will your headline and advertising copy say?
- What will your illustration and signature look like?
- How will you design the advertisement and organize your presentation?

Analyze What type of print advertisement will best attract your target audience?

glencoe.com

Activity
Get a worksheet activity about designing print ads.

Evaluate
Download a rubric you can use to evaluate your project.

DECA Connection

DECA Event Role Play

Concepts in this chapter are related to DECA competitive events that involve either an interview or role play.

Performance Indicators The performance indicators represent key skills and knowledge. Your key to success in DECA competitive events is relating them to concepts in this chapter.

- Explain the components of advertisements.
- Explain the importance of coordinating elements in advertisements.
- Explain the nature of effective written communication.
- Edit and revise written work consistent with professional standards.
- Orient new employees.

DECA Prep

Role Play Practice role-playing with the DECA Connection competitive-event activity at the end of this chapter. More information on DECA events can be found on DECA's Web site.

ENGAGE

Visual Literacy

Read the chapter opener photo caption question to students: ***Think of a print ad you have seen recently. What makes it effective?*** Students may mention one or all of the four elements of an advertisement—layout, color, typeface, and type size. They may suggest that any one of these elements or a combination of these elements is what makes the ad effective. Ask these guiding questions to focus the discussion about advertising.

Guiding Questions

List What types of advertising make up print advertising?	newspaper, magazine, direct-mail, directory, outdoor, and transit
Evaluate What are some advantages of advertising in a newspaper?	Because a newspaper's distribution is known, advertisers can target their advertising to people living in certain areas or with certain interests. Responses to newspaper ads and coupon sales are dated and easily tracked.

Discovery Project

The Print Advertisement Ask students where they typically see print advertisements. Students may mention newspaper, magazine, direct-mail, directory, outdoor, and transit ads. Then ask them the Discovery Project Essential Question: ***What key components make a print advertisement effective?*** Answers will vary but may include layout, color, typeface, and type size, all of which are important to making a print ad effective (logo). They might also mention headline, copy, illustrations, and signature as important parts to an effective ad. Ask students to share what they typically look at first when viewing a print ad. Students might suggest the headline, illustrations, copy, or the signature.

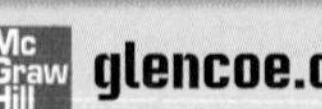

glencoe.com

Discovery Project Resources Send students to the Online Learning Center to download a rubric to evaluate their projects.

ENGAGE

Introduce the Chapter

Chapter 20 provides an in-depth look at print advertising. These main concepts are introduced and discussed:

- Advertising campaigns
- Advertising agencies
- Headlines
- Copy
- Illustrations
- Signatures
- Layout
- Color
- Typeface
- Type size

Discussion Starter

Tell students that as a member of a marketing team, they might be asked their opinion about various aspects of an advertising campaign that is in development. Ask: ***What elements contribute to effective print advertisements?*** Students may suggest headline, copy, illustrations, signature, layout, color, typeface, or type size. Now list common consumer products or the names of national chain retailers for the class to read and ask: ***What advertising have you seen that promotes these products or stores?*** Students may mention print ads in newspapers or magazines, or television ads. Ask: ***What brands do you associate with memorable advertising campaigns?*** Answers will vary but should include well-known brands or products that are heavily advertised.

DECA Connection

Discuss the performance indicators listed in the DECA Connection feature. Explain to students that performance indicators tell them how to demonstrate their acquired skills and knowledge through individual or team competitive events.

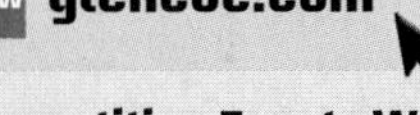

Competitive Events Workbook For more DECA Role Plays, send students to the Online Learning Center to download the Competitive Events Workbook.

PRINT RESOURCES

- **Student Edition**
- **Teacher Edition**
- **Student Activity Workbook with Academic Integration** includes worksheets and activities correlated to the text.
- **Mathematics for Marketing Workbook** provides math activities for every unit in the text.

TECHNOLOGY TOOLBOX

- **Connect**
- **ConnectPlus**
- **ExamView Assessment Suite** is a comprehensive solution for creating, administering, and scoring tests.

Online Learning Center provides a variety of resources to enrich and enhance learning.

SECTION, CHAPTER, AND UNIT RESOURCES

- **Graphic Organizers** for organizing text concepts visually.
- **Digital Nation Activities** and **Green Marketer Activities** extend learning beyond the text features.
- **Career Chatroom Career Profiles** allow students to explore different marketing occupations in depth.
- **After You Read Answer Keys** for students to check their answers.
- **Discovery Project Rubrics** and **Marketing Internship Project Rubrics** for students to evaluate their projects.

PROGRAM RESOURCES

- **Student Activity Workbook with Academic Integration Teacher Annotated Edition** includes annotated answers for the activities and worksheets.
- **Marketing Research Project Workbook** provides a step-by-step approach for students to complete their own marketing research studies.
- **School-to-Career Activity Workbook** helps students relate their class work to on-the-job experience and involves work-site analysis and working with mentors.
- **Competitive Events Workbook** helps prepare students for state and national marketing education competitions.
- **Inclusion in the Marketing Education Classroom** provides teaching resources for working with students with special needs.
- **PowerPoint Presentations** provides visual teaching aids and assessments for this chapter.

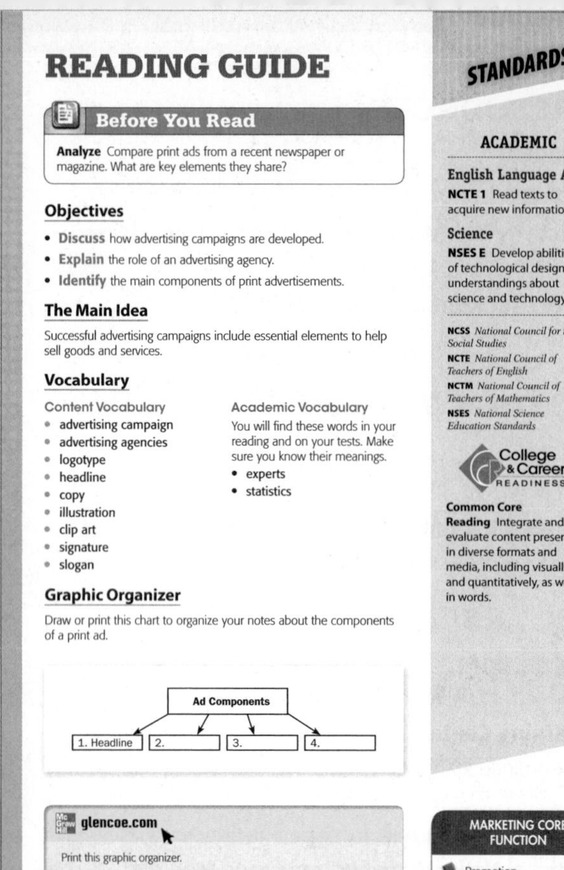

READING GUIDE

Before You Read

Analyze Compare print ads from a recent newspaper or magazine. What are key elements they share?

Objectives

- **Discuss** how advertising campaigns are developed.
- **Explain** the role of an advertising agency.
- **Identify** the main components of print advertisements.

The Main Idea

Successful advertising campaigns include essential elements to help sell goods and services.

Vocabulary

Content Vocabulary

- advertising campaign
- advertising agencies
- logotype
- headline
- copy
- illustration
- clip art
- signature
- slogan

Academic Vocabulary

You will find these words in your reading and on your tests. Make sure you know their meanings.

- experts
- statistics

Graphic Organizer

Draw or print this chart to organize your notes about the components of a print ad.

Ad Components: 1. Headline | 2. | 3. | 4.

glencoe.com

Print this graphic organizer.

STANDARDS

ACADEMIC

English Language Arts

NCTE 1 Read texts to acquire new information.

Science

NSES E Develop abilities of technological design, understandings about science and technology.

NCSS *National Council for the Social Studies*
NCTE *National Council of Teachers of English*
NCTM *National Council of Teachers of Mathematics*
NSES *National Science Education Standards*

College & Career READINESS

Common Core
Reading Integrate and evaluate content presented in diverse formats and media, including visually and quantitatively, as well as in words.

MARKETING CORE FUNCTION

Promotion

466 | Unit 6 · Promotion

Section 20.1

Elements of Advertising

THE ADVERTISING CAMPAIGN

To advertise a product or service, a company must plan an advertising campaign. An **advertising campaign** is a group of advertisements, commercials, and related promotional materials and activities that are designed as part of a coordinated advertising plan to meet the specific goals of a company.

An advertising campaign involves the creation and coordination of a series of advertisements placed in various types of media. Broadcast, print, Internet, outdoor, and specialty advertisements are organized around a particular theme. The theme of an advertising campaign is the central message that a company hopes to communicate to potential customers. The theme can be used to promote a specific product or service or a mix of the company's various products and services.

> "To advertise a product or service, a company must plan an advertising campaign."

The size and the financial resources of a business determine whether an advertising campaign is developed by an in-house advertising department, a few designated individuals, or an advertising agency. Advertising agencies from outside the company can be full-service or limited-service. These distinctions indicate the agency's level of involvement in the creation and production of the advertisement. Regardless of how it is developed, an advertising campaign should be part of a promotional effort that includes personal selling, public relations, and sales promotion.

Planning an integrated advertising campaign involves a series of steps:

1. **Identify the target audience** Advertisers analyze the market for a product or service and determine which potential customers should receive messages.
2. **Determine objectives** An advertiser identifies the objectives, such as increasing brand awareness or sales, changing customer attitudes, or increasing knowledge about the product.
3. **Establish the budget** Advertisers decide what to spend on advertising over a set period of time. It is important to make sure that advertising dollars are spent as effectively as possible.
4. **Develop the message** Advertisers develop the overall theme and messages based on the features, benefits, and uses of a particular product or service. The message can also be used to highlight a company's unique mix of products and services.
5. **Select the media** The target audience and available funds determine the best media to use, such as TV, radio, Internet, or print. Selections are based upon which media will have the best chance to reach the target audience and stay within the budget.
6. **Evaluate the campaign** Advertisers use market research to see if the campaign met its objectives and if the advertising messages were well received. Metrics, such as improvement in sales, increases in sales leads, and response rates for direct mail may be used to determine if a print advertising campaign was successful.

As You Read

Reflect What elements of graphic design have you noticed in ads?

Chapter 20 · Print Advertisements | 467

ENGAGE

Anticipation Activity

Improving Student Achievement Have students choose a familiar product, and then have them imagine a new product based on the familiar product. Tell students to choose a name for the new product and develop an idea for a print advertisement that includes a photo or illustration, copy, and a catchy slogan. Have them draw a layout of the advertisement. Then ask volunteers to share their advertisements.

Objectives

- **Discuss** how advertising campaigns are developed. Identify the target audience, determine objectives, establish the budget, develop the message, select the media, evaluate the campaign.
- **Explain** the role of an advertising agency. Agencies set objectives, develop advertising messages and strategies, complete media plans, select media, and coordinate sales promotion and public relations
- **Identify** the main components of print advertisements. headline, copy illustrations, and signature

Graphic Organizer

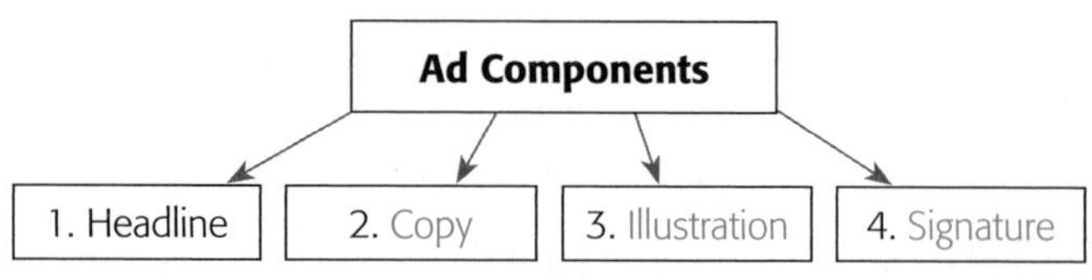

glencoe.com

iWB

Graphic Organizer Send students to the Online Learning Center to print this graphic organizer.

EXPLORE

Before You Read

Read the Before You Read question aloud: ***Compare print ads from a recent newspaper or magazine. What are key elements they share?*** Students may recognize that the ads all contain headlines, copy, illustrations, and a signature. Ask: ***Which element(s) do you find most interesting? Why?*** Answers will vary but should include an explanation of why they find the element(s) interesting. Sample answer: I like the way the car is photographed because it emphasizes the unique lines and details.

Preteaching Vocabulary

Have students go to the Online Learning Center at glencoe.com for the Chapter 20 Preteaching Vocabulary games.

Content Vocabulary

Tell students to write a paragraph in which they discuss how the Content Vocabulary terms are interrelated. Sample paragraph: Advertising campaigns are often created and developed by advertising agencies. Print ads developed as part of a campaign typically include elements such as logotypes, headlines, copy, illustrations, signatures, and slogans. Illustrations are generally made up of photos, drawings, or clip art. Ask volunteers to share their paragraphs with the rest of the class.

Academic Vocabulary

Experts—Usage Divide the class into small groups and have them develop lists of experts. Lists can include trades people such as plumbers, electricians, and carpenters or professionals such as Web site designers, computer programmers, doctors, dentists, and lawyers. After groups develop their lists, work together as a class to combine the lists into one class list. Ask: ***What is it that makes these people experts?*** They have a great amount of knowledge and skill in their particular area.

Statistics—Usage Ask students: ***How have you heard the term* statistics *used?*** Some may say that they have heard it used to describe numbers that track situations such as baseball or basketball statistics. Tell students that statistics are often used in advertising to make a point.

MINI CLIP

ELL: Previewing a Text
Go to the Online Learning Center for a video in which a teacher points out strategies to increase comprehension.

Elements of Advertising

THE ADVERTISING CAMPAIGN

Tell students that the right advertising campaign can make a product successful. Ask these guiding questions to focus the discussion.

Guiding Questions

Identify What are the steps involved in planning an integrated advertising campaign?	(1) Identify the target audience; 2) Determine objectives; (3) Establish the budget; (4) Develop the message; (5) Select the media; (6) Evaluate the campaign
Explain What determines whether an advertising campaign is developed in-house or by an advertising agency?	The size and financial resources of a business determine where and how the advertising campaign is developed.
Analyze Why is it important to analyze an advertising campaign?	Students should recognize that analysis is important so the company can know the effectiveness of the campaign.

As You Read

Read students the As You Read question: ***What elements of graphic design have you noticed in ads?*** Successful ads contain a headline, copy, illustrations, a signature, a slogan, and disclosures and use color and layout to attract attention.

Expert Advice

Read the quote to students:

> **"To advertise a product or service, a company must plan an advertising campaign."**

Ask students: ***What might happen if a company came out with a new product but did not advertise it?*** The product would not sell because no one would know about it, and the company would lose money because they wouldn't have paying customers to make up for what was spent on developing or manufacturing the product.

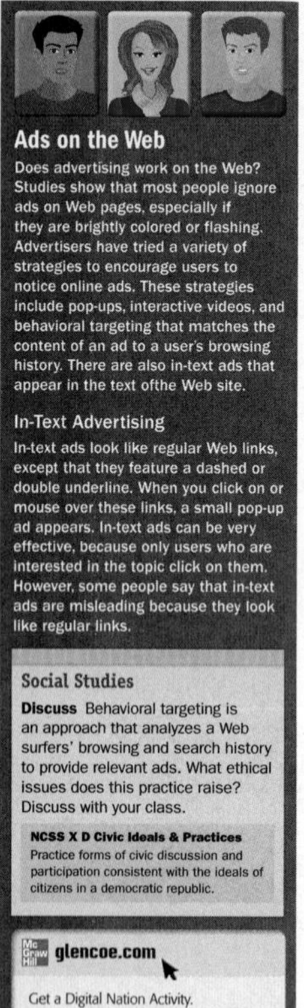

DIGITAL NATION

Ads on the Web

Does advertising work on the Web? Studies show that most people ignore ads on Web pages, especially if they are brightly colored or flashing. Advertisers have tried a variety of strategies to encourage users to notice online ads. These strategies include pop-ups, interactive videos, and behavioral targeting that matches the content of an ad to a user's browsing history. There are also in-text ads that appear in the text ofthe Web site.

In-Text Advertising

In-text ads look like regular Web links, except that they feature a dashed or double underline. When you click on or mouse over these links, a small pop-up ad appears. In-text ads can be very effective, because only users who are interested in the topic click on them. However, some people say that in-text ads are misleading because they look like regular links.

Social Studies

Discuss Behavioral targeting is an approach that analyzes a Web surfers' browsing and search history to provide relevant ads. What ethical issues does this practice raise? Discuss with your class.

NCSS X D Civic Ideals & Practices Practice forms of civic discussion and participation consistent with the ideals of citizens in a democratic republic.

glencoe.com

Get a Digital Nation Activity.

ADVERTISING AGENCIES

Advertising agencies are independent businesses that specialize in developing ad campaigns and crafting the ads for clients. Depending on the scope and size of the advertising campaign and the needs of the business, agencies can serve as a full-service agency or a limited-service agency. There are also new models that advertising agencies can follow.

Types of Advertising Agencies

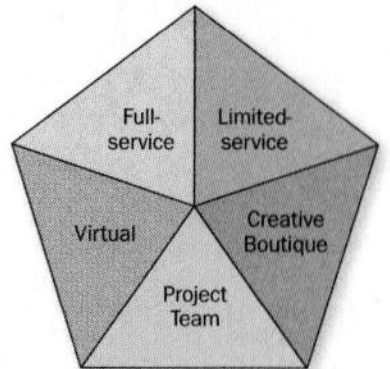

Full-service agencies plan an entire advertising campaign by setting objectives, developing advertising messages and strategies, and completing media plans. They also select media and coordinate related activities such as sales promotion and public relations.

Larger businesses often select a full-service agency to be the agency of record to handle all aspects of the campaign. The agency of record does all the necessary research, media selection, copy development, and artwork. Advertising agencies employ specialists, such as copywriters, graphic artists, media **experts**, marketing researchers, and legal advisers to help with the development and execution of campaigns.

Limited-service agencies specialize in one aspect of the campaign, such as creative services, media planning, or media buying for an advertising campaign. Larger companies are increasingly selecting specialists, such as those who concentrate only on Internet advertising, to develop different aspects of an advertising campaign. Global consumer brands also make use of specialty agencies to develop or tailor campaigns to specific countries, ethnic groups, or other target markets.

Technology and e-commerce opportunities have led many businesses to employ in-house staff for some advertising functions, such as Web-site development and maintenance. Some companies assist in-house resources with the work of freelance professionals or limited-service agencies.

NEW MODELS FOR ADVERTISING AGENCIES

Some new models for advertising agencies include several business formats. They are creative boutiques, project team agencies, and virtual agencies.

A creative boutique is a specialized service agency that helps businesses with creative production. In a creative boutique, the advertiser develops the message and copy but outsources the design and production of the advertisement. This type of organization enables the advertiser to create ads more quickly than a traditional agency could.

Agencies that are organized around a project team provide research, copywriting, creative execution, and media placement without the overhead of a larger agency. Teams can come together to do one project, and then move on to the next when the ad campaign is complete.

In a virtual agency, one individual coordinates the work of a network of experienced freelancers. A freelancer is a self-employed person who sells work or services by the hour, day, or job, rather than working on a regular salary basis for one employer. One of the benefits of this type of agency is that the agency has lower overhead expenses, which means lower costs for the client.

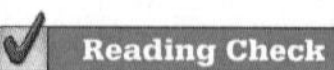

Reading Check

Recall What are the types of advertising agencies?

DEVELOPING PRINT ADVERTISEMENTS

Although they are only one part of an advertising campaign, print advertisements are very important to most campaigns. Print advertisements have four key elements: headline, copy, illustrations, and signature (see **Figure 20.1** on page 470).

Some advertisements also include a company's slogan, logo, and, if required, product disclosures. A **logotype** or logo is a graphic symbol for a company, brand, or organization. It can be used separately or in combination with a signature.

Ads that must include mandatory disclosures, terms, and conditions may display them on the bottom of a print advertisement. For example, a car or truck ad that advertises better gas mileage must disclose the Environmental Protection Agency's (EPA) estimated mileage at the bottom of the ad.

WORLD MARKET

SOUTH AFRICA

Gems

The ancient Greeks valued them as the "tears of the Gods." People in the Dark Ages swallowed them to cure illness. Medieval knights wore them under their armor for protection. Diamonds have been prized for thousands of years. Today's advertisers promote diamonds with an appeal to emotions and the excitement of spectacular discoveries.

African Treasure South Africa supplies half the global demand for diamonds. It also claims some of the world's rarest diamonds. A seven-carat, flawless blue diamond was unearthed in its Cullinan mine in 2008. It sold for a record $9.5 million. In 1905, it produced the largest diamond ever found. Experts cut more than 100 diamonds from this massive gemstone, including the Great Star of Africa and the Lesser Star of Africa. Both are part of the British Crown Jewels.

Science

Compare Imagine you are working for an advertising agency. You are working with a company that sells natural diamonds. Research the differences between natural diamonds and synthetic diamonds. Create an ad that features this distinction.

NSES A Develop abilities necessary to do scientific inquiry, understandings about scientific inquiry.

Here are some entry-level phrases that are used in conversations about marketing all over the world.

English	Afrikaans
Hello	Hállo
Goodbye	Tótsiens
How are you?	Hoe gáán dit?
Thank you	Dánkie
You're welcome	Jy is wélkom

EXPLAIN

DIGITAL NATION

Social Studies Answer Read the Social Studies Activity to students: Behavioral targeting is an approach that analyzes a Web surfers' browsing and search history to provide relevant ads. ***What ethical issues does this practice raise?*** collecting information about Web activity is an invasion of privacy; Internet users are bombarded with unwanted advertisements that try to induce them to spend money they may or may not have, which could create issues with debt.

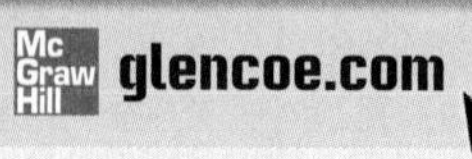

glencoe.com

Worksheet Activity Send students to the Online Learning Center to get a Digital Nation worksheet activity.

ADVERTISING AGENCIES

Ask these guiding questions to focus the discussion on advertising agencies.

Guiding Questions

Explain What do full-service advertising agencies do?	Plan an entire campaign: set objectives, develop messages and strategies, complete media plans, select media, coordinate related activities
Analyze What are the advantages of using a full-service advertising agency?	Full-service agencies offer one-stop advertising shopping and offer all services necessary to develop a campaign.

ELABORATE

Graphic Organizer

Display this diagram. Ask students to describe the different types of advertising agencies. Possible answers are provided.

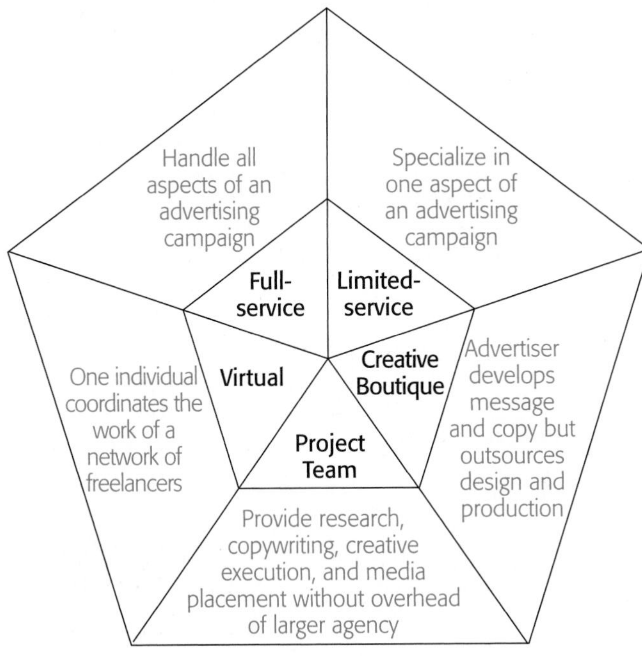

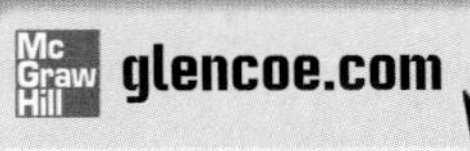

iWB

Graphic Organizer Send students to the Online Learning Center to print this graphic organizer.

Critical Thinking

Have students locate and study the Web sites of three different advertising agencies. Students should choose one of the agencies and write a half-page essay in which they describe the overall message the Web site sends to potential customers. Have students discuss how the copy and visuals used on the home page of the Web site support that message. Students will have a variety of opinions about how the copy and visuals support (or don't support) the particular message on their selected Web sites. Some sites are very edgy or forward-looking. Other sites may have a "traditional" look and lack appeal for savvy consumers. Ask students to share their essays with the class.

Mini Projects

Enrichment

Develop an Ad Divide the class into groups of four or five. Tell groups that they manage the creative services department at an advertising agency. Their department, which includes copywriters and graphic designers, is responsible for presenting ideas for an advertising campaign to a client. Tell students the client has invented a new product. They are to create a name for the product and develop ideas for a photo or illustration, copy, and a catchy slogan. Groups should prepare and give brief presentations to express their ideas. Presentations should demonstrate an understanding of the tasks involved in building and advertising campaign. Presentations should include a name for the client's product, ideas for a photo or illustration, copy, and a catchy slogan.

Parts of a Team Organize the class into small groups. Have students discuss the different departments of an advertising agency such as copywriting, graphic arts, media, research, and legal. Have students share with their group which department of an advertising agency they would like to work in and in what capacity. Ask each group member to consider if he or she would make the most valuable contribution in a creative, research, media, or client role. Based on their answers, encourage students to identify the skills they would need to develop to succeed in their chosen role. Graphic arts role-playing might need a strong art background; copywriters might need a strong language arts background, and so on.

WORLD MARKET

SCIENCE

Organize students into pairs to identify the differences between synthetic and natural diamonds. Have each pair create a two-column chart and label the columns Synthetic Diamonds and Natural Diamonds. Put together a class chart based on the pairs' charts. Ask: ***Which of these qualities would you focus on in your ad for natural diamonds?*** natural diamonds are created deep in the earth over millions of years and synthetic diamonds are created in laboratories. The flaws and blemishes sometimes found in natural diamonds add to their natural beauty.

Reading Check Answer

Read the Reading Check question to students: ***What are the types of advertising agencies?*** Advertising agencies consist of full-service, limited-service, creative boutique, project team, and virtual.

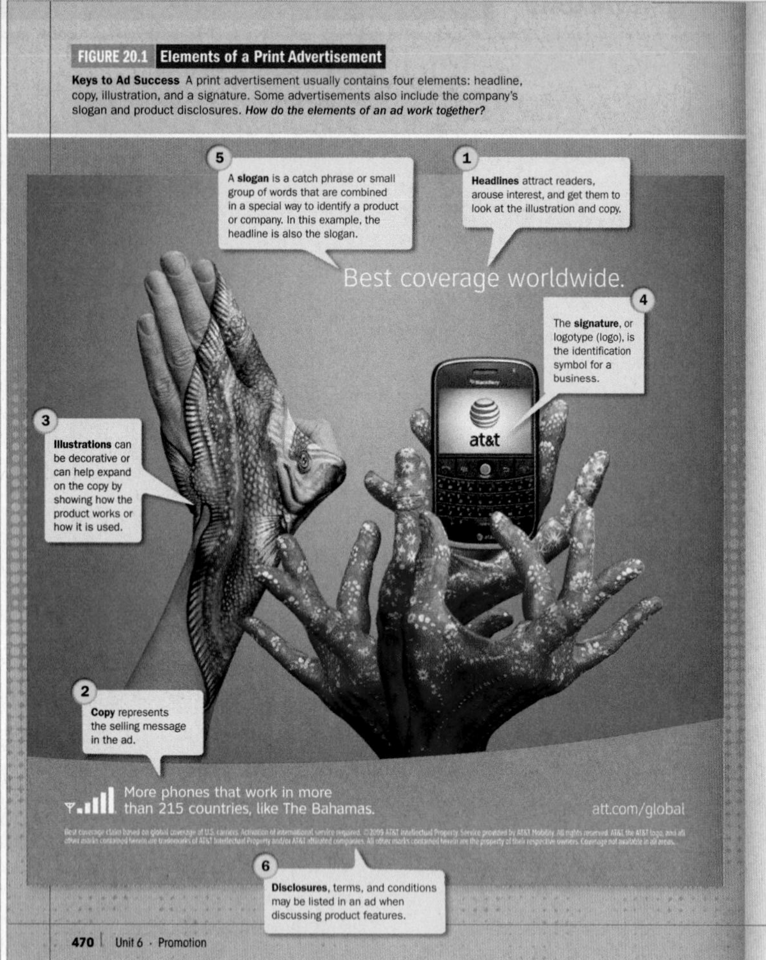

5
A **slogan** is a catch phrase or small group of words that are combined in a special way to identify a product or company. In this example, the headline is also the slogan.
1
Headlines attract readers, arouse interest, and get them to look at the illustration and copy.
Best coverage worldwide.
4
The **signature**, or logotype (logo), is the identification symbol for a business.
3
Illustrations can be decorative or can help expand on the copy by showing how the product works or how it is used.
at&t
2
Copy represents the selling message in the ad.
More phones that work in more than 215 countries, like The Bahamas.
att.com/global
6
Disclosures, terms, and conditions may be listed in an ad when discussing product features.

FIGURE 20.1 Elements of a Print Advertisement

Keys to Ad Success A print advertisement usually contains four elements: headline, copy, illustration, and a signature. Some advertisements also include the company's slogan and product disclosures. ***How do the elements of an ad work together?***

Each key element enhances the overall theme and promotes the product. The four fundamental elements of a print advertisement are applicable for ads in other media, too. As you read this section, think of ways these concepts would apply to preparing television, radio, and Internet ads.

HEADLINE

The **headline** is the phrase or sentence that captures the readers' attention, generates interest, and entices them to read the rest of the ad. Headlines quickly grab attention to a product. Headlines are responsible for the overall effectiveness of most advertising campaigns. Many experts believe that every print ad, including brochures, flyers, newspaper ads, and magazine ads, needs a headline. A headline leads readers into the ad's illustration. It makes them want to read the copy to learn more about the product's benefits.

PURPOSE OF HEADLINES

Headlines must be attention-getters or the ad may not be read. More than 80 percent of the people who look at an advertisement just read the headline. Research shows that words such as *free, new, now,* and *your* attract attention.

Effective headlines target an audience. They have advertising appeal and provide reasons for purchasing a good or service. The motivation for purchasing helps to identify potential customers. Headlines appeal to people by using a variety of motivators, such as profit, love, fear, fun, and vanity. Effective headlines allow the advertised product to project an image for the potential customer.

A headline provides a benefit for the reader. It promises something that matches a need or want. Benefits might include more miles per gallon, better service, or fewer cavities.

Headlines lead to the copy and illustration. Headlines are often written so that readers grasp the entire point of the ad simply by viewing the headline, seeing the illustration, and reading a few words of copy. Other times, headlines have a sub-headline to either clarify or expand on the main idea expressed in the headline. Sub-headlines are usually found in smaller type close to the headline. Powerful headlines draw potential customers into reading the copy.

WRITING EFFECTIVE HEADLINES

Before writing a headline, a copywriter must know the needs of the target market. These needs might relate to price, delivery, performance, reliability, service, or quality. The headline must identify a benefit of the product.

Effective headlines stress these benefits by making a promise, asking a question, posing a challenge, or using a testimonial. Key words are often used in headlines to link the benefits in a personal way to the reader. Research has found that the words used most frequently in successful headlines include *you, your, how,* and *new.*

Most headlines are brief and usually consist of five to fifteen words. Studies show that people have difficulty processing more than seven words at one time. One effective and short headline is for Sure® deodorant: "Works all day. Just like you." It is possible to create longer headlines that are effective if they are striking or touch on specific emotions. A headline used by DeBeers® diamonds reads: "When She Describes This Anniversary To Her Friends, She'll Start With 'Once Upon A Time.'"

Catchy Headlines

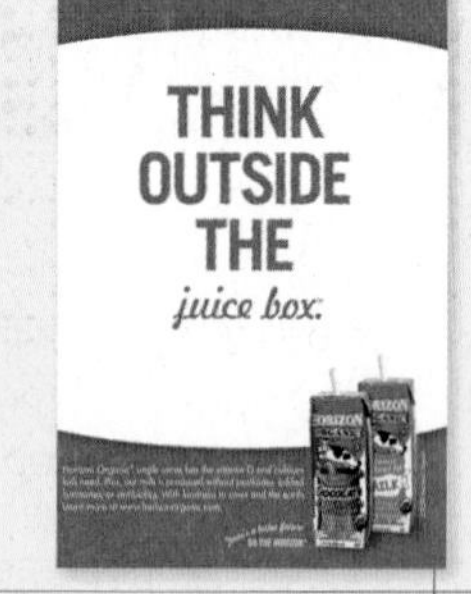

An effective headline grabs attention in print advertisements. ***Explain why headlines are so important in a print ad.***

EXPLAIN

Visual Literacy

Figure 20.1 Caption Answer Read the caption question to students: ***How do the elements of an ad work together?*** Each key element—headline, illustration, signature, copy, work together to enhance the overall theme and promotes the product. When a slogan and disclosure are added, the message is extended and reinforced. Ask: ***In your opinion, what are the two most important elements necessary in a print ad?*** Student opinions will vary, but should show a rationale to why they chose these elements as the most important. Possible answer: a headline and an illustration are the best way to grab the reader's attention—with a visual image and a catchy phrase to make a connection in the reader's mind. This is also, in print, the traditional approach. Ask: ***Do the key elements work together in this ad effectively to portray the company as a global provider?*** Answers will vary. Possible answer: Yes, the painted hands depicting a fish and coral to communicate a visually effective message. Ask: ***What elements stand out as being the most effective?*** Students should explain why the elements work together. For example, the headline and the slogan are the same. The illustration of the hands alluding to a scene from a coral reef complements the copy referring to the Bahamas, which has extensive coral reefs. The global message works.

Critical Thinking

Ask students to discuss each of the key elements presented and defined in the advertisement on this page. Ask: ***Which elements do you think are the most effective? Why?*** Students may mention any of the elements, but should provide a rationale for their answers. Then ask: ***Are there any elements in the ad that you think can be improved? If so, which one(s)? How would you improve it (them)?*** Students should offer thoughtful answers and the reasoning behind them. Have students work in six groups. Each group is to create one element for a print ad. For example, there would be one group for headlines, illustrations, the signature, copy, a slogan, and disclosures. As a class, you may choose the product type that you will use. Then, have each group create their assigned element. As a class, create one ad from the elements.

MINI CLIP

Reading: Obstacles to Achievement

Go to the Online Learning Center to view a video clip in which teachers work together to help students master specific standards.

ELABORATE

Mini Projects

Differentiated Instruction

Students with Learning Disabilities To reinforce students' understanding of headlines, ask: ***What are the characteristics of effective headlines?*** Write students' answers for the class to read. Answers should include: Brief, fewer than seven words; grab and hold the reader's attention; contain the words *you, your, how,* and *new;* appeal to an immediate need; identify a benefit of the product or service; evoke emotion; use a familiar saying with a twist; make use of opposites. Ask: ***Does the headline in the ad on page 470 contain these characteristics?*** Students' answers will vary; some may think the ad does contain the characteristics, while others may not. Encourage them to explain their answers.

Interpersonal Learners Tell students to imagine that they are members of an advertising agency team working on a campaign for a new client. Present a product or service with which students are familiar (possibilities include: MP3 player, DVDs, soft drinks, haircuts, and so on). Then lead a brainstorming session in which students develop headlines and sub-headlines for print advertisements for that product or service. Ask a volunteer to write the headlines and sub-headlines for the rest of the class to read. Have the class vote on the best headline and sub-headline for the product or service.

Visual Literacy

Catchy Headlines Caption Answer Read the caption question to students: ***Explain why headlines are so important in a print ad.*** The headline is the phrase or sentence that captures the readers' attention, generates interest, and entices them to read the rest of the ad. Headlines are responsible for the overall effectiveness of an ad. Then have students write their own headlines for products that are in your classroom (books, globes, chairs, desks, and so on). Encourage them to make their headlines capture the readers' attention, generate interest, and entice readers to read the rest of the ad.

VIRTUAL BUSINESS

PROMOTION

Introduce students to the concept of promotion using Knowledge Matters' Virtual Business Retailing visual simulation, *Promotion*. In this simulation, students will learn that promotion is the way in which stores actively communicate with their customers.

e MARKETING

Augmented Reality and Mash-ups

Augmented Reality (AR) is technology that permits readers to see expanded aspects of an illustration through a simulator, which may include 3D, holograms, or the ability to see oneself using a product. A web cam computer connection is required. Imagine an illustration or product coming off the page into a virtual reality. A sunglasses company using augmented reality on its Web site allows viewers to see themselves trying on different virtual sunglasses. USPS Priority Mail uses augmented reality on its Web site to permit viewers to compare the item to be shipped with the various boxes offered by USPS. The user clicks on different size boxes, which appear transparent, to see which size box best fits the item to be shipped.

Innovate and Create

Have students conduct an Internet search to find examples of augmented reality and mash-ups. Once they have a handle on how they work, have students work in groups to create an ad campaign that uses augmented reality or cut and paste mash-ups. They can begin with a current advertisement or create a completely new one. Final projects should be shared with classmates in an oral report. The ad campaign must contain augmented reality or cut and paste mash-ups. Any current advertisement could be used as the basis for the ad campaign, as long as it has elements that can be augmented. Students may elect to make use of a tie-in with a gaming site that matches the ad's theme. For example, if an advertisement is for Georgia peaches or California grapes, a tie-in with Farmville would be a perfect tie-in. Students should note that their newly designed ads could be shared with friends via Facebook or as part of Farmville's site. .

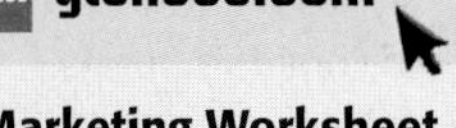

eMarketing Worksheet Activity Send students to the Online Learning Center to download an eMarketing worksheet activity.

Good Copy Is Simple and Direct

Each element of an ad enhances the overall theme and promotes the product. ***How are these three Western Union ads similar to each other?***

In a recent study, creative directors from several major advertising agencies analyzed award-winning print advertisements to determine what their headlines had in common. They discovered that 32 percent of the headlines used familiar sayings—with a twist. For example, "When it rains, it pours®" (Morton® salt). About 23 percent of the headlines made use of opposites, for example, "Eats Gravel. Sips Fuel" (Chevy Silverado truck).

COPY

The **copy** is the selling message of a written advertisement. The headline of your copy should identify a need for the customer. The copy then should detail how the product meets the customer's needs. As with headlines, copy should be based on market research and the business objectives for the advertising campaign. For example, the objectives may be to introduce a new product, build an image, attract new customers, answer inquiries, or generate sales to existing customers.

Here are some tips to write compelling, effective copy:

1. Your copy should be conversational and written in a very personal, friendly style. Keep your copy personal by using familiar language and casual phrases and terms.
2. Good copy is simple and direct. Copy can vary from a few words to several paragraphs. Copy does not need to be extensive to get a message across. It shows how using a product can help a customer or solve a problem.
3. Copy should appeal to the senses. Through the words, the customer should be able to see, hear, touch, taste, or even smell a product. This can be done through using descriptive adjectives and action words.
4. Your copy should have news value by providing specific information. It should tell the *who, what, when, where, why,* and *how* of your product. Remember that facts about your product are more powerful than claims. Use case histories, examples, **statistics**, performance figures, dates, and quotes from experts whenever possible.
5. Your copy should generate interest, encourage awareness, and create desire. Key words used in the copy, such as *easy, guaranteed, hurry, now, price,* and *save* establish an immediate connection with a reader. Customers also enjoy being on the cutting edge when using innovative products, and words such as *new, improved,* and *introducing* give that impression.
6. Advertising copy should provide a personal call to action now or in the near future. It should always be written in the second person and in the active rather than the passive voice. For example, you would write, "This item will help you," rather than the more passive phrase, "You will be helped by this item." Words such as *last chance, limited supply,* or *special bonus offer* help create a sense of urgency and need for immediate action.

A call for action tells the reader to buy your product, visit your store or Web site, or contact the business or organization. Asking for immediate action is especially important to local advertisers. For example, most print ads in local newspapers seek immediate action for sale items or special events. On the other hand, most national advertisers are not looking for immediate action, but seek action in the near future. They desire to keep the product name in front of the public by building brand awareness for new prospects and brand loyalty for current customers.

Good copywriters write in short sentences, sentence fragments, or bulleted lists, if there is a lot of information. Try to avoid the use of commas. Long sentences and too many commas distract readers. White space in the copy breaks up the text and creates an illusion of shorter sentences and fewer words. Print ads with less copy and more white space have higher recall rates.

ILLUSTRATION

The **illustration** is the photograph, drawing, or other graphic elements that is used in an advertisement. An illustration should be clear enough to attract, hold attention, and even encourage action. It also integrates the headline and copy. The illustration and the headline motivate the consumer to read at least the first sentence of the copy.

EXPLAIN

COPY

Tell students that print advertisements contain copy, which is the selling message of a written advertisement. Then ask these guiding questions to focus the discussion on advertising copy.

Guiding Questions

Identify What are six tips for writing compelling, effective copy?	Be conversational and written in a personal, friendly manner; be simple and direct; appeal to the senses; have news value by providing specific information; generate interest; provide a personal call to action.
Explain What is a call for action? What words are often used to create a sense of urgency?	A call for action tells the reader to buy a product, visit a store or Web site, or contact a business or organization. Words used include *last chance, limited supply,* and *special bonus.*

Visual Literacy

Good Copy Is Simple and Direct Caption Answer Read the photo caption question to students: ***How are these Western Union ads similar to each other?*** They all ask a question and give Yes! as the answer. Ask students: ***How does the signature provide instant recognition?*** Students should recognize that the signature includes Western Union's corporate logo.

Critical Thinking

Organize students into pairs to design and develop a signature for a company of their choosing. It can be an existing company or a company of their own creation. Ask pairs to share their signatures with the class. Signatures for national companies should contain the name of the company and the corporate symbol and slogan. If the company is local, the signature should contain the company's name, address, telephone number, business hours, map and directions, and slogan.

ELABORATE

Graphic Organizer

Display this T-chart. After students have read the information about copy and illustration in the text, call on volunteers to identify characteristics of effective copy and illustration in print advertisements. Possible answers:

Copy	Illustration
• conversational and written in a personal, friendly manner • simple and direct • appeals to the senses • has news value by providing specific information • generates interest • provides a personal call to action	• attracts attention • holds attention • encourages action • integrates headline and copy • helps to motivate consumer to read at least the first sentence of the copy

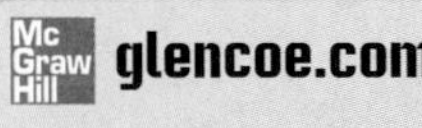

Graphic Organizer Send students to the Online Learning Center to print this graphic organizer.

Critical Thinking

Have students look at the advertisements reprinted in this chapter or at other ads you have brought to class. Have students describe how the characteristics they listed in the Graphic Organizer activity above are reflected in the ads. Ask students to pay particular attention to how the headlines, copy, and illustrations work together in especially effective ads. Copy: conversational and written in a personal, friendly manner; simple and direct; appeals to the senses; has news value by providing specific information; generates interest; provides a personal call to action. Illustration: attracts attention; holds attention; encourages action; integrates headline and copy; helps to motivate consumer to read at least the first sentence of the copy.

VIRTUAL BUSINESS

ADVANCED PROMOTION

Introduce the concept of advanced promotion using Knowledge Matters' Virtual Business Retailing visual simulation, *Advanced Promotion*. In this simulation, students will learn about additional sales and merchandise promotion activities that a storeowner or manager can use to attain the stated goals of a sales promotion.

Mini Projects

Differentiated Instruction

Linguistic Learners To help students better understand how advertisements should be written to attract attention, have students rewrite the following sentences in the active voice: 1. Gillette® brings you the next revolution in shaving closeness. Sample rewritten answer: Try Gillette's next revolution in shaving closeness—you've never felt anything as close as this! 2. One hundred twenty images from Professional Photos are profiled in this coffee-table book and companion CD-ROM. Sample rewritten answer: Imagine, one hundred twenty professional quality images showcased in this huge book. This offer also includes a CD-ROM that allows you to view these images in crystal clear digital format. 3. A V8 engine, air conditioning, and many other luxury amenities are included as standard features of this new car. Sample rewritten answer: This new car has a V8 engine, air conditioning, and so many other luxury amenities as standard features that we don't have space to list them all.

Visual Learners Have students collect and critique a variety of print ads and discuss the use of active and passive voices. Students can choose to do a one-page written analysis or a five-minute oral presentation. Analyses should be written using good grammar and spelling. All information in a paragraph should relate to one idea and all details in the paragraph are relevant to the idea. Transitions show connections of cause and effect, time, and place. Presentations should be well-planned and include graphics (when presented in computer slideshows, on posters, or by other visual means).

English Language Learners Collect several print ads depicting action. Find simple ads that show verbs in action where you can re-enact the event, or illustrate the action. For example, pouring a cup of coffee, jumping hurdles, and so on. Have students identify the verbs and the subjects. Tell students that using a sentence with an active voice means that the verb tells the action performed by the subject. For example, *She poured the coffee.* A sentence with a passive voice has the action performed on the subject. For example, *The coffee was poured by the girl.* Have students write passive and active sentences for their ads. Sentences will vary depending upon the ads chosen and the action shown in each ad.

The illustration and its graphic elements send a message that is hard to communicate with words alone. For example, illustrations show the product, how it works, and its safety features. Illustrations should also project the desired image or benefit such as convenience, entertainment, or status.

Sometimes consumers need to see the product in use. For example, models might wear featured clothing items. Businesses also need to choose images that will not become outdated too soon. Illustrations should be selected and evaluated periodically to match and convey the desired business image.

Photographs are effective in advertisements when a sense of reality is necessary. It is important for consumers to see how some products look or how they are used. Consumer products such as cars, computers, cosmetics, electronic equipment, furniture, sporting equipment, and vacation resorts are often depicted in photographs.

Drawings can show a part of a product that the reader would not normally see. Cut-away drawings and illustrations of products and equipment help reveal important features not visible in a photograph. They also help the reader understand how a product is made and works.

Illustrations should be balanced with other ad components and take up about one-third of an entire ad's space. Headlines should also use one-third of the ad's space, with the remaining one-third used for copy and the signature.

Businesses often use clip art in their print ads. **Clip art** includes inexpensive or free images, stock drawings, and photographs. Suppliers, manufacturers, or trade associations can provide clip art for print ads. When clip art is not appropriate, professionals may be hired to photograph or illustrate situations or products.

SIGNATURE

Print ads are not complete without the name of the advertiser, or sponsor. The **signature** (name of the advertiser) or logotype (logo) is the distinctive identification symbol for a business. The signature usually appears at the bottom of an ad. A well-designed signature gets instant recognition for a business. No advertisement is complete without it.

In national ads, the signature is the name of the firm. It may also include the corporate symbol and slogan. The signature in local advertisements usually includes the business's name, address, telephone number, business hours, map and directions, or slogan. Many advertisers also include their Web-site address for contact information.

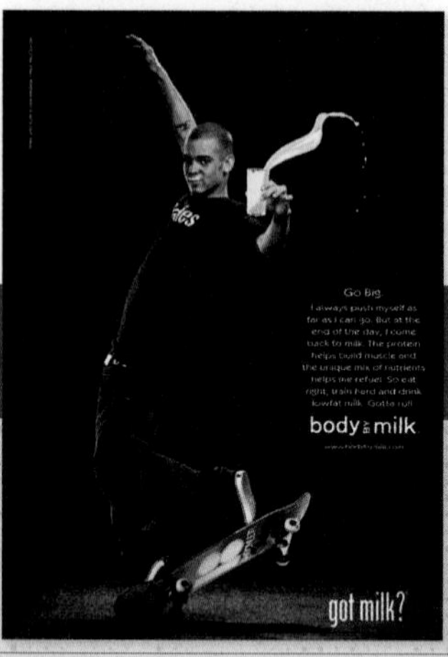

Got Milk?

The use of celebrities or athletes is an effective way to attract viewers to read the copy. ***Who do you think the target market might be for this ad?***

SLOGAN

A **slogan** is a catchy phrase or words that identify a product or company. These advertising slogans have the power to attract attention and arouse interest for the company or its product. To support a firm's signature, many businesses create and use slogans that will help their customers identify the firm and its image.

Here are some literary devices that copywriters use when developing slogans for advertising campaigns:

- **Alliteration** This device uses repeating initial consonant sounds: "Welcome to the World Wide Wow" (AOL).
- **Paradox** This is a statement that is a seeming contradiction that could be true: "The taste you love to hate" (Listerine® mouthwash).
- **Rhyme** Slogans might use rhyming words or phrases: "Give a hoot, don't pollute" (United States Forest Service).
- **Pun** This technique is a humorous use of a word that suggests two or more of its meanings or the meaning of another word similar in sound: "Time to Re-Tire" (Fisk Tires).
- **Play on words** This device cleverly uses words to mean something else: "Let your fingers do the walking" (*Yellow Pages®*).

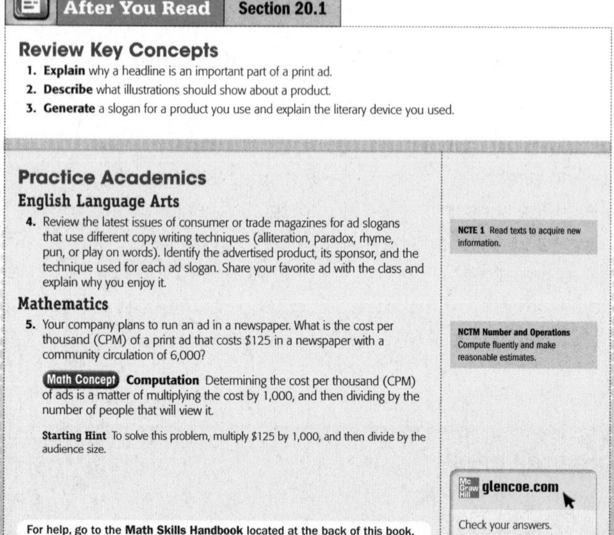

After You Read Section 20.1

Review Key Concepts

1. **Explain** why a headline is an important part of a print ad.
2. **Describe** what illustrations should show about a product.
3. **Generate** a slogan for a product you use and explain the literary device you used.

Practice Academics

English Language Arts

4. Review the latest issues of consumer or trade magazines for ad slogans that use different copy writing techniques (alliteration, paradox, rhyme, pun, or play on words). Identify the advertised product, its sponsor, and the technique used for each ad slogan. Share your favorite ad with the class and explain why you enjoy it.

NCTE 1 Read texts to acquire new information.

Mathematics

5. Your company plans to run an ad in a newspaper. What is the cost per thousand (CPM) of a print ad that costs $125 in a newspaper with a community circulation of 6,000?

Math Concept **Computation** Determining the cost per thousand (CPM) of ads is a matter of multiplying the cost by 1,000, and then dividing by the number of people that will view it.

Starting Hint To solve this problem, multiply $125 by 1,000, and then divide by the audience size.

NCTM Number and Operations Compute fluently and make reasonable estimates.

For help, go to the **Math Skills Handbook** located at the back of this book.

glencoe.com

Check your answers.

ELABORATE

Mini Project

Differentiated Instruction

Students with Learning Disabilities To help students better understand the different elements of a print advertisement, distribute a number of print ads to students. Provide students with a supply of sticky notes that they can write on and attach to the ads. Have students identify and label these parts of the ads: headline, copy, illustration, and signature. Ask students: ***What is a headline?*** A headline is the phrase or sentence that captures the reader's attention, generates interest, and entices them to read the rest of the ad. ***What is copy?*** Copy is the selling message of a written advertisement. ***What is the illustration?*** The illustration is the photograph, drawing, or other graphic elements that is used in an advertisement. ***What is the signature?*** The signature is the name of the advertiser or the company's logo.

Visual Literacy

Got Milk? Caption Answer Read the caption question to students: ***After reading the copy, who do you think the target market might be for this ad?*** The skateboarder suggests that the ad is aimed at young males. Then ask: ***What is the slogan used for this ad?*** Got milk? ***What is the headline?*** Go Big. Ask: ***Which tip(s) for writing compelling, effective copy does this ad follow?*** conversational and written in a personal, friendly manner; simple and direct; appeals to the senses; has news value by providing specific information; generates interest; provides a personal call to action.

Critical Thinking

Have students locate a print advertisement and television advertisement for the same product. Ask students to analyze the different advertisements by answering questions such as: ***How are the ads the same? How are they different? Is the copy similar for both ads? If not, how does it differ?*** You might have students create a T-chart and put similarities in one column and differences in the other column.

EVALUATE

Graphic Organizer

Display this diagram. Ask students to name the literary devices often used by copywriters when developing slogans for advertising campaigns. Write the literary devices in the outside shapes of the diagram. Then ask:
What is alliteration? use of repeating initial consonant sounds
What is a paradox? a seeming contradiction that could be true
What is a rhyme? phrases that have similarity in sound
What is a pun? funny use of a word with two or more meanings
What is a play on words? use of words to mean something else

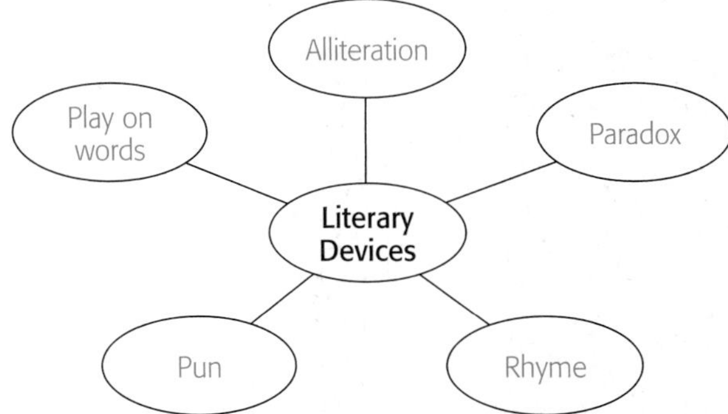

glencoe.com

iWB

Graphic Organizer Send students to the Online Learning Center to print this graphic organizer.

Mini Project

Enrichment

Create Slogans Organize the class into pairs or small groups. Provide each group with a product or service for which they will create an advertisement. Have groups create an advertisement for their product or service that includes a slogan; however, slogans should not be put on the ads at this point. Groups should create at least one slogan for each of these literary devices: alliteration, paradox, rhyme, pun, and play on words. After groups have created their advertisements and slogans, have them read the slogans to the class and have the class vote on the best slogan for the advertisement. Then have groups finalize the ads with the selected slogans and post the ads throughout the classroom.

After You Read **Section 20.1**

Review Key Concepts

1. The headline captures the reader's attention, arouses, their interest, and entices them to read the rest of the ad.
2. Illustrations should transmit a message that would be difficult to communicate with words alone. It could show the product, how it works, safety features, or its benefits.
3. Slogans will vary but should use one of the following literary devices: alliteration, paradox, rhyme, pun, or play on words.

Practice Academics

English Language Arts

4. Accept all reasonable and complete responses that use proper grammar and spelling. Each headline must use a different copywriting technique. (alliteration, paradox, rhyme, pun, or play on words). The advertised product, its sponsor, and the technique used for each ad headline must be identified.

Mathematics

5. \$20.83 (\$125 × 1,000 ÷ 6,000).

glencoe.com

Answer Key Send students to the Online Learning Center to check their answers.

READING GUIDE

Before You Read

Predict How might the use of color in a print ad affect a viewer's reaction?

Objectives

- **Explain** the principles of preparing an ad layout.
- **List** advantages and disadvantages of using color in advertising.
- **Describe** how typefaces and sizes add variety and emphasis to print advertisements.

The Main Idea

Advertisers must understand effective design principles when developing ad layouts in order to quickly attract the attention of a targeted audience.

Vocabulary

Content Vocabulary
- ad layout
- advertising proof

Academic Vocabulary

You will find these words in your reading and on your tests. Make sure you know their meanings.
- technique
- emphasis

Graphic Organizer

Draw or print this chart for taking notes on the principles of ad design.

Tips for Developing Effective Ad Layouts
1. Leave white (unused) space.
2. ______
3. ______
4. ______

glencoe.com

Print this graphic organizer.

STANDARDS

ACADEMIC

English Language Arts
NCTE 1 Read texts to acquire new information.

Science
NSES E Develop abilities of technological design, understandings about science and technology.

NCSS *National Council for the Social Studies*
NCTE *National Council of Teachers of English*
NCTM *National Council of Teachers of Mathematics*
NSES *National Science Education Standards*

College & Career READINESS

Common Core
Writing Produce clear and coherent writing in which the development, organization, and style are appropriate to task, purpose, and audience.

MARKETING CORE FUNCTION

Promotion

m.e. Section 20.2 Advertising Layout

PRINT ADVERTISING LAYOUTS

An **ad layout** is a sketch that shows the general arrangement and appearance of a finished ad. It clearly indicates the position of the headline, illustration, copy, and signature.

There are different sources for ad layout services, including newspaper salespeople, magazine representatives, and advertising agency personnel including art directors, copy editors, or account executives. In addition, desktop publishing programs are useful for smaller businesses.

You do not need to be an artist to develop an ad layout. You submit a rough draft of an idea, and the vendor creates a final ad based upon your information. You do need to make sure, however, that all the information is correct.

As You Read

Evaluate How do businesses assess the effectiveness of their advertisements?

COMPONENTS OF EFFECTIVE AD LAYOUTS

Ad layouts should be prepared in the same size as the final advertisement. Newspapers and magazines offer certain rates on pre-calculated ad sizes. Typical ad sizes are: $\frac{1}{16}$ page, $\frac{1}{8}$ page, $\frac{1}{4}$ page, $\frac{1}{2}$ page, and full page.

The illustrations should be large enough to show the product in use and grab attention through size, humor, or dramatic content. Print ads that feature large visuals (60 to 70 percent of the total ad) are the best attention-getters. The image projected in the layout should be appropriate for the target audience.

> "Visual elements like color, different typefaces, and font sizes bring print advertisements to life."

NO ONE GROWS KETCHUP LIKE HEINZ.

HEINZ. GROWN, NOT MADE.

Focal Point

A single visual is a basic advertising layout design. *How does this ad design create a memorable image for the viewer?*

ENGAGE

Anticipation Activity

Improving Student Achievement Have students work in pairs or small groups to select a product and create an ad for it. The ad should be exciting, subtle, or something in between. Have them choose a color palette to express that concept. Ask: ***Why did you choose these colors? What concept were you trying to communicate?*** Students should explain their color choices and how it conveys their concept. Ask the class if they think the concept was accurately conveyed.

Objectives

- **Explain** the principles of preparing an ad layout. An ad layout should be the same size as the final ad with illustrations large enough to show product, focal point
- **List** advantages and disadvantages of using color in advertising. advantages—more realistic, visually appealing, commands attention, can increase readership; disadvantage—increased cost
- **Describe** how typefaces and sizes add variety and emphasis to print advertisements. Large, boldface, and uppercase type is strong and powerful and implies shouting. Small, lightface, lowercase type is delicate and implies whispering.

Graphic Organizer

Tips for Developing Effective Ad Layouts

1. Leave white (unused) space.
2. Make illustrations large enough to grab attention.
3. Color is more realistic and visually appealing.
4. Employ distinctive and appropriate type faces and sizes.

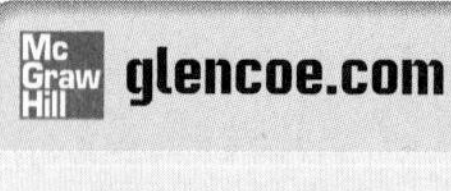

Graphic Organizer Send students to the Online Learning Center to print this graphic organizer.

EXPLORE

Before You Read

Read the Before You Read question aloud: ***How might the use of color in a print ad affect a viewer's reaction?*** Explain to students that warm colors such as red, orange, and yellow make things appear to advance, or move forward, and cool colors such as blues and greens make things appear to recede. ***How do colors affect your reaction to an ad?*** Students should explain which colors appeal to them and which colors "turn them off."

Preteaching Vocabulary

Have students go to the Online Learning Center at glencoe.com for the Chapter 20 Preteaching Vocabulary games.

Content Vocabulary

Write the key terms *ad layout* and *advertising proof* for the class to read. Ask students to guess what the meanings of the terms might be. Then ask volunteers to look up the definitions of the terms in the glossary or in a dictionary and to share them with the class. An *ad layout* is a sketch that shows the general arrangement and appearance of a finished ad. An *advertising proof* is a representation of an ad that shows exactly how it will appear in print.

Academic Vocabulary

Technique—Synonyms Display the term *technique* and ask students to share ways they have seen it used. Ask: ***What are some synonyms for this term?*** method, procedure, skill, routine Ask volunteers to use the term in an original sentence. Sample: My sister is learning Indian cooking techniques from a class at the recreation center. Our teachers use a variety of techniques to make sure all of the students benefit from the lesson.

Emphasis—Multiple Meanings Write the term *emphasis* for the class to read. Then read to students the following definitions of the term: (1) special importance; (2) forcefulness; (3) spoken stress on a word. Ask: ***Which of the three definitions do you think is the one used in this section on advertising layout? Why?*** Students might make a case for either definition 1 or definition 2. Adding emphasis to a layout can be done by giving special importance to an element or by forcefully presenting a product.

PROFESSIONAL DEVELOPMENT **MINI CLIP**

Reading: Strategic Readers
Go to the Online Learning Center to view a video clip in which an author discusses strategic readers.

Section 20.2

Advertising Layout

PRINT ADVERTISING LAYOUTS

Ask these guiding questions to focus the discussion on print advertising layouts.

Guiding Questions

Identify What are some different sources for ad layout services?	newspaper salespeople, magazine representatives, ad agency personnel such as art directors, copy editors, account executives
Explain Why is a balance of white space and color desired in a print advertisement?	A balance highlights the image that you want the consumer to notice.

As You Read

Read students the As You Read question: ***How do businesses assess the effectiveness of their advertisements?*** Businesses measure the effectiveness of their advertisements by the number of responses and, ultimately, by the increase in sales generated by the ads.

Expert Advice

Read the quote to students:

> **"Visual elements like color, different typefaces, and font sizes bring print advertisements to life."**

Have students look through this chapter in their textbooks. Ask: ***Do you think the color, typefaces, and font sizes help make this text visually interesting?*** Students' answers should reflect honesty and an understanding of the concepts.

Visual Literacy

Focal Point Caption Answer Read the caption question to students: ***How does this ad design create a memorable image for the viewer?*** It's humorous and clever to see a ketchup bottle sliced like a tomato; the design is simple with emphasis on the image; the sliced bottle reflects the grown, not manufactured, image the company wants to project.

The ad should make generous use of white or unused space for a clean look. A proper balance of white space and color highlights the image or drawing that you want the consumer to notice. White space also helps to make copy legible and creates an "eye flow" for the ad. The typeface, style of printing type, and size should be easy to read and appropriate for the target audience.

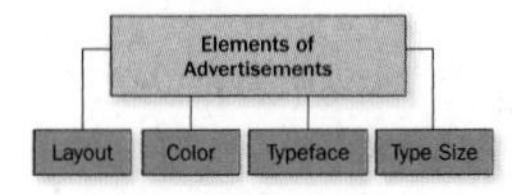

TYPES OF ADVERTISING LAYOUTS

There are several popular types of ad layouts that designers use in print advertisements. The best ads contain a focal point and lines of force that guide the reader to the copy through photographs and illustrations.

The single-visual layout design is a **technique** that uses a single illustration as a focal point with a very short headline and little copy. It is a simple, basic design but creates a powerful image.

The top-heavy layout places the illustration in the upper half to upper two-thirds of the space or on the left side of the layout. In this layout a strong headline is placed before or after the illustration, and the copy follows.

The illustrated layout uses photos or other images to show how a product can be used—or to illustrate additional technical concepts. An illustrated layout often gets attention by its dramatic presentation, the kinds of illustrations, or by using humor.

The Ogilvy layout, named after advertising expert David Ogilvy, arranges each ad element into a specific order. The elements are presented from top to bottom, in the order most people view them. Research shows that most people view ads in the following order: illustration, photo caption, headline, copy, and signature.

The Z layout is organized with the most important items an advertiser wants viewers to see (often the headline) placed on the top of the Z. Since a reader's eye will normally follow the path of the Z, the illustrations and copy are on the line going down. The signature and "call to action" are at the bottom of the Z in the lower right corner.

MARKETING CASE STUDY

AT & T Hands On

AT&T's popular "Hands" ads show off the company's international presence in the wireless communication industry. In these creative print ads, hands are painted and posed in unusual ways to hint at the many parts of the world where customers can use AT&T's wireless service. (See Figure 20.1 on page 470.)

Worth a Thousand Words

The images use visual clues to represent different global regions. In one picture, a left hand is shaped and colored like an angel fish, while several right hands depict an orange reef with an AT&T phone sitting on top. Another ad shows two hands painted as elephants, holding a phone between them. Unique in the world of print ads, the AT&T "Hands" ads rely on the relationship between illustration and copy.

English Language Arts

Create Think of a product that you use often. Design a print ad that incorporates the use of the product. Be sure to combine the elements of illustration and copy in your design.

NCTE 4 Use written language to communicate effectively.

COLOR IN PRINT ADVERTISEMENTS

A color ad is usually more realistic and visually appealing than a black-and-white advertisement. In fact, research proves that color newspaper ads can increase the readership of ad copy by as much as 80 percent over black-and-white ads. In addition, studies have also shown that full-color ads are often more cost effective than two-color ads (usually black and another color) because of their increased response rates.

Although color commands the viewer's attention by adding excitement and realism, each added color raises the cost of the advertisement. Adding another color can increase costs by as much as 35 percent. When businesses use color in advertisements, the added cost must be continually measured against the desired results.

Advertisers must consider the appropriate colors for the product and target market. For example, red is used for passion, excitement, and power. It is often used in automobile and food advertising. Also, when developing ads for global markets or ethnic groups in the United States, advertisers must be sensitive to the different meanings that color conveys to people of various cultures and countries.

TYPEFACES FOR PRINT ADVERTISEMENTS

Many typefaces and type sizes are effective for use in print advertisements. Advertisers make sure to select styles and type sizes that are distinctive, yet appropriate for the business and specific target audience.

The look and appearance (design) of the type is called the "typeface." A complete set of letters in a specific size and typeface is called a "font." The appearance of the typeface affects the entire character of an advertisement.

An advertiser would choose a large, bold typeface in a headline when the goal is to convey the message forcefully. A smaller, lighter typeface might be selected when the words in a headline are to be conveyed more gently or subtly. In general, print advertisers should use one typeface for headlines and prices, and another typeface for copy.

A Different League

This ad demonstrates several components of an effective advertising layout. ***What principles of advertising layout are represented in this ad?***

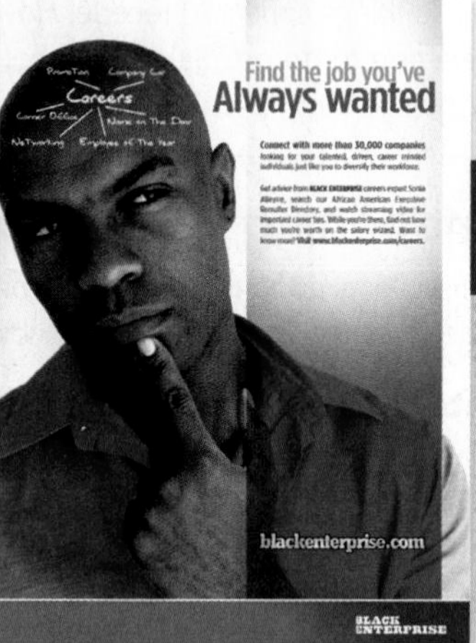

478 | Unit 6 · Promotion

Chapter 20 · Print Advertisements | 479

EXPLAIN

MARKETING CASE STUDY

English Language Arts Answer Students' advertisements will vary but should incorporate the use of the product. They should also use the elements of illustration (a photograph, drawing, or other graphic element) and copy (the selling message of a written advertisement). After students have completed their ads, have them share the ads with the class. Have volunteers from the class point out how use of the product was incorporated into the ad and describe the use of illustration and design.

Critical Thinking

Have students refer to Figure 20.1 on page 470. After reading the Marketing Case Study about the AT&T "Hands" ad, read the last sentence, ***Unique in the world of print ads, the AT&T "Hands" ads rely on the relationship between illustration and copy***. Explain that though there is very little copy, the headline, illustration, and other ad elements are tied together by the words, *worldwide* and *global.* Ask: ***What other qualities make this ad unique?*** Answers will vary but may include that the painted hands and the artwork is in itself unique; the artwork on the hands represent something technological and manmade, while the fish and coral represent something natural Ask: ***What other relationships can you identify?*** The use of the bars parallels the shape of the hands—one tall shape on the left, and several expanding shapes on the right.

ELABORATE

Graphic Organizer

Display this chart. As you discuss the elements of advertisements with students, have them provide facts. Possible answers:

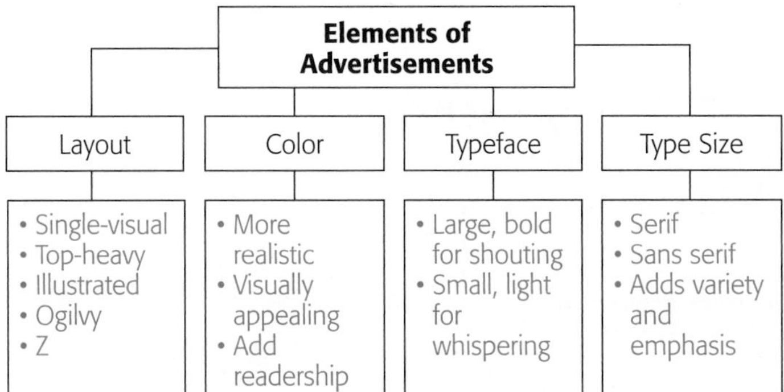

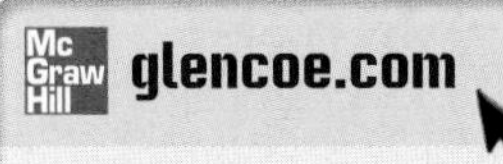

Graphic Organizer Send students to the Online Learning Center to print this graphic organizer.

Mini Projects

Differentiated Instruction

Students with Learning Disabilities For added practice identifying fonts, have students look through various textbooks, library books, magazines, and other printed materials readily available in the classroom. Ask them to look at the way fonts are used in the printed materials. Have them keep track of when and where serif fonts are used and sans serif fonts are used. Then have the class work together to develop a chart that indicates the most common places serif fonts are used and the most common places that sans serif fonts are used. serif fonts are often used for the body of the text; sans serif fonts are often used in headlines and captions.

Interpersonal/Linguistic Discuss with students the different types of advertising layouts—single-visual, top-heavy, illustrated, Ogilvy, and Z. Bring to class a number of different magazines, newspapers, and flyers. Have students work in pairs to find examples of each of the different types of layouts. Then have pairs show their advertisements to the class and explain why they fit a particular layout. After the presentations, ask the class: ***Which layout seems to be the most popular? Why do you think this is so?*** Answers will depend on which layout is present in the most examples. Students should provide a rationale for the popularity of the different layout types.

Critical Thinking

Point out to students that color is not always required for an ad to be effective. Ask them to look in newspapers and magazines to find ads they think work effectively in black and white and to share them with the class. Encourage students to support their opinions with specific examples. Suggest to students that they look for ads that have a strong call to action—ads that announce sales or provide a coupon for a substantial savings on a product with which most people are familiar. Ask: ***Why might a black-and-white ad with a coupon be more effective than a black-and-white ad that simply advertises a product?*** The ads with coupons have a strong call to action and people will want to read them and answer the call to action for the benefits it provides.

Mini Project

Differentiated Instruction

Visual/Kinesthetic Learners Bring in a variety of advertisements from diverse print sources, focusing on design and ad elements with or lacking bright colors. Set up several ads strategically around the room, creating stations. Place several ads at each station, along with printed questions, to include: ***What is your reaction to the color?*** Answers will vary depending on the ads chosen. Students may suggest that the color is pleasing because it is bright, colorful, attracts attention, and adds emphasis to the advertisement. Ask: ***Who might this ad appeal to?*** Possible answers: people with a youthful attitude; people attracted to bright colors.

Visual Literacy

A Different League Caption Answer Read the photo caption question to students: ***What principles of advertising layout are represented in this ad?*** Answers may include: the ad shows the illustrated layout with a large photo and another illustration showing the ad's intent (inside his head and his thoughts); the large font size used in the headline on the second line emphasizes the idea of what a person *Always wanted* (to represent his dreams and desires); there is a lot of copy, but it easy to read and speaks directly to the intended audience; the Web address is mentioned twice; the signature identifies the company by using their recognizable logo; the ad contains a focal point; visuals match the target audience; type and type placement aid the reader; appropriate use of color.

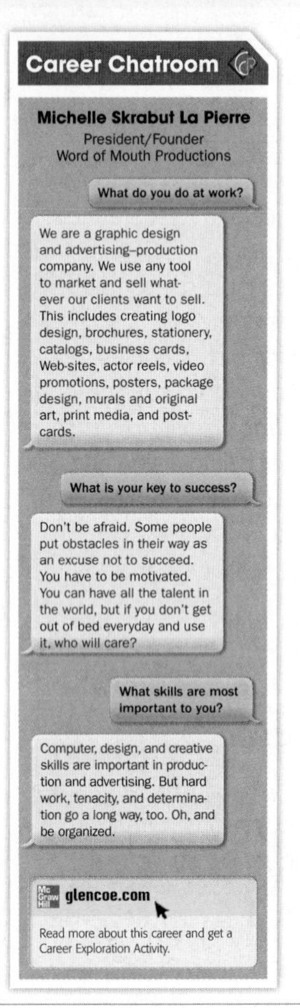
Career Chatroom

Michelle Skrabut La Pierre
President/Founder
Word of Mouth Productions

What do you do at work?

We are a graphic design and advertising–production company. We use any tool to market and sell whatever our clients want to sell. This includes creating logo design, brochures, stationery, catalogs, business cards, Web-sites, actor reels, video promotions, posters, package design, murals and original art, print media, and post-cards.

What is your key to success?

Don't be afraid. Some people put obstacles in their way as an excuse not to succeed. You have to be motivated. You can have all the talent in the world, but if you don't get out of bed everyday and use it, who will care?

What skills are most important to you?

Computer, design, and creative skills are important in production and advertising. But hard work, tenacity, and determination go a long way, too. Oh, and be organized.

glencoe.com

Read more about this career and get a Career Exploration Activity.

TYPE SIZES FOR PRINT ADS

Type size is measured in points. There are 12 points to one pica, and 6 picas to 1 inch. So a point is about $\frac{1}{72}$ of an inch. Word-processing program allows you to select type size.

One way to classify typefaces is serif or sans serif. A serif typeface has short crosslines at the upper and lower ends of the letters. Times Roman and Palatino are two commonly used serif fonts. Here are examples of these fonts in 10-point and 24-point type. Can you see the crosslines at the top and bottom of the letters T and P?

Times Roman, 10-point

Times Roman, 24-point

Palatino, 10-point

Palatino, 24-point

A sans serif font is one that is *sans* (French for "without") any crosslines. These fonts are popular because their simple design makes them very easy to read. Some common sans serif fonts are Arial, Helvetica, and Futura. Here are examples:

Arial, 10-point

Helvetica, 16-point

Futura, 24-point

The preferences and characteristics of the target market will dictate the choice of the type size. A study found that one-third of readers over 65 do not read ads because the type is too small. This means that a 14-point font would be a better choice than a 10-point font for ads designed to reach readers over 65. Many companies use serif typefaces and 12-point font sizes in most ad copy. Type that is too small or difficult to read will lower the readership of an ad.

You can add variety and **emphasis** by using different sizes of typefaces, italics, boldface, and combinations of capital and lowercase letters. The message remains the same, but capitalizing different words may change the effect on the viewer.

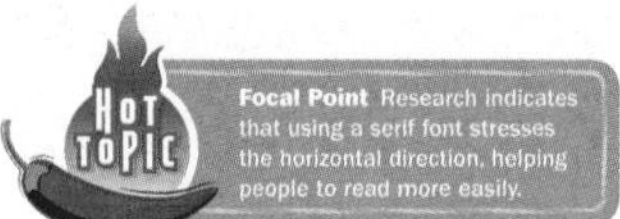

Focal Point Research indicates that using a serif font stresses the horizontal direction, helping people to read more easily.

CHECKING ADVERTISING PROOFS

When designers create advertisements, an advertising proof is developed. The **advertising proof** is a presentation of an ad that shows exactly how it will appear in print. Most proofs are developed and delivered in a digital format, which saves time and money.

The advertising proof is sent to the advertiser for review and approval. Before giving final approval, the advertiser makes an evaluation based on the following criteria:

- The ad should be bold enough to stand out on a page, even if it is placed next to other ads.
- The overall layout should look clean and uncluttered and should guide the reader through the copy.
- The typefaces and type sizes should be easy to read and help to emphasize the message.
- The signature should be apparent and distinctive.
- The intended message and image projected must be appropriate for the target audience.

In addition, it is important to make sure that all prices printed in an ad are accurate and that all brand names and company names are spelled correctly. Any errors found in the proof must be marked and returned for correction before the ad is finally published.

After You Read Section 20.2

Review Key Concepts

1. **Explain** how to create a focal point and eye movement using a Z ad layout.
2. **Describe** how to select the size and type of a typeface.
3. **List** three things that you should look for in an advertising proof.

Practice Academics

English Language Arts

4. Conduct research on popular advertising campaigns from the past. Select one of these advertising campaigns and write a one-page newspaper editorial in reaction to it. Be sure to mention the company, name of the campaign, and the year or years that the campaign ran.

NCTE 1 Read texts to acquire new information.

Mathematics

5. You must create a Web banner advertisement for a new hybrid automobile. If the Web banner advertisement has a click-through rate of one percent and is sent to 55,000 people, how many people will visit the banner Web site?

NCTM Number and Operations Compute fluently and make reasonable estimates.

Math Concept **Computation** It is necessary to convert percents to their decimal equivalent before using them in computations.

Starting Hints Divide one percent by 100 to get a decimal. Multiply the decimal by the number of people who received the ad to determine the number of visitors.

For help, go to the **Math Skills Handbook** located at the back of this book.

glencoe.com

Check your answers.

480 | Unit 6 · Promotion

Chapter 20 · Print Advertisements | 481

ELABORATE

Reinforce Vocabulary

Serif and Sans Serif—Origin Point out to students that serif typefaces were invented to aid the reader. The serifs added to the letters are designed to help the word hold together so that it appears as a unit, which makes it easier for the brain to recognize and read. Tell students that serif typefaces are often used with running text such as the paragraphs in books. *Sans* is the French word for *without*. Sans serif typefaces are often used in picture captions, callouts, and headlines.

Focal Point Have students survey at least ten print products. These can be books, newspapers, magazines, posters, flyers, and so on. Ask them to keep track of the number of print items that use serif fonts and the number that use sans serif fonts. Tally the class results.

Career Chatroom

Use these questions to focus the discussion about the Career Chatroom feature.

Guiding Questions

Analyze What does Ms. La Pierre mean when she says, "Don't be afraid"?	Try new things. Don't make excuses. Be motivated to do the best you can do.
Predict What skills and attributes should you develop for success in advertising and production?	computer, design, and creative skills and hard work, tenacity, and determination

glencoe.com

Career Exploration Send students to the Online Learning Center to read more about this career and to get a Career Exploration activity.

EVALUATE

Graphic Organizer

Display this diagram. Ask students to provide additional criteria an advertiser should use in reviewing and checking advertising proofs. Remind students that the primary objective in checking proofs is to find and eliminate any errors. Possible answers:

Criteria for Checking Advertising Proofs

- Ad should be bold enough to stand out on a page, even if placed next to other ads.
- Overall layout looks clean and uncluttered and should guide the reader through the copy.
- Typefaces and type sizes should be easy to read and help to emphasize the message.
- Signature should be apparent and distinctive.
- Intended message and image projected must be appropriate for the target audience.

glencoe.com

iWB

Graphic Organizer Send students to the Online Learning Center to print this graphic organizer.

Mini Project

Extension

Research Photos Have students explore commercial and other photo sources online using a search engine to find images that could be used in certain ad situations to evoke emotions. Ask them to find photos that could be used to convey comfort, excitement, sadness, happiness, sorrow, and other emotions. Have students print or make copies of the photos and create a paper or digital photo album with the photos labeled with the appropriate emotion. (Tell students to look carefully at the copyright information on any Web site they use. They should be sure it is allowable for them to use the photos in a school setting.) Have students share their photo albums with the class. Ask the class to make suggestions about what kinds of products or services might be advertised with a particular photo. For example, a photo of a happy couple might be used to advertise a jeweler who sells engagement rings.

After You Read Section 20.2

Review Key Concepts

1. Create a Z layout by placing the most dominant item (typically the headline) on top of the Z. Then place copy and illustrations on the diagonal line of the Z, and your signature and call to action at the bottom of the Z in the right corner.
2. The size of the typeface should be distinctive, yet appropriate for the business and target audience.
3. When checking an advertising proof, you should make sure all prices are accurate and that all brand names and company names are spelled correctly. In addition, the following should be considered: The ad should be bold enough to stand out on a page, even if it is placed next to other ads. The overall layout should look clean and uncluttered and should guide the reader through the copy. The typefaces and type sizes should be easy to read and help to emphasize the message. The signature should be apparent and distinctive. The intended message and image projected must be appropriate for the target audience.

Practice Academics

English Language Arts

4. Students must identify one of the top advertising campaigns. The completed one-page report should list the company, name of the campaign, the year or years that the campaign ran.

Mathematics

5. 550 (55,000 × .01)

glencoe.com

Answer Key Send students to the Online Learning Center to check their answers.

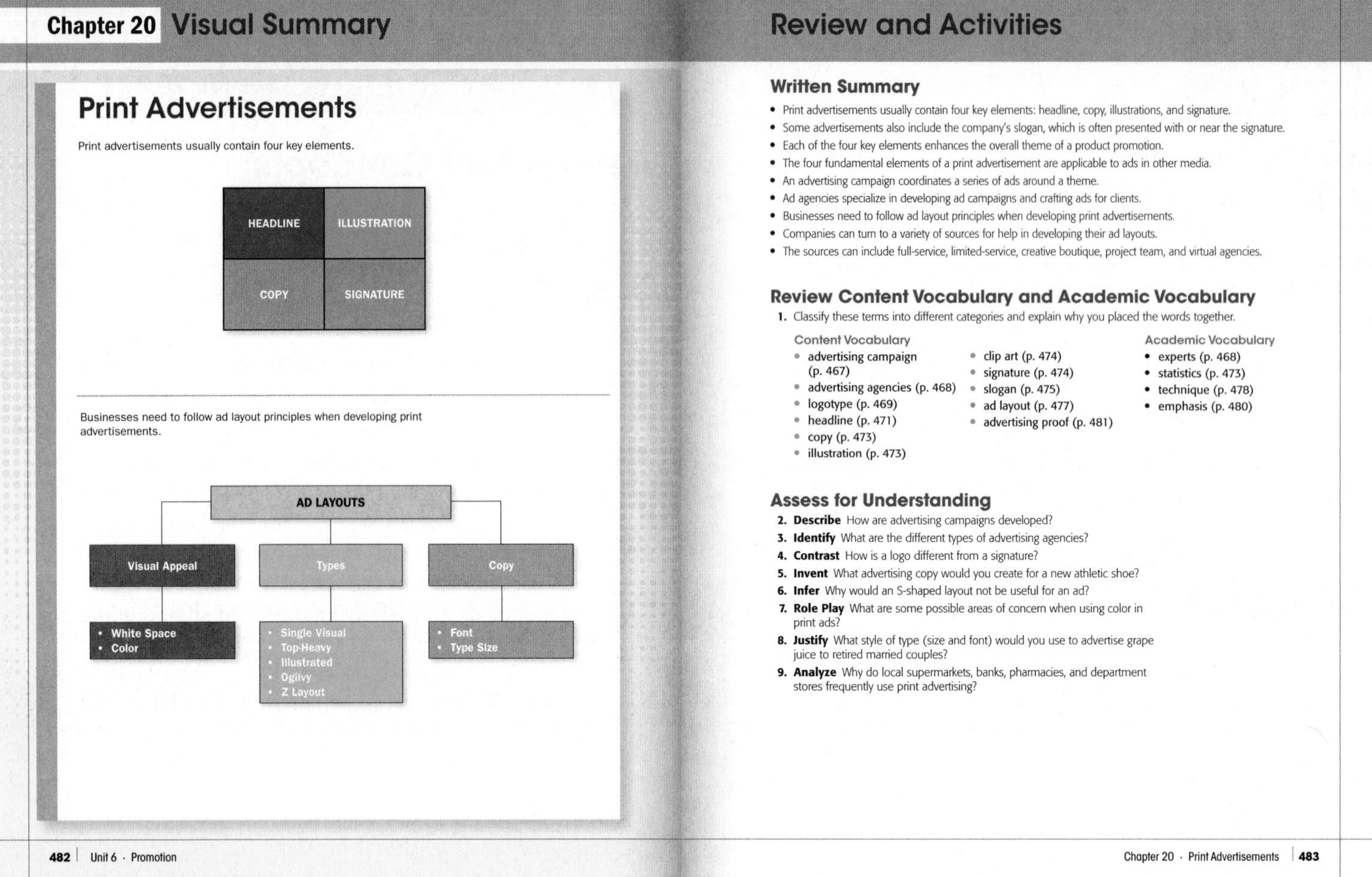

Chapter 20 Visual Summary

Print Advertisements

Print advertisements usually contain four key elements.

Businesses need to follow ad layout principles when developing print advertisements.

482 | Unit 6 · Promotion

Review and Activities

Written Summary

- Print advertisements usually contain four key elements: headline, copy, illustrations, and signature.
- Some advertisements also include the company's slogan, which is often presented with or near the signature.
- Each of the four key elements enhances the overall theme of a product promotion.
- The four fundamental elements of a print advertisement are applicable to ads in other media.
- An advertising campaign coordinates a series of ads around a theme.
- Ad agencies specialize in developing ad campaigns and crafting ads for clients.
- Businesses need to follow ad layout principles when developing print advertisements.
- Companies can turn to a variety of sources for help in developing their ad layouts.
- The sources can include full-service, limited-service, creative boutique, project team, and virtual agencies.

Review Content Vocabulary and Academic Vocabulary

1. Classify these terms into different categories and explain why you placed the words together.

Content Vocabulary
- advertising campaign (p. 467)
- advertising agencies (p. 468)
- logotype (p. 469)
- headline (p. 471)
- copy (p. 473)
- illustration (p. 473)
- clip art (p. 474)
- signature (p. 474)
- slogan (p. 475)
- ad layout (p. 477)
- advertising proof (p. 481)

Academic Vocabulary
- experts (p. 468)
- statistics (p. 473)
- technique (p. 478)
- emphasis (p. 480)

Assess for Understanding

2. **Describe** How are advertising campaigns developed?
3. **Identify** What are the different types of advertising agencies?
4. **Contrast** How is a logo different from a signature?
5. **Invent** What advertising copy would you create for a new athletic shoe?
6. **Infer** Why would an S-shaped layout not be useful for an ad?
7. **Role Play** What are some possible areas of concern when using color in print ads?
8. **Justify** What style of type (size and font) would you use to advertise grape juice to retired married couples?
9. **Analyze** Why do local supermarkets, banks, pharmacies, and department stores frequently use print advertising?

Chapter 20 · Print Advertisements | 483

EVALUATE

Visual Summary

Express Creativity Ask students to develop their own visual summary of a concept in the chapter. Encourage students to use different formats for their visual summaries, such as a storyboard, a timeline, a table, a tree diagram, or a word web. Visual summaries will vary depending on the concept depicted. Questions to ask when assessing a visual summary include:

- Is the summary clear, economical, and simple?
- Are any important steps left out?
- Are steps or concepts arranged in the same order as the original?
- Does the summary reveal a pattern that connects the details?
- Does the summary locate and highlight the most important information?

Review Content Vocabulary and Academic Vocabulary

1. Classifications will vary, however students should provide a reasonable explanation for their classifications. Sample answer:

   Advertising a Product: advertising campaign, advertising agencies

   Elements of Print Advertisements: logotype, headline, copy, illustration, clip art, signature, slogan

   Developing the Advertisement: ad layout, advertising proof

   Explanation: Advertising campaigns and advertising agencies are used to advertise or promote products and services. Logotype, headline, copy, illustration, clip art, signature, and slogan are all used in the creation of an advertisement. Ad layouts and advertising proofs are part of the development process for creating advertisements.

EVALUATE

Assess for Understanding

2. An advertising campaign depends on its scope, size, and the size of the business. Smaller firms may develop the campaign "in-house" using individuals or their own advertising department. Larger companies often designate all or a part of the campaign to a full- or limited-service agency. Planning the campaign involves these steps: identify the target audience; determine objectives; establish the budget; develop the message; select the media; and evaluate the campaign.

3. Types of advertising agencies include: full-service, limited-service, creative boutique, project team, and virtual.

4. A logo is a graphic symbol for a company, brand, or organization. The signature is the distinctive identification for a business, often the name of the advertiser.

5. Students' copy will vary. However, copy should follow these guidelines: copy should be conversational and written in a very personal, friendly manner; good copy is simple and direct; copy should appeal to the senses; copy should have news value by providing specific information.

6. Answers will vary. Sample answer: The eye does not naturally follow an S shape when reading or scanning a page, so the S layout would not have information in the order a person would normally look at it.

7. Adding more colors can increase costs by 35 percent. Cultural differences pertaining to color may have unintended results in certain target markets and with global commerce.

8. Students should suggest using a sans serif font in at least 14 point for the advertisement.

9. The primary trading area is well known, which allows these businesses to target customers effectively. Many people read print media, flyers, circulars, daily and weekly newspapers, so there is an immediate response to coupons, special events, and sales. These businesses mass market their products and print advertising can reach all customers in the area.

21st Century Skills

Critical Thinking Skills

10. Ads and the Law One of the most successful print advertising campaigns is the "Got Milk?" campaign. These ads are developed on behalf of America's Milk Processors Board and are paid for by individual dairy producers. Producers are charged a per-head fee on cattle to pay for the campaign. That means dairy producers were charged more if they had more cattle. Discuss whether this payment method is fair.

Financial Literacy Skills

11. The Cost of Advertising A small, independently owned business has hired a full-service advertising agency to develop an advertising campaign. The advertising agency will charge $3,500 a month to run the campaign. If the campaign runs for a year, what will be the yearly contracted amount? What will it cost the business each quarter?

e-Marketing Skills

12. Online Advertising Imagine that you work for a local travel agency. You are considering placing Internet display ads on several travel Web sites. Your manager agrees about the need for advertising but is not convinced that the Internet is the best medium. Use what you know about advertising to convince your manager to follow through with this ad campaign.

- Identify the strengths of Internet advertisements.
- Explain the features of Internet ads that cannot be replicated in print.
- Find examples of Internet ads for an agency that will develop the ad.
- Present the examples of Internet ads to your manager for feedback.

Build Academic Skills

English Language Arts

13. Advertising Layout Skills There are several popular types of ad layouts that designers use in print advertisements. Review newspapers and magazines to research and find print advertisements. Select a print ad for each layout design. Organize your materials and give a presentation on how each ad represents a different layout design.

NCTE 1 Read texts to acquire new information.

Science

14. Science, Technology, and Ads Marketers use scientific data to design advertising campaigns. Examples include personal data mining; analyzing keywords and phrases from Internet searches; calculating direct-mail response rates; and researching purchase behavior. Identify the use of a scientific principle or technological innovation that has application for print advertising. Share an ad that features this principle or feature.

NSES E Develop abilities of technological design, understandings about science and technology.

Mathematics

15. Calculate Advertising Credit Your home store has an arrangement with a manufacturer of patio furniture. The store receives a 4-percent advertising credit on total yearly sales. What is your advertising credit on sales totaling $68,000?

NCTM Number and Operations Compute fluently and make reasonable estimates.

Math Concept **Computation** A percent discount is usually calculated as an amount off an original price, not an amount off an already discounted price. To figure the amount of a discount, convert fractions and percents to decimals, and multiply.

For help, go to the **Math Skills Handbook** located at the back of this book.

Standardized Test Practice

Directions Read the following questions. On a separate sheet of paper, write the best possible answer for each one.

1. Which of the following provides the selling message in a print advertisement?
   A. Copy
   B. Headline
   C. Illustration
   D. Signature
2. Clip art in a print ad can include images, stock drawings, and photographs.
   T
   F
3. The sketch that shows the general arrangement and appearance of a finished ad is known as the __________.

Test-Taking Tip
Look for key words in test directions, such as *choose, describe, explain, compare, identify, similar, except,* and *not.*

DECA Connection Role Play

Manager Small Hotel

Situation Your hotel is located in the historic district of a popular tourist destination. It has 30 guest rooms in a building and has been in operation for 145 years. The hotel has recently been renovated and redecorated. Bookings run at near capacity during the spring and fall months. Bookings during the summer and winter months are not as good. They reach about 70 percent of capacity. You advertise in upscale lifestyle magazines and in magazines that appeal to the traveling public.

You recently hired a new employee (judge) for your assistant manager position. You plan to train the new employee (judge) in all aspects of the hotel operation. You have assigned the new employee (judge) the task of creating a magazine advertisement that announces the hotel's redecoration. Before the new employee (judge) begins working on the advertisement, you are to meet with the employee (judge) to explain print advertisements and their components.

Activity You are to explain to the new employee (judge) each of the components of print advertisements and the importance of coordinating those elements. You are also to explain the importance of ensuring that the copy is correct and that the advertisement meets the standards of your hotel.

Evaluation You will be evaluated on how well you meet the following performance indicators:

1. Explain the components of advertisements.
2. Explain the importance of coordinating elements in advertisements.
3. Explain the nature of effective written communication.
4. Edit and revise written work consistent with professional standards.
5. Orient new employees.

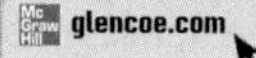
glencoe.com

Role Plays Download the Competitive Events Workbook for more Role-Play practice.

EVALUATE

21st Century Skills

Critical Thinking Skills

10. Answers will vary but students should be able to state pros for the mandatory assessments, for example, the ad promotes the use of milk, and indirectly benefits milk sales for individual farmers. The cons are that the ads infringe on free speech rights by requiring farmers to pay for them. Recent U.S. District Court decisions have held that the ads do violate free speech rights, but litigation has been ongoing over the years in this case and in others related to generic advertising campaigns.

Financial Literacy Skills

11. Yearly cost is $42,000 (12 months × $3,500/month). The quarterly cost is $10,500 ($42,000/4 quarters).

e-Marketing Skills

12. Students should recall from Chapter 19 that Internet ads include opt-in e-mail ads, search engine and banner ads, rich-media and video ads, and social-media advertising. Social-media ads, in particular, allow companies to develop advertising messages, to create customer profiles, to develop sales leads, to provide special offers, and to maintain customer feedback about the image and performance of their products. Rich-media and video ads offer animation and sound with interactive features to deliver advertising messages, which print ads cannot do. Students should locate examples of Internet ads for an agency that will develop the ad and present the examples.

EVALUATE

Build Academic Skills

English Language Arts

13. Accept all correctly identified advertising layouts. Each ad selected should represent one of the different ad layout designs (single visual, top heavy, illustrated, Oglivy, and Z layout designs).

Science

14. Accept all reasonable answers that identify a scientific principle or technology that is currently being used to assist with print advertising or advertising campaigns.

Mathematics

15. $2,720 ($68,000 × .04 = $2,720)

Standardized Test Practice

1. A Copy
2. True
3. ad layout

DECA Connection Role Play

Evaluations will be based on these performance indicators:

1. **Explain the components of advertisements.** The elements of a print advertisement include: *headlines,* which attract readers, arouse interest, and get them to look at the illustration and copy; *copy* represents the selling message in the ad; the *signature,* or logotype, is the identification symbol for a business; a *slogan* is a catch phrase or small group of words that are combined in a way that identifies a product or company; *disclosures,* which include terms and conditions, are included in some advertisements; *illustrations* help expand on the copy by showing how the product works or how it is used.
2. **Explain the importance of coordinating elements in advertisements.** The four main elements of advertisements—layout, color, typeface, and type size—must work together (coordinate) to create the most effective advertisement possible. If the type is too big or the colors clash, for example, it will affect the layout and interest level of the ad. The four elements must be balanced for the ad to grab the interest of the target audience.
3. **Explain the nature of effective written communication.** Basic considerations in effective written communication include: know your audience; know your purpose; and know your subject. Using language effectively and organizing your thoughts are also important to effective written communication.
4. **Edit and revise written work consistent with professional standards.** Students should demonstrate how they would check a written communication for spelling and grammar errors and to make sure all prices, dates, and so on are correct.
5. **Orient new employees.** Students should show how they would train new employees in all aspects of the business, or in the parts of the business that the employee will be involved in. They should develop training manuals and interactive presentations as appropriate. They need to be able to answer any questions the new employees might have about the company.

glencoe.com

Role Plays For more DECA Role Plays, send students to the Online Learning Center to download the Competitive Events Workbook.

UNIT 6 **Marketing Internship Project**

Promotional Campaign for a Hybrid Automobile

The next generation of automobiles is hybrid. What kind of promotional campaign would be most effective to reach the target market for this product?

Scenario

Your advertising agency has an automobile company as a potential client. It is coming out with a new hybrid automobile that will be in direct competition with the Toyota® Prius and other hybrid automobiles in that price range, such as the Ford® Fusion Hybrid and Honda® Civic Hybrid. The promotional campaign must be exciting, creative, and engaging.

You must decide how the advertising dollars should be spent. Which media should make up the promotional mix? Who makes up the target market? The theme for the promotional campaign must speak to that target market.

The Skills You'll Use

Academic Skills Reading, writing, social studies, researching, and analyzing

Basic Skills Speaking, listening, thinking, and interpersonal

Technology Skills Word processing, spreadsheet, presentation, telecommunications, and the Internet

NCTE 4 Use written language to communicate effectively.
NCTE 7 Conduct research and gather, evaluate, and synthesize data to communicate discoveries.

Your Objective

Your objective is to design an effective promotional campaign to introduce your client's new hybrid automobile to the target market.

STEP 1 Do Your Research

Conduct research to find out about hybrid automobiles and people who buy them. How do hybrid cars function? What are the features and benefits of owning one? Study the promotional efforts of hybrid automobile manufacturers. What models are in the price range of your major competitor? As you conduct your research, answer these questions:

- What are the major hybrid automobiles in the same price range?
- What political, economic, socio-cultural, and technological factors may shed light on how the creative promotional campaign should be designed?
- Who is the target market for a hybrid automobile?
- What media and messages are competitors using to sell their hybrid automobiles?

Write a summary of your research.

STEP 2 Plan Your Project

Now that you have completed your research, you need to begin planning your project.

- Create a name for the new hybrid automobile and draft a theme that will be used for all promotional materials.
- Conduct a PEST analysis.
- Create a profile of a potential hybrid automobile customer.
- List and design materials that will be part of your promotional mix.
- Prepare a calendar of events to indicate when each phase of the promotional campaign should take place.
- Write a press release for the introduction of the new hybrid.
- Provide rationale for your plan with supporting research and a budget for your client's approval.
- Present your ideas in a written report.

STEP 3 Connect with Your Community

- Interview a trusted adult in your community who drives a hybrid car. Find out what he or she likes and dislikes about hybrid cars.
- Interview a retail car sales associate to learn the features and benefits of hybrid automobiles.
- Take notes during the interviews, and transcribe your notes after the interviews.

STEP 4 Share What You Learn

Assume your class is your client's marketing department staff that will decide if your advertising agency will get the job.

- Present your findings in an oral presentation. Be prepared to answer questions.
- Use software to create a slide presentation to complement your oral report. Include one slide in your presentation for each topic in your written report.
- Present samples of the promotional mix.

STEP 5 Evaluate Your Marketing and Academic Skills

Your project will be evaluated based on the following:

- The promotional campaign's theme and how it relates to the suggested target market
- The customer profile, calendar of events, press release, and promotional budget
- The coordination among the many facets of the promotional plan
- Creativity in the sample materials that are part of the promotional mix
- Research data to support the rationale for your plan
- Organization and continuity of presentation
- Mechanics—presentation and neatness
- Speaking and listening skills

MARKETING CORE FUNCTIONS
Promotion
Market Planning

Marketing Internship Project Checklist

Plan
- ✓ Conduct research on companies that make and sell hybrid automobiles.
- ✓ Design a comprehensive promotional campaign for a new hybrid automobile.

Write
- ✓ Explain how results of the PEST analysis will help you design an effective promotional campaign.
- ✓ Describe your ideas for your promotional campaign in a written report.
- ✓ Write a press release for the introduction of the new hybrid automobile.

Present
- ✓ Present research supporting your rationale for the theme and budget of the promotional campaign.
- ✓ Present your promotional campaign.
- ✓ Present samples of the promotional mix (e.g., magazine ad, television commercial, Web site, and/or social media connection).

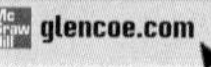
glencoe.com

Evaluate Download a rubric you can use to evaluate your final project.

my marketing portfolio

Internship Report Once you have completed your Marketing Internship Project and oral presentation, put your written report and a few printouts of key slides from your oral presentation in your Marketing Portfolio.

Research and Design a Promotional Campaign Do research and create the promotional mix for a product of your choice. Consider a smartphone, surfboard, jeans, sports apparel or equipment, or a food product. Does your research data support the rationale for the theme of the promotional campaign? Are your sample promotional materials creative and directed to a specific target market? Are your budget and calendar of events realistic? Is the campaign coordinated? Prepare a written report and an oral presentation.

486 | Unit 6 · Promotion   Unit 6 · Promotion | 487

EVALUATE

Anticipation Activity

Project Objective Read the project objective aloud to students: ***Design an effective promotional campaign to introduce your client's new hybrid automobile to the target market.*** Then ask students to think about what they learned about the promotional mix in Unit 6. Remind them of these key points:

- The promotional mix includes personal selling, advertising, direct marketing, sales promotion, and public relations.
- The steps of developing a promotional mix are: (1) Identify the target market; (2) determine objectives; (3) design promotional message; (4) select promotional activities; (5) allocate budget amounts; and (6) measure results.

Ask students: ***What are examples of consumer promotions?*** Strategies that encourage customers to buy a product include coupons, premiums, incentives, product samples, sponsorships, tie-ins, product placement, loyalty marketing, and POP displays.

Ask students: ***What are the elements of a print/online advertisement?*** Advertisements have four key elements: headline, copy, illustrations, and signature; some also include a company's slogan, logo, and, product disclosures.

Graphic Organizer

Display this diagram. Ask students to name different brands of hybrid automobiles. Possible answers:

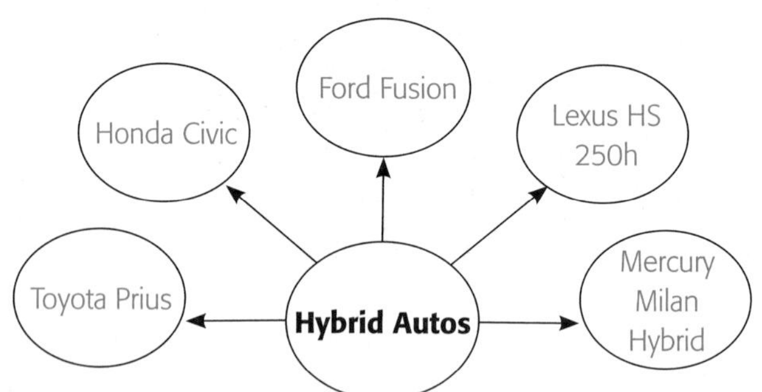

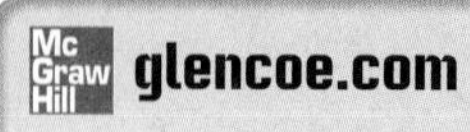
glencoe.com iWB

Graphic Organizer Send students to the Online Learning Center to print this graphic organizer.

EVALUATE

STEP 1 Do Your Research

Tell students that there are many places to find information they can use to develop a promotional campaign. Students can use library and Internet resources, but they should also talk to people in the community. Encourage students to seek the opinions and ideas of trusted people they know. Other people can bring new perspectives and ideas about promotional and advertising campaigns as well as customer preferences and the typical consumers who buy hybrid automobiles.

STEP 2 Plan Your Project

Students should create a customer profile and PEST analysis before designing a promotional campaign. Students should explain why they chose the target market, the name and theme for the promotional campaign and provide information about a calendar of events and a press release. Students' explanation of their promotional campaigns should include the research and a budget.

STEP 3 Connect with Your Community

Explain to students that connecting with members of the community is a great way to build relationships. Tell them that young people who have relationships with caring, responsible, and competent adults are more likely to achieve success in life than those who do not. Encourage students to take part in opportunities for adults to serve as mentors, coaches, advocates, and advisors, both formally and informally.

STEP 4 Share What You Learn

Students should present their ideas in a written report and oral presentation with presentation software. They should have at least one slide in their presentation for each key topic in the written report. Encourage students to speak clearly, use appropriate grammar and vocabulary, and actively engage the audience by making and maintaining eye contact and using movement (facial expressions, posture, gestures) to focus attention and interest.

STEP 5 Evaluate Your Marketing and Academic Skills

Have students use the Marketing Internship Project Checklist to help them to plan, write, and present their reports. Exemplary written reports will include information that clearly supports a central thesis, a single, distinct focus, generally well-developed ideas, well-phrased sentences that flow smoothly and are varied in length and structure, consistently precise word choice, and few, if any, errors in grammar, spelling, and mechanics.

Evaluation Rubric Send students to the Online Learning Center to get a rubric to evaluate their projects.

Culminating Activity

Explain to students that the choice of media to use for advertising in a promotional campaign is somewhat dependent on the target market for the product being promoted. If the product is a toy for children, a commercial for the toy would most likely be placed on television and not on the radio, since few children listen to that medium. Ask students: ***Generally, what might be the most effective media to use for each of these age groups: teens, 20–40-year-olds, and elders?*** A teen target market would likely be viewing the Internet, television, and teen magazines. The 20-to-40 age segment may use a combination of television, radio, the Internet, newspapers, and certain magazines. Online advertising might be not be viewed by the elderly, but newspaper, radio, and television ads may yield more results. The Internet provides interactivity. Newspaper ads can deliver more detailed information. Radio and television advertising speaks to a captive audience that must watch or listen to ads—however, many viewers switch channels or use TiVo to bypass commercials.

my marketing portfolio

Internship Report Have students put their written reports and printouts of key slides from their oral presentations in their marketing portfolio.

Research and Design a Promotional Campaign Direct students to select a product of their choice, such as a smartphone, surfboard, jeans, sports apparel or equipment, or a food product, and then research and create a promotional campaign for it. Students' completed promotional campaigns should include all of the elements and answer all of the questions included in the Marketing Internship Project on this page. This additional activity can build relevance for students who are motivated to learn about other specific business and industries. Relevance shifts the focus to what motivates individual students to learn.

UNIT 7

Distribution

PLANNING GUIDE AND RESOURCES

	Print	Digital
Unit 7 Distribution		Unit 7 Fast Files: Marketing Internship Project Activity Connect Online Learning Center through glencoe.com
Chapter 21 **Channels of Distribution**	Student Activity Workbook: Chapter 21 DECA Connection Role Play; Chapter 21 Vocabulary Activity; Section Note Taking Activities; Chapter Academics Activity; Section Study Skills Activities; Section Real-World Applications Activities Mathematics for Marketing Workbook Marketing Research Project Workbook School-to-Career Activity Workbook	Unit 7 Fast Files: Chapter 21 Discovery Project Worksheet and Rubric; Chapter 21 Green Marketer Activity; Chapter 21 Digital Nation Activity; Section Graphic Organizers; Section Outlines with Key Terms and Definitions; Section Summaries ExamView Assessment Suite, Chapter 21 Connect Online Learning Center through glencoe.com
Chapter 22 **Physical Distribution**	Student Activity Workbook: Chapter 22 DECA Connection Role Play; Chapter 22 Vocabulary Activity; Section Note Taking Activities; Chapter Academics Activity; Section Study Skills Activities; Section Real-World Applications Activities Mathematics for Marketing Workbook Marketing Research Project Workbook School-to-Career Activity Workbook	Unit 7 Fast Files: Chapter 22 Discovery Project Worksheet and Rubric; Chapter 22 Green Marketer Activity; Chapter 22 Digital Nation Activity; Section Graphic Organizers; Section Outlines with Key Terms and Definitions; Section Summaries ExamView Assessment Suite, Chapter 22 Connect Online Learning Center through glencoe.com
Chapter 23 **Purchasing**	Student Activity Workbook: Chapter 23 DECA Connection Role Play; Chapter 23 Vocabulary Activity; Section Note Taking Activities; Chapter Academics Activity; Section Study Skills Activities; Section Real-World Applications Activities Mathematics for Marketing Workbook Marketing Research Project Workbook School-to-Career Activity Workbook	Unit 7 Fast Files: Chapter 23 Discovery Project Worksheet and Rubric; Chapter 23 Green Marketer Activity; Chapter 23 Digital Nation Activity; Section Graphic Organizers; Section Outlines with Key Terms and Definitions; Section Summaries ExamView Assessment Suite, Chapter 23 Connect Online Learning Center through glencoe.com
Chapter 24 **Stock Handling and Inventory Control**	Student Activity Workbook: Chapter 24 DECA Connection Role Play; Chapter 24 Vocabulary Activity; Section Note Taking Activities; Chapter Academics Activity; Section Study Skills Activities; Section Real-World Applications Activities Mathematics for Marketing Workbook Marketing Research Project Workbook School-to-Career Activity Workbook	Unit 7 Fast Files: Chapter 24 Discovery Project Worksheet and Rubric; Chapter 24 Green Marketer Activity; Chapter 24 Digital Nation Activity; Section Graphic Organizers; Section Outlines with Key Terms and Definitions; Section Summaries ExamView Assessment Suite, Chapter 24 Connect Online Learning Center through glencoe.com

McGRAW-HILL PROFESSIONAL DEVELOPMENT

Perkins IV has placed more emphasis than ever on providing quality professional development for Career and Technology educators. The legislation mandates that the focus of professional development be the integration and reinforcement of academic competencies in order to improve student achievement. Specifically, Perkins requires measurements of students' academic success. McGraw-Hill answers the challenge for strong and effective professional development with a five-prong **Online Professional Development for Integrating Academics.**

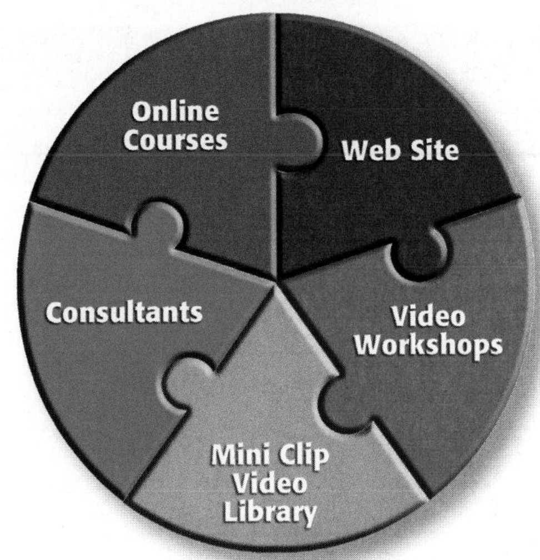

For pricing and ordering information contact your McGraw-Hill Sales Representative.

VIDEO LIBRARY

The McGraw-Hill Professional Development Mini-Clip Video Library, referenced for your convenience at the point of use, provides teaching strategies to strengthen academic and learning skills. Go to the Online Learning Center to view these professional development video clips for Unit 7:

Chapter 21: Channels of Distribution

- **Reading: Lesson Reflections:** A narrator discusses various instructional strategies suitable for use with English learners. (p. 493)
- **ELL: Academic Language:** Authors discuss the importance of addressing academic language when teaching English language learners. (p. 503)

Chapter 22: Physical Distribution

- **Reading: Prereading Strategies:** A teacher assesses students' prior knowledge about a text selection. (p. 521)
- **Reading: Vocabulary:** An author describes the critical importance of academic language. (p. 525)

Chapter 23: Purchasing

- **Reading: Preparing to Read:** A teacher uses multiple instructional strategies to prepare students to read a persuasive essay. (p. 537)
- **Math: Multiple Approaches to Problem Solving:** A teacher and students discuss various options of problem solving and then apply one, working backward, to a problem. (p. 540)

Chapter 24: Stock Handling and Inventory Control

- **Reading: During and After Reading:** A teacher models reading for her students and then has them practice what a good reader thinks about. (p. 557)
- **ELL: Modeling the Concept:** Students use manipulatives to model a problem and clarify content concepts. (p. 565)

UNIT OVERVIEW

Sections	Objectives	Common Core State Standards College and Career Readiness
Section 21.1 **Distribution**	• Explain the concept of a channel of distribution. • Identify channel members. • Compare different channels of distribution.	• **Writing** Produce clear and coherent writing in which the development, organization, and style are appropriate to task, purpose, and audience.
Section 21.2 **Distribution Planning**	• Explain distribution planning. • Name and describe the three levels of distribution intensity. • Explain the effect of the Internet on distribution planning. • Describe the challenges of international distribution planning.	• **Writing** Produce clear and coherent writing in which the development, organization, and style are appropriate to task, purpose, and audience.
Section 22.1 **Transportation**	• Describe the nature and scope of physical distribution. • Identify transportation systems and services that move products from manufacturers to consumers. • Name the different kinds of transportation service companies.	• **Writing** Conduct short as well as more sustained research projects based on focused questions, demonstrating understanding of the subject under investigation.
Section 22.2 **Inventory Storage**	• Explain the concept and function of inventory storage. • Identify the types of warehouses. • Discuss distribution planning for international markets.	• **Writing** Conduct short as well as more sustained research projects based on focused questions, demonstrating understanding of the subject under investigation. • **Writing** Write informative/explanatory texts to examine and convey complex ideas and information clearly and accurately through the effective selection, organization, and analysis of content.

Sections	Objectives	Common Core State Standards College and Career Readiness
Section 23.1 **The Role of the Buyer**	• Define the terms used to describe organizational buyers. • Explain how planning purchases differs between an industrial market and a resellers' market. • Describe the six-month merchandising plan and explain its calculations. • Explain the concept of chain-store buying.	• **Speaking and Listening** Prepare for and participate effectively in a range of conversations and collaborations with diverse partners, building on others' ideas and expressing their own clearly and persuasively.
Section 23.2 **The Purchasing Process**	• List the three types of purchase situations. • Explain the criteria for selecting suppliers. • Name the factors involved in negotiating terms of a sale. • Describe the various Internet purchasing methods.	• **Writing** Write informative/explanatory texts to examine and convey complex ideas and information clearly and accurately through the effective selection, organization, and analysis of content. • **Writing** Write narratives to develop real or imagined experiences or events using effective technique, well-chosen details, and well-structured event sequences.
Section 24.1 **Stock Handling**	• Describe the receiving process. • Explain stock handling techniques used in receiving deliveries.	• **Reading** Read closely to determine what the text says explicitly and to make logical inferences from it. • **Writing** Conduct short as well as more sustained research projects based on focused questions, demonstrating understanding of the subject under investigation.
Section 24.2 **Inventory Control**	• Describe the process for providing effective inventory management. • Explain the types of inventory control systems. • Relate customer service to distribution. • Analyze sales information to determine inventory turnover. • Discuss technology and inventory management.	• **Writing** Conduct short as well as more sustained research projects based on focused questions, demonstrating understanding of the subject under investigation.

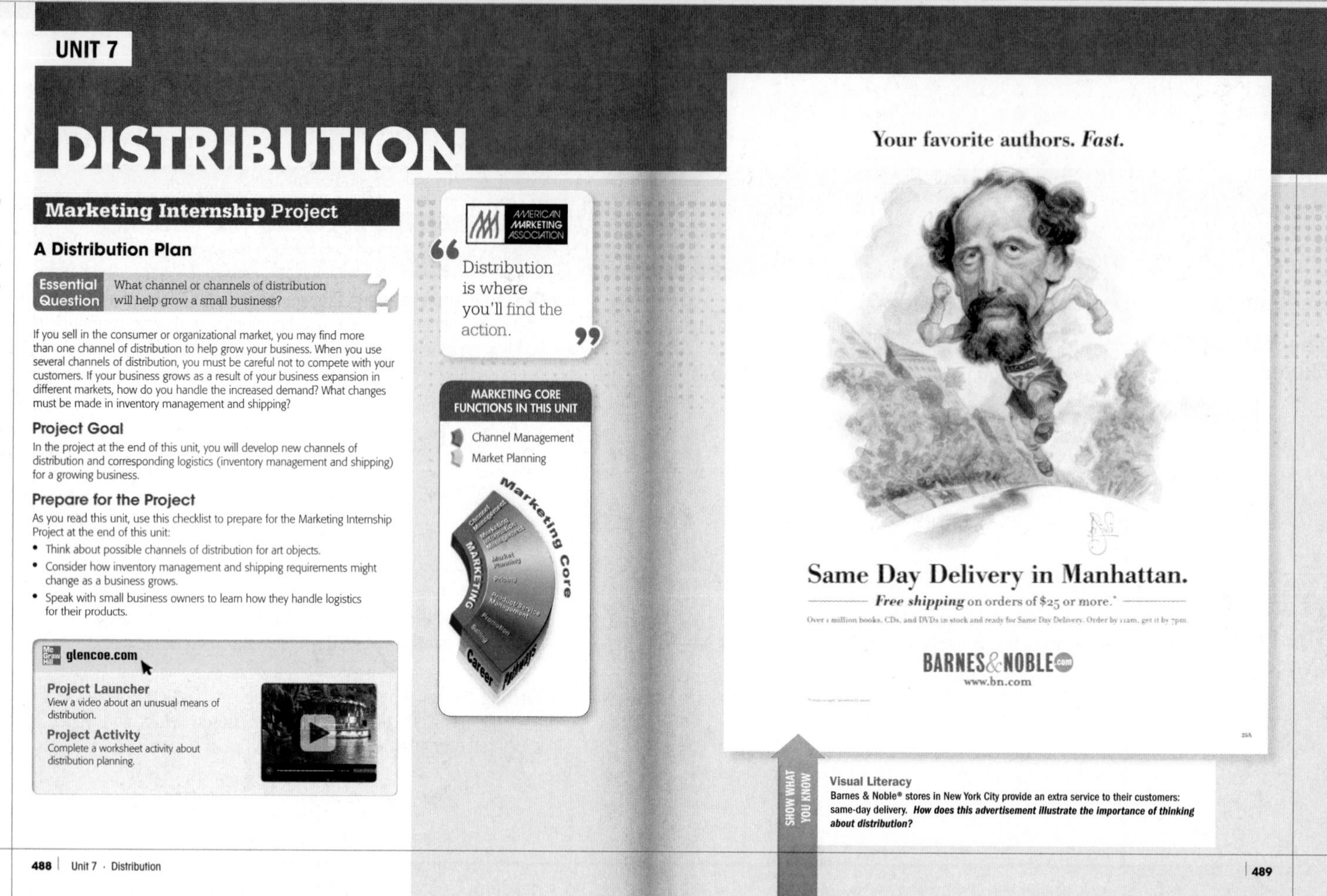

UNIT 7

DISTRIBUTION

Marketing Internship Project

A Distribution Plan

Essential Question What channel or channels of distribution will help grow a small business?

If you sell in the consumer or organizational market, you may find more than one channel of distribution to help grow your business. When you use several channels of distribution, you must be careful not to compete with your customers. If your business grows as a result of your business expansion in different markets, how do you handle the increased demand? What changes must be made in inventory management and shipping?

Project Goal

In the project at the end of this unit, you will develop new channels of distribution and corresponding logistics (inventory management and shipping) for a growing business.

Prepare for the Project

As you read this unit, use this checklist to prepare for the Marketing Internship Project at the end of this unit:

- Think about possible channels of distribution for art objects.
- Consider how inventory management and shipping requirements might change as a business grows.
- Speak with small business owners to learn how they handle logistics for their products.

glencoe.com

Project Launcher View a video about an unusual means of distribution.

Project Activity Complete a worksheet activity about distribution planning.

AMERICAN MARKETING ASSOCIATION

"Distribution is where you'll find the action."

MARKETING CORE FUNCTIONS IN THIS UNIT

- Channel Management
- Market Planning

Marketing Core
MARKETING
Career Pathways

Your favorite authors. Fast.
Same Day Delivery in Manhattan.
Free shipping on orders of $25 or more.*
Over 1 million books, CDs, and DVDs in stock and ready for Same Day Delivery. Order by 11am, get it by 7pm.
BARNES&NOBLE.com
www.bn.com

SHOW WHAT YOU KNOW

Visual Literacy Barnes & Noble® stores in New York City provide an extra service to their customers: same-day delivery. ***How does this advertisement illustrate the importance of thinking about distribution?***

488 | Unit 7 · Distribution

489

ENGAGE

Introduce the Unit

Unit 7 explores the basics of buying and distribution.

Chapter 21 explains how products are distributed and sold—the place decision.

Chapter 22 focuses on the nature and scope of physical distribution, such as transportation, systems, and storage.

Chapter 23 examines the purchasing function as part of marketing.

Chapter 24 discusses stock handling, inventory control, and stock management.

Build Background

Ask students to choose a product they might buy at a local retail store. Have them name steps to get that product from the manufacturer to the customer. Ask students: ***Why is having an efficient distribution system vital?*** Without an efficient distribution system, products would not arrive in the right quantity and at the right time for customers.

Visual Literacy

Photo Caption Answer Read the copy on the ad to students. Then read the photo caption and the photo caption question to students: ***How does this advertisement illustrate the importance of thinking about distribution?*** Answers will vary. Accept all reasonable answers. Sample answer: Most bookstores offer shipping, but very few offer same-day shipping. Most consumers would not expect to get same-day delivery of books so this ad is effective at getting the message about this unique service across. Ask students to evaluate the visual components of the advertisement. Ask volunteers to explain how the visual aspects of the advertisement complement the text of the advertisement. The image of author Dickens running through Central Park is a funny way to imagine and depict how the book store will make same-day book deliveries in Manhattan. The headline "Your favorite authors. Fast." complements the illustration and the message about the service offered.

ENGAGE

Marketing Internship Project Preview

Read students the Marketing Internship Project Essential Question: ***What channel or channels of distribution will help grow a small business?*** Because students are just starting to learn about channels of distribution, they will likely not know the specific answer to this question, which is that the right channels of distribution will reach target markets in the most efficient and cost-effective way. However, students should know that shipping, via any mode of transportation, is part of distribution. Explain to students that they will learn about distribution and different channels of distribution while studying this unit. Tell students that when they are finished studying this unit, they will ask questions to find answers about creating a distribution plan to expand an artist's business. As they study each chapter in the unit, they can prepare for the Unit Project by thinking of possible channels of distribution for art objects.

glencoe.com

Marketing Internship Project Resources Send students to the Online Learning Center to watch a video and download a worksheet activity related to the topic of the Unit Project.

Read the American Marketing Association quote to students:

"Distribution is where you'll find the action."

Explain to students that the AMA's Resource Library provides information through articles and resources that address the functions of marketing. Content about the channel management function examines issues of concern to distributors:

The Importance of Distribution Efforts to ensure that brands are available to end users mean that product distribution is a critical element in a brand's success.

Managers should spend time evaluating the impact of their changes in distribution strategy.

Ask students: ***Why do managers need to be aware of changes in distribution strategies?*** Pricing changes can affect profits as customers may react to price increases. The effects of changing distribution strategies would affect profits and pricing if a new shipping method costs more in exchange for the advantage of faster delivery. Conversely, arranging for a less expensive method of shipping could mean lost customers if products were delivered late or damaged.

MARKETING CORE FUNCTIONS IN THIS UNIT

Point out to students that Chapters 21, 22, 23, and 24 will touch on two of the seven marketing core functions. Describe each of these marketing functions to students to prepare them to start studying this unit.

Channel Management or Distribution is the process of deciding how to get goods into customer's hands.

Market Planning involves understanding the concepts and strategies used to develop and target specific marketing strategies to a select audience.

MARKETING RESEARCH

PROJECT WORKBOOK

The purpose of the Marketing Research Project Workbook is to provide a step-by-step approach for students to conduct their own marketing research study. Each chapter is devoted to key elements in the research process. Each chapter builds upon the previous chapters, and by the end of the book, students will have completed an in-depth marketing research study, complete with rationale for all decisions, a report of the findings and conclusions, recommendations based on the original research problem and study objectives, and an annotated bibliography.

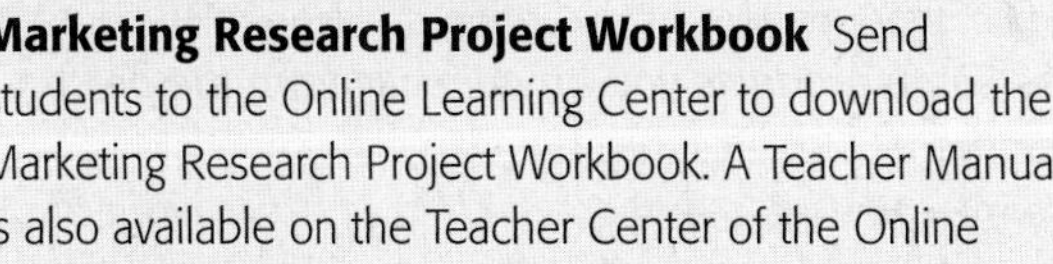
glencoe.com

Marketing Research Project Workbook Send students to the Online Learning Center to download the Marketing Research Project Workbook. A Teacher Manual is also available on the Teacher Center of the Online Learning Center.

Chapter 21 | Section 21.1 Distribution | Section 21.2 Distribution Planning

channels of distribution

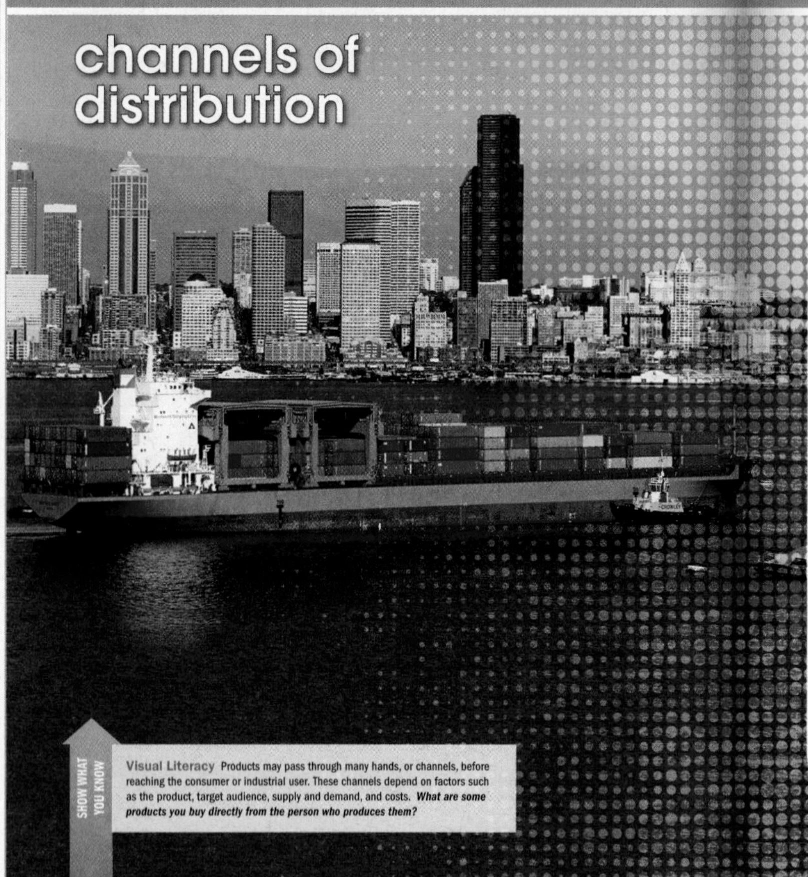

SHOW WHAT YOU KNOW

Visual Literacy Products may pass through many hands, or channels, before reaching the consumer or industrial user. These channels depend on factors such as the product, target audience, supply and demand, and costs. ***What are some products you buy directly from the person who produces them?***

Discovery Project

From Producer to Final User

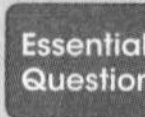

Essential Question How is a product moved from the manufacturer to the customer?

Project Goal

Select a product and describe how and by whom that product is transported from the manufacturer to the customer. You might select a type of produce, a computer, a digital SLR camera, a smartphone, a car, or any other product. Then visualize the path that product will take to reach the end user. (Hint: See **Figures 21.1** and **21.2** on pages 496–497.) Conduct additional research as necessary. Write a detailed report of how the product moves from manufacturer to the consumer.

Ask Yourself...

- What key words will you use to initiate your research?
- Would the channels of distribution for this product be different than for other products?
- Who would determine the channels of distribution for this product?

Analyze What are some criteria that would determine the channels used to distribute a product?

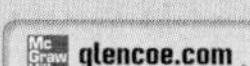

glencoe.com

Activity
Get a worksheet activity about channels of distribution.

Evaluate
Download a rubric you can use to evaluate your project.

DECA Connection

DECA Event Role Play

Concepts in this chapter are related to DECA competitive events that involve either an interview or role play.

Performance Indicators The performance indicators represent key skills and knowledge. Your key to success in DECA competitive events is relating them to concepts in this chapter.

- Explain the nature of channels of distribution.
- Explain the nature of channel-member relationships.
- Explain the nature and scope of channel management.
- Explain legal considerations in channel management.
- Explain ethical considerations in channel management.

DECA Prep

Role Play Practice role-playing with the DECA Connection competitive-event activity at the end of this chapter. More information about DECA events can be found on DECA's Web site.

Chapter 21 · Channels of Distribution | 491

ENGAGE

Visual Literacy

Read the chapter opener photo caption question to students: ***What are some products you buy directly from the person who produces them?*** Students may mention such products as produce from a farmers market, baked goods from a bakery, or electricity from an electrical utilities company. Ask these guiding questions to activate prior knowledge.

Guiding Questions

Recall What are the four Ps of the marketing mix?	product, place, price, and promotion
Analyze Which of the four Ps deals with distribution planning? Explain your rationale.	place, because it deals with decisions as to how the product will be distributed in order to reach a business's customers

Discovery Project

From Producer to Final User Ask students the Discovery Project Essential Question to focus their thinking on how products are transported: ***How is a product moved from the manufacturer to the customer?*** Students should recognize that it depends on the product, distance, and the customer. For example, large products might be shipped by train or ship and then by truck to a local store where they are purchased by customers. Also, items purchased online from a manufacturer might be sent directly to the customer. Ask students to share different ways they have received goods. Answers may include: purchasing items at a store, receiving items through the mail, and receiving items by a package delivery system.

glencoe.com

Discovery Project Resources Send students to the Online Learning Center to download a rubric to evaluate their projects.

ENGAGE

Introduce the Chapter

Chapter 21 provides fundamental information about channels of distribution. These main concepts are introduced and discussed:

- Channel members
- Direct and indirect channels
- Channels of distribution for consumer products and services
- Channels of distribution for industrial products and services
- Distribution planning
- Multiple channels
- Control versus costs
- Distribution intensity
- Legal and ethical considerations
- Distribution in foreign markets

Discussion Starter

Channels of Distribution Bring a cotton T-shirt to class. Ask students to brainstorm all the elements and steps involved in bringing it to market. As students name the steps and elements, display their answers in a time-line format. Add any steps the students leave out. Answers may include: raw cotton in the field, farmer's harvest and labor, making the raw material into fabric, collecting and delivering fabric to a manufacturer, and producing, warehousing, distributing, and selling the shirt. Ask: ***What might happen to this time line if there was a strike among shippers?*** There would be delays in the delivery of raw cotton to the fabric manufacturer, the shipping of fabric to the shirt manufacturer, the shipping of the shirt to warehouse, and the shipping from the warehouse to the store.

DECA Connection

Discuss the performance indicators listed in the DECA Connection feature. Explain to students that performance indicators tell them how to demonstrate their acquired skills and knowledge through individual or team competitive events.

glencoe.com

Competitive Events Workbook For more DECA Role Plays, send students to the Online Learning Center to download the Competitive Events Workbook.

PROGRAM RESOURCE ORGANIZER

PRINT RESOURCES

- **Student Edition**
- **Teacher Edition**
- **Student Activity Workbook with Academic Integration** includes worksheets and activities correlated to the text.
- **Mathematics for Marketing Workbook** provides math activities for every unit in the text.

TECHNOLOGY TOOLBOX

- **Connect**
- **ConnectPlus**
- **ExamView Assessment Suite** is a comprehensive solution for creating, administering, and scoring tests.

glencoe.com

Online Learning Center provides a variety of resources to enrich and enhance learning.

SECTION, CHAPTER, AND UNIT RESOURCES

- **Graphic Organizers** for organizing text concepts visually.
- **Digital Nation Activities** and **Green Marketer Activities** extend learning beyond the text features.
- **Career Chatroom Career Profiles** allow students to explore different marketing occupations in depth.
- **After You Read Answer Keys** for students to check their answers.
- **Discovery Project Rubrics** and **Marketing Internship Project Rubrics** for students to evaluate their projects.

PROGRAM RESOURCES

- **Student Activity Workbook with Academic Integration Teacher Annotated Edition** includes annotated answers for the activities and worksheets.
- **Marketing Research Project Workbook** provides a step-by-step approach for students to complete their own marketing research studies.
- **School-to-Career Activity Workbook** helps students relate their class work to on-the-job experience and involves work-site analysis and working with mentors.
- **Competitive Events Workbook** helps prepare students for state and national marketing education competitions.
- **Inclusion in the Marketing Education Classroom** provides teaching resources for working with students with special needs.
- **PowerPoint Presentations** provides visual teaching aids and assessments for this chapter.

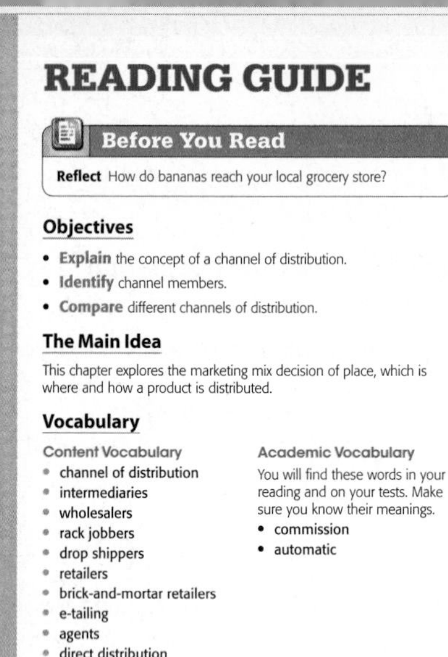

READING GUIDE

Before You Read

Reflect How do bananas reach your local grocery store?

Objectives

- **Explain** the concept of a channel of distribution.
- **Identify** channel members.
- **Compare** different channels of distribution.

The Main Idea

This chapter explores the marketing mix decision of place, which is where and how a product is distributed.

Vocabulary

Content Vocabulary
- channel of distribution
- intermediaries
- wholesalers
- rack jobbers
- drop shippers
- retailers
- brick-and-mortar retailers
- e-tailing
- agents
- direct distribution
- indirect distribution

Academic Vocabulary

You will find these words in your reading and on your tests. Make sure you know their meanings.
- commission
- automatic

Graphic Organizer

Draw or print this chart for listing routes to distribute products.

Routes Taken to Distribute Products

Consumer Products	Industrial Products
A.	A.
B.	B.
C.	C.
D.	D.
E.	

glencoe.com

Print this graphic organizer.

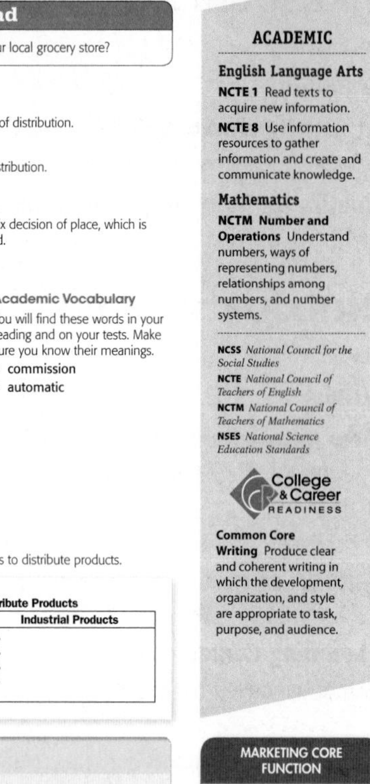

STANDARDS

ACADEMIC

English Language Arts

NCTE 1 Read texts to acquire new information.

NCTE 8 Use information resources to gather information and create and communicate knowledge.

Mathematics

NCTM Number and Operations Understand numbers, ways of representing numbers, relationships among numbers, and number systems.

NCSS *National Council for the Social Studies*
NCTE *National Council of Teachers of English*
NCTM *National Council of Teachers of Mathematics*
NSES *National Science Education Standards*

College & Career READINESS

Common Core
Writing Produce clear and coherent writing in which the development, organization, and style are appropriate to task, purpose, and audience.

MARKETING CORE FUNCTION

Channel Management

Section 21.1 Distribution

DISTRIBUTION: HOW IT WORKS

How do you get somebody to buy your product? By marketing it! Another important question is: "How does the product get to your customers?" The answer relates to the place decision, one of the four Ps of the marketing mix.

The **channel of distribution** is the path a product takes from its producer or manufacturer to the final user. When the product is purchased for use in a business, the final user is classified as an industrial user. When the product is purchased for personal use, the final user is classified as a consumer.

> "To make a place decision, marketers must decide on a channel of distribution."

Using shampoo as an example, you can see how the same product may be classified as both a consumer and an industrial product. Manufacturers of shampoo sell their products to the customer through retail stores. They may also sell shampoo to hair salons and hotel chains as an industrial product for use in a business.

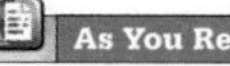

As You Read

Apply Select a product. Which channel of distribution does your product follow?

CHANNEL MEMBERS

Businesses involved in sales transactions that move products from the manufacturer to the final user are **intermediaries** or middlemen. Intermediaries reduce the number of contacts required to reach the final user of the product.

Suppose four customers wanted to buy a digital camera made by Nikon®. If Nikon sold directly to them, it would have to make four separate sales transactions. By using an intermediary, such as a video store, the number of contacts with sales transactions Nikon must make would be reduced to one.

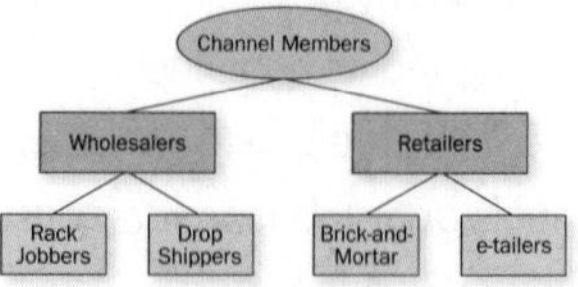

Intermediaries are classified on the basis of whether they take ownership (title) of goods and services. Merchant intermediaries take title. Agent intermediaries do not. Agent intermediaries, usually called "agents," receive a **commission**. The two major types of merchant intermediaries are known as *wholesalers* and *retailers*.

WHOLESALERS

Businesses that buy large quantities of goods from manufacturers, store the goods, and then resell them to retailers are called **wholesalers**. Wholesalers may be called "distributors" when their customers are professional or commercial users, manufacturers, governments, institutions, or other wholesalers. In either case, they take title to the goods that they buy for resale.

Two types of wholesalers are rack jobbers and drop shippers. **Rack jobbers** manage inventory and merchandising for retailers by counting stock, filling the shelves when needed, and maintaining store displays. They provide the racks for display of products in a retail store. They bill the retailer only for the goods sold, not for all the items on display.

ENGAGE

Anticipation Activity

Improving Student Achievement Manufacturers must make decisions about how best to reach their customers so that their products are available where their customers shop. Ask students all the different ways they can purchase a computer. Answer: in a retail store, from a printed catalog, from an online store that carries computers, or directly from a manufacturer's Web site

Objectives

- **Explain** the concept of a channel of distribution. A channel of distribution is the path a product takes from its producer or manufacturer to the final user.
- **Identify** channel members. manufacturer, final user, intermediaries (wholesalers, retailers) and agents (brokers, independent manufacturers' representatives)
- **Compare** different channels of distribution. Direct distribution is the most common channel in the industrial market. Direct distribution is not the most common channel in retail.

Graphic Organizer

Routes Taken to Distribute Products

Consumer Products	Industrial Products
A. Manufacturer/Producer Directly to Consumer	**A.** Manufacturer/Producer Directly to Industrial Users
B. Manufacturer/Producer to Retailer to Consumer	**B.** Manufacturer/Producer to Industrial Distributors to Industrial Users
C. Manufacturer/Producer to Wholesaler to Retailer to Consumer	**C.** Manufacturer/Producer to Agents to Industrial Distributors to Industrial Users
D. Manufacturer/Producer to Agents to Wholesaler to Retailer to Consumer	**D.** Manufacturer/Producer to Agents to Industrial Users

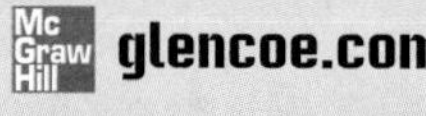

glencoe.com

Graphic Organizer Send students to the Online Learning Center to print this graphic organizer.

EXPLORE

Before You Read

Read the Before You Read question aloud: ***How do bananas reach your local grocery store?*** Sample answer: Bananas are picked on a plantation and shipped by truck to a port, where they are distributed by ship, train, or truck to a regional warehouse and then by truck to a local grocery store. Ask: ***Who sold the bananas to the grocery store?*** a produce wholesaler, or if it is a very large store chain, possibly the actual banana farmer

Preteaching Vocabulary

Have students go to the Online Learning Center at glencoe.com for the Chapter 21 Preteaching Vocabulary games.

Content Vocabulary

Instruct students to write a paragraph in which they discuss how the vocabulary terms are interrelated. Sample answer: A channel of distribution is the path a product takes from its producer or manufacturer to the final user. Members of the channel include intermediaries, wholesalers, rack jobbers, drop shippers, retailers, brick-and-mortar retailers, and agents. Online retailing, called e-tailing, is also a member of the channel; this shopping outlet is called the e-marketplace. There are direct and indirect channels of distribution, and there are a number of types of distribution such as exclusive, integrated, selective, and intensive distribution.

Academic Vocabulary

Automatic—Synonyms Tell students that *automatic* can refer to something done unconsciously or involuntarily, such as breathing or eyelid blinking, or it can refer to something done or produced by a machine. Have students create a list of synonyms for automatic. instinctive, unthinking, knee-jerk, mechanical, robotic, spontaneous. Read the following sentence to students: ***The hotel placed automatic retail machines on each floor so guests can purchase snacks and beverages 24 hours a day.*** Ask students to name the synonym that best fits the use of *automatic* in this sentence. mechanical

PROFESSIONAL DEVELOPMENT **MINI CLIP**

Reading: Lesson Reflections

Go to the Online Learning Center to view a video clip in which a narrator discusses various instructional strategies suitable for use with English learners.

Section 21.1 Distribution

DISTRIBUTION: HOW IT WORKS

Explain to students that distribution is an important part of marketing. Recall the four Ps of the marketing mix—product, place, price, and promotion. Companies make "place decisions" when planning how best to distribute their products in order to reach their customers.

Guiding Questions

Explain What is an industrial user? What is a consumer?	An industrial user is the final user of a product that is purchased to be used in a business. A consumer is the final user of a product.
Contrast What is the difference between wholesalers and retailers?	Wholesalers buy large quantities of goods from manufacturers, store the goods, and then resell them to retailers. Retailers sell goods to the final consumer for personal use.

As You Read

Read students the As You Read question: ***Select a product. Which channel of distribution does your product follow?*** Manufacturer/Producer Directly to Consumer; Manufacturer/Producer to Retailer to Consumer; Manufacturer/Producer to Wholesaler to Retailer to Consumer; Manufacturer/Producer to Agents to Wholesaler to Retailer to Consumer; or Manufacturer/Producer to Agents to Retailer to Consumer.

Expert Advice

Read the quote to students:

> **"To make a place decision, marketers must decide on a channel of distribution."**

Ask students: ***How are channels of distribution and place connected?*** Manufacturers must know how to get their product to consumers, which involves knowing where the consumer will purchase the product and the best way to get the product to that point.

Drop shippers own the goods they sell, but they do not physically handle the actual products. They deal in bulk, or large quantities of items, such as coal, lumber, and chemicals that require special handling. Drop shippers sell the goods to other businesses and have the producer ship the merchandise directly to the buyers.

RETAILERS

Retailers sell goods to the final consumer for personal use. Traditional retailers, called **brick-and-mortar retailers**, sell goods to customers from their own physical stores. These retail stores buy their products from manufacturers or wholesalers. They serve as the final link or path between the manufacturer and consumer. To build good customer relationships, they may offer special services, such as credit or delivery. Big box stores, such as Costco, straddle a line between being a wholesaler and a retailer, as they might sell products at close-to-wholesale prices directly to the public.

A number of non-store retailing operations serve the customer. These operations include online retailing (or e-tailing), direct mail and catalog retailing, TV home shopping, and **automatic** retailing (vending machines).

Online retailing, or **e-tailing**, involves retailers selling products over the Internet to the customer. Some e-tailing companies are found only on the Internet, such as amazon.com or overstock.com.

Almost all major brick-and-mortar and catalog retailers also sell their products online. This area of marketing is growing faster than any other.

Direct mail and catalogs also reach the final consumer. Many large brick-and-mortar retailers produce their own catalogs to reach consumers who prefer shopping at home. There are also catalog houses that buy goods from different manufacturers and display them in a catalog for sale to the customer. Most catalogs also offer the option of ordering online.

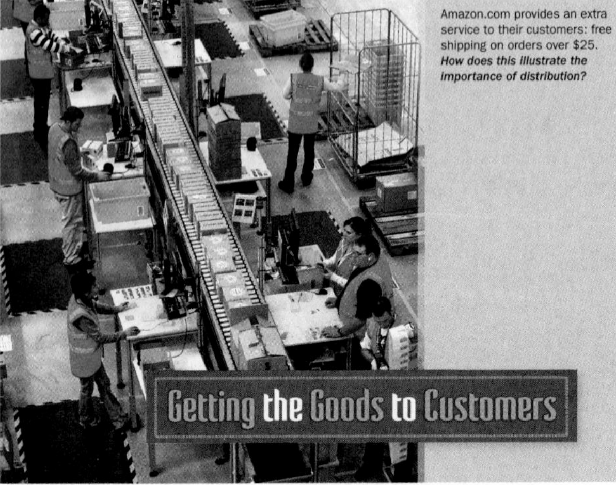

Amazon.com provides an extra service to their customers: free shipping on orders over $25. ***How does this illustrate the importance of distribution?***

Television home shopping networks are TV stations that sell products to consumers. These networks buy the products in set quantities and sell them via television programs. Consumers phone in their orders while watching shows.

Vending service companies buy manufacturers' products, such as drinks, snacks, and travelers' items, and then sell them through vending machines. These companies place their vending machines in stores, office buildings, hospitals, airports, schools, and other institutions at no charge.

AGENTS

Unlike wholesalers and retailers, agents do not own the goods they sell. **Agents** act as intermediaries by bringing buyers and sellers together. There are two different types of agents: manufacturers' representatives and brokers.

INDEPENDENT MANUFACTURERS' REPRESENTATIVES

Independent manufacturers' representatives work with several related (but noncompeting) manufacturers in a specific industry. They are not on any manufacturer's payroll. Instead, they are paid commissions based on what they sell.

An independent manufacturers' agent might carry a line of fishing rods from one manufacturer. He or she may buy lures from a second manufacturer and nets from a third manufacturer.

BROKERS

A broker's principal function is to bring buyers and sellers together in order for a sale to take place. Brokers usually do not have a continued relationship with either party. They negotiate the sale, receive a commission, and then look for other customers. Food brokers, however, represent several manufacturers of products sold in supermarkets, convenience stores, and other specialty food stores.

DIRECT AND INDIRECT CHANNELS

Channels of distribution are classified as direct or indirect. **Direct distribution** occurs when the producer sells goods or services directly to the customer with no intermediaries. **Indirect distribution** involves one or more intermediaries. Consumer markets and industrial markets use both direct and indirect channels of distribution. (See **Figures 21.1** and **21.2** on pages 496 and 497.)

Reading Check

Contrast What is the difference between direct and indirect distribution?

Pottery Barn® began as a retail store and then began e-tailing with its own Web site. ***What advantages and disadvantages do brick-and-mortar stores give a company?***

EXPLAIN

Activate Prior Learning

The Four Ps of the Marketing Mix Ask students to recall the four Ps of the marketing mix. product, price, place, and promotion Ask: ***What is place in terms of the marketing mix?*** The means of getting the product into the customer's hands is the place element of the marketing mix. Knowing where one's customers shop helps marketers make the place decision. Place strategies determine how and where a product will be distributed. For global companies, it may mean making decisions about which products will be sold in which countries and which retail outlets or other means of selling the product will best reach the customer. Marketers need to determine whether the product can be sold directly to the customer, via the Internet, through catalogs, or through a reseller.

Visual Literacy

Getting the Goods to Customers Caption Answer Read the caption and question to students: Amazon.com provides an extra service to their customers: free shipping on orders over $25. ***How does this illustrate the importance of distribution?*** Sample answer: Free shipping entices customers to purchase even when they cannot be physically present at the brick-and-mortar store. Convenience and reliability are keys to sustaining business in the e-tailing environment.

Critical Thinking

Ask students: ***What do you think is the cause-and-effect relationship of a reliable channel of distribution and sales as opposed to an unreliable channel of distribution and sales?*** Students should recognize that a reliable channel of distribution will help to increase sales and an unreliable channel of distribution will hurt sales.

ELABORATE

Critical Thinking

Ask students if they think that a company such as Hershey Foods Corporation in Hershey, Pennsylvania, would be willing to distribute candy bars directly to their high school student store and sporting events. Ask: ***Why or why not?*** Have students give reasons for their responses. Most students should recognize that the Hershey Foods Corporation would not want to deal with such a small operation as a local high school because the paperwork and shipping would be too costly and time consuming. Hershey might sell to the high school if it sold candy by the truckload, which is impractical for the high school.

Mini Projects

Enrichment

Write an Essay Ask students to imagine that the intermediaries they have come to rely on have disappeared overnight. Have them write a one-page essay on what would happen within a year to the variety of goods available to consumers and to production capabilities. Students might suggest that the variety of goods available to consumers would be reduced and production capabilities would be limited, unless they could use the Internet to generate enough business from manufacturers. Essays should consist of unified paragraphs. All information in a paragraph relates to one idea and no details in the paragraph are irrelevant to the idea. Essays should be free of grammar and spelling errors.

Conduct an Analysis Have students conduct a comparative shopping analysis and purchase plan for one book of their choice at the following locations: a local brick-and-mortar bookstore, an online store, a local used bookstore, and an online used bookstore. Students should research a variety of measures such as price (including taxes and shipping), time of delivery, condition of purchase (see the product's description on sites for used books), convenience factor, and so on. Ask students to record their data in a spreadsheet and to indicate their proposed purchase plan. Have students share their spreadsheets and purchase plans with the class. Ask students for the rationale behind their purchase plan.

Graphic Organizer

Display this chart. Ask students to provide descriptions for Rack Jobbers, Drop Shippers, Brick-and-Mortar, and e-tailers. Possible answers:

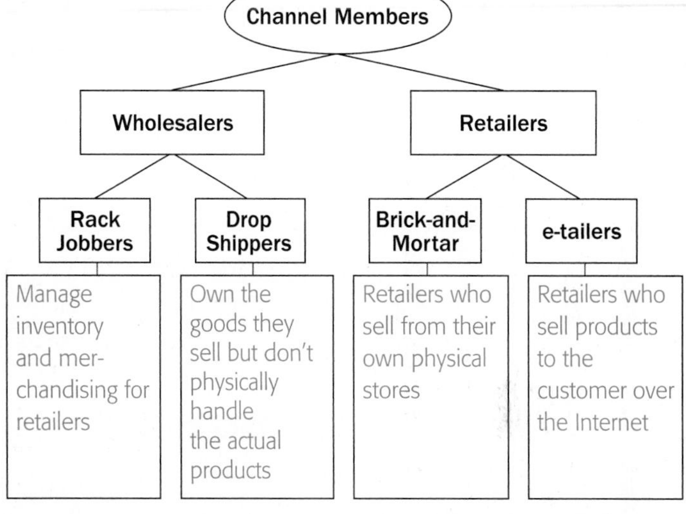

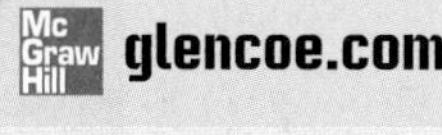

Graphic Organizer Send students to the Online Learning Center to print this graphic organizer.

Reading Check Answer

Read the Reading Check question to students: ***What is the difference between direct and indirect distribution?*** Direct distribution occurs when the producer sells goods or services directly to the customer with no intermediaries. Indirect distribution involves one or more intermediaries.

Visual Literacy

E-Tailing, Etc. Caption Answer Read the photo caption question to students: ***What advantages and disadvantages do brick-and-mortar stores give a company?*** Advantages: They serve as the final link or path between the manufacturer and consumer. To build good customer relationships, they may offer special services. Big box stores straddle a line between wholesale and retail, as they might sell products at close-to-wholesale prices directly to the public. Customers have the opportunity to see products up close. Disadvantages: Prices may be higher to pay for the overhead necessary to have a brick-and-mortar site.

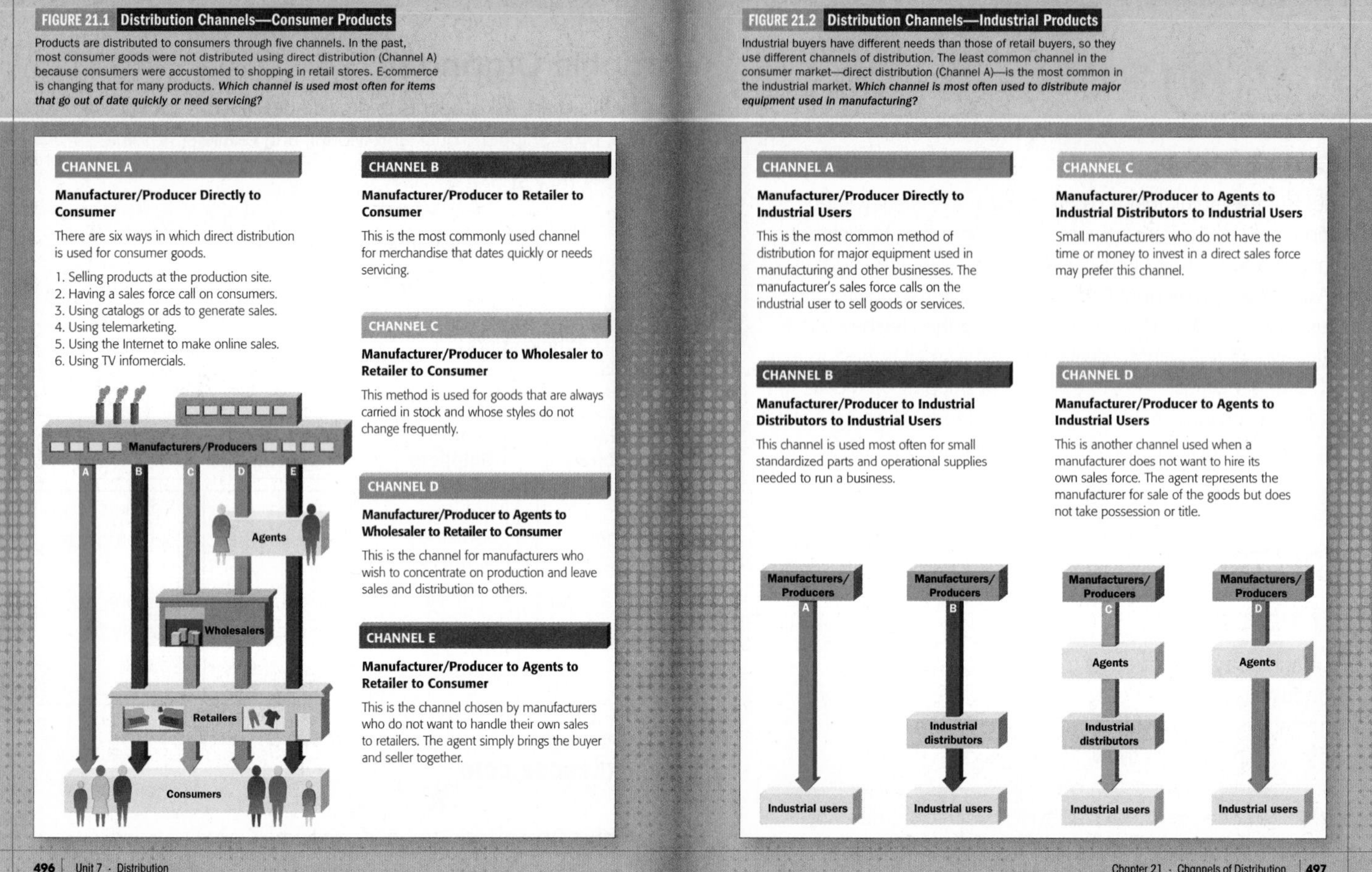

FIGURE 21.1 Distribution Channels—Consumer Products

Products are distributed to consumers through five channels. In the past, most consumer goods were not distributed using direct distribution (Channel A) because consumers were accustomed to shopping in retail stores. E-commerce is changing that for many products. ***Which channel is used most often for items that go out of date quickly or need servicing?***

CHANNEL A

Manufacturer/Producer Directly to Consumer

There are six ways in which direct distribution is used for consumer goods.

1. Selling products at the production site.
2. Having a sales force call on consumers.
3. Using catalogs or ads to generate sales.
4. Using telemarketing.
5. Using the Internet to make online sales.
6. Using TV infomercials.

CHANNEL B

Manufacturer/Producer to Retailer to Consumer

This is the most commonly used channel for merchandise that dates quickly or needs servicing.

CHANNEL C

Manufacturer/Producer to Wholesaler to Retailer to Consumer

This method is used for goods that are always carried in stock and whose styles do not change frequently.

CHANNEL D

Manufacturer/Producer to Agents to Wholesaler to Retailer to Consumer

This is the channel for manufacturers who wish to concentrate on production and leave sales and distribution to others.

CHANNEL E

Manufacturer/Producer to Agents to Retailer to Consumer

This is the channel chosen by manufacturers who do not want to handle their own sales to retailers. The agent simply brings the buyer and seller together.

FIGURE 21.2 Distribution Channels—Industrial Products

Industrial buyers have different needs than those of retail buyers, so they use different channels of distribution. The least common channel in the consumer market—direct distribution (Channel A)—is the most common in the industrial market. ***Which channel is most often used to distribute major equipment used in manufacturing?***

CHANNEL A

Manufacturer/Producer Directly to Industrial Users

This is the most common method of distribution for major equipment used in manufacturing and other businesses. The manufacturer's sales force calls on the industrial user to sell goods or services.

CHANNEL B

Manufacturer/Producer to Industrial Distributors to Industrial Users

This channel is used most often for small standardized parts and operational supplies needed to run a business.

CHANNEL C

Manufacturer/Producer to Agents to Industrial Distributors to Industrial Users

Small manufacturers who do not have the time or money to invest in a direct sales force may prefer this channel.

CHANNEL D

Manufacturer/Producer to Agents to Industrial Users

This is another channel used when a manufacturer does not want to hire its own sales force. The agent represents the manufacturer for sale of the goods but does not take possession or title.

496 | Unit 7 · Distribution

Chapter 21 · Channels of Distribution | 497

EXPLAIN

Visual Literacy

Figure 21.1 Caption Answer Read the figure caption question to students: ***Which channel is used most often for items that go out of date quickly or need servicing?*** Channel B—Manufacturer/Producer to Retailer to Consumer Then ask these guiding questions to take a closer look at distribution channels for consumer goods.

Guiding Questions

List What are six ways in which direct distribution is used for consumer goods?	selling products at production site; having salesperson call on consumers; using catalogs to generate sales; telemarketing; online sales via the Internet; infomercials
Determine What channel would be used by a manufacturer who wished to concentrate on production and leave sales and distribution to others?	They would most likely use Channel D—Manufacturer/Producer to Agents to Wholesaler to Retailer to Consumer

Critical Thinking

Explain to students that small retailers often cannot match the deep discounts and low prices offered by large retail operations based on their ability to buy directly from the manufacturer. Have students consider and list ways a smaller retailer could compete to keep or gain customers from large chain retail stores. After students have created their lists, ask them to read their lists. Create a class list and display it for all the students to read. Answers may include: offer a different selection of merchandise, use a theme, and emphasize personal customer service.

ELABORATE

Visual Literacy

Figure 21.2 Caption Answer Read the figure caption question to students: ***Which channel is most often used to distribute major equipment used in manufacturing?*** Channel A—Manufacturer/Producer Directly to Industrial Users Then ask these guiding questions.

Guiding Questions

Explain Which channel would be used by a manufacturer/producer that makes small standardized parts?	They would use Channel B—Manufacturer/Producer to Industrial Distributors to Industrial Users.
Discuss What else might manufacturers offer to retailers?	product information, display materials, and advertising ideas

Mini Projects

Enrichment

Research Paths of Distribution for Consumer Products Divide the class into small groups. Have each group choose a consumer product that interests them and research its path of distribution. Then have students use the information they collect to create a visual map of the distribution channels used to get the product to consumers. Maps can be created on poster board using paint or ink, or students can use graphic design software to create their visuals. Have groups share their maps with the class and then post them around the room.

Research Paths of Distribution for Industrial Products Divide the class into small groups. Have each group choose an industrial product and research its path of distribution. Have students interview industrial users to learn how they get their products. Prior to the interviews, students should create a list of question to ask the industrial user. Students should take notes during the interview. Then have students use the information they collect from the interview to create a visual map of the distribution channels used to get the product to industrial users. Maps can be created on poster board using paint or ink or students can use graphic design software to create their visuals. Have groups share their maps with the class and then post them around the room.

Graphic Organizer

Have students fill in this Distribution Channel Members outline using stores, wholesalers, retailers, merchant intermediaries, rack jobbers, agent intermediaries, drop shippers, intermediaries, direct mailers, and independent manufacturers' representatives.

Distribution Channel Members
I. Intermediaries
 A. Agent Intermediaries
  1. Independent manufacturer's representative
 B. Merchant Intermediaries
  1. Wholesalers
   a. Rack jobbers
   b. Drop shippers
  2. Retailers
   a. Stores
   b. Direct mail operations

Graphic Organizer

Display this diagram and use it to to help students compare distribution channels for consumer products and for industrial products. Ask: ***What are the five members of the consumer products distribution channel?*** Manufacturer/Producer, Agents, Wholesalers, Retailers, Consumers Ask students to tell you what order to place them in on the diagram. Then ask: ***What are the four members of the industrial products distribution channel?*** Manufacturer/Producer, Agents, Industrial Distributors, Industrial Users Ask students to tell you what order to place them in on the diagram. Ask: ***Why do you think there are fewer members in the industrial channel?*** Sample answer: Industrial buyers have different needs from those of retail buyers.

Consumer	Industrial
Manufacturer/Producer	Manufacturer/Producer
↓ Agents	↓ Agents
↓ Wholesalers	↓ Industrial Distributors
↓ Retailers	↓
↓ Consumers	Industrial Users

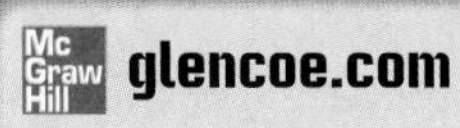

Graphic Organizer Send students to the Online Learning Center to print this graphic organizer.

The GREEN Marketer

Eating Local

Eating local means choosing to eat food produced on farms or ranches near home. Local food is fresher, supports local businesses, and uses less fuel for transportation from farm to consumer.

Local Advantage Restaurants that support local and organic farms have a competitive edge with many of today's consumers. Restaurateurs who buy locally often serve seasonal foods that appeal to adventurous diners. They also proudly list suppliers' names on their menus so that customers know exactly where the food was grown.

English Language Arts/Writing

Discuss Describe possible benefits to a restaurant owner of buying directly from a farmer rather than through a food wholesaler.

NCTE 12 Use language to accomplish individual purposes.

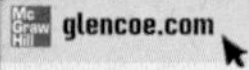

glencoe.com

Get an activity on green marketing.

EXAMPLES OF CHANNELS OF DISTRIBUTION

Different channels of distribution are generally used to reach the customer in the consumer and industrial markets.

When selling to the industrial market, a manufacturer would sell paper napkins to industrial distributors who, in turn, would sell the napkins to restaurants.

When selling to the consumer market, the company would sell napkins to a wholesaler or use food brokers to sell to retailers, such as grocery stores or party supply shops.

Not every option works best for every product or company. Despite the potential for success, a product can fail with the wrong channel of distribution.

DISTRIBUTION CHANNELS FOR CONSUMER PRODUCTS AND SERVICES

Few consumer products are marketed using direct distribution (Channel A) because most consumers have become accustomed to shopping in retail stores. The most common indirect channel in the consumer market is Producer to Retailer to Consumer (Channel B).

MANUFACTURER/PRODUCER DIRECTLY TO CONSUMER (CHANNEL A)

Direct distribution can be used in six different ways to deliver products to consumers:

1. Selling products at the production site. Examples include factory outlets or farmers' roadside stands.
2. Having a sales force call on consumers at home. Examples include Avon® and Tupperware®.
3. Using catalogs or ads to generate sales.
4. Calling consumers on the telephone (telemarketing). (The National Do Not Call registry has limited this method.)
5. Using the Internet to make online sales.
6. Using TV infomercials.

In this channel, there are no middlemen. That means the prices a customer pays can be low. Retailers do not have to pay rent for a store that houses the goods, agents do not have to be paid commission, and wholesalers do not have to negotiate prices and shipping with retailers and agents. All of these processes increase the final price of the product for the consumer.

MANUFACTURER/PRODUCER TO RETAILER TO CONSUMER (CHANNEL B)

This channel is used most often for products that become out of date quickly or need regular servicing. Clothing and automobiles are sold this way. Chain stores and online retailers use this channel. Retailers do not have to involve agents or wholesalers to acquire their products. The distribution of a product from the manufacturer or producer to the retailer is quick and efficient. The short length of this channel makes it easy for consumers to stay up to date with a company's products at a relatively low price.

Channel A Dell Computers uses channel partnership because it sells via the Internet, so it needs assistance from shippers like FedEx and UPS.

MANUFACTURER/PRODUCER TO WHOLESALER TO RETAILER TO CONSUMER (CHANNEL C)

This method of distribution is most often used for staple goods, which are items that are always carried in stock and whose styles do not change frequently. The manufacturer sells to the wholesaler, who then handles the sales, warehousing, and distribution of the goods to retailers. Consumer goods sold this way include supermarket items, flowers, candy, and stationery supplies.

MANUFACTURER/PRODUCER TO AGENTS TO WHOLESALER TO RETAILER TO CONSUMER (CHANNEL D)

Manufacturers who prefer to concentrate on production and leave sales and distribution to others use this channel. The agent sells to wholesalers who are involved in storage, sale, and transportation to retailers. The retailer then sells to consumers.

MARKETING CASE STUDY

DirecTV's NFL Sunday Ticket

Football fans are a passionate bunch. Few things are more important to them than their favorite games. Sunday is the big day for professional football. Highlighting fans' football fever, DirecTV® created a TV commercial with a comedian as the "NFL Sunday Ticket" self-help counselor. Celebrities like LL Cool J, Eli Manning, and Peyton Manning also appeared in the ads. DirecTV promoted its product as the ultimate way to deliver the games to viewers.

Delivering More Action

With so many games on any given Sunday, football fans are used to doing a lot of channel flipping. The DirecTV spots advertise the Sunday Ticket service as a way for viewers to watch up to eight games simultaneously on a single television. All games are in high-definition, and DirecTV can deliver them to many brands of cell phones.

Mathematics

Compute Analyze this information: there are 32 teams in the NFL. There are 16 games in the regular season. There are 17 weeks of games. Each team has a bye week during which they do not play a game. How many teams have a bye week each week?

NCTM Problem Solving Solve problems that arise in mathematics and in other contexts.

EXPLAIN

The GREEN Marketer

English Language Arts/Writing Answer Read the statement to students: ***Describe possible benefits to a restaurant owner of buying directly from a farmer rather than through a food wholesaler.*** Fresher food, lower cost, and a personal relationship with the seller. Ask: ***What channel is represented by the restaurant owner buying directly from a farmer?*** This is Channel B, manufacturer/producer to retailer to consumer. Ask students: ***How could Channel A be represented if the farmer is manufacturer/producer?*** Consumers would have to buy directly from the farmer, either at a farm or a farmers market.

glencoe.com

Worksheet Activity Send students to the Online Learning Center to get a Green Marketer worksheet activity.

Mini Project

Differentiated Instruction

Mathematical Learners

Tell students to assume that the manufacturer sells an item to two chain stores. The first chain store gets 50 percent off the list price. The second chain store does not get 50 percent off the list price, but rather gets the standard 40 percent off and an additional 10 percent off for doing its own distribution. Ask: ***Do the two discounts amount to the same dollar amount? Explain your answer.*** No; the amounts differ because the discounts apply in sequence—if the list price is \$75.59, then the first chain store pays \$37.80 (\$75.59 × 0.50 = \$37.80) and the second chain store pays \$40.82 (\$75.59 × 0.60 = \$45.35; \$45.35 × 0.90 = \$40.82).

ELABORATE

Channel A Have students research other well-known manufacturer/producers to learn what channel(s) they generally use to get their products to consumers. Ask students to share their findings with the rest of the class.

MARKETING CASE STUDY

Mathematics Answer Two teams have byes each week of the season. Tell students that the Marketing Case Study states that with Sunday Ticket, viewers can watch any of up to eight games being played at the same time.

Graphic Organizer

Display these charts. Cross out the members that do not belong in a particular channel.

Distribution Channels—Consumer Products

A	B	C	D	E
Manufacturer/ Producer	Manufacturer/ Producer	Manufacturer/ Producer	Manufacturer/ Producer	Manufacturer/ Producer
~~Agents~~	~~Agents~~	~~Agents~~	Agents	Agents
~~Wholesalers~~	~~Wholesalers~~	Wholesalers	Wholesalers	~~Wholesalers~~
~~Retailers~~	Retailers	Retailers	Retailers	Retailers
Consumers	Consumers	Consumers	Consumers	Consumers

Distribution Channels—Industrial Products

A	B	C	D
Manufacturer/ Producer	Manufacturer/ Producer	Manufacturer/ Producer	Manufacturer/ Producer
~~Agents~~	~~Agents~~	Agents	Agents
~~Industrial Distributors~~	Industrial Distributors	Industrial Distributors	~~Industrial Distributors~~
Industrial Users	Industrial Users	Industrial Users	Industrial Users

glencoe.com iWB

Graphic Organizer Send students to the Online Learning Center to print this graphic organizer.

e MARKETING

Digital Distribution

When studying channels of distribution, a new option is now available—digital distribution. Digital distribution is a form of direct distribution whereby the product is sold via the Internet in a digital format. For example, Netflix® offers its customer streaming of movies and television online. Customers just need to connect to the Internet to take advantage of this service. Square Enix, maker of role playing videogames is looking to go digital. Rather than buying games in a brick and mortar retailer, Square Enix wants to go change to a direct digital channel of distribution. It could then sell separate chapters of a game for $5 each via the Internet.

Innovate and Create

Ask students what other products are available via digital distribution. Almost all computer software can be purchased via digital distribution. All special applications on smartphones are examples of digital distribution. Games on the Internet (i.e., Bridge) are sold via digital distribution. You pay a fee to play Bridge with other people around the world or with a robot. Physical products are also utilizing digital distribution for sales of related merchandise. For example, the Kindle™ and Nook e-readers sell digital books that can be downloaded onto those devices.

glencoe.com

eMarketing Worksheet Activity Send students to the Online Learning Center to download an eMarketing worksheet activity.

MANUFACTURER/PRODUCER TO AGENTS TO RETAILER TO CONSUMER (CHANNEL E)

Manufacturers who do not want to handle their sales to retailers use this channel. The agent brings the buyer and seller together. Expensive cookware, meat, cosmetics, and many supermarket items are sold this way. It may be more cost-effective for the company to use agents to sell its products. This choice allows the company's manufacturers to spend time and money creating the best products possible.

DISTRIBUTION CHANNELS FOR INDUSTRIAL PRODUCTS AND SERVICES

Industrial users shop differently and have different needs than consumers, so they use different channels of distribution. The least-used channel in the consumer market—direct distribution (Channel A)—is the most used channel in the industrial market. Often, a business or industry's needs are defined by the products or services it provides. These groups do not have to shop around for different products like consumers do. They already know which products they need.

MANUFACTURER/PRODUCER DIRECTLY TO INDUSTRIAL USERS (CHANNEL A)

This method of distribution is most often used for major equipment used in manufacturing and other businesses. The manufacturer's sales force calls on the industrial user to sell goods or services. For example, a Xerox® sales representative sells copier machines directly to manufacturers and commercial businesses.

MANUFACTURER/PRODUCER TO INDUSTRIAL DISTRIBUTORS TO INDUSTRIAL USERS (CHANNEL B)

This channel is used most often for small standardized parts and operational supplies needed to run a business. Industrial wholesalers (distributors) take ownership of the products, stock them, and sell them as needed to industrial users. A restaurant-supply wholesaler buys pots, pans, utensils, serving pieces, and paper products from various manufacturers to sell to restaurant owners. The industrial user is able to choose from a variety of small standardized products for its business. It would cost a lot of time and money for an industrial user to shop at many different manufacturers or producers.

There are five channels of distribution to transfer goods from producer to consumer. ***Which channel was most likely used to transfer the goods like the high-end cosmetics in this photo?***

MANUFACTURER/PRODUCER TO AGENTS TO INDUSTRIAL DISTRIBUTORS TO INDUSTRIAL USERS (CHANNEL C)

Small manufacturers may prefer to use the services of an agent, who represents the manufacturer for sale of the goods. The agent coordinates a large supply of the product. The agent does not take possession or title of the goods, but sells the goods to the industrial wholesaler. The wholesaler in turn stores, resells, and ships them to the industrial user. Agents can work for several producers at one time.

MANUFACTURER/PRODUCER TO AGENTS TO INDUSTRIAL USERS (CHANNEL D)

Some manufacturers cannot afford a sales force, and other manufacturers simply do not want to manage a sales force. These manufacturers use agents to sell their products to industrial users, but they cut out the distributor and ship their merchandise directly to the industrial users. This method keeps distribution costs low. Many types of industrial products are distributed in this manner, including construction equipment, farm products, and dry goods.

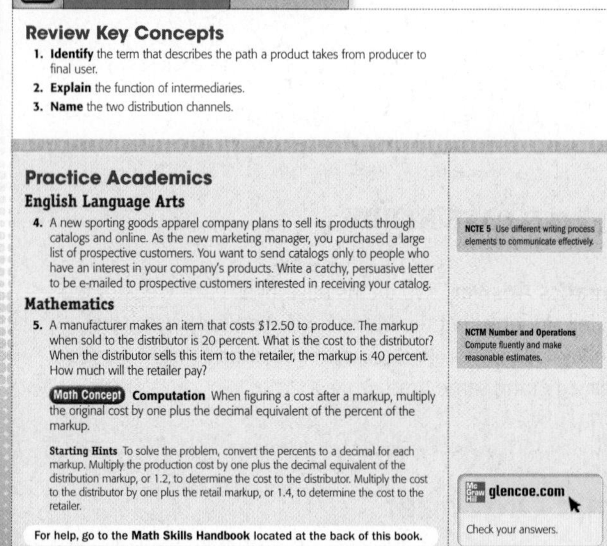

After You Read | **Section 21.1**

Review Key Concepts

1. **Identify** the term that describes the path a product takes from producer to final user.
2. **Explain** the function of intermediaries.
3. **Name** the two distribution channels.

Practice Academics

English Language Arts

4. A new sporting goods apparel company plans to sell its products through catalogs and online. As the new marketing manager, you purchased a large list of prospective customers. You want to send catalogs only to people who have an interest in your company's products. Write a catchy, persuasive letter to be e-mailed to prospective customers interested in receiving your catalog.

NCTE 5 Use different writing process elements to communicate effectively.

Mathematics

5. A manufacturer makes an item that costs $12.50 to produce. The markup when sold to the distributor is 20 percent. What is the cost to the distributor? When the distributor sells this item to the retailer, the markup is 40 percent. How much will the retailer pay?

Math Concept **Computation** When figuring a cost after a markup, multiply the original cost by one plus the decimal equivalent of the percent of the markup.

Starting Hints To solve the problem, convert the percents to a decimal for each markup. Multiply the production cost by one plus the decimal equivalent of the distribution markup, or 1.2, to determine the cost to the distributor. Multiply the cost to the distributor by one plus the retail markup, or 1.4, to determine the cost to the retailer.

NCTM Number and Operations Compute fluently and make reasonable estimates.

For help, go to the **Math Skills Handbook** located at the back of this book.

glencoe.com

Check your answers.

ELABORATE

Visual Literacy

Distribution Channels Caption Answer Read the photo caption question to students: ***Which channel was most likely used to transfer the goods in this photo?*** Channel E—Manufacturer/Producer to Agents to Retailer to Consumer. Then ask these guiding questions to focus the discussion on distribution.

Guiding Questions

Explain Why do manufacturers/producers of items such as cookware, meat, and cosmetics use Channel E?	It may be more cost-effective for the company to use agents to sell its products. By using Channel E the manufacturers can spend more time and money creating better products.
Determine Years ago, salesmen went door-to-door selling encyclopedias and vacuum cleaners. What channel of distribution does this represent?	Channel A—Manufacturer/Producer Directly to Consumer

Critical Thinking

This activity will help students better understand the role of agents in the various distribution channels. Tell students that many of the distribution channels for both consumer and industrial products rely on the services of agents. Ask: ***What do real estate agents do?*** They find buyers for sellers and sellers for buyers, tasks for which they receive a commission. Real estate agents deal with the buying and selling of property. Then ask: ***In general, do the real estate agents own the property they deal with?*** No, they are sales agents for the people who wish to sell their property—the agents bring buyers and sellers together. Ask: ***How are real estate agents similar to agents who are members of distribution channels?*** Agents also act as intermediaries bringing buyers and sellers together; they typically do not own the merchandise they are looking to sell; and they often work for a commission.

EVALUATE

DISTRIBUTION CHANNELS FOR INDUSTRIAL PRODUCTS AND SERVICES

Ask students these guiding questions to direct a discussion on industrial distribution channels.

Guiding Questions

Identify What is the most used channel in the industrial market and the least used channel in the consumer market?	Channel A—direct distribution
Explain Why is direct distribution the most commonly used distribution channel in the industrial market?	Products sold by manufacturers to other manufacturers in the industrial market are often very specialized or very expensive. Thus, direct contact is necessary for a sale to take place.
Determine Which industrial distribution channel would you use for the following: a bull dozer used for making highways; fresh corn; handmade chairs from a small manufacturer; a powerful blow dryer for a beauty shop?	bulldozer—Channel A; fresh corn—Channel D; handmade chairs from a small manufacturer—Channel C; a powerful blow dryer for a beauty shop—Channel B

Reinforce Vocabulary

Industrial—Root Meaning Display the term *industrial* for the class. Ask students what the root word is. industry Then ask: ***What does the term* industry *mean?*** manufacturing or production done on a large scale Ask students to provide examples of industry. Sample answers: large companies such as Ford®, Starbucks®, or Microsoft®. Then ask: ***How does distribution of industrial products differ from distribution of consumer products?*** Answers may include: industrial distribution has fewer channels, and the end user of industrial items are not the consumers.

After You Read Section 21.1

Review Key Concepts

1. The path a product takes from producer to final user is the channel of distribution.
2. The function of intermediaries is to reduce the number of contacts required to reach the final user of the product.
3. Channels of distribution are either direct or indirect.

Practice Academics

English Language Arts

4. Letters should be catchy, persuasive, and formatted for sending via e-mail. Accept all reasonable answers; letters should use proper grammar, spelling, and punctuation.

Mathematics

5. The cost to the distributor is \$15.00 (\$12.50 × 1.2 = \$15.00). The cost to the retailer is \$21.00 (\$15.00 × 1.4 = \$21.00).

glencoe.com

Answer Key Send students to the Online Learning Center to check their answers.

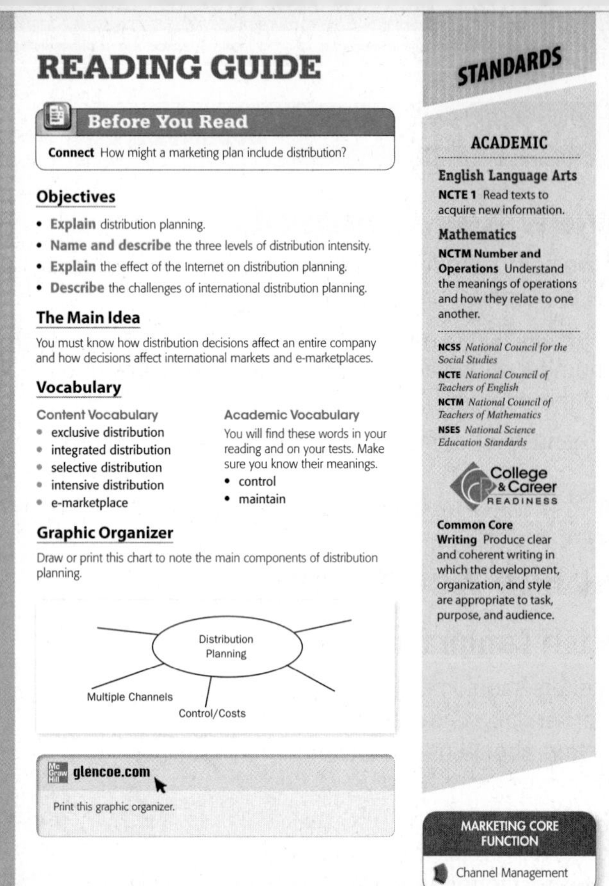
READING GUIDE

Before You Read

Connect How might a marketing plan include distribution?

Objectives

- **Explain** distribution planning.
- **Name and describe** the three levels of distribution intensity.
- **Explain** the effect of the Internet on distribution planning.
- **Describe** the challenges of international distribution planning.

The Main Idea

You must know how distribution decisions affect an entire company and how decisions affect international markets and e-marketplaces.

Vocabulary

Content Vocabulary
- exclusive distribution
- integrated distribution
- selective distribution
- intensive distribution
- e-marketplace

Academic Vocabulary

You will find these words in your reading and on your tests. Make sure you know their meanings.
- control
- maintain

Graphic Organizer

Draw or print this chart to note the main components of distribution planning.

glencoe.com

Print this graphic organizer.

STANDARDS

ACADEMIC

English Language Arts

NCTE 1 Read texts to acquire new information.

Mathematics

NCTM Number and Operations Understand the meanings of operations and how they relate to one another.

NCSS National Council for the Social Studies
NCTE National Council of Teachers of English
NCTM National Council of Teachers of Mathematics
NSES National Science Education Standards

College & Career READINESS

Common Core
Writing Produce clear and coherent writing in which the development, organization, and style are appropriate to task, purpose, and audience.

MARKETING CORE FUNCTION

Channel Management

Distribution Planning

Section 21.2

UNDERSTANDING DISTRIBUTION PLANNING

Distribution planning involves decisions about a product's physical movement and transfer of ownership from producer to consumer. This chapter focuses on transfer of ownership issues. Distribution decisions affect a firm's marketing program. Some of the major considerations are the use of multiple channels, **control** versus costs, intensity of distribution desired, and involvement in e-commerce.

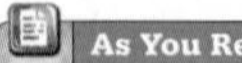

As You Read

Analyze How does the Internet facilitate channels of distribution?

MULTIPLE CHANNELS

A producer uses multiple channels when its product fits the needs of both industrial and consumer markets. For example, a snack food company sells its pretzels, drinks, and cookies to supermarkets, movie theaters, stadiums, and other sports arenas. It also sells to schools, colleges, and hospitals. Each new market poses questions regarding the exact channel of distribution needed to reach it.

CONTROL VERSUS COSTS

All manufacturers and producers must weigh the control they want to have over the distribution of their products versus their costs and profitability. Many businesses have sales representatives who work directly for the company, but there are costs to maintain a sales force. A company can also use a network of independent agents and distributors, but that might result in less control over where its products and services are sold and for how much.

WHO DOES THE SELLING?

A manufacturer must decide how much control it wants over its sales function. It can use its own sales force, or it may decide to hire agents to do the selling.

A direct sales force is costly. In-house sales representatives are on the company payroll, receive employee benefits, and are reimbursed for expenses. The manufacturer, though, has complete control over them. It can establish sales quotas and easily monitor each sales representative's performance.

> "Distribution planning involves decisions about a product's physical movement and transfer of ownership from producer to consumer."

With an agent, a manufacturer loses some of its control over how sales are made. This is because agents work independently, running their own businesses. The agent's interests may not always be exactly the same as those of the manufacturer.

However, the relative cost of using agents can be lower than hiring an in-house sales staff. No employee benefits or expenses must be paid because agents are independent businesspeople. Another benefit is that agents are typically paid a set percentage based on what they sell. This ensures that the cost of selling a product or service is always the same in relation to sales generated.

ENGAGE

Anticipation Activity

Improving Student Achievement Tell students that distributors in all industries tend to experience pressure from both customers and vendors. Ask: ***Why do you think distributors might feel pressure from both sides?*** Vendors want their products sold as soon as possible for as much money as they can get; customers want the best price they can get and quick delivery.

Objectives

- **Explain** distribution planning. It involves the physical movement and transfer of ownership of products from producer to consumer
- **Name** and describe the three levels of distribution intensity. exclusive, selective, and intensive
- **Explain** the effect of the Internet on distribution planning. A greater proportion of trade takes place via the Internet.
- **Describe** the challenges of international distribution planning. requires that businesses adjust their distribution systems

Graphic Organizer

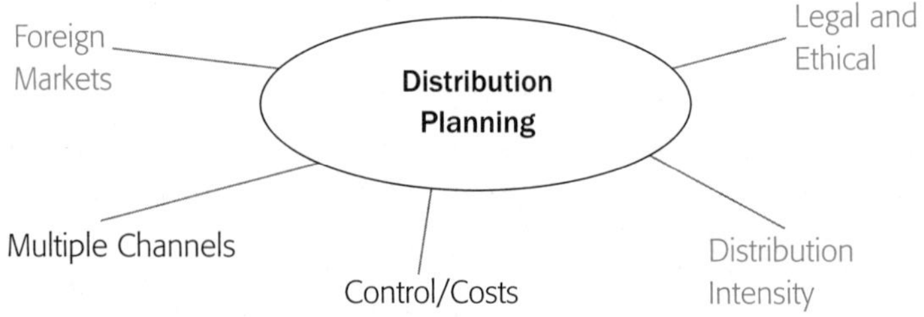

glencoe.com iWB

Graphic Organizer Send students to the Online Learning Center to print this graphic organizer.

EXPLORE

Before You Read

Read the Before You Read question aloud: ***How might a marketing plan include distribution?*** Marketing plans include: marketing strategies, which include the marketing mix (product, price, place, and promotion—the four Ps). Place includes distribution of the product to the consumer. ***Ask students how important distribution would be to the marketing plan.*** It's very important; if the consumer can't get the product, the marketing plan will fail. Also, the cost of distribution must be accounted for in the plan.

Preteaching Vocabulary

Have students go to the Online Learning Center at glencoe.com for the Chapter 21 Preteaching Vocabulary games.

Content Vocabulary

Display the words *exclusive*, *integrated*, *selective*, and *intensive* for the students to read. Ask volunteers to offer definitions for the words. exclusive—available to one company or in one area; integrated—combined; selective—applying only to some, not to all; intensive—making heavy use of Tell students to keep these definitions in mind as they read the section on distribution planning and learn about the different types of distribution.

Academic Vocabulary

Control—Usage Have students volunteer sentences in which they use the term *control* (noun). Ask the class to determine whether the term was used correctly. Tell students that the term means the ability to manage or exercise power over something. Sample answers: The owner had control over unnecessary spending. The store owner had to give up some control to the new manager.

Maintain—Usage Have students volunteer sentences in which they use the term *maintain*. Ask the class to determine whether the term was used correctly. Tell students that in marketing, retailers may have to buy and maintain (or keep) a minimum amount of a product to get the best prices.

MINI CLIP

ELL: Academic Language
Go to the Online Learning Center for a video in which authors discuss the importance of addressing academic language when teaching English language learners.

Distribution Planning

UNDERSTANDING DISTRIBUTION PLANNING

Ask students to recall the members of the distribution channels for consumer products. manufacturer/producer, agents, wholesalers, retailers, consumers Then ask students to recall the members of the distribution channels for industrial products. manufacturer/producer, agents, industrial distributors, industrial users Tell students that as products flow through these channels, transfer of ownership takes place. Then ask these guiding questions on distribution planning.

Guiding Questions

Provide Examples In addition to snack foods, what products fit the needs of both industrial and consumer markets?	Sample answer: Tires are sold to retailers for purchase by consumers, but they are also sold to car makers to be put on new cars as they are built.
Analyze Why might a producer give up control over sales?	It is less expensive to hire agents to sell products than to have an in-house sales force. Hiring agents means giving up some control over the process.

As You Read

Read students the As You Read question: ***How does the Internet facilitate channels of distribution?*** E-marketplaces provide one-stop shopping and substantial savings for B2B operations. Online catalogs make it easy for corporate buyers to compare prices and get the best deal for their money.

Expert Advice

Read the quote to students:

> **“Distribution planning involves decisions about a product's physical movement and transfer of ownership from producer to consumer.”**

Ask students to provide examples of transfer of ownership. Answers may include: selling a car to a buyer, selling a house, and so on. Ask: ***Have you ever thought that when you purchase an item in a store there is a transfer of ownership?*** Explain to students that when a product goes through the channels of distribution, there are sometimes multiple transfers of ownership.

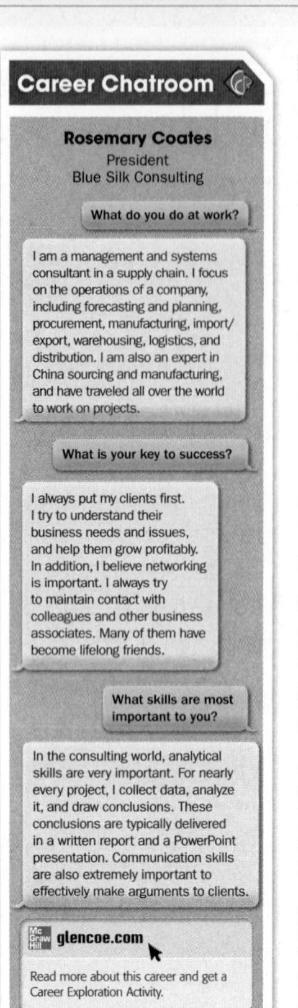

Career Chatroom
Rosemary Coates
President
Blue Silk Consulting
What do you do at work?
I am a management and systems consultant in a supply chain. I focus on the operations of a company, including forecasting and planning, procurement, manufacturing, import/export, warehousing, logistics, and distribution. I am also an expert in China sourcing and manufacturing, and have traveled all over the world to work on projects.
What is your key to success?
I always put my clients first. I try to understand their business needs and issues, and help them grow profitably. In addition, I believe networking is important. I always try to maintain contact with colleagues and other business associates. Many of them have become lifelong friends.
What skills are most important to you?
In the consulting world, analytical skills are very important. For nearly every project, I collect data, analyze it, and draw conclusions. These conclusions are typically delivered in a written report and a PowerPoint presentation. Communication skills are also extremely important to effectively make arguments to clients.
glencoe.com
Read more about this career and get a Career Exploration Activity.

DISTRIBUTION INTENSITY

Distribution intensity depends on how widely a product will be distributed. There are three levels of distribution intensity: exclusive, selective, and intensive.

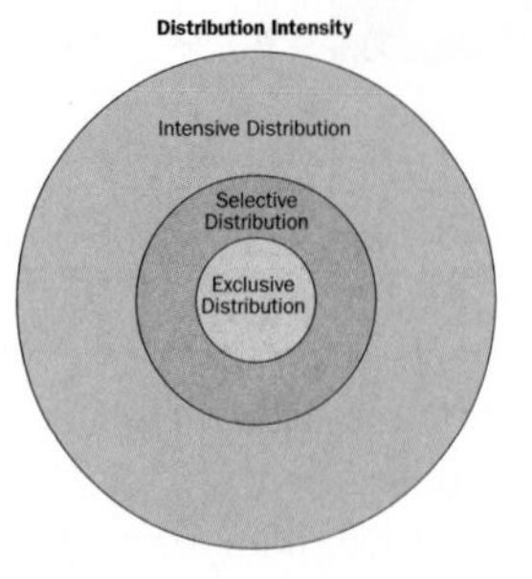

EXCLUSIVE DISTRIBUTION

Exclusive distribution involves distribution of a product in protected territories in a given geographic area. Dealers are assured that they are the only ones within a certain geographic radius that have the right to sell the manufacturer's or wholesaler's products. Prestige, image, channel control, and a high profit margin for both the manufacturer and intermediaries are among the reasons that companies choose this distribution strategy.

The exclusive distribution method also encourages distributors to advertise the products they sell and to provide any customer service that might be necessary after the sale. Franchised operations use exclusive distribution planning. An example of this kind of franchised operation is a distributor that supplies a specific name-brand item to all the stores in a particular region.

In addition, wholesalers may sponsor voluntary groups in which a retailer agrees to buy and **maintain** a minimum inventory of the wholesaler's products. One example of a voluntary group sponsored by a wholesaler is the National Auto Parts Association (NAPA). Retailers affiliated with NAPA buy most of their stock directly from NAPA and participate in its promotions.

Some manufacturers own and run their own retail operations. This variation on exclusive distribution is **integrated distribution**. The manufacturer acts as wholesaler and retailer for its own products. For example, Gap® Inc. sells its clothing in company-owned retail stores.

SELECTIVE DISTRIBUTION

Selective distribution means that a limited number of outlets in a given geographic area sell a manufacturer's product. The goal is to select channel members that can maintain the image of the product. These channel members are also good credit risks, aggressive marketers, and good inventory planners.

Intermediaries are selected for their ability to cater to the final users that the manufacturer wants to attract. For example, designers Armani and Vera Wang sell their clothing only through stores that appeal to the affluent customers who buy their merchandise. They do not sell goods in a chain store or a variety store.

INTENSIVE DISTRIBUTION

Intensive distribution involves the use of all suitable outlets to sell a product. The objective is complete market coverage, and the ultimate goal is to sell to as many customers as possible, in all the various locations they shop. A good example of this is motor oil. Motor oil is marketed in quick-lube shops, farm stores, auto-parts retailers, supermarkets, drugstores, hardware stores, warehouse clubs, and other mass merchandisers to reach the maximum number of customers.

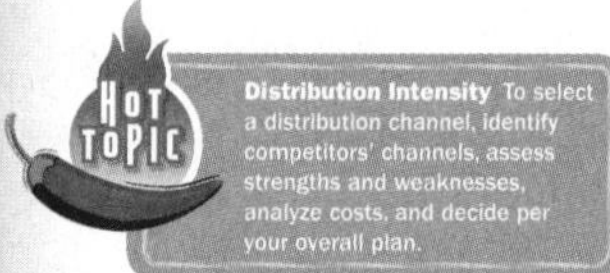

HOT TOPIC
Distribution Intensity To select a distribution channel, identify competitors' channels, assess strengths and weaknesses, analyze costs, and decide per your overall plan.

E-COMMERCE

E-commerce actually means "electronic commerce." E-commerce is the process in which products are sold to customers and industrial buyers over electronic systems such as the Internet. You already learned that e-tailing is retail selling via the Internet. This online shopping outlet is called the **e-marketplace**. The amount of business that is now conducted electronically has grown immensely in recent years with widespread Internet usage and the popularity of Web sites that have become online marketplaces.

Travel industry researchers estimate that more than half of all travel bookings were made online in 2010. Consumers have also become accustomed to buying books, toys, and other goods on the Internet. This trend has led to the term "Black Monday," which refers to the first Monday after the start of the holiday shopping season. This Monday after Thanksgiving is the day on which consumer Web site traffic in the United States is traditionally the busiest of the year.

E-marketplaces for business-to-business (B2B) operations provide one-stop shopping and substantial savings for industrial buyers. Online catalogs of products supplied by different companies make it easier for corporate buyers to compare prices and get the best deal.

E-marketplaces provide smaller businesses with the exposure that they could not get elsewhere. Small businesses can also use social networking sites such as Twitter® and Facebook® to share information about their products. These sites allow consumers to see what is available for sale at a company's store. The company can reach consumers directly through the use of the Internet.

In each of the past five years, a greater proportion of B2B trade has taken place via the Internet. For example, many companies with locations in different parts of the country find it more efficient to use dedicated Web sites for restocking and tracking of their office supply needs. This trend is expected to continue in the future.

Reading Check

Identify What are the three levels of distribution intensity?

504 | Unit 7 · Distribution

Chapter 21 · Channels of Distribution | 505

EXPLAIN

Career Chatroom

Use these questions to focus the discussion about the Career Chatroom feature.

Guiding Questions

Explain Why should international traders travel?	Cultural differences influence the way companies do business.
Predict What analytical skills would you need?	Data collection, data analysis, drawing conclusion

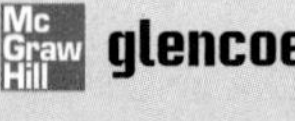

glencoe.com

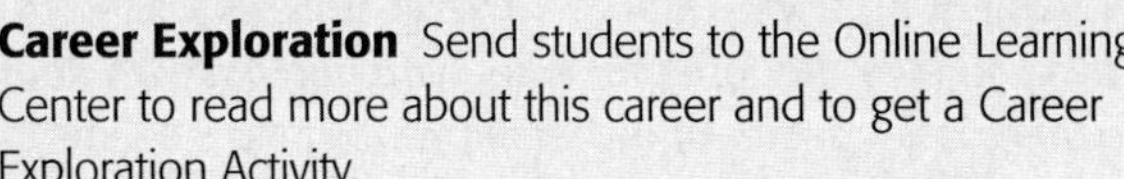

Career Exploration Send students to the Online Learning Center to read more about this career and to get a Career Exploration Activity.

Mini Project

Enrichment

Research Sales Have students go online to find at least three real-world examples of companies that employ manufacturer's agents/representatives (those who work for several producers and carry noncompetitive, complementary merchandise) and selling agents (who represent a single producer). Have them create a table that indicates the company name, industry, and how they handle their sales. Sample table:

Company	Industry	How Sales are Handled

Then ask students how it would affect manufacturer's agents/representatives and agents if a company opened outlet stores for direct sales to the consumer. this would drastically cut down on sales opportunities for the manufacturers' agents/representatives and agents.

ELABORATE

DISTRIBUTION INTENSITY

Ask these guiding questions to focus the discussion on distribution intensity.

Guiding Questions

Identify What are the benefits of exclusive distribution?	Benefits include prestige, image, channel control, and a high profit margin for the manufacturer and intermediaries.
Explain What is integrated distribution?	It is a variation on exclusive distribution in which the manufacturers own and run their own retail operations.
Analyze Why would a manufacturer choose selective distribution?	A manufacturer that wanted to maintain the image of its product and to hand pick distributors of the product would likely choose selective distribution.

Critical Thinking

Tell students to imagine that they have created a new product. Ask: ***What factors would you need to consider before creating a distribution plan?*** They need to consider cost, expenses, brand image, accessibility, and place. Tell them that by knowing these factors, they can begin to generate the appropriate distribution plan. Then tell students that the trend toward manufacturers opening their own stores (such as those in outlet malls) to sell their products is on the upswing. Ask students to speculate how this kind of distribution might help independent retailers increase product awareness. The advertising done by the manufacturer's stores would increase the public's awareness of that brand, which would benefit all retailers that sell that brand.

Graphic Organizer

Display this target diagram. Ask students to explain each type of distribution. Possible answers:

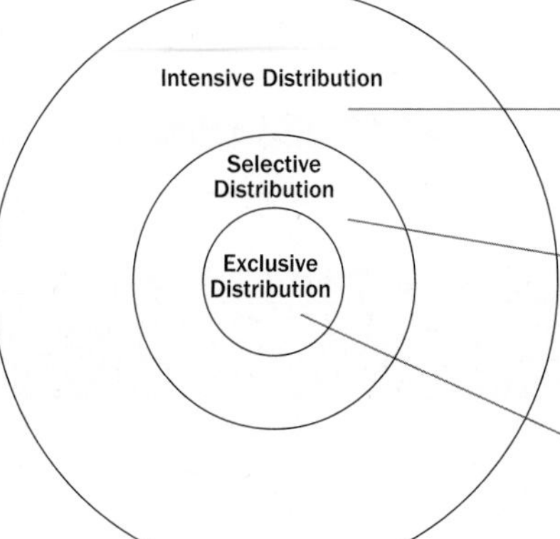

involves the use of all suitable outlets to sell a product

involves a limited number of outlets in a given geographic area sell a manufacturer's product

involves distribution of a product in protected territories in a given geographic area

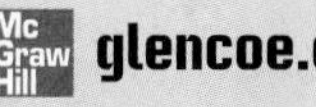

Graphic Organizer Send students to the Online Learning Center to print this graphic organizer.

Distribution Intensity Have students visit local stores and ask whether they have exclusive distribution rights on any products. If so, have students ask what the products are. Ask students to share their findings with the class.

Reading Check Answer

Read the Reading Check question to students: ***What are the three levels of distribution intensity?*** exclusive, selective, and intensive Then ask: ***What is integrated distribution?*** It is a variation on exclusive distribution in which the manufacturer acts as wholesaler and retailer for its own products.

LEGAL AND ETHICAL CONSIDERATIONS IN DISTRIBUTION

In most cases, businesses may use whatever channel arrangement they desire. Laws affecting channels generally prevent exclusionary tactics that might keep other companies from using a desired channel of distribution.

The Clayton Antitrust Act of 1914 prevents exclusive arrangements that substantially lessen competition, create a monopoly, or in which one party did not commit to the agreement voluntarily.

Antitrust laws help to ensure that companies compete fairly with one another for the benefit of consumers. If competing businesses are on an even playing field, it helps ensure that their customers get the best possible deals on products and services.

Some distribution practices meet legal requirements but may be ethically questionable. The American Marketing Association (AMA) Code of Ethics lists the following responsibilities in the area of distribution:

- Not manipulating the availability of a product for purpose of exploitation
- Not using coercion in the marketing channel
- Not exerting undue influence over the reseller's decision to handle the product

Reading Check

Evaluate Is it legal to tell a customer you do not have a product even when you do?

Intensive Distribution

Palm® distributes cell phones through several different retail and e-tail stores. ***What benefits does intensive distribution provide for Palm?***

palm prē

Full featured for the full-on life.

Vivid touchscreen
View web pages[1], photos, and videos on a bright, responsive display.

Slide-out keyboard
Type away on a full QWERTY keyboard whenever you need it.

Palm® webOS™ platform
Get more done and have more fun with the amazingly powerful Palm webOS.

Work and play
Access your business and personal contacts, information, or events, all at once.[2]

DISTRIBUTION PLANNING FOR FOREIGN MARKETS

Foreign market environments require that businesses adjust their distribution systems. They also give businesses a chance to experiment with different distribution strategies. For example, when McDonald's® first enters a foreign market, it opens company-owned stores to familiarize the consumer with its products and store atmosphere. This means the company is both the producer and the retailer. After company-owned stores have opened the market, the company switches over to selling franchises. At that point, the company acts as both producer and agent, and the franchisee is the retailer.

Cultural considerations should also be weighed when planning distribution in world markets. For example, when Reebok® wanted to sell athletic shoes in Europe, it studied European culture and found that Europeans visit sporting goods stores far less often than Americans. The company decided to distribute Reebok's shoes through hundreds of traditional retail shoe outlets instead of sporting goods stores. Within one year of adopting this distribution strategy, Reebok's sales in France doubled.

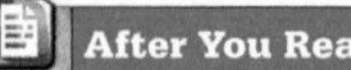

After You Read **Section 21.2**

Review Key Concepts

1. **Explain** why a company would decide to use multiple distribution channels.
2. **List** the reasons a company would choose a direct sales force.
3. **Name** two advantages that e-commerce provides for B2B sales.

Practice Academics

English Language Arts

4. As secretary for the local association of retail florists, you have been asked by the association president to write to a local wholesale florist who has been selling to the final consumer. Give at least two reasons in your letter why the retail florists are upset about this.

NCTE 12 Use language to accomplish individual purposes.

Mathematics

5. Assume Manufacturer A had sales of $2,500,000 and sales expenses of 6 percent for outside sales agents. Manufacturer B, a rival company, had sales of $4,250,000 for the same period. Its sales expenses were $400,500. Which company had the lower rate of sales expenses?

NCTM Number and Operations Understand meanings of operations and how they relate to one another.

Math Concept **Relationships Among Numbers** Determining the significance of numbers can be critical to problem solving.

Starting Hints To solve the problem, write the sales expenses as decimals. Multiply the decimal by the respective total sales. Compare both numbers to determine which company had the lower rate of sales expenses.

For help, go to the **Math Skills Handbook** located at the back of this book.

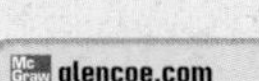

glencoe.com

Check your answers.

ELABORATE

LEGAL AND ETHICAL CONSIDERATIONS IN DISTRIBUTION

Ask students if they are aware that there are laws that govern distribution channels and other business issues such as monopolies. Then ask these guiding questions to focus the discussion on laws and ethics in distribution.

Guiding Questions

Explain What does the Clayton Antitrust Act of 1914 prevent?	exclusive arrangements that substantially lessen competition, create a monopoly, or in which one party did not commit to the agreement voluntarily
Differentiate What is the difference between practices that are illegal and those that are unethical?	Illegal practices can result in jail time or heavy fines. Unethical acts probably cannot be prosecuted or monitored.

Reading Check Answer

Read the Reading Check question to students: ***Is it legal to tell a customer you do not have a product even when you do?*** According to the AMA Code of Ethics, it is unethical to manipulate the availability of a product for the purpose of exploitation. It is also unethical to lie to a customer.

Mini Project

Enrichment

Interview Retailers Have students interview local retailers or wholesalers about ethical issues they have come across regarding product distribution. Students might work in pairs to develop a list of questions. Then have students set up an appointment to speak to the business owner or manager. After students have conducted their interviews, ask them to share their results with the class. Answers might include such issues as environmental responsibility in using local producers to cut down on the amount of fuel that is used to transport products.

EVALUATE

DISTRIBUTION PLANNING FOR FOREIGN MARKETS

Tell students that when companies in the United States decide to do business in foreign countries, they must conduct intensive cultural studies of those countries to learn the customs and to avoid insulting the people of the country. This information can affect the way the products are distributed and marketed. Ask students these guiding questions to focus a discussion about distribution planning and foreign markets.

Guiding Questions

Explain Why would a company like McDonald's® open a company-owned store when first entering a foreign market?	allows the company to familiarize the consumer with its products and store atmosphere; the company to familiarize itself with the population.
Determine In the case presented in the text, how was McDonald's both the producer and the retailer?	Owning their own stores and selling directly to the consumer made them both producer and retailer.
Predict What might have been the outcome if Reebok® had not studied European culture before marketing their shoes in Europe?	If they had sold the shoes in sporting goods stores, they might not have been successful in the European market.

Mini Project

Extension

Inventory Products Have students take an inventory of products in their homes that are made in foreign countries. Products can be clothing, electronics, even automobiles. Ask students to create a table that lists the products in one column and the country of origin in the other column. (See sample table below.) Then have them select one product to research. Ask them to describe the distribution process for that product's trip to the United States and to their local retailer. Sample answer for a car made in Mexico: Channel B—Manufacturer/Producer to Retailer to Consumer.

Product	Country of Origin
Car	Mexico
Computer	Japan

After You Read Section 21.2

Review Key Concepts

1. A producer uses multiple channels when its product fits the needs of both industrial and consumer markets.
2. A company would choose a direct sales force when they want complete control over the sales; when they want to establish sales quotas; and when they want to monitor each sales representative's performance.
3. E-marketplaces for B2B operations provide one-stop shopping and substantial savings for industrial buyers. Online catalogs of products supplied by different companies make it easier for corporate buyers to compare prices and get the best deal. E-marketplaces provide smaller businesses with the exposure that they could not get elsewhere.

Practice Academics

English Language Arts

4. Reasons might include the retailers cannot match the wholesalers' prices to the customer and the wholesaler is taking customers away from the retail florists. Accept all reasonable answers; letters should use proper grammar, spelling, and punctuation.

Mathematics

5. Manufacturer A had the lowest rate of sales expenses—6% as compared to 9.4% for Manufacturer B. (Manufacturer B = $400,500 ÷ $4,250,000 = .094)

glencoe.com

Answer Key Send students to the Online Learning Center to check their answers.

Chapter 21 Visual Summary

Channels of Distribution

Manufacturers or producers may choose one or more paths (channels) to distribute products to the final user.

Manufacturer/Producer

Agent

Wholesaler

Industrial Distributor

Retailer

Consumer

Business/Industrial User

A B C D E D C B A

Review and Activities

Written Summary

- Manufacturers or producers may choose one or more paths (channels) to distribute products to the final user.
- The channels used to distribute consumer products usually differ from those used to distribute to the industrial market.
- Manufacturers or producers may use multiple channels of distribution to reach different markets. Product distribution in foreign markets often requires special planning.
- Distribution intensity may be exclusive, selective, or intensive.

Review Content Vocabulary and Academic Vocabulary

1. Explain how each term relates to the subject of the chapter or the unit.

Content Vocabulary
- channel of distribution (p. 493)
- intermediaries (p. 493)
- wholesalers (p. 493)
- rack jobbers (p. 493)
- drop shippers (p. 494)
- retailers (p. 494)
- brick-and-mortar retailers (p. 494)
- e-tailing (p. 494)
- agents (p. 495)
- direct distribution (p. 495)
- indirect distribution (p. 495)
- exclusive distribution (p. 504)
- integrated distribution (p. 505)
- selective distribution (p. 505)
- intensive distribution (p. 505)
- e-marketplace (p. 505)

Academic Vocabulary
- commission (p. 493)
- automatic (p. 494)
- control (p. 503)
- maintain (p. 504)

Assess for Understanding

2. **Explain** What is the place decision?
3. **Name** What is another term for intermediaries?
4. **Identify** What are two types of intermediaries?
5. **List** What are four non-store retailing methods?
6. **Distinguish** What are the most common methods of distribution for consumer products and for industrial products?
7. **Generate** What are some questions to consider in establishing a distribution plan?
8. **Contrast** When would it be beneficial to use exclusive distribution rather than intensive distribution?
9. **Describe** What is the difference between the cost of having a direct sales force and the cost of using independent sales agents?

EVALUATE

Visual Summary

Express Creativity Ask students to develop their own visual summary of a concept in the chapter. Encourage students to use different formats for their visual summaries, such as a storyboard, a timeline, a table, a tree diagram, or a word web. Visual summaries will vary depending on the concept depicted and the visual manner in which it is depicted. Questions to ask when assessing a visual summary include:

- Is the summary clear, economical, and simple?
- Are any important steps left out?
- Are steps or concepts arranged in the same order as the original?
- Does the summary reveal a pattern that connects the details?
- Does the summary locate and highlight the most important information?

Review Content Vocabulary and Academic Vocabulary

1. A **channel of distribution** is the path a product takes from its producer or manufacturer to the final user. Members of the channel include **intermediaries**, **wholesalers**, **rack jobbers**, **drop shippers**, **retailers**, **brick-and-mortar retailers**, and **agents**. Online retailing, called **e-tailing**, is also a member of the channel; this online shopping outlet is called the **e-marketplace**. There are **direct** and **indirect channels of distribution** and there are a number of types of distribution such as **exclusive**, **integrated**, **selective**, and **intensive distribution**. Channel members called agents receive **commissions**. **Automatic** retailing (vending machines) is a type of non-store retailing operations. **Control** versus costs is a consideration when making distribution decisions. Wholesalers may sponsor voluntary groups in which a retailer agrees to buy and **maintain** a minimum inventory of the wholesaler's products.

EVALUATE

Assess for Understanding

2. A place decision means deciding how a product will reach the customer, that is, what channel or channels of distribution will be utilized.
3. Another name for intermediaries is middlemen.
4. Two types of intermediaries are merchant intermediaries and agent intermediaries.
5. Non-store retailing methods include vending machines, direct mail and catalog retailing, TV home shopping, and online retailing.
6. The most common method of distribution for consumer products is producer to retailer to consumer (Channel B). The most common method in the industrial market is direct distribution (Channel A).
7. Key questions include the use of multiple channels, control of sales versus cost of sales, intensity of distribution desired, and use of e-commerce.
8. Prestige, image, channel control, and a high profit margin for both the manufacturer and intermediaries are reasons to choose this distribution strategy. This method of distribution also encourages distributors to advertise the products and provide necessary after-sales customer service.
9. A direct sales force is usually more expensive than sales agents. An in-house or direct sales force gives the producer more control over the product than they get with sales agents.

Chapter 21 Review and Activities

21st Century Skills

Communication

10. **Distribution in Other Cultures** Identify a company. Explain how it might want to distribute its products in another country. Select the country and explain why you chose the distribution channel.

Financial Literacy Skills

11. **Distribution Planning** It costs you $4.95 to make a graphic t-shirt. You are considering selling the shirts to wholesalers and retail stores. A wholesaler will buy 500 shirts for $3595. Retail stores will buy 100 shirts for $645. What will your profit be per shirt from each distribution channel?

Everyday Ethics

12. **Power Source** More than half the electricity generated in the United States comes from coal. It is extracted through traditional mining and by mountaintop removal, a process that blasts away the tops of mountains to reach the underlying veins of this fossil fuel. However, mountaintop removal damages the environment in ways that cannot be undone. Discuss whether it is ethical to blast away mountaintops to make the production and distribution of coal easier.

e-Marketing Skills

13. **E-Commerce and Distribution** Conduct research on the effect of e-commerce on the channels of distribution used for consumer and industrial products. Write a report summarizing current information about types of products sold and dollar sales figures for those products.

Build Academic Skills

Science

14. **The Impact of Technology** The process of distributing products uses a wide range of technologies. From the vehicles used to transport goods to the Internet and e-commerce, there are many ways to reduce costs and modify product distribution. What are some technologies or gadgets you use that may be helpful to distributors? Share your ideas with your class.

NSES A Develop abilities necessary to do scientific inquiry, understandings about scientific inquiry.

Social Studies

15. **Planning for Global Distribution** You have just been hired as a marketing consultant for an automobile accessories manufacturing company that wishes to expand its business worldwide. Your job is to develop a plan for sales and distribution of their products in the global market. Research the steps that must be taken to begin selling the company's products in European, Asian, and South American countries. Describe what considerations should be given to differences in culture. Write a two-page report on your findings.

NCSS V B Individuals, Groups, & Institutions Analyze group and institutional influences on people, events, and elements of culture in both historical and contemporary settings.

Mathematics

16. **Calculate Savings** The price of a best-selling DVD is $19.00 at a local store. You can purchase the same DVD through an e-tailer for $10.20 plus 20 percent for shipping charges. How much will you save by purchasing the DVD through the e-tailer?

NCTM Number and Operations Compute fluently and make reasonable estimates.

Math Concept **Computations** Calculating the amount saved by purchasing one product instead of another involves comparison.

For help, go to the **Math Skills Handbook** located at the back of this book.

Standardized Test Practice

Directions Read the following questions. On a separate piece of paper, write the best possible answer for each one.

1. In distributing products from the producer to the consumer, which of the following could be a channel member?
   A. Wholesaler
   B. Retailer
   C. Agent
   D. All of the above
2. True or false? Direct distribution occurs when goods are sold by the producer directly to the consumer.
   T
   F
3. The businesses that move products from the manufacturer to the final user are called ________.

Test-Taking Tip
In a true or false test, every part of a true statement must be true. If any part of the statement is false, the answer has to be false.

DECA Connection Role Play

Owner
Wholesale Kitchen Appliance Company

Situation Your company sells the finest kitchen appliances available. You have agreements with all of the appliance manufacturers whose appliances your company offers for sale that you have selective distribution of their appliances.

Earlier this week you finalized an agreement to become the exclusive distributor for the most sought-after brand of European kitchen appliances. The European brand represents a significant financial investment for your company. You feel that the investment is worthwhile because of the quality of the appliances and the prestige of distributing these appliances. Your exclusive distribution rights mean that your company will be the only one in this country to sell the European brand.

You are very happy about selling the European appliance line and the potential it offers your company. You have called a special staff meeting to announce that your company is the country's exclusive distributor of the European appliance line.

Activity You are to explain to your employees (judge) the significance of your company being the exclusive distributor of the European appliances line. You must also explain exclusive distribution and how it differs from the selective distribution of your other appliance lines.

Evaluation You will be evaluated on how well you meet the following performance indicators:

1. Explain the nature of channels of distribution.
2. Explain the nature of channel-member relationships.
3. Explain the nature and scope of channel management.
4. Explain legal considerations in channel management.
5. Explain ethical considerations in channel management.

Download the Competitive Events Workbook for more Role-Play Practice.

21st Century Skills

Communication

10. Accept all reasonable answers; students should use proper grammar, spelling, and punctuation. Students' answers will vary but should show an understanding of the effects of the distribution channels. A sample answer might be to select China as the country in which to distribute products, and then choose either channel D or E so that the products go through an agent before going to the retailer and consumer. An agent is important in international sales because it is necessary to go through someone who understands the culture where the products will be sold.

Financial Literacy Skills

11. Profit from wholesaler = $2.24 ($3595 ÷ 500 = $7.19; $7.19 − 4.95 = $2.24). Profit from retailer = $1.50 ($645 ÷ 100 = $6.45; $6.45 − 4.95 = $1.50).

Everyday Ethics

12. Answers will vary, but students should provide a rationale for their answers. Sample answers: Students who consider it to be ethical to mine by removing mountaintops might suggest that this type of mining helps to keep the cost of the fuel down and therefore makes it more affordable for those who use it. Those who think it is unethical to mine this way will likely cite the irreversible damage to the environment as their reasoning.

e-Marketing Skills

13. Students should use online or current library sources for their research. They should gather information and organize it in a logical order. Use criteria similar to the following to evaluate students' reports:
Are the sources current?
Are the sources cited in the report?
Does the report include a thesis statement?
Is the thesis statement supported throughout the report?
Are sentences logical and well-composed?
Are there grammar or spelling errors?

EVALUATE

Build Academic Skills

Science

14. Students might discuss the use of computers and different apps on smartphones. Encourage students to think creatively and come up with some outside-the-box ideas for distributing products.

Social Studies

15. Students' reports should cover a number of topics such as trade agreements, trade barriers, economic factors, political factors, trade regulations and laws, socio-cultural factors, technological factors, product adaptation or customization (you might refer students to Chapter 4, Global Analysis, for some background information).

Mathematics

16. \$6.76 [\$19.00 – (\$10.20 + ([\$10.20 × .20])) = \$19.00 – (\$10.20 + 2.04) = \$19.00 – 12.24 = \$6.76]

Standardized Test Practice

1. D All of the above
2. T
3. intermediaries or middlemen

DECA Connection Role Play

Evaluations will be based on these performance indicators:

1. **Explain the nature of channels of distribution.** The channel of distribution is the path a product takes from its producer or manufacturer to the final user. When the product is purchased for use in a business, the final user is classified as an industrial user. When the product is purchased for personal use, the final user is classified as a consumer.
2. **Explain the nature of channel-member relationships.** Businesses involved in sales transactions that move products from the manufacturer to the final user are intermediaries or middlemen. Intermediaries reduce the number of contacts required to reach the final user of the product.
3. **Explain the nature and scope of channel management.** Distribution planning involves decisions about a product's physical movement and transfer of ownership from producer to consumer. Distribution decisions affect a firm's marketing program. Some of the major considerations are the use of multiple channels, control versus costs, intensity of distribution desired, and involvement in e-commerce.
4. **Explain legal considerations in channel management.** In most cases, businesses may use whatever channel arrangement they desire. Laws affecting channels generally prevent exclusionary tactics that might keep other companies from using a desired channel. The Clayton Antitrust Act of 1914 prevents exclusive arrangements that substantially lessen competition, create a monopoly, or in which one party did not commit to the agreement voluntarily. These laws help companies compete with each other for the benefit of consumers. A fair playing field will ensure that customers get the best possible deals on products.
5. **Explain ethical considerations in channel management.** The American Marketing Association (AMA) Code of Ethics lists the following responsibilities in the area of distribution: Not manipulating the availability of a product for purpose of exploitation; not using coercion in the marketing channel; not exerting undue influence over the reseller's decision to handle the product.

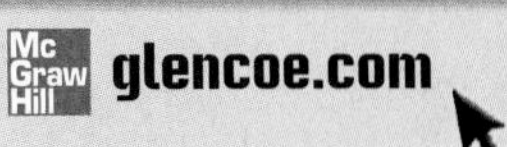

Role Plays For more DECA Role Plays, send students to the Online Learning Center to download the Competitive Events Workbook.

Chapter 22 Section 22.1 Transportation Section 22.2 Inventory Storage

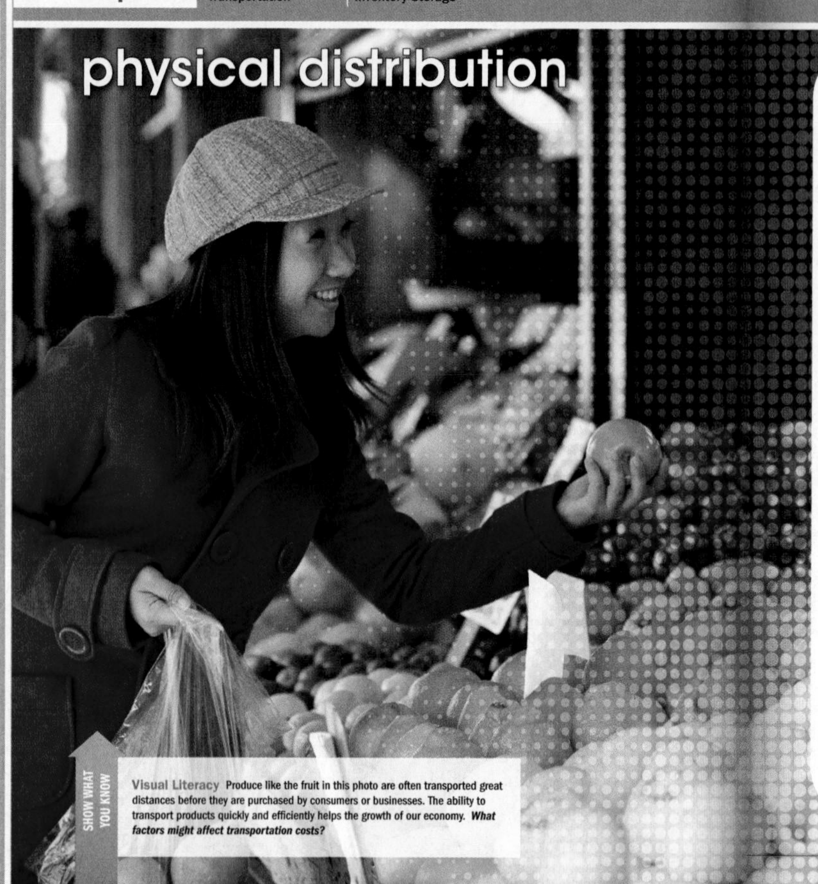

SHOW WHAT YOU KNOW

Visual Literacy Produce like the fruit in this photo are often transported great distances before they are purchased by consumers or businesses. The ability to transport products quickly and efficiently helps the growth of our economy. ***What factors might affect transportation costs?***

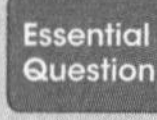

Discovery Project

Transportation Systems

Essential Question What factors must companies consider when transporting goods?

Project Goal

Assume that you are employed by a furniture manufacturer that sells its products nationwide. You have been asked to evaluate your current truck transportation system. The company is deciding between a common carrier, its own fleet, or a combination of both to transport its products. You have been asked to prepare a written report that identifies the pros and cons for each transportation option.

Ask Yourself...

- Why are trucks used for the distribution of your product?
- What are the advantages for using a common carrier, your own fleet, or both?
- What are the disadvantages for using a common carrier, your own fleet, or both?
- How will you organize your written report?

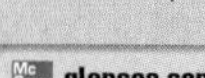

Organize and Interpret Summarize your research by explaining which form of transportation is the best for your company and why.

glencoe.com

Activity
Get a worksheet activity about distributing products.

Evaluate
Download a rubric you can use to evaluate your project.

DECA Connection

DECA Event Role Play

Concepts in this chapter are related to DECA competitive events that involve either an interview or role play.

Performance Indicators The performance indicators represent key skills and knowledge. Your key to success in DECA competitive events is relating them to concepts in this chapter.

- Select the best shipping method.
- Explain the role of distribution centers.
- Explain the storage process in warehouse operations.
- Explain distribution issues and trends.
- Discuss shipping methods used with food products.

DECA Prep

Role Play Practice role-playing with the DECA Connection competitive-event activity at the end of this chapter. More information about DECA events can be found on DECA's Web site.

Chapter 22 · Physical Distribution | 513

ENGAGE

Visual Literacy

Discuss with students that having a product people want to buy is only part of being successful in business—you also must be able to get it to them when they want it, and at a reasonable cost. Ask students: ***What factors might affect transportation costs?*** Answers may include distance, weight of goods, and type of transportation used. Ask: ***What do you think is the most expensive way of shipping an item such as a laptop computer? What might be the least expensive?*** Students may suggest that air transportation is the most expensive, and the least expensive would be by train or ship. Then ask these guiding questions.

Guiding Questions

Define What is channel management?	Channel management is the process of deciding how to get goods into customer's hands.
Analyze How do tariffs affect international trade?	They constitute a tax on imports, they increase the price.

Discovery Project

Transportation Systems To get students thinking about distribution issues, ask them the Discovery Project Essential Question: ***What factors must companies consider when transporting goods?*** distance, speed, cost, type of goods, when the goods are needed Ask students to give examples of situations in which each of these factors would be important. Create a table and fill it in with the examples. Sample answer: Under the Types of Goods heading, students might suggest livestock, perishable items such as milk, eggs, or fresh produce, and flammable liquids such as gasoline.

glencoe.com

Discovery Project Resources Send students to the Online Learning Center to download a rubric to evaluate their projects.

ENGAGE

Introduce the Chapter

Chapter 22 discusses the physical distribution of goods and the factors that companies must consider when making transportation and storage decisions. These main concepts are introduced and discussed:

- Types of transportation systems
- Advantages and disadvantages of different transportation systems
- Transportation service companies
- Types of storage facilities
- Distribution planning for international markets

Discussion Starter

Examples of Distribution and Storage Initiate a discussion about the various types of physical distribution available to businesses. Compile a list and display it for students to read. Answers may include trucks, trains, ships, and airplanes. Then ask students to define product storage and encourage them to discuss how companies store products. Storage refers to holding goods until they are sold. Students may suggest that these products are kept in warehouses or in storage areas within retail stores. Some products require special handling during this time, such as refrigeration.

DECA Connection

Discuss the performance indicators listed in the DECA Connection feature. Explain to students that performance indicators tell them how to demonstrate their acquired skills and knowledge through individual or team competitive events.

glencoe.com

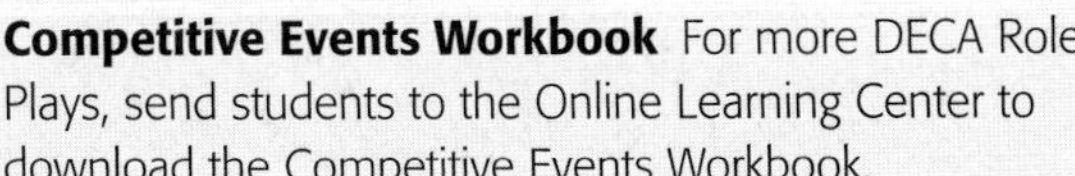

Competitive Events Workbook For more DECA Role Plays, send students to the Online Learning Center to download the Competitive Events Workbook.

PRINT RESOURCES

- **Student Edition**
- **Teacher Edition**
- **Student Activity Workbook with Academic Integration** includes worksheets and activities correlated to the text.
- **Mathematics for Marketing Workbook** provides math activities for every unit in the text.

TECHNOLOGY TOOLBOX

- **Connect**
- **ConnectPlus**
- **ExamView Assessment Suite** is a comprehensive solution for creating, administering, and scoring tests.

glencoe.com

Online Learning Center provides a variety of resources to enrich and enhance learning.

SECTION, CHAPTER, AND UNIT RESOURCES

- **Graphic Organizers** for organizing text concepts visually.
- **Digital Nation Activities** and **Green Marketer Activities** extend learning beyond the text features.
- **Career Chatroom Career Profiles** allow students to explore different marketing occupations in depth.
- **After You Read Answer Keys** for students to check their answers.
- **Discovery Project Rubrics** and **Marketing Internship Project Rubrics** for students to evaluate their projects.

PROGRAM RESOURCES

- **Student Activity Workbook with Academic Integration Teacher Annotated Edition** includes annotated answers for the activities and worksheets.
- **Marketing Research Project Workbook** provides a step-by-step approach for students to complete their own marketing research studies.
- **School-to-Career Activity Workbook** helps students relate their class work to on-the-job experience and involves work-site analysis and working with mentors.
- **Competitive Events Workbook** helps prepare students for state and national marketing education competitions.
- **Inclusion in the Marketing Education Classroom** provides teaching resources for working with students with special needs.
- **PowerPoint Presentations** provides visual teaching aids and assessments for this chapter.

READING GUIDE

Before You Read

Connect What channels of transportation are used to deliver your favorite products to you?

Objectives

- **Describe** the nature and scope of physical distribution.
- **Identify** transportation systems and services that move products from manufacturers to consumers.
- **Name** the different kinds of transportation service companies.

The Main Idea

Success in today's business environment requires companies to deliver products efficiently and effectively to their customers around the world.

Vocabulary

Content Vocabulary
- physical distribution
- transportation
- common carriers
- contract carriers
- private carriers
- exempt carriers
- ton-mile
- carload
- freight forwarders

Academic Vocabulary

You will find these words in your reading and on your tests. Make sure you know their meanings.
- regulate
- options

Graphic Organizer

Draw or print this chart to list the advantages and disadvantages of each type of transportation system.

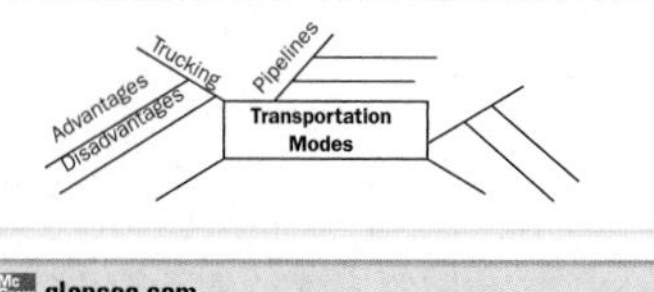

Print this graphic organizer.

STANDARDS

ACADEMIC

English Language Arts
NCTE 1 Read texts to acquire new information.

Science
NSES E Develop abilities of technological design, understandings about science and technology.

NCSS *National Council for the Social Studies*
NCTE *National Council of Teachers of English*
NCTM *National Council of Teachers of Mathematics*
NSES *National Science Education Standards*

College & Career READINESS

Common Core
Writing Conduct short as well as more sustained research projects based on focused questions, demonstrating understanding of the subject under investigation.

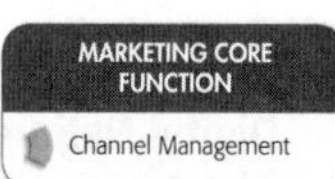

MARKETING CORE FUNCTION

Channel Management

m.e. Section 22.1 Transportation

THE NATURE AND SCOPE OF PHYSICAL DISTRIBUTION

Physical distribution comprises activities for delivering the right amount of product to the right place at the right time. Physical distribution is a key link between a business and its customers. Physical distribution ensures that products reach final customers by using a network of distributors, warehouses, and retailers. Customer satisfaction depends upon the success of this process.

> "After a company chooses its channels of distribution, it decides how to move its products through those channels."

The global market is a competitive, rapidly changing place. Business owners and managers have many ways to help assure continued success in the global and domestic markets. They can store goods in convenient locations. They can also create fast, reliable means of getting the goods to customers.

Physical distribution is also known as logistics. It involves order processing, transportation, storage, stock handling, as well as inventory control of materials and products. The purchase of a product initiates the movement of products through a physical distribution system. Marketing experts believe that between 20–25 percent of the value of a product includes physical distribution costs. Physical distribution is the third-largest expense for most businesses. This expense is surpassed only by the costs of material and labor.

Physical distribution can be viewed as a system of links for the efficient movement of products from warehouse to retailer to customer. The links include customer service, transportation, storage, order processing, inventory, and packaging. When setting their distribution goals, business owners need to ask themselves questions about these links. What level of customer service should be provided? How will the products be shipped? Where will the goods be located? How many warehouses should be used? How should orders be handled? How much inventory should be kept at each location? What kinds of protective packaging and handling are required?

Each link in the system affects the other links. For example, a business that provides customized personal computers may transport finished products by air rather than by truck. Faster delivery times may allow lower inventory costs, which would make up for the higher cost of air transport.

Businesses need to make the physical distribution system as efficient and cost effective as possible. At the same time, physical distribution needs to be coordinated with other business functions, such as purchasing, finance, production, packaging, and promotion. Suppose a business has planned to launch promotional ads for a new product available on a certain date. If the distribution system is unreliable, the product may not arrive at stores in time. This error will cost the business customers and cause the business to lose credibility.

As You Read

Predict Consider the effects of changing the transportation system a business always uses.

ENGAGE

Anticipation Activity

Improving Student Achievement Have students imagine that they own a shoe factory and must get 200 pairs of shoes transported to a shoe store 450 miles away. Ask: ***How might you do this?*** Answers may include truck, train, or air carrier.

Objectives

- **Describe** the nature and scope of physical distribution. processing, transporting, storing, stock handling, inventory
- **Identify** transportation systems and services that move products from manufacturers to consumers. trucking, railroads, waterways, pipelines, and air carriers
- **Name** the different kinds of transportation service companies. USPS, express delivery services, bus package carriers, freight forwarders

Graphic Organizer

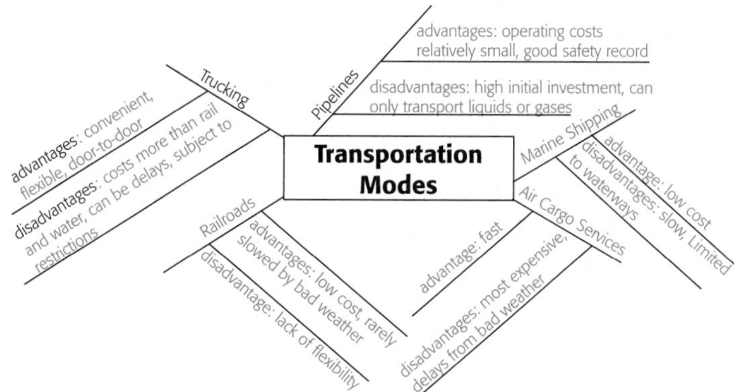

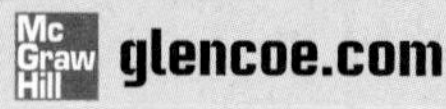

Graphic Organizer Send students to the Online Learning Center to print this graphic organizer.

EXPLORE

Before You Read

Read the Before You Read question aloud: ***What channels of transportation are used to deliver your favorite products to you?*** Accept all reasonable responses that speculate on how the products arrived at their places of purchase. For example, electronic devices might be shipped to a central warehouse by rail and then to local stores by truck. Perishable food products are shipped in refrigerated trucks.

Preteaching Vocabulary

Have students go to the Online Learning Center at glencoe.com for the Chapter 22 Preteaching Vocabulary games.

Content Vocabulary

Organize students into pairs. Have each pair choose two of the four types of carriers (common carriers, contract carriers, private carriers, and exempt carriers). Instruct each pair to write a sentence contrasting two types of carriers. Have students share their sentences with the class. Private carriers transport goods for a single company, while contract carriers provide equipment and drivers for specific routes agreed upon with the shipper.

Academic Vocabulary

Regulate—Word Origin Display the word *regulate* for the students to read. Explain that *regulate* comes from the Latin word *regula,* which means "rule." This forms the basis of today's meaning for *regulate,* "to govern or direct according to rule."

Options—Denotative Meaning Display the word *options* for the students to read. Explain that *options* means "choices" or "alternatives." Ask students: ***When you got up this morning, what options did you have?*** Answers may include what to wear; what to eat for breakfast; and how to get to school.

Section 22.1

Transportation

THE NATURE AND SCOPE OF PHYSICAL DISTRIBUTION

Ask these guiding questions to discuss physical distribution.

Guiding Questions

Apply Give an example of a situation in which a business would want to coordinate physical distribution with promotion.	If a department store is having a back-to-school clothing sale, it would want to make certain the store is well-stocked for the sale.
Analyze In what types of situation might a business want to use a relatively slow means of transportation?	When the business can save money by doing so, particularly for inexpensive products that can be stored for extended periods of time.

Expert Advice

Read the quote to students:

"After a company chooses its channels of distribution, it decides how to move its products through those channels."

Ask: ***Why must a company choose its distribution channels before it decides how to move products through those channels?*** The type of channel determines how products can be moved.

As You Read

Read students the As You Read question: ***Consider the effects of changing the transportation system a business always uses.*** Effects can be extensive. Warehouses might need to be moved to meet the needs of the new system. For example, when going from transporting by truck to a combination of railroad and truck, goods will have to be shipped to a location where they can be off-loaded from train cars. It also might be necessary to adjust to stricter scheduling. Ask students: ***What do you think might be a reason that a company would change the way it transports goods?*** Sample answer: to save money, because the current method is not meeting company needs (for example, too many delays are occurring, resulting in goods arriving after they were promised).

TYPES OF TRANSPORTATION SYSTEMS

Transportation is the marketing function of moving a product from the place where it is made to the place where it is sold. It is estimated that up to 8 percent of a company's sales revenue is spent on transportation.

There are three factors that affect transportation costs. First is the distance between the source and the destination. Second is the means of transportation. Third is the size and quantity of the product to be shipped.

Since transportation costs are a significant part of each sale, manufacturers, wholesalers, and retailers look for the most cost-effective delivery methods. An efficient distribution system moves products with minimal handling to minimize costs and maximize customer satisfaction.

Decisions made about transportation are closely related to several other distribution issues. Access to appropriate transportation plays a part in choosing a location for a business or facility.

The means of transportation, such as air, water, or land, may determine the form of packing materials used. The means of transportation may also affect the size and frequency of shipments. Transportation costs may be reduced by sending larger shipments less frequently. However, it is also necessary to consider the costs of maintaining extra inventory. The connection among these decisions means that careful planning and scheduling can help save on transportation costs.

There are five major transportation systems, or modes, used move products: trucks, railroads, waterways, pipelines, and air carriers.

In many cases, there are several sources and many destinations for the same product. This adds a significant level of complexity to the challenge of minimizing transportation costs. The percentage of freight carried by each transportation mode is shown in **Figure 22.1**.

FIGURE 22.1 Transportation Systems

This pie chart shows the percentage of freight shipped by each type of single-mode transportation in the United States. ***Why do you think the percentage of freight carried by trucks is so large?***

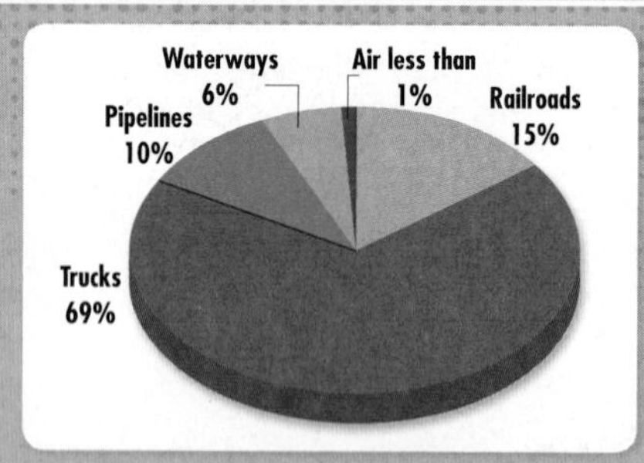

TRUCKING

Trucks, or motor carriers, are the most frequently used transportation mode. Trucks are readily available and ideally suited for transporting goods over short distances. They carry higher-valued products that are expensive for a business to keep in inventory. They also carry products with a limited shelf life, such as produce, meat, and dairy products. Lightweight shipments transported over moderate distances are generally handled by trucks. Nearly 80 percent of those shipments weigh less than 1,000 pounds each. Businesses use trucks for virtually all intracity (within a city) shipping and for 26 percent of the intercity (between cities) freight traffic in the United States.

State and federal transportation agencies **regulate** motor carriers used for interstate (between states) commerce. They regulate the number of hours motor carrier operators can drive without stopping and the length of rest periods. State transportation agencies regulate fuel taxes, safety issues, and rates charged for intrastate (within a state) trucking.

TYPES OF CARRIERS

Businesses that use trucks to move their products have several different **options**. They can use for-hire carriers, private carriers, or a combination of both. For-hire carriers include common carriers and contract carriers.

Common carriers are trucking companies that provide transportation services to any business in their operating area for a fee. Common carriers must treat all customers equally. Less-than-truckload carriers provide shipments in which freight from multiple shippers are consolidated into a single truckload. Carriers can change their rates or geographical areas, as long as they do not charge rates that are different from their published rates. More than one-third of all motor freight is handled by common carriers.

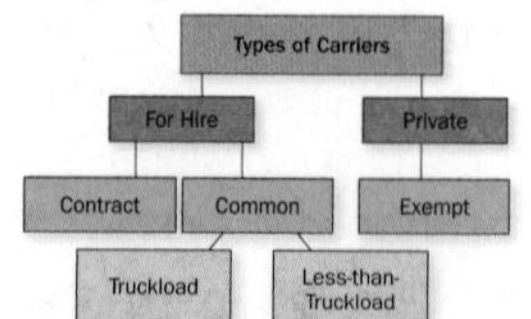

The physical movement of products involves transportation. It is estimated that up to 8 percent of a company's sales revenue is spent on transportation. ***Why is an effective transportation system important for a company?***

EXPLAIN

Graphic Organizer

Display the following illustration to focus the discussion on the three factors that affect transportation costs.

Distance Between Source and Destination

Means of Transportation

Size and Quantity of Product Being Shipped

= Total Transportation Costs

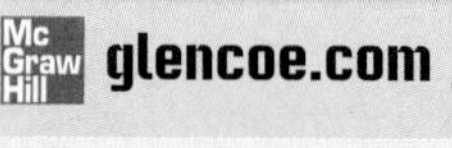

Graphic Organizer Send students to the Online Learning Center to print this graphic organizer.

Visual Literacy

Figure 22.1 Caption Answer Read the caption question to students: ***Why do you think the percentage of freight carried by trucks is so large?*** Trucks can provide door-to-door delivery and are fairly rapid, reducing the need for businesses to maintain large inventories. Ask: ***According to this chart, which transportation system carries one and one-half times as much as pipelines?*** railroads To help students understand how charts and graphs are created, ask: ***Why do you think the total percentages in this chart add up to 101 percent?*** The person who compile the information and created the chart rounded each percentage to the nearest whole number.

Reinforce Vocabulary

Contract Carriers—Denotative Meaning Explain to students that the word *contract* means "a legally binding agreement between two or more parties." A contract carrier enters into such an agreement with the shipper.

ELABORATE

TYPES OF TRANSPORTATION SYSTEMS

To focus the discussion on transportation systems, ask these guiding questions.

Guiding Questions

Draw Conclusions A motorcycle is shipped from a southern city where it was manufactured to a warehouse in Cleveland, Ohio, a distance of 850 miles. It is then shipped to a local motorcycle dealership 75 miles from the warehouse. One leg of this trip was by rail. Which leg do you think was by truck? Why?	The second one. Heavy products, such as motorcycles, are shipped more economically by rail. However, a truck has greater flexibility to transport the motorcycle from the warehouse to a local dealership.
Infer What do you think the word *common* means in the term *common carrier?*	It means "public," or "relating to the community at large." A common carrier is one that anyone can hire.

Critical Thinking

Display these two prefixes for the class to read: *intra-* and *inter-*. Ask for a volunteer to explain the difference. *Intra-* means "within" or "inside," and *inter-* means "between" or "among." Remind students that intrastate commerce is commerce that occurs within a single state. Interstate commerce is commerce that occurs between two states or among several states.

Graphic Organizer

Display the diagram to illustrate the relationship among the different types of carriers. Tell students that they see a truck that says "Target" on its side. What category of carrier is this? private Then tell students they see a truck that says "Schneider," a major trucking company, on its side. What category is this? for hire (common, truckload)

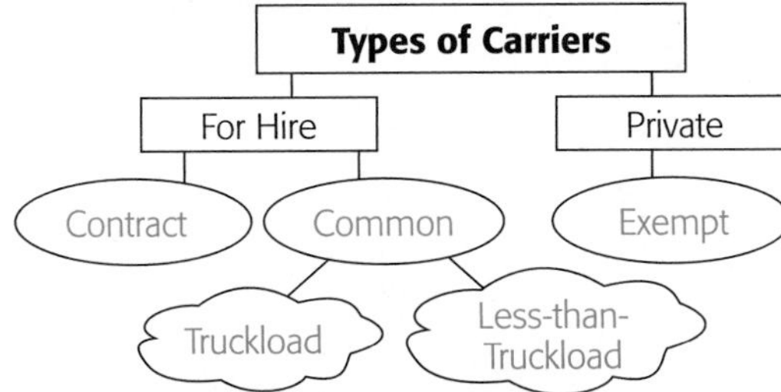

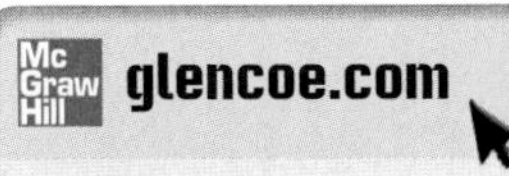

iWB

Graphic Organizer Send students to the Online Learning Center to print this graphic organizer.

Visual Literacy

Transportation Function Caption Answer Read the caption question to students: ***Why is an effective transportation system important for a company?*** In order to be competitive in today's marketplace, a company must be able to move goods at as low a cost as possible.

Critical Thinking

Display a model of a semi-truck. Discuss with students that this type of truck consists of two parts: the front part, called the tractor, and the back part, or semi-trailer (or simply trailer). The trailer itself does not have a front axle. A good portion of its weight is supported by the tractor. This is why it has the name *semi.* Ask students: ***What do you think is an advantage of using semi-trucks rather than trucks that are a single unit?*** Possible answers: The tractor can be attached to different kinds of trailers as needed; the trailer can be unhooked from the tractor which simplifies loading and unloading; the semi is more maneuverable and can turn corners more easily than if it were a single unit.

Mini Projects

Extension

Identifying Different Types of Semi-Trailers Have students work in pairs to create a list of the different types of semi-trailers. Types might include vans (enclosed boxes), tankers, refrigerated trailers, flatbeds, and auto transports. Then have them create a collage of these trailers. The collage should contain either a photo or a drawing of each trailer type. Next to each trailer, have students include images of the kinds of products it could haul. Collages will vary. Sample images may include a photo of a gas pump next to a tanker, new or damaged vehicles next to an auto transport, horses or cows next to a livestock trailer, and bales of hay next to a flatbed truck.

Calculating Percentage of Truck Traffic Have students work independently to determine the percentage of truck traffic on a nearby interstate. Students should count the total number of vehicles along with the number of trucks. Students then should calculate the percentage of all vehicles that are trucks. Have students report their percentages to the class.

Illustrating Percentage of Different Types of Trailers As a class, discuss the different types of trailers that semi-trucks may be towing. Have students count the number of trailers of each type traveling along a local interstate over a specific time period. Students should use this data to create a pie chart that graphically illustrates the percentage of each type of trailer. Students' pie charts should show the percentage of each type of trailer, such as vans, tankers, and flatbeds, seen along a local interstate during a specific time period. The chart should be easy to understand and clearly labeled.

Contract carriers are for-hire trucking companies that provide equipment and drivers for specific routes, according to agreements between the carrier and the shipper. A contract carrier can provide services on a one-time basis or on a continuing basis.

Contract carriers negotiate fee agreements with each customer and usually transport goods for more than one business. Contract carriers can legally charge different rates to each business. However, they must file their contracts with the appropriate state or federal regulatory agency.

When using for-hire carriers, a business does not need to invest in transportation equipment. However, for-hire carriers offer less flexibility for rush deliveries, direct shipments, and special pick-ups or handling.

PRIVATE CARRIERS

Private carriers are trucking companies that transport goods for an individual business. A company can own or lease transportation equipment. In many cases, the carrier's primary business is not transportation. For example, a grocery store chain may own and operate a private fleet to deliver produce and goods to its stores. Significant capital investment is needed to own a private fleet.

Cost is a major factor in selecting transportation. Starting a private-carrier operation requires a large investment in equipment and facilities. Private carriers allow a business to have control over equipment, maintenance, availability, routes, delivery times, and handling procedures. A business can also quickly change schedules, routes, and delivery times to meet customers' needs.

Many businesses use a combination of private and for-hire carriers. They may use their own trucks for local deliveries and common or contract carriers for shipments beyond their local service areas.

Exempt carriers are trucking companies that are free (exempt) from direct regulation of rates and operating procedures. This exemption allows their rates to be lower than those of common carriers.

MARKETING CASE STUDY

UPS Races with NASCAR

Most of the advertising done by international delivery service UPS® is serious and businesslike. It communicates the benefits of using "Brown" and how it can help companies succeed. One ad campaign, though, took a more light-hearted tone. It put a NASCAR® driver to the test against UPS drivers.

Taking Brown for a Spin

In the four-part series of ads, a well-known race car driver is challenged by UPS drivers to "race the truck." Eventually, the race car driver ends up driving the brown truck on a NASCAR track. The series not only promoted the UPS service and told the story of how fast it is, but it also tied in with the UPS sponsorship of the NASCAR racer.

English Language Arts

Investigate Identify three other brands that are sponsors of NASCAR vehicles. Discuss possible values these sponsorships have for each company.

NCTE 1 Read texts to acquire new information.

Local transportation firms may also receive exempt status if they make short-distance deliveries within specified trading areas in cities. In most cases, exempt carriers transport agricultural products.

ADVANTAGES AND DISADVANTAGES OF TRUCK TRANSPORTATION

Trucks are a convenient form of transportation. They can pick up products from a manufacturer, wholesaler, or retailer and deliver them door-to-door to just about any location. Trucks can make rapid deliveries, which reduces the need for businesses to carry large inventories between shipments.

Some disadvantages of trucks are that they cost more to operate than rail and water carriers. Trucks are susceptible to delays due to traffic jams, road conditions, and severe weather. Trucks are also subject to size and weight restrictions, which can vary from state to state, making interstate travel difficult in some situations.

RAILROADS

Railroads are another major form of transportation in the United States. Trains transport nearly 15 percent of the total ton-miles of freight shipped in the United States. A **ton-mile** is the movement of one ton (2,000 pounds) of freight one mile. Rail transportation is typically used for long-distance shipping. It is less expensive than air transportation. The delivery speed of rail transportation is comparable to the delivery speed of trucks over long distances. Rail transportation is faster than marine waterway transportation. Deregulation and the introduction of larger-capacity freight cars have created opportunities in areas previously dominated by motor carriers.

Trains are excellent for moving heavy and bulky freight, such as coal, steel, lumber, and grain. Specialized rail cars also haul certain products over long distances. For example, refrigerated cars keep perishable products such as milk, fruit, and vegetables from spoiling. Tankers haul combustible or hazardous materials, such as chemicals. Rail cars with ramps can transport automobiles.

PRICING AND DELIVERY SERVICES

Shippers pay lower rail transportation rates if they fill an entire boxcar. A **carload** is the minimum number of pounds of freight needed to fill a boxcar. Carload weights are established for different classifications of goods. Once a shipment reaches the minimum weight, the shipper pays the lower rate, regardless of the physical size of the shipment.

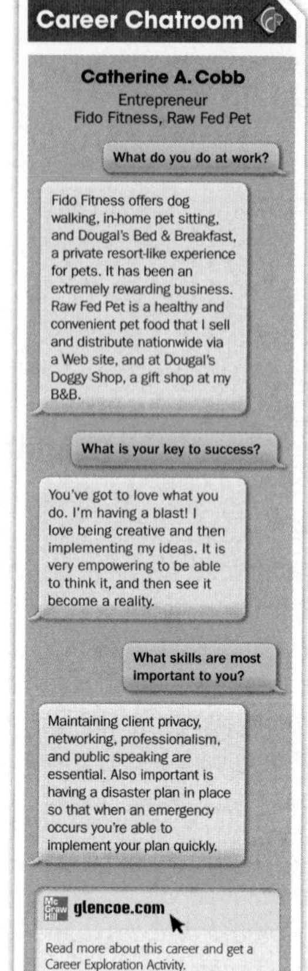
Career Chatroom

Catherine A. Cobb
Entrepreneur
Fido Fitness, Raw Fed Pet

What do you do at work?

Fido Fitness offers dog walking, in-home pet sitting, and Dougal's Bed & Breakfast, a private resort-like experience for pets. It has been an extremely rewarding business. Raw Fed Pet is a healthy and convenient pet food that I sell and distribute nationwide via a Web site, and at Dougal's Doggy Shop, a gift shop at my B&B.

What is your key to success?

You've got to love what you do. I'm having a blast! I love being creative and then implementing my ideas. It is very empowering to be able to think it, and then see it become a reality.

What skills are most important to you?

Maintaining client privacy, networking, professionalism, and public speaking are essential. Also important is having a disaster plan in place so that when an emergency occurs you're able to implement your plan quickly.

glencoe.com

Read more about this career and get a Career Exploration Activity.

EXPLAIN

PRIVATE CARRIERS

To focus the discussion on private carriers, ask these guiding questions.

Guiding Questions

Describe What is the major drawback to a company owning a private fleet?	It requires significant capital investment.
Analyze In spite of the difficulties, why do many companies decide to maintain their own fleets?	The company can maintain control over equipment, availability, routes, delivery times, and so on, and therefore better meet customer needs.
Infer What do you think might be an advantage to a company leasing the transportation equipment it needs, rather than purchasing it?	Possible answers: It can adjust the amount of equipment based on current needs; it does not have to worry about maintenance.

MARKETING CASE STUDY

English Language Arts Answer Students should list three brands that are sponsors of NASCAR®vehicles. Brands may include Coca-Cola®, Gillette®, Nationwide®, and Office Depot®. Students should explain the possible value of sponsorship for each company. For example, the National Guard might sponsor a car because research has shown that the NASCAR audience has a relatively high percentage of young people who are interested in joining the Guard. Typically, businesses will invest in a sponsorship if their target market is included in the audience at a relatively high percentage.

ELABORATE

Reinforce Vocabulary

Exempt carriers—Usage Discuss with students that the word *exempt* means "released from a liability or requirement to which others are subject." Ask: ***Have you ever been exempt from a requirement at school?*** Possible response: Yes, I did not have to take physical education class during the semester after I broke my leg. Discuss that some carriers are exempt from specific regulations and operating procedures.

RAILROADS

Trains are often used to carry bulky freight over long distances. Ask these guiding questions to focus the discussion on railroads.

Guiding Questions

Explain Why are rates higher for less-than-carload shipments than for carload shipments?	For less-than-carload shipments, partial carloads have to be unloaded at each destination, taking extra time and additional labor expenses.
Draw Conclusions Why is rail transportation typically used for long-distance shipping?	The speed of rail transportation is comparable to that of trucks over long distances. Rail transportation is faster than marine waterways..

Career Chatroom

Focus the Career Chatroom discussion concerning Catherine A. Cobb by asking students these guiding questions.

Guiding Questions

Analyze How does Catherine Cobb explain her success?	She loves what she does and enjoys being creative and implementing ideas.
Infer Why do you think Cobb sees public speaking as an important skill?	Possible answer: She may need to speak to dog owners and other groups about her services.

 **glencoe.com** 

Career Exploration Send students to the Online Learning Center to find more information about this career and to get a Career Exploration activity.

e MARKETING

Online Games

Online games are virtual games that players enjoy through membership in the virtual community. Physical distribution of the product is nonexistent because everything involved in the game is online. For example, Bridge (card game) players from around the world may play Bridge with one another through an online Bridge site. Since Bridge is a card game, language is not a barrier for players. Cards are displayed and a simple mouse click allows players to bid and select the cards they want to play when it is their turn. Free-to-play online games, like Farmville (published by Zynga®, an American company), make money by selling virtual products to players to use on their virtual farm. Players from around the world have joined Farmville to have fun buying virtual cows, flowers, barns, tractors, corn, and the like for their virtual farms.

Innovate and Create

Ask students if they have played any online games and what their experiences were with those online sites. Inquire if the sites were free and if they had to pay, what they paid for and how they paid. Have students work in a group to design an online game based on a current game they play or create an entirely new, simple game that could be played by others their age around the world. Ask them to include all the factors they have to consider since the game would be played in other countries as well as in the United States. Students' online games will vary. If students are having difficulty, suggest childhood games such as Candyland, or Monopoly. Some students may even think up a game similar to Club Penguin, a popular online game and community for children. Some factors they may have to consider is how to provide directions in different languages, the familiarity of game characters and settings with players from other countries (i.e., Monopoly site may have to change from Atlantic City to a site in another country), rewards to earn virtual money, purchasing virtual money to buy special items for use in the virtual game, and payment options that would work in countries around the world.

 **glencoe.com** 

eMarketing Worksheet Activity Send students to the Online Learning Center to download an eMarketing worksheet activity.

The term *less-than-carload* refers to a freight shipment that falls short of the minimum weight requirements to fill a boxcar. Rates charged for less-than-carload shipments are more expensive, because partial carloads have to be unloaded at each destination. The extra unloading time and labor increase the shipping rates for less-than-carload amounts.

ADVANTAGES AND DISADVANTAGES OF RAILROAD TRANSPORTATION

Railroads are one of the lowest-cost transportation modes, because trains carry large quantities at relatively low per-unit costs. Trains require 50 to 70 percent less energy than a motor carrier to transport freight, and they are seldom slowed or stopped by bad weather. This makes trains one of the safest modes of transportation.

The biggest disadvantage of rail transport is the lack of flexibility in terms of delivery locations. Trains can pick up and deliver goods only at designated stations along rail lines.

MARINE SHIPPING

Barges and container ships transport merchandise within the United States and around the world. Container ships carry their loads in either 20- or 40-foot-long standardized truck-size containers.

WATERWAYS

Inland shipping is shipping from one port to another on connecting rivers and lakes. The St. Lawrence Seaway, the Great Lakes, and the Mississippi and Ohio Rivers are all inland shipping routes.

Intracoastal shipping is the shipping of goods on inland and coastal waterways between ports along the same coast. For example, shipments can be sent from Virginia to North Carolina through the Dismal Swamp Canal.

International waterways are the oceans, seas, and rivers that connect continents and countries. Almost all overseas nonperishable freight, such as heavy equipment, steel, ore, forest products, grain, and petroleum is transported by container ships and barges because of the low cost.

ADVANTAGES AND DISADVANTAGES OF MARINE SHIPPING

The biggest advantage of marine transportation is the low cost. However, they are also the slowest form of transportation.

Marine shipping has other disadvantages. Buyers that are located far from the port city must have products off-loaded from container ships onto railroad cars or motor carriers to reach their destination. This added cost of distribution reduces some of the cost advantages of marine shipping.

Two Is Better Than One

Intermodal transportation combines two or more modes of transportation to get products to the customer. ***Why might a company use both marine and road shipping methods?***

Marine shipping is affected by bad weather and seasonal conditions. Great Lakes shipping, for example, is closed for two to three months in the winter.

INTERMODAL TRANSPORTATION

Intermodal transportation combines two or more transportation modes to maximize the advantages of each. Piggyback service involves carrying loaded truck trailers over land on railroad flatcars. Trucks then take the trailers to their final destinations. Fishyback service involves shipping loaded truck trailers over water on ships and barges. Piggyback and fishyback services combine all the advantages of truck transportation with the lower costs of rail and marine transportation.

PIPELINES

Pipelines are usually owned by the company using them, and in these instances, they are considered private carriers. There are more than 200,000 miles of pipelines within the United States.

Pipelines are most frequently used to transport oil and natural gas. They move crude oil from oil fields to refineries, where it is processed. The refined products, such as gasoline, are then trucked to retail outlets such as your local gasoline station.

Miles and Miles The U.S. has the largest transportation system in the world with 4 million miles of roads and railroad tracks that could circle the world 7 times.

ADVANTAGES AND DISADVANTAGES OF PIPELINES

The construction of pipelines requires a high initial investment, but operational costs are relatively small. Pipeline transportation has the best safety record among all major transportation systems. Products carried through pipelines move slowly but continuously and suffer minimal product damage or theft. These products are not subject to delivery delays due to bad weather.

The risk of a pipeline leak is low, but when a leak does occur, the damage to the environment can be extensive.

AIR CARGO SERVICES

Currently, air cargo services are less than 1 percent of the total ton-miles of freight shipped. High-value, low-weight, time-critical items, such as overnight mail, are often shipped by air. Certain high-value products, such as emergency parts, instruments, and medicines, may also be shipped by air. Air cargo has space and weight restraints, so most products that are transported in smaller containers are well suited for this form of shipment.

Specialized firms offer ground support to businesses that use air cargo services. These firms collect shipments from businesses and deliver them to the air terminal where they are loaded onto commercial airliners or specialized air cargo planes.

The Federal Aviation Administration (FAA) regulates air transportation, but airlines and air transport companies set their own rates. Air cargo service carriers offer such things as wide-bodied jets that can ship more goods and specialized packaging designed to help prevent damage.

ADVANTAGES AND DISADVANTAGES OF AIR TRANSPORTATION

The greatest advantage for air transportation is its speed. A fast delivery time allows businesses to satisfy customers who need something quickly. It also reduces inventory expenses and storage costs.

The greatest disadvantage of air transportation is its cost. It is by far the most expensive form of distribution. Air cargo rates are at least twice as costly as truck rates. Other disadvantages of air cargo services include mechanical breakdowns and delays in delivery caused by bad weather. Although it is a rare occurrence, airlines can be disrupted by terrorism or suspected terrorism.

Reading Check

Recall What are the five transportation systems used to move products?

EXPLAIN

MARINE SHIPPING

Ask these guiding questions to encourage students to discuss marine shipping.

Guiding Questions

Identify Which of these is an example of inland shipping: Transporting cars across Lake Michigan or transporting wheat down the Mississippi River?	Both are examples of inland shipping, both involve transporting goods from one port to another on connecting rivers and lakes.
Draw Conclusions Why is it a relatively easy process to transfer goods from trucks to container ships?	Container ships can carry either 20- or 40-foot long standardized truck-size containers.
Evaluate Which of the disadvantages of marine shipping do you think is the most significant? Why?	The biggest disadvantage may be the requirement that both ends of the shipping route be accessible by seaport.

Visual Literacy

Two Is Better Than One Caption Answer Read the caption question to students: ***Why might a company use both marine and road shipping methods?*** Because waterways provide a relatively inexpensive shipment method, goods might be shipped to the port closest to the final destination. At that point, the goods could be transferred to motor carrier. ***How might this same method be used with rail shipping?*** Goods could be shipped to the rail depot closest to the final destination where they could be transferred to motor carrier.

Critical Thinking

Display a map of the world for the class. Ask: ***What would be an example of inland shipping?*** Milwaukee to Chicago ***An example of intracoastal shipping?*** New York to Charleston ***An example of international shipping?*** New York to Liverpool, England

ELABORATE

PIPELINES

Ask these guiding questions to encourage students to discuss pipelines.

Guiding Questions

Summarize How are both pipelines and trucks used to get gasoline to its final destination?	Pipelines move crude oil from oil fields to refineries. Trucks are typically used to get the refined gasoline to retail outlets.
Synthesize A company's executives are concerned about the cost of installing a new oil pipeline. How would you convince them to do so?	An oil pipeline is a relatively cheap and safe transportation method. It also is reliable and not subject to delivery delays due to bad weather.

Miles and Miles Discuss with students that most highways are built and maintained by tax dollars, both at the state and federal level. Federal tax on gasoline is 18.4 cents per gallon and federal tax on diesel fuel (the fuel use by semis) is 24.4 cents a gallon. The average state gasoline tax is 18.6 while the average state tax on diesel fuel is 19.1 cents per gallon. A big portion of truck operating costs is purchasing fuel, and a large part of fuel cost is taxes.

AIR CARGO SERVICES

Ask these guiding questions to focus the discussion on air cargo services.

Guiding Questions

Recall What types of items are most likely to be shipped using an air cargo service?	items that are time-critical, high-value, and low-weight
Make a Decision You run a small manufacturing plant. A piece of equipment has broken. You can get a replacement by air cargo in 24 hours for $1200 or by truck in 72 hours for $450. What will you do?	Calculate the income lost from not being able to use the equipment for an additional 48 (72–24) hours. If the cost is more than $750 ($1200–$450), you should have the part shipped by air. .

Reading Check Answer

Read the Reading Check question to students: ***What are the five transportation systems used to move products?*** trucks, railroads, marine shipping, pipelines, and air cargo services Ask students: ***Which of these systems has the best safety record?*** pipelines

Critical Thinking

Discuss with students that this section is concerned with physical distribution systems. Ask: ***Can you think of another type of distribution system that is commonly used?*** electronic distribution, primarily over the Internet Ask: ***What kinds of products can you receive by this type of distribution?*** computer software, data files containing books and music Then ask: ***What are the requirements of this type of distribution?*** access to a computer; access to a network, such as the Internet; and appropriate software, such as a Web browser or e-mail Encourage students to discuss products they have purchased and then received electronically.

MINI CLIP

Reading: Prereading Strategies
Go to the Online Learning Center to view a video clip in which a teacher assesses students' prior knowledge about a text selection.

Mini Projects

Enrichment

Government Regulations on Physical Distribution Systems Instruct students to investigate how federal agencies have placed new regulations on physical distribution systems since the September 11, 2001 terrorist attacks. Have students choose one transportation system and prepare a five-minute presentation on their findings. The Container Security Initiative allows U.S. Customs and Border Protection to work with foreign customs offices to examine cargo at overseas ports before it is loaded onto vessels bound for the United States.

Analyzing the Impact of the St. Lawrence Seaway The St. Lawrence Seaway allows ship travel between the Atlantic and the Great Lakes. Have students write a 2–3 page report summarizing the Seaway's history and analyzing its importance to international shipping. Students should discuss how years of planning culminated in the Seaway's opening in 1959. It constitutes a 2,300 mile marine highway running between the United States and Canada. In 2009, over 3.5 million tons of freight were transported on the Seaway. Reports should also contain a map illustrating the Seaway's route.

TRANSPORTATION SERVICE COMPANIES

Transportation service companies handle small- and medium-size packages. Some examples of these companies are the U.S. Postal Service®, express delivery services, bus package carriers, and freight forwarders.

U.S. POSTAL SERVICE

More than two centuries have passed since Benjamin Franklin was appointed the first Postmaster General in 1775. Today, the U.S. Postal Service is a primary source for shipping small packages by parcel post or first-class mail. Parcel post is used for shipping packages weighing up to 70 pounds and no larger than 130 inches in combined length and girth. With nearly 220,000 vehicles, The U.S. Postal Service boasts the largest civilian ground fleet in the world. The U.S. Postal Service also ships via international and domestic express mail, and they offer special services for commercial customers. If a package is sent cash on delivery (COD), the recipient must pay to receive the package.

A New Approach

Some people prefer to print their own shipping labels. The U.S. Postal Service makes it possible for customers to pay for and print shipping labels online. ***How does this service help customers with their shipping needs?***

For an extra fee, parcel post can be insured against loss or damage. Parcel post can also be express-mailed at higher rates to guarantee next-day delivery. The U. S. Postal Service has a Click-N-Ship® online service that prints shipping labels and accepts payment for packages shipped to domestic and international locations.

EXPRESS DELIVERY SERVICES

Express delivery services specialize in delivering small, lightweight packages, envelopes, and high-priority mail usually weighing less than 150 pounds. Express delivery companies, such as FedEx®, DHL®, and the United Parcel Service®, offer door-to-door pick-up, delivery, and COD services. Shipments can be made nationally or internationally by airplane, truck, bus, or train. Rates are based on speed of delivery, size and weight of package, distance to be sent, and type of service to be used. Regular service usually takes from two to three days; more expensive next-day service is also available.

During the last 40 years, express carriers have become important players in physical distribution. Their role is likely to become even more important as technology continues to make an impact on global economy and the world market place. FedEx began operations in 1971. After decades of purchasing and merging with other businesses, FedEx now transports over 3 million shipments daily. It has the world's largest civil fleet of 658 aircraft, 280,000 employees, and more than 1,300 service centers serving 220 countries and territories. In addition, FedEx provides integrated logistics and technology solutions, and international logistics and trade information technology.

DHL, a pioneering express delivery carrier, started shipping from San Francisco to Honolulu in 1969. It was the first carrier to introduce express international shipping via airplane to Eastern Europe in 1983 and to China in 1986. DHL is the largest company specializing in international express shipping. It sends packages to approximately 120,000 destinations in more than 220 countries.

BUS PACKAGE CARRIERS

Bus package carriers provide same-day or next-day package delivery service to businesses in cities and towns along their scheduled routes. For example, Greyhound's PackageXpress®, delivers packages weighing less than 100 pounds and smaller than 30″ × 47″ × 82″ in size.

The cost of bus package transportation services depends on the weight of the package, the distance it will travel, and service level. Daily buses run to larger cities, such as Boston, Chicago, New York and San Francisco. This provides opportunities for some businesses to move their products quickly and at reasonable rates.

FREIGHT FORWARDERS

Freight forwarders are private companies that combine less-than-carload or less-than-truckload shipments from several businesses and deliver them to their destinations. They gather small shipments into larger lots, and then hire a carrier to move them, usually at reduced rates. By combining shipments, freight forwarders often obtain truckload or carload rates and can lower transportation costs for shippers. Freight forwarders also provide logistical services that help businesses select the best transportation methods and routes.

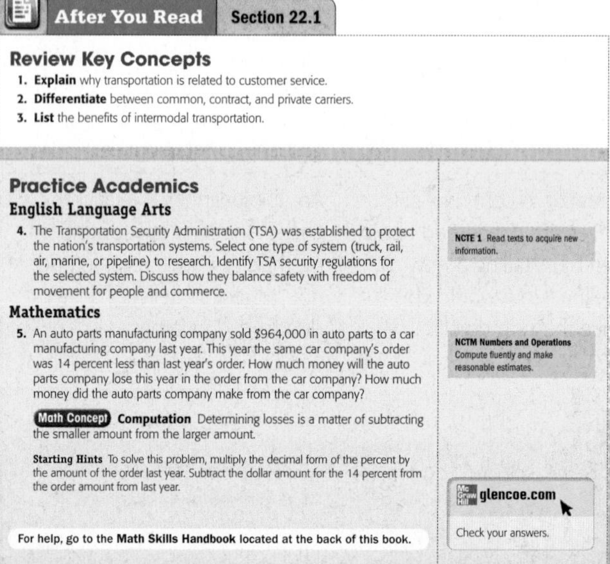

After You Read | **Section 22.1**

Review Key Concepts

1. **Explain** why transportation is related to customer service.
2. **Differentiate** between common, contract, and private carriers.
3. **List** the benefits of intermodal transportation.

Practice Academics

English Language Arts

4. The Transportation Security Administration (TSA) was established to protect the nation's transportation systems. Select one type of system (truck, rail, air, marine, or pipeline) to research. Identify TSA security regulations for the selected system. Discuss how they balance safety with freedom of movement for people and commerce.

NCTE 1 Read texts to acquire new information.

Mathematics

5. An auto parts manufacturing company sold $964,000 in auto parts to a car manufacturing company last year. This year the same car company's order was 14 percent less than last year's order. How much money will the auto parts company lose this year in the order from the car company? How much money did the auto parts company make from the car company?

NCTM Numbers and Operations Compute fluently and make reasonable estimates.

Math Concept **Computation** Determining losses is a matter of subtracting the smaller amount from the larger amount.

Starting Hints To solve this problem, multiply the decimal form of the percent by the amount of the order last year. Subtract the dollar amount for the 14 percent from the order amount from last year.

For help, go to the **Math Skills Handbook** located at the back of this book.

glencoe.com

Check your answers.

ELABORATE

Graphic Organizer

Display this chart. Add to the chart by having students provide a brief description of each type.

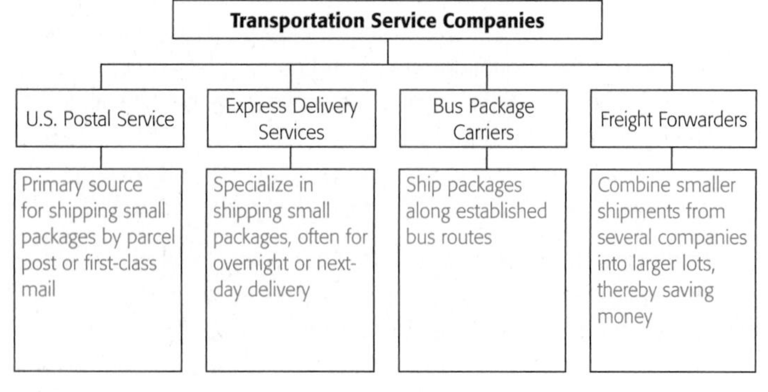
Transportation Service Companies
U.S. Postal Service
Express Delivery Services
Bus Package Carriers
Freight Forwarders
Primary source for shipping small packages by parcel post or first-class mail
Specialize in shipping small packages, often for overnight or next-day delivery
Ship packages along established bus routes
Combine smaller shipments from several companies into larger lots, thereby saving money

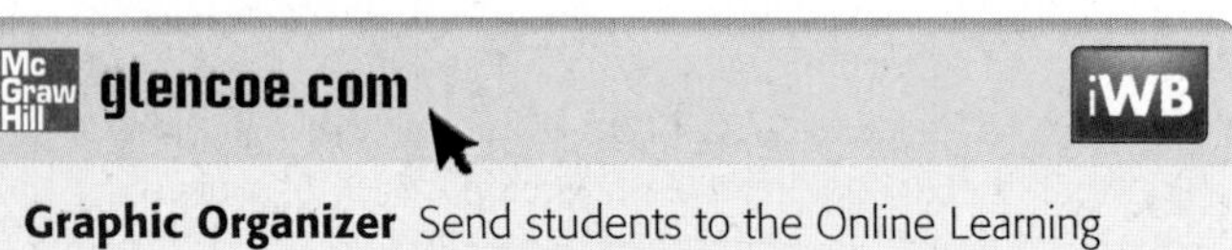
glencoe.com
iWB

Graphic Organizer Send students to the Online Learning Center to print this graphic organizer.

Visual Literacy

A New Approach Caption Answer Read the caption question to students: ***How does this service help customers with their shipping needs?*** It is very customer oriented because customers can save time and fuel by printing their own shipping labels. As more people work from home and telecommute, this service is a helpful way to promote using the U.S. Postal Service for shipping needs.

Critical Thinking

Ask: ***How do you think e-commerce has affected companies such as UPS® and FedEx®?*** Their business has increased because goods purchased online must be shipped to individuals' homes, which is the type of service common carriers specialize in. Then ask: ***Do you think the use of these companies by e-commerce outlets will increase even more in the future? Why or why not?*** Answers will vary. If the use of the e-commerce continues to increase, the amount of goods shipped will also increase.

EVALUATE

TRANSPORTATION SERVICE COMPANIES

Ask these guiding questions to focus the discussion of transportation service companies.

Guiding Questions

Contrast How is using a bus package carrier different from using an express delivery service?	It provides less flexibility because the package is carried along a bus route according to the regular schedule.
Synthesize The textbook says that FedEx offers "trade information technology." What do you think might be some features of trade information technology?	Possible answer: computer software that allows FedEx to determine any regulations, import taxes, and quotas involved in shipping an item to a specific country and the logistics involved in doing so.

Mini Projects

Differentiated Instruction

Verbal/Linguistic Learners Have students interview a local business owner who regularly uses transportation service companies. Instruct students to ask what factors, such as timeliness or package size, determine which service is best in each specific case. Have students write a paragraph describing their findings. Students should discuss how various circumstances help the business owner decide which service to use. For example, if a package does not need to arrive for 3–4 days, it might be sent USPS priority mail, which is relatively inexpensive. However, if a package must arrive the next business day, it might be sent via an express delivery service, even though this involves an additional expense.

Visual Learners Instruct students to choose a express delivery service, such as UPS, FedEx, or DHL. Then have them conduct research on the company's print, television, and Web ads. Students should prepare an illustrated presentation in which they evaluate the effectiveness of the ads. They also should state each ad's target market. Students' presentations will vary depending on the express delivery service chosen. For example, because DHL's target market is business people involved in international commerce, DHL ads emphasize its extensive experience in this area. DHL sponsors a Formula 1 car, tying into its promotion that "Speed is our business."

After You Read Section 22.1

Review Key Concepts

1. Transportation is related to customer service because choosing the right mode of transportation can make a product more affordable for a customer or can make the product more desirable (for example, if it arrives faster or on time.)
2. Common carriers provide truck transportation services to any business in their operating area for a fee. Contract carriers are for-hire trucking companies that provide equipment and drivers for specific routes, according to agreements between the carrier and the shipper. Private carriers transport goods for an individual business.
3. Intermodal transportation such as piggyback or fishyback services combine the advantages of truck transportation with the lower costs of rail and marine transportation.

Practice Academics

English Language Arts

4. The students must identify one system, its related security regulations, and explain how these measures are implemented. They should also explain how the regulations allow for the free movement of people and commerce. For example, for rail traffic, the TSA has extensive requirements for moving hazardous materials. The TSA's Surface Transportation Security Inspection Program (STSI) has over 100 inspectors assigned to 18 field offices across the country. The TSA's Visible Intermodal Protection Response (VIPR) teams can quickly raise the security level anywhere in the country, if necessary. Canine teams engage in the detection of explosives.

Mathematics

5. \$134,960 (964,000 × 0.14), \$829,040 (964,000 − 134,960)

glencoe.com

Answer Key Send students to the Online Learning Center to check their answers.

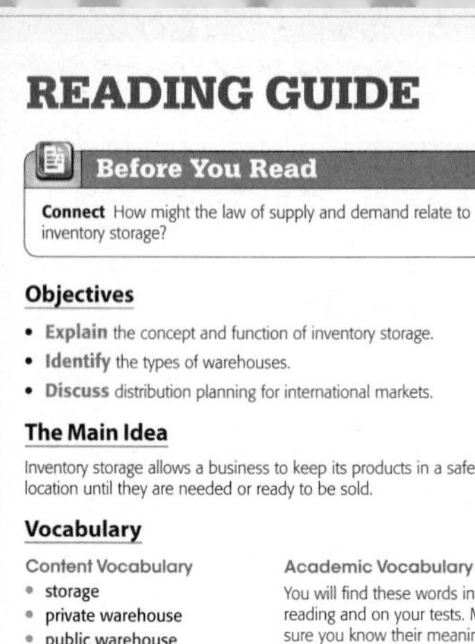

READING GUIDE

Before You Read

Connect How might the law of supply and demand relate to inventory storage?

Objectives

- **Explain** the concept and function of inventory storage.
- **Identify** the types of warehouses.
- **Discuss** distribution planning for international markets.

The Main Idea

Inventory storage allows a business to keep its products in a safe location until they are needed or ready to be sold.

Vocabulary

Content Vocabulary
- storage
- private warehouse
- public warehouse
- distribution center
- bonded warehouse

Academic Vocabulary

You will find these words in your reading and on your tests. Make sure you know their meanings.
- ensures
- restrict

Graphic Organizer

Draw this chart to take notes about different types of warehouses.

glencoe.com

Print this graphic organizer.

STANDARDS

ACADEMIC

English Language Arts

NCTE 1 Read texts to acquire new information.

Science

NSES E Develop abilities of technological design, understandings about science and technology.

NCSS *National Council for the Social Studies*
NCTE *National Council of Teachers of English*
NCTM *National Council of Teachers of Mathematics*
NSES *National Science Education Standards*

College & Career READINESS

Common Core

Writing Conduct short as well as more sustained research projects based on focused questions, demonstrating understanding of the subject under investigation.

Writing Write informative/explanatory texts to examine and convey complex ideas and information clearly and accurately through the effective selection, organization, and analysis of content.

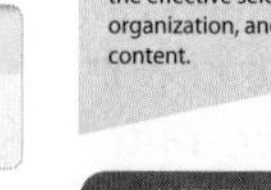

MARKETING CORE FUNCTION

Channel Management

Section 22.2 Inventory Storage

THE STORAGE OF GOODS

Storage is part of a marketing function and refers to the holding of goods until they are sold. The amount of goods stored is called an "inventory." The storage function facilitates the movement of products through the distribution channel as products are sold.

There are many reasons why storing goods is an essential activity for most businesses. First of all, products are stored until orders are received from customers. Products might also need to be stored because production has exceeded consumption, or demand decreases.

> "Products are produced in large quantities, but they must be stored until they are sold."

Sometimes, agricultural commodities such as corn, wheat, and soybeans may only be available during certain seasons. Commodity storage makes these products available year-round and **ensures** that their price remains relatively stable.

Some purchasers buy in quantity to get discounts on their purchases, and then store the items until they are needed. Finally, products are stored at convenient locations to provide faster delivery to customers.

Storing products adds time and place utility to them. Products must be available for customers when and where they want them. The costs involved in storing products include space, equipment, and personnel. Storage also means spending money (or capital) on inventory rather than investing it in another activity that could provide a larger return.

Businesses balance product storage costs against the possibility of not having products available for customers when they want to buy them. Most products are stored in warehouses, or facilities, in which goods are received, identified, sorted, stored, and dispatched for shipment.

Internet-based stores do not require physical retail space, but still require warehouses to store goods. This kind of warehouse fills orders directly from customers.

As You Read

Connect What products that you use do not need to be stored?

PRIVATE WAREHOUSES

A **private warehouse** is a storage facility designed to meet the specific needs of its owner. Any producer, wholesaler, or retailer has the option of owning a private warehouse.

A private warehouse is valuable for companies that move a large volume of products. Specialized conditions, such as a temperature-controlled environment, may be built into the facility. Private warehouses often house other parts of the business operation, such as offices.

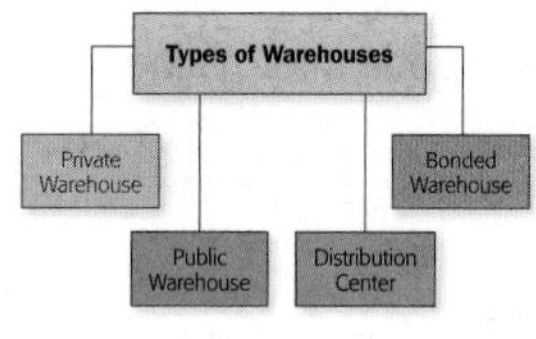

ENGAGE

Anticipation Activity

Improving Student Achievement Ask students: *Have you ever stored anything in a public storage facility? If so, how did it work?* Responses will vary; typically storage facility renters pay a fee and get a small storage space, often for temporary use.

Objectives

- **Explain** the concept and function of inventory storage. designed to facilitate the movement of products through the distribution channel as products are sold
- **Identify** the types of warehouses. private warehouses, public warehouses, distribution centers, bonded warehouses
- **Discuss** distribution planning for international markets. know about and follow all applicable regulations, be familiar with the country's physical transportation systems

Graphic Organizer

Private Warehouse
- Used only by owner
- For large volumes
- May house other parts of the business

Stores products until needed

Public Warehouse
- Offered to anyone for a fee
- Typically offers other services
- Mainly for low- to medium-volume storage needs

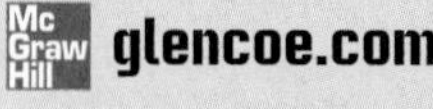

glencoe.com

Graphic Organizer Send students to the Online Learning Center to print this graphic organizer.

EXPLORE

Before You Read

Read the Before You Read question aloud: ***How might the law of supply and demand relate to inventory storage?*** When demand is up, there will be virtually no inventory because goods will be sold as soon as they become available. When demand is down, especially if this occurs unexpectedly, the amount of inventory is likely to rise. Since storage costs money, businesses will lower prices to encourage consumers to purchase goods.

Preteaching Vocabulary

Have students go to the Online Learning Center at glencoe.com for the Chapter 22 Preteaching Vocabulary games.

Content Vocabulary

Display each word and read sentences from this section that contain them. For *storage*, you might read: ***Businesses balance product storage costs against the possibility of not having products available for customers when they want to buy them.*** Ask a volunteer to define this word based on its context. space in which products are stored Tell students that as they read this section, they will learn more about word meanings.

Academic Vocabulary

Ensure—Similar Words Write *ensure* and *insure* for students to read. Tell students that many people confuse these words. Explain that *insure* primarily refers to financially protecting property. Read aloud this example: ***I insured my bike for $500.*** Then explain that *ensure* means "to make sure or guarantee." Read this aloud: ***I always lock my bike to ensure that it will not be stolen.***

Restrict—Word Origin Write *restrict* for the class to read. Explain that it comes from the Latin word *restringere*, which means "to draw tight." Therefore, *restrict* can mean "to physically tighten something." In another sense, however, it can mean "to limit the availability of something while excluding certain groups."

PROFESSIONAL DEVELOPMENT **MINI CLIP**

Reading: Vocabulary
Go to the Online Learning Center for a video in which an author describes the importance of academic language.

Section 22.2

Inventory Storage

THE STORAGE OF GOODS

Present these guiding questions to focus the discussion.

Guiding Questions

Analyze What do the owners of a small company need to consider in deciding whether to build their own warehouse?	They should consider capital investment and maintenance costs and the convenience of having closer inventory control.
Synthesize Unlike soybeans, tomatoes are not considered a commodity. Why not? How does this affect the market?	Tomatoes cannot be stored as long. Prices tend to rise when tomatoes are scarcer or need to be shipped long distances.

Expert Advice

"Products are produced in large quantities, but they must be stored until they are sold."

Ask students: ***Why do most factories produce products in large quantities?*** Large-scale production increases efficiency.

As You Read

Read the As You Read question aloud: ***What products that you use do not need to be stored?*** Nearly all products need to be produced in large quantities in order to be cost effective.

Graphic Organizer

Use this graphic organizer to review different types of warehouses.

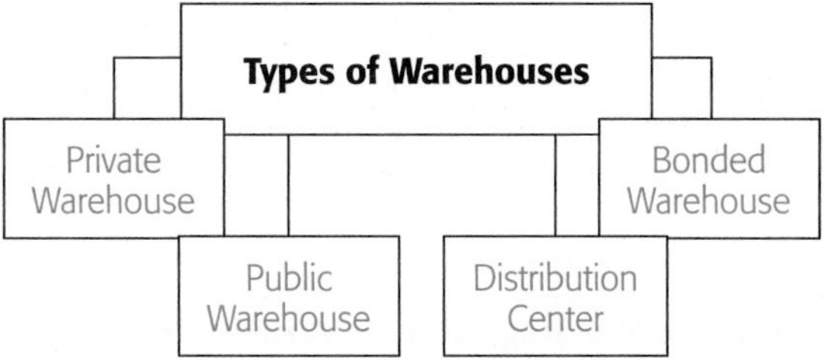

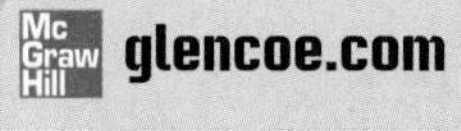

glencoe.com iWB

Graphic Organizer Send students to the Online Learning Center to print this graphic organizer.

A disadvantage is that private warehouses are costly to build and maintain. In a recent survey, large retailers reported spending 51 percent of their total physical distribution costs on warehouse expenses. Transportation costs accounted for the remaining 49 percent. Private warehouses should be considered only when a significant amount of merchandise needs to be stored. Doing so makes the total operating costs of private warehouses lower than the operating costs of public warehouses.

Economic Impact Industry and household spending on transportation accounts for nearly 10 percent of the U.S. gross domestic product.

PUBLIC WAREHOUSES

A **public warehouse** is a storage and handling facility offered to any individual or company that will pay for its use. Public warehouses rent storage space. They may also provide additional services to businesses, such as shipment consolidation, receiving, unloading, inspecting, reshipping, order filling, and truck terminal operation services.

Public warehouses are helpful to businesses that have low- to medium-volume storage needs or seasonal production.

There are five types of public warehouses:

1. **Bulk storage warehouses** keep products only in bulk form, such as chemical and oil.
2. **Cold storage warehouses** handle perishables, such as fruits, vegetables, and frozen products.
3. **Commodity warehouses** store agricultural products, such as, tobacco, cotton, or grain.
4. **General merchandise warehouses** handle products that do not require specialized handling.
5. **Household goods warehouses** store personal property storage, household articles, and furniture.

DISTRIBUTION CENTERS

A **distribution center** is a warehouse designed to speed delivery of goods and to minimize storage costs. The main focus in a distribution center is on sorting and moving products, not on storing them. Distribution centers are planned around markets rather than transportation requirements. They can cut costs by reducing the number of warehouses and eliminating excessive inventory.

Storage activity facilitates the movement of products through the distribution channel. ***What is the purpose of storage?***

Some businesses, such as paint companies Sherwin-Williams and Benjamin Moore, use their distribution centers to physically change the product for the final customer. Their distribution centers perform additional functions such as mixing ingredients, labeling, and repackaging for shipments to retailers.

Every distribution center has its own methods and systems of operation. A typical center may employ an unloader, a receiver, a hauler, a put-away driver, a replenishment driver, an order filler, and a loader.

- The unloader unloads trucks and breaks down pallets.
- The receiver inventories and tags unloaded pallets using a mobile cart computer unit and printer.
- A hauler transports received pallets, with equipment, from the receiving dock to the storage racks.
- A put-away driver loads the product into racks with a forklift.
- The replenishment driver pulls a product from the racks, with a forklift, and prepares it for the order filler.
- The order filler locates the ordered product and moves it to a designated location.
- The loader wraps the pallets and loads the trucks.
- The cycle begins again with the unloader.

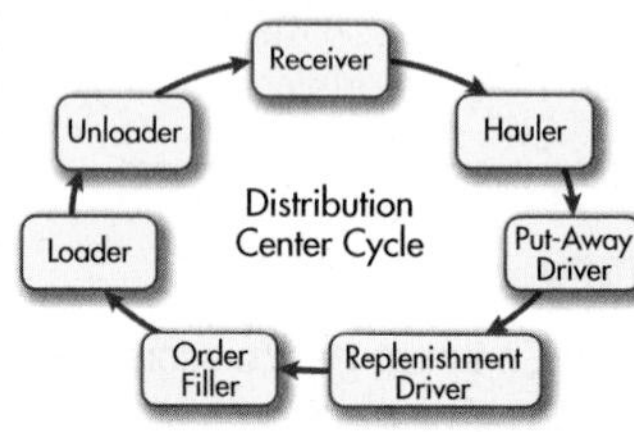

The name by which the distribution center is known is based on the purpose of the operation. A retail distribution center distributes goods to retail stores. An order fulfillment center distributes goods directly to consumers.

Distribution centers also consolidate large orders from many sources and redistribute them as separate orders for individual accounts or stores in a chain. Merchandise stays a short time in a distribution center.

WORLD MARKET
INDIA

Transporting Beauty

The saying, "A woman's hair is her crowning glory," has been around since ancient times. In India, human hair ranks as the "crowning" export. The country's hair business took off in the 1960s and now makes more than $300 million annually. Before reaching the market, the hair is collected by the ton from barber shops, villages, and temples. Then it is sorted, washed, dried, and bundled into varying lengths. The 6- to 45-inch tresses are then shipped to Asia, Europe, and North America.

Faith to Fashion Many celebrities seek this natural hair. One source is found at Hindu temples where women shave their heads as an act of sacrifice, known as *tonsuring*. They believe that losing their hair "unloads" their pride to God. What do they think of these women in other countries wearing the hair as extensions and wigs? "I think it's wonderful. Why not? I have no need for it," says one devotee.

Social Studies
In India, some cut their hair to overcome pride. Westerners do the opposite. Discuss how each of these practices relates to its culture.

NCSS IV C Individual Development & Identity Describe the ways family, religion, gender, ethnicity, nationality, socioeconomic status, and other group and cultural influences contribute to the development of a sense of self.

Here are some entry-level phrases that are used in conversations about marketing all over the world.

English	Hindi
Hello/Goodbye	Namaste
Yes/No	Ji ha/Ji nahi
Please	Kripaya
Thank you	Dhanyavad
You're welcome	Koi bat nahi

EXPLAIN

Economic Impact Encourage students to discuss whether they think this percentage is likely to increase or decrease over the next decade. Some students may think it will decrease because more purchases, such as books and magazines, are being delivered electronically.

Visual Literacy

The Importance of Storage Caption Answer Read the caption question to students: ***What is the purpose of storage?*** to hold goods until they are sold Tell students that businesses must continually assess the risks involved in storing goods in a warehouse such as the one shown here. Ask: ***What kinds of risks do you think the manager of this warehouse must be aware of?*** fire; natural disasters such as flooding; theft; loss of goods because of misplacement; and worker injury due to improper handling of goods or misuse of equipment.

DISTRIBUTION CENTERS

Ask these guiding questions to focus the discussion on distribution centers.

Guiding Questions

Recall How do distribution centers help reduce costs?	Distribution centers reduce the number of warehouses a company needs to maintain. They also help to eliminate excessive inventory that may be held in multiple warehouses.
Make Decisions A chain of hobby stores is planning to set up a distribution center. What should determine where the distribution center is built?	Ideally, a distribution center should be built in a place that is central to where the chain's retail stores are located.

ELABORATE

Critical Thinking

Explain to students that some city zoning laws allow running a business from home, but not using the home for inventory storage. Ask: ***Where might small home business owners store their inventory?*** at a general merchandise or household goods warehouse Then ask: ***How would this affect their prices?*** It would increase prices. The business owner would need to pay for storage instead of doing it for free in their home, and the added cost would be passed on to their customers.

Graphic Organizer

Use this diagram to discuss the cycle goods go through in a distribution center. Ask: ***What is the first step in the cycle?*** using the unloader to get goods off trucks Choose a specific product, such as a refrigerator or a television, and have students trace it through the entire distribution center cycle.

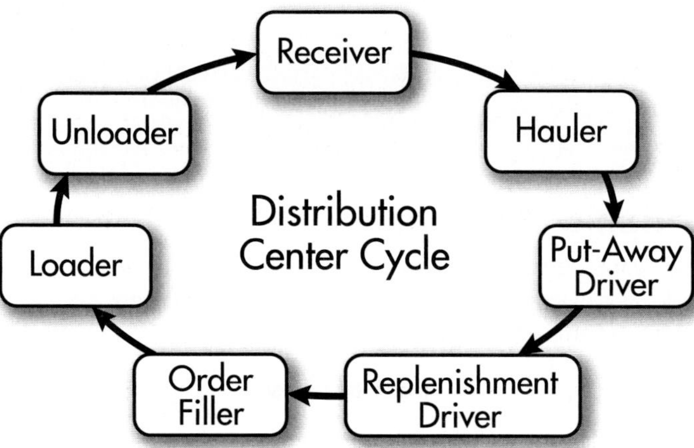

Graphic Organizer Send students to the Online Learning Center to print this graphic organizer.

WORLD MARKET
SOCIAL STUDIES

Students' discussions should focus on how cultural values indicate which behaviors reflect humility and which reflect pride. In Western culture, allowing hair to grow long as an expression of humility extends back many centuries. Some believe that long, and in particular unkempt hair, indicates a lack of concern about physical appearance, and therefore an overcoming of pride and being humbled before God. In India, women see beautiful hair as something to be proud of. Therefore, shaving it represents surrendering to God.

Mini Projects

Differentiated Instruction

English Language Learners Have students create a poster that explains the five types of public warehouses. Students should use their own words to write a brief description for each type of warehouse. In addition, they should draw images of the kinds of goods that would be stored in that type of warehouse. For example, under "Commodities Warehouse," they might draw pictures of wheat and cotton. Student posters should contain the names of each of the five types of warehouses, a brief description of each, and appropriate images of the kinds of goods stored in that type of warehouse.

Kinesthetic Learners Organize students into groups of three or four. Tell them they have just purchased a public warehouse and want to encourage small businesses to rent storage space in their building. Each group of students should work as a team to develop a television ad that explains the advantages of renting space at their warehouse and also describes the specific services they provide. Encourage students to use creativity that will attract the viewers' attention and still get the main points across. Have students present their commercials to the class. Students' commercials should explain the advantages of renting warehouse space rather than maintaining a private warehouse. Advantages might include less capital layout and avoiding maintenance issues. The commercials should also explain the types of services the warehouse provides to small businesses, such as receiving, unloading, and order filling.

DIGITAL NATION

Amazon Ships Fastest

Slow, unreliable shipping is one of the most frequent complaints from online shoppers. America's largest online retailer, Amazon.com, excels at speedy delivery. Its network of fulfillment centers combines the functions of warehouse and distribution center.

Sort, Scan, Send

Technology, including scanners and sorting machines, helps workers locate and combine a huge variety of items into single orders for shipping. One end of the fulfillment center houses the inventory, while the other end handles scanning, packaging, gift wrapping, and shipping. Amazon also uses software that determines the right size box for each item based on size and weight. This reduces packaging waste. Amazon is so efficient at fulfillment that it even rents its warehousing and distribution services to other companies.

Mathematics

Compute Last year Amazon shipped a hardcover book in a box that was 12″ long, 8″ wide, and 4″ deep. Now it uses a 10″ × 7″ × 2″ sleeve for shipping. Calculate the cardboard savings in square inches.

NCTM Number and Operations Compute fluently and make reasonable estimates.

glencoe.com

Get a Digital Nation Activity.

BONDED WAREHOUSES

Bonded warehouses are public or private warehouses that store products that require payment of a federal tax. Imported or domestic products cannot be removed until the required tax is paid. Although they are charged storage fees, businesses can save on taxes by taking goods out of storage only when needed.

Reading Check

Recall What are some types of storage facilities available to businesses?

DISTRIBUTION PLANNING FOR INTERNATIONAL MARKETS

Distribution is of critical importance in global marketing. The U.S. Department of Commerce estimates that for every $1 billion worth of U.S. products sold abroad, 19,000 jobs are supported at home. Exports support one-sixth of the total manufacturing and agricultural output of the United States. In other words, 17 percent of everything made or grown in the U.S. is shipped to other countries.

However, selling to customers in the international marketplace requires more planning than selling to domestic customers. Businesses that sell internationally must follow U.S. export laws as well as the import laws of the countries to which they are selling. Some countries also have laws that **restrict** how products may be transported to and within those countries. Businesses frequently have to deal with conflicting bureaucratic regulations, multiple language barriers, and complex negotiations.

Extensive distribution planning is needed in a global marketplace. Consider the example of high-tech, complex products. The parts used to manufacture items such as automobiles, computers, wireless phones, and jet airliners are made in several countries. The parts are then shipped to other countries for final assembly, and the finished product is shipped to still more destinations. All these stages of production require that a manufacturer plan effectively. A company needs to make sure not only that the process is efficient and cost-effective but also that it follows the various rules and regulations of all the countries involved.

In order to deliver their goods successfully, businesses must understand other countries' physical transportation systems. In the U.S. or Europe, it might take only a day or two for an shipment to get from the manufacturing plant to the store by rail or truck.

In some less-developed nations, however, the air-cargo or rail systems may not be reliable enough to assure delivery of goods in a timely and efficient manner. Other countries may not have the networks of roads and highways needed to support dependable truck deliveries. In some parts of the world, for example, many consumer goods are still transported to market by bicycle or cart.

It is also important to understand how retail institutions in other countries differ from American retail institutions. Consider all the different kinds of food that are available in grocery stores near you. Many of the items we take for granted, such as milk, cheese, eggs, and frozen foods, may be hard to find in stores in less-developed countries.

In some parts of the world, electricity is still unreliable, even in the bigger cities. As a result, retailers in remote locations are left with little or no capacity to refrigerate or freeze items that can easily spoil. This lack of storage facilities means that supermarkets, which are so common in the U.S., are rare in developing countries.

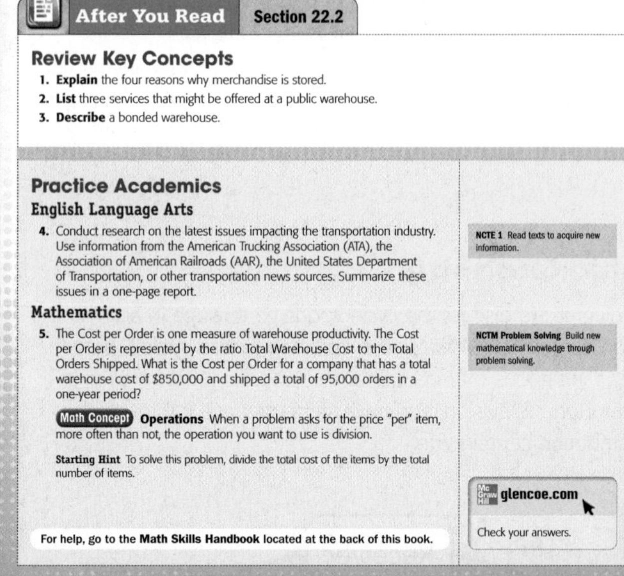

After You Read Section 22.2

Review Key Concepts

1. **Explain** the four reasons why merchandise is stored.
2. **List** three services that might be offered at a public warehouse.
3. **Describe** a bonded warehouse.

Practice Academics

English Language Arts

4. Conduct research on the latest issues impacting the transportation industry. Use information from the American Trucking Association (ATA), the Association of American Railroads (AAR), the United States Department of Transportation, or other transportation news sources. Summarize these issues in a one-page report.

NCTE 1 Read texts to acquire new information.

Mathematics

5. The Cost per Order is one measure of warehouse productivity. The Cost per Order is represented by the ratio Total Warehouse Cost to the Total Orders Shipped. What is the Cost per Order for a company that has a total warehouse cost of $850,000 and shipped a total of 95,000 orders in a one-year period?

NCTM Problem Solving Build new mathematical knowledge through problem solving.

Math Concept **Operations** When a problem asks for the price "per" item, more often than not, the operation you want to use is division.

Starting Hint To solve this problem, divide the total cost of the items by the total number of items.

glencoe.com

Check your answers.

For help, go to the **Math Skills Handbook** located at the back of this book.

ELABORATE

DIGITAL NATION

Mathematics Answer The surface area of the original box is 2 (12″ × 8″) + 2 (12″ × 4″) + 2 (8″ × 4″) = 352 in². The surface area of the new sleeve is 2 (10″ × 7″) + 2 (10″ × 2″) + 2 (7″ × 2″) = 208 in². The cardboard savings is 144 in² (352 − 208.) Discuss that the feature states that Amazon rents out its warehousing and distribution services to other companies. Ask students: ***What does this tell you about the efficiency of Amazon's fulfillment center?*** Amazon would not be renting out these services if it could not make money doing so. The fact that it can provide the services at a reasonable price and still make a profit testifies to the fulfillment center's efficiency.

Worksheet Activity Send students to the Online Learning Center to get a Digital Nation worksheet activity.

Graphic Organizer

Display this diagram to refresh students' memories as to the challenges of international shipping. Ask students to define tariff, quota, and embargo.

Trade Barriers

Tariff	tax on imports
Quota	limit, either based on quantity or monetary value, on importing specific goods
Embargo	ban on importing specific goods

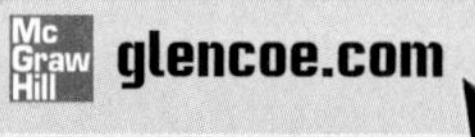

Graphic Organizer Send students to the Online Learning Center to print this graphic organizer.

EVALUATE

DISTRIBUTION PLANNING FOR INTERNATIONAL MARKETS

Explain to students that companies that distribute their goods outside their home country must have an extensive understanding of both export and import laws. Ask these guiding questions to focus the discussion on distribution planning for international markets.

Guiding Questions

Describe About what percentage of the manufacturing and agricultural output of the United States do exports support?	about 17 percent (1/6)
Analyze Why is it vital that companies understand a country's physical transportation system if they are going to be successful in delivering goods in that country?	They must know what types of transportation to use to get goods to their destination in a timely and efficient manner.
Apply What might be an example of an export law? An import law?	An example of an export law is a law that prohibits certain types of weapons from being shipped out of a country. An example of an import law is a law that restricts what kinds of produce can enter a country.

Mini Project

Extension

Drop-Shipping Goods Explain to students that in certain situations, some companies choose to drop-ship goods. When goods are drop-shipped, they are shipped directly from the manufacturer or distributor to the consumer. Have students work with partners to list the advantages and disadvantages of drop-shipping. Have each pair share their lists with the class. Advantages—The business does not have to pay for storage, and it is free to focus on selling goods rather than shipping them. Disadvantages—The business becomes dependent on the distributor or manufacturer for shipping. It may cost more to have each item shipped to a separate address. A business may also want to stockpile goods; for example, to prepare for high demand of seasonal products.

After You Read Section 22.2

Review Key Concepts

1. Students should list any four of these reasons for storing merchandise: facilitate delivery to purchaser, production has outpaced demand, products require seasonal storage, to take advantage of quantity purchases, and to be located close to purchasers.
2. Students should list any three of these services that might be offered at a public warehouse: shipment consolidation, receiving, unloading, inspecting, reshipping, order filling, and truck terminal operation services.
3. A bonded warehouse can be either a public or private warehouse that stores products that require the payment of a federal tax. Products cannot be removed until the required tax is paid.

Practice Academics

English Language Arts

4. Students should write a one-page report summarizing a current issue that is impacting the transportation industry. For example, in November of 2008, the TSA issued rules codifying the scope of TSA's inspection program and specifying extensive chain of custody and control requirements for hazardous materials security. The industry reacted, stating that they were unable to comply with these rules in the allotted time frame. In response to this complaint, the effective date for the new regulations was extended.

Mathematics

5. $8.95 per item per year (850,000/95,000)

glencoe.com

Send students to the Online Learning Center to check their answers.

Chapter 22 Visual Summary

Physical Distribution

Physical distribution or logistics involves transportation, storage, order processing, stock handling, and inventory control.

Transportation → Storage (Order Processing, Stock Handling, Inventory Control) → Transportation

The different kinds of transportation systems include trucking, railroads, marine shipping, pipelines, and air cargo services.

Transportation Systems: Trucking, Railroads, Marine Shipping, Pipelines, Air Cargo

530 | Unit 7 · Distribution

Review and Activities

Written Summary

- Physical distribution links a business and its customers.
- Physical distribution comprises all the activities that help to ensure that the right amount of product is delivered to the right place at the right time
- Physical distribution is also known as logistics.
- It involves transporting, storing, order processing, stock handling, and inventory control of materials and products.
- The different kinds of transportation include marine, air, pipeline, and land transportation, which includes both trucking and railroads.
- Storage is the marketing function of holding goods until they are sold.
- Storing goods is an essential activity for most businesses.
- Products are stored in warehouses or distribution centers until orders are received from customers.
- Globalization is increasing the importance of international distribution.

Review Content Vocabulary and Academic Vocabulary

1. Use each of these vocabulary terms in a written sentence.

Content Vocabulary
- physical distribution (p. 515)
- transportation (p. 516)
- common carriers (p. 517)
- contract carriers (p. 518)
- private carriers (p. 518)
- exempt carriers (p. 518)
- ton-mile (p. 519)
- carload (p. 519)
- freight forwarders (p. 523)
- storage (p. 525)
- private warehouse (p. 525)
- public warehouse (p. 526)
- distribution center (p. 526)
- bonded warehouse (p. 528)

Academic Vocabulary
- regulate (p. 517)
- options (p. 517)
- ensures (p. 525)
- restrict (p. 528)

Assess for Understanding

2. **Summarize** What is the nature and scope of physical distribution?
3. **Name** What are the transportation systems and services used to move products from manufacturers to consumers?
4. **List** What are the different kinds of transportation service companies?
5. **Justify** Why is inventory storage important in marketing?
6. **Distinguish** What are the different types of warehouses?
7. **Contrast** What makes a distribution center different from other types of warehouses?
8. **Role-Play** What factors will you discuss with your manager when considering whether to expand distribution to countries abroad?
9. **Create** What would a map of a transportation system look like for an orange that is sold at your local grocery store?

Chapter 22 · Physical Distribution | 531

EVALUATE

Visual Summary

Express Creativity Ask students to create a visual summary that illustrates a concept in the chapter. Encourage students to use different formats for their visual summaries, such as a slide show, graphic organizer, or poster. Visual summaries will vary depending on the concept depicted. Questions to ask when assessing a visual summary include:

- Is the summary clear, economical, and simple?
- Are any important steps or concepts left out?
- Are steps or concepts arranged in the same order as the original?
- Does the summary reveal a pattern that connects the details?
- Does the summary locate and highlight the most important information?

Review Content Vocabulary and Academic Vocabulary

1. **Physical distribution** requires the use of **transportation** to deliver the right amount of product. **Common carriers** provide transportation services to any business for a fee whereas **contract carriers** provide equipment and drivers for specific routes. When a trucking company transports goods for an individual business, it is a **private carrier.** Trucking companies that carry agricultural products are often **exempt carriers.** Rail transportation costs are often specified by the **ton-mile.** The minimum pounds of freight needed to fill a boxcar is called a **carload. Freight forwarders** gather small shipments into larger lots.

   Private warehouses provide **storage** for their owners whereas **public warehouses** rent space. Big-box stores such as Walmart and Target keep costs down by having their own **distribution centers.** Businesses use **bonded warehouses.** It is important for the government to **regulate** interstate commerce. One **option** for shipping goods is to use a common carrier. Using an overnight courier can **ensure** the customer fast delivery.

   Governments have the ability to **restrict** imports.

EVALUATE

Assess for Understanding

2. Physical distribution involves order processing (initiates the movement of products), transportation (physical movement of products), storage (facilitates the movement of products as products are sold), stock handling (receiving, checking, and marking items for sales), and inventory control (keeping products in sufficient quantities).

3. Major transportation systems include motor carriers, railroads, waterways, pipelines, and air carriers; service carriers include for-hire carriers, private carriers, or a combination of both.

4. The different kinds of transportation service companies are U.S. Postal Service, express delivery services, bus package carriers, and freight forwarders.

5. Inventory storage is important because it is vital that product is ready when the customer wants to purchase it. However, in order to be efficient, every attempt is made to have it just at the time it is needed.

6. Types of warehouses include private warehouses, public warehouses, distribution centers, and bonded warehouses.

7. A distribution center is different from other warehouses because it is designed to speed goods on their way, with a minimum of storage costs. Distribution centers focus on sorting and moving products, not on storing them.

8. Selling internationally is more complex than selling domestically. Companies must follow both U.S. export laws and the import laws of countries in which they are selling. They also have to follow any laws that restrict how products can be transported. Problems can include extensive bureaucratic regulations, language barriers, and difficulties in negotiating in a different culture. In some less developed countries, physical transportation systems may be unreliable or nonexistent, and retailers may not have access to refrigeration.

9. Answers will vary. If the orange was grown in Florida, it might have been stored for a short period in a local warehouse before being shipped by rail to a chain supermarket distribution center. From there, it might have traveled by truck to the local supermarket.

Chapter 22 Review and Activities

21st Century Skills

Everyday Ethics

10. **Damaged Merchandise** You work in a distribution center. A carton containing several items has been damaged during an incoming shipment. As you fill out a damaged merchandise form, a coworker suggests that you take some of the items, since they may not be missed. How do you think management would view this suggestion? How do you view it? Discuss with a partner.

Financial Literacy Skills

11. **U-Pick-Up** You can have camping equipment shipped directly to your home for $12.75 or have it delivered to an outdoor store that is 45 miles from your house. Your truck gets 18 miles/gal, and gas costs $2.75/gallon. Calculate what it would cost for you to drive to pick up your item. Would you save more if you picked it up yourself or paid for the shipping costs?

e-Marketing Skills

12. **Research Rates** Imagine that you are employed in a manufacturing firm that ships small electric motors weighing 25 pounds to locations in the United States. Investigate how much it would cost to send one package from your location to Chicago, Illinois. The shipment must arrive within five days either by the U.S. Postal Service or an express delivery service such as FedEx or United Parcel Service.
    - List the steps that you must take to send the package through the Postal Service.
    - List the steps that you must take to send the package through an express delivery service.
    - What were the lowest costs for each?
    - What additional services were available for you to purchase?

Build Academic Skills

English Language Arts

13. **Trucking Regulations** Conduct research about the advantages and disadvantages of federal regulation of the trucking industry. Write a 100-word paper summarizing your findings.

NCTE 4 Use written language to communicate effectively.

Science

14. **Wireless Technology** Radio frequency identification, satellite communications, and cellular networks are used for physical distribution systems and inventory storage. Describe how one of these forms of technology is used in the delivery of products or inventory storage. Present a short description of how this technology is used in shipping to your class.

NSES E Develop abilities of technological design, understandings about science and technology.

Mathematics

15. **Calculate Savings** A large manufacturer can save 25 percent by using a distribution service instead of a private warehouse. The cost of the distribution service would total $55,450. How much money will the manufacturer save by using the distribution service?

NCTM Number and Operations Compute fluently and make reasonable estimates.

Math Concept **Computation** Calculating the amount saved by using one service instead of another is a matter of comparing the numbers.

For help, go to the **Math Skills Handbook** located at the back of this book.

Standardized Test Practice

Directions Read the following questions. On a separate piece of paper, write the best possible answer for each one.

1. Which of the following single modes of transportation moves the largest percentage of freight in ton miles?
   A. Air
   B. Pipelines
   C. Railroads
   D. Trucks
2. Physical distribution is the marketing function of moving a product from the place where it is made to the place where it will be sold.
   T
   F
3. The activity that refers to the holding of goods until they are sold is known as ________.

Test-Taking Tip
When studying for a test, write important ideas, definitions, and formulas on flash cards.

DECA Connection Role Play

Shipping/Receiving Manager
Online Gourmet Food Retailer

Situation The best-selling products for your company are cheeses and spices. Small producers that have limited production capabilities make the cheeses. The cheeses are all produced from certified organic ingredients. Cheese is considered a perishable product; therefore, it requires special handling for storage and shipping.

The spices you sell include both well-known and rare varieties. All of the spices are of the highest quality and arrive fresh from their producers in sealed glass jars. Spices are not as perishable as the cheeses you sell, but they do need to be shipped to your customers while they are very fresh. For that reason, you stock only limited quantities of each variety.

Your customers understand that they may have to wait a couple of days for their spice orders. Customers feel that the quality and freshness are worth the brief delay. You are in the process of training a new employee (judge) in your department.

Activity You are to explain to the new employee (judge) the importance of proper storage of each of the gourmet food items. You are to also explain the equally important factor of selecting the best shipping method for each item.

Evaluation You will be evaluated on how well you meet the following performance indicators:

1. Select the best shipping method.
2. Explain the role of distribution centers.
3. Explain the storage process in warehouse operations.
4. Explain distribution issues and trends.
5. Discuss shipping methods used with food products.

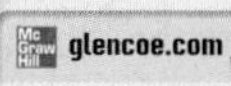

glencoe.com

Download the Competitive Events Workbook for more Role-Play Practice.

EVALUATE

21st Century Skills

Everyday Ethics

10. Management would see it as theft and possibly a reason for termination. Partners might discuss that the goods do not belong to them and therefore it would be wrong to take them. If they were caught, they could lose their jobs and be forced to leave under serious allegations. The distribution center may be required to return any damaged goods in order to be reimbursed.

Financial Literacy Skills

11. It would cost $6.88 in gas to pick it up at the store. Therefore, it would be cheaper to pick it up at the store than to have it shipped to your home (cost to ship to store = 45/18 × 2.75 = $6.88).

e-Marketing Skills

12. Costs of each delivery service will vary based upon the location, but student should be able to list the steps that need to be taken to send the package to Chicago, Illinois. The required steps typically include filling out a form with the package's place of origin and final destination, its weight, a contact phone number, and so on. Additional services could include insurance against breakage or loss, packaging services, print labeling services, and priority shipping arrangements to allow the package to be delivered more quickly.

EVALUATE

Build Academic Skills

English Language Arts

13. Students should write a 100-word paper summarizing the advantages and disadvantages of federal regulation of the trucking industry. Advantages include that regulations improve safety, such as rules regarding mandatory rest periods, regulations for hauling hazardous materials, and drug and alcohol testing. However, obeying the regulations adds to transportation costs, which is then passed on the consumer.

Science

14. Students should present a brief description of how wireless technologies, such as RFI, satellite communications, and cellular networks, are used in physical distribution systems and inventory storage. RFI can be used to quickly and accurately check and record the contents of shipments. Many professionals who are involved in transporting goods, such as long-haul truck drivers, communicate with their companies via laptop computers and satellite communications. Warehouse workers can use cellular phone and networks to communicate with one another.

Mathematics

15. $18,483.33

Standardized Test Practice

1. D (Trucks)
2. False (Transportation is the marketing function of moving a product from the place where it is made to the place where it will be sold.)
3. storage

DECA Connection Role Play

Evaluations will be based on these performance indicators:

1. **Select the best shipping method.** Shipping choices vary depending on the desired delivery time, cost, type of goods, weight of goods, whether the goods must be shipped over water, etc. When goods are being shipped over water, marine shipping is more economical, but slower than using an air carrier. The USPS provides parcel post, first-class mail, and express mail. Express delivery services specialize in delivering small, lightweight packages and envelopes. Bus package carriers provide same-day or next-day delivery, allowing packages to be moved quickly at reasonable rates. Freight forwarders are private firms that combine less-than-carload or less-than-truckload shipments from several businesses and deliver them to customers. These services can help lower transportation costs for the shipper.
2. **Explain the role of distribution centers.** The role of distribution centers is to speed delivery of goods and to minimize storage costs. The main focus of a distribution center is sorting and moving products, not storing them.
3. **Explain the storage process in warehouse operations.** Companies store goods so that they will have products available for customers when and where they are needed. Options include private warehouses, which are designed to meet the specific needs of the owner; public warehouses, in which storage and handling are provided to any individual or company willing to pay for the service; distribution centers, which are designed to speed delivery of goods and minimize storage costs; and bonded warehouses, which store products that require payment of federal tax. The products cannot be removed from the warehouse until the required tax is paid.
4. **Explain distribution issues and trends.** Issues and trends in distribution involve ongoing increases in online purchases, digital distribution, and international trade.
5. **Discuss shipping methods used with food products.** Food products must be kept at the proper temperature. For example, foods such as dairy products and fresh produce must be transported in refrigerated cars to prevent spoilage. Some foods, such as milk and oils, may be transported in bulk containers.

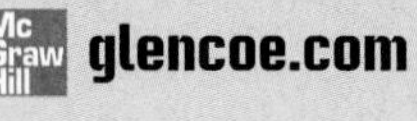

Role Plays For more DECA Role Plays, send students to the Online Learning Center to download the Competitive Events Workbook.

purchasing

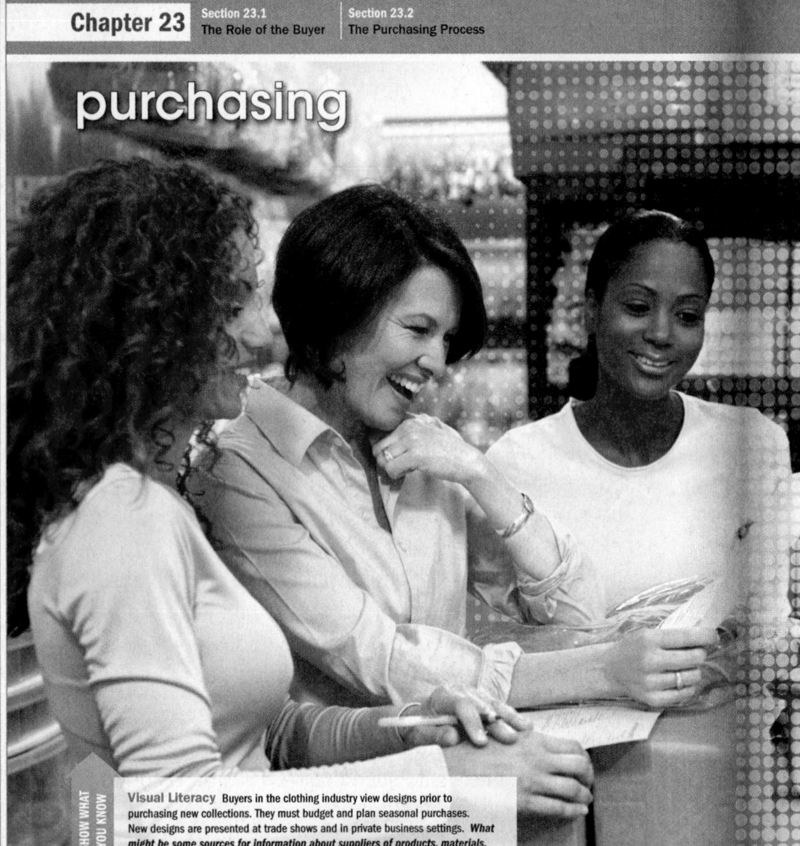

SHOW WHAT YOU KNOW

Visual Literacy Buyers in the clothing industry view designs prior to purchasing new collections. They must budget and plan seasonal purchases. New designs are presented at trade shows and in private business settings. ***What might be some sources for information about suppliers of products, materials, and services?***

Discovery Project

From Producer to Final User

Essential Question How does a buyer at a retail store plan purchases for upcoming resale?

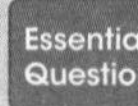

Project Goal

You and a partner are buyers for a retail store or chain of stores. Select a product or group of products for resale at the store. With your partner, learn all you can about how to plan a purchasing program for the coming months or season. Conduct research and also interview at least three store buyers or managers. Share your purchasing plan with the class.

Ask Yourself...

- What will you investigate in your research?
- What questions will you ask buyers and managers during your interviews?
- What information is contained in a purchasing plan?

Solve Problems What are some criteria you would use for selecting goods for purchase?

glencoe.com

Activity
Get a worksheet activity about planning purchases.

Evaluate
Download a rubric you can use to evaluate your project.

DECA Connection

DECA Event Role Play

Concepts in this chapter are related to DECA competitive events that involve either an interview or role play.

Performance Indicators The performance indicators represent key skills and knowledge. Your key to success in DECA competitive events is relating them to concepts in this chapter.

- Explain the nature and scope of purchasing.
- Place order/reorders.
- Persuade others.
- Select vendors.
- Evaluate vendor performance.

DECA Prep

Role Play Practice role-playing with the DECA Connection competitive-event activity at the end of this chapter. More information on DECA events can be found on DECA's Web site.

Chapter 23 · Purchasing | 535

ENGAGE

Visual Literacy

Ask students: ***What might be some sources for information about suppliers of products, materials, and services?*** magazines, journals, and Web sites that cater to a specific trade, such as athletic wear or home furnishings, trade shows, fellow buyers Then ask these guiding questions to activate prior knowledge.

Guiding Questions

List What are the five rights of merchandising?	(1) right goods; (2) right time; (3) right place; (4) right price; (5) right quantity
Analyze What part of the marketing plan contains sales forecasts? What should a company do if it fails to meet a specific sales forecast?	The implementation portion contains the sales forecast. If a company fails to meet sales forecasts, managers should attempt to determine why and, if appropriate, take corrective action to modify future forecasts.

Discovery Project

From Producer to Final User To start a discussion about purchasing, ask students the Discovery Project Essential Question: ***How does a buyer at a retail store plan purchases for upcoming resale?*** A buyer for a retail store would likely plan purchases of goods to be sold in coming months by preparing a six-month merchandise plan, which would be based on past sales, changing market conditions, and so on. Factors such as the types of products, available capital, space for storage, available sources, and delivery time affect merchandise plans.

glencoe.com

Discovery Project Resources Send students to the Online Learning Center to download a rubric to evaluate their projects.

ENGAGE

Introduce the Chapter

Chapter 23 discusses how different types of buyers make purchasing decisions along with the tools and resources they use in making these decisions. These main concepts are introduced and discussed:

- Fundamentals of planning purchases
- The six-month merchandise plan
- How to calculate figures such as open-to-buy and beginning-of-the-month inventory
- Planning purchases for chain-store operations
- Centralized and decentralized buying
- Government and institutional markets
- Types of purchase situations
- Selecting suppliers
- Negotiating terms
- Internet purchasing

Discussion Starter

Importance of Planning Purchases Ask students if they would enjoy shopping—with someone else's money. Then ask if any of them have ever considered becoming a buyer, either one who buys goods for a retail store or one who buys goods to operate a business. Point out that two types of buyers—industrial and resale buyers—will be discussed here. Encourage students to discuss what they think each job entails and to give their opinions as to whether the job would be fun, interesting, or challenging.

DECA Connection

Discuss the performance indicators listed in the DECA Connection feature. Explain to students that performance indicators tell them how to demonstrate their acquired skills and knowledge through individual or team competitive events.

Competitive Events Workbook For more DECA Role Plays, send students to the Online Learning Center to download the Competitive Events Workbook.

PRINT RESOURCES

- **Student Edition**
- **Teacher Edition**
- **Student Activity Workbook with Academic Integration** includes worksheets and activities correlated to the text.
- **Mathematics for Marketing Workbook** provides math activities for every unit in the text.

TECHNOLOGY TOOLBOX

- **Connect**
- **ConnectPlus**
- **ExamView Assessment Suite** is a comprehensive solution for creating, administering, and scoring tests.

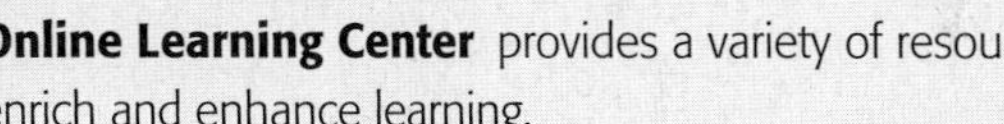

Online Learning Center provides a variety of resources to enrich and enhance learning.

SECTION, CHAPTER, AND UNIT RESOURCES

- **Graphic Organizers** for organizing text concepts visually.
- **Digital Nation Activities** and **Green Marketer Activities** extend learning beyond the text features.
- **Career Chatroom Career Profiles** allow students to explore different marketing occupations in depth.
- **After You Read Answer Keys** for students to check their answers.
- **Discovery Project Rubrics** and **Marketing Internship Project Rubrics** for students to evaluate their projects.

PROGRAM RESOURCES

- **Student Activity Workbook with Academic Integration Teacher Annotated Edition** includes annotated answers for the activities and worksheets.
- **Marketing Research Project Workbook** provides a step-by-step approach for students to complete their own marketing research studies.
- **School-to-Career Activity Workbook** helps students relate their class work to on-the-job experience and involves work-site analysis and working with mentors.
- **Competitive Events Workbook** helps prepare students for state and national marketing education competitions.
- **Inclusion in the Marketing Education Classroom** provides teaching resources for working with students with special needs.
- **PowerPoint Presentations** provides visual teaching aids and assessments for this chapter.

READING GUIDE

Before You Read

Connect What happens when you cannot find a product you need at a store because it is sold out?

Objectives

- **Define** the terms used to describe organizational buyers.
- **Explain** how planning purchases differs between an industrial market and a resellers' market.
- **Describe** the six-month merchandising plan and explain its calculations.
- **Explain** the concept of chain-store buying.

The Main Idea

Purchasing for a business is important, because the costs of running a business are affected by the buyer and by the services needed to run the business.

Vocabulary

Content Vocabulary
- organizational buyers
- wholesale and retail buyers
- six-month merchandise plan
- open-to-buy (OTB)
- centralized buying
- decentralized buying

Academic Vocabulary

You will find these words in your reading and on your tests. Make sure you know their meanings.
- predicts
- technical

Graphic Organizer

Draw or print this chart to write two or three sentences describing these markets: industrial, resellers, government, and institutional.

Market	Notes
Industrial	
Resellers	
Government	
Institutional	

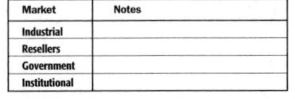

glencoe.com

Print this graphic organizer.

STANDARDS

ACADEMIC

English Language Arts
NCTE 5 Use different writing process elements to communicate effectively.

Mathematics
NCTM Problem Solving Solve problems that arise in mathematics and in other contexts.
NCTM Algebra Represent and analyze mathematical situations and structures using algebraic symbols.

NCSS National Council for the Social Studies
NCTE National Council of Teachers of English
NCTM National Council of Teachers of Mathematics
NSES National Science Education Standards

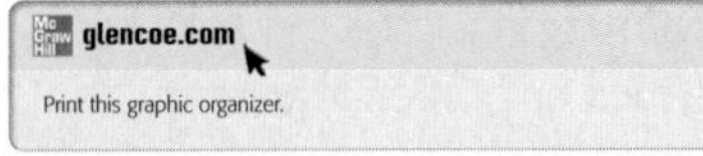

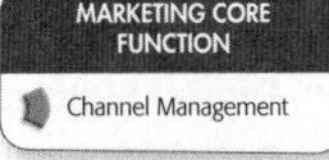

Common Core
Speaking and Listening Prepare for and participate effectively in a range of conversations and collaborations with diverse partners, building on others' ideas and expressing their own clearly and persuasively.

MARKETING CORE FUNCTION
Channel Management

m.e. Section 23.1

The Role of the Buyer

PLANNING PURCHASES

Organizational buyers purchase goods for business purposes, usually in much larger quantities than purchased by the average consumer. They must have knowledge about the products they buy and understand the operations of their firm. Knowledge of the manufacturing and service operations is especially important.

As You Read

Compare Identify the similarities and differences of the four markets.

INDUSTRIAL MARKETS

In manufacturing and service businesses, the people responsible for purchasing may be known as *purchasing managers, industrial buyers,* or *procurement managers.*

Although their specific job titles may vary, all of these individuals share the same function in common—to purchase goods and services for use by the business.

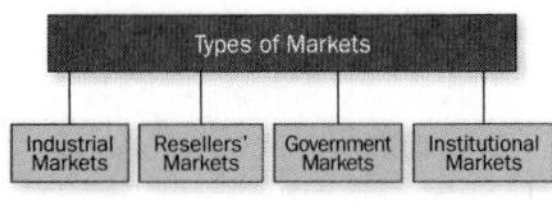

In manufacturing businesses, planning purchases often requires industrial buyers to be directly involved with production planning.

Consider the following case of a purchasing manager for a manufacturer that makes specialty clothing designed for outdoor activities. This example will help give you an idea of the various duites and responsibilities involved in planning purchases for a business.

Initially, the purchasing manager reviews the company's master production schedule for details of production needed to meet sales requirements. Let's say that the marketing department **predicts** that the company will be able to sell 500 of the manufacturer's Style Number 1900 jackets in the coming season.

The purchasing manager must know exactly how much fabric, insulation, and thread and how many zippers it will take to produce a single Style Number1900 jacket. This list is called a "bill of materials." The total of all the materials necessary to make one jacket can then be multiplied by 500. The resulting figure will show exactly what needs to be purchased in order to produce the number of jackets that will meet the sales goal.

> "Having a handle on business trends that affect a buyer's industry is important, especially when buying for resale purposes."

In order to determine when to buy the items needed, the purchasing manager would be responsible for materials requirement planning (MRP). MRP includes a **technical** analysis of when to make the purchases so they are available when needed, according to the production schedule. The purchasing manager must therefore know the capacity of the manufacturing facility. The individual must make sure the company has enough room to house all the supplies and raw materials and the inventory of finished goods.

ENGAGE

Anticipation Activity

Improving Student Achievement Organize students into teams of five. Each team should research the purchases needed to open a 50-seat restaurant. Have teams present a list of goods to purchase, a proposed budget, and a list of vendors to contact.

Objectives

- **Define** the terms used to describe organizational buyers. Purchasing managers, procurement managers, and industrial buyers each obtain goods and services either for business use or to resell.
- **Explain** how planning purchases differs between an industrial market and a reseller's market. industrial—based on business needs; reseller's—based on consumer wants, needs
- **Describe** the six-month merchandising plan and explain its calculations. It is the sales for next six-month period and it includes projected sales, BOM, reductions, and purchases.
- **Explain** the concept of chain-store buying. Allows the chain to forge a unified image and obtain quantity discounts.

Graphic Organizer

Market	Notes
Industrial	called purchasing managers, industrial buyers, or procurement managers; buy goods and services for use in the business
Resellers	can be wholesale or retail buyers; buy for resell; must forecast customer's needs and wants
Government	buy for federal, state, and local agencies; make up one of the largest single markets in the world
Institutional	consist of institutions and nonprofit organizations; may buy for internal use or for use in the production of their own goods or services

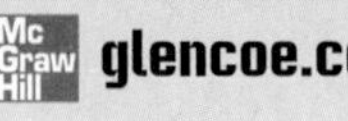

Graphic Organizer Send students to the Online Learning Center to print this graphic organizer.

EXPLORE

Before You Read

Read the Before You Read question aloud: ***What happens when you cannot find a product you need at a store because it is sold out?*** Sample answers: I look for the product in another store. In the future, I may not return to the sold-out store because I don't want to take a chance that they might be sold out again. Then ask: ***What does this tell you about the importance of a retail store having knowledgeable buyers?*** Knowledgeable buyers are vital if a store is going to be competitive in the marketplace.

Preteaching Vocabulary

Have students go to the Online Learning Center at glencoe.com for the Chapter 23 Preteaching Vocabulary games.

Content Vocabulary

Tell students to work individually to write a quiz consisting of six true/false questions, one for each of the Content Vocabulary words. When finished, students should trade questions with a partner and take one another's quizzes. Sample question: While wholesale buyers are a type of organizational buyer, retail buyers are not. (False—both are types of organizational buyers)

Academic Vocabulary

Predicts—Usage Display the word *predicts* for the class and ask: ***What does it mean when a weather forecaster predicts tomorrow's weather?*** The forecaster attempts to tell what the weather will be like in the future, based on current conditions, conditions in surrounding areas, science, past experience, and so on. Discuss that, like the weather forecaster, we try to make predictions based on a variety of factors, including our past experiences and events happening around us.

Technical—Denotative Meaning Display the word *technical* and explain that it means "to have specialized, usually practical knowledge." Read aloud this sentence: ***Purchasing managers must make a technical analysis of which materials are required to manufacture a specific product.*** Discuss that the manager must have *specialized* knowledge that is applied in a *practical* way (to make a list of needed materials).

Reading: Preparing to Read
Go to the Online Learning Center for a video in which a teacher uses multiple instructional strategies to prepare students to read a persuasive essay.

The Role of the Buyer

PLANNING PURCHASES

Ask these guiding questions to focus the discussion on planning purchases.

Guiding Questions

Describe What kinds of knowledge must an organizational buyer have?	product knowledge and an understanding of manufacturing and service operations
Contrast Why does an industrial buyer often have to be directly involved in production planning?	The industrial buyer must know details such as how much will be manufactured and when, so they will know which materials to order.
Infer In the term *procurement manager,* what do you think the word *procurement* means?	buying or obtaining the materials, products, and supplies needed to run a business

As You Read

Read to students the As You Read statement: ***Identify the similarities and differences of the four markets.*** **Similarities**: All require buyers to be knowledgeable about their products, the operations of their firms, and current trends. They also must plan far in advance of the selling season. **Differences**: Industrial buyers purchase goods to be used in the manufacturing process and therefore frequently are directly involved with production planning. Wholesale and retail buyers purchase goods for resale. Unlike industrial buyers, government buyers and institutional buyers purchase goods for use by local, state, and federal governmental agencies and nonprofit organizations.

Expert Advice

Read the quote to students:

> **"Having a handle on business trends that affect a buyer's industry is important, especially when buying for resale purposes."**

Tell students that this quote emphasizes how important it is for buyers to stay on "the cutting edge." Ask students: ***If you were a buyer for a sporting goods store, what kinds of trends would you watch for?*** increases or decreases in the percentage of Internet sales, changes in the popularity of certain sports, and changes in technology of equipment, such as new technologies in fishing reels.

Timelines and delivery of all supplies must be followed and checked on a regular basis to maintain the master production schedule. This ensures that everything is as it should be for manufacturing to progress at an appropriate rate.

RESELLERS' MARKETS

The resellers' market is found in wholesaling and retailing operations where the person responsible for purchasing is simply called a "buyer." **Wholesale and retail buyers** purchase goods for resale. They forecast customers' needs and buy the necessary products. All buyers must plan far in advance of the selling season to know how much of each item to purchase.

Buy to Sell Buyers decide which goods are best, choose suppliers, negotiate prices, and award contracts ensuring the product's timely receipt.

SIX-MONTH MERCHANDISE PLAN

Buyers plan their purchases by preparing a **six-month merchandise plan**, which is the budget that estimates planned purchases for a six-month period. (See **Figure 23.1** on page 540 for a nearly completed merchandise plan.)

The first figure calculated on a merchandise plan is the planned sales figure. In most cases, buyers determine this figure by using the previous year's monthly sales figures. Then they adjust them to reflect the firm's current-year sales goal.

Suppose sales for a particular month last year totaled $100,000, and this year's goal is to increase sales by 10 percent. This year's planned sales for the month would be calculated as follows:

Desired increase: $100,000 × .10 = $10,000

Planned sales: $100,000 + $10,000 = $110,000

You could also reach the same result in a single step:

$100,000 × 1.10 = $110,000

Purchasing and inventory control go hand in hand. Buyers need to know what sells and what does not. Companies need to figure out their projected sales to order the correct quantities of merchandise. ***What can happen if a this dress shop runs out of a popular dress just before prom season?***

The company goal for the current year is derived from a study of last year's sales, current market and economic conditions, and an analysis of the competition. Projection of accurate planned sales figures is important because all other figures on the merchandise plan are computed on the basis of this figure.

Buyers must ensure that there is enough stock to accommodate the planned sales volume. This is also known as *beginning-of-the-month (BOM) inventory*. To project this figure, a buyer checks the previous year's records for how much stock was needed in relation to monthly sales. Sales were $40,000 in a given month, and the BOM stock value for that month was $120,000. Therefore, the stock-to-sales ratio is 3 to 1. The buyer can apply that same ratio to the planned figure for another month if both economic and market conditions are similar.

Here is how the BOM figure on the merchandise plan is calculated. Suppose the stock-to-sales ratio is 2:1 (usually reported as 2). This means that to accommodate a given sales volume, twice that amount of stock must be kept on hand. In other words, BOM inventory should be twice the amount of anticipated sales. If sales are $5,000, then the BOM would be $10,000.

The end-of-the-month (EOM) stock figure is closely related to the BOM stock figure. The BOM stock figure for any given month is the EOM stock figure for the previous month.

Planned retail reductions take into account reductions in the selling price, shortages of merchandise caused by clerical errors, employee theft, and customer shoplifting. Such reductions in earnings and merchandise shortages ultimately affect the amount of money that must be planned for purchases.

Planned retail reductions can be calculated in two different ways. One is to calculate reductions as a percentage of planned sales. Suppose planned reductions have historically been 10 percent of planned sales. If planned sales for the month are $25,000, planned reductions for that month would be calculated as follows:

$25,000 × .10 = $2,500

MARKETING CASE STUDY

Frito-Lay Buys Local

When you buy a bag of chips and crunch into them, you are eating a product that started out as a potato in the ground—from California, Texas, or other states. That was the idea behind Frito-Lay's "Local" campaign, which speaks to the trend of buying products obtained from local suppliers.

Meet the Suppliers

"While Lay's Potato Chips have been one of the most popular snacks since they were introduced, what people might not realize is how many communities across the country play a role in the creation of America's favorite potato chip," said a Frito-Lay vice president. The company purchases potatoes from 80 different farms in 27 states. Some of the actual farmers appeared in Lay's TV ads, which emphasized the notion that the company is "closer to home than people might expect."

English Language Arts/Writing

Discuss You are the buyer for a competing potato chip manufacturer and have decided to buy potatoes from local growers. What type of purchase is buying potatoes for potato chips? What information would you need before you could plan your purchase?

NCTE 1 Read texts to acquire new information.

EXPLAIN

Activate Prior Knowledge

Reteach Wholesale versus Retail Ask students: ***What is the difference between wholesale and retail buyers?*** Wholesale buyers sell goods that will be resold. Retail buyers sell to the final customer.

Buy to Sell Display a list of these responsibilities of buyers: (1) Choose goods to buy; (2) Choose suppliers; (3) Negotiate prices; (4) Award contracts, making certain goods will be received when needed.

Critical Thinking

Discuss the roles of a buyer. Ask students: ***Which responsibilities of a buyer do you think would be the most difficult to meet? Why?*** I think it would be hard to choose what goods to buy, especially in a trendy market such as a boutique clothing store. Styles change quickly, and it would be difficult to stay on top of the latest fashions.

Visual Literacy

Buy to Sell Caption Answer Read the caption question to students: ***What can happen if this dress shop runs out of a popular dress just before prom season?*** Consumers might go to another store or the Internet to look for the product. If they are satisfied with this new source, they might become loyal to it and not return to the original store. Ask: ***Has this, or a similar situation ever happened to you? What did you do?*** Yes, I wanted to buy a particular digital camera, but the store I usually go to was sold out. The salesperson said they should have another shipment in a week, but I needed the camera for a birthday party, so I went to another store. I would have looked on the Web, but I did not have time to wait for delivery. Then ask: ***Have you shopped at the store since that time? If not, what might it take to get you back into that store?*** The point that students should understand is that if a store loses a customer because it does not have what the customer wants, it may be difficult to get the customer to return to the store.

ELABORATE

SIX-MONTH MERCHANDISE PLAN

Discuss with students that clearly-stated goals help buyers focus on where they are heading. To encourage a discussion of the six-month merchandise plan, ask these guiding questions.

Guiding Questions

Analyze Why is it important that the projection of the planned sales figures be reasonably accurate?	If these figures are not reasonably accurate, there will be problems with the entire plan because all other figures are computed from these figures.
Predict Describe a situation in which one year ago, a store had monthly sales for March of $85,000 and beginning-of-the-month stock value of $250,000. For this year, the planned March sales were increased by 6 percent, but the BOM stock was unchanged. What might happen?	Possible answer: The planned sales figure might not be reached because the BOM inventory does not support the increase in sales.

Critical Thinking

Lead a discussion about the implications of a poorly planned six-month merchandise plan. Point out that having too much or too little inventory can be a major problem for a business as it affects sales and profit. Encourage students to discuss the kinds of difficulties that might occur. If there is too much inventory, capital resources are tied up, preventing the money from being spent in other ways. Inventory must be stored, which is expensive. Prices will probably have to be reduced to get rid of excess inventory, thereby reducing or eliminating profits. If there is too little inventory, consumers are likely to go where the selection is better, and may not return, even if selections improve at a later time.

MARKETING CASE STUDY

English Language Arts/Writing Answer Students should state that buying potatoes is an industrial purchase. Information might include answers to these questions: Can suppliers provide the type and quality of potatoes needed? Can they provide the necessary quantities? Could suppliers deliver potatoes, or would the buyer have to hire someone to do this? Another consideration would be whether suppliers could supply potatoes year-round as needed by the manufacturer, or whether the manufacturer needs storage facilities. The second option might allow the manufacturer to save money on potatoes, but it would increase overhead for storage.

Graphic Organizer

Display this graphic organizer. Then work with students to fill in four common causes of retail reduction.

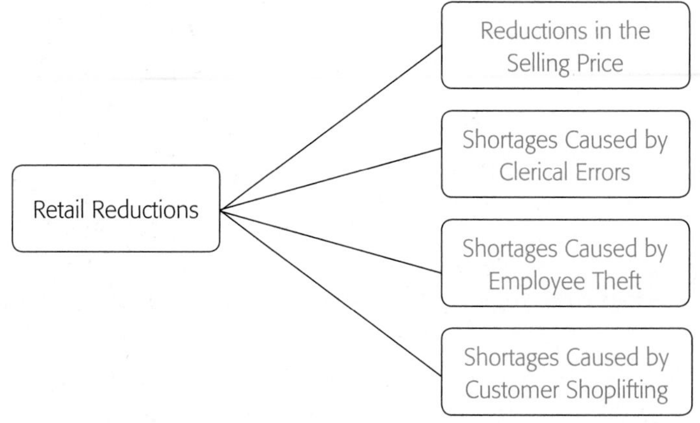

Graphic Organizer Send students to the Online Learning Center to print this graphic organizer.

Mini Project

Differentiated Instruction

Verbal Learners Organize the class into pairs. One student in each pair should teach the other how to perform each of these calculations: (1) Planned sales; (2) Beginning-of-the-month (BOM) inventory; (3) End-of-the-month (EOM) inventory; (4) Planned retail reductions based on a percentage of planned sales. Encourage students to make up their own figures. Pairs should take turns explaining each of the listed calculations. Sample: The beginning-of-the-month inventory is calculated using the ratio from the previous year. So, if planned sales for a month are $85,000 and the BOM ratio is 3:1, the BOM inventory should be $255,000 (85,000 × 3).

Extension

Researching Trade Shows Point out to students that many wholesale and retail buyers keep up with their markets by attending trade shows. Have students choose a retail market in which they are interested and research trade shows aimed at that market. Instruct students to create a listing of the major shows. Each listing should contain: the name of the trade show, a brief description of the show, the location of the next show, and the date(s) for the next show. Each listing should contain the specified information. For example, jewelers and gemstone dealers from around the world attend the Tucson JOGS Jewelry & Gem Show every winter to buy and sell gemstones and finished jewelry

FIGURE 23.1 Six-Month Merchandise Plan

This nearly completed model merchandise plan is based on the following assumptions: Sales are expected to increase by 10 percent over last year; last year's stock-to-sales ratios should be used to complete this year's BOM stock figures; this year's planned reductions should be 5 percent lower than last year's; and the planned BOM for August is $264,000. ***What are the planned purchase figures for May through July?***

Spring Season 20___ Department Toys No. 6124

		February	March	April	May	June	July	Total
Sales	Last year	82,000	96,000	90,000	100,000	94,000	80,000	
	Plan	90,200	105,600	99,000	110,000	103,400	88,000	
	Actual							
Retail Stock BOM	Last year	328,000	336,000	297,000	360,000	291,400	224,000	
	Plan	360,800	369,600	326,700	396,000	320,540	246,400	
	Actual							
Retail Reductions	Last year	12,300	14,400	13,500	15,000	14,100	12,000	
	Plan	11,685	13,680	12,825	14,250	13,395	11,400	
	Actual							
Purchases	Last year	N/A	N/A	N/A	N/A	N/A	N/A	
	Plan	110,685	76,380	181,125				
	Actual							

Some companies set goals of reducing planned reductions from the previous year. Assume that a firm's goal is to reduce this year's planned reductions by 5 percent from last year's figure. Last year's reductions totaled $700; therefore this year's planned reductions would be figured this way:

Desired decrease: $700 × .05 = $35

Planned reductions: $700 – $35 = $665

This result could also be reached in a single step: $700 × .95 = $665

The planned purchase entry shows the retail-dollar purchase figures that a firm needs to achieve its sales and inventory projections for each month. Planned sales, BOM stock, and reductions are all necessary for determining planned purchases (P). That includes planned sales (PS), planned EOM/BOM stock, and planned reductions (R).

The formula for planned purchases is:

(PS + EOM stock + R) – BOM stock = P

Assume that planned sales are $10,000, planned EOM stock is $25,000, planned reductions are $500, and BOM stock is $20,000. Using the formula, planned purchases would be calculated this way:

($10,000 + $25,000 + $500) – $20,000 =

$35,500 – $20,000 = $15,500

OPEN-TO-BUY

During the buying season, a buyer may want to know the **open-to-buy (OTB)**, which is the amount of money a retailer has left for buying goods after considering all purchases received, on order, and in transit.

OTB is calculated this way:

P – (goods received + goods ordered) = OTB

Assume that merchandise received against the planned purchase figure just calculated is $6,500 so far, and merchandise on order against it is $2,000. The present OTB would be as follows:

$15,500 – ($6,500 + $2,000) = OTB

$15,500 – $8,500 = $7,000

This $7,000 figure represents the retail value of the goods that the buyer may purchase at the time. However, the problem is not solved here.

There is a way to determine the actual money the buyer has to spend. You must calculate the markup percentage used by the buyer and deduct that figure from the retail value. Assume that the markup percentage is 45 percent, based on the retail value of the merchandise.

Here is the formula for determining the OTB at cost:

100% – markup % =

% attributed to cost of the item

% attributed to cost × retail value =

OTB at cost

100% – 45% markup = 55% (cost)

55% (cost) × $7,000 (retail) =

$3,850 OTB at cost

Therefore, in the end, the buyer has $3,850 to spend with all other costs considered. You can see how this extra step makes a big difference in the final amount.

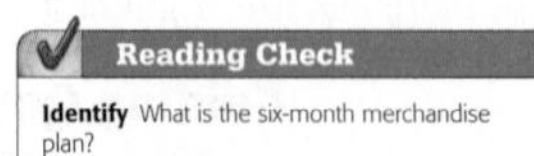

Reading Check

Identify What is the six-month merchandise plan?

Buyers need to understand their customers and the products they sell in order to make purchasing decisions. ***How can the knowledge of a company's customers and products improve a buyer's purchasing power?***

EXPLAIN

Visual Literacy

Figure 23.1 Caption Answer

Read the caption question to students: ***What are the planned purchase figures for May through July?*** May: $48,790; June: $42,655; July: $117,000 Ask students: ***Assume that the planned Retail Stock BOM for February is $315,700. What stock-to-sales ratio would this be?*** 3.5:1 Then ask: ***How does this stock-to-sales ratio compare with the one shown for February in this figure?*** Because the ratio in the table is 4:1, a BOM of $315,700 would be 0.5 percent less.

PROFESSIONAL DEVELOPMENT **MINI CLIP**

Math: Multiple Approaches to Problem Solving

Go to the Online Learning Center to view a video clip in which a teacher and students discuss various options of problem solving and then apply one, working backward, to a problem.

Critical Thinking

After students have studied Figure 23.1, point out that the plan covers the months February through July. Tell students that some retail markets are very active only at certain times of the year. The market for candy, for example, centers on holidays such as Halloween and Valentine's Day. In such cases, it is important for buyers to be able to project sales by the month because the variation from month-to-month can be great. Ask: ***What other retail markets might vary greatly depending on the time of year?*** bedding plants are typically purchased in the spring; winter clothing sales are higher in the late summer and fall; school supply sales are up during the weeks before and after the start of the school year.

Reinforce Vocabulary

Open-to-Buy—Usage Explain that in this situation, *open* refers to money that is available for use in purchasing new inventory. Likewise, the term *open stock* is stock that is available for consumers to purchase. Ask: ***Can you think of other situations in which*** **open** ***is used in this sense?:*** The pool has open swimming from 1:00 to 5:00.

ELABORATE

OPEN-TO-BUY

Ask these guiding questions to focus the discussion on the topic of open-to-buy.

Guiding Questions

Explain Why must the cost of goods on order be taken into account when determining the open-to-buy number?	Goods have already been ordered, but not paid for; their cost must be subtracted to determine, how much money is left for additional purchases.
Calculate Assume that a buyer's planned purchase figure is \$35,500. Goods already received are \$20,000 and goods on order are \$4,000. The markup is 40 percent, based on the retail value of the merchandise. What is the actual amount of money the buyer has left to spend?	First calculate the retail cost of the goods that can still be purchased: (35,500 – 20,000 – 4,000) = \$11,500. Then, determine the markup and subtract it from 100. Multiply this cost percentage by the retail value of the goods: 11,500 × (1.00 – 0.40) = \$6,900.

Reading Check Answer

Read the Reading Check question to students: ***What is the six-month merchandise plan?*** It is a budget that estimates planned purchases for a six-month period.

Visual Literacy

Purchasing Power Caption Answer

Read the caption question to students: ***How can the knowledge of a company's customers and products improve a buyer's purchasing power?*** A buyer's knowledge of the company's customers helps the buyer to understand the kinds of products or services that will appeal to that customer. For example, older customers are more likely to want clothes that are more conservative and can be worn for a longer time period to a variety of functions. Younger customers may want clothes that are trendier and may only wear the clothes for a relatively short time period. A buyer must be aware of the products the company is currently selling in order to purchase new products that will complement, but not duplicate, current products.

e MARKETING

Meta Markets

A Meta Market is a special market found on the Web that caters to a specific event or industry. Complementary products are included in the Meta Market. A Meta Market can be established for business-to-consumer (B2C) and for business-to-business (B2B). Meta Markets create a one-stop shopping for consumers. For example, there could be a Meta Market for anglers that include businesses that sell boats, fishing poles, line, reels, and other equipment and accessories. B2B Meta Markets generally center around an industry, such as the chemical industry or auto industry. B2B companies can get rid of excess inventory by trading items with other vendors and can easily attract new buyers who visit a Meta Market.

Innovate and Create

Have students assume they are wedding planners or event planners for a business. They must put together all the details for an upcoming event. For a wedding the details will include: purchasing flowers, wedding invitations, favors, and a wedding cake, as well as finding the right venue, DJ, and caterer. For a business conference the details may include: catering food, finding a meeting site, ordering audio-visual equipment, arranging travel plans for participants, and organizing activities for the spouses of the conference attendees. After students conduct all the research for one of the above events, have them create a Meta Market Web site for other event planners to use in order to make their job easier. What complementary vendors would they include in their Meta Market for Event Planners? There is a Meta Market for weddings already in existence for consumers to use called "the knot," which you can view to see the vendors included. Students may add additional businesses such as photographers, videographers, bridal shops, and mother-of-the-bride dress shops. For event planning for business conferences, students may include hotels, airlines, restaurants, caterers, and local sightseeing companies.

glencoe.com

eMarketing Worksheet Activity Send students to the Online Learning Center to download an eMarketing worksheet activity.

PLANNING PURCHASES FOR A CHAIN-STORE OPERATION

The buying process for all branches in a chain store operation is usually done in a central location, such as company headquarters. This process is called **centralized buying**. Buyers will purchase all the items for a department or part of a department. There may be three buyers for women's shoes—one for casual shoes, another for traditional shoes, and still another for better shoes. To coordinate the efforts of those three buyers, there would be a merchandise or division manager. This person would oversee all shoe buyers, which may include those for men's, children's, and women's shoes.

Chain stores use centralized buying to create a unified image for the chain. Another benefit of centralized buying is quantity discounts. Stores can negotiate with vendors because of the large volume of goods that they purchase at one time.

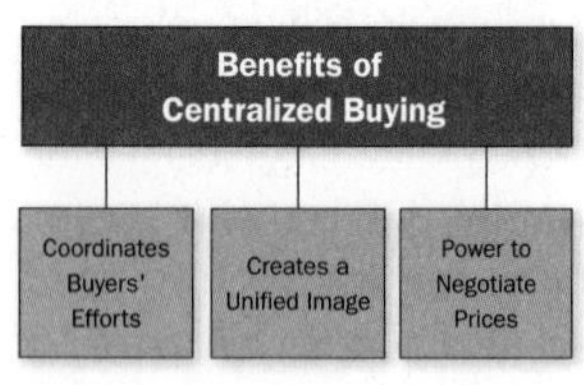

DECENTRALIZED BUYING

Sometimes chain stores want to have special goods in their stores that are not available elsewhere in the chain. In these cases, local store managers or their designated buyers are authorized to make special purchases for their individual stores. This is **decentralized buying**. Decentralization occurs when authority for retail decisions is made at lower levels in the organization.

Retailers constantly make trade-offs between efficiency and sales potential. Centralized buying is more efficient and decentralized buying has more sales potential. This potential is due to the decisions that tailor merchandise to local markets.

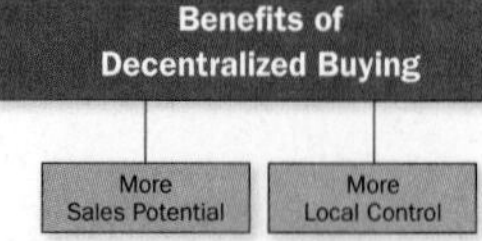

Practice

On a separate sheet of paper, practice the following calculations that are necessary for creating a six-month merchandise plan:

1. Last March a shop had sales of $7,300. The owner's goal is to increase sales by 8 percent for this year. What would be the planned sales for this March?
2. Last year's BOM for March was $10,950. Calculate the stock-to-sales ratio.
3. What should be the BOM stock figure for this March?
4. Planned reductions have historically been 10 percent of sales. Using this figure, what would be the planned reductions for this March? The owner would like to cut planned reductions by 5 percent this year. Last year's reductions for the month were $750. Therefore, what would be this year's target figure?
5. Using the figures given or calculated in numbers 1, 3, and 4, determine the planned purchases for the shop if the EOM stock figure for March is $12,000.
6. Assuming merchandise received and ordered amounted to $1,850, what would be the open-to-buy position at retail?
7. The customary markup for an item is 60 percent. What is OTB at cost?

Check your answers.

GOVERNMENT MARKETS

There are also buyers for government markets. Federal, state, and local agencies are the government units responsible for purchasing goods and services for their specific markets. There are approximately 85,000 government units in the United States. These include the departments of sanitation, public libraries, and local school boards.

Government markets make up one of the largest single markets for retail goods and services in the world. In the United States, the federal government is a huge consumer of goods, ranging from food for school lunches to military equipment. No one federal agency is responsible for all government buying.

INSTITUTIONAL MARKETS

One final segment of the market includes institutions and nonprofit organizations that do not compete in the business world in the same way retailers and wholesalers do. These institutions include hospitals, museums, libraries, prisons, schools, colleges, places of worship, civic clubs, and various foundations that do not work solely for profit.

Many institutions and nonprofit organizations have unique buying needs. Some of these organizations may purchase goods and services for use in the production of their own goods or services.

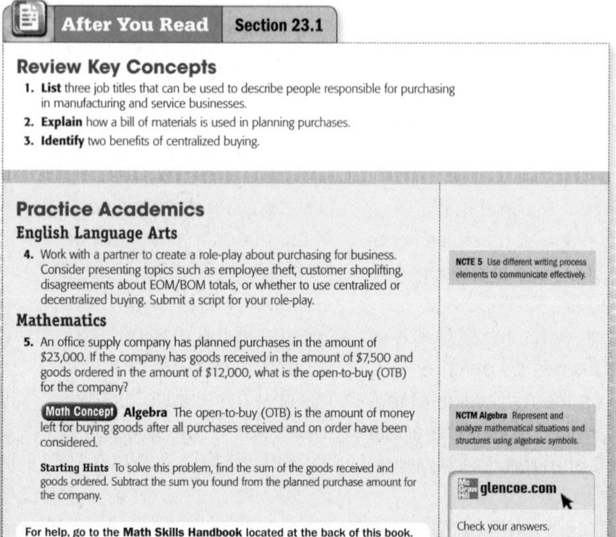

After You Read | **Section 23.1**

Review Key Concepts

1. **List** three job titles that can be used to describe people responsible for purchasing in manufacturing and service businesses.
2. **Explain** how a bill of materials is used in planning purchases.
3. **Identify** two benefits of centralized buying.

Practice Academics

English Language Arts

4. Work with a partner to create a role-play about purchasing for business. Consider presenting topics such as employee theft, customer shoplifting, disagreements about EOM/BOM totals, or whether to use centralized or decentralized buying. Submit a script for your role-play.

NCTE 5 Use different writing process elements to communicate effectively.

Mathematics

5. An office supply company has planned purchases in the amount of $23,000. If the company has goods received in the amount of $7,500 and goods ordered in the amount of $12,000, what is the open-to-buy (OTB) for the company?

Math Concept **Algebra** The open-to-buy (OTB) is the amount of money left for buying goods after all purchases received and on order have been considered.

NCTM Algebra Represent and analyze mathematical situations and structures using algebraic symbols.

Starting Hints To solve this problem, find the sum of the goods received and goods ordered. Subtract the sum you found from the planned purchase amount for the company.

For help, go to the **Math Skills Handbook** located at the back of this book.

glencoe.com

Check your answers.

ELABORATE

Reinforce Vocabulary

Decentralized Buying—Prefixes The prefix *de-* means "opposite of." Thus, *decentralized* means "not centralized." Ask for examples of other words that use the *de-* prefix. deodorize, deflate, decompose

Answers to Practice 1

1. Planned sales for this March = $7,884 (7300 × .08) + 7300
2. Stock-to-sales ratio = 1.5 (10950/7300)
3. BOM stock figure for March = $11,826 (7884 × 1.5)
4. Reductions at 10% of sales = $788.40 (7884 × 0.10); Reductions by 5% from last year = $712.50 (750 × .05 = 37.50, 750 – 37.50 = 712.50)
5. Planned purchases = $8,846.40 [P = (7884 + 12,000 + 788.40) – 11,826]
6. OTB at retail = $6, 996.40 (8,846.40 – 1850)
7. OTB at cost = $2,798.56 (1.00 – 0.60 = .40, 6996.40 × .400

PLANNING PURCHASES FOR A CHAIN-STORE OPERATION

Tell students that most chains keep a tight rein on their individual stores, including the kinds of goods these stores offer for sale. To focus student discussion on planning purchases for chain-store operations, ask students these guiding questions.

Guiding Questions

Recall How are purchases for chain store operations typically made?	They are typically made at a single central location such as company headquarters.
Make Judgments What might be a disadvantage if individual chain stores made their own buying decisions?	The overall unifying image of the chain may get lost; the stores might not get the same quantity discounts.

EVALUATE

Graphic Organizer

To encourage a discussion of centralized versus decentralized buying, display this cause-and-effect diagram. Ask students to provide reasons that centralized buying occurs. Possible answers:

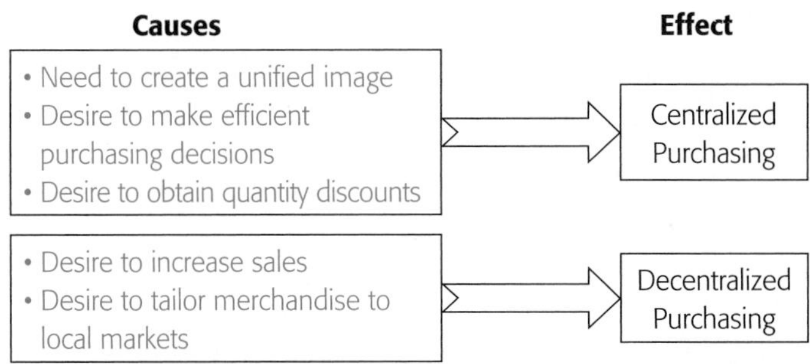

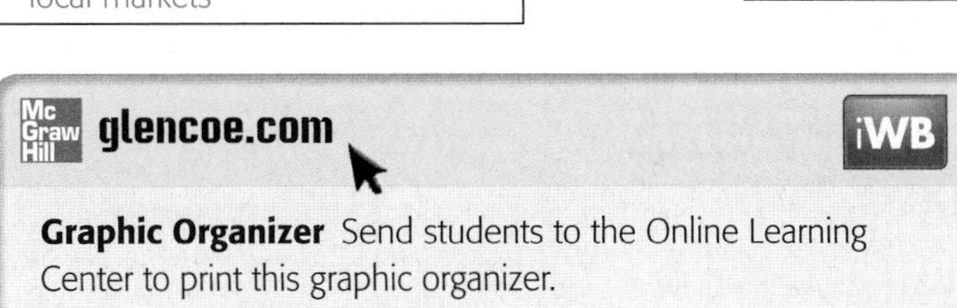

glencoe.com iWB

Graphic Organizer Send students to the Online Learning Center to print this graphic organizer.

Activate Prior Knowledge

Reteach Public Sector and Private Sector Remind students that government-financed agencies are part of the public sector. This sector purchases approximately one-third of all goods and services sold in the United States. Those businesses not associated with government agencies are part of the private sector. While the purpose of most private sector businesses is to make a profit, some of them, such as the International Red Cross, may operate like businesses, but are not intended to earn a profit.

Mini Project

Differentiated Instruction

Kinesthetic Learners Pair students and tell them they work for a large chain clothing store. One student is the store manager; the other is sales manager. The store is in a college town and the sales manager is often asked for specific clothing brands geared toward this market. Currently, all clothing is centrally purchased, and the store has little control over its inventory. Have students role-play a discussion in which the sales manager encourages the store manager to make a more decentralized purchases. The sales manager should discuss how decentralized purchases will give the store more appeal in the market, which will result in more sales. The manager should state the advantages of centralized buying, such as setting a specific brand image and obtaining quantity discounts.

After You Read Section 23.1

Review Key Concepts

1. Three job titles that can be used to describe people responsible for purchasing in manufacturing and service businesses include: purchasing managers, industrial buyers, and procurement managers.
2. A bill of materials gives the total of all materials necessary to make one item. This can be multiplied by the total number of items to determine the exact quantity of materials that must be purchased.
3. Centralized buying helps to create a unified image for the chain; merchandise can be transferred from one store to another where it is selling better; and quantity discounts can be negotiated due to large-volume purchases.

Practice Academics

English Language Arts

4. Students should submit a detailed, well-written script for a role-play in which they discuss making purchases for a business. Topics covered might include reductions related to customer shoplifting, employee theft, and how to establish BOM totals. In addition, students may choose to have a debate over the topics of centralized and decentralized purchasing. For example, one partner might believe that in order to meet local needs, the store needs to engage in some decentralized buying, while the other partner might support centralized buying in order to maintain the chain's brand.

Mathematics

5. The open-to-buy is \$3,500.
(23,000 – 7,500 – 12,000)

glencoe.com

Answer Key Send students to the Online Learning Center to check their answers.

READING GUIDE

Before You Read

Connect How do you decide where to buy products that are offered at different stores?

Objectives

- **List** the three types of purchase situations.
- **Explain** the criteria for selecting suppliers.
- **Name** the factors involved in negotiating terms of a sale.
- **Describe** the various Internet purchasing methods.

The Main Idea

The details of the purchasing process help describe the buyer's job responsibilities.

Vocabulary

Content Vocabulary
- want slips
- consignment buying
- memorandum buying
- reverse auction

Academic Vocabulary

You will find these words in your reading and on your tests. Make sure you know their meanings.
- evaluates
- journals

Graphic Organizer

Draw or print this chart to write in three types of purchase situations and four criteria for selecting suppliers.

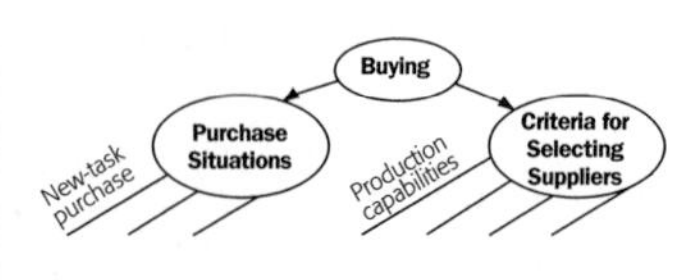

glencoe.com

Print this graphic organizer.

STANDARDS

ACADEMIC

English Language Arts
NCTE 12 Use language to accomplish individual purposes.

Mathematics
NCTM Problem Solving Solve problems that arise in mathematics and in other contexts.

NCSS *National Council for the Social Studies*
NCTE *National Council of Teachers of English*
NCTM *National Council of Teachers of Mathematics*
NSES *National Science Education Standards*

Common Core
Writing Write informative/explanatory texts to examine and convey complex ideas and information clearly and accurately through the effective selection, organization, and analysis of content.
Writing Write narratives to develop real or imagined experiences or events using effective technique, well-chosen details, and well-structured event sequences.

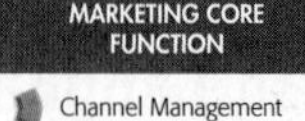

Section 23.2 The Purchasing Process

UNDERSTANDING THE PROCESS

The ways that buyers select suppliers, how the terms are negotiated, and how the Internet is used are all factors that affect the entire buying or purchasing process. In addition, there are many types of purchase situations.

As You Read

Compare Consider the differences between the types of purchase situations.

TYPES OF PURCHASE SITUATIONS

How difficult is the task of a purchasing manager or a buyer? The answer depends on which type of purchase situation is considered. Let's review the three types of purchase situations: new task purchase, modified rebuy, and straight rebuy.

NEW-TASK PURCHASE

In a new-task purchase situation, a purchase is made for the first time. It can be triggered by a formerly unrecognized need, a new manufacturing process, or organizational change. This can be the most complicated buying situation, because it involves a first-time purchase. In a retail or wholesale operation, salespeople prepare **want slips**, which are customer requests for items not carried in the store. The buyer **evaluates** want slips to determine if the requests warrant the purchase of new merchandise.

> "The level of difficulty for a buyer varies depending on the type of purchasing situation."

MODIFIED REBUY

In a modified-rebuy situation, the buyer has had experience buying the good or service, but some aspect of the purchase changes. Perhaps the buyer is purchasing from a new vendor because the previous vendor went out of business or increased prices significantly. Other reasons for investigating new vendors may come from an analysis of the competition through comparison shopping. Buyers may also analyze current trade information found in trade publications or trade shows.

Finally, retail buyers may hire the services of a resident buying office. Resident buying offices are retailers' representatives in a geographic area where many suppliers of a given product are located. New York City's garment district, for example, is a central market for clothing. Resident buying offices send information to retail buyers on a regular basis. They inform buyers about new merchandise offerings, closeouts, or fashion trends.

STRAIGHT REBUY

In a straight-rebuy situation, the buyer routinely orders the goods and services purchased from the same vendor(s) as in the past. Staple goods such as office supplies fall into the straight-rebuy category for wholesale and retail buyers. The purchase of certain manufacturing supplies may be considered a straight rebuy.

SELECTING SUPPLIERS

The criteria for selecting suppliers fall into a few key categories. They include production capabilities, past experiences, product quality, special buying arrangements, special services, and negotiated terms such as pricing.

ENGAGE

Anticipation Activity

Improving Student Achievement Organize students in groups and explain they are going off to college. They want to rent a house rather than live in a dorm. Have them determine how they will establish their needs, determine available housing, and reach a final decision.

Objectives

- **List** the three types of purchase situations. new-task purchase, modified rebuy, straight rebuy
- **Explain** the criteria for selecting suppliers production capabilities, past experiences, product quality, special buying arrangements, special services, negotiated terms
- **Name** the factors involved in negotiating terms of a sale. dating terms, delivery arrangements, discounts
- **Describe** the various Internet purchasing methods. Web sites for direct purchases, electronic exchanges, online auctions

Graphic Organizer

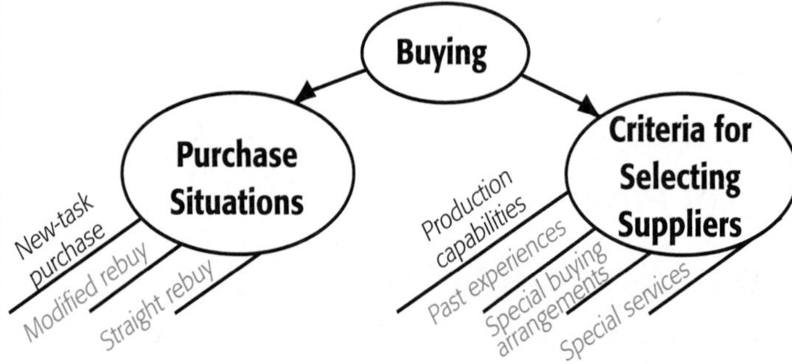

glencoe.com iWB

Graphic Organizer Send students to the Online Learning Center to print this graphic organizer.

EXPLORE

Before You Read

Read the Before You Read question aloud: ***How do you decide where to buy products that are offered at different stores?*** Sample answers: If it is a large item, such as an expensive electronic device, I watch the ads and go to a store that offers a good price. If it is a small item or something I need quickly, such as a gift, I go to the store that is most convenient. Then ask: ***How do you decide when to purchase an item online rather than at a brick-and-mortar store?*** Sample answers: When I don't have time to shop or cannot find an item locally. Sometimes I buy an item online if it is less expensive, but I have to be careful to factor in any shipping charges.

Preteaching Vocabulary

Have students go to the Online Learning Center at glencoe.com for the Chapter 23 Preteaching Vocabulary games.

Content Vocabulary

Display the following terms for students to read: *want slips, consignment buying, memorandum buying, reverse auction.* Go around the classroom, assigning each student a number from 1 to 4. Assign students the term that corresponds to their number (for example, the student with number 3 would be assigned *memorandum buying*). Display the following sentence for the class to read: ***How does this term affect the buying process?*** Each student should use his or her assigned term to write a single sentence that answers this question. When students are finished, ask for volunteers to read their sentences aloud. Sample sentence: Buyers use want slips to help determine which products to order.

Academic Vocabulary

Evaluates—Usage Explain to students that *evaluates* means "to determine the significance, worth, or condition of." Display these three sentences and ask students whether each sentence is concerned with an object or event's *significance,* its *worth,* or its *condition:*

1. She evaluates the book as being in poor shape. condition
2. The American historian evaluates the Continental Congress as an important turning point. significance 3. My realtor evaluates the house at $135,000. worth

Journals—Denotative Meaning Tell students that a *journal* typically is a record of current transactions or events. Explain that people in business often keep journals to record transactions. Be sure to emphasize that a journal is a record of transactions or events as they happen.

The Purchasing Process

UNDERSTANDING THE PROCESS

Ask these guiding questions to focus student discussion on different purchase situations.

Guiding Questions

Analyze Why might a buyer hire the services of a resident buying office?	Resident buying offices are often located close to many suppliers; because they specialize in a particular product, they can provide inside information, such as fashion trends and closeouts.
Apply Assume that you are a leisure wear buyer for a large department store. You are going through a stack of want slips. What determines whether you order any of the requested products?	Possible answers: The number of customers requesting a specific product, its availability, whether the product will continue to be popular or is just a fad.

As You Read

Read the As You Read statement aloud: ***Consider the differences between the types of purchase situations.*** New-task purchases require the most research and time because the buyer has no previous experience; modified rebuys require some time because a change in buying patterns has occurred; straight rebuys are routine and therefore require little of the buyer's time.

Expert Advice

Read the quote to students:

"The level of difficulty for a buyer varies depending on the type of purchasing situation."

Describe these two purchasing situations. In the first, a buyer is purchasing basic supplies for an office. In the second case, a buyer is purchasing cameras that use the latest digital technology. Ask: ***Which of these purchases is likely to be more difficult and time-consuming? Why?*** The second, because the buyer must determine types of cameras to purchase, where the best prices can be obtained, and so on. The first buyer will probably purchase the office supplies from the company's regular vendor.

PRODUCTION CAPABILITIES

When dealing with a source for the first time, buyers may request specific information about the source's production capabilities. They may even visit a facility in person to see it in operation. Buyers may ask for business references to determine the source's reputation in the industry. These factors would be extremely important when selecting suppliers and transportation businesses as partners in a just-in-time production arrangement.

Issues of production capabilities for some companies go beyond the actual physical plant and focus on ethical and social issues. Companies may require a review of facilities to ensure that they are not operating sweatshops. Sweatshops are factories characterized by poor working conditions and negligent treatment of employees. Being associated with a sweatshop can be very damaging to a company's reputation.

Some companies also try to determine whether suppliers are following green environmental practices. The popularity of green marketing has led more companies to take environmental concerns very seriously.

PAST EXPERIENCES

Many buyers maintain resource files and **journals** that document past experiences with vendors. All basic information, such as products carried, prices, delivery and dating terms, and the names of sales representatives, is recorded. Buyers also note evaluations of products, delivery performance, and customer service.

A major factor in selecting a supplier is the quality of goods it offers. Retail buyers keep accurate records of customer returns and the reasons for the returns. Returns relating to the quality of the goods may cause buyers to stop doing business with the supplier. It is important to clearly define standards of quality for products that buyers will purchase from suppliers. Standards should be explained to suppliers so they understand the criteria by which product quality is measured.

SPECIAL BUYING ARRANGEMENTS

Most suppliers may have specific policies regarding merchandise returns and sales arrangements. Two special types of sales and return policies are consignment buying and memorandum buying.

Clothes you buy in the United States are often manufactured abroad. Hong Kong is a central market for the garment industry. ***Look at the tags on a few items of clothing (at home or at a store). List the countries where the clothes were made.***

In **consignment buying**, goods are paid for only after the final customer purchases them. The supplier owns the goods until the wholesaler or retailer sells them. Many suppliers offer consignment buying as an incentive when introducing a new line of goods. However, a problem can arise with consignment buying when merchandise is stolen or damaged, raising the question of who must pay.

Memorandum buying occurs when the supplier agrees to take back any unsold goods by a certain pre-established date. The buyer pays for all the goods purchased but is later reimbursed for all the goods returned under the terms of the agreement. This buying arrangement allows for returns.

SPECIAL SERVICES

Businesses today demand more services from their suppliers. Almost all retailers demand that manufacturers place universal product codes (UPCs) on goods. Having the codes on all products saves the retailer time because individual items do not have to be marked with a price. The codes also allow retailers to track inventory easily as each sale is immediately recorded electronically in a central database.

See the Latest To get the most from trade shows sponsored by vendors and industry associations, a buyer should have an action plan.

NEGOTIATED TERMS

Buyers must negotiate prices, dating terms, delivery arrangements, and discounts. Discounts are any reductions from the quoted price. Such reductions are generally granted for the buyer's performance of certain functions. These are discussed in Chapter 26.

Dating terms include when a bill must be paid and the discount permitted for paying early. There are several dating variations for specific situations. A company may allow the dating terms to take effect later than the invoice date. This is known as advance dating. It is sometimes offered to businesses as an incentive to buy before the buying season.

Reading Check

List What are the criteria for selecting a supplier?

The GREEN Marketer

Walmart Checks Green Credentials

How can companies be sure that products and supplies they buy are made without harm to workers or the environment? In 2009, Walmart® introduced an original solution with its "Sustainability Index." Walmart asked suppliers how their actions affect the environment and local communities. Suppliers were given a survey. It assessed energy and climate, material efficiency, natural resources, and people and community.

Supplier Comparison The company prints this supplier information on product labels. This allows customers to compare the environmental impact of different items. In the long-term, there will be a global database with this type of information from all types of companies. This database will have information that will help consumers.

Mathematics

Calculate A study shows that consumers are willing to pay up to 15 percent more for green products. If a bottle of Clorox® Green Works cleaner costs $3.49, and a bottle of standard Clorox cleaner costs $2.99, will the green cleaner sell well?

NCTM Problem Solving Solve problems that arise in mathematics and in other contexts.

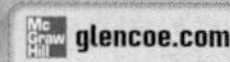

Get an activity on green marketing.

546 | Unit 7 · Distribution

Chapter 23 · Purchasing | 547

EXPLAIN

Graphic Organizer

Display this graphic organizer. Encourage the class to discuss the importance of the criteria used to choose a buyer. Possible answers:

Criteria for Selecting Suppliers

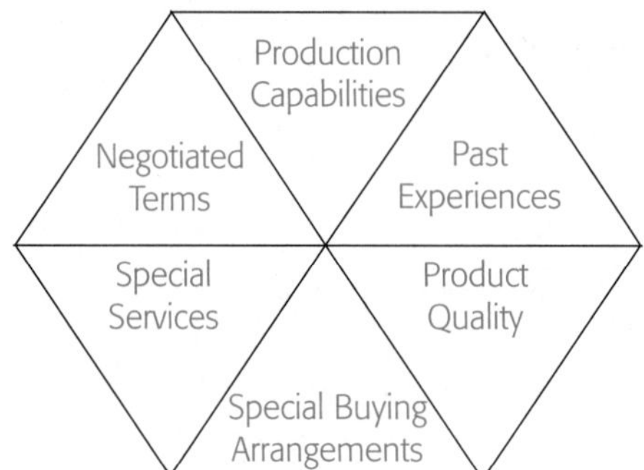

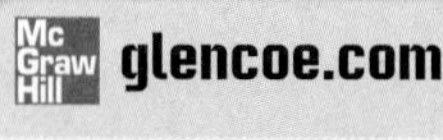

Graphic Organizer Send students to the Online Learning Center to print this graphic organizer.

Visual Literacy

Country of Origin Caption Answer

Read the question to students: ***Look at the tags on a few items of clothing (at home or at a store). List the countries in which the clothes were made.*** Lists will vary, but may include China, India, Indonesia, Vietnam, Jordan, Mongolia, Ukraine. Ask students: ***Have you heard of any bad publicity that some clothing or toy manufacturers have received regarding the mistreatment of workers in other countries? If so, what have you heard?*** I've heard that some companies make employees work long hours for little money and that some companies hire underage workers.

VIRTUAL BUSINESS

PURCHASING

Introduce students to the concept of purchasing using Knowledge Matters' Virtual Business Retailing visual simulation, *Purchasing*. In this simulation, students will learn that purchasing inventory for a store is an important and complicated job.

ELABORATE

PRODUCTION CAPABILITIES

Ask these questions to focus discussion on production capabilities.

Guiding Questions

Explain What are three methods a buyer might use to evaluate a potential product source?	request information about the source's production capabilities; ask for business references; visit the production facility
Draw Conclusions Why would a company want to avoid purchasing products made in sweatshops?	The company might not want to profit from poor working conditions. Purchasing goods from sweatshops can also lead to negative publicity.

Critical Thinking

Ask students: ***Why are a supplier's production capabilities especially important in just-in-time production arrangements?*** If the supplier is unable to provide the product when it is needed, the company can be left without any product. Because the company is using just-in-time production, it has no inventory to fall back on.

SPECIAL BUYING ARRANGEMENTS

Ask these guiding questions to help students explore these special buying arrangements.

Guiding Questions

Analyze Who do you think benefits more from memorandum buying—the supplier or the buyer? Why?	The buyer does, because the goods can be returned for a previously agreed-upon price if they are not sold.
Judge Imagine a supplier has consigned a $300 bracelet to a jewelry store. The bracelet is stolen in a burglary. Who should be out the $300—the supplier or the jewelry store owner? Why?	It may seem that because the bracelet still belonged to the supplier, the supplier should suffer the loss. However, in most situations, the entity that actually holds the goods is responsible for insuring them against loss.

See the Latest Tell students that they are buyers for a furniture store and are attending a large trade show. They realize they can only visit about one-fourth of all the booths. How would they decide which to visit?

Reading Check Answer

Read the Reading Check question to students: ***What are the criteria for selecting a supplier?*** The criteria include whether the supplier's production capabilities are adequate for the buyer's needs; past experience with the supplier; quality of products; whether the supplier can meet any specific buying arrangements; what kinds of special services the supplier can provide; and the terms the supplier is willing to offer.

The GREEN Marketer

Mathematics Answer No, it may not sell well. Consumers are willing to pay up to 15 percent more for green products. The price for Clorox cleaner is $2.99, and 15 percent more would be $3.44. Clorox Green Works costs $3.49, which is four cents over the maximum. Have students work with partners to research the information Walmart requests from suppliers to obtain its Sustainability Index. When they are finished, ask students to report their findings to the class. To obtain a Sustainability Index for each supplier, Walmart asks questions that focus on four areas: energy and climate, material efficiency, natural resources, and people and community.

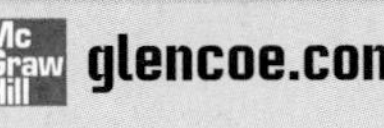

Activity Worksheet Send students to the Online Learning Center to download a Green Marketer activity worksheet.

Mini Project

Differentiated Instruction

Cooperative Learning Tell students that they are buyers for a large toy store. Students should conduct research to locate a new toy that they think will be especially popular next holiday season. Students should use a word processor to create a table that contains a list of questions they would ask potential suppliers of this toy. When students are finished creating their tables, they should exchange them with a partner. Each partner should evaluate the other's table for completeness, appropriateness of the questions, and correct spelling and grammar. Based on partner feedback, students should make any needed corrections. Students' tables should contain questions such as: What are your production capabilities? Do you have any references? What special services can you offer?

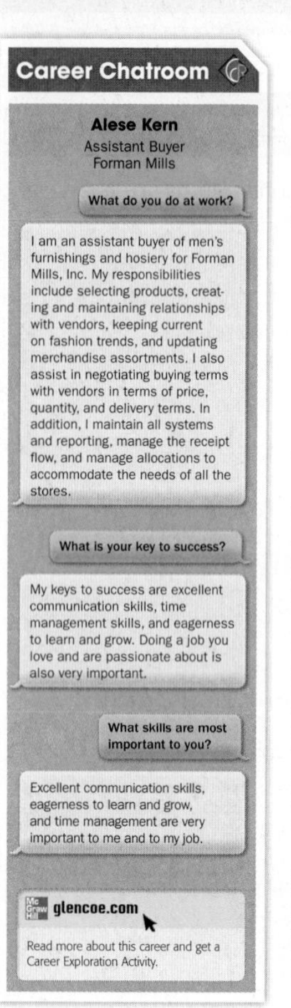
Career Chatroom

Alese Kern
Assistant Buyer
Forman Mills

What do you do at work?

I am an assistant buyer of men's furnishings and hosiery for Forman Mills, Inc. My responsibilities include selecting products, creating and maintaining relationships with vendors, keeping current on fashion trends, and updating merchandise assortments. I also assist in negotiating buying terms with vendors in terms of price, quantity, and delivery terms. In addition, I maintain all systems and reporting, manage the receipt flow, and manage allocations to accommodate the needs of all the stores.

What is your key to success?

My keys to success are excellent communication skills, time management skills, and eagerness to learn and grow. Doing a job you love and are passionate about is also very important.

What skills are most important to you?

Excellent communication skills, eagerness to learn and grow, and time management are very important to me and to my job.

glencoe.com

Read more about this career and get a Career Exploration Activity.

An invoice may be dated January 15 and include the following advance dating terms: 2/10, net 30, as of March 1.

In other situations, additional days may be granted for the discount (called "extra dating"). This special dating may be used to encourage a buyer to purchase new merchandise. In still another situation, the terms begin when the buyer's firm receives the goods, which is ROG dating (receipt of goods).

INTERNET PURCHASING

Business-to-business (B2B) e-commerce has revolutionized the purchasing function for businesses in the industrial and reseller markets. The volume of B2B transactions is much higher than all other types of online transactions combined. The main reason for this is that a lot more steps are involved in the manufacture of a product than in the sale to a customer. For example, a computer maker uses parts from several different suppliers, all of which require separate B2B transactions. However, only one transaction is needed to complete a sale to the customer. As a result, organizational buyers account for 80 percent of the total dollar value of all transactions conducted online.

The trend toward increased use of online buying is expected to continue. This is partly because organizational buyers have come to depend heavily on timely information from suppliers. Supplier information can be easily and quickly communicated via the Internet. Another advantage of online purchasing is that it dramatically reduces marketing costs for many types of goods and services.

B2B e-commerce transactions cover all aspects of a company's purchasing needs, from office supplies such as paper and staples to raw materials needed for manufacturing. Electronic procurement software and the Internet together make the process more efficient. Before e-commerce became possible, a company may have employed a large purchasing department to order supplies and other materials in person, over the phone, or through the mail. They would have to personally track and account for many individual purchases, which can result in errors and delays. Web-based systems make procurement simpler and more cost-effective.

Most companies have their own Web sites from which other companies may make purchases directly. Growing in popularity, however, are electronic exchanges where registered users can buy and sell their goods online. Most of these exchanges are in specific industries, such as Converge IT Product Procurement, an open market for electronic components, computer products, and networking equipment.

Another Internet purchasing trend involves online auction companies. An auction usually involves a seller setting an asking price and buyers trying to outbid each other. In other cases, a reverse auction takes place. In a **reverse auction**, companies post what they want to buy, and suppliers bid for the contract.

Purchasing online through third parties has both advantages and disadvantages. The biggest advantage is lower prices. However, as with most businesses on the Internet, privacy is a problem. Some companies fear that competitors will know how much was paid for materials and supplies.

In order to address privacy concerns, some companies, like Intel and General Electric®, began operating reverse auctions. GE expanded its trading process network (TPN) to serve other companies, and later sold the division to a private buyer, GXS, which services 70 percent of Fortune 500 companies.

Another problem with the online purchasing process, especially in a reverse auction, is that unknown companies could artificially deflate prices by bidding low prices. Such a practice would benefit buyers but cause bad relationships with suppliers.

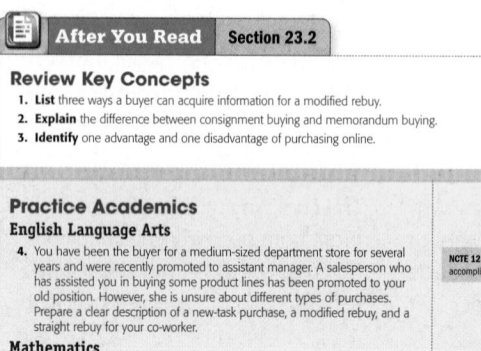

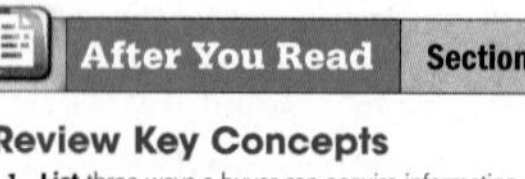

Review Key Concepts

1. **List** three ways a buyer can acquire information for a modified rebuy.
2. **Explain** the difference between consignment buying and memorandum buying.
3. **Identify** one advantage and one disadvantage of purchasing online.

Practice Academics

English Language Arts

4. You have been the buyer for a medium-sized department store for several years and were recently promoted to assistant manager. A salesperson who has assisted you in buying some product lines has been promoted to your old position. However, she is unsure about different types of purchases. Prepare a clear description of a new-task purchase, a modified rebuy, and a straight rebuy for your co-worker.

NCTE 12 Use language to accomplish individual purposes.

Mathematics

5. Vendor A sells 144 (1 gross) coffee bowls at $685.50 with free shipping. Dating terms are 2/10, net 30. Vendor A is offering a 2 percent discount on the cost of one gross. Vendor B's offer is $5.25 per bowl for one gross, with shipping charges of $25, and payment is COD. Which vendor is offering the better deal?

NCTM Problem Solving Solve problems that arise in mathematics and in other contexts.

Math Concept **Operations** Knowing which operations to use, and when to use them, is critical in problem solving.

Starting Hints To solve this problem, determine the discount applied to Vendor A by multiplying the total cost of the bowls by .02 to determine the discount. Subtract the value of the discount from the total cost to determine Vendor A's price. Multiply Vendor B's price by 144 to determine the cost for a gross of their bowls, and add the cost of shipping to determine the total price.

For help, go to the **Math Skills Handbook** located at the back of this book.

glencoe.com

Check your answers.

548 | Unit 7 · Distribution

Chapter 23 · Purchasing | 549

ELABORATE

Career Chatroom

Ask students these guiding questions.

Guiding Questions

Recall What are Alese Kern's most important skills?	communication skills, eagerness to learn and grow, time management
Infer What does managing allocations to meet needs mean?	It may be to keep track variations in the stores among needed merchandise

glencoe.com

Career Exploration Send students to the Online Learning Center to get a Career Exploration activity.

Graphic Organizer

To focus discussion on the advantages of business-to-business e-commerce, display this chart. Emphasize that B2B e-commerce has taken over organizational purchasing because it does an exceptional job of meeting the needs of organizational buyers. Have students research companies on the Internet that give examples of how they provide timely information, reduce market costs, and cover all areas of purchasing.

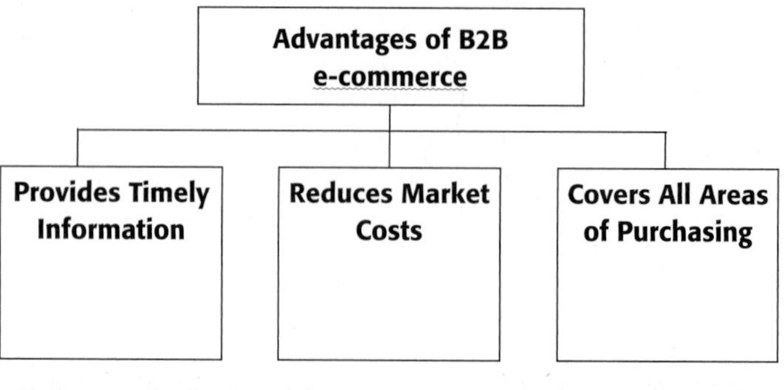

glencoe.com

Graphic Organizer Send students to the Online Learning Center to print this graphic organizer.

EVALUATE

INTERNET PURCHASING

Discuss that as e-commerce has grown, a number of services, including electronic exchanges and auction sites, have flourished. To encourage students to discuss Internet purchasing, ask these guiding questions.

Guiding Questions

Analyze Why are electronic exchanges growing in popularity?	They provide an efficient means for members of a specific industry to buy and sell goods.
Contrast How is a reverse auction different from a traditional auction?	Rather than suppliers offering goods and buyers bidding, companies post what they need and suppliers do the bidding.
Synthesize The textbook states: "… buyers have come to depend heavily on timely supplier information." What makes the Internet such a good resource?	Unlike other methods of updating supplier information, such as through phone calls or printed catalogs, Web sites can be updated whenever necessary, and changes appear immediately.

Mini Projects

Enrichment

Investigating the Advantages of Using an Electronic Exchange Have students imagine they are buyers for a large retail store such as a furniture warehouse or remodeling company. Students should research electronic exchanges to which they could belong. Have students choose the exchange that best meets their business's needs and write a report on the features it offers to retail buyers. Reports will vary depending on the business. For example, FurnitureNet offers access to 160 furniture makers in a single forum. FurnitureNet claims to help "reduce paperwork, data entry, errors, faxes, and phone calls while accelerating order processing to shorten delivery cycles."

Participating in Auctions To help students experience the auction and reverse auction, divide the class into two groups. Have one group decide on an item they want to buy and the other decide on an item they want to sell. Have each group conduct an auction. After the two auctions are completed, ask students to write a paragraph or two on each type of auction, describing their similarities and differences. Similarities: Both involve auctioning goods or services. Differences: In traditional auctions, suppliers offer goods whereas in a reverse auction, companies post what they want to buy.

After You Read — Section 23.2

Review Key Concepts

1. A buyer can acquire information for a modified rebuy by analyzing competition by comparison shopping, by analyzing current information found in trade publications or at trade shows, or by hiring the services of a resident buying office.
2. Consignment goods are paid for when they are purchased from the reseller. Memorandum goods are paid for when purchased from the supplier, but the price of unsold goods may be refunded to the reseller.
3. Advantages include timely supplier information, reduction of costs, and ease. Disadvantages include potential privacy issues and not being familiar with the company from which goods are being purchased.

Practice Academics

English Language Arts

4. New-task purchase: A purchase is made for the first time, possibly triggered by a formerly unrecognized need, a new manufacturing process, or an organizational change. This can be the most complicated buying situation. The buyer typically must locate a vendor, evaluate the product's quality, negotiate a price, and so on. Modified-rebuy: The buyer has had experience buying the goods or service, but some aspect of the purchase changes. For example, the buyer might need to locate a new vendor because the previous vendor is no longer carrying the needed product. Straight-rebuy: The buyer routinely orders goods and services purchased from the same vendor(s) as in the past.

Mathematics

5. Vendor A (Vendor A = $685.50 \times 0.98 = \$671.79$; Vendor B = $5.25 \times 144 + 25 = \$781$)

glencoe.com

Send students to the Online Learning Center to check their answers.

Chapter 23 Visual Summary

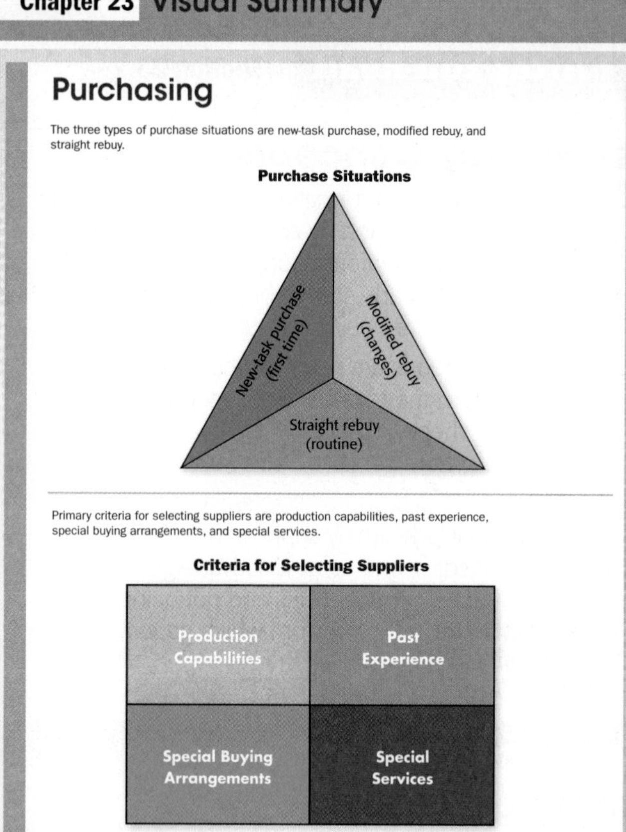

Purchasing
The three types of purchase situations are new-task purchase, modified rebuy, and straight rebuy.
Purchase Situations
New-task purchase (first time)
Modified rebuy (changes)
Straight rebuy (routine)
Primary criteria for selecting suppliers are production capabilities, past experience, special buying arrangements, and special services.
Criteria for Selecting Suppliers
Production Capabilities
Past Experience
Special Buying Arrangements
Special Services

Review and Activities

Written Summary

- Organizational buyers in industrial and resellers' (wholesale and retail) markets purchase goods in much greater quantities than the average consumer.
- Buyers for government markets make purchases of goods and services for one of the largest single markets in the world.
- The three types of purchase situations are new-task purchase, modified rebuy, and straight rebuy.
- The primary criteria for selecting suppliers are production capabilities, past experience, special buying arrangements (such as consignment buying and memorandum buying), and special services.
- The Internet has revolutionized purchasing in the industrial and resellers' markets.
- Online buying is expected to grow in the coming years.

Review Content Vocabulary and Academic Vocabulary

1. Use each of these vocabulary terms in a written sentence.

Content Vocabulary
- organizational buyers (p. 537)
- wholesale and retail buyers (p. 538)
- six-month merchandise plan (p. 538)
- open-to-buy (OTB) (p. 540)
- centralized buying (p. 542)
- decentralized buying (p. 542)
- want slips (p. 545)
- consignment buying (p. 547)
- memorandum buying (p. 547)
- reverse auction (p. 549)

Academic Vocabulary
- predicts (p. 537)
- technical (p. 537)
- evaluates (p. 545)
- journals (p. 546)

Assess for Understanding

2. **List** What are three titles for manufacturing or service business buyers?
3. **Identify** What type of planning is used to guide purchasing by organizational buyers and by resellers?
4. **Explain** What is a six-month merchandise plan?
5. **Justify** Why should chain stores use centralized buying?
6. **Contrast** What are the differences between the three types of purchasing situations?
7. **Create** What is a list of criteria you might use to evaluate suppliers?
8. **Decide** As the owner of an independent music store, will you use consignment buying or memorandum buying? Why?
9. **Consider** How would selling be different if the Internet could not be used?

EVALUATE

Visual Summary

Express Creativity Ask students to create a visual summary that illustrates a concept in the chapter. Encourage students to use different formats for their visual summaries, such as a Venn diagram, table, or poster. Visual summaries will vary depending on the concept depicted. Questions to ask when assessing a visual summary include:

- Is the summary clear, economical, and simple?
- Are any important steps or concepts left out?
- Are steps or concepts arranged in the same order as the original?
- Does the summary reveal a pattern that connects the details?
- Does the summary locate and highlight the most important information?

Review Content Vocabulary and Academic Vocabulary

1. **Organizational buyers,** such as **wholesale and retail buyers,** typically purchase goods in much larger quantities than the average consumer. Developing a **six-month merchandise plan** allows a buyer to establish a budget. The **open-to-buy** tells a buyer how much is left to spend. In an attempt to meet as many customer needs as possible, chain stores may use a combination of **centralized buying** and **decentralized buying.** If a customer asks a salesperson for an item the store does not carry, the salesperson may fill out a **want slip**. In **consignment buying**, goods are paid for only after the final customer purchases them whereas in **memorandum buying**, the supplier agrees to take back any unsold goods. When buyers post what they want to buy and different suppliers bid on the contract, a **reverse auction** is occurring. The buyer **predicts** what consumers will want in the future. Determining the materials required to make a specific product requires **technical** knowledge. A buyer **evaluates** want slips collected to help in determining what products to order. Many buyers keep **journals** on vendors.

EVALUATE

Assess for Understanding

2. Three job titles that describe people responsible for purchasing in manufacturing and service businesses are: purchasing managers, industrial buyers, and procurement managers.

3. Organizational buyers plan purchases by reviewing the company's master production schedule to determine purchasing requirements. Resellers plan purchases by establishing a six-month merchandise plan. In most cases, this plan is based on the previous year's monthly sales figures for the same time period.

4. A six-month merchandise plan is a budget that estimates planning for a six-month period. It contains figures such as last year's sales figures, planned sales figures, retail stock BOM, retail reductions, and purchases.

5. Centralized buying helps to create a unified image for the chain, merchandise can be transferred from one store to another where it is selling better, and quantity discounts can be negotiated due to large volume purchases.

6. In a new-task purchase situation, a purchase is made for the first time, possibly triggered by a formerly unrecognized need, a new manufacturing process, or organizational change. This can be the most complicated buying situation, because it involves a first-time purchase. In a modified-rebuy situation, the buyer has had experience buying the good or service, but some aspect of the purchase changes. In a straight-rebuy situation, the buyer routinely orders the goods and services purchased from the same vendor(s) as in the past.

7. Criteria that could be used to evaluate suppliers include: production capabilities, product quality, past experiences with that supplier, any special buying arrangements that are required, and special services that the supplier can provide.

8. Accept any answer for which the student provides appropriate reasons. An advantage to consignment buying is that the owner would only pay when goods were sold. However, suppliers generally only offer the consignment option under special circumstances, such as when introducing a new line of goods. In addition, problems can arise if merchandise is damaged, lost, or stolen. Memorandum buying has the advantage that the supplier will buy back unsold goods at a pre-established price; however, this price might be less than what the buyer originally paid.

9. Answers may include: supplier information would not be quickly and easily available online; purchasing would be more expensive because more time and labor would be involved; the ability to automate regular purchases through the Internet would not be available; buyers probably would not have access to as wide a variety of products as they do through the Internet.

Chapter 23 Review and Activities

21st Century Skills

People Skills

10. Supervisor as Teacher You are the supervisor of cashiers in a retail store. Today you observed one of the cashiers making mistakes keying in SKU codes when an item will not scan. When you asked her if she was having trouble keying in the codes, she said she was not having any trouble: "The customers like me to check them out fast, so if I make a mistake keying in all those numbers, I don't worry about it." Create a role-play script in which you explain the importance of correct SKU entry to this employee.

Financial Literacy Skills

11. Discounts and Profits You purchase computer components for resale at a trade discount of 40 percent. If you buy a monitor with a retail price of $450, what is your discount? What is your net cost? When you resell the monitor for $450, what will be your gross profit?

Everyday Ethics

12. Green Initiatives The eco-friendly, low-energy fluorescent bulb is replacing the standard light bulb. The European Union banned retailers from purchasing any more standard bulbs, so stores have hoarded them in stock. The fluorescents are more expensive. However, they use 80 percent less energy and last eight to ten years. Not everyone agrees with the EU's choice to ban the bulbs. Discuss with your class whether green initiatives should be mandatory.

e-Marketing Skills

13. Researching Web Sites Choose a product that you find interesting and might want to market in the future. Search out pages from at least six Web sites that look most interesting. Evaluate the pages, then describe what you believe are the best aspects of all of the sites you have reviewed.

Build Academic Skills

English Language Arts

14. Observing and Reporting You are a salesperson in a specialty clothing store. Over the past month, about ten people have asked about a line of clothing that your store does not carry. You have filled out several want slips and left them with the buyer. However, this new line has not been added to the store's stock. You feel sure that adding these items would increase sales. Write an e-mail message to the buyer stating why you believe adding these items would increase sales.

NCTE 12 Use language to accomplish individual purposes.

Science

15. Technology Investigate the ways in which technology is improving the coordination of products in supply chains. You may wish to research the use of Global Positioning Systems, Portable Digital Assistants, or tracking devices as they relate to supply chains. Share with your class one innovation you find interesting.

NSES A Develop abilities necessary to do scientific inquiry, understandings about scientific inquiry.

Mathematics

16. Calculate a Sales Total You prepare a purchase order for the following: 130 pants at $14.15 each, 58 pants at $16.99 each, 74 pants at $21.30 each, and 45 pants at $23.80 each. What is the total cost of the merchandise?

NCTM Problem Solving Apply and adapt a variety of appropriate strategies to solve problems.

Math Concept **Multi-Step Problems** When a word problem involves multiple steps, it is helpful to outline the information you know before you solve.

For help, go to the **Math Skills Handbook** located at the back of this book.

Standardized Test Practice

Directions Read the following questions. On a separate piece of paper, write the best possible answer for each one.

1. Planned retail reductions take into account:
   - **A.** Reductions in the selling price
   - **B.** Shortages of merchandise caused by clerical mistakes
   - **C.** Employee theft
   - **D.** Customer shoplifting
   - **E.** All of the above
2. A want slip must be completed before purchasing goods in a straight-buy situation.
   - T
   - F
3. The beginning-of-the-month and end-of-the-month inventories are indicated by the abbreviations ________ and ________.

Test-Taking Tip

If each item on a test is worth the same number of points, skip questions that are confusing, and then come back to them after you have answered all the rest of the questions.

DECA Connection Role Play

Buyer
Coat & Jacket Department

Situation You are a buyer for a local department store. While at market recently, you viewed a new line of jackets manufactured by a vendor that your store has not used before. The sample jackets are of high quality and excellent construction. The styling of the jackets reflects the latest in teen fashion trends. Everything about the jacket line makes you want to purchase them for your store. The jackets show every sign of becoming best sellers.

Store buying policy is that all new vendors must be reviewed before orders can be placed with them, and that the merchandise manager (judge) must approve all orders before ordering from a new vendor. You have informally asked other buyers about the vendor's reputation and determined that other buyers view the vendor as reliable, that samples reflect the actual quality of items, and that the vendor ships as promised.

You want to add these jackets to your fall merchandise purchases. You would like to purchase a limited quantity of several styles from the jacket line. Before doing so you must discuss the purchase with your merchandise manager (judge) to win approval for the purchase.

Activity You are to discuss this situation with your merchandise manager (judge) and persuade the merchandise manager that the jackets will be a wise and profitable purchase for your department and store.

Evaluation You will be evaluated on how well you meet the following performance indicators:

1. Explain the nature and scope of purchasing.
2. Place order/reorders.
3. Persuade others.
4. Select vendors.
5. Evaluate vendor performance.

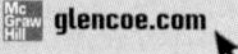

Role Plays Download the Competitive Events Workbook for more Role-Play practice.

EVALUATE

21st Century Skills

People Skills

10. Students should present a skit in which the supervisor emphasizes the importance of keying in the correct SKU code. The supervisor should explain that these codes are used to update the store's inventory. These inventory numbers are then used to automatically reorder product when the current stock gets below a certain level. If SKU numbers are incorrectly entered, the inventory will be off and replacement stock will not be ordered. This can lead to the store being out of some items that customers want. If the store cannot fill customer needs, they will go elsewhere, decreasing the store's sales and potentially leading to the necessity of reducing the number of employees.

Financial Literacy Skills

11. The discount is $180 (450 × .40), the net cost is $270 (450 × .60), and the gross profit is $180.

Everyday Ethics

12. Students should discuss the positives and negatives of banning retailers from purchasing standard incandescent light bulbs. Even though fluorescent bulbs are much more efficient and longer lasting, some consumers object to the higher cost. Opinions on whether or not it is the government's responsibility to force consumers and business owners to conserve energy and behave ethically is a matter of debate. Some people think it is vital that the earth's resources be conserved and that we owe this to future generations. Others believe that if people understand the consequences of their actions, most will make environmentally conscious choices, which is preferable to the government forcing regulations on its citizens. Some students may think it is acceptable for retailers to hoard incandescent bulbs because they are only responding to their customers' wishes. Others may think these businesses are behaving irresponsibly.

EVALUATE

e-Marketing Skills

13. Students should choose a product that they might want to market in the future and then evaluate six Web sites that offer the product. They should evaluate the sites and describe what they believe are the sites' best assets. For example, if they chose sites that sell tennis rackets, the sites might compare the brands each one offers. In addition, they might evaluate sites as to price and information provided on each racquet, such as size, the type of material used in the frame, the type of grip, and so on.

Build Academic Skills

English Language Arts

14. Students should write an e-mail to the buyer specifically stating why they think the store should add this new line to its stock. They might state that numerous customers have requested these items and, in fact, have told the salesperson they are going to other stores to purchase the clothing. Students also might say that they are concerned these customers will not return to their store in the future to buy other clothing.

Science

15. Answers will vary. Global positioning systems can be used to track entire orders so that both suppliers and purchasers know where a shipment is at any given time, exactly when it is expected to be delivered, and if there are any unexpected delays, such as weather issues.

Mathematics

16. \$5,472.12 (130 × 14.15) + (58 × 16.99) + (74 × 21.30) + (45 × 23.80)

Standardized Test Practice

1. E (All of the above)
2. False
3. BOM; EOM

DECA Connection Role Play

Evaluations will be based on these performance indicators:

1. **Explain the nature and scope of purchasing.** Organizational buyers purchase goods for business purposes and typically buy in large quantities. In manufacturing businesses, industrial buyers must review the company's master production schedule to determine what supplies are needed and when they are needed. Wholesale and retail buyers, on the other hand, purchase goods for resale. They must be able to forecast customers' needs and to decide how much of each item to purchase.
2. **Place order/reorders.** Students should be able to explain how a merchandise plan can help in estimating planned purchases for a six-month period. Buyers determine estimated sales figures based on the previous year's figures, adjusted to reflect the current-year sales goals. Buyers must then order enough stock to accommodate the planned sales volume.
3. **Persuade others.** Students should be able to persuade others to agree with them by clearly stating reasons for their points-of-view. For example, they should be able to persuade a buyer that the buyer ought to purchase items that customers have been requesting by explaining how doing so will increase company sales.
4. **Select vendors.** The key criteria for selecting a vendor include production capabilities, past experiences with that vendor, product quality, special buying arrangements, special services, and negotiated terms, such as pricing. It is vital that the buyer make certain the vendor is capable of producing the specified goods when needed. This is especially important in just-in-time production arrangements.
5. **Evaluate vendor performance.** Buyers must continually evaluate their vendors and the market as a whole to make certain that the vendors they are using are meeting the company's needs. They must make certain product is being delivered at the needed times, the quality and prices are acceptable, and so forth. If conditions change, such as competitors offering lower prices, the buyer must determine whether the advantages of switching to another vendor are worth any perceived disadvantages.

Mc Graw Hill **glencoe.com** 

Role Plays For more DECA Role Plays, send students to the Online Learning Center to download the Competitive Events Workbook.

stock handling and inventory control

SHOW WHAT YOU KNOW **Visual Literacy** Proper procedures for stock handling allow businesses to move products to customers in a timely and efficient manner. The receiving process is an important part of inventory management and control. ***How does the effective handling of stock relate to customer service?***

Discovery Project

Technology for Stock and Inventory

Essential Question How can technology improve stock and inventory procedures?

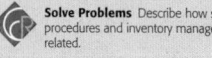

Project Goal

You are employed as a supply chain executive for a large retail chain that sells musical instruments. You have been asked to research a technology or technological process that could improve stock handling and inventory control for your firm. You will give an oral presentation about the technology to senior management for possible implementation.

Ask Yourself...

- How does technology affect stock handling and inventory control?
- What are the advantages of using a selected technology or process?
- What are the disadvantages of using a selected technology or process?
- How will you organize your oral report?

Solve Problems Describe how stock handling procedures and inventory management are related.

glencoe.com

Activity
Get a worksheet activity about stock and inventory.

Evaluate
Download a rubric you can use to evaluate your project.

DECA Connection

DECA Event Role Play

Concepts in this chapter are related to DECA competitive events that involve either an interview or role play.

Performance Indicators The performance indicators represent key skills and knowledge. Your key to success in DECA Competitive events is relating them to concepts in this chapter.

- Explain stock handling techniques used in receiving deliveries.
- Describe inventory control systems.
- Maintain inventory control systems.
- Motivate team members.
- Foster positive working relationships.

DECA Prep

Role Play Practice role-playing with the DECA Connection competitive-event activity at the end of this chapter. More information on DECA events can be found on DECA's Web site.

Chapter 24 · Stock Handling and Inventory Control | 555

ENGAGE

Visual Literacy

Read the chapter opener photo caption question to students: ***How does the effective handling of stock relate to customer service?*** Businesses must manage stock so that customers have the merchandise they want when they want it. Having too little stock results in lost sales and dissatisfied customers. Then ask these guiding questions.

Guiding Questions

Explain Recall a time when you went to a store to purchase a particular item, but the store was out of the item. How did you feel when the item was not in stock?	Encourage students to share their feelings about not being able to purchase the item when they needed it or about having to travel to another store to purchase the item.
Make a Judgment What kinds of reasons are given to customers when items are out of stock? Do you feel these are valid?	Reasons may include: shipment is late, supplier is out of the item, we forgot to reorder, and so on. Some may be considered valid—forgetting to reorder is not.

Discovery Project

Technology for Stock and Inventory Ask students the Discovery Project Essential Question: ***How can technology improve stock and inventory procedures?*** Answers may include: Technology can help keep track of the amount of stock and alert the buyer when particular items need to be reordered, thus keeping stock on hand for when customers need it. Ask students to discuss the importance of having a product when a customer wants it or needs it. Students should recognize that having the right product at the right time is one of the factors that keep businesses operating. If customers can't get what they need when they need it, they will take their business elsewhere.

glencoe.com

Discovery Project Resources Send students to the Online Learning Center to download a rubric to evaluate their projects.

ENGAGE

Introduce the Chapter

In this chapter students will learn the key functions involved in the distribution system of stock handling and inventory control. These main concepts are introduced and discussed:

- Steps in the receiving process of merchandise
- Inventory control
- Types of inventory systems
- Unit and dollar control of inventory
- Stock turnover
- Stock management
- Technology and inventory systems

Discussion Starter

Inventory Control Ask students to provide a definition for *inventory.* Inventory can include raw materials, parts purchased from suppliers, manufactured sub-assemblies, work-in-process, packaging materials, or finished goods. Now have students imagine that they have a business making homemade cookies to sell at local farmers markets. Ask: ***What items would you need to consider when developing a system to control your inventory?*** Answers may include: ingredients for the cookies, packaging materials, cleaning supplies, and so on. Ask: ***How would you ensure that you have all of the items you need when you need them?*** Students may suggest that for a business this size, a simple list of items on hand and a grocery list for items needed might be all of the inventory control they would need.

DECA Connection

Discuss the performance indicators listed in the DECA Connection feature. Explain to students that performance indicators tell them how to demonstrate their acquired skills and knowledge through individual or team competitive events.

glencoe.com

Competitive Events Workbook For more DECA Role Plays, send students to the Online Learning Center to download the Competitive Events Workbook.

PRINT RESOURCES

- **Student Edition**
- **Teacher Edition**
- **Student Activity Workbook with Academic Integration** includes worksheets and activities correlated to the text.
- **Mathematics for Marketing Workbook** provides math activities for every unit in the text.

TECHNOLOGY TOOLBOX

- **Connect**
- **ConnectPlus**
- **ExamView Assessment Suite** is a comprehensive solution for creating, administering, and scoring tests.

glencoe.com

Online Learning Center provides a variety of resources to enrich and enhance learning.

SECTION, CHAPTER, AND UNIT RESOURCES

- **Graphic Organizers** for organizing text concepts visually.
- **Digital Nation Activities** and **Green Marketer Activities** extend learning beyond the text features.
- **Career Chatroom Career Profiles** allow students to explore different marketing occupations in depth.
- **After You Read Answer Keys** for students to check their answers.
- **Discovery Project Rubrics** and **Marketing Internship Project Rubrics** for students to evaluate their projects.

PROGRAM RESOURCES

- **Student Activity Workbook with Academic Integration Teacher Annotated Edition** includes annotated answers for the activities and worksheets.
- **Marketing Research Project Workbook** provides a step-by-step approach for students to complete their own marketing research studies.
- **School-to-Career Activity Workbook** helps students relate their class work to on-the-job experience and involves work-site analysis and working with mentors.
- **Competitive Events Workbook** helps prepare students for state and national marketing education competitions.
- **Inclusion in the Marketing Education Classroom** provides teaching resources for working with students with special needs.
- **PowerPoint Presentations** provides visual teaching aids and assessments for this chapter.

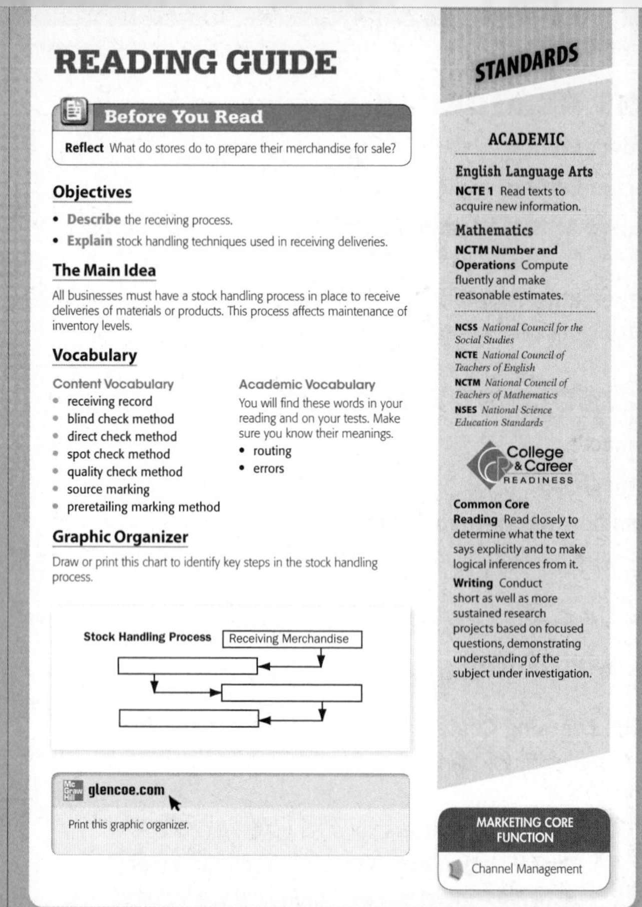

READING GUIDE

Before You Read

Reflect What do stores do to prepare their merchandise for sale?

Objectives

- **Describe** the receiving process.
- **Explain** stock handling techniques used in receiving deliveries.

The Main Idea

All businesses must have a stock handling process in place to receive deliveries of materials or products. This process affects maintenance of inventory levels.

Vocabulary

Content Vocabulary
- receiving record
- blind check method
- direct check method
- spot check method
- quality check method
- source marking
- preretailing marking method

Academic Vocabulary

You will find these words in your reading and on your tests. Make sure you know their meanings.
- routing
- errors

Graphic Organizer

Draw or print this chart to identify key steps in the stock handling process.

Stock Handling Process → Receiving Merchandise

glencoe.com

Print this graphic organizer.

STANDARDS

ACADEMIC

English Language Arts

NCTE 1 Read texts to acquire new information.

Mathematics

NCTM Number and Operations Compute fluently and make reasonable estimates.

NCSS *National Council for the Social Studies*
NCTE *National Council of Teachers of English*
NCTM *National Council of Teachers of Mathematics*
NSES *National Science Education Standards*

College & Career READINESS

Common Core

Reading Read closely to determine what the text says explicitly and to make logical inferences from it.

Writing Conduct short as well as more sustained research projects based on focused questions, demonstrating understanding of the subject under investigation.

MARKETING CORE FUNCTION

Channel Management

Section 24.1 Stock Handling

STOCK HANDLING

Manufacturing companies depend on suppliers to deliver parts or raw materials used in making finished products accurately and on time. When these parts or materials are delivered to the warehouse, plant, or store, they must be received into stock. Information about them must be recorded and tracked. For example, a door-handle manufacturer has a contract with an automobile assembly plant to supply door handles for pickup trucks. The manufacturer delivers door handles almost every day to keep pace with production at the assembly plant.

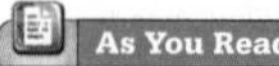

As You Read

Sequence What happens after a business receives the products it orders?

The parts or raw materials used in making finished products must be tracked just as retailers track the merchandise they receive. The steps in the stock handling process include receiving goods; checking them; marking them with information, if necessary; and delivering them to a place where they will be used, stored, or displayed for sale. The receiving clerk checks in the door handles at the truck assembly plant. He or she must make sure that the correct part has been delivered in the right quantity. This clerk must also be sure that the door handles get to the assembly line in time to be installed on the truck doors. The receiving clerk also records that information about the parts in the system. This ensures that inventory levels are correct and that the accounts payable department knows to pay the invoice from the door-handle manufacturer.

Incoming raw materials, parts, or merchandise are received, inspected, and recorded. ***Why is receiving stock or merchandise an important step in the stock handling process?***

556 | Unit 7 · Distribution

Chapter 24 · Stock Handling and Inventory Control | 557

ENGAGE

Anticipation Activity

Improving Student Achievement Tell students to imagine they are in charge of receiving shipments at a grocery store. Have them brainstorm how they might handle a shipment upon arrival. Verify that the shipment is complete, make sure nothing is broken, put prices on the items, and put the items in the store or in the storage area. Ask: ***Why do you think these steps are important?*** It is important to know if you received what you ordered and if it is in good condition, and to make sure the items are accurately priced before they are displayed or stored.

Objectives

- **Describe** the receiving process. Stock is received, checked, and, in retail settings, often marked with a price before it goes to the sales area. Raw materials are received, checked, marked with information, and delivered to be used, stored, or sold.
- **Explain** stock handling techniques used in receiving deliveries. Information about received goods is recorded manually or electronically.

Graphic Organizer

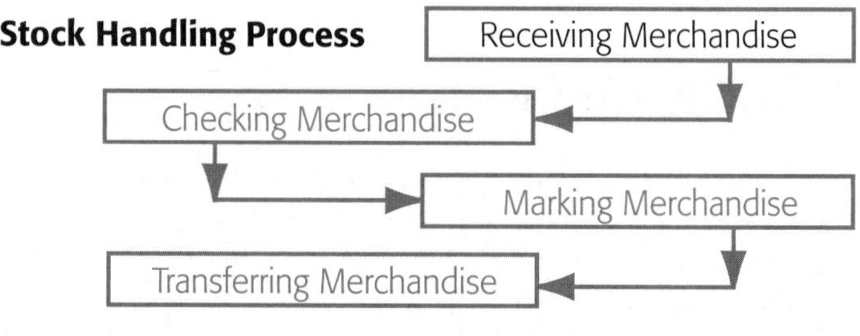

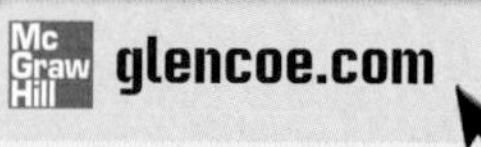

glencoe.com

iWB

Graphic Organizer Send students to the Online Learning Center to print this graphic organizer.

EXPLORE

Before You Read

Read the Before You Read question aloud: ***What do stores do to prepare their merchandise for sale?*** These activities include receiving merchandise that was ordered; checking orders for damages, quality, and completeness; marking or pricing the merchandise, if necessary; and displaying merchandise in a specific selling location within the store.

Preteaching Vocabulary

Have students go to the Online Learning Center at glencoe.com for the Chapter 24 Preteaching Vocabulary games.

Content Vocabulary

Have students write down each Content Vocabulary term and then write a prediction for what the term means or how it will be used in the section. Ask volunteers to read their predictions. receiving record—a form filled out when a shipment arrives and is checked; blind check method—writing down the items and quantities in a shipment; direct check method—checking off a shipment by looking at the invoice; spot check method—checking off a shipment by randomly looking at only parts of it; quality check method—carefully checking the workmanship of items in a shipment; source marking—marking an item's price before delivering it to the retailer; preretailing marking method—pricing information is marked in advance

Academic Vocabulary

Routing—Context Read the following sentences to students: "The apron includes the receiving number, the department number, and the purchase order number. It also includes terms on the purchase order and on the invoice, routing information, and the date the shipment was checked." Ask: ***What does the term*** routing ***mean in this context?*** It refers to the route the information should follow.

Errors—Synonyms Students are likely familiar with the term *errors.* Ask students to brainstorm a list of synonyms for the term. Display the list for the class to read. Answers may include mistakes, blunders, inaccuracies, or bloopers.

Reading: During and After Reading
Go to the Online Learning Center for a video clip in which a teacher models reading for her students and then has them practice what a good reader thinks about.

Stock Handling

STOCK HANDLING

Explain to students that efficiently and accurately handling stock can make or break a business. If stock is not handled properly when received, business owners will not know what stock they have on hand, which could jeopardize sales. Then ask students these guiding questions to focus your discussion on stock handling.

Guiding Questions

Identify What are the steps in the stock handling process?	1) receiving goods; 2) checking them; 3) marking them with information, if necessary; 4) delivering them to a place where they will be used, stored, or displayed for sale
Predict What might happen if a receiver does not accurately enter shipment information into the system?	Items might be reordered because they are not showing in the system; vendors might not get paid; customers might not receive their items.

As You Read

Read students the As You Read question: ***What happens after a business receives the products it orders?*** steps include in-store logistics such as receiving the merchandise, checking it for damages, and moving it for sale or storing it in a location within the store.

Visual Literacy

Receiving Merchandise Caption Answer Read the photo caption question to students: ***Why is receiving stock or merchandise an important step in the stock handling process?*** The receiving process is important to inventory control because it ensures that ordered stock or merchandise has been received, checked, and moved to a sales location. Improper receiving can lead to out-of-stock situations, inflated inventories, and financial losses.

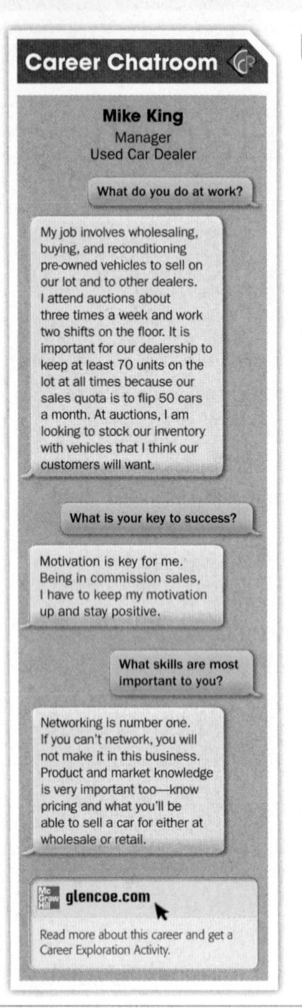
Career Chatroom

Mike King
Manager
Used Car Dealer

What do you do at work?

My job involves wholesaling, buying, and reconditioning pre-owned vehicles to sell on our lot and to other dealers. I attend auctions about three times a week and work two shifts on the floor. It is important for our dealership to keep at least 70 units on the lot at all times because our sales quota is to flip 50 cars a month. At auctions, I am looking to stock our inventory with vehicles that I think our customers will want.

What is your key to success?

Motivation is key for me. Being in commission sales, I have to keep my motivation up and stay positive.

What skills are most important to you?

Networking is number one. If you can't network, you will not make it in this business. Product and market knowledge is very important too—know pricing and what you'll be able to sell a car for either at wholesale or retail.

glencoe.com

Read more about this career and get a Career Exploration Activity.

RECEIVING MERCHANDISE

Stock or merchandise ordered by a business is received and checked. The store manager or owner should be aware of the shipping date and can prepare for receipt of the merchandise. In retail settings, the items are often marked with a selling price before they are transferred to the sales area. In larger businesses, several people might perform this function. In smaller businesses, a salesperson, manager, or even the owner may do this job. Retail chain stores often schedule weekly deliveries of ordered inventory to arrive at each store on a predetermined day of the week. Knowing when the merchandise will arrive can help in scheduling extra staff.

> **“Whether a business receives raw materials, parts, or merchandise for resale, it needs a process to handle the items.”**

FACILITIES

The location of the storage area for received products depends on the type and size of the business. Smaller businesses may use a backroom or may even place items in store aisles when they are received. Most businesses, however, reserve a specific area for receiving activities. These activities may include unpacking, pricing, assembly, and disposal of shipping materials.

Large businesses and chain stores sometimes have separate warehouses or distribution centers where merchandise is received and stored. Then it is taken to the department or branch store that needs it. Facilities such as these have large bays with loading docks that open at the height of the truck bed for easy unloading. Loading docks usually have covered or enclosed platforms to protect merchandise from weather damage.

RECEIVING RECORDS

A **receiving record** is information recorded by businesses about the goods they receive. The information can be recorded either manually or electronically. Hand-held laser scanners and imagers can capture signatures, take images, and read product codes. Mobile computers can capture images to document shipment damage and signatures to reduce shrinkage, or the loss of goods, at the receiving dock.

The amount and type of information recorded depends on the needs of the business. The information can include the following:

- A receiving number
- The person who received the shipment
- The shipper of the merchandise
- The place from which the goods were shipped
- The name of the carrier
- The number of the carrier
- The number of items delivered
- The weight of items delivered
- The condition of the goods received
- Shipping charges
- The department or store that ordered the merchandise
- The date the shipment was received

Each set of goods received is assigned a receiving number. Some businesses include this number on a record called an "apron." An apron is a form that is attached to the invoice that accompanies the goods received before they move through checking and marking. The apron system helps prevent duplicate payment of invoices because the invoice is only paid when the proper information is recorded on the apron.

The receiving number may be called an "apron number." In retail businesses, a store's buyer may prepare the apron. For example, Lydia buys scarves for a women's clothing shop. She prepares apron forms for a shipment of scarves when they arrive. These forms will travel with the scarves as they are inspected, priced, prepared for display, and placed on the sales floor. The apron lists the steps the scarves take to reach the selling floor. It includes:

- The receiving number
- The department number
- The purchase order number
- The terms on the purchase order and invoice
- **Routing** information
- The date the shipment was checked

CHECKING MERCHANDISE

Merchandise is checked to verify quantity and condition. Cartons are checked for damage and the goods are sorted and counted. Some businesses use specially trained employees called "receivers" to inspect and record newly arrived merchandise.

In the past, checking merchandise was a time- and labor-intensive process. Today, however, electronic data interchange systems minimize the time required for this process. For example, the door-handle manufacturer's distribution center can notify the truck assembly plant in advance with information about which cartons of door handles to expect each day and the contents of each carton. Upon receipt at the assembly plant, coded shipping-box labels are electronically scanned. This scan identifies the carton's contents, and the information is automatically transferred to an inventory management computer system.

METHODS OF CHECKING

Careful checking practices can save a business large amounts of money. There are four methods that are frequently used to check merchandise: the blind check, the direct check, the spot check, and the quality check.

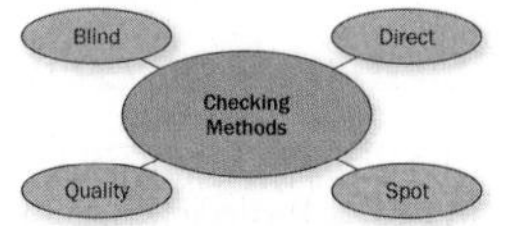

The **blind check method** requires the receiver to write the description of the merchandise, count the quantities received, and list them on a blank form or dummy invoice. The list or dummy invoice is then compared to the actual invoice after the blind check is made. The blind check method is considered the most accurate checking method, but it can be time-consuming. The blind check method is used when the merchandise needs to be moved quickly to the sales floor, and the actual invoice has not yet been received from the seller. Invoices often follow the shipment of goods by two or more days.

EXPLAIN

Expert Advice

Read the quote to students:

> **“Whether a business receives raw materials, parts, or merchandise for resale, it needs a process to handle the items.”**

Ask students: ***Could the same process be used to handle raw materials, parts, and merchandise?*** Yes, but different items would all need to be checked, marked appropriately, and delivered to where they will be used, stored, or displayed for sale.

Critical Thinking

Ask students: ***When an order for materials or products is received, what are some problems that might occur at delivery?*** missing purchase order or packing list, partial shipment, duplicate shipments, missing shipment, wrong item/model, or damaged merchandise

Career Chatroom 

Use these guiding questions to focus the discussion about the Career Chatroom feature.

Guiding Questions

Explain Why is motivation important for salespeople?	If they are commissioned, they have to be motivated to sell in order to get paid.
Analyze Why should a car salesperson network?	Networking involves talking to people, some of whom might want to buy a car.

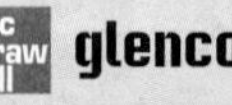
glencoe.com

Career Exploration Send students to the Online Learning Center to read more about this career and to get a Career Exploration Activity.

ELABORATE

RECEIVING MERCHANDISE

Ask students what they think might be involved in receiving a shipment of goods at a store. Students may suggest counting the items delivered or matching the items to the packing slip. Tell students that careful documentation must be part of the receiving process for a company to be able to track its merchandise.

Guiding Questions

Explain What information might be included on a receiving record?	a receiving number; person who received the shipment; shipper of the merchandise; place from which the goods were shipped; name and number of the carrier, number of items delivered; weight of items delivered; condition of the goods received; shipping charges; department or store that ordered the merchandise; date shipment received
Analyze Why might it be impractical to have an off-site storage area for a small business?	If a customer needs an item that is not on the store shelves but is in the storage area, the salesperson could not leave the store to retrieve the item and therefore might lose a sale. There would be an extra cost involved in renting an off-site storage area, and it would also cost extra to transport items to and from the storage area.

Critical Thinking

Have students think of some ways that receiving, checking, marking, and transferring merchandise would be handled on these products: flowers and plants; produce; seafood and red meat; and animals received in a pet store. Students should recognize that all of these products would probably need to be more closely inspected than some other products that are easier to check, such as packaged products.

Activate Prior Knowledge

Have students create a bulleted list of five costs that a business incurs from carrying inventory. cost of moving inventory in warehouse; cost of tracking receipts; overhead costs of warehouse where inventory is stored; insurance and taxes on inventory; physical inventory counting methods; shrinkage and obsolescence; return on investment ratio from holding stock

Graphic Organizer

Display this diagram. Ask students to name the four methods of checking merchandise. blind, direct, spot, and quality Write these methods in the center column of boxes. Then ask students to supply facts about each of the methods. Possible answers:

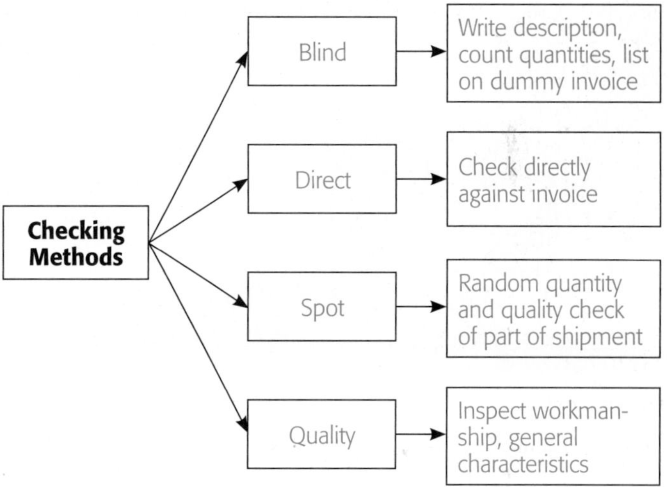

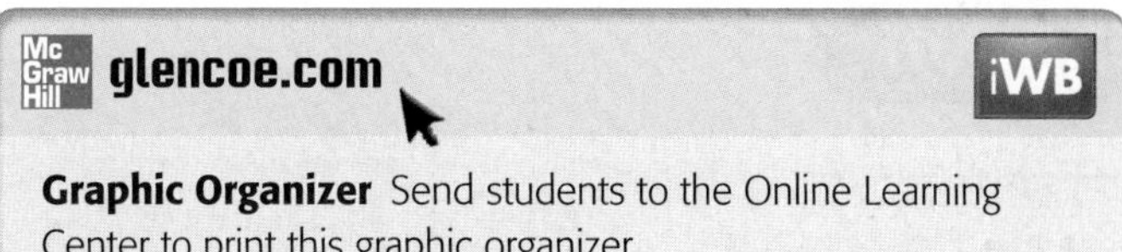

Graphic Organizer Send students to the Online Learning Center to print this graphic organizer.

VIRTUAL BUSINESS

PURCHASING

Introduce students to the concept of purchasing using Knowledge Matters' Virtual Business Retailing visual simulation, *Purchasing*. In this simulation, students will learn that purchasing inventory for a store is an important and complicated job.

MERCHANDISING

Introduce students to the concept of merchandising using Knowledge Matters' Virtual Business Retailing visual simulation, *Merchandising*. In this simulation, students will explore merchandising and its importance to store sales and profits.

With the **direct check method**, the merchandise is checked directly against the actual invoice or purchase order. This procedure is faster than the blind check method, but **errors** may not be found if the invoice itself is incorrect. Some receivers do not completely check the total number of items once they see the amount listed on the invoice. If the amount looks correct, they may not bother to take an actual count.

The **spot check method** is a random check of one carton in a shipment (such as one out of every 20). The carton is checked for quantity, and then one product in the carton is inspected for quality. When the contents are as stated on the invoice, the remaining cartons are assumed to be in the same condition. Spot checking is often used for supermarket and pharmaceutical deliveries.

The **quality check method** is done to inspect the workmanship and general characteristics of the received merchandise. Although a receiver can do a quality check, a buyer often performs this check. The merchandise is checked to determine whether the quality of the goods received matches the quality of the products that were ordered.

This type of check is usually done for products such as furniture and products with artistic value, such as vases and paintings. If the goods are damaged, a damage report is prepared. Damaged goods should not be discarded without the authorization of the supplier.

RETURNING MERCHANDISE

There are many reasons a business might return merchandise. In addition to damage, items can be received that were not ordered. Sometimes a decision to cancel an order was made after the items were shipped. Sometimes orders are delivered to the wrong client, too many or too few items are sent, or they arrive late. All incorrect items, damaged merchandise, and items ordered but not received are identified and reported according to the policies of the business. When this is done, the business can get proper credit or adjustments from the carrier or the seller.

Upon return of the merchandise, the seller issues a credit memorandum. A credit memorandum is notification that the buyer's account has been credited for the value of the returned merchandise.

The Blind Check

This method of checking merchandise is time-consuming, but is considered the most accurate. ***If this method is time-consuming and accurate, why must the merchandise still be checked?***

The Direct Check Method

This checking method checks merchandise directly against the actual invoice or purchase order. ***How can errors still occur with this checking method?***

MARKING MERCHANDISE

After it has been received and checked, merchandise must be marked with the selling price and other information. Different methods may be used for various kinds of merchandise. The most common method of marking merchandise is with a UPC barcode. However, a hand-operated pricing machine or pricing tickets can be used as well. Barcoding allows customers to spend less time when purchasing items at checkout.

Universal Product Codes (UPCs) are also widely used in business to monitor sales as they take place. Barcoding allows manufacturers and retailers to track merchandise and decide when to order more products or to reduce inventories. (See **Figure 24.1** on page 562.)

Barcode History First used commercially in 1967, the UPC barcode was invented in 1948 by Bernard Silver and Norman Woodland from the Drexel Institute of Technology.

UPCs originate with the Uniform Code Council (UCC). The UCC establishes and promotes standards for product identification and related electronic communication. Manufacturers pay an annual fee to the UCC for permission to use the UPC system.

Source marking is a method used by sellers or manufacturers to mark the price before delivering the merchandise to the retailer. UPCs are often used for source marking. Merchandise can then be moved directly from the receiving area to the sales floor. The UPCs are scanned at the checkout area, and the price stored in the computer for that code is entered for the sale. Many businesses receive goods that are preticketed with prices and UPCs.

Some businesses, such as American Apparel®, use a newer type of barcode on individual products in its distribution system and retail store network. These electronic product codes (EPCs) are also called Radio Frequency Identification (RFID) tags. EPC tags can send and receive data using radio waves. Item-level EPC tags have the potential to help retailers better manage inventory and improve accuracy at the point of sale.

EXPLAIN

Mini Project

Enrichment

Identify Criteria Divide the class into small groups. Then read the following scenario to students: You work for a manufacturer that ships products for domestic as well as international markets. Management has asked you to list criteria to consider when selecting a freight carrier to move its products to market and to help control the inventory. Ask: ***What criteria would you use to select a carrier? Work together with your group to create a list of criteria.*** Assess the places to which each freight carrier delivers, in order to make sure the manufacturer's products can get to wherever they need to go. Also, different freight carriers have varying price structures based on size of shipments, distance, number of destinations, and so on. Criteria for deciding which freight carrier could best help the manufacturer with inventory control include availability of computerized inventory tracking systems; electronic data interchange; and so on.

Visual Literacy

The Blind Check Caption Answer Read the caption question to students: ***If this method is time-consuming and accurate, why must the merchandise still be checked?*** There still has to be a record that shows whether the shipment is complete and in good condition. Then ask these guiding questions to focus a discussion on checking merchandise.

Guiding Questions

Analyze How can carefully checking shipments save a business money?	The business would not pay for items that they did not receive or that were not in good condition.
Predict Which method of checking do you think is used most often? Why?	direct check method—quick but does not check the entire shipment; spot check method—fastest, but entire shipment is not checked

ELABORATE

Visual Literacy

The Direct Check Method Caption Answer Read the photo caption question to students: ***How can errors still occur with this checking method?*** Errors can occur with direct checking if the invoice itself is incorrect. Ask students: ***Why might some receivers not completely check the total number of items once they see the amount listed on the invoice?*** They may trust their judgment—if the amount looks correct, they don't need to check everything; it may take too much time, which costs the company.

Graphic Organizer

Display this diagram. Point out to students that it is the responsibility of the receiver to determine whether a shipment is correct and whether it should be returned in part or in whole. Ask students to provide valid reasons for returning a shipment. Possible answers:

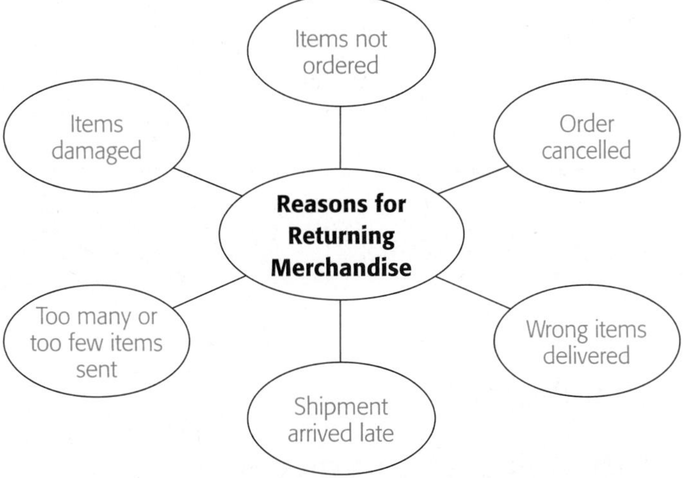

iWB

Graphic Organizer Send students to the Online Learning Center to print this graphic organizer.

Barcode History Have students research the history of the barcode to learn what it was used for initially. Ask them to research current uses for barcode technology.

MARKING MERCHANDISE

Ask students to think about a store where they shop. Ask: ***What type of marking does the store use?*** Universal Product Code or price tickets Ask: ***Which method do you prefer to use? Why?*** Answers may include: I prefer UPC pricing, because it is computerized and more efficient. Price tickets are more user friendly—the price is actually on the merchandise. Then ask these guiding questions.

Guiding Questions

Analyze Why might source marking be popular with small retailers?	It saves a business time and money to have prices already marked when the merchandise arrives at the store.
Compare and Contrast What are the differences and similarities of UPC marking and price ticket marking?	Price tickets are done manually, while UPC codes are computerized. UPC codes might be completed preretail, while price tickets are done in the store.

Graphic Organizer

Display this graphic organizer and discuss with students the different methods of marking merchandise and the benefits of each method. Sample answer:

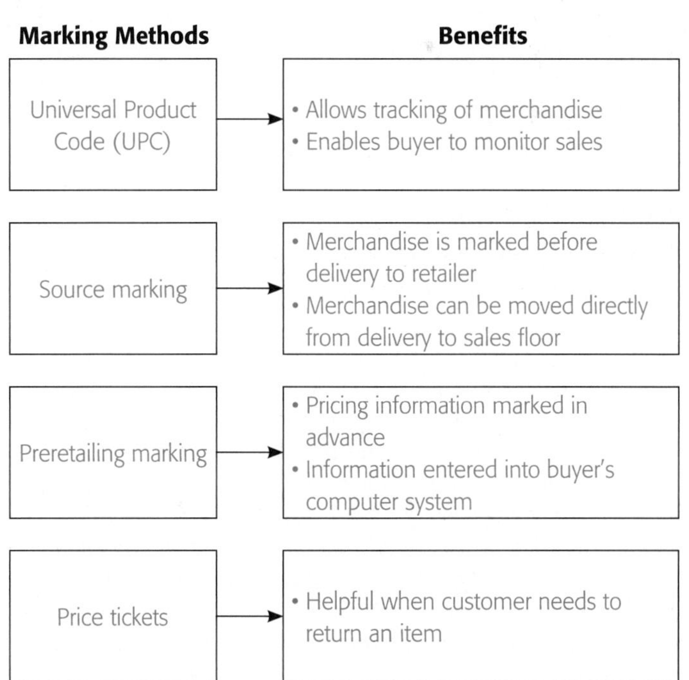

Marking Methods
Benefits
Universal Product Code (UPC)
• Allows tracking of merchandise
• Enables buyer to monitor sales
Source marking
• Merchandise is marked before delivery to retailer
• Merchandise can be moved directly from delivery to sales floor
Preretailing marking
• Pricing information marked in advance
• Information entered into buyer's computer system
Price tickets
• Helpful when customer needs to return an item

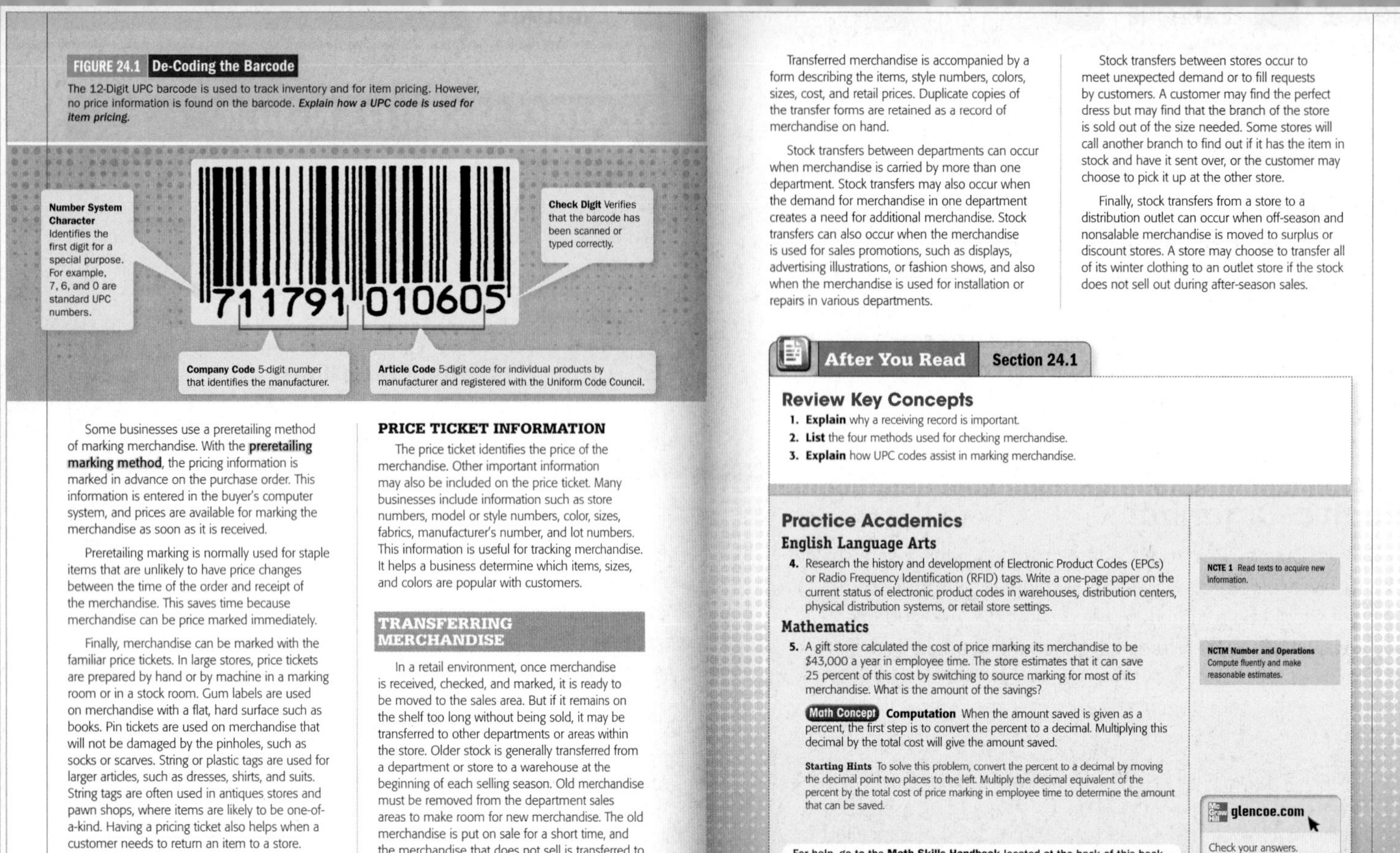

FIGURE 24.1 **De-Coding the Barcode**

The 12-Digit UPC barcode is used to track inventory and for item pricing. However, no price information is found on the barcode. ***Explain how a UPC code is used for item pricing.***

Number System Character Identifies the first digit for a special purpose. For example, 7, 6, and 0 are standard UPC numbers.
7 11791 010605
Check Digit Verifies that the barcode has been scanned or typed correctly.
Company Code 5-digit number that identifies the manufacturer.
Article Code 5-digit code for individual products by manufacturer and registered with the Uniform Code Council.

Some businesses use a preretailing method of marking merchandise. With the **preretailing marking method**, the pricing information is marked in advance on the purchase order. This information is entered in the buyer's computer system, and prices are available for marking the merchandise as soon as it is received.

Preretailing marking is normally used for staple items that are unlikely to have price changes between the time of the order and receipt of the merchandise. This saves time because merchandise can be price marked immediately.

Finally, merchandise can be marked with the familiar price tickets. In large stores, price tickets are prepared by hand or by machine in a marking room or in a stock room. Gum labels are used on merchandise with a flat, hard surface such as books. Pin tickets are used on merchandise that will not be damaged by the pinholes, such as socks or scarves. String or plastic tags are used for larger articles, such as dresses, shirts, and suits. String tags are often used in antiques stores and pawn shops, where items are likely to be one-of-a-kind. Having a pricing ticket also helps when a customer needs to return an item to a store.

PRICE TICKET INFORMATION

The price ticket identifies the price of the merchandise. Other important information may also be included on the price ticket. Many businesses include information such as store numbers, model or style numbers, color, sizes, fabrics, manufacturer's number, and lot numbers. This information is useful for tracking merchandise. It helps a business determine which items, sizes, and colors are popular with customers.

TRANSFERRING MERCHANDISE

In a retail environment, once merchandise is received, checked, and marked, it is ready to be moved to the sales area. But if it remains on the shelf too long without being sold, it may be transferred to other departments or areas within the store. Older stock is generally transferred from a department or store to a warehouse at the beginning of each selling season. Old merchandise must be removed from the department sales areas to make room for new merchandise. The old merchandise is put on sale for a short time, and the merchandise that does not sell is transferred to a warehouse or distribution center.

Transferred merchandise is accompanied by a form describing the items, style numbers, colors, sizes, cost, and retail prices. Duplicate copies of the transfer forms are retained as a record of merchandise on hand.

Stock transfers between departments can occur when merchandise is carried by more than one department. Stock transfers may also occur when the demand for merchandise in one department creates a need for additional merchandise. Stock transfers can also occur when the merchandise is used for sales promotions, such as displays, advertising illustrations, or fashion shows, and also when the merchandise is used for installation or repairs in various departments.

Stock transfers between stores occur to meet unexpected demand or to fill requests by customers. A customer may find the perfect dress but may find that the branch of the store is sold out of the size needed. Some stores will call another branch to find out if it has the item in stock and have it sent over, or the customer may choose to pick it up at the other store.

Finally, stock transfers from a store to a distribution outlet can occur when off-season and nonsalable merchandise is moved to surplus or discount stores. A store may choose to transfer all of its winter clothing to an outlet store if the stock does not sell out during after-season sales.

After You Read | **Section 24.1**

Review Key Concepts

1. **Explain** why a receiving record is important.
2. **List** the four methods used for checking merchandise.
3. **Explain** how UPC codes assist in marking merchandise.

Practice Academics

English Language Arts

4. Research the history and development of Electronic Product Codes (EPCs) or Radio Frequency Identification (RFID) tags. Write a one-page paper on the current status of electronic product codes in warehouses, distribution centers, physical distribution systems, or retail store settings.

NCTE 1 Read texts to acquire new information.

Mathematics

5. A gift store calculated the cost of price marking its merchandise to be $43,000 a year in employee time. The store estimates that it can save 25 percent of this cost by switching to source marking for most of its merchandise. What is the amount of the savings?

NCTM Number and Operations Compute fluently and make reasonable estimates.

Math Concept **Computation** When the amount saved is given as a percent, the first step is to convert the percent to a decimal. Multiplying this decimal by the total cost will give the amount saved.

Starting Hints To solve this problem, convert the percent to a decimal by moving the decimal point two places to the left. Multiply the decimal equivalent of the percent by the total cost of price marking in employee time to determine the amount that can be saved.

For help, go to the **Math Skills Handbook** located at the back of this book.

glencoe.com

Check your answers.

562 | Unit 7 · Distribution

Chapter 24 · Stock Handling and Inventory Control | 563

ELABORATE

Visual Literacy

Figure 24.1 Caption Answer Read the caption question to students: ***Explain how a UPC code is used for item pricing.*** UPCs are often used for source marking, a method used by sellers or manufacturers to mark the price before delivering the merchandise to the retailer. Merchandise can then be moved directly from the receiving area to the sales floor. The UPCs are scanned at the checkout area, and the price stored in the computer for that code is entered for the sale. Many businesses receive goods that are preticketed with prices and UPCs. Ask students: ***From a business perspective, what are some advantages of using UPC pricing?*** It saves the business the time of pricing each item individually. That time saved ultimately saves the business money. Then ask students: ***From a consumer standpoint, are there disadvantages to using UPC pricing?*** The UPC prices sometimes do not reflect any sales or discounts that the business may be offering. In such a case, the code has to be manually entered into the computer at checkout so that the correct price is reflected.

Mini Project

Differentiated Instruction

Kinesthetic Learners Cut construction paper into "price tickets." Distribute the tickets to students. Have students select an item within the classroom such as a backpack Then have students complete a "price ticket" for each item. Tickets should include information such as: price, store number, model or style numbers, color, size, fabrics, manufacturer's number, and lot numbers. Have students compare price tickets for the same items.

Price:
Store No.:
Model:
Color:
Size:
Fabric:
Manufacturer's No.:
Lot:

EVALUATE

TRANSFERRING MERCHANDISE

Ask students these guiding questions to direct a discussion on transferring merchandise.

Guiding Questions

Explain Why might merchandise be transferred between departments?	same merchandise is carried by more than one department; demand for merchandise in one department creates a need for additional merchandise; merchandise is used for sales promotions; merchandise is used for installation or repairs
Analyze Why is it important to move older, unsold stock off of the store shelves?	The space taken up by the older stock should be used to display new stock, which will likely generate more customer interest than the older stock.

Mini Project

Extension

Create Store Policies Ask students to imagine that they are in the process of opening a new store in their community. They realize that they need to set some store policies before they are up and running. Have students work together in pairs or small groups to determine answers to the following questions:

- What criteria would you use to select a shipping company to deliver your goods?
- Where would you store merchandise that does not fit on the store shelves?
- What information would you need on your receiving records?
- Which method of checking merchandise would you use?
- What return policies would your store have?
- How would your merchandise be marked—UPC or price ticket?
- What policies for transferring merchandise would you have?

Ask groups to share their answers with the rest of the class. Allow the class to ask questions for clarification. Groups should be prepared to offer a rationale for their answers if asked by the class. Answers will vary depending on the type of store students choose to discuss. Accept all answers that demonstrate an understanding of the concepts.

After You Read Section 24.1

Review Key Concepts

1. A receiving record describes the goods received by a business. It is important because it serves as a permanent record of delivery.
2. Blind check, direct check, spot check, and quality check are used for checking merchandise.
3. UPC barcodes allow the store to track sales and inventory levels. They also allow customers to spend less time at check out when purchasing items.

Practice Academics

English Language Arts

4. Accept all reasonable and complete responses that use proper grammar, mechanics, and are of proper length. The students must identify at least one application of electronic product code usage. Examples may include the use of RFID tags in warehouse management systems or distribution centers at the carton or pallet level. They should also be able to find examples of how UPCs are currently being used at the product or item level to better address ordering and product availability, assist with inventory control, speed check-outs at POS terminals, and assist with perpetual inventory systems.

Mathematics

5. \$10,750 (\$43,000 × 0.25).

 glencoe.com 

Answer Key Send students to the Online Learning Center to check their answers.

READING GUIDE

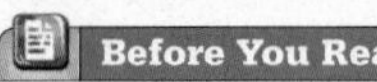

Before You Read

Connect Think about a time you went to a store, and an item you wanted was not available. How did you react?

Objectives

- **Describe** the process for providing effective inventory management.
- **Explain** the types of inventory control systems.
- **Relate** customer service to distribution.
- **Analyze** sales information to determine inventory turnover.
- **Discuss** technology and inventory management.

The Main Idea

Inventory owned by a business represents a capital investment until the products are sold. Effective inventory management and accurate inventory systems increase profits.

Vocabulary

Content Vocabulary

- inventory
- inventory management
- just-in-time (JIT) inventory system
- perpetual inventory system
- physical inventory system
- cycle counts
- stockkeeping unit (SKU)
- dollar control
- unit control
- inventory turnover
- basic stock list
- model stock list
- never-out list
- real-time inventory systems

Academic Vocabulary

You will find these words in your reading and on your tests. Make sure you know their meanings.

- complex
- authorized

Graphic Organizer

Draw or print this chart to take notes on inventory systems.

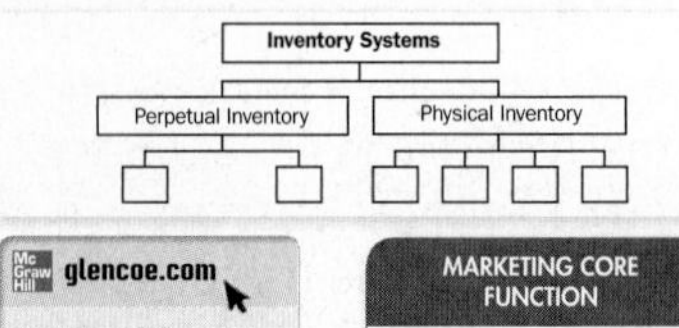

glencoe.com

Print this graphic organizer.

MARKETING CORE FUNCTION

Channel Management

STANDARDS

ACADEMIC

English Language Arts

NCTE 1 Read texts to acquire new information.

NCTE 12 Use language to accomplish individual purposes.

Math

NCTM Problem Solving Solve problems that arise in mathematics and in other contexts.

Social Studies

NCSS V B Individuals, Groups, & Institutions Analyze group and institutional influences on people, events, and elements of culture in both historical and contemporary settings.

NCSS *National Council for the Social Studies*
NCTE *National Council of Teachers of English*
NCTM *National Council of Teachers of Mathematics*
NSES *National Science Education Standards*

College & Career READINESS

Common Core
Writing Conduct short as well as more sustained research projects based on focused questions, demonstrating understanding of the subject under investigation.

m.e. Section 24.2 Inventory Control

INVENTORY MANAGEMENT

One of the major expenses of running a business is the purchasing of merchandise, or the items bought for reselling to customers. The amount of merchandise on hand at any particular time is known as inventory. The inventory managed by a business depends on the type of business. The business may be a producer (such as a farming enterprise), a manufacturer (such as an automobile company), a wholesaler, or a retailer. Based on the type of business, **inventory** can include raw materials, parts purchased from suppliers, manufactured sub-assemblies, work-in-process, packaging materials, or finished goods. Wholesalers' and retailers' inventories include all merchandise available for resale.

As You Read

Understand Why must businesses maintain proper inventories?

Inventory management is the process of buying and storing materials and products while controlling costs for ordering, shipping, handling, and storage. Inventory management is usually the responsibility of the supply chain manager. This person's job is to maintain just the right level of inventory to meet the supply-and-demand needs of a business. Having the wrong merchandise in stock, holding too many slow-selling items, or not storing enough fast-selling items are challenges faced by the supply chain manager every day.

Unnecessarily high inventories can create many problems for a business. In addition to using up storage space, personnel costs increase for security and warehouse staff, as do inventory insurance premiums, which may lead to increased interest expenses. Businesses can lose money, and profits may decrease.

> **"Products are purchased in large quantities to lower costs and ensure availability, but they must be stored until they are sold."**

DISTRIBUTION, INVENTORY MANAGEMENT, AND CUSTOMER SERVICE

The most important goal of any business is to meet the needs of its customers. Businesses must manage inventory so that customers have the merchandise that they want when they want it. Having too little inventory results in lost sales and dissatisfied customers. Every business must carry the desired products in sufficient quantities. Every business must provide quality customer service if the overall business is to be successful.

JUST-IN-TIME INVENTORY

A **just-in-time (JIT) inventory system** controls the flow of parts and materials into assembly and manufacturing plants. A JIT inventory system coordinates demand and supply so that suppliers deliver parts and raw materials just before they are needed for use. This system allows plants to keep only small stocks on hand to avoid tying up money and inventory space.

Electronic data interchanges (EDI) tell suppliers and transportation companies which items are needed and when to deliver them to meet production needs. Suppliers deliver parts on a schedule so they arrive just in time for use in the production process. A late shipment can bring an entire manufacturing operation to a standstill.

ENGAGE

Anticipation Activity

Improving Student Achievement Have students imagine they are managers of a restaurant. Ask: ***Why might it be challenging to track the inventory in this type of store?*** The variety and quantity of ingredients used in each menu offering cannot easily be scanned and tracked in a computer.

Objectives

- **Describe** the process for providing effective inventory management. controlling costs for ordering, shipping, storage
- **Explain** the types of inventory control systems. perpetual: constantly tracks inventory; physical: counts inventory visually
- **Relate** customer service to distribution. If orders are not filled and goods are not delivered, customers will not be happy
- **Analyze** sales information to determine inventory turnover. monitoring plans: basic stock list, model stock list, never-out list
- **Discuss** technology and inventory management. real-time inventory management connects applications, data, and users

Graphic Organizer

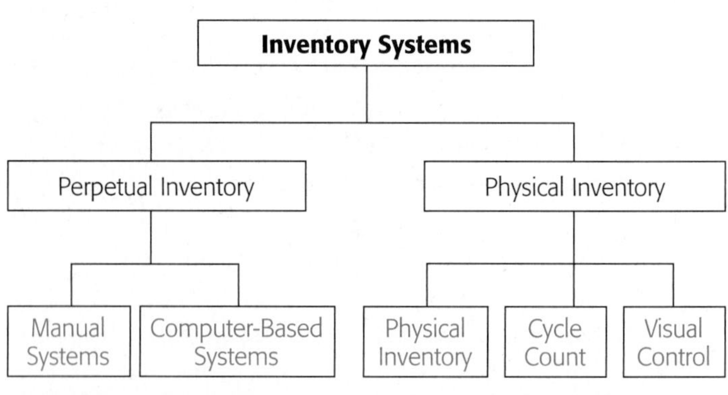

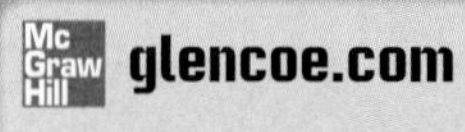

Graphic Organizer Send students to the Online Learning Center to print this graphic organizer.

EXPLORE

Before You Read

Read the Before You Read question aloud: ***Think about a time you went to a store, and an item you wanted was not available. How did you react?*** Students will likely express a range of emotions including frustration, unhappiness, and disappointment because the item they wanted to purchase was unavailable. Ask: ***Would this incident cause you to reconsider doing business at that store? Why or why not?*** Some students might be annoyed by the inconvenience and cost (time, money, gas) to go to a store and not find what they wanted.

Preteaching Vocabulary

Have students go to the Online Learning Center at glencoe.com for the Chapter 24 Preteaching Vocabulary games.

Content Vocabulary

Have students work together to create flashcards of the Content Vocabulary terms. Students should write each term on the front of a card or small piece of paper and write the definition on the back. Then have pairs use the cards to quiz each other.

Academic Vocabulary

Complex—Synonyms Display the term *complex* for the class to read. Ask students to supply synonyms for the term. Display the list. Synonyms may include: difficult, complicated, and intricate. Then ask volunteers to use the term in a sentence. It was difficult to attach the new screen door because of the *complex* directions supplied by the manufacturer. The *complex* workings of human anatomy boggle my mind.

Authorized—Context Display this sentence for the class to read: The city authorized the building of a new parking lot. Ask students to define the term *authorized* based on its use in this sentence. Answers should include approved, endorsed, granted permission for, or allowed.

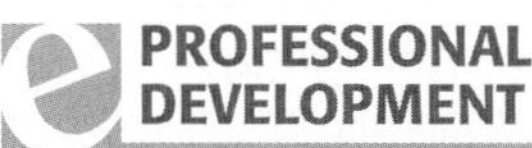

ELL: Using Manipulatives
Go to the Online Learning Center to view a video clip in which students use manipulatives to model a problem and clarify content concepts.

Inventory Control

INVENTORY MANAGEMENT

Ask these guiding questions to focus the discussion about inventory management.

Guiding Questions

Analyze What problems might be caused by having too much inventory on hand?	uses up storage space, increases costs for security and warehouse personnel, increases inventory insurance premiums, can increase interest expenses
Predict What might happen if a company had too many slow-selling items and not enough fast-selling items in its inventory?	The business might not have on hand what the customers really want and therefore might lose business.

As You Read

Read students the As You Read question: ***Why must businesses maintain proper inventories?*** businesses need inventory so that customers have the merchandise they want when they want it.

Expert Advice

Read the quote to students:

> **“Products are purchased in large quantities to lower costs and ensure availability, but they must be stored until they are sold.”**

Ask students: ***For what kinds of stores might purchasing and storing large quantities be a negative rather than a positive?*** independent stores that cannot afford to purchase large quantities; small stores with limited storage space

DIGITAL NATION

Netflix: Success in the Long Tail

Traditional retailers need a high inventory-turnover rate to stay in business. But innovative online businesses such as Netflix.com, a DVD rental service, make money by stocking both popular *and* unpopular items. How do they do it?

Niche Products Mean Profit

Netflix® offers more than 100,000 movie titles, including little-known and less-popular films. Because Netflix offers so many movies, the combined demand for those "unpopular" items makes up a large portion of its revenue. By making specialty movies available, Netflix helps more viewers discover them. This, in turn, allows these movies to gain a larger audience and become more popular. Consumer demand for a wide range of specialty items, rather than a narrow range of best sellers, is known in marketing as *the long tail.*

English Language Arts

Imagine that you are running a local DVD/CD rental store. What could you do to compete with Netflix? Write a paragraph with your ideas that includes ideas for stocking.

NCTE 12 Use language to accomplish individual purposes.

glencoe.com 

Get a Digital Nation activity.

QUICK RESPONSE DELIVERY

Quick response delivery (QRD) systems apply just-in-time principles to retailers. Sometimes retailers allow manufacturers or vendors to manage their inventory by sharing point-of-sale information. QRD programs shorten the time between when a product is made, distributed, and sold by letting the suppliers stock and reorder merchandise. Quick response programs assure that merchandise is restocked to correct levels at precisely the time when the additional stock is needed. This helps retail businesses avoid out-of-stock situations and reduce inventory holding costs.

CHALLENGES OF INVENTORY MANAGEMENT

Inventory management is **complex** because a business has to correctly anticipate demand for its products. At the same time, a business has to keep overall inventory investment as low as possible.

Retail businesses are expected to do the following:

- Maintain the right quantities of merchandise without running out of stock.
- Keep a wide product assortment (with low investment) without compromising customer needs and wants.
- Purchase merchandise at large volumes to gain the lowest prices while not buying more than it will sell.
- Pay attention to what customers are buying and what they are not buying.
- Keep a current inventory on hand.

Good inventory management balances the costs of maintaining a large inventory with the benefits of maintaining a large inventory. The costs of inventory include not only the cost of the items in stock but also the costs of storage, insurance, and taxes. Inventory ties up working capital, which is money that could be used for other purposes. It is not effective for a company to maintain large inventory holdings if money could be spent more effectively to benefit the business somewhere else. Effective inventory management helps increase working capital and allows a business to pay for other business expenses.

Reading Check

Contrast How is just-in-time inventory different from quick response delivery?

Depending on the type of business, inventory can represent raw materials, parts, work-in-progress, sub-assemblies, and finished goods. ***Why is inventory control so important?***

INVENTORY SYSTEMS

Two methods of tracking inventory are the perpetual inventory system and the physical inventory system.

PERPETUAL INVENTORY SYSTEM

A **perpetual inventory system** tracks the number of items in inventory on a constant basis. The system tracks all new items purchased and returned, as well as sales of current stock. An up-to-date count of inventory is maintained for purchases and returns of merchandise, sales and sales returns, sales allowances, and transfers to other stores and departments. Reordering and restocking items whenever quantities become low can help avoid loss of sales. This system tracks sales and other transactions as they occur.

MANUAL SYSTEMS

In a manual system, employees gather paper records of sales and enter that information into the inventory system. These records can include receiving department records, sales checks, price tickets, cash register receipts, stock transfer requests, and other documents used for coding and tabulation.

Employees use computer-generated merchandise tags are used to record information about the vendor, date of receipt, department, product classification, price, color, size, and style. The merchandise tags from items sold are sent in batches to a company-owned tabulating facility or to an independent computer service organization. Here, the coded information is analyzed through the use of computer software.

COMPUTER-BASED SYSTEMS

Computer-based systems for controlling inventory are increasingly popular, even among smaller businesses. They are also faster and more accurate than manual systems. Employees at a point-of-sale terminal use hand-held laser guns, stationary lasers, light pens, or slot scanners. These feed sales transaction data directly from Universal Product Codes (UPCs), sales checks, or merchandise tags into a computer. Businesses then print the information for review and action.

Electronic Data Interchange (EDI) involves computer-to-computer information exchanges and relays of sales information directly to a supplier. The supplier uses the sales transaction data to ship additional items automatically.

WMS The use of headsets allows employees to keep both of their hands free for other warehouse tasks.

EXPLAIN

DIGITAL NATION

English Language Arts Answer Read the English Language Arts/Writing Activity to students: Imagine that you are running a local DVD/CD rental store. ***What could you do to compete with Netflix®?*** You could stock less-popular titles, as Netflix does. You could charge less per DVD/CD than Netflix, since your customers do not have to pay for postage. You could advertise that your customers can get their movies right away, rather than waiting for them to arrive in the mail.

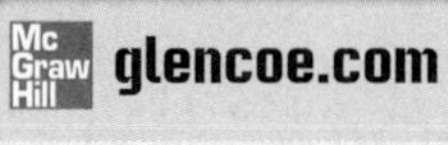

Worksheet Activity Send students to the Online Learning Center to get a Digital Nation worksheet activity.

Activate Prior Knowledge

Barcodes In the previous section, students learned about Universal Product Codes (UPC), or barcodes. Ask: ***Why are barcodes so important in today's business environment?*** They allow sales transaction data to be fed directly into a computer for efficient record-keeping and inventory control. They allow manufacturers and retailers to track merchandise and decide when to order more products or when to reduce inventories.

Reading Check Answer

Read the Reading Check question to students: ***How is just-in-time inventory different from quick response delivery?*** Just-in-time inventory systems control the flow of parts and materials into assembly and manufacturing plants. Quick response delivery applies just-in-time principles to retailers.

ELABORATE

Visual Literacy

Inventory Control Caption Answer Read the caption question to students: ***Why is inventory control so important?*** The purpose behind inventory control is to maintain just the right level of inventory to meet the supply-and-demand needs of a business. Having the wrong merchandise in stock, holding too many slow-selling items, or not storing enough fast-selling items can cost the business money. Unnecessarily large inventories can also cause the company to lose money. Having too little inventory can result in lost sales and dissatisfied customers.

INVENTORY SYSTEMS

Tell students that tracking inventory is extremely important for both big and small businesses. There are tracking systems available that will fit the budget of any business. Then ask these guiding questions to focus the discussion on inventory systems.

Guiding Questions

Describe What are the perpetual inventory system and the physical inventory system?	Perpetual: tracks the number of items in inventory on a constant basis. Physical: stock is visually inspected or actually counted to determine the quantity on hand.
Compare and Contrast What are the similarities and differences between manual and computer-based inventory systems?	Both systems collect inventory data from sales checks and merchandise tags, both use computers to analyze the data collected. Manual systems collect paper records and other information to be entered into the inventory system; computer-based systems use computer input devices

WMS Have students research Warehouse Management Systems and create a two-column list of pros and cons. If possible, have them interview workers at a local business that uses WMS. Have students add the workers' opinions to the list of pros and cons.

Mini Projects

Enrichment

Manual Inventory Systems To help students better understand what goes into tracking inventory, divide the class into pairs and have pairs work together to inventory the items in your classroom. Students should manually write down a description of each item (teacher desk, chair, student desks, textbooks, and so on) and the quantity of each item. Then have students enter the information into a computer spreadsheet application. Finally, have students analyze the information collected. Are there enough of each item? Are there too many? Ask students to share their results with the class.

Computer-Based Inventory Systems Have students visit a local store that uses a scanning process at checkout. Have students talk with a store manager or owner and ask him or her to explain the scanning process. Students might ask questions such as: What information does the scanner collect? Is it tied to inventory control? Does it automatically order items that are low in stock? Have students write a one-page report of their findings to share with the class. Reports should be well-written and free of grammar and spelling errors.

Critical Thinking

Discuss with students the advantages of paperless operations to inventory management controls and timely and accurate inventory records. Remind students that there are a number of possible ways to monitor inventory including the use of UPC data, receiving records, sales checks, price tickets, cash register receipts, stock transfer records, and so on. Ask: ***Why are paperless processes important in today's business environment?*** They simplify file systems and reduce file space. They are cost-effective because they save on paper, paper storage, and document removal. They also allow a business to easily project an environmentally friendly image.

PHYSICAL INVENTORY SYSTEM

Under a physical inventory system, information about stock levels is not continually maintained. A **physical inventory system** is an inventory system in which stock is visually inspected or actually counted to determine the quantity on hand.

Inventory data can be captured in many ways, from high-tech methods to manual counts. Some of the most popular methods for larger retailers are scanned bar codes and keypad entry onto hand-held devices.

For most businesses, the process of identifying and counting all items is time consuming. Therefore, inventory is usually counted when the quantity of merchandise is at its lowest point.

Even if a perpetual inventory system is used, physical inventories are still conducted periodically or on a regular annual basis. A physical inventory allows a business to calculate its income tax, determine the correct value of its ending inventory, identify any stock shortages, and plan future purchases. There are several methods used.

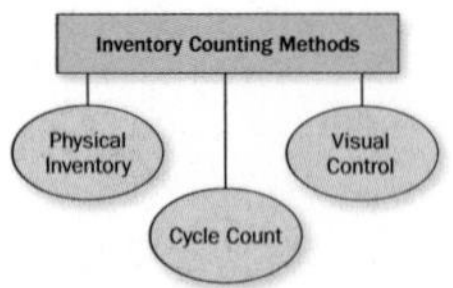

INVENTORY COUNTING METHODS

To count inventory, businesses often use a combination of methods. A business can have its regular employees count the inventory, or the process can be conducted by an outside inventory service company. Major national retailers typically have thousands of items stocked in many different locations around the country. These large chains of stores tend to use outside companies, such as Washington Inventory Services, RGIS, or smaller regional or local firms. After the counting is completed, the total value of the inventory is then determined. This value is reported on the business's financial statements.

PHYSICAL INVENTORY METHOD

The most popular method of inventory management is to physically count the inventory. Most businesses do this once a year. Others do this on a semiannual, quarterly, or more frequent basis. Inventory clerks usually work in pairs. One counts merchandise, while the other one records the count. Physical inventories are usually wall-to-wall store inventories, which often require that the business close temporarily to conduct the inventory.

CYCLE COUNT METHOD

Many businesses use cycle counts either in combination with an annual physical inventory or alone to track inventory. **Cycle counts** involve a portion of the inventory being counted each day by stockkeeping units so that the entire inventory is accounted for on a regular basis. With this method, the entire inventory is never counted at one time.

A **stockkeeping unit (SKU)** is coded information for a specific product used for inventory control. Each product has a unique series of numbers and letters embedded in the code. For example 59G10-1 may be a code for specific shirt. The 59 may represent the brand, the "G" is the color green, the "10" is the size, and the "1" is the season. Businesses develop their own codes based on the information they need for inventory control purposes.

A variation of the cycle method is used by manufacturers' representatives when they visit a business on a regular basis, take the stock count, and write a new order. Unwanted merchandise is removed from stock and returned to the manufacturer through a predetermined, **authorized** procedure.

VISUAL CONTROL METHOD

Visual control is a method used to monitor physical inventory levels. Smaller businesses place stock cards on pegboards with stock number information and descriptions for each item displayed. The stock cards specify the number of each item to be kept in stock. This method can be inaccurate because it does not account for misplaced merchandise. The amount to reorder is the difference between the number on hand and the specified number to be stocked. The number to stock may be an estimate of sales for a typical period of time.

TRENDS IN INVENTORY METHODS

As businesses become increasingly competitive, more efficient and effective inventory management methods will be developed. This will surely include recording inventories by using SKU or UPC codes, greater use of technology in taking inventories, increased use and frequency of cycle counts by SKU, increased use of Internet technologies to link with vendors, and increased vendor participation.

Most businesses use both systems. The perpetual system gives an up-to-date inventory record throughout the year. The physical system gives an accurate count that can be compared to the perpetual records to identify any errors or problems.

The perpetual inventory records help the business track sales and manage its merchandise. After a physical inventory is taken, the ending inventory amount becomes the beginning inventory for the year that follows. Purchases by the business during the year are added to this amount, while sales are subtracted. Ending inventory is calculated in the example that follows:

Number of Items for 1/1/20_ _ to 6/30/20_ _		
Beginning inventory, 1/1/20_ _		1,000
Net purchases (purchases less purchases and allowances returned)	+ 300	
Merchandise available for sale		1,300
Less net sales (sales less returns and allowances)	− 1,050	
Ending inventory, 6/30/20_ _		250

Sometimes, the ending inventory shown in the perpetual inventory system does not match the physical count of inventory. When the physical count shows less merchandise than is supposed to be in inventory, a stock shortage or shrinkage has occurred. Theft, receiving errors, incorrect counting, and selling errors can cause shortages for a business.

In the example, the ending inventory figure of 250 items is the perpetual inventory. It is possible that this is not the most accurate count. If the physical inventory system showed ending inventory of 225, a stock shortage of 25 would have occurred. It is not until the physical inventory is taken that the company really knows if its ending inventory records are correct. The perpetual inventory can be used as an estimation.

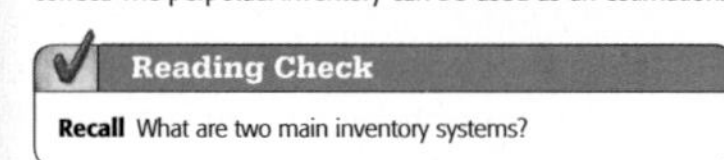

Reading Check

Recall What are two main inventory systems?

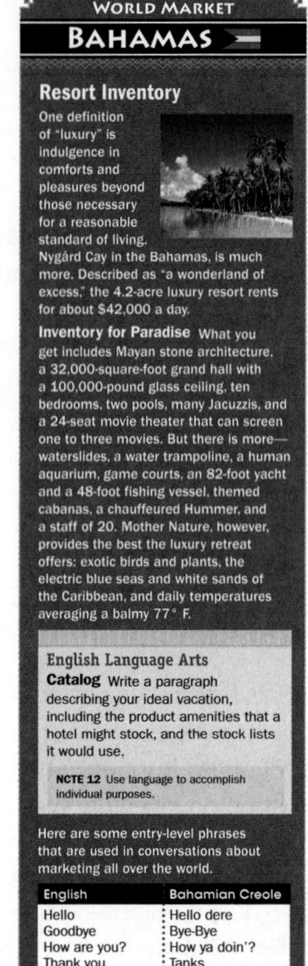

WORLD MARKET

BAHAMAS

Resort Inventory

One definition of "luxury" is indulgence in comforts and pleasures beyond those necessary for a reasonable standard of living. Nygård Cay in the Bahamas, is much more. Described as "a wonderland of excess," the 4.2-acre luxury resort rents for about $42,000 a day.

Inventory for Paradise What you get includes Mayan stone architecture, a 32,000-square-foot grand hall with a 100,000-pound glass ceiling, ten bedrooms, two pools, many Jacuzzis, and a 24-seat movie theater that can screen one to three movies. But there is more—waterslides, a water trampoline, a human aquarium, game courts, an 82-foot yacht and a 48-foot fishing vessel, themed cabanas, a chauffeured Hummer, and a staff of 20. Mother Nature, however, provides the best the luxury retreat offers: exotic birds and plants, the electric blue seas and white sands of the Caribbean, and daily temperatures averaging a balmy 77° F.

English Language Arts

Catalog Write a paragraph describing your ideal vacation, including the product amenities that a hotel might stock, and the stock lists it would use.

NCTE 12 Use language to accomplish individual purposes.

Here are some entry-level phrases that are used in conversations about marketing all over the world.

English	Bahamian Creole
Hello	Hello dere
Goodbye	Bye-Bye
How are you?	How ya doin'?
Thank you	Tanks
You're welcome	Ya're wery velcome

EXPLAIN

PHYSICAL INVENTORY SYSTEM

Ask these guiding questions to focus student discussion.

Guiding Questions

Identify What are three inventory counting systems?	physical inventory, cycle count, and visual control
Similarities and Differences How are perpetual inventory systems and physical inventory systems alike? How are they different?	Both types of systems track the number of items in inventory, both can be manual or computer-based; Perpetual inventory systems constantly track inventory; Physical inventory systems track inventory periodically

Graphic Organizer

Display this diagram. Ask students to describe the three inventory counting systems. Possible answers:

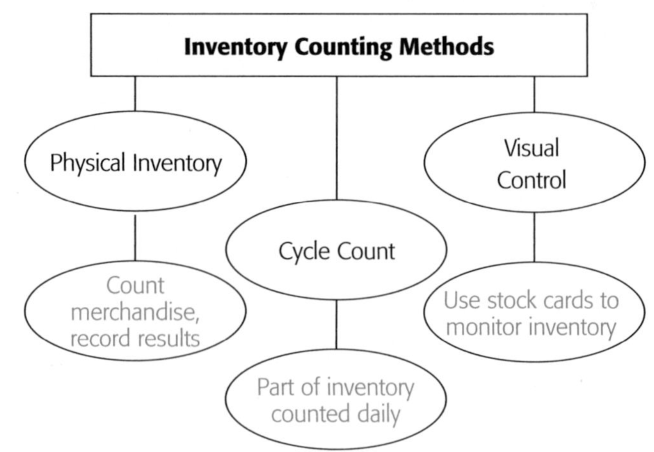

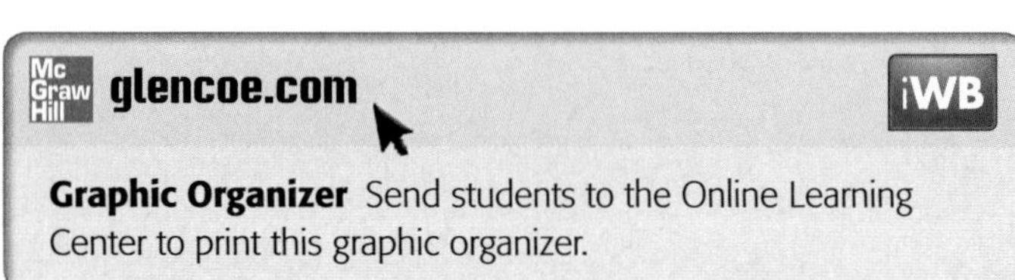

glencoe.com

iWB

Graphic Organizer Send students to the Online Learning Center to print this graphic organizer.

ELABORATE

Graphic Organizer

Display this table. Have pairs work together to generate a list of types of goods that each of these types of businesses would keep in their inventory. Possible answers:

Manufacturing	Wholesaling	Retailing	Service	Extraction
• raw materials • parts purchased from suppliers • work-in-process	• finished goods • packaging materials	• finished goods • packaging materials	• finished goods • amenities	• machinery • tools

 **glencoe.com** 

Graphic Organizer Send students to the Online Learning Center to print this graphic organizer.

Mini Project

Extension

Research Barcodes Remind students that barcodes are used not just to scan merchandise at the checkout counter, but also to track inventory. Have students research to learn what the 13 numbers in a barcode represent. Then ask them to create a visual representation of the information they gather. The first two digits give country information. The next five digits identify manufacturers from throughout the world who have registered their own unique code with regional authorities like the Uniform Code Council. The next five digits are assigned to individual products by each manufacturer. The first twelve numbers are used to mathematically come up with the 13th number, or check digit, which verifies that a product has been scanned correctly. Sample visual representation:

Country information	Manufacturer	Product	Check digit
12	34567	89123	4

TRENDS IN INVENTORY METHODS

Ask these guiding questions to focus the discussion.

Guiding Questions

Determine Why do most companies use both the perpetual and physical inventory systems?	The perpetual system gives an up-to-date inventory record throughout the year. The physical system gives an accurate count that can be compared to the perpetual records to identify any discrepancies or problems.
Predict What could result if a company used only a perpetual inventory system and did not use a physical inventory system?	If a physical inventory is not used, a company may not be aware of stock shortages due to employee and customer theft, receiving errors, incorrect counting, and selling errors.

Reading Check Answer

Read the Reading Check question to students: ***What are two main inventory systems?*** Two main systems are perpetual and physical inventory systems.

WORLD MARKET
ENGLISH LANGUAGE ARTS

Ask students to write a paragraph describing their ideal vacation. They should include product amenities the hotel might stock and the stock lists it would use. After students have completed their paragraphs, display a stock list for the class to view. Ask students to share their stock lists, and add their answers to the displayed list. Ask: ***What amenities might the hotel have that are not included on the stock list?*** swimming pools, concierge service, golf courses, shops, restaurants, exercise equipment, cable television, Internet connection, and so on.

STOCK CONTROL

Stock control involves monitoring stock levels and investments in stock so that a business runs efficiently. Monitoring systems include dollar versus unit control methods, inventory turnover calculations, and three stock lists.

DOLLAR VERSUS UNIT CONTROL

Inventory management involves both dollar control and unit control of merchandise held in inventory. **Dollar control** represents the planning and monitoring of the total inventory investment made by a business during a stated period of time. A business's dollar control of inventory involves information about the amount of purchases, sales, dollar value of beginning and ending inventory, and stock shortages. This information helps a business determine the cost of goods sold and the amount of gross profit or loss during a given period of time. By subtracting operating expenses from the gross profit, the business can determine its net profit or loss.

Unit control is a stock control method that measures the amounts of merchandise a business handles during a stated period of time. Unit control allows a business to adjust inventory to sales. Unit control lets the business determine how to spend money available under a planned budget. In a unit control inventory system, merchandise is tracked by stockkeeping unit. Tracking the SKUs gives valuable sales information on those items that are successful and those that are not selling. A business can use this information to make better merchandising decisions. Sales promotions can be run to sell slow-moving items or to spotlight popular ones.

Unit-control records also allow purchasing personnel to see what brands, sizes, colors, and price ranges are popular. By keeping track of this information, buyers can understand customer preferences and order accordingly. Finally, unit-control records specify when items need to be ordered. When a minimum stock amount is reached, an order is placed for more stock. This system ensures that adequate assortments are available and helps avoid out-of-stock situations.

MARKETING CASE STUDY

Fiesta Movement

The Ford® Motor Company's Fiesta subcompact car was first produced in 1976. Although it was produced by a United States automaker, it was very popular in Europe. In fact, it has only been available in the United States as an import since the 1980s. That situation changed in 2010. Ford decided to start selling the Fiesta to U.S. consumers.

New Marketing Mix

Ford introduced the Fiesta to U.S. consumers through social media. Rather than simply using a blog post, tweet, or Facebook® status update, the company did something different. It started a movement. The Fiesta Movement involved 100 people in the United States who used social media in a variety of ways. They were given Fiestas 18 months before the car was available to the general public. They blogged, tweeted, and posted pictures of the car on social networks. This resulted in a 38% increase in brand awareness without any money spent on advertising.

English Language Arts

Evaluate Ford changed the way it interacted with its customers during the Fiesta Movement. It allowed its customers to communicate and spread influence on its behalf. Discuss the risks and benefits of Ford's use of social media.

NCSS V B Individuals, Groups, & Institutions Analyze group and institutional influences on people, events, and elements of culture in both historical and contemporary settings.

INVENTORY TURNOVER

The most effective way to measure how well inventory is being managed is to look at inventory turnover. **Inventory turnover** is the number of times the average inventory has been sold and replaced in a given period of time. The higher the inventory-turnover rate, the more times the goods were sold and replaced. For example, imagine that you own a swimsuit shop that regularly orders 100 swimsuits per order. The stock sells out quickly during July but more slowly in August. Your inventory turnover rate is higher in July.

In retailing and wholesaling operations, the key is moving inventory so there is cash available to buy more fast-selling merchandise. High turnover rates mean that merchandise is selling quickly. That means higher profit for the business because its money is not tied up in inventory.

Inventory turnover is also a good measure of success for businesses to use in evaluating suppliers and products from year to year. Businesses use industry inventory-turnover rates to compare a particular business with the operations of similar businesses.

Inventory-turnover rates by industry are available from trade associations and commercial publishers. One such publisher is Dun & Bradstreet, which publishes Industry Norms and Key Business Ratios. Inventory-turnover rates can be calculated in dollars (retail or cost) or in units.

CALCULATING TURNOVER RATES

Turnover rates are a measure of how well a business is managing its assets and inventory. Retailers that want to learn the rate at retail compute their inventory turnover rate as follows:

$$\frac{\text{Net sales (in retail dollars)}}{\text{Average inventory on hand (in retail dollars)}}$$

When net sales during a period are $49,500 and average inventory is $8,250, the inventory turnover is 6:

$$\frac{\$49{,}500}{\$8{,}250} = 6$$

To determine the average inventory, use inventory amounts for each of the months included in the time period being considered. Total these, as shown in the second column below, and then calculate the average.

Month	Inventory	Net Sales
January	$50,000	$10,000
February	55,000	15,000
March	68,000	20,000
April	64,000	19,000
May	63,000	21,000
June	60,000	20,000
Totals	$360,000	$105,000

To get the average inventory for the six-month period, divide by the number of months:

$$6 = \frac{\$360{,}000}{\$60{,}000}$$

Finally, to calculate inventory turnover, divide total net sales (see the third column above) by average inventory:

$$\frac{\$105{,}000}{\$60{,}000} = 1.75$$

This figure means that the average inventory was sold and replaced 1.75 times during the six-month period.

Inventory-turnover rates can also be calculated at cost and unit levels. When only cost information about inventory is available, inventory turnover can be calculated with this formula:

$$\frac{\text{Cost of goods sold}}{\text{Average inventory (at cost) on hand for a given time period}}$$

When a business wants to look at the number of items carried in relation to the number of items sold, it calculates its stock-turnover rates in units with this formula:

$$\frac{\text{Number of SKUs sold}}{\text{Average SKUs on hand (for a given time period)}}$$

570 | Unit 7 · Distribution

Chapter 24 · Stock Handling and Inventory Control | 571

EXPLAIN

STOCK CONTROL

Ask these questions to focus the discussion about stock control methods.

Guiding Questions

Analyze What are the benefits of a unit control method?	adjust inventory to sales; lets the business decide how to spend within a budget; use tracking information to make decisions; purchasing personnel can see what brands, sizes, colors, and price ranges are popular
Predict Since stock is an investment, what might be the result of having too much stock?	the company's return on investment may not be high; resources might not be available for other things

MARKETING CASE STUDY

English Language Arts Answer Students may suggest that Ford® took a big risk not knowing what the bloggers and tweeters would say about the Fiesta. If they didn't like the car, it would have been bad advertising for Ford. Benefits might include the low cost of advertising (giving away the cars) and the increase in brand awareness. Ask students whether they think other companies will use similar marketing techniques to promote their products. Have them offer a rationale for their answers. Ford's success in using social media to increase brand awareness will likely cause other companies to use similar techniques. Social media has become a powerful communication device.

ELABORATE

Mini Projects

Enrichment

Research Inventory Systems Have students locate and read an article on inventory systems. They may find articles online or in trade journals in the library. Ask students to write a 200-word summary of the article, including the title of the article, the source, and the date of publication. Use the following criteria to help evaluate the essays: Do the paragraphs have a topic sentence? Do supporting details enhance the main idea? Are all opinions supported by details?

Route Inventory Movement Divide the class into pairs. Assign pairs to create a floor plan of a warehouse that stores inventory for a business. Maps should include an area where physical inventory resides, a delivery area, and an area for receiving inventory shipments. Then have students draw a route that indicates the safest and quickest way from receiving an order to picking it up and dropping it off at the delivery area. Have pairs share their floor plans with the class. If possible, post the plans around the classroom.

Create an Inventory Spreadsheet Have students create their own inventory figures for a 12-month period and develop a spreadsheet with vertical columns that include: month, average inventory, and net sales. Once they have created the spreadsheet, have them find the inventory turnover rate for the 12-month period.

Critical Thinking

Display this formula for inventory turnover rates:

$$\frac{\text{Net sales (in retail dollars)}}{\text{Average inventory on hand (in retail dollars)}}$$

Now pose the following problem to students: ***What is the inventory turnover when the net sales during a period are $23,500 and average inventory is $3,550?*** Ask a volunteer to come to the board to solve the problem. 23,500 ÷ 3,550 = 6.6 Divide the class into pairs and have pairs generate their own problems for determining inventory turnover rates. Ask pairs to display their problems and have volunteers solve them.

e MARKETING

E-Procurement Platform

E-procurement (electronic procurement) involves buying and selling products through the Internet. Members of the e-procurement platform are registered buyers and sellers. In many cases the buyer selects the preferred vendors to participate in the e-procurement platform. All aspects of the purchase are computerized and completed on the Internet, such as negotiating, getting approval, processing purchases and invoices, and making payments. In this supplier exchange, computerized supply chain management may be integrated so that vendors can automatically ship goods when the buyer's stock records reach a certain level. E-procurement can also involve finding new suppliers (e-sourcing), sending information and pricing based on request (e-tendering), getting purchasing information (e-informing), and buying through specific buying communities (e-marketsites).

Innovate and Create

Tell students to research the benefits of e-procurement. Then have them role play to convince a purchasing agent for a small manufacturing company that e-procurement is the way to go. Some of the benefits of e-procurement are: improved productivity through automation, reduced paperwork, and purchasing standardization. Human errors are greatly reduced and orders are processed quickly. Inventory management is improved.

E-procurement is especially good for novice purchasing agents. Less training is needed. The role plays should be evaluated based on the students' knowledge of the subject matter (e-procurement and its benefits), as well as their communication skills and ability to respond to objections or questions.

glencoe.com

eMarketing Worksheet Activity Send students to the Online Learning Center to download an eMarketing worksheet activity.

STOCK LISTS

There are three plans used to monitor different types of goods—staple items, fashionable items, and very popular items. They are the basic stock list, model stock list, and never-out list.

A **basic stock list** is used for those staple items that should always be in stock. This list specifies products that a store should always carry based upon the type of business. A basic stock list in a men's clothing store would include items such as T-shirts, underwear, and dress socks. The basic stock list at a card store would include birthday cards, blank cards, thank you cards, and cards for special occasions, such as weddings and anniversaries.

A basic stock list specifies the minimum amount of merchandise that should be on hand for particular products. It is based on expected sales for a given period. It shows the quantity of items that should be reordered, as well as the colors, styles, and sizes that should be carried.

Retailers assign each product a code for ease in recording when the products are purchased and sold.

A **model stock list** is used for fashionable merchandise. Fashion items change relatively rapidly; therefore, these lists are less specific than basic stock lists. The information contained in model stock lists identifies goods by general classes (blouses, skirts, dresses, slacks) and style categories (short sleeve, long sleeve), sizes, materials, colors, and price lines. Style numbers are not included because each manufacturer's style numbers change each year. Although model stock lists identify how many of each type of item should be purchased, the buyer must actually select specific models at the market. A **never-out list** is used for best-selling products that make up a large percentage of sales volume. Items are added to or taken off the list as their popularity increases or declines.

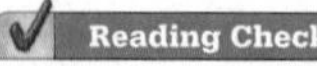

Reading Check

Recall What are the three types of stock lists?

New electronic processes and systems can assist with inventory management and improve customer service. ***How can electronic systems such as Quick Response Delivery lead to better customer service?***

THE IMPACT OF TECHNOLOGY

Sophisticated information-gathering hardware and software has been developed to track items from the purchase order to the final customer sale. **Real-time inventory systems** use Internet technology that connects applications, data, and users in real time. This technology allows a company to constantly track every product it sells. Each product is tracked from when it is manufactured, to when it arrives in the warehouse, to when the customer orders it online, to when it arrives at the buyer's door. These systems and technologies include:

- Standardized shipping container marking (SCM) as a way to identify case and case contents.
- Radio frequency identification (RFID) to allow retailers to track and authenticate pallets, cartons, and products without relying on barcodes.
- Warehouse Management Systems (WMS) utilizing radio frequency (RF) terminals, pick-to-light terminals (PTL), and voice-directed small computers with headsets to locate stored items quicker and to improve accuracy.
- Universal Product Codes (UPCs) with standard product identifier barcode symbols to capture SKU-level information at the point of sale.
- Quick Response Delivery (QRD) computer systems to replenish inventory based upon consumer demand and point-of-sale information.
- Electronic Data Interchange (EDI) transactions to exchange standard business transactions or information by electronic computer-to-computer transfers, requiring little or no human intervention.

After You Read **Section 24.2**

Review Key Concepts

1. **Describe** the difference between a perpetual and a physical inventory.
2. **List** the three different inventory counting methods.
3. **Explain** how to calculate stock turnover rates.

Practice Academics

English Language Arts

4. Investigate smart cards or radio frequency identification (RFID) tags and write a one-page report on the current usage of RFID technology in retail stores.

Mathematics

5. Calculate the inventory turnover for a company that has annual net sales totaling $240,000 and an average inventory on hand of $160,000 throughout the year. What does your answer represent?

Math Concept **Problem Solving** The inventory-turnover rate is a measure of how often the average inventory is sold and replaced during a given time period. Dividing the net sales by the cost of the average inventory on hand yields the inventory-turnover rate.

Starting Hint To solve this problem, divide the total net sales by the average inventory on hand to determine the turnover rate.

For help, go to the **Math Skills Handbook** located at the back of this book.

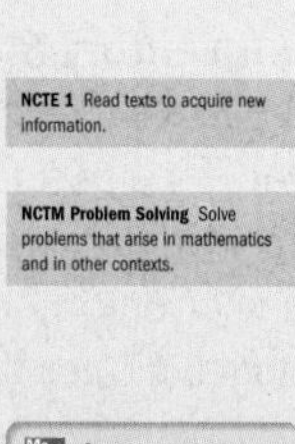

NCTE 1 Read texts to acquire new information.

NCTM Problem Solving Solve problems that arise in mathematics and in other contexts.

glencoe.com Check your answers.

ELABORATE

Reading Check Answer

Read the Reading Check question to students: ***What are the three types of stock lists?*** a basic stock list, a model stock list, a never-out stock list

Visual Literacy

Using Technology Caption Answer Read the caption question to students: ***How can electronic systems such as Quick Response Delivery lead to better customer service?*** Because Quick Response Delivery systems replenish inventory based on consumer demand and point of sale information, customers should always be able to find the items they are looking for.

Graphic Organizer

Display this diagram. Ask students to provide the different types of stock lists and details about each. Possible answers:

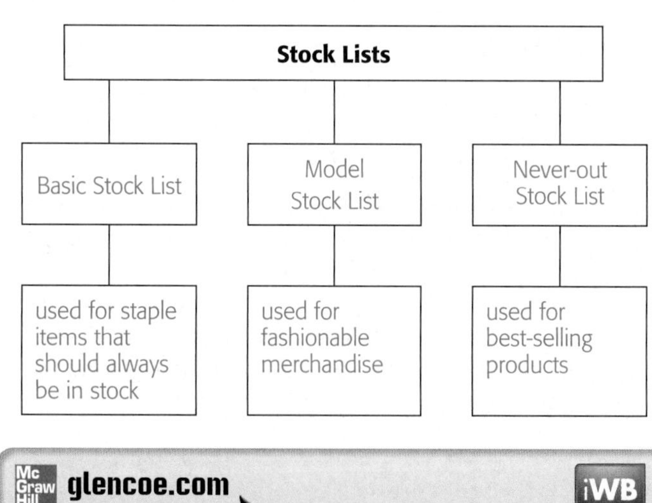

glencoe.com iWB

Graphic Organizer Send students to the Online Learning Center to print this graphic organizer.

EVALUATE

THE IMPACT OF TECHNOLOGY

Tell students that technology is constantly changing the way inventory is controlled—the more sophisticated technology becomes, the more accurate inventory control becomes. Ask these guiding questions to focus the discussion about technology's impact on inventory control.

Guiding Questions

Describe What is a real-time inventory system?	an inventory system that uses Internet technology that connects applications, data, and users in real time; allows a company to constantly track every product it sells; products are tracked every step of the process
Distinguish Imagine that a coworker has shown some confusion about the difference between just-in-time inventory systems and quick response delivery. How would you explain?	Just-in-time inventory systems control the flow of parts and materials into assembly and manufacturing plants. Quick response delivery applies just-in-time principles to replenish inventory based upon consumer demand.

Mini Projects

Differentiated Instruction

Visual Learners Divide the class into six groups. Assign each group one of the main concepts in this section—stock turnover, dollar control, unit control, perpetual inventory system, physical inventory system, and technology. Have groups design an outline, graphic organizer, or symbolic drawing that represents the concept. Then have groups use their visuals to review the concept with the rest of the class.

Gifted Learners Have students locate a local business willing to discuss its inventory system. Students should then set up an appointment to see how the business's inventory works. In advance of the appointment, students should create a list of questions to ask their contact at the business. Questions might include: What type of inventory system do you use? Is it manual or computer-based? Do you use a perpetual inventory system, a physical inventory system, or both? What kind of counting system do you use: physical inventory, cycle count, or visual control? After the appointment, have students write a summary of their findings to share with the class.

After You Read Section 24.2

Review Key Concepts

1. A perpetual inventory system tracks the number of items in inventory on a constant basis. Under a physical inventory system, stock is visually inspected or actually counted to determine the quantity on hand.
2. Counting methods include physical inventory, cycle counts, and visual control.
3. When a store wants to look at the number of items carried in relation to the number of items sold, it uses this formula: Cost of goods sold ÷ average inventory on hand (at cost). When a store wants to calculate its inventory turnover rates in units, it uses this formula: Number of units ÷ average inventory on hand in units.

Practice Academics

English Language Arts

4. Accept all reasonable answers on how smart cards or radio frequency identification tags technology are used in retail stores. Students should include the source(s) of the information, summarize the activity (pricing, inventory control, marketing research, and so on), use correct grammar and spelling, and submit papers that are one-page in length.

Mathematics

5. 1.5 ($240,000 ÷ $160,000). This figure means the average inventory was sold and replaced 1.5 times during the annual period.

glencoe.com

Answer Key Send students to the Online Learning Center to check their answers.

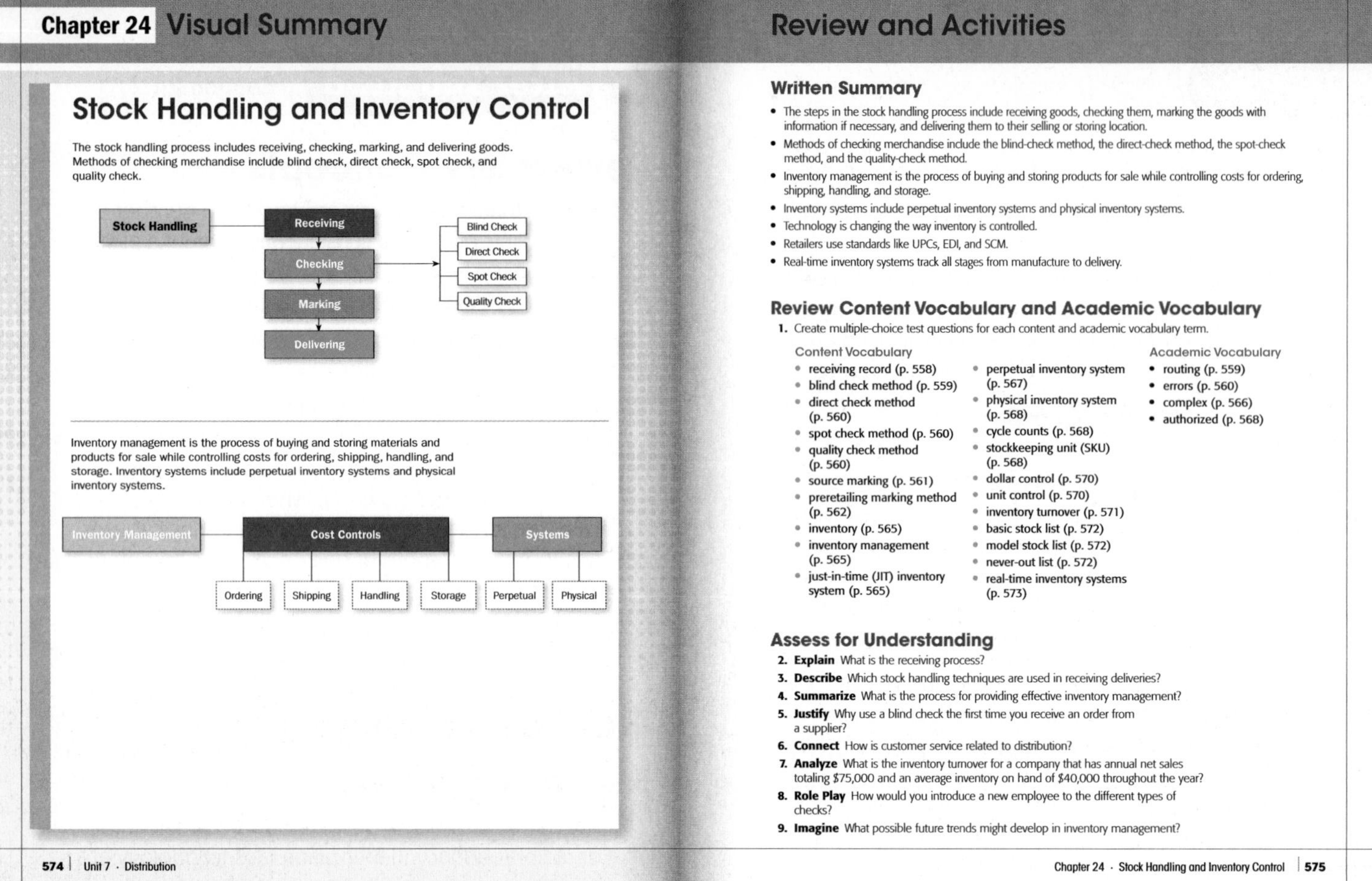

Chapter 24 Visual Summary

Stock Handling and Inventory Control

The stock handling process includes receiving, checking, marking, and delivering goods. Methods of checking merchandise include blind check, direct check, spot check, and quality check.

Inventory management is the process of buying and storing materials and products for sale while controlling costs for ordering, shipping, handling, and storage. Inventory systems include perpetual inventory systems and physical inventory systems.

574 | Unit 7 · Distribution

Review and Activities

Written Summary

- The steps in the stock handling process include receiving goods, checking them, marking the goods with information if necessary, and delivering them to their selling or storing location.
- Methods of checking merchandise include the blind-check method, the direct-check method, the spot-check method, and the quality-check method.
- Inventory management is the process of buying and storing products for sale while controlling costs for ordering, shipping, handling, and storage.
- Inventory systems include perpetual inventory systems and physical inventory systems.
- Technology is changing the way inventory is controlled.
- Retailers use standards like UPCs, EDI, and SCM.
- Real-time inventory systems track all stages from manufacture to delivery.

Review Content Vocabulary and Academic Vocabulary

1. Create multiple-choice test questions for each content and academic vocabulary term.

Content Vocabulary
- receiving record (p. 558)
- blind check method (p. 559)
- direct check method (p. 560)
- spot check method (p. 560)
- quality check method (p. 560)
- source marking (p. 561)
- preretailing marking method (p. 562)
- inventory (p. 565)
- inventory management (p. 565)
- just-in-time (JIT) inventory system (p. 565)
- perpetual inventory system (p. 567)
- physical inventory system (p. 568)
- cycle counts (p. 568)
- stockkeeping unit (SKU) (p. 568)
- dollar control (p. 570)
- unit control (p. 570)
- inventory turnover (p. 571)
- basic stock list (p. 572)
- model stock list (p. 572)
- never-out list (p. 572)
- real-time inventory systems (p. 573)

Academic Vocabulary
- routing (p. 559)
- errors (p. 560)
- complex (p. 566)
- authorized (p. 568)

Assess for Understanding

2. **Explain** What is the receiving process?
3. **Describe** Which stock handling techniques are used in receiving deliveries?
4. **Summarize** What is the process for providing effective inventory management?
5. **Justify** Why use a blind check the first time you receive an order from a supplier?
6. **Connect** How is customer service related to distribution?
7. **Analyze** What is the inventory turnover for a company that has annual net sales totaling $75,000 and an average inventory on hand of $40,000 throughout the year?
8. **Role Play** How would you introduce a new employee to the different types of checks?
9. **Imagine** What possible future trends might develop in inventory management?

Chapter 24 · Stock Handling and Inventory Control | 575

EVALUATE

Visual Summary

Express Creativity Ask students to develop their own visual summary of a concept in the chapter. Encourage students to use different formats for their visual summaries, such as a storyboard, a timeline, a table, a tree diagram, or a word web. Visual summaries will vary depending on the concept depicted. Questions to ask when assessing a visual summary include:

- Is the summary clear, economical, and simple?
- Are any important steps left out?
- Are steps or concepts arranged in the same order as the original?
- Does the summary reveal a pattern that connects the details?
- Does the summary locate and highlight the most important information?

Review Content Vocabulary and Academic Vocabulary

1. Multiple-choice questions will vary. Sample questions:

Information on a receiving record can include
   a. a receiving number.
   b. the name of the carrier.
   c. the number of items delivered.
   d. all of the above.

The **blind check method** requires the receiver to
   a. write the description of the merchandise.
   b. randomly check one carton in a shipment.
   c. disregard a count on the quantities received.
   d. list items on a just-in-time device

With the **direct check method**, the merchandise is checked
   a. against the actual invoice or purchase order.
   b. against a list provided by the ordering department.
   c. against a dummy invoice.
   d. against the shipping contract.

EVALUATE

Assess for Understanding

2. The steps in the process include receiving goods, checking them, marking the goods with information, if necessary, and delivering them to a place where they will be used, stored, or displayed for sale.

3. A receiving record is made about the condition and status of the goods as they are received. The information can be recorded either manually or electronically. Hand-held laser scanners and imagers can capture signatures, take images, and read product codes. Mobile computers can capture images to document shipment damage and signatures to reduce shrinkage at the receiving dock. The amount and type of information recorded depends on the needs of the business.

4. Effective inventory management is the process of buying and storing products for sale while controlling costs for ordering, shipping, handling, and storage. Businesses can lose money without an effective system.

5. The blind check is the most accurate checking method because it requires the receiver to write the description of the merchandise, count the quantities received, and list them on a blank form or dummy invoice. This dummy invoice can then be compared to the supplier's invoice to check for accuracy. It will help determine whether future shipments from this supplier will need to be checked as thoroughly.

6. Businesses must manage inventory so that customers have the merchandise they want when they want it. Having too little inventory results in lost sales and dissatisfied customers.

7. Inventory turnover rate:

$$\frac{\text{Net sales}}{\text{Average inventory on hand}} = \frac{\$75{,}000}{\$40{,}000} = 1.875$$

8. Answers may include demonstrating the four different techniques for checking while the new employee watches, and then having the new employee demonstrate the checking methods on new shipments.

9. Answers may include the following: Standardized shipping container marking (SCM) as a way to identify case and case contents. Radio frequency identification (RFID) to allow retailers to track and authenticate pallets, cartons, and products without relying on bar code labeling. Warehouse Management Systems (WMS) utilizing radio frequency (RF) terminals, pick-to-light terminals (PTL), and voice-directed small computers with headsets to locate stored items quicker and to improve accuracy. UPC codes with standard product identifier barcode symbols to capture SKU-level information at the point of sale. Quick Response Delivery (QRD) computer systems to replenish inventory based upon consumer demand and point of sale information. Electronic Data Interchange (EDI) transactions to exchange standard business transactions or information by electronic computer to computer transfers, requiring little or no human intervention.

21st Century Skills

Communication Skills

10. Explaining Damages You are a receiver in a warehouse. You know that a coworker has been damaging incoming merchandise through deliberate and careless behavior. However, your manager suspects that you are at fault and has approached you about these events. How would you handle this situation? Role play the situation with a partner.

Financial Literacy Skills

11. Calculating Unit-Turnover Rates You manage a ski shop at a resort and have been asked to compare your store's average turnover rate in units to a competitor's rate for a six-month period. For the time period, your store sold 50 pairs of skis, while your competitor sold 100 pairs of the same ski. Using the following chart, determine which store has a better turnover rate for this item.

	Your Store (SKU on hand)	Your Competitor
Oct	40	125
Nov	30	75
Dec	20	50
Jan	15	50
Feb	10	35
March	5	25

e-Marketing Skills

12. Smartphones Imagine that you work for a technology firm that manufactures smartphones with digital-camera and Web-browser features. Investigate the process of using your smartphone to launch 2-D barcodes to cosmetic retailers. Keeping the retailers' needs in mind, consider the following questions:

- What advantages do 2-D barcodes offer relative to 12-digit barcodes?
- What steps must you take to sell the concept?
- What benefits might 2-D barcodes have?
- What technological improvements must your smartphones have to read 2-D barcodes?

Build Academic Skills

Science

13. Interactive Barcodes Two-dimensional (2-D) barcodes are similar to UPC codes, but are interactive and can store additional information, such as a Web site or an e-mail address. Conduct research to learn how this emerging technology might be used to benefit businesses. Describe in writing how 2-D bar codes could improve one aspect of a local business.

NSES E Develop abilities of technological design, understandings about science and technology.

English Language Arts

14. Quick Response Delivery Systems Many retailers are letting their suppliers manage their inventory by sharing point-of-sale information through electronic data exchanges. Conduct research on quick response systems and vendor managed inventory. Discuss the benefits and risks of this approach.

NCTE 3 Apply strategies to interpret texts.

Mathematics

15. Inventory Turnover For a six-month period, a company had an inventory-turnover rate of 4, and the cost of the average inventory on hand was $14,725. What were the net sales for this company during this six-month period?

NCTM Algebra Represent and analyze mathematical situations and structures using algebraic symbols.

Math Concept **Analyzation** The inventory-turnover rate is a measure of how often the average inventory is sold and replaced during a given time period.

For help, go to the **Math Skills Handbook** located at the back of this book.

Standardized Test Practice

Directions Read the following questions. On a separate sheet of paper, write the best possible answer for each one.

1. Which of the following methods of checking inventory includes inspecting workmanship and the general characteristics of the received merchandise?
   A. Blind check method
   B. Direct check method
   C. Quality check method
   D. Spot check method
2. A perpetual inventory system tracks the number of items in inventory on a constant basis.
   T
   F
3. The number of times the average inventory has been sold and replaced in a given period of time is called ________.

Test-Taking Tip
At the beginning of a test, review it quickly to see what kinds of questions are on the test to help plan your time. You may find multiple choice, matching, true or false, short answer, extended response, and essay questions.

DECA Connection Role Play

New Manager
Small Hotel

Situation The housekeeping staff have mentioned that several key supplies for the guest rooms, public spaces, and meeting rooms have run very low before being reordered. These supplies are necessary for the smooth running of the hotel and for guest convenience. When reorders are placed for those supplies, they must be delivered by rush delivery. This increases shipping costs, which increases the cost of supplies to the hotel.

Just yesterday you observed two boxes in a corner of the hotel's receiving dock. As you investigated the contents of the boxes, you found that one box contained a reorder of guest room bars of soap, and the other contained a reorder of hotel logo note pads. You have had complaints from customers attending meetings at the hotel that packages are not ready for them when they arrive.

You have researched the problem and determined that the cause of the problem is poor inventory control of hotel supplies and inefficient procedures for receiving deliveries.

Activity You are to meet with the hotel's operations manager (judge) to discuss the situation. You will discuss the need for proper inventory control, the types of inventory control systems suitable for the hotel, and the maintenance of the inventory control system. You will also review procedures for receiving packages.

Evaluation You will be evaluated on how well you meet the following performance indicators:

1. Explain stock-handling techniques used in receiving deliveries.
2. Describe inventory control systems.
3. Maintain inventory control systems.
4. Motivate team members.
5. Foster positive working relationships.

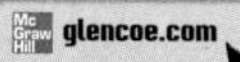

glencoe.com

Download the Competitive Events Workbook for more Role-Play practice.

EVALUATE

21st Century Skills

Communication Skills

10. Accept all reasonable responses. Suggestions include avoid becoming angry and indignant. Your communication should be clear and thoughtful, but also tactful. You might offer to be observed during the receiving process for verification of your skills. You might also suggest the possibility that the other receiver might need additional training and supervision to resolve the problem.

Financial Literacy Skills

11. Answer: Total units for six-month period ÷ 6 to get average on hand ÷ by units sold.

Number of SKUs sold
Average SKUs on hand (for a given time period)
Total the units on hand
Turnover rate for your store = 2.5. (50 units sold ÷ 20 unit average for period = 2. 5).
Turnover rate for competitor = 1.66 (100 units sold ÷ 60 unit average for period = 1.66)
Your store had better managed the inventory for this item.

e-Marketing Skills

12. Implementation steps: You might consider a trade booth at a convention to demonstrate how the smartphone would work in the retail sector. The next step might include pilot testing the smartphone in several different stores and locations. The final step might include promotion and public relations of the smartphone in the pilot location followed by implementation of 2-D barcodes for cosmetic products for a large chain of stores.

Benefits: With a camera and web browser you could create an interactive exchange between the manufacturer and potential customer. The camera would allow the 2-D barcode to be captured. The Web browser would direct the customer to a Web site for the product. The 2-D barcode could also provide the location of the potential customer and purchase history.

EVALUATE

Build Academic Skills

Science

13. Accept all reasonable answers that list possible benefits of 2-D barcodes. Answers may include opportunities to interact with consumers across any media, such as posters, videogames, store displays, and screens. 2-D barcodes on products could enable consumers to use cell phones or PDAs to connect to a company Web site or collect an email address for future promotions. In Japan, 2-D codes are used to pay bills and download videos.

English Language Arts

14. Responses will vary but should include analysis of the risks and benefits of both quick response delivery systems and vendor managed inventory. Research should come from trusted Web sites or from interviews with inventory control managers who utilize these systems.

Mathematics

15. The net sales were $88,350 ($x \div \$14{,}725 = 6$; $x = \$14{,}725 \times 6 = \$88{,}350$).

Standardized Test Practice

1. C Quality check method
2. True
3. turnover

DECA Connection Role Play

Evaluations will be based on these performance indicators:

1. **Explain stock handling techniques used in receiving deliveries.** Stock or merchandise ordered by a business is received and checked. The store manager should be aware of the shipping date. In retail settings, the items are often marked with a selling price before they are transferred to the sales area. In larger businesses, several people might perform this function. In smaller businesses, a salesperson, manager, or even the owner may do this job.
2. **Describe inventory control systems.** A *perpetual inventory system* tracks the number of items in inventory on a constant basis. The system tracks all new items purchased and returned, as well as sales of current stock. An up-to-date count of inventory is maintained for purchases and returns of merchandise, sales and sales returns, and transfers. Reordering and restocking items whenever quantities become low can help avoid loss of sales. Under a *physical inventory system*, information about stock levels is not continually maintained. With a physical inventory system, stock is visually inspected or counted to determine the quantity on hand.
3. **Maintain inventory control systems.** Businesses must: maintain the right quantities of merchandise without running out of stock; keep a wide product assortment without compromising customer needs and wants; purchase merchandise at large volumes to gain the lowest prices while not buying more than it will sell; pay attention to what customers are buying; and keep a current inventory on hand.
4. **Motivate team members.** Model the kind of behavior you want to see in employees; publicly reward employees who have done a good job; share ideas; ask for their ideas; show them respect.
5. **Foster positive working relationships.** Find common interests; communicate openly; work together sharing ideas; encourage and motivate one another.

glencoe.com

Role Plays For more DECA Role Plays, send students to the Online Learning Center to download the Competitive Events Workbook.

UNIT 7 **Marketing Internship Project**

A Distribution Plan for a Growing Business

An artist who makes and ships small art objects has simple distribution needs. How might this entrepreneur manage an expanding business and distribution?

Scenario

For several years an artist who designs small wooden sculptures has been selling art items at local arts and crafts fairs as well as through mail order. The orders are easily packaged and shipped via the U.S. Postal Service. However, after visiting a trade show, this artist was commissioned to mass-produce replicas of one sculpture for a retail chain store with locations throughout the United States. This expansion requires mass production using materials similar to wood, a new inventory management system, and a review of current shipping methods.

The artist has hired your firm to handle the details. Your firm has contracted with a manufacturer to make the replicas but now sees an opportunity to sell replicas of the artist's other designs through new channels of distribution.

The Skills You'll Use

Academic Skills Reading, writing, social studies, researching, and analyzing

Basic Skills Speaking, listening, thinking, and interpersonal

Technology Skills Word processing, spreadsheet, presentation, telecommunications, and the Internet

NCTE 4 Use written language to communicate effectively.
NCTE 7 Conduct research and gather, evaluate, and synthesize data to communicate discoveries.

Your Objective

Your objective is to prepare a plan to help grow this artist's business by developing new channels of distribution and planning the logistics required to expand this business.

STEP 1 Do Your Research

Conduct research to identify competitors in the market and find out what channels of distribution they use to sell their products. As you conduct your research, answer these questions:

- Who makes up the target markets for the company's products?
- What channels of distribution will reach those target markets?
- How will the products be stored, inventoried, and shipped?
- Does the company have other companies that handle the logistics (inventory management and shipping)?
- Does the company use the U.S. Postal Service for shipping?

Write a summary of your research.

STEP 2 Plan Your Project

Now that you have completed your research, you need to begin planning your project.

- Research different channels of distribution that could be used to sell the artist's work.
- Select one or two target markets.
- Decide on the channels of distribution that would be used to reach those target markets.
- Create a diagram or flowchart to illustrate the channels of distribution you select.
- Develop a written plan for warehousing, distribution, and shipping to those target markets.

STEP 3 Connect with Your Community

- Visit a local art gallery or curio shop and ask the business owner or manager how distribution and shipping are handled.
- Take notes during your interview, and transcribe the notes after your interview.

STEP 4 Share What You Learn

Assume your class is your company's sales staff that will be responsible for presenting this plan to the artist for approval.

- Present your findings in an oral presentation. Be prepared to answer questions.
- Display and explain the diagram or flowchart illustrating suggested channels of distribution.
- Use software to create a slide presentation to accompany your oral presentation. Include one slide for each topic in your written plan.

STEP 5 Evaluate Your Marketing and Academic Skills

Your project will be evaluated based on the following:

- Knowledge of the market
- Understanding of various channels of distribution that can be used to sell products
- Suggestions for handling the logistics for the expanded business
- Research data to support the rationale for your plan
- Organization and continuity of presentation
- Mechanics—presentation and neatness
- Speaking and listening skills

MARKETING CORE FUNCTIONS
Channel Management
Market Planning

Marketing Internship Project Checklist

Plan
- ✓ Conduct research on companies that sell products similar to the artists's creations.
- ✓ Design a plan to grow the artist's business through new channels of distribution.

Write
- ✓ Write a summary of your research.
- ✓ Transcribe your interview notes.
- ✓ Write a plan that includes your reccommendations for warehousing, distribution, and shipping.
- ✓ Design a visual to illustrate the channels of distribution.

Present
- ✓ Present research that supports your rationale for new channels of distribution for specific target markets.
- ✓ Present your logistics plan for warehousing, distribution, and shipping.

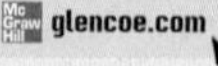
glencoe.com

Evaluate Download a rubric you can use to evaluate your final project.

my marketing portfolio

Internship Report Once you have completed your Marketing Internship Project and oral presentation, put your written report and a few printouts of key slides from your oral presentation in your Marketing Portfolio.

Research and Design a Distribution Plan Research and create a distribution plan for a bakery that makes breads and desserts. It has purchased a facility to make these items in large quantities. What are the potential target markets? What channels of distribution are needed? Who are the competitors in the new channels of distribution? What logistical plan do you have for inventory management of baking supplies and finished products? What shipping methods do you recommend? Will you hire a logistics company or handle everything yourself? Prepare a written report and an oral presentation.

578 | Unit 7 · Distribution

Unit 7 · Distribution | 579

EVALUATE

Anticipation Activity

Project Objective Read the project objective aloud to students: ***Prepare a plan to help grow this artist's business by developing new channels of distribution and planning the logistics required to expand this business.*** Ask students to think about what they learned about distribution (channel management) in Unit 7. Remind them of these key points:

- Distribution planning involves decisions about a product's physical movement and transfer of ownership.
- Other logistics considerations include purchasing, inventory, warehousing, and budgeting.

Ask students: ***What is the goal of a distribution plan?*** get products into customers' hands; considerations include the use of multiple channels, control versus costs, intensity of distribution, e-commerce

Ask students: ***Why should you examine the target market, or customer, before making decisions about distribution?*** A product can fail with the wrong channel of distribution. Certain channels are more effective for reaching certain customers. To reach customers in the consumer market, the indirect distribution is used to distribute products to retail stores. To reach the industrial market, direct and indirect channels of distribution are implemented.

Graphic Organizer

Display this chart. Ask students to name the types of retailers that might sell or distribute art objects such as sculptures. Possible answers:

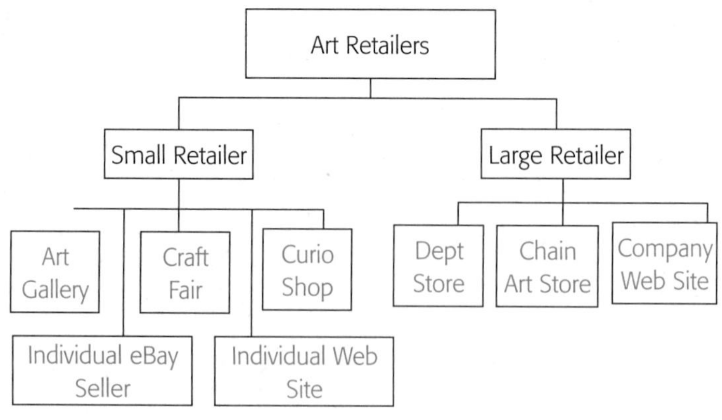

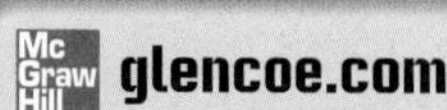

glencoe.com iWB

Graphic Organizer Send students to the Online Learning Center to print this graphic organizer.

EVALUATE

STEP 1 Do Your Research

Tell students that there are many places to find information they can use to develop a distribution plan. Students can use library and Internet resources, but they should also talk to people in the community. Encourage students to seek the opinions and ideas of trusted people they know. Other people can bring new perspectives and ideas about channels of distribution as well as target markets and logistics that relate to distributing art objects in the current marketplace.

STEP 2 Plan Your Project

Students should create a list of competitors and target markets before creating the distribution plan. Students should explain why they chose the channels of distribution and provide information about the best channels to reach customers. Students' explanation of their distribution plan should include warehousing, distribution, and shipping plans.

STEP 3 Connect with Your Community

Explain to students that connecting with members of the community is a great way to build relationships. Tell them that young people who are capable of building relationships with caring, responsible, and competent adults are more likely to achieve success in life. Encourage students to take part in opportunities for adults to serve as mentors, coaches, advocates, and advisors, both formally and informally.

STEP 4 Share What You Learn

Students should present their ideas in a written report and oral presentation with presentation software. They should have at least one slide in their presentation for each key topic in the written report. Encourage students to speak clearly, use appropriate grammar and vocabulary, and actively engage the audience by making and maintaining eye contact and using movement (facial expressions, posture, gestures) to focus attention and interest.

STEP 5 Evaluate Your Marketing and Academic Skills

Have students use the Marketing Internship Project Checklist to help them to plan, write, and present their reports. Exemplary written reports will include information that clearly supports a central thesis, a single, distinct focus, generally well-developed ideas, well-phrased sentences that flow smoothly and are varied in length and structure, consistently precise word choice, and few, if any, errors in grammar, spelling, and mechanics.

glencoe.com

Evaluation Rubric Send students to the Online Learning Center to get a rubric to evaluate their projects.

Culminating Activity

Explain to students that there are many shipping options for small businesses that distribute art objects. Besides the U.S. Postal Service, there are a number of private parcel carriers in competition with the long-established USPS. These include express carriers for overnight and expedited service, such as FedEx®, UPS®, and DHL®. Ask students: ***What are some factors to compare when choosing a shipping company?*** Sample factors may include: (1) prices for package weight and measurement; (2) delivery speed options: same day, overnight, 2-day, 3-day, extended time; (3) discounts for volume, business vs. individual, promotions; (4) service to cities, states, countries; (5) customer service; (6) reliability; (7) insurance costs.

my marketing portfolio

Internship Report Have students put their written reports and printouts of key slides from their oral presentations in their marketing portfolio.

Research and Design a Distribution Plan Direct students to research and consider a target market for a bakery that makes breads and desserts in large quantities, and then design a distribution plan for the products. Students' completed distribution plans should include all of the elements and answer all of the questions included in the Marketing Internship Project on this page. This additional activity can build relevance for students who are motivated to learn about other specific businesses and industries. Relevance shifts the focus to what motivates individual students to learn.

UNIT 8

Pricing

PLANNING GUIDE AND RESOURCES

	Print	Digital
Unit 8 Pricing		Unit 8 Fast Files: Marketing Internship Project Activity Connect Online Learning Center through glencoe.com
Chapter 25 **Price Planning**	Student Activity Workbook: Chapter 25 DECA Connection Role Play; Chapter 25 Vocabulary Activity; Section Note Taking Activities; Chapter Academics Activity; Section Study Skills Activities; Section Real-World Applications Activities Mathematics for Marketing Workbook Marketing Research Project Workbook School-to-Career Activity Workbook	Unit 8 Fast Files: Chapter 25 Discovery Project Worksheet and Rubric; Chapter 25 Green Marketer Activity; Chapter 25 Digital Nation Activity; Section Graphic Organizers; Section Outlines with Key Terms and Definitions; Section Summaries ExamView Assessment Suite, Chapter 25 Connect Online Learning Center through glencoe.com
Chapter 26 **Pricing Strategies**	Student Activity Workbook: Chapter 26 DECA Connection Role Play; Chapter 26 Vocabulary Activity; Section Note Taking Activities; Chapter Academics Activity; Section Study Skills Activities; Section Real-World Applications Activities Mathematics for Marketing Workbook Marketing Research Project Workbook School-to-Career Activity Workbook	Unit 8 Fast Files: Chapter 26 Discovery Project Worksheet and Rubric; Chapter 26 Green Marketer Activity; Chapter 26 Digital Nation Activity; Section Graphic Organizers; Section Outlines with Key Terms and Definitions; Section Summaries ExamView Assessment Suite, Chapter 26 Connect Online Learning Center through glencoe.com
Chapter 27 **Pricing Math**	Student Activity Workbook: Chapter 27 DECA Connection Role Play; Chapter 27 Vocabulary Activity; Section Note Taking Activities; Chapter Academics Activity; Section Study Skills Activities; Section Real-World Applications Activities Mathematics for Marketing Workbook Marketing Research Project Workbook School-to-Career Activity Workbook	Unit 8 Fast Files: Chapter 27 Discovery Project Worksheet and Rubric; Chapter 27 Green Marketer Activity; Chapter 27 Digital Nation Activity; Section Graphic Organizers; Section Outlines with Key Terms and Definitions; Section Summaries ExamView Assessment Suite, Chapter 27 Connect Online Learning Center through glencoe.com

McGRAW-HILL PROFESSIONAL DEVELOPMENT

Perkins IV has placed more emphasis than ever on providing quality professional development for Career and Technology educators. The legislation mandates that the focus of professional development be the integration and reinforcement of academic competencies in order to improve student achievement. Specifically, Perkins requires measurements of students' academic success. McGraw-Hill answers the challenge for strong and effective professional development with a five-prong **Online Professional Development for Integrating Academics.**

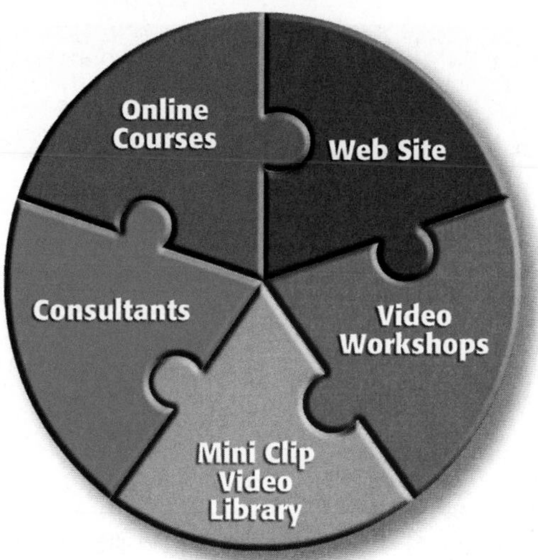

For pricing and ordering information contact your McGraw-Hill Sales Representative.

VIDEO LIBRARY

The McGraw-Hill Professional Development Mini-Clip Video Library, referenced for your convenience at the point of use, provides teaching strategies to strengthen academic and learning skills. Go to the Online Learning Center to view these professional development video clips for Unit 8:

Chapter 25: Price Planning

- **Reading: Building Vocabulary:** A teacher introduces and plays two vocabulary building games with students. (p. 585)
- **Math: Independent and Dependent Events:** An algebra teacher explains independent and dependent events. (p. 588)

Chapter 26: Pricing Strategies

- **Math: Communication in Mathematics:** An expert explains the importance of student communication in the mathematics classroom. (p. 609)
- **ELL: Strategies for English Language Learners:** An author discusses strategies for teaching English language learners. (p. 617)

Chapter 27: Pricing Math

- **ELL: Words and Pictures:** Use media examples to teach students new vocabulary. (p. 627)
- **Math: Ways of Working: Solving Equations:** Teachers build understanding of equation-solving processes. (p. 633)

UNIT OVERVIEW

Sections	Objectives	Common Core State Standards College and Career Readiness
Section 25.1 **Price Planning Issues**	• Recognize the different forms of pricing. • Explain the importance of pricing. • List the goals of pricing. • Differentiate between market share and market position.	• **Reading** Read closely to determine what the text says explicitly and to make logical inferences from it; cite specific textual evidence when writing or speaking to support conclusions drawn from the text.
Section 25.2 **Price Planning Factors**	• List the four market factors that affect price planning. • Analyze demand elasticity and supply-and-demand theory. • Explain how government regulations affect price planning.	• **Speaking and Listening** Prepare for and participate effectively in a range of conversations and collaborations with diverse partners, building on others' ideas and expressing their own clearly and persuasively.
Section 26.1 **Basic Pricing Policies**	• Name three pricing policies used to establish a base price. • Explain two polar pricing policies for introducing a new product. • Explain the relationship between pricing and the product life cycle.	• **Writing** Write narratives to develop real or imagined experiences or events using effective techniques, well-chosen details, and well-structured event sequences.
Section 26.2 **Pricing Process Strategies**	• Describe pricing strategies that adjust the base price. • List the steps involved in determining a price. • Explain the use of technology in the pricing function.	• **Writing** Write narratives to develop real or imagined experiences or events using effective techniques, well-chosen details, and well-structured event sequences.

Sections	Objectives	Common Core State Standards College and Career Readiness
Section 27.1 **Calculating Prices**	• Explain how a company's profit is related to markup. • Use the basic formula for calculating a retail price. • Calculate dollar and percentage markup based on cost or retail. • Calculate markdowns in dollars and percentages. • Calculate maintained markup in dollars and percentages.	• **Reading** Read closely to determine what the text says explicitly and to make logical inferences from it; cite specific textual evidence when writing or speaking to support conclusions drawn from the text.
Section 27.2 **Calculating Discounts**	• Utilize a general procedure for figuring discounts and net prices. • Calculate discounts in dollars and percentages. • Calculate net amount.	• **Writing** Conduct short as well as more sustained research projects based on focused questions, demonstrating understanding of the subject under investigation.

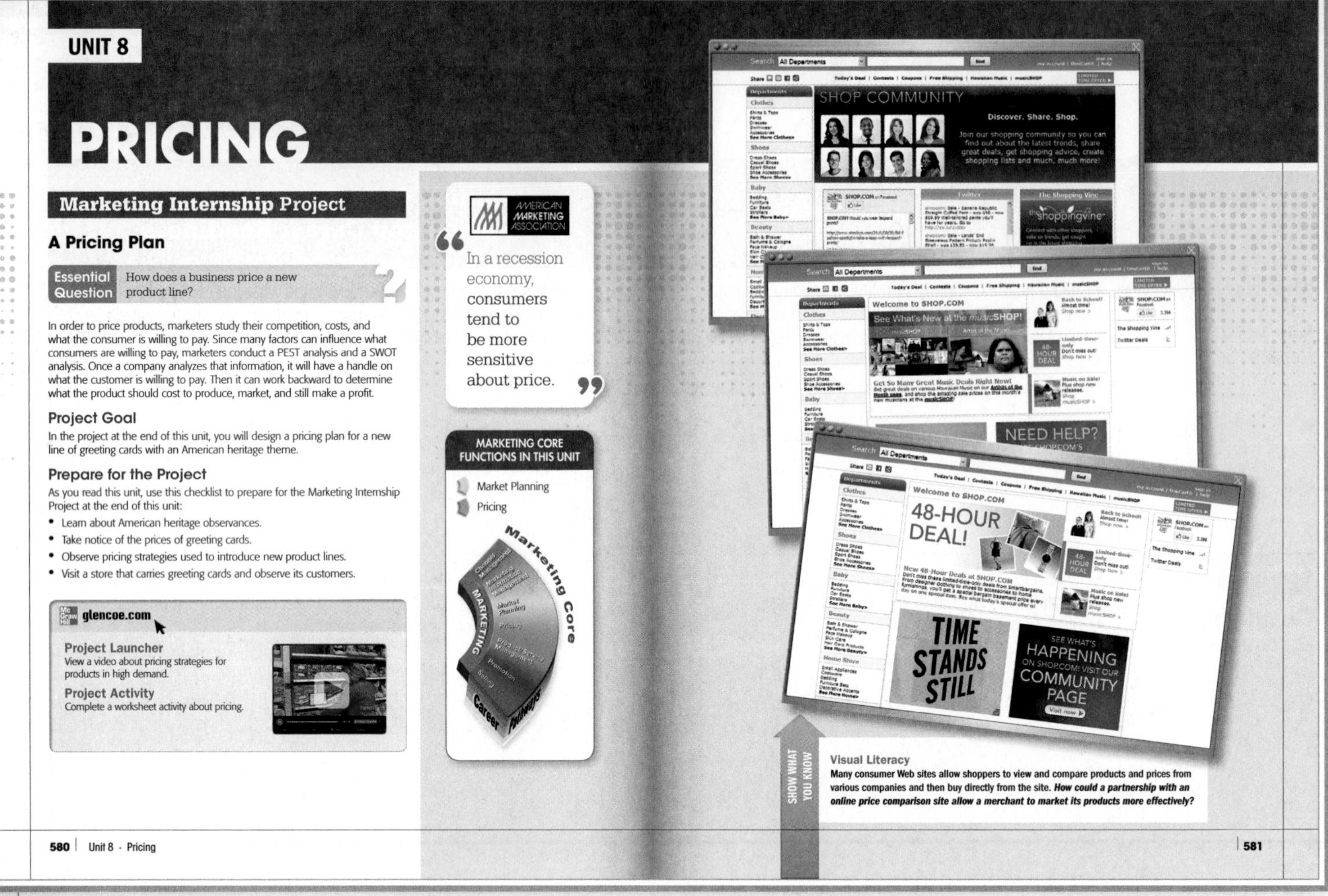
UNIT 8

PRICING

Marketing Internship Project

A Pricing Plan

Essential Question How does a business price a new product line?

In order to price products, marketers study their competition, costs, and what the consumer is willing to pay. Since many factors can influence what consumers are willing to pay, marketers conduct a PEST analysis and a SWOT analysis. Once a company analyzes that information, it will have a handle on what the customer is willing to pay. Then it can work backward to determine what the product should cost to produce, market, and still make a profit.

Project Goal

In the project at the end of this unit, you will design a pricing plan for a new line of greeting cards with an American heritage theme.

Prepare for the Project

As you read this unit, use this checklist to prepare for the Marketing Internship Project at the end of this unit:

- Learn about American heritage observances.
- Take notice of the prices of greeting cards.
- Observe pricing strategies used to introduce new product lines.
- Visit a store that carries greeting cards and observe its customers.

glencoe.com

Project Launcher View a video about pricing strategies for products in high demand.

Project Activity Complete a worksheet activity about pricing.

AMERICAN MARKETING ASSOCIATION

"In a recession economy, consumers tend to be more sensitive about price."

MARKETING CORE FUNCTIONS IN THIS UNIT

- Market Planning
- Pricing

SHOW WHAT YOU KNOW

Visual Literacy
Many consumer Web sites allow shoppers to view and compare products and prices from various companies and then buy directly from the site. ***How could a partnership with an online price comparison site allow a merchant to market its products more effectively?***

580 | Unit 8 · Pricing

581

ENGAGE

Introduce the Unit

Unit 8 examines pricing principles and practices.

Chapter 25 explores the importance of price and factors that affect the pricing decision.

Chapter 26 explains pricing policies and strategies as well as how pricing decisions are made.

Chapter 27 teaches pricing computations and calculating markups, markdowns, and discounts, and discusses the profit-and-loss statement connection to pricing.

Build Background

Ask students what would happen to a local store if it charged the same amount for its goods as it pays for them. Answers may include that the business would lose money because there would be no money left for operating expenses. Ask students: ***What are some factors that might affect the price of a product?*** the wholesale price, the markup, the desired profit, whether a store is upscale or discount, the price charged by competitors, and the current economic environment

Visual Literacy

Photo Caption Answer Read the copy on the ad to students. Then read the photo caption and the photo caption question to students: ***How could a partnership with an online price comparison site allow a merchant to market its products more effectively?*** Answers will vary. Accept all reasonable answers. Sample answer: A business that creates a partnership with an online price comparison site like shop.com is opening itself up to the opportunity to achieve sales it might not have otherwise achieved because its products are exposed to customers who might have never otherwise learned about the products.

ENGAGE

Marketing Internship Project Preview

Read students the Marketing Internship Project Essential Question: ***How does a business price a new product line?*** Because students are just starting to learn about pricing, they will likely not know the specific answer to this question, which is to create a pricing plan based on factors that affect price. However, students should know that a retailer's cost (high or low) for a product can directly affect the price the retailer charges to customers. Explain to students that they will learn how businesses set prices for goods and services while studying this unit. Tell students that when they are finished studying this unit, they will ask questions to find answers about pricing a new line of American heritage greeting cards. As they study each chapter in the unit, they can prepare for the Unit Project by thinking of the heritage observances in the United States and the current prices of greeting cards.

 **glencoe.com**

Marketing Internship Project Resources Send students to the Online Learning Center to watch a video and download a worksheet activity related to the topic of the Unit Project.

Read the American Marketing Association quote to students:

AMERICAN MARKETING ASSOCIATION

> ❝ In a recession economy, consumers tend to be more sensitive about price. ❞

Explain to students that the AMA's Resource Library provides information through articles and other resources that address the functions of marketing. Content about the pricing function may examine pricing strategies of an economic environment:

Comparing Options As households try to save money, it is important to convey value effectively. Direct comparisons to other brands are particularly effective in a recession, since shoppers tend to compare options.

Alternative Sizes Consider alternative sizes and price points. As shoppers gravitate toward the two ends of the value spectrum (budget brands and premium indulgences), they also move toward extremes in packaging size.

Ask students: ***What are examples of using alternative sizes as a pricing strategy?*** Products might be offered in multi-packs at a reduced unit price. For example, discounters such as Costco and Smart & Final sell extra-large boxes of food items at a reduced unit prices to encourage sales.

MARKETING CORE FUNCTIONS IN THIS UNIT

Point out to students that Chapters 25, 26, and 27 will touch on two of the seven marketing core functions. Describe each of these marketing functions to students to prepare them to start studying this unit.

 **Market Planning** involves understanding the concepts and strategies used to develop and target specific marketing strategies to a select audience.

 **Pricing** decisions dictate how much to charge for goods and services in order to make a profit.

MARKETING RESEARCH

PROJECT WORKBOOK

The purpose of the Marketing Research Project Workbook is to provide a step-by-step approach for students to conduct their own marketing research study. Each chapter is devoted to key elements in the research process. Each chapter builds upon the previous chapters, and by the end of the book, students will have completed an in-depth marketing research study, complete with rationale for all decisions, a report of the findings and conclusions, recommendations based on the original research problem and study objectives, and an annotated bibliography.

 **glencoe.com**

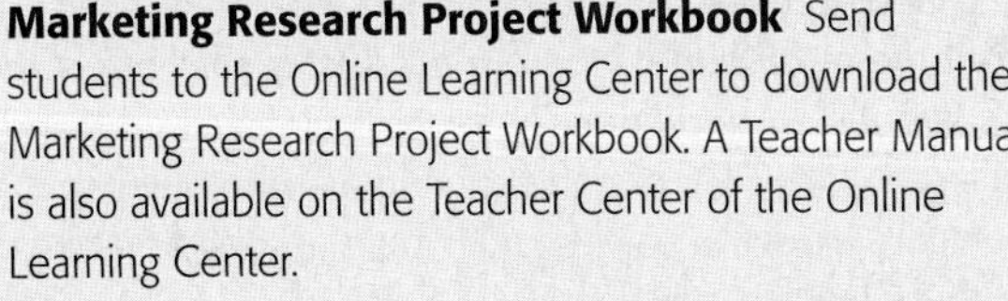

Marketing Research Project Workbook Send students to the Online Learning Center to download the Marketing Research Project Workbook. A Teacher Manual is also available on the Teacher Center of the Online Learning Center.

price planning

SHOW WHAT YOU KNOW

Visual Literacy Furniture retailers target different age groups of males, females, and families because their needs and budgets differ. Furniture products for young families are different than furniture products for older men and women. ***How might the retail outlet where a product is sold affect the product's suggested retail price?***

Discovery Project

Analysis of Pricing Products

Essential Question What factors go into pricing grooming products for teenagers?

Project Goal

Work with a partner to analyze the prices of grooming and beauty products for a specific target market. Compare competing companies that sell similar products for that target market. The products may be cosmetics, grooming aids, or skin care for males or females. Check them out online and in different types of retail outlets (pharmacies, supermarkets, department stores). Analyze the prices and explain the goals and factors that must have been considered when pricing these products.

Ask Yourself...

- How will you select a specific target market?
- How will you decide on which product lines to research?
- How will you analyze the goals and factors that go into pricing products?
- How will you organize and present your report?

Analyze and Interpret Provide research to back up your analysis of goals and factors that go into pricing beauty and grooming products.

glencoe.com

Activity
Get a worksheet activity about pricing products.

Evaluate
Download a rubric you can use to evaluate your project.

DECA Connection

DECA Event Role Play

Concepts in this chapter are related to DECA competitive events that involve either an interview or role play.

Performance Indicators The performance indicators represent key skills and knowledge. Your key to success in DECA Competitive events is relating them to concepts in this chapter.

- Explain factors affecting pricing decisions.
- Select an approach for setting a base price (cost, demand, competition).
- Set prices.
- Explain the nature of overhead/ operating costs.
- Maintain collaborative partnerships with colleagues.

DECA Prep

Role Play Practice role-playing with the DECA Connection competitive-event activity at the end of this chapter. More information on DECA events can be found on DECA's Web site.

ENGAGE

Visual Literacy

Read the chapter opener photo caption questions to students: ***How might the retail outlet where a product is sold affect the product's suggested retail price?*** The store's image and clientele dictate different prices. For example, customers who buy furniture at a discount store expect to pay less than at an upscale furniture store. Then ask these guiding questions.

Guiding Questions

Contrast How is price competition different from nonprice competition?	Price competition focuses on offering the lowest price for a product. Nonprice competition focuses factors such as service, financing, and business location.
Explain What is price gouging? Give an example of when price gouging might occur.	pricing products unreasonably high when the need is great or consumers do not have other choices Example: Raising the price of food after an earthquake.

Discovery Project

Analysis of Pricing Products Hold up examples of three or four grooming products geared toward teens, such as shampoo, body wash, and deodorant. Ask students the Discovery Project Essential Question: ***What factors go into pricing grooming products for teenagers?*** Answers may include prices charged by the competitors and how much teens are willing to pay. Then ask: ***Does price play an important role in which grooming products you purchase? Why?*** Sample answer: It plays a small role. There are certain brands that I like, but I try to buy them only on sale.

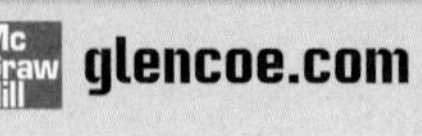

Discovery Project Resources Send students to the Online Learning Center to download a rubric to evaluate their projects.

ENGAGE

Introduce the Chapter

Chapter 25 provides students with an overview of price planning issues and factors. These main concepts are introduced and discussed:

- Relationship of product and value
- Various forms of price
- Importance of price
- Goals of pricing
- Market factors affecting price
- Legal and ethical considerations for pricing

Discussion Starter

Determining Price Ask students what the sayings "put a price on it" and "name your price" mean to them. Answers will vary. "Name your price" can mean "I want this item so badly, I'll pay anything." Then ask: ***How do you determine what a product is worth to you?*** Students may say that it depends on whether the product is something they truly need or just something they want. It also might depend on how much money they have available. Tell students that in this chapter they will learn how businesses make pricing decisions.

DECA Connection

Discuss the performance indicators listed in the DECA Connection feature. Explain to students that performance indicators tell them how to demonstrate their acquired skills and knowledge through individual or team competitive events.

glencoe.com

Competitive Events Workbook For more DECA Role Plays, send students to the Online Learning Center to download the Competitive Events Workbook.

PROGRAM RESOURCE ORGANIZER

PRINT RESOURCES

- **Student Edition**
- **Teacher Edition**
- **Student Activity Workbook with Academic Integration** includes worksheets and activities correlated to the text.
- **Mathematics for Marketing Workbook** provides math activities for every unit in the text.

TECHNOLOGY TOOLBOX

- **Connect**
- **ConnectPlus**
- **ExamView Assessment Suite** is a comprehensive solution for creating, administering, and scoring tests.

glencoe.com

Online Learning Center provides a variety of resources to enrich and enhance learning.

SECTION, CHAPTER, AND UNIT RESOURCES

- **Graphic Organizers** for organizing text concepts visually.
- **Digital Nation Activities** and **Green Marketer Activities** extend learning beyond the text features.
- **Career Chatroom Career Profiles** allow students to explore different marketing occupations in depth.
- **After You Read Answer Keys** for students to check their answers.
- **Discovery Project Rubrics** and **Marketing Internship Project Rubrics** for students to evaluate their projects.

PROGRAM RESOURCES

- **Student Activity Workbook with Academic Integration Teacher Annotated Edition** includes annotated answers for the activities and worksheets.
- **Marketing Research Project Workbook** provides a step-by-step approach for students to complete their own marketing research studies.
- **School-to-Career Activity Workbook** helps students relate their class work to on-the-job experience and involves work-site analysis and working with mentors.
- **Competitive Events Workbook** helps prepare students for state and national marketing education competitions.
- **Inclusion in the Marketing Education Classroom** provides teaching resources for working with students with special needs.
- **PowerPoint Presentations** provides visual teaching aids and assessments for this chapter.

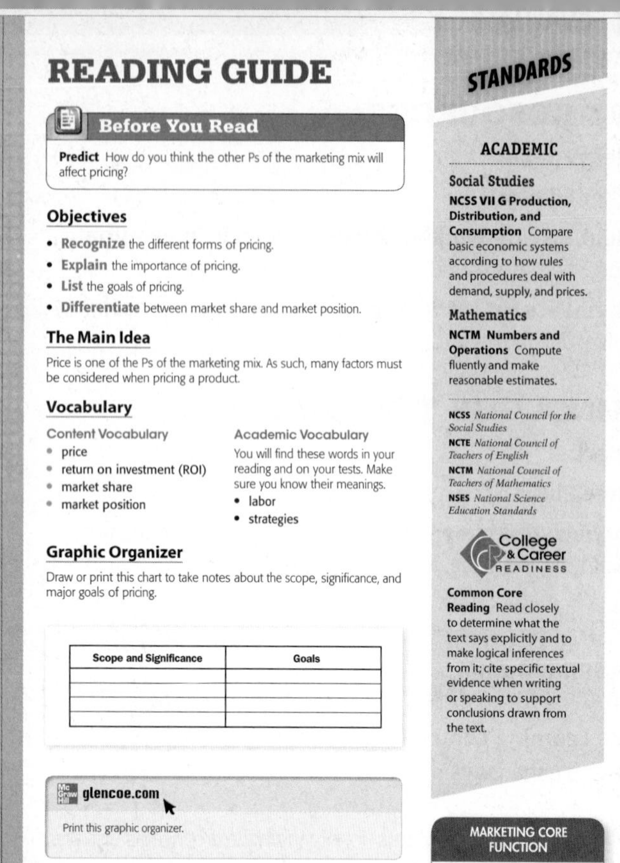

READING GUIDE

Before You Read

Predict How do you think the other Ps of the marketing mix will affect pricing?

Objectives

- **Recognize** the different forms of pricing.
- **Explain** the importance of pricing.
- **List** the goals of pricing.
- **Differentiate** between market share and market position.

The Main Idea

Price is one of the Ps of the marketing mix. As such, many factors must be considered when pricing a product.

Vocabulary

Content Vocabulary
- price
- return on investment (ROI)
- market share
- market position

Academic Vocabulary
You will find these words in your reading and on your tests. Make sure you know their meanings.
- labor
- strategies

Graphic Organizer

Draw or print this chart to take notes about the scope, significance, and major goals of pricing.

Scope and Significance	Goals

glencoe.com

Print this graphic organizer.

STANDARDS

ACADEMIC

Social Studies

NCSS VII G Production, Distribution, and Consumption Compare basic economic systems according to how rules and procedures deal with demand, supply, and prices.

Mathematics

NCTM Numbers and Operations Compute fluently and make reasonable estimates.

NCSS *National Council for the Social Studies*
NCTE *National Council of Teachers of English*
NCTM *National Council of Teachers of Mathematics*
NSES *National Science Education Standards*

College & Career READINESS

Common Core

Reading Read closely to determine what the text says explicitly and to make logical inferences from it; cite specific textual evidence when writing or speaking to support conclusions drawn from the text.

MARKETING CORE FUNCTION

Pricing

584 | Unit 8 · Pricing

Section 25.1 Price Planning Issues

WHAT IS PRICE?

Price is the value in money (or its equivalent) placed on a good or service. It is usually expressed in monetary terms, such as $40 for a sweater. Price may also be expressed in nonmonetary terms, such as free goods or services in exchange for the purchase of a product. As the payment given in exchange for transfer of ownership, price forms the essential basis of commercial transactions.

The oldest form of pricing is the barter system. Bartering involves the exchange of a good or service for another product. It does not involve the use of money. You may remember offering your friend a bag of chips for his cheese and crackers when you were in elementary school. That was bartering. Today's methods are more sophisticated, but the principle is the same. For example, a business might exchange some of its products for advertising space in a magazine or newspaper. Some companies will also exchange advertising spots on their Web pages as a form of bartering, or an equal trade.

As You Read

Analyze What role does price play in marketing planning?

RELATIONSHIP OF PRODUCT VALUE

The value that a customer places on an item or service can make the difference between spending $25,000 or $80,000 on a new automobile, or $20 or $150 on a concert ticket. Value is a matter of anticipated satisfaction. If consumers believe they will gain a great deal of satisfaction from a product, they will place a high value on it. They will also be willing to pay a high price.

A seller must be able to gauge where a product will rank in the customer's estimation. Sellers try to decide whether it will be valued much, valued little, or valued somewhere in between. This information can then be considered in the pricing decision. The seller's objective is to set a price high enough for the company to make a profit but not so high that it exceeds the value potential customers place on the product.

Cost and Price An item's cost may have little to do with its price if price depends on what the market will pay.

VARIOUS FORMS OF PRICE

Price is involved in every marketing exchange. The fee you pay a dentist to clean your teeth, the amount you pay for a new pair of shoes, and minor charges such as bridge tolls and bus fares are all prices. Rent is the monthly price of an apartment. Interest is the price of a loan. Dues are the price of membership. Tuition is the price you pay for an education. Wages, salaries, commissions, and bonuses are the various prices that businesses pay workers for their **labor**. Price comes in many forms and goes by many names.

> "Pricing helps define a company's image and reflects what customers expect to pay."

Chapter 25 · Price Planning | 585

ENGAGE

Anticipation Activity

The Importance of Price Ask students: ***Have you ever purchased a hamburger or fries from a fast-food restaurant's value (or dollar) menu? What type of customer is the restaurant is appealing to?*** someone who wants to save money ***How important is price when you decide where to buy food?*** students may say price is most important; others may say they would pay more for convenience or quality

Objectives

- **Recognize** the different forms of pricing. product price, rent, fee, tuition, commission, interest, salary, dues, wage, bonus
- **Explain** the importance of pricing. It helps establish and maintain a firm's image, competitive edge, and profits.
- **List** the goals of pricing. earning a profit, gaining market share, and meeting the competition
- **Differentiate** between market share and market position. Market share: firm's percentage of total sales volume for all competitors in a given market. Market position: relative standing a firm has in a given market when compared to its competitors.

Graphic Organizer

Scope and Significance	Goals
Value in money (or equivalent) for a good or service	Earn a profit
Price comes in various forms, including rent, salary, wage, and interest	Gain market share
Price affects profits	Meet the competition
Price affects a company's image and competitive edge	Establishes brand

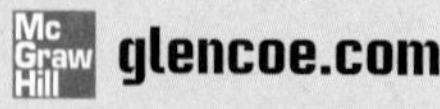

glencoe.com

iWB

Graphic Organizer Send student to the Online Learning Center to print this graphic organizer.

EXPLORE

Before You Read

Read the Before You Read question aloud: ***How do you think the other Ps of the marketing mix will affect pricing?*** Factors such as product features and improvements add to cost and therefore can increase price. This is why a simpler version of a product, such as a dishwasher, is less expensive than one that has additional features such as a heavy-duty cycle and power-saving features. If a product is difficult to find in a specific location or must be shipped from far away, price can increase. Promotion, or advertising, can be very expensive and frequently results in higher prices.

Preteaching Vocabulary

Have students go to the Online Learning Center at glencoe.com for the Chapter 25 Preteaching Vocabulary games.

Content Vocabulary

Instruct students to write each Content Vocabulary word on an index card. As they read this section, have them add a definition to each card. When finished, have students work with a partner to compare their definitions.

Academic Vocabulary

Labor—Synonyms Write the word *labor* on the board. Ask for synonyms for the word. Possible answers: work, job, employment. Then read aloud this sentence: ***Wages, salaries, commissions, and bonuses are the various prices that businesses pay employees for their labor.*** Ask: ***Which of these synonyms fits best in this sentence?*** work

Strategies—Word Origin Explain to students that the word *strategy* comes from the Greek *stratēgía,* which means "generalship." This meaning came about because strategy originally referred to developing tactics related to warfare. Today it refers to developing any type of tactic or approach, and is often used when discussing business tactics.

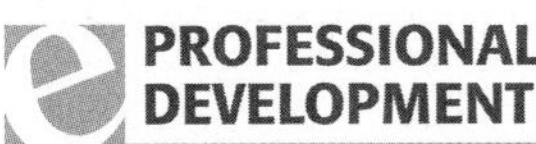

PROFESSIONAL DEVELOPMENT **MINI CLIP**

Reading: Building Vocabulary
Go to the Online Learning Center to view a video clip in which a teacher introduces and plays two vocabulary building games with students.

Price Planning Issues

WHAT IS PRICE?

Explain to students that because price is at the center of commercial transactions, it is vital to understand its role in the marketplace. Ask these guiding questions to focus the discussion on price.

Guiding Questions

Describe What is an example of a non-monetary price?	exchanging food with a friend; agreeing to do a chore at home in exchange for a privilege
Analyze What is an advantage to bartering? What is a disadvantage?	Possible advantage: You may get a better deal than if you paid money. Possible disadvantage: You may not find someone who will barter for what you want.
Evaluate Think of something you purchased in the last week or so. Do you think you got good value for your money? Why or why not?	people think they received good value for their money if they gained satisfaction from the product

As You Read

Read students the As You Read question: ***What role does price play in marketing planning?*** Components of marketing planning must be taken into account when determining price. For example, whether the product is value-oriented or geared to a more upscale market plays a role in pricing and in how the product will be promoted. The product's quality, distribution methods, competitor pricing, and advertising all affect the final price.

Cost and Price Ask students: ***What product have you purchased recently where the price you paid had little to do with the item's actual cost?***

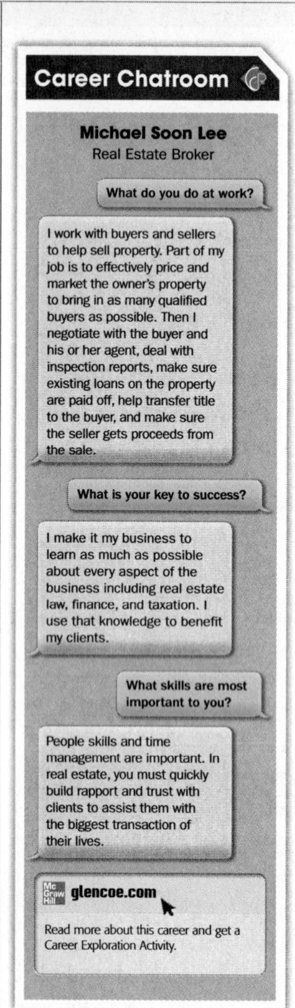

Career Chatroom

Michael Soon Lee
Real Estate Broker

What do you do at work?

I work with buyers and sellers to help sell property. Part of my job is to effectively price and market the owner's property to bring in as many qualified buyers as possible. Then I negotiate with the buyer and his or her agent, deal with inspection reports, make sure existing loans on the property are paid off, help transfer title to the buyer, and make sure the seller gets proceeds from the sale.

What is your key to success?

I make it my business to learn as much as possible about every aspect of the business including real estate law, finance, and taxation. I use that knowledge to benefit my clients.

What skills are most important to you?

People skills and time management are important. In real estate, you must quickly build rapport and trust with clients to assist them with the biggest transaction of their lives.

glencoe.com

Read more about this career and get a Career Exploration Activity.

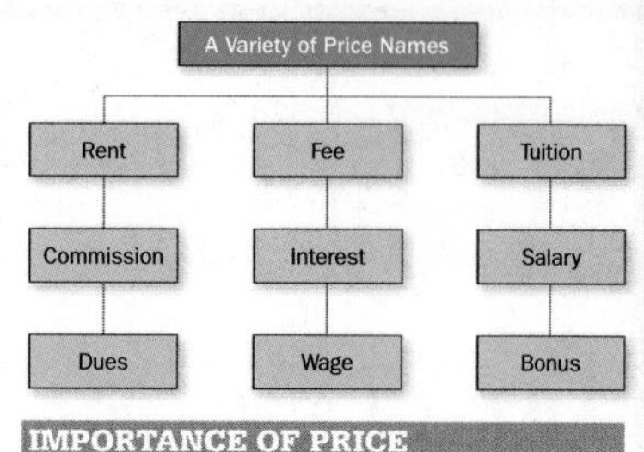

IMPORTANCE OF PRICE

Price is an important factor in the success or failure of a business. Setting a price may seem like a simple task, but there is much more involved than just adding a few dollars to the wholesale cost. A well-planned pricing strategy should result in fair and appropriate prices. Appropriate pricing helps establish and maintain a firm's image, competitive edge, and profits.

Many customers use price to make judgments about products and the companies that make them. A higher price may mean better quality from an upscale store or company to some customers. To other customers, a lower price means more value for their money.

Advertising **strategies** are closely aligned to a company's image. Walmart's® low-price policy is the main focus of its advertising strategy. Some retailers stress that they offer the lowest prices in town. Others promise that they will beat any other store's prices. In such cases, price plays an important role in establishing the edge a firm enjoys over its competition.

Finally, price helps determine profits. Marketers know that sales revenue is equal to price times the quantity sold. In theory, sales revenue can be increased either by selling more items or by increasing the price per item. However, the number of items sold may not increase or they may even remain stable if prices are raised. **Figure 25.1** shows what may happen.

It is also important to remember that an increase in price can increase profits only if costs and expenses can be maintained. You will explore this factor in Section 25.2.

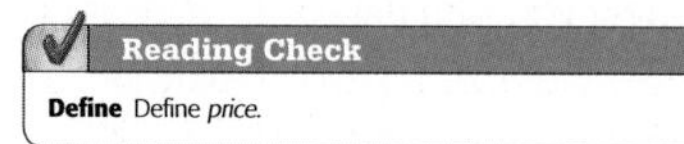

Reading Check

Define Define *price.*

FIGURE 25.1 Projected Effects of Different Prices on Sales

An increase in the price of an item may not produce an increase in sales revenue. ***Explain why an increase in price does not always mean an increase in revenue.***

Price per Item	Quantity Sold	Sales Revenue
$50	200	$10,000
$45	250	$11,250
$40	280	$11,200
$35	325	$11,375
$30	400	$12,000
$25	500	$12,500

GOALS OF PRICING

Marketers are concerned with earning a profit, or return on investment, as their primary goal of doing business. There are times when other pricing goals become important. Gaining market share and meeting the competition are the other main goals of doing business.

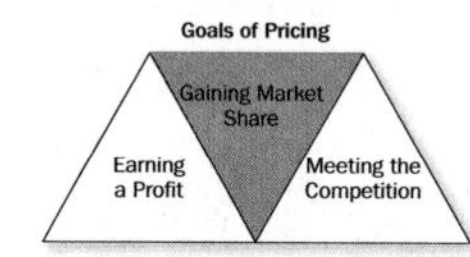

EARNING A PROFIT

Return on investment (ROI) is a calculation that is used to determine the relative profitability of a product. The formula used for calculating the rate of return on investment is as follows:

Rate of Return = Profit/Investment

Profit is another word for *return*, which explains the expression return on investment. Assume your company sells watches to retailers for $9 each. Your cost to make and market the watches is $7.50 per unit. Remember that profit is money earned by a business minus costs and expenses, so that your profit on each watch is $1.50:

$$\$9.00 - \$7.50 = \$1.50$$

Your rate of return is 20 percent:

$$\$1.50/\$7.50 = .20$$

A company may price its products to achieve a certain return on investment. Let's say that you run a watch company. Your company wants to achieve a return on investment of at least 25 percent on a new model. To determine the price at which the new watch would have to sell, you would begin by working backward. Start with a target price, which is the price at which you want to sell the watch. Then determine how your company can get costs down so the price will bring your target return.

EXPLAIN

Career Chatroom

Focus the Career Chatroom discussion concerning Michael Soon Lee by asking students these guiding questions.

Guiding Questions

Explain What does Lee do that will benefit his clients?	learns about finance, law, and business of real estate
Analyze Why hire Lee?	He brings in qualified buyers

glencoe.com

Career Exploration Send students to the Online Learning Center to find more information about this career and to get a Career Exploration activity.

Knowledge Matters

VIRTUAL BUSINESS

PRICING

Introduce students to the concept of pricing using Knowledge Matters' Virtual Business Retailing visual simulation, *Pricing*. In this simulation, students will learn that pricing is a vital concern for business owners.

SUPPLY AND DEMAND

Introduce the concept of supply and demand to students using Knowledge Matters' Virtual Business Retailing visual simulation, *Supply and Demand*. In this simulation, students will learn about the factors of supply and demand and what happens in businesses when these factors are out of balance.

Reading Check Answer

Read the Reading Check question to students: ***Define price.*** Price is the value in money (or its equivalent) placed on a good or service.

ELABORATE

IMPORTANCE OF PRICE

To focus the discussion on price, ask these guiding questions.

Guiding Questions

Explain What does appropriate pricing accomplish?	It helps establish and maintain a company's image, competitive edge, and profits.
Characterize What are two ways in which consumers make judgments based on price?	Some people think a higher price means better quality. Others think a lower price means they are getting more value for their money.
Synthesize Barb wins a smartphone in a contest. She leaves it in an unlocked car and it is stolen. Barb's brother, James, works part-time to earn the money to buy a smartphone, takes care of it, and has it for years. What conclusions might you draw?	Possible answer: The value that a person places on goods is related to how much (or how little) the person paid to obtain the goods.

Visual Literacy

Figure 25.1 Caption Answer Read the caption question to students: ***Explain why an increase in price does not always mean an increase in revenue.*** The number of people willing to pay the higher price may decrease, causing the quantity sold to decline enough to result in a loss of revenue. Ask students: ***If a company wants to increase revenue without increasing a product's price, what might it do?*** Possible answers: Improve its market share by creative advertising; emphasize its product's quality; draw attention to any unique features that set it apart from the competition.

Critical Thinking

Use the data in Figure 25.1 to display a line graph. Then ask: ***What factor is not represented in this graph that can increase the profitability of selling larger quantities of goods at lower prices?*** This graph does not take into account that when producing larger quantities of goods, costs and expenses typically drop. For example, when producing 200 items, costs and expenses per item might be $38, whereas when producing 500 items, they might drop to $34 per item.

Reinforce Vocabulary

Return on Investment (ROI)—Denotative Meaning Write *return on investment* for students to view. Tell students that this term refers to a calculation that is used to determine the relative profitability of a product. Explain that in this situation, the word *return* means the "yield (in profit or interest) that is paid for labor, investment, or other expenditure."

GOALS OF PRICING

Ask these guiding questions to focus the discussion on the goals of pricing.

Guiding Questions

Define What is another word for profit?	return, or return on investment
Analyze A company sells a smartphone for $105. The phone costs the company $80 to make. However, a competitor has started selling a similar phone for $75. What options does the company have?	can reduce its costs to a level where it can compete and still make a profit; use advertising to convince consumers its product is superior; quit making the phone and focus on other products
Formulate A company makes a bird house that sells for $16. The cost of making it has increased from $13 to $14.50. How is this going to affect the ROI?	The ROI will be reduced from about 23 percent $\left(\frac{3}{13}\right)$ to about 10 percent $\left(\frac{1.50}{14.50}\right)$.

Mini Projects

Extension

Using Microsoft Excel to Calculate ROI This mini project requires the student to have a working knowledge of Microsoft Excel, including the ability to enter simple formulas. Have students determine how to use Excel to calculate return on investment (ROI). Instruct students to create a worksheet that performs this calculation. Have students make up their own data to test the worksheet to make certain it works properly. Then have students give a short presentation explaining the steps they used in Excel to calculate ROI. In their presentations, students should demonstrate how to enter profit in one column, costs in a second column, and then divide the profit by the costs (investment) to obtain the ROI.

Exploring Microsoft Excel's What-If Analysis This mini project requires students to be comfortable using Excel for tasks such as entering formulas to calculate ROI. Instruct students to use Excel's Help feature (or other appropriate resource) to learn how to use its What-If analysis. Explain that this feature allows the user to determine outcomes based on different variables. For example, you can calculate a product's ROI based on different values for cost. Have students create several scenarios that make use of What-If analysis. Then have them write a brief report explaining how What-If analysis can be useful in determining ROI under varying conditions. Reports should explain how What-If analysis can be useful in determining how changing variables such as price and cost can affect outcomes such as return on investment.

Take into consideration the suggested retail price you think consumers are willing to pay for the watch. Target pricing will then take on another dimension. Chapter 26 discusses more about target pricing for the customer.

GAINING MARKET SHARE

A business may forgo immediate profits for long-term gains in some other area. One goal, for example, might be to take business away from competitors. The business is trying to increase its market share in this case. For example, in 2009 Walmart sold over 100 toys for $10 each in an effort to garner market share from its major competitor Toys "R" Us® during the holiday season. **Market share** is a firm's percentage of the total sales volume generated by all competitors in a given market.

Businesses constantly study their market share to see how well they are doing with a given product in relation to their competitors. Visualize the total market as a pie. Each pie slice represents each competitor's share of that market. The biggest slice of the pie represents the firm that has the largest percentage of the total sales volume.

MARKET POSITION

Marketers are also interested in their market position. **Market position** is the relative standing a competitor has in a given market in comparison to its other competitors. To monitor market position, a firm must keep track of the changing size of the market and the growth of its competitors. Competitors are ranked according to their total sales volume. Thus, the company or brand with the highest sales volume would be ranked number one. Avis® car rental service used its rank of 2nd place to its advantage in one of its oldest running ad campaigns, which stated: "We're number two so we try harder." Since then Avis has grown and is now ranked number one in on-airport auto rentals. See **Figure 25.2**.

IMPROVING MARKET SHARE AND MARKET POSITION

Pricing is one means of improving market share and market position. Other means of accomplishing the same goals may involve increased advertising expenditures, changes in product design, and new distribution outlets. For example, during the holiday season, Toys "R" Us opened mall-based kiosks in order to increase its share of the toy market.

FIGURE 25.2 Car Rental Market Share

The graph shows that Avis Budget group has the largest share of market in on-airport car rentals. Thus is it is ranked number one in that category. ***What is the market position of all the car rental competitors shown in the chart?***

2.1%
11.2%
31.5%
28.6%
26.6%

- Avis Budget Group
- Hertz
- Enterprise/Alamo/National
- Dollar Thrifty
- Other

MEETING THE COMPETITION

Some companies simply aim to meet the prices of their competition. They either follow the industry leader or calculate the average price, and then position their product close to that figure. Airline pricing appears to follow this pattern. Most airlines charge around the same price for the service provided.

How else do you compete when you do not want to rely on price alone? You compete on the basis of other factors in the marketing mix.

These nonprice competing factors might include quality or uniqueness of product, convenience of business location or hours, and level of service. For example, TD Bank is open seven days a week and offers hours from 8:30 A.M. until 8:00 P.M. during weekdays. Automobile manufacturers are now competing with warranties and maintenance agreements, some offering coverage for five or ten years, or 50,000 or 100,000 miles, respectively. A computer store may offer free installation of software and training to teach you how to use your new software.

After You Read **Section 25.1**

Review Key Concepts

1. **Explain** the relationship between product value and price in a consumer's mind.
2. **Explain** why a higher price does not always bring in higher sales revenue.
3. **Identify** other ways, besides price, that marketers have to accomplish the goal for improving market share.

Practice Academics

Social Studies

4. What problems might a company face when trying to compete with price in a different country? Create a list of possible issues and compare it with a partner. Discuss why your lists are similar or different.

Mathematics

5. A skincare company has developed a new line of lotion. Each bottle of lotion costs $10.00 to make and market, and it is sold for $28.50. What is the rate of return on investment?

Math Concept **Rate of Return** The rate of return measures the profitability of a product. The return on an investment is calculated by dividing the profits by the cost of the investment.

Starting Hints To solve this problem, subtract the cost of making the lotion from the selling price to determine profit. Divide the profit by the cost of making the lotion to get the rate of return in decimal form. Multiply the decimal rate of return by 100 to convert it to a percent.

For help, go to the **Math Skills Handbook** located at the back of this book.

NCSS VII G Production, Distribution, and Consumption Compare basic economic systems according to how rules and procedures deal with demand, supply, prices, the role of government, banks, labor and labor unions, savings and investments, and capital.

NCTM Number and Operations Understand numbers, ways of representing numbers, relationships among numbers, and number systems.

glencoe.com

Check your answers.

ELABORATE

GAINING MARKET SHARE

To focus the discussion on how companies work to increase market share, ask these guiding questions.

Guiding Questions

Analyze A company reports that its market share is $2,400,000. What is the problem with this figure?	Market share is always reported as a percentage. Without knowing the total revenues for all competitors, it is impossible to determine market share from this number.
Synthesize What risks was Sony taking when it reduced the price of PlayStation 2 to $99? Do you think it was appropriate for Sony to take these risks?	Sony was risking that it would lose more money than it could afford and that consumers would not switch to its product because of a strong preference for the Nintendo Wii™.

VIRTUAL BUSINESS

ANALYZING THE COMPETITION

Introduce the concept of analyzing the competition to students using Knowledge Matters' Virtual Business Retailing visual simulation, *Analyzing the Competition*. In this simulation, students will learn how to determine who the competition is, competitive analysis, and how competition affects a business.

PROFESSIONAL DEVELOPMENT **MINI CLIP**

Math: Independent and Dependent Events

Go to the Online Learning Center to view a video clip in which an algebra teacher explains independent and dependent events.

EVALUATE

MEETING THE COMPETITION

Use these guiding questions to focus the discussion on these methods of competition.

Guiding Questions

Identify What are the three ways that a product can compete other than price?	It can be superior to the competition, it can be more widely available, and its can be better advertised.
Draw Conclusions Imagine that you are marketing a tennis ball that costs 20 percent more than the top-selling ball. However, you know that your ball has a better "bounce" than the competitor's ball. What is your primary challenge?	You must convince consumers that your ball is superior enough for them to pay more for it. Possible ways of doing this might include television and Web ads that illustrate this difference.
Correlate Think of a product that you use several times a week. How does this product compete based on "place"?	Students might say they prefer a specific sports drink and that it available at most convenience stores, making it easy to purchase.

Mini Projects

Differentiated Instruction

Visual Learners Have students investigate the market share for each of three video game companies. Students might choose Nintendo® Wii, Sony® PlayStation, and Microsoft® Xbox. Students should create a pie chart showing the portion of total revenues obtained by each of their chosen companies. The chart should be clearly labeled. For example, in the first five months of 2010, both the Wii and Xbox were at 34 percent and PlayStation was at 32 percent.

Verbal/Linguistic Learners Instruct students to investigate the Web sites and social networking sites of two major airlines. Then have them write a brief report explaining what they learned about how these airlines are competing in the marketplace. They should focus on nonprice methods of competition. Reports should discuss nonprice competition methods, such as an emphasis on accumulating points that can be redeemed for free tickets, the ability to receive e-mail notification of delayed flights or special fares, or an airline's high percentage of on-time flights.

After You Read Section 25.1

Review Key Concepts

1. Value is a matter of anticipated satisfaction. If a product is highly valued the price can be a little higher, which is the case in very popular items like the iPod or certain video games. If a product is not of much value in a consumer's mind, the price cannot be very high. For example, an older version of a computer game may be valued much lower than the current version. Thus, the price for the older version must be lower.
2. Since fewer customers buy a product at a higher price, the volume is lower and so is sales revenue.
3. Other means of improving market share include increasing advertising expenditures, changing product design, and obtaining new distribution outlets.

Practice Academics

Social Studies

4. Accept all reasonable answers. A company that wants to compete with price in a foreign country may run across problems with government regulations prohibiting such a practice, tariffs which increase product costs, low-cost local labor that makes competition difficult, and a population that chooses to purchase domestically made goods whenever possible.

Mathematics

5. 185% $\left(\frac{18.50}{10} = 1.85\right)$

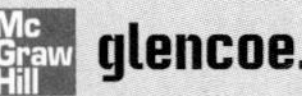

Answer Key Send students to the Online Learning Center to check their answers.

READING GUIDE

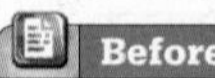

Before You Read

Predict What are some factors that might influence prices?

Objectives

- **List** the four market factors that affect price planning.
- **Analyze** demand elasticity and supply-and-demand theory.
- **Explain** how government regulations affect price planning.

The Main Idea

Pricing requires the examination of many factors. Skipping even one aspect of the pricing process could cost a business millions of dollars in lost sales, fines, and/or lawsuits.

Vocabulary

Content Vocabulary
- break-even point
- demand elasticity
- law of diminishing marginal utility
- price fixing
- price discrimination
- unit pricing
- loss leader

Academic Vocabulary

You will find these words in your reading and on your tests. Make sure you know their meanings.
- constant
- equate

Graphic Organizer

Draw or print this chart to note factors that affect price and legal and ethical considerations in pricing.

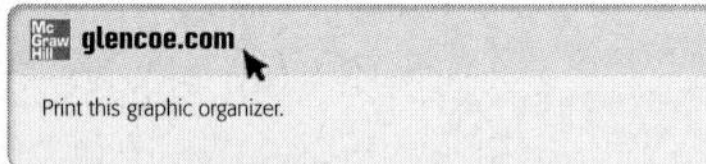

Factors that Affect Price	Legal & Ethical Considerations
Costs and Expenses	Price Fixing

glencoe.com

Print this graphic organizer.

STANDARDS

ACADEMIC

Social Studies

NCSS VII B Production, Distribution, and Consumption Analyze the role that supply and demand, prices, incentives, and profits play in determining what is produced and distributed in a competitive market system.

NCSS VI C Power, Authority, and Governance Analyze and explain ideas and mechanisms to meet needs and wants of citizens, regulate territory, manage conflict, establish order and security, and balance competing conceptions of a just society.

Mathematics

NCTM Problem Solving Solve problems that arise in mathematics and in other contexts.

Common Core

Speaking and Listening Prepare for and participate effectively in a range of conversations and collaborations with diverse partners, building on others' ideas and expressing their own clearly and persuasively.

MARKETING CORE FUNCTION

Pricing

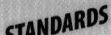

m.e. Section 25.2 Price Planning Factors

MARKET FACTORS AFFECTING PRICES

How do businesses make pricing decisions? The answer is not simple. **Constant** changes in the marketplace force businesses to review pricing decisions frequently. There are four key market factors that must be considered when reviewing and establishing prices. They are costs and expenses, supply and demand, consumer perceptions, and competition.

Most price planning begins with an analysis of costs and expenses. Many of these are related to current market conditions. For example, the cost of raw materials may increase a manufacturer's costs to make an item.

As You Read

Connect Relate the goals of pricing to the factors involved in making a pricing decision.

COSTS AND EXPENSES

Today's economic environment is competitive and becoming more globalized. To compete, businesses must constantly monitor, analyze, and project prices and sales in the light of costs and expenses. They do this because sales, costs, and expenses combine to determine a firm's profit. Many factors have to be considered when raising or lowering prices. This is true even if the impulse to increase or decrease is a direct and seemingly logical reaction to events in the marketplace.

RESPONSES TO INCREASING COSTS AND EXPENSES

When oil prices go up, you will often see an increase in rates charged by airlines, shipping companies, and gas stations. How else could businesses maintain their profit margins? Let's look at other options.

Some businesses have found that price is so important in the marketing strategy of a product that they hesitate to make any price changes. They will reduce the size of an item before they will change its price. A candy manufacturer might reduce a candy bar from 4 to 3.5 ounces instead of increasing its price.

> "Pricing decisions involve extensive analysis of many factors."

Another option manufacturers have for keeping prices to a minimum is to drop features that their customers do not value. Some airlines have stopped serving meals and offer only beverages. Eliminating a small portion of its service helps a company stay competitive.

Some manufacturers respond to higher costs and expenses by adding more features or upgrading the materials in order to justify a higher price. For example, the Ford® Motor Company designed more comfortable supercabs on some of its trucks and charged more for those models.

RESPONSES TO LOWER COSTS AND EXPENSES

Prices may occasionally drop because of decreased costs and expenses. Aggressive firms are constantly looking for ways to increase efficiency and decrease costs. Improved technology and less expensive materials may help create better-quality products at lower costs. For example, the prices of personal computers and high-definition televisions have fallen because of improved technology.

ENGAGE

Anticipation Activity

Improving Student Achievement Have the class list items whose prices they know. Examples may include video games, shoes, movies, and energy drinks. Write each item and its price on the board. Ask: *How do you think these prices are determined?* Retailers set prices based on the cost of goods purchased for resale, competitors' prices, and what people are willing to pay.

Objectives

- **List** the four market factors that affect price planning. costs and expenses, supply and demand, consumer perceptions, competition
- **Analyze** demand elasticity and supply-and-demand theory. demand elasticity: the degree to which demand for a product is affected by price supply-and-demand theory: general rule that demand tends to go up when price goes down
- **Explain** how government regulations affect price planning. Federal laws control what companies can charge. Example: Consumer Goods Pricing Act prohibits manufacturers from forcing retailers to charge a specific price.

Graphic Organizer

Factors that Affect Price	Legal & Ethical Considerations
Costs and expenses	Price fixing
Supply and demand	Price discrimination
Consumer perceptions	Resale price maintenance
Competition	Price advertising

glencoe.com

Graphic Organizer Send student to the Online Learning Center to print this graphic organizer.

EXPLORE

Before You Read

Read the Before You Read question aloud: ***What are some factors that might influence prices?*** Answers may include: economic conditions, supply and demand, competition, how much people are willing to pay, and how much retailers and manufacturers need to charge to make a profit.

Preteaching Vocabulary

Have students go to the Online Learning Center at glencoe.com for the Chapter 25 Preteaching Vocabulary games.

Content Vocabulary

Write the content vocabulary terms and definitions on strips of paper. Place them in a container. Have volunteers draw the strips of paper and read them out loud. Challenge students to match each term with the correct definition.

Academic Vocabulary

Constant—Denotative Meaning Write the word *constant* on the board. Read the statement: ***Constant changes in the marketplace force businesses to review pricing decisions frequently.*** Explain that in this sentence, *constant* means "continual," "invariable," or "unending." Have volunteers come up with original sentences using a form of *constant* in the same sense. Examples: The constant pounding of the rain against the window kept me awake last night. My parents constantly remind me to get my homework done.

Equate—Prior Knowledge Ask students: ***In math class, what does the word*** equation ***mean?*** a statement in which two expressions are equal to one another Ask: ***Based on this, what do you think the verb*** equate ***means?*** to make equal Then ask: ***How might you use*** equate ***in a sentence?*** Paying more money for a product does not necessarily equate better quality.

Critical Thinking

Have students imagine they are buying a book from an online book store. Ask: ***What expenses would the company incurred in shipping the book to you?*** The book must be pulled from inventory, packaged, and delivered to a shipping service. The company must pay the shipping service for transporting the book. Ask: ***How would these expenses change if you owned a reading device such as the Kindle?*** The company must maintain a server from which the book could be downloaded. The file must be uploaded to the server.

Price Planning Factors

MARKET FACTORS AFFECTING PRICES

To focus the discussion of market factors that affect price, present these guiding questions.

Guiding Questions

Recall What is usually the first step in price planning?	analyzing costs and expenses
Apply Imagine a scenario in which there is a shortage of coffee beans because a disease affecting bean crops has caused yields to drop. A coffee company does not want to increase its prices. What else might it do to maintain its current profit margin?	Possible answers: It could reduce container sizes, use less expensive packaging, or reduce advertising expenses.
Deduce Why have the prices of personal computers dropped in recent years?	Technological improvements have allowed computers to be manufactured at a lower cost; to remain competitive, companies have reduced prices.

Expert Advice

Read the quote to students:

“ Pricing decisions involve extensive analysis of many factors. ”

Describe a scenario in which StreetWize Skateboards has introduced a high-end board that sells for 30 percent more than its previous most expensive product. However, sales have been sluggish. What factors might not have been taken into account when the decision was made to add this product to the StreetWize line? Possible answers include whether there is consumer demand for a skateboard in this price range; whether consumers will understand why the board is worth the price; if competitors have products in this price range, how well they are selling; and the state of the economy at the time.

The GREEN Marketer

Eco-Luxury at a Premium Price

Upscale green consumers are willing to pay more for eco-friendly goods so they can enjoy the good life and remain supportive of environmental initiatives. "Eco-luxury" products come in all types: ecologically managed spa vacations, organic French linen sheets, hybrid cars from Lexus® and Mercedes®, and more.

A Growing Market With pricey products like these, companies are tapping into the burgeoning luxury market. They also attract earth-conscious consumers looking for a sustainable splurge. Customers may be willing to spend more money on these products because of their environmental friendliness.

Mathematics

Calculate A Lexus LS Hybrid gets 20 miles per gallon (mpg), and a Lexus LS gets 16 mpg. If the Lexus LS hybrid costs $106,000 and the LS costs $73,000, how much will the buyer pay for each gallon of gas saved in 4 years (10,000 miles/yr)?

NCTM Problem Solving Solve problems that arise in mathematics and in other contexts.

glencoe.com

Get an activity on green marketing.

BREAK-EVEN POINT

Manufacturers are always concerned with making a profit. They are especially concerned when marketing a new product and when trying to establish a new price. In these circumstances, manufacturers carefully analyze their costs and expenses in relation to unit and dollar sales. To do this, they calculate their break-even point.

The **break-even point** is the point at which sales revenue equals the costs and expenses of making and distributing a product. After this point is reached, businesses begin to make a profit on the product.

Suppose a toy manufacturer plans to make 100,000 dolls that will be sold at $6 each to retailers and wholesalers. The cost of making and marketing the dolls is $4.50 per unit, or $450,000 for the 100,000 dolls. How many dolls must the toy manufacturer sell to cover its costs and expenses? To calculate the break-even point, divide the total amount of costs and expenses by the selling price:

$$\$450{,}000 \div \$6 = 75{,}000$$

SUPPLY AND DEMAND

Demand tends to go up when price goes down, and down when price goes up. This statement is accurate as a general rule. However, demand for some products does not respond to changes in price. The degree to which demand for a product is affected by its price is called **demand elasticity**. Products have either elastic demand or inelastic demand. Chapter 5 examined supply-and-demand theory in detail.

ELASTIC DEMAND

Elastic demand refers to situations in which a change in price creates a change in demand. Changes in the price of steak can serve as an example. If the price of steak were $8 per pound, few people would buy steak. If the price were to drop to $5, $3, and finally $2 per pound, however, demand would increase at each price level.

LAW OF DIMINISHING MARGINAL UTILITY

These increases would not continue indefinitely, however. At some point, they would be limited by another economic law. The **law of diminishing marginal utility**, which states that consumers will buy only so much of a given product, even though the price is low. Let's say that detergent went on sale, and you bought five bottles of it. Three weeks later a new sale is announced for the same detergent, but you already have enough to last for months. You do not need to take advantage of the new sale.

INELASTIC DEMAND

Inelastic demand refers to situations in which a change in price has very little effect on demand for a product. If milk prices were to increase, parents with young children may still pay the higher price. During the holiday season, you may see parents willing to pay a higher price for a popular toy than they would normally pay. Since there is no substitute for that toy, it is an example of inelastic demand.

FACTORS INFLUENCING DEMAND ELASTICITY

Five factors determine whether demand is elastic or inelastic. They are brand loyalty, price relative to income, availability of substitutes, luxury versus necessity, and urgency of purchase. See **Figure 25.3** on page 594 for details.

CONSUMER PERCEPTIONS

Consumer perceptions about the relationship between price and quality or other values also play a role in price planning. Some consumers **equate** quality with price. They believe a high price reflects high quality. A high price may also suggest status, prestige, and exclusiveness. Sometimes a higher-priced item may be the better choice. However, consumers should be aware that many businesses sell identical items for significantly different prices.

Some businesses create the perception that a particular product is worth more than others by limiting the supply of the item in the market. They do this by coming out with a limited edition of a certain model and charging a higher price. Why? The reasoning is that the value of the item will increase as a result of its exclusiveness.

Personalized service can add to a consumer's perceptions about price. Many consumers are willing to pay more for items purchased from certain businesses because of the service those businesses might offer.

Businesses can charge slightly higher prices because consumers are willing to pay for the added service. Five-star restaurants offer fancy place settings, well-designed interiors, and an attentive wait staff to make your dining experience more elegant.

COMPETITION

Price must be evaluated in relation to the target market, as one of the four Ps of the marketing mix. A company can use a lower price when its target market is price conscious, such as senior citizens on fixed incomes. When its target market is not price conscious, a company can resort to various forms of nonprice competition.

Nonprice competition minimizes price as a reason for purchasing. It creates a distinctive product through product availability and customer service. The more unusual a product is perceived to be by consumers, the greater the marketer's freedom to set prices above those of competitors.

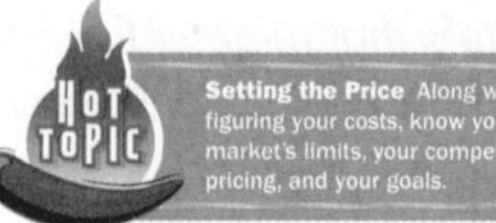

Setting the Price Along with figuring your costs, know your market's limits, your competitors' pricing, and your goals.

Marketers change prices to reflect consumer demand, cost, or competition. When products are very similar, price often becomes the sole basis on which customers make their decisions. Shoppers are more likely to buy less expensive brands if they see no difference between products. Competitors watch each other closely. When one company changes its prices, other companies usually react.

When competitors engage in a battle to attract customers by lowering prices, a price war results. Price wars are good for consumers, who can take advantage of lower prices. However, the lower prices reduce profit margins and can lead to business failure. In 2009, Amazon®, Walmart®, and Target® tried to outdo each other by reducing the price on selected popular books to below $9. None of these companies made money on those books, and their price war hurt the publishing industry, as well as retail book stores.

Reading Check

Explain When might demand for a product go up?

EXPLAIN

The GREEN Marketer

Mathematics Answer The buyer will pay $66 for each gallon of gas saved. $([106{,}000 - 73{,}000] / [10{,}000 \times \frac{4}{20} - 10{,}000 \times \frac{4}{16}])$

Use these guiding questions to discuss this topic in more detail.

Guiding Questions

Draw Conclusions You are marketing environmentally friendly Caribbean vacations. What might be some features of such a vacation?	Hotel rooms use solar energy for hot water, restaurant food is locally grown and organic
Analyze What are the two components of "eco-luxury" products?	They are luxurious and they are geared toward causing less environmental damage than other similar products.

Reinforce Vocabulary

Law of Diminishing Marginal Utility—Analyzing Term Components Writing the term *law of diminishing marginal utility* for students to view. Explain that it is often possible to determine the meaning of a term by analyzing its components. Discuss the meaning of each of these words:

- Law—rule
- Diminishing—becoming smaller or less
- Marginal—close to the lower limit
- Utility—usefulness

Therefore, this rule says there comes a point at which buying more of a product becomes of little use, regardless of how low the price.

Critical Thinking

Take a rubber band and stretch it. Then take a piece of rope and try to stretch it. Compare these two items to elasticity of demand. The purchase of expensive food items, such as steak and lobster, can be thought of as being elastic, just like the rubber band. These purchases typically expand or contract depending on the overall economy. Other products, such as milk and bread, are similar to the rope. People consider these items necessities and demand remains relatively constant. Encourage students to list other items in these categories.

ELABORATE

Graphic Organizer

Reteach the Theory of Supply and Demand Ask students: ***What did you learn about supply and demand in Chapter 5?*** Supply: As the price of a product increases, the quantity supplied generally rises. Demand: As the price of a product increases, the quantity demanded generally falls. Display this graphic organizer. Instruct students to label these components on the following Supply and Demand graph: Demand Curve, Supply Curve, and Equilibrium Point.

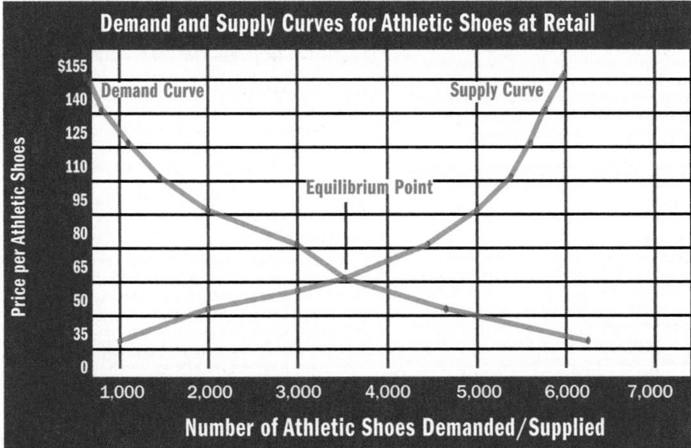

glencoe.com iWB

Graphic Organizer Send student to the Online Learning Center to print this Supply and Demand graph.

CONSUMER PERCEPTIONS

Ask these guiding questions to focus the discussion on this topic.

Guiding Questions

Draw Conclusions What is an example of a high-priced product that is high quality? What is an example of a high-priced product that is not necessarily high quality?	paying more for sports equipment equates to higher quality; With clothing, may pay for a brand name
Make Judgments Imagine that a toy company deliberately limits the supply of a popular doll during the holidays to drive up its price. Do you think this is ethical? Why or why not?	Yes, because the doll is not a necessity and stores are only charging what customers are willing to pay.

Critical Thinking

Describe this scenario: A family wins a raffle sponsored by a charitable organization. The prize is a sports car that the family does not want. The family decides to sell the car. Ask: ***How do you think potential buyers will perceive this car? How will that affect the price the family can get?*** Any potential buyer will probably expect a significant discount off the dealer's price because the buyer will perceive the car as being used. ***What do you think the family should do to determine an appropriate price?*** The family should find out what the dealership would charge for the car and then determine the discount they need to offer in order to obtain a buyer.

COMPETITION

Remind students that competition is at the heart of the free enterprise system. Then ask these guiding questions to focus the discussion on the role competition plays in the marketplace.

Guiding Questions

Analyze Explain why this statement true: *The more unusual a product is perceived to be by consumers, the greater the marketer's freedom to set prices above those of competitors.*	If consumers think a product is special or difficult to get, they will see it as valuable and will be willing to pay more.
Synthesize How would consumers be affected in the short term by a price war? How might they be affected in the long term?	short term: save money; long term: pay higher prices if competition is eliminated

Setting the Price Ask students what they think is meant by the phrase "know your market's limits"?

Reading Check Answer

Read the Reading Check question to students: ***When might demand for a product go up?*** Demand tends to go up when price goes down.

FIGURE 25.3 Demand Elasticity

Demand elasticity varies with five factors: brand loyalty, price relative to income, availability of substitutes, luxury versus necessity, and urgency of purchase. ***How does demand elasticity work?***

1. **Brand Loyalty** Some consumers will not accept a substitute product, even though there are many competing brands. In such situations, demand becomes inelastic because customers are loyal to one brand.
2. **Price Relative to Income** If the price increase is significant relative to one's income, demand is likely to be elastic.
3. **Availability of Substitutes** When substitutes are readily available, demand becomes more elastic.

4. **Luxury Versus Necessity** When a product is a necessity (such as medicine for a sick person) demand tends to be inelastic. When a product is a luxury, like a diamond necklace, demand tends to be elastic.

5. **Urgency of Purchase** If a purchase must be made immediately, demand tends to be inelastic.

LEGAL AND ETHICAL CONSIDERATIONS FOR PRICING

Marketers must be aware of their rights and responsibilities regarding price fixing, price discrimination, resale price maintenance, minimum pricing, unit pricing, and price advertising. Laws have been enacted involving pricing practices, but ethical pricing considerations are also important.

PRICE FIXING

Price fixing occurs when competitors agree on certain price ranges within which they set their own prices. Price fixing can be proven only when there is evidence of collusion. This means that there was communication among the competing firms to establish a price range. Price fixing is illegal because it eliminates competition. The federal law against price fixing is the Sherman Antitrust Act of 1890. This law also outlawed monopolies.

PRICE DISCRIMINATION

Price discrimination occurs when a firm charges different prices to similar customers in similar situations. The Clayton Antitrust Act of 1914 defines price discrimination as creating unfair competition. It also protects against monopolies. The Robinson-Patman Act was passed in 1936 to strengthen the provisions of the Clayton Act. The Robinson-Patman Act prohibits sellers from offering one customer one price and another customer a different price if both customers are buying the same product in similar situations. The Robinson-Patman Act was intended to help smaller retailers compete with the large chain stores.

UNIT PRICING

A number of states have passed laws to make it easier for consumers to compare similar goods that are packaged in different sizes or come in different forms. **Unit pricing** allows consumers to compare prices in relation to a standard unit of measure, such as an ounce or a pound. For example, the unit for canned foods may be ounces or pounds. Food stores post unit prices on labels affixed to store shelves.

For example, if you want to buy frozen orange juice, you may find a 6-ounce can that cost $.64, which equals $3.42 per quart. A 12-ounce can of frozen orange juice in another brand may cost $.89. The unit price for the larger container of juice is listed as $2.38 per quart. Here, the larger container is cheaper per quart.

Remember that foods that cost less per unit are not always the better buy. The larger size is not a good buy if you can't use it before it spoils.

RESALE PRICE MAINTENANCE

Manufacturers' resale price maintenance policies have come under scrutiny by legal authorities. Historically, manufacturers would set a retail price for an item and force retailers to sell it at that price. The manufacturer would punish retailers that sold the item for a lower price by withholding deliveries or refusing promised discounts or allowances. This practice of punishing retailers was outlawed in 1975 in the Consumer Goods Pricing Act.

A manufacturer may suggest resale prices in its advertising, price tags, and price lists. There can even be an agreement to fix the maximum retail price as long as the price agreement is not an "unreasonable restraint of trade" or considered "anti-competitive." A business cannot coerce, or force, current customers into adhering to such prices. It can tell customers in advance that they will not be permitted to sell its products if they break the established pricing policy.

EXPLAIN

Visual Literacy

Figure 25.3 Caption Answer Read the caption question to students: ***How does demand elasticity work?*** Demand elasticity works by determining in which situations a change in price will result in a change in demand. The more elastic the demand, the more likely sales will fluctuate with changes in price. Use these guiding questions to focus the discussion about demand elasticity

Guiding Questions

Recall If a person is loyal to a particular brand, how does that affect demand elasticity?	Demand becomes inelastic.
Analyze Why does the urgency of a purchase tend to make demand inelastic?	If you must have a product immediately, you will pay almost any price that is asked.

Mini Project

Differentiated Instruction

Interpersonal Learners
Have students conduct a poll on the brand loyalty of 30 to 40 adults. Students should ask each person: ***To what product do you have the greatest loyalty?*** When finished, students should divide the products into categories. The categories might include food, clothing, toiletries, cosmetics, cars, cleaning products, and so on. Students then should create a line graph showing the number of people loyal to each product category. Have students share their graphs with the class. Students should categorize the 30 to 40 responses they obtain and then use this data to generate a line graph. As students share their graphs with the class, encourage the class to analyze the results. For example, do people tend to be more loyal to one type of product more than another? What conclusions might a marketing professional draw from these results?

ELABORATE

Graphic Organizer

Display this graphic organizer. Fill it in with student-generated examples.

Brand Loyalty
Always buy Apple Computers rather than PCs

Urgency of Purchase
Airline loses luggage while on trip to Europe

Factors that Determine Demand Elasticity

Price Relative to Income
Senior citizen on Social Security stops going to movies when price increases

Luxury Versus Necessity
Need formula for infant

Availability of Substitutes
Price of butter rises, so some consumers switch to margarine

glencoe.com iWB

Graphic Organizer Send student to the Online Learning Center to print this graphic organizer.

LEGAL AND ETHICAL CONSIDERATIONS FOR PRICING

Ask these guiding questions to focus the discussions.

Guiding Questions

Identify What is price fixing?	Businesses that are competing with one another agree on a price.
Synthesize Why might a manufacturer want to enforce a resale price maintenance policy? Why might a retailer not want to follow such a policy?	The manufacturer might want to keep prices up to establish the value of its products. The retailer might want to lower the price to be more competitive.

e MARKETING

Cost Per Impression

Cost Per Impression (CPI) or Cost Per thousand impressions (CPM) is used to measure Web traffic in order to determine the cost of an e-marketing campaign. A flat rate is given to the advertiser for Web banners, text links, and e-mail advertising when CPI or CPM is used as the basis for pricing. In this method, when an ad is seen on a viewer' screen, you count that appearance as one impression. When using CPM an advertiser is quoted a rate of $10 it means that the cost per impression is actually $0.010 ($10 divided by 1,000 = $0.010).

Innovate and Create

Have students research and report on other terms used in conjunction with pricing for online advertising. Tell them to prepare a short, written summary of their findings and to note which method they would recommend for a big multinational company and for a small, local restaurant. Other terms used in conjunction with pricing for online advertising include: Cost Per Click (CPC), which can be a flat rate or a bid-based rate; Cost Per Lead (CPL), Cost Per Sale (CPS), Dynamic Cost Per Thousand, revenue per thousand impressions (RPM) and Cost Per Action. Affiliate advertising involves a click through to another web site of an affiliate partner (retargeting). In this model, some type of pay per performance may be used for the cost per click. Bid-based models depend on the level of competition among advertisers, which may vary based on the key words used in the advertisement. Accept all reasonable answers for each type of business. Theoretically, large companies would prefer cost per thousand, while a small local restaurant might prefer some type of cost per click.

glencoe.com

eMarketing Worksheet Activity Send students to the Online Learning Center to download an eMarketing worksheet activity.

UNFAIR TRADE PRACTICES

Unfair Trade Practices Law, also known as *Minimum Price Law*, prevents large companies with market power from selling products at very low prices. If they did this, it would drive out competition. In general, the federal law prohibits pricing that has a predatory intent or that harms competition or consumers.

Many states have enacted "sales below cost" or "unfair sales" statutes that may prohibit certain below-cost pricing, even though they would be permitted under federal law. The state laws were enacted to prevent retailers from selling goods below cost plus a percentage for expenses and profit. Some states have passed such laws that cover all products, while others have included only specific products, such as gas, milk, or insurance.

In states where minimum price laws are not in effect, an item priced at or below cost to draw customers into a store is called a **loss leader**. This means the business takes a loss on the item to lead customers into the store. Retailers use popular, well-advertised products as loss leaders. Their hope is that customers will buy other items at regular prices while shopping.

PRICE ADVERTISING

The Federal Trade Commission (FTC) has developed strict guidelines for advertising prices. For exmaple, the FTC's price advertising guidelines forbid a company from advertising a price reduction unless the original price was offered to the public on a regular basis for a reasonable and recent period of time. Another rule says that a company may not claim that its prices are lower than its competitors' prices without proof based on a significant number of items.

Also, a premarked or list price cannot be used as the reference point for a new sale price unless the item has actually been presented for sale at that price.

Bait-and-switch advertising, in which a business advertises a low price for an item that it ultimately has no intention of selling, is not just unethical, it is illegal. For example, when a customer comes in and asks for the advertised item, salespeople switch the customer to a higher-priced item by saying that the advertised product is out of stock or of poor quality.

MARKETING CASE STUDY

Shoppers' Response to Higher Prices

Food shoppers reacted poorly to a $0.25 increase in ConAgra Foods' Banquet® Meals. The increase in price was due to increased costs on food products in that product line. Banquet frozen meals sold for $1.00 in food stores before the price increase. When the price went up to $1.25, sales of Banquet frozen meals dropped significantly.

ConAgra Foods' Response

ConAgra Foods decided to take measures to get the suggested retail price of Banquet meals back to the original $1.00 price point. It removed foods that were costly, such as barbecued chicken, and replaced brownies with mashed potatoes. It also created new entrees with meat patties, beans, and rice. Portions were reduced to cut costs too.

Social Studies

ConAgra Foods' Banquet Meals were priced too highly for their market. However, their price increase may have been successful if it was smaller. Consider the effects of changing the price to $1.10. Discuss with a partner whether you think customers would still have purchased the meals.

NCSS VII B Production, Distribution, and Consumption Analyze the role that supply and demand, prices, incentives, and profits play in determining what is produced and distributed in a competitive market system.

PRICING ETHICS

Most ethical pricing considerations arise when interpreting pricing laws. Some businesses, such as computer chip makers and pharmaceutical companies, spend a lot of money for research and development of new products. Once the product is actually created, its manufacturing cost may be relatively small. When you compare the selling price of a computer chip to the cost of manufacturing it, the price may seem unusually high. However, if the costs of developing the chip are also taken into account, the selling price may seem to be more reasonable.

Price gouging is when a price is set higher than normal for a product or service that is suddenly in high demand. Gouging is unethical and against the law in many states, especially when it happens during a state of emergency as a result of a natural disaster or labor strike.

In the wake of a natural disaster, essentials such as food, water, ice, power generators, lanterns, lumber, and hotel rooms may be in very short supply. Charging excessive prices for these necessities following a disaster is always unethical and usually illegal. For example, raising the price of a hotel room from $100 to $500 following a hurricane would be price gouging.

After You Read Section 25.2

Review Key Concepts

1. **Identify** four pricing options a business might consider in response to increased costs and expenses.
2. **List** five factors that affect demand elasticity.
3. **Name** the government agency that regulates price advertising.

Practice Academics

Social Studies

4. Identify the federal laws involved in the following situations: (a) price fixing; (b) price discrimination; and (c) resale price maintenance.

Mathematics

5. You work for a company that makes and sells watches. Calculate the break-even point for a watch that costs $14 to make and market, and that will be sold for $40. The total quantity that will be sold at that price is 100,000 watches.

Math Concept **Computing the Break-Even Point** The break-even point is the point at which revenue equals the costs of production and distribution. To determine the break-even point, first compute the total production and distribution costs for all products. Dividing the total cost of production by the selling price will yield the number of products that must be sold to break even.

Starting Hints To solve this problem, multiply $14, the cost to make one watch, by the total number of watches produced to determine the total cost of production. Divide total production costs by selling price, $40, to get break-even point.

For help, go to the **Math Skills Handbook** located at the back of this book.

NCSS VI C Power, Authority, & Governance Analyze and explain ideas and mechanisms to meet needs and wants of citizens, regulate territory, manage conflict, establish order and security, and balance competing conceptions of a just society.

NCTM Problem Solving Solve problems that arise in mathematics and in other contexts.

glencoe.com

Check your answers.

ELABORATE

UNFAIR TRADE PRACTICES

Discuss with students that balancing our free enterprise system with the need to protect against unfair trade practices is a challenge. Ask these guiding questions to focus the discussion on unfair trade practices law.

Guiding Questions

Explain Why is the Unfair Trade Practices Law also known as the Minimum Price Law?	In order to protect smaller businesses, it sets minimum prices companies can charge.
Judge You are a legislator in a state that is discussing passing a "sales below cost" statute. Would you be for or against such a law? Why?	Possible answer: I would be for the law because predatory pricing can destroy small businesses, which communities need.

MARKETING CASE STUDY

Social Studies Answer Students' opinions will vary. Possible answer: If the competitors' price was still $1.00 and the Banquet meals were not seen as being superior, most consumers would probably buy the cheaper meals. Then ask: ***Do you think ConAgra made the right decision in making changes to get the price back down to $1.00?*** Answers will vary. Possible answer: I think it was a good idea to remove the more expensive foods, but reducing the portion size might annoy consumers.

EVALUATE

Graphic Organizer

Display the table. Ask students to offer details.

FTC Guidelines for Advertising Prices

- Cannot advertise a price reduction unless product was previously offered at original price
- Cannot say your prices are lower than competitors' prices without proof
- Cannot use premarked or list price as reference for sale price unless item was actually sold at that price
- Cannot use bait-and-switch advertising

 **glencoe.com** 

Graphic Organizer Send students to the Online Learning Center to print this graphic organizer.

PRICING ETHICS

The word *ethics* refers to rules of conduct that a society accepts as being morally correct. Ask these guiding questions to focus the discussion of pricing ethics.

Guiding Questions

Debate Because of a state-wide drought, a farmer receives twice as much money as last year for her corn crop. Is this farmer price gouging? Why or why not?	No, because the farmer is simply getting the market price—she did not require anyone to pay this price. It is likely she also suffered from the drought and had a small yield.
Predict A pharmaceutical company spends hundreds of thousands of dollars to develop a diabetes drug that costs pennies to manufacture. What might happen if the company is only allowed to charge consumers slightly over the manufacturing costs?	The company might stop developing new drugs because it would not be able to afford the research and development costs.

 **After You Read** **Section 25.2**

Review Key Concepts

1. In response to increased costs and expenses, pricing options a business might consider are: pass the increase onto the consumer, reduce the size of the item or drop features to maintain the price, increase features or upgrade materials in order to justify a higher price.
2. Five factors that affect demand elasticity are: brand loyalty, price relative to income, availability of substitutes, luxury versus necessity, and urgency of purchase.
3. The Federal Trade Commission regulates price advertising.

Practice Academics

Social Studies

4. The federal laws involved in the following situations are: (a) price fixing—Sherman Antitrust Act; (b) price discrimination—Clayton Antitrust Act and Robinson Patman Act (c) resale price maintenance—Unfair Trade Practices Law (also known as the Minimum Price Law).

Mathematics

5. 35,000 watches

 **glencoe.com**

Send students to the Online Learning Center to check their answers.

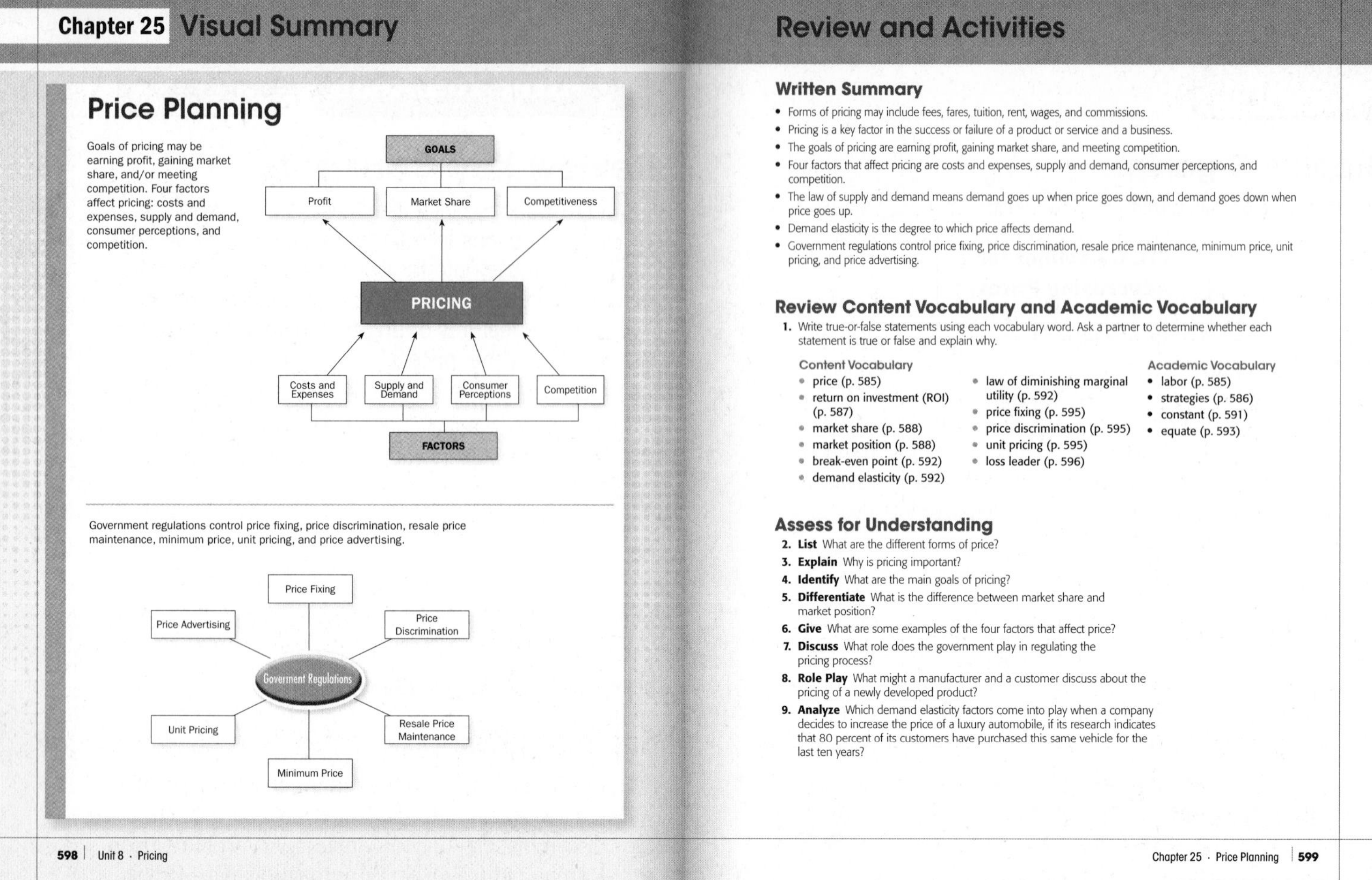

Chapter 25 Visual Summary

Price Planning

Goals of pricing may be earning profit, gaining market share, and/or meeting competition. Four factors affect pricing: costs and expenses, supply and demand, consumer perceptions, and competition.

GOALS
Profit
Market Share
Competitiveness
PRICING
Costs and Expenses
Supply and Demand
Consumer Perceptions
Competition
FACTORS

Government regulations control price fixing, price discrimination, resale price maintenance, minimum price, unit pricing, and price advertising.

Price Fixing
Price Advertising
Price Discrimination
Government Regulations
Unit Pricing
Resale Price Maintenance
Minimum Price

598 | Unit 8 · Pricing

Review and Activities

Written Summary

- Forms of pricing may include fees, fares, tuition, rent, wages, and commissions.
- Pricing is a key factor in the success or failure of a product or service and a business.
- The goals of pricing are earning profit, gaining market share, and meeting competition.
- Four factors that affect pricing are costs and expenses, supply and demand, consumer perceptions, and competition.
- The law of supply and demand means demand goes up when price goes down, and demand goes down when price goes up.
- Demand elasticity is the degree to which price affects demand.
- Government regulations control price fixing, price discrimination, resale price maintenance, minimum price, unit pricing, and price advertising.

Review Content Vocabulary and Academic Vocabulary

1. Write true-or-false statements using each vocabulary word. Ask a partner to determine whether each statement is true or false and explain why.

Content Vocabulary
- price (p. 585)
- return on investment (ROI) (p. 587)
- market share (p. 588)
- market position (p. 588)
- break-even point (p. 592)
- demand elasticity (p. 592)
- law of diminishing marginal utility (p. 592)
- price fixing (p. 595)
- price discrimination (p. 595)
- unit pricing (p. 595)
- loss leader (p. 596)

Academic Vocabulary
- labor (p. 585)
- strategies (p. 586)
- constant (p. 591)
- equate (p. 593)

Assess for Understanding

2. **List** What are the different forms of price?
3. **Explain** Why is pricing important?
4. **Identify** What are the main goals of pricing?
5. **Differentiate** What is the difference between market share and market position?
6. **Give** What are some examples of the four factors that affect price?
7. **Discuss** What role does the government play in regulating the pricing process?
8. **Role Play** What might a manufacturer and a customer discuss about the pricing of a newly developed product?
9. **Analyze** Which demand elasticity factors come into play when a company decides to increase the price of a luxury automobile, if its research indicates that 80 percent of its customers have purchased this same vehicle for the last ten years?

Chapter 25 · Price Planning | 599

EVALUATE

Visual Summary

Express Creativity Ask students to create a visual summary that illustrates a concept in the chapter. Encourage students to use different formats for their visual summaries, such as a storyboard, a timeline, a table, or a word web. For example, students might use a cause-and-effect diagram when summarizing government regulations. Visual summaries will vary depending on the concept depicted and the visual manner in which it is depicted. Questions to ask when assessing a visual summary include:

- Is the summary clear, economical, and simple?
- Are any important steps left out?
- Are steps or concepts arranged in the same order as the original?
- Does the summary reveal a pattern that connects the details?
- Does the summary locate and highlight the most important information?

Review Content Vocabulary and Academic Vocabulary

1. True-or-false statements will vary. Sample statements:
Price is always stated in monetary terms. (False—Price can be expressed in non-monetary terms.)
The calculation used to determine the relative profitability of a product is its **return on investment (ROI)**. (True)
Market share is a firm's percentage of total sales volume for all competitors in a given market. (True)
Market position is used to determine the point at which sales revenue equals costs and expenses of production. (False—Market position is a firm's relative standing in comparison to competitors.)
A product's **break-even point** is calculated by subtracting all expenses from the product's cost. (False—The break-even point is calculated by adding the total costs and expenses of producing a product and dividing that figure by the product's selling price.)
Demand elasticity is the degree to which product demand is affected by price. (True)
The **law of diminishing marginal utility** states that people will buy any amount of a product as long as the price is very low. (False—The law of diminishing marginal utility states that people will buy only so much of a product, even if the price is extremely low.)
Price fixing is illegal because it makes it difficult to import products. (False—Price fixing is illegal because it eliminates competition.)

EVALUATE

Assess for Understanding

2. Different forms of pricing are fees, tolls, fares, rent, interest, dues, tuition, wages, salaries, commissions, and bonuses.
3. Pricing can determine the success or failure of a business as a result of its effect on a firm's image, competitive edge, and profits.
4. The main goals of pricing are earning a profit, gaining market share, and meeting competition.
5. Market share is the percentage of the total sales volume generated by competitors, whereas market position is a firm's rank compared to that of competitors.
6. Factors affecting prices are: costs and expenses—cost of electricity may rise; supply and demand—supply of tomatoes may drop because of a new disease; consumer perceptions—consumers may be willing to pay more for a particular make of car because they see it as being of better quality; competition—a company may follow suit when a competitor lowers a product's price.
7. Government regulations attempt to ensure legal and ethical pricing practices. For example, the Sherman Antitrust Act outlaws monopolies and the Robinson-Patman Act prohibits sellers from offering one customer one price and another customer a different price if circumstances are similar.
8. Accept all reasonable answers. Students might discuss the product's target market, the product's features, the product's price, its major competitors and what prices they charge, features that differentiate the product from its competitors, consumer loyalty to the brand in general, and so on.
9. In theory, demand should go down because the price went up. However, since it is a luxury automobile, factors of demand elasticity could come into play. Price relative to income may not be enough for loyal customers to buy another vehicle, and if they are so loyal that they would not consider a substitute, they would pay the higher price. They may also consider a car a necessity if they are in a certain line of work, like real estate agents or car services that drive customers in their vehicles.

Chapter 25 Review and Assessment

21st Century Skills

Ethical Skills

10. Price Wars Research historical examples and current examples of price wars. Consider the effect of price wars on consumers, the companies involved, and the industry. What ethical dilemmas are involved for companies that consider engaging in price wars?

Financial Literacy Skills

11. Home Business Profits Assume that you make and sell jewelry that you create from your own designs. You operate the business from your home, so you currently do not have to pay rent or utilities on office space. It costs you $8.00 for materials, and you sell the jewelry for $20. If you make 100 jewelry items, when do you break even? Of what significance is the break-even point to making a profit?

Everyday Ethics

12. Used Car Trends Car shoppers who want to save money might ask, "What about a used car?" Buyers, however, could find themselves stuck with many car problems if they do not do their homework. A mechanic should evaluate the car, and a background report should be done. Read the contract before signing. Remember, "The big print typically gives, the little print typically takes away." Discuss whether it is ethical for used car salespeople to put constrictive terms and conditions into the fine print at the end of a contract.

e-Marketing Skills

13. Online Pricing Online merchants constantly study their competitors' prices. Assume you work for an online merchant that sells computers. Research the prices of three comparable computers. Write a report on your price analysis and recommendations for pricing those items on your company Web site.

Build Academic Skills

Social Studies

14. Economics Printers are priced quite reasonably in relation to the cost of making and marketing them. Research how companies that make printers cover their costs and remain profitable. Consider the accessories that a printer needs in the course of its daily use. Select a model of printer and estimate how much it would cost over the course of a year.

NCSS VII B Production, Distribution, and Consumption Analyze the role that supply and demand, prices, incentives, and profits play in determining what is produced and distributed in a competitive market system.

Science

15. Scientific Inquiry Research natural disasters such as major hurricanes. What products were in demand before and after the disaster? How did companies that sell those products price them? Create a graph that shows the supply and demand curves for such products before and after a disaster.

NSES A Develop abilities necessary to do scientific inquiry, understandings about scientific inquiry.

Mathematics

16. Return on Investment A toy company has launched a new product that has a manufacturing cost of $5.75 and a marketing cost of $3.00. The toy is being sold for $14.50. What is the return on investment (ROI) for the product? (Round your answer to the nearest whole percent.)

NCTM Numbers and Operations Compute fluently and make reasonable estimates.

Math Concept **Computation** The ROI is calculated by dividing the profits by the cost of investment.

For help, go to the **Math Skills Handbook** located at the back of this book.

Standardized Test Practice

Directions Read the following questions. On a separate sheet of paper write the best possible answer for each one.

1. A firm's percentage of the total sales volume generated by all competitors in a given market is
   A. market position.
   B. market share.
   C. its breakeven point.
   D. market demand.
2. When a product is a necessity, demand tends to be elastic.
   T
   F
3. A calculation that is used to determine the relative profitability of a product is called ________.

Test-Taking Tip

If you want to use a calculator at a testing site, make sure it is authorized. Also, make sure other electronic devices, such as phones and pagers, are turned off.

DECA Connection Role Play

Owner
Cleaning Service

Situation Your company specializes in cleaning for businesses. You and your business partner (judge) have been in business for five years. You employ 15 employees. You train each cleaning employee to clean the business thoroughly and to treat the customer's property with care and respect. You provide all of the equipment and supplies for normal cleaning tasks.

Most of your customers use your service daily. Because of the number of cleaners you employ and the time involved at each business, you are unable to accept new customers except when an existing customer leaves your service. Because of the quality and care your service offers, you are able to charge top-dollar prices.

You have been considering expanding your business. A custom homebuilder has approached you. The builder would like to explore the possibility of having your service clean the completed homes. You and your partner (judge) have many things to consider before accepting or declining the builder's offer. One of the factors you must carefully consider is the pricing of your company services for the proposed cleanings.

Activity You are to discuss with your partner (judge) some of the factors in terms of cost, demand, and competition that must be considered before pricing the proposed cleanings.

Evaluation You will be evaluated on how well you meet the following performance indicators:

1. Explain factors affecting pricing decisions.
2. Select an approach for setting a base price (cost, demand, competition).
3. Set prices.
4. Explain the nature of overhead/operating costs.
5. Maintain collaborative partnerships with colleagues.

glencoe.com

Download the Competitive Events Workbook for more Role-Play practice.

EVALUATE

Ethical Skills

10. Accept all reasonable answers. Research will reveal price wars in the airline industry, home scanners, supermarkets, books, as well as other products. Consumers will benefit from lower prices, the companies involved will lose money, and the industry can be hurt because consumers may expect those low prices to continue. An ethical dilemma for companies that consider engaging in price wars may be the aftermath from it. Some smaller companies that cannot compete may go under. Consumers may not trust the company's pricing policies because they will think the original prices were too high and unfair, compared to the lower prices offered during a price war.

Financial Literacy Skills

11. Yes, you will start making a profit after selling 40 jewelry pieces ($8.00 × 100 pieces of jewelry = $800 divided by $20 sale price = 40).

Everyday Ethics

12. Student responses as to whether it is ethical to put constrictive terms and conditions into the fine print at the end of a contract will vary. However, students should be aware that it is their responsibility to thoroughly read all contracts. If they do not understand part of the contract, they should ask a reliable and knowledgeable person to help them, even if it means losing a car they want to buy.

e-Marketing Skills

13. Reports will vary depending on the computers researched. Accurate research and analysis for the prices of three comparable computers, along with recommendations for pricing the computers on the company Web site, should be included in the written report.

EVALUATE

Build Academic Skills

Social Studies

14. The primary way that printer manufacturers remain profitable is by selling the ink or toner required to use their printers. This is particularly true for color inkjet printers. For example, a color inkjet printer may sell for only $89. However, the ink cartridges cost about $20 each and only print about 450 pages. Therefore, if an individual prints 200 pages a month (2400 a year), at the end of a year, about $106 has been spent on ink, more than the cost of the printer.

Science

15. Students should create a graph showing the supply and demand for specific products before and after a natural disaster. They also should discuss how these products were priced both before and after the disaster. Products that will increase in demand include bottled water, basic food supplies (especially those that do not require refrigeration or other special handling), batteries, portable generators, cleaning supplies such as bleach, and building supplies such as lumber, plywood, and window glass.

Mathematics

16. 66 percent ([14.50 – 8.75])/8.75)

Standardized Test Practice

1. B market share
2. False
3. return on investment (ROI)

DECA Connection Role Play

Evaluations will be based on these performance indicators:

1. **Explain factors affecting pricing decisions.** A major factor affecting price is the perceived value of the product, which is a matter of the customer's anticipated satisfaction. In addition, costs and expenses, supply and demand, the degree of elasticity in the demand, consumer perceptions, competition, and possible legal implications, all affect price.
2. **Select an approach for setting a base price (cost, demand, competition).** The students should be able to examine the specific market situation and select an appropriate approach for setting a base price. For example, in a situation where demand is inelastic, such as when a popular toy is seen as highly desirable, pricing may go up considerably. However, if there are many substitutes for a product, demand will be elastic and prices will drop. Competition can lead to prices being lower to gain market share, but companies must take care that they are still receiving an appropriate return on their investment.
3. **Set prices.** The student should be able to establish prices based on the approach selected. For examples, if price is based on costs and expenses, these values are used to calculate it and profit is then added on to achieve the final price. If a store emphasizes its competitiveness, price may be primarily determined by what other businesses are charging.
4. **Explain the nature of overhead/operating costs.** Overhead/ operating costs include items such as store rental (or mortgage) costs, utilities, property taxes, maintenance, advertising expenses, etc.
5. **Maintain collaborative partnerships with colleagues.** Students should be able to work together when performing tasks such as calculating break-even points, analyzing factors affecting price, determining demand elasticity, and setting prices.

Mc Graw Hill 

Role Plays For more DECA Role Plays, send students to the Online Learning Center to download the Competitive Events Workbook.

pricing strategies

SHOW WHAT YOU KNOW

Visual Literacy The retail market for fashion accessories is extremely competitive. The pricing model depends not only on the cost, but on what consumers are willing to pay to be in style. ***What pricing strategies would you use when deciding on the price of a popular fashion accessory?***

Discovery Project

Pricing Electronics

Essential Question How do you set the price for a new electronic product?

Project Goal

Work with a partner to decide on a price for a new electronic game console that is breaking into the lucrative gaming market. Major players in this market are Xbox and Playstation. Assume the new game console is similar to these. Go online or in person to a store that sells electronic games consoles to see how they are priced. Identify the product's life cycle. Determine the pricing strategies used to market electronic games. Also consider marketing the new electronic product in another country with an emerging market for these games. Summarize your findings in a report.

Ask Yourself...

- How will you find businesses that sell electronic game consoles?
- How will you conduct research on their pricing strategies?
- How will you decide on the price for a new product?
- How will you organize and present your report?

Synthesize and Present Research Synthesize your research by summarizing your findings and providing the rationale for your suggested retail price of a new electronic game console.

glencoe.com

Activity
Get a worksheet activity about pricing.

Evaluate
Download a rubric you can use to evaluate your project.

DECA Connection

DECA Event Role Play

Concepts in this chapter are related to DECA competitive events that involve either an interview or role play.

Performance Indicators The performance indicators represent key skills and knowledge. Your key to success in DECA competitive events is relating them to concepts in this chapter.

- Select an approach for setting a base price (cost, demand, competition).
- Describe pricing strategies.
- Set prices.
- Organize information.
- Adjust prices to maximize profitability.

DECA Prep

Role Play Practice role-playing with the DECA Connection competitive-event activity at the end of this chapter. More information on DECA events can be found on DECA's Web site.

ENGAGE

Visual Literacy

Ask students: ***What pricing strategies would you use when deciding on the price of popular fashion accessory?*** Sample answer: If the item is in high demand, and customers will pay, then competitive pricing above the competition might be profitable. Pricing below the competition and discount pricing may be profitable for a popular item like a bag that is made of inexpensive materials. Then ask these guiding questions.

Guiding Questions

Define What is meant by demand elasticity? What is an example?	It is the extent to which demand for a product is affected by its price. Example: If the price of spinach goes up dramatically, demand will drop because consumers can substitute other greens.
Analyze What are the three goals of pricing?	earning a profit, gaining market share, meeting the competition

Discovery Project

Pricing Electronics To help students begin to think about the pricing strategies used in business, ask students the Discovery Project Essential Question: ***How do you set the price for a new electronic product?*** Encourage students to take a "big-picture" view as they discuss their options. Ask: ***Would you want everyone to own the product? Or would you want to price it high so that consumers would believe the product is better than other products in its category?*** Students should recognize that marketing people take all these ideas into consideration when pricing a volatile product such as the latest electronic gaming console.

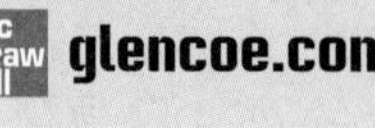

Discovery Project Resources Send students to the Online Learning Center to download a rubric to evaluate their projects.

ENGAGE

Introduce the Chapter

Chapter 26 discusses the methods companies use to set product prices and the factors and company policies that can affect pricing. These main concepts are introduced and discussed:

- Demand-oriented pricing
- Competition-oriented pricing
- Cost-oriented pricing
- One-price versus flexible-price policy
- Pricing during product life cycle
- Pricing strategies for adjusting the base price
- Product mix strategies
- Promotional pricing
- The six steps in the pricing process
- Pricing technology

Discussion Starter

Have students work as a group on a collaborative list of items whose prices they know have increased or decreased over time. Examples might include laptops, DVD players, video games, gasoline, and cars. As they name the items, write a plus or minus after each item to indicate whether the price has increased or decreased. Ask students why they think these prices have fluctuated. Answers will vary. Some items, such laptops and DVD players, have decreased as the prices of the technologies they use have dropped. For example, the price of flat screen televisions has decreased dramatically in recent years. Others, such as the cost of cars, have gone up because of general inflation and possibly an increase in available features, such as GPS technology.

DECA Connection

Discuss the performance indicators listed in the DECA Connection feature. Explain to students that performance indicators tell them how to demonstrate their acquired skills and knowledge through individual or team competitive events.

 **glencoe.com** 

Competitive Events Workbook For more DECA Role Plays, send students to the Online Learning Center to download the Competitive Events Workbook.

PROGRAM RESOURCE ORGANIZER

PRINT RESOURCES

- **Student Edition**
- **Teacher Edition**
- **Student Activity Workbook with Academic Integration** includes worksheets and activities correlated to the text.
- **Mathematics for Marketing Workbook** provides math activities for every unit in the text.

TECHNOLOGY TOOLBOX

- **Connect**
- **ConnectPlus**
- **ExamView Assessment Suite** is a comprehensive solution for creating, administering, and scoring tests.

 **glencoe.com** 

Online Learning Center provides a variety of resources to enrich and enhance learning.

SECTION, CHAPTER, AND UNIT RESOURCES

- **Graphic Organizers** for organizing text concepts visually.
- **Digital Nation Activities** and **Green Marketer Activities** extend learning beyond the text features.
- **Career Chatroom Career Profiles** allow students to explore different marketing occupations in depth.
- **After You Read Answer Keys** for students to check their answers.
- **Discovery Project Rubrics** and **Marketing Internship Project Rubrics** for students to evaluate their projects.

PROGRAM RESOURCES

- **Student Activity Workbook with Academic Integration Teacher Annotated Edition** includes annotated answers for the activities and worksheets.
- **Marketing Research Project Workbook** provides a step-by-step approach for students to complete their own marketing research studies.
- **School-to-Career Activity Workbook** helps students relate their class work to on-the-job experience and involves work-site analysis and working with mentors.
- **Competitive Events Workbook** helps prepare students for state and national marketing education competitions.
- **Inclusion in the Marketing Education Classroom** provides teaching resources for working with students with special needs.
- **PowerPoint Presentations** provides visual teaching aids and assessments for this chapter.

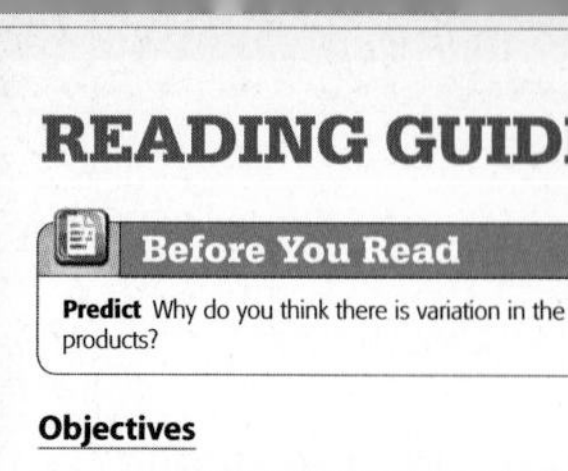

READING GUIDE

Before You Read

Predict Why do you think there is variation in the prices of products?

Objectives

- **Name** three pricing policies used to establish a base price.
- **Explain** two polar pricing policies for introducing a new product.
- **Explain** the relationship between pricing and the product life cycle.

The Main Idea

It is important to establish a base price from which price adjustments can be made. Various situations and company policies can affect the pricing of a product.

Vocabulary

Content Vocabulary

- markup
- one-price policy
- flexible-price policy
- skimming pricing
- penetration pricing

Academic Vocabulary

You will find these words in your reading and on your tests. Make sure you know their meanings.

- relation
- allocated

Graphic Organizer

Draw or print this chart to take notes about the pricing policies that can affect the base price of a product.

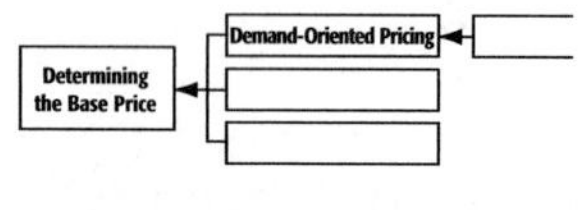

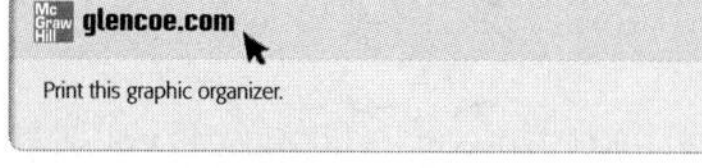

glencoe.com

Print this graphic organizer.

STANDARDS

ACADEMIC

English Language Arts

NCTE 12 Use language to accomplish individual purposes.

Mathematics

NCTM Number and Operations Understand numbers, ways of representing numbers, relationships among numbers, and number systems.

NCTM Problem Solving Apply and adapt a variety of appropriate strategies to solve problems.

NCSS *National Council for the Social Studies*
NCTE *National Council of Teachers of English*
NCTM *National Council of Teachers of Mathematics*
NSES *National Science Education Standards*

Common Core
Writing Write narratives to develop real or imagined experiences or events using effective technique, well-chosen details, and well-structured event sequences.

MARKETING CORE FUNCTIONS

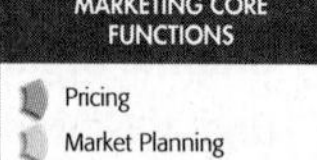

Pricing
Market Planning

Section 26.1

Basic Pricing Policies

BASIC PRICING CONCEPTS

Demand, competition, and cost all influence pricing policies and are important in establishing a base price for a product. Each factor is the basis for the three strategies used for setting base prices: demand-oriented pricing, competition-oriented pricing, and cost-oriented pricing.

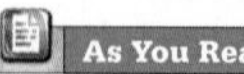

As You Read

Analyze Consider policies and situations that marketers use to establish the base price for new and old products.

DEMAND-ORIENTED PRICING

Marketers who use demand-oriented pricing attempt to determine what consumers are willing to pay for specific goods and services. The key to this method of pricing is the consumer's perceived value of the item. The price must be in line with this perception, or the item will be priced too high or too low for the target market. Inappropriate pricing could cause the product to fail.

Demand-oriented pricing relies on the basic premises of supply-and-demand theory and on demand elasticity factors. The higher the demand, the more a business can charge for a good or service. This is true even though the good or service and its cost do not change.

COMPETITION-ORIENTED PRICING

Marketers may elect to take one of three actions after learning the competitors' prices: price above the competition, price below the competition, or price in line with the competition (going-rate pricing). In this pricing method, there is no **relation** between cost and price or between demand and price.

Competitive-bid pricing, one type of competition-oriented pricing strategy, determines the price for a product based on bids submitted by competitors to a company or government agency. In such cases, some companies will try to enter the lowest bid in order to obtain the contract.

> "A major factor in determining the profitability of any product is establishing a base price."

COST-ORIENTED PRICING

In cost-oriented pricing, marketers first calculate the costs of acquiring or making a product and their expenses of doing business. Then they add their projected profit margin to these figures to arrive at a price. Resellers use different terminology than used by manufacturers and service businesses in the process.

RESELLERS

Resellers calculate prices using the concept of markup. **Markup**, generally expressed as a percentage, is the difference between an item's cost and sale price. For example, if an item costs \$10 and the percentage of markup on cost is 40 percent, the retail price would be \$14 (\$10 × .40 = \$4; \$10 + \$4 = \$14).

Markup pricing is used primarily by wholesalers and retailers, who are involved in acquiring goods for resale. The markup on products must be high enough to cover the expenses of running the business and must include the intended profit. However, retailers must make sure the intended profit does not exceed a reasonable price.

ENGAGE

Anticipation Activity

Improving Student Achievement Have students choose a product they purchase regularly. Have them brainstorm a list of reasons the product's price might go up. increase in production costs, scarcity, increased demand, new markets

Objectives

- **Name** three pricing policies used to establish a base price. demand-oriented, competition-oriented, and cost-oriented pricing
- **Explain** two popular pricing policies for introducing a new product. skimming pricing, penetration pricing
- **Explain** the relationship between pricing and the product life cycle. Stages—introduction, growth, maturity, decline. Pricing during each stage depends on original method. In penetration pricing, for example, the goal is to keep volume up as long as possible during growth cycle to keep cost per unit down.

Graphic Organizer

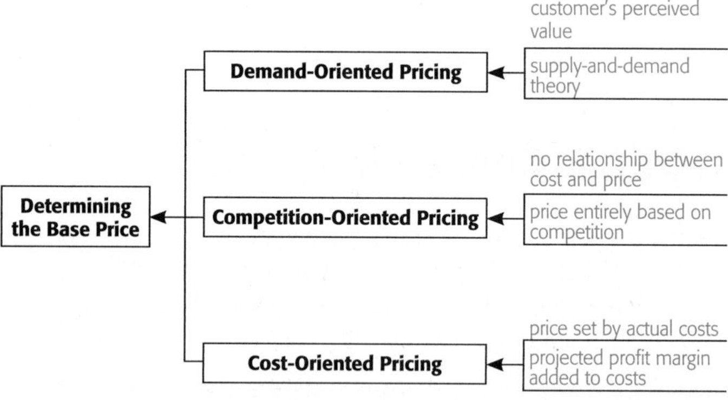

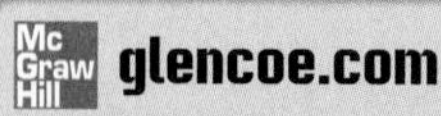

glencoe.com

Graphic Organizer Send students to the Online Learning Center to print this graphic organizer.

EXPLORE

Before You Read

Read the Before You Read question aloud: ***Why do you think there is variation in the prices of products?*** differences in production costs, competition, variations in demand, the product's current position in the product life cycle, and various pricing strategies Then ask: ***When have you seen a product's price vary? Why do you think it varied?*** The cost of the soft drink I like varies depending on whether I buy it in a convenience store or a supermarket. Supermarkets deal in large quantities of goods, so they can afford to sell at lower prices.

Preteaching Vocabulary

Have students go to the Online Learning Center at glencoe.com for the Chapter 26 Preteaching Vocabulary games.

Content Vocabulary

Have students place each content vocabulary word into one of these categories: (1) Basic pricing concepts; (2) Pricing policies; (3) Pricing of new products. (1) markup; (2) one-price policy, flexible-price policy; (3) skimming pricing, penetration pricing

Academic Vocabulary

Relation—Synonyms Display this sentence for the class to read: ***There is a relationship between the cost of a product and its retail price.*** Ask students: ***What are some synonyms for*** relation? association, connection, link, correlation

Allocated—Denotative Meaning Explain that *allocated* means "set apart for a special purpose." Ask: ***How might a school use the word*** allocated ***in reference to government money?*** The new funding is allocated for the computer lab.

Basic Pricing Policies

BASIC PRICING CONCEPTS

Explain to students that marketers understand the concepts and strategies involved in setting prices. Ask these guiding questions.

Guiding Questions

Recall In demand-oriented pricing, how are prices set?	Price is based on consumers' perceived value of a product..
Contrast How is competition-oriented pricing different from cost-oriented pricing?	In competition-oriented pricing, competitors' prices are the main factor. In cost-oriented pricing, price is based on cost, expenses, and profit margin.
Predict Each of a town's gas stations charges the same price per gallon. What might happen if one cut the price by 2 cents?	The others may also lower prices. If this continues and profit margins are small, the price could drop below cost.

As You Read

Read students the As You Read question: ***Consider policies and situations that marketers use to establish the base price for new and old products.*** Demand, competitor's prices, and costs are all considered when establishing a product's base price. A business must decide whether to have a one-price or flexible-price policy. The product's position in its life cycle is also a factor in establishing the base price.

Expert Advice

"A major factor in determining the profitability of any product is establishing a base price."

Ask: ***What might happen if a retailer underestimates demand and sets a price too low?*** The retailer might quickly run out of the product and make less profit than what may have been possible.

Critical Thinking

Describe a scenario in which students run a home cleaning business. They rent an office and have four employees who travel to homes in a company van. Ask: ***What are some fixed expenses? Variable expenses?*** Fixed expenses—rent, utilities, van payments, insurance. Variable expenses—labor, cleaning supplies, fuel, maintenance.

MANUFACTURERS AND SERVICE BUSINESSES

Manufacturers and service businesses use a more sophisticated pricing method than markup pricing. They do this because all fixed and variable expenses are calculated separately. Fixed expenses are those expenses that do not change based on production. Fixed expenses include things such as rent, interest on loans, executives' salaries, advertising, and insurance. Variable expenses are associated with the production of the good or service. These include costs related to labor and supplies. When a manufacturer is running at full capacity, the percentage of fixed expenses **allocated** to each product becomes smaller. This permits the manufacturer to charge a lower unit price for goods. **Figure 26.1** shows how a manufacturer may determine the price for a jacket.

Manufacturers also consider the prices they will charge resellers (wholesalers and retailers) for their products to set a base price. This can be done in two ways. You can work backward from the final retail price to find the price for the wholesalers. Or, you can do this in reverse, by working forward from costs and expenses to the final retail price. These two methods are illustrated in **Figure 26.1.**

The second table of information in Figure 26.1 lists the steps in working backward. The suggested retail price is established first on the basis of consumer demand and competition. Next, the markups desired by the wholesalers and retailers are deducted sequentially from the suggested retail price. Finally, the base price that the manufacturer will charge the wholesaler is determined. Note that the price to the wholesaler must be high enough to cover the manufacturer's costs, any expenses, and the intended profit.

Figure 26.1 also shows the steps for working forward from the manufacturer's cost. Expenses and intended profit must be considered, and then the wholesaler's and retailer's markups are added to the manufacturer's price to arrive at the base selling price. Competition and consumer demand may be left out of the pricing decision if the price is set at this point.

Pricing Food Products

This ConAgra Foods® ad suggests that its products' prices will help generate sales volume for a retailer. ***Which method of calculating a price to charge retailers did this manufacturer most likely use? Explain.***

FIGURE 26.1 Calculating the Unit Price, Wholesale Price, and Retail Price

Pricing a Jacket Manufacturers take cost of materials, labor, expenses, and intended profit into consideration when determining the unit price for an item. When calculating the wholesale price, the manufacturer subtracts all the markups for channel members. When calculating the retail price, the manufacturer calculates all of its costs, then calculates resellers' markups to determine the price that retailers will charge their customers.

UNIT PRICE FOR A JACKET	
Materials *(fabric, insulation, thread, zipper, pockets)*	$12.00
Labor *(piecework)*	$2.00
Fixed expenses *(overhead)*	$.75
Intended profit margin	$4.25
Price to business customer	$19.00

CALCULATING THE WHOLESALE PRICE	
Manufacturer's suggested retail price *(MSRP)*	$100
Retailer's markup *(40% of retail price)*	– $40
Wholesaler's price to retailer *(subtract retailer's markup from MSRP)*	= $60
Wholesaler's markup *(20% of wholesale price)*	– $12
Manufacturer's price to wholesaler * *(subtract wholesaler's markup from wholesaler's price)*	= $48
* *This amount must cover costs, expenses, and profit for the manufacturer.*	

CALCULATING THE RETAIL PRICE	
Cost of producing the item	$40
Manufacturer's expenses and intended profit *(20% of cost)*	+ $8
Manufacturer's price to wholesaler *(Cost plus expenses and intended profit margin)*	= $48
Wholesaler's markup *(25% of price wholesaler paid for item)*	+ $12
Wholesaler's price to retailer *(Manufacturer's price to wholesaler + markup)*	= $60
Retailer's markup *(66.67% based on price paid to wholesaler)*	+ $40
Retailer's base price to consumer	= $100

EXPLAIN

MANUFACTURERS AND SERVICE BUSINESSES

To focus the discussion on how manufacturers and service businesses set prices, ask the following guiding questions.

Guiding Questions

Recall Why do manufacturers use a more sophisticated pricing method than markup pricing?	They calculate all fixed and variable expenses separately.
Analyze Why do manufacturers want to run their plants at full capacity as much as possible?	The percentage of fixed expenses allocated to each product becomes smaller.
Contrast How are the two methods that manufacturers can use when calculating resell prices different from one another?	In the first, manufacturers work backward from the final retail price. In the second method, they work forward from costs.

Visual Literacy

Pricing Food Products Caption Answer Read the caption question to students: ***Which method of calculating a price to charge retailers did this manufacturer most likely use? Explain.*** The manufacturer most likely calculated the prices backward from the retail price because it was intent on making sure the final retail price was what consumers were willing to pay. The manufacturer probably started with the retail price and calculated what retailers would mark it up to get to the allowable production cost. The ingredients in the products or the packaging had to be figured to arrive at that price.

VIRTUAL BUSINESS

PRICING

Introduce students to the concept of pricing using Knowledge Matters' Virtual Business Retailing visual simulation, *Pricing*. In this simulation, students will learn that pricing is a vital concern for business owners.

ELABORATE

Visual Literacy

Figure 26.1 Calculating the Unit Price, Wholesale Price, and Retail Price The top table demonstrates working backward from the retail price. The bottom table shows how to work forward from the production cost. Ask: ***What problem would this manufacturer have if its costs and expenses totaled $50?*** It would be losing money.

CALCULATING THE WHOLESALE PRICE	
Manufacturer's suggested retail price *(MSRP)*	$100
Retailer's markup *(40% of retail price)*	– $40
Wholesaler's price to retailer *(subtract markup from MSRP)*	= $60
Wholesaler's markup *(20% of wholesale price)*	– $12
Manufacturer's price to wholesaler * *(subtract wholesaler's markup from wholesaler's price)* * *This amount must cover costs, expenses, and profit*	= $48

CALCULATING THE RETAIL PRICE	
Cost of producing the item	$40
Manufacturer's expenses and intended profit *(20% of cost)*	– $8
Manufacturer's price to wholesaler *(Cost plus expenses and intended profit margin)*	= $48
Wholesaler's markup *(25% of price wholesaler paid for item)*	+ $12
Wholesaler's price to retailer *(Price to wholesaler + markup)*	= $60
Retailer's markup *(66.67% based on price paid to wholesaler)*	+ $40
Retailer's base price to consumer	= $100

Mini Project

Differentiated Instruction

Logical Learners Have students work independently to develop their own versions of the second and third tables in Figure 26.1. First, they should choose a product with which they are reasonably familiar. Based on their knowledge, they should create (1) a table that calculates the product's wholesale price; and (2) a table that calculates the product's retail price. The wholesaler's markup should be 25% and the retailer's markup should be 40%. Student tables will vary depending on the product chosen. The student should list all costs, expenses, and a profit for the manufacturer. The first table should work backward from the MSRP, while the second table should start with the manufacturer's costs.

e MARKETING

Online Reverse Auctions

In online reverse auctions the seller bids based on the criteria set up by the buyer. In essence the buyer is requesting a quote from the seller. Once all the quotes are in from various sellers, the buyer can decide which seller is offering the best price and deal. The lowest bidder may not always be offering the best deal because there may be other considerations, such as delivery time, the company's reputation, and production capabilities. Online reverse auctions are used for e-procurement by large companies. Special software for reverse auctions help buyers compare vendor offerings by showing the bids side by side in a chart format, which makes comparisons easy. One of the most popular Web sites that sell products using reverse auction pricing is eBay

Innovate and Create

Ask students to compare a regular auction with a reverse auction by conducting two auctions; a regular auction and a reverse auction for a truckload of peaches. Let half of the class act as buyers and the other half as sellers. Conduct a regular auction with the buyers quoting prices for the truckload of peaches with the bidding set to begin at $150 and watch as the price goes up in a regular auction. Then conduct a reverse auction where a company that makes jams is looking to purchase a truckload of peaches. Now the sellers are the ones bidding. Note how the bids go down in price. Ask students: If you were the farmer selling peaches, which auction method would you prefer and if you were the company making jams, which auction method would you prefer? Answers will vary. Sample answer: Farmers selling peaches would prefer the regular auction because they would get a higher price for their peaches as buyers would increase their offers to win the bid. Jam makers would prefer the reverse auction because farmers would bid against each other by lowering their prices to win the bid. With regard to how they would come up with a minimum price from which to begin bidding for a product of their choice, accept all reasonable figures and methods for selecting that price.

glencoe.com

eMarketing Worksheet Activity Send students to the Online Learning Center to download an eMarketing worksheet activity.

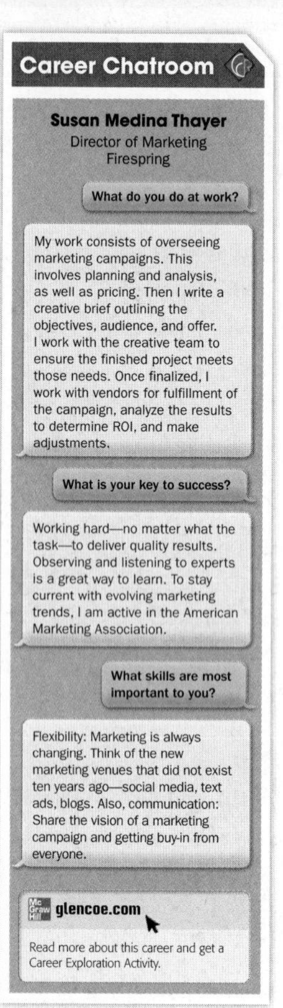

Career Chatroom

Susan Medina Thayer
Director of Marketing
Firespring

What do you do at work?

My work consists of overseeing marketing campaigns. This involves planning and analysis, as well as pricing. Then I write a creative brief outlining the objectives, audience, and offer. I work with the creative team to ensure the finished project meets those needs. Once finalized, I work with vendors for fulfillment of the campaign, analyze the results to determine ROI, and make adjustments.

What is your key to success?

Working hard—no matter what the task—to deliver quality results. Observing and listening to experts is a great way to learn. To stay current with evolving marketing trends, I am active in the American Marketing Association.

What skills are most important to you?

Flexibility: Marketing is always changing. Think of the new marketing venues that did not exist ten years ago—social media, text ads, blogs. Also, communication: Share the vision of a marketing campaign and getting buy-in from everyone.

glencoe.com

Read more about this career and get a Career Exploration Activity.

ESTABLISHING THE BASE PRICE

To establish the base price or price range for a good or service, three different pricing approaches are useful.

Cost-oriented pricing helps marketers determine the price floor for a product. This is the lowest price at which it can be offered and still be profitable.

Demand-oriented pricing determines a price range for the product that is defined by the price floor and the ceiling price. This is the highest amount consumers would pay.

Competition-oriented pricing may be used to ensure that the final price is in line with the company's pricing policies. For example, a retail store may set a policy to always offer prices that are lower than its competitors' prices. Combining pricing considerations offers a good range within which a company can establish its base price. If a company decides to go with the competition-oriented pricing strategy, it still knows how much it can lower its prices if necessary. It can lower its prices based on the cost-oriented pricing figures.

Reading Check

Recall Identify three types of pricing.

PRICING POLICIES AND PRODUCT LIFE CYCLE

A basic pricing decision every business must make is to choose between a one-price policy and a flexible-price policy. A business also needs to consider how a new product will be introduced. That choice will determine the pricing decisions that follow throughout the product's life cycle.

ONE-PRICE VERSUS FLEXIBLE-PRICE POLICY

A **one-price policy** is one in which all customers are charged the same prices. Prices are quoted to customers using signs and price tags. Deviations from a one-price policy are not allowed. Most retail stores employ a one-price policy. A one-price policy offers consistency and reliability. It also allows retailers to estimate sales and profits because they know the set price.

A **flexible-price policy** is one in which customers pay different prices for the same type or amount of merchandise. This kind of policy permits customers to bargain for merchandise. This means the customer can negotiate a price rather than pay a fixed price established by the seller. Most retail stores avoid using flexible pricing because it can cause legal problems, and it may keep some customers away.

A flexible-price strategy is common for goods such as used cars, artwork, antiques, furniture, and selected jewelry. One disadvantage of a flexible-price policy is that it does not offer consistent profits. It can be difficult to estimate sales revenue because of the flexible nature of the price. However, with computer technology and huge databases, such estimations may become more feasible.

PRODUCT LIFE CYCLE

Products move through four stages: introduction, growth, maturity, and decline. Pricing plays an important role in this sequence.

NEW PRODUCT INTRODUCTION

A business may price a new product above, in line with, or below its competitors' prices. This choice depends on the philosophy of the business and on market conditions. When a going-rate strategy is not used to introduce a new product, two methods may be used: skimming pricing or penetration pricing.

Method 1 Skimming pricing is a pricing policy that sets a very high price for a new product. This kind of policy can be used any time demand is greater than supply. Such a policy is designed to capitalize on the high demand for a product during its introductory period.

Businesses that use this method recognize that the price will have to be lowered once the market for the product shifts to more price-conscious customers. While the product is hot, the business will enjoy a high profit margin. Another advantage of skimming pricing is that the price may be lowered without insulting the target market. One disadvantage of skimming pricing is that the high initial price generally attracts competition. Also, if the initial price is far above what consumers pay, sales will be lost and profits diminished.

Pricing Electronics

Computers, cameras, and other electronic items quickly go out of date as new technology emerges and becomes more common. ***How does this rapid product life cycle affect pricing?***

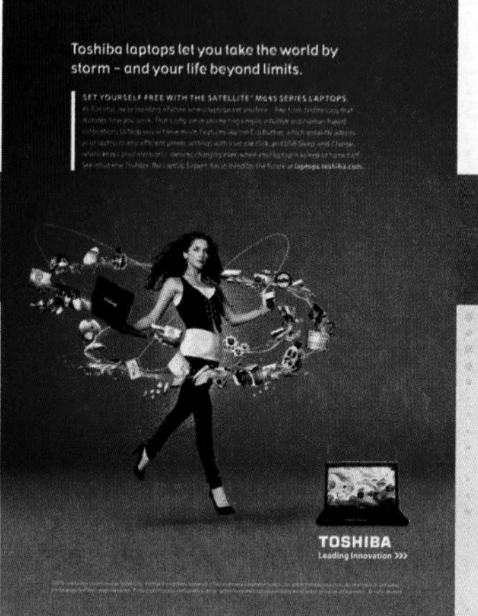

EXPLAIN

Career Chatroom

Focus the discussion by asking these guiding questions.

Guiding Questions

Describe What does Susan Medina Thayer's work involve?	overseeing marketing campaigns, planning, analysis, pricing
Analyze Why is Thayer's activity in the AMA important?	It helps her stay on top of current market trends.

 **glencoe.com** 

Career Exploration Send students to the Online Learning Center to find more information about this career and to get a Career Exploration activity.

ESTABLISHING THE BASE PRICE

Ask these guiding questions to focus the discussion.

Guiding Questions

Explain Why is it important that a business know the price floor for a product?	The price floor lets the business know the lowest price at which it can still make a profit.
Draw Conclusions Why do most retail stores combine various pricing considerations when making pricing decisions?	Combining approaches offers flexibility and gives the business a good range within which to set the price.

Reading Check Answer

Read the Reading Check question to students: ***Identify three types of pricing.*** demand-oriented pricing, competition-oriented pricing, cost-oriented pricing

ELABORATE

Reinforce Vocabulary

Flexible-price policy—Denotative Meaning Discuss that *flexible* means "yielding to influence" or "characterized by a ready capability to adapt to new or changing requirements." Tell students that a *flexible-price policy* is pricing that can change depending on customers' influence, in particular their bargaining ability.

PRICING POLICIES AND PRODUCT LIFE CYCLE

Ask these guiding questions to focus the discussion on pricing policies and product life cycle.

Guiding Questions

Draw Conclusions What type of consumer is likely to purchase a product that has been priced using a skimming pricing strategy?	Possible answer: Someone who has disposable income and likes to be on the "cutting edge," that is, they want to have the newest and trendiest products.
Make a Judgment An auto dealership advertises that it has a one-price, rather than a flexible-price, policy. However, it also advertises that it has the lowest prices around. Would you like to shop for a car at this dealership? Why or why not?	Answers will vary. Sample answer: Yes, I would, because at other dealerships I might have to bargain in order to get a good price. Whenever I bargain, I feel that I do not get as good a price as other people.

Critical Thinking

Describe a scenario in which an antique dealer is offered $250 for an oak dresser that is priced at $290. Ask students: ***What factors do you think might enter into whether or not the dealer accepts this price?*** what the dealer paid for the dresser; how high the shop's fixed expenses are; whether this type of dresser is currently in demand; how long the dealer has owned the dresser; and whether or not the dealer is anxious to sell the dresser for other reasons, such as a shortage of space or a need to obtain capital quickly

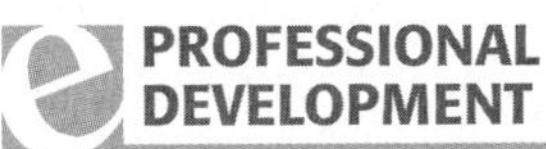

MINI CLIP

Math: Communication in Mathematics
Go to the Online Learning Center to view a video clip in which an expert explains the importance of student communication in the mathematics classroom.

Visual Literacy

Pricing Electronics Caption Answer Read the caption question to students: ***How does this rapid product life cycle affect pricing?*** New products generally have higher prices than older products. Then ask: ***Based on supply and demand theory, why is it possible for businesses to charge high prices when a new technology first becomes available?*** because demand is typically higher than supply

Mini Projects

Extension

Bidding on a Snow Removal Project Tell students to imagine they run a snow removal company. A local supermarket is accepting bids from companies to keep its parking lot clear of snow this winter. As the manager of the company, you want the supermarket's business and plan to submit a bid. Ask students to work in small groups to brainstorm ideas on how to ensure that they will get the supermarket's business. Have students select one idea they think is the most feasible, and then present their ideas to the class in an oral report. First we would determine the base cost of removing the snow, including labor, gasoline, equipment expenses, and so on. Then we would try to determine what competitors' bids might be. We could do this by checking ads or calling competitors and asking what they would charge for a lot the size of the supermarket lot. We would then try to place our bid above the base cost but below what the competition would be likely to bid.

Analyzing Competition-Oriented Pricing Describe this scenario: Mega Micro Electronics Store has a policy that it will not be undersold. If the consumer finds a product priced lower at a competitor's store, Mega Micro will honor that price. Therefore, Mega Micro often makes little money on larger items. However, Mega Micro teaches its sales associates to work hard at selling product accessories. These accessories have a much higher markup than larger products and are rarely, if ever, on sale. Instruct students to write a paragraph in which they take a position either for or against this strategy. In their paragraph, they should give specific reasons for their positions. Mega Micro's pricing strategies. Sample answer: I think it is a good strategy. Consumers compare prices on large purchases, and if Mega Micro guarantees the best prices on these products, they are likely to go there. However, most consumers do not compare prices on accessories because they see them as being relatively inexpensive and often purchase them on the spur of the moment.

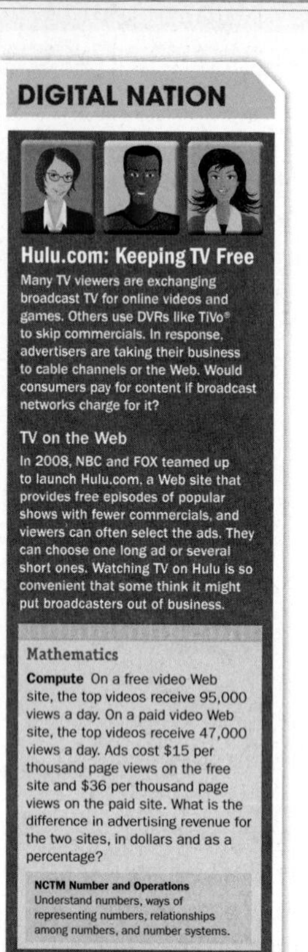
DIGITAL NATION

Hulu.com: Keeping TV Free

Many TV viewers are exchanging broadcast TV for online videos and games. Others use DVRs like TiVo® to skip commercials. In response, advertisers are taking their business to cable channels or the Web. Would consumers pay for content if broadcast networks charge for it?

TV on the Web

In 2008, NBC and FOX teamed up to launch Hulu.com, a Web site that provides free episodes of popular shows with fewer commercials, and viewers can often select the ads. They can choose one long ad or several short ones. Watching TV on Hulu is so convenient that some think it might put broadcasters out of business.

Mathematics

Compute On a free video Web site, the top videos receive 95,000 views a day. On a paid video Web site, the top videos receive 47,000 views a day. Ads cost $15 per thousand page views on the free site and $36 per thousand page views on the paid site. What is the difference in advertising revenue for the two sites, in dollars and as a percentage?

NCTM Number and Operations Understand numbers, ways of representing numbers, relationships among numbers, and number systems.

glencoe.com

Get a Digital Nation activity.

Method 2 Penetration pricing is the opposite of skimming pricing: The price for a new product is set very low. The purpose of penetration pricing is to encourage as many people as possible to buy the product, and thus penetrate the market. This type of pricing is most effective in the sale of price-sensitive products (items with elastic demand). SONY® used a penetration-pricing strategy when it introduced its first PlayStation® game console.

To penetrate the market quickly with penetration pricing, mass production, distribution, and promotion must be incorporated into the marketing strategy. The product should take hold in a short period of time. This allows the marketer to save money on fixed expenses (through mass production) and to increase the profit margin (through volume sales).

The biggest advantage of penetration pricing is its ability to capture a large number of customers in a relatively short period of time. This blocks competition from other companies.

If the product is not in high demand, however, the lower price will cause the marketer to suffer a bigger loss than it would have if a higher initial price had been set.

Price Policy Points Price carefully. With underpricing, your market thinks the product is not very good. With overpricing, the competition is boosted.

PRICING DURING THE PRODUCT STAGES

Pricing during subsequent periods in a product's life cycle is determined by which pricing method was originally used—skimming or penetration. Sales increase rapidly during the penetration stage, and total costs per unit decrease because the volume absorbs fixed costs. The main goal of marketers is to keep products in this stage as long as possible.

Sales of products introduced with skimming pricing must be monitored. Once sales begin to level off, the price should be lowered for the price-conscious target market.

Very little price change will be made in the growth stage for products introduced with penetration pricing. When demand decreases and sales begin to level off, competition is generally very keen. Marketers look for new market segments to hold the prices for their products. They may look for other distribution outlets or suggest additional uses for a product.

The marketer's goal during the maturity stage is to stretch the life of a product. Some companies do this by reducing their prices. Others revise products by adding new features or improvements. Companies may also look for new target markets. Another option is to seek new markets in other nations in the global marketplace. Products that have been sold in the United States for many years may be in the introductory or growth stage in other places. By using such techniques, marketers can significantly extend a product's life cycle. The maturity stage may last a long time. When efforts are not successful, however, a product moves into decline.

Sales decrease and profit margins are reduced in the decline stage. Like the maturity stage, the decline stage can last for a long time. Companies are forced to reduce the price to generate sales. To maintain profitability, marketers reduce manufacturing costs or cut back on advertising and promotional activities. Once a product is no longer profitable, it is phased out. However, discontinuing a product does not necessarily mean a company no longer earns revenue from the product. Some discontinued products, especially those used in business and industrial settings, may continue to earn money through support services such as selling supplies and service and repair contracts.

After You Read | **Section 26.1**

Review Key Concepts

1. **Name** the types of businesses that use markup to determine prices.
2. **Explain** why manufacturers consider the final consumer with a suggested retail price when calculating the price to charge wholesalers.
3. **List** the advantages of using a one-price policy.

Practice Academics

English Language Arts

4. Write a paragraph to reflect your opinion of flexible pricing policies from a customer's point of view.

NCTE 12 Use language to accomplish individual purposes.

Mathematics

5. Apply the "pricing backward from retail price" approach to calculate the manufacturer's price to a wholesaler for a product that has a suggested retail price of $300. Assume that the retailer's markup on the retail price is 40 percent, and the wholesaler's markup is 20 percent.

Math Concept **Backward Pricing** To determine the manufacturer's price, work backward from the retail price. Subtract the retailer's and wholesaler's markup from the manufacturer's suggested retail price.

Starting Hints To solve this problem, multiply the retail price by the decimal equivalent of 40 percent to determine the retailer's markup. Subtract the value of the retailer's markup from the retail price. This will give the wholesaler's price. Multiply the wholesaler's price by the decimal equivalent of the wholesaler's markup, 20 percent, and subtract this amount from the wholesaler's price to determine the manufacturer's price.

NCTM Problem Solving Apply and adapt a variety of appropriate strategies to solve problems.

For help, go to the **Math Skills Handbook** located at the back of this book.

glencoe.com

Check your answers.

ELABORATE

DIGITAL NATION

Mathematics Answer Ad revenues for the free site are $1,425 (95 × $15). Ad revenues for the paid site are $1,692 (47 × $36). The paid site earns $267, or 18.74%, more in ad revenue than the paid site. Ask students: ***Why are many advertisers choosing to take their business to the Web?*** Many consumers are choosing to watch television shows on Web sites such as Hulu.com because of its convenience. In addition, there are generally fewer commercials, and viewers can often select the ads.

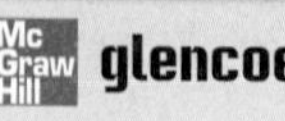

glencoe.com

Worksheet Activity Send students to the Online Learning Center to get a Digital Nation worksheet activity.

Price Policy Points Tell students that they really want to get a particular brand of designer jeans that sell for $130 at the local mall. One day after school, a friend says that they know someone who can get the jeans for $55. Ask students: ***What would you think of this bargain price? Why?*** Then ask: ***How does underpricing an item affect the way you view it?***

EVALUATE

PRICING DURING THE PRODUCT STAGES

Ask these guiding questions to focus the discussion of pricing during different product stages.

Guiding Questions

List What are three things marketers might do to help keep an item, such as a new type of floor cleaner, selling well during the maturity stage?	Answers will vary. They might look for new uses for the product. Perhaps the floor cleaner can be used for other kinds of cleaning tasks.
Explain As the penetration stage continues, what happens to the total costs per unit? Why?	Total costs per unit drop because the increased volume greatly reduces the fixed costs per unit.
Apply Your store applied a skimming pricing policy to a new type of athletic shoe. As this shoe continues through its life cycle, why is vital that you keep an eye on sales volume?	As soon as sales begin to level off, the price should be lowered so that more price-conscious consumers will buy it—in this way, the sales volume can continue to remain high.

Mini Project

Differentiated Instruction

Interpersonal Learning Organize students into groups of two or three. Have each group think of a product that uses a new technology. For example, they may pick a smartphone that has features that were not previously available. Students should then choose three or four similar products; however, these other products should have been on the market for a while and use technology that is not brand new. Have students conduct research to determine the prices of all products. Then have students prepare a presentation about how product prices varied depending on where they were in the product life cycle. Presentations will vary depending on the product chosen. For example, newer laptops may have higher prices because their processors typically run at faster speeds and they have more internal memory than laptops that have been on the market for a while. In addition, they may come with software that is more current.

After You Read — Section 26.1

Review Key Concepts

1. Markup is used primarily by wholesalers and retailers who are involved in acquiring goods for resale.
2. Manufacturers will often do research to determine the price the final consumer is willing to pay for an item. That price becomes the manufacturer's suggested retail price (list price) from which the company expects wholesalers and retailers to take their customary markups. Customary markups are well known in each industry.
3. The advantages of using a one-price policy are that they offer consistency and reliability, which allows retailers to estimate sales and profit because they know the set price.

Practice Academics

English Language Arts

4. Accept all reasonable responses. Some students like to haggle over a price because they enjoy the challenge, while other may not like to haggle. They might find a flexible pricing policy to be intimidating and uncomfortable.

Mathematics

5. $144 (300 – [300 × 0.4] – [300 – (300 × .4)] × 0.2)

 **glencoe.com** 

Answer Key Send students to the Online Learning Center to check their answers.

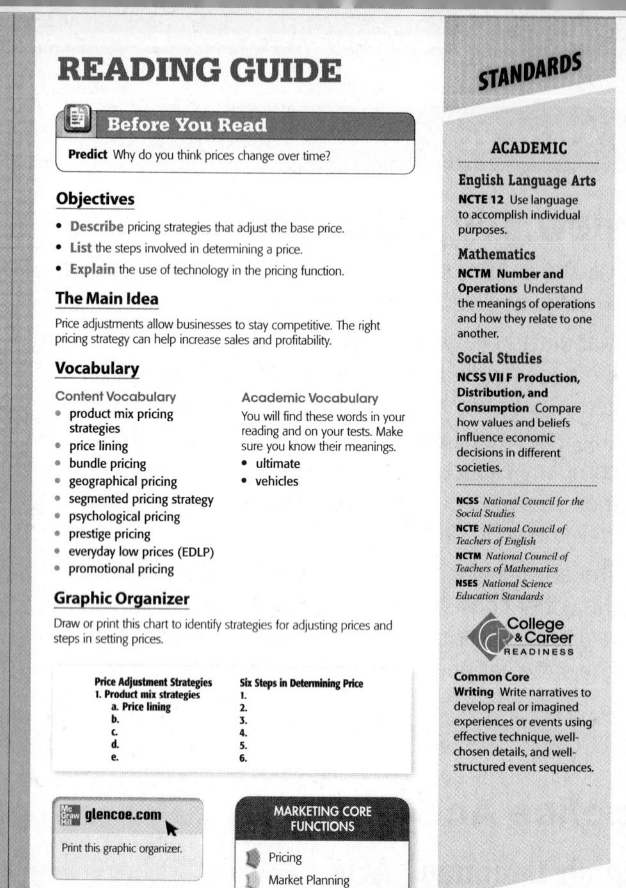

READING GUIDE

Before You Read

Predict Why do you think prices change over time?

Objectives

- **Describe** pricing strategies that adjust the base price.
- **List** the steps involved in determining a price.
- **Explain** the use of technology in the pricing function.

The Main Idea

Price adjustments allow businesses to stay competitive. The right pricing strategy can help increase sales and profitability.

Vocabulary

Content Vocabulary
- product mix pricing strategies
- price lining
- bundle pricing
- geographical pricing
- segmented pricing strategy
- psychological pricing
- prestige pricing
- everyday low prices (EDLP)
- promotional pricing

Academic Vocabulary

You will find these words in your reading and on your tests. Make sure you know their meanings.
- ultimate
- vehicles

Graphic Organizer

Draw or print this chart to identify strategies for adjusting prices and steps in setting prices.

Price Adjustment Strategies	Six Steps in Determining Price
1. Product mix strategies	1.
a. Price lining	2.
b.	3.
c.	4.
d.	5.
e.	6.

glencoe.com

Print this graphic organizer.

MARKETING CORE FUNCTIONS
- Pricing
- Market Planning

STANDARDS

ACADEMIC

English Language Arts
NCTE 12 Use language to accomplish individual purposes.

Mathematics
NCTM Number and Operations Understand the meanings of operations and how they relate to one another.

Social Studies
NCSS VII F Production, Distribution, and Consumption Compare how values and beliefs influence economic decisions in different societies.

NCSS National Council for the Social Studies
NCTE National Council of Teachers of English
NCTM National Council of Teachers of Mathematics
NSES National Science Education Standards

College & Career READINESS

Common Core
Writing Write narratives to develop real or imagined experiences or events using effective technique, well-chosen details, and well-structured event sequences.

612 | Unit 8 · Pricing

Section 26.2 Pricing Process Strategies

ADJUSTING THE BASE PRICE

To adjust base prices, marketers use the following pricing strategies: product mix, geographical, international, segmented, psychological, promotional pricing, discounts and/or allowances. Businesses can remain competitive by using these strategies in the appropriate situations.

As You Read

Connect Note pricing strategy examples from your own observations as a consumer.

PRODUCT MIX STRATEGIES

Product mix pricing strategies involve adjusting prices to maximize the profitability for a group of products rather than for just one item. One product may have a small profit margin, while another may be high to balance the effect of the lower-priced one. These strategies include price lining, optional product pricing, captive product pricing, by-product pricing, and bundle pricing.

PRICE LINING

Price lining is a pricing technique that sets a limited number of prices for specific groups or lines of merchandise. A store might price all its blouses at $25, $35, and $50. Marketers must be careful to make the price differences great enough to represent low, middle, and high-quality items. Price lines of $25, $26, $27, and $28, for example, would confuse customers because they would have difficulty figuring out their basis.

An advantage of price lining is that the target market is fully aware of the price range of products in a given store. In addition, price lining makes merchandising and selling easier for salespeople who can readily draw comparisons between floor and ceiling prices.

OPTIONAL PRODUCT

Optional product pricing involves setting prices for accessories or options sold with the main product. One example is options for cars. All options need to be priced so that a final price for the main product can be established.

" Marketers can use specific pricing strategies to fit different economic and market conditions. "

CAPTIVE PRODUCT

Captive product pricing sets the price for one product low but makes up for it by pricing the supplies needed to use that product high. Ink-jet printers are low in price, but the ink cartridges required for the printers have high markups.

BY-PRODUCT

By-product pricing helps businesses get rid of excess materials used in making a product by using low prices. Wood chips that are residual by-products from making furniture may be sold at a very low price to other manufacturing companies that use wood chips in making their products.

BUNDLE PRICING

With **bundle pricing**, a company offers several complementary, or corresponding, products in a package that is sold at a single price. The one price for all the complementary products that go with the main item is lower than if a customer purchased each item separately. An example of bundle pricing is when computer companies include software in the sale price of a computer.

Chapter 26 · Pricing Strategies | 613

ENGAGE

Anticipation Activity

Improving Student Achievement Have students list items they have bought at discounted or promotional prices. smartphones, clothes, toiletries, and so on As you write down the items for the class to read, ask students why they think the products were offered at special prices.

Objectives

- **Describe** pricing strategies that adjust the base price. product mix, geographical, international, segmented, psychological, promotional pricing, discounts, and/or allowances
- **List** the steps involved in determining a price. (1) establish pricing objectives; (2) determine costs; (3) estimate demand; (4) study competition; (5) decide pricing strategy; (6) set prices
- **Explain** the use of technology in the pricing function. smart pricing based on data; communicating prices to customers through the use of electronic shelves, digital price labels, and scanning kiosks

Graphic Organizer

Price Adjustment Strategies	Six Steps in Determining Price
1. Product mix strategies	**1.** Establish pricing objectives
a. Price lining	**2.** Determine costs
b. Optional product	**3.** Estimate demand
c. Captive product	**4.** Study competition
d. By-product	**5.** Decide on a pricing strategy
e. Bundle pricing	**6.** Set prices

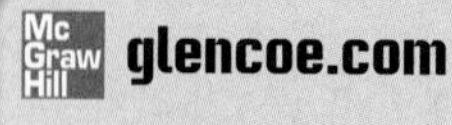

Graphic Organizer Send students to the Online Learning Center to print this graphic organizer.

EXPLORE

Before You Read

Read the Before You Read question aloud: ***Why do you think prices change over time?*** Prices change because costs change and competition changes, consumers' wants and needs change, as do the goals and objectives of a company. When a product is first introduced, the price is often set high to attract those who are interested in the latest fashion, technology, and so on. As consumers see the product as being more readily available, the price typically drops.

Preteaching Vocabulary

Have students go to the Online Learning Center at glencoe.com for the Chapter 26 Preteaching Vocabulary games.

Content Vocabulary

Display the following words for the class to read: *product mix, pricing strategies, price lining, bundle pricing, geographical pricing, segmented pricing strategy, psychological pricing,* and *prestige pricing*. Have students work individually to create sentence stems using these words. Then have them trade work with another student and complete their partners' sentences. Sample sentence stem: A store that prices all best-selling books at $12, $16, or $22 is engaging in __________. (answer: price lining)

Academic Vocabulary

Ultimate—Word Origin Display the word *ultimate* for the class to read. Tell students that ultimate comes from the Latin word *ultimatus*, which means "last" or "final." Ask students how this is related to our use of ultimate today. We sometimes use ultimate to mean last, for example in the sentence "Our ultimate goal is to have the report completed by next week." However, we also use it to mean "best or most extreme," as in the sentence "She made the ultimate sacrifice."

Vehicles—Alternate Meanings Display the word *vehicles* for the class to read. Discuss with students that in its most literal sense, vehicles are means of transportation, such as cars and trucks. Then ask: ***What might be a more abstract definition of vehicles?*** means by which things are conveyed or transmitted

Pricing Process Strategies

PRODUCT MIX STRATEGIES

Explain to students that product mix strategies help businesses remain profitable in a volatile marketplace. To focus your discussion on this topic, ask these guiding questions.

Guiding Questions

Analyze A restaurant offers a dozen different meals each night. Depending on the expense of its ingredients and the time required to make it, each meal is assigned one of three prices: $12.95, 16.95 or 21.95. What pricing technique is the restaurant using?	price lining
Make Judgments How do you think consumers feel when they buy a product that uses captive product pricing?	Consumers may become annoyed or angry because they may think they were trapped into buying a product that requires overly expensive supplies.

As You Read

Read the As You Read statement aloud: ***Note pricing strategy examples from your own observations as a consumer.*** Encourage students to keep a list of times they have encountered the pricing strategies discussed in this section. When finished with the section, have volunteers share their lists with the class.

Expert Advice

Read the quote to students:

> **"Marketers can use specific pricing strategies to fit different economic and market conditions."**

Tell students one specific pricing strategy is "everyday low prices." Ask students: ***In what kind of economic conditions do you think the everyday low prices strategy would do best? Why?*** when economic conditions are uncertain or the economy is relatively weak.

Bundling helps businesses sell items (parts of the package) that they may not have sold otherwise. As such, bundling increases a company's sales and revenue.

GEOGRAPHICAL PRICING

Geographical pricing refers to price adjustments required because of different shipping agreements. The FOB (Free On Board) origin or point-of-production shipping arrangement would not require a price adjustment because the customer pays the shipping charges. With FOB destination pricing, the seller pays for the shipping and assumes responsibility for the shipment until it reaches the buyer. When determining the price to charge a buyer, shipping charges must be included in the calculations and the adjustment to the base price.

INTERNATIONAL PRICING

When doing business internationally, marketers need to set prices that take into consideration costs, consumers, competition, laws, regulations, economic conditions, and the monetary exchange rate. Costs may include shipping, tariffs, or other charges. Consumers' income levels, perceptions, and lifestyles determine adjustments to the price.

The country's distribution system is another factor because in some countries, several resellers may be involved to get the products to the final consumers.

SEGMENTED PRICING STRATEGIES

A **segmented pricing strategy** uses two or more different prices for a product, though there is no difference in the item's cost. This strategy helps businesses optimize profits and compete effectively. Four factors can help marketers use segmented pricing strategies:

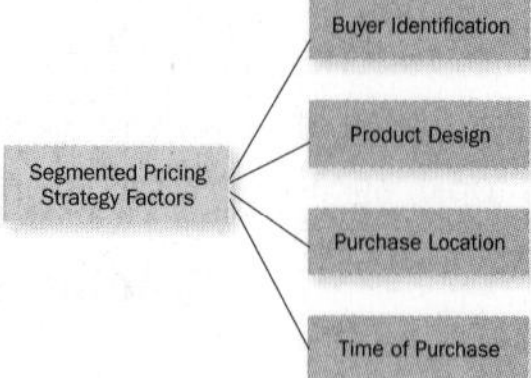

BUYER IDENTIFICATION

Recognizing a buyer's sensitivity to price (demand elasticity) is one way to identify a customer segment. For example, to attract customers on fixed incomes, some businesses offer senior citizen and student discounts. Airlines offer different classes of travel—first class and coach. First-class travelers pay a significantly higher price to get to the same destination. Another segment may be based on purchases. Companies may offer incentives to loyal customers to encourage them to do more business with them. Some supermarkets and pharmacies have customer loyalty programs whereby loyal customers pay less on selected merchandise.

PRODUCT DESIGN

Manufacturers may also create different prices for different product styles that do not reflect the cost of making the item. Instead, the demand for a given style is the cause of the difference in price. For example, a red-colored washer and dryer may be priced higher than a white set.

PURCHASE LOCATION

Purchase location involves pricing according to where a product is sold and the location of the good or service. Tickets for Broadway shows in New York City will be priced higher than those for the same show when it goes on the road.

TIME OF PURCHASE

Some types of businesses experience highs and lows in sales activity. During peak times, they are able to charge more because of increased demand. Telephone companies often charge more for long-distance calls made during business hours, a peak time.

PSYCHOLOGICAL PRICING STRATEGIES

Psychological pricing strategies are pricing techniques that help create an illusion for customers. They are often based on a buyer's motivation for making a purchase and purchasing habits. For price-conscious customers, five cents could make a difference in the price they are willing to pay. Among common psychological pricing techniques are odd-even pricing, prestige pricing, multiple-unit pricing, and everyday low prices (EDLPs).

ODD-EVEN PRICING

A technique that involves setting price figures that end in either odd or even numbers is known as *odd-even pricing.* This strategy is based on the psychological principle that odd numbers ($0.79, $9.95, $699, $1.99) convey a bargain image.

MARKETING CASE STUDY

Caribou Coffee at Home

When budgets tighten and people can't afford specially made coffee, they tend to make coffee at home, rather than buying it at a coffee house. The Caribou Coffee™ Company sells its classic coffee blends at Caribou Coffee locations and supermarkets across the country as well as online. This allows their customers to enjoy their quality coffee at a lower cost.

Segmented Pricing

A 12-ounce bag of Caribou Blend coffee costs $9.99 ($0.83 per ounce) in the supermarket. However, a 1-pound bag of the same coffee costs $10.99 ($0.69 per ounce) online. Buying coffee in a local supermarket is faster than waiting for an online purchase to arrive, so the cost is slightly higher. Caribou Blend coffee may also cost more in a supermarket located in Los Angeles than in a supermarket located in Cleveland. The difference in price is due to the purchase location.

English Language Arts

Location and Pricing What are some of the reasons purchase location might affect the price of a product? Identify another marketing campaign that relies on segmented pricing.

NCTE 12 Use language to accomplish individual purposes.

WORLD MARKET AUSTRALIA

uSocial™ Marketing

An online marketing agency called "uSocial" prides itself on being unique. It is not unlike the continent it calls home, Australia. The company came up with a brainstorm: Why not sell "friends" to Facebook® members, one of the world's top social networking sites? As members use it, they create a "friend's list."

Got Friends? With more than 250 million users worldwide, Facebook has become "an extremely effective marketing tool," states uSocial's CEO, particularly if you have a big friend's list. For those without many friends, uSocial offers package deals and sells friends by the thousands. Buy 1,000 friends for under $200. Marketing researchers and Facebook, who prohibits its members from profiting commercially from personal profiles, are watching.

Social Studies

Evaluate Discuss with your class how you would react to an offer from uSocial. Assume that you can easily afford the price of the service.

NCSS X D Civic Ideals & Practices Practice forms of civic discussion and participation consistent with the ideals of citizens in a democratic republic.

Here are some entry-level phrases that are used in conversations about marketing all over the world.

English	Strine (Aussie-speak)
Hello	G'day
Goodbye	Goodbye
How are you?	How are ya?
Thank you	Thanks
You're welcome	No worries

EXPLAIN

MARKETING CASE STUDY

English Language Arts Answer Read aloud this question to students: ***What are some of the reasons purchase location might affect the price of a product?*** Overhead might be considerably more at one location than another; one location might be more convenient or in a more-affluent neighborhood and thus draw consumers with more disposable income. Another example of segmented pricing might involve sports equipment. For example, a golfer would expect to pay more for golf balls at a country club's pro shop than for the same golf balls at a discount store.

Critical Thinking

Ask students: ***Have you ever forgotten to pack an item, such as a toothbrush, for an airplane trip? Would you expect to pay more or less for the toothbrush at an airport store than at a local drug store? Why?*** I would expect to pay more at the airport because I am paying for the convenience. The airport store does not have anywhere near the volume of sales as the local drug store and probably has greater expenses for the amount of floor space.

Reinforce Vocabulary

Psychological pricing—Denotative Meaning Explain that since *psychological* means "having to do with the mind or emotions," the denotative meaning of *psychological pricing* is pricing that attempts to influence the mind or emotions. Ask students: ***Do you think marketers are taking unfair advantage of consumers when they use psychological pricing? Why or why not?*** Sample answer: No, even though consumers may be making decisions for emotional reasons, emotions enter into purchasing choices in many ways, for example, by the décor of a shop or the friendliness of salespeople.

ELABORATE

SEGMENTED PRICING STRATEGIES

Segmented pricing strategies often depend on what consumers in a particular location or situation will pay. Ask these guiding questions.

Guiding Questions

Draw a Conclusion Why might a flower shop charge more for roses on February 14 than on February 18?	The "time of purchase" factor allows the florist to charge more on Valentine's Day (February 14) due to increased demand.
Make a Connection How is demand elasticity connected to buyer identification?	Identifying customers who are particularly influenced by price reductions (demand elasticity) can help to determine who should be offered discounts.

Graphic Organizer

Display this diagram of the four segmented pricing strategy factors. As the diagram is completed, discuss examples of each factor.

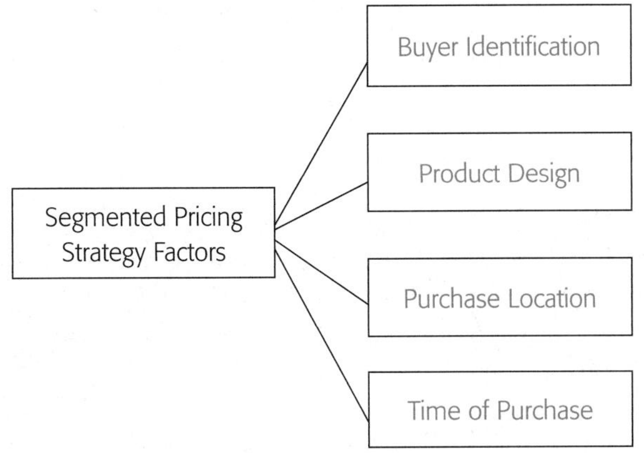

iWB

Graphic Organizer Send students to the Online Learning Center to print this graphic organizer.

Critical Thinking

Tell students that a small, independent online store has a CD by a band whose music is not yet available from a digital music provider. The price is listed at $3 more than at a local chain retail outlet, but free shipping is included. Ask students to list reasons why they might prefer to order from the online site. convenience of delivery; a desire to patronize the independent store rather than the chain retailer.

WORLD MARKET
SOCIAL STUDIES

Students' discussions should focus on how they feel about the concept of buying Facebook friends (or Twitter followers). Some students may think that the purpose of social networking is not to see how many friends you can accumulate, but the quality of these friendships. Others may think it is just part of a competition—to see who can have the most friends.

Mini Project

Enrichment

Examining Social Network Marketing Discuss with students that businesses such as uSocial have found ways to make money off social networking sites. However, companies such as Facebook are upset because they do not want their sites taken over by other people using them for profit. Have students organize into pairs and debate this topic. One person should be in favor of letting businesses such as uSocial profit from social networking sites, and the other student should be against it. Each student should conduct research to come up with specific reasons for their opinion. Students should present their debates to the class. Students should participate in a debate in which they present the pros and cons for allowing businesses such as uSocial to profit from social networking sites. The pro side is that it creates buzz for the network and supports free enterprise by encouraging entrepreneurs to come up with creative services for individuals and businesses using these sites. The con side is that these sites are primarily intended to encourage social interaction, not to make money for businesses.

Even numbers ($10, $50, $100) convey a quality image. Marketers use the odd-even technique to project an image. Some companies use even numbers as part of promotional campaigns. For example, Subway's® $5 foot-long sandwich became the focus of an advertising campaign. McDonald's® and Burger King® offered $1 meal promotions, which convey a value-pricing strategy.

PRESTIGE PRICING

Prestige pricing sets higher-than-average prices to suggest status and high quality to the consumer. Many customers assume that higher prices mean better quality. Rolls-Royce® automobiles, Waterford® crystal, and Rolex® watches are all prestige-priced products.

MULTIPLE-UNIT PRICING

Some businesses have found that pricing items in multiples, such as three for $1.00, is better than selling the same items at $.34 each. Multiple-unit pricing suggests a bargain and helps to increase sales volume.

EVERYDAY LOW PRICES

Everyday low prices (EDLP) are low prices set on a consistent basis with no intention of raising them or offering discounts in the future. Everyday low prices are not as deeply discounted as promotional prices, which creates sales stability. Other benefits include reduced promotional expenses and reduced losses due to discounting.

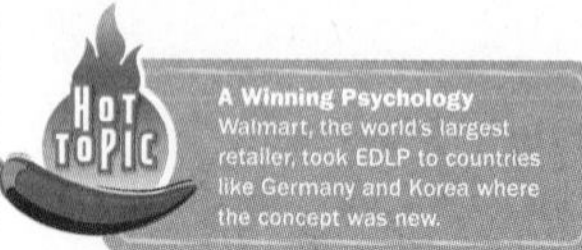

A Winning Psychology Walmart, the world's largest retailer, took EDLP to countries like Germany and Korea where the concept was new.

PROMOTIONAL PRICING

Promotional pricing is generally used in conjunction with sales promotions wherein prices are reduced for a short period of time. Common types of promotional pricing are loss leader pricing (discussed in Chapter 25), special-event pricing, and rebates and coupons.

LOSS LEADER PRICING

Loss leader pricing is used to increase store traffic by offering very popular items of merchandise for sale at below-cost prices. The theory behind this practice is that customers will be attracted by the low price. Once in the store, they will buy regularly priced merchandise in addition to the loss leader item.

SPECIAL-EVENT PRICING

In special-event pricing, items are reduced in price for a short period of time, based on a specific event. For example, stores may promote back-to-school, Presidents' Day, or anniversary sales. Manufacturers offer special promotions to wholesalers and retailers willing to advertise or promote a manufacturer's products.

REBATES AND COUPONS

Rebates are partial refunds provided by the manufacturer to consumers. To receive the rebate, a customer buys the product, and then sends in a rebate form along with the product's proof of purchase and a store receipt. Manufacturers offer rebates to wholesalers and retailers for purchasing certain quantities of goods before the manufacturer runs a special product promotion. Coupons allow customers to take reductions at the time of purchase. Coupons may be found in newspapers, advertisements, product packages, and even on sales receipts printed by retailers, such as supermarkets.

DISCOUNTS AND ALLOWANCES

Discount pricing involves the seller offering reductions from the usual price. Such reductions are generally granted in exchange for the buyer performing certain actions. These include cash discounts, quantity discounts, trade discounts, seasonal discounts, and special allowances.

CASH DISCOUNTS

Cash discounts are offered to buyers to encourage them to pay their bills quickly. Terms are generally written on the invoice. For example, 2/10, net 30 means that a 2 percent discount is granted if the bill is paid in ten days.

QUANTITY DISCOUNTS

Quantity discounts are offered to buyers for placing large orders. Sellers benefit from large orders through the lower selling costs involved in one transaction, as opposed to several small transactions. Quantity discounts also offer buyers an incentive to purchase more merchandise than they originally intended to purchase.

Two types of quantity discounts are noncumulative and cumulative. Noncumulative quantity discounts are offered on one order, while cumulative quantity discounts are offered on all orders over a specified period of time.

Cumulative discounts may be granted for purchases made over six months. For example, all purchases for that period are used to determine the quantity discount offered. In other cases, buyers may be required to sign a contract that guarantees a certain level of business. Advertisers who agree to use a specified number of column inches in their newspaper ads might be charged cheaper contract rates. Generally, the more you advertise, the less you pay per column inch.

TRADE DISCOUNTS

Trade discounts are not really discounts at all but, rather, the way manufacturers quote prices to wholesalers and retailers. Many manufacturers establish suggested retail prices, or list prices, for their items. They grant discounts from the list price to members of the channel of distribution. A manufacturer might grant wholesalers a 40 percent discount from the list price and retailers a 30 percent discount.

The manufacturer might also quote the discounts in series, such as 25 percent and 10 percent for retailers and wholesalers, respectively. Series, or chain, discounts are calculated in sequence, with discounts taken on the declining balance as shown below. The example is based on a list price of $50.

Retailer's discount

$50 × .25 = $12.50

Cost to retailer

$50 – $12.50 = $37.50

Wholesaler's discount

$37.50 × .10 = $3.75

Cost to wholesaler

$37.50 – $3.75 = $33.75

In series discounts, note that the wholesaler's discount is based on the retailer's discount, not the original list price.

SEASONAL DISCOUNTS

Seasonal discounts are offered to buyers willing to buy at a time outside the customary buying season. Manufacturers offer discounts to obtain orders for seasonal merchandise early so that production facilities and labor can be used throughout the year.

Other businesses use seasonal discounts to cut anticipated costs. For example, many retailers drastically reduce prices on swimsuits after the summer season. A good time to buy a winter coat is in the spring, when retailers sell them at a discount. Such retailers prefer to sell this merchandise at a lower markup than pay the costs of warehousing it until the following year. A variation on this device is used by vacation resorts. They offer vacationers lower rates to encourage use of resort facilities during the off season. For example, a ski resort may offer attractive rates during the summer months.

ALLOWANCES

Trade-in allowances go directly to the buyer. Customers are offered a price reduction if they sell back an old model of the product they are purchasing. Consumers are generally offered trade-in allowances when purchasing new cars or major appliances. Companies usually get such allowances when purchasing machinery or equipment. Occasionally, real estate transactions may use a trade-in allowance approach. Buyers may offer a house or other piece of property as partial payment for a different property.

Reading Check

Analyze Would a higher price benefit a high-end product?

EXPLAIN

Graphic Organizer

Display this graphic organizer on psychological pricing strategies. Have students enter a brief description of each pricing strategy.

Odd-Even Pricing	odd numbers: bargain image; even numbers: quality image
Prestige Pricing	High prices often suggest higher quality and status.
Multiple-Unit Pricing	Bundling items may suggest increased value to customers.
Everyday Low Price	Consistent low prices appeal to cost-conscious consumers

→ **Psychological Pricing Strategies Goal**: to create a specific illusion in a customer

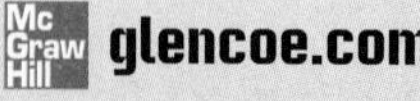

glencoe.com

Graphic Organizer Send students to the Online Learning Center to print this graphic organizer.

A Winning Psychology Ask students: ***Why is everyday low pricing such a powerful psychological concept for consumers?*** Then ask: ***Do you think there is a specific group of consumers who are particularly attracted to EDLP?***

Reinforce Vocabulary

Prestige pricing—Connotative Meanings The word *prestige* means "standing or estimation in the eyes of people." Prestige pricing suggests some purchases are based on what others will think, not because a consumer truly wants or needs the product. Ask students: ***Have you ever been influenced by prestige pricing? If so, how?*** Students may say they purchased an item they knew was overpriced, but they were influenced by a desire to show it off to their friends.

ELABORATE

PROMOTIONAL PRICING

Ask these questions to focus the discussion on promotional pricing.

Guiding Questions

Explain How is promotional pricing different from an everyday low price strategy?	Unlike everyday low prices, promotional pricing generally last for a short period of time.
Analyze Do you think a boutique clothing store would be likely to use loss leader pricing? Why or why not?	No, because boutiques do not attract customers with low pricing; they draw customers by appealing to a niche market.
Apply Would you rather have a coupon for $2 off a product or a $3 rebate? Why?	With a coupon, you don't have to fill out a form, mail it in, and wait to get your money back.

Reading Check Answer

Read the Reading Check question to students: ***Would a higher price benefit a high-end product?*** Possibly; many consumers equate price with quality and therefore will automatically think they are purchasing a better product if they pay more. Ask students: ***Have you ever paid more for a product because you thought its quality was better than less expensive products? Do you think the extra cost was worth it? Why or why not?*** Yes, I paid more to buy a certain brand of running shoes. The shoes lasted longer than less expensive shoes.

DISCOUNTS AND ALLOWANCES

Ask these questions to focus discussion on discounts and allowances.

Guiding Questions

Explain What are trade discounts?	the percentage manufacturers take off suggested retail prices (or list prices) when selling to wholesalers and retailers
Apply Businesses that sign a contract guaranteeing three minutes of advertising over 24 hours get a 25 percent discount off the regular 30-second rate of $1,000. How much money can a business save by buying three minutes at a time?	The business will save $1,500. (6 × 1000 × 0.25)

Critical Thinking

Tell students the following joke: ***A customer comments that a store's price for a specific television is $50 less than the closest competitor's price. The store owner says the reason is that even though she buys the TVs for $655, she is able to sell them for only $640. The customer asks how this is possible. The store owner's response is:* Volume!** Ask Students: ***What makes this joke funny?*** No matter how much volume you have, you cannot make money if you are selling an item for less than what you paid for it; in fact, the more you sell in such cases, the more money you lose.

PROFESSIONAL DEVELOPMENT **MINI CLIP**

ELL: Strategies for English Language Learners
Go to the Online Learning Center to view a video clip in which an author discusses strategies for teaching English language learners.

Mini Projects

Enrichment

Creating an Ad Using a Psychological Pricing Strategy Organize students into groups of two or three. Instruct each group to choose one of the methods of psychological pricing discussed here. The group should then price and promote a product using its chosen technique. Students should develop either store signs, TV ads, or Internet ads for their promotion. Have the groups present their promotions to the class. The class should then determine which of the psychological pricing strategies was used in the ad. Students should create and present a promotion that uses one of these strategies: odd-even pricing, prestige pricing, multiple unit pricing, or everyday low prices. The class should then identify the psychological pricing strategy that was used and the strategy's purpose.

Examining Odd-Even Pricing Have students check the prices of 100 items at a supermarket or discount store and keep track of how many items have odd-numbered prices and how many have even-numbered prices. Have students report their numbers to the class. The class should total the numbers and then calculate the percentage of odd-numbered prices and the percentage of even-numbered prices. Encourage students to draw a conclusion based on their results. Each student should report to the class how many odd-numbered and even-numbered prices they find out of 100 products. The class should then total the percentage of odd and even prices. Conclusions will vary. The greater percentage of prices will probably be odd, because most supermarkets and discount stores want to project a value-conscious image.

THE PRICING PROCESS AND RELATED TECHNOLOGY

As one of the four Ps of the marketing mix, pricing is the most flexible because ongoing pricing strategies and prices can be changed quickly.

DETERMINING PRICES

Six steps are used to determine prices: establish pricing objectives, determine costs, estimate demand, study the competition, decide on a pricing strategy, and set prices.

STEP 1: ESTABLISH PRICING OBJECTIVES

Pricing objectives must conform to the company's overall goals: making profit, improving market share, and meeting the competition. Pricing objectives should be specific, time sensitive, realistic, and measurable. Increasing sales of a given product is not a good pricing objective. Increasing unit or dollar sales by 20 percent in one year compared with the previous year is better because it is time-sensitive (one year), specific, and measurable (20 percent increase). At the end of one year, a company can evaluate and make revisions if the pricing objective was not met.

STEP 2: DETERMINE COSTS

For wholesalers and retailers, money owed to vendors plus freight charges equals the cost of an item. Service providers must consider the cost of supplies plus the cost of performing the service. The cost of materials and labor used in a manufactured product make up the item's cost. A business must keep accurate records and understand that changes in costs and in economic conditions may affect its **ultimate** pricing decision.

STEP 3: ESTIMATE DEMAND

Marketers study the size of the market to determine the total number of possible customers for a given product. From their basic research, marketers estimate the percentage of potential customers who might buy that new product. Much of this analysis is based on supply-and-demand theory and exceptions due to demand elasticity.

STEP 4: STUDY THE COMPETITION

You need to investigate what prices your competitors are charging for similar goods and services. Businesses subscribe to services that provide competitive information on a daily basis. In today's computer age, it is easy to go online to check out competitors' prices.

STEP 5: DECIDE ON A PRICING STRATEGY

You need to revisit the pricing objectives and decide on a pricing strategy or strategies that will help you accomplish your objectives. Everything you learned in this section will help you in this endeavor. However, you must remember that as economic and market conditions change, strategies may require changes too.

STEP 6: SET PRICES

Setting the published price that you see on price tickets, Web sites, price sheets, catalogs, and promotional materials is the final step. It is important that all the above steps are carefully considered. Customers' reactions to price changes must be considered before marketers decide if and when to change their published prices.

PRICING TECHNOLOGY

Technology applications for pricing are evident in the data that are now made available to marketers when making pricing decisions. They are also evident in the tools and **vehicles** for providing price information to customers.

SMART PRICING

Smart pricing allows marketers to make intelligent pricing decisions based on enormous amounts of data. Web-based pricing technology crunches this data into timely, usable information. Software that combines sales data with inventory data results in pricing recommendations, which the pricing team can accept, revise, or reject. Previous sales data are compared with current sales data. This comes from from the store's point-of-sale system. They are also compared with its merchandising system, which includes all items' inventory levels. All these data help to set prices for new merchandise, and when to take markdowns, if any, on current merchandise in stock. This system gives this company the ability to adjust prices according to changing market conditions.

COMMUNICATING PRICES TO CUSTOMERS

Electronic gadgets provide customers with real-time pricing information. Retailers that invest in electronic shelves and digital price labels can change prices quickly and easily. They also can alert in-store shoppers to deals based on customers' buying habits.

Kiosks in retail stores allow customers to scan a product to determine its price. In supermarket chains, customers scan their own merchandise and pay for the products without the assistance of a clerk. With these new technological advances, older price-marking techniques, such as printed price tags, are quickly becoming a thing of the past in certain industries.

RFID TECHNOLOGY

Advanced technology that may revolutionize pricing and inventory control is called "radio frequency identification," or RFID. RFID is wireless technology that involves tiny chips embedded in products. A chip has an antenna, a battery, and a memory chip filled with a description of the item for sale.

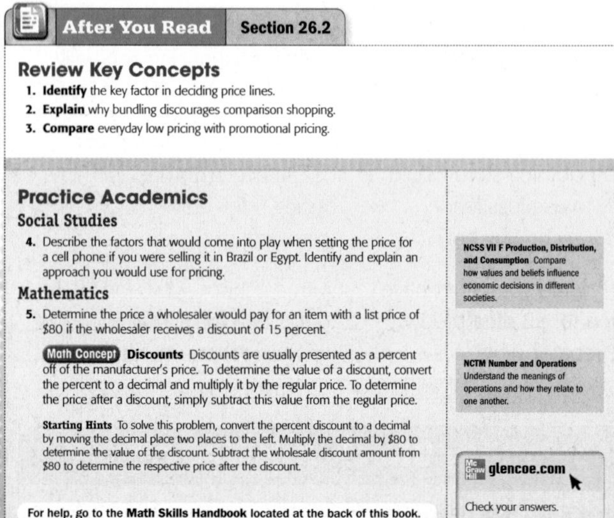

After You Read | Section 26.2

Review Key Concepts

1. **Identify** the key factor in deciding price lines.
2. **Explain** why bundling discourages comparison shopping.
3. **Compare** everyday low pricing with promotional pricing.

Practice Academics

Social Studies

4. Describe the factors that would come into play when setting the price for a cell phone if you were selling it in Brazil or Egypt. Identify and explain an approach you would use for pricing.

Mathematics

5. Determine the price a wholesaler would pay for an item with a list price of $80 if the wholesaler receives a discount of 15 percent.

Math Concept **Discounts** Discounts are usually presented as a percent off of the manufacturer's price. To determine the value of a discount, convert the percent to a decimal and multiply it by the regular price. To determine the price after a discount, simply subtract this value from the regular price.

Starting Hints To solve this problem, convert the percent discount to a decimal by moving the decimal place two places to the left. Multiply the decimal by $80 to determine the value of the discount. Subtract the wholesale discount amount from $80 to determine the respective price after the discount.

For help, go to the **Math Skills Handbook** located at the back of this book.

NCSS VII F Production, Distribution, and Consumption Compare how values and beliefs influence economic decisions in different societies.

NCTM Number and Operations Understand the meanings of operations and how they relate to one another.

glencoe.com

Check your answers.

ELABORATE

Activate Prior Knowledge

Looking at the Place of Price in the Marketing Mix To remind students of the importance of price in the marketing mix, review the four Ps. Emphasize that price is an important factor in controlling how customers respond to specific products and how they respond to the businesses selling them.

MARKETING MIX			
P	PRODUCT	P	PLACE
P	PRICE	P	PROMOTION

DETERMINING PRICES

Ask students the following guiding questions to focus on this topic.

Guiding Questions

Analyze Why is it important that a pricing objectives be time sensitive? Give an example of time-sensitive pricing objective.	Without a specific date, it is impossible to determine if a goal has been met. Example: Dollar sales on laundry products will increase by 8 percent next quarter as compared to the previous quarter.
Predict What might happen if a company underestimates the demand for a product when setting its price?	Possible answer: The price might get set too low and the company might quickly sell out of the product and lose a chance to make additional profits.

EVALUATE

Graphic Organizer

Display this graphic to help students better understand the purpose of the six steps used to determine price.

Step 1 Establish Objectives Should make profit, improve market share meet competition

Step 2 Determine Costs Depends on whether wholesaler, retailer, or service provider

Step 3 Estimate Demand Estimate number of potential customers

Step 4 Study Competition Investigate competitors' prices for similar products and services

Step 5 Decide on Strategy Revisit objectives to help in choosing strategy

Step 6 Set Prices

glencoe.com

Graphic Organizer Send students to the Online Learning Center to print this graphic organizer.

PRICING TECHNOLOGY

Ask these questions to focus the discussion on pricing technology.

Guiding Questions

Recall What are some data used in smart pricing decisions?	current sales data, previous sales data, inventory data
Synthesize How might RFID technology revolutionize the way consumer purchases are handled at checkout counters?	RFID uses a special chip to transmit information such as prices. This wireless technology can quickly read large numbers of items in a shopping cart.

Mini Project

Extension

Looking at Advantages and Disadvantages of Electronic Shelves Have students investigate electronic shelf technology and create a table listing its advantages and disadvantages. Student tables should list some of the following: Advantages: saves costs of labor involved in manually update shelf prices; allows price changes to be immediately displayed; prevents discrepancies between shelf price and the POS price. Disadvantages: requires a large initial investment and specific technologies such as specialized communication networks.

After You Read Section 26.2

Review Key Concepts

1. The key factor in deciding price lines is the differential between the levels of pricing. The prices within the line must be far enough apart so that the customer can perceive that there are significant differences between the groups.
2. Bundling discourages comparison shopping because the grouping of products in the package may differ among competitors, making it difficult to see which one is the better deal.
3. In everyday low pricing, the prices are low and they remain low with no intention of changing them in the future. In promotional pricing, prices are lowered for a short period of time, after which they go back up to the original price when the promotion is over.

Practice Academics

Social Studies

4. In both Brazil and Egypt, many factors would come into play when setting the price for a cell phone. Competition, local laws, the country's infrastructure, economic conditions, monetary exchange rates, tariffs, and distribution systems would have to be considered. Ultimately, the price customers are able and willing to pay would also have to be considered. The cell phone features required for them to work in each country may have a bearing on the final price. In addition, in some cases, land lines may not be available, limiting the consumer's options.

Mathematics

5. $68 ($80 × 0.15 = $12; $80 - $12 = $68)

glencoe.com

Send students to the Online Learning Center to check their answers.

Pricing Strategies

The three types of pricing are demand-based, cost-based, and competition-based. All can be used to establish the base price.

TYPES of PRICING

Demand-Based

Cost-Based

Competition-Based

BASE PRICE

Adjustments to the base price can be made using these strategies: product mix, geographical, international, segmented, psychological, promotional, and discounted.

Product Mix

Discounted

Geographical

Promotional

BASE PRICE

International

Psychological

Segmented

Written Summary

- Establishing a base price for a product can be accomplished by combining cost-oriented, demand-oriented, and competition-oriented policies, and considering resellers' needs.
- Businesses must decide whether to use a one-price policy or a flexible price policy.
- The product life cycle should be considered in the pricing process. Two polar pricing strategies for the introduction of a product are skimming pricing and penetration pricing.
- Once a base price is established, price adjustments are made using pricing strategies: product mix pricing, geographical pricing, international pricing, segmented pricing, psychological pricing, promotional pricing, and discounts and allowances.
- Six steps to determine prices are establishing pricing objectives, determining costs, estimating demand, studying competition, deciding on a strategy, and setting actual price.
- Pricing technology has revolutionized the way businesses make pricing decisions.

Review Content Vocabulary and Academic Vocabulary

1. Create multiple-choice test questions for each content and academic vocabulary term.

Content Vocabulary

- markup (p. 605)
- one-price policy (p. 608)
- flexible-price policy (p. 608)
- skimming pricing (p. 609)
- penetration pricing (p. 610)
- product mix pricing strategies (p. 613)
- price lining (p. 613)
- bundle pricing (p. 613)
- geographical pricing (p. 614)
- segmented pricing strategy (p. 614)
- psychological pricing (p. 615)
- prestige pricing (p. 616)
- everyday low prices (EDLP) (p. 616)
- promotional pricing (p. 616)

Academic Vocabulary

- relation (p. 605)
- allocated (p. 606)
- ultimate (p. 618)
- vehicles (p. 618)

Assess for Understanding

2. **Identify** What are three ways to find a base price?
3. **Explain** Why does pricing change during a product's life cycle?
4. **Contrast** What is the major difference in the two polar pricing strategies for introducing a new product?
5. **Suggest** How can the six types of pricing strategies be used to adjust the base price?
6. **Sequence** What are six steps in the pricing process?
7. **Imagine** What kinds of new technology are used in pricing?
8. **Define** What is the definition of the term *psychological pricing*?
9. **Calculate** Forty percent of your customers place large orders during a 3-month period, while the remaining customers place smaller orders over a 12-month period. Which will you offer all your customers: cumulative or noncumulative quantity discounts? Why?

EVALUATE

Visual Summary

Express Creativity Ask students to create a visual summary that illustrates a concept in the chapter. Encourage students to use different formats for their visual summaries, such as a slide show, graphic organizer, or poster. Visual summaries will vary depending on the concept depicted. Questions to ask when assessing a visual summary include:

- Is the summary clear, economical, and simple?
- Are any important steps or concepts left out?
- Are steps or concepts arranged in the same order as the original?
- Does the summary reveal a pattern that connects the details?
- Does the summary locate and highlight the most important information?

Review Content Vocabulary and Academic Vocabulary

1. Multiple-choice questions will vary. Sample questions:
   The difference between an item's cost and its sale price is its
   a. expenses.
   b. markup.
   c. penetration price.
   d. price line.
   If a company is charging every customer the same price for its products, the business is using
   a. everyday low pricing.
   b. a flexible-price policy.
   c. a one-price policy.
   d. penetration pricing.
   When a business allows customers to bargain for the best prices they can get, the business is using
   a. everyday low pricing.
   b. a flexible-price policy.
   c. a one-price policy.
   d. penetration pricing.

EVALUATE

Assess for Understanding

2. Three ways to find a base price are cost-oriented pricing, the lowest price at which a product can be offered and still be profitable; demand-oriented pricing, which determines a price range for the product that is defined by the price floor and the ceiling price; and competition-oriented pricing, which ensure the final price is in line with the company's pricing policies.

3. Pricing in subsequent stages during a product's life cycle is dependent upon whether skimming or penetration pricing was used in the product's introduction. With skimming pricing, prices can be lowered as more competitors enter the market. With penetration pricing, the main goal is to keep products in this stage as long as possible.

4. The major difference is that skimming pricing sets the price high to draw on those who are interested in having the latest product, while penetration pricing aims to sell as many items as possible.

5. Product mix is used to adjust prices to maximize the profitability of a group of products, rather than just one item. Geographical pricing adjusts the price according to different shipping agreements. International pricing adjusts the price according to local considerations, such as competition, laws, regulations, economic conditions, and the monetary exchange rate. Segmented pricing strategies use two or more different prices for a product, even though there is no difference in the item's cost. Psychological pricing strategies help create an illusion for customers, such as that they are getting an usually good deal. Promotional pricing usually involves prices being reduced for a short period of time. Discount pricing involves the seller offering reductions from the usual price, usually in return for the buyer performing certain actions, such as buying a certain quantity of the product.

6. Six steps in the pricing process are: (1) Establish pricing objectives; (2) determine costs; (3) estimate demand; (4) study competition; (5) decide on a pricing strategy; (6) set prices.

7. Responses should show an understanding of how technology is used in pricing. Examples include smart pricing software which provides businesses with an enormous amount of data to help make pricing decisions; electronic shelves and digital pricing labels, kiosks for customers to check prices, self-service checkout counters, and radio frequency identification technology (RFID).

8. Psychological pricing strategies involve pricing a product to create a specific illusion in the customer's mind. One example would be to make a product seem to be cheaper by setting the price at $4.95 instead of $5.00.

9. Accept all reasonable answers. Cumulative quantity discounts would benefit 60 percent of the company's customers because they place orders over the year. Noncumulative discounts would benefit 40 percent of the company's customers that place large orders during a short period of time (3 months).

21st Century Skills

Problem-Solving Skills

10. **Selling Toys** Use the steps in determining price to set a price for a children's toy that you think will be popular during the holiday season. The economy is in a recession, so the pricing objective is to sell this toy at a reasonable price. The cost to manufacture the toy is $2.15. Remember the manufacturer needs to cover its expenses and make a profit (20%) on this item and so do the wholesalers (25% markup) and retailers (66.7% markup). Show your calculations and how you used the six steps in determining the final price to the customer.

Financial Literacy Skills

11. **How Much to Charge?** You have determined that consumers are willing to pay only $25 for a widget. If wholesaler's markup is 20 percent and retailer's markup is 40 percent, what price should you charge wholesalers for a widget? What does that price have to cover?

e-Marketing Skills

12. **Pricing Technology** Research smart pricing technology. Cite where and how it is used, and especially look at how it may be used with online ads found on search engines. You may want to consider the questions below as you conduct your research. Prepare a written report on your findings.
    - How are customers affected by this technology?
    - How are businesses affected by this technology?
    - What are some advantages and disadvantages of the smart pricing technologies you found in your research?
    - How might businesses use their pricing strategies as an advertising strategy?
    - How do smart pricing techniques fit into a rapidly expanding global economy?

Build Academic Skills

Social Studies

13. **Economics** For a fund raising project, you ordered 50 items at $5, 25 items at $8 and 25 items $10. You are not sure all these items will sell well. Explain the markup, selling price, and pricing strategy you suggest to make at a minimum profit of $700.

NCSS VII B Production, Distribution, and Consumption Analyze the role that supply and demand, prices, incentives, and profits play in determining what is produced and distributed in a competitive market system.

Science

14. **Scientific Inquiry** Conduct research on the price 20 teens are willing to pay for a concert ticket for three different popular groups. Analyze your findings to determine the ceiling and floor prices. Report your findings in a chart and note the price you would recommend for each group's next tour.

NSES A Develop abilities necessary to do scientific inquiry, understandings about scientific inquiry.

Mathematics

15. **Calculate Incentive Discounts** Promotional discounts are given to stores by manufacturers to place products in preferred locations or to pay for ads, displays, or in-store demonstrations. What is the percent discount to stock an item that has a purchase amount of $10,800 and a discount amount of $600? (Round your answer to the nearest whole percent.)

NCTM Number and Operations Compute fluently and make reasonable estimates.

Math Concept **Percent Discount** When a discount is given in a dollar amount, it can be converted to a percent by dividing the dollar value of the discount by the purchase amount and then multiplying by 100.

For help, go to the **Math Skills Handbook** located at the back of this book.

Standardized Test Practice

Directions Read the following questions. On a separate sheet of paper, write the best possible answer for each one.

1. If you want to capture a large number of customers in a relatively short period of time when introducing a new product, you would use
   A. cost-oriented pricing
   B. flexible pricing
   C. skimming pricing
   D. penetration pricing
2. An effective price-lining policy for jackets would be $50, $52, and $55.
   T
   F
3. __________ are partial refunds provided by the manufacturer to consumers.

Test-Taking Tip

Just before taking a test, avoid talking to other students. Text anxiety can be contagious.

DECA Connection Role Play

Consultant
New Business Owners

Situation You are consulting for a company that offers advice and assistance to prospective new business owners. Your current client (judge) is planning to open a business that will provide various errand services to customers in the community. Some of the services the client (judge) plans to provide include collecting mail and packages while customers are away, dog walking, grocery shopping, picking-up dry cleaning, and other related errands. Your research of the planned target market indicates that the residents are primarily working couples that do not have a lot of free time.

The client (judge) has limited business experience and is eager for the business to succeed. Your client (judge) is uncertain about the pricing of the services of the new business and has questions about pricing strategies and determining prices for the services. You are meeting with your client (judge) later today to discuss pricing for the services of the proposed business.

Activity You are to discuss with your client (judge) the steps in determining prices for the proposed services and some pricing strategies appropriate for the new business.

Evaluation You will be evaluated on how well you meet the following performance indicators:

1. Select an approach for setting a base price (cost, demand, competition).
2. Describe pricing strategies.
3. Set prices.
4. Organize information.
5. Adjust prices to maximize profitability.

Download the Competitive Events workbook for more Role-Play practice.

EVALUATE

21st Century Skills

Problem-Solving Skills

10. Accept all reasonable answers, as long as each of the six steps is covered in the answer: establish pricing objective (reasonable MSRP), determine cost ($2.15), estimate demand (popular), study competition (not known), decide on a pricing strategy (odd-even) and set prices. If students price forward their calculations would be: $2.15 × 20% = $.43; manufacturer's price to wholesaler $2.58 ($2.15 + $.43); wholesaler's markup $0.65 ($2.58 × 25%) and price to retailer $3.23 ($2.58 + $0.65); retailer's markup $2.15 ($3.23 × 66.7%) and base price to customer $5.38. Use odd-even pricing to set price $5.39 price to final consumer, which meets the pricing objective of being reasonably priced.

Financial Literacy Skills

11. The lowest price you can charge wholesalers is $12 ($25 × .40 = $10; $25 − 10 = $15; $15 × .20 = $3; $15 − $3 = $12). The $12 must cover the manufacturer's cost, expenses, and intended profit.

e-Marketing Skills

12. Students should create a written report that discusses smart pricing. In the report, they should discuss where and how smart pricing is used, its advantages and disadvantages, how both customers and businesses are affected by the technology, and so on. Smart pricing combines sales data, inventory data, and a number of other factors to make pricing recommendations that managers can then either accept or reject. With search engines, prices may be lowered if an ad receives a low number of clicks. Google, for example, has developed a service called AdWords, which uses smart pricing to assign a specific value to each click-through an ad receives, based on variety of factors. These factors are designed to determine the likelihood that a specific click will lead to a Web site purchase.

EVALUATE

Build Academic Skills

Social Studies

13. Accept all answers that arrive at a minimum $700 profit. A simple solution is to mark up all items 100 percent based on the cost. The $5 item's selling price would be $10, the $8 item —$16, and the $10 item —$20, which would be an example of price lining strategy. Students who take into account that not all the items will sell well may suggest a bundle pricing strategy that will group the two better selling items with the $5 item; in which case the packaged selling price could be $30. ($5 + $8 = $13 cost plus $17 markup = $30; $5 + 10 = 15 cost plus a $15 markup). In this case, the profit would be $100 more than with the price lining strategy.

Science

14. Students should conduct research to determine what 20 teens are willing to pay for a concert ticket for three different popular groups. They then should analyze the results of their research to determine the ceiling and floor prices. Students should create a chart that visually illustrates their findings, and use this chart to recommend what each group should charge for tickets during their next tour.

Mathematics

15. 6% (600/10,800 = .055, rounds to 6%)

Standardized Test Practice

1. C (penetration pricing)
2. F (False. The prices are too close together to differentiate the price lines.)
3. Rebates

DECA Connection Role Play

Evaluations will be based on these performance indicators:

1. **Select an approach for setting a base price (cost, demand, competition).** While cost, demand, and competition are taken into account when setting prices, one approach usually predominates. When demand-oriented pricing is used, marketers attempt to determine what consumers are willing to pay for specific goods or services. The price must be in line with the consumer's perceived value of the item. With competition-oriented pricing, marketers set the price in relationship to competitors' price. With cost-oriented pricing, marketers calculate the costs of acquiring or making the product and the expenses of doing business and then add on the projected profit margin to arrive at the price.
2. **Describe pricing strategies.** Product mix pricing strategies involve adjusting prices to maximize the profitability for an entire group of products, rather than just one item. Geographical pricing involves price adjustments required because of different shipping agreements. International pricing involves setting prices that take into consideration such factors as costs, competition, laws, economic conditions, etc., in different countries. A segmented pricing strategy uses two or more different prices for a product, although there is no difference in the item's cost.
3. **Set prices.** Prices should be set using a six step process: (1) Establish pricing objectives; (2) Determine costs; (3) Estimate demand; (4) Study competition; (5) Decide on a pricing strategy; (6) Set prices
4. **Organize information.** Students should be able to organize needed information, such as cost of producing items, expenses, markup, etc., in order to calculate results such as unit prices, wholesale prices, and retail prices.
5. **Adjust prices to maximize profitability.** A important method of maximizing profitability is by using a segmented pricing strategy. One segmented pricing strategy factor is buyer identification. Another segmented pricing strategy is to set different prices for products that are essentially the same, but have a slightly different style, color, etc. Purchase location is an important segmented pricing strategy. A fourth segmented pricing strategy is the time of purchase. An example of this is the rise in the price of roses around Valentine's Day.

Mc Graw Hill 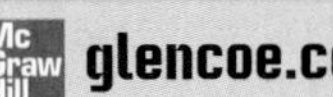

Role Plays For more DECA Role Plays, send students to the Online Learning Center to download the Competitive Events Workbook.

Chapter 27 | Section 27.1 Calculating Prices | Section 27.2 Calculating Discounts

pricing math

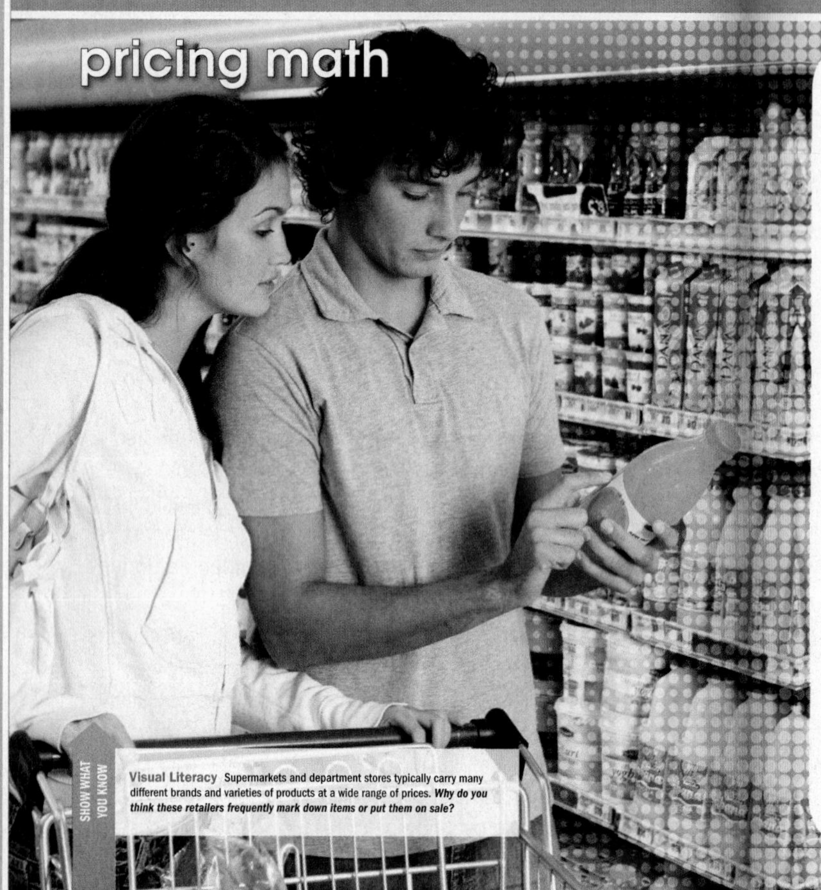

SHOW WHAT YOU KNOW

Visual Literacy Supermarkets and department stores typically carry many different brands and varieties of products at a wide range of prices. ***Why do you think these retailers frequently mark down items or put them on sale?***

Discovery Project

Pricing Markups and Discounts

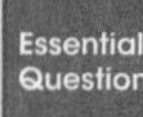

Essential Question How do retailers calculate original markups, knowing that prices will be reduced later in the season?

Project Goal

Work with a partner to analyze a retailer's original prices and subsequent discounts on ten items. Assume the retailer purchased 200 of each of those ten items. In scenario #1, 75 percent of those items sold at the original price and the remainder sold at the reduced price. In Scenario #2, assume the opposite was true. So, 25 percent sold at the original price and 75 percent sold at the reduced price. Determine the difference in sales revenue. If the cost of each item was 50 percent of the original retail price, what was the original dollar markup? (original price – cost = dollar markup). Once the discount was taken, what was the dollar markup on each item (reduced price – cost = dollar markup)?

Ask Yourself...

- How will you find stores that are discounting their goods?
- How will you decide on which goods to use for this project?
- What computer software program could help you do the calculations for this assignment?
- How will you analyze and report your findings?

Synthesize and Present Research Synthesize your research by analyzing the two scenarios and showing the dollar effect each has on the retailer. Discuss what your analysis says about setting original prices when you know the prices will be reduced later in the season.

glencoe.com

Activity
Get a worksheet activity about markups and discounts.

Evaluate
Download a rubric you can use to evaluate your project.

DECA Connection

DECA Event Role Play

Concepts in this chapter are related to DECA competitive events that involve either an interview or role play.

Performance Indicators The performance indicators represent key skills and knowledge. Your key to success in DECA competitive events is relating them to concepts in this chapter.

- Identify factors affecting a business's profit.
- Determine cost of product (breakeven, ROI, markup).
- Demonstrate responsible behavior.
- Adjust prices to maximize profitability.
- Describe the nature of profit and loss statements.

DECA Prep

Role Play Practice role-playing with the DECA Connection competitive-event activity at the end of this chapter. More information on DECA events can be found on DECA's Web site.

Chapter 27 · Pricing Math | 625

ENGAGE

Visual Literacy

Read the chapter opener photo caption to students: ***Why do you think these retailers frequently mark down items or put them on sale?*** Retailers mark down merchandise to move merchandise quickly and to remain competitive in the marketplace. Then ask these guiding questions.

Guiding Questions

List What are the steps in converting $\frac{2}{3}$ to a decimal?	Divide 2 by 3, which is 0.666 (a repeating decimal.) Round off to 0.67.
Explain What do resellers consider when determining an item's markup?	Resellers must consider the cost of acquiring the item and expenses required to run the business. They then add the intended profit to get the final markup.

Discovery Project

Pricing Markups and Discounts To get students thinking about the strategies behind pricing markups and discounts, read aloud the Discovery Project Essential Question: ***How do retailers calculate original markups, knowing prices will be reduced later in the season?*** Discuss how retailers must accurately estimate what percentage of items will sell at each price point. Estimates are typically based on past experience with similar products under similar market conditions.

glencoe.com

Discovery Project Resources Send students to the Online Learning Center to download a rubric to evaluate their projects.

ENGAGE

Introduce the Chapter

Chapter 27 discusses how prices are set and discounts are determined. These major concepts are presented:

- Basic markup calculations
- Percentage markup
- Cost method of pricing
- Retail method of pricing
- Calculations for lowing prices
- Planning for stock shortages
- Calculating discounts
- Employee and vendor discounts
- Potential pitfalls of discount pricing

Discussion Starter

Profit and Markup Display an abbreviated income statement for the students to view. You may want to refer to the income statement in **Figure 27.1** as a guideline. Next to the statement, put the parts of a retail price that correspond to items on the statement. For example, next to Sales Revenue, put an arrow and note *Retail Price*; next to Gross Profit, note *Markup*. Point out that that if you multiply Retail Price by the number of items sold, you will get the Sales Revenue. Ask students: ***How is markup related to gross profit?*** The gross profit and markup percentages are the same. Then ask: ***How is the net profit related to gross profit?*** Net profit equals gross profit minus expenses.

DECA Connection

Discuss the performance indicators listed in the DECA Connection feature. Explain to students that performance indicators tell them how to demonstrate their acquired skills and knowledge through individual or team competitive events.

 **glencoe.com** 

Competitive Events Workbook For more DECA Role Plays, send students to the Online Learning Center to download the Competitive Events Workbook.

PRINT RESOURCES

- **Student Edition**
- **Teacher Edition**
- **Student Activity Workbook with Academic Integration** includes worksheets and activities correlated to the text.
- **Mathematics for Marketing Workbook** provides math activities for every unit in the text.

TECHNOLOGY TOOLBOX

- **Connect**
- **ConnectPlus**
- **ExamView Assessment Suite** is a comprehensive solution for creating, administering, and scoring tests.

 **glencoe.com** 

Online Learning Center provides a variety of resources to enrich and enhance learning.

SECTION, CHAPTER, AND UNIT RESOURCES

- **Graphic Organizers** for organizing text concepts visually.
- **Digital Nation Activities** and **Green Marketer Activities** extend learning beyond the text features.
- **Career Chatroom Career Profiles** allow students to explore different marketing occupations in depth.
- **After You Read Answer Keys** for students to check their answers.
- **Discovery Project Rubrics** and **Marketing Internship Project Rubrics** for students to evaluate their projects.

PROGRAM RESOURCES

- **Student Activity Workbook with Academic Integration Teacher Annotated Edition** includes annotated answers for the activities and worksheets.
- **Marketing Research Project Workbook** provides a step-by-step approach for students to complete their own marketing research studies.
- **School-to-Career Activity Workbook** helps students relate their class work to on-the-job experience and involves work-site analysis and working with mentors.
- **Competitive Events Workbook** helps prepare students for state and national marketing education competitions.
- **Inclusion in the Marketing Education Classroom** provides teaching resources for working with students with special needs.
- **PowerPoint Presentations** provides visual teaching aids and assessments for this chapter.

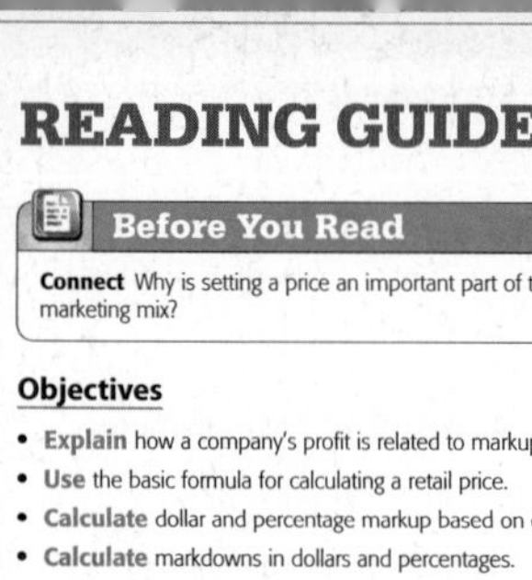

READING GUIDE

Before You Read

Connect Why is setting a price an important part of the marketing mix?

Objectives

- **Explain** how a company's profit is related to markup.
- **Use** the basic formula for calculating a retail price.
- **Calculate** dollar and percentage markup based on cost or retail.
- **Calculate** markdowns in dollars and percentages.
- **Calculate** maintained markup in dollars and percentages.

The Main Idea

Pricing and profit have a direct relationship to each other. Retailers use different formulas for calculating prices, markups, and markdowns.

Vocabulary

Content Vocabulary
- gross profit
- maintained markup

Academic Vocabulary
You will find these words in your reading and on your tests. Make sure you know their meanings.
- convert
- visual

Graphic Organizer

Draw or print this chart to insert the formula for calculating a retail price in the middle circle. Use outer circles to note other formulas.

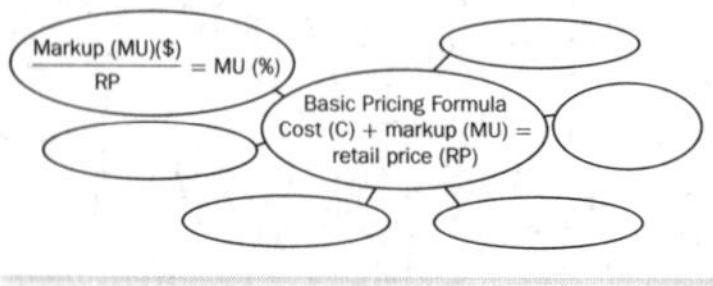

glencoe.com

Print this graphic organizer.

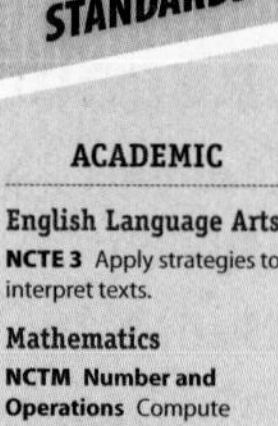

ACADEMIC

English Language Arts
NCTE 3 Apply strategies to interpret texts.

Mathematics
NCTM Number and Operations Compute fluently and make reasonable estimates.
NCTM Problem Solving Apply and adapt a variety of appropriate strategies to solve problems.

NCSS *National Council for the Social Studies*
NCTE *National Council of Teachers of English*
NCTM *National Council of Teachers of Mathematics*
NSES *National Science Education Standards*

Common Core
Reading Read closely to determine what the text says explicitly and to make logical inferences from it; cite specific textual evidence when writing or speaking to support conclusions drawn from the text.

MARKETING CORE FUNCTION
Pricing

Section 27.1 Calculating Prices

PROFIT AND MARKUP

A businessperson says, "We made a profit of $50 from buying the radio for $100 and selling it for $150." The businessperson is only partially correct. The difference between the retail price of $150 (which is equal to 100 percent) and the $100 cost ($66\frac{2}{3}$ percent) is the markup, or margin, of $50 ($33\frac{1}{3}$ percent), not the profit.

As You Read

Analyze How do you think profit relates to markup on prices?

Profit is the amount left over from revenue after the costs of the merchandise and expenses have been paid. The markup (margin) on an item, however, is the same as gross profit. **Gross profit** is the difference between sales revenue and the cost of goods sold. Expenses must still be deducted in order to get net (actual) profit. Therefore, a business must have a markup that is high enough to cover expenses and provide the profit needed to be successful when deciding on a price.

Let's compare profit with retail markup by using the above figures and sales of 300 radios. Look at **Figure 27.1** on page 628 for this comparison. On an income statement, sales revenue would be $45,000 (100 percent), less cost of goods sold of $30,000 ($66\frac{2}{3}$ percent), which would equal gross profit of $15,000 ($33\frac{1}{3}$ percent). If expenses were $9,000 (20 percent), the gross profit ($33\frac{1}{3}$ percent) would be enough to cover expenses and earn a net profit before taxes of $6,000 or $13\frac{1}{3}$ percent ($6,000 divided by $45,000; or $33\frac{1}{3}$ percent – 20 percent).

BASIC MARKUP CALCULATIONS

Retailers and wholesalers use the same formulas to calculate markup. We will use only retail prices here to make these formulas easier to understand. Note, however, that wholesale prices can be substituted in any of the markup formulas.

> "Retail price and markup correlate with a business's income statement."

The most basic pricing formula is the one for calculating retail price. It states in mathematical terms the relationship that has been discussed in the last two chapters. Retail price is a combination of cost and markup. Knowing these two figures will enable you to calculate retail price. Here's how:

Cost (C) + markup (MU) = retail price (RP)

For example,

$14 (C) + $6 (MU) = $20 (RP)

Two other formulas can be derived from this basic formula—cost and markup.

Retail price (RP) – markup (MU) = cost (C)

$20 (RP) – $6 (MU) = $14 (C)

Retail price (RP) – cost (C) = markup (MU)

$20 (RP) – $14 (C) = $6 (MU)

You will rely on these three formulas throughout this chapter. The formulas and their terms will be cited in abbreviated form (for example, C + MU = RP).

ENGAGE

Anticipation Activity

Improving Student Achievement Organize students into groups and tell them to determine the cost of a week-long vacation for the group. They should consider airfare, lodging, car rental, and meals. Then have them calculate both a discount of 15 percent and a markup of 15 percent.

Objectives

- **Explain** how a company's profit is related to markup. Markup is the same as gross profit, or profit before expenses are deducted.
- **Use** the basic formula for calculating a retail price. Retail price = cost + markup
- **Calculate** dollar and percentage markup based on cost or retail. See pages 627–633
- **Calculate** markdowns in dollars and percentages. See pages 634–635
- **Calculate** maintained markup in dollars and percentages. See pages 635–636

Graphic Organizer

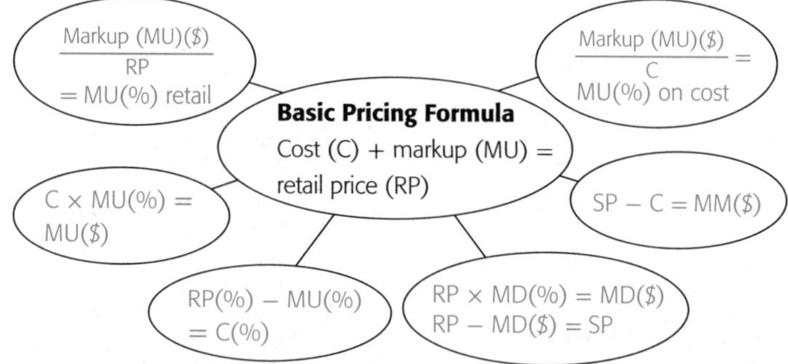

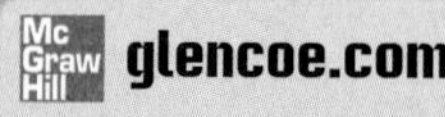

Graphic Organizer Send students to the Online Learning Center to print this graphic organizer.

EXPLORE

Before You Read

Read the Before You Read question aloud: ***Why is setting a price an important part of the marketing mix?*** It is important that customers see prices as being fair, or they may go elsewhere to shop. In addition, the price must be appropriate. Appropriate pricing establishes and maintains a firm's image, competitive edge, and profits. Ask: ***How might maintaining a firm's image be related to maintaining its competitive edge?*** They are most closely related in retail situations in which a store tries to have the lowest prices—for example, when a retail store advertises it will match any competitor's prices.

Preteaching Vocabulary

Have students go to the Online Learning Center at glencoe.com for the Chapter 27 Preteaching Vocabulary games.

Content Vocabulary

Student pairs should locate the terms *gross profit* and *maintained markup* in this section. They should come up with a brief definition for each term based on its context. Encourage students to use as few words as possible in their definitions. Have the class evaluate the definitions as to their clarity and brevity.

Academic Vocabulary

Convert—Synonyms Read aloud the following sentence: ***You can convert the markup on retail to the markup on cost.*** Ask: ***What are some synonyms for the word* convert *in this sentence?*** change, switch, exchange Reread the sentence and ask students which of these words fits the best in this sentence. change

Visual—Usage Display the word *visual* for the class. Explain that visual means "of," "relating to," or "used in vision." Discuss that we often use this word to mean photos, illustrations, graphs, slide shows, and other aids that help people use their sight to understand the ideas being presented.

PROFESSIONAL DEVELOPMENT **MINI CLIP** 

ELL: Words and Pictures
Go to the Online Learning Center for a video clip on using media examples to teach students new vocabulary.

Section 27.1 Calculating Prices

PROFIT AND MARKUP

Ask these guiding questions to discuss profit and markup.

Guiding Questions

Analyze As a fund raiser, your club sells 40 pizzas for $10 each. The club purchased these pizzas for $5.50. Your friend says, "This is great, we made $400 on the fund raiser." Do you agree? Why or why not?	No, because the friend forgot to subtract the cost of the 40 pizzas ($220) from the amount made ($400). The club actually made $180 (400 – 220 = 180).
Apply What are two formulas that could be derived from this one: RP = C + MU($)	C = RP – MU$ MU$ = RP – C

Activate Prior Knowledge

Practice Model how to convert percentages, decimals, and fractions by using a calculator. Display the following values for the students to copy. Have students complete each sequence so that the equivalent fractions, decimals, and percentages are listed. Complete the first one for the students.

$\mathbf{\frac{1}{3}}$ (0.333, $33\frac{1}{3}$ percent)
0.4 ($\frac{2}{5}$, 40 percent)
80 percent (0.8, $\frac{4}{5}$)
0.667 ($\frac{2}{3}$, $66\frac{2}{3}$ percent)

As You Read

Read students the As You Read question: ***How do you think profit relates to markup on prices?*** The amount by which a product is marked up determines the gross profit (the profit before any expenses are deducted.) Therefore, the higher the markup, the greater the profit.

Expert Advice

Read the quote to students:

> **"Retail price and markup correlate with a business's income statement."**

Ask: ***If a business increases its markup, how is retail price affected?*** It goes up. Then ask: ***How are sales revenues affected?*** Since sales revenues are based on retail sales, they also go up.

FIGURE 27.1 How an Income Statement Relates to Markup

Income Statement and Retail Pricing When retailers and wholesalers set the prices on their goods, they consider the effect the prices will have on their bottom line—profit. Markup on all products must ultimately cover their costs and expenses. Let's look at how retail pricing and markup correlate with an income statement. ***What part of the income statement relates to markup?***

Sales Revenue of $30,000 represents 100 percent of the money a firm has to run its business.

Cost of Goods Sold is the cost to purchase or make items for sale. In this example, the cost of goods sold is 47.5 percent of the money the firm generated from sales revenue. ($14,250 divided by $30,000 = .475 or 47.5%)

Income Statement		
Sales Revenue 500 items @ $60/item	$30,000	100%
Cost of Goods Sold 500 items @ $28.50/item	$14,250	47.5%
Gross Profit	$15,750	52.5%
Less Expenses	$11,250	37.5%
Net Profit (before taxes)	$ 4,500	15.0%

Gross Profit or Gross Margin is the difference between sales revenue and cost of goods sold: $30,000 – $14,250 = $15,750. The gross profit high enough to cover expenses and leave money left over for profit. In this case, it represents 52.5 percent of total sales revenue ($14,250 divided by $30,000 = .525 = 52.5%). Note that the gross profit and markup percentages are the same.

Net Profit (before taxes) is the amount left over from revenue after the cost of the merchandise sold and expenses are paid. Net profit before taxes is 15 percent of total sales revenue ($4,500 divided by $30,000 = .15 = 15%).

Retail Pricing	
$60 RP	100%
$28.50 C	47.5%
$31.50 MU	52.5%

Expenses include salaries, rent, utilities, and other costs of running a business. In this case, expenses represented 37.5 percent of sales revenue ($11,250 divided by $30,000 = .375 or 37.5%).

Retail Pricing Chart Note that the markup of $31.50 × 500 = $15,750, which is the same as the gross profit on the Income Statement.

PRACTICE 1

Use the retail price formula and its variations to do the following problems.

1. A jacket costs $50, and the markup is $49.99. What is its retail price?
2. A pen has a retail price of $2.49, and its markup is $0.83. What is its cost?

glencoe.com

Find answers to all Practice activities.

PERCENTAGE MARKUP

In the Practice examples, markup was expressed as a dollar amount. In most business situations, however, the markup figure is generally expressed as a percentage. We will distinguish between these two forms of markup (dollar and percentage) throughout the rest of the chapter. In calculations, dollar markup will be represented with the abbreviation MU($) and percentage markup with the abbreviation MU(%).

Expressing markup in either dollar or percentage form is not the only choice that wholesalers and retailers have in making markup calculations. They may also decide to compute their markup on either cost or retail price if they choose to use the percentage form.

Most choose to base the markup on retail price for three reasons. First, the markup on the retail price sounds like a smaller amount. This sounds better to customers who know the markup percentage and makes the price seem reasonable.

Second, future markdowns and discounts are calculated on a retail basis. Third, profits are generally calculated on sales revenue. It makes sense to base markup on retail prices when comparing and analyzing data that play a role in a firm's profits.

Any person working in business or retail will find the skill of being able to calculate percentage markup very valuable. Here are the steps for calculating the percentage markup on retail. They will be easier to follow if we use an example. Assume that you want to calculate the percentage markup on a pair of brass bookends that Chris's Specialty Store stocks for $49.50 (cost) and sells for $82.50 (retail price).

STEP 1 Determine the dollar markup.
RP – C = MU($)
$82.50 – $49.50 = $33.00

The GREEN Marketer

Saving Green by Buying Green

Do companies that make sustainable products have to charge higher prices? Not necessarily. Peet's® Coffee charges the same price for its Fair Trade Blend as it does for its Peet's signature blend. The Fair Trade Blend allows for a living wage for Costa Rican farmers. Sneakers from Simple® Shoes and jeans from Levi's® Eco line are also sustainable products. They are made with organic cotton, yet they cost the same as conventional styles.

Profit Trade-Off Many businesses accept a lower profit margin on their green products. These products may have a higher wholesale cost. However, this higher cost is offset by the chance to win over "green" consumers. This strategy pays off with an expanded customer base.

Mathematics

Compute If the ingredients for a bag of Newman's Own Organics cookies cost $0.89 with Fair Trade cocoa, and $0.81 with conventional cocoa, what is the cost difference for 12,000 bags? If wholesale markup is 35 percent, what would Newman's Own® charge retailers for a bag of Fair Trade cocoa cookies?

NCTM Problem Solving Solve problems that arise in mathematics and in other contexts.

glencoe.com

Get an activity on green marketing.

EXPLAIN

Graphic Organizer

Use this graphic organizer to review the three main goals of pricing. Emphasize that setting the right price, one that is not too high or too low, is vital if a business is to maintain its position in the marketplace.

Goals of Pricing

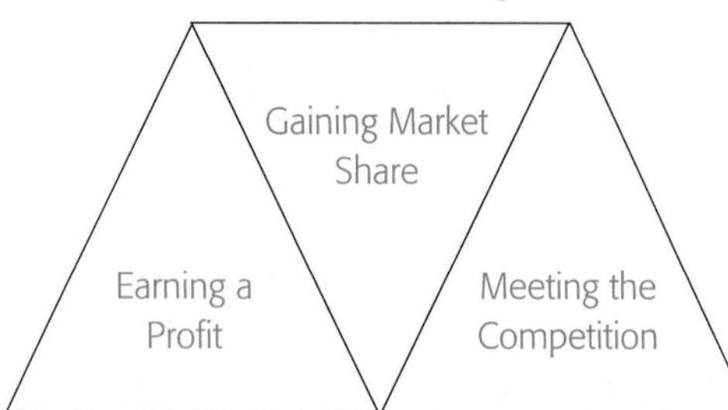

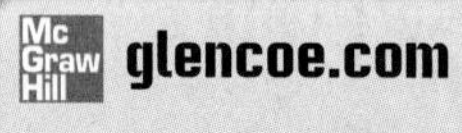

Graphic Organizer Send students to the Online Learning Center to print this graphic organizer.

Visual Literacy

Figure 27.1 Caption Answer Read the caption question to students: ***What part of the income statement relates to markup?*** Gross profit, because it is determined by subtracting the cost of the goods sold by the sales revenue. Ask: ***Why is gross profit an important number on the income statement?*** Cost of goods is an unavoidable cost to the business. The business must buy or manufacture goods before they can be sold. Expenses, however, are more discretionary, even though they may be necessary. Therefore, if the manager of the business prepares a "pro forma" income statement, the gross profit number tells the manager how much he or she can spend on such things as marketing and still make a profit.

VIRTUAL BUSINESS

PRICING

Introduce students to the concept of pricing using Knowledge Matters' Virtual Business Retailing visual simulation, *Pricing*. In this simulation, students will learn that pricing is a vital concern for business owners.

ELABORATE

Critical Thinking

Display the following expression for the class: RP = C + MU
Ask students to explain the steps needed to rearrange the equation so that Cost (C) is alone on the left side of the formula.
RP – MU = C + MU – MU (Subtract MU from both sides)
RP – MU = C *or* C = RP – MU

ANSWERS TO PRACTICE 1

1. Retail price = $99.99 (50 + 49.99)
2. Cost = $1.66 (2.49 – 0.83)

PERCENTAGE MARKUP

Ask these questions to focus class discussion on percentage markup.

Guiding Questions

Judge Of the three reasons most retailers choose to base markup on retail price, rather than on cost, which is the most important? Why?	Basing markup on the retail price makes the percentage smaller and looks better to the consumer. Charging $50 for shoes a retailer paid $25 for is a 100% wholesale markup but only 50% retail.
Synthesize Many retailers base markups on retail price because future markdowns are calculated based on retail price. Why is this valid?	Using the same basis to make both markups and markdowns allows them to be directly compared.

Mini Project

Extension

Fair Trade Organizations Have students research Web sites of nonprofit organizations that certify products as Fair Trade and give presentations explaining how these groups work. Presentations will vary. An example is TransFair USA, which licenses its Fair Trade Certified label for display on products that meet strict standards. These standards include a guaranteed floor price, safe working conditions with no child labor, and sustainable farming methods.

Graphic Organizer

This diagram shows the three basic ways to perform markup. Point out how the different methods affect the final retail price.

Pair of Jeans:
Wholesale Price (Cost): $25.50

Markup Based on Dollar Amount ($)	**Markup Based on Percentage (%) of Wholesale Price (C)**	**Markup Based on Percentage (%) of Retail Price (RP)**
Markup = $20.00 Retail Price = $45.50	Markup on Cost = 60% Retail Price = $40.80	Markup on Retail Price = 60% Retail Price = $63.75

glencoe.com iWB

Graphic Organizer Send students to the Online Learning Center to print this graphic organizer.

The GREEN Marketer

Mathematics Answer The cost difference is $960. The cost difference per package is $0.08, and $0.08 × 12,000 = $960. The company would charge $1.20 per bag; $0.89 × 1.35 = $1.20.

 **glencoe.com** 

Activity Worksheet Send students to the Online Learning Center to download a Green Marketer activity worksheet.

Extension

Ask students: ***If you were a retailer, would you accept a smaller profit in order to sell Fair Trade cocoa and coffee? Why or why not?*** Sample answer: Yes, because I want farmers to make a living wage so that they can continue to grow their products and support their families. Remind students that in Chapter 23 they learned that consumers are willing to pay an average of 15 percent more for green products. Ask: ***If both the regular and Fair Trade cocoa have a wholesale markup of 35 percent, would the price of the Fair Trade cocoa fall within this 15 percent guideline?*** Yes, because the Fair Trade cocoa costs 9.1 percent more than the regular cocoa.

STEP 2 To change the dollar markup to the percentage markup, divide it by the retail price. The result will be a decimal.
MU($) ÷ RP = MU(%) on retail
$33.00 divided by $82.50 = .4

STEP 3 Change the decimal to a percentage by shifting the decimal point two places to the right. This figure is the percentage markup on retail.
.40 = 40%

Retailers may find the percentage markup on cost to be helpful. The calculation is the same, except for Step 2. Using the same facts from above, you calculate the percentage markup on cost as follows:

STEP 1 Determine the dollar markup.
RP − C = MU($)
$82.50 − $49.50 = $33.00

STEP 2 To change the dollar markup to the percentage markup, divide by cost.
MU($) ÷ C = MU(%) on cost
$33.00 divided by $49.50 = .6667

STEP 3 Change the decimal to a percentage. This figure is the percentage markup on cost. .6667 = 66.67%

PRACTICE 2

Calculate markup percentages; round your answers to the tenths place.

1. The retail price of an alarm clock is $39.99, and its cost to the retailer is $20. (A) What is the markup percentage based on its cost? (B) Based on its retail price?
2. A pair of slippers costs a retailer $7.50, and its markup is $5.49. (A) What is the markup percentage based on its cost? (B) Based on its retail price?
3. A camera's retail price is $249.99, and its markup is $112.50. (A) What is the markup percentage based on its cost? (B) Based on its retail price?

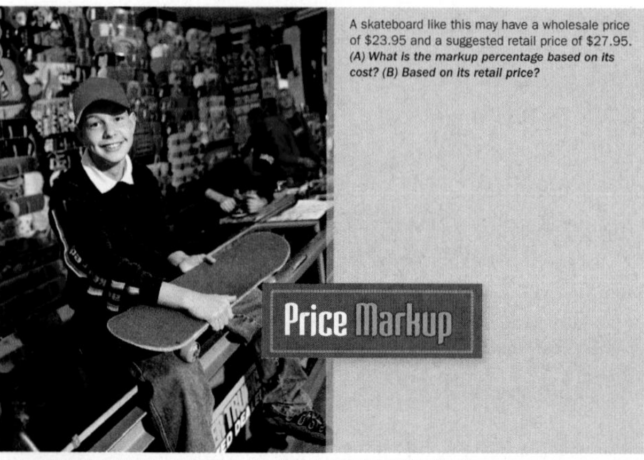

A skateboard like this may have a wholesale price of $23.95 and a suggested retail price of $27.95. ***(A) What is the markup percentage based on its cost? (B) Based on its retail price?***

FIGURE 27.2 Markup Equivalents

Markup Equivalents Table This sample markup equivalents table allows users to convert markups on retail to markups on cost and vice versa. ***A 20-percent markup on retail is equal to what markup percent based on cost?***

Markup on Retail	Markup on Cost	Markup on Retail	Markup on Cost
4.8%	5.0%	25.0%	33.3%
5.0	5.3	26.0	35.0
6.0	6.4	27.0	37.0
7.0	7.5	27.3	37.5
8.0	8.7	28.0	39.0
9.0	10.0	28.5	40.0
10.0	11.1	29.0	40.9
10.7	12.0	30.0	42.9
11.0	12.4	31.0	45.0
11.1	12.5	32.0	47.1
12.0	13.6	33.3	50.0
12.5	14.3	34.0	51.5
13.0	15.0	35.0	53.9
14.0	16.3	35.5	55.0
15.0	17.7	36.0	56.3
16.0	19.1	37.0	58.8
16.7	20.0	37.5	60.0
17.0	20.5	38.0	61.3
17.5	21.2	39.0	64.0
18.0	22.0	39.5	65.5
18.5	22.7	40.0	66.7
19.0	23.5	41.0	70.0
20.0	25.0	42.0	72.4
21.0	26.6	42.8	75.0
22.0	28.2	44.4	80.0
22.5	29.0	46.1	85.0
23.0	29.9	47.5	90.0
23.1	30.0	48.7	95.0
24.0	31.6	50.0	100.0

630 | Unit 8 · Pricing

EXPLAIN

Graphic Organizer

Display this example to calculate percentage markup on retail.

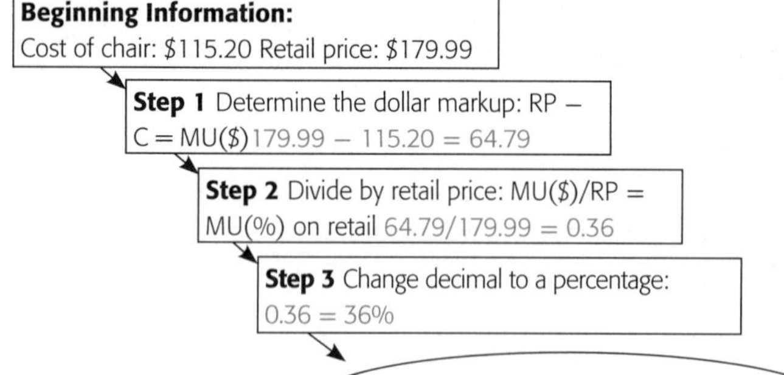

Beginning Information:
Cost of chair: $115.20 Retail price: $179.99
Step 1 Determine the dollar markup: RP − C = MU($) 179.99 − 115.20 = 64.79
Step 2 Divide by retail price: MU($)/RP = MU(%) on retail 64.79/179.99 = 0.36
Step 3 Change decimal to a percentage: 0.36 = 36%
Percentage Markup on Retail = 36%

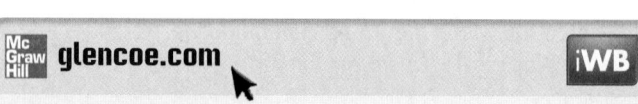

Graphic Organizer Send students to the Online Learning Center to print this graphic organizer.

Visual Literacy

Price Markup Caption Answer Read the questions: *(A) What is the markup percentage based on its cost?* 4.00/23.95 = 16.7% *(B) Based on its retail price?* *14.3%*

ANSWERS TO PRACTICE 2

1. (A) Markup percentage based on cost = 100% (19.99/20); (B) Markup percentage based on retail price = 50% (19.99/39.99)
2. (A) Markup percentage based on cost = 73.2% (5.49/7.50); (B) Markup percentage based on retail price = 42.3% (5.49/12.99)
3. (A) Markup percentage based on cost = 81.8% (112.50/137.49); (B) Markup percentage based on retail price = 45% (112.50/249.99)

ELABORATE

Graphic Organizer

Display these sample steps to calculate percentage markup on cost.

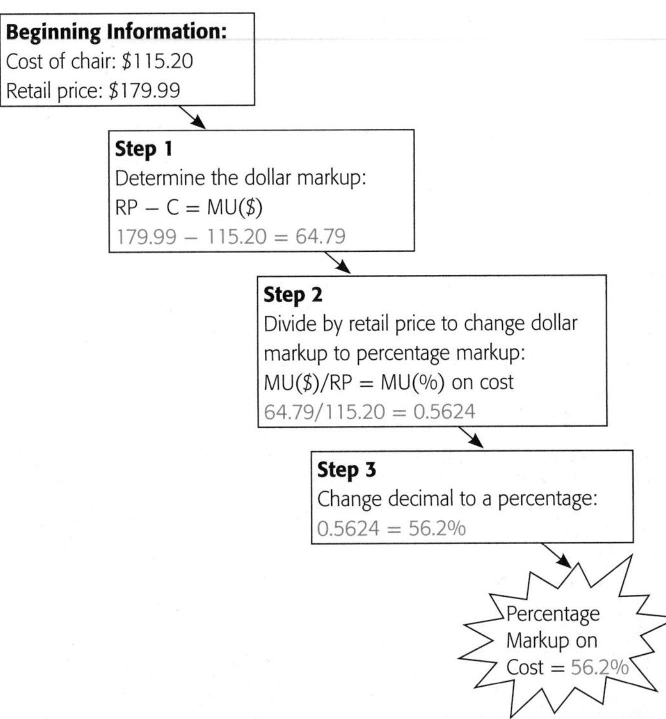

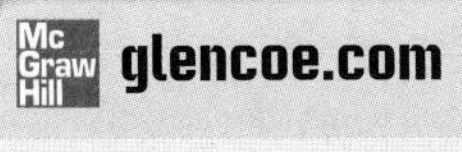 glencoe.com  iWB

Graphic Organizer Send students to the Online Learning Center to print this graphic organizer.

Visual Literacy

Figure 27.2 Caption Answer Read the caption question to students: ***A 20-percent markup on retail is equal to what markup percent based on cost?*** 25 percent markup based on cost Then ask: ***A 20-percent markup based on cost is equal to what markup percent based on retail?*** 16.7 percent markup based on retail

Critical Thinking

Ask students why an oil painting in an art gallery might be marked up 50 percent or more on a price basis while items such as sheets and towels, for example, would be marked up at a much lower percentage. The oil painting is a one-of-a-kind item, and the gallery only has one chance to sell it. A store selling sheets and towels, on the other hand, would have many units of the same item in stock and would sell them to many different customers. Stores might compete with one another to sell sheets and towels at the lowest price; because the oil painting is unique, it cannot be directly compared with other merchandise.

e MARKETING

Search Engine Pricing Model

Search engines offer advertisers the ability to place contextual ads (only text) that will appear when queries are made. Key words in the contextual ad are used to match queries with advertisers. Search engine ads contain a heading, text, and a URL, which will send the viewer to the advertiser's Web site. The relevancy of the key words and Web site are important for search engine advertising because they are the basis of where an ad will be placed in the listing. Advertisers can also pay for placement of their search engine ad, in which case they will be identified as "paid search" or "sponsored links." Advertisers that pay for inclusion are often charged on a pay-per-click basis. To arrive at the cost per click, advertisers bid on key words that are relevant to the audience they want to reach (their target market). Advertisers provide their host with the maximum amount they are willing to pay per click for key words. The popularity of the key words and other factors such as relevancy determines where the ad will be placed in the search results.

Innovate and Create

For additional clarification of search engine pricing, have students research Google and Yahoo! to see sample key words per-click rates. Students should select key words for a business or product of their choice to calculate a monthly cost for their paid search advertisement. Students should prepare a short written report on their findings. Reports on key word per-click rates will vary depending on the key words selected for comparison. To estimate the monthly cost of the paid search advertisement, multiply the maximum cost-per-click rate times the number of times the ad may be clicked. For example: cost-per-click recommended is $1.28 × 271 (number of times ad may be clicked) = $346.88 monthly cost of the paid search advertisement.

 glencoe.com

eMarketing Worksheet Activity Send students to the Online Learning Center to download an eMarketing worksheet activity.

MARKUP EQUIVALENTS TABLE

You would notice a correlation between the two markup figures if you calculated several problems using the formulas for computing percentage markup based on cost and retail. This correlation led marketers to develop a calculation aid called a "Markup Equivalents Table." A portion of this table is shown in **Figure 27.2** on page 631. The table lists markup percentages based on retail and the equivalent percentages based on cost. To use the table, locate the percentage markup on retail and read its cost equivalent in the adjacent column.

Practice 3

Use the markup equivalents table in Figure 27.2 to answer the following questions:

1. When the markup on retail is 37.5 percent, what is its equivalent markup on cost?
2. The markup on cost is 33.3 percent. What is its equivalent markup on retail?
3. The markup on cost is 50 percent. What is its equivalent markup on retail?

COST METHOD OF PRICING

Sometimes marketers know only the cost of an item and its markup on cost. In such a situation, they use the cost method of pricing.

Consider a board game that a toy store buys for $8.50 and sells for cost plus a 40-percent markup on cost. To arrive at the retail price, follow these steps:

STEP 1 Determine the dollar markup on cost. Multiply the cost by the percentage markup on cost in decimal form.
C × MU(%) = MU($)
$8.50 × .40 = $3.40

STEP 2 Add the dollar markup to the cost to get the retail price.
C + MU($) = RP
$8.50 + $3.40 = $11.90

Many times the situation is not that simple. Suppose you have the cost, but the only markup figure you know is the markup on retail. What do you do? You cannot use the markup percentage on retail to calculate the markup in dollars unless you know the retail price. This is a good time to use the Markup Equivalents Table in **Figure 27.2**.

You can **convert** the markup on retail to the markup on cost and apply it to the cost of the item to arrive at the markup in dollars.

Here is an example: A marketer knows that the customary markup for a particular cosmetics firm is 33.3 percent, based on retail and that the cost of its most popular lipstick is $8.00. To calculate the lipstick's retail price, follow these steps:

STEP 1 Use the markup equivalents table to get all the information in the same form (cost). Find the cost equivalent of a 33.3-percent markup on retail.

Markup Percent on Retail	Markup Percent on Cost
32.0	47.1
33.3	50.0
34.0	51.5

STEP 2 Calculate the dollar markup on cost.
C × MU(%) = MU($)
$8.00 × .50 = $4.00

STEP 3 Then calculate the retail price.
C + MU($) = RP
$8.00 + $4.00 = $12.00

RETAIL METHOD OF PRICING

There is another way to calculate the retail price when all you know are cost and the markup on retail. In this situation, you would use the retail method. This method is based on converting the information that you already have into retail figures.

Here is another example. The owner of a sporting goods store wants to know what the markup and retail price should be for a sun visor that costs $6.75. The customary markup for most items, based on the retail price, is 40 percent. Below are the calculations you would use in this situation.

STEP 1 Determine what percentage of the retail price is equal to cost. This is a matter of subtracting the known retail markup percent from 100 percent, which represents the retail price.
RP(%) – MU(%) = C(%)
100% – 40% = 60%

STEP 2 To determine the retail price, divide the cost by the decimal equivalent of the percentage calculated in Step 1.
$6.75 divided by .60 = $11.25

MARKETING CASE STUDY

Priced at 99¢!

Stores such as Dollar Tree®, Everthing's A Dollar®, and 99¢ Only Store® are successful dollar-store chains. These companies' stores offer name-brand and private-label food and beverages, health and beauty aids, household goods, toys, and more at $1 or less per item. How do they do it? Selling low-cost closeout, overstock, and regular merchandise in volume helped boost annual sales.

Selling Strategies

In addition to a frugal management culture that counts pennies, cutting-edge warehouse and in-store stock-tracking and technology have served to keep low pricing and high profits on track. 99¢ Only Stores founder David Gold and his team are also master marketers, coming up with "99¢" promotions, such as celebrating the 99th birthday of public figures and selling a high-priced item like an iPod nano for 99 cents to the first nine customers at a new store opening.

Mathematics

Compute What is the retail price of a T-shirt with a markup of 40 percent and a closeout wholesale cost of 70 cents? Would the T-shirt be priced right for a dollar-store?

NCTM Number and Operations Compute fluently and make reasonable estimates.

FIGURE 27.3 Retail Box

The Retail Method To compute the retail price using the retail method, fill in the boxes following the letter sequence (J-O). Note that the box labeled "J" (RP%) is always 100 percent. The amounts that go in the boxes labeled K (MU%) and O (C$) are known figures. ***Why is this retail box an example of the retail method for calculating markup?***

	$	%		$	%
Retail Price	M 11.25	J 100	Retail Price	M	J 100
Markup	N 4.50	K 40	Markup	N	K
Cost	O 6.75	L 60	Cost	O	L

Computation: L = J – K L = 100 – 40 = 60%
M = O ÷ L M = $6.75 ÷ .60 = $11.25
N = M – O N = $11.25 – $6.75 = $4.50

Check: M × K = N 11.25 × .40 = $4.50

EXPLAIN

Answers to Practice 3

1. 60%
2. 50%
3. 100%

MARKETING CASE STUDY

Mathematics Answer The retail price would be .70 + (.70 × .40), or $0.98, which is less than the $1.00 maximum at a dollar store.

Extension Ask students: What is the maximum wholesale price for a dollar-store item if the markup on cost is 60 percent? 62 cents ([C + C × .60] = 1.00)

COST METHOD OF PRICING

Ask these guiding questions to focus the discussion on the cost method of pricing.

Guiding Questions

Explain You know only the cost of an item and its percentage markup on cost. In your own words, explain how you would calculate the retail price.	(1) Multiply the cost by the percentage markup on cost. (2) To get the final retail price, add this amount to the cost.
Apply Give an example of a specific situation in which the markup equivalents table would be useful.	Possible answer: You know the cost of a bottle of laundry detergent and you know that this brand of detergent is always marked up 55 percent, based on retail.

ELABORATE

Graphic Organizer

Display these sample steps to show the cost method of pricing.

Beginning Information:
Cost of shampoo: \$1.80
Markup on cost: 75%

Step 1
Determine the dollar markup on cost:
C × MP(%) = MU(\$)
\$1.80 × .75 = \$1.35

Step 2
Add the dollar markup to the cost to get retail price
C + MU(\$) = RP
\$1.80 + \$1.35 = \$3.15

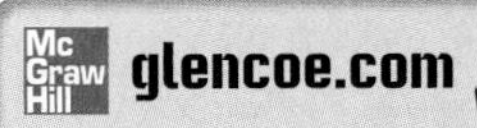

iWB

Graphic Organizer Send students to the Online Learning Center to print this graphic organizer.

Activate Prior Knowledge

Practice Tell students that a product originally cost \$75.49 and had a markup of \$38.41. But the cost of purchasing the product has gone up 10%, and the selling price must be increased accordingly. Have students work in pairs to determine the new selling price and markup using the original markup percentage. The new selling price is \$125.39; the new markup is \$42.35. The new cost is \$75.49 × 1.10 = \$83.04. The original markup on cost is 51% (\$38.51/\$75.49.) The new markup is therefore \$42.35 (\$83.04 × 0.51 = \$42.35.) The new selling price is \$83.04 + \$42.35 = \$125.39.

Critical Thinking

Ask students: ***Why might a retail business make its markup percentages proprietary information?*** Answers may include: The business would not want customers to know its markup percentages because customers might think the prices were too high. It would not want competing stores to know because then they would know what prices the store was paying to wholesalers. It would not want vendors to know because it might become more difficult to get manufacturers and wholesalers to compete directly with one another.

Graphic Organizer

Display these sample steps to show how to convert the markup on retail to the markup on cost and apply it to the cost of an item.

Beginning Information:
Cost of chair: \$115.20
Retail markup: 37.5%

Step 1
Use the markup equivalents table to get cost percentage:
C(%) = 60

Step 2
Calculate the dollar markup on cost:
C × MU(%) = MU(\$)
115.20 × .60 = \$69.12

Step 3
Calculate the retail price:
C + MU(\$) = RP
\$115.20 + \$69.12 = \$184.32

iWB

Graphic Organizer Send students to the Online Learning Center to print this graphic organizer.

Visual Literacy

Figure 27.3 Caption Answer Ask students: ***Why is this retail box an example of the retail method for calculating markup?*** because all figures are converted to retail figures for computation purposes Then ask: ***Why is the step "L = J − K" necessary?*** You do not want to multiply the cost by the markup percentage, but rather the difference between it and the total (100 percent).

MINI CLIP

Math: Ways of Working: Solving Equations
Go to the Online Learning Center to view a video in which teachers build understanding of equation-solving processes.

STEP 3 Calculate the dollar markup.
RP – C = MU($)
$11.25 – $6.75 = $4.50

STEP 4 Check your work by multiplying the retail price you calculated in Step 2 by the percentage markup on retail price given originally. The answer will match the dollar markup you calculated in Step 3, if your retail price is correct.
RP × MU(%) = MU($)
$11.25 × .40 = $4.50

You can use a **visual** device called the "retail box" (see **Figure 27.3** on page 633) to help you remember this sequence of calculations. This retail box organizes your information and makes it simple to check your work.

PRACTICE 4

Calculate retail price and markup in these two problems by using the retail method. Then double-check your answers to see if your retail price is correct.

1. (A) Find the retail price and (B) dollar markup for a box of cereal that costs $3.41 and has a 5 percent markup on retail. (C) Double-check your answer.
2. A golf bag costs the retailer $75.60 and has a 60 percent markup on retail. Calculate this golf bag's (A) retail price and (B) dollar markup. (C) Double-check your answer.

Reading Check

Recall Explain the cost method of pricing.

CALCULATIONS FOR LOWERING PRICES

When a business lowers its prices, new sale prices and new markups must be calculated. Let's look at the steps used in calculating markdowns (lowered prices), maintained markups, and the actual sale prices derived from these calculations. Businesses also need to figure out how to price merchandise left in stock, and how to minimize the effects of theft and employee errors.

MARKDOWNS

To reduce the quantity of goods in stock, businesses will sometimes mark down merchandise by a certain percentage (MD[%]). They advertise the markdown percentages, such as 20 to 40 percent off.

LOWERING PRICES

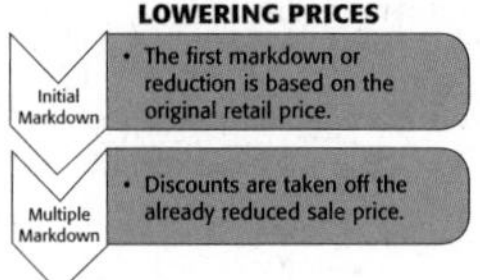
Initial Markdown
• The first markdown or reduction is based on the original retail price.
Multiple Markdown
• Discounts are taken off the already reduced sale price.

CALCULATING MARKDOWN PERCENTAGES

To calculate a percentage markdown, the dollar markdown is divided by the original price. For example, assume an item had an original price of $25 and a sale price of $19.99. A retailer can advertise the $19.99 sale price as 20 percent off. Here are the calculations: $25 (original price) – $19.99 (sale price) = $5 (markdown); $5 (markdown) divided by $25 (original price) = .2 = 20 percent.

INITIAL MARKDOWN

The first markdown or reduction is based on the original retail price. For example, a music store sells CDs for $16. The store wants to mark down the CDs by 25 percent to make room for new products. An easy way to arrive at the sale price for the CDs is to consider what percentage of the original price will equal the sale price. The procedure requires two steps, but the percentage calculation is so easy that you can probably do it in your head and save some time. Here are the steps involved:

STEP 1 Determine what percentage of the original price will equal the sale price. This is simply a matter of subtracting the markdown percentage from 100 percent.
RP(%) – MD(%) = SP(%)
100% – 25% = 75%

STEP 2 To find the sale price, multiply the retail price by the decimal equivalent of the percentage calculated in Step 1.
RP × SP(%) = SP
$16 × .75 = $12

MULTIPLE MARKDOWNS

When multiple markdowns are considered due to special sales promotions, you take the discounts off the already reduced sale price. For example, assume an item that had an original price of $60 was marked down 20 percent. Customers were offered an additional 15 percent discount off the reduced price. The price customers would pay for that item would be $40.80.

To arrive at $40.80, calculate the first sale price ($60 × .80 = $48), and then calculate the next markdown based on the already reduced price to get the final sale price the customer would pay ($48 sale price × .85 = $40.80).

PRACTICE 5

Calculate the markdowns, markdown percentages, and sale prices.

1. A $59.99 item is marked down to $41.99. (A) What is the dollar markdown? (B) What is the markdown percentage?
2. A suit that sells for $350 is to be marked down by 15 percent, and customers with a coupon can take an additional markdown of 20 percent. (A) How much does a customer pay without a coupon? (B) With a coupon?

MAINTAINED MARKUP

When a retailer marks down goods, the markup and markup percentage change. The difference between an item's final sale price and its cost is called the **maintained markup**.

Initial markups need to be higher than maintained markups if a retailer is to meet revenue and profit goals. The initial markup for an item must reflect the fact that during a selling season there will be shrinkage, breakage, employee discounts, and end-of-season markdowns.

Early Bird

On Black Friday retailers offer "early bird specials" in conjunction with other promotions to entice shoppers to shop in the morning. ***With large discounts, a consumer may pay only $25 for a sweater that originally sold for $79. How can a retailer offer such big discounts and remain in business?***

634 | Unit 8 · Pricing   Chapter 27 · Pricing Math | 635

EXPLAIN

Activate Prior Knowledge

Review Pricing During the Product Life Cycle Remind students of how pricing is related to the product life cycle. This topic was covered in Chapter 26. Ask students to recall the stages of the product life cycle. introduction, growth, maturity, and decline Ask students: ***During which stages do prices typically remain stable?*** introduction and growth Then ask students: ***During which stage are prices reduced? Why?*** Prices are reduced during the maturity stage because companies want to stretch this stage as long as possible.

ANSWERS TO PRACTICE 4

1. (A) Retail price = $3.59 (100% – 5% = 95%; 3.41/.95 = 3.59); (B) Dollar markup = $0.18 (3.59 – 3.41); (C) Double-check: 3.59 = 3.41 + (3.59 × 0.05)
2. (A) Retail price = $189 (100% – 60% = 40%; 75.60 / .40 = 189); (B) Dollar markup = $113.40 (189 – 75.60); (C) Double-check: 189 = 75.60 + (189 × .60)

Reading Check Answer

Read the Reading Check statement to students: ***Explain the cost method of pricing.*** Multiply cost by the markup on cost to get the markup in dollars. Add the markup in dollars to the cost to get the retail price.

ELABORATE

Graphic Organizer

Display the following steps to show students a second method of calculating the retail price from the cost and the markup on retail.

Beginning Information:
Cost of chair: $115.20
Retail markup: 37.5%

Step 1
Subtract known retail markup from 100%:
RP(%) – MU(%) = C(%)
100 – 37.5% = 62.5%

Step 2
Divide the cost by the decimal equivalent of the percentage:
C/C(%)/100 = RP
$115.20/(62.5/100) = $184.32

Retail Price
= $184.32

 glencoe.com 

Graphic Organizer Send students to the Online Learning Center to print this graphic organizer.

Graphic Organizer

To illustrate for students how product reductions are performed, display the following graphic. Make certain students understand that subsequent reductions are based on the sale price, not on the original retail price.

LOWERING PRICES

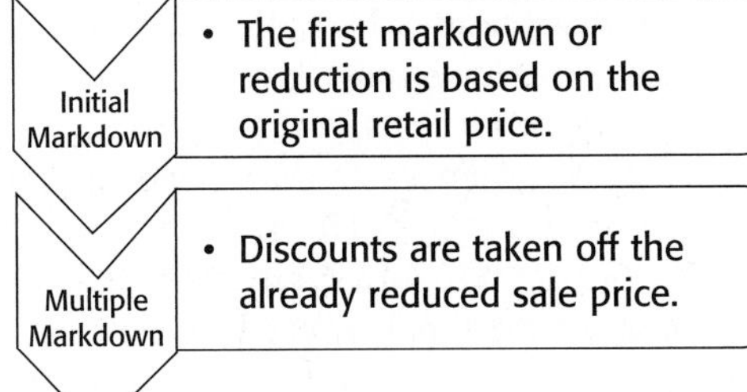
Initial Markdown
• The first markdown or reduction is based on the original retail price.
Multiple Markdown
• Discounts are taken off the already reduced sale price.

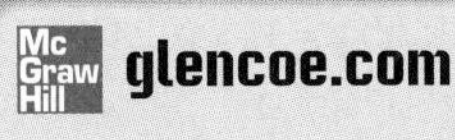 

Graphic Organizer Send students to the Online Learning Center to print this graphic organizer.

CALCULATIONS FOR LOWERING PRICES

Ask these guiding questions to focus the discussion on calculations for lowering prices.

Guiding Questions

Recall Why do businesses mark down goods?	to reduce the quantity of the goods in stock
Synthesize A store owner marks down a $600 television by 25%. A second store owner marks down the same $600 television by 15% and later marks it down by another 10%. Will both televisions end up being the same price? Why or why not?	No, because at Store 2, the second markdown is taken on the already reduced price. The sale price at Store 1 will be $450, while at Store 2 it will be $459. Store 1: 600 × 0.75 = $450 Store 2: (600 × 0.85) × 0.90 = $459

ANSWERS TO PRACTICE 5

1. (A) Dollar markdown = $18.00 (59.99 – 41.99);
   (B) Markdown percentage = 30% (18/59.99)
2. (A) Price without coupon = $297.50 (350 × [1 – 0.15]);
   (B) Price with coupon = $238.00 (297.50 × [1 – .2])

Reinforce Vocabulary

Maintained Markup—Denotative Meaning Explain to students that in this situation, the word *maintained* means "preserved" or "sustained." Therefore, a maintained markup is a markup that is still preserved.

Visual Literacy

Early Bird Caption Answer Read the caption question to students: ***With large discounts, a consumer may pay only $25 for a sweater that originally sold for $79. How can a retailer offer such big discounts and remain in business?*** Typically, retailers heavily advertise those items that are being sold at large markdowns. Consumers are drawn to the store by these large markdowns and then purchase other items that are not as heavily discounted. Even if they do not purchase these less-discounted items on Black Friday, the discounts consumers receive that day give them a positive image of the store, which increases the likelihood they will return later during the holiday season.

A maintained markup represents the weighted average markup for an item. This is calculated as:

(Total actual revenues received – the cost of goods sold) divided by total actual revenues received.

Price Appeal Prestige pricing is a case of a markup that suggests a high level of quality or status for a product.

Businesses must plan ahead for markdowns. Careful planning helps businesses to remain profitable and competitive in the marketplace. Reductions in the original retail price include employee discounts, shrinkage, damaged goods allowances, and special sales events. For businesses to enjoy the profit margin needed to be successful, they must take these factors into account.

The concept of maintained markup becomes extremely important in planning the original price of the item and all future markdowns.

Let's consider an example. Assume that a video game that cost Zap Electronics $25 to manufacture and originally sold for $50 is marked down 20 percent. The maintained markup (expressed in both dollars and as a percentage) is calculated as follows:

STEP 1 Calculate the new sale price.
100% – 20% = 80%
$50 × .80 = $40

STEP 2 To determine the maintained markup in dollars (MM$), subtract the cost from the sale price.
SP – C = MM($)
$40 – $25 = $15

STEP 3 To determine the maintained markup percentage, divide the maintained markup in dollars by the sale price. *Note:* Round percents to the tenths place.
MM($) ÷ SP = MM(%)
$15 ÷ $40 = .3750
.375 = 37.5%

PRACTICE 6

Now try the same type of computation on your own.

A piece of luggage that costs the retailer $65 to stock sells for $139.99 (retail price). The retailer wants to mark down the luggage by 25 percent. (A) Determine the sale price and (B) maintained markup in dollars, and then (C) calculate the maintained markup percentage. Round the markup percentage to the tenths place.

Anti-theft devices such as these security towers at this store's entrance help prevent stock shortages. ***What other measures can be taken to reduce a shortage in stock?***

MERCHANDISE REMAINING IN STOCK

Consider a store that sells sweaters, coats, and gloves. When spring arrives, the retailer may be left with unsold merchandise. How does the store determine prices for items returned to inventory? The main consideration is the value of the merchandise. For example, if the store's cost to purchase a sweater from the manufacturer is $40, a 25 percent markup would result in a selling price of $50. This is a simple process if the cost to the store for sweaters is consistent. However, other factors can complicate pricing for inventory remaining in stock. If the cost of sweaters varies, a price planner must consider how much of each type of sweater has been purchased at each cost level. The store then applies the retail method of inventory planning, which takes into account the average cost to the store of all merchandise.

PLANNING FOR STOCK SHORTAGES

When a retailer purchases merchandise from a supplier or manufacturer and various factors prevent the store from recording a sale, profits are negatively affected. Issues such as theft, shoplifting, damaged merchandise, errors in inventory tracking, and mistakes at the checkout counter cost retailers millions of dollars a year in lost sales revenue.

As a result, all businesses take steps to try to limit the problem. You may have noticed anti-theft devices in stores. These can take the form of electronic tags and detectors, special mirrors, and security cameras. Stores should be sure that employees have up-to-date training on stocking and point-of-sale systems. Retailers should also track the rate of "inventory shrinkage" and use this data to help set prices. Stores may choose to mark up merchandise by a greater percentage to account for a high rate of shrinkage.

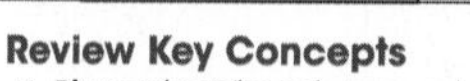

After You Read | **Section 27.1**

Review Key Concepts

1. **Discuss** why retailers prefer to use markup percent based on the retail price instead of the markup percent on cost.
2. **Identify** when the markup equivalents chart is used to calculate retail prices.
3. **Explain** when the initial markup is the same as the maintained markup.

Practice Academics

English Language Arts

4. Explain the relationship between retail pricing and an income statement. Provide an example.

NCTE 3 Apply strategies to interpret texts.

Mathematics

5. You own a kitchen supply store. What is the retail price of an item that costs the business $45 and has a markup of $25?

Math Concept **Backward Pricing** Markups can be represented as a percent or a dollar value. If the markup is in the form of a percentage, multiplication is used. When it is represented as a dollar amount, simple addition can be used.

Starting Hint To solve this problem, add the amount of the markup to the cost to determine the retail price.

NCTM Problem Solving Apply and adapt a variety of appropriate strategies to solve problems.

For help, go to the **Math Skills Handbook** located at the back of this book.

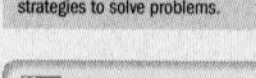

glencoe.com

Check your answers.

ELABORATE

Price Appeal Remind students of the three strategies used for setting prices that were covered in Chapter 26: demand-oriented pricing, competition-oriented pricing, cost-oriented pricing.

ANSWERS TO PRACTICE 6

1. (A) Sale price = $104.99 (139.99 × [1 – .25]);
(B) Maintained markup = $39.99 (104.99 – 65);
(C) Maintained markup % = 38.1% (39.99/104.99)

Visual Literacy

Stock Shortage Prevention Caption Answer Read the caption question to students: ***What other measures can be taken to reduce a shortage in stock?*** Answers may include: surveillance cameras, mirrors that allow employees to see around displays, security personnel, well-trained sales associates who know how to watch for shoplifting, posted signs stating the store will prosecute all shoplifters, and keeping small and expensive items in locked display cases.

Activate Prior Knowledge

Reteach Return on Investment Review with students that businesses are concerned with their rate of return on investment. This number is important even when items are marked down. The rate of return on investment is determined by dividing the net profit by cost plus expenses. Present students with this scenario: An item has a retail price of $52.15 cost is $28.40 and expenses are $10.25. Ask students: ***Using these numbers, how would you calculate return on investment?***

Net profit: $52.15 – ($28.40 + $10.25) = $13.50

Return on investment: $13.50 / ($28.40 + $10.25) = 0.3492, or 34.9%

EVALUATE

Graphic Organizer

Display these steps to show how to determine maintained markup.

Beginning Information:
Toy cost: $30.00
Toy retail price: $60.00
Marked down: 10%

Step 1
Calculate new sale price:
100% − 10% = 90%
$60.00 × .90 = $54

Step 2
To determine maintained markup in dollars, subtract cost from sale price:
SP − C = MM($)
$54 − $30 = $24

Step 3 To determine percentage, divide the maintained markup in dollars by sale price:
MM($)/SP = MM(%)
$24/$54 = .4444
.4444 = 44.4%

Maintained Markup = 44.4%

glencoe.com

Graphic Organizer Send students to the Online Learning Center to print this graphic organizer.

PLANNING FOR STOCK SHORTAGES

Ask these guiding questions to focus the discussion on planning for stock shortages.

Guiding Questions

Contrast How are clerical errors different from inventory shrinkage?	Clerical errors are accidental, while shrinkage due to theft is deliberate.
Apply You manage a store. You notice a large number of employee errors. What would you do to reduce the errors?	Thorough, ongoing training can reduce many errors. Employees must learn to follow store procedures exactly.

After You Read Section 27.1

Review Key Concepts

1. Retailers prefer markup percent based on retail price because the markup on retail price sounds like a smaller amount and makes the price seem more reasonable to the consumer. Future markdowns and discounts are calculated on a retail basis. Profits are generally calculated on sales revenue.
2. The markup equivalents chart is used to calculate retail prices when you know the cost and you know the percent of markup you want based on retail price.
3. When no markdowns are taken, the initial markup and maintained markup are the same.

Practice Academics

English Language Arts

4. An income statement is affected by retail pricing because the higher the markup percentage, the greater the sales revenue, which affects both the gross profit (profit before expenses) and the net profit (profit after expenses). For example, if markup based on retail is increased by 10 percent, sales revenues will increase by 10 percent. If cost and expenses remain the same, net profit also will increase by 10 percent.

Mathematics

5. $70 (45 + 25)

glencoe.com

Answer Key Send students to the Online Learning Center to check their answers.

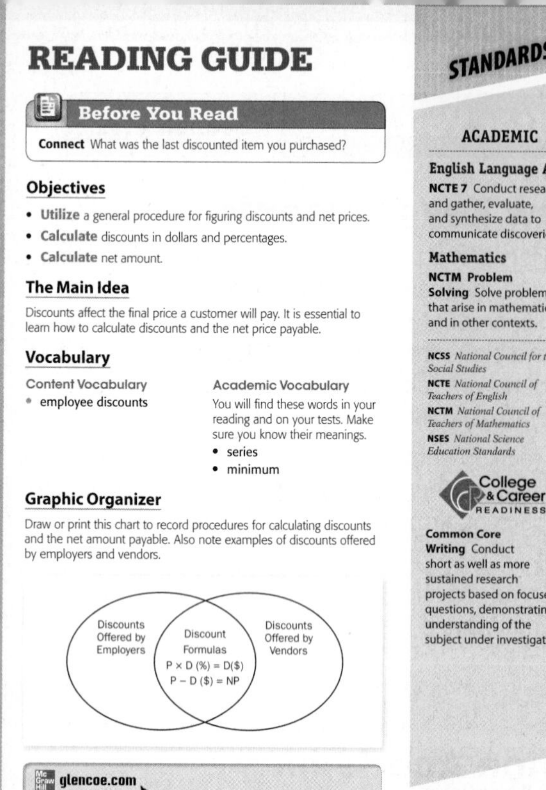

READING GUIDE

STANDARDS

Before You Read

Connect What was the last discounted item you purchased?

Objectives

- **Utilize** a general procedure for figuring discounts and net prices.
- **Calculate** discounts in dollars and percentages.
- **Calculate** net amount.

The Main Idea

Discounts affect the final price a customer will pay. It is essential to learn how to calculate discounts and the net price payable.

Vocabulary

Content Vocabulary

- employee discounts

Academic Vocabulary

You will find these words in your reading and on your tests. Make sure you know their meanings.

- series
- minimum

Graphic Organizer

Draw or print this chart to record procedures for calculating discounts and the net amount payable. Also note examples of discounts offered by employers and vendors.

Discounts Offered by Employers | Discount Formulas $P \times D(\%) = D(\$)$ $P - D(\$) = NP$ | Discounts Offered by Vendors

glencoe.com

Print this graphic organizer.

ACADEMIC

English Language Arts

NCTE 7 Conduct research and gather, evaluate, and synthesize data to communicate discoveries.

Mathematics

NCTM Problem Solving Solve problems that arise in mathematics and in other contexts.

NCSS *National Council for the Social Studies*
NCTE *National Council of Teachers of English*
NCTM *National Council of Teachers of Mathematics*
NSES *National Science Education Standards*

College & Career READINESS

Common Core
Writing Conduct short as well as more sustained research projects based on focused questions, demonstrating understanding of the subject under investigation.

MARKETING CORE FUNCTION

Pricing

Section 27.2

Calculating Discounts

DISCOUNTS

Recall that a discount is a reduction in the price of goods and services sold to customers. You already know markdowns are essentially discounts offered to retail customers. Retailers also offer discounts to their employees as a job benefit. Manufacturers and other vendors offer discounts to their customers to encourage prompt payment and stimulate business. Below is a review of how discounts are calculated.

> "Discounts and allowances are price adjustments given to employees for purchases and also offered by vendors to their customers."

When you want to calculate the discount in dollars and the net price, follow the steps below.

STEP 1 Multiply the price (P) by the discount percentage [D(%)] to get the dollar amount of the discount [D($)].
$P \times D(\%) = D(\$)$

STEP 2 Subtract the discount from the price to get the net price (NP), or the amount that the customer will actually pay.
$P - D(\$) = NP$
Here is an example: A business is offering a 35 percent discount on an item that sells for $150.
$\$150 \times .35 = \$52.50$
$\$150 - 52.50 = \$97.50$

When you simply want to know the net amount due, multiply the price by the net price's percentage equivalent, as follows:

STEP 1 Subtract the discount percent from 100 percent. This figure represents the net price's percentage equivalent (NPPE).
$100\% - D(\%) = NPPE$
$100\% - 35\% = 65\%$

STEP 2 Then multiply the original price by that net price's equivalent percentage to get the net price.
$P \times NPPE = NP$
$\$150 \times .65 = \$97.50$

As You Read

Compare How do you decide between using net amounts and calculating discounts?

EMPLOYEE DISCOUNTS

Discounts offered by employers to their workers are **employee discounts**. Employee discounts encourage employees to buy and use their company's products. In so doing, businesses hope employees will project confidence in and enthusiasm for those products. This is especially important for the sales staff and customer service representatives, so they can speak about the products from firsthand experience. Employee discounts can range from 10 percent to 30 percent for entry-level employees and as high as 50 percent or more for top-level executives. Some companies even offer discounts to family members of their employees.

ENGAGE

Anticipation Activity

Improving Student Achievement Have students recall situations in which they purchased goods at a discount off the regular price. Ask students how they determined the price of the goods—guessing, estimating, or calculating.

Objectives

- **Utilize** a general procedure for figuring discounts and net prices. Multiply the price by the discount percentage and subtract this amount from the price
- **Calculate** discounts in dollars and percentages. Discount($) = Discount(%) × Price; Discount(%) = Discount($) / Price
- **Calculate** net amount. $100\% - D(\%) = NPPE$; $P \times NPPE = NP$

Graphic Organizer

Discounts Offered by Employers
Employee Discounts

Discount Formulas
$P \times D(\%) = D(\$)$
$P - D(\$) = NP$

Discounts Offered by Vendors
Trade Discounts
Quantity Discounts
Promotional Discounts
Seasonal Discounts

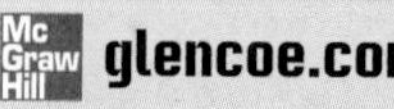

Graphic Organizer Send students to the Online Learning Center to print this graphic organizer.

EXPLORE

Before You Read

Read the Before You Read question aloud: ***What was the last discounted item you purchased?*** Answers will vary. Sample answer: I bought a digital camera at 25% off. Then ask: ***Did you buy it because it was discounted, or would you have bought it anyway?*** Sample answer: Yes, it was a major purchase and I went to a specific store because they had the item on sale.

Preteaching Vocabulary

Have students go to the Online Learning Center at glencoe.com for the Chapter 27 Preteaching Vocabulary games.

Content Vocabulary

Display the term *employee discounts* for the class to read. Ask: ***What does the word* discounts *mean?*** reductions from regular or list prices Ask: ***How do you think employee discounts are calculated?*** They are based on a percentage of the regular price.

Academic Vocabulary

Series—Usage Explain that the word *series* can be defined as "a number of things of the same class coming one after another." As an example, ask a volunteer to list the prime numbers (2, 3, 5, 7, 11, 13...) Tell students that in this section they will learn how series of numbers can be used to calculate price discounts.

Minimum—Word Origin Explain that the word *minimum* comes from the Latin *minimus,* which means "smallest" or "least." Ask volunteers to form sentences using the word minimum. Sample sentences: The minimum age for voting is 18. We hope to raise a minimum of $200 at the bake sale.

Section 27.2 Calculating Discounts

DISCOUNTS

Expert Advice

"Discounts and allowances are price adjustments given to employees for purchases, and also offered by vendors to their customers."

Ask students: ***Have you ever had a job where you received an employee discount? If so, what conditions were attached to using the discount privilege?*** Commonly, such discounts can be used only by employees and possibly immediate family members.

As You Read

Read the As You Read question aloud: ***How do you decide between using net amounts and calculating discounts?*** When you do not need to know the dollar amount of the discount, you can simply use the formula that calculates the net amount

Graphic Organizer

Display these sample steps to show how to calculate a discount in dollars along with an item's net price.

Beginning Information:
Cost of pizza: $7.50
Discount: 15%

Step 1 Determine dollar amount of discount:
P × D(%) = D($)
$7.50 × 0.15 = $1.13

Step 2 Determine net price after discount:
P – D($) = NP
$7.50 – $1.13 = $6.37

Discount = $1.13
Net Price = $6.37

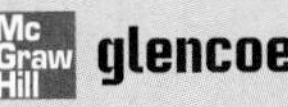

Graphic Organizer Send students to the Online Learning Center to print this graphic organizer.

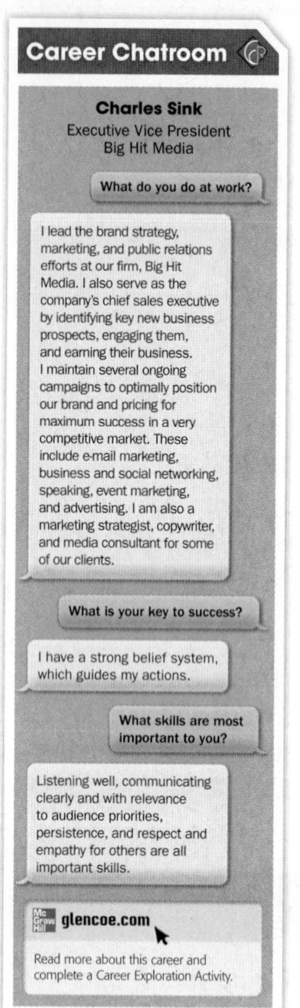
Career Chatroom

Charles Sink
Executive Vice President
Big Hit Media

What do you do at work?

I lead the brand strategy, marketing, and public relations efforts at our firm, Big Hit Media. I also serve as the company's chief sales executive by identifying key new business prospects, engaging them, and earning their business. I maintain several ongoing campaigns to optimally position our brand and pricing for maximum success in a very competitive market. These include e-mail marketing, business and social networking, speaking, event marketing, and advertising. I am also a marketing strategist, copywriter, and media consultant for some of our clients.

What is your key to success?

I have a strong belief system, which guides my actions.

What skills are most important to you?

Listening well, communicating clearly and with relevance to audience priorities, persistence, and respect and empathy for others are all important skills.

glencoe.com

Read more about this career and complete a Career Exploration Activity.

DISCOUNTS BY VENDORS

Some common types of discounts offered by manufacturers and distributors are cash, trade, quantity, seasonal, and promotional (see Chapter 26). These discounts are part of the place or promotion decision in the marketing mix. Those who offer discounts also need to consider the long-term effects of their pricing decisions, not just the quick sale.

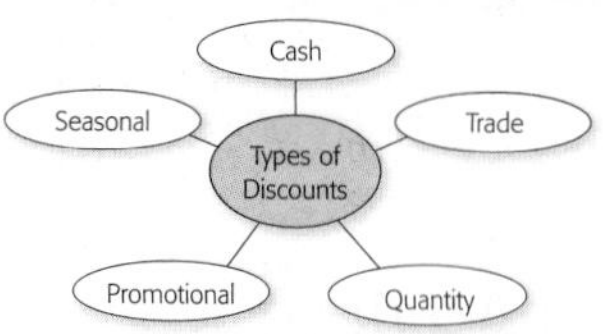

CASH DISCOUNTS

Chapter 26 explains that a cash discount is a discount offered to buyers to encourage them to pay their bills quickly. Consider the invoice terms 3/15, net 60.

Recall that the first number (3) represents the percentage of the discount applicable to the invoice total. When that total is $1,000, and the customer takes advantage of the discount, the calculations are as follows:

STEP 1 Determine the dollar discount.
P × D(%) = D($)
$1,000 × .03 = $30

STEP 2 Determine the net price.
P – D($) = NP
$1,000 – $30 = $970

Cash discounts can also be calculated on a unit basis. The net unit price for 100 items at $10 each is determined as follows:

STEP 1 Determine the dollar discount.
P × D(%) = D($)
$10.00 × .03 = $.30

STEP 2 Determine the net price.
P – D($) = NP
$10.00 – $.30 = $9.70

The net amount payable by the customer would still be the same, of course: $970 ($9.70 × 100). If you wanted to determine the net price quickly, subtract 3 percent from 100 percent and take 97 percent of $10 ($10 × .97 = $9.70).

HOT TOPIC
Discounts When retailers offer discounts and sales to tempt consumers, they might *not* be building long-term customer relationships.

TRADE DISCOUNTS

Trade discounts are based on manufacturers' list prices. They are the way manufacturers quote prices to wholesalers and retailers. They are called "trade discounts" because different prices are offered to different lines of trade (for example, wholesalers versus retailers) in a **series**, such as 40 percent and 20 percent. The 40-percent discount is offered to the retailer, and the series of discounts, 40 percent and 20 percent, are offered to the wholesaler. To figure 40 percent and 20 percent trade discounts for a wholesaler's invoice totaling $8,450, you would do the following:

STEP 1 Determine the first dollar discount.
P × D(%) = D($)
$8,450 × .40 = $3,380

STEP 2 Determine the declining balance.
P – D($) = DB
$8,450 – $3,380 = $5,070

STEP 3 Take the second discount off the declining balance in Step 2.
DB × D (%) = D($)
$5,070 × .20 = $1,014

STEP 4 Determine the net price.
DB – D($) = NP($)
$5,070 – $1,014 = $4,056

Sometimes retailers or wholesalers want to calculate the net unit price of individual items listed on an invoice. In those cases, using the result of subtracting the discounts from 100 percent would be faster. Assuming one of the items on that above invoice was $84.50, you would multiply $84.50 × .60 = $50.70. Then you would multiply $50.70 × .80 = $40.56 (net unit price).

PRACTICE 7

Determine the amounts payable by the following customers.

1. A&B Trucking receives an invoice in the amount of $675,000, showing the terms 2/10, net 30. The invoice lists eight trucks at $84,375 each. (A) If A&B takes advantage of the discount, what will be the net amount due on the invoice? (B) The net price per truck?
2. Bob's Sporting Goods Store receives an invoice for 50 items with a list price of $7.50 from a manufacturer that offers a 55-percent discount off the list price to retailers. (A) What is the discount? (B) What is the amount payable to the manufacturer?
3. A manufacturer gives wholesalers discounts of 40 percent and 15 percent. The invoice received by J&G Wholesaler totals $560,000. What is the net amount payable to the manufacturer?

QUANTITY DISCOUNTS

Quantity discounts are offered to buyers for placing large orders. Sellers benefit from large orders because the selling costs for one transaction are lower than for several small transactions. Quantity discounts are meant to encourage buyers to buy in bulk. These discounts may be quoted either as a percentage of the price or as part of a quantity price list like this:

No. of items	1–24	25–48	49–72
Unit price	$0.95	$0.90	$0.85

Using the above table, if you purchased 50 items, you would pay $0.85 each. Your total bill would be $42.50 ($.85 × 50).

Sometimes businesses offer cumulative quantity discounts, whereby a certain **minimum** purchase must be made during a specified period of time for the discount to be activated. A firm may offer a 2-percent cumulative quantity discount to any company that purchases $3,000 worth of products in a six-month period. If a company's purchases total $2,500 during that period, no discount is given. If they total $4,000, however, the discount is allowed.

EXPLAIN

Graphic Organizer

Display the diagram and review the various discounts offered by vendors.

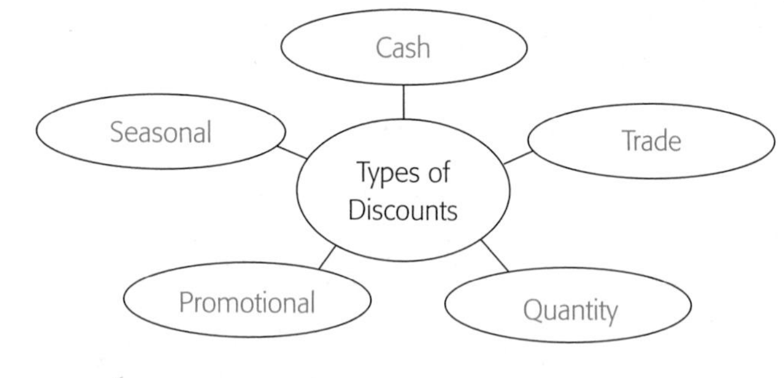

Discounts Read aloud the Hot Topic statement. Ask students whether they think this statement is true. Encourage them to give reasons for their responses.

Career Chatroom

Focus the Career Chatroom discussion concerning Charles Sink by asking students these guiding questions.

Guiding Questions

Recall What are Charles Sink's three responsibilities as chief sales executive?	He identifies new business prospects, engages them, and earns their business.
Analyze What does Sink mean by "optimally position our brand and pricing"?	He means potential customers must see Big Hit Media as being able to meet their needs at an appropriate price.

glencoe.com

Career Exploration Send students to the Online Learning Center to find more information about this career and to get a Career Exploration activity.

ELABORATE

DISCOUNTS BY VENDORS

Ask these guiding questions to focus the discussion on vendor discounts.

Guiding Questions

Analyze What is meant by the term *trade discount?* Why are these discounts listed in a series?	Trade discounts are the different ways that prices are quoted. For example, a manufacturer might give retailers a 25% discount, with an additional 15% off for wholesalers.
Draw Conclusions For a buyer, what advantage does a cumulative quantity discount have over a straight quantity discount?	With a straight quantity discount, the buyer must purchase all items at the same time. With a cumulative quantity discount, purchases can be spread over a specified time period.

Graphic Organizer

Display these sample steps to show how to calculate a trade discount based on a series.

Beginning Information:
Invoice: $380.000
(wholesalers receive discounts of 45% and 15%)

Step 1 Determine first dollar discount
P × D(%) = D($)
$380,000 × .45 = $171,000

Step 2 Determine declining balance:
P – D($) = DB
$380,000 – $171,000 = $209,000

Step 3 Determine second dollar discount
DB × D(%) = D($)
$209,000 × .15 = $31,350

Step 4 Determine the net price:
DB – D($) = NP($)
$209,000 – $31,350 = $177,650

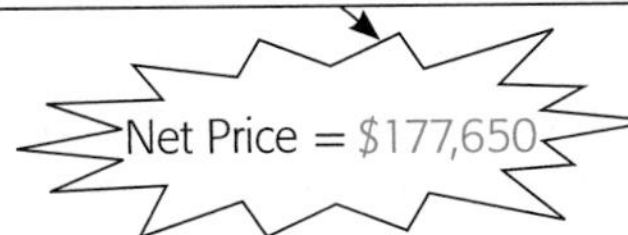

glencoe.com iWB

Graphic Organizer Send students to the Online Learning Center to print this graphic organizer.

ANSWERS TO PRACTICE 7

1. Net amount due on the invoice = $661,500 (675,000 × [1 – .02]); Net price per truck = $82,687.50 (661,500/8)
2. (A) Discount = $206.25 (7.50 × 50 × 0.55); Amount payable to the manufacturer = $168.75 (7.50 × 50 – 206.25)
3. Net amount payable the manufacturer = $285,600 (560,000 – [560,000 × .40] = $336,000; $336,000 – (336,000 × .15) = $285,600

Mini Projects

Differentiated Instruction

Cooperative Learners Have students work in teams of three or four to develop their own quantity discount plan for T-shirts to be sold at their school store. The target market consists of school sports teams and team supporters. The cost per T-shirt will be $10. Students should then determine the markup and retail price for each shirt. They then should determine quantity discounts. For example, they may choose to have three categories of discounts: 10–20 shirts, 21–50 shirts, and over 50 shirts. Students should summarize their discount pricing plans in chart form. A simple drawing of the proposed T-shirt should appear at the top of the chart. Students should prepare a written report explaining the rationale for their pricing plan. Student reports should contain a chart listing the T-shirt's retail price along with quantity discounts. A drawing of the T-shirt should appear at the top of the chart. The reports should include a rationale for the pricing plan.

Logical Learners To encourage students to develop their understanding of the formulas used in calculating discounts, read aloud Problem 3 in Practice 7. Then ask: ***Do you think you can write a single-step formula that solves this problem?*** Have students work individually to create their formulas. When finished, have them compare their formulas with a partner. There are several ways students can combine the four steps under Trade Discounts into a single formula. Possible answer: Net amount = $560,000 – ($560,000 × 0.40 + $560,000 × [1 – 0.40] × 0.15)

For example, let's say a manufacturer offers a 5-percent cumulative quantity discount for purchases that total at least $5,000 in a three-month period. Suppose Kathy's Flowers placed the following orders:

January 15: $1,000; February 28: $2,000; March 10: $3,000. The total purchases of $6,000 would meet the dollar requirement within the three-month period. Thus, Kathy's net amount payable would be $5,700 ($1,000 + $2,000 + $3,000 = $6,000 × .95 = $5,700). If Kathy's Flowers had not placed the March 10 order, the total for the three-month period would be only $3,000, so no discounts would be permitted.

PROMOTIONAL DISCOUNTS

Promotional discounts are given to businesses that agree to advertise or in some other way promote a manufacturer's products. When the promotional discount is quoted as a percentage, it is calculated in the same way as a cumulative discount.

Sometimes, marketers are granted a dollar amount as a promotional discount. In such cases, they may want to determine the net purchase price or the percentage of the promotional discount for themselves.

Consider an example. The Cycle Shop buys Speedy bicycles for $10,000 and is granted a $250 promotional discount for displaying the bikes in its store window during the month of March. To determine the percentage discount, follow these steps:

STEP 1 Divide the dollar discount by the original price. The answer will be a decimal.
D($) divided by P = D(%)
$250 ÷ $10,000 = .025

STEP 2 Change the decimal to a percentage by shifting the decimal point two places to the right. This figure is the percentage discount. When necessary, round the percentage to the tenths place.
.025 = 2.5%

SEASONAL DISCOUNTS

Sellers offer seasonal discounts to encourage buyers to purchase goods long before the actual consumer buying season. Purchasing beach towels before January 27 or ski apparel before May 1 might qualify retailers for seasonal discounts.

Seasonal discounts are calculated in the same way as other discounts. PNC Inc. offers an 8-percent seasonal discount to all buyers that purchase winter coats before June 1. An order placed on May 20 for $1,500 worth of parkas would qualify for the discount. However, if that order was placed on June 15, PNC Inc. would not grant the 8-percent discount.

PRACTICE 8

Now solve these problems involving quantity, promotional, and seasonal discounts.

1. Suppose a firm is required to buy $10,000 worth of goods by September 15 in order to qualify for a 10-percent cumulative quantity discount. (A) Would a firm that purchased $8,000 worth of goods on September 1 get the discount? (B) What about one that purchased $11,500 worth on September 30?
2. A manufacturer offers a retailer $3,867 as a promotional discount for advertising a certain product. What is the percentage discount if the total invoice was $128,900?
3. Regal Shoe Company offers retailers a 5-percent discount for placing orders by May 1. A retailer takes advantage of the offer and purchases $829,500 worth of shoes by the cutoff date. What is the net amount payable on the invoice?

POTENTIAL PITFALLS OF DISCOUNT PRICING

Customers love discounts, but what about the retailers and manufacturers? Some analysts argue about the effects of discounts on short-term sales, longer term profits, brand loyalty, and overall supply chain costs for retailers and manufacturers.

Discounts are a staple of business strategy for many retail companies. Discounting in the United States has been built into the retail cycle. However, small retail businesses should make sure that they go about the discounting process in an intelligent fashion. Retailers should beware of overusing discounts. Economists and business owners have noted that discount periods do increase sales volume, but frequent sales tend to numb customer response over time.

Retailers should study historic customer response, inventory levels, competitor pricing, seasonal cycles, and other factors to determine the level of discount to offer. Some businesses are able to dramatically increase their sales volume through discounts of 20 percent or less.

Other businesses may have to offer discounts of 40-50 percent in order to see meaningful increases in traffic. Still other retailers employ a price philosophy that emphasizes every-day low prices in the hopes that the increased volume will make up for the small profit margin on individual sales.

Manufacturers, too, should be very careful in establishing discounts for their products. Price promotions offered by manufacturers may set a precedent, and customers may make purchases based on price rather than company loyalty. Poorly-planned discount sales can lead to price wars with competitors and can tarnish the image of the company offering the discount.

After You Read **Section 27.2**

Review Key Concepts

1. **Explain** why employers offer employee discounts.
2. **Identify** what the number "3" represents in invoice terms 3/10, net 45.
3. **Discuss** why vendors offer seasonal discounts.

Practice Academics

English Language Arts

4. Collectibles vary in price based on certain criteria. Select a collectible to research, such as coins, dolls, comic books, or baseball cards. What criteria are used to put a price on a collectible? Summarize your findings in a written report.

NCTE 7 Conduct research and gather, evaluate, and synthesize data to communicate discoveries.

Mathematics

5. How much would you charge a customer who purchased 30 items, based on the following quantity price list?

Number of items:	0–12	13–36	37–49	50–74
Unit price:	$6.50	$6.25	$6.00	$5.75

Math Concept **Quantity Pricing** When pricing is based on the number of items purchased, the first step is determining the number of items bought or sold. Once the quantity is known, multiplication is used to calculate the total cost.

Starting Hints To solve this problem, determine the price of each item when 30 are purchased. Multiply the individual price by 30 to determine the total cost.

NCTM Problem Solving Solve problems that arise in mathematics and in other contexts.

For help, go to the **Math Skills Handbook** located at the back of this book.

glencoe.com

Check your answers.

ELABORATE

PROMOTIONAL DISCOUNTS

Ask these guiding questions to focus the discussion on promotional discounts.

Guiding Questions

Explain What does a manufacturer get in return for giving a business a promotional discount?	The business agrees to advertise or in some other way promote the manufacturer's products.
Apply You manage a grocery store. The manufacturer of a new cereal has offered you a 15% discount on your next order if you agree to position this cereal on an end-cap (at the end of an aisle) for two weeks. Why might you accept this offer? Why might you turn it down?	You might do it to increase your profit on the cereal. However, end-cap space is limited, and you might have better offers from other vendors.

ANSWERS TO PRACTICE 8

1. (A) No, because the minimum quantity is $10,000.
(B) No, because the purchase had to be made by September 15 to get the discount.
2. Percentage discount = 3% (3,867/128,900)
3. Net amount payable = $788,025
(829,500 × [1 − .05])

Reinforce Vocabulary

Have students locate a word in this chapter with which they are unfamiliar (or are uncertain of its definition). Then have them attempt to write a definition of the word based on its context in the text. When they are finished, they should look up the word in a dictionary and compare its dictionary definition with the definition they developed.

EVALUATE

POTENTIAL PITFALLS OF DISCOUNT PRICING

Ask these guiding questions to focus the discussion on the potential pitfalls of discount pricing.

Guiding Questions

Analyze What are some factors retailers should look at when determining what level of discount to offer?	customers' past response to various discount levels, competitor pricing, seasonal cycles
Judge The management of a major retail store is debating whether to have periodic sales with deeply discounted prices on popular items or to go with everyday low pricing on all items. What are some advantages and disadvantages of each strategy?	Periodic sales on popular items can draw large numbers; however, consumers may learn to shop at the store only during sales. Everyday low prices attract consumers who do not want to watch for sales, and increases in volume may make up for a small profit margin.

Critical Thinking

After students have read about the various types of discounts, give them a clue, such as those listed below, associated with each type of discount. Have them tell you which type of discount the clue illustrates:

a. 1–12 items at 8 cents each, 13–20 items at 6 cents each quantity discount

b. 15 percent off if you buy your back-to-school stock in May seasonal discount

c. 30 percent off anything you can wear on the job employee discount

d. $4,300 off your total purchase if you feature the item in a newspaper ad promotional discount

Mini Project

Enrichment

Ideas for Promotional Discounts Tell students to imagine they work for a vendor that sells a specific brand of high-end sports equipment to retailers. Have students write a report explaining creative promotional discounts to offer the retailers. Student reports should list various types of promotional discounts. For example, if they are handling soccer equipment, the vendor might offer a discount if the retailer agrees to supply a local youth team with free equipment. The store might get discounts for highlighting the equipment on its Web site and displaying it at the front of the store.

After You Read Section 27.2

Review Key Concepts

1. Offering discounts encourages employees to buy and use the products in the hope that they will then project confidence in the products and enthusiasm when selling those products.
2. The number "3" indicates that the buyer will receive a 3 percent discount if the invoice is paid within 10 days.
3. Vendors offer seasonal discounts to encourage buyers to purchase goods long before the consumer buying season.

Practice Academics

English Language Arts

4. Reports will vary depending on the type of collectible covered, but students should specifically state those factors that can affect a particular collectible's price. For example, many factors can affect the price of a collectible postage stamp. The rarity of the stamp is of prime importance. Its condition is categorized in a number of ways that affect its value. For example, it might be described as being mint, very fine, fine, and so on. In addition, the condition might indicate whether the stamp has ever been "hinged" and whether it is cancelled. The type of cancellation can also affect value.

Mathematics

5. The customer should be charged $187.50 ($30 \times \$6.25$).

glencoe.com

Send students to the Online Learning Center to check their answers.

Pricing Math

The cost method of pricing and the retail method of pricing are used to calculate markups.

Cost Method of Pricing — Markup Equivalents Table Converts Markups on Retail to Markups on Cost and Vice Versa — Retail Method of Pricing

A variety of discounts are offered to vendors as well as employees.

DISCOUNTS
- EMPLOYEE
- VENDOR
  - Cash
  - Trade
  - Quantity
  - Promotional
  - Seasonal

Written Summary

- Gross profit on an income statement is the same as gross margin or markup in pricing.
- The basic formula for markup is Cost + Markup = Retail Price.
- To calculate a markdown, multiply the markdown percent by the retail price. To arrive at the sale price, subtract the dollar markdown from the original retail price.
- Maintained markup is the difference between sale price and cost.
- One procedure for calculating discounts is to multiply the price by the discount percentage, and then subtract that amount from the original price to find the net price.
- Cash discounts are offered to customers with dating terms such as 2/10, net 30. The 2 represents the discount percentage.
- Quantity discounts may be quoted on a quantity price list that provides unit prices for specific quantities purchased.

Review Content Vocabulary and Academic Vocabulary

1. Write true-or-false statements using each vocabulary word. Ask a partner to determine whether each statement is true or false and explain why.

Content Vocabulary	Academic Vocabulary
• gross profit (p. 627)	• convert (p. 633)
• maintained markup (p. 635)	• visual (p. 634)
• employee discounts (p. 639)	• series (p. 641)
	• minimum (p. 641)

Assess for Understanding

2. **Connect** How does profit relate to markup?
3. **Identify** What is the formula that calculates retail price?
4. **Explain** How are dollar and percentage markups calculated?
5. **Process** How do you calculate the discount and net price for a $45 item with a 15 percent discount, and also calculate just the net price?
6. **Calculate** A company is granted a $150 promotional discount for including a product in its flyer. What is the percentage of the discount of a $5,000 invoice?
7. **Identify** Which two groups get trade discounts off the manufacturer's list price?
8. **Define** What is *gross profit*?
9. **Compute** You buy a case of 48 headphones for $240 and sell all of them for $10 each. What is the markup percentage based on retail? What is the percentage of total sales revenue that is the gross profit?

EVALUATE

Visual Summary

Express Creativity Ask students to create a visual summary that illustrates a concept in the chapter. Encourage students to use different formats for their visual summaries, such as a chart, graphic organizer, or poster. Visual summaries will vary depending on the concept depicted. Questions to ask when assessing a visual summary include:

- Is the summary clear, economical, and simple?
- Are any important steps or concepts left out?
- Are steps or concepts arranged in the same order as the original?
- Does the summary reveal a pattern that connects the details?
- Does the summary locate and highlight the most important information?

Review Content Vocabulary and Academic Vocabulary

1. True-or-false sentences will vary. Sample sentences:

   When calculating **gross profit,** you subtract cost of goods sold from sales revenue, and you do not subtract any expenses. (True)

   Calculating **maintained markup** helps a marketer make certain revenue and profit goals are still being met, even after multiple markdowns. (True)

   If you like the products a store sells you can ask for an **employee discount** just by being a loyal customer. (False; you have to work there to get a discount.)

EVALUATE

Assess for Understanding

2. Markup is the same as gross profit, or profit before expenses are deducted.

3. Retail price (RP) = Cost (C) + Markup (MU)

4. Dollar markup (MU$) = Retail price (RP) – Cost (C); Percentage markup (MU%) on retail = Dollar markup (MU$)/ Retail price (RP)

5. Discount = 45 × (0.15) = $6.75; Net price = 45 – 6.75 = $38.25; 45 × (1 – .15) = $38.25

6. 150/5,000 = 0.03 = 3% discount

7. Wholesalers and retailers get trade discounts off the manufacturer's list price.

8. Gross profit is the difference between sales revenue and the cost of goods sold. Gross profit does not take into account expenses.

9. Cost = $5 (240/48). Markup percentage based on retail = 50% (10 – 5)/10. Percentage of total sales revenue that is the gross profit = 50% (480 – 240)/480

21st Century Skills

Communication Skills

10. **Borrowing a Discount** You work at a clothing store that offers a 15-percent employee discount. One of the items you and your five friends need for your Halloween costumes is sold at your store. Your friends want you to buy that item in their respective sizes with your employee discount. However, your store policy does not allow this. How would you explain this to your friends?

Financial Literacy Skills

11. **Actual Cost** Determine the cost for each of the following items. Use the markup equivalents chart to convert the markup on cost to the markup on retail in order to do your calculations.

Item	Markup on Cost	Suggested Retail Price	Cost
Model #510	50%	$15.00	?
Model #512	25%	$72.50	?
Model #514	100%	$99.99	?

Everyday Ethics

12. **Special Discounts** Many supermarkets offer special discounts on selected items to customers who have frequent-shopper cards. Due to privacy concerns, some customers do not want their purchases traced through such a program. However, they do not want to pay higher prices. One customer with a card pays $2.25 for the loaf of bread, but a customer without the card pays $3.59. What advantage does the card-carrying customer have by percentage? Discuss whether this price advantage is fair.

e-Marketing Skills

13. **Budgeting Small Favors** Conduct research online to find a favor (small gift) for a charity golf tournament. All 100 participants will receive this favor, and you would like it to be imprinted with the name of the charity. Your budget is $750, but if you spend less, more money goes to the charity. Be sure to include shipping charges and taxes in your calculations, as well as imprint charges. Present three favors, along with your calculations in a chart, and your recommendation in an oral report.

Build Academic Skills

English Language Arts

14. **Language Arts** Prepare a written advertisement for a special sale on boots and include the total discount savings in dollars and percentage. The original retail price of the boots was $250. The first markdown taken two weeks ago was a 10-percent markdown. Now the store is offering a 20-percent markdown off the already reduced price. Show your calculations in the advertisement.

NCTE 5 Use different writing process elements to communicate effectively.

Science

15. **Scientific Inquiry** Conduct research to analyze price discounting strategies used by supermarkets and other food stores located geographically close to one another. Are they discounting the same or different products? How much of a discount are they offering? Report your findings and analysis in a written report.

NSES A Develop abilities necessary to do scientific inquiry, understandings about scientific inquiry.

Mathematics

16. **Calculate Percentage Markup** A card store buys boxes of candy for $5.50 and puts a $4.49 markup on each box. (A) What is the percentage markup on the cost? (B) What is the percentage markup on retail?

NCTM Number and Operations Compute fluently and make reasonable estimates.

Math Concept **Computation** When a markup is given as a dollar amount, dividing the markup value by the cost gives the percentage markup in decimal form.

For help, go to the **Math Skills Handbook** located at the back of this book.

Standardized Test Practice

Directions Read the following questions. On a separate sheet of paper, write the best possible answer for each one.

1. What is the maintained markup percentage for an item that cost a retailer $37 with an original retail price of $85 that was later marked down 15 percent?
   - **A.** 48.0%
   - **B.** 48.8%
   - **C.** 56.5%
   - **D.** 72.3%
2. The markup percentage equivalent for a 100-percent markup on cost is a 50-percent markup retail.
   - T
   - F
3. The difference between sales revenue and the cost of goods sold is ________.

Test-Taking Tip

When studying in small groups, make sure your study group includes only students who are serious about studying. Some should be at your level of ability or better.

DECA Connection Role Play

Owner
Specialty Shop

Situation Your store sells leather briefcases, purses, and small leather goods. You sell only high-quality items made by established vendors. Your business is successful. You are not content to allow the shop to rest on its reputation.

Always seeking opportunities to add items related to your basic stock items, you recently met a local artist who hand-paints original designs on silk scarves. The artist is seeking a retail outlet to sell the scarves. The artist works with rectangular and square-shaped scarves. The artist will sell the rectangles to your shop for $30.00 each and the squares for $45.00 each. You view this as a great opportunity for your business since the artist is willing to sell to your shop exclusively.

You have decided that you will be able to attain a higher markup on the scarves than on your basic stock items. Your normal markup on basic stock items is 40%. Because of the exclusive nature of the scarves, you feel that you can easily set the retail prices at $70.00 for the rectangles and $90.00 for the squares. Your assistant manager (judge) has asked to explain why you plan to use a higher markup on these items.

Activity You are to explain to the assistant manager (judge) how the additional markup on the scarves can benefit the store's overall profitability and help cover overhead and operating costs.

Evaluation You will be evaluated on how well you meet the following performance indicators:

1. Identify factors affecting a business's profit.
2. Determine cost of product (breakeven, ROI, markup).
3. Demonstrate responsible behavior.
4. Adjust prices to maximize profitability.
5. Describe the nature of profit and loss statements.

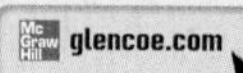

Download the Competitive Events Workbook for more Role-Play practice.

EVALUATE

Communication Skills

10. Answers will vary. The best approach is to explain the situation to your friends directly, without being defensive. You could simply state that the discount is only given to employees, not to family or friends. It is a perk for working at the store. Your employer is entitled to make a profit on goods that are being purchased for others' use. In addition, if your employer found out that you had purchased goods for friends, you could be disciplined, or even fired.

Financial Literacy Skills

11. $10.05 (15 – [15 × 0.33]; 15 – 4.95 = 10.05)
$58 (72.50 – [72.50 × 0.20]; 72.50 – 14.50 = 58)
$49.99 (99.99 – [99.99 × 0.50]; 99.99 – 50 = 49.99)

Everyday Ethics

12. The customer using the frequent-shopper card saves $1.34, or 37.3%. Answers to the second part of the question will vary. Some students may feel that the store should not require customers to give up information about their purchases in order to get a discount. Others may state that the store is not requiring customers to use the cards. Each side is getting something when the customer uses the card—the customer is getting savings and the store, while reducing its profit, is getting information which may be useful for gaining future profits. Many consumers are willing to make this trade-off to save money.

e-Marketing Skills

13. Students should prepare an oral report in which they present three different favors, each of which would cost $750 or less for 100 items (including imprinting, shipping charges, and any required taxes). In the report, they should recommend which item they think should be purchased. Students should aim to locate an appropriate favor that is $7.50 or less per item. For example, a carton of 50 golf tees personalized with the charity's name is $3.95. Total cost would be $395 plus shipping and handling. Other possible gifts might include inexpensive hats, golf towels, golf balls, and so on.

EVALUATE

Build Academic Skills

English Language Arts

14. Students should create an advertisement for a special sale on boots. The ad should explain that the original retail price was $250. It should indicate that the price was previously reduced by 10% to $225 (250 – 250 × .10). Now an additional 20% is being taken off the previous sale price, making the new sale price $180 (225 – 225 × .20). The advertisement should emphasize what a good deal this new reduced price is.

Science

15. Reports will vary depending on the stores' research and their geographical location. Many stores discount similar items because loss-leaders tend to be items in high demand, such as dairy products and cereals. In addition, vendors may offer stores discounts on the same items, such as a specific brand of soft drink. Students should state the percentages of the discounts in their reports.

Mathematics

16. (A) Percentage markup on cost = 81.6% (4.49/5.50);
(B) Percentage markup on retail = 44.9% (4.49/[5.50 + 4.49])

Standardized Test Practice

1. B (48.8%)
2. True
3. gross profit

DECA Connection Role Play

Evaluations will be based on these performance indicators:

1. **Identify factors affecting a business's profit.** A major factor affecting a business's profit is the markup percentage. Other factors affecting a business's profit include the ability to get appropriate discounts from vendors and suppliers, the ability of the business to keep shrinkage and damage to a minimum and to efficiently manage inventory, and the ability of the business to mark down merchandise when appropriate while still keeping a maintained markup.
2. **Determine cost of product (breakeven, ROI, markup).** The breakeven point for an item is calculated by adding together the costs of the merchandise and any expenses related to it. The price is determined by adding markup to this amount. The return on investment, or net profit, is determined by subtracting the costs and expenses from the price.
3. **Demonstrate responsible behavior.** Students should be able to demonstrate responsible behavior in a variety of situations. For example, they should be able to explain to friends that they cannot give them an employee discount that they receive from a part-time job when the friends are not entitled to such a discount.
4. **Adjust prices to maximize profitability.** In order to make a profit, businesses must set their prices high enough to cover the costs and expenses associated with merchandise and also include markup. When establishing price, marketers must take into account costs and expenses, the value of the merchandise as perceived by the consumer, competitors' prices, etc. In order to remain profitable and competitive, marketers must know when to mark down merchandise.
5. **Describe the nature of profit and loss statements.** The profit and loss, or income, statement provides a summary of income and expenses during a specific time period. Students should be able to explain how markup is related to this statement. When establishing markup, retailers and wholesalers must set a price that takes into account costs, expenses, and adds to that total a projected profit margin.

Role Plays For more DECA Role Plays, send students to the Online Learning Center to download the Competitive Events Workbook.

UNIT 8 **Marketing Internship Project**

A Pricing Plan for New Greeting Cards

Greeting cards for Americans can be multicultural, celebrating diverse heritages. How would you design and price a new line of American heritage cards?

Scenario

Your company specializes in greeting cards and related specialties. Its Web site has an e-greeting card capability. Also, retail stores that carry your cards are listed online. The company is considering a new line of paper greeting cards that celebrate American heritages.

The suggested retail price for this new line of cards is between $.99 and $5.99. The retailer's markup will be between 40 and 50 percent of the suggested retail price. The cost of printing the cards depends on the size and quality of paper used. Overhead and marketing expenses also affect pricing. Your company wants a gross profit of 40 percent for e-greeting cards and paper greeting cards sold to retailers. You need to calculate the minimum and maximum costs per card to achieve the gross profit goal for your pricing plan.

The Skills You'll Use

Academic Skills Reading, writing, social studies, researching, and analyzing

Basic Skills Speaking, listening, thinking, and interpersonal

Technology Skills Word processing, spreadsheet, presentation, telecommunications, and the Internet

NCTE 7 Conduct research and gather, evaluate, and synthesize data to communicate discoveries.
NCTE 9 Develop an understanding of diversity in language use across cultures.

Your Objective

Your objective is to design and price a potentially profitable new line of greeting cards that feature monthly American heritage observances.

STEP 1 Do Your Research

Conduct research to find out the months during which various American heritages are observed or celebrated. Identify competing greeting card companies, as well as retailers and Internet companies that sell greeting cards. As you conduct your research, answer these questions:

- What are the competitors' retail prices for paper and e-greeting cards?
- Which American heritages do the competitors' cards celebrate?
- What are the political, economic, socio-cultural, and technological factors that could impact the designs, pricing, and marketing of American heritage-themed greeting cards?
- What do the product costs have to be in order to price the new line competitively?

Write a summary of your research.

STEP 2 Plan Your Project

Now that you have completed your research, you need to begin planning your project.

- Conduct a PEST analysis.
- Conduct a SWOT analysis to identify the strengths, weaknesses, opportunities, and threats involved with this new greeting card line.
- Design sample greeting cards that feature various American heritages.
- Write a pricing plan for the new line of greeting cards by using your knowledge of pricing strategies and profit margins to decide how the greeting cards should be priced.
- Write a rationale for your plan with supporting research and suggestions for marketing the new product line.

STEP 3 Connect with Your Community

- Interview the owner or manager of a store that carries greeting cards to see where your new product line might fit in the store's merchandising scheme.
- Take notes during your interview, and transcribe your notes after your interview.
- Test your sample greeting card designs and suggested retail prices on ten people to see how receptive they are to your ideas.

STEP 4 Share What You Learn

Assume your class is the product manager and staff that will decide if your plan has the potential to be implemented by the company.

- Present your findings in an oral presentation. Be prepared to answer questions.
- Use software to create a slide presentation to accompany your oral presentation. Include one slide for each topic in your pricing plan and written rationale.
- Share your greeting card designs.

STEP 5 Evaluate Your Marketing and Academic Skills

Your project will be evaluated based on the following:

- Your product designs with regard to cultural diversity within the United States
- Your pricing plan's potential for being profitable
- Accurate calculations to determine the cost necessary to achieve suggested retail prices
- Research data to support the rationale for your plan
- Organization and continuity of presentation
- Mechanics—presentation and neatness
- Speaking and listening skills

MARKETING CORE FUNCTIONS
- Market Planning
- Pricing

Marketing Internship Project Checklist

Plan
- ✓ Conduct research on companies that make and sell greeting cards in retail stores and on the Internet.
- ✓ Conceive a pricing plan for a new line of greeting cards that you design for a specific target market.

Write
- ✓ Write a pricing plan for the new line of greeting cards, using your knowledge of pricing strategies and profit margins.
- ✓ Explain how the results of the PEST analysis help you decide on prices.
- ✓ Explain supporting research and suggestions for marketing the new product line.

Present
- ✓ Present research that supports your rationale for pricing strategies and product designs.
- ✓ Present your pricing plan.
- ✓ Display samples of your greeting card designs.

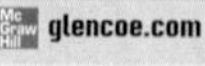

Evaluate Download a rubric you can use to evaluate your final project.

my marketing portfolio

Internship Report Once you have completed your Marketing Internship Project and oral presentation, put your written report and a few printouts of key slides from your oral presentation in your Marketing Portfolio.

Research and Develop a Pricing Plan Research and create a complementary product line with an American heritage theme for kites, flags, figurines, coffee mugs, T-shirts, or other products that target a specific ethnic group. Does your research data support the rationale for the product line and suggested pricing plan? Is your pricing plan calculated correctly and does it achieve a satisfactory profit margin? Are your product designs culturally appropriate for the target market? Prepare a written report and an oral presentation.

EVALUATE

Anticipation Activity

Project Objective Read the project objective aloud to students: ***Design and price a potentially profitable new line of greeting cards that feature monthly American heritage observances.*** Then ask students to think about what they learned about pricing in Unit 8. Remind them of these key points:

- Four market factors that affect price planning are costs and expenses, supply and demand, consumer perceptions, and competition.
- The steps in determining a price include: (1) Establish pricing objectives; (2) determine costs; (3) estimate demand; (4) study competition; (5) decide on a pricing strategy; and (6) set prices.

Ask students: ***What is the goal of pricing?*** Earning a profit is one goal, but two other pricing goals are gaining market share and meeting the competition.

Ask students: ***How is profit related to markup?*** Gross profit is the difference between sales revenue and cost of goods sold. Expenses must be deducted to arrive at net (actual) profit. The markup on a product must be high enough to cover expenses and provide a profit.

Graphic Organizer

Display this table. Name American heritage observances.

Jan	
Feb	Black History Month
Mar	Irish-American Heritage Month
Apr	
May	Jewish-American Heritage Month
June	Caribbean-American Heritage Month
July	
Aug	
Sept	National Hispanic Heritage Month
Oct	National Hispanic Heritage Month
Nov	National American-Indian Heritage Month
Dec	

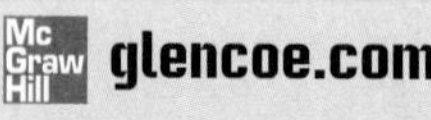

Graphic Organizer Send students to the Online Learning Center to print this graphic organizer.

EVALUATE

STEP 1 Do Your Research

Tell students that there are many places to find information they can use to design a greeting card line and develop a pricing plan for it. Students can use library and Internet resources, but they should also talk to people in the community. Encourage students to seek the opinions and ideas of trusted people they know. Other people can bring new perspectives and ideas about designing and developing a pricing plan as well as factors that affect pricing.

STEP 2 Plan Your Project

Students should conduct a PEST analysis before designing their cards and creating a pricing plan. Students should explain why they chose their designs and prices, and provide information about their pricing strategies and profit margins. Students' explanation of their pricing plans should include supporting research, marketing suggestions, and a SWOT analysis for the new greeting card line.

STEP 3 Connect with Your Community

Explain to students that connecting with members of the community is a great way to build relationships. Tell them that young people who are capable of building relationships with caring, responsible, and competent adults are more likely to achieve success. Encourage students to take part in opportunities for adults to serve as mentors, coaches, advocates, and advisors, both formally and informally.

STEP 4 Share What You Learn

Students should present their ideas in a written report and oral presentation with presentation software. They should have at least one slide in their presentation for each key topic in the written report. Encourage students to speak clearly, use appropriate grammar and vocabulary, and actively engage the audience by making and maintaining eye contact and using movement (facial expressions, posture, gestures) to focus attention and interest.

STEP 5 Evaluate Your Marketing and Academic Skills

Have students use the Marketing Internship Project Checklist to help them to plan, write, and present their reports. Exemplary written reports will include information that clearly supports a central thesis, a single, distinct focus, generally well-developed ideas, well-phrased sentences that flow smoothly and are varied in length and structure, consistently precise word choice, and few, if any, errors in grammar, spelling, and mechanics.

glencoe.com

Evaluation Rubric Send students to the Online Learning Center to get a rubric to evaluate their projects.

Culminating Activity

Explain to students that pricing laws and ethics should also be considered when evaluating the merits of a pricing plan. As discussed in Chapter 25, federal and state governments have enacted laws to prohibit price fixing and discrimination, such as the Clayton Antitrust Act, the Sherman Antitrust Act, and the Robinson-Patman Act. Ask students: ***What are some ways to ensure that a product's price is legally and ethically compliant?*** Do not make agreements with competitors to set prices to eliminate competition. Do not offer a special advantageous price to one retailer, and then offer a higher price to another. Be sure there is a unit price breakdown for the retailer to display. To adhere to ethical pricing practices, if your product becomes a top seller, do not set a price higher than normal and "price gouge."

my marketing portfolio

Internship Report Have students put their written reports and printouts of key slides from their oral presentations in their marketing portfolio.

Research and Develop a Pricing Plan Direct students to select a product line, such as kites, flags, figurines, coffee mugs, T-shirts, or other product, and then research and develop a pricing plan for the line that targets a specific ethnic group. Students' completed pricing plans should include all of the elements and answer all of the questions included in the Marketing Internship Project on this page. This additional activity can build relevance for students who are motivated to learn about pricing for other types of products.

UNIT 9

Marketing Information Management

PLANNING GUIDE AND RESOURCES

	Print	Digital
Unit 9 Marketing Information Management		Unit 9 Fast Files: Marketing Internship Project Activity Connect Online Learning Center through glencoe.com
Chapter 28 **Marketing Research**	Student Activity Workbook: Chapter 28 DECA Connection Role Play; Chapter 28 Vocabulary Activity; Section Note Taking Activities; Chapter Academics Activity; Section Study Skills Activities; Section Real-World Applications Activities Mathematics for Marketing Workbook Marketing Research Project Workbook School-to-Career Activity Workbook	Unit 9 Fast Files: Chapter 28 Discovery Project Worksheet and Rubric; Chapter 28 Green Marketer Activity; Chapter 28 Digital Nation Activity; Section Graphic Organizers; Section Outlines with Key Terms and Definitions; Section Summaries ExamView Assessment Suite, Chapter 28 Connect Online Learning Center through glencoe.com
Chapter 29 **Conducting Marketing Research**	Student Activity Workbook: Chapter 29 DECA Connection Role Play; Chapter 29 Vocabulary Activity; Section Note Taking Activities; Chapter Academics Activity; Section Study Skills Activities; Section Real-World Applications Activities Mathematics for Marketing Workbook Marketing Research Project Workbook School-to-Career Activity Workbook	Unit 9 Fast Files: Chapter 29 Discovery Project Worksheet and Rubric; Chapter 29 Green Marketer Activity; Chapter 29 Digital Nation Activity; Section Graphic Organizers; Section Outlines with Key Terms and Definitions; Section Summaries ExamView Assessment Suite, Chapter 29 Connect Online Learning Center through glencoe.com

McGRAW-HILL PROFESSIONAL DEVELOPMENT

Perkins IV has placed more emphasis than ever on providing quality professional development for Career and Technology educators. The legislation mandates that the focus of professional development be the integration and reinforcement of academic competencies in order to improve student achievement. Specifically, Perkins requires measurements of students' academic success. McGraw-Hill answers the challenge for strong and effective professional development with a five-prong **Online Professional Development for Integrating Academics.**

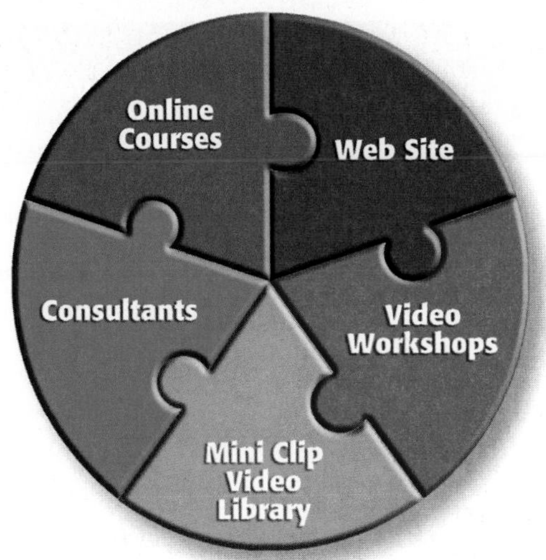

For pricing and ordering information contact your McGraw-Hill Sales Representative.

VIDEO LIBRARY

The McGraw-Hill Professional Development Mini-Clip Video Library, referenced for your convenience at the point of use, provides teaching strategies to strengthen academic and learning skills. Go to the Online Learning Center to view these professional development video clips for Unit 9:

Chapter 28: Marketing Research

- **ELL: Providing Clear Directions:** A teacher provides clear written directions for an assignment and checks for student understanding. (p. 655)
- **Reading: Planning for Future Instruction:** Teachers plan for future instruction by developing strategies for nonfiction text. (p. 663)

Chapter 29: Conducting Marketing Research

- **ELL: Low-Risk Environment:** An author discusses the importance of creating a low-risk environment for English language learners. (p. 679)
- **ELL: Elaborating on Student Responses:** A teacher uses explanatory language to elaborate on a student response and places it in the context of the lesson. (p. 689)

UNIT OVERVIEW

Sections	Objectives	Common Core State Standards College and Career Readiness
Section 28.1 **Marketing Information**	• Describe the purpose of marketing research. • Explain the characteristics and purposes of a marketing information system. • Identify procedures for gathering information using technology.	• **Writing** Conduct short as well as more sustained research projects based on focused questions, demonstrating understanding of the subject under investigation.
Section 28.2 **Issues in Marketing Research**	• Identify the methods of conducting marketing research. • Discuss trends and limitations in marketing research.	• **Writing** Present arguments to support claims in an analysis of substantive topics or texts, using valid reasoning and relevant evidence. • **Writing** Conduct short research projects based on focused questions, demonstrating understanding of the subject under investigation.

Sections	Objectives	Common Core State Standards College and Career Readiness
Section 29.1 **Marketing Research**	• Explain the steps in designing and conducting marketing research. • Compare primary and secondary data. • Collect and interpret marketing information. • Identify the elements in a marketing research report.	• **Writing** Write informative/explanatory texts to examine and convey complex ideas and information clearly and accurately through the effective selection, organization, and analysis of content.
Section 29.2 **The Marketing Survey**	• Design a marketing research survey. • Administer a marketing research survey.	• **Writing** Conduct short as well as more sustained research projects based on focused questions, demonstrating understanding of the subject under investigation.

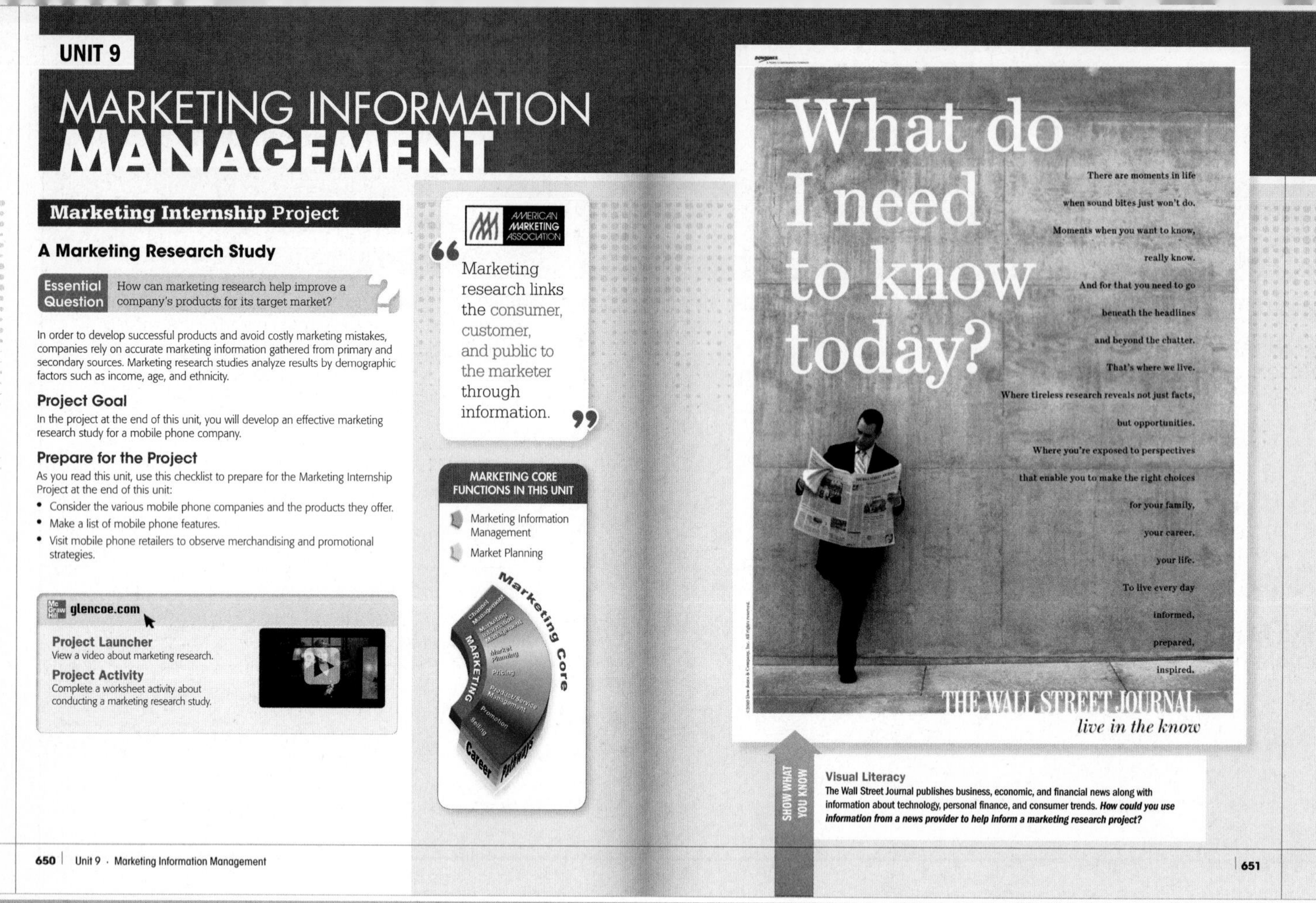

UNIT 9

MARKETING INFORMATION MANAGEMENT

Marketing Internship Project

A Marketing Research Study

Essential Question How can marketing research help improve a company's products for its target market?

In order to develop successful products and avoid costly marketing mistakes, companies rely on accurate marketing information gathered from primary and secondary sources. Marketing research studies analyze results by demographic factors such as income, age, and ethnicity.

Project Goal

In the project at the end of this unit, you will develop an effective marketing research study for a mobile phone company.

Prepare for the Project

As you read this unit, use this checklist to prepare for the Marketing Internship Project at the end of this unit:

- Consider the various mobile phone companies and the products they offer.
- Make a list of mobile phone features.
- Visit mobile phone retailers to observe merchandising and promotional strategies.

glencoe.com

Project Launcher
View a video about marketing research.

Project Activity
Complete a worksheet activity about conducting a marketing research study.

AMERICAN MARKETING ASSOCIATION

"Marketing research links the consumer, customer, and public to the marketer through information."

MARKETING CORE FUNCTIONS IN THIS UNIT

- Marketing Information Management
- Market Planning

Marketing Core
MARKETING
Career Pathways

What do I need to know today?
There are moments in life
when sound bites just won't do.
Moments when you want to know,
really know.
And for that you need to go
beneath the headlines
and beyond the chatter.
That's where we live.
Where tireless research reveals not just facts,
but opportunities.
Where you're exposed to perspectives
that enable you to make the right choices
for your family,
your career,
your life.
To live every day
informed,
prepared,
inspired.
THE WALL STREET JOURNAL.
live in the know

SHOW WHAT YOU KNOW

Visual Literacy
The Wall Street Journal publishes business, economic, and financial news along with information about technology, personal finance, and consumer trends. ***How could you use information from a news provider to help inform a marketing research project?***

650 | Unit 9 · Marketing Information Management

651

ENGAGE

Introduce the Unit

Unit 9 explores the function of marketing information management, including marketing research and the marketing research process.

Chapter 28 discusses the process of marketing research done through systematic gathering, recording, and analysis of data to make sound marketing decisions.

Chapter 29 examines the five steps of conducting marketing research: problem definition, obtaining data, data analysis, recommending solutions, and implementing findings.

Build Background

Ask students why marketing information is essential to business success. Discuss their ideas in class. Answers will vary but may note that marketing information systems can help businesses predict and solve the problems they face. Ask students: ***What are some methods that businesses use to collect marketing information about their products and customers?*** Marketing information can be collected from various sources, including research studies, surveys, focus groups, interviews, online forms, ratings, observation, etc.

Visual Literacy

Photo Caption Answer Read the copy on the ad to students. Then read the photo caption and the photo caption question to students: ***How could you use information from a news provider to help inform a marketing research project?*** Answers will vary. Accept all reasonable answers. Sample answer: News providers frequently publish information that could be used to inform a market research project. For example, if you were researching the automotive industry for a client, it would be in your interest to stay abreast of all news related to that industry. Many news sources publish articles about the automobile industry. Ask students to evaluate the visual components of the advertisement. Ask volunteers to explain how the visual aspects of the advertisement complement the text of the advertisement. The demographic shown in the ad is a businessman who subscribes to The Wall Street Journal. Businesspeople have long been the target market for this newspaper. The headline "What do I need to know today" and the slogan "live in the know" each use the word ***know,*** impressing that you can know what you need to know each day and live in the know if you read this newspaper. The copy of the ad implies that the being in the know will help you to make the right decisions every day.

ENGAGE

Marketing Internship Project Preview

Read students the Marketing Internship Project Essential Question: ***How can marketing research help improve a company's products for its target market?*** Because students are just starting to learn about marketing research, they will likely not know the specific answer to this question, which is to develop an effective marketing research study. However, students should know that getting feedback on products from customers or potential customers can provide valuable information that a company can use to make product improvements. Explain to students that they will learn how companies plan and conduct marketing research while studying this unit. Tell students that when they are finished studying this unit, they will ask questions to find answers about developing a marketing research study for a cell phone company. As they study each chapter in the unit, they can prepare for the Unit Project by thinking of various mobile phone companies and mobile phone features.

Marketing Internship Project Resources Send students to the Online Learning Center to watch a video and download a worksheet activity related to the topic of the Unit Project.

Read the American Marketing Association quote to students:

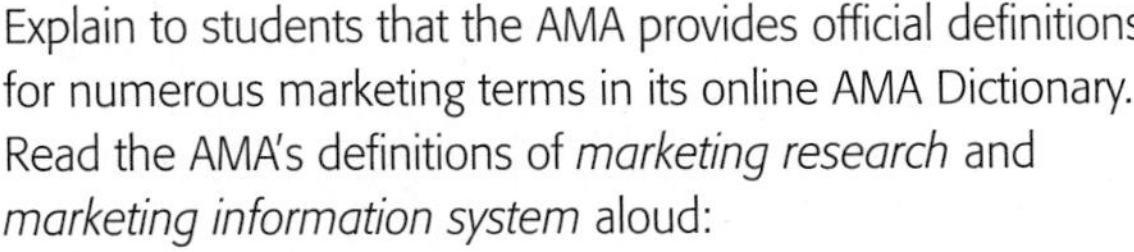

> "Marketing research links the consumer, customer, and public to the marketer through information."

Explain to students that the AMA provides official definitions for numerous marketing terms in its online AMA Dictionary. Read the AMA's definitions of *marketing research* and *marketing information system* aloud:

Market Research The systematic gathering, recording, and analyzing of data for a target market.

Marketing Information System A set of procedures and for the planned collection and analysis of information to make marketing decisions.

Ask students: ***What is the difference between market research and a marketing information system?*** Marketing research yields information that builds a bridge connecting marketers with consumers. A marketing information system is the overall process by which the marketing research is gathered and analyzed in order to inform marketing decisions.

MARKETING CORE FUNCTIONS IN THIS UNIT

Point out to students that Chapters 28 and 29 will touch on two of the seven marketing core functions. Describe each of these marketing functions to students to prepare them to start studying this unit.

Marketing Information Management involves gathering, storing, and analyzing information about customers, trends, and competing products.

Market Planning involves understanding the concepts and strategies used to develop and target specific marketing strategies to a select audience.

MARKETING RESEARCH
PROJECT WORKBOOK

The purpose of the Marketing Research Project Workbook is to provide a step-by-step approach for students to conduct their own marketing research study. Each chapter is devoted to key elements in the research process. Each chapter builds upon the previous chapters, and by the end of the book, students will have completed an in-depth marketing research study, complete with rationale for all decisions, a report of the findings and conclusions, recommendations based on the original research problem and study objectives, and an annotated bibliography.

Marketing Research Project Workbook Send students to the Online Learning Center to download the Marketing Research Project Workbook. A Teacher Manual is also available on the Teacher Center of the Online Learning Center.

marketing research

SHOW WHAT YOU KNOW

Visual Literacy Marketing research is the process of obtaining information needed to make effective marketing decisions. Marketers use this information to create business plans, solve problems, and make decisions about products. ***What kinds of business decisions do you think marketers make as a result of conducting marketing research?***

Discovery Project

The Purpose of Marketing Research

Essential Question How can research be used to gain data about marketing opportunities?

Project Goal

You and a classmate are employed to perform marketing research for a new electronic product that your team identifies. Your team has been asked to conduct a research project to gain information about the potential market for the product. You have been asked to provide a written report to management about the target market for the product. You will also report on some marketing information systems and methods used in marketing research.

Ask Yourself...

- What is your product, who uses your product, and what competitive products currently exist?
- Where will your potential customers purchase the product?
- What types of media (print, broadcast, electronic) do your potential customers use?
- How will you organize your written report?

Synthesize and Present Research Synthesize your research by reporting about the target market for the product and some marketing information systems and methods used in marketing research.

glencoe.com

Activity
Get a worksheet activity about marketing research.

Evaluate
Download a rubric you can use to evaluate your project.

DECA Connection

DECA Event Role Play
Concepts in this chapter are related to DECA competitive events that involve either an interview or role play.

Performance Indicators The performance indicators represent key skills and knowledge. Your key to success in DECA competitive events is relating them to concepts in this chapter.

- Explain the nature of marketing research.
- Explain the nature of marketing research problems/issues.
- Assess information needs.
- Explain the nature of marketing research in a marketing information management system.
- Prepare simple written reports.

DECA Prep
Role Play Practice role-playing with the DECA Connection competitive-event activity at the end of this chapter. More information on DECA events can be found on DECA's Web site.

ENGAGE

Visual Literacy

Read the chapter opener photo caption question to students: ***What kinds of business decisions do you think marketers make as a result of conducting marketing research?*** Marketing research is used to gather information to help make decisions about customer preferences, product features, market size and potential, competitive products, buying cycles, and public perceptions of companies. Then ask these guiding questions.

Guiding Questions

Identify What are the four Ps of the marketing mix?	product, place, price, and promotion
Predict How might marketing research benefit from each of the four Ps?	product—test product features; place—determine buying cycles, understand how the company is perceived by the public; price—determine market size and potential; promotion—determine buying cycles

Discovery Project

The Purpose of Marketing Research Ask students if they have ever participated in a market research survey and the types of questions they were asked. Then ask students the Discovery Project Essential Question: ***How can research be used to gain data about marketing opportunities?*** It can be used to obtain information about the preferences, opinions, habits, trends, and plans of current and potential customers. Marketers use that information to plan marketing strategies.

 **glencoe.com** 

Discovery Project Resources Send students to the Online Learning Center to download a rubric to evaluate their projects.

ENGAGE

Introduce the Chapter

Chapter 28 explains the purpose of marketing research and identifies ways to gathering information and methods of conducting research. These main concepts are introduced and discussed:

- Defining marketing research
- The importance of marketing research
- Users of marketing research
- Marketing information systems
- Technology and marketing research
- Attitude research
- Market intelligence
- Media research
- Product research
- Trends in marketing research
- Limitations of marketing research

Discussion Starter

Gathering Information Discuss with students the factors that influence their purchasing decisions. Ask: ***How would the companies that make the products you buy benefit from understanding the reasons behind your purchasing decisions?*** Students might suggest that if the companies knew why they purchased the products, they might make changes to the product, place, price, or promotion to gain more customers. Ask: ***What factors are important for companies to know?*** With regard to customers, companies need to know consumers' attitudes and preferences and how the company is perceived by customers. Tell students that in this chapter they will learn how companies compile and use such information in marketing their products and services.

DECA Connection

Discuss the performance indicators listed in the DECA Connection feature. Explain to students that performance indicators tell them how to demonstrate their acquired skills and knowledge through individual or team competitive events.

 **glencoe.com** 

Competitive Events Workbook For more DECA Role Plays, send students to the Online Learning Center to download the Competitive Events Workbook.

PROGRAM RESOURCE ORGANIZER

PRINT RESOURCES

- **Student Edition**
- **Teacher Edition**
- **Student Activity Workbook with Academic Integration** includes worksheets and activities correlated to the text.
- **Mathematics for Marketing Workbook** provides math activities for every unit in the text.

TECHNOLOGY TOOLBOX

- **Connect**
- **ConnectPlus**
- **ExamView Assessment Suite** is a comprehensive solution for creating, administering, and scoring tests.

 **glencoe.com** 

Online Learning Center provides a variety of resources to enrich and enhance learning.

SECTION, CHAPTER, AND UNIT RESOURCES

- **Graphic Organizers** for organizing text concepts visually.
- **Digital Nation Activities** and **Green Marketer Activities** extend learning beyond the text features.
- **Career Chatroom Career Profiles** allow students to explore different marketing occupations in depth.
- **After You Read Answer Keys** for students to check their answers.
- **Discovery Project Rubrics** and **Marketing Internship Project Rubrics** for students to evaluate their projects.

PROGRAM RESOURCES

- **Student Activity Workbook with Academic Integration Teacher Annotated Edition** includes annotated answers for the activities and worksheets.
- **Marketing Research Project Workbook** provides a step-by-step approach for students to complete their own marketing research studies.
- **School-to-Career Activity Workbook** helps students relate their class work to on-the-job experience and involves work-site analysis and working with mentors.
- **Competitive Events Workbook** helps prepare students for state and national marketing education competitions.
- **Inclusion in the Marketing Education Classroom** provides teaching resources for working with students with special needs.
- **PowerPoint Presentations** provides visual teaching aids and assessments for this chapter.

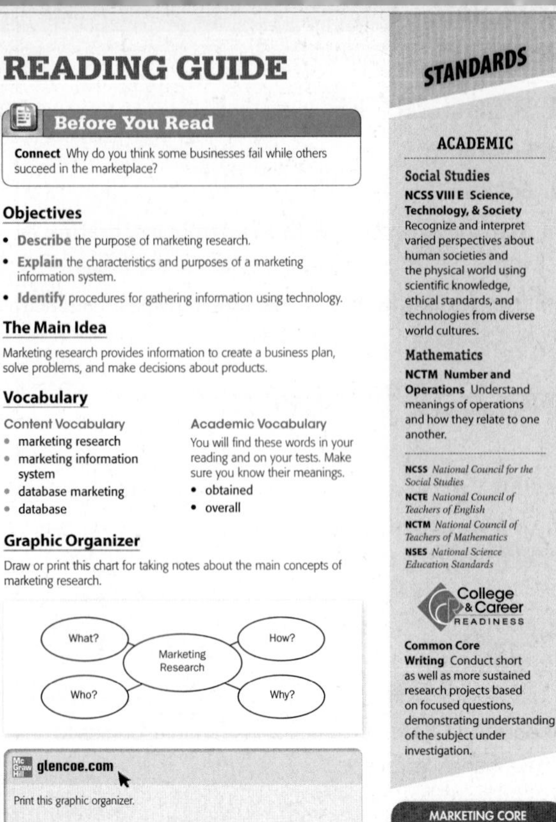

READING GUIDE

Before You Read

Connect Why do you think some businesses fail while others succeed in the marketplace?

Objectives

- **Describe** the purpose of marketing research.
- **Explain** the characteristics and purposes of a marketing information system.
- **Identify** procedures for gathering information using technology.

The Main Idea

Marketing research provides information to create a business plan, solve problems, and make decisions about products.

Vocabulary

Content Vocabulary
- marketing research
- marketing information system
- database marketing
- database

Academic Vocabulary

You will find these words in your reading and on your tests. Make sure you know their meanings.
- obtained
- overall

Graphic Organizer

Draw or print this chart for taking notes about the main concepts of marketing research.

What? How? Marketing Research Who? Why?

glencoe.com

Print this graphic organizer.

STANDARDS

ACADEMIC

Social Studies

NCSS VIII E Science, Technology, & Society Recognize and interpret varied perspectives about human societies and the physical world using scientific knowledge, ethical standards, and technologies from diverse world cultures.

Mathematics

NCTM Number and Operations Understand meanings of operations and how they relate to one another.

NCSS *National Council for the Social Studies*
NCTE *National Council of Teachers of English*
NCTM *National Council of Teachers of Mathematics*
NSES *National Science Education Standards*

College & Career READINESS

Common Core

Writing Conduct short as well as more sustained research projects based on focused questions, demonstrating understanding of the subject under investigation.

MARKETING CORE FUNCTION

Marketing Information Management

Section 28.1 Marketing Information

DEFINING MARKETING RESEARCH

A major health and beauty manufacturer marketed its brand of toothpaste in overseas markets. The brand was advertised in Southeast Asia by saying that "it whitens teeth." However, sales were disappointingly low. What went wrong?

Even though the product had a global focus, it did not have global appeal, at least not in Southeast Asia. Careful marketing research would have revealed that, as a cultural tradition, much of the local population chews betel nuts, which blacken teeth. Few Southeast Asians purchased the product.

> "Success in business relies on effective marketing research."

Marketing research involves the process and methods used to gather information, analyze it, and report findings related to marketing goods and services. Businesses use marketing research to identify marketing opportunities, solve marketing problems, implement marketing plans, and monitor marketing performance.

Marketing research can apply to any aspect of marketing. Coca-Cola®, a food-and-beverage manufacturer, might research the potential sales and market for a new product line of fruit drinks. Wells Fargo®, a bank, might conduct customer satisfaction research on the quality of its mortgage lending service.

Market research and marketing research are often confused. *Market* research is a narrow concept that deals specifically with the gathering of information about a market's size and trends. *Marketing* research is a broader concept that includes a wider range of activities. While it may involve market research, marketing research is a more general, systematic process that can be applied to a variety of marketing issues. Marketing research includes areas such as research into new products, and new methods of distribution, such as through the Internet.

The main purpose of marketing research is to obtain information. Researchers need to know about the preferences, opinions, habits, trends, and plans of current and potential customers. This information helps marketers in many ways. Before developing a product, marketers conduct research to determine the product that customers want. The research minimizes potential losses when introducing the new product. Consumers accept only one out of every ten new products introduced into the marketplace. So, it is important to gain information about consumer likes and dislikes.

Marketing research is used by companies to do the following:

- Determine consumers' attitudes and preferences.
- Test product features.
- Determine market size and growth potential.
- Learn about competitive products.
- Determine buying cycles.
- Understand how the company is perceived by the public.

As You Read

Analyze Compare and contrast the terms *market research* and *marketing research.*

ENGAGE

Anticipation Activity

Improving Student Achievement Divide the class into small groups. Have each group choose two products–one that is successful and one that failed in the marketplace (students can do an online search for "failed products"). Have groups brainstorm how marketing research might have contributed to the success and failure of the products. As a class, have students consider how consumers' attitudes and preferences might have been taken into consideration regarding the failed products.

Objectives

- **Describe** the purpose of marketing research. gathering and analyzing information and reporting findings related to marketing goods and services
- **Explain** the characteristics and purposes of a marketing information system. generates, stores, analyzes, and distributes information for use in marketing and other business decisions
- **Identify** procedures for gathering information using technology. Technology is used to generate, store, analyze, and distribute marketing information.

Graphic Organizer

Marketing Research

What?
- Customer profile data
- Company results
- Competitive results
- Government data

How?
- Marketing information systems
- Database marketing

Who?
- Company's staff, in-house research departments
- Outside research companies
- Trade associates
- Nonprofit organizations

Why?
- Determine consumer's attitudes and preferences
- Determine market size and growth potential
- Learn about competition
- Understand a company's place in the market

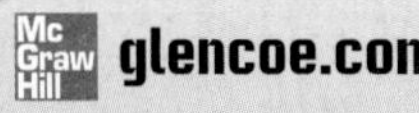

glencoe.com

Graphic Organizer Send students to the Online Learning Center to print this graphic organizer.

EXPLORE

Before You Read

Ask students the Before You Read question: ***Why do you think some businesses fail while others succeed in the marketplace?*** A business may fail because of poor marketing research, bad location, underfinancing, poor customer service, and so on. Successful businesses have good products, good customer service, good marketing research, and so on.

Preteaching Vocabulary

Have students go to the Online Learning Center at glencoe.com for the Chapter 28 Preteaching Vocabulary games.

Content Vocabulary

Have students write a paragraph explaining how the vocabulary terms are related. Sample: Marketing research is the process and methods used to gather and analyze information and report findings on marketing goods and services. A marketing information system is a set of procedures that generates, stores, analyzes, and distributes information for making marketing and other business decisions. Database marketing designs, creates, and manages customer lists. A database collects data generated by the marketing information system.

Academic Vocabulary

Obtained—Synonyms Display the vocabulary term *obtained* and ask students to provide synonyms for the root word *obtain*. get, find, gain, take, acquire Display their answers for the rest of the class. Ask volunteers to use the term in original sentences.

Overall—Usage Display the vocabulary term *overall* and ask volunteers to define it. general, inclusive, total, whole, complete; a one-piece garment worn to protect clothing from dirt or wear Read the sentence from the text that contains the term *overall*: ***Most marketing information systems rely heavily on data about current customers, overall product sales reports, and inventory levels.*** Ask students to identify the best definition for this use of *overall*. complete or total

PROFESSIONAL DEVELOPMENT MINI CLIP

ELL: Providing Clear Directions
Go to the Online Learning Center to view a video clip in which a teacher provides clear written directions for an assignment and checks for student understanding.

Marketing Information

DEFINING MARKETING RESEARCH

Ask these questions to focus the discussion on marketing research.

Guiding Questions

Identify Why do companies use marketing research?	determine consumers' attitudes and preferences; test product features; determine market size and growth potential; learn about competitive products; determine buying cycles; understand how the company is perceived by the public
Analyze What do companies need to know about their customers?	They need to know the preferences, opinions, habits, trends, and plans of current and potential customers.

As You Read

Read students the As You Read question: ***Compare and contrast the terms* market *and* marketing research.** *Market* represents the people who share similar needs and wants and are capable of buying products. *Marketing research* represents the process and methods used to gather information, analyze it, and report findings related to marketing goods and services to a particular market.

Expert Advice

Read the quote to students:

> **"Success in business relies on effective marketing research."**

Ask students: ***Do you think all existing businesses conducted marketing research before starting the business? Why or why not?*** Possible answers: Yes, because they have been successful and are still in business. No, because their business isn't doing well or it already has closed.

Career Chatroom

Denise Gavilan
Principal
Gavilan Marketing & PR

What do you do at work?

My firm provides associations, nonprofits, and corporations with marketing, communications, and public relations services. I develop multi-faceted campaigns that utilize direct mail, e-mail, Web sites, advertising, public relations, and social media to disseminate messages to target audiences. I also write message points and sales copy to support each campaign, manage timelines and budgets, work with clients to identify and research target audiences, work with graphic designers to create print materials and online information.

What is your key to success?

Providing sound, research-based advice to clients that will help drive the decision making for the campaigns. Also being creative in the approach and realistic in projecting outcomes. Be honest, always, and proofread, proofread, proofread!

What skills are most important to you?

Strategic planning skills are critical. This means having the ability to think through every aspect of a marketing and communications campaign to see how all elements work together.

glencoe.com

Read more about this career and get a Career Exploration Activity.

WHY IS MARKETING RESEARCH IMPORTANT?

Businesses that do not pay attention to different markets and to what consumers are buying and why are likely to make costly mistakes. Because of the high failure rate of new products, marketing research can make or break a business plan.

The information **obtained** from research helps businesses increase sales and profits. Research answers questions about what products to produce, at what price to sell the products, who will buy the products, and how to promote the products.

Research also helps businesses solve marketing problems and gauge the potential of new product ideas. For example, Stouffer's® spent almost 13 years doing marketing research and development before starting its Lean Cuisine™ product line. Stouffer's studied consumers' interest in health and dieting. They conducted consumer panels to find out what dieters liked and disliked about diet meals. Using the information, the company developed its product, tested its package design, and held pilot sales of the product in several large cities before national distribution. The product was a tremendous success, with more than $125 million in sales after the first year of national distribution.

Research also helps a company keep track of what is happening with its current markets. Through research, a company can determine its major competitors, what its competitors are offering, which products consumers prefer, and if customers are satisfied with those products.

DETERMINING THE VALUE OF INFORMATION

Information can be useful, but what determines its real value to a business? The value of information is generally determined by the following:

- A company's ability and willingness to act on the information.
- The accuracy of the information.
- The level of uncertainty that would exist without the information.
- The amount of variation in the possible results.
- The level of risk consumers are willing to take on a new product or service.
- The reaction of competitors to any decision improved by the information.
- The cost of the information in terms of time and money.

WHO USES MARKETING RESEARCH?

Small businesses usually do not have separate research specialists or departments. There, marketing research is done informally by the owners, managers, and employees. A small business would likely find large-scale marketing research too costly. Instead they may depend on friends, family, or their customers to point out what is working and what is not. However, small businesses have access to the ever-growing amount of information available on the Internet.

If it is in their budget, some businesses may hire outside service providers who specialize in marketing research. Sometimes actual costs and findings are shared by a number of companies in large syndicated research studies. Larger companies often have in-house research departments and marketing personnel to plan and conduct marketing research. There are more than 2,000 research companies in the U.S. Full-service companies design and conduct surveys, tabulate and analyze data, and prepare reports.

Interviewing-services companies collect data through interviews. Some interviewing companies specialize in multilingual survey services.

An initial search online will reveal a seemingly endless variety of research collection tactics. For example, a restaurant may offer a free appetizer to customers who complete a telephone or online survey about their dining experience. You may have noticed an increasing number of pop-up surveys on the Web sites you visit.

Trade associations representing various manufacturers, wholesalers, and retailers conduct marketing research. For example, industry trade associations, such as the National Retail Federation, collect industry data to help their members understand the markets for their products. Nonprofit organizations, such as hospitals, conduct patient satisfaction surveys to improve on programs and services. State and federal government agencies conduct research to gather information on a variety of issues and concerns.

The National Retail Federation conducts an annual *Holiday Consumer Intentions and Actions* survey. ***Why do national associations conduct marketing research surveys?***

656 | Unit 9 · Marketing Information Management

Chapter 28 · Marketing Research | 657

EXPLAIN

Career Chatroom 

Use these questions to focus the discussion on this Career Chatroom feature.

Guiding Questions

Describe How is marketing research used?	to provide research-based advice; to drive client decision making
Explain Why is strategic planning important?	prices or product information in ads may be incorrect

 **glencoe.com** 

Career Explorations Send students to the Online Learning Center to read more about this career and to get a Career Exploration Activity.

WHY IS MARKETING RESEARCH IMPORTANT?

Ask students if they have ever had to write a paper that required them to do research. Ask: ***Why was the research important?*** to learn as much as possible about the topic; to help make decisions about what information to include and what could be left out; to cross-check resources to verify accuracy Ask these guiding questions about marketing research.

Guiding Questions

Explain Why is the information obtained from research important?	It helps businesses increase sales and profits.
Determine Why would a business analyze the cost of research information to determine its value?	If the information is too costly in terms of time and/or money, it would not benefit the company to use the information.

ELABORATE

WHO USES MARKETING RESEARCH?

Ask students if they have ever participated in a survey. Ask: ***How was the survey conducted?*** by telephone; in person in front of a store; online Ask: ***What do you think the survey information was used for?*** to improve customer service; to get ideas for new products Then ask these guiding questions about the uses of marketing research.

Guiding Questions

Identify What services do full-service research companies provide?	design and conduct surveys, tabulate and analyze data, and prepare reports
Analyze Why would a restaurant offer a free appetizer or dessert in exchange for completing a survey?	The free appetizer or dessert serves as a reward for completing the survey. Without such an incentive, customers may not even consider the restaurant's survey request..
Synthesize When might a business use information collected by a trade association?	when the information collected might be better than what the business could collect on its own.

Critical Thinking

Ask students if they have ever tried a new product and disliked it. Ask them to brainstorm reasons the company thought their product would be successful. Display their answers for the class. Answers may include: they may have tested it in limited markets; it may be based on a successful product; it might be similar to a competitor's product. Ask: ***Do you think thorough marketing research might have provided the company with the information it needed to determine whether to introduce the product? Why or why not?*** Students may suggest that even thorough marketing research is not a guarantee that a product will be successful, but it is a step toward knowing how the product might do in the marketplace.

VIRTUAL BUSINESS

MARKET RESEARCH

Introduce students to the concept of market research using Knowledge Matters' Virtual Business Retailing visual simulation, Market Research. In this simulation, students learn how to collect market information and how to use the information to make their business more successful.

Visual Literacy

The Most Popular Toys Caption Answer Read the caption question to students: ***Why do national associations conduct marketing research surveys?*** Possible answers: The information they collect can be beneficial to small businesses that do not have budgets to conduct marketing research; to improve on programs and services; and to increase the profits of their member companies.

Mini Projects

Enrichment

Using Marketing Research Ask the class to brainstorm types of organizations other than individual companies that would use marketing research. nonprofit organizations, religious organizations, schools, community organizations, hospitals, and so on Then have students focus on marketing research for their own school. Ask: ***What kinds of information might the school collect?*** noise and traffic survey among local residents; ways to communicate with parents; needs of teachers and students; and so on Have student groups create a survey for one of the target groups—students, parents, family members, local residents, teachers, other staff. Have groups share their surveys and discuss how each target groups' opinions could help the school function better and which target group's opinions should be most important.

Define Marketing Research Ask students to brainstorm new product ideas. Tell them they have one year before the launch of their new product. Ask: ***Which factors must be researched before you begin product development?*** target market; competing products; feasibility; and so on Ask: ***What information must be collected from consumers?*** Students may suggest: age, income level, ethnic background, occupation, attitudes, lifestyle, and geographic residence. As a class, compile the list of questions and rank them in order of importance.

MARKETING INFORMATION SYSTEMS

The data collected in marketing research must be sorted and stored so that the results can be put to good use. Many businesses have sophisticated marketing information systems. These systems are used to organize, collect, and store marketing research data for future decisions. A **marketing information system** is a set of procedures and methods that regularly generates, stores, analyzes, and distributes information for making marketing and other business decisions. Timely marketing information provides a basis for decisions about product development or improvement, pricing, packaging, distribution, media selection, and promotion.

Most marketing information systems rely heavily on data about current customers, **overall** product sales reports, and inventory levels. Marketers use marketing information systems to design advertising campaigns, develop promotional plans, and sell directly to customers. (See **Figure 28.1**.) Data that should be part of a marketing information system include the following:

- Customer profile data, such as the results of previous marketing studies regarding buying behavior, shopping patterns, customer demographics, and lifestyles research.
- Company records, such as sales results, expenses, supplier data, and production schedules.
- Competitors' records, such as their prices, products, and market share.
- Government data, such as price trends, new regulations and laws, and economic projections.
- Marketing research reports that are produced and sold by research firm.

DATABASE MARKETING

Information technologies have made the collection and analysis of data for decision making much easier. **Database marketing**, or customer relationship management (CRM), is a process of designing, creating, and managing customer lists. These customer lists contain information about individuals' characteristics and transactions with a business.

Customer lists are developed from customer touch points, such as face-to-face sales, direct-mail responses, telephone or e-mail purchases, service requests, or Web-site visits. Marketing lists can also be obtained through third-party companies that specialize in selling databases of names and addresses to specific markets. Once a customer list is developed, marketers can use it for locating, selecting, and targeting customers with special programs and services.

CONSUMER DATABASES

Information about consumers and their buying habits are stored in computer databases. A **database** is simply a collection of related information about a specific topic. Typical sources from which the information is obtained are charity donation forms, application forms for any free product or contest, product warranty cards, subscription forms, and credit application forms.

REI®, an outdoor recreational products retailer, has a database of people to whom it sends its catalogs. American Express® maintains a database of its card members and their addresses. This database also includes what they buy, where they buy it, where they dine out, and how much money they spend. The company uses the information to send their card members special, customized offers on products, hotels, restaurants, and travel.

Reading Check

Recall What are some marketing information systems?

FIGURE 28.1 Obtaining Market Research Data

Public and private organizations provide valuable information for exploring the market potential for products and services. ***Why is the data found in this chart, for example, important for marketing information systems?***

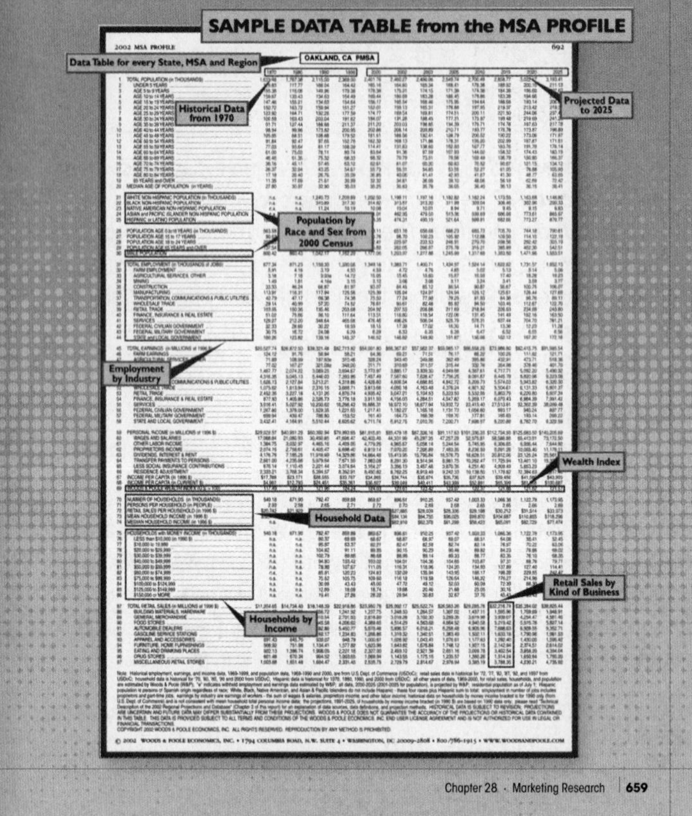

EXPLAIN

MARKETING INFORMATION SYSTEMS

Ask these guiding questions about marketing information systems.

Guiding Questions

Define What is database marketing?	a process of designing, creating, and managing customer lists
Identify What data should be included in a marketing information system?	customer profile data, company records, competitor's records, government data, research reports
Analyze What are some uses for a customer list?	locating, selecting, and targeting customers with special programs

Reading Check Answer

Ask the question: ***What are some marketing information systems?*** A marketing information system is a set of procedures and methods that generates, stores, analyzes, and distributes information for use in marketing and other business decisions.

Mini Project

Enrichment

Research Products Have students select a product currently on the market that they believe has room for improvement. Then have them research the product and write a one-page report outlining a marketing research plan to improve the product's sales. Have students share their reports with the class. Reports will vary but should focus on one topic, and all sentences in the paragraph should support that topic.

ELABORATE

Visual Literacy

Figure 28.1 Caption Answer Read the caption question to students: ***Why is the data found in this chart, for example, important for marketing information systems?*** The data in this chart are important to companies for the purpose of making marketing and other business decisions. Then ask these guiding questions to focus a discussion on obtaining market research data.

Guiding Questions

List What are the customer touch points, or sources, from which customer lists are developed?	face-to-face sales, direct-mail responses, telephone or e-mail purchases, service requests, Web site visits
Identify What kinds of data are presented in this table?	historical data, projected data, population by race and sex, employment by industry, household data, households by income, wealth index, retail sales
Predict How might the information in this table be used to help market products?	Information on population by race and sex might be used when marketing products that can be specific to gender, such as personal grooming products.

Critical Thinking

Share with students the following scenario: Results You'll Love Foods has hired the marketing firm Jaime works for to conduct a survey to learn what 20- to 30-year-old women want in a nutrition bar. The research team has written a 20-minute survey and sent Jaime and his coworker, Elisa, to the mall to interview young women. When Jaime tells shoppers how long the survey will take, they don't want to participate. Elisa doesn't seem to be having trouble getting people to participate in the survey during their lunch break, so Jaime asks how she does it. Elisa tells Jaime that she tells people the survey will take only five minutes. When the people realize they have already spent ten minutes with the survey, she tells them they are almost finished. Ask students: ***Do you think Elisa's behavior is ethical? Why or why not?*** Students should realize that intentionally misleading people is unethical. Tell students that when Jaime and Elisa return to the office, Jaime's survey results will be very different from Elisa's results. Ask: ***How should Jaime handle this?*** Students may suggest that Jaime tell his supervisor that Elisa misled people to get them to participate in the survey, or they might recommend that Jaime wait for his supervisor to ask why Elisa did better than he did.

Graphic Organizer

Display this diagram. Ask students to provide details for each type of data. Possible answers:

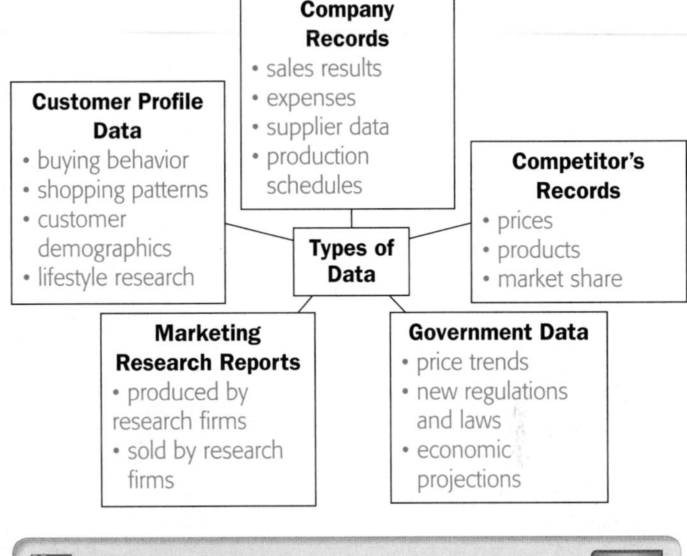

glencoe.com iWB

Graphic Organizer Send students to the Online Learning Center to print this graphic organizer.

Mini Project

Extension

Discuss Database Marketing Lead a discussion about supermarket rewards cards as an example of database marketing. Ask students: ***What types of information may be collected from supermarket rewards cards?*** Answers may include household demographics, lifestyle, and purchasing behavior. Then ask: ***How many of you use supermarket rewards cards or know someone who does?*** Students may or may not be familiar with the cards. For those who are familiar with the cards ask: ***Did you know that the supermarket was collecting this information when you signed up for the card?*** Then ask: ***Does knowing that your purchases are being tracked make you more or less likely to use the card?*** Answers will vary depending on students' feelings.

USING TECHNOLOGY TO GATHER INFORMATION

Specialized equipment, loyalty programs, and computer software are increasingly used to gather database information. Barcode scanners at point-of-sale terminals provide information on sold merchandise and existing inventory levels.

CUSTOMER LOYALTY PROGRAMS

Many businesses create special loyalty programs to assist in data collection by providing "valued customer cards" to customers.

A loyalty program offers discounts and other rewards to encourage customers to shop at a particular retailer. This concept benefits both the retailer and the customer. Customers who participate in loyalty programs can save money, and as a result, they are likely to return to the same retailer. Examples include Staples® *Teacher* and Ace® *Hardware Reward* programs. Customers who choose to enroll in such programs fill out an application that generally requires a minimal amount of identifying or demographic data, such as their name and address. In return, the customer is given a loyalty program card.

The cards are visually similar to credit or debit cards. Loyalty cards may also be called rewards cards, points cards, advantage cards, or club cards. Cards usually have a barcode or magnetic stripe for easy scanning. Small key ring cards are often used for convenience and easy access. Cardholders are typically entitled to either a discount on the current purchase, or an allowance of points that can be used for future purchases. The business in turn collects data on household demographics, lifestyles, and purchase behavior.

Loyalty The first loyalty card program was started by the Safeway® supermarket chain in 1998 to track customer purchase behavior.

COMPUTER SOFTWARE

Existing company software can track activity online and combine that information with existing customer databases.

COOKIES

Online retailers may automatically upload small data files called "cookies" to customers' computers. Cookies keep track of how often and how much time a person spends at a Web site or views an ad. Businesses use this type of data to target an audience with ads for products. The ads can then appear at certain times and in specific geographical locations.

DATA-MINING SOFWARE

Data-mining software can be purchased from specialized companies to analyze existing and external business databases. For example, sales of a product during a particular period can be compared with sales when the product is moved or displayed in a different store location. Data-mining software also collects information from other customer databases to match and identify patterns that help businesses promote their products or advertise them in more timely or effective ways.

CONSUMER PRIVACY

Privacy is a central element of the Federal Trade Commission's (FTC) consumer protection mission. In recent years, advances in computer technology have changed the way information is collected. Technology has helped make it possible for detailed information about people to be compiled and shared with greater ease and cost effectiveness than ever before. This provides benefits for society as a whole and for individual consumers as well. For example, it is easier for law enforcement to track down criminals and for banks to prevent fraud. Consumers can learn about new products and services, which allows them to make better-informed purchasing decisions.

As personal information becomes more accessible, it is important that everyone—companies, associations, government agencies, and consumers—take precautions to protect against the misuse of personal information. Another part of the FTC's mission is to educate consumers and businesses about the importance of personal information privacy, including the security of personal information. Under the FTC Act, the Commission guards against unfairness and deception by enforcing companies' privacy promises about how they collect, use, and secure consumers' personal information.

Many companies that collect information about their customers sell the information to others. New homeowners may find their mailboxes are loaded with offers from landscapers and furniture stores. This is likely because the mortgage companies sold the homeowners' information to local businesses that specialize in home and garden services. This exchange of information among businesses has led to complaints of invasion of privacy.

Other businesses offer clients the choice of being added to mailing lists. Some businesses, such as Yahoo!®, go a step further and have strict bans on selling data from customer registration lists. The government, however, has regulations regarding protecting the privacy of consumers. For example, banks and hospitals offer detailed privacy statements that ensure the protection of clients' personal information. Marketers often defend the need to gather information about customers and their buying habits by stating that this data helps improve customer service.

After You Read **Section 28.1**

Review Key Concepts

1. **Explain** why marketing research is important.
2. **Identify** what organizations conduct marketing research.
3. **Describe** a customer database.

Practice Academics

Social Studies

4. Conduct research to acquire information about the concept of database marketing. Write a one-page paper on how database marketing improves customer relationships.

NCSS VIII E Science, Technology, & Society Recognize and interpret varied perspectives about human societies and the physical world using scientific knowledge, ethical standards, and technologies from diverse world cultures.

Mathematics

5. You work for a medical supplies company that spends $38,000 annually for researching new product ideas. $5,700 of that money was spent researching a new tool for surgery. What percentage of the overall research dollars does this represent?

Math Concept **Number and Operations: Percents** A percent is a ratio that compares values to 100. A percent can also be thought of as a part of a whole. When figuring what percentage a value is of another value, divide the part by the whole. This gives the decimal equivalent of the percent.

NCTM Number and Operations Understand meanings of operations and how they relate to one another.

Starting Hints To solve this problem, divide $5,700 by the total amount spent on researching new product ideas to get the decimal equivalent of the percent. Multiply the decimal by 100 to get the percent it represents.

For help, go to the **Math Skills Handbook** located at the back of this book.

glencoe.com

Check your answers.

ELABORATE

Loyalty Have students ask loyalty card holders whether information gathered through these programs influences their use of the card.

Mini Project

Differentiated Instruction

Verbal/Linguistic Learners Have students research the concept of customer relationship management (CRM). Then have them write a paper on the benefits and strategies of business-to-consumer relationships.

USING TECHNOLOGY TO GATHER INFORMATION

Ask these guiding questions to focus the discussion about technology and information gathering.

Guiding Questions

Identify What are cookies and what is their purpose?	small data files uploaded by online retailers, which allow the retailers to keep track of how often and how much time a person spends at a Web site or views an ad.
Critique Do you think it is ethical for companies to collect personal information about their customers and to sell that information to others? Explain your answer.	Students' opinions will vary but should be backed up by sound reasoning and examples, if possible.

EVALUATE

Graphic Organizer

Display this outline framework. Compile student answers and add them to the framework. Possible answers:

Using Technology to Gather Information

I. Customer Loyalty Programs
  A. Rewards customers
  B. Encourages loyal buying behavior

II. Computer Software
  A. Cookies
  1. Small data files uploaded to customer's computers by online retailers
  2. Track how often and how much time a person spends at a Web site or views an ad
  B. Data-mining software
  1. Analyzes existing and external databases
  2. Collects information from other customer databases to match and identify patterns of customer behavior

III. Consumer Privacy
  A. Technology allows for ease of gathering and sharing personal information
  1. Advantages
  a. Easier to track down criminals and prevent bank fraud
  b. Consumers can learn about new products and services
  2. Disadvantages
  a. Misuse of personal information

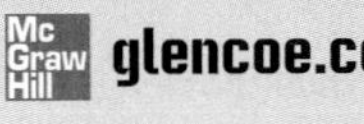

glencoe.com iWB

Graphic Organizer Send students to the Online Learning Center to print this graphic organizer.

After You Read Section 28.1

Review Key Concepts

1. Marketing research is important because it can be used to identify marketing opportunities, solve marketing problems, implement marketing plans, and monitor marketing performance.
2. Individual businesses, various manufacturers, wholesalers, retailers, departments within local, state, and federal governments, and nonprofit organizations all conduct marketing research.
3. Information about consumers and their buying habits are stored in customer databases.

Practice Academics

Social Studies

4. Accept all reasonable and complete responses that use proper grammar, mechanics, and are of proper length. The students must demonstrate an understanding of database marketing and be able to identify several benefits and strategies to achieve effective CRM.

Mathematics

5. 15% ($5,700 ÷ $38,000).

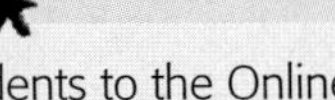

glencoe.com

Answer Key Send students to the Online Learning Center to check their answers.

READING GUIDE

Before You Read

Predict What would happen if marketing research was not used in product development?

Objectives

- **Identify** the methods of conducting marketing research.
- **Discuss** trends and limitations in marketing research.

The Main Idea

Different types of marketing research improve a business's ability to solve problems and successfully market products and services.

Vocabulary

Content Vocabulary

- quantitative research
- qualitative research
- attitude research
- market intelligence
- media research
- product research

Academic Vocabulary

You will find these words in your reading and on your tests. Make sure you know their meanings.

- anticipate
- associated

Graphic Organizer

Draw or print this chart to note the differences between quantitative research and qualitative research.

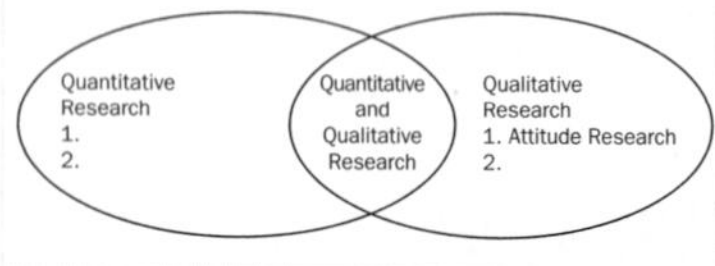

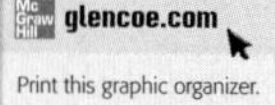

Print this graphic organizer.

MARKETING CORE FUNCTION

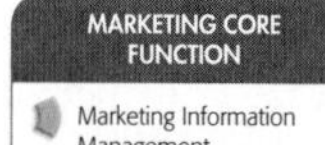

Marketing Information Management

STANDARDS

ACADEMIC

English Language Arts

NCTE 7 Conduct research and gather, evaluate, and synthesize data to communicate discoveries.

NCTE 8 Use information resources to gather information and create and communicate knowledge.

NCTE 9 Develop an understanding of diversity in language use across cultures.

Mathematics

NCTM Problem Solving Solve problems that arise in mathematics and in other contexts.

NCTM Problem Solving Apply and adapt a variety of appropriate strategies to solve problems.

NCSS *National Council for the Social Studies*
NCTE *National Council of Teachers of English*
NCTM *National Council of Teachers of Mathematics*
NSES *National Science Education Standards*

Common Core

Writing Arguments to support claims in an analysis of substantive topics or texts, using valid reasoning and relevant evidence.

Writing Conduct short research projects based on focused questions, demonstrating understanding of the subject under investigation.

m.e. Section 28.2 Issues in Marketing Research

TYPES OF MARKETING RESEARCH

Marketing research is usually divided into two broad types of research: quantitative and qualitative. **Quantitative research** answers questions that begin with "how many" or "how much." To help you remember, think of the word "quantity," which is an amount or a number of something. Quantitative research usually gathers information from large samples of people. Quantitative research uses surveys or questionnaires to obtain numbers and responses of people to certain activities. The surveys can be answered independently or by an interviewer. They can be answered either in writing or orally.

Qualitative research focuses on smaller numbers of people (usually fewer than 100) and tries to answer questions that begin with "why" or "how." Qualitative research relies heavily on in-depth, one-on-one interviews, small group settings, and observations. Rather than prepared survey questions constructed ahead of time, this research uses focused discussions about a topic. Qualitative research is not limited to products. It is also conducted to answer questions about attitudes and behaviors, market segments, advertising media, brands, prices, employees, and every other aspect of marketing.

Most marketing research combines quantitative and qualitative methods. Sometimes many companies or organizations share actual costs and findings to perform marketing research in large syndicated research studies.

As You Read

Identify What types of marketing research do successful businesses use?

ATTITUDE RESEARCH

Attitude research, also known as *opinion research*, is designed to obtain information on how people feel about certain products, services, companies, or ideas. Attitude research is used in marketing to ascertain opinions among consumers and the public in general. It is also used within organizations when employee attitude surveys are conducted. Satisfaction studies conducted by mail surveys or telephone interviews are the most common ways to get at individuals' opinions. Customers are usually asked to rate "how satisfied" they are with a good or service they purchased or used.

> **"The type of research that businesses conduct depends on the problem that they are trying to solve."**

Opinion polls are another example of attitude research. An opinion poll is a survey of public opinion from a particular population sample. Carefully designed questions are asked of the sample group, then the answers are compiled to represent the opinions of a population. Gallup Consulting® conducts opinion polls on politics, elections, business and the economy, social issues, and public policy. Based on random samples of the population, opinion poll results can be generalized for the entire population. A business considering a major expansion might be interested in the attitude of the general population toward the economy.

ENGAGE

Anticipation Activity

Improving Student Achievement Bring a number of magazines to class. Have small student groups look through a magazine and choose a product advertisement. Have groups brainstorm types of marketing research they could conduct to help market this product. Then have groups choose the research method they think would work best for their particular product and to present it, along with their rationale, to the class. Ask: ***Why might different types of marketing research work better for different products?*** Attitude research might work for a product that has been on the market a long time so marketers can learn consumers' opinions and likes and dislikes about a product so improvements can be made.

Objectives

- **Identify** the methods of conducting marketing research. attitude and opinion research, market intelligence, media research, product research
- **Discuss** trends and limitations in marketing research. Trends—global marketplace, use of Internet and external information in managing a business, total quality management. Limitations—money, time, number of personnel needed to conduct research.

Graphic Organizer

Quantitative Research
1. Surveys
2. Questionnaires

Quantitative and Qualitative Research
1. Media research
2. Product research
3. Market intelligence
4. Forecasting

Qualitative Research
1. Attitude Research
2. Opinion research

Graphic Organizer Send students to the Online Learning Center to print this graphic organizer.

EXPLORE

Before You Read

Ask: ***What would happen if marketing research was not used in product development?*** Products developed without data from marketing research are not likely to be successful. Students should be able to connect successful products to research used to guide product development.

Preteaching Vocabulary

Have students go to the Online Learning Center at glencoe.com for the Chapter 28 Preteaching Vocabulary games.

Content Vocabulary

Display the Content Vocabulary terms for the class to read: *quantitative research, qualitative research, attitude research, market intelligence, media research, and product research.* Now have students group the terms in the most logical manner. Sample word groups: quantitative research and qualitative research—media research, product research, market intelligence; qualitative research—attitude research

Academic Vocabulary

Anticipate—Usage Display the term *anticipate* for the class to read. Ask volunteers to use the term in a sentence. Sample sentence: We anticipate having a good vacation this summer. Then ask a volunteer to define *anticipate* in his or her own words. Possible definitions: to be fairly certain something will happen; to look forward to something.

Associated—Usage Display the term *associated* for the class to read. Then write the following synonyms: *affiliated, allied, connected, coupled, linked, and related.* Now read the following sentence to students: ***During the research, they may be asked about the extent to which they noticed the ad, remembered it, and associated it with the advertised brand.*** Then ask students: ***Which synonym best fits the way the term*** associated ***is used in this sentence?*** Possible answers: connected, linked, related.

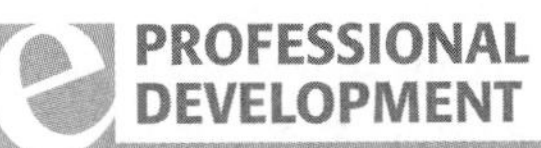

PROFESSIONAL DEVELOPMENT **MINI CLIP**

Reading: Planning for Future Instruction
Go to the Online Learning Center to view a video clip in which teachers plan for future instruction by developing strategies for nonfiction text.

Section 28.2

Issues in Marketing Research

TYPES OF MARKETING RESEARCH

Tell students that marketing research can help to ensure that a business is successful. Ask these guiding questions to focus the discussion on marketing research.

Guiding Questions

Identify What is the purpose of attitude research?	to obtain information about how people feel about products, services, companies, or ideas
Compare How are quantitative and qualitative research different?	Quantitative research answers questions that begin with "how many" or "how much." It usually gathers information from large samples through surveys or questionnaires. Qualitative research answers questions that begin with "why" or "how" and usually relies on one-on-one interviews, small group settings, and observations. It gathers information from smaller groups.

As You Read

Read the As You Read question aloud: ***What types of marketing research do successful businesses use?*** Successful businesses usually combine both quantitative and qualitative research. The specific type of research is dependent on the information that needs to be collected or problem that needs to be solved.

Expert Advice

Read the quote to students:

"The type of research that businesses conduct depends on the problem that they are trying to solve."

Ask students: ***Which type of research would you use (qualitative or quantitative) to research the need for a new product? Why?*** Answers: I would use quantitative research to gather input from as many people as possible. I would use qualitative research to gain an understanding of how the product might meet customers' needs.

MARKET INTELLIGENCE

Market intelligence, also known as *market research*, is concerned with the size and location of a market, the competition, and segmentation within the market for a particular product. Businesses use existing market data and new research to assemble a profile of present and potential customers, competitors, and the overall industry. Market intelligence helps define potential target markets for a particular good or service and helps identify how to reach potential customers.

A company's current sales and projected sales data are part of market intelligence. Sales data help businesses project the potential sales for a product and **anticipate** problems related to future sales. Sales trends for various products may also be compared to determine whether a product's sales are increasing or declining.

SALES FORECASTING

Business owners need to make predictions in order to plan investments, launch new products, and decide when to stop producing products. For most businesses, sales forecasting is crucial.

Sales forecasting is an attempt to estimate the future sales of an existing product. A company calculates a total estimate of the market for a product, analyzes its own sales and the sales of its competitors, and then estimates its individual share of the market. The share that is assigned to a particular company is called its "market share," or sales penetration of the market.

Based on these research findings, a business can then take steps to try to increase its market share. Businesses can increase their sales penetration by making changes in the product, its pricing, promotion efforts, or distribution strategy.

Estimation of market share and research into market segmentation are used for new products in both consumer and industrial markets. The goal of market share and segmentation studies is to investigate potential markets and define the specific characteristics of the target market.

Businesses often use software to assist with sales and market forecasting. These computer programs are able to analyze current market data and then use this information to predict future sales.

Syndicated Research Firms

There are more than 2,000 research companies in the United States, categorized as either interviewing services or full-service companies. ***Based upon content in this ad, what kind of market research services are offered by Zoomerang™?***

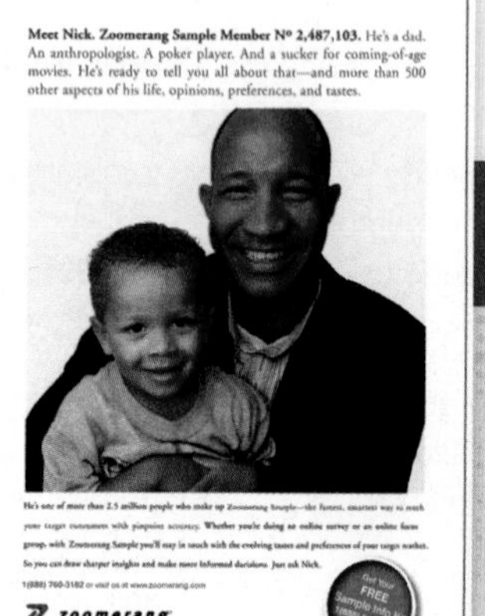

Meet Nick. Zoomerang Sample Member Nº 2,487,103. He's a dad. An anthropologist. A poker player. And a sucker for coming-of-age movies. He's ready to tell you all about that—and more than 500 other aspects of his life, opinions, preferences, and tastes.
So you can draw sharper insights and make more informed decisions. Just ask Nick.
zoomerang
Get Your FREE Sample Info Kit

ECONOMIC FORECASTING

Economic forecasting is an attempt to predict the future economic conditions of a city, a region, a country, or other part of the world. This kind of research requires extensive knowledge of economic statistics and trend indicators.

Several federal agencies collect information on key economic indicators. Economic indicators are used in the analysis of past and current economic performance to help predict future performance. These indicators include new building construction, industrial production, the stock market, inflation and interest rates, money supply, and consumer and producer price indexes.

Most businesses rely on government data to predict economic conditions, and then they adjust their business activities depending on the economic outlook. Businesses use this information to help plan for long-range expansion. This research helps to determine whether to cut costs when unfavorable economic conditions are predicted. These conditions may include higher interest rates or raw materials costs.

Private companies, such as Woods and Poole Economics®, specialize in long-term economic and demographic projections. The database contains projections through the year 2040 for every state, region, county, and metropolitan statistical area (MSA). This information helps marketing researchers analyze the makeup of the population. To do this, they collect information about age, race, gender, employment by industry, personal and household income, and retail sales by type of business.

MEDIA RESEARCH

Media research, also known as *advertising research*, focuses on issues of media effectiveness, selection, frequency, and ratings. Businesses conduct research to determine which media are most effective for getting an advertising message to a particular market.

Media research is used to measure brand awareness, advertisement recall, brand image, effectiveness of advertising copy, and audience size. These studies are used to measure attitudes and opinions toward a brand and its image. They also measure how well individual ads are remembered, and whether print, broadcast, or Internet advertising increased product sales.

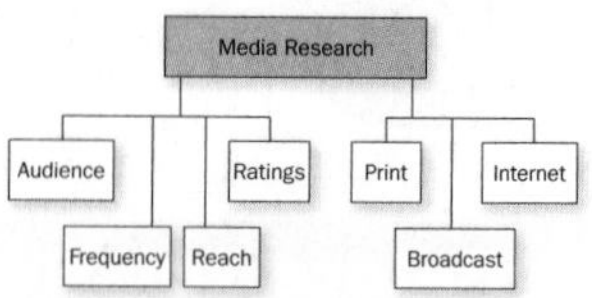

MEDIA ADVERTISING MEASURES

Important statistics for media measurement include *audience, frequency, reach,* and *ratings*. Audience is the number of homes or people exposed to a particular advertising medium. Frequency is the number of times a viewer in the audience sees or hears an ad. Reach is the percentage of the target audience that will see or hear an ad at least once. Ratings are the total number of audience impressions delivered over a set period of time.

To obtain these important media advertising measures, businesses request information from the print, broadcast, and electronic media of interest to them. In most cases, the information received would include a rate card. The rate card lists the advertising costs, its circulation or viewership figures, deadline dates, and other requirements for submission of an advertisement. Other information might involve the age, income, interests, hobbies, occupations, and attitudes of readers, subscribers, or viewers. Another way to measure advertising research on the various media is to subscribe to *Standard Rate and Data Service®* (SRDS), which publishes media rates and data for the advertising industry.

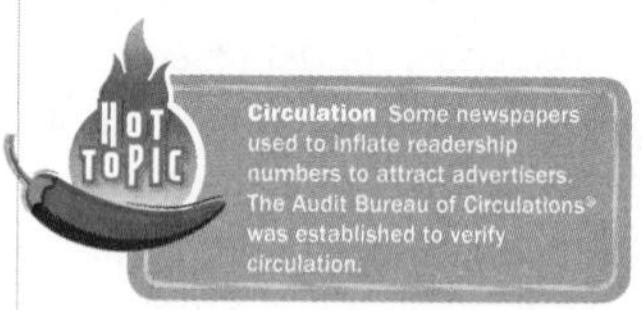

Circulation Some newspapers used to inflate readership numbers to attract advertisers. The Audit Bureau of Circulations® was established to verify circulation.

EXPLAIN

MARKET INTELLIGENCE

Ask these guiding questions to focus the discussion on market intelligence.

Guiding Questions

Explain What is the purpose behind market intelligence?	Market data can be used to assemble a profile of present and potential customers, competitors, and the overall industry. Market data can also help define potential target markets for a particular good or service and help identify potential customers.
Hypothesize How do you think businesses use the concept of sales forecasting in their marketing?	to predict future sales of an existing or new product; to calculate market share for the company

Visual Literacy

Syndicated Research Firms Caption Answer Read the caption question to students. ***Based upon content in this ad, what kind of market research services are offered by Zoomerang™?*** Zoomerang is a full-service company. Ask: ***What criteria did you use to make your decision?*** Since this ad is not an interview, that makes Zoomerang a full-service company.

Critical Thinking

Ask students to imagine that they own a small business. Sales have been down for the past year. They have decided to conduct marketing research to find out what customers are looking for in an attempt to boost sales. Ask: ***Should you consider quantitative or qualitative research?*** quantitative research Ask: ***Why?*** Sample answers: It is easier to conduct than qualitative research; it uses surveys and questionnaires, which take less effort on the part of the company.

ELABORATE

MEDIA RESEARCH

Tell students that media research is also known as advertising research. Ask: ***Why do you think it is called advertising research?*** Students will likely suggest that it focuses on advertising in the different media. Then ask these guiding questions to focus the discussion on media research.

Guiding Questions

Identify What does media research study?	brand awareness, effectiveness of advertising copy, and audience size for a particular type of advertising
Analyze Why might a marketer want to know the occupation of media viewers?	Possible answers: it might give them an idea of how much money they make and have to spend, or what their interests might be.
Evaluate Which statistic—audience, frequency, reach, or ratings—do you think is most important to a marketer? Why?	Students may suggest any of the statistics as being most important but should back up their answer with logical reasoning.

Graphic Organizer

Display this diagram. Ask students to provide details about the statistics for media measurement. Possible answers:

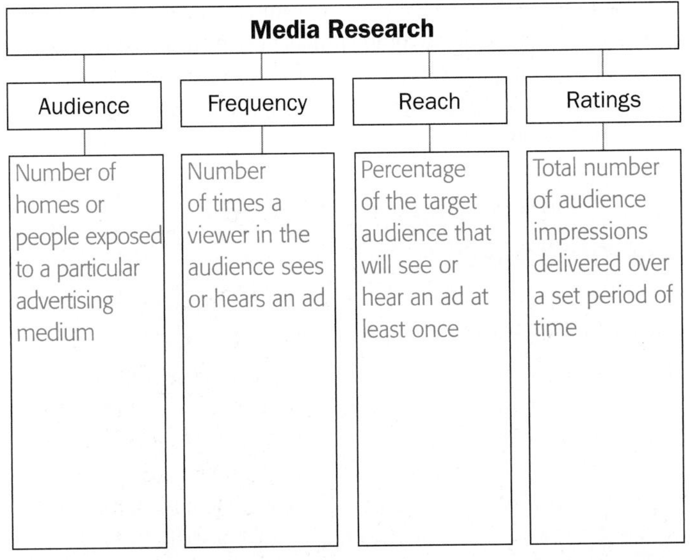
Media Research
Audience
Frequency
Reach
Ratings
Number of homes or people exposed to a particular advertising medium
Number of times a viewer in the audience sees or hears an ad
Percentage of the target audience that will see or hear an ad at least once
Total number of audience impressions delivered over a set period of time

Mc Graw Hill
glencoe.com
iWB

Graphic Organizer Send students to the Online Learning Center to print this graphic organizer.

HOT TOPIC

Circulation Have students choose several nationally distributed newspapers as well as your local newspaper(s) and find the circulation or readership numbers. Ask students to determine which newspaper might be the best for a national company to advertise in and which would be the best for a local company to advertise in.

Mini Project

Enrichment

Analyze a Market Intelligence Report Make copies of a market research report covering a specific industry such as consumer electronics, cosmetics, or juice drinks. Have students read the report and write notes on the type of information included. Information may include sales data, sales forecasts, customer demographics, and competitor profiles. Ask: ***What information is included in the report?*** Information will depend on the report selected. Display students' answers for the class to read. Tell students that many companies pay large amounts of money to purchase market information. Ask: ***Why do you think companies find market information so valuable?*** Students should recognize that the more information a company has, the better chance they have of being successful and increasing their profit margin. Have students keep the market research report and work in class to create a brief summary of the key points in the report. Summaries will depend on the information contained in the report. Students should include the main points in the report, use proper grammar, and avoid spelling errors.

Critical Thinking

Divide the class into small groups. Have groups choose one type of marketing research and write a one-page report describing a scenario that uses that type of marketing research. Groups can choose to use qualitative or quantitative research or they can be more specific and use attitude research, opinion research, media research, or product research. Encourage groups to be creative but realistic in the ways they use the research. After groups have written their papers, ask a volunteer from each group to share the papers with the class. Groups should be prepared to answer questions from the class about the papers.

RESEARCHING PRINT MEDIA

Marketing researchers can use different techniques to discover people's reactions to an advertisement. To determine the ad's effectiveness, readers are asked specific questions. They may be asked about the extent to which they noticed the ad, remembered it, and **associated** it with the advertised brand. The ad is also measured on its ability to change the consumer's beliefs, attitudes, or intended behavior.

Using consumer panels is another technique for measuring print advertising effectiveness. Consumer panels, also called "focus groups," are groups of people who are questioned periodically to provide information on research issues. A consumer panel can be comprised of a cross-section of people or individuals who share common characteristics, such as senior citizens, single parents, college-educated adults, or teenagers. Oral, written, or observed behavioral responses are recorded to indicate panel members' reactions to an advertisement.

Readership in print media is measured by surveys or estimated by circulation. Established in 1914, the Audit Bureau of Circulations® is a nonprofit organization of advertisers, advertising agencies, newspaper, and magazine publishers. It provides audits on average circulation, average print, and online readership circulation, total combined audiences, and total Web-site users for newspapers and magazines.

Mediamark Research and Intelligence® (MRI) and the Simmons Market Research Bureau® are syndicated research companies. They provide audience and media data. MRI's *Survey of the American Consumer*™ is a source of audience data for the U.S. consumer magazine industry. Simmons provides *Shopper Behavior Graphics*™, which provides data for retail mailing lists and computer software for media behavior. These companies conduct reading studies to see if participants can recall a magazine logotype, have read the magazine, and can remember where they read it during a recent period.

MARKETING CASE STUDY

Giant Eagle's Fuelperks

The grocery store chain Giant Eagle® recently started selling more than food and pharmacy items. They now have GetGo® fuel stations at or near many of their locations. Giant Eagle offers fuel discounts to customers through their fuelperks! program. Customers scan their Giant Eagle Advantage Card® when they shop at Giant Eagle. With fuelperks! customers earn 10 cents per gallon off fuel with every $50 spent at Giant Eagle.

The Next Step

Due to the success of the fuelperks! program, Giant Eagle now offers its customers another discount called foodperks!® Customers who use the foodperks! program can save money on their purchases in the grocery store. For every 10 gallons of gas a customer pumps at GetGo, he or she receives a one-percent discount on his or her next grocery purchase. Customers save money on both food and fuel. Giant Eagle is able to track and monitor its customers' purchases and offer discounts and coupons when they complete a transaction.

Math

Calculate You recently signed up for a Giant Eagle Advantage card and began earning fuelperks! discounts. You spent $263.82 on groceries in the past month. Regular unleaded gas is sold at $2.89 per gallon at your local GetGo. How much will you pay per gallon if you use your Fuelperks discount?

NCTM Problem Solving Solve problems that arise in mathematics and in other contexts.

RESEARCHING BROADCAST MEDIA

Most broadcast ad testing research is done on television commercials. Testing research can use quantitative or qualitative research techniques, such as personal interviews, theater tests, in-home testing, or focus groups, to get reaction to planned TV advertisements.

Nielsen Media Research, Inc.®, provides audience measurement information for the television industry. Nielsen estimates the audience by measuring a national sample of the viewing habits of 26,000 people in 10,000 homes. Nielsen's measurement information is recorded by "people meters" on TV sets, set tuning meters, and diaries that monitor program viewing.

Nielsen counts the number of viewers in meter-equipped households to get the number of households using TV, the share of the audience that is tuned to a particular station, and the rating, or percentage of viewers, for a particular television program at a particular time. Broadcast, cable network operators, satellite providers, program developers, distributors, and advertisers use this information to decide on which television programs to advertise.

The Arbitron Ratings Company® assembles important data on radio advertising. Arbitron produces radio audience measurements and sells software that analyzes advertising expenditure data. Arbitron surveys radio listeners to obtain the size and audience in 276 local markets serving 4,600 radio stations. It also has developed a "portable people meter" to compile audio broadcasts from a variety of broadcast media. The information provides audience listening data to a station and identifies tuned-in programs.

RESEARCHING INTERNET MEDIA

The effectiveness of Internet advertising is often measured with tracking studies. Tracking studies can be either Web-centric or user-centric. The Web-centric method logs the total number of people who have visited a Web site or views an online ad. The *interaction, click-through,* and *dwell rates* for particular ads are stored on the Internet provider's network. Advertisers can then decide on the Web site or online advertising that was most effective.

The user-centric method focuses on demographic and lifestyle profiling. It often involves metering software placed in ads that track computer usage and Web-site visits. User-centric surveys and tracking software identify the types of people visiting a Web site to get audience and lifestyle profiles. Advertisers can then reach a particular audience based upon a person's Web-surfing behavior.

DIGITAL NATION

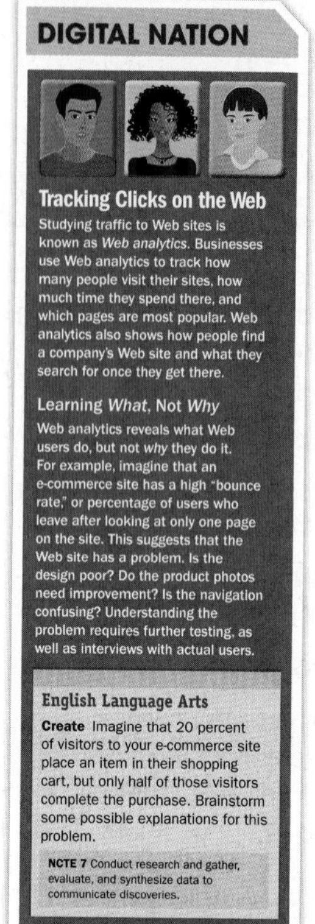

Tracking Clicks on the Web

Studying traffic to Web sites is known as *Web analytics*. Businesses use Web analytics to track how many people visit their sites, how much time they spend there, and which pages are most popular. Web analytics also shows how people find a company's Web site and what they search for once they get there.

Learning *What*, Not *Why*

Web analytics reveals what Web users do, but not *why* they do it. For example, imagine that an e-commerce site has a high "bounce rate," or percentage of users who leave after looking at only one page on the site. This suggests that the Web site has a problem. Is the design poor? Do the product photos need improvement? Is the navigation confusing? Understanding the problem requires further testing, as well as interviews with actual users.

English Language Arts

Create Imagine that 20 percent of visitors to your e-commerce site place an item in their shopping cart, but only half of those visitors complete the purchase. Brainstorm some possible explanations for this problem.

NCTE 7 Conduct research and gather, evaluate, and synthesize data to communicate discoveries.

glencoe.com

Get a Digital Nation Worksheet activity.

EXPLAIN

MARKETING CASE STUDY

Math Answer $2.39 per gallon ($263.82 ÷ 50 = 5.28; $2.89 – .50 = $2.39) Have students work in pairs to create additional math problems based on Giant Eagle's customer discounts. Ask pairs to exchange problems and then solve them.

Critical Thinking

Provide students with practice in calculating the market share of a company. Tell students that market share is calculated by dividing the company's total sales by the total market sales. The result is the company's market share. Then ask students to solve the following problem: ***A popcorn company's yearly sales are $250 million. The total popcorn market is $5 billion. What is the popcorn company's market share?*** The company's market share is 5 percent ($250 million ÷ $5 billion = 0.05 or 5 percent).

Activate Prior Knowledge

Have students imagine that they are advertisers. Ask them to choose a product and create an ad for the product using construction paper, magazine clippings, markers, graphic software, and so on. Remind students of the elements of a print advertisement: headline, copy, signature, illustration, and slogan.

Mini Project

Enrichment

Media Research Make transparencies of ten advertisements from a print magazine or newspaper. Allow students to view each ad for about five to ten seconds before switching to the next one. After students have viewed all of the ads, have them write down the subject of as many of the ads as they can remember. Then ask them to remember details, such as illustrations, colors, slogans, and so on. Lead a discussion about which ads stuck in students' minds the most and why. Compile the class results in a visual display.

ELABORATE

Graphic Organizer

Display this diagram. Ask students to provide details about the different types of media. Possible answers:

Media Research		
Print	Broadcast	Internet
To determine an ad's effectiveness, readers may be asked about the extent to which they noticed the ad, remembered it, and associated it with the advertised brand.	Nielsen Media Research, Inc.®, provides audience measurement information for the television industry. Companies use this information to determine which television programs to advertise on.	The effectiveness of Internet advertising is often measured with tracking studies, which can be Web-centric or user-centric. Advertisers use this information to determine the most effective online advertising.

 **glencoe.com** 

Graphic Organizer Have students go to the Online Learning Center to print a graphic organizer like the one above and use it to write notes about markets.

DIGITAL NATION

English Language Arts Answer Read the English Language Arts Activity to students: ***Imagine that 20 percent of visitors to your e-commerce site place an item in their shopping cart, but only half of those visitors complete the purchase. Brainstorm some possible explanations for this problem.*** The checkout process might be confusing or have technical flaws, such as inaccurate form fields or slow processing times. High fees for shipping or handling could be catching shoppers off guard. The process may be insecure, driving away security-conscious customers. Items may be frequently out of stock.

 **glencoe.com** 

Worksheet Activity Send students to the Online Learning Center to get a Digital Nation worksheet activity.

e MARKETING

Web Page Surveys

Visitors to Web sites are often invited to participate in marketing research studies. A pop-up window invites visitors to take the survey at the end of their visit to the site. Customer satisfaction is often the main theme of Web page surveys—that is, satisfaction with the Web site or the company's products and services. Advanced analytics can include tracking studies, whereby the visitor's navigation on the Web site is correlated with the questionnaire data to get a more complete picture of the visitor's experience.

Innovate and Create

Ask students if they ever participated in a Web survey. For students who have participated, ask them to share their experience with the class. Have them indicate what they liked and disliked about their experience. Conduct a discussion about the advantages and disadvantages of Web surveys. Have students prepare a 10-question customer satisfaction survey for a company of their choice. The objective can be customer satisfaction with the website or the company's products. Have them save their questionnaires for review in Chapter 29 where they will revise the questions based on what learn about effective survey question techniques. Students' experiences with Web surveys will determine how much they share with classmates. Advantages of Web surveys may include: cost is low because the survey is administered online (no postage or printing costs); larger samples can be used without an increase in cost; questions that do not pertain the participant can be programmed so they are skipped, making the questionnaire easier to administer and complete. Disadvantages may include: sample may not be representative of the target population because anyone who clicks on the Web site may complete the survey and it is easy for participants to quit the survey before completion.

 **glencoe.com** 

eMarketing Worksheet Activity Send students to the Online Learning Center to download an eMarketing worksheet activity.

PRODUCT RESEARCH

Product research centers on evaluating product design, package design, product usage, and consumer acceptance of new and existing products. Many new products and their packages are designed, tested, changed, and introduced each year. Product research is also conducted to collect information about competing products.

NEW PRODUCT RESEARCH

Concept testing is typically used in the early stages of product development. Concept testing attempts to get information on the product, pricing, advertising, and product positioning before product introduction. Concept testing, product positioning, and pricing studies are frequently done with focus groups or in-depth interviews to get initial consumer reaction to a description of a product, rather than to particular product.

Early product development also focuses on brand research. Brand research uses word and personality association techniques to develop brand names. Branding research attempts to develop product names that will closely relate to consumers' feelings and attitudes about the product. After a new product has been developed, other marketing research methods are used.

Product placement tests are a way of measuring new product acceptance. One type of product placement test has consumers try a product and give their opinions as to quality and performance. Product testers are asked questions about specific aspects of the product. A tester of body lotion may be asked about the lotion's texture, scent, consistency, oiliness, and absorption into the skin. Another method of product placement is to place products on retail shelves to observe the rate of customer sales.

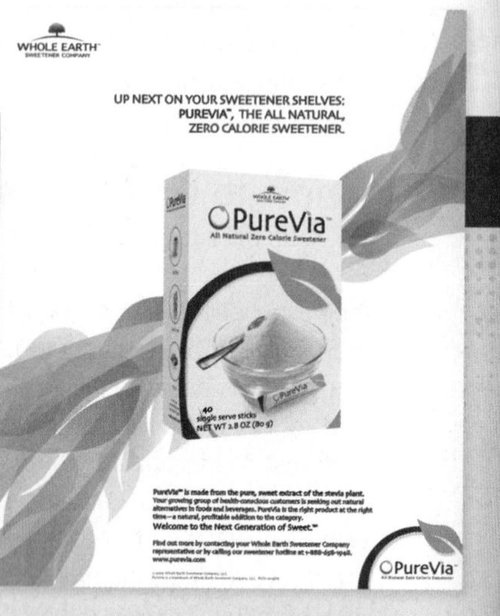

New Product Introduction

PureVia™ did extensive product research before introducing its new product to the market. ***What kind of information is obtained from customer satisfaction surveys?***

Choice studies or blind tests are sometimes used for new products. A choice study or blind test allows a product or package to be evaluated without the aid of brand names. The products are packaged generically and identified by letter or number. Consumer panels (focus groups) or individuals give feedback on new products.

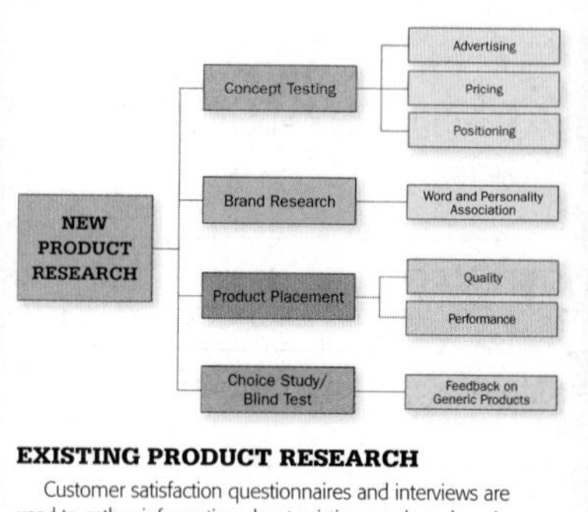

EXISTING PRODUCT RESEARCH

Customer satisfaction questionnaires and interviews are used to gather information about existing goods and services for both the industrial and consumer markets. Industrial satisfaction surveys focus on products utilized by business and manufacturing firms. Customer satisfaction surveys provide a rich data source for businesses interested in customer attitudes toward existing retail products and services.

A consumer who makes a major purchase may be contacted by a firm that specializes in customer satisfaction studies. A leading company in this field is J.D. Power and Associates, which is well-known for its ratings on vehicle quality, reliability, and dependability. If you buy a new car, you may get a follow-up phone call, e-mail, or letter from J.D. Power asking about your buying experience and your impressions of the quality of your vehicle. The company compiles research gained from thousands of these customer surveys into data showing which automakers offer the most reliable and dependable models. Information like this can help guide consumers in their buying decisions. It can also assist automakers in determining what factors are most important to their customers.

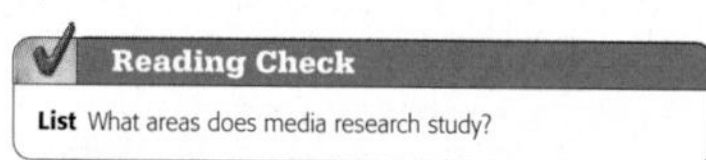

Reading Check

List What areas does media research study?

WORLD MARKET

SOUTH KOREA

Brave New Robots

For decades inventors have been dreaming up mechanical gizmos to perform the tedious tasks of daily life. The dream became a reality with robotics. In fact, the robotics industry may eventually rival the automobile and computer industries.

Dream Machines Hoping to create a billion-dollar industry, South Korea has ambitious plans for two robot theme parks and a variety of "service robots" to work in housekeeping, school teaching, firefighting, and elderly care fields. The Korea Advancement Institute of Science and Technology partnered with a U.S. robotics company to produce a robot called "Einstein HUBO" (humanoid robot). Designed with Einstein's face, it moves, talks, recognizes facial expressions, and even "flashes a dashing smile."

Here are some entry-level phrases that are used in conversations about marketing all over the world.

English	Korean
Hello	Anyonghashimnika
Bye	Anyonghekashipsheo
Yes/No	Nay/Anyo
Please	Butakhamnida
Thank you	Kamsahamnida
You're welcome	Chunmaneyo

English Language Arts

Write Korea hopes to develop a "wearable robot." Conduct research on this product. Write ten questions for a focus group testing this new product.

NCTE 8 Use information resources to gather information and create and communicate knowledge.

EXPLAIN

PRODUCT RESEARCH

Ask these questions to focus the discussion about product research.

Guiding Questions

Identify What are the four types of new product research?	concept testing, brand research, product placement, and choice study/blind test
Analyze How does new product research differ from existing product research?	New product research gets initial reaction to a description of a product to help the manufacturer know whether it is feasible to market it. Existing product research provides information about whether existing products should be modified.

Visual Literacy

New Product Introduction Caption Answer Read the caption question to students: ***What kind of information is obtained from customer satisfaction surveys?*** Customer satisfaction surveys provide a data source for businesses interested in retail customer attitudes toward existing products and services.

Critical Thinking

Have students talk to the manager of a local supermarket to discuss which products have been test marketed in the store within the past few years. Students should obtain answers to these questions: How was your store chosen to participate in the test? How did the manufacturer promote the products? Are the products now sold regularly in the store? How was customer feedback solicited on these products? Were changes made to the product as a result of the customer feedback? Have students summarize their findings in a one-page report and then share their findings with the class.

ELABORATE

Reading Check Answer

Read the Reading Check question to students: ***What areas does media research study?*** Media research studies statistics for audience, frequency, reach, and ratings. It also researches information from print, broadcast, and Internet media.

Mini Projects

Enrichment

Research Consumer Privacy Have students search current newspapers, magazines, and online media for stories involving consumer privacy issues. Article topics may include litigation over privacy issues, new technology that affects consumer privacy, or new laws concerning privacy. After students have shared their articles with the class, have a class "debate" about the issues shared in the articles. For example, if there is litigation over someone being filmed without their knowledge or permission and posted on a Web site that has sponsors, ask which side students are on. Should people be able to film and post whatever they want without regard for someone's privacy? Why or why not? Have students share their feelings about consumer privacy issues.

Participate in Online Surveys Ask students to find an online survey site and take one or more surveys on the site. Then have students write a one-page analysis in which they share their findings. Analyses should answer the following questions: Did you have to register on the site in order to take the surveys? What kind of information did you have to submit to register? What incentives were you offered to take the surveys? How do you think the company will use the information you submitted in the survey? Analyses will vary but should answer the questions listed. Ask volunteers to share their analyses with the class.

WORLD MARKET
ENGLISH LANGUAGE ARTS

Ask students to work with a partner to discuss the possibility of a "wearable robot" and to develop ten questions about the topic. Then display students' questions for the class to read and discuss. Ask students: ***How would you go about setting up a focus group to ask these questions?*** Students might suggest finding people with an interest in robots and asking them to participate in the focus group. If possible, have students ask several people the questions generated about robots. Compile the class results.

Graphic Organizer

Display this diagram. Ask students what type of research tool is used to collect data for these two groups. Then ask students to provide details about the research tools. Possible answers:

Graphic Organizer Send students to the Online Learning Center to print this graphic organizer.

TRENDS IN MARKETING RESEARCH

The nature and scope of marketing research is rapidly changing to keep pace with a changing marketplace. The trend toward a global marketplace means increased international competition for U.S. companies, which must improve or change products frequently to hold on to their customers.

In this environment product quality and customer satisfaction are the keys to business success. To maintain customer satisfaction, companies need to understand their customers' needs. They also need information that tells them how well they are meeting those needs. Research that measures these qualities has become the fastest growing form of marketing research.

Another important trend is the use of both internal and external information in managing a business. Total quality management (TQM) programs place a premium on gathering and using database research in improving business operations.

MARKETING RESEARCH IN A GLOBAL MARKETPLACE

A company doing business internationally must consider different countries' cultures that could affect a product's success. This factor requires research to determine the cultural preferences and traditions of the parts of the world in which they want to market their products.

GLOBAL STRATEGIES

Different strategies are used based on the part of the world in which the company is marketing. A fast food company like McDonald's® focuses on marketing popular domestic items with a twist that appeal to the diners in the international location. For example, the menu at a McDonald's in India might feature a Maharaja Mac®, which is a Big Mac® made of lamb or chicken meat because most Hindu people do not eat beef.

GOING GLOBAL WITH THE 4 P'S

The four Ps of marketing—product, price, placement, and promotion—are all affected as a company transitions into the global marketplace.

- **Product** A global company is one that can create a single product and only have to alter certain elements for different markets. For example, Coca-Cola® uses the same bottle shape for all markets, but they change the bottle size and the language on the packaging.
- **Price** Price will always vary from market to market. Price is affected by the costs of local product development, ingredients, and delivery.
- **Placement** Placement decisions must take into account the product's position in the marketplace. For example, a high-end product would not be distributed at a "dollar store" in the U.S. Conversely, a product promoted as a low-cost option in France would not be sold in an expensive boutique.
- **Promotion** Promotion, especially advertising, is generally the largest expense in a global company's marketing budget. If the goal of a global company is to send the same message worldwide, then delivering that message in a relevant, engaging, and cost-effective way is the challenge.

LIMITATIONS OF MARKETING RESEARCH

Few companies can conduct as much marketing research as they would like to conduct. The amount of information that can be gathered is limited by the amount of money and time a company can afford to spend on the equipment and number of personnel needed to conduct the research.

Marketing managers make multiple and overlapping strategic decisions in the process of identifying and satisfying customer needs. They make decisions about potential opportunities, target market selection, market segmentation, planning and implementing marketing programs, marketing performance, and control.

Marketing research information also has its limitations. The decisions are complicated by interactions between the controllable marketing variables of product, pricing, promotion, and distribution.

Marketing managers must also factor into this mix the consumers themselves. Customers in a test-market situation may say they like a particular product, and they may indicate that they would strongly consider buying it, but there is no guarantee they will actually purchase the product when it goes on the market.

In addition, fast-changing markets may not allow time for research. There is a time lag between identifying the need for a product, collecting the marketing research, and presenting the findings so the business can decide whether to produce the product. Business conditions, customer buying habits, and customer preferences can change.

Despite these limitations, marketing research provides valuable information. Businesses will continue to rely on marketing research to obtain the best possible information about customers and the marketplace.

After You Read **Section 28.2**

Review Key Concepts

1. **Differentiate** between attitude and market intelligence research.
2. **Explain** the purpose of media research.
3. **Explain** the purpose of product research.

Practice Academics

English Language Arts

4. Perform library or online research to investigate a country of your choice and develop a two-page paper on its location, demographics, traditions, lifestyles, and culture. Include recommendations for conducting market research in your selected country.

NCTE 9 Develop an understanding of diversity in language use across cultures.

Mathematics

5. You plan to purchase a health club targeted to professionals aged 22 to 55 in your town. Research shows that 3,250 households in your target market spend $900 a year on fitness activities. There is one other health club that serves 30 percent of your target market. What would be your annual sales forecast for the center?

Math Concept **Problem Solving: Multi-Step Problems** When solving problems that require multiple steps, list the information given and the information for which you will be solving. This will clarify the relationship between the two.

Starting Hints To solve this problem, determine the percent of households you hope to service by subtracting 30 percent from the total market of 100 percent. Multiply the decimal equivalent of this percent by the total number of households to determine the number of households in the target market. Multiply the number of households in the target market by the amount they spend on fitness activities each year to determine the annual sales forecast.

NCTM Problem Solving Apply and adapt a variety of appropriate strategies to solve problems.

For help, go to the **Math Skills Handbook** located at the back of this book.

glencoe.com

Check your answers.

ELABORATE

Mini Project

Differentiated Instruction

Students with Learning Disabilities To help students recall topics discussed in this section, ask: ***What are the four types of marketing research? Provide an example for each type.*** Attitude and opinion research—political surveys; market research—economic forecasting; media research—Nielsen ratings or Internet tracking; and product research—new product test marketing or product usage surveys. Then lead a discussion comparing and contrasting Web-centric and user-centric tracking. Divide the class into small groups and have them write down examples of when each type of study would be appropriate. Ask groups to share their examples with the class. Web-centric—comparing hits on a company's Web site versus hits on their competitors' sites; user-centric—studying which Web sites are popular among a demographic.

TRENDS IN MARKETING RESEARCH

Ask these questions to focus the discussion about trends in marketing research.

Guiding Questions

Identify What are two trends facing marketing research today?	(1) a global marketplace; and (2) the use of both internal and external information in managing a business
Explain What must companies do to maintain customer satisfaction?	understand customers' needs; know how they are meeting those needs
Predict Why must a company doing business internationally consider different countries' cultures?	Products must appeal to the consumers in the market without offending or insulting them; understand that what appeals to one culture may not appeal to another.

EVALUATE

LIMITATIONS OF MARKETING RESEARCH

Ask these questions to focus the discussion.

Guiding Questions

List What do marketing managers make decisions about in the process of identifying and satisfying customer needs?	potential opportunities, target market selection, market segmentation, planning and implementing marketing programs, marketing performance
Analyze Why are customers themselves a limitation to marketing research information?	Their buying habits and preferences can change.

Graphic Organizer

Display this diagram. Ask students to provide details about the global marketplace for each of the four Ps. Possible answers:

GOING GLOBAL WITH THE FOUR Ps

P PRODUCT	P PLACEMENT
P PRICE	P PROMOTION

P PRODUCT

- Single product modified for different markets

P PRICE

- Affected by costs of local product development, ingredients, and delivery

P PLACEMENT

- Takes into account the product's position in the marketplace

P PROMOTION

- Largest expense in a global company's marketing budget
- Message must be delivered in a relevant, engaging, and cost-effective way worldwide

glencoe.com  iWB

Graphic Organizer Send students to the Online Learning Center to print this graphic organizer.

After You Read Section 28.2

Review Key Concepts

1. Attitude research, also known as opinion research, is designed to obtain information on how people feel about certain products, services, companies, or ideas. Market intelligence, also known as market research, is concerned with the size and location of a market, the competition, and segmentation within the market for a particular product or service.
2. Businesses often conduct media research to determine which media are most effective for getting an advertising message to a particular market.
3. The purpose of product research is to evaluate product design, package design, product usage, and consumer acceptance of new and existing products.

Practice Academics

English Language Arts

4. Accept all reasonable answers. Students should include the source(s) for the information, the selected country, its demographics (age and size of population, ethnicity, gender, and so on), its traditions, lifestyles, and culture. Recommendations for conducting research should also be included.

Mathematics

5. \$2,047,500 (100% − 30% = 70%; .70 × 3,250 × \$900)

glencoe.com 

Send students to the Online Learning Center to check their answers.

Marketing Research

Marketing information is used to identify marketing opportunities, solve marketing problems, implement marketing plans, and monitor marketing performance.

MARKETING RESEARCH
Identify Marketing Opportunities
Monitor Marketing Performance
Solve Marketing Problems
Implement Marketing Plans

Marketing research methods include attitude research, market intelligence, media research, and product research.

MARKETING RESEARCH METHODS
Attitude Research
Opinion Polls
Satisfaction Surveys
Product Research
New Products
Existing Products
Market Intelligence
Sales Forecasting
Economic Forecasting
Media Research
Print
Broadcast
Internet

Written Summary

- Marketing research involves the marketing function that links the consumer, customer, and public to the marketer through information.
- Marketing information is used to identify marketing opportunities, solve marketing problems, implement marketing plans, and monitor marketing performance.
- A marketing information system is a set of procedures and methods that regularly generates, stores, analyzes, and distributes marketing information for use in making marketing decisions.
- Marketing research is usually divided into two broad types of research: quantitative and qualitative.
- Marketing research involves the process and methods used to gather information, analyze it, and report findings related to marketing goods and services.
- The nature and scope of marketing research are rapidly changing to keep pace with a changing marketplace.
- Marketing research information provides much information but does have limitations.

Review Content Vocabulary and Academic Vocabulary

1. Write your own definition for each content and academic vocabulary term.

Content Vocabulary
- marketing research (p. 655)
- marketing information system (p. 658)
- database marketing (p. 658)
- database (p. 658)
- quantitative research (p. 663)
- qualitative research (p. 663)
- attitude research (p. 663)
- market intelligence (p. 664)
- media research (p. 665)
- product research (p. 668)

Academic Vocabulary
- obtained (p. 656)
- overall (p. 658)
- anticipate (p. 664)
- associated (p. 666)

Assess for Understanding

2. **Identify** What is the purpose of marketing research?
3. **Characterize** What are the characteristics and purposes of a marketing information system?
4. **Sequence** What are the procedures for gathering information using technology?
5. **Contrast** How does quantitative research differ from qualitative research?
6. **Explain** What are the methods of conducting marketing research?
7. **Suggest** What is one trend affecting marketing research?
8. **Define** How do you define the term *market intelligence*?
9. **Create** How might one limitation of marketing research affect a business? (Identify the limitation.)

EVALUATE

Visual Summary

Express Creativity Ask students to develop their own visual summary of a concept in the chapter. Encourage students to use different formats for their visual summaries, such as a storyboard, a timeline, a table, a tree diagram, or a word web. Visual summaries will vary depending on the concept depicted. Questions to ask when assessing a visual summary include:

- Is the summary clear, economical, and simple?
- Are any important steps left out?
- Are steps or concepts arranged in the same order as the original?
- Does the summary reveal a pattern that connects the details?
- Does the summary locate and highlight the most important information?

Review Content Vocabulary and Academic Vocabulary

1. **Marketing research** involves the process and methods used to gather information, analyze it, and report findings. A **marketing information system** is a set of procedures and methods that regularly generates, stores, analyzes, and distributes information for making marketing decisions. **Database marketing** is a process of designing, creating, and managing customer lists. A **database** is a collection of related information about a specific topic. **Quantitative research** answers questions that begin with "how many." **Qualitative research** focuses on smaller numbers of people and tries to answer questions that begin with "why." **Attitude research** is designed to obtain information on how people feel about products, companies, or ideas. **Market intelligence** is concerned with the size and location of a market, the competition, and segmentation within the market for a product. **Media research** focuses on issues of media effectiveness, selection, frequency, and ratings. **Product research** centers on evaluating product design, package design, product usage, and consumer acceptance of new and existing products.

EVALUATE

Assess for Understanding

2. The purpose of marketing research is to gather information, analyze it, and report findings related to the marketing of goods and services.

3. Marketing information systems include sets of procedures and methods that regularly generate, store, analyze, and distribute information for making marketing and other business decisions. Marketers use marketing information systems in many ways, including designing advertising campaigns, developing promotional plans, and selling directly to customers.

4. Procedures used to collect information include specialized equipment at POS terminals, loyalty programs, and internal company software and purchased data-mining software.

5. Quantitative research answers questions that start with "how many" or "how much." This type of research usually gathers information by surveys from large samples of people. Qualitative research focuses on smaller numbers of people (usually fewer than 100) and tries to answer "why" or "how questions."

6. There are four types of marketing research: attitude and opinion research, marketing intelligence, media research, and product research. Information can be collected in a variety of ways such as surveys, interviews, tracking studies, focus groups, and observations.

7. Any of the following are trends affecting marketing research: the global marketplace, the use of internal and external information in managing a business, and total quality management.

8. Market intelligence is information about the size and location of a market, the competition, and the segmentation within the market for a particular product or service.

9. Any of the following are examples of marketing research limitations: time, money, and the number of personnel available to conduct the research. Faulty or limited research can affect sales, advertising expenditures, new product development and the overall success or failure of the business.

21st Century Skills

Teamwork Skills

10. **Honest Answers?** You have a part-time job in the marketing research department of a large corporation. You and three coworkers are gathering information through mailed surveys. Your supervisor wants each of you to complete at least 30 surveys a day, which can be difficult. One coworker adds responses to some incomplete surveys that have missing responses in order to reach the quota of 30 surveys. What should you do? Discuss with a partner.

Financial Literacy Skills

11. **Calculating Household Market Research** You work for a full-service marketing research firm. You have been asked to calculate the total amount spent on market research. If $753 is spent on each of 2,400 households, what is the total amount?

e-Marketing Skills

12. **Mobile Phone Research** Imagine that you are employed in an interviewing-services research firm that collects data through the Internet, by telephone, by mail, and by in-person interviews. You are assigned to investigate the use of mobile phones for collecting interview data for clients. Investigate the process and benefits of using mobile phones for data collection.
    - List the steps that you must take to sell the concept to your clients.
    - What potential benefits might data collection by mobile phone give clients?
    - What are some methods you could use to collect data on mobile phones?
    - How can customers' information be studied and analyzed on a large scale?

Build Academic Skills

Social Studies

13. **Data-Mining Technologies** Perform library and online research using at least three different sources of information on data-mining technologies and software applications. Compare and contrast the views of marketing professionals with privacy advocates on the benefits and disadvantages of data mining. Identify the sources used and outline the benefits and disadvantages in a one-page outline.

NCSS VIII E Science, Technology, & Society Recognize and interpret varied perspectives about human societies and the physical world using scientific knowledge, ethical standards, and technologies from diverse world cultures.

English Language Arts

14. **Nature and Scope of Marketing Research** Review a current or online article from *The Wall Street Journal, Inc., BusinessWeek, Forbes, Money, Advertising Age, Brandweek,* or your local newspaper. Find one current marketing research activity and write a one-page report on the nature and scope of the activity.

NCTE 1 Read texts to acquire new information.

Mathematics

15. **Calculating Costs for Direct Mail** Your company plans to send a marketing questionnaire to 40 percent of the names on a mailing list of 20,000 people. The mailing list was purchased from another company for $0.20 per name. Each questionnaire costs $0.10 to print; mailing costs are $0.55 each; and the cost of writing the questionnaire, analyzing the information, and preparing the report is $15,000. What is the total cost?

NCTM Problem Solving Build new mathematical knowledge through problem solving.

Math Concept **Multi-Step Problems** When solving problems that require multiple steps, make a list of the information given in the problem and information for which you are solving. This will clarify the relationship between the two.

For help, go to the **Math Skills Handbook** located at the back of this book.

Standardized Test Practice

Directions Read the following questions. On a separate piece of paper, write the best possible answer for each one.

1. Which of the following types of marketing research includes information about sales and economic forecasting?
   A. Attitude and opinion research
   B. Market intelligence
   C. Media research
   D. Product research
2. The amount of research information collected is limited by time, money, and personnel.
   T
   F
3. What type of research answers the questions of "how many" and "how much"?

Test-Taking Tip

To cope with the stress of taking a test, view the test as an opportunity to show how much you have studied and to receive a reward for the work you have done.

DECA Connection Role Play

Business Information Manager Catalog/Online Gifts Company

Situation You work for a well-established gift items business. The company has been in business for more than 40 years. During the early years, business was conducted exclusively through a mail-order catalog. Then the Internet led the business to add a Web site and online catalog for customer orders.

Business is good, but the rising costs of paper, printing, and postage are causing management to make a careful assessment of the print catalog that is mailed to customers six times a year. The big questions are the following: Should the company stop production of the print catalog and do business from only the Web-site catalog? Or should the company publish the print catalog less frequently? Or should the company continue to publish the catalog as it is now?

The company president (judge) has asked you to assess the situation and make recommendations about the print catalog. Before you can make any recommendations about this issue you must have additional information. You know that your company will need to conduct some marketing research in order to make an informed decision about the print catalog. You feel that this important decision warrants the hiring of a marketing research firm.

Activity You are to list several points that need to be addressed and note how marketing research can help provide the information your company needs. You will then present your ideas and information to the company president (judge).

Evaluation You will be evaluated on how well you meet the following performance indicators:

1. Explain the nature of marketing research.
2. Explain the nature of marketing research problems/issues.
3. Assess information needs.
4. Explain the nature of marketing research in a marketing information management system.
5. Prepare simple written reports.

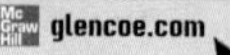

Download the Competitive Events Workbook for more Role-Play practice.

EVALUATE

Teamwork Skills

10. Answers may include: Communicate to your co-worker about how important accuracy is to the data collection process. False reporting errors might jeopardize the employment of the entire part-time staff. If the pattern continues, you need to report the incident to your immediate supervisor. If reporting is necessary, your communication should be done in a private location, be clear and thoughtful, and honestly tell what happened.

Financial Literacy Skills

11. $1,807,200 (2,400 households × $753)

e-Marketing Skills

12. Process steps: You might consider a booth at a research convention to demonstrate how mobile phones would work in data collection. You might develop a whitepaper for free distribution on the benefits of mobile phone data collection. The next step might include pilot testing mobile phone data collection for a client. Benefits and limitations: With a mobile phone you might get higher response rates than a mailed or Internet survey. Since more people are using mobile phones and dropping land lines you might get a better representative sample of the population. Mobile phones provide real time answers and actual locations of people during specific times of the day. As with any survey, some potential interviewees will resent the intrusion on their time and will be non-respondents.

EVALUATE

Build Academic Skills

Social Studies

13. Accept all reasonable answers that list possible benefits and disadvantages of data mining technologies and software applications. Students should identify at least three sources of information and a one-page outline of their findings.

English Language Arts

14. Accept all reasonable answers that identify the article and source of information. Acceptable answers include: articles dealing with attitude or opinion, market intelligence, media, or product research activities.

Mathematics

15. \$24,200 (cost of mailing list: 20,000 × \$0.20 = \$4,000; printing costs: \$0.10 × (.40 × 20,000) = \$800; mailing costs: \$0.55 × (.40 × 20,000) = \$4,400; cost of writing, analyzing, and preparing report: \$15,000; total cost: \$4,000 + \$800 + \$4,400 + \$15,000 = \$24,200)

Standardized Test Practice

1. B Market intelligence
2. True
3. Quantitative research

DECA Connection Role Play

Evaluations will be based on these performance indicators:

1. **Explain the nature of marketing research.** Marketing research involves the process and methods used to gather information, analyze it, and report findings related to marketing goods and services. Businesses use marketing research to identify marketing opportunities, solve marketing problems, implement plans, and monitor performance.
2. **Explain the nature of marketing research problems/issues.** Marketing research issues include the global marketplace, the use of internal and external information in a business, and total quality management. Marketing research limitations include money, time, and the number of personnel needed to conduct the research.
3. **Assess information needs.** Research answers questions about what products to produce, at what price to sell the products, who will buy the products, and how to promote the products. Through research, a company can determine its major competitors, what its competitors are offering, which products consumers prefer, and if customers are satisfied with those products.
4. **Explain the nature of marketing research in a marketing information management system.** Many businesses have sophisticated marketing information systems. These systems are used to organize, collect, and store marketing research data for future decisions. A marketing information system is a set of procedures and methods that regularly generates, analyzes, and distributes information for making marketing decisions. Timely marketing information provides a basis for decisions about product development, pricing, packaging, distribution, media selection, and promotion.
5. **Prepare simple written reports.** Reports should be written with the target audience in mind. Factual information should be cited in the report. Information should be presented in a clear, logical format. All sentences in the paragraph should support that topic. Graphics should be used to illustrate information if possible.

Role Plays For more DECA Role Plays, send students to the Online Learning Center to download the Competitive Events Workbook.

conducting marketing research

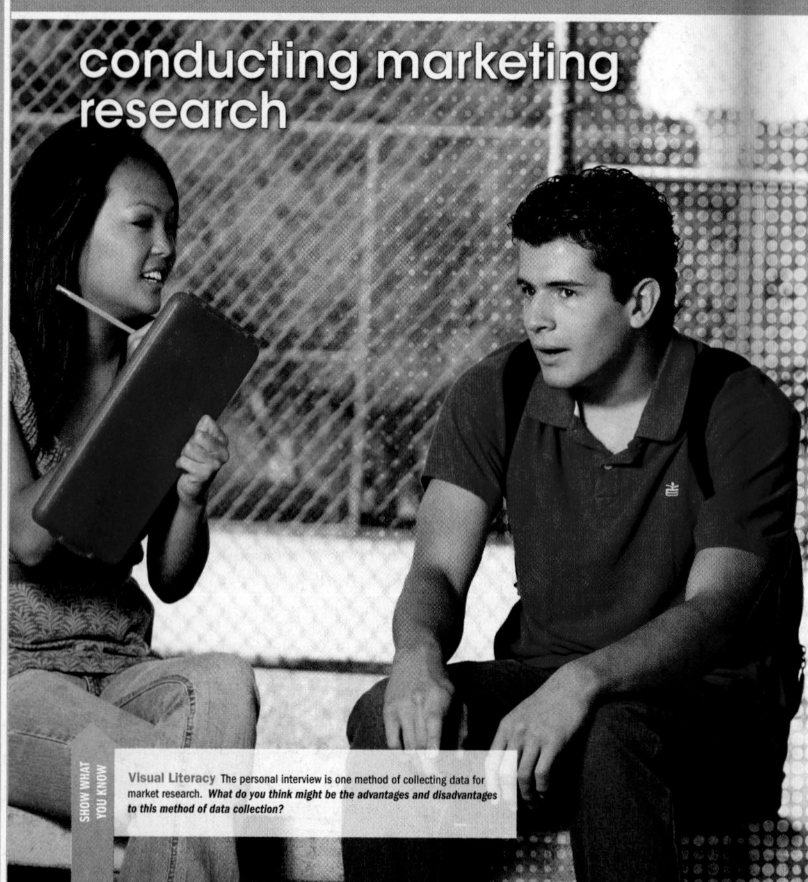

SHOW WHAT YOU KNOW **Visual Literacy** The personal interview is one method of collecting data for market research. ***What do you think might be the advantages and disadvantages to this method of data collection?***

Discovery Project

The Marketing Survey

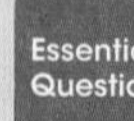

Essential Question How can marketing surveys obtain important data for identifying customer's needs and wants?

Project Goal

You and a classmate have been hired to conduct marketing research for a vacation home manufacturer. Your team has been asked to develop a ten-question survey to gather information to identify people who currently own a home in your area, their willingness to purchase a vacation home, and their basic demographics. You have been asked to design a survey that addresses this information for the company.

Ask Yourself...

- What questions will your team ask on the survey?
- How will you determine home ownership and vacation home interest?
- What types of demographic questions will you ask?
- How will you organize your survey instrument?

Synthesize and Present Research Synthesize your research by designing a ten-question survey that identifies people who currently own a home in your area and their willingness to purchase a vacation home.

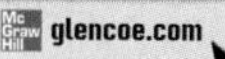

glencoe.com

Activity
Get a worksheet activity about marketing surveys.

Evaluate
Download a rubric you can use to evaluate your project.

DECA Connection

DECA Event Role Play

Concepts in this chapter are related to DECA competitive events that involve either an interview or role play.

Performance Indicators The performance indicators represent key skills and knowledge. Your key to success in DECA competitive events is relating them to concepts in this chapter.

- Describe methods to design research studies.
- Describe options businesses use to obtain marketing-research data (e.g., primary and secondary research).
- Discuss the nature of sampling plans (i.e., who, how many, how chosen).
- Evaluate questionnaire design (e.g., types of questions, question wording, routing, sequencing, length, layout).
- Explain the use of descriptive statistics in marketing decision making.

DECA Prep

Role Play Practice role-playing with the DECA Connection competitive-event activity at the end of this chapter. More information on DECA events can be found on DECA's Web site.

ENGAGE

Visual Literacy

Read the chapter opener photo caption question to students: ***What do you think might be the advantages and disadvantages of this method of data collection?*** Advantages: The survey taker can personalize questions based on the interviewee. Respondents can offer more in-depth answers. Disadvantages: Surveys may not cover a representative sample of the population. Interviewees may answer based on what they think the survey taker wants to hear. Then ask these guiding questions.

Guiding Questions

Define What is marketing research?	the process of obtaining information needed to make effective marketing decisions
Explain Why do companies use marketing research?	to determine consumer's attitudes and preferences; test product features; determine market size and growth potential; learn about competitive products; understand how the company is perceived by the public

Discovery Project

The Marketing Survey Ask students if they have ever filled out a marketing survey. Ask what kinds of questions the survey contained. Then ask them the Discovery Project Essential Question: ***How can marketing surveys obtain important data for identifying customers' needs and wants?*** Students should recall from Chapter 28 that marketing surveys are specially designed to obtain specific information needed by companies. Surveys provide many types of data, such as personal information and demographics, which help companies better serve their customers and increase profits.

glencoe.com

Discovery Project Resources Send students to the Online Learning Center to download a rubric to evaluate their projects.

ENGAGE

Introduce the Chapter

Chapter 29 introduces students to the methods used to collect data for marketing research. These main concepts are introduced and discussed:

- Marketing research process
- Sources of primary data
- Sources of secondary data
- Constructing questionnaires
- Administering questionnaires
- Mailed surveys
- E-mail and Web surveys
- In-person surveys

Discussion Starter

Marketing Research Ask students to brainstorm ways in which businesses decide to introduce new products and eliminate old ones. Students may suggest that if sales of a certain product are declining, the business will no longer sell it. Ask students: ***What might prompt a restaurant to add low-fat meals to its menu?*** Answers may include requests from customers and concern for customers' health. Then ask: ***How can the restaurant determine if its customers are pleased with this addition?*** The restaurant can ask the customers and calculate sales for the new menu items. Tell students that getting feedback on menu items from customers is a form of marketing research. Tell students that in this chapter they will learn different methods businesses use to conduct marketing research.

DECA Connection

Discuss the performance indicators listed in the DECA Connection feature. Explain to students that performance indicators tell them how to demonstrate their acquired skills and knowledge through individual or team competitive events.

glencoe.com

Competitive Events Workbook For more DECA Role Plays, send students to the Online Learning Center to download the Competitive Events Workbook.

PRINT RESOURCES

- **Student Edition**
- **Teacher Edition**
- **Student Activity Workbook with Academic Integration** includes worksheets and activities correlated to the text.
- **Mathematics for Marketing Workbook** provides math activities for every unit in the text.

TECHNOLOGY TOOLBOX

- **Connect**
- **ConnectPlus**
- **ExamView Assessment Suite** is a comprehensive solution for creating, administering, and scoring tests.

glencoe.com

Online Learning Center provides a variety of resources to enrich and enhance learning.

SECTION, CHAPTER, AND UNIT RESOURCES

- **Graphic Organizers** for organizing text concepts visually.
- **Digital Nation Activities** and **Green Marketer Activities** extend learning beyond the text features.
- **Career Chatroom Career Profiles** allow students to explore different marketing occupations in depth.
- **After You Read Answer Keys** for students to check their answers.
- **Discovery Project Rubrics** and **Marketing Internship Project Rubrics** for students to evaluate their projects.

PROGRAM RESOURCES

- **Student Activity Workbook with Academic Integration Teacher Annotated Edition** includes annotated answers for the activities and worksheets.
- **Marketing Research Project Workbook** provides a step-by-step approach for students to complete their own marketing research studies.
- **School-to-Career Activity Workbook** helps students relate their class work to on-the-job experience and involves work-site analysis and working with mentors.
- **Competitive Events Workbook** helps prepare students for state and national marketing education competitions.
- **Inclusion in the Marketing Education Classroom** provides teaching resources for working with students with special needs.
- **PowerPoint Presentations** provides visual teaching aids and assessments for this chapter.

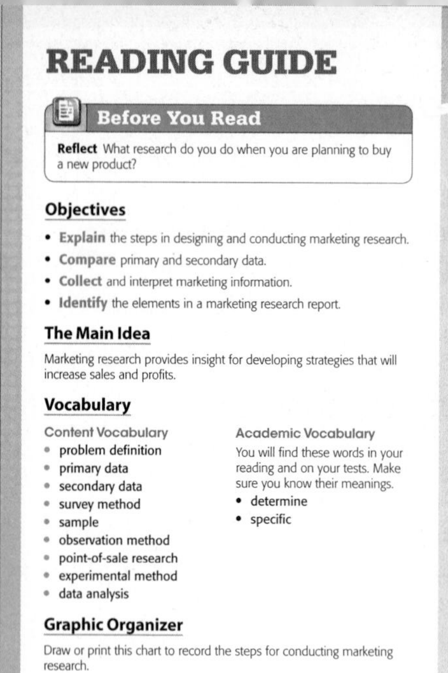

READING GUIDE

Before You Read

Reflect What research do you do when you are planning to buy a new product?

Objectives

- **Explain** the steps in designing and conducting marketing research.
- **Compare** primary and secondary data.
- **Collect** and interpret marketing information.
- **Identify** the elements in a marketing research report.

The Main Idea

Marketing research provides insight for developing strategies that will increase sales and profits.

Vocabulary

Content Vocabulary
- problem definition
- primary data
- secondary data
- survey method
- sample
- observation method
- point-of-sale research
- experimental method
- data analysis

Academic Vocabulary

You will find these words in your reading and on your tests. Make sure you know their meanings.
- determine
- specific

Graphic Organizer

Draw or print this chart to record the steps for conducting marketing research.

The Marketing Research Process

Step 1: Define the Problem

glencoe.com

Print this graphic organizer.

STANDARDS

ACADEMIC

English Language Arts

NCTE 8 Use information resources to gather information and create and communicate knowledge.

Mathematics

NCTM Number and Operations Understand the meanings of operations and how they relate to one another.

Science

NSES E Develop abilities of technological design, understandings about science and technology.

NCSS *National Council for the Social Studies*
NCTE *National Council of Teachers of English*
NCTM *National Council of Teachers of Mathematics*
NSES *National Science Education Standards*

College & Career READINESS

Common Core
Writing Write informative/explanatory texts to examine and convey complex ideas and information clearly and accurately through the effective selection, organization, and analysis of content.

MARKETING CORE FUNCTION

Marketing Information Management

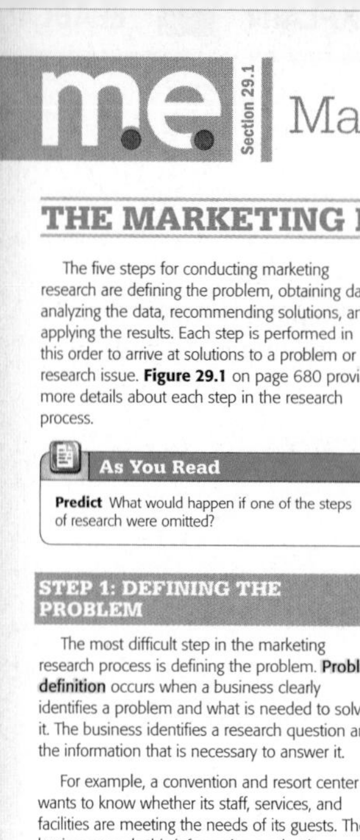

Section 29.1 | Marketing Research

THE MARKETING RESEARCH PROCESS

The five steps for conducting marketing research are defining the problem, obtaining data, analyzing the data, recommending solutions, and applying the results. Each step is performed in this order to arrive at solutions to a problem or research issue. **Figure 29.1** on page 680 provides more details about each step in the research process.

As You Read

Predict What would happen if one of the steps of research were omitted?

STEP 1: DEFINING THE PROBLEM

The most difficult step in the marketing research process is defining the problem. **Problem definition** occurs when a business clearly identifies a problem and what is needed to solve it. The business identifies a research question and the information that is necessary to answer it.

For example, a convention and resort center wants to know whether its staff, services, and facilities are meeting the needs of its guests. The business needs this information so that it can continually improve its services as a resort and convention destination.

> "Conducting marketing research improves decision making and creates opportunities."

With the problem defined, the researcher can create objectives for the study that will help answer the research problem. Objectives might include determining customer satisfaction in the following categories: reservation procedures, accommodations, guest services, and meeting and recreational facilities.

The actual questions that will be included in the research instrument are formulated by first considering the objectives. You will learn more about writing questions later in this chapter. For now, you should know that objectives and questions must correlate with one another. Here are two examples:

- **Objective:** Determine the level of guest satisfaction with the resort and convention center's facilities.
  Question: On a scale of 1 to 5, with 1 being very poor and 5 being excellent, how would you rate the quality of the meeting facilities? (Please offer a rating for each of the facilities you used.)
- **Objective:** Determine levels of satisfaction with the resort and convention staff services.
  Question: On a five-point scale, with 1 being very unsatisfied to 5 being very satisfied, how would you rate the staff's courtesy? How would you rate the staff's friendliness?

These questions are necessary so that guests' ratings of the center's facilities and staff services can be analyzed separately. If each question was not included in the research instrument, each of the objectives could not be accomplished.

Every business faces limits in the form of time and financial resources. Therefore, all companies need to obtain the information necessary to solve the problems they identify and make the marketing decisions that are most important.

ENGAGE

Anticipation Activity

Improving Student Achievement Read this scenario to students: A bakery owner wants to expand to include breakfast and lunch menu items. Ask: ***How can she decide whether her target market of middle-class, two-income families would support the expansion?*** informal interviews and/or a printed survey for customers to complete

Objectives

- **Explain** the steps in designing and conducting marketing research. define the problem, obtain data, analyze data, recommend solutions, apply the results
- **Compare** primary and secondary data. primary: the problem under study; secondary: another purpose
- **Collect** and interpret marketing information. data-collecting methods are survey, observation, and experimental methods
- **Identify** the elements in a marketing research report. title page; acknowledgments; table of contents; list of tables, figures, charts, and graphs; introduction; review of the research; procedures used; findings; recommendations; summary and conclusions; appendixes; and bibliography

Graphic Organizer

The Marketing Research Process

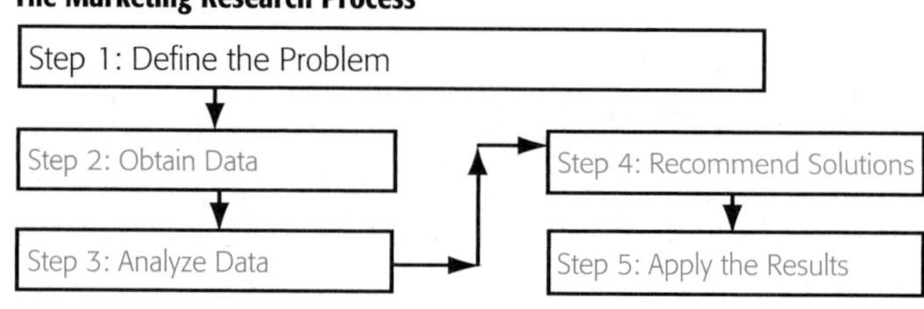

Graphic Organizer Send students to the Online Learning Center to print this graphic organizer.

EXPLORE

Before You Read

Read the question aloud: ***What research do you do when you are planning to buy a new product?*** check prices for similar products at various retailers; go to Web sites that offer product information and evaluations to customers; ask friends and family if they have knowledge about the product Ask: ***What are the ultimate criteria for making your purchase?*** information collected from the various sources; cost; and friends' influence

Preteaching Vocabulary

Have students go to the Online Learning Center at glencoe.com for the Chapter 29 Preteaching Vocabulary games.

Content Vocabulary

Display the Content Vocabulary terms for the class. Then read the glossary definitions in a different order. As you read the definitions, ask students to identify which term goes with each definition.

Academic Vocabulary

Determine—Alternate Meanings Display the Academic Vocabulary term *determine* and ask students to provide its meaning. to find out something; to set limits on something; to decide something; to influence something Then read the following sentence: A marketing information system is an internal way of collecting data to measure monthly sales, determine the geographic distribution of customers, track customer buying patterns, and identify popular items on the market. Ask: ***Which definition is correct for the way the term is used in the sentence?*** to find out something

Specific—Synonyms Display the term *specific* for the class to read. Ask students to find and list synonyms for *specific*. exact, precise, definite, particular Read the sentence from the text that includes the term: ***Such data may include population demographics, specific markets, industries, products, economic news, export information, and legislative trends.*** Then ask volunteers to use the term in original sentences.

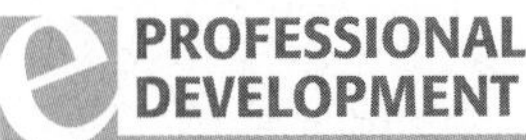

PROFESSIONAL DEVELOPMENT **MINI CLIP**

ELL: Low-Risk Environment
Go to the Online Learning Center to view a video clip in which an author discusses the importance of creating a low-risk environment for English language learners.

Marketing Research

THE MARKETING RESEARCH PROCESS

Explain to students that the marketing research process includes five steps that help researchers arrive at solutions to a problem or research issue. Then ask these guiding questions to focus the discussion about the marketing research process.

Guiding Questions

Identify What are the five steps of the marketing research process?	define the problem, obtain data, analyze the data, recommend solutions, apply the results
Explain When does problem definition occur?	when a business clearly identifies a problem and what is needed to solve it
Analyze Why must research questions correlate to objectives?	The objectives are used to develop the questions so that the questions are actually asking for the desired information.

As You Read

Read students the As You Read question: ***What would happen if one of the steps of research were omitted?*** Students should recognize that all the steps must be followed to make the marketing research process, and ultimately the overall results of the research, more powerful and effective.

Expert Advice

Read the quote to students:

> **"Conducting marketing research improves decision making and creates opportunities."**

Ask students: ***How does conducting marketing research improve decision making?*** It collects a variety of information pertinent to the decision so that the decision maker is more informed. Then ask: ***How does conducting marketing research create opportunities?*** It gives businesses insights, which can be used to create or improve products and promotional campaigns. Research can also help uncover needs and wants that are not being fulfilled, which are opportunities a company might be able to capitalize on.

FIGURE 29.1 The Marketing Research Process

Five Research Steps Marketing research helps businesses find solutions to problems. There are five steps in the marketing research process. It begins with defining the problem or research issue. It ends with applying the results of the research. Following the steps in sequence is important because each step depends on the steps that come before it. ***What can researchers do after the data are analyzed?***

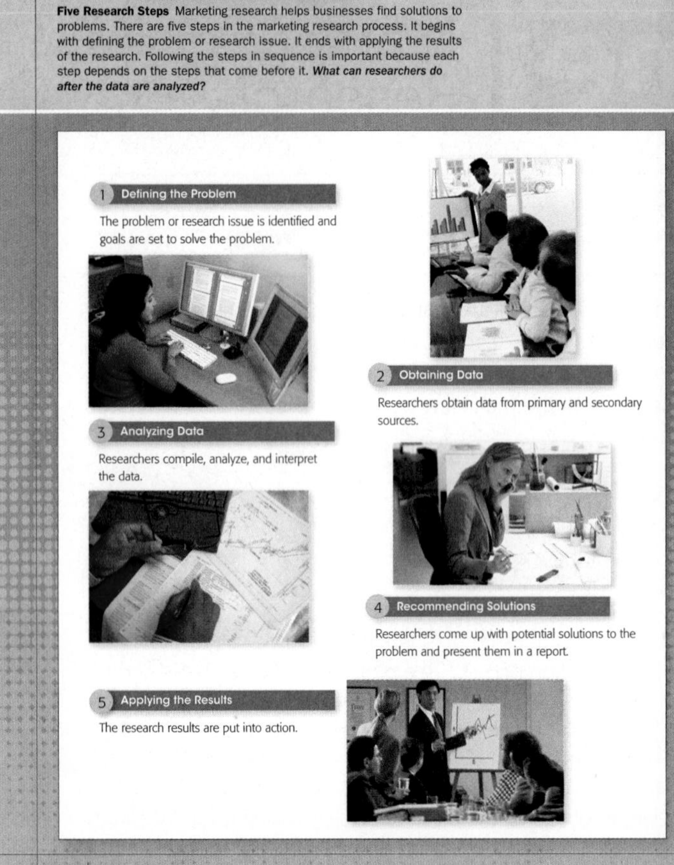

1 Defining the Problem
The problem or research issue is identified and goals are set to solve the problem.
2 Obtaining Data
Researchers obtain data from primary and secondary sources.
3 Analyzing Data
Researchers compile, analyze, and interpret the data.
4 Recommending Solutions
Researchers come up with potential solutions to the problem and present them in a report.
5 Applying the Results
The research results are put into action.

STEP 2: OBTAINING DATA

The second step in the marketing research process is obtaining data. During this second step, data are collected and examined in terms of the problem or problems being studied. The word *data* means facts. There are two types of data used in marketing research: primary and secondary. **Primary data** are data obtained for the first time and used specifically for the particular problem or issue under study. **Secondary data** have already been collected for some purpose other than the current study. Secondary data are less expensive to collect than primary data. Therefore, it is most cost effective for a company to first decide what secondary data it can use.

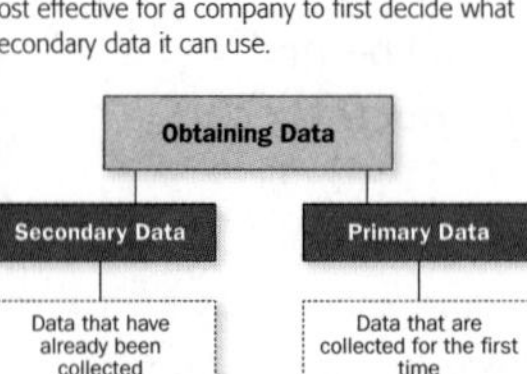

SOURCES OF SECONDARY DATA

Secondary data are obtained from both internal sources (inside the company) and external sources (outside the company). An excellent source of internal secondary data is the marketing information system of a business. A marketing information system is an internal way to collect data used to measure monthly sales, **determine** the geographic distribution of customers, track customer buying patterns, and identify popular items on the market. Secondary data are usually collected from a number of sources.

Internet Sources

The Internet has increased the availability of secondary data from a variety of sources. Some secondary information is available for free through a company's home page. A company's description of its products, services offered, locations, sales revenue, number of employees, product specifications, and pricing is often available. However, Web site information is used primarily for promotional purposes. So, any information obtained from Web sites should be verified through other, more objective sources.

MARKETING CASE STUDY

Palm Prē with the "Flow"

Smartphone maker Palm, Inc.®, needed to make a splash in the competitive smartphone market with its new Prē phone, which takes aim at the best-selling iPhone® and Blackberry® devices. So, it created a quiet, subtle ad campaign around a woman who tells viewers of the phone's benefits. One commercial in particular, though, went beyond subtle understatement.

Going with the Flow

In the "Flow" spot, a woman sits on a stone in the middle of a beautiful green field. She is surrounded by hundreds of people in orange suits doing choreographed movements. The screen switches to aerial views, revealing patterns and wave-like movements the dancers are creating, as the woman asks, "Isn't it beautiful when life simply flows together?"

English Language Arts

Analyze Define the problem that marketers might have identified as step two of the marketing research process for the Palm Prē product. List methods of obtaining marketing research data that Palm most likely used to find out which features shoppers want in a new smartphone. In what ways do you think Palm's commercial reflects marketing research for the product and its potential customer base?

NCTE 8 Use information resources to gather information and create and communicate knowledge.

EXPLAIN

Visual Literacy

Figure 29.1 Caption Answer Read the caption question to students: ***What can researchers do after the data are analyzed?*** Researchers can come up with potential solutions to the problem and present them in a report. Then ask students these guiding questions to focus the discussion about marketing research.

Guiding Questions

List What are the five steps of the marketing research process?	defining the problem, obtaining data, analyzing data, recommending solutions, applying the results
Predict What might happen if the data for a research problem were not thoroughly analyzed?	The recommended solutions might be faulty, and the applied results might not have the desired outcome.

Mini Project

Enrichment

Define the Problem To help students better understand *Step 1: Defining the Problem*, have the class brainstorm five or six issues that need to be addressed at your school. Issues might include such things as adding more lockers, keeping trash picked up, offering more nutritious snacks, and so on. Compile a list of the issues they bring up, and then have them vote on the four most pressing problems. Then divide the class into four groups and assign one of the problems to each group. Have groups set goals to solve the problem and present their solutions to the class. As groups are presenting their solutions, have the rest of the class imagine that they are the school board and are considering the merit of each group's solution. Tell students that the school board can only address one of the problems at this time. Based on the solutions presented, have the class vote on which problem to address. Tell students that the school board has limited funds but might be able to address additional problems if the solutions involve less time, money, or resources. Have groups revise their solutions based on these criteria. Ask groups to share their revised solutions with the class.

ELABORATE

STEP 2: OBTAINING DATA

Explain that data collected in marketing research must relate to the problem being studied. Then ask these guiding questions.

Guiding Questions

Explain Why is it more cost effective for a company to use secondary data?	Secondary data have already been collected, so it is less expensive to use those figures than it is to gather primary data.
Discuss What is the purpose of a marketing information system?	A marketing information system is a way to collect data used to measure sales, determine the geographic distribution of customers, track buying patterns, and identify popular items on the market.

Graphic Organizer

Display this diagram. Ask: ***What are the sources of secondary data?*** Answers are provided in the graphic below. Then ask: ***What are the sources of primary data?*** Answers are provided in the graphic below. Write students' answers in the diagram.

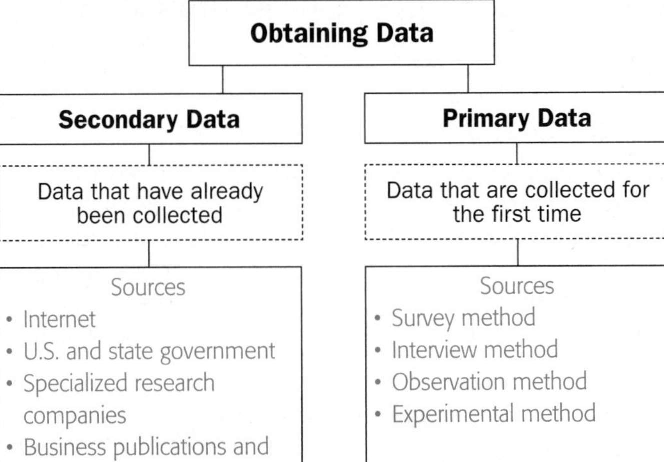

iWB

Graphic Organizer Send students to the Online Learning Center to print this graphic organizer.

Critical Thinking

Ask students to determine whether the follow data are primary or secondary sources.

- A personal interview response to a new iPod® packaging design (primary)
- A U.S. government demographic report (secondary)
- Statistics from the Small Business Administration on the number of small business start-ups (secondary)
- Apple's® five-year sales figures (secondary)
- Marketing research conducted by Kellogg's® for a new breakfast cereal (primary)
- A jewelry store's customer buying records (secondary)
- Census data from the state of Oregon (secondary)
- An opinion research poll conducted by Hewlett Packard® for a new computer it plans to introduce next year (primary)
- A supermarket survey conducted by a representative of a new ice cream manufacturer (primary)
- Statistics from a magazine on population growth in the U.S. (secondary)

To extend this activity, divide the class into groups and have groups create lists of data sources. Then have groups exchange lists and identify the sources as primary or secondary.

MARKETING CASE STUDY

English Language Arts Answer Marketers might have felt that they needed to get people to pay attention to their contribution to the smartphone market. Palm may have used secondary sources of information about features customers want in a smartphone. Palm may be targeting more mature smartphone users with their quiet, subtle ads. Their research may have found that there is an older target market for smartphones. The common in-your-face ads tend to appeal to a younger customer base. The more subtle commercials will likely appeal to a more mature customer base.

Digital dossiers, which provide company profiles on public corporations, income statements, and balance sheets, are available online for a fee. Business clearinghouses, such as Hoover's™ Online, Dow Jones Factiva®, Standard and Poor's NetAdvantage®, LexisNexis®, and Mergent Online™, are a few examples.

U.S. and State Government Sources

State departments of commerce and small business development centers can provide useful information. Data collected by U.S. government agencies can be accessed on the Internet for free or for a small fee. Such data may include population demographics, specific markets, industries, products, economic news, export information, and legislative trends. The Small Business Administration, U.S. Department of Commerce, U.S. Census Bureau, U.S. Securities and Exchange Commission, and the Bureau of Labor Statistics can also provide secondary data.

The *United States Census* and the *Statistical Abstract of the United States* contain hundreds of tables, graphs, and charts that can be useful when analyzing information. These publications feature data such as income, personal expenditures, age, and family size, in areas as small in size as ZIP code areas.

Specialized Research Companies

An active and growing number of specialized research companies, or syndicated services, also offer secondary data for business needs in print and electronic formats. Specialized companies sell demographic data, five-year forecasts, consumer purchase information, business data, census information, and consumer classification reports to businesses.

An example is Mediamark Research and Intelligence (MRI), which provides comprehensive demographic, lifestyle, product usage, and exposure data to all forms of advertising media. MRI is the nation's leading producer of multimedia audience research for advertisers, agencies, and magazines. The company also provides research for consumer marketing, brand loyalty, promotional opportunities, trade marketing services, and many other types of market research services.

Business Publications and Trade Organizations

Business publications, such as *Forbes, Business Week*, the *Wall Street Journal*, and *Marketing Management Journal*, are also good sources of secondary data. National and statewide trade associations often publish secondary data in articles, reports, and books.

Important information can be obtained from a variety of secondary data sources like this Web site. ***What benefits and risks are involved in the use of secondary data?***

Examples of trade associations that provide marketing research include the Advertising Research Foundation, American Association for Public Opinion Research, American Marketing Association, Council of American Survey Research Organizations, and the Marketing Research Association. Check the *Small Business Sourcebook* or the *Encyclopedia of Business Information Sources* for major books, trade journals, and organizations in **specific** business categories.

Advantages of Secondary Data

The greatest advantage of secondary data is that it can be obtained easily. Secondary data are on the Internet, and often available free of charge. The data are also in corporate, public, and college libraries. The data are also available for purchase from syndicated services. The U.S. Census Bureau can provide nationwide data that would cost any firm a great deal of time and money to research on its own.

Disadvantages of Secondary Data

There are two major disadvantages associated with secondary data. First, the existing data may not be suitable or specific for the problem under study. For example, little or no secondary data exist for new or innovative products.

The other disadvantage is that secondary data may sometimes be inaccurate. Federal census data are collected every ten years. As a result, projections based on the most the recent census may not be correct for the current year. Despite these limitations, a business should first investigate free or low-cost secondary data to solve a marketing problem.

SOURCES OF PRIMARY DATA

When marketing researchers cannot find information they need from secondary data, they collect primary data. Primary research data can be obtained through company research projects or specialized research organizations (see **Figure 29.2**). Large companies often have their own marketing research staff to conduct primary research. However, both large and small companies use research organizations. National research organizations contract with businesses and organizations to provide attitude and opinion, market, media, and product research services. The Nielsen Company®, Kantar Group®, Arbitron Inc.®, J.D. Power and Associates®, and Opinion Research Corporation® are some of the leading research organizations in the U.S. Primary data are collected using three methods: the survey method, the observation method, and the experimental method.

FIGURE 29.2 Primary Data Collection Methods

Collecting Primary Data This chart shows the methods used to collect primary data by market research firms. ***Why do you think Internet surveys have replaced the telephone as the most popular method of data collection?***

Method of Survey Data Collection	Used by Marketing Research Firms	
	2007	2008
Internet	30%	46%
Telephone	42%	33%
Mall Intercept	NA	7%
Mail	6%	7%
Mobile Phone	0%	4%
In-Person	NA	0%
Hybrid (combines two or more methods)	NA	3%

EXPLAIN

Mini Projects

Enrichment

Research a Competitor Have students select a company that has a Web site, and then imagine that they work for a competing company. Tell students to search the Web site and collect data that might help their own business. Ask students to write a thorough report about the company using data they collect from the Web site. Have them include suggestions for their own company's improvement based on the information obtained. Ask volunteers to share their reports with the class.

List Objective Source Have students work together in groups to create a list of sources they might use to verify data collected from a company's Web site. Then have groups share their lists and compile a class list. Possible answers: Business clearinghouses, such as Hoover's™ Online, Dow Jones Factiva®, Standard and Poor's NetAdvantage®, LexisNexis®, and Mergent Online™.

Visual Literacy

Secondary Research Data Caption Answer Read the caption question to students: ***What benefits and risks are involved in the use of secondary data?*** Benefits—the data have already been collected; secondary data are less expensive to collect than primary data; secondary data are readily available online. Risks—information available on company Web sites should be verified through objective sources. Ask students these guiding questions about secondary data.

Guiding Questions

Describe What types of data are available in the *United States Census* and the *Statistical Abstract of the United States*?	income, personal expenditures, age, and family size by ZIP code
Analyze Why might a company purchase data from a specialized research company?	The research company likely has more resources than the purchasing company; it would cost the purchasing company more to conduct their own research.

ELABORATE

Critical Thinking

Ask students to suggest secondary sources where they might obtain information for the following scenarios:

- A company wants to know if consumers will continue to purchase 35mm cameras five years from now. Possible answer: visit the Web sites of 35 mm camera makers and find their projected sales for the next five years.
- A company wants to determine whether there is a demand for household cleaners in the international market. Possible answer: visit the Web site of one or more household cleaner manufacturers and find where they sell their products in the global market.
- A clothing company wants to know its chief competitor's current prices for long-sleeved T-shirts. Possible answer: visit the competitor's Web site and find the prices for the T-shirts.

Graphic Organizer

Display this diagram. Ask students: ***What are the advantages of using secondary data?*** Answers are provided in the graphic below. Then ask: ***What are the disadvantages of using secondary data?*** Answers are provided in the graphic below. Possible answers:

Secondary Data

Advantages	Disadvantages
• Easily obtained • Often available free of charge • Available on Internet, in corporate, public, and college libraries • Available for purchase from syndicated services • Available from U.S. Census Bureau	• Existing data may not be suitable or specific for the problem under study • Little or no secondary data exist for new or innovative products • Secondary data may sometimes be inaccurate

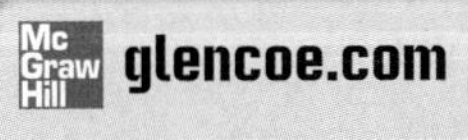

iWB

Graphic Organizer Send students to the Online Learning Center to print this graphic organizer.

Mini Projects

Extension

Devise a Scenario Divide the class into small groups. Ask students to create a scenario in which a small company might benefit from hiring a research organization to collect primary data. Sample scenario: A company needs to collect information about people's interest in outdoor sports in a nearby town where the company plans to open a new sporting goods store.

Research an Organization Have students select a national research organization such as The Nielsen Company®, Kantar Group®, Arbitron Inc.®, J.D. Power and Associates®, and Opinion Research Corporation®. Ask them to research the organization and write a review of the organization's services, fees, and special interests.

Visual Literacy

Figure 29.2 Caption Answer Read the caption question to students: *Why do you think Internet surveys have replaced the telephone as the most popular method of data collection?* Internet-based research allows for real-time data collection, multiple-choice questions, and open-ended, text-based answers. They are also less intrusive than phone calls. The national do-not-call list also makes telephone solicitation illegal if the person called has registered and is on the list. Then ask these guiding questions to help students better understand Figure 29.2.

Guiding Questions

Identify In addition to Internet, which methods of survey data collection increased in use from 2007 to 2008 (do not include those listed NA in 2007)?	mail and mobile phone
Predict Notice that in-person data collection was used 0% by marketing research firms in 2008. Why do you think this is so?	In-person data collection is probably more expensive and more time consuming than other methods, which makes it less cost effective.

The Survey Method

The **survey method** is a research technique in which information is gathered from people through the use of surveys or questionnaires. The surveys can be answered independently or by an interviewer, either in writing or orally. It is the most frequently used way of collecting primary data.

When designing a survey, marketers determine the number of people to include in a survey. Researchers can survey the entire target population if it is small. This is called a "census." However, researchers usually cannot survey the entire target population because it is too large, and time and money are limited. Instead, researchers use a sample of the target population to get results.

A **sample** is a part of the target population that represents the entire population. The size of the sample depends on the amount of money the company has to spend and the degree of accuracy that is needed. Generally, the larger the sample, the more accurate are the results.

After determining the size of the population to survey, a marketer must decide what type of survey to conduct. Surveys can be conducted in person, by phone (using personal calls and prerecorded messages), by mail (regular and email), or by using the Internet. When the marketer decides exactly how to conduct the survey, he or she then writes the questions according to the type of survey that will be used.

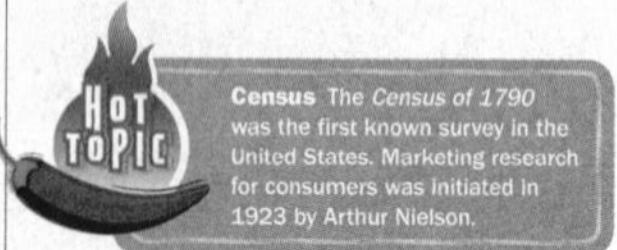

Census *The Census of 1790* was the first known survey in the United States. Marketing research for consumers was initiated in 1923 by Arthur Nielson.

Internet, Mail, and Telephone Surveys

Internet surveys are now the primary way of collecting primary data. Internet-based research allows for real-time data collection, multiple-choice questions, and open-ended, text-based answers. They are also less intrusive than phone calls.

E-mail surveys are surveys sent to a sample of people who are on a list of electronic-mail addresses. Respondents reply through e-mail. A *Web survey* is a survey uploaded to a Web site. People are asked to participate by visiting the designated Web site to answer questions online.

Data collection with e-mail and Web surveys is quick, since responses are automatically tabulated when they are completed. Disadvantages include having e-mail addresses and lists that are not accurate. Also, some people dislike receiving uninvited e-mail surveys, or lack computer proficiency or access to the Web. These disadvantages contribute to low response rates.

A standard *mail survey* is efficient and relatively inexpensive. Respondents are generally honest in their responses. Respondents are not interrupted with a phone call or e-mail message, and they can complete the survey at their leisure.

The *telephone survey* is a quick way to reach a potentially large audience (96 percent of households have phones). The use of mobile and smartphones for survey research is increasingly being used. However, the telephone method is somewhat limited by *Do Not Call* registry rules.

To increase response rates, some companies combine techniques, such as mail, Internet, and telephone invitations to take part in surveys.

The Interview Method

The personal interview involves questioning people face-to-face for a period of 10 to 30 minutes. Interviews can be conducted in individual homes and offices. But to reduce costs, researchers usually conduct interviews at central locations. Because centralized personal interviews first began in shopping malls, they are called "mall intercept interviews." A major advantage of interviews is that it is easier to get people to respond to personal interviews than to Internet, telephone, or mail surveys.

Another form of personal interview is the focus group interview. A focus group interview involves 8 to 12 people who are brought together to evaluate advertising, a particular product, package design, or a specific marketing strategy under the direction of a skilled moderator.

The moderator must direct the discussion to accomplish the objectives of the study. Focus group facilities usually include conference and observation rooms with audio and video equipment.

The Observation Method

The **observation method** is a research technique in which the actions of people are watched and recorded either by cameras or by observers. Properly performed and recorded observations supply better results than those obtained with survey techniques.

Mystery shopping is a form of observation that views interactions between customers and employees. A mystery shopper is a researcher who poses as a customer and goes into a business to observe employees and operations. A restaurant, for example, might want to observe the wait staff in their approach, sales presentation, product knowledge, and suggestion selling techniques.

Observation research is faster than conducting personal interviews, plus people are unaware that they are being observed, so they are acting as they normally would. This type of research is also cost effective.

Point-of-sale research is a powerful form of research that combines natural observation with personal interviews to explain buying behavior. Point-of-sale researchers observe shoppers to decide which ones to choose as research subjects. Participants can be chosen based upon variables, such as time of day (morning, afternoon, or evening) or the product that was purchased.

After observation, researchers approach the selected shoppers and ask them questions. Shoppers can easily remember the reason why they purchased a product because they have just made the decision to buy. Researchers might also gain additional input from other family members or shopping companions.

The Experimental Method

The **experimental method** is a research technique in which a researcher observes the results of changing one or more marketing variables while keeping all the other variables constant under controlled conditions. The experimental approach can be used to test new package designs, media usage, and new promotions.

For example, a manufacturer may want to compare two different colors for its new laundry detergent packaging. One group of consumers is shown the proposed package color. The other group is shown the same product with different package colors. Each group's responses are measured and recorded. Because only the package colors have been changed, the different responses are attributed to the color.

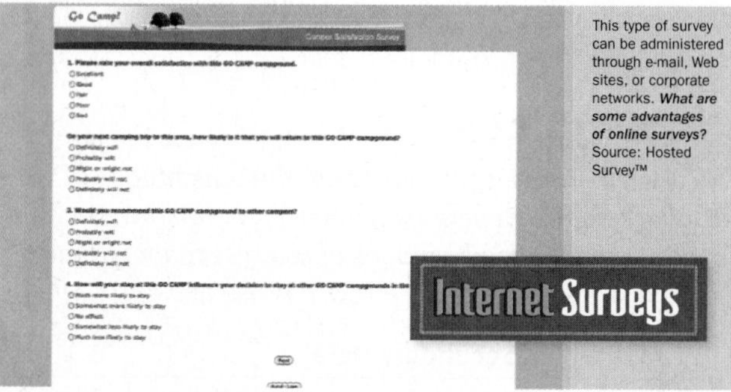

This type of survey can be administered through e-mail, Web sites, or corporate networks. ***What are some advantages of online surveys?*** Source: Hosted Survey™

EXPLAIN

Critical Thinking

Ask students to brainstorm examples of data that could be obtained only through primary research. Display students' answers for everyone to read. Answers may include: customers' satisfaction with products or services, future buying plans, personal brand preferences, and so on.

Census Have students visit the U.S. Census Bureau's Web site and create a list of the different types of information posted there. Then ask students to research Arthur Nielsen to learn whether he is associated with the company that conducts ratings of television programs.

Mini Projects

Enrichment

Research a Focus Group Ask students: ***What criteria might companies use to select participants for a focus group?*** Answers may include: geographic location, gender, or age. Now have students work in small groups to find online or other focus groups and give a brief oral summary of what they found. Ask: ***Have any of you ever participated in a focus group? If so, how would you describe the experience?*** Encourage students to share their experiences in as much detail as possible.

Conduct Mall Intercept Survey Have students work in small groups to develop three questions to use in a mall intercept survey. Questions should ask participants if they have ever participated in a mall interview before and what the experience was like. Compile the questions into a class list and have the class choose the three best questions to use in the survey. Then ask volunteers to use the questions to interview people at a mall. (Students should obtain permission from their parents, the school, and mall officials before conducting interviews.) Have interviewers share their experiences and data with the class.

ELABORATE

Mini Project

Extension

Investigate Attitude and Opinion Research Have students investigate how three different companies conduct attitude and opinion research. Make sure students include at least one local business in their exploration, such as a grocery store, post office, or restaurant. For local businesses, students may visit the business and interview a manager. For other businesses, have students look online for examples of attitude and opinion surveys. Have students write a one-page report detailing their findings. Reports should answer these questions: Do all of these businesses conduct research in the same way? If not, how do their approaches differ? Ask volunteers to share their reports with the class.

Graphic Organizer

Display this graphic organizer. Ask: ***What are the four sources of primary data?*** Survey Method, Interview Method, Observation Method, and Experimental Method. Label the four satellite shapes with these sources. Then ask students to provide details for each of the methods. Sample answers are provided in the graphic organizer.

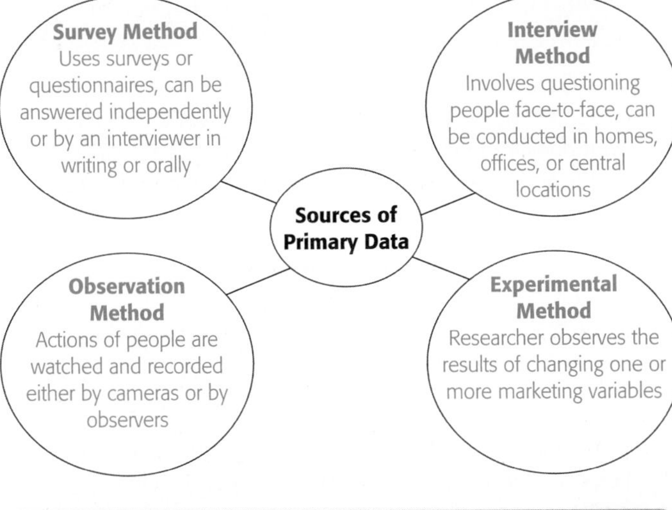
Survey Method
Uses surveys or questionnaires, can be answered independently or by an interviewer in writing or orally
Interview Method
Involves questioning people face-to-face, can be conducted in homes, offices, or central locations
Sources of Primary Data
Observation Method
Actions of people are watched and recorded either by cameras or by observers
Experimental Method
Researcher observes the results of changing one or more marketing variables

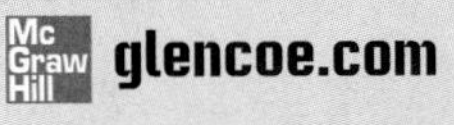
glencoe.com

iWB

Graphic Organizer Send students to the Online Learning Center to print this graphic organizer.

Critical Thinking

Tell students that they work for an ice cream company that would like to conduct mall intercept interviews. Have students identify at least three central locations that might be ideal for gathering customer feedback. Answers may include: at the food court, near an ice cream store, in the center of the mall, outside a large anchor store, and so on.

Visual Literacy

Internet Surveys Caption Answer Read the caption question to students: ***What are some advantages of online surveys?*** They allow for real-time data collection, multiple-choice questions, and open-ended, text-based answers; and they are less intrusive than phone calls. Ask students: ***Have you ever participated in an online survey? If so, share your experience with the class.*** Encourage students who have participated in online surveys to share what the survey was about and whether they found the experience to be pleasant or unpleasant. Also, ask if the students received any incentive for answering the survey. Then ask these guiding questions to stimulate discussion about Internet surveys.

Guiding Questions

Explain What are some advantages and disadvantages of Internet surveys?	Advantages: data collection is quick; responses are automatically tabulated when they are completed. Disadvantages: e-mail addresses and lists may not be accurate; some people dislike receiving uninvited e-mail surveys; some people lack computer proficiency or access to the Web.
Compare and Contrast How are e-mail surveys and Web surveys alike? How are they different?	Both are conducted online and allow for real-time data collection, multiple-choice questions, and open-ended, text-based answers. E-mail surveys are sent to a sample of people who are on a list of electronic-mail addresses. Web surveys are uploaded to Web sites where people visit to complete the survey.

Knowledge Matters

VIRTUAL BUSINESS

MARKET RESEARCH

Introduce students to the concept of market research using Knowledge Matters' Virtual Business Retailing visual simulation, Market Research. In this simulation, students learn how to collect market information and how to use the information to make their business more successful.

Experimental research can provide useful information. However, it is used less frequently than other methods. It is used less often because people usually respond differently in actual buying situations.

Impact of Technology

Computer technologies have had a tremendous impact on marketing research. Quantitative and qualitative survey research can be done on the Internet through e-mail and Web surveys, computer-aided Web interviewing, and focus group sessions. Audio-visual effects, graphics, company logos, and brands can be included in Internet surveys.

Computer-assisted, telephone-dialing surveys allow a prerecorded voice to qualify a respondent, and then to ask a series of survey questions. Automated dialers can be used to increase the number of telephone survey responses by placing multiple calls and automatically rejecting those with busy signals, answering machines, and voicemail.

Fax broadcasting allows businesses to send questionnaires to a select group of fax numbers. Interactive voice response is similar to voicemail as callers are greeted by a recorded voice that leads them through a series of questions. Responders use the telephone keypad to provide their answers.

STEP 3: ANALYZING THE DATA

The third step in the marketing research process is data analysis. **Data analysis** is the process of compiling, analyzing, and interpreting the results of primary and secondary data collection.

A-P Super Service, Inc., created a customer survey about the quality and efficiency of the auto mechanics' repair service. A-P Super Service received 120 completed surveys. Answers were organized so that the percentage of men and women responding to each question was clearly shown. Data were cross-tabulated to determine such things as how men and women differ in their perceptions of the service. The answers to a question about the quality of service might be presented as shown in the following table. The number of respondents is given in parentheses after the question.

Question: How would you rate the quality of service provided by A-P Super Service, Inc.? (N = 120)

Rating	Men	Women
Excellent	30%	60%
Good	15%	10%
Average	20%	20%
Fair	20%	5%
Poor	15%	5%

As you can see, female customers of A-P Super Service, Inc., have a more favorable impression of the quality of service than the male customers have. This information shows the owner that the shop's image among its male customers needs to be improved.

DATA MINING

Data mining is a computer process that uses statistical methods to extract new information from large amounts of data. A database may contain subtle relationships or patterns that only a mathematical search process can identify. Competitive, demographic, site, and location data obtained through data mining assists in forecasting and predicting sales opportunities.

Data mining also allows researchers to generate lists of potential survey respondents and to design surveys for primary data collection. Marketing information data is stored, sorted, and used to improve new and existing products and services.

STEP 4: RECOMMENDING SOLUTIONS TO THE PROBLEM

Conclusions drawn from research are usually presented in an organized and detailed written report. Recommendations must be clear and well supported by the research data. A typical research report includes the following elements:

- Title page
- Acknowledgments of people who assisted in the research effort
- Table of contents
- List of tables, figures, charts, and graphs
- Introduction (includes the problem under study, its importance, definitions, limitations of the study, and basic assumptions)
- Review of the research information (including the results of any secondary data reviewed for the research effort)
- Procedures used (research technique or techniques used to obtain primary data)
- Findings
- Recommendations
- Summary and conclusions
- Appendixes
- Bibliography

STEP 5: APPLYING THE RESULTS

In evaluating any research, managers may find that the study was inconclusive and that additional research is needed. They may also conclude that the research suggests specific changes or new courses of action.

After the research has been completed and any actions are taken, a business should carefully monitor the results of those changes. A business needs to know whether the specific actions taken are successful. The research effort can be considered a success if the resulting decisions lead to higher profits in the form of increased sales, greater efficiency, or reduced expenses.

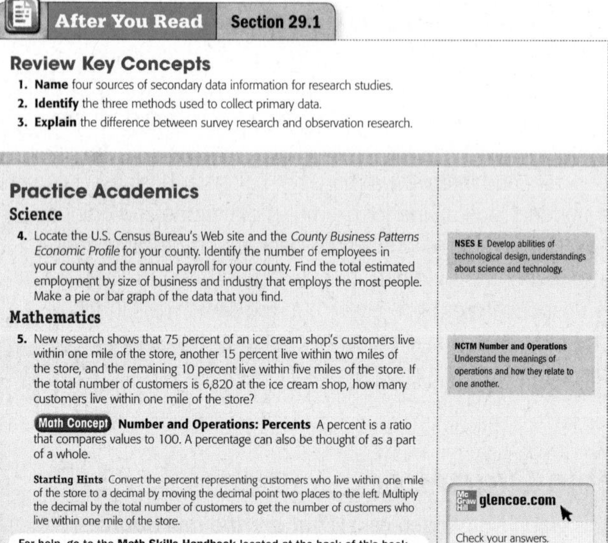

After You Read | **Section 29.1**

Review Key Concepts

1. **Name** four sources of secondary data information for research studies.
2. **Identify** the three methods used to collect primary data.
3. **Explain** the difference between survey research and observation research.

Practice Academics

Science

4. Locate the U.S. Census Bureau's Web site and the *County Business Patterns Economic Profile* for your county. Identify the number of employees in your county and the annual payroll for your county. Find the total estimated employment by size of business and industry that employs the most people. Make a pie or bar graph of the data that you find.

Mathematics

5. New research shows that 75 percent of an ice cream shop's customers live within one mile of the store, another 15 percent live within two miles of the store, and the remaining 10 percent live within five miles of the store. If the total number of customers is 6,820 at the ice cream shop, how many customers live within one mile of the store?

Math Concept **Number and Operations: Percents** A percent is a ratio that compares values to 100. A percentage can also be thought of as a part of a whole.

Starting Hints Convert the percent representing customers who live within one mile of the store to a decimal by moving the decimal point two places to the left. Multiply the decimal by the total number of customers to get the number of customers who live within one mile of the store.

For help, go to the **Math Skills Handbook** located at the back of this book.

NSES E Develop abilities of technological design, understandings about science and technology.

NCTM Number and Operations Understand the meanings of operations and how they relate to one another.

glencoe.com

Check your answers.

ELABORATE

Mini Projects

Differentiated Instruction

Interpersonal Learners Divide the class into small groups. Have them discuss the process of data analysis and devise a method to teach the concept. Students might use visuals, repetition, or other ideas. Ask a volunteer from each group to explain the concept to the class. The process involves compiling, analyzing, and interpreting results of primary and secondary data collection. This data may be organized into a chart or other visual aid to clearly present the results.

Students with Learning Disabilities Divide the class into small groups. Have groups work together to learn the Content and Academic Vocabulary terms for this section (see vocabulary list on page 678). Students might make a card game in which they write the words and definitions on separate index cards and then match each word to its definition. After they learn the words, have students use them in original sentences.

STEP 3: ANALYZING THE DATA

Tell students that collecting data is only part of the puzzle for arriving at a solution for the defined problem—the data have to be analyzed. Ask: ***What does it mean to analyze data?*** to compile, analyze, and interpret the results of the data collection Then ask these guiding questions about data analysis.

Guiding Questions

Define What is data mining?	a computer process that uses statistical methods to extract new information from large amounts of data
Explain What is the purpose of data mining?	It assists in predicting sales opportunities. It allows researchers to generate lists of survey respondents and to design surveys for primary data collection. Marketing information data are stored, sorted, and used to improve products and services.
Analyze How does data mining aid in data analysis?	It helps analyze data by extracting new information that only a mathematical search can identify.

EVALUATE

Graphic Organizer

Display this graphic organizer Ask students: ***What are the five steps of the marketing research process?*** Step 1: Defining the Problem; Step 2: Obtaining Data; Step 3: Analyzing Data; Step 4: Recommending Solutions; and Step 5: Applying the Results. Then ask students to provide details about each step. Sample answers are provided in the graphic organizer.

Step 5: Applying the Results Monitor changes made based on research results

Step 4: Recommending Solutions Present clear and well-supported conclusions in organized, detailed report

Step 3: Analyzing Data Compile, analyze, and interpret the results of primary and secondary data collection

Step 2: Obtaining Data Collect primary and secondary data; examine data in terms of problem(s) being studied; secondary data more cost effective; primary data may be more reliable

Step 1: Defining the Problem Identify a research question and the information that is necessary to answer it; create objectives that will help answer the problem; use objectives to construct questions

 **glencoe.com** 

Graphic Organizer Send students to the Online Learning Center to print this graphic organizer.

Critical Thinking

Divide the class into small groups. Ask students the following question: ***After completing all five steps of the marketing research process, how will a company know if its research effort was a success?*** Have groups discuss the question and list as many answers as they can. Then have the groups come together and generate a class list of answers to the question. Answers may include: The company should monitor the decisions made as a result of the research; if the decisions lead to increased profits through better sales, increased efficiency, or reduced expenses, then the research was successful.

 **After You Read** Section 29.1

Review Key Concepts

1. Answers may include any four of the following: a business's marketing information system, Internet resources, government sources, specialized research companies, business publications and trade organizations.
2. The three methods of collecting primary data are the survey method, the observation method and the experimental method.
3. The survey method gathers information through surveys or questionnaires. The observation method collects data by observing people.

Practice Academics

Science

4. Answers are dependent on information specific to your county. Students should identify the number of employees in your county and the annual payroll for your county, find the total estimated employment by size of business and industry that employs the most people, and make a pie chart or bar graph of the data that they find.

Mathematics

5. The answer is 5,115 (6,820 × .75).

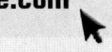

 **glencoe.com** 

Answer Key Send students to the Online Learning Center to check their answers.

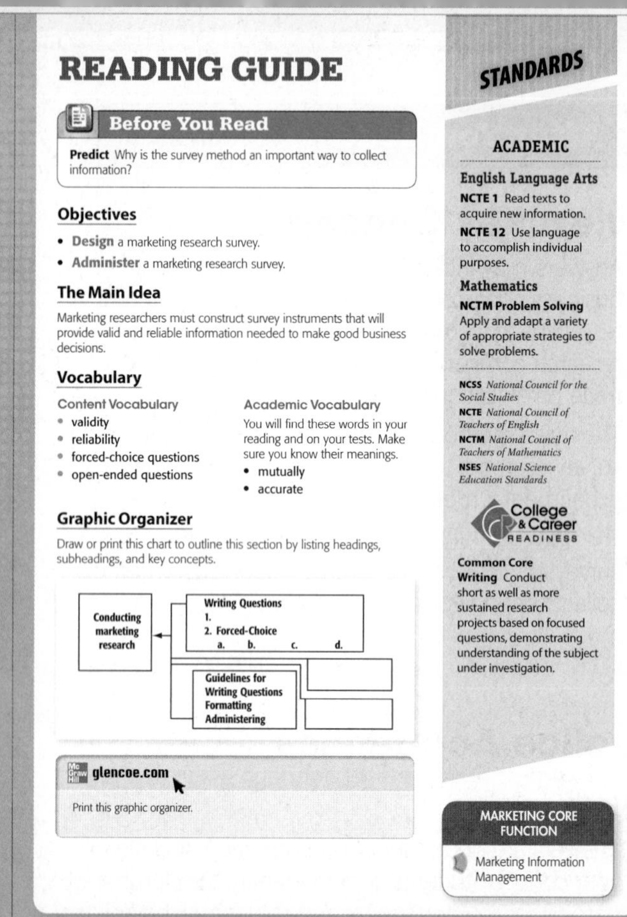

READING GUIDE

Before You Read

Predict Why is the survey method an important way to collect information?

Objectives

- **Design** a marketing research survey.
- **Administer** a marketing research survey.

The Main Idea

Marketing researchers must construct survey instruments that will provide valid and reliable information needed to make good business decisions.

Vocabulary

Content Vocabulary
- validity
- reliability
- forced-choice questions
- open-ended questions

Academic Vocabulary

You will find these words in your reading and on your tests. Make sure you know their meanings.
- mutually
- accurate

Graphic Organizer

Draw or print this chart to outline this section by listing headings, subheadings, and key concepts.

Conducting marketing research | Writing Questions 1. 2. Forced-Choice a. b. c. d. | Guidelines for Writing Questions Formatting Administering

glencoe.com

Print this graphic organizer.

STANDARDS

ACADEMIC

English Language Arts

NCTE 1 Read texts to acquire new information.

NCTE 12 Use language to accomplish individual purposes.

Mathematics

NCTM Problem Solving Apply and adapt a variety of appropriate strategies to solve problems.

NCSS *National Council for the Social Studies*
NCTE *National Council of Teachers of English*
NCTM *National Council of Teachers of Mathematics*
NSES *National Science Education Standards*

College & Career READINESS

Common Core
Writing Conduct short as well as more sustained research projects based on focused questions, demonstrating understanding of the subject under investigation.

MARKETING CORE FUNCTION

Marketing Information Management

Section 29.2

The Marketing Survey

CONSTRUCTING THE QUESTIONNAIRE

A questionnaire is a set of questions used to generate data in order to answer the research problem and accomplish the objectives of the study. Questionnaires should provide data that have validity.

A questionnaire has **validity** when the survey questions measure what was intended to be measured. For example, a researcher designs a questionnaire to measure customer satisfaction with a hotel's lodging services. Questionnaires that are poorly written or that do not address lodging services will not have validity.

As You Read

Compare What are the similarities between written survey instruments and scripted interviews?

Research questionnaires should also have reliability. **Reliability** exists when a research technique produces nearly identical results in repeated trials. Reliability requires that the questions ask for the same type of information from all the respondents.

Questions should be clear and easily understood so that all participants understand the question in the same way. Asking a question in a restaurant survey such as "Was your food hot?" would not yield a reliable answer. "Hot" could be interpreted as either the level of spiciness or the temperature of the food.

A valid and reliable questionnaire must be well written, correctly formatted, and properly administered. A questionnaire directed at hotel guests may not be appropriate for the purchaser of a new vehicle. It is also important to ask questions only of customers who have actually used the product or service in question.

> "A well-constructed survey motivates people to complete questions and provide accurate information."

TYPES OF QUESTIONS

Survey questions can be either open-ended or forced-choice. **Forced-choice questions** ask respondents to choose answers from possibilities given on a questionnaire. Forced-choice questions are the simplest questions to write and also the easiest to tabulate. They can be two-choice, multiple-choice, or rating-scale questions. A two-choice question might ask respondents to provide a simple yes-or-no answer or to choose between one of two given answers. A multiple-choice question presents a short list of answers from which to choose. A rating-scale question asks for a ranking, such as "between 1 and 5." Respondents may also be asked to rank a list of specific activities or task in order of preference.

Open-ended questions ask respondents to construct their own response to a question. "What changes or additions to your hotel room would you recommend?" is an example of an open-ended question.

Some surveys have a space for general comments or suggestions. This type of open-ended question allows respondents to give opinions in their own words. Open-ended questions generate a wide variety of responses that are sometimes difficult to categorize and tabulate. As a result, most researchers prefer forced-choice questions.

ENGAGE

Anticipation Activity

Improving Student Achievement Have students brainstorm a list of three problems for which a business might use marketing research. Display each problem as a column heading. Sample problems: to find out customers' satisfaction with a product; to learn whether a new product might be successful. Then have each student choose one of the problems and write three questions that could be asked about the problem on a research questionnaire. Write their questions in the appropriate column. Then ask: ***Are the questions open-ended or forced-choice?*** Answers will vary depending on the type of questions students came up with.

Objectives

- **Design** a marketing research survey. A valid and reliable questionnaire must have questions that are well written and correctly formatted.
- **Administer** a marketing research survey. Basic guidelines include deadlines for completion and clear, concise instructions.

Graphic Organizer

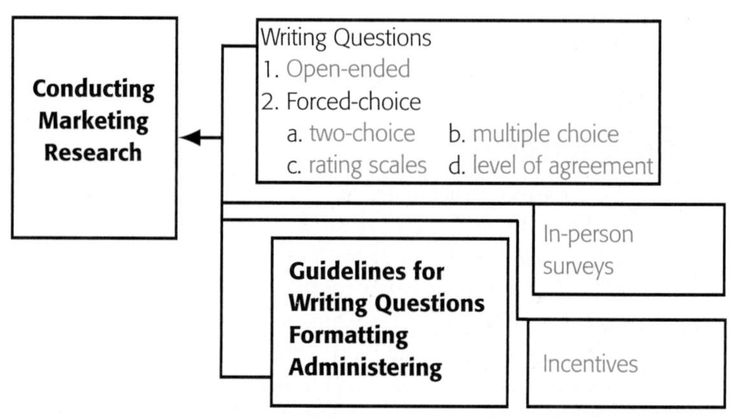

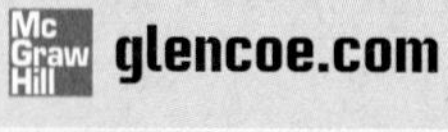

glencoe.com

iWB

Graphic Organizer Send students to the Online Learning Center to print this graphic organizer.

EXPLORE

Before You Read

Read the question aloud: ***Why is the survey method an important way to collect information?*** Surveys can be collected in organized and systematic ways to gather information about customer demographics, reasons for purchases, income levels, knowledge of competitor's products, and customer satisfaction.

Preteaching Vocabulary

Have students go to the Online Learning Center at glencoe.com for the Chapter 29 Preteaching Vocabulary games.

Content Vocabulary

Display the vocabulary terms for the class: *validity*, *reliability*, *forced-choice questions*, and *open-ended questions*. Ask students to predict the meanings of the terms. validity—questions asked on a questionnaire measure what was intended to be measured; reliability—a research technique produces nearly identical results in repeated trials; forced-choice questions—questions that ask respondents to choose answers from possibilities given on a questionnaire; open-ended questions—questions that require respondents to construct their own answers

Academic Vocabulary

Mutually—Usage Read the following sentence to students: ***When constructing multiple-choice questions, it is important to make the options mutually exclusive and comprehensive enough to include every possible response.*** Tell students that in this sentence, *mutually* must be paired with *exclusive* to understand the usage. The term *mutually exclusive*, in terms of writing multiple-choice questions, means that the answers cannot all be true at the same time. To help students better understand this concept, display the days of the week for everyone to view. Ask students: ***Which is your favorite day of the week?*** Help students understand that there can be only one true answer to the question—the options are mutually exclusive.

PROFESSIONAL DEVELOPMENT **MINI CLIP** 

ELL: Elaborating on Student Responses
Go to the Online Learning Center to view a video in which a teacher uses explanatory language to elaborate on a student response and places it in the context of the lesson.

Section 29.2

The Marketing Survey

CONSTRUCTING THE QUESTIONNAIRE

Explain to students that constructing a good questionnaire involves much more than just writing some questions. Ask these guiding questions to focus the discussion on questionnaire construction.

Guiding Questions

Explain When does a research questionnaire have validity and reliability?	A questionnaire has validity when the questions measure what was intended to be measured. Reliability exists when a research technique produces nearly identical results in repeated trials.
Differentiate What is the difference between forced-choice questions and open-ended questions?	Forced-choice questions ask respondents to choose answers from possibilities provided on the questionnaire. Open-ended questions ask respondents to construct their own response to a question.

As You Read

Read the As You Read question aloud: ***What are the similarities between written survey instruments and scripted interviews?*** They both represent organized methods to ensure that the research questions are asked in a complete and well-defined systematic manner. Both methods usually survey a sample of the population and include some type of incentive to participate.

Expert Advice

Read the quote to students:

> **“A well-constructed survey motivates people to complete questions and provide accurate information.”**

Ask students: ***Why would a well-constructed survey motivate people to complete it?*** If a survey seems too difficult or too confusing, people will not bother to complete it.

YES/NO QUESTIONS

Two-choice questions give the respondent only two options, usually yes or no. Yes-or-no questions should be used only when asking for a response on one issue. You could use a yes-or-no question to ask questions like these:

"Did you have a problem during your stay?"

☐ **YES** ☐ **NO**

"If **YES**, did you report it to the staff?

☐ **YES** ☐ **NO**

You would not ask: "Did you have a problem and did you report it?" The customer may have different answers for the two issues that the question addresses.

Having a question that asks about more than one issue decreases validity and reliability. Yes-or-no questions are most often used as filter questions. Filter questions help to guide respondents to answer only those questions that apply. In cases in which there is a range of choices and yes-or-no questions are not appropriate, you would use multiple-choice questions or rating-scale questions for your survey.

MULTIPLE-CHOICE QUESTIONS

Multiple-choice questions give the respondent several choices. When constructing multiple-choice questions, it is important to make the options **mutually** exclusive and comprehensive enough to include every possible response.

In order to be sure that all options are covered, many surveys have a space for the option "other." For example, a car rental company might ask its customers the following question:

When you have a choice of the car rental companies listed below, which do you prefer? (check one)

☐ Alamo	☐ Hertz
☐ Avis	☐ National
☐ Budget	☐ Thrifty
☐ Dollar	☐ Other ______
☐ Enterprise	

Offering the choice of "other" increases the reliability of a questionnaire. If "other" was not an option, respondents who use an unlisted car rental service might not give an answer at all, or they might choose an inaccurate answer from the list based on their limited choices. Either of these actions by respondents would result in misleading survey results.

RATING-SCALE QUESTIONS

Other forced-choice questions may ask respondents to rate a product or service based upon a scale. A variety of customer conditions, perceptions, and situations can be measured using rating scales.

Some of the most common rating scales measure levels of agreement, beliefs, frequency, importance, quality, satisfaction, and use. Examples of wording include a satisfaction scale that ranges from *completely satisfied* to *completely dissatisfied*, a quality scale that ranges from *excellent* to *poor*, or an amount-of-use scale that ranges from *never use* to *frequently use*.

Some questionnaires ask respondents to rate a product or service based on a percentage scale, on which 100 would be a perfect score. Others ask for ratings based on a numerical scale. Many consumer Web sites ask users to give products they purchase ratings of between 1 and 5 stars.

Research indicates that questionnaires which use five-point and seven-point rating scales result in the most reliability and validity. The following is an example of a five-point rating questionnaire used to rate the quality of front desk staff.

How would you rate the quality of service provided by the hotel's front desk?

	Excellent	Very Good	Good	Fair	Poor
Courtesy	5 ☐	4 ☐	3 ☐	2 ☐	1 ☐
Speed at check-in	5 ☐	4 ☐	3 ☐	2 ☐	1 ☐
Check-out process	5 ☐	4 ☐	3 ☐	2 ☐	1 ☐
Accuracy of bill	5 ☐	4 ☐	3 ☐	2 ☐	1 ☐

RATING SCALE STATEMENTS

In some surveys respondents answer statements rather than questions. They respond to belief or behavior statements to describe their attitudes, opinions, or preferences. A seven-point rating scale for a level of agreement rating scale might include *completely agree* (CA), *somewhat agree* (SA), *agree* (A) *neither agree nor disagree* (N), *disagree* (D) *somewhat disagree* (SD), and *completely disagree* (SD).

Below are examples of statements that might be used to measure attitudes and opinions in a health-care questionnaire. The respondents relate their personal experiences to the statements when responding.

As you can see, if someone had to answer yes or no to these questions, the researcher might not get an **accurate** picture. That is why it is often easier to use descriptive statements for research on attitudes and opinions.

Indicate your level of agreement with the following statements:

Completely Agree	Somewhat Agree	Agree	Neither Agree Nor Disagree	Disagree	Somewhat Disagree	Completely Disagree
"I am extremely health conscious."						
CA ☐	SA ☐	A ☐	N ☐	D ☐	SD ☐	CD ☐
"I do not like vegetables."						
CA ☐	SA ☐	A ☐	N ☐	D ☐	SD ☐	CD ☐
"Eating low-cholesterol foods is important to me."						
CA ☐	SA ☐	A ☐	N ☐	D ☐	SD ☐	CD ☐
"The cafeteria should serve heart-healthy foods."						
CA ☐	SA ☐	A ☐	N ☐	D ☐	SD ☐	CD ☐

Lost Respondents

This graph shows the number of people who do not complete a survey based upon the number of survey questions. ***Based upon the data provided in this graph, what implications about survey research rates can you draw?***

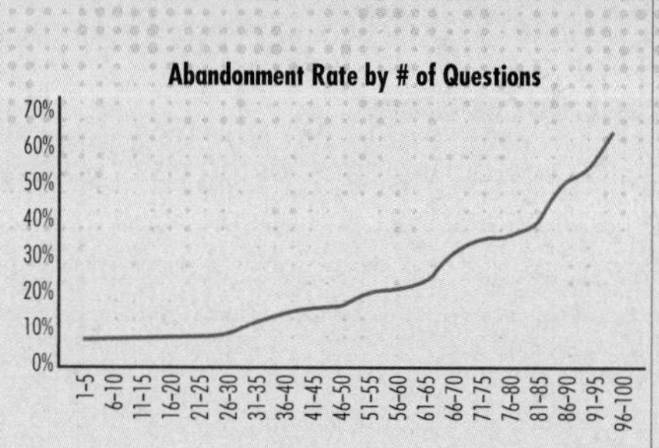

EXPLORE

Graphic Organizer

Display this chart. Ask students to provide other type questions discussed in the text. Possible answers:

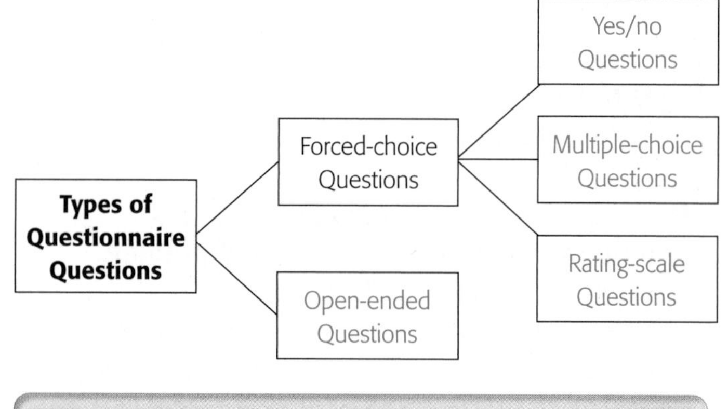

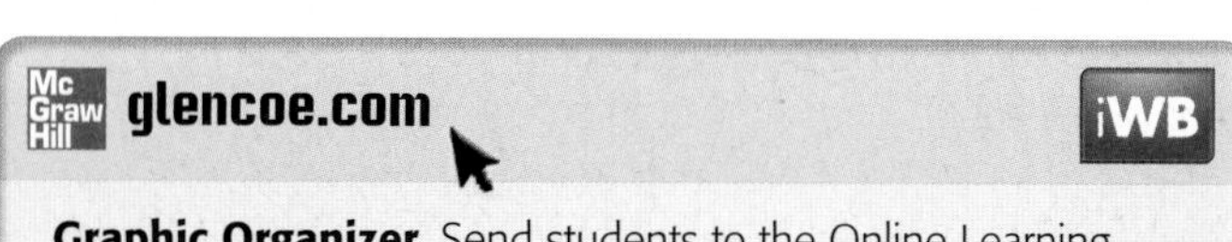

Graphic Organizer Send students to the Online Learning Center to print this graphic organizer.

Critical Thinking

To help students better understand the concept of yes/no questions, provide them with the following example questions and ask them to explain why the questions are poorly constructed. Then ask students to rewrite and improve the questions.

- ***Was your hotel experience enjoyable and problem-free?*** The respondent may have different answers to "enjoyable" and "problem-free" but they are being asked to answer both in one question. Improvement: Was your hotel experience enjoyable? Was your hotel experience problem-free?
- ***Do you support the mayor's view on education?*** The question assumes the respondent already knows the mayor's view on education. Improvement: The mayor's official view on education is ____. Do you support her view on education?
- ***Will you ever return to Los Angeles?*** The respondent may not know his future plans. Improvement: Do you plan to return to Los Angeles within the next year?

EXPLAIN

Mini Projects

Extension

Write Multiple-Choice Questions Bring to class examples of multiple-choice surveys from the Internet. Have students guess what kind of company distributed each survey. Then ask students to guess the problem the survey was designed to address. Next, ask students to select a topic that interests them. Have them create their own survey about this topic to distribute to classmates. The survey should include 10–20 multiple-choice questions. Have students distribute the survey and compile the results. Ask students to share their results with the class.

Write Rating-Scale Questions Ask students to consider the following scenario: A small bookstore has been losing money since a larger bookstore opened in the same area. Some customers have mentioned that the new bookstore has a coffee bar and a reading lounge—things the small bookstore does not have. The owners are willing to expand their small bookstore, but need to know what customers really want. Ask students what questions the owners should ask if they distribute a survey to their current customers. Then have students write five rating-scale questions to be used in the survey.

Visual Literacy

Lost Respondents Caption Answer Read the caption question to students. ***Based upon the data provided in this graph, what implications about survey research rates can you draw?*** The graph shows that the longer the survey, the higher the abandonment rate. Students should conclude that shorter questionnaires are more likely to be answered by respondents.

RATING SCALE STATEMENTS

Ask these guiding questions about rating scale statements.

Guiding Questions

Explain Why is it often easier to use descriptive statements for research on attitudes and opinions?	It is difficult to get an accurate picture or a person's attitudes or opinions with yes or no questions.
Predict Which would be easier to analyze the answers to yes/no questions or the answers to rating-scale questions?	It is more difficult to analyze the answer to rating-scale questions because there are more possible answers.

e MARKETING

Web Panels—Online Focus Groups

Consumer Web panel research is conducted by marketing research firms with access to a representative population in a geographic area. Since the marketing research firm has the demographic information of its panel members, the sample can be statistically accurate for any target population regarding age, gender, marital status, education level, etc. Online focus groups are essentially forum discussion groups (chat rooms) that take place online led by trained moderators. Effective online focus groups are usually limited to ten or fewer pre-selected participants. Open-ended discussion question scripts usually work best and allow the moderator to interject questions in response to what is discussed by the participants. Online focus groups are easily recorded so marketers can study transcripts of the sessions.

Innovate and Create

Have students design an online focus group for a topic of their choice. They should base their research on a specific research question and objectives. Their script (open-ended questions) needs to be correlated with the objectives in order to produce the information needed to answer the research question. For this exercise to be effective, it is best to keep the research question simple, appropriate for teens, and of interest to students. A research question may be "How can the school lunch program be improved? Or "How can school spirit be improved?" Objectives for the each of those studies may be to determine: current satisfaction; areas that need to be addressed; ideas for improving the current programs; and how students can be instrumental in implementing those ideas. The written report should include: research methodology, the specific research question, objectives, sample script (questions), findings, conclusions, and recommendations.

glencoe.com

eMarketing Worksheet Activity Send students to the Online Learning Center to download an eMarketing worksheet activity.

The GREEN Marketer

Convincing the Green Consumer

Consumers' spending does not always match their attitudes. Many Americans say they value environmentalism, yet relatively few buy green products. Market research shows that consumers are more likely to switch to green items, however, if they are told about their specific benefits.

Package Benefits Seventh Generation®, for example, states on its packaging that if every family replaced just one roll of nonrecycled toilet paper with a recycled roll, we could save 448,000 trees every year.

English Language Arts

Create You have agreed to write a level-of-agreement survey for Ranch Market to assess consumers' environmental attitudes. First, write three statements to assess beliefs or opinions. Next write three statements that assess whether consumers would buy green products at the market.

NCTE 12 Use language to accomplish individual purposes.

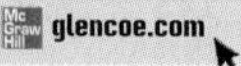 glencoe.com

Get an activity on green marketing.

BASIC GUIDELINES FOR WRITING QUESTIONS

Each question should be written clearly and as briefly as possible. Use the same rating scales for all similar questions. It is important not to ask leading questions, which suggest a correct answer. An example of a leading question is: "Do you prefer X or the more reasonably priced Z?" The phrase "more reasonably priced" could influence the respondents to answer Z.

You should avoid any bias, which is a systematic error introduced by encouraging one outcome or answer over the others. It is also important to avoid questions that might cause a respondent to guess at the meaning of your question. The following is an example of a question that might cause a respondent to guess:

How many students in your high school drink coffee on a daily basis?

- ☐ Less than 10
- ☐ 10–49
- ☐ 50–99
- ☐ 100–149
- ☐ 150–199
- ☐ over 200

Without asking every student in school, the respondent cannot answer the question without guessing.

When a survey questionnaire is finished, it is a good idea to pretest the wording of the questions. This pretest allows for correction of any misleading questions, directions, or problems on the questionnaire.

FORMATTING

Questionnaires must have good visual appearance and ample white space for respondents. Different colors and typefaces can add to the design appeal, but use no more than two different ink colors and typefaces. The preferred color for most surveys is black on light paper and an easy-to-read font, such as Times Roman.

The questionnaire should be short enough to be answered quickly. Distinct headings should be placed on all individual survey sections. Numbers should be placed on all individual questions. If your questionnaire requires more than one page, place a note on the bottom of each page to continue to the next page.

It is good practice to vary the format between the questions and the options. For example, you might set the questions in sentence format and options to questions or statements capitalized or set in boldface type. Another format would be to set the questions in sentence format and boldface type with options in sentence format. Questions and multiple-choice answer selections should be short. Instructions and other text used in the survey should use common language so they will be understood by respondents. Varying the format is also a good way to keep the survey interesting for the respondents.

You should place boxes ☐, circles ○, or brackets [ ] next to your possible options. These symbols tell the respondents where they should place their answers.

CONTENT FORMATTING

Directions for completing written surveys must be clear for each section or group of questions. All of the questions need to be numbered. Questions generally follow a sequence starting with screening questions, and then leading to more specific questions.

Screening questions are asked at the beginning of the survey. For example, if an interviewer wanted to study the views of young adults, he or she might ask, "Are you between the ages of 18 and 29?" If the respondent answers yes, the interviewer administers the survey. If the answer is no, then the person would not be included in the study. Such information is placed at the beginning of a questionnaire only to "screen" or qualify a respondent. General and specific questions about the business are asked next.

Demographic questions are used to identify such traits as gender, age, ethnic background, income, and education. Demographic questions can help a business to determine, for example, that most of its customers live in the Northeast, are between the ages of 30 and 55, and have incomes between $45,000 and $65,000. Demographic profiles are typically grouped together at the end of a questionnaire. This is because respondents are more likely to answer personal questions after completing the other questions.

Lastly, many surveys provide an open-end section for comments and suggestions. Companies frequently ask permission to follow-up and provide a contact point, if respondents desire additional information.

 **Reading Check**

Recall What are three types of questions used on surveys?

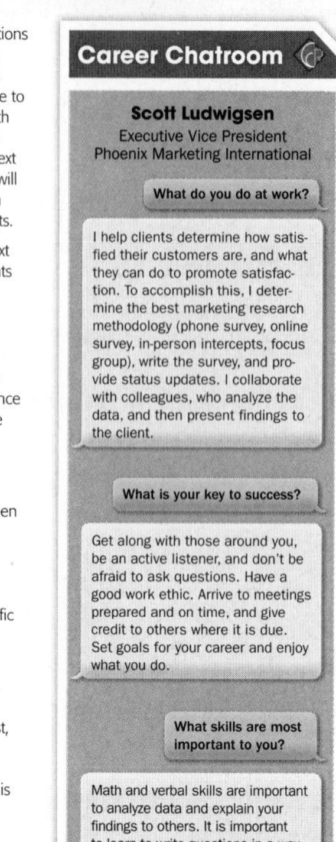

Career Chatroom

Scott Ludwigsen
Executive Vice President
Phoenix Marketing International

What do you do at work?

I help clients determine how satisfied their customers are, and what they can do to promote satisfaction. To accomplish this, I determine the best marketing research methodology (phone survey, online survey, in-person intercepts, focus group), write the survey, and provide status updates. I collaborate with colleagues, who analyze the data, and then present findings to the client.

What is your key to success?

Get along with those around you, be an active listener, and don't be afraid to ask questions. Have a good work ethic. Arrive to meetings prepared and on time, and give credit to others where it is due. Set goals for your career and enjoy what you do.

What skills are most important to you?

Math and verbal skills are important to analyze data and explain your findings to others. It is important to learn to write questions in a way that will not bias responses.

glencoe.com

Read more about this career and complete a Career Exploration Activity.

EXPLAIN

The GREEN Marketer

English Language Arts Answer Read the English Language Arts Activity: ***You have agreed to write a level-of-agreement survey for Ranch Market to assess consumers' environmental attitudes. First, write three statements to assess beliefs or opinions. Next write three statements that assess whether consumers would buy green products at the market.*** Statements may assess their values ("The environment is important to me"), identity, and opinions. Statements should focus on behavior: "I always choose green products over conventional ones" or "I would pay more for green products at Ranch Market."

 **glencoe.com**

Worksheet Activity Send students to the Online Learning Center to get a Green Marketer worksheet activity.

BASIC GUIDELINES FOR WRITING QUESTIONS

Tell students that there are a number of guidelines that must be followed to create the best survey possible. Ask students these questions to focus the discussion about guidelines for writing questions.

Guiding Questions

Decide Determine whether the following question is a leading question: "How many people in your neighborhood are renters?" Explain your decision.	No, a leading question suggests a correct answer. This question will probably require guessing on the respondents' part.
Analyze Why is it important that questions be written clearly and as briefly as possible?	Possible answers: Respondents are more likely to understand the question if it is written clearly and more likely to complete a survey if the questions aren't too long.

ELABORATE

Graphic Organizer

Display this chart. Record students' answers in a list. Possible answers:

Formatting Questionnaires
1. Provide good visual appearance and ample white space.
2. Use different colors and typefaces.
3. Use black ink on white paper and easy-to-read font.
4. Make it short enough to be answered quickly.
5. Place distinct headings on all individual survey sections.
6. Number individual questions.
7. Place a note to remind respondents to go to next page if needed.
8. Vary the format between questions and options.
9. Provide clear directions for each section or group of questions.
10. Include screening questions if appropriate.
11. Include demographic questions if needed.
12. Provide for comments and suggestions if desired.

 **glencoe.com**  iWB

Graphic Organizer Send students to the Online Learning Center to print this graphic organizer.

Critical Thinking

To reinforce students' understanding of appropriate formatting techniques for questionnaires, have them list five ways to strengthen the visual appearance of a questionnaire. Answers may include: provide ample white space, use different colors, use different typefaces, use black ink on white paper, and use an easy-to-read font. Then have students find or create an example of a well-formatted questionnaire and an example of a poorly-formatted questionnaire. Have students write a two- or three-sentence critique of each questionnaire and share them with the class. Critiques will vary but should show students' understanding of what a well-formatted questionnaire should look like. Then share with students this scenario: Your coworker has developed a survey but the appearance and content are too casual. They would be appropriate for friends, but not for a formal survey. Write a memo to your coworker tactfully explaining how the survey could be revised. Memos should be tactful but clearly explain why the survey is too casual.

Mini Project

Enrichment

Analyze Online Surveys Have students locate and take an Internet survey designed specifically for teens. After they complete the survey, have them print out a copy to bring to class. Divide the class into groups, and have groups analyze the survey questions. Students should determine the types of questions used, whether there are leading questions, if the wording is clear, and so on.

Career Chatroom

Use these questions to focus the discussion about the feature.

Guiding Questions

Explain What does Mr. Ludwigsen mean when he says to "be an active listener"?	Remind students that in Chapter 8 they learned how to be an effective (active) listener. Active listeners identify the purpose, look for a plan, give feedback, search for a common interest, evaluate the message, listen for more than verbal content, listen for a conclusion, and take notes.
Analyze Why do you think the first skill Mr. Ludwigsen mentioned is "get along with those around you"?	Possible answer: In any business you must be able to get along with those around you to be able to build good working relationships and provide customers with what they need.

 **glencoe.com**

Career Exploration Send students to the Online Learning Center to find more information about this career and to get a Career Exploration activity.

Reading Check Answer

Read the Reading Check question to students: ***What are three types of questions used on surveys?*** yes/no questions, multiple choice, and rating scale questions

ADMINISTERING QUESTIONNAIRES

The response rate for most surveys is only ten percent or less, so proper administration can improve response rates. All surveys should have deadlines for completion. All surveys should also include clear and concise instructions on how to complete the questionnaire. These must be very easy to understand, so use short sentences and basic vocabulary.

Types of Surveys	
Mailed Surveys	E-mail Surveys
In-Person Surveys	Web Surveys

MAILED SURVEYS

A mailed questionnaire should be sent first-class with a hand-signed cover letter, and it should be personalized if the potential respondent is known. First impressions are important, so make the envelope stand out. Envelopes with bulk mail permits or generic labels are perceived as unimportant. This will generally produce a lower response rate.

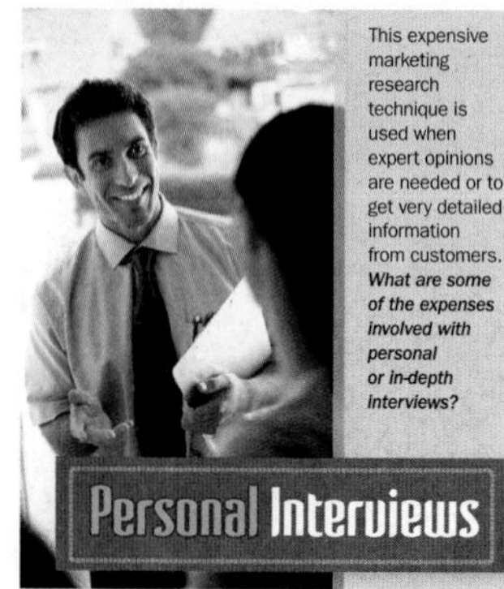

This expensive marketing research technique is used when expert opinions are needed or to get very detailed information from customers. ***What are some of the expenses involved with personal or in-depth interviews?***

Include a well-written cover letter. The respondent's next impression comes from the cover letter. The cover letter provides your best opportunity to convince the respondent to complete the survey. The cover letter or introductory remarks should explain the purpose of the survey. It also should clearly state the deadline for returning the questionnaire. A postage-paid return envelope should be included with the questionnaire for the respondent's convenience. However, you should also print the return address on the questionnaire itself because questionnaires are easily separated from the reply envelopes.

E-MAIL AND WEB SURVEYS

As with traditional mailed surveys, e-mail and Web surveys should be brief. E-mail and Web surveys should limit the number of screens that respondents have to scroll through to answer questions or statements.

Graphics and images can enhance the appearance of a Web survey. However, too many graphics or excessive use of animation can be distracting. Annoyed respondents are not likely to complete the survey. Internet surveys should allow respondents to stop and complete the survey at a later time.

IN-PERSON SURVEYS

Questionnaires that are not mailed should have a brief explanation of the survey's purpose placed on the questionnaire itself. A plan should be established for selecting participants in an unbiased way. Whether done in the repondent's home, over the phone, or in a mall, it is important that the interviewer be skilled and discreet. The interviewer should have the ability to answer questions from the respondents. The interviewer should recognize when it may be appropriate to ask more complex or sensitive questions.

Personal interviews can provide very detailed information, but they require special training to conduct effectively, can be time-consuming, and might be difficult to analyze and interpret.

Personal interviews can be useful when you need to collect detailed information from a relatively small group of people. Interviews can be used to explore issues and options to a greater extent than written surveys. In a personal interview, reactions to visual materials, such as ads or actual product samples, can be collected.

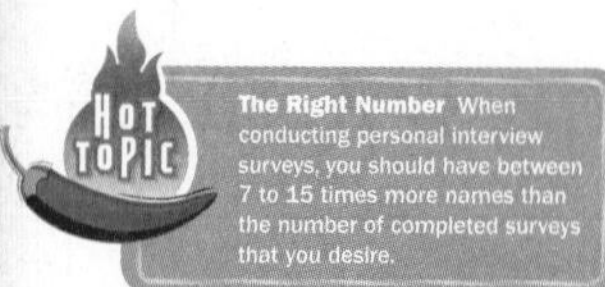

HOT TOPIC
The Right Number When conducting personal interview surveys, you should have between 7 to 15 times more names than the number of completed surveys that you desire.

INCENTIVES

Many marketing researchers offer incentives and set deadlines for completing surveys to increase response rates. For example, to get a quicker response, a company may enter the first 100 respondents into a drawing for a cash prize; or each participant may receive a gift card or a discount on the company's product. Other incentives might include token gifts such as notepads, pens, refigerator magnets, mini calendars, key rings, participation in a raffle or lottery, or a donation to a charity in the respondent's name. Studies have shown that incentives do work to increase response rates, so it may be a wise investment for companies to consider.

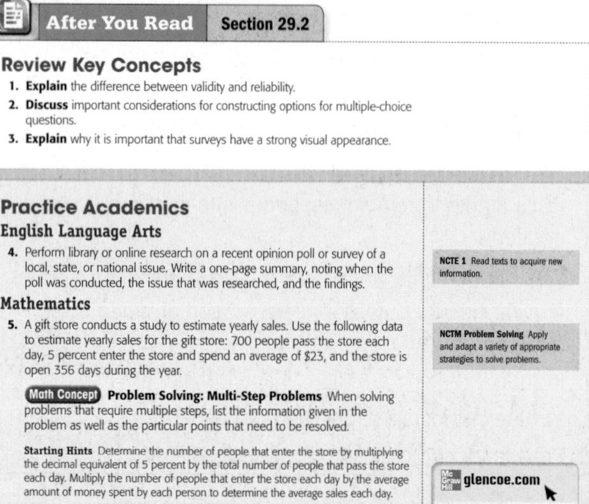

After You Read Section 29.2

Review Key Concepts

1. **Explain** the difference between validity and reliability.
2. **Discuss** important considerations for constructing options for multiple-choice questions.
3. **Explain** why it is important that surveys have a strong visual appearance.

Practice Academics

English Language Arts

4. Perform library or online research on a recent opinion poll or survey of a local, state, or national issue. Write a one-page summary, noting when the poll was conducted, the issue that was researched, and the findings.

NCTE 1 Read texts to acquire new information.

Mathematics

5. A gift store conducts a study to estimate yearly sales. Use the following data to estimate yearly sales for the gift store: 700 people pass the store each day, 5 percent enter the store and spend an average of $23, and the store is open 356 days during the year.

NCTM Problem Solving Apply and adapt a variety of appropriate strategies to solve problems.

Math Concept **Problem Solving: Multi-Step Problems** When solving problems that require multiple steps, list the information given in the problem as well as the particular points that need to be resolved.

Starting Hints Determine the number of people that enter the store by multiplying the decimal equivalent of 5 percent by the total number of people that pass the store each day. Multiply the number of people that enter the store each day by the average amount of money spent by each person to determine the average sales each day.

For help, go to the **Math Skills Handbook** located at the back of this book.

glencoe.com

Check your answers.

ELABORATE

Visual Literacy

Personal Interviews Caption Answer Read the caption question to students: ***What are some of the expenses involved with personal or in-depth interviews?*** Answers may include: Paying for training for the interviewers, analyzing the data, and transportation. Ask: ***Have you ever participated in a personal interview? If so, where was it conducted?*** Students may have participated in mall-intercept interviews or other types of store-related or on-the-street interviews.

Critical Thinking

Ask students to imagine that they are going to conduct a survey to learn where hip, young people like to shop for clothing. Ask: ***What type of survey would you create? Explain your answer.*** Answers may include: an online survey because hip, young people often spend time on the Internet; a mall-intercept because you can talk to the people face-to-face and determine whether they really are hip and young. Ask students to share their answers and reasoning with the class.

ADMINISTERING QUESTIONNAIRES

Ask students these guiding questions to focus the discussion on administering questionnaires.

Guiding Questions

Identify What two things must surveys always have?	deadlines for completion and clear and concise instructions
Analyze What are some benefits of in-person surveys?	They can provide very detailed information; they can be used to explore issues and options to a greater extent than written surveys; reactions to visual materials can be collected.

EVALUATE

The Right Number Ask students to do online research to find the results of completed surveys. Have them find the response rate to the surveys and compare to the average response rate of ten percent or less.

Graphic Organizer

Display this diagram. After students have read the Administering Questionnaires section, ask them to provide details for administering each of the three types of surveys discussed in the text. Write their answers in the diagram. Possible answers:

Administering Questionnaires

Mailed Surveys	E-mail and Web Surveys	In-person Surveys
• Include well-written, hand-signed cover letter • Personalize letter if possible • Send first class • Explain purpose of survey • Include postage-paid return envelope	• Make them brief • Limit the number of screens respondents must scroll through • Use graphics and animations carefully	• Include explanation of purpose • Conduct interview skillfully and discreetly • Recognize when appropriate to ask more complex or sensitive questions

 **glencoe.com** 

Graphic Organizer Send students to the Online Learning Center to print this graphic organizer.

After You Read Section 29.2

Review Key Concepts

1. Validity is when the questions asked measure what was intended to be measured. Reliability exists when a research technique produces nearly identical results in repeated trials.
2. Options must be mutually exclusive and comprehensive enough to include every possible response.
3. Questionnaires must have an excellent visual appearance and design to appeal to respondents.

Practice Academics

English Language Arts

4. Answers will vary depending on the issues students choose to research. Accept all reasonable answers that list when the poll was conducted, identifies the issue, and summarizes the findings.

Mathematics

5. \$286,580 (700 × .05 × 23 × 356)

 **glencoe.com**

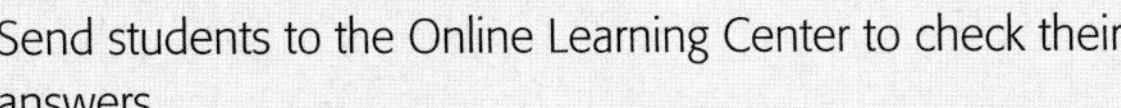

Send students to the Online Learning Center to check their answers.

Review and Activities

Written Summary

- The five steps that a business follows when conducting marketing research are defining the problem, obtaining data, analyzing data, recommending solutions, and applying results.
- Steps are performed sequentially to find solutions or research an issue.
- Questionnaires should provide data that are valid and reliable.
- Marketing surveys may include open-ended and forced-choice questions.
- Forced-choice questions include yes/no, multiple-choice, rating scale, and level of agreement questions.
- To obtain unbiased data and increase response rates, market researchers must follow guidelines when constructing, formatting, and administering surveys.

Review Content Vocabulary and Academic Vocabulary

1. Write each of the vocabulary terms below on an index card, and the definitions on separate index cards. Work in pairs or small groups to match each term to its definition.

Content Vocabulary
- problem definition (p. 679)
- primary data (p. 681)
- secondary data (p. 681)
- survey method (p. 684)
- sample (p. 684)
- observation method (p. 685)
- point-of-sale research (p. 685)
- experimental method (p. 685)
- data analysis (p. 686)
- validity (p. 689)
- reliability (p. 689)
- forced-choice questions (p. 689)
- open-ended questions (p. 689)

Academic Vocabulary
- determine (p. 681)
- specific (p. 683)
- mutually (p. 690)
- accurate (p. 691)

Assess for Understanding

2. **Sequence** What are the steps for designing and conducting marketing research?
3. **Define** What do the terms *primary data* and *secondary data* mean?
4. **Explain** How do marketers apply the data-analysis process to collect marketing information?
5. **List** What are the elements in a marketing research report?
6. **Evaluate** What are important design features for constructing a marketing research survey?
7. **Identify** What procedures are used to administer a marketing research survey?
8. **Contrast** What is the difference between the definitions of *open-ended questions* and *forced-choice questions?*
9. **Provide** What is an example of interviewer bias being introduced into a questionnaire?

696 | Unit 9 · Marketing Information Management

Chapter 29 · Conducting Marketing Research | 697

EVALUATE

Visual Summary

Express Creativity Ask students to develop their own visual summary of a concept in the chapter. Encourage students to use different formats for their visual summaries, such as a storyboard, a timeline, a table, a tree diagram, or a word web. Visual summaries will vary depending on the concept depicted. Questions to ask when assessing a visual summary include:

- Is the summary clear, economical, and simple?
- Are any important steps left out?
- Are steps or concepts arranged in the same order as the original?
- Does the summary reveal a pattern that connects the details?
- Does the summary locate and highlight the most important information?

Review Content Vocabulary and Academic Vocabulary

1. **problem definition**—process by which a business identifies a problem

   primary data—data obtained for the first time and used for an issue under study

   secondary data—data that have been collected for some other purpose

   survey method—a technique in which information is gathered through the use of surveys

   sample—a part of the target population

   observation method—technique in which people's actions are watched

   point-of-sale research—research that combines natural observation with personal interviews

   experimental method—technique in which a researcher observes the results of changing one or more marketing variables

   data analysis—process of compiling, analyzing, and interpreting the results data collection

   validity—when questions asked on a questionnaire measure what was intended to be measured

EVALUATE

Review Content Vocabulary and Academic Vocabulary *(continued)*

reliability—when a technique produces nearly identical results in repeated trials

forced-choice questions—questions that ask respondents to choose answers from a questionnaire

open-ended questions—questions that require respondents to construct their own answers.

Assess for Understanding

2. The five steps for designing and conducting marketing research are: (1) defining the problem; (2) obtaining data; (3) analyzing data; (4) recommending solutions; and (5) applying the results.
3. Primary data are obtained to address the problem under study. Secondary data are collected for some other purpose and are also readily available at little or no cost, should be used before primary data.
4. Marketers compile, analyze, and interpret marketing information to better understand the market and to increase sales and profitability.
5. The elements in a marketing research report include: title page; acknowledgments; table of contents; list of tables, figures, charts, and graphs; introduction; review of the research; procedures used; findings; recommendations; summary and conclusions; appendixes; and bibliography.
6. Important design features for constructing a marketing research survey include: excellent visual appearance and ample white space; use of dark ink; easy-to-read typefaces; surveys that are designed to be short; all sections are identified; all questions are numbered; questions are short; use of common language; and use of symbols for answers.
7. Procedures to administer a survey include the following for mailed questionnaires: use cover letter, explain the purpose, indicate deadline, and use a postage-paid return envelope. For Internet surveys: limit the screens, use graphics, allow respondents to stop and complete survey later. For in-person surveys: state purpose, select people in an unbiased way. All methods can use incentives and deadlines to encourage rapid and completed surveys.
8. Open-ended questions require respondents to construct their own answers, while forced-choice questions ask respondents to choose answers from possibilities provided on a questionnaire.
9. Answer should demonstrate an understanding of the concept of bias; bias could be introduced by asking leading questions, or asking questions that require respondents to guess the answer.

Chapter 29 Review and Activities

21st Century Skills

Communication Skills

10. Information Mining Interview an owner or manager of a company in your community to discover how the company collects demographic information about its customers. Write a two-page outline identifying the company, the person interviewed, how customer information (name, address, phone numbers, occupations, age, spending patterns, and so on) is collected. Explain how the information is used for marketing purposes.

Financial Literacy Skills

11. Calculating Personal Interviewing Costs What are the per-person costs to complete a personal-interview survey for 100 people, given the following costs: $600 for travel and meals expenses; $3,800 for interviewer wages; $200 for printing survey instruments; and $750 for data entry and analysis?

Everyday Ethics

12. Spa Trends The term "spa" originated from the name of the Belgian town Spa, known for its healing mineral baths. A new market for spas is teenagers. More than 30 percent of spas offer teen packages. Popular treatments include facials, head-and-shoulder massage, and manicures. Gather primary data by interviewing five teenagers on what spa services they would want and how much they would spend for the services. Consider if targeting teens who have limited funds is ethical. Summarize your findings and opinions in a one-page report.

e-Marketing Skills

13. Internet Research Imagine you and a classmate are employed by a marketing research firm. The firm uses Internet survey research for product satisfaction studies. Your team has been assigned to develop a ten-question satisfaction survey about a product of your choice.

- List the techniques that you must use to develop an Internet survey.
- Identify the types of questions your team will use to complete the Internet survey.

Build Academic Skills

English Language Arts

14. Research Services Perform online research, locating the Web page of *Quirk's Marketing Research Review* to find a marketing research firm in your city or state that performs marketing research. Identify the research that is done by the firm and the services that the firm provides to clients in a one-page outline.

NCTE 1 Read texts to acquire new information.

English Language Arts

15. Marketing Research Trends Perform library or online research about a recent trend in marketing research. Identify the name of the article, its source, and the marketing research trend. Write a one-page summary of the research trend that you investigated.

NCTE 3 Apply strategies to interpret texts.

Mathematics

16. Internet Survey Costs Calculate the total cost to complete an Internet survey for 50,000 people, given the following costs: $250 to create/deliver the survey, and $0.02 per person to convert data.

NCTM Number and Operations Compute fluently and make reasonable estimates.

Math Concept **Problem Solving: Calculating Costs** When calculating business costs, be sure to include all components that contribute to the cost. Per-person costs need to be distinguished from costs that are not related to head count.

For help, go to the **Math Skills Handbook** located at the back of this book.

Standardized Test Practice

Directions Read the following questions. On a separate piece of paper, write the best possible answer for each one.

1. Which of the following marketing research methods combines natural viewing with personal interviews to get people to explain buying behavior?
   A. Experimental method
   B. Observation method
   C. Point-of-sale method
   D. Survey method
2. Forced-choice questions ask respondents to construct their own responses to a question.
   T
   F
3. When survey questions measure what was intended to be measured, the survey is said to have ________.

Test-Taking Tip

Look for key words in test directions and test questions, such as *choose, describe, explain, compare, identify, similar, except, not,* and *but,* to help guide your responses.

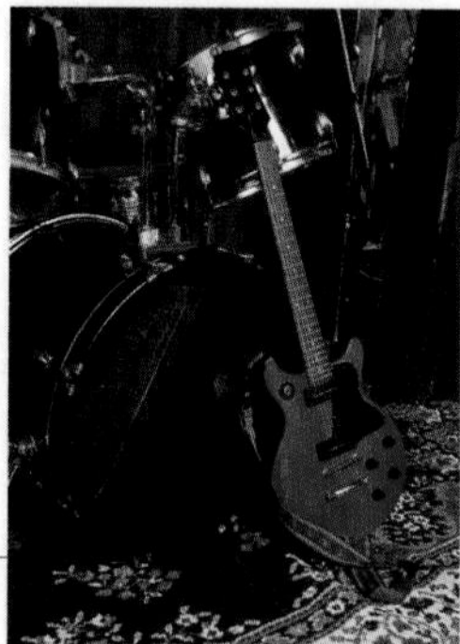

DECA Connection Role Play

Marketing Research Consultant
Popular Band

Situation You are working with the manager of a band (judge) that is popular among teens. The band recently completed a nationwide tour. The tour was a huge success, playing to sold-out audiences at each venue. The band-related merchandise sold at the concerts was also a huge success.

The band manager (judge) is considering adding concert and band merchandise that fans could purchase on the band's Web site. The addition of merchandise sales to the Web site will require hiring personnel to process and ship items, and to manage the merchandise sales. The band members agree that the idea is a good one and worth trying.

Before beginning the merchandise sales, the manager (judge) and band want to gather information about whether fans would buy merchandise from the Web site and, if so, what types of merchandise would they be likely to purchase. The band manager (judge) has decided to ask fans visiting the band's Web site to complete a questionnaire about buying band merchandise from the Web site.

Activity You are to prepare recommendations about the design of the questionnaire. Your recommendations should include the types of questions that should be asked, the length of the questionnaire, and the formatting. You will then present your recommendations to the band manager (judge).

Evaluation You will be evaluated on how well you meet the following performance indicators:

1. Describe methods to design research studies.
2. Describe options businesses use to obtain marketing-research data.
3. Discuss the nature of sampling plans (i.e., who, how many, how chosen).
4. Evaluate questionnaire design.
5. Explain the use of descriptive statistics in marketing decision making.

Download the Competitive Events Workbook for more Role-Play practice.

EVALUATE

Communication Skills

10. Accept all reasonable responses that identify the person interviewed, the local company, and how the company collects demographic information on its customers (name, address, phone numbers, occupation, age, spending patterns, and so on) and how the information is used. All outlines should be well-organized, use proper grammar, and be free of spelling errors.

Financial Literacy Skills

11. $53.50 per interviewee ($600 + $3,800 + $200 + $750 = $5350 ÷ 100).

Everyday Ethics

12. Reports should summarize students' findings from their survey of five teens and should include primary data collected, as well as a discussion about the ethics of targeting teens with limited funds. Ethical opinions will vary and should be supported with reasonable arguments. Reports should be one-page in length and be free of grammatical and spelling errors.

e-Marketing Skills

13. Accept all reasonable answers for teams that develop a ten-question Internet survey. The survey must be well-designed. Questions must be properly formatted, grammatically correct, and be free of spelling errors. Possible techniques: surveys should limit the number of screens that respondents have to scroll through to answer questions or statements; limited use of distracting graphics or animation; Internet surveys should allow respondents to stop and complete the survey at a later time.

EVALUATE

Build Academic Skills

English Language Arts

14. Accept all reasonable answers that identify the name of the research company, research performed, and cover the marketing research services provided to clients. Outline reports should be one-page in length, use proper grammar, and be free of spelling errors.

15. Accept all reasonable answers that identify the name of the article, source of information, and a recent trend in marketing research. Summary reports should be one-page in length, use proper grammar, and be free of spelling errors.

Mathematics

16. $1,250.00 (50,000 × $0.02 + $250)

Standardized Test Practice

1. C Point-of-sale method

2. False

3. validity

DECA Connection Role Play

Evaluations will be based on these performance indicators:

1. **Describe methods to design research studies.** The five steps for conducting marketing research are defining the problem, obtaining data, analyzing the data, recommending solutions, and applying the results. Each step is performed in this order to arrive at solutions to a problem or issue.
2. **Describe options businesses use to obtain marketing-research data.** Primary data are obtained for the first time and used specifically for the problem or issue under study. Sources include: surveys, interviews, observations, and experiments. Secondary data have already been collected. Sources include: Internet sites, U.S. and state government sources, specialized research companies, and business publications and trade organizations.
3. **Discuss the nature of sampling plans.** A sample is a part of the target population that represents the entire population. The size of the sample depends on how much a company can spend and the accuracy needed. Generally, a larger sample gives more accurate results.
4. **Evaluate questionnaire design.** Questionnaires must have good visual appearance and ample white space. Different colors and typefaces can add to the design appeal, but no more than two ink colors and typefaces should be used. The preferred color for most surveys is black with an easy-to-read font. The questionnaire should be short enough to answer quickly. Distinct headings should be placed on all sections. Numbers should be placed on all individual questions. If the questionnaire requires more than one page, a note should be placed on the bottom of each page to continue to the next page.
5. **Explain the use of descriptive statistics in marketing decision making.** In evaluating statistics, managers may find that the research was inconclusive and that more is needed. Or they may find that the research suggests specific courses of action. After the research has been completed and changes made, a business should carefully monitor the results. A business needs to know if the specific actions taken are successful. The research effort can be deemed a success if resulting decisions lead to greater profits through better sales, increased efficiency, or reduced expenses.

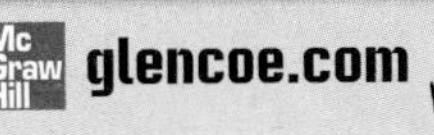

Role Plays For more DECA Role Plays, send students to the Online Learning Center to download the Competitive Events Workbook.

UNIT 9 **Marketing Internship Project**

Research Study on Mobile Phones

Companies look to consumers for feedback on new products. How can marketing research help in that endeavor?

Scenario

Your marketing research company has been hired to study a specific target market for mobile phones—teenagers. The client's objective for doing the study is to develop products specifically designed for the teenage market.

You need to find out how teens use their cell phones, what features are most important to them, how best to promote a new phone, and who pays for the phones. The results of the study will be used to design a new cell phone and a marketing plan for it.

The Skills You'll Use

Academic Skills Reading, writing, social studies, researching, and analyzing

Basic Skills Speaking, listening, thinking, and interpersonal

Technology Skills Word processing, presentation, spreadsheet, telecommunication, and the Internet

NCTE 7 Conduct research and gather, evaluate, and synthesize data to communicate discoveries.
NCTE 8 Use information resources to gather information and create and communicate knowledge.

Your Objective

Your objective is to develop an effective marketing research study on teenaged cell phone users for your client, a mobile phone company.

STEP 1 Do Your Research

Conduct research on cell phones. Find out about all the features, prices, and promotional materials used by mobile phone companies to target teens. Also, look for issues related to cell phones and teenagers. As you conduct your research, answer these questions:

- Which mobile phone companies specifically target teens and how do they do so?
- What main features are found on the majority of cell phones?
- What are the current prices for mobile phones?
- What are the current issues (in the media) regarding teens and cell phone usage?

Write a summary of your research.

STEP 2 Plan Your Project

Now that you have completed your research, you need to begin planning your project.

- Define the research issue (problem) and objectives for the marketing research study.
- Conduct secondary research on cell phones and teens.
- Review marketing research methods to decide which one will work best.
- Develop questions for use in the marketing research study.
- Conduct primary research.
- Write a report that summarizes your research, defines the research issue, details the study's objectives, includes the questions asked in the study, reports the results of the study, analyzes the data generated by the study, and makes recommendations for marketing strategies.

STEP 3 Connect with Your Community

- Interview one or more trusted adults at home, at school, at work or in your community. Find out what issues concern them regarding teen cell phone usage.
- Take notes during your interviews and transcribe your notes after your interviews.
- Visit a store that sells mobile phones to review the products and promotional materials used to target teens.
- Observe people using their cell phones to see how, when, and where they use them.

STEP 4 Share What You Learn

Assume your class is the client's staff who will apply the results of your study.

- Present your results in an oral presentation. Be prepared to answer questions.
- Present your written report, complete with recommendations and suggested marketing strategies.
- Use software to create a slide presentation to accompany your oral presentation. Include one slide for each topic in your written report.

STEP 5 Evaluate Your Marketing and Academic Skills

Your project will be evaluated based on the following:

- The marketing research study's design (problem and methodology)
- Secondary and primary research findings
- Analysis of findings and recommendations for the client
- Samples of suggested ideas
- Organization and continuity of presentation
- Mechanics—presentation and neatness
- Speaking and listening skills

MARKETING CORE FUNCTIONS

Marketing Information Management

Market Planning

Marketing Internship Project Checklist

Plan

✓ Conduct secondary research on how teens use mobile phones, parents' concerns, and marketing strategies used to target teens.

✓ Conduct a marketing research study on teens and cell phones.

Write

✓ Create a written report, complete with recommendations and suggested marketing strategies.

✓ Explain the findings and analysis of the data.

Present

✓ Present a marketing research problem and methodology used to conduct the study.

✓ Present findings and recommendations.

✓ Display ideas for implementing the recommendations.

glencoe.com

Evaluate Download a rubric you can use to evaluate your final project.

my marketing portfolio

Internship Report Once you have completed your Marketing Internship Project and oral presentation, put your written report and a few printouts of key slides from your oral presentation in your Marketing Portfolio.

Marketing Research Study for a New Client Conduct a marketing research study for a new client of your choice. Consider companies that target teens or choose a different target market. Your new client could be a retail store that wants to change its product offerings or a video game company that wants consumer input for designing new games. Define the problem, obtain the data, analyze the data, report your findings, make recommendations, and include samples of your suggestions.

EVALUATE

Anticipation Activity

Project Objective Read the project objective aloud to students: ***Develop an effective marketing research study on teenaged cell phone users for your client, a mobile phone company.*** Ask students to think about what they learned about the marketing research process in Unit 9. Remind them of these key points:

- The marketing research process should be followed sequentially for best results: Define the problem; obtain data; analyze data; recommend solutions; and implement findings.
- There are two types of marketing research data: primary and secondary.

Ask students: ***What is the most difficult step in the marketing research process and what is involved?*** Defining the problem is the most difficult step. A business identifies a problem, a research question, and the information needed to answer it. The researcher then creates objectives that can be adapted into survey questions.

Ask students: ***What is the difference between primary and secondary data?*** Primary data is obtained for the first time and used specifically for the issue under study. Secondary data has been previously collected for another purpose and is less expensive.

Graphic Organizer

Display this diagram. Ask students to name preferred cell phone features and brands. Possible answers:

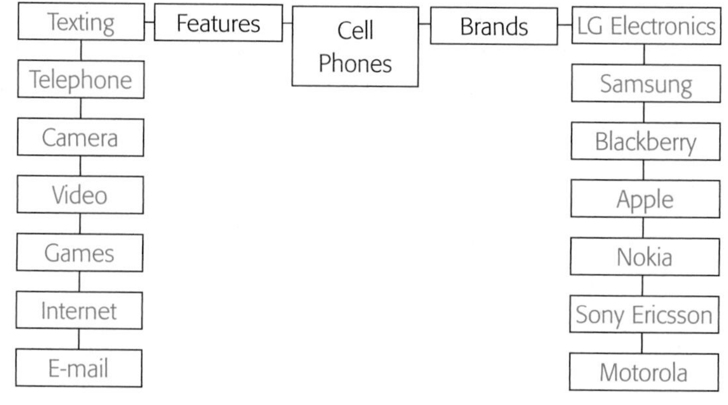

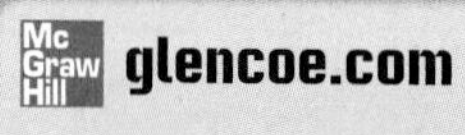

glencoe.com iWB

Graphic Organizer Send students to the Online Learning Center to print this graphic organizer.

EVALUATE

STEP 1 Do Your Research

Tell students that there are many places to find information they can use to develop a marketing research study. Students can use library and Internet resources, but they should also talk to people in the community. Encourage students to seek the opinions and ideas of trusted people they know. Other people can bring new perspectives and ideas about marketing research studies as well as the best sources for primary and secondary research on teens and their cell phones.

STEP 2 Plan Your Project

Students should find out about the features, prices, and promotional materials used by competitors as well as current issues related to teens and mobile phones before developing their marketing research study. Students should explain why they decided to use the research methodology for their study. Students' explanation of their marketing research study should include research questions, data, an analysis of the data, and recommendations for marketing strategies.

STEP 3 Connect with Your Community

Explain to students that connecting with members of the community is a great way to build relationships. Tell them that young people who are capable of building relationships with caring, responsible, and competent adults are more likely to achieve success. Encourage students to take part in opportunities for adults to serve as mentors, coaches, advocates, and advisors, both formally and informally.

STEP 4 Share What You Learn

Students should present their ideas in a written report and oral presentation with presentation software. They should have at least one slide in their presentation for each key topic in the written report. Encourage students to speak clearly, use appropriate grammar and vocabulary, and actively engage the audience by making and maintaining eye contact and using movement (facial expressions, posture, gestures) to focus attention and interest.

STEP 5 Evaluate Your Marketing and Academic Skills

Have students use the Marketing Internship Project Checklist to help them to plan, write, and present their reports. Exemplary written reports will include information that clearly supports a central thesis, a single, distinct focus, generally well-developed ideas, well-phrased sentences that flow smoothly and are varied in length and structure, consistently precise word choice, and few, if any, errors in grammar, spelling, and mechanics.

glencoe.com

Evaluation Rubric Send students to the Online Learning Center to get a rubric to evaluate their projects.

Culminating Activity

Explain to students that, as one source for obtaining data in the marketing research process, research questionnaires must be valid and reliable. It is important to avoid including biased questions that would invalidate a questionnaire or survey and, thus, would produce flawed data, analysis, and recommendations. Ask students: ***What are important factors for achieving valid and reliable results from a questionnaire?*** The questionnaire should be well written with clear, understandable questions and directions. The same questions should be asked of all respondents. Questions can be open-ended or forced-choice, e.g., yes/no and multiple choice. The same ranking or rating scales should be used for all similar questions. Do not ask leading questions that encourage one answer over another. Questions should not elicit a guessed answer. All mail-in or Internet surveys should have a deadline.

my marketing portfolio

Internship Report Have students put their written reports and printouts of key slides from their oral presentations in their marketing portfolio.

Marketing Research Study for a New Client Direct students to select a company that targets teens or another demographic, and then use the steps of the marketing research process to create a marketing research study. Students' completed marketing research studies should include all of the elements and answer all of the questions included in the Marketing Internship Project on this page. This additional activity can build relevance for students who are motivated to learn about other specific businesses and industries. Relevance shifts the focus to what motivates individual students to learn.

UNIT 10 Product and Service Management

PLANNING GUIDE AND RESOURCES

	Print	Digital
Unit 10 Product and Service Management		Unit 10 Fast Files: Marketing Internship Project Activity Connect Online Learning Center through glencoe.com
Chapter 30 **Product Planning**	Student Activity Workbook: Chapter 30 DECA Connection Role Play; Chapter 30 Vocabulary Activity; Section Note Taking Activities; Chapter Academics Activity; Section Study Skills Activities; Section Real-World Applications Activities Mathematics for Marketing Workbook Marketing Research Project Workbook School-to-Career Activity Workbook	Unit 10 Fast Files: Chapter 30 Discovery Project Worksheet and Rubric; Chapter 30 Green Marketer Activity; Chapter 30 Digital Nation Activity; Section Graphic Organizers; Section Outlines with Key Terms and Definitions; Section Summaries ExamView Assessment Suite, Chapter 30 Connect Online Learning Center through glencoe.com
Chapter 31 **Branding, Packaging, and Labeling**	Student Activity Workbook: Chapter 31 DECA Connection Role Play; Chapter 31 Vocabulary Activity; Section Note Taking Activities; Chapter Academics Activity; Section Study Skills Activities; Section Real-World Applications Activities Mathematics for Marketing Workbook Marketing Research Project Workbook School-to-Career Activity Workbook	Unit 10 Fast Files: Chapter 31 Discovery Project Worksheet and Rubric; Chapter 31 Green Marketer Activity; Chapter 31 Digital Nation Activity; Section Graphic Organizers; Section Outlines with Key Terms and Definitions; Section Summaries ExamView Assessment Suite, Chapter 31 Connect Online Learning Center through glencoe.com
Chapter 32 **Extended Product Features**	Student Activity Workbook: Chapter 32 DECA Connection Role Play; Chapter 32 Vocabulary Activity; Section Note Taking Activities; Chapter Academics Activity; Section Study Skills Activities; Section Real-World Applications Activities Mathematics for Marketing Workbook Marketing Research Project Workbook School-to-Career Activity Workbook	Unit 10 Fast Files: Chapter 32 Discovery Project Worksheet and Rubric; Chapter 32 Green Marketer Activity; Chapter 32 Digital Nation Activity; Section Graphic Organizers; Section Outlines with Key Terms and Definitions; Section Summaries ExamView Assessment Suite, Chapter 32 Connect Online Learning Center through glencoe.com

McGRAW-HILL PROFESSIONAL DEVELOPMENT

Perkins IV has placed more emphasis than ever on providing quality professional development for Career and Technology educators. The legislation mandates that the focus of professional development be the integration and reinforcement of academic competencies in order to improve student achievement. Specifically, Perkins requires measurements of students' academic success. McGraw-Hill answers the challenge for strong and effective professional development with a five-prong **Online Professional Development for Integrating Academics.**

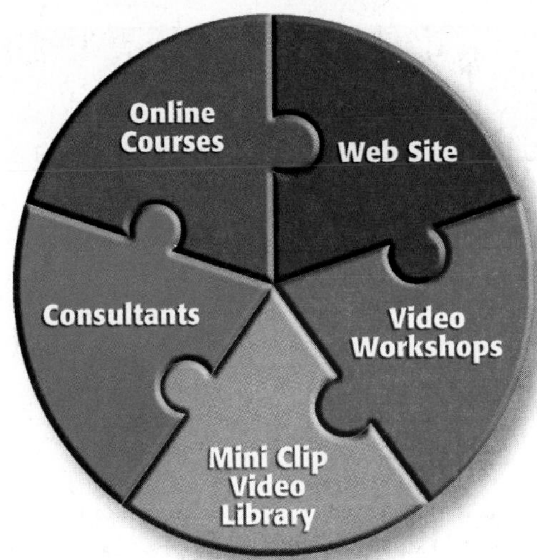

For pricing and ordering information contact your McGraw-Hill Sales Representative.

VIDEO LIBRARY

The McGraw-Hill Professional Development Mini-Clip Video Library, referenced for your convenience at the point of use, provides teaching strategies to strengthen academic and learning skills. Go to the Online Learning Center to view these professional development video clips for Unit 10:

Chapter 30: Product Planning
- **Reading: Planning and Classroom Management:** An educator discusses instructional strategies that support a differentiated classroom. (p. 709)
- **Reading: Options for Learning:** Two teachers explain to their students multiple ways to read and respond to the assigned text. (p. 721)

Chapter 31: Branding, Packaging, and Labeling
- **Reading: Focus Lesson:** A teacher models how to find the main idea or theme of a selection by identifying the major and minor details. (p. 731)
- **ELL: Comprehension and English Language Learners:** An author discusses comprehension strategies for English language learners. (p. 739)

Chapter 32: Extended Product Features
- **Reading: During and After Reading:** A teacher models reading for her students and then has them practice what a good reader thinks about. (p. 761)
- **ELL: Providing Clear Directions:** A teacher provides clear written and oral directions for a classroom assignment and checks student understanding. (p. 767)

UNIT OVERVIEW

Sections	Objectives	Common Core State Standards College and Career Readiness
Section 30.1 **Product Development**	• Describe the steps in product planning. • Explain how to develop, maintain, and improve a product mix.	• **Reading** Interpret words and phrases as they are used in a text, including determining technical, connotative, and figurative meanings, and analyze how specific word choices shape meaning or tone.
Section 30.2 **Sustaining Product Sales**	• Identify the four stages of the production life cycle. • Describe product positioning techniques.	• **Reading** Integrate and evaluate content presented in diverse formats and media, including visually and quantitatively, as well as in words.
Section 31.1 **Branding**	• Discuss the nature, scope, and importance of branding in product planning. • Identify the various branding elements. • List three different types of brands. • Explain how branding strategies are used to meet sales and company goals.	• **Writing** Conduct short as well as more sustained research projects based on focused questions, demonstrating understanding of the subject under investigation.
Section 31.2 **Packaging and Labeling**	• Explain the functions of product packaging. • Identify the functions of labels.	• **Reading** Read closely to determine what the text says explicitly and to make logical inferences from it; cite specific textual evidence when writing or speaking to support conclusions drawn from the text.

Sections	Objectives	Common Core State Standards College and Career Readiness
Section 32.1 **Warranties**	• Identify different types of warranties. • Explore the importance of warranties in product planning. • Identify the major provisions of product safety legislation. • Explain consumer responsibilities and rights related to product performance.	• **Reading** Interpret words and phrases as they are used in a text, including determining technical, connotative, and figurative meanings, and analyze how specific word choices shape meaning or tone.
Section 32.2 **Credit**	• Describe the importance of credit. • Explain various sources of consumer credit. • Identify the types of credit accounts extended to consumers. • Discuss how businesses use trade credit.	• **Reading** Determine central ideas or themes of a text and analyze their development; summarize the key supporting details and ideas.

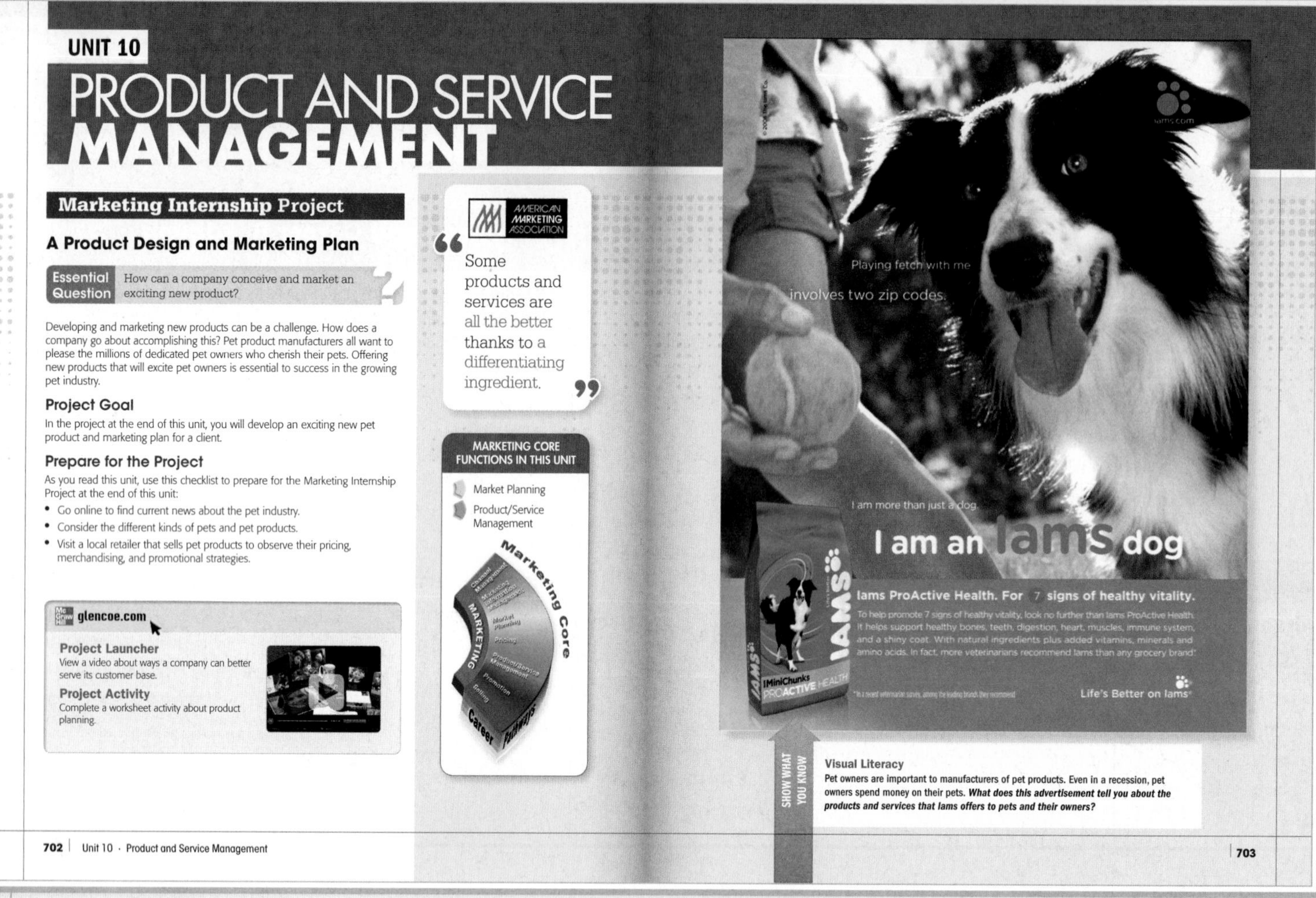

ENGAGE

Introduce the Unit

Unit 10 discusses the decisions a business makes in the production and sales of its products.

Chapter 30 explains how businesses plan their products to produce and sell.

Chapter 31 explores the nature and scope of branding in product planning.

Chapter 32 examines the various types of warranties and credit offerings provided by businesses to support products.

Build Background

Ask students why businesses need to introduce new products while keeping other products. List their answers on the board. Answers will vary but may note that new products add to a company's overall sales and boost market share. Varying an original or existing product can lead to more sales with new products accounting for more than 35 percent of sales. Ask students: ***Why is product planning important?*** It allows businesses to coordinate existing products and features, add new products, and discontinue products that no longer sell.

Visual Literacy

Photo Caption Answer Read the copy on the ad to students. Then read the photo caption and the photo caption question to students: ***What does this advertisement tell you about the products and services that Iams offers to pets and their owners?*** Answers will vary. Accept all reasonable answers. Sample answer: The ad communicates visually and verbally to conscientious pet owners that Iams® pet food offers "7 signs of healthy vitality" for their dogs. Ask students to evaluate the visual components of the advertisement. Ask volunteers to explain how the visual aspects of the advertisement complement the text of the advertisement. The image of the healthy, perky, and well-cared-for border collie, an energetic breed, next to the master's hand holding a ball, ready to play fetch, communicates to dog owners that Iams will impart health and vitality to their dogs. The natural green color scheme also echoes this healthful message. The humorous headline spoken by the dog, "playing fetch with me involves two ZIP codes," coordinates with the visual image, denoting that Iams provides the nutrition and energy that allows the dog to run and play. Other text reiterates this message. The play-on-words slogan, "I am more than just a dog, I am an Iams dog," supports the concept that the Iams brand is the definition of a healthy, happy dog.

ENGAGE

Marketing Internship Project Preview

Read students the Marketing Internship Project Essential Question: ***How can a company conceive and market an exciting new product?*** Because students are just starting to learn about developing new products, they will likely not know the specific answer to this question, which is follow steps for developing a product and marketing plan. However, students should know that research on current products and their marketing strategies can inform new product development. Explain to students that they will learn how businesses develop new products while studying this unit. Tell students that when they are finished studying this unit, they will ask questions to find answers about developing and marketing a new or improved pet product. As they study each chapter in the unit, they can prepare for the Unit Project by thinking about types of pets and pet products.

glencoe.com

Marketing Internship Project Resources Send students to the Online Learning Center to watch a video and download a worksheet activity related to the topic of the Unit Project.

Read the American Marketing Association quote to students:

“Some products and services are all the better thanks to a differentiating ingredient.”

Explain to students that the AMA's Resource Library provides information through articles and resources that address the functions of marketing. Content about the product/service management function discusses developing and marketing successful products:

Ingredient Branding If differentiation matters to consumers, there are extra profits to be had, not just from the brand the consumers are buying, but for the B2B brand that makes the consumer product so desirable.

Think Intel® for Dell® and Nutrasweet® for soda. The ingredient is marketed as the differentiator, providing the characteristic that can make a product desirable.

Ask students: ***Why would a differentiating quality make a new or updated product more desirable to consumers?*** Differentiation can create consumer interest in a quality not possessed by a competitor's similar product.

MARKETING CORE FUNCTIONS IN THIS UNIT

Point out to students that Chapters 30, 31, and 32 will touch on two of the seven marketing core functions. Describe each of these marketing functions to students to prepare them to start studying this unit.

Product/Service Management involves obtaining, developing, maintaining, and improving a product or a product mix in response to marketing opportunities.

Market Planning involves understanding the concepts and strategies used to develop and target specific marketing strategies to a select audience.

MARKETING RESEARCH

PROJECT WORKBOOK

The purpose of the Marketing Research Project Workbook is to provide a step-by-step approach for students to conduct their own marketing research study. Each chapter is devoted to key elements in the research process. Each chapter builds upon the previous chapters, and by the end of the book, students will have completed an in-depth marketing research study, complete with rationale for all decisions, a report of the findings and conclusions, recommendations based on the original research problem and study objectives, and an annotated bibliography.

glencoe.com

Marketing Research Project Workbook Send students to the Online Learning Center to download the Marketing Research Project Workbook. A Teacher Manual is also available on the Teacher Center of the Online Learning Center.

Chapter 30 | Section 30.1 Product Development | Section 30.2 Sustaining Product Sales

product planning

SHOW WHAT YOU KNOW

Visual Literacy Businesses plan, position, and manage the new and existing goods and services they create. The product planning process also includes determining the right product mix and product mix strategies. ***What do you think is necessary to make a new product successful?***

Discovery Project

New Product Plan

Essential Question How do businesses develop a new product and position it for sale?

Project Goal

Assume that you and a classmate are employed in research and product development for a large consumer products manufacturer. Your team has developed a new consumer product. Management has asked your team to design a plan to identify, place, and sell the new product.

Ask Yourself...

- What is your product and its target market?
- How will you define your product by price and quality?
- What are your product's features and benefits?
- How will your product be viewed by competitors?

Synthesize and Present Research Synthesize your research by designing a product plan that identifies, places, and sells the new product.

glencoe.com

Activity
Get a worksheet activity about product planning.

Evaluate
Download a rubric you can use to evaluate your project.

DECA Connection

DECA Event Role Play

Concepts in this chapter are related to DECA competitive events that involve either an interview or role play.

Performance Indicators The performance indicators represent key skills and knowledge. Your key to success in DECA competitive events is relating them to concepts in this chapter.

- Explain the nature and scope of the product/service management function.
- Identify the impact of product life cycles on marketing decisions.
- Explain the concept of product mix.
- Demonstrate adaptability.
- Make oral presentations.

DECA Prep

Role Play Practice role-playing with the DECA Connection competitive-event activity at the end of this chapter. More information on DECA events can be found on DECA's Web site.

Chapter 30 · Product Planning | 705

ENGAGE

Visual Literacy

Read the chapter opener photo caption question to students: ***What do you think is necessary to make a new product successful?*** Businesses plan, position, and manage the new and existing goods and services they create. The product planning process also includes determining the right product mix and product mix strategies. Then ask these guiding questions.

Guiding Questions

List When conducting product research, what are some aspects of the product that are evaluated?	product design, package design, product usage, consumer acceptance
Analyze What are the goals of the product/service management function of the marketing core?	to obtain, develop, maintain, and improve a product or a product mix in response to market opportunities

Discovery Project

New Product Plan To get students thinking about how new products enter the marketplace, ask the Discovery Project Essential Question: ***How do businesses develop a new product and position it for sale?*** Businesses follow a process that usually involves seven key steps, starting with generating ideas and ending with evaluating customer acceptance of the final product. Businesses position products by identifying customer needs, developing a product that meets those needs, identifying how their product compares to the competition, and creating a product image that appeals to consumers.

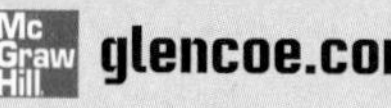

Discovery Project Resources Send students to the Online Learning Center to download a rubric to evaluate their projects.

ENGAGE

Introduce the Chapter

Chapter 30 introduces students to the nature and scope of product planning. These main concepts are introduced and discussed:

- The product mix and the importance of product mix strategies
- The impact of product mix strategies on product planning
- Product items and lines
- The seven key steps in new product development
- Development of existing products
- Deletion of products or product lines
- The product life cycle
- Product positioning
- Category management
- Use of planograms

Discussion Starter

Building a Brand Ask students to name a clothing brand they like. Then ask: ***What characterizes that brand, such as style, colors, and where it is sold?*** Answers will vary. Sample answer: My favorite clothing brand has a vintage look with faded colors and lots of texture. The brand is sold mainly in mall department stores. ***What are some of the brand's more subtle characteristics, such as the messages the clothes symbolize?*** Sample answer: The clothes are casual, but well-made and relatively expensive. They suggest a relaxed lifestyle but also indicate that the wearer is concerned with quality. Tell students that in this chapter they will learn how brands are developed and positioned in the marketplace.

DECA Connection

Discuss the performance indicators listed in the DECA Connection feature. Explain to students that performance indicators tell them how to demonstrate their acquired skills and knowledge through individual or team competitive events.

glencoe.com

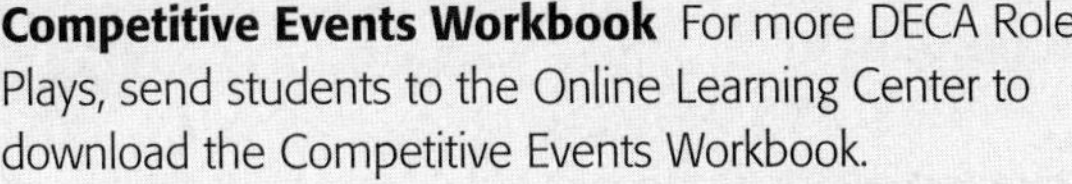

Competitive Events Workbook For more DECA Role Plays, send students to the Online Learning Center to download the Competitive Events Workbook.

PRINT RESOURCES

- **Student Edition**
- **Teacher Edition**
- **Student Activity Workbook with Academic Integration** includes worksheets and activities correlated to the text.
- **Mathematics for Marketing Workbook** provides math activities for every unit in the text.

TECHNOLOGY TOOLBOX

- **Connect**
- **ConnectPlus**
- **ExamView Assessment Suite** is a comprehensive solution for creating, administering, and scoring tests.

glencoe.com

Online Learning Center provides a variety of resources to enrich and enhance learning.

SECTION, CHAPTER, AND UNIT RESOURCES

- **Graphic Organizers** for organizing text concepts visually.
- **Digital Nation Activities** and **Green Marketer Activities** extend learning beyond the text features.
- **Career Chatroom Career Profiles** allow students to explore different marketing occupations in depth.
- **After You Read Answer Keys** for students to check their answers.
- **Discovery Project Rubrics** and **Marketing Internship Project Rubrics** for students to evaluate their projects.

PROGRAM RESOURCES

- **Student Activity Workbook with Academic Integration Teacher Annotated Edition** includes annotated answers for the activities and worksheets.
- **Marketing Research Project Workbook** provides a step-by-step approach for students to complete their own marketing research studies.
- **School-to-Career Activity Workbook** helps students relate their class work to on-the-job experience and involves work-site analysis and working with mentors.
- **Competitive Events Workbook** helps prepare students for state and national marketing education competitions.
- **Inclusion in the Marketing Education Classroom** provides teaching resources for working with students with special needs.
- **PowerPoint Presentations** provides visual teaching aids and assessments for this chapter.

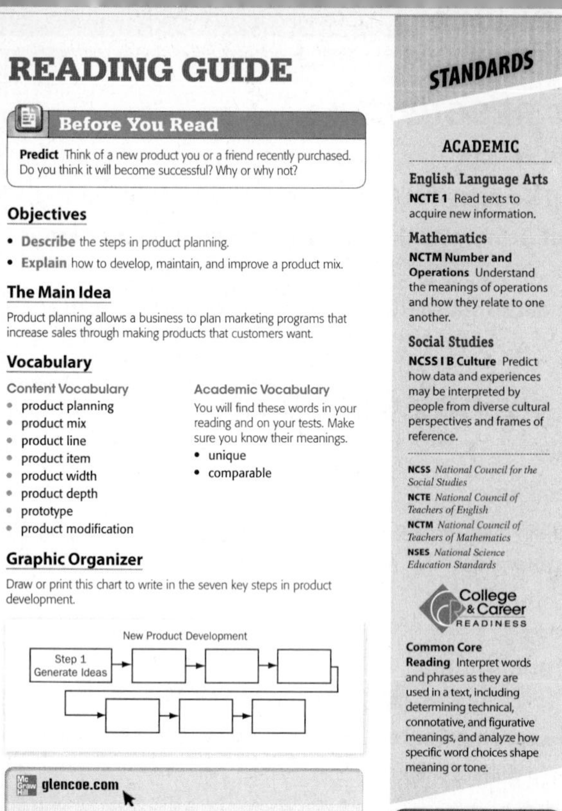

READING GUIDE

Before You Read

Predict Think of a new product you or a friend recently purchased. Do you think it will become successful? Why or why not?

Objectives

- **Describe** the steps in product planning.
- **Explain** how to develop, maintain, and improve a product mix.

The Main Idea

Product planning allows a business to plan marketing programs that increase sales through making products that customers want.

Vocabulary

Content Vocabulary
- product planning
- product mix
- product line
- product item
- product width
- product depth
- prototype
- product modification

Academic Vocabulary

You will find these words in your reading and on your tests. Make sure you know their meanings.
- unique
- comparable

Graphic Organizer

Draw or print this chart to write in the seven key steps in product development.

New Product Development

Step 1 Generate Ideas

glencoe.com

Print this graphic organizer.

STANDARDS

ACADEMIC

English Language Arts

NCTE 1 Read texts to acquire new information.

Mathematics

NCTM Number and Operations Understand the meanings of operations and how they relate to one another.

Social Studies

NCSS I B Culture Predict how data and experiences may be interpreted by people from diverse cultural perspectives and frames of reference.

NCSS *National Council for the Social Studies*
NCTE *National Council of Teachers of English*
NCTM *National Council of Teachers of Mathematics*
NSES *National Science Education Standards*

College & Career READINESS

Common Core
Reading Interpret words and phrases as they are used in a text, including determining technical, connotative, and figurative meanings, and analyze how specific word choices shape meaning or tone.

MARKETING CORE FUNCTION

Product and Service Management

Section 30.1

Product Development

PRODUCT PLANNING

A product can be a tangible item (Apple iPad™), a service (Twitter® micro-blogging service), an idea (a plan for a public relations campaign), an abstract belief (obtain a good education), or a combination of all of these concepts. A product includes its physical features, the seller's reputation, the seller's services, and the way the product is viewed by people.

Product planning involves making decisions about the features and services of a product or idea that will help sell that product. These decisions relate to product features, such as packaging, labeling, and branding. They also relate to services, such as product warranties, that are necessary to support the product.

Product planning allows a business to coordinate existing products and features offered to customers. It also allows them to add new products and delete products that no longer appeal to customers. Product planning requires creativity as well as the ability to interpret current customer needs and forecast new trends.

As You Read

Analyze What marketing activities must occur prior to launching a new product?

PRODUCT MIX

The **product mix** includes all the different products that a company makes or sells. A large manufacturer may have a variety of products in different categories. For example, Kraft Foods© has hundreds of products in the areas of snacks, beverages, cheese, groceries, and convenience meals. Kraft's major brands include Kraft®, Maxwell House®, Nabisco®, Oscar Mayer®, Oreo®, and Philadelphia® products.

Retailers frequently sell more than one product brand. Doing so helps prevent companies from depending on just one product. It also helps companies keep up with the ever-changing marketplace and with diverse customers. For example, a large appliance store might sell LG®, Panasonic®, Sharp®, Sony®, and Toshiba® television sets. Retail stores must plan their product mix carefully because most cannot carry all the product brands that may be available.

> "A product is anything a person receives in an exchange."

Stores need to offer a good selection, but adding more product brands may not result in increased sales. In fact, adding too many brands may result in fewer sales. The added brands may not be as popular as those already in stock.

VARIATIONS IN PRODUCT MIXES

Have you ever heard of *Grand' Mère*® or *Trakinas*®? Both are brands that Kraft sells outside the United States. *Grand' Mère* is a popular coffee in France. *Trakinas* is a cookie sold in Argentina, Brazil, and China. Kraft has a diverse international market. So, Kraft carries product mixes for different cultures and customer needs around the world.

Even similar types of businesses in the domestic market offer different product mixes. The Gap® and Men's Wearhouse® are both apparel stores, yet they offer different product mixes. The Men's Wearhouse focuses on a mix of classic attire for business. The Gap carries a product mix of more casual, trendsetting clothing.

ENGAGE

Anticipation Activity

Improving Student Achievement Have students work in groups to choose a type of retail store to open. First have each group create a list of four categories of merchandise the store will carry. Then have the groups determine types and quantities of products to carry within each category.

Objectives

- **Describe** the steps in product planning. Product planning involves making decisions about what features, such as packaging, labeling, and branding, should be used in selling a business's products, services, or ideas.
- **Explain** how to develop, maintain, and improve a product mix. To make product mix decisions, a business must take an objective look at sales as well as factors such as current trends. A product that has been successful in the past may not continue to thrive if it fails to respond to changing consumer needs.

Graphic Organizer

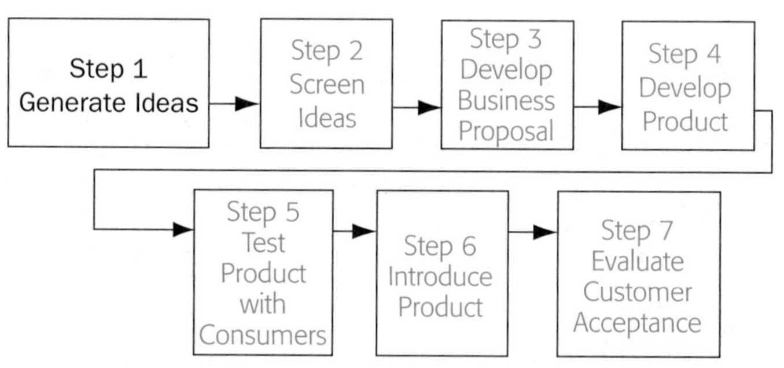

 glencoe.com 

Graphic Organizer Send students to the Online Learning Center to print this graphic organizer.

EXPLORE

Before You Read

Read the question aloud: *Think of a new product you or a friend recently purchased. Do you think it will become successful? Why or why not?* Sample answer: My family recently bought a "no-bark" collar for our puppy, who barks a lot. Whenever the dog barks, the collar lets out a high-pitched squeal that dogs don't like. However, our puppy barks just as much as before. Based on our experience, I don't think the product will be successful.

Preteaching Vocabulary

Have students go to the Online Learning Center at glencoe.com for the Chapter 30 Preteaching Vocabulary games.

Content Vocabulary

Have students create sentence stems for each of the Content Vocabulary words. Then have them complete a classmate's sentences. Sample stem: When a manufacturer makes five types of shampoo, this is an example of ________. (product depth)

Academic Vocabulary

Unique—Usage Display this sentence: *The product is very unique.* Ask: *Do you think* unique *is used properly?* No, because *unique* means "one of a kind." A thing is either unique or not unique. It cannot be "very one of a kind." Adjectives such as *very* and *most* cannot be used with unique.

Graphic Organizer

Display this diagram. Discuss with students that every product is much more than just its physical features.

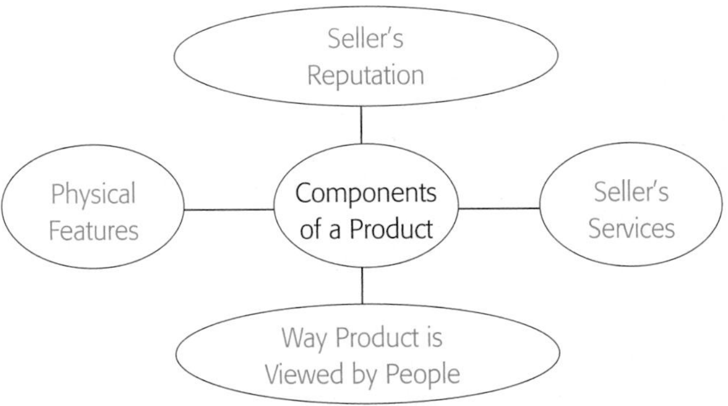

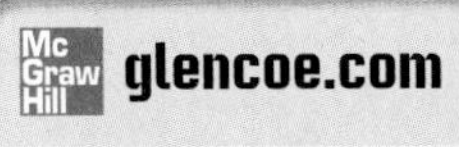
glencoe.com  iWB

Graphic Organizer Send students to the Online Learning Center to print this graphic organizer.

PRODUCT PLANNING

Ask these guiding questions on the topic of product planning.

Guiding Questions

Describe Give an example of each of the following: a tangible product, a service, a product that is an idea, and a product that is an abstract belief.	Possible answers: tangible—skateboard; service—Google; idea—political campaign plan; abstract belief—citizens should vote in elections
Categorize A manufacturer promises to replace the product if it breaks. Is this an example of a product feature, the seller's reputation, or seller services?	seller services
Infer Why might it not be a good idea for a store to increase the number of brands it offers?	Possible answers: Added items may not be as popular as current brands and may take up valuable space; too many brands may confuse customers' buying decisions.

As You Read

Read students the As You Read question: *What marketing activities must occur prior to launching a new product?* The product should be evaluated by focus groups to provide additional input into final product design; it may be test-marketed to determine whether consumers will accept it; and the product must be advertised to make consumers aware of its features and benefits.

Expert Advice

"A product is anything a person receives in an exchange."

Ask: *What is the last exchange you made?* Sample answer: I bought lunch in the cafeteria. Ask: *What did you receive? What did you give?* Sample answer: I received a chef's salad, and I gave money. Discuss exchanges in which students did not give money. Perhaps they traded clothing or gadgets with a friend or did chores at home in exchange for being allowed to borrow the family car.

All the different products and brands that a company makes is its product mix. ***How does a product line differ from a product item?***

The type and number of products to be carried must be based on the objectives of the business, the image the business wants to project, and the market it is trying to reach. This makes product mixes **unique** to each business.

PRODUCT ITEMS AND LINES

A **product line** is a group of closely related products manufactured or sold by a business. Examples include all the car models produced by the Lincoln® division of the Ford Motor Company® or all the cereals produced by Kellogg's®.

A **product item** is a specific model, brand, or size of a product within a product line. Typically, retailers carry several product items for each product line they sell. A Harley-Davidson® motorcycle dealer might carry several Softail® models, such as the Fat Boy®, Softail Deluxe®, or Heritage Softail® Classic.

PRODUCT WIDTH AND PRODUCT DEPTH

The width and depth of a company's product offerings define a product mix. **Product width** refers to the number of different product lines a business manufactures or sells. A retailer that sells three brands of jeans—Lee®, Levi's® and Wrangler®—has a product width of three.

Product depth refers to the number of items offered within each product line. The product depth is the number of sizes, price ranges, colors, fabric type, and styles for each brand of jeans.

Product mix strategies vary with the type of business. Red Lobster® restaurants specialize in seafood dinners. They have considerable product depth within a narrow product line (seafood entrées). Other restaurants may offer broader menus that include steak, chicken, pork, and pasta dinners, as well as seafood. Their product mix may have greater width but less depth than Red Lobster's product mix.

Both manufacturers and retailers must decide on the width and depth of their product mix. To determine its product mix, a business needs to identify its target market, its competitors, and the image it wants to project. After a target market and an image are identified, a business must determine which product lines and items to manufacture or sell. Businesses must also periodically review whether its existing product lines need to be expanded, modified, decreased, or eliminated.

 **Reading Check**

Contrast What is the difference between product planning and product mix?

PRODUCT MIX STRATEGIES

A product mix strategy is a plan for determining which products a business will manufacture or stock. Businesses can use different product mix strategies depending on their resources and objectives. Some businesses develop completely new products to add to their existing product lines. Others expand or modify their current product lines. Sometimes businesses drop existing products to allow for new product offerings.

To make these decisions, a business must take an objective look at sales as well as other factors such as current trends. A product that has experienced success in the past may not continue to thrive if it fails to respond to changing consumer wants and needs.

DEVELOPING NEW PRODUCTS

New product development is an important business strategy for large consumer product manufacturers. The W.E. Kellogg Institute for Food and Nutrition Research has 400,000 square feet devoted to global product development. The Institute has office space, innovation labs, research facilities, an experimental production area, and a pilot plant for its cereal and snack lines.

Successful new products can add substantially to a company's overall sales and boost its market share. (See **Figure 30.1** on page 710.) Often a slight variation of the original or existing product can lead to increased sales.

Procter & Gamble® (P&G) is the number one U.S. manufacturer of personal care and household products. It devotes roughly 15 percent of its research and development budget to developing new products. Innovative P&G products that have created new consumer-goods categories include Febreze® Air Fresheners, the Swiffer® dry-mop system, and the Olay® anti-aging cosmetic line.

According to one study, new products (those less than five years old) account for about 35 percent of total sales for major consumer and industrial goods companies. New products can help a company's image by building the company's reputation among customers as an innovator and leader. In addition, a new product may increase markups and profits to sellers. This is because prices on new products tend to be 10 to 15 percent higher than that of some older, **comparable** products.

DIGITAL NATION

The Wisdom of Crowds

"Crowdsourcing" is a popular new approach to product development that uses social media to gather ideas from customers. To encourage customers to comment, companies set up blogs, Facebook® pages, Twitter® feeds, online polls, and even dedicated Web sites. Many companies ask for feedback about a specific idea or part of the business.

Free Ideas Pour In

Coffee chain Starbucks® created Mystarbucksidea.com, where tens of thousands of customers posted and voted on ideas for new drinks, food, and merchandise. They also vented frustrations and shared solutions to problems. Some customers even posted money-saving ideas, such as saving paper by turning off automatic receipt printing. The site also included a blog on which Starbucks explained how it implemented customers' ideas.

English Language Arts

Create Imagine that 22,000 people vote for a drink recipe submitted to a coffee company's Web site. What should the company do to test the idea? Write a paragraph with your ideas.

NCTE 12 Use language to accomplish individual purposes.

glencoe.com

Get a Digital Nation Worksheet Activity.

EXPLAIN

Visual Literacy

Product Mix Caption Answer Read the caption question to students: ***How does a product line differ from a product item?*** A product line is a group of closely related products manufactured or sold by a business. A product item is a specific model, brand, or size of a product within a product line. Then ask: ***Why do you think Frito-Lay® has such a large variety of products?*** to appeal to different customer preferences and needs Encourage students to choose two of the products in this photo and contrast their target markets. Sample answer: the Fritos appeal to customers who prefer corn chips, while the Lays appeal to customers who prefer potato chips. Other customers prefer chips that are baked rather than fried.

Critical Thinking

Have students think of a food product that they or someone they know consumes often. Ask them to list what might be some other products in this product line. Answers will vary. Sample answer: If an individual consumes ice cream cones, other products in the line might include frozen yogurt, ice cream bars, and frozen fruit bars.

Reinforce Vocabulary

Product Line—Multiple Meanings Explain to students that the word *line* has many meanings. For example, it can refer to a thread, string, cord, or rope. It also can refer to a boundary or division. However, when used in marketing, line has a special meaning: merchandise or services of the same general class that are manufactured or sold by a business.

ELABORATE

Critical Thinking

Ask students to consider the following scenario: You decide to start a pet store. What do you need to consider when determining the width and depth of product offerings? For example, are there other places where people can buy pet food in the neighborhood? What brands of pet food should you carry? Where do people buy or adopt pets? Should the store offer pet grooming? Sample answer: The amount of available shelf space is central in determining the width and depth of the pet food product lines. Different brands attract different customers. Some are more cost -conscious while others might emphasize high-quality ingredients. Within each line, there are products designed to meet the needs of pets of different ages or conditions (puppy, senior, overweight, and so on) and different tastes.

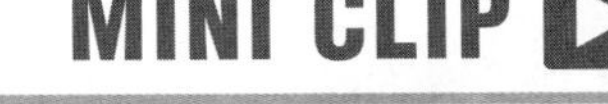

PROFESSIONAL DEVELOPMENT MINI CLIP

Reading: Planning and Classroom Management
Go to the Online Learning Center to view a video clip in which an educator discusses instructional strategies that support a differentiated classroom.

Mini Projects

Extension

Examining a Product Line Instruct students to research a pet food line to determine how it differentiates itself from other products on the market. Have students create a chart showing the line's product mix. Charts will vary depending on the chosen product line. For example, Nutura Pet Products positions itself as a leader in the area of all-natural, healthful pet foods. Its brands include Evo, which contains meat-based proteins and fats; California Natural, designed for pets with food sensitivities; and Karma, featuring organic ingredients.

Expanding a Product Line Divide the class into four groups and have them examine the products in an existing pet food line. Instruct students to develop an idea for a new product that will fit into the existing line. Have students write a paragraph describing the product and explaining why they propose that it be added to the product line. Students' new products will vary depending on the existing line they choose. Students' paragraphs should explain how the product is different from any of the existing products, and how it attempts to meet a consumer need that the existing products do not.

Reading Check Answer

Read the question to students: ***What is the difference between product planning and product mix?*** Product planning refers to making decisions about the features and services of a product or idea that will help sell that product. A product mix is all the different products that a company makes or sells. Emphasize that in planning a new product, a company must always consider how it will fit into the existing product mix.

PRODUCT MIX STRATEGIES

Ask these questions to focus the discussion on product mix strategies.

Guiding Questions

Explain Why might a product that has been successful in the past experience a sudden drop in sales?	The product may not be responding to changing consumer wants and needs. For example, there might be a new competing product that has better or additional features.
Analyze How can new products increase sellers' profits?	Products less than five years old account for about 35 percent of total sales. In addition, the price of a new product tends to be 10 to 15 percent higher than that of older, comparable products.
Infer How can introducing a new product help a company's image?	Consumers may see the company as an innovator or leader and may want to purchase its products; they may even be willing to pay a premium for them.

DIGITAL NATION

English Language Arts Answer The company should make sure the product fits into its overall marketing strategy. The product should be tested to determine any qualities consumers like or dislike. The company should determine whether the product matches current market trends. It also must be determined whether the product can be mass produced at an appropriate cost while still maintaining its quality.

glencoe.com

Worksheet Activity Send students to the Online Learning Center to get a Digital Nation worksheet activity.

FIGURE 30.1 Top Innovations of the Decade

New Ideas These ten innovations have significantly changed the world of marketing. ***Why are new and innovative products and ideas so important?***

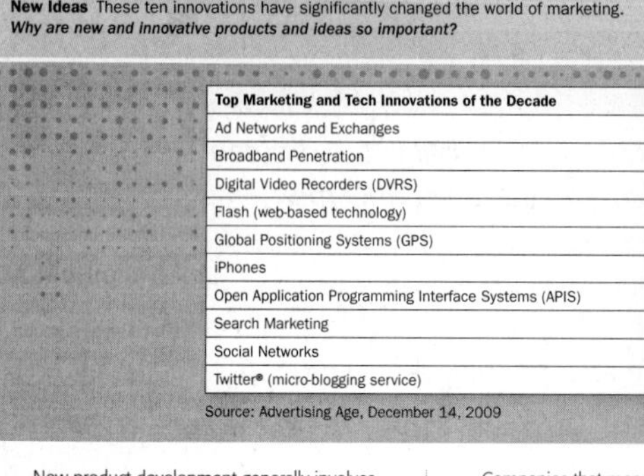

Top Marketing and Tech Innovations of the Decade
Ad Networks and Exchanges
Broadband Penetration
Digital Video Recorders (DVRS)
Flash (web-based technology)
Global Positioning Systems (GPS)
iPhones
Open Application Programming Interface Systems (APIS)
Search Marketing
Social Networks
Twitter® (micro-blogging service)

Source: Advertising Age, December 14, 2009

New product development generally involves seven key steps (see **Figure 30.2**):

1. Generating ideas
2. Screening ideas
3. Developing a business proposal
4. Developing the product
5. Testing the product with consumers
6. Introducing the product (commercialization)
7. Evaluating customer acceptance

GENERATING IDEAS

Creativity is essential for new product development. New product ideas come from a variety of sources, including customers, competitors, channel members, and company employees. Current and existing customers are frequently involved in focus groups and consumer panels. These groups are created to generate new product ideas in as many categories as possible.

Many companies that manufacture consumer packaged goods use a task force approach to new product development. With this approach, employees from departments such as marketing, sales, manufacturing, finance, and research and development, take a new concept from the idea stage through the seven steps of product development.

Companies that manufacture and sell industrial products may establish venture teams that are independent of any particular department. Venture teams normally develop new products that are not part of the company's existing business.

Best Buy®, a consumer electronics firm, involves employees working in idea incubators. Idea incubator teams often include salespeople, computer programmers, and engineers who brainstorm ideas. Team members work and live together in housing complexes for several weeks and exit with ideas for new products, services, and processes.

Microsoft® has developed product ideas using Windows Live® with actual users. The company maps user activities, tests new ideas, and runs statistical tests with controlled scientific experiments on new product ideas.

SCREENING IDEAS

During the screening process, ideas for products are evaluated. This process is done early on, before significant resources like time and money are used up. New product ideas are matched against the company's overall strategy, which defines customers, target markets, competitors, and existing competitive strengths.

FIGURE 30.2 The Steps in New Product Development

From Ideas to New Products There are several key steps for new product development. ***How does an idea lead to a new product or service?***

Steps 1 and 2
GENERATING AND SCREENING IDEAS

Generating ideas involves tracking cultural trends and observing customer behaviors. Screening ideas for new products includes eliminating possibilities until one or two ideas are selected for development.

Steps 3, 4, 5
WRITING A BUSINESS PROPOSAL/ DEVELOPING THE PRODUCT/ TESTING THE PRODUCT

A business proposal evaluates the proposed product in terms of size of market, potential sales, costs, profit potential, technology, the competition, and the level of risk involved. During the development and testing stage, a prototype is made and tested.

Step 6
INTRODUCING THE PRODUCT

If customer response is favorable, the product is introduced into the marketplace.

Step 7
EVALUATING CUSTOMER ACCEPTANCE

After the product has been introduced, marketers track customer acceptance.

EXPLAIN

Activate Prior Knowledge

Reviewing New Product Research Display this diagram to refresh students' memories concerning the different components of new product research that were discussed in Chapter 28.

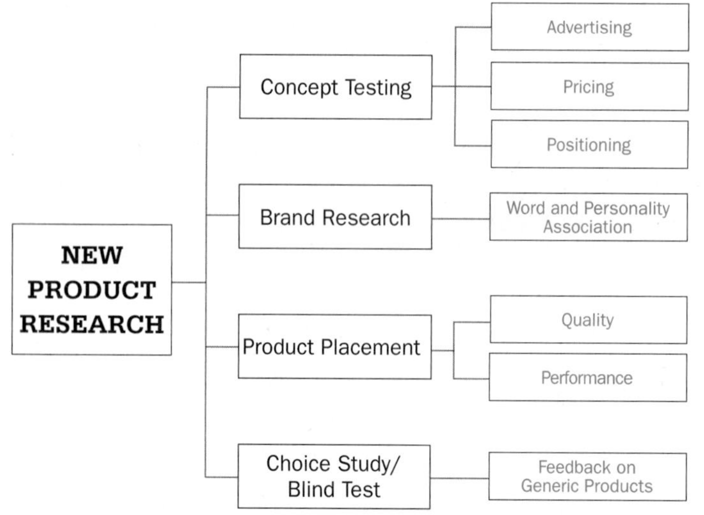

Visual Literacy

Figure 30.1 Caption Answer Read the caption question to students: ***Why are new and innovative products and ideas so important?*** Innovations can make marketing strategies more effective by better meeting the needs and wants of today's consumers. In addition, new products represent a large part of the sales revenue of companies. Ask for volunteers to list products they have recently seen or heard about that they think are truly innovative. Encourage them to discuss what made the product innovative. Sample answer: I saw an ad for a metal door handle that automatically sanitizes itself after each use. I thought this was a great idea for places like public restrooms, schools, and hospitals, especially with the increased concern about the spread of infections.

VIRTUAL BUSINESS

ANALYZING THE COMPETITION

Introduce the concept of analyzing the competition to students using Knowledge Matters' Virtual Business Retailing visual simulation, *Analyzing the Competition*. In this simulation, students will learn how to determine who the competition is, competitive analysis, and how competition affects a business.

ELABORATE

Mini Project

Differentiated Instruction

Logical Learners Ask students to review the innovations in Figure 30.1 and choose the one they think has had the greatest impact on marketing. Have them prepare a persuasive speech explaining the reasons for their choice. Speeches will vary depending on the innovation they choose. For example, if they choose broadband penetration, they might emphasize how it has led to more video and animation on the Web, which has greatly increased the power of online advertising.

GENERATING IDEAS

Ask these questions to focus the discussion on generating ideas.

Guiding Questions

List What are four possible sources of new product ideas?	customers, competitors, channel members, employees
Draw Conclusions Why do product development task forces typically include employees from a variety of departments?	Different backgrounds and training enable employees to point out a product's specific strengths and weaknesses.
Synthesize Why are venture teams typically independent of any particular department within a company?	Because they are developing new products, the team needs to be free of existing departmental influences.

Visual Literacy

Figure 30.2 Caption Answer Read the question: ***How does an idea lead to a new product or service?*** The idea is the critical first step in new product development—a process that perceives a need and a way to fill it. If the idea passes the screening process, a product is developed, tested, and introduced. Then ask: ***What is the purpose of the last step in the new product development process?*** The last step evaluates not only how customers accepted the product but also the marketing strategies used to introduce it.

Critical Thinking

Offer this scenario: One member of a product development team has a very logical way of thinking while another is very creative. Ask: ***What would each team member be more qualified to do, generate ideas or screen them? Why?*** The logical thinker would be better at screening ideas because that person would know whether an idea was practical. The creative thinker would be better at generating ideas because of that person's ability to see creative solutions.

e MARKETING

Online Idea Generation

Getting ideas for new products has been made easier with e-marketing. Companies solicit product ideas from outsiders and customers via Web sites. Connect & Develop is Procter and Gamble's® (P&G) source for innovation from outsiders. If an idea is selected from P&G's research and development team, the innovator becomes a partner with P&G. P&G also lets Web site visitors share their ideas without compensation. General Electric® and Pepsi-Co® go a step further by sponsoring competitions for fledgling entrepreneurs. General Electric accepts ideas at its "ecomagination" Web site, where people can evaluate the ideas and vote on them. PepsiCo's competition centers around start-up companies involved in social media, mobile marketing, and other digital platforms.

Companies can get immediate feedback about product ideas via the Internet. Social media sites, like Facebook, can even help launch a new product. Ford® unveiled its 2011 Ford Explorer on Facebook and saw its share of SUV shoppers increase dramatically on that day.

Innovate and Create

Ask students if they ever voted for a new M&M® candy color or a new Crayola® crayon color. Ask if they ever considered entering a new Ben & Jerry's® ice cream flavor at its Web site. Discuss the benefits of recruiting outsiders and especially current customers to generate new product ideas. Answers will vary regarding students' participation in voting for M&M or Crayola colors. Some of the benefits of recruiting outsiders, especially current customers to generate new product ideas are the low cost, number of creative ideas that can be generated, the customer engagement factor, and use of the competition for marketing purposes.

glencoe.com

eMarketing Worksheet Activity Send students to the Online Learning Center to download an eMarketing worksheet activity.

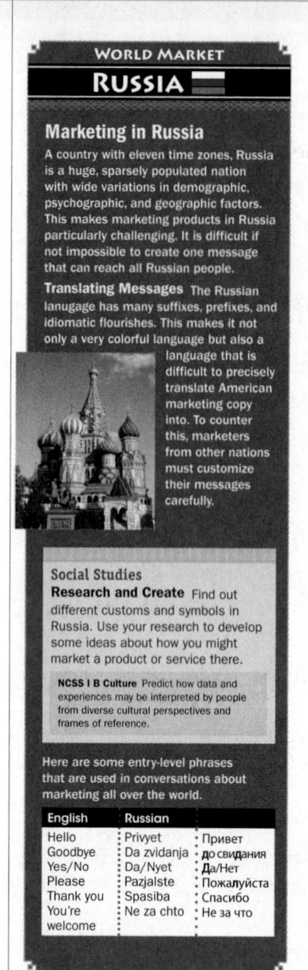

WORLD MARKET

RUSSIA

Marketing in Russia

A country with eleven time zones, Russia is a huge, sparsely populated nation with wide variations in demographic, psychographic, and geographic factors. This makes marketing products in Russia particularly challenging. It is difficult if not impossible to create one message that can reach all Russian people.

Translating Messages The Russian lanugage has many suffixes, prefixes, and idiomatic flourishes. This makes it not only a very colorful language but also a language that is difficult to precisely translate American marketing copy into. To counter this, marketers from other nations must customize their messages carefully.

Social Studies

Research and Create Find out different customs and symbols in Russia. Use your research to develop some ideas about how you might market a product or service there.

NCSS I B Culture Predict how data and experiences may be interpreted by people from diverse cultural perspectives and frames of reference.

Here are some entry-level phrases that are used in conversations about marketing all over the world.

English	Russian	
Hello	Privyet	Привет
Goodbye	Da zvidanja	до свидания
Yes/No	Da/Nyet	Да/Нет
Please	Pazjalste	Пожалуйста
Thank you	Spasiba	Спасибо
You're welcome	Ne za chto	Не за что

During the screening process, marketers evaluate new ideas for potential conflicts with existing products. What would a manufacturer of digital thermometers do if a new way to measure body temperature were invented? Suppose the invention was a disposable plastic strip that turned colors depending on body heat. Would the new product be in conflict with the existing product such as a digital thermometer?

A screening might involve concept testing with consumers. Consumers would identify qualities they like and dislike about the new concept, and whether they would buy such a product. If the company planned to market the new product globally, opinions from proposed foreign markets should be obtained.

The purpose of the screening stage is to find the products that deserve further study. A large number of products are rejected in the screening stage, making it an important early step.

DEVELOPING A BUSINESS PROPOSAL

Marketers evaluate a product idea that makes it through the screening process in terms of its profit potential. A business proposal is developed to evaluate the new product. Marketers must consider the size of the market, potential sales, costs, profit potential, technological trends, overall competitive environment, and level of risk.

During this stage, the company must also consider production requirements. How long will it take to create and introduce the new product? Can it be produced efficiently and at a competitive price? The business must plan a program to study the realities of making and marketing the new product.

DEVELOPING THE PRODUCT

During product development, the new product idea takes on a physical shape, and marketers develop a marketing strategy. The company makes plans relating to production, packaging, labeling, branding, promotion, and distribution.

During this phase of product development, technical evaluations are made to see whether the company can produce the new product and whether it is practical to do so. The Ben & Jerry's® ice cream company had difficulties when it first developed Cherry Garcia ice cream. The original idea was to add whole chocolate-coated cherries to the ice cream. But the whole cherries were too large to go through the production machinery, which caused the chocolate to break off the cherries. After numerous tests, the company finally added the cherries and the chocolate separately.

In addition to detecting difficulties with product production, a business must conduct tests on products to see how they will hold up during normal and not-so-normal use by the consumer.

A new product may be tested for durability in the lab. Testers use machines and experiments that will reproduce the actions or motions that the product will undergo during use. Technical problems should be detected at this stage so that they can be corrected before full-scale production begins.

Millions of dollars can be spent on this stage of product development for testing, prototypes, and research. A **prototype** is a model of the new product. Usually only a few models are made at first, as the business tests the idea and makes changes to improve the final product. A concept car is an example of a prototype.

New Product Launches Every year more than 30,000 new food, tobacco, health, and beauty products are introduced in North America.

The government requires extensive scientific testing in various stages for some products, such as prescription drugs and genetically engineered food products. These tests end with testing on human beings to determine side effects and problems with a product's safety. Getting final approval from the government for use by the general public can take years.

TESTING THE PRODUCT WITH CONSUMERS

New products are usually test-marketed in certain geographic areas to see whether consumers will accept them. Larger companies establish research and development departments that work with marketing staff, marketing research staff, and outside research companies to develop and test new products.

For example, PepsiCo® developed a low-calorie soft drink for the European market. Because international customers typically do not like diet beverages, the company spent more than two years testing the drink with different flavors. Finally, one flavor combination met the company's goal of having at least 40 percent of potential consumers choose Pepsi Max® over a competitor's product.

Not every new product must be test-marketed. A focus-group evaluation during development can provide additional input into final product design, revealing potential problems before production.

In some cases, the costs of test marketing, focus-groups, or direct-marketing tests may be too high. Marketers may skip the testing of other products because they do not yet have a product to be evaluated. Sometimes a company delays test marketing to keep information away from competitors. Such information might help competitors get a similar product on the market.

INTRODUCING THE PRODUCT

This stage is also called "commercialization." Introducing a new product can be expensive. For example, to convince adults to use Crest Whitening Expressions® toothpaste in cinnamon, citrus, and herbal mint flavors, Procter & Gamble spent about $80 million on a marketing campaign.

New products must be advertised to introduce their benefits to consumers. A new or revised distribution network may be needed. The company may need to develop training programs for its sales force.

To pay these costs, the company must get its new products into the market as quickly as possible. The first company to introduce a new product has an advantage in acquiring customers and in building brand loyalty.

EVALUATING CUSTOMER ACCEPTANCE

The purpose of this step is to evaluate customer acceptance of the product and the marketing strategies used to introduce the product. Scanning equipment and computer systems can be used to compile large amounts of sales and market data on existing and new products. From this information, customized reports can be prepared. These reports help answer key questions such as:

- How often do customers buy the new product?
- When did customers last buy the new product?
- Where are the best customers for our new product?
- What new products are customers buying?

EXPLAIN

Activate Prior Knowledge

To help students better understand the World Market feature, ask them to list examples of demographic factors (age, gender, income), psychographic factors (attitudes, values, opinions), and geographic factors (location).

WORLD MARKET

SOCIAL STUDIES

Have students research Russian customs and symbols to come up with ideas for marketing a specific product or service. For example, the Matryoshka doll (nesting doll) is a well-known symbol of Russian culture. Students might come with an idea to create customized Matryoshka dolls that are tied in with a contemporary sports or cultural event in Russia.

Mini Project

Differentiated Instruction

Cooperative Learners Have students work in pairs to generate three ideas for pet food products. The pair should establish a focus group of several fellow students. Students should present their product ideas to the focus group. The focus group should discuss what they liked and disliked about the products, any improvements they might suggest, and so on. Have students summarize what they learned from the focus group in a one-page report. Each pair should present their pet food ideas to their focus group. The focus group should analyze the ideas and state what they like and dislike about them. The students' final report should summarize the focus group feedback and discuss how the pair might improve their products based on this feedback.

ELABORATE

Graphic Organizer

Display this business proposal graphic organizer and ask volunteers to list all information that must be included.

Business Proposal

- Market size
- Potential sales
- Cost
- Profit potential
- Technological trends
- Overall competitive environment
- Level of risk
- Production requirements
- Time needed to create and introduce product
- Production efficiency
- Competitiveness of projected price

 **glencoe.com**  iWB

Graphic Organizer Send students to the Online Learning Center to print this graphic organizer.

DEVELOPING THE PRODUCT

Ask these questions to encourage discussion of product development.

Guiding Questions

Recall What are some tasks performed during product development?	Companies make production plans, conduct technical evaluations, and develop a marketing strategy.
Analyze What is the purpose of a prototype?	for testing to determine whether any changes need to be made
Draw Conclusions Why is it important to identify technical issues in product development rather than after production begins?	If technical problems are not found until after production begins, it is likely that large amounts of time and money will be wasted.

New Product Launches It has been estimated that for every 3,000 new product ideas, only one is ultimately successful. Ask students: ***Why do you think the success rate is so low?***

INTRODUCING THE PRODUCT

Remind students that because developing new products is incredibly expensive, companies are dedicated to getting these products introduced as quickly as possible. Ask these guiding questions to focus the discussion on product introduction.

Guiding Questions

Explain Why do you think that introducing a product is also called "commercialization"?	This is when the product enters the marketplace and becomes available to be sold for a profit.
Analyze What are advantages to being the first on the market with a new product?	The first company to put a product on the market has the advantages of acquiring a customer base and building brand loyalty.
Synthesize Why do you think many customers will be loyal to the first company to get a new product on the market?	Possible answer: Customers may see this company as being an innovator and therefore think the company's product is superior to competitors' products that follow it.

Mini Projects

Differentiated Instruction

Visual Learners Have students create posters illustrating the seven key steps in new product development. Instruct students to write each step on the poster, and then tell them to create drawings or insert images from magazines, the Internet, or other sources to illustrate each step. Display the posters where the rest of the class can view them. Students' illustrated posters should explain the seven key steps in product development. For example, a student might insert an image of a scientist working in a research lab for the Developing the Product step.

Verbal/Linguistic Learners Have students use appropriate sources to research hybrid cars. Ask students why they believe the hybrid car was introduced and to account for the length of time it took for hybrids to be produced. Have students summarize their findings in a brief report. Sample reports may include the following information: One reason the hybrid was introduced was the growing number of consumers concerned with pollution caused by petroleum products and the challenges in getting these products to the marketplace. Reasons for the length of time it took for hybrid cars to enter the marketplace include the difficulties in dealing with performance issues, such as range and acceleration rates; concerns about whether consumers would be willing to buy them, particularly with their higher price tags; and the challenges involved in supplying spare parts and trained mechanics to work on the cars.

DEVELOPING EXISTING PRODUCTS

Companies constantly review their product mix to see if they can further expand their product lines or modify existing products. They do this to build on an already established image, to appeal to new markets, and to increase sales and profits.

One disadvantage of adding new product versions and products to a company's product mix is cost. The additions increase inventory, promotion, storage, and distribution costs. New products also may take sales away from existing products. A brand or corporate name is usually placed on the new product. If the product is unpopular, poorly made, or harmful, all products with the corporate name may suffer. However, the disadvantages usually do not keep a company from improving its existing products.

LINE EXTENSIONS

Companies can expand product offerings by adding new product lines, items, or services, which may or may not be related to current products. Consider the varieties of Tylenol®. Some varieties include Tylenol Flu, Tylenol Cold, Tylenol PM, and Tylenol Allergy Sinus. These products also come in a variety of forms, such as tablets, caplets, and gel caps. Each of these products is a line extension of the original Tylenol headache pain product.

A line extension is intended to be a different product that appeals to somewhat different needs of consumers. In essence, the company wants to provide a wider range of choices to increase product depth within a line. Line extensions are easy to market because customers are already familiar with the original product on which the extension is based.

PRODUCT MODIFICATIONS

A **product modification** is an alteration in a company's existing product. Modified products may be offered in new and different varieties, formulations, colors, styles, features, or sizes. Product modifications are a relatively quick and easy way to add new products to a company's product line. When modifying a product, the old product may be phased out. Packaging can also be modified to appeal to consumers and attract them to the new product.

DELETING A PRODUCT OR PRODUCT LINE

Sometimes companies decide that they will no longer produce or sell a particular product or even a whole product line. There can be many reasons for this move.

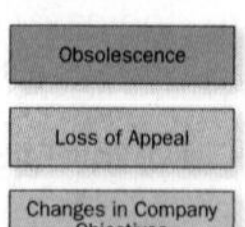

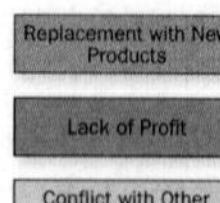

OBSOLESCENCE

Changes in technology have caused many products to be discontinued over time. An obsolete item is something that is no longer useful. For example, some analysts say telephone land lines are on their way to obsolescence. Music listening devices have evolved from 45 RPM records and $33\frac{1}{3}$ RPM albums, eight-track tapes, cassette tapes, and CDs to MP3 players and computer downloads.

LOSS OF APPEAL

As consumer tastes change, companies drop products that no longer appeal to old tastes and interests. For example, new video games with better visual effects and improved interactive features replace earlier versions to spark continued customer interest and appeal. Older products or versions may have some lasting loyalties that generate revenue, but the manufacturers must decide whether these benefits are worth the expense of keeping the item in their product mixes.

CHANGES IN COMPANY OBJECTIVES

Sometimes a product or entire product mix does not match a company's current objectives. After operating in Japan for 30 years, the Wendy's® hamburger chain closed its 70 restaurants there. While still looking at international expansion, the company focused on Yoshinoya® and other restaurants. The company closed its outlets and discontinued its product in this market to meet new company objectives.

LACK OF PROFIT

Product developers may drop products when sales reach such a low level that the return on sales does not meet company objectives.

CONFLICT WITH OTHER PRODUCTS IN THE LINE

Sometimes products take business away from other products in the same product line. Increased sales of one product can cause decreased sales of another product in that line.

REPLACEMENT WITH NEW PRODUCTS

To encourage retailers to cover costs of putting a new product onto limited shelf space, manufacturers pay slotting fees or allowances. A slotting fee is a cash premium a manufacturer pays to a retailer for the costs involved with placing a new product on its shelves.

Slotting fees may pay for a retailer's discounted specials on a new product, store shelf space, penalties for poor sales, advertising, and display costs. Slotting fees for consumer products range from a few thousand dollars to more than $100,000 per product.

According to a Federal Trade Commission study, a nationwide product launch might cost more than $2 million in slotting fees alone. Slotting fees help the retailer balance the costs associated with accepting a new product. A retailer must mark down eliminated products and pay for software, labor, and materials to change price labels and enter a new product into the inventory.

After You Read **Section 30.1**

Review Key Concepts

1. **Differentiate** between product depth and product width.
2. **Name** the types of criteria used to screen new product ideas.
3. **List** four reasons for expanding a product line.

Practice Academics

English Language Arts

4. Perform online or library research to obtain information about slotting fees. Write a one- or two-page paper on the advantages and disadvantages of slotting fees from a manufacturer's and a retailer's perspective.

NCTE 1 Read texts to acquire new information.

Mathematics

5. A towel manufacturing company had total sales of $34,250 in 2009. In 2010, the company's total sales were $42,780. What is the percentage increase in sales from 2009 to 2010?

Math Concept **Percent Increase** A percent is a ratio that compares values to 100. Percents represent parts of a whole. When determining the percentage of an increase in values, such as sales, first determine the nominal increase by subtracting. Convert that to a decimal number by division.

Starting Hints To solve this problem, subtract the total sales in 2009 from the total sales in 2010. Divide the difference by the total sales in 2009 to determine the decimal equivalent of the percentage increase.

NCTM Number and Operations Understand the meanings of operations and how they relate to one another.

For help, go to the **Math Skills Handbook** located at the back of this book.

glencoe.com

Check your answers.

ELABORATE

Graphic Organizer

Display this Venn diagram. Ask students to write characteristics of line extensions and product modifications in the appropriate circles. Ask for ways in which both are similar, and write these in the overlapping area.

Line Extensions	Both	Product Modifications
• Different products appeal to somewhat different customer needs • Increase product depth within a line	• Build on already established image • Meet customer needs • Appeal to new markets • Increase sales and profits	• Change to an existing product • May offer new colors, sizes, or features • Relatively quick and easy

glencoe.com

Graphic Organizer Send students to the Online Learning Center to print this graphic organizer.

DEVELOPING EXISTING PRODUCTS

Tell students that companies can save considerable time and money by further developing products in which they have already invested. Ask these guiding questions to focus class discussion on developing existing products.

Guiding Questions

Analyze What are some reasons that companies may be hesitant to add new products to a company's existing product mix?	New product additions add to costs; they may take sales away from existing products; if there are problems with the new product, all products associated with the company may suffer.
Make Judgments Which do you think would be easier to market: a line extension or an existing product that has been modified? Why?	Possible answer: An existing product. Consumers are likely already aware of the basic product, so they would only need to be convinced that the modifications make the product more desirable.

EVALUATE

Graphic Organizer

Display this graphic. As you discuss each of these reasons a product might be discontinued, ask for volunteers to give examples.

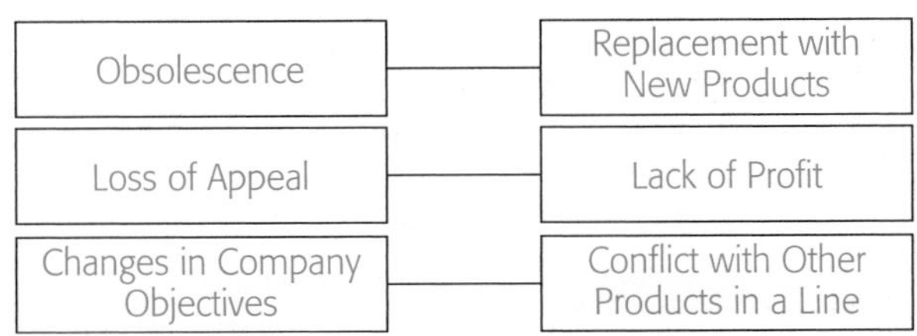

 glencoe.com  iWB

Graphic Organizer Send students to the Online Learning Center to print this graphic organizer.

DELETING A PRODUCT OR PRODUCT LINE

Ask these questions to focus student discussion on product deletion.

Guiding Questions

Recall What is primary cause of obsolescence?	technological advances
Analyze Why do retailers frequently charge slotting fees for putting a new product on their shelves?	The new product takes up additional space; it must be advertised and specials may be offered; displays may have to be set up; and the store risks losing money on the product.
Synthesize A clothing manufacturer has deleted a particular sweater from its product line. What is the most likely reason?	Loss of appeal—clothing styles change so often that manufacturers must constantly remove outdated items to keep their lines current.

Mini Project

Enrichment

Analyzing Obsolescence Have pairs of students create lists of products they think will become obsolete in the next ten years and the reasons why. When they are done, have each pair share their list. Sample answers: printed maps (due to GPS technology); wireless phones without Internet or e-mail access; CDs and DVDs (due to increased online streaming and downloading and the use of digital media players).

After You Read — Section 30.1

Review Key Concepts

1. Product depth refers to the number of items offered within each product line whereas product width refers to the number of different product lines a business manufactures or sells.
2. Criteria used to screen new product ideas include: Is the product in line with the company's overall strategy, which defines customers, target markets, competitors, and existing competitive strengths? Are there any potential conflicts with existing products? Has the product been tested with consumers, and, if so, did they like it and would they buy it?
3. Four reasons to expand a product line are to build on an already established image, to appeal to new markets, to increase sales and profits, and for the company to be seen as an innovator in the field.

Practice Academics

English Language Arts

4. Retailers state that because shelf space is scarce, slotting fees help share the risk of the failure of a new product between them and the manufacturer. A disadvantage is that retailers must take markdowns on discontinued items. The advantage for manufacturers is that they get shelf space and access to consumers. However, paying for slotting fees causes them to raise the prices they charge retailers for their products. Small manufacturers state that high slotting fees make it difficult, if not impossible, for them to compete with larger companies.

Mathematics

5. 25% ([42,780 – 34,250]/34,250)

Answer Key Send students to the Online Learning Center to check their answers.

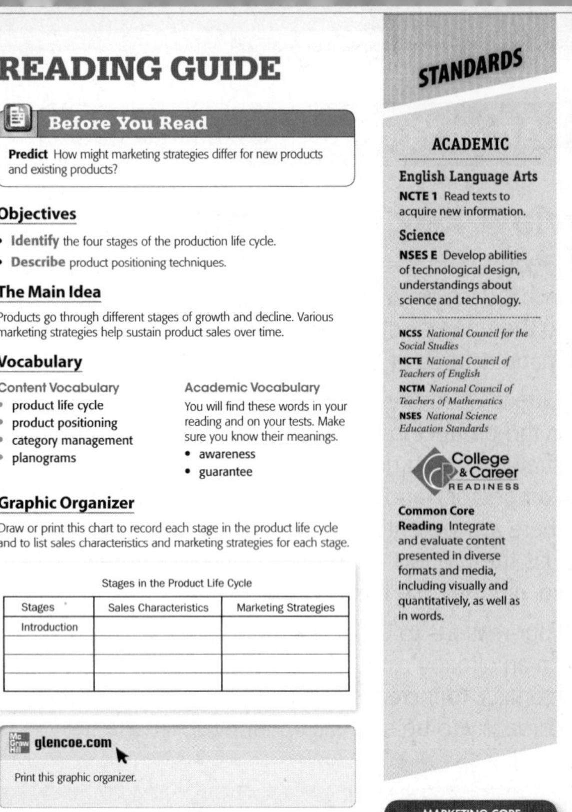

READING GUIDE

Before You Read

Predict How might marketing strategies differ for new products and existing products?

Objectives

- **Identify** the four stages of the production life cycle.
- **Describe** product positioning techniques.

The Main Idea

Products go through different stages of growth and decline. Various marketing strategies help sustain product sales over time.

Vocabulary

Content Vocabulary
- product life cycle
- product positioning
- category management
- planograms

Academic Vocabulary

You will find these words in your reading and on your tests. Make sure you know their meanings.
- awareness
- guarantee

Graphic Organizer

Draw or print this chart to record each stage in the product life cycle and to list sales characteristics and marketing strategies for each stage.

Stages in the Product Life Cycle

Stages	Sales Characteristics	Marketing Strategies
Introduction		

glencoe.com

Print this graphic organizer.

STANDARDS

ACADEMIC

English Language Arts

NCTE 1 Read texts to acquire new information.

Science

NSES E Develop abilities of technological design, understandings about science and technology.

NCSS *National Council for the Social Studies*
NCTE *National Council of Teachers of English*
NCTM *National Council of Teachers of Mathematics*
NSES *National Science Education Standards*

College & Career READINESS

Common Core
Reading Integrate and evaluate content presented in diverse formats and media, including visually and quantitatively, as well as in words.

MARKETING CORE FUNCTION

Product/Service Management

716 | Unit 10 · Product and Service Management

Section 30.2 Sustaining Product Sales

THE PRODUCT LIFE CYCLE

The **product life cycle** represents the stages that a product goes through during its life. There are four basic stages of the product life cycle: introduction, growth, maturity, and decline (see **Figure 30.3** on page 718). The product life cycle has an impact on the marketing strategy and the product mix. The length of a product life cycle varies with the product. For example, products purchased for events, such as decorations and gift wrap, have very short life cycles. Appliances, automobiles, and some consumer food and household products have much longer life cycles. At each stage in the product life cycle, marketers must adjust their product mix and their marketing strategies to ensure continued sales.

As You Read

Connect Think of a product you recently purchased. Why did you select that product instead of another similar product?

MANAGING IN THE INTRODUCTION STAGE

When the product is introduced to the market, a company focuses its efforts on promotion and production. The major goal is to draw the customer's attention to the new product. The company works to build its sales by increasing product **awareness** and develop a market for the product. Special promotions get the customer to try the new product. There may also be increased costs due to new packaging and distribution expenses. This is also the time when intellectual property protection such as patents and trademarks are obtained. Because of these activities, the costs of introducing a product are high. Therefore, introduction is usually the least profitable stage of the life cycle.

MANAGING IN THE GROWTH STAGE

In the growth stage, the company seeks to build brand preference and increase market share. During the growth phase of the product life cycle, the product is enjoying success. This is demonstrated through increasing sales and profits. Much of the target market knows about and buys the product. Advertising now focuses on consumer satisfaction, rather than on the benefits of new products.

> "A product has a life cycle with several stages: introduction, growth, maturity, and decline."

By this time, the competition is aware of the success of the product. The competition is also likely to offer new products in order to compete. To keep its product sales growing, the company may enter into price competition or introduce new models. The company may also decide to modify the existing product to offer more benefits than the competition offers.

MANAGING IN THE MATURITY STAGE

A product reaches the maturity stage when its sales decrease or slow down. The product has more competition now, or most of the target market consumers already own the product. Advertising continues to reinforce the product brand, but the promotional costs are lower than in the introduction stage.

Chapter 30 · Product Planning | 717

ENGAGE

Anticipation Activity

Improving Student Achievement Have students think of one product that has been around most of their lives—for example, Coca-Cola® or Barbie®. Then ask students to describe the different ways in which the product was marketed at different times. Explain that products go through the life stages of introduction, growth, maturity, and decline, and require different marketing strategies in each cycle.

Objectives

- **Identify** the four stages of the production life cycle. introduction, growth, maturity, decline
- **Describe** product positioning techniques. Products can be positioned by price and quality, features and benefits, in relation to the competition, and in relation to other products in a line.

Graphic Organizer

Stages in the Product Life Cycle

Stages	Sales Characteristics	Marketing Strategies
Introduction	Least profitable stage; consumers still learning	Special promotions; focus on benefits
Growth	Increasing sales and profits	Focus on consumer satisfaction; competitive pricing; new models
Maturity	Sales slow; increased competition or market saturation	Reinforce brand; anti-competition spending; slotting fees may rise
Decline	Sales fall and profits may be smaller than expenses	Ads reduced; may sell, license, discount, or regionalize product

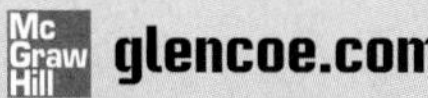

glencoe.com

Graphic Organizer Send students to the Online Learning Center to print this graphic organizer.

EXPLORE

Before You Read

Read the Before You Read question aloud: ***How might marketing strategies differ for new products and existing products?*** Marketing for new products is geared toward making the target market aware of the product and possibly offering special promotion to encourage consumers to try the product. With an existing product, marketing strategies emphasize new features. For products that were first on the market but now have competitors, ads might emphasize the company's innovativeness. Any advantages the product has over the competition are also emphasized.

Preteaching Vocabulary

Have students go to the Online Learning Center at glencoe.com for the Chapter 30 Preteaching Vocabulary games.

Content Vocabulary

Have students create a two-column chart on a blank sheet of paper. Ask them to write each of the four vocabulary words in the first column. Then have students scan this section to locate each term and write a quick definition of the word in the second column. As they read through the section, they should modify or expand on the definitions as needed.

Academic Vocabulary

Awareness—Suffixes Display the word *awareness* for the class, and underline the suffix *-ness*. Explain that *aware* means "having or showing realization or knowledge." Then explain that the suffix *-ness* means "state of" or "condition of." Ask: ***What does awareness mean?*** the state of having realization or knowledge. Display the following words for the class. Have the students add *-ness* and provide a definition for each: *calm*, *quiet*, and *happy*. Sample definitions: calmness—the state of being calm, not anxious; quietness—the state of being quiet, lack of noise; happiness—the state of being happy, agreeable feeling or condition.

Guarantee—Multiple Usages Explain to students that *guarantee* can be used as either a noun or a verb. As a noun, it means "an assurance for the fulfillment of a condition." As a verb, it means "to assume responsibility for the quality or performance of." Read aloud this sentence: ***There is no guarantee that the sales on this product will remain steady.*** Ask: ***Does this sentence use guarantee as a noun or a verb?*** noun Then ask for a sentence that uses it as a verb. Sample sentence: I guarantee that this car will get at least 30 miles per gallon on the highway.

Sustaining Product Sales

THE PRODUCT LIFE CYCLE

Use these questions to focus discussion on the product life cycle.

Guiding Questions

Recall Give an example of a product with a relatively short life cycle and one that typically has a long life cycle.	short: wedding decorations; long: cars, large appliances
Analyze A new kitchen cleaning product is in the introduction stage and sales are occurring at projected levels. Do you think the company will make a strong profit during this stage? Why or why not?	No, because high costs of promotion at this stage cut into profits. The company may also offer discounts to encourage consumers to try the product.
Draw Conclusions TV ads for a product consist of testimonials from satisfied buyers. What stage is the product probably in? Explain.	The product is probably in the growth stage, because ads in this stage focus on customer satisfaction.

As You Read

Read the As You Read question aloud: ***Think of a product you recently purchased. Why did you select that product instead of another similar product?*** Answers will vary but may include low cost, better quality, specific features, product placement, advertisements, and so on. Then ask: ***Of all the reasons you might select one product over another, which one do you think is most important? Why?*** Answers will vary. Sample answer: Product features, because if the product does not meet my needs, I will not be happy with it, regardless of its price or quality.

Expert Advice

"A product has a life cycle with several stages: introduction, growth, maturity, and decline."

Explain that the product life cycle is based on the biological life cycle. Display a two-column table. For each stage of the product life cycle in the left column, place the corresponding plant life cycle stage in the right column. Introduction—seed is planted; Growth—seed sprouts; Maturity—plant is full-grown; Decline—plant shrinks and dies

During this stage, a company spends more of its marketing dollars fighting off the competition, which now has similar products. Because of competing brands, the product loses market share and has lower profits.

Slotting fees may rise during this stage as the company seeks to maintain its market share. At this stage, the company has to decide whether it can continue to improve the product to maintain market share and extend the life of the product.

MANAGING IN THE DECLINE STAGE

During the decline stage, sales fall. Profits reach the point where they are smaller than the expenses. Management needs to decide how long it will continue to support the product.

In the decline stage, advertising and promotional costs are reduced to maximize profits on declining sales. If the company believes that the product has reached the end of its life cycle, the company deletes the product entirely from its product mix.

Besides dropping the product, the company can use other product mix strategies to try to gain further sales from a declining product. These strategies include selling or licensing the product, recommitting to the product line, discounting the product, regionalizing the product, and updating or altering the product.

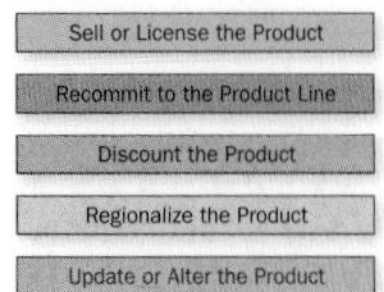

SELL OR LICENSE THE PRODUCT

Many companies sell or license their poorly performing products to risk-taking companies. Risk-taking companies try to revitalize the product by changing the product's image or introducing it to a new market. By rejuvenating products, companies may regain lost market share and generate more profit.

FIGURE 30.3 Understanding the Product Life Cycle

Product Stages The life cycle of a product can be divided into four stages: introduction, growth, maturity, and decline. ***Why are sales relatively slow during the maturity stage?***

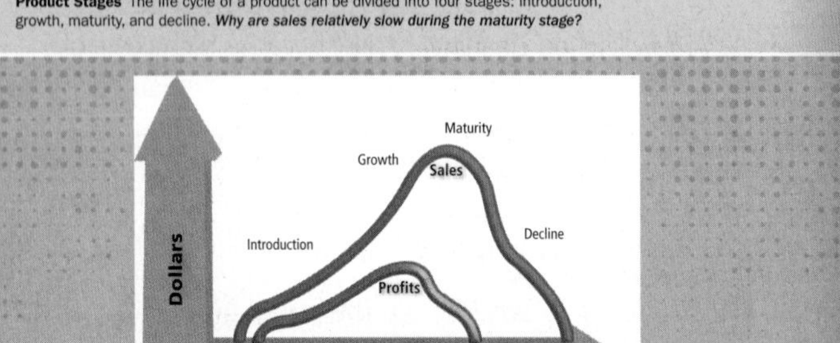

RECOMMIT TO THE PRODUCT LINE

Some companies decide that a declining product has other possible uses that can help improve sales. Knox® lost sales as people spent less time making fancy gelatin desserts. The company found a new use for the product that appealed to a different market. By adding Knox gelatin to JELL-O® mixes, it allowed consumers to make hand-held desserts. The new JELL-O Jigglers® desserts are especially popular with children. This new use for the product helped Knox improve its sales.

Even with recommitment and advertising of new product uses, there is no **guarantee** that a product will continue to have enough sales. Eventually, a company may need to discontinue the product.

DISCOUNT THE PRODUCT

Many declining product lines can be saved from deletion by discounting them to compete with cheaper store brands or private brands. Companies that discount declining products often advertise with phrases such as "compare and save" to stimulate sales.

REGIONALIZE THE PRODUCT

Sometimes companies decide to sell declining products only in the geographical areas where there is strong customer loyalty. By marketing its product only in those areas, the company avoids the cost of national advertising and distribution.

UPDATE OR ALTER THE PRODUCT

Certain products can be altered or modernized to avoid deletion. Some products can be redesigned, packaged differently, or reformulated. An example of an updated product is baking soda.

Baking soda, as its name suggests, was traditionally used for baking cakes. As this purpose declined, product developers and marketers found new ways to use baking soda: an odor-removing agent (e.g., cat litter) and cleanser (e.g., toothpaste and household cleaners). Tide® laundry detergent—originally available only in powder form in a box—was reformulated in liquid form and repackaged in a plastic bottle. The liquid product appealed to new and existing customers alike. By modernizing and altering product lines, the company expanded into a new area and avoided a product deletion of an existing product.

Companies spend large amounts of money to develop and promote consumer and industrial products. As a result, they are reluctant to delete products without trying one of the above strategies. When products must be dropped, a company needs to plan the move carefully to avoid disappointing customers and damaging the company's image.

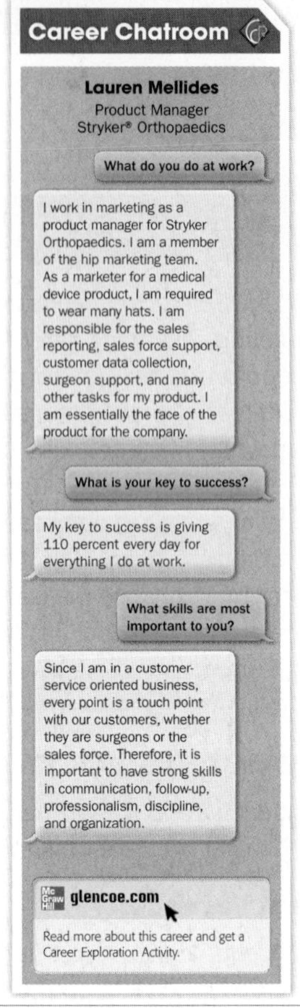

Career Chatroom
Lauren Mellides
Product Manager
Stryker® Orthopaedics
What do you do at work?
I work in marketing as a product manager for Stryker Orthopaedics. I am a member of the hip marketing team. As a marketer for a medical device product, I am required to wear many hats. I am responsible for the sales reporting, sales force support, customer data collection, surgeon support, and many other tasks for my product. I am essentially the face of the product for the company.
What is your key to success?
My key to success is giving 110 percent every day for everything I do at work.
What skills are most important to you?
Since I am in a customer-service oriented business, every point is a touch point with our customers, whether they are surgeons or the sales force. Therefore, it is important to have strong skills in communication, follow-up, professionalism, discipline, and organization.
glencoe.com
Read more about this career and get a Career Exploration Activity.

EXPLAIN

Critical Thinking

Ask students to contrast how marketing dollars are spent during the introductory stage with how they are spent during the maturity stage. Introductory stage: ads describe the product's features to the target market; maturity stage: ads are used to fight off the competition.

Mini Project

Enrichment

Managing a Product during the Maturity Stage Have groups of students discuss the way Coke™ is managed in its maturity stage. Students should answer questions such as: ***What products must Coke compete against?*** Pepsi®, other colas and beverages ***What promotional campaigns has Coke put in place to manage against the competition?*** contests such as prizes linked to bottle caps ***What other strategies has Coke put in place to manage against the competition?*** requiring that it be served exclusively in some restaurants

MANAGING IN THE DECLINE STAGE

Knowing how to handle a product's decline keeps companies relevant to the marketplace. To discuss different strategies for handling the decline stage, ask students these guiding questions.

Guiding Questions

Recall What happens to profits during the decline stage?	They weaken until eventually they reach the point where they are smaller than the expenses.
Describe Why are promotional costs reduced during the decline stage?	to maximum profits as sales decline
Apply Give an example of a situation in which a company might choose to regionalize a product. Explain why this choice might be made.	Examples will vary. Possible answer: A soft drink might only be profitable in the Southeast. To maximize its profits, the company might discontinue it everywhere but in the Southeast.

ELABORATE

Graphic Organizer

Display the following graphic organizer, and ask students to fill in the boxes with strategies for managing products in the decline stage.

Managing Products in Decline

Sell or License the Product
Recommit to the Product Line
Discount the Product
Regionalize the Product
Update or Alter the Product

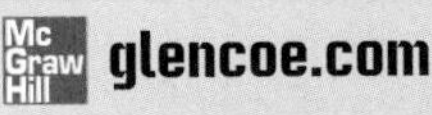

glencoe.com iWB

Graphic Organizer Send students to the Online Learning Center to print this graphic organizer.

Visual Literacy

Figure 30.3 Caption Answer Read the question to students: ***Why are sales relatively slow during the maturity stage?*** Many people in the target market may already own the product, or there may be more competition for the product. Then ask these guiding questions.

Guiding Questions

Summarize Once a product's sales slow down, what decision must management make?	Management must decide whether to continue supporting the product.
Analyze At what two points are sales and profits fairly equal? Why?	during the introduction, due to low sales and high advertising costs, and during the decline, because sales are dropping

Mini Projects

Differentiated Instruction

English Language Learners Have student partners come up with a one-sentence summary explaining Figure 30.3. Then instruct them to work as a group to develop a summary and display it for the class. Sample summary: Figure 30.3 shows how the four product stages are related to the time a product has been in the market and the amount of profit it earns.

Cooperative Learners Instruct small groups of students to pick a product that appears to be in the decline stage. Tell them their task is to update or alter the product to appeal to more customers. Students should brainstorm a list of ideas for achieving this goal. Have each group present their product to the class, describe their ideas, and explain how these ideas will increase sales. Students' ideas should be appropriate for the product and likely to increase sales by improving quality or encouraging consumers to use it for a new purpose. One example might be a computer redesigned with recycled parts, which would appeal to consumers interested in protecting the environment.

Career Chatroom

Focus the discussion concerning Lauren Mellides by asking students these guiding questions.

Guiding Questions

Describe What does Lauren Mellides's team market?	medical device products related to the hip
Analyze What skills does Mellides say are particularly important to her?	communication, follow-up, professionalism, discipline, and organization
Infer Mellides is responsible for "surgeon support." What do you think this means?	Possible answer: Mellides must answer any technical questions surgeons may have, such as exact product specifications.

glencoe.com

Career Exploration Send students to the Online Learning Center to find more information about this career and to get a Career Exploration activity.

PRODUCT POSITIONING

The purpose of product positioning is to create an image of a product that appeals to consumers. The goal is to set the product apart from the competition. **Product positioning** refers to the efforts a business makes to identify, place, and sell its products in the marketplace. To position products, businesses identify customer needs and determine how their products compare to the competition. Many strategies are used to position products.

POSITIONING BY PRICE AND QUALITY

Companies can position their products in a product line on the basis of price and quality. A company may offer an economy line, a mid-priced line, and a luxury line. Positioning by price and quality stresses high price as a symbol of quality or low price as an indication of a good value.

The Ford Motor Company® deliberately positions its Focus® as an economical compact car while still emphasizing quality. Ford positions its Mustang® as a high-performance car. Promotional efforts are aimed at creating price and quality images for these products. This strategy enables Ford to give each of its products a unique position in the marketplace.

POSITIONING BY FEATURES AND BENEFITS

Products can be associated with a general feature, attribute, or customer benefit. For example, Rockport® shoes are positioned as always comfortable, regardless of active, casual, or dress use.

Companies frequently position their products to highlight a unique or perceived characteristic. Axe®, a line of personal care products for men, was first introduced in France in 1983. The product was introduced in the United States in 2003 and now sells in more than 60 countries. Advertising for the product is adventurous and unconventional.

The product line includes cologne sticks, body sprays, and shower gels. It is promoted with bold product names and unique fragrances. Axe is positioned to give guys the edge in the dating game. These product features and its perceived unique characteristic have made it one of the world's most popular male grooming brands.

POSITIONING IN RELATION TO THE COMPETITION

Some businesses position their products to compete directly with the products of other companies. Positioning in relation to the competition is a common strategy when a firm is trying to establish an advantage over another firm. It is not always a good idea to compete head-to-head with the industry leader. It might be better to compete as the underdog. Southwest Airlines® does a good job of doing that by telling potential customers that the airline is the low-fare alternative to other larger airlines.

New Product Failures Every year between 60 and 80 percent of new grocery store products fail.

POSITIONING IN RELATION TO OTHER PRODUCTS IN A LINE

Individual products may be positioned in relation to other products in the same line. Starting with the original iPod® fit-in-your-pocket music player, Apple has introduced other handheld players that not only store songs and playlists, but also have added features. The iPod nano® plays music and shoots video. The iPod touch® is a music player and a pocket computer with a 3.5 inch screen for playing portable games and viewing movies. Each product has unique features and benefits, but each appeals to the different needs of customers.

Reading Check

Contrast How is positioning a product in relation to competition different from positioning it in relation to other products in a line?

CATEGORY MANAGEMENT

Many manufacturers and retailers are adopting a process for marketing and selling their products known as *category management*. **Category management** is a process that involves managing product categories as individual business units. A category may include a group of product lines with the same target market and distribution channels. The process is designed to put manufacturers and retailers in touch with customer needs.

The category manager is responsible for all the brands for one generic product category, such as foods, beverages, or health and beauty products. The category manager is responsible for the profits or losses of the product mix and product lines in the category. The position evolved out of the position of product manager. A product manager handles a particular product and has more direct interaction with the company's sales force. A category manager is responsible for a generic category and has more interaction with other managers from finance, production, and research and development.

The manufacturer can customize a product mix within a category according to customer preference on a store-by-store basis. Using scanned data on product sales and other market data, manufacturers assist retailers with their product mix. In examining product mix, a manufacturer determines which of its products a particular retailer does not carry. It also identifies products that would have strong sales potential for both the retailer and the manufacturer. This analysis helps the manufacturer recommend an optimum product mix by projecting sales volume and profits for a retailer. The manufacturer then suggests adding or deleting certain items to its product mix. If the category manager feels that one product is decreasing sales of other products in the same category, this one product may be discontinued.

Another way manufacturers can help retailers is through **planograms**. A planogram is a computer-developed diagram that shows retailers how and where products within a category should be displayed on a shelf at individual stores. A planogram is shown in **Figure 30.4** (page 722).

MARKETING CASE STUDY

Style Meets Sound

Roxy® is a brand of Quiksilver®, Inc., a sports/casual lifestyle company that produces and distributes a mix of apparel, footwear, and other products for the youth market and board culture. The Roxy brand targets active, fashion-conscious young women. While exploring new product concepts, Roxy decided to partner with sound specialist JBL®, Inc., to create a new market category of portable audio products.

Uniquely Positioned

As Roxy's director of entertainment and sports marketing observes, music is a huge part of everyday living for most young people, and "Listening to music with great sound technology makes all the difference." So, the two companies developed a unique collection of stylish and colorful headphones—some with velvet earpieces—that also deliver high-quality sound. With this positioning strategy, Roxy and JBL plan to deliver more chic tech to the market.

English Language Arts

Collaborate Work with a partner to think of a new sports or music-related product. Write a summary of how you would *position* this product in the market for success.

NCTE 4 Use written language to communicate effectively.

EXPLAIN

Graphic Organizer

Display this diagram to discuss different product positioning strategies.

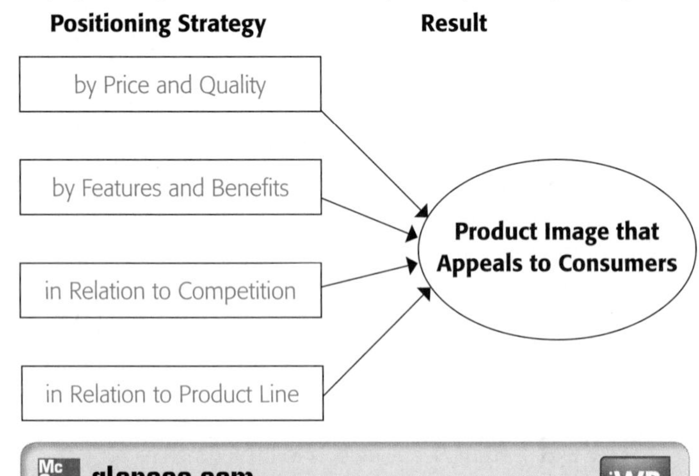

glencoe.com iWB

Graphic Organizer Send students to the Online Learning Center to print this graphic organizer.

PRODUCT POSITIONING

Knowing exactly how a product is to be positioned allows marketers to determine the best way to promote it. To focus discussion on product positioning, ask the following guiding questions.

Guiding Questions

Recall What is the primary goal of product positioning?	to set the product apart from the competition
Apply A pet food manufacturer has dog food for puppies, for active adult dogs, and for indoor dogs. It is now adding a food designed to meet the needs of senior dogs. How is it positioning this product?	It is positioning it in relation to other products in its line. Previously there was no dog food aimed specifically at older dogs.

ELABORATE

Mini Project

Enrichment

Analyzing Product Positioning Ask students to bring ads to class illustrating product positioning for personal care products. Have them give presentations on how the product is positioned in the ad they brought in. Students should state how the ad positions the product by price, quality, features, benefits, or in relation to the competition or other products in the same line.

New Product Failures Encourage students to discuss why they think new product failures are so high. For example, one product might be seen as overpriced for its quality (incorrect "Positioning by Price and Quality") and another might be seen as being too similar to another product in the same line (incorrect "Positioning in Relation to Other Products in a Line"). Also discuss that products often fail for a combination of reasons.

Reading Check Answer

Read the question to students: ***How is positioning a product in relation to competition different from positioning it in relation to other products in a line?*** When positioning a product in relation to the competition, a company is competing with the competition's products. When positioning a product in relation to other products in a line, a company is trying to meet a customer need that is not met by other products in the line.

MINI CLIP

Reading: Options for Learning
Go to the Online Learning Center to view a video clip in which two teachers explain to their students multiple ways to read and respond to the assigned text.

CATEGORY MANAGEMENT

Discuss that an important goal of category management is to put manufacturers and retailers in closer touch with the needs of the customer. Ask these guiding questions to focus the discussion on category management.

Guiding Questions

Recall How can the term *category* be defined?	group of product lines with the same target market and distribution channels
Contrast How is a category manager different from a product manager?	A category manager is responsible for all the brands for one generic product category, such as beauty products, and is responsible for the profits or losses of that product mix and profit lines in that category. A product manager handles a specific product and has more direct interaction with the company's sales force.
Draw Conclusion How can a manufacturer help a store customize its product mix within a specific category?	The manufacturer can use scanned data on product sales and other market data to examine the current product mix and use this information to identify those products that would have strong sales potential in that location. Using this analysis, the manufacturer can recommend products to be added or deleted.

Reinforce Vocabulary

Planogram—Analyzing Word Components Display the term *planogram* and divide it into syllables for the class to read. Explain that sometimes you can approximate a word's meaning by looking at its components. Planogram has two basic parts: *plan* and *gram*. The word *plan* can be defined as "a method for achieving an end." The suffix *-gram* means "drawing, writing or record." So a planogram is a drawing that provides a method for showing how products should be displayed in a store.

MARKETING CASE STUDY

English Language Arts Answer
Students should work with a partner to think of a product related to sports, music, or an integration of both. For example, students may suggest smartphones that offer the same kind of stylish appearance as the headphones developed by Roxy and JBL. Use these guiding questions to discuss this marketing case study in more detail.

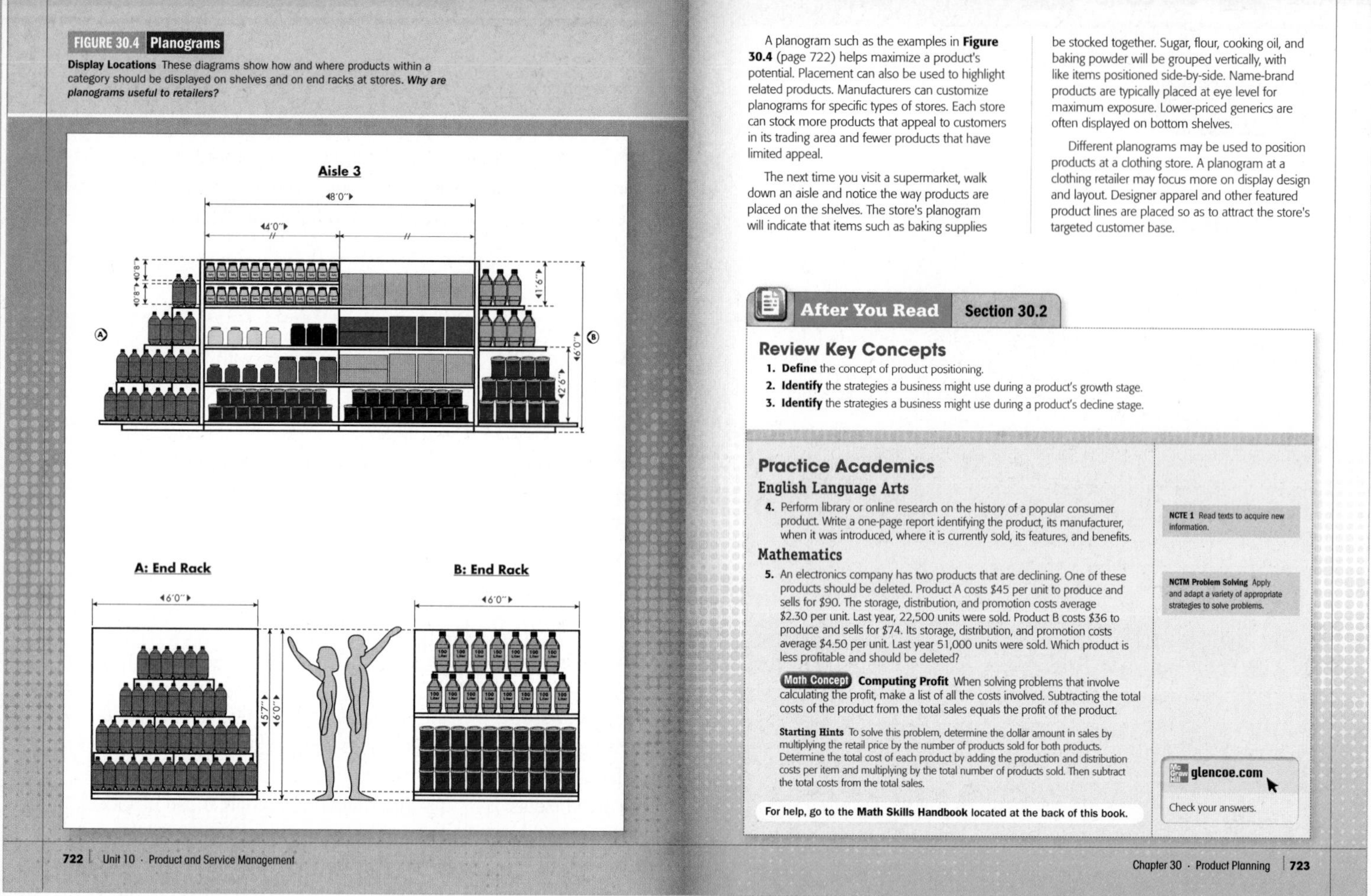

FIGURE 30.4 **Planograms**

Display Locations These diagrams show how and where products within a category should be displayed on shelves and on end racks at stores. ***Why are planograms useful to retailers?***

A planogram such as the examples in **Figure 30.4** (page 722) helps maximize a product's potential. Placement can also be used to highlight related products. Manufacturers can customize planograms for specific types of stores. Each store can stock more products that appeal to customers in its trading area and fewer products that have limited appeal.

The next time you visit a supermarket, walk down an aisle and notice the way products are placed on the shelves. The store's planogram will indicate that items such as baking supplies be stocked together. Sugar, flour, cooking oil, and baking powder will be grouped vertically, with like items positioned side-by-side. Name-brand products are typically placed at eye level for maximum exposure. Lower-priced generics are often displayed on bottom shelves.

Different planograms may be used to position products at a clothing store. A planogram at a clothing retailer may focus more on display design and layout. Designer apparel and other featured product lines are placed so as to attract the store's targeted customer base.

After You Read **Section 30.2**

Review Key Concepts

1. **Define** the concept of product positioning.
2. **Identify** the strategies a business might use during a product's growth stage.
3. **Identify** the strategies a business might use during a product's decline stage.

Practice Academics

English Language Arts

4. Perform library or online research on the history of a popular consumer product. Write a one-page report identifying the product, its manufacturer, when it was introduced, where it is currently sold, its features, and benefits.

NCTE 1 Read texts to acquire new information.

Mathematics

5. An electronics company has two products that are declining. One of these products should be deleted. Product A costs $45 per unit to produce and sells for $90. The storage, distribution, and promotion costs average $2.30 per unit. Last year, 22,500 units were sold. Product B costs $36 to produce and sells for $74. Its storage, distribution, and promotion costs average $4.50 per unit. Last year 51,000 units were sold. Which product is less profitable and should be deleted?

NCTM Problem Solving Apply and adapt a variety of appropriate strategies to solve problems.

Math Concept **Computing Profit** When solving problems that involve calculating the profit, make a list of all the costs involved. Subtracting the total costs of the product from the total sales equals the profit of the product.

Starting Hints To solve this problem, determine the dollar amount in sales by multiplying the retail price by the number of products sold for both products. Determine the total cost of each product by adding the production and distribution costs per item and multiplying by the total number of products sold. Then subtract the total costs from the total sales.

For help, go to the Math Skills Handbook located at the back of this book.

glencoe.com

Check your answers.

722 Unit 10 · Product and Service Management

Chapter 30 · Product Planning 723

ELABORATE

Visual Literacy

Figure 30.4 Caption Answer Read the caption question to students: ***Why are planograms useful to retailers?*** They maximize a product's potential. Placement of a product can also be used to highlight other products that can be used in conjunction with a product. Use these guiding questions to examine the planograms in more detail.

Guiding Questions

Describe What kinds of information can be obtained from the top diagram?	aisle number, overall height and width of shelves, heights and widths of individual shelves, individual product positioning
Draw Conclusions Why do you think the man and woman are positioned in the center of the lower diagram with their arms extended?	Businesses try not to place merchandise outside customers' reach. This diagram is designed to show how high the average man and woman can reach.

Critical Thinking

Ask students: ***Why might a retail chain want all of its stores to use the same planograms?*** Possible answers: So that customers know where a particular product is found, regardless of what store they are in; to give stores a uniform appearance; because corporate managers may be better able to develop the planograms than the local store managers can; because they might have agreements with manufacturers and/or vendor that specify how particular products are to be displayed. Then ask: ***Why might a chain store manager want to customize planograms for their particular store rather than simply use the ones sent from corporate headquarters?*** Possible answers: To customize them to local needs and tastes; to highlight those products that sell well locally.

EVALUATE

Mini Projects

Extension

Explaining the Advantages of Using Planograms Describe a scenario in which students are assistant managers at an independent discount store that does not use planograms. The store manager has asked them to research planograms and prepare a presentation discussing the advantages that using planograms could offer the store. Instruct students to prepare a visual presentation on this topic. Have them conduct research on the Internet to learn more about the advantages of using planograms. Encourage students to create a slide show to accompany their presentations. Presentations will vary. Students may include such advantages as: Shelf space is limited, and therefore valuable, so it must be used wisely; planograms encourage the consistent use of shelf space; planograms are customer-centered, making it easier for customers to locate and compare products; because they are visual, planograms are relatively easy for all employees to understand and implement when stocking shelves; using planograms simplifies customizing product arrangement based on local needs.

Investigating Planogram Software Tell students that as assistant managers at an independent discount store, they have been assigned the task of choosing the software their store will use to develop planograms. Students should research the different types of software available and choose the product they think will best meet the store's needs. They should then write a short report discussing why they chose this product and explaining some of its features. If possible, students should include screen shots in their reports. Student reports should explain what planogram software product they think will best meet their store's needs and provide an overview of the product's features. For example, SmartDraw is a relatively easy-to-use, inexpensive software application that allows the user to create visual diagrams, including planograms, either from scratch or by using templates.

After You Read — Section 30.2

Review Key Concepts

1. In product positioning, a business attempts to identify, place, and sell its products in the marketplace. In order to properly position products, businesses must identify customer needs and determine how their products compare to the competition.
2. During the growth stage, the business works to build brand preference and increase market share. It may enter into price competition with other businesses with similar products, introduce new models, or modify the existing product to offer more benefits than the competition.
3. During the decline stage, the business might reduce advertising and promotional costs to maximize profits, or even delete the product entirely from its product mix. Other strategies are to sell or license the product, recommit to the product line, discount the product, regionalize the product, and update or alter the product.

Practice Academics

English Language Arts

4. Students should write a one-page report identifying a popular consumer product, its manufacturer, when it was introduced, and its features and benefits. Answers will vary depending on the product selected. For example, the George Foreman Grill® was introduced in 1994. It entered the indoor grilling market early. It has continued to grow as the company added grills of various sizes, built on customers' growing desire to cook and eat healthy foods, and consistently added new features. Today's George Foreman Grills are available at a variety of stores, including department stores, discount stores, and on the Web.

Mathematics

5. Product A is less profitable and should be deleted. Product A: $90 - (45 + 2.30) \times 22{,}500 = \$960{,}750$; Product B: $(74 - [36 + 4.50]) \times 51{,}000 = \$1{,}708{,}500$

glencoe.com

Send students to the Online Learning Center to check their answers.

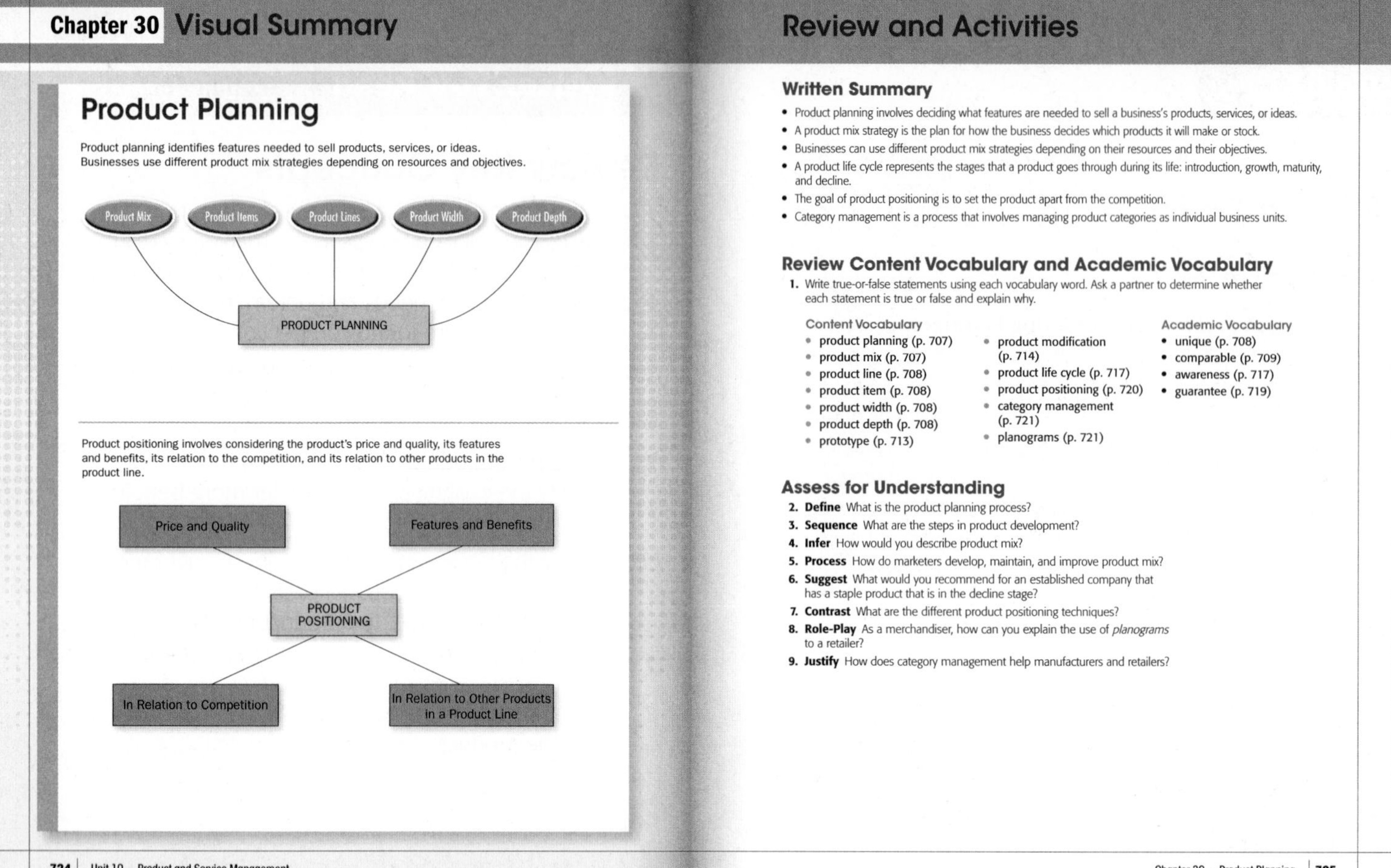

Chapter 30 Visual Summary

Product Planning

Product planning identifies features needed to sell products, services, or ideas. Businesses use different product mix strategies depending on resources and objectives.

Product Mix
Product Items
Product Lines
Product Width
Product Depth
PRODUCT PLANNING

Product positioning involves considering the product's price and quality, its features and benefits, its relation to the competition, and its relation to other products in the product line.

Price and Quality
Features and Benefits
PRODUCT POSITIONING
In Relation to Competition
In Relation to Other Products in a Product Line

724 | Unit 10 · Product and Service Management

Review and Activities

Written Summary

- Product planning involves deciding what features are needed to sell a business's products, services, or ideas.
- A product mix strategy is the plan for how the business decides which products it will make or stock.
- Businesses can use different product mix strategies depending on their resources and their objectives.
- A product life cycle represents the stages that a product goes through during its life: introduction, growth, maturity, and decline.
- The goal of product positioning is to set the product apart from the competition.
- Category management is a process that involves managing product categories as individual business units.

Review Content Vocabulary and Academic Vocabulary

1. Write true-or-false statements using each vocabulary word. Ask a partner to determine whether each statement is true or false and explain why.

Content Vocabulary
- product planning (p. 707)
- product mix (p. 707)
- product line (p. 708)
- product item (p. 708)
- product width (p. 708)
- product depth (p. 708)
- prototype (p. 713)
- product modification (p. 714)
- product life cycle (p. 717)
- product positioning (p. 720)
- category management (p. 721)
- planograms (p. 721)

Academic Vocabulary
- unique (p. 708)
- comparable (p. 709)
- awareness (p. 717)
- guarantee (p. 719)

Assess for Understanding

2. **Define** What is the product planning process?
3. **Sequence** What are the steps in product development?
4. **Infer** How would you describe product mix?
5. **Process** How do marketers develop, maintain, and improve product mix?
6. **Suggest** What would you recommend for an established company that has a staple product that is in the decline stage?
7. **Contrast** What are the different product positioning techniques?
8. **Role-Play** As a merchandiser, how can you explain the use of *planograms* to a retailer?
9. **Justify** How does category management help manufacturers and retailers?

Chapter 30 · Product Planning | 725

EVALUATE

Visual Summary

Express Creativity Ask students to create a visual summary that illustrates a concept in the chapter. Encourage students to use different formats for their visual summaries, such as a table, a Venn diagram, a hierarchy chart, or a word web. Visual summaries will vary depending on the concept depicted and the visual manner in which it is depicted. Questions to ask when assessing a visual summary include:

- Is the summary clear, economical, and simple?
- Are any important steps or concepts left out?
- Are steps or concepts arranged in the same order as the original?
- Does the summary reveal a pattern that connects the details?
- Does the summary locate and highlight the most important information?

Review Content Vocabulary and Academic Vocabulary

1. True-or-false sentence will vary. Sample sentences:
Product planning involves deciding how a product will be advertised (False: Product planning involves making decisions about the features and services that will help sell the product.)
A company's **product mix** consists of the different product lines it makes or sells. (False: A company's product mix consists of all the products it makes or sells.)
In order for a group of products to make up a **product line**, all the products must be closely related to one another. (True)
A 16-ounce bag of Lays Wavy Original Potato Chips is an example of a **product item**. (True)
The terms **product width** and **product line** mean the same thing. (False: Product width refers to the number of different product lines a business manufactures or sells.)
If a discount store sells five brands of food processors, its **product depth** in this area is five. (False: If a discount store sells five brands of food processors, its product width in this area is five.)

EVALUATE

Review Content Vocabulary and Academic Vocabulary *(continued)*

When a company is developing a new product, having a **prototype** is helpful in determining whether the final product will be successful. (True)

If an existing snowmobile is altered so that it has more comfortable seating, this is an example of **product modification**. (True)

When a product's sales start to slow down, it has reached the maturity stage of the **product life cycle**. (True)

Proper **product positioning** requires that a company accurately identify customer needs. (True)

In **category management**, each model of a particular product is managed as an individual business unit. (False: In category management, each category of a product is managed as an individual business unit.)

Planograms are useful in helping marketers determine what stage of the product life cycle a particular product is in. (False: Planograms show how and where products within a category should be displayed.)

All products, even **unique** ones, have a product life cycle. (True)

If two companies are selling **comparable** products, they are likely to compete for the same target market. (True)

Awareness of the needs of a product's target market is vital if a product is to succeed. (True)

No matter how hard a company works to promote a product, there is no **guarantee** the product will be successful. (True)

Assess for Understanding

2. The product planning process entails making decisions about the features and services of a product that will help to sell it. These decisions involve product features, such as packaging, labeling, and branding. They also include making decisions concerning product services, such as product warranties, that are necessary to support the product. It requires creativity and the ability to understand current customer needs and spot new trends.

3. The steps in product development include: generating ideas, screening ideas, developing a business proposal, developing the product, testing the product with consumers, introducing the product, and evaluating customer acceptance.

4. The product mix consists of all the different products a company makes or sells.

5. To develop, maintain, and improve product mix, marketers must carefully examine sales as well as factors such as current trends. A product that has been successful in the past may not continue to thrive if it fails to respond to changing consumer needs. Marketers develop product mix by introducing new products; they maintain the mix by staying competitive, for example, by offering discounts; and they improve the product mix by addressing unmet consumer needs.

6. Suggestions may include selling or licensing the product, recommitting to the product, discounting or regionalizing it, modernizing it, or altering it.

7. Product positioning techniques are to stress price and quality, stress product features and benefits, stress unique characteristics, compare the product to the competition, and show a relationship to other products in the line.

8. Explain to the retailer that the planogram shows exactly how and where products in a particular category should be displayed on shelves and end racks in the store. This makes for consistent stocking and helps the customer by placing similar products together.

9. Because category management involves managing product categories as individual business units, it is designed to put manufacturers and retailers in closer touch with customer needs.

21st Century Skills

Communication Skills

10. **Customer Complaints** You are the store manager for a grocery store that has recently changed merchandise locations. You are confronted by a frustrated customer who cannot find a desired product and complains that the new layout is not logical. What can you do to assist the customer and to encourage continued shopping?

Financial Literacy Skills

11. **Calculating Gross Profit** What is the gross profit from 420 products that cost $1.30 to produce and sell for $2.00? What is the gross profit? What is the difference in percent between these totals?

e-Marketing Skills

12. **Product Line Extensions** Imagine that you are employed in research and development for a large food manufacturer. The firm uses online research to review product lines of major food manufacturers for possible product ideas. You have been assigned to review one of the following Web sites (Campbell's®, J.M. Smucker®, Hershey® Foods, Kellogg's®, H.J. Heinz®, General Mills®, Kraft®, Del Monte®, or Stouffer®) and identify five products and the product line extensions for each product.
    - Who is the manufacturer and what five products were reviewed?
    - List the product line extension for each of the five products.

Build Academic Skills

English Language Arts

13. **Technology in Automobiles** Conduct research on an existing or planned technology that is developed for automobiles today. Identify the name of your source(s) and prepare a written report of 150–200 words about how the technology has impacted driving, vehicular safety, or the environment.

NCTE 1 Read texts to acquire new information.

Science

14. **Virtual Product Development** New high-tech products are being developed by coordinating software with electrical and mechanical design disciplines. Perform library or online research about virtual product development. Identify the name of the article, its source, and explain how scientists and engineers can speed delivery of new products to market. Write a one-page summary describing your research.

NSES E Develop abilities of technological design, understandings about science and technology.

Mathematics

15. **Slotting Fees** Retailers sometimes charge manufacturers slotting fees for helping to introduce merchandise. Assume that a small retail chain charges $2,000 per store for a new brand of sandwich bread, while a mass market merchandiser charges $10,000 per store for the same product. To how many stores could you sell your brand of sandwich bread if your company has a slotting allowance budget of $60,000 and must include at least two mass market stores?

NCTM Number and Operations Compute fluently and make reasonable estimates.

Math Concept **Calculating Fees** Calculating fees is done by multiplying the dollar amount of fees by the number of stores that will be charged a fee.

For help, go to the **Math Skills Handbook** located at the back of this book.

Standardized Test Practice

Directions Read the following questions. On a separate piece of paper, write the best possible answer for each one.

1. During which phase of the product life cycle would improving the product be a good strategy?
   A. Introduction Stage
   B. Growth Stage
   C. Maturity Stage
   D. Decline Stage
2. Product depth refers to the number of different product lines a business manufactures or sells.
   T
   F
3. All the different products that a company makes or sells are called ________.

Test-Taking Tip
Read and consider all of the answer choices before you choose the best response to the question. Examine each answer choice and think about how each differs from the others.

DECA Connection Role Play

Manager
Supermarket

Situation You are a manager of a large supermarket that is part of a regional chain. Your chain of supermarkets has been in business for many years. The supermarkets have a reputation for providing excellent customer service and extensive product width and depth. Prices at the stores are known to be somewhat higher than at similar supermarkets and higher than at discount supermarkets. Your customers know that they will find the exact item they want at your store.

Within the last year, a chain of upscale supermarkets has opened stores in your region. The chain sells many of the same products as your chain in their modern, clean, well-lit, and appealing stores. The competing chain does things differently from yours. Their product prices are significantly lower, and their product width and depth are much narrower than your chain's. Since the opening of your competitor's stores, sales at stores in your chain have declined notably.

In order to meet the competition's pricing, management of your chain has decided to narrow the product depth of many of the product lines you carry. This means that some product sizes will no longer be stocked in your stores. Your chain will carry only the best-selling sizes in most of your product lines.

Activity You are to discuss the product changes at this week's staff (judge) meeting. Your explanation should address the product changes, the reason for them, and a way to explain the changes to customers.

Evaluation You will be evaluated on how well you meet the following performance indicators:

1. Explain the nature and scope of the product/service management function.
2. Identify the impact of product life cycles on marketing decisions.
3. Explain the concept of product mix.
4. Demonstrate adaptability.
5. Make oral presentations.

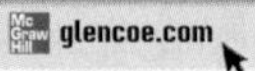
glencoe.com

Download the Competitive Events Workbook for more Role-Play practice.

EVALUATE

Communication Skills

10. Students should be tactful in their responses to the customer. They might help the customer locate needed item, or find an employee to do so. They might try explaining the purpose behind the changes and express the feeling that while change can be difficult, the manager hopes the customer will find the new arrangement helpful in the long run.

Financial Literacy Skills

11. Gross profit is $294.00. (420 × [2.00 – 1.30])

e-Marketing Skills

12. Answers will vary depending on the food manufacturer chosen. For the chosen manufacturer, students should review five products and list product line extensions for each of those products. For example, Campbell® Soup Company has Campbell's Condensed soups, Campbell's Microwavable soups, Campbell's Chunky soups, Campbell's Select Harvest soups, and Campbell's Healthy Request soups. Under Campbell's Healthy Request soups, there are Chicken Noodle, Chicken Corn Chowder, Sirloin Burger, and Savory Vegetable.

EVALUATE

Build Academic Skills

English Language Arts

13. Reports will vary depending on the technology chosen by the students. Sample answer: One newer technology involves the use of onboard cameras to help drivers view blind spots and keep an eye on any children in the back seat. Some cars are being designed to parallel park themselves. This convenient feature uses electronically assisted steering to maneuver into the parking space and front and rear ultrasonic sensors to avoid hitting any objects that may be in the way.

Science

14. One of the most important ways to speed the delivery of new products to market is through the use of rapid prototyping. This includes equipment that generates a prototype of a product while it is still in the design stage. This allows engineers to determine at a relatively early point whether a particular product will meet the specified needs. This prototyping is often done in conjunction with computer-aided design (CAD) software. The specifications provided by the software are used to generate the prototype, which may be fabricated out of a variety of substances, such as cardboard, plastic, or metal.

Mathematics

15. At most, 22 stores—2 mass market stores and 20 small retail chain stores.

Standardized Test Practice

1. B (Growth Stage)
2. F (Product width refers to the number of different product lines a business manufactures or sells.)
3. product mix

DECA Connection Role Play

Evaluations will be based on these performance indicators:

1. **Explain the nature and scope of the product/service management function.** One method of managing products is through the use of category management. This involves managing product categories as individual business units. A category may include a group of product lines with the same target market and distribution channels. An important goal of category management is to increase the degree to which manufacturers and retailers are in touch with customer needs
2. **Identify the impact of product life cycles on marketing decisions.** When a product is new, proper marketing decisions, such as extensive promotions, discounts, and coupons, can help it receive a favorable consumer response. Once a product reaches the maturity stage, promotions are primarily geared toward combating competitors, for example by pointing out new product features. As the product declines, advertising and promotional costs are reduced to maximize profits. The company may decide to sell or license the product; recommit to the product line, for example by finding new uses for the product; discounting or regionalizing the product; or updating or altering it.
3. **Explain the concept of product mix.** Product mix includes all the different products that a company makes or sells. For example, a grocery store may sell a particular brand, style, and flavor of potato chips in four different sizes. Each of these is a component of the product mix.
4. **Demonstrate adaptability.** Students should demonstrate adaptability by explaining how they would adjust to a changing market, an aging product line, and so forth. For example, one way to keep customers from switching to a competitor who has lower prices is to narrow the depth of product lines you carry, thereby allowing for a reduction in prices.
5. **Make oral presentations.** Students should be able to make well organized, interesting oral presentations. For example, students should be able to present a well reasoned and thorough explanation of why a particular business is changing its product mix.

Mc Graw Hill **glencoe.com** 

Role Plays For more DECA Role Plays, send students to the Online Learning Center to download the Competitive Events Workbook.

branding, packaging, and labeling

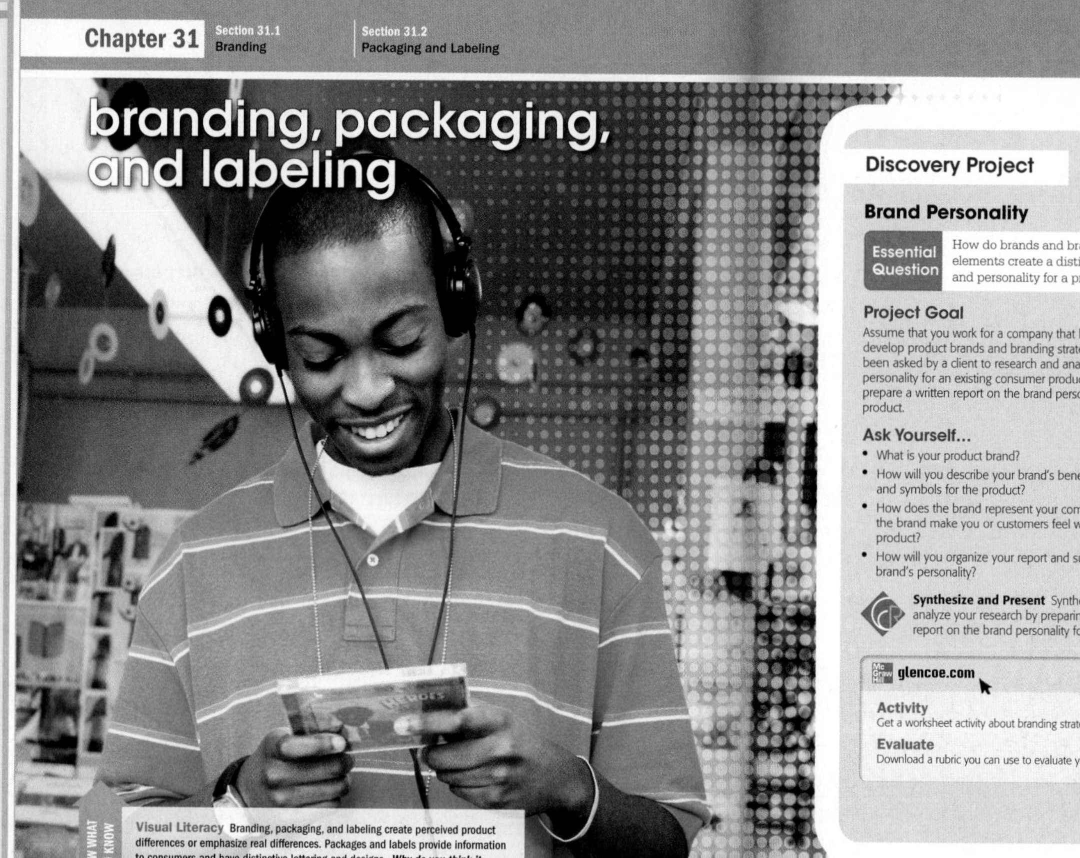

SHOW WHAT YOU KNOW **Visual Literacy** Branding, packaging, and labeling create perceived product differences or emphasize real differences. Packages and labels provide information to consumers and have distinctive lettering and designs. ***Why do you think it might be important for a product to have a specific brand, package, and label?***

Discovery Project

Brand Personality

Essential Question How do brands and branding elements create a distinct image and personality for a product?

Project Goal

Assume that you work for a company that helps clients develop product brands and branding strategies. You have been asked by a client to research and analyze the brand personality for an existing consumer product. You are to prepare a written report on the brand personality for the product.

Ask Yourself...

- What is your product brand?
- How will you describe your brand's benefits, features, and symbols for the product?
- How does the brand represent your company? How does the brand make you or customers feel when using its product?
- How will you organize your report and summarize the brand's personality?

Synthesize and Present Synthesize and analyze your research by preparing a written report on the brand personality for the product.

glencoe.com

Activity
Get a worksheet activity about branding strategies.

Evaluate
Download a rubric you can use to evaluate your project.

DECA Connection

DECA Event Role Play

Concepts in this chapter are related to DECA competitive events that involve either an interview or role play.

Performance Indicators The performance indicators represent key skills and knowledge. Your key to success in DECA competitive events is relating them to concepts in this chapter.

- Explain the nature of corporate branding.
- Describe factors used by businesses to position corporate brands.
- Explain the nature of product/service branding.
- Develop strategies to position a product/business.
- Describe the nature of product bundling.

DECA Prep

Role Play Practice role-playing with the DECA Connection competitive-event activity at the end of this chapter. More information on DECA events can be found on DECA's Web site.

ENGAGE

Visual Literacy

Read the chapter opener photo caption question to students: ***Why do you think it might be important for a product to have a specific brand, package, and label?*** A brand identifies a product and sets it apart from its competitors. A package represents the final appearance of a product and must appeal to the customer. A label informs customers about a product's contents and gives directions for use. These elements work together to create an image for a product. Then ask these guiding questions.

Guiding Questions

Recall At what point do marketers make decisions about a product's brand, package, and label?	These decisions are made during the product planning phase.
Explain What is product planning?	Product planning involves making decisions about what features should be used in selling a business's products, services, or ideas.

Discovery Project

Brand Personality Have students brainstorm any brands they can think of. Ask: ***Why do those brands come to mind?*** Students may say they use those brands, that family members and friends use them, or that they have seen or heard those brands advertised. Then ask the Discovery Project Essential Question: ***How do brands and branding elements create a distinct image and personality for a product?*** Brands are developed to target customers' needs and preferences. The target audience should feel that a brand is created just for them. Branding elements include brand names, trade names, brand marks, trade characters, and trademarks. These elements often combine to form a firm's corporate symbol or name.

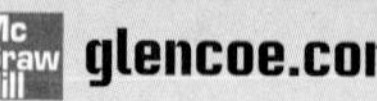

Discovery Project Resources Send students to the Online Learning Center to download a rubric to evaluate their projects.

ENGAGE

Introduce the Chapter

Chapter 31 explains the role of branding in product planning and the functions of product packaging and labeling. These main concepts are introduced and discussed:

- Elements of branding
- Brands and product planning
- Generating brand names
- Types of brands
- Brand extension
- Brand licensing
- Mixed brands
- Co-branding
- Functions of packaging
- Contemporary packaging issues
- Labeling

Discussion Starter

Brand Names Ask students to brainstorm brand names of products they use. Then ask students to consider whether they would buy another product because they are familiar with the brand name. Answers will vary. Emphasize to students how powerful a brand name can be. To reinforce this concept, ask students if there are products for which they will only buy one brand. For example, they might only buy Hostess® snack cakes rather than another brand like Little Debbie®. Ask: ***Why will you only use that brand of product?*** Answers may include quality, taste, habit, price, and so on. Remind them of the power of a brand name.

DECA Connection

Discuss the performance indicators listed in the DECA Connection feature. Explain to students that performance indicators tell them how to demonstrate their acquired skills and knowledge through individual or team competitive events.

glencoe.com

Competitive Events Workbook For more DECA Role Plays, send students to the Online Learning Center to download the Competitive Events Workbook.

PRINT RESOURCES

- **Student Edition**
- **Teacher Edition**
- **Student Activity Workbook with Academic Integration** includes worksheets and activities correlated to the text.
- **Mathematics for Marketing Workbook** provides math activities for every unit in the text.

TECHNOLOGY TOOLBOX

- **Connect**
- **ConnectPlus**
- **ExamView Assessment Suite** is a comprehensive solution for creating, administering, and scoring tests.

glencoe.com

Online Learning Center provides a variety of resources to enrich and enhance learning.

SECTION, CHAPTER, AND UNIT RESOURCES

- **Graphic Organizers** for organizing text concepts visually.
- **Digital Nation Activities** and **Green Marketer Activities** extend learning beyond the text features.
- **Career Chatroom Career Profiles** allow students to explore different marketing occupations in depth.
- **After You Read Answer Keys** for students to check their answers.
- **Discovery Project Rubrics** and **Marketing Internship Project Rubrics** for students to evaluate their projects.

PROGRAM RESOURCES

- **Student Activity Workbook with Academic Integration Teacher Annotated Edition** includes annotated answers for the activities and worksheets.
- **Marketing Research Project Workbook** provides a step-by-step approach for students to complete their own marketing research studies.
- **School-to-Career Activity Workbook** helps students relate their class work to on-the-job experience and involves work-site analysis and working with mentors.
- **Competitive Events Workbook** helps prepare students for state and national marketing education competitions.
- **Inclusion in the Marketing Education Classroom** provides teaching resources for working with students with special needs.
- **PowerPoint Presentations** provides visual teaching aids and assessments for this chapter.

READING GUIDE

Before You Read

Connect What influences your decision to purchase a product?

Objectives

- **Discuss** the nature, scope, and importance of branding in product planning.
- **Identify** the various branding elements.
- **List** three different types of brands.
- **Explain** how branding strategies are used to meet sales and company goals.

The Main Idea

A company name and its products should project a positive image. An important part of product and service management is to select, promote, and protect the company image and personality of its brands.

Vocabulary

Content Vocabulary
- brand
- brand name
- trade name
- brand mark
- trade character
- trademark
- national brands
- private distributor brands
- generic brands
- brand extension
- brand licensing
- mixed brand
- co-branding

Academic Vocabulary

You will find these words in your reading and on your tests. Make sure you know their meanings.
- component
- distinctive

Graphic Organizer

Draw or print this chart to take notes on the branding process.

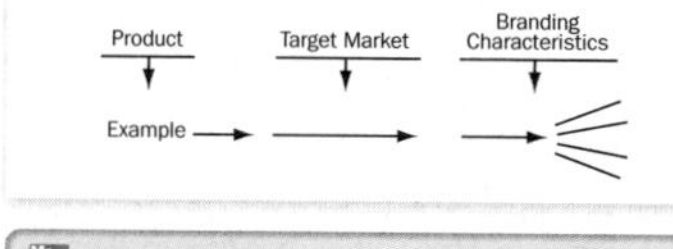

glencoe.com

Print this graphic organizer.

STANDARDS

ACADEMIC

English Language Arts

NCTE 1 Read texts to acquire new information.

NCTE 12 Use language to accomplish individual purposes.

Mathematics

NCTM Number and Operations Understand meanings of operations and how they relate to one another.

NCSS *National Council for the Social Studies*
NCTE *National Council of Teachers of English*
NCTM *National Council of Teachers of Mathematics*
NSES *National Science Education Standards*

Common Core

Writing Conduct short as well as more sustained research projects based on focused questions, demonstrating understanding of the subject under investigation.

MARKETING CORE FUNCTION

Product/Service Management

m.e. Section 31.1 Branding

BRANDING

Branding is an important **component** of the product planning process. A **brand** is a name, term, design, symbol, or combination of these elements that identifies a business, product, or service, and sets it apart from its competitors.

Developing a brand strategy can be one of the most challenging steps in the process. However, it is a crucial step when creating a company identity. A brand consistently and repeatedly tells customers and prospective customers why they should buy the company's products or services.

A brand can be used to identify one product, a family of related products, or all products of a company. Brands suggest a product's benefits, features, or qualities. For example, a company may want to develop a brand that suggests quality and reliability. Another company may want to develop a brand that suggests fun and excitement.

When a company defines its brand strategy and uses it in every interaction with its market, the company strengthens its message and its relationships. Brands are important assets and powerful tools for marketing and selling products.

As You Read

Analyze Why are brands so important to the success of a business?

ELEMENTS OF BRANDING

Brands are developed to target customers' needs and preferences. The target audience should feel that a brand is created just for them. Branding elements include brand names, trade names, brand marks, trade characters, and trademarks. These elements often combine to form a firm's corporate symbol or name.

Successful brands have tremendous value and frequently become global brands. Global brands appeal to consumers across cultural or political boundaries. For example, Coca-Cola® is an effective global brand. The brand projects an image of consistent quality, but it adapts its beverages to consumer needs within individual countries.

BRAND NAME

A **brand name**, or product brand, is a word, group of words, letters, or numbers that represent a product or service. An effective brand name should be easily pronounced, **distinctive**, and recognizable. Brand names are heavily marketed and are important company assets. Examples of brand names include Ford Focus®, Pepsi®, Barbie®, and Big Mac®. (See **Figure 31.1** on page 734.)

> "Branding gives a company and its products distinct personalities."

TRADE NAME

A **trade name**, or corporate brand, identifies and promotes a company or a division of a particular corporation. The trade name is the legal name of the business. Trade names reflect the quality, value, and reliability of the organization. Trade names are used for investors, media, governmental purposes, and to support a company's product brands. Procter & Gamble®, IBM®, Disney®, Kellogg's®, Nike,® and Google® are trade names, or corporate brands. Trade names are legally protected and rarely change. If a trade name does change, it most often occurs because of a corporate merger or an acquisition.

ENGAGE

Anticipation Activity

Improving Student Achievement Ask students: ***How do brands affect your purchasing choices?*** Sample answers: I choose certain brands because of their reputation for high quality. I don't care about brands; I just buy whatever's on sale. Then ask: ***How do packaging and labeling affect your purchasing choices?*** Students may or may not be aware of ways in which they are influenced by these elements.

Objectives

- **Discuss** the nature, scope, and importance of branding in product planning. brands target customers' needs; elements of branding may form a corporate symbol; effective brands have great value
- **Identify** the various branding elements. brand name, trade name, brand mark, trade character, trademark
- **List** three different types of brands. national, private distributor, generic
- **Explain** how branding strategies are used to meet sales and company goals. brand extension, brand licensing, mixed-brand strategy, co-branding

Graphic Organizer

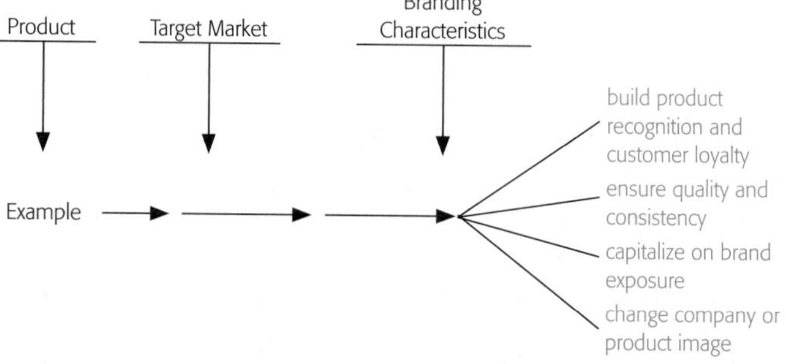

glencoe.com iWB

Graphic Organizer Send students to the Online Learning Center to print this graphic organizer.

EXPLORE

Before You Read

Read the Before You Read question aloud: ***What influences your decision to purchase a product?*** Answers may include: advertisements, price, product reputation, friends, family, or brands they have used in the past. Display students' answers for the class to read. Ask: ***Which of these items has the strongest influence on what you purchase?*** Students may mention any of the influences listed; ask them to explain their answers.

Preteaching Vocabulary

Have students go to the Online Learning Center at glencoe.com for the Chapter 31 Preteaching Vocabulary games.

Content Vocabulary

Instruct students to write a paragraph in which they discuss how the vocabulary terms are interrelated. Sample answer: All of the terms listed are related to product branding. Brand name, trade name, brand mark, trade character, and trademark are all elements of branding. National brands, private distributor brands, and generic brands are types of brands. Brand extension, brand licensing, mixed brand, and co-branding are branding strategies. Ask volunteers to share their paragraphs with the rest of the class.

Academic Vocabulary

Component—Synonyms Display the term *component* for the class to read. Have students work together in pairs to develop a list of synonyms for the term *component.* element, piece, section, part, module, factor Then read the following sentence to students: Branding is an important component of the product planning process. Ask: ***Which synonym for* component *best fits its use in this sentence?*** part, element

Distinctive—Definitions Display the term *distinctive* for the class to read. Ask volunteers to find definitions for the term *distinctive.* serving to identify or different from others Ask: ***Why might this term be used to describe a brand name?*** Brand names should serve to identify the product and be different from other brand names.

MINI CLIP

Reading: Focus Lesson
Go to the Online Learning Center to view a video clip in which a teacher models how to find the main idea or theme of a selection by identifying the major and minor details.

Branding

BRANDING

Remind students that they learned in Chapter 30 that product planning involves making decisions about the features and services of a product or idea that will help sell that product. These decisions relate to product features, such as packaging, labeling, and branding. Then ask these guiding questions to focus the discussion about branding.

Guiding Questions

Define What is a brand?	a name, term, design, symbol, or combination of these elements that identifies a business, product, or service, and sets it apart from its competitors
Identify What are the elements of branding?	brand names, trade names, brand marks, trade characters, and trademarks
Distinguish What is the difference between a brand name and a trade name?	A brand name is a word, group of words, letters, or numbers that represent a product or service. A trade name identifies and promotes a company or a division of a particular corporation.

As You Read

Read students the As You Read question: ***Why are brands to important to the success of a business?*** Answers may include: successful brands have tremendous value and frequently become global brands; brands help a company strengthen its message and relationships; brands make a product and company recognizable.

Expert Advice

Read the quote to students:

> **"Branding gives a company and its products distinct personalities."**

Ask students: ***How does a brand give a product a distinct personality?*** Possible answer: Brands are one-of-a-kind so there would be only one of a specific product with that brand, which gives the product a distinct personality.

BRAND MARK, TRADE CHARACTER, AND TRADEMARK

A **brand mark** incorporates a unique symbol, coloring, lettering, or design element. A brand mark is visually recognizable. Examples of brand marks are the Apple® Computer's apple or McDonald's® golden arches. A **trade character** is a specific type of brand mark, one with human form or characteristics. Some examples of trade characters include Betty Crocker's Jolly Green Giant®, Keebler Elves®, and the Pillsbury Doughboy®.

A **trademark** is a brand name, brand mark, trade name, trade character, or a combination of these elements that is registered with the federal government and has legal protection. Trademarks are used to prevent other companies from using a similar element that might be confused with the trademarked one. The U.S. Patent and Trademark Office grants trademark rights. Disputes regarding trademarks are settled in federal courts.

Trademarks are followed by a registered trademark symbol (®). Examples include Kellogg's Rice Krispies® cereal, and the Visa® credit card. Unregistered trademarks are followed by another symbol (™) and have limited protections. When elements of branding are registered as trademarks, they cannot be used or misused by other companies.

IMPORTANCE OF BRANDS IN PRODUCT PLANNING

Branding establishes an image for a product or company and projects that image to its customers and the marketplace. Companies should put careful consideration into developing their brand name and brand image. The use of brands is important in product planning for several reasons:

- **To build product recognition and customer loyalty**—It is important that customers easily recognize a company's branded products when they make repeat purchases.
- **To ensure quality and consistency**—Through branding, companies communicate to customers consistent quality and performance, purchase after purchase. Branding suggests consistency. For example, nine out of ten people will pay 25 percent more to buy GE's Soft White® light bulbs rather than another brand. The GE Soft White brand is perceived to be of higher quality and a better value than lower-priced competitors.

Trade Characters

Trade characters like the Michelin® man help build successful brands for their product categories. ***Why might companies use trade characters when advertising their brands?***

- **To capitalize on brand exposure**—Branding helps companies extend their products or services into new target markets. It also helps introduce new product lines or categories. When Burger King® announced the BK Veggie™ burger, the company wanted to target new customers. Customers and prospects are more willing to try new products that carry a familiar brand name.
- **To change company or product image**—With careful planning, companies can also adjust or reposition a corporate or product brand's image to expand sales. For example, Aol.® changed its logotype AOL to Aol., and its brand symbol from a triangle to various backgrounds. The company used the new brand mark and the redesigned backgrounds of a fish, skateboarder, monster, and other objects to update, change, and re-energize the image for one of the first Internet service providers. The new brand mark and its different backgrounds project a new company image about the breadth of its services.

GENERATING BRAND NAMES

An estimated 75 percent of all companies introduce a new product name every year. The U.S. Patent and Trademark Office registers more than 400,000 trademarks per year. It is understandable why some companies find it increasingly difficult to secure desirable corporate or product names.

Some companies use computer software programs that specialize in generating brand names. These programs will check to see if a name is already owned and trademarked by another company. Other companies hire branding agencies, naming consultants, or public relations firms to generate and check the availability of brand names.

Branding is so important to product planning that more than 60 percent of all companies conduct market research to test new brand names before they are released. After a name has been generated and researched, companies will then conduct brand-loyalty research to gauge the brand's effectiveness.

Once established, brand names are carefully protected. New brand names may be created when a business adds new product lines, seeks a new domestic or international market, or attempts to update its existing brand image. Brand names can also change as a result of trademark lawsuits and court decisions.

TYPES OF BRANDS

Manufacturers, wholesalers, and retailers brand their products. As a result, there are three classifications of brands.

Career Chatroom

Lauren Tesar
Associate Brand Manager
FUZE Beverage

What do you do at work?

I plan and manage strategic marketing efforts, which help build brand awareness and loyalty. Projects involve development and management of brand positioning and identity in line with brand vision. My duties include analyzing market trends, brainstorming with my team, developing promotional plans, outsourcing projects, and communicating programs to sales and field organizations. Brand management is exciting because we are involved in every step of the marketing process—from identifying consumer needs to developing new products to communicating our message through advertising.

What is your key to success?

Eagerness to learn and having a positive outlook on life is essential.

What skills are most important to you?

Passion for what you do and teamwork is important. The foundation of quality marketing comes from believing in the brand vision. Bringing strategies to life is only made possible through the support of your team.

glencoe.com

Read more about this career and get a Career Exploration Activity.

EXPLAIN

Mini Project

Extension

Understand Trademarks Discuss with students some well-known trademarks. You might want to bring to class some examples of well-known trademarks such as a logo, as well as more unusual trademarks such as color. Then ask students to think of companies that have successfully trademarked sounds, colors, or smells. Examples may include: the song "Sweet Georgia Brown" trademarked by the Harlem Globetrotters basketball team, the color pink for Owens-Corning's fiberglass insulation, and plumeria scent for sewing thread. Ask: ***What makes these elements distinct enough to trademark?*** Divide the class into small groups and have them list elements that should qualify for a trademark and elements that should not qualify for a trademark. Have each groups present their lists, and then lead a discussion about where the line should be drawn.

Visual Literacy

Trade Characters Caption Answer Read the caption question to students: ***Why might companies use trade characters when advertising their brands?*** Trade characters help to build identity and recognition to a brand name. Trade characters are often incorporated into print and broadcast advertising campaigns to help create a product image and appeal for the product that can be effective over time.

Critical Thinking

Display some brand names that have a brand mark or trade character. Ask students to identify the brand marks or trade characters. Then display some brand names that do not have brand marks or trade characters. Ask students to give suggestions for brand marks or trade characters for these items. Remind students that the brand marks or trade characters should not be too complicated. In general, the simpler the brand marks and trade characters, the easier they are to remember and the more recognizable they are.

ELABORATE

Graphic Organizer

Display this diagram. Ask students: ***What are four reasons the use of brands is important in product planning?*** Then say: Provide details for each reason. Write students' answers in the displayed diagram. Sample answers are provided in the diagram below.

Importance of Brands in Product Planning

To build product recognition and customer loyalty	To ensure quality and consistency	To capitalize on brand exposure	To change company or product image
Customers must easily recognize a company's branded products when they make repeat purchases.	Branding suggests consistency in quality and performance.	Branding helps companies extend their products or services into new target markets and to introduce new product lines or categories.	Companies can adjust or reposition a corporate or product brand's image to expand sales

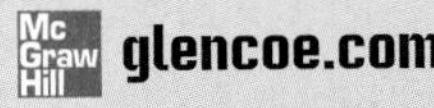
glencoe.com

iWB

Graphic Organizer Send students to the Online Learning Center to print this graphic organizer.

Critical Thinking

Have students brainstorm new products that have come out in the past year. Display their list for the all the students to read. Then ask: ***Are these products extensions of existing products or are they new products? Is the brand name based on an existing product or entirely new?*** Have students explain their responses. Then ask students why they think the companies might have chosen the brand names. Divide the class into small groups. Provide each group with a foreign language dictionary. Have groups choose one of the product names on the list and to come up with a brand name to use for the product in a foreign language. Remind students to take into account what the name will sound like or mean in another language. Ask groups to share their foreign language brand names.

Mini Projects

Differentiated Instruction

Students with Learning Disabilities Ask students to create a list of ten branded products that they know of and to then list another brand of that product if possible. Sample answers: toothpaste—Crest® and Colgate®; potato chips—Lay's® and Pringles®.

Logical Learners Ask students to make three columns on a sheet of paper. In the first column, have students list products for which they only buy one brand, for example, many consumers always buy Coca-Cola®. In the second column, have them list products for which they will buy any brand. In the third column, have students list products for which they will buy a store brand or generic brand. Then ask students to write a paragraph explaining the rationale behind their decision-making process. Ask volunteers to share their charts and paragraphs with the class.

Career Chatroom

Use these questions to focus the discussion about the Career Chatroom feature.

Guiding Questions

Explain Why does Ms. Tesar consider brand management to be exciting?	Brand management is a part of every step in the marketing process—from identifying consumer needs to developing new products to communicating the company's messages through advertising.
Explain According to Ms. Tesar, what is the source of the foundation of quality marketing?	believing in the brand vision
Analyze If you were to have a job interview with Ms. Tesar, what kind of attitude should you show?	Possible answer: a very positive outlook on life.

glencoe.com

Career Exploration Send students to the Online Learning Center to find more information about this career and to get a Career Exploration activity.

There is one for each type of company that brands its products: national brands (manufacturers), private distributor brands (wholesalers and retailers), and generic brands.

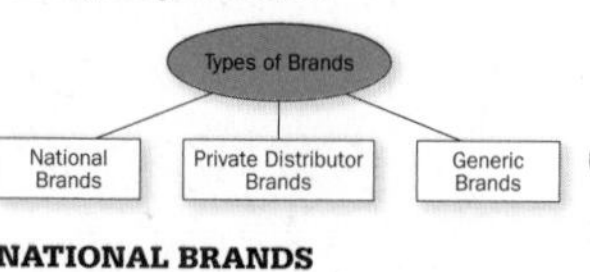

NATIONAL BRANDS

National brands, also known as *producer brands*, are owned and initiated by national manufacturers or by companies that provide services. Some national brands for goods include Hershey Foods®, Colgate-Palmolive®, Whirlpool®, Sunoco®, and Ford®. Some service companies that generate national brands are Delta Airlines®, Hilton Hotels®, Avis® rent-a car, Wells Fargo® banking services, and AFLAC® insurance.

THE IMPORTANCE OF NATIONAL BRANDS

National brands generate the majority of sales for most consumer product categories. Approximately 65 percent of all appliances, 78 percent of all food products, 80 percent of all gasoline, and 100 percent of all cars are national brands.

HOT TOPIC
Branding Style The Helvetica font was created more than 50 years ago by the Haas type foundry in Switzerland and is used for most corporate brand names and logos.

Electronic technologies have created a new category of national brand—the Internet brand. There are Internet brands for both consumer goods and services. Internet consumer product brands include Amazon® and eBay®. Internet service brands include Google®, Bing®, and MSN® search engines, and social media brands such as Facebook®, Twitter®, YouTube®, and LinkedIn®.

National brands are also associated with an image. They appeal to consumers who believe that a national brand will have consistent standards of quality, dependability, performance, and reliability.

PRIVATE DISTRIBUTOR BRANDS

Private distributor brands, known as *private brands, store brands, dealer brands*, or *private labels*, are developed and owned by wholesalers and retailers. The manufacturer's name may not appear on the product.

Private distributor brands include Radio Shack® electronic items, Nordstrom's Caslon® women's apparel, and Walmart's Great Value® food and general merchandise product brands. Private distributor brands appeal to customers who want the quality and performance of national brands at a lower price. Some private brands, such as Sears' Craftsman® tools, have become so popular and respected that they rival national brands in sales and customer recognition.

Many large supermarket and retail chains have private distributor brands. In the United States, more than 800 categories of private label goods exist in clothing, food products, paper products, medications, vitamins, and pet foods.

THE INCREASING POPULARITY OF PRIVATE BRANDS

Private distributor brands are increasing their global market share in most product categories. Private brands represent 45 percent of the market in Switzerland, 28 percent in Great Britain, 19 percent in Canada, and 16 percent in the U.S.

Private brands are popular with retailers because they usually carry higher gross margins. For example, 7 Eleven® sells 180 private label items priced up to 20 percent lower than national brands. Thus, they are more profitable than national brands. Also, because private brands are not sold at competitors' stores, they help cultivate customer loyalty.

GENERIC BRANDS

Generic brands are products that do not carry a company identity. The packaging for generic products simply describes the item, such as "pancake mix" or "paper towels." Generic brands are generally sold in supermarkets and discount stores. These unbranded products are often priced 30 to 50 percent lower than manufacturer brands and 10 to 15 percent lower than private distributor brands. Companies that manufacture and sell generic brands do not heavily advertise or promote these products and, therefore, can pass on savings to customers.

Generic products include more than 300 product categories, including vitamins, auto parts, food staples, and pharmaceuticals. Generic products are offered in more than 250 retail chains in the United States, and more than 75 percent of all U.S. supermarkets carry generic items.

Reading Check

Explain What is the difference between a brand mark and a trademark?

FIGURE 31.1 Top Global Brands

Global Recognition Some brands that are recognized around the world are a company's most valuable asset. ***What is the brand value of the top five global brands?***

Rank	Name of Brand	Brand Value ($ millions)	Country of Ownership
1	Coca-Cola	70,452	USA
2	IBM	64,727	USA
3	Microsoft	60,895	USA
4	Google	43,557	USA
5	GE	42,808	USA
6	McDonald's	33,578	USA
7	Intel	32,015	USA
8	Nokia	29,495	Finland
9	Disney	28,731	USA
10	Hewlett-Packard	26,867	USA

Source: Interbrand Study Best Global Brands 2010

Private distributor brands are growing in importance. ***What are some of the reasons behind this trend?***

EXPLAIN

Visual Literacy

Figure 31.1 Caption Answer Read the caption questions to students: ***What is the brand value of the top five global brands?*** $264,986 ($millions) or $264.986 billion [$66,667 + 59,031 + 56,647 + 47,777 + 34,864 = $264,986 ($millions). Then ask these guiding questions to help students learn more about the top global brands.

Guiding Questions

Explain How many brands in the top ten are from countries other than the USA? What are the countries?	Two brands are from other countries—Finland and Japan.
Calculate What is the difference in brand value between the number 1 ranked brand and the number 10 ranked brand?	$38,220 ($millions) [66,667 – 28,447]
Analyze How many of the top 10 brands are food-related? What are the brands?	Two are food-related—Coca-Cola® and McDonald's®.

Branding Style Ask students why they think Helvetica is so popular with corporate brand names and logos. Then have students go online to research to find a brand name or logo that uses a serif font.

Critical Thinking

Bring to class examples of brand-name, store-brand, and generic products. Also bring an example of a repositioned brand, showing it before and after the change. Then have students choose a brand they think is outdated and write up a plan to reposition it, including changes to brand name, image, brand mark or trade character, and advertising. Ask students to share their changes with the class.

ELABORATE

Critical Thinking

Display the following categories for the students to copy: Food, Appliances, Gasoline, and Automobiles. Then have students brainstorm brand names for each category and ask the volunteer to write students' answers under the appropriate head. Students should list both national and private distributor brands. After the category lists are complete, have students figure the percentages of national versus private distributor brands for each category. Then have them compare the percentages to those presented in the text: 78 percent of all food products are national brands; 65 percent of appliances are national brands; 80 percent of all gasoline; and 100 percent of all cars are national brands.

Graphic Organizer

Display this diagram After students have read the appropriate sections, ask them to supply details about each type of brand. Sample answers are provided in the graphic organizer below.

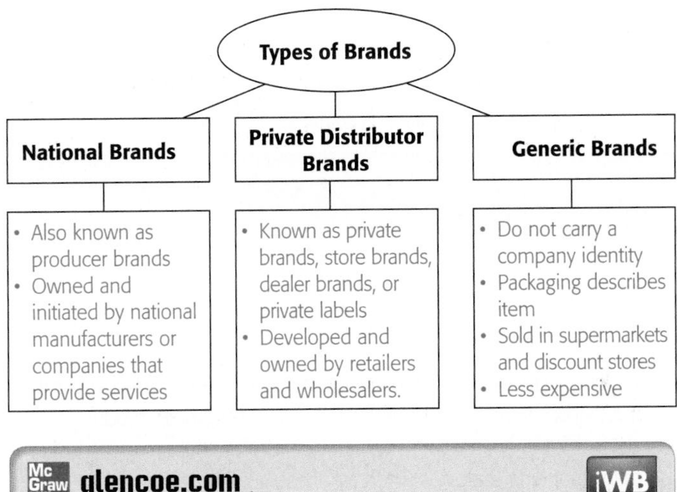

glencoe.com **iWB**

Graphic Organizer Send students to the Online Learning Center to print this graphic organizer.

PRIVATE DISTRIBUTOR BRANDS

Ask students to define the *term private distributor brands.* Private distributor brands are brands that are developed and owned by wholesalers and retailers. Then ask: ***Where can you find private distributor brands?*** These brands can be found in most supermarkets, and many other retail stores. Then ask these guiding questions to focus the discussion about private distributor brands.

Guiding Questions

List What are some other names for private distributor brands?	private brands, store brands, dealer brands, or private labels
Explain Why do customers purchase private distributor brands?	They want the quality and performance of national brands at a lower price.
Analyze Why would retailers carry private distributor brands in addition to national brands?	Private brands are popular with retailers because they usually carry higher gross margins. Therefore, they are more profitable than national brands. Also, because private brands are not sold at competitors' stores, they help cultivate customer loyalty.

Reading Check Answer

Read the Reading Check question to students: ***What is the difference between a brand mark and a trademark?*** A brand mark incorporates a unique symbol, coloring, lettering, or design element to make a company visually recognizable. A trademark is a brand mark that is legally protected because it is registered with the federal government.

Visual Literacy

Private Brands Caption Answer Read the caption and question to students: ***Private distributor brands are growing in importance. What are some of the reasons behind this trend?*** The perception of private brands is changing. Many people now view them to be of equal or similar quality to national brands, but typically available at a lower cost. Ask students: ***Do you typically purchase national brands, private brands, generic brands, or a combination?*** Students should consider all of their purchases before answering this question.

BRANDING STRATEGIES

Companies develop and rely on a variety of branding strategies to meet sales and company objectives. Some of these strategies include brand extensions, brand licensing, mixed branding, and co-branding. Effective use of different brand strategies can increase sales of branded products and maximize company profits.

BRAND EXTENSION

Brand extension is a branding strategy that uses an existing brand name to promote a new or improved product in a company's product line. For example, Ocean Spray® extended its cranberry juice drink product line by adding flavors, including Cran®Apple, Cran®Cherry, and Cran®Grape fruit blends. Launching new products is costly, and the failure rate for new products is high. Sometimes companies can reduce this risk by using an already established brand name.

A risk that companies face when they employ a brand extension strategy is overextending a product line and diluting or weakening the brand. When does brand dilution occur? If a brand includes too many products, the original brand and other selections in the product line may lose recognition and appeal with customers.

BRAND LICENSING

Brand licensing is a legal authorization by a brand owner to allow another company (the licensee) to use its brand, brand mark, or trade character for a fee. The agreement explains all the terms and conditions under which the brand may be used.

Companies license their brands to increase revenue sources, enhance company image, and sell more of their core products. For example, the National Football League® (NFL) has a licensing arrangement with EA SPORTS®. EA SPORTS uses NFL team names, logos, and individual players in their video games to try to attract customers. Licensed products must always support the brand strategy and image of the company—in this case, the NFL grants the license to use its name.

MARKETING CASE STUDY

EA's Branding Savvy

Electronic Arts' (EA) is one of the world's leading electronic-games companies. Its branding strategies have long included brand licensing and co-branding. They are essential components of its marketing plan and concept development process. Forging partnerships with sports organizations as well as consumer products, such as Dr. Pepper®, EA has depended on such strategic alliances to reach fans.

Virtual Competition

The company's popular game brand EA SPORTS™ was one of the first to tap into the lucrative gaming software and online gaming markets. EA developed cool action-game franchises, such as NBA Live, NASCAR Thunder™, and SSX for snowboarding. Partnering with Major League Gaming, the largest professional video game league in the world, EA can provide online tournament functionality for many of its sports titles. As EA's president says, EA is ushering in "a new era of video game competition."

English Language Arts

Create Think of a theme for a new electronic-game series. Write a one-page description of the game concept and include your ideas for co-branding or licensing for this new product.

NCTE 12 Use language to accomplish individual purposes.

MIXED BRANDS

Some manufacturers and retailers use a mixed brand strategy to sell products. A **mixed brand** strategy offers a combination of manufacturer, private distributor, and generic brands to consumers.

A manufacturer of a national brand agrees to make a product for sale under another company's brand. For example, Michelin® manufactures its own brand of tires as well as tires for sale at Sears under the Sears brand name. A mixed-brand strategy enables a business to maintain brand loyalty through its national brand and reach several different target markets through private brands. This strategy increases its overall product mix. It can maximize its profits by selling a private brand product without damaging the reputation and the sales of its national brand product.

CO-BRANDING

A **co-branding** strategy combines one or more brands in the manufacture of a product or in the delivery of a service. For example, Smucker's® sugar-free preserves are made with Splenda®. This strategy enables companies to capitalize on the popularity of other companies' goods and services to reach new customers and ideally increase sales for both companies' brands.

To ensure that all partners benefit from co-branding, it is essential that potential partners are compatible. The partners do not need to be the same size or have comparable reputations. Co-branding can work with one or several partners. Co-branding can also work when two or more retailers share the same location. For example, Starbucks Coffee® has an agreement with Barnes & Noble® to establish coffee shops inside their bookstores.

After You Read | **Section 31.1**

Review Key Concepts

1. **Explain** the difference between a brand name and a trade name.
2. **Describe** brand extension and brand licensing.
3. **Define** mixed branding and co-branding.

Practice Academics

English Language Arts

4. Conduct research to obtain information about why multinational companies, such as Kellogg's®, Procter & Gamble®, and others, often use different brand names for the same product sold in various countries. Prepare a one-page written report on your findings.

NCTE 1 Read texts to acquire new information.

Mathematics

5. Compare the brand values of two paper-products companies. Company A has a brand value of $1.95 billion and Company B has a brand value of $1.3 billion. How many times greater is the brand value of A than B?

Math Concept **Division** When determining how many times greater a value is compared to another value, the operation to use is division.

Starting Hints To solve this problem, divide Company A's brand value of $1.95 billion by Company B's brand value to determine the answer.

NCTM Number and Operations Understand meanings of operations and how they relate to one another.

For help, go to the **Math Skills Handbook** located at the back of this book.

glencoe.com

Check your answers.

ELABORATE

MARKETING CASE STUDY

English Language Arts Answer Students should be creative in their thinking about a new electronic-game series. The one-page description of the game should also include how they would co-brand or license the product.

Extend the Concept Ask students: ***What would be the benefit in granting licensing for your game to other companies?*** Sample answer: Selling the licenses will generate money for your company and you will also get a percentage of sales from the licensees. It will also allow for wider distribution of the game and therefore generate additional revenue. Refer students to the Marketing Case Study. Ask: ***What deductions can you make from the following sentence?*** **Forging partnerships with sports organizations as well as consumer products, such as Dr. Pepper®, EA® Sports has depended on such strategic alliances to reach fans.** Students may say these alliances may result in more attention from the public, free advertising for the company, and increased revenue.

BRANDING STRATEGIES

Ask students to recall the definition of *brand*. a name, term, design, symbol, or combination of these elements that identifies a business, product, or service, and sets it apart from its competitors Explain that companies often use many branding strategies. Then ask these guiding questions.

Guiding Questions

Identify What are the branding strategies used to increase sales and maximize profits?	brand extension, brand licensing, mixed brands, and co-branding
Compare What is the difference between brand licensing and brand extension?	Brand licensing is legal authorization allowing another company to use a brand, brand mark, or trade character for a fee. Brand extension uses an existing brand name to promote a new or improved product in a product line.
Predict When might a company use a mixed brand strategy?	when a company wants to maintain brand loyalty through a national brand and reach a larger market through private brands

EVALUATE

Graphic Organizer

Display this diagram. Then ask students to supply details about each type of brand. Write their answers in the third row of boxes under the appropriate head. Sample answers are provided in the graphic below.

Branding Strategies

Brand Extension	Brand Licensing	Mixed Brands	Co-Branding
• Uses an existing brand name to promote a new or improved product in a company's product line • Can overextend product line and dilute the brand	• Legally allows another company to use a brand, brand mark, or trade character for a fee • Can increase revenue sources, enhance company image, sell more core products	• Offers a combination of manufacturer, private distributor, and generic brands to customers • Enables a business to maintain brand loyalty through a national brand and reach other target markets through private brands	• Combines one or more brands in the manufacture of a product or in the delivery of a service • Can work with one or several partners • Partners must be compatible

 glencoe.com  iWB

Graphic Organizer Send students to the Online Learning Center to print this graphic organizer.

Mini Projects

Extension

Interview Consumers Ask students to interview a friend, family member, or other person they know about a brand that they have remained loyal to over the years. Before the interview, have students develop questions to ask the interviewee. Possible questions: What is it about the brand that has made you stay loyal? How has the brand changed over the years? Do you plan to continue using this product? Why or why not? Have students summarize their interviews in a half-page report. Ask volunteers to share their reports with the class.

Identify Brand Elements Bring to class a number of print and online advertisements. Have students work together in pairs to identify the following: brand name, trade name, brand mark, trade character, or trademark. Then have students determine whether it is a national brand or a private distributor brand. Ask students to share their results with the class.

 **After You Read** Section 31.1

Review Key Concepts

1. A brand name, or product brand, is a word, group of words, letters, or numbers that represent a product or service. A trade name, or corporate brand, identifies and promotes a company or a division of a particular corporation. The trade name is the legal name of the business.
2. Brand extension is a branding strategy that uses an existing brand name to promote a new or improved product in a company's product line. Brand licensing is a legal authorization by a brand owner to allow another company (the licensee) to use its brand, brand mark, or trade character for a fee. The agreement explains all the terms and conditions under which the brand may be used.
3. A mixed brand strategy offers a combination of manufacturer, private distributor, and generic brands to consumers. A co-branding strategy combines one or more brands in the manufacture of a product or in the delivery of a service.

Practice Academics

English Language Arts

4. Students' papers should point out that large companies have traditionally attempted to build brand equity in different countries by addressing advertising and promotions based upon the unique culture of the country. With the rise of a global economy, however, many companies see the advantage of having a single brand.

Mathematics

5. Company A's brand value is 1.5 times greater $(1.95 \div 1.3)$.

 glencoe.com 

Answer Key Send students to the Online Learning Center to check their answers.

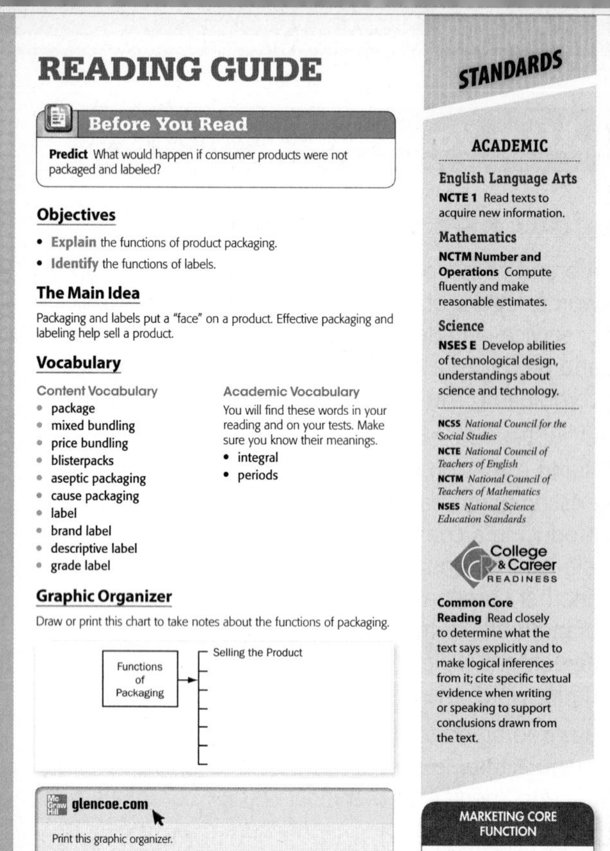

READING GUIDE

Before You Read

Predict What would happen if consumer products were not packaged and labeled?

Objectives

- **Explain** the functions of product packaging.
- **Identify** the functions of labels.

The Main Idea

Packaging and labels put a "face" on a product. Effective packaging and labeling help sell a product.

Vocabulary

Content Vocabulary
- package
- mixed bundling
- price bundling
- blisterpacks
- aseptic packaging
- cause packaging
- label
- brand label
- descriptive label
- grade label

Academic Vocabulary

You will find these words in your reading and on your tests. Make sure you know their meanings.
- integral
- periods

Graphic Organizer

Draw or print this chart to take notes about the functions of packaging.

Functions of Packaging → Selling the Product

glencoe.com

Print this graphic organizer.

STANDARDS

ACADEMIC

English Language Arts

NCTE 1 Read texts to acquire new information.

Mathematics

NCTM Number and Operations Compute fluently and make reasonable estimates.

Science

NSES E Develop abilities of technological design, understandings about science and technology.

NCSS *National Council for the Social Studies*
NCTE *National Council of Teachers of English*
NCTM *National Council of Teachers of Mathematics*
NSES *National Science Education Standards*

College & Career READINESS

Common Core

Reading Read closely to determine what the text says explicitly and to make logical inferences from it; cite specific textual evidence when writing or speaking to support conclusions drawn from the text.

MARKETING CORE FUNCTION

Product/Service Management

738 | Unit 10 · Product and Service Management

PACKAGING

A **package** is the physical container or wrapping for a product. A package represents the size, shape, and final appearance of a product at the time of sale. A product's package is an **integral** part of product planning. It is estimated that 10 percent of a product's retail price is spent on the actual package, its design, and development.

As You Read

Connect Consider how product packaging and labeling help you as a consumer.

FUNCTIONS OF PACKAGING

Aside from holding products, packaging fulfills several functions. Those functions include selling the product, communicating product identity, providing information, meeting customer needs, protecting consumers, protecting the product, and theft reduction.

SELLING THE PRODUCT

Customer reaction to a product's package and its brand name is an important factor in its success or failure in the marketplace. Attractive, colorful, and visually appealing packages have promotional value and can carry important messages about the product's performance, features, and benefits. A well-designed package is a powerful point-of-purchase selling device. In today's self-service environments, an attractive package can make a product stand out from its competition.

Sometimes marketers package, or bundle, two or more different goods or services in one package. This is known as **mixed bundling**. For example, airlines often bundle airfare, lodging, and car rental packages together for vacationers.

> "Innovative product packages and clear labels can lead to double-digit sales growth."

Price bundling occurs when two or more similar products are placed on sale for one package price. Price and mixed bundling provide cheaper prices for the goods and services than if they were purchased separately.

A container's design can minimize sales lost to competitors' products. It can even create new sales opportunities. Pump soap containers were designed to be neater, cleaner, and easier to use than bar soaps. These new containers have not replaced bar soaps. Instead, they provide a choice for customers. Pump-type dispensers created new sales and started an entire new line of soap products.

COMMUNICATING PRODUCT IDENTITY

Packages can promote an image such as prestige, convenience, or status. How does packaging communicate with consumers? The design, color, words, and labels on the package all talk to the consumer.

Color is one of the main design elements for packages because it can attract attention and project an image. For example, research indicates that red packaging communicates vitality, sensibility, and dependability. Yellow makes packages look larger and conveys the image of sun, warmth, happiness, and newness. Blue packaging conveys an image of cleanliness, and feelings of knowledge, confidence, and credibility. Green projects a natural and healthy image. White packaging implies freshness, while black implies status, quality, and richness.

Chapter 31 · Branding, Packaging, and Labeling | 739

ENGAGE

Anticipation Activity

Improving Student Achievement Bring to class a number of products without their packaging. Ask students to brainstorm different types of packaging for the product. Ask: ***What is the goal of the packaging?*** Possible answers: promote and sell the product, define product identity, provide information, express benefits and features, ensure safe use, and protect the product. Then ask students what they would put on a label for the product. Possible answers: information about the product, directions for use, ingredients or contents, safety warnings, and so on.

Objectives

- **Explain** the functions of product packaging. promotes and sells the product, defines product identity, provides information, expresses benefits and features, ensures safe use, and protects the product
- **Identify** the functions of labels. inform customers about a product's contents and give directions for use; protect businesses from legal liability if a consumer is injured using its product

Graphic Organizer

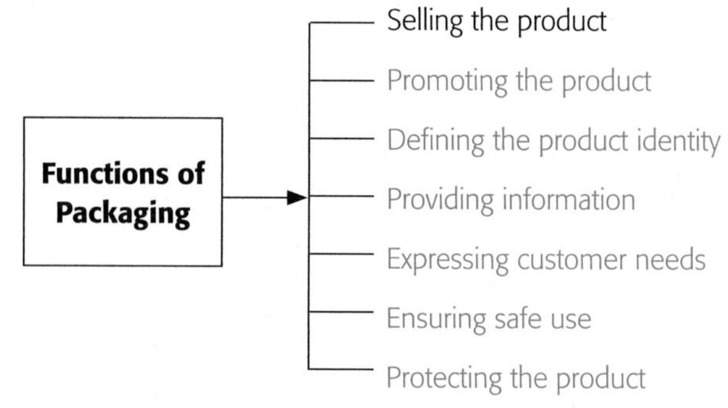

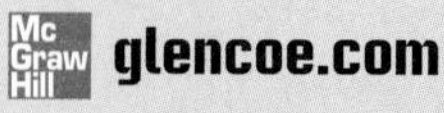

iWB

Graphic Organizer Send students to the Online Learning Center to print this graphic organizer.

EXPLORE

Before You Read

Read the Before You Read question aloud: ***What would happen if consumer products were not packaged or labeled?*** Possible answers: Consumers might not know what the product is for or know how to use it. They wouldn't know who made it in case they had questions about the product. Ask students whether they typically read the labels on the products they purchase. If so, why? If not, why not? Students may read the information to learn about the product before they buy it, to compare two or more products, to learn about warranties, and so on.

Preteaching Vocabulary

Have students go to the Online Learning Center at glencoe.com for the Chapter 31 Preteaching Vocabulary games.

Content Vocabulary

Divide the class into pairs or small groups. Have each team write definitions for the Content Vocabulary terms, using dictionaries or the glossary in the back of the textbook. Then have teams write a sentence for each term. Sentences will vary but should show an understanding of the terms. Ask volunteers to share their sentences with the class.

Academic Vocabulary

Integral—Usage Display the term *integral* and ask students to predict what it means. Then ask a volunteer to look it up and share the definition. necessary, essential, complete Read the following sentence to students: A product's packaging is an integral part of product planning. Then ask: ***Does the sentence make sense if you exchange the word* integral *for* necessary?** Students should recognize that the meaning of the sentence does not change. Ask volunteers to share original sentences using the term *integral*.

Periods—Meaning Display this sentence: Aseptic packaging utilizes a technology that keeps foods fresh without refrigeration for extended periods. Ask: ***What is the meaning of the term* periods *in this sentence?*** amounts of time Ask students to create other sentences using this meaning of the term *periods.*

PROFESSIONAL DEVELOPMENT

MINI CLIP

ELL: Comprehension and English Language Learners
Go to the Online Learning Center to view a video clip in which an author discusses comprehension strategies for English language learners.

Packaging and Labeling

PACKAGING

Ask students if they have ever considered what goes into planning the packaging for a product. Tell them that packaging has more functions than they may be aware of. Then ask these guiding questions to focus the discussion about packaging.

Guiding Questions

Identify What functions does packaging fulfill?	selling the product, communicating product identity, providing information, meeting customer needs, protecting consumers, protecting the product, and theft reduction
Explain What elements of packaging communicate with consumers?	design, color, words, and labels
Predict How might a container's design minimize sales lost to competitor's products?	Possible answers: Consumers might find some packaging to be easier to open or easier to reseal. They might find some packaging to be more durable than others. All of these factors could affect a consumer's purchasing decisions.

As You Read

Read students the As You Read question: ***Consider how product packaging and labeling help you as a consumer.*** They make it easier to make buying decisions by providing information such as directions for a product's care, use, and proper storage as well as listing ingredients and safety warnings.

Expert Advice

Read the quote to students:

“Innovative product packages and clear labels can lead to double-digit sales growth.”

Ask students: ***How do you think innovative product packages can lead to double-digit growth?*** Possible answers: Some people may purchase the product just because of its cool packaging or because the packaging is environmentally friendly. Then ask: ***How do you think clear labels can lead to double-digit growth?*** Possible answer: Clear labels won't detract from the appearance of the product, making the product more visually appealing.

PROVIDING INFORMATION

A package provides useful information for the customer. Many package labels give directions for using a product, the contents, product guarantees, nutritional information, instructions for care, and warnings about potential hazards.

MEETING CUSTOMER NEEDS

When designing packages, product planners analyze customer lifestyles and create packaging for customer convenience, functionality, and family size. To improve convenience, Nabisco® created its patented resealable opening for its Chips Ahoy!® cookies. Customer demands for a better way to use all of the contents led to the Heinz Ketchup® upside-down bottle.

Product packages also come in various sizes for different market segments. Family packs meet the needs of larger families, while smaller packages are made for individuals. Some examples include multipacks of beverages such as soda and juice, bulk sizes of paper packages, single-serving cans of soup, and family meals at fast-food outlets.

PROTECTING CONSUMERS

A package can also improve product safety. For example, many products that were formerly packaged in glass now come in plastic containers.

To avoid misuse or product tampering, over-the-counter medications and cosmetics are sold in tamper-resistant containers. Airtight containers are used to protect against spoilage of perishable food, such as dairy, fruit, meat, and vegetable products.

Many products are packaged in childproof containers that feature sealed lids that are more difficult to open. This reduces the chances of accidental spills and poisonings. Product planners must consider these factors, or companies risk of losing business and harming their brand images.

PROTECTING THE PRODUCT

A package must protect a product during shipping, storage, and display. The package design should also prevent or discourage tampering, prevent shoplifting, and protect against breakage. **Blisterpacks** are packages with preformed plastic molds surrounding individual items arranged on a backing. "Packing peanuts" are a loose-fill packaging and cushioning material used to prevent damage to products during shipping. Packing peanuts may be reused or recycled.

Sending the Message

The design, color, words, and labels on a package all help to communicate product identity to consumers. ***What kind of identity and image is projected by this product's package?***

Stores must strike a balance between product protection and consumer frustration with packages that are difficult to open. Because of governmental concerns about consumer injuries when trying to open clamshell-type packages, Best Buy®, Amazon®, and other leading retailers are working on simpler, easier-to-open package designs.

THEFT REDUCTION

Packaging may also help reduce theft. Some packages, for example, are intentionally made larger than the product. Consider software packages, where the packaging is much larger than the discs inside. This larger packaging makes it more difficult for a thief to steal it . Electronic anti-theft devices are often attached to packages.

CONTEMPORARY PACKAGING ISSUES

Product packaging offers companies unique opportunities to incorporate the latest technologies and address lifestyle changes, as well as environmental, social, and political concerns.

ASEPTIC PACKAGING

Aseptic packaging uses technology that keeps foods fresh without refrigeration for long **periods**. The process involves separately sterilizing the package and the food product, and then filling and sealing the package in a sterile environment. Examples of aseptic packaging include paperboard boxes for juices, puddings, syrups, flavored milks, and liquid eggs. Aseptic packages are convenient because they can be stored unopened or can be refrigerated in the package.

ENVIRONMENTAL PACKAGING

Companies are developing packages that respond to consumer demand for environmentally sensitive designs. Public opinion surveys show that most Americans support less wasteful packaging and better recycling efforts. For example, several local and state governments have proposed fees on disposable plastic bags that are used to carry purchases.

In response to consumer concerns, companies are promoting reusable shopping bags and making more space-saving packages. Such packages may be biodegradable, reusable, recyclable, and safer for the environment.

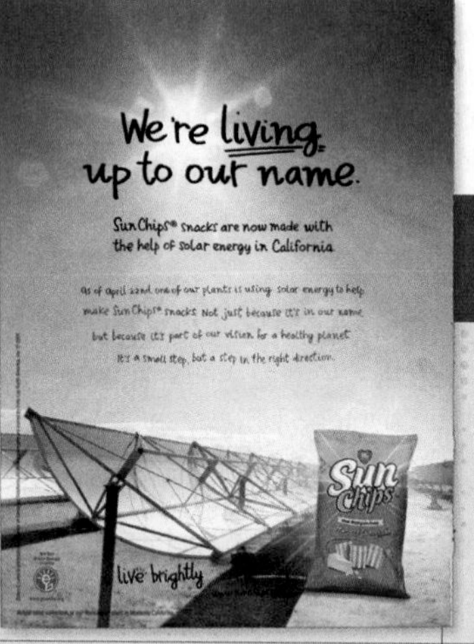

Helping the Environment

This advertisement promotes how this company uses solar energy and how it will help make a greener planet. ***How could a manufacturer benefit from focusing its marketing messages on environmental concerns?***

EXPLAIN

Mini Projects

Differentiated Learning

Kinesthetic Learners Bring to class examples of product packaging that provides a lot of information, such as food packaging or medicine packaging. Divide the class into small groups and give each group a product package. Ask: ***What information is required by law?*** Ask groups to write down the information on their package that is required by law. Then ask: ***How do companies indicate which information is most important?*** Have groups list all the information they can find on their package and present their findings to the class.

Students with Learning Disabilities Bring to class a product package. Hold up the package and point to different information on the package. Ask: ***What type of information is this?*** Continue to point to different types of information and to ask students to identify them.

Visual Literacy

Sending the Message Caption Answer Read the caption question to students: ***What kind of identity and image is projected by this product's package?*** Research indicates that red packaging and bold red lettering communicates vitality, sensibility, and dependability. The product is identified as a convenient, healthy, practical way of obtaining the required daily servings of vegetables. Then ask these guiding questions to focus the discussion on packaging.

Guiding Questions

Explain What do the following packaging colors communicate: yellow, blue, green, and white?	Yellow—makes packages look larger; conveys the image of sun, warmth, happiness, and newness. Blue—conveys cleanliness, and feelings of knowledge, confidence, and credibility. Green—projects a natural and healthy image. White—implies freshness.
Predict What emotions might a black package evoke?	Black—implies status, quality, richness, sadness, sophistication.

ELABORATE

Critical Thinking

Read the following scenario to students: A company wants to increase sales of its peanut butter. All of its competitors sell peanut butter in jars, and it wants to take a new, bold packaging stand. Ask: ***What other packaging could the company consider?*** Display the answers as students provide them. Sample answers: a toothpaste-like tube, individual serving packets, and so on. Now divide the class into pairs or small groups. Have each pair create a three-column table. In the left column they should list the answers that are written in the display. In the second column they should list reasons the packaging WOULD work. In the third column they should list reasons the packaging WOULD NOT work. Ask pairs to share their reasoning with the class.

Graphic Organizer

Display this graphic. Review with students the Functions of Packaging listed on pages 739–741.

Graphic Organizer Send students to the Online Learning Center to print this graphic organizer.

CONTEMPORARY PACKAGING ISSUES

Ask students to recall the seven functions of packaging (selling the product, communicating product identity, providing information, meeting customer needs, protecting consumers, protecting the product, and theft reduction). Tell students there is more to consider when developing packaging than these seven functions. Then ask these guiding questions to focus the discussion about packaging issues.

Guiding Questions

Identify What are three contemporary packaging issues?	Possible answers: packaging that addresses the latest technologies, lifestyle changes, as well as environmental, social, and political concerns; aseptic packaging, environmental packaging, cause packaging.
Differentiate What is the difference between environmental packaging and cause packaging?	Environmental packaging responds to consumer demands for environmentally sensitive designs. Cause packaging occurs when companies use their packages to promote social and political causes.
Evaluate How has aseptic packaging impacted your life?	Sample answer: It allows me to bring unrefrigerated juice, milk, yogurt, and pudding in my lunch bag.

Reinforce Vocabulary

Aseptic—Word Origin Display the term *aseptic* for the class to read. Tell students that the term aseptic is often used by doctors and other medical personnel. The term originates from a Greek term that means "not to decay." To have an aseptic atmosphere or package means it is free from any disease-causing microorganisms. Ask: ***Why is it important to have aseptic packaging for items such as puddings, liquid eggs, and flavored milks?*** Students should recognize that keeping consumers safe and healthy should be of primary concern to providers of food products. Using aseptic packaging helps to ensure that the product is free of disease-causing microorganisms and safe for consumption.

Visual Literacy

Helping the Environment Caption Answer Read the caption question to students: ***How could a manufacturer benefit from focusing its marketing messages on environmental concerns?*** Consumers may be more likely to purchase products made by a company that they perceive as being responsive to their concerns about environmental issues. Companies that brand themselves as being eco-friendly might be able to reach new target markets for their products.

Coca-Cola® introduced a new plastic bottle in 2010 that is partially made from sugarcane and molasses. The PlantBottle™ is recyclable and uses a renewable resource—plants. It is made with 30-percent plant material and reduces carbon emissions by up to 25 percent, compared with petroleum-based PET plastic bottles.

Many companies that manufacture spray products, such as hair products and air fresheners, have switched from using aerosol cans to pump dispensers. These containers do not release ozone-destroying chlorofluorocarbons, or CFCs, into the atmosphere.

CAUSE PACKAGING

Some companies are also using their packages to promote social and political causes. This practice is known as **cause packaging**. The issues promoted on the packages may be totally unrelated to the products inside.

Ben & Jerry's ice cream cartons promote saving the rain forests and express opposition to the use of bovine growth hormone to stimulate milk production in cows. Another example is the internationally recognized symbol of breast cancer awareness—a pink ribbon. Because the symbolic pink ribbon is in the public domain, it has been seen on a wide variety of products, from body wash to portable DVD players to cookie cutters.

Printing messages on packages encourages consumers to participate in or think about issues. In many ways, cause packaging is also a company's effort to differentiate its products from those of its competitors.

Reading Check

Explain What is the difference between mixed bundling and price bundling?

LABELING

A **label** is an information tag, wrapper, seal, or imprinted message that is attached to a product or its package. The main function of a label is to inform customers about a product's contents and give directions for use. Labels also protect businesses from legal liability if a consumer is injured during the use of its product. Fear of litigation (law suits), consumer pressure, government regulation, and concern for consumer safety are all factors that have compelled manufacturers to place more detailed information on labels. There are three kinds of labels: brand, descriptive, and grade.

Three Kinds of Labels
Brand Label
Descriptive Label
Grade Label

The **brand label** gives the brand name, trademark, or logo. For example, some bananas are stickered with the Chiquita® brand label. Although this is an acceptable form of labeling, it supplies insufficient product information. The U.S. government may approve laser-etched labels. This technology, already used in many countries, allows companies to place produce look-up codes (PLUs), brand names, logos, and country-of-origin information on fruits and vegetables. The process is designed to help track and trace produce-borne illnesses.

A **descriptive label** gives information about the product's use, construction, care, performance, and other features. For example, food labels include product illustrations, weight statements, dating and storage information, ingredients, product guarantees, and the manufacturer's name and address. Product illustrations must represent what is in the package. Weight statements give the net weight of the entire product minus the package or liquid in which it is packed.

Date and storage information is necessary for food items. Date information includes the "packed on" date (date food was packed), the "sell by" date (last date product should be sold), the "best if used by" date (last date for use for top quality), and the expiration date (date after which the product should not be used). Storage information tells how the product should be stored to have the least waste and best quality. Descriptive labels do not necessarily always contain all the information that consumers need when making a buying decision.

Nonfood labels usually provide consumers with instructions for the proper use and care of products. They also give manufacturers a convenient place to communicate warranty information and product use warnings. Notices of electrical hazard, flammability, and poisonous ingredients are required on the labels of certain categories of products. Labels might also contain symbols that give basic instructions on how to wash, cook, or care for the product.

Labels also include the manufacturer's name and address, so consumers can write for more information or to register a complaint. Many labels also include the company's Web address, encouraging consumers to visit for more information. Some labels include a customer-service phone number that consumers can use for questions or problems.

A **grade label** states the quality of the product. For example, eggs are grade-labeled AA, A, and B; corn and wheat are grade-labeled 1 and 2; and canned fruit is often grade-labeled A, B, or C. Beef is graded as prime, choice, or select.

Now, even our cap is pain-free.

As always, Aleve is 100% Acetaminophen Free.

ALEVE

Meeting Customer Needs

Packaging designers look at how customers interact and use products. ***Why is it necessary to study customer lifestyles?***

LABELING LAWS

Labeling laws have been enacted to prevent manufacturers from misleading consumers with deceptive or incomplete packaging labels.

Many package labels must now meet local, state, and federal standards. Federal laws require that the name and address of the manufacturer, packer, or distributor, and the quantity of contents appear on labels.

The Fair Packaging and Labeling Act (FPLA) of 1966 established mandatory labeling requirements and authorized the U.S. Food and Drug Administration (FDA) and the Federal Trade Commission (FTC) to establish packaging regulations. A 1992 amendment to the FPLA called for packages of selected products to include metric measurements. The amendment, which went into effect in 1994, requires that product weight be listed in American and metric weights and measures.

In today's global marketplace, companies must also consider the labeling laws of other countries. Some countries require bilingual labels. Others require that every ingredient in a product be listed on the label.

EXPLAIN

Mini Projects

Extension

Promote a Cause Have students bring in ads or packaging that show companies promoting a cause. Have students share their examples and explain what the product is, the cause being promoted, and whether they see any connection.

Find a Cause Have students select a cause they feel strongly about and a product they believe would be a good match with that cause. Have students create a label for the product that shows the cause being promoted. Ask students to share their labels and explain why they believe the product is a good match for the cause.

Write a Letter Ask students to write a letter to the company that manufactures the product they chose for the activity Find a Cause above. In the letters, students should try to persuade the company president or board to promote their cause through cause packaging. Ask volunteers to read their letters to the class.

Critical Thinking

Go online to find examples of brands or products and the causes they promote. Then create a worksheet with a list of brands or products on one side and the causes they promote on the other side. Have students match which brands/products they think go with each cause. Provide students with the correct answers and discuss if each brand/product is related to the cause on its packaging. Ask students if they believe companies should use their product packaging to promote social or political causes. Then have students to make a list of causes they think would be acceptable to the general public, and a list of causes they think are too controversial to be used on packaging.

Reading Check Answer

Read the Reading Check question to students: ***What is the difference between mixed bundling and price bundling?*** Mixed bundling is the packaging of two very different goods or services together. Price bundling occurs when two or more similar products are packaged together and sold for one price.

ELABORATE

LABELING

Ask students if they have ever been attracted to a product simply because of the label. Tell students that labels can promote interest in a product, but their main function is to provide information. Then ask these guiding questions to focus the discussion about labels.

Guiding Questions

Define What is a label?	an information tag, wrapper, seal, or imprinted message that is attached to a product or its package
Identify What are three types of labels?	brand labels, descriptive labels, grade labels
Explain Why do companies place detailed labels on their products?	Fear of litigation, consumer pressure, government regulation, and concern for consumer safety have compelled manufacturers to place more detailed information on labels.
Analyze Labeling laws have been enacted to prevent manufacturers from misleading consumers with deceptive or incomplete packaging labels. Why would manufacturers deceive or mislead consumers?	Possible answer: Telling the complete truth might cause consumers to not purchase a product, which would cut into a company's sales and profits.

Visual Literacy

Meeting Customer Needs Caption Answer Read the caption question to students: ***Why is it necessary to study customer lifestyles?*** Customer lifestyles tell us what product modifications or changes need to be made for people at different times in their lives and to address customer's needs. For example, the need for functionality and convenience (larger handles, oversized caps, and ribbed closures) are more important for the elderly, while larger product package sizes are required for young parents with children.

e MARKETING

Domain Name—A Branding Tool

A domain name (or host name) is the alphanumeric name that begins the web address or URL. It is used to identify a computer on the Internet. Domain names for .com, .org, .biz, .net, .info, and .name must be registered with accredited registrars and their resellers. The agency that approves resellers is ICANN.org. Domain names are crucial to businesses because they provide the means for visitors to find companies' Web sites on the Internet. The company's trademark is often its name. Thus, it is important to register a business's domain name before someone else does. "Cybersquatting" is a term used for people who register domain names in order to resell them at a profit.

Innovate and Create

Have students research prices for existing domain names that are being resold. You may want to provide a few examples, such as "marketing clubs" and "soda pop." The site that provides this service is WHOIS Lookup and Domain Name Search. Have students share their findings with classmates. What was the highest price anyone found for a domain name? Did anyone find a domain name that does not have any cybersquatters? Have students discuss why domain names are important as a branding tool and ask them to create a domain name that they may be able to resell in the future. The prices students find for domain names will vary. You may want to create a chart of the prices found listing the domain names and respective prices from the highest to the lowest price found. Have students analyze the list when discussing the importance of domain names as a branding tool. The domain names students create can be checked out on WHOIS Lookup and Domain Name Search to see if it already exists. A domain name for a local business that does not already have one would end in .com or .biz.

 **glencoe.com** 

eMarketing Worksheet Activity Send students to the Online Learning Center to download an eMarketing worksheet activity.

Green Yogurt

A new breed of businesspeople is combining profit with progress. Take Gary Hirshberg, whc transformed Stonyfield Farm from a tiny farming school in New Hampshire into the leading organic yogurt brand in the United States. The company buys milk from family farms, donates 10 percent of profits to environmental groups, and offsets its CO_2 emissions—all while still making a profit.

Eco-Packaging Before many others did it, this company evaluated its own carbon footprint. As part of its mission, Stonyfield set up a sustainable packaging team to create the most environmentally sustainable product packaging possible. Their goal is to achieve 100 percent sustainable packaging. Packaging has been reduced by about 1 million pounds per year.

Science

Ask Find out the meaning of the term ***carbon footprint*** and how packaging impacts it. Do research to find three products with "green" packaging and explain what qualifies their packaging as sustainable.

NSES E Develop abilities of technological design, understandings about science and technology.

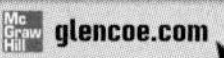 glencoe.com

Get an activity on green marketing.

THE FDA

The federal Nutrition Labeling and Education Act of 1990 protects consumers from deceptive labeling. This act, administered by the FDA, requires that labels give nutritional information on how a food fits into an overall daily diet. Labels must clearly state the amount of calories, fat, carbohydrates, sodium, cholesterol, and protein in each serving. Labels must also state the percentage of a daily intake of 2,000 calories. The act also regulates health claims in that it allows the use of only certain descriptive words on labels. These words include *light* and *lite, free* (as in *fat free, salt free, cholesterol free*), *low, reduced,* and *good source of.*

The FDA also requires that U.S. manufacturers of certain products place health warnings on their packages. Beginning in 1989, all alcoholic beverage labels had to carry the following statements: "According to the Surgeon General, women should not drink alcoholic beverages during pregnancy because of the risk of birth defects. Consumption of alcoholic beverages impairs the ability to drive a car or operate machinery and may cause health problems." Similar warnings of health risks are required on cigarette package labels.

In 2009, the FDA issued regulations regarding the labeling of products made with genetically engineered animals. Companies are not required to label food products containing genetically modified organisms. Such labeling is voluntary.

THE FEDERAL TRADE COMMISSION

The Federal Trade Commission is responsible for regulating labeling and monitoring advertising that is false or misleading.

The Care Labeling Rule of 1972 requires that care labels be placed in textile clothing. This rule ensures that specific information about the care of garments be detailed on labels, including information related to washing, drying, and ironing.

The FTC released guidelines in 1992 for companies to follow when making environmental claims on labels. Previously, many environmental terms had definitions that were not clear. When using the term *recycled* to describe the content of its products, a company must demonstrate proof of the claim. It must prove that it has retrieved or recovered a certain amount of scraps or materials from the waste stream.

The term *recyclable* can be used only if the product or package can be reused as raw material for a new product or package. The terms *ozone safe* and *ozone friendly* can be used only if the products do not contain any ozone-depleting chemicals. The terms *degradable, biodegradable,* and *photodegradable* can be used only if the product will decompose into elements found in nature within a short time after disposal.

U.S. DEPARTMENT OF AGRICULTURE

Increasing sales of organic foods led the U.S. Department of Agriculture (USDA) to issue legal standards, certification requirements, and penalties for misuse of organic labels. The Organic Foods Production (OFPA) Act of 1990, as amended, requires labeling based on the percentage of organic ingredients in a product.

Organic foods are produced without hormones, antibiotics, herbicides, insecticides, chemicals, genetic modification, or germ-killing radiation. The required product labeling and ingredients differ for foods marketed as *100 percent organic, organic* or *made with organic ingredients.* The USDA Organic label requires both products and producers to be certified.

The Country of Origin Labeling (COOL) Act of 2002 is also administered by the USDA and requires that a country-of-origin label be placed on all fruits, vegetables, peanuts, meats, and fish.

The Food Allergen Labeling and Consumer Protection Act (FALCPA) of 2004 applies to consumer packaged foods regulated by the FDA. The FDA does not regulate meat, poultry, and egg products. This is the job of the Food Safety and Inspection Service (FSIS). The FSIS has established policies for processors to voluntarily add FSIS-approved allergen statements to the labeling of meat, poultry, and egg products. This can help allergen-sensitive individuals to make informed food choices for all foods, including those not regulated by the FDA.

After You Read | **Section 31.2**

Review Key Concepts

1. **Differentiate** between a label and a brand label.
2. **Identify** the types of information found on a food label.
3. **Name** three federal agencies that regulate packaging and labeling.

Practice Academics

English Language Arts

4. Perform library or online research on one of the federal labeling laws as explained in this chapter. Write a one-page report on the purpose of the law, its provisions, and penalties for violating the law.

NCTE 1 Read texts to acquire new information.

Mathematics

5. The newest law firm in town paid a total of $33,860 to a marketing firm for the research and development of the firm's corporate trade name and trademark. From this budget, a Web-site developer was paid $9,475 for her creative work on the project. Her salary was what percentage of the entire amount?

Math Concept **Division** When solving problems that involve percents, it is usually a matter of dividing one value by another.

Starting Hints To solve this problem, divide the salary of the Web-site developer by the total amount paid to the marketing firm to determine what percent the developer's salary was of the total.

NCTM Number and Operations Compute fluently and make reasonable estimates.

For help, go to the **Math Skills Handbook** located at the back of this book.

glencoe.com

Check your answers.

ELABORATE

The GREEN Marketer

Science Answer A carbon footprint is the amount of carbon dioxide or greenhouse gases released into the atmosphere by a product (including its manufacture), event, or organization. Students may visit local stores or go online to find products with "green" packaging. Sustainable packaging reduces ecological impact and meets current needs without compromising the ability of future generations to meet their needs.

 glencoe.com 

Worksheet Activity Send students to the Online Learning Center to get a Green Marketer worksheet activity.

Mini Projects

Extension

Research Laws Have students go the FDA Web site and read the Federal Nutrition Labeling and Education Act. Have students research the act and write a one-page report summarizing the major points of the act that affect labeling. Have interested students give oral presentations. Encourage students to use visuals to enhance their presentations.

Label Laws Make a list of federal, state, and local laws that govern product labels. Assign a law to each student and have students research the law, including the requirements of the law, when it was established, products affected by the law, and any court cases regarding the law. Have students present their findings in an oral report. Students should include a visual that shows the part of the label to which the law pertains.

EVALUATE

Graphic Organizer

Display this diagram. Ask students to identify the three agencies that make laws regarding U.S. product labels. FDA, Federal Trade Commission, U.S. Department of Agriculture Then ask students to provide details about the agencies and list them in the appropriate boxes. Sample answers are provided in the diagram below.

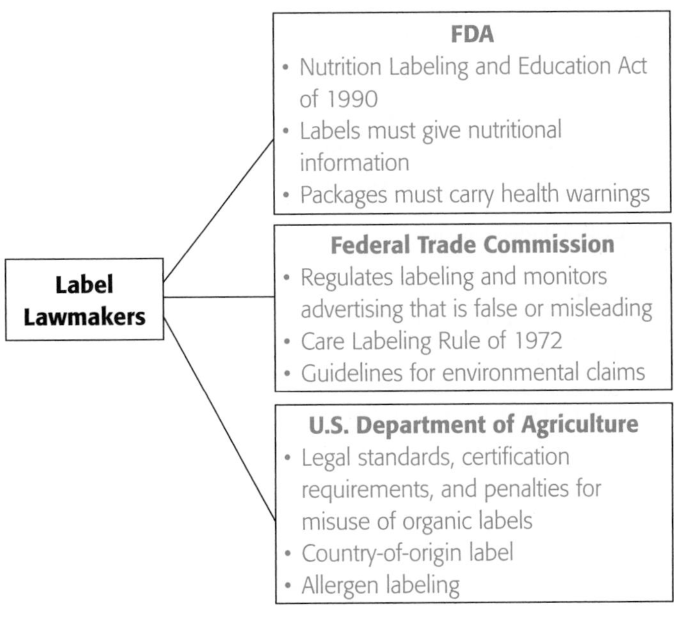
Label Lawmakers
FDA
• Nutrition Labeling and Education Act of 1990
• Labels must give nutritional information
• Packages must carry health warnings
Federal Trade Commission
• Regulates labeling and monitors advertising that is false or misleading
• Care Labeling Rule of 1972
• Guidelines for environmental claims
U.S. Department of Agriculture
• Legal standards, certification requirements, and penalties for misuse of organic labels
• Country-of-origin label
• Allergen labeling

Critical Thinking

Discuss with students what issues might occur if product labels were not regulated by law. Ask students to share their thoughts. Possible issues: people would buy products that didn't live up to the claims on the label; people would become sick or die because of allergic reactions to ingredients not listed on the label; it might not be possible to track down the producer or manufacturer of the product. Ask: ***Do you think it is worth it to have government regulations regarding product labels?*** Students should recognize the advantages to consumers of having label information regulated by government agencies.

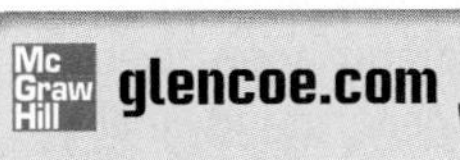
glencoe.com

iWB

Graphic Organizer Send students to the Online Learning Center to print this graphic organizer.

After You Read — Section 31.2

Review Key Concepts

1. A label is an information tag, wrapper, seal, or imprinted message that is attached to a product or its package. The main function of a label is to inform customers about a product's contents and give directions for use. The brand label gives the brand name, trademark, or logo. Although this is an acceptable form of labeling, it supplies insufficient product information.
2. Food labels include product illustrations, weight statements, dating and storage information, ingredients, product guarantees, and the manufacturer's name and address.
3. U.S. Food and Drug Administration, Federal Trade Commission, and U.S. Department of Agriculture

Practice Academics

English Language Arts

4. Students may select one of the laws mentioned in the section, such as the Fair Packaging and Labeling Act, to research. One-page reports should include information about the purpose of the law, its provisions, and penalties for violating the law.

Mathematics

5. 28% ($\$9,475 \div \$33,860 = 0.279$).

glencoe.com

Answer Key Send students to the Online Learning Center to check their answers.

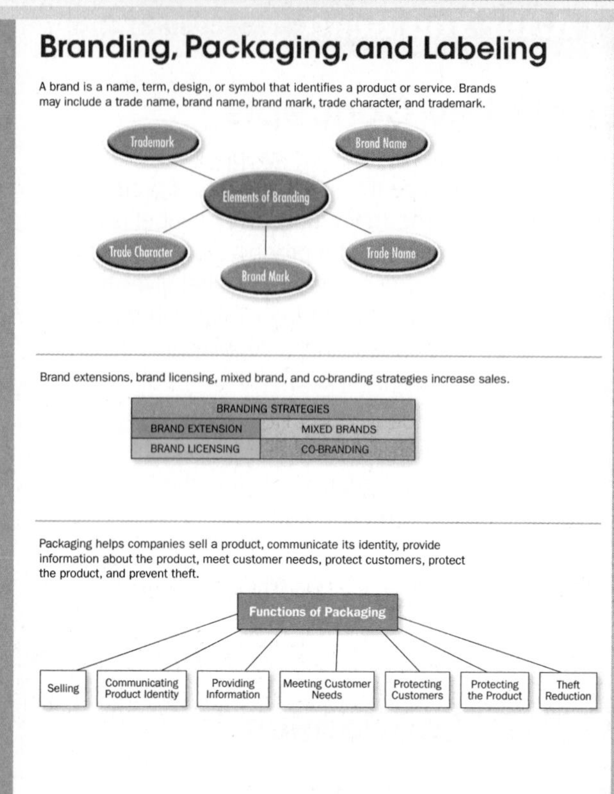
Chapter 31 Visual Summary
Branding, Packaging, and Labeling
A brand is a name, term, design, or symbol that identifies a product or service. Brands may include a trade name, brand name, brand mark, trade character, and trademark.
Trademark
Brand Name
Elements of Branding
Trade Character
Brand Mark
Trade Name
Brand extensions, brand licensing, mixed brand, and co-branding strategies increase sales.
BRANDING STRATEGIES
BRAND EXTENSION
MIXED BRANDS
BRAND LICENSING
CO-BRANDING
Packaging helps companies sell a product, communicate its identity, provide information about the product, meet customer needs, protect customers, protect the product, and prevent theft.
Functions of Packaging
Selling
Communicating Product Identity
Providing Information
Meeting Customer Needs
Protecting Customers
Protecting the Product
Theft Reduction
746 | Unit 10 · Product and Service Management

Review and Activities

Written Summary

- A brand is a name, term, design, or symbol (or combination of these elements) that identifies a product or service.
- Brands can include a trade name, brand name, brand mark, trade character, and trademark.
- Branding strategies include brand extensions, brand licensing, mixed branding, and co-branding.
- Effective use of brand strategies can increase sales of branded products and maximize company revenues.
- The functions of packaging include promoting and selling the product, defining product identity, providing information, expressing benefits and features to customers, ensuring safe use, and protecting the product.
- The main function of a label is to inform customers about a product's contents and give directions for use.
- Labels also protect businesses from legal liability that may occur if a consumer misuses the product.

Review Content Vocabulary and Academic Vocabulary

1. Label each of these content and vocabulary terms as a noun, verb, or adjective.

Content Vocabulary
- brand (p. 731)
- brand name (p. 731)
- trade name (p. 731)
- brand mark (p. 732)
- trade character (p. 732)
- trademark (p. 732)
- national brands (p. 734)
- private distributor brands (p. 735)
- generic brands (p. 735)
- brand extension (p. 736)
- brand licensing (p. 736)
- mixed brand (p. 737)
- co-branding (p. 737)
- package (p. 739)
- mixed bundling (p. 739)
- price bundling (p. 739)
- blisterpacks (p. 740)
- aseptic packaging (p. 741)
- cause packaging (p. 742)
- label (p. 742)
- brand label (p. 742)
- descriptive label (p. 742)
- grade label (p. 743)

Academic Vocabulary
- component (p. 731)
- distinctive (p. 731)
- integral (p. 739)
- periods (p. 741)

Assess for Understanding

2. **Explain** What are the nature, scope, and importance of branding in product planning?
3. **Contrast** What are the differences between the various branding elements?
4. **Identify** What are three different types of brands?
5. **Apply** How are branding strategies used to meet sales and company goals?
6. **Demonstrate** What are the functions of product packaging?
7. **Justify** What are the functions of labels?
8. **Define** What are the definitions of the terms *descriptive label* and *grade label*?
9. **Consider** Why is packaging important to product planning?

Chapter 31 · Branding, Packaging, and Labeling | 747

EVALUATE

Visual Summary

Express Creativity Ask students to develop their own visual summary of a concept in the chapter. Encourage students to use different formats for their visual summaries, such as a storyboard, a timeline, a table, a tree diagram, or a word web. Visual summaries will vary depending on the concept depicted and the visual manner in which it is depicted. Questions to ask when assessing a visual summary include:

- Is the summary clear, economical, and simple?
- Are any important steps left out?
- Are steps or concepts arranged in the same order as the original?
- Does the summary reveal a pattern that connects the details?
- Does the summary locate and highlight the most important information?

Review Content Vocabulary and Academic Vocabulary

1. **brand**—noun or verb; **brand name**—noun; **trade name**—noun; **brand mark**—noun; **trade character**—adjective or noun; **trademark**—adjective or noun; **national brands**—noun; **private distributor brands**—noun; **generic brands**—noun; **brand extension**—adjective or noun; **brand licensing**—noun or verb; **mixed brand**—adjective or noun; **co-branding**—adjective (adverb) or verb; **package**—noun or verb; **mixed bundling**—noun or verb; **price bundling**—noun or verb; **blisterpacks**—adjective; **aseptic packaging**—adjective; **cause packaging**—adjective or noun; **label**—noun or verb; **brand label**—adjective or noun; **descriptive label**—adjective or noun; **grade label**—adjective or noun; **component**—noun; **distinctive**—adjective; **integral**—adjective; **periods**—noun

EVALUATE

Assess for Understanding

2. Brands are developed to target customers' needs and preferences and include elements such as brand names, trade names, brand marks, trade characters, and trademarks. These elements are often combined to form a firm's corporate symbol or name. Effective brands have tremendous value and frequently become global brands.

3. Brand names, brand marks, and trade names are unique symbols, colors, words, lettering, and design elements that distinguish a product as belonging to and visually recognizable as the product of a certain company. Trademarks are registered with the federal government and are legally protected trade names, brand names, and/or brand marks.

4. National brands, private distributor brands, and generic brands are three different types of brands.

5. Brand extension is a strategy that uses an existing brand name to promote a new or improved product in a company's product line. Brand licensing is a legal licensing agreement for which the licensing company receives a fee, such as a royalty, in return for the authorization. Mixed brands offer a combination of manufacturer, private distributor, and generic brands. A co-branding strategy combines one or more brands in the manufacture of a product or in the delivery of a service.

6. Packaging helps promote and sell the product, define the product's identity, provide information about the product, express its benefits and features, ensure safe use, and protect the product.

7. Many package labels give directions for using the product as well as information about its contents, product guarantees, nutritional value, or potential hazards.

8. A descriptive label gives information about the product's use, construction, care, performance, and other features. A grade label is specific to the quality of the product, especially when placed on a food label. For example, eggs, grains, fruit, and beef have specific grades that may be on a grade label.

9. Packaging is important in a company's product planning because the packaging is part of the overall branding and defines the product identity, providing information and expressing benefits and features that will define the product and increase the company's brand name.

21st Century Skills

Teamwork Skills

10. Products and Brand Extensions You and a classmate work for a consumer products manufacturer. You have been asked by management to identify the products offered in a competitor's branded product line. Use the Internet and corporate Web sites to find out the brand extensions within the brand line. With your partner, prepare a written report about the products, the number of brand extensions, and various features of the products.

Financial Literacy Skills

11. Calculating Barcode Costs A global company wants to design a barcode that is fun and memorable as part of a new package. If design costs for an exclusive barcode total $4,000, what percentage does this represent for a package that costs $50,000 to develop?

Everyday Ethics

12. Truth in Labeling The FDA has developed guidelines for *voluntary* labeling on genetically modified products. Do you believe it is the obligation of a grocery store to label its fruits and vegetables as genetically engineered or otherwise? Write a two-paragraph statement expressing your opinion.

e-Marketing Skills

13. Guide to Environmental Labels You are a product planner for a large food manufacturer. You are to go to the Consumer Reports® Greener Choices™ Web site to get an expert opinion on eco-labels for the food category. Select one product from the food category. Identify one eco-label for a specific product and the certifying agency or organization. List five other products that may also carry this eco-label. What product did you investigate in the food category?

Build Academic Skills

English Language Arts

14. Brand Licensing Use publications, such as *Brandweek, AdWeek, BusinessWeek,* and entertainment and sports publications, or online research to investigate brand licensing arrangements in the sports or entertainment fields. Identify the name of your source(s) and prepare a one-page report that summarizes the arrangement, the parties and companies involved, and length of the licensing agreement.

NCTE 1 Read texts to acquire new information.

Science

15. Environmental Packaging Marketers are increasingly using packaging materials that are reusable, recyclable, and safer for the environment. Perform library or online research about the science and technologies used to recycle one selected item (paper, cardboard, glass, plastic, wood or another packaging material of your choice) used in product packaging. Identify the name of the article, its publisher, the packaging material investigated, and explain the recycling process for it. Write a one-page summary describing the process.

NSES E Develop abilities of technological design, understandings about science and technology.

Mathematics

16. Private Distributor Brands Some larger U.S. stores have created private distributor brands for their stores. This allows them to sell goods at a lower retail price. At one such store, its private distributor brand accounts for 60 percent of total annual sales. If the total annual sales were $86,450,735, what were the sales for the private distributor brand?

NCTM Number and Operations Compute fluently and make reasonable estimates.

Math Concept **Calculating Percent** Calculate percent by multiplying the total sales dollar amount by the decimal form of the percent given.

For help, go to the **Math Skills Handbook** located at the back of this book.

Standardized Test Practice

Directions Read the following questions. On a separate piece of paper, write the best possible answer for each one.

1. Which of the following is a name, term, design, symbol, or combination of these elements that defines a product and distinguishes it from its competitors?
   A. Brand
   B. Brand mark
   C. Trademark
   D. Trade character
2. Generic brands carry company identity on the package.
   T
   F
3. An information tag, wrapper, seal, or imprinted message attached to a product is known as a(n) ________.

Test-Taking Tip

Have a nutritious meal and avoid junk food before taking a test. Studies show that you need good nutrition to concentrate and perform at your best.

DECA Connection Role Play

Representative Business Advice Company

Situation You represent a company that specializes in advising businesses about overcoming their business challenges. Your current client (judge) is the sales manager for a local office supply chain. The chain sells all of the major national brand products.

The chain recently began selling a limited range of products produced for the company and sold with the company name on the packages. Some of the products include office paper, pens, markers, pencils, paper clips, staplers and staples, and other small office products. The store brand products are of excellent quality, made from recycled materials where possible, and sell for less than the national brands.

However, the store products are not selling very well. The sales manager (judge) has asked you study the situation and make recommendations. Your study has shown that the products, while having the store name, have few identifying factors on the packaging and no coordination of the packaging of various products. You think the office supply chain needs to establish a company brand identity that can be extended to the packaging of the store brand products.

Activity You are to meet with the sales manager (judge) to explain your findings and recommend that the office supply chain establish a company brand. You are to also explain branding and its importance to the business and sales of the store brand products.

Evaluation You will be evaluated on how well you meet the following performance indicators:

1. Explain the nature of corporate branding.
2. Describe factors used by businesses to position corporate brands.
3. Explain the nature of product/service branding.
4. Develop strategies to position a product/business.
5. Describe the nature of product bundling.

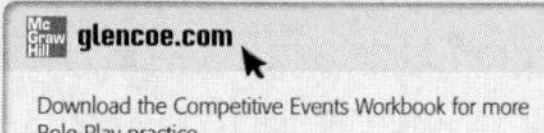

Download the Competitive Events Workbook for more Role-Play practice.

EVALUATE

Teamwork Skills

10. Answers will vary. Students should work together in pairs to search the Internet and corporate Web sites to identify the products offered in a competitor's branded product line. Written reports should identify the products, brand extensions, and various features of the products.

Financial Literacy Skills

11. 8% ($4,000 ÷ $50,000)

Everyday Ethics

12. Students may or may not believe it is the obligation of a grocery store to label its fruits and vegetables as genetically engineered. Accept all answers that logically support the opinions stated.

e-Marketing Skills

13. Students should go to the ConsumerReports® Greener Choices™ Web site, select one food product, identify one eco-label for the product and the certifying agency or organization, and then list five other products that may also carry this eco-label.

EVALUATE

Build Academic Skills

English Language Arts

14. Online research should include the name of the source and a summary report that highlights the entertainment or sports arrangement between all parties and companies, as well as the term length of the licensing agreement. Reports should follow proper mechanics and be free of grammatical and spelling errors. Examples could include television commercials using popular songs as part of their advertising campaign.

Science

15. Accept all reasonable reports that discuss the uniqueness of the product packaging that is reusable, recyclable, and safer for the environment. Summaries should include the name of the article, its publisher, the packaging material investigated, and explain the recycling process for the packaging.

Mathematics

16. $51,870,441 ($86,450,735 × .60)

Standardized Test Practice

1. B brand mark
2. F
3. label

DECA Connection Role Play

Evaluations will be based on these performance indicators:

1. **Explain the nature of corporate branding.** A brand can be used to identify one product, a family of related products, or all products of a company. Brands suggest a product's benefits, features, or qualities. When a company defines its brand strategy and uses it in every interaction with its market, the company strengthens its message and its relationships. Brands are important assets and powerful tools for marketing and selling products.
2. **Describe factors used by businesses to position corporate brands.** Companies use a variety of branding strategies to meet sales and company objectives. Some of these strategies include brand extensions, brand licensing, mixed branding, and co-branding. Effective use of different brand strategies can increase sales and maximize profits.
3. **Explain the nature of product/service branding.** Brands are developed to target customers' needs and preferences. The target audience should feel that a brand is created just for them. Branding elements include brand names, trade names, brand marks, trade characters, and trademarks. These elements often combine to form a firm's corporate symbol or name.
4. **Develop strategies to position a product/business.** It is important that customers easily recognize a company's branded products when they make repeat purchases. Through branding, companies communicate to customers consistent quality and performance, purchase after purchase. Branding suggests consistency. Branding helps companies extend their products or services into new target markets. It also helps introduce new product lines or categories. With careful planning, companies can also adjust or reposition a corporate or product brand's image to expand sales.
5. **Describe the nature of product bundling.** Sometimes marketers package, or bundle, two or more different goods or services in one package. This is known as mixed bundling. For example, airlines often bundle airfare, lodging, and car rental packages together for vacationers. Price bundling occurs when two or more similar products are placed on sale for one package price. Price and mixed bundling provide cheaper prices for the goods and services than if they were purchased separately.

glencoe.com

Role Plays For more DECA Role Plays, send students to the Online Learning Center to download the Competitive Events Workbook.

extended product features

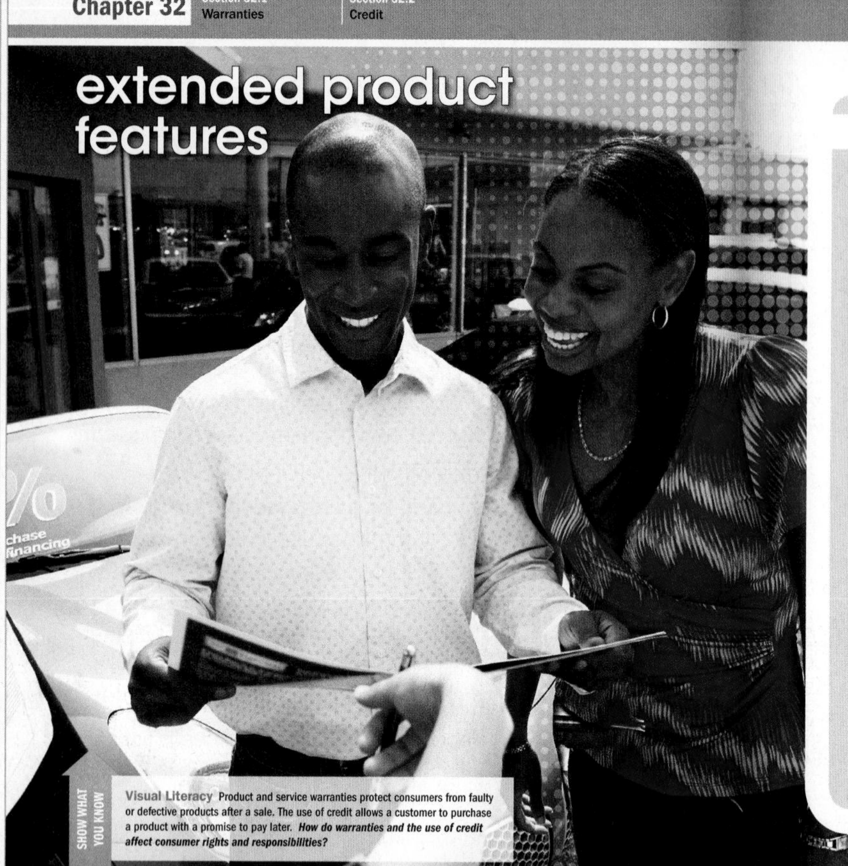

SHOW WHAT YOU KNOW **Visual Literacy** Product and service warranties protect consumers from faulty or defective products after a sale. The use of credit allows a customer to purchase a product with a promise to pay later. ***How do warranties and the use of credit affect consumer rights and responsibilities?***

Discovery Project

Planning Extended Product Features

Essential Question How do warranties and credit affect product and service management?

Project Goal

Assume that you and a classmate work for a company that helps clients develop and offer extended product features for higher-priced electronic products. You have been asked by a client to analyze an existing consumer electronic product. You will suggest five extended product and service features that should be offered as part of its product and service management plan. You are to prepare a written report on the extended product features that you would recommend for the product.

Ask Yourself...

- What is your consumer electronic product?
- What extended product features will you recommend?
- What extended service features will you recommend?
- How will you organize your report and summarize your recommendations?

Synthesize and Present Synthesize your research and analysis by describing the extended product features that you would recommend for the product and the importance of warranties and use of credit in a written report.

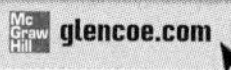

glencoe.com

Activity
Get a worksheet activity about extended product features.

Evaluate
Download a rubric you can use to evaluate your project.

DECA Connection

DECA Event Role Play

Concepts in this chapter are related to DECA competitive events that involve either an interview or role play.

Performance Indicators The performance indicators represent key skills and knowledge. Your key to success in DECA competitive events is relating them to concepts in this chapter.

- Discuss the nature of environmental law.
- Explain the nature of agency relationships.
- Discuss legal issues affecting businesses.
- Identify legal considerations for granting credit.
- Determine creditworthiness of customers/client.

DECA Prep

Role Play Practice role-playing with the DECA Connection competitive-event activity at the end of this chapter. More information on DECA events can be found on DECA's Web site.

Chapter 32 · Extended Product Features | 751

ENGAGE

Visual Literacy

Read the chapter opener photo caption question to students: ***How do warranties and the use of credit affect consumer rights and responsibilities?*** Consumers have the right to expect products to function as the manufacturer or seller says they will. They have the responsibility to follow directions provided with products and to pay credit bills according to any specified agreements. Then ask the following questions.

Guiding Questions

Define What does the term *product feature* mean?	any attribute or characteristic of a product
Analyze What is the purpose of the Food and Drug Administration? The Consumer Product Safety Commission?	FDA: regulate the labeling and safety of foods, drugs, and cosmetics; CPSC: oversee the safety of products such as toys, electronics, and household furniture

Discovery Project

Planning Extended Product Features Ask students the Discovery Project Essential Question: ***How do warranties and credit affect product and service management?*** Companies offer extended product features in order to improve customer satisfaction and thereby increase sales. However, such features need to be carefully managed. For example, a company has to charge enough for an extended warranty to cover the cost of honoring it. Likewise, sales may increase when customers are allowed to pay for products over a specified period of time, but it may cost a company money to grant credit. All these factors must be weighed against the company's goals and the benefits of offering extended features.

glencoe.com

Discovery Project Resources Send students to the Online Learning Center to download a rubric to evaluate their projects.

ENGAGE

Introduce the Chapter

Chapter 32 introduces the concept of extended product features. These major concepts are discussed.

- Warranties and product planning
- Express warranties
- Implied warranties
- Extended warranties
- Consumer laws and agencies
- Federal and state statutes related to consumer safety
- Consumer rights and responsibilities
- The role of credit in the marketplace
- The different types of credit accounts
- Legislation affecting credit

Discussion Starter

The Importance of Warranties Explain to students that a warranty is a promise or guarantee given to a customer that a product will meet certain standards. Have students suggest ways warranties might help in marketing a product. Display a list of student suggestions for the class to read. Possible suggestions: Warranties can reassure consumers that products will perform as advertised, that consumers are spending their money wisely, and that consumers will not be burdened with unexpected repair bills. In situations where consumers see competing products as being similar in terms of quality and features, a strong warranty can set one product apart from another.

DECA Connection

Discuss the performance indicators listed in the DECA Connection feature. Explain to students that performance indicators tell them how to demonstrate their acquired skills and knowledge through individual or team competitive events.

Competitive Events Workbook For more DECA Role Plays, send students to the Online Learning Center to download the Competitive Events Workbook.

PROGRAM RESOURCE ORGANIZER

PRINT RESOURCES

- **Student Edition**
- **Teacher Edition**
- **Student Activity Workbook with Academic Integration** includes worksheets and activities correlated to the text.
- **Mathematics for Marketing Workbook** provides math activities for every unit in the text.

TECHNOLOGY TOOLBOX

- **Connect**
- **ConnectPlus**
- **ExamView Assessment Suite** is a comprehensive solution for creating, administering, and scoring tests.

glencoe.com

Online Learning Center provides a variety of resources to enrich and enhance learning.

SECTION, CHAPTER, AND UNIT RESOURCES

- **Graphic Organizers** for organizing text concepts visually.
- **Digital Nation Activities** and **Green Marketer Activities** extend learning beyond the text features.
- **Career Chatroom Career Profiles** allow students to explore different marketing occupations in depth.
- **After You Read Answer Keys** for students to check their answers.
- **Discovery Project Rubrics** and **Marketing Internship Project Rubrics** for students to evaluate their projects.

PROGRAM RESOURCES

- **Student Activity Workbook with Academic Integration Teacher Annotated Edition** includes annotated answers for the activities and worksheets.
- **Marketing Research Project Workbook** provides a step-by-step approach for students to complete their own marketing research studies.
- **School-to-Career Activity Workbook** helps students relate their class work to on-the-job experience and involves work-site analysis and working with mentors.
- **Competitive Events Workbook** helps prepare students for state and national marketing education competitions.
- **Inclusion in the Marketing Education Classroom** provides teaching resources for working with students with special needs.
- **PowerPoint Presentations** provides visual teaching aids and assessments for this chapter.

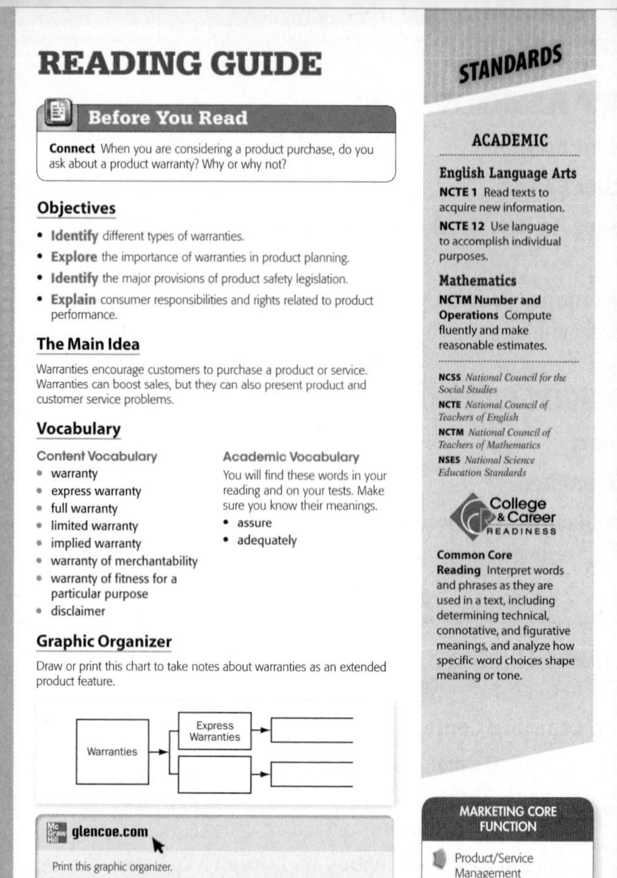
READING GUIDE

Before You Read

Connect When you are considering a product purchase, do you ask about a product warranty? Why or why not?

Objectives

- **Identify** different types of warranties.
- **Explore** the importance of warranties in product planning.
- **Identify** the major provisions of product safety legislation.
- **Explain** consumer responsibilities and rights related to product performance.

The Main Idea

Warranties encourage customers to purchase a product or service. Warranties can boost sales, but they can also present product and customer service problems.

Vocabulary

Content Vocabulary
- warranty
- express warranty
- full warranty
- limited warranty
- implied warranty
- warranty of merchantability
- warranty of fitness for a particular purpose
- disclaimer

Academic Vocabulary

You will find these words in your reading and on your tests. Make sure you know their meanings.
- assure
- adequately

Graphic Organizer

Draw or print this chart to take notes about warranties as an extended product feature.

Warranties → Express Warranties → ; →

glencoe.com

Print this graphic organizer.

STANDARDS

ACADEMIC

English Language Arts

NCTE 1 Read texts to acquire new information.

NCTE 12 Use language to accomplish individual purposes.

Mathematics

NCTM Number and Operations Compute fluently and make reasonable estimates.

NCSS National Council for the Social Studies
NCTE National Council of Teachers of English
NCTM National Council of Teachers of Mathematics
NSES National Science Education Standards

College & Career READINESS

Common Core Reading Interpret words and phrases as they are used in a text, including determining technical, connotative, and figurative meanings, and analyze how specific word choices shape meaning or tone.

MARKETING CORE FUNCTION

Product/Service Management

Section 32.1 Warranties

WARRANTIES

Warranties and guarantees emerged as ways to protect consumer rights. A **warranty** is a promise or guarantee given to a customer that a product will meet certain standards. Typically, these standards apply to materials, workmanship, and performance. A warranty is an extended product feature that is offered after a sale. Warranties often determine the likelihood of repeat sales.

A *guarantee* is another term for warranty. A guarantee is generally provided by manufacturers, while the majority of warranties are provided by retailers or distributors. The major difference between a guarantee and a warranty is the promotional value of the promise. The term *guarantee* (or *guaranteed*) is usually used in conjunction with promotional phrases, such as *money-back guarantee, results guaranteed, guaranteed for 1,000 hours of use,* or *satisfaction guaranteed.*

A warranty, on the other hand, is usually framed as a series of specific promises. An example is a statement such as the following: "Norm's Body Shop will repair any defects in workmanship billed on the repair invoice unless caused by or damaged from unreasonable use, maintenance, or care of the vehicle, excluding paint work if the vehicle's original finish is defective."

Typical warranties set time or use limits for coverage and restrict the seller's liability. The most familiar language is usually found in auto warranties: "Warranty ends at 36 months or 36,000 miles, whichever occurs first."

As You Read

Analyze Why are warranties and guarantees both essential components of product and service planning?

WARRANTIES AND PRODUCT PLANNING

Warranties are an important element of product planning because they help increase sales and profits. Businesses are not required by law to issue warranties. However, most do issue warranties to **assure** their customers that their products and services meet quality standards.

> "Retailers view warranties as a way to increase profits without sacrificing shelf space."

Customers often make purchasing decisions based on warranties and the coverage provided. Many customers perceive longer warranty coverage periods for products to imply better quality over similar products that have shorter warranty periods.

For some companies, such as car makers, warranties play a prominent role in their product advertising. Warranties are also significant to businesses for the following reasons:

- They direct a company to focus on customer satisfaction.
- They require a company to adhere to performance standards.
- They generate customer feedback.
- They encourage quality in product development.
- They boost promotional efforts.

Warranties come in two different forms: express and implied. These forms, in turn, each include specific types.

ENGAGE

Anticipation Activity

Improving Student Achievement Remind students that product features can be the physical attributes of a product. Discuss that products also can have extended features. Have students brainstorm ways a product's features can be extended.

Objectives

- **Identify** different types of warranties. express warranties (full and limited warranties); implied warranties (warranties of merchantability, warranties of fitness); extended warranties
- **Explore** the importance of warranties in product planning. They help increase sales and profits.
- **Identify** the major provisions of product safety legislation. Products must be safe, adequately labeled, properly advertised.
- **Explain** consumer responsibilities and rights related to product performance. Consumers are responsible for reading and following all safety instructions provided with the product. Consumers can sue manufacturers when the warranty terms of a product are not met.

Graphic Organizer

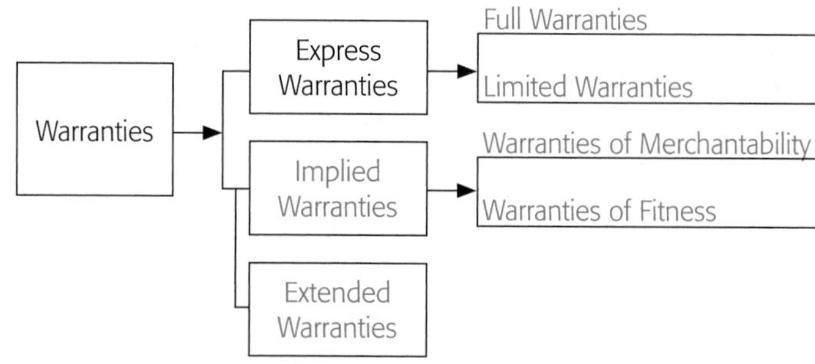

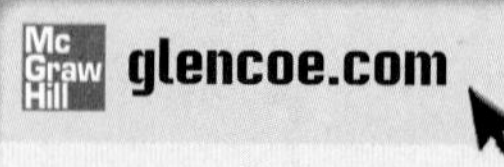

iWB

Graphic Organizer Send students to the Online Learning Center to print this graphic organizer.

EXPLORE

Before You Read

Read the question aloud: ***When you are considering a product purchase, do you ask about a product warranty? Why or why not?*** Sample answer: I ask about warranties when I'm buying an expensive item, such as an electronic gadget or a sports accessory, because I want to make sure that it will work. If it breaks or doesn't work, I want to be able to return it to the store.

Preteaching Vocabulary

Have students go to the Online Learning Center at glencoe.com for the Chapter 32 Preteaching Vocabulary games.

Content Vocabulary
Warranty means "a guarantee that a product will meet certain standards." Display these terms: *express warranty*, *full warranty*, *limited warranty*, and *implied warranty*. Have each student look up one of the adjectives used with the terms, and based on its meaning, write a definition for that term. Ask for volunteers to read their definitions. Sample answer: One meaning for *express* is "explicitly stated," so an express warranty is one that explicitly states what is covered.

Academic Vocabulary
Assure—Synonyms Display the word *assure* and ask: ***What are some synonyms for* assure?** promise, reassure, ensure, guarantee Point out that some of these words contain the word *sure*, which means "marked by or given to feelings of certainty."

Adequately—Usage Read this sentence: ***Products must be safe, adequately labeled, and properly advertised.*** Tell students that *adequate*, when used as an adjective, means "sufficient to meet a need." Ask students to volunteer to read sentences using *adequately* as an adverb. Sample answer: She didn't adequately prepare for the test, so she got a poor grade.

Graphic Organizer

Display this graphic organizer to explain how warranties came into being. Explain that warranties help assure consumers that they will get their money's worth when buying a product.

Cause		Effect
Consumers often had no recourse when products and services did not live up to their promises	→	Companies began issuing warranties

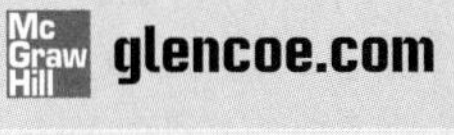

Graphic Organizer Send students to the Online Learning Center to print this graphic organizer.

Warranties

WARRANTIES

Explain that warranties are considered extended product features because they are not physical components. Ask these questions.

Guiding Questions

Recall What is the purpose of a warranty?	A warranty protects the rights of the consumer.
Summarize What are some ways in which warranties help businesses?	Warranties make a company focus on performance and customer satisfaction and also generate feedback, encourage quality, and boost promotional efforts.
Contrast What is the primary difference between a guarantee and a warranty?	A guarantee contains a promotional phrase such as "satisfaction guaranteed." Warranties contain specific promises such as "We will repair any defects."

As You Read

Read students the As You Read question: ***Why are warranties and guarantees both essential components of product and service planning?*** Without warranties and guarantees, consumers would not be sure they had any recourse if a product did not perform as promised. However, because of their reassurances, warranties and guarantees boost the likelihood consumers will make purchases, increasing a business's sales and profits. Describe a scenario in which students must purchase a new coat or a smartphone. Each costs the same amount. Ask: ***Would you rather have a warranty for the coat or for the phone? Why?*** Sample answer: the phone—because of the large number of complex components, electronics are more likely to have defects than clothing.

Expert Advice

"Retailers view warranties as a way to increase profits without sacrificing shelf space."

Ask: ***Why do you think "without sacrificing shelf space" is an important part of this quote?*** Marketers must try to obtain the highest possible profit for each unit of retail space. Anything that can increase profits without taking up room is seen as important.

EXPRESS WARRANTIES

An **express warranty** is one that is clearly stated, in writing or verbally, to encourage a customer to make a purchase. A written warranty must be easily accessible and can appear in a number of places. It may appear on the product packaging, in the product literature, in an advertisement, or as part of a point-of-purchase display. The warranty must always be clearly worded so that customers can easily understand its terms. Some warranties ask customers to submit a product registration card or to register the product online. Spoken warranties, however, even if clearly worded, may not be enforceable unless they are also in writing.

Here is an example of how an express warranty works. A broadcast advertisement shows that a portable MP3 player will operate while the user jogs with it. You purchase the player and discover right away that it shorts out when you jog. You are entitled to whatever relief the warranty specifies. Now imagine that the MP3 package features a photo of a runner using the product in the rain. You found that the product shorts out in the rain. Again, you are entitled to warranty relief because the illustration on the package is equivalent to a promise of performance, even though the promise is not a written one.

Occasionally you may come across a lifetime guarantee. This may sound like a promise for complete product replacement for as long as an individual owns it. However, this is rarely the case. *Lifetime* refers to the amount of time the product is reasonably expected to last. Or, it may refer to the duration of ownership. For example, a muffler shop may offer a lifetime guarantee on a new muffler. The lifetime guarantee only applies as long as the customer owns the vehicle that received the new muffler. Once the vehicle is sold to a new owner, the lifetime guarantee is null and void.

FULL WARRANTY

A **full warranty** is a warranty that covers the repair or replacement of any defect in a product. If the product is found to be defective within the warranty period, it will be repaired or replaced at no cost to the purchaser. A manufacturer who offers a full warranty agrees to repair a defective product "within a reasonable time and without charge." Defective products must be replaced or a full refund offered if the product does not work after a reasonable number of repairs.

4 kids. 11 grandchildren.
9 cars. 2 dogs. 3 remodels. 66 vacations.
1 roof.

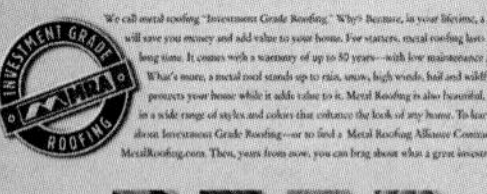

Visit www.MetalRoofing.com

A Roof with Coverage

A 50-year warranty on a metal roof appeals to consumers who want low-maintenance roofing. ***How might a 50-year warranty also boost promotional efforts?***

LIMITED WARRANTY

A **limited warranty** is a written guarantee that may exclude certain parts of the product from coverage or require the customer to bear some of the expense for repairs resulting from defects. For example, a limited warranty could specify that the manufacturer will pay for replacement parts but charge the customer for labor or shipping.

IMPLIED WARRANTIES

Most major consumer purchases are covered by written manufacturer warranties after a purchase for a certain period of time (usually 90 days up to one year). When there are no written warranties, implied warranty laws apply. An **implied warranty** is one that takes effect automatically by state law whenever a purchase is made. There are two types of implied warranties: a warranty of merchantability and a warranty of fitness for a particular purpose.

WARRANTY OF MERCHANTABILITY

A **warranty of merchantability** is the seller's promise that the product sold is fit for its intended purpose. Some examples of sellers' promises are a gasoline-powered lawnmower that will cut the grass and an electric table saw that will cut wood.

WARRANTY OF FITNESS

A **warranty of fitness for a particular purpose** is used when the seller advises a customer that a product is suitable for a particular use, and the customer acts on that advice. A customer, for example, might buy a small truck based on a salesperson's recommendation that it will pull a trailer of a certain weight. The dealership must take back the truck and refund the buyer's money if it turns out that the truck cannot tow the anticipated load.

WARRANTY DISCLAIMERS

Warranties often have disclaimers. A **disclaimer** is a statement that contains exceptions to and exclusions from a warranty.

Businesses use disclaimers to limit damages that can be recovered by a customer. A common type of disclaimer limits recovery to a refund of the purchase price. It can specifically exclude any other costs paid, by the owner as a result of product failure. Another common disclaimer waives customers' rights under implied-warranty laws.

Extended Warranties

Extended warranties are beneficial to businesses and consumers. ***List several consumer benefits of extended service warranties.***

EXPLAIN

EXPRESS WARRANTIES

To focus the discussion on express warranties, ask these guiding questions.

Guiding Questions

Recall True or false: Spoken warranties may not be enforceable.	True (unless they are also in writing)
Draw Conclusions The fan in your home's furnace has failed. The new fan comes with a lifetime guarantee. What does this most likely mean?	The fan is guaranteed for as long as the furnace lasts.
Make Judgments The lifetime-guarantee brakes in your car wore out. The new brakes were free, but you had to pay for installation. What kind of warranty is this?	Limited, because while the brakes were covered, the cost of the labor for their installation was not.

Visual Literacy

A Roof with Coverage Caption Answer Read the caption question to students: ***How might a 50-year warranty also boost promotional efforts?*** Such warranties increase the value of a home when it is sold. Just like having quality physical features, such as high-quality windows and siding, can add to the value of a home, so can having extensive warranties for home components. Ask: ***What other parts of a home might come with warranties?*** Answers may include: siding, windows, furnace and air conditioning units, and some appliances.

Reinforce Vocabulary

Limited Warranty—Connotative Meaning Tell students that for many consumers, the term *limited warranty* has a negative connotation. They become suspicious that the components which are most likely to fail are the ones that will not be covered by the warranty. Explain to students that when purchasing a product with a limited warranty, they should be especially careful to determine what parts are *not* covered by the warranty.

ELABORATE

Visual Literacy

Extended Warranties Caption Answer Read the caption question to students: ***List several consumer benefits of extended service warranties.*** Saves costly repair bills; simplifies making arrangements for a repair; provides access to factory-trained experts; product will be replaced if repair is not possible. Then ask: ***Can you think of any potential disadvantages to extended service warranties?*** The primary disadvantage is that the cost of the extended service warranty may be considerably more than just paying for repairs as needed.

IMPLIED WARRANTIES

Explain to students that implied warranties are established by state law and therefore vary from state-to-state. Ask these guiding questions.

Guiding Questions

Describe Under what conditions do implied warranty laws apply?	when there is no written warranty
Analyze How does a warranty of merchantability protect consumers?	It promises that a product is fit for its intended purpose.
Apply In what type of situation might a seller give a customer a warranty of fitness for a particular purpose?	Responses should state that the seller promised the buyer that the product was suitable for a stated purpose. For example, if the seller states that a particular paint can be used on a plastic table, but it later peels off, the warranty of fitness would not have been met.

Critical Thinking

As you read the sample warranty, ask students to keep the following phrases in mind: (1) promises to repair defects in materials; (2) under certain conditions; and (3) within a certain time period. Then have the class brainstorm limited warranty language for a wireless phone. Sample limited warranty: This product is warranted to be free from manufacturing defects for a period of one year from the date of purchase, subject to the following: that it is not misused and/or taken apart and that it is not used for commercial purposes. This warranty does not cover failure caused by build-up of food matter or water deposits. If this appliance becomes defective under the terms of this one-year warranty, we will repair it free of charge, including materials and labor, or replace it at our nearest Authorized Service Center.

WARRANTY DISCLAIMERS

Ask these questions to focus the discussion on warranty disclaimers.

Guiding Questions

Explain Why do warranties often have disclaimers?	to protect businesses by limiting the damages that can be recovered
Infer Why do warranty disclaimers often limit the company's liability to the cost of the product? What might happen if they did not?	Possible answer: The company wants to limit its liability. Without this disclaimer, consumers might seek compensation for all damages caused by a product failure.

Mini Projects

Enrichment

Comparing Warranties Instruct students to find two products that are similar in features and cost. Have them conduct research to compare the warranties offered with the products. Then have students write a brief paragraph stating whether there are any differences in the warranties, and if there are, whether they think these differences would affect purchasing decisions. Students should compare the warranties offered with two similar products, such as appliances, electronic equipment, or vehicles. Students should evaluate whether they think any differences would affect purchasing decisions.

Interviewing a Consumer about Warranty Experiences Have students interview an adult who has purchased a product or service that did not live up to its warranty. Prior to the interview, students should prepare a list of questions to ask the adult about his or her experience. Sample questions might include: How do you believe the product did not live up to its warranty? Was the warranty clearly written? What did you do when you realized there was a problem? How was the situation resolved? Were you satisfied with the result? Then have students prepare a brief presentation in which they summarize their interview. When students are finished with their presentation, encourage the class to discuss whether they think the manufacturer or retailer handled the situation appropriately. Answers will vary, but should include a description of the situation, the resolution, and the adult's response to the resolution.

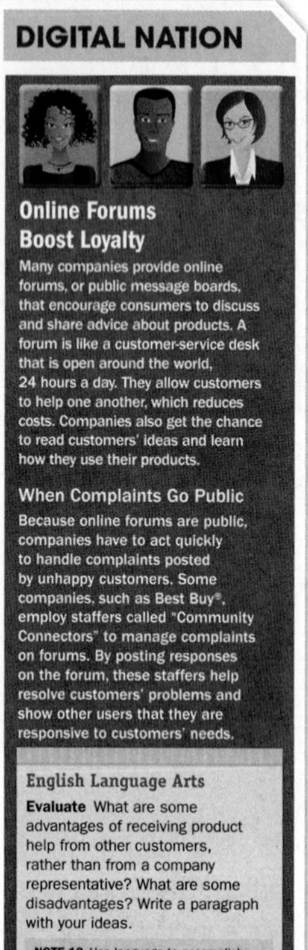

DIGITAL NATION

Online Forums Boost Loyalty

Many companies provide online forums, or public message boards, that encourage consumers to discuss and share advice about products. A forum is like a customer-service desk that is open around the world, 24 hours a day. They allow customers to help one another, which reduces costs. Companies also get the chance to read customers' ideas and learn how they use their products.

When Complaints Go Public

Because online forums are public, companies have to act quickly to handle complaints posted by unhappy customers. Some companies, such as Best Buy®, employ staffers called "Community Connectors" to manage complaints on forums. By posting responses on the forum, these staffers help resolve customers' problems and show other users that they are responsive to customers' needs.

English Language Arts

Evaluate What are some advantages of receiving product help from other customers, rather than from a company representative? What are some disadvantages? Write a paragraph with your ideas.

NCTE 12 Use language to accomplish individual purposes.

glencoe.com

Get a Digital Nation Activity.

EXTENDED WARRANTIES

Extended warranties or service contracts provide repairs or preventive maintenance for a specified length of time beyond a product's normal warranty period. Customers pay extra for this contract at the time of purchase or shortly afterward. Costs range from a few dollars on a low-cost item to hundreds or even thousands of dollars on a higher-priced item, such as a car. There is often a deductible amount, which the customer pays before work is performed.

Extended warranties are beneficial to both businesses and customers. Businesses benefit by receiving additional money (and more profit, if the product performs as expected) on the original sale of a product. Customers benefit from the assurance of long-term satisfaction with their purchase.

There are also disadvantages to service contracts. Some repairs are covered under the standard manufacturer's warranty, so the customer pays for something that is already available. It is also not unusual for customers to forget that they purchased a service contract if service is needed.

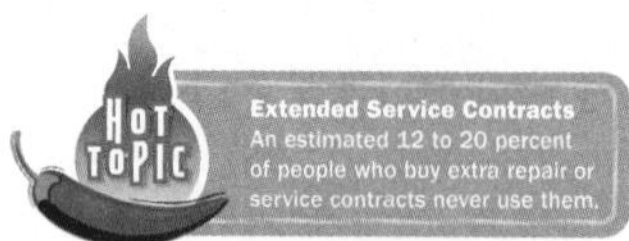
HOT TOPIC
Extended Service Contracts
An estimated 12 to 20 percent of people who buy extra repair or service contracts never use them.

OTHER EXTENDED PRODUCT FEATURES

Product planners may also create extended product features to boost customer satisfaction. These features include delivery, installation, billing, service after the sale, directions for use, technical assistance, and training.

Businesses gain feedback by conducting customer-service and satisfaction surveys. After an initial purchase, customers are frequently asked to submit product registration cards. This is a way to gain customer data and ideas for product and service improvements. If privacy is a concern, read the fine print. In many cases, only minimal information, if any, is required to qualify for warranties.

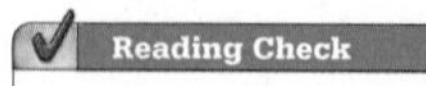

Reading Check

Recall How do warranties affect product planning?

CONSUMER LAWS AND AGENCIES

Businesspeople need a working knowledge of relevant federal, state, and local laws. Manufacturers must be sure that their products meet all legal requirements. Products must be safe, **adequately** labeled, and properly advertised. If they are not, the manufacturer could face fines or product recalls.

Larger companies often employ consumer affairs or legislative specialists to advise management about legal requirements. Smaller companies may join trade associations to stay informed about existing and pending laws that affect their products.

FEDERAL STATUTES

Some products are regulated by more than one agency. Making sure products meet all federal product safety standards is an important function of product planning. For example, cars and trucks have their emission standards set by the Environmental Protection Agency (EPA). Their price stickers are regulated by the Federal Trade Commission (FTC). Any potentially dangerous design flaws are investigated by the National Highway Traffic Safety Administration.

MAGNUSON-MOSS CONSUMER PRODUCT WARRANTY ACT

Many of the warranty features have their origins in a federal statute—the Magnuson-Moss Consumer Product Warranty Act of 1975. This statute governs written warranties for all consumer products costing $15 or more. It sets minimum standards for such warranties, rules for making them available before a product is sold, and provisions for lawsuits against manufacturers if a warranty is not fulfilled. The FTC enforces this act.

CONSUMER PRODUCT SAFETY ACT

Other federal statutes help to protect consumers by requiring companies to manufacture and sell safe products. The Consumer Product Safety Act of 1972, for example, established the Consumer Product Safety Commission (CPSC). This agency monitors the safety of more than 15,000 nonfood items, including toys; household, outdoor, sports, recreation, and specialty products; and appliances. The agency issues standards for the construction, testing, packaging, and performance of these products. When the CPSC finds any product defective or dangerous, it can:

- Issue a product safety alert.
- Require warning labels on the product.
- Recall the product and order repairs.
- Withdraw the product or prohibit its sale.

Since its inception, the CPSC has recalled more than 5,000 products. CPSC studies have found that less than 5 percent of recalled toys, 60 percent of child safety seats, and 90 percent of major appliances are returned for repairs and replacement. Notices for unsafe products are communicated through the media and placed in all U.S. Postal Service offices.

CONSUMER PRODUCT SAFETY IMPROVEMENT ACT

High lead-content paint used in children's toys imported into the United States and other product safety issues led to the passage of the Consumer Product Safety Improvement Act of 2008. This law requires third-party testing of children's products (used by children 12 years of age or younger) including toys, cribs, small parts, baby bouncers, walkers, and strollers.

FOOD, DRUG, AND COSMETIC ACT

The Food, Drug, and Cosmetic Act of 1938 is a federal statute designed to ensure that products are "safe." Safe, in this case, means pure, wholesome, and effective. This law covers features such as informative labels and truthful advertising. The Food and Drug Administration is responsible for the safety of drugs, medical devices, foods, and some food supplements. It also enforces the act. The agency regulates the advertising and sale of imported and exported items. These items include foods, drugs, cosmetics, medical devices, animal drugs, animal feed, and products that emit radiation.

756 | Unit 10 · Product and Service Management

Chapter 32 · Extended Product Features | 757

EXPLAIN

DIGITAL NATION

English Language Arts Answer Instruct students to write a paragraph discussing some of the advantages and disadvantages of receiving product help from other consumers, rather than from a company representative. Advantages might include that customers are more likely to be receptive to ideas from fellow consumers; sharing ideas builds a sense of community; and encouraging consumers to help each other saves the company money. A disadvantage may be that some ideas are poorly thought out or simply incorrect.

glencoe.com

Worksheet Activity Send students to the Online Learning Center to get a Digital Nation worksheet activity.

Critical Thinking

Ask students: ***What does the term* quality control *mean?*** Quality control is a system that makes certain manufactured products meet specified requirements Lead a discussion about why product warranties would encourage quality control. Possible answer: It is less expensive for a company to produce a quality product than to repair or replace a defective one.

HOT TOPIC

Extended Service Contracts Read this statement to the students: ***An estimated 12 to 20 percent of people who buy extra repair or service contracts never use them.*** Ask: ***Why do you think this is?*** Then ask: ***What does this fact mean to the company?***

ELABORATE

EXTENDED WARRANTIES

Discuss with students that many companies offer extended warranties on major purchases such as cars, electronic devices, and appliances. To focus the discussion on extended warranties, ask these questions.

Guiding Questions

Explain Why are extended warranties also called service contracts?	For a fee, they provide for repairs and preventive maintenance for a specified length of time beyond the normal warranty period.
Analyze Why do you think companies offer extended warranties?	Companies typically make money from them because the cost of the warranties is greater than the cost of supplying the required maintenance and repair services.
Apply Imagine that you are buying a tablet computer. The salesperson encourages you to buy the extended warranty. Would you? Why or why not?	Sample answer: No, because the computer already comes with a basic warranty, and the computer probably won't fail until after the extended warranty expires.

OTHER EXTENDED PRODUCT FEATURES

Ask these questions to focus discussion on other extended features.

Guiding Questions

Recall What extended product features, other than warranties, do product planners frequently offer?	free delivery, installation, service after the sale, directions for use, technical assistance, and training
Analyze How might product planners use the information customers provide on product registration cards?	They can get ideas for product and service improvements, and they can obtain data about who is buying their products.

Reading Check Answer

Read the Reading Check question to students: ***How do warranties affect product planning?*** When product planning includes the creation of a well-written warranty, consideration of features and services can significantly increase sales and profits.

Graphic Organizer

Reviewing the Duties of the FDA AND CPSC To remind students of the duties of the FDA and the CPSC, display this Venn diagram and ask students to fill it in. Answers are shown in the diagram below.

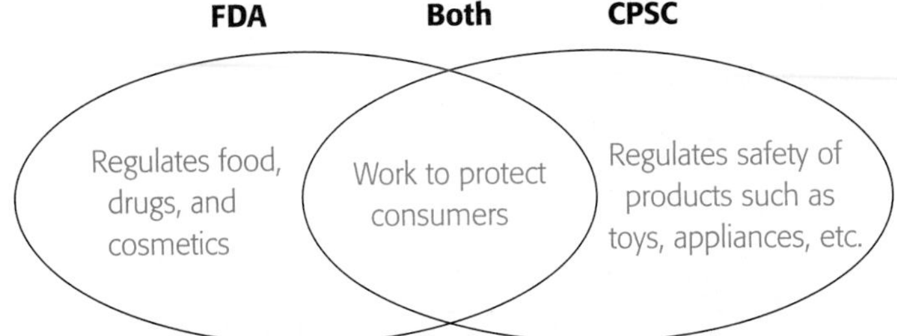

Graphic Organizer Send students to the Online Learning Center to print this graphic organizer.

CONSUMER LAWS AND AGENCIES

To focus discussion on consumer laws, ask these guiding questions.

Guiding Questions

Recall What are three ways vehicles are regulated by the federal government?	EPA: emissions standards; FTC: price stickers; National Highway Traffic Safety Administration: design flaws
Analyze What might a small company do to make sure it complies with laws that apply to its products?	It might join trade associations that help members stay informed about existing and pending laws.

Mini Project

Enrichment

Making a Public Service Announcement for a Product Recall Have student pairs research a recent product recall and create a public service announcement explaining it. These PSAs should state the product(s) being recalled, the reason for the recall, and how consumers should proceed. Have students present their announcements to the class. Students PSAs will vary but should explain the details of a product recall that has occurred in the past few years. Recalled products may include vehicles, parts, toys, food, or medicine.

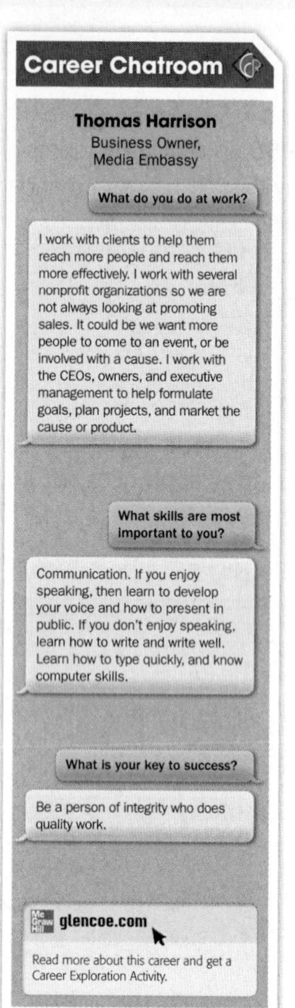

Career Chatroom
Thomas Harrison
Business Owner,
Media Embassy
What do you do at work?
I work with clients to help them reach more people and reach them more effectively. I work with several nonprofit organizations so we are not always looking at promoting sales. It could be we want more people to come to an event, or be involved with a cause. I work with the CEOs, owners, and executive management to help formulate goals, plan projects, and market the cause or product.
What skills are most important to you?
Communication. If you enjoy speaking, then learn to develop your voice and how to present in public. If you don't enjoy speaking, learn how to write and write well. Learn how to type quickly, and know computer skills.
What is your key to success?
Be a person of integrity who does quality work.
glencoe.com
Read more about this career and get a Career Exploration Activity.

STATE STATUTES

The most common form of state consumer protection regulation affects service businesses. Most states require certain individuals to meet training requirements. For example, many health-care professionals must be licensed or state certified before legally practicing in those professions. The process usually involves testing and payment of a fee.

LEMON LAWS

Nearly all states have lemon laws to protect customers. Lemon laws are statutes designed to protect consumers from poorly built cars. Under most lemon laws, a car is a lemon if it is out of service at least 30 days during the first year of ownership, or if four attempts have been made to fix the same problem. Lemon owners are entitled to a refund or a comparable replacement car.

Many states have incorporated arbitration programs into their lemon laws. In arbitration, an impartial third party decides if the vehicle is a lemon and the amount of the refund. In most cases, the arbitrator's ruling is not binding on the parties. The owner can sue the carmaker if he or she is not satisfied with the outcome. The benefit of arbitration is that it saves all parties the delays and costs often associated with a lawsuit.

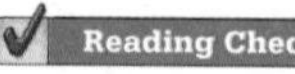

Reading Check

Define What is the Consumer Product Safety Act?

CONSUMER RIGHTS AND RESPONSIBILITIES

Consumers can take several steps when they have not been adequately protected by a warranty:

- Contact the business via phone, letter, or e-mail.
- Contact the local, state, or federal offices that can assist with consumer complaints.
- Take legal action if all else fails.

Consumers can sue manufacturers or retailers on at least three grounds: breach of federal law (written warranty), breach of state law (implied warranty), and negligence. *Negligence* means failure to take proper or reasonable care. When a company does not fulfill its warranty or shows carelessness, consumers have the right to go to court.

Courts have held manufacturers, retailers, and food suppliers liable for defects in products or when injury or illness is caused by use of the product. Class action suits are lawsuits filed by more than one party. It is estimated that Bridgestone/Firestone® spent more than $1.5 billion in product recalls and legal fees on cases related to SUV rollover accidents.

Products should be tested thoroughly. Manufacturers should pay attention to product and package design and provide warnings on the package and labels about any potential hazards. When a manufacturer suspects a problem with a product, it may be more cost effective to recall that product than to risk liability and a damaged reputation.

Private distributors can limit their liability by questioning manufacturers before accepting a product for sale. They should obtain the manufacturer's test data and determine the company's ability to stand behind the product before it is put on store shelves.

Businesses should encourage their customers to be responsible consumers and remind them of their duty to be informed. Customers are responsible for reading and following the safety directions provided with products. This is especially important with items for children, such as car seats, cribs, and toys.

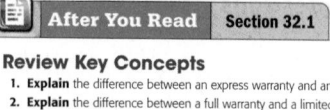

After You Read **Section 32.1**

Review Key Concepts

1. **Explain** the difference between an express warranty and an implied warranty.
2. **Explain** the difference between a full warranty and a limited warranty.
3. **Describe** a warranty disclaimer.

Practice Academics

English Language Arts

4. Select a household item such as an appliance, electronic device, or other item that comes with a warranty. Write a one-page paper that identifies the product, type of warranty (full or limited), the terms of the warranty, and whether or not the warranty is appropriate for this type of product.

NCTE 1 Read texts to acquire new information.

Mathematics

5. You work for a telecommunications company that has an annual marketing budget of $3,560,700. The company spent a total of $1,250,420 on print ads that include a written warranty for service. What percentage of the total marketing budget was spent on the ads? (Round your answer to the nearest whole percent.)

NCTM Number and Operations Compute fluently and make reasonable estimates.

Math Concept **Percents** A percent problem compares a part to a whole. Percent can be determined by using division.

Starting Hints To solve this problem, divide the amount spent on print ads, $1,250,420, by the total amount of money in the marketing budget. This gives you the equivalent decimal value. Multiply the decimal value by 100 to get the percent.

For help, go to the **Math Skills Handbook** located at the back of this book.

glencoe.com

Check your answers.

ELABORATE

STATE STATUTES

Ask these guiding questions to focus the discussion on state statutes related to consumer protection.

Guiding Questions

Recall Why do states require that certain professionals, such as dental hygienists and hairdressers, be licensed or state certified?	States do this to protect consumers from untrained or unqualified service providers.
Recall Why do most states include arbitration programs in lemon laws?	They can save the delays and costs often associated with lawsuits.
Infer What events do you think led to the passage of state lemon laws?	Consumer complaints to state legislators that manufacturers and/or dealers were not handling problems with new cars to the consumers' satisfaction.

Career Chatroom

Focus the Career Chatroom discussion by asking students these guiding questions.

Guiding Questions

Explain Why is communication so important in Harrison's job?	Because he works with clients to help them reach their audiences.
Infer Why do you think integrity is an important key to success?	Because then clients will trust you and then keep coming back.

glencoe.com

Career Exploration Send students to the Online Learning Center to find more information about this career and to get a Career Exploration activity.

EVALUATE

Mini Project

Differentiated Instruction

Writing an Essay on Teacher Certification Ask students why states require teachers to be certified. Possible answer: to make certain teachers meet certain basic requirements, such as level of education. Have students research what *certified* means. Possible answer: to state or confirm that something is true. Then have students write essays defending their answer to this question: ***If an individual is certified, does that mean the person is a good teacher?*** Essays should state whether students believe state certification means an individual is a good teacher and provide specific reasons why or why not.

Critical Thinking

Ask: ***Why do you think statutes designed to protect consumers from poorly built cars are called "lemon laws" and not "orange laws" or "apple laws"?*** One definition of *lemon* is "an unsatisfactory or defective product." This likely comes from the lemon's sour taste.

Reading Check Answer

Read the question to students: ***What is the Consumer Product Safety Act?*** This act established the Consumer Product Safety Commission, which monitors the safety of non-food items such as toys, sports and recreation products, and appliances

CONSUMER RIGHTS AND RESPONSIBILITIES

Ask these questions to focus on consumer rights and responsibilities.

Guiding Questions

Recall What steps should you take if you think you have not been adequately protected by a product or service warranty?	(1) Contact the business; (2) Contact government agencies that assist consumers; (3) If all else fails, take legal action.
Infer What might be an advantage to being part of a class action suit rather than suing a manufacturer individually?	Class action suits can reduce legal costs and increase credibility because of the number of people involved.

After You Read Section 32.1

Review Key Concepts

1. An express warranty is a warranty that is clearly stated, either in writing or verbally, to encourage a customer to make a purchase. An implied warranty is one that takes effect automatically by state law when a purchase is made.
2. A full warranty is one that completely covers the repair or replacement of any defect in a consumer product. A limited warranty may exclude certain parts of the product from coverage or require the customer to bear some of the expense for repairs resulting from defects.
3. A warranty disclaimer is a statement that contains exceptions to and exclusions from a warranty.

Practice Academics

English Language Arts

4. Students should write a one-page paper in which they discuss a specific product, the type of warranty it comes with, the terms of the warranty, and whether the warranty is appropriate for this type of product. For example, a GE® 22-cubic-foot refrigerator with bottom freezer comes with a one-year limited warranty that covers functional parts and labor costs, but does not cover food spoilage. An extended warranty for up to 15 years is available at an additional cost. It covers functional parts and labor costs and includes a $100 allowance for food spoilage.

Mathematics

5. 35% ($1,250,420/$3,560,700)

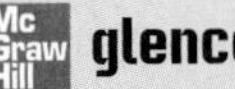

glencoe.com

Answer Key Send students to the Online Learning Center to check their answers.

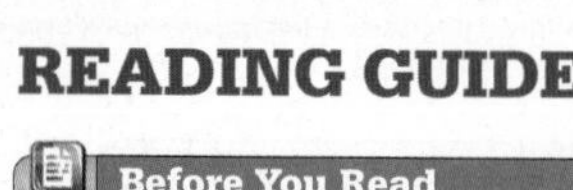

READING GUIDE

Before You Read

Predict What might happen if consumers could not use credit cards to pay for purchases?

Objectives

- **Describe** the importance of credit.
- **Explain** various sources of consumer credit.
- **Identify** the types of credit accounts extended to consumers.
- **Discuss** how businesses use trade credit.

The Main Idea

Extending credit to customers and accepting credit cards for purchases are important to product planning. Using credit wisely can benefit a business and its customers.

Vocabulary

Content Vocabulary
- credit
- 30-day accounts
- installment accounts
- revolving accounts
- budget accounts

Academic Vocabulary

You will find these words in your reading and on your tests. Make sure you know their meanings.
- exceeded
- enable

Graphic Organizer

Draw or print this chart to take notes about the features of credit.

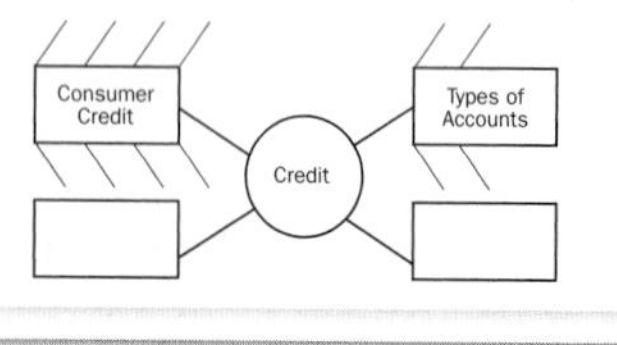

Print this graphic organizer.

STANDARDS

ACADEMIC

English Language Arts

NCTE 1 Read texts to acquire new information.

Mathematics

NCTM Problem Solving Apply and adapt a variety of appropriate strategies to solve problems.

NCTM Problem Solving Solve problems that arise in mathematics and in other contexts.

NCSS *National Council for the Social Studies*
NCTE *National Council of Teachers of English*
NCTM *National Council of Teachers of Mathematics*
NSES *National Science Education Standards*

Common Core
Reading Determine central ideas or themes of a text and analyze their development; summarize the key supporting details and ideas.

MARKETING CORE FUNCTION

Product/Service Management

Section 32.2 Credit

CREDIT AND ITS IMPORTANCE

Credit is essentially loaned money, providing the opportunity for businesses or individuals to obtain products or money in exchange for a promise to pay later. Credit allows most consumers to make major purchases, such as homes, automobiles, appliances, furniture, and recreational vehicles.

Consumers also use credit to make less costly purchases, such as meals, clothing, groceries, and movies. Credit cards are convenient, easy to use, and more secure than carrying cash. However, if credit cards are not managed carefully, it can be easy for consumers to lose track of spending.

The use of credit is essential to the United States and global economies. Federal Reserve Board and U.S. Census data indicate that the average American adult carries more than $3,752 in revolving debt (mainly credit cards), and average household debt exceeds $7,394.

As You Read

Connect What are the advantages and disadvantages of using credit for purchases?

THE ROLE OF CREDIT

Businesses and consumers alike use credit to purchase goods and services. Credit is also used between manufacturers, wholesalers, and retailers to buy materials, equipment, supplies, and services for their businesses or to sell to other businesses.

Millions of people and thousands of businesses would not be able to buy necessary goods and services without credit. By extending credit to its customers, a business provides an incentive to purchase and enhances its sales and profits.

CONSUMER CREDIT

Companies that offer credit, such as banks, retail stores, and oil companies, typically issue credit cards. Federal Reserve surveys indicate that about 75 percent of U.S. households have at least one credit card. However, the average cardholder has about 3.5 credit cards.

> "Does a credit card offering $10,000 of credit sound better than one offering $10,000 of debt?"

Customers fill out credit applications to provide information about their sources of income and credit history. If they meet the company's lending requirements, they receive a credit card and agree to a credit contract that establishes the rules governing the use of the card. These rules include interest rates on outstanding balances. Consumers should read the fine print carefully. Frequently, the card issuers include disclaimers that allow them to change the terms at any time.

Credit cards are issued with credit limits based on customers' ability to pay, their payment histories, and credit score (see **Figure 32.1** on page 762). A credit limit is a preapproved dollar amount. Customers can accumulate balances up to that amount. Credit limits can range from as little as $500 for first-time cardholders to thousands of dollars.

Purchases made by credit cards go through a computerized preapproval process prior to the purchase. This assures the store or company that a customer has not **exceeded** his or her credit limit.

ENGAGE

Anticipation Activity

Improving Student Achievement Ask students to brainstorm two lists: The first list should be things people often buy on credit. Sample answers: houses, cars, appliances The second list should be things that businesses buy on credit. Sample answers: manufacturing materials, products for resale

Objectives

- **Describe** the importance of credit. Credit allows consumers and businesses to obtain goods and services when they need them rather than waiting until they can pay the full amount.
- **Explain** various sources of consumer credit. bank credit cards, store and gasoline credit cards, travel and entertainment cards, secured and unsecured loans
- **Identify** the types of credit accounts extended to consumers. regular, installment, revolving, budget
- **Discuss** how businesses use trade credit. to buy goods and services where payment terms are agreed upon by both parties

Graphic Organizer

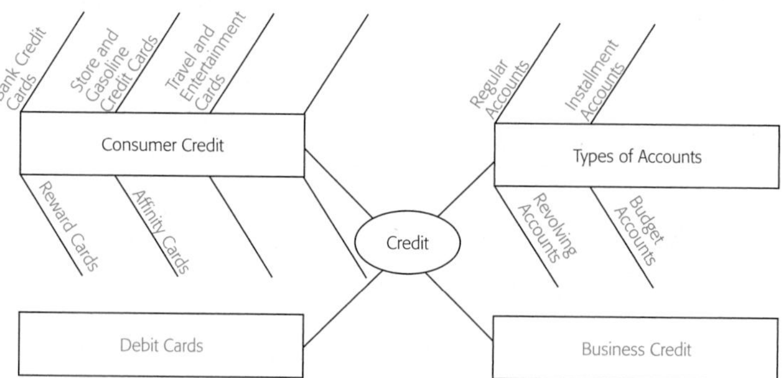

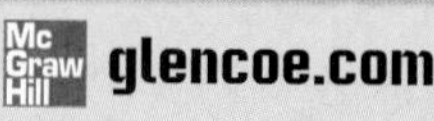

Graphic Organizer Send students to the Online Learning Center to print this graphic organizer.

EXPLORE

Before You Read

Read the Before You Read question aloud: ***What might happen if consumers could not use credit cards to pay for purchases?*** Consumers would have to wait until they could pay cash. For example, if a refrigerator quit working, a consumer would not be able to purchase a new one if the needed cash was not available. Extending credit encourages consumers to make purchases now instead of later, which can help increase a business's profits.

Preteaching Vocabulary

Have students go to the Online Learning Center at glencoe.com for the Chapter 32 Preteaching Vocabulary games.

Content Vocabulary

Display the word *credit* for the class to read. Discuss that the word *credit* can have several meanings. For example, it can mean "acknowledgement of work done," as in the sentence: ***She received credit for writing that report.*** However, in business the word *credit* often refers to borrowed money, as in the sentence: ***He purchased the car on credit.*** Read aloud the remaining Content Vocabulary terms. Discuss that each term refers to a type of credit account that students will learn about in this section.

Academic Vocabulary

Exceeded—Alternate Meanings Display the word *exceeded* for the class to read. Explain that two meanings of exceeded are "was superior to" or "gone over the limit of." Read aloud the sentence: ***The customer had exceeded his credit limit.*** Ask students: ***Which of these definitions best fits the use of exceeded in this sentence?*** second one

Enables—Examine Word Components Display the word *enables* for the class to read, and underline the prefix *en-*. Explain that *able* means "having sufficient power, skill, or resources to." Also explain that the prefix *en-* means "cause to be" or "provide with." Ask: ***Based on these definitions, how might you define* enables?** provides sufficient resources to make something possible

PROFESSIONAL DEVELOPMENT **MINI CLIP**

Reading: During and After Reading

Go to the Online Learning Center to view a video clip in which a teacher models reading for her students and then has them practice what a good reader thinks about.

Credit

CREDIT AND ITS IMPORTANCE

Use these guiding questions to focus the discussion about credit.

Guiding Questions

Recall What are some examples of companies that offer credit?	banks, retail stores, oil companies
Analyze Why might a consumer use a credit card to pay for small purchases, such as an $8.00 lunch or a parking fee?	Possible answers: convenience, not having to carry cash, reward points
Draw Conclusions How does a retail store know that a customer has exceeded the limit on a credit card? What will the store do if this happens?	The retail store uses a computerized preapproval process. If there is a problem with the card, the store will refuse to accept it.

As You Read

Read the As You Read question aloud: ***What are the advantages and disadvantages of using credit for purchases?*** Advantages: allows buyer to make purchases when needed and pay later; provides an incentive to make purchases which increases a business's profits; some credit cards provide special incentives, such as frequent flyer miles. Disadvantages: can encourage consumers to overspend; if the balance is not paid in full within the allotted time, consumers must pay interest on the balance.

Expert Advice

Read the quote to students:

“Does a credit card offering $10,000 of credit sound better than one offering $10,000 of debt?”

Ask: ***Why do most people think $10,000 of credit sounds better than $10,000 of debt?*** When you receive credit for something, such as writing a report, you see this as positive, while debt is seen as being or as a burden. Explain that this is why credit card companies send cardholders letters with messages such as "Congratulations! Your credit limit has just been increased!" Credit card companies want customers to feel they are being rewarded for good behavior.

FIGURE 32.1 Credit Scores

Calculating Your Score A credit score is a number usually between 350 (poor) and 850 (excellent). The number represents the risk in lending money and is used to determine credit limits offered to consumers. ***Why are the five categories represented in the chart important factors in determining a credit score?***

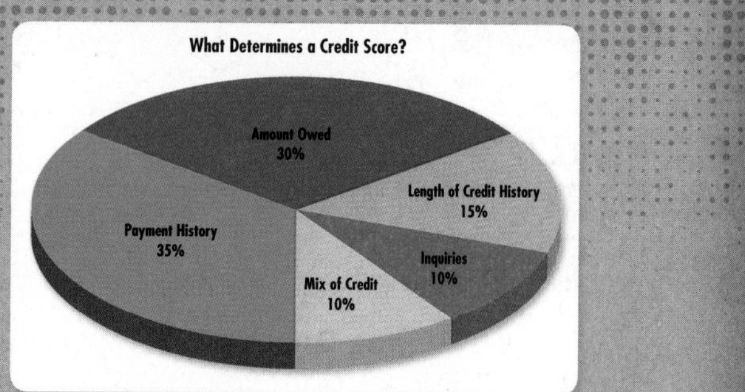

BANK CREDIT CARDS

Banks or their subsidiaries issue bank credit cards. Visa® and MasterCard® sponsor bank credit cards, but these companies do not issue them directly. Banks that issue credit cards set their own fees and interest rates. Examples of such banks are Chase® and Bank of America®.

An annual fee is a flat yearly charge similar to a membership fee. Annual fees vary from card to card, so it is important to comparison shop when deciding on a credit card. Interest rates are tied to other lending rates such as the prime rate or the Treasury bill rate. These are called "variable-rate plans." Other plans, which are not specifically tied to changes in other rates, are called "fixed-rate plans."

Retailers who belong to a bank credit card system either electronically process credit card sales or mail the credit card forms to the bank for payment. First, the bank deducts a service fee from the sale amount. Then it remits the balance to the retailer.

STORE AND GASOLINE CREDIT CARDS

Some businesses are large enough to offer their own credit cards, known as *proprietary* or *house* cards. Examples of national chains that issue credit cards are JC Penney®, Nordstrom®, and Target®.

Examples of gasoline cards are Shell® and Sunoco Rewards® cards. They offer cash rebates on gas purchases at affiliated stations and allow customers to track gasoline purchases separately.

Usually, proprietary cards do not have an annual fee, but they do have high interest rates. A business prefers customers to use proprietary cards because it receives income from finance charges, usually generated from the interest charged. Finance charges on unpaid credit card balances are very expensive. Depending on an applicant's credit history, annual percentage rates (APRs) can range from 13.99 percent to 22.99 percent or more on purchases. Cash advance rates can be as high as 24.99 percent.

TRAVEL AND ENTERTAINMENT CARDS

Travel and entertainment cards, such as American Express®, are issued to pay for airline, hotel, and other business-related expenses. These types of cards are often accepted for other types of goods and services. They have annual fees and service charges, and often require that transaction balances be paid in full each month. Travel and entertainment credit card companies charge retailers higher service fees than credit card companies do for processing the payment. Some businesses choose not to pay these fees, so these cards are not universally accepted.

REWARD CARDS

Reward cards are credit cards that offer some type of reward or incentive to consumers who use them. Rebates, awards, or points are offered when credit purchases are made. These cards are often co-branded and offer rewards in cash, airline miles, hotel discounts, or special offers.

Some reward cards offer special services. For example, the Visa® Signature card shown in the ad below offers benefits such as concierge services and other special offers. Card members can use the Visa Signature concierge service to make travel arrangements, buy event tickets, make restaurant reservations, and arrange for business services.

Individuals who plan to carry balances on a reward credit card should search for a card with the lowest interest rate. Consumers who pay the balance every month may find that reward cards offer the best deal.

AFFINITY CARDS

Affinity cards are credit cards issued by banks to show a consumer's loyalty to a team, school, charity, business, or other organization. The organization solicits its members or customers. The card issuer returns a percentage (usually less than one percent) of the interest to the organization and gives reward points or miles to the customer.

DEBIT CARDS

A debit card is like a mobile automated teller machine (ATM). Consumers authorize the seller to withdraw funds directly from their bank accounts at the time of sale. About 29 percent of all consumer transactions are made with debit cards.

Signature debit cards require a signature on the receipt when you make a purchase. The purchase is processed through a card-processing network like Visa or MasterCard, and money is deducted from the user's account in a couple of days.

Credit Card Rewards

This ad describes the benefits Visa Signature card members can get when staying at certain hotels. ***What target markets might be particularly interested in the special features of this particular credit card?***

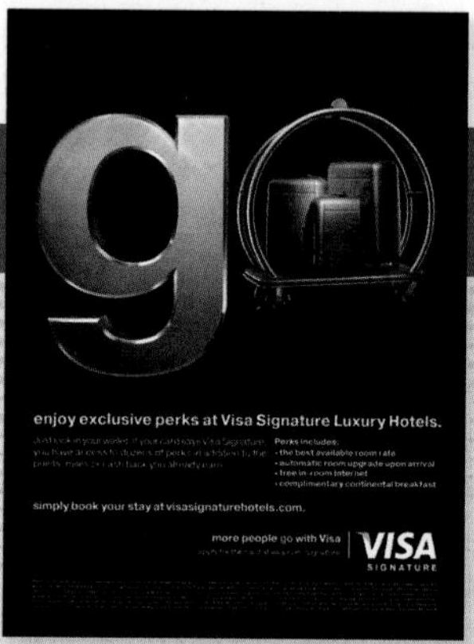

EXPLAIN

Figure 32.1 Caption Answer Read the caption question to students: ***Why are the five categories represented in the chart important factors in determining a credit score?*** Each influences the likelihood that a consumer will pay debts on time. Use these guiding questions to discuss credit scores in more detail.

Guiding Questions

Analyze Why do you think "Payment History" makes up the largest percentage?	If consumers have paid their debts in the past, they are likely to do so in the future.
Draw Conclusions What do you think would be covered in the category "Mix of Credit"?	Possible answers: different categories of cards, other secured and unsecured loans.
Summarize Based on this pie chart, what would you suggest that a person do if they wanted to raise their credit score?	Always make payments on time, and try to decrease the amount of money owed.

BANK CREDIT CARDS

Tell students that bank cards are the most common kind of credit card. Use these questions to focus the discussion on bank credit cards.

Guiding Questions

Recall Who sets the fees and interest rates for a bank credit card?	the bank that issues the card
Analyze If all consumers paid off their credit card balances every month, would banks still be able to make money from their credit cards? If so, how?	Yes, because banks charge retailers a service fee, and some banks also require their cardholders to pay a yearly service fee.
Infer Why might a bank offer a variable-rate plan rather than a fixed-rate plan?	Because the bank's interest rate will vary depending on the current cost of borrowing money, the bank's profit will remain the same (assuming the markup is unchanged).

ELABORATE

Critical Thinking

Discuss with students that some credit card companies promote their cards as status symbols. For example, American Express® offers tiers of membership: the green card, the gold card, the platinum card, the blue card, and the Centurion Card (offered by invitation only). Ask students: ***Why do you think some companies want consumers to see these cards as status symbols?*** Sample answers: It makes them feel special; they want others to recognize their affluence or importance; they enjoy the privileges that come with certain types of cards. Then ask students: ***Besides the prestige of carrying a special credit card, what other benefits might the cardholder enjoy?*** Possible answers: special product offers and special services, such as exclusive discounts, concierge services, tickets to popular concerts or sporting events, or preferred seating at shows Then ask: ***What criteria might credit card companies use to determine whether a customer should be issued a special or hard-to-get credit cards?*** Answer: personal income, credit rating, customer loyalty, past credit history with the credit card company, and purchases made with the credit card

STORE AND GASOLINE CREDIT CARDS

Discuss with students that many larger businesses offer their own credit cards, typically decorated with the company name and logo. To focus the discussion on store and gasoline credit cards, ask students these guiding questions.

Guiding Questions

Recall When retail businesses offer their own credit cards, what are these cards called?	proprietary cards or house cards
Analyze Why does a business prefer that customers use its proprietary card rather than a bank credit card?	The business receives income from the finance charges, usually generated from the interest charged.
Apply A cashier at a discount store tells you that you can save 10 percent on today's purchase if you sign up for the store's proprietary credit card. How would you respond?	Responses will vary. Sample answers: I would say that I have a credit card and do not need another one. I might ask about the annual interest rate, and if it is not lower than my current credit card's rate, I would decline.

Mini Projects

Extension

Creating a Brochure Explaining Credit Scores Tell students they have been assigned the job of developing a brochure that explains how credit scores are determined. Have students use a word processing or page layout program to create an attractively illustrated brochure. The brochure should be written in easy-to-understand language. Encourage students to include a pie chart that illustrates the weight of each credit score component. For example, payment history makes up about 35 percent of the total score. Students should create a clearly written, illustrated brochure explaining credit scores. The brochure might explain that the scores are based on payment history (about 35%), how much is owed (about 30%), length of credit history (about 15%), new credit (about 10%) and other factors (about 10%).

Learning about Credit Scores Have students research agencies that publish credit reports. Instruct them to choose one credit reporting agency and summarize the contents of what is found in a personal credit report from that agency. Have students report on their findings in class and lead a discussion on the uses of consumer credit reports. Students' oral reports will vary depending on the credit reporting agency chosen. For example, a credit report from Equifax contains personal information obtained from credit applications you have filled out; details about credit accounts opened in your name, including balances, dates opened, credit limits, and whether you have made payments on time. It also includes inquiries about the accounts that have been made in the last two years and matters of public record, such as bankruptcies and overdue child support payments.

Visual Literacy

Credit Card Rewards Caption Answer Read the caption question to students: ***What target markets might be particularly interested in the special features of this particular credit card?*** People who travel a lot, especially for business, might be interested in staying at more luxurious hotels than they might otherwise choose. Other consumers might think that the benefits of using this card would offer them the only way they could ever afford such an expensive vacation. Advertising these features encourages consumers to use the card and serves as a reminder of the card's benefits.

PIN type debit cards are scanned electronically at the point of sale. Such transactions require the customer to enter a PIN number. With PIN debit cards the money is deducted from the bank account immediately. Some cards work both ways.

SPECIAL CUSTOMER CARDS

While neither a credit nor a debit card, these special customer cards **enable** customers to receive reward points or a percentage of money back in rewards on purchases made at sponsoring stores. Examples of these cards include Best Buy's Reward Zone® program and the Winn-Dixie® Customer Reward Card. Customers can use the reward points stored on the card for cash discounts, coupons, and prizes on future purchases at the sponsoring store.

SECURED AND UNSECURED LOANS

Loans are also a form of credit. Consumers and businesses can obtain secured loans and unsecured loans to use for the purchase of goods and services.

In secured loans, something of value, such as real estate or property, motor vehicles, machinery, or merchandise, is pledged as *collateral*. Collateral is security used to protect the interests of the lender. The collateral helps to ensure that a loan will be repaid. If the loan is not repaid by the borrower, the lender keeps the pledged collateral items to cover the debt.

Consumers and businesses can also obtain unsecured loans, which represent a written promise to repay a loan. Unsecured loans do not require collateral to protect the interests of the lender. Instead, unsecured loans rely on the excellent credit reputation of the borrower who pledges in writing to repay the loan. In either case, a credit contract is signed to detail payment terms and penalties for not meeting those terms.

TYPES OF CREDIT ACCOUNTS

Four major consumer credit plans are in use today: regular or 30-day accounts, installment accounts, revolving accounts, and budget accounts. The dollar amount a customer pays to use credit is called the "finance charge." A finance charge may include interest costs and other charges associated with transactions.

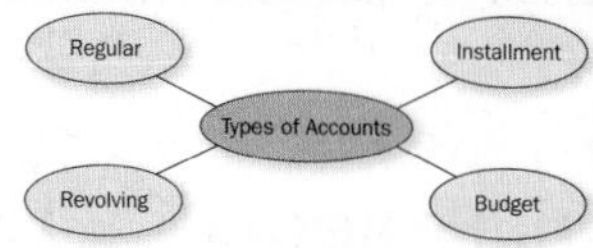

REGULAR

Regular charge accounts, or **30-day accounts**, enable customers to charge purchases during a month and pay the balance in full within 30 days after they are billed. There is no finance charge for this type of plan as long as the bill is paid on time.

INSTALLMENT ACCOUNTS

Installment accounts, or time-payment plans, allow for payment over a period of time. Installment accounts are normally used for large purchases, such as a college education, appliances, cars, furniture, and vacation travel. Installment accounts offer a certain interest rate over a set period of time. Installment accounts sometimes require a down payment and a separate contract for each purchase.

REVOLVING ACCOUNTS

Revolving accounts are charge accounts offered by a retailer that sets the credit limit and payment terms. The minimum payment is usually a certain percentage on the balance owed or a minimum dollar amount, such as $15. The customer can choose to pay more than the minimum payment to reduce the balance owed. An interest charge is added to the unpaid balance for the billing period.

Customers can make purchases up to the credit limit when using a revolving account. Under most credit card arrangements, regular accounts become revolving accounts if the full amount is not paid for the billing period. Most billing cycles are 25-day periods.

BUDGET ACCOUNTS

Budget accounts allow account holders to pay for purchases over a specific period of time without incurring a finance charge. The most common interest-free time period is 90 days, but can be a year or longer. Some retailers who handle expensive products, such as furniture and appliances, offer budget accounts. Budget accounts do not require the customer to pay any interest charges if the amount owed is paid within the interest-free time period. Finance charges are applied if the amount is not paid within the specified time period. Offering budget accounts is a way that a company can stay competitive.

BUSINESS CREDIT

Banks were once the primary source of money to help businesses support their operations. However, banks are now likely to lend only to well-established companies. A business can apply for a line of credit from a bank. This type of loan allows a company to borrow up to a certain amount of money from the bank and pay it back regularly over time. A business may be able to borrow using its assets as security or collateral. If the company does not pay back the loan, the bank can then take away those assets.

Another way that businesses can borrow is more similar to the way consumer credit works. Business credit, or trade credit, involves companies extending loans to other companies. It is a source of short-term financing provided by a company within the same industry. If a company needs certain goods or services, a supplier agrees to deliver them and to allow the company to pay within a certain amount of time.

Imagine you have a business that makes and sells custom team logo apparel to various schools in your area. You need a supply of t-shirts, sweatshirts, hats, and jackets in various colors along with ink and fabric to create the logos. A supplier agrees to let you purchase the materials you need as long as you pay within 90 days after delivery. This arrangement gives you time and money to create, manufacture, and market your products and pay your bill to the supplier out of your sales revenue.

Business or trade credit is similar to consumer credit in that businesses extend loans for goods and services. A supplier sells raw materials, equipment, and inventory to a business that agrees to pay with credit. Unlike consumer credit, trade credit does not involve the use of a credit card. Letters of credit and credit memorandums or drafts are used in trade credit arrangements. The parties involved agree to payment terms.

Reading Check

Analyze What is the difference between consumer and business credit?

WORLD MARKET

FRANCE

Tour de Paris

Cycling has taken Paris by storm. In 2007, the City of Lights rolled out a bicycle-sharing program called *Vélib*—from *velos* for bicycle and *liberté* for liberty. Thousands of bicycles in hundreds of kiosks are stationed every two or three streets for easy pickup and drop-off. Tourists and locals can bypass taxis and the metro by riding bikes throughout the 20 districts of Paris.

24/7 All it takes to become a *Vélibien* is a credit card and a subscription. Subscriptions range from one day at US$1.48 to a year at US$43.02. The first half-hour is free. This service includes online subscription sign-up, 230 miles of bike paths, free 24-hour service, and a Web site with weather forecast.

Mathematics

Compute The *Vélib* program has been a success for the city's finances. If you subscribed for a 10-day stay in Paris, about how much would you pay?

NCTM Problem Solving Solve problems that arise in mathematics and in other contexts.

Here are some entry-level phrases that are used in conversations about marketing all over the world.

English	French
Hello	Bonjour
Goodbye	Au revoir
How are you?	Comment allez-vous?
Thank you	Merci
You're welcome	De rien

EXPLAIN

SECURED AND UNSECURED LOANS

Tell students that lenders make their money by charging people to borrow money, just like retailers make their money by selling products and services. To focus the discussion on secured and unsecured loans, ask these guiding questions.

Guiding Questions

Explain What is the difference between a secured loan and an unsecured loan?	Secured loan: Something of value, such as a car, is pledged as collateral to protect the lender. Unsecured loan: The borrower only provides the lender with a written promise to pay.
Analyze How do lenders attempt to make certain that their unsecured loans will be paid back?	They check to make certain the borrower has an excellent credit reputation.

Graphic Organizer

Display this diagram and discuss the different types of credit accounts. Ask students to name each account type and write it in one of the shapes.

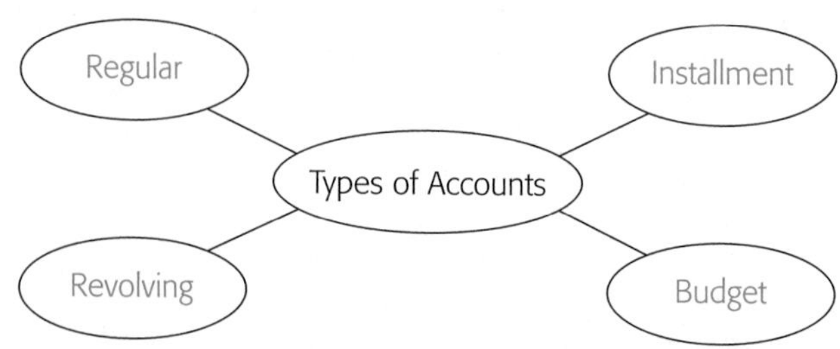

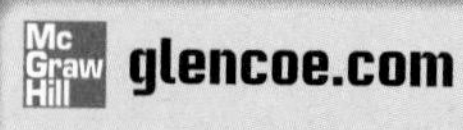

Graphic Organizer Send students to the Online Learning Center to print this graphic organizer.

ELABORATE

TYPES OF CREDIT ACCOUNTS

Ask these guiding questions to discuss the types of credit accounts.

Guiding Questions

Recall Why are regular credit accounts also called 30-day accounts?	The balance must be paid in full within 30 days after billing or finance charges will be added.
Compare and Contrast In what ways are installment and budget accounts similar? How are they different?	While both allow for payment over time, installment accounts charge interest. However, budget accounts do not charge interest if the balance is paid within a specified time period.

Reading Check Answer

Read the Reading Check question to students: ***What is the difference between consumer and business credit?*** Unlike consumer credit, business credit does not involve the use of a card. Trade credit typically involves credit memorandums, letters of credit, and credit drafts.

WORLD MARKET MATHEMATICS

The cost for 10 days would be $14.80 ($1.48 × 10). Use these questions to discuss Vélib in more detail.

Guiding Questions

Analyze Why might people use this service over cars, buses, or trains?	convenience; affordability; flexibility; more eco-friendly than motor vehicles
Predict Do you think this program would work in the U.S.? Why or why not?	Sample answer: No, because cities here are more spread out and less safe for cyclists.

Mini Project

Differentiated Instruction

Logical Learners Have pairs of students conduct a debate for and against credit cards. Instruct students to present the pros and cons discussed in this section. The pro side might state that credit is necessary to our economy; the con side might say it encourages people to live beyond their means.

e MARKETING

Mobile Alerts

Extended product features now include many online services such as mobile alerts. Mobile alerts are messages sent to customers via their mobile phone to tell them about something important. For example, airlines send mobile alerts when there is a change in flight times and banks send mobile alerts when a customer's balance is low or when a direct deposit has been made in the customer's account. Customers can opt in to mobile alerts for the purpose of learning about new products, special promotions, and other offers. Mobile phone companies offer mobile alerts sent by the government in case of terrorist acts, weather disasters, and Amber alerts. Mobile phone customers can opt out from receiving those alerts. Search engine providers, such as Yahoo! and Google offer mobile alerts as well for stock quotes, weather, horoscope information, sports, and a lot more.

Innovate and Create

Discuss how mobile alerts could be considered an extended product feature. Brainstorm ideas on how other businesses could make use of mobile alerts. Answers will vary. Anything that helps create customer satisfaction can be considered an extended product feature. Some possible answers for ideas for businesses' use of mobile alerts are: service providers (i.e., doctors, hair salons) sending mobile alerts to remind customers, clients and patients of appointments; pharmacies could send mobile alerts when it is time to renew a prescription; stores could send mobile alerts when there is a product recall; schools could send mobile alerts for school closings due to inclement weather.

glencoe.com

eMarketing Worksheet Activity Send students to the Online Learning Center to download an eMarketing worksheet activity.

LEGISLATION AFFECTING CREDIT

Federal laws, rules, and regulations are designed to protect consumers, their credit standing, and their rights when using credit. Government regulations require businesses to inform consumers about the use of credit. Businesses must also establish procedures for notification, billing, and debt-collection activities.

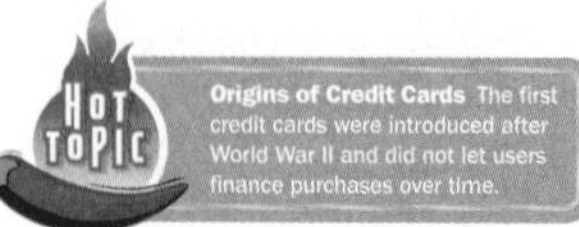

HOT TOPIC
Origins of Credit Cards The first credit cards were introduced after World War II and did not let users finance purchases over time.

The Truth in Lending Act of 1968 requires that lenders disclose information about annual percentage rates, the name of the company extending credit, the amount financed, the total purchase price minus any down payments and taxes, the actual finance charge in dollars, a payment schedule, and late payment penalties.

The Fair Credit Reporting Act of 1971 requires that a lender report the name and address of the credit bureau used when a consumer is denied credit. The act gives consumers the opportunity to check their credit histories for errors that prevent them from obtaining credit.

The Fair Credit Billing Act of 1974 requires lenders to correct billing errors within 90 days of a consumer complaint, limits cardholder liability, and dictates that consumers be given a statement of their credit rights.

The Equal Credit Opportunity Acts of 1975 and 1976 set guidelines for the review of applications for credit. These acts also prohibit discrimination based on age, gender, race, religion, or marital status.

The Fair Debt Collection Practices Act of 1978 establishes required conduct for debt collectors and prevents harassing or abusing customers to collect debts.

MARKETING CASE STUDY

Rewarding Credit

Consumers wanting to avoid credit-card expenses may choose to cut back on charging purchases. However, because rewards credit cards offer incentives, or rewards, many cardholders are inclined to continue using them. Rewards include cash-back rebates, gas rebates, airline tickets, or even gift cards and specialty items.

Reward or Penalty?

The typical rewards card comes with higher interest rates. But the wise consumer will pay off a balance in full before the next bill, so no interest accrues. Also, restrictions usually apply to redeeming rewards. However, newer cards, such as the Capital One® Venture card, streamlined the terms so that redemption is easier. With no limits on when, where, or how to earn miles, no blackout dates, and a simple points formula, the company hopes customers take advantage of the rewards perks.

Mathematics

Compute You earn two mileage points per dollar on purchases charged to your rewards card. You just charged $1,565 for computer equipment. How many miles did you earn?

NCTM Problem Solving Solve problems that arise in mathematics and in other contexts.

The Fair Credit and Charge Card Disclosure Act of 1988 requires credit card issuers to provide information about the costs of credit and charge accounts. This information helps consumers better understand the terms of their credit cards. It is also aimed at preventing card issuers from surprising consumers with hidden fees and other charges.

The Fair and Accurate Credit Transactions Act of 2003 requires businesses to verify identities and addresses before opening accounts to fight identity theft. Consumers can correct errors more easily in their credit files, opt-out of sharing their information for marketing purposes, and are entitled to a free credit report once a year.

The Credit Card Accountability, Responsibility and Disclosure (CARD) Act of 2009 makes significant changes in how consumers access and use their credit cards. It establishes how interest is charged and how interest rates change. It also limits credit card fees and requires a 45-day notice of increases in rates, fees, and finance charges.

The CARD Act requires a creditor to send a bill to a card holder at least three weeks before payment is due on an account. Bills must include details about the length of time needed to pay off the balance. In addition, anyone under the age of 21 must obtain a co-signer or provide proof that the applicant can make payments.

After You Read Section 32.2

Review Key Concepts

1. **Explain** why credit is an important extended product feature.
2. **Discuss** the difference between a credit card and a debit card.
3. **Explain** how travel and entertainment charge cards differ from bank, store, and gasoline credit cards.

Practice Academics

English Language Arts

4. Perform library or online research on how to use credit responsibly. Write a one-page report on how consumers can maintain the best possible credit scores.

NCTE 1 Read texts to acquire new information.

Mathematics

5. Your local grocery store offers "store dollars" for every $100 spent in the store. For every $100 you spend at the grocery store, you earn 5 store dollars. If the average person spends $400 at the grocery store each month, how many months would it take to earn 60 store dollars?

Math Concept **Multi-Step Problems** When solving problems that require multiple steps, make a list of the information given in the problem, as well as the information for which you will be solving. This will make the relationships between what you are looking for and what is given clear.

Starting Hints To solve this problem, divide the average monthly amount spent at the store by $100. Multiply this number by the amount earned in store dollars per $100 spent at the store. This is the number of store dollars earned per month. Divide 60 store dollars by the number of store dollars earned each month to find out how many months it will take.

NCTM Problem Solving Apply and adapt a variety of appropriate strategies to solve problems.

For help, go to the **Math Skills Handbook** located at the back of this book.

glencoe.com

Check your answers.

ELABORATE

Graphic Organizer

Display this graphic organizer. Have students describe each legislative act and write their responses in the correct locations.

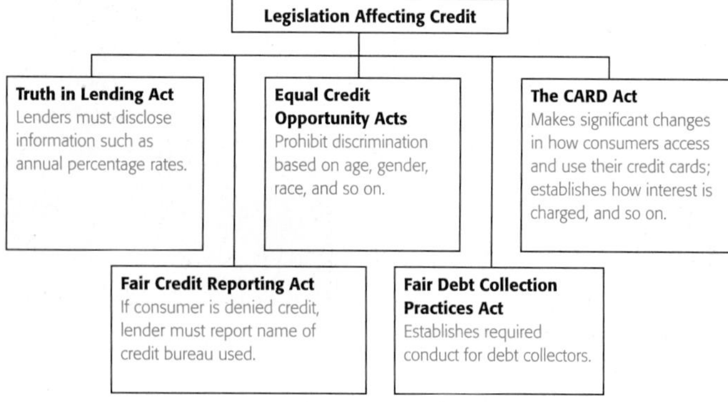

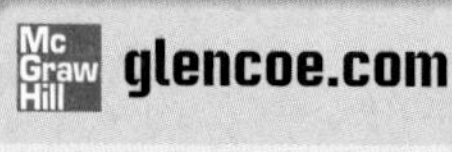

glencoe.com  iWB

Graphic Organizer Send students to the Online Learning Center to print this graphic organizer.

LEGISLATION AFFECTING CREDIT

To focus the discussion on legislation affecting credit, ask these guiding questions.

Guiding Questions

Recall What is the purpose of federal laws and regulations involving credit?	to protect consumers, their credit standings, and their rights when using credit
Analyze Why do you think the Fair Credit Billing Act of 1974 limits a cardholder's liability?	Possible answer: Cardholders may not know that someone is fraudulently using the card, and therefore have no way to stop it.
Synthesize Why are the provisions in the Fair and Accurate Credit Transactions Act of 2003 important to cardholders?	Possible answers: They help to prevent identity theft; consumers can monitor their credit reports without paying a fee.

EVALUATE

Origins of Credit Cards Explain that early credit cards could only be used at the store or gas station that issued them. Ask: ***Why would a business issue this type of card?*** Then ask: ***Why would customers want these proprietary cards if the bill had to be paid in full each month?***

MARKETING CASE STUDY

Mathematics Answer You earned 3,130 miles (1,565 x 2). Use these questions to further discuss this Marketing Case Study.

Guiding Questions

Explain If customers could pay cash, why might they choose to use rewards cards?	to get incentives such as cash-back rebates, free airline tickets, and travel discounts
Apply If you use a rewards card, what should you do to get the most out of it? Why?	You should pay it off each month because it typically carries a high interest rate.

PROFESSIONAL DEVELOPMENT **MINI CLIP**

ELL: Providing Clear Directions
Go to the Online Learning Center to view a video in which a teacher provides clear written and oral directions for a classroom assignment and checks student understanding.

Mini Project

Differentiated Instruction

Cooperative Learners Have students write multiple-choice questions about laws affecting credit. Then ask for volunteers to answer them. Questions should require an understanding of laws designed to protect consumers and regulate creditors.

After You Read Section 32.2

Review Key Concepts

1. Credit is an important extended product feature because it allows most consumers to make major purchases such as homes, automobiles, and appliances when needed in exchange for a promise to pay later. It also makes purchasing less costly day-to-day items more convenient.
2. A credit card is basically a loan. Credit cards are issued with a credit limit based on customers' ability to pay and their payment history. Debit cards allow funds to be withdrawn directly from a checking account and transferred to the place of purchase.
3. Travel and entertainment cards have annual fees, while regular credit cards may or may not have these fees. They often require transaction balances to be paid in full each month, while credit card balances can be paid off over time, but interest is charged on any remaining balance. Travel and entertainment cards also charge retailers higher service fees than regular credit card companies.

Practice Academics

English Language Arts

4. Suggestions may include: try to pay off the card's balance each month and at the least, always make more than the minimum monthly payment; do not open too many cards; live within your means; do not charge items you know you cannot afford; learn to recognize what you truly need and what you simply want.

Mathematics

5. 3 months ($400/$100 = 4; 4 × 5 = 20 store dollars per month; 60 store dollars/20 store dollars per month =3 months)

glencoe.com

Send students to the Online Learning Center to check their answers.

Chapter 32 Visual Summary

Extended Product Features

A product's express or implied warranty can influence a customer's decision to make a purchase. Federal and state laws regulate warranties.

Credit enables businesses or individuals to obtain products or money in exchange for a promise to pay later. There are many forms of consumer credit.

768 | Unit 10 · Product and Service Management

Review and Activities

Written Summary

- Customers often base their purchasing decisions on the availability of warranties.
- Knowledge of relevant federal, state, and local laws regarding warranties is essential for product planning.
- Credit enables businesses or individuals to obtain products or money in exchange for a promise to pay later.
- The use of credit is essential to our economy.
- Government regulations protect consumers and their use of credit.

Review Content Vocabulary and Academic Vocabulary

1. Arrange the vocabulary terms below into groups of related words. Explain why you put the words together.

Content Vocabulary
- warranty (p. 753)
- express warranty (p. 754)
- full warranty (p. 754)
- limited warranty (p. 755)
- implied warranty (p. 755)
- warranty of merchantability (p. 755)
- warranty of fitness for a particular purpose (p. 755)
- disclaimer (p. 755)
- credit (p. 761)
- 30-day accounts (p. 764)
- installment accounts (p. 764)
- revolving accounts (p. 764)
- budget accounts (p. 764)

Academic Vocabulary
- assure (p. 753)
- adequately (p. 757)
- exceeded (p. 761)
- enable (p. 763)

Assess for Understanding

2. **Identify** What are the different types of warranties?
3. **Justify** Why are product warranties important in product planning?
4. **Explain** What are the major provisions of product safety legislation?
5. **Connect** How are consumer responsibilities and rights related to product performance?
6. **Find** What are the sources for consumer and business credit?
7. **Contrast** What are the differences in the types of credit accounts extended to consumers?
8. **Define** What is the definition of the term *disclaimer*?
9. **Process** How do businesses use trade credit?

Chapter 32 · Extended Product Features | 769

EVALUATE

Visual Summary

Express Creativity Ask students to create a visual summary that illustrates a concept in the chapter. Encourage students to use different formats for their visual summaries, such as a table, a cause-and-effect diagram, or a word web. Visual summaries will vary depending on the concept depicted and the visual manner in which it is depicted. Questions to ask when assessing a visual summary include:

- Is the summary clear, economical, and simple?
- Are any important steps or concepts left out?
- Are steps or concepts arranged in the same order as the original?
- Does the summary reveal a pattern that connects the details?
- Does the summary locate and highlight the most important information?

Review Content Vocabulary and Academic Vocabulary

1. Students should arrange vocabulary terms into groups of related words as shown in the examples below:
Warranty: express warranty, full warranty, limited warranty, implied warranty, warranty of merchantability, warranty of fitness for a particular purpose, disclaimer, assure
Credit: 30-day accounts, installment accounts, revolving accounts, budget accounts, exceeded, enables

EVALUATE

Assess for Understanding

2. Different types of warranties include express warranties (including full and limited warranties), implied warranties (including warranties of merchantability and warranties of fitness), and extended warranties.

3. Product warranties are important because a well-written warranty can increase product sales and therefore company profits.

4. Products must be safe, adequately labeled, and properly advertised. If a product is defective or dangerous, a product safety alert may be issued, warning labels may be required, the product may be recalled, or it may be prohibited from being sold.

5. If products do not perform as warranted, consumers can sue manufacturers or retailers on breach of federal law, breach of state law, and negligence. Consumers are responsible for reading and following the safety directions provided with products.

6. Sources for consumer credit include bank credit cards, store and gasoline credit cards, travel and entertainment cards, and secured and unsecured loans. Businesses often borrow money to pay for goods, services, manufacturing supplies, and so on. Trade credit arrangements include credit memorandums, letters of credit, and credit drafts.

7. Regular charge accounts enable customers to charge purchases during a month and pay the balance in full within 30 days after they are billed without a finance charge. Installment accounts allow for payment over a specified period of time. Revolving accounts establish a set credit limit and payment terms. Budget accounts allow for the payment of a purchased item over a certain time period without any finance charges.

8. A disclaimer is a statement that contains exceptions to and exclusions from a warranty.

9. Businesses use trade credit to buy goods and services. For example, they may buy products from a supplier on credit with the agreement they will pay the entire invoiced amount within 90 days.

College & Career READINESS

21st Century Skills

Problem-Solving Skills

10. Conduct a search of available credit cards. Choose a type of card (balance transfer, low-interest, cash-back, reward, frequent flyer, pre-paid, or secured credit) to investigate. Review a total of three different cards offered for the card type you selected and recommend the best choice. Identify the type of card, three cards of that type, your choice of card, and your rationale for choosing the card. Provide a one-page outline of the results and your recommendation.

Financial Literacy Skills

11. Calculating Payments Assume that a consumer has a credit card balance and wants to pay only a minimum monthly payment. What is the monthly minimum payment for a balance of $2354.00 with a 17.99 percent annual interest rate?

e-Marketing Skills

12. Product Safety Imagine you are employed in product planning for a large children's toy manufacturer. Go to the Consumer Product Safety Commission Web site to investigate a toy product that was recently recalled. Select one children's toy product and find out its manufacturer, the date and reasons for the recall, and available remedies for consumers who have purchased the product. Summarize your findings in a one-page written report that includes this information:

- Name of the product
- Date of recall
- Manufacturer
- Reasons for the recall
- Available remedies for purchasers

Build Academic Skills

English Language Arts

13. Extended Product Warranties Conduct research on the advantages and disadvantages of extended product warranties or service contracts. Identify the name of your source(s). Prepare a one-page report that summarizes the advantages and disadvantages of extended product warranties.

NCTE 1 Read texts to acquire new information.

Social Studies

14. Better Business Bureaus Better Business Bureaus are organizations that seek to resolve problems that arise from purchases made by businesses and consumers. Perform library or online research on a Better Business Bureau located within your state. Identify its name, location, goals, and services provided to consumers. Summarize your findings in a one-page written report.

NCSS V G Individuals, Groups, & Institutions Analyze the extent to which groups and institutions meet individual needs and promote the common good in contemporary and historical settings.

Mathematics

15. Consolidating Debt A household has $14,000 in credit card debt and pays 3 percent per month interest on all credit card payments. The family gets an offer for a new credit card. It promises no minimum payment for three months on all balance transfers, and then a 5-percent interest rate thereafter. Assuming that the household pays only the interest each month on a $14,000 balance, under which scenario will the customer spend less money over a year?

NCTM Algebra Represent and analyze mathematical situations and structures using algebraic symbols.

Math Concept **Interest Rates** Credit card interest rates are based on a percentage of the credit card's monthly balance. When figuring the total amount of interest paid each year, it is important to understand that the interest rate might not be applicable for the entire year.

For help, go to the **Math Skills Handbook** located at the back of this book.

Standardized Test Practice

Directions Read the following questions. On a separate piece of paper, write the best possible answer for each one.

1. Which of the following warranties guarantees that if a product is found defective within the warranty period, it will be repaired or replaced at no cost to the purchaser?

A. Full warranty
B. Implied warranty
C. Limited warranty
D. Warranty of merchantability

2. Credit allows businesses or individuals to obtain products or money in exchange for a promise to pay later.

T
F

3. A credit card issued by banks to demonstrate a consumer's loyalty to a team, university, charity, business, or other organization is known as a(n) _________ card.

Test-Taking Tip

Before the test, study over a few days or weeks, continually reviewing class material. Do not wait until the night before and try to learn everything at once.

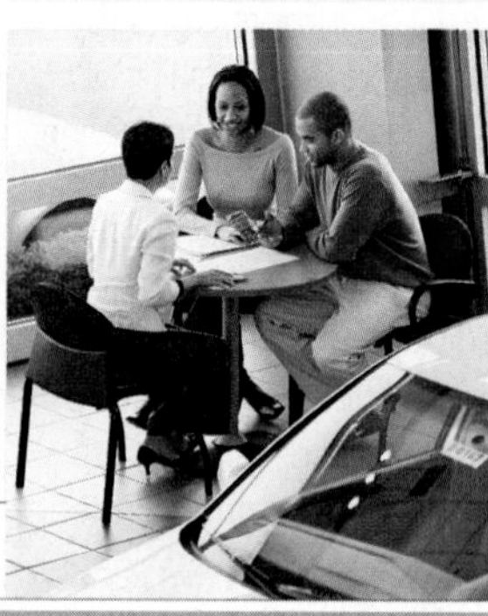

DECA Connection Role Play

Credit Evaluator Automobile Dealership

Situation You work for a business that sells new and used automobiles. The business is large and well-established, having been in business for more than 20 years. Your job is to work with the company sales associates to establish the credit worthiness of customers applying for company credit to purchase automobiles. Most customers use some type of credit to make automobile purchases. Many customers arrange financing for their purchases through their banks or credit unions. Many other customers decide to finance their purchases through your company. Before extending credit to a customer, it is important to determine whether the customer is a credit risk. Management has recently hired a new sales associate (judge). It is your job to explain the role of credit in your business to the new sales associate (judge).

Activity You are to meet with the new sales associate (judge) to explain the role credit plays in your business and its importance to both your business and your customers. You are also to explain the importance of establishing the creditworthiness of customers and the legal considerations for granting credit.

Evaluation You will be evaluated on how well you meet the following performance indicators:

- Discuss the nature of environmental law.
- Explain the nature of agency relationships.
- Discuss legal issues affecting businesses.
- Identify legal considerations for granting credit.
- Determine creditworthiness of customers/clients.

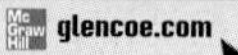

glencoe.com

Download the Competitive Events Workbook for more Role-Play practice.

EVALUATE

21st Century Skills

Problem-Solving Skills

10. Students should write a one-page outline in which they analyze a specific type of card, such as low-interest or reward cards. Within this group, they should review three different cards and recommend the one they think is the best choice. They should provide a rationale for their choice.

Financial Literacy Skills

11. Multiply your outstanding balance by your percent annual interest rate. So, you owe $2354.00 on a card with 17.99 percent interest rate, the equation would be $2,354 \times 0.1799 = \$423.48$.

e-Marketing Skills

12. Reports should include the product's name, date of recall, manufacturer, reasons for the recall, and the remedies available to purchasers. For example, in September of 2010, "Love Tester" Mood Rings, distributed by D&D Distributing-Wholesale, were recalled because of high lead levels. Purchasers could take the product to the store where it was purchased to receive a full refund or a replacement product.

EVALUATE

Build Academic Skills

English Language Arts

13. Student reports should summarize the advantages and disadvantages of extended product warranties. In their reports, students should identify the sources of their information. For example, ConsumerReports.org states that as products, particularly cars, have become more reliable, items are unlikely to break down during the extended warranty period. The warranties typically cost more than the consumer will recover and often include fine-print terms that disqualify claims. Instead of purchasing extended warranties, ConsumerReports.org suggests buying reliable brands and following the usage and maintenance instructions.

Social Studies

14. Student reports should state the name, location, goals, and services provided to consumers by a Better Business Bureau within their state. For example, the Better Business Bureau in Atlanta, Georgia seeks to create "an ethical marketplace where buyers and sellers can trust each other." Those businesses that meet the BBB's standards are invited to join. The BBB site contains current consumer news, alerts, FTC articles, and so on. It also allows consumers to file online complaints against specific businesses.

Mathematics

15. They are better off to stay with the current card paying 3% interest each month. That amount comes to $5,040 a year. The new card offer would have the family paying $6,300 over a 12-month period.

Standardized Test Practice

1. A (Full warranty)
2. T
3. affinity

DECA Connection Role Play

Evaluations will be based on these performance indicators:

1. **Discuss the nature of environmental law.** Governmental environmental laws are designed to protect the air, water, ground, etc. For example, the Environmental Protection Agency (EPA) sets emission standards for cars and trucks.
2. **Explain the nature of agency relationships.** Federal and state agencies have laws that protect consumers and the environment. On the federal level, the EPA protects the environment; the CPSC monitors the safety of thousands of non-food items, such as toys and appliances; and FDA is responsible for the safety of food and drugs. Most state laws, on the other hand, are designed to protect consumers and often affect service businesses.
3. **Discuss legal issues affecting businesses.** Businesses must follow environmental laws and safety regulations that apply to their industry. They also must comply with any licensing or certification requirements. Most states have implied warranty laws that take effect whenever a purchase is made. Businesses must follow legal requirements for notification, billing, and debt collection activities, follow laws such as the Truth in Lending Act of 1968, the Fair Credit Reporting Act of 1971, etc.
4. **Identify legal considerations for granting credit.** Government regulations require businesses to inform consumers about the use of credit. They must establish procedures for notification, billing, and debt collection activities. The Truth in Lending Act of 1968 requires that lenders disclose information about annual percentage rates, amount financed, etc. The Fair Credit Reporting Act of 1971 requires the lender to report the name of the credit bureau used when denying credit to a consumer. The Fair Credit Opportunity Acts of 1975 and 1976 forbid discrimination when granting credit.
5. **Determine creditworthiness of customers/clients.** Lenders grant credit based on what they perceive as the consumer's ability to repay the loan. An important component of issuing credit is the consumer's credit score which is a number between 350 (poor) and 850 (excellent) designed to measure the risk in lending money and is used in establishing the credit limits offered to consumers.

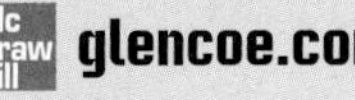

Role Plays For more DECA Role Plays, send students to the Online Learning Center to download the Competitive Events Workbook.

UNIT 10 **Marketing Internship Project**

Create a Design for a New Pet Product

Pet product companies embrace pet owners' desire to create a great life for their pets. What new products would you create to appeal to both pets and pet owners?

Scenario

The pet industry is growing every year. U.S. pet owners spend more than $45 billion on their pets annually. Pet food sales account for $17 billion, while the rest of the sales are for pet clothing, accessories, toys, medicine, grooming, and pet services. Research indicates that pet owners "humanize" pets, which means they are treated like family members. This booming industry includes pet hotels and spas, magazines for pet owners, Animal Planet® on television, and even Web sites for sharing photos and videos of pets via a social network.

A pet product company wants your marketing firm to capitalize on the booming pet economy by creating an exciting new product and a marketing plan to launch it.

The Skills You'll Use

Academic Skills Reading, writing, social studies, and research

Basic Skills Speaking, listening, thinking, and interpersonal

Technology Skills Word processing, presentation software, spreadsheet, telecommunication, and the Internet

NCTE 4 Use written language to communicate effectively.
NCTE 7 Conduct research and gather, evaluate, and synthesize data to communicate discoveries.

Your Objective

Your objective is to conceive a new or improved pet product for your client and prepare a marketing plan.

STEP 1 Do Your Research

- Research all aspects of the pet industry, looking for trends in pet food, medicine, services, clothing, toys, and accessories.
- Research current political, economic, socio-cultural, and technological factors that may affect the pet industry.
- Study current advertisements and packaging of pet products.
- Visit online sites that have a pet theme.
- Visit Web sites for pet food manufacturers (e.g., Nestle's Ralston Purina®) pet stores (e.g., PetSmart®), pet sections of supermarkets, and pet e-tailers (e.g., PetCo®).
- Find independent social media sites for pet owners.
- Research potential competitors and pricing of competitive products.

Write a summary of your research.

STEP 2 Plan Your Project

Now that you have completed your research, you need to begin planning your project.

- Develop your new product concept by following the steps for product development.
- Develop a marketing plan that includes the following: objectives, situation analysis (environmental scan and SWOT analysis) to support your new product concept, identification of the target market, marketing mix details (product, place, price, and promotion), as well as your ideas for implementation, evaluation, and control.
- Design product packaging and promotional materials.

STEP 3 Connect with Your Community

- Interview one or more trusted adults who are pet owners to identify any unmet needs and to get ideas about the best way to communicate with them about a new product (e.g., social media, magazines, television). Describe your product idea to these pet owners and ask for feedback.
- Interview pet store owners or managers to find out which products sell the most and how to get shelf space for a new pet product. Describe your product idea and ask for feedback.

STEP 4 Share What You Learn

Assume your class is the client's executives—the decision makers.

- Present your research findings and ideas in an oral presentation. Be prepared to answer questions.
- Describe your new product idea and your marketing plan and display your packaging and promotional materials.
- Use software to create a slide presentation to accompany your oral presentation. Include one slide for each topic in your marketing plan.

STEP 5 Evaluate Your Marketing and Academic Skills

Your project will be evaluated based on the following:

- Knowledge of the pet market
- Comprehensive PEST and SWOT analyses
- Proper use of marketing terminology
- Product feasibility and rationale for it
- Organization and continuity of presentation
- Mechanics—presentation and neatness
- Speaking and listening skills

MARKETING CORE FUNCTIONS
- Product/Service Management
- Market Planning

Marketing Internship Project Checklist

Plan
- ✓ Research the current pet market and successful pet products.
- ✓ Brainstorm ideas to capitalize on current trends in the pet market.

Write
- ✓ Describe your research findings and create a marketing plan outline with all essential components in a written report.
- ✓ Explain how the results of the PEST and SWOT analyses helped you conceive the new product and develop the marketing plan.

Present
- ✓ Present your idea for a new pet product with rationale supported by your research.
- ✓ Present your marketing plan with a specific target market, price, place, and promotion ideas for the product.
- ✓ Display sample packaging for your product and promotional materials.

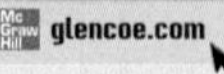

Evaluate Download a rubric you can use to evaluate your final project.

my marketing portfolio

Internship Report When you have completed your Marketing Internship Project and oral presentation, put your written report and a few printouts of key slides from your oral presentation in your marketing portfolio.

Design a New Product in a Different Industry Design a new product based on a trend in a consumer or an organizational market. Conduct an environmental scan (PEST analysis) to support your idea. Then conduct a SWOT analysis for the company that will make the product. To test your product concept, conduct marketing research. Prepare a marketing plan, complete with your target market and your ideas for the marketing mix (product, place, price, and promotion). Prepare a written report and an oral presentation.

EVALUATE

Anticipation Activity

Project Objective Read the project objective aloud to students: ***Conceive a new or improved pet product for your client and prepare a marketing plan.*** Then ask students to think about what they learned about product planning in Unit 10. Remind them of these key points:

- Product planning involves making decisions about what features should be used in selling a business's products, services, or ideas.
- Product planning for a new or improved product should also consider branding strategies as well as extended product features.

Ask students: ***What are the steps in new product development?*** (1) Generate ideas; (2) screen ideas; (3) develop a business proposal; (4) develop the product; (5) test the product with consumers; (6) introduce the product; and (7) evaluate customer acceptance.

Ask students: ***Why is branding important in product planning?*** Branding helps build product recognition and customer loyalty. It ensures quality and consistency. Branding can help companies extend products into new target markets and introduce new product lines.

Graphic Organizer

Display this diagram. Then ask students to name categories of pet products. Possible answers:

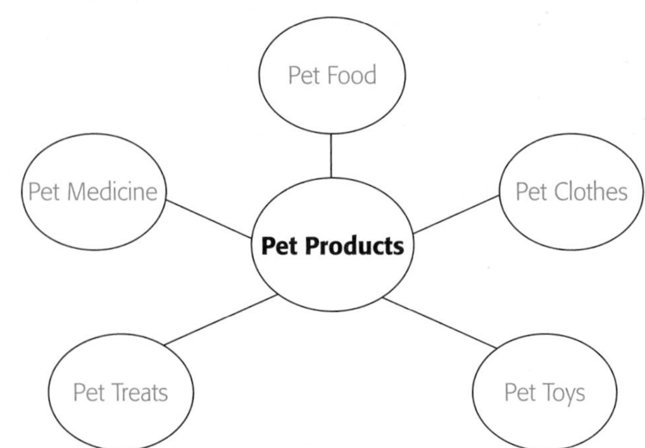

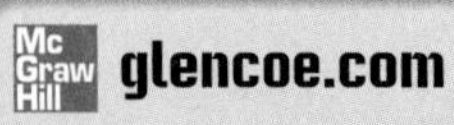

iWB

Graphic Organizer Send students to the Online Learning Center to print this graphic organizer.

EVALUATE

STEP 1 Do Your Research

Tell students that there are many places to find information they can use to conceive of a new or improved pet product. Students can use library and Internet resources, but they should also talk to people in the community. Encourage students to seek the opinions and ideas of trusted people they know. Other people can bring new perspectives and ideas about trends and preferences in pet products and advertising as well as the PEST factors that affect the pet industry.

STEP 2 Plan Your Project

Students should create a product plan using the steps of the product development process before designing product packaging and outlining a marketing plan for the product. Students should explain why they chose their particular pet product, providing information about the target market. Students' explanation of the marketing mix should include all four Ps: product, price, place, and promotion.

STEP 3 Connect with Your Community

Explain to students that connecting with members of the community is a great way to build relationships. Tell them that young people who are capable of building relationships with caring, responsible, and competent adults are more likely to achieve success. Encourage students to take part in opportunities for adults to serve as mentors, coaches, advocates, and advisors, both formally and informally.

STEP 4 Share What You Learn

Students should present their ideas in a written report and oral presentation with presentation software. They should have at least one slide in their presentation for each key topic in the written report. Encourage students to speak clearly, use appropriate grammar and vocabulary, and actively engage the audience by making and maintaining eye contact and using movement (facial expressions, posture, gestures) to focus attention and interest.

STEP 5 Evaluate Your Marketing and Academic Skills

Have students use the Marketing Internship Project Checklist to help them to plan, write, and present their reports. Exemplary written reports will include information that clearly supports a central thesis, a single, distinct focus, generally well-developed ideas, well-phrased sentences that flow smoothly and are varied in length and structure, consistently precise word choice, and few, if any, errors in grammar, spelling, and mechanics.

Evaluation Rubric Send students to the Online Learning Center to get a rubric to evaluate their projects.

Culminating Activity

Explain to students that federal statutes, such as the Magnuson-Moss Consumer Product Warranty Act, the Consumer Product Safety Act, and the Federal Food, Drug, and Cosmetic Act (FFDCA), legislated for consumer products also apply to pet products. Students should consider these laws when planning for their new or improved pet product. Ask students: ***What are some specific examples of situations in which these laws might affect a pet product?*** Answers will vary and may require research. Sample answer: The laws regarding warranties apply to all products. The FFDCA requires that pet foods, like human foods, be safe to eat, produced under sanitary conditions, contain no harmful substances, and be truthfully labeled. Canned pet foods must be processed free of viable microorganisms. Recently, toxic chemicals like lead, cadmium, mercury, and arsenic have been found present in certain pet toys and accessories, especially those made in China. However, there is debate as to whether certain amounts of such chemicals pose a health threat. Pet protection organizations support stronger laws to ensure safer pet products. In addition, some manufacturers are voluntarily developing products according to more stringent guidelines.

my marketing portfolio

Internship Report Have students put their written reports and printouts of key slides from their oral presentations in their marketing portfolio.

Design a New Product in a Different Industry Direct students to select a new product based on a market trend and write a marketing plan for it. Students should conduct a PEST analysis, SWOT analysis, and marketing research. Students' completed marketing plans should include all of the elements and answer all of the questions included in the Marketing Internship Project on this page. This additional activity can build relevance for students who are motivated to learn about other specific businesses and industries.

UNIT 11 Entrepreneurship and Finance

PLANNING GUIDE AND RESOURCES

	Print	Digital
Unit 11 Entrepreneurship and Finance		Unit 11 Fast Files: Marketing Internship Project Activity Connect Online Learning Center through glencoe.com
Chapter 33 **Entrepreneurial Concepts**	Student Activity Workbook: Chapter 33 DECA Connection Role Play; Chapter 33 Vocabulary Activity; Section Note Taking Activities; Chapter Academics Activity; Section Study Skills Activities; Section Real-World Applications Activities Mathematics for Marketing Workbook Marketing Research Project Workbook School-to-Career Activity Workbook	Unit 11 Fast Files: Chapter 33 Discovery Project Worksheet and Rubric; Chapter 33 Green Marketer Activity; Chapter 33 Digital Nation Activity; Section Graphic Organizers; Section Outlines with Key Terms and Definitions; Section Summaries ExamView Assessment Suite, Chapter 33 Connect Online Learning Center through glencoe.com
Chapter 34 **Risk Management**	Student Activity Workbook: Chapter 34 DECA Connection Role Play; Chapter 34 Vocabulary Activity; Section Note Taking Activities; Chapter Academics Activity; Section Study Skills Activities; Section Real-World Applications Activities Mathematics for Marketing Workbook Marketing Research Project Workbook School-to-Career Activity Workbook	Unit 11 Fast Files: Chapter 34 Discovery Project Worksheet and Rubric; Chapter 34 Green Marketer Activity; Chapter 34 Digital Nation Activity; Section Graphic Organizers; Section Outlines with Key Terms and Definitions; Section Summaries ExamView Assessment Suite, Chapter 34 Connect Online Learning Center through glencoe.com
Chapter 35 **Developing a Business Plan**	Student Activity Workbook: Chapter 35 DECA Connection Role Play; Chapter 35 Vocabulary Activity; Section Note Taking Activities; Chapter Academics Activity; Section Study Skills Activities; Section Real-World Applications Activities Mathematics for Marketing Workbook Marketing Research Project Workbook School-to-Career Activity Workbook	Unit 11 Fast Files: Chapter 35 Discovery Project Worksheet and Rubric; Chapter 35 Green Marketer Activity; Chapter 35 Digital Nation Activity; Section Graphic Organizers; Section Outlines with Key Terms and Definitions; Section Summaries ExamView Assessment Suite, Chapter 35 Connect Online Learning Center through glencoe.com
Chapter 36 **Financing the Business**	Student Activity Workbook: Chapter 36 DECA Connection Role Play; Chapter 36 Vocabulary Activity; Section Note Taking Activities; Chapter Academics Activity; Section Study Skills Activities; Section Real-World Applications Activities Mathematics for Marketing Workbook Marketing Research Project Workbook School-to-Career Activity Workbook	Unit 11 Fast Files: Chapter 36 Discovery Project Worksheet and Rubric; Chapter 36 Green Marketer Activity; Chapter 36 Digital Nation Activity; Section Graphic Organizers; Section Outlines with Key Terms and Definitions; Section Summaries ExamView Assessment Suite, Chapter 36 Connect Online Learning Center through glencoe.com

McGRAW-HILL PROFESSIONAL DEVELOPMENT

Perkins IV has placed more emphasis than ever on providing quality professional development for Career and Technology educators. The legislation mandates that the focus of professional development be the integration and reinforcement of academic competencies in order to improve student achievement. Specifically, Perkins requires measurements of students' academic success. McGraw-Hill answers the challenge for strong and effective professional development with a five-prong **Online Professional Development for Integrating Academics.**

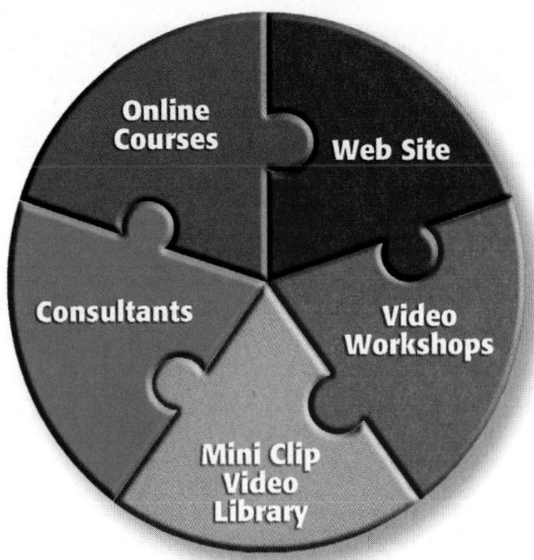

For pricing and ordering information contact your McGraw-Hill Sales Representative.

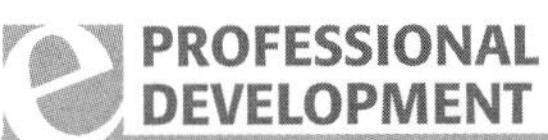

VIDEO LIBRARY

The McGraw-Hill Professional Development Mini-Clip Video Library, referenced for your convenience at the point of use, provides teaching strategies to strengthen academic and learning skills. Go to the Online Learning Center to view these professional development video clips for Unit 11:

Chapter 33: Entrepreneurial Concepts

- **ELL: Strategies for English Language Learners:** An author discusses strategies for teaching English language learners. (p. 779)
- **ELL: Reading Aloud:** A teacher reads aloud, modeling fluency, pronunciation, expression, and comprehension strategies. (p. 785)

Chapter 34: Risk Management

- **Reading: Focus Lesson:** A teacher models how to find the main idea or theme of a selection by identifying the major and minor details. (p. 800)
- **Reading: Differentiated Instruction:** An expert discusses elements of a differentiated classroom. (p. 803)

Chapter 35: Developing a Business Plan

- **ELL: Collaborative Work:** Students work in groups to complete a science lab and then use academic vocabulary to discuss and record their findings. (p. 819)
- **ELL: Understanding Proficiency:** An author discusses proficiency and describes the various levels of proficiency that can be applied to English learners. (p. 829)

Chapter 36: Financing the Business

- **ELL: Understanding Proficiency:** An author discusses proficiency and describes the various levels of proficiency that can be applied to English learners. (p. 848)
- **Reading: Connecting the Pieces:** A teacher helps students develop predictions and inferences. (p. 854)

UNIT OVERVIEW

Sections	Objectives	Common Core State Standards College and Career Readiness
Section 33.1 **Entrepreneurship**	• Define entrepreneurship. • Describe the advantages of entrepreneurship. • Explain the risks of entrepreneurship. • List the characteristics and skills of entrepreneurs. • Understand the importance of small business in various economies.	• **Reading** Read closely to determine what the text says explicitly and to make logical inferences from it; cite specific textual evidence when writing or speaking to support conclusions drawn from the text.
Section 33.2 **Business Ownership**	• Identify the forms of business ownership. • Name the legal steps to take in establishing a business.	• **Reading** Integrate and evaluate content presented in diverse formats and media, including visually and quantitatively, as well as in words.
Section 34.1 **Business Risk Management**	• Explain the nature and scope of risk management. • Identify the various types of business risks.	• **Reading** Read closely to determine what the text says explicitly and to make logical inferences from it; cite specific textual evidence when writing or speaking to support conclusions drawn from the text.
Section 34.2 **Handling Business Risks**	• Explain effective security and safety precautions, policies, and procedures. • Describe the various ways businesses can manage risk. • Explain the concept of insurance.	• **Reading** Integrate and evaluate content presented in diverse formats and media, including visually and quantitatively, as well as in words.

Sections	Objectives	Common Core State Standards College and Career Readiness
Section 35.1 **The Business Plan**	• Explain the purpose and importance of a business plan. • Identify external planning considerations.	• **Reading** Interpret words and phrases as they are used in a text, including determining technical, connotative, and figurative meanings, and analyze how specific word choices shape meaning or tone.
Section 35.2 **Marketing and Financial Plans**	• Explain a business's organizational plan. • Construct a marketing plan. • Describe financing sources for businesses. • Identify the financial elements of a business plan.	• **Reading** Read closely to determine what the text says explicitly and to make logical inferences from it; cite specific textual evidence when writing or speaking to support conclusions drawn from the text.
Section 36.1 **Financial Analysis**	• Explain the purpose of financial documents. • Develop a personal financial statement. • Determine start-up costs for a business.	• **Reading** Integrate and evaluate content presented in diverse formats and media, including visually and quantitatively, as well as in words.
Section 36.2 **Financial Statements**	• Estimate business income and expenses. • Prepare an income statement. • Create a balance sheet. • Interpret a cash flow statement.	• **Writing** Conduct short as well as more sustained research projects based on focused questions, demonstrating understanding of the subject under investigation.

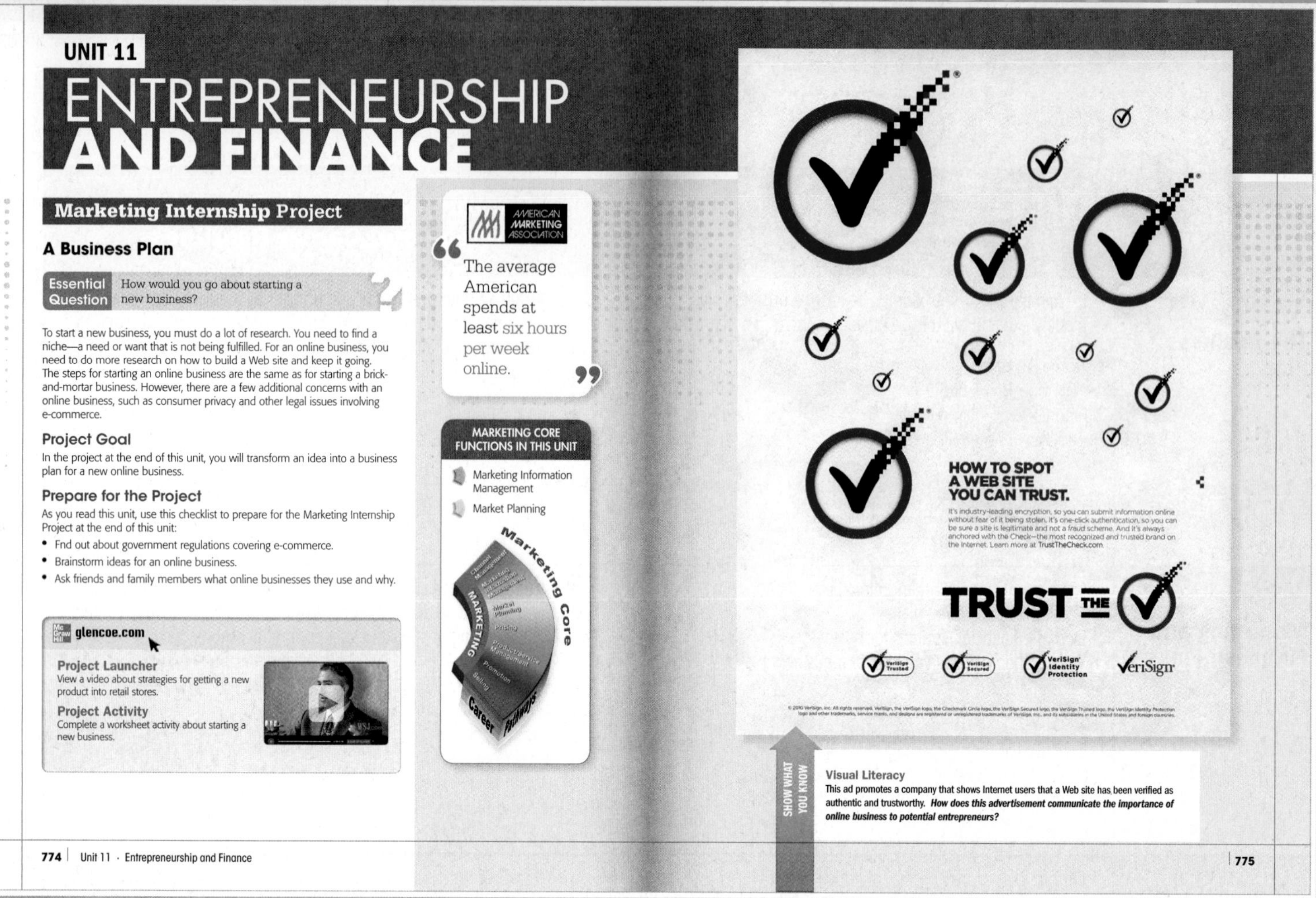

UNIT 11

ENTREPRENEURSHIP AND FINANCE

Marketing Internship Project

A Business Plan

Essential Question How would you go about starting a new business?

To start a new business, you must do a lot of research. You need to find a niche—a need or want that is not being fulfilled. For an online business, you need to do more research on how to build a Web site and keep it going. The steps for starting an online business are the same as for starting a brick-and-mortar business. However, there are a few additional concerns with an online business, such as consumer privacy and other legal issues involving e-commerce.

Project Goal

In the project at the end of this unit, you will transform an idea into a business plan for a new online business.

Prepare for the Project

As you read this unit, use this checklist to prepare for the Marketing Internship Project at the end of this unit:

- Fnd out about government regulations covering e-commerce.
- Brainstorm ideas for an online business.
- Ask friends and family members what online businesses they use and why.

glencoe.com

Project Launcher View a video about strategies for getting a new product into retail stores.

Project Activity Complete a worksheet activity about starting a new business.

AMERICAN MARKETING ASSOCIATION

"The average American spends at least six hours per week online."

MARKETING CORE FUNCTIONS IN THIS UNIT

- Marketing Information Management
- Market Planning

SHOW WHAT YOU KNOW

Visual Literacy This ad promotes a company that shows Internet users that a Web site has been verified as authentic and trustworthy. ***How does this advertisement communicate the importance of online business to potential entrepreneurs?***

774 | Unit 11 · Entrepreneurship and Finance

775

ENGAGE

Introduce the Unit

Unit 11 examines entrepreneurship and financial planning.

Chapter 33 explores the process of starting a business.

Chapter 34 discusses the economic, natural, and human risks involved with business ownership.

Chapter 35 explains how to create a business plan to give an overview of the proposed business to potential investors and lenders.

Chapter 36 teaches how to identify capital needs for a business.

Build Background

Ask students why entrepreneurship and small businesses are important for the U.S. economy. Answers may note that entrepreneurship promotes growth in the marketplace and provides jobs. Income from jobs provides money for consumer spending on products and services, and tax revenue for government services. Ask students: ***What are useful qualities that entrepreneurs need to be successful?*** They include determination, self-motivation, self-confidence, organizational skills, leadership ability, self-discipline, creativity, willingness to work hard and accept risk, and social skills.

Visual Literacy

Photo Caption Answer Read the copy on the ad to students. Then read the photo caption and the photo caption question to students: ***How does this advertisement communicate the importance of online business to potential entrepreneurs?*** Answers will vary. Accept all reasonable answers. Sample answer: The advertiser uses the check mark, a familiar symbol that is integrated into VeriSign's logo. This ad communicates that by using VeriSign's encryption technology, small businesses can thrive and expand because they can be assured that their customers' personal information is safe and secure thanks to VeriSign encryption technology. Ask students to evaluate the visual components of the advertisement. Ask volunteers to explain how the visual aspects of the advertisement complement the text of the advertisement. The slogan is Trust the Check and the checkmark is the logo. This is the logo that consumers see when they visit a site that uses VeriSign encryption technology. The headline "How to Spot a Web Site You Can Trust" is meant to communicate that the presence of the VeriSign check logo means that the Web site can be trusted.

ENGAGE

Marketing Internship Project Preview

Read students the Marketing Internship Project Essential Question: ***How would you go about starting a new business?*** Because students are just starting to learn about entrepreneurship, they will likely not know the specific answer to this question, which is choose an idea and create a business plan. However, students should know that an entrepreneur would need a good product or service and a good plan. Explain to students that they will learn about creating a business plan while studying this unit. Tell students that when they are finished studying this unit, they will ask questions to find answers about transforming an idea into a business plan for a new online business. As they study each chapter in the unit, they can prepare for the Unit Project by thinking of ideas for online businesses and asking friends and family about the online businesses they use.

Marketing Internship Project Resources Send students to the Online Learning Center to watch a video and download a worksheet activity related to the topic of the Unit Project.

Read the American Marketing Association quote to students:

“The average American spends at least six hours per week online.”

Explain to students that the AMA provides official definitions for numerous marketing terms in its online AMA Dictionary. Read the AMA's definitions of *e-commerce* and *online marketing* aloud:

E-Commerce A term referring to a wide variety of Internet-based business models. Typically, an e-commerce strategy incorporates various elements of the marketing mix to drive users to a Web site for the purpose of purchasing a product.

Online Marketing A term referring to the Internet and e-mail aspects of a marketing campaign. This can incorporate banner ads, e-mail marketing and search engine optimization.

Ask students: ***How has e-commerce and online marketing helped to expand opportunities for entrepreneurs?*** With Americans using the Internet on the average of six hours a week, the Internet has become a low-overhead retail environment. Businesses can target specific markets using proven online marketing strategies.

MARKETING CORE FUNCTIONS IN THIS UNIT

Point out to students that Chapters 33, 34, 35, and 36 will touch on two of the seven marketing core functions. Describe each of these marketing functions to students to prepare them to start studying this unit.

Marketing Information Management involves gathering, storing, and analyzing information about customers, trends, and competing products.

Market Planning involves understanding the concepts and strategies used to develop and target specific marketing strategies to a select audience.

MARKETING RESEARCH

PROJECT WORKBOOK

The purpose of the Marketing Research Project Workbook is to provide a step-by-step approach for students to conduct their own marketing research study. Each chapter is devoted to key elements in the research process. Each chapter builds upon the previous chapters, and by the end of the book, students will have completed an in-depth marketing research study, complete with rationale for all decisions, a report of the findings and conclusions, recommendations based on the original research problem and study objectives, and an annotated bibliography.

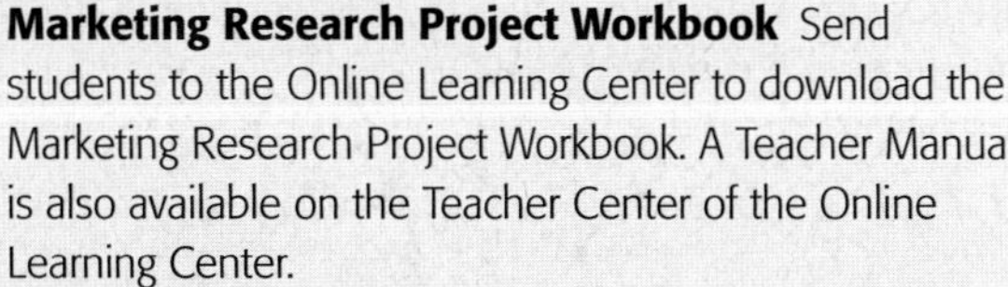

Marketing Research Project Workbook Send students to the Online Learning Center to download the Marketing Research Project Workbook. A Teacher Manual is also available on the Teacher Center of the Online Learning Center.

Chapter 33 Section 33.1 Entrepreneurship | Section 33.2 Business Ownership

entrepreneurial concepts

SHOW WHAT YOU KNOW

Visual Literacy Do you like to plan your own day and make your own decisions? If so, you might like to own your own company and be the boss. You might even have an interest in a subject that you could use to start the business. ***What are some questions you would need to answer before deciding to start up your own business?***

Discovery Project

Planning a Start-Up Business

Essential Question Where can you find answers to questions you might have about starting your own business?

Project Goal

Work with a partner as you begin planning how to start a business. Choose a business. Begin with your own list of the questions that you think will need to be answered as you develop your plan. Then use the Internet to do your research. Use key words such as *how to start a business, starting a small business,* and *becoming an entrepreneur.* Next contact several local business owners and request interviews with them about how to start a business. Write a report describing what you have learned about starting up your own business.

Ask Yourself...

- What questions will you ask business owners during your interviews?
- What do small business owners need to know when they are starting a business?
- What are some of the steps you could take to increase the likelihood that your business would succeed?
- How will you describe your findings?

Synthesize and Present Research Synthesize your research by writing a report describing what you have learned about starting up your own business.

glencoe.com

Activity
Get a worksheet activity about entrepreneurship.

Evaluate
Download a rubric you can use to evaluate your project.

DECA Connection

DECA Event Role Play

Concepts in this chapter are related to DECA competitive events that involve either an interview or role play.

Performance Indicators The performance indicators represent key skills and knowledge. Your key to success in DECA competitive events is relating them to concepts in this chapter.

- Explain the types of business ownership.
- Describe legal issues affecting businesses.
- Explain the organizational design of businesses.
- Explain how organizations adapt to today's markets.
- Demonstrate responsible behavior.

DECA Prep

Role Play Practice role-playing with the DECA Connection competitive-event activity at the end of this chapter. More information on DECA events can be found on DECA's Web site.

Chapter 33 · Entrepreneurial Concepts | 777

ENGAGE

Visual Literacy

Read the chapter opener photo caption question to students: ***What are some questions you would need to answer before deciding to start up your own business?*** Sample answers: Am I willing to work 12 to 16 hours a day, six days a week and on holidays, to make my business work? Do I enjoy competition? Am I prepared to lose some or all of my savings? Do I have the skills and expertise necessary to make a business succeed? Then ask these guiding questions.

Guiding Questions

Recall What are three basic functions of the manager of a business?	planning, organizing, controlling
Analyze What interpersonal skills does an entrepreneur need for building good relationships?	Possible answers: self-esteem, self-awareness, positive attitude, initiative, responsibility, self-control, creativity, time management, stress management, assertiveness, and flexibility.

Discovery Project

Planning a Start-Up Business Start a discussion that connects students to the Discovery Project Essential Question: ***Where can you find answers to questions you might have about starting your own business?*** Students may suggest the Internet as a good source for information about starting your own business. Specific places to look for answers may include the U.S. Small Business Administration, county government offices, the state's Department of Commerce, and so on. Ask students whether they know anyone who has started a business. Have students share what the person did to get the business started.

glencoe.com

Discovery Project Resources Send students to the Online Learning Center to download a rubric to evaluate their projects.

ENGAGE

Introduce the Chapter

Chapter 33 introduces entrepreneurship and all of its aspects. These main concepts are introduced and discussed:

- Advantages of entrepreneurship
- Disadvantages of entrepreneurship
- Entrepreneurship as a career choice
- Trends in entrepreneurship
- Business ownership opportunities
- Forms of business organization
- Legal steps to establishing a business

Discussion Starter

Entrepreneurs Ask students: ***Have any of you had your own baby-sitting service, lawn mowing service, dog-walking service, or other enterprise in which you were self-employed?*** Ask those who have been self-employed to share their experiences. Ask them to share the advantages and disadvantages of being self-employed. Advantages may include: personal freedom, personal satisfaction, increased self-esteem, increased income, free to set own work schedule and make own decisions, free to try out new ideas. Disadvantages may include: high level of stress, possible setbacks, risk of failure, potential loss of income, long and irregular hours, need to multitask, need for strong self-discipline. Ask students: ***Did you feel the advantages of working for yourself outweighed the disadvantages?*** Then ask them to explain their answers. Students will have different reasons for their thoughts and feelings. Encourage them to be honest about why they feel the way they do.

DECA Connection

Discuss the performance indicators listed in the DECA Connection feature. Explain to students that performance indicators tell them how to demonstrate their acquired skills and knowledge through individual or team competitive events.

glencoe.com

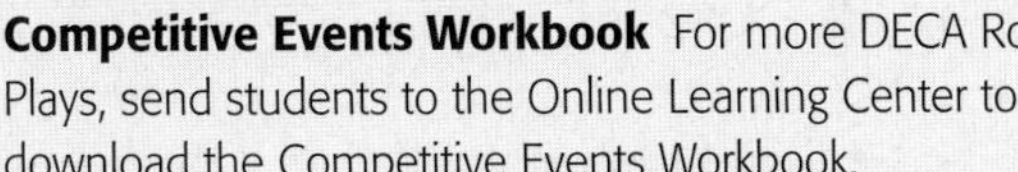

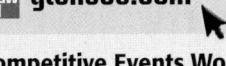

Competitive Events Workbook For more DECA Role Plays, send students to the Online Learning Center to download the Competitive Events Workbook.

PROGRAM RESOURCE ORGANIZER

PRINT RESOURCES

- **Student Edition**
- **Teacher Edition**
- **Student Activity Workbook with Academic Integration** includes worksheets and activities correlated to the text.
- **Mathematics for Marketing Workbook** provides math activities for every unit in the text.

TECHNOLOGY TOOLBOX

- **Connect**
- **ConnectPlus**
- **ExamView Assessment Suite** is a comprehensive solution for creating, administering, and scoring tests.

glencoe.com

Online Learning Center provides a variety of resources to enrich and enhance learning.

SECTION, CHAPTER, AND UNIT RESOURCES

- **Graphic Organizers** for organizing text concepts visually.
- **Digital Nation Activities** and **Green Marketer Activities** extend learning beyond the text features.
- **Career Chatroom Career Profiles** allow students to explore different marketing occupations in depth.
- **After You Read Answer Keys** for students to check their answers.
- **Discovery Project Rubrics** and **Marketing Internship Project Rubrics** for students to evaluate their projects.

PROGRAM RESOURCES

- **Student Activity Workbook with Academic Integration Teacher Annotated Edition** includes annotated answers for the activities and worksheets.
- **Marketing Research Project Workbook** provides a step-by-step approach for students to complete their own marketing research studies.
- **School-to-Career Activity Workbook** helps students relate their class work to on-the-job experience and involves work-site analysis and working with mentors.
- **Competitive Events Workbook** helps prepare students for state and national marketing education competitions.
- **Inclusion in the Marketing Education Classroom** provides teaching resources for working with students with special needs.
- **PowerPoint Presentations** provides visual teaching aids and assessments for this chapter.

READING GUIDE

Before You Read

Connect Think of some successful entrepreneurs. What are possible reasons for their success?

Objectives

- **Define** entrepreneurship.
- **Describe** the advantages of entrepreneurship.
- **Explain** the risks of entrepreneurship.
- **List** the characteristics and skills of entrepreneurs.
- **Understand** the importance of small business in various economies.

The Main Idea

Entrepreneurship has many advantages, including personal freedom and financial reward. It also has disadvantages, such as accepting risk.

Vocabulary

Content Vocabulary
- entrepreneurship
- entrepreneurs

Academic Vocabulary

You will find these words in your reading and on your tests. Make sure you know their meanings.
- indication
- domestic

Graphic Organizer

Draw or print this chart to list the characteristics of entrepreneurship.

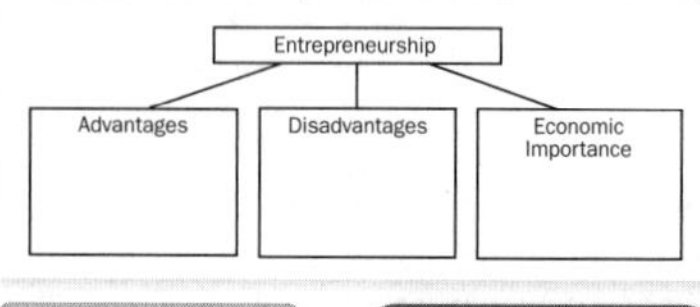

Print this graphic organizer.

MARKETING CORE FUNCTIONS

- Marketing Information Management
- Market Planning

STANDARDS

ACADEMIC

English Language Arts
NCTE 5 Use different writing process elements to communicate effectively.

Social Studies
NCSS III H People, Places, & Environments Examine, interpret, and analyze physical and cultural patterns and their interactions, such as land use, settlement patterns, cultural transmission of customs and ideas, and ecosystem changes.

Mathematics
NCTM Measurement Understand measurable attributes of objects and the units, systems, and processes of measurement.

NCSS *National Council for the Social Studies*
NCTE *National Council of Teachers of English*
NCTM *National Council of Teachers of Mathematics*
NSES *National Science Education Standards*

Common Core
Reading Read closely to determine what the text says explicitly and to make logical inferences from it; cite specific textual evidence when writing or speaking to support conclusions drawn from the text.

me. Section 33.1 Entrepreneurship

WHAT IS ENTREPRENEURSHIP?

Entrepreneurship is the process of starting and operating your own business. **Entrepreneurs** are people who create, launch, organize, and manage a new business and take the risk of business ownership. You are an entrepreneur if you have provided babysitting services or cut someone's lawn for pay. Entrepreneurs often have an idea, or business concept, that drives their business. An entrepreneur combines this vision with the means to manufacture the product (or provide the service) and market it. The contributions entrepreneurs make to the economy both within and outside the United States can be remarkable.

As You Read

Connect Compare the characteristics of an entrepreneur to your own personality. Would you make a good entrepreneur?

The results of entrepreneurship can change our lives in other ways, too. Consider these examples:

- Henry Ford introduced the mass production of vehicles by making them affordable to average people. His entrepreneurship revolutionized transportation and transformed lifestyles.
- William Hewlett and David Packard started a small business in Packard's garage near Stanford University in California. They invented the floppy memory disk and the first pocket calculator. Their business grew into the giant Hewlett-Packard Corporation. Hewlett-Packard produces a vast array of computer products, including laser printers. These products changed the speed with which people process information.

These entrepreneurs became famous and wealthy as a result of starting and growing their businesses. However, it is important to recognize that not all entrepreneurs achieve such success.

Some entrepreneurs start companies simply because they want to be their own bosses and make their own business decisions.

> "Entrepreneurs make major contributions to our economy by providing jobs for their employees."

ADVANTAGES OF ENTREPRENEURSHIP

The advantages of entrepreneurship can include personal freedom, personal satisfaction, increased self-esteem, and increased income. Entrepreneurs set their own work schedules and make their own decisions. They are able to try out their own new ideas, direct their energies into business activities, and take control of their businesses and their work settings.

Many business owners are willing to put in the extra effort to make their businesses succeed because of financial rewards. With success often comes money, and this potential motivates many entrepreneurs.

DISADVANTAGES OF ENTREPRENEURSHIP

Being an entrepreneur has disadvantages, too. These include a high level of stress, possible setbacks, the risk of failure, potential loss of income, long and irregular hours, and the need to handle multiple tasks.

ENGAGE

Anticipation Activity

Improving Student Achievement Ask students to name reasons people become entrepreneurs. able to set own work hours, be own boss, make all decisions, and so on Then ask: ***How might altruism (acting for the good of others) affect one's choice to be an entrepreneur?*** An entrepreneur may give back to the community in various ways.

Objectives

- **Define** entrepreneurship. the process of starting and operating your own business
- **Describe** the advantages of entrepreneurship. personal freedom, personal satisfaction, increased self-esteem, increased income
- **Explain** the risks of entrepreneurship. high level of stress, possible setbacks, risk of failure, potential loss of income
- **List** the characteristics and skills of entrepreneurs. organized, determined, self-confident, leadership ability, self-disciplined
- **Understand** the importance of small business. generate growth at a faster rate than larger businesses, provide 80 percent of new jobs annually

Graphic Organizer

Entrepreneurship

Advantages	Disadvantages	Economic Importance
1. Personal freedom 2. Personal satisfaction 3. Increased self-esteem 4. Increased income 5. Set own work schedule 6. Make own decisions	1. High level of stress 2. Risk of failure 3. Possible setbacks 4. Potential loss of income 5. Long and irregular hours 6. Need to handle multiple tasks 7. Need for self-discipline	1. Major contributions to economy 2. Contributions are remarkable 3. Small businesses generate economic growth faster than larger companies 4. New businesses create 80% of new jobs

iWB

Graphic Organizer Send students to the Online Learning Center to print this graphic organizer.

EXPLORE

Before You Read

Read the Before You Read question aloud: ***Think of some successful entrepreneurs. What are possible reasons for their success?*** Students may recognize that successful entrepreneurs will have similar qualities and characteristics, such as strong self-discipline, creativity, self-motivation, and a willingness to work hard. Ask students if they think they have the qualities and characteristics needed to be a successful entrepreneur. Students may or may not feel they have what it takes. Ask volunteers how they might go about acquiring the necessary qualities and characteristics.

Preteaching Vocabulary

Have students go to the Online Learning Center at glencoe.com for the Chapter 33 Preteaching Vocabulary games.

Content Vocabulary

Ask students to write a paragraph discussing how the Content Vocabulary terms are different. Entrepreneurship is the process of starting and operating a new business. Entrepreneurs are people who create, launch, organize, and manage a business and take the risks of ownership. Ask volunteers to share their paragraphs.

Academic Vocabulary

Indication—Synonyms Display the term *indication* and ask volunteers to suggest synonyms for it. suggestion, warning, hint, sign, signal Now read this sentence: ***This information should give you a good indication of whether you are ready to be a small business owner.*** Ask: ***Which synonym best fits the way the term*** indication ***is used in the sentence?*** hint, sign, or signal

Domestic—Synonyms Display the term *domestic* and ask volunteers to suggest synonyms for it. family, home, household, national, local, internal Now read this: ***Entrepreneurs and small businesses play a key role in the domestic and global economy.*** Ask: ***Which synonym best fits the way the term*** domestic ***is used in the sentence?*** national, local, or internal

MINI CLIP

ELL: Strategies for English Language Learners
Go to the Online Learning Center to view a video clip in which an author discusses strategies for teaching English language learners.

Entrepreneurship

WHAT IS ENTREPRENEURSHIP?

Tell students that some of the biggest companies in the world were started by entrepreneurs. Then ask these guiding questions to focus the discussion about entrepreneurship.

Guiding Questions

Explain What are some ways that teens can be entrepreneurs?	Possible answers: baby-sitting, lawn-mowing, dog-walking, or delivery service.
Analyze What personal characteristic(s) would a person need to be able to set their own work schedule but still accomplish what needs to get done?	Students should recognize that this would require strong personal motivation, self-discipline, and self-control.

As You Read

Read students the As You Read question: ***Compare the characteristics of an entrepreneur to your own personality. Would you make a good entrepreneur?*** Have students write out the personal skills and characteristics that they think would help them be a successful entrepreneur. Then have them compare their list with the characteristics and skills listed in the text. Ask volunteers to share how they think they measured up.

Expert Advice

Read the quote to students:

> **"Entrepreneurs make major contributions to our economy by providing jobs for their employees."**

Ask students: ***Have you ever worked for an entrepreneur or know someone who has?*** If students are unsure of the answer, tell them a small to medium company that has only one owner is likely run by an entrepreneur. Encourage students to share any experiences they are aware of. Ask: ***Do you think you would like to work for an entrepreneur? Why or why not?*** Possible answers: Students may say they think it would be a very good place to learn about a business, or they may think an entrepreneur might be very demanding of his or her employees.

The GREEN Marketer

Selling Eco-Fashion

Everything old is new again, at least in the world of eco-fashion. Turning yesterday's trash into today's ready-to-wear is the trend. Environmental entrepreneurs are developing businesses with earth-friendly names, such as "Save the Planet" and "Greenloop." They build their marketing plans around green products. They attract customers who want to do good as well as look good in clothes made from recycled wares and natural fibers.

Raw Material Worn tires and old denim take shape as ultra-cool sneakers. Fabric made from wood, bamboo, or corn turns into high-end haute couture. Reclaimed Coke® cans add sparkle when recycled as sequins. For the conscientious shopper, dressing "green" means wearing conviction with style.

English Language Arts

Create Think of an object at home that could be recycled as a product for a new business venture. Describe in writing the new product and business, along with the pros and cons of starting the new business.

NCTE 5 Use different writing process elements to communicate effectively.

glencoe.com

Get an activity on green marketing.

Most new businesses have a restricted cash flow because of start-up costs. As a result, an entrepreneur may not meet his or her personal financial needs during the first year of operation, or even longer. Increased income comes only when the business succeeds.

Entrepreneurs are not 40-hours-per-week people. To succeed, they must meet the needs of the marketplace. This often means long and irregular hours.

Running a business requires doing many tedious, time-consuming tasks. To save money, new business owners may do many of these jobs themselves. Among the tasks they may perform is time-consuming paperwork. This paperwork includes tending to accounts payable, accounts receivable, payroll, and government forms.

THE RISKS OF ENTREPRENEURSHIP

Starting a new business requires a major commitment of time, money, and effort. A new business owner must be a risk taker. It is often necessary to quit a job, work long hours, invest savings, and borrow money—all with no guarantee that the new business will succeed. The amount of money you would need to start a new business depends on many factors, such as the type of business and the location. There are many stories about people starting a business on a shoestring (very little money). However, most small business owners underestimate how much capital they will need to start a new business and make it successful.

If you plan to start a business, it is always better to save up the money you will need to get started or borrow as little as possible. More than half of all new businesses fail within two to three years. Therefore, careful planning is essential to help you avoid facing a huge debt.

ENTREPRENEURSHIP AS A CAREER CHOICE

Being an entrepreneur can be exciting and greatly rewarding, but it is not for everyone. Those who succeed have certain skills and personal characteristics that enable them to meet the challenges of business ownership.

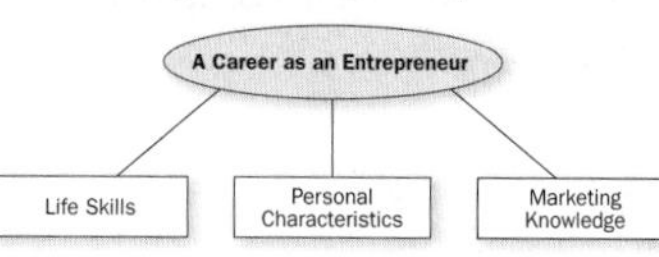

First, entrepreneurs must have the skills necessary to run their business. Beyond specific skills, most successful entrepreneurs share a number of characteristics:

Characteristics of Successful Entrepreneurs

- Determination
- Self-motivation, self-discipline, and self-confidence
- Strong organizational skills
- Leadership ability
- Creativity
- Willingness to work hard
- Spirit of adventure
- Good social skills

DO YOU HAVE WHAT IT TAKES?

You can answer this question by doing a self-evaluation—an assessment of your personal qualities, abilities, interests, and skills. The self-evaluation in **Figure 33.1** on page 782 was developed by the Small Business Administration (SBA). Think about each queston and write your honest answers on paper. Answering "yes" to most or all of these questions suggests that you may have the right characteristics for success.

Before you start a business, ask family members, friends, and other businesspeople that are in the same or a similar business about their experiences. Do research on the type of business you want to start. All this information should give you a good **indication** of whether you are ready to join the millions of small-business owners in the United States.

MARKETING AND ENTREPRENEURSHIP

Entrepreneurs may have the business and technical skills they need to produce and provide a quality product or service. However, they may overlook the importance of marketing. Entrepreneurs who possess a good understanding of marketing have an advantage over those who do not.

Here are some helpful resources. The American Marketing Association has a special interest group devoted to helping entrepreneurs develop marketing skills—the Marketing and Entrepreneur Special Interest Group. The National Federation of Independent Businesses (NFIB) has the "Business Toolkit," an award-winning online library of management information.

Reading Check

Summarize What are some risks of being an entrepreneur?

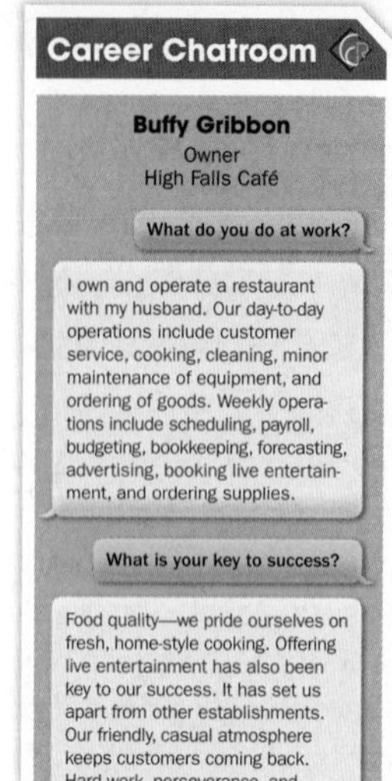

Career Chatroom

Buffy Gribbon
Owner
High Falls Café

What do you do at work?

I own and operate a restaurant with my husband. Our day-to-day operations include customer service, cooking, cleaning, minor maintenance of equipment, and ordering of goods. Weekly operations include scheduling, payroll, budgeting, bookkeeping, forecasting, advertising, booking live entertainment, and ordering supplies.

What is your key to success?

Food quality—we pride ourselves on fresh, home-style cooking. Offering live entertainment has also been key to our success. It has set us apart from other establishments. Our friendly, casual atmosphere keeps customers coming back. Hard work, perseverance, and keeping costs down have worked to make us a success.

What skills are most important to you?

Communication is important. We have to communicate with customers so they are happy and come back, *and* with our staff, so they help our business flourish. We also deal with vendors and salespeople. Without strong communication, things would not run smoothly.

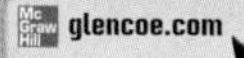

glencoe.com

Read more about this career and get a Career Exploration Activity.

EXPLAIN

The GREEN Marketer

English Language Arts Answer Read the activity to students: *Think of an object at home that could be recycled as a product for a new business venture. Describe in writing the new product and business, along with the pros and cons of starting the new business.* After writing their descriptions, have students share their ideas with the class. Possible answers: using old jeans to make stylish purses or satchels, using yard waste to create compost to sell to gardeners, and so on. Ask students to share the pros and cons of starting a new business. Pros may include: working for yourself, making your own decisions. Cons may include: working lots of hours to make the business successful, taking a financial risk, and so on.

glencoe.com

Worksheet Activity Send students to the Online Learning Center to get a Green Marketer worksheet activity.

ENTREPRENEURSHIP AS A CAREER CHOICE

Ask students if they had ever thought of starting their own business (entrepreneurship) as a career choice. Answers will vary; students may or may not have thought about being a business owner. Most students will likely think of more traditional career choices, which involve working for someone else. Then ask these guiding questions to focus the discussion about entrepreneurship as a career choice.

Guiding Questions

List What are characteristics of successful entrepreneurs?	determination, self-motivation, self-discipline, self-confidence, strong organizational skills, leadership ability, creativity, willingness to work hard, spirit of adventure, good social skills
Examine Why would entrepreneurs who have a good understanding of marketing have an advantage over those who do not?	Possible answer: Those who understand marketing know the best ways to let consumers know about their products and services, which will help to increase business.

ELABORATE

Mini Projects

Enrichment

Determine Skills and Attributes Have students choose a specific type of entrepreneurship such as opening a Web design company. Ask them to list both the specific skills and general attributes needed to succeed in this business. Answers may include: artistic ability, proficiency in using necessary Web site development software, ability to understand and interpret customers' needs and wants, and so on.

Research an Entrepreneur Ask students to use online or print sources to research a well-known entrepreneur. In a two-page expository essay, have them explain the steps the entrepreneur took to build his or her business, the entrepreneur's personal attributes, and his or her specific skills. When students are finished, have them summarize the information for the class. Ask: ***What attributes do these entrepreneurs have in common?*** Answers may include: determination, self-motivation, self-discipline, leadership ability, ability to make own decisions, able to take advice from others, access to funding, and so on.

Graphic Organizer

Display this diagram. Ask students to provide information to fill in the diagram. Sample answers are provided below.

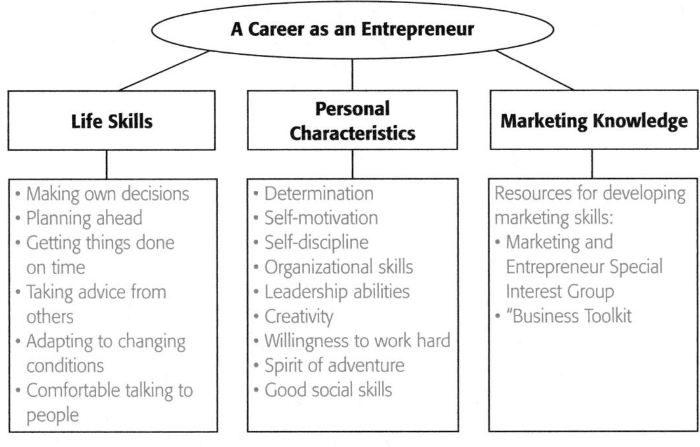

glencoe.com iWB

Graphic Organizer Send student to the Online Learning Center to print this graphic organizer.

Critical Thinking

Divide the class into small groups. Ask each group to determine what kind of business(es) they could open and run based on the skill sets of group members. Ask: ***How will you go about determining the kind of business you could open?*** Students may suggest that they will have each group member list his or her skills, and then combine the skills into one list. They may then use that list to determine the type(s) of business they could open and run successfully. To arrive at their answer, they should also identify the skills necessary for different types of businesses, and compare those skills to the group members' skills. When groups have arrived at an answer, have them share their answers and reasoning with the class.

Reading Check Answer

Read the Reading Check question to students: ***What are some risks of being an entrepreneur?*** Risks of being an entrepreneur may include: having to quit your job; investing your own money; and possibly borrowing money to open and run a business, knowing that only half of new businesses survive for four years. Ask: ***Are you willing to take these risks in order to be an entrepreneur?*** Encourage students to think seriously about the risks involved in entrepreneurship.

Career Chatroom

Use these questions to focus the discussion about the Career Chatroom feature.

Guiding Questions

List What is included in the day-to-day operations for Ms. Gribbon?	customer service, cooking, cleaning, minor maintenance of equipment, and ordering of goods
Analyze Which of the day-to-day operations listed would be part of most enterprises?	customer service; perhaps ordering of goods and cleaning
Predict What might the day-to-day operations for your business look like?	Answers will vary based on the type of business, but customer service should always be listed.

glencoe.com

Career Exploration Send students to the Online Learning Center to find more information about this career and to get a Career Exploration activity.

FIGURE 33.1 Self-Evaluation

Know Yourself A clear understanding of your strengths and skills will help you decide whether to pursue entrepreneurship. ***What do your answers say about you?***

The first eight questions relate to your personality characteristics.	**YES**	**NO**
1. Do you like to make your own decisions?	___	___
2. Do you enjoy competition?	___	___
3. Do you have willpower and self-determination?	___	___
4. Do you plan ahead?	___	___
5. Do you like to get things done on time?	___	___
6. Can you take advice from others?	___	___
7. Can you adapt to changing conditions?	___	___
8. Are you comfortable talking to people you do not know or have just met?	___	___
The next series of questions relates to your physical, emotional, and financial well-being.		
9. Do you understand that owning your own business may entail working 12 to 16 hours a day, probably six days a week and maybe on holidays?	___	___
10. Do you have the physical stamina to handle a business?	___	___
11. Do you have the emotional strength to withstand the strain?	___	___
12. Are you prepared to lower your living standard for several months or years?	___	___
13. Are you prepared to lose your savings?	___	___
14. Do you know which skills and areas of expertise are critical to the success of your business?	___	___
15. Do you have these skills?	___	___
16. Does your idea for a business use these skills?	___	___
17. Can you find the people who have the expertise you lack?	___	___
18. Do you know why you are considering this business?	___	___
19. Will your business meet your career aspirations?	___	___

TRENDS IN ENTREPRENEURSHIP

Entrepreneurs and small-to-medium businesses play a key role in the **domestic** economy and the global economy. They generate growth at a much faster rate than other larger and more established businesses. Consider these statistics:

- Eighty percent of the new jobs created annually come from businesses that are less than five years old.
- Ninety percent of all U.S. businesses have fewer than 20 employees.
- Firms with fewer than 500 employees were responsible for 50 percent of the gross domestic product (GDP).
- About one in ten adults in the United States are planning to start a new business.
- As many as 25 percent of all U.S. workers are self-employed.

Several trends in the marketplace have fostered the growth of entrepreneurship. These trends include the availability of technology, increased global communication, the rise of the Internet and e-commerce, and an increasingly diversified society and market. The U.S. Small Business Administration (SBA) provides loans to help small businesses in the competitive global economy. The SBA Web site provides business owners with helpful information. This includes access to government services, help with regulations, and applications for help, money, and training. The SBA is also providing more opportunities to work with government buyers and ways to compete in international markets.

After You Read | Section 33.1

Review Key Concepts

1. **Compare** being an entrepreneur with being an employee.
2. **List** the personal characteristics required of an entrepreneur that describe you.
3. **Explain** how small businesses contribute to the U.S. economy.

Practice Academics

Social Studies

4. You have decided to become an entrepreneur. You want to investigate types of business that are socially responsible, environmentally sensitive, personally interesting, and financially rewarding. Research at least three types of business that you believe would meet these criteria. Read business magazines, research online, and interview business owners. Write a report explaining why one of these types of business would be satisfying to you.

Mathematics

5. You live in a city known for entrepreneurship. The city had 1,600 new business start-ups in one year. How many new start-ups is this per week?

Math Concept **Measuring Time** Determining the frequency of events over a certain time period is usually accomplished with division.

Starting Hints Divide the total number of start-ups by 52, the number of weeks in a year, to determine how many businesses start up each week.

For help, go to the **Math Skills Handbook** located at the back of this book.

NCSS III H People, Places, & Environments Examine, interpret, and analyze physical and cultural patterns and their interactions, such as land use, settlement patterns, cultural transmission of customs and ideas, and ecosystem changes.

NCTM Measurement Understand measurable attributes of objects and the units, systems, and processes of measurement.

glencoe.com Check your answers.

ELABORATE

Visual Literacy

Figure 33.1 Caption Answer Read the caption and question to students: ***A clear understanding of your strengths and skills will help you decide whether to pursue entrepreneurship. What do your answers say about you?*** Students should identify any strengths or weaknesses that might affect their decision to run a small business. Then ask these guiding questions to focus students' attention on the self-evaluation.

Guiding Questions

Identify What types of questions are represented in this self-evaluation?	The questions relate to personality characteristics and to physical, emotional, and financial well-being.
Examine Why should you consider your emotional well-being when thinking about becoming an entrepreneur?	Students should recognize that emotional strain can be even more debilitating than physical strain. If a person does not consider the emotional side of owning and operating a business, he or she may find it to be far more difficult than originally thought.

Graphic Organizer

Display this diagram. Have students refer to Figure 33.1 and categorize items 9–19 as either physical, emotional, financial, or a combination of those. Write the item numbers in the appropriate places in the diagram. Sample answers are provided below.

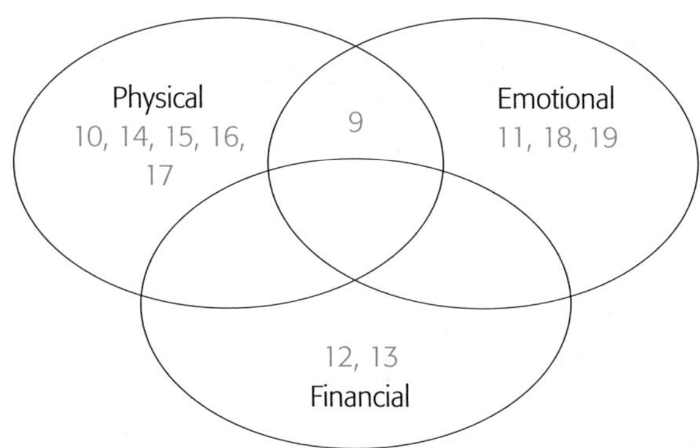

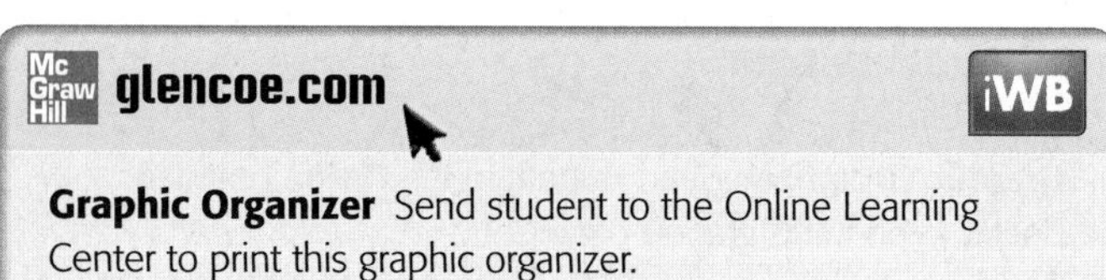

EVALUATE

Critical Thinking

Have students create a checklist to use when seeking partners with whom to start a business. Students should first consider their own strengths and weaknesses, then list the characteristics and skills they think are necessary for a business partner to have. Help students recognize that they will need to look for a partner with characteristics that complement their own. Sample answers: I have weak math skills, so I'll seek a business partner who's good at accounting and bookkeeping. I'm good at carrying out great ideas but I'm not very creative, so I need a business partner who's creative and will come up with great ideas for me to carry out.

TRENDS IN ENTREPRENEURSHIP

Ask students: ***In addition to this class, where might you find information about starting up your own business?*** Answers may include print and online business publications, and from entrepreneurs in the community. Tell them that there are agencies such as the U.S. Small Business Administration that offer information for business start-ups. Then ask students these guiding questions to direct a discussion on trends in entrepreneurship.

Guiding Questions

Identify What is the domestic economy?	In this context, it is the economy of the United States.
Explain What role do entrepreneurs and small business play in the domestic and global economies?	They generate growth at a much faster rate than other larger and more established businesses.
Calculate What percentage of adults in the United States is planning to start a new business?	about 10 percent
Synthesize How might the availability of technology, increased global communication, the rise of the Internet and e-commerce, and an increasingly diversified society and market lead to growth in entrepreneurship?	Possible answers: in many cases, not much money is required to start an online business; small businesses can do business around the world; with a diversified market, many different types of businesses can be successful.

After You Read — Section 33.1

Review Key Concepts

1. Entrepreneurs organize, manage, and assume the risk of owning and operating a business. Employees work for owners.
2. Lists may include: determined, self-motivated, self-confident, organized, having leadership ability, self-disciplined, creative, willing to work hard, willing to take risks, and having good social skills.
3. Firms with fewer than 500 employees were responsible for 50 percent of the gross domestic product (GDP).

Practice Academics

Social Studies

4. Students should read business magazines, conduct online research, and interview business owners to investigate types of businesses that are socially responsible, environmentally sensitive, personally interesting, and financially rewarding. They should research at least three types of businesses that they believe would meet these criteria and then write a report explaining why one of these types of businesses would be satisfying to them.

Mathematics

5. 30 or 31 ($1{,}600 \div 52 = 30.77$).

glencoe.com

Answer Key Send students to the Online Learning Center to check their answers.

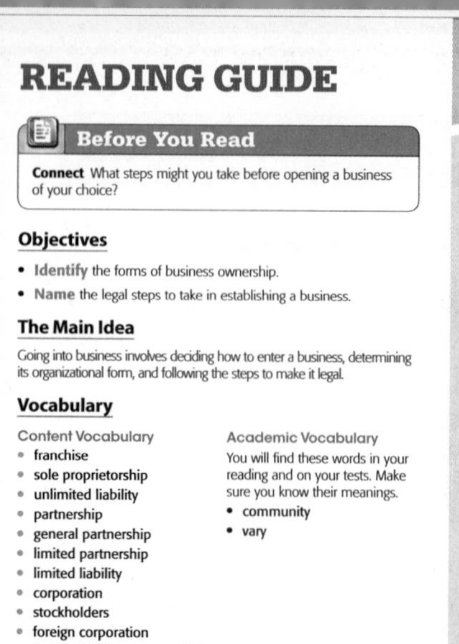

READING GUIDE

Before You Read

Connect What steps might you take before opening a business of your choice?

Objectives

- **Identify** the forms of business ownership.
- **Name** the legal steps to take in establishing a business.

The Main Idea

Going into business involves deciding how to enter a business, determining its organizational form, and following the steps to make it legal.

Vocabulary

Content Vocabulary
- franchise
- sole proprietorship
- unlimited liability
- partnership
- general partnership
- limited partnership
- limited liability
- corporation
- stockholders
- foreign corporation
- limited liability company (LLC)
- Doing Business As (DBA)
- Articles of Incorporation

Academic Vocabulary

You will find these words in your reading and on your tests. Make sure you know their meanings.
- community
- vary

Graphic Organizer

Draw or print this chart to write down the steps to establish a new business.

glencoe.com

Print this graphic organizer.

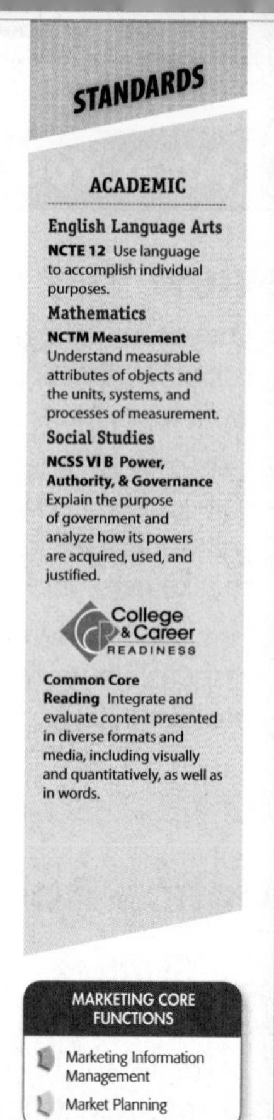

STANDARDS

ACADEMIC

English Language Arts
NCTE 12 Use language to accomplish individual purposes.

Mathematics
NCTM Measurement Understand measurable attributes of objects and the units, systems, and processes of measurement.

Social Studies
NCSS VI B Power, Authority, & Governance Explain the purpose of government and analyze how its powers are acquired, used, and justified.

College & Career READINESS

Common Core
Reading Integrate and evaluate content presented in diverse formats and media, including visually and quantitatively, as well as in words.

MARKETING CORE FUNCTIONS
- Marketing Information Management
- Market Planning

Section 33.2 Business Ownership

BUSINESS OWNERSHIP OPPORTUNITIES

You may become an entrepreneur if you (1) purchase an existing nonfranchise business, (2) take over the family business, (3) start a new business, or (4) purchase a franchise business.

As You Read

Connect Compare the pros and cons of the four forms of business organization.

PURCHASE AN EXISTING NONFRANCHISE BUSINESS

When an entrepreneur buys an existing nonfranchise business, there is usually little or no help from the previous owner. The buyer must investigate why the business was sold. Business records, the condition of the property, and inventory must be closely examined. The reputation of the business in the **community** must be considered. In some cases, the new owner may contract the services of the previous owner to assist with management during a transition period.

TAKE OVER A FAMILY BUSINESS

Similar considerations for purchasing an existing business apply to taking over a family business. Will the fact that the previous owner is a family member help or hurt the new owner? The new owner must explore potential conflicts with family members. Succession planning (transition to the next generation), managing growth, and family relations may be challenging when taking over and running a family business.

> "There are four ways to start a business."

START A NEW BUSINESS

Starting a new business gives an entrepreneur great freedom of choice. The new business owner can start the business of his or her choice and plan it from the ground up. He or she can decide where it is located, what it sells, and how it is organized. There are no old debts to settle and no bad reputation to overcome. On the other hand, it is up to the new owner to establish the business's reputation and build a customer base.

PURCHASE A FRANCHISE

A **franchise** is a legal agreement to sell a parent company's product or services in a designated geographic area. McDonald's Corporation and Taco Bell® are examples of companies that sell franchises. They are franchisors. The franchisee (the person buying the business) has to invest money to buy the franchise. The franchisee also pays an annual fee and a share of the profits. In exchange, the franchisor provides a well-known name, a business plan, advertising, and the proven methods and products of the parent company.

In franchise businesses, new business owners have a lot of help. The business planning is done by the franchisor. Planning includes management training, merchandising, and day-to-day operations.

A disadvantage of franchising is the initial cost. A large amount of capital is needed to purchase most franchises. The franchisee must also pay high initial fees to begin operations. Many franchisors are very strict about how the franchise is run.

Reading Check

Contrast How are nonfranchise and franchise businesses similar? How are they different?

ENGAGE

Anticipation Activity

Improving Student Achievement Distribute sections of the newspaper to students. Challenge them to a ten-minute brainstorming session to come up with imaginative ideas for potential business ventures based on articles, photos, and ads. Answers may include: gourmet food store, photography service, delivery service, construction company, and so on. Then have students focus on the "business for sale" section of the classified ads in the newspaper. Ask them to select an ad and create a list of things they would consider before buying the business. They might consider whether they would need a partner to make the business work, whether they have enough money to do the job right, and so on.

Objectives

- **Identify** the forms of business ownership. purchase an existing nonfranchise business, take over the family business, start a new business, or purchase a franchise business
- **Name** the legal steps to take in establishing a business. register the business, file Articles of Incorporation or Articles of Organization, obtain necessary licenses, get federal tax number

Graphic Organizer

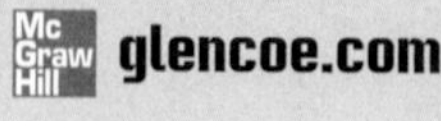

glencoe.com iWB

Graphic Organizer Send students to the Online Learning Center to print this graphic organizer.

EXPLORE

Before You Read

Read the Before You Read question aloud: ***What steps might you take before opening a business of your choice?*** Answers may include: a study of businesses that would fulfill a need; evaluating the competition; available funding; personal skills; willingness to commit to entrepreneurship; and necessary legal steps. Then ask: ***Why is it important to do some background research before committing to open a business?*** Students should recognize that every business poses a financial risk. The better prepared you are, the better chance you have of having a successful business.

Preteaching Vocabulary

Have students go to the Online Learning Center at glencoe.com for the Chapter 33 Preteaching Vocabulary games.

Content Vocabulary

Have students create a table with the heads *Business Ownership Opportunities, Forms of Business Organization,* and *Legal Steps to Establishing a Business.* Have students put each content vocabulary term under the head where it fits best. Business Ownership Opportunities—franchise. Forms of Business Organization— sole proprietorship, unlimited liability, partnership, general partnership, limited partnership, limited liability, corporation, stockholders, foreign corporation, limited liability company (LLC). Legal Steps to Establishing a Business—Doing Business As, Articles of Incorporation.

Academic Vocabulary

Vary—Origin Display the term *vary* for the class to read. Tell students that the term is from the Latin term for "various" and from the Middle English for "to undergo change." From this information, ask students to supply a definition for the term. Possible answers: to make or cause changes to occur or to add variety. Ask volunteers to use the term in original sentences. Sample answer: The steps vary depending on whether the business will be a sole proprietorship, partnership, corporation, or limited liability company.

ELL: Reading Aloud
Go to the Online Learning Center to view a video clip in which a teacher reads aloud, modeling fluency, pronunciation, expression, and comprehension strategies.

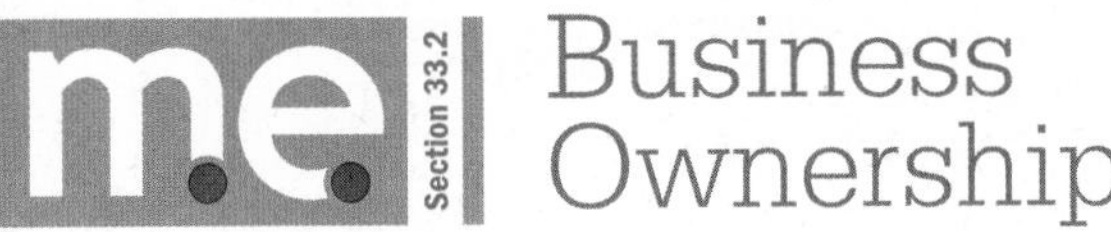

Business Ownership

BUSINESS OWNERSHIP OPPORTUNITIES

Ask these questions to focus discussion on business ownership.

Guiding Questions

Identify What are the four types of business opportunities?	purchase an existing nonfranchise business; take over a family business; start a new business; purchase a franchise
Evaluate What are some benefits of buying a franchise?	The franchisee gets a well-known name, a business plan, advertising, proven methods and products, and lots of help.

As You Read

Read students the As You Read question: ***Compare the pros and cons of the four forms of business organization.*** A sole proprietorship gives an entrepreneur the greatest control and all profits, but it exposes the owner to greater risks. A partnership shares decision-making, profits, and losses. A corporation is owned by stockholders who may not be involved in the day-to-day decision-making but are responsible for losses only to the level of his or her investment. In a limited liability company (LLC), owners have only limited liability.

Expert Advice

"There are four ways to start a business."

Ask students: ***What are the four ways to start a business?*** purchase an existing nonfranchise business, take over a family business, start a new business, purchase a franchise

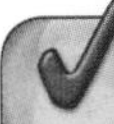

Reading Check Answer

Read the Reading Check question to students: ***How are nonfranchise and franchise businesses similar? How are they different?*** They are similar in that they are both businesses that must be run according to legal requirements. Owners must also purchase supplies, hire employees, and so on. Franchise owners get more help than nonfranchise owners—the franchisor does the business planning, which includes management training, merchandising, and day-to-day operations. Nonfranchise owners must do this on their own.

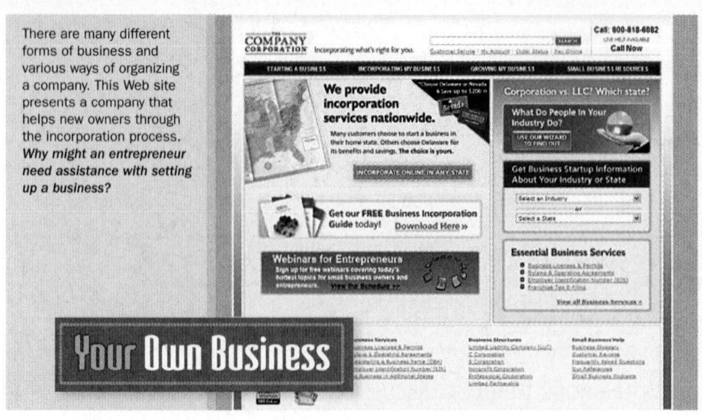

There are many different forms of business and various ways of organizing a company. This Web site presents a company that helps new owners through the incorporation process. ***Why might an entrepreneur need assistance with setting up a business?***

FORMS OF BUSINESS ORGANIZATION

The choice of which legal organization or structure a new business should have is a critical decision. It may make the difference between the success or failure of the business. The form determines how fast business decisions are implemented and how well the business competes in the marketplace. There are four possible forms of business organization (see **Figure 33.2** on page 788): sole proprietorship, partnership, corporation, and limited liability company (LLC).

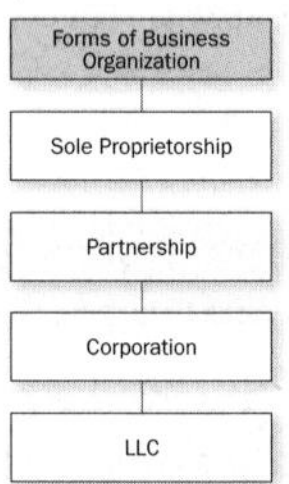

The choice depends on the financial and tax situation of the owner, the type of business, the number of employees who will be hired, and the level of risk involved in the new business. As a business grows, these factors may change and may require reorganization. A business could start out as a sole proprietorship, grow into a partnership, and ultimately become a corporation.

SOLE PROPRIETORSHIP

A **sole proprietorship** is a business that is owned and operated by one person. This is the most common form of business ownership. Approximately 70 percent of all U.S. businesses are sole proprietorships. Sole proprietors usually have a special skill by which they can earn a living. For example, plumbers, contractors, and many entrepreneurs who start Web-site businesses are often sole proprietors. The sole proprietor must provide the money and management skill to run the business. In return for all this responsibility, the sole proprietor is entitled to all the profits.

Advantages A sole proprietorship is relatively easy to start. The sole proprietor provides the money to start the business. For instance, a plumber buys tools and a truck, leases work space and buys office supplies, and spends money to advertise the business. A sole proprietorship is generally taxed less than other forms of business, and there is greater freedom from government regulation. Because the owner is usually the only investor in the business, that person is entitled to all the profits. A sole proprietorship also gives the owner great control over the business.

Disdvantages The primary disadvantage of a sole proprietorship is financial. The owner is responsible for all business debts and any legal judgments against the company. If the business does not do well, its debts may exceed its assets. If that happens, creditors can claim the owner's personal assets, such as a home, cars, and savings. The owner of a sole proprietorship has **unlimited liability**, which means that the owner's financial liability is not limited to investments in the business. It extends to include whether the owner can personally make payments on any debts owed by the business.

THE PARTNERSHIP

A **partnership** is a legal agreement between two or more people to be jointly responsible for the success or failure of a business. Partnerships represent about 10 percent of U.S. businesses. Common partnerships in your community may include real estate agencies, law offices, and medical offices.

A partnership is formed by a partnership agreement, usually prepared by an attorney, which specifies the responsibilities of each partner. Partners share the profits if the business is a success and the losses if it fails. Profits are usually divided according to the amount of time and money each partner invests. There are two kinds of partnerships: general and limited.

GENERAL PARTNERSHIP

In a **general partnership**, each partner shares in the profits and losses. As in the sole proprietorship, partners have shared unlimited liability for the company's debts. Also, each partner's share of the business profits is taxed as personal income.

MARKETING CASE STUDY

Flat-Rate Shipping from the U.S. Postal Service

One of the frustrations of online shopping, for both buyers and sellers, is the sometimes-complex nature of figuring out shipping costs.

A recent ad campaign by the United States Postal Service® put the focus on its flat-rate shipping service. The campaign focused on how it could benefit businesses by making everything simpler.

Keeping It Simple

In one ad, a postal carrier visits two partners who own a hobby shop. Their new toy robot kit is a huge hit, but they are struggling with shipping. The carrier shows them a flat-rate box, which is the perfect size for the robot, and which will cost them the same amount of postage no matter where they send it. The carrier tells them that with the U.S. Postal Service, shipping is simple: 'With a flat-rate box from the Postal Service – if it fits, it ships!'

English Language Arts

Analyze Discuss the advantages and disadvantages of a flat-rate shipping method for entrepreneurs, especially for planning a partnership business.

NCTE 12 Use language to accomplish individual purposes.

EXPLAIN

Visual Literacy

Your Own Business Caption Answer Read the caption question to students: ***Why might an entrepreneur need assistance with setting up a business?*** Students might conclude that there are many tasks involved in setting up a business, and outsourcing or delegating those tasks may reduce the amount of time or ease the workload of the entrepreneur. Also, before an entrepreneur can officially open the doors of a new business, he or she must take specific steps to legally establish and protect the business. These steps vary depending on whether the business will be a sole proprietorship, partnership, corporation, or limited liability company.

Extend the Activity Have students interview an entrepreneur in your community. Instruct them to find out whether the entrepreneur had help when starting up the business and if so, what kind of help was required. Ask students to share their findings with the rest of the class.

FORMS OF BUSINESS ORGANIZATION

Tell students that there are several ways to organize a business. Some ways allow the owner(s) exclusive control, while other ways allow for much less control. Then ask these guiding questions to focus the discussion on forms of business organization.

Guiding Questions

Identify What are the four forms of business organization?	sole proprietorship, partnership, corporation, and a limited liability company
Compare the advantages of sole proprietorship and a partnership.	Sole proprietorship: easy to start, money comes from sole proprietor, generally taxed less, all profits go to the sole proprietor, who has control over the business. Partnership: combines the skills of the owners, more capital may be available, each partner has a voice in decisions, taxed on profits, and less regulated than corporations.

ELABORATE

Graphic Organizer

Display this diagram. Ask students to provide details for each type of business organization. Write students' answers in the diagram. Sample answers are provided.

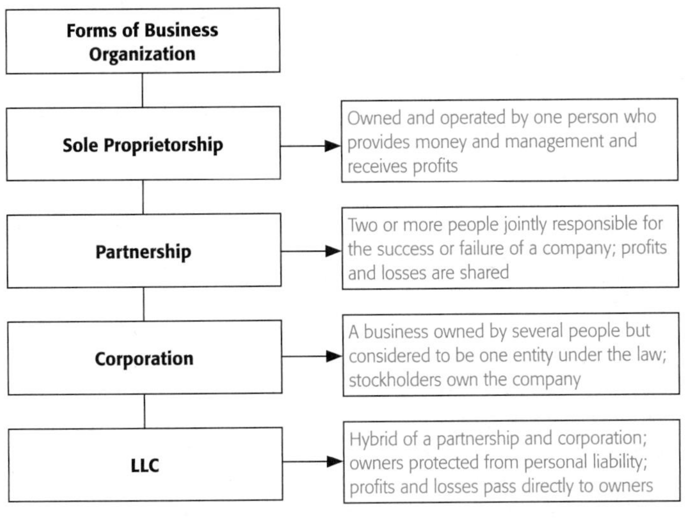
Forms of Business Organization
Sole Proprietorship
Owned and operated by one person who provides money and management and receives profits
Partnership
Two or more people jointly responsible for the success or failure of a company; profits and losses are shared
Corporation
A business owned by several people but considered to be one entity under the law; stockholders own the company
LLC
Hybrid of a partnership and corporation; owners protected from personal liability; profits and losses pass directly to owners

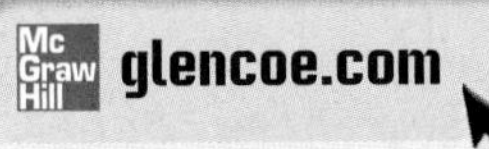
glencoe.com

iWB

Graphic Organizer Send students to the Online Learning Center to print this graphic organizer.

Critical Thinking

Divide the class into pairs. Have each pair imagine that one of them is an entrepreneur who has hired the other one to give advice about the most appropriate form of business ownership for a business opportunity. Have pairs work together to research, write, and perform a role play in which they present a question-and-answer session about the various forms of business ownership. Role plays should include an analysis of the advantages and disadvantages of the various forms of legal ownership. Students should present a business scenario and recommend a suitable legal form for the business.

Mini Projects

Differentiated Instruction

Gifted Learners Read to students the following scenario: You have an idea for a consumer product—a special backpack that has a separate section for trash items. The "trash can" is designed to keep odors and bacteria to a minimum. You are going to develop the backpack in your home, then find a manufacturing facility and hire employees after you have secured funding. In two paragraphs, describe your strategy for using the most appropriate legal form of business ownership at each stage of the development of the company. Sample answer: During the development of the backpack, you do not incur liability and you probably do not have employees, so a simple structure, the sole proprietorship, is appropriate. When you are manufacturing the product and hiring employees, you want to protect yourself from unlimited liability, so the corporate form or the limited liability company is appropriate.

Logical Learners Ask students to recall the self-evaluation survey they completed in Figure 33.1 on page 782. Ask: ***Which of the four forms of business organization would best suit your personality as revealed in the self-evaluation?*** Ask students to explain their answers for the class. Students should identify specific personality traits and the form of business organization that best suits those personality traits.

MARKETING CASE STUDY

English Language Arts Answer Students may suggest that the flat-rate shipping would make running a business much easier. It would also make predicting expenses easier. On the other hand, if the flat-rate costs more than weighing each item individually for shipping, it could cut into profits. If the general partner in a limited partnership opted for flat-rate shipping and it was actually more expensive than regular shipping, the other partner(s) would not get a say in the matter. However, the other partner(s) would have to accept a lower profit margin due to higher shipping expenses.

FIGURE 33.2 Business Organization

The Four Forms of Business Ownership The legal organization of a business is a key decision for an entrepreneur. It determines how fast business decisions can be made, how well the business will compete in the marketplace, and how quickly it can raise money. ***Which form of business ownership is easiest to establish?***

SOLE PROPRIETORSHIP

A sole proprietorship gives an entrepreneur the greatest control over business decisions and all the profits. It also exposes the owner to greater risks.

PARTNERSHIP

Partners share decision-making responsibility as well as the business's profits and losses. In a limited partnership, a limited partner is responsible for losses only to the level of his or her investment in the business. The general partner is fully responsible for losses.

CORPORATION

Corporations are owned by stockholders, who may range in number from one to millions. Each stockholder owns a portion of the business and is responsible for losses only to the level of his or her investment. In a corporation, the owners may not be involved in the day-to-day decision making for the business. With this type of organization, the benefits and risks are shared among the stockholders. Corporations can raise money relatively easily, but the decision-making process can be slow.

LIMITED LIABILITY COMPANY

The limited liability company (LLC) is a combination of a partnership and a corporation. Its owners (members) have only limited liability, and it has tax benefits not available to a corporation.

LIMITED PARTNERSHIP

In a **limited partnership**, each limited partner is liable for any debts only up to the amount of his or her investment in the company. Every limited partnership, however, must have at least one general partner who has unlimited liability. In exchange for limited liability, the limited partners have no voice in the management of the partnership. **Limited liability** means that the personal assets of the owners cannot be taken if a company does not meet its financial obligations or if it gets into legal trouble. The withdrawal of a limited partner does not dissolve the partnership.

Advantages A partnership combines the skills of the owners. It may make more capital available, allowing easier operation and expansion. Each partner has a voice in the management of the business. A partnership is taxed solely on the profits of the business and regulated less heavily than a corporation.

Disdvantages The owners may not always agree on business decisions, yet the actions of one partner are legally binding on the other partners. This means that all partners must assume their share of the business debt. They must also be responsible for the shares of any partners who cannot pay. Finally, the business is dissolved if one partner dies. It can be reorganized as a new partnership, but the process is time consuming and costly.

THE CORPORATION

A **corporation** is a legal entity created by either a state or a federal statute, authorizing individuals to operate an enterprise. In other words, a corporation is a business that is owned by several people but is considered to be just one person or entity under the law. A corporation has several unique features:

- **Legal permission to operate** To operate a business as a corporation, the owners must file an application with state officials for permission. Once the application is approved, this document becomes the corporation's charter.
- **Separate legal entity** A corporation is a separate legal entity that is created by law. A corporation can borrow money, sign contracts, buy or sell property, and sue and be sued in court.
- **Stockholders** **Stockholders** are the owners of a corporation and have limited liability. The ownership of a corporation is divided into shares of stock. The corporation can raise money by selling stocks.
- **Board of Directors** Stockholders own the corporation, but often they do not manage it. Instead, the stockholders elect a board of directors that is responsible for major decisions that affect the company.

Corporations also offer owners limited liability. Unlike a partnership, a corporation is not affected by the death, incapacity, or bankruptcy of an officer or a shareholder.

TYPES OF CORPORATIONS

The two main types of corporations are private and public corporations. A public corporation is a business entity created by the federal, state, or local government. This group can include incorporated cities as well as school, transit, and sanitation districts.

A private corporation is formed by private persons. It includes closely held corporations or "close corporations." This category also includes publicly held corporations. These are sometimes called "public corporations" even though they are subject to different rules than the public corporations described above.

A closely held corporation is owned by a few persons or a family. Shares or stocks of a closely held corporation are not sold to the public. On the other hand, a publicly held corporation is one whose stock (shares) is owned by a large group of people. Selling stock helps a corporation raise capital. In the United States, stocks or shares of a publicly held corporation are usually sold on the New York Stock Exchange (NYSE), Euronext™, the American Stock Exchange (AMEX®), or the National Association of Securities Dealers Automated Quotations (NASDAQ®) system.

If a corporation succeeds, the value of the stock rises, and stockholders benefit. Stockholders own their shares with limited liability. For example, if a stockholder purchases $1,000 worth of Dell Computers stock and the company fails, the investor would lose the investment amount but would not be responsible for the company's debt.

EXPLAIN

Visual Literacy

Figure 33.2 Caption Answer Read the caption question to students: ***Which form of business ownership is easiest to establish?*** Sole proprietorship is the easiest to establish. Ask: ***Which form of business ownership allows for the quickest decision making?*** Sole proprietorship makes it easiest and quickest to make decisions. Then ask these guiding questions to focus students' attention on the four forms of business ownership.

Guiding Questions

Explain What is a limited partner responsible for?	A limited partner is responsible for losses only to the level of his or her investment in the business.
Analyze In which of the four forms of business organization does the owner have the least amount of control? Why?	Because of the structure of a corporation, the owners may not be involved in day-to-day operations.

Mini Project

Differentiated Learning

Interpersonal Learners Divide the class into four groups. Assign each group one of the four forms of business organization. Have group members work together to make sure each member of their group understands and can explain the form of business organization assigned to their group. Then have groups develop a lesson to teach the form of business organization to the rest of the class. Encourage groups to develop learning objectives so they can focus their teaching and to use a mix of visual and auditory teaching methods. If time and resources allow, students might create their presentations using presentation software. When presentations are complete, have each group teach their assigned form of business organization to the rest of the class. Allow the class time to ask questions for clarification and understanding.

ELABORATE

Graphic Organizer

Display a table like the one below. At the top, write *Organization Form, Advantages,* and *Disadvantages.* In the left-column, write *Sole Proprietorship, Partnership, Corporation,* and *LLC.* Ask students to provide advantages and disadvantages for each organization type. Write students' answers in the table. Sample answers are provided.

Organization Form	Advantages	Disadvantages
Sole Proprietorship	• Easy to start • Taxed less than other forms of business • More freedom from regulation • Owner entitled to all profits • Owner has control	• Owner responsible for all debts and legal judgments • Liability extends to owner's total ability to make payments
Partnership	• Combines skills of owners • May make more capital available • Each partner has a voice in management • Taxed only on profits • Less regulated than corporations	• Owners may not always agree on decisions • Actions of one partner legally binding on all partners • Business dissolved if one partner dies
Corporation	• Each owner has limited liability • Easier to raise capital • Owners can enter or exit by selling stock • Management is shared	• Formation is complex • Accounting and record keeping complicated • Increased regulation by government • Shareholders taxed on dividends and profits
LLC	• Hybrid of partnership and corporation • Allowed in all states • Owners or members protected from personal liability • Profits and losses pass directly to owners without taxation of the entity	• Federal government does not recognize as a classification for tax purposes • Must file a corporation, partnership, or sole proprietorship tax return

 **glencoe.com** 

Graphic Organizer Send student to the Online Learning Center to print this graphic organizer.

Critical Thinking

Bring to class some "businesses for sale" ads for sole proprietorships from a local or national newspaper. Read the ads to students and ask them to generate a list of the things they would consider before buying each business. Answers may include: money needed to invest, products sold, legal requirements for start-up, and location.

e MARKETING

Pure Play Businesses

A pure play business is one that did not have a physical presence before opening on the Web. Its business is conducted solely on the Internet. Originally designed as an online bookstore, Amazon.com is an example of a pure play business. Now it is a multinational online retailer that sells books and a host of different products, such as video games, apparel, toys, software, electronics, and furniture. Netflix® and eBay® are also pure play businesses.

Brick and mortar businesses that have a presence on the Internet utilize multi-channel marketing. Most large retailers, like Walmart®, Kmart®, and Best Buy® offer multiple channels for customers to shop. Customers can shop in the brick and mortar store or online via the company's Web site.

Innovate and Create

Have students work in groups and research the steps involved in opening a pure play business and also what is involved in selling goods on Amazon.com. Let students decide which avenue they would take if they wanted to start selling goods or services online. Have students share their group's decision and rationale in an oral report and a one-page written report. Research into opening a pure play business may include the following topics: obtaining a vendor's license, registering a domain name, finding wholesalers, designing your Web site, which may involve purchasing software or hiring a Web site designer (be sure the Web site can facilitate online payment), selecting a hosting service, deciding on shipping requirements and inventory methods (or find wholesalers that drop ship), develop a marketing plan and a means to get your site viewed on search engines, research federal internet laws, as well as state and local regulations, and federal, state, and local tax requirements. If selling internationally, you must also know international trade laws. To sell on Amazon.com or eBay.com the process is less complicated. However, these sites do charge a fee for transactions made on their Web sites. When evaluating the group's oral and written reports, include a rubric for the required research which should be evident in the rationale for the method selected for starting an online business.

 **glencoe.com** 

eMarketing Worksheet Activity Send students to the Online Learning Center to download an eMarketing worksheet activity.

FORMING A CORPORATION

Forming a corporation is a complicated process. An entrepreneur must determine the company's internal corporate structure. This is defined by its bylaws, and the processes for selecting a board of directors and electing officers. The officers handle the day-to-day operations. In small corporations, members of the board of directors are usually elected as the officers of the corporation.

An entrepreneur must also choose the state in which to incorporate (establish) the company. For small companies, it is generally best to do this in the state where the company will do business. A **foreign corporation** is one that is incorporated under the laws of a state that differs from the one in which it does business. *Foreign* in this context means another state, not another country. Foreign corporations must register with each state in which they intend to do business.

Advantages Each owner has limited liability. It is easier to raise capital with corporations than with other forms of business. Capital is often needed for expansion. Owners can easily enter or exit the business simply by buying or selling stock. Management is shared. Each area of the business is handled by someone with expertise in that area.

Disadvantages The process of formation can be complex, and the accounting and record keeping can be complicated. Government regulation is increased. There are taxable corporate profits, which means shareholders are taxed on dividends they earn and on profits made from the sale of a stock.

LIMITED LIABILITY COMPANY

The **limited liability company (LLC)** is a relatively new form of business organization that is a hybrid of a partnership and a corporation. LLCs are now allowed in all 50 states. The LLC is sometimes incorrectly called a "limited liability corporation," instead of company. The federal government does not recognize an LLC as a classification for federal tax purposes. Thus, an LLC must file a corporation, partnership, or sole proprietorship tax return. Its owners, or members, are protected from personal liability. All profits and losses pass directly to the owners without taxation of the entity itself.

Reading Check

Summarize What are the forms of business organization?

LEGAL STEPS TO ESTABLISHING A BUSINESS

Before an entrepreneur can officially open the doors of a new business, he or she must take specific steps to legally establish and protect the business. These steps **vary** depending on whether the business will be a sole proprietorship, partnership, a corporation, or a limited liability company.

New business owners may wish to consult an accountant, attorney, or other business advisor to determine the best organization for a new business. When a corporation is formed, the laws of many states require that an attorney be hired. An attorney can guide the entrepreneur through the complicated process of incorporation. The entrepreneur must check the laws of the state in which she or he is incorporating.

To form a sole proprietorship or partnership, a business owner must file for a DBA at the local county clerk's office. A **DBA (Doing Business As)** is the registration by which the county government officially recognizes that a new proprietorship or partnership exists.

A DBA also protects the name of the business for a certain number of years. This name protection applies only to the county where the business is registered. There is usually a filing fee for registration.

To form a corporation, an entrepreneur must file Articles of Incorporation with the Corporation and Securities Bureau in the state's Department of Commerce. **Articles of Incorporation** identify the name and address of a new corporation, its purpose, and the names of the initial directors. They also include the amount of stock that will be issued to each director. There is a filing fee, but the business becomes protected. No other business may register under that business's name. The forms, applications, and information on filing fees can be obtained from the state's Department of Commerce.

An LLC is established by filing Articles of Organization with the state. This document describes the LLC and lists the names of its members and initial managers. Many states also require LLCs to have an operating agreement. For the company to have the tax advantage of an LLC, this document must show that the company is distinct from a corporation.

Depending on the type of business and where it is located, a new owner may have to obtain one or more licenses in order to operate.

Licenses establish minimum standards of education and training for people who practice in a particular profession. They also regulate where businesses can locate, and they protect neighborhoods and the environment.

Individual states license many businesses and occupations, such as doctors, accountants, cosmetologists, barbers, marriage counselors, and pharmacists. Licensing is done to protect the public from unqualified people practicing in a business. Licensing also helps maintain the health and welfare of the citizens.

In addition to state licenses, the community may require special local licenses or permits to comply with zoning ordinances, building codes, and safety standards.

After You Read **Section 33.2**

Review Key Concepts

1. **Name** the four ways to become a business owner.
2. **List** the four legal forms of business organization and note which is the most common.
3. **Name** an advantage of a limited liability company.

Practice Academics

Social Studies

4. The U.S. government protects copyrights, trademarks, and patents for new businesses. Research these terms on the Internet and write a description of the type of protection provided for each.

Mathematics

5. A friend who just opened a new business works 12 hours a day, 5 days a week, 50 weeks a year. How many hours does this person work annually? To how many 40-hour workweeks is this equivalent?

Math Concept **Solving Time Problems** When solving problems that ask for values associated with time periods, know the equivalent measurements. For example, there are 24 hours in a day, 7 days in a week, and 52 weeks in a year.

Starting Hints Multiply the number of hours worked each day by the number of days worked each week, and then the number of weeks worked each year to determine the total number of hours worked in a year. Divide the total hours worked in a year by 40 to determine the number of 40-hour workweeks.

For help, go to the **Math Skills Handbook** located at the back of this book.

NCSS VI B Power, Authority, & Governance Explain the purpose of government and analyze how its powers are acquired, used, and justified.

NCTM Measurement Understand measurable attributes of objects and the units, systems, and processes of measurement.

glencoe.com Check your answers.

ELABORATE

Critical Thinking

Have students create a chart that compares each type of business organization—sole proprietorship, partnership, corporation, and LLC. Students should use these headings to compare the types of businesses: Initial Investment, Level of Risk, Taxes, Ease/Difficulty of Starting a Business.

Reading Check Answer

Read the Reading Check question to students: ***What are the forms of business organization?*** The forms of business organization include sole proprietorship, the partnership (general partnership and limited partnership), the corporation, and limited liability company.

LEGAL STEPS TO ESTABLISHING A BUSINESS

Tell students that there are a number of legal requirements that must be met before opening a business. Then ask these guiding questions to focus the discussion on legal steps to establishing a business.

Guiding Questions

Explain What are Articles of Incorporation?	documents that must be filed with the Corporation and Securities Bureau in the state's Department of Commerce; they identify the name and address of a new corporation, its purpose, the names of initial directors, and the amount of stock that will be issued to each director
Evaluate List the four forms of business organization in order from easiest to most difficult to establish. Explain your reasoning.	Sole proprietorships and partnerships are the easiest to establish; corporations and LLCs require more extensive legal effort to establish

EVALUATE

Graphic Organizer

Display this diagram. Ask students to provide the steps for establishing each form of business organization. List students' answers in the diagram. Sample answers are provided.

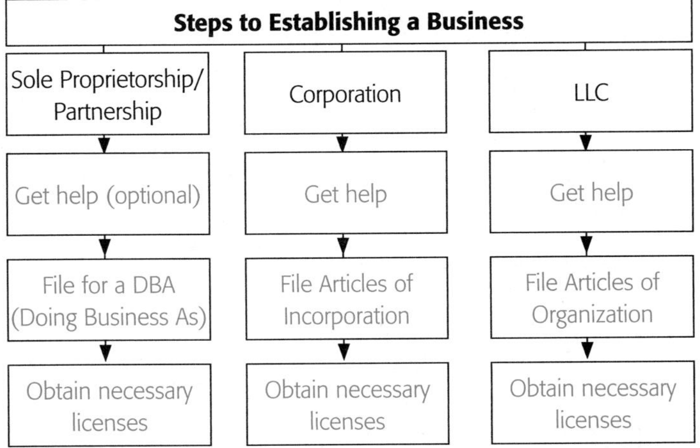

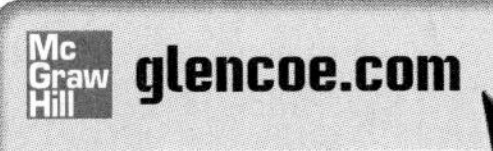 **glencoe.com** 

Graphic Organizer Send student to the Online Learning Center to print this graphic organizer.

Mini Projects

Extension

Research Online Businesses Have students research the regulations required for registering businesses that conduct operations over the Internet. Encourage students to choose one company or organization which conducts its business over the Internet and describe at least two characteristics of that business that relate to the Internet. For example, Amazon.com advertises and sells books and other items online. Have students summarize their findings in a one-page report to share with the class.

Interview an Entrepreneur Have students make an appointment to speak with a business owner in your area. Before the interview, students should create a list of questions to ask the owner. Questions should focus on how the business is structured (sole proprietorship, partnership, corporation, or LLC) and what legal requirements the owner(s) followed to establish the business. Tell students to take notes during the interview. Then have them write a summary of the interview. Ask volunteers to share their summaries with the class.

 **After You Read** **Section 33.2**

Review Key Concepts

1. Four ways to become a business owner are: start a new business, purchase a franchise, purchase an existing nonfranchise business, and take over a family business.
2. Four legal forms of business organization are sole proprietorship, partnership, corporation, and limited liability company. Sole proprietorship is the most common form of business organization.
3. Advantages of a limited liability company: It has certain tax benefits, and its owners are shielded from personal liability.

Practice Academics

Social Studies

4. A trademark is a symbol, word, phrase, or design that identifies the source of goods; it can be used legally only by the owner of the trademark. A copyright protect an original artistic or literary work. A patent protects an invention.

Mathematics

5. The friend works 3,000 hours annually, which is the equivalent of 75 40-hour workweeks. (12 × 5 × 50 = 3,000; 3,000 ÷ 40 = 75)

 **glencoe.com**

Answer Key Send students to the Online Learning Center to check their answers.

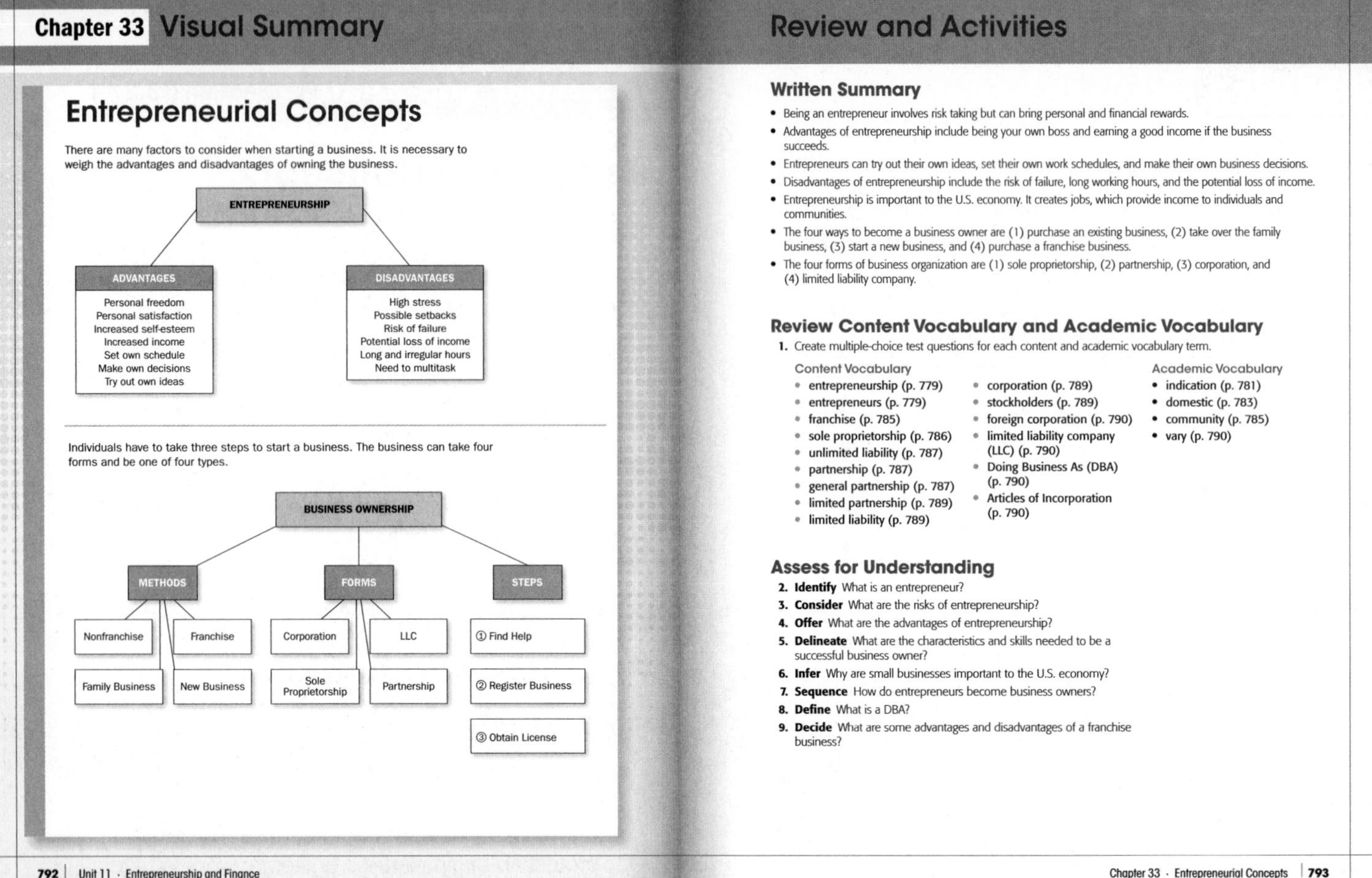

Chapter 33 Visual Summary

Entrepreneurial Concepts

There are many factors to consider when starting a business. It is necessary to weigh the advantages and disadvantages of owning the business.

Individuals have to take three steps to start a business. The business can take four forms and be one of four types.

792 | Unit 11 · Entrepreneurship and Finance

Review and Activities

Written Summary

- Being an entrepreneur involves risk taking but can bring personal and financial rewards.
- Advantages of entrepreneurship include being your own boss and earning a good income if the business succeeds.
- Entrepreneurs can try out their own ideas, set their own work schedules, and make their own business decisions.
- Disadvantages of entrepreneurship include the risk of failure, long working hours, and the potential loss of income.
- Entrepreneurship is important to the U.S. economy. It creates jobs, which provide income to individuals and communities.
- The four ways to become a business owner are (1) purchase an existing business, (2) take over the family business, (3) start a new business, and (4) purchase a franchise business.
- The four forms of business organization are (1) sole proprietorship, (2) partnership, (3) corporation, and (4) limited liability company.

Review Content Vocabulary and Academic Vocabulary

1. Create multiple-choice test questions for each content and academic vocabulary term.

Content Vocabulary
- entrepreneurship (p. 779)
- entrepreneurs (p. 779)
- franchise (p. 785)
- sole proprietorship (p. 786)
- unlimited liability (p. 787)
- partnership (p. 787)
- general partnership (p. 787)
- limited partnership (p. 789)
- limited liability (p. 789)
- corporation (p. 789)
- stockholders (p. 789)
- foreign corporation (p. 790)
- limited liability company (LLC) (p. 790)
- Doing Business As (DBA) (p. 790)
- Articles of Incorporation (p. 790)

Academic Vocabulary
- indication (p. 781)
- domestic (p. 783)
- community (p. 785)
- vary (p. 790)

Assess for Understanding

2. **Identify** What is an entrepreneur?
3. **Consider** What are the risks of entrepreneurship?
4. **Offer** What are the advantages of entrepreneurship?
5. **Delineate** What are the characteristics and skills needed to be a successful business owner?
6. **Infer** Why are small businesses important to the U.S. economy?
7. **Sequence** How do entrepreneurs become business owners?
8. **Define** What is a DBA?
9. **Decide** What are some advantages and disadvantages of a franchise business?

Chapter 33 · Entrepreneurial Concepts | 793

EVALUATE

Visual Summary

Express Creativity Ask students to develop their own visual summary of a concept in the chapter. Encourage students to use different formats for their visual summaries, such as a storyboard, a timeline, a table, a tree diagram, or a word web. Visual summaries will vary depending on the concept depicted and the visual manner in which it is depicted. Questions to ask when assessing a visual summary include:

- Is the summary clear, economical, and simple?
- Are any important steps left out?
- Are steps or concepts arranged in the same order as the original?
- Does the summary reveal a pattern that connects the details?
- Does the summary locate and highlight the most important information?

Review Content Vocabulary and Academic Vocabulary

1. Multiple-choice questions will vary. Sample questions:

   Entrepreneurship is
   a. a legal agreement to sell a parent company's product or services in a designated geographic area.
   b. the process of starting and operating your own business.
   c. a business that is owned and operated by one person.
   d. a legal agreement between two or more people to be jointly responsible for the success or failure of a business.

   Entrepreneurs create, launch, organize, and manage
   a. a business for someone else.
   b. large projects for their employers.
   c. a new business and take the risk of business ownership.
   d. an established business.

   A **franchise** is
   a. a legal agreement to sell a parent company's product or services in a designated geographic area.
   b. the process of starting and operating your own business.
   c. a business that is owned and operated by one person.
   d. a legal agreement between two or more people to be jointly responsible for the success or failure of a business.

EVALUATE

Assess for Understanding

2. An entrepreneur is someone who creates, launches, organizes, and manages a new business and takes the risk of business ownership.

3. The risks of entrepreneurship include potential failure, loss of income, and poor health.

4. Advantages of entrepreneurship include personal freedom, satisfaction, increased income, and increased self-esteem.

5. Determination, self-motivation, self-discipline, self-confidence, strong organizational skills, leadership ability, creativity, willingness to work hard, spirit of adventure, and good social skills are characteristics and skills needed to be a successful business owner.

6. Small businesses produce 50 percent of the GDP, and they generate growth at a faster rate than other larger and more established businesses.

7. Entrepreneurs can become business owners by starting a new business, purchasing a franchise, purchasing an existing business, or taking over a family business.

8. A DBA (Doing Business As) is the registration by which the county government officially recognizes that a new proprietorship or partnership exists.

9. Some advantages of a franchise business include: the franchisor provides a well-known name, a business plan, advertising, and the proven methods and products of the parent company; new business owners have a lot of help; the business planning is done by the franchisor; planning includes management training, merchandising, and day-to-day operations. Disadvantages include: the initial cost; a large amount of capital is needed to purchase most franchises; the franchisee must also pay high initial fees to begin operations; many franchisors are very strict about how the franchise is run.

Chapter 33 Review and Activities

21st Century Skills

Social Responsibility Skills

10. **Social Responsibility** You have decided to become an entrepreneur. You know that you will have to learn a great deal to run a business. However, you have also become very interested in social responsibility and environmental concerns. Conduct research on what businesses are doing to preserve the environment and be more socially responsible. Write a description of how you would plan your own business, addressing these concerns.

Financial Literacy Skills

11. **Expenses** You and a friend are considering a business picking up and delivering clothing for a local cleaning service. Your major expense would be for the purchase of a used van. Suppose that you have located a suitable van at a local dealer priced at $6,000. If you can pay 20 percent down, find out the interest rate a local bank or credit union would charge for a loan. How much would the monthly payments be and for how many months?

Everyday Ethics

12. **Finding a Need** In 1981, an attorney established a company called CMG Worldwide after he realized that many deceased celebrities had no one to safeguard their interests. CMG negotiates the use of clients' names and images in a variety of commercial contracts, from TV ads to posters and T-shirts. Elvis Presley, CMG's first client, brings in more than $50 million each year. Other CMG clients include Babe Ruth, Ella Fitzgerald, Duke Ellington, Mark Twain, and Marilyn Monroe. Even if a client's estate or family approved, should a deceased celebrity represent a product he or she would not have liked when alive? Express your opinion in a brief paragraph.

e-Marketing Skills

13. **e-Marketing Problems** Investigate the difficulties faced by new online businesses. Research on the Internet, using key words such as *e-marketing problems* and *online marketing problems*. List the problems, starting with what you believe would be the most difficult, ending the list with the easiest problem to solve.

Build Academic Skills

Social Studies

14. **Matching Interests** Interview an entrepreneur who owns and operates a retail business that you think might be interesting. Ask questions about what the owner likes and dislikes about owning a business. Ask how he or she got started in business and what knowledge, skills, and personal qualities are important for success. As you listen, you may think of and ask other questions. Prepare a written summary of your interview.

NCSS VII D Production, Distribution, and Consumption Describe relationships among the various economic institutions that comprise economic systems such as households, business firms, banks, government agencies, labor unions, and corporations.

English Language Arts

15. **Business Organization** Conduct Internet research to learn how to form either a partnership or a corporation. You can find information by searching with key words such as *forming a partnership*, and *forming a corporation*. Write a one- or two-page report on your findings.

NCTE 4 Use written language to communicate effectively.

Mathematics

16. **Calculate Profit** A clothing company had a sales revenue of $4,000,000 last year. Its profit was $2,500,000. Of that profit, 20 percent was allocated for new equipment. How much is left after the purchase of the new equipment?

NCTM Algebra Represent and analyze mathematical situations and structures using algebraic symbols.

Math Concept **Solving Multi-Step Problems** When solving problems that require multiple steps, make a list of the information given in the problem, as well as the information for which you will be solving. This will make clear the relationships between what you are looking for and what is given.

For help, go to the **Math Skills Handbook** located at the back of this book.

Standardized Test Practice

Directions Read the following questions. On a separate piece of paper, write the best possible answer for each one.

1. A corporation is owned by the
   - **A.** members
   - **B.** board of directors
   - **C.** stockholders
   - **D.** partners
2. A limited liability company (LLC) is a cross between a partnership and a corporation.
   T
   F
3. The most common form of business ownership is a ________.

Test-Taking Tip

If you do not know the answer on multiple-choice and true/false questions, always guess if there is no penalty for wrong answers, but never guess if there is a penalty.

DECA Connection Role Play

Consultant
Start-Up Company

Situation You are a consultant for a business that advises potential entrepreneurs about realizing their dream of owning their own business. Today you are going to meet with a new client (judge). The new client (judge) is a jewelry designer who works with sterling silver and semi-precious stones. The jewelry designer (judge) has been making jewelry as a hobby for the past three years. The jewelry designer (judge) has sold his/her jewelry to family, friends, and at craft fairs. The jewelry designer's (judge's) reputation for beautiful and unique designs has spread throughout your community.

Customer demand for the jewelry has increased to the point where the designer (judge) feels that the time has come to open his/her own shop. The jewelry designer (judge) has found a perfect location for a shop. The building has space for a workroom and a showroom/sales area. The building is located in an area that is adjacent to the shops of other artists.

The reasonable rent has convinced the designer (judge) that the time is right to open the business. The jewelry designer (judge) has little business experience and has many questions for you. Today's meeting will focus on some basics of business ownership.

Activity You are to discuss with the jewelry designer (judge) the types of business ownership and organizational design for the proposed business, as well as some of the legal issues that affect businesses.

Evaluation You will be evaluated on how well you meet the following performance indicators:

1. Explain the types of business ownership.
2. Describe legal issues affecting businesses.
3. Explain the organizational design of businesses.
4. Explain how organizations adapt to today's markets.
5. Demonstrate responsible behavior.

Download the Competitive Events Workbook for more Role-Play practice.

EVALUATE

21st Century Skills

Social Responsibility Skills

10. Students' descriptions will vary but should address how they would plan their business to be socially responsible and not harmful to the environment. They might discuss such things as giving back to the community and using environmentally friendly cleaning supplies or fuels.

Financial Literacy Skills

11. The interest rate on a loan for $4,800 will vary by bank or credit union depending on current rates. The monthly payments and length of the loan will also vary.

Everyday Ethics

12. Students' paragraphs will vary but should indicate whether they feel it is ethical to use a deceased celebrity to promote a product he or she may not have liked. Students may point out that it might be difficult or impossible to determine whether the deceased would or would not have liked the product.

e-Marketing Skills

13. e-Marketing problems will vary but may include: cybercrime; inability of customer to touch and feel the product; low-speed Internet connections; and outdated technology. Students should list the problems from most-difficult-to-fix to easiest-to-fix.

EVALUATE

Build Academic Skills

Social Studies

14. Written summaries should contains answers to questions regarding what the owner likes and dislikes about owning a business, how he or she got started in business, and what knowledge, skills, and personal qualities are important for success.

English Language Arts

15. Reports should contain information on forming a partnership or corporation. Information might include: choosing a business name, registering the business, creating an agreement among owners, obtaining appropriate licenses, and so on.

Mathematics

16. The answer is $2,000,000 ($2,500,000 × .80).

Standardized Test Practice

1. C (stockholders)
2. T
3. sole proprietorship

DECA Connection Role Play

Evaluations will be based on these performance indicators:

1. **Explain the types of business ownership.** Types of business ownership include purchase of an existing nonfranchise business, takeover of a family business, starting a new business, or purchasing a franchise.
2. **Describe legal issues affecting businesses.** Before an entrepreneur can officially open the doors of a new business, he or she must take specific steps to legally establish and protect the business. These steps vary depending on whether the business will be a sole proprietorship, partnership, corporation, or limited liability company. To form a sole proprietorship or partnership, a business owner must file for a DBA at the local county clerk's office. To form a corporation, an entrepreneur must file Articles of Incorporation with the Corporation and Securities Bureau in the state's Department of Commerce. An LLC is established by filing Articles of Organization with the state.
3. **Explain the organizational design of businesses.** A sole proprietorship is a business that is owned and operated by one person. A partnership is a legal agreement between two or more people to be jointly responsible for the success or failure of a business. A corporation is a legal entity created by either a state or a federal statute, authorizing individuals to operate an enterprise. The limited liability company (LLC) is a relatively new form of business organization that is a hybrid of a partnership and a corporation.
4. **Explain how businesses adapt to today's markets.** There are a number of methods companies use to adapt to today's markets. They may conduct various types of research to learn what consumers want or need and then determine how to implement changes based on company goals and budget.
5. **Demonstrate responsible behavior.** Demonstrations will vary but may include students providing appropriate information to the jewelry designer—information that will help him or her determine what type of business to pursue, how to organize the business, and certain legal matters.

Mc Graw Hill **glencoe.com**

Role Plays For more DECA Role Plays, send students to the Online Learning Center to download the Competitive Events Workbook.

risk management

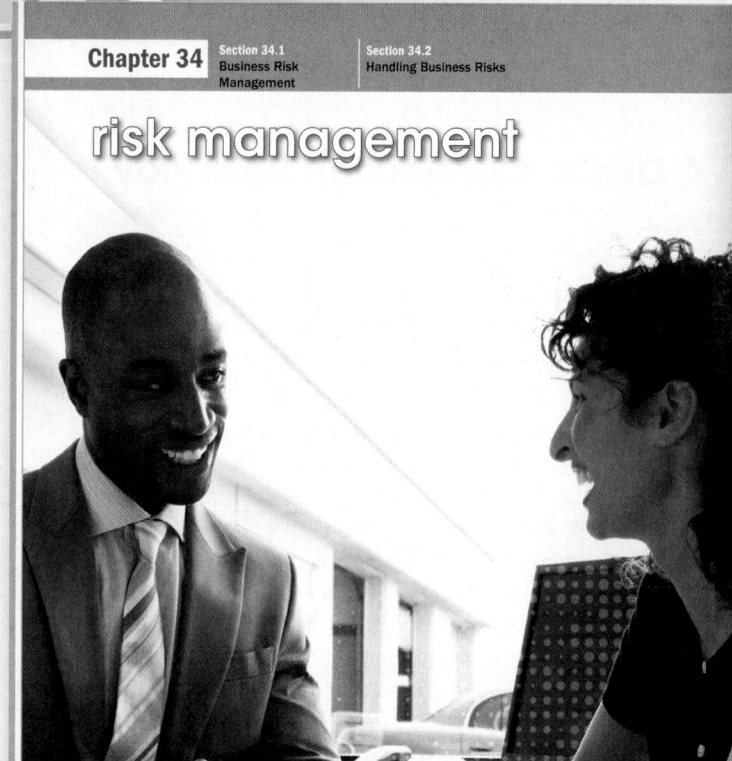

SHOW WHAT YOU KNOW

Visual Literacy Risk is part of doing business. Managing risk is part of the planning process for every business. Risk management strives to prevent risks that can be avoided. It also aims to minimize the risks that are beyond the control of a business. ***What kinds of risks might be avoided and minimized for a business?***

Discovery Project

Retail Risks

Essential Question How does a business manage its risks?

Project Goal

You and a classmate work for a company that helps clients develop risk management plans for retailers. The client has asked you to plan an internal theft and shoplifting prevention plan. Research some strategies that stores use to prevent internal theft and shoplifting. You are to prepare a written report on the specific measures that your team would recommend for handling retail theft.

Ask Yourself...

- How will you find out about other stores' policies and strategies?
- What general policies and procedures regarding retail theft would you recommend?
- What specific measures would you recommend to handle internal theft?
- What specific measures would you recommend to handle shoplifting?
- How will you organize your report and summarize your recommendations?

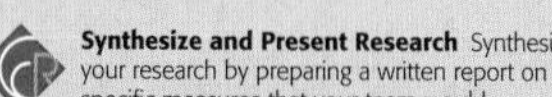

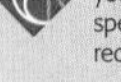

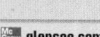

Synthesize and Present Research Synthesize your research by preparing a written report on the specific measures that your team would recommend for handling retail theft.

glencoe.com

Activity
Get a worksheet activity about risk management.

Evaluate
Download a rubric you can use to evaluate your project.

DECA Connection

DECA Event Role Play

Concepts in this chapter are related to DECA competitive events that involve either an interview or role play.

Performance Indicators The performance indicators represent key skills and knowledge. Your key to success in DECA competitive events is relating them to concepts in this chapter.

- Determine the factors affecting business risk.
- Follow established security procedures/policies.
- Identify the key loss prevention methods retailers use to reduce shrinkage.
- Describe the concept of insurance.
- Explain the nature of risk management.

DECA Prep

Role Play Practice role-playing with the DECA Connection competitive-event activity at the end of this chapter. More information on DECA events can be found on DECA's Web site.

ENGAGE

Visual Literacy

Read the chapter opener photo caption question to students: ***What kinds of risks might be avoided and minimized for a business?*** Answers may include: Risks involving natural disasters can be minimized by purchasing insurance. Risks involving stealing by customers and employees can be minimized by proper security measures. Then ask these guiding questions.

Guiding Questions

Identify What are some of the external factors posing threats or risks that might be listed in a SWOT analysis?	Possible answers: strong competition, recession, government regulations, lifestyle and population changes.
Analyze What governmental agencies work to reduce risks to workers?	Possible answer: OSHA sets workplace safety guidelines.

Discovery Project

Retail Risks Start a discussion about the Discovery Project Essential Question: ***How does a business manage its risks?*** First the business must identify those risks. For example, a retail store might be concerned with internal theft and shoplifting. The store then can choose the methods it uses to handle the risks, such as risk prevention and control, risk transfer, risk retention, and risk avoidance. For example, shoplifting might be handled by risk prevention and control while natural disasters might be managed by risk transfer (buying insurance).

glencoe.com

Discovery Project Resources Send students to the Online Learning Center to download a rubric to evaluate their projects.

ENGAGE

Introduce the Chapter

Chapter 34 introduces students to the concept of business risk and what can be done to manage these risks. These major concepts are discussed:

- Definition of risk management
- Economic risks
- Natural risks
- Human risks
- Risk prevention and control
- Risk transfer
- Property and liability insurance
- Risk retention
- Risk avoidance

Discussion Starter

Being Aware of Risks Ask students to give examples of risks they take in their own lives. Display their risk examples for the class. Have students discuss ways they work to minimize these risks. They may, for example, try to eat right in order to stay healthy and study hard to maintain good grades. Discuss that each time we step into a car, we risk being involved in an accident. Ask: ***What can drivers do to lower the risk of an accident?*** Possible answers: Obey traffic laws and use defensive driving techniques; avoid distractions such as cell phones and other electronic devices. Ask: ***What are some ways we try to reduce damages if an accident should occur?*** We use seatbelts, drive cars that have safety features, and have insurance.

DECA Connection

Discuss the performance indicators listed in the DECA Connection feature. Explain to students that performance indicators tell them how to demonstrate their acquired skills and knowledge through individual or team competitive events.

glencoe.com

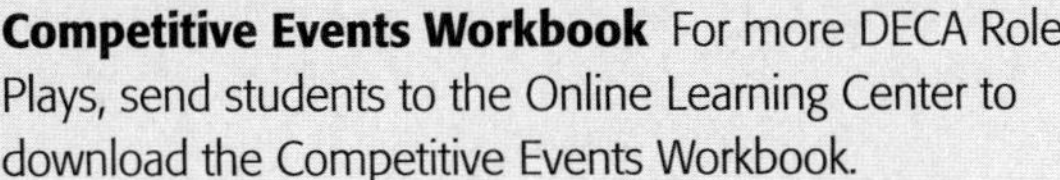

Competitive Events Workbook For more DECA Role Plays, send students to the Online Learning Center to download the Competitive Events Workbook.

PRINT RESOURCES

- **Student Edition**
- **Teacher Edition**
- **Student Activity Workbook with Academic Integration** includes worksheets and activities correlated to the text.
- **Mathematics for Marketing Workbook** provides math activities for every unit in the text.

TECHNOLOGY TOOLBOX

- **Connect**
- **ConnectPlus**
- **ExamView Assessment Suite** is a comprehensive solution for creating, administering, and scoring tests.

glencoe.com

Online Learning Center provides a variety of resources to enrich and enhance learning.

SECTION, CHAPTER, AND UNIT RESOURCES

- **Graphic Organizers** for organizing text concepts visually.
- **Digital Nation Activities** and **Green Marketer Activities** extend learning beyond the text features.
- **Career Chatroom Career Profiles** allow students to explore different marketing occupations in depth.
- **After You Read Answer Keys** for students to check their answers.
- **Discovery Project Rubrics** and **Marketing Internship Project Rubrics** for students to evaluate their projects.

PROGRAM RESOURCES

- **Student Activity Workbook with Academic Integration Teacher Annotated Edition** includes annotated answers for the activities and worksheets.
- **Marketing Research Project Workbook** provides a step-by-step approach for students to complete their own marketing research studies.
- **School-to-Career Activity Workbook** helps students relate their class work to on-the-job experience and involves work-site analysis and working with mentors.
- **Competitive Events Workbook** helps prepare students for state and national marketing education competitions.
- **Inclusion in the Marketing Education Classroom** provides teaching resources for working with students with special needs.
- **PowerPoint Presentations** provides visual teaching aids and assessments for this chapter.

READING GUIDE

Before You Read

Predict What are some possible risks for businesses?

Objectives

- **Explain** the nature and scope of risk management.
- **Identify** the various types of business risks.

The Main Idea

Risk is part of doing business. Businesses manage risks to benefit public interest, safety, and the environment and to comply with existing laws.

Vocabulary

Content Vocabulary
- business risk
- risk management
- economic risks
- natural risks
- human risks

Academic Vocabulary

You will find these words in your reading and on your tests. Make sure you know their meanings.
- stress
- internal

Graphic Organizer

Draw or print this chart to identify business risks and provide examples of those risks.

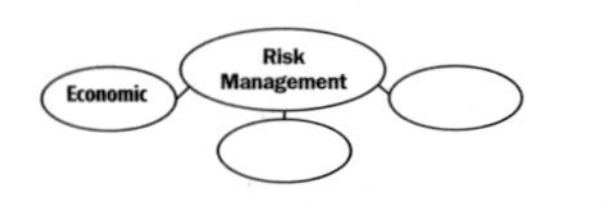

Print this graphic organizer.

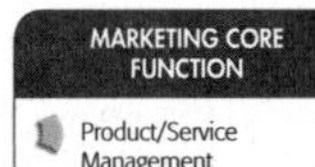

STANDARDS

ACADEMIC

English Language Arts

NCTE 1 Read texts to acquire new information.

NCTE 12 Use language to accomplish individual purposes.

Mathematics

NCTM Number and Operations Compute fluently and make reasonable estimates.

Social Studies

NCSS X D Civic Ideals & Practices Practice forms of civic discussion and participation consistent with the ideals of citizens in a democratic republic.

NCSS *National Council for the Social Studies*
NCTE *National Council of Teachers of English*
NCTM *National Council of Teachers of Mathematics*
NSES *National Science Education Standards*

Common Core
Reading Read closely to determine what the text says explicitly and to make logical inferences from it; cite specific textual evidence when writing or speaking to support conclusions drawn from the text.

m.e. Section 34.1

Business Risk Management

WHAT IS RISK MANAGEMENT?

The primary goal of every business is to make a profit. However, there is no guarantee that this will happen. A business may experience a lower return on investment than was expected. The business may experience a loss after all the expenses have been paid. The possibility of financial loss is what is known as *business risk*. A **business risk** is a situation that can lead to financial gain, loss, or failure. A business cannot eliminate all risk, but marketers can use their planning skills to reduce and manage their risks.

According to the American Risk and Insurance Association, **risk management** is the systematic process of managing an organization's risks to achieve objectives in a manner consistent with public interest, human safety, environmental needs, and the law. Risks are managed by using the best available marketing information, analyzing opportunities, and making wise decisions.

As You Read

Analyze Is it possible for a business to eliminate business risks?

TYPES OF BUSINESS RISKS

Risks to businesses come in many forms. Economic, natural, and human risks are among the types of risks that a business may experience.

ECONOMIC RISKS

Economic risks are risks that result from changes in overall business conditions. These changes can include the level or type of competition, changing consumer lifestyles, population changes, limited usefulness or style of some products, product obsolescence, government regulation, inflation, or recession.

Failure to keep up with competition may lead to lost sales and economic risk. Foreign competition is also a threat. Products can often be produced and sold for less than similar domestic products.

> "Risk management is an around-the-clock, every day-of-the-year concern for businesses."

Consumer lifestyles and population changes are other economic risks facing modern businesses if they fail to adapt goods or services to meet customers' changing interests and needs.

The limited usefulness or style of some products is another potential economic risk. Prices are frequently reduced on products to sell them at the end of the season. Every price reduction reduces both revenue and profits.

Some products inevitably become obsolete or outdated. Known as *product obsolescence*, this type of economic risk frequently concerns businesses that depend on the latest trends to market goods and services. Obsolescence occurs because new products are constantly being developed, and new trends are being started. When a new product is hipper, faster, more convenient, or more efficient than its earlier versions, the older product becomes obsolete.

Changes in the general business environment caused by inflation or recession can also present economic risks for retail businesses. For example, businesses in a geographic area experiencing high unemployment will suffer because consumers will likely cut back on purchases.

ENGAGE

Anticipation Activity

Improving Student Achievement To prepare for reading this section, have students work in groups of five or six to compose their own tales about Sad Sam's Service Station, a place where everything seems to go wrong. Encourage students to incorporate a wide variety of disasters involving employees, customers, the weather, and so on. Have each group share its story and categorize the risks under the headings *economic, natural,* and *human.*

Objectives

- **Explain** the nature and scope of risk management. Risk management refers to systematically managing an organization's risks to achieve objectives in a manner consistent with public interest, human safety, environmental needs, and the law.
- **Identify** the various types of business risks. Types of business risks include economic risks, natural risks, and human risks.

Graphic Organizer

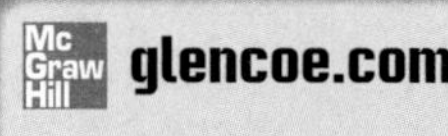

Graphic Organizer Send students to the Online Learning Center to print this graphic organizer.

EXPLORE

Before You Read

Read the Before You Read question aloud: ***What are some possible risks for businesses?*** Risks may include: a competitor coming up with better or less-expensive products; company products becoming obsolete; a natural disaster, such as a flood or earthquake, that causes costly damage; a company may be required to recall an unsafe product, which can be financially disastrous and damaging to the company's reputation.

Preteaching Vocabulary

Have students go to the Online Learning Center at glencoe.com for the Chapter 34 Preteaching Vocabulary games.

Content Vocabulary

Display the word *risk* for the class to read. Explain that it can be defined as "the possibility of loss or injury." Then read aloud each of the Content Vocabulary terms. Point out that each one contains the word *risk.* Discuss that in this section, students will learn about the wide variety of risks that confront businesses.

Academic Vocabulary

Stress—Usage Display the word *stress* for the class to read. Then read aloud this sentence: ***Restaurants have safety programs that stress the importance of proper food handling.*** Ask: ***Is stress used as a noun or a verb in this sentence?*** verb Then ask: ***Can you think of a sentence that uses stress as a noun?*** Sample sentence: The assistant manager was under stress to complete the project on time.

Internal—Antonyms Display the word *internal* for the class to read. Ask students: ***What are some antonyms for* internal?** external, outside, outer Then display a large circle and write *internal* inside of it; then write *external* in the area outside of the circle. Discuss that events occurring within a company are internal, while events occurring anywhere else are external.

Critical Thinking

Display headlines and articles from local print or online news publications that address current business conditions. Lead a discussion about the general business environment in your area. Ask students if business is going through an inflationary or a recessionary period and have them describe some of the risks associated with these factors. Point out that recessions often lead to higher unemployment, which leads to lower revenues for local businesses, which in turn feeds higher unemployment as businesses cut costs and lay off workers.

WHAT IS RISK MANAGEMENT?

Tell students that the purpose of risk management is to reduce or manage the chances for losses. Ask these guiding questions.

Guiding Questions

Recall What is business risk?	the possibility of financial loss
Analyze How can population changes lead to economic risk? Give an example of a situation in which this might occur.	Different demographics have different purchasing patterns. A skateboard shop might do well if lots of teens live nearby, but in an older community, it might fail.
Synthesize Why is it important that a business have the best available marketing information when attempting to manage risks?	Without it, a business cannot make wise decisions. If poor decisions are made, products are likely to fail, causing the company to lose money.

Critical Thinking

Bring in items such as cassette tapes as examples of product obsolescence. Ask how product obsolescence is an economic risk. Businesses can get stuck with merchandise they cannot sell.

As You Read

Read students the As You Read question: ***Is it possible for a business to eliminate business risks?*** No, because risk is inevitable in our world. Ask: ***What can responsible business owners do about risk?*** They can work to reduce and manage it. For example, they can reduce risk through rigorous employee training and manage risk by purchasing insurance.

Expert Advice

"Risk management is an around-the-clock, every day-of-the-year concern for businesses."

Ask: ***What might happen if a company does not constantly watch for risks that must be managed?*** The company will probably lose sales and profits, and has a strong chance of failure.

Government Regulations

Government laws and regulations can also result in economic risks. Laws that require businesses to pay for such things as special licenses or permits, street and sewer improvements, special assessments for environmental clean-ups, parking, and general upkeep may contribute to reduced profits.

Another risk is product recall. A product recall is a request to return to the maker a part of a product or an entire product. This usually occurs when safety is in question. A recall is an effort to limit liability and to avoid or curb negative publicity.

Product recalls, or even the threat of recalls, by government agencies can affect sales and profits. Companies experience additional expenses because product recalls require notification to all owners through paid media outlets, customer mailings, and provisions for free repair and replacement parts.

In addition to expensive repairs and replacements, companies with recalled products that caused injuries or deaths face high legal costs and injury claim settlements. These companies may also suffer from damaged reputations, which can be costly to rebuild.

NATURAL RISKS

Natural risks are risks that are caused by natural occurrences. They can result in loss or damage of property and may cause a business to shut down for a period of time. Common natural risks include catastrophes such as floods, tornadoes, hurricanes, fires, lightning, droughts, and earthquakes.

Some risks that are caused by people are also natural risks: Power outages, civil unrest, oil spills, arson, terrorism, and even war are classified as natural risks. Businesses can insure against unexpected losses from some natural risks, but not all. For example, a typical business insurance policy may not cover damage caused by acts of war or riots; special insurance may be required to cover regional threats such as earthquakes or floods.

Weather is an example of a natural risk. Some businesses and products depend on predictable weather for success. Ski resorts depend on normal snowfall levels to operate ski lifts, sell lodging and ski packages, and fill restaurants. A mild winter season or below-normal snowfall represents lost revenues and a natural risk for ski resorts.

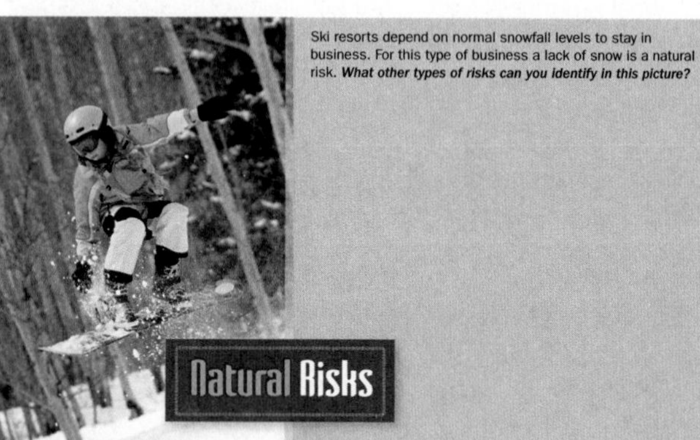

Ski resorts depend on normal snowfall levels to stay in business. For this type of business a lack of snow is a natural risk. ***What other types of risks can you identify in this picture?***

Protecting business property against the risk of loss by fire is a direct way to manage risk. Installing smoke detectors, portable fire extinguishers, and automatic sprinklers, for example, can help to protect staff, property, and revenue.

HUMAN RISKS

Human risks are risks caused by employee dishonesty, errors, mistakes, and omissions as well as the unpredictability of customers or the workplace itself. Human risks range from internal risks and customer theft to employee- and customer-related injuries.

HUMAN RISKS	
Theft	Environment
Employees	Computers

Internal and Customer Theft

A National Retail Security Survey of 106 retail chains found that overall theft in the United States was estimated at over $36 billion a year. Total theft represented 1.51 percent of retail sales and continues to grow every year. Employee theft represents the largest share of retailer unexplained losses.

The most common employee theft includes not processing transactions or not scanning items for people at cash registers. Other types of employee theft include making false merchandise returns, gift card fraud, embezzlement, and stealing merchandise.

Customer theft is a loss caused by shoplifting, fraudulent activities, or nonpayment. The National Retail Federation has estimated that shoplifting alone adds 3 to 4 percent to the cost of each product just to cover losses. This loss is passed on to all of us in the form of higher prices to cover inventory shortages, pay for security personnel, and install theft-prevention systems. Additional examples of customer dishonesty include the nonpayment of accounts, and paying for goods and services with fraudulent checks, credit cards, or gift cards.

Employee Risks

Employees represent another human risk for business by engaging in fraudulent or improper business practices. For example, members of management at the energy trading giant Enron Corporation and its accounting firm, Arthur Andersen LLP, used questionable accounting techniques that inflated profits and hid losses. These fraudulent practices resulted in the company declaring bankruptcy, which became one of the largest bankruptcies in U.S. history. Thousands of Enron

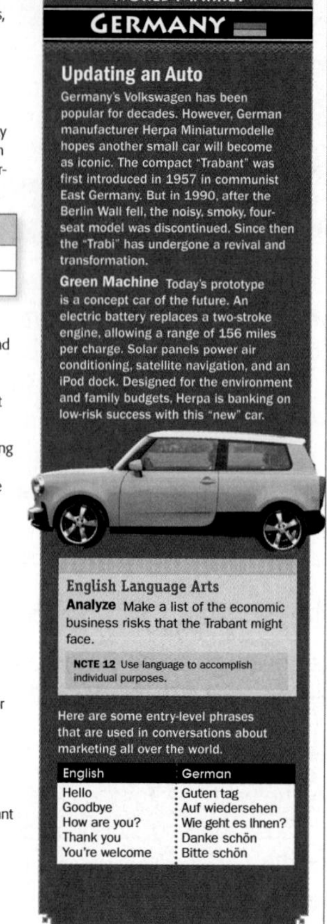

WORLD MARKET

GERMANY

Updating an Auto

Germany's Volkswagen has been popular for decades. However, German manufacturer Herpa Miniaturmodelle hopes another small car will become as iconic. The compact "Trabant" was first introduced in 1957 in communist East Germany. But in 1990, after the Berlin Wall fell, the noisy, smoky, four-seat model was discontinued. Since then the "Trabi" has undergone a revival and transformation.

Green Machine Today's prototype is a concept car of the future. An electric battery replaces a two-stroke engine, allowing a range of 156 miles per charge. Solar panels power air conditioning, satellite navigation, and an iPod dock. Designed for the environment and family budgets, Herpa is banking on low-risk success with this "new" car.

English Language Arts

Analyze Make a list of the economic business risks that the Trabant might face.

NCTE 12 Use language to accomplish individual purposes.

Here are some entry-level phrases that are used in conversations about marketing all over the world.

English	German
Hello	Guten tag
Goodbye	Auf wiedersehen
How are you?	Wie geht es Ihnen?
Thank you	Danke schön
You're welcome	Bitte schön

800 | Unit 11 · Entrepreneurship and Finance

Chapter 34 · Risk Management | 801

EXPLAIN

Government Regulations

Discuss with students that virtually all businesses are subject to some government laws and regulations, all of which come with a cost, leading to increased economic risk. To focus the discussion on how government laws and regulations can result in economic risks, ask these guiding questions.

Guiding Questions

Identify What are two ways that government regulations can result in economic risks?	Licenses, permits, and assessments for street and sewer improvements can reduce profits; product recalls can be expensive.
Infer Why do you think even the threat of a product recall can affect sales and profits?	If consumers hear that a product may be recalled, they might think it is dangerous or poorly made and not buy it.

Visual Literacy

Natural Risks Caption Answer Read the caption question to students: ***What other types of risks can you identify in this picture?*** Answers may include: avalanches, severe winter storms, falling trees, snowboarder using improper techniques leading to injury, snowboarder running into trees or other hazards such as large chunks of ice or equipment failure. After students are finished listing the risks, have them separate the risks into two categories: natural risks and human risks. Natural risks: avalanches, winter storms, and falling trees. Human risks: running into trees, improper snowboarding techniques, improperly checking equipment.

Reading: Focus Lesson

Go to the Online Learning Center to view a video clip in which a teacher models how to find the main idea or theme of a selection by identifying the major and minor details.

ELABORATE

NATURAL RISKS

Ask these guiding questions to focus the discussion on natural risks.

Guiding Questions

List What are three risks caused by people that are considered to be natural risks?	Possible answers: power outages, civil unrest, oil spills, arson, terrorism, and war
Apply An insurance company has written a policy for your company warehouse that covers fire loss and damage. In what ways might the insurance company require you to protect this warehouse before it will implement the policy?	Requirements might include: installation and maintenance of smoke detectors, automatic sprinklers; and fire extinguishers; training employees in fire prevention; creating and practicing evacuation plans; having security staff monitor the premises; and requiring that inventory and equipment be stored properly.
Make Judgments Why do you think insurance policies typically do not cover damages caused by acts of war?	Possible answer: Such damages could be extremely extensive and prohibitively expensive for insurance companies to cover.

Critical Thinking

Discuss with students that there has been some discussion in the insurance industry about whether acts of terrorism, such as the terrorist attacks of September 11, 2001, should be considered acts of war. Ask students: ***Do you think damage incurred in these attacks should be considered acts of war and therefore not covered by the typical insurance policy? Why or why not?*** Responses will vary, but students should provide logical reasons for their responses. In general, the insurance industry has not viewed such events as acts of war and has paid policies related to damage caused by terrorism.

Mini Project

Extension

Summarizing the Sarbanes-Oxley Act of 2002 Have students conduct research to learn more about the Sarbanes-Oxley Act of 2002 and write a brief summary explaining why the act was implemented and how it helps public companies better manage business risk. Students' summaries should explain that the act was passed as a result of scandals involving companies such as Enron and WorldComm that led to investors losing billions of dollars. The act mandated reforms that enhance financial disclosures and fight corporate and accounting fraud.

Reinforce Vocabulary

Human Risks—Usage Display the term *human risks* for the class to read. Emphasize that human risks include not only deliberate actions, but also accidental behavior and damages caused by individuals forgetting to perform specific actions.

HUMAN RISKS

To focus the discussion on human risks, ask these guiding questions.

Guiding Questions

Recall What makes up the largest share of retailer unexplained losses?	employee theft
Summarize How does shoplifting increase product prices for all consumers?	Stores must raise prices due to resulting inventory shortages and the need for security and theft-prevention systems.
Draw Conclusions Why is it vital that companies make sure their accountants follow proper business practices?	Poor accounting procedures can cause profits and losses to be improperly stated and can result in charges of fraud.

WORLD MARKET

ENGLISH LANGUAGE ARTS

Lists might include: The Trabant has a poor reputation from previous times, it is small, and consumers might not want a car with a range of only 156 miles. Ask these questions to further explore this topic.

Guiding Questions

Explain Why is the Trabant called a "green machine"?	It has features that reduce its environmental impact, such as an electric battery and solar panels.
Make Judgments Which of Trabant's features do you think will appeal to consumers the most? Which of its drawbacks do you think will consumers find most serious?	Answers will vary. Its gasoline engine might appeal to consumers the most; however, it can only travel 156 miles before requiring recharging.

DIGITAL NATION

When Employees Tweet Too Much

More and more workers have personal Twitter accounts, blogs, and Facebook pages. This can be a benefit to companies if employees speak highly of their employers. But it can be a PR nightmare if paid employees waste time, criticize their employer, reveal company secrets, or pose as official spokespeople. In 2009, two employees at a pizza chain posted a YouTube video that showed them tampering with customers' food. The video had a million views in less than a week.

Facebooking on Work Time

Companies are now adopting policies about how employees should act when they post comments, videos, or photos to the Web. Many policies prohibit workers from criticizing the company, using its logo, or discussing clients or work projects. Most policies also remind employees to save social media activities for personal time.

Social Studies

Evaluate Do you think it is fair for companies to tell workers what they can and cannot do on social media sites? Discuss with your class.

NCSS X D Civic Ideals & Practices Practice forms of civic discussion and participation consistent with the ideals of citizens in a democratic republic.

glencoe.com

Get a Digital Nation Worksheet Activity.

employees lost their jobs, and many people lost savings they had invested in Enron stock. In addition, Arthur Andersen LLP, previously one of the top five accounting firms in the United States, lost its auditing license and sold its assets to competitors.

Skills and Working Environment

In a restaurant, failing to properly cook or handle food can lead to customers becoming ill or hospitalized. To reduce risks of this type, many companies have created safety programs that **stress** the importance of proper food handling.

Customer or employee accidents are potential human risks. Commercial airlines, for example, prepare crews for mechanical-related emergencies but also for human risks. A passenger might fall in the aisle, break an arm, and sue the airline. Retail businesses take precautions to keep customers safe when rain, ice, or liquid cleaners create slippery floors. An employee might be injured on the job by faulty machinery or improperly built structures. Employee illnesses could also be caused by toxic fumes or other environmental hazards.

Another potential risk faced by employers is the threat of sexual harassment, stalking, or physical violence. Violent crime in the workplace accounts for 15 percent of the violent acts experienced by U.S. residents age 12 or older. Trade associations, such as the Food Marketing Institute®, provide materials to help businesses assess policies and practices dealing with workplace violence.

Handling Risks Risk management started with insurance protection against natural disasters. Now it includes electronic security, information technology, legal compliance, strategic planning, workplace threats, and worker safety.

Computer-Related Crime

"Cybercrime" has emerged as a significant new risk for businesses. Employees who use their company's network to visit untrusted Web sites can mistakenly download "malware," or malicious computer software. Malware programs, including "worms" and "viruses," can be disastrous to information and communication systems and **internal** computer networks. Computer worms and viruses are often spread through unwanted or "spam" e-mail. Some spam is harmless, but e-mail attacks containing malicious links have been known to infect millions of computers and disable entire networks.

Individuals may also illegally penetrate, or "hack," the security of computer systems to gain access or information for mischievous or criminal purposes. Hacking may include industrial espionage, such as stealing proprietary company information, client lists, or bank accounts.

Computer crime is committed by many kinds of people, from current or past employees to professional gangs of cyber-thieves. Protecting a business from computer crime requires a secure computer network that utilizes passwords, encoded firewall programs, and virus detectors. It requires being vigilant about scanning for operational or human security risks that affect technology. It is also important to stay current on security alerts released by software publishers.

In order to avoid becoming the victims of cybercrime, businesses must install reputable and up-to-date antivirus software on their computer systems. Employers need to train staff on privacy policies and the proper handling of confidential information related to voicemail, e-mail, and Internet use. Companies also need their employees to be on the lookout for potential issues such as "phishing." A common scam involves official-looking requests for information that are actually fraudulent. A business should always verify that such requests are legitimate before giving out account numbers. All these steps are necessary to help minimize the risk of computer intrusion, customer identity theft, and information theft.

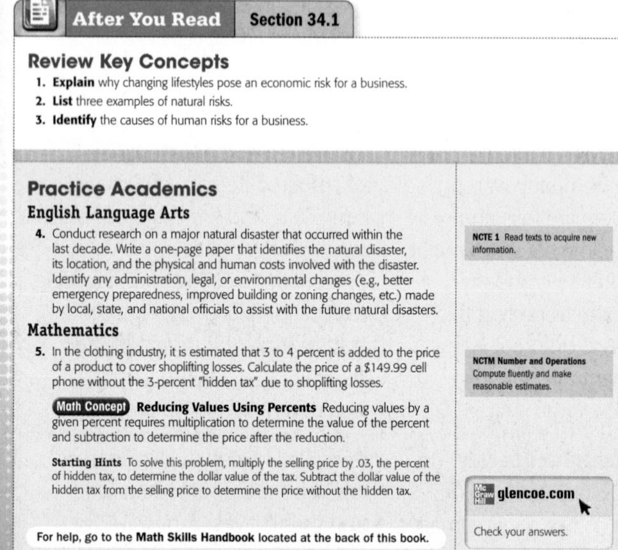
After You Read Section 34.1

Review Key Concepts

1. **Explain** why changing lifestyles pose an economic risk for a business.
2. **List** three examples of natural risks.
3. **Identify** the causes of human risks for a business.

Practice Academics

English Language Arts

4. Conduct research on a major natural disaster that occurred within the last decade. Write a one-page paper that identifies the natural disaster, its location, and the physical and human costs involved with the disaster. Identify any administration, legal, or environmental changes (e.g., better emergency preparedness, improved building or zoning changes, etc.) made by local, state, and national officials to assist with the future natural disasters.

NCTE 1 Read texts to acquire new information.

Mathematics

5. In the clothing industry, it is estimated that 3 to 4 percent is added to the price of a product to cover shoplifting losses. Calculate the price of a $149.99 cell phone without the 3-percent "hidden tax" due to shoplifting losses.

Math Concept **Reducing Values Using Percents** Reducing values by a given percent requires multiplication to determine the value of the percent and subtraction to determine the price after the reduction.

Starting Hints To solve this problem, multiply the selling price by .03, the percent of hidden tax, to determine the dollar value of the tax. Subtract the dollar value of the hidden tax from the selling price to determine the price without the hidden tax.

NCTM Number and Operations Compute fluently and make reasonable estimates.

For help, go to the **Math Skills Handbook** located at the back of this book.

glencoe.com

Check your answers.

802 | Unit 11 · Entrepreneurship and Finance

Chapter 34 · Risk Management | 803

ELABORATE

DIGITAL NATION

Social Studies Answer Encourage the class to discuss this question: ***Do you think it is fair for companies to tell workers what they can and cannot do on social media sites?*** Some students may say that companies should not regulate what workers do in their personal time. Others may say it is wrong for employees to use company assets for non-work purposes.

Extend Have the class develop a policy on employee use of company computers and networks. Policies may include: Employees may only use social media on personal time; workers may not use company resources to criticize the company; employees may not discuss clients or work projects.

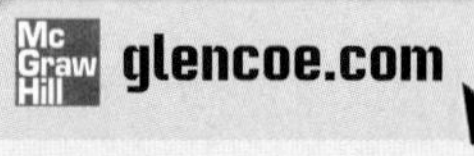

Worksheet Activity Send students to the Online Learning Center to get a Digital Nation worksheet activity.

Handling Risks Ask students: ***What kinds of risks might a company face that are related to information technology?***

Critical Thinking

Ask students: ***What kinds of protection do you have on computers in your school or home?*** Answers might include anti-virus and spyware software, firewalls, internet filters, and so on. Then ask: ***Do you think this protection is adequate? Why or why not?*** Answers will vary. Possible answer: I think so because as far as I know, we've never had a security problem.

VIRTUAL BUSINESS

RISKS AND SURPRISES

Introduce the concept of risks and surprises to students using Knowledge Matters' Virtual Business Retailing visual simulation, *Risks and Surprises*. In this simulation, students will learn about the types of risks that businesses face and how to manage them.

EVALUATE

PROFESSIONAL DEVELOPMENT **MINI CLIP**

Reading: Differentiated Instruction
Go to the Online Learning Center for a video in which an expert discusses elements of a differentiated classroom.

Mini Projects

Differentiated Instruction

Visual Learners Have students work in pairs to create a poster that shows examples of various economic, natural, and human risks. You may want to supply magazines from which students can cut photos or illustrations. Students may also include their own drawings. Instruct students to title their posters and label the different risk categories. Posters should contain photos, drawings, or other visual representations of the different types of business risks. Posters should have titles and their components should be clearly labeled.

Verbal/Linguistic Learners Tell students they have been assigned to write a pamphlet to help small businesses keep their computer networks free of malicious software and security breaches. Have students use the knowledge they have gained in this chapter, along with additional information they obtain from research, to create the pamphlet. Students' pamphlets should discuss ways small businesses can protect their computer systems and networks. Examples may include backing up all data and storing it off-site; installing software to protect against viruses, worms, and spyware; installing firewalls to prevent unauthorized access; and requiring account names and passwords to access company networks and databases.

Gifted Learners Have students locate and obtain a copy of an article geared toward business professionals that discusses business risk. Have students write a 100- to 200-word abstract and outline of the article. Ask students to prepare a brief oral presentation on what they learned from the article. Students' abstracts, outlines, and presentations will vary depending on the article chosen. For example, numerous articles have been written about the risk involved in international business due to widespread corruption in specific areas of the world. Such corruption causes governments to be unstable, discourages economic growth, distorts product prices, and makes local legal and judicial systems unreliable. Because of these situations, companies must carefully evaluate the potential benefits against the risk of such business ventures.

After You Read Section 34.1

Review Key Concepts

1. Changing lifestyles are a risk because if businesses fail to adapt goods and services to meet these changing interests and needs, they probably will not survive due to drops in sales.
2. Examples may include floods, tornadoes, hurricanes, fires, lightning, droughts, and earthquakes.
3. Causes for human risks include employee dishonesty, errors, mistakes, omissions, and the unpredictability of customers or the workplace itself.

Practice Academics

English Language Arts

4. Answers will vary depending on which natural disaster was researched. Students' papers should discuss the physical and human costs of the natural disaster and any administration, legal, or environmental changes made by local, state, and national officials to assist with future natural disasters.

Mathematics

5. \$145.49 (\$149.99 – [149.99 × 0.03])

glencoe.com

Answer Key Send students to the Online Learning Center to check their answers.

READING GUIDE

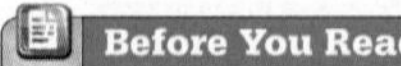

Before You Read

Predict What are some of the methods businesses use to handle risks?

Objectives

- **Explain** effective security and safety precautions, policies, and procedures.
- **Describe** the various ways businesses can manage risk.
- **Explain** the concept of insurance.

The Main Idea

Businesses use various strategies to help prevent, avoid, and protect against accidents, injuries, fires, thefts, defective products, and environmental and other disasters.

Vocabulary

Content Vocabulary
- insurance policy
- extended coverage
- fidelity bonds
- performance bonds

Academic Vocabulary

You will find these words in your reading and on your tests. Make sure you know their meanings.
- undergo
- devices

Graphic Organizer

Draw this chart and fill in the boxes with different methods of handling risk.

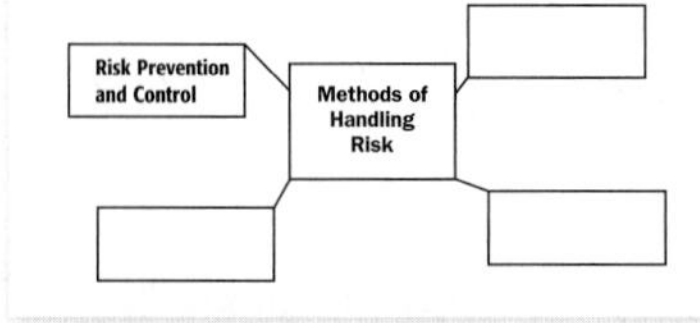

glencoe.com

Print this graphic organizer.

STANDARDS

ACADEMIC

English Language Arts

NCTE 1 Read texts to acquire new information.

NCTE 7 Conduct research and gather, evaluate, and synthesize data to communicate discoveries.

Mathematics

NCTM Number and Operations Understand numbers, ways of representing numbers, relationships among numbers, and number systems.

NCSS *National Council for the Social Studies*
NCTE *National Council of Teachers of English*
NCTM *National Council of Teachers of Mathematics*
NSES *National Science Education Standards*

Common Core
Reading Integrate and evaluate content presented in diverse formats and media, including visually and quantitatively, as well as in words.

MARKETING CORE FUNCTION

Product/Service Management

m.e. Section 34.2 Handling Business Risks

WAYS OF HANDLING BUSINESS RISKS

There are four basic ways that businesses can handle risks: risk prevention and control, risk transfer, risk retention, and risk avoidance. An effective risk prevention program for a business should use a combination of all these methods.

RISK PREVENTION AND CONTROL

Business risks can be handled through prevention and control. Many common types of risks can be controlled and minimized by screening and training employees, providing safe working conditions and sufficient safety instruction, preventing external theft, and by deterring employee theft.

As You Read

Identify Consider some ways a business might manage or protect itself from risks.

SCREENING AND TRAINING EMPLOYEES

The best way to prevent the human risk of employee carelessness and incompetence is through effective employee screening, orientation, and training. Background screening on all job applications, checking references, requiring driver licenses, and verifying citizenship are often used to assist in new employee selection. Many employers also use pre-employment tests for basic and technical skills to find the right people. Larger companies and some smaller ones now require prospective employees to **undergo** testing for illegal drugs before being hired. Substance abuse can lead to increased human risk by causing employees to be careless and more likely to ignore or forget safety rules.

> "Risk managers must develop effective programs and techniques for a variety of risks."

When employees begin a new job, orientation, training, and instruction is normally provided. The training may be brief verbal instruction or extensive training that lasts several weeks or months. Workers should be trained in the policies, procedures, and processes dealing with human risks. This can minimize the risk of lost sales through human errors, mistakes, or omissions.

PROVIDING SAFE CONDITIONS AND SAFETY INSTRUCTION

According to the most recent U.S. Bureau of Labor Statistics, there were over 5,071 workplace deaths in the United States due to unintentional injuries. The rate of fatal injuries for U.S. workers was 3.6 fatalities for 100,000 workers.

Nonfatal workplace injuries and illnesses involved 3.7 million workers. Over half of these injuries required days away from work, job transfers, or job restrictions.

Based on these numbers alone, it is clear that safety and health information must be provided to all employees. When all employees receive safety instruction and have safe working conditions, the potential for on-the-job accidents is greatly reduced.

To manage such risks, businesses should design all employee work zones and customer selling areas for efficient foot traffic and storage. They can also provide training on proper ways to safely lift, store, and deliver merchandise.

ENGAGE

Anticipation Activity

Improving Student Achievement Have students work in small groups to identify how their school administration protects the school against natural risks and human risks. Have them list safety-related rules and regulations they follow in the school environment and describe ways these rules are communicated.

Objectives

- **Explain** effective security and safety precautions, policies, and procedures. (See pages 805–807.)
- **Describe** the various ways businesses can manage risk. risk prevention and control, risk transfer (insurance, warranties), risk retention (assuming the loss), and risk avoidance (anticipating risks)
- **Explain** the concept of insurance. to transfer the risk of a potential loss from the business to the insurance company

Graphic Organizer

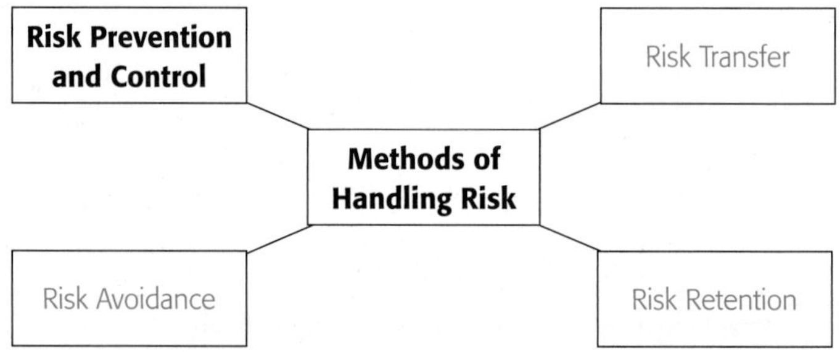

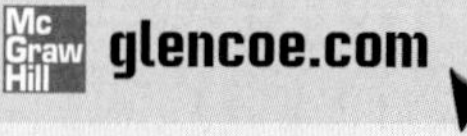

Graphic Organizer Send students to the Online Learning Center to print this graphic organizer.

EXPLORE

Before You Read

Read the question: ***What are some of the methods businesses use to handle risks?*** risk prevention and control, risk transfer, risk retention, and risk avoidance
Then ask: ***What are some things your family uses to handle risks?*** home and car insurance; safety belts and child restraint systems in the car; smoke alarms and fire extinguishers at home; surge protectors around electronics

Preteaching Vocabulary

Have students go to the Online Learning Center at glencoe.com for the Chapter 34 Preteaching Vocabulary games.

Content Vocabulary

Display the terms *fidelity bonds* and *performance bonds*. Explain that a bond is an insurance agreement that will be paid if a third party acts in certain way or does not complete a specified task.

Academic Vocabulary

Undergo—Usage Display the word *undergo* and explain that it can mean "to pass through." As an example, read aloud this sentence: ***The office building will undergo renovations in the fall.*** However, *undergo* is often used to indicate submitting to or enduring something unpleasant. As an example, read aloud this sentence: ***She must undergo a tonsillectomy on Monday.***

Graphic Organizer

Display this graphic organizer and have students provide answers in the ovals on the left.

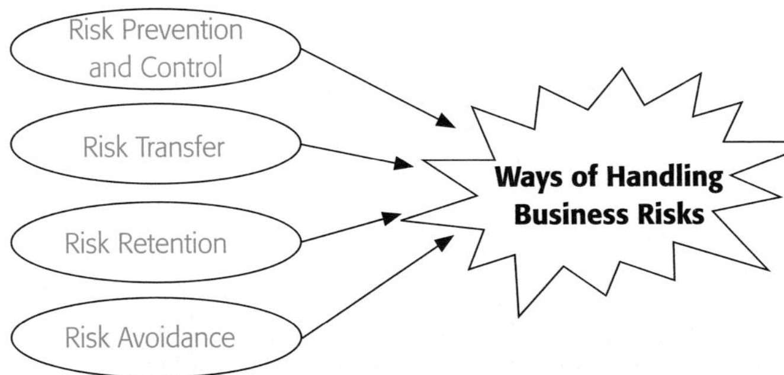

Graphic Organizer Send students to the Online Learning Center to print this graphic organizer.

Handling Business Risks

WAYS OF HANDLING BUSINESS RISK

Tell students that many business risks can be prevented or controlled by following certain basic guidelines. Then use these guiding questions to focus the discussion on handling business risks.

Guiding Questions

Explain Why do many companies require potential employees to submit to drug testing?	Substance abuse can increase human risk by making workers careless and more likely to ignore or forget safety rules.
Apply You have been hired for the summer to work on the grounds crew for your school. What kinds of safety training would you expect to get in training sessions?	Sample answers: I would expect to be taught how to properly use all equipment; how to prepare the grounds before mowing; and when to use safety gear such as ear protection. I would expect to learn basic first aid and what to do in case of an emergency.

As You Read

Read the As You Read question aloud: ***Consider some ways a business might manage or protect itself from risks.*** Risk prevention and control: checking the references of potential employees; risk transfer: purchasing property insurance; risk retention: assuming the loss when a certain percentage of goods are damaged before being sold; risk avoidance: deciding not to manufacturer certain items, such as ladders, because the potential risks appear to be high when compared to the potential benefits.

Expert Advice

Read the quote to students:

“Risk managers must develop effective programs and techniques for a variety of risks.”

Ask: ***What kinds of skills do you think a good risk manager would have?*** Possible answers: problem solving, critical thinking, conflict management, planning, and analytical skills.

Many companies address workplace health and safety by developing programs that includes these strategies:

- Creating committees to check for hazards
- Correcting hazards before accidents occur
- Complying with all state and federal health and safety regulations
- Investigating and recording all workplace incidents and accidents
- Providing protective clothing and equipment
- Placing first-aid kits near workstations
- Posting directions to nearby health-care facilities
- Offering employee classes in first aid and CPR
- Tracking workdays missed due to accidents or injuries
- Scheduling regular safety meetings and trainings
- Distributing written safety and health plans
- Offering incentives for improved safety records
- Addressing workplace threats such as sexual harassment or violence
- Communicating business standards and policies

CONTROLLING EMPLOYEE THEFT

One of the most costly forms of human risk is theft by employees and customers. Employee theft represents the greatest part of all unexplained business losses due to theft. The most recent National Retail Security Survey estimated that internal theft from retail stores costs Americans more than $15.5 billion each year.

Most employee theft occurs at the point-of-sale (POS) terminal, or cash register. To protect against employee theft, many businesses have installed POS terminals that generate reports that monitor cash discrepancies, cash register transactions, employees' discounts, gift-card purchases, refunds by employees, merchandise returns, sales reports, and void transfers. By analyzing these data, businesses can improve the chances of catching dishonest employees.

Closed-circuit television systems also lower the risk of employee theft. These systems include hidden cameras operated and observed by security personnel in a control room and backed up with recording equipment.

MARKETING CASE STUDY

Insuring Sports and Events

Most companies must sign up for standard liability coverage to do business as usual. This is especially important if they have employees and deal with the public. However, some businesses and organizations cannot be covered by standard policies. Instead, they are insured by companies that specialize in niche markets like sports and events.

Risky Business

For protection that goes beyond kneepads and helmets, insurance companies such as Sportsinsurance.com or Nationwide® provide liability coverage for all kinds of sports. These sports include football, soccer, baseball, basketball, extreme sports, and more. Owners and organizers need insurance for themselves, their teams and leagues, their athletes, their employees, and even their volunteers at events, sports camps, and tournaments. With so much money invested in sports activities, insurance is a safe bet in case bad weather, accidents, and injuries put employees on the "DL" (disabled list).

English Language Arts

Compose Conduct research to find out whether your school needs insurance for hosting a sports event, such as a championship football game. What kind of coverage must the school have?

NCTE 7 Conduct research and gather, evaluate, and synthesize data to communicate discoveries.

PREVENTING SHOPLIFTING

Shoplifting is external theft that involves stealing merchandise from a business. It is estimated that shoplifting causes one-third of lost inventory.

To deter shoplifting, businesses can educate employees about shoplifting prevention guidelines. Adequately lighting store layouts, storing expensive items in locked display cases, or tagging products with electronic anti-theft **devices** can reduce shoplifting. Many stores use digital video cameras, electronic gates, and wall or ceiling mirrors to cut down on the risk of theft.

Many states have passed strict laws regarding shoplifting. However, apprehending shoplifters is a significant risk. Businesses can be sued for allegations of false arrest, false imprisonment, malicious prosecution, excessive use of force, or physical assault. To limit their liability, retailers must educate themselves and their employees about acceptable shoplifter detention policies.

REDUCING WORKPLACE THREATS

Violent crime in the workplace is real. It is estimated that more than 2 million personal thefts and more than 200,000 car thefts occur annually at work. Employees also experience incidents of sexual harassment and stalking while working.

Robbery is stealing of money or merchandise by violence or threat. Many police departments provide instruction on how to prevent and handle armed robberies. Businesses can lower their workplace threat risks and protect their employees by taking the following steps:

- Developing and communicating workplace violence policies
- Training employees on how to handle incidents
- Increasing lighting in and outside
- Limiting the amount of money kept on hand
- Handling bank deposits discreetly
- Installing cameras
- Hiring security guards and extra employees to assure double coverage
- Installing bulletproof glass in cashier cubicles
- Opening back doors only for freight or trash
- Installing switches for remotely locking doors
- Making sure doors are locked and alarms are set

RISK TRANSFER

Some business risks can be handled by transferring the risk of loss to another business or party. Risk transfer methods include purchasing insurance, promoting product and service warranties, and transferring risk through business ownership.

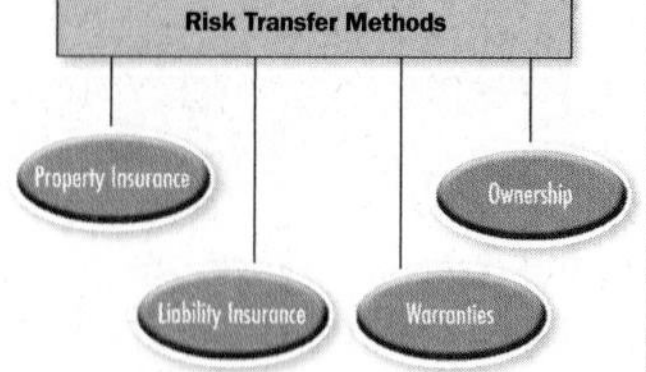

PURCHASING INSURANCE

A business can insure property and people against potential loss by purchasing insurance policies. An **insurance policy** is a contract between a business and an insurance company to cover a specific business risk. A business can buy an insurance package that combines two or more types of insurable risks of loss.

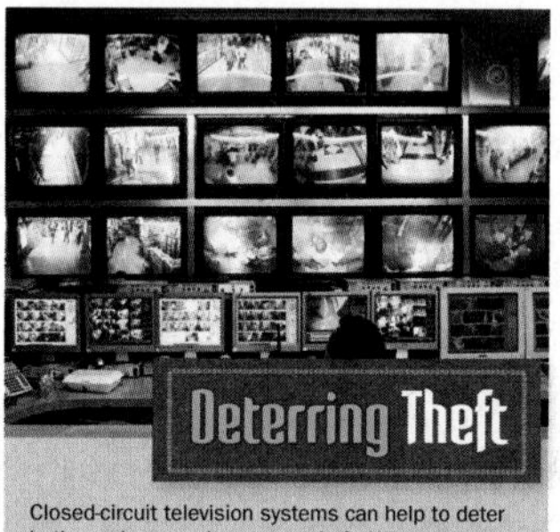

Closed-circuit television systems can help to deter both employee and customer theft. ***What other systems do retailers use to help prevent theft?***

EXPLAIN

Mini Project

Enrichment

Researching OSHA Have students research information about OSHA, the U.S. Department of Labor Occupational Safety & Health Administration. Have students visit OSHA's Web site, choose one section of the site, and summarize its contents in a five-minute oral presentation. Students should give an oral presentation in which they summarize one section of the OSHA Web site. For example, OSHA provides regulations for safety and health standards for shipyard employment. These regulations cover such topics as the safe use of liquids such as paint, paint removers, and toxic cleaning solvents; standards covering welding, cutting, and heating; and standards covering scaffolding, ladders, and illumination.

MARKETING CASE STUDY

English Language Arts Answer

Students' responses will vary depending on the school's coverage. Generally, schools have liability coverage for coaches and other hired professionals, athletes, volunteers, and spectators. Ask these guiding questions to further explore this topic.

Guiding Questions

List What are some examples of situations in which a school might need coverage?	Sample answers: Spectators are injured when a bleacher collapses; an athlete's injured knee is further injured when an athletic trainer treats it inappropriately
Infer Why do insurers offer insurance to niche markets?	to meet specialized insurance needs, such as policies to protect special events

ELABORATE

Activate Prior Knowledge

Reteach the Capabilities of Point-of-Sale Systems Remind students of the changes brought about in the retail industry by the introduction of point-of-sale systems (discussed in Chapter 16). Not only do they perform the functions of traditional cash registers, they also submit data for inventory tracking. An important benefit is that it becomes much harder for employees to steal from businesses. When POS systems are used along with "exception reporting," which analyzes transactions and looks for anything unusual, businesses can see a significant reduction in employee theft.

CONTROLLING EMPLOYEE THEFT

Ask these questions to focus discussion on controlling employee theft.

Guiding Questions

Recall Where does most employee theft occur?	at the POS terminal or cash register
Analyze How can a POS system help managers detect employee theft?	by generating reports that monitor cash discrepancies, cash register transactions, merchandise returns
Make Judgments Some people think closed-circuit TV systems are an invasion of privacy. Do you agree or disagree? Why?	Answers will vary, but students should provide logical reasons. Most students will probably agree that cameras should not be used in locations where privacy is expected, such as dressing rooms and restrooms.

Graphic Organizer

Display this graphic organizer. Have students provide the four methods of transferring business risk.

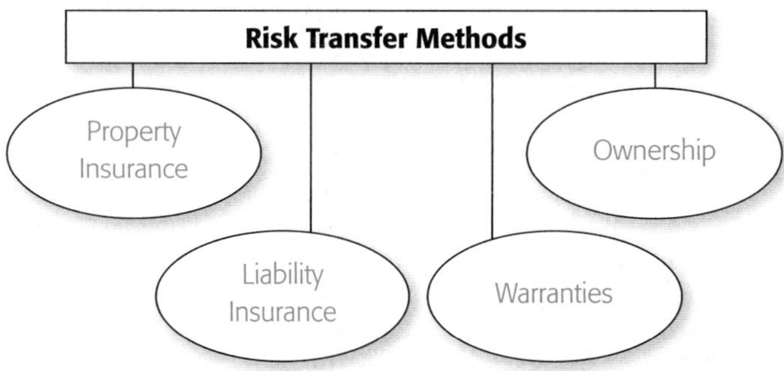

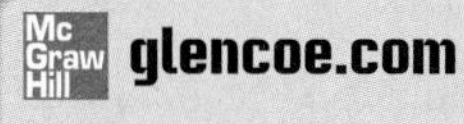

glencoe.com  iWB

Graphic Organizer Send students to the Online Learning Center to print this graphic organizer.

Mini Projects

Enrichment

Interviewing a Manager of a Convenience Store Instruct students to interview the manager of a local convenience store. Before conducting the interview, have students come up with a list of questions to ask the manager, such as: How do you screen potential employees? How do you train employees? What are some measures you have taken to ensure employee and customer safety? Then have students prepare a brief oral presentation in which they summarize what they learned from the interview. Students' interviews should summarize what the manager stated about how employees are trained, what kinds of measures the store takes to ensure employee and customer safety, and so on. For example, training might include how to limit the amount of cash in a cash drawer and what to do in case of an emergency.

Presenting a Workshop on Preventing Shoplifting Organize students into groups of three or four. One member of the group should be assigned the role of presenter. This individual will present a workshop on shoplifting to a group of department store sales associates, played by the remaining group members. Encourage students to be interactive in their presentations—for example, the presenter might recruit an audience member to assist in acting out a shoplifting scene. The presenter should instruct the employees on how to identify a shoplifter and what steps to take when they suspect a customer is shoplifting. Each group's presentation should explain the exact steps a sales associate should take when confronted with a shoplifting situation. The presenter also should explain how to use tools such as mirrors to help identify shoplifters.

Visual Literacy

Deterring Theft Caption Answer Read the caption and question to students: ***What other systems do retailers use to help prevent theft?*** Answers may include: adequate lighting systems; electronic anti-theft devices; electronic gates; wall and ceiling mirrors; POS systems that track cash, purchases, and inventory. Then ask: ***While placing items in locked display cases can deter theft, why might retailers want to limit their use of this method?*** It might discourage customers from purchasing these goods if they must hunt for a salesperson to unlock the case.

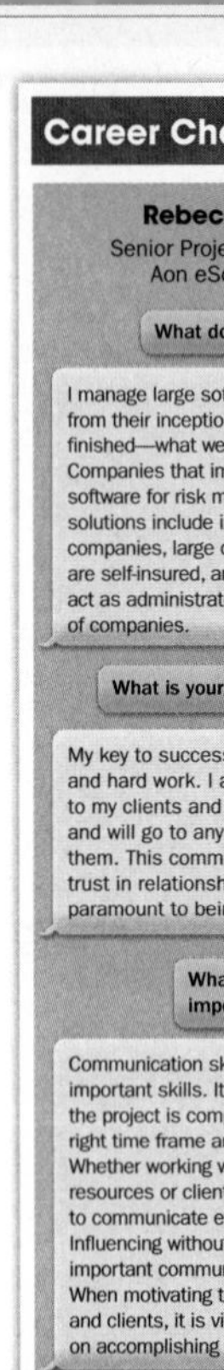
Career Chatroom

Rebecca Gill
Senior Project Manager
Aon eSolutions

What do you do at work?

I manage large software projects from their inception until they are finished—what we call "go-live." Companies that implement our software for risk management solutions include insurance companies, large organizations that are self-insured, and companies that act as administrators for a collection of companies.

What is your key to success?

My key to success is dedication and hard work. I am committed to my clients and team members, and will go to any length to support them. This commitment fosters trust in relationships, which is paramount to being successful.

What skills are most important to you?

Communication skills are the most important skills. It is critical that the project is completed within the right time frame and within budget. Whether working with internal resources or clients, it is essential to communicate effectively. Influencing without authority is an important communication skill. When motivating team members and clients, it is vital to have buy-in on accomplishing overall goals.

glencoe.com

Read more about this career and get a Career Exploration Activity.

Insurance companies estimate the probability of loss due to natural risks, such as fire, lightning, and wind damage, and human risks, such as theft and vandalism. The insurance company then looks at the business's location, past experience, limits, and type of business to determine an insurance rate.

A business located in a neighborhood with a higher crime rate is charged higher rates for insurance coverage. This business has a higher likelihood of making a claim against the insurance company for losses.

PROPERTY INSURANCE

One of the most common forms of business insurance is property insurance. Property insurance covers the loss of or damage to buildings, equipment, machinery, merchandise, furniture, and fixtures. Coverage can be purchased for up to the full replacement value of the building or inventory, or for a portion of the replacement value.

Property insurance policies can be purchased with optional extended coverage endorsements. An **extended coverage** endorsement provides protection against types of loss that may not be covered under a basic property insurance policy.

Extended coverage may include off-premise property, rental cars, valuable papers and records, fire department service charges, water leakage, sewer back-ups, and personal property of others, including theft. Property insurance typically includes the following features:

- **Replacement Cost Coverage** This reimburses the business owner for the replacement cost of buildings and other personal property. A co-insurance penalty may apply if the insured business purchases less coverage than the reconstruction value of property. This means, for example, that the insurance company might pay 80 percent of the covered items, and the insured pays the balance.
- **Automatic Increase Protection** This policy feature adjusts the coverage to compensate for inflation on both the building and its contents.
- **Business Interruption** This feature compensates a business for loss of income during the time after a catastrophe when repairs are being made to a building. This coverage will also reimburse other expenses that continue during the repair period, such as interest on loans, taxes, rent, advertising, and salaries.

LIABILITY INSURANCE

Business liability insurance protects a business against damages for which it may be held legally liable, such as an injury to a customer or damage to property of others.

808 | Unit 11 · Entrepreneurship and Finance

Transferring Risk

Insurance policies are a way of transferring risk from the business owner to an insurance company. How much you pay for such insurance depends on how high the risk of loss appears to the insurer. ***How can an insurer help a business determine its insurance needs?***

Chapter 34 · Risk Management | 809

EXPLAIN

Graphic Organizer

Display this graphic organizer. Ask students to provide descriptions of each feature. Sample answers are provided below.

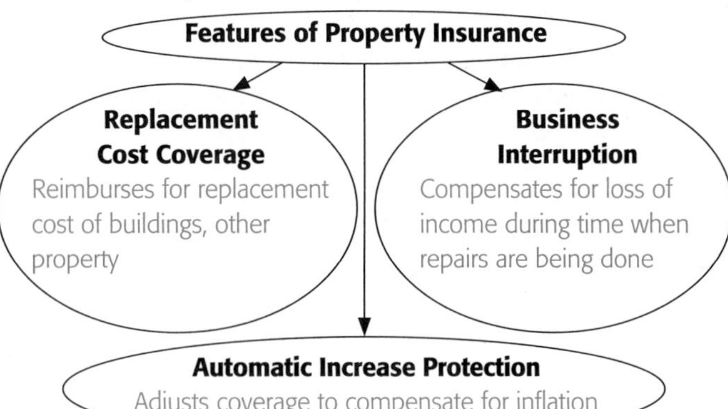

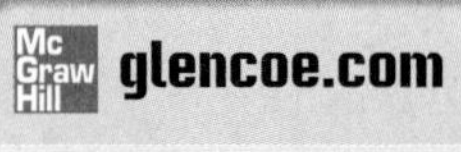
glencoe.com iWB

Graphic Organizer Send students to the Online Learning Center to print this graphic organizer.

Career Chatroom

Focus the Career Chatroom discussion by asking students these guiding questions.

Guiding Questions

Explain Why does Rebecca Gill say that commitment to those she works with is essential to her success?	Commitment fosters trust in relationships.
Infer What does Gill mean when she says ". . . it is vital to have buy-in on accomplishing overall goals"?	If team members and clients do not feel like they are a part of a project and committed to its goals, it will not succeed.

glencoe.com

Career Exploration Send students to the Online Learning Center to find more information about this career and to get a Career Exploration activity.

ELABORATE

PROPERTY INSURANCE

Discuss that property insurance is common because everyone wants to be protected against the loss of major possessions. To focus discussion on property insurance, ask these guiding questions.

Guiding Questions

Recall What is covered by property insurance?	loss or damage to buildings, equipment, machinery, merchandise, fixtures, and so on
Analyze When purchasing insurance, why might a business owner want to make certain the policy has business interruption insurance?	so the owner will not be out the entire amount of lost income should the business be unable to operate for a period of time
Predict What might happen if a business's policy did not include automatic increase protection?	If damage occurred to covered property, the insurance might only pay its value at the time the policy was purchased. If the value had increased since then, the business might lose a considerable amount of money.

Visual Literacy

Transferring Risk Caption Answer Read the caption question: ***How can an insurer help a business determine its insurance needs?*** Because insurers are aware of specific business risks, they can readily describe them to business managers or owners. Insurers can help determine the cost of losses; for example, they could help figure the actual profit that would be lost if a business had to close for one month. Then ask: ***Besides asking an insurer, how else might a business owner determine what kinds of insurance to purchase?*** Answers will vary. The owner might ask owners or managers of similar businesses about the types of insurance they carry.

Mini Project

Extension

Learning about Actuarial Science Discuss with students that actuaries are professionals who evaluate the likelihood of specific undesirable events occurring and work to decrease the impact of these events. Have students research actuarial science and why it is vital to the insurance industry. Then have students write a report describing what they learn. Students' one-page reports should explain actuarial science and discuss why actuaries are important to the insurance industry.

e MARKETING

Phishing and Identity Theft

Phishing is obtaining personal information via the Internet or by telephone and using it for illegitimate purposes. Phishing often involves an e-mail sent from what appears to be a legitimate company that requests an individual to update his or her account information. The data collected through phishing is often used for identity theft. Identity theft is stealing a person's personal data such as social security number, telephone, address, credit card number, and other information. The Federal Trade Commission's Web site provides consumers and businesses with suggestions and regulations for identity theft protection and protocol.

Innovate and Create

Part of risk management involves preventing cyber-thieves from gaining access to customers' records. Businesses are required to implement Identity Theft Prevention Programs. The Federal Trade Commission publishes a guideline called "Red Flags Rule" and provides an online template to help businesses comply. Have students visit the FTC's Web site to review the "Red Flags Rule" template. Have students assume they work for an online business that takes phone orders, such as an online florist. Have students work in groups to complete the Red Flags Rule compliance template for a specific online business that takes phone orders. Accept all reasonable answers. The "Red Flags Rule template includes: Part A: Is your business or organization at low risk for identity theft? Part B: Designing an Identity Theft Prevention Program for Businesses or Organizations at Low Risk, which has four basic steps: Step 1 Identifying relevant red flags; Step 2 Detecting red flags; Step 3 Responding to red flags; and Step 4 Administering your program.

glencoe.com

eMarketing Worksheet Activity Send students to the Online Learning Center to download an eMarketing worksheet activity.

Primary business liability insurance is usually provided for claims up to $1 million. This type of insurance may be extended to cover business premises, company operations, customer medical expenses, and product and advertising liability claims.

Product liability insurance protects against business losses resulting from personal injury or property damage caused by products manufactured or sold by a business. Many businesses purchase product liability insurance to protect against potential customer claims. They may choose to do so even though private laboratories and government agencies may have tested the products extensively.

Fidelity bonds provide insurance that protects a business from employee dishonesty. Businesses usually require employees who handle money, such as bank tellers and cashiers, to be bonded. If a bonded employee steals money or merchandise, the bonding company pays the loss. Individuals who are to be bonded are subject to background checks before a bond is issued.

The bankruptcy or insolvency of a contractor during a construction contract will likely cause a project to be delayed. This will lead to additional expenses for another contractor to finish the work. Therefore, it is not uncommon to require contractors to provide insurance. **Performance bonds**, also called surety bonds, provide financial protection for losses that might occur when a construction project is not finished due to a contractor's impaired financial condition.

Owners or managers of a business may purchase life insurance. A sole proprietor (individual business owner) is usually required to have life insurance in order to borrow money. The policy will guarantee that there will be money to pay off the sole proprietor's debts and obligations if he or she dies. Life insurance for a business partner can provide the money needed for other partners to continue the business. This occurs when the insured partner dies if the other partners are named as beneficiaries and receive proceeds from the policy.

Credit insurance protects a business from losses on credit extended to customers. Credit life insurance pays off the balance due for loans granted by banks, credit unions, and other financial institutions if the borrower dies.

Workers' compensation insurance covers employees who suffer job-related injuries and illness. This insurance covers medical care, a portion of lost wages, and permanent disability. It also protects employers from lawsuits that may be filed by an employee injured on the job.

All states have specific workers' compensation insurance coverage. These requirements are based on the number of employees and prescribed time periods.

PROMOTING PRODUCT AND SERVICE WARRANTIES

Warranties are promises made by a manufacturer or distributor with respect to the duration of performance and quality of a product. Businesses can transfer risks by informing customers about existing manufacturer warranties for defective products and required repairs. They can also offer extended product and service warranties that lengthen the warranty period through third-party service and repair providers.

TRANSFERRING RISKS THROUGH BUSINESS OWNERSHIP

The type of business ownership determines the amount of risk that is managed. In a sole proprietorship, the individual owner assumes all risks. Partnerships enable the partners to share in the business risks. Corporations allow the stockholders, as owners, to share the business risks. The corporate form of ownership offers the most protection from losses.

Reading Check

List What are the ways for businesses to transfer risk?

RISK RETENTION

In some cases, it is impossible for businesses to prevent or transfer certain types of risks. Therefore, they retain or assume financial responsibility for the consequences of loss. This process is called "risk retention." A business has to assume the loss—or retain the risk—if customer trends change and merchandise remains unsold. Most retailers assume the loss of a certain percentage of goods due to damage or theft.

It is possible to underestimate the risk, such as when merchandise is purchased in anticipation of high demand, but weather, fashion trends, or customers' purchasing habits change. A business may attempt to generate a profit by taking a risk, such as purchasing land for future development or sale through subdivision.

RISK AVOIDANCE

Certain risks can be avoided by anticipating the risks and rewards in advance. Risk avoidance means that a business refuses to engage in a particular activity, such as producing or selling a certain product or offering a particular service.

Avoidance may seem like a good strategy to avoid all risks. However, avoiding risks also means missing out on the potential gain that accepting or retaining the risk may have offered.

Market research can lead businesses to conclude that the investment risk in some goods or services is not worth the potential gain. All business decisions should be made with the consideration of both potential benefits and potential risks. Avoiding unacceptable business risks should be a key consideration in any marketing decision.

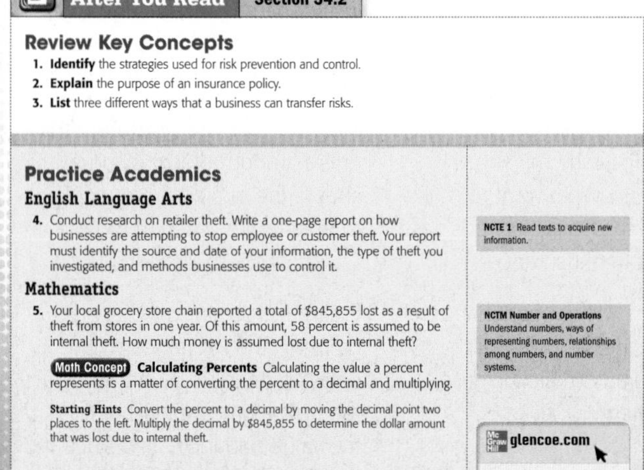
After You Read Section 34.2

Review Key Concepts

1. **Identify** the strategies used for risk prevention and control.
2. **Explain** the purpose of an insurance policy.
3. **List** three different ways that a business can transfer risks.

Practice Academics

English Language Arts

4. Conduct research on retailer theft. Write a one-page report on how businesses are attempting to stop employee or customer theft. Your report must identify the source and date of your information, the type of theft you investigated, and methods businesses use to control it.

Mathematics

5. Your local grocery store chain reported a total of $845,855 lost as a result of theft from stores in one year. Of this amount, 58 percent is assumed to be internal theft. How much money is assumed lost due to internal theft?

Math Concept **Calculating Percents** Calculating the value a percent represents is a matter of converting the percent to a decimal and multiplying.

Starting Hints Convert the percent to a decimal by moving the decimal point two places to the left. Multiply the decimal by $845,855 to determine the dollar amount that was lost due to internal theft.

For help, go to the **Math Skills Handbook** located at the back of this book.

NCTE 1 Read texts to acquire new information.

NCTM Number and Operations Understand numbers, ways of representing numbers, relationships among numbers, and number systems.

glencoe.com

Check your answers.

ELABORATE

Graphic Organizer

Display this Venn diagram. Ask students to list characteristics of fidelity bonds and performance bonds and characteristics of both.

Fidelity Bonds	Both	Performance Bonds
• Protect against employee dishonesty • Often required for employees who handle money	• Provide a business with protection	• Provide financial protection for losses if project is not finished because of contractor's impaired financial condition

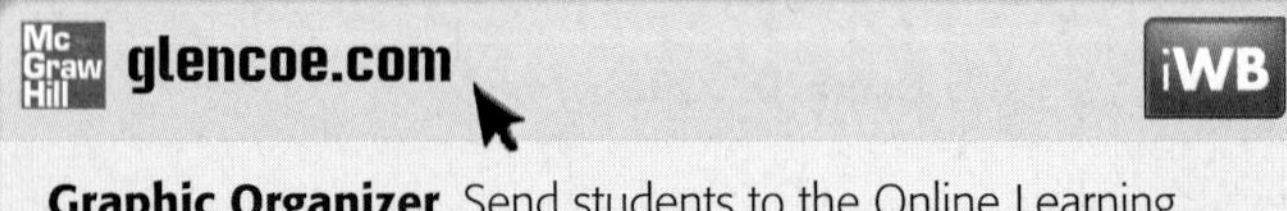

Graphic Organizer Send students to the Online Learning Center to print this graphic organizer.

Reinforce Vocabulary

Performance bonds—Denotative Meaning Display the term *performance bonds* for the class to read. Tell students that in this situation the word *performance* means "the fulfillment of a claim, promise or request." Therefore, a performance bond protects the insured if the specified fulfillment does not occur.

Critical Thinking

Ask students: ***What is the difference in risk between a partnership and a corporation?*** In a partnership, partners share the risks. In a corporation, the stockholders (owners) share the risks. Then ask: ***If you were starting a new business with several partners and wanted to protect yourself as much as possible against risks, what kind of ownership would you choose?*** corporation

VIRTUAL BUSINESS

SECURITY

Introduce the concept of security to students using Knowledge Matters' Virtual Business Retailing visual simulation, *Security*. In this simulation, students will learn how theft affects a business and how much businesses lose to theft each year.

EVALUATE

Reading Check Answer

Read the Reading Check question to students: ***What are the ways for businesses to transfer risk?*** Ways to transfer risk include purchasing property and liability insurance, promoting product and service warranties, and transferring risk through business ownership.

Mini Project

Extension

Examining Risk in Different Types of Business Ownership Have students prepare oral presentations on the three types of business ownership presented here: sole proprietorships, partnerships, and corporations. Students should discuss the liabilities of business owners in each situation. In particular, they should present the ways in which corporations protect their owners from personal liability. Students' presentations should define each type of ownership and owner liability. In a sole proprietorship, the owner can be held personally liable. Likewise, in a partnership, each individual partner is liable. However, in most situations, if a corporation goes bankrupt, stockholders cannot be held liable for its debts. This is because the law sees a corporation as an artificial being with the same rights and responsibilities as an individual person.

RISK RETENTION

Explain that the word *retention* means "the act of keeping possession of something." Ask these guiding questions to focus on risk retention.

Guiding Questions

Recall What is risk retention?	assuming financial responsibility for the consequences of losses
Analyze Why might a business retain a risk rather than handle it by another method such as transferring it?	A business may retain risk when there are no other options—for example, insurance might not be available for a specific risk.
Predict What might happen if a business underestimates a particular risk?	The business may suffer serious losses, and may even fail.

After You Read Section 34.2

Review Key Concepts

1. Strategies used for risk prevention and control include screening and training employees, providing safe conditions and sufficient safety instruction, preventing external theft, and deterring employee theft.
2. The purpose of an insurance policy is to transfer risk from the business to an insurance company.
3. Three different ways a business can transfer risks are by purchasing insurance, promoting product and service warranties, and transferring risk through business ownership.

Practice Academics

English Language Arts

4. Students should write a one-page report on how businesses are attempting to stop employee or customer theft. The report must identify the source and date of the information, the type of theft being investigated, and methods used by business to control it. For example, a report on preventing employee theft might include information such as: employers should carefully screen potential employees by verifying references, employment histories, and any education claims. They should increase the perception that any employee theft will be caught, carefully educate all employees on what constitutes fraud, and develop audits that focus on high-risk areas, such as expense reporting and payroll.

Mathematics

5. \$490,595.90 (\$845,855 × 0.58)

glencoe.com

Send students to the Online Learning Center to check their answers.

Risk Management

Business risks fall into three categories: economic, natural, and human.

RISK MANAGEMENT TYPES

- ECONOMIC
  - Government Regulations
- NATURAL
  - Weather
  - Natural Disasters
- HUMAN
  - Theft
  - Environment
  - Employees
  - Computer

There are four strategies businesses use to manage risk: prevention and control, transfer, retention, and avoidance.

RISK MANAGEMENT STRATEGIES

- PREVENTION AND CONTROL
  - Training
  - Safe Environment
- TRANSFER
  - Insurance
  - Warranties
- RETENTION
  - Assume Financial Responsibility
- AVOIDANCE
  - Careful Consideration

Written Summary

- Business risks can lead to financial gain, loss, or failure.
- Risk management is the process of managing risk in an ethical way.
- Business risks fall into three categories: economic, natural, and human.
- Businesses manage risks of financial loss through loss prevention and control, transfer, retention, and avoidance.
- Safe working conditions, external and internal theft control, insurance, warranties, and ownership changes are risk management techniques.

Review Content Vocabulary and Academic Vocabulary

1. Write true-or-false statements using each vocabulary word. Ask a partner to determine whether each statement is true or false and explain why.

Content Vocabulary

- business risk (p. 799)
- risk management (p. 799)
- economic risks (p. 799)
- natural risks (p. 800)
- human risks (p. 801)
- insurance policy (p. 807)
- extended coverage (p. 808)
- fidelity bonds (p. 810)
- performance bonds (p. 810)

Academic Vocabulary

- stress (p. 802)
- internal (p. 802)
- undergo (p. 805)
- devices (p. 807)

Assess for Understanding

2. **Explain** What are the nature and scope of risk management?
3. **Identify** What are the various types of business risks?
4. **Describe** How do safety procedures and policies help a business reduce risk?
5. **Consider** Which security policies and procedures would you use as a business owner?
6. **Suggest** How can businesses manage risks?
7. **Define** What is the concept of insurance?
8. **Justify** Why do businesses need risk management?
9. **Role Play** How can you convince a customer to use product and service warranties for a product that is advertised for its quality of construction and durability?

EVALUATE

Visual Summary

Express Creativity Ask students to create a visual summary that illustrates a concept in the chapter. Encourage students to use different formats for their visual summaries, such as a graph, a cause-and-effect diagram, or a poster. Visual summaries will vary depending on the concept depicted and the visual manner in which it is depicted. Questions to ask when assessing a visual summary include:

- Is the summary clear, economical, and simple?
- Are any important steps or concepts left out?
- Are steps or concepts arranged in the same order as the original?
- Does the summary reveal a pattern that connects the details?
- Does the summary locate and highlight the most important information?

Review Content Vocabulary and Academic Vocabulary

1. Students should write true-or-false statements for each vocabulary word. Sample statements are shown below:

   Business risk can lead to the failure of a company. (True)

   In order to engage in **risk management,** it is vital to have the best available marketing information. (True)

   Civil unrest and terrorism are examples of **economic risks.** (False—natural risks)

   Floods and hurricanes are categorized as **natural risks.** (True)

   An increase in the level of competition is an example of a **human risk.** (False—economic risk)

   When a jewelry store purchases an **insurance policy,** the store is engaging in risk avoidance. (False—risk transfer)

   A business purchases **extended coverage** because its basic insurance policy does not cover flooding. (True)

   Fidelity bonds are also called surety bonds. (False—Performance bonds)

EVALUATE

Assess for Understanding

2. Risk management is the systematic process of managing an organization's risks to achieve objectives in a manner consistent with public interest, human safety, environmental needs, and the law.

3. Types of business risks include economic risks (such as competition), natural risks (such as fires), and human risks (such as employee theft).

4. Safety procedures and policies help a business reduce risks because they help communicate to all employees specific ways to minimize risk in these areas. For example, an employee who is properly trained in the use of a forklift is much less likely to have an accident than one who is not. Installation and maintenance of appropriate safety devices and equipment can also reduce property damage and prevent injuries in the event of natural risks such as power outages and fires.

5. Sample answer: I would install POS terminals that generate reports which monitor cash discrepancies, cash register transactions, employee discounts, gift-card purchases, and refunds by employees. I also would install closed-circuit television systems to monitor both employees and customers. To deter shoplifting, I would educate employees about shoplifting prevention procedures, install adequate lighting and mirrors in strategic locations, and store expensive items in locked display cases and/or tag them with anti-theft devices.

6. The four basic ways that businesses can handle risks are: risk prevention and control, risk transfer, risk retention, and risk avoidance. Businesses can manage risk by using the best available marketing information, analyzing opportunities, and making wise decisions.

7. The concept of insurance is that a business purchases an insurance policy in order to transfer specific risk(s) to the insurer.

8. Businesses need risk management to reduce or control situations which might lead to financial loss or failure. Economic, natural, and human risks can be minimized or managed through a variety of techniques, such as having high-quality market information, properly training employees, and purchasing insurance.

9. Sample answer: I would tell the customer that even though this product has a high quality rating, it is inevitable that problems may occur with some individual items. Consumers can protect themselves against these unexpected occurrences by purchasing an extended warranty. This can protect them against unexpected repair bills.

Chapter 34 Review and Activities

21st Century Skills

Social Responsibility

10. **Healthful Habits** Conduct research on the importance of hygiene in food-service establishments. Identify the kinds of risks faced by employees and customers. Provide a one-page memo to staff explaining the importance of personal hygiene. Include recommendations for good practice in the workplace to protect coworkers and the general public.

Financial Literacy Skills

11. **Calculating Theft Costs** Assume that you would like to purchase a Kindle® e-reader that retails for $259. It was estimated in 2009 that about 1.51 percent of retail sales was lost to overall theft. What would your e-reader cost, if 1.51 percent were not added to its price due to theft? How much would you save?

e-Marketing Skills

12. **Workplace Threats** Imagine that you work for a risk management firm. You have been asked by a client to design a workplace safety plan for a quick-serve restaurant that employs late-night and early-morning employees. Perform Internet research on workplace security and make five recommendations regarding worker safety and operational safety. Outline your recommendations in a one-page written report.
    - What specific recommendations will you make for worker safety?
    - What specific recommendations will you make for operational safety?
    - How will you implement these recommendations?

Build Academic Skills

English Language Arts

13. **Extended Product Warranties** Conduct research on the advantages and disadvantages of extended product warranties. Identify the name of your source(s) and prepare a one-page report that summarizes the advantages and disadvantages of extended product warranties.

NCTE 1 Read texts to acquire new information.

Science

14. **Business and the Environment** The U.S. Environmental Protection Agency (EPA) plays a significant role in preventing, correcting, and eliminating potential environmental risks. Conduct research using the EPA's Web site. Describe a recent action or situation involving a business and actions taken by the agency to protect the public interest. Identify the business name, location, situation, and actions planned or taken to protect consumers. Summarize your findings in a one-page written report.

NSES E Develop abilities of technological design, understandings about science and technology.

Mathematics

15. **Calculate Losses from Theft** Calculate the amount of net sales lost to an electronics store with annual sales of $8,359,000 and a shoplifting rate of 3.2 percent.

NCTM Algebra Represent and analyze mathematical situations and structures using algebraic symbols.

Math Concept **Calculating Losses** Solutions to problems that ask values of losses are most often given as a percent. Convert the percent to a decimal number and multiply to find the dollar value.

For help, go to the **Math Skills Handbook** located at the back of this book.

Standardized Test Practice

Directions Read the following questions. On a separate piece of paper, write the best possible answer for each one.

1. A business that provides safe working conditions and safety instruction is handling risks by which of the following methods?
   A. Risk avoidance
   B. Risk prevention
   C. Risk retention
   D. Risk transfer
2. Customer dishonesty is an example of a natural risk.
   T
   F
3. The possibility of financial loss is what is known as a(n) ________.

Test-Taking Tip
When answering multiple-choice questions, ask yourself if each option is true or false. This may help you find the best answer if you are not sure.

DECA Connection Role Play

Employee
Dry Cleaners

Situation Assume the role of an experienced employee of a dry cleaning establishment. The store has been in business for 40 years. It has an outstanding reputation. The store also handles specialty cleaning of leather items, quilts, and bridal gowns. You are training a new counter person (judge). You mention that the owners carry insurance on the building and equipment, and on the items they clean. The new employee (judge) wants to know why the business carries so much insurance when it has a good reputation.

Activity You are to explain to the new employee (judge) why the dry cleaner carries insurance and some of the risks that can be protected against by purchasing insurance.

Evaluation You will be evaluated on how well you meet the following performance indicators:

1. Determine the factors affecting business risk.
2. Follow established security procedures/policies.
3. Identify the key loss prevention methods retailers use to reduce shrinkage.
4. Describe the concept of insurance.
5. Explain the nature of risk management.

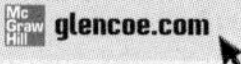

Download the Competitive Events Workbook for more Role-Play practice.

EVALUATE

21st Century Skills

Social Responsibility

10. Students should prepare a one-page memo to the staff at a food-service establishment explaining the importance of proper personal hygiene. It should mention the risks that could result from failing to follow appropriate cleanliness guidelines, and recommend specific practices in the workplace to protect coworkers and the general public.

Financial Literacy Skills

11. It would have cost $255.09. ($259 – [$259 × 0.0151]) The amount saved would be $3.91. ($259 × 0.0151)

e-Marketing Skills

12. Students should write a one-page report outlining a workplace safety plan for a quick-serve restaurant. The report should present five specific recommendations regarding worker safety and operational safety. The report also should discuss how the recommendations are to be implemented. Possible recommendations might include: assigning specific individuals the responsibility of regularly checking for hazards; having a plan for correcting hazards before accidents occur; scheduling regular safety meetings and trainings and making certain all employees are formally trained in using equipment and that written instructions on equipment use are available to all employees; making certain first-aid kits are near workstations; posting directions to nearby health facilities; and enforcing safety rules such as keeping all exterior doors locked.

EVALUATE

Build Academic Skills

English Language Arts

13. Students' reports should be one page in length and summarize the advantages and disadvantages of extended product warranties. In their reports, students should identify the sources of their information. ConsumerReports.org, for example, states that products, particularly cars, have become more reliable and are unlikely to break down during the extended warranty period. The warranties typically cost more than the consumer will recover and often include fine-print terms that disqualify claims. Instead of purchasing extended warranties, ConsumerReports.org suggests buying reliable brands and following the usage and maintenance instructions.

Science

14. Students' reports should be one page in length and summarize a recent situation in which the EPA took action against a business to protect the public interest. The student should identify the business's name and location, along with the specific actions planned or taken to protect consumers. For example, in September 2010, the EPA issued an Administrative Penalty Order against Tony's Fine Foods, based on Sacramento, California. The EPA fined Tony's over $90,000. The EPA stated that Tony's had leaked approximately 360 gallons of anhydrous ammonia into the air from a pressure relief valve in a warehouse, resulting in the evacuation of four nearby schools and numerous residences. Specifically, Tony's was accused of failing to provide critical information regarding the leak to the proper authorities, thereby diminishing the community's ability to respond to the emergency.

Mathematics

15. The amount of net sales lost annually is $267,488. ($8,359,000 × 0.032)

Standardized Test Practice

1. B (Risk prevention)
2. F (Customer dishonesty is an example of a human risk.)
3. business risk

DECA Connection Role Play

Evaluations will be based on these performance indicators:

1. **Determine the factors affecting business risk.** The possibility of financial loss is called business risk. Economic risks occur when there are changes in overall business conditions, such as the level or type of competition, changes in consumer lifestyles, population changes, limited usefulness of some products, product obsolescence, government regulation, inflation, or recession. Natural risks include loss or damage of property resulting from catastrophes such as floods, tornadoes, fires, earthquakes, power outages, civil unrest, war, etc. Human risks include employee dishonesty, errors, mistakes, omission, etc.
2. **Follow established security procedures/policies.** Established security procedures and policies include thoroughly screening and training employees, providing safe conditions and safety instruction, controlling employee theft, working to prevent shoplifting, and reducing workplace threats
3. **Identify the key loss prevention methods used by retailers to reduce shrinkage.** Employee theft can be reduced by installing video cameras and POS terminals that generate reports on cash register transactions, discrepancies, void transfers, etc. Shoplifting can be reduced by educating employees about prevention guidelines, adequately lighting store layouts, storing expensive items in locked display cases, tagging products with electronic anti-theft devices, and using video cameras, electronic gates, and wall or ceiling mirrors.
4. **Describe the concept of insurance.** Insurance is designed to transfer specific business risks from a business to an insurance company. Purchasing an insurance policy allows a business to insure property and people against potential loss.
5. **Explain the nature of risk management.** Risk management involves systematically managing an organization's risks to achieve objectives in a manner consistent with public interest, human safety, environmental needs, and the law. Risks are managed by using the best available marketing information, analyzing opportunities, and making wise decisions.

glencoe.com

Role Plays For more DECA Role Plays, send students to the Online Learning Center to download the Competitive Events Workbook.

developing a business plan

SHOW WHAT YOU KNOW

Visual Literacy A business plan includes a plan for making a new business succeed. It includes a philosophy and mission statement, describes an organizational scheme, identifies various marketing strategies, and provides a detailed financial plan. ***Why must entrepreneurs research all available sources of funding and opportunities to raise capital?***

Discovery Project

Start-Up Planning

Essential Question How does an entrepreneur develop a business plan?

Project Goal

You and a classmate are partners in a proposed new product or service business. The first step in developing a business plan is to describe the type of business and complete a team self-analysis. The team must also develop and agree on an organization and marketing plan for the business. Your team must prepare a written report that describes the business, its organization, and marketing plans.

Ask Yourself...

- How will your team describe the product/service and analyze the team's special skills?
- How will your team organize the new business?
- What pricing policies and promotional strategies will your team use?
- How will your team organize the written plan for these three sections of a business plan?

Synthesize and Present Synthesize your research by describing in a report the important elements in your business plan including the description and analysis, organization, and marketing plans.

glencoe.com

Activity
Get a worksheet activity about business plans.

Evaluate
Download a rubric that you can use to evaluate your project.

DECA Connection

DECA Event Role Play

Concepts in this chapter are related to DECA competitive events that involve either an interview or role play.

Performance Indicators The performance indicators represent key skills and knowledge. Your key to success in DECA competitive events is relating them to concepts in this chapter.

- Assess personal interests and skills needed for success in business.
- Identify a company's unique selling proposition.
- Conduct an environmental scan to obtain business information.
- Conduct market analysis.
- Describe factors that affect the business environment.

DECA Prep

Role Play Practice role-playing with the DECA Connection competitive-event activity at the end of this chapter. More information on DECA events can be found on DECA's Web site.

ENGAGE

Visual Literacy

Read the chapter opener photo caption question to students: ***Why must entrepreneurs research all available sources of funding and opportunities to raise capital?*** It is important because this is how they can get the best and most realistic deal for their company. Then ask these guiding questions.

Guiding Questions

List What are some advantages and disadvantages of entrepreneurship?	Advantages include: freedom, personal satisfaction, increased self-esteem, increased income. Disadvantages include: high level of stress, risk of failure, potential loss of income.
Make a Judgment In your opinion, do the advantages of entrepreneurship outweigh the disadvantages? Why or why not?	Sample answer: the advantages outweigh the disadvantages because you can be your own boss and make your own decisions.

Discovery Project

Start-Up Planning Ask students if they have ever been in a disorganized store. Ask: ***What do you think contributed to the store's disorganization?*** Possible answers: the owner is a disorganized person; the owner didn't have a plan for the business; there wasn't enough staff to keep things organized. Then ask them the Discovery Project Essential Question: ***How does an entrepreneur develop a business plan?*** Business plan formats can vary, but they must be well organized and easy to read. Plans should contain: description and analysis, organizational plan, marketing plan, and financial plan. The business plan must convince investors and lenders that an idea will be profitable. It must identify legal procedures for establishing the business, and identify the activities necessary to operate a profitable business.

glencoe.com

Discovery Project Resources Send students to the Online Learning Center to download a rubric to evaluate their projects.

ENGAGE

Introduce the Chapter

In this chapter, students are introduced to the business plan. These main concepts are introduced and discussed:

- Description and analysis
- Type of business
- Business philosophy
- Product and service plan
- Self-analysis
- Trading area analysis
- Market segment analysis
- Operational plan
- Organizational plan
- Marketing plan
- Financial plan

Discussion Starter

Description and Analysis Ask students if they have ever tried to get to a new place without directions. Ask: *How did you do? Were you able to find the place without difficulty?* Tell students that a business plan is similar to directions or a road map to a new destination. The business plan helps people choose the best ways of creating their business. Ask students what they think an entrepreneur might need to know before starting up a business. Answers may include: what products to buy; what prices to charge; where to locate the business; how to get money to start the business; who the customers will be; and people they will need to hire. Tell students that a good business plan will contain answers to these questions.

DECA Connection

Discuss the performance indicators listed in the DECA Connection feature. Explain to students that performance indicators tell them how to demonstrate their acquired skills and knowledge through individual or team competitive events.

 **glencoe.com** 

Competitive Events Workbook For more DECA Role Plays, send students to the Online Learning Center to download the Competitive Events Workbook.

PROGRAM RESOURCE ORGANIZER

PRINT RESOURCES

- **Student Edition**
- **Teacher Edition**
- **Student Activity Workbook with Academic Integration** includes worksheets and activities correlated to the text.
- **Mathematics for Marketing Workbook** provides math activities for every unit in the text.

TECHNOLOGY TOOLBOX

- **Connect**
- **ConnectPlus**
- **ExamView Assessment Suite** is a comprehensive solution for creating, administering, and scoring tests.

 **glencoe.com** 

Online Learning Center provides a variety of resources to enrich and enhance learning.

SECTION, CHAPTER, AND UNIT RESOURCES

- **Graphic Organizers** for organizing text concepts visually.
- **Digital Nation Activities** and **Green Marketer Activities** extend learning beyond the text features.
- **Career Chatroom Career Profiles** allow students to explore different marketing occupations in depth.
- **After You Read Answer Keys** for students to check their answers.
- **Discovery Project Rubrics** and **Marketing Internship Project Rubrics** for students to evaluate their projects.

PROGRAM RESOURCES

- **Student Activity Workbook with Academic Integration Teacher Annotated Edition** includes annotated answers for the activities and worksheets.
- **Marketing Research Project Workbook** provides a step-by-step approach for students to complete their own marketing research studies.
- **School-to-Career Activity Workbook** helps students relate their class work to on-the-job experience and involves work-site analysis and working with mentors.
- **Competitive Events Workbook** helps prepare students for state and national marketing education competitions.
- **Inclusion in the Marketing Education Classroom** provides teaching resources for working with students with special needs.
- **PowerPoint Presentations** provides visual teaching aids and assessments for this chapter.

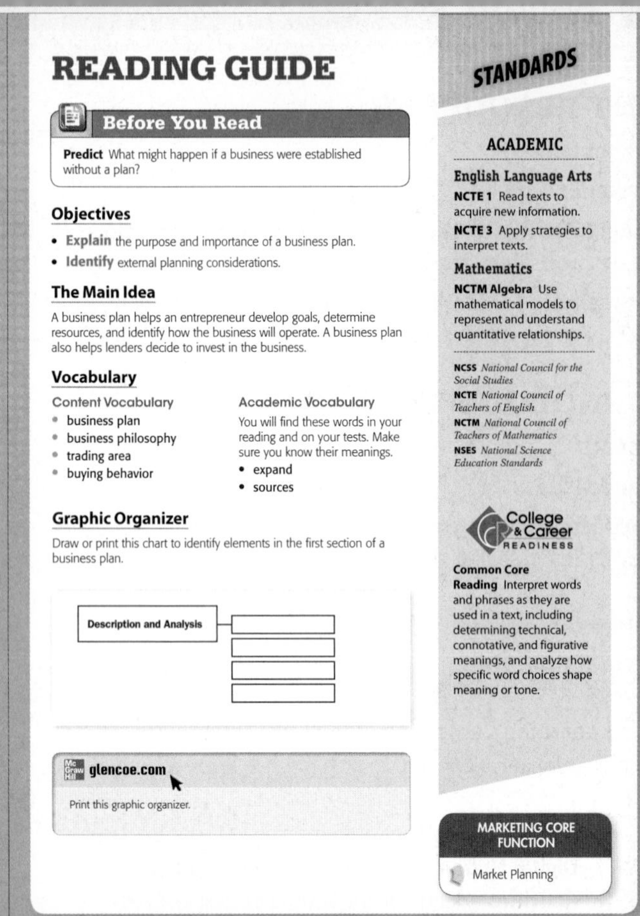

READING GUIDE

Before You Read

Predict What might happen if a business were established without a plan?

Objectives

- **Explain** the purpose and importance of a business plan.
- **Identify** external planning considerations.

The Main Idea

A business plan helps an entrepreneur develop goals, determine resources, and identify how the business will operate. A business plan also helps lenders decide to invest in the business.

Vocabulary

Content Vocabulary
- business plan
- business philosophy
- trading area
- buying behavior

Academic Vocabulary

You will find these words in your reading and on your tests. Make sure you know their meanings.
- expand
- sources

Graphic Organizer

Draw or print this chart to identify elements in the first section of a business plan.

glencoe.com

Print this graphic organizer.

STANDARDS

ACADEMIC

English Language Arts

NCTE 1 Read texts to acquire new information.

NCTE 3 Apply strategies to interpret texts.

Mathematics

NCTM Algebra Use mathematical models to represent and understand quantitative relationships.

NCSS *National Council for the Social Studies*
NCTE *National Council of Teachers of English*
NCTM *National Council of Teachers of Mathematics*
NSES *National Science Education Standards*

College & Career READINESS

Common Core
Reading Interpret words and phrases as they are used in a text, including determining technical, connotative, and figurative meanings, and analyze how specific word choices shape meaning or tone.

MARKETING CORE FUNCTION

Market Planning

DEVELOPING THE BUSINESS PLAN

If you want to establish a business, you will need financial help. A business plan helps you to secure that assistance. A **business plan** is a proposal that outlines a strategy to turn a business idea into a reality. It describes a business opportunity, such as a new business or plans to **expand** an existing one, to potential investors and lenders. Investors will review the business plan before granting you credit or start-up capital. In addition to obtaining capital, a business plan guides you in opening the business and operating it after the start-up phase.

Your business plan must convince investors and lenders that your business idea will be profitable. It must identify procedures necessary to legally establish the business. It also works as a management tool to identify the activities necessary to operate a profitable business.

Although formats of business plans vary, the outline shown in **Figure 35.1** on page 820 is an excellent model to follow. A plan for a proposed business must be well organized and easy to read. It should contain four main sections:

- Description and analysis
- Organizational plan
- Marketing plan
- Financial plan

As You Read

Predict List three questions a lender might ask an entrepreneur about his or her business philosophy before providing a business loan.

DESCRIPTION AND ANALYSIS

The description and analysis section introduces the business concept. This section clearly identifies the products and services the business will sell. It explains your business philosophy. It presents a personal self-analysis that describes your business experience, education, and training. This section of your business plan also includes a trading area and market segment analysis. It presents an operational plan for the proposed location.

> "A written plan for starting and operating a successful new business is essential."

When preparing your plan, be as factual as possible. A business description should answer questions like these about your company:

- Is it a new or established business?
- How long you have been in business?
- Is it a corporation, sole proprietorship or partnership?
- What expertise do you bring to the company?
- Is it retail, wholesale, service, or manufacturing?
- How many employees do you have?
- What is your general management structure like?

For small business and entrepreneurship information, consult magazines such as *Black Enterprise, Entrepreneur, Fast Company, Home Business,* and *Inc.* Also try Internet resources, such as *BusinessWeek Online* and *SmallBizResources.*

818 | Unit 11 · Entrepreneurship and Finance

Chapter 35 · Developing a Business Plan | 819

ENGAGE

Anticipation Activity

Improving Student Achievement Divide the class into small groups. Have groups do online research to find samples or templates of business plans. Ask groups to provide titles for the different sections to the plans as you display them for the class to read. Then, as you point to each section, ask: ***What is the importance of this section in the business plan?*** Sample answer: Self-analysis is important for the entrepreneur to evaluate strengths and weaknesses and to plan for continued personal development.

Objectives

- **Explain** the purpose and importance of a business plan. It is a proposal that outlines a strategy to turn a business idea into a reality. It is presented to potential investors and lenders who will consider it before granting credit for start-up capital.
- **Identify** external planning considerations. trading area analysis: geographic, demographic, and economic data; competitive analysis; market segment analysis

Graphic Organizer

Description and Analysis
- Type of business
- Business philosophy
- Product and service plan
- Self-analysis
- Trading area analysis
- Market segment analysis
- Operational plan

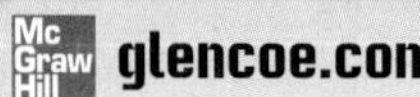

Graphic Organizer Send students to the Online Learning Center to print this graphic organizer.

EXPLORE

Before You Read

Read the Before You Read question aloud: ***What might happen if a business were established without a plan?*** The owner would be unable to convince potential lenders that he or she is organized and had thought through the start-up end of the business, and would be unlikely to obtain funding. Tell students to imagine that they were willing to invest in a start-up company. Ask: ***What would you want to know about the owner and his or her background before you loaned money for the business or invested money in it?*** Sample answers: the owner's strengths and weaknesses; how he or she plans to overcome the weaknesses; credit history; the success rate of other business ventures.

Preteaching Vocabulary

Have students go to the Online Learning Center at glencoe.com for the Chapter 35 Preteaching Vocabulary games.

Content Vocabulary

Instruct students to write a paragraph in which they discuss how the vocabulary terms are interrelated. Possible answer: Business philosophy, trading area, and buying behavior are all discussed as part of the business plan. Ask volunteers to share their paragraphs with the rest of the class.

Academic Vocabulary

Expand—Synonyms Display *expand* and have students develop a list of synonyms for the word: enlarge, increase, magnify, inflate, develop Then have students determine which synonym could be used to replace *expand* in this sentence: ***A business plan describes a business opportunity such as a new business or plans to expand an existing one.*** increase, develop

Sources—Synonyms Display the term *sources* and have the class develop a list of synonyms for it:. basis, resource, cause, informant. Then have students determine which synonym could replace *sources* in this sentence: ***Industry trade and professional associations can also be rich sources of data.*** resources

MINI CLIP

ELL: Collaborative Work

Go to the Online Learning Center to view a video clip in which students work in groups to complete a science lab and then use academic vocabulary to discuss and record their findings.

The Business Plan

Section 35.1

DEVELOPING THE BUSINESS PLAN

Tell students that a business plan outlines the strategy that will turn an idea into a reality. Then ask these guiding questions to focus the discussion on developing the business plan.

Guiding Questions

List What are the four main sections a business plan should contain?	description and analysis, organizational plan, marketing plan, and financial plan
Identify In addition to helping obtain capital, what does a business plan provide?	a guide to opening the business and operating it after the start-up phase
Examine Why must a business plan convince lenders and/or investors that your business will be profitable?	Lenders want assurance that they will get their money back; investors want to know that they will make money on their investment.
Predict Under what conditions would you not need financial help to establish a business?	Possible answer: If the entrepreneur had already saved up the necessary capital, he or she would not need financial help.

As You Read

Read students the As You Read question: ***List three questions a lender might ask an entrepreneur about his or her business philosophy before providing a business loan.*** Possible answers: What do you see as your business's role in the marketplace? What is your mission statement? What roles do employees play in your business plan?

Expert Advice

Read the quote to students:

> **“A written plan for starting and operating a successful new business is essential.”**

Ask students: ***Why is a written plan essential?*** Possible answer: Lenders and potential investors must see that the owner is organized and has thought through all aspects of the business.

FIGURE 35.1 **Outline for a Business Plan**

The Business Plan A business plan is a written plan prepared for a new business. ***What is the purpose of the plan for a potential investor or lender?***

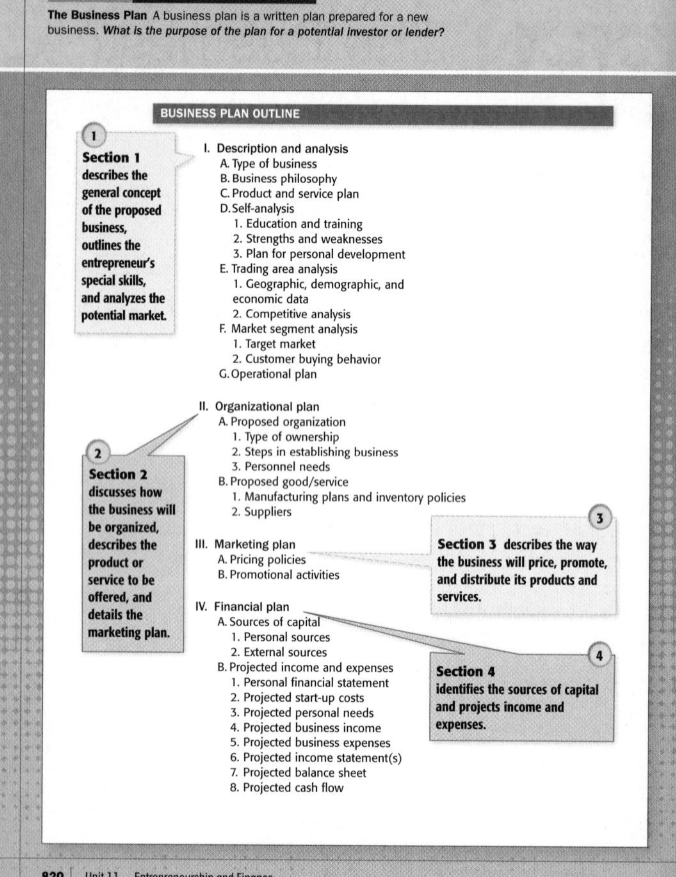

BUSINESS PLAN OUTLINE
1 Section 1 describes the general concept of the proposed business, outlines the entrepreneur's special skills, and analyzes the potential market.
I. Description and analysis
A. Type of business
B. Business philosophy
C. Product and service plan
D. Self-analysis
1. Education and training
2. Strengths and weaknesses
3. Plan for personal development
E. Trading area analysis
1. Geographic, demographic, and economic data
2. Competitive analysis
F. Market segment analysis
1. Target market
2. Customer buying behavior
G. Operational plan
2 Section 2 discusses how the business will be organized, describes the product or service to be offered, and details the marketing plan.
II. Organizational plan
A. Proposed organization
1. Type of ownership
2. Steps in establishing business
3. Personnel needs
B. Proposed good/service
1. Manufacturing plans and inventory policies
2. Suppliers
3 Section 3 describes the way the business will price, promote, and distribute its products and services.
III. Marketing plan
A. Pricing policies
B. Promotional activities
4 Section 4 identifies the sources of capital and projects income and expenses.
IV. Financial plan
A. Sources of capital
1. Personal sources
2. External sources
B. Projected income and expenses
1. Personal financial statement
2. Projected start-up costs
3. Projected personal needs
4. Projected business income
5. Projected business expenses
6. Projected income statement(s)
7. Projected balance sheet
8. Projected cash flow

820 | Unit 11 · Entrepreneurship and Finance

Industry trade and professional associations can also be rich **sources** of data. Entrepreneurs can obtain research results and data from local chambers of commerce, local and county government offices, and state economic development agencies and boards. The U.S. Small Business Administration and its resource partner, the Senior Corps of Retired Executives (SCORE®), can refer you to potential sources of information and classes for aspiring entrepreneurs. Many community colleges and universities also have small business development centers or agencies. These places provide information, referrals, and resources to develop a winning business plan.

TYPE OF BUSINESS

A business plan begins with a description of the type of business you have or plan to start. In part of the plan, you will present marketing research data and review significant trends that will influence the success of your proposed business. You should also provide an explanation of how a current or changing situation has created an opportunity for your business to fulfill consumer demand.

BUSINESS PHILOSOPHY

In the company description, you state your business philosophy. A **business philosophy** contains beliefs on how a business should be run. It also demonstrates an understanding of the business's role in the marketplace. The business philosophy reveals your attitude toward your customers, employees, and competitors. A business philosophy should also include a mission statement and a vision statement. A mission statement expresses the specific aspirations of the company. A vision statement states the scope and purpose of the company.

PRODUCT AND SERVICE PLAN

After identifying a business philosophy, you describe the product and/or service that will be offered. You will explain the potential consumer benefits and why your product or service will be successful. Include as many facts, trends, and statistics as you can, and be thorough in your research and documentation. Unsupported data, speculation, and personal assumptions will not convince investors and lenders to lend you money.

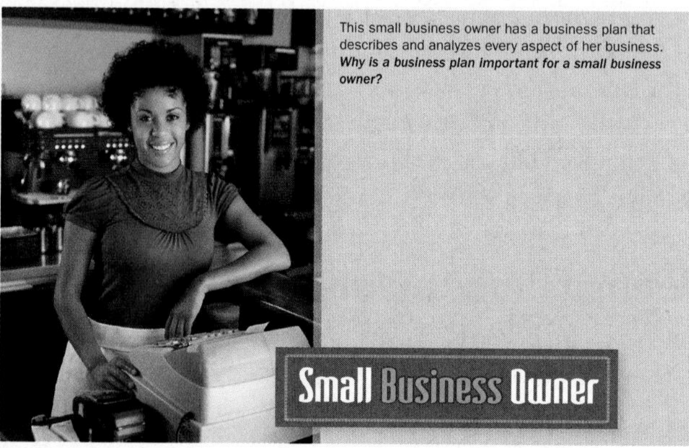

This small business owner has a business plan that describes and analyzes every aspect of her business. ***Why is a business plan important for a small business owner?***

Chapter 35 · Developing a Business Plan | 821

EXPLAIN

Visual Literacy

Figure 35.1 Caption Answer Read the caption question to students: ***What is the purpose of the plan for a potential investor or lender?*** The plan must convince investors and lenders that the business idea will be profitable. Then ask these guiding questions.

Guiding Questions

Identify What areas are considered when developing the projected income and expenses for a business?	Areas include a personal financial statement as well as projected start-up costs, personal needs, business income, business expenses, income statement(s), balance sheet, and cash flow.
Make a Judgment Which part of the business plan might be of most interest to lenders and investors? Why?	The financial plan likely would be of the most interest because they are interested in making money on their investments and in getting back (with interest) the money they are considering lending.

Critical Thinking

To help students understand the business plan outline presented in Figure 35.1, ask: ***What might happen if a business did not have an organizational or marketing plan?*** Answers may include: Lack of an organizational plan might delay start-up while the owner tried to determine what to do next. Lack of a marketing plan would make it difficult to price products or services and plan promotional activities. Then ask: ***Why should a business plan be a continuous work-in-progress?*** Students should recognize that the market, business, and competition are dynamic. A business plan needs to be revised to account for ongoing changes. Have students debate which part of the business plan is most important. Ask students to provide sound reasoning. Help them understand that each part is equally important.

VIRTUAL BUSINESS

TURNAROUND

Introduce the concept of turnaround using Knowledge Matters' Virtual Business Retailing visual simulation, *Turnaround.* In this simulation, students will learn how to diagnose business problems and apply turnaround strategies to set the business back on the right track.

ELABORATE

Mini Projects

Differentiated Instruction

Kinesthetic Learners Divide the class into pairs and have them develop role plays in which one student plays the part of an entrepreneur and the other acts as an investor or lender. The entrepreneur should pitch a new business to the investor or lender in an attempt to convince that person to provide funding. Entrepreneurs should give their business a name, explain what the business is, explain to the lender or investor what will be included in the business plan, and explain why it is important to read the business plan. Students who play the investor or lender should be prepared to ask questions of the entrepreneur that will provide additional background information.

Students with Learning Difficulties Have students write a four paragraph self-analysis. The first paragraph should include their education and training. The second paragraph should explore their strengths. The third should describe their weaknesses, and the fourth should outline their plan for personal development.

Visual Literacy

Small Business Owner Read the caption question to students: ***Why is a business plan important for a small business owner?*** Answers may include: business owners need a business plan to convince lenders and investors that they are a good risk; a plan that is flexible enough to adjust to a changing economy provides focus. Then ask these guiding questions to help students better understand the concept of a business plan.

Guiding Questions

Define What is a business philosophy?	beliefs on how a business should be run; it demonstrates an understanding of the business's role in the marketplace
Explain What is included under the head Type of Business on a business plan?	description of the type of business, marketing research data, significant trends that will influence the business, explanation of how a current or changing situation has created an opportunity for the business to fulfill consumer demand
Examine Why should an entrepreneur include facts, trends, and statistics in the Product and Service Plan section of a business plan?	Including this information tells potential investors and lenders that the entrepreneur has done his or her homework. It shows that the entrepreneur understands his or her industry, and is formulating plans for how to use the knowledge to benefit the business.

Graphic Organizer

Display this diagram. Ask students to provide the titles for the four parts of the business plan. Description and analysis, organizational plan; marketing plan; financial plan. Write students' answers in the diagram. Then ask: ***What are main elements of each part of the business plan?*** Answers are provided below. Ask: ***Why do you think each part of the business plan has the same amount of space on the diagram?*** Students should recognize that it is because each part is equally important.

Parts of the Business Plan

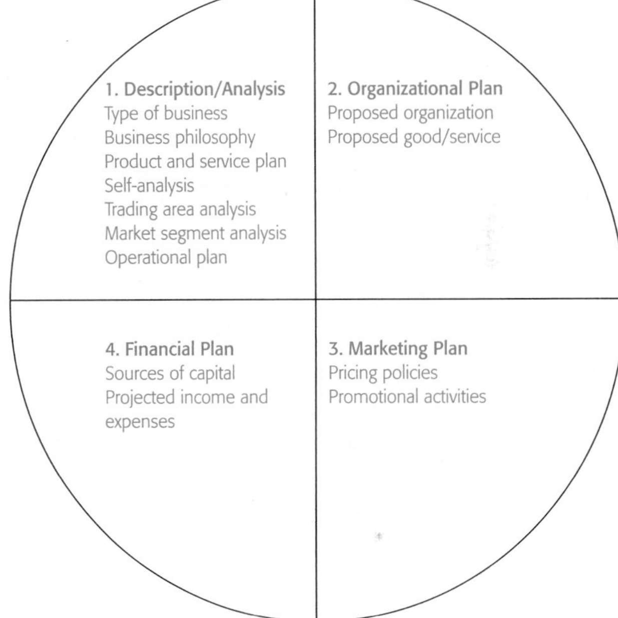

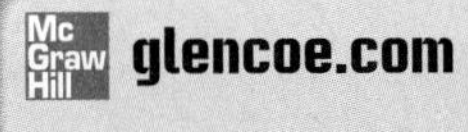

iWB

Graphic Organizer Send students to the Online Learning Center to print this graphic organizer.

Critical Thinking

Ask students to consider the following business philosophies and discuss what kind of business each philosophy would be appropriate for: 1. We get it there on time. a delivery service 2. We provide the highest-quality product. Any kind of product-based company—electronics, housewares, furniture, restaurants, and so on. 3. We pamper the customer. This would work well for service-based businesses such as hair salons, restaurants, or hotels, but would also work for a product-based business that values its customers.

Extend the Concept Bring to class a variety of ads that show a business philosophy. Have students read the ads and determine the philosophy of the business. Ask students to share their insights with the class.

SELF-ANALYSIS

The next part of the business plan includes a self-analysis—a description of your personal education and professional training, an appraisal of your strengths and weaknesses, and any plans you have for continued personal and professional development.

EDUCATION AND TRAINING

Indicate any education and training that has prepared you to operate the new business you are planning. For example, if you are planning to open a tax preparation business, you should highlight your bachelor's degree in accounting along with your state-issued license to work as a Certified Public Accountant. If you have worked for another company that prepares tax returns, you should also be sure to highlight that experience.

Your education and work experience show potential lenders that you understand the industry you hope to enter. They demonstrate your interest in your chosen field and your commitment to succeeding in it. They also show that you have the skills required to run a successful business.

SPECIAL STRENGTHS

Many businesses require the owner or operator to have a special license. For example, the owner of an adult foster care center, an automotive repair shop, or a styling salon is required to possess a special occupational license. Special certification is also required for operators of child day care, construction, and electrical businesses.

In this part of the business plan, you should highlight all the professional licenses, certifications, skills, and strengths that you have obtained. You should also explain how they will be useful in starting up and operating the proposed business.

You should also clearly describe any personal traits and work habits that you believe will help you manage the business. Examples of leadership activities, personal initiatives, and willingness to work hard add strength to your business plan. Be sure to mention any involvement in professional organizations that might reflect well on your ability to successfully operate your own business. Also note your involvement in any relevant volunteer activities that can help demonstrate your sense of commitment and responsibility.

MARKETING CASE STUDY

The KGB Plan: Got Questions?

If you are having trouble remembering the name of that actor in the TV show you watched as a kid, you might try a Google search or another online service, such the KGB (Knowledge Generated Bureau). Send a text message and get an answer on your cell phone. Unlike free search engines, however, "KGB agents" respond for 99 cents per question.

Targeting Texters

KGB has been in the directory assistance business since 1992. Because customer behavior changed, they changed. KGB decided to expand its business plan to keep up with the changes in customer activities: People don't call for information anymore, they text. CEO Bruce Stewart explains the KGB philosophy: "We wanted to rebrand the KGB—we're democratizing information." And as part of its marketing plan, a series of TV commercials depict people in humorous situations desperately in need of an answer.

English Language Arts

Collaborate With a partner, write a hypothetical Description and Analysis for the first section of this company's business plan. Refer to **Figure 35.1** and conduct Internet research as needed.

NCTE 7 Conduct research and gather, evaluate, and synthesize data to communicate discoveries.

PLAN FOR PERSONAL DEVELOPMENT

You should also describe how you will acquire the needed skills that you might currently lack or need to improve. Needed skills can be gained through additional training or membership in trade associations. Skills may also be acquired by hiring or partnering with other professionals to assist you in managing the business. Plans for continuing personal development show your intent to improve on your existing skills and abilities as a business owner.

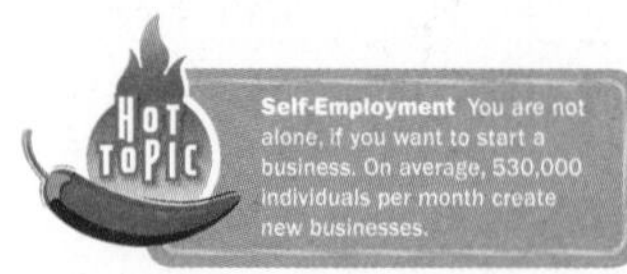

HOT TOPIC
Self-Employment You are not alone, if you want to start a business. On average, 530,000 individuals per month create new businesses.

TRADING AREA ANALYSIS

The trading area analysis part of the plan defines your trading area. A **trading area** is the geographical area from which a business draws its customers. Before going into business, you must analyze the trading area to become familiar with geographic, demographic, and economic data, and with the competition.

It is very important that you do this research and analysis before choosing where you will conduct business. Your location is likely to become a long-term financial commitment that will be difficult to change if it does not work out.

Information about the population in your trading area is available from your local chamber of commerce or state department of commerce. You can also consult the most recent local U.S. Census data in your library or on the Internet.

GEOGRAPHIC, DEMOGRAPHIC, AND ECONOMIC DATA

Geographic data include population distribution figures, or how many people live in a certain area. Demographics are identifiable and measurable population statistics, such as age, gender, marital status, and race/ethnicity. Knowing the demographics of a trading area helps to identify market trends that have a direct impact on a business.

Prevailing economic conditions are crucial factors affecting any business. National and state economic conditions affect businesses by increasing or decreasing the demand or need for products or services.

The GREEN Marketer

Green Building = Smart Business

Having an eco-friendly location can help a business's image and its bottom line. In fact, many new companies plan for "green" building sites in their business plans, flying their "green" colors to draw customers.

Good Habits Businesses can dramatically reduce costs by increasing building insulation, planting native plants for shade and beauty, using solar panels, and opening blinds to increase available sunlight. Employees can get involved, too, by recycling waste and shutting off computers and task lights at the end of each workday.

Science

Create Imagine that you are planning to open a restaurant in your town. Describe the area and the type of building you have chosen, and explain your choice. Brainstorm ten ways to "green" your operation.

NSES F Develop understanding of personal and community health; population growth; natural resources; environmental quality; natural and human-induced hazards; science and technology in local, national, and global challenges.

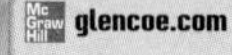

glencoe.com

Get an activity on green marketing.

EXPLORE

SELF-ANALYSIS

Tell students that potential lenders and investors want to know about not only the business they will be funding but also about the entrepreneur they will be funding. Then ask these guiding questions to focus the discussion on a self-analysis.

Guiding Questions

Explain Why would potential lenders and investors want to know the background of the entrepreneur(s) heading the business?	They need to make sure the entrepreneur(s) is able to run the business efficiently and to make a profit. The entrepreneur's background is important to determining whether the business will be a success.
Predict Why is personal development an important part of the self-analysis?	Entrepreneurs must keep abreast of the trends and changes in their business in order to be successful. Having a plan shows intent to improve and learn and keep up with the needs of the business.

MARKETING CASE STUDY

English Language Arts Answer Answers may include: Type of business—information provider. Business philosophy—make information available to everyone. Product and service plan—provide the best answers possible as quickly as possible. Self-analysis—strong background in general education provides broad base of resources from which to provide information, weak in business management skills and knowledge, need to partner with someone who has these strengths and take business courses at local college. Trading area analysis—geographic area is limited only by availability of cell phone service, service will appeal to people who communicate by texting, price is competitive. Market segment analysis—target market includes all who communicate by text messaging, customers will be comfortable making purchases by credit card over their cell phones or smartphones. Operational plan—business will be based in a call center with access to high-speed Internet service to locate and provide information as quickly as possible.

EXPLAIN

TRADING AREA ANALYSIS

Ask these guiding questions to focus the discussion on trading areas.

Guiding Questions

Define What is a trading area?	the geographical area from which a business draws its customers
Explain What types of data are included in a trading area analysis?	geographic, demographic, economic, and competitive
Deduce Why should you know a trading area's demographics?	Demographics can help identify current market trends that have a direct impact on a business.
Evaluate Why is economic data an important part of the trading area analysis?	Prevailing economic conditions affect businesses by increasing or decreasing the demand or need for products or services.
Distinguish What is the difference between geographic data and demographic data?	Geographic data include population distribution, or how many people live in an area. Demographics refer to population statistics, such as age, gender, marital status, and ethnicity.

Critical Thinking

Have students generate a list of popular local businesses. Then have small groups classify the businesses according to their trading areas. For example, stores selling popular music might have the same trading area, but stores selling groceries would have a different trading area. Ask each group to write a paragraph explaining each trading area. Have groups share their insights with the class.

Self-Employment Tell students that each year more than six million people create new businesses. Have students suggest advantages of being their own boss (make your own decisions, create your own schedule, and so on), as well as the possible disadvantages (financial risk, long hours, and so on). Some students may find it exciting to imagine running a business on their own; others may feel intimidated by it and would prefer the relative security of working for someone else.

Graphic Organizer

Display this diagram. Ask students to think of two small businesses in their community that compete with each other. Then ask students to determine answers to these questions:

- How does the business differentiate itself from the competition?
- Hoes does it keep abreast of the competition?
- What indirect competition does it face?

Write students' answers in the diagram. Sample answers are below.

	Business A: Sam's Grocery	Business B: Mom's Food Mart
How does it differentiate itself from the competition?	Tells customers they'll get the best deal in town.	Tells customers the products are chosen especially for them by a loving mom.
Hoes does it keep abreast of the competition?	Reads the competition's ads in the local newspaper.	Visits the competition's store on a regular basis.
What indirect competition does it face?	New chain store offers online purchasing and delivery services.	New chain store offers online purchasing and delivery services.

Graphic Organizer Send students to the Online Learning Center to print this graphic organizer.

The GREEN Marketer

Science Answer Read the activity: *Imagine that you are planning to open a restaurant in your town. Describe the area and the type of building you have chosen, and explain your choice. Brainstorm ten ways to "green" your operation.* Students should explain why the neighborhood and facility they choose would be appropriate. Green ideas include using eco-friendly interior supplies; choosing green power; serving local, organic food; and recycling and composting. The restaurant could communicate these efforts via its Web site, signage, menus, and staff.

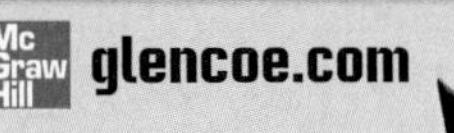

Worksheet Activity Send students to the Online Learning Center to get a Green Marketer worksheet activity.

Economic factors include business growth projections, trends in employment, interest rates, economic statistics, stock market forecasts, and governmental regulations. Tax increases or decreases levied by the local, state, and federal governments affect consumer buying power.

It is important to include and analyze the disposable income potential of consumers in your trading area. Disposable income is the personal income remaining from wages after all taxes are taken out. Disposable income is also called "buying income."

A special measurement called a "buying power index" (BPI) has been developed to help new business owners determine the buying power for a given target market. The BPI index factors total population, total income, and total retail sales figures. These figures are used to determine an overall indicator of an area's sales potential. A market can be a state, region, county, or metropolitan statistical area (MSA). These factors are then expressed as a percentage of total potential U.S. sales. You can find more information on buying power indexes in *Demographics USA*, which is published annually by Trade Dimensions International.

An excellent source of information on local economic conditions is your local bank. Bank officials often have business projections for major geographical areas and for most types of businesses located in their immediate area.

In addition, the Small Business Administration (SBA) has provided funding for over 1,000 small business development centers (SBDCs) housed in leading universities, colleges, and economic development agencies. Millions of rural and urban entrepreneurs have received no-cost consulting services and low-cost training from SBDCs. Other good sources of information are business publications available at public libraries, colleges, and universities, or on the Internet.

COMPETITIVE ANALYSIS

As a new business owner, you must analyze your competition. List all the competitors in your trading area: their products, prices, locations, quality of products, strengths, and weaknesses. Try to estimate your competitors' sales volume.

It is also helpful to identify how competitors promote and sell their products. These factors can help demonstrate how a business will be different and better than the competition.

Information about competitors can be found through annual reports and business publications, such as those published by Dun & Bradstreet®, and from the Internet, local chambers of commerce, trade associations, and the *Yellow Pages*.

MARKET SEGMENT ANALYSIS

A business plan contains a market segment analysis: a description of your target market and the buying behavior of your potential customers.

TARGET MARKET

A target market is a group of people identified as those most likely to become customers. They are the people that you want to reach with your business. A target market is identified by common geographic characteristics such as region, county size, size of city, density of population, and climate of the area. Target markets can also be categorized by demographic characteristics such as age, gender, marital status, family size, income, occupation, education, religion, culture, or ethnic background.

Target Market Characteristics

Geographic Characteristics	Demographic Characteristics	
• Region	• Age	• Occupation
• County Size	• Gender	• Education
• City Size	• Marital Status	• Religion
• Population Density	• Family Size	• Culture
• Climate	• Income	• Ethnicity

Businesses carefully identify target markets so they can meet the needs and wants of different individuals for their goods and services. Your task as an entrepreneur is to decide which market to target and how to do it. The challenging part here is how to reach your target market. You have many options available to you in terms of advertising and promotion.

CUSTOMER BUYING BEHAVIOR

After you have identified the target market, explain how the buying behavior of potential customers will be a good match for your products and services. **Buying behavior** is the process that individuals use to decide what they will buy, where they will buy it, and from whom they will buy it.

OPERATIONAL PLAN

The operational plan explains where a business is located—at home or in a bought or leased facility away from home. This section also describes competing and complementary businesses, hours of operation, visibility, customer safety and accessibility, and how zoning regulations will be met for the business.

Operational Plan	
Location	Visibility
Other Businesses	Customer Safety
Hours	Zoning

LOCATION OF THE BUSINESS

The location of your business is largely determined by the products and services that you plan to provide and your personal preferences.

Is it important for you to be in close proximity to family members and friends? Do you want to locate in your community or away from where you currently live?

Other intangible issues such as atmosphere of the community, character of the neighborhood, commuting and travel distance, working hours, and other preferences enter into any location decision.

Entrepreneurs who offer contracted services, such as computer, child care, housekeeping, technical, or online services, can locate their business in an existing residence. Home-based businesses have distinct cost advantages for any entrepreneur. But many new businesses need to consider other location options away from a home or residence.

If another business location is needed, should you buy, lease, or build a facility? The advantages of leasing often outweigh the other options for most new businesses. With leasing, you avoid a large initial cash outlay. Another benefit is that your risk is reduced by the shorter time commitment. Also, your lease expenses are tax deductible. The process of buying or building is more complex and almost always requires major financing.

Regardless of whether you buy, lease, or build, you need to compare certain terms of each method of financing for your place of business.

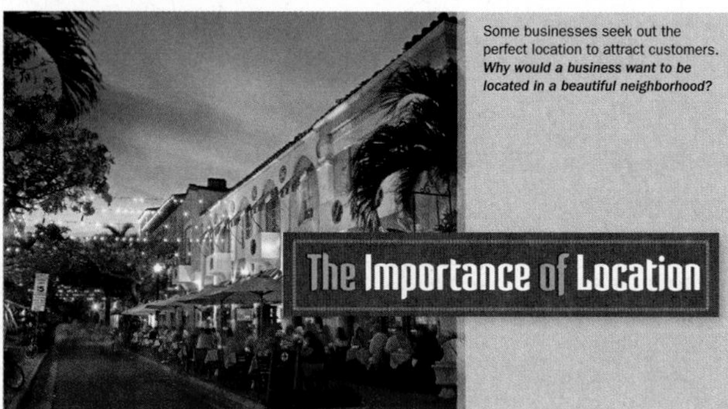

Some businesses seek out the perfect location to attract customers. ***Why would a business want to be located in a beautiful neighborhood?***

EXPLAIN

Graphic Organizer

Display this chart. Ask students to provide specific details for each of the types of data. Sample answers are provided below.

Types of Data

Geographic	Demographic	Economic
• Population distribution figures or how many people live in a certain area	• Age • Gender • Marital status • Race/ethnicity	• Business growth projections • Trends in employment • Interest rates • Economic statistics • Stock market forecasts • Governmental regulations

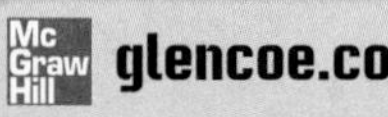 glencoe.com  iWB

Graphic Organizer Send students to the Online Learning Center to print this graphic organizer.

Critical Thinking

Have students compute the buying power index for G City. Display the following formula and information for the class:

Buying Power Index =
.5 × Area's Percentage for U.S. Effective Buying Power
+ .3 × Area's Percentage of U.S. Retail Sales
+ .2 × Area's Percentage of U.S. Population

G City Percentage of U.S. Effective Buying Power = .0103
G City Percentage of U.S. Retail Sales = .0099
G City Percentage of U.S. Population = .008
Buying Power Index = .00972 [(.5 × .0103) + (.3 × .0099) + (.2 × .008) = .00515 + .00297 + .0016 = .00972]

VIRTUAL BUSINESS

LOCATION SELECTION

Introduce the concept of location selection to students using Knowledge Matters' Virtual Business Retailing visual simulation, *Location Selection*. In this simulation, students will learn the importance of choosing a location for a retail store.

ELABORATE

Mini Projects

Enrichment

Interview a Local Banker Divide the class into pairs. Have each pair work together to develop interview questions to ask a local banker about local economic conditions. Students may want to ask about such things as the buying power index or projections for major geographical areas and for business in your area. Then have pairs make an appointment to interview someone at a local bank. Interviews can be conducted in person or over the phone. During the interview, students should take notes so they remember the interviewee's answers to the questions. After the interview, have students write a one-page summary of their interview and include answers to all of their interview questions as well as any other information the interviewee offered. Ask pairs to share their reports with the class.

Analyze the Competition Tell students to imagine that they are opening a new business. Have them determine the kind of business and the products and/or services they will provide. Then have students go online to locate and analyze a competing company. Have students locate a company Web page and use other sources such as annual reports, business publications, local chambers of commerce, trade associations, and the *Yellow Pages* to determine the following information for the competing company: Products, Prices, Location, Quality of Products, Strengths, Weaknesses, Sales Volume, and Promotion Strategies. Have students use the information to write a one-page analysis of the company. Ask students to share their analyses and to suggest what effect the information would have on their own business strategies.

Activate Prior Knowledge

Ask students to recall the definition of *target market.* a group of people identified as those most likely to become customers To reinforce the concept, have students look at their class as a whole. Divide the class into small groups and have them imagine that a company that sells clothing with the school logo and colors has targeted their class. What are some facts the company can use in its marketing effort? Ask the groups to share their ideas with the class. Possible answers: gender, age, interests, and region.

Graphic Organizer

Display this diagram. Ask students to explain what an operational plan for a business is. It explains where a business is located—at home or in a bought or leased facility away from home. Ask students what items must be a part of their operational plan. List students' answers in the diagram. Answers are provided below.

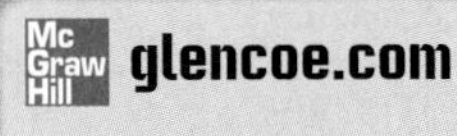

Graphic Organizer Send students to the Online Learning Center to print this graphic organizer.

Visual Literacy

The Importance of Location Caption Answer Read the caption question to students: ***Why would a business want to be located in a beautiful neighborhood?*** Possible answers: Beautiful neighborhoods will likely draw more affluent people; people will feel safer in a beautiful neighborhood; pleasant work environment. Then ask these guiding questions to focus on the location of a business.

Guiding Questions

Identify What intangible issues must be considered when deciding on a location for a business?	atmosphere of the community, character of the neighborhood, commuting and travel distance, working hours, and other preferences
Explain What determines the location of a business?	the products and services that will be provided and the personal preferences of the business owner
Analyze Why do the advantages of leasing a business location often outweigh other options such as buying or building a facility?	With leasing, a large initial cash outlay is avoided; the risk is reduced by a shorter time commitment; securing a lease is not as complex or expensive as buying or building a facility.

Those terms include monthly rent, utilities, other required payments, and the length of commitment.

For risk management purposes, you must investigate insurance policies. You must be sure that appropriate coverage is provided by you or the owner. An attorney should review any lease or contract before you sign it. An attorney can also help you to fully understand your obligations. He or she can negotiate the best possible terms before finalizing the lease agreement.

COMPETING AND COMPLEMENTARY BUSINESSES

There are many things to consider when selecting a location. Before you decide on location, consider the number and size of potential competitors in the area. If your business is similar in size and merchandise to your competitors, you may want to locate near them. Nearness to competitors can encourage comparison shopping and generate customer traffic. For example, restaurants and auto dealers are often located in close proximity to each other to attract targeted customers.

On the other hand, a larger business that offers more variety than the competition should be able to generate its own customers and, therefore, can be situated away from the competition. A complementary business is one that helps generate store traffic. A shoe store located next to a clothing store is an example of a complementary business.

HOURS OF OPERATION

The nature of your business will determine your location. This will help you decide whether you locate the business in your home, a freestanding location, mall, or neighborhood shopping center. That location, in turn, will determine your hours of operation and the number of customers who will see and patronize your business.

If you are a home-based or a free-standing business, you can determine your own hours of operation based on the needs of your customers. A business in a shopping mall or center needs to adhere to regular hours dictated by the mall or shopping center management.

Online businesses normally have extended hours of operation. For many businesses, the hours of operation can differentiate a business from the competition.

VISIBILITY

Restaurants, convenience stores, gas stations, and other businesses that rely on high visibility or prime locations may spend the extra money to locate in a high-traffic location. Such a high-traffic site may not be a priority for other businesses, and location savings might be better used for advertising, promotion, and other expenses.

CUSTOMER SAFETY

Customer safety is essential for all businesses. Customers should never have to think about whether they will have a safe experience while making a purchase or while waiting for a service to be performed.

Businesses need to protect themselves from potential lawsuits by making sure that customers are kept safe during business transactions. Therefore, a business plan should also include customer safety considerations.

Research the community's crime rate. You do not want to open your business where customers feel uncomfortable or are hesitant to visit. You can obtain crime rate information from the local police department, or you can conduct a city-specific search online.

Find out whether the fire department is a volunteer or municipal fire department. Then contact the fire department to inquire about safety codes that apply to your business. Use this research to help determine the location of your business.

CUSTOMER ACCESSIBILITY

Make sure your customers can get to your location easily. Identify the highways, streets, and public transportation options that are available to arrive at your site.

- Will traffic routes or congestion be an obstacle?
- Is there sufficient free parking or paid parking for a reasonable fee?
- Are the entrances, facilities, and parking accessible to customers with physical limitations?

ZONING AND OTHER REGULATIONS

After considering personal preferences, ownership options, hours of operation, visibility, customer safety and accessibility, you are ready to select a specific site location. You need to learn about any local ordinances or laws that may affect your business.

Research and learn about any restrictions that might prevent you from locating your business in a particular area. Zoning regulations vary among states and regions, and may change over time. Plans to build or renovate an office or building will require appropriate building permits. Operating a regulated business, such as a service station, requires local zoning approvals as well as state or federal licenses or permits.

After You Read | **Section 35.1**

Review Key Concepts

1. **List** the four major parts of a business plan.
2. **Explain** why aspiring entrepreneurs should conduct a self-analysis as part of a business plan.
3. **Discuss** why knowledge about disposable income of potential customers is an important part of a business plan.

Practice Academics

English Language Arts

4. Conduct research on geographic, demographic, and economic data for a geographical area (village, city, county, region, or state) by reading city, county, or state government, local chamber of commerce, regional economic development agency, or U.S. Census publications. Write a one-page report that identifies geographic data on your selected community, demographic data such as age, gender, population, racial/ethnic, and educational statistics; and economic data such as income, major industries, labor force participation rates, levels of employment, labor force participation rates, and major industries.

NCTE 1 Read texts to acquire new information.

Mathematics

5. Compute the buying power index for town B, given the following formula and information.
   Buying Power Index = .5 × Area's Percentage for U.S. Effective Buying Power
   + .3 × Area's Percentage of U.S. Retail Sales
   + .2 × Area's Percentage of U.S. Population
   Town B Percentage of U.S. Effective Buying Power = .025
   Town B Percentage of U.S. Retail Sales = .005
   Town B Percentage of U.S. Population = .006

NCTM Algebra Use mathematical models to represent and understand quantitative relationships.

Math Concept **Buying Power Index Formula** The buying power index formula involves a number of different variables. To solve for the buying power index, substitute the known value for the variables and multiply.

Starting Hints To solve this problem, write out the buying power index formula. Insert the given percentages for town B in the formula, and multiply to determine the buying power index.

For help, go to the **Math Skills Handbook** located at the back of this book.

glencoe.com

Check your answers.

ELABORATE

Critical Thinking

Explain to students that auto dealers often locate their businesses near their competitors. Ask: ***What kind of location do auto dealers typically prefer?*** Most dealerships prefer to be near competitors. They are often near freeways or on major streets for high visibility. Ask: ***Why do you think so many auto dealers are located next to each other?*** Students might suggest that each dealer sells a different brand of auto, and customers may shop with their minds set on a particular brand. Locating near other auto dealers offers convenience to shoppers and provides visibility. Test driving a variety of vehicles is more convenient.

Activate Prior Knowledge

Ask students to recall the purpose of a business plan. Students should mention that a business plan is a proposal that outlines a strategy to turn business ideas into a reality. It describes a business opportunity, such as a new business or plans to expand an existing one, to potential investors and lenders. The four main parts of a business plan are the description and analysis, organizational plan, marketing plan, and financial plan.

Mini Projects

Extension

Marketing to Differences Tell students that even though a professional 40-year-old man with children and a 20-year-old man with no children might both buy computers, businesses market computers differently to the two consumers. Have students discuss the potential differences in marketing to these two people. Sample answer: The 20-year-old man might be sold on real-time e-mail access to friends and a powerful game package, while the 40-year-old man might be more interested in online shopping and resources to help his children with their school work.

Location Analysis Have students list five different types of successful businesses in their community and analyze why each one is located where it is. Tell them to consider such things as accessibility to the public, to suppliers, and to transit routes. Sample answers: Businesses value low space costs, good transit access, and visibility to the public. A fast-food restaurant might be located near a highway exit. A gas station might be located on a corner in order to make it easier for customers to get there from different directions.

EVALUATE

Graphic Organizer

Display this diagram. Have the class work together to select a type of business for which to develop an operational plan. Students may suggest clothing stores, fast-food restaurants, movie theaters, and so on. List the type of business in the title. Then have students suggest a location, competing businesses, hours of operation, visibility issues, customer safety issues, customer accessibility issues and zoning and other regulations and necessary solutions. Write students' answers in the diagram. Sample answers are provided below for an athletic shoe store.

Operational Plan for an Athletic Shoe Store Business

Location	the local mall
Competing Businesses	the large department stores that anchor the mall
Hours of Operation	10:00 a.m. to 7:00 p.m. every day
Visibility	located near a sporting goods store that sells some clothing but no shoes
Customer Safety	good lighting in store; mounted mirrors to increase visibility of interior of store; clean, well-maintained aisles
Customer Accessibility	wide, clear aisles; wheelchair ramp to door of store; large parking area shared by other mall occupants
Zoning and Other Regulations	mall zoned for retail sales; additional regulations written into lease agreement with mall owners

 **glencoe.com** 

Graphic Organizer Send students to the Online Learning Center to print this graphic organizer.

Critical Thinking

Tell students that there are many types of software available that can walk you through the development of a business plan step-by-step. Business plan software helps organize all of the information needed and by using a "question/answer" approach to help draft the document. Ask: ***What might be a downside of using business plan software?*** Possible answer: Investors and lenders might recognize the "cookie cutter" approach to the business plan and feel the entrepreneur took a shortcut to develop the plan. They might feel that the entrepreneur would take other shortcuts that would be harmful to the business.

 **After You Read** **Section 35.1**

Review Key Concepts

1. The four major parts of a business plan are description and analysis, organizational plan, marketing plan, and financial plan.
2. The self-analysis shows the entrepreneur's strengths and weaknesses. It allows him or her to plan ways to acquire the needed skills that are lacking or to improve in certain areas. Plans for continuing personal development show potential lenders and investors your intent to improve on your existing skills and abilities as a business owner.
3. Disposable income is the personal income remaining from wages after all taxes are taken out. Disposable income is also known as "buying income" because this is the money consumers have to spend on the products and services offered by businesses.

Practice Academics

English Language Arts

4. Reports will vary depending on area selected. Reports should be organized, concise, and free of spelling and grammatical errors. Students should include information about age, gender, population, racial/ethnic, and educational statistics; and economic data such as income, labor force participation rates, levels of employment, and major industries.

Mathematics

5. Town B Buying Power Index = .0152 [(.5 × .025) + (.3 × .005) + (.2 × .006) = .0152]

 **glencoe.com**

Answer Key Send students to the Online Learning Center to check their answers.

READING GUIDE

Before You Read

Predict What do lenders want to see in the organizational, marketing, and financial sections of a business plan?

Objectives

- **Explain** a business's organizational plan.
- **Construct** a marketing plan.
- **Describe** financing sources for businesses.
- **Identify** the financial elements of a business plan.

The Main Idea

The organizational plan explains to investors how a business will function. The marketing plan explains how it will market its products. The financial plan projects its future profitability.

Vocabulary

Content Vocabulary
- job descriptions
- organization chart
- equity capital
- debt capital
- collateral
- credit union

Academic Vocabulary

You will find these words in your reading and on your tests. Make sure you know their meanings.
- authority
- funding

Graphic Organizer

Draw or print this chart to describe the three business plan components explained in this section.

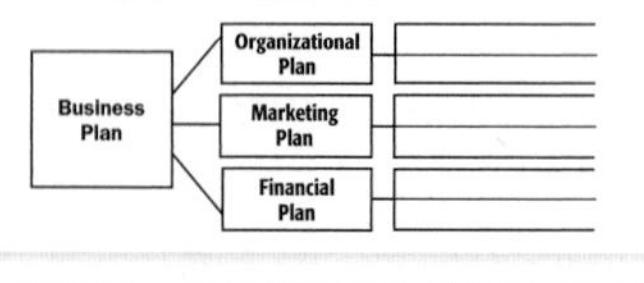

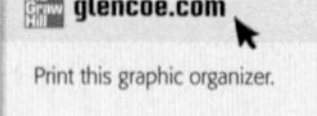

glencoe.com

Print this graphic organizer.

STANDARDS

ACADEMIC

English Language Arts
NCTE 3 Apply strategies to interpret texts.

Mathematics
NCTM Number and Operations Understand numbers, ways of representing numbers, relationships among numbers, and number systems.

NCSS *National Council for the Social Studies*
NCTE *National Council of Teachers of English*
NCTM *National Council of Teachers of Mathematics*
NSES *National Science Education Standards*

College & Career READINESS

Common Core
Reading Read closely to determine what the text says explicitly and to make logical inferences from it; cite specific textual evidence when writing or speaking to support conclusions drawn from the text.

MARKETING CORE FUNCTION

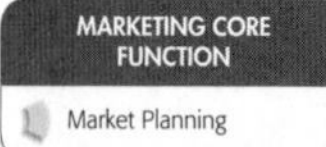

Market Planning

m.e. Section 35.2 Marketing and Financial Plans

ORGANIZATIONAL, MARKETING, AND FINANCIAL PLANS

A business plan explains to a potential lender or investor how you will organize, market, and finance a new business. The organizational plan describes your current and anticipated staffing needs. It describes how you will manufacture or purchase the goods you plan to sell. An organizational plan also includes a description of the products you plan to make or the services you will offer. It also lists potential suppliers and inventory policies.

The marketing plan details your proposed pricing policies and promotional activities. Your financial plan indicates sources of capital and projects the future profitability of the business.

As You Read

Analyze What marketing activities would you include in a business plan for a new business?

ORGANIZATIONAL PLAN

The organizational section of your business plan is a blueprint for the structure of your proposed business. You must construct a clear, solid foundation around which to build your business.

PROPOSED ORGANIZATION

There are three main types of business ownership structures: sole proprietorships, partnerships, and corporations. In this part of the plan, you identify which type you have chosen and explain why. The form of business ownership will have an impact on the rest of the business plan.

ESTABLISHING YOUR BUSINESS

Next you outline the steps to establish your business. The specific steps taken will depend on the type of business ownership you select.

> "A business plan is a guide for organizing, marketing, and financing a business."

PERSONNEL NEEDS

Potential investors and lenders need to know that you can identify essential jobs for the business so that it will operate efficiently and successfully. List staffing needs in the business plan and identify the people who will perform those jobs.

Many new businesses begin as one-person operations. It is not unusual for an entrepreneur to handle all business functions from advertising and promotion to management to financial oversight. The selected organizational structure must be able to allow for more employees and more specialization of duties as the business grows.

JOB DESCRIPTIONS

Job descriptions are written statements listing the requirements of a particular job and the skills needed to fulfill those requirements. Each job description includes the purpose, qualifications and skills, duties, equipment, and expected working conditions. Detailed job descriptions help employees know exactly what is expected of them. Job descriptions also help measure their performance against those expectations.

ENGAGE

Anticipation Activity

Improving Student Achievement Display a three-column chart with the columns labeled *Organizational Plan, Marketing Plan,* and *Financial Plan.* Have students brainstorm topics that would fit in these categories, and write their answers in the chart. Sample answers: Organizational Plan—proposed organization, products, and services; Marketing Plan—pricing policies, promotional activities; Financial Plan—equity capital, debt capital.

Objectives

- **Explain** a business's organizational plan. a blueprint or foundation for the structure of the proposed business
- **Construct** a marketing plan. outlines the way a business will price, promote, and distribute products
- **Describe** financing sources for businesses. equity capital is raised by selling part interest in company; debt capital is borrowed and must be repaid
- **Identify** the financial elements of a business plan. start-up costs, personal and external sources of capital, projected income and expenses for first three years

Graphic Organizer

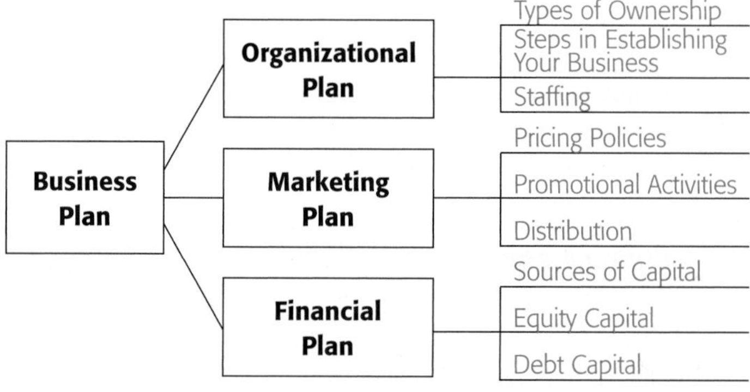

glencoe.com

Graphic Organizer Send students to the Online Learning Center to print this graphic organizer.

EXPLORE

Before You Read

Read the Before You Read question aloud: ***What do lenders want to see in the organizational, marketing, and financial sections of a business plan?*** Possible answers: organizational plan—proposed organization and proposed product and service; marketing plan—pricing policies and promotional activities; financial plan—how the business will be funded, with equity and/or debt capital.

Preteaching Vocabulary

Have students go to the Online Learning Center at glencoe.com for the Chapter 35 Preteaching Vocabulary games.

Content Vocabulary

Instruct students to write the content vocabulary terms and their definitions on index cards. Then have students place those terms in the order in which they would appear in a business plan. Possible answer: job descriptions, organization chart, equity capital, debt capital, collateral, credit union.

Academic Vocabulary

Authority—Usage Display the term *authority* for the class. Read the following sentence to students: ***An organization chart is a diagram of the company's departments and jobs with lines of authority clearly shown.*** Ask: ***What is the meaning of the term* authority *as it is used in this sentence?*** someone who has power over the personnel below them in the organization chart Ask students to provide an original example for this use of the term *authority.* Sample answer: The manager has authority over the clerks in her department.

Funding—Usage Display the term *funding* for the class. Then read the following sentence to students: ***Capital is the funding needed to finance the operation of a business.*** Ask students: ***What is the meaning of the term* funding *as it is used in this sentence?*** financial support Then, to ensure students' understanding of the term, ask them to use the term *funding* in original sentences. Sample answer: I hope my parents will be able to provide some of the funding I'll need for college.

MINI CLIP

ELL: Understanding Proficiency
Go to the Online Learning Center to view a video in which an author discusses proficiency and describes the various levels of proficiency that can be applied to English learners.

Marketing and Financial Plans

ORGANIZATIONAL, MARKETING, AND FINANCIAL PLANS

Tell students that a business plan could be likened to a recipe: the more detailed it is, the better the final product turns out. Then ask students these guiding questions to focus the discussion on organizational, marketing, and financial plans for business.

Guiding Questions

Explain Why is it important to develop a strong organizational plan for a business?	It is the blueprint for the structure of the proposed business. The business must be constructed on a clear, solid foundation.
Analyze Why must an entrepreneur develop detailed job descriptions?	A job description includes the purpose, qualifications, skills, duties, equipment, and working conditions for a particular job. It helps employees know what is expected of them and helps the employer measure employee performance.

As You Read

Read the As You Read question aloud: ***What marketing activities would you include in a business plan for a new business?*** The marketing plan would detail the proposed pricing policies and promotional activities. Then ask: ***What would the financial plan include?*** The financial plan would include an explanation of the monies needed to start and operate the business and the source(s) of the monies.

Expert Advice

Read the quote to students:

> **" A business plan is a guide for organizing, marketing, and financing a business. "**

Ask students: ***What do you think might happen if a business started up without a business plan?*** Possible answers: The business could fail, lenders and investors may not want to provide funding, the business would be disorganized, and so on.

ORGANIZATION CHART

Once you have completed the job descriptions, you will develop an organization chart. This will establish the chain of command within your business. An **organization chart** is a diagram of the company's departments and jobs with lines of **authority** clearly shown. An organization chart tells employees to whom they report and to whom they can turn with problems or questions. It also establishes department responsibilities.

OUTSIDE EXPERTS

Sometimes outside professional help is needed to get a business started and keep it growing. Trained professionals can help you avoid mistakes that could damage your prospects for success. If you decide to use outside professionals, identify them and their responsibilities on your organization chart. Professionals who can help include accountants, attorneys, bankers, and insurance agents. Technical assistance is often needed to negotiate loans, complete tax returns, and provide risk management services.

New business owners must become familiar with laws about child labor, equal opportunity employment, health and safety, payment of wages, unemployment and workers' disability insurance. State agencies such as state departments of civil rights, commerce, labor, licensing, and regulation publish many inexpensive or free publications. They also offer technical assistance to help new entrepreneurs understand various employment laws, rules, and regulations.

PROPOSED PRODUCT AND SERVICE

The organizational plan should include information on the types of products and services you will offer. It should also include your potential suppliers, manufacturing plans if required, and inventory policies. Your investors or lenders will also want to know the associated costs for your proposed product or service.

If you are selling a product, you will need to develop a plan that details all of the purchasing or manufacturing requirements as well as the anticipated costs. You need to show how you will manage the products you purchase or manufacture. For example, how much will you keep on hand? How will you keep track of what to order and what has been sold? Where will you store the products that you have in stock?

Your inventory system depends on the size and scope of your proposed business. Trade associations and many suppliers can give suggestions for the best inventory control system for your business.

For a service business, you need to develop an organizational plan that addresses who will provide the service to your customers and how the services will be provided. In your plan, state the services and estimate the costs of providing services.

Reading Check

Define What is an organizational chart?

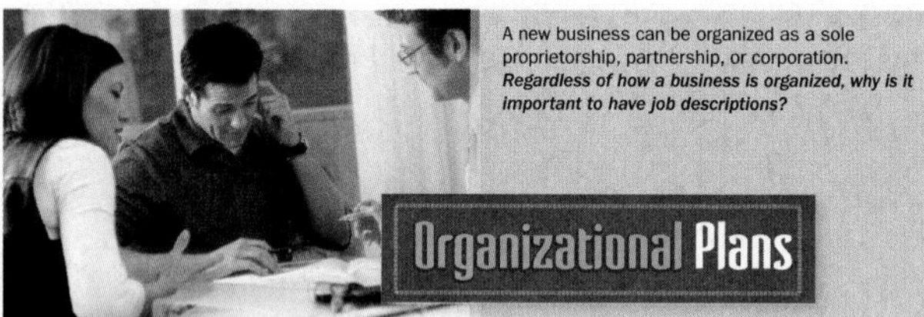

A new business can be organized as a sole proprietorship, partnership, or corporation. ***Regardless of how a business is organized, why is it important to have job descriptions?***

MARKETING PLAN

You are now ready to develop your marketing policies. This is the way you will price, promote, and distribute your products. You should state the promotional strategies that you will use and explain your marketing mix.

PRICING POLICIES

Your business plan must outline your pricing policies. You must set a price high enough to cover your costs and make a profit, but competitive enough to attract customers. The three important factors in determining pricing are: costs, demand, and the competition. Each factor needs to be investigated and detailed in your pricing strategy.

PROMOTIONAL ACTIVITIES

Once pricing policies have been established, you need to describe your promotional activities. Identify how to reach the greatest number of potential customers in your target market in the most efficient and effective way.

The simplest method of promoting a business is by providing quality products and services to customers. Satisfied customers generate word-of-mouth advertising when they talk to their friends. This type of social marketing attracts additional customers because people usually trust the opinion of friends.

Visibility comes from the promotional mix. A firm's promotional mix includes advertising, public relations, promotions, and personal selling. Your marketing plan will outline the mix that will be most effective in persuading wholesalers, retailers, and consumers to do business with you.

A convincing business plan provides a rationale for the selection of activities and the related costs. You need to present a budget for promotion and a list of promotional activities you intend to use.

Reading Check

Identify What are the three considerations when price planning?

FINANCIAL PLAN

In the financial section of a business plan, lenders and investors can see what monies are needed to start and operate the business. They will also review the entrepreneur's statements of personal and external sources of capital. In addition, the financial section contains statements of projected income and expenses for at least the first three years of operation.

Capital is the **funding** needed to finance the operation of a business. It includes all goods used to produce other goods. In business, capital may include owned property as well as cash resources. In this chapter, the term *capital* refers to anything that can be converted into money.

Entrepreneurs usually need a large amount of capital to open a business. There are several ways to raise capital (see **Figure 35.2** on page 833).

The method used to raise capital and its repayment depends on how the capital will be used. Capital for operating expenses and inventory is usually repaid within a year. Money used to build facilities and purchase equipment is normally repaid over a longer period of time.

EQUITY CAPITAL

Money raised from within a company or from selling part of an owner's share is **equity capital**. The advantage of using equity capital is that you do not need to repay the money or pay interest. However, the buyer becomes a co-owner in the business. The larger the share of your business that you sell, the more control you hand over to your buyers/investors. Equity capital sources include personal savings, partners, and shareholders.

EXPLAIN

Graphic Organizer

Display this graphic organizer. Ask students to suggest what should be included in an organizational plan for proposed products and services. Write students' answers in the surrounding shapes. Possible answers are provided below.

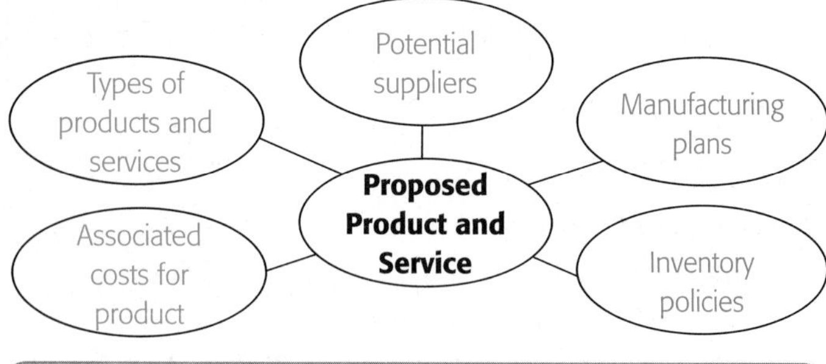

glencoe.com

Graphic Organizer Send students to the Online Learning Center to print this graphic organizer.

Visual Literacy

Organizational Plans Caption Answer Read the caption question to students. ***Regardless of how a business is organized, why is it important to have job descriptions?*** Answers may include: Job descriptions tell potential lenders and investors that the entrepreneur has spent time looking ahead to see what future needs might be. A job description includes the purpose, qualifications, skills, duties, equipment, and expected working conditions for a particular job. The description helps employees know what is expected of them and helps the employer measure the employee's performance.

Reading Check Answer

Read the Reading Check question to students: ***What is an organizational chart?*** An organizational chart is a diagram of the company's departments and jobs with lines of authority clearly shown. It tells employees who they report to and to whom they can turn with problems and questions. It also establishes department responsibilities. Have students work in pairs to develop an organizational chart for your school. Have them start with the superintendent or principal at the head and then include others such as teachers, maintenance workers, office staff, and students.

ELABORATE

Critical Thinking

Organize the class into small groups. Ask groups to come up with an example of a business they would like to start. It may be a sporting goods store or a coffee house or another idea they might have. Then have each group list all the information they would need to gather on their product or service before starting a business. Lists will vary depending on the product or service chosen. Make sure groups include information on inventory needed, methods of storing and tracking the inventory, services provided, and the methods for providing the services. Have groups share their completed lists with the class.

MARKETING PLAN

Tell students that the marketing plan consists of policies to price, promote, and distribute a business's products or services. Then ask students these guiding questions to focus the discussion on the marketing plan.

Guiding Questions

List What is included in a firm's promotional mix?	advertising, public relations, promotions, and personal selling
Identify What are the two parts to the marketing plan?	The marketing plan needs to include pricing policies and promotional activities.
Explain What is the simplest way to promote a business?	provide quality products and services to customers
Examine What is word-of-mouth advertising and why is it effective?	Word-of-mouth advertising occurs when satisfied customers tell their friends and family about the products or services. This attracts additional customers because people usually trust their friends and family.

Reading Check Answer

Read the Reading Check question to students: ***What are the three considerations when price planning?*** costs, demand, competition Ask: ***Why should costs, demand, and the competition be considered when planning prices?*** Costs should be considered because you must price items higher than your cost to make a profit. Demand should be considered because if no one wants your product, you will have to price it low to get people interested in it; however, if demand is high, you can price it higher. Competition should be considered because if you price the same item higher than a competitor, consumers will buy from your competitor.

FINANCIAL PLAN

Tell students that a financial section may be the most important part of a business plan. Ask: ***Why do you think this is so?*** If there is no plan to acquire the money needed to open and operate the business, there will be no business. Then ask students these guiding questions to focus the discussion on the financial section of a business plan.

Guiding Questions

Identify What is capital?	the funding needed to finance the operation of a business
Explain What is the purpose of the financial sections of a business plan?	It allows lenders and investors to see what monies are needed to start and operate the business.
Analyze Why would money used to build facilities and purchase equipment be repaid over periods of longer than a year?	Possible answer: These expenses are greater than day-to-day operating expenses and will take more time to pay off.

Graphic Organizer

Display this diagram. Ask students to name the two different types of capital. equity capital and debt capital Ask: ***What are the sources of equity capital?*** personal savings, partners, shareholders Then ask: ***What are the sources of debt capital?*** banks, credit unions, suppliers and previous owners Add students' answers to the diagram.

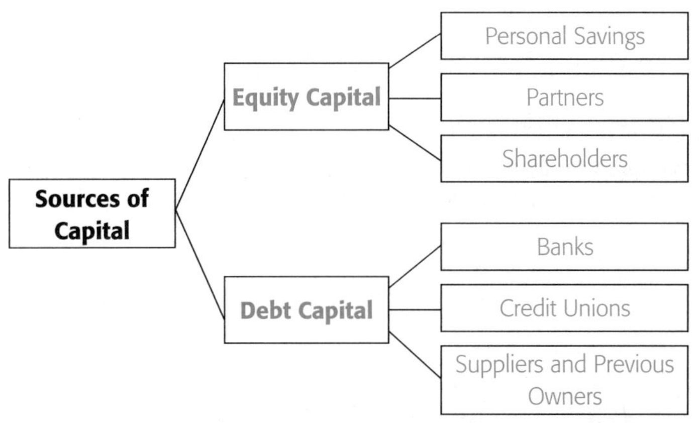

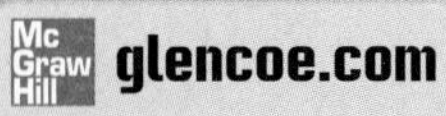

Graphic Organizer Send students to the Online Learning Center to print this graphic organizer.

PERSONAL SAVINGS

The most common method of financing a business is personal savings. Although you may not prefer this option, you probably cannot avoid investing part of your savings. Starting any new business involves risk. Your prospective investors and lenders will expect you to share in that risk.

PARTNERS

A partnership is another way to raise capital for your business. Partners may contribute their own money or have access to other sources. As with equity investors, you may have to share control of the business if you accept partners.

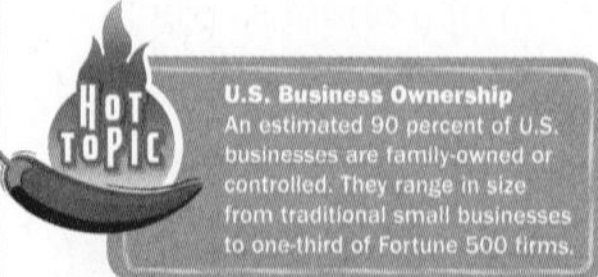

U.S. Business Ownership An estimated 90 percent of U.S. businesses are family-owned or controlled. They range in size from traditional small businesses to one-third of Fortune 500 firms.

SHAREHOLDERS

Forming a corporation is another method of raising capital. You need to incorporate and obtain a charter to operate as a corporation. You sell stock to shareholders as a way of raising capital.

A corporation can raise large amounts of money, because shareholders have the opportunity to share in the growth and profits of a successful business. However, they lose only their original investment if the business is unsuccessful. Shareholders influence general corporate policy decisions. However, as long as you hold a majority of the shares, you control the corporation's daily activities.

DEBT CAPITAL

Debt capital is a term used to describe borrowed funds that must be repaid. Some debt capital sources are banks, credit unions, the Small Business Administration, friends, relatives, suppliers, and previous business owners.

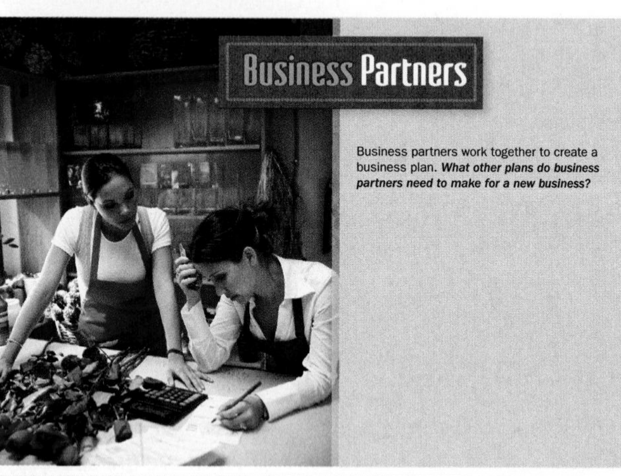

Business Partners

Business partners work together to create a business plan. ***What other plans do business partners need to make for a new business?***

Debt capital can work to your advantage when you finance a new business. Borrowing money and repaying it on a timely basis builds a good credit rating. In turn, a good credit rating makes it easier to borrow additional money. Although interest must be paid with the loan, that interest becomes a tax-deductible business expense.

Also, by financing with debt capital, you do not share control of the business with lenders. Since they are simply a source of financing for your company, your lenders do not have any input on the way you run the business.

There is a major disadvantage to using debt capital, however. If you are not able to pay back your debt, you could be forced into bankruptcy. That does not necessarily mean the business must close, but creditors might take control of the company away from the owner.

BANKS

Commercial banks are a common source of business financing. Although banks may be hesitant to lend money to start-up companies, they routinely lend to businesses that are established and which have a proven record of success. Banks know their local areas and economies well and offer a number of different loans and services with competitive and government-regulated terms.

Approximately 12 percent of businesses use commercial bank loans to finance their companies. Bank loans guaranteed by the government make up make up another 1 percent of start-up financing.

To evaluate the credit worthiness of a business owner, banks rely on criteria known as the six Cs of credit: character, capability, capital, collateral, coverage, and conditions.

FIGURE 35.2 Sources of Funding

Financing a Business There are several methods and sources for financing new businesses. The most common source is personal/family savings. ***Why do you think personal or family savings is a major way of financing a new business?***

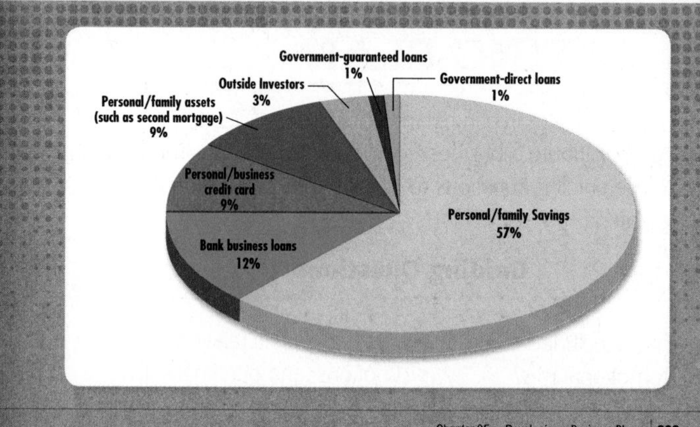

832 | Unit 11 · Entrepreneurship and Finance

Chapter 35 · Developing a Business Plan | 833

EXPLAIN

Visual Literacy

Business Partners Caption Answer Read the caption question to students: ***What other plans do business partners need to make for a new business?*** Answers may include: financial and marketing plans (which are part of the business plan); plans for scheduling employees; plans for future growth; plans to expand the product line.

U.S. Business Ownership Instruct students to conduct an Internet search to identify six family-owned businesses. Have students categorize the companies according to type (such as technology, food, apparel, and so on) and according to size. Have students construct a chart in which to display their findings and to share their charts with the class.

Mini Projects

Enrichment

Reasons to Invest Ask students: ***If you were an investor asked to put money into a business that did not have a business plan, what factors would determine whether or not you would invest?*** Answers may include: whether the potential owner is starting a new business or buying an existing business; if buying an existing business, whether the existing business is successful; the potential owner's experience with the type of business; local market needs for the business. Then ask: ***Why would it make a difference if the business is brand new or existing?*** A brand new business has no track record for income, while an existing business might be successful and have a better chance of not only surviving but remaining successful.

Pros and Cons of Equity Capital Ask students to create a list of advantages and disadvantages of using equity capital to finance a business. Advantages: the business owner does not have to pay back or pay interest. Disadvantages: the owner might lose personal savings; taking on partners or shareholders may decrease the amount of control the business owner has.

ELABORATE

Visual Literacy

Figure 35.2 Caption Answer Read the caption question to students: ***Why do you think personal or family savings is a major way of financing a new business?*** Personal and family savings are readily available, and the business owner would not have to convince strangers (bank, credit, union, shareholder, and so on) that he or she is a good risk; family members often want to be helpful. Then ask these guiding questions about sources of funding.

Guiding Questions

Rank List sources of funding from most popular to least popular.	personal/family savings; bank business loans; personal/business credit card; personal/family assets; outside investors; government-guaranteed loans; government-direct loans
Identify Which of the sources of income are used equally often?	personal/business credit cards and personal/family assets at 9% each; government/guaranteed loans and government/direct loans at 1% each
Analyze What sources of funding are used by only 5% of business owners?	a combination of outside investors (3%), government/guaranteed loans, (1%) and government/direct loans (1%)

Critical Thinking

Ask students: ***Why might lenders and investors read the financial section of a business plan more closely than other parts of the plan?*** Sample answer: They want to make sure the business is profitable so that they do not lose money. Then ask: ***Before taking on a financial partner, what might the business owner want to know about the person?*** Possible answer: the person's background, education, work experience, business philosophy, and financial situation.

VIRTUAL BUSINESS

BUSINESS PLAN ANALYSIS

Introduce the concept of business plan analysis to students using Knowledge Matters' Virtual Business Retailing visual simulation, *Business Plan Analysis*. In this simulation, students will study business plans and explore the reasons for preparing a business plan.

FINANCING

Introduce students to the concept of financing using Knowledge Matters' Virtual Business Retailing visual simulation, Financing. In this simulation, students will learn about and evaluate different financing methods to finance their start-up business.

e MARKETING

Online Business Models

There are many types of businesses on the Web. They include marketplace exchanges, such as Orbitz®; direct buying and selling, such as CarsDirect®; the name-your-price model, such as Priceline®; auction sites, such as eBay; brokers to handle transactions, such as PayPal®; search engines or portals, such as Yahoo!®; digital product online businesses, such as the Apple® iTunes Music Store; online subscription services, such as Netflix®; digital games, such as Club Penguin; networking services, such as Classmates and LinkedIn; and other social media sites, such as Twitter and Facebook.

Innovate and Create

Assign groups of students an online business model to research and then report their findings. They should look for case studies and current information on the businesses. Ask them to assess the market leader's business plan—what makes it work so well? Students' oral and written reports should be evaluated based on the extent of accurate and current research, for which documentation is provided. Their assessment of the market leader's business plan should include analysis of each section of a business plan: description and analysis, organizational plan, marketing plan, and financial plan.

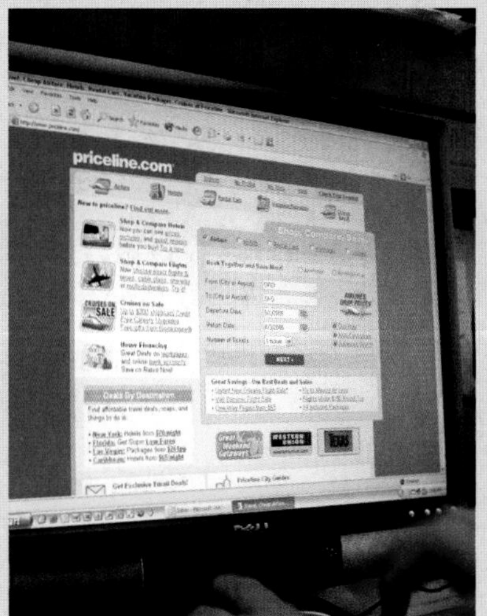

eMarketing Worksheet Activity Send students to the Online Learning Center to download an eMarketing worksheet activity.

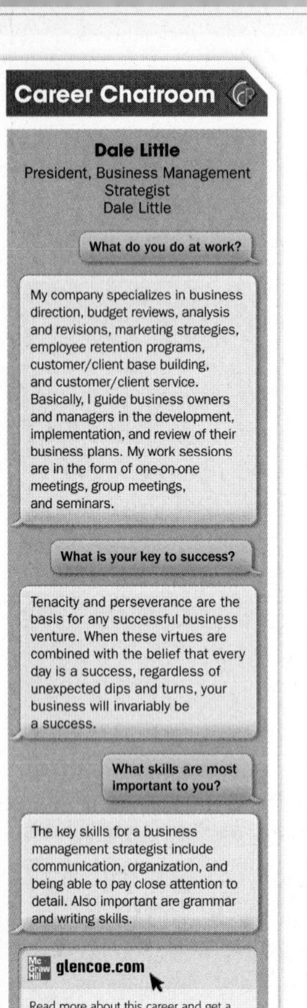

Career Chatroom

Dale Little
President, Business Management Strategist
Dale Little

What do you do at work?

My company specializes in business direction, budget reviews, analysis and revisions, marketing strategies, employee retention programs, customer/client base building, and customer/client service. Basically, I guide business owners and managers in the development, implementation, and review of their business plans. My work sessions are in the form of one-on-one meetings, group meetings, and seminars.

What is your key to success?

Tenacity and perseverance are the basis for any successful business venture. When these virtues are combined with the belief that every day is a success, regardless of unexpected dips and turns, your business will invariably be a success.

What skills are most important to you?

The key skills for a business management strategist include communication, organization, and being able to pay close attention to detail. Also important are grammar and writing skills.

glencoe.com

Read more about this career and get a Career Exploration Activity.

- **Character and Capability** A résumé of your previous training and related work experience, including professional and personal references, will answer questions about your character and capability. Your personal credit history will also be reviewed to see if you regularly pay your bills on time.
- **Capital** How much of your own money, or capital, is to be invested in your new business? Banks, like other potential investors, will want to know how much capital you are willing to invest into your new venture.
- **Collateral** What assets (anything of value that you own) can be used as collateral for a loan? **Collateral** is something of value that you pledge as payment for a loan in case of default. Lenders usually require that the value of the collateral be greater than the amount of the loan. Examples of collateral include bonds, equipment, real estate, stocks, and vehicles. Some businesses may use accounts receivable, which is the sum of money owed to a business by its customers, as collateral. Banks want to know that your loan will be repaid, even if your business fails.
- **Coverage and Conditions** Banks will want to know the amount of insurance coverage that you carry. Also, what are the general circumstances of your business? How will the money help you grow your business, strengthen your market position, and make more money? This is outlined in the description and analysis section of your business plan.

CREDIT UNIONS

A **credit union** is a cooperative association formed by groups of employees for the benefit of its members. Compared to commercial banks, credit unions often charge lower interest rates on loans. To borrow money from a credit union, however, you must be a member. Credit unions often accept memberships for family members. Check with your parents, guardians, and credit union staff to determine your eligibility. Credit unions also use the six Cs of credit to decide whether they will accept your loan application.

SUPPLIER AND PREVIOUS OWNERS

Suppliers often provide low-cost loans for purchasing inventory, furniture, fixtures, and equipment on a delayed payment basis. This method of raising capital can improve your credit rating and stretch available cash.

If you purchase an existing business, consider the previous owner as a potential source of capital. Many sole proprietors want to see their businesses continue after they retire. Previous owners may provide you with a loan and a favorable repayment plan to get started. The rates on this type of loan are often lower than rates from a bank or credit union.

FINANCIAL STATEMENTS

After you have identified a potential source or sources of capital, the last part of your business plan requires development of projected income and expenses. This part of the business plan normally includes the following financial statements:

- Personal financial statement
- Projected start-up costs
- Projected personnel needs
- Projected business income
- Projected business expenses
- Projected income statement(s)
- Projected balance sheet
- Projected cash flow

Your financial statements display your personal financial records along with the projected income and expenses of your proposed business. A list of projected start-up costs shows how much money is needed to get your business going. A balance sheet can help you show how you plan to manage your company's finances. Estimates of projected income and cash flow are also especially important because they show your ability to pay back a loan or offer a return on investments.

Realistic projections of income and expenses in financial statements help to convince investors to loan you money for your new business. It can be challenging to obtain the money to start up a new company, but a solid business plan and detailed projections can overcome those challenges.

After You Read | **Section 35.2**

Review Key Concepts

1. **Identify** the three main types of ownership.
2. **Explain** why personnel needs are identified in a business plan.
3. **Name** the six Cs of credit.

Practice Academics

English Language Arts

4. Perform library or online research on a favorite product. Find out the company that makes it and what types of activities are included in the company's marketing plan for that product. Write a one-page summary describing the marketing plan. Also make recommendations for a revised marketing plan.

NCTE 3 Apply strategies to interpret texts.

Mathematics

5. A relative decides to loan you $16,000 with a simple interest rate of 5.5 percent, payable one year after the start of your new Internet business. How much will you owe at the end of the year?

Math Concept **Interest Rates** Interest is paid when money is loaned. Interest rates are expressed as percents of the money that was borrowed.

Starting Hints Convert the percent to a decimal by moving the decimal point two places to the left. Multiply the dollar amount that was borrowed by the decimal equivalent of the percent plus one to determine the total amount owed after one year.

NCTM Number and Operations Understand numbers, ways of representing numbers, relationships among numbers, and number systems.

glencoe.com

Check your answers.

For help, go to the **Math Skills Handbook** located at the back of this book.

ELABORATE

Career Chatroom

Use these guiding questions to focus the discussion about the Career Chatroom feature.

Explain What are tenacity and perseverance, and why are they important?	These traits involve persistence and determination. They ensure completion and follow-through.
Analyze What skills would you need to work for Dale Little?	focus on details, verbal and written communication skills, organization

 **glencoe.com** 

Career Exploration Send students to the Online Learning Center to find more information about this career and to get a Career Exploration activity.

Mini Project

Extension

Agree or Disagree Ask students: ***Should state economic development agencies use public dollars to create economic development loans for small businesses?*** Have students who say *yes* to this question stand on one side of the room, and have students who say *no* stand on the other side. Those who are undecided should stand in the middle. Ask someone on the *yes* side to give a reason for this opinion. Possible reason: new business expansions create jobs and help the economy. If this reasoning makes someone on the no side change his or her mind or convinces someone in the middle, have the person on the *no* side or person in the middle move to the *yes* side. Then have someone on the *no* side provide a reason for this opinion. Possible reason: the government would be using public tax dollars and public employees to aid private businesses. If the reasoning convinces someone on the *yes* side to change his or her mind or convinces someone in the middle, have those people move to the *no* side. Continue the activity until all have shared their reasons and there is no more movement from one side to the other.

EVALUATE

Critical Thinking

Have each student brainstorm a list of five or more reasons that other people should invest in a business they might like to start. Ask them to assemble the parts of the list into a short argument that they could use to pitch the idea to someone who might lend them the money. Students should include the six Cs (character, capability, capital, collateral, coverage, and conditions) in their reasons. Ask students to present their arguments to the class. Ask the class to offer constructive feedback. Lists and arguments may vary depending on the type of business selected, the student's perception of the growth potential for the business, and to whom they plan to make their pitch.

Graphic Organizer

Display this diagram. Ask students to list the different financial statements that are normally included in financial section of a business plan. Write students' answers in the surrounding shapes. Answers are provided below.

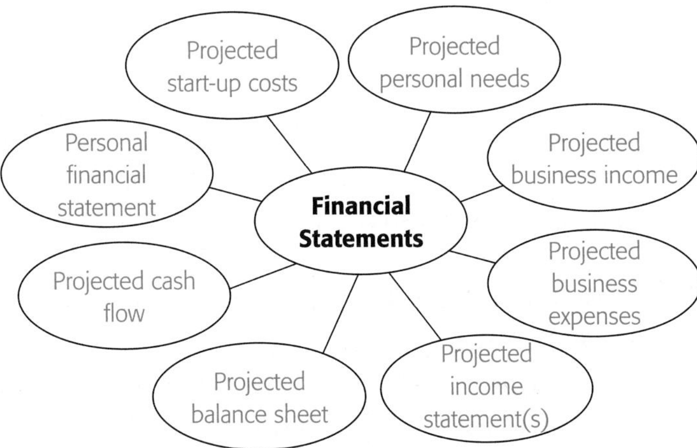

glencoe.com iWB

Graphic Organizer Send students to the Online Learning Center to print this graphic organizer.

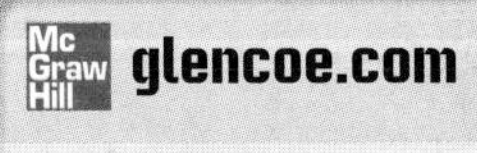

VIRTUAL BUSINESS

FINANCIAL STATEMENTS

Introduce the concept of financial statements to students using Knowledge Matters' Virtual Business Retailing visual simulation, *Financial Statements*. In this simulation, students will learn that business owners must have accurate and timely information about the financial status of their business to make the best decisions.

After You Read Section 35.2

Review Key Concepts

1. The three main types of business ownership structures are sole proprietorships, partnerships, and corporations.
2. Potential investors and lenders need to know that the entrepreneur can identify essential jobs for the business so that it will operate efficiently and successfully.
3. The six Cs of credit include: character, capability, capital, collateral, coverage, and conditions.

Practice Academics

English Language Arts

4. Summaries and recommendations will vary. Students should identify a favorite product, find out the company that makes it and what types of activities are included in the company's marketing plan for that product. They should write a one-page summary describing the marketing plan and make recommendations for a revised marketing plan.

Mathematics

5. \$16,880 (\$16,000 × 1.055)

glencoe.com

Send students to the Online Learning Center to check their answers.

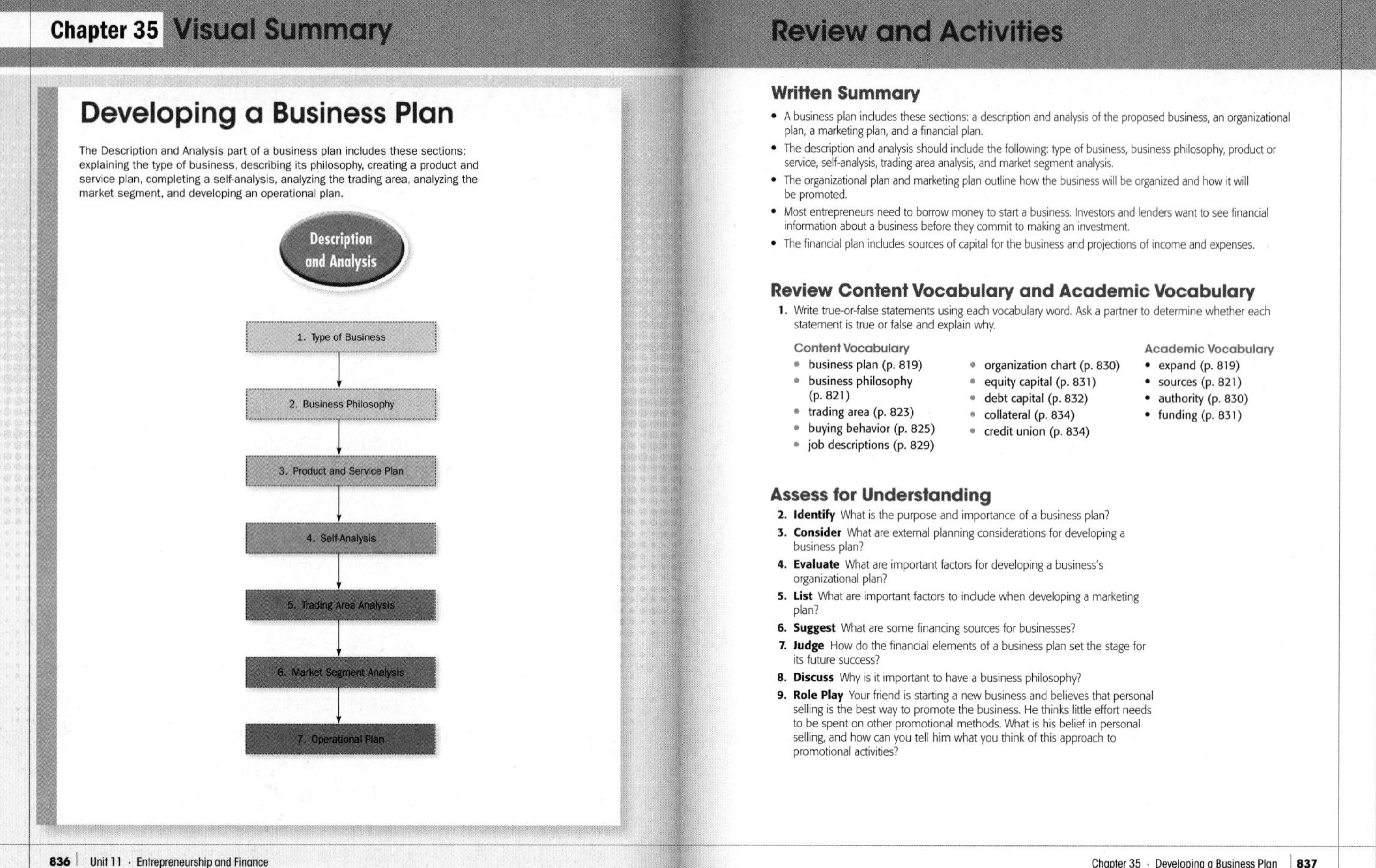

Chapter 35 Visual Summary

Developing a Business Plan

The Description and Analysis part of a business plan includes these sections: explaining the type of business, describing its philosophy, creating a product and service plan, completing a self-analysis, analyzing the trading area, analyzing the market segment, and developing an operational plan.

836 | Unit 11 · Entrepreneurship and Finance

Review and Activities

Written Summary

- A business plan includes these sections: a description and analysis of the proposed business, an organizational plan, a marketing plan, and a financial plan.
- The description and analysis should include the following: type of business, business philosophy, product or service, self-analysis, trading area analysis, and market segment analysis.
- The organizational plan and marketing plan outline how the business will be organized and how it will be promoted.
- Most entrepreneurs need to borrow money to start a business. Investors and lenders want to see financial information about a business before they commit to making an investment.
- The financial plan includes sources of capital for the business and projections of income and expenses.

Review Content Vocabulary and Academic Vocabulary

1. Write true-or-false statements using each vocabulary word. Ask a partner to determine whether each statement is true or false and explain why.

Content Vocabulary
- business plan (p. 819)
- business philosophy (p. 821)
- trading area (p. 823)
- buying behavior (p. 825)
- job descriptions (p. 829)
- organization chart (p. 830)
- equity capital (p. 831)
- debt capital (p. 832)
- collateral (p. 834)
- credit union (p. 834)

Academic Vocabulary
- expand (p. 819)
- sources (p. 821)
- authority (p. 830)
- funding (p. 831)

Assess for Understanding

2. **Identify** What is the purpose and importance of a business plan?
3. **Consider** What are external planning considerations for developing a business plan?
4. **Evaluate** What are important factors for developing a business's organizational plan?
5. **List** What are important factors to include when developing a marketing plan?
6. **Suggest** What are some financing sources for businesses?
7. **Judge** How do the financial elements of a business plan set the stage for its future success?
8. **Discuss** Why is it important to have a business philosophy?
9. **Role Play** Your friend is starting a new business and believes that personal selling is the best way to promote the business. He thinks little effort needs to be spent on other promotional methods. What is his belief in personal selling, and how can you tell him what you think of this approach to promotional activities?

Chapter 35 · Developing a Business Plan | 837

EVALUATE

Visual Summary

Express Creativity Ask students to develop their own visual summary of a concept in the chapter. Encourage students to use different formats for their visual summaries, such as a storyboard, a timeline, a table, a tree diagram, or a word web. Visual summaries will vary depending on the concept depicted and the visual manner in which it is depicted. Questions to ask when assessing a visual summary include:

- Is the summary clear, economical, and simple?
- Are any important steps left out?
- Are steps or concepts arranged in the same order as the original?
- Does the summary reveal a pattern that connects the details?
- Does the summary locate and highlight the most important information?

Review Content Vocabulary and Academic Vocabulary

1. True-or-false statements will vary. Sample statements:

   A **business plan** is a strategy to turn an idea into a reality. (True)

   A **business philosophy** is a strategy for growing a business. (False—It contains beliefs on how a business should be run along with mission and vision statements.)

   A **trading area** refers to all the locations from which customers are drawn. (True)

   Buying behavior tells what, where, and from whom people will make purchases. (True)

   Job descriptions describe a company's departments. (False—They are written statements about the requirements for jobs.)

   An **organization chart** includes job requirements. (False—It is a diagram of a company with lines of authority clearly shown.)

   Money raised from within a company is **equity capital.** (True)

   Debt capital is money raised by selling part of an owner's share. (False—It is borrowed funds that must be repaid.)

EVALUATE

Assess for Understanding

2. A business plan is a proposal that outlines a strategy to turn a business idea into a reality. It describes a business opportunity, such as a new business or plans to expand an existing one, to potential investors and lenders. Investors will review the business plan before granting credit or start-up capital. In addition to obtaining capital, a business plan provides guides for opening the business and operating it after the start-up phase.

3. External planning considerations include: trading area analysis; geographic, demographic, and economic data; competitive analysis; and market segment analysis.

4. The organizational section of a business plan is a blueprint or foundation for the structure of the proposed business. Important factors for developing the plan include: the steps to establish the business, personnel needs, job descriptions, organization chart, outside experts, and proposed product and/or service.

5. The marketing plan should include pricing policies and promotional activities. It should describe how the business will price, promote, and distribute its products and services.

6. Examples of financing sources include personal/family savings, bank loans, personal credit card loans, outside investors, and government loans.

7. The financial elements of a business plan contain start-up costs, personal and exterior sources of capital, and projected income and expenses for the first three years of operation. The necessary start-up capital must be in place to help ensure the future success of the company.

8. A business philosophy contains beliefs on how a business should be run. It also demonstrates an understanding of the business's role in the marketplace. The business philosophy reveals your attitude toward your customers, employees, and competitors. A business philosophy should also include a mission statement and a vision statement. A mission statement expresses the specific aspirations of the company. A vision statement states the scope and purpose of the company.

9. The friend needs to be made aware that visibility comes from the promotional mix. A firm's promotional mix includes advertising, public relations, promotions, and personal selling. The marketing plan will outline the mix that will be most effective in persuading wholesalers, retailers, and consumers to do business with you. If the marketing plan includes only personal selling, the chances of getting the start-up capital necessary to fund the business are very slight. Lenders are aware that there needs to be a mix of promotional activities to induce consumers to purchase your goods and/or services.

21st Century Skills

Social Responsibility Skills

10. Labor laws dealing with child labor, equal opportunity employment, health and safety, payment of wages, unemployment, and workers' disability insurance have been passed to protect employees. Conduct research dealing with a specific labor law in your state. Identify the labor law that you researched and prepare a one-page report on the purpose of the law and what protections are provided for employees.

Financial Literacy Skills

11. Calculating Employee Wages Assume that you had an employee that was paid $10.80 an hour during the week and time and one-half time on Sunday. If the employee worked four hours on Wednesday, three and a half hours on Thursday, six hours on Saturday, and four hours on Sunday, what was the total gross wages before any deductions?

Everyday Ethics

12. A Medical Business "You're sick, we're quick," says a slogan announcing a newer healthcare business, the Minute Clinic. Staffed by either a nurse practitioner or physician's assistant, the clinics are located in drugstores and shopping centers. They treat walk-ins with routine problems for minimal cost. The clinics have begun to attract public attention. Some critics, however, call this type of medical care "inappropriate." Write a paragraph explaining what the clinic's business philosophy might be, and express your opinion about the clinic's pros and cons.

e-Marketing Skills

13. Small Business Resources You are an intern for a small business development center at a community college. Your supervisor asked you to prepare a list of five Internet resources for small business owners in the areas of promotion and financing. You are to identify the URLs for each Internet resource and provide a brief summary of the resource materials.

Build Academic Skills

English Language Arts

14. The Need for Occupational Licensing Small business owner/operators and their employees often need to be licensed before they can open or work in a regulated industry. Perform library or online research on occupational licensing or licensure. Identify the reasons that governmental agencies require special licenses. Summarize your findings in a one-page written report.

NCTE 1 Read texts to acquire new information.

English Language Arts

15. Business Structure Perform online or library research on multi-level marketing and how some companies use it. Write a two-paragraph description of this type of marketing structure for a company that could be used in a business plan.

NCTE 3 Apply strategies to interpret texts.

Mathematics

16. Calculate Buying Power Index Determine the buying power indexes for Johnstown and Milton. Which location is more favorable for a new business?
Buying Power Index = .5 × Area's Percentage for U.S. Effective Buying Power
+ .3 × Area's Percentage of U.S. Retail Sales
+ .2 × Area's Percentage of U.S. Population

Johnstown Percentage of:	Milton Percentage of:
• U.S. Effective Buying Power = .0251	• U.S. Effective Buying Power = .0181
• U.S. Retail Sales = .0183	• U.S. Retail Sales = .018
• U.S. Population = .025	• U.S. Population = .0154

Math Concept **Representation** The buying power index is determined by multiplying a given constant by several variables, usually given as percents.

NCTM Algebra Represent and analyze mathematical situations and structures using algebraic symbols.

For help, go to the **Math Skills Handbook** located at the back of this book.

Standardized Test Practice

Directions Read the following questions. On a separate piece of paper, write the best possible answer for each one.

1. Which part of a business plan contains information about the trading area and target market?
   - **A.** Description and analysis
   - **B.** Financial plan
   - **C.** Marketing plan
   - **D.** Organizational plan
2. A market segment analysis describes your trading area.
   - T
   - F
3. Something of value pledged as payment for a loan in case of default is ________.

Test-Taking Tip
Study for tests over a few days or weeks and continually review class material. Do not wait until the night before or try to learn everything at once.

DECA Connection Role Play

Loan Officer
Bank

Situation You are the loan officer for a bank. Your community has many aspiring new business owners. Many prospective business owners are unsure about the steps to take to give their new businesses the best chance of succeeding.

The community merchants and your bank have formed a business development committee. You are the bank's representative on the committee. The goal of the committee is to offer advice and answer questions for prospective entrepreneurs. Committee members offer advice on an individual basis and also give talks to groups of interested individuals.

Since you work for the bank, you have been designated as the provider of information about business plans, their importance, and use in helping a new business succeed. You are preparing to meet with an aspiring business owner (judge). The prospective new business owner (judge) would like to own a business, but is unsure about which type of business. The prospective new business owner (judge) has work experience, but is still in the thinking stages of planning for a new business and has many questions about preparing a business plan.

Activity You are to discuss business plans in general with the prospective new business owner (judge). Then you are to discuss the new business owner's (judge's) interests, skills, and the types of businesses being considered.

Evaluation You will be evaluated on how well you meet the following performance indicators:

1. Assess personal interests and skills needed for success in business.
2. Identify a company's unique selling proposition.
3. Conduct an environmental scan to obtain business information.
4. Conduct market analysis.
5. Describe factors that affect the business environment.

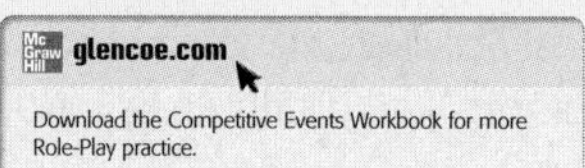

Download the Competitive Events Workbook for more Role-Play practice.

EVALUATE

Social Responsibility Skills

10. Answers are dependent on the particular laws in your state. Reports should state the purpose of the law, whether it deals with child labor, equal opportunity employment, health and safety, payment of wages, unemployment, workers' disability insurance, or another topic. Reports should clearly state what protections the law provides for employees.

Financial Literacy Skills

11. Answer is $210.60 [(4 + 3.5 + 6) × $10.80 + (4 × $16.20) = $145.80 + $64.80].

Everyday Ethics

12. Business philosophies may suggest that the company is trying to meet the needs of the population who cannot afford traditional medical care or those who do not have a personal physician. Students' opinions may include: the business meets the needs of a specific part of the population; traditional medical care—having one primary care physician—is not a reality for many who cannot afford or do not have medical insurance; this source of medical care meets their needs.

e-Marketing Skills

13. Sample answer: The U.S. Small Business Administration offers information on financial assistance for borrowers and prospective lenders, contract opportunities, disaster assistance, counseling and assistance, special audiences, laws and regulations, compliance and online training on topics such as starting a business, business planning, finance and accounting, marketing and advertising, business management, government contracting, and surviving a slow economy. Students should provide similar information for at least five different Internet resources.

EVALUATE

Build Academic Skills

English Language Arts

14. Occupational licensure varies from state to state but, in general, occupations that can be hazardous to the employee or to the public are licensed. For example, the occupations of asbestos professionals, medical personnel, toxic waste handlers, and food services are licensed by the state. Students should identify the reasons governmental agencies require special licenses and summarize their findings in a one-page written report.

English Language Arts

15. Students' descriptions should mention that in multi-level marketing, the sales force is compensated for sales they personally generate and also for the sales of others they recruit, which creates multiple levels of compensation. Descriptions for how this marketing structure could be used in a business plan may include suggestions such as including it in the business philosophy.

Mathematics

16. Johnstown Buying Power Index = .02304 (.5 × .0251) + (.3 × .0183) + (.2 × .025) = .02304; Milton Buying Power Index = .01753 (.5 × .0181) + (.3 × .018) + (.2 × .0154) = .01753

Standardized Test Practice

1. A. Description and Analysis
2. F
3. collateral

DECA Connection Role Play

Evaluations will be based on these performance indicators:

1. **Assess personal interests and skills needed for success in business.** Entrepreneurs who want to be successful in business should assess their life skills, personal characteristics, and marketing knowledge to learn whether they have what it takes to be a successful entrepreneur. Some characteristics they should assess include: determination, self-motivation, self-discipline, self-confidence, strong organizational skills, leadership ability, creativity, willingness to work hard, spirit of adventure, and good social skills.
2. **Identify a company's unique selling proposition.** This should include an explanation of how a company plans to meet consumers' needs in a way that other companies cannot. Ideas may include how the product or service is distributed to the consumers, how the product or service is priced, or how it is serviced after purchase.
3. **Conduct an environmental scan to obtain business information.** An environmental scan is conducted to analyze outside influences that may have an impact on an organization. It typically includes four areas: political, economic, socio-cultural, and technological information. Understanding how each of these areas is changing or is likely to change in the future can lead to a better appreciation of potential opportunities or threats for the company.
4. **Conduct market analysis.** The best way for businesses to make a connection with customers is to know these people well. This means knowing where they live, their income level, age, ethnic background, activities, values, and what interests them. Such information can help identify groups of people who have things in common. Market analysis can provide a company with this information.
5. **Describe factors that affect the business environment.** Business environments can be affected by a variety of political, economic, socio-cultural, and technological factors.

glencoe.com

Role Plays For more DECA Role Plays, send students to the Online Learning Center to download the Competitive Events Workbook.

financing the business

Visual Literacy Start-up money is needed to make a good idea grow into a prosperous business. Most entrepreneurs must borrow the money or capital from commercial banks, credit unions, investors, and other lenders. ***What do you think must be done to convince a lender to provide funding for a new business?***

SHOW WHAT YOU KNOW

Discovery Project

Preparing Financial Documents

Essential Question How does an entrepreneur develop the necessary financial documents for a business plan?

Project Goal

You and a classmate are partners in a proposed new product or service business. Your team must choose the new business, and then research and prepare a written report that includes a personal financial statement, estimates the start-up costs, develops an income statement, balance sheet, and a cash flow statement for that business.

Ask Yourself...

- How will your team decide upon the type of new business you will develop?
- How will your team develop a personal financial statement and estimate start-up costs?
- How will your team complete the income statement for the business?
- How will your team complete a balance sheet and a cash flow statement?
- How will your team organize the financial section of a business plan?

Synthesize Research and Present Synthesize your research by describing and preparing important financial documents required in business plans when financing a new business.

glencoe.com

Activity Get a worksheet activity about financial documents.

Evaluate Download a rubric that you can use to evaluate your project.

DECA Connection

DECA Event Role Play

Concepts in this chapter are related to DECA competitive events that involve either an interview or role play.

Performance Indicators The performance indicators represent key skills and knowledge. Your key to success in DECA competitive events is relating them to concepts in this chapter.

- Explain the role of finance in business.
- Set financial goals.
- Describe the nature of cash flow statements.
- Explain the nature of balance sheets.
- Describe the nature of income statements.

DECA Prep

Role Play Practice role-playing with the DECA Connection competitive-event activity at the end of this chapter. More information on DECA events can be found on DECA's Web site.

ENGAGE

Visual Literacy

Read the chapter opener photo caption question to students: ***What do you think must be done to convince a lender to provide funding for a new business?*** Possible answer: You must show that you have carefully projected the potential income the business could generate and estimated business expenses, possibly by examining similar businesses. You should have a repayment plan, show that the business will have a reasonable profit margin, and have a convincing marketing plan. Then ask these guiding questions.

Guiding Questions

Explain What is the purpose of a business plan?	to outline a strategy for turning a business idea into a reality
Analyze What is a credit score?	a number that is designed to represent the risk involved in lending money

Discovery Project

Preparing Financial Documents Start a discussion about the Discovery Project Essential Question: ***How does an entrepreneur develop the necessary financial documents for a business plan?*** Different documents require different techniques to develop. In addition, different businesses have different financial needs. When creating a personal financial statement, for example, the entrepreneur will need to refer to past expenses, such as utilities, rent, food bills, and so on. The entrepreneur must be familiar with the contents and format of documents such as income statements and balance sheets. Determining start-up and on-going costs requires knowledge of the business and the types of one-time and continuing expenses that will be required.

Discovery Project Resources Send students to the Online Learning Center to download a rubric to evaluate their projects.

ENGAGE

Introduce the Chapter

Chapter 36 explains to students the steps in determining how to finance a business. These major concepts are discussed:

- The financial component of the business plan
- Creating a personal financial statement
- Estimating start-up costs
- Estimating business income and expenses
- Preparing an income statement
- Calculating gross and net profits
- Creating a balance sheet
- Creating a cash flow statement

Discussion Starter

Developing a Sample Personal Budget Work with the class to develop a sample personal budget for a college student for one month, listing their assets and liabilities (debts). Ask: ***What expenses do you think the student would have?*** Answers may include: tuition, rent, food, books, gasoline, entertainment, and so on. Encourage students to make rough estimates of the costs of each of these items. Display their estimates in a list for the class to read. Then repeat the process by asking students to list the assets a typical student might have, such as a car or laptop computer. Tell students that this information can be used to prepare a personal financial statement.

DECA Connection

Discuss the performance indicators listed in the DECA Connection feature. Explain to students that performance indicators tell them how to demonstrate their acquired skills and knowledge through individual or team competitive events.

glencoe.com

Competitive Events Workbook For more DECA Role Plays, send students to the Online Learning Center to download the Competitive Events Workbook.

PROGRAM RESOURCE ORGANIZER

PRINT RESOURCES

- **Student Edition**
- **Teacher Edition**
- **Student Activity Workbook with Academic Integration** includes worksheets and activities correlated to the text.
- **Mathematics for Marketing Workbook** provides math activities for every unit in the text.

TECHNOLOGY TOOLBOX

- **Connect**
- **ConnectPlus**
- **ExamView Assessment Suite** is a comprehensive solution for creating, administering, and scoring tests.

glencoe.com

Online Learning Center provides a variety of resources to enrich and enhance learning.

SECTION, CHAPTER, AND UNIT RESOURCES

- **Graphic Organizers** for organizing text concepts visually.
- **Digital Nation Activities** and **Green Marketer Activities** extend learning beyond the text features.
- **Career Chatroom Career Profiles** allow students to explore different marketing occupations in depth.
- **After You Read Answer Keys** for students to check their answers.
- **Discovery Project Rubrics** and **Marketing Internship Project Rubrics** for students to evaluate their projects.

PROGRAM RESOURCES

- **Student Activity Workbook with Academic Integration Teacher Annotated Edition** includes annotated answers for the activities and worksheets.
- **Marketing Research Project Workbook** provides a step-by-step approach for students to complete their own marketing research studies.
- **School-to-Career Activity Workbook** helps students relate their class work to on-the-job experience and involves work-site analysis and working with mentors.
- **Competitive Events Workbook** helps prepare students for state and national marketing education competitions.
- **Inclusion in the Marketing Education Classroom** provides teaching resources for working with students with special needs.
- **PowerPoint Presentations** provides visual teaching aids and assessments for this chapter.

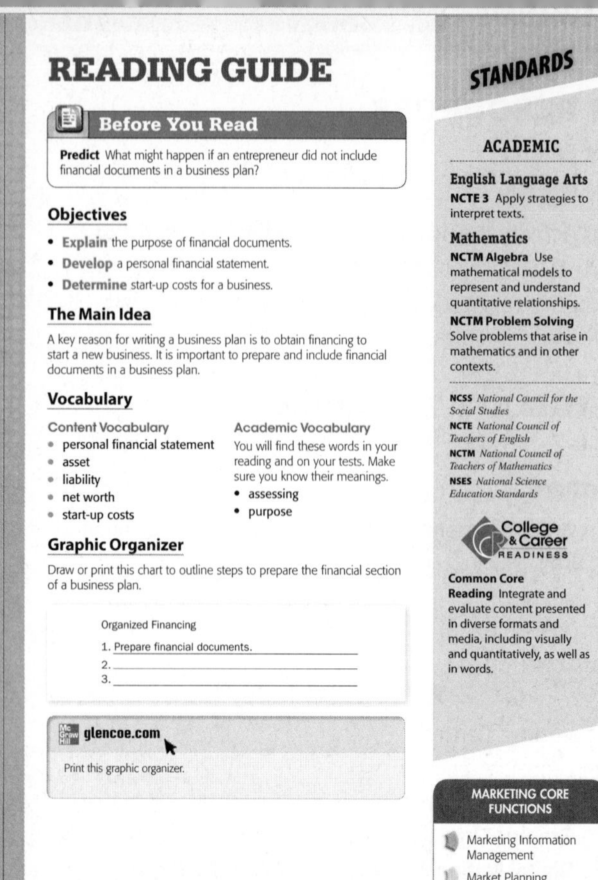

READING GUIDE

Before You Read

Predict What might happen if an entrepreneur did not include financial documents in a business plan?

Objectives

- **Explain** the purpose of financial documents.
- **Develop** a personal financial statement.
- **Determine** start-up costs for a business.

The Main Idea

A key reason for writing a business plan is to obtain financing to start a new business. It is important to prepare and include financial documents in a business plan.

Vocabulary

Content Vocabulary
- personal financial statement
- asset
- liability
- net worth
- start-up costs

Academic Vocabulary

You will find these words in your reading and on your tests. Make sure you know their meanings.
- assessing
- purpose

Graphic Organizer

Draw or print this chart to outline steps to prepare the financial section of a business plan.

Organized Financing
1. Prepare financial documents.
2.
3.

glencoe.com

Print this graphic organizer.

STANDARDS

ACADEMIC

English Language Arts
NCTE 3 Apply strategies to interpret texts.

Mathematics
NCTM Algebra Use mathematical models to represent and understand quantitative relationships.
NCTM Problem Solving Solve problems that arise in mathematics and in other contexts.

NCSS *National Council for the Social Studies*
NCTE *National Council of Teachers of English*
NCTM *National Council of Teachers of Mathematics*
NSES *National Science Education Standards*

College & Career READINESS

Common Core
Reading Integrate and evaluate content presented in diverse formats and media, including visually and quantitatively, as well as in words.

MARKETING CORE FUNCTIONS
- Marketing Information Management
- Market Planning

842 | Unit 11 · Entrepreneurship and Finance

THE FINANCIAL PART OF A BUSINESS PLAN

Financial information is a major component of a business plan. In a business plan, you need to include financial documents that describe your personal finances as well as the financial needs of the business. By preparing financial statements, you determine the amount of money needed to operate the business as well as the amount that needs to be borrowed, if any.

As You Read

Analyze Assume that you are completing a business plan. Why do you think that it is necessary to include personal and start-up financial statements in the plan?

When you borrow money, the lender will want proof that you are able to repay the loan. The lender examines your credit history, collateral, and the prospects for business success. The financial documents included in your business plan show that you are able to pay off the loan.

There are five important financial documents normally included in a business plan:

- the personal financial statement
- start-up cost estimate
- income statement
- balance sheet
- cash flow statement

In this section, you learn about developing a personal financial statement and estimating start-up costs.

> "A business plan helps obtain financing to start a new business."

THE PERSONAL FINANCIAL STATEMENT

A **personal financial statement** is a summary of your current personal financial condition. It is an important document to include in a business plan. You will need it when applying for additional money or capital to finance a new business. The personal financial statement gives a snapshot of your net worth at a particular point in time by looking at your assets and liabilities.

An **asset** is anything of monetary value that a person owns, such as cash, checking and savings accounts, real estate, or stocks. A **liability** is a debt that you owe to others, such as a car payment, credit card debt, rental payments, or taxes. A personal financial statement shows potential lenders that you have some money at risk as well as in your proposed business.

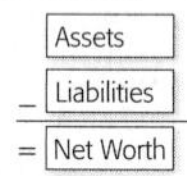

ASSETS

The first step in developing a personal financial statement is to identify assets. Be realistic about the current value of your assets. For example, if you have a car worth $11,700, do not round it up to $12,000.

Be sure to list all your cash assets (checking and savings accounts), any investments (bonds, insurance policies, mutual funds, and stocks), and personal assets (cars, clothing, furniture, and residence, if owned). Estimate the present value of each item. A lender will look for assets that could be sold to pay off the business loan if a new business fails. Provide a total value for each asset and a grand total for all assets.

Chapter 36 · Financing the Business | 843

ENGAGE

Anticipation Activity

Improving Student Achievement Divide students into four groups, each representing a type of business: manufacturing, wholesale, retail, or service. Give each group ten minutes to brainstorm a list of capital requirements for its start-up business.

Objectives

- **Explain** the purpose of financial documents. Financial documents provide an overall picture of how well a business is doing or how well a new business is projected to do, where money is coming from, how it is being spent, and so on.
- **Develop** a personal financial statement. It should summarize net worth at a particular time by listing assets and liabilities.
- **Determine** start-up costs for a business. Costs such as one-time costs and continuing costs must be estimated.

Graphic Organizer

Organized Financing

1. Prepare financial documents.
2. Prepare personal financial statement.
3. Prepare start-up costs worksheet.
4. Prepare personal living expenses worksheet.

Graphic Organizer Send students to the Online Learning Center to print this graphic organizer.

EXPLORE

Before You Read

Read the Before You Read question aloud: ***What might happen if an entrepreneur did not include financial documents in a business plan?*** The entrepreneur would not be able to predict how viable the proposed business might be. Any organization that the entrepreneur approached for a loan would not consider making the loan without the required financial documents. Then ask: ***What do you think would happen if the documents were completed, but appeared to be hastily prepared without much thought?*** If the entrepreneur approached a lender, the loan officer would probably be experienced enough to realize the documents were poorly prepared. The loan officer might deny the loan or insist that the documents be modified before reviewing them again.

Preteaching Vocabulary

Have students go to the Online Learning Center at glencoe.com for the Chapter 36 Preteaching Vocabulary games.

Content Vocabulary

Tell students they are going to create a dictionary of financial terms related to business. Have students write each Content Vocabulary term on an index card. As they encounter each term in their reading, have them add a definition to the term's card. Encourage them to create cards for additional terms they do not understand.

Academic Vocabulary

Assessing—Denotative Display the word *assessing* and then read aloud this sentence: ***By assessing start-up costs before getting involved in a new business, you are protecting yourself and helping to ensure the viability of the proposed business.*** Explain that *assessing* here means "determining the amount or value of." By assessing start-up costs, the entrepreneur is estimating how much these costs will be.

Purpose—Synonyms Display *purpose* and have students list some synonyms for that word. intent, goal, reason, objective Read this sentence: ***The purpose of start-up money is to get a business going.*** Ask: ***Which synonyms most closely match the meaning of* purpose *in this sentence?*** Goal, objective

Critical Thinking

Ask: ***If you were starting a small business, who would you rely on to help prepare the financial section of the business plan?*** Possible answers include someone they know who is a banker or accountant or who runs a successful small business.

Financial Analysis

THE FINANCIAL PART OF A BUSINESS PLAN

Explain that a financial statement can give a potential business owner a chance to objectively examine the possibilities of success.

Guiding Questions

Recall How can the financial part of a business plan help determine how much money you might need to borrow?	The difference between your start-up costs and expenses and what you have shows how much you need to get from elsewhere.
Analyze You are going to ask your bank for a loan to start a business. What will the bank consider in deciding whether to make the loan?	Factors include credit history, collateral, and prospects for the new business. Your financial documents will help to evaluate your chances of success.
Predict If your personal financial statement shows liabilities greater than your assets, do you think a bank would give you a loan to start a business? Why or why not?	Sample answer: No, because the total value of my possessions, cash, and savings is less than the total amount of money I owe. In such a case, it would be difficult to pay off a loan from the bank.

As You Read

Read students the As You Read question: ***Assume that you are completing a business plan. Why do you think that it is necessary to include personal and start-up financial statements in the plan?*** It is important that you have a clear idea concerning the amount of money required to cover start-up costs and personal expenses; in addition, if you are applying for a loan, the lender must have this information in order to make an informed decision about whether to grant the loan.

Expert Advice

Read the quote to students:

"A business plan helps obtain financing to start a new business."

Ask: ***Why is financial information a vital part of a business plan?*** It helps both the entrepreneur and any potential lenders determine whether the business is a reasonable risk.

This sample worksheet can be used to show an entrepreneur's personal net worth. ***Why is the personal financial statement an important part of a business plan?***

Personal Financial Statement
Name: __________ Date: __________

Assets	
Cash	$____
Savings Account	$____
Checking Account	
Savings Bonds	$____
Stocks and Bonds	$____
Mutual Funds	$____
Cash Value of Life Insurance	$____
Vehicles (owned not financed)	$____
Real Estate	$____
Retirement Accounts (401K or IRAs)	$____
Other Assets	$____
Total Assets	$____
Liabilities	
Accounts Payable (i.e. credit cards)	$____
Contracts Payable (i.e. car loans)	$____
Notes Payable (i.e. student loans)	$____
Taxes Payable	$____
Real Estate/Mortgage Loans	$____
Other Liabilities	$____
Total Liabilities	$____
Total Assets	$____
Less Total Liabilities	$____
Net Worth	$____

Financial Statement

LIABILITIES

Next list your monthly liabilities or debt. These include payments for automobile loans, credit card accounts, mortgage loans, and rental payments. Calculate a total for each type of liability and a grand total for all of your liabilities.

NET WORTH

Next calculate your personal net worth. Your **net worth** is the difference between assets and liabilities. To find a business's net worth, subtract its debts from its assets. For corporations, net worth is called "stockholders' equity." For partnerships and sole proprietorships, it is called "owner's equity."

Your personal financial statement is one way to determine if you and your business are good credit risks. A lender will want a personal credit report to determine how well you have paid past debts.

A lender will also need a copy of your personal tax returns for the past three to five years. Past tax returns show how you earned money in the past.

You may plan to continue working at another job. If so, the lender will be interested in whether the income can cover your personal expenses until your new business becomes profitable.

Practice 1: Develop a Personal Financial Statement

1. You have assets of $15,000 (car), $5,000 (savings), $1,000 (cash value of life insurance), $1,700 (cash), and personal property worth $2,500. What are your total assets?
2. You have liabilities of $10,000 (car loan), $5,000 (student loan), and $1,500 (credit card balances). What are your total liabilities?
3. What is your net worth?

Check your answers to all Practice sets.

ESTIMATING START-UP COSTS

How do you estimate how much capital is needed to start a business? **Start-up costs** are projections of how much money a new business owner needs for the business's first year of operation. Then, for that first year of operation, your income goal should be to reach a break-even point. The break-even point is reached when enough money is received to pay all operating expenses, including your salary, and to pay debt obligations.

The Small Business Administration (SBA) provides forms and worksheets to help new business owners. A worksheet like the one shown in **Figure 36.1** on page 846 can help determine start-up costs for a new business. A start-up cost estimate can also be used to project on-going operating costs after the business gets off the ground.

By **assessing** start-up costs before getting involved in a new business, you are protecting yourself and helping to ensure the viability of the proposed business. Start-up costs vary, depending on the type of business.

Practice 2: Determine Start-Up Costs

Your business has one-time costs of $25,000 and average monthly costs of $3,600. What are your total costs for the first quarter of operation? Using the same average monthly costs, what are your total costs for the year?

The amount of start-up money needed varies, but it is based on factors such as:

- **The nature of the proposed business** Manufacturing, wholesale, and retail businesses all have different needs and requirements.
- **The size of the business** Smaller businesses usually do not require as much money to start as larger ones.
- **The amount and kind of inventory needed** For example, it is much more costly to purchase inventory for a large supermarket than for a neighborhood convenience store.
- **The estimated time between starting the business and earning income** For example, a home-based accountant may start earning income within weeks, but a large accounting firm may not see a profit for many months or longer.

MARKETING CASE STUDY

Good Samaritans + Smartphones

A vision of Web developer Jason Kiesel, CitySourced started up from a meager investment of $100,000, small change in the world of new high-tech businesses. Recognized as a finalist at TechCrunch50, the CitySourced smartphone application was designed to improve communities.

Neighborhood Watch 2.0

As a "real-time civic engagement tool," the app allows citizens to identify urban blight, such as graffiti, trash, potholes, broken streetlights, stray shopping carts, and more. With a photo function, you take a picture of the problem and send it off with data to City Hall where participating governments process the report for resolution. Launched in large cities in California and other states, CitySourced's time- and money-saving concept is a civic-minded innovation.

Mathematics

Create and Calculate Think of a business you could launch that would require minimal start-up costs. Describe and name your business. Make a list of the equipment and supplies you might need to start, and then calculate that total cost.

NCTM Problem Solving Solve problems that arise in mathematics and in other contexts.

EXPLAIN

Visual Literacy

Financial Statement Caption Answer Read the caption question to students: ***Why is the personal financial statement an important part of a business plan?*** The personal financial statement breaks down assets and liabilities in a clear and easy-to-understand format; therefore, it simplifies understanding an individual's net worth, and it shows how that net worth was determined. Then ask: ***In which category would you place a truck you owned?*** The truck is an asset. Then ask: ***In which category would you place a bank loan you had on the truck?*** A bank loan is a liability.

Reinforce Vocabulary

Net Worth—Denotative Meaning Explain to students that in business, the term *net* means "free from all charges or deductions" and *worth* can be defined as "value." Therefore, *net worth* refers to something's value after any charges or deductions have been made.

Activate Prior Knowledge

Recalling the Components of a Credit Score Remind students that one factor lenders use when determining whether to loan money is the individual's credit score. Use the following diagram to help students recall how credit scores are calculated.

What Determines a Credit Score?

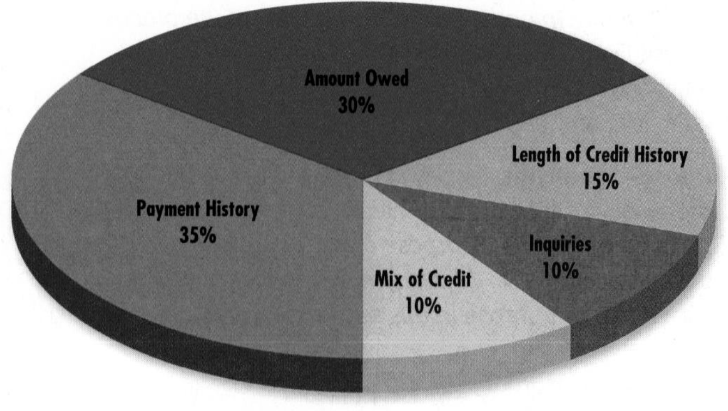

ELABORATE

NET WORTH

Explain to students that net worth is your equity after the total of all your liabilities has been subtracted from your assets.

Guiding Questions

Identify What document can be used to calculate your net worth?	personal financial statement
Analyze Why do corporations use the term *stockholders' equity* for *net worth*?	The term *equity* refers to monetary value; stockholders' equity refers to the monetary value of the stockholders' share of a corporation.
Apply What might a bank ask you to bring in to help determine whether you are a good risk for a loan to start a new business?	The bank will want to see your recent tax returns and personal financial statement and obtain a credit report.

ANSWERS TO PRACTICE 1

1. Total assets are $25,200 ($15,000 + $5,000 + $1,000 + 1,700 + $2,500 = $25,200)
2. Total liabilities are $16,500 ($10,000 + $5,000 + $1,500 = $16,500)
3. Net worth is $8,700 ($25,200 – $16,500 = $8,700)

ESTIMATING START-UP COSTS

Emphasize to students that start-up costs vary greatly depending on the type of business. To focus the discussion on estimating start-up costs, ask these guiding questions.

Guiding Questions

Define What does the term "break-even point" mean?	The break-even point is the point at which enough money is coming in to cover all expenses.
Analyze How might the inventory a business requires affect the amount of start-up money it needs? Provide an example.	The capital required will depend on the cost and quantity of the items needed. For example, a furniture store needs a greater investment in inventory than does a coffee house.
Make Judgments You are estimating start-up costs for a potential start-up business. Would you rather underestimate or overestimate them? Why?	If you underestimate them, the business may fail due to inadequate capital to cover expenses for the first year. If you overestimate them, the bank might think the business is not viable and not give you a loan.

ANSWERS TO PRACTICE 2

The total costs for the first quarter (3 months) are $35,800 [$25,000 + ($3,600 × 3) = $35,800]. The total costs for the year are $68,200 [$25,000 + ($3,600 × 12) = $68,200].

MARKETING CASE STUDY

Mathematics Answer Students should list needed equipment and supplies and estimate their start-up costs. Sample answer: I could start a dog-walking business. I might need to buy leashes, water containers, and bags for cleaning up after the dogs. I also might need money for advertising. Total start-up costs might be $100–$150. Use these questions to further discuss the feature.

Guiding Questions

Infer Why is CitySourced called a "civic-minded" app?	It encourages citizens to report urban blight so that the authorities can address the issues.
Elaborate What might be some apps that could be created for your city or area?	Examples will vary. One app might help with traffic and parking issues during large public gatherings such as concerts and sporting events.

FIGURE 36.1 **Start-Up Costs Worksheet**

Estimating Start-Up Costs The SBA has developed a worksheet for estimating start-up costs and operating expenses for new businesses. ***Why is a start-up worksheet helpful to an entrepreneur?***

ESTIMATED MONTHLY EXPENSES			
Item	Your estimate of monthly expenses based on sales of $_____ per year	Your estimate of how much cash you need to start your business (See column 3)	What to put in column 2. (These figures are typical for one kind of business. You will have to decide how many months to allow for your business.)
	Column 1	Column 2	Column 3
Salary of owner	$	$	2 times column 1
All other salaries and wages			3 times column 1
Rent			3 times column 1
Advertising			3 times column 1
Delivery expenses			3 times column 1
Supplies			3 times column 1
Telephone and Internet			3 times column 1
Other utilities			3 times column 1
Insurance			Payment required by insurance company
Taxes, including Social Security			4 times column 1
Interest			3 times column 1
Maintenance			3 times column 1
Legal and other professional fees			3 times column 1
Miscellaneous			3 times column 1
STARTING COSTS YOU ONLY HAVE TO PAY ONCE			Leave column 2 blank
Fixtures and equipment			See separate worksheet
Decorating and remodeling			Talk it over with a contractor
Installation of fixtures and equipment			Talk to suppliers from whom you buy these
Starting inventory			Supplies will probably help you estimate this
Deposits with public utilities			Find out from utility companies
Legal and other professional fees			Lawyer, accountant, and so on
Licenses and permits			Find out from city offices what you need
Advertising and promotion			Estimate what you'll use for opening
Accounts receivable			What you need to buy more stock until credit customers pay
Cash			For unexpected expenses or losses, special purchases, etc.
Other			Make a separate list and enter total
TOTAL ESTIMATED CASH YOU NEED TO START	$	$	Add up all the numbers in column 2

- **The operating expenses** Operating costs must be paid before any income is received from sales.
- **Start-up expenses** Some are one-time costs while others are continuing costs that occur on an ongoing basis after the initial business start-up.
- **One-time costs** These are expenses that will not be repeated after you open the business. Examples include licenses, permits, telephone installation deposits, and charges for installation of equipment, fixtures, and machinery.
- **Continuing costs** These are expenses you will pay throughout the life of the business. Examples of continuing costs are payroll, monthly rent, advertising, supplies, insurance, repairs, maintenance, and taxes. Most businesses are not profitable immediately, so include at least three months of continuing costs when estimating the amount of cash you will need to get started.

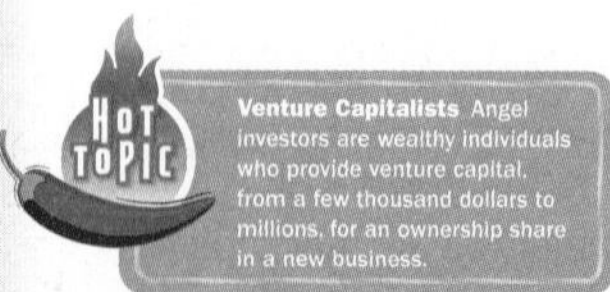

Venture Capitalists Angel investors are wealthy individuals who provide venture capital, from a few thousand dollars to millions, for an ownership share in a new business.

Information is available from several reliable sources to help plan financial needs. (See **Figure 36.2**.) The Small Business Administration (SBA) provides information to people who want to start a new business. The SBA offers a wide variety of loan programs. These programs help small businesses borrow money from traditional lenders at reasonable interest rates. The National Federation of Independent Business (NFIB) has a section on its Web site devoted to helping entrepreneurs develop a budget specific to the needs of new small business owners. Similarly, the U.S. Chamber of Commerce Small Business Nation Web site features a Start Up Toolkit for new business owners.

You can also get estimates of start-up costs from people who are already in a similar business or from a trade association. State and local government agencies, such as a state department of commerce and local chamber of commerce, are valuable sources of cost information.

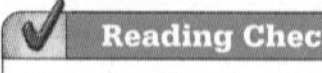

Reading Check

Understand How do start-up costs differ from personal costs?

FIGURE 36.2 **Financing Sources**

Finding Funding There are many different sources for funding new businesses. ***What is the difference between a primary and a secondary source of funding?***

Primary Sources		**Secondary Sources**	
Long-term financing	***Short-term financing***	***Long-term financing***	***Short-term financing***
• Personal financing • Family and friends • Private investors • Equity financing • Leasing • Credit unions • SBA LowDoc	• Personal financing • Family and friends • Credit cards • Credit unions • Trade credit • Banks • SBA Microloans • SBA LowDoc	• Business alliances • SBA regular 7(a) program • Venture capital • SBICs • State and local public financing • Franchising • Asset-based financing	• SBA CAPLines • Consumer finance companies • Commercial finance companies • State and local public financing

EXPLAIN

Visual Literacy

Figure 36.1 Caption Answer Read the caption question to students: ***Why is a start-up worksheet helpful to an entrepreneur?*** It helps the entrepreneur predict the one-time start-up costs as well as the ongoing costs of a new business. It encourages the entrepreneur to approach the task in an organized fashion and makes certain that all components of costs are covered.

Extension Tell students that they are business consultants, and entrepreneurs come to them with questions regarding starting a business. Ask them to generate a list of questions new business owners might bring to the consultants' attention. Display their questions in a list and discuss them as a class. Questions might include: How can I estimate advertising costs? What types of insurance do I need? Where can I get advice concerning the quantity of starting inventory needed?

Mini Project

Differentiated Instruction

Verbal/Linguistic Learners Explain that a business and finance dictionary can help de-mystify business jargon. Have students work independently to find a reputable, free online business dictionary. Then have them share their findings and explain their choices. Each student should share the name and Web address of an online business dictionary and explain reasons for that choice. For example, AllBusiness's Business Glossary provides clear definitions for thousands of terms.

ELABORATE

Critical Thinking

Ask these questions to focus discussion on factors determining the amount of start-up money needed.

Topic	Question
The nature of the proposed business	*Would a manufacturing plant or a retail store have greater start-up costs? Why?* A manufacturing plant would have more costs because it would need more expensive equipment.
The amount and kind of inventory needed	*How do you think a business such as a car dealership might afford a substantial inventory?* Businesses that carry expensive inventory often obtain financing from the manufacturer. The business can use sales revenue to repay the loans or purchase additional inventory.
The estimated time between starting the business and earning income	*Give an example of a situation in which there might be a lengthy wait between start-up and receiving any earned income.* Possible answer: a manufacturing firm
Operating expenses	*What kinds of operating expenses might a bicycle repair shop have?* utilities such as electricity, water, and telephone service; rent or mortgage payments, taxes, and so on
One-time costs	*A hair stylist is opening her own salon. What are some of the one-time costs she might have?* licensing fees, permits, utility deposits, fees for installation of equipment and fixtures such as washers, dryers, and sinks
Continuing costs	*An insurance firm has a three-floor office with 50 employees. What do you think would be this company's largest continuing expense?* payroll

Venture Capitalists Tell students: Angel investors are wealthy individuals who provide venture capital, from a few thousand dollars to millions, for an ownership share in a new business.

Reading Check Answer

Read the Reading Check question to students: ***How do start-up costs differ from personal costs?*** Start-up costs are those expenses related to the business itself, such as purchasing inventory or remodeling a retail store. Personal costs are expenses related to living, such as rent and utilities. Personal costs would occur even if no business was being started.

Visual Literacy

Figure 36.2 Caption Answer Read the caption question to students: ***What is the difference between a primary and a secondary source of funding?*** A primary source of financing has the borrower using personal means to acquire funding. A secondary source of financing relies on outside lenders to provide the funds for a new business. Ask students: ***Would you prefer to use primary or secondary sources of financing to start a new business? Explain you answer.*** Sample answer: I would prefer to use a primary source, such as my local bank, because I want to establish a good relationship with them, and the bank would give me a fair interest rate.

Mini Project

Extension

Investigating Angel Investors Tell students that there are Web sites devoted to matching up individuals needing money for new or existing businesses with angel investors. Instruct students to investigate one of these sites. Have them write a one-paragraph summary explaining the site's features. Instruct students to include descriptions of any fees the Web site charges for its services. Paragraphs will vary depending on the Web site reviewed. For example, the Web site gobignetwork.com is designed to match up businesses of various sizes with venture capitalists and others offering loans. The site's monthly fees start at about $50 and one-time fees are about $250. In addition, the site offers information on starting a business, templates for various financial documents, and so on.

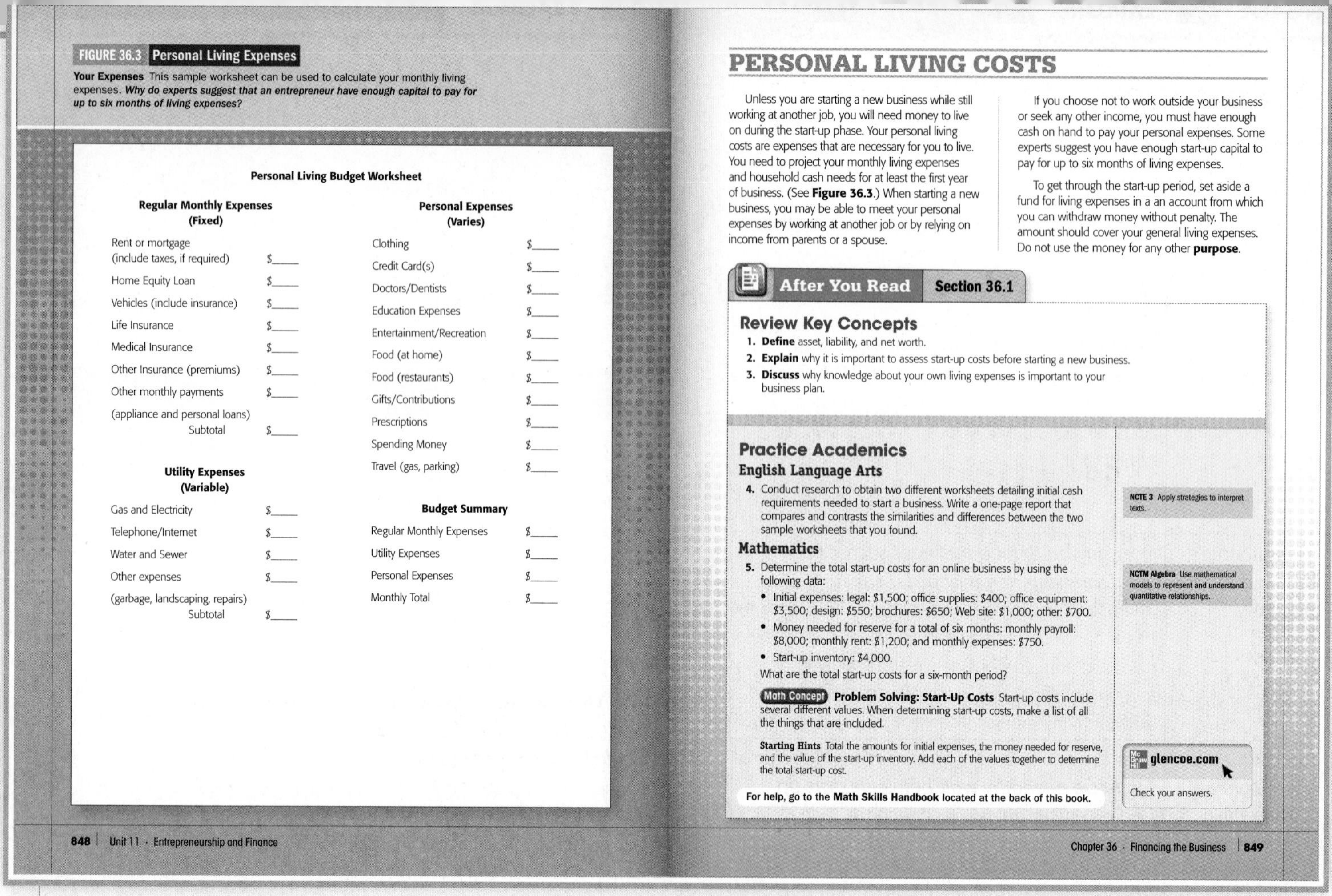

FIGURE 36.3 Personal Living Expenses

Your Expenses This sample worksheet can be used to calculate your monthly living expenses. ***Why do experts suggest that an entrepreneur have enough capital to pay for up to six months of living expenses?***

Personal Living Budget Worksheet

Regular Monthly Expenses (Fixed)	
Rent or mortgage (include taxes, if required)	$____
Home Equity Loan	$____
Vehicles (include insurance)	$____
Life Insurance	$____
Medical Insurance	$____
Other Insurance (premiums)	$____
Other monthly payments (appliance and personal loans)	$____
Subtotal	$____

Utility Expenses (Variable)	
Gas and Electricity	$____
Telephone/Internet	$____
Water and Sewer	$____
Other expenses (garbage, landscaping, repairs)	$____
Subtotal	$____

Personal Expenses (Varies)	
Clothing	$____
Credit Card(s)	$____
Doctors/Dentists	$____
Education Expenses	$____
Entertainment/Recreation	$____
Food (at home)	$____
Food (restaurants)	$____
Gifts/Contributions	$____
Prescriptions	$____
Spending Money	$____
Travel (gas, parking)	$____

Budget Summary	
Regular Monthly Expenses	$____
Utility Expenses	$____
Personal Expenses	$____
Monthly Total	$____

PERSONAL LIVING COSTS

Unless you are starting a new business while still working at another job, you will need money to live on during the start-up phase. Your personal living costs are expenses that are necessary for you to live. You need to project your monthly living expenses and household cash needs for at least the first year of business. (See **Figure 36.3**.) When starting a new business, you may be able to meet your personal expenses by working at another job or by relying on income from parents or a spouse.

If you choose not to work outside your business or seek any other income, you must have enough cash on hand to pay your personal expenses. Some experts suggest you have enough start-up capital to pay for up to six months of living expenses.

To get through the start-up period, set aside a fund for living expenses in a an account from which you can withdraw money without penalty. The amount should cover your general living expenses. Do not use the money for any other **purpose**.

After You Read | **Section 36.1**

Review Key Concepts

1. **Define** asset, liability, and net worth.
2. **Explain** why it is important to assess start-up costs before starting a new business.
3. **Discuss** why knowledge about your own living expenses is important to your business plan.

Practice Academics

English Language Arts

4. Conduct research to obtain two different worksheets detailing initial cash requirements needed to start a business. Write a one-page report that compares and contrasts the similarities and differences between the two sample worksheets that you found.

NCTE 3 Apply strategies to interpret texts.

Mathematics

5. Determine the total start-up costs for an online business by using the following data:
   - Initial expenses: legal: $1,500; office supplies: $400; office equipment: $3,500; design: $550; brochures: $650; Web site: $1,000; other: $700.
   - Money needed for reserve for a total of six months: monthly payroll: $8,000; monthly rent: $1,200; and monthly expenses: $750.
   - Start-up inventory: $4,000.

   What are the total start-up costs for a six-month period?

NCTM Algebra Use mathematical models to represent and understand quantitative relationships.

Math Concept **Problem Solving: Start-Up Costs** Start-up costs include several different values. When determining start-up costs, make a list of all the things that are included.

Starting Hints Total the amounts for initial expenses, the money needed for reserve, and the value of the start-up inventory. Add each of the values together to determine the total start-up cost.

For help, go to the **Math Skills Handbook** located at the back of this book.

glencoe.com Check your answers.

ELABORATE

Visual Literacy

Figure 36.3 Caption Answer Read the caption question to students: ***Why do experts suggest that an entrepreneur have enough capital to pay for up to six months of living expenses?*** It typically takes that long for a business to generate enough income to cover living expenses; in some cases, it can take considerably longer. To further examine this worksheet, ask students the following guiding questions.

Guiding Questions

Identify Under what heading would you place snow removal expenses?	utility expenses
Analyze Why do you think life insurance is listed under Regular Monthly Expenses rather than Personal Expenses?	It is a fixed expense—it does not vary from one month to the next.

Critical Thinking

Ask students: ***What might be some of the advantages of borrowing money from a friend or relative when starting a small business?*** Possible answers: They might loan you money when a bank refuses, and they might charge you a lower interest rate; they might be more understanding if you made a late payment. ***What might be some of the disadvantages?*** Possible answers: If the business fails and you are unable to repay them, it might damage your relationship with them and hurt them financially; they may unexpectedly need the money and you might not be able to give it to them. Encourage the class to debate the pros and cons of borrowing start-up money from friends or family members.

ELL: Understanding Proficiency

Go to the Online Learning Center to view a clip in which an author discusses proficiency and describes the various levels of proficiency that can be applied to English learners.

EVALUATE

Critical Thinking

Which of the three categories of expenses listed in Figure 36.3 would probably be easiest to reduce? Why? personal expenses, because an individual has more control over spending on many of those items

PERSONAL LIVING COSTS

Discuss with students that start-up money for a new business is not enough; you also must be able to meet your personal expenses.

Guiding Questions

Describe When starting a new business, what are three ways an individual might obtain personal living expenses if they do not want to borrow money?	Answers may include: saving an adequate amount before starting the business; continuing to work at a paying job while starting the business; relying on income from a spouse or other relative.
Apply A relative is starting a sporting goods store and is trying to decide how much to set aside for living expenses. What would you recommend?	Possible answer: The person should have enough set aside to cover living expenses and household cash for at least the first year of the business.
Draw Conclusions An entrepreneur is opening a specialty jewelry store. Even though she knows money will be tight, she is not working a second job. Why do you think she made this decision?	Possible answer: She thinks the business will have a better chance of succeeding if she devotes all her energy to it. A part-time job could bring in more income but reduce her focus on the new business.

Mini Project

Enrichment

Learning from an Entrepreneur Have students arrange an interview with a successful entrepreneur of a small business, such as a restaurant or retail shop, to discuss how that person got started. Students should prepare a list of questions such as: Did you estimate your start-up costs accurately? If you did not, did it affect your business? Did you have to change your standard of living when you first started your business? If so, how? Have students prepare a brief oral presentation on what they learned from the interview. Students' presentations will vary. They should be able to use information gathered from the interview to explain what they learned about starting a business.

After You Read — Section 36.1

Review Key Concepts

1. Asset: anything of monetary value that you own; liability: a debt that you owe to others; net worth: the difference between assets and liabilities
2. You need to accurately assess start-up costs so that you can protect yourself by having adequate capital and help to ensure the viability of the proposed business.
3. It is important to know about your own living expenses because if you are not going to continue to work at another job or get living expenses from elsewhere, you need to have money to live on until the businesses starts producing enough to cover your expenses. It is a good idea to project your monthly living expenses and household cash needs for at least the first year of business.

Practice Academics

English Language Arts

4. Students should conduct research to locate two different worksheets that help in determining initial cash requirements needed to start a business, and then write a one-page report comparing and contrasting the worksheets. For example, the Missouri Small Business & Technology Development Centers and SCORE both provide such worksheets. Both are similar, including places for expenses such as advertising and promotion, legal fees, and utility deposits. The SCORE worksheet provided more detail and had the expenses divided into categories, such as "Capital Equipment List" and "Advertising and Promotional Expenses." It also had a "Sources of Capital" section.

Mathematics

5. Total start-up costs for a six-month period: $72,000. ($1,500 + $400 + $3,500 + $550 + $650 + $1,000 + $700 + [$8,000 × 6] + [$1,200 × 6] + [$750 × 6] + $4,000)

 **glencoe.com** 

Answer Key Send students to the Online Learning Center to check their answers.

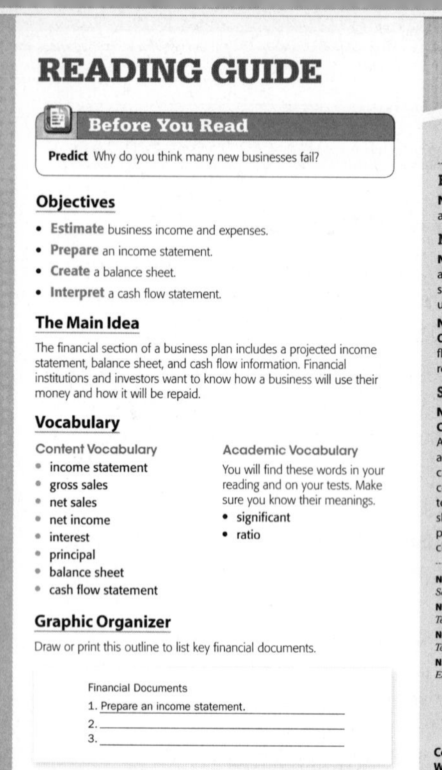
READING GUIDE

Before You Read

Predict Why do you think many new businesses fail?

Objectives

- **Estimate** business income and expenses.
- **Prepare** an income statement.
- **Create** a balance sheet.
- **Interpret** a cash flow statement.

The Main Idea

The financial section of a business plan includes a projected income statement, balance sheet, and cash flow information. Financial institutions and investors want to know how a business will use their money and how it will be repaid.

Vocabulary

Content Vocabulary
- income statement
- gross sales
- net sales
- net income
- interest
- principal
- balance sheet
- cash flow statement

Academic Vocabulary

You will find these words in your reading and on your tests. Make sure you know their meanings.
- significant
- ratio

Graphic Organizer

Draw or print this outline to list key financial documents.

Financial Documents
1. Prepare an income statement.
2. ________
3. ________

glencoe.com

Print this graphic organizer.

MARKETING CORE FUNCTIONS
- Marketing Information Management
- Market Planning

STANDARDS

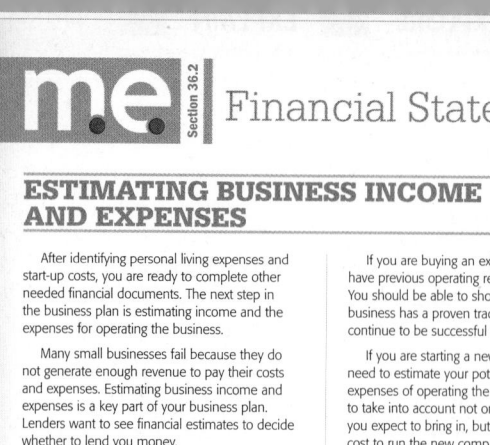

ACADEMIC

English Language Arts

NCTE 1 Read texts to acquire new information.

Mathematics

NCTM Algebra Represent and analyze mathematical situations and structures using algebraic symbols.

NCTM Number and Operations Compute fluently and make reasonable estimates.

Social Studies

NCSS II B Time, Continuity, & Change Apply key concepts such as time, chronology, causality, change, conflict, and complexity to explain, analyze, and show connections among patterns of historical change and continuity.

NCSS *National Council for the Social Studies*
NCTE *National Council of Teachers of English*
NCTM *National Council of Teachers of Mathematics*
NSES *National Science Education Standards*

College & Career READINESS

Common Core
Writing Conduct short as well as more sustained research projects based on focused questions, demonstrating understanding of the subject under investigation.

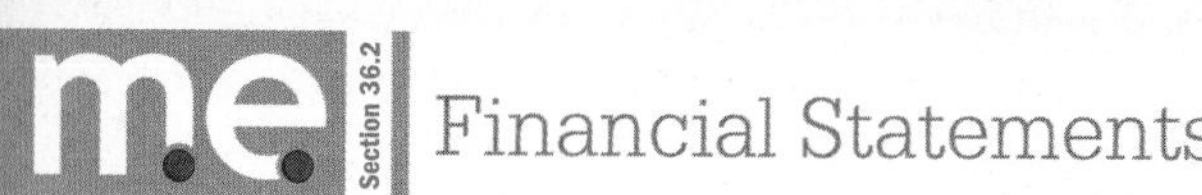

Financial Statements

ESTIMATING BUSINESS INCOME AND EXPENSES

After identifying personal living expenses and start-up costs, you are ready to complete other needed financial documents. The next step in the business plan is estimating income and the expenses for operating the business.

Many small businesses fail because they do not generate enough revenue to pay their costs and expenses. Estimating business income and expenses is a key part of your business plan. Lenders want to see financial estimates to decide whether to lend you money.

If you are buying an existing business, you will have previous operating results to use as a guide. You should be able to show lenders that the business has a proven track record and that it will continue to be successful under your ownership.

If you are starting a new business, you will need to estimate your potential revenue and the expenses of operating the business. You will need to take into account not only how much money you expect to bring in, but also how much it will cost to run the new company.

PREPARING AN INCOME STATEMENT

The financial document used to calculate revenue, costs, and expenses is the income statement. The **income statement** is a summary of income and expenses during a specific period such as a month, a quarter, or a year. This statement is often called a "profit-and-loss statement."

The income statement for an existing business shows the previous year's income, costs, and expenses. The income statement for a new or planned business estimates earnings and expenses for the first few months (or the first year) of operation. **Figure 36.4** on page 853 shows a sample projected quarterly income statement. Refer to this figure as you read about the parts of the income statement.

> "Lenders want financial documents that are logical and realistic."

Income statements have several major parts: total and net sales, cost of goods sold, gross profit, expenses of operating the business, net income from operations, other income or expenses, net profit before income taxes, and net profit after income taxes. Each item on the income statement is added to or subtracted from total sales to find the amount of net profit or loss.

Total Sales
– Returns and Allowances
Net Sales
– Cost of Goods Sold
Gross Profit
– Operating Expenses
Net Income from Operations
– Other Expenses (Interest)
Net Profit (Loss) Before Taxes
– Taxes
Net Profit (Loss) After Taxes

Now we will see how to determine the different amounts for each part of the income statement.

ENGAGE

Anticipation Activity

Improving Student Achievement Tell students that estimating is a crucial skill for forecasting the financial section of the business plan. Ask students what factors would help in estimating revenue for a new business.

Objectives

- **Estimate** business income and expenses. projects both the potential revenue and the cost of operating the business
- **Prepare** an income statement. summarizes income and expenses over a specified time period
- **Create** a balance sheet. lists a business's assets, liabilities, and owner's equity
- **Interpret** a cash flow statement. indicates when cash is expected to come in and when it is expected to be paid out

Graphic Organizer

Financial Documents

1. Prepare an income statement.
2. Prepare a balance sheet.
3. Prepare a cash flow statement.

glencoe.com

iWB

Graphic Organizer Send students to the Online Learning Center to print this graphic organizer.

EXPLORE

Before You Read

Read the Before You Read question aloud: ***Why do you think many new businesses fail?*** Many new businesses fail because the timing or amounts of revenues and expenditures are different from those planned. As a result, they are unable to pay their costs and expenses.

Preteaching Vocabulary

Have students go to the Online Learning Center at glencoe.com for the Chapter 36 Preteaching Vocabulary games.

Content Vocabulary

Display the terms *principal* and *interest.* Ask: ***How are these words related?*** The principal is multiplied by the interest rate to determine the amount of interest the lender charges per year. Explain that *principal* refers to the amount of money borrowed, while *interest* refers to the money paid for the use of that money. Then ask: ***What is the difference between the terms* interest *and* interest rate?** The interest rate is the percentage used to determine the amount of interest owed. For example, if a loan's principal is $200 and the interest rate is 6 percent, you would pay $12 in interest to borrow the money for one year.

Academic Vocabulary

Significant—Denotative Meaning Display the word *significant* for the class. Read aloud this sentence: ***The marketing plan was a significant factor in the business's success.*** Then explain that the word *significant* means "having or likely to have influence or effect." Ask for a volunteer to use this definition to reword the sentence. Sample sentence: The marketing plan had an influence on the business's success.

Ratio—Word Origin Display the word *ratio* for the class to read. Explain that *ratio* comes from the Latin word *ratiō*, which means "a reckoning, account, or calculation." This has led to today's meaning of ratio as a "relationship in quantity, amount, or size between two or more things."

Financial Statements

ESTIMATING BUSINESS INCOME AND EXPENSES

Use these guiding questions to focus the discussion on estimating business income and expenses.

Guiding Questions

Explain Why is an income statement also called a "profit-and-loss statement"?	The statement determines whether a business made a profit or had a loss.
Analyze When asking a lender for a loan, what is an advantage that purchasing an existing business has over starting a new business?	With an existing business, you have previous sales and expense records to show the lender. With a new business, these values must be estimated.
Solve A business has sales of $8,450, cost of goods sold of $4,600, returns and allowances of $370, and operating expenses of $1,090. What is its net income from operations?	The business's net income from operations is $2,390 ($8,450 − $4,600 − $370 − $1,090 = $2,390).

Critical Thinking

Remind students that calculating sales volume for a service business involves establishing an hourly rate and multiplying that by the hours worked annually and then dividing the result by 12 to determine a monthly income figure. Tell students that a local home cleaning business, Mighty Maids, charges $20 for each hour of cleaning performed by one worker. If the business has 6 workers, each of whom averages 8 hours a day for 240 days a year, what is the total income per month? $19,200. ($20 × 6 × 8 × 240/12 = $19,200. Remind students that a new service business cannot charge more than the industry average unless it offers something extra.

Expert Advice

"Lenders want financial documents that are logical and realistic."

Tell students to imagine that they are lenders. Ask: ***How might you determine if a business's financial documents are logical and realistic?*** You might be able to compare the business's financial documents with the documents of a similar business that you have financed in the past. You also might be able to conduct research, for example on the Internet, to determine whether the numbers given in the financial documents appear to be reasonable.

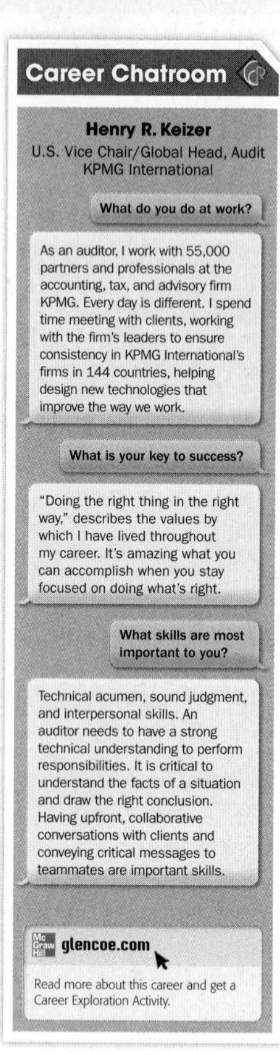

Career Chatroom

Henry R. Keizer
U.S. Vice Chair/Global Head, Audit
KPMG International

What do you do at work?

As an auditor, I work with 55,000 partners and professionals at the accounting, tax, and advisory firm KPMG. Every day is different. I spend time meeting with clients, working with the firm's leaders to ensure consistency in KPMG International's firms in 144 countries, helping design new technologies that improve the way we work.

What is your key to success?

"Doing the right thing in the right way," describes the values by which I have lived throughout my career. It's amazing what you can accomplish when you stay focused on doing what's right.

What skills are most important to you?

Technical acumen, sound judgment, and interpersonal skills. An auditor needs to have a strong technical understanding to perform responsibilities. It is critical to understand the facts of a situation and draw the right conclusion. Having upfront, collaborative conversations with clients and conveying critical messages to teammates are important skills.

glencoe.com

Read more about this career and get a Career Exploration Activity.

ESTIMATING TOTAL SALES

The income generated by a business depends on the yearly volume of sales. Most new businesses grow slowly in the beginning. Therefore, be conservative in estimating your first-year sales.

Suppose you are starting a new T-shirt printing business. You have a contract for 2,000 shirts, which you will sell at $8 each wholesale. Your estimated total sales will be $16,000. If you think you could produce and sell ten times that number during your first year, you would estimate your total sales at $160,000.

It is important to calculate and verify a reasonable estimated sales volume. Compare it with projected industry figures for your business size and location. Trade associations, bankers, and industry publications can help you make sales and income estimates.

The accuracy of your sales estimates will also depend on the quality of your market analysis. Losses rather than profits are common during the first year of business. In your business plan, you will need to show how you will cover any losses by investing more capital or reducing your operating expenses.

CALCULATING NET SALES

The total of all sales for a given period of time is called **gross sales**. Your gross sales will simply be the total of all cash sales if your company sells only on a cash basis. Your company may accept credit cards, sell gift certificates, or offer merchandise on account. All of these different types of sales transactions must be totaled to arrive at gross sales.

Most businesses have some customer returns and allowances (credit granted to customers for damaged or defective goods kept by the customer). Therefore, the gross sales figure does not reflect the actual income from sales. The total of all sales returns, discounts, and allowances is subtracted from gross sales to get net sales. The **net sales** is the amount left after gross sales have been adjusted for returns and allowances. Look at **Figure 36.4** to find the net sales for each month.

COST OF GOODS SOLD

The total amount spent to produce or to purchase the goods that are sold is called the "cost of goods sold." Stock on hand is counted and calculated to determine beginning and ending inventory amounts. To calculate cost of goods sold, add goods purchased during the period to the beginning inventory value. Then subtract the amount of the ending inventory.

FIGURE 36.4 Projected Quarterly Income Statement

Financial Statement An income statement summarizes a business's income and expenses for a specific period of time. It gives a snapshot of the business's health and shows profits or losses. ***Without a history how might a new business gather the information needed to project income and expenses?***

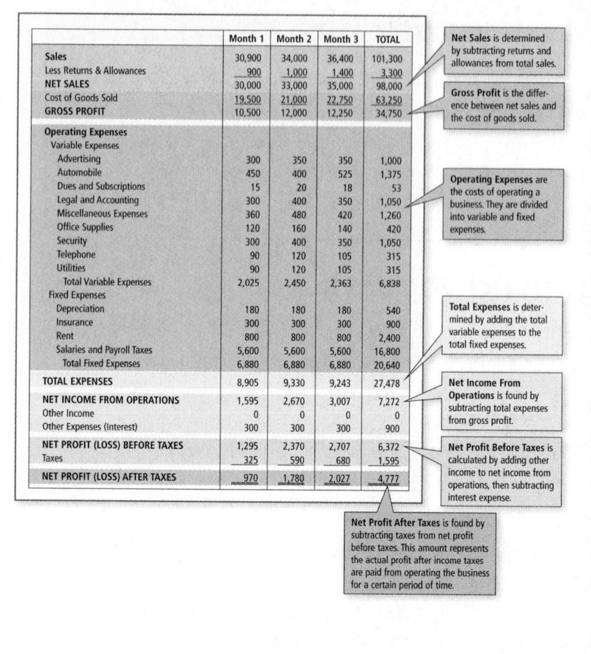

	Month 1	Month 2	Month 3	TOTAL
Sales	30,900	34,000	36,400	101,300
Less Returns & Allowances	900	1,000	1,400	3,300
NET SALES	30,000	33,000	35,000	98,000
Cost of Goods Sold	19,500	21,000	22,750	63,250
GROSS PROFIT	10,500	12,000	12,250	34,750
Operating Expenses				
Variable Expenses				
Advertising	300	350	350	1,000
Automobile	450	400	525	1,375
Dues and Subscriptions	15	20	18	53
Legal and Accounting	300	400	350	1,050
Miscellaneous Expenses	360	480	420	1,260
Office Supplies	120	160	140	420
Security	300	400	350	1,050
Telephone	90	120	105	315
Utilities	90	120	105	315
Total Variable Expenses	2,025	2,450	2,363	6,838
Fixed Expenses				
Depreciation	180	180	180	540
Insurance	300	300	300	900
Rent	800	800	800	2,400
Salaries and Payroll Taxes	5,600	5,600	5,600	16,800
Total Fixed Expenses	6,880	6,880	6,880	20,640
TOTAL EXPENSES	8,905	9,330	9,243	27,478
NET INCOME FROM OPERATIONS	1,595	2,670	3,007	7,272
Other Income	0	0	0	0
Other Expenses (Interest)	300	300	300	900
NET PROFIT (LOSS) BEFORE TAXES	1,295	2,370	2,707	6,372
Taxes	325	590	680	1,595
NET PROFIT (LOSS) AFTER TAXES	970	1,780	2,027	4,777

Net Sales is determined by subtracting returns and allowances from total sales.
Gross Profit is the difference between net sales and the cost of goods sold.
Operating Expenses are the costs of operating a business. They are divided into variable and fixed expenses.
Total Expenses is determined by adding the total variable expenses to the total fixed expenses.
Net Income From Operations is found by subtracting total expenses from gross profit.
Net Profit Before Taxes is calculated by adding other income to net income from operations, then subtracting interest expense.
Net Profit After Taxes is found by subtracting taxes from net profit before taxes. This amount represents the actual profit after income taxes are paid from operating the business for a certain period of time.

EXPLAIN

ESTIMATING TOTAL SALES

To focus discussion on how a business's sales can be estimated, ask students these guiding questions.

Guiding Questions

Explain Why is it a good idea to be conservative in estimating a new business's first-year sales?	Most businesses grow slowly in the beginning.
Analyze What sources might be helpful in estimating first-year sales for a skateboarding shop?	bankers, owners of similar businesses, trade associations, industry publications, and so on
Solve You estimate you will sell 250 skateboards at a cost of $75 each during your first month of business with a 10 percent increase each month. What will be your income for the first two months?	month 1: $18,750 (250 × $75); month 2: $20, 625 (250 + [250 × .10] × $75); total for the two months: $39,375

Career Chatroom

Focus the Career Chatroom discussion concerning Henry R. Keizer by asking students these guiding questions.

Describe As an auditor, what does Henry R. Keizer do?	He ensures proper record keeping and consistency among financial documents in KPMG International's firms.
Infer Why do you think Keizer says, "An auditor needs to have a strong technical understanding to perform responsibilities"?	If an auditor does not have a strong technical understanding, the auditor will not be able to spot errors and inconsistencies.

glencoe.com

Career Exploration Send students to the Online Learning Center to find more information about this career and to get a Career Exploration activity.

ELABORATE

Reinforce Vocabulary

Gross Sales—Multiple Meanings Explain to students that in business situations, *gross* is typically used to mean "a total that is exclusive of any deductions." Therefore, gross sales are sales from which deductions, such as returns and allowances, have not been subtracted. Discuss that gross has a number of other meanings. It can mean 12 dozen (or 144) items. It can also mean coarse or crude.

CALCULATING NET SALES

Explain that net sales will vary depending on returns and allowances.

Guiding Questions

List What types of sales transactions are totaled to obtain gross sales?	cash sales, credit card sales, gift certificates, merchandise offered on account
Compare How is an allowance different from a return?	With a return, the customer gives the item back to the store for a refund. With an allowance, the customer keeps the item and gets a credit for the item being damaged or defective.

Critical Thinking

Explain that many stores, including chain stores, typically do not count gift certificates or gift cards when calculating gross sales. Instead, they add these sales when the cards are redeemed. Ask: ***What are some reasons stores might do this?*** A card might be redeemed at a different store from where it was purchased, and the redeemed value of the card might be split over several purchases.

Visual Literacy

Figure 36.4 Caption Answer Read the caption question: ***Without a history how might a new business gather the information needed to project income and expenses?*** The owner might obtain information from owners of similar businesses, trade organizations and magazines, lenders, governmental and non-profit organizations devoted to helping small businesses, and so on. To further discuss this projected quarterly income statement, ask these guiding questions.

Guiding Questions

Identify During what month were office supplies the highest? During what month were utilities the lowest?	Office supplies were the highest during month 2. Utilities were the lowest during month 1.
Anlayze Which are greater, variable or fixed expenses? By how much?	The fixed expenses are greater by $13,802 ($20,640 − $6,838 = $13,802).

Mini Projects

Enrichment

Examining a Company's Quarterly Income Statement Instruct students to locate a public company's quarterly income statement. Encourage them to choose a company with which they are familiar. Have them examine the statement. Tell them not to worry if they do not understand every component of the statement, but they should be able to determine the basics, such as net sales, cost of goods sold, operating expenses, net income, and so on. Then have students write a paragraph summarizing the income statement. In their summaries, they should state whether the company showed a profit or a loss. Students should write a one-paragraph summary of a quarterly income statement for a company of their choosing. In their summaries, they should list some of the numbers given in the statement, such as gross profit, operating expenses, and net income from operations. Students should also specify whether the company showed a profit or a loss.

Asking for a Start-Up Loan Organize students into pairs. Tell the pairs that they are going to act out a scenario in which a young entrepreneur approaches a lender for a loan to start a new business. To start with, each pair should come up with an idea for the business and create the financial documents, such as a start-up costs worksheet and a projected quarterly income statement, which the lender will want to see. In addition, they should come up with a list of questions that the lender is likely to ask the potential business owner. Sample questions might include: How will the money you want to borrow make your business profitable? How will the business repay the loan? What experience do you have in this area of business? Each pair should then act out the meeting between the entrepreneur and the lender. Students should present a skit in which a young entrepreneur asks a lender for money to start a new business. The entrepreneur should have the appropriate financial documents prepared for the lender's examination. The lender should ask questions concerning the financial aspects of the business, and the entrepreneur should respond appropriately.

VIRTUAL BUSINESS

FINANCING

Introduce students to the concept of financing using Knowledge Matters' Virtual Business Retailing visual simulation, *Financing*. In this simulation, students will learn about and evaluate different financing methods to finance their start-up business.

DIGITAL NATION

Keeping the Books Online

Did you know that you can use software without having it installed on your computer? With Web-based software, you visit a Web site, set up an account, and start using the software directly through your Web browser. If you have tried Yahoo! Mail, Hotmail, or Gmail, you have already used Web-based software. Commercial Web-based software is especially popular for accounting and financial tasks, such as tracking income and expenses, doing payroll, generating invoices, and preparing tax returns.

A Click Away

Web-based software has many plusses. Files are stored on secure servers, protecting them from being lost or stolen. Manufacturers also upgrade software automatically when new features are released. The biggest plus is that users can access their files through the Internet from anywhere.

Mathematics

Calculate Imagine you run a business and have 24 employees with e-mail accounts. Your business pays $56.99 a month for every five inboxes. How much would your yearly fixed expenses decrease if you were to switch to free Web-based e-mail?

NCTM Number and Operations Compute fluently and make reasonable estimates.

glencoe.com

Get a Digital Nation Activity.

Beginning Inventory
+ Net Purchases, or Production Costs
Subtotal
– Ending Inventory
Cost of Goods Sold

Most service businesses do not provide goods to their customers. Therefore, they do not have to determine the cost of goods sold. Their gross profit is the same as net sales. Other businesses that produce or purchase products to sell must calculate the cost of goods sold.

DETERMINING GROSS PROFIT

Gross profit or gross margin on sales is the difference between the net sales and the cost of goods sold. The formula for calculating gross profit is:

Net Sales
– Cost of Goods Sold
Gross Profit

Once you know the cost of goods sold, calculate your gross profit by subtracting the cost of goods sold from net sales.

DETERMINING BUSINESS EXPENSES

The next major part of the income statement is the operating expenses. Operating expenses are the costs of operating the business, including variable and fixed expenses.

CALCULATING VARIABLE EXPENSES

Variable expenses change from one month to the next and fluctuate depending upon the sales volume of the business. Variable expenses include advertising, office supplies, and utilities. Variable expenses are often calculated as a percentage of some baseline amount. Advertising expenses, for example, may average 5 percent of total sales.

CALCULATING FIXED EXPENSES

Fixed expenses are costs that remain the same for a period of time. These types of expenses stay fixed for months, regardless of sales volume. Depreciation, insurance, rent, salaries, and payroll taxes are examples of fixed expenses.

Depreciation is a complicated fixed expense. Depreciation represents the amount by which an asset's value has fallen because of age, wear, or deterioration in a given period of time. IRS laws and rules govern the time period over which assets can be depreciated. An accountant can also determine the asset depreciation schedule and amounts to use for listing assets on income tax returns.

Projecting other fixed expenses usually is easier because you simply add all of your fixed costs, such as rent or insurance.

CALCULATING PAYROLL EXPENSES

To calculate payroll expenses, you must first estimate the number of employees you need to operate your business. Then research typical salaries in your area for the work the employees will perform. You can get help with salary information by consulting your state employment security agency (SESA) office. You can also review the help-wanted ads online and in the newspaper for similar jobs. You can also use the minimum wage as a starting point and decide how much more to pay for more skilled workers. A skilled worker should have a higher salary than an unskilled worker.

Payroll records are important to your employees and to your company. They are also used to prepare income tax returns. Your banker, an accountant, or a computer software publisher can set up a system to calculate, record, and issue payroll checks.

Your payroll records may be part of a cash disbursements journal where you keep records of all cash payments. You may prefer to keep payroll records in a separate payroll journal. Use a separate record for each employee. Each record will show one employee's pay period, hours worked, earnings, deductions, and net pay.

The amount earned by an employee is that person's gross pay. Net pay is what the employee receives after deductions for taxes, insurance, and voluntary deductions. Nancy Baker earns $11 an hour and worked 40 hours during the week; therefore, her gross pay is $440 ($11 × 40 hours).

Nancy's deductions total $125.66, so you would calculate her net pay by subtracting the deductions from her gross pay:

$440 – $125.66 = $314.34 (net pay)

Tax tables are available for calculating the amount to be deducted from each employee's pay for local, state, and federal income tax. The percentage of gross pay to be deducted for FICA (Social Security and Medicare taxes) changes frequently. Get the latest information from your local Social Security office.

Example: Find the net pay for Rosarita Ramirez, who worked a total of 44 hours during a week at $13 per hour. She is paid time-and-a-half for overtime (hours beyond 40 hours in a week). Her deductions totaled $105.25 for the week.

STEP 1 **Calculate the gross pay.**
$520.00 ($13 × 40 hours)
+ 78.00 ($13 × 4 hours × 1.5)
$598.00 (gross pay)

STEP 2 **Subtract deductions.**
$598.00 (gross pay)
– 105.25 (total deductions)
$492.75 (net pay)

In estimating your total payroll expenses, you need to use current tax rates for local, state, and federal income taxes. Remember that, as the employer, you will also pay FICA and unemployment payroll taxes on your employees' earnings. You need to include those tax amounts in your total payroll expense estimate.

CALCULATING TOTAL EXPENSES

Once you have calculated all your operating (variable and fixed) expenses, you are ready to total your expenses. To calculate total expenses, add the variable expenses to the fixed expenses.

Total Variable Expenses
+ Total Fixed Expenses
Total Expenses

NET INCOME FROM OPERATIONS

After calculating your total expenses, the next step is to calculate net income from business operations. **Net income** is the amount left after the total expenses are subtracted from gross profit. The formula for calculating net income from operations is:

Gross Profit on Sales
– Total Expenses
Net Income from Operations

Suppose you own the "I Can Do That" Home Remodeling Company, which had gross profit on sales of $153,156 during the year. Your total operating expenses for the year were $88,991, so your net income from operations was:

$153,156 – $88,991 = $64,165

EXPLAIN

DIGITAL NATION

Mathematics Answer Yearly fixed expenses would decrease by $3,419.40. The business currently pays $284.95 ($56.99 × 5) a month or $3,419.40 (12 × $284.95) a year.

Guiding Questions

List examples of Web-based software.	Yahoo! Mail, Hotmail, Gmail
Analyze Why might a company use Web-based software?	online access from anywhere; files are stored on secure servers; software updates are automatic

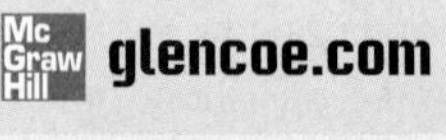

Worksheet Activity Send students to the Online Learning Center to get a Digital Nation worksheet activity.

Critical Thinking

Describe a situation in which a young electrician decides to start her own business. The bank is willing to give her a loan to finance the start-up costs but insists that she purchase life insurance. Ask: ***Why do you think the bank makes life insurance a requirement?*** The bank wants to make sure that the loan will be repaid if something happens to the electrician.

MINI CLIP

Reading: Connecting the Pieces
Go to the Online Learning Center to view a video clip in which a teacher helps students develop predictions and inferences.

ELABORATE

DETERMINING BUSINESS EXPENSES

Discuss that the income statement breaks operating expenses into variable (those that change from month to month) and fixed (those that do not change). To focus discussion on determining these expenses, ask these guiding questions.

Guiding Questions

Recall What is depreciation and what type of expense is it?	Depreciation is the amount by which an asset's value has fallen because of age, wear, or deterioration in a given period of time. It is a fixed expense.
Analyze The owner of a new landscaping business plans to hire 10 workers. What are some ways in which the owner might determine how much to pay these workers?	The owner might consult the state employment security agency office and review help wanted ads for similar jobs. Another method is to start with the minimum wage and, depending on each worker's skills, decide the additional value of that worker.
Infer Employers are required to pay FICA and unemployment payroll taxes on their employees' earnings. How does this requirement affect the income of a self-employed business owner?	Because business owners are self-employed, they must pay these taxes on their own income. This requirement reduces the amount of their income.

Mini Project

Differentiated Instruction

Logical Learners Ask students to create a spreadsheet with an income statement for a hypothetical business. Students should use spreadsheet software such as Microsoft Excel to create the spreadsheet. The spreadsheet should contain formulas that automatically calculate the needed results. Students should review the differences between variable expenses and fixed expenses before they begin. Students should use application software such as Microsoft Excel to create a spreadsheet that can produce an income statement for a hypothetical business. All the needed calculations should be performed by formulas built into the spreadsheet.

e MARKETING

Internet-Based Accounting

Internet-based accounting or e-accounting is virtual recordkeeping and backup of financial data. It is a form of Cloud Computing. E-accounting service providers have multiple servers, software, and backup capabilities. A general ledger is often the first step in setting up an e-accounting platform for a business where all transactions are recorded by transmitting the data to the off-site firm. Invoicing and bill paying can be handled along with financial reporting and analysis. Benefits of having financial records maintained off-site include cost, safety, and ease of operation. A business does not have to employ an IT person and does not have to invest in expensive computer equipment. It must simply pay the e-accounting firm for its services. The off-site firm has many technical experts to monitor Internet viruses and has many ways of backing up data so they are not lost. To input and retrieve data, employees log into a secure off-site account with their passwords.

Innovate and Create

Have students conduct research online banking. How are the services similar to e-accounting? Discuss why banks should consider entering the e-accounting market by targeting business customers. Online banking services include direct deposit for employee pay, ATMs, mobile alerts, electronic bill payments, and electronic fund transfers. Businesses already use these services. With online banking and mobile services, banks already have the technology to provide e-accounting services. To enter the Internet-based accounting market, a bank would have to create software and accounting platforms to match the same services as the e-accounting firms now offer. Most of today's financial transactions and government reporting are already handled electronically, so it would be an easy transition to offer additional services.

glencoe.com

eMarketing Worksheet Activity Send students to the Online Learning Center to download an eMarketing worksheet activity.

During the first year of operation, a business may have a net loss from operations. A net loss results when total expenses are larger than the gross profit on sales. The financial plan should address how the business intends to pay its debts in the short term.

CALCULATING OTHER INCOME

In the Net Income From Operations section, list money earned from sources other than sales. You may earn dividends on stocks or interest on accounts. **Interest** is the money paid for the use of money borrowed or invested. It is likely that you will use some of this money during the year. Therefore, you need to calculate interest only on the amount that is actually on deposit. Because of the time value of money, the money you have now is worth more than the same amount in the future. This is due to the interest it can earn. Unless the interest income that you expect to earn is **significant**, you may want to list this amount as zero in your business plan.

CALCULATING OTHER EXPENSES

The amount you borrow to start your business is called the **principal**. Interest is expressed as a percentage of the principal and is called the "rate of interest." For example, if you borrow $100 at 6 percent, the principal is $100 and the rate of interest is 6 percent. To find the amount of interest for one year, multiply the principal (p) times the rate of interest (r) times the length of time (t):

$$i = prt$$

$$(\$100 \times .06 \times 1 = \$6)$$

You would pay $6 in interest in the previous example.

The units in the rate of interest and time must agree. That is, if the rate of interest is expressed in years, then the time must be expressed in years as well. Both may be expressed in months. Check this before you do your math so that your answers will be correct. If the rate is given without reference to a time period, you can assume that it is for one year.

Suppose you are quoted a yearly rate and need to convert it to a monthly rate. There are 12 months in a year, so you would divide the yearly rate by 12 to get the monthly rate. When you are quoted a monthly rate and want to convert it to a yearly rate, multiply the monthly rate by 12.

Once you decide how much money you will need to borrow and how long it will take you to repay the loan, you can calculate your total annual (or monthly) interest. This amount is listed on the financial statement as Other Expenses (Interest).

NET PROFIT OR LOSS BEFORE TAXES

Net profit or net loss before taxes is calculated by adding other income to net income from operations, and then subtracting other expenses from the total.

Net Income from Operations
\+ Other Income
Subtotal
– Other Expenses
Net Profit (or Loss) Before Taxes

PRACTICE 3: COMPLETE AN INCOME STATEMENT

Using the income statement shown below, answer the following questions:

1. How much did Mountain Air Bikes pay for the bikes it sold?
2. How much was the gross profit for the year?
3. How much were total operating expenses?
4. Which operating expense was the most costly?
5. How much net income was earned during the year?

Mountain Air Bikes
Income Statement for the Year Ended December 31, 2—

Net Sales	$ 202,736
Cost of Goods Sold	$ 124,375
Gross Profit	$?
Operating Expenses	
Salaries	$ 28,022
Rent	$ 14,211
Utilities	$ 5,214
Advertising	$ 3,422
Total Operating Expenses	$?
Net Income From Operations	$?

NET PROFIT OR LOSS AFTER TAXES

Net profit (or loss) after taxes is the amount of money left over after federal, state, and local taxes are subtracted. You may be familiar with the more common term for this concept: the "bottom line." A traditional income statement shows all revenues and expenses over a specified time period with the result on the bottom line of the report. This amount represents the actual profit from operating the business for a certain period of time. The revenues are sometimes called the "top line" figures.

The projected income statement should be done on a monthly basis for new businesses. After the first year, projected income statements can be prepared on a quarterly basis.

The steps that follow are a summary of how to prepare a monthly projected income statement.

STEP 1 Estimate total sales.

STEP 2 Subtract sales discounts, returns, and allowances from total sales to calculate net sales.

STEP 3 List the estimated cost of goods sold.

STEP 4 Subtract the cost of goods sold from net sales to find gross profit on sales.

STEP 5 List each monthly operating expense, categorizing each as a variable or fixed expense.

STEP 6 Total the monthly operating expenses.

STEP 7 Subtract total operating expenses from gross profit on sales to find net income from operations. Put parentheses around any projected losses; for example, a projected loss of $1,000 would be identified as ($1,000).

STEP 8 Add other income such as interest on bank deposits and subtract other expenses, such as interest expense, from net income from operations. The result is net profit (or loss) before income taxes.

STEP 9 Estimate total taxes on the net income and subtract that amount from net profit. The result is net profit (or loss) after taxes.

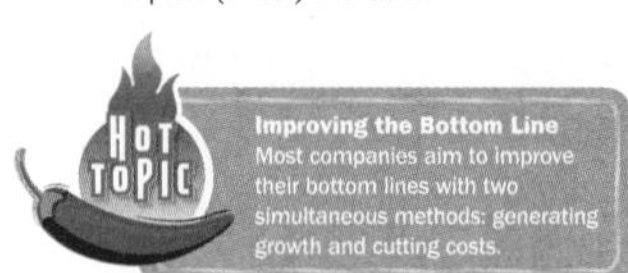
HOT TOPIC
Improving the Bottom Line
Most companies aim to improve their bottom lines with two simultaneous methods: generating growth and cutting costs.

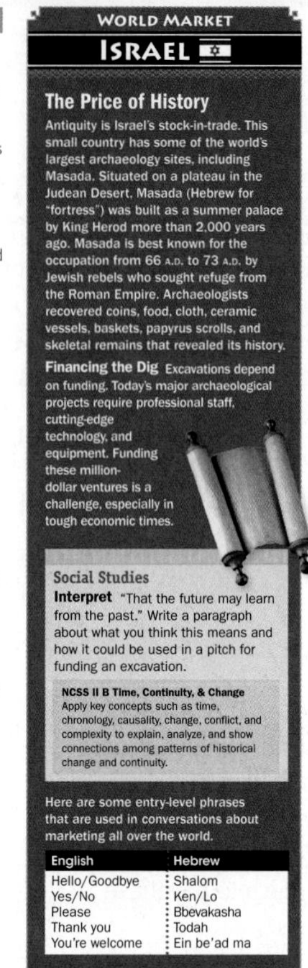
WORLD MARKET

ISRAEL

The Price of History

Antiquity is Israel's stock-in-trade. This small country has some of the world's largest archaeology sites, including Masada. Situated on a plateau in the Judean Desert, Masada (Hebrew for "fortress") was built as a summer palace by King Herod more than 2,000 years ago. Masada is best known for the occupation from 66 A.D. to 73 A.D. by Jewish rebels who sought refuge from the Roman Empire. Archaeologists recovered coins, food, cloth, ceramic vessels, baskets, papyrus scrolls, and skeletal remains that revealed its history.

Financing the Dig Excavations depend on funding. Today's major archaeological projects require professional staff, cutting-edge technology, and equipment. Funding these million-dollar ventures is a challenge, especially in tough economic times.

Social Studies

Interpret "That the future may learn from the past." Write a paragraph about what you think this means and how it could be used in a pitch for funding an excavation.

NCSS II B Time, Continuity, & Change Apply key concepts such as time, chronology, causality, change, conflict, and complexity to explain, analyze, and show connections among patterns of historical change and continuity.

Here are some entry-level phrases that are used in conversations about marketing all over the world.

English	Hebrew
Hello/Goodbye	Shalom
Yes/No	Ken/Lo
Please	Bbevakasha
Thank you	Todah
You're welcome	Ein be'ad ma

EXPLAIN

Graphic Organizer

Display this diagram. Discuss the different types of income and expenses that should be listed under Determining Net Income from Operations. Ask students to give examples and write them on the diagram.

Determining Net Income from Operations

- **Calculate Other Income**
  Examples:
  Dividends on stocks
  Interest on money on deposit
- **Calculate Other Expenses**
  Example:
  Interest on loans

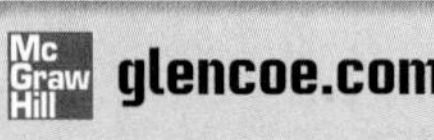

glencoe.com iWB

Graphic Organizer Send students to the Online Learning Center to print this graphic organizer.

CALCULATING OTHER EXPENSES

To focus discussion on calculating the other expenses that are used when determining net income from operations, ask students these guiding questions.

Guiding Questions

Recall You borrow $350 from the bank at 8 percent interest. What is the $350 called? What is the 8 percent called?	The $350 is the principal; the 8 percent is the rate of interest.
Apply Your friend has a credit card that charges a monthly interest rate of 1.5 percent. He says he plans to only make minimum payments on his balance of $600. After all, he says, even if the balance remains at $600, he will only pay $9 in interest for the entire year. How would you respond?	Remind him that 1.5 is the *monthly* rate. The interest rate is actually 18 percent (1.5 × 12) per year. This means that on a $600 balance, he would be paying $108 in interest.

ELABORATE

Reinforce Vocabulary

Principal—Homonyms Display the word *principal* and explain that homonyms are words that sound alike but have different meanings. Remind students that in business, the word *principal* refers to the amount of a loan. Ask: ***Can you think of a homonym for the word principal?*** principle Write *principle* next to *principal*. Then ask: ***What does principle mean?*** a fundamental law, doctrine, or assumption

Answers to Practice 3

1. Mountain Air Bikes paid $124,375 for the bikes sold.
2. Gross profit was $78,361 ($202,736 – $124,375 = $78, 361).
3. Total operating expenses were $50,869 ($28,022 + $14,211 + $5,214 + $3,422 = $50,869).
4. Salaries were the most costly operating expense.
5. Net income is $27,492 ($78, 361 – $50,869 = $27,492).

NET PROFIT OR LOSS AFTER TAXES

Remind students that net profit can be determined only after all taxes are subtracted. Ask these questions to discuss this topic with students.

Guiding Questions

Recall How do you indicate a loss on an income statement?	You place the number in parentheses.
Draw Conclusions Why is net profit after taxes also referred to as the "bottom line"?	because this number comes at the end, or bottom, of the income statement
Infer Why do you think income statements should be completed monthly for new businesses but quarterly after the first year?	When a business is first getting started, it is important to be able to quickly deal with any financial difficulties..

Improving the Bottom Line Read the text to the students: ***Most companies aim to improve their bottom lines with two simultaneous methods: generating growth and cutting costs.*** Ask: ***What are some ways a company might generate growth?*** Then ask: ***What are some ways it might cut costs?***

Mini Projects

Differentiated Instruction

Cooperative Learners Have students work independently to create a matching quiz. The quiz should have the names of 8 to 10 computations in the left column. The right column should contain the same number of formulas, in mixed order. Students should take the quiz by drawing a line from the name of each computation to its formula. For example, students would draw a line from "Total Expenses" to the formula "Total Variable Expenses + Total Fixed Expenses." When students are finished creating their quizzes, have them trade with a classmate and take one another's quizzes. Each student should create a matching quiz that tests the quiz-takers knowledge of the formulas presented so far in this chapter. When finished, students should go over the results and review any items they missed.

Verbal/Linguistic Learners Remind students that *acronym* means "a word formed from the beginning letters of a name or term." An example is NOPAT, which stands for "net operating profit after taxes." Explain that the business world is filled with acronyms and abbreviations. Have student use the Internet and other appropriate resources to create a list of acronyms and abbreviations related to business finances. Students' lists should contain business-related acronyms and abbreviations, along with each one's meaning.

English Language Learners Have students create a two-column chart. In the first column, have them list the financial documents discussed in this chapter. In the second column, have them use their own words to explain the reasons for including that document as part of the financial section of a business plan. Students' two-column charts should list the required financial documents in the left column, and the reason each document is required in a business plan in the right column. For example, a start-up costs worksheet is required so that all costs involved in developing the new business can be accounted for and estimated.

World Market
Social Studies

Students should write a paragraph on what they think "That the future may learn from the past" means and how the statement could be used to generate funds for an archaeological excavation. Students' paragraphs might explain that understanding how people lived, the forms of government they implemented, and how their marketplaces functioned can help us understand how we might implement structures that have historically been useful and avoid those that have not.

THE BALANCE SHEET

A **balance sheet** is a summary of a business's assets, liabilities, and owner's equity.

ASSETS

Assets are anything of monetary value that you own. They are classified as current or fixed.

- Current assets are cash and anything of value that can be converted into cash in a year. Examples of current assets are cash in the bank, accounts receivable (money owed to you by your customers), and inventory.
- Fixed assets are used over a period of years to operate your business. Fixed assets cannot normally be changed into cash within a year. Examples of fixed assets include land, buildings, equipment, furniture, and fixtures. The assets of the business are needed to operate the business. When borrowing money to start a business, assets are also often used as collateral for the loan.

LIABILITIES

Liabilities are listed in another section of the balance sheet. Liabilities are the amounts that the business owes—for example, money owed for merchandise purchased. Liabilities are classified as either current or long-term.

- Current liabilities are the debts the business must pay during the upcoming business year. Examples of current liabilities are accounts payable (money owed to suppliers), notes payable (money owed to a bank), taxes payable, and money owed to employees for salaries.
- Long-term liabilities are debts that are due after 12 months. Some examples are mortgages and long-term loans.

EQUITY

Equity, or net worth, is the third section of the balance sheet. When you start a new business, you will likely invest personal savings in the business. The amount of the savings is your equity, or ownership interest, in the business. The money invested will be used to buy assets and to operate the business.

The assets owned by the business and the debts the business owes affect your equity. Remember, net worth is the difference between the assets of a business and its liabilities: Assets − Liabilities = Net Worth (Equity).

ANALYSIS OF FINANCIAL STATEMENTS

Lenders use **ratio** analysis to determine how a business is performing compared to other businesses in the industry. Ratios indicate whether a business has too much debt, is carrying too much inventory, or is not making enough gross profit. Information on the balance sheet and the income statement may be used to calculate these ratios. Lenders use ratio analysis to determine whether a business would be a good investment risk and whether its revenues could repay a loan.

Figures on the balance sheet show you the amount of your ownership interest (owner's or stockholders' equity) and the financial strength of a business on a given date. The data on the income statement shows how well the business is operating over a period of time. You may need information from both statements to calculate ratios.

A number of sources and directories exist to help you determine the common business ratios for your type of business. These include *Financial Studies of Small Business* published by the Financial Research Associates, *Industry Norms and Key Business Ratios* by Dun & Bradstreet, and *Almanac of Business and Industrial Financial Ratios* by Leo Troy.

LIQUIDITY RATIOS

Liquidity ratios analyze the ability of a firm to meet its current debts. One liquidity ratio is *current ratio*. Its formula is: current assets divided by current liabilities. The *acid test ratio*, or quick ratio, determines if a company can meet its short-term cash needs. Its formula is: cash plus marketable securities plus accounts receivables divided by current liabilities. In both cases, it is better to have high ratios of assets to liabilities.

ACTIVITY RATIOS

Activity ratios determine how quickly assets can be turned into cash. One such ratio is the *accounts receivable turnover*. This indicates the number of days it takes to collect the money owed by customers. To calculate this ratio, divide net sales by average trade receivables. In this case, it is better to have a lower ratio.

The *stock turnover ratio* measures how many days it takes to turn over (sell) the inventory. Too much inventory ties up cash that can be used to grow the business. The basic formula for this ratio is: cost of goods sold divided by average inventory.

PROFITABILITY RATIOS

Profitability ratios measure how well the company has operated during the past year. One ratio is *profit margin on sales*, which shows the rate of profit in percentages. This information is found on the income statement. Its formula is: net income divided by net sales. Another profitability ratio is the *rate of return on assets*, which shows how well you are doing when compared to other companies. The formula for this ratio is: net income divided by average total assets.

Reading Check

Explain Why do lenders use ratio analysis?

PRACTICE 4: COMPLETE A BALANCE SHEET

Using the balance sheet shown below, answer the following questions:

1. How much are the total assets for Mountain Air Bikes?
2. How much are the total liabilities?
3. What is Mountain Air's net worth?

Mountain Air Bikes
Balance Sheet December 31, 2---

Current Assets	
Cash	$ 10,000
Accounts Receivable	15,000
Inventory	68,000
Fixed Assets	
Building	120,000
Equipment	80,000
Vehicles	30,000
Total Assets	$?
Current Liabilities	
Notes Payable	$ 3,000
Accounts Payable	12,000
Salaries Payable	5,000
Taxes Payable	1,000
Long-Term Liabilities	
Notes Payable	90,000
Total Liabilities	$?
Net Worth	$?

CASH FLOW STATEMENT

A **cash flow statement** is a monthly plan that tracks when cash is expected to come into the business and when cash is expected to be paid out. A cash flow statement helps you determine whether you will have enough money to pay your bills on time. Businesses need cash to pay bills and their employees, and to use for unexpected expenses. The cash flow statement itemizes how much cash you started with, what your projected cash expenditures are, and how and when you plan to receive cash. It also shows when you will need to find additional funds and when you will have cash remaining. Most lenders will require you to estimate the business's cash flow for the first year of operation.

CASH PAYMENTS

When operating a business, one of your largest payments of cash will be for merchandise. You will most likely have to pay for part of the merchandise in cash and part of it on credit.

When estimating sales for the income statement, you include both cash and credit sales. In contrast, the cash flow statement shows only the amount you expect to receive in cash (for cash sales and payments for credit sales) during the month.

EXPLAIN

Graphic Organizer

Display this diagram. Use it to trace through the steps in creating a balance sheet.

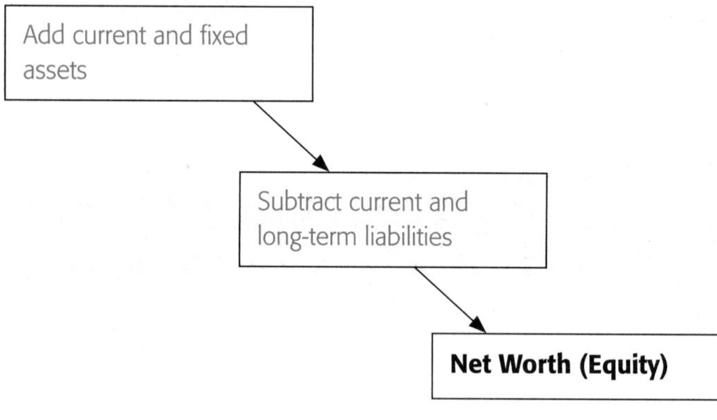

 **glencoe.com**  iWB

Graphic Organizer Send students to the Online Learning Center to print this graphic organizer.

THE BALANCE SHEET

Explain that the purpose of the balance sheet is to compare, or "balance," a business's assets with its liabilities. To focus discussion on the balance sheet, ask these guiding questions.

Guiding Questions

Explain Why is equity listed in the third section of a balance sheet, below assets and liabilities?	because the amount of equity, or net worth, is obtained by subtracting liabilities from assets
Contrast How is a current asset different from a fixed asset? Provide examples of each type of asset.	Current assets include cash and anything that can be converted into cash in a year. Example: accounts receivable. Fixed assets are items needed to operate a business and cannot quickly be converted into cash. Examples: land, buildings, equipment

ELABORATE

Critical Thinking

Ask students: ***Why are the accounts receivable turnover ratio and the stock turnover ratio both referred to as "activity ratios"?*** They both indicate how much activity there is in a business—the first one indicates activity in cash flow; the second indicates activity in inventory.

Graphic Organizer

Display this diagram. Have students identify the ratios for each situation on the left, and then write them in on the right.

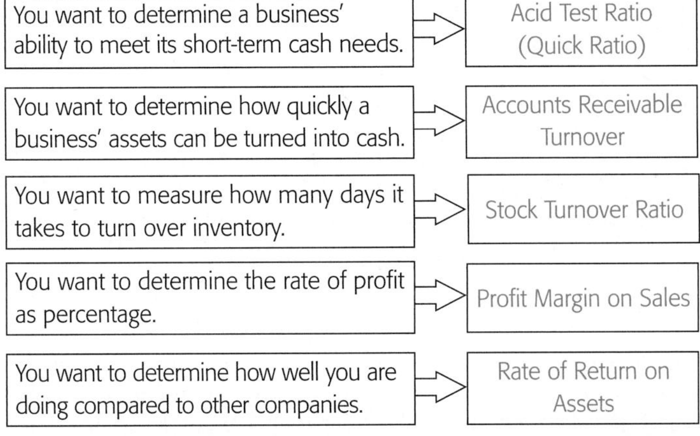
You want to determine a business' ability to meet its short-term cash needs.
Acid Test Ratio (Quick Ratio)
You want to determine how quickly a business' assets can be turned into cash.
Accounts Receivable Turnover
You want to measure how many days it takes to turn over inventory.
Stock Turnover Ratio
You want to determine the rate of profit as percentage.
Profit Margin on Sales
You want to determine how well you are doing compared to other companies.
Rate of Return on Assets

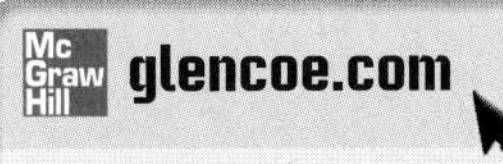
glencoe.com

iWB

Graphic Organizer Send students to the Online Learning Center to print this graphic organizer.

Mini Project

Differentiated Instruction

Logical Learners Have pairs of students create an outline of the information under "The Balance Sheet" heading. Students should first determine the major points and then fill in related minor details. The outline should be logically organized and thorough. The first part might look similar to the following:

I. Balance Sheet: Summary of assets, liabilities, and equity
II. Assets
- A. Current assets
  1. Anything that can be converted into cash in a year
  2. Example: accounts receivable
- B. Fixed assets
  1. Used long-term in operation of a business
  2. Cannot normally be quickly changed to cash
  3. Example: buildings, fixtures

Reading Check Answer

Read the question: ***Why do lenders use ratio analysis?*** The lender can determine if the business has too much debt or too much inventory, or is not making enough gross profit compared to other businesses in the industry.

Answers to Practice 4

Mountain Air Bikes
Balance Sheet December 31, 20–

Current Assets	
Cash	$ 10,000
Accounts Receivable	15,000
Inventory	68,000
Fixed Assets	
Building	120,000
Equipment	80,000
Vehicles	30,000
Total Assets	$323,000
Current Liabilities	
Notes Payable	$ 3,000
Accounts Payable	12,000
Salaries Payable	5,000
Taxes Payable	1,000
Long-Term Liabilities	
Notes Payable	90,000
Total Liabilities	$111,000
Net Worth	$212,000

1. Total assets are $323,000. ($10,000 + $15,000 + $68,000 + $120,000 + $80,000 + $30,000)
2. Total liabilities are $111,000. ($3,000 + $12,000 + $5,000 + $1,000 + $90,000)
3. Net worth is $212,000. ($323,000 – $111,000)

CASH FLOW STATEMENT

Ask these guiding questions to focus the discussion about cash flow statements.

Guiding Questions

Recall How long of a period does a cash flow statement cover?	one month
Analyze What are the basic components of a cash flow statement?	(1) amount you start with; (2) cash you expect to receive; (3) cash you expect to pay out; (4) projected amount left at the end of month

You may receive payment for most of your credit sales 30 days after the sales. You will also need to calculate your monthly costs for operating the business.

PREPARING A CASH FLOW STATEMENT

Use the following steps to prepare a cash flow statement:

STEP 1 Add the total cash on hand (in bank accounts) and money received from any loans to find your total start-up money.

STEP 2 Subtract the start-up costs to determine the amount of cash left for operation.

STEP 3 Enter the estimated cash you expect to receive from cash sales and credit sales for each month during the first year. Enter income amounts from business investments or additional loans.

STEP 4 Add all sources of cash receipts to find the total cash income for the month.

STEP 5 List the cost of goods you will buy for your inventory. Separate purchases for which you will pay cash and purchases you will make on credit, which you will pay for the next month.

For example, on the cash flow statement, the payment for goods bought on credit in Month 1 were purchased prior to the opening of the business. Add the cash and credit purchases to find the total cost of inventory purchases.

STEP 6 List the expenses you expect to pay during the month. These amounts are the same as those listed on the income statement, except for the depreciation expense.

Depreciation is a means of spreading the cost of an asset over a period of years. The amount of depreciation is not an actual payment made by the business, so it is not listed on the cash flow statement.

STEP 7 Total all expenses for the month.

STEP 8 List amounts that will be paid out for capital expenditures. A capital expenditure is money paid for an asset used to operate the business. The purchase of a delivery truck would be a capital expenditure.

STEP 9 List any other payments that will be made, such as repayment of the principal and interest for the loan.

STEP 10 Add all the cash expenditures (cost of inventory purchased, expenses, capital expenditures, and other payments).

Subtract the total cash payments from the total cash received during the month to determine net cash flow.

The amount of any cash payments that are higher than cash receipts should be placed in parentheses to show a loss.

STEP 11 Add the beginning cash balance from the start-up column to the net cash flow for the month.

The result is the cash surplus for the month. When the costs of operating the business are higher than income added to the beginning of the cash balance, the business will have a deficit instead of a surplus.

In that case, the business will need additional cash for its operations. This amount is listed on the Cash Needs line.

The income statement does not take into account how long it may take a business to collect the cash from sales made on credit.

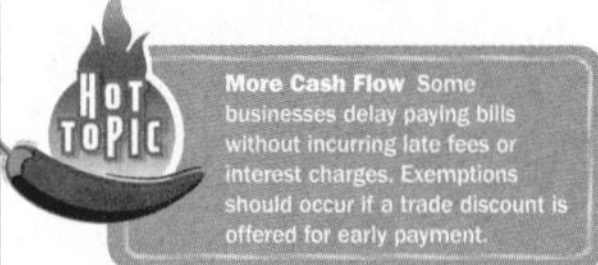

More Cash Flow Some businesses delay paying bills without incurring late fees or interest charges. Exemptions should occur if a trade discount is offered for early payment.

Reading Check

Recall What is the purpose of a cash flow statement?

LOANS

What can you do if your cash flow statement indicates you will need additional money during the year? You should be able to borrow money if your business has potential and your balance sheet shows enough assets to serve as collateral.

A loan can help you keep the business going during the start-up period and during slow sales months. When your cash flow projections indicate that you need to borrow money to meet monthly expenses, you will want to include monthly payments on the loan as a part of your cash needs for the rest of the year.

PRACTICE 5: INTERPRET A CASH FLOW STATEMENT

1. You have total cash of $23,000 to start your business and start-up costs of $12,000. What amount of cash is available for operating the business?
2. Suppose cash income for the first three months is $100, $750, and $980. Total expenses for these same months are $4,800, $3,400, and $2,700. What is the cash flow for each month?
3. What is the cumulative amount of cash available at the end of each month?

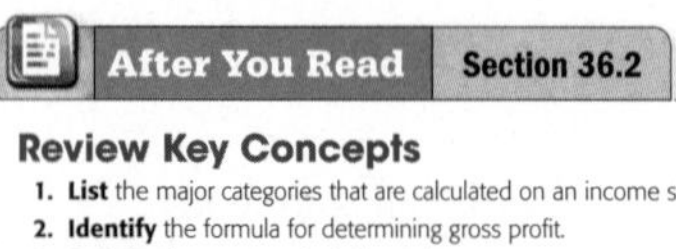

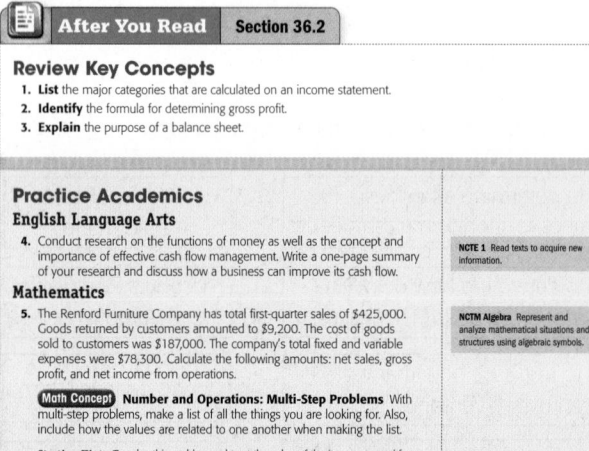

After You Read Section 36.2

Review Key Concepts

1. **List** the major categories that are calculated on an income statement.
2. **Identify** the formula for determining gross profit.
3. **Explain** the purpose of a balance sheet.

Practice Academics

English Language Arts

4. Conduct research on the functions of money as well as the concept and importance of effective cash flow management. Write a one-page summary of your research and discuss how a business can improve its cash flow.

NCTE 1 Read texts to acquire new information.

Mathematics

5. The Renford Furniture Company has total first-quarter sales of $425,000. Goods returned by customers amounted to $9,200. The cost of goods sold to customers was $187,000. The company's total fixed and variable expenses were $78,300. Calculate the following amounts: net sales, gross profit, and net income from operations.

NCTM Algebra Represent and analyze mathematical situations and structures using algebraic symbols.

Math Concept **Number and Operations: Multi-Step Problems** With multi-step problems, make a list of all the things you are looking for. Also, include how the values are related to one another when making the list.

Starting Hints To solve this problem, subtract the value of the items returned from the total sales to calculate the net sales. Subtract the cost of goods sold and goods returned from the net sales to determine the gross profits. Subtract the value of fixed costs and variable expenses from the gross profit to calculate the net income from operations.

For help, go to the **Math Skills Handbook** located at the back of this book.

glencoe.com

Check your answers.

ELABORATE

PREPARING A CASH FLOW STATEMENT

To focus discussion on preparing a cash flow statement, ask these guiding questions.

Guiding Questions

Recall What is a capital expenditure?	money paid for an asset used to operate a business
Analyze When you list the cost of goods you plan to buy this month, why should you separate cash purchases from purchases made on credit?	You only enter those purchases that will be paid for this month—credit purchases will not be paid for until next month.
Summarize Under what circumstances will a deficit occur?	A deficit occurs if the total cash received is less than the total cash paid.

Critical Thinking

Describe to students the following scenario. Your friend Tom has a lawn care business. He complains about his cash flow problems—it seems that he does not receive payment until about 60 days after he performs the work. In the meantime, he is short on cash to pay his monthly expenses. You look at his books and discover he sends out bills about every 45 days, usually about 30 days after the yard work is completed. Ask students: ***What would you suggest to Tom to improve his cash flow situation?*** He should send out bills more quickly after he completes the work. Students might suggest he try to bill clients within a week of performing the work.

Knowledge Matters

VIRTUAL BUSINESS

FINANCIAL STATEMENTS

Introduce the concept of financial statements to students using Knowledge Matters' Virtual Business Retailing visual simulation, *Financial Statements*. In this simulation, students will learn that business owners must have accurate and timely information about the financial status of their business to make the best decisions.

EVALUATE

More Cash Flow Tell students that the ability of a business owner or manager to negotiate terms with suppliers and manufacturers can save the business money in many ways. For example, it can allow the business to keep a larger inventory on hand, thereby drawing more potential customers.

Reading Check Answer

Ask the question: What is the purpose of a cash flow statement? It helps you determine whether you will have enough money to pay your bills on time.

LOANS

Ask these guiding questions to focus discussion on short-term loans.

Guiding Questions

Recall If you need to borrow money for your business's start-up period, what will a lender consider in deciding whether to give you a loan?	the business's potential and whether the balance sheet shows enough assets to serve as collateral
Apply You have just completed a cash flow statement for next month and discover that your new business will be $1,200 short of covering its expenses. What should you do?	You should immediately look for ways of coming up with the $1,200, for example, by borrowing the money from a lender.

Answers to Practice 5

1. The amount of cash available for business operations is $11,000. ($23,000 – $12,000)
2. The cash flow is as follows: month 1: –$4,700 ($100 – $4,800); month 2: –$2,650 ($750 – $3,400); month 3: –$1,720 ($980 – $2,700).
3. The cumulative cash available at the end of each month is as follows: month 1: $6,300 ($11,000 – $4,700); month 2: $3,650 ($6,300 – $2,650); month 3: $1,930 ($3,650 – $1,720).

After You Read — Section 36.2

Review Key Concepts

1. The major categories calculated on an income statement are total sales, net sales, cost of goods sold, gross profit, business expenses (operating expenses and fixed expenses), net income from operations, net profit or loss before taxes, net profit or loss after taxes.
2. The formula for determining gross profit is: Gross Profit = Net Sales – Cost of Goods Sold.
3. The purpose of a balance sheet is to provide a summary of a business's assets, liabilities, and owner's equity.

Practice Academics

English Language Arts

4. Students should write a one-page summary explaining the functions of money and the concept and importance of effective cash flow management. The report also should discuss how a business can improve its cash flow. Cash flow statements are vital to businesses because they help in determining when cash is expected to come in and when it will need to be paid out. This allows the business to determine if there will be enough cash to pay bills and employees, and also to cover any unexpected expenses that may occur. By creating a cash flow statement, you can determine if it might be necessary to locate funds elsewhere, for example by obtaining a short-term bank loan, before the situation becomes a crisis. Ways of improving cash flow are to invoice as soon as the work is done, to offer discounts for quick payment, to keep close track of any accounts that are overdue and attempt to collect them as quickly as possible, and to not pay your bills until they are actually due.

Mathematics

5. Net sales = $415,800 ($425,000 – $9,200). Gross profit = $228,800 ($415,800 – $187,000). Net income from operations = $150,500 ($228,800 – $78,300).

glencoe.com

Send students to the Online Learning Center to check their answers.

Chapter 36 Visual Summary

Financing the Business

Personal financial statements, start-up costs estimates, income statements, balance sheets, and cash flow statements are essential financial documents that are used in running a business.

Liquidity ratios, activity ratios, and profitability ratios tell lenders about a business's debt, inventory, and profit.

Review and Activities

Written Summary

- Five important financial documents are the personal financial statement, the start-up cost estimate, the income statement, the balance sheet, and the cash flow statement.
- The personal financial statement is a summary of your current personal financial condition.
- Start-up costs are a projection of how much initial money you will need for your first and continuing years of operation.
- You also need to estimate your personal living expenses.
- The next step is to estimate the money you expect to earn and to spend operating your business.
- The income statement is the financial document used to calculate a business's revenue, costs, and expenses.
- A balance sheet is a summary of a business's assets, liabilities, and owner's equity.
- A cash flow statement is a monthly plan that indicates when you anticipate cash coming into the business and when you expect to pay out cash.
- A cash flow statement shows whether you will have enough money to pay your bills.

Review Content Vocabulary and Academic Vocabulary

1. Arrange the vocabulary terms below into groups of related words. Explain why you put the words together.

Content Vocabulary
- personal financial statement (p. 843)
- asset (p. 843)
- liability (p. 843)
- net worth (p. 844)
- start-up costs (p. 845)
- income statement (p. 851)
- gross sales (p. 852)
- net sales (p. 852)
- net income (p. 855)
- interest (p. 856)
- principal (p. 856)
- balance sheet (p. 858)
- cash flow statement (p. 859)

Academic Vocabulary
- assessing (p. 845)
- purpose (p. 849)
- significant (p. 856)
- ratio (p. 858)

Assess for Understanding

2. **Discuss** What is the purpose of preparing financial documents?
3. **Explain** What is a personal financial statement?
4. **Determine** How do you determine start-up costs for a business?
5. **Estimate** How do you estimate business income and expenses?
6. **Develop** How do you create an income statement?
7. **Create** How do you create a balance sheet?
8. **Define** What is the definition of the term *net income*?
9. **Analyze** Your friend is starting a new business and believes that a cash flow statement is the same as an income statement. How do you analyze the difference and explain a cash flow statement?

EVALUATE

Visual Summary

Express Creativity Ask students to create a visual summary that illustrates a concept in the chapter. Encourage students to use different formats for their visual summaries, such as tables with callouts, diagrams, or illustrated posters. Visual summaries will vary depending on the concept depicted and the visual manner in which it is depicted. Questions to ask when assessing a visual summary include:

- Is the summary clear, economical, and simple?
- Are any important steps or concepts left out?
- Are steps or concepts arranged in the same order as the original?
- Does the summary reveal a pattern that connects the details?
- Does the summary locate and highlight the most important information

Review Content Vocabulary and Academic Vocabulary

1. Students should arrange the vocabulary terms into groups of related words. Possible groups:

   Personal financial statement—asset, liability, net worth, start-up costs, assessing.

   Income statement—gross sales, net sales, net income, interest, significant, principal.

   Other financial statements—balance sheet, ratio, cash flow statement.

EVALUATE

Assess for Understanding

2. The financial documents related to a business plan are necessary to determine the amount of money needed to operate the business as well as the amount that needs to be borrowed, if any. These documents can show whether a particular business will be viable. Financial documents allow business owners to get an overall picture of how well a business is doing, where money is coming from, how it is being spent, the types of assets, and so on.

3. A personal financial statement is a summary of your current personal financial condition and gives a snapshot of your net worth at a specific point in time by listing assets and liabilities.

4. You determine start-up costs by projecting how much money a new business requires for its first year of operation. The goal should be to have the business reach the break-even point by the end of the year. Factors to consider when calculating start-up costs include the nature and size of the business, the amount and kind of inventory needed, the estimated time between starting the business and earning income, operating expenses, start-up expenses, one-time costs, and continuing costs.

5. To calculate business income, you need to estimate total sales. You can then compare this estimate with projected industry figures for your business's size and location. You then must subtract estimated amounts for customer returns and allowances and subtract the cost of goods sold. Expenses that must be estimated include variable expenses and fixed expenses, including payroll expenses. Variable expenses are often calculated as a specific percentage of some baseline amount. In order to calculate payroll expenses, you must estimate the number of employees along with their salaries or hourly wages.

6. You calculate total sales and then subtract returns and allowances to obtain net sales. You then subtract cost of goods sold to get gross profit and subtract operating expenses from that to obtain net income from operations. You then subtract other expenses, such as interest on borrowed money, to obtain net profit (loss) before taxes. Lastly, you subtract taxes to get net profit (loss) after taxes.

7. When creating a balance sheet, you add up all current and fixed assets; such as cash, buildings, and office equipment; and then subtract liabilities, such as loans and accounts payable. The result gives the business's net worth.

8. Net income is the amount left after the total expenses are subtracted from gross profit.

9. An income statement summarizes income and expenses during a specific time period, such as a quarter. A cash flow statement is a monthly plan that keeps track of when cash is expected to come in and when expenses will need to be paid, and helps in determining whether there is enough money to pay bills when they are due.

21st Century Skills

Problem-Solving Skills

10. **Building a Business** Start-up costs are an important consideration when starting a new business. A close friend is starting a new landscaping business around an inland lake used by summer vacationers. He believes that he will not need extra capital for personal living expenses, since the business will generate immediate revenue to cover all living and business expenses. What problems can you foresee and what advice would you give to your friend?

Financial Literacy Skills

11. **Monthly Living Costs** Assume that you share an apartment with a roommate, dividing all rent, utility, and food expenses equally. Personal expenses are paid separately. For the past month, you and your roommate had the following expenses: apartment rent \$650; utilities \$60; and food expenses \$170. Your own personal expenses totaled \$245. What are your total living expenses for the month?

e-Marketing Skills

12. **Franchising Opportunities** Imagine that you are an aspiring entrepreneur investigating franchise business opportunities. Find the Web site for the International Franchise Association and browse its pages. Write a one-page summary that describes one specific franchising opportunity you found, including the kind of franchise (goods or services business), its potential for growth, and capital requirements for potential franchise owners.
    - What franchise business opportunity did you investigate?
    - What additional resources are available on the Web site that would be useful to an aspiring entrepreneur?
    - What is the growth potential for the business?
    - What are the capital requirements for franchise owners?

Build Academic Skills

English Language Arts

13. **Education for Entrepreneurs** The level of education attained by U.S. entrepreneurs can make a difference when starting a business. Perform library or online research on levels of education possessed by entrepreneurs. Identify any relationships that may or may not exist between a person's level of schooling and willingness to start a new business. Summarize your findings in a one-page written report.

NCTE 1 Read texts to acquire new information.

English Language Arts

14. **Investigating Start-Up Costs** Conduct research on the start-up costs required for a specific type of business. Research people in business, suppliers, trade associations, Service Corps of Retired Executives (SCORE), the Small Business Administration, chambers of commerce, start-up guides, and business publications. Identify multiple resources and prepare a one-page report on the projected start-up costs for the selected business.

NCTE 3 Apply strategies to interpret texts.

Mathematics

15. **Planning Monthly Expenses** Suppose that you are renting an apartment and earn a yearly salary of \$43,200. Financial planning experts suggest that you spend no more than 30 percent of your monthly income on either rent or a mortgage. What is the most that you should spend on rent?

NCTM Number and Operations Compute fluently and make reasonable estimates.

Math Concept **Problem Solving: Budgeting Rent** Calculate 30 percent of your monthly income to determine the maximum amount of rent you should pay.

For help, go to the **Math Skills Handbook** located at the back of this book.

Standardized Test Practice

Directions Read the following questions. On a separate piece of paper, write the best possible answer for each one.

1. Which of the following is a summary of income and expenses during a specific period, such as a month, quarter or year?
   A. Balance Sheet
   B. Cash Flow Statement
   C. Income Statement
   D. Personal Financial Statement
2. Net income is the amount left after total expenses are subtracted from gross profit.
   T
   F
3. The money that is paid for the use of money borrowed or invested is known as _________.

Test-Taking Tip

If you have time at the end of a test, check your answers and solutions. Make sure you answered each part of every question and that your answers all seem reasonable.

DECA Connection Role Play

Certified Public Accountant, Owner Accounting Firm

Situation You are the owner of a new business. As a Certified Public Accountant, you have worked for a general accounting firm for the past three years. You used that time to gain experience and to save money to open your business. Your business specialty is preparing financial documents for small businesses. You perform complete bookkeeping functions for your clients, prepare selected financial statements, and offer advice and guidance about the preparation and uses of business financial statements.

This afternoon you are going to meet with the new owner (judge) of a lawn and garden supply store. The new owner (judge) has recently purchased the business from the longtime previous owner. The new owner (judge) worked at the business for two years before deciding to make the purchase. For the past three years, the business has made little profit. The new owner (judge) realizes that it is necessary to make changes in the business's operation. The new owner (judge) has hired you to prepare several financial statements relating to the business. You have prepared a cash flow statement, balance sheet, and an income statement.

Activity You are to explain to the new owner (judge) about the information contained in each statement. You are to also explain how to use that information as a tool to guide the business to greater profitability.

Evaluation You will be evaluated on how well you meet the following performance indicators:

1. Explain the role of finance in business.
2. Set financial goals.
3. Describe the nature of cash flow statements.
4. Explain the nature of balance sheets.
5. Describe the nature of income statements.

Download the Competitive Events Workbook for more Role-Play practice.

EVALUATE

21st Century Skills

Problem-Solving Skills

10. I would tell my friend that starting a small business is not like working as an employee for someone else. First of all, there will be start-up expenses. Even if my friend already has some equipment, he probably needs to advertise, equipment requires maintenance and repairs, and there will be other ongoing expenses, such as gasoline. In addition, there may be permit and licensing fees. People typically expect to have 30 days to pay their bills, so there will be some delay before he actually receives any money. It also may take some time for customers to start the service—people often want to make certain a business is stable and reliable before they switch to it. I would advise my friend to have at least three or four months' worth of living expenses available before starting the business.

Financial Literacy Skills

11. Total living expenses = \$685. ([\$650 + \$60 + \$170]/2 + 245)

e-Marketing Skills

12. Students should write a one-page summary that describes a specific franchise opportunity that they have investigated and includes information such as the type of franchise, its potential for growth, and the capital requirements for becoming a franchise owner. For example, the Maid Brigade is a service franchise that provides professional home cleaning. It provides exclusive territories of at least 10,000 qualified households, training with corporate experts, webinars, conferences, and so on. Start-up costs are around \$45,000, with an initial investment from about \$60,000 to \$143,000.

EVALUATE

Build Academic Skills

English Language Arts

13. Students should perform library or online research on levels of education possessed by entrepreneurs and identify any relationships that may or may not exist between a person's level of schooling and willingness to start a new business. Students' findings should be summarized in a one-page written report.

English Language Arts

14. Students should prepare a one-page report on the projected start-up costs for a specific business of their choice. In developing their reports, students should research people in the business, suppliers, trade associations, organizations such as Service Corps of Retired Executives (SCORE), the Small Business Administration, chambers of commerce, and any appropriate start-up guides and business publications.

Mathematics

15. The most that you should spend on rent is $1,080. ($43,200/12 × 0.30)

Standardized Test Practice

1. C (Income Statement)
2. T
3. interest

DECA Connection Role Play

Evaluations will be based on these performance indicators:

1. **Explain the role of finance in business.** Managing finances is vital in determining the amount of money a business needs to operate, how much profit it should be able to generate, and the amount of money that needs to be borrowed, if any. There are five important financial documents that should be included in a business plan to help in determining the business' financial needs: personal financial statement, start-up cost estimate, income statement, balance sheet, and cash flow statement.
2. **Set financial goals.** The student should be able to set appropriate financial goals, such as keeping personal expenses within a budgeted amount, increasing gross sales, etc.
3. **Describe the nature of cash flow statements.** A cash flow statement is a monthly plan that tracks when cash is expected to come into a business and when cash is expected to be paid out. A cash flow statement helps you determine whether you will have enough money to pay your bills on time.
4. **Explain the nature of balance sheets.** A balance sheet is a summary of a business' assets, liabilities, and owner's equity. The assets are anything of monetary value that the business owns and can be divided into current assets and fixed assets. Liabilities are the amounts that a business owes and are classified as either current or long-term. Equity is net worth. Therefore, Assets – Liabilities = Equity (Net Worth).
5. **Describe the nature of income statements.** An income statement is a summary of income and expenses during a specific period such as a month, a quarter, or a year. Parts of an income statement include: total and net sales, cost of goods sold, gross profit, expenses of operating the business, net income from operations, other income or expenses, net profit before income taxes, and net profit after income taxes.

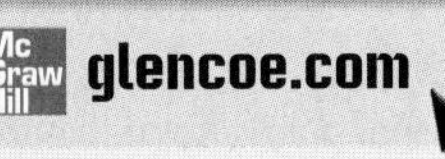

Role Plays For more DECA Role Plays, send students to the Online Learning Center to download the Competitive Events Workbook.

UNIT 11 **Marketing Internship Project**

A Business Plan for a New Online Business

Entrepreneurs continue to start up new online businesses. How can you make your dream to become an entrepreneur come true?

Scenario

Each year, more and more entrepreneurs are starting up online e-tail businesses instead of brick-and-mortar retail businesses. Bank loan departments receive applications from these entrepreneurs every week.

As an employee working in a bank's loan department, you have reviewed many loan requests for small businesses. Your supervisor asked you to prepare a sample business plan for an online business to use as a guideline for reviewing loans. In so doing, you realized you had a dream of your own—to be an entrepreneur. Growing up in a digital world, you find an online business appealing, especially for your first venture.

The Skills You'll Use

Academic Skills Reading, writing, social studies, researching, and analyzing

Basic Skills Speaking, listening, thinking, and interpersonal

Technology Skills Word processing, presentation, spreadsheet, telecommunication, and the Internet

NCTE 4 Use written language to communicate effectively.
NCTE 7 Conduct research and gather, evaluate, and synthesize data to communicate discoveries.

Your Objective

Your objective is to transform an idea into a business plan for a new online business.

STEP 1 Do Your Research

Conduct research to find out about online businesses. How are they the same as brick-and-mortar businesses and how are they different? For example, how are sales taxes and consumer privacy handled? Spend time researching your interests and current trends to come up with a viable online business idea. As you conduct your research, answer these questions:

- What type of online business has the potential for success?
- What costs are involved in starting an online business?
- What political, economic, socio-cultural, and technological factors (PEST) could affect your online business?
- What are the strengths, weaknesses, opportunities and threats of your proposed online business? (SWOT analysis)

Write a summary of your reseach.

STEP 2 Plan Your Project

Now that you have completed your research, you need to begin planning your project.

- Choose an online business and provide rationale for it.
- Conduct a PEST and a SWOT analysis.
- Decide on the organization and vendors needed.
- Develop a marketing plan for the business.
- Determine the capital needed.
- Prepare proposed financial statements.
- Write a business plan that includes all of this information .

STEP 3 Connect with Your Community

- Visit online businesses on the Internet to see how they are set up.
- Visit government Web sites to learn about government rules and regulations for online businesses.
- Interview trusted adults who might be potential customers of your proposed business to see if your product or service is something they would buy online.
- Take notes during your interviews and transcribe your notes after the interviews.

STEP 4 Share What You Learn

Assume your class is a committee in a bank that decides on small business loans.

- Present your business plan in an oral presentation. Be prepared to answer questions.
- Use presentation software to create a slide presentation to accompany your oral presentation. Include one slide for each topic in your business plan.

STEP 5 Evaluate Your Marketing and Academic Skills

Your project will be evaluated based on the following:

- The business selected as well as the rationale and organization for it
- Your proposed marketing plan
- The capital needed and proposed financial statements
- Organization and continuity of your presentation
- Mechanics—presentation and neatness
- Speaking and listening skills

MARKETING CORE FUNCTIONS

Marketing Information Management

Market Planning

Marketing Internship Project Checklist

Plan

✓ Conduct research on online businesses—products sold, government rules, and special considerations, such as payment options and consumer privacy issues.

✓ Conduct PEST and SWOT analyses.

Write

✓ Write a comprehensive business plan and marketing plan for your online business.

✓ Prepare proposed financial statements.

✓ Explain how the results of the PEST and SWOT analyses help you conceive the new product and develop the marketing plan.

Present

✓ Present research to support the rationale for your online business.

✓ Present your marketing plan for the proposed business.

✓ Present your financial plan for the proposed business.

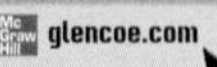
glencoe.com

Evaluate Download a rubric you can use to evaluate your final project.

my marketing portfolio

Internship Report Once you have completed your Marketing Internship Project and oral presentation, put your written report and a few printouts of key slides from your oral presentation in your Marketing Portfolio.

Create a Virtual Business With a virtual online business, you do not have to purchase supplies. Some virtual businesses exist as games on Facebook or on their own Web sites. Think of an appealing game in which players can buy virtual products. How can you inspire players to return your Web site? What business plan do you need? How do you develop marketing and financial plans? What competition will you have? What political, environmental, socio-cultural, and technological factors should you consider? What is your SWOT analysis? Prepare a written report and an oral presentation.

866 | Unit 11 · Entrepreneurship and Finance

Unit 11 · Entrepreneurship and Finance | 867

EVALUATE

Anticipation Activity

Project Objective Read the project objective aloud to students: ***Transform an idea into a business plan for a new online business.*** Then ask students to think about what they learned about entrepreneurship and business plans in Unit 11. Remind them of these key points:

- An entrepreneur creates, launches, organizes, and manages a new business, and takes the risk of ownership.
- A business plan is a proposal outlining a strategy to turn a business idea into a reality. It contains four parts: (1) Description and analysis, (2) organizational plan, (3) marketing plan, and (4) financial plan.

Ask students: ***What are the forms of business organization and which one is most common?*** They are sole proprietorship, partnership, corporation, and limited liability company (LLC). The sole proprietorship, a business owned and operated by one person, is the most common. Many Web-site businesses are organized as sole proprietorships.

Ask students: ***What is the purpose of a business plan?*** It presents a description with goals, determines resources, and identifies how a business will operate. Potential investors and lenders consider it before extending credit or capital.

Graphic Organizer

Display this table. Ask students to name online retailers, national or local, who may or may not also have bricks-and-mortar stores. Possible answers:

Online Businesses	Type of Business
Amazon.com	Books, music, etc.
Macys.com	Apparel, housewares
Staples.com	Office supplies
Petco.com	Pet supplies
Overstock.com	Various
Sephora.com	Makeup, skin care
Zappos.com	Shoes
Patagonia.com	Outdoor gear

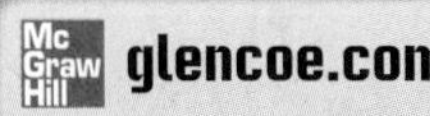
glencoe.com

Graphic Organizer Send students to the Online Learning Center to print this graphic organizer.

EVALUATE

STEP 1 Do Your Research

Tell students that there are many places to find information they can use to develop a business plan for a new online business. Students can use library and Internet resources, but they should also talk to people in the community. Encourage students to seek the opinions and ideas of trusted people they know. Other people can bring new perspectives and ideas about online businesses and costs as well as the political, socio-cultural, and technological factors that affect online retail businesses.

STEP 2 Plan Your Project

Students should create PEST and SWOT analyses before deciding on an organization type and marketing plan. Students should explain why they chose their particular online business and provide information about its target market. Students' explanation of their new idea for their business and its business plan should include information regarding financial statements and capital needed.

STEP 3 Connect with Your Community

Explain to students that connecting with members of the community is a great way to build relationships. Tell them that young people who are capable of building relationships with caring, responsible, and competent adults are more likely to achieve success. Encourage students to take part in opportunities for adults to serve as mentors, coaches, advocates, and advisors, both formally and informally.

STEP 4 Share What You Learn

Students should present their ideas in a written report and oral presentation with presentation software. They should have at least one slide in their presentation for each key topic in the written report. Encourage students to speak clearly, use appropriate grammar and vocabulary, and actively engage the audience by making and maintaining eye contact and using movement (facial expressions, posture, gestures) to focus attention and interest.

STEP 5 Evaluate Your Marketing and Academic Skills

Have students use the Marketing Internship Project Checklist to help them to plan, write, and present their reports. Exemplary written reports will include information that clearly supports a central thesis, a single, distinct focus, generally well-developed ideas, well-phrased sentences that flow smoothly and are varied in length and structure, consistently precise word choice, and few, if any, errors in grammar, spelling, and mechanics.

glencoe.com

Evaluation Rubric Send students to the Online Learning Center to get a rubric to evaluate their projects.

Culminating Activity

Explain to students that lenders and investors evaluate whether a new business is risky while reviewing a business plan and before providing funds to entrepreneurs. Students should consider and research the risk factors for the online business they have chosen. Ask students: ***What would a lender or investor want to know regarding a new venture?*** A lender or investor would want to know how the money will boost the business's profits. Also, how and when will the owner repay the business loan? Does the entrepreneur know anything about the new business or have training or experience in the field? Also, how successful are similar businesses?

my marketing portfolio

Internship Report Have students put their written reports and printouts of key slides from their oral presentations in their marketing portfolio.

Create a Virtual Business Direct students to select a game as a virtual business, and then create a business plan for it. Students' completed business plans should include all of the elements and answer all of the questions included in the Marketing Internship Project on this page. This additional activity can build relevance for students who are motivated to learn about other specific businesses and industries. Relevance shifts the focus to what motivates individual students to learn.

UNIT 12 Career Development

PLANNING GUIDE AND RESOURCES

	Print	Digital
Unit 12 Career Development		Unit 12 Fast Files: Marketing Internship Project Activity Connect Online Learning Center through glencoe.com
Chapter 37 **Identifying Career Opportunities**	Student Activity Workbook: Chapter 37 DECA Connection Role Play; Chapter 37 Vocabulary Activity; Section Note Taking Activities; Chapter Academics Activity; Section Study Skills Activities; Section Real-World Applications Activities Mathematics for Marketing Workbook Marketing Research Project Workbook School-to-Career Activity Workbook	Unit 12 Fast Files : Chapter 37 Discovery Project Worksheet and Rubric; Chapter 37 Green Marketer Activity; Chapter 37 Digital Nation Activity; Section Graphic Organizers; Section Outlines with Key Terms and Definitions; Section Summaries ExamView Assessment Suite, Chapter 37 Connect Online Learning Center through glencoe.com
Chapter 38 **Finding and Applying for a Job**	Student Activity Workbook: Chapter 38 DECA Connection Role Play; Chapter 38 Vocabulary Activity; Section Note Taking Activities; Chapter Academics Activity; Section Study Skills Activities; Section Real-World Applications Activities Mathematics for Marketing Workbook Marketing Research Project Workbook School-to-Career Activity Workbook	Unit 12 Fast Files: Chapter 38 Discovery Project Worksheet and Rubric; Chapter 38 Green Marketer Activity; Chapter 38 Digital Nation Activity; Section Graphic Organizers; Section Outlines with Key Terms and Definitions; Section Summaries ExamView Assessment Suite, Chapter 38 Connect Online Learning Center through glencoe.com

McGRAW-HILL PROFESSIONAL DEVELOPMENT

Perkins IV has placed more emphasis than ever on providing quality professional development for Career and Technology educators. The legislation mandates that the focus of professional development be the integration and reinforcement of academic competencies in order to improve student achievement. Specifically, Perkins requires measurements of students' academic success. McGraw-Hill answers the challenge for strong and effective professional development with a five-prong **Online Professional Development for Integrating Academics.**

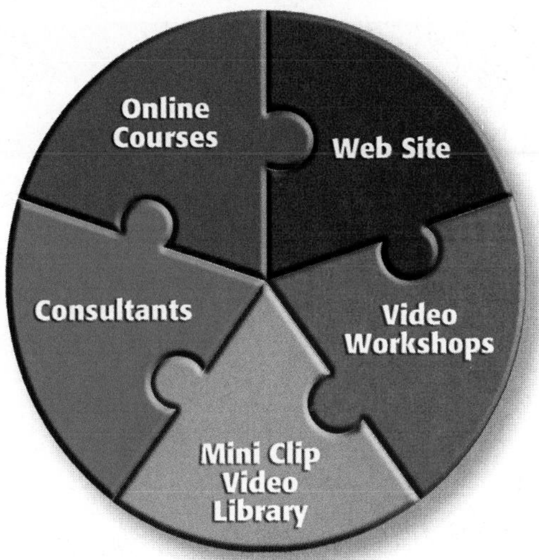

For pricing and ordering information contact your McGraw-Hill Sales Representative.

VIDEO LIBRARY

The McGraw-Hill Professional Development Mini-Clip Video Library, referenced for your convenience at the point of use, provides teaching strategies to strengthen academic and learning skills. Go to the Online Learning Center to view these professional development video clips for Unit 12:

Chapter 37: Identifying Career Opportunities

- **ELL: Graphic Organizers:** Use graphic organizers to distinguish between major and minor details. (p. 873)
- **Reading: Another Point of View:** Teachers discuss collaboration on standards-based instruction. (p. 883)

Chapter 38: Finding and Applying for a Job

- **ELL: Level 1 Proficiency:** An author discusses Level 1 proficiency English learners. (p. 904)
- **Reading: Planning and Management:** An expert discusses the role of the teacher in presenting standards to students. (p. 906)

UNIT OVERVIEW

Sections	Objectives	Common Core State Standards College and Career Readiness
Section 37.1 **Define Goals**	• Assess your goals, values, interests, skills, and aptitudes. • Appraise your personality. • Complete a career assessment. • Locate career research resources. • Develop a plan to reach your career goals.	• **Reading** Read and comprehend complex literary and informational texts independently and proficiently.
Section 37.2 **Careers in Marketing**	• Explain the importance of marketing careers to the U.S. economy.	• **Reading** Determine central ideas or themes of a text and analyze their development; summarize the key supporting details and ideas.

Sections	Objectives	Common Core State Standards College and Career Readiness
Section 38.1 **Finding a Job**	• Identify a variety of sources for job leads. • Describe the best ways to develop job leads.	• **Reading** Interpret words and phrases as they are used in a text, including determining technical, connotative, and figurative meanings, and analyze how specific word choices shape meaning or tone.
Section 38.2 **Applying for a Job**	• Name the legal document needed to begin working. • Write a letter of application and complete an application form. • Write a résumé and a cover letter. • Prepare for an interview.	• **Reading** Integrate and evaluate content presented in diverse formats and media, including visually and quantitatively, as well as in words.

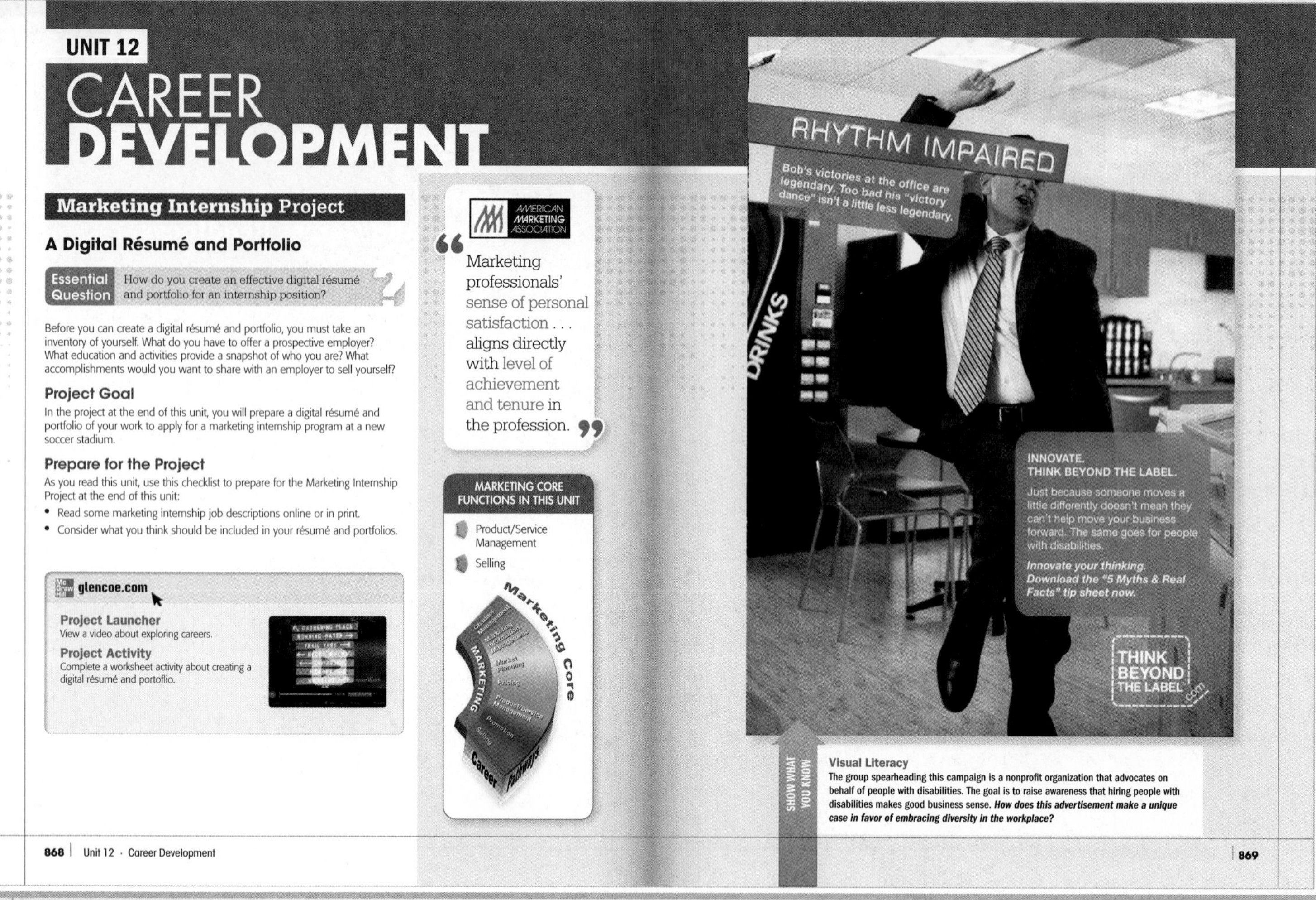
UNIT 12

CAREER DEVELOPMENT

Marketing Internship Project

A Digital Résumé and Portfolio

Essential Question How do you create an effective digital résumé and portfolio for an internship position?

Before you can create a digital résumé and portfolio, you must take an inventory of yourself. What do you have to offer a prospective employer? What education and activities provide a snapshot of who you are? What accomplishments would you want to share with an employer to sell yourself?

Project Goal

In the project at the end of this unit, you will prepare a digital résumé and portfolio of your work to apply for a marketing internship program at a new soccer stadium.

Prepare for the Project

As you read this unit, use this checklist to prepare for the Marketing Internship Project at the end of this unit:

- Read some marketing internship job descriptions online or in print.
- Consider what you think should be included in your résumé and portfolios.

glencoe.com

Project Launcher
View a video about exploring careers.

Project Activity
Complete a worksheet activity about creating a digital résumé and portfolio.

AMERICAN MARKETING ASSOCIATION

"Marketing professionals' sense of personal satisfaction . . . aligns directly with level of achievement and tenure in the profession."

MARKETING CORE FUNCTIONS IN THIS UNIT

- Product/Service Management
- Selling

RHYTHM IMPAIRED

Bob's victories at the office are legendary. Too bad his "victory dance" isn't a little less legendary.

INNOVATE.
THINK BEYOND THE LABEL.

Just because someone moves a little differently doesn't mean they can't help move your business forward. The same goes for people with disabilities.

Innovate your thinking.
Download the "5 Myths & Real Facts" tip sheet now.

THINK BEYOND THE LABEL.com

SHOW WHAT YOU KNOW

Visual Literacy
The group spearheading this campaign is a nonprofit organization that advocates on behalf of people with disabilities. The goal is to raise awareness that hiring people with disabilities makes good business sense. ***How does this advertisement make a unique case in favor of embracing diversity in the workplace?***

868 | Unit 12 · Career Development

869

ENGAGE

Introduce the Unit

Unit 12 examines the process of planning and developing a career.

Chapter 37 explains how to identify and research career possibilities and discusses preparation of a plan of action once a career is chosen.

Chapter 38 explores some proven methods for conducting a job search.

Build Background

Ask students to name some occupational areas or fields in marketing. List their ideas on the board. Answers will vary but may include advertising, customer service, e-commerce, fashion merchandising, international marketing, marketing research, product management, public relations, sales, sports marketing. Ask students: ***What skills are useful for a career in marketing?*** Basic skills include writing, researching, communication, analytical skills, critical thinking, social and interpersonal skills, and others.

Visual Literacy

Photo Caption Answer Read the copy on the ad to students. Then read the photo caption and the photo caption question to students: ***How does this advertisement make a unique case in favor of embracing diversity in the workplace?*** Answers will vary. Accept all reasonable answers. Sample answer: Think Beyond the Label is using humor to illustrate that there are many different kinds of people with disabilities and that they can all make a valid contribution in the workplace. Ask students to evaluate the visual components of the advertisement. Ask volunteers to explain how the visual aspects of the advertisement complement the text of the advertisement. The image of Bob dancing his victory dance with the text RHYTHM IMPAIRED and THINK BEYOND THE LABEL reinforces that there are many different types of disabilities and that people with disabilities should not be judged for their disabilities. Their contributions to the workplace are as important as anyone's.

ENGAGE

Marketing Internship Project Preview

Read students the Marketing Internship Project Essential Question: ***How do you create an effective digital résumé and portfolio for an internship position?*** Because students are just starting to learn about developing résumés, they will likely not know the specific answer to this question, which is to prepare a résumé according to specific formats and create a portfolio. However, students should know that there is a difference between preparing traditional paper and digital résumés. Explain to students that they will learn about formatting styles and "selling" oneself as a job candidate while studying this unit. Tell students that when they are finished studying this unit, they will ask questions to find answers about creating an effective digital résumé and portfolio for an internship position at a soccer stadium. As they study each chapter in the unit, they can prepare for the Unit Project by thinking of information they would include on their résumés.

 **glencoe.com**

Marketing Internship Project Resources Send students to the Online Learning Center to watch a video and download a worksheet activity related to the topic of the Unit Project.

Read the American Marketing Association quote to students:

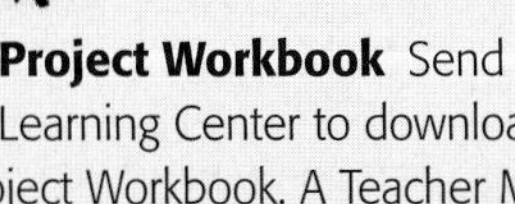

> "Marketing professionals' sense of personal satisfaction ... aligns directly with level of achievement and tenure in the profession."

Explain to students that the AMA Web site provides a variety of resources that address careers in marketing in its Career Management section. In addition, a resource called "Students Ask the Expert" provides real-world insight. For example:

Question How do I determine which section of marketing is right for me if I have not had experience?

Answer Most curricula will have an introduction to marketing course that will explain career options and help you decide.

Ask students: ***What questions about a career in marketing do you have?*** Have the class choose questions to submit to the AMA Students Ask the Expert feature or ask a marketing professional to speak with your class.

MARKETING CORE FUNCTIONS IN THIS UNIT

Point out to students that Chapters 37 and 38 will touch on two of the seven marketing core functions. Describe each of these marketing functions to students to prepare them to start studying this unit.

 **Product/Service Management** involves obtaining, developing, maintaining, and improving a product or a product mix in response to marketing opportunities.

 **Selling** is offering customers in any market the right product or service, and requires intense business development to employ concepts and strategies that work.

MARKETING RESEARCH PROJECT WORKBOOK

The purpose of the Marketing Research Project Workbook is to provide a step-by-step approach for students to conduct their own marketing research study. Each chapter is devoted to key elements in the research process. Each chapter builds upon the previous chapters, and by the end of the book, students will have completed an in-depth marketing research study, complete with rationale for all decisions, a report of the findings and conclusions, recommendations based on the original research problem and study objectives, and an annotated bibliography.

 **glencoe.com**

Marketing Research Project Workbook Send students to the Online Learning Center to download the Marketing Research Project Workbook. A Teacher Manual is also available on the Teacher Center of the Online Learning Center.

identifying career opportunities

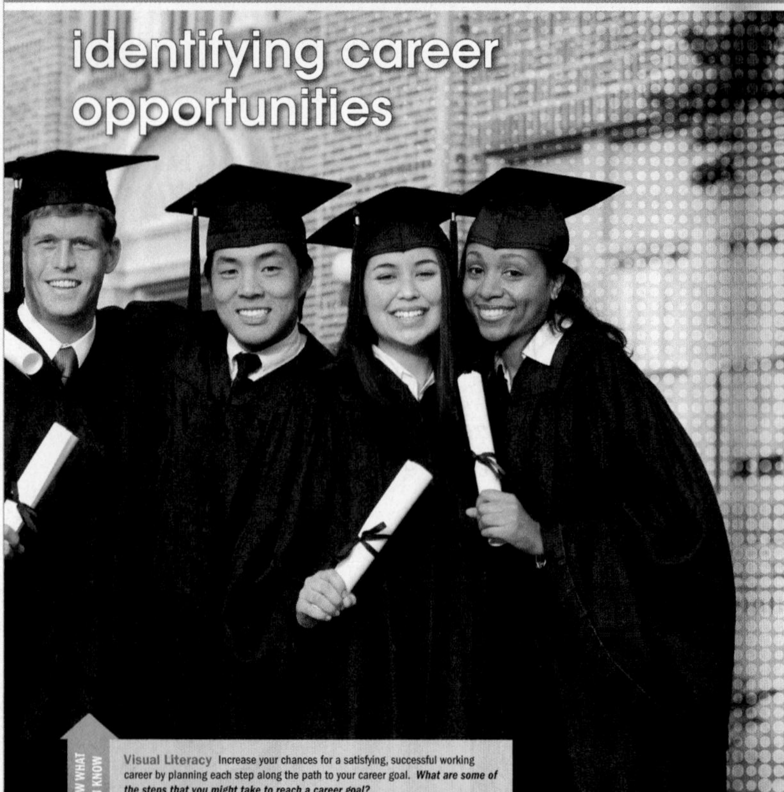

SHOW WHAT YOU KNOW

Visual Literacy Increase your chances for a satisfying, successful working career by planning each step along the path to your career goal. ***What are some of the steps that you might take to reach a career goal?***

Discovery Project

Begin a Personal Career Profile

Essential Question How would your personal information help you choose and prepare for a career?

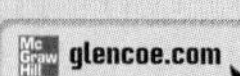

Project Goal

Begin writing personal information that will help you choose and prepare for a career. List some of your values (things that are important to you) and your interests. Describe your personality. Define your preferences for working with other people, data (information), and things. Describe your skills and aptitudes (activities that are easy for you to learn). Finally, estimate how much education and training (in years) you are willing to complete in order to reach your career goal. (Look at **Figure 37.1** on page 878 to help you complete your own Personal Career Profile.)

Ask Yourself...

- How will you understand and describe your values and interests?
- How will you describe honestly your own personality?
- How will you know your preferences for working with people, data, and things?
- How will you identify your skills and aptitudes?
- How much time are you willing to devote to additional education and training?

Synthesize and Present Research Synthesize your research and self-analysis by beginning your own Personal Career Profile.

glencoe.com

Activity
Get a worksheet activity about career opportunities.

Evaluate
Download a rubric that you can use to evaluate your project.

DECA Connection

DECA Event Role Play

Concepts in this chapter are related to DECA competitive events that involve either an interview or role play.

Performance Indicators The performance indicators represent key skills and knowledge. Your key to success in DECA competitive events is relating them to concepts in this chapter.

- Identify sources of career information.
- Assess personal strengths and weaknesses.
- Describe techniques for obtaining work experience.
- Explain possible advancement patterns for jobs.
- Utilize resources that can contribute to professional development.

DECA Prep

Role Play Practice role-playing with the DECA Connection competitive-event activity at the end of this chapter. More information on DECA events can be found on DECA's Web site.

ENGAGE

Visual Literacy

Read the chapter opener photo caption question to students: ***What are some of the steps that you might take to reach a career goal?*** Answers may include: define goals, conduct a self-assessment, identify career choices and gather information on each, evaluate choices, make a decision, plan how you will reach your goal. Ask these guiding questions. Keep a list of questions that arise during the discussion, and return to them as you work through the chapter.

Guiding Questions

Explain Based on what you have learned about marketing, are you interested in pursuing a career in marketing?	Encourage students to honestly consider whether a career in marketing would be a good fit for them. Ask for the reasoning behind their thoughts.
Evaluate How do your personal skills and abilities match up to a career in marketing?	Students should conduct a mini self-assessment and base their answers on what they have learned about the marketing industry.

Discovery Project

Begin a Personal Career Profile Ask students if they know people who are unhappy in their jobs. Ask why they think they are unhappy. Answers may include: the job does not line up with their interests, they work too many hours, they are not happy with the way the company is run, and so on. Then ask them the Discovery Project Essential Question: ***How would your personal information help you choose and prepare for a career?*** Students should recognize that knowing such things as your values, personal goals, interests, personality traits, preferences for working with people, skills, abilities, and aptitudes can help them focus on the path to a career that fits well with their personal attributes. Tell students that if they do not look at their own personal information, they might end up in a career they are not happy with.

glencoe.com

Discovery Project Resources Send students to the Online Learning Center to download a rubric to evaluate their projects.

ENGAGE

Introduce the Chapter

In Chapter 37 students will examine factors that will affect and influence their career decisions and plans. These main concepts are introduced and discussed:

- Defining personal goals
- Conducting a self-assessment
- Identifying career choices
- Gathering career information
- Evaluating career choices
- Formulating planning goals
- Continuing professional development
- Evaluating careers in marketing
- Categorizing skill levels
- Identifying occupational areas

Discussion Starter

Career Choices Ask students to share with the class information about jobs they have had. Have them evaluate such things as: What factors in a job make it satisfying? What kind of skills or preparation did they need to do the job? Did they need to know basic math operations? Then ask them to discuss any training they might have had for the jobs. Ask students: ***What criteria would you use to find a job that is right for you?*** Answers may include: finding a job that's interesting, that offers room for growth, meets financial needs, makes use of skills and abilities, and so on.

DECA Connection

Discuss the performance indicators listed in the DECA Connection feature. Explain to students that performance indicators tell them how to demonstrate their acquired skills and knowledge through individual or team competitive events.

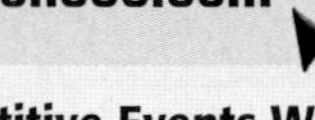

Competitive Events Workbook For more DECA Role Plays, send students to the Online Learning Center to download the Competitive Events Workbook.

PRINT RESOURCES

- **Student Edition**
- **Teacher Edition**
- **Student Activity Workbook with Academic Integration** includes worksheets and activities correlated to the text.
- **Mathematics for Marketing Workbook** provides math activities for every unit in the text.

TECHNOLOGY TOOLBOX

- **Connect**
- **ConnectPlus**
- **ExamView Assessment Suite** is a comprehensive solution for creating, administering, and scoring tests.

glencoe.com

Online Learning Center provides a variety of resources to enrich and enhance learning.

SECTION, CHAPTER, AND UNIT RESOURCES

- **Graphic Organizers** for organizing text concepts visually.
- **Digital Nation Activities** and **Green Marketer Activities** extend learning beyond the text features.
- **Career Chatroom Career Profiles** allow students to explore different marketing occupations in depth.
- **After You Read Answer Keys** for students to check their answers.
- **Discovery Project Rubrics** and **Marketing Internship Project Rubrics** for students to evaluate their projects.

PROGRAM RESOURCES

- **Student Activity Workbook with Academic Integration Teacher Annotated Edition** includes annotated answers for the activities and worksheets.
- **Marketing Research Project Workbook** provides a step-by-step approach for students to complete their own marketing research studies.
- **School-to-Career Activity Workbook** helps students relate their class work to on-the-job experience and involves work-site analysis and working with mentors.
- **Competitive Events Workbook** helps prepare students for state and national marketing education competitions.
- **Inclusion in the Marketing Education Classroom** provides teaching resources for working with students with special needs.
- **PowerPoint Presentations** provides visual teaching aids and assessments for this chapter.

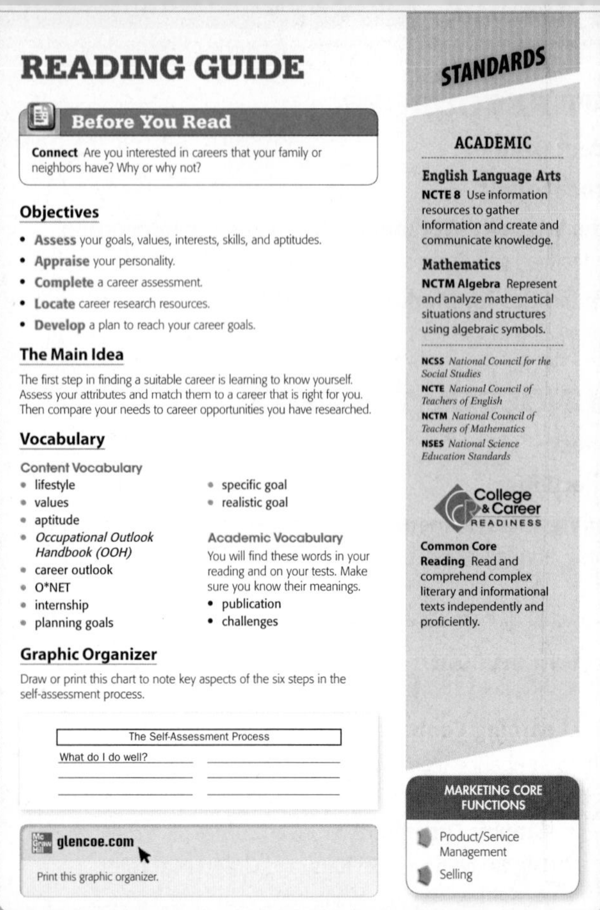

READING GUIDE

STANDARDS

Before You Read

Connect Are you interested in careers that your family or neighbors have? Why or why not?

Objectives

- **Assess** your goals, values, interests, skills, and aptitudes.
- **Appraise** your personality.
- **Complete** a career assessment.
- **Locate** career research resources.
- **Develop** a plan to reach your career goals.

The Main Idea

The first step in finding a suitable career is learning to know yourself. Assess your attributes and match them to a career that is right for you. Then compare your needs to career opportunities you have researched.

Vocabulary

Content Vocabulary

- lifestyle
- values
- aptitude
- *Occupational Outlook Handbook (OOH)*
- career outlook
- O*NET
- internship
- planning goals
- specific goal
- realistic goal

Academic Vocabulary

You will find these words in your reading and on your tests. Make sure you know their meanings.

- publication
- challenges

Graphic Organizer

Draw or print this chart to note key aspects of the six steps in the self-assessment process.

The Self-Assessment Process

What do I do well?

glencoe.com

Print this graphic organizer.

ACADEMIC

English Language Arts

NCTE 8 Use information resources to gather information and create and communicate knowledge.

Mathematics

NCTM Algebra Represent and analyze mathematical situations and structures using algebraic symbols.

NCSS *National Council for the Social Studies*

NCTE *National Council of Teachers of English*

NCTM *National Council of Teachers of Mathematics*

NSES *National Science Education Standards*

College & Career READINESS

Common Core

Reading Read and comprehend complex literary and informational texts independently and proficiently.

MARKETING CORE FUNCTIONS

Product/Service Management

Selling

872 | Unit 12 · Career Development

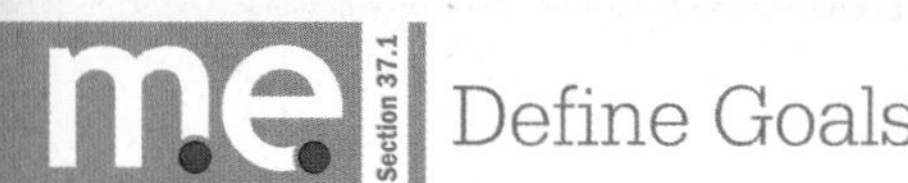

Section 37.1 Define Goals

CHOOSING A CAREER

A career often includes a series of increasingly responsible jobs in one field or in related fields. Choosing a career requires careful thought and preparation. This six-step process can help guide you in making important career decisions:

1. Define your personal (lifestyle) goals.
2. Conduct a self-assessment.
3. Identify possible career choices and gather information on each choice.
4. Evaluate your choices.
5. Make your decision.
6. Plan how you will reach your goal.

As You Read

Compare Which of the six self-assessment areas will have the greatest impact on your career choice?

DEFINE YOUR PERSONAL GOALS

The first step in choosing a career requires that you do some reflecting. You need to think about what kind of life you think you would like to have. The type of life you would like to live is your personal **lifestyle**. What type of lifestyle do you want? How do you want to spend your time, energy, and money? The answers to these questions will help you set personal goals. Reaching these goals can help make possible the life you want to have in the future.

> "Your career is the work you will do to earn a living over a period of years."

Your career choice will affect your lifestyle. Some careers will fit your personal goals better than others. If spending time with family is important to you, then you probably will not want a career that requires a lot of travel or weekend work. Religious observations may require that you not work certain days or times. Knowing your personal goals will help you find a career that adds to your lifestyle.

As a student, your life revolves around school, friends, and family. As an adult, your lifestyle will be influenced by these factors:

- Where you live (city, suburbs, or rural area)
- Type of housing in which you live
- Cultural environment in which you live, including the shopping and leisure activities you enjoy
- Your mode of transportation
- Relationships with your family and friends
- Work you do to earn a living

Your career is the key to your lifestyle because it will provide the funds needed to support your lifestyle. Before you can determine whether a career will be a good match with your personal goals, you need to identify and assess your goals.

CONDUCT A SELF-ASSESSMENT

Be prepared to record your findings in a notebook. Label the notebook "Self-Assessment File." Summarize your various assessments in paragraph form or, where appropriate, by using a rating scale.

YOUR VALUES

Values are beliefs that guide the way we live. Just as people have different abilities and personalities, they also have different values. Defining your system of values is essential in choosing a career.

Chapter 37 · Identifying Career Opportunities | 873

ENGAGE

Anticipation Activity

Improving Student Achievement Have students create a collaborative list of facets of jobs such as work hours, training, travel, independence, daily tasks, environmental factors, and amount of responsibility. Ask students to share which kind of work environment they would prefer.

Objectives

- **Assess** your goals, values, interests, and aptitudes. A self-assessment will help you learn about yourself in these areas.
- **Appraise** your personality. Personality tests can help you identify your personality type.
- **Complete** a career assessment. assessment should include values, interests, skills and aptitudes, personality, work environment preferences, and relationship preferences
- **Locate** career research resources. library, Internet, informational interviews, professional and trade organizations, work experience
- **Develop** a plan to reach your career goals. formulate planning goals, determine professional development, outline your plan

Graphic Organizer

The Self-Assessment Process	
What do I do well?	What do I believe?
What interests me?	What am I like?
Where do I work?	Do I like working with others?

glencoe.com

Graphic Organizer Send students to the Online Learning Center to print this graphic organizer.

EXPLORE

Before You Read

Read the Before You Read question aloud: ***Are you interested in careers that your family or neighbors have? Why or why not?*** Some students may say yes if the work seems exciting, rewarding, or lucrative. Others may say no if the work seems boring, requires too much travel, too much time at a desk, or if the company is too big or too small. Ask students to share their thoughts about jobs they have had or would like to have. Ask: ***What about the job appeals to you?*** Sample answers: fun work environment, friendly coworkers, a good supervisor, flexible schedule, good pay, challenging work, and so on.

Preteaching Vocabulary

Have students go to the Online Learning Center at glencoe.com for the Chapter 37 Preteaching Vocabulary games.

Content Vocabulary

Provide students with a card or small piece of paper for each Content Vocabulary term. Have students write a term on one side of the card and the definition for the term on the other side of the card. Then have students work with a partner to quiz each other on the correct definitions of the terms.

Academic Vocabulary

Publication—Usage Display *publication* and ask students if they have heard the term before. If so, ask: ***What do you think*** publication ***means?*** Answers may include: newspaper, magazine, book, and so on. Ask students to share original sentences in which they use the term *publication* correctly.

Challenges—Synonyms Tell students that the term *challenges* can be either a noun or a verb. Have students work together in pairs to develop a list of synonyms for the noun *challenge*. test, contest, experiment, trial Then have them list synonyms for the verb *challenge*. defy, dare, confront, face Read this sentence to students: ***Those who have met the challenges of a career are usually happy to talk about it.*** Ask: ***What is the meaning of the term*** challenge ***in this sentence?*** test or trial

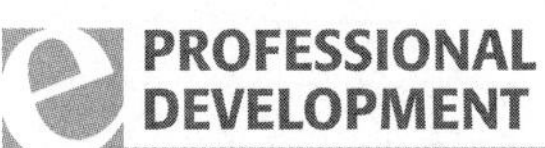

PROFESSIONAL DEVELOPMENT **MINI CLIP**

ELL: Graphic Organizers
Go to the Online Learning Center for a clip on using graphic organizers to distinguish between major and minor details.

Section 37.1

Define Goals

CHOOSING A CAREER

Tell students that choosing a career can be one of the most exciting times of their lives. Because a career is so important to most people, they should take the time to carefully work through the process of choosing a career. Then ask these guiding questions to focus the discussion about choosing a career.

Guiding Questions

List What are the six steps that can help guide you in making important career decisions?	(1) define your personal goals; (2) conduct a self-assessment; (3) identify possible career choices and gather information on each; (4) evaluate your choices; (5) make your decision; (6) plan how you will reach your goal
Analyze How are personal goals related to a career choice?	Possible answer: Goals tell where you want to be at a particular time in the future. Your career can help you meet your goals.

As You Read

Read students the As You Read question: ***Which of the six self-assessment areas will have the greatest impact on your career choice?*** Self-assessment areas discussed are values, interests, skills and aptitudes, personality, work environment preferences, and relationship preferences. All are important, so answers will depend on the individual students. Accept all reasonable answers.

Expert Advice

Read the quote to students:

> **“Your career is the work you will do to earn a living over a period of years.”**

Ask students: ***Do you think you will have the same career for as long as you work? Why or why not?*** Possible answers: it would be boring to do the same thing for so many years; it depends on the level of education and training that may or may not be available during the working years; people rarely have the same career for their entire working life; it would be more interesting and challenging to change careers.

The GREEN Marketer

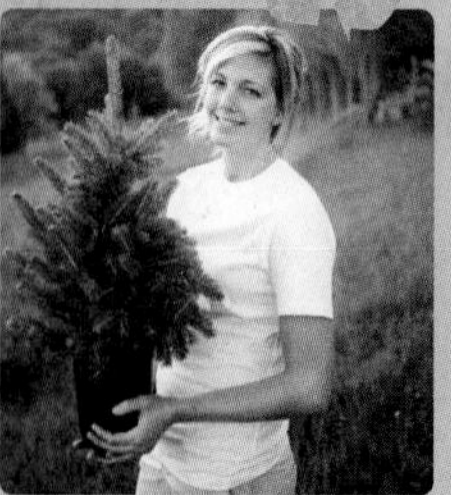

Does Your Job Match Your Values?

Socially responsible companies strive to care for the earth, workers, and customers. Before applying for a job, careful job seekers research a company, including its green credentials.

Get the Answers Does the employer strive to reduce pollution and waste? Does the company support community organizations? Do managers communicate openly with workers? Knowing the answers to these questions can help you find the company that will be the best fit for you.

Social Studies

Evaluate Brainstorm ten values that are important to you in your career. For each value, write one question that you might research or ask in a job interview to see if the company is the right match for you.

NCSS IX D Global Connections Analyze the causes, consequences, and possible solutions to persistent, contemporary, and emerging global issues, such as health, security, resource allocation, economic development, and environmental quality.

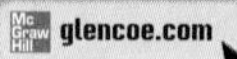

glencoe.com

Get an activity on green marketing.

Identify your values by focusing on the beliefs and actions that are important to you. If you are willing to work very hard to succeed, then you value achievement. Another possible value is the opportunity to express yourself.

YOUR INTERESTS

Most people spend 30 to 40 years working. It makes sense to choose work that interests you. Defining your interests, can help you gain a clearer picture of a career that will be fulfilling. To start evaluating your interests, write down what you like to do, such as leisure, school, social, and athletic activities.

You can also take a career interest survey. From a long list of activities, rate how much you like doing each of them. There are no right or wrong answers. Your score can help you find potential career matches. Go online to find a survey, or ask your school counselor or marketing teacher for information.

YOUR SKILLS AND APTITUDES

To be successful in any career, you need specific skills and aptitudes. An **aptitude** may be an ability or natural talent, or it may be the potential to learn a certain skill. Pursuing a career without the aptitude for the required skills may be a struggle and lead to disappointment. Once you know what skills are required to perform a job, you can determine if you have the aptitude to acquire those skills. For example, do you find it easy to sell goods to raise funds for your DECA chapter or another group? Are you good at organizing committees and inspiring others? Is math easy for you? Have you won prizes for your creativity? List your skills and aptitudes in your self-assessment file. Update your list as you develop new skills.

YOUR PERSONALITY

Your personality is the combination of all of the unique qualities that make you who you are. Understanding your personality characteristics can help you determine the types of work situations that will suit you best. Personality tests, available online and through your guidance counselor, can help you identify your personality type. For example, do you find stress to be an enjoyable challenge, or do you avoid it? Remember that there is no right or wrong kind of personality, just different kinds of people.

YOUR WORK ENVIRONMENT PREFERENCES

Your work environment refers to where you work. Work environment includes the physical location and its working conditions. Sights, sounds, and smells are all part of the working conditions.

You do not have to know all your preferences about working conditions now, but you should start thinking about them. For example, do you prefer to work indoors or outdoors? Do you like silence, or would you prefer some background noise?

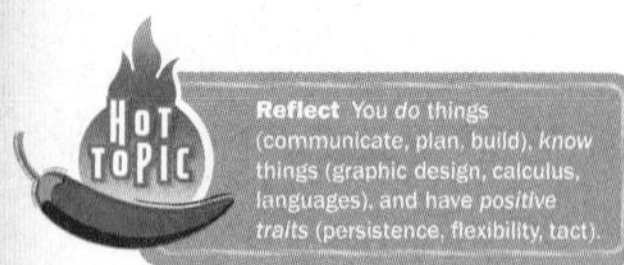

Reflect You *do* things (communicate, plan, build), *know* things (graphic design, calculus, languages), and have *positive traits* (persistence, flexibility, tact).

YOUR RELATIONSHIP PREFERENCES

All jobs require working with information and ideas, people, or objects (things) individually or in combination. Any career you choose will likely involve an overlap of these categories. It is important to think about which interests you most. Do you like working with others or alone? Are you comfortable handling interpersonal conflicts at work? The answers to these questions can help you understand your relationship preferences.

IDENTIFY CAREER CHOICES AND GATHER INFORMATION

To research careers, you will need to gather information from a variety of sources. You will find current information at libraries or on the Internet. You can also learn a great deal through informational interviews, professional and trade organizations, and actual work experience.

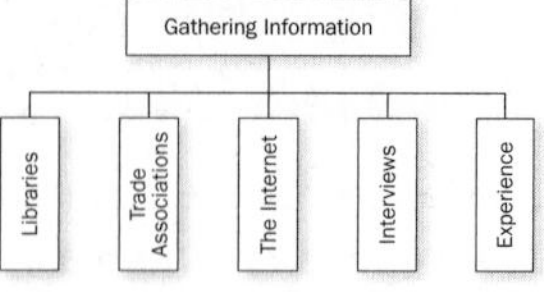

LIBRARIES

The *Occupational Outlook Handbook (OOH)* is available online and in libraries. The ***Occupational Outlook Handbook (OOH)*** describes what workers do on the job, working conditions, the training and education required, earnings, and expected job prospects in a wide range of occupations. The U.S. Department of Labor publishes an updated edition of the *OOH* every two years. The *OOH Quarterly* is published four times each year.

Living in the city can be exciting yet demanding. A rural setting offers a quieter, more relaxed lifestyle. ***In which setting would you feel most comfortable, urban or rural?***

EXPLAIN

The GREEN Marketer

Social Studies Answer Read the Social Studies Activity to students: ***Brainstorm ten values that are important to you in your career. For each value, write one question that you might research or ask in a job interview to see if the company is the right match for you.*** Sample answers: Values might include integrity, diversity, learning, helping others, recognition, environmentalism, or others of students' choosing. Sample questions: Does the company emphasize diversity in its hiring? How is excellent performance recognized in the organization? Could you describe the company's environmental initiatives?

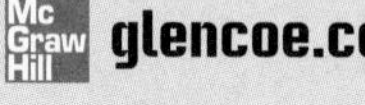

glencoe.com

Worksheet Activity Send students to the Online Learning Center to get a Green Marketer worksheet activity.

Mini Project

Enrichment

Research a Career Give students the following scenario: ***All his life, Jarrod's family has encouraged him to become a teacher. There are a number of teachers in Jarrod's family and they tell him he will enjoy the long vacations, interacting with the students, and feeling like he has made a difference in the world. Jarrod became an elementary school teacher and enjoyed it for a while. But he has become frustrated by the children's dependence on him and on the amount of paperwork and preparation time that are necessary to do the job well. He is considering changing careers, but isn't sure what he wants to do.*** Then ask students: ***Where should Jarrod start?*** Have students brainstorm a list of questions they could ask Jarrod to get him thinking about a new career. Sample questions: What are your interests? Are you interested in working with people, or by yourself? Where would you like to live? How can you apply your teaching skills to another career?

ELABORATE

Critical Thinking

Name a specific job in the field of marketing, such as Director of Public Relations for a local sports team. Ask students: ***How would you describe the skills, preferences, and lifestyle of a person with this job?*** Descriptions may include an outgoing person who loves sports, doesn't mind working evenings and weekends, and manages others well. Ask: ***Why did you describe the person the way you did?*** Students may say that a director of public relations for a sports team would need to be outgoing and love sports and, because games are often in the evenings and on weekends, would not mind working at those times.

Graphic Organizer

Display this diagram. Ask students to name the six parts of a self-assessment listed in the text. Values, interests, skills and aptitudes, personality, work environment preferences, and relationship preferences. Write students' answers in the diagram.

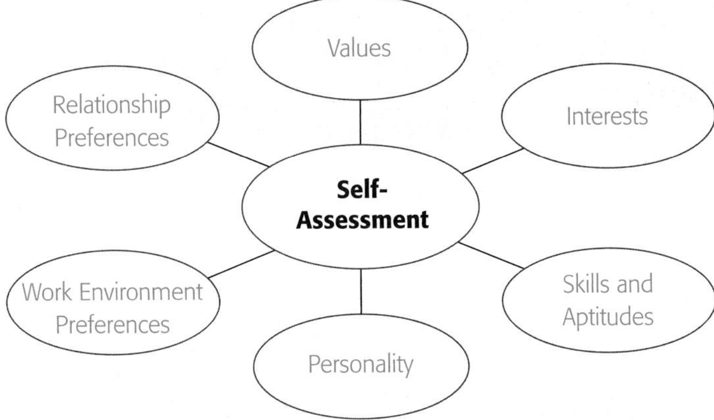

iWB

Graphic Organizer Send students to the Online Learning Center to print this graphic organizer.

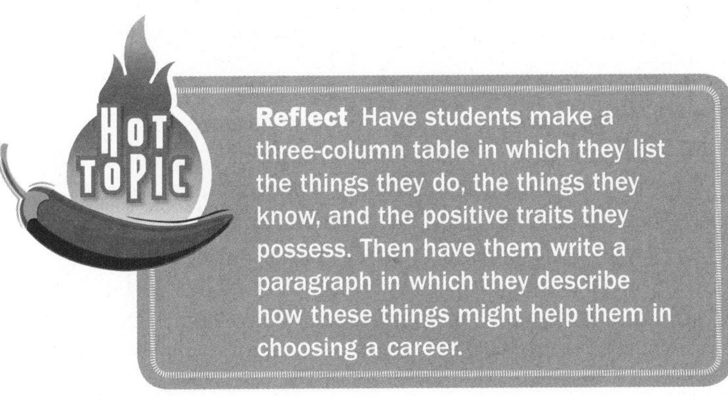

Reflect Have students make a three-column table in which they list the things they do, the things they know, and the positive traits they possess. Then have them write a paragraph in which they describe how these things might help them in choosing a career.

Mini Projects

Enrichment

Complete a Self-Assessment Have students go online to find different Web sites that offer free personality and career assessments. Have students complete at least one assessment. Ask: ***Did your findings surprise you? Or, did your findings confirm what you already knew about yourself?*** Encourage students to answer honestly. Then have students write a short paragraph in which they describe the results of their self-assessment and whether the results surprised them or confirmed what they already knew.

Think About Careers Ask students to use the results from the self-assessment they completed in the activity above and compare the results with careers that interest them. Ask students to write a paragraph in which they explain whether they think the results of the self-assessment show that they would be a good match for a career that interests them.

Visual Literacy

City or Country? Caption Answer Read the caption question to students: ***In which setting would you feel more comfortable, urban or rural?*** Answers will depend on students' preferences. Ask volunteers to share reasons for their choices. Sample answers: I prefer to be in a remote, secluded environment. I like to be where the action is. I feel energized when I'm around lots of people.

Critical Thinking

Synthesize Information After students have read the section under Your Interests, ask them to imagine doing their favorite hobby for a living. Ask them to explain in a one-paragraph response how they could use their hobby in a career. Sample answers: Someone who enjoys playing computer games could study programming and become a game creator or tester; someone who enjoys cooking could take culinary classes and become a chef.

Draw Conclusions Ask students to brainstorm reasons it is important to research a career outlook for more than one career. Possible responses: It is easier to get a job in a growing field. If a career outlook is decreasing, so will the number of job opportunities in that field. It makes more sense to train for a career in a stable or growing field.

These **publications** provide valuable information on the number and types of jobs available in any field. This is known as the **career outlook**.

PROFESSIONAL AND TRADE ASSOCIATIONS

Professional and trade associations serve individuals and businesses with common interests. These are excellent sources for current information about careers in many professions.

Association members work in or are associated with the same industry. Some associations serve individuals in particular careers, such as the American Marketing Association or the Direct Marketing Association. These associations promote pooling of resources, technology cooperation, and common standards. Information is distributed in newsletters, journals, and reports and online.

THE INTERNET

O*NET, the Occupational Information Network, is the primary source for occupational information in the United States. The O*NET database includes information on skills, abilities, knowledge, work activities, and interests associated with occupations. The O*NET site provides information on how to use the O*NET database.

You can also find a wealth of resources for research from America's Career InfoNet Web site. The College Board also has a section on its Web site devoted to helping you research careers.

INFORMATIONAL INTERVIEWS

You may want to set up an informational interview with a professional who works in a field that interests you. You can learn about the demands, opportunities, and day-to-day realities of a career from an experienced person. Those who have met the **challenges** of a career are usually happy to talk about it.

Ask your teacher, counselor, family, and friends if they know people in the community who enjoy talking with young people about their work. You may also want to contact the public affairs or public relations officer at a professional association. Ask about career nights or other opportunities where you can speak with people who are currently working in the field.

Before any interview, prepare a list of questions that you want to ask. Here are some suggestions:

- How do you spend most of your time on the job?
- Which work activities do you like most?
- What skills will I need to do this type of work?
- What skills will I need to advance?
- What education and training will I need?
- Can I complete some of the training on the job?
- How much time do you spend working with ideas and information? With people? With objects?
- Will there be an increase in job opportunities in this field over the next several years?
- What impact will automation and new technology have on job opportunities in the next few years?

ON-THE-JOB EXPERIENCE

Many students work part-time after school, on weekends, or during the summer. An entry-level position in a field that interests you will offer you great experience. On-the-job experience offers many benefits that allow you to:

- Try out some of the work activities in your career field and decide how much you like doing them.
- Experience the work environment.
- Develop work habits that will help you succeed in your career.
- Broaden your understanding of the world of work and smooth the transition from school to work.
- Make career contacts who can serve as mentors or assist you when you are searching for a job.
- Build up your résumé, which will grow as you gain more working experience.

You may also explore an internship program. An **internship** offers students direct work experience and exposure to various aspects of a career, either with or without pay. Professional association and government Web sites usually have links to internship possibilities.

The value of an internship is in the experience and the contacts that you make. Employers seriously consider internship experience when reviewing candidates. It demonstrates high interest and a willingness to put in time to gain valuable experience. It gives you a definite competitive edge over applicants who do not have internship experience.

EVALUATE YOUR CHOICES

Once you identify one or more interesting careers, you can compare and contrast a potential career with your self-assessment. This evaluation can help determine whether a career that seems interesting is a good match.

Organize your task before you begin. Gather all your self-assessment notes and research on various careers. Create a personal career profile. Use an evaluation format that allows you to compare your self-assessment side-by-side with a particular career assessment (see **Figure 37.1** on page 878).

On the left side of the profile, write down all the information about yourself. Then make a copy of this form for each of your researched career choices. Using these copies, refer to your notes to fill in the career information on the right side of the profile form. Reread all the information.

It may also help to get some feedback on the information you have compiled. Share your profile with a friend, family member, teacher, or someone else you trust. Ask that person whether your self-assessment is accurate and whether the careers you have researched seem right for you.

The following questions will guide you as you evaluate your choices.

- Do the work values in this field match my personal values?
- If I am successful in this career, will I be able to achieve my personal lifestyle goals?
- Do the responsibilities match my skills and aptitudes?
- How well is this career suited to my personality?
- Does the work environment suit my work environment preferences?
- Does the career offer the kinds of work relationships I am seeking?

You may notice that many of these questions are similar to those you might ask during an informational interview with someone who works in a particular field. You may possess skills and aptitudes suited to many different careers, but an honest self-evaluation will help you determine which career is most suitable for you.

Reading Check

Summarize What are some helpful sources of information about careers?

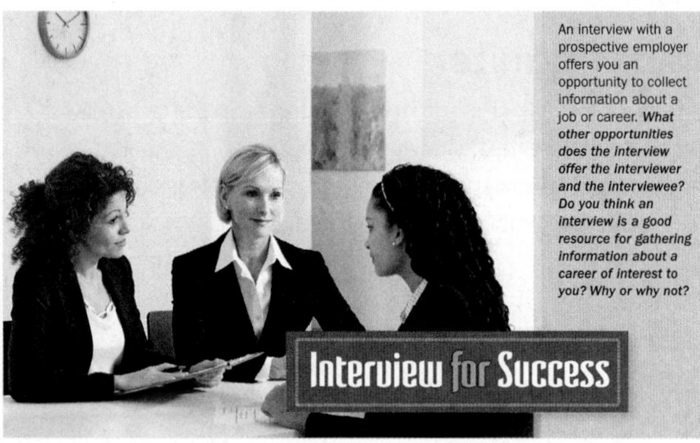

An interview with a prospective employer offers you an opportunity to collect information about a job or career. ***What other opportunities does the interview offer the interviewer and the interviewee? Do you think an interview is a good resource for gathering information about a career of interest to you? Why or why not?***

EXPLAIN

Critical Thinking

Read the following scenario to students: *If your career goal is a high-level job in any area of marketing, you will need to continue your education into college, and probably beyond a bachelor's degree to an MBA or other graduate degree. But what if you have already begun your career path and do not have time for college or an advanced degree? An online degree program could be the solution. Bachelor's, master's, and doctoral degrees are all available online. Taking classes online often means students download lectures to view at their own pace and to fit their own schedules. Students receive and submit assignments and get instructor feedback by e-mail. They have access to online research libraries as well as to other students with whom they can discuss course content.* Ask students: ***What are three advantages and three disadvantages of an online degree program?*** Answers may include: Advantages—working at your own pace, studying according to your schedule, not having to commute. Disadvantages—not being face-to-face with teachers or other students, not getting immediate feedback from the instructor, having to be self-disciplined.

Mini Projects

Extension

Informational Interviews Contact local businesses and ask if they would allow your students to shadow an employee for half a day or a full day. Prior to the shadow day, have students create a list of questions they can use for an informational interview with the person they shadow. If businesses are reluctant to participate, tell them that the shadow program could bring them some very positive publicity. The program can be very beneficial to both the businesses and the students.

On-the-Job Experience Have students locate a business that could provide work experience in their chosen career field. Then have students call to find out if that company offers internships. If the company does offer internships, students should find out to whom they should write a letter to request an internship. Have them write a one-page letter requesting an internship. In the letter students should explain the reasons behind their request, list skills and aptitudes that they feel would help them in this career field, and provide information about future career plans.

ELABORATE

Critical Thinking

Ask students: ***What kinds of career materials do you think you might find at your local or school library?*** Items that can be found at libraries include computer stations for Internet research, business magazines and other periodicals and newspapers, and books on résumé writing. Remind students that libraries can be useful places to find up-to-date career data, and that most libraries have computer stations that can be used to access the Internet.

Graphic Organizer

Display this diagram. Ask students to provide two sources of career information for each resource. Write students' answers in the diagram. Sample answers are provided below.

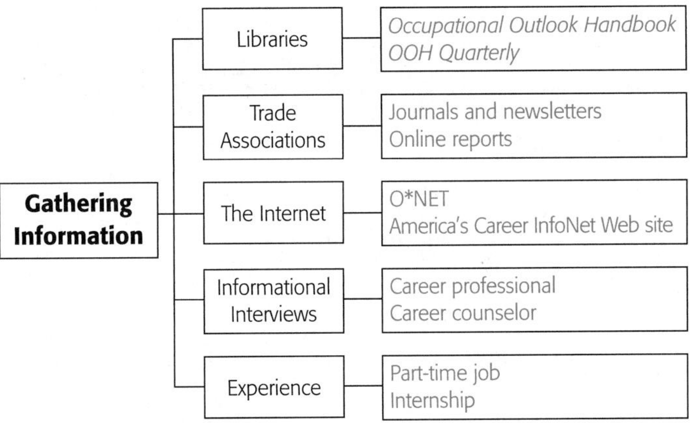

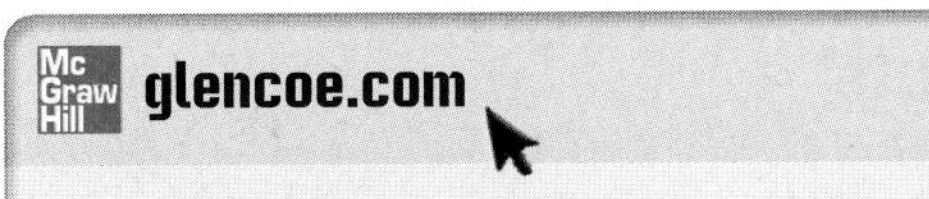

Graphic Organizer Send students to the Online Learning Center to print this graphic organizer.

Mini Project

Enrichment

Identify and Research Marketing Careers Have students do online or other research to create a list of careers related to the field of marketing. Display a collaborative list of students' answers. Careers may include: advertisers, marketers, promotions specialists, public relations specialists, sales managers, and others. Then have students choose one of the marketing careers from the collaborative list or another marketing career, and conduct research to find the following information: nature of the work, work environment, education and training, other qualifications, certification and advancement, job outlook, and earnings. Students might use online or library resources such as the *Occupational Outlook Handbook* to find this information. Then have students write a one-page report that summarizes their findings. Students' reports will vary depending on the career they researched.

Reading Check Answer

Read the Reading Check question to students: ***What are some helpful sources of information about careers?*** Sources include the Internet, libraries, professional and trade associations, informational interviews, and on-the-job experience.

Visual Literacy

Interview for Success Caption Answer Read the caption questions to students. ***What other opportunities does the interview offer the interviewer and the interviewee? Do you think an interview is a good resource for gathering information about a career of interest to you? Why or why not?*** Answers will vary. Students may recognize that an interview provides an opportunity to learn the day-to-day realities of a job and the demands and possibilities of the career from someone with experience.

FIGURE 37.1 Personal Career Profile

Is It a Match? A personal career profile helps you compare your self-assessment with a particular career. ***Based on this career profile, how does Joan Smith's personal information match the information about a teaching career? Rank each category from 1 to 5, with 5 being the best match.***

Name Joan Smith Date September 4, 20--

Personal Information	Career Information	Match (1–5, with 5 being the best match)
Your Values: The value scales I took showed that I like to help other people (humanitarianism). I like to be a leader. Doing creative things is fun, too.	**Values:** As a teacher I would have a chance to help others—that's what it's all about. Teachers certainly have plenty of opportunities to be leaders, too. Teachers also need to be creative!	
Your Interests: My hobby interests have always been photography, reading, and theater. My career interest survey showed that I might like a career in leading/influencing, selling, the arts, or maybe a humanitarian career.	**Career Duties and Responsibilities:** As a teacher, I would present information, and direct student discussions and activities in class. I would help each student individually, too. (Maybe I could teach marketing or general business.) A teacher's working conditions would be good in most schools. (Summers off!)	
Your Personality: I like people, and I have a good attitude toward learning. I have an open mind. I'm enthusiastic, too. However, I don't have the energy and drive that some people have. I don't know if I could work night after night.	**Type of Personality Needed:** A teacher must like kids, even when they aren't very likeable. I would have to prepare my lessons every day—couldn't just forget about them. Teachers need to be organized, too.	
Data-People-Things Preferences: I think I like working with people most of all. I wouldn't want to be stuck in an office all day with only "data" to talk to. I also wouldn't like working only with things. Some data would be all right, though.	**Data-People-Things Relationships:** Teachers work mostly with people—their students, the principal, parents. They work with data (information), too, though. I don't think they work much with things.	
Skills and Aptitudes: I may have some natural teaching skills—the kids at the YMCA always come to me for help. I helped several kids in Miss Moore's class. Business classes are easy for me.	**Skills and Aptitudes Needed:** Being able to present information so students can understand it is a very important skill. Of course, you must know your subject. An appetite for learning new approaches to teaching is important, too.	
Education/Training Acceptable: I sure never thought I would go to college—I never even liked doing the homework in high school. However, here I am a senior with no real prospects of a good job. Maybe college is the answer.	**Education/Training Required:** Four years of college (it sounds like forever, but I guess it does go fast) are required before you can begin teaching in most states. Some states require course work beyond that.	

DEVELOPING AN ACTION PLAN

A plan does not guarantee success, but it can help you to achieve success. A plan helps you remember what needs to be done and when. A plan also helps you prioritize, or put tasks in order. A plan outlines the steps that you need to follow to reach your ultimate goal.

In order to begin developing a plan, you must first complete a self-evaluation to determine your strengths, weaknesses, interests, skills, aptitudes, values, lifestyle goals, and work environment preferences. Then you will research possible career paths, identify possible career choices, gather information, and evaluate each of your choices.

Once you have completed your self-evaluation and researched your potential career options, you will have laid the groundwork to move forward. You will then be ready to make a career decision, develop your career action plan, and begin to act on your plan.

FORMULATE PLANNING GOALS

The small steps you take to get from where you are now to where you want to be in the future are called **planning goals**. They allow you to take charge of your life by helping you make decisions. Planning goals give your life a sense of direction and move you steadily toward your ultimate career goal. Every time you reach a goal, you gain confidence to move on to the next one.

A plan gives you a feeling of accomplishment. As you complete each part of your plan, you can cross it off, apply what you've learned, and move forward to the next step. Any progress you make toward your ultimate goal can also be rewarding in itself. With each step, you develop a better understanding of who you are and what you are best suited to do.

MARKETING CASE STUDY

Selling Digital Cameras

CASIO®

Casio's ***Exilim*** camera line was first launched in 2002. Since then, all Exilim cameras have been thinner and smaller than most others on the market. Some are very small, about the size of a credit card, while others are larger digital devices for professional use. This strategy has helped Casio cameras win the J.D. Power customer satisfaction award.

Who Will Buy Them?

To sell these digital cameras, the marketers at Casio target different consumers. To do this, they highlight the features of each type of camera based on who is likely to use it. The high-end EX-F1 model is marketed to professional photographers. The middle-of-the-road Zoom models are targeted for the majority of consumers.

English Language Arts

Research Write a paragraph about how you would gather information about becoming a marketing manager for a digital camera company.

NCTE 8 Use information resources to gather information and create and communicate knowledge.

EXPLAIN

Visual Literacy

Figure 37.1 Caption Answer Read the question: *Based on this profile, how does Joan Smith's personal information match the information about a teaching career? Rank each category from 1 to 5, with 5 being the best match.* Most students will agree that the strongest career matches are the Values, Interests, and Skills and Aptitudes sections. The weakest match is Education/Training Acceptable. Then use these questions to discuss the career profile.

Guiding Questions

Explain How do the personal Data-People-Things Preferences measure up to the Data-People-Things Relationships?	They seem to be a good fit. Preferences list working with people over working with things or data. Teachers work with people more than things or data.
Evaluate Do you think the personal information in the career profile is honest?	It appears to be honest because the information in the Education/Training Acceptable section is not very flattering.

Mini Projects

Enrichment

Write a Self-Assessment Have students choose a job that interests them, and have them write a self-assessment that states why they would be a good fit for that job. Have students list all their resources and attach any job ads used as source material. Encourage students to share their source materials and resources in class. Explain that self-assessments can help prepare them for a job interview for that particular career.

Role Play an Interview Organize the class into pairs. Have each pair develop a role play in which one student gives an interview for an internship to the other student. Students should identify the job for which the student is interviewing. The interviewer should ask questions such as "What skills do you already have that will help you do this job?" and "What kind of training have you had that has prepared you for this position?" Ask students to present their role plays to the class. Then ask the class to determine, based on answers provided during the interview, whether the student would be a good candidate for the internship. Ask them to give the reasoning for their answers.

ELABORATE

Graphic Organizer

Display this graphic organizer. Ask students to provide, in order, the steps to developing a career action plan. Write students' answers in the diagram. Answers are provided in the diagram below.

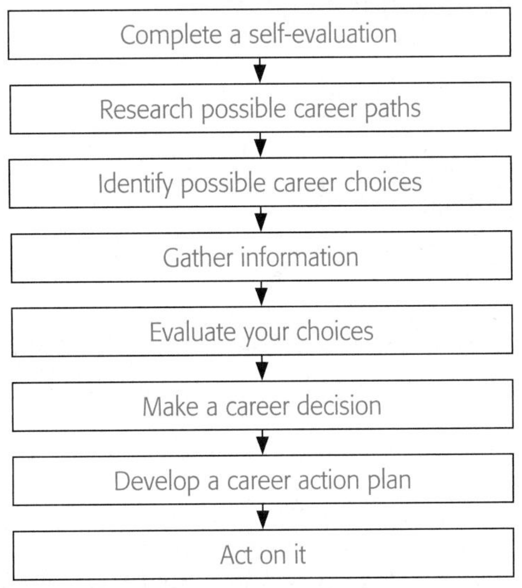
Develop an Action Plan
Complete a self-evaluation
Research possible career paths
Identify possible career choices
Gather information
Evaluate your choices
Make a career decision
Develop a career action plan
Act on it

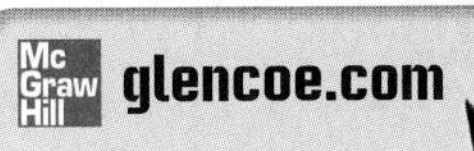
glencoe.com

iWB

Graphic Organizer Have students go to the Online Learning Center to print this graphic organizer.

MARKETING CASE STUDY

English Language Arts Answer Students may suggest using libraries, professional and trade associations, the Internet, information interviews, or on-the-job experience for gathering information about becoming a marketing manager for a digital camera company.

Extend the Concept Ask students: ***What skills and aptitudes would you need to be a marketing manager for a digital camera company?*** Answers may include: ability to work well with others; strong communication skills; working knowledge of photography trends and the latest camera equipment.

eMARKETING

Lawful Data Mining of Blogs for Employment Screening

Employers can gain a wealth of knowledge about prospective employees by accessing information contained in their blogs on social networks, such as Facebook, MySpace, and Windows Live Spaces. Why? Because anyone can read those blogs if they are part of the social networks and have permission. Most social network sites allow users to post personal information, interests, hobbies, relationship status, and political beliefs. Courts have ruled that using Internet searches for employment decisions is okay as long as employers comply with the terms of use outlined in the agreement. The reasoning behind the legal decisions is that information posted on the Internet becomes public and privacy is lost. Employers may review employee blogs as well. To do so without any complications, employers may seek consent from employees. Also, since race, age, gender, and religion may not be considered during the employment process, employers should be sure to state that those topics may not be used in data mining of employees or job applicants.

Innovate and Create

Discuss why employers should conduct lawful mining of social networks when researching potential and current employees. What information might help them decide between two candidates for employment or promotions? Since students know that employers may conduct an Internet searches when considering them for employment, what might they consider to avoid being rejected before getting an interview? Employers would be negligent if they did not use all the resources available when considering a new employee. Internet searches are inexpensive and readily available. They are a great tool for studying job applicants and current employees. Positive information about job candidates could include volunteer work or recommendations from friends. Negative information may include partying habits, comments about other workers and working conditions, or sharing of bad habits. Job applicants should not post anything on a blog that they would not say to a prospective or current employer; they should not post anything too personal or revealing; and they should not post any negative or angry comments.

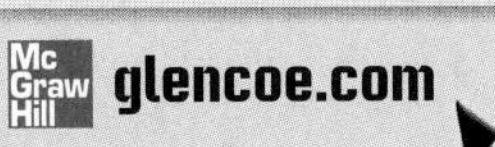
glencoe.com

eMarketing Worksheet Activity Send students to the Online Learning Center to download an eMarketing worksheet activity.

BE SPECIFIC

Make your planning goals as specific as possible. A **specific goal** is stated in exact terms and includes some details.

"I want to be successful," is not specific. "I want to complete my class in marketing this semester and earn at least a 'B'" is specific. This type of specific planning goal moves you forward toward your ultimate goal. When you are specific about your goals, you are more likely to formulate a plan to reach those goals.

BE REALISTIC

Planning goals must also be realistic. A **realistic goal** is one that you have a reasonable chance of achieving.

Think about all of the different skills and aptitudes that you possess. They will guide you in identifying both your ultimate career goal and your planning goals. Careful self-assessment can help you to focus on being realistic.

WORK BACKWARD

When you set your planning goals, you should work backward:

- Begin with your ultimate career goal.
- Decide what objectives you must accomplish along the way to achieve your ultimate goal.
- Determine the necessary medium- term goals.
- Determine the necessary short- term goals.

For example, suppose your ultimate career goal is to become a sustainable-design architect. A long-term goal may be to work for a top "green" architectural firm. In order to earn the credentials you will need to get such an opportunity, you might want to set a medium-term goal of earning your college degree in architecture. Another medium-term goal might be to start earning credentials. For example, you could set a goal to pass the U.S. Green Building Council's performance-based rating system to gain Leadership in Energy and Environmental Design (LEED) accreditation.

In order to prepare for your medium-term goals, you could set a short-term goal of working for a sustainable-housing construction company. This could start out as an unpaid internship designed to gain experience. Then, after you have gained experience as an intern, your next goal could be to get hired for a paid position with the company. Another short-term goal may be to investigate the type of specialized training you will need. There are many ways to do this. For example, you could subscribe to architectural trade publications and listservs or keep up-to-date by reading books and blogs about sustainable building.

Having a progressive series of goals allows you to test your ultimate career goal and make corrections or adjustments along the way. As you make progress toward your career goal, your experiences may reinforce your career decision or lead you to change your career goal. You may even discover another career that you find more interesting.

Think back to the example of wanting a career in "green" architecture. Based on your hands-on work experience in at the sustainable-housing construction company, for instance, you may discover that you would prefer a career working as a sustainable-design contractor rather than becoming an sustainable-design architect. Having a progressive series of goals allows you to adjust your path and your ultimate career goal at any point along the way.

PROFESSIONAL DEVELOPMENT

Whatever your career choice, you will need a plan of action to reach your goal. Your plan must include the concepts and strategies needed for personal and professional growth. Professional development is the process of obtaining the skills, qualifications, and experiences to continue to make progress in your chosen career.

Choosing education is much like choosing a career. Follow the complete decision-making process to select the best school and program for you. Your school counselor, library, and Web sites will have useful information.

Professionals must upgrade their existing skills and acquire new ones. Changes brought about by technology and global competition make lifelong learning key to any successful career.

If you are planning for education and training beyond high school, consider the following questions:

- What is my ultimate career goal?
- What courses can I take now that will help me to reach that career goal?
- What futher education and training are required?
- How much of this education and training must I complete before I enter this career?
- Where can I get this education and training?
- How much will this education and training cost, and how will I get the money?
- How much education and training can I get on the job?

OUTLINING YOUR PLAN

After you have answered these questions, begin writing your personal plan of action. Write down all of your goals, the dates that you plan to begin and reach each goal. Identify the skills you will need to improve progression in your career. Outline both the work experience goals and the educational goals you will need to achieve to meet your ultimate career goal. Be realistic about the timing of each step of your plan. Know that you will likely revise it as your situation changes and evolves. This will help keep you on track toward your ultimate career goal—the one that turns your dream lifestyle into reality.

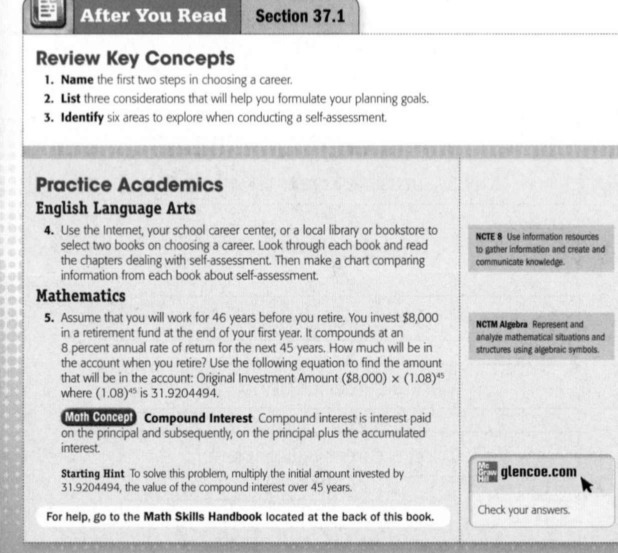

After You Read | **Section 37.1**

Review Key Concepts

1. **Name** the first two steps in choosing a career.
2. **List** three considerations that will help you formulate your planning goals.
3. **Identify** six areas to explore when conducting a self-assessment.

Practice Academics

English Language Arts

4. Use the Internet, your school career center, or a local library or bookstore to select two books on choosing a career. Look through each book and read the chapters dealing with self-assessment. Then make a chart comparing information from each book about self-assessment.

NCTE 8 Use information resources to gather information and create and communicate knowledge.

Mathematics

5. Assume that you will work for 46 years before you retire. You invest $8,000 in a retirement fund at the end of your first year. It compounds at an 8 percent annual rate of return for the next 45 years. How much will be in the account when you retire? Use the following equation to find the amount that will be in the account: Original Investment Amount ($8,000) × $(1.08)^{45}$ where $(1.08)^{45}$ is 31.9204494.

NCTM Algebra Represent and analyze mathematical situations and structures using algebraic symbols.

Math Concept **Compound Interest** Compound interest is interest paid on the principal and subsequently, on the principal plus the accumulated interest.

Starting Hint To solve this problem, multiply the initial amount invested by 31.9204494, the value of the compound interest over 45 years.

For help, go to the **Math Skills Handbook** located at the back of this book.

glencoe.com

Check your answers.

ELABORATE

Critical Thinking

Ask students to explain how setting career goals can be like a roadmap. Sample answers: A roadmap helps you reach a destination, which is your goal. Sometimes there is more than one way to reach the destination. Then ask: ***What might the landmarks in a career plan be?*** Sample answer: When you get directions to a place, there are usually landmarks along the way to help you know you are going in the right direction. Landmarks in a career plan are short- and medium-term goals that help you reach your long-term goal, which is the final destination.

Extend the Concept Explain to students that people often use roadmaps even though they have written directions as well. In the same way, visualizing the distance between your goals on your career plan can help you decide which path to take to reach your goal.

BE SPECIFIC

Tell students that the small steps you take to get from where you are now to where you want to be are called planning goals, which give a sense of direction to your journey toward your career goal. Then ask these guiding questions about formulating planning goals.

Guiding Questions

Explain What does it mean to be specific when formulating planning goals?	It is stated in exact terms and includes some details. You know when you have achieved a specific goal and can move on to the next goal.
Examine What is a realistic goal?	It is one that you have a good chance of achieving. Look at your skills and aptitudes to set realistic goals that you can actually achieve.
Analyze Why should you work backward when formulating planning goals?	Begin with your ultimate career goal and then work backward to determine the objectives you must meet along the way to achieve your ultimate goal.

EVALUATE

PROFESSIONAL DEVELOPMENT

Ask students: ***What is a plan of action?*** A plan of action shows how you will meet your goals. Tell students that they will need a plan of action to meet their career goals. Then ask students these guiding questions to direct a discussion about professional development.

Guiding Questions

List What questions should you ask yourself if you are planning for education and training after high school?	What is my ultimate career goal? What courses can I take now that will help me to reach that career goal? What further education and training is required? How much of this education and training must I complete before I enter this career? Where can I get this education and training? How much will this education and training cost, and how will I get the money? How much education and training can I get on the job?
Explain How is choosing education like choosing a career?	You must follow a similar decision-making process to determine how to reach your ultimate goal; in the case of education—graduation; in the case of a career—your dream job.
Synthesize How might you be able to get on-the-job training and get paid for it?	A paid internship would provide on-the-job training and a wage.

Reinforce Vocabulary

Upgrade—Usage Read the following sentence to students: ***Professionals must upgrade their existing skills and acquire new ones***. Ask students what it means to upgrade. In this case, it means to improve the quality of existing skills. Ask: ***Do you think you would be willing to constantly upgrade your skills to stay on top of your job? Why or why not?*** Some students will feel the constant upgrading is like continuing to go to school and probably will not care for the idea. Others will recognize upgrading as a means to reaching their career goals.

After You Read Section 37.1

Review Key Concepts

1. The first two steps in choosing a career are to define your personal (lifestyle) goals and conduct a self-assessment.
2. Considerations that help formulate planning goals are: be specific, be realistic, and work backward. Other considerations include training and education; costs; time frames; and short-, medium-, and long-term goals.
3. Areas to explore when conducting a self-assessment include: values, skills, aptitudes, personality, work environment preferences, and relationship preferences.

Practice Academics

English Language Arts

4. Students should create a chart that compares the elements of a self-assessment from two different books or other resources.

Mathematics

5. $255,363.59 ($8,000 × 31.9204494).

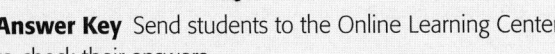

glencoe.com

Answer Key Send students to the Online Learning Center to check their answers.

READING GUIDE

Before You Read

Connect What do you already know about careers in marketing?

Objectives

- **Explain** the importance of marketing careers to the U.S. economy.

The Main Idea

When considering a marketing career, learn about the requirements, opportunities, rewards, and trends. The more information you have, the easier it will be to make a career.

Vocabulary

Content Vocabulary
- occupational area

Academic Vocabulary

You will find these words in your reading and on your tests. Make sure you know their meanings.
- subordinate
- monitored

Graphic Organizer

Draw or print this chart to write down questions about a marketing career..

Questions About a Marketing Career

1. ____________
2. Are there many jobs available?
3. ____________

glencoe.com

Print this graphic organizer.

STANDARDS

ACADEMIC

Mathematics

NCTM Problem Solving Solve problems that arise in mathematics and in other contexts.

Social Studies

NCSS VI B Power, Authority, & Governance Explain the purpose of government and analyze how its powers are acquired, used, and justified.

NCSS *National Council for the Social Studies*
NCTE *National Council of Teachers of English*
NCTM *National Council of Teachers of Mathematics*
NSES *National Science Education Standards*

College & Career READINESS

Common Core
Reading Determine central ideas or themes of a text and analyze their development; summarize the key supporting details and ideas.

MARKETING CORE FUNCTIONS
- Product/Service Management
- Selling

Section 37.2 Careers in Marketing

IS A MARKETING CAREER FOR YOU?

The skills and knowledge you gain from studying marketing can also help you in school and on the job. These skills include writing, researching, communication, and analytical skills, among others.

As You Read

Identify What are three pros and three cons of a career in marketing?

AN OVERVIEW OF MARKETING CAREERS

Marketing provides perhaps the greatest diversity of opportunities of any career field—from purchasing merchandise, to selling, to designing ads, to steering the company as president. More than 30 million Americans earn a living in marketing. Job growth in marketing careers is expected to exceed 12 percent for the next ten years. Careers in marketing include an array of activities required to develop, promote, and distribute goods and services to consumers. When considered in this broad sense, marketing activities account for about one in every three American jobs.

BENEFITS OF A MARKETING CAREER

The most obvious benefit of a career in marketing is the opportunity to make an above-average income. Even for an entry-level or **subordinate** position, potential earnings are excellent. Due to the high visibility of many marketing positions, there are usually more opportunities to advance than in almost any other area of business. People who work in marketing frequently present and shape their ideas in meetings with company managers and executives.

> "As you study marketing, you have the opportunity to evaluate marketing as a potential career."

People who work in sales get constant feedback in the form of sales figures that are reviewed by management. People who work in advertising may develop ad campaigns that are acclaimed by professional associations. Promotions tend to come faster in marketing than in many other careers. However, a career in marketing can be stressful. There are pressures to succeed, and the results of one's efforts are highly visible.

EMPLOYMENT TRENDS IN MARKETING

The U.S. Bureau of Labor Statistics (BLS) projects that employment in marketing and sales will continue at a high level. The rapid growth of e-commerce provides many opportunities. However, Department of Labor projections indicate that competition for managerial jobs in marketing-related fields will be keen in most industries.

The rise in the number of single-person households, changes in recreational activities, and the increase in foreign competition are all **monitored** through market research and marketing information systems. To track these developing trends, companies are expanding their marketing programs and staffs.

Reading Check

Connect How many Americans earn a living in careers in marketing?

ENGAGE

Anticipation Activity

Improving Student Achievement Have students brainstorm a list of marketing jobs. Ask a volunteer to keep a list of the jobs as they are named. Sample jobs: marketing manager, advertising executive, public relations specialist. Ask students to rank the jobs in order from those that make the most money to those that make the least money. Then ask: ***How do you think the salary is determined for these jobs?*** level of education or training, level of responsibility, commissions

Objective

- **Explain** the importance of marketing careers to the U.S. economy. More than 30 million Americans earn a living in marketing. Job growth in marketing careers is expected to exceed 12 percent for the next 10 years. Careers in marketing include activities required to develop, promote, and distribute goods and services to consumers. When considered in this broad sense, marketing activities account for about one in every three American jobs.

Graphic Organizer

Questions About a Marketing Career

1. Is there opportunity to make an above average income?
2. Are there many jobs available?
3. Is there diversity in the career opportunities?

iWB

Graphic Organizer Send students to the Online Learning Center to print this graphic organizer.

EXPLORE

Before You Read

Read the Before You Read question aloud: ***What do you already know about careers in marketing?*** Answers will depend on students' familiarity with careers in marketing. List all marketing jobs students are aware of and then lead a discussion by asking about each job: ***What do you know about this job?*** Have students share as much detail as they can.

Preteaching Vocabulary

Have students go to the Online Learning Center at glencoe.com for the Chapter 37 Preteaching Vocabulary games.

Content Vocabulary

Display the term *occupational area* and ask students what they think it means. Possible answer: a group of similar occupations. Explain that an occupational area is a job category that involves similar interests and skills. Then have volunteers use the term in sentences. Sample: I'm thinking about a banking career, so I plan to research the occupational area of financial services.

Academic Vocabulary

Subordinate—Synonyms Ask students to supply synonyms for the term *subordinate.* lesser, minor, inferior, lower, secondary, assistant Ask students to explain the meaning of *subordinate* in this sentence: ***Even for an entry-level subordinate position, potential earnings are excellent.*** assistant, lower

Monitored—Usage Display the term *monitored* and have students use it in a sentence. Samples: A monitor allows you to look at your work or a game on a computer. A hall monitor watches to make sure people follow the rules in the hallways. Tell students that when something is monitored, it is watched carefully. Read this sentence: ***The rise in the number of single-person households, changes in recreational activities, and the increase in foreign competition are all monitored through market research and marketing information systems.*** Ask students: ***Why do you think these incidents would be monitored through market research?*** They can help marketers learn how people are spending their money.

MINI CLIP

Reading: Another Point of View
Go to the Online Learning Center for a video discussing teacher collaboration on standards-based instruction.

Careers in Marketing

IS A MARKETING CAREER FOR YOU?

Ask these guiding questions on the economic benefits of careers in marketing.

Guiding Questions

Identify What skills and knowledge gained from studying marketing can help you in school and on the job?	Written and verbal communication, critical thinking, research skills, analytical skills, and so on
Analyze Why is it easier to get promotions in the field of marketing than in some other fields?	Marketers often present in front of executives who see their skills and potential. This shows who is worthy of a promotion.

As You Read

Read students the As You Read question: ***What are three pros and three cons of a career in marketing?*** Possible answers: The most obvious benefit of a career in marketing is the opportunity to make an above-average income. There are usually more opportunities to advance in a marketing career than in almost any other area of business. A career in marketing can be stressful, however, because there are pressures to succeed, and results of one's efforts are highly visible.

Expert Advice

“As you study marketing, you have the opportunity to evaluate marketing as a potential career.”

Ask students: ***Considering what you know now about marketing, does marketing as a potential career interest you?*** Encourage students to be honest about their answers. Ask volunteers to explain why they feel they way they do.

Reading Check Answer

Read the question to students: ***How many Americans earn a living in careers in marketing?*** Answer: more than 30 million.

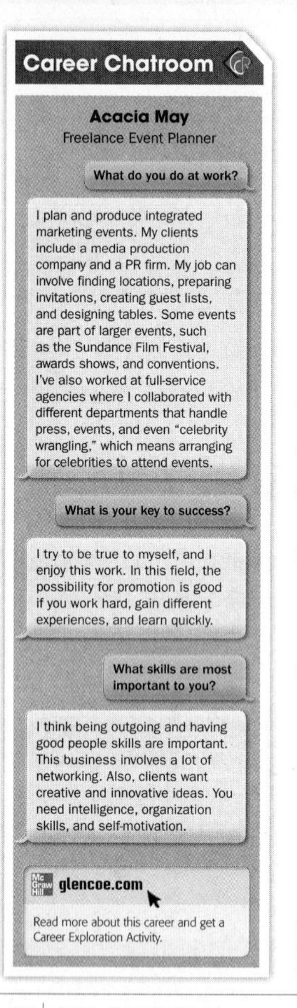
Career Chatroom

Acacia May
Freelance Event Planner

What do you do at work?

I plan and produce integrated marketing events. My clients include a media production company and a PR firm. My job can involve finding locations, preparing invitations, creating guest lists, and designing tables. Some events are part of larger events, such as the Sundance Film Festival, awards shows, and conventions. I've also worked at full-service agencies where I collaborated with different departments that handle press, events, and even "celebrity wrangling," which means arranging for celebrities to attend events.

What is your key to success?

I try to be true to myself, and I enjoy this work. In this field, the possibility for promotion is good if you work hard, gain different experiences, and learn quickly.

What skills are most important to you?

I think being outgoing and having good people skills are important. This business involves a lot of networking. Also, clients want creative and innovative ideas. You need intelligence, organization skills, and self-motivation.

glencoe.com

Read more about this career and get a Career Exploration Activity.

JOB LEVELS IN MARKETING

Many jobs exist within each of the occupational areas, or career applications, of marketing. Jobs in each marketing area can be categorized according to five skill levels.

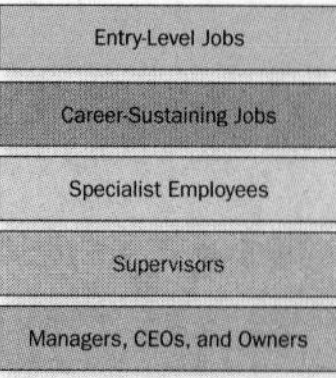

- **Entry level jobs** usually require no prior experience and involve limited decision-making skills.
- **Career-sustaining jobs** require a higher level of skill and more decision making than entry-level jobs.
- **Marketing specialist employees** must show leadership ability and make many decisions on a daily basis. Being a marketing specialist is usually a long-term career goal.
- **Marketing supervisors** must have good management skills, the ability to make many decisions on a daily basis, and excellent marketing skills. This is the highest career level to which many people aspire. The prestige and income are generally quite high, and there is less risk involved than at the top management level.
- **Managers and CEOs/owners** are at the top level. People at this level are capable of running an entire company or a significant part of it. They must be highly skilled in a number of areas. They are responsible for the final success of the enterprise.

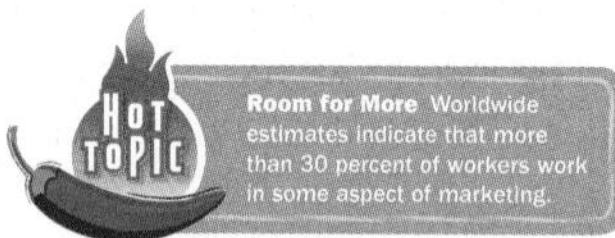

Room for More Worldwide estimates indicate that more than 30 percent of workers work in some aspect of marketing.

Reading Check

Compare Which marketing job level would you prefer?

OCCUPATIONAL AREAS

An **occupational area** is a category of jobs that involve similar interests and skills. Focusing on one or two areas makes it much easier to find information about the career area that most interests you. Here are some career areas within the field of marketing:

- Advertising
- Customer Service
- E-Commerce
- Entrepreneur
- Fashion Merchandising
- Financial Services
- Food Marketing
- Importing/Exporting
- International Marketing
- Marketing Research
- Pharmaceutical/Medical Marketing
- Product Management
- Professional Sales
- Public Relations
- Real Estate
- Restaurant Management
- Retail Management
- Sales Management
- Service Marketing
- Sports Marketing
- Travel/Tourism/Hospitality Marketing

After You Read **Section 37.2**

Review Key Concepts

1. **Name** three benefits of a career in marketing.
2. **Identify** and rank the ten major areas that you should consider when investigating careers. (Rank 1 as your highest priority and 10 your lowest priority.)
3. **List** five resources for researching careers.

Practice Academics

Social Studies

4. Select one of the following agencies to research: Federal Communications Commission, Federal Reserve board, Federal Trade Commission, Food and Drug Administration, or Internal Revenue Service. Write a one-page report on the agency and what it does. Explain how the agency impacts economic, market, and employment trends.

NCSS VI B Power, Authority, & Governance Explain the purpose of government and analyze how its powers are acquired, used, and justified.

Mathematics

5. You receive an offer for a job in marketing that pays $42,500, plus the eligibility for a 12-percent bonus annually. Calculate the total annual salary assuming you are also paid a 12-percent bonus.

Math Concept **Percent Problems** To calculate a 12-percent bonus, multiply the decimal form of the percent by the salary. Then add this amount to the annual salary to find the salary plus the bonus amount.

Starting Hints Multiply the annual amount of pay for the job, $42,500, by 12 percent to determine the bonus amount. Add the amount of the bonus to the annual pay to calculate the total annual salary.

NCTM Problem Solving Solve problems that arise in mathematics and in other contexts.

For help, go to the Math Skills Handbook located at the back of this book.

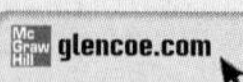
glencoe.com

Check your answers.

EXPLAIN

Career Chatroom

Use these questions to focus the discussion about the Career Chatroom feature.

Explain If you were going to interview for a job as an event planner, what skills would you need to possess?	outgoing, good people skills, creativity, innovation, intelligence, organization skills, self-motivation
Apply What would you tell a friend in this industry if he or she wants a promotion?	work hard, gain different experience, and learn quickly

glencoe.com

Career Exploration Send students to the Online Learning Center to find more information about this career and to get a Career Exploration activity.

Room for More Remind students that more than 30 million Americans earn a living in marketing. Job growth in marketing careers is expected to exceed 12 percent for the next 10 years. Careers in marketing include an array of activities required to develop, promote, and distribute goods and services to consumers. When considered in this broad sense, marketing activities account for about one in every three American jobs. Have students choose one other industry and determine the percentage of workers that work in that industry.

Reading Check Answer

Read the question to students: ***Which marketing job level would you prefer?*** Answers may include: entry-level, career-sustaining, specialist, supervisors, or managers, CEOs, or owners. Ask students to give the rationale behind their choices.

ELABORATE

Graphic Organizer

Display this graphic organizer. Ask students to provide the different levels of jobs in marketing and to provide two facts about each level. Write students' answers in the diagram. Sample answers are provided below.

Job Levels in Marketing

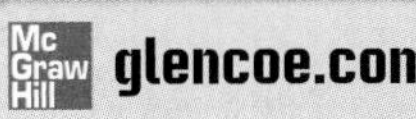 glencoe.com  iWB

Graphic Organizer Have students go to the Online Learning Center to print this graphic organizer.

Mini Projects

Extension

Research Employment Trends in Marketing Have students choose one of the occupational areas and find projections for the area and for specific jobs within the area. Projections should be for the next 5, 10, and 20 year periods. Remind students of places to find the information, such as the U.S. Bureau of Labor Statistics Web site. Ask students to share their findings with the rest of the class.

Research a Career Have students pick a career in marketing or a career of their choice. Instruct them to write a two-page report in which they discuss the projected outlook for the job, responsibilities for the job, salary range, training and education needed, and opportunities for advancement. Ask volunteers to share their reports with the class.

 **After You Read** **Section 37.2**

Review Key Concepts

1. Benefits include varied and interesting work, good salary, room for advancement, and perks.
2. Accept any order, but rankings should include personal lifestyle goals, values, interests, skills, aptitudes, personality, environmental and relationship preferences, careers goals, and employment trends.
3. Resources may include: persons working in a particular field, the *Occupational Outlook Handbook*, Department of Labor brochures, training courses and seminars, internships, and trade associations and Web sites.

Practice Academics

Social Studies

4. Students should write a one-page report on the agency of their choice. Reports should explain how the agency impacts economic, market, and employment trends.

Mathematics

5. $47,600 [$42,500 + ($42,500 × .12)]

 glencoe.com 

Answer Key Send students to the Online Learning Center to check their answers.

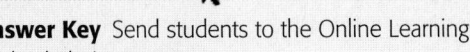

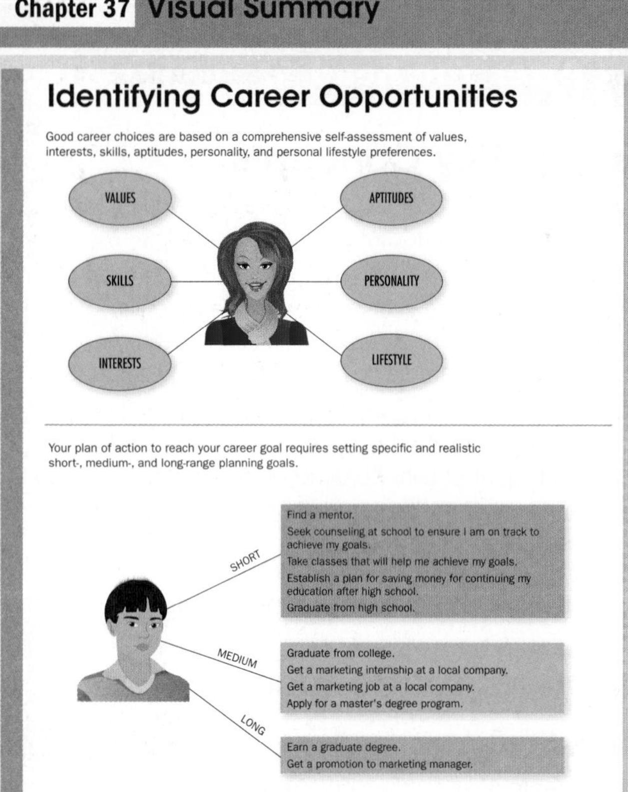
Chapter 37 Visual Summary

Identifying Career Opportunities

Good career choices are based on a comprehensive self-assessment of values, interests, skills, aptitudes, personality, and personal lifestyle preferences.

VALUES
APTITUDES
SKILLS
PERSONALITY
INTERESTS
LIFESTYLE

Your plan of action to reach your career goal requires setting specific and realistic short-, medium-, and long-range planning goals.

SHORT
Find a mentor.
Seek counseling at school to ensure I am on track to achieve my goals.
Take classes that will help me achieve my goals.
Establish a plan for saving money for continuing my education after high school.
Graduate from high school.

MEDIUM
Graduate from college.
Get a marketing internship at a local company.
Get a marketing job at a local company.
Apply for a master's degree program.

LONG
Earn a graduate degree.
Get a promotion to marketing manager.

886 | Unit 12 · Career Development

Review and Activities

Written Summary

- Career choices are based on a comprehensive self-assessment of values, interests, skills, aptitudes, personality, and personal lifestyle preferences.
- Career planning includes looking at work values, lifestyle fit, and the education and training required. It also includes learning about the duties and skills required, and looking at helpful personality traits, work environment, and work relationships.
- A plan of action to reach a career goal requires setting specific and realistic short-, medium-, and long-range planning goals.
- Consider the benefits, employment trends, occupational areas, and job levels in marketing.

Review Content Vocabulary and Academic Vocabulary

1. Write each of the vocabulary terms below on an index card, and the definitions on separate index cards. Work in pairs or small groups to match each term to its definition.

Content Vocabulary
- lifestyle (p. 873)
- values (p. 873)
- aptitude (p. 874)
- *Occupational Outlook Handbook (OOH)* (p. 875)
- career outlook (p. 876)
- O*NET (p. 876)
- internship (p. 876)
- planning goals (p. 879)
- specific goal (p. 880)
- realistic goal (p. 880)
- occupational area (p. 885)

Academic Vocabulary
- publication (p. 876)
- challenges (p. 876)
- subordinate (p. 883)
- monitored (p. 883)

Assess for Understanding

2. **Contrast** What are values, lifestyle goals, interests, and aptitudes?
3. **Reflect** Why is it important to assess values, lifestyle goals, interests, and aptitudes when choosing a career?
4. **Identify** What are two methods for appraising your personality?
5. **Explain** What is a work environment?
6. **Consider** What areas should be investigated when completing a career assessment?
7. **Search** What are two online and two library career research resources?
8. **Role Play** How can you explain to a peer the purpose a personal career profile serves?
9. **Imagine** What is the most obvious benefit of a career in marketing?

Chapter 37 · Identifying Career Opportunities | 887

EVALUATE

Visual Summary

Express Creativity Ask students to develop their own visual summary of a concept in the chapter. Encourage students to use different formats for their visual summaries, such as a storyboard, a timeline, a table, a tree diagram, or a word web. Visual summaries will vary depending on the concept depicted and the visual manner in which it is depicted. Questions to ask when assessing a visual summary include:

- Is the summary clear, economical, and simple?
- Are any important steps left out?
- Are steps or concepts arranged in the same order as the original?
- Does the summary reveal a pattern that connects the details?
- Does the summary locate and highlight the most important information?

Review Content Vocabulary and Academic Vocabulary

1. Terms and definitions may include:
lifestyle—the type of life you would like to live
values—beliefs that guide the way we live
aptitude—an ability, natural talent, or potential to learn a certain skill
Occupational Outlook Handbook (OOH)—describes what workers do on the job, working conditions, training and education required, and expected job prospects
career outlook—number and types of jobs available in any given field
O*NET—Occupational Information Network, the primary source of occupational information in the United States
internship—offers students direct work experience and exposure to various aspects of a career, either with or without pay
planning goals—the small steps you take to get from where you are now to where you want to be
specific goal—stated in exact terms and includes some details
realistic goal—a goal that you have a reasonable chance of achieving
occupational area—a category of jobs that involve similar interests and skills

EVALUATE

Assess for Understanding

2. Values are beliefs that guide how a person lives. Lifestyle goals include where people choose to live, how they relate to others, and how they earn a living. Interests are things that a person enjoys doing in his or her leisure time. Aptitudes are a person's natural abilities. These factors should be considered to better choose a satisfying career.

3. It is important to assess values, lifestyle goals, interests, and aptitudes when choosing a career so that you can find a career that matches what you know about yourself. For example, a vegetarian is not likely to consider a career as a butcher.

4. You can appraise your personality by taking a personality test or by listing your own personality traits.

5. A work environment is the place and conditions in which a person works. The categories involved in relationship preferences are whether you prefer working with data (information), things, or other people.

6. A career assessment should investigate the areas of personal values, personality, education, lifestyle goals, interests, skills, and aptitudes.

7. Online career resources may include the OOH online and O*NET. Besides free Internet access, libraries also have books, trade magazines, pamphlets, films, videos, and special references with information about careers.

8. A personal career profile can help a person easily see if his or her own interests match those of a successful worker in that field.

9. The most obvious benefit of a career in marketing is the opportunity to make an above-average income.

21st Century Skills

Communication Skills

10. Requesting an Informational Interview Write a script for what you would say in a telephone call requesting an informational interview. What impression would you want to make? Describe the tone of voice and manner of speaking you would use to make that impression.

Financial Literacy Skills

11. Calculating Payroll Taxes You are an assistant marketing manager for Big 12 Sporting Goods. Your gross monthly income is $4,900. Use the Internet to locate (1) the IRS monthly payroll tax table, (2) the payroll tax for your state, (3) the Social Security tax rate, and (4) the Medicare tax rate. What will be the amount of the payroll check you will receive each month? If you owned your own business and paid yourself a salary, how much more would be deducted from a $4,900 gross salary?

Everyday Ethics

12. Real World or Not? Are you interested in a career in television—with real people? Although reality shows have been around for decades in various forms, they usually refer to a particular type of program produced since 2000. Programming usually involves a competition between "real" people that awards career opportunities, a monetary payoff, or both to the winners. Reality shows have become a mainstay in American culture, as this headline notes, "History Channel stays the reality course." The channel's scheduled programs include a number of educational reality shows. Critics say reality TV brings out the worst in its participants. Create an idea or theme for a reality show that you think would bring out the best.

e-Marketing Skills

13. Defining e-Marketing Skills Use the Internet to locate blogs, Web sites, and articles that discuss e-marketing skills. Then write a half-page report in which you discuss the most important e-marketing skills and how you may go about developing these skills.

Build Academic Skills

English Language Arts

14. Personal Career Profile Research a career of your choice using the Internet. Then prepare a *Personal Career Profile* that compares all of the qualities you included in your self-assessment with the career you researched. (See **Figure 37.1** for an example.)

NCTE 8 Use information resources to gather information and create and communicate knowledge.

Social Studies

15. Develop a Plan of Action Follow the suggestions discussed in this chapter as you write a personal *Plan of Action* that will help you achieve your planning goals in the next several years. Remember to be as specific as possible.

NCSS IV F Individual Development & Identity Analyze the role of perceptions, attitudes, values, and beliefs in the development of personal identity.

Mathematics

16. Distinguishing Wages If the average national wage for an employee with a bachelor's degree is $52,000, while the average wage for an employee with a master's degree is $67,000, how much more does the person with the master's degree earn? (Provide your answer in dollars and in percentage.)

Math Concept **Determining Differences** Determining the difference between two numbers is a matter of subtracting the smaller amount from the larger amount.

NCTM Number and Operations Compute fluently and make reasonable estimates.

For help, go to the **Math Skills Handbook** located at the back of this book.

Standardized Test Practice

Directions Read the following questions. On a separate piece of paper, write the best possible answer for each one.

1. O*NET is:
   - **A.** a TV network.
   - **B.** a program for searching the Internet.
   - **C.** the Occupational Information Network.
   - **D.** a Web site that displays NFL football scores.
2. Self-employed persons that operate their own small businesses must pay higher Social Security and Medicare taxes than employees of a company.

   T

   F
3. The _________ _________ _________, published by the U.S. Department of Labor, describes what workers do on the job, working conditions, the training and education needed, earnings, and expected job prospects in a wide range of occupations.

Test-Taking Tip

Even though your first choice is often correct, do not be afraid to change an answer if, after you think about it, it seems wrong to you.

DECA Connection Role Play

Employee
Career Guidance Company

Situation Your company specializes in offering advice and assistance to individuals who are entering the workforce for the first time or are seeking to change career fields. Some of the services your company offers include résumé review, advice about gaining relevant work experience, and exploration of career paths for job advancement.

At this point in time, the economy of your area is weak. There have been layoffs at many businesses throughout the area, and most others are not hiring new employees. Unemployment is high, and there are few jobs available. For each career position available, there are at least five applicants. Some of those applicants have several years of experience. The job market is particularly difficult for individuals entering the workforce for the first time.

Your current client (judge) is young and has limited work experience. The client (judge) is uncertain about the type of job he/she is seeking. The client (judge) is also interested in a job that will offer a career path and is seeking advice about creating a standout resume.

Activity You are to meet with the client (judge) and explain some sources of career information, ways to gain work experience, and advancement patterns along career paths.

Evaluation You will be evaluated on how well you meet the following performance indicators:

1. Identify sources of career information.
2. Assess personal strengths and weaknesses.
3. Describe techniques for obtaining work experience.
4. Explain possible advancement patterns for jobs.
5. Utilize resources that can contribute to professional development.

Download the Competitive Events Workbook for more Role-Play practice.

EVALUATE

Communication Skills

10. Scripts will vary but should contain questions such as: How do you spend most of your time on the job? Which work activities do you like most? What skills will I need to do this type of work? What skills will I need to advance? What education and training will I need? Can I complete some of the training on the job? How much time do you spend working with ideas and information? With people? With objects? Will there be an increase in job opportunities in this field over the next several years? What impact will automation and new technology have on job opportunities in the next few years? Tone of voice and manner of speaking should be professional, without the use of slang.

Financial Literacy Skills

11. Calculating Payroll Taxes Payroll tax rates and tables change periodically as taxes are increased or reduced. Current tax rates and tables can be found on the Internal Revenue Service (IRS) Web site and other Web sites. At the time of publication, Federal Income Tax Withholding on $4900 per month was $820.15. State income taxes (rates varied by state) were additional, as were Social Security tax (12.4%) and Medicare (2.9%). Entrepreneurs (self-employed owners of small businesses) were taxed an additional 15.3%.

Everyday Ethics

12. Students should create an idea or theme for a reality show that brings out the best in people. Ideas should show students' creativity and may include such things as following a person for a week to see how many good deeds they do for others, finding the best volunteer in the country, or a program with a theme of "pay it forward."

e-Marketing Skills

13. Students may mention various e-Marketing skills such as blogging, collaborating with others, successful e-mailing, and so on. Half-page reports should include skills students consider to be the most important and a description of how the students might go about developing these skills. For example, students may read a book on blogging to learn the do's and don'ts of successful blogging.

EVALUATE

Build Academic Skills

English Language Arts

14. Each student's career profile will be unique. However, the elements of the profile should appear similar to those in Figure 37.1.

Social Studies

15. Plans should include an ultimate career goal and realistic, specific long-, medium-, and short-term goals that will lead toward the ultimate goal. They should include the type and amount of education and training, along with the work experience that will help achieve the ultimate goal.

Mathematics

16. The person with a master's degree earns an average of $15,000 or about 22% more than a person with a bachelor's degree.

Standardized Test Practice

1. C (the Occupational Information Network)
2. T
3. *Occupational Outlook Handbook (OOH)*

DECA Connection Role Play

Evaluations will be based on these performance indicators:

1. **Identify sources of career information.** Libraries, trade associations, the Internet, informational interviews, and experience are all sources of career information. Publications such as the *Occupational Outlook Handbook* and networks such as O*NET are excellent sources of career information.
2. **Assess personal strengths and weaknesses.** In addition to listing strengths and weaknesses, students should list their values, interests, skills and aptitudes, personality, work environment preferences, and relationship preferences.
3. **Describe techniques for obtaining work experience.** On-the-job training, internships, volunteering, and work experience programs are some techniques for obtaining work experience.
4. **Explain possible advancement patterns for jobs.** There are a number of qualities and behaviors employers look for when considering promotions or advancements. They may include: seniority, knowledge and competence, willingness to learn, initiative, perseverance, cooperativeness, and thinking skills.
5. **Utilize resources that can contribute to professional development.** Lifelong learning is key to any successful career. College courses, industry-based training, and seminars offer opportunities to upgrade existing skills and acquire new ones.

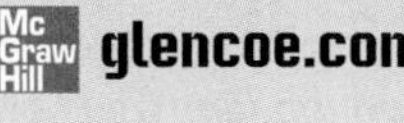

Role Plays For more DECA Role Plays, send students to the Online Learning Center to download the Competitive Events Workbook.

finding and applying for a job

SHOW WHAT YOU KNOW

Visual Literacy Finding job leads, attending job fairs, going through the application process, and getting interviews is a job in itself. These activities require more time than you might expect. ***What might be some good sources for finding job leads?***

Discovery Project

Begin Your Career Portfolio

Essential Question What is a career portfolio and how can it help develop a career and life plan?

Project Goal

A career portfolio is an organized scrapbook of information about you and your best work, presented in an attractive and professional way. A good career portfolio is an essential tool for college and employment interviews. This project is just the beginning. At the end of this chapter, you will further develop your career portfolio. Go online to research ways to format and organize your portfolio and get ideas to get you started. You may find some sample career portfolios that can be helpful, too. After your research, begin to develop an outline of what will become your own career portfolio.

Ask Yourself...

- How will you format your career portfolio?
- How will you organize it?
- What should be included?
- Where will you find the information to be included?

Synthesize and Present Research Synthesize your research by creating a format for a career portfolio, and begin to develop an outline of what will become your own career portfolio.

glencoe.com

Activity
Get a worksheet activity about preparing a career portfolio.

Evaluate
Download a rubric that you can use to evaluate your project.

DECA Connection

DECA Event Role Play

Concepts in this chapter are related to DECA competitive events that involve either an interview or role play.

Performance Indicators The performance indicators represent key skills and knowledge. Your key to success in DECA competitive events is relating them to concepts in this chapter.

- Utilize job search strategies.
- Complete a job application.
- Interview for a job.
- Prepare a résumé.
- Write a letter of application.

DECA Prep

Role Play Practice role-playing with the DECA Connection competitive-event activity at the end of this chapter. More information on DECA events can be found on DECA's Web site.

ENGAGE

Visual Literacy

Read the chapter opener photo caption question to students: ***What might be some good sources for finding job leads?*** people you know, such as family members, friends, parents of friends, teachers, coaches, school counselors, former employers Then ask these guiding questions to activate prior knowledge. Tell students that they learned the answers to these questions in Chapter 37.

Guiding Questions

Explain Why is your career key to your life style?	It provides the funds necessary to support your lifestyle.
Analyze How has the rapid growth of e-commerce affected jobs in marketing and sales?	It has increased the variety of opportunities in these fields and kept the number of available jobs at a high level.

Discovery Project

Begin Your Career Portfolio Start a discussion about the Discovery Project Essential Question: ***What is a career portfolio and how can it help develop a career and life plan?*** A career portfolio is a collection of materials that projects an image of you, your skills, and your accomplishments. It lists your education, projects you have completed, and contains extensive samples of your work. Some career portfolios are dynamic, with visual images and video presentations. A career portfolio can help you develop your career and life plan by telling others about your capabilities. Ask students: ***How could you make your career portfolio stand out from those of other job candidates?*** Answers will vary, but encourage students to be creative.

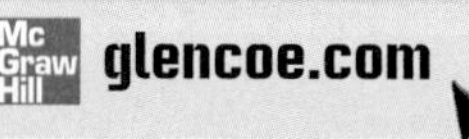

Discovery Project Resources Send students to the Online Learning Center to download a rubric to evaluate their projects.

ENGAGE

Introduce the Chapter

Chapter 38 helps students explore the process of finding and applying for a job. These major concepts are discussed:

- Finding job openings
- Networking
- Following up on job leads
- Getting a work permit
- The importance of using standard English
- Filling out an application form
- Writing a cover letter
- Preparing a résumé
- Differences between electronic résumés and traditional print résumés
- Appropriate conduct during an interview
- Appropriate follow-up after an interview

Discussion Starter

Planning for Success Discuss with students that everyone has a better chance at success with the proper planning. While this is true in business in general, it is also true of people marketing themselves to find the right job. Ask students: ***Have you planned how you would market yourself to a potential employer? What kinds of skills might you emphasize?*** Answers will vary, but may include knowing how to sell merchandise or being a good team player. Then ask: ***What have you learned in this course that might help you market yourself?*** Answers may include: marketing, selling, promotion, pricing, and planning skills; interpersonal skills; communication skills; management skills; and so on.

DECA Connection

Discuss the performance indicators listed in the DECA Connection feature. Explain to students that performance indicators tell them how to demonstrate their acquired skills and knowledge through individual or team competitive events.

 **glencoe.com** 

Competitive Events Workbook For more DECA Role Plays, send students to the Online Learning Center to download the Competitive Events Workbook.

PROGRAM RESOURCE ORGANIZER

PRINT RESOURCES

- **Student Edition**
- **Teacher Edition**
- **Student Activity Workbook with Academic Integration** includes worksheets and activities correlated to the text.
- **Mathematics for Marketing Workbook** provides math activities for every unit in the text.

TECHNOLOGY TOOLBOX

- **Connect**
- **ConnectPlus**
- **ExamView Assessment Suite** is a comprehensive solution for creating, administering, and scoring tests.

 **glencoe.com** 

Online Learning Center provides a variety of resources to enrich and enhance learning.

SECTION, CHAPTER, AND UNIT RESOURCES

- **Graphic Organizers** for organizing text concepts visually.
- **Digital Nation Activities** and **Green Marketer Activities** extend learning beyond the text features.
- **Career Chatroom Career Profiles** allow students to explore different marketing occupations in depth.
- **After You Read Answer Keys** for students to check their answers.
- **Discovery Project Rubrics** and **Marketing Internship Project Rubrics** for students to evaluate their projects.

PROGRAM RESOURCES

- **Student Activity Workbook with Academic Integration Teacher Annotated Edition** includes annotated answers for the activities and worksheets.
- **Marketing Research Project Workbook** provides a step-by-step approach for students to complete their own marketing research studies.
- **School-to-Career Activity Workbook** helps students relate their class work to on-the-job experience and involves work-site analysis and working with mentors.
- **Competitive Events Workbook** helps prepare students for state and national marketing education competitions.
- **Inclusion in the Marketing Education Classroom** provides teaching resources for working with students with special needs.
- **PowerPoint Presentations** provides visual teaching aids and assessments for this chapter.

READING GUIDE

Before You Read

Connect Find out how family members and friends found their jobs, and the job-hunting techniques they used.

Objectives

- **Identify** a variety of sources for job leads.
- **Describe** the best ways to develop job leads.

The Main Idea

It is important to know how to locate job leads. This will help you find a job in your chosen career.

Vocabulary

Content Vocabulary
- job lead
- networking
- public employment agencies
- private employment agencies
- staffing/temporary agencies

Academic Vocabulary

You will find these words in your reading and on your tests. Make sure you know their meanings.
- contacting
- pursuing

Graphic Organizer

Draw or print this chart to write in six types of sources for job leads.

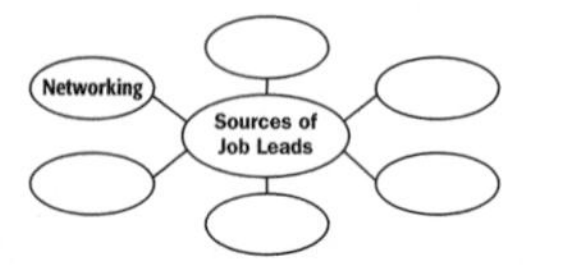

Print this graphic organizer.

MARKETING CORE FUNCTIONS

- Product/Service Management
- Selling

STANDARDS

ACADEMIC

English Language Arts

NCTE 12 Use language to accomplish individual purposes.

Social Studies

NCSS I F Culture Interpret patterns of behavior reflecting values and attitudes that contribute or pose obstacles to cross-cultural understanding.

NCSS VI D Power, Authority, & Governance Compare and analyze the ways nations and organizations respond to conflicts between forces of unity and forces of diversity.

Mathematics

NCTM Problem Solving Apply and adapt a variety of appropriate strategies to solve problems.

NCSS *National Council for the Social Studies*
NCTE *National Council of Teachers of English*
NCTM *National Council of Teachers of Mathematics*
NSES *National Science Education Standards*

Common Core

Reading Interpret words and phrases as they are used in a text, including determining technical, connotative, and figurative meanings, and analyze how specific word choices shape meaning or tone.

m.e. Section 38.1 Finding a Job

FINDING JOB OPENINGS

How do you uncover job opportunities? The best way to start is by **contacting** all of the sources available to you that might produce a job lead. A **job lead** is information about a job opening, perhaps providing some indication about the type of work and who to contact. You need to follow up on minor leads and research information about a company. Finding the right job requires getting leads and following up on them.

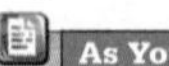

As You Read

Connect Think about which sources for job leads would be most productive for you.

NETWORKING

Often the best sources for job leads are people you know. Consider family, friends, and schoolmates and their families. You may also want to contact former employers, coaches, and teachers or professors. Local business owners and professionals can also be good sources. You might talk to members of a religious or community group to which you belong, and even acquaintances. All of these people form your network.

Networking is the art of building alliances. Finding contacts among people in your network is the most effective way to find a job. Most businesses welcome applications from friends of employees because they trust their employees' opinions. Make a list of all your contacts, including addresses, phone numbers, and e-mail addresses. Keep this list current, and add to it as your career and education progress.

Let your contacts know you are seeking employment and the type of work for which you are suited. Explain what you have to offer, and the types of companies or careers that interest you.

> "Developing effective job-search and interview skills will help you make the most of your time and effort when job hunting."

Politely ask your contacts if they would be comfortable letting you know if they hear of any openings. They may not immediately know of the perfect job for you, but they can keep you in mind and even ask their friends and coworkers about openings. Networking is a mutual exchange, so be prepared to help them in return. Always let them know when you have responded to one of their leads and thank them for helping you.

Social networks on the Internet like Facebook®, and LinkedIn®, a professional network, are other options when searching for job leads.

SCHOOL COUNSELOR

When you are building your network, include your school guidance counselor. Local businesses frequently call school counselors for names of qualified students for part-time or temporary jobs.

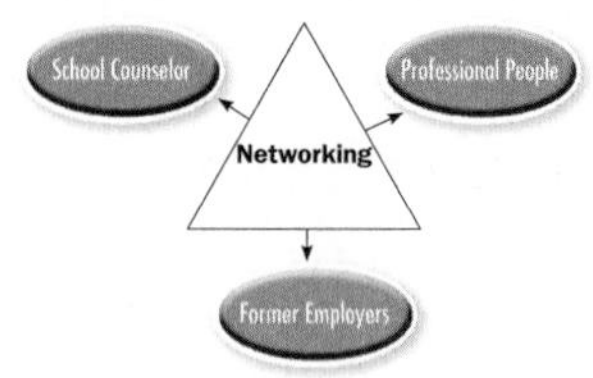

ENGAGE

Anticipation Activity

Improving Student Achievement Ask students: ***Who is currently working?*** Then ask: ***How did you obtain your job?*** If no one is working, ask students how they could begin looking for a job. Their answers will help you introduce the concept of networking, as well as other means of developing job leads, such as online job postings, newspaper ads, signs in store windows, and so on.

Objectives

- **Identify** a variety of sources for job leads. family, friends, friends' families, classmates, teachers, coaches, school counselors, former employers, and so on.
- **Describe** the best ways to develop job leads. Tell everyone in your network that you are seeking employment, what you have to offer, and the type of work you want.

Graphic Organizer

glencoe.com

Graphic Organizer Send students to the Online Learning Center to print this graphic organizer.

EXPLORE

Before You Read

Read the instructions: ***Find out how family members and friends found their jobs, and the job-hunting techniques they used.*** Have each student obtain this information from ten people. Then have the class categorize how respondents found their jobs. Categories might include: Newspaper Ad, Friend, or Online Posting. Use the total number of responses that fall into each category to create a pie chart. Lead a discussion by asking: ***What does this pie chart tell you about how people find jobs?*** Responses will vary based on results.

Preteaching Vocabulary

Have students go to the Online Learning Center at glencoe.com for the Chapter 38 Preteaching Vocabulary games.

Content Vocabulary

Have students write sentences describing how each of the content vocabular terms is related to the topic of this section, Finding Job Openings. Sample: When finding job openings, you should use networking to get job leads from people you know.

Academic Vocabulary

Contacting—Usage Display the word *contacting* and read aloud this sentence: ***One way of uncovering job opportunities is by contacting all of the sources you think might produce a job lead.*** Ask: ***Based on this sentence, what do you think*** **contacting** ***means?*** getting in touch with, communicating with

Pursuing—Synonyms Display the word *pursuing,* and ask students to list some synonyms. engaging in, working at, taking up Ask students for examples of sentences using *pursuing*, and then have them replace the word with a synonym.

Activate Prior Knowledge

Review the Six-Step Process in Making Career Decisions
Ask students to list the steps covered in Chapter 37. Discuss that in order to ask for help in your job search, you must know what kind of job you want.

1. Define your personal (lifestyle) goals.
2. Conduct a self-assessment.
3. Identify possible career choices and gather information on each choice.
4. Evaluate your choices.
5. Make your decision.
6. Plan how you will reach your goal.

Section 38.1

Finding a Job

FINDING JOB OPENINGS

Ask these questions to focus the discussion on finding job openings.

Guiding Questions

Analyze Why should you always follow up on job leads, even if they seem unlikely?	Following leads can expand your network and help you learn about other openings.
Apply Jennifer needs work, but she hides the fact that she has just lost her job. What advice might you give her?	Jennifer needs to tell everyone she is looking for a new job because her network may be her best chance to find one.

Mini Project

Differentiated Instruction

Kinesthetic Learners Have partners conduct role plays in which one is a school counselor and the other is a student who needs a career plan. Role plays will vary. Students should include a discussion on identifying short- and long-term goals.

As You Read

Read the statement: ***Think about which sources for job leads would be most productive for you.*** Have students create a list of sources and then share them. Sources may include friends, parents, teachers, counselors, Web sites, and newspaper ads..

Expert Advice

“ Developing effective job-search and interview skills will help you make the most of your time and effort when job hunting. ”

Tell students that looking for a job can be thought of as dropping a pebble in a pond. Ask: ***Do you think this is a good analogy? Why or why not?*** Sample answer: Yes, because as you tell people you need work and they tell others, the word spreads like a wave until you have a wide circle (or network) of people who can help you.

PROFESSIONALS YOU KNOW

You probably have occasional contact with professional people in your personal life—doctors, teachers, dentists, or lawyers. If you have good relationships with these people, they will probably be happy to help you in your job search. Since they are part of your network, you can ask them about people to contact, job prospects, or advice about the career you are **pursuing**.

FORMER EMPLOYERS

Whether you worked full-time, part-time, or in a temporary position, former employers may be good sources of job leads. They will likely help you find a job if they were pleased with your work.

Why Network? CareerXRoad's "Annual Sources of Hire Survey" reports that referrals, especially from employees, made up 27.3 percent of all new hires.

COOPERATIVE EDUCATION AND WORK EXPERIENCE PROGRAMS

Cooperative education teachers have contacts in the business community because they place and supervise students in part-time jobs. Students enrolled in cooperative work experience programs receive course credit and are sometimes paid as well.

SEARCHING THE INTERNET

Employers use the Internet extensively, and millions of jobs are posted at any given time. In addition to searching company Web sites for openings, search for opportunities on Craigslist, Yahoo! HotJobs and Monster.com. For jobs in marketing, also check MarketingJobs.com. There are also many professional associations that serve the marketing field. Those include the American Marketing Association, the Direct Marketing Association, the Public Relations Society of America, and the International Association of Business Communicators. Check the listings on their local chapter Web sites, too.

On employment Web sites, search for listings that are no more than a month old. Many job search engines and Web sites enable you to search by location, job type, industry, date of posting, and even salary. Some enable you to sign up for an e-mail alert to notify you when positions are posted. Check to see if there is a charge for this service. It is a great way to learn about opportunities as soon as they become available.

NEWSPAPERS AND MAGAZINES

For many years, the "Help Wanted" section of local newspapers was perhaps the best place to find job openings. While many employers have moved their job listings to their own Web sites or other online job-listing sites, do not overlook your local newspaper. These Help Wanted sections also provide information about the local job market. You will learn the qualifications required for different types of jobs. You may find information about salaries and benefits as well.

Follow up immediately on every ad that might lead to the job you want. Be aware, however, if an ad requires you to pay money or enroll in a course; it may be a disguised attempt to sell something rather than a genuine job offer.

In business newspapers and magazines, look for ads or articles about local and regional companies that are expanding, opening a new office, entering a new market, or introducing a new product. These companies are likely to be hiring. Many professionals depend on their association's magazine to alert them to job openings. Look online or in libraries for such publications.

EMPLOYMENT AGENCIES

Employment and temporary staffing agencies match workers with jobs. Most cities have several types of employment agencies. **Public employment agencies** are supported by state or federal taxes and offer free services to both job applicants and employers. **Private employment agencies** and **staffing/temporary agencies**, which are not supported by taxes, must earn a profit to stay in business. They charge a fee for their services, which is paid by either the job applicant or the employer.

Public employment agencies are identified by the names of the states in which they are located. The Texas Employment Commission and the California Employment Development Department are examples. In some cities, the state employment service is the only one available. When you fill out an application form at the public employment agency near you, you will be interviewed to determine your qualifications and interests. The agency will call you if it finds a job that is a good match. You will be told about the company and the duties of the job, and then referred for an interview if you are interested.

Many times, private employment agencies have job leads that are not listed with public agencies. Remember, however, that private agencies charge a fee if they succeed in placing you in a job. Make sure you know who is expected to pay the fee—it might be you. This would be stated in a contract you would be asked to sign. The employer will sometimes pay the fee for matching workers with higher-level jobs. The employee usually pays the placement fee for an entry-level job. The fee is usually a percentage of the salary for the first several months or even the first full year of employment.

MARKETING CASE STUDY

Monster Motivates

monster
Your calling is calling

For one ad campaign, the online job search site Monster.com took an emotional and an inspirational approach to marketing its services. The company built a campaign called "Monster Works for Me," which included TV, radio, print, and Internet ads. Online ads in the campaign were scattered across a wide array of sites, including eBay, ESPN, MSN, and Hoovers.

Reaching the Job Seeker

One commercial featured the voices of various workers, explaining why they work: "I work for the future," "I work to create style," "I work because I care," "I work for my family." The spots portrayed a job as more than just a way to make money, but also a way to express passion—stressing that Monster.com is a better way for people to find the job that is right for them.

English Language Arts

Create Think of a marketing job that you might pursue as a "passion." Find listings for similar jobs online. Then write a complete listing for the job you would like to have.

NCTE 12 Use language to accomplish individual purposes.

EXPLAIN

Why Network? Read the statement: ***CareerXRoad's "Annual Sources of Hire Survey" reports that referrals, especially from employees, made up 27.3 percent of all new hires.*** Ask students: ***What can you infer from this statement?***

Reinforce Vocabulary

Public Employment Agencies—Alternate Meanings Display the term *public employment agencies* and underline the word *public.* Tell students that *public* can have several meanings. A public restaurant is open to anyone. However, *public* can also mean "relating to the government." This is its meaning in the term *public employment agencies*—agencies run by the government and funded by taxes.

SEARCHING THE INTERNET

Tell students that to use the Internet effectively, they need to know where the jobs they might want are likely to be posted. To focus the discussion on using the Internet to look for a job, ask these guiding questions.

Guiding Questions

Explain What is the advantage of signing up to receive an e-mail alert when a job meeting your specifications is posted?	You will hear about the job immediately and therefore can apply very quickly.
Contrast How is MarketingJobs.com different from Web sites such as Craigslist and Monster.com?	MarketingJobs.com is specifically aimed at jobs in the marketing field. Craigslist and Monster.com post all types of jobs.
Infer Why do you think employers are increasingly turning to the Web, rather than posting ads in newspapers or trade journals when trying to fill positions?	Possible answers: It is easy and fast; more and more potential employees search for jobs on the Internet; digital résumés can be searched electronically.

ELABORATE

NEWSPAPERS AND MAGAZINES

Tell students that print advertising can provide helpful job leads. Ask these questions to focus discussion on newspapers and magazines.

Guiding Questions

Recall What kinds of information can you get from the "Help Wanted" section of your local newspaper?	information about the job market in your area, the salaries and benefits offered, and the qualifications required for different types of jobs
Draw Conclusions An ad states you can earn $10 an hour working from home. To prepare, you have to take a course costing $400. Would you do it? Why or why not?	No, because the business probably is not legitimate. They may have only a few jobs, while many more people sign up for the course. The business probably makes money by selling the course.
Infer Other than reading the help wanted ads, how might you use your local newspaper to learn about businesses that are likely to be hiring new employees?	Newspapers often print stories about local businesses expanding, companies opening local branches, and businesses introducing new products. These companies are likely to need more employees.

Graphic Organizer

To explain the two basic types of employment agencies, display this Venn diagram. Have students explain ways in which these types of agencies differ, and write their responses in the appropriate circle. Then ask them to name ways in which they are similar, and write their responses in the space where the circles overlap.

Public Employment Agencies	Both	Private Employment Agencies & Staffing/Temporary Agencies
• Supported by state or federal taxes • Services are free to both job applicants and employers	• Help workers find jobs • Help employers find qualified workers	• Must earn a profit to stay in business • Charge fees, which are paid by either the job applicant or the employer

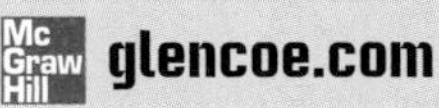

glencoe.com iWB

Graphic Organizer Send students to the Online Learning Center to print this graphic organizer.

Mini Projects

Differentiated Instruction

Verbal/Linguistic Learners Have students explore online and newspaper job ads. Have them use these ads to come up with a list of phrases used to describe specific jobs. Then have them create a table in which they list six to eight phrases in the left column. In the right column, instruct them to describe in their own words what each phrase means. To get students started, display this example:

Phrase	What I Think It Means
We're looking for sales reps who are self-starters.	Applicants must be able to work with little supervision or direction.

When students are finished with their tables, encourage them to share some of the phrases and their interpretations with the class. Interpretations will vary but should be based on phrases from actual job advertisements.

Musical Learners Organize students into groups of three or four. Tell students that they are entrepreneurs who are starting an online job site. Have the group members work together to create a musical jingle that advertises their site. The jingle should be entertaining and describe the site's features and benefits. Encourage students to perform their jingles for the class. Students' musical jingles should describe the features and benefits of their new online job site and explain how their site can help both job hunters and employers.

MARKETING CASE STUDY

English Language Arts Answer Have students search the Internet for job listings that are similar to a job that they think would allow them to pursue their passion. Instruct students to use the contents of these job listings to write a complete listing for their ideal job. Use the following guiding questions to further discuss this marketing case study.

Guiding Questions

Infer On an emotional level, why do you think the Monster ad campaign was successful?	Possible answer: It appealed to people's desire to obtain a job that allowed them to express their passion.
Make Judgments Do you think Monster's slogan "Your calling is calling" is well chosen? Why or why not?	Sample answer: Yes, because it tells job seekers that Monster can help them find a meaningful job.

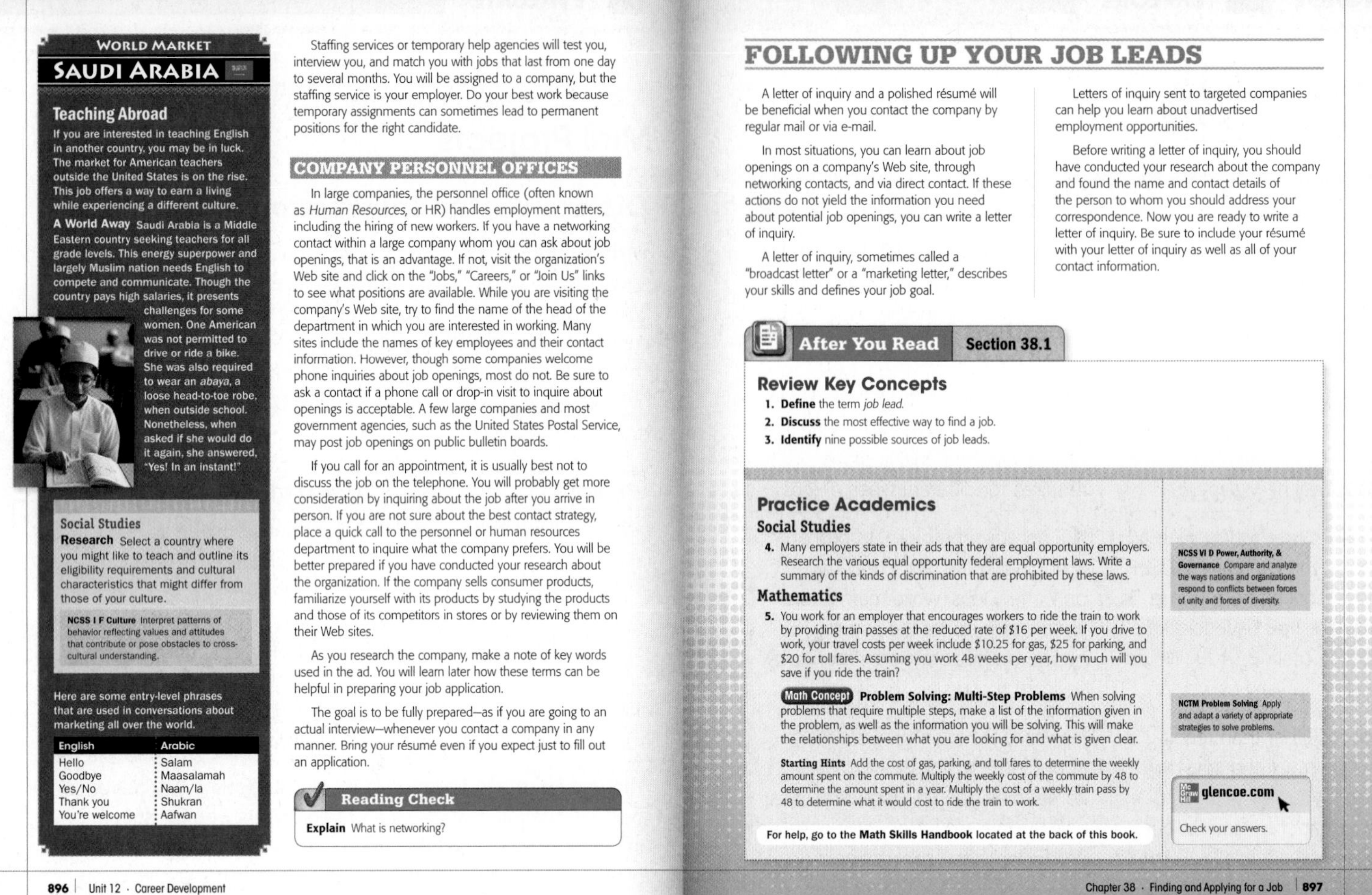

WORLD MARKET

SAUDI ARABIA

Teaching Abroad

If you are interested in teaching English in another country, you may be in luck. The market for American teachers outside the United States is on the rise. This job offers a way to earn a living while experiencing a different culture.

A World Away Saudi Arabia is a Middle Eastern country seeking teachers for all grade levels. This energy superpower and largely Muslim nation needs English to compete and communicate. Though the country pays high salaries, it presents challenges for some women. One American was not permitted to drive or ride a bike. She was also required to wear an *abaya*, a loose head-to-toe robe, when outside school. Nonetheless, when asked if she would do it again, she answered, "Yes! In an instant!"

Social Studies

Research Select a country where you might like to teach and outline its eligibility requirements and cultural characteristics that might differ from those of your culture.

NCSS I F Culture Interpret patterns of behavior reflecting values and attitudes that contribute or pose obstacles to cross-cultural understanding.

Here are some entry-level phrases that are used in conversations about marketing all over the world.

English	Arabic
Hello	Salam
Goodbye	Maasalamah
Yes/No	Naam/la
Thank you	Shukran
You're welcome	Aafwan

Staffing services or temporary help agencies will test you, interview you, and match you with jobs that last from one day to several months. You will be assigned to a company, but the staffing service is your employer. Do your best work because temporary assignments can sometimes lead to permanent positions for the right candidate.

COMPANY PERSONNEL OFFICES

In large companies, the personnel office (often known as *Human Resources*, or HR) handles employment matters, including the hiring of new workers. If you have a networking contact within a large company whom you can ask about job openings, that is an advantage. If not, visit the organization's Web site and click on the "Jobs," "Careers," or "Join Us" links to see what positions are available. While you are visiting the company's Web site, try to find the name of the head of the department in which you are interested in working. Many sites include the names of key employees and their contact information. However, though some companies welcome phone inquiries about job openings, most do not. Be sure to ask a contact if a phone call or drop-in visit to inquire about openings is acceptable. A few large companies and most government agencies, such as the United States Postal Service, may post job openings on public bulletin boards.

If you call for an appointment, it is usually best not to discuss the job on the telephone. You will probably get more consideration by inquiring about the job after you arrive in person. If you are not sure about the best contact strategy, place a quick call to the personnel or human resources department to inquire what the company prefers. You will be better prepared if you have conducted your research about the organization. If the company sells consumer products, familiarize yourself with its products by studying the products and those of its competitors in stores or by reviewing them on their Web sites.

As you research the company, make a note of key words used in the ad. You will learn later how these terms can be helpful in preparing your job application.

The goal is to be fully prepared—as if you are going to an actual interview—whenever you contact a company in any manner. Bring your résumé even if you expect just to fill out an application.

Reading Check

Explain What is networking?

FOLLOWING UP YOUR JOB LEADS

A letter of inquiry and a polished résumé will be beneficial when you contact the company by regular mail or via e-mail.

In most situations, you can learn about job openings on a company's Web site, through networking contacts, and via direct contact. If these actions do not yield the information you need about potential job openings, you can write a letter of inquiry.

A letter of inquiry, sometimes called a "broadcast letter" or a "marketing letter," describes your skills and defines your job goal.

Letters of inquiry sent to targeted companies can help you learn about unadvertised employment opportunities.

Before writing a letter of inquiry, you should have conducted your research about the company and found the name and contact details of the person to whom you should address your correspondence. Now you are ready to write a letter of inquiry. Be sure to include your résumé with your letter of inquiry as well as all of your contact information.

After You Read | **Section 38.1**

Review Key Concepts

1. **Define** the term *job lead*.
2. **Discuss** the most effective way to find a job.
3. **Identify** nine possible sources of job leads.

Practice Academics

Social Studies

4. Many employers state in their ads that they are equal opportunity employers. Research the various equal opportunity federal employment laws. Write a summary of the kinds of discrimination that are prohibited by these laws.

NCSS VI D Power, Authority, & Governance Compare and analyze the ways nations and organizations respond to conflicts between forces of unity and forces of diversity.

Mathematics

5. You work for an employer that encourages workers to ride the train to work by providing train passes at the reduced rate of $16 per week. If you drive to work, your travel costs per week include $10.25 for gas, $25 for parking, and $20 for toll fares. Assuming you work 48 weeks per year, how much will you save if you ride the train?

Math Concept **Problem Solving: Multi-Step Problems** When solving problems that require multiple steps, make a list of the information given in the problem, as well as the information you will be solving. This will make the relationships between what you are looking for and what is given clear.

Starting Hints Add the cost of gas, parking, and toll fares to determine the weekly amount spent on the commute. Multiply the weekly cost of the commute by 48 to determine the amount spent in a year. Multiply the cost of a weekly train pass by 48 to determine what it would cost to ride the train to work.

NCTM Problem Solving Apply and adapt a variety of appropriate strategies to solve problems.

For help, go to the **Math Skills Handbook** located at the back of this book.

glencoe.com

Check your answers.

ELABORATE

WORLD MARKET

SOCIAL STUDIES

Students should select a country where they would like to teach, and then outline the eligibility requirements and any cultural characteristics that might differ from those in their culture. For example, in certain countries it might be necessary to speak one or more local languages, while in others it might be acceptable to only speak English. Cultural characteristics might involve individuals dressing as the local people do and possibly adhering to local customs, such as the requirement that women not appear in public unaccompanied or that individuals not eat certain types of foods.

COMPANY PERSONNEL OFFICES

Discuss with students that a company's personnel office typically lists job openings on the company's Web site. To focus the discussion on company personnel offices, ask these guiding questions.

Guiding Questions

Recall You are applying for a job with an e-commerce company that sells pet supplies. How might you best learn about the company's products?	You could visit the company's Web site and study the products and product information. You also should visit competitor's Web sites to learn how their products vary and try to determine the company's strengths and weaknesses.
Decide If you want to contact a large company about a job, but are not sure about the best contact strategy, what might you do?	You could place a quick call to the personnel or human resources department to ask about the best contact strategy.

EVALUATE

Critical Thinking

Ask students: ***Why do you think some businesses refer to their personnel departments as human resources?*** It shows they see employees as a resource their company needs to compete, just as the business needs other resources such as raw materials and products.

Mini Project

Enrichment

Researching Government Job Web Sites Ask students to research two local, state, or federal job search Web sites. Have them summarize the contents and characteristics of both in a bulleted list. An example of one site is IowaJobs.org, which is maintained by Iowa WorkForce Development. This state agency allows visitors to search for jobs by title, location, and pay rate.

Reading Check Answer

Read the question to students: ***What is networking?*** the art of building alliances. Ask: ***What is an alliance?*** a bond between individuals, families, friends, coworkers, and so on Then ask: ***Why do you think it is important to have alliances when you are job hunting?*** When people are allied with you, they help and support you. If they know you are looking for a job, they will watch for openings they think might interest you.

FOLLOWING UP YOUR JOB LEADS

Ask these questions to focus discussion on following up on job leads.

Guiding Questions

List What are three common ways of finding out about job openings in a specific company?	going to the company's Web site; through networking contacts; direct contact (with the company's human resources department)
Analyze Why might you send a letter of inquiry to a company?	You may want to work for that specific company, for example, because you think it is a particularly good match for your skills, and you haven't been able to find any postings for suitable jobs.

After You Read Section 38.1

Review Key Concepts

1. A job lead is information about a job opening, perhaps providing some indication about the type of work and whom to contact.
2. The most effective way to find a job is through contacts among members of your network, which includes people you know, such as family, friends, classmates, former employers, teachers, coaches, and so on.
3. Sources of job leads include family and friends, school counselors, professional people, former employers, cooperative education and work experience programs, Internet Web sites, newspaper ads, employment agencies, and company personnel offices.

Practice Academics

Social Studies

4. Students should write a summary discussing the various equal opportunity federal employment laws. Kinds of discrimination that are prohibited by these laws include race, color, religion, gender, and national origin. Qualified individuals cannot be discriminated against on the basis of disability, and the employer must make reasonable accommodations to any known physical or mental limitations of an otherwise qualified individual with a disability. Employers also cannot discriminate based on age or genetic information.

Mathematics

5. Savings will be \$1,884. ([{10.25 + \$25 + \$20} – 16] × 48) = \$1,884

glencoe.com

Answer Key Send students to the Online Learning Center to check their answers.

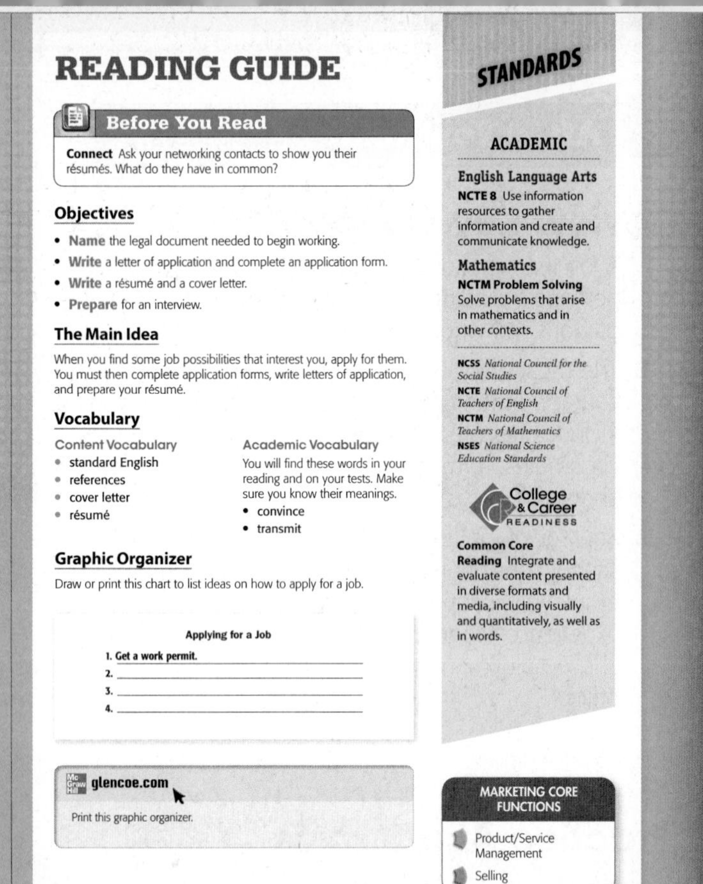

READING GUIDE

Before You Read

Connect Ask your networking contacts to show you their résumés. What do they have in common?

Objectives

- **Name** the legal document needed to begin working.
- **Write** a letter of application and complete an application form.
- **Write** a résumé and a cover letter.
- **Prepare** for an interview.

The Main Idea

When you find some job possibilities that interest you, apply for them. You must then complete application forms, write letters of application, and prepare your résumé.

Vocabulary

Content Vocabulary
- standard English
- references
- cover letter
- résumé

Academic Vocabulary

You will find these words in your reading and on your tests. Make sure you know their meanings.
- convince
- transmit

Graphic Organizer

Draw or print this chart to list ideas on how to apply for a job.

Applying for a Job
1. Get a work permit.
2. ______
3. ______
4. ______

glencoe.com

Print this graphic organizer.

STANDARDS

ACADEMIC

English Language Arts

NCTE 8 Use information resources to gather information and create and communicate knowledge.

Mathematics

NCTM Problem Solving Solve problems that arise in mathematics and in other contexts.

NCSS *National Council for the Social Studies*
NCTE *National Council of Teachers of English*
NCTM *National Council of Teachers of Mathematics*
NSES *National Science Education Standards*

College & Career READINESS

Common Core
Reading Integrate and evaluate content presented in diverse formats and media, including visually and quantitatively, as well as in words.

MARKETING CORE FUNCTIONS
- Product/Service Management
- Selling

m.e. Section 38.2 Applying for a Job

GETTING A WORK PERMIT

In some states, work permits are required for minors (ages 12–17). The permit must specify the exact duties and hours of work. Both the employer and the worker fill out sections of an application for the permit. The employer, worker, and the worker's parent or guardian must sign the application before a work permit is issued.

Laws vary from state to state but generally, minors under 18 years of age must attend school to get a work permit. If a student graduates from high school before age 18, he or she is no longer required to obtain a work permit.

Ask your marketing teacher or counselor whether you will need a work permit and, if so, where you can get one. A designated school official usually issues work permits. Check this now so you can avoid possible delays when you are ready to work.

As You Read

Analyze Study the résumé in this text to become familiar with their form and content.

APPLYING FOR A JOB

Companies are looking for the most qualified people to fill their jobs. The decision to hire is based on three main criteria:

1. How well can you do the job?
2. How willing are you to do the job?
3. How well will you fit in?

The decision about whether to hire you will depend on information you provide in your résumé, application form, and interview. The way you present the information and yourself is also very important.

> "A work permit establishes that it is legal for a young worker to do the type of work offered."

Many employers ask job applicants for a résumé. Some request that applicants fill out an application form. Some require both. Throughout this course, you have been building your employment portfolio with examples of some of your best marketing-related efforts. You will want to add a copy of your résumé to your portfolio.

Employers may administer one or more employment tests to applicants. Most companies today do background checks for any criminal activity. A background check may also be done to verify your education and previous employment. Some companies might also require some type of drug testing.

USING STANDARD ENGLISH

Standard English is the formal style of writing and speaking that you have learned in school. This style is called "standard" because the words and structure mean the same thing to everyone.

ENGAGE

Anticipation Activity

Improving Student Achievement Give each student a copy of a generic job application form or one from a familiar local business. Have students fill out the application for a specific job (for example, a retail sales associate or coffee barista). Allow them to use any resources they may have with them (such as address books). Allow 10 to 15 minutes for this activity.

Objectives

- **Name** the legal document needed to begin working work permit
- **Write** a letter of application and complete an application form. See pages 900 to 901.
- **Write** a résumé and a cover letter. See pages 901 to 904.
- **Prepare** for an interview. See pages 904 to 908.

Graphic Organizer

Applying for a Job

1. **Get a work permit.**
2. Fill out an application form.
3. Write and submit a cover letter.
4. Write and submit a résumé.

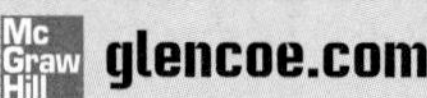

Graphic Organizer Send students to the Online Learning Center to print this graphic organizer.

EXPLORE

Before You Read

Read the question aloud: ***Ask your networking contacts to show you their résumés. What do they have in common?*** They are clearly written, error-free, use standard English, and contain objectives, contact information, and job and education histories. Ask students: ***If you were an interviewer, what would give you a positive impression of a résumé?*** It would be error-free, concise, easy to read, and contain pertinent information.

Preteaching Vocabulary

Have students go to the Online Learning Center at glencoe.com for the Chapter 38 Preteaching Vocabulary games.

Content Vocabulary

Have students write a paragraph on how these terms are related. Sample answer: Cover letters and résumés must use standard English, or the formal English we learn in school. A résumé may include references, or individuals who will recommend me.

Academic Vocabulary

Convince—Word Origin Display the word *convince*. Explain that it comes from the Latin word *convincere,* which means "to refute" or "to prove." Ask how this Latin meaning could lead to today's definition of *convince*: "to overcome by argument." Possible answer: When you convince someone, you get them to agree with you by presenting, or arguing, your point of view.

Transmit—Word Components Display the word *transmit,* dividing it into the syllables *trans* and *mit.* Explain that the prefix *trans-* means "beyond" or "across." Therefore, transmit means "to convey or send from one person or place to another."

GETTING A WORK PERMIT

Use these questions to focus the discussion on work permits.

Guiding Questions

Identify What laws might a state have concerning when and where a minor can work?	Laws might restrict hours, times of day, and working conditions for minors.
Draw Conclusions Why is a parent or guardian required to sign work permit applications?	It is important that parents and guardians approve that their children are working.

m.e. Section 38.2 Applying for a Job

As You Read

Read students the As You Read statement: ***Study the résumé in this text to become familiar with its form and content.*** Ask students: ***Why do you think items in a résumé are typically listed in the order shown in Figure 38.1?*** Answers will vary. Placing identification and contact information at the top makes it easy to locate. Having Objective come next sets the stage for the remaining information. Experience and Education are of prime importance in determining whether the candidate is qualified, so they are listed immediately below Objective.

APPLYING FOR A JOB

Use these questions to focus the discussion on applying for a job.

Guiding Questions

List What are three ways in which employers typically obtain the information they use to determine who to hire?	résumé, application form, and interview
Analyze Why do you think employers are concerned with how well a job candidate will fit into their workplace?	Employers know that different kinds of workers do better in certain environments. Some workers do best in a structured environment, while others need more freedom.
Summarize Why is it vital to use standard English whenever you communicate with a potential employer?	Employers want to hire well-educated individuals who will represent the company in a professional manner.

Expert Advice

"A work permit establishes that it is legal for a young worker to do the type of work offered."

Ask students: ***What might happen if states did not have laws governing when and where minors can work?*** Minors might work such long hours that it affected their school work; if their family was facing financial hardship, minors might feel pressured to work long hours to help out financially; minors might be exposed to dangerous working conditions for which they are not adequately prepared.

DIGITAL NATION

Your Web Presence

Who are you online? Potential employers want to know! Today many employers "google" the names of job applicants to find out more about them. Everything you write online, from blog comments to restaurant reviews, may be visible in search results. Your Facebook or MySpace profile and names of your friends may also appear.

Polishing Your Online Credentials

Job seekers can use their visibility on the Web to their advantage. Interested in a career in sports marketing? Set up a Twitter feed to network with others in the field. Want to work at a certain company? Blog about it to show how you could be an asset. Many job seekers create profiles on professional networking sites such as LinkedIn.com. Some set up their own portfolio Web sites to showcase their work.

English Language Arts

Evaluate You want to hire a marketing assistant. You use a search engine to find the name of a candidate but find poorly written, critical comments on blogs and social networks. What would you do? Why?

NCTE 8 Use information resources to gather information and create and communicate knowledge.

glencoe.com

Get a Digital Nation Activity.

Therefore, everything you write and say to a prospective employer should be in standard English. Standard English employs correct grammar, spelling, pronunciation, and usage. The repeated use of interjections, such as "you know" or "like," is not advisable. Nonstandard pronunciations are also undesirable.

Employers will have several opportunities to evaluate your communication skills. Your letter of application or résumé will indicate your writing skills. Finally, when you are interviewed, the employer will evaluate your verbal communication skills. He or she will also take note of your ability to listen and interact in a businesslike manner.

FILLING OUT APPLICATION FORMS

Most application forms are short (from one to four pages) and ask similar questions. More and more companies and organizations are asking applicants to complete online forms. Companies usually design their own application forms, so you may find differences among various applications.

The application form provides information about your qualifications so company personnel can determine whether to interview you. The first rule of filling out an application form is to complete the form neatly and spell all words correctly. Whenever possible, ask a family member or trusted friend to check your application for errors or omissions. If you complete the form at the place of employment, use a pen with blue or black ink. Do not use colored inks.

Answer every question that applies to you. Write "N/A" for those questions that are not applicable. This shows that you did not overlook the item.

Use your full name, not a nickname, on the form. On most applications, your first name, middle initial, and last name are requested. Provide your complete address, including your ZIP code.

List a specific job title if asked about your job preference. Do not write "anything" as an answer. Employers expect you to know what type of work you can and want to do.

Most application forms include a section on education. Write the names of all the schools you have attended and the dates of attendance. There will also be a section on previous work experience. As a student, you may not have had much work experience. However, you can include short-term or unpaid jobs. Fill out this section in reverse chronological order. Begin with your current or most recent job and end with your first job.

Be prepared to list several **references**. Your references are people who know your work habits and personal traits well and will recommend you for the job. Make sure you ask permission of your references before listing them on an application form. Try to use professional references, such as your teachers, friends established in business, or former employers. Do not list classmates, relatives, or personal friends. Sign your name using your first name, middle initial, and last name. Your signature should be written, never typed or printed.

WRITING COVER LETTERS

A **cover letter** is a letter written by a job applicant to introduce the applicant to an employer and, hopefully, convince the employer to read the résumé. The cover letter should describe why the applicant is the best person to fill a specific job opening. Writing a cover letter is like writing a sales pitch about yourself. Your goal is to **convince** an employer that you are the best person to fill a specific job opening. Your cover letter should reflect your understanding of the company and how you may be able to meet its needs. Cover letters can be submitted via mail, e-mail, or fax. They usually accompany a résumé. A cover letter should be personalized for each position and addressed to an individual. Tell why you are interested in the position and describe your special qualifications for it.

Write a first draft to get down most of the main points. Next, revise your letter until you are pleased with the end result. Ask a teacher, parent or guardian, or friend in business to read and critique your letter. Then put the final touches on it and print out a copy.

Describe how you learned about the job opening in the first paragraph. The second paragraph should contain a description of how your education and experience qualify you for the job. Emphasize facts that make you especially well qualified for the job. Do not repeat the information in the résumé; instead, describe how that experience or education qualifies you for this position. If you have a lot to say about both your education and job experience, use a separate paragraph for each. Mention classes you have taken that are related to the job.

Finally, in your last paragraph, ask for an interview at the employer's convenience. State when you will be available, and provide your telephone number and e-mail address. If your e-mail address is unusual or quirky, create one with a mature name to use for your job search.

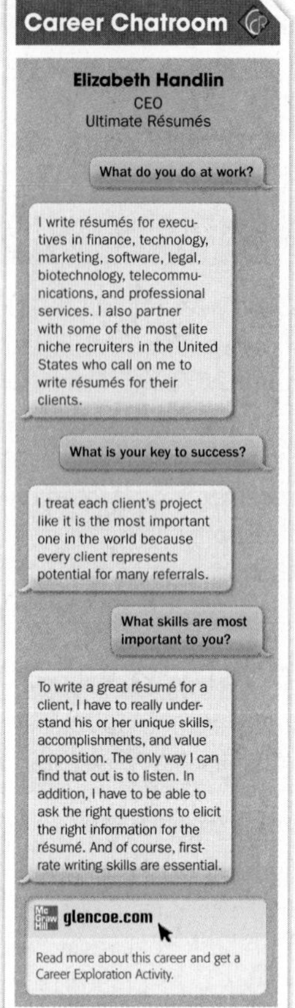

Career Chatroom

Elizabeth Handlin
CEO
Ultimate Résumés

What do you do at work?

I write résumés for executives in finance, technology, marketing, software, legal, biotechnology, telecommunications, and professional services. I also partner with some of the most elite niche recruiters in the United States who call on me to write résumés for their clients.

What is your key to success?

I treat each client's project like it is the most important one in the world because every client represents potential for many referrals.

What skills are most important to you?

To write a great résumé for a client, I have to really understand his or her unique skills, accomplishments, and value proposition. The only way I can find that out is to listen. In addition, I have to be able to ask the right questions to elicit the right information for the résumé. And of course, first-rate writing skills are essential.

glencoe.com

Read more about this career and get a Career Exploration Activity.

EXPLAIN

DIGITAL NATION

English Language Arts Answer Students might choose to take the candidate out of the running, or ask him or her directly about the comments to gauge the response. Remind students of the possibility that the comments were written by another person with the same name. To further explore creating a Web presence, ask these guiding questions.

Guiding Questions

Recall Why do many employers "google" job applicants?	They want to see what they can learn about the applicant by looking online.
Apply How might you use Twitter, Facebook, or LinkedIn to increase your chances of obtaining a specific job?	Answers will vary. For example, you could use Facebook to discuss your knowledge about a specific area of marketing.

FILLING OUT APPLICATION FORMS

Ask these questions to focus discussion on filling out job applications.

Guiding Questions

Recall What is the first rule of filling out an application form?	Complete the form neatly and spell all words correctly.
Infer Why do you think a company might require you to fill out an application even if you have already provided a cover letter and résumé?	The company may want to make sure you have provided all necessary information; it may want it in a standardized format for easier reference.

Critical Thinking

Ask students: ***What are some qualities employers look for on job applications?*** honesty, legibility, complete and accurate information

ELABORATE

Mini Projects

Enrichment

Talking about Facebook Describe for students a scenario in which a friend is applying for a job. They know the friend's Facebook page contains content a potential employer might view negatively. For example, it contains photos of the friend acting immaturely, and it is filled with grammar and spelling errors. Have students write a paragraph on what they might say to their friend. Sample paragraph: I would explain that employers often search social networking sites to learn more about job applicants. I would suggest that poor grammar and spelling and casual photos do not reflect well on my friend and should maybe be removed from Facebook for the time being.

Examining LinkedIn.com Explain that LinkedIn is often described as a business social networking site. Have students go to LinkedIn and examine some of its features. Then have them describe ways in which marketing professionals might use LinkedIn to advance their careers. Students should give a brief presentation describing how LinkedIn can help marketing professionals network with others. By creating a profile, professionals can share their goals, job experiences, accomplishments, and samples of their work.

WRITING COVER LETTERS

Ask these questions to focus the discussion on writing cover letters.

Guiding Questions

Recall What is the purpose of a cover letter?	It introduces a job applicant to an employer and convinces the employer to read the applicant's résumé.
Analyze How can a cover letter be thought of as a sales pitch for yourself?	Its purpose is to emphasize why you are the best candidate for the position you are applying for.
Summarize What should the three paragraphs of a cover letter contain?	(1) how you learned about the job opening; (2) a description of how your education and experience make you especially well qualified for the job; (3) a request for an interview

Career Chatroom

Focus the Career Chatroom discussion concerning Elizabeth Handlin by asking students these guiding questions.

Guiding Questions

Describe What is Elizabeth Handlin's job?	She writes résumés for executives in a variety of professions.
Analyze What are some of the skills that are most important to her?	listening carefully, knowing what questions to ask, having first-rate writing skills
Infer What do you think she means by "niche recruiters"?	people who recruit professionals for highly specialized positions

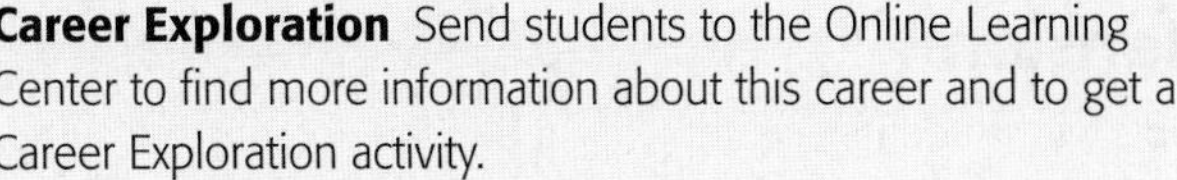

glencoe.com

Career Exploration Send students to the Online Learning Center to find more information about this career and to get a Career Exploration activity.

Many companies receive dozens of cover letters with résumés every week. Businesses that advertise jobs in the newspaper or online may receive hundreds of letters. Businesses interview only a small portion of those who write—those who qualify for the position and make an effective written presentation. Your cover letter can give you a big advantage over other applicants. Take the time to develop an effective letter of which you are really proud. Once you write a letter, you can adapt it for other jobs, personalizing the details to each position.

As with any sales pitch, a good first impression counts. Use the spell-check function of your word processing program to eliminate any spelling errors. Then proofread it with your own eyes because a computer will not know that you meant "from" instead of "form," or "manager" instead of "manger." Before you send your letter, have another person review it for accuracy.

Your letter must not only be neat and clear but also follow the rules outlined in this section. Be sure to include all the elements of a business letter, including the salutation and a formal closing.

Print your cover letter with black ink on white or off-white paper. Use paper that matches the kind you use for your résumé. Keep in mind that colored paper does not fax well. For electronic submission, be sure to apply the formatting suggestions that are discussed in the next section for your *electronic* cover letter.

PREPARING RÉSUMÉS

A cover letter and a résumé convey your qualifications in writing and sell your abilities. You can see an example of a traditional printed résumé in **Figure 38.1**. A **résumé** is a brief summary of personal information, education, skills, work experience, activities, and interests. A résumé organizes job-related facts about you and saves the employer time before and during an interview.

When you send an employer a résumé, include a cover letter. The résumé makes filling out job applications a simpler process because you have already organized all the information. Many people prepare a résumé as the first step in the job application process.

Even if you are not hired, many employers will keep your résumé on file for a certain period of time. If they have an opening for which you qualify in the future, they might call you.

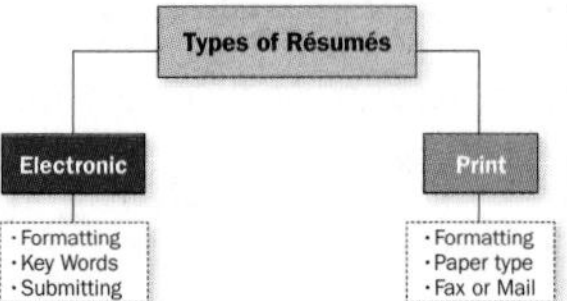

ELECTRONIC RÉSUMÉS

If you are applying for a position online, you may be required to submit an electronic résumé. Compose your electronic résumé using a word processing program.

ELECTRONIC FORMATTING ISSUES

The format of your electronic résumé should be text only. Save your résumé as a text-only file; this is the easiest way to **transmit** and read electronic files. Avoid bold type, italics, and underlining, which do not transmit well and make your résumé difficult to read. Stick to a commonly used traditional font, such as Times New Roman. Keep the font size between 12 and 14 points. Do not use tabs; use the space bar instead.

USING KEY WORDS

Companies that accept résumés electronically often search for job qualifications by looking for key words. It is very likely that a computer program, not a person, will first scan your résumé. The computer scans, or searches, for key words and phrases, and the résumé is summarized and ranked among other qualified candidates.

Because of this, it is important to use key words to describe what you can do. What are key words? Key words consist primarily of nouns. They are usually divided into three categories: job title, industry, and personal traits. You will have a list of key words or phrases from the initial research you did about the company, the industry, and the job.

FIGURE 38.1 Résumé

What Information Should You Include? Your résumé should show off your education, skills, and experience in the best way possible, using one page or a maximum of two pages. ***What are some tips for writing a résumé?***

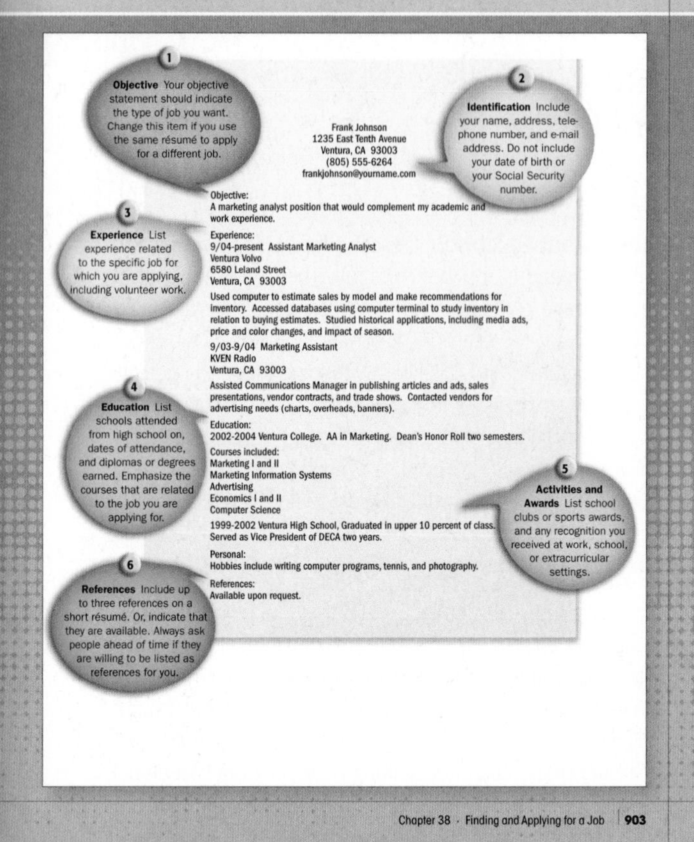

EXPLAIN

Reinforce Vocabulary

Résumé—Usage Display the word *résumé* for the class to read. Then write the word *resume* next to it. Pronounce both words aloud and make certain that students can correctly pronounce *résumé.* Point out that the difference between these two words is the accents in *résumé.* Explain that *résumé* is a French word. Emphasize to students that they must always correctly include these accents when writing *résumé.* Not only is it incorrect to not include the accents, but if you leave them out, the reader might think you mean the word *resume.*

Extension

Discuss with students how they might add the accents to *résumé* when using a word processing program. For example, when using Microsoft Word 2007 or Microsoft Word 2010, they can add the accents by clicking the *Insert* tab, opening the *Symbol* dialog box, and locating the *é* symbol.

PREPARING RÉSUMÉS

Tell students that having a well-written résumé simplifies completing other documents, such as cover letters and job applications. To focus the discussion on preparing résumés, ask students these guiding questions.

Guiding Questions

List What are some of the sections included in a traditional résumé?	Identification (Personal Information), Objective, Work Experience, Education, Skills, Activities and Interests (Personal Information), References
Contrast How is a résumé different from a cover letter?	A résumé contains information, such as work experience and education, which is needed when applying for any job. A cover letter explains why the applicant is particularly well suited to a specific job.

ELABORATE

Graphic Organizer

To discuss the similarities and differences between electronic résumés and print résumés, display this graphic organizer. Have volunteers list the characteristics and features of each résumé type and write them in the correct box.

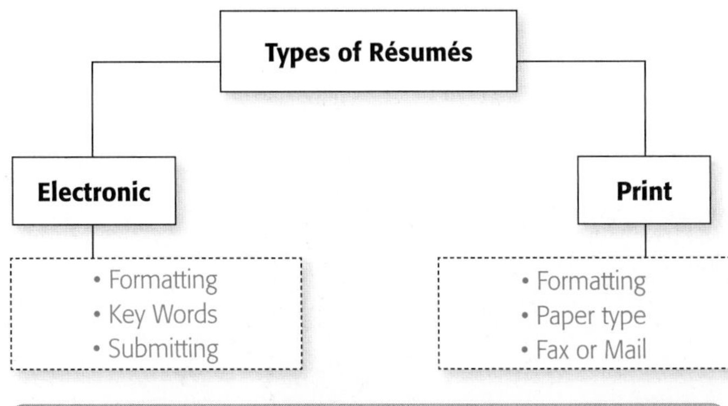

iWB

Graphic Organizer Send students to the Online Learning Center to print this graphic organizer.

ELECTRONIC RÉSUMÉS

Remind students that, like print résumés, electronic résumés are typically created using word processing programs. To focus the discussion on electronic résumés, ask students these guiding questions.

Guiding Questions

Recall True or false: When creating an electronic résumé, you should include items like bulleted lists and bold type to make the document look professional.	False. Formatting such as bulleted lists and bold type may not transmit properly and therefore can make the resulting résumé difficult to read.
Analyze How can you create a list of key words?	You can create the list based on words and phrases you encountered during your initial research of the industry and the types of jobs in which you are interested.
Predict When writing your résumé, you do not include key words related to the type of position you want. What might happen as a result?	When the résumé is electronically scanned, no key words will be found, so your résumé will not be flagged as a match for jobs in which you might be interested.

Critical Thinking

Ask students to discuss some common ways of submitting application forms and résumés. Have them speculate on why companies increasingly use high-tech recruitment and screening measures. Common documents can be submitted via mail, fax machines, Web sites, e-mail, or in person. Web-based recruitment is popular with companies who want to save time and money and quickly locate qualified candidates. Applicants and the documents they submit can be electronically screened to promptly weed out unqualified candidates.

Visual Literacy

Figure 38.1 Caption Answer Read the caption question to students: *What are some tips for writing a résumé?* Keep it as short as you can and still include the necessary information; be accurate; organize information into clearly defined sections; if it is an electronic résumé, save it as a text-only file and do not use formatting such as bold type or tabs; make certain it is error-free, grammatically correct, and use Standard English. To further discuss information to include in a résumé, ask these guiding questions.

Guiding Questions

Analyze What part of your résumé should typically change depending on the job you are applying for? Why?	The objective statement should change to match the job description.
Infer Professional résumé writers agree that you should not include the word "I" in your résumé. Why do you think this is?	Avoiding the use of the word "I" takes the narrator out of the résumé and instead focuses on the action.

Mini Projects

Differentiated Instruction

Verbal/Linguistic Learners Have students write a paper with tips for writing electronic résumés (e-résumés). Explain that the paper should discuss the e-résumé's organization, proper formatting, and the importance of key words. Students should explain that the résumé should showcase the applicant's education, skills, and experience in a maximum of two pages. They also should discuss the importance of using key words so that if the résumé is scanned, it will be seen as a match.

Cooperative Learners Tell students that one way to come up with key words is to examine ads or listings. Have partners choose a specific job and then examine online listings for that job to create a list of key words. When done, have students share their lists with the class. Lists will vary depending on the jobs chosen. Key words for a sales position might include: sales associate, high energy, outgoing, self-motivated, service-oriented, communication skills, flexible hours, and so on.

The information you gained from the Internet, publications, or networking will help you figure out which key words to use.

It is important to include industry-specific jargon, as many employers will search by industry language. Be sure to spell out all acronyms. For example, mention your membership in the American Marketing Association, not just AMA. You might not be considered for a job for which you are qualified if key words do not appear on your résumé.

Confidentiality is an issue when you post your résumé on the Internet. Remember that once posted on a career Web site, your résumé is a public document that is out of your control. You will need to provide information so that a potential employer can contact you. Usually, you have the option of limiting your personal information by including only an e-mail address or post office box. Since most employers prefer to contact applicants by telephone or e-mail, make sure your voice mail greeting is professional and brief. Check your messages and e-mails daily so you can respond promptly. Before e-mailing your résumé to employers, e-mail a copy to yourself so that you can review the message.

HOW TO SUBMIT YOUR RÉSUMÉ

When you have completed your cover letter and résumé, you can submit them as part of an e-mail. You can "cut and paste" the résumé into the body of an e-mail message rather than including it as an attached file. An attached file can be difficult to read unless it is created in a word processing program designated by the employer. Also, some employers may be hesitant to open file attachments because of the risk of computer viruses. Some companies will specify what type of electronic form they prefer; read online submission directions carefully to avoid having your résumé rejected.

TRADITIONAL PRINT RÉSUMÉS

In addition to your electronic résumé, prepare a print résumé. You can use it for positions that require a cover letter and résumé to be mailed or faxed. It is also a good idea to keep printed versions of your documents in case your computer files are ever erased or corrupted. If you print your own résumé, use black ink on white or off-white paper. Ideally, the paper should match the kind you use for your cover letter. Some applicants use local printing companies to print their résumés. If you have your résumé printed in this manner, inquire about prices and ask to look at samples of actual résumés. Shop around. Some printing companies offer package deals that include matching paper for your cover letters as well as envelopes.

PRINT FORMATTING ISSUES

As you can see in **Figure 38.1** on p. 903, the format of a résumé helps organize the material and enables the reader to find the information easily. You can review additional styles and formatting options for printed résumés. Look at the many résumé sample books that can be found in your library or bookstore. Many online job search sites also feature samples and free advice about preparing résumés and cover letters. Enter "résumé samples" on your favorite search engine to find many sites where you can view résumés. Many of these Web sites are free, but some do charge for samples. Some students hire writers to help them develop their résumés. You can find these experts in traditional or online *Yellow Pages*. Online résumé writing services can also be a resource. Prices, quality, and turnaround times vary; again, shop around.

PREPARING FOR AN INTERVIEW

What happens during an interview is usually what determines an employer's choice of one applicant over another applicant. It is critical to prepare yourself carefully for your interview. Your plan should include three steps: preparing for the interview, conducting yourself properly during the interview, and following up after the interview.

The employer's first impression of you will have a significant impact on his or her hiring decision. Appropriate dress and grooming, body language that shows confidence, and use of standard English all combine to make a good first impression.

DRESS AND GROOMING

More recently employers in many offices and stores have adopted a dress code known as *business casual*. This does not mean, however, that you should dress casually for an interview. It is better to take extra time and effort to make a good impression by dressing in a more formal way.

Your clothes should be neat, clean, and wrinkle-free for every interview. In some cases, appropriate interview dress depends on the job. In sales, for example, people dress formally and conservatively to make a good impression on customers.

Regardless of its style, your hair should be clean and neat. The interviewer will be observing you to see how well you will fit in, so a moderate hairstyle is prudent.

Employers will notice hands—be sure they are clean and your nails are neatly trimmed. Nail polish, if worn, should be clear or a pale, subtle color. Extravagant jewelry can be distracting. Too much makeup can also distract the interviewer. Avoid wearing perfume or cologne as well. Strong scents can be overwhelming and distracting, and some people are allergic to them.

THINGS TO KNOW

When you get a call from a company for an interview appointment, write down the date and time and the name of the interviewer. Check the spelling and make sure you can pronounce the interviewer's name correctly. Ask the receptionist for the pronunciation if it is unfamiliar to you.

Preparation is essential to a good interview. Research the types of questions you expect to be asked, and have a friend, family member, or teacher role-play the interview with you. Practicing your answers and then reviewing how you did is a good way to become more comfortable.

Before you get to your actual interview, take time to carefully review your résumé. Be ready to answer any questions about your education, work experience, and other qualifications.

The research you have conducted about a company will again come in handy in an interview situation. Your knowledge of the business will help you make a better impression. You will be able to speak intelligently about the company's products and operations. It will show that you are interested in the firm.

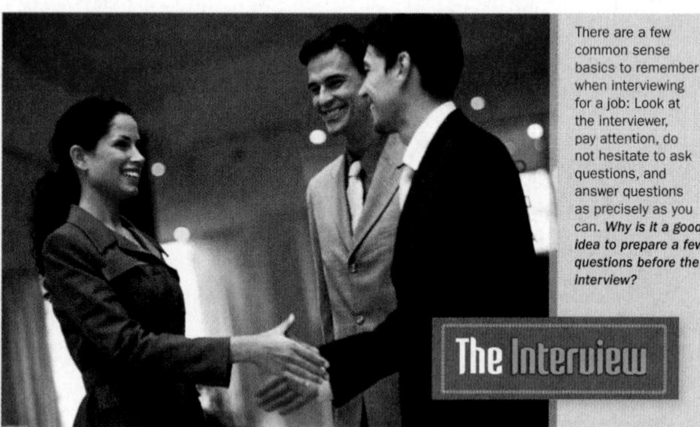

There are a few common sense basics to remember when interviewing for a job: Look at the interviewer, pay attention, do not hesitate to ask questions, and answer questions as precisely as you can. ***Why is it a good idea to prepare a few questions before the interview?***

EXPLAIN

Critical Thinking

Tell students to contemplate this scenario: A human resources manager receives a student's résumé with blatantly false information. The position requires a high school diploma, and the candidate has not graduated from high school. Ask: ***How might the human resources manager respond to such an applicant?*** Have students share their thoughts with the class. If the manager determines that part of the résumé is false, he or she is likely to become suspicious of the entire résumé and disqualify the applicant. Or, the manager may decide to disqualify the applicant based solely on one piece of false information.

PROFESSIONAL DEVELOPMENT **MINI CLIP**

ELL: Level 1 Proficiency

Go to the Online Learning Center for a video clip in which an author discusses Level 1 proficiency English learners.

HOW TO SUBMIT YOUR RÉSUMÉ

Tell students that the more times they submit electronic résumés and cover letters, the more comfortable they will become doing so. To focus the discussion on how to submit résumés, ask these guiding questions.

Guiding Questions

Explain Why is it important to read a company's online submission directions carefully before submitting a résumé?	If you submit your résumé incorrectly, it is likely to be rejected.
Analyze Why is it generally not a good idea to send your résumé as an attached file, unless you specifically have been instructed to do so?	An attached file can be difficult to read if the recipient does not have the appropriate software program. Some employers may be hesitant to open attachments because of the risk of computer viruses.

ELABORATE

TRADITIONAL PRINT RÉSUMÉS

Ask these questions to encourage discussion of traditional résumés.

Guiding Questions

Identify Under what circumstances do you need a print résumé?	when you need to mail or fax the résumé; it is also a good idea to take a copy to job interviews
Summarize Where might you look to examine some sample résumés?	online job search sites, the library, book stores, friends or families who have copies of successful résumés
Draw Conclusions Why do you think some job seekers hire professional résumé writers to help them develop their résumés?	Some people may need help with writing and organizing information; if the job seeker is applying for a high-level position, he or she may feel they need professional input.

PREPARING FOR AN INTERVIEW

Ask these questions to encourage discussion of interview preparation.

Guiding Questions

List What are the three basic steps in the interview process?	(1) prepare for the interview; (2) conduct yourself properly during the interview; (3) follow up after the interview
Explain What should you do if you are unsure how to pronounce your interviewer's name?	Ask the receptionist for the pronunciation.
Analyze Why is the interview such a critical step in the job-seeking process?	It is usually the interview that helps the employer determine which applicant to hire.
Infer Why should you dress formally for a job interview, even if the workplace is one in which people dress casually?	You want to make a good impression, and you cannot go wrong by dressing more formally than others; dressing formally shows respect.

Critical Thinking

Ask students: ***Do you think it is right for an interviewer to judge a candidate based on his or her attire and appearance?*** Encourage students to discuss their responses. Possible answers: Yes, because an employee represents the company. If a potential employee takes the time and effort to make a good appearance, the interviewer may conclude that the same effort will be applied toward the job.

Critical Thinking

Tell students that companies often must juggle filling a position quickly with finding the "perfect" candidate. Ask students to consider the following statement: ***Hiring the right person is better than hiring someone right away.*** Have students brainstorm and discuss the advantages and disadvantages of this job recruitment philosophy. Advantages of waiting include that the company may find someone who will have a strong, positive influence on other employees and be extremely productive for the company. Disadvantages are that the "perfect" person may never come along and important opportunities may be missed while the position remains vacant.

Visual Literacy

The Interview Caption Answer Read the caption question to students: ***Why is it a good idea to prepare a few questions before the interview?*** You are likely to be nervous during the interview, especially at the beginning. Preparing a few questions makes it easier to relax and allows you to present a more confident image. Instruct students to examine the photo. Ask: ***What image does the young woman's body language project?*** Because she is standing erect and holding out her hand, she projects attentiveness and confidence. Because she is smiling, she gives a friendly impression.

Mini Projects

Differentiated Instruction

Verbal/Linguistic Learners Instruct students to use the tips listed here to create an electronic résumé (e-résumé) for themselves. Encourage students to go online to obtain additional tips. They may want to create a résumé that could accompany the cover letter they previously created. Remind students to include key words that are appropriate for the type of job listed in the objective statement. When students are finished, have students trade e-résumés with a partner and provide constructive feedback. Then have them modifications to their résumés based on this feedback. E-résumés should be error-free and grammatically correct, be properly formatted, contain all necessary information, and be organized similarly to Figure 38.1. They should contain key words appropriate for the objective statement. Feedback from students' partners should be included if appropriate.

Kinesthetic Learners Organize students into groups of three. The first student is the narrator, the second one demonstrates proper dress and grooming for a job interview, and the third one demonstrates improper dress and grooming. Have each group prepare a skit in which the narrator analyzes the students' appearance for the class. Skits will vary. Sample: a properly dressed job seeker might wear a solid-colored shirt, a tie, pressed slacks, and leather shoes, while an improperly dressed job seeker might wear a decorated T-shirt, worn jeans, and flip-flops.

The following questions are often asked of job applicants during interviews. Write the answers to these questions, and then practice answering them. Ask a family member, teacher, or friend to help you by asking the questions and giving you feedback on your anwers.

- Why do you want to work for this company?
- Do you want permanent or temporary work?
- Why do you think you can do this job?
- What jobs have you had? Why did you leave?
- What classes did you like best in school?
- In what school activities have you participated?
- What do you want to be doing in five years?
- Do you prefer working alone or with others?
- What are your main strengths and weaknesses?
- What salary do you expect?
- What grades have you received in school?
- How do you feel about working overtime?
- How many days were you absent from school last year?
- Why should I hire you?
- When can you begin work?

Under federal law, employers cannot make employment decisions on the basis of race or ethnicity, gender, religion, marital status, age, country of origin, sexual orientation, or physical and/or mental status. A job interviewer should not ask questions about these topics.

The law requires employers to give every job applicant the same consideration. This concept is known as equal opportunity. Questions asked during a job interview should address only the factors that relate to the ability of an applicant to carry out the work required.

The interviewer may unknowingly ask you an unlawful question, or that person may ask you a lawful question using the wrong words. In an interview setting, it is often best to give an answer based on the *intent* of the question.

For example, you may be asked whether you are a United States citizen. It is not legal to ask that question. However, it *is* legal to ask whether you are authorized to work in the United States. In such a case, it is usually best to respond to the question as if it had been worded properly.

Ability

Federal law makes it illegal to discriminate in hiring decisions based on a disability, unless it would cause the employer significant hardship. ***What qualities do many disabled people have that would make them good employees?***

If asked unlawful questions, you have three choices, with the last choice being the most sensible:

1. You can answer truthfully if you feel your answer will not harm you.
2. You can say the question is inappropriate because of laws against discrimination in hiring (though this may prevent you from getting the job).
3. You can sidestep the question and base your answer on the requirements of the job and your ability to perform it.

APPROPRIATE CONDUCT DURING AN INTERVIEW

Always go alone to a job interview. If someone must accompany you on the day of the interview, ask that person to wait for you outside in a public location. Plan to arrive for your interview five to ten minutes early. Always allow some extra time in case you run into delays. Do not be too early, though. Waiting outside the interviewer's door for half an hour is not comfortable for you or the employer.

Turn off your cell phone before you enter the building where the interview will take place. A ringing cell phone during the interview will likely disqualify you. If your watch beeps, do not wear it.

Before you meet the interviewer, you may meet a receptionist, administrative assistant, or other employee. Be courteous and polite to anyone you meet. These people might be your future co-workers.

If you have not already completed an application form, you may be asked to do so before or after the interview. Be prepared by bringing a good pen or two with black or blue ink. You may also need to supply your Social Security number and your references. Bring along several copies of your résumé to the interview to leave with your interviewer(s). Your résumé will also help you to fill out an application form. A zippered folder is handy for carrying pens, copies of your résumé, and your list of references.

Remain standing until you are asked to sit down. Sit up straight, leaning forward slightly toward the interviewer to show interest. Relax and focus on your purpose to make the best impression.

Place your purse or briefcase on the floor by your chair. Never put anything on the interviewer's desk, even if there is room. This may appear disrespectful or too casual.

It is normal to feel a little nervous at the beginning of an interview. You will relax as the interview progresses. Keep your hands in your lap, and try to keep them still. Never place your hands on the interviewer's desk. Look the interviewer in the eye most of the time and listen to him or her carefully. Be careful not to interrupt when the interviewer is speaking. Be confident, smile, and be yourself. The employer has taken the time to interview you because he or she has confidence that you are a qualified candidate.

WHAT TO SAY IN AN INTERVIEW

Most interviewers begin by asking specific questions. Answer each question honestly. If you do not know the answer to a particular question, say so. The interviewer will probably be able to tell if you try to fake an answer. Keep your answers short and to the point.

Two particular questions often cause problems for young job applicants. These questions are: "What type of work would you like to do?" and "What compensation (wage or salary) do you expect?" You can answer the first question by giving the name of the specific job you want. The question about expected employment compensation is a little more difficult if you do not have a specific wage or salary in mind. The best approach is to do your research before the interview to find out the wages usually pay for the type of work for which you are applying. Once you have this information, you can answer with a range of pay suitable for the job.

Wages and benefits are usually discussed toward the end of an interview. If your interviewer does not mention pay, wait until the interview is almost over. Then ask how much the job pays. If you know that there will be a second interview before the job is offered, you may wait until then to ask about salary. You may also want to ask about benefits if you are applying for a full-time permanent job. Benefits may include paid vacation time, sick days, holidays, and insurance coverage.

EXPLAIN

Critical Thinking

Ask students: ***Why is it important to actually practice your answers to the questions in the left column on page 906 with someone such as a friend or family member?*** Practicing out loud allows you to determine exactly how you want to word your answer and how the answer will sound. In addition, the other person can provide you with helpful feedback.

Extend Have students write out their answers to each question. Students should answer the questions as if they are interviewing for a specific job at a specific company. When they are finished, ask for volunteers to share their answers with the class. Then have the class discuss the answers and offer constructive feedback.

Visual Literacy

Ability Caption Answer Read the caption question to students: ***What qualities do many people with disabilities possess that would make them good employees?*** Possible answers: flexibility, persistence, and good problem solving skills. Then ask: ***Why do you think a person with a disability might be more likely to have qualities such as flexibility and good problem solving skills than some people without disabilities?*** Possible answer: Because they may have had to deal with uncommon challenges in their lives, and they have learned to create solutions to challenges and to be flexible when faced with extraordinary situations.

MINI CLIP 

Reading: Planning and Management
Go to the Online Learning Center for a video clip on the role of the teacher in presenting standards to students.

ELABORATE

APPROPRIATE CONDUCT DURING AN INTERVIEW

Tell students that if they get a job interview, it is because the employer believes they are qualified to take the next step in the hiring process. To focus the discussion on appropriate conduct during an interview, ask students these guiding questions.

Guiding Questions

Explain Why should you try to arrive five to ten minutes early for an interview? Why do you not want to arrive too early?	You want to allow enough time in case of any delays. Arriving too early can create awkwardness as you wait.
Analyze How should you respond if you are asked what wage you expect to receive?	You should conduct research ahead of time to determine the typical wage range for this type of work and respond with those numbers.
Draw Conclusions A job candidate fidgets during an interview and does not look the interviewer in the eye. What conclusions might the interviewer draw from this behavior?	The interviewer would probably conclude that the candidate was nervous and unsure of himself, and possibly poorly prepared.
Apply You are concerned that you will be nervous during your interview. What can you do to help yourself minimize this feeling?	You can go to the interview well prepared, sit up straight, keep your hands on your lap and try to keep them still, and focus on the conversation.

Mini Project

Extension

Creating a Storyboard about Looking for a Job Have students create a storyboard that tells the story of how a young adult finds his or her first marketing job. The storyboard should start out with the steps in the beginning of the job-seeking process, such as networking and following up on various leads. It should conclude with the person obtaining a new position. Encourage students to be creative in illustrating their storyboards. Students should create a storyboard that traces a young adult through the job-seeking process. It should illustrate each step, such as searching for jobs on the Internet and in newspapers, writing a résumé, writing a cover letter in response to an ad, preparing for a job interview, and so on.

e MARKETING

Internet Employment Agencies (Online Job Searching)

Internet employment agencies are online companies that help applicants and employers find each other. Monster.com® and Career Builder.com™ are examples of Internet Employment Agencies. You can find a wealth of information about job hunting from these sites. For example, at Monster you can search for a job by state, industry, category, posting date, career level, experience level, education level, and job type. The site also offer advice on resume writing, job hunting strategies, interviewing, salary and benefits, as well as career development.

Innovate and Create

Have students search the Internet for Internet employment agencies and make a list of the sites they found. Ask them to select the one they would use if they were looking for a job right now and to provide rationale for their selection. Some Internet employment agencies are: Monster®, Yahoo! HotJobs®, JobCentral, CollegeRecruiter®, CareerBuilder™, JobFox™, Indeed®, Simply Hired®, Jobing, and Net Temps. The site selected and rationale should make sense based on their current job needs (i.e., temporary employment, part-time employment, level of experience, and career interest).

Mc Graw Hill **glencoe.com**

eMarketing Worksheet Activity Send students to the Online Learning Center to download an eMarketing worksheet activity.

The interviewer will expect you to ask some questions. This shows the interviewer that you have done your research and are interested in learning more. Job applicants often ask questions like those listed below:

- Why is the position vacant?
- What are the typical responsibilities for this position?
- Would I work individually or with a team?
- With what other areas of the company would I interact on a regular basis?
- What type of training or orientation would I receive?
- What are some of the issues the new hire will need to address immediately?
- Please tell me about the department in which I would work.
- What is the typical career path for someone starting in this position? What are the opportunities for advancement and what skills would be required?
- Will I have regular evaluations or reviews?
- What is the company's structure?
- To whom would I report?
- Will I need to take any tests as part of the interview process?
- What is the dress code?
- What are the hours of work?
- Would I be expected to work on weekends?
- Does the position require any travel?
- Is overtime common on this job?
- What benefits do you offer?
- When will you make your hiring decision?

CLOSING THE INTERVIEW

At the close of the interview, one of several things can happen. You may be offered the job, or you may be told that you will not be hired. More likely, however, you will be told that a decision will be made later. You may be asked to a second interview with someone else in the company, such as a department head. This usually means you have made a good impression in your first interview, and your chances of being offered the job are good.

If you are interested in the position, let the interviewer know. You can ask if another interview is required. Be a good salesperson and say something like, "I am very impressed with what I've seen and heard here today, and I am confident that I could do an excellent job in the position you've described to me. When might you be in a position to make an offer?" If an offer is extended, accept it only if you are ready. If you are sure that you want it, accept it on the spot. If you want some time to think it over, be courteous and tactful in asking for that time. It is not unreasonable to want to think about this decision before making a commitment. Set a date when you can answer (usually 24 to 48 hours).

You will be able to sense when the interview is almost over. Then you should stand, smile, and thank your interviewer for his or her time and consideration. Shake hands and go. Be sure to thank the receptionist or administrative assistant on your way out.

FOLLOWING UP AFTER AN INTERVIEW

A thank-you letter or e-mail is an appropriate way to follow up most interviews. Thank the employer and reaffirm your interest in the job.

Include any information that you may have forgotten to mention during the interview that will help qualify you for the position. Your letter may be either handwritten or typed, but it must be neat.

Many employers check references and call your school for a recommendation. This may take several days. Unless you were told not to call, it is all right to telephone the employer five or six days after the interview. Ask to speak with the person who interviewed you. Then give your name and ask if he or she has made a decision on the job. This will let the employer know that you are still interested.

If you are not selected for the job, try not to be discouraged. Do not take it personally. Learn from the experience. You will be better prepared next time.

Reading Check

Recall What is usually the best way to handle interview questions unrelated to your ability to carry out the work required?

AFTER YOU ARE HIRED

After you begin a new job, there are several steps you can take to enhance your career growth and future job searches:

- Thank all those who interviewed you.
- Analyze employer expectations in the business environment.
- Identify skills needed to enhance career progression.
- List accomplishments and awards received individually or as part of a team.
- If applicable, keep samples of your work (but get written permission from your employer first).
- Save copies of reviews and evaluations.
- Take advantage of any opportunity to learn new skills or receive training.
- Build your networking contacts.
- Volunteer for committee responsibilities unrelated to your job which may help you stand out in the company and may uncover your next career step.
- Be a team player and work to the best of your ability.

After You Read Section 38.2

Review Key Concepts

1. **List** the basic categories of information to include in a résumé.
2. **Name** three steps to achieve a successful interview.
3. **Describe** how to learn about a company in order to prepare for an interview.

Practice Academics Skills

English Language Arts

4. Find three job leads, including at least one in marketing. Prepare a résumé for one of these jobs. Use the format of the résumé in Figure 38.1, but include information only about yourself.

NCTE 8 Use information resources to gather information and create and communicate knowledge.

Mathematics

5. You want to determine the take-home pay for a new job offer. The job pays $18 per hour for 40 hours, plus an additional 5 hours per week at time-and-a-half. You will work 50 weeks per year. If the combined withholding of taxes on your pay is 28 percent, what will your total annual net pay be?

NCTM Problem Solving Solve problems that arise in mathematics and in other contexts.

Math Concept **Problem Solving: Multi-Step Problems** When solving problems that require multiple steps, make a list of information given in the problem, as well as information you will be solving. This will make the relationships between what you are looking for and what is given clear.

Starting Hints To solve this problem, multiply the base pay by 1.5 to determine the value of time-and-a-half. Multiply the value of time-and-a-half by 5 and add it to $18 times 40 to determine the weekly salary. Multiply the weekly salary by 50 to determine the annual salary. Multiply the yearly salary by 0.72 to calculate the value after taxes.

For help, go to the **Math Skills Handbook** located at the back of this book.

glencoe.com

Check your answers.

ELABORATE

CLOSING THE INTERVIEW

To focus the discussion on closing the interview, ask these guiding questions.

Guiding Questions

Recall What are three things that might happen at the close of an interview?	You are offered the job, you are told you will not be hired, or you are told that a decision will be made later.
Analyze What are you selling during a job interview? How can you be a good salesperson?	You are selling yourself. You can indicate that you are impressed by what you learned during the interview and are sure you could do an excellent job in the position being filled.

FOLLOWING UP AFTER AN INTERVIEW

Explain to students that following up after an interview shows your potential employer that you have a strong desire to get the job. To focus the discussion on following up after an interview, ask these guiding questions.

Guiding Questions

Recall True or false: You should not e-mail a thank-you note after an interview, but rather send a printed letter by mail.	False. E-mailing a thank-you note is acceptable.
Analyze How can you avoid being discouraged when you do not get a job for which you interviewed?	It is important to not take it personally. You should remind yourself that the interview was a learning experience that will help you do better next time.

EVALUATE

Critical Thinking

Ask students to think of reasons job candidates might not be offered an employment opportunity. Have them write down their reasons and share them with the class. Reasons may include: the candidate did not have all the required skills; another candidate had additional skills that the interviewer thought might be useful; the candidate did not seem to be well-informed about the company; the candidate did not listen carefully; the candidate answered the questions with little thought.

Reading Check Answer

Read the Reading Check question to students: ***What is usually the best way to handle interview questions unrelated to your ability to carry out the work required?*** It is usually best to sidestep inappropriate or illegal questions, and base your answer on the requirements of the job and your ability to perform it.

AFTER YOU ARE HIRED

Tell students that prioritizing tasks and goals at a new job requires some thought. To focus the discussion on the steps to take after being hired, ask students these guiding questions.

Guiding Questions

Explain Why would you want to thank everyone who interviewed you?	You want to let them know that you appreciate this opportunity. In addition, these same people may decide your future.
Analyze Why should you continue networking, even after obtaining a job?	Creating a strong network improves your position in your career and helps you move to more advanced positions.
Make Judgments Of the items listed in this section, which do you think is most important in enhancing your career growth? Why?	Answers will vary. Possible answers: "Analyze employer expectations in the business environment" is most important. If you do not do this correctly, you will not know what is expected of you.

Critical Thinking

Ask students why a job seeker should avoid making statements such as "I was lucky enough …" or "I don't mean to brag, but …" during an interview. Students should not label their successes as a matter of luck, but rather as a result of their skills and hard work. An interview is not a time to rely on modesty, but rather is a chance for them to be their own best salespeople. It is important that they discuss their strengths and accomplishments as they related to the possible position at hand.

Mini Project

Extension

Creating a Career Timeline Have students create and illustrate a hypothetical career timeline from now through their retirement, including education, job opportunities and advancements, and location moves. Timelines should include potential education, job opportunities, and promotions students think may await them as they progress through their careers.

After You Read Section 38.2

Review Key Concepts

1. Basic information includes personal identification, your objective, experience, education, activities and awards, and references.
2. Three steps toward a successful interview include preparation, appropriate conduct, and follow-up with a thank-you letter or phone call.
3. Ways to learn about a company include reading company brochures, catalogs, quarterly reports, and online articles, visiting the company's Web site, and asking members of your network.

Practice Academics

English Language Arts

4. Students should prepare a properly formatted résumé for a job they have chosen from three different job leads. Students should format the résumé as shown in Figure 38.1, but the résumé should contain information about themselves, such as their objective, education, and work experience.

Mathematics

5. Annual salary after taxes is \$30,780 ([18 × 40] + [18 × 1.5 × 5] × 50 × 0.72 = \$30,780).

glencoe.com

Send students to the Online Learning Center to check their answers.

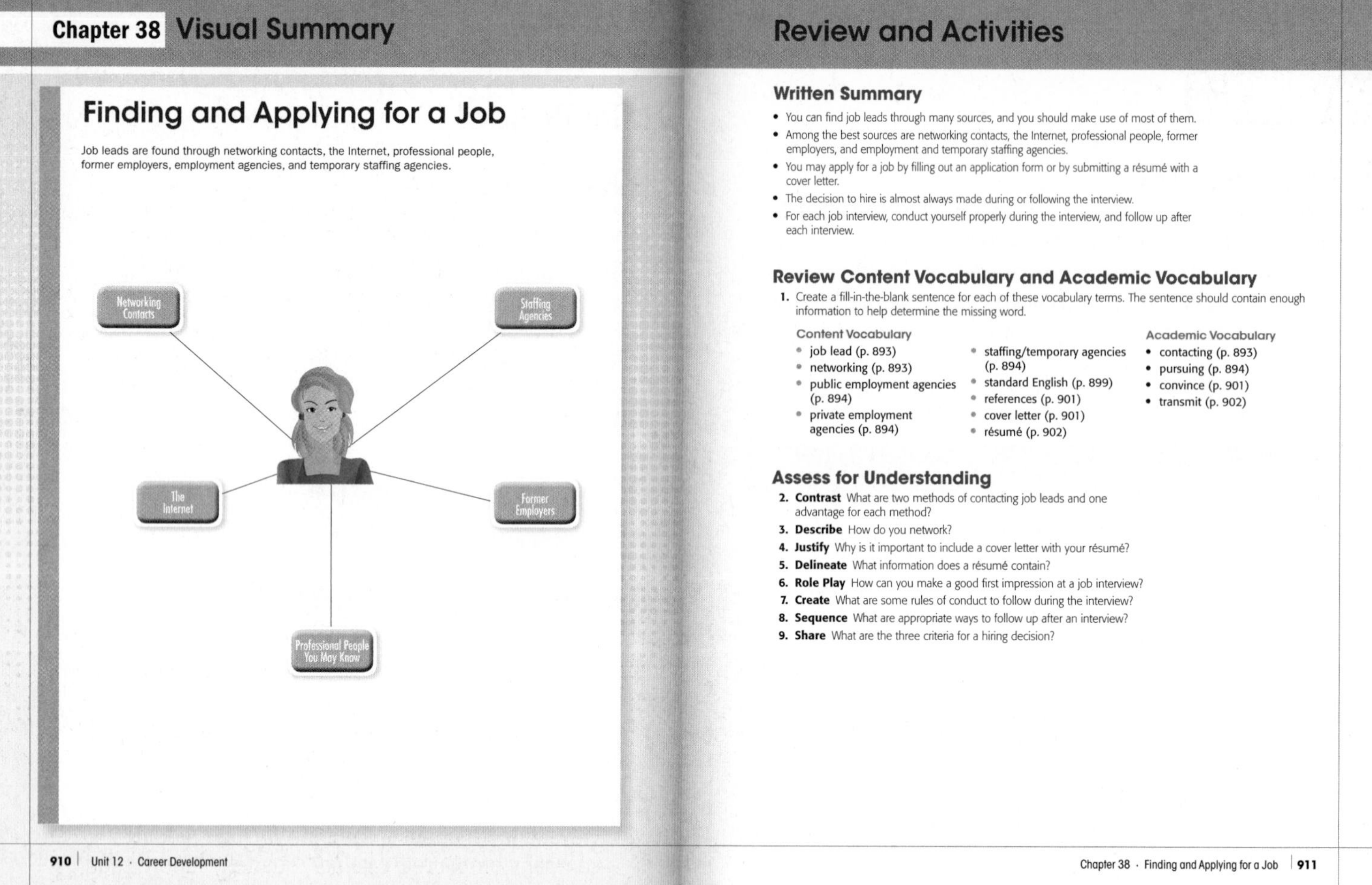

Chapter 38 Visual Summary

Finding and Applying for a Job

Job leads are found through networking contacts, the Internet, professional people, former employers, employment agencies, and temporary staffing agencies.

910 | Unit 12 · Career Development

Review and Activities

Written Summary

- You can find job leads through many sources, and you should make use of most of them.
- Among the best sources are networking contacts, the Internet, professional people, former employers, and employment and temporary staffing agencies.
- You may apply for a job by filling out an application form or by submitting a résumé with a cover letter.
- The decision to hire is almost always made during or following the interview.
- For each job interview, conduct yourself properly during the interview, and follow up after each interview.

Review Content Vocabulary and Academic Vocabulary

1. Create a fill-in-the-blank sentence for each of these vocabulary terms. The sentence should contain enough information to help determine the missing word.

Content Vocabulary
- job lead (p. 893)
- networking (p. 893)
- public employment agencies (p. 894)
- private employment agencies (p. 894)
- staffing/temporary agencies (p. 894)
- standard English (p. 899)
- references (p. 901)
- cover letter (p. 901)
- résumé (p. 902)

Academic Vocabulary
- contacting (p. 893)
- pursuing (p. 894)
- convince (p. 901)
- transmit (p. 902)

Assess for Understanding

2. **Contrast** What are two methods of contacting job leads and one advantage for each method?
3. **Describe** How do you network?
4. **Justify** Why is it important to include a cover letter with your résumé?
5. **Delineate** What information does a résumé contain?
6. **Role Play** How can you make a good first impression at a job interview?
7. **Create** What are some rules of conduct to follow during the interview?
8. **Sequence** What are appropriate ways to follow up after an interview?
9. **Share** What are the three criteria for a hiring decision?

Chapter 38 · Finding and Applying for a Job | 911

EVALUATE

Visual Summary

Express Creativity Ask students to create a visual summary that illustrates a concept in the chapter. Encourage students to use different formats for their visual summaries, such as hierarchy charts, annotated illustrations, and Venn diagrams. Visual summaries will vary depending on the concept depicted and the visual manner in which it is depicted. Questions to ask when assessing a visual summary include:

- Is the summary clear, economical, and simple?
- Are any important steps or concepts left out?
- Are steps or concepts arranged in the same order as the original?
- Does the summary reveal a pattern that connects the details?
- Does the summary locate and highlight the most important information?

Review Content Vocabulary and Academic Vocabulary

1. Students should write fill-in-the-blank sentences for the vocabulary terms. Sample sentences:

A(n) _________ provides you with information about a job opening. (job lead)

_________ involves establishing relationships and alliances between yourself and others around you. (Networking)

_________ help workers find jobs and are funded with tax dollars. (Public employment agencies)

_________ and _________ charge fees to fill job positions. (Private employment agencies; staffing/temporary agencies)

When you write in the formal style you learned in school, you are using _________. (standard English)

When you list _________ on a job application, you should include people who know about both your work habits and your personal traits. (references)

A(n) _________ should describe why you are particularly well suited for a specific job, whereas a(n) _________ should contain general information, such as personal information, education, and skills, that would be pertinent when applying for any job. (cover letter; résumé)

EVALUATE

Assess for Understanding

2. Students should state two methods of contacting job leads, such as by phone, e-mail, responding to a Web site listing, and regular mail. Students also should state advantages of their chosen method. For example, e-mail is fast and most professionals appreciate receiving messages via e-mail because of its efficiency.

3. You network by building relationships with people whom you interact with on a regular basis, such as teachers, counselors, classmates, friends, friends of parents, and so on. When looking for a job, it is important to tell all these people that you are seeking employment and the type of work you would like to obtain.

4. A cover letter introduces you to the employer and is intended to convince the employer to read your résumé. It should also reflect your understanding of the company and show that you are the best person to fill the job.

5. A résumé should contain your personal identification and contact information, your job or career objective, experience, education, activities and awards, and your references.

6. Answers may include: dress conservatively and be well groomed, go to the interview alone, arrive a few minutes early, turn off your cell phone, be courteous, bring copies of your résumé, remain standing until you are asked to sit, and respect the interviewer's personal space.

7. Answers may include: sit up straight, leaning forward slightly toward the interviewer, keep your hands on your lap, look your interviewer in the eye most of the time, listen carefully, answer questions carefully and thoroughly, use standard English, be confident, and smile.

8. Write a thank-you letter or e-mail and reaffirm your interest in the job. Include any information you may have forgotten to mention during the interview. Unless you were told not to call, it is acceptable to call five or six days after the interview to ask if a decision has been made concerning the job.

9. Three criteria for hiring are: how well you can do the job, how willing you are to do the job, and how well you will fit in.

Chapter 38 Review and Activities

21st Century Skills

People Skills

10. The Interview Prepare a study sheet listing questions that you may be asked during an interview and the answers that you would give. Also, list questions that you would plan to ask an interviewer.

Financial Literacy Skills

11. Salary Options Following an interview for a job in sales, you are offered the job and told that you may have your choice of two methods of calculating your pay. Either you will be paid a straight salary of $800 per week or a base salary of $500 per week, plus commissions of 12 percent of sales. In your last job, you sold $4,000 a week. Assuming you will continue to sell at least that amount, which salary option should you take? What is the difference between the two?

e-Marketing Skills

12. Marketing Yourself You know that the process of applying for a employment is a job in itself. You have to convince an employer that you can perform the duties and carry out the responsibilities in a way that satisfies the company and helps make the company profitable. You do this by writing a convincing résumé and accompanying cover letter. You continue marketing yourself by performing well during your interviews. Write a one-page report describing how you will go about marketing yourself to an employer.

- What research will you perform before drafting your résumé and cover letter?
- How will you prepare ahead of time for your interview?
- What skills and character traits will you highlight in your documents and during the interview?
- What steps will you take after the interview to ensure that you leave a good impression?

Build Academic Skills

English Language Arts

13. Following Up an Interview You have just been interviewed for a job that you believe you would enjoy and that you think you could do very well. Write a thank-you letter to the interviewer. Remember to keep your letter brief and to the point.

NCTE 12 Use language to accomplish individual purposes.

Social Studies

14. Gender Equity Use the Internet to research gender pay equity in the United States. Write a one-page report on the history of this issue and current developments.

NCSS IV C Individual Development & Identity Describe the ways family, religion, gender, ethnicity, nationality, socioeconomic status, and other group and cultural influences contribute to the development of a sense of self.

Mathematics

15. Average Rate of Pay You work full time for a local department store as a manager. For three days a week, you work a standard nine-to-five shift. For two days a week, you work a split shift. Your pay is $20 per hour. However, on the two days you work a split shift, you receive an 8-percent pay differential, which makes your pay $21.60 per hour for those two 8-hour days. What is your average rate of pay for the 40-hour week?

Math Concept **Number and Operations: Averages** You can determine an average by adding all the values and dividing by the number of values added. When calculating average pay, be sure to calculate the correct totals before dividing.

NCTM Number and Operations Compute fluently and make reasonable estimates.

For help, go to the **Math Skills Handbook** located at the back of this book.

Standardized Test Practice

Directions Read the following questions. On a separate piece of paper, write the best possible answer for each one.

1. Employers most often make hiring decisions based on:
   A. how well you can do the job.
   B. how willing you are to do the job.
   C. how well you fit in.
   D. all of the above.
2. Key words are an important part of preparing electronic résumés.
   T
   F
3. The decision of whether to hire a job applicant is often made during the ________.

Test-Taking Tip

Start early. Make sure that you have sufficient time to study so that you are well prepared for the test.

DECA Connection Role Play

Marketing Student High School Class

Situation As part of your marketing class, you are able to earn an extra unit of credit if you find and secure a part-time job related to the field of marketing. Your teacher has provided information about the types of jobs that are acceptable in order to earn the extra credit. You have never applied for a job before now. The only job you have had is babysitting for neighbors. You know that there are several things you need to consider before you apply for a job and several things you can do to enhance your chances of being hired. A family friend (judge) works in the human resources department of a local business. Your friend (judge) has agreed to assist you in your job search, and to help you prepare to apply for your first job. Your friend (judge) has suggested that you meet this afternoon to discuss your job preparation efforts.

Activity You are to discuss with your friend (judge) your preparations for your search for your first job. Be sure to mention your résumé preparation and job application letter. You are also to discuss your preparations for using job-search strategies, completing job applications, and preparation for the interview process.

Evaluation You will be evaluated on how well you meet the following performance indicators:

1. Utilize job search strategies.
2. Complete a job application.
3. Interview for a job.
4. Prepare a résumé.
5. Write a letter of application.

Download the Competitive Events Workbook for more Role-Play practice.

EVALUATE

21st Century Skills

People Skills

10. Extensive lists of questions frequently asked of job applicants and questions applicants can ask to show interest in the company appear under the headings Things To Know and What to Say in an Interview in Section 38.2.

Financial Literacy Skills

11. You should take the base salary with commissions, which is $180 more per week than the straight salary. Salary amount = $800 week. Commission amount = 500 + (4,000 × 0.12) = $980.

e-Marketing Skills

12. Accept all reasonable answers. Students should specifically state what research they would perform on the company, such as examining its Web site for company goals, current projects, and so on. They should explain how they would prepare for the interview, such as writing an appropriate cover letter and résumé and dressing appropriately. They should indicate those skills and character traits that would make them good job candidates, such as being team players, having experience in marketing and selling, and so on. In addition, they should indicate what steps they would take after the interview, such as writing thank-you letters and reiterating their interest in the position.

EVALUATE

Build Academic Skills

English Language Arts

13. Students should write a thank-you note that uses proper grammar, spelling, and punctuation. The note should be brief and thank the interviewer for taking the time to consider him or her for the position. It should reaffirm the student's interest in the job. Students also may present any information that they forgot to mention during the interview that would help qualify them for the position.

Social Studies

14. Students should write a one-page report on the history of gender pay equity and discuss current developments on this topic. The paper should use proper grammar, spelling, and punctuation. The Equal Pay Act of 1963 prohibits sex discrimination in the payment of wages to women and men performing substantially equal work. In 2009, median pay for men working full-time was $47,127 and for women it was $36,278.

Mathematics

15. Average rate of pay (hourly) for the 40-hour week is $20.64. $([20 \times 3 \times 8] + [21.60 \times 2 \times 8] / 40) = \$20.64$.

Standardized Test Practice

1. D (all of the above)

2. T

3. interview

DECA Connection Role Play

Evaluations will be based on these performance indicators:

1. **Utilize job search strategies.** The student should be able to search for jobs using a variety of strategies, such as networking with friends, family members, former employers, etc.; getting help from teachers and school counselors; searching the Internet; including online job sites; checking newspaper and magazine ads and articles; and investigating employment agencies.
2. **Complete a job application.** The student should be able to properly complete a job application by writing clearly and without spelling errors, answering every question thoroughly and accurately, providing a complete list of schools and work experiences, and supplying a list of references.
3. **Interview for a job.** The student should be able to properly interview for a job. The student should dress properly; research the company and the types of questions that are likely to be asked; go to the interview alone; be courteous, polite, and a careful listener; answer all questions honestly; and follow up properly by sending a thank-you note.
4. **Prepare a résumé.** The student should be able to write a concise, error-free résumé. The résumé should include a brief summary of personal information, the student's objective, education, skills, work experience, activities, and interests. It also should organize job-related facts about the student.
5. **Write a letter of application.** The student should be able to write a concise, error-free letter of application. The letter should state the exact job being applied for and also state why the student is especially well suited for this job. The letter should supplement, but not duplicate, the résumé.

glencoe.com

Role Plays For more DECA Role Plays, send students to the Online Learning Center to download the Competitive Events Workbook.

UNIT 12 **Marketing Internship Project**

A Digital Résumé for a Marketing Internship

How would you prepare a digital résumé and portfolio for a marketing internship position?

Scenario

A new professional soccer stadium will be opening in your community. There are several internships available in advertising, marketing, sales, and public relations. The job description for this stadium's internship program states that applicants must be able to prioritize assignments, attend to details, and handle several tasks at one time. Other qualities required are excellent interpersonal and communications skills. The intern must demonstrate professionalism, courtesy, and high motivation to learn. Interns may be asked to work on projects such as event planning, community relations, as well as conduct surveys and help with pre-game and post-game activities.

The Skills You'll Use

Academic Skills Reading, writing, social studies, researching, and analyzing

Basic Skills Speaking, listening, thinking, and interpersonal

Technology Skills Word processing, spreadsheet, presentation, telecommunications, and the Internet

NCTE 4 Use written language to communicate effectively.
NCTE 7 Conduct research and gather, evaluate, and synthesize data to communicate discoveries.

Your Objective

Your objective is to prepare a digital résumé and portfolio to apply for a marketing internship program at a new soccer stadium.

STEP 1 Do Your Research

Conduct research to find job descriptions and requirements for marketing internship programs. Identify the key words that you should include in your digital résumé. Search for specific sports-team job opportunities to further refine the key words for your résumé. As you conduct your research, answer these questions:

- What key words and other information should you include in your résumé?
- What digital media have other applicants used to apply for marketing positions?
- What digital medium should you use to prepare your résumé and portfolio?

Write a summary of your research.

STEP 2 Plan Your Project

Now that you have completed your research, you need to begin planning your project.

- Research required skills and job description characteristics for a marketing internship position.
- Assess your skills, knowledge, and personal characteristics for inclusion in your résumé.
- Decide on the digital medium to use to prepare your résumé and present your portfolio of marketing projects.
- Use what you learn to prepare your résumé and digital portfolio.

STEP 3 Connect with Your Community

- Interview a human resources manager to find out what should be included in a résumé so that it stands out from others in the pool of applicants.
- Interview a marketing manager of a local business to determine which aspects of marketing appeal to you.
- Take notes during your interviews and transcribe your notes after your interviews.

STEP 4 Share What You Learn

Assume that your class is the human resources staff for the new professional soccer team's stadium. The staff is responsible for selecting the marketing interns for in-person interviews.

- Present your résumé and digital portfolio in an oral presentation. Be prepared to answer questions
- Present a hard copy of your résumé and portfolio for further evaluation.

STEP 5 Evaluate Your Marketing and Academic Skills

Your project will be evaluated based on the following:

- Your résumé and portfolio for a marketing internship program
- Your understanding of the online job application process
- Selection and use of digital media for your résumé and portfolio
- Research on marketing internship requirements
- Organization and continuity of presentation
- Mechanics—presentation and neatness
- Speaking and listening skills.

MARKETING CORE FUNCTIONS
- Product/Service Management
- Selling

Marketing Internship Project Checklist

Plan
- ✓ Conduct research on marketing internship programs.
- ✓ Design your own résumé and portfolio in a digital medium.

Write
- ✓ Explain the job descriptions and requirements for marketing internship programs you find.
- ✓ Write your résumé and create your portfolio.

Present
- ✓ Present your résumé and portfolio.
- ✓ Explain why you selected the digital media you used in your portfolio.

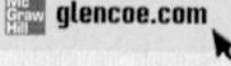

glencoe.com

Evaluate Download a rubric you can use to evaluate your final project.

my marketing portfolio

Internship Report Once you have completed your Marketing Internship Project and oral presentation, put your written report and a few printouts of key slides from your oral presentation in your Marketing Portfolio.

Résumé and Portfolio Do research on a career of your choice. Learn the job requirements and necessary skills. Build a résumé and a portfolio for an internship for that career. Find out which related companies are hiring interns. Apply for an internship with one of the companies. What kind of résumé will you prepare? What key words will you include in your résumé? How will you present your résumé—in hard copy or digitally? What will you include in your portfolio? How will you prepare your portfolio for that position? Submit a hard copy of your résumé and portfolio. Decide what you will do after submitting your résumé and portfolio to follow up.

914 | Unit 12 · Career Development

Unit 12 · Career Development | 915

EVALUATE

Anticipation Activity

Project Objective Read the project objective aloud to students: ***Prepare a digital résumé and portfolio to apply for a marketing internship program at a new soccer stadium.*** Then ask students to think about what they learned about career development and résumés in Unit 12. Remind them of these key points:

- Choosing a suitable career requires self-assessment.
- A résumé is a summary of personal information, education, skills, work experience, and activities.

Ask students: ***How do you choose a career?*** (1) Define lifestyle goals; (2) Conduct a self-assessment; (3) Identify possible career choices and gather information on each; (4) Evaluate choices; (5) Make your decision; (6) Plan how to reach your goal.

Ask students: ***What type of résumé would you submit online?*** Submit an electronic résumé as text only, or as a PDF or Word document, using Times New Roman 12-point font and no special formatting. You can also send it as an e-mail attachment. Use key words corresponding to the job description so scanners will find the words and rank you as a qualified candidate.

Graphic Organizer

Display this graphic organizer. Ask students to name specific skills needed for a sports marketing internship. Answers will vary but may include:

Skills
Interpersonal skills
Communication skills
Technology skills
Academic skills

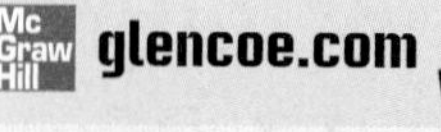

glencoe.com iWB

Graphic Organizer Send students to the Online Learning Center to print this graphic organizer.

EVALUATE

STEP 1 Do Your Research

Tell students that there are many places to find information they can use to develop a digital résumé and portfolio. Students can use library and Internet resources, but they should also talk to people in the community. Encourage students to seek the opinions and ideas of trusted people they know. Other people can bring new perspectives and ideas about developing effective résumés and portfolios as well as the right key words and media to use for applying to a marketing internship at a soccer stadium.

STEP 2 Plan Your Project

Students should research required skills and job descriptions for a sports marketing internship and perform a self-assessment before preparing résumés and portfolios. Students should explain why they focused on certain skills and personal qualifications for their résumés and provide information about their self-assessments. Students' explanation of their résumés and portfolios should include a discussion of the media chosen for their portfolios.

STEP 3 Connect with Your Community

Explain to students that connecting with members of the community is a great way to build relationships. Tell them that young people who are capable of building relationships with caring, responsible, and competent adults are more likely to achieve success. Encourage students to take part in opportunities for adults to serve as mentors, coaches, advocates, and advisors, both formally and informally.

STEP 4 Share What You Learn

Students should present their résumés and portfolios with an oral presentation with a digital medium. Encourage students to speak clearly, use appropriate grammar and vocabulary, and actively engage the audience by making and maintaining eye contact and using movement (facial expressions, posture, gestures) to focus attention and interest.

STEP 5 Evaluate Your Marketing and Academic Skills

Have students use the Marketing Internship Project Checklist to help them to plan, write, and give their presentations. Exemplary résumés and portfolios will include information that reflects the content presented in the unit, incorporating generally well-developed ideas, well-phrased sentences that flow smoothly and are varied in length and structure, consistently precise word choice, and few, if any, errors in grammar, spelling, and mechanics.

glencoe.com

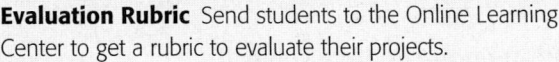

Evaluation Rubric Send students to the Online Learning Center to get a rubric to evaluate their projects.

Culminating Activity

Explain to students that submitting a résumé and portfolio is just the beginning of the job application process. Once candidates are selected from all submissions, a human resources representative sets up a preliminary interview with each candidate. Ask students: ***If an employer asked you to identify the most relevant qualification cited in your résumé for this internship, what would you say?*** Answers will vary. Accept all reasonable answers that also provide a correlation to specific duties of an intern at a soccer stadium. Sample answers may focus on past experience with school sporting events; advanced skills with computer applications; people skills and experience dealing with customer service gained from after-school jobs; expert knowledge regarding the sport of soccer; communication skills, both written and verbal; public relations experience through school activities; or another relevant qualification or skill.

my marketing portfolio

Internship Report Have students put their written reports and printouts of key slides from their oral presentations in their marketing portfolio.

Résumé and Portfolio Direct students to select a career of their choice and learn about the job requirements and necessary skills, and then build a résumé and portfolio for an internship for that career, and then apply for an internship with a company offering an internship in that field. Students' completed résumés, portfolios, and applications should include all of the elements and answer all of the questions included in the Marketing Internship Project on this page. This additional activity can build relevance for students who are motivated to learn about other specific business and industries. Relevance shifts the focus to what motivates individual students to learn.

Making Career Choices

A career differs from a job in that it is a series of progressively more responsible jobs in one field or a related field. You will need to learn some special skills to choose a career and to help you in your job search. Choosing a career and identifying career opportunities require careful thought and preparation. To aid you in making important career choices, follow these steps:

Steps to Making a Career Decision

1. Conduct a self-assessment to determine your:
   - values
   - lifestyle goals
   - interests
   - skills and aptitudes
   - personality
   - work environment preferences
   - relationship preferences
2. Identify possible career choices based on your self-assessment.
3. Gather information on each choice, including future trends.
4. Evaluate your choices based on your self-assessment.
5. Make your decision.

After you make your decision, plan how you will reach your goal. It is best to have short-term, medium-term, and long-term goals. In making your choices, explore the future opportunities in this field or fields over the next several years. What impact will new technology and automation have on job opportunities in the next few years? Remember, if you plan, you make your own career opportunities.

Personal Career Portfolio

You will want to create and maintain a personal career portfolio. In it you will keep all the documents you create and receive in your job search:

- Contact list
- Résumé
- Letters of recommendation
- Employer evaluations
- Awards
- Evidence of participation in school, community, and volunteer activities
- Notes about your job search
- Notes made after your interviews

Career Research Resources

In order to gather information on various career opportunities, there are a variety of sources to research:

- **Libraries.** Your school or public library offers good career information resources. Here you will find books, magazines, pamphlets, films, videos, and special reference materials on careers. In particular, the U.S. Department of Labor publishes three reference books that are helpful: the *Dictionary of ccupational Titles (DOT),* which describes about 20,000 jobs and their relationships with data, people, and things; the *Occupational Outlook Handbook (OOH),* with information on more than 200 occupations; and the *Guide for Occupational Exploration (GOE),* a reference that organizes the world of work into 12 interest areas that are subdivided into work groups and subgroups.

- **The Internet.** The Internet is becoming a primary source of research on any topic. It is especially helpful in researching careers.
- **Career Consultations.** Career consultation, an informational interview with a professional who works in a career that interests you, provides an opportunity to learn about the day-to-day realities of a career.
- **On-the-Job Experience.** On-the-job experience can be valuable in learning firsthand about a job or career. You can find out if your school has a work-experience program, or look into a company or organization's internship opportunities. Interning gives you direct work experience and often allows you to make valuable contacts for future full-time employment.

The Job Search

To aid you in your actual job search, there are various sources to explore. You should contact and research all the sources that might produce a job lead, or information about a job. Keep a contact list as you proceed with your search. Some of these resources include:

- **Networking with family, friends, and acquaintances.** This means contacting people you know personally, including school counselors, former employers, and professional people.
- **Cooperative education and work-experience programs.** Many schools have such programs in which students work part-time on a job related to one of their classes. Many also offer work-experience programs that are not limited to just one career area, such as marketing.
- **Newspaper ads.** Reading the Help Wanted advertisements in your local papers will provide a source of job leads, as well as teach you about the local job market.
- **Employment agencies.** Most cities have two types of employment agencies, public and private. These employment agencies match workers with jobs. Some private agencies may charge a fee, so be sure to know who is expected to pay the fee and what the fee is.
- **Company personnel offices.** Large and medium-sized companies have personnel offices to handle employment matters, including the hiring of new workers. You can check on job openings by contacting the office by telephone or by scheduling a personal visit.
- **Searching the Internet.** Cyberspace offers multiple opportunities for your job search. Web sites, such as Hotjobs.com or Monster.com, provide lists of companies offering employment. There are tens of thousands of career-related Web sites, so the challenge is finding those that have jobs that interest you and that are up-to-date in their listings. Companies that interest you may have a Web site, which will provide valuable information on their benefits and opportunities for employment.

Applying for a Job

When you have contacted the sources of job leads and found some jobs that interest you, the next step is to apply for them. You will need to complete application forms, write letters of application, and prepare your own résumé. Before you apply for a job, you will need to have a work permit if you are under the age of 18 in most states. Some state and federal labor laws designate certain jobs

as too dangerous for young workers. Laws also limit the number of hours of work allowed during a day, a week, or the school year. You will also need to have proper documentation, such as a green card if you are not a U.S. citizen.

Job Application

You can obtain the job application form directly at the place of business, by requesting it in writing, or over the Internet. It is best if you can fill the form out at home, but some businesses require that you fill it out at the place of work.

Fill out the job application forms neatly and accurately, using standard English, the formal style of speaking and writing you learned in school. You must be truthful and pay attention to detail in filling out the form.

Personal Fact Sheet

To be sure that the answers you write on a job application form are accurate, make a personal fact sheet before filling out the application:

- Your name, home address, and phone number
- Your Social Security number
- The job you are applying for
- The date you can begin work
- The days and hours you can work
- The pay you want
- Whether or not you have been convicted of a crime
- Your education
- Your previous work experience
- Your birth date
- Your driver's license number if you have one
- Your interests and hobbies, and awards you have won
- Your previous work experience, including dates
- Schools you have attended
- Places you have lived
- Accommodations you may need from the employer
- A list of references—people who will tell an employer that you will do a good job, such as relatives, students, former employers, and the like

Letters of Recommendation

Letters of recommendation are helpful. You can request teachers, counselors, relatives, and other acquaintances who know you well to write these letters. They should be short, to the point, and give a brief overview of your assets. A brief description of any of your important accomplishments or projects should follow. The letter should end with a brief description of your character and work ethic.

Letter of Application

Some employees prefer a letter of application, rather than an application form. This letter is like writing a sales pitch about yourself. You need to tell why you are the best person for the job, what special qualifications you have, and include all the information usually found on an application form. Write the letter in standard English, making certain that it is neat, accurate, and correct.

Résumé

The purpose of a résumé is to make an employer want to interview you. A résumé tells prospective employers what you are like and what you can do for them. A good résumé summarizes you in a one- or two-page outline. It should include the following information:

1. **Identification.** Include your name, address, telephone number, and e-mail address.
2. **Objective.** Indicate the type of job you are looking for.
3. **Experience.** List experience related to the specific job for which you are applying. List other work if you have not worked in a related field.
4. **Education.** List schools attended from high school on, dates of attendance, and diplomas or degrees earned. You may also include courses related to the job you are applying for.
5. **References.** Include up to three references or indicate that they are available. Always ask people ahead of time if they are willing to be listed as references for you.

A résumé that you put online or send by e-mail is called an *electronic résumé.* Some Web sites allow you to post them on their sites without charge. Employers access these sites to find new employees. Your electronic résumé should follow the guidelines for a regular one. It needs to be accurate. Stress your skills and sell yourself to prospective employers.

Cover Letter

If you are going to get the job you want, you need to write a great cover letter to accompany your résumé. Think of a cover letter as an introduction: a piece of paper that conveys a smile, a confident hello, and a nice, firm handshake. The cover letter is the first thing a potential employer sees, and it can make a powerful impression. The following are some tips for creating a cover letter that is professional and gets the attention you want:

- **Keep it short.** Your cover letter should be one page, no more.
- **Make it look professional.** These days, you need to type your letter on a computer and print it on a laser printer. Do not use an inkjet printer unless it produces extremely crisp type. Use white or buff-colored paper; anything else will draw the wrong kind of attention. Type your name, address, phone number, and e-mail address at the top of the page.
- **Explain why you are writing.** Start your letter with one sentence describing where you heard of the opening. "Joan Wright suggested I contact you regarding a position in your marketing department," or "I am writing to apply for the position you advertised in the Sun City Journal."
- **Introduce yourself.** Give a short description of your professional abilities and background. Refer to your attached résumé: "As you will see in the attached résumé, I am an experienced editor with a background in newspapers, magazines, and textbooks." Then highlight one or two specific accomplishments.
- **Sell yourself.** Your cover letter should leave the reader thinking, "This person is exactly what we are looking for." Focus on what you can do for the company. Relate your skills to the skills and responsibilities mentioned in the job listing. If the ad mentions solving problems, relate a problem you solved at school or work. If the ad mentions specific skills or knowledge required, mention your mastery of these in your letter. (Also be sure these skills are included on your résumé.)
- **Provide all requested information.** If an ad asks for "salary requirements" or "salary history," include this information in your cover letter. However, you do not have to give specific numbers. It is okay to say, "My wage is in the range of $10 to $15 per hour." If the employer does not ask for this information, do not offer it.

Career Skills Handbook

- **Ask for an interview.** You have sold yourself, now wrap it up. Be confident, but not pushy. "If you agree that I would be an asset to your company, please call me at [insert your phone number]. I am available for an interview at your convenience." Finally, thank the person. "Thank you for your consideration. I look forward to hearing from you soon." Always close with a "Sincerely," followed by your full name and signature.
- **Check for errors.** Read and re-read your letter to make sure each sentence is correctly worded and there are no errors in spelling, punctuation, or grammar. Do not rely on your computer's spell checker or grammar checker. A spell check will not detect if you typed "tot he" instead of "to the." It is a good idea to have someone else read your letter, too. He or she might notice an error you overlooked.

Interview

Understanding how to best prepare for and follow up on interviews is critical to your career success. At different times in your life, you may interview with a teacher or professor, a prospective employer, a supervisor, or a promotion or tenure committee. Just as having an excellent résumé is vital for opening the door, interview skills are critical for putting your best foot forward and seizing the opportunity to clearly articulate why you are the best person for the job.

Research the Company

Your ability to convince an employer that you understand and are interested in the field you are interviewing to enter is important. Show that you have knowledge about the company and the industry. What products or services does the company offer? How is it doing? What is the competition? Use your research to demonstrate your understanding of the company.

Prepare Questions for the Interviewer

Prepare interview questions to ask the interviewer. Some examples include:

- "What would my responsibilities be?"
- "Could you describe my work environment?"
- "What are the chances to move up in the company?"
- "Do you offer training?"
- "What can you tell me about the people who work here?"

Dress Appropriately

You will never get a second chance to make a good first impression. Nonverbal communication is 90 percent of communication, so dressing appropriately is of the utmost importance. Every job is different, and you should wear clothing that is appropriate for the job for which you are applying. In most situations, you will be safe if you wear clean, pressed, conservative business clothes in neutral colors. Pay special attention to grooming. Keep makeup light and wear very little jewelry. Make certain your nails and hair are clean, trimmed, and neat. Do not carry a large purse, backpack, books, or coat. Simply carry a pad of paper, a pen, and extra copies of your résumé and letters of reference in a small folder.

Exhibit Good Behavior

Conduct yourself properly during an interview. Go alone; be courteous and polite to everyone you meet. Relax and focus on your purpose: to make the best possible impression.

- Be on time.
- Be poised and relaxed.
- Avoid nervous habits.
- Avoid littering your speech with verbal clutter such as "you know," "um," and "like."
- Look your interviewer in the eye and speak with confidence.
- Use nonverbal techniques to reinforce your confidence, such as a firm handshake and poised demeanor.
- Convey maturity by exhibiting the ability to tolerate differences of opinion.
- Never call anyone by a first name unless you are asked to do so.
- Know the name, title, and the pronunciation of the interviewer's name.
- Do not sit down until the interviewer does.
- Do not talk too much about your personal life.
- Never bad-mouth your former employers.

Be Prepared for Common Interview Questions

You can never be sure exactly what will happen at an interview, but you can be prepared for common interview questions. There are some interview questions that are illegal. Interviewers should not ask you about your age, gender, color, race, or religion. Employers should not ask whether you are married or pregnant, or question your health or disabilities.

Take time to think about your answers now. You might even write them down to clarify your thinking. The key to all interview questions is to be honest, and to be positive. Focus your answers on skills and abilities that apply to the job you are seeking. Practice answering the following questions with a friend:

- "Tell me about yourself."
- "Why do you want to work at this company?"
- "What did you like/dislike about your last job?"
- "What is your biggest accomplishment?"
- "What is your greatest strength?"
- "What is your greatest weakness?"
- "Do you prefer to work with others or on your own?"
- "What are your career goals?" or "Where do you see yourself in five years?"
- "Tell me about a time that you had a lot of work to do in a short time. How did you manage the situation?"
- "Have you ever had to work closely with a person you didn't get along with? How did you handle the situation?"

After the Interview

Be sure to thank the interviewer after the interview for his or her time and effort. Do not forget to follow up after the interview. Ask, "What is the next step?" If you are told to call in a few days, wait two or three days before calling back.

Career Skills Handbook

If the interview went well, the employer may call you to offer you the job. Find out the terms of the job offer, including job title and pay. Decide whether you want the job. If you decide not to accept the job, write a letter of rejection. Be courteous and thank the person for the opportunity and the offer. You may wish to give a brief general reason for not accepting the job. Leave the door open for possible employment in the future.

Follow Up With a Letter

Write a thank-you letter as soon as the interview is over. This shows your good manners, interest, and enthusiasm for the job. It also shows that you are organized. Make the letter neat and courteous. Thank the interviewer. Sell yourself again.

Accepting a New Job

If you decide to take the job, write a letter of acceptance. The letter should include some words of appreciation for the opportunity, written acceptance of the job offer, the terms of employment (salary, hours, benefits), and the starting date. Make sure the letter is neat and correct.

Starting a New Job

Your first day of work will be busy. Determine what the dress code is and dress appropriately. Learn to do each task assigned properly. Ask for help when you need it. Learn the rules and regulations of the workplace.

You will do some paperwork on your first day. Bring your personal fact sheet with you. You will need to fill out some forms. Form W-4 tells your employer how much money to withhold for taxes. You may also need to fill out Form I-9. This shows that you are allowed to work in the United States. You will need your Social Security number and proof that you are allowed to work in the United States. You can bring your U.S. passport, your Certificate of Naturalization, or your Certificate of U.S. Citizenship. If you are not a permanent resident of the United States, bring your green card. If you are a resident of the United States, you will need to bring your work permit on your first day. If you are under the age of 16 in some states, you need a different kind of work permit.

You might be requested to take a drug test as a requirement for employment in some states. This could be for the safety of you and your coworkers, especially when working with machinery or other equipment.

Important Skills and Qualities

You will not work alone on a job. You will need to learn skills for getting along and being a team player. There are many good qualities necessary to get along in the workplace. They include being positive, showing sympathy, taking an interest in others, tolerating differences, laughing a little, and showing respect. Your employer may promote you or give you a raise if you show good employability skills. You must also communicate with your employer. For example, if you will be sick or late to work, you should call your employer as soon as possible.

There are several qualities necessary to be a good employee and get ahead in your job:

- be cooperative
- possess good character
- be responsible
- finish what you start

- work fast but do a good job
- have a strong work ethic
- work well without supervision
- work well with others
- possess initiative
- show enthusiasm for what you do
- be on time
- make the best of your time
- obey company laws and rules
- be honest
- be loyal
- exhibit good health habits

Leaving a Job

If you are considering leaving your job or are being laid off, you are facing one of the most difficult aspects in your career. The first step in resigning is to prepare a short resignation letter to offer your supervisor at the conclusion of the meeting you set up with him or her. Keep the letter short and to the point. Express your appreciation for the opportunity you had with the company. Do not try to list all that was wrong with the job.

You want to leave on good terms. Do not forget to ask for a reference. Do not talk about your employer or any of your coworkers. Do not talk negatively about your employer when you apply for a new job.

If you are being laid off or face downsizing, it can make you feel angry or depressed. Try to view it as a career-change opportunity. If possible, negotiate a good severance package. Find out about any benefits you may be entitled to. Perhaps the company will offer job-search services or consultation for finding new employment.

Take Action!

It is time for action. Remember the networking and contact lists you created when you searched for this job. Reach out for support from friends, family, and other acquaintances. Consider joining a job-search club. Assess your skills. Upgrade them if necessary. Examine your attitude and your vocational choices. Decide the direction you wish to take and move on!

Number and Operations

▶ ***Understand numbers, ways of representing numbers, relationships among numbers, and number systems***

Fraction, Decimal, and Percent

A percent is a ratio that compares a number to 100. To write a percent as a fraction, drop the percent sign, and use the number as the numerator in a fraction with a denominator of 100. Simplify, if possible. For example, $76\% = \frac{76}{100}$, or $\frac{19}{25}$. To write a fraction as a percent, convert it to an equivalent fraction with a denominator of 100. For example, $\frac{3}{4} = \frac{75}{100}$, or 75%. A fraction can be expressed as a percent by first converting the fraction to a decimal (divide the numerator by the denominator) and then converting the decimal to a percent by moving the decimal point two places to the right.

Comparing Numbers on a Number Line

In order to compare and understand the relationship between real numbers in various forms, it is helpful to use a number line. The zero point on a number line is called the origin; the points to the left of the origin are negative, and those to the right are positive. The number line below shows how numbers in fraction, decimal, percent, and integer form can be compared.

$-\frac{1}{2}$ 0.25 75% 2.5

−3 −2 −1 0 1 2 3

Percents Greater Than 100 and Less Than 1

Percents greater than 100% represent values greater than 1. For example, if the weight of an object is 250% of another, it is 2.5, or $2\frac{1}{2}$, times the weight.

Percents less than 1 represent values less than $\frac{1}{100}$. In other words, 0.1% is one tenth of one percent, which can also be represented in decimal form as 0.001, or in fraction form as $\frac{1}{1{,}000}$. Similarly, 0.01% is one hundredth of one percent or 0.0001 or $\frac{1}{10{,}000}$.

Ratio, Rate, and Proportion

A ratio is a comparison of two numbers using division. If a basketball player makes 8 out of 10 free throws, the ratio is written as 8 to 10, 8:10, or $\frac{8}{10}$. Ratios are usually written in simplest form. In simplest form, the ratio "8 out of 10" is 4 to 5, 4:5, or $\frac{4}{5}$. A rate is a ratio of two measurements having different kinds of units—cups per gallon, or miles per hour, for example. When a rate is simplified so that it has a denominator of 1, it is called a unit rate. An example of a unit rate is 9 miles per hour. A proportion is an equation stating that two ratios are equal. $\frac{3}{18} = \frac{13}{78}$ is an example of a proportion. The cross products of a proportion are also equal. $\frac{3}{18} = \frac{13}{78}$ and $3 \times 78 = 18 \times 13$.

Representing Large and Small Numbers

In order to represent large and small numbers, it is important to understand the number system. Our number system is based on 10, and the value of each place is 10 times the value of the place to its right.

The value of a digit is the product of a digit and its place value. For instance, in the number 6,400, the 6 has a value of six thousands and the 4 has a value of four hundreds. A place value chart can help you read numbers. In the chart, each group of three digits is called a period. Commas separate the periods: the ones period, the thousands period, the millions period, and so on. Values to the right of the ones period are decimals. By understanding place value you can write very large numbers like 5 billion and more, and very small numbers that are less than 1, like one-tenth.

Scientific Notation

When dealing with very large numbers like 1,500,000, or very small numbers like 0.000015, it is helpful to keep track of their value by writing the numbers in scientific notation. Powers of 10 with positive exponents are used with a decimal between 1 and 10 to express large numbers. The exponent represents the number of places the decimal point is moved to the right. So, 528,000 is written in scientific notation as 5.28×10^5. Powers of 10 with negative exponents are used with a decimal between 1 and 10 to express small numbers. The exponent represents the number of places the decimal point is moved to the left. The number 0.00047 is expressed as 4.7×10^{-4}.

Factor, Multiple, and Prime Factorization

Two or more numbers that are multiplied to form a product are called factors. Divisibility rules can be used to determine whether 2, 3, 4, 5, 6, 8, 9, or 10 are factors of a given number. Multiples are the products of a given number and various integers.

For example, 8 is a multiple of 4 because $4 \times 2 = 8$. A prime number is a whole number that has exactly two factors: 1 and itself. A composite number is a whole number that has more than two factors. Zero and 1 are neither prime nor composite. A composite number can be expressed as the product of its prime factors. The prime factorization of 40 is $2 \times 2 \times 2 \times 5$, or $2^3 \times 5$. The numbers 2 and 5 are prime numbers.

Integers

A negative number is a number less than zero. Negative numbers like −8, positive numbers like +6, and zero are members of the set of integers. Integers can be represented as points on a number line. A set of integers can be written {..., −3, −2, −1, 0, 1, 2, 3, ...} where ... means "continues indefinitely."

Real, Rational, and Irrational Numbers

The real number system is made up of the sets of rational and irrational numbers. Rational numbers are numbers that can be written in the form *a/b* where *a* and *b* are integers and $b \neq 0$. Examples are 0.45, $\frac{1}{2}$, and $\sqrt{36}$. Irrational numbers are non-repeating, non-terminating decimals. Examples are $\sqrt{71}$, π, and 0.020020002....

Complex and Imaginary Numbers

A complex number is a mathematical expression with a real number element and an imaginary number element. Imaginary numbers are multiples of *i*, the "imaginary" square root of −1. Complex numbers are represented by $a + bi$, where *a* and *b* are real numbers and *i* represents the imaginary element. When a quadratic equation does not have a real number solution, the solution can be represented by a complex number. Like real numbers, complex numbers can be added, subtracted, multiplied, and divided.

Vectors and Matrices
A matrix is a set of numbers or elements arranged in rows and columns to form a rectangle. The number of rows is represented by m and the number of columns is represented by n. To describe the number of rows and columns in a matrix, list the number of rows first using the format $m \times n$. Matrix A below is a 3×3 matrix because it has 3 rows and 3 columns. To name an element of a matrix, the letter i is used to denote the row and j is used to denote the column, and the element is labeled in the form $a_{i,j}$. In matrix A below, $a_{3,2}$ is 4.

$$\text{Matrix A} = \begin{pmatrix} 1 & 3 & 5 \\ 0 & 6 & 8 \\ 3 & 4 & 5 \end{pmatrix}$$

A vector is a matrix with only one column or row of elements. A transposed column vector, or a column vector turned on its side, is a row vector. In the example below, row vector b' is the transpose of column vector b.

$$b = \begin{pmatrix} 1 \\ 2 \\ 3 \\ 4 \end{pmatrix}$$

$$b' = \begin{pmatrix} 1 & 2 & 3 & 4 \end{pmatrix}$$

Understand meanings of operations and how they relate to one another

Properties of Addition and Multiplication
Properties are statements that are true for any numbers. For example, $3 + 8$ is the same as $8 + 3$ because each expression equals 11. This illustrates the Commutative Property of Addition. Likewise, $3 \times 8 = 8 \times 3$ illustrates the Commutative Property of Multiplication.

When evaluating expressions, it is often helpful to group or associate the numbers. The Associative Property says that the way in which numbers are grouped when added or multiplied does not change the sum or product. The following properties are also true:

- **Additive Identity Property:** When 0 is added to any number, the sum is the number.
- **Multiplicative Identity Property:** When any number is multiplied by 1, the product is the number.
- **Multiplicative Property of Zero:** When any number is multiplied by 0, the product is 0.

Rational Numbers
A number that can be written as a fraction is called a rational number. Terminating and repeating decimals are rational numbers because both can be written as fractions.

Decimals that are neither terminating nor repeating are called irrational numbers because they cannot be written as fractions. Terminating decimals can be converted to fractions by placing the number (without the decimal point) in the numerator. Count the number of places to the right of the decimal point, and in the denominator, place a 1 followed by a number of zeros equal to the number of places that you counted. The fraction can then be reduced to its simplest form.

Writing a Fraction as a Decimal

Any fraction $\frac{a}{b}$, where $b \neq 0$, can be written as a decimal by dividing the numerator by the denominator. So, $\frac{a}{b} = a \div b$. If the division ends, or terminates, when the remainder is zero, the decimal is a terminating decimal. Not all fractions can be written as terminating decimals. Some have a repeating decimal. A bar indicates that the decimal repeats forever. For example, the fraction $\frac{4}{9}$ can be converted to a repeating decimal, $0.\overline{4}$

Adding and Subtracting Like Fractions

Fractions with the same denominator are called like fractions. To add like fractions, add the numerators and write the sum over the denominator. To add mixed numbers with like fractions, add the whole numbers and fractions separately, adding the numerators of the fractions, then simplifying if necessary. The rule for subtracting fractions with like denominators is similar to the rule for adding. The numerators can be subtracted and the difference written over the denominator. Mixed numbers are written as improper fractions before subtracting. These same rules apply to adding or subtracting like algebraic fractions. An algebraic fraction is a fraction that contains one or more variables in the numerator or denominator.

Adding and Subtracting Unlike Fractions

Fractions with different denominators are called unlike fractions. The least common multiple of the denominators is used to rename the fractions with a common denominator. After a common denominator is found, the numerators can then be added or subtracted. To add mixed numbers with unlike fractions, rename the mixed numbers as improper fractions. Then find a common denominator, add the numerators, and simplify the answer.

Multiplying Rational Numbers

To multiply fractions, multiply the numerators and multiply the denominators. If the numerators and denominators have common factors, they can be simplified before multiplication. If the fractions have different signs, then the product will be negative. Mixed numbers can be multiplied in the same manner, after first renaming them as improper fractions. Algebraic fractions may be multiplied using the same method described above.

Dividing Rational Numbers

To divide a number by a rational number (a fraction, for example), multiply the first number by the multiplicative inverse of the second. Two numbers whose product is 1 are called multiplicative inverses, or reciprocals. $\frac{7}{4} \times \frac{4}{7} = 1$. When dividing by a mixed number, first rename it as an improper fraction, and then multiply by its multiplicative inverse. This process of multiplying by a number's reciprocal can also be used when dividing algebraic fractions.

Adding Integers

To add integers with the same sign, add their absolute values. The sum takes the same sign as the addends. An addend is a number that is added to another number (the augend). The equation $-5 + (-2) = -7$ is an example of adding two integers with the same sign. To add integers with different signs, subtract their absolute values. The sum takes the same sign as the addend with the greater absolute value.

Subtracting Integers

The rules for adding integers are extended to the subtraction of integers. To subtract an integer, add its additive inverse. For example, to find the difference $2 - 5$, add the additive inverse of 5 to 2: $2 + (-5) = -3$. The rule for subtracting integers can be used to solve real-world problems and to evaluate algebraic expressions.

Additive Inverse Property

Two numbers with the same absolute value but different signs are called opposites. For example, −4 and 4 are opposites. An integer and its opposite are also called additive inverses. The Additive Inverse Property says that the sum of any number and its additive inverse is zero. The Commutative, Associative, and Identity Properties also apply to integers. These properties help when adding more than two integers.

Absolute Value

In mathematics, when two integers on a number line are on opposite sides of zero, and they are the same distance from zero, they have the same absolute value. The symbol for absolute value is two vertical bars on either side of the number. For example, $|-5| = 5$.

Multiplying Integers

Since multiplication is repeated addition, $3(-7)$ means that −7 is used as an addend 3 times. By the Commutative Property of Multiplication, $3(-7) = -7(3)$. The product of two integers with different signs is always negative. The product of two integers with the same sign is always positive.

Dividing Integers

The quotient of two integers can be found by dividing the numbers using their absolute values. The quotient of two integers with the same sign is positive, and the quotient of two integers with a different sign is negative. $-12 \div (-4) = 3$ and $12 \div (-4) = -3$. The division of integers is used in statistics to find the average, or mean, of a set of data. When finding the mean of a set of numbers, find the sum of the numbers, and then divide by the number in the set.

Adding and Multiplying Vectors and Matrices

In order to add two matrices together, they must have the same number of rows and columns. In matrix addition, the corresponding elements are added to each other. In other words $(a + b)_{ij} = a_{ij} + b_{ij}$. For example,

$$\begin{pmatrix}1 & 2\\2 & 1\end{pmatrix}+\begin{pmatrix}3 & 6\\0 & 1\end{pmatrix}=\begin{pmatrix}1+3 & 2+6\\2+0 & 1+1\end{pmatrix}=\begin{pmatrix}4 & 8\\2 & 2\end{pmatrix}$$

Matrix multiplication requires that the number of elements in each row in the first matrix is equal to the number of elements in each column in the second. The elements of the first row of the first matrix are multiplied by the corresponding elements of the first column of the second matrix and then added together to get the first element of the product matrix. To get the second element, the elements in the first row of the first matrix are multiplied by the corresponding elements in the second column of the second matrix then added, and so on, until every row of the first matrix is multiplied by every column of the second. See the example below.

$$\begin{pmatrix}1 & 2\\3 & 4\end{pmatrix}\times\begin{pmatrix}3 & 6\\0 & 1\end{pmatrix}=\begin{pmatrix}(1\times3)+(2\times0) & (1\times6)+(2\times1)\\(3\times3)+(4\times0) & (3\times6)+(4\times1)\end{pmatrix}=\begin{pmatrix}3 & 8\\9 & 22\end{pmatrix}$$

Vector addition and multiplication are performed in the same way, but there is only one column and one row.

Permutations and Combinations

Permutations and combinations are used to determine the number of possible outcomes in different situations. An arrangement, listing, or pattern in which order is important is called a permutation. The symbol P(6, 3) represents the number of permutations of 6 things taken 3 at a time. For P(6, 3), there are $6 \times 5 \times 4$ or 120 possible outcomes. An arrangement or listing where order is not important is called a combination. The symbol C(10, 5) represents the number of combinations of 10 things taken 5 at a time. For C(10, 5), there are $(10 \times 9 \times 8 \times 7 \times 6) \div (5 \times 4 \times 3 \times 2 \times 1)$ or 252 possible outcomes.

Powers and Exponents

An expression such as $3 \times 3 \times 3 \times 3$ can be written as a power. A power has two parts, a base and an exponent. $3 \times 3 \times 3 \times 3 = 3^4$. The base is the number that is multiplied (3). The exponent tells how many times the base is used as a factor (4 times). Numbers and variables can be written using exponents. For example, $8 \times 8 \times 8 \times m \times m \times m \times m \times m$ can be expressed 8^3m^5. Exponents also can be used with place value to express numbers in expanded form. Using this method, 1,462 can be written as $(1 \times 10^3) + (4 \times 10^2) + (6 \times 10^1) + (2 \times 10^0)$.

Squares and Square Roots

The square root of a number is one of two equal factors of a number. Every positive number has both a positive and a negative square root. For example, since $8 \times 8 = 64$, 8 is a square root of 64. Since $(-8) \times (-8) = 64$, -8 is also a square root of 64. The notation $\sqrt{\ }$ indicates the positive square root, $-\sqrt{\ }$ indicates the negative square root, and $\pm\sqrt{\ }$ indicates both square roots. For example, $\sqrt{81} = 9$, $-\sqrt{49} = -7$, and $\pm\sqrt{4} = \pm2$. The square root of a negative number is an imaginary number because any two factors of a negative number must have different signs, and are therefore not equivalent.

Logarithm

A logarithm is the inverse of exponentiation. The logarithm of a number x in base b is equal to the number n. Therefore, $b^n = x$ and $\log bx = n$. For example, $\log_4(64) = 3$ because $4^3 = 64$. The most commonly used bases for logarithms are 10, the common logarithm; 2, the binary logarithm; and the constant e, the natural logarithm (also called $ln(x)$ instead of $\log_e(x)$). Below is a list of some of the rules of logarithms that are important to understand if you are going to use them.

$$\log_b(xy) = \log_b(x) + \log_b(y)$$

$$\log_b(x/y) = \log_b(x) - \log_b(y)$$

$$\log_b(1/x) = -\log_b(x)$$

$$\log_b(x)y = y\log_b(x)$$

Compute fluently and make reasonable estimates

Estimation by Rounding

When rounding numbers, look at the digit to the right of the place to which you are rounding. If the digit is 5 or greater, round up. If it is less than 5, round down. For example, to round 65,137 to the nearest hundred, look at the number in the tens place. Since 3 is less than 5, round down to 65,100. To round the same number to the nearest ten thousandth, look at the number in the thousandths place. Since it is 5, round up to 70,000.

Finding Equivalent Ratios

Equivalent ratios have the same meaning. Just like finding equivalent fractions, to find an equivalent ratio, multiply or divide both sides by the same number. For example, you can multiply 7 by both sides of the ratio 6:8 to get 42:56. Instead, you can also divide both sides of the same ratio by 2 to get 3:4. Find the simplest form of a ratio by dividing to find equivalent ratios until you can't go any further without going into decimals. So, 160:240 in simplest form is 2:3. To write a ratio in the form *1:n,* divide both sides by the left-hand number. In other words, to change 8:20 to *1:n,* divide both sides by 8 to get 1:2.5.

Front-End Estimation

Front-end estimation can be used to quickly estimate sums and differences before adding or subtracting. To use this technique, add or subtract just the digits of the two highest place values, and replace the other place values with zero. This will give you an estimation of the solution of a problem. For example, 93,471 – 22,825 can be changed to 93,000 – 22,000 or 71,000. This estimate can be compared to your final answer to judge its correctness.

Judging Reasonableness

When solving an equation, it is important to check your work by considering how reasonable your answer is. For example, consider the equation $9\frac{3}{4} \times 4\frac{1}{3}$. Since $9\frac{3}{4}$ is between 9 and 10 and $4\frac{1}{3}$ is between 4 and 5, only values that are between 9×4 or 36 and 10×5 or 50 will be reasonable. You can also use front-end estimation, or you can round and estimate a reasonable answer. In the equation 73×25, you can round and solve to estimate a reasonable answer to be near 70×30 or 2,100.

Algebra

▶ *Understand patterns, relations, and functions*

Relation

A relation is a generalization comparing sets of ordered pairs for an equation or inequality such as $x = y + 1$ or $x > y$. The first element in each pair, the x values, forms the domain. The second element in each pair, the y values, forms the range.

Function

A function is a special relation in which each member of the domain is paired with exactly one member in the range. Functions may be represented using ordered pairs, tables, or graphs. One way to determine whether a relation is a function is to use the vertical line test. Using an object to represent a vertical line, move the object from left to right across the graph. If, for each value of x in the domain, the object passes through no more than one point on the graph, then the graph represents a function.

Linear and Nonlinear Functions

Linear functions have graphs that are straight lines. These graphs represent constant rates of change. In other words, the slope between any two pairs of points on the graph is the same. Nonlinear functions do not have constant rates of change. The slope changes along these graphs. Therefore, the graphs of nonlinear functions are *not* straight lines. Graphs of curves represent nonlinear functions. The equation for a linear function can be written in the form $y = mx + b$, where m represents the constant rate of change, or the slope. Therefore, you can determine whether a function is linear by looking at the equation. For example, the equation $y = \frac{3}{x}$ is nonlinear because x is in the denominator and the equation cannot be written in the form $y = mx + b$. A nonlinear function does not increase or decrease at a constant rate. You can check this by using a table and finding the increase or decrease in y for each regular increase in x. For example, if for each increase in x by 2, y does not increase or decrease the same amount each time, the function is nonlinear.

Linear Equations in Two Variables

In a linear equation with two variables, such as $y = x - 3$, the variables appear in separate terms and neither variable contains an exponent other than 1. The graphs of all linear equations are straight lines. All points on a line are solutions of the equation that is graphed.

Quadratic and Cubic Functions

A quadratic function is a polynomial equation of the second degree, generally expressed as $ax^2 + bx + c = 0$, where a, b, and c are real numbers and a is not equal to zero. Similarly, a cubic function is a polynomial equation of the third degree, usually expressed as $ax^3 + bx^2 + cx + d = 0$. Quadratic functions can be graphed using an equation or a table of values. For example, to graph $y = 3x^2 + 1$, substitute the values –1, –0.5, 0, 0.5, and 1 for x to yield the point coordinates (–1, 4), (–0.5, 1.75), (0, 1), (0.5, 1.75), and (1, 4).

Plot these points on a coordinate grid and connect the points in the form of a parabola. Cubic functions also can be graphed by making a table of values. The points of a cubic function from a curve. There is one point at which the curve changes from opening upward to opening downward, or vice versa, called the point of inflection.

Slope

Slope is the ratio of the rise, or vertical change, to the run, or horizontal change of a line: slope = rise/run. Slope (m) is the same for any two points on a straight line and can be found by using the coordinates of any two points on the line:

$$m = \frac{y_2 - y_1}{x_2 - x_1}, \text{ where } x_2 \neq x_1$$

Asymptotes

An asymptote is a straight line that a curve approaches but never actually meets or crosses. Theoretically, the asymptote meets the curve at infinity. For example, in the function $f(x) = \frac{1}{x}$, two asymptotes are being approached: the line $y = 0$ and $x = 0$. See the graph of the function below.

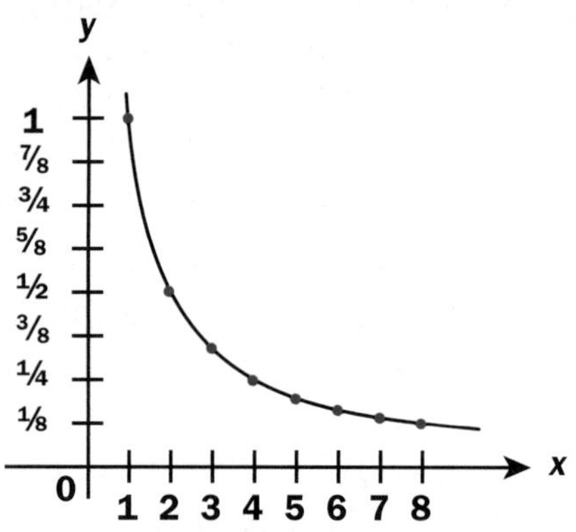

Represent and analyze mathematical situations and structures using algebraic symbols

Variables and Expressions

Algebra is a language of symbols. A variable is a placeholder for a changing value. Any letter, such as x, can be used as a variable. Expressions such as $x + 2$ and $4x$ are algebraic expressions because they represent sums and/or products of variables and numbers. Usually, mathematicians avoid the use of i and e for variables because they have other mathematical meanings ($i = \sqrt{-1}$ and e is used with natural logarithms). To evaluate an algebraic expression, replace the variable or variables with known values, and then solve using order of operations. Translate verbal phrases into algebraic expressions by first defining a variable: Choose a variable and a quantity for the variable to represent. In this way, algebraic expressions can be used to represent real-world situations.

Constant and Coefficient

A constant is a fixed value unlike a variable, which can change. Constants are usually represented by numbers, but they can also be represented by symbols. For example, π is a symbolic representation of the value 3.1415.... A coefficient is a constant by which a variable or other object is multiplied. For example, in the expression $7x^2 + 5x + 9$, the coefficient of x^2 is 7 and the coefficient of x is 5. The number 9 is a constant and not a coefficient.

Monomial and Polynomial

A monomial is a number, a variable, or a product of numbers and/or variables such as 3×4. An algebraic expression that contains one or more monomials is called a polynomial. In a polynomial, there are no terms with variables in the denominator and no terms with variables under a radical sign. Polynomials can be classified by the number of terms contained in the expression. Therefore, a polynomial with two terms is called a binomial ($z^2 - 1$), and a polynomial with three terms is called a trinomial ($2y^3 + 4y^2 - y$). Polynomials also can be classified by their degrees. The degree of a monomial is the sum of the exponents of its variables. The degree of a nonzero constant such as 6 or 10 is 0. The constant 0 has no degree. For example, the monomial $4b^5c^2$ had a degree of 7. The degree of a polynomial is the same as that of the term with the greatest degree. For example, the polynomial $3x^4 - 2y^3 + 4y^2 - y$ has a degree of 4.

Equation

An equation is a mathematical sentence that states that two expressions are equal. The two expressions in an equation are always separated by an equal sign. When solving for a variable in an equation, you must perform the same operations on both sides of the equation in order for the mathematical sentence to remain true.

Solving Equations with Variables

To solve equations with variables on both sides, use the Addition or Subtraction Property of Equality to write an equivalent equation with the variables on the same side. For example, to solve $5x - 8 = 3x$, subtract $3x$ from each side to get $2x - 8 = 0$. Then add 8 to each side to get $2x = 8$. Finally, divide each side by 2 to find that $x = 4$.

Solving Equations with Grouping Symbols

Equations often contain grouping symbols such as parentheses or brackets. The first step in solving these equations is to use the Distributive Property to remove the grouping symbols. For example $5(x + 2) = 25$ can be changed to $5x + 10 = 25$, and then solved to find that $x = 3$.

Some equations have no solution. That is, there is no value of the variable that results in a true sentence. For such an equation, the solution set is called the null or empty set, and is represented by the symbol $\varnothing$ or $\{\}$. Other equations may have every number as the solution. An equation that is true for every value of the variable is called the identity.

Inequality

A mathematical sentence that contains the symbols $<$ (less than), $>$ (greater than), $\leq$ (less than or equal to), or $\geq$ (greater than or equal to) is called an inequality. For example, the statement that it is legal to drive 55 miles per hour or slower on a stretch of the highway can be shown by the sentence $s \leq 55$. Inequalities with variables are called open sentences. When a variable is replaced with a number, the inequality may be true or false.

Solving Inequalities

Solving an inequality means finding values for the variable that make the inequality true. Just as with equations, when you add or subtract the same number from each side of an inequality, the inequality remains true. For example, if you add 5 to each side of the inequality $3x < 6$, the resulting inequality $3x + 5 < 11$ is also true. Adding or subtracting the same number from each side of an inequality does not affect the inequality sign. When multiplying or dividing each side of an inequality by the same positive number, the inequality remains true. In such cases, the inequality symbol does not change. When multiplying or dividing each side of an inequality by a negative number, the inequality symbol must be reversed. For example, when dividing each side of the inequality $-4x \geq -8$ by -2, the inequality sign must be changed to $\leq$ for the resulting inequality, $2x \leq 4$, to be true. Since the solutions to an inequality include all rational numbers satisfying it, inequalities have an infinite number of solutions.

Representing Inequalities on a Number Line

The solutions of inequalities can be graphed on a number line. For example, if the solution of an inequality is $x < 5$, start an arrow at 5 on the number line, and continue the arrow to the left to show all values less than 5 as the solution. Put an open circle at 5 to show that the point 5 is *not* included in the graph. Use a closed circle when graphing solutions that are greater than or equal to, or less than or equal to, a number.

Order of Operations

Solving a problem may involve using more than one operation. The answer can depend on the order in which you do the operations. To make sure that there is just one answer to a series of computations, mathematicians have agreed upon an order in which to do the operations. First simplify within the parentheses, often called graphing symbols, and then evaluate any exponents. Then multiply and divide from left to right, and finally add and subtract from left to right.

Parametric Equations

Given an equation with more than one unknown, a statistician can draw conclusions about those unknown quantities through the use of parameters, independent variables that the statistician already knows something about. For example, you can find the velocity of an object if you make some assumptions about distance and time parameters.

Recursive Equations

In recursive equations, every value is determined by the previous value. You must first plug an initial value into the equation to get the first value, and then you can use the first value to determine the next one, and so on. For example, in order to determine what the population of pigeons will be in New York City in three years, you can use an equation with the birth, death, immigration, and emigration rates of the birds. Input the current population size into the equation to determine next year's population size, then repeat until you have calculated the value for which you are looking.

▶ *Use mathematical models to represent and understand quantitative relationships*

Solving Systems of Equations

Two or more equations together are called a system of equations. A system of equations can have one solution, no solution, or infinitely many solutions. One method for solving a system of equations is to graph the equations on the same coordinate plane. The coordinates of the point where the graphs intersect is the solution. In other words, the solution of a system is the ordered pair that is a solution of all equations. A more accurate way to solve a system of two equations is by using a method called substitution. Write both equations in terms of y. Replace y in the first equation with the right side of the second equation. Check the solution by graphing. You can solve a system of three equations using matrix algebra.

Graphing Inequalities

To graph an inequality, first graph the related equation, which is the boundary. All points in the shaded region are solutions of the inequality. If an inequality contains the symbol $\leq$ or $\geq$, then use a solid line to indicate that the boundary is included in the graph. If an inequality contains the symbol $<$ or $>$, then use a dashed line to indicate that the boundary is not included in the graph.

▶ *Analyze change in various contexts*

Rate of Change

A change in one quantity with respect to another quantity is called the rate of change. Rates of change can be described using slope:

$$\text{slope} = \frac{\text{change in } y}{\text{change in } x}$$

You can find rates of change from an equation, a table, or a graph. A special type of linear equation that describes rate of change is called a direct variation. The graph of a direct variation always passes through the origin and represents a proportional situation. In the equation $y = kx$, k is called the constant of variation. It is the slope, or rate of change. As x increases in value, y increases or decreases at a constant rate k, or y varies directly with x. Another way to say this is that y is directly proportional to x. The direct variation $y = kx$ also can be written as $k = \frac{y}{x}$. In this form, you can see that the ratio of y to x is the same for any corresponding values of y and x.

Slope-Intercept Form

Equations written as $y = mx + b$, where m is the slope and b is the y-intercept, are linear equations in slope-intercept form. For example, the graph of $y = 5x - 6$ is a line that has a slope of 5 and crosses the y-axis at $(0, -6)$. Sometimes you must first write an equation in slope-intercept form before finding the slope and y-intercept. For example, the equation $2x + 3y = 15$ can be expressed in slope-intercept form by subtracting $2x$ from each side and then dividing by 3: $y = -\frac{2}{3}x + 5$, revealing a slope of $-\frac{2}{3}$ and a y-intercept of 5. You can use the slope-intercept form of an equation to graph a line easily. Graph the y-intercept and use the slope to find another point on the line, then connect the two points with a line.

Geometry

Analyze characteristics and properties of two- and three-dimensional geometric shapes and develop mathematical arguments about geometric relationships

Angles

Two rays that have the same endpoint form an angle. The common endpoint is called the vertex, and the two rays that make up the angle are called the sides of the angle. The most common unit of measure for angles is the degree. Protractors can be used to measure angles or to draw an angle of a given measure. Angles can be classified by their degree measure. Acute angles have measures less than 90° but greater than 0°. Obtuse angles have measures greater than 90° but less than 180°. Right angles have measures of 90°.

Triangles

A triangle is a figure formed by three line segments that intersect only at their endpoints. The sum of the measures of the angles of a triangle is 180°. Triangles can be classified by their angles. An acute triangle contains all acute angles. An obtuse triangle has one obtuse angle. A right triangle has one right angle. Triangles can also be classified by their sides. A scalene triangle has no congruent sides. An isosceles triangle has at least two congruent sides. In an equilateral triangle all sides are congruent.

Quadrilaterals

A quadrilateral is a closed figure with four sides and four vertices. The segments of a quadrilateral intersect only at their endpoints. Quadrilaterals can be separated into two triangles. Since the sum of the interior angles of all triangles totals 180°, the measures of the interior angles of a quadrilateral equal 360°. Quadrilaterals are classified according to their characteristics, and include trapezoids, parallelograms, rectangles, squares, and rhombuses.

Two-Dimensional Figures

A two-dimensional figure exists within a plane and has only the dimensions of length and width. Examples of two-dimensional figures include circles and polygons. Polygons are figures that have three or more angles, including triangles, quadrilaterals, pentagons, hexagons, and many more. The sum of the angles of any polygon totals at least 180° (triangle), and each additional side adds 180° to the measure of the first three angles. The sum of the angles of a quadrilateral, for example, is 360°. The sum of the angles of a pentagon is 540°.

Three-Dimensional Figures

A plane is a two-dimensional flat surface that extends in all directions. Intersecting planes can form the edges and vertices of three-dimensional figures or solids. A polyhedron is a solid with flat surfaces that are polygons.

Polyhedrons are composed of faces, edges, and vertices and are differentiated by their shape and by their number of bases. Skew lines are lines that lie in different planes. They are neither intersecting nor parallel.

Congruence

Figures that have the same size and shape are congruent. The parts of congruent triangles that match are called corresponding parts. Congruence statements are used to identify corresponding parts of congruent triangles. When writing a congruence statement, the letters must be written so that corresponding vertices appear in the same order. Corresponding parts can be used to find the measures of angles and sides in a figure that is congruent to a figure with known measures.

Similarity

If two figures have the same shape but not the same size they are called similar figures. For example, the triangles below are similar, so angles *A*, *B*, and *C* have the same measurements as angles *D*, *E*, and *F*, respectively. However, segments *AB*, *BC*, and *CA* do not have the same measurements as segments *DE*, *EF*, and *FD* , but the measures of the sides are proportional.

For example, $\frac{\overline{AB}}{\overline{DE}} = \frac{\overline{BC}}{\overline{EF}} = \frac{\overline{CA}}{\overline{FD}}$.

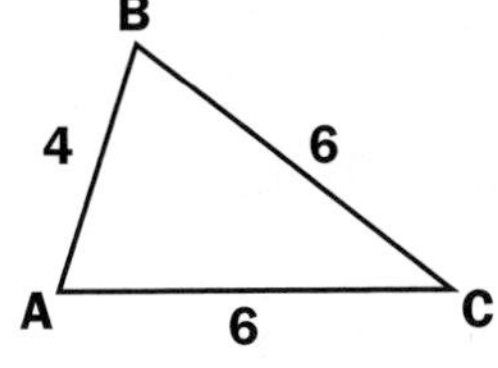

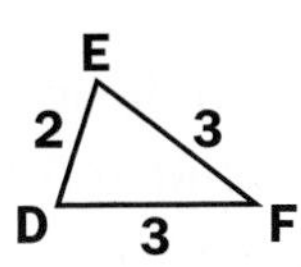

Solid figures are considered to be similar if they have the same shape and their corresponding linear measures are proportional. As with two-dimensional figures, they can be tested for similarity by comparing corresponding measures. If the compared ratios are proportional, then the figures are similar solids. Missing measures of similar solids can also be determined by using proportions.

The Pythagorean Theorem

The sides that are adjacent to a right angle are called legs. The side opposite the right angle is the hypotenuse.

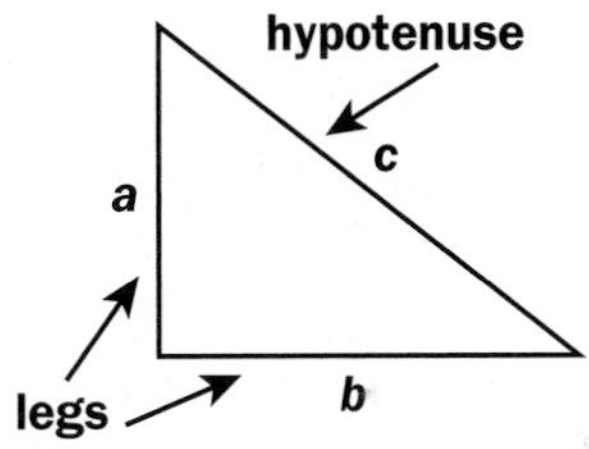

The Pythagorean Theorem describes the relationship between the lengths of the legs a and b and the hypotenuse c. It states that if a triangle is a right triangle, then the square of the length of the hypotenuse is equal to the sum of the squares of the lengths of the legs. In symbols, $c^2 = a^2 + b^2$.

Sine, Cosine, and Tangent Ratios

Trigonometry is the study of the properties of triangles. A trigonometric ratio is a ratio of the lengths of two sides of a right triangle. The most common trigonometric ratios are the sine, cosine, and tangent ratios. These ratios are abbreviated as *sin*, *cos*, and *tan*, respectively.

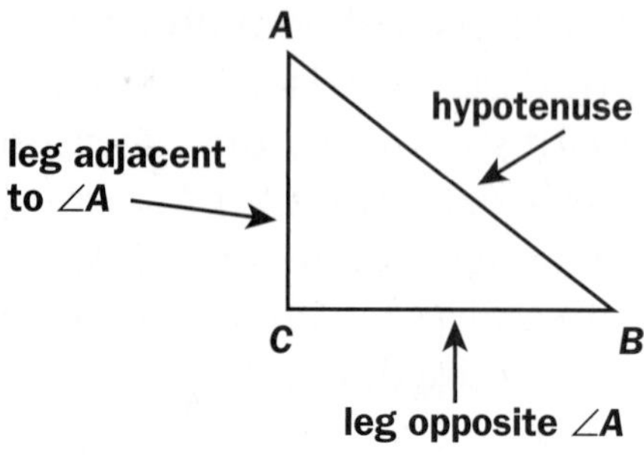

If $\angle A$ is an acute angle of a right triangle, then

$$\sin \angle A = \frac{\text{measure of leg opposite } \angle A}{\text{measure of hypotenuse}},$$

$$\cos \angle A = \frac{\text{measure of leg adjacent to } \angle A}{\text{measure of hypotenuse}}, \text{ and}$$

$$\tan \angle A = \frac{\text{measure of leg opposite } \angle A}{\text{measure of leg adjacent to } \angle A}.$$

Specify locations and describe spatial relationships using coordinate geometry and other representational systems

Polygons

A polygon is a simple, closed figure formed by three or more line segments. The line segments meet only at their endpoints. The points of intersection are called vertices, and the line segments are called sides. Polygons are classified by the number of sides they have. The diagonals of a polygon divide the polygon into triangles. The number of triangles formed is two less than the number of sides. To find the sum of the measures of the interior angles of any polygon, multiply the number of triangles within the polygon by 180. That is, if n equals the number of sides, then $(n - 2)$ 180 gives the sum of the measures of the polygon's interior angles.

Cartesian Coordinates

In the Cartesian coordinate system, the y-axis extends above and below the origin and the x-axis extends to the right and left of the origin, which is the point at which the x- and y-axes intersect. Numbers below and to the left of the origin are negative. A point graphed on the coordinate grid is said to have an x-coordinate and a y-coordinate. For example, the point (1,–2) has as its x-coordinate the number 1, and has as its y-coordinate the number –2. This point is graphed by locating the position on the grid that is 1 unit to the right of the origin and 2 units below the origin.

The x-axis and the y-axis separate the coordinate plane into four regions, called quadrants. The axes and points located on the axes themselves are not located in any of the quadrants. The quadrants are labeled I to IV, starting in the upper right and proceeding counterclockwise. In quadrant I, both coordinates are positive. In quadrant II, the x-coordinate is negative and the y-coordinate is positive. In quadrant III, both coordinates are negative. In quadrant IV, the x-coordinate is positive and the y-coordinate is negative. A coordinate graph can be used to show algebraic relationships among numbers.

Apply transformations and use symmetry to analyze mathematical situations

Similar Triangles and Indirect Measurement

Triangles that have the same shape but not necessarily the same dimensions are called similar triangles. Similar triangles have corresponding angles and corresponding sides. Arcs are used to show congruent angles. If two triangles are similar, then the corresponding angles have the same measure, and the corresponding sides are proportional. Therefore, to determine the measures of the sides of similar triangles when some measures are known, proportions can be used.

Transformations

A transformation is a movement of a geometric figure. There are several types of transformations. In a translation, also called a slide, a figure is slid from one position to another without turning it. Every point of the original figure is moved the same distance and in the same direction. In a reflection, also called a flip, a figure is flipped over a line to form a mirror image. Every point of the original figure has a corresponding point on the other side of the line of symmetry. In a rotation, also called a turn, a figure is turned around a fixed point. A figure can be rotated 0°–360° clockwise or counterclockwise. A dilation transforms each line to a parallel line whose length is a fixed multiple of the length of the original line to create a similar figure that will be either larger or smaller.

Use visualizations, spatial reasoning, and geometric modeling to solve problems

Two-Dimensional Representations of Three-Dimensional Objects

Three-dimensional objects can be represented in a two-dimensional drawing in order to more easily determine properties such as surface area and volume. When you look at the triangular prism, you can see the orientation of its three dimensions, length, width, and height. Using the drawing and the formulas for surface area and volume, you can easily calculate these properties.

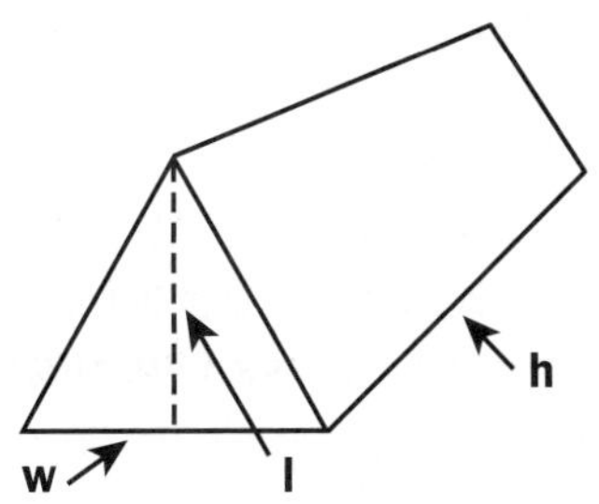

Another way to represent a three-dimensional object in a two-dimensional plane is by using a net, which is the unfolded representation. Imagine cutting the vertices of a box until it is flat then drawing an outline of it. That's a net. Most objects have more than one net, but any one can be measured to determine surface area. Below is a cube and one of its nets.

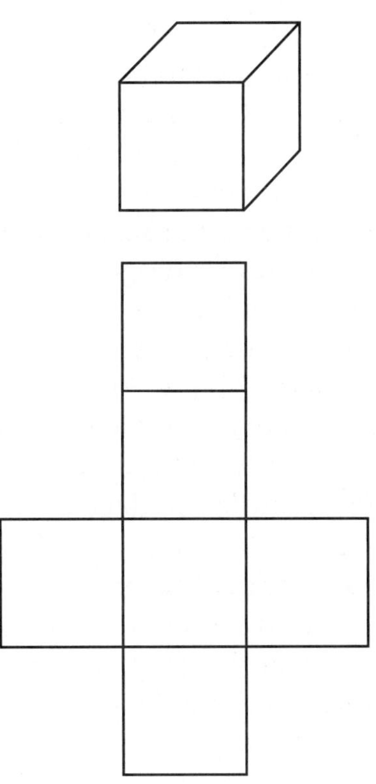

Measurement

Understand measurable attributes of objects and the units, systems, and processes of measurement

Customary System

The customary system is the system of weights and measures used in the United States. The main units of weight are ounces, pounds (1 equal to 16 ounces), and tons (1 equal to 2,000 pounds). Length is typically measured in inches, feet (1 equal to 12 inches), yards (1 equal to 3 feet), and miles (1 equal to 5,280 feet), while area is measured in square feet and acres (1 equal to 43,560 square feet). Liquid is measured in cups, pints (1 equal to 2 cups), quarts (1 equal to 2 pints), and gallons (1 equal to 4 quarts). Finally, temperature is measured in degrees Fahrenheit.

Metric System

The metric system is a decimal system of weights and measurements in which the prefixes of the words for the units of measure indicate the relationships between the different measurements. In this system, the main units of weight, or mass, are grams and kilograms. Length is measured in millimeters, centimeters, meters, and kilometers, and the units of area are square millimeters, centimeters, meters, and kilometers. Liquid is typically measured in milliliters and liters, while temperature is in degrees Celsius.

Selecting Units of Measure

When measuring something, it is important to select the appropriate type and size of unit. For example, in the United States it would be appropriate when describing someone's height to use feet and inches. These units of height or length are good to use because they are in the customary system, and they are of appropriate size. In the customary system, use inches, feet, and miles for lengths and perimeters; square inches, feet, and miles for area and surface area; and cups, pints, quarts, gallons or cubic inches and feet (and less commonly miles) for volume. In the metric system use millimeters, centimeters, meters, and kilometers for lengths and perimeters; square units millimeters, centimeters, meters, and kilometers for area and surface area; and milliliters and liters for volume. Finally, always use degrees to measure angles.

Apply appropriate techniques, tools, and formulas to determine measurements

Precision and Significant Digits

The precision of measurement is the exactness to which a measurement is made. Precision depends on the smallest unit of measure being used, or the precision unit. One way to record a measure is to estimate to the nearest precision unit. A more precise method is to include all of the digits that are actually measured, plus one estimated digit. The digits recorded, called significant digits, indicate the precision of the measurement. There are special rules for determining significant digits. If a number contains a decimal point, the number of significant digits is found by counting from left to right, starting with the first nonzero digit.

If the number does not contain a decimal point, the number of significant digits is found by counting the digits from left to right, starting with the first digit and ending with the last nonzero digit.

Surface Area

The amount of material needed to cover the surface of a figure is called the surface area. It can be calculated by finding the area of each face and adding them together. To find the surface area of a rectangular prism, for example, the formula $S = 2lw + 2lh + 2wh$ applies. A cylinder, on the other hand, may be unrolled to reveal two circles and a rectangle. Its surface area can be determined by finding the area of the two circles, $2\pi r^2$, and adding it to the area of the rectangle, $2\pi rh$ (the length of the rectangle is the circumference of one of the circles), or $S = 2\pi r^2 + 2\pi rh$. The surface area of a pyramid is measured in a slightly different way because the sides of a pyramid are triangles that intersect at the vertex. These sides are called lateral faces and the height of each is called the slant height. The sum of their areas is the lateral area of a pyramid. The surface area of a square pyramid is the lateral area $\frac{1}{2}bh$ (area of a lateral face) times 4 (number of lateral faces), plus the area of the base. The surface area of a cone is the area of its circular base (πr^2) plus its lateral area (πrl, where l is the slant height).

Volume

Volume is the measure of space occupied by a solid region. To find the volume of a prism, the area of the base is multiplied by the measure of the height, $V = Bh$. A solid containing several prisms can be broken down into its component prisms. Then the volume of each component can be found and the volumes added. The volume of a cylinder can be determined by finding the area of its circular base, πr^2, and then multiplying by the height of the cylinder. A pyramid has one-third the volume of a prism with the same base and height. To find the volume of a pyramid, multiply the area of the base by the pyramid's height, and then divide by 3. Simply stated, the formula for the volume of a pyramid is $V = \frac{1}{3}bh$. A cone is a three-dimensional figure with one circular base and a curved surface connecting the base and the vertex. The volume of a cone is one-third the volume of a cylinder with the same base area and height. Like a pyramid, the formula for the volume of a cone is $V = \frac{1}{3}bh$. More specifically, the formula is $V = \frac{1}{3}\pi r^2 h$.

Upper and Lower Bounds

Upper and lower bounds have to do with the accuracy of a measurement. When a measurement is given, the degree of accuracy is also stated to tell you what the upper and lower bounds of the measurement are. The upper bound is the largest possible value that a measurement could have had before being rounded down, and the lower bound is the lowest possible value it could have had before being rounded up.

Data Analysis and Probability

▶ ***Formulate questions that can be addressed with data and collect, organize, and display relevant data to answer them***

Histograms

A histogram displays numerical data that have been organized into equal intervals using bars that have the same width and no space between them. While a histogram does not give exact data points, its shape shows the distribution of the data. Histograms also can be used to compare data.

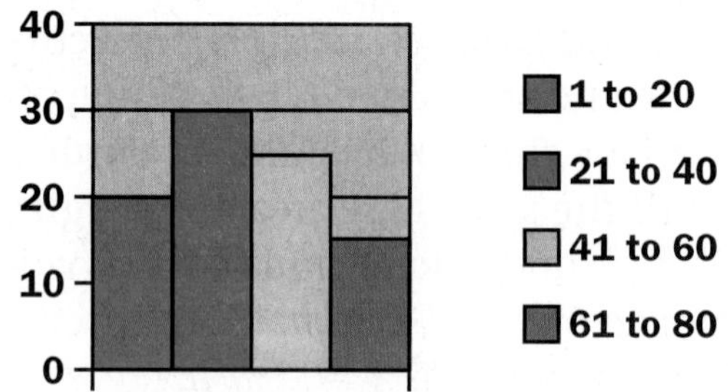

Box-and-Whisker Plot

A box-and-whisker plot displays the measures of central tendency and variation. A box is drawn around the quartile values, and whiskers extend from each quartile to the extreme data points. To make a box plot for a set of data, draw a number line that covers the range of data. Find the median, the extremes, and the upper and lower quartiles. Mark these points on the number line with bullets, then draw a box and the whiskers. The length of a whisker or box shows whether the values of the data in that part are concentrated or spread out.

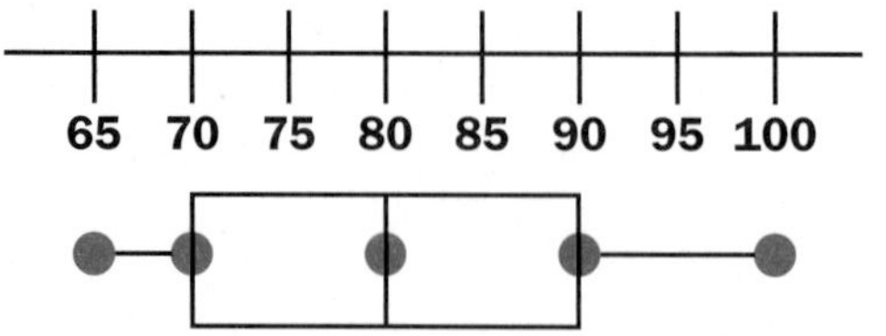

Scatter Plots

A scatter plot is a graph that shows the relationship between two sets of data. In a scatter plot, two sets of data are graphed as ordered pairs on a coordinate system. Two sets of data can have a positive correlation (as x increases, y increases), a negative correlation (as x increases, y decreases), or no correlation (no obvious pattern is shown). Scatter plots can be used to spot trends, draw conclusions, and make predictions about data.

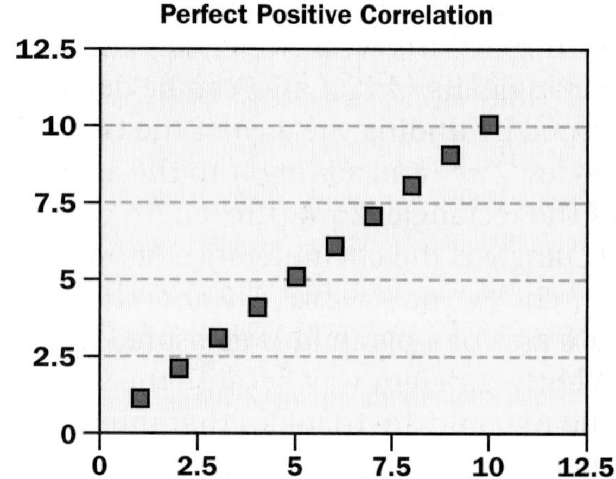

Randomization

The idea of randomization is a very important principle of statistics and the design of experiments. Data must be selected randomly to prevent bias from influencing the results. For example, you want to know the average income of people in your town but you can only use a sample of 100 individuals to make determinations about everyone. If you select 100 individuals who are all doctors, you will have a biased sample. However, if you chose a random sample of 100 people out of the phone book, you are much more likely to accurately represent average income in the town.

Statistics and Parameters

Statistics is a science that involves collecting, analyzing, and presenting data. The data can be collected in various ways—for example through a census or by making physical measurements. The data can then be analyzed by creating summary statistics, which have to do with the distribution of the data sample, including the mean, range, and standard error. They can also be illustrated in tables and graphs, like box-plots, scatter plots, and histograms. The presentation of the data typically involves describing the strength or validity of the data and what they show. For example, an analysis of ancestry of people in a city might tell you something about immigration patterns, unless the data set is very small or biased in some way, in which case it is not likely to be very accurate or useful.

Categorical and Measurement Data

When analyzing data, it is important to understand if the data is qualitative or quantitative. Categorical data is qualitative and measurement, or numerical, data is quantitative. Categorical data describes a quality of something and can be placed into different categories. For example, if you are analyzing the number of students in different grades in a school, each grade is a category. On the other hand, measurement data is continuous, like height, weight, or any other measurable variable. Measurement data can be converted into categorical data if you decide to group the data. Using height as an example, you can group the continuous data set into categories like under 5 feet, 5 feet to 5 feet 5 inches, over 5 feet five inches to 6 feet, and so on.

Univariate and Bivariate Data

In data analysis, a researcher can analyze one variable at a time or look at how multiple variables behave together. Univariate data involves only one variable, for example height in humans. You can measure the height in a population of people then plot the results in a histogram to look at how height is distributed in humans. To summarize univariate data, you can use statistics like the mean, mode, median, range, and standard deviation, which is a measure of variation. When looking at more than one variable at once, you use multivariate data. Bivariate data involves two variables. For example, you can look at height and age in humans together by gathering information on both variables from individuals in a population. You can then plot both variables in a scatter plot, look at how the variables behave in relation to each other, and create an equation that represents the relationship, also called a regression. These equations could help answer questions such as, for example, does height increase with age in humans?

Select and use appropriate statistical methods to analyze data

Measures of Central Tendency

When you have a list of numerical data, it is often helpful to use one or more numbers to represent the whole set. These numbers are called measures of central tendency. Three measures of central tendency are mean, median, and mode. The mean is the sum of the data divided by the number of items in the data set. The median is the middle number of the ordered data (or the mean of the two middle numbers). The mode is the number or numbers that occur most often. These measures of central tendency allow data to be analyzed and better understood.

Measures of Spread
In statistics, measures of spread or variation are used to describe how data are distributed. The range of a set of data is the difference between the greatest and the least values of the data set. The quartiles are the values that divide the data into four equal parts. The median of data separates the set in half. Similarly, the median of the lower half of a set of data is the lower quartile. The median of the upper half of a set of data is the upper quartile. The interquartile range is the difference between the upper quartile and the lower quartile.

Line of Best Fit
When real-life data are collected, the points graphed usually do not form a straight line, but they may approximate a linear relationship. A line of best fit is a line that lies very close to most of the data points. It can be used to predict data. You also can use the equation of the best-fit line to make predictions.

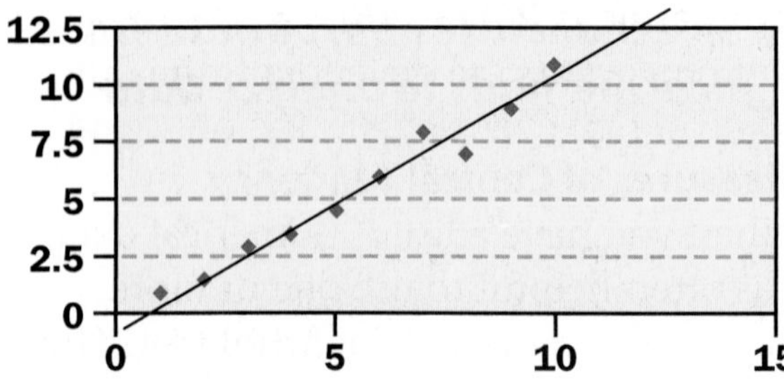

Stem and Leaf Plots
In a stem and leaf plot, numerical data are listed in ascending or descending order. The greatest place value of the data is used for the stems. The next greatest place value forms the leaves. For example, if the least number in a set of data is 8 and the greatest number is 95, draw a vertical line and write the stems from 0 to 9 to the left of the line. Write the leaves from to the right of the line, with the corresponding stem. Next, rearrange the leaves so they are ordered from least to greatest. Then include a key or explanation, such as 1|3 = 13. Notice that the stem-and-leaf plot below is like a histogram turned on its side.

0|8
1|3 6
2|5 6 9
3|0 2 7 8
4|0 1 4 7 9
5|1 4 5 8
6|1 3 7
7|5 8
8|2 6
9|5

Key: **1|3 = 13**

Develop and evaluate inferences and predictions that are based on data

Sampling Distribution
The sampling distribution of a population is the distribution that would result if you could take an infinite number of samples from the population, average each, and then average the averages. The more normal the distribution of the population, that is, how closely the distribution follows a bell curve, the more likely the sampling distribution will also follow a normal distribution. Furthermore, the larger the sample, the more likely it will accurately represent the entire population. For instance, you are more likely to gain more representative results from a population of 1,000 with a sample of 100 than with a sample of 2.

Validity

In statistics, validity refers to acquiring results that accurately reflect that which is being measured. In other words, it is important when performing statistical analyses, to ensure that the data are valid in that the sample being analyzed represents the population to the best extent possible. Randomization of data and using appropriate sample sizes are two important aspects of making valid inferences about a population.

Understand and apply basic concepts of probability

Complementary, Mutually Exclusive Events

To understand probability theory, it is important to know if two events are mutually exclusive, or complementary: the occurrence of one event automatically implies the non-occurrence of the other. That is, two complementary events cannot both occur. If you roll a pair of dice, the event of rolling 6 and rolling doubles have an outcome in common (3, 3), so they are not mutually exclusive. If you roll (3, 3), you also roll doubles. However, the events of rolling a 9 and rolling doubles are mutually exclusive because they have no outcomes in common. If you roll a 9, you will not also roll doubles.

Independent and Dependent Events

Determining the probability of a series of events requires that you know whether the events are independent or dependent. An independent event has no influence on the occurrence of subsequent events, whereas, a dependent event does influence subsequent events. The chances that a woman's first child will be a girl are $\frac{1}{2}$, and the chances that her second child will be a girl are also $\frac{1}{2}$ because the two events are independent of each other. However, if there are 7 red marbles in a bag of 15 marbles, the chances that the first marble you pick will be red are $\frac{7}{15}$ and if you indeed pick a red marble and remove it, you have reduced the chances of picking another red marble to $\frac{6}{14}$.

Sample Space

The sample space is the group of all possible outcomes for an event. For example, if you are tossing a single six-sided die, the sample space is {1, 2, 3, 4, 5, 6}. Similarly, you can determine the sample space for the possible outcomes of two events. If you are going to toss a coin twice, the sample space is {(heads, heads), (heads, tails), (tails, heads), (tails, tails)}.

Computing the Probability of a Compound Event

If two events are independent, the outcome of one event does not influence the outcome of the second. For example, if a bag contains 2 blue and 3 red marbles, then the probability of selecting a blue marble, replacing it, and then selecting a red marble is $P(A) \times P(B) = \frac{2}{5} \times \frac{3}{5}$ or $\frac{6}{25}$.

If two events are dependent, the outcome of one event affects the outcome of the second. For example, if a bag contains 2 blue and 3 red marbles, then the probability of selecting a blue and then a red marble without replacing the first marble is $P(A) \times P(B \text{ following } A) = \frac{2}{5} \times \frac{3}{4}$ or $\frac{3}{10}$. Two events that cannot happen at the same time are mutually exclusive. For example, when you roll two number cubes, you cannot roll a sum that is both 5 and even. So, $P(A \text{ or } B) = \frac{4}{36} + \frac{18}{36}$ or $\frac{11}{18}$.

Glossary

How To Use This Glossary

- Content vocabulary terms in this glossary are words that relate to this book's content. They are **highlighted yellow** in your text.
- Words in this glossary that have an asterisk (*) are academic vocabulary terms. These words help you with your understanding in all your school subjects and are often used on tests. They are **boldfaced black** in your text.

A

accounting The discipline that keeps track of a company's financial situation. (p. 128)

accounting program A program that can store and retrieve financial records and process all business transactions automatically. (p. 214)

* **accurate** Conforming exactly or almost exactly to fact or a standard; characterized by perfect conformity to fact or truth. (p. 691)

* **achieve** To gain with effort. (p. 245)

Ad Council A nonprofit organization that helps produce public service advertising campaigns for government agencies and other qualifying groups. (p. 148)

ad layout A sketch that shows the general arrangement and appearance of a finished ad. (p. 477)

* **adaptation** A company's use of an existing product or promotion from which changes are made to better suit the characteristics of a country or region. (p. 99)

* **adequate** Enough to meet a purpose; acceptable. (p. 757)

adjacent colors Those that are located next to each other on the color wheel and share the same undertones; also called analogous colors. (p. 430)

* **administration** The persons (or committees or departments etc.) who make up a body for the purpose of tending to or supervising something. (p. 137)

advertising A form of nonpersonal promotion in which companies pay to promote ideas, goods, or services in a variety of media outlets. (pp. 396, 441)

advertising agency An independent business that specializes in developing ad campaigns and crafting the ads for clients. (p. 468)

advertising campaign A group of advertisements, commercials, and related promotional materials and activities that are designed as part of a coordinated advertising plan to meet the specific goals of a company. (p. 467)

advertising proof A presentation of an ad that shows exactly how it will appear in print. (p. 481)

agent One who acts as an intermediary by bringing buyers and sellers together. (p. 495)

agreement A specific commitment that each member of a team makes to the group. (p. 243)

* **allocate** Distribute according to a plan or set apart for a special purpose. (p. 606)

allowance Partial return of a sale price for merchandise the customer has kept, for example if there is a defect. (p. 370)

* **analyze** Consider in detail in order to discover essential features or meaning. (p. 214)

* **anticipate** Act in advance of; deal with ahead of time. (p. 664)

* **appreciate** To recognize with gratitude; be grateful for. (p. 349)

* **approach** Ideas or actions intended to deal with a problem or situation. (p. 61)

aptitude An ability or natural talent, or the potential to learn a certain skill. (p. 874)

* **area** A part of a structure having some specific characteristic or function. (p. 369)

Articles of Incorporation Identifies the name and address of a new corporation, its purpose, the names of the initial directors, and the amount of stock that will be issued to each director. (p. 790)

aseptic packaging Packaging that utilizes a technology that keeps foods fresh without refrigeration for extended periods. (p. 741)

assertiveness Acting in a bold or self-confident manner. (p. 235)

* **assess** Place a value on; judge the worth of something. (p. 845)

asset Anything of monetary value that a person owns, such as cash, checking and savings accounts, real estate, or stocks. (p. 843)

* **associate** Make a logical or causal connection. (p. 666)

* **assure** To inform positively or to reinforce with certainty and confidence. (p. 753)

* **astute** Marked by practical intelligence. (p. 310)

* **attitude** A complex mental state involving beliefs and feelings and values and dispositions to act in certain ways. (p. 47)

attitude research Also known as opinion research; designed to obtain information on how people feel about certain products, services, companies, or ideas. (p. 663)

audience The number of homes or people exposed to an ad. (p. 453)

* **authority** The power to make decisions and tell others what to do. (p. 830)

* **authorize** To give or delegate power or authority. (p. 568)

* **automatic** Acting or operating in a manner essentially independent of external influence or control. (p. 494)

* **automatically** In a mechanical manner; by a mechanism. (p. 373)
* **awareness** Having knowledge of. (p. 717)

B

balance of trade The difference in value between exports and imports of a nation. (p. 87)
balance sheet A summary of a business's assets, liabilities, and owner's equity. (p. 858)
bar graph A drawing made up of parallel bars whose lengths correspond to what is being measured. (p. 180)
barrier An obstacle that interferes with the understanding of a message. (p. 191)
basic stock list A stock list used for staple items that should always be in stock. (p. 572)
* **benefits** Those things that aid or promote well-being. (p. 13)
Better Business Bureau (BBB) Nonprofit organization that set up self-regulation among businesses. Business members must "agree to follow the highest principles of business ethics and voluntary self-regulation, and have a proven record of marketplace honesty and integrity." (p. 150)
blind check method A method of checking whereby the receiver writes the description of the merchandise, counts the quantities received, and lists them on a blank form or dummy invoice. The list is then compared to the actual invoice after the blind check is made. (p. 559)
blisterpack A package with a preformed plastic mold surrounding individual items arranged on a backing. (p. 740)
blog Personal Web site where an individual shares thoughts, pictures, and comments with visitors. (p. 449)
bonded warehouse A public or private warehouse that stores products requiring payment of a federal tax. (p. 528)
boomerang method A method of answering objections by bringing the objection back to the customer as a selling point. (p. 331)
brand A name, term, design, symbol, or combination of these elements that identifies a business, product, or service, and sets it apart from its competitors. (p. 731)
brand extension A branding strategy that uses an existing brand name to promote a new or improved product in a company's product line. (p. 736)
brand label The information tag on a product or package that gives the brand name, trademark, or logo. (p. 742)
brand licensing A legal authorization by a brand owner to allow another company (the licensee) to use its brand, brand mark, or trade character for a fee. (p. 736)
brand mark Incorporates a unique symbol, coloring, lettering, or design element that is easily visible. (p. 732)
brand name A word, group of words, letters, or numbers that represents a product or service. (p. 731)
break-even point The point at which sales revenue equals the costs and expenses of making and distributing a product. (p. 592)
brick-and-mortar retailer A traditional retailer who sells goods to customers from a physical store. (p. 494)
broadcast media Radio and television. (p. 446)
budget account A credit account that allows for the payment of a purchased item over a certain time period without a finance charge. (p. 764)
bundle pricing Pricing method in which a company offers several complementary, or corresponding, products in a package that is sold at a single price. (p. 613)
business cycle Recurring changes in economic activity. (p. 75)
business philosophy A company's stated beliefs on how its business should be run. (p. 821)
business plan A proposal that outlines a strategy to turn a business idea into a reality. (p. 819)
business risk The potential for financial gain, loss, or failure. (pp. 117, 799)
buying behavior The process that individuals use to decide what they will buy, where they will buy it, and from whom they will buy it. (p. 825)
buying motive A reason a customer buys a product. (p. 302)
buying signals Things customers say or do to indicate a readiness to buy. (p. 341)

C

call report A written report that documents a sales representative visit with a customer, including the purpose and outcome of the visit. (p. 280)
career outlook The number and types of jobs available in any field. (p. 876)
carload Minimum number of pounds of freight needed to fill a boxcar. (p. 519)
cash flow statement A monthly plan that tracks when cash is expected to come into the business and when it is expected to be paid out. (p. 859)
cash-on-delivery (COD) sale A transaction that occurs when a customer pays for merchandise at the time of delivery. (p. 369)
category management A process that involves managing product categories as individual business units. (p. 721)
cause packaging Packaging that promotes social and political causes. (p. 742)
centralized buying The buying process for all branches in a chain-store operation done in a central location. (p. 542)
* **challenge** A demanding or stimulating situation. (p. 876)
channel of distribution The path a product takes from its producer or manufacturer to the final user. (p. 493)
channels/media The avenues through which messages are delivered. (p. 191)
circle graph A pie-shaped figure that shows the relative sizes of the parts of a whole. (p. 181)
clip art Inexpensive or free images, stock drawings, and photographs. (p. 474)

closing the sale Obtaining positive agreement from a customer to buy. (p. 341)

co-branding A strategy that combines one or more brands in the manufacture of a product or in the delivery of a service. (p. 737)

cold call A sales visit without an appointment. (p. 285)

cold canvassing The process of locating as many potential customers as possible without checking leads beforehand. (p. 304)

* **collate** To assemble in proper sequence. (p. 323)

collateral Something of value that you pledge as payment for a loan in case of default. (p. 834)

color wheel Illustrates the relationships among colors. (p. 430)

command economy A system in which a country's government makes all economic decisions regarding what, how, and for whom. (p. 64)

* **commission** A fee for services rendered based on a percentage of an amount received or collected or agreed to be paid (as distinguished from a salary). (p. 493)

* **commit** To give entirely to a specific activity or cause. (p. 342)

common carrier Trucking company that provides transportation services to any business in their operating area for a fee. (p. 517)

communication The process of exchanging messages between a sender and a receiver. (p. 191)

communications program A computer program that enables users to communicate with other users through their computers. (p. 216)

* **community** A district where people live; occupied primarily by private residences. (p. 785)

* **comparable** Conforming in most respects; able to be compared. (p. 709)

* **compensate** To make up for shortcomings or a feeling of inferiority by exaggerating good qualities. (p. 332)

competition A business relation in which parties compete to gain customers. (p. 115)

complementary colors Colors that are opposite each other on the color wheel and create high contrast. (p. 430)

* **complex** Complicated in structure; consisting of interconnected parts. (p. 566)

* **component** Something determined in relation to something that includes it. (p. 731)

* **concentrate** To direct one's attention on something. (p. 378)

* **concept** An abstract or general idea inferred or derived from specific instances. (p. 419)

* **conduct** To direct or take part in the operation or management of something. (p. 8)

* **conflict** A disagreement or argument about something important. (p. 245)

consensus A decision about which all members of a team approve. (p. 243)

consignment buying A buying process in which goods are paid for only after the final customer purchases them. (p. 547)

* **consist** Be composed or made up of. (p. 219)

* **constant** Continually recurring or continuing without interruption. (p. 591)

consumer market Consumers who purchase goods and services for personal use. (p. 17)

consumer price index (CPI) Measures the change in price over a period of time of 400 specific retail goods and services used by the average urban household. (p. 73)

Consumer Product Safety Commission (CPSC) Responsible for overseeing the safety of products such as toys, electronics, and household furniture. (p. 140)

consumer promotions Sales strategies that encourage customers and prospects to buy a product or service. (p. 406)

* **contact** To be in or establish communication with. (p. 893)

contract carrier A for-hire trucking company that provides equipment and drivers for specific routes, per agreements between the carrier and the shipper. (p. 518)

contract manufacturing Hiring a foreign manufacturer to make your products according to your specifications. (p. 94)

* **control** The power to direct or determine. (p. 503)

controlling The process of setting standards and evaluating performance. (p. 257)

* **convert** Change from one system to another or to a new plan or policy. (p. 633)

* **convince** Make someone agree, understand, or realize the truth or validity of something. (p. 901)

copy The selling message of a written advertisement. (p. 473)

copyright Anything that is authored by an individual, such as writings (books, magazine articles, etc.), music, and artwork. (p. 115)

* **corporate** Of or belonging to a corporation, a business firm whose articles of incorporation have been approved in some state. (p. 97)

corporation A legal entity created by either a state or federal statute, authorizing individuals to operate an enterprise. (p. 789)

cost per thousand (CPM) The media-measurement cost of exposing 1,000 readers or viewers to an advertising impression. (p. 453)

coupon A certificate that entitles a customer to a cash discount on goods or services. (p. 406)

cover letter A letter written by a job applicant to introduce the applicant to an employer in the hopes of convincing the employer to read the résumé. (p. 901)

* **create** To make or cause to be or to become (p. 7)

credit Loaned money in exchange for the promise to pay later. (p. 761)

credit union A cooperative association formed by groups of employees to serve as a financial organization and offer lower rates for the benefit of its members. (p. 834)

cross-training Preparing to do many different activities, such as for tasks on a team. (p. 243)

* **crucial** Of the greatest importance. (p. 454)

customer benefit Advantage or personal satisfaction a customer will get from a good or service. (p. 301)

customer profile Information about the target market, such as age, gender, income level, marital status, ethnic background, geographic residence, attitudes, lifestyle, and behavior. (p. 20)

customer relationship management (CRM) A system that involves finding customers and keeping them satisfied. (p. 277)

customization Creating specially designed products or promotions for certain countries or regions. (p. 101)

cycle count An inventory system involving a small portion of the inventory each day that is counted by stockkeeping units so that the entire inventory is accounted for on a regular basis. (p. 568)

D

data analysis The process of compiling, analyzing, and interpreting the results of primary and secondary data collection. (p. 686)

database A collection of related information about a specific topic. (p. 658)

database marketing Also known as customer relationship management (CRM); a process of designing, creating, and managing customer lists. (p. 658)

database program An application that stores and organizes information, like a filing cabinet. (p. 213)

DBA (Doing Business As) The registration by which the county government officially recognizes that a new proprietorship or partnership exists. (p. 790)

debt capital Borrowed funds, from sources such as banks, friends, and suppliers, that must be repaid. (p. 832)

decentralized buying The buying process in which local store managers or designated buyers are authorized to make special purchases for their individual stores. (p. 542)

decimal number Another way to write a fraction or mixed number whose denominator is a power of 10. (p. 167)

demand Consumer willingness and ability to buy products. The law of demand is the economic principle that price and demand move in opposite directions. (p. 119)

demand elasticity The degree to which demand for a product is affected by its price. (p. 592)

demographics Statistics that describe a population in terms of personal characteristics, such as age, gender, income, marital status, and ethnic background. (p. 44)

* **demonstrate** To show by one's behavior, attitude, or external attributes. (p. 233)

denominator The bottom number of a fraction, which represents how many parts in a whole. (p. 166)

depression A period of prolonged recession. (p. 76)

derived demand Demand in the organizational market that is based on, or derived from, the demand for consumer goods and services. (p. 125)

descriptive label A label that gives information about the product's use, construction, care, performance, and other features. (p. 742)

desktop publishing program A computer program that enables users to edit and manipulate both text and graphics in one document. (p. 215)

* **determine** Decide upon or fix definitely. (p. 681)

* **device** A machine or piece of equipment that does a particular job. (p. 807)

digits The ten basic symbols in our numbering system: 0, 1, 2, 3, 4, 5, 6, 7, 8, and 9. Each digit represents a number and can be combined to represent larger numbers. (p. 165)

direct check method A method of checking in which the merchandise is checked directly against the actual invoice or purchase order. (p. 560)

direct close A method in which the salesperson asks for the sale, when the buying signal is very strong. (p. 344)

direct distribution A channel of distribution that occurs when the producer sells goods or services directly to the customer with no intermediaries. (p. 495)

direct marketing A type of advertising that sends a promotional message to a targeted group of prospects and customers rather than to a mass audience. (p. 396)

disclaimer A statement that contains exceptions to and exclusions from a warranty. (p. 755)

discretionary income The money left after paying for basic living necessities, such as food, shelter, and clothing. (p. 45)

display The visual and artistic aspects of presenting a product or service to a target group of customers to encourage a purchase. (p. 419)

disposable income The money left after taking out taxes. (p. 45)

* **distinct** Serving to distinguish or identify a species or group. (p. 731)

distraction Something that competes with the message for the listener's attention. (p. 195)

* **distribution** The commercial activity of transporting and selling goods from a producer to a consumer. (p. 406)

distribution center A warehouse designed to speed delivery of goods and to minimize storage costs. (p. 526)

dollar control Represents the planning and monitoring of the total inventory investment made by a business during a stated period of time. (p. 570)

* **domestic** Produced in a particular country; of concern to or concerning the internal affairs of a nation. (p. 783)

domestic business A business that sells its products only in its own country. (p. 123)

drop shipper One who owns the goods he or she sells, but does not physically handle the actual products. (p. 494)

E

economic risk A risk that results from changes in overall business conditions. (p. 799)

economy The organized way a nation provides for the needs and wants of its population. (p. 61)

* **edit** Prepare for publication or presentation by correcting, revising, or adapting. (p. 215)

* **element** An important basic part of something complicated, for example, a system or plan. (p. 21)
e-marketplace An online shopping outlet. (p. 505)
embargo A total ban on specific goods coming into or leaving a country. (p. 89)
emotional barrier A bias against a sender's opinions that prevent a listener from understanding. (p. 195)
emotional motive A feeling expressed by a customer through association with a product. (p. 302)
empathy An understanding of a person's situation or frame of mind. (p. 239)
* **emphasis** Special importance or attention that is given to one thing. (p. 480)
employee discount A discount offered to workers by their employers. (p. 639)
empowerment Encouraging team members to contribute to and take responsibility for the management process. (p. 254)
* **enable** To make capable or able for some task. (p. 764)
endless chain method When salespeople ask previous customers for names of potential customers. (p. 303)
* **enhance** To increase; to make better or more attractive. (p. 199)
* **ensure** To make certain of something. (p. 525)
enterprise resource planning (ERP) Software used to integrate all parts of a company's business management, including planning, manufacturing, sales, marketing, invoicing, payroll, inventory control, order tracking, customer service, finance, and human resources. (p. 220)
entrepreneur Someone who creates, launches, organizes, and manages a new business and takes the risk of business ownership. (p. 779)
entrepreneurship The skills of people who are willing to invest their time and money to run a business; the process of starting and operating your own business. (pp. 62, 779)
enumeration A listing of items in order. (p. 200)
Environmental Protection Agency (EPA) Protects human health and our environment. Its responsibilities include monitoring and reducing air and water pollution and overseeing recycling and hazardous waste disposal. (p. 142)
Equal Employment Opportunity Commission (EEOC) Responsible for the fair and equitable treatment of employees with regard to hiring, firing, and promotions. (p. 141)
* **equate** Make equal, uniform, corresponding, or matching. (p. 593)
* **equip** To provide with something, usually for a specific purpose. (p. 427)
equity Equal rights and opportunities for everyone. (p. 237)
equity capital Money raised from within a company or from selling part of an owner's share. (p. 831)
* **error** A wrong action attributable to bad judgment or ignorance or inattention. (p. 560)
* **estimate** Judge tentatively or judge to be probable. (p. 175)
e-tailing Online retailing that involves retailers selling products over the Internet to customers. (p. 494)
ethics Guidelines for good behavior; the basic values and moral principles that guide the behavior of individuals and groups. (pp. 150, 236)
European Union (EU) Europe's trading bloc. (p. 90)
* **evaluate** To judge the worth or value of something. (p. 545)
everyday low prices (EDLP) Low prices set on a consistent basis with no intention of raising them or offering discounts in the future. (p. 616)
* **exceed** To be or do something to a greater extent; go beyond. (p. 761)
exclusive distribution Distribution that involves distributing a product in protected territories in a given geographic area. (p. 504)
excuse A reason given when a customer has no intention of buying in retail-sales situations. (p. 327)
executive summary A brief overview of the entire marketing plan. (p. 37)
exempt carrier A trucking company that is free from direct regulation of rates and operating procedures. (p. 518)
exit interview An opportunity for an employee and a manager to obtain valuable feedback when an employee leaves the company. (p. 265)
* **expand** To make something become larger in size and fill more space. (p. 819)
* **expansion** A time when the economy is expanding. (p. 75)
experimental method A research technique in which a researcher observes the results of changing one or more marketing variables while keeping all the other variables constant under controlled conditions. (p. 685)
* **expert** A person with special knowledge or ability who performs skillfully. (p. 468)
exports Goods and services sold to other countries. (p. 8)
express warranty A warranty clearly stated in writing or offered verbally to encourage a customer to make a purchase. (p. 754)
extended coverage A property insurance endorsement that provides protection against types of loss that may not be covered under a basic property insurance policy. (p. 808)
extended product feature Intangible attribute related to the sale of a product that customers find important. (p. 301)
extensive decision making A type of customer decision making used when there has been little or no previous experience with an item offered for sale. (p. 287)

F

* **factor** Anything that contributes causally to a result. (p. 31)
factors of production Resources that are comprised of land, labor, capital, and entrepreneurship. (p. 61)
feature-benefit selling Matching the characteristics of a product to a customer's needs and wants. (p. 299)

Federal Trade Commission (FTC) Enforces the principles of a private-enterprise system and protects consumers from unfair or deceptive business practices. (p. 143)

feedback A receiver's response to a message. (p. 191)

fidelity bond A bond that provides insurance that protects a business from employee dishonesty. (p. 810)

finance The function of business that involves money management. (p. 128)

firewall A hardware and software checkpoint for all requests for or inputs of data, incoming and outgoing. (p. 223)

fixtures Permanent or movable store furnishings that hold and display merchandise. (p. 423)

flexibility The ability to adapt to changing circumstances. (p. 235)

flexible-price policy A policy in which customers pay different prices for the same type or amount of merchandise. (p. 608)

flextime A system that allows workers to choose their work hours. (p. 147)

focal point An area in a display that attracts attention first. (p. 431)

Food and Drug Administration (FDA) Regulates the labeling and safety of food, drugs, and cosmetics sold throughout the United States. (p. 140)

forced-choice question A question that asks respondents to choose an answer from possibilities given on a questionnaire. (p. 689)

foreign corporation One that is incorporated under the laws of a state that differs from the one in which it does business. (p. 790)

foreign direct investment (FDI) The establishment of a business in a foreign country. (p. 95)

formal balance Created in a display by placing large items with large items and small items with small items. (p. 431)

* **formula** A group of symbols that make a mathematical statement. (p. 172)

for-profit business A business that seeks to make a profit from its operations. (p.124)

fraction Number used to describe or compare parts of a whole. (p. 166)

franchise A legal agreement to sell a parent company's product or services in a designated geographic area. (p. 785)

free on board (FOB) A delivery arrangement that means the price for goods includes delivery at the seller's expense to a specified point and no farther. (p. 383)

free trade Commercial exchange between nations that is conducted on free market principles, without regulations. (p. 88)

freight forwarder A private company that combines less-than-carload or less-than-truckload shipments from several businesses and delivers them to their destinations. (p. 523)

frequency The number of times an audience sees or hears an advertisement. (p. 453)

full warranty A written guarantee that if a product is found to be defective within the warranty period, it will be repaired or replaced at no cost to the purchaser. (p. 754)

* **funding** Money provided for a specific purpose, such as capital to finance the operation of a business. (p. 831)

G

gauge To form a judgment of something uncertain or variable. (p. 336)

general partnership A type of business ownership in which each partner shares in the profits and losses. (p. 787)

generalization A statement that is accepted as true by most people. (p. 200)

* **generate** To bring into existence; produce. (p. 124)

generic brand A product that does not carry a company identity. (p. 735)

geographical pricing Price adjustments required because of different shipping agreements. (p. 614)

geographics Segmentation of the market based on where people live. (p. 46)

global business A business that sells its products in more than one country. (p. 123)

globalization Selling the same product and using the same promotion methods in all countries. (p. 99)

goods Tangible items that have monetary value and satisfy one's needs and wants. (p. 7)

grade label A label that states the quality of the product, such as eggs. (p. 743)

graphics and design program Software application for creating and modifying images. (p. 215)

green marketing When companies engage in the production and promotion of environmentally safe products. (p. 148)

greeting approach A retail approach method in which the salesperson welcomes the customer to the store. (p. 308)

gross domestic product (GDP) The output of goods and services produced by labor and property located within a country. (p. 72)

gross national product (GNP) The total dollar value of goods and services produced by a nation, including goods and services produced abroad by U.S. citizens and companies. (p. 72)

gross profit The difference between sales revenue and the cost of goods sold. (p. 627)

gross sales The total of all sales for a given period of time. (p. 852)

* **guarantee** A pledge that something will happen or that something is true. (p. 719)

H

headline The phrase or sentence in an advertisement-that captures the readers' attention, generates interest, and entices them to read the rest of the ad. (p. 471)

home page The entry point for a Web site, giving general information to introduce the company, person, or product. (p. 216)

horizontal organization A type of management style in which top management shares decision making with self-managing teams of workers who set their own goals and make their own decisions. (p. 254)

human risk Risk caused by employee dishonesty, errors, mistakes, and omissions, as well as the unpredictability of customers or the workplace. (p. 801)

hypertext markup language (HTML) The specific, detailed, and complicated code used to create a Web page. (p. 216)

hypertext transfer protocol (HTTP) The technology that links documents together on the Web. (p. 222)

I

* **identify** To ascertain the origin, nature, or definitive characteristics of. (p. 257)

illustration The photograph, drawing, or other graphic element that is used in an advertisement. (p. 473)

* **impact** A strong effect or influence. (p. 13)

implied warranty A warranty that takes effect automatically by state law whenever a purchase is made. (p. 755)

imports Goods and services purchased from other countries. (p. 85)

impression A single exposure to an advertising message. (p. 453)

incentive A higher-priced product, award, or gift card that is earned and given away through contests, sweepstakes, special offers, and rebates. (p. 408)

income statement A summary of income and expenses during a specific period such as a month or year. (p. 851)

* **indicate** To make a sign that something will happen, is true, or exists. (p. 781)

indirect distribution A channel of distribution that involves one or more intermediaries. (p. 495)

* **individual** A single human being as contrasted with a social group or institution. (p. 255)

industry A group of establishments primarily engaged in producing or handling the same product or group of products or in rendering the same services. (p. 125)

inflation Rising prices. (p. 73)

informal balance Achieved in a display by placing several small items with one large item within the display. (p. 431)

infrastructure The physical development of a country, such as roads, ports, and utilities. (pp. 61, 85)

initiative Taking action and doing what needs to be done without being asked. (p. 233)

installment account A time-payment plan that allows for payment over a period of time. (p. 764)

institutional advertising Advertising designed to create a favorable image for a company and foster goodwill in the marketplace. (p. 441)

institutional promotion A promotional method used to create a favorable image for a business, help it advocate for change, or take a stand on trade or community issues. (p. 395)

insurance policy A contract between a business and an insurance company to cover a specific business risk. (p. 807)

* **integral** Forming an essential part of something and needed to make it complete. (p. 739)

integrated distribution A type of distribution in which manufacturers own and run their own retail operations, acting as wholesaler and retailer for their own products. (p. 505)

intensive distribution Distribution that involves the use of all suitable outlets to sell a product. (p. 505)

* **interact** To act together or toward others or with others. (p. 116)

interactive kiosk An interactive point-of-purchase display that is a free-standing, full-service retail location. (p. 425)

interest The money paid for the use of money borrowed or invested. (p. 856)

* **interface** To join by means of a computer and any other entity, such as a printer or human operator. (p. 279)

intermediary Middleman business involved in sales transactions that move products from the manufacturer to the final user. (p. 493)

* **internal** Occurring within an institution or community. (p. 803)

international trade The exchange of goods and services among nations. (p. 85)

Internet An electronic communications network that connects computer networks and organizational computer facilities around the world. (p. 222)

Internet advertising The form of advertising that uses either e-mail or the World Wide Web. (p. 448)

internship Direct work in a job that allows the person to get experience, either with or without pay. (p. 876)

inventory Amount of merchandise on hand at any particular time, including raw materials, parts from suppliers, manufactured subassemblies, work-in-process, packing materials, or finished goods. (p. 565)

inventory management The process of buying and storing materials and products while controlling costs for ordering, shipping, handling, and storage. (p. 565)

inventory turnover The number of times the average inventory has been sold and replaced in a given period of time. (p. 571)

invest To commit (money or capital) in order to gain a financial return. (p. 75)

invoice Itemized list of goods that include prices, terms of sale, total, taxes and fees, and amount due. (p. 382)

J

jargon A specialized vocabulary used by members of a particular group. (p. 196)

job description A written statement listing the requirements of a particular job and the skills needed to fulfill those requirements. (p. 829)

job lead Information about a job opening, perhaps providing some indication about the type of work and who to contact. (p. 893)

joint venture A business enterprise that a domestic company and a foreign company undertake together. (p. 94)

* **journal** A ledger in which transactions have been recorded as they occurred. (p. 546)

just-in-time (JIT) inventory system A system that controls and coordinates the flow of parts and materials into assembly and manufacturing plants so that suppliers deliver parts and raw materials just before they are needed for use. (p. 565)

K

kiosk A point-of-purchase display that is a stand-alone structure. (p. 411)

L

label An information tag, wrapper, seal, or imprinted message that is attached to a product or its package. (p. 742)

labor Productive work (especially physical work done for wages). (p. 585)

law of diminishing marginal utility An economic law that states that consumers will buy only so much of a given product, even if the price is low. (p. 592)

layaway Removing merchandise from stock and keeping it in a separate area until the customer pays for it. (p. 369)

layman's terms Words that the average customer can understand. (p. 322)

liability A debt owed to others, such as a car payment, credit card debt, or taxes. (p. 843)

licensing Letting another company, or licensee, use a trademark, patent, special formula, company name, or some other intellectual property for a fee or royalty. (p. 93)

lifestyle The type of life you would like to live. (p. 873)

limited decision making Used when a person buys goods and services that he or she has purchased before but not regularly. (p. 287)

limited liability A type of investment in which the personal assets of the owners cannot be taken if a company does not meet its financial obligations or if it gets into legal trouble. (p. 789)

limited liability company (LLC) A relatively new form of business organization that is a hybrid of a partnership and a corporation. (p. 790)

limited partnership A type of business ownership in which each limited partner is liable for any debts only up to the amount of his or her investment in the company. (p. 789)

limited warranty A written guarantee that may exclude certain parts of the product from coverage or require the customer to bear some of the expense for repairs resulting from defects. (p. 755)

line graph A line (or lines) that joins points representing changes in a quantity over a specific period of time. (p. 180)

* **link** An instruction that connects one part of a program or an element on a list to another program or list. (p. 222)

* **logotype** A graphic symbol for a company, brand, or organization; logo. (p. 469)

* **longevity** Having a long life or existence. (p. 299)

loss leader An item priced at or below cost to draw customers into a store. (p. 596)

loyalty marketing program A marketing program that rewards customers by offering incentives for repeat purchases, such as a frequent flyer. (p. 410)

M

maintain To keep in a certain state, position, or activity. (p. 504)

maintained markup The difference between an item's final sale price and its cost. (p. 635)

major Significant; of considerable importance. (p. 180)

management The process of achieving company goals by effective use of resources through planning, organizing, and controlling. (pp. 128, 253)

market All people who share similar needs and wants and who have the ability to purchase a given product. (p. 17)

market economy An economic system in which there is no government involvement in economic decisions. (p. 63)

market intelligence Also known as market research; concerned with the size and location of a market, the competition, and segmentation within the market for a particular product. (p. 664)

market position The relative standing a competitor has in a given market in comparison to its other competitors. (p. 588)

market segmentation The process of classifying people who form a given market into even smaller groups. (p. 43)

market share A company's percentage of the total sales volume generated by all companies that compete in a given market (pp. 18, 588)

marketing The activity, set of institutions, and processes for creating, communicating, delivering, and exchanging offerings that have value for customers, clients, partners, and society at large. (p. 7)

marketing concept The idea that a business should strive to satisfy customers' needs and wants while generating a profit for the business. (p. 10)

marketing information system A set of procedures and methods that regularly generates, stores, analyzes, and distributes information for making marketing and other business decisions. (p. 658)

marketing mix The four basic marketing strategies called the four P's: product, place, price, and promotion. (p. 20)

marketing plan A formal, written document that directs a company's activities for a specific period of time. (p. 37)

marketing research The process and methods used to gather information, analyze it, and report findings related to marketing goods and services. (p. 655)

marketing strategy Identifies target markets and sets marketing mix choices that focus on those markets. (p. 39)

markup The difference between an item's cost and sale price. (p. 605)
marquee A canopy that extends over a store's entrance. (p. 420)
mass marketing Using a single marketing strategy to reach all customers. (p. 49)
media The agencies, means, or instruments used to convey messages to the public. (p. 442)
media/channels The avenues through which messages are delivered. (p. 191)
media planning The process of selecting the appropriate advertising media and deciding the time or space in which ads should appear to accomplish a marketing objective. (p. 451)
media research Also known as advertising research; focuses on issues of media effectiveness, selection, frequency, and ratings. (p. 665)
memorandum buying The buying process in which the supplier agrees to take back any unsold goods by a pre-established date. (p. 547)
merchandise approach A retail-sales method, also called the theme approach, in which the salesperson makes a comment or asks a question about a product in which the customer shows an interest. (p. 309)
merchandising Coordinating sales and promotional plans with buying and pricing. (p. 298)
* **method** A way of doing something, especially a systematic way. (p. 71)
middle management The type of management that implements the decisions of top management and plans how the departments under them can work to reach top management's goals. (p. 253)
* **minimum** The smallest possible quantity. (p. 641)
mini-national A midsize or smaller company that has operations in foreign countries. (p. 95)
mission statement A description of the ultimate goals of a company. (p. 258)
mixed brand A strategy that offers a combination of manufacturer, private distributor, and generic brand to consumers. (p. 737)
mixed bundling Packaging two or more different goods or services in one package. (p. 739)
mixed number A whole number and a fraction. (p. 166)
model stock list A stock list that is used for fashionable merchandise. (p. 572)
* **monitor** To keep an eye on; keep under surveillance. (p. 883)
monopoly Exclusive control over a product or the means of producing it. (p. 117)
multinational A large corporation that has operations in several countries. (p. 95)
* **mutual** Concerning each of two or more things; especially given or done in return. (p. 690)

N

national brand Also known as producer brand, this is owned and initiated by a national manufacturer or by a company that provides services. (p. 734)
natural risk A risk that is caused by natural occurrences, such as floods, fires, and earthquakes. (p. 800)
negotiation The process of working with parties in conflict to find a resolution. (p. 238)
net income The amount left after total expenses are subtracted from gross profit. (p. 855)
net sales The amount left after gross sales have been adjusted for returns and allowances. (p. 852)
net worth The difference between assets and liabilities. (p. 844)
* **network** A communication system consisting of a group of broadcasting stations that all transmit the same program. (p. 446)
networking The art of building alliances. (p. 893)
never-out list A stock list used for best-selling products that make up a large percentage of sales volume. (p. 572)
news release An announcement sent to the appropriate media outlets. (p. 399)
nonprice competition When businesses choose to compete on the basis of factors that are not related to price, including the quality of the products, service, financing, business location, and reputation. (p. 116)
nonprofit organization A group that functions like a business but uses the money it makes to fund the cause identified in its charter. (p. 124)
nonverbal communication Expressing oneself without the use of works, such as with facial expressions, eye movement, and hand motions. (p. 310)
North American Free Trade Agreement (NAFTA) An international trade agreement among the United States, Canada, and Mexico. (p. 91)
numerator The top number of a fraction, which represents the number of parts being considered. (p. 166)

O

objection A concern, hesitation, doubt, complaint, or other reason a customer has for not making a purchase. (p. 327)
objection analysis sheet A document that lists common objections and possible responses to them. (p. 328)
objective The goal intended to be attained. (p. 458)
observation method A research technique in which the actions of people are watched and recorded, either by cameras or by observers. (p. 685)
* **obtain** Come into possession of. (p. 656)
occupational area A category of jobs that involve similar interests and skills. (p. 885)
Occupational Information Network (O*NET) A database that is the primary source for occupational information in the United States; contains information on skills, abilities, knowledge, work activities, and interests associated with occupations. (p. 876)
Occupational Outlook Handbook (OOH) A publication available online and in libraries that describes what workers do, working conditions, the training and education required, earnings, and expected job prospects in a wide range of occupations. (p. 875)
Occupational Safety and Health Administration (OSHA) Sets guidelines for workplace safety and environmental concerns and enforces those regulations. (p. 142)

on-approval sale An agreement that allows a customer to take merchandise home for further consideration. (p. 369)

one-price policy A policy in which all customers are charged the same prices. (p. 608)

open-ended question A question that requires more than a "yes" or "no" answer and requires respondents to construct their own response. (pp. 313, 689)

opening cash fund A limited amount of money in the cash register at the beginning of business. (p. 376)

open-to-buy (OTB) The amount of money a retailer has left for buying goods after considering all purchases received, on order, and in transit. (p. 540)

* **option** The act of choosing or selecting. (p. 517)

organization chart A diagram of a company's departments and jobs with lines of authority clearly shown. (p. 830)

organizational buyer One who purchases goods for business purposes, usually in greater quantities than that of the average consumer. (p. 537)

organizational market Also known as business-to-business (B2B), this includes all businesses that buy products for use in their operations. (p. 17)

organizational selling Sales exchanges that occur between two or more companies or business groups. (p. 285)

organizing Establishing a time frame in which to achieve a goal, assigning employees to the project, and determining a method for approaching the work. (p. 257)

* **overall** Including everything; regarded as a whole; general. (p. 656)

* **overseas** In a foreign country. (p. 382)

P

package The physical container or wrapping for a product. (p. 739)

* **paraphrase** To express the same message in different words. (p. 330)

partnership A legal agreement between two or more people to be jointly responsible for the success or failure of a business. (p. 787)

patent A document granting an inventor sole rights to an item or an idea. (p. 114)

patronage motive A reason for remaining a loyal customer of a company. (p. 302)

penetration pricing Setting the price for a new product very low to encourage as many as possible to buy the product. (p. 610)

* **perceive** To become aware of through the senses. (p. 233)

* **percent** A proportion multiplied by 100. (p. 178)

percentage A number expressed as parts per 100. (p. 178)

performance bond Also called a surety bond, a bond that provides financial protection for losses that might occur when a construction project is not finished due to a contractor's impaired financial condition. (p. 810)

performance standard An expectation for performance that reflects the plan's objectives. (p. 40)

* **period** An amount of time during which something happens. (p. 741)

perpetual inventory system An inventory system that tracks the number of items in inventory on a constant basis; tracking sales and other transactions as they occur. (p. 567)

* **perquisite** An incidental benefit awarded for certain types of employment (especially if it is regarded as a right). (p. 289)

* **perseverance** The act of persisting; continuing or repeating behavior. (p. 346)

personal financial statement A summary of one's current personal financial condition listing assets and liabilities. (p. 843)

personal selling Any form of direct contact between a salesperson and a customer. (p. 285)

persuade To convince someone to change an opinion in order to get him or her to do what you want. (p. 199)

PEST analysis Scanning of outside influences on an organization. (p. 34)

physical distribution Activities for delivering the right amount of product to the right place at the right time. (p. 515)

physical feature Tangible attribute that helps explain how a product is constructed. (p. 301)

physical inventory system An inventory system in which stock is visually inspected or actually counted to determine the quantity on hand. (p. 568)

planning Setting goals and determining how to reach them. (p. 257)

planning goals Small steps taken to get from where you are to where you want to be in your career. (p. 879)

planogram A computer-developed diagram that shows retailers how and where products within a category should be displayed on a shelf at individual stores. (p. 721)

podcast Any brief digital broadcast that includes audio, images, and video delivered separately or in combination. (p. 448)

point-of-purchase display (POP) A standalone structure that serves as a customer sales promotion device. (p. 424)

point-of-sale research Powerful form of research that combines natural observation with personal interviews to explain buying behavior. (p. 685)

point-of-sale system A combination of a cash register with a computer, making it possible to capture information about the transaction at the time of sale and apply it to different functions. (p. 374)

* **policy** A plan or course of action, as of a business, intended to influence and determine decisions, actions, and other matters. (p. 147)

* **potential** Expected to become or be; in prospect. (p. 85)

* **predict** To state, tell about, or make known in advance, especially on the basis of special knowledge. (p. 537)

premium Low cost item given to consumers at a discount or for free. (p. 407)

preretailing marking method A method of marking in which the pricing information is marked in advance on the purchase order, then entered into the buyer's computer system, and prices are available for marking as soon as merchandise is received. (p. 562)

presentation software Computer software that produces slide shows or multimedia presentations. (p. 215)

* **pre-sold** Refers to sales that are due to promotional efforts before a customer comes to a store. (p. 285)

prestige pricing Higher-than-average prices to suggest status and high quality to the customer. (p. 616)

price The value in money or its equivalent placed on a good or service. (p. 585)

price bundling When two or more similar products are placed on sale for one package price. (p. 739)

price competition A focus on the sale price of a product. The assumption is that, all other things being equal, consumers will buy the products that are lowest in price. (p. 116)

price discrimination When a firm charges different prices to similar customers in similar situations. (p. 595)

price fixing A situation that occurs when competitors agree on certain price ranges within which they set their own prices. (p. 595)

price gouging Pricing products unreasonably high when the need is great or when consumers do not have other choices. (p. 151)

price lining A pricing technique that sets a limited number of prices for specific groups or lines of merchandise. (p. 613)

primary data Data obtained for the first time and used specifically for the particular problem or issue under study. (p. 681)

principal The amount of money needed to start a business. (p. 856)

* **principle** A basic generalization that is accepted as true and that can be used as a basis for reasoning or conduct. (p. 429)

print media Advertising in newspapers, magazines, direct mail, signs, and billboards. (p. 442)

private carrier A trucking company that transports goods for an individual business. (p. 518)

private distributor brand Known as private brand, store brand, dealer brand, or private label, this is developed and owned by wholesalers and retailers. (p. 734)

private employment agency An employment agency not supported by taxes that must earn a profit to stay in business; it charges a fee for its services, paid either by the job applicant or the employer. (p. 894)

private enterprise Business ownership by ordinary people, not the government. (p. 113)

private sector Businesses not associated with government agencies. (p. 124)

private warehouse A storage facility designed to meet the specific needs of its owner. (p. 525)

problem definition Occurs when a business clearly identifies a problem and what is needed to solve it. (p. 679)

* **process** A particular course of action intended to achieve a result. (p. 191)

producer price index (PPI) Measures wholesale price levels in the economy. (p. 73)

product depth The number of items offered within each product line. (p. 708)

product feature Basic, physical, or extended attribute of a product or purchase. (p. 299)

product item A specific model, brand, or size of a product within a product line. (p. 708)

product life cycle The stages that a product goes through during its life. (p. 717)

product line A group of closely related products manufactured or sold by a business. (p. 708)

product mix All the different products that a company makes or sells. (p. 707)

product mix pricing strategy Adjusting prices to maximize the profitability for a group of products rather than for just one item. (p. 613)

product modification An alteration in a company's existing product. (p. 714)

product planning Making decisions about the features and services of a product or idea that will help sell the product. (p. 707)

product positioning The efforts a business makes to identify, place, and sell its products in the marketplace. (p. 720)

product promotion A promotional method used by businesses to convince prospects to select their goods or services instead of a competitor's brands. (p. 395)

product research Research that centers on evaluating product design, package design, product usage, and consumer acceptance of new and existing products. (p. 668)

product width The number of items offered within each product line. (p. 708)

production The process of creating, growing, manufacturing, or improving on goods and services. (p.127)

productivity Output per worker hour that is measured over a defined period time. (p. 71)

profit The money earned from conducting business after all costs and expenses have been paid. (p. 118)

* **project** To put or send forth. (p. 419)

promotion Decisions about advertising, personal selling, sales promotion, and public relations used to attract customers. (p. 395)

promotional advertising Advertising designed to increase sales. (p. 441)

promotional mix A cost-effective combination of advertising, selling, sales promotion, direct marketing, and public relations strategies used to reach company goals. (p. 396)

promotional pricing Used in conjunction with sales promotions when prices are reduced for a short period of time. (p. 616)

promotional tie-in Activity that involves sales promotions between one or more retailers or manufacturers; also called cross-promotion or cross-selling. (p. 409)

proportion The relationship between and among objects in a display. (p. 431)

* **proprietary** Made or produced or distributed by one having exclusive rights. (p. 94)

props Properties that are items or physical objects that hold the merchandise on display or support the display setting. (p. 428)

prospect A sales lead; a potential customer. (p. 303)

prospecting Looking for new customers. (p. 303)

protectionism A government's establishment of economic policies that systematically restrict imports in order to protect domestic industries. (p. 89)

prototype A model of a new product, usually made before the product is manufactured. (p. 713)

psychographics Grouping people with similar attitudes, interests, and opinions, as well as lifestyles and shared values. (p. 47)

psychological pricing Pricing techniques that create an illusion for customers. (p. 615)

public employment agency An employment agency supported by state or federal taxes that offers free services to both job applicants and employers. (p. 894)

public relations Activities that help an organization to influence a target audience. (p. 397)

public sector Government-financed agencies, such as the Environmental Protection Agency. (p. 124)

public warehouse A storage and handling facility offered to any individual or company that will pay for its use. (p. 526)

* **publication** A copy of a printed word offered for distribution. (p. 876)

publicity Bringing news or newsworthy information about an organization to the public's attention. (p. 399)

pull policy A type of promotion by manufacturers that directs promotional activities toward consumers. (p. 403)

* **purchase** To acquire by means of a financial transaction. (p. 113)

purchase order (PO) A legal contract between a buyer and seller that lists the quantity, price, and description of the products ordered, along with the terms of payment and delivery. (p. 381)

* **purpose** What something is used for. (p. 849)

* **pursue** To carry further or go in search of. (p. 894)

push policy A type of promotion in which manufacturers use a mix of advertising, personal selling, and trade discounts with partners in the distribution channel to "push" the product through to the retailer. (p. 403)

Q

qualitative research Marketing research that focuses on smaller numbers of people and tries to answer questions that begin with "why" or "how." (p. 663)

quality check method A checking method that inspects workmanship and general characteristics of the received merchandise. (p. 560)

quantitative research Marketing research that answers questions that begin with "how many" or "how much." (p. 663)

quota A limit on either the quantity or the monetary value of a product that may be imported. (p. 88)

R

rack jobber One who manages inventory and merchandising for retailers by counting stock, filling the shelves when needed, and maintaining store displays. (p. 493)

* **range** An amount or extent of variation; complete group that is included between two points on a scale of measurement or quality. (p. 44)

* **rapport** A feeling of sympathetic and mutual understanding. (p. 307)

* **ratio** A relationship between the sizes of two numbers or amounts. (p. 858)

rational motive A conscious, logical reason for a purchase. (p. 302)

realistic goal A goal that you have a reasonable chance of achieving. (p. 880)

real-time inventory system A system that uses Internet technology that connects applications, data, and users in real time. (p. 573)

receiving record Information recorded by businesses about they goods they receive. (p. 558)

recession A period of economic slowdown that lasts for at least two quarters, or six months. (p. 75)

recovery The term that signifies a period of renewed economic growth following a recession or depression. (p. 76)

reference Someone who knows your work habits and personal traits and will recommend you for a job. (p. 901)

referral A recommendation of another person who might buy the product being sold. (p. 303)

* **region** An area; place; space. Often refers to a geographic area. (p. 443)

* **register** To record in writing or enroll. (p. 408)

* **regulate** To bring into conformity with rules or principles. (p. 517)

* **relation** A logical or natural association between two or more things; relevance of one to another; connection (p. 605)

reliability When a research technique produces nearly identical results in repeated trials; the trait of being dependable. (p. 689)

remedial action A means of encouraging appropriate workplace behavior in order to improve employee performance. (p. 264)

* **require** Consider as obligatory, useful, just, or proper. (p. 258)

resources All the things used in producing goods and services; a source of aid or support that may be drawn upon when needed. (pp. 61, 253)

* **respond** To reply or show a response or a reaction to something. (p. 192)

* **restrict** To place limits on. (p. 528)

résumé A brief summary of personal information, education, skills, work experience, activities, and interests. (p. 902)

retailer A business that buys goods from wholesalers or directly from manufacturers and resells them to consumers. (pp. 126, 494)

return on investment (ROI) A financial calculation that is used to determine the relative profitability of a product. (p. 587)

reverse auction An auction in which companies post online what they want to buy, and suppliers bid for the contract. (p. 549)

revolving account A charge account offered by a retailer that sets the credit limit and payment terms. (p. 764)

risk management The systematic process of managing an organization's risks to achieve objectives in a manner consistent with public interest, human safety, environmental needs, and the law. (p. 799)

* **role** The actions and activities assigned to or required or expected of a person or group. (p. 147)

routine decision making A type of customer decision making used when a person needs little information about a product he or she is buying. (p. 288)

* **routing** Sending via a specific route. (p. 559)

RPN A reverse-entry method used in calculators, in which the operators follow the operands. (p. 175)

S

sales check A written record of a sales transaction that includes such information as the date, items purchased, prices, sales tax, and total amount due. (p. 365)

sales forecast The projection of probable, future sales in units or dollars. (p. 40)

sales promotion All marketing activities, other than personal selling, advertising, and public relations, that are directed at business or retail customers to boost sales. (p. 397)

sales promotions Incentives that encourage customers to buy products or services. (p. 405)

sales quota A dollar or unit sales goal set for the sales staff to achieve in a specified period of time. (p. 281)

sales tax A percentage fee levied by the government on the sale of goods and services. (p. 370)

sample Part of a target population that represents the entire population. (p. 684)

scarcity The difference between wants and needs and available resources. (p. 62)

secondary data Data already collected for some purpose other than the current study. (p. 681)

Securities and Exchange Commission (SEC) Regulator of the sale of securities (stocks and bonds). It is responsible for issuing licenses to brokerage firms and financial advisers and investigates any actions among corporations that affect the value of stocks. (p. 142)

segmented pricing strategy A strategy that uses two or more different prices for a product, though there is no difference in the item's cost. (p. 614)

selective distribution Distribution in which a limited number of outlets in a given geographic area sell a manufacturer's product. (p. 505)

self-esteem How you perceive your worth or value as a person. (p. 233)

selling point The function of a product feature and its benefit to a customer. (p. 301)

* **sequence** An order of steps; serial arrangement in which things follow in logical order or a recurrent pattern. (p. 200)

* **series** Similar things placed in order or happening one after another. (p. 641)

service approach A retail-selling method in which salespeople ask customers if they need assistance. (p. 309)

service close A closing method in sales in which services that overcome obstacles or problems are explained. (p. 345)

services Intangible items that have monetary value and satisfy your needs and wants. (p. 7)

setting Where communication takes place, including place, time, sights, and sounds. (p. 191)

* **shadowing** Spending time in the workplace with someone as he or she goes through a normal workday. (p. 297)

signature The name of the advertiser or logotype that is the distinctive identification symbol for a business. (p. 474)

* **significant** Of great importance. (p. 856)

* **similar** Having the same or some of the same characteristics. (p. 17)

site map An outline of what can be found on each page within a Web site. (p. 223)

situation analysis The study of the internal and external factors that affect marketing strategies. (p. 37)

six-month merchandise plan The budget that estimates planned purchases for a six-month period. (p. 538)

skimming pricing A pricing policy that sets a very high price for a new product. (p. 609)

slogan A catchy phrase or words that identify a product or company. (p. 475)

social media Electronic media that allows people with similar interests to participate in a social network. (p. 397)

sole proprietorship A business that is owned and operated by one person. (p. 786)

* **solidify** To make strong or united. (p. 278)

* **source** A person, plan, or thing that provides something needed. (p. 821)

source marking Method used by sellers or manufacturers to mark the price before delivering the merchandise to the retailer. (p. 561)

specialty media Relatively inexpensive useful items featuring an advertiser's name or logo; also called giveaways or advertising specialties. (p. 449)

* **specific** Stated explicitly or in detail. (p. 683)

specific goal A goal stated in exact terms and including some details. (p. 880)

spot check method A random checking method of one carton in a shipment for quantity, and one item in the carton is inspected for quality; if the item is as stated on invoice, remaining cartons are assumed to be in the same condition. (p. 560)

spreadsheet program A computer program that organizes, calculates, and analyzes numerical data. (p. 214)
staffing/temporary agency An employment agency not supported by taxes that must earn a profit to stay in business; it charges a fee for its services, paid either by the job applicant or the employer. (p. 894)
standard English The formal style of writing and speaking learned in school. (p. 899)
standing-room-only close A closing method in sales used when a product is in short supply or when the price will be going up. (p. 344)
start-up costs Projections of how much money a new business owner needs for the business's first year of operation. (p. 845)
* **statistic** A number that represents facts or that describes a situation. (p. 473)
stockholder An owner of a corporation with limited liability. (p. 789)
stockkeeping unit (SKU) A unit or group of related items. (p. 568)
storage The holding of goods until they are sold. (p. 525)
store layout Ways that stores use floor space to facilitate and promote sales and serve customers. (p. 421)
storefront A business's exterior, including the sign, marquee, outdoor lighting, banners, awnings, windows, and exterior design of the building. (p. 420)
* **strategy** An elaborate and systematic plan of action. (p. 586)
* **stress** To single out as important. (p. 802)
* **structure** An organization or system that is made up of many parts that work together. (p. 136)
* **subordinate** Having less power or authority than someone else. (p. 883)
substitution method Recommending a different product that would still satisfy the customer's needs. (p. 331)
suggestion selling Selling additional goods or services to the customer. (p. 359)
superior-point method A technique of overcoming objections by permitting the salesperson to acknowledge objections as valid, yet still offset them with other features and benefits. (p. 332)
supervisory-level management Type of management in which managers supervise the employees who carry out the tasks determined by middle and top management. (p. 253)
supply The amount of goods producers are willing to make and sell. (p. 119)
* **survey** A gathering of a sample of data or opinions considered to be representative of a whole. (p. 166)
survey method A research technique in which information is gathered from people through the use of surveys and questionnaires. (p. 684)
* **swatch** A sample piece of fabric. (p. 323)
SWOT analysis An assessment that lists and analyzes the company's strengths and weaknesses. SWOT is an acronym for strengths, weaknesses, opportunities, and threats. (p. 31)

T

* **target** Something or someone to be affected by an action or development. (p. 401)
target market The group of people most likely to become customers, identified for a specific marketing program. (p. 18)
tariff A tax on imports. (p. 88)
teamwork Work done by a group of people to achieve a common goal. (p. 243)
* **technical** Of or relating to proficiency in a practical skill. (p. 537)
* **technique** A method of doing something using a special skill. (p. 478)
* **technology** The practical application of science to commerce or industry or practical problems. (p. 31)
telecommuting Working at home, usually on a computer. Employees can send completed tasks by e-mail or mail-in disk. (p. 147)
telemarketing Telephone solicitation to make a sale. (p. 286)
terms for delivery The final delivery arrangement made between the buyer and seller. (p. 382)
* **theory** A belief; an abstract thought or idea. (p. 65)
third-party method A technique that involves using another customer or neutral person who can give a testimonial about the product. (p. 333)
30-day account A regular charge account that enables customers to charge purchases during a month and pay the balance in full within 30 days after they are billed. (p. 764)
till The cash drawer of a cash register. (p. 375)
time management Budgeting your time to accomplish tasks on a certain schedule. (p. 234)
ton-mile Movement of one ton (2,000 pounds) of freight one mile. (p. 519)
top management Those who make decisions that affect the whole company. (p. 253)
trade character A specific type of brand mark, one with human form or characteristics. (p. 732)
trade name Corporate brand; identifies and promotes a company or division of a particular corporation. (p. 731)
trade promotions Sales promotions designed to get support for a product from manufacturers, wholesalers, and retailers. (p. 405)
trademark A word, name, symbol, sound, brand name, brand mark, trade name, trade character, color, or a combination of these elements that identifies a good or service and cannot be used by anyone but the owner because it is registered with the federal government and has legal protection. (pp. 114, 732)
trading area The geographical area from which a business draws its customers. (p. 823)
* **tradition** A specific practice of long standing. (p. 382)
traditional economy An economic system in which habits, traditions, and rituals answer the basic questions of what, how, and for whom. (p. 63)
* **transfer** To move from one place to another. (p. 368)

transit advertising Advertisement seen on public transportation. (p. 445)

* **transmit** To send from one person or place to another. (p. 902)

transportation The marketing function of moving a product from the place it's made to where it is sold. (p. 516)

* **trend** A general direction in which something tends to move; current style or inclination. (p. 123)

triadic colors Three colors equally spaced on the color wheel, such as red, yellow, and blue. (p. 430)

trial close An initial effort to close a sale. (p. 342)

U

* **ultimate** Furthest or highest in degree or order; utmost or extreme. (p. 618)

* **undergo** To experience something, often unpleasant. (p. 805)

uniform resource locator (URL) The protocol used to identify and locate Web pages on the Internet; Web address. (p. 222)

* **unique** Radically distinctive and without equal. (p. 708)

unit control A stock control method that measures the amounts of merchandise a business handles during a stated period of time. (p. 570)

unit pricing A pricing method that allows consumers to compare prices in relation to a standard unit or measure. (p. 595)

Universal Product Code (UPC) A combination barcode and number used to identify a product and manufacturer that must be on every item sold by the manufacturer. (p. 374)

unlimited liability A type of investment in which the business owner's financial liability is not limited to investments in the business, but extends to his or her total ability to make payments. (p. 787)

utility An added value in economic terms; an attribute of goods or services that makes them capable of satisfying consumers' wants and needs. (p. 14)

V

* **validity** When the questions in a questionnaire measure what was intended to be measured; the quality of being logically valid or effective. (p. 689)

values Beliefs that guide the way we live. (p. 873)

* **vary** To be different; to change. (p. 790)

* **vehicle** A medium for the expression or achievement of something. (p. 618)

vertical organization A hierarchical, up-and-down structure in which the tasks and responsibilities of each level are clearly defined. (p. 253)

* **via** By way of. (p. 396)

* **visual** Able to be seen. (p. 634)

visual merchandising Coordinating all the physical elements in a place of business to project an image to customers. (p. 419)

* **volume** The property of something that is great in magnitude. (p. 349)

W

want slip Customer request for an item or items not carried in the store. (p. 545)

warranty A promise or guarantee given to a customer that a product will meet certain standards. (p. 753)

warranty of fitness for a particular purpose A warranty that is used when the seller advises a customer that a product is suitable for a particular use, and the customer acts on that advice. (p. 755)

warranty of merchantability A seller's promise that the product sold is fit for its intended purpose. (p. 755)

which close A closing method in sales that encourages a customer to make a decision between two items. (p. 344)

whistle-blowing Reporting an illegal action of one's employer. (p. 153)

wholesale and retail buyers Buyers who purchase goods for resale. (p. 538)

wholesaler A business that obtains goods from manufacturers and resells them to organizational users, other wholesalers, and retailers, also called distributors. (pp. 126, 493)

Wi-Fi Wireless fidelity; the technology that creates a wireless Internet connection with radio frequencies. (p. 217)

word-processing program An application that creates text documents that may contain a few graphics. (p. 213)

World Trade Organization (WTO) A global coalition of nations that makes the rules governing international trade. (p. 90)

World Wide Web A part of the Internet and a collection of interlinked electronic documents. (p. 222)

Index

C

D

G

H

Index

M

Q

R

S

T

Photo Credits

All AMA logos are "Used by permission of American Marketing Association."
All DECA logos are "Used by permission of DECA Inc."
All Marketing Core graphics are "Used by permission. Copyright MBA Research, Columbus, Ohio."

Abbreviation key: MH=The McGraw-Hill Companies

Cover (from left to right, top to bottom)Anthony Bradshaw/Getty Images, (2 5 7 13 14 24 34)Karen Gonzalez/MH, (3)Christine Balderas/Getty Images, (4)Rubberball Photography/Veer, (6)Image Source/Getty Images, (8)Digital Vision/Getty Images, (9)PhotoAlto Photography/Veer, (10)Nicholas Eveleigh/Getty Images, (11 17 28 33)giraffarte/iStockphoto, (12)fotog/Getty Images, (15 22)Flickr/Getty Images, (16 25 37)Photodisc/Getty Images, (18)Digitaler Lumpensammler/Getty Images, (19)Brand X Pictures/PunchStock, (20)Yellowdog Productions/Getty Images, (21)Image Source Photography/Veer, (23)Thomas Hawk/Getty Images, (26)Artville/Getty Images, (27)Hola Images/Getty Images, (29 32)Royalty-Free/CORBIS, (30)Miemo Penttinen/Getty Images, (31) Photo 24/Getty Images, (35)Kraig Scarbinsky/Getty Images, (36)Andrew Dernie/Getty Images, (38)Image Source/Alamy Images; **ix** Spencer Platt/Getty Images; **v** Steven Puetzer/Getty Images; **x** Steve Allen/Getty Images; **xi** Blend Images/Getty Images; **xii** Jon Feingersh/Getty Images; **xiii** Car Culture/CORBIS; **xv** Mark Scott/Getty Images; **2** Used by permission of International Coffee & Tea, LLC.; **3** Used by permission of International Coffee & Tea, LLC.; **4** Chris Cooper-Smith/Alamy; **8** U.S. Department of Agriculture; **9** By permission of Block & DeCorso Advertising.; **14** Jelly Belly Candy Company; **19** Courtesy of Campbell Soup Company; **20** Used by permission of State Farm. Copyright Lars Topelmann; **22** (l b)Eric J. Neeb/MH, (r)Courtesy of Campbell Soup Company, (t)MBI/Alamy, **27** Lifesize/Getty Images; **28** Steven Puetzer/Getty Images; **32** Horizon Organic; **35** Bellurget Jean Louis/Getty Images; **36** (t)giraffarte/iStockphoto, (cl)Comstock Images, (c)Karen Gonzalez/MH, (cr)Punchstock, (b)EPSON exceed your vision is a registered logo mark of Seiko Epson Corporation; **40** Digital Vision/Getty Images; **44** Randy Faris/CORBIS; **45** (l)Hola Images/Getty Images; **45** (c)Brand X Pictures/Getty Images, (r)BananaStock/Alamy; **53** Punchstock; **54** Superstock; **56** Reprinted with permission of The Wall Street Journal, Copyright © 2010 Dow Jones & Company, Inc. All Rights Reserved Worldwide.; **57** Copyright The LEGO Group. Used with permission.; **58** Chuck Franklin/Alamy; **62** Marc Romanelli/Getty Images; **63** Used by permission of Tourism NT.; **64** travelib bhutan/Alamy; **66** Pat Tuson/Alamy; **67** Kathy deWitt/Alamy; **68** Well-Pict Berries; **73** Bloomberg via Getty images; **81** Blend Images/Alamy; **82** Celine Ramoni/Getty Images; **86** Photodisc/Getty Image; **87** Courtesy of the Center for Disease Control; **90** Tetra Images/Getty Images; **96** Used by permission of Research in Motion Ltd.; **98** Used by permission of Zurich North American Insurance.; **100** (t)Jack Sullivan/Alamy, (tc) Stuwdamdorp/Alamy, (bc)Used by permission of General Mills., (b) Henry Westheim Photography/Alamy; **105** Noel Hendrickson/Getty Images; **106** Matt Gary/Getty Images; **108** Produced by Food Alliance, www.FoodAlliance.org.; **109** Aquafina and Ecofina Bottle are registered trademarks of Pepsico, Inc. Used with permission.; **110** Patrick Bennett/CORBIS; **113** Simon Jarratt/CORBIS; **114** Mario Tama/Getty Images; **115** Ethan Miller/Getty Images; **117** Car Culture/CORBIS; **118** Axel Koester/CORBIS; **124** Used by permission of American Red Cross.; **125** blickeinkel/Alamy; **128** Copyright 2010 California Milk Advisory Board. An instrumentality of the California Department of Food and Agriculture.; **133** © Shannon Thompson; **134** Photodisc/Getty Images; **137** U.S. General Services Administration; **138** Olaf Doering/Alamy; **139** giraffarte/iStockphoto; **141** (t)Burke Triolo Productions/Getty Images, (c)Keigh Leighton/Alamy; **141** (b)A9999 DB CDC James Gathany/dpa/CORBIS; **142** Jose Luis Pelaez, Inc./Blend Images/CORBIS; **143** Advertisement reprinted with permission of The California Raisin Marketing Board.; **144** Photodisc/Getty Images; **149** Used by permission of The Hershey Company.; **150** General Motors LLC. Used with permission, GM Media Archives.; **151** Bloomberg/Getty Images; **157** Juice Images/Alamy; **158** Jeff Greenberg/PhotoEdit; **160** Reprinted with permission of The Wall Street Journal, Copyright © 2010 Dow Jones & Company, Inc. All Rights Reserved Worldwide.; **161** Reprinted with permission. © 2010 Wells Fargo Bank, N.A. All rights reserved.; **162** Ariel Skelley/Blend Images/CORBIS; **167** JupiterImages/Getty Images; **171** Used by permission of Geico.; **172** Nicolas Russell/Getty Images; **177** Stockbyte/Getty Images; **187** Jose Luis Pelaez Inc/Getty Images; **188** ColorBlind Images/Getty Images; **192** PhotosIndia.com LLC/Alamy; **193** Nancy Brown/Getty Images; **195** (l)Nicole Hill/Getty Images, (c) Somos Images/Alamy, (r)Johner Images/Alamy; **201** Radius Images/Getty Images; **202** Scott Quinn Photography/Getty Images; **204 206** giraffarte/iStockphoto; **209** foodfolio/Alamy; **210** Klaus Tiedge/Getty Images; **214** Jose Luis Pelaez, Inc./CORBIS; **215** Used by permission of Intuit, Inc., (inset)Alex and Laila/Getty Images; **216** (t)Kim Kulish/CORBIS, (b)allfive/Alamy; **219** David Williams/Alamy; **220** Tetra Images/Getty Images; **221** (t)Erik Dreyer/Getty Images, (tc) Photographer's Choice/Getty Images, (inset)Photodisc/Getty Images, (b) Blend Images/Getty Images; **224** Tony French/Alamy; **228** Brand X Pictures/PunchStock; **230** Blend Images/Getty Images; **234** John Lund/Drew Kelly/age Fotostock; **235** Martin Child/Getty Images; **236** giraffarte/iStockphoto; **238** BananaStock/SuperStock; **242** Lifesize/Getty Images; **244** (l)Hill Street Studios/Getty Images, (r)BananaStock/JupiterImages; **249** Margo Silver/Getty Images; **250** Reggie Casagrande/Getty Images; **254** (t)Stockbyte/Getty Images, (b)Image Source/Getty Images; **258** (l)F1online digitale Bildagentur GmbH/Alamy Images, (c) David Raymer/CORBIS, (r)LWA-JDC/CORBIS; **259** Bloomberg/Getty Images; **261** Fuse/Getty Images; **262** Kent Smith/Getty Images; **263** JupiterImages/ Comstock Images/Alamy; **269** Yellow Dog Productions/Getty Images; **270** Ilene MacDonald/Alamy; **272** Reprinted with permission of The Wall Street Journal, Copyright © 2010 Dow Jones & Company, Inc. All Rights Reserved Worldwide.; **273** Used with permission of Stokely-Van Camp, Inc.; **274** Digital Vision/Getty Images; **278** Used by permission of Lucky Brand.; **279** Eric J. Neeb/MH; **280** vario images GmbH & Co.KG/Alamy; **281** giraffarte/iStockphoto; **282** Cultra/Getty Images; **286** Thinkstock/Punchstock; **288** Ingram Publishing/SuperStock; **293** Digital Vision/Getty Images; **294** age Fotostock/SuperStock; **298** We would like to acknowledge and thank Phillips-Van Heusen Corporation, the owner of the IZOD trademark.; **299** Getty Images/Uppercut RF; **300** Used by permission of Skyway Luggage Company.; **301** Keith Brofsky/Getty Images; **304** Thinkstock Images/Getty Images; **308** Blend Images/Getty Images; **309** Hill Street Studios/Gary Kious/Getty Images; **312** Used by permission of Kyocera Mita.; **317** Ingram Publishing/Fotosearch; **318** Purestock/Getty Images; **322** Steve Hix/Somos Images/CORBIS; **324** Fuse/Getty Images; **327** Masterfile; **329** Tim Boyle/Getty Images; **330** RL Productions/Getty Images; **332** Pierre Arsenault/Alamy; **337** amanaimages/Getty Images; **338** Fuse/Getty Images; **341** C. Borland/PhotoLink/Getty Images; **342** altrendo images/Getty Images; **343** Steve Cole/Getty Images; **344** Neville Elder/CORBIS; **345** Hans Neleman/Getty Images; **351** (t)Tomas Hudcovic/isifa/Getty Images, (c)Lifesize/Getty Images, (b)John Kelly/Getty Images; **352** Used by permission of L.L.Bean. Copyright LLBean.; **353** Frances Roberts/Alamy; **354** Bambu Productions/Getty Images; **355** Blend Images/Getty Images; **361** travelstock.ca/Alamy; **362** Juice Images/Alamy; **367** giraffarte/iStockphoto; **376** Used by permission of Wendy's International.; **378** AFP/AFP/Getty Images; **383** Fuse/Getty

Images; **387** Tooga/Getty Images; **388** Lana Sundman/Alamy; **390** Reprinted with permission of The Wall Street Journal, Copyright © 2010 Dow Jones & Company, Inc. All Rights Reserved Worldwide.; **391** Used by permission of Ben & Jerry's.; **392** Comstock Images/Getty Images; **395** Used by permission of J.D. Power and Associates.; **396** Juice Images/CORBIS; **401** (l)Rock Band logo used with permission by Harmonix Music Systems, Inc. All rights reserved., (r)Colin Young-Wolff/PhotoEdit; **407** Ethan Miller/Getty Images; **408** Jeff Greenberg/Alamy; **409** Cate Gillon/Getty Images; **410** Bloomberg via Getty Images; **415** Nikreates/Alamy; **416** Atlantide Phototravel/CORBIS; **420** Andrew Resek/MH; **421** (t)Spencer Platt/Getty Images, (b)Michael Newman/PhotoEdit; **422** Jayme Thornton/Getty Images; **423** Rachel Weill/Getty Images; **424** Jeff Greenberg/Alamy; **428** Purestock/Getty Images; **432** cultura/CORBIS; **436** Rob Melnychuk/Getty Images; **438** Alamy Images; **442 443** Mark Andersen/Getty Images; **446** Kaveh Kazemi/Getty Images; **447** Justin Sullivan/Getty Images; **448** Used by permission of Company C.; **449** Used by permission of J.D. Power and Associates.; **455** Fuse/Getty Images; **456** Courtesy of Garmin International.; **458** OJO Images Ltd/Alamy; **463** Tetra Images/CORBIS; **465** Moment/Getty Images; **468** giraffarte/iStockphoto; **469** Dimitri Vervitsiotis/Getty Images; **470** Andric (Photography)/Guido Daniele (Painting); **471** Used by permission Horizon and Hoffman Lewis. Copyright 2010., (inset)John E. Kelly/Getty Images; **472** The WESTERN UNION name, logo and related trademarks and service marks, owned by Western Union Holdings, Inc., are used with permission.; **474** Used by Permission of Deutsch Inc. as Agent for National Fluid Milk Processor Promotion Board; **477** Used by permission of H.J. Heinz Company.; **478** Courtesy of AT&T Intellectual Property. Used with permission.; **479** Used by permission of Black Enterprise.; **483** nagelestock.com/Alamy; **486** Bryan Mitchell/Getty Images; **488** Reprinted with permission of The Wall Street Journal, Copyright © 2010 Dow Jones & Company, Inc. All Rights Reserved Worldwide.; **489** © Barnes & Noble .com. Reprinted by permission.; **490** Paul A. Souders/CORBIS; **494** Apex News and Pictures Agency/Alamy; **495** Mira/Alamy; **498** Hill Street Studios/Getty Images; **499** (l)Used by permission of DIRECTV., (r)Comstock/Getty Images; **500** YOSHIKAZU TSUNO/AFP/Getty Images; **506** Used by permission of Palm Inc.; **511** Judith Collins/Alamy; **513** Brand X Pictures/Getty Images; **517** Walter Hodges/Photodisc/ Getty Images; **518** Rick Havner/AP Photo; **520** Steve Allen/Getty Images; **522** Comstock/PunchStock; **523** Ingram Publishing/Alamy; **526** Ray Juno/CORBIS; **527** Photodisc/Getty Images; **528** giraffarte/iStockphoto; **534** LWA/CORBIS; **538** Digital Vision/Getty Images; **539** Courtesy of Frito-Lay North America.; **541** Tanya Constantine/Digital Vision/Getty Images; **546** Dejan Patic/Getty Images; **547** Jose Luis Pelaez/Getty Images; **553** Thomas Northcut/Getty Images; **554** Adam Frieberg/CORBIS; **557** Erik Isakson/Getty Images; **560** RL Productions/Getty Images; **561** Inti St. Clair/Digital Vision/Getty Images; **562** Photodisc/Imagestate; **566** giraffarte/iStockphoto; **567** Digital Vision/Getty Images; **569** Royalty-Free/CORBIS; **570** Jim West/Alamy; **572** Andersen Ross/Getty Images; **577** Chris Stein/Getty Images; **578** John Burke/Getty Images; **580** Reprinted with permission of The Wall Street Journal, Copyright © 2010 Dow Jones & Company, Inc. All Rights Reserved Worldwide.; **581** Used by permission of Shop.com.; **582** Photographer's Choice RF/Getty Images; **592** Bryan Mitchell/Getty Images; **594** (t)Richard Levine/Alamy, (c)Ryan McVey/Getty Images, (b) Steve Allen/Getty Images; **596** Used by permission of ConAgra Foods.; **601** Eye-Stock/Alamy; **602** Blend Images/Getty Images; **606** Used by permission of ConAgra Foods.; **609** Permission granted by Toshiba America Information Systems, Inc.; **610** giraffarte/iStockphoto; **614** Used by permission of Caribou Coffee.; **615** Blend Images/Getty Images; **623** LWA/Sharie Kennedy/Getty Images; **624** Photodisc/Getty Images; **629** Photodisc/Getty Images; **630** Andreas Pollok/Getty Images; **632** MH; **635** Matthew Staver/Bloomberg via Getty Images; **636** age Fotostock; **647** Photographer's Choice RF/Getty Images; **648** Barry Austin Photography/Getty Images; **650** Used by permission of Peggy Collins, eHow Presenter, www.powercurvecommunications.com <http://www.powercurvecommunications; **651** Reprinted with permission of The Wall Street Journal, Copyright © 2010 Dow Jones & Company, Inc. All Rights Reserved Worldwide.; **652** Jon Feingersh/Getty Images; **657** AP Photo/Mark Lennihan; **664** Used by permission of Market Tools, Inc.; **667** giraffarte/iStockphoto; **666** Used by permission of Giant Eagle, Inc.; **668** Image Courtesy of Merisant Company. Copyright 2009 Merisant Company.; **669** Nigel Treblin/AFP/Getty Images; **675** C Squared Studios/Getty Images; **676** Richard G. Bingham II/Alamy; **680** (tl)David Young-Wolff/PhotoEdit, (tr)Stockbyte/Getty Images, (cr)Royalty-free/CORBIS, (bl)Gary Conner/Index Stock Imagery, (br)Joseph Pobereskin/Getty Images; **681** Used by permission of Palm Inc.; **682** U.S. Census Bureau/U.S. Department of Commerce; **685** Used by permission of Hostedware Corporation, www.hostedware.com.; **692** Getty Images; **694** Flying Colours Ltd/Getty Images; **699** JupiterImages/Getty Images; **700** Radius Images/Jupiter Images; **702** Reprinted with permission of The Wall Street Journal, Copyright © 2010 Dow Jones & Company, Inc. All Rights Reserved Worldwide.; **703** Used by permission of Procter & Gamble.; **704** Car Culture/CORBIS; **708** Stephen Hilger/Bloomberg/Getty Images; **709** giraffarte/iStockphoto; **711** (t)jeremy sutton-hibbert/Alamy, (tc)Mark Richards/PhotoEdit, (bc)Daniel Acker/Bloomberg/Getty Images, (b)Jeff Greenberg/Age Fotostock; **712** Travelif/Getty Images; **721** Used by permission of Harmon International; **727** Mike Kemp/Getty Images; **728** Blend Images/Getty Images; **732** Used by permission of Bayer Healthcare LLC.; **735** Nick Ut/AP Photo; **740** Courtesy of Campbell Soup Company; **741** Provided courtesy of Frito-Lay North America, Inc.; **743** Used by permission of Bayer Healthcare LLC.; **744** Creatas/PunchStock; **749** foodfolio/Alamy; **750** Radius Images/Getty Images; **754** Phil Banko Photography (photograph)/Reprinted by permission of the Metal Roofing Alliance (advertisement); **755** Courtesy: Electrolux Major Appliances North America.; **756** giraffarte/iStockphoto; **763** Used by permission of VISA, Inc.; **765** Creative Crop/Getty Images; **766** Daniel Sicolo/Design Pics/CORBIS; **771** Digital Vision/Getty Images; **772** Juniors Bildarchiv/Alamy; **774** Reprinted with permission of The Wall Street Journal, Copyright © 2010 Dow Jones & Company, Inc. All Rights Reserved Worldwide.; **775** Used by permission of VeriSign Inc.; **776** Ariel Skelley/Blend Images/CORBIS; **780** Image property of Little Earth Productions, Inc.; **786** Used by permission. The Company Corporation - Incorporate.com.; **788** (l)Jupiter Images/Getty Images, (r)Thomas Barwick/Getty Images; **795** Roger T. Schmidt/Getty Images; **796** Radius Images/Getty Images; **800** John Kelly/Getty Images; **801** Andreas Rentz/Getty Images; **802** giraffarte/iStockphoto; **806** Nationwide, Nationwide Insurance, On Your Side, The Framework are service marks of Nationwide Mutual Insurance Company.; **807** Andrea Pistolesi/Getty Images; **809** Used by permission of Zurich North American Insurance.; **815** Manchan/Getty Images; **816** Juice Images/Alamy; **821** Brand X Pictures/Getty Images; **823** Lester Lefkowitz/Getty Images; **825** Angelo Cavalli/Getty Images; **830** Jim Craigmyle/CORBIS; **832** Hola Images/Getty Images; **839** Bill O'Leary/The Washington Post/Getty Images; **840** Jamie Grill/Getty Images; **845** Used by permission of CitiSourced.; **854** giraffarte/iStockphoto; **857** Burke/Triolo/Brand X Pictures/JupiterImages; **865** OJO Images/Getty Images; **866** Monkey Business Images/Cutcaster; **868** Reprinted with permission of The Wall Street Journal, Copyright © 2010 Dow Jones & Company, Inc. All Rights Reserved Worldwide.; **869** Used by permission of Health Disability Advocates.; **870** Mark Scott/Getty Images; **874** John Kelly/Getty Images; **875** rubberball/Getty Images; **877** Nick White and Fiona Jackson-Downes/Getty Images; **879** Used by permission of Casio America.; **886** giraffarte/iStockphoto; **889** Caroline von Tuempling/Getty Images; **890** Denkou Images/Alamy; **895** Used by permission of Monster.; **896** Robin Laurance/Age Fotostock; **902** giraffarte/iStockphoto; **907** PhotoAlto/Age Fotostock; **908** Jeff Topping/AFP/Getty Images; **912** giraffarte/iStockphoto; **914** Doug Pensinger/Getty Images; **915** Stockbyte/Getty Images.